THE HBJ ANTHOLOGY OF DRAMA

THE HBJ ANTHOLOGY OF DRAMA

W · B · WORTHEN

NORTHWESTERN UNIVERSITY

HARCOURT BRACE COLLEGE PUBLISHERS

FORT WORTH PHILADELPHIA SAN DIEGO NEW YORK ORLANDO AUSTIN SAN ANTONIO

TORONTO MONTREAL LONDON SYDNEY TOKYO

PUBLISHER	*Ted Buchholz*
ACQUISITIONS EDITOR	*Stephen T. Jordan*
DEVELOPMENTAL EDITOR	*Karl Yambert*
PROJECT EDITOR	*Steve Norder*
PRODUCTION MANAGER	*Jane Tyndall Ponceti*
DESIGNER	*Linda Wooton Miller*
PHOTO EDITOR	*Lili Weiner*
TYPOGRAPHER	*TypeLink, Inc.*

✣ ABOUT THE ARTIST ✣

STEPHEN ALCORN is an internationally known painter and printmaker. While born in the United States, he spent his formative years in Florence, Italy, where he first became acquainted, at a very early age, with the art of printmaking. Major American and European publishers alike have made extensive use of his prints and paintings, and his work hangs in many important private and permanent collections throughout the world. Alcorn currently is working on an Abraham Lincoln anthology to be published by HBJ in the fall of 1993. He lives with his wife and two daughters in Cambridge, New York, and dedicates the linocuts in this volume to Tiberio Antinori.

Literary and illustration credits begin on p. 1051.

Address for Editorial Correspondence: Harcourt Brace College Publishers, 301 Commerce Street, Suite 3700, Fort Worth, TX 76102.

Address for Orders: Harcourt Brace & Company, 6277 Sea Harbor Drive, Orlando, FL 32887. 1-800-782-4479, or 1-800-433-0001 (in Florida).

ISBN: 0-15-500006-3

Library of Congress Catalog Card Number: 92-081339

Printed in the United States of America

3 4 5 6 7 8 9 0 1   048   9 8 7 6 5 4 3 2

STUDYING DRAMA IS MORE THAN READING PLAYS; IT REQUIRES US TO STUDY THE theaters where plays were produced, the cultures that framed those theaters, and the critical and interpretive history that has framed the meanings of drama over time. What distinguishes THE HBJ ANTHOLOGY OF DRAMA is its sense that the meaning of drama arises in two contexts: in the play's original theater and the society that sustained it and in *our* culture where the play continues to live both as literature and as theatrical performance.

❋ ❋ ❋ THE HBJ ANTHOLOGY OF DRAMA offers a collection of classic plays from the European and American repertory, as well as a challenging body of new plays. It is organized into units focusing on significant moments in history of Western drama and theater: Athens in the fifth century B.C., England in the late Middle Ages and Renaissance, France and England in the late seventeenth century, industrial Europe from 1850 to 1950, twentieth-century America, and the contemporary world stage. Such lists of traditionally significant plays often seem — and become in practice — prescriptive. Throughout, however, the book raises the opportunity to question the making of such canons, and "canonicity" provides the organizing theme of the final unit.

❋ ❋ ❋ THE HBJ ANTHOLOGY OF DRAMA responds to the ways that drama and theater are studied and taught today. Its thirty-eight plays (and one screenplay) include a substantial selection of Greek drama (four plays), medieval and Renaissance drama (four plays), and Restoration and Neoclassical drama (three plays); it provides a wide-ranging survey of modern European plays (seven plays), an excellent introduction to American drama (twelve plays), and an unusually rich selection of contemporary drama drawn from the United States, Europe, Latin America, and Africa (sixteen plays and one screenplay). THE HBJ ANTHOLOGY OF DRAMA is designed to be used in a variety of drama and theater courses: in general surveys of drama and theater, in courses on tragedy and/or comedy, or in classes on tradition and innovation in the modern theater. More than most anthologies, THE HBJ ANTHOLOGY OF DRAMA enables students and teachers to explore the issues of representation in the theater, the ways that culture shapes issues of identity, of gender and power, of race. Some of these issues are raised in later units, in plays like Jean Genet's *The Blacks*, Ntozake Shange's *spell #7*, Caryl Churchill's *Vinegar Tom*, Manuel Puig's *The Kiss of the Spider Woman*, Wole Soyinka's *Death and the King's Horseman*, Luis Valdez's *Los Vendidos*, Brian Friel's *Translations*, Maria Irene Fornes's *Mud*, and David Henry Hwang's *M. Butterfly*. However, plays such as Aristophanes' *Lysistrata*, William Shakespeare's *The Tempest*, Aphra Behn's *The Rover*, Henrik Ibsen's *A Doll House*, Susan Glaspell's *Trifles*, or Eugene O'Neill's *The Emperor Jones* allow students and instructors to explore identity, power, and other issues throughout the history of Western drama and theater.

✤   ✤   ✤   Each unit begins with an extensive introduction, placing drama in the context of a particular historical era and using illustrations of theater design to develop a precise sense of stage practice. Each play is accompanied by a brief biography of the playwright and a short introduction to the play. Each unit concludes with a selection of critical readings, including essays that reflect the esthetic and cultural concerns of the period. The past, though, is not static. We create and recreate it in relation to the present, that is, in relation to our own understanding, beliefs, and circumstances. Each unit, then, concludes with a "Contemporary Perspectives" essay by an important scholar, critic, or theater practitioner. These essays renovate traditional thinking about drama and theater in relation to literary history, theater practice, questions of social practice and empowerment, and issues of gender, race, ethnicity, and sexuality. THE HBJ ANTHOLOGY OF DRAMA includes classic essays by Aristotle, Sir Philip Sidney, Friedrich Nietzsche, Émile Zola, Mikhail Bakhtin, Northrop Frye, Roland Barthes, Bertolt Brecht, Antonin Artaud, Arthur Miller, Raymond Williams, George Steiner, Martin Esslin, and others. It also includes recent interventions by Sue-Ellen Case, Lynda E. Boose, Katharine Maus, Michael Goldman, Amiri Baraka, Fredric Jameson, and Lynda Hart. Presenting drama and theater in relation to the community of the past and the community of the present, the twenty-seven critical readings — including four reviews of recent plays — focus our attention on how drama contributes to the richly contested field of contemporary culture.

✳ ✳ ✳   Finally, THE HBJ ANTHOLOGY OF DRAMA is designed for both beginning and advanced students. An extensive photo essay traces the development of performance style and theater design, and also provides a glimpse of some memorable productions of the twentieth century. An introduction to writing about drama and theater furnishes beginning students with an outline of the formal and rhetorical practices used in writing about plays. This book also includes a useful glossary of dramatic, theatrical, and literary terms; an extensive bibliography of drama and theater history and theory, and of works about plays and playwrights included in the volume; and a selected list of video, film, and sound recordings. As a whole, THE HBJ ANTHOLOGY OF DRAMA provides a wide-ranging survey of Western drama and theater, one that both presents traditional issues and provides the materials to interrogate that tradition.

— W.B.W.
1 9 9 2

✢ ACKNOWLEDGMENTS ✢

MY SINCERE THANKS TO STEPHEN T. JORDAN OF HARCOURT BRACE JOVANOVICH FOR suggesting this project and for shepherding it through its many incarnations. Thanks, too, to Karl Yambert and Steve Norder, also of HBJ, and to Elizabeth Alvarez and Carla Clardy, for their valuable and careful editing of the manuscript; to Eleanor Garner for undertaking the difficult task of obtaining permissions; to Linda Wooton Miller for designing the book's visual layout and overall look; to Jane Tyndall Ponceti for overseeing the production; and to Lili Weiner for assembling the photo essay. I would also like to thank the many people who read and commented on the manuscript, making it more accurate and useful for instructors: Stanton B. Garner, Jr., of the University of Tennessee; Josephine Lee of Smith College; Don Moore of Louisiana State University; and Cyndia Susan Clegg of Pepperdine University. I am very much indebted to Sharon Mazer of Vassar College for writing the instructor's manual and for many helpful suggestions about the contents and orientation of the anthology as a whole. I am especially grateful to Oscar G. Brockett of the University of Texas at Austin and to Janelle Reinelt of California State University at Sacramento, who allowed me to think out loud about what a book such as this might accomplish. Finally, I would like to thank Denise Sechelski for providing the critical perspective that only another teacher of drama can give.

— W. B. W.

CONTENTS

Preface to Instructors and Students v

INTRODUCTION: DRAMA, THEATER, AND CULTURE 1

Reading Drama and Seeing Theater 3

Drama and Theater in History 5

Dramatic Genres 7

Dramatic Form 8

The Stage in Critical Practice 9

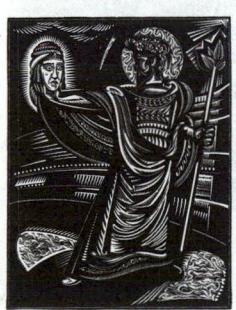

UNIT I: DRAMA AND THEATER IN CLASSICAL ATHENS 11

AESCHYLUS	*Agamemnon* 23
SOPHOCLES	*Oedipus Rex* 43
EURIPIDES	*The Bacchae* 61
ARISTOPHANES	*Lysistrata* 80

CRITICAL CONTEXTS	ARISTOTLE, from *The Poetics* 98
	FRIEDRICH NIETZSCHE, from *The Birth of Tragedy* 107
CONTEMPORARY PERSPECTIVES	SUE-ELLEN CASE, from *"Classic Drag: The Greek Creation of Female Parts"* 111

Unit II:
Drama and Theater in Medieval and Renaissance England 117

Anonymous · *Everyman* 134

Christopher Marlowe · *Doctor Faustus* 145

William Shakespeare · *King Lear* 171

William Shakespeare · *The Tempest* 215

Critical Contexts · Sir Philip Sidney, from *Apology for Poetry* 243

Mikhail Bakhtin, from *Rabelais and His World* 244

Alvin B. Kernan, from *The Playwright as Magician* 247

Contemporary Perspectives · Lynda E. Boose, from *"The Father and the Bride in Shakespeare"* 250

Unit III:
Drama and Theater in the Late Seventeenth Century:
Restoration England and Louis XIV's France 261

Molière · *Tartuffe* 273

Jean Racine · *Phaedra* 302

Aphra Behn · *The Rover* 321

Critical Contexts · Jean Chapelain, *Summary of a Poetics of the Drama* 354

Northrop Frye, from *Anatomy of Criticism* 355

Contemporary Perspectives · Katharine Eisaman Maus, from *"'Playhouse Flesh and Blood:' Sexual Ideology and the Restoration Actress"* 362

Unit IV:
Drama and Theater in Modern Europe 369

HENRIK IBSEN	*A Doll House* 381 —
AUGUST STRINDBERG	*Miss Julie* 406
ANTON CHEKHOV	*The Cherry Orchard* 429
WILLIAM BUTLER YEATS	*On Baile's Strand* 449
BERNARD SHAW	*Major Barbara* 459
LUIGI PIRANDELLO	*Six Characters in Search of an Author* 492 —
BERTOLT BRECHT	*Mother Courage and Her Children* 515
CRITICAL CONTEXTS	ÉMILE ZOLA, from *Naturalism in the Theatre* 543
	BERTOLT BRECHT, *"Theater for Pleasure or Theater for Instruction"* 549
	ROLAND BARTHES, *"The Tasks of Brechtian Criticism"* 553
CONTEMPORARY PERSPECTIVES	MICHAEL GOLDMAN, *"The Ghost of Joy: Romanticism and the Forms of Modern Drama"* 557

Unit V:
Drama and Theater in The United States 567

SUSAN GLASPELL	*Trifles* 577
EUGENE O'NEILL	*The Emperor Jones* 583
TENNESSEE WILLIAMS	*The Glass Menagerie* 595 —
ARTHUR MILLER	*The Crucible* 621

AMIRI BARAKA / LEROI JONES   *Dutchman* 659

LUIS VALDEZ   *Los Vendidos* 668

NTOZAKE SHANGE   *spell #7* 673

SAM SHEPARD   *True West* 693

CRITICAL CONTEXTS   ARTHUR MILLER, *"Tragedy and the Common Man"* 713

GEORGE STEINER, from *The Death of Tragedy* 715

RAYMOND WILLIAMS, from *Modern Tragedy* 718

CONTEMPORARY PERSPECTIVES   AMIRI BARAKA / LEROI JONES, *"The Revolutionary Theatre"* 728

UNIT VI:
DRAMA AND THEATER TODAY: THE WORLD STAGE 731

JEAN GENET   *The Blacks* 740

SLAWOMIR MROZEK   *Striptease* 763

SAMUEL BECKETT   *Happy Days* 769

HAROLD PINTER   *The Homecoming* 781

ATHOL FUGARD, JOHN KANI,
WINSTON NTSHONA   *Sizwe Bansi Is Dead* 804

WOLE SOYINKA   *Death and the King's Horseman* 820

CARYL CHURCHILL   *Vinegar Tom* 844

BRIAN FRIEL   *Translations* 862

MANUEL PUIG   *Kiss of the Spider Woman* 886
(screenplay by Leonard Schrader)

CRITICAL CONTEXTS   ANTONIN ARTAUD, from *The Theater and Its Double* 912

MARTIN ESSLIN, from *The Theatre of the Absurd* 918

FREDRIC JAMESON, from *"Postmodernism and Consumer Society"* 922

CONTEMPORARY PERSPECTIVES   LYNDA HART, from *"Performing Feminism"* 925

Unit VII:
Drama and Theater Today:
Popular Arts and the Canon(s) of Theater 929

Maria Irene Fornes   *Mud* 934

William M. Hoffman   *As Is* 944

David Henry Hwang   *M. Butterfly* 962

David Mamet   *Speed-the-Plow* 985

Critical Contexts   Wendell V. Harris, *"Canonicity"* 1003

Theatrical Perspectives   Michael Feingold, review of *Mud* 1013

Walter Goodman, review of *As Is* 1013

Frank Rich, review of *M. Butterfly* 1014

Frank Rich, review of *Speed-the-Plow* 1016

Appendix   *Writing About Drama and Theater* 1019

Glossary 1027

Bibliography 1036

Handlist of Video, Film, and Sound Recordings of Plays 1049

Credits 1051

THE HBJ ANTHOLOGY OF DRAMA

INTRODUCTION: DRAMA,
THEATER, AND CULTURE

F THE MANY KINDS OF
literature, drama is perhaps the most immediately involved in the life of its community. Drama shares with such other literary modes as lyric poetry, the novel, the epic, and romance the ability to represent and challenge social, political, philosophical, and esthetic attitudes. But unlike most literature, drama has generally been composed for performance, confronting the audience in the public, sociable confines of a theater.

To understand DRAMA, we need to understand THEATER, because the theater forges the active interplay between drama and its community.[1] On a practical level, for instance, the community must determine where drama will take place, and it is in the theater that a space is carved out for dramatic performance. Not surprisingly, the place of the theater in a city's social and physical geography often symbolizes drama's place in the culture at large. In classical Athens, the theater adjoined a sacred precinct, and plays were part of an extensive religious and civic festival. Greek drama accordingly engages questions of moral, political, and religious authority. In seventeenth-century Paris, the close affiliation between the theater and the court of Louis XIV is embodied in the drama's concern with power, authority, and the regulation of rebellious passions. In the United States today, most live theater takes place either in the privileged setting of colleges and universities, or in the "theater districts" of major cities, competing for an audience alongside movie theaters, nightclubs, and other entertainments. Drama also seems to be struggling to define itself as at once part of an established cultural tradition reaching back to Aeschylus and as part of the live diversity of contemporary popular culture. Social attitudes are reflected in the theater in other ways, too; during performance, the theater constructs its own "society" of performers and spectators. Staging a play puts it immediately into a dynamic social exchange: the interaction between dramatic characters, between characters and the actors who play them, between the performers and the audience, between the drama onstage and the drama of life outside the theater.

The Greek word for "theater" — *theatron* — means "seeing place," and plays performed in the theater engage their audiences largely through visual means. Less than a century ago, live plays could be seen only on the stage; today, most of us see drama in a variety of media: on film and television as well as in the theater. Yet for the past five hundred years or so we have also had access to plays in another, nontheatrical venue: by reading them in books. To see a play performed and to read it in a book are two very different activities, but these distinct experiences of drama can be made to enrich one another in a number of ways.

In the theater, a dramatic text is fashioned into an event, something existing in space and time. The space of the stage, with whatever setting is devised, becomes the place of the drama. The characters are embodied by specific individuals. How a given actor interprets a role tends to shape the audience's sense of that dramatic character; for the duration of the play, it is difficult to imagine another kind of performance, a different Oedipus, Lear, or Miss Julie than the one standing before us in the flesh. The drama onstage is also bound by the temporal exigencies of performance. The process of performance is irreversible; for the duration of the performance, each moment becomes significant and yet unrecoverable —

READING
DRAMA AND
SEEING
THEATER

---

[1]Terms are defined in the **Glossary**.

we can't flip back a few pages to an earlier scene, or rewind the videotape. When a company puts a play into stage production, it inevitably confronts these material facts of the theater: a specific cast of actors, a given theatrical space, so much money to spend, and the necessity of transforming the rich possibilities offered by the play into a clear and meaningful performance. To make the drama active and concrete, theatrical production puts a specific interpretation of the play on the stage. Whether or not to play Caliban in Shakespeare's *The Tempest* as a native of the West Indies; whether to play Torvald Helmer in Ibsen's *A Doll House* as a patriarchal autocrat or as someone bewildered by a changing world; whether to set *Phaedra* in a classical, neoclassical, or a modern setting; whether to use cross-gender or intercultural casting in *The Homecoming* — these are some of the kinds of questions that a production must face, and how the production decides such issues inevitably leads the audience toward a particular sense of the play. Everything that happens onstage becomes meaningful for an audience, something to interpret. Even apparently irrelevant facts — a short actor cast to play King Lear in Shakespeare's play, or a beautiful actress playing Brecht's Mother Courage — become part of the audience's experience of the play, particularizing the play, lending it a definite flavor and meaning.

Reading plays presents us with a different experience of the drama. Reading plays is, first of all, a relatively recent phenomenon. In early theaters, like those of classical Athens and Rome, medieval Europe, and even Renaissance Europe of the sixteenth century, drama was almost entirely a theatrical mode, rather than a mode of literature. Although the texts of plays were written down, by and large, audiences came into contact with drama primarily through theatrical performance. By the late sixteenth century, though, the status of drama began to change. The recovery and prestige of Greek and Latin literature led to pervasive familiarity with classical texts, including plays. Throughout Europe, schooling was conducted mainly in Latin, and the plays of Roman playwrights like Plautus, Terence, and Seneca were frequently used to teach Latin grammar and rhetoric; these plays were widely imitated by playwrights writing drama in vernacular languages for emerging secular, commercial theaters. Printing made it possible to disseminate texts more widely, and plays slowly came to be regarded as worthy of publication and preservation in book form. By the late nineteenth century, widespread literacy created a large reading public and a great demand for books; continued improvements in printing technology provided the means to meet the demand. Playwrights often published their plays as books before they could be produced onstage, with some profound effects. The detailed narrative stage directions in plays by Bernard Shaw, Eugene O'Neill, or Henrik Ibsen, for instance, are useful to a stage director and set designer, but they principally fill in a kind of novelistic background for the reading audience who will experience the play only on the page.

Theater audiences are bound to the temporality and specificity of the stage, but readers have the freedom to compose the play in much more varied ways. A reader can pause over a line, teasing out possible meanings, in effect stopping the progress of the play. Readers are not bound by the linear progress of the play's action, in that they can flip back and forth in the play, looking for clues, confirmations, or connections. Nor are readers bound by the stringent physical economy of the stage, the need to embody the characters with individual actors, to specify the dramatic locale as a three-dimensional space. While actors and directors must decide on a specific interpretation of each moment and every character in the play, readers can keep several competing interpretations alive in the imagination at the same time.

Both ways of thinking about drama are demanding, and students of drama should try to develop a sensitivity to both approaches. Treating the play like a novel or poem, decomposing and recomposing it critically, leads to a much fuller sense of the play's potential meanings, its gaps and inconsistencies; it allows us to question the text without the need to come to definite conclusions. Treating the play as a design for the stage forces us to make commitments, to articulate and defend a particular version of the play, and to find ways of making those meanings active onstage, visible in performance. As readers, one way to develop a sense of the reciprocity between stage and page is to think of the play as constructed mainly of actions, not of words. Think of seeing a play in an unknown language: the *action* of the play would still emerge in its larger outlines, carried by the deeds of the characters. Not knowing the words would not prevent the audience from understanding what a character is doing onstage — threatening, lying, persuading, boasting.

When reading a play, it is easy to be seduced by the text, to think of the play's language as mainly narrative, describing the attitudes of the character. For performers onstage, however, speech — language in action — is always a way of doing something. One way for readers to attune themselves to this active quality of dramatic writing is to ask questions of the text from the point-of-view of performers or characters. What do I — Lysistrata, Everyman, Miranda — want in this speech? How can I use this speech to help me get it? What am I trying to do by speaking in this way? Although questions like these are still removed from the actual practice of performance, they can help readers unfamiliar with drama begin to read plays in theatrical terms.

Another way to enrich the reading experience of drama is to imagine staging the play: How could the design of the set, the movements of the actors, the pacing of the scenes affect the play's meaning, make the play mean something in particular? Questions of this kind can help to make the play seem more concrete, but they have one important limitation. When asking questions like these, it is tempting to imagine the play being performed in today's theaters, according to our conventions of acting and stagecraft, and within the social and cultural context that frames the theater now. To imagine the play on our stage is, of course, to produce it in our contemporary idiom, informed by our notions both of theater and of the world our theater represents. However, while envisioning performance, we should also imagine the play in the circumstances of its original theater, a theater located in a different culture and possibly sharing few practices of stagecraft with the modern theater. How would King Lear's nighttime scenes on the stormy heath — "Blow, winds, and crack your cheeks. Rage, blow" — have appeared on the Globe theater's empty platform stage on a sunny afternoon in London in the summer of 1605? Are there ways in which Shakespeare's text capitalizes on this dissonance between the fictive setting and the visible circumstances of the stage? In a theater where a complete, "realistic" illusion was not possible (and, possibly, not even desirable), how does Shakespeare's play turn the conditions of theatrical performance to dramatic advantage? Both reading drama and staging drama involve a complex double-consciousness, inviting us to see the plays with contemporary questions in mind, while at the same time imagining them on their original stages. In this doubleness lies an important dramatic principle: plays can speak to us in our theater but perhaps always retain something of their original accents.

DRAMA AND THEATER IN HISTORY

Throughout its development in Western culture, dramatic art has changed as the theater's place in the surrounding society has changed. The categories that we apply to drama and theater today — art *vs.* entertainment, popular *vs.* classic, literary *vs.* theatrical — are categories of relatively recent vintage. They imply ways of thinking about drama and theater that are foreign to the function of theater in many other cultures. Much as drama and theater today emerge in relation to other media of dramatic performance like film and television, so in earlier eras the theater defined itself in relation to other artistic, social, and religious institutions. Placed in a different sphere of culture, drama and theater gained a different kind of significance than they have in the United States today.

Drama and theater often arise in relation to religious observance. In ancient Egypt, for instance, religious rituals involved the imitation of events in a god's or goddess's life. In Greece, drama may have had similar origins; by the sixth century B.C., the performance of plays had become part of a massive religious festival celebrating the god Dionysus. The plays performed in this theater — including those of Aeschylus, Sophocles, Euripides, and Aristophanes gathered here — were highly wrought and intellectually, morally, and esthetically complex and demanding works. Aristotle classes drama among other forms of poetry, but in classical Athens these plays occupied a very different position in the spectrum of culture than do drama or "art" today, precisely because of their central role in the City Dionysia. The Roman theater set drama in the context of a much greater variety of performance — chariot racing, juggling, gladiatorial shows — and while plays were performed on religious holidays, drama was more clearly related to secular entertainments than it had been in Athens. Theater waned in Europe with the decline of the Roman Empire and the systematic efforts of the Catholic church to prevent theatrical performance. Yet, when theater was revived in the late Middle Ages, it emerged with the support of the church itself. By the year 1000, brief dramatizations illustrated the liturgy of the Catholic Mass; by the fourteenth century, a full range of dramatic forms — plays dramatizing the lives of saints, morality plays, narrative plays on Christian history — was used to illustrate Christian doctrine and to celebrate important days in the Christian year. Like plays in classical Athens, these plays were produced through community effort rather than by specialized "theaters" in the modern sense. Although we now regard medieval drama as extraordinarily rich and complex "literature," in its own era it was part of a different strand of culture, sharing space with other forms of pageantry and religious celebration, rather than being read with the poetry of Chaucer or Dante.

Secular performance did, of course, take place in classical and medieval Europe, including improvised farces on contemporary life, fairground shows, puppetry, mimes, and other quasi-dramatic events. Many plays were performed only on religious occasions, though, and their performers were usually itinerant, lacking the social and institutional support that would provide them with lasting and continuous existence. Only in the Renaissance of the fifteenth and sixteenth centuries did the Western theater begin to assume the function it has today: a fully secular, profit-making, commercial enterprise. Although Renaissance theaters continually vied with religious and state officials for the freedom to practice their trade, by the sixteenth century, the European theater was part of a secular entertainment market, competing with bear-baiting, animal shows, athletic contests, public executions, royal and civic pageants, public preaching, and many other attractions to draw a paying public. The theater emerged in this period as a distinct institution, supported by its own income; the theater became a trade, a profession, a business, rather than a necessary function of the state or of religious worship. Indeed, if drama in classical Athens was conceived more as religious ritual than as "art" in a modern sense, drama in Renaissance London was classed mainly as popular "entertainment." The theater only gradually became recognized as an arena for "literary" accomplishment, for literary status in this period was reserved mainly for skill demonstrated in forms like the sonnet, the prose romance, or the epic — forms that could win the author a measure of aristocratic prestige and patronage. As part of the motley, vulgar world of the public theater, plays were not considered serious, permanent literature.

However, the desire to transform drama from ephemeral theatrical "entertainment" into permanent literary "art" begins to be registered in the Renaissance. The poet and playwright Ben Jonson included plays in the 1616 edition of his *Works*, insisting on the literary importance of the volume by publishing it in the large, FOLIO format generally reserved for classical authors. In 1623, seven years after his death, William Shakespeare's friends and colleagues published a similar, folio-sized collection of his plays, a book that was reprinted several times throughout the seventeenth century. By the 1660s and 1670s, writers at the court of Louis XIV in Paris could achieve both literary and social distinction as dramatists; Jean Racine's reputation as a playwright, in part at least, helped to win his appointment as Louis's royal historiographer. Yet, despite many notable exceptions, the theatrical origins of drama prevented contemporary plays from being regarded as "literature" — although plays from earlier eras were increasingly republished and gradually seen to have "literary" merit. Indeed, by the nineteenth century, contemporary plays often achieved "literary" recognition by avoiding the theater altogether. English poets like Lord Byron and Percy Bysshe Shelley, for instance, wrote plays that were in many ways unstageable, and so preserved them from degrading contact with the tawdry stage. The English critic Charles Lamb remarked in a famous essay that he preferred reading Shakespeare's plays to seeing them in the theater; for Lamb, the practical mechanics of acting and the stage intruded on the experience of the drama's poetic dimension. In fact, the great playwrights of the late nineteenth century — Henrik Ibsen, Anton Chekhov, August Strindberg, and even the young Bernard Shaw — carved a space for themselves as dramatists by writing plays *in opposition* to the values of their contemporary audiences and to the practice of their contemporary theater — a strategy that would have seemed unimaginable to Aeschylus, Shakespeare, or even Molière. To bring their plays successfully to the stage, new theaters and new theater practices had to be devised, and a new audience had to be found, or made.

This split between the "literary drama" and the "popular theater" has become the condition of twentieth-century drama and theater: plays of the artistic AVANT-GARDE are more readily absorbed into the CANON of literature, while more conventional entertainments — television screenplays, for instance — remain outside it. The major modern playwrights from Ibsen to Luigi Pirandello to Samuel Beckett first wrote for small theaters and were produced by experimental companies playing to coterie audiences on the fringes of the theatrical "mainstream." This sense of modernist "art" as opposed to the values of bourgeois culture was not confined to drama and theater. Modernist fiction and poetry, cubist and abstract painting and sculpture, modern dance, and modern music all developed a new formal complexity, thematic abstraction, and critical self-consciousness in opposition to the sentimental superficiality they found in conventional art forms. This modernist tendency has itself produced a kind of reaction, a desire to bring the devices of popular culture and mass culture into drama, as a way of altering the place of the theater in society and changing the relationship between the spectators and the stage. Bertolt Brecht's ALIENATION EFFECT, Samuel Beckett's importation of circus and film clowns to absurdist theater, or Wole Soyinka's interweaving of African ritual and fourth-wall realism in *Death and the King's Horseman* are all examples of this reaction. For the theater has been challenged by film and television to define its space in contemporary culture, and, given the pervasive availability of other media, theater has increasingly seemed to occupy a place akin to that of opera, among the privileged, elite forms of "high culture." As a result, innovation in today's theater often takes place on the margins or fringes of mainstream theater and mainstream culture: in smaller companies experimenting with new performance forms, in subversive theaters confronting political oppression in many parts of the world, in theaters working to form a new audience and a new sense of theater by conceiving new forms of drama.

Dramatic Genres

Perhaps because its meaning must emerge rapidly and clearly in performance, drama tends to be compressed and condensed; its characters tend toward types, and its action tends toward certain general patterns as well. It is conventional to speak of these kinds of drama as

GENRES, each with its own identifying formal structure and typical themes. Following Aristotle's *Poetics*, for example, TRAGEDY is usually considered to concern the fate of an individual hero, singled out from the community through circumstances and through his or her own actions. In the course of the drama, the hero's course of action entwines with events and circumstances beyond his or her control. As a result, the hero's final downfall — usually, but not always, involving death — seems at once both chosen and inevitable. COMEDY, on the other hand, focuses on the fortunes of the community itself. While the hero of tragedy is usually unique, the heroes of comedy often come in pairs — the lovers who triumph over their parents in romantic comedies, the dupe and the trickster at the center of more ironic or satirical comic modes. While tragedy points toward the hero's downfall or death, comedy generally points toward some kind of broader reform or remaking of society, usually signalled by a wedding or other celebration at the end of the play.

To speak of genre in this way, though, is to suggest that these ideal critical abstractions actually exist in some form, exemplified more or less adequately by particular plays. In fact, terms like *tragedy* and *comedy*, or MELODRAMA, TRAGICOMEDY, FARCE, and others, arise from our efforts to find continuities between extraordinarily different kinds of drama: between plays written in different theaters, for different purposes, to please different audiences, under different historical pressures. When we impose these terms in a prescriptive way, we usually find that the drama eludes them or even calls them into question. Aristotle's brilliant sense of Greek tragedy in the *Poetics*, for instance, hardly "applies" with equal force to Greek plays as different as *Agamemnon*, *Oedipus Rex*, and *The Bacchae*, let alone later plays like *King Lear* or *Miss Julie*. In his essay, "Tragedy and the Common Man," Arthur Miller tries to preserve "tragedy" for modern drama by redefining Aristotle's description of the hero of tragedy. Instead of Aristotle's hero — a man (not a woman) of an elevated social station — Miller argues that the modern hero should be an average, "common" man (not a woman), precisely because the "best families" do not seem normative to us or representative of our basic values. Our exemplary characters are taken from the middle classes. Yet to redefine the hero in this way calls Aristotle's other qualifications — the notion of the hero's character and actions, the meaning of the tragic "fall" — into question as well, forcing us to redefine Aristotelian tragedy in ways that make it something entirely new, something evocative in modern terms.

In approaching the question of genre, then, it is often useful to avoid asking how a play exemplifies the universal and unchanging features of tragedy or comedy. Instead, one could ask how a play or a theater *invents* tragedy or comedy for its contemporary audience. What terms does the drama present, what formal features does it use, to represent human experience? How do historically "local" genres — Renaissance REVENGE TRAGEDY, French NEOCLASSICAL DRAMA, modern THEATER OF THE ABSURD — challenge, preserve, or redefine broader notions of genre?

DRAMATIC FORM

In about 335 B.C., Aristotle's *Poetics* set down the formal elements of drama, and the influence of Aristotle's description has been massive: today we still speak of dramatic form in terms of its PLOT, CHARACTERS, LANGUAGE, THEME, and its performative elements, what Aristotle called MUSIC and SPECTACLE. Any student of drama can profit by thinking about how these formal elements function in a given play. How are the incidents of the play — its plot — arranged? What effects are achieved by *this* ordering, rather than by another? How does the plot relate to the play's narrative story, which includes events dating from before the play begins? How does the plot, the structure of the events — Nora Helmer's first act in *A Doll House* is to enter the house, and her last act is to leave it — develop the play's themes? We might then ask how the play defines its characters. What elements of human experience—family history, psychological motivation, public action—seem to be most prominent in a play's conception of "character"? How do the formal conventions of characterization—blank verse in Shakespeare's plays; the densely imagistic, jazzy language of Shange's *spell #7*—affect our reading of the characters and our understanding of them as representations of human beings?

Although Aristotle presents these elements of drama as distinct, in practice they are mutually defining, making it very difficult to speak of them separately. A play's language, for example, can be analyzed purely for its verbal and rhetorical features, but it is more interesting to ask how the language affects our understanding of the characters or invests the play with certain thematic possibilities. Similarly, while we may regard a play's themes as inside the play, they actually arise only in our interpretation of the play. The themes are something we create by asking certain questions about the play's plotting, its characterization, its use of language. The artificiality of separating these features becomes especially clear when we turn to a play's performative or theatrical dimension. Although Aristotle suggests that a play's literary dimension and its theatrical dimensions are independent, to get a real sense of drama we must see the play both as literature and as theater. We must assess how an audience's sense of the play's plot, characters, and themes are shaped by the kinds of spectacle demanded by the play and provided by the theater. The "meaning" of Greek drama cannot be separated from its conditions of performance: the religious festival, the huge amphitheater, the masked actors, the singing, dancing chorus. The barren "great stage of fools" of *King Lear*, Phaedra's claustral chamber, Winnie's mound of earth in *Happy Days*: these elements of the theatrical spectacle are not outside the meaning of the drama; they are its means, the vehicle for achieving that meaning on the stage.

THE STAGE IN CRITICAL PRACTICE

In a book like this one—indeed, in any book—it is difficult to convey a real sense of the power of theater. It is possible, though, to imagine this experience and to discuss it through the materials collected here: dramatic texts, descriptions of stage practice, illustrations of theaters, photographs, essays. However, an obstacle to understanding arises from a split between the disciplines we use to understand drama and theater. At many colleges and universities, this split is represented in the geography of the campus itself, where the English or Literature departments, which teach dramatic literature, are housed in one building, and the Theater or Drama department, which teaches acting, directing, design, and which actually stages the plays, is housed in another. "Literary" approaches to drama focus our attention initially, sometimes exclusively, on the text of a play and train the complex strategies of poetics and poetic interpretation on it. Such interpretation regards the dramatic text as incomplete and specifies the text's range of possible meanings by placing it in various textual and cultural contexts; in a sense, the negotiation between the text and these contexts determines what we can say the play *means*.

"Theatrical" approaches to drama tend to see a play in terms of stage practice, both in the terms of the play's original production and in the light of performance practice today. This approach interrogates the play's staging: how it can be set, what obstacles it presents to acting and casting, what the dramatic effects of costume and design will be. "Theatrical" interpretation regards the dramatic text as an incomplete design for performance and trains the complex machinery of stage representation—directing, acting, design, costuming— on the task of fleshing the script out as performed action. The meaning of the play in this regard emerges from what we can make the play *do*.

The literary and theatrical approaches to drama and theater share the assumption that plays are not fully meaningful in themselves; they share the sense that the meaning of drama emerges from the kinds of questions we ask of it, the contexts—literary, historical, theoretical, theatrical — in which we can make it perform, and make it mean something in particular. Although each approach can seem needlessly mysterious, involving its own specialized language and critical practice, its own set of "right" questions and "right" answers, this book has been assembled with the conviction that the literary and the theatrical approaches are necessary complements to each other. Thinking about drama requires us to think about how plays perform as literature, in culture and history, and on the stage.

I

DRAMA AND THEATER
IN CLASSICAL ATHENS

REAT DRAMA ARISES WHERE
the theater occupies an important place in the life of the community. In many respects,
Western understanding of drama originated in classical Athens of the fifth century
(500-400) B.C. where the theater played a central role in politics, religion, and society. The
Athenian stage invented forms of tragedy and comedy that persist to the present day. In
tragedy, the Greeks dramatized climactic events in the lives of legendary heroes from prehistory and myth, bringing ethical problems of motive and action to the stage. In comedy,
the theater staged satiric portraits of the life of the POLIS (the city-state), vividly depicting the
energetic conflicts of contemporary Athens in matters of politics, war, education—even
the arts of drama. Playwrights through the long history of the theater have continued to find
in Greek drama both a model and a point of resistance against which to practice their own
craft—see, for example, Jean Racine's *Phaedra* or Bernard Shaw's *Major Barbara* in this
volume. And we need only recall Sigmund Freud's understanding of the "Oedipus complex" to sense the influence of models of action derived from the Greek theater on later
Western culture.

Athens and Sparta were dominant rival powers in fifth-century Greece, which comprised many small independent city-states, each with its own political and cultural institutions, form of government, and alliances. Dramatic performances took place under a variety of circumstances in all Greek cities, but drama as we know it developed in Athens.
Dramatic performance in Athens was part of citywide religious festivals honoring the god
Dionysus, the most important being the CITY DIONYSIA. Plays were produced in contests,
in which playwrights, actors, and choruses competed for prizes and for distinction among
their fellow citizens. These contests, held in an outdoor amphitheater adjoining the sacred
temple of the god, followed several days of religious parades and sacrifices. This connection
between early drama and religion suggests that the essential nature of Greek drama lies in
its supposed "origins" in religious ritual. But the City Dionysia was also a massive civic
spectacle that went far beyond religious worship, emphasizing the theater's implication in
other areas of public life. Dramatic performance contributed to this celebration of Athens'
economic power, cultural accomplishment, and military might. The City Dionysia united
religion and politics, enabling Athenians to celebrate both Dionysus and the achievements
of their *polis*.

THE CITY DIONYSIA

The City Dionysia was the most prominent of the four religious festivals honoring
Dionysus held between December and April in Athens and in the surrounding province of
Attica. Although its purpose was primarily a religious one, the City Dionysia was structured
around a series of contests between individual citizens and between major Athenian social
groups—the ten (later twelve to fifteen) "tribes" that formed the city's basic political and
military units. Dramatic performance was introduced to the City Dionysia during the sixth
century B.C. and became the centerpiece of the elaborate festival. Each year a city magistrate, or ARCHON, honored selected wealthy citizens by choosing them to finance one of
the three principal tragic dramatists competing for a prize at the festival. Each sponsor,
called a CHOREGOS, was responsible for hiring the CHORUS of young men who sang and
danced in the plays. He also hired musicians and provided costumes and other support for
the playwright to whom he was assigned. Later in the period, the state also assigned the

leading actor to the *choregos* as well, and this actor also competed for a prize. The play-wright was responsible for training the chorus and the actors, and for some of the acting himself, and he shared his prize with the *choregos*.

Taking place over several days in late March or early April, the City Dionysia opened with a lavish parade of religious officials and dramatic performers through the city, followed by religious observances and sacrifices held in the theater. Athens also received its annual tribute of goods, money, and slaves from subject and allied states at this time, and war orphans raised at state expense also were displayed to the audience. After this display of religious worship and civic pride, two days were then devoted to contests of DITHYRAMBS, hymns sung and danced by a large chorus. Each of Athens' tribes sponsored two choruses: one consisting of fifty men, another consisting of fifty boys. The city's politics revolved around the tribes, and their contribution to the festival was prominent in this contest, too. The dithyrambic contest involved a thousand Athenian citizens directly in the perfor-mance. Following the dithyrambs, the main dramatic contest began. The competing play-wrights each produced a TRILOGY of tragedies, staged over three days. A trilogy could take a single theme or series of events as its subject (like the three plays of Aeschylus' *Oresteia*, 458 B.C.), or present three distinct, unrelated dramas. A rugged farce called a SATYR PLAY followed the performance of each complete trilogy; these plays parodied a god's activities using actors dressed as satyrs — half-man, half-goat. After 486 B.C., comedies were also awarded prizes, but it is unclear whether the comedies were performed on a single day or spread over several days. Prominent citizens representing each of the tribes served as judges and awarded prizes to the playwrights, their *choregoi*, and the actors.

THE THEATER OF DIONYSUS

The Greek theater was a public spectacle, a kind of cross between Inauguration Day, the Super Bowl, the Academy Awards, Memorial Day, and a major religious holiday. Plays were first produced in the AGORA (marketplace), which often served as a performance place for festivals in Athens and elsewhere. The size and importance of the City Dionysia, how-ever, required a separate site, and a theater was built on the slope of the Acropolis, near the precinct of Dionysus. The original theater, a ring of wooden seats facing a circular floor, was later refined, enlarged, and constructed of stone. By the time of Aeschylus, Euripides, Sophocles, and Aristophanes, the Athenian theater had achieved its basic design: a circular floor for dancing and acting, ringed by a hillside AMPHITHEATER and backed by a low, rectangular building.

The focus of the classical amphitheater — which seated about 14,000 people — was the round ORCHESTRA ("dancing place"), containing the central altar of Dionysus, at which the festival sacrifices were performed. The dithyrambic choruses performed their ecstatic dances in the *orchestra*, and the bulk of the action of the plays took place there as well. Facing the *orchestra*, the hillside was divided into wedge-shaped seating areas. The citizens sat on wooden benches with their tribes: leaders and priests in the front of the sections, women perhaps toward the rear or possibly in a separate section. *Metics* (resident aliens) and visitors were probably seated in a separate area. Special front and center seats were reserved for the judges and the priests of Dionysus.

Behind the *orchestra*, a low building called the SKENE faced the audience. Although the *skene* became a permanent stone structure in the fourth century B.C., in the fifth century it was a temporary wooden building, used for changing masks and possibly also for changing costumes. Playwrights quickly found the theatrical potential latent in the *skene's* facade and set of doors — through these doors the audience heard Agamemnon being mur-dered in his bath, or saw eyeless Oedipus return to confront the Chorus and his future in

EARLY AMPHITHEATER DESIGN

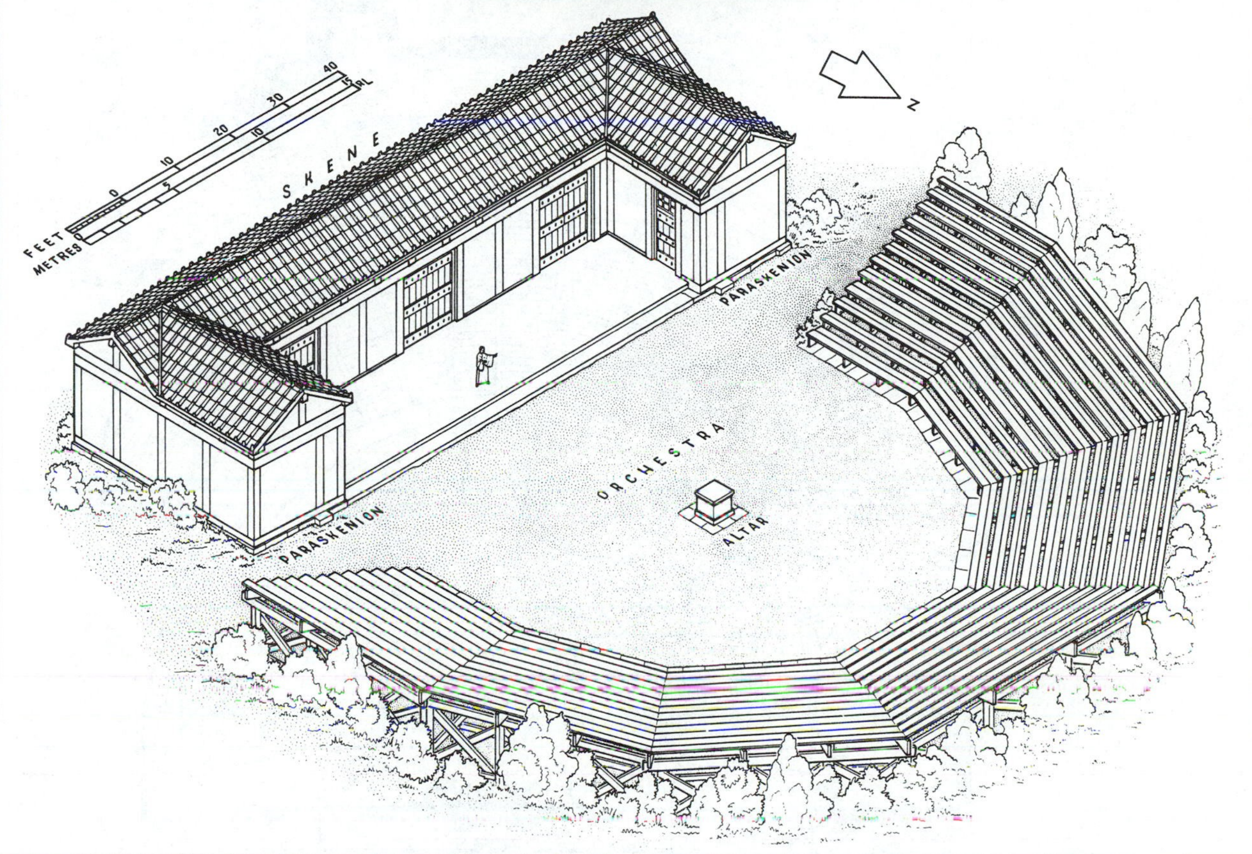

*This drawing is an artist recreation of an early theater in
Eretria, Greece. Notice that the seating is constructed
of wooden benches and the skene
is a temporary structure.*

exile. In Aeschylus' *Agamemnon*, the Watchman awaits the signal fires on the palace roof, and in performance he may have waited on the roof of the *skene*. The theater also used some machinery for scenic effects: a rolling platform used to bring objects or bodies from the *skene* into the *orchestra*; a crane (**MACHINA**) to raise or lower characters — the gods, for instance — from the *orchestra* over the roof of the *skene*; and possibly painted panels to indicate the play's setting or location.

The experience of theater in classical Athens was in some ways akin to participation in other institutions of civic life. Athens was a participatory democracy for its citizens, though citizenship was restricted to adult male Athenians: women, foreigners, slaves, freed slaves, and children were not citizens. Citizens sat in the assembly to discuss and vote on matters of state policy, and they were eligible to serve in all public and military offices as well. Attendance at the City Dionysia was, then, like other aspects of Athenian public life, a privilege and an obligation mainly reserved for citizens. Citizens received tickets to the

THEATER OF DIONYSUS GROUND PLAN

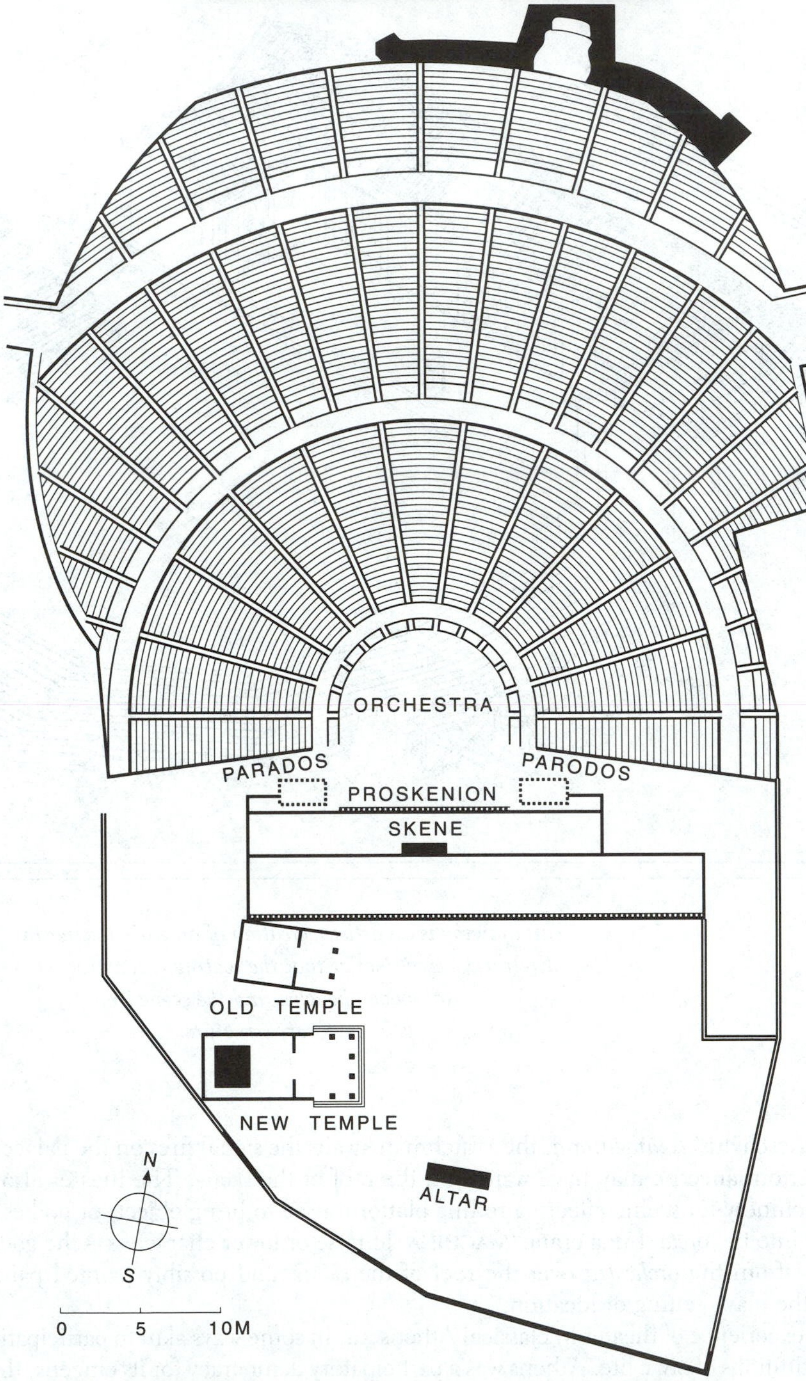

ORCHESTRA

PARADOS   PARODOS

PROSKENION

SKENE

OLD TEMPLE

NEW TEMPLE

ALTAR

N

S

0   5   10M

*This drawing illustrates the ground plan of the sacred precinct of Dionysus in
Athens in the fourth century B.C. Notice that the theater is much larger than
the earlier theater at provincial Eretria. The large and permanent skene was
constructed after the fifth century B.C.*

festival from neighborhood officials; tickets may have been awarded on the basis of participation in other civic obligations — serving in the courts, the assembly, the army. At the theater, citizens sat together with members of their tribe. In a sense, the theater offered a visual map of the organization of Athenian society, for the tribes formed the basis of political participation outside the theater: the Athenian Assembly and the army were similarly arranged by tribe. Organized by tribes, with precedence given to religious officials and with inferior status or nonparticipation accorded to noncitizens such as women, slaves, and foreigners, the theater of Dionysus mirrored the structure of Athenian society.

The fifth century B.C. was the era of Athens' greatest political power and cultural vitality and an era of intense reciprocity between Athenian theater and society. Yet the tension manifest in Greek drama perhaps points to the precarious stability of the Athenian *polis*. The Athenian maritime empire, forged after the defeat of massive Persian forces in 479, was resisted by the smaller Greek states and opposed by Athens' chief rival, the military state of Sparta. Following a long period of hostility and skirmishing, Athens and Sparta declared war against each other in 431 B.C., resulting in Athens' utter defeat in 404. Athenian democracy was replaced by an oppressive oligarchy, the Thirty Tyrants. Although the tyrants were rapidly overthrown and democracy restored, Athens never regained the dynamic cultural life and political power it enjoyed during the fifth century. And although dramatic performance continued after the restoration of democracy, the theater's central role in the *polis* seems to have declined after the Spartan victory. Yet, the theater became one of Greece's most widely disseminated cultural products. When Alexander the Great conquered Greece, the Near East, and northern Africa, he took Greek culture — including theater and drama — with him throughout his empire. And when the Roman Empire later absorbed Alexander's former dominions, it appropriated Greek dramatic traditions, the design of Greek theaters, and the arts and religion of Greece, as well.

DRAMA AND PERFORMANCE

In his *Poetics*, Aristotle suggests that drama originated in the singing of the dithyrambic choruses; a masked actor was first used to respond to the chorus as an individualized "character" in the mid-sixth century B.C., an innovation attributed to the playwright Thespis, about whom little else is known. Aeschylus was the first to use two actors, probably taking one of the parts himself; in the 460s, Sophocles introduced a third actor and was successfully imitated by Aeschylus in his *Oresteia* in 458 B.C. In general, classical tragedy can be performed with three actors, and comedy with four, though each actor may play several parts. All of the performers in the Greek theater — the dramatists, actors, musicians, and chorus members — were male citizens of Athens, as was the bulk of the audience. The dramatic choruses were perhaps composed of young men between the age of seventeen, when military training began, and twenty-one, when Athenian men entered into adulthood.

The chorus of tragedy both sang and danced, and it was expected to perform with grace and precision. Actors and choruses wore full-head masks made of painted linen or lightweight wood. The main characters' masks were individualized, but the members of the chorus all wore identical masks, giving a special force to the conflict between the unique claims of the protagonist and the more diffuse claims of his society. Costuming in comedy was somewhat more complex. Aristophanes' plays suggest that the chorus at times wore animal masks. The comic protagonists' masks, though, were again individualized; since Aristophanes often put his contemporaries in his plays — Socrates in *Clouds*, for instance, or Euripides in *Frogs* — the masks probably resembled these citizens quite closely. Comic actors often sported a leather **PHALLUS**, clearly visible in statues depicting comic actors and of much dramatic use in plays like *Lysistrata*.

CHORUS OF SATYRS

Vase painting showing actors apparently in a satyr play. Note that the central seated figure of Dionysus (holding the polelike thyrsus) is surrounded by actors holding their masks. The older, bearded actor to the right of Dionysus, wearing the lion skin over his shoulder, is apparently

WOMEN IN THE ATHENIAN THEATER

In Athenian tragedy and comedy, female characters were played by men. Not only did men sponsor and write the plays, but the "women" onstage were literally men in disguise. Yet, many plays throw the theatrical convention of men playing women into relief. In *The Bacchae*, Pentheus is possessed by Dionysus when he dresses up as a woman and admires his good looks; in *Lysistrata*, the Spartan woman Lampito is closely and physically examined by Lysistrata and the other women in ways that focus the audience's attention precisely on the fact that the woman is being played by a man. Drama, then, participated fully in Athens' denial of equality to women. Athena says as much in Aeschylus' *The Eumenides* when she judges Orestes' murder of his mother as a lesser crime than Clytaemnestra's murder of her husband. Looking closely at both the drama and its performance can help us to see how justice, power, and gender came to be arranged in Athenian society.

Yet although the theater — like Athenian society — was a male-dominated institution, Greek drama repeatedly inquires into the nature of gendered behavior and uses female characters to focus some of its most challenging questions. Given the absence of women from the stage and their marginal status in the theater and in the state, it is fascinating to

*playing Hercules, the protagonist of the play. The other, younger and
beardless figures may compose the chorus. While Hercules holds an
individualized mask, the chorus members all hold masks similar to each
other, and they wear costumes suggestive of satyrs.*

note how many plays turn on the action of female characters. Women were not themselves
citizens of Athens, and their prerogatives in the *polis* were defined only through marriage.
Yet many of the plays raise critical moral, ethical, and political problems through the
actions of women—Clytaemnestra and Cassandra in Aeschylus' *Agamemnon*, Agave in
Euripides' *The Bacchae*, and the women of Aristophanes' *Lysistrata* and *Assembly of
Women*. Although Aristotle probably voices his contemporaries' views when he remarks in
The Poetics that "a woman can be good, or a slave, although one of these classes [women] is
inferior and the other, as a class, worthless," the theater stages women in ways that implicitly challenge the authority of this "natural" connection between the good, the legitimate,
and the masculine.

Formally, Greek tragedy is organized somewhat differently than modern plays are, for
Greek drama is based on the singing and dancing of the chorus, for whom many of the
plays were named. Most plays begin with a **PROLOGUE**, like the Watchman's speech at the

FORMS OF GREEK DRAMA

ALTHOUGH MANY OF THEIR TRADI-tions were absorbed from Greece, the Romans developed a distinctive theater, quite different from the Athenian stage. From its beginnings, Roman theater was more varied than the Greek stage, including acrobatics, juggling, athletic events, gladiatorial combats, and skits. In the sixth and seventh centuries B.C., Rome was a relatively unimportant town, ruled by the Etruscan kingdoms of northern Italy. In 509, the Romans drove out the Etruscans and founded a republic; the republic expanded its influence throughout the fourth century B.C. and eventually came to control many territories once governed by the Greeks and by Alexander. Much as the Romans absorbed other Greek cultural institutions, they also absorbed Greek theater and drama, which were first performed in Rome in the mid-third century, in 240 B.C. As Rome's political influence expanded, particularly under the Roman Empire (27 B.C.–A.D. 476), the Romans disseminated their characteristic cultural institutions—including theater and drama—throughout Europe, North Africa, and the Middle East.

Like the Greeks, the Romans associated the drama with festivals, but the Romans not only produced plays on festival occasions throughout the year,

ROMAN DRAMA and THEATER

they also developed a much wider variety of theatrical entertainments, of which drama was only a small part. Some of the Roman entertainments descended from the sixth-century *ludi Romani*, which included chariot racing, boxing, and other athletic contests, and Greek drama was first performed in Rome at these games. Moreover, Greek drama not only competed with other nondramatic entertainment, it also was rivalled by an indigenous dramatic form, known as **ATELLAN FARCE**. Associated with the town of Atella (near present-day Naples), these farces were probably improvised comic skits, involving stock characters and played by masked actors.

After the introduction of tragedy and comedy to the *ludi Romani* in 240 B.C., dramatic performances were introduced to several other festivals, and by 179 B.C., drama was being performed at major religious festivals throughout the year: at the *ludi Romani* honoring Jupiter in September, at a second festival consecrated to Jupiter in November, at festivals honoring Flora and the Great Mother in April, and at a festival honoring Apollo in July. Dramatic performances, though still associated with festivals, were much more common in Rome than in fifth-century Athens, not only because special celebrations sometimes

included theatrical performance, but also because any disruption in the rituals connected with the festivals required that the entire festival be repeated, including the dramatic performances.

Given the variety of entertainments offered in Rome—including the chariot races and gladiatorial combats that became increasingly popular in the later Empire, especially after A.D. 300—it is not surprising that the Romans built several different kinds of entertainment buildings, stadiums and racecourses as well as theaters. Yet until 55 B.C., theaters in Rome were temporary, built and taken down for each festival. In the first century B.C., the Romans began to build permanent theaters with some regularity. Like their Greek predecessors, the Roman theaters were outdoor amphitheaters, but the Romans built their theaters on level ground, and their superior engineering—particularly the Romans' use of arches in construction—enabled them to build much more massive buildings. Roman theaters were generally three stories in height. A rectangular stage house, or **SCAENA** stood—like the Greek *skene*—behind the semicircular orchestra and faced a steeply tiered semicircular auditorium. The facade of the *scaena* was elaborately ornamented with columns and porticos. The Romans built theaters of stone and built them throughout the Empire; many of the Greek theaters that remain today were refurbished and redesigned by the Romans.

Although the Romans continued to

opening of *Agamemnon*, followed by the **PARADOS** (entrance) of the singing and dancing chorus. Several **EPISODES** follow, in which the central characters engage one another and the chorus; the chorus itself often sings (and dances) several **ODES**, which are used to enunciate and enlarge on the play's pivotal issues, and the Chorus often becomes a decisive character in the play, as it does in Aeschylus' *Eumenides* or Euripides' *The Bacchae*. The choral odes are written in lyric meters different from the meters used for the characters' speeches. The play's **CATASTROPHE**, or downturn, marks some change in the hero's status

perform plays from the Greek theater, they also developed a native strain of drama represented in the plays of Plautus, Terence, and Seneca. Titus Maccius Plautus (c. 254–c. 184 B.C.) is probably the most influential Roman comic playwright. His earliest surviving plays date from 205 B.C., or about 35 years after Greek drama was first introduced to Rome; Plautus is thought to have based many of his comedies on Greek New Comedy, but none of these prototypes survive. Plautus is thought to have written more than one hundred comedies, many of which—*Amphitryon*, *The Braggart Warrior*, *The Rope*, and *The Menaechmus Twins*, for example—established the formal conventions of later comedy. Publius Terentius Afer (c. 195–159 B.C.)—usually called Terence—was probably born in Carthage and brought to Rome as a slave. Unlike the prolific Plautus, Terence wrote only six comedies, all of which survive, and strove throughout his career to adapt Greek originals to the Roman stage: *The Woman of Andros*, *Mother-in-Law*, *Self-Tormentor*, *Eunuch*, *Phormio*, and *The Brothers*. The plays of Plautus and Terence have been particularly influential on the form and structure of later European comedy; not only did they establish many of the forms and character types developed by later playwrights, but in the late Middle Ages and Renaissance, their plays were often used to teach Latin in the schools, giving rise to generations of playwrights—including William Shakespeare, Christopher Marlowe, and Molière—who found in

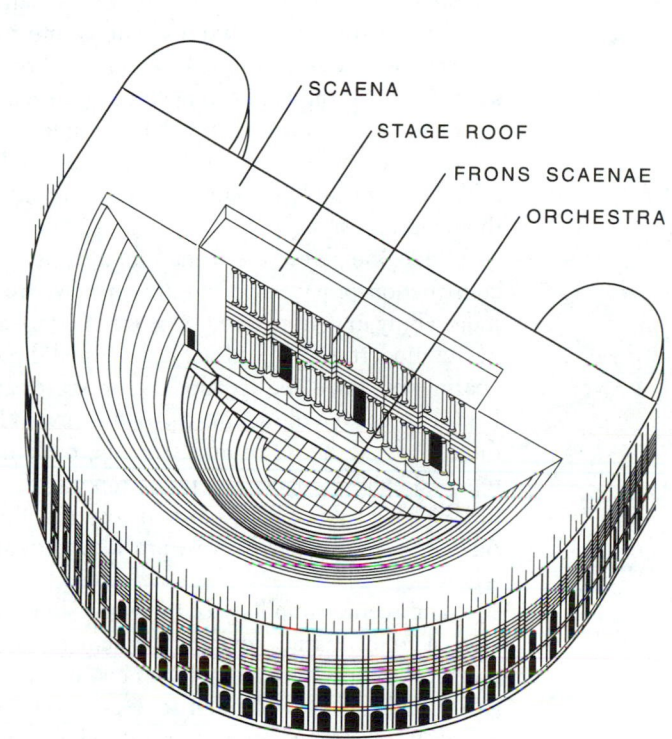

SCAENA
STAGE ROOF
FRONS SCAENAE
ORCHESTRA

THEATER OF MARCELLUS IN ROME, BUILT 13–11 BC.

Roman drama a form for their own contemporary plays.

The only surviving Roman tragedies were written by Lucius Annaeus Seneca (5 B.C.–A.D. 65). Seneca's tragedies were adapted from Greek plays but tend to be more sensational and violent; indeed, it is doubtful if they were performed in the theater. Although only nine of Seneca's plays survive—The Trojan Women, Medea, Oedipus,

Phaedra, *Thyestes*, *Hercules on Oeta*, *Hercules Mad*, *The Phoenecian Women*, *Agamemnon*—Senecan tragedy also exerted an important influence on later drama, especially in the English Renaissance, where Senecan tragedy provided a prototype for the nascent English drama of the sixteenth century.

and is followed by the departure of the characters from the stage and the EXODOS, or final song, dance, and departure of the chorus. Comedy—at least for Aristophanes, whose plays are the only surviving comedies from the period—is structured similarly, though Aristophanes' plays usually include a long PARABASIS, a choral ode delivered to the audience discussing political issues, and a final KOMOS, a scene of choral dancing and revelry.

This formal description, however, hardly accounts for the real and continued power of Greek drama, which arises from an intense and economical relationship between (1) a situation, usually at the point of climax as the play opens, (2) a complex of characters, each with distinctive goals and motives, (3) a chorus used both as a character and as a commentator on the action, and (4) a series of incidents that precipitates a crisis and brings the meaning of the PROTAGONIST's actions into focus. Aristotle termed this crisis the PERIPETEIA, or "reversal," in the external situation or fortunes of the main character, and he argued that it should be accompanied by an act of ANAGNORISIS, or "recognition," in which the character responds to this change. Indeed, Aristotle argued that when the pressure of the tragic action produces a close relationship between reversal and recognition, it instills in the audience intense feelings of fear and pity and then effects CATHARSIS, a purgation of these emotions.

Since the plays were written for a contest, it is not surprising that their language and construction provide opportunity for powerful acting—particularly since the plays were judged only in performance. And yet the stage action of Greek drama is hardly spectacular in the modern sense. Although the visual dimension of Agamemnon's descent from the chariot onto the blood-red tapestry, or Agave's appearance with the severed head of her son Pentheus, or even the aching gait of the men in *Lysistrata* is critical to any understanding of these plays, scenes of murder, suicide, or battle usually take place offstage, to be vividly reported by messengers—as in the reports of Iokaste's death and Oedipus's blinding, or of the Bacchae tearing Pentheus to pieces with their hands. Cassandra's graphic prophecy of Agamemnon's murder likewise provides a brutal counterpoint to the slaughter taking place offstage.

The scenic simplicity of the Greek theater enabled playwrights to achieve a special kind of concentration, one that capitalized on the special circumstances of the open-air, festival theater. Greek comedy has come down to us in the work of only two playwrights, Aristophanes and Menander (c. 342–c. 291 B.C.). While Aristophanes' plays—usually called OLD COMEDY—are energetic and sometimes ribald comedies lampooning the Athenian *polis* and its leading citizens, Menander's comedies—called NEW COMEDY—are more generally concerned with the mores and manners. Menander wrote more than one hundred plays, but only one of his comedies—*The Grouch*—survives. Menander's plays were often focused on a comic conflict between parents and children, devising situations and characters that forged an important link between the Greek and Roman theaters and helped to establish the enduring traditions of stage comedy. While the comedies center on the life of the community, the stage action of Greek tragedy focuses on the relation between the hero's intention, action, and consequence in ways that typically pit the hero's greatest talents against his unavoidable destiny, his society, his family, and himself. This recipe has provided—in plays from the era of Aeschylus, Sophocles, and Euripides to our own—the substance of tragic drama. The characteristic concerns of Greek drama speak undeniably of classical Athens, but the plays also represent trials of decision, suffering, and desperation with a power and purpose that continue to speak to us in accents very much our own.

AESCHYLUS

Aeschylus (c. 523–456 B.C.), whose life spanned the first half of the fifth century, witnessed Athens' chief political and military conflicts and became its preeminent dramatist. His epitaph suggests that he fought at the battle of Marathon against the Persians, and the detailed description of the naval battle at Salamis in his play *The Persians* implies that he may have fought there as well. Aeschylus added the second actor to dramatic performance, only one of his many achievements in the theater. He won his first victory as a playwright at the City Dionysia in 484 B.C., and in 472 B.C. he produced *The Persians*, for which Pericles served as his sponsoring *choregos*. In 468 B.C. he was defeated by Sophocles but was again victorious with his trilogy *The Oresteia* and the accompanying satyr play *Proteus* (now lost) in 458. Aeschylus died in Sicily in 456 B.C. Of about seventy plays that Aeschylus is said to have written, seven survive: *The Suppliants*, *The Persians*, *The Seven Against Thebes*, *Prometheus Bound*, *Agamemnon*, *The Libation Bearers*, and *The Eumenides*.

Agamemnon

Agamemnon is the first of three plays — including *The Libation Bearers* and *The Eumenides* — collectively called *The Oresteia* (458 B.C.). Working from the model of Homer's *Odyssey*, Aeschylus fashioned a complex and original narrative of injustice and retribution, relying on events and characters well-known to his Athenian audience. Indeed, *The Oresteia* depends on the audience's understanding of events that took place a generation before the opening of *Agamemnon*. In the previous generation, the two sons of Pelops — Atreus and Thyestes — began a bitter feud for control of Argos. Thyestes disputed his brother's claim to the throne and seduced his wife; for this he was exiled, but he later returned to Argos with his children to ask Atreus' forgiveness. Atreus received his brother but had the children secretly murdered and baked into a dish that he served to Thyestes. When the truth was revealed to him, Thyestes fled with his one remaining child, Aegisthus, leaving a terrible curse on Atreus, his family, and his descendants.

This curse gives rise to the action of *The Oresteia*, for Aeschylus shows how murder and revenge are played out across the next two generations of the house of Atreus — involving Thyestes' son, Aegisthus; Atreus' two sons, Menelaus and Agamemnon; and Agamemnon's wife, Clytaemnestra, and their children, Iphigeneia, Electra, and Orestes.

The force of much of Aeschylus' drama lies in a powerful economy of action and character, everywhere visible in *Agamemnon*. *Agamemnon* opens with a watchman awaiting the signal fire that

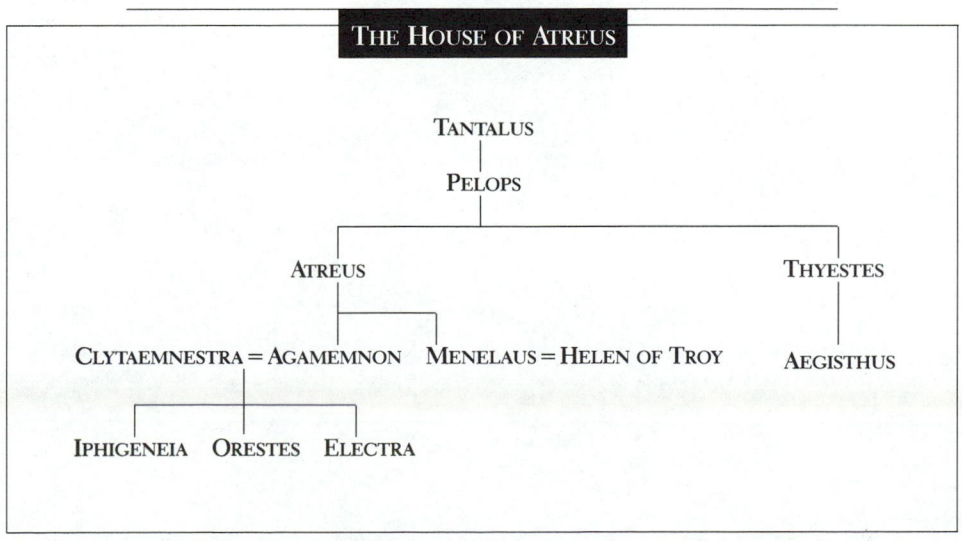

THE HOUSE OF ATREUS

TANTALUS

PELOPS

ATREUS   THYESTES

CLYTAEMNESTRA = AGAMEMNON   MENELAUS = HELEN OF TROY   AEGISTHUS

IPHIGENEIA   ORESTES   ELECTRA

will announce the end of the war on Troy and the return of Agamemnon. This nighttime scene immediately invests the play with a dark sense of foreboding. The opening lyrics of the chorus provide the context for Agamemnon's arrival by recounting the events of ten years before, when Agamemnon, to secure favorable winds for sailing against Troy, sacrificed his own daughter Iphigeneia. Clytaemnestra, eager to punish Agamemnon for his brutal murder of their daughter, is recognized at once as a deceptive and powerful queen, feared by the Argive elders of the chorus. Cassandra's curse — that her prophecies will never be believed — is appallingly enacted before us at the moment of Agamemnon's murder, and Aegisthus appears as a kind of thug, dehumanized by his cruel and vengeful mission. For a modern audience, the most problematic character is Agamemnon himself, seen onstage in only one scene. Yet this brief scene testifies to the intricate knotting of history and temperament in the design of Aeschylus' tragedy. We see Agamemnon's lordly ambition for success and glory, his malleability, and his insensitivity to his own wrongdoing. Treading on the crimson tapestries, Agamemnon follows a trail of blood leading him into the house of Atreus, to his accounting for the murder of Iphigeneia, to Aegisthus' fulfillment of Thyestes' curse, and to his own death.

The cycle of retribution continues in the remaining plays of the cycle. In *The Libation Bearers*, Agamemnon's son, Orestes, returns to Argos from exile, where he had been sent by Aegisthus and Clytaemnestra, in order to avenge the murder of his father. He arrives in secret and surprises his sister, Electra (and the chorus of slave women bearing libations), at Agamemnon's grave. Brother and sister vow to avenge Agamemnon's death. Returning to the palace, they murder Aegisthus, and then Orestes executes justice on his mother, Clytaemnestra, as well. But this act summons the Furies (or Eumenides), horrible demons who haunt and torment Orestes for his crime. The final play, *The Eumenides*, follows Orestes' search for purification. He first appeals to Apollo to release him and then to Athena. Athena calls the Furies and Orestes to a trial before a jury of mortal Athenian judges. Casting her tie-breaking vote for Orestes, Athena releases him from the Furies; to placate them, she invites them to serve as the honorary deities of Athens itself. The terrible curse of the house of Atreus is finally healed by redefining the process of justice. Revenge is replaced by the code of law.

AGAMEMNON

Aeschylus

TRANSLATED BY ROBERT FAGLES

— CHARACTERS —

WATCHMAN	CHORUS, THE OLD MEN OF ARGOS	TIME AND SCENE: *A night in the tenth and final autumn of the Trojan war. The house of Atreus in Argos. Before it, an altar stands unlit; a watchman on the high roofs fights to stay awake.*
CLYTAEMNESTRA	AND THEIR LEADER	
HERALD	ATTENDANTS OF CLYTAEMNESTRA	
AGAMEMNON	AND OF AGAMEMNON,	
CASSANDRA	BODYGUARD OF AEGISTHUS	
AEGISTHUS		

WATCHMAN: Dear gods, set me free from all the pain,
  the long watch I keep, one whole year awake . . .
  propped on my arms, crouched on the roofs of Atreus
  like a dog.
          I know the stars by heart,
5 the armies of the night, and there in the lead
  the ones that bring us snow or the crops of summer,
  bring us all we have —
  our great blazing kings of the sky,
  I know them, when they rise and when they fall . . .
10 and now I watch for the light, the signal-fire
  breaking out of Troy, shouting Troy is taken.
  So she commands, full of her high hopes.
  That woman — she manoeuvres like a man.

  And when I keep to my bed, soaked in dew,
15 and the thoughts go groping through the night
  and the good dreams that used to guard my sleep . . .
  not here, it's the old comrade, terror, at my neck.
  I mustn't sleep, no —

(Shaking himself awake.)

          Look alive, sentry.
  And I try to pick out tunes, I hum a little,
20 a good cure for sleep, and the tears start,
  I cry for the hard times come to the house,
  no longer run like the great place of old.

  Oh for a blessed end to all our pain,
  some godsend burning through the dark —

(Light appears slowly in the east; he struggles to his feet and scans it.)

          I salute you!
25 You dawn of the darkness, you turn night to day —
  I see the light at last.
  They'll be dancing in the streets of Argos
  thanks to you, thanks to this new stroke of —
          Aieeeeee!
  There's your signal clear and true, my queen!
30 Rise up from bed — hurry, lift a cry of triumph
  through the house, praise the gods for the beacon,
  if they've taken Troy . . .
          But there it burns,

fire all the way. I'm for the morning dances.
Master's luck is mine. A throw of the torch
has brought us triple-sixes — we have won!   35
My move now —

(Beginning to dance, then breaking off, lost in thought.)

          Just bring him home. My king,
I'll take your loving hand in mine and then . . .
the rest is silence. The ox is on my tongue.
Aye, but the house and these old stones,
give them a voice and what a tale they'd tell.   40
And so would I, gladly . . .
I speak to those who know; to those who don't
my mind's a blank. I never say a word.

(He climbs down from the roof and disappears into the palace through a side entrance. A CHORUS, *the old men of Argos who have not learned the news of victory, enters and marches round the altar.)*

CHORUS: Ten years gone, ten to the day
  our great avenger went for Priam —   45
    Menelaus and lord Agamemnon,
  two kings with the power of Zeus,
  the twin throne, twin sceptre,
  Atreus' sturdy yoke of sons
  launched Greece in a thousand ships,   50
  armadas cutting loose from the land,
  armies massed for the cause, the rescue —

(From within the palace CLYTAEMNESTRA *raises a cry of triumph.)*

  the heart within them screamed for all-out war!
  Like vultures robbed of their young,
    the agony sends them frenzied,   55
  soaring high from the nest, round and
  round they wheel, they row their wings,
  stroke upon churning thrashing stroke,
  but all the labour, the bed of pain,
    the young are lost forever.   60
  Yet someone hears on high — Apollo,
  Pan or Zeus — the piercing wail
  these guests of heaven raise,
  and drives at the outlaws, late
  but true to revenge, a stabbing Fury!   65

---

8 **our great blazing kings** major constellations that demarcate the seasons

35 **triple-sixes** a winning throw of dice

(CLYTAEMNESTRA *appears at the doors and pauses with her entourage.*)

So towering Zeus the god of guests
drives Atreus' sons at Paris,
all for a woman manned by many
the generations wrestle, knees
70   grinding the dust, the manhood drains,
the spear snaps in the first blood rites
    that marry Greece and Troy.
And now it goes as it goes
and where it ends is Fate.
75   And neither by singeing flesh
nor tipping cups of wine
nor shedding burning tears can you
enchant away the rigid Fury.

(CLYTAEMNESTRA *lights the altar-fires.*)

We are the old, dishonoured ones,
80   the broken husks of men.
Even then they cast us off,
the rescue mission left us here
to prop a child's strength upon a stick.
What if the new sap rises in his chest?
85   He has no soldiery in him,
    no more than we,
and we are aged past ageing,
gloss of the leaf shrivelled,
three legs at a time we falter on.
90   Old men are children once again,
    a dream that sways and wavers
into the hard light of day.
                              But you,
daughter of Leda, queen Clytaemnestra,
what now, what news, what message
95   drives you through the citadel
    burning victims? Look,
the city gods, the gods of Olympus,
gods of the earth and public markets—
all the altars blazing with your gifts!
100   Argos blazes! Torches
race the sunrise up her skies—
drugged by the lulling holy oils,
    unadulterated,
run from the dark vaults of kings.
105   Tell us the news!
What you can, what is right—
Heal us, soothe our fears!
Now the darkness comes to the fore,
now the hope glows through your victims,
110   beating back this raw, relentless anguish
    gnawing at the heart.

(CLYTAEMNESTRA *ignores them and pursues her rituals; they assemble for the opening chorus.*)

O but I still have power to sound the god's command at the
    roads
that launched the kings. The gods breathe power through
    my song,

my fighting strength, Persuasion grows with the years—
I sing how the flight of fury hurled the twin command,   115
    one will that hurled young Greece
and winged the spear of vengeance straight for Troy!
The kings of birds to kings of the beaking prows, one black,
    one with a blaze of silver
        skimmed the palace spearhand right   120
        and swooping lower, all could see,
            plunged their claws in a hare, a mother
        bursting with unborn young—the babies spilling,
quick spurts of blood—cut off the race just dashing
    into life!
Cry, cry for death, but good win out in glory in the end.   125
But the loyal seer of the armies studied Atreus' sons,
two sons with warring hearts—he saw two eagle-kings
    devour the hare and spoke the things to come,
'Years pass, and the long hunt nets the city of Priam,
    the flocks beyond the walls,   130
a kingdom's life and soul—Fate stamps them out.
Just let no curse of the gods lour on us first,
    shatter our giant armour
        forged to strangle Troy. I see
            pure Artemis bristle in pity—   135
            yes, the flying hounds of the Father
        slaughter for armies . . . their own victim . . . a
        woman
trembling young, all born to die—She loathes the eagles'
    feast!'
Cry, cry for death, but good win out in glory in the end.

'Artemis, lovely Artemis, so kind   140
to the ravening lion's tender, helpless cubs,
the suckling young of beasts that stalk the wilds—
    bring this sign for all its fortune,
        all its brutal torment home to birth!
I beg you, Healing Apollo, soothe her before   145
her crosswinds hold us down and moor the ships too long,
pressing us on to another victim . . .
    nothing sacred, no,
        no feast to be eaten
            the architect of vengeance   150

(*Turning to the palace.*)

        growing strong in the house
        with no fear of the husband
here she waits
the terror raging back and back in the future
    the stealth, the law of the hearth, the mother—   155
        Memory womb of Fury child-avenging
        Fury!'
So as the eagles wheeled at the crossroads,
Calchas clashed out the great good blessings mixed with
    doom
    for the halls of kings, and singing with our fate
we cry, cry for death, but good win out in glory in the end.   160

Zeus, great nameless all in all,
if that name will gain his favour,
    I will call him Zeus.

---

89 **three legs** a reference to the use of a walking stick as a third leg in old age

126 **the loyal seer** Calchas, who foretold much hardship at the outset of the Trojan War

165 I have no words to do him justice,
weighing all in the balance,
all I have is Zeus, Zeus—
lift this weight, this torment from my spirit,
cast it once for all.

170 He who was so mighty once,
storming for the wars of heaven,
he has had his day.
And then his son who came to power
met his match in the third fall
175 and he is gone. Zeus, Zeus—
raise your cries and sing him Zeus the Victor!
You will reach the truth:

Zeus has led us on to know,
the Helmsman lays it down as law
that we must suffer, suffer into truth.
180 We cannot sleep, and drop by drop at the heart
the pain of pain remembered comes again,
and we resist, but ripeness comes as well.
From the gods enthroned on the awesome rowing-bench
there comes a violent love.

185 So it was that day the king,
the steersman at the helm of Greece,
would never blame a word the prophet said—
swept away by the wrenching winds of fortune
he conspired! Weatherbound we could not sail,
190 our stores exhausted, fighting strength hard-pressed,
and the squadrons rode in the shallows off Chalkis
where the riptide crashes, drags,

and winds from the north pinned down our hulls at Aulis,
port of anguish . . . head winds starving,
195 sheets and the cables snapped
and the men's minds strayed,
the pride, the bloom of Greece
was raked as time ground on,
ground down, and then the cure for the storm
200 and it was harsher—Calchas cried,
'My captains, Artemis must have blood!'—
so harsh the sons of Atreus
dashed their sceptres on the rocks,
could not hold back the tears,

205 and I still can hear the older warlord saying,
'Obey, obey, or a heavy doom will crush me!—
Oh but doom *will* crush me
once I rend my child,
the glory of my house—
210 a father's hands are stained,
blood of a young girl streaks the altar.
Pain both ways and what is worse?
Desert the fleets, fail the alliance?
No, but stop the winds with a virgin's blood,
215 feed their lust, their fury?—feed their fury!—
Law is law!—
Let all go well.'

And once he slipped his neck in the strap of Fate,
his spirit veering black, impure, unholy,

once he turned he stopped at nothing,
seized with the frenzy 220
blinding driving to outrage—
wretched frenzy, cause of all our grief!
Yes, he had the heart
to sacrifice his daughter,
to bless the war that avenged a woman's loss, 225
a bridal rite that sped the men-of-war.
'My father, father!'—she might pray to the winds;
no innocence moves her judges mad for war.
Her father called his henchmen on,
on with a prayer, 230
'Hoist her over the altar
like a yearling, give it all your strength!
She's fainting—lift her,
sweep her robes around her,
but slip this strap in her gentle curving lips . . . 235
here, gag her hard, a sound will curse the house'—

and the bridle chokes her voice . . . her saffron robes
pouring over the sand
her glance like arrows showering
wounding every murderer through with pity
clear as a picture, live, 240
she strains to call their names . . .
I remember often the days with father's guests
when over the feast her voice unbroken,
pure as the hymn her loving father
bearing third libations, sang to Saving Zeus— 245
transfixed with joy, Atreus' offspring
throbbing out their love.

What comes next? I cannot see it, cannot say.
The strong techniques of Calchas do their work.
But Justice turns the balance scales, 250
sees that we suffer
and we suffer and we learn.
And we will know the future when it comes.
Greet it too early, weep too soon.
It all comes clear in the light of day. 255
Let all go well today, well as she could want,

(*Turning to* CLYTAEMNESTRA.)

our midnight watch, our lone defender,
single-minded queen.
LEADER: We've come,
Clytaemnestra. We respect your power.
Right it is to honour the warlord's woman 260
once he leaves the throne.
But why these fires?
Good news, or more good hopes? We're loyal,
we want to hear, but never blame your silence.
CLYTAEMNESTRA: Let the new day shine—as the proverb
says—
glorious from the womb of Mother Night. 265

(*Lost in prayer, then turning to the* CHORUS.)

You will hear a joy beyond your hopes.
Priam's citadel—the Greeks have taken Troy!

245 **third libations** offered to Zeus, following libations to the gods of
Olympus and the spirits of the dead

LEADER: No, what do you mean? I can't believe it.
CLYTAEMNESTRA: Troy is ours. Is that clear enough?
LEADER: The joy of it,
270   stealing over me, calling up my tears—
CLYTAEMNESTRA: Yes, your eyes expose your loyal hearts.
LEADER: And you have proof?
CLYTAEMNESTRA: I do,
    I must. Unless the god is lying.
LEADER: That,
    or a phantom spirit sends you into raptures.
275 CLYTAEMNESTRA: No one takes me in with visions—senseless
        dreams.
LEADER: Or giddy rumour, you haven't indulged yourself—
CLYTAEMNESTRA: You treat me like a child, you mock me?
LEADER: Then when did they storm the city?
CLYTAEMNESTRA: Last night, I say, the mother of this
        morning.
280 LEADER: And who on earth could run the news so fast?
CLYTAEMNESTRA: The god of fire—rushing fire from Ida!
    And beacon to beacon rushed it on to me,
    my couriers riding home the torch.
                              From Troy
    to the bare rock of Lemnos, Hermes' Spur,
285   and the Escort winged the great light west
    to the Saving Father's face, Mount Athos hurled it
    third in the chain and leaping Ocean's back
    the blaze went dancing on to ecstasy—pitch-pine
    streaming gold like a new-born sun—and brought
290   the word in flame to Mount Makistos' brow.
    No time to waste, straining, fighting sleep,
    that lookout heaved a torch glowing over
    the murderous straits of Euripos to reach
    Messapion's watchmen craning for the signal.
295 Fire for word of fire! tense with the heather
    withered gray, they stack it, set it ablaze—
    the hot force of the beacon never flags,
    it springs the Plain of Asôpos, rears
    like a harvest moon to hit Kithairon's crest
300   and drives new men to drive the fire on.
    That relay pants for the far-flung torch,
    they swell its strength outstripping my commands
    and the light inflames the marsh, the Gorgon's Eye,
    it strikes the peak where the wild goats range—
305   my laws, my fire whips that camp!
    They spare nothing, eager to build its heat,
    and a huge beard of flame overcomes the headland
    beetling down the Saronic Gulf, and flaring south
    it brings the dawn to the Black Widow's face—
310   the watch that looms above your heads—and now
    the true son of the burning flanks of Ida
    crashes on the roofs of Atreus' sons!
    And I ordained it all.
    Torch to torch, running for their lives,
315   one long succession racing home my fire.
                              One,
    first in the laps and last, wins out in triumph.

281 **Ida** mountain near Troy   286 **Saving Father's face** Mount Athos, a
seat of Zeus the Savior in northern Greece   309 **Black Widow's face**
"Spider Mountain," perhaps the citadel of Mycenae

There you have my proof, *my* burning sign, I tell you—
    the power my lord passed on from Troy to me!
LEADER: We'll thank the gods, my lady—first this story,
    let me lose myself in the wonder of it all!   320
    Tell it start to finish, tell us all.
CLYTAEMNESTRA: The city's ours—in our hands this very day!
    I can hear the cries in crossfire rock the walls.
    Pour oil and wine in the same bowl,
    what have you, friendship? A struggle to the end.   325
    So with the victors and the victims—the outcries,
    you can hear them clashing like their fates.

    They are kneeling by the bodies of the dead,
    embracing men and brothers, infants over
    the aged loins that gave them life, and sobbing,   330
    as the yoke constricts their last free breath,
    for every dear one lost.
                    And the others,
    there, plunging breakneck through the night—
    the labour of battle sets them down, ravenous,
    to breakfast on the last remains of Troy.   335
    Not by rank but chance, by the lots they draw,
    they lodge in the houses captured by the spear,
    settling in so soon, released from the open sky,
    the frost and dew. Lucky men, off guard at last,
    they sleep away their first good night in years.   340
    If only they are revering the city's gods,
    the shrines of the gods who love the conquered land,
    no plunderer will be plundered in return.
    Just let no lust, no mad desire seize the armies
    to ravish what they must not touch—   345
    overwhelmed by all they've won!
                              The run for home
    and safety waits, the swerve at the post,
    the final lap of the gruelling two-lap race.
    And even if the men come back with no offence
    to the gods, the avenging dead may never rest—   350
    Oh let no new disaster strike! And here
    you have it, what a woman has to say.
    Let the best win out, clear to see.
    A small desire but all that I could want.
LEADER: Spoken like a man, my lady, loyal,   355
    full of self-command. I've heard your sign
    and now your vision.

(Reaching towards her as she turns and re-enters the palace.)

                    Now to praise the gods.
    The joy is worth the labour.
CHORUS: O Zeus my king and Night, dear Night,
    queen of the house who covers us with glories,   360
    you slung your net on the towers of Troy,
    neither young nor strong could leap
    the giant dredge net of slavery,
        all-embracing ruin.
    I adore you, iron Zeus of the guests   365
    and your revenge—you drew your longbow
    year by year to a taut full draw
    till one bolt, not falling short
    or arching over the stars,
        could split the mark of Paris!   370

The sky stroke of god! — it is all Troy's to tell,
but even I can trace it to its cause:
god does as god decrees.
    And still some say
375 that heaven would never stoop to punish men
who trample the lovely grace of things
untouchable. How wrong they are!
    A curse burns bright on crime —
      full-blown, the father's crimes will blossom,
380   burst into the son's.
Let there be less suffering . . .
give us the sense to live on what we need.

      Bastions of wealth
      are no defence for the man
385   who treads the grand altar of Justice
        down and out of sight.

Persuasion, maddening child of Ruin
overpowers him — Ruin plans it all.
And the wound will smoulder on,
390   there is no cure,
a terrible brilliance kindles on the night.
He is bad bronze scraped on a touchstone:
put to the test, the man goes black.
    Like the boy who chases
395   a bird on the wing, brands his city,
        brings it down and prays,
but the gods are deaf
to the one who turns to crime, they tear him down.

      So Paris learned:
400   he came to Atreus' house
      and shamed the tables spread for guests,
        he stole away the queen.

And she left her land *chaos*, clanging shields,
companions tramping, bronze prows, men in bronze,
405   and she came to Troy with a dowry, death,
strode through the gates
      defiant in every stride,
as prophets of the house looked on and wept,
'Oh the halls and the lords of war,
410   the bed and the fresh prints of love.
I *see* him, unavenging, unavenged,
the stun of his desolation is so clear —
    he longs for the one who lies across the sea
until her phantom seems to sway the house.

415   Her curving images,
      her beauty hurts her lord,
      the eyes starve and the touch
        of love is gone,

'and radiant dreams are passing in the night,
420 the memories throb with sorrow, joy with pain . . .
    it is pain to dream and see desires
slip through the arms,
      a vision lost for ever
winging down the moving drifts of sleep.'
425 So he grieves at the royal hearth
    yet others' grief is worse, far worse.
All through Greece for those who flocked to war

they are holding back the anguish now,
    you can feel it rising now in every house;
I tell you there is much to tear the heart.   430

      They knew the men they sent,
      but now in place of men
      ashes and urns come back
        to every hearth.

War, War, the great gold-broker of corpses   435
holds the balance of the battle on his spear!
Home from the pyres he sends them,
    home from Troy to the loved ones,
heavy with tears, the urns brimmed full,
    the heroes return in gold-dust,   440
dear, light ash for men; and they weep,
they praise them, 'He had skill in the swordplay,'
    'He went down so tall in the onslaught,'
'All for another's woman.' So they mutter
in secret and the rancour steals   445
towards our staunch defenders, Atreus' sons.

      And there they ring the walls, the young,
      the lithe, the handsome hold the graves
      they won in Troy; the enemy earth
        rides over those who conquered.   450

The people's voice is heavy with hatred,
now the curses of the people must be paid,
and now I wait, I listen . . .
    there — there is something breathing
under the night's shroud. God takes aim   455
    at the ones who murder many;
the swarthy Furies stalk the man
gone rich beyond all rights — with a twist
    of fortune grind him down, dissolve him
into the blurring dead — there is no help.   460
The reach for power can recoil,
the bolt of god can strike you at a glance.

      Make me rich with no man's envy,
      neither a raider of cities, no,
      nor slave come face to face with life   465
        overpowered by another.

(Speaking singly.)

  — Fire comes and the news is good,
    it races through the streets
but is it true? Who knows?
Or just another lie from heaven?   470

  — Show us the man so childish, wonderstruck,
    he's fired up with the first torch,
then when the message shifts
he's sick at heart.

           — Just like a woman
to fill with thanks before the truth is clear.   475

  — So gullible. Their stories spread like wildfire,
    they fly fast and die faster;
rumours voiced by women coming to nothing.
LEADER: Soon we'll know her fires for what they are,
her relay race of torches hand-to-hand —   480

know if they're real or just a dream,
the hope of a morning here to take our senses.
I see a herald running from the beach
and a victor's spray of olive shades his eyes
485 and the dust he kicks, twin to the mud of Troy,
shows he has a voice—no kindling timber
on the cliffs, no signal-fires for him.
He can shout the news and give us joy,
or else . . . please, not that.
                                    Bring it on,
490 good fuel to build the first good fires.
And if anyone calls down the worst on Argos
let him reap the rotten harvest of his mind.

(The HERALD *rushes in and kneels on the ground.)*

HERALD: Good Greek earth, the soil of my fathers!
Ten years out, and a morning brings me back.
495 All hopes snapped but one—I'm home at last.
Never dreamed I'd die in Greece, assigned
the narrow plot I love the best.
                                    And now
I salute the land, the light of the sun,
our high lord Zeus and the king of Pytho—
500 no more arrows, master, raining on our heads!
At Scamander's banks we took our share,
your longbow brought us down like plague.
Now come, deliver us, heal us—lord Apollo!
Gods of the market, here, take my salute.
505 And you, my Hermes, Escort,
loving Herald, the herald's shield and prayer!—
And the shining dead of the land who launched the armies,
warm us home . . . we're all the spear has left.
You halls of the kings, you roofs I cherish,
510 sacred seats—you gods that catch the sun,
if your glances ever shone on him in the old days,
greet him well—so many years are lost.
He comes, he brings us light in the darkness,
free for every comrade, Agamemnon lord of men.

515 Give him the royal welcome he deserves!
He hoisted the pickaxe of Zeus who brings revenge,
he dug Troy down, he worked her soil down,
the shrines of her gods and the high altars, gone!—
and the seed of her wide earth he ground to bits.
520 That's the yoke he claps on Troy. The king,
the son of Atreus comes. The man is blest,
the one man alive to merit such rewards.

Neither Paris nor Troy, partners to the end,
can say their work outweighs their wages now.
525 Convicted of rapine, stripped of all his spoils,
and his father's house and the land that gave it life—
he's scythed them to the roots. The sons of Priam
pay the price twice over.
LEADER: Welcome home
from the wars, herald, long live your joy.

499-502 **the king of Pytho . . . plague** at Troy, when Agamemnon
refused to release a daughter of Apollo's priest, Apollo ("king of Pytho")
visited a plague upon the Greeks by shooting his arrows among
them   528 **pay the price twice over** in ancient Greek law, double damages were the penalty for theft

HERALD: *Our* joy—
now I could die gladly. Say the word, dear gods.   530
LEADER: Longing for your country left you raw?
HERALD: The tears fill my eyes, for joy.
LEADER: You too,
down the sweet disease that kills a man
with kindness . . .
HERALD: Go on, I don't see what you—
LEADER: Love
for the ones who love you—that's what took you.
HERALD: You mean   535
the land and the armies hungered for each other?
LEADER: There were times I thought I'd faint with longing.
HERALD: So anxious for the armies, why?
LEADER: For years now,
only my silence kept me free from harm.
HERALD: What,
with the kings gone did someone threaten you?
LEADER: So much . . .   540
now as you say, it would be good to die.
HERALD: True, we *have* done well.
Think back in the years and what have you?
A few runs of luck, a lot that's bad.
Who but a god can go through life unmarked?   545
A long, hard pull we had, if I would tell it all.
The iron rations, penned in the gangways
hock by jowl like sheep. Whatever miseries
break a man, our quota, every sun-starved day.

Then on the beaches it was worse. Dug in   550
under the enemy ramparts—deadly going.
Out of the sky, out of the marshy flats
the dews soaked us, turned the ruts we fought from
into gullies, made our gear, our scalps
crawl with lice.
                        And talk of the cold,   555
the sleet to freeze the gulls, and the big snows
come avalanching down from Ida. Oh but the heat,
the sea and the windless noons, the swells asleep,
dropped to a dead calm . . .

But why weep now?   560
It's over for us, over for them.
The dead can rest and never rise again;
no need to call their muster. We're alive,
do we have to go on raking up old wounds?
Good-bye to all that. Glad I am to say it.   565

For us, the remains of the Greek contingents,
the good wins out, no pain can tip the scales,
not now. So shout this boast to the bright sun—
fitting it is—wing it over the seas and rolling earth:

'Once when an Argive expedition captured Troy   570
they hauled these spoils back to the gods of Greece,
they bolted them high across the temple doors,
the glory of the past!'
                        And hearing that,
men will applaud our city and our chiefs,
and Zeus will have the hero's share of fame—   575
he did the work.
                        That's all I have to say.

LEADER: I'm convinced, glad that I was wrong.
Never too old to learn; it keeps me young.

(CLYTAEMNESTRA *enters with her women.*)

First the house and the queen, it's their affair,
but I can taste the riches.

580   CLYTAEMNESTRA: I cried out long ago! —
for joy, when the first herald came burning
through the night and told the city's fall.
And there were some who smiled and said,
'A few fires persuade you Troy's in ashes.
585   Women, women, elated over nothing.'

You made me seem deranged.
For all that I sacrificed — a woman's way,
you'll say — station to station on the walls
we lifted cries of triumph that resounded
590   in the temples of the gods. We lulled and blessed
the fires with myrrh and they consumed our victims.

(*Turning to the* HERALD.)

But enough. Why prolong the story?
From the king himself I'll gather all I need.
Now for the best way to welcome home
my lord, my good lord . . .
595   No time to lose!
What dawn can feast a woman's eyes like this?
I can see the light, the husband plucked from war
by the Saving God and open wide the gates.

Tell him that, and have him come with speed,
600   the people's darling — how they long for him.
And for his wife,
may he return and find her true at hall,
just as the day he left her, faithful to the last.
A watchdog gentle to him alone,

(*Glancing towards the palace.*)

savage
605   to those who cross his path. I have not changed.
The strains of time can never break our seal.
In love with a new lord, in ill repute I am
as practised as I am in dyeing bronze.

That is my boast, teeming with the truth.
610   I am proud, a woman of my nobility —
I'd hurl it from the roofs!

(*She turns sharply, enters the palace.*)

LEADER: She speaks well, but it takes no seer to know
she only says what's right.

(*The* HERALD *attempts to leave; the leader takes him by the arm.*)

Wait, one thing.
Menelaus, is he home too, safe with the men?
615   The power of the land — dear king.
HERALD: I doubt that lies will help my friends,
in the lean months to come.
LEADER: Help us somehow, tell the truth as well.
But when the two conflict it's hard to hide —
out with it.

580 **I can taste the riches** *according to custom, the bearer of good news
was rewarded*

HERALD: He's lost, gone from the fleets!   620
He and his ship, it's true.
LEADER: After you watched him
pull away from Troy? Or did some storm
attack you all and tear him off the line?
HERALD: There,
like a marksman, the whole disaster cut to a word.
LEADER: How do the escorts give him out — dead or alive?   625
HERALD: No clear report. No one knows . . .
only the wheeling sun that heats the earth to life.
LEADER: But then the storm — how did it reach the ships?
How did it end? Were the angry gods on hand?
HERALD: This blessed day, ruin it with *them*?   630
Better to keep their trophies far apart.

When a runner comes, his face in tears,
saddled with what his city dreaded most,
the armies routed, two wounds in one,
one to the city, one to hearth and home . . .   635
our best men, droves of them, victims
herded from every house by the two-barb whip
that Ares likes to crack,
                         that charioteer
who packs destruction shaft by shaft,
careering on with his brace of bloody mares —   640
when he comes in, I tell you, dragging that much pain,
wail your battle-hymn to the Furies, and high time!
But when he brings salvation home to a city
singing out her heart —
how can I mix the good with so much bad   645
and blurt out this? —
                    'Storms swept the Greeks,
and not without the anger of the gods!'

Those enemies for ages, fire and water,
sealed a pact and showed it to the world —
they crushed our wretched squadrons.
                              Night looming,   650
breakers lunging in for the kill
and the black gales come brawling out of the north —
ships ramming, prow into hooking prow, gored
by the rush-and-buck of hurricane pounding rain
by the cloudburst —
                    ships stampeding into the darkness,   655
lashed and spun by the savage shepherd's hand!

But when the sun comes up to light the skies
I see the Aegean heaving into a great bloom
of corpses . . . Greeks, the pick of a generation
scattered through the wrecks and broken spars.   660

But not us, not our ship, our hull untouched.
Someone stole us away or begged us off.
No mortal — a god, death grip on the tiller,
or lady luck herself, perched on the helm,
she pulled us through, she saved us. Aye,   665
we'll never battle the heavy surf at anchor,
never shipwreck up some rocky coast.

But once we cleared that sea-hell, not even
trusting luck in the cold light of day,

648 **fire and water** *lightning and the sea*

670 we battened on our troubles, they were fresh—
the armada punished, bludgeoned into nothing.
And now if one of them still has the breath
he's saying *we are lost.* Why not?
We say the same of him. Well,
here's to the best.
675   And Menelaus?
Look to it, he's come back, and yet . . .
if a shaft of the sun can track him down,
alive, and his eyes full of the old fire—
thanks to the strategies of Zeus, Zeus
680 would never tear the house out by the roots—
then there's hope our man will make it home.

You've heard it all. Now you have the truth.

(Rushing out.)

CHORUS: Who—what power named the name that drove your
fate?—
what hidden brain could divine your future,
685 steer that word to the mark,
to the bride of spears,
the whirlpool churning armies,
Oh for all the world a Helen!
Hell at the prows, hell at the gates
690 hell on the men-of-war,
from her lair's sheer veils she drifted
launched by the giant western wind,
and the long tall waves of men in armour,
huntsmen trailing the oar-blades' dying spoor
695 slipped into her moorings,
Simois' mouth that chokes with foliage,
bayed for bloody strife,
for Troy's Blood Wedding Day—she drives her word,
her burning will to the birth, the Fury
700 late but true to the cause,
to the tables shamed
and Zeus who guards the hearth—
the Fury makes the Trojans pay!
Shouting their hymns, hymns for the bride
705 hymns for the kinsmen doomed
to the wedding march of Fate.
Troy changed her tune in her late age,
and I think I hear the dirges mourning
'Paris, born and groomed for the bed of Fate!'
710 They mourn with their life breath,
they sing their last, the sons of Priam
born for bloody slaughter.

So a man once reared
a lion cub at hall, snatched
715 from the breast, still craving milk
in the first flush of life.
A captivating pet for the young,
and the old men adored it, pampered it
in their arms, day in, day out,
720 like an infant just born.
Its eyes on fire, little beggar,
fawning for its belly, slave to food.

But it came of age
and the parent strain broke out

and it paid its breeders back.   725
Grateful it was, it went
through the flock to prepare a feast,
an illicit orgy—the house swam with blood,
none could resist that agony—
massacre vast and raw!   730
From god there came a priest of ruin,
adopted by the house to lend it warmth.
And the first sensation Helen brought to Troy . . .
call it a spirit
shimmer of winds dying   735
glory light as gold
shaft of the eyes dissolving, open bloom
that wounds the heart with love.
But veering wild in mid-flight
she whirled her wedding on to a stabbing end,   740
slashed at the sons of Priam—hearthmate, friend to the
death,
sped by Zeus who speeds the guest,
a bride of tears, a Fury.

There's an ancient saying, old as man himself:
men's prosperity   745
never will die childless,
once full-grown it breeds.
Sprung from the great good fortune in the race
comes bloom on bloom of pain—
insatiable wealth! But not I,   750
I alone say this. Only the reckless act
can breed impiety, multiplying crime on crime,
while the house kept straight and just
is blessed with radiant children.

But ancient Violence longs to breed,   755
new Violence comes
when its fatal hour comes, the demon comes
to take her toll—no war, no force, no prayer
can hinder the midnight Fury stamped
with parent Fury moving through the house.   760

But Justice shines in sooty hovels,
loves the decent life.
From proud halls crusted with gilt by filthy hands
she turns her eyes to find the pure in spirit—
spurning the wealth stamped counterfeit with praise,   765
she steers all things towards their destined end.

(AGAMEMNON enters in his chariot, his plunder borne before him by his entourage; behind him, half hidden, stands CASSANDRA. The old men press towards him.)

Come, my king, the scourge of Troy,
the true son of Atreus—
How to salute you, how to praise you
neither too high nor low, but hit   770
the note of praise that suits the hour?
So many prize some brave display,
they prefer some flaunt of honour
once they break the bounds.
When a man fails they share his grief,   775
but the pain can never cut them to the quick.

725 **it paid its breeders back** on reaching maturity, children customarily made thank offerings to their parents

When a man succeeds they share his glory,
torturing their faces into smiles.
But the good shepherd knows his flock.
780 When the eyes seem to brim with love
  and it is only unction, fawning,
he will know, better than we can know.
That day you marshalled the armies
all for Helen — no hiding it now —
785 I drew you in my mind in black;
you seemed a menace at the helm,
  sending men to the grave
to bring her home, that hell on earth.
But now from the depths of trust and love
790 I say Well fought, well won —
  the end is worth the labour!
Search, my king, and learn at last
who stayed at home and kept their faith
  and who betrayed the city.

AGAMEMNON: First,
795 with justice I salute my Argos and my gods,
my accomplices who brought me home and won
my rights from Priam's Troy — the just gods.
No need to hear our pleas. Once for all
they consigned their lots to the urn of blood,
800 they pitched on death for men, annihilation
for the city. Hope's hand, hovering
over the urn of mercy, left it empty.
Look for the smoke — it is the city's seamark,
building even now.
                               The storms of ruin live!
805 Her last dying breath, rising up from the ashes
sends us gales of incense rich in gold.

For that we must thank the gods with a sacrifice
our sons will long remember. For their mad outrage
of a queen we raped their city — we were right.
810 The beast of Argos, foals of the wild mare,
thousands massed in armour rose on the night
the Pleiades went down, and crashing through
their walls our bloody lion lapped its fill,
gorging on the blood of kings.
                               Our thanks to the gods,
815 long drawn out, but it is just the prelude.

(CLYTAEMNESTRA *approaches with her women; they are carrying
dark red tapestries.* AGAMEMNON *turns to the leader.*)

And your concern, old man, is on my mind.
I hear you and agree, I will support you.
How rare, men with the character to praise
a friend's success without a trace of envy,
820 poison to the heart — it deals a double blow.
Your own losses weigh you down but then,
look at your neighbour's fortune and you weep.
Well I know. I understand society,
the flattering mirror of the proud.
                               My comrades . . .

they're shadows, I tell you, ghosts of men   825
who swore they'd die for me. Only Odysseus:
I dragged that man to the wars but once in harness
he was a trace-horse, he gave his all for me.
Dead or alive, no matter, I can praise him.

And now this cause involving men and gods.   830
We must summon the city for a trial,
found a national tribunal. Whatever's healthy,
shore it up with law and help it flourish.
Wherever something calls for drastic cures
we make our noblest effort: amputate or wield   835
the healing iron, burn the cancer at the roots.

Now I go to my father's house —
I give the gods my right hand, my first salute.
The ones who sent me forth have brought me home.

(*He starts down from the chariot, looks at* CLYTAEMNESTRA,
stops, and offers up a prayer.)

Victory, you have sped my way before,   840
now speed me to the last.

(CLYTAEMNESTRA *turns from the king to the* CHORUS.)

CLYTAEMNESTRA: Old nobility of Argos
gathered here, I am not ashamed to tell you
how I love the man. I am older,
and the fear dies away . . . I am human.
Nothing I say was learned from others.   845
This is my life, my ordeal, long as the siege
he laid at Troy and more demanding.
                               First,
when a woman sits at home and the man is gone,
the loneliness is terrible,
unconscionable . . .   850
and the rumours spread and fester,
a runner comes with something dreadful,
close on his heels the next and his news worse,
and they shout it out and the whole house can hear;
and wounds — if he took one wound for each report   855
to penetrate these walls, he's gashed like a dragnet,
more, if he had only died . . .
for each death that swelled his record, he could boast
like a triple-bodied Geryon risen from the grave,
'Three shrouds I dug from the earth, one for every body 860
that went down!'
                               The rumours broke like fever,
broke and then rose higher. There were times
they cut me down and eased my throat from the noose.
I wavered between the living and the dead.

(*Turning to* AGAMEMNON.)

                               And so
our child is gone, not standing by our side,   865
the bond of our dearest pledges, mine and yours;
by all rights our child should be here . . .
Orestes. You seem startled.
You needn't be. Our loyal brother-in-arms

799-802 **they consigned . . . empty** Athenian citizens voted in law cases
by placing one hand over each of two urns and dropping a voting-pebble
into either the urn for acquittal or the urn for condemnation   810 **the
wild mare** the Trojan Horse

826-8 **Only Odysseus . . . trace-horse** to try to evade conscription for the
Trojan War, Odysseus feigned madness, but performed loyally once at
war   859 **Geryon** a three-bodied giant killed by Heracles

870 will take good care of him, Strophios the Phocian.
He warned from the start we court two griefs in one.
You risk all on the wars—and what if the people
rise up howling for the king, and anarchy
should dash our plans?

                        Men, it is their nature,
875 trampling on the fighter once he's down.
Our child is gone. That is my self-defence
and it is true.

                For me, the tears that welled
like springs are dry. I have no tears to spare.
I'd watch till late at night, my eyes still burn,
880 I sobbed by the torch I lit for you alone

(Glancing towards the palace.)

I never let it die . . . but in my dreams
the high thin wail of a gnat would rouse me,
piercing like a trumpet—I could see you
suffer more than all
885 the hours that slept with me could ever bear.

I endured it all. And now, free of grief,
I would salute that man the watchdog of the fold,
the mainroyal, saving stay of the vessel,
rooted oak that thrusts the roof sky-high,
890 the father's one true heir.
Land at dawn to the shipwrecked past all hope,
light of the morning burning off the night of storm,
the cold clear spring to the parched horseman—
O the ecstasy, to flee the yoke of Fate!
895 It is right to use the titles he deserves.
Let envy keep her distance. We have suffered
long enough.

(Reaching towards AGAMEMNON.)

                Come to me now, my dearest,
down from the car of war, but never set the foot
that stamped out Troy on earth again, my great one.

900 Women, why delay? You have your orders.
Pave his way with tapestries.

(They begin to spread the crimson tapestries between the king and
the palace doors.)

                        Quickly.
Let the red stream flow and bear him home
to the home he never hoped to see—Justice,
lead him in!
                Leave all the rest to me.
905 The spirit within me never yields to sleep.
We will set things right, with the god's help.
We will do whatever Fate requires.
AGAMEMNON: There
is Leda's daughter, the keeper of my house.
And the speech to suit my absence, much too long.
910 But the praise that does us justice,
let it come from others, then we prize it.
                                This—
you treat me like a woman. Grovelling, gaping up at me—

908 **Leda** visited by Zeus in the form of a swan, Leda conceived both
Clytaemnestra and Helen

what am I, some barbarian peacocking out of Asia?
Never cross my path with robes and draw the lightning.
Never—only the gods deserve the pomps of honour   915
and the stiff brocades of fame. To walk on them . . .
I am human, and it makes my pulses stir
with dread.
                Give me the tributes of a man
and not a god, a little earth to walk on,
not this gorgeous work.   920
There is no need to sound my reputation.
I have a sense of right and wrong, what's more—
heaven's proudest gift. Call no man blest
until he ends his life in peace, fulfilled.
If I can live by what I say, I have no fear.   925
CLYTAEMNESTRA: One thing more. Be true to your ideals and
    tell me—
AGAMEMNON: True to my ideals? Once I violate them I am
    lost.
CLYTAEMNESTRA: Would you have sworn this act to god in a
    time of terror?
AGAMEMNON: Yes, if a prophet called for a last, drastic rite.
CLYTAEMNESTRA: But Priam—can you see him if he had your   930
    success?
AGAMEMNON: Striding on the tapestries of god, I see him
    now.
CLYTAEMNESTRA: And *you* fear the reproach of common
    men?
AGAMEMNON: The voice of the people—aye, they have
    enormous power.
CLYTAEMNESTRA: Perhaps, but where's the glory without a
    little gall?
AGAMEMNON: And where's the woman in all this lust for   935
    glory?
CLYTAEMNESTRA: But the great victor—it becomes him to
    give way.
AGAMEMNON: Victory in this . . . war of ours, it means so
    much to you?
CLYTAEMNESTRA: O give way! The power is yours if you
    surrender,
all of your own free will, to me!
AGAMEMNON: Enough.
If you are so determined—   940

(Turning to the women, pointing to his boots.)

Let someone help me off with these at least.
Old slaves, they've stood me well.
                        Hurry,
and while I tread his splendours dyed red in the sea,
may no god watch and strike me down with envy
from on high. I feel such shame—   945
to tread the life of the house, a kingdom's worth
of silver in the weaving.

(He steps down from the chariot to the tapestries and reveals
CASSANDRA, dressed in the sacred regalia, the fillets, robes, and
sceptre of Apollo.)

                        Done is done.
Escort this stranger in, be gentle.
Conquer with compassion. Then the gods
shine down upon you, gently. No one chooses   950

the yoke of slavery, not of one's free will—
and she least of all. The gift of the armies,
flower and pride of all the wealth we won,
she follows me from Troy.
                              And now,
955 since you have brought me down with your insistence,
just this once I enter my father's house,
trampling royal crimson as I go.

(*He takes his first steps and pauses.*)

CLYTAEMNESTRA: There is the sea
and who will drain it dry? Precious as silver,
inexhaustible, ever-new, it breeds the more we reap it—
960 tides on tides of crimson dye our robes blood-red.
Our lives are based on wealth, my king,
the gods have seen to that.
Destitution, our house has never heard the word.
I would have sworn to tread on legacies of robes,
965 at one command from an oracle, deplete the house—
suffer the worst to bring that dear life back!

(*Encouraged,* AGAMEMNON *strides to the entrance.*)

When the root lives on, the new leaves come back,
spreading a dense shroud of shade across the house
to thwart the Dog Star's fury. So you return
970 to the father's hearth, you bring us warmth in winter
like the sun—
                    And you are Zeus when Zeus
tramples the bitter virgin grape for new wine
and the welcome chill steals through the halls, at last
the master moves among the shadows of his house,
    fulfilled.

(AGAMEMNON *goes over the threshold; the women gather up the tapestries while* CLYTAEMNESTRA *prays.*)

975 Zeus, Zeus, master of all fulfilment, now fulfil our
        prayers—
speed our rites to their fulfilment once for all!

(*She enters the palace, the doors close, the old men huddle in terror.*)

CHORUS: Why, why does it rock me, never stops,
this terror beating down my heart,
        this seer that sees it all—
980 it beats its wings, uncalled unpaid
thrust on the lungs
the mercenary song beats on and on
singing a prophet's strain—
        and I can't throw it off
985 like dreams that make no sense,
and the strength drains
that filled the mind with trust,
and the years drift by and the driven sand
        has buried the mooring lines
990 that churned when the armoured squadrons cut for Troy . . .
and now I believe it, I can prove he's home,
        my own clear eyes for witness—
                              Agamemnon!

Still it's chanting, beating deep so deep in the heart
this dirge of the Furies, oh dear god,
not fit for the lyre, its own master   995
    it kills our spirit
kills our hopes
and it's real, true, no fantasy—
        stark terror whirls the brain
                and the end is coming   1000
                Justice comes to birth—
I pray my fears prove false and fall
and die and never come to birth!
Even exultant health, well we know,
    exceeds its limits, comes so near disease   1005
it can breach the wall between them.

Even a man's fate, held true on course,
in a blinding flash rams some hidden reef;
but if caution only casts the pick of the cargo—
one well-balanced cast—   1010
the house will not go down, not outright;
labouring under its wealth of grief
the ship of state rides on.

Yes, and the great green bounty of god,
sown in the furrows year by year and reaped each fall   1015
can end the plague of famine.

But a man's life-blood
    is dark and mortal.
Once it wets the earth
what song can sing it back?   1020
Not even the master-healer
    who brought the dead to life—
Zeus stopped the man before he did more harm.

Oh, if only the gods had never forged
the chain that curbs our excess,   1025
    one man's fate curbing the next man's fate,
my heart would outrace my song, I'd pour out all I feel—
        but no, I choke with anguish,
                mutter through the nights.
Never to ravel out a hope in time   1030
and the brain is swarming, burning—

(CLYTAEMNESTRA *emerges from the palace and goes to* CASSANDRA, *impassive in the chariot.*)

CLYTAEMNESTRA: Won't you come inside? I mean you,
    Cassandra.
Zeus in all his mercy wants you to share
some victory libations with the house.
The slaves are flocking. Come, lead them   1035
up to the altar of the god who guards
our dearest treasures.
                    Down from the chariot,
this is no time for pride. Why even Heracles,
they say, was sold into bondage long ago,
he had to endure the bitter bread of slaves.   1040

969 **Dog Star** Sirius, whose rising commonly marks the hot "dog days" of summer

995 **not fit for the lyre** the lyre-god, Apollo, required songs of joy, not mourning   1021 **the master-healer** the physician Asclepius, who restored a dead man to life and was struck dead in consequence by Zeus   1038-40 **Why even Heracles . . . slaves** as punishment, Heracles was sold in bondage by Hermes to Omphale, queen of Lydia

But if the yoke descends on you, be grateful
for a master born and reared in ancient wealth.
Those who reap a harvest past their hopes
are merciless to their slaves.
                       From us
1045   you will receive what custom says is right.

(CASSANDRA *remains impassive.*)

LEADER: It's *you* she is speaking to, it's all too clear.
    You're caught in the nets of doom—obey
    if you can obey, unless you cannot bear to.
CLYTAEMNESTRA: Unless she's like a swallow, possessed
1050   of her own barbaric song, strange, dark.
    I speak directly as I can—she must obey.
LEADER: Go with her. Make the best of it, she's right.
    Step down from the seat, obey her.
CLYTAEMNESTRA: Do it *now*—
    I have no time to spend outside. Already
1055   the victims crowd the hearth, the Navelstone,
    to bless this day of joy I never hoped to see!—
    our victims waiting for the fire and the knife,
    and you,
    if you want to taste our mystic rites, come now.
    If my words can't reach you—

(*Turning to the* LEADER.)

1060   Give her a sign,
    one of her exotic handsigns.
LEADER: I think
    the stranger needs an interpreter, someone clear.
    She's like a wild creature, fresh caught.
CLYTAEMNESTRA: She's mad,
    her evil genius murmuring in her ears.
1065   She comes from a *city* fresh caught.
    She must learn to take the cutting bridle
    before she foams her spirit off in blood—
    and that's the last I waste on her contempt!

(*Wheeling, re-entering the palace. The* LEADER *turns to*
CASSANDRA, *who remains transfixed.*)

LEADER: Not I, I pity her. I will be gentle.
1070   Come, poor thing. Leave the empty chariot—
    Of your own free will try on the yoke of Fate.
CASSANDRA: Aieeeeee! Earth—Mother—
               Curse of the Earth—Apollo Apollo!
LEADER: Why cry to Apollo?
    He's not the god to call with sounds of mourning.
CASSANDRA: Aieeeeee! Earth—Mother—
1075   Rape of the Earth—Apollo Apollo!
LEADER: Again, it's a bad omen.
    She cries for the god who wants no part of grief.

(CASSANDRA *steps from the chariot, looks slowly towards the rooftops of the palace.*)

CASSANDRA: God of the long road,
          Apollo *Apollo* my destroyer—
1080   you destroy me once, destroy me twice—
LEADER: She's about to sense her own ordeal, I think.
    Slave that she is, the god lives on inside her.

1055 **the Navelstone** an allusion to Apollo's "World Navel," a stone
erected at Delphi

CASSANDRA: God of the iron marches,
          Apollo *Apollo* my destroyer—
    where, where have you led me now? what house—   1085
LEADER: The house of Atreus and his sons. Really—
    don't you know? It's true, see for yourself.
CASSANDRA: No . . . the house that hates god,
    an echoing womb of guilt, kinsmen
        torturing kinsmen, severed heads,   1090
    slaughterhouse of heroes, soil streaming blood—
LEADER: A keen hound, this stranger.
    Trailing murder, and murder she will find.
CASSANDRA: See, my witnesses—
    I trust to them, to the babies   1095
        wailing, skewered on the sword,
    their flesh charred, the father gorging on their parts—
LEADER: We'd heard your fame as a seer,
    but no one looks for seers in Argos.
CASSANDRA: Oh no, what horror, what new plot,   1100
    new agony this?—
    it's growing, massing, deep in the house,
        a plot, a monstrous—*thing*
            to crush the loved ones, no,
        there is no cure, and rescue's far away and—   1105
LEADER: I can't read these signs; I knew the first,
    the city rings with them.
CASSANDRA: You, you godforsaken—you'd do *this*?
    The lord of your bed,
    you bathe him . . . his body glistens, then—   1110
            how to tell the climax?—
          comes so quickly, see,
    hand over hand shoots out, hauling ropes—
                       then lunge!
LEADER: Still lost. Her riddles, her dark words of god—
    I'm groping, helpless.
CASSANDRA: No no, look *there*!—   1115
    what's that? some net flung out of hell—
    No, *she* is the snare,
    the bedmate, deathmate, murder's strong right arm!
        Let the insatiate discord in the race
    rear up and shriek 'Avenge the victim—stone them dead!'   1120
LEADER: What Fury is this? Why rouse it, lift its wailing
    through the house? I hear you and lose hope.
CHORUS: Drop by drop at the heart, the gold of life ebbs out.
    We are the old soldiers . . . wounds will come
    with the crushing sunset of our lives.   1125
    Death is close, and quick.
CASSANDRA: Look out! *look out!*—
    Ai, drag the great bull from the mate!—
    a thrash of robes, she traps him—
    writhing—
        black horn glints, twists—
                 she gores him through!
        And now he buckles, look, the bath swirls red—   1130
    There's stealth and murder in the cauldron, do you hear?
LEADER: I'm no judge, I've little skill with the oracles,
    but even I know danger when I hear it.
CHORUS: What good are the oracles to men? Words, more
    words,
    and the hurt comes on us, endless words   1135
    and a seer's techniques have brought us
    terror and the truth.

CASSANDRA: The agony — O I am breaking! — Fate's so hard,
    and the pain that floods my voice is mine alone.
1140   Why have you brought me here, tormented as I am?
    Why, unless to die with him, why else?
LEADER AND CHORUS: Mad with the rapture — god speeds
    you on
        to the song, the deathsong,
    like the nightingale that broods on sorrow,
1145   mourns her son, her son,
    her life inspired with grief for him,
    she lilts and shrills, dark bird that lives for night.
CASSANDRA: The nightingale — O for a song, a fate like hers!
    The gods gave her a life of ease, swathed her in wings,
1150   no tears, no wailing. The knife waits for me.
    They'll splay me on the iron's double edge.
LEADER AND CHORUS: Why? — what god hurls you on, stroke
    on stroke
        to the long dying fall?
    Why the horror clashing through your music,
1155   terror struck to song? —
    why the anguish, the wild dance?
    Where do your words of god and grief begin?
CASSANDRA: Ai, the wedding, wedding of Paris,
    death to the loved ones. Oh Scamander,
1160   you nursed my father . . . once at your banks
    I nursed and grew, and now at the banks
    of Acheron, the stream that carries sorrow,
    it seems I'll chant my prophecies too soon.
LEADER AND CHORUS: What are you saying? Wait, it's clear,
1165   a child could see the truth, it wounds within,
        like a bloody fang it tears —
    I hear your destiny — breaking sobs,
        cries that stab the ears.
CASSANDRA: Oh the grief, the grief of the city
1170   ripped to oblivion. Oh the victims,
    the flocks my father burned at the wall,
       rich herds in flames . . . no cure for the doom
    that took the city after all, and I,
    her last ember, I go down with her.
1175 LEADER AND CHORUS: You cannot stop, your song goes on —
    some spirit drops from the heights and treads you down
        and the brutal strain grows —
    your death-throes come and come and
        I cannot see the end!
1180 CASSANDRA: Then off with the veils that hid the fresh
    young bride —
    we will see the truth.
    Flare up once more, my oracle! Clear and sharp
    as the wind that blows towards the rising sun,
    I can feel a deeper swell now, gathering head
1185   to break at last and bring the dawn of grief.
    No more riddles. I will teach you.
    Come, bear witness, run and hunt with me.
    We trail the old barbaric works of slaughter.

    These roofs — look up — there is a dancing troupe
1190   that never leaves. And they have their harmony

1145 **her son** Itys, son of Philomela, the mother was transformed into a nightingale after she inadvertently tricked her husband, Tereus, into eating their son's flesh

but it is harsh, their words are harsh, they drink
beyond the limit. Flushed on the blood of men
their spirit grows and none can turn away
their revel breeding in the veins — the Furies!
They cling to the house for life. They sing,   1195
sing of the frenzy that began it all,
strain rising on strain, showering curses
on the man who tramples on his brother's bed.

There. Have I hit the mark or not? Am I a fraud,
a fortune-teller babbling lies from door to door?   1200
Swear how well I know the ancient crimes
that live within this house.
LEADER: And if I did?
Would an oath bind the wounds and heal us?
But you amaze me. Bred across the sea,
your language strange, and still you sense the truth   1205
as if you had been here.
CASSANDRA: Apollo the Prophet
introduced me to his gift.
LEADER: A *god* — and moved with love?
CASSANDRA: I was ashamed to tell this once,
but now . . .
LEADER: We spoil ourselves with scruples,   1210
long as things go well.
CASSANDRA: He came like a wrestler,
magnificent, took me down and breathed his fire
through me and —
LEADER: You bore him a child?
CASSANDRA: I yielded,
then at the climax I recoiled — I deceived Apollo!
LEADER:
But the god's skills — they seized you even then?   1215
CASSANDRA: Even then I told my people all the grief to come.
LEADER: And Apollo's anger never touched you? — is it
    possible?
CASSANDRA: Once I betrayed him I could never be believed.
LEADER: We believe you. Your visions seem so true.
CASSANDRA: Aieeeee! —
the pain, the terror! the birth-pang of the seer   1220
who tells the truth —
        it whirls me, oh,
the storm comes again, the crashing chords!
Look, you see them nestling at the threshold?
Young, young in the darkness like a dream,
like children really, yes, and their loved ones   1225
brought them down . . .
        their hands, they fill their hands
with their own flesh, they are serving it like food,
holding out their entrails . . . now it's clear,
I can see the armfuls of compassion, see the father
reach to taste and —
        For so much suffering,   1230
I tell you, someone plots revenge.
A lion who lacks a lion's heart,
he sprawled at home in the royal lair
and set a trap for the lord on his return.
My lord . . . I must wear his yoke, I am his slave.   1235
The lord of the men-of-war, he obliterated Troy —
he is so blind, so lost to that detestable hellhound
who pricks her ears and fawns and her tongue draws out

her glittering words of welcome—
                              No, he cannot see
1240 the stroke that Fury's hiding, stealth, and murder.
What outrage—the woman kills the man!
                              What to call
that . . . monster of Greece, and bring my quarry down?
Viper coiling back and forth?
                    Some sea-witch?—
Scylla crouched in her rocky nest—nightmare of sailors?
1245 Raging mother of death, storming deathless war against
the ones she loves!
                And how she howled in triumph,
boundless outrage. Just as the tide of battle
broke her way, she seems to rejoice that he
is safe at home from war, saved for her.
1250 Believe me if you will. What will it matter
if you won't? It comes when it comes,
and soon you'll see it face to face
and say the seer was all too true.
You will be moved with pity.
LEADER: Thyestes' feast,
1255 the children's flesh—that I know,
and the fear shudders through me. It's true,
real, no dark signs about it. I hear the rest
but it throws me off the scent.
CASSANDRA: Agamemnon.
You will see him dead.
LEADER: Peace, poor girl!
Put those words to sleep.
1260 CASSANDRA: No use,
the Healer has no hand in this affair.
LEADER: Not if it's true—but god forbid it is!
CASSANDRA: You pray, and they close in to kill!
LEADER: What man prepares this, this dreadful—
CASSANDRA: Man?
You *are* lost, to every word I've said.
1265 LEADER: Yes—
I don't see who can bring the evil off.
CASSANDRA: And yet I know my Greek, too well.
LEADER: So does the Delphic oracle,
but he's hard to understand.
CASSANDRA: His *fire*!—
1270 sears me, sweeps me again—the torture!
Apollo Lord of the Light, you burn,
you blind me—
            Agony!
                  She is the lioness,
she rears on her hind legs, she beds with the wolf
when her lion king goes ranging—
                            she will kill me—
Ai, the torture!
1275   She is mixing her drugs,
adding a measure more of hate for me.
She gloats as she whets the sword for him.
He brought me home and we will pay in carnage.

Why mock yourself with these—trappings, the rod,
1280 the god's wreath, his yoke around my throat?
Before I die I'll tread you—

1244 **Scylla** a many-headed monster who terrorized sailors

(*Ripping off her regalia, stamping it into the ground.*)
                        Down, out,
die die die!
Now you're down. I've paid you back.
Look for another victim—I am free at last—
make her rich in all your curse and doom.

(*Staggering backwards as if wrestling with a spirit tearing at her robes.*)

                              See,   1285
Apollo himself, his fiery hands—I feel him again,
he's stripping off my robes, the Seer's robes!
And after he looked down and saw me mocked,
even in these, his glories, mortified by friends
I loved, and they hated me, they were so blind   1290
to their own demise—
                  I went from door to door,
I was wild with the god, I heard them call me
'Beggar! Wretch! Starve for bread in hell!'

And I endured it all, and now he will
extort me as his due. A seer for the Seer.   1295
He brings me here to die like this,
not to serve at my father's altar. No,
the block is waiting. The cleaver steams
with my life blood, the first blood drawn
for the king's last rites.

(*Regaining her composure and moving to the altar.*)
                  We will die,   1300
but not without some honour from the gods.
There will come another to avenge us,
born to kill his mother, born
his father's champion. A wanderer, a fugitive
driven off his native land, he will come home   1305
to cope the stones of hate that menace all he loves.
The gods have sworn a monumental oath: as his father lies
upon the ground he draws him home with power like a
  prayer.

Then why so pitiful, why so many tears?
I have seen my city faring as she fared,   1310
and those who took her, judged by the gods,
faring as they fare. I must be brave.
It is my turn to die.

(*Approaching the doors.*)

I address you as the Gates of Death.
I pray it comes with one clear stroke,   1315
no convulsions, the pulses ebbing out
in gentle death. I'll close my eyes and sleep.
LEADER: So much pain, poor girl, and so much truth,
  you've told so much. But if you *see* it coming,
  clearly—how can you go to your own death,   1320
  like a beast to the altar driven on by god,
  and hold your head so high?
CASSANDRA: No escape, my friends,
not now.
LEADER: But the last hour should be savoured.
CASSANDRA: My time has come. Little to gain from flight.
LEADER: You're brave, believe me, full of gallant heart.   1325

CASSANDRA: Only the wretched go with praise like that.
LEADER: But to go nobly lends a man some grace.
CASSANDRA: My noble father—you and your noble children.

(She nears the threshold and recoils, groaning in revulsion.)

LEADER: What now? what terror flings you back?
    Why? Unless some horror in the brain—
1330 CASSANDRA: Murder.
    The house breathes with murder—bloody shambles!
LEADER: No, no, only the victims at the hearth.
CASSANDRA: I know that odour. I smell the open grave.
LEADER: But the Syrian myrrh, it fills the halls with
    splendour,
    can't you sense it?
CASSANDRA:
1335   Well, I must go in now,
    mourning Agamemnon's death and mine.
    Enough of life!

(Approaching the doors again and crying out.)

              Friends—I cried out,
    not from fear like a bird fresh caught,
    but that you will testify to *how* I died.
1340   When the queen, woman for woman, dies for me,
    and a man falls for the man who married grief.
    That's all I ask, my friends. A stranger's gift
    for one about to die.
LEADER: Poor creature, you
    and the end you see so clearly. I pity you.
1345 CASSANDRA: I'd like a few words more, a kind of dirge,
    it is my own. I pray to the sun,
    the last light I'll see,
    that when the avengers cut the assassins down
    they will avenge me too, a slave who died,
    an easy conquest.
1350   Oh men, your destiny.
    When all is well a shadow can overturn it.
    When trouble comes a stroke of the wet sponge,
    and the picture's blotted out. And that,
    I think that breaks the heart.

(She goes through the doors.)

1355 CHORUS: But the lust for power never dies—
    men cannot have enough.
    No one will lift a hand to send it
    from his door, to give it warning,
    'Power, never come again!'
1360   Take this man: the gods in glory
    gave him Priam's city to plunder,
    brought him home in splendour like a god.
    But now if he must pay for the blood
        his fathers shed, and die for the deaths
1365   he brought to pass, and bring more death
    to avenge his dying, show us one
        who boasts himself born free
    of the raging angel, once he hears—

(Cries break out within the palace.)

AGAMEMNON: Aagh!
    Struck deep—the death-blow, deep—
LEADER: Quiet. Cries,
    but who? Someone's stabbed—

AGAMEMNON: Aaagh, again . . .   1370
    second blow—struck home.
LEADER: The work is done,
    you can feel it. The king, and the great cries—
    Close ranks now, find the right way out.

(But the old men scatter, each speaks singly.)

CHORUS: —I say send out heralds, muster the guard,
    they'll save the house.

              —And I say rush in now,   1375
    catch them red-handed—butchery running on their
    blades.

    —Right with you, do something—now or never!

    —Look at them, beating the drum for insurrection.

                     —Yes,
    we're wasting time. They rape the name of caution,
    their hands will never sleep.

              —Not a plan in sight.   1380
    Let men of action do the planning, too.

    —I'm helpless. Who can raise the dead with words?

    —What, drag out our lives? bow down to the tyrants,
    the ruin of the house?

            —Never, better to die
    on your feet than live on your knees.

                —Wait,   1385
    do we take the cries for signs, prophesy like seers
    and give him up for dead?

            —No more suspicions,
    not another word till we have proof.

            —Confusion
    on all sides—one thing to do. See how it stands
    with Agamemnon, once and for all we'll see—   1390

*(He rushes at the doors. They open and reveal a silver cauldron
that holds the body of* AGAMEMNON *shrouded in bloody robes,
with the body of* CASSANDRA *to his left and* CLYTAEMNESTRA
*standing to his right, sword in hand. She strides towards the
chorus.)*

CLYTAEMNESTRA: Words, endless words I've said to serve the
    moment—
    now it makes me proud to tell the truth.
    How else to prepare a death for deadly men
    who seem to love you? How to rig the nets
    of pain so high no man can overleap them?   1395
    I brooded on this trial, this ancient blood feud
    year by year. At last my hour came.
    Here I stand and here I struck
    and here my work is done.
    I did it all. I don't deny it, no.   1400
    He had no way to flee or fight his destiny—

(Unwinding the robes from AGAMEMNON'S *body, spreading
them before the altar where the old men cluster around them,
unified as a chorus once again.)*

    our never-ending, all embracing net, I cast it
    wide for the royal haul, I coil him round and round

1405 in the wealth, the robes of doom, and then I strike him
once, twice, and at each stroke he cries in agony —
he buckles at the knees and crashes here!
And when he's down I add the third, last blow,
to the Zeus who saves the dead beneath the ground
I send that third blow home in homage like a prayer.

1410 So he goes down, and the life is bursting out of him —
great sprays of blood, and the murderous shower
wounds me, dyes me black and I, I revel
like the Earth when the spring rains come down,
the blessed gifts of god, and the new green spear
1415 splits the sheath and rips to birth in glory!

So it stands, elders of Argos gathered here.
Rejoice if you can rejoice — I glory.
And if I'd pour upon his body the libation
it deserves, what wine could match my words?
1420 It is right and more than right. He flooded
the vessel of our proud house with misery,
with the vintage of the curse and now
he drains the dregs. My lord is home at last.
LEADER: You appal me, you, your brazen words —
exulting over your fallen king.
1425 CLYTAEMNESTRA: And you,
you try me like some desperate woman.
My heart is steel, well you know. Praise me,
blame me as you choose. It's all one.
Here is Agamemnon, my husband made a corpse
1430 by this right hand — a masterpiece of Justice.
Done is done.
CHORUS: Woman! — what poison cropped from the
soil
or strained from the heaving sea, what nursed you,
drove you insane? You brave the curse of Greece.
You have cut away and flung away and now
1435 the people cast you off to exile,
broken with our hate.
CLYTAEMNESTRA: And now you sentence me? —
you banish *me* from the city, curses breathing
down my neck? But *he* —
name one charge you brought against him then.
1440 He thought no more of it than killing a beast,
and his flocks were rich, teeming in their fleece,
but he sacrificed his own child, our daughter,
the agony I laboured into love
to charm away the savage winds of Thrace.
1445 Didn't the law demand you banish him? —
hunt him from the land for all his guilt?
But now you witness what I've done
and you are ruthless judges.
                              Threaten away!
I'll meet you blow for blow. And if I fall
1450 the throne is yours. If god decrees the reverse,
late as it is, old men, you'll learn your place.
CHORUS: Mad with ambition,
               shrilling pride! — some Fury
crazed with the carnage rages through your brain —
1455   I can see the flecks of blood inflame your eyes!
But vengeance comes — you'll lose your loved ones,
stroke for painful stroke.

CLYTAEMNESTRA: Then learn this, too, the power of my
oaths.
By the child's Rights I brought to birth,
by Ruin, by Fury — the three gods to whom   1460
I sacrificed this man — I swear my hopes
will never walk the halls of fear so long
as Aegisthus lights the fire on my hearth.
Loyal to me as always, no small shield
to buttress my defiance.
                              Here he lies.   1465
He brutalized me. The darling of all
the golden girls who spread the gates of Troy.
And here his spear-prize . . . what wonders she beheld! —
the seer of Apollo shared my husband's bed,
his faithful mate who knelt at the rowing-benches,   1470
worked by every hand.
                    They have their rewards.
He as you know. And she, the swan of the gods
who lived to sing her latest, dying song —
his lover lies beside him.
She brings a fresh, voluptuous relish to my bed!   1475
CHORUS: Oh quickly, let me die —
no bed of labour, no, no wasting illness . . .
bear me off in the sleep that never ends,
               now that he has fallen,
now that our dearest shield lies battered —   1480
    Woman made him suffer,
               woman struck him down.

Helen the wild, maddening Helen,
one for the many, the thousand lives
you murdered under Troy. Now you are crowned   1485
with this consummate wreath, the blood
that lives in memory, glistens age to age.
Once in the halls she walked and she was war,
angel of war, angel of agony, lighting men to death.
CLYTAEMNESTRA: Pray no more for death, broken   1490
as you are. And never turn
    your wrath on her, call her
the scourge of men, the one alone
who destroyed a myriad Greek lives —
Helen the grief that never heals.   1495
CHORUS: The *spirit*! — you who tread
the house and the twinborn sons of Tantalus —
you empower the sisters, Fury's twins
               whose power tears the heart!
Perched on the corpse your carrion raven   1500
    glories in her hymn,
               her screaming hymn of pride.
CLYTAEMNESTRA: Now you set your judgement straight,
you summon *him*! Three generations
    feed the spirit in the race.   1505
Deep in the veins he feeds our bloodlust —
aye, before the old wound dies
it ripens in another flow of blood.
CHORUS: The great curse of the house, the spirit,
dead weight wrath — and you can praise it!   1510

1472 **the swan** the bird of Apollo, reputed to sing only when about to
die   1497 **the twinborn sons of Tantalus** here, Agamemnon and
Menelaus

Praise the insatiate doom that feeds
relentless on our future and our sons.
Oh all through the will of Zeus,
the cause of all, the one who works it all.
1515   What comes to birth that is not Zeus?
Our lives are pain, what part not come from god?

Oh my king, my captain,
how to salute you, how to mourn you?
What can I say with all my warmth and love?
1520   Here in the black widow's web you lie,
gasping out your life
in a sacrilegious death, dear god,
reduced to a slave's bed,
my king of men, yoked by stealth and Fate,
1525   by the wife's hand that thrust the two-edged sword.
CLYTAEMNESTRA: You claim the work is mine, call me
Agamemnon's wife—you are so wrong.
Fleshed in the wife of this dead man,
the spirit lives within me,
1530   our savage ancient spirit of revenge.
In return for Atreus' brutal feast
he kills his perfect son—for every
murdered child, a crowning sacrifice.
CHORUS: And *you*, innocent of his murder?
1535   And who could swear to that? and how? . . .
and still an avenger could arise,
bred by the fathers' crimes, and lend a hand.
He wades in the blood of brothers,
stream on mounting stream—black war erupts
1540   and where he strides revenge will stride,
clots will mass for the young who were devoured.

Oh my king, my captain,
how to salute you, how to mourn you?
What can I say with all my warmth and love?
1545   Here in the black widow's web you lie,
gasping out your life
in a sacrilegious death, dear god,
reduced to a slave's bed,
my king of men, yoked by stealth and Fate,
1550   by the wife's hand that thrust the two-edged sword.
CLYTAEMNESTRA: No slave's death, I think—
no stealthier than the death he dealt
our house and the offspring of our loins,
Iphigeneia, girl of tears.
1555   Act for act, wound for wound!
Never exult in Hades, swordsman,
here you are repaid. By the sword
you did your work and by the sword you die.
CHORUS: The mind reels—where to turn?
1560   All plans dashed, all hope! I cannot think . . .
the roofs are toppling, I dread the drumbeat thunder
the heavy rains of blood will crush the house
the first light rains are over—
Justice brings new acts of agony, yes,
1565   on new grindstones Fate is grinding sharp the sword of
Justice.
Earth, dear Earth,
if only you'd drawn me under
long before I saw him huddled

in the beaten silver bath.
Who will bury him, lift his dirge?   1570

(*Turning to* CLYTAEMNESTRA.)

You, can you dare *this*?
To kill your lord with your own hand
then mourn his soul with tributes, terrible tributes—
do his enormous works a great dishonour.
This god-like man, this hero. Who at the grave   1575
will sing his praises, pour the wine of tears?
Who will labour there with truth of heart?
CLYTAEMNESTRA: This is no concern of yours.
The hand that bore and cut him down
will hand him down to Mother Earth.   1580
This house will never mourn for him.
Only our daughter Iphigeneia,
by all rights, will rush to meet him
first at the churning straits,
the ferry over tears—   1585
she'll fling her arms around her father,
pierce him with her love.
CHORUS: Each charge meets counter-charge.
None can judge between them. Justice.
The plunderer plundered, the killer pays the price.   1590
The truth still holds while Zeus still holds the throne:
the one who acts must suffer—
that is law. Who can tear from the veins
the bad seed, the curse? The race is welded to its ruin.
CLYTAEMNESTRA: At last you see the future and the truth!   1595
But I will swear a pact with the spirit
born within us. I embrace his works,
cruel as they are but done at last,
if he will leave our house
in the future, bleed another line   1600
with kinsmen murdering kinsmen.
Whatever he may ask. A few things
are all I need, once I have purged
our fury to destroy each other—
purged it from our halls.

(AEGISTHUS *has emerged from the palace with his bodyguard
and stands triumphant over the body of* AGAMEMNON.)

AEGISTHUS: O what a brilliant day   1605
it is for vengeance! Now I can say once more
there are gods in heaven avenging men,
blazing down on all the crimes of earth.
Now at last I see this man brought down
in the Furies' tangling robes. It feasts my eyes—   1610
he pays for the plot his father's hand contrived.

Atreus, this man's father, was king of Argos.
My father, Thyestes—let me make this clear—
Atreus' brother challenged him for the crown,
and Atreus drove him out of house and home   1615
then lured him back, and home Thyestes came,
poor man, a suppliant to his own hearth,
to pray that Fate might save him.
                              So it did.
There was no dying, no staining our native ground

1585 **the ferry** Charon's ferry across the River Styx into the underworld

1620   with *his* blood. Thyestes was the guest,
       and this man's godless father—

(Pointing to AGAMEMNON.*)*

       the zeal of the host outstripping a brother's love,
       made my father a feast that seemed a feast for gods,
       a love feast of his children's flesh.
                                    He cuts
1625   the extremities, feet and delicate hands
       into small pieces, scatters them over the dish
       and serves it to Thyestes throned on high.
       He picks at the flesh he cannot recognize,
       the soul of innocence eating the food of ruin—
       look,

(Pointing to the bodies at his feet.)

1630   that feeds upon the house! And then,
       when he sees the monstrous thing he's done, he shrieks,
       he reels back head first and vomits up that butchery,
       tramples the feast—brings down the curse of Justice:
       'Crash to ruin, all the race of Pleisthenes, crash down!'

1635   So you see him, down. And I, the weaver of Justice,
       plotted out the kill. Atreus drove us into exile,
       my struggling father and I, a babe-in-arms,
       his last son, but I became a man
       and Justice brought me home. I was abroad
1640   but I reached out and seized my man,
       link by link I clamped the fatal scheme
       together. Now I could die gladly, even I—
       now I see this monster in the nets of Justice.

       LEADER: Aegisthus, you revel in pain—you sicken me.
1645   You say you killed the king in cold blood,
       single-handed planned his pitiful death?
       I say there's no escape. In the hour of judgement,
       trust to this, your head will meet the people's
       rocks and curses.

       AEGISTHUS: You say! you slaves at the oars—
1650   while the master on the benches cracks the whip?
       You'll learn, in your late age, how much it hurts
       to teach old bones their place. We have techniques—
       chains and the pangs of hunger,
       two effective teachers, excellent healers.
1655   They can even cure old men of pride and gall.
       Look—can't you see? The more you kick
       against the pricks, the more you suffer.

       LEADER: You, pathetic—
       the king had just returned from battle.
1660   You waited out the war and fouled his lair,
       you planned my great commander's fall.

       AEGISTHUS: Talk on—
       you'll scream for every word, my little Orpheus.
       We'll see if the world comes dancing to your song,
       your absurd barking—snarl your breath away!
1665   I'll make you dance, I'll bring you all to heel.

       LEADER: *You* rule Argos? You who schemed his death
       but cringed to cut him down with your own hand?

1634 **Pleisthenes** an unidentified ancestral figure, perhaps Atreus or
Pelops   1662 **Orpheus** a musician who enchanted even rocks and trees
with his lyre

AEGISTHUS: The treachery was the woman's work, clearly.
       I was a marked man, his enemy for ages.
       But I will use his riches, stop at nothing   1670
       to civilize his people. All but the rebel:
       him I'll yoke and break—
       no cornfed colt, running free in the traces.
       Hunger, ruthless mate of the dark torture-chamber,
       trains her eyes upon him till he drops!   1675

       LEADER: Coward, why not kill the man yourself?
       Why did the woman, the corruption of Greece
       and the gods of Greece, have to bring him down?
       Orestes—
                    If he still sees the light of day,
       bring him home, good Fates, home to kill   1680
       this pair at last. Our champion in slaughter!

AEGISTHUS: Bent on insolence? Well, you'll learn, quickly.
       At them, men—you have your work at hand!

(His men draw swords; the old men take up their sticks.)

       LEADER: At them, first at the hilt, to the last man—
       AEGISTHUS:
       First at the hilt, I'm not afraid to die.   1685

       LEADER: It's death you want and death you'll have—
       we'll make that word your last.

*(*CLYTAEMNESTRA *moves between them, restraining*
AEGISTHUS.*)*

CLYTAEMNESTRA: No more, my dearest,
       no more grief. We have too much to reap
       right here, our mighty harvest of despair.
       Our lives are based on pain. No bloodshed now.   1690

       Fathers of Argos, turn for home before you act
       and suffer for it. What we did was destiny.
       If we could end the suffering, how we would rejoice.
       The spirit's brutal hoof has struck our heart.
       And that is what a woman has to say.   1695
       Can you accept the truth?

*(*CLYTAEMNESTRA *turns to leave.)*

AEGISTHUS: But these . . . mouths
       that bloom in filth—spitting insults in my teeth.
       You tempt your fates, you insubordinate dogs—
       to hurl abuse at me, your master!

       LEADER: No Greek
       worth his salt would grovel at your feet.   1700

AEGISTHUS: I—I'll stalk you all your days!
       LEADER: Not if the spirit brings Orestes home.
AEGISTHUS: Exiles feed on hope—well I know.
       LEADER: More,
       gorge yourself to bursting—soil justice, while you can.

AEGISTHUS: I promise you, you'll pay, old fools—in good   1705
       time, too!

       LEADER: Strut on your own dunghill, you cock beside your
       mate.

CLYTAEMNESTRA: Let them howl—they're impotent. You and
       I have power now.
       We will set the house in order once for all.

*(They enter the palace; the great doors close behind them; the old
men disband and wander off.)*

SOPHOCLES

Like Aeschylus, Sophocles (c. 496–406 B.C.) had an important career in the civic life of Athens as well as in the theater. He was treasurer for the Athenian imperial league, and served as one of ten generals who led a campaign against Samos, an island threatening to secede from the Athenian alliance. In 411 B.C., he was appointed to a committee called to examine Athens' disastrous military campaign in Sicily. Sophocles' greatest achievements, though, were in the theater. Sophocles is responsible for introducing a third actor into dramatic performance, an innovation rapidly imitated by other playwrights, including Aeschylus and Euripides. He also enlarged the size of the chorus from twelve to fifteen men. Sophocles won his first victory, against Aeschylus, in 468 B.C.; he was victorious twenty-four times in his career and never finished lower than second in the dramatic competition. Of the one hundred twenty plays attributed to Sophocles, only seven survive: *Ajax, Trachiniae, Antigone, Oedipus Rex, Electra, Philoctetes,* and *Oedipus at Colonus.* Fragments of a satyr play, *The Trackers,* also remain. The three "Theban" plays—*Antigone, Oedipus Rex,* and *Oedipus at Colonus*—are thematically related, but, unlike *The Oresteia* of Aeschylus, were not composed as a single trilogy. *Antigone,* a play about Oedipus' daughters after his banishment from Thebes, was composed around the year 441 B.C.; *Oedipus Rex* was first produced sometime shortly after the declaration of war with Sparta in 431 B.C.; and *Oedipus at Colonus* was first produced after Sophocles' death and Athens' defeat.

Oedipus Rex

Oedipus Rex is framed by two acts of identification, recognition, and acknowledgment. The action of the play is about the deepening and horrible understanding of what it means for the hero to recognize who he is, what it means to *be* Oedipus.

In his *Poetics,* written nearly a century later (about 335 B.C.), Aristotle frequently refers to *Oedipus Rex* as a definitive example of the form and purpose of tragedy. Modern audiences, though, sometimes find the play baffling, in part because the prophecy delivered to Oedipus' parents, Laïos and Iokaste—that their son will murder his father and marry his mother—seems to rob Oedipus of the ability to act, to decide his fate through his own deeds. The tension between destiny and discovery is central to the play, and to understand it, we should pay attention to the function of the oracle at Delphi both in the Greek world and in *Oedipus Rex.* The Greeks consulted the oracle at Delphi on a variety of matters, ranging from personal decisions to problems of state. In the play, Laïos and Iokaste, for example, have consulted the oracle to learn the future of their child, and Oedipus turns to Delphi to find out whether Polybos is actually his father; at the same time, the oracle also speaks on important public issues—about the cause of the plague afflicting Thebes and about what should be done with Oedipus after his blinding. Sophocles lived in an era of increasing skepticism, when political conflict and the rise of rhetorical training raised questions about the nature and significance of truth—even the truth of oracular revelation. It is not surprising that characters in *Oedipus Rex* frequently question such prophecy or have difficulty learning how to accept and interpret it—as when Oedipus flees Corinth to avoid murdering his father.

Critical as the prophecy is to Oedipus' life, Oedipus' deeds are really at issue in *Oedipus Rex.* Sophocles chooses to begin and end his drama on the day of Oedipus' discovery of his own identity. The play focuses less on the prophecy than on the course and meaning of Oedipus' actions, on *how* he comes to recognize himself as the criminal he seeks. Oedipus arrives at this recognition only through an extraordinary effort of action and decision: Oedipus calls for the exile of Laïos' murderer; he insults Teiresias when the prophet tries to evade his questions; he accuses Kreon; he threatens the old shepherd with torture in order to learn the truth of his birth. The oracle says that Oedipus will commit his terrible crimes of murder and incest, but Oedipus *chooses* the relentless, brutal pursuit of the truth himself, even to the point of his own incrimination and destruction. The tragedy of *Oedipus Rex* lies in the fearsome turn of events caused by Oedipus' inflexible compulsion to discover the truth.

Aristotle considers the hero of tragedy at some length, in terms that are at once compelling and confusing, particularly in the case of Oedipus. Aristotle suggests in his *Poetics* that the hero of tragedy should be "a man who is neither a paragon of virtue and justice nor undergoes the change to misfortune through any real badness or wickedness but because of some mistake," a description that leads some to look for the cause of this error within Oedipus' character, in a so-called "tragic flaw." But, in fact, when he says that the character's "mistake" — or HAMARTIA — is not the result of "any real badness or wickedness," Aristotle seems to deny that the hero's downfall is the effect of any moral "flaw" at all. It might help us to remember that to his audience, Oedipus may have seemed to share some typically "Athenian" characteristics. Oedipus' passion for inquiry, his abrupt decisiveness, and his impulsive desire to act were seen as the stereotypical traits of Athenian citizens and of Athens as a city. Far from being "flaws," these are just the qualities that made Oedipus (and Athens) successful. What is "tragic" about Oedipus' fate in *Oedipus Rex* is the way that his own surest strengths, the aggressive, pragmatic qualities that enabled him to outwit the Sphinx, lead, on this one occasion, to his destruction. Oedipus' "mistake" is neither a moral failing nor a deed that he might have avoided; it is simply that he is Oedipus and acts like Oedipus — intelligent, masterful, assertive, impatient, impulsive. The tragedy lies in the way that acting like Oedipus leads him, as it has always led him in the past, to the discovery of the truth he seeks, this time with ruinous consequences.

OEDIPUS REX

Sophocles

TRANSLATED BY DUDLEY FITTS AND ROBERT FITZGERALD

— CHARACTERS —

OEDIPUS	MESSENGER
A PRIEST	SHEPHERD OF LAÏOS
KREON	SECOND MESSENGER
TEIRESIAS	CHORUS OF THEBAN ELDERS
IOKASTE	CHORAGOS

SCENE: *Before the palace of Oedipus, King of Thebes. A central door and two lateral doors open onto a platform which runs the length of the façade. On the platform, right and left, are altars; and three steps lead down into the "orchestra," or chorus-ground. At the beginning of the action these steps are crowded by suppliants who have brought branches and chaplets of olive leaves and who lie in various attitudes of despair.* OEDIPUS *enters.*

— PROLOGUE —

OEDIPUS: My children, generations of the living
  In the line of Kadmos, nursed at his ancient
    hearth:
  Why have you strewn yourselves before these altars
  In supplication, with your boughs and garlands?
5 The breath of incense rises from the city
  With a sound of prayer and lamentation.
  Children,
  I would not have you speak through messengers,
  And therefore I have come myself to hear you —
10 I, Oedipus, who bear the famous name.

(To a PRIEST*)*

  You, there, since you are eldest in the company,
  Speak for them all, tell me what preys upon you,
  Whether you come in dread, or crave some
    blessing:
  Tell me, and never doubt that I will help you
15 In every way I can; I should be heartless
  Were I not moved to find you suppliant here.
PRIEST: Great Oedipus, O powerful King of Thebes!
  You see how all the ages of our people
  Cling to your altar steps: here are boys
20 Who can barely stand alone, and here are priests
  By weight of age, as I am a priest of God,
  And young men chosen from those yet unmarried;
  As for the others, all that multitude,
  They wait with olive chaplets in the squares,
25 At the two shrines of Pallas, and where Apollo
  Speaks in the glowing embers.
  Your own eyes
  Must tell you: Thebes is tossed on a murdering sea
  And can not lift her head from the death surge.
30 A rust consumes the buds and fruits of the earth;
  The herds are sick; children die unborn,
  And labor is vain. The god of plague and pyre
  Raids like detestable lightning through the city,
  And all the house of Kadmos is laid waste,
35 All emptied, and all darkened: Death alone
  Battens upon the misery of Thebes.

  You are not one of the immortal gods, we know;
  Yet we have come to you to make our prayer
  As to the man surest in mortal ways

And wisest in the ways of God. You saved us   40
From the Sphinx, that flinty singer, and the tribute
We paid to her so long; yet you were never
Better informed than we, nor could we teach you;
A god's touch, it seems, enabled you to help us.

Therefore, O mighty power, we turn to you: 45
Find us our safety, find us a remedy,
Whether by counsel of the gods or of men.
A king of wisdom tested in the past
Can act in a time of troubles, and act well.
Noblest of men, restore   50
Life to your city! Think how all men call you
Liberator for your boldness long ago;
Ah, when your years of kingship are remembered,
Let them not say *We rose, but later fell* —
Keep the State from going down in the storm!   55
Once, years ago, with happy augury,
You brought us fortune; be the same again!
No man questions your power to rule the land:
But rule over men, not a dead city!
Ships are only hulls, high walls are nothing,   60
When no life moves in the empty passageways.
OEDIPUS: Poor children! You may be sure I know
All that you longed for in your coming here.
I know that you are deathly sick; and yet,
Sick as you are, not one is as sick as I.   65
Each of you suffers in himself alone
His anguish, not another's; but my spirit
Groans for the city, for myself, for you.

I was not sleeping, you are not waking me.
No, I have been in tears for a long while   70
And in my restless thought walked many ways.
In all my search I found one remedy,
And I have adopted it: I have sent Kreon,
Son of Menoikeus, brother of the Queen,
To Delphi, Apollo's place of revelation,   75
To learn there, if he can,
What act or pledge of mine may save the city.
I have counted the days, and now, this very day,
I am troubled, for he has overstayed his time.
What is he doing? He has been gone too long.   80
Yet whenever he comes back, I should do ill
Not to take any action the god orders.

PRIEST: It is a timely promise. At this instant
    They tell me Kreon is here.
85 OEDIPUS: O Lord Apollo!
    May his news be fair as his face is radiant!
PRIEST: Good news, I gather: he is crowned with bay,
    The chaplet is thick with berries.
OEDIPUS: We shall soon know;
90   He is near enough to hear us now.

(Enter KREON.)

    O Prince:
    Brother: son of Menoikeus
    What answer do you bring us from the God?
KREON: A strong one. I can tell you, great afflictions
95   Will turn out well, if they are taken well.
OEDIPUS: What was the oracle? These vague words
    Leave me still hanging between hope and fear.
KREON: Is it your pleasure to hear me with all these
    Gathered around us? I am prepared to speak,
100   But should we not go in?
OEDIPUS: Speak to them all.
    It is for them I suffer, more than for myself.
KREON: Then I will tell you what I heard at Delphi.
    In plain words
105   The god commands us to expel from the land of Thebes
    An old defilement we are sheltering.
    It is a deathly thing, beyond cure;
    We must not let it feed upon us longer.
OEDIPUS: What defilement? How shall we rid ourselves of it?
110 KREON: By exile or death, blood for blood. It was
    Murder that brought the plague-wind on the city.
OEDIPUS: Murder of whom? Surely the god has named him?
KREON: My lord: Laïos once ruled this land,
    Before you came to govern us.
115 OEDIPUS: I know;
    I learned of him from others; I never saw him.
KREON: He was murdered; and Apollo commands us now
    To take revenge upon whoever killed him.
OEDIPUS: Upon whom? Where are they? Where shall we find
    a clue
120   To solve that crime, after so many years?
KREON: Here in this land, he said. Search reveals
    Things that escape an inattentive man.
OEDIPUS: Tell me: Was Laïos murdered in his house,
    Or in the fields, or in some foreign country?
125 KREON: He said he planned to make a pilgrimage.
    He did not come home again.
OEDIPUS: And was there no one,
    No witness, no companion, to tell what happened?
KREON: They were all killed but one, and he got away
130   So frightened that he could remember one thing only.
OEDIPUS: What was that one thing? One may be the key
    To everything, if we resolve to use it.
KREON: He said that a band of highwaymen attacked them,
    Outnumbered them, and overwhelmed the King.
135 OEDIPUS: Strange, that a highwayman should be so daring —
    Unless some faction here bribed him to do it.
KREON: We thought of that. But after Laïos' death
    New troubles arose and we had no avenger.
OEDIPUS: What troubles could prevent your hunting down the
    killers?

KREON: The riddling Sphinx's song   140
    Made us deaf to all mysteries but her own.
OEDIPUS: Then once more I must bring what is dark to light.
    It is most fitting that Apollo shows,
    As you do, this compunction for the dead.
    You shall see how I stand by you, as I should,   145
    Avenging this country and the god as well,
    And not as though it were for some distant friend,
    But for my own sake, to be rid of evil.
    Whoever killed King Laïos might — who knows? —
    Lay violent hands even on me — and soon.   150
    I act for the murdered king in my own interest.

    Come, then, my children: leave the altar steps,
    Lift up your olive boughs!
    One of you go
    And summon the people of Kadmos to gather here.   155
    I will do all that I can; you may tell them that.

(Exit a PAGE.)

    So, with the help of God.
    We shall be saved — or else indeed we are lost.
PRIEST: Let us rise, children. It was for this we came,
    And now the King has promised it.   160
    Phoibos has sent us an oracle; may he descend
    Himself to save us and drive out the plague.

(Exeunt OEDIPUS *and* KREON *into the palace by the central
door. The* PRIEST *and the* SUPPLIANTS *disperse right and left.
After a short pause the* CHORUS *enters the* orchestra.)

PARODOS

Strophe 1

CHORUS: What is God singing in his profound
    Delphi of gold and shadow?
    What oracle for Thebes, the sunwhipped city?   165

Fear unjoints me, the roots of my heart tremble.

Now I remember, O Healer, your power and wonder:
Will you send doom like a sudden cloud, or weave it
Like nightfall of the past?

Speak to me, tell me, O   170
Child of golden Hope, immortal Voice.

Antistrophe 1

Let me pray to Athene, the immortal daughter of Zeus,
And to Artemis her sister
Who keeps her famous throne in the market ring,

And to Apollo, archer from distant heaven —   175

O gods, descend! Like three streams leap against
The fires of our grief, the fires of darkness;
Be swift to bring us rest!

As in the old time from the brilliant house
Of air you stepped to save us, come again!   180

Strophe 2

Now our afflictions have no end,
Now all our stricken host lies down
And no man fights off death with his mind;

The noble plowland bears no grain,
185 And groaning mothers can not bear—

See, how our lives like birds take wing,
Like sparks that fly when a fire soars,
To the shore of the god of evening.

Antistrophe 2

The plague burns on, it is pitiless,
190 Though pallid children laden with death
Lie unwept in the stony ways,

And old gray women by every path
Flock to the strand about the altars

There to strike their breasts and cry
195 Worship of Phoibos in wailing prayers:
Be kind, God's golden child!

Strophe 3

There are no swords in this attack by fire,
No shields, but we are ringed with cries.

Send the besieger plunging from our homes
200 Into the vast sea-room of the Atlantic
Or into the waves that foam eastward of Thrace—

For the day ravages what the night spares—

Destroy our enemy, lord of the thunder!
Let him be riven by lightning from heaven!

Antistrophe 3

205 Phoibos Apollo, stretch the sun's bowstring,
That golden cord, until it sing for us,
Flashing arrows in heaven!
Artemis, Huntress,
Race with flaring lights upon our mountains!

210 O scarlet god, O golden-banded brow,
O Theban Bacchos in a storm of Maenads,

(Enter OEDIPUS, *center.)*

Whirl upon Death, that all the Undying hate!
Come with blinding torches, come in joy!

SCENE I

OEDIPUS: Is this your prayer? It may be answered. Come,
Listen to me, act as the crisis demands,
And you shall have relief from all these evils.

Until now I was a stranger to this tale,
5 As I had been a stranger to the crime.
Could I track down the murderer without a clue?
But now, friends,
As one who became a citizen after the murder,
I make this proclamation to all Thebans:

10 If any man knows by whose hand Laïos, son of Labdakos,
Met his death, I direct that man to tell me everything,
No matter what he fears for having so long withheld it.
Let it stand as promised that no further trouble
Will come to him, but he may leave the land in safety.

15 Moreover: If anyone knows the murderer to be foreign,
Let him not keep silent: he shall have his reward from me.

However, if he does conceal it; if any man
Fearing for his friend or for himself disobeys this edict,
Hear what I propose to do:

I solemnly forbid the people of this country, 20
Where power and throne are mine, ever to receive that
    man
Or speak to him, no matter who he is, or let him
Join in sacrifice, lustration, or in prayer.
I decree that he be driven from every house,
Being, as he is, corruption itself to us: the Delphic 25
Voice of Apollo has pronounced this revelation.
Thus I associate myself with the oracle
And take the side of the murdered king.
As for the criminal, I pray to God—
Whether it be a lurking thief, or one of a number— 30
I pray that that man's life be consumed in evil and
    wretchedness.
And as for me, this curse applies no less
If it should turn out that the culprit is my guest here,
Sharing my hearth.
You have heard the penalty. 35

I lay it on you now to attend to this
For my sake, for Apollo's, for the sick
Sterile city that heaven has abandoned.
Suppose the oracle had given you no command:
Should this defilement go uncleansed for ever? 40
You should have found the murderer: your king,
A noble king, had been destroyed!
Now I,
Having the power that he held before me,
Having his bed, begetting children there 45
Upon his wife, as he would have, had he lived—
Their son would have been my children's brother,
If Laïos had had luck in fatherhood!
(And now his bad fortune has struck him down)—
I say I take the son's part, just as though 50
I were his son, to press the fight for him
And see it won! I'll find the hand that brought
Death to Labdakos' and Polydoros' child,
Heir of Kadmos' and Agenor's line.
And as for those who fail me, 55
May the gods deny them the fruit of the earth,
Fruit of the womb, and may they rot utterly!
Let them be wretched as we are wretched, and worse!

For you, my loyal Thebans, and for all
Who find my actions right, I pray the favor 60
Of justice, and of all the immortal gods.
CHORAGOS: Since I am under oath, my lord, I swear
I did not do the murder, I can not name
The murderer. Phoibos ordained the search;
Why did he not say who the culprit was? 65
OEDIPUS: An honest question. But no man in the world
Can make the gods do more than the gods will.
CHORAGOS: There is an alternative, I think—
OEDIPUS: Tell me.
Any or all, you must not fail to tell me. 70
CHORAGOS: A lord clairvoyant to the lord Apollo,
As we all know, is the skilled Teiresias.
One might learn much about this from him, Oedipus.

OEDIPUS: I am not wasting time:
75   Kreon spoke of this, and I have sent for him —
      Twice, in fact; it is strange that he is not here.
CHORAGOS: The other matter — that old report — seems
      useless.
OEDIPUS: What was that? I am interested in all reports.
CHORAGOS: The King was said to have been killed by
      highwaymen.
80 OEDIPUS: I know. But we have no witnesses to that.
CHORAGOS: If the killer can feel a particle of dread,
      Your curse will bring him out of hiding!
OEDIPUS: No.
      The man who dared that act will fear no curse.

(*Enter the blind seer* TEIRESIAS, *led by a* PAGE.)

85 CHORAGOS: But there is one man who may detect the
      criminal.
      This is Teiresias, this is the holy prophet
      In whom, alone of all men, truth was born.
OEDIPUS: Teiresias: seer: student of mysteries,
      Of all that's taught and all that no man tells,
90   Secrets of Heaven and secrets of the earth:
      Blind though you are, you know the city lies
      Sick with plague; and from this plague, my lord,
      We find that you alone can guard or save us.

      Possibly you did not hear the messengers?
95   Apollo, when we sent to him,
      Sent us back word that this great pestilence
      Would lift, but only if we established clearly
      The identity of those who murdered Laïos.
      They must be killed or exiled.
100   Can you use
      Birdflight or any art of divination
      To purify yourself, and Thebes, and me
      From this contagion? We are in your hands.
      There is no fairer duty
105   Than that of helping others in distress.
TEIRESIAS: How dreadful knowledge of the truth can be
      When there's no help in truth! I knew this well,
      But did not act on it: else I should not have come.
OEDIPUS: What is troubling you? Why are your eyes so cold?
110 TEIRESIAS: Let me go home. Bear your own fate, and I'll
      Bear mine. It is better so: trust what I say.
OEDIPUS: What you say is ungracious and unhelpful
      To your native country. Do not refuse to speak.
TEIRESIAS: When it comes to speech, your own is neither
      temperate
115   Nor opportune. I wish to be more prudent.
OEDIPUS: In God's name, we all beg you —
TEIRESIAS: You are all ignorant.
      No; I will never tell you what I know.
      Now it is my misery; then it would be yours.
120 OEDIPUS: What! You do know something, and will not tell us?
      You would betray us all and wreck the State?
TEIRESIAS: I do not intend to torture myself, or you.
      Why persist in asking? You will not persuade me.
OEDIPUS: What a wicked old man you are! You'd try a stone's
125   Patience! Out with it. Have you no feeling at all?
TEIRESIAS: You call me unfeeling. If you could only see
      The nature of your own feelings . . .

OEDIPUS: Why,
      Who would not feel as I do? Who could endure
      Your arrogance toward the city?   130
TEIRESIAS: What does it matter?
      Whether I speak or not, it is bound to come.
OEDIPUS: Then, if 'it' is bound to come, you are bound to
      tell me.
TEIRESIAS: No, I will not go on. Rage as you please.
OEDIPUS: Rage? Why not!   135
      And I'll tell you what I think:
      You planned it, you had it done, you all but
      Killed him with your own hands: if you had eyes,
      I'd say the crime was yours, and yours alone.
TEIRESIAS: So? I charge you, then,   140
      Abide by the proclamation you have made:
      From this day forth
      Never speak again to these men or to me;
      You yourself are the pollution of this country.
OEDIPUS: You dare say that! Can you possibly think you have   145
      Some way of going free, after such insolence?
TEIRESIAS: I have gone free. It is the truth sustains me.
OEDIPUS: Who taught you shamelessness? It was not your
      craft.
TEIRESIAS: You did. You made me speak. I did not want to.
OEDIPUS: Speak what? Let me hear it again more clearly.   150
TEIRESIAS: Was it not clear before? Are you tempting me?
OEDIPUS: I did not understand it. Say it again.
TEIRESIAS: I say that you are the murderer whom you seek.
OEDIPUS: Now twice you have spat out infamy. You'll pay
      for it!
TEIRESIAS: Would you care for more? Do you wish to be really 155
      angry?
OEDIPUS: Say what you will. Whatever you say is worthless.
TEIRESIAS: I say you live in hideous shame with those
      Most dear to you. You can not see the evil.
OEDIPUS: Can you go on babbling like this for ever?
TEIRESIAS: I can, if there is power in truth.   160
OEDIPUS: There is:
      But not for you, not for you,
      You sightless, witless, senseless, mad old man!
TEIRESIAS: You are the madman. There is no one here
      Who will not curse you soon, as you curse me.   165
OEDIPUS: You child of total night! I would not touch you;
      Neither would any man who sees the sun.
TEIRESIAS: True: it is not from you my fate will come.
      That lies within Apollo's competence,
      As it is his concern.   170
OEDIPUS: Tell me, who made
      These fine discoveries? Kreon? Or someone else?
TEIRESIAS: Kreon is no threat. You weave your own doom.
OEDIPUS: Wealth, power, craft of statesmanship!
      Kingly position, everywhere admired!   175
      What savage envy is stored up against these,
      If Kreon, whom I trusted, Kreon my friend,
      For this great office which the city once
      Put in my hands unsought — if for this power
      Kreon desires in secret to destroy me!   180

      He has brought this decrepit fortune-teller, this
      Collector of dirty pennies, this prophet fraud —
      Why, he is no more clairvoyant than I am!

Tell us:
185 Has your mystic mummery ever approached the truth?
When that hellcat the Sphinx was performing here,
What help were you to these people?
Her magic was not for the first man who came along:
It demanded a real exorcist. Your birds—
190 What good were they? or the gods, for the matter of that?
But I came by,
Oedipus, the simple man, who knows nothing—
I thought it out for myself, no birds helped me!
And this is the man you think you can destroy,
195 That you may be close to Kreon when he's king!
Well, you and your friend Kreon, it seems to me,
Will suffer most. If you were not an old man,
You would have paid already for your plot.
      CHORAGOS: We can not see that his words or yours
200 Have been spoken except in anger, Oedipus,
And of anger we have no need. How to accomplish
The god's will best: that is what most concerns us.
      TEIRESIAS: You are a king. But where argument's concerned
I am your man, as much a king as you.
205 I am not your servant, but Apollo's.
I have no need of Kreon's name.

Listen to me. You mock my blindness, do you?
But I say that you, with both your eyes, are blind:
You can not see the wretchedness of your life,
210 Nor in whose house you live, no, nor with whom.
Who are your father and mother? Can you tell me?
You do not even know the blind wrongs
That you have done them, on earth and in the world
      below.
But the double lash of your parents' curse will whip you
215 Out of this land some day, with only night
Upon your precious eyes.
Your cries then—where will they not be heard?
What fastness of Kithairon will not echo them?
And that bridal-descant of yours—you'll know it then,
220 The song they sang when you came here to Thebes
And found your misguided berthing.
All this, and more, that you can not guess at now,
Will bring you to yourself among your children.

Be angry, then. Curse Kreon. Curse my words.
225 I tell you, no man that walks upon the earth
Shall be rooted out more horribly than you.
      OEDIPUS: Am I to bear this from him?—Damnation
Take you! Out of this place! Out of my sight!
      TEIRESIAS: I would not have come at all if you had not
      asked me.
230 OEDIPUS: Could I have told that you'd talk nonsense, that
      You'd come here to make a fool of yourself, and of me?
      TEIRESIAS: A fool? Your parents thought me sane enough.
      OEDIPUS: My parents again!—Wait: who were my parents?
      TEIRESIAS: This day will give you a father, and break your
      heart.
235 OEDIPUS: Your infantile riddles! Your damned abracadabra!
      TEIRESIAS: You were a great man once at solving
      riddles.
      OEDIPUS: Mock me with that if you like; you will find it true.
      TEIRESIAS: It was true enough. It brought about your ruin.
      OEDIPUS: But if it saved this town?

TEIRESIAS (to the PAGE): Boy, give me your hand.   240
OEDIPUS: Yes, boy; lead him away.
   —While you are here
We can do nothing. Go; leave us in peace.
TEIRESIAS: I will go when I have said what I have to say.
How can you hurt me? And I tell you again: 245
The man you have been looking for all this time,
The damned man, the murderer of Laïos,
That man is in Thebes. To your mind he is foreign-born,
But it will soon be shown that he is a Theban,
A revelation that will fail to please.   250
A blind man,
Who has his eyes now; a penniless man, who is rich now;
And he will go tapping the strange earth with his staff.
To the children with whom he lives now he will be
Brother and father—the very same; to her   255
Who bore him, son and husband—the very same
Who came to his father's bed, wet with his father's blood.

Enough. Go think that over.
If later you find error in what I have said,
You may say that I have no skill in prophecy.   260

(Exit TEIRESIAS, led by his PAGE. OEDIPUS goes into the palace.)

ODE I

Strophe 1

CHORUS: The Delphic stone of prophecies
Remembers ancient regicide
And a still bloody hand.
That killer's hour of flight has come.
He must be stronger than riderless   265
Coursers of untiring wind,
For the son of Zeus armed with his father's thunder
Leaps in lightning after him;
And the Furies hold his track, the sad Furies.

Antistrophe 1

Holy Parnassos' peak of snow   270
Flashes and blinds that secret man,
That all shall hunt him down:
Though he may roam the forest shade
Like a bull gone wild from pasture
To rage through glooms of stone.   275
Doom comes down on him; flight will not avail him;
For the world's heart calls him desolate,
And the immortal voices follow, for ever follow.

Strophe 2

But now a wilder thing is heard
From the old man skilled at hearing Fate in the wingbeat of   280
   a bird.
Bewildered as a blown bird, my soul hovers and can not
   find
Foothold in this debate, or any reason or rest of mind.
But no man ever brought—none can bring
Proof of strife between Thebes' royal house,
Labdakos' line, and the son of Polybos;
And never until now has any man brought word   285
Of Laïos' dark death staining Oedipus the King.

Antistrophe 2

Divine Zeus and Apollo hold
Perfect intelligence alone of all tales ever told;
290 And well though this diviner works, he works in his own
          night;
No man can judge that rough unknown or trust in second
          sight,
For wisdom changes hands among the wise.
Shall I believe my great lord criminal
At a raging word that a blind old man let fall?
295 I saw him, when the carrion woman faced him of old,
Prove his heroic mind. These evil words are lies.

SCENE II

KREON: Men of Thebes:
    I am told that heavy accusations
    Have been brought against me by King Oedipus.

    I am not the kind of man to bear this tamely.

5   If in these present difficulties
    He holds me accountable for any harm to him
    Through anything I have said or done—why, then,
    I do not value life in this dishonor.

    It is not as though this rumor touched upon
10   Some private indiscretion. The matter is grave.
    The fact is that I am being called disloyal
    To the State, to my fellow citizens, to my friends.
CHORAGOS: He may have spoken in anger, not from his
        mind.
KREON: But did you not hear him say I was the one
15   Who seduced the old prophet into lying?
CHORAGOS: The thing was said: I do not know how seriously.
KREON: But you were watching him! Were his eyes steady?
    Did he look like a man in his right mind?
CHORAGOS: I do not know.
20   I can not judge the behavior of great men.
    But here is the King himself.

(*Enter* OEDIPUS.)

OEDIPUS: So you dared come back.
    Why? How brazen of you to come to my house,
    You murderer!
25   Do you think I do not know
    That you plotted to kill me, plotted to steal my throne?
    Tell me, in God's name: am I coward, a fool,
    That you should dream you could accomplish this?
    A fool who could not see your slippery game?
30   A coward, not to fight back when I saw it?
    You are the fool, Kreon, are you not? hoping
    Without support or friends to get a throne?
    Thrones may be won or bought: you could do neither.
KREON: Now listen to me. You have talked; let me talk, too.
35   You can not judge unless you know the facts.
OEDIPUS: You speak well: there is one fact; but I find it hard
    To learn from the deadliest enemy I have.
KREON: That above all I must dispute with you.
OEDIPUS: That above all I will not hear you deny.
40   KREON: If you think there is anything good in being stubborn
    Against all reason, then I say you are wrong.

OEDIPUS: If you think a man can sin against his own kind
    And not be punished for it, I say you are mad.
KREON: I agree. But tell me: what have I done to you?
OEDIPUS: You advised me to send for that wizard, did you   45
    not?
KREON: I did. I should do it again.
OEDIPUS: Very well. Now tell me:
    How long has it been since Laïos—
KREON: What of Laïos?
OEDIPUS: Since he vanished in that onset by the road?   50
KREON: It was long ago, a long time.
OEDIPUS: And this prophet,
    Was he practicing here then?
KREON: He was; and with honor, as now.
OEDIPUS: Did he speak of me at that time?   55
KREON: He never did;
    At least, not when I was present.
OEDIPUS: But . . . the enquiry?
    I suppose you held one?
KREON: We did, but we learned nothing.   60
OEDIPUS: Why did the prophet not speak against me then?
KREON: I do not know; and I am the kind of man
    Who holds his tongue when he has no facts to go on.
OEDIPUS: There's one fact that you know, and you could
        tell it.
KREON: What fact is that? If I know it, you shall have it.   65
OEDIPUS: If he were not involved with you, he could not say
    That it was I who murdered Laïos.
KREON: If he says that, you are the one that knows it!—
    But now it is my turn to question you.
OEDIPUS: Put your questions. I am no murderer.   70
KREON: First, then: You married my sister?
OEDIPUS: I married your sister.
KREON: And you rule the kingdom equally with her?
OEDIPUS: Everything that she wants she has from me.
KREON: And I am the third, equal to both of you?   75
OEDIPUS: That is why I call you a bad friend.
KREON: No. Reason it out, as I have done.
    Think of this first: Would any sane man prefer
    Power, with all a king's anxieties,
    To that same power and the grace of sleep?   80
    Certainly not I.
    I have never longed for the king's power—only his rights.
    Would any wise man differ from me in this?
    As matters stand, I have my way in everything
    With your consent, and no responsibilities.   85
    If I were king, I should be a slave to policy.
    How could I desire a sceptre more
    Than what is now mine—untroubled influence?
    No, I have not gone mad; I need no honors,
    Except those with the perquisites I have now.   90
    I am welcome everywhere; every man salutes me,
    And those who want your favor seek my ear,
    Since I know how to manage what they ask.
    Should I exchange this ease for that anxiety?
    Besides, no sober mind is treasonable.   95
    I hate anarchy
    And never would deal with any man who likes it.
    Test what I have said. Go to the priestess
    At Delphi, ask if I quoted her correctly.

100 And as for this other thing: If I am found
Guilty of treason with Teiresias,
Then sentence me to death. You have my word
It is a sentence I should cast my vote for—
But not without evidence!

105 You do wrong
When you take good men for bad, bad men for good.
A true friend thrown aside—why, life itself
Is not more precious!
In time you will know this well:

110 For time, and time alone, will show the just man,
Though scoundrels are discovered in a day.
CHORAGOS: This is well said, and a prudent man would
ponder it.
Judgments too quickly formed are dangerous.
OEDIPUS: But is he not quick in his duplicity?

115 And shall I not be quick to parry him?
Would you have me stand still, hold my peace, and let
This man win everything, through my inaction?
KREON: And you want—what is it, then? To banish me?
OEDIPUS: No, not exile. It is your death I want,

120 So that all the world may see what treason means.
KREON: You will persist then? You will not believe me?
OEDIPUS: How can I believe you?
KREON: Then you are a fool.
OEDIPUS: To save myself?

125 KREON: In justice, think of me.
OEDIPUS: You are evil incarnate.
KREON: But suppose that you are wrong?
OEDIPUS: Still I must rule.
KREON: But not if you rule badly.

130 OEDIPUS: O city, city!
KREON: It is my city, too!
CHORAGOS: Now, my lords, be still. I see the Queen,
Iokastê, coming from her palace chambers;
And it is time she came, for the sake of you both,

135 This dreadful quarrel can be resolved through her.

(*Enter* IOKASTE.)

IOKASTE: Poor foolish men, what wicked din is this?
With Thebes sick to death, is it not shameful
That you should rake some private quarrel up?

(*To* OEDIPUS.)

Come into the house.

140 And you, Kreon, go now:
Let us have no more of this tumult over nothing.
KREON: Nothing? No, sister: what your husband plans for me
Is one of two great evils: exile or death.
OEDIPUS: He is right.

145 Why, woman I have caught him squarely
Plotting against my life.
KREON: No! Let me die
Accurst if ever I have wished you harm!
IOKASTE: Ah, believe it, Oedipus!

150 In the name of the gods, respect this oath of his
For my sake, for the sake of these people here!

Strophe 1

CHORAGOS: Open your mind to her, my lord. Be ruled by
her, I beg you!

OEDIPUS: What would you have me do?
CHORAGOS: Respect Kreon's word. He has never spoken like
a fool,
And now he has sworn an oath.   155
OEDIPUS: You know what you ask?
CHORAGOS: I do.
OEDIPUS: Speak on, then.
CHORAGOS: A friend so sworn should not be baited so,
In blind malice, and without final proof.   160
OEDIPUS: You are aware, I hope, that what you say
Means death for me, or exile at the least.

Strophe 2

CHORAGOS: No, I swear by Helios, first in Heaven!
May I die friendless and accurst,
The worst of deaths, if ever I meant that!   165
It is the withering fields
That hurt my sick heart:
Must we bear all these ills,
And now your bad blood as well?
OEDIPUS: Then let him go. And let me die, if I must,   170
Or be driven by him in shame from the land of Thebes.
It is your unhappiness, and not his talk,
That touches me.
As for him—
Wherever he goes, hatred will follow him.   175
KREON: Ugly in yielding, as you were ugly in rage!
Natures like yours chiefly torment themselves.
OEDIPUS: Can you not go? Can you not leave me?
KREON: I can.
You do not know me; but the city knows me,   180
And in its eyes I am just, if not in yours.

(*Exit* KREON.)

Antistrophe 1

CHORAGOS: Lady Iokastê, did you not ask the King to go to
his chambers?
IOKASTE: First tell me what has happened.
CHORAGOS: There was suspicion without evidence; yet
it rankled
As even false charges will.   185
IOKASTE: On both sides?
CHORAGOS: On both.
IOKASTE: But what was said?
CHORAGOS: Oh let it rest, let it be done with!
Have we not suffered enough?   190
OEDIPUS: You see to what your decency has brought you:
You have made difficulties where my heart saw none.

Antistrophe 2

CHORAGOS: Oedipus, it is not once only I have told you—
You must know I should count myself unwise
To the point of madness, should I now forsake you—   195
You, under whose hand,
In the storm of another time,
Our dear land sailed out free.
But now stand fast at the helm!

IOKASTE: In God's name, Oedipus, inform your wife as well: 200
Why are you so set in this hard anger?

OEDIPUS: I will tell you, for none of these men deserves
   My confidence as you do. It is Kreon's work,
   His treachery, his plotting against me.
205 IOKASTE: Go on, if you can make this clear to me.
   OEDIPUS: He charges me with the murder of Laïos.
   IOKASTE: Has he some knowledge? Or does he speak from
      hearsay?
   OEDIPUS: He would not commit himself to such a charge,
      But he has brought in that damnable soothsayer
210   To tell his story.
   IOKASTE: Set your mind at rest.
      If it is a question of soothsayers, I tell you
      That you will find no man whose craft gives knowledge
      Of the unknowable.

215   Here is my proof:
      An oracle was reported to Laïos once
      (I will not say from Phoibos himself, but from
      His appointed ministers, at any rate)
      That his doom would be death at the hands of his own
         son —
220   His son, born of his flesh and of mine!

      Now, you remember the story: Laïos was killed
      By marauding strangers where three highways meet;
      But his child had not been three days in this world
      Before the King had pierced the baby's ankles
225   And left him to die on a lonely mountainside.
      Thus, Apollo never caused that child
      To kill his father, and it was not Laïos' fate
      To die at the hands of his son, as he had feared.
      This is what prophets and prophecies are worth!
230   Have no dread of them.
      It is God himself
      Who can show us what he wills, in his own way.
   OEDIPUS: How strange a shadowy memory crossed my mind,
      Just now while you were speaking; it chilled my heart.
235 IOKASTE: What do you mean? What memory do you speak of?
   OEDIPUS: If I understand you, Laïos was killed
      At a place where thee roads meet.
   IOKASTE: So it was said;
      We have no later story.
240 OEDIPUS: Where did it happen?
   IOKASTE: Phokis, it is called: at a place where the Theban
      Way
      Divides into the roads toward Delphi and Daulia.
   OEDIPUS: When?
   IOKASTE: We had the news not long before you came
245   And proved the right to your succession here.
   OEDIPUS: Ah, what net has God been weaving for me?
   IOKASTE: Oedipus! Why does this trouble you?
   OEDIPUS: Do not ask me yet.
      First, tell me how Laïos looked, and tell me
250   How old he was.
   IOKASTE: He was tall, his hair just touched
      With white; his form was not unlike your own.
   OEDIPUS: I think that I myself may be accurst
      By my own ignorant edict.
255 IOKASTE: You speak strangely.
      It makes me tremble to look at you, my King.
   OEDIPUS: I am not sure that the blind man can not see.
      But I should know better if you were to tell me —

IOKASTE: Anything — though I dread to hear you ask it.
OEDIPUS: Was the King lightly escorted, or did he ride   260
   With a large company, as a ruler should?
IOKASTE: There were five men with him in all: one was
      a herald;
   And a single chariot, which he was driving.
OEDIPUS: Alas, that makes it plain enough!
   But who —   265
   Who told you how it happened?
IOKASTE: A household servant,
   The only one to escape.
OEDIPUS: And is he still
   A servant of ours?   270
IOKASTE: No; for when he came back at last
   And found you enthroned in the place of the dead king,
   He came to me, touched my hand with his, and begged
   That I would send him away to the frontier district
   Where only the shepherds go —   275
   As far away from the city as I could send him.
   I granted his prayer; for although the man was a slave,
   He had earned more than this favor at my hands.
OEDIPUS: Can he be called back quickly?
IOKASTE: Easily.   280
   But why?
OEDIPUS: I have taken too much upon myself
   Without enquiry; therefore I wish to consult him.
IOKASTE: Then he shall come.
   But am I not one also   285
   To whom you might confide these fears of yours?
OEDIPUS: That is your right; it will not be denied you,
   Now least of all; for I have reached a pitch
   Of wild foreboding. Is there anyone
   To whom I should sooner speak?   290
   Polybos of Corinth is my father.
   My mother is a Dorian: Meropê.
   I grew up chief among the men of Corinth
   Until a strange thing happened —
   Not worth my passion, it may be, but strange.   295

At a feast, a drunken man maundering in his cups
Cries out that I am not my father's son!
I contained myself that night, though I felt anger
And a sinking heart. The next day I visited
My father and mother, and questioned them. They   300
   stormed,
Calling it all the slanderous rant of a fool;
And this relieved me. Yet the suspicion
Remained always aching in my mind;
I knew there was talk; I could not rest;
And finally, saying nothing to my parents,   305
I went to the shrine at Delphi.

The god dismissed my question without reply;
He spoke of other things.
Some were clear,
Full of wretchedness, dreadful, unbearable: 310
As, that I should lie with my own mother, breed
Children from whom all men would turn their eyes;
And that I should be my father's murderer.

I heard all this, and fled. And from that day
Corinth to me was only in the stars   315

Descending in that quarter of the sky,
As I wandered farther and farther on my way
To a land where I should never see the evil
Sung by the oracle. And I came to this country
320 Where, so you say, King Laïos was killed.

I will tell you all that happened there, my lady.

There were three highways
Coming together at a place I passed;
And there a herald came towards me, and a chariot
325 Drawn by horses, with a man such as you describe
Seated in it. The groom leading the horses
Forced me off the road at his lord's command;
But as this charioteer lurched over towards me
I struck him in my rage. The old man saw me
330 And brought his double goad down upon my head
As I came abreast.
He was paid back, and more!
Swinging my club in this right hand I knocked him
Out of his car, and he rolled on the ground.
335 I killed him.
I killed them all.
Now if that stranger and Laïos were — kin,
Where is a man more miserable than I?
More hated by the gods? Citizen and alien alike
340 Must never shelter me or speak to me —
I must be shunned by all.
And I myself
Pronounced this malediction upon myself!

Think of it: I have touched you with these hands,
345 These hands that killed your husband. What defilement!

Am I all evil, then? It must be so,
Since I must flee from Thebes, yet never again
See my own countrymen, my own country,
For fear of joining my mother in marriage
350 And killing Polybos, my father.
Ah,
If I was created so, born to this fate,
Who could deny the savagery of God?

O holy majesty of heavenly powers!
355 May I never see that day! Never!
Rather let me vanish from the race of men
Than know the abomination destined me!
CHORAGOS: We too, my lord, have felt dismay at this.
But there is hope: you have yet to hear the shepherd.
360 OEDIPUS: Indeed, I fear no other hope is left me.
IOKASTE: What do you hope from him when he comes?
OEDIPUS: This much:
If his account of the murder tallies with yours,
Then I am cleared.
365 IOKASTE: What was it that I said
Of such importance?
OEDIPUS: Why, 'marauders', you said,
Killed the King, according to this man's story.
If he maintains that still, if there were several,
370 Clearly the guilt is not mine: I was alone.
But if he says one man, singlehanded, did it,
Then the evidence all points to me.

IOKASTE: You may be sure that he said there were several;
And can he call back that story now? He can not.
The whole city heard it as plainly as I. 375
But suppose he alters some detail of it:
He can not ever show that Laïos' death
Fulfilled the oracle: for Apollo said
My child was doomed to kill him; and my child —
Poor baby! — it was my child that died first. 380

No. From now on, where oracles are concerned,
I would not waste a second thought on any.
OEDIPUS: You may be right.
But come: let someone go
For the shepherd at once. This matter must be settled. 385
IOKASTE: I will send for him.
I would not wish to cross you in anything,
And surely not in this. — Let us go in.

(Exeunt into the palace.)

ODE II

Strophe 1

CHORUS: Let me be reverent in the ways of right,
Lowly the paths I journey on; 390
Let all my words and actions keep
The laws of the pure universe
From highest Heaven handed down.
For Heaven is their bright nurse,
Those generations of the realms of light; 395
Ah, never of mortal kind were they begot,
Nor are they slaves of memory, lost in sleep:
Their Father is greater than Time, and ages not.

Antistrophe 1

The tyrant is a child of Pride
Who drinks from his great sickening cup 400
Recklessness and vanity,
Until from his high crest headlong
He plummets to the dust of hope.
That strong man is not strong.
But let no fair ambition be denied; 405
May God protect the wrestler for the State
In government, in comely policy,
Who will fear God, and on His ordinance wait.

Strophe 2

Haughtiness and the high hand of disdain
Tempt and outrage God's holy law; 410
And any mortal who dares hold
No immortal Power in awe
Will be caught up in a net of pain:
The price for which his levity is sold.
Let each man take due earnings, then, 415
And keep his hands from holy things,
And from blasphemy stand apart —
Else the crackling blast of heaven
Blows on his head, and on his desperate heart.
Though fools will honor impious men, 420
In their cities no tragic poet sings.

Antistrophe 2

Shall we lose faith in Delphi's obscurities,
We who have heard the world's core
Discredited, and the sacred wood
425   Of Zeus at Elis praised no more?
The deeds and the strange prophecies
Must make a pattern yet to be understood.
Zeus, if indeed you are lord of all,
Throned in light over night and day,
430   Mirror this in your endless mind:
Our masters call the oracle
Words on the wind, and the Delphic vision blind!
Their hearts no longer know Apollo,
And reverence for the gods has died away.

SCENE III

(*Enter* IOKASTE.)

IOKASTE: Princes of Thebes, it has occurred to me
   To visit the altars of the gods, bearing
   These branches as a suppliant, and this incense.
   Our King is not himself: his noble soul
5   Is overwrought with fantasies of dread,
   Else he would consider
   The new prophecies in the light of the old.
   He will listen to any voice that speaks disaster,
   And my advice goes for nothing.

(*She approaches the altar, right.*)

10   To you, then, Apollo,
   Lycéan lord, since you are nearest, I turn in prayer.

   Receive these offerings, and grant us deliverance
   From defilement. Our hearts are heavy with fear
   When we see our leader distracted, as helpless sailors
15   Are terrified by the confusion of their helmsman.

(*Enter* MESSENGER.)

MESSENGER: Friends, no doubt you can direct me:
   Where shall I find the house of Oedipus,
   Or, better still, where is the King himself?
CHORAGOS: It is this very place, stranger; he is inside.
20   This is his wife and mother of his children.
MESSENGER: I wish her happiness in a happy house,
   Blest in all the fulfillment of her marriage.
IOKASTE: I wish as much for you: your courtesy
   Deserves a like good fortune. But now, tell me:
25   Why have you come? What have you to say to us?
MESSENGER: Good news, my lady, for your house and your
     husband.
IOKASTE: What news? Who sent you here?
MESSENGER: I am from Corinth.
   The news I bring ought to mean joy for you,
30   Though it may be you will find some grief in it.
IOKASTE: What is it? How can it touch us in both ways?
MESSENGER: The word is that the people of the Isthmus
   Intend to call Oedipus to be their king.
IOKASTE: But old King Polybos — is he not reigning still?
35   MESSENGER: No. Death holds him in his sepulchre.
IOKASTE: What are you saying? Polybos is dead?

MESSENGER: If I am not telling the truth, may I die myself.
IOKASTE (*to a* MAIDSERVANT): Go in, go quickly; tell this to
   your master.

   O riddlers of God's will, where are you now!
   This was the man whom Oedipus, long ago,   40
   Feared so, fled so, in dread of destroying him —
   But it was another fate by which he died.

(*Enter* OEDIPUS, *center.*)

OEDIPUS: Dearest Iokastê, why have you sent for me?
IOKASTE: Listen to what this man says, and then tell me
   What has become of the solemn prophecies.   45
OEDIPUS: Who is this man? What is his news for me?
IOKASTE: He has come from Corinth to announce your
   father's death!
OEDIPUS: Is it true, stranger? Tell me in your own words.
MESSENGER: I can not say it more clearly: the King is dead.
OEDIPUS: Was it by treason? Or by an attack of illness?   50
MESSENGER: A little thing brings old men to their rest.
OEDIPUS: It was sickness, then?
MESSENGER: Yes, and his many years.
OEDIPUS: Ah!
   Why should a man respect the Pythian hearth, or   55
   Give heed to the birds that jangle above his head?
   They prophesied that I should kill Polybos,
   Kill my own father; but he is dead and buried,
   And I am here — I never touched him, never,
   Unless he died of grief for my departure,   60
   And thus, in a sense, through me. No. Polybos
   Has packed the oracles off with him underground.
   They are empty words.
IOKASTE: Had I not told you so?
OEDIPUS: You had; it was my faint heart that betrayed me.   65
IOKASTE: From now on never think of those things again.
OEDIPUS: And yet — must I not fear my mother's bed?
IOKASTE: Why should anyone in this world be afraid,
   Since Fate rules us and nothing can be foreseen?
   A man should live only for the present day.   70

   Have no more fear of sleeping with your mother:
   How many men, in dreams, have lain with their mothers!
   No reasonable man is troubled by such things.
OEDIPUS: That is true; only —
   If only my mother were not still alive!   75
   But she is alive. I can not help my dread.
IOKASTE: Yet this news of your father's death is wonderful.
OEDIPUS: Wonderful. But I fear the living woman.
MESSENGER: Tell me, who is this woman that you fear?
OEDIPUS: It is Meropê, man; the wife of King Polybos.   80
MESSENGER: Meropê? Why should you be afraid of her?
OEDIPUS: An oracle of the gods, a dreadful saying.
MESSENGER: Can you tell me about it or are you sworn
   to silence?
OEDIPUS: I can tell you, and I will.
   Apollo said through his prophet that I was the man   85
   Who should marry his own mother, shed his father's blood
   With his own hands. And so, for all these years
   I have kept clear of Corinth, and no harm has come —
   Though it would have been sweet to see my parents again.
MESSENGER: And is this the fear that drove you out of   90
   Corinth?

OEDIPUS: Would you have me kill my father?
MESSENGER: As for that
    You must be reassured by the news I gave you.
OEDIPUS: If you could reassure me, I would reward you.
95 MESSENGER: I had that in mind, I will confess: I thought
    I could count on you when you returned to Corinth.
OEDIPUS: No: I will never go near my parents again.
MESSENGER: Ah, son, you still do not know what you are
    doing—
OEDIPUS: What do you mean? In the name of God tell me!
100 MESSENGER: —If these are your reasons for not going home.
OEDIPUS: I tell you, I fear the oracle may come true.
MESSENGER: And guilt may come upon you through your
    parents?
OEDIPUS: That is the dread that is always in my heart.
MESSENGER: Can you not see that all your fears are
    groundless?
105 OEDIPUS: Groundless? Am I not my parents' son?
MESSENGER: Polybos was not your father.
OEDIPUS: Not my father?
MESSENGER: No more your father than the man speaking to
    you.
OEDIPUS: But you are nothing to me!
110 MESSENGER: Neither was he.
OEDIPUS: Then why did he call me son?
MESSENGER: I will tell you:
    Long ago he had you from my hands, as a gift.
OEDIPUS: Then how could he love me so, if I was not his?
115 MESSENGER: He had no children, and his heart turned to
    you.
OEDIPUS: What of you? Did you buy me? Did you find me by
    chance?
MESSENGER: I came upon you in the woody vales of
    Kithairon.
OEDIPUS: And what were you doing there?
MESSENGER: Tending my flocks.
120 OEDIPUS: A wandering shepherd?
MESSENGER: But your savior, son, that day.
OEDIPUS: From what did you save me?
MESSENGER: Your ankles should tell you that.
OEDIPUS: Ah, stranger, why do you speak of that childhood
    pain?
125 MESSENGER: I pulled the skewer that pinned your feet
    together.
OEDIPUS: I have had the mark as long as I can remember.
MESSENGER: That was why you were given the name you
    bear.
OEDIPUS: God! Was it my father or my mother who did it?
    Tell me!
130 MESSENGER: I do not know. The man who gave you to me
    Can tell you better than I.
OEDIPUS: It was not you that found me, but another?
MESSENGER: It was another shepherd gave you to me.
OEDIPUS: Who was he? Can you tell me who he was?
135 MESSENGER: I think he was said to be one of Laïos' people.
OEDIPUS: You mean the Laïos who was king here years ago?
MESSENGER: Yes; King Laïos; and the man was one of his
    herdsmen.
OEDIPUS: Is he still alive? Can I see him?
MESSENGER: These men here
140   Know best about such things.

OEDIPUS: Does anyone here
    Know this shepherd that he is talking about?
    Have you seen him in the fields, or in the town?
    If you have, tell me. It is time things were made plain.
CHORAGOS: I think the man he means is that same shepherd   145
    You have already asked to see. Iokastê perhaps
    Could tell you something.
OEDIPUS: Do you know anything
    About him, Lady? Is he the man we have summoned?
    Is that the man this shepherd means?   150
IOKASTE: Why think of him?
    Forget this herdsman. Forget it all.
    This talk is a waste of time.
OEDIPUS: How can you say that,
    When the clues to my true birth are in my hands?   155
IOKASTE: For God's love, let us have no more questioning!
    Is your life nothing to you?
    My own is pain enough for me to bear.
MESSENGER: You need not worry. Suppose my mother a
    slave,
    And born of slaves: no baseness can touch you.   160
IOKASTE: Listen to me, I beg of you: do not do this thing!
OEDIPUS: I will not listen; the truth must be made known.
IOKASTE: Everything that I say is for your own good!
OEDIPUS: My own good
    Snaps my patience, then; I want none of it.   165
IOKASTE: You are fatally wrong! May you never learn who you
    are!
OEDIPUS: Go, one of you, and bring the shepherd here.
    Let us leave this woman to brag of her royal name.
IOKASTE: Ah, miserable!
    That is the only word I have for you now.   170
    That is the only word I can ever have.

(Exit into the palace.)

CHORAGOS: Why has she left us, Oedipus? Why has she gone
    In such a passion of sorrow? I fear this silence:
    Something dreadful may come of it.
OEDIPUS: Let it come!   175
    However base my birth, I must know about it.
    The Queen, like a woman, is perhaps ashamed
    To think of my low origin. But I
    Am a child of Luck; I can not be dishonored.
    Luck is my mother; the passing months, my brothers,   180
    Have seen me rich and poor.
    If this is so,
    How could I wish that I were someone else?
    How could I not be glad to know my birth?

ODE III

Strophe

CHORUS: If ever the coming time were known   185
    To my heart's pondering,
    Kithairon, now by Heaven I see the torches
    At the festival of the next full moon,
    And see the dance, and hear the choir sing
    A grace to your gentle shade: 190
    Mountain where Oedipus was found,
    O mountain guard of a noble race!

May the god who heals us lend his aid,
And let that glory come to pass
195   For our King's cradling-ground.

Antistrophe

Of the nymphs that flower beyond the years,
Who bore you, royal child,
To Pan of the hills or the timberline Apollo,
Cold in delight where the upland clears,
200   Or Hermês for whom Kyllenês heights are piled?
Or flushed as evening cloud,
Great Dionysos, roamer of mountains,
He—was it he who found you there,
And caught you up in his own proud
205   Arms from the sweet god-ravisher
Who laughed by the Muses' fountains?

SCENE IV

OEDIPUS: Sirs: though I do not know the man,
   I think I see him coming, this shepherd we want:
   He is old, like our friend here, and the men
   Bringing him seem to be servants of my house.
5   But you can tell, if you have ever seen him.

(Enter SHEPHERD *escorted by servants.)*

CHORAGOS: I know him, he was Laïos' man. You can trust
   him.
OEDIPUS: Tell me first, you from Corinth: is this the shepherd
   We were discussing?
MESSENGER: This is the very man.
10   OEDIPUS (*to* SHEPHERD): Come here. No, look at me. You
   must answer
   Everything I ask.—You belonged to Laïos?
SHEPHERD: Yes: born his slave, brought up in his house.
OEDIPUS: Tell me: what kind of work did you do for him?
SHEPHERD: I was a shepherd of his, most of my life.
15   OEDIPUS: Where mainly did you go for pasturage?
SHEPHERD: Sometimes Kithairon, sometimes the hills
   near-by.
OEDIPUS: Do you remember ever seeing this man out there?
SHEPHERD: What would he be doing there? This man?
OEDIPUS: This man standing here. Have you ever seen him
   before?
20   SHEPHERD: No. At least, not to my recollection.
MESSENGER: And that is not strange, my lord. But I'll refresh
   His memory: he must remember when we two
   Spent three whole seasons together, March to September,
   On Kithairon or thereabouts. He had two flocks;
25   I had one. Each autumn I'd drive mine home
   And he would go back with his to Laïos' sheepfold.—
   Is this not true, just as I have described it?
SHEPHERD: True, yes; but it was all so long ago.
MESSENGER: Well, then: do you remember, back in those
   days,
30   That you gave me a baby boy to bring up as my own?
SHEPHERD: What if I did? What are you trying to say?
MESSENGER: King Oedipus was once that little child.
SHEPHERD: Damn you, hold your tongue!

OEDIPUS: No more of that!
   It is your tongue needs watching, not this man's.   35
SHEPHERD: My King, my Master, what is it I have done
   wrong?
OEDIPUS: You have not answered his question about the boy.
SHEPHERD: He does not know . . . He is only making
   trouble . . .
OEDIPUS: Come, speak plainly, or it will go hard with you.
SHEPHERD: In God's name, do not torture an old man!   40
OEDIPUS: Come here, one of you; bind his arms behind him.
SHEPHERD: Unhappy king! What more do you wish to learn?
OEDIPUS: Did you give this man the child he speaks of?
SHEPHERD: I did.
   And I would to God I had died that very day.   45
OEDIPUS: You will die now unless you speak the truth.
SHEPHERD: Yet if I speak the truth, I am worse than dead.
OEDIPUS (*to* ATTENDANT): He intends to draw it out,
   apparently—
SHEPHERD: No! I have told you already that I gave him the
   boy.
OEDIPUS: Where did you get him? From your house? 50
   From somewhere else?
SHEPHERD: Not from mine, no. A man gave him to me.
OEDIPUS: Is that man here? Whose house did he belong to?
SHEPHERD: For God's love, my King, do not ask me any
   more!
OEDIPUS: You are a dead man if I have to ask you again.
SHEPHERD: Then . . . Then the child was from the palace of   55
   Laïos.
OEDIPUS: A slave child? or a child of his own line?
SHEPHERD: Ah, I am on the brink of dreadful speech!
OEDIPUS: And I of dreadful hearing. Yet I must hear.
SHEPHERD: If you must be told, then . . .
   They said it was Laïos' child;   60
   But it is your wife who can tell you about that.
OEDIPUS: My wife!—Did she give it to you?
SHEPHERD: My lord, she did.
OEDIPUS: Do you know why?
SHEPHERD: I was told to get rid of it.   65
OEDIPUS: Oh heartless mother!
SHEPHERD: But in dread of prophecies . . .
OEDIPUS: Tell me.
SHEPHERD: It was said that the boy would kill his own father.
OEDIPUS: Then why did you give him over to this old man?   70
SHEPHERD: I pitied the baby, my King,
   And I thought that this man would take him far away
   To his own country.
   He saved him—but for what a fate!
   For if you are what this man says you are,   75
   No man living is more wretched than Oedipus.
OEDIPUS: Ah God!
   It was true!
   All the prophecies!
   —Now,   80
   O Light, may I look on you for the last time!
   I, Oedipus,
   Oedipus, damned in his birth, in his marriage damned,
   Damned in the blood he shed with his own hand!

(He rushes into the palace.)

ODE IV

Strophe 1

85 CHORUS: Alas for the seed of men.

What measure shall I give these generations
That breathe on the void and are void
And exist and do not exist?

Who bears more weight of joy
90   Than mass of sunlight shifting in images,
Or who shall make his thought stay on
That down time drifts away?

Your splendor is all fallen.

O naked brow of wrath and tears,
95   O change of Oedipus!
I who saw your days call no man blest—
Your great days like ghosts gone.

Antistrophe 1

That mind was a strong bow.

Deep, how deep you drew it then, hard archer,
100   At a dim fearful range,

And brought dear glory down!

You overcame the stranger—
The virgin with her hooking lion claws—
And though death sang, stood like a tower
105   To make pale Thebes take heart.

Fortress against our sorrow!

True king, giver of laws,
Majestic Oedipus!
No prince in Thebes had ever such renown,
110   No prince won such grace of power.

Strophe 2

And now of all men ever known
Most pitiful is this man's story:
His fortunes are most changed, his state
Fallen to a low slave's
115   Ground under bitter fate.

O Oedipus, most royal one!
The great door that expelled you to the light
Gave at night—ah, gave night to your glory:
As to the father, to the fathering son.

120   All understood too late.

How could that queen whom Laïos won,
The garden that he harrowed at his height,
Be silent when that act was done?

Antistrophe 2

But all eyes fail before time's eye,
125   All actions come to justice there.
Your bed, your dread sirings,
Are brought to book at last.

Child by Laïos doomed to die,
Then doomed to lose that fortunate little death,

Would God you never took breath in this air   130
That with my wailing lips I take to cry:

For I weep the world's outcast.

I was blind, and now I can tell why:
Asleep, for you had given ease of breath
To Thebes, while the false years went by.   135

EXODUS

(*Enter, from the palace,* SECOND MESSENGER.)

SECOND MESSENGER: Elders of Thebes, most honored in this
    land,
What horrors are yours to see and hear, what weight
Of sorrow to be endured, if, true to your birth,
You venerate the line of Labdakos!
I think neither Istros nor Phasis, those great rivers,   140
Could purify this place of all the evil
It shelters now, or soon must bring to light—
Evil not done unconsciously, but willed.

The greatest griefs are those we cause ourselves.
CHORAGOS: Surely, friend, we have grief enough already;   145
    What new sorrow do you mean?
SECOND MESSENGER: The Queen is dead.
CHORAGOS: O miserable Queen! But at whose hand?
SECOND MESSENGER: Her own.
The full horror of what happened you can not know,   150
For you did not see it; but I, who did, will tell you
As clearly as I can how she met her death.

When she had left us,
In passionate silence, passing through the court,
She ran to her apartment in the house,   155
Her hair clutched by the fingers of both hands.
She closed the doors behind her; then, by that bed
Where long ago the fatal son was conceived—
That son who should bring about his father's death—
We heard her call upon Laïos, dead so many years,   160
And heard her wail for the double fruit of her marriage,
A husband by her husband, children by her child.

Exactly how she died I do not know:
For Oedipus burst in moaning and would not let us
Keep vigil to the end: it was by him   165
As he stormed about the room that our eyes were caught.
From one to another of us he went, begging a sword,
Hunting the wife who was not his wife, the mother
Whose womb had carried his own children and himself.
I do not know: it was none of us aided him,   170
But surely one of the gods was in control!
For with a dreadful cry
He hurled his weight, as though wrenched out of himself,
At the twin doors: the bolts gave, and he rushed in.
And there we saw her hanging, her body swaying   175
From the cruel cord she had noosed about her neck.
A great sob broke from him, heartbreaking to hear,
As he loosed the rope and lowered her to the ground.

I would blot out from my mind what happened next!
For the King ripped from her gown the golden brooches   180

That were her ornament, and raised them, and plunged
   them down
Straight into his own eyeballs, crying, 'No more,
No more shall you look on the misery about me,
The horrors of my own doing! Too long you have known
185   The faces of those whom I should never have seen,
Too long been blind to those for whom I was searching!
From this hour, go in darkness!' And as he spoke,
He struck at his eyes — not once, but many times;
And the blood spattered his beard,
190   Bursting from his ruined sockets like red hail.

So from the unhappiness of two this evil has sprung,
A curse on the man and woman alike. The old
Happiness of the house of Labdakos
Was happiness enough: where is it today?
195   It is all wailing and ruin, disgrace, death — all
The misery of mankind that has a name —
And it is wholly and for ever theirs.
CHORAGOS: Is he in agony still? Is there no rest for him?
SECOND MESSENGER: He is calling for someone to open the
   doors wide
200   So that all the children of Kadmos may look upon
His father's murderer, his mother's — no,
I can not say it!
And then he will leave Thebes,
Self-exiled, in order that the curse
205   Which he himself pronounced may depart from the house.
He is weak, and there is none to lead him,
So terrible is his suffering.
But you will see:
Look, the doors are opening; in a moment
210   You will see a thing that would crush a heart of stone.

(The central door is opened; OEDIPUS, blinded, is led in.)

CHORAGOS: Dreadful indeed for men to see.
Never have my own eyes
Looked on a sight so full of fear.

Oedipus!
215   What madness came upon you, what daemon
Leaped on your life with heavier
Punishment than a mortal man can bear?
No: I can not even
Look at you, poor ruined one.
220   And I would speak, question, ponder,
If I were able. No.
You make me shudder.
OEDIPUS: God.   God.
Is there a sorrow greater?
225   Where shall I find harbor in this world?
My voice is hurled far on a dark wind.
What has God done to me?
CHORAGOS: Too terrible to think of, or to see.

Strophe 1

OEDIPUS: O cloud of night,
230   Never to be turned away: night coming on,
I can not tell how: night like a shroud!

My fair winds brought me here.
O God. Again
The pain of the spikes where I had sight,

The flooding pain   235
Of memory, never to be gouged out.
CHORAGOS: This is not strange.
You suffer it all twice over, remorse in pain,
Pain in remorse.

Antistrophe 1

OEDIPUS: Ah dear friend   240
Are you faithful even yet, you alone?
Are you still standing near me, will you stay here,
Patient, to care for the blind?
The blind man!
Yet even blind I know who it is attends me,   245
By the voice's tone —
Though my new darkness hide the comforter.
CHORAGOS: Oh fearful act!
What god was it drove you to rake black
Night across your eyes?   250

Strophe 2

OEDIPUS: Apollo. Apollo. Dear
Children, the god was Apollo.
He brought my sick, sick fate upon me.
But the blinding hand was my own!
How could I bear to see   255
When all my sight was horror everywhere?
CHORAGOS: Everywhere; that is true.
OEDIPUS: And now what is left?
Images? Love? A greeting even,
Sweet to the senses? Is there anything?   260
Ah, no, friends: lead me away.
Lead me away from Thebes.
Lead the great wreck
And hell of Oedipus, whom the gods hate.
CHORAGOS: Your misery, you are not blind to that.   265
Would God you had never found it out!

Antistrophe 2

OEDIPUS: Death take the man who unbound
My feet on the hillside
And delivered me from death to life! What life?
If only I had died,   270
This weight of monstrous doom
Could not have dragged me and my darlings down.
CHORAGOS: I would have wished the same.
OEDIPUS: Oh never to have come here
With my father's blood upon me! Never   275
To have been the man they call his mother's husband!
Oh accurst! Oh child of evil,
To have entered that wretched bed —
The selfsame one!
More primal than sin itself, this fell to me.   280
CHORAGOS: I do not know what words to offer you.
You were better dead than alive and blind.
OEDIPUS: Do not counsel me any more. This punishment
That I have laid upon myself is just.
If I had eyes,   285
I do not know how I could bear the sight
Of my father, when I came to the house of Death,
Or my mother: for I have sinned against them both
So vilely that I could not make my peace

290 By strangling my own life
Or do you think my children,
Born as they were born, would be sweet to my eyes?
Ah never, never! Nor this town with its high walls,
Nor the holy images of the gods.

295 For I,
Thrice miserable!—Oedipus, noblest of all the line
Of Kadmos, have condemned myself to enjoy
These things no more, by my own malediction
Expelling that man whom the gods declared
300 To be a defilement in the house of Laïos.
After exposing the rankness of my own guilt,
How could I look men frankly in the eyes?
No, I swear it,
If I could have stifled my hearing at its source,
305 I would have done it, and made all this body
A tight cell of misery, blank to light and sound:
So I should have been safe in my dark mind
Beyond external evil.
Ah Kithairon!
310 Why did you shelter me? When I was cast upon you,
Why did I not die? Then I should never
Have shown the world my execrable birth.

Ah, Polybos! Corinth, city that I believed
The ancient seat of my ancestors: how fair
315 I seemed, your child! And all the while this evil
Was cancerous within me!
For I am sick
In my own being, sick in my origin,

O three roads, dark ravine, woodland and way
320 Where three roads met: you, drinking my father's blood,
My own blood, spilled by my own hand: can you remember
The unspeakable things I did there, and the things
I went on from there to do?
O marriage, marriage!
325 The act that engendered me, and again the act
Performed by the son in the same bed—
Ah, the net
Of incest, mingling fathers, brothers, sons,
With brides, wives, mothers: the last evil
330 That can be known by men: no tongue can say
How evil!
No. For the love of God, conceal me
Somewhere far from Thebes; or kill me; or hurl me
Into the sea, away from men's eyes for ever.
335 Come, lead me. You need not fear to touch me.
Of all men, I alone can bear this guilt.

(*Enter* KREON.)

CHORAGOS: Kreon is here now. As to what you ask,
He may decide the course to take. He only
Is left to protect the city in your place.
340 OEDIPUS: Alas, how can I speak to him? What right have I
To beg his courtesy whom I have deeply wronged?
KREON: I have not come to mock you, Oedipus,
Or to reproach you, either.

(*To* ATTENDANTS)

—You, standing there:
345 If you have lost all respect for man's dignity,

At least respect the flame of Lord Helios:
Do not allow this pollution to show itself
Openly here, an affront to the earth
And Heaven's rain and the light of day. No, take him
Into the house as quickly as you can. 350
For it is proper
That only the close kindred see his grief.
OEDIPUS: I pray you in God's name, since your courtesy
Ignores my dark expectation, visiting
With mercy this man of all men most execrable: 355
Give me what I ask—for your good, not for mine.
KREON: And what is it that you turn to me begging for?
OEDIPUS: Drive me out of this country as quickly as may be
To a place where no human voice can ever greet me.
KREON: I should have done that before now—only, 360
God's will had not been wholly revealed to me.
OEDIPUS: But his command is plain: the parricide
Must be destroyed. I am that evil man.
KREON: That is the sense of it, yes; but as things are,
We had best discover clearly what is to be done. 365
OEDIPUS: You would learn more about a man like me?
KREON: You are ready now to listen to the god.
OEDIPUS: I will listen. But it is to you
That I must turn for help. I beg you, hear me.

The woman in there— 370
Give her whatever funeral you think proper:
She is your sister.
—But let me go, Kreon!
Let me purge my father's Thebes of the pollution
Of my living here, and go out to the wild hills, 375
To Kithairon, that has won such fame with me,
The tomb my mother and father appointed for me,
And let me die there, as they willed I should.
And yet I know
Death will not ever come to me through sickness 380
Or in any natural way: I have been preserved
For some unthinkable fate. But let that be.

As for my sons, you need not care for them.
They are men, they will find some way to live.
But my poor daughters, who have shared my table, 385
Who never before have been parted from their father—
Take care of them, Kreon; do this for me.
And will you let me touch them with my hands
A last time, and let us weep together?
Be kind, my lord, 390
Great prince, be kind!
Could I but touch them.
They would be mine again, as when I had my eyes.

(*Enter* ANTIGONE *and* ISMENE, *attended.*)

Ah, God!
Is it my dearest children I hear weeping? 395
Has Kreon pitied me and sent my daughters?
KREON: Yes, Oedipus: I knew that they were dear to you
In the old days, and you must love them still.
OEDIPUS: May God bless you for this—and be a friendlier
Guardian to you than he has been to me! 400

Children, where are you?
Come quickly to my hands: they are your brother's—

Hands that have brought your father's once clear eyes
To this way of seeing—
405   Ah dearest ones,
I had neither sight nor knowledge then, your father
By the woman who was the source of his own life!
And I weep for you—having no strength to see you—,
I weep for you when I think of the bitterness
410   That men will visit upon you all your lives.
What homes, what festivals can you attend
Without being forced to depart again in tears?
And when you come to marriageable age,
Where is the man, my daughters, who would dare
415   Risk the bane that lies on all my children?
Is there any evil wanting? Your father killed
His father; sowed the womb of her who bore him;
Engendered you at the fount of his own existence!

That is what they will say of you.

420   Then, whom
Can you ever marry? There are no bridegrooms for you,
And your lives must wither away in sterile dreaming.

O Kreon, son of Menoikeus!
You are the only father my daughters have,
425   Since we, their parents, are both of us gone for ever.
They are your own blood: you will not let them
Fall into beggary and loneliness;
You will keep them from the miseries that are mine!
Take pity on them; see, they are only children,
430   Friendless except for you. Promise me this,
Great Prince, and give me your hand in token of it.

(KREON *clasps his right hand.*)

Children:
I could say much, if you could understand me,

But as it is, I have only this prayer for you:
Live where you can, be as happy as you can—   435
Happier, please God, than God has made your father.
KREON: Enough. You have wept enough. Now go within.
OEDIPUS: I must; but it is hard.
KREON: Time eases all things.
OEDIPUS: You know my mind, then?   440
KREON: Say what you desire.
OEDIPUS: Send me from Thebes!
KREON: God grant that I may!
OEDIPUS: But since God hates me . . .
KREON: No, he will grant your wish.   445
OEDIPUS: You promise?
KREON: I can not speak beyond my knowledge.
OEDIPUS: Then lead me in.
KREON: Come now, and leave your children.
OEDIPUS: No! Do not take them from me!   450
KREON: Think no longer
That you are in command here, but rather think
How, when you were, you served your own destruction.

(*Exeunt into the house all but the* CHORUS; *the* CHORAGOS
chants directly to the audience.)

CHORAGOS: Men of Thebes: look upon Oedipus.

This is the king who solved the famous riddle   455
And towered up, most powerful of men.
No mortal eyes but looked on him with envy,
Yet in the end ruin swept over him.

Let every man in mankind's frailty
Consider his last day; and let none   460
Presume on his good fortune until he find
Life, at his death, a memory without pain.

EURIPIDES

Euripides (c. 484–406 B.C.) was the youngest of the three tragic playwrights whose plays remain today. Although he first competed in the City Dionysia in 455 B.C., and won his first victory in 441 B.C., he won only four victories in his lifetime and left Athens about the year 408 B.C. for the court of King Archileus of Macedon, where he died. We do not know why Euripides won so infrequently, but his tragedies are much more bitter and ironic than those of Aeschylus or Sophocles, brilliantly unfolding the selfish capriciousness of gods and heroes alike. Of the roughly ninety plays Euripides is thought to have written, eighteen survive, and most of these were written and produced during the war with Sparta: *Alcestis*, *Medea*, *Heracleidae*, *Hippolytus*, *Cyclops* (a satyr play), *Heracles*, *Iphigeneia in Tauris*, *Helen*, *Hecuba*, *Andromache*, *The Trojan Women*, *Ion*, *The Suppliant Women*, *Orestes*, *Electra*, *The Phoenician Women*. Three additional plays — *Iphigeneia at Aulis*, *The Bacchae*, and *Alcmaeon at Corinth* (now lost) — were written in Macedon and brought to Athens by the play-wright's son Euripides the Younger. This trilogy, produced after Euripides' death, won him his final prize at the City Dionysia.

The Bacchae

The Bacchae is a touchstone for students of drama in its depiction of Dionysus, the god celebrated at the City Dionysia and perhaps glorified in some sense by the invention of drama itself. Dionysus figured in a variety of ritual passion plays about his death and rebirth, but Euripides' play is important precisely because it is not a passion play, a solely religious or ritual drama celebrating the god's sacred activities. *The Bacchae* is a secular play concerning the conflict between Dionysus the god and Pentheus, king of Thebes. Although many legends describe the origins of Dionysus, Euripides trains our attention on Dionysus' semimortal origins and his challenge to Pentheus. In his opening speech, Dionysus recalls the troubling uncertainty of his origins. Dionysus' mother, Semele, claimed to have been seduced by Zeus. Her father, Cadmus, and the citizens of Thebes, though, refused to believe her and shunned her when she became pregnant. In anger, Zeus appeared as a thunderbolt and destroyed her. The god Hermes, however, rescued the unborn Dionysus from the ashes of his mother and sewed him into Zeus' thigh until he was ready to be born. As Dionysus informs us, both he and Semele were dishonored by the mysterious circumstances of his birth: she was shamed, and he is not yet recognized as a legitimate divinity. In *The Bacchae* — the title refers to the chorus of his ecstatic female worshippers — Dionysus returns to Thebes to establish his rites, confronting and destroying his cousin Pentheus in the process.

It is important to recognize that Dionysus is not simply a god of wine, though intoxication points to the kind of religious experience that Dionysus offers. For Dionysus was associated with the changing of the seasons, an embodiment of the force of nature itself. In *The Bacchae*, a herdsman watches the secret rites of the women who worship Dionysus, and the women seem at one with nature itself. But when the Bacchae spy him, this power takes on a different dimension, and they fall on his herds with enormous strength, tearing his cattle to pieces with their hands. The power of Dionysus is the power to create and to destroy. Possessed by Dionysus, the Bacchae embody the force of nature in all its incomprehensibility. The Bacchae are possessed by a power — nature, Dionysus — beyond human understanding and, so, beyond human categories of good and evil.

The terrible duality of Dionysus' power gives rise to the deeply ironic tone of *The Bacchae*. Dionysus' changeable nature is deftly opposed to the rational singlemindedness of Pentheus. Characterizing Pentheus, Euripides at first seems to side with Dionysus, for next to the mystery of the god — a power that turns the elderly Cadmus and Teiresias into youthful revelers — Pentheus' rigid decorum seems petty, even blasphemous. But Euripides refuses to limit the power of Dionysus, to make the god easily acceptable to his audience by making his power conform readily to our sense of justice. For example, when Dionysus "possesses" Pentheus, we can see this change in Pentheus' character clearly in the theater. Pentheus not only assumes the disguise of the female Bacchae, he becomes feminized, taking on precisely those "feminine" characteristics he had criticized in Dionysus and his worshippers. This transformation points out — as Friedrich Nietzsche suggests in *The Birth of Tragedy* —

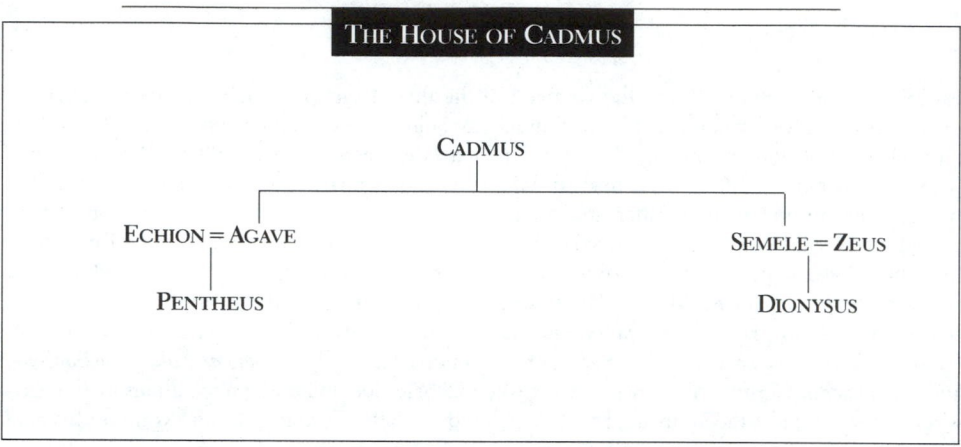

another feature of Dionysus' power, its ability to break down the construct of identity, of the self. Yet, while the intoxicated Bacchae celebrate the freedom of this surrender, it too has its terrible side. For to lose the boundaries of the self is to be destroyed, and Pentheus' transformation into one of Dionysus' revelers is, in the end, the first step toward his final undoing. The irony of Dionysus' power is perhaps best revealed in the play's climactic scene, when Agave enters holding her son's head, ripped from his body by her own hands. Possessed by the god, she believes she is holding the head of a mountain lion; as the god's power leaves her, she awakens to see the head of the son she has killed. This is a stunning, appalling recognition. Like Pentheus, who is both empowered and destroyed in his possession by Dionysus, Agave is destroyed by the recognition of what Dionysus' power has led her to become. Yet even Pentheus' death and the dishonoring of his household do not satisfy Dionysus: he exiles Agave and transforms Cadmus into a serpent. The power of the god is awesome, beyond the terms (such as divine law *vs.* human law, nature *vs.* culture, the irrational *vs.* the rational) that we might use to explain and justify it. In *The Bacchae,* Dionysus remains a figure of terror and wonder.

THE BACCHAE

Euripides

TRANSLATED BY WILLIAM ARROWSMITH

— CHARACTERS —

DIONYSUS (*also called* BROMIUS,
   EVIUS, *and* BACCHUS)
CHORUS OF ASIAN BACCHAE
   (*followers of* DIONYSUS)
TEIRESIAS
CADMUS
PENTHEUS
ATTENDANT

FIRST MESSENGER
SECOND MESSENGER
AGAVE
CORYPHAEUS
   (*chorus leader*)

SCENE: *Before the royal palace at Thebes. On the left is the way to Cithaeron; on the right, to the city. In the center of the orchestra stands, still smoking, the vine-covered tomb of Semele, mother of Dionysus.*

Enter DIONYSUS. *He is of soft, even effeminate, appearance. His face is beardless; he is dressed in a fawn-skin and carries a thyrsus (i.e., a stalk of fennel tipped with ivy leaves). On his head he wears a wreath of ivy, and his long blond curls ripple down over his shoulders. Throughout the play he wears a smiling mask.*

DIONYSUS: I am Dionysus, the son of Zeus,
come back to Thebes, this land where I was born.
My mother was Cadmus' daughter, Semele by name,
midwived by fire, delivered by the lightning's
   blast.
5   And here I stand, a god incognito,
disguised as man, beside the stream of Dirce
and the waters of Ismenus. There before the palace
I see my lightning-married mother's grave,
and there upon the ruins of her shattered house
10 the living fire of Zeus still smolders on
in deathless witness of Hera's violence and rage
against my mother. But Cadmus wins my praise:
he has made this tomb a shrine, sacred to my mother.
It was I who screened her grave with the green
of the clustering vine.
15   Far behind me lie
those golden-rivered lands, Lydia and Phrygia,
where my journeying began. Overland I went,
across the steppes of Persia where the sun strikes hotly
down, through Bactrian fastness and the grim waste
20 of Media. Thence to rich Arabia I came;
and so, along all Asia's swarming littoral
of towered cities where Greeks and foreign nations,
mingling, live, my progress made. There
I taught my dances to the feet of living men,
25 establishing my mysteries and rites
that I might be revealed on earth for what I am:
a god.
       And thence to Thebes.
              This city, first
in Hellas, now shrills and echoes to my women's cries,
their ecstasy of joy. Here in Thebes
30 I bound the fawn-skin to the women's flesh and armed
their hands with shafts of ivy. For I have come
to refute that slander spoken by my mother's sisters—
those who least had right to slander her.
They said that Dionysus was no son of Zeus,
35 but Semele had slept beside a man in love

and fathered off her shame on Zeus—a fraud, they
   sneered,
contrived by Cadmus to protect his daughter's name.
They said she lied, and Zeus in anger at that lie
blasted her with lightning.
             Because of that offense
I have stung them with frenzy, hounded them from home 40
up to the mountains where they wander, crazed of mind,
and compelled to wear my orgies' livery.
Every woman in Thebes—but the women only—
I drove from home, mad. There they sit,
rich and poor alike, even the daughters of Cadmus, 45
beneath the silver firs on the roofless rocks.
Like it or not, this city must learn its lesson:
it lacks initiation in my mysteries;
that I shall vindicate my mother Semele
and stand revealed to mortal eyes as the god 50
she bore to Zeus.
           Cadmus the king has abdicated,
leaving his throne and power to his grandson Pentheus;
who now revolts against divinity, in *me*;
thrusts *me* from his offerings; forgets *my* name
in his prayers. Therefore I shall *prove* to him 55
and every man in Thebes that I am god
indeed. And when my worship is established here,
and all is well, then I shall go my way
and be revealed to other men in other lands.
But if the men of Thebes attempt to force 60
my Bacchae from the mountainside by threat of arms,
I shall marshal my Maenads and take the field.
To these ends I have laid my deity aside
and go disguised as man.

(*He wheels and calls offstage.*)

           On, my women,
women who worship me, women whom I led 65
out of Asia where Tmolus heaves its rampart
over Lydia!
         On, comrades of my progress here!

---

6 **Dirce** a spring symbolically associated with Thebes

62 **Maenads** women participants in orgiastic Dionysian rites 66
Tmolus mountain in Asia Minor

Come, and with your native Phrygian drum—
Rhea's drum and mine—pound at the palace doors
70 of Pentheus! Let the city of Thebes behold you,
while I return among Cithaeron's forest glens
where my Bacchae wait and join their whirling dances.

(Exit DIONYSUS *as the* CHORUS OF ASIAN BACCHAE *comes dancing in from the right. They are dressed in fawn-skins, crowned
with ivy, and carry thyrsi, timbrels, and flutes.)*

CHORUS: Out of the land of Asia,
down from holy Tmolus,
75 speeding the service of god,
for Bromius we come!
Hard are the labors of god;
hard, but his service is sweet.
Sweet to serve, sweet to cry:

$\qquad\qquad\qquad\qquad$ *Bacchus!   Evohé!*
— You on the streets!
$\qquad\qquad$ — You on the roads!
80 $\qquad\qquad\qquad\qquad$ — Make way!
— Let every mouth be hushed. Let no ill-omened words
profane your tongues.
$\qquad\qquad$ — Make way! Fall back!
$\qquad\qquad\qquad\qquad$ — Hush.
— For now I raise the old, old hymn to Dionysus.

— Blessèd, blessèd are those who know the mysteries of
god.
85 — Blessèd is he who hallows his life in the worship of god,
he whom the spirit of god possesseth, who is one
with those who belong to the holy body of god.
— Blessèd are the dancers and those who are purified,
who dance on the hill in the holy dance of god.
90 — Blessèd are they who keep the rite of Cybele the Mother.
— Blessèd are the thyrsus-bearers, those who wield in their
hands
the holy wand of god.
— Blessèd are those who wear the crown of the ivy of god.
— Blessèd, blessèd are they: Dionysus is their god!

95 — On, Bacchae, on, you Bacchae,
bear your god in triumph home!
Bear on the god, son of god,
escort your Dionysus home!
Bear him down from Phrygian hill,
100 attend him through the streets of Hellas!

— So his mother bore him once
in labor bitter; lightning-struck,
forced by fire that flared from Zeus,
consumed, she died, untimely torn,
105 in childbed dead by blow of light!
Of light the son was born!

— Zeus it was who saved his son;
with speed outrunning mortal eye,
bore him to a private place,

bound the boy with clasps of gold; 110
in his thigh as in a womb,
concealed his son from Hera's eyes.

— And when the weaving Fates fulfilled the time,
the bull-horned god was born of Zeus. In joy
he crowned his son, set serpents on his head— 115
wherefrom, in piety, descends to us
the Maenad's writhing crown, her *chevulure* of snakes.

— O Thebes, nurse of Semele,
crown your hair with ivy!
Grow green with bryony! 120
Redden with berries! O city,
with boughs of oak and fir,
come dance the dance of god!
Fringe your skins of dappled fawn
with tufts of twisted wool! 125
Handle with holy care
the violent wand of god!
And let the dance begin!
He is Bromius who runs
to the mountain!
$\qquad\qquad\qquad$ *to the mountain!* 130
where the throng of women waits,
driven from shuttle and loom,
possessed by Dionysus!

— And I praise the holies of Crete,
the caves of the dancing Curetes, 135
there where Zeus was born,
where helmed in triple tier
around the primal drum
the Corybantes danced. They,
they were the first of all 140
whose whirling feet kept time
to the strict beat of the taut hide
and the squeal of the wailing flute.
Then from them to Rhea's hands
the holy drum was handed down; 145
but, stolen by the raving Satyrs,
fell at last to me and now
accompanies the dance
which every other year
celebrates your name: 150
Dionysus!

— He is sweet upon the mountains. He drops to the earth
from the running packs.
He wears the holy fawn-skin. He hunts the wild goat
and kills it. 155
He delights in the raw flesh.
He runs to the mountains of Phrygia, to the mountains
of Lydia he runs!
He is Bromius who leads us! *Evohé!*

— With milk the earth flows! It flows with wine! 160
It runs with the nectar of bees!

69 **Rhea** Cretan goddess, mother of Zeus   71 **Cithaeron** mountain of
Boeotia, sacred to Zeus and site where the infant Oedipus was
exposed   76 **Bromius** Bacchus   79 **Evohé** a cry by worshippers   90
Cybele the Mother a fertility goddess, often identified with Rhea

117 **chevulure** hairdo   120 **bryony** a vine   135 **Curetes** Cretan priests
of Rhea   139 **Corybantes** attendants or priests of Cybele, noted for
their orgiastic rites

—Like frankincense in its fragrance
is the blaze of the torch he bears.
Flames float out from his trailing wand
165   as he runs, as he dances,
    kindling the stragglers,
    spurring with cries,
and his long curls stream to the wind!

—And he cries, as they cry, *Evohé!*—
170   On, Bacchae!
    On, Bacchae!
Follow, glory of golden Tmolus,
    hymning god
    with a rumble of drums,
175 with a cry, *Evohé!* to the Evian god,
with a cry of Phrygian cries,
when the holy flute like honey plays
the sacred song of those who go
to the mountain!
            to the mountain!

180 —Then, in ecstasy, like a colt by its grazing mother,
the Bacchante runs with flying feet, she leaps!

(*The* CHORUS *remains grouped in two semicircles about the orchestra as* TEIRESIAS *makes his entrance. He is incongruously dressed in the bacchant's fawn-skin and is crowned with ivy. Old and blind, he uses his thyrsus to tap his way.*)

TEIRESIAS: Ho there, who keeps the gates?
                Summon Cadmus—
Cadmus, Agenor's son, the stranger from Sidon
who built the towers of our Thebes.
                Go, someone.
185 Say Teiresias wants him. He will know what errand
brings me, that agreement, age with age, we made
to deck our wands, to dress in skins of fawn
and crown our heads with ivy.

(*Enter* CADMUS *from the palace. Dressed in Dionysiac costume and bent almost double with age, he is an incongruous and pathetic figure.*)

CADMUS: My old friend,
I knew it must be you when I heard your summons.
190 For there's a wisdom in his voice that makes
the man of wisdom known.
            But here I am,
dressed in the costume of the god, prepared to go.
Insofar as we are able, Teiresias, we must
do honor to this god, for he was born
195 my daughter's son, who has been revealed to men,
the god, Dionysus.
            Where shall we go, where
shall we tread the dance, tossing our white heads
in the dances of god?
            Expound to me, Teiresias.
For in such matters you are wise.
            Surely
200 I could dance night and day, untiringly
beating the earth with my thyrsus! And how sweet it is
to forget my old age.
TEIRESIAS: It is the same with me.
I too feel young, young enough to dance.

CADMUS: Good. Shall we take our chariots to the mountain?
TEIRESIAS: Walking would be better. It shows more honor   205
to the god.
CADMUS: So be it. I shall lead, my old age
conducting yours.
TEIRESIAS: The god will guide us there
with no effort on our part.
CADMUS: Are we the only men
who will dance for Bacchus?
TEIRESIAS: They are all blind.
Only we can see.
CADMUS: But we delay too long.   210
Here, take my arm.
TEIRESIAS: Link my hand in yours.
CADMUS: I am a man, nothing more. I do not scoff
at heaven.
TEIRESIAS: We do not trifle with divinity.
No, we are the heirs of customs and traditions
hallowed by age and handed down to us   215
by our fathers. No quibbling logic can topple *them*,
whatever subtleties this clever age invents.
People may say: "Aren't you ashamed? At your age,
going dancing, wreathing your head with ivy?"
Well, I am *not* ashamed. Did the god declare   220
that just the young or just the old should dance?
No, he desires his honor from all mankind.
He wants no one excluded from his worship.
CADMUS: Because you cannot see, Teiresias, let me be
interpreter for you this once. Here comes   225
the man to whom I left my throne, Echion's son,
Pentheus, hastening toward the palace. He seems
excited and disturbed. Yes, listen to him.

(*Enter* PENTHEUS *from the right. He is a young man of athletic build, dressed in traditional Greek dress; like* DIONYSUS, *he is beardless. He enters excitedly, talking to the attendants who accompany him.*)

PENTHEUS: I happened to be away, out of the city,
but reports reached me of some strange mischief here,   230
stories of our women leaving home to frisk
in mock ecstasies among the thickets on the mountain,
dancing in honor of the latest divinity,
a certain Dionysus, whoever he may be!
In their midst stand bowls brimming with wine.   235
And then, one by one, the women wander off
to hidden nooks where they serve the lusts of men.
Priestesses of Bacchus they claim they are,
but it's really Aphrodite they adore.
I have captured some of them; my jailers   240
have locked them away in the safety of our prison.
Those who run at large shall be hunted down
out of the mountains like the animals they are—
yes, my own mother Agave, and Ino
and Autonoë, the mother of Actaeon.   245
In no time at all I shall have them trapped
in iron nets and stop this obscene disorder.

---

245 **Actaeon** a cousin of Pentheus who angered Aphrodite, who in consequence turned Actaeon into a stag so that he was torn to pieces by his own dogs on Cithaeron

I am also told a foreigner has come to Thebes
from Lydia, one of those charlatan magicians,
250 with long yellow curls smelling of perfumes,
with flushed cheeks and the spells of Aphrodite
in his eyes. His days and nights he spends
with women and girls, dangling before them the joys
of initiation in his mysteries.
255 But let me bring him underneath that roof
and I'll stop his pounding with his wand and tossing
his head. By god, I'll have his head cut off!
And *this* is the man who claims that Dionysus
is a god and was sewn into the thigh of Zeus,
260 when, in point of fact, that same blast of lightning
consumed him and his mother both for her lie
that she had lain with Zeus in love. Whoever
this stranger is, aren't such impostures,
such unruliness, worthy of hanging?

(For the first time he sees TEIRESIAS *and* CADMUS *in their
Dionysiac costumes.)*

                              What!
265 But this is incredible! Teiresias the seer
tricked out in a dappled fawn-skin!
                    And *you,*
you, my own grandfather, playing at the bacchant
with a wand!
                    Sir, I shrink to see your old age
so foolish. Shake that ivy off, grandfather!
Now drop that wand. Drop it, I say.

(He wheels on TEIRESIAS.*)*

270   Aha,
I see: this is *your* doing, Teiresias.
Yes, you want still another god revealed to men
so you can pocket the profits from burnt offerings
and bird-watching. By heaven, only your age
275 restrains me now from sending you to prison
with those Bacchic women for importing here to Thebes
these filthy mysteries. When once you see
the glint of wine shining at the feasts of women,
then you may be sure the festival is rotten.
280 CORYPHAEUS: What blasphemy! Stranger, have you no respect
for heaven? For Cadmus who sowed the dragon teeth?
Will the son of Echion disgrace his house?
TEIRESIAS: Give a wise man an honest brief to plead
and his eloquence is no remarkable achievement.
285 But you are glib; your phrases come rolling out
smoothly on the tongue, as though your words were wise
instead of foolish. The man whose glibness flows
from his conceit of speech declares the thing he is:
a worthless and a stupid citizen.
                    I tell you,
290 this god whom you ridicule shall someday have
enormous power and prestige throughout Hellas.
Mankind, young man, possesses two supreme blessings.
First of these is the goddess Demeter, or Earth —
whichever name you choose to call her by.
295 It was she who gave to man his nourishment of grain.
But after her there came the son of Semele,
who matched her present by inventing liquid wine

as his gift to man. For filled with that good gift,
suffering mankind forgets its grief; from it
comes sleep; with it oblivion of the troubles 300
of the day. There is no other medicine
for misery. And when we pour libations
to the gods, we pour the god of wine himself
that through his intercession man may win
the favor of heaven.
              You sneer, do you, at that story 305
that Dionysus was sewed into the thigh of Zeus?
Let me teach you what that really means. When Zeus
rescued from the thunderbolt his infant son,
he brought him to Olympus. Hera, however,
plotted at heart to hurl the child from heaven. 310
Like the god he is, Zeus countered her. Breaking off
a tiny fragment of that ether which surrounds the world,
he molded from it a dummy Dionysus.
This he *showed* to Hera, but with time men garbled
the word and said that Dionysus had been *sewed* 315
into the thigh of Zeus. This was their story,
whereas, in fact, Zeus *showed* the dummy to Hera
and gave it as a hostage for his son.
                              Moreover,
this is a god of prophecy. His worshippers,
like madmen, are endowed with mantic powers. 320
For when the god enters the body of a man
he fills him with the breath of prophecy.
                              Besides,
he has usurped even the functions of warlike Ares.
Thus, at times, you see an army mustered under arms
stricken with panic before it lifts a spear. 325
This panic comes from Dionysus.
                              Someday
you shall even see him bounding with his torches
among the crags at Delphi, leaping the pastures
that stretch between the peaks, whirling and waving
his thyrsus: great throughout Hellas.
                    Mark my words, 330
Pentheus. Do not be so certain that power
is what matters in the life of man; do not mistake
for wisdom the fantasies of your sick mind.
Welcome the god to Thebes; crown your head;
pour him libations and join his revels. 335
    Dionysus does not, I admit, *compel* a woman
to be chaste. Always and in every case
it is her character and nature that keeps
a woman chaste. But even in the rites of Dionysus,
the chaste woman will not be corrupted.
                    Think: 340
you are pleased when men stand outside your doors
and the city glorifies the name of Pentheus.
And so the god: he too delights in glory.
But Cadmus and I, whom you ridicule, will crown
our heads with ivy and join the dances of the god — 345
an ancient foolish pair perhaps, but dance
we must. Nothing you have said would make me
change my mind or flout the will of heaven.
You are mad, grievously mad, beyond the power
of any drugs to cure, for you are drugged 350
with madness.

CORYPHAEUS: Apollo would approve your words.
Wisely you honor Bromius: a great god.
CADMUS:

My boy,
Teiresias advises well. Your home is here
with us, with our customs and traditions, not
355 outside, alone. Your mind is distracted now,
and what you think is sheer delirium.
Even if this Dionysus is no god,
as you assert, persuade yourself that he is.
The fiction is a noble one, for Semele will seem
360 to be the mother of a god, and this confers
no small distinction on our family.

You saw
that dreadful death your cousin Actaeon died
when those man-eating hounds he had raised himself
savaged him and tore his body limb from limb
365 because he boasted that his prowess in the hunt surpassed
the skill of Artemis.

Do not let this fate be yours.
Here, let me wreathe your head with leaves of ivy.
Then come with us and glorify the god.
PENTHEUS: Take your hands off me! Go worship your
Bacchus,
370 but do not wipe your madness off on me.
By god, I'll make him pay, the man who taught you
this folly of yours.

(He turns to his attendants.)

Go, someone, this instant,
to the place where this prophet prophesies.
Pry it up with crowbars, heave it over,
375 upside down; demolish everything you see.
Throw his fillets out to wind and weather.
That will provoke him more than anything.
As for the rest of you, go and scour the city
for that effeminate stranger, the man who infects our
women
380 with this strange disease and pollutes our beds.
And when you take him, clap him in chains
and march him here. He shall die as he deserves—
by being stoned to death. He shall come to rue
his merrymaking here in Thebes.

(Exeunt attendants.)

TEIRESIAS: Reckless fool,
385 you do not know the consequences of your words.
You talked madness before, but this is raving
lunacy!
Cadmus, let us go and pray
for this raving fool and for this city too,
pray to the god that no awful vengeance strike
from heaven.
390 Take your staff and follow me.
Support me with your hands, and I shall help you too
lest we stumble and fall, a sight of shame,
two old men together.
But go we must,
acknowledging the service that we owe to god,

Bacchus, the son of Zeus.
And yet take care   395
lest someday your house repent of Pentheus
in its sufferings. I speak not prophecy
but fact. The words of fools finish in folly.

(Exeunt TEIRESIAS *and* CADMUS. PENTHEUS *retires into the
palace.)*

CHORUS: —Holiness, queen of heaven,
Holiness on golden wing   400
who hover over earth,
do you hear what Pentheus says?
Do you hear his blasphemy
against the prince of the blessèd,
the god of garlands and banquets,   405
Bromius, Semele's son?
These blessings he gave:
laughter to the flute
and the loosing of cares
when the shining wine is spilled   410
at the feast of the gods,
and the wine-bowl casts its sleep
on feasters crowned with ivy.

—A tongue without reins,
defiance, unwisdom—   415
their end is disaster.
But the life of quiet good,
the wisdom that accepts—
these abide unshaken,
preserving, sustaining   420
the houses of men.
Far in the air of heaven,
the sons of heaven live.
But they watch the lives of men.
And what passes for wisdom is not;   425
unwise are those who aspire,
who outrange the limits of man.
Briefly, we live. Briefly,
then die. Wherefore, I say,
he who hunts a glory, he who tracks   430
some boundless, superhuman dream,
may lose his harvest here and now
and garner death. Such men are mad,
their counsels evil.

—O let me come to Cyprus,   435
island of Aphrodite,
homes of the loves that cast
their spells on the hearts of men!
Or Paphos where the hundred-
mouthed barbarian river   440
brings ripeness without rain!
To Pieria, haunt of the Muses,
and the holy hill of Olympus!
O Bromius, leader, god of joy,
Bromius, take me there!   445
There the lovely Graces go,

442 **Pieria** a region in northern Greece

and there Desire, and there
the right is mine to worship
as I please.

450 —The deity, the son of Zeus,
in feast, in festival, delights.
He loves the goddess Peace,
generous of good,
preserver of the young.

455 To rich and poor he gives
the simple gift of wine,
the gladness of the grape.
But him who scoffs he hates,
and him who mocks his life,

460 the happiness of those
for whom the day is blessed
but doubly blessed the night;
whose simple wisdom shuns the thoughts
of proud, uncommon men and all

465 their god-encroaching dreams.
But what the common people do,
the things that simple men believe,
    I too believe and do.

(As PENTHEUS *reappears from the palace, enter from the left several attendants leading* DIONYSUS *captive.*)

ATTENDANT: Pentheus, here we are; not empty-handed either.

470 We captured the quarry you sent us out to catch.
But our prey here was tame: refused to run
or hide, held out his hands as willing as you please,
completely unafraid. His ruddy cheeks were flushed
as though with wine, and he stood there smiling,

475 making no objection when we roped his hands
and marched him here. It made me feel ashamed.
"Listen, stranger," I said, "I am not to blame.
We act under orders from Pentheus. He ordered
your arrest."

        As for those women you clapped in chains

480 and sent to the dungeon, they're gone, clean away,
went skipping off to the fields crying on their god
Bromius. The chains on their legs snapped apart
by themselves. Untouched by any human hand,
the doors swung wide, opening of their own accord.

485 Sir, this stranger who has come to Thebes is full
of many miracles. I know no more than that.
The rest is your affair.

PENTHEUS: Untie his hands.
We have him in our net. He may be quick,
but he cannot escape us now, I think.

(While the servants untie DIONYSUS' hands, PENTHEUS *attentively scrutinizes his prisoner. Then the servants step back, leaving* PENTHEUS *and* DIONYSUS *face to face.*)

                            So,

490 you *are* attractive, stranger, at least to women—
which explains, I think, your presence here in Thebes.
Your curls are long. You do not wrestle, I take it.
And what fair skin you have—you must take care of it—
no daylight complexion; no, it comes from the night
when you hunt Aphrodite with your beauty.

495   Now then,
who are you and from where?

DIONYSUS: It is nothing
to boast of and easily told. You have heard, I suppose,
of Mount Tmolus and her flowers?

PENTHEUS: I know the place.
It rings the city of Sardis.

DIONYSUS: I come from there.
My country is Lydia.

PENTHEUS: Who is this god whose worship   500
you have imported into Hellas?

DIONYSUS: Dionysus, the son of Zeus.
He initiated me.

PENTHEUS:

                You have some local Zeus
who spawns new gods?

DIONYSUS: He is the same as yours—
the Zeus who married Semele.

PENTHEUS: How did you see him?
In a dream or face to face?

DIONYSUS: Face to face.   505
He gave me his rites.

PENTHEUS: What form do they take,
these mysteries of yours?

DIONYSUS: My hair is holy.
My curls belong to god.

(PENTHEUS *shears away the god's curls.*)

PENTHEUS: Second, you will surrender
your wand.

DIONYSUS: You take it. It belongs to Dionysus.

(PENTHEUS *takes the thyrsus.*)

PENTHEUS: Last, I shall place you under guard and confine   510
you in the palace.

DIONYSUS: The god himself will set me free
whenever I wish.

PENTHEUS: You will be with your women in prison
when you call on him for help.

DIONYSUS: He is here now
and sees what I endure from you.

PENTHEUS: Where is he?
I cannot see him.

DIONYSUS: With me. Your blasphemies   515
have made you blind.

PENTHEUS: (*to attendants*)   Seize him. He is mocking me
and Thebes.

DIONYSUS: I give you sober warning, fools:
place no chains on *me*.

PENTHEUS: But *I* say: chain him.
And I am the stronger here.

DIONYSUS: You do not know
the limits of your strength. You do not know   520
what you do. You do not know who you are.

PENTHEUS: I am Pentheus, the son of Echion and Agave.

DIONYSUS: Pentheus: you shall repent that name.

PENTHEUS: Off with him.
Chain his hands; lock him in the stables by the palace.
Since he desires the darkness, give him what he wants.   525
Let him dance down there in the dark.

(As *the attendants bind* DIONYSUS' *hands, the* CHORUS *beats on its drums with increasing agitation as though to emphasize the sacrilege.*)

As for these women,
your accomplices in making trouble here,
I shall have them sold as slaves or put to work
at my looms. That will silence their drums.

(Exit PENTHEUS.)

DIONYSUS: I go,
530   though not to suffer, since that cannot be.
But Dionysus whom you outrage by your acts,
who you deny is god, will call you to account.
When you set chains on me, you manacle the god.

(Exeunt attendants with DIONYSUS captive.)

CHORUS:
—O Dirce, holy river,
535   child of Achelöus' water,
yours the springs that welcomed once
divinity, the son of Zeus!
For Zeus the father snatched his son
from deathless flame, crying:
540   *Dithyrambus, come!*
Enter my male womb.
I name you Bacchus and to Thebes
proclaim you by that name.
But now, O blessèd Dirce,
545   you banish me when to your banks I come,
crowned with ivy, bringing revels.
O Dirce, why am I rejected?
By the clustered grapes I swear,
by Dionysus' wine,
550   someday you shall come to know
the name of *Bromius!*

—With fury, with fury, he rages,
Pentheus, son of Echion,
born of the breed of Earth,
555   spawned by the dragon, whelped by Earth!
Inhuman, a rabid beast,
a giant in wildness raging,
storming, defying the children of heaven.
He has threatened me with bonds
560   though my body is bound to god.
He cages my comrades with chains;
he has cast them in prison darkness.
O lord, son of Zeus, do you see?
O Dionysus, do you see
565   how in shackles we are held
unbreakably, in the bonds of oppressors?
Descend from Olympus, lord!
Come, whirl your wand of gold
and quell with death this beast of blood
570   whose violence abuses man and god
outrageously.

—O lord, where do you wave your wand
among the running companies of god?
There on Nysa, mother of beasts?

There on the ridges of Corycia?   575
Or there among the forests of Olympus
where Orpheus fingered his lyre
and mustered with music the trees,
mustered the wilderness beasts?
O Pieria, you are blessed!   580
Evius honors you. He comes to dance,
bringing his Bacchae, fording the race
where Axios runs, bringing his Maenads
whirling over Lydias,
generous father of rivers   585
and famed for his lovely waters
that fatten a land of good horses.

(Thunder and lightning. The earth trembles. The CHORUS is
crazed with fear.)

DIONYSUS (from within): Ho!
Hear me! Ho, Bacchae!
Ho, Bacchae! Hear my cry!   590
CHORUS: Who cries?
Who calls me with that cry
of Evius? Where are you, lord?
DIONYSUS: Ho! Again I cry—
the son of Zeus and Semele!   595
CHORUS: O lord, lord Bromius!
Bromius, come to us now!
DIONYSUS: *Let the earthquake come! Shatter the floor of the*
world!
CHORUS: —Look there, how the palace of Pentheus totters.
—Look, the palace is collapsing!   600
—Dionysus is within. Adore him!
—We adore him!
—Look there!
—Above the pillars, how the great stones
gape and crack!
—Listen. Bromius cries his victory!
DIONYSUS: *Launch the blazing thunderbolt of god! O*   605
lightnings,
come! Consume with flame the palace of Pentheus!

(A burst of lightning flares across the façade of the palace and
tongues of flame spurt up from the tomb of Semele. Then a great
crash of thunder.)

CHORUS: Ah,
look how the fire leaps up
on the holy tomb of Semele,
the flame of Zeus of Thunders,   610
his lightnings, still alive,
blazing where they fell!
Down, Maenads,
fall to the ground in awe! He walks
among the ruins he has made!   615
He has brought the high house low!
He comes, our god, the son of Zeus!

(The CHORUS falls to the ground in oriental fashion, bowing their
heads in the direction of the palace. A hush; then DIONYSUS appears, lightly picking his way among the rubble. Calm and smiling
still, he speaks to the CHORUS with a solicitude approaching banter.)

---

535 **Achelöus** a river flowing to the Ionian Sea   540 **Dithyrambus**
"Twice Born," an epithet of Dionysus, referring to his second birth,
from the thigh of Zeus   574 **Nysa** mountain on which the infant
Dionysus was raised by nymphs and after which he was named

575 **Corycia** a nymph associated with Mount Parnassus   581 **Evius**
Dionysus

DIONYSUS: What, women of Asia? Were you so overcome
with fright
you fell to the ground? I think then you must have seen
620   how Bacchus jostled the palace of Pentheus. But come,
rise.
Do not be afraid.
CORYPHAEUS: O greatest light of our holy revels,
how glad I am to see your face! Without you I was lost.
DIONYSUS: Did you despair when they led me away to cast me
down
in the darkness of Pentheus' prison?
CORYPHAEUS: What else could I do?
625   Where would I turn for help if something happened to you?
But how did you escape that godless man?
DIONYSUS: With ease.
No effort was required.
CORYPHAEUS: But the manacles on your wrists?
DIONYSUS: There I, in turn, humiliated him, outrage for
outrage.
He seemed to think that he was chaining me but never
once
630   so much as touched my hands. He fed on his desires.
Inside the stable he intended as my jail, instead of me,
he found a bull and tried to rope its knees and hooves.
He was panting desperately, biting his lips with his teeth,
his whole body drenched with sweat, while I sat nearby,
635   quietly watching. But at that moment Bacchus came,
shook the palace and touched his mother's grave with
tongues
of fire. Imagining the palace was in flames,
Pentheus went rushing here and there, shouting to his
slaves
to bring him water. Every hand was put to work: in vain.
640   Then, afraid I might escape, he suddenly stopped short,
drew his sword and rushed to the palace. There, it seems,
Bromius had made a shape, a phantom which resembled me,
within the court. Bursting in, Pentheus thrust and stabbed
at that thing of gleaming air as though he thought it me.
645   And then, once again, the god humiliated him.
He razed the palace to the ground where it lies, shattered
in utter ruin—his reward for my imprisonment.
At that bitter sight, Pentheus dropped his sword, exhausted
by the struggle. A man, a man, and nothing more,
yet he presumed to wage a war with god.
650   For my part,
I left the palace quietly and made my way outside.
For Pentheus I care nothing.
But judging from the sound
of tramping feet inside the court, I think our man
will soon be here. What, I wonder, will he have to say?
655   But let him bluster. I shall not be touched to rage.
Wise men know constraint: our passions are controlled.

(Enter PENTHEUS, *stamping heavily, from the ruined palace.*)

PENTHEUS: But this is mortifying. That stranger, that man
I clapped in irons, has escaped.

(*He catches sight of* DIONYSUS.)

What! *You?*
Well, what do you have to say for yourself?
How did you escape? Answer me.

DIONYSUS: Your anger   660
walks too heavily. Tread lightly here.
PENTHEUS: *How did you escape?*
DIONYSUS: Don't you remember?
Someone, I said, would set me free.
PENTHEUS: Someone?
But who? Who is this mysterious someone?
DIONYSUS: [He who makes the grape grow its clusters   665
for mankind.]
PENTHEUS: A splendid contribution, that.
DIONYSUS: You disparage the gift that is his chiefest glory.
PENTHEUS: [If I catch him here, he will not escape my anger.]
I shall order every gate in every tower
to be bolted tight.
DIONYSUS: And so? Could not a god   670
hurdle your city walls?
PENTHEUS: You are clever—very—
but not where it counts.
DIONYSUS: Where it counts the most,
there I *am* clever.

(*Enter a* MESSENGER, *a herdsman from Mount Cithaeron.*)

But hear this messenger
who brings you news from the mountain of Cithaeron.
We shall remain where we are. Do not fear: 675
we will not run away.
MESSENGER: Pentheus, king of Thebes,
I come from Cithaeron where the gleaming flakes of snow
fall on and on forever—
PENTHEUS: Get to the point.
What is your message, man?
MESSENGER: Sir, I have seen
the holy Maenads, the women who ran barefoot   680
and crazy from the city, and I wanted to report
to you and Thebes what weird fantastic things,
what miracles and more than miracles,
these women do. But may I speak freely
in my own way and words, or make it short?   685
I fear the harsh impatience of your nature, sire,
too kingly and too quick to anger.
PENTHEUS: Speak freely.
You have my promise: I shall not punish you.
Displeasure with a man who speaks the truth is wrong.
However, the more terrible this tale of yours,   690
that much more terrible will be the punishment
I impose upon that man who taught our womenfolk
this strange new magic.
MESSENGER: About that hour
when the sun lets loose its light to warm the earth,
our grazing herds of cows had just begun to climb   695
the path along the mountain ridge. Suddenly
I saw three companies of dancing women,
one led by Autonoë, the second captained
by your mother Agave, while Ino led the third.
There they lay in the deep sleep of exhaustion,   700
some resting on boughs of fir, others sleeping
where they fell, here and there among the oak leaves—
but all modestly and soberly, not, as you think,
drunk with wine, nor wandering, led astray
by the music of the flute, to hunt their Aphrodite   705
through the woods.

But your mother heard the lowing
of our horned herds, and springing to her feet,
gave a great cry to waken them from sleep.
And they too, rubbing the bloom of soft sleep
710 from their eyes, rose up lightly and straight—
a lovely sight to see: all as one,
the old women and the young and the unmarried girls.
First they let their hair fall loose, down
over their shoulders, and those whose straps had slipped
715 fastened their skins of fawn with writhing snakes
that licked their cheeks. Breasts swollen with milk,
new mothers who had left their babies behind at home
nestled gazelles and young wolves in their arms,
suckling them. Then they crowned their hair with leaves,
720 ivy and oak and flowering bryony. One woman
struck her thyrsus against a rock and a fountain
of cool water came bubbling up. Another drove
her fennel in the ground, and where it struck the earth,
at the touch of god, a spring of wine poured out.
725 Those who wanted milk scratched at the soil
with bare fingers and the white milk came welling up.
Pure honey spurted, streaming, from their wands.
If you had been there and seen these wonders for yourself,
you would have gone down on your knees and prayed
to the god you now deny.
730   We cowherds and shepherds
gathered in small groups, wondering and arguing
among ourselves at these fantastic things,
the awful miracles those women did.
But then a city fellow with the knack of words
735 rose to his feet and said: "All you who live
upon the pastures of the mountain, what do you say?
Shall we earn a little favor with King Pentheus
by hunting his mother Agave out of the revels?"
Falling in with his suggestion, we withdrew
740 and set ourselves in ambush, hidden by the leaves
among the undergrowth. Then at a signal
all the Bacchae whirled their wands for the revels
to begin. With one voice they cried aloud:
"O Iacchus! Son of Zeus!" "O Bromius!" they cried
745 until the beasts and all the mountain seemed
wild with divinity. And when they ran,
everything ran with them.
                                    It happened, however,
that Agave ran near the ambush where I lay
concealed. Leaping up, I tried to seize her,
750 but she gave a cry: "Hounds who run with me,
men are hunting us down! Follow, follow me!
Use your wands for weapons."
                                    At this we fled
and barely missed being torn to pieces by the women.
Unarmed, they swooped down upon the herds of cattle
755 grazing there on the green of the meadow. And then
you could have seen a single woman with bare hands
tear a fat calf, still bellowing with fright,
in two, while others clawed the heifers to pieces.
There were ribs and cloven hooves scattered everywhere,
760 and scraps smeared with blood hung from the fir trees.

And bulls, their raging fury gathered in their horns,
lowered their heads to charge, then fell, stumbling
to the earth, pulled down by hordes of women
and stripped of flesh and skin more quickly, sire,
765 than you could blink your royal eyes. Then,
carried up by their own speed, they flew like birds
across the spreading fields along Asopus' stream
where most of all the ground is good for harvesting.
Like invaders they swooped on Hysiae
770 and on Erythrae in the foothills of Cithaeron.
Everything in sight they pillaged and destroyed.
They snatched the children from their homes. And when
they piled their plunder on their backs, it stayed in place,
untied. Nothing, neither bronze nor iron,
775 fell to the dark earth. Flames flickered
in their curls and did not burn them. Then the villagers,
furious at what the women did, took to arms.
And *there*, sire, was something terrible to see.
For the men's spears were pointed and sharp, and yet
780 drew no blood, whereas the wands the women threw
inflicted wounds. And then the men *ran*,
routed by women! Some god, I say, was with them.
The Bacchae then returned where they had started,
by the springs the god had made, and washed their hands
785 while the snakes licked away the drops of blood
that dabbled their cheeks.
                                    Whoever this god may be,
sire, welcome him to Thebes. For he is great
in many other ways as well. It was he,
or so they say, who gave to mortal men
790 the gift of lovely wine by which our suffering
is stopped. And if there is no god of wine,
there is no love, no Aphrodite either,
nor other pleasure left to men.

(Exit MESSENGER.*)*

CORYPHAEUS: I tremble
to speak the words of freedom before the tyrant.
But let the truth be told: there is no god
795 greater than Dionysus.

PENTHEUS: Like a blazing fire
this Bacchic violence spreads. It comes too close.
We are disgraced, humiliated in the eyes
of Hellas. This is no time for hesitation.

(He turns to an ATTENDANT.*)*

You there. Go down quickly to the Electran gates
800 and order out all heavy-armored infantry;
call up the fastest troops among our cavalry,
the mobile squadrons and the archers. We march
against the Bacchae! Affairs are out of hand
when we tamely endure such conduct in our women.
805

(Exit ATTENDANT.*)*

DIONYSUS: Pentheus, you do not hear, or else you disregard
my words of warning. You have done me wrong,
and yet, in spite of that, I warn you once
again: do not take arms against a god.

---

723 **fennel** a plant from which thyrsi were commonly made   744 **Iacchus** Dionysus   769–70 **Hysiae . . . Erythrae** two villages   800 **Electran gates** the seven gates of Thebes

810 Stay quiet here. Bromius will not let you
drive his women from their revels on the mountain.
PENTHEUS: Don't you lecture me. You escaped from prison.
Or shall I punish you again?
DIONYSUS: If I were you,
I would offer him a sacrifice, not rage
815 and kick against necessity, a man defying
god.
PENTHEUS: I shall give your god the sacrifice
that he deserves. His victims will be his women.
I shall make a great slaughter in the woods of Cithacron.
DIONYSUS: You will all be routed, shamefully defeated,
820 when their wands of ivy turn back your shields
of bronze.
PENTHEUS: It is hopeless to wrestle with this man.
Nothing on earth will make him hold his tongue.
DIONYSUS: Friend,
you can still save the situation.
PENTHEUS: How?
By accepting orders from my own slaves?
DIONYSUS: No.
825 I undertake to lead the women back to Thebes.
Without bloodshed.
PENTHEUS: This is some trap.
DIONYSUS: A trap?
How so, if I save you by my own devices?
PENTHEUS: I know.
You and they have conspired to establish your rites
forever.
DIONYSUS: True, I *have* conspired—with god.
830 PENTHEUS: Bring my armor, someone. And *you* stop talking.

(PENTHEUS *strides toward the left, but when he is almost off-stage,* DIONYSUS *calls imperiously to him.*)

DIONYSUS: *Wait!*
Would you like to *see* their revels on the mountain?
PENTHEUS: I would pay a great sum to see that sight.
DIONYSUS: Why are you so passionately curious?
PENTHEUS: Of course
I'd be sorry to see them drunk—
835 DIONYSUS: But for all your sorrow,
you'd like very much to see them?
PENTHEUS: Yes, very much.
I could crouch beneath the fir trees, out of sight.
DIONYSUS: But if you try to hide, they may track you down.
PENTHEUS: Your point is well taken. I will go openly.
840 DIONYSUS: Shall I lead you there now? Are you ready to go?
PENTHEUS: The sooner the better. The loss of even a moment
would be disappointing now.
DIONYSUS: First, however,
you must dress yourself in women's clothes.
PENTHEUS: *What?*
You want *me*, a man, to wear a woman's dress. But why?
845 DIONYSUS: If they knew you were a man, they would kill you
instantly.
PENTHEUS: True. You are an old hand at cunning, I see.
DIONYSUS: Dionysus taught me everything I know.
PENTHEUS: Your advice is to the point. What I fail to see
is what we do.
DIONYSUS: I shall go inside with you
and help you dress.

PENTHEUS: Dress? In a *woman's* dress, 850
you mean? I would die of shame.
DIONYSUS: Very well.
Then you no longer hanker to see the Maenads?
PENTHEUS: What is this costume I must wear?
DIONYSUS: On your head
I shall set a wig with long curls.
PENTHEUS: And then?
DIONYSUS: Next, robes to your feet and a net for your hair. 855
PENTHEUS: Yes? Go on.
DIONYSUS: Then a thyrsus for your hand
and a skin of dappled fawn.
PENTHEUS: I could not bear it.
I *cannot* bring myself to dress in women's clothes.
DIONYSUS: Then you must fight the Bacchae. That means
bloodshed.
PENTHEUS: Right. First we must go and reconnoiter. 860
DIONYSUS: Surely a wiser course than that of hunting bad
with worse.
PENTHEUS: But how can we pass through the city
without being seen?
DIONYSUS: We shall take deserted streets.
I will lead the way.
PENTHEUS: Any way you like,
provided those women of Bacchus don't jeer at me. 865
First, however, I shall ponder your advice,
whether to go or not.
DIONYSUS: Do as you please.
I am ready, whatever you decide.
PENTHEUS: Yes.
Either I shall march with my army to the mountain
or act on your advice.

(Exit PENTHEUS *into the palace.*)

DIONYSUS: Women, our prey now thrashes 870
in the net we threw. He shall see the Bacchae
and pay the price with death.
O Dionysus,
now action rests with you. And you are near.
Punish this man. But first distract his wits;
bewilder him with madness. For sane of mind 875
this man would never wear a woman's dress;
but obsess his soul and he will not refuse.
After those threats with which he was so fierce,
I want him made the laughingstock of Thebes,
paraded through the streets, a woman.
Now 880
I shall go and costume Pentheus in the clothes
which he must wear to Hades when he dies, butchered
by the hands of his mother. He shall come to know
Dionysus, son of Zeus, consummate god,
most terrible, and yet most gentle, to mankind. 885

(Exit DIONYSUS *into the palace.*)

CHORUS: —When shall I dance once more
with hare feet the all-night dances,
tossing my head for joy
in the damp air, in the dew,
as a running fawn might frisk
for the green joy of the wide fields, 890
free from fear of the hunt,

895 free from the circling beaters
and the nets of woven mesh
and the hunters hallooing on
their yelping packs? And then, hard pressed,
she sprints with the quickness of wind,
bounding over the marsh, leaping
to frisk, leaping for joy,
900 gay with the green of the leaves,
to dance for joy in the forest,
to dance where the darkness is deepest,
    where no man is.

—What is wisdom? What gift of the gods
905 is held in honor like this:
to hold your hand victorious
over the heads of those you hate?
Honor is precious forever.

—Slow but unmistakable
910 the might of the gods moves on.
It punishes that man,
infatuate of soul
and hardened in his pride,
who disregards the gods.
915 The gods are crafty:
they lie in ambush
a long step of time
to hunt the unholy.
Beyond the old beliefs,
920 no thought, no act shall go.
Small, small is the cost
to believe in this:
whatever is god is strong;
whatever long time has sanctioned,
925 that is a law forever;
the law tradition makes
is the law of nature.

—What is wisdom? What gift of the gods
is held in honor like this:
930 to hold your hand victorious
over the heads of those you hate?
Honor is precious forever.

—Blessèd is he who escapes a storm at sea,
who comes home to his harbor.
935 —Blessèd is he who emerges from under affliction.
—In various ways one man outraces another in the
race for wealth and power.
—Ten thousand men possess ten thousand hopes.
—A few bear fruit in happiness; the others go awry.
940 —But he who garners day by day the good of life,
he is happiest. Blessèd is he.

(Re-enter DIONYSUS from the palace. At the threshold he turns
and calls back to PENTHEUS.)

DIONYSUS: Pentheus if you are still so curious to see
forbidden sights, so bent on evil still,
come out. Let us see you in your woman's dress,
945 disguised in Maenad clothes so you may go and spy
upon your mother and her company.

(Enter PENTHEUS from the palace. He wears a long linen dress
which partially conceals his fawn-skin. He carries a thyrsus in his

hand; on his head he wears a wig with long blond curls bound by
a snood. He is dazed and completely in the power of the god who
has now possessed him.)

                          Why,
    you look exactly like one of the daughters of Cadmus.
PENTHEUS: I seem to see two suns blazing in the heavens.
    And now two Thebes, two cities, and each
    with seven gates. And you—you are a bull   950
    who walks before me there. Horns have sprouted
    from your head. Have you always been a beast?
    But now I see a bull.
DIONYSUS: It is the god you see.
    Though hostile formerly, he now declares a truce
    and goes with us. You see what you could not   955
    when you were blind.
PENTHEUS: (coyly primping) Do I look like anyone?
    Like Ino or my mother Agave?
DIONYSUS: So much alike
    I almost might be seeing one of them. But look:
    one of your curls has come loose from under the snood
    where I tucked it.
PENTHEUS: It must have worked loose   960
    when I was dancing for joy and shaking my head.
DIONYSUS: Then let me be your maid and tuck it back.
    Hold still.
PENTHEUS: Arrange it. I am in your hands
    completely.

(DIONYSUS tucks the curl back under the snood.)
DIONYSUS: And now your strap has slipped. Yes,
    and your robe hangs askew at the ankles.
PENTHEUS: (bending backward to look)   I think so.   965
    At least on my right leg. But on the left the hem
    lies straight.
DIONYSUS: You will think me the best of friends
    when you see to your surprise how chaste the Bacchae are.
PENTHEUS: But to be a real Bacchante, should I hold
    the wand in my right hand? Or this way?
DIONYSUS: No.   970
    In your right hand. And raise it as you raise
    your right foot. I commend your change of heart.
PENTHEUS: Could I lift Cithaeron up, do you think?
    Shoulder the cliffs, Bacchae and all?
DIONYSUS: If you wanted.
    Your mind was once unsound, but now you think   975
    as sane men do.
PENTHEUS: Should we take crowbars with us?
    Or should I put my shoulder to the cliffs
    and heave them up?
DIONYSUS: What? And destroy the haunts
    of the nymphs, the holy groves where Pan plays
    his woodland pipe?
PENTHEUS: You are right. In any case,   980
    women should not be mastered by brute strength.
    I will hide myself beneath the firs instead.
DIONYSUS: You will find all the ambush you deserve,
    creeping up to spy on the Maenads.
PENTHEUS: Think.
    I can see them already, there among the bushes,   985
    mating like birds, caught in the toils of love.

DIONYSUS: Exactly. This is your mission: you go to watch.
You may surprise them—or they may surprise you.
PENTHEUS: Then lead me through the very heart of Thebes,
990   since I, alone of all this city, dare to go.
DIONYSUS: You and you alone will suffer for your city.
A great ordeal awaits you. But you are worthy
of your fate. I shall lead you safely there;
someone else shall bring you back.
PENTHEUS: Yes, my mother.
DIONYSUS: An example to all men.
995 PENTHEUS: It is for that I go.
DIONYSUS: You will be carried home—
PENTHEUS: O luxury!
DIONYSUS: cradled in your mother's arms.
PENTHEUS: You will spoil me.
DIONYSUS: I *mean* to spoil you.
PENTHEUS: I go to my reward.
DIONYSUS: You are an extraordinary young man, and you go
1000   to an extraordinary experience. You shall win
a glory towering to heaven and usurping
god's.

(*Exit* PENTHEUS.)

      Agave and you daughters of Cadmus,
reach out your hands! I bring this young man
to a great ordeal. The victor? Bromius,
1005 Bromius—and I. The rest the event shall show.

(*Exit* DIONYSUS.)

CHORUS: —Run to the mountain, fleet hounds of madness!
Run, run to the revels of Cadmus' daughters!
Sting them against the man in women's clothes,
the madman who spies on the Maenads, who peers
1010 from behind the rocks, who spies from a vantage!
His mother shall see him first. She will cry
to the Maenads: "Who is this spy who has come
to the mountains to peer at the mountain-revels
of the women of Thebes? What bore him, Bacchae?
1015 This man was born of no woman. Some lioness
give him birth, some one of the Libyan gorgons!"

—O Justice, principle of order, spirit of custom,
come! Be manifest; reveal yourself with a sword!
Stab through the throat that godless man,
1020 the mocker who goes, flouting custom and outraging god!
O Justice, stab the evil earth-born spawn of Echion!

—Uncontrollable, the unbeliever goes,
in spitting rage, rebellious and amok,
madly assaulting the mysteries of god,
1025 profaning the rites of the mother of god.
Against the unassailable he runs, with rage
obsessed. Headlong he runs to death.
For death the gods exact, curbing by that bit
the mouths of men. They humble us with death
1030 that we remember what we are who are not god,
but men. We run to death. Wherefore, I say,
accept, accept:

humility is wise; humility is blest.
But what the world calls wise I do not want.
Elsewhere the chase. I hunt another game,   1035
those great, those manifest, those certain goals,
achieving which, our mortal lives are blest.
Let these things be the quarry of my chase:
purity; humility; an unrebellious soul,
accepting all. Let me go the customary way,   1040
the timeless, honored, beaten path of those who walk
with reverence and awe beneath the sons of heaven.

—O Justice, principle of order, spirit of custom,
come! Be manifest; reveal yourself with a sword!
Stab through the throat that godless man,   1045
the mocker who goes, flouting custom and outraging
    god!
O Justice, destroy the evil earth-born spawn of Echion!

—O Dionysus, reveal yourself a bull! Be manifest,
a snake with darting heads, a lion breathing fire!
O Bacchus, come! Come with your smile!   1050
Cast your noose about this man who hunts
your Bacchae! Bring him down, trampled
underfoot by the murderous herd of your Maenads!

(*Enter a* MESSENGER *from Cithaeron.*)

MESSENGER: How prosperous in Hellas these halls once were,
this house founded by Cadmus, the stranger from Sidon   1055
who sowed the dragon seed in the land of the snake!
I am a slave and nothing more, yet even so
I mourn the fortunes of this fallen house.
CORYPHAEUS: What is it?
Is there news of the Bacchae?
MESSENGER: This is my news:
Pentheus, the son of Echion, is dead.   1060
CORYPHAEUS: All hail to Bromius! Our god is a great god!
MESSENGER: What is this you say, women? You dare to
    rejoice
at these disasters which destroy this house?
CORYPHAEUS: I am no Greek. I hail my god
in my own way. No longer need I   1065
shrink with fear of prison.
MESSENGER: If you suppose this city is so short of men—
CORYPHAEUS: Dionysus, Dionysus, not Thebes,
has power over me.
MESSENGER: Your feelings might be forgiven, then. But this,   1070
this exultation in disaster—it is not right.
CORYPHAEUS: Tell us how the mocker died.
How was he killed?
MESSENGER: There were three of us in all: Pentheus and I,
attending my master, and that stranger who volunteered   1075
his services as guide. Leaving behind us
the last outlying farms of Thebes, we forded
the Asopus and struck into the barren scrubland
of Cithaeron.
            There in a grassy glen we halted,
unmoving, silent, without a word,   1080
so we might see but not be seen. From that vantage,
in a hollow cut from the sheer rock of the cliffs,

1016 **Libyan gorgons** three monstrous sisters with snakes for hair; anyone
who looked directly at Medusa, one of the gorgon sisters, turned to stone

1056 **the dragon seed** from dragon's teeth sown by Cadmus grew men
who helped him build and populate Thebes

a place where water ran and the pines grew dense
with shade, we saw the Maenads sitting, their hands
1085 busily moving at their happy tasks. Some
wound the stalks of their tattered wands with tendrils
of fresh ivy; others, frisking like fillies
newly freed from the painted bridles, chanted
in Bacchic songs, responsively.
                        But Pentheus—
1090 unhappy man—could not quite see the companies
of women. "Stranger," he said, "from where I stand,
I cannot see these counterfeited Maenads.
But if I climbed that towering fir that overhangs
the banks, then I could see their shameless orgies
better."
1095   And now the stranger worked a miracle.
Reaching for the highest branch of a great fir,
he bent it down, down, down to the dark earth,
till it was curved the way a taut bow bends
or like a rim of wood when forced about the circle
1100 of a wheel. Like that he forced that mountain fir
down to the ground. No mortal could have done it.
Then he seated Pentheus at the highest tip
and with his hands let the trunk rise straightly up,
slowly and gently, lest it throw its rider.
1105 And the tree rose, towering to heaven, with my master
huddled at the top. And now the Maenads saw him
more clearly than he saw them. But barely had they seen,
when the stranger vanished and there came a great voice
out of heaven—Dionysus', it must have been—
1110 crying: "Women, I bring you the man who has mocked
at you and me and at our holy mysteries.
Take vengeance upon him." And as he spoke
a flash of awful fire bound earth and heaven.
The high air hushed, and along the forest glen
1115 the leaves hung still; you could hear no cry of beasts.
The Bacchae heard that voice but missed its words,
and leaping up, they stared, peering everywhere.
Again that voice. And now they knew his cry,
the clear command of god. And breaking loose
1120 like startled doves, through grove and torrent,
over jagged rocks, they flew, their feet maddened
by the breath of god. And when they saw my master
perching in his tree, they climbed a great stone
that towered opposite his perch and showered him
1125 with stones and javelins of fir, while the others
hurled their wands. And yet they missed their target,
poor Pentheus in his perch, barely out of reach
of their eager hands, treed, unable to escape.
Finally they splintered branches from the oaks
1130 and with those bars of wood tried to lever up the tree
by prying at the roots. But every effort failed.
Then Agave cried out: "Maenads, make a circle
about the trunk and grip it with your hands.
Unless we take this climbing beast, he will reveal
1135 the secrets of the god." With that, thousands of hands
tore the fir tree from the earth, and down, down
from his high perch fell Pentheus, tumbling
to the ground, sobbing and screaming as he fell,
for he knew his end was near. His own mother,
1140 like a priestess with her victim, fell upon him
first. But snatching off his wig and snood

so she would recognize his face, he touched her cheeks,
screaming, "No, no, Mother! I am Pentheus,
your own son, the child you bore to Echion!
Pity me, spare me, Mother! I have done a wrong,   1145
but do not kill your own son for my offense."
But she was foaming at the mouth, and her crazed eyes
rolling with frenzy. She was mad, stark mad,
possessed by Bacchus. Ignoring his cries of pity,
she seized his left arm at the wrist; then, planting   1150
her foot upon his chest, she pulled, wrenching away
the arm at the shoulder—not by her own strength,
for the god had put inhuman power in her hands.
Ino, meanwhile, on the other side, was scratching off
his flesh. Then Autonoë and the whole horde   1155
of Bacchae swarmed upon him. Shouts everywhere,
he screaming with what little breath was left,
they shrieking in triumph. One tore off an arm,
another a foot still warm in its shoe. His ribs
were clawed clean of flesh and every hand   1160
was smeared with blood as they played ball with scraps
of Pentheus' body.
                        The pitiful remains lie scattered,
one piece among the sharp rocks, others
lying lost among the leaves in the depths
of the forest. His mother, picking up his head,   1165
impaled it on her wand. She seems to think it is
some mountain lion's head which she carries in triumph
through the thick of Cithaeron. Leaving her sisters
at the Maenad dances, she is coming here, gloating
over her grisly prize. She calls upon Bacchus: 1170
he is her "fellow-huntsman," "comrade of the chase,
crowned with victory." But all the victory
she carries home is her own grief.
                                    Now,
before Agave returns, let me leave
this scene of sorrow. Humility,   1175
a sense of reverence before the sons of heaven—
of all the prizes that a mortal man might win,
these, I say, are wisest; these are best.

(*Exit* MESSENGER.)

CHORUS: —We dance to the glory of Bacchus!
     We dance to the death of Pentheus,   1180
     the death of the spawn of the dragon!
          He dressed in woman's dress;
          he took the lovely thyrsus;
          it waved him down to death,
               led by a bull to Hades.   1185
     Hail, Bacchae! Hail, women of Thebes!
     Your victory is fair, fair the prize.
               this famous prize of grief!
     Glorious the game! To fold your child
     in your arms, streaming with his blood!   1190
CORYPHAEUS: But look: there comes Pentheus' mother,
     Agave,
running wild-eyed toward the palace.
                        —Welcome,
welcome to the reveling band of the god of joy!

(*Enter* AGAVE *with other Bacchantes. She is covered with blood
and carries the head of* PENTHEUS *impaled upon her thyrsus.*)

AGAVE: Bacchae of Asia —
CHORUS: Speak, speak.
1195   AGAVE: We bring this branch to the palace,
       this fresh-cut spray from the mountains.
       Happy was the hunting.
CHORUS: I see.
       I welcome our fellow-reveler of god.
AGAVE: The whelp of a wild mountain lion,
1200   and snared by me without a noose.
       Look, look at the prize I bring.
CHORUS: Where was he caught?
AGAVE: On Cithaeron —
CHORUS: On Cithaeron?
AGAVE: Our prize was killed.
CHORUS: Who killed him?
AGAVE: I struck him first.
1205   The Maenads call me "Agave the blest."
CHORUS: And then?
AGAVE: Cadmus' —
CHORUS: Cadmus'?
AGAVE: Daughters.
       After me, they reached the prey.
       After me. Happy was the hunting.
CHORUS: Happy indeed.
AGAVE: Then share my glory,
       share the feast.
1210   CHORUS: Share, unhappy woman?
AGAVE: See, the whelp is young and tender.
       Beneath the soft mane of its hair,
       the down is blooming on the cheeks.
CHORUS: With that mane he *looks* a beast.
1215   AGAVE: Our god is wise. Cunningly, cleverly,
       Bacchus the hunter lashed the Maenads
       against his prey.
CHORUS: Our king is a hunter.
AGAVE: You praise me now?
CHORUS: I praise you.
AGAVE: The men of Thebes —
CHORUS: And Pentheus, your son?
1220   AGAVE: Will praise his mother. She caught
       a great quarry, this lion's cub.
CHORUS: Extraordinary catch.
AGAVE: Extraordinary skill.
CHORUS: You are proud?
AGAVE: Proud and happy.
       I have won the trophy of the chase,
1225   a great prize, manifest to all.
CORYPHAEUS: Then, poor woman, show the citizens of
       Thebes
       this great prize, this trophy you have won
       in the hunt.

(AGAVE *proudly exhibits her thyrsus with the head of* PENTHEUS
impaled upon the point.)

AGAVE: You citizens of this towered city,
       men of Thebes, behold the trophy of your women's
1230   hunting! *This* is the quarry of our chase, taken
       not with nets nor spears of bronze but by the white
       and delicate hands of women. What are they worth,
       your boastings now and all that uselessness
       your armor is, since we, with our bare hands,

captured this quarry and tore its bleeding body   1235
limb from limb?
                    —But where is my father Cadmus?
He should come. And my son. Where is Pentheus?
Fetch him. I will have him set his ladder up
against the wall and, there upon the beam,
nail the head of this wild lion I have killed   1240
as a trophy of my hunt.

(Enter CADMUS, *followed by* ATTENDANTS *who bear upon a bier
the dismembered body of* PENTHEUS.)

CADMUS: Follow me, attendants.
Bear your dreadful burden in and set it down,
there before the palace.

(The ATTENDANTS *set down the bier.*)

                    This was Pentheus
whose body, after long and weary searchings
I painfully assembled from Cithaeron's glens   1245
where it lay, scattered in shreds, dismembered
throughout the forest, no two pieces
in a single place.
          Old Teiresias and I
had returned to Thebes from the orgies on the mountain
before I learned of this atrocious crime   1250
my daughters did. And so I hurried back
to the mountain to recover the body of this boy
murdered by the Maenads. There among the oaks
I found Aristaeus' wife, the mother of Actaeon,
Autonoë, and with her Ino, both   1255
still stung with madness. But Agave, they said,
was on her way to Thebes, still possessed.
And what they said was true, for there she is,
and not a happy sight.
AGAVE: Now, Father,
yours can be the proudest boast of living men.   1260
For you are now the father of the bravest daughters
in the world. All of your daughters are brave,
but I above the rest. I have left my shuttle
at the loom; I raised my sight to higher things —
to hunting animals with my bare hands.
                              You see?   1265
Here in my hands I hold the quarry of my chase,
a trophy for our house. Take it, Father, take it.
Glory in my kill and invite your friends to share
the feast of triumph. For you are blest, Father,
by this great deed I have done.
CADMUS: This is a grief   1270
so great it knows no size. I cannot look.
This is the awful murder your hands have done.
This, this is the noble victim you have slaughtered
to the gods. And to share a feast like this
you now invite all Thebes and me?
                              O gods,   1275
how terribly I pity you and then myself.
Justly — too, too justly — has lord Bromius,
this god of our own blood, destroyed us all,
every one.
AGAVE: How scowling and crabbed is old age
in men. I hope my son takes after his mother   1280

and wins, as she has done, the laurels of the chase
when he goes hunting with the younger men of Thebes.
But all my son can do is quarrel with god.
He should be scolded, Father, and you are the one
1285   who should scold him. Yes, someone call him out
so he can see his mother's triumph.
CADMUS: Enough. No more.
When you realize the horror you have done,
you shall suffer terribly. But if with luck
your present madness lasts until you die,
1290   you will seem to have, not having, happiness.
AGAVE: Why do you reproach me? Is there something wrong?
CADMUS: First raise your eyes to the heavens.
AGAVE: There.
But why?
CADMUS: Does it look the same as it did before?
Or has it changed?
AGAVE: It seems — somehow — clearer,
brighter than it was before.
1295   CADMUS: Do you still feel
the same flurry inside you?
AGAVE: The same — flurry?
No, I feel — somehow — calmer. I feel as though —
my mind were somehow — changing.
CADMUS: Can you still hear me?
Can you answer clearly?
AGAVE: No. I have forgotten
what we were saying, Father.
1300   CADMUS: Who was your husband?
AGAVE: Echion — a man, they said, born of the dragon seed.
CADMUS: What was the name of the child you bore your
        husband?
AGAVE: Pentheus.
CADMUS: And whose head do you hold in your hands?
AGAVE: (averting her eyes) A lion's head — or so the hunters
        told me.
1305   CADMUS: Look directly at it. Just a quick glance.
AGAVE: What is it? What am I holding in my hands?
CADMUS: Look more closely still. Study it carefully.
AGAVE: No! O gods, I see the greatest grief there is.
CADMUS: Does it look like a lion now?
AGAVE: No, no. It is —
Pentheus' head — I hold —
1310   CADMUS: And mourned by me
before you ever knew.
AGAVE: But who killed him?
Why am I holding him?
CADMUS: O savage truth,
what a time to come!
AGAVE: For god's sake, speak.
My heart is beating with terror.
CADMUS: You killed him.
You and your sisters.
1315   AGAVE: But where was he killed?
Here at home? Where?
CADMUS: He was killed on Cithaeron,
there where the hounds tore Actaeon to pieces.
AGAVE: But why? Why had Pentheus gone to Cithaeron?
CADMUS: He went to your revels to mock the god.
AGAVE: But we —
what were we doing on the mountain?

CADMUS: You were mad.   1320
The whole city was possessed.
AGAVE: Now, now I see:
Dionysus has destroyed us all.
CADMUS: You outraged him.
You denied that he was truly god.
AGAVE: Father,
where is my poor boy's body now?
CADMUS: There it is.
I gathered the pieces with great difficulty.   1325
AGAVE: Is his body entire? Has he been laid out well?
CADMUS: [All but the head. The rest is mutilated
   horribly.]
AGAVE: But why should Pentheus suffer for my crime?
CADMUS: He, like you, blasphemed the god. And so
the god has brought us all to ruin at one blow,   1330
you, your sisters, and this boy. All our house
the god has utterly destroyed and, with it,
me. For I have no sons left, no male heir;
and I have lived only to see this boy,
this branch of your own body, most horribly   1335
and foully killed.

(He turns and addresses the corpse.)

                  — To you my house looked up.
Child, you were the stay of my house; you were
my daughter's son. Of you this city stood in awe.
No one who once had seen your face dared outrage
the old man, or if he did, you punished him.   1340
Now I must go, a banished and dishonored man —
I, Cadmus the great, who sowed the soldiery
of Thebes and harvested a great harvest. My son,
dearest to me of all men — for even dead,
I count you still the man I love the most —   1345
never again will your hand touch my chin;
no more, child, will you hug me and call me
"Grandfather" and say, "Who is wronging you?
Does anyone trouble you or vex your heart, old man?
Tell me, Grandfather, and I will punish him."   1350
No, now there is grief for me; the mourning
for you; pity for your mother; and for her sisters,
sorrow.
        If there is still any mortal man
who despises or defies the gods, let him look
on this boy's death and believe in the gods.   1355
CORYPHAEUS: Cadmus, I pity you. Your daughter's son
has died as he deserved, and yet his death
bears hard on you.

[At this point there is a break in the manuscript of nearly fifty
lines. The following speeches of AGAVE and CORYPHAEUS and the
first part of DIONYSUS' speech have been conjecturally reconstructed from fragments and later material which made use of the
Bacchae. Lines which can plausibly be assigned to the lacuna are
otherwise not indicated. My own inventions are designed, not to
complete the speeches, but to effect a transition between the fragments, and are bracketed. — TRANS.]

AGAVE: O Father, now you can see
how everything has changed. I am in anguish now,
tormented, who walked in triumph minutes past,
exulting in my kill. And that prize I carried home   1360

with such pride was my own curse. Upon these hands
I bear the curse of my son's blood. How then
with these accursed hands may I touch his body?
1365 How can I, accursed with such a curse, hold him
to my breast? O gods, what dirge can I sing
[that there might be] a dirge [for every]
broken limb?

. . . .

Where is a shroud to cover up his corpse?
O my child, what hands will give you proper care
1370 unless with my own hands I lift my curse?

(She lifts up one of PENTHEUS' limbs and asks the help of
CADMUS in piecing the body together. She mourns each piece
separately before replacing it on the bier.)

Come, Father. We must restore his head
to this unhappy boy. As best we can, we shall make
him whole again.
            —O dearest, dearest face!
Pretty boyish mouth! Now with this veil
1375 I shroud your head, gathering with loving care
these mangled bloody limbs, this flesh I brought
    to birth.

. . . .

CORYPHAEUS: Let this scene teach those [who see these
        things:
    Dionysus is the son] of Zeus.

(Above the palace DIONYSUS appears in epiphany.)

DIONYSUS: [I am Dionysus,
    the son of Zeus, returned to Thebes, revealed,
1380 a god to men.] But the men [of Thebes] blasphemed me.
    They slandered me; they said I came of mortal man,
    and not content with speaking blasphemies,
    [they dared to threaten my person with violence.]
    These crimes this people whom I cherished well
1385 did from malice to their benefactor. Therefore,
    I now disclose the sufferings in store for them.
    Like [enemies], they shall be driven from this city
    to other lands; there, submitting to the yoke
    of slavery, they shall wear out wretched lives,
1390 captives of war, enduring much indignity.

(He turns to the corpse of PENTHEUS.)

This man has found the death which he deserved,
torn to pieces among the jagged rocks.
You are my witnesses: he came with outrage;
he attempted to chain my hands, abusing me
1395 [and doing what he should least of all have done.]
And therefore he has rightly perished by the hands
of those who should the least of all have murdered him.
What he suffers, he suffers justly.
                    Upon you,
Agave, and on your sisters I pronounce this doom:
1400 you shall leave this city in expiation
of the murder you have done. You are unclean,
and it would be a sacrilege that murderers
should remain at peace beside the graves [of those
whom they have killed].

(He turns to CADMUS.)

. . . .

        Next I shall disclose the trials
which await this man. You, Cadmus, shall be changed   1405
to a serpent, and your wife, the child of Ares,
immortal Harmonia, shall undergo your doom,
a serpent too. With her, it is your fate
to go a journey in a car drawn on by oxen,
leading behind you a great barbarian host.   1410
For thus decrees the oracle of Zeus.
With a host so huge its numbers cannot be counted,
you shall ravage many cities; but when your army
plunders the shrine of Apollo, its homecoming
shall be perilous and hard. Yet in the end   1415
the god Ares shall save Harmonia and you
and bring you both to live among the blest.
    So say I, born of no mortal father,
Dionysus, true son of Zeus. If then,
when you would not, you had muzzled your madness,   1420
you should have an ally now in the son of Zeus.
CADMUS: We implore you, Dionysus. We have done wrong.
DIONYSUS: Too late. When there was time, you did not know
    me.
CADMUS: We have learned. But your sentence is too harsh.
DIONYSUS: I am a god. I was blasphemed by you.   1425
CADMUS: Gods should be exempt from human passions.
DIONYSUS: Long ago my father Zeus ordained these things.
AGAVE: It is fated, Father. We must go.
DIONYSUS: Why then delay?
    For you must go.
CADMUS: Child, to what a dreadful end
    have we all come, you and your wretched sisters   1430
    and my unhappy self. An old man, I must go
    to live a stranger among barbarian peoples, doomed
    to lead against Hellas a motley foreign army.
    Transformed to serpents, I and my wife,
    Harmonia, the child of Ares, we must captain   1435
    spearsmen against the tombs and shrines of Hellas.
    Never shall my sufferings end; not even
    over Acheron shall I have peace.
AGAVE: (embracing Cadmus)   O Father,
    to be banished, to live without you!
CADMUS: Poor child,
    like a white swan warding its weak old father,   1440
    why do you clasp those white arms about my neck?
AGAVE: But banished! Where shall I go?
CADMUS: I do not know,
    my child. Your father can no longer help you.
AGAVE: Farewell, my home! City, farewell.
    O bridal bed, banished I go,   1445
    in misery, I leave you now.
CADMUS: Go, poor child, seek shelter in Aristaeus' house.
AGAVE: I pity you, Father.
CADMUS: And I pity you, my child,
    and I grieve for your poor sisters. I pity them.
AGAVE: Terribly has Dionysus brought   1450
    disaster down upon this house.

1438 **Acheron** a river in Hades

DIONYSUS: I was terribly blasphemed,
  my name dishonored in Thebes.
AGAVE: Farewell, Father.
CADMUS: Farewell to you, unhappy child.
1455   Fare well. But you shall find your faring hard.

    (*Exit* CADMUS.)

AGAVE: Lead me, guides, where my sisters wait,
  poor sisters of my exile. Let me go
  where I shall never see Cithaeron more,
  where that accursed hill may not see me,

where I shall find no trace of thyrsus!   1460
  That I leave to other Bacchae.

(*Exit* AGAVE *with* ATTENDANTS.)

CHORUS: The gods have many shapes.
  The gods bring many things
  to their accomplishment.
  And what was most expected   1465
  has not been accomplished.
  But god has found his way
  for what no man expected.
    So ends the play.

ARISTOPHANES

Aristophanes (c. 450–c. 388 B.C.) pursued his career as a playwright throughout the Peloponnesian War. As he observed the decline and defeat of Athens, his comedies relentlessly attacked the war and the individuals and attitudes that supported it. Aristophanes first entered the City Dionysia in 427 B.C. and first won in 426 B.C. with a now-lost play that satirized the policies and character of the military leader Cleon. Many of Aristophanes' plays — *Birds*, *Lysistrata*, *Assembly of Women* — use a utopian premise to criticize the war, but in other plays, Aristophanes lampoons other aspects of city life. In *Frogs*, for instance, a pompous Aeschylus and an embittered Euripides come from Hades to vie with one another once again; in *Clouds*, Aristophanes ridicules the sophists — professional teachers of rhetoric — for their ability to argue any side of an issue, and he particularly singles out Socrates for blame. The impact of Aristophanes' comedy on Athens should not be underestimated. In Plato's *Apology*, Socrates cites Aristophanes' portrayal of him in *Clouds* as one of the factors that turned Athenian sentiment against him, resulting in his trial and sentence of execution. Aristophanes' plays include *Acharnians*, *Knights*, *Clouds*, *Wasps*, *Peace*, *Birds*, *Lysistrata*, *Women Celebrating the Thesmophoria*, *Frogs*, *Assembly of Women*, and *Plutus*.

Lysistrata

Lysistrata is one of several plays critical of Athens' war with Sparta. Produced in 411 B.C., it follows shortly on a disastrous phase of the war for Athens. Two years earlier, the Athenian raid on Sicily had failed, and the navy was decimated, leaving Athens vulnerable to attack by Sparta. Although the navy was rebuilt before Sparta mounted its final assault, Athens fell to Sparta in 404 B.C.

Lysistrata explores the premise that the women of Greece — drawn from all the major city-states and regions — could unite to oppose the war. Led by the Athenian Lysistrata (her name means "disband the army"), the women barricade themselves on the Acropolis, withholding sex from the men until peace can be declared. Aristophanes provides each of his women with the physical attributes and accent typical of her region. The large and powerful Spartan woman Lampito, for example, is both an expert in the Spartan rump-kicking dance and speaks in what was — to an Athenian audience — an outlandish accent (to make this clear for English-speaking readers, this translation gives Lampito a Scots accent).

Lysistrata addresses the politics of its era in a variety of ways. It is, of course, a passionate plea for peace, concluding with a scene of comic feasting and dancing enjoyed by all the characters in the play, Athenians and Spartans, men and women. For modern audiences, though, the play's connection between gender and politics may seem more immediate. On one hand, the play implies an equality between men and women. The women claim that the morality of their domestic sphere is superior to the military morality pursued by the men, and to get the women back, the men are forced to compromise with them. On the other hand, although *Lysistrata* seems to provide women with political power, their power resides wholly in their sexuality; they can interrupt, but not change, the fact that they are the property of men. The Theater of Dionysus could not, of course, put women on the stage, and Lysistrata, Lampito, Calonice, and the rest — even the naked girl Reconciliation — were all played by men in padded costumes. We might also take this stage convention as an indication of the place of gender in the politics of Athens and its theater: women's concerns are only represented or impersonated by men. In the play and in the *polis*, women were defined principally through their relation to men. The limited influence women could exert was subordinate to the civil power that Aristophanes and his audience took to be the "natural" preserve of the male audience. Despite the play's earthy humor and apparent feminism, *Lysistrata* documents the actual status of women in classical Athens; their power is restricted to the sphere of the *oikos*, or home, and can be practiced only through their subservience to men, who — as citizens — finally can command women's bodies, the home, and the state as well.

LYSISTRATA

Aristophanes

TRANSLATED BY ALAN H. SOMMERSTEIN

— CHARACTERS —

LYSISTRATA
CALONICE   *Athenian women*
MYRRHINE
LAMPITO, *a Spartan woman*
CHORUS OF OLD MEN
CHORUS OF OLD WOMEN
STRATYLLIS, *leader of the Women's Chorus*
A MAGISTRATE, *member of the Committee of Ten for the Safety of the State*
FIVE YOUNG WOMEN
CINESIAS, *husband to Myrrhine*
BABY, *son to Cinesias and Myrrhine*
A SPARTAN HERALD

A SPARTAN AMBASSADOR
AN ATHENIAN NEGOTIATOR
TWO LAYABOUTS
DOORKEEPER, *of the Acropolis*
TWO DINERS
ISMENIA, *a Boeotian woman*
A CORINTHIAN WOMAN
RECONCILIATION, *maidservant to Lysistrata*
FOUR SCYTHIAN POLICEMEN
A SCYTHIAN POLICEWOMAN
ATHENIAN CITIZENS, SPARTAN AMBASSADORS,
ATHENIAN AND SPARTAN WOMEN, SLAVES, *etc.*

— ACT ONE —

SCENE: *In front of the entrance to the Athenian Acropolis. At the back of the stage stands the Great Gateway (the Propylaea); to the right, a stretch of the Acropolis wall with a little shrine to Athena Niké (Victory) built into it; to the left, a statue of the tyrannicides Harmodius and Aristogeiton. It is early morning.*

(LYSISTRATA *is standing in front of the Propylaea looking, with increasing impatience, to see if anyone is coming.*)

LYSISTRATA: (*stamping her foot and bursting into impatient speech*) Just think if it had been a Bacchic celebration they'd been asked to attend — or something in honour of Pan or Aphrodite — particularly Aphrodite! You wouldn't have been
5   able to move for all the drums. And now look — not a woman here!

(*Enter* CALONICE.)

Ah! here's one at last. One of my neighbours, I — Why, hello, Calonice.
CALONICE: Hello, Lysistrata. What's bothering you, dear? Don't
10   screw up your face like that. It really doesn't suit you, you know, knitting your eyebrows up like a bow or something.
LYSISTRATA: Sorry, Calonice, but I'm furious. I'm disappointed in womankind. All our husbands think we're such clever villains —
15 CALONICE: Well, aren't we?
LYSISTRATA: And here I've called a meeting to discuss a very important matter, and they're all still fast asleep!
CALONICE: Don't worry, dear, they'll come. It's not so easy for a wife to get out of the house, you know. They'll all be rushing
20   to and fro for their husbands, waking up the servants, putting the baby to bed or washing and feeding it —
LYSISTRATA: Damn it, there are more important things than that!
CALONICE: Tell me, Lysistrata dear, what is it you've summoned
25   this meeting of the women for? Is it something big?
LYSISTRATA: Very.
CALONICE: (*thinking she detects a significant intonation in that word*) Not thick as well?

LYSISTRATA: As a matter of fact, yes.
CALONICE: Then why on earth aren't they here?   30
LYSISTRATA: (*realizing she has been misleading*) No, not that kind of thing — well, not exactly. If it had been, I can assure you, they'd have been here as quick as you can bat an eyelid. No, I've had an idea, which for many sleepless nights I've been tossing to and fro —   35
CALONICE: Must be a pretty flimsy one, in that case.
LYSISTRATA: Flimsy? Calonice, we women have the salvation of Greece in our hands.
CALONICE: In our hands? We might as well give up hope, then.
LYSISTRATA: The whole future of the City is up to us. Either the   40 Peloponnesians are all going to be wiped out —
CALONICE: Good idea, by Zeus!
LYSISTRATA: — and the Boeotians be destroyed too —
CALONICE: Not all of them, please! Do spare the eels.
LYSISTRATA: — and Athens — well, I won't say it, but you know   45 what might happen. But if all the women join together — not just us, but the Peloponnesians and Boeotians as well — then we can save Greece.
CALONICE: The women! — what could they ever do that was any use? Sitting at home putting flowers in their hair, putting on   50 cosmetics and saffron gowns and Cimberian see-through shifts, with slippers on our feet?
LYSISTRATA: But don't you see, that's exactly what I mean to use to save Greece. Those saffron gowns and slippers and see-through dresses, yes, and our scent and rouge as well.   55
CALONICE: How are you going to do that?
LYSISTRATA: I am going to bring it about that the men will no longer lift up their spears against one another —
CALONICE: I'm going to get some new dye on my yellow gown!
LYSISTRATA: — nor take up their shields —   60
CALONICE: I'll put on a see-through right away!
LYSISTRATA: — or their swords.
CALONICE: Slippers, here I come!

---

44 **eels** Boeotia was well-known for its seafood

LYSISTRATA: *Now* do you think the women ought to be here by
65   now?

CALONICE: By Zeus, yes — they ought to have taken wing and
flown here.

LYSISTRATA: No such luck, old girl; what do you expect? —
they're Athenian, and everything they do too late. But really —
70   for nobody to have come at all! None from the Paralia, none
of the Salaminians —

CALONICE: Oh, they'll have been on the go since the small
hours. *(Aside)* They probably will too.

LYSISTRATA: And the ones I was most counting on being here
75   first — the Acharnians — they haven't come either.

CALONICE: Well, as to that, I did see Theagenes' wife consulting
the shrine of Hecate in front of her door, so I imagine she's
going to come.

(Enter, from various directions, MYRRHINE *and other women.)*

Ah, here are some coming — and here are some more. Ugh!
80   *(puckering up her nose)* where do this lot come from?

LYSISTRATA: Ponchidae.

CALONICE: I can well believe it!

MYRRHINE: *(a little out of breath)* We're not late, are we,
Lysistrata?

*(*LYSISTRATA *frowns and says nothing.)*

85   Well? Why aren't you saying anything?

LYSISTRATA: Myrrhine, I don't think much of people who come
this late when such an important matter is to be discussed.

MYRRHINE: *(lamely)* Well, I had some difficulty finding my girdle in the dark. If it is so important, don't let's wait for the rest;
90   tell us about it now.

LYSISTRATA: Let's just wait a moment. The Boeotian and Peloponnesian women should be here any time now.

MYRRHINE: Good idea. Ah, here comes Lampito!

(Enter LAMPITO, *with several other Spartan women, their dresses
fringed at the bottom with sheepskin, and with representatives
from Corinth and Boeotia.)*

LYSISTRATA: Welcome, Lampito, my dear. How are things in
95   Sparta? Darling, you look simply beautiful. Such colour,
such resilience! Why, I bet you could throttle a bull.

LAMPITO: Sae cuid you, my dear, if ye were in training. Dinna
ken, I practise rump-jumps every day.

LYSISTRATA: *(prodding her)* And such marvellous tits, too.

100   LAMPITO: *(indignantly)* I'd thank ye not tae treat me as though
ye were just aboot tae sacrifice me.

LYSISTRATA: Where's this other girl come from?

LAMPITO: *(presenting* ISMENIA) By the Twa Gudes, this is the
Boeotian Ambassadress that's come tae ye.

105   LYSISTRATA: *(inspecting* ISMENIA) I should have known — look
what a fertile vale she's got there!

CALONICE: Yes, and with all the grass so beautifully cropped,
too!

LYSISTRATA: And this one?

110   LAMPITO: Och, she's a braw bonny lass — a Corinthian.

CALONICE: Yes, I can see why you call her that! *(indicating a
prominent part of the Corinthian's person).*

LAMPITO: Who's the convener of this female assembly?

LYSISTRATA: I am.

LAMPITO: Then tell us the noo what ye have tae say.   115

MYRRHINE: Yes, dear, tell us what this important business is.

LYSISTRATA: I will tell you. But before I do, I want to ask you just
one little question.

MYRRHINE: By all means.

LYSISTRATA: The fathers of your children — don't you miss them   120
when they're away at the war? I know not one of you has a
husband at home.

CALONICE: I know, my dear. My husband has been away for five
months, five months, my dear, in Thrace I think, keeping an
eye on our general there.   125

MYRRHINE: And mine has been in Pylos for the last seven
months.

LAMPITO: And as for my mon, if he ever turns up at home, it's
anely to pit a new strap on his shield and fly off again.

LYSISTRATA: That's what it's like. There isn't anyone even to   130
have an affair with — not a sausage! Talking of which, now the
Milesians have rebelled, we can't even get our six-inch
Ladies' Comforters which we used to keep as leather rations
for when all else failed. Well then, if I found a way to do it,
would you be prepared to join with me in stopping the war?   135

MYRRHINE: By the Holy Twain, I would! Even if I had to take off
my cloak this very day and — drink!

CALONICE: And so would I — even if I had to cut myself in two,
like a flatfish, and give half of myself for the cause.

LAMPITO: And I too, if I had tae climb tae the top o' Taygetus, so   140
I cuid see the licht o' peace whenas I got there.

LYSISTRATA: Then I will tell you my plan: there is no need to
keep it back. Ladies, if we want to force our husbands to make
peace, we must give up — *(She hesitates.)*

CALONICE: What must we give up? Go on.   145

LYSISTRATA: Then you'll do it?

CALONICE: If need be, we'll lay down our lives for it.

LYSISTRATA: Very well then. We must give up — sex.

*(Strong murmurs of disapproval, shaking of heads, etc. Several of
the company begin to walk off.)*

Why are you turning away from me? Where are you going?
What's all this pursing of lips and shaking of heads mean?   150
You're all going pale — I can see tears! Will you do it or won't
you? Answer!

MYRRHINE: I won't do it. Better to let the war go on.

CALONICE: I won't do it either. Let the war go on.

LYSISTRATA: Weren't you the flatfish who was ready to cut herself   155
in half a moment ago?

CALONICE: I still am! I'll do that, or walk through the fire, or
anything — but give up sex, never! Lysistrata, darling, there's
just nothing like it.

LYSISTRATA: *(to* MYRRHINE) How about you?   160

MYRRHINE: I'd rather walk through the fire too!

LYSISTRATA: I didn't know we women were so beyond redemption. The tragic poets are right about us after all: all we're
interested in is having our fun and then getting rid of the
baby. My Spartan friend, will you join me? Even if it's just the   165
two of us, we might yet succeed.

LAMPITO: Well — it's a sair thing, the dear knows, for a woman
tae sleep alone wi'oot a prick — but we maun do it, for the sake
of peace.

---

103 **Twa Gudes** to a Spartan, this means Castor and Polydeuces (Pollux)

136 **Holy Twain** to an Athenian, Demeter and her daughter, Persephone

170 LYSISTRATA: *(enthusiastically embracing her)* Lampito, darling, you're the only real woman among the lot of them.

CALONICE: But look, suppose we did give up — what you said — which may heaven forbid — but if we did, how would that help to end the war?

175 LYSISTRATA: How? Well, just imagine: we're at home, beautifully made up, wearing our sheerest lawn negligées and nothing underneath, and with our — our triangles carefully plucked; and the men are all like ramrods and can't wait to leap into bed, and then we absolutely refuse — that'll make

180 them make peace soon enough, you'll see.

LAMPITO: Din ye mind how Menelaus threw away his sword when he saw but a glimpse of Helen's breasties?

CALONICE: But look, what if they divorce us?

LYSISTRATA: Well, that wouldn't help them much, would it?

185 Like Pherecrates says, it would be no more use than skinning the same dog twice.

CALONICE: *(misunderstanding her)* You know what you can do with those imitation dogskin things. Anyway, what if they take hold of us and drag us into the bedroom by force?

190 LYSISTRATA: Cling to the door.

CALONICE: And if they hit us and force us to let go?

LYSISTRATA: Why, in that case you've got to be as damned unresponsive as possible. There's no pleasure in it if they have to use force and give pain. They'll give up trying soon enough.

195 And no man is ever happy if he can't please his woman.

CALONICE: Well — if you really think it's a good idea — we agree.

LAMPITO: And we'll do the same thing and see if we can persuade oor men tae mak peace and mean it. But I dinna see how ye're ever going to get the Athenian riff-raff tae see sense.

200 LYSISTRATA: We will, you'll see.

LAMPITO: Not sae lang as their warships have sails and they have that bottomless fund o' money in Athena's temple.

LYSISTRATA: Oh, don't think we haven't seen to that! We're going to occupy the Acropolis. While we take care of the sexual side

205 of things, so to speak, all the older women have been instructed to seize the Acropolis under pretence of going to make sacrifices.

LAMPITO: A guid notion; it sounds as if it will wark.

LYSISTRATA: Well then, Lampito, why don't we confirm the

210 whole thing now by taking an oath?

LAMPITO: Tell us the aith and we'll sweir.

LYSISTRATA: Well spoken. Officeress!

(Enter a SCYTHIAN POLICEWOMAN, *with bow and arrows and a shield. She stares open-eyed about her.)*

Stop gawping like an idiot! Put your shield face down in front of you — so. Now someone give me the limbs of the sacrificial

215 victim.

(The severed limbs of a ram are handed to her.)

CALONICE: *(interrupting)* Lysistrata, what sort of oath is this you're giving us?

LYSISTRATA: Why, the one that Aeschylus talks about somewhere, 'filling a shield with blood of fleecy sheep.'

220 CALONICE: But Lysistrata, this oath is about peace! We can't possibly take it over a shield.

181-82 **Din ye . . . breasties** when he was about to kill her at Troy for her infidelity 185 **Pherecrates** a contemporary comic writer 218 **Aeschylus** in his *Seven Against Thebes*

LYSISTRATA: What do you suggest, then?

CALONICE: Well, if we could slaughter a full-grown cock . . .

LYSISTRATA: You've got a one-track mind.

CALONICE: Well, how *are* you going to take the oath, then? 225

MYRRHINE: I've got an idea, if you like. Put a large black cup on the ground, and pour some Thasian vine's blood into it, and then we can swear over the cup that we won't — put any water in.

LAMPITO: Whew, that's the kind of aith I like! 230

LYSISTRATA: A cup and a wine-jar, somebody!

(These are brought. Both are of enormous size.)

CALONICE: My dears, isn't it a whopper? It cheers you up even to touch it!

LYSISTRATA: Put the cup down, and take up the sacrificial jar.

(The attendant elevates the jar, and LYSISTRATA *stretches out her hands towards it and prays.)*

O holy Goddess of Persuasion, and thou, O Lady of the Loving Cup, receive with favour this sacrifice from your servants the women of Greece. Amen. 235

(The attendant begins to pour the wine into the cup.)

CALONICE: What lovely red blood! And how well it flows!

LAMPITO: And how sweet it smells forby, by Castor!

MYRRHINE: *(pushing to the front)* Let me take the oath first! 240

CALONICE: Not unless you draw the first lot, you don't!

LYSISTRATA: Lampito and all of you, take hold of the cup. One of you repeat the oath after me, and everybody else signify assent.

(All put their hands on the cup. CALONICE *comes forward; and as she repeats each line of the following oath, all the others bow their heads.)*

LYSISTRATA: I will not allow either boyfriend or husband — 245

CALONICE: I will not allow either boyfriend or husband —

LYSISTRATA: — to approach me in an erect condition. Go on!

CALONICE: — to approach me in an — erect — condition — help, Lysistrata, my knees are giving way! *(She nearly faints, but recovers herself.)* 250

LYSISTRATA: And I will live at home without any sexual activity —

CALONICE: And I will live at home without any sexual activity —

LYSISTRATA: — wearing my best make-up and my most seductive dresses — 255

CALONICE: — wearing my best make-up and my most seductive dresses —

LYSISTRATA: — to inflame my husband's ardour.

CALONICE: — to inflame my husband's ardour.

LYSISTRATA: But I will never willingly yield to his desires. 260

CALONICE: But I will never willingly yield to his desires.

LYSISTRATA: And should he force me against my will —

CALONICE: And should he force me against my will —

LYSISTRATA: I will be wholly passive and unresponsive.

CALONICE: I will be wholly passive and unresponsive. 265

LYSISTRATA: I will not raise my legs towards the ceiling.

CALONICE: I will not raise my legs towards the ceiling.

LYSISTRATA: I will not take up the lion-on-a-cheese-grater position.

CALONICE: I will not take up the lion-on-a-cheese-grater 270 position.

LYSISTRATA: As I drink from this cup, so will I abide by this oath.
CALONICE: As I drink from this cup, so will I abide by this oath.
LYSISTRATA: And if I do not abide by it, may the cup prove to be
275   filled with water.
CALONICE: And if I do not abide by it, may the cup prove to be
filled with water.
LYSISTRATA: *(to the others)* Do you all join in this oath?
ALL: We do.

(CALONICE drinks from the cup.)

280   LYSISTRATA: *(taking the cup)* I'll dispose of the sacred remains.
MYRRHINE: Not all of them, my friend — let's share them, as
friends should.

*(LYSISTRATA drinks part of the remaining wine and, with some
reluctance, hands the rest to MYRRHINE. As she is drinking it off
a shout of triumph is heard backstage.)*

LAMPITO: What was that?
LYSISTRATA: What I said we were going to do. The Citadel of
285   Athena is now in our hands. Well then, Lampito, you'll be
wanting to go and see to your side of the business at home; but
you'd better leave your friends here *(indicating the other Peloponnesian women)* as hostages with us. We'll go up on to the
Acropolis now and join the others — the first thing we must do
290   is bar the doors. *(Exit LAMPITO.)*
CALONICE: Won't the men be coming soon to try to get us out?
LYSISTRATA: They can if they like — it won't bother me. Doesn't
matter what they threaten to do — even if they try to set fire to
the place — they won't make us open the gates except on our
295   own terms.
CALONICE: No, by Aphrodite, they won't. We must show that
it's not for nothing that women are called impossible.

*(All the women retire into the Acropolis, and the gates are closed
and barred. Enter the CHORUS OF MEN, twelve in number, advanced in years, carrying heavy logs and pitchers — the latter
containing, as we shall see, lighted embers.)*

LEADER: *(recitative)* Keep moving, Draces, even if the weight
Of olive wood is hurting your poor shoulder.
300   CHORUS: Incredible! Impossible!
Our women, if you please!
We've kept and fed within our doors
A pestilent disease!

They've seized our own Acropolis,
305   With bars they've shut the gate!
They hold the statue of the Maid,
Protectress of our state!

Come on and let us hurry there
And put these logs around,
310   Smoke out the whole conspiracy
From Pallas' sacred ground!

With one accord we vote that all
Have forfeited their life,
And first in the indictment-roll
315   (Who else?) stands Lycon's wife.

LEADER: And shall these females hold the sacred spot
That mighty King Cleomenes could not?
CHORUS: The grand old Spartan king,
He had six hundred men,
He marched them into the Acropolis   320
And he marched them out again.
And he entered breathing fire,
But when he left the place
He hadn't washed for six whole years
And had hair all over his face.   325

We slept before the gates;
We wore our shields asleep;
We all of us laid siege to him
In units twenty deep.
And the King came out half starved,   330
And wore a ragged cloak,
And 'I surrender — let me go!'
Were all the words he spoke.

Now the enemies of the gods
And of Euripides   335
Have seized the Acropolis and think
They can beat us to our knees.
Well, we swear that they will not,
And we will take them on,
Or else we never fought and beat   340
The Medes at Marathon.
LEADER: I doubt if I have any hope
Of hauling these logs up the slope.
My legs they are wonky,
I haven't a donkey,   345
But somehow I'll just have to cope.

And I'd better make sure that I've got
Some fire still left in my pot;
For it would be so sad
If I thought that I had   350
And I found in the end that I'd not.

*(He blows on the embers in the pitcher. A pungent smoke arises,
which hurts his eyes.)*

Yow!
This smoke is so stinging and hot.
I think a mad dog in disguise
Has jumped up and bitten my eyes!   355
With precision more fine
One might call it a swine,
'Cos just look what it's done to my styes.

But come, let us go to the aid
Of Pallas the Warrior-Maid;   360
For now is the time,
As to glory we climb,
And we must not, must not be afraid.

(Blows on the embers again.)

Yow!
This smoke fairly has me dismayed.   365

---

306 **the Maid** Athena, also called "the Protectress" and "Pallas"   315
Lycon's wife a lady noted for her immorality

317 **Cleomenes** a Spartan king who occupied the Acropolis nearly a
century before the events of *Lysistrata*

Ah, that's woken the old flame up all right, the gods be praised! Now, suppose we put the logs down here, and put tapers into the pots, lighting them first of all of course, and then go for the door like a battering ram? We'll call on them to
370 let the bars down, and if they refuse, then we'll set fire to all the doors and smoke them out. Let's put this stuff down first.

(They lay down the logs. The LEADER *has some difficulty in sorting out his logs and his pitcher.)*

Ugh! Can the generals in Samos hear us? Will some of them come and help? Well, at least these things aren't crushing my backbone any longer. *(He puts a taper into his pitcher.)* It's up
375 to you now, pot; let's have the coal burning, and let me be the fist to have my taper alight. *(Turning towards the shrine of Victory)* Our Lady of Victory, be with us now, and may we set up a trophy to thee when we have conquered the audacious attempt of the women to occupy thy holy Acropolis.

(The CHORUS OF MEN *continue to make preparations. Just now, however, the voices of the* CHORUS OF OLD WOMEN, *also twelve in number, are heard in the distance.)*

380 STRATYLLIS: *(off)*
   I think I see the smoke and vapour rising.
   The fire has started, ladies; we must hasten.
   CHORUS OF WOMEN: *(off, approaching)*
      Come, come and help
385   Before our friends are fried.
      Some evil men
   Have lit a fire outside.

      Are we too late?
   It's early in the day,
390   But at the spring
   We suffered great delay.

      The jostling slaves,
   The crash as pitchers fall,
      The crush, the noise —
395   It's no damn fun at all.

   But now I come with water to the aid
   Of thy beleaguered servants, holy Maid!

(Hereabouts the WOMEN *begin to enter, carrying pitchers full of water.)*

      Some frail old men
   Approach with limping gait,
400   And carry logs
   Of an enormous weight.

      Dire threats they make,
   Our friends they hope to see
      Roasted alive.
405   O Maid, this must not be!

      No, may they save
   All Greece from war insane,
      For that is why
   They occupy thy fane.

410 If seeds of fire around thy hill are laid,
   Bear water with thy servants, holy Maid!

---

*(*STRATYLLIS, *at the* WOMEN's *head, almost collides with the* MEN, *who were just about to begin their rush at the doors.)*

STRATYLLIS: Hold it! What do you think you're up to, you scoundrels?

(The LEADER *tries to protest.)*

   If you were honest, or had any respect for the gods, you
   wouldn't be doing what you're doing now.   415
LEADER: This is the end! A swarm of women come as reinforcements!
STRATYLLIS: What are you so frightened for? We don't outnumber you, after all. Still, remember you haven't seen the millionth part of us yet!   420
LEADER: *(to his neighbour)* Are we going to let them go on blethering like this? Shouldn't we be bringing down our logs on their backs rather? *(All the* MEN *put down their pitchers.)*
STRATYLLIS: *(to her followers)* Put down your jars too. We don't want any encumbrances in case it comes to a fight.   425
LEADER: *(raising his fist)* Someone ought to give them a Bupalus or two on the jaw — that might shut them up for a bit.
STRATYLLIS: *(presenting her cheek to him)* All right; there you are; hit me; I won't shy away. Only, if you do, no dog will ever grab your balls again!   430
LEADER: If you don't shut up, you old crone, I'll knock the stuffing out of you!
STRATYLLIS: If you so much as touch me with the tip of your finger —
LEADER: All right, suppose I do; what then?   435
STRATYLLIS: I'll bite your chest and tear out your inside!
LEADER: *(with calculated insolence)* Euripides was right! 'There is no beast so shameless as a woman'!
STRATYLLIS: *(with cold determination)* Rhodippe! Everybody! Take up — jars! *(They do so.)*   440
LEADER: Damn you, what have you brought water for?
STRATYLLIS: Well, how about *you*, you warmed-up corpse? What's that fire for? Your funeral?
LEADER: No — those pals of yours, for their funeral.
STRATYLLIS: And we've got the water here to put your fire out!   445
LEADER: Put our fire out?
STRATYLLIS: You'll see!

(She prepares to throw the contents of her pitcher on the wood, but the LEADER *keeps her off with his lighted taper.)*

LEADER: I'm just making up my mind whether to give *you* a roasting.
STRATYLLIS: You wouldn't happen to have any soap, would you?   450
   How would you like a bath?
LEADER: A bath, you toothless wonder?
STRATYLLIS: A bridal bath, if you like.
LEADER: Of all the barefaced —
STRATYLLIS: I'm not a slave, you know.   455
LEADER: I'll shut your big mouth.
STRATYLLIS: If you try, you'll never sit on a jury again.
LEADER: Come on, let's set fire to her hair!
STRATYLLIS: Over to you, water!

(The WOMEN *all empty their pitchers over the* MEN, *who are thus thoroughly drenched.)*

---

372 **Samos** an island in the Aegean that was the headquarters of the Athenian navy

427 **Bupalus** a sculptor ridiculed by the satirist Hipponax as the recipient of blows to the jaw

460   MEN: Help, I'm soaking!
WOMEN: *(with affected concern)* Was it hot?
MEN: No, it certainly was not!
    What're you doing? Let me go!
WOMEN: *(continuing to wet them)* We're watering you to make
465   you grow.
MEN: Stop it! Stop! I'm numb with cold!
WOMEN: Well, if I may make so bold,

(pointing to the MEN's fires)

    Warm yourselves before the grate.
MEN: Stop it! Help! Help! Magistrate!

(As if in answer to their call, an elderly MAGISTRATE of severe appearance enters, attended by four SCYTHIAN POLICEMEN. The WOMEN put down their empty pitchers and await developments. The MAGISTRATE has not, in fact, come in answer to the MEN's appeal, and he at first takes no notice of their bedraggled appearance. Of the WOMEN he takes no notice at all.)

470   MAGISTRATE: I hear it's the same old thing again—the un-
    bridled nature of the female sex coming out. All their banging
    of drums in honour of that Sabazius god, and singing to
    Adonis on the roofs of houses, and all that nonsense. I re-
475   member once in the Assembly—Demostratus, may he come
    to no good end, was saying we ought to send the expedition to
    Sicily, and this woman, who was dancing on the roof, she
    cried, 'O woe for Adonis!', and then he went on and said we
    should include some heavy infantry from Zacynthus, and the
    woman on the roof—she'd had a bit to drink, I fancy—she
480   shouted, 'Mourn for Adonis, all ye people!' But the damnable
    scoundrel from Angeriae just blustered on and on. Anyway
    (rather lamely) that's the sort of outrage that women get up to.
LEADER: Wait till you hear what this lot have done. We have
    been brutally assaulted, and what is more, we have been
485   given an unsolicited cold bath out of these pots *(kicking one of
    them and breaking it)*, and all our clothes are wringing wet.
    Anybody would think we were incontinent!
MAGISTRATE: Disgraceful. Disgraceful. But by Poseidon the
    Shipbuilder, I'm not surprised. Look at the way we pander to
490   the women's vices—we positively teach them to be wicked.
    That's why we get this kind of conspiracy. Think of when we
    go to the shops, for example. We might go to the goldsmith's
    and say, 'Goldsmith, the necklace you made for my wife—
    she was dancing last night and the clasp came unstuck. Now
495   I've got to go off to Salamis; so if you've got time, could you go
    down to my place tonight and put the pin back in the hole for
    her?' Or perhaps we go in to a shoemaker's, a great strapping
    well-hung young fellow, and we say, 'Shoemaker, the toe-
    strap on my wife's sandal is hurting her little toe—it's rather
500   tender, you know. Could you go down around lunchtime per-
    haps and ease the strap off for her, enlarge the opening a
    little?' And now look what's happened! I, a member of the
    Committee of Ten, having found a source of supply for tim-
    ber to make oars, and now requiring money to buy it, come to
505   the Acropolis and find the women have shut the doors in my
    face! No good standing around. Fetch the crowbars, some-

body, and we'll soon put a stop to this nonsense. *(To two of the
POLICEMEN)* What are you gawping at, you fool? And you?
Dreaming about pubs, eh?

(Crowbars are brought in.)

    Let's get these bars under the doors and lever them up. I'll help.   510

*(They begin to move the crowbars into position, when
LYSISTRATA, CALONICE and MYRRHINE open the gates and come
out.)*

LYSISTRATA: No need to use force. I'm coming out of my own
    free will. What's the use of crowbars? It's intelligence and
    common sense that we need, not violence.
MAGISTRATE: You disgusting creature! Officer!—take her and
    tie her hands behind her back.   515
LYSISTRATA: By Artemis, if he so much as touches me, I'll teach
    him to know his place!

(The POLICEMAN hesitates.)

MAGISTRATE: Frightened, eh? Go on, the two of you, up-end
    her and tie her up!
CALONICE: *(interposing herself between SECOND POLICEMAN   520
    and LYSISTRATA)* If you so much as lay a finger on her, by
    Pandrosus, I'll hit you so hard you'll shit all over the place.
MAGISTRATE: Obscene language! Officer! *(To THIRD POLICE-
    MAN)* Tie this one up first, and stop her mouth.
MYRRHINE: *(interposing herself between THIRD POLICEMAN and   525
    CALONICE)* By the Giver of Light, if you touch her, you'll
    soon be crying out for a cupping-glass!
MAGISTRATE: What's all this? Officer! *(To FOURTH POLICEMAN)*
    Get hold of her. I'm going to stop this relay some time.
STRATYLLIS: *(intervening in her turn)* By the Bull Goddess, if   530
    you go near her, I'll make you scream! *(Giving an exemplary
    tug to FOURTH POLICEMAN's hair.)*
MAGISTRATE: Heaven help me, I've no more archers! Well, we
    mustn't let ourselves be worsted by women. Come on, offi-
    cers, we'll charge them, all together.   535
LYSISTRATA: If you do, by the Holy Twain, you'll find out that
    we've got four whole companies of fighting women in there,
    fully armed.
MAGISTRATE: *(calling her bluff)* Twist their arms behind them,
    officers.   540

*(The POLICEMEN approach the four women with intent to do
this.)*

LYSISTRATA: *(to the women inside)* Come out, the reserve! Let-
    tuce-seed-pancake-vendors of the Market Square! Inn-
    keepers, bakers and garlic-makers! Come to our help! *(Four
    bands of women emerge from the Acropolis.)* Drag them along!
    Hit them! Shout rude words in their faces!   545

*(The POLICEMEN are quickly brought to the ground, and
punched and kicked as they lie there.)*

    All right—withdraw—no plunder will be taken.

(The women retire into the Acropolis.)

MAGISTRATE: *(his hand to his head)* My bowmen have been ut-
    terly defeated!

---

472 **Sabazius** an Asiatic god, often identified with Dionysus and wor-
shipped mainly by women   473 **Adonis** a youth beloved by Aphrodite
who died young and was honored yearly in a women's festival

522 **Pandrosus** Artemis, who is also the Giver of Light and the Bull
Goddess

LYSISTRATA: Well, what did you expect? Did you think we were
550　slaves?—or that women couldn't have any stomach for
a fight?

MAGISTRATE: I must admit I thought they only had one for
booze.

LEADER: Our noble magistrate, why waste your words
555　On these sub-human creatures? Know you not
How we were given a bath when fully clothed,
And that without the benefit of soap?

STRATYLLIS: Well, he who uses force without good reason
Should not complain on getting a black eye.
560　We only want to stay at home content
And hurting no-one; but if you provoke us,
You'll find you're stirring up a hornets' nest!

CHORUS OF MEN: Monsters, enough!—our patience now is
gone.
565　　It's time for you to tell
Why you are barricaded here upon
　　Our hallowed citadel.

LEADER: (to MAGISTRATE) Now question her, and test her out,
and never own she's right:
570　It's shameful to surrender to a girl without a fight.

MAGISTRATE: (to LYSISTRATA) Well, the first thing I want to
know is—what in Zeus' name do you mean by shutting and
barring the gates of our own Acropolis against us?

LYSISTRATA: We want to keep the money safe and stop you from
575　waging war.

MAGISTRATE: The war has nothing to do with money—

LYSISTRATA: Hasn't it? Why are Peisander and the other office-
seekers always stirring things up? Isn't it so they can take a few
more dips in the public purse? Well, as far as we're concerned
580　they can do what they like; only they're not going to lay their
hands on the money in there.

MAGISTRATE: Why, what are you going to do?

LYSISTRATA: Do? Why, we'll be in charge of it.

MAGISTRATE: *You* in charge of *our* finances?

585　LYSISTRATA: Well, what's so strange about that? We've been in
charge of all your housekeeping finances for years.

MAGISTRATE: But that's not the same thing.

LYSISTRATA: Why not?

MAGISTRATE: Because the money here is needed for the war!

590　LYSISTRATA: Ah, but the war itself isn't necessary.

MAGISTRATE: Not necessary! How is the City going to be saved
then?

LYSISTRATA: We'll save it for you.

MAGISTRATE: You!!!

595　LYSISTRATA: Us.

MAGISTRATE: This is intolerable!

LYSISTRATA: It may be, but it's what's going to happen.

MAGISTRATE: But Demeter!—I mean, it's against nature!

LYSISTRATA: (very sweetly) We've got to save you, after all, Sir.

600　MAGISTRATE: Even against my will?

LYSISTRATA: That only makes it all the more essential.

MAGISTRATE: Anyway, what business are war and peace of yours?

LYSISTRATA: I'll tell you.

MAGISTRATE: (restraining himself with difficulty) You'd better
605　or else.

LYSISTRATA: I will if you'll listen and keep those hands of yours
under control.

MAGISTRATE: I can't—I'm too livid.

STRATYLLIS: (interrupting) It'll be you that regrets it.

MAGISTRATE: I hope it's you, you superannuated crow! (To　610
LYSISTRATA) Say what you have to say.

LYSISTRATA: In the last war we were too modest to object to anything you men did—and in any case you wouldn't let us say a
word. But don't think we approved! We knew everything that
was going on. Many times we'd hear at home about some　615
major blunder of yours, and then when you came home we'd
be burning inside but we'd have to put on a smile and ask what
it was you'd decided to inscribe on the pillar underneath the
Peace Treaty.—And what did my husband always say?—
'Shut up and mind your own business!' And I did.　620

STRATYLLIS: *I* wouldn't have done!

MAGISTRATE: (ignoring her—to LYSISTRATA) He'd have given
you one if you hadn't!

LYSISTRATA: Exactly—so I kept quiet. But sure enough, next
thing we knew you'd take an even sillier decision. And if I so　625
much as said, 'Darling, why are you carrying on with this silly
policy?' he would glare at me and say, 'Back to your weaving,
woman, or you'll have a headache for a month. "Go and
attend to your work; let war be the care of the menfolk."'

MAGISTRATE: Quite right too, by Zeus.　630

LYSISTRATA: Right? That we should not be allowed to make the
least little suggestion to you, no matter how much you mis-
manage the City's affairs? And now, look, every time two people meet in the street, what do they say? 'Isn't there a man in
the country?' and the answer comes, 'Not one.' That's why we　635
women got together and decided we were going to save
Greece. What was the point of waiting any longer, we asked
ourselves. Well now, we'll make a deal. You listen to us—and
we'll talk sense, not like you used to—listen to us and keep
quiet, as we've had to do up to now, and we'll clear up the　640
mess you've made.

MAGISTRATE: Insufferable effrontery! I will not stand for it!

LYSISTRATA: (magisterially) Silence!

MAGISTRATE: You, confound you, a woman with your face
veiled, dare to order me to be silent! Gods, let me die!　645

LYSISTRATA: Well, if that's what's bothering you—

(During the ensuing trio the women put a veil on the MAGIS-
TRATE's head, and give him a sewing-basket and some uncarded
wool.)

　　With veiling bedeck
　　Your head and your neck,
　And then, it may be, you'll be quiet.

MYRRHINE:　This basket fill full—　650

CALONICE:　By carding this wool—

LYSISTRATA: Munching beans—they're an excellent diet.

　　So hitch up your gown
　　And really get down
　To the job—you could do with some　655
　　　slimmin'.
　　And keep this refrain
　　Fixed firm in your brain—

628-29 "Go . . . menfolk" from the *Iliad*, Hector's parting—and
final—words to his wife at Troy

ALL: That war is the care of the *women!*

(During the song and dance of the women the MAGISTRATE *has been sitting, a ludicrous figure, with not the least idea what to do with the wool. During the following chorus, fuming, he tears off the veil, flings away wool and basket, and stands up.)*

660 STRATYLLIS: Come forward, ladies: time to lend a hand
Of succour to our heroine's brave stand!

CHORUS OF WOMEN: I'll dance for ever, never will I tire,
To aid our champions here.
For theirs is courage, wisdom, beauty, fire;
665 And Athens hold they dear.

STRATYLLIS: *(to* LYSISTRATA*)* Now, child of valiant ancestors of stinging-nettle stock,
To battle! — do not weaken, for the foe is seized with shock.

LYSISTRATA: If Aphrodite of Cyprus and her sweet son Eros still
670 breathe hot desire into our bosoms and our thighs, and if they still, as of old, afflict our men with that distressing ailment, club-prick — then I prophecy that before long we women will be known as the Peacemakers of Greece.

MAGISTRATE: Why, what will you do?

675 LYSISTRATA: Well, for one thing, there'll be no more people clomping round the Market Square in full armour, like lunatics.

CALONICE: By Aphrodite, never a truer word!

LYSISTRATA: You see them every day — going round the vegeta-
680 ble and pottery stalls armed to the teeth. You'd think they were Corybants!

MAGISTRATE: Of course: that's what every true Athenian ought to do.

LYSISTRATA: But a man carrying a shield with a ferocious
685 Gorgon on it — and buying minnows at the fishmonger's! Isn't it ridiculous?

CALONICE: Like that cavalry captain I saw, riding round the market with his lovely long hair, buying a pancake from an old stallholder and stowing it in his helmet! And there was a
690 Thracian too — coming in brandishing his light-infantry equipment for all the world as if he were a king or something. The fruiteress fainted away with fright, and he annexed everything on her stall!

MAGISTRATE: But the international situation at present is in a
695 hopeless muddle. How do you propose to unravel it?

LYSISTRATA: Oh, it's dead easy.

MAGISTRATE: Would you explain?

LYSISTRATA: Well, take a tangled skein of wool for example. We take it so, put it to the spindle, unwind it this way, now that
700 way. *(miming with her fingers)* That's how we'll unravel this war, if you'll let us. Send ambassadors first to Sparta, this way, then to Thebes, that way —

MAGISTRATE: Are you such idiots as to think that you can solve serious problems with spindles and bits of wool?

705 LYSISTRATA: As a matter of fact, it might not be so idiotic as you think to run the whole City entirely on the model of the way we deal with wool.

MAGISTRATE: How d'you work that out?

LYSISTRATA: The first thing you do with wool is wash the grease
710 out of it; you can do the same with the City. Then you stretch

681 **Corybants** priests of Cybele, who wore full armor during their ceremonies

out the citizen body on a bench and pick out the burrs — that is, the parasites. After that you prise apart the club-members who form themselves into knots and clots to get into power, and when you've separated them, pick them out one by one. Then you're ready for the carding: they can all go into the 715 basket of Civic Goodwill — including the resident aliens and any foreigners who are your friends — yes, and even those who are in debt to the Treasury! Not only that. Athens has many colonies. At the moment these are lying around all over the place, like stray bits and pieces of the fleece. You should pick 720 them up and bring them here, put them all together, and then out of all this make an enormous great ball of wool — and from that you can make the People a coat.

MAGISTRATE: Burrs — balls of wool — nonsense! What right have you to talk about these things? What have you done for 725 the war effort?

LYSISTRATA: Done, you puffed-up old idiot! We've contributed to it twice over and more. For one thing, we've given you sons, and then had to send them off to fight.

MAGISTRATE: Enough, don't let's rub the wound. 730

LYSISTRATA: For another, we're in the prime of our lives, and how can we enjoy it? Even if we've got husbands, we're war widows just the same. And never mind us — think of the un-married ones, getting on in years and with never a hope — that's what really pains me. 735

MAGISTRATE: But for heaven's sake, it's not only women that get older.

LYSISTRATA: Yes, I know, but it's not the same thing, is it? A man comes home — he may be old and grey — but he can get him-self a young wife in no time. But a woman's not in bloom for 740 long, and if she doesn't succeed quickly, there's no one will marry her, and before long she's going round to the fortune-tellers to ask them if she's any chance.

MAGISTRATE: That's right — any man who's still got a serviceable — 745

(Whatever he was going to say, it is drowned by music. During the following trio the women supply him with two half-obols, a filleted head-dress and a wreath, and dress him up as a corpse.)

LYSISTRATA: Shut up! It's high time that you died.
You'll find a fine coffin outside.
Myself I will bake
Your Cerberus-cake,
And here is the fare for the ride. 750

CALONICE: Look, here are your fillets all red —

LYSISTRATA: So why do you wait?
You'll make Charon late!
Push off! Don't you realize? You're dead!

MAGISTRATE: *(spluttering with rage)* This is outrageous! I shall 755 go at once and show my colleagues what these women have done to me.

LYSISTRATA: What's your complaint? You haven't been properly laid out? Don't worry; we'll be with you early the day after tomorrow to complete the funeral! 760

749 **Cerberus-cake** a cake placed with the dead with which to distract Cerberus, the hound guarding the gates of Hades   750 **fare for the ride** a coin with which to pay Charon, who ferried the dead across the River Styx to Hades

(The MAGISTRATE *goes out.* LYSISTRATA, CALONICE *and* MYR-
RHINE *go back into the Acropolis.*)

LEADER: No time to laze; our freedom's now at risk;
　　Take off your coats, and let the dance be brisk!
CHORUS OF MEN: There's more in this than meets the eye,
　　　Or so it seems to me.
765　The scum will surface by and by:
　　　It stinks of Tyranny!

　　Those Spartan rogues are at their games
　　　(Their agent's Cleisthenes)—
　　It's them that's stirring up these dames
770　　To seize our jury fees!
LEADER: Disgraceful!—women venturing to prate
　　In public so about affairs of State!
　　They even (men could not be so naive)
　　The blandishments of Sparta's wolves believe!
775　The truth the veriest child could surely see:
　　This is a Monarchist Conspiracy.
　　I'll fight autocracy until the end:
　　My freedom I'll unswervingly defend.
　　As once our Liberators did, so now
780　'I'll bear my sword within a myrtle bough,'
　　And stand beside them, thus.

(He places himself beside the statue of Harmodius and Aristogeiton, imitating the attitude of the latter.)

　　　　　And from this place
　　I'll give this female one upon the face!

(He slaps STRATYLLIS *hard on the cheek.*)

STRATYLLIS: (giving him a blow in return that sends him reel-
　　ing) Don't trifle with us, rascals, or we'll show you
785　Such fisticuffs, your mothers will not know you!
CHORUS OF WOMEN: My debt of love today
　　　To the City I will pay,
　　And I'll pay it in the form of good advice;
　　　For the City gave me honour
790　　(Pallas' blessing be upon her!),
　　And the things I've had from her deserve their price.

　　　For at seven years or less
　　　I became a girl priestess
　　In the Erechthean temple of the Maid;
795　　And at ten upon this hill
　　　I made flour in the mill
　　For the cakes which to our Lady are displayed.

　　　Then I went to Brauron town
　　　And put on a yellow gown
800　To walk in the procession as the Bear;
　　　To complete my perfect score
　　　I the sacred basket bore
　　At Athena's feast when I was young and fair.

768 **Cleisthenes** Athenian statesman and well-known homosexual
770 **jury fees** a main source of income for older men, and stored in the
Citadel on the Acropolis　779 **Liberators** Harmodius and Aristogeiton,
who tried to assassinate the last Tyrant of Athens in 514 B.C.　798-800
Brauron town . . . the Bear a reference to a festival for Artemis, who
evidently supplanted a local bear-goddess　802 **sacred basket** containing objects sacred to Athena and a great honor for an Athenian girl to
carry in a festival

STRATYLLIS: See why I think I have a debt to pay?
　　'But women can't talk politics,' you say.　　　　805
　　Why not? What is it you insinuate?
　　That we contribute nothing to the State?
　　Why, we give more than you! See if I lie:
　　We cause men to be born, you make them die.
　　What's more, you've squandered all the gains of old,　810
　　The Persians' legacy, the allies' gold;
　　And now, the taxes you yourselves assess
　　You do not pay. Who's got us in this mess?
　　Do you complain? Another grunt from you,
　　And you will feel the impact of this shoe!　　　815

(She takes off her shoe and hits the MEN'S LEADER with it.)

MEN: Assault! Assault! This impudence
　　　Gets yet more aggravated.
　　Why don't we act in self-defence?
　　　Or are we all castrated?
LEADER: Let's not be all wrapped up, let's show we're men,　820
　　Not sandwiches! Take off your cloaks again!
CHORUS OF MEN: Come, party-sandalled men of war,
　　　The tyrants' foes in days of yore,
　　　　Those days when we were men;
　　　The time has come to grow new wings　　　825
　　　And think once more of martial things;
　　　　We must be young again.
LEADER: If once we let these women get the semblance of a
　　　start,
　　Before we know, they'll be adept at every manly art.
　　They'll build a navy, quickly master strategy marine,　830
　　And fight against the City's fleet, just like that Carian
　　　queen.
　　And if to form a cavalry contingent they decide,
　　They'd soon be teaching our equestrian gentry how to ride!
　　For riding on cock-horses suits a woman best of all;
　　Her seat is sure, and when it bolts she doesn't often fall.　835
　　Just look at Micon's painting, and you'll see the sort of
　　　thing:
　　The Amazonian cavalry engaging Athens' king.
　　I think that we should seize them now, that's what we ought
　　　to do,
　　And shove them in the stocks—and I will start by seizing
　　　you!

(He grabs STRATYLLIS by the scruff of the neck but is forced to let
her go by a well-aimed bite.)

WOMEN: Our anger now is all afire,　　　　840
　　　And, by the Holy Twain,
　　We'll give you such a dose of ire
　　　You'll scream and scream again.
STRATYLLIS: Take off your coats and feel the heart beneath:
　　We're women, and our wrath is in our teeth!　　845
CHORUS OF WOMEN: The man who lays a hand on me
　　　Will never more eat celery
　　　　Or beans—he won't be able.
　　I burn with anger: I will strike

831 **Carian queen** Artemisia, who distinguished herself against the Athenian navy at Salamis in 480 B.C.　836 **Micon's painting** a fresco depicting the battle between Theseus and the Amazons

850 And smash his bloody eggs, just like
         The beetle in the fable.
STRATYLLIS: Friend Lampito from Sparta and Ismenia from
         the north
      Are still alive, and so I scorn the threats you vomit forth.
      You cannot hurt us, though you pass your motions six
         times o'er:

(Pointing at a well-known politician in the audience)

855 You're hated by the People here and by the folks next door.
      The other day I asked a friend to share a sacred meal
      To Hecate; my friend (she is a rich Boeotian eel)
      Sent word to say, 'I cannot come, my dear; forgive me,
         please;
      I can't get through to Athens 'cause of You Know Who's
         decrees.'
860 These damn decrees will never stop, until we make a
         frontal
      Assault on you and grab your legs and make you horizontal!

*(Each of the women grabs a man by the leg and brings him to the
ground. The* MEN, *defeated, retire down stage; the* WOMEN *move
closer to the Acropolis gates.)*

— ACT TWO —

SCENE I:

The same. It is five days later.

*(*LYSISTRATA *comes out of the Acropolis, in great agitation.)*

STRATYLLIS: *(in tragic tones)* Lady who did this daring plot
         invent,
      Why from thy fortress com'st thou grim-look'd out?
LYSISTRATA: It is the thoughts of evil women's minds
      That makes me wander restless to and fro.
5 WOMEN: What sayest thou?
LYSISTRATA: 'Tis true, 'tis true.
STRATYLLIS: But what hath caused it? Speak; we are thy
         friends.
LYSISTRATA: Silence is hard, but it were shame to speak.
STRATYLLIS: Hide not the ill that we are suffering from.
10 LYSISTRATA: I will but one word speak: 'tis sex-starvation.
WOMEN: Alas, great Zeus!
LYSISTRATA: Why cry to Zeus? for 'tis natural. *(In her ordinary
      voice)* I just can't keep them to their vow of abstinence any
      longer. They're deserting. One I caught clearing out the
15 stopped-up hole in the wall near Pan's Grotto — another let-
      ting herself down by a rope — another leaving her post as sen-
      try — and there was even one yesterday who was trying to fly
      down on sparrow-back — aiming straight for the nearest
      pimpshop! I was able to grab her by the hair and pull her
20 back. And they invent every kind of excuse just to be allowed
      to go home. Here's one now. *(To* FIRST WOMAN, *who is trying
      to leave the Acropolis swiftly and stealthily)* Hey, you, where
      do you think you're going?

FIRST WOMAN: I want to go home. I've got some fleeces there
      from Miletus, and the moths will be eating them up.   25
LYSISTRATA: No nonsense about moths! Go back inside.
FIRST WOMAN: But I promise you, I swear, I'll come right back.
      I'll only spread it out on the bed.
LYSISTRATA: No you won't; you're not going anywhere.
FIRST WOMAN: Am I to leave my fleeces to be destroyed, then?   30
LYSISTRATA: *(unyielding)* If necessary, yes.
SECOND WOMAN: *(rushing out of the Acropolis)* Help! My flax,
      my Amorgian flax! I left it at home without taking the bark off!
LYSISTRATA: Here's another — flax this time. *(To* SECOND
      WOMAN) Come back.   35
SECOND WOMAN: But by Artemis I will, as soon as I've stripped
      it off!
LYSISTRATA: No. Once I let you strip anything off, they'll all be
      wanting to.
THIRD WOMAN: *(coming out as if heavily pregnant)* Not yet,   40
      holy Eilithuia, not yet! Wait till I've got somewhere where it's
      lawful to give birth!
LYSISTRATA: What's all this nonsense?
THIRD WOMAN: Can't you see? I'm in labour!
LYSISTRATA: But you weren't even pregnant yesterday!   45
THIRD WOMAN: Well, I am today! Lysistrata, let me go home
      right away. The midwife's waiting.
LYSISTRATA: What do you think you're talking about? *(Pokes her
      stomach.)* Rather hard, isn't it? What have you got there?
THIRD WOMAN: Hard? — yes, of course — it's — it's a baby, a boy. 50
LYSISTRATA: *(tapping it)* Nonsense! It's made of bronze — and
      hollow — Let's have a look at it.

(Dives under THIRD WOMAN'S *dress and emerges with an enormous bronze helmet.)*

      Athena's sacred helmet! What were you trying to kid me, say-
      ing you were pregnant?
THIRD WOMAN: But I am, I swear.   55
LYSISTRATA: What's this, then?
THIRD WOMAN: Well, I thought — if I found it coming upon me
      before I got out of the Acropolis — I could nest in the helmet
      like the pigeons do, and give birth there.
LYSISTRATA: No good trying to get out of it. You're caught. You 60
      can stay here until the day your baby *(pointing to the helmet)*
      is named.

(Two more women rush out of the Acropolis.)

FOURTH WOMAN: I can't sleep in there any longer! I've seen the
      Guardian Serpent!
FIFTH WOMAN: I can't either! Those owls are keeping me awake 65
      with their infernal hooting!
LYSISTRATA: *(stopping them firmly)* Tall tales will get you no-
      where, ladies. I know you miss your husbands; but don't you
      realize they miss you as well? Think of the sort of nights they'll
      be spending! Be strong, sisters; you won't have to endure   70
      much longer. There is an oracle *(unrolls a scroll)* that we will
      triumph if only we don't fall out among ourselves. I have
      it here.

(The women all gather round.)

850-51 **smash . . . fable** in Aesop's fable, an eagle steals the beetle's
young, and the beetle retaliates by destroying the eagle's eggs

41 **Eilithuia** goddess of childbirth   41-42 **somewhere . . . birth** that is,
not on the Acropolis, which was sacred ground   64 **Guardian Serpent**
symbolic of Athena's protection and supposed to dwell on the Acropolis

FIFTH WOMAN: What does it say?

75 LYSISTRATA: Listen. *(Reads)* 'When that the swallows escape
　　from the hoopoes and gather together,
　　Keeping away from the cock-birds, then trouble and sorrow
　　will perish,
　　Zeus will make high into low—'

THIRD WOMAN: What, will we be on top when we do it?

80 LYSISTRATA: 'But if the swallows rebel and fly from the sacred
　　enclosure,
　　Then will it manifest be that there is no creature more
　　sex-mad.'

FIFTH WOMAN: Pretty blunt, isn't it? So help us the gods, we
　　won't give up the fight now. Let's go inside. It would be dis-
　　graceful, my dears, wouldn't it, to flag or fail now we've heard
85　　what the oracle says.

*(They all go into the Acropolis. The two CHORUSES move to the
centre of the stage, facing each other.)*

MEN: I feel a rather pressing need
　　To exercise my tongue:
　　I'll tell a little fairy tale
　　I heard when I was young.

90　　Well, once upon a time there was
　　A wise young man who fled
　　From women and from marriage, and
　　He roamed the hills instead.

　　He hunted hares with nets, and had
95　　A faithful little hound,
　　And hated girls so much he ne'er
　　Came back to his native ground.

　　Yes, he was truly wise, this lad,
　　Loathed women through and through,
100　　And following his example we
　　Detest the creatures too.

LEADER: *(to STRATYLLIS)* Give us a kiss.
STRATYLLIS: *(slapping him)* You can take this!
LEADER: *(raising his tunic and kicking her)* That's got you there.
105 STRATYLLIS: *(giggling)* Look at that hair!
MEN: A sign of valour is such hair
　　Upon the crotch, you know;
　　Myronides had lots of it,
　　And so had Phormio.

110 WOMEN: I'll tell a little tale myself
　　(I like this little game)
　　About a man who had no home,
　　And Timon was his name.

　　He lived among the thorns and briars,
115　　And never served on juries;
　　Some said his mother really was
　　A sister of the Furies.

　　This Timon went away and lived
　　So far from mortal ken

Not out of hate for women but　　　　　　　　　　120
　　Because of hate for men.

He loathed them for their wickedness,
　　Their company abhorred,
And cursed them loud and long and deep—
　　But *women* he adored.　　　　　　　　　　　125

STRATYLLIS: *(to leader)* One on the cheek! *(Slaps him.)*
LEADER: *(in mockery)* Oh, how I shriek!
STRATYLLIS: Let's have a go! *(Prepares to kick him.)*
LEADER: Think what you'll show!

(STRATYLLIS hastily lets her skirt fall again.)

WOMEN: At least, despite our age, it's not　　　　130
　　With hirsute mantle fringed:
　　With utmost care and frequently
　　Our triangles are singed.

*(LYSISTRATA appears on the battlements. She looks away to the
right, and cries out.)*

LYSISTRATA: Women! Women! Come here, quickly!

*(Several women join her, among them CALONICE and
MYRRHINE.)*

CALONICE: What is it dear? What are you shouting for?　　135
LYSISTRATA: A man! There's a man coming—and by the look of
　　him he's equipped for the Mysteries of Aphrodite!
CALONICE: Aphrodite, Lady of Cyprus, Paphos and Cythera', as
　　thou hast gone with us till now, so aid us still!—Where is he,
　　whoever he is?　　　　　　　　　　　　　　　　　　140
LYSISTRATA: There, down by the shrine of Chloe.
CALONICE: So he is; but who on earth is he?
LYSISTRATA: Have a look, all of you. Does anyone know him?
MYRRHINE: Yes, by Zeus! It's Cinesias, my husband!
LYSISTRATA: Well, dear, you know what you have to do: keep　　145
　　him on toast. Tantalize him. Lead him on. Say no, say yes.
　　You can do anything—except what you swore over the cup
　　not to do.
MYRRHINE: Don't worry, I'll do as you say.
LYSISTRATA: I'll stay here and start the process of toasting. Off　　150
　　you go.

(All go within except LYSISTRATA.)

(Enter, right, CINESIAS and a SLAVE, the latter carrying a BABY.)

CINESIAS: Gods help me, I'm so bloody stretched out I might
　　just as well be on the rack!
LYSISTRATA: Who goes there?
CINESIAS: Me.　　　　　　　　　　　　　　　　　　　155
LYSISTRATA: A man?
CINESIAS: I certainly am!
LYSISTRATA: Well, off with you.
CINESIAS: Who do you think you are, sending me away?
LYSISTRATA: I'm on guard duty.　　　　　　　　　　　160
CINESIAS: Well—for the god's sake—ask Myrrhine to come out
　　to me.
LYSISTRATA: You want me to get you Myrrhine? Who might
　　you be?
CINESIAS: Her husband—Cinesias from Paeonidae.　　　165
LYSISTRATA: Cinesias! That name we know well. It's for ever in
　　your wife's mouth. She can't eat an egg or an apple but she
　　says, 'Here's to my love Cinesias.'

75-76 **When that . . . together** a reference to the story of Tereus' lustful pursuit of Procne, even after he was transformed into a hoopoe and
she into a swallow　108 **Myronides** victorious Athenian general　109
Phormio victorious Athenian admiral　118 **Timon** famous misanthrope

CINESIAS: (breathing more rapidly) Gods!

170 LYSISTRATA: It's true, I swear by Aphrodite. And if we happen to get talking about our husbands, she always says, 'The rest are nothing to my Cinesias!'

CINESIAS: Bring her to me! Bring her to me!

LYSISTRATA: Well, aren't you going to give me anything?

175 CINESIAS: If you want. Look, this is all I've got; catch.

(Throws up a purse of silver.)

LYSISTRATA: Thanks. I'll go and get her. (She disappears.)

CINESIAS: Quickly, please! I've no joy in life any longer since she left home. It pains me to enter the place, it all seems so empty—and my food doesn't agree with me. I'm perma-
180   nently rigid!

MYRRHINE: (appearing on the battlements, pretending to talk to somebody within) I love him, I love him! But he won't love me. Don't ask me to go out to him.

CINESIAS: Myrrie darling, why on earth not? Come down here.

185 MYRRHINE: No, I won't.

CINESIAS: Aren't you going to come down when I call you, Myrrhine?

MYRRHINE: You don't really want me.

CINESIAS: What! I'm dying for love of you.

190 MYRRHINE: I'm going. (Turns to go back inside.)

CINESIAS: No—don't—listen to your child!

(The SLAVE caresses the BABY without result.)

Come on, damn you—say 'mama'! (Strikes the BABY.)

BABY: Mama, mama, mama!

CINESIAS: What's wrong with you? Surely you can't harden your
195   heart against your baby! It's five days now since he had a bath or a feed.

MYRRHINE: I pity him all right. His father hasn't looked after him very well.

CINESIAS: For heaven's sake, won't you come down to your
200   own child?

MYRRHINE: How powerful motherhood is! My feelings compel me. I will come down. (She leaves the battlements.)

CINESIAS: I think she looks much younger and more beautiful than she was! And all this spurning and coquetting—why, it
205   just inflames my desire even more!

MYRRHINE: (coming out and taking the BABY in her arms) Come on there, darling, you've got a bad daddy, haven't you? Come on, do you want a little drink, then? (She feeds him.)

CINESIAS: Tell me, darling, why do you behave like this and shut
210   yourself up in there with the other women? Why do you give me pain—and yourself too? (Attempts to caress her breast.)

MYRRHINE: Keep your hands off me!

CINESIAS: And our things at home—they belong to you as well as me—they're going to ruin!

215 MYRRHINE: (playing with the BABY) I don't care!

CINESIAS: What, you don't care if the chickens are pulling all your wool to pieces?

MYRRHINE: No, I don't.

CINESIAS: And what about the rites of Aphrodite? How long is it
220   since you performed them? (Puts his arm around her.) Come along home.

MYRRHINE: (wriggling free) No, I won't. Not until you stop the war and make peace.

CINESIAS: Then, if you want, we'll do that.

MYRRHINE: Then, if you want, I'll go home. Till then, I've   225
sworn not to.

CINESIAS: But won't you let me make love to you? It's been such a long time!

MYRRHINE: No. Mind you, I'm not saying I don't love you . . .

CINESIAS: You do, Myrrie love? Why won't you let me, then?   230

MYRRHINE: What, you idiot, in front of the baby?

CINESIAS: No—er—Manes, take it home.

(The SLAVE departs with the BABY.)

All right, darling, it's out of the way. Let's get on with it.

MYRRHINE: Don't be silly, there's nowhere we can do it here.

CINESIAS: What's wrong with Pan's Grotto?   235

MYRRHINE: And how am I supposed to purify myself before going back into the Acropolis? It's sacred ground, you know.

CINESIAS: Why, there's a perfectly good spring next to it.

MYRRHINE: You're not asking me to break my oath!

CINESIAS: On my own head be it. Don't worry about that,   240
darling.

MYRRHINE: All right, I'll go and get a camp bed.

CINESIAS: Why not on the ground?

MYRRHINE: By Apollo—I love you very much—but not on the ground! (She goes into the Acropolis.)   245

CINESIAS: Well, at least she does love me, that I can be sure of.

MYRRHINE: (returning with a bare camp bed) Here you are. You just lie down, while I take off my—Blast it! We need a—what do you call it?—a mattress.

CINESIAS: Mattress? I certainly don't!   250

MYRRHINE: In the name of Artemis, you're not proposing we should do it on the cords!

CINESIAS: At least give us a kiss first.

MYRRHINE: (doing so) There. (She goes.)

CINESIAS: Mmmm! Come back quickly!   255

MYRRHINE: (returning with a mattress) There. Now just lie down, and I'll—But look, you haven't got a pillow!

CINESIAS: I don't want one. (He lies down on the mattress.)

MYRRHINE: But I do! (She goes in.)

CINESIAS: This is a Heracles' supper and no mistake!   260

MYRRHINE: (returning with a pillow) Lift up your head. So.

CINESIAS: That's everything.

MYRRHINE: Everything?

CINESIAS: Yes. Come to me now, precious.

MYRRHINE: (her back to him) I'm just undoing my bra. Remem-   265
ber, don't let me down on what you said about making peace.

CINESIAS: May Zeus strike me dead if I do!

MYRRHINE: But look now, you haven't got a blanket!

CINESIAS: But I don't want one! All I want is you, darling!

MYRRHINE: In a moment, love. I'll just pop in for the blanket.   270

(Goes into the Acropolis.)

CINESIAS: These bedclothes will be the end of me!

MYRRHINE: (returning with a blanket and a box of ointment) Lift yourself up.

CINESIAS: You can see very well I did that long ago.

MYRRHINE: Do you want me to anoint you?   275

CINESIAS: No, dammit, I don't!

MYRRHINE: Too bad, then, because I'm going to anyway.

260 **Heracles' supper** a stock bit in comedies in which the ravenous Heracles is cheated of his dinner

CINESIAS: *(aside)* Zeus, make her spill the stuff!

MYRRHINE: Hold out your hand and you can rub it on.

280 CINESIAS: *(smelling the ointment)* I don't care for it. I only like sexy ones, and besides, this positively reeks of prevarication!

MYRRHINE: *(pretending to sniff it in her turn)* Why, silly me, I brought the wrong one!

CINESIAS: Well, never mind, darling, let it be.

285 MYRRHINE: Don't talk such nonsense. *(She goes in with the box.)*

CINESIAS: Curse whoever invented these ointments!

MYRRHINE: *(returning with another unguent in a bottle)* Here you are, take this bottle.

290 CINESIAS: I've got one already and it's fit to burst! *(indicating what he is referring to.)* Come here and lie down, damn you, and stop this stupid game.

MYRRHINE: I will, I swear it by Artemis. I've got both my shoes off now. But darling, don't forget about making peace.

295 CINESIAS: I'll —

(MYRRHINE runs off into the Acropolis and the gates slam behind her.)

She's gone! She's been having me on! Just when I was all ripe for her, she ran away! *(Bursts into sorrowful song.)*

Oh what, tell me what, can this woeful laddie do?
And who, tell me who, can this woeful laddie screw?
300 Philostratus, I need you, do come and help me quick:
Could I please hire a nurse for my poor young orphan prick?

CHORUS OF MEN: It's clear, my poor lad, that you're in a baddish way.
And I pity you — O alack and well-a-day!
What heart, what soul, what bollocks could long endure this plight,
305 Having no one to screw in the middle of the night?

CINESIAS: O Zeus! Hear me, Zeus! I am suffering tortures dire.

MEN: It's that female's fault; she inflamed you with false fire.
I think she is a villain and deserves to suffer death!

WOMEN: She's a heroine, and I will praise her while I've breath.

310 MEN: A heroine you call her? — to that I'll ne'er agree.
I'll tell you just what I would really like to see:
To see a whirlwind catch her, just like a heap of hay,
And to waft her aloft, take her up, up and away.

Then let the whirlwind drop, after tossing her around
315 Till giddy and dizzy she falls back to the ground,
Where suddenly she finds that there still is more in store:
We'd be queuing and screwing a dozen times or more.

SCENE II:

The same.

(Enter severally a HERALD from Sparta and the Athenian MAGISTRATE we met before. Both appear to be suffering from acute priapism but the HERALD is ineffectually endeavouring to conceal the fact.)

HERALD: Where are the lairds o' the Athenian council, or the Executive Committee? I wuid hae words wi' them.

MAGISTRATE: *(guffawing)* Ha! ha! ha! What are you — a man or a phallic symbol?

HERALD: My dear lad, I'm a herald, and I'm come frae Sparta 5 tae talk aboot peace.

MAGISTRATE: *(pointing)* Which is why you've got a spear under your clothes, I suppose?

HERALD: *(turning his back on him)* No, I hanna.

MAGISTRATE: What have you turned round for, then? Why are 10 you holding your cloak in that funny way? Did you get a rupture on the way here?

HERALD: *(to himself)* By Castor, the man's senile!

MAGISTRATE: Why, you rascal, you've got prickitis!

HERALD: No, I hanna. Dinna be stupid. 15

MAGISTRATE: Well, what's that, then?

HERALD: It's a standard Spartan cipher rod.

MAGISTRATE: *(indicating his counter-part)* Yes, and so is this. You needn't think I'm a fool; you can tell me the truth. What is the present situation in Sparta? 20

HERALD: Tae be colloquial, things ha' reached a total cock-up. All our allies ha' risen, and we canna get hold o' Pellene.

(Looks longingly at the WOMEN'S CHORUS.)

MAGISTRATE: What's the cause of it all? Do you think Pan was responsible?

HERALD: Pan? Och, no, it was Lampito, and then a' the ither 25 women — almost as though there were some kind of plot in it — they a' pit up a Keep Oot notice over their whatnots.

MAGISTRATE: So how are you getting on?

HERALD: Verra badly, verra badly. We a' bend double as we walk roond the toon, as though we were carrying lamps. D'ye ken, 30 the women won't even let us sae much as touch their knobs, till we a' consent tae mak a general peace for the whole of Greece.

MAGISTRATE: Ah, now I see the plot! They're all in it — all the women everywhere. Tell your people at once to send dele- 35 gates here with full powers to negotiate for peace. I'll go and tell the Council to choose delegates to represent Athens. When they see my — my cipher rod I don't think they'll hesitate a moment.

HERALD: That's a' fine by me. I'll fly. 40

(Exeunt severally.)

(The two CHORUSES advance.)

LEADER: There is no beast more stubborn than a woman,
And neither fire nor leopard is more shameless.

STRATYLLIS: If you know that, why do you hate us so?
We would be faithful friends, if you would let us.

LEADER: Women I loathe, both now and evermore. 45

STRATYLLIS: Well, as you please. But really, you look stupid
Without your coat. Come on now, put it on.
Or no, I know, I'll put your coat on for you.

LEADER: *(when she has done so)* That was a good turn that you did to me,
And I was wrong to yield to wrath and doff it. 50

17 **Spartan cipher rod** Spartans wrote coded messages on strips wound around a rod; these were then decoded by the recipient by winding them around an identical rod   22 **Pellene** both a city considering an alliance with Sparta against Athens and an infamous woman of pleasure

300 **Philostratus** a pimp

STRATYLLIS: There, you look better now, and not so comic.
  And now, if you'll keep still, I'll take that gnat
  Out of your eye.
LEADER: A gnat! that's what it was
  Was biting me! Come, dig it out and show me.
55 I've had these bites for hours and hours and hours.
STRATYLLIS: All right. (*She explores his eye carefully; he
  winces.*)
            You *are* a difficult old man.
  Great Zeus, it's monstrous! Look, just look at it!
  It must be from the Marsh of Marathon!
60 LEADER: Thank you so much. The gnat was digging deep,
  And now the tears are streaming from my eyes.
STRATYLLIS: Don't worry, I've a handkerchief to wipe them —
  You *are* a bad old man, you know — and now
  I'll kiss you.
LEADER: No, you don't.
ALL THE WOMEN: Oh, yes, we do!

(*And each of them kisses one of the* MEN.)

65 LEADER: Damn you, you wheedlers! Still the saying's true —
  We can't live with you, we can't live without you!
  Let us make peace, that's what we ought to do;
  You won't hit us, we promise not to flout you;
  Let us all form a single happy ring
70 And in that union our next number sing.

(*The two* CHORUSES *join hands and are from now on united in a
single chorus. They sing the following two songs together.*)

      No citizen need fear that we
        Will dent his reputation;
      We rather think you've had enough
        Of toil and tribulation.

75   So what we'll do is not to jest
        Or try to be buffoons;
      Instead we'd like to publicize
        Some unexpected boons.

      If anyone is short of drachs,
80   Two hundred (say) and twenty,
      Just call on us, because we've got
        Good money-bags in plenty.

      It's true they have no cash inside;
        Still, I should not complain:
85   That means that you will never need
        To pay it back again!

I'm entertaining some friends from Carystus tonight,
    tonight,
The table's prepared and you'll find the menu just right,
    just right.
There's plenty of soup and I've sacrificed a sow, a sow,
90 And — I think I can smell it — the pork should be roasting
    now, 'sting now.
You'd best be quick; it's a well-attended affair, affair,
So bath the kids and then get along right there, right there.
Walk in — no questions — pretend that you're in your own
    place, own place;
There's just one thing: the door will be shut in your face,
    your face.

(*Enter a group of* SPARTAN AMBASSADORS, *again looking very
distended.*)

LEADER: Here come our bearded Spartan friends. Why,   95
    anyone would swear
  That each of them was carrying a pig-pen under there!
  Welcome, gentlemen. How are you?
AMBASSADOR: I dinna need tae answer that in words; ye can see
  for yersel's how we are.
LEADER: Whew! You're certainly under severe tension — I   100
  should say things were quite inflammatory.
AMBASSADOR: And that's no lie. We dinna mind where, we
  dinna mind how, but we maun hae peace!

(*Enter several* ATHENIAN NEGOTIATORS.)

LEADER: Ah, here are our true-born Athenian representatives.
  Look as if they'd dropped from a great height and broken their   105
  backs, the way they're bending over. Yes, definitely a case of
  dropsy, I'd say. And look how they're holding their clothes
  miles away from their bodies!
NEGOTIATOR: Will somebody tell us where Lysistrata is? We're
  at the *point* of collapse.   110
LEADER: You've both got the same thing, I think. When does it
  get you worst? In the small hours?
NEGOTIATOR: Not just then — all the time — and it's killing us.
  If we don't make peace right away, we shall all end up screwing Cleisthenes.   115

(*The* SPARTAN AMBASSADORS *take off their coats.*)

LEADER: I shouldn't do that if I were you. You wouldn't want
  your sacred emblems mutilated, would you?
NEGOTIATOR: (*to* AMBASSADOR) They're right, you know.
AMBASSADOR: I'm thinking so too. Here, let's pit them on again.
NEGOTIATOR: Well now, old chap, this is a pretty pass we've all   120
  come to!
AMBASSADOR: Not sae bad as it wuid be, my dear fellow, if one
  of those amateur sculptors saw us like this.
NEGOTIATOR: Anyway, to business. What are you here for?
AMBASSADOR: Tae mak peace.   125
NEGOTIATOR: That's good to hear. So are we. Why don't we ask
  Lysistrata to come out? She's the only one who can reconcile
  us properly.
AMBASSADOR: Ay, by the Twa Gudes, Lysistratus, Lysistrata,
  Lysistratum, masculine, feminine or neuter, I couldna care   130
  less, sae we can bring this war to an end!

(*Music. The Propylaea opens wide, and* LYSISTRATA *appears,
magnificently arrayed.*)

NEGOTIATOR: No need to summon her, it seems; here she is!
CHORUS: Mighty lady with a mission —
    Paragon of common sense —
    Running fount of erudition —   135
      Miracle of eloquence!
        Greece is torn, and would be healed;
        War is rife — let peace be sealed;
        Thou hast conquered by thy charm;
        Make the cities all disarm.   140

117 **sacred emblems mutilated** a reference to the recent mutilation by
vandals of the heads and phalluses of all the statues of Hermes in Athenian streets

Mighty lady with a mission—
Paragon of common sense—
Running fount of erudition—
Miracle of eloquence!

145 LYSISTRATA: It's not hard, if you catch them when they're
aroused but not satisfied. We'll soon see. Reconciliation!

(An extremely beautiful and totally unclothed girl enters from
the Acropolis.)

Bring the Spartans to me first of all. Don't be rough or
brusque; handle them very gently, not in the brutal way men
lay hold on us, but the way a lady should—very civilized.

(RECONCILIATION goes up to one of the SPARTAN AMBASSADORS
and offers him her hand. He refuses.)

150 Well, if he won't give you his hand, try that leather thing.
That's right. Now the Athenians. You can take hold of anything they offer you. Now you, Spartans, stand on this side of
me, and you, Athenians, on the other side, and listen to what
I have to say.

(The AMBASSADORS and NEGOTIATORS, guided by RECONCILIA-
TION, take their places on either side of LYSISTRATA.)

155 I am a woman, but I am not brainless:
I have my share of native wit, and more,
Both from my father and from other elders
Instruction I've received. Now listen, both:
Hard will my words be, but not undeserved.

160 You worship the same gods at the same shrines,
Use the same lustral water, just as if
You were a single family—which you are—
Delphi, Olympia, Thermopylae—
How many other Panhellenic shrines

165 Could I make mention of, if it were needed!
And yet, although the Mede is at our gates,
You ruin Greece with mad intestine wars.
This is my first reproach to both of you.

NEGOTIATOR: (who has been eyeing RECONCILIATION all

170 through this speech) I hope she doesn't take much longer. I
doubt if this giant carrot will stand it.

LYSISTRATA: The next is for the Spartans. Know you not
How Pericleidas came to Athens once,
And sat a suppliant at our holy altar,

175 In scarlet uniform and death-white face,
Beseeching us to send a force to help you?
For then two perils threatened you at once:
The Helots, and Poseidon with his earthquake.
So Cimon took four thousand infantry

180 And saved the Spartan people from destruction.
This, Spartans, the Athenians did for you:
Is it then just to ravage Athens' land?

NEGOTIATOR: Yes, Lysistrata, they're in the wrong.

AMBASSADOR: We are. But by the Twa Gudes, she's a fine

185 bottom.

LYSISTRATA: Think not, Athenians, you are guiltless either.
Remember once you had to dress like slaves,
Until the Spartans came in force, and slew

The foreign mercenaries of Hippias
And many of his allies and confederates. 190
They fought for you alone upon that day
And set you free, removed your servile cloak
And clothed you with Democracy again.

AMBASSADOR: (still intent on RECONCILIATION) I havena seen a
bonnier lass. 195

NEGOTIATOR: Nor I a shapelier cunt.

LYSISTRATA: So why on fighting are your hearts so set?
For each of you is in the other's debt.
Why don't you make peace? What's the problem?

AMBASSADOR: (who has got hold of RECONCILIATION; both he 200
and his opposite number map out their demands on her person) We will, if ye'll give us back this little promontory.

NEGOTIATOR: Which one, sir?

AMBASSADOR: Pylos. We've set oor hearts on it and been prod-
prodding at it for years. 205

NEGOTIATOR: By Poseidon, you shan't have it!

LYSISTRATA: Give it them.

NEGOTIATOR: Who will we have left to stimulate, then? To revolt, I mean.

LYSISTRATA: Well, you ask for somewhere else in exchange. 210

NEGOTIATOR: Very well . . . give us (mapping the areas out)
first of all the Echinian Triangle here, then the Malian
Gulf—I mean the one round behind, of course—and
lastly—er—the Long Legs—I mean the Long Walls of
Megara. 215

AMBASSADOR: Are ye crazy? There's naething left!

LYSISTRATA: Come now, don't quarrel over a pair of legs—I
mean walls.

NEGOTIATOR: I'm ready to go back to my husbandry now.

AMBASSADOR: And I'm wanting tae do some manuring. 220

LYSISTRATA: Time enough for that when you've made peace. If
that's what you want to do, go and have a conference with
your allies and agree it with them.

NEGOTIATOR: Allies, ma'am?—look at the state we're in! We
know what the allies will say—the same as we do: 'Peace! 225
Peace! Bed! Bed!'

AMBASSADOR: And oors the same.

NEGOTIATOR: And we certainly needn't ask the Carystians.

LYSISTRATA: Fine then. Now we had better ratify the treaty in the
usual way. The women will entertain you in the Acropolis; 230
they have plenty of good food in their picnic baskets. And over
that you can clasp hands and take the oaths. And then, let
everyone take his wife and live happily ever after!

NEGOTIATOR: Let's go right away.

AMBASSADOR: Lead the way, my dear. 235

NEGOTIATOR: Yes, and quickly.

(All except the CHORUS go inside.)

CHORUS: Embroidered upholstery—magnificent cloaks—
Fine ornaments fashioned of gold:
If your daughter is chosen the Basket to bear,
Don't ask where these items are sold. 240

For all that I've got for the taking is yours;
The seals on the boxes are weak;

178 Helots Spartan serfs, who rebelled following an earthquake in 464 B.C.

189 Hippias an Athenian ruler dethroned by a coalition of Athenian
nobles and Spartans   228 Carystians a notoriously lustful folk

Remove them, and then from whatever's inside
Take just what it is that you seek.

245 There's one little thing I should warn you of first,
For if not, I'd be being unfair:
That unless you have got sharper eyesight than me,
You'll find there ain't anything there!

If anyone who's short of bread
250 Has slaves and kids that must be fed,
I've got some loaves of finest milling,
Quadruple size, and very filling.

Let any who provisions lack
Come round to me with bag or sack;
255 My servant is enjoined by me
To give them all these loaves for free.

One thing I should have said before —
They'd better not come near the door;
I have a dog who at the sight
260 Of strangers will not bark but bite.

(Some LAYABOUTS come in, and begin pounding on the Acropolis gates.)

FIRST LAYABOUT: Open up! Open up!
DOORKEEPER: (coming to the door) Get away from here!
FIRST LAYABOUT: (to his companions) What are you waiting for?
(To the DOORKEEPER and others inside) Do you want me to
265 burn you up with my torch? No, on second thoughts, that's
an absolute comic cliché and I won't do it.

(Protests from the audience.)

Oh — very well — to please you, I'll go through with it.
SECOND LAYABOUT: And we'll be with you.
DOORKEEPER: (coming out) Get off with you! I'll pull your long
270 hair out! Shoo! Get out of the way of the Spartans — the banquet's nearly over, and they'll soon be coming out!

(He drives them away and goes back inside. Presently the door
opens, and two well-fed ATHENIAN DINERS emerge.)

FIRST DINER: Never known a party like it. The Spartans were
the life and soul of it, weren't they? And we were pretty clever,
considering how sozzled we were.
275 SECOND DINER: Not surprising really. We couldn't be as stupid
as we are when we're sober. If the Athenians took my advice
they'd always get drunk when going on diplomatic missions.
As it is, you see, we go to Sparta sober, and so we're always
looking for catches. We don't hear what they do say, and we
280 hunt for implications in what they don't say — and we bring
back quite incompatible reports of what went on. And yet we
only have to have a few, and everything's all right. Even if one
of them starts singing 'Telamon' when he should be singing
'Cleitagora,' all we do is slap him on the back and swear that
285 'Telamon' was just what was wanted!

(They go out. The LAYABOUTS return.)

DOORKEEPER: Here come these no-goods again. Bugger off, all
of you!
FIRST LAYABOUT: We'd better. They're coming out. (They run off.)

282-85 **Even if . . . wanted** a reference to an after-dinner singing game

(ENTER ATHENIANS and SPARTANS, one of whom carries
bagpipes.)

SPARTAN: Here, my dear fellow, tak the pipes, and I'll dance a
reel and sing a song in honour of the Athenians and of oursel's 290
forby.
ATHENIAN: Yes, do. There's nothing I enjoy so much as a good
old Spartan dance.

(The PIPER takes the pipes and strikes up. The SPARTAN dances a
solo as he sings.)

Raise the song o' Sparta's fame,
And tae valiant Athens' name 295
Kindle an undying flame,
Holy Memory.

How they focht in days of yore
Off the Artemisium shore —
They were few, the Medes were more — 300
Theirs the victory!

While we Spartans quit oor hame —
Boarlike from oor mouths ran faem —
Brave our King, and high our aim —
'Hellas shall be free!' 305

Nocht cuid frighten us that day,
Nocht cuid mak us run away,
And we won renown for aye
At Thermopylae.

Artemis the Virgin Queen, 310
Huntress in the wuids sae green,
Come and bless this happy scene,
Come, we call on thee!

Pour thy grace upon oor peace;
Make the artful foxes cease; 315
Let guidwill and love increase
And prosperity!

(The Propylaea opens wide, and LYSISTRATA appears, flanked by
all the Athenian and Spartan women.)

LYSISTRATA: Well, gentlemen, it's all happily settled. Spartans,
here are your wives back. And here are yours. Now form up
everyone, two by two, and let us have a dance of thanksgiving. 320
And may the gods vouchsafe to give us sense
Ne'er to repeat our former dire offence!
CHORUS: Come, let us on the Graces call,
Apollo next who healeth all,
On Artemis and Hera too, 325
On Bacchus and his Maenad crew,
And most on Zeus above:

Let all the gods come witness now
The making of our solemn vow
To stay our hands from mutual war 330
And keep the peace for evermore
Made by the power of Love.

298 **How . . . yore** the following lines allude to the Spartan attempt to
block the Persian (Mede) advance at Thermopylae and to the Athenian
naval victory at Artemisium in 480 B.C.

O great Apollo, hail!
O let it be that we
335   May win the victory!
O great Apollo, hail!
O great Apollo, hail!
Evoi! Evoi! Evoi!

(The CHORUS *dance joyfully out. The* ATHENIANS *and* SPARTANS *and their wives remain.)*

LYSISTRATA: *(recitative)* To hail the peace for which we've
    pined so long,
340   There's time, I fancy, for another song!
SPARTAN:

(As a spectacular dance is performed by a soloist and everyone else dances in the background)

Muse, now be Sparta praisin',
Muse, Phoebus' name be raisin',
And in her temple brazen
    Let Pallas hear:
345 Come, sons of Tyndareus's,
Castor and Polydeuces,
Favourites of a' the Muses,
    Famed far and near.

    Dance, dance tae Sparta's might!
350   Swing, swing yer sheepskins light!
    Let's praise oor noble city,
    Home o' songs and dances pretty—

Home of the sacred chorus,
Home of our sires before us,
355 Stout shield and mantle o'er us,
    Sparta the brave!

Girls, shake your pretty tresses,
Whirl roond yer Doric dresses,
See your display expresses
360   Joy and relief:
Joy at the end o' slaughter—
See, Leda's beauteous daughter,
Purer than mountain water,
    Helen's the chief.

365   Dance, dance for Helen fair!
    Smooth, smooth yer flowing hair!
    Tak off wi' both yer feet and
    Stamp on every ither beat and
Pray that Athena never
370 Her link tae Sparta sever,
May she protect for ever
    Sparta the brave!

(All kneel facing the shrine of Victory.)

ALL: Athena, hail, thou Zeus-born Maid!
  Who war and death in Greece hast stayed:
375 Hail, fount from whom all blessings fall;
  All hail, all hail, Protectress of us all!

(General dance.)

98

✦ CRITICAL CONTEXTS ✦

ARISTOTLE

(384–322 B.C.)

FROM *The Poetics*

(c. 335 B.C.)

TRANSLATED BY
GERALD F. ELSE

BORN NEAR MACEDONIA, *Aristotle entered the Academy in Athens at the age of seventeen to study with Plato. After Plato's death, Aristotle conducted research in natural history—mainly botany and zoology—throughout the Aegean region and served as the tutor of the young Alexander the Great in Macedon, before returning to Athens to found the Lyceum in 355 B.C.*

Aristotle wrote extensively on topics ranging from ethics, rhetoric, and metaphysics to physics and natural history. In The Poetics, he analyzes the field of poetry into different "species" or genres (epic, tragedy, comedy, dithyramb) and attempts to discover the basic features of each. The Poetics demonstrates Aristotle's extensive knowledge of drama, which he uses to refine a keen sense of the form and purpose of tragedy. We should remember that The Poetics *was written sometime after 335 B.C., roughly a century after the height of the Athenian theater. And although* The Poetics *is the cornerstone of Western dramatic criticism, the meaning of several of Aristotle's key terms—*MIMESIS *(imitation), catharsis (purgation),* HAMARTIA *(error)—remain controversial.*

Basic considerations

The art of poetic composition in general and its various species, the function and effect of each of them; how the plots should be constructed if the composition is to be an artistic success; how many other component elements are involved in the process, and of what kind; and similarly all the other questions that fall under this same branch of inquiry—these are the problems we shall discuss; let us begin in the right and natural way, with basic principles.

Epic composition, then; the writing of tragedy, and of comedy also; the composing of dithyrambs; and the greater part of the making of music with flute and lyre: these are all in point of fact, taken collectively, imitative processes. They differ from each other, however, in three ways, namely by virtue of having (1) different means, (2) different objects, and (3) different methods of imitation.

The differentiation according to medium

First, in the same way that certain people imitate a variety of things by means of shapes and colors, making visible replicas of them (some doing this on the basis of art, others out of habit), while another group produces its mimicry with the voice, so in the case of the arts we just mentioned: they all carry on their imitation through the media of rhythm, speech, and melody, but with the latter two used separately or together. Thus the arts of flute and lyre music, and any others of similar nature and effect such as the art of the panpipe, produce their imitation using melody and rhythm alone, while there is another which does so using speeches or verses alone, bare of music, and either mixing the verses with one another or employing just one certain kind—an art which is, as it happens, nameless up to the present time. In fact we could not even assign a common name to the mimes of Sophron and Xenarchus and the Socratic discourses; nor again if somebody should compose his imitation in trimeters or elegiac couplets or certain other verses of that kind; (Except people do link up poetic composition with verse and speak of "elegiac poets," "epic poets," not treating them as poets by virtue of their imitation, but employing the term as a common appellation going along with the use of verse. And in fact the name is also applied to anyone who treats a medical or scientific topic in verses, yet Homer and Empedocles actually have nothing in common except their verse; hence the proper term for the one is "poet," for the other, "science-writer" rather than "poet.") and likewise if someone should mix all the kinds of verse together in composing his imitation, as Chaeremon composed a *Centaur* using all the verses.

Such is the disjunction we feel is called for in these cases. There are on the other hand certain arts which use all the aforesaid media, I mean such as rhythm, song, and verse. The composition of dithyrambs and of nomes does so, and both tragedy and comedy. But there is a difference in that some of these arts use all the media at once while others use them in different parts of the work.

These then are the differentiations of the poetic arts with respect to the media in which the poets carry on their imitation.

Since those who imitate imitate men in action, and these must necessarily be either worthwhile or worthless people (for definite characters tend pretty much to develop in men of action), it follows that they imitate men either better or worse than the average, as the painters do—for Polygnotus used to portray superior and Pauson inferior men; and it is evident that each of the forms of imitation afore-mentioned will include these differentiations, that is, will differ by virtue of imitating objects which are different in this sense. Indeed it is possible for these dissimilarities to turn up in flute and lyre playing, and also in prose dialogues and bare verses: thus Homer imitated superior men and Hege-mon of Thasos, the inventor of parody, and Nicochares, the author of the *Deiliad*, inferior ones; likewise in connection with dithyrambs and nomes, for one can make the imitation the way Tim-otheus and Philoxenus did their Cyclopes. Finally, the difference between tragedy and comedy coin-cides exactly with the master-difference: namely the one tends to imitate people better, the other one people worse, than the average.

The objects of imitation

The third way of differentiating these arts is by the mode of imitation. For it is possible to imitate the same objects, and in the same media, (1) by narrating part of the time and dramatizing the rest of the time, which is the way Homer composes (mixed mode), or (2) with the same person continuing without change (straight narrative), or (3) with all the persons who are performing the imitation acting, that is, carrying on for themselves (straight dramatic mode).

The modes of imitation

Poetic imitation, then, shows these three *differentiae*, as we said at the beginning: in the media, objects, and modes of imitation. So in one way Sophocles would be the same (kind of) imitator as Homer, since they both imitate worthwhile people, and in another way the same as Aristophanes, for they both imitate people engaged in action, doing things. In fact some authorities maintain that that is why plays are called dramas, because the imitation is of men acting (*drôntas*, from *drân*, 'do, act'). It is also the reason why both tragedy and comedy are claimed by the Dorians: comedy by the Megarians, both those from hereabouts, who say that it came into being during the period of their democracy, and those in Sicily, and tragedy by some of those in the Peloponnese. They use the names "comedy" and "drama" as evidence; for they say that *they* call their outlying villages *kômai* while the Athenians call theirs "demes" (*dêmoi*)—the assumption being that the participants in comedy were called *kômôidoi* not from their being revelers but because they wandered from one village to another, being degraded and excluded from the city—and that they call "doing" or "acting" *drân* while the Athenians designate it by *prattein*.

Jottings, chiefly on comedy

So much, then, for the *differentiae* of imitation, their number and identity. As to the origin of the poetic art as a whole, it stands to reason that two operative causes brought it into being, both of them rooted in human nature. Namely (1) the habit of imitating is congenital to human beings from childhood (actually man differs from the other animals in that he is the most imitative and learns his first lessons through imitation), and so is (2) the pleasure that all men take in works of imitation. A proof of this is what happens in our experience. There are things which we see with pain so far as they themselves are concerned but whose images, even when executed in very great detail, we view with pleasure. Such is the case for example with renderings of the least favored animals, or of cadavers. The cause of this also is that learning is eminently pleasurable not only to philosophers but to the rest of mankind in the same way, although their share in the pleasure is restricted. For the reason they take pleasure in seeing the images is that in the process of viewing they find themselves learning, that is, reckoning what kind a given thing belongs to: "This individual is a So-and-so." Because if the viewer happens not to have seen such a thing before, the reproduction will not produce the pleasure *qua* reproduction but through its workmanship or color or something else of that sort.

Since, then, imitation comes naturally to us, and melody and rhythm too (it is obvious that verses are segments of the respective rhythms), in the beginning it was those who were most gifted in these respects who, developing them little by little, brought the making of poetry into being out of improvisations. And the poetic enterprise split into two branches, in accordance with the two kinds of character. Namely, the soberer spirits were imitating noble actions and the actions of noble persons, while the cheaper ones were imitating those of the worthless, producing lampoons and invectives at

The origin and development of poetry

first just as the other sort were producing hymns and encomia. (. . .) In them (i.e., the invectives), in accordance with what is suitable and fitting, iambic verse also put in its appearance; indeed that is why it is called "iambic" now, because it is the verse in which they used to "iambize," that is, lampoon, each other. And so some of the early poets became composers of epic, the others of iambic, verses.

Now it happens that we cannot name anyone before Homer as the author of that kind of poem (i.e., an iambic poem), though it stands to reason that there were many who were; but from Homer on we can do so: thus his *Margites* and other poems of that sort. However, just as on the serious side Homer was most truly a poet, since he was the only one who not only composed well but constructed dramatic imitations, so too he was the first to adumbrate the forms of comedy by producing a (1) dramatic presentation, and not of invective but of (2) the ludicrous. For as the *Iliad* stands in relation to our tragedies, so the *Margites* stands in relation to our comedies.

Once tragedy and comedy had been partially brought to light, those who were out in pursuit of the two kinds of poetic activity, in accordance with their own respective natures, became in the one case comic poets instead of iambic poets, in the other case producers of tragedies instead of epics, because these genres were higher and more esteemed than the others. Now to review the question whether even tragedy is adequate to the basic forms or not—a question which is (can be) judged both by itself, in the abstract, and in relationship to our theater audiences—that is another story. However that may be, it did spring from an improvisational beginning (both it and comedy: the one from those who led off the dithyramb, the other from those who did so for the phallic performances [?] which still remain on the program in many of our cities); it did expand gradually, each feature being further developed as it appeared; and after it had gone through a number of phases it stopped upon attaining its full natural growth. Thus Aeschylus was the first to expand the troupe of assisting actors from one to two, shorten the choral parts, and see to it that the dialogue takes first place; (. . .) at the same time the verse became iambic trimeter instead of trochaic tetrameter. For in the beginning they used the tetrameter because the form of composition was "satyr-like," that is, more given over to dancing, but when speech came along the very nature of the case turned up the appropriate verse. For iambic is the most speech-like of verses. An indication of this is that we speak more iambics than any other kind of verse in our conversation with each other, whereas we utter hexameters rarely, and when we do we abandon the characteristic tone-pattern of ordinary speech.

Further, as to plurality of episodes and the other additions which are recorded as having been made to tragedy, let our account stop here; for no doubt it would be burdensome to record them in detail.

Comedy

Comedy is as we said it was, an imitation of persons who are inferior; not, however, going all the way to full villainy, but imitating the ugly, of which the ludicrous is one part. The ludicrous, that is, is a failing or a piece of ugliness which causes no pain or destruction; thus, to go no farther, the comic mask is something ugly and distorted but painless.

Now the stages of development of tragedy, and the men who were responsible for them, have not escaped notice, but comedy did escape notice in the beginning because it was not taken seriously. (In fact it was late in its history that the presiding magistrate officially "granted a chorus" to the comic poets; until then they were volunteers.) Thus comedy already possessed certain defining characteristics when the first "comic poets," so-called, appear in the record. Who gave it masks, or prologues, or troupes of actors and all that sort of thing, is not known. The composing of plots came originally from Sicily; of the Athenian poets, Crates was the first to abandon the lampooning mode and compose arguments, that is, plots, of a general nature.

Epic and tragedy

Well then, epic poetry followed in the wake of tragedy up to the point of being a (1) good-sized (2) imitation (3) in verse (4) of people who are to be taken seriously; but in its having its verse unmixed with any other and being narrative in character, there they differ. Further, so far as its length is concerned tragedy tries as hard as it can to exist during a single daylight period, or to vary but little, while the epic is not limited in its time and so differs in that respect. Yet originally they used to do this in tragedies just as much as they did in epic poems.

The constituent elements are partly identical and partly limited to tragedy. Hence anybody who knows about good and bad tragedy knows about epic also; for the elements that the epic possesses appertain to tragedy as well, but those of tragedy are not all found in the epic.

Our discussions of imitative poetry in hexameters, and of comedy, will come later; at present let us deal with tragedy, recovering from what has been said so far the definition of its essential nature, as it was in development. Tragedy, then, is a process of imitating an action which has serious implications, is complete, and possesses magnitude; by means of language which has been made sensuously attractive, with each of its varieties found separately in the parts; enacted by the persons themselves and not presented through narrative; through a course of pity and fear completing the purification of tragic acts which have those emotional characteristics. By "language made sensuously attractive" I mean language that has rhythm and melody, and by "its varieties found separately" I mean the fact that certain parts of the play are carried on through spoken verses alone and others the other way round, through song.

Tragedy and its six constituent elements

Now first of all, since they perform the imitation through action (by acting it), the adornment of their visual appearance will perforce constitute some part of the making of tragedy; and song-composition and verbal expression also, for those are the media in which they perform the imitation. By "verbal expression" I mean the actual composition of the verses, and by "song-composition" something whose meaning is entirely clear.

Next, since it is an imitation of an action and is enacted by certain people who are performing the action, and since those people must necessarily have certain traits both of character and thought (for it is thanks to these two factors that we speak of people's actions also as having a defined character, and it is in accordance with their actions that all either succeed or fail); and since the imitation of the action is the plot, for by "plot" I mean here the structuring of the events, and by the "characters" that in accordance with which we say that the persons who are acting have a defined moral character, and by "thought" all the passages in which they attempt to prove some thesis or set forth an opinion — it follows of necessity, then, that tragedy as a whole has just six constituent elements, in relation to the essence that makes it a distinct species; and they are plot, characters, verbal expression, thought, visual adornment, and song-composition. For the elements by which they imitate are two (i.e., verbal expression and song-composition), the manner in which they imitate is one (visual adornment), the things they imitate are three (plot, characters, thought), and there is nothing more beyond these. These then are the constituent forms they use.

The greatest of these elements is the structuring of the incidents. For tragedy is an imitation not of men but of a life, an action, and they have moral quality in accordance with their characters but are happy or unhappy in accordance with their actions; hence they are not active in order to imitate their characters, but they include the characters along with the actions for the sake of the latter. Thus the structure of events, the plot, is the goal of tragedy, and the goal is the greatest thing of all.

The relative importance of the six elements

Again: a tragedy cannot exist without a plot, but it can without characters: thus the tragedies of most of our modern poets are devoid of character, and in general many poets are like that; so also with the relationship between Zeuxis and Polygnotus, among the painters: Polygnotus is a good portrayer of character, while Zeuxis' painting has no dimension of character at all.

Again: if one strings end to end speeches that are expressive of character and carefully worked in thought and expression, he still will not achieve the result which we said was the aim of tragedy; the job will be done much better by a tragedy that is more deficient in these other respects but has a plot, a structure of events. It is much the same case as with painting: the most beautiful pigments smeared on at random will not give as much pleasure as a black-and-white outline picture. Besides, the most powerful means tragedy has for swaying our feelings, namely the peripeties and recognitions, are elements of the plot.

Again: an indicative sign is that those who are beginning a poetic career manage to hit the mark in verbal expression and character portrayal sooner than they do in plot construction; and the same is true of practically all the earliest poets.

So plot is the basic principle, the heart and soul, as it were, of tragedy, and the characters come second: (. . .) it is the imitation of an action and imitates the persons primarily for the sake of their action.

Third in rank is thought. This is the ability to state the issues and appropriate points pertaining to a given topic, an ability which springs from the arts of politics and rhetoric; in fact the earlier poets made their characters talk "politically," the present-day poets rhetorically. But "character" is that kind of utterance which clearly reveals the bent of a man's moral choice (hence there is no character in that class of utterances in which there is nothing at all that the speaker is choosing or rejecting), while "thought" is the passages in which they try to prove that something is so or not so, or state some general principle.

Fourth is the verbal expression of the speeches. I mean by this the same thing that was said earlier, that the "verbal expression" is the conveyance of thought through language: a statement which has the same meaning whether one says "verses" or "speeches."

The song-composition of the remaining parts is the greatest of the sensuous attractions, and the visual adornment of the dramatic persons can have a strong emotional effect but is the least artistic element, the least connected with the poetic art; in fact the force of tragedy can be felt even without benefit of public performance and actors, while for the production of the visual effect the property man's art is even more decisive than that of the poets.

General principles of the tragic plot

With these distinctions out of the way, let us next discuss what the structuring of the events should be like, since this is both the basic and the most important element in the tragic art. We have established, then, that tragedy is an imitation of an action which is complete and whole and has some magnitude (for there is also such a thing as a whole that has no magnitude). "Whole" is that which has beginning, middle, and end. "Beginning" is that which does not necessarily follow on something else, but after it something else naturally is or happens; "end," the other way round, is that which naturally follows on something else, either necessarily or for the most part, but nothing else after it; and "middle" that which naturally follows on something else and something else on it. So, then, well-constructed plots should neither begin nor end at any chance point but follow the guidelines just laid down.

Furthermore, since the beautiful, whether a living creature or anything that is composed of parts, should not only have these in a fixed order to one another but also possess a definite size which does not depend on chance—for beauty depends on size and order; hence neither can a very tiny creature turn out to be beautiful (since our perception of it grows blurred as it approaches the period of imperceptibility) nor an excessively huge one (for then it cannot all be perceived at once and so its unity and wholeness are lost), if for example there were a creature a thousand miles long—so, just as in the case of living creatures they must have some size, but one that can be taken in in a single view, so with plots: they should have length, but such that they are easy to remember. As to a limit of the length, the one is determined by the tragic competitions and the ordinary span of attention. (If they had to compete with a hundred tragedies they would compete by the water clock, as they say used to be done [?].) But the limit fixed by the very nature of the case is: the longer the plot, up to the point of still being perspicuous as a whole, the finer it is so far as size is concerned; or to put it in general terms, the length in which, with things happening in unbroken sequence, a shift takes place either probably or necessarily from bad to good fortune or from good to bad—that is an acceptable norm of length.

But a plot is not unified, as some people think, simply because it has to do with a single person. A large, indeed an indefinite number of things can happen to a given individual, some of which go to constitute no unified event; and in the same way there can be many acts of a given individual from which no single action emerges. Hence it seems clear that those poets are wrong who have composed *Heracleïds*, *Theseïds*, and the like. They think that since Heracles was a single person it follows that the plot will be single too. But Homer, superior as he is in all other respects, appears to have grasped this point well also, thanks either to art or nature, for in composing an *Odyssey* he did not incorporate into it everything that happened to the hero, for example how he was wounded on Mt. Parnassus or how he feigned madness at the muster, neither of which events, by happening, made it at all necessary or probable that the other should happen. Instead, he composed the *Odyssey*—and the *Iliad* similarly—around a unified action of the kind we have been talking about.

A poetic imitation, then, ought to be unified in the same way as a single imitation in any other mimetic field, by having a single object: since the plot is an imitation of an action, the latter ought to be both unified and complete, and the component events ought to be so firmly compacted that if any one of them is shifted to another place, or removed, the whole is loosened up and dislocated; for an element whose addition or subtraction makes no perceptible extra difference is not really a part of the whole.

From what has been said it is also clear that the poet's job is not to report what has happened but what is likely to happen: that is, what is capable of happening according to the rule of probability or necessity. Thus the difference between the historian and the poet is not in their utterances being in verse or prose (it would be quite possible for Herodotus' work to be translated into verse, and it would not be any the less a history with verse than it is without it); the difference lies in the fact that the historian speaks of what has happened, the poet of the kind of thing that *can* happen. Hence also poetry is a more philosophical and serious business than history; for poetry speaks more of universals, history of particulars. "Universal" in this case is what kind of person is likely to do or say certain kinds of things, according to probability or necessity; that is what poetry aims at, although it gives its persons particular names afterward; while the "particular" is what Alcibiades did or what happened to him.

In the field of comedy this point has been grasped: our comic poets construct their plots on the basis of general probabilities and then assign names to the persons quite arbitrarily, instead of dealing with individuals as the old iambic poets did. But in tragedy they still cling to the historically given names. The reason is that what is possible is persuasive; so what has not happened we are not yet ready to believe is possible, while what has happened is, we feel, obviously possible: for it would not have happened if it were impossible. Nevertheless, it is a fact that even in our tragedies, in some cases only one or two of the names are traditional, the rest being invented, and in some others none at all. It is so, for example, in Agathon's *Antheus* — the names in it are as fictional as the events — and it gives no less pleasure because of that. Hence the poets ought not to cling at all costs to the traditional plots, around which our tragedies are constructed. And in fact it is absurd to go searching for this kind of authentication, since even the familiar names are familiar to only a few in the audience and yet give the same kind of pleasure to all.

So from these considerations it is evident that the poet should be a maker of his plots more than of his verses, insofar as he is a poet by virtue of his imitations and what he imitates is actions. Hence even if it happens that he puts something that has actually taken place into poetry, he is none the less a poet; for there is nothing to prevent some of the things that have happened from being the kind of things that can happen, and that is the sense in which he is their maker.

Simple and complex plots

Among simple plots and actions the episodic are the worst. By "episodic" plot I mean one in which there is no probability or necessity for the order in which the episodes follow one another. Such structures are composed by the bad poets because they are bad poets, but by the good poets because of the actors: in composing contest pieces for them, and stretching out the plot beyond its capacity, they are forced frequently to dislocate the sequence.

Furthermore, since the tragic imitation is not only of a complete action but also of events that are fearful and pathetic, and these come about best when they come about contrary to one's expectation yet logically, one following from the other; that way they will be more productive of wonder than if they happen merely at random, by chance — because even among chance occurrences the ones people consider most marvelous are those that seem to have come about as if on purpose: for example the way the statue of Mitys at Argos killed the man who had been the cause of Mitys' death, by falling on him while he was attending the festival; it stands to reason, people think, that such things don't happen by chance — so plots of that sort cannot fail to be artistically superior.

Some plots are simple, others are complex; indeed the actions of which the plots are imitations already fall into these two categories. By "simple" action I mean one the development of which being continuous and unified in the manner stated above, the reversal comes without peripety or recognition, and by "complex" action one in which the reversal is continuous but with recognition or peripety or both. And these developments must grow out of the very structure of the plot itself, in such a way that on the basis of what has happened previously this particular outcome follows either by necessity or in accordance with probability; for there is a great difference in whether these events happen because of those or merely after them.

"Peripety" is a shift of what is being undertaken to the opposite in the way previously stated, and that in accordance with probability or necessity as we have just been saying; as for example in the *Oedipus* the man who has come, thinking that he will reassure Oedipus, that is, relieve him of his fear with respect to his mother, by revealing who he once was, brings about the opposite; and in the *Lynceus*, as he (Lynceus) is being led away with every prospect of being executed, and Danaus pursuing him with every prospect of doing the executing, it comes about as a result of the other things that have happened in the play that *he* is executed and Lynceus is saved. And "recognition" is, as indeed the name indicates, a shift from ignorance to awareness, pointing in the direction either of close blood ties or of hostility, of people who have previously been in a clearly marked state of happiness or unhappiness.

The finest recognition is one that happens at the same time as a peripety, as is the case with the one in the *Oedipus*. Naturally, there are also other kinds of recognition: it is possible for one to take place in the prescribed manner in relation to inanimate objects and chance occurrences, and it is possible to recognize whether a person has acted or not acted. But the form that is most integrally a part of the plot, the action, is the one aforesaid; for that kind of recognition combined with peripety will excite either pity or fear (and these are the kinds of action of which tragedy is an imitation according to our definition), because both good and bad fortune will also be most likely to follow that kind of event. Since, further, the recognition is a recognition of persons, some are of one person by the other one only (when it is already known who the "other one" is), but sometimes it is necessary for both persons to go through a recognition, as for example Iphigenia is recognized by her brother through the sending of the letter, but of him by Iphigenia another recognition is required.

These then are two elements of plot: peripety and recognition; third is the *pathos*. Of these, peripety and recognition have been discussed; a *pathos* is a destructive or painful act, such as deaths on stage, paroxysms of pain, woundings, and all that sort of thing.

The tragic side of tragedy: pity and fear and the patterns of the complex plot

The "parts" of tragedy which should be used as constituent elements were mentioned earlier; (. . .) but what one should aim at and what one should avoid in composing one's plots, and whence the effect of tragedy is to come, remains to be discussed now, following immediately upon what has just been said.

Since, then, the construction of the finest tragedy should be not simple but complex, and at the same time imitative of fearful and pitiable happenings (that being the special character of this kind of poetry), it is clear first of all that (1) neither should virtuous men appear undergoing a change from good to bad fortune, for that is not fearful, nor pitiable either, but morally repugnant; nor (2) the wicked from bad fortune to good — that is the most untragic form of all, it has none of the qualities that one wants: it is productive neither of ordinary sympathy nor of pity nor of fear — nor again (3) the really wicked man changing from good fortune to bad, for that kind of structure will excite sympathy but neither pity nor fear, since the one (pity) is directed towards the man who does not deserve his misfortune and the other (fear) towards the one who is like the rest of mankind — what is left is the man who falls between these extremes. Such is a man who is neither a paragon of virtue and justice nor undergoes the change to misfortune through any real badness or wickedness but because of some mistake; one of those who stand in great repute and prosperity, like Oedipus and Thyestes: conspicuous men from families of that kind.

So, then, the artistically made plot must necessarily be single rather than double, as some maintain, and involve a change not from bad fortune to good fortune but the other way round, from good fortune to bad, and not thanks to wickedness but because of some mistake of great weight and consequence, by a man such as we have described or else on the good rather than the bad side. An indication comes from what has been happening in tragedy: at the beginning the poets used to "tick off" whatever plots came their way, but nowadays the finest tragedies are composed about a few houses: they deal with Alcmeon, Oedipus, Orestes, Meleager, Thyestes, Telephus, and whichever others have had the misfortune to do or undergo fearful things.

Thus the technically finest tragedy is based on this structure. Hence those who bring charges against Euripides for doing this in his tragedies are making the same mistake. His practice is correct in the way that has been shown. There is a very significant indication: on our stages and in the competitions, plays of this structure are accepted as the most tragic, *if* they are handled successfully, and Euripides, though he may not make his other arrangements effectively, still is felt by the audience to be the most tragic, at least, of the poets.

Second comes the kind which is rated first by certain people, having its structure double like the *Odyssey* and with opposite endings for the good and bad. Its being put first is due to the weakness of the audiences; for the poets follow along, catering to their wishes. But this particular pleasure is not the one that springs from tragedy but is more characteristic of comedy.

Now it is possible for the fearful or pathetic effect to come from the actors' appearance, but it is also possible for it to arise from the very structure of the events, and this is closer to the mark and characteristic of a better poet. Namely, the plot must be so structured, even without benefit of any visual effect, that the one who is hearing the events unroll shudders with fear and feels pity at what happens: which is what one would experience on hearing the plot of the *Oedipus*. To set out to achieve this by means of the masks and costumes is less artistic, and requires technical support in the staging. As for those who do not set out to achieve the fearful through the masks and costumes, but only the monstrous, they have nothing to do with tragedy at all; for one should not seek any and every pleasure from tragedy, but the one that is appropriate to it.

Since it is the pleasure derived from pity and fear by means of imitation that the poet should seek to produce, it is clear that these qualities must be built into the constituent events. Let us determine, then, which kinds of happening are felt by the spectator to be fearful, and which pitiable. Now such acts are necessarily the work of persons who are near and dear (close blood kin) to one another, or enemies, or neither. But when an enemy attacks an enemy there is nothing pathetic about either the intention or the deed, except in the actual pain suffered by the victim; nor when the act is done by "neutrals"; but when the tragic acts come within the limits of close blood relationship, as when brother kills or intends to kill brother or do something else of that kind to him, or son to father or mother to son or son to mother—those are the situations one should look for.

Now although it is not admissible to break up the transmitted stories—I mean for instance that Clytemestra was killed by Orestes, or Eriphyle by Alcmeon—one should be artistic both in inventing stories and in managing the ones that have been handed down. But what we mean by "artistic" requires some explanation.

It is possible, then, (1) for the act to be performed as the older poets presented it, knowingly and wittingly; Euripides did it that way also, in Medea's murder of her children. It is possible (2) to refrain from performing the deed, with knowledge. Or it is possible (3) to perform the fearful act, but unwittingly, then recognize the blood relationship later, as Sophocles' Oedipus does; in that case the act is outside the play, but it can be in the tragedy itself, as with Astydamas' Alcmeon, or Telegonus in the *Wounding of Odysseus*. A further mode, in addition to these, is (4) while intending because of ignorance to perform some black crime, to discover the relationship before one does it. And there is no other mode besides these; for one must necessarily either do the deed or not, and with or without knowledge of what it is.

Of these modes, to know what one is doing but hold off and not perform the act (no. 2) is worst: it has the morally repulsive character and at the same time is not tragic; for there is no tragic act. Hence nobody composes that way, or only rarely, as, for example, Haemon threatens Creon in the *Antigone*. Performing the act (with knowledge) (no. 1) is second (poorest). Better is to perform it in ignorance and recognize what one has done afterward (no. 3); for the repulsive quality does not attach to the act, and the recognition has a shattering emotional effect. But the best is the last (no. 4): I mean a case like the one in the *Cresphontes* where Merope is about to kill her son but does not do so because she recognizes him first; or in *Iphigenia in Tauris* the same happens with sister and brother; or in the *Helle* the son recognizes his mother just as he is about to hand her over to the enemy.

The reason for what was mentioned a while ago, namely that our tragedies have to do with only a few families, is this: It was because the poets, when they discovered how to produce this kind of effect in their plots, were conducting their search on the basis of chance, not art; hence they have been forced to focus upon those families which happen to have suffered tragic happenings of this kind.

Enough, then, concerning the structure of events and what traits the tragic plots should have. As for the characters, there are four things to be aimed at. First and foremost, that they be good. The persons will have character if in the way previously stated their speech or their action reveals the moral quality of some choice, and good character if a good choice. Good character exists, moreover, in each category of persons: a woman can be good, or a slave, although one of these classes (*sc.* women) is inferior and the other, as a class, worthless. Second, that they be appropriate; for it is possible for a character to be brave, but inappropriately to a woman. Third is likeness to human nature in general; for this is different from making the character good and appropriate according to the criteria previously mentioned. And fourth is consistency. For even if the person being imitated is inconsistent, and that kind of character has been taken as the theme, he should be inconsistent in a consistent fashion.

Pity and fear and the tragic act

The tragic characters

An example of moral depravity that accomplishes no necessary purpose is the Menelaus in Euripides' *Orestes*; of an unsuitable and inappropriate character, the lamentation of Odysseus in the *Scylla* and the speech of Melanippe; and of the inconsistent, Iphigenia at Aulis; for the girl who pleads for her life is in no way like the later one.

In character portrayal also, as in plot construction, one should always strive for either the necessary or the probable, so that it is either necessary or probable for that kind of person to do or say that kind of thing, just as it is for one event to follow the other. It is evident, then, that the dénouements of plots also should come out of the character itself, and not from the "machine" as in the *Medea* or with the sailing of the fleet in the *Aulis*. Rather the machine should be used for things that lie outside the drama proper, either previous events that a human being cannot know, or subsequent events which require advance prophecy and exposition; for we grant the gods the ability to foresee everything. But let there be no illogicality in the web of events, or if there is, let it be outside the play like the one in Sophocles' *Oedipus*.

Since tragedy is an imitation of persons who are better than average, one should imitate the good portrait painters, for in fact, while rendering likenesses of their sitters by reproducing their individual appearance, they also make them better-looking; so the poet, in imitating men who are irascible or easygoing or have other traits of that kind, should make them, while still plausibly drawn, morally good, as Homer portrayed Achilles as good yet like other men.

Techniques of recognition

What recognition is generically, was stated earlier; now as to its varieties: First comes the one that is least artistic and is most used, merely out of lack of imagination, that by means of tokens. Of these some are inherited, like "the lance that all the Earth-born wear," or "stars" such as Carcinus employs in his *Thyestes*; some are acquired, and of those some are on the body, such as scars, others are external, like the well-known amulets or the recognition in the *Tyro* by means of the little ark. There are better and poorer ways of using these; for example, Odysseus was recognized in different ways by means of his scar, once by the nurse and again by the swineherds. Those that are deliberately cited for the sake of establishing an identity, and all that kind, are less artistic, while those that develop naturally but unexpectedly, like the one in the foot-washing scene, are better.

Second poorest are those that are contrived by the poet and hence are inartistic; for example the way, in the *Iphigenia*, she recognizes that it is Orestes: *she* was recognized by means of the letter, but *he* goes out of his way to say what the poet, rather than the plot, wants him to say. Thus this mode is close kin to the error mentioned above: he might as well have actually worn some tokens. Similarly, in Sophocles' *Tereus*, the "voice of the shuttle."

Third poorest is that through recollection, by means of a certain awareness that follows on seeing or hearing something, like the one in the *Cypriotes* of Dicaeogenes where the hero bursts into tears on seeing the picture, and the one in Book 8 of the *Odyssey*: Odysseus weeps when he hears the lyre-player and is reminded of the War; in both cases the recognition follows.

Fourth in ascending order is the recognition based on reasoning; for example in the *Libation-Bearers*: "Somebody like me has come; nobody is like me but Orestes; therefore he has come." And the one suggested by the sophist Polyidus in speaking of the *Iphigenia*: it would have been natural, he said, for Orestes to draw the conclusion (aloud): "My sister was executed as a sacrifice, and now it is my turn." Also in the *Tydeus* of Theodectes: "I came expecting to find my son, and instead I am being destroyed myself." Or the one in the *Daughters of Phineus*: when they see the spot they reflect that it was indeed their fate to die here; for they had been exposed here as babies also. There is also one based on mistaken inference on the part of the audience, as in *Odysseus the False Messenger*. In that play, that he and no one else can string the bow is an assumption, a premise invented by the poet, and also his saying that he would recognize the bow when in fact he had not seen it; whereas the notion that he (the poet) had made his invention for the sake of the other person who would make the recognition, that is a mistaken inference.

The best recognition of all is the one that arises from the events themselves; the emotional shock of surprise is then based on probabilities, as in Sophocles' *Oedipus* and in the *Iphigenia*; for it was only natural that she should wish to send a letter. Such recognitions are the only ones that dispense with artificial inventions and visible tokens. And second-best are those based on reasoning. . . .

THROUGHOUT HIS CAREER, THE GERMAN PHILOSOPHER AND POET FRIEDRICH NIETZSCHE CRIT-icized the limitations of modern conceptual and moral categories. This revolutionary subversion of the premises of philosophy forms the core of his most famous works— The Gay Science *(1882),* Also Spoke Zarathustra *(1883–1892), and* Beyond Good and Evil *(1886). In* The Birth of Tragedy *(1872), Nietzsche argues that Greek tragedy arose from the collision between Athenian rationalism—symbolized by Apollo, Socrates, and Euripides—and an earlier, irrational mysticism, symbolized by Dionysus. Although Nietzsche's reading of Greek history has been generally discredited, the essay offers a powerful and influential reading of the tension between the rational and irrational informing Greek drama. Nietzsche was admired by several modern playwrights represented in this volume, including Bernard Shaw, August Strindberg, and Eugene O'Neill.*

FRIEDRICH NIETZSCHE
(1844–1900)

FROM *The Birth of Tragedy*
(1872)

TRANSLATED BY
WALTER KAUFMANN

Section 1

We shall have gained much for the science of aesthetics, once we perceive not merely by logical inference, but with the immediate certainty of vision, that the continuous development of art is bound up with the *Apollinian* and *Dionysian* duality—just as procreation depends on the duality of the sexes, involving perpetual strife with only periodically intervening reconciliations. The terms Dionysian and Apollinian we borrow from the Greeks, who disclose to the discerning mind the profound mysteries of their view of art, not, to be sure, in concepts, but in the intensely clear figures of their gods. Through Apollo and Dionysus, the two art deities of the Greeks, we come to recognize that in the Greek world there existed a tremendous opposition, in origin and aims, between the Apollinian art of sculpture, and the nonimagistic, Dionysian art of music. These two different tendencies run parallel to each other, for the most part openly at variance; and they continually incite each other to new and more powerful births, which perpetuate an antagonism, only superficially reconciled by the common term "art"; till eventually, by a metaphysical miracle of the Hellenic "will," they appear coupled with each other, and through this coupling ultimately generate an equally Dionysian and Apollinian form of art—Attic tragedy.

In order to grasp these two tendencies, let us first conceive of them as the separate art worlds of *dreams* and *intoxication*. These physiological phenomena present a contrast analogous to that existing between the Apollinian and the Dionysian. It was in dreams, says Lucretius, that the glorious divine figures first appeared to the souls of men; in dreams the great shaper beheld the splendid bodies of superhuman beings; and the Hellenic poet, if questioned about the mysteries of poetic inspiration, would likewise have suggested dreams and he might have given an explanation like that of Hans Sachs in the *Meistersinger:*

> The poet's task is this, my friend,
> to read his dreams and comprehend.
> The truest human fancy seems
> to be revealed to us in dreams:
> all poems and versification
> are but true dreams' interpretation.

The beautiful illusion of the dream worlds, in the creation of which every man is truly an artist, is the prerequisite of all plastic art, and, as we shall see, of an important part of poetry also. In our dreams we delight in the immediate understanding of figures; all forms speak to us; there is nothing unimportant or superfluous. But even when this dream reality is most intense, we still have, glimmering through it, the sensation that it is *mere appearance*: at least this is my experience, and for its frequency—indeed, normality—I could adduce many proofs, including the sayings of the poets.

Philosophical men even have a presentiment that the reality in which we live and have our being is also mere appearance, and that another, quite different reality lies beneath it. Schopenhauer actually indicates as the criterion of philosophical ability the occasional ability to view men and things as mere phantoms or dream images. Thus the aesthetically sensitive man stands in the same relation to the reality of dreams as the philosopher does to the reality of existence; he is a close and willing observer, for these images afford him an interpretation of life, and by reflecting on these processes he trains himself for life.

It is not only the agreeable and friendly images that he experiences as something universally intelligible: the serious, the troubled, the sad, the gloomy, the sudden restraints, the tricks of accident, anxious expectations, in short, the whole divine comedy of life, including the inferno, also pass before him, not like mere shadows on a wall — for he lives and suffers with these scenes — and yet not without that fleeting sensation of illusion. And perhaps many will, like myself, recall how amid the dangers and terrors of dreams they have occasionally said to themselves in self-encouragement, and not without success: "It is a dream! I will dream on!" I have likewise heard of people who were able to continue one and the same dream for three and even more successive nights — facts which indicate clearly how our innermost being, our common ground, experiences dreams with profound delight and a joyous necessity.

This joyous necessity of the dream experience has been embodied by the Greeks in their Apollo: Apollo, the god of all plastic energies, is at the same time the soothsaying god. He, who (as the etymology of the name indicates) is the "shining one," the deity of light, is also ruler over the beautiful illusion of the inner world of fantasy. The higher truth, the perfection of these states in contrast to the incompletely intelligible everyday world, this deep consciousness of nature, healing and helping in sleep and dreams, is at the same time the symbolical analogue of the soothsaying faculty and of the arts generally, which make life possible and worth living. But we must also include in our image of Apollo that delicate boundary which the dream image must not overstep lest it have a pathological effect (in which case mere appearance would deceive us as if it were crude reality). We must keep in mind that measured restraint, that freedom from the wilder emotions, that calm of the sculptor god. His eye must be "sunlike," as befits his origin; even when it is angry and distempered it is still hallowed by beautiful illusion. And so, in one sense, we might apply to Apollo the words of Schopenhauer when he speaks of the man wrapped in the veil of *māyā* [illusion]: "Just as in a stormy sea that, unbounded in all directions, raises and drops mountainous waves, howling, a sailor sits in a boat and trusts in his frail bark: so in the midst of a world of torments the individual human being sits quietly, supported by and trusting in the *principium individuationis*." In fact, we might say of Apollo that in him the unshaken faith in this *principium* and the calm repose of the man wrapped up in it receive their most sublime expression; and we might call Apollo himself the glorious divine image of the *principium individuationis*, through whose gestures and eyes all the joy and wisdom of "illusion," together with its beauty, speak to us.

In the same work Schopenhauer has depicted for us the tremendous *terror* which seizes man when he is suddenly dumbfounded by the cognitive form of phenomena because the principle of sufficient reason, in some one of its manifestations, seems to suffer an exception. If we add to this terror the blissful ecstasy that wells from the innermost depths of man, indeed of nature, at this collapse of the *principium individuationis*, we steal a glimpse into the nature of the *Dionysian*, which is brought home to us most intimately by the analogy of intoxication.

Either under the influence of the narcotic draught, of which the songs of all primitive men and peoples speak, or with the potent coming of spring that penetrates all nature with joy, these Dionysian emotions awake, and as they grow in intensity everything subjective vanishes into complete self-forgetfulness. In the German Middle Ages, too, singing and dancing crowds, ever increasing in number, whirled themselves from place to place under this same Dionysian impulse. In these dancers of St. John and St. Vitus, we rediscover the Bacchic choruses of the Greeks, with their prehistory in Asia Minor, as far back as Babylon and the orgiastic Sacaea. There are some who, from obtuseness or lack of experience, turn away from such phenomena as from "folk-diseases," with contempt or pity born of the consciousness of their own "healthy-mindedness." But of course such poor wretches have no idea how corpselike and ghostly their so-called "healthy-mindedness" looks when the glowing life of the Dionysian revelers roars past them.

Under the charm of the Dionysian not only is the union between man and man reaffirmed, but nature which has become alienated, hostile, or subjugated, celebrates once more her reconciliation with her lost son, man. Freely, earth proffers her gifts, and peacefully the beasts of prey of the rocks and desert approach. The chariot of Dionysus is covered with flowers and garlands; panthers and tigers walk under its yoke. Transform Beethoven's "Hymn to Joy" into a painting; let your imagination conceive the multitudes bowing to the dust, awestruck — then you will approach the Dionysian. Now the slave is a free man; now all the rigid, hostile barriers that necessity, caprice, or "impudent convention" have fixed between man and man are broken. Now, with the gospel of universal harmony, each one feels himself not only united, reconciled, and fused with his neighbor, but as one with him, as if the veil of *māyā* had been torn aside and were now merely fluttering in tatters before the mysterious primordial unity.

In song and in dance man expresses himself as a member of a higher community; he has forgotten how to walk and speak and is on the way toward flying into the air, dancing. His very gestures express enchantment. Just as the animals now talk, and the earth yields milk and honey, supernatural sounds emanate from him, too: he feels himself a god, he himself now walks about enchanted, in ecstasy, like the gods he saw walking in his dreams. He is no longer an artist, he has become a work of art: in these paroxysms of intoxication the artistic power of all nature reveals itself to the highest gratification of the primordial unity. The noblest clay, the most costly marble, man, is here kneaded and cut, and to the sound of the chisel strokes of the Dionysian world-artist rings out the cry of the Eleusinian mysteries: "Do you prostrate yourselves, millions? Do you sense your Maker, world?" . . .

The tradition is undisputed that Greek tragedy in its earliest form had for its sole theme the sufferings of Dionysus and that for a long time the only stage hero was Dionysus himself. But it may be claimed with equal confidence that until Euripides, Dionysus never ceased to be the tragic hero; that all the celebrated figures of the Greek stage — Prometheus, Oedipus, etc. — are mere masks of this original hero, Dionysus. That behind all these masks there is a deity, that is one essential reason for the typical "ideality" of these famous figures which has caused so much astonishment. Somebody, I do not know who, has claimed that all individuals, taken as individuals, are comic and hence untragic — from which it would follow that the Greeks simply *could* not suffer individuals on the tragic stage. In fact, this is what they seem to have felt; and the Platonic distinction and evaluation of the "idea" and the "idol," the mere image, is very deeply rooted in the Hellenic character.

Using Plato's terms we should have to speak of the tragic figures of the Hellenic stage somewhat as follows: the one truly real Dionysus appears in a variety of forms, in the mask of a fighting hero, and entangled, as it were, in the net of the individual will. The god who appears talks and acts so as to resemble an erring, striving, suffering individual. That he *appears* at all with such epic precision and clarity is the work of the dream-interpreter, Apollo, who through this symbolic appearance interprets to the chorus its Dionysian state. In truth, however, the hero is the suffering Dionysus of the Mysteries, the god experiencing in himself the agonies of individuation, of whom wonderful myths tell that as a boy he was torn to pieces by the Titans and now is worshiped in this state as Zagreus. Thus it is intimated that this dismemberment, the properly Dionysian *suffering*, is like a transformation into air, water, earth, and fire, that we are therefore to regard the state of individuation as the origin and primal cause of all suffering, as something objectionable in itself. From the smile of this Dionysus sprang the Olympian gods, from his tears sprang man. In this existence as a dismembered god, Dionysus possesses the dual nature of a cruel, barbarized demon and a mild, gentle ruler. But the hope of the epopts [initiates] looked toward a rebirth of Dionysus, which we must now dimly conceive as the end of individuation. It was for this coming third Dionysus that the epopts' roaring hymns of joy resounded. And it is this hope alone that casts a gleam of joy upon the features of a world torn asunder and shattered into individuals; this is symbolized in the myth of Demeter, sunk in eternal sorrow, who *rejoices* again for the first time when told that she may *once more* give birth to Dionysus. This view of things already provides us with all the elements of a profound and pessimistic view of the world, together with the *mystery doctrine of tragedy*: the fundamental knowledge of the oneness of everything existent, the conception of individuation as the primal cause of evil, and of art as the joyous hope that the spell of individuation may be broken in augury of a restored oneness.

We have already suggested that the Homeric epos is the poem of Olympian culture, in which this culture has sung its own song of victory over the terrors of the war of the Titans. Under the predominating influence of tragic poetry, these Homeric myths are now born anew; and this metempsychosis reveals that in the meantime the Olympian culture also has been conquered by a still more profound view of the world. The defiant Titan Prometheus has announced to his Olympian tormentor that some day the greatest danger will menace his rule, unless Zeus should enter into an alliance with him in time. In Aeschylus we recognize how the terrified Zeus, fearful of his end, allies himself with the Titan. Thus the former age of the Titans is once more recovered from Tartarus and brought to the light.

Section 10

The philosophy of wild and naked nature beholds with the frank, undissembling gaze of truth the myths of the Homeric world as they dance past: they turn pale, they tremble under the piercing glance of this goddess — till the powerful fist of the Dionysian artist forces them into the service of the new deity. Dionysian truth takes over the entire domain of myth as the symbolism of *its* knowledge which it makes known partly in the public cult of tragedy and partly in the secret celebrations of dramatic mysteries, but always in the old mythical garb.

What power was it that freed Prometheus from his vultures and transformed the myth into a vehicle of Dionysian wisdom? It is the Heraclean power of music: having reached its highest manifestation in tragedy, it can invest myths with a new and most profound significance. This we have already characterized as the most powerful function of music. For it is the fate of every myth to creep by degrees into the narrow limits of some alleged historical reality, and to be treated by some later generation as a unique fact with historical claims: and the Greeks were already fairly on the way toward restamping the whole of their mythical juvenile dream sagaciously and arbitrarily into a historico-pragmatical *juvenile history*. For this is the way in which religions are wont to die out: under the stern, intelligent eyes of an orthodox dogmatism, the mythical premises of a religion are systematized as a sum total of historical events; one begins apprehensively to defend the credibility of the myths, while at the same time one opposes any continuation of their natural vitality and growth; the feeling for myth perishes, and its place is taken by the claim of religion to historical foundations. This dying myth was now seized by the new-born genius of Dionysian music; and in these hands it flourished once more with colors such as it had never yet displayed, with a fragrance that awakened a longing anticipation of a metaphysical world. After this final effulgence it collapses, its leaves wither, and soon the mocking Lucians of antiquity catch at the discolored and faded flowers carried away by the four winds. Through tragedy the myth attains its most profound content, its most expressive form; it rises once more like a wounded hero, and its whole excess of strength, together with the philosophic calm of the dying, burns in its eyes with a last powerful gleam.

What did you want, sacrilegious Euripides, when you sought to compel this dying myth to serve you once more? It died under your violent hands — and then you needed a copied, masked myth that, like the ape of Heracles, merely knew how to deck itself out in the ancient pomp. And just as the myth died on you, the genius of music died on you, too. Though with greedy hands you plundered all the gardens of music, you still managed only copied, masked music. And because you had abandoned Dionysus, Apollo abandoned you: rouse all the passions from their resting places and conjure them into your circle, sharpen and whet a sophistical dialectic for the speeches of your heroes — your heroes, too, have only copied, masked passions and speak only copied, masked speeches. . . .

CONTEMPORARY
PERSPECTIVES

A *PROMINENT SCHOLAR
and theoretician of feminism and theater, Sue-Ellen Case examines the
complicity of traditional theatrical practices — cross-dressing in the Greek theater, for example — in the
patriarchal structure of Western culture. Professor Case has written many influential studies of gender,
sexuality, and theater and is the author of* Feminism and Theatre *(1988).*

SUE-ELLEN CASE

FROM *"Classic Drag:
The Greek Creation of
Female Parts"*
(1985)

From a feminist perspective, the initial observations about the history of theatre noted the absences of women within the tradition. Since traditional scholarship has focused on evidence related to written texts, the absence of women playwrights became central to early feminist investigations. The fact that there was no significant number of extant texts written by women for the stage until the seventeenth century produced a rather astounding sense of absence in the classical traditions of the theatre. The silence of women's voices in these traditions led feminist historians who were interested in women playwrights to concentrate on periods in which they did emerge: primarily the seventeenth century in England, the nineteenth century in America, and the twentieth century in Europe and America. These studies produced a number of new anthologies of plays by women and biographies of women playwrights that began to appear in the early seventies.

Work on the classical periods became possible by studying the image of women within plays written by men. Many scholars attribute the beginning to this type of textual discovery to the popular book by Kate Millett entitled *Sexual Politics* (1970). Millett's book illustrated a way to recognize and interpret the images of women in male literature as misogynistic. *Sexual Politics* offered a way to read against texts by becoming aware of their gendered bias and, as the title suggests, to foreground the notion that art is not distinct from politics. While Millett's book concentrated on describing the images of women, other early works such as Judith Fetterly's *The Resisting Reader* articulated a posture for resisting reading texts by men as they were conventionally read. Fetterly outlined ways to read against texts to discover the feminist subtext latent in such subversions. Works on images of women still predominate in the feminist criticism of historical texts. Numerous re-visions of Aeschylus and Shakespeare are currently being produced. The images are commonly identified as being one of two basic types: positive roles, which depict women as independent, intelligent, and even heroic and a surplus of misogynistic roles commonly identified as the Bitch, the Witch, the Vamp, or the Virgin/Goddess. These roles reflect the perspective of the playwright or of the theatrical tradition on women. Originally, feminist historians used these theatrical images of women as evidence of the kind of lives actual women might have lived in the period. For example, what the characters and situations of Medea or Phaedra might tell us about the lives of powerful women in Greece. This approach was useful because traditional socio-economic histories tend to exhibit the same absence of women as does the literature. In the seventies, groundbreaking work on women in history was done in both realms: the socio-historical evidence identified in theatrical texts, and the publication of newly-collated documents on laws, social practices, and economic restrictions on women in history. This work enabled feminist critics and historians to produce a new kind of cultural analysis, which is based on the interplay of cultural phenomena, such as plays, theatre practice, and socio-economic evidence, to discover the nature of women's lives in the classical periods.

Yet the discovery of the complicity of art with political projects, as well as the complicity of traditional history with the patriarchy led to new discoveries which reverse the original interpretations of these documents. The feminist critic may no longer believe that the portrayal of women in classical plays by men relates to the lives of actual women. Instead, the feminist critic may assume that the images of women in these plays represent a fiction of women constructed by the patriarchy. This assumption originates in a central practice within classical cultures: the division between private and public life. The public life becomes privileged in the classical plays and histories, while the private life remains relatively invisible. The new feminist analyses prove that this division is gender-specific, i.e., the public life is the property of men and women are relegated to the invisible private sphere. The result of the suppression of actual women in the classical world created the invention of a representation of the gender "Woman" within the culture. This "Woman" appeared on the stage, in the myths, and in the plastic arts, representing the patriarchal values attached to the gender of "Woman" while suppressing the experiences, stories, feelings, and fantasies of actual women.[1] The new feminist approach to these cultural fictions divides this "Woman" as a male-produced fiction from historical women, insisting that there is little connection between the two categories. Within theatre practice, the clearest illustration of this division is in the tradition of the all-male stage. "Woman" was played by male actors in drag, while actual women were banned from the stage. The classical acting practice reveals the construction of the fictional gender created by the patriarchy. The classical plays and theatrical conventions can now be regarded as allies in the project of suppressing actual women and replacing them with the masks of patriarchal production.

The beginning of the activity and literature known as theatre is traditionally assigned to the plays and practices of the Athenian festivals of Dionysos in sixth and fifth century B.C. Our notions of plays, acting, physical theatre space, costume, mask, and relation of play to audience begin with these Athenian festivals. In the sixth century, both women and men participated in these ceremonies, but by the fifth century, when the ceremonies were becoming what is known as theatre, women disappeared from the practice. Scholars do not record any evidence for specific laws or codes forbidding women to appear in the songs and dances, nor is there any evidence for the specific date or occasion of the beginning of their omission. Margarete Bieber, a recognized authority on this history, merely notes that it was part of "Attic morality" which "banished women from public life."[2] This implies, then, that the reason for this practice must be sought in the emerging cultural codes of Athens, rather than in specific political or theatrical practices. Three elements of Athenian culture help to understand the emerging theatrical practice: the new economic practices, the new cultural project and the new genealogy of the gods. The intersection of all of these elements will be theatrically legitimatized in the text of *The Oresteia*.

Among the new economic practices, the rise of the family unit radically altered the role of women in Greek public life. Ironically, the important role women began to assume within the family unit was the cause of their removal from public life. The family unit became the new site for the creation and transmission of personal wealth. With the rise of the *polis*, the large network inherent in aristocracies gave way to single families. The rise of metals as commodities and the small-scale cultivation of land made it possible for individuals to control their own wealth. Yet while ownership became more individual and located within the family unit, it was limited to the male gender. Women were restricted to limited conditions of ownership and exchange. For example, women could only enter into inheritance transactions in the absence of a male and women were not allowed to barter for property over one medimnos (bushel). Within this new economy, women became a medium of exchange and marriage became an institution of ownership.[3] In fact, the word for marriage, *ekdosis*, meant loan—women were loaned to their husbands by their fathers, and in the case of a divorce, they were returned to their fathers.

With this change in the organization of wealth came a concomitant change in the organization of political units. The *oikos*, or household, became the basic unit for citizenship.[4] Citizenship was dependent upon family lines—a son was granted citizenship only if his parents were citizens, but without a son the parents could not retain their citizenship. This new condition for citizenship led to the strict definition and regulation of the sex life of the woman. The mother/wife assumed a new moral/legal dimension for the legitimacy and security of heirs and, by extension, political membership in the *polis*. Clear lines of reproduction were vital to the *polis*, making adultery a crime against society, rather than a sign of personal transgression. At the same time that the household became controlled by needs of the state, its activities became totally separate from those which were considered the business of the state, the mark of the citizen, or the activities of public life. Nancy Hartsock,

[1]See Teresa de Lauretis, *Alice Doesn't: Feminism, Semiotics, Cinema* (Bloomington: Indiana University Press, 1984), for a thorough development of the concept of "Woman."

[2]Margarete Bieber, *The History of the Greek and Roman Theatre* (Princeton: Princeton University Press, 1939), p. 9.

[3]See Gayle Rubin, "The Traffic in Women: Notes on the 'Political Economy' of Sex," in *Toward an Anthropology of Women*, ed. Rayna R. Reiter (New York: Monthly Review Press, 1975) for a discussion of women as a medium of exchange through the institution of marriage and kinship laws.

[4]Marilyn Arthur, "'Liberated' Women: The Classical Era," in *Becoming Visible: Women in European History*, eds. Renate Bridenthal and Claudia Koonz (Boston: Houghton Mifflin, 1977), pp. 67–68.

in her book *Money, Sex and Power*, describes it this way: the Greeks defined the household as a private, apolitical space from the public, political space of the *polis*. "The result was a theorization of politics and political power as activities that occurred in a masculine arena characterized by freedom from necessary labor, dominance of intellect or soul," while the domestic space was defined by necessary labor and as a place where bodily needs were dominant.[5] Since Athenian women were confined to the house (explicitly in the laws of Solon), they were removed from the public life of the intellect and the soul and confined to the world of domestic labor, childbearing, and concomitant sexual activities. Actual women disappeared from the public life of the *polis*, lost their economic and legal powers and became objects of exchange. Within the socio-economic life of the *polis*, it is not surprising that their participation in the Dionysian festivals was restricted to private practices, resulting in their eventual exclusion from the stage.

Alongside these new legal and economic practices came new cultural institutions. Athens created new architecture, new religions, new myths, and the practice of theatre. These cultural institutions became allied with the suppression of women by creating the new gender role of "Woman" that would privilege the masculine gender and oppress the feminine one. At base, the new cultural categories of gender were constructed as categories of difference and polarity.[6] "Woman" appeared as the opposite of man. This move can best be seen in the new myths and architectural depictions of the amazons. The image of amazons is central to the female gender conflated with the outsider and with polar differences from the Greek male citizen. The amazons, dangerous but defeated, reverse the "natural" gender roles. They are warriors who force men to do "women's" work, such as child rearing, while the women go off to war.[7] The amazons also embody other myths of gender reversal—they keep female babies and dispose of the male ones, while the custom was to dispose of female babies.[8] Moreover, the word "amazon" (no breast) ties such practices to a biological, secondary sex characteristic specific to the female. The new architecture of the Acropolis, the civic center of Athens, displays the downfall of the amazons and the rise of Athena. Central to the new political order, then, is the demise of these women who would defy correct gender associations and the rise of a woman who would enforce the new image of "Woman" in the *polis*. This demise of the old images of women and the rise of Athena are central themes in *The Oresteia*.

The genealogy of the gods provides the mytho-historical context for this creation of the new "Woman." The history of the gods explains why genders are opposite, locked in conflict, and why the male gender must defeat the former female one. The myth of the first earth-mother-goddess, Gaia, is a story of the dangers of her womb—the story of her children is one of murders and castrations. It concludes with the final conquest by Zeus, who swallows his wife Metis in order to gain her power of reproduction and then gives birth to Athena. Athena represents the end of the dangers of the womb, for she has no mother (breaking with matriarchal and female-identification), has no sexuality (she remains a virgin), defeats the amazons, allies herself with the reign of Zeus and Apollo, and thereby brings order to Athens. About this same time, Dionysos, a new god, appears in Athens and usurps the role of fertility and sexuality which the earlier female goddesses had retained. This male usurpation of female fertility will later be idealized by Plato in his famous midwife metaphor, while the assimilation of female sexuality will be usurped by boys in the social practice of male homosexuality (also later idealized by Plato). The genealogy of the gods thus divides female sexuality from power, assimilating female sexuality in the figure of Dionysos and isolating power in the image of the motherless virgin, Athena.

The rise of drama, within the Athenian state festivals dedicated to the celebration of Dionysos, places theatre securely within this new patriarchal institution of gender wars. Theatre must be gender-specific to the male and enact the suppression of actual women as well as the representation of the new "Woman." The maenads (the female celebrants of the Dionysian festivals) must dance into

---

[5]Nancy Hartsock, *Money, Sex and Power: Toward a Feminist Historical Materialism* (New York: Longman, 1983), p. 187.

[6]Page duBois, *Centaurs and Amazons* (Ann Arbor: University of Michigan Press, 1982), p. 2.

[7]William Blake Tyrell, *Amazons: A Study in Athenian Mythmaking* (Baltimore: The Johns Hopkins University Press, 1984), p. 47.

[8]Tyrell, p. 55.

oblivion, while the satyrs (the male celebrants) must become the first choruses of the drama. "The singer Arion is said to have given to the singers of the dithyramb . . . the costume of the satyrs. The practice of representing someone other than oneself grew out of this ecstasy and led to the mimic art of the actors."[9] In other words, the power of representation was given only to the male celebrants. The invention of acting was gender-specific—the actor was the satyr. The gender-specific quality of the actor in the satyr play was even underscored by his wearing of the leather phallus. Yet in order to dramatize the battle of the genders, the female must somehow be represented: the male actor would need to perform the female role. Though scholars and theatre historians never mention this strange phenomenon in more than passing remarks, Bieber does note one specific problem for male actors in their representation of women: on the vases, the maenads seem to be in a state of ecstasy—to play maenads, the male actors needed the comprehension of the religious emotion felt by these women.[10] Yet a more central problem emerges: how does one depict a woman? How does the male actor signal to the audience that he is a woman? Along with the female costume of the shorter tunic and the female mask with longer hair, he might have indicated through gesture, movement, and vocal intonation that the character was female. In considering this portrayal, it is important to remember that the notion of the female derived from the male point of view, which remained alien to female experience and reflected the perspective of her gendered opposite. This vocabulary of gestures initiated the image of "Woman" as she is seen on the stage—institutionalized through patriarchal culture and represented by male-originated signs of her appropriate gender behavior. Moreover, the practice of male actors playing women probably encouraged the creation of female roles which lent themselves to generalization and stereotype. The depiction and development of female characters in the written texts must have accommodated the practice of their representation onstage. Though all characters were formalized and masked, the cross-gender casting for female characters distinguished them in kind from the male characters. A subtextual message was delivered about the nature of the female gender, its behavior, appearance, and formal distance from the representation of the male.

The Athenian theatre practice created a political and aesthetic arena for ritualized and codified gender behavior, linking it to civic privileges and restrictions. The elevation of this gender principle to the term "classic" canonizes it as a paradigmatic element of the history of theatre, connoting the expulsion of women from the canon and the ideal. The etymology of "classic," connoting class, indicates that this expulsion is also related to the economic and legal privileges of the "first class"—a class to which women were denied admittance. The consonance of aesthetic criteria with economic ones becomes clear in the term itself. In each of the cultures which has produced "classics" for the stage (not only the Athenian, but the Roman and the Elizabethan) women were denied access to the stage and to legal and economic enfranchisement. These same production values are embedded in the texts of these periods. Female characters are derived from the absence of actual women on the stage and from the reasons for their absence. Each culture which valorizes the reproduction of those "classic" texts actively participates in the same patriarchal subtext which created those female characters as "Woman." Though we cannot examine a production of the Greek classics, we can examine one of the "classic" texts produced for the Dionysian festivals and reproduced in the history of theatrical productions, history, and criticism within our own contemporary culture. The trilogy of *The Oresteia* exhibits all of the themes and practices discussed above. Moreover, its elevated position in the canon illustrates its lasting value. A feminist reading of *The Oresteia* illustrates the defeat of the old matriarchal genealogy, the nature of "Woman" as portrayed on the stage, the rise of Athena, and the legacy of the suppression of actual women.

The Oresteia   Many feminist critics and historians have analyzed *The Oresteia* as a text central to the formalization of misogyny. Simone de Beauvoir and Kate Millett describe it as the mythical rendering of a patriarchal takeover. Nancy Hartsock argues that it associates the female gender with sexuality and nature, those forces that must be tamed in outside activities and within the inner person for the survival of the *polis*.[11] Hartsock describes *The Oresteia* within the dramatic festivals that are themselves associated with male gender activities. The drama, like the four-horse chariot race, is a contest. It formalizes

---

[11]Hartsock, p. 192.

agons (contests) and the notion of winners and losers. The festivals associate the heroic ideal of valor in battle with the peacetime ideal of rhetorical and dramatic competition.[12] The subject of the drama is the subject of war — the male warrior hero. When this *agon* is inscribed with the conflicts of gender, the dramatic dice are loaded for the same gender-specific hero to win. *The Oresteia* enacts the "battle of the sexes," using Athenian cultural and political codes to prescribe that women must lose the battle.

Early in the first play of the trilogy, *Agamemnon*, the chorus of old men explicates the dramatic situation within the perspective of male-female problems. The old men describe a promiscuous woman (Helen) as the cause of the Trojan war in which Agamemnon is presently engaged and they tell of the war fleet launched by Agamemnon's sacrifice of his virgin-daughter Iphigenia. The Trojan war and the relationship of Agamemnon and Clytemnestra are already fraught with conflicts embedded in gender roles. Then the chorus prepares the audience for the entrance of Clytemnestra by linking gender with certain attributes of character. They suggest that steady resolve and intensity of purpose are gender-specific when they refer to the male (inner) strength of Clytemnestra (line 10).[13] Within this context Clytemnestra enters, played by a man. After s/he speaks, the chorus congratulates her for thinking like a man and dismisses her announcement of the end of the war as just "like a woman to take rapture before fact" (line 483). These lines presume certain gender roles regarding the judgment of evidence and decision-making. Within the theatre practice, they also play with a certain level of irony since a man in drag plays a woman who "thinks like a man." Clearly, the primary referent is the male. The notion of female, like the notion of the amazon, disrupts the male order. Clytemnestra is introduced as a figure of that disruption. The absence of the male king has provided her with "unnatural" political power. In his absence, she has taken a male lover. By this act, she disrupts the gender code of female sexuality, for the tradition was that women were to remain monogamous even during ten year wars. The chorus treats Clytemnestra's liaison as dangerous. Yet when Agamemnon enters with his sexual war booty, Cassandra, the implication of social disruption is not in the text. In fact, the dramatic pathos of the drama favors Agamemnon, despite his treatment of women as evidenced by his rape of Cassandra or his murder of Iphigenia.

Cassandra provides the Athenian image of the woman in the public arena (even though she is played by a man). She has certain privileges of belonging (she is the priestess of Apollo which assures her of sexual liaisons with citizens of rank such as Agamemnon), but she does not have the privilege of effective public speech because of her prior refusal to be violated by Apollo. Cassandra's entrance, as an outsider, as Agamemnon's booty, mute to Clytemnestra and expelled from effective dialogue, even portrayed by a male actor, projects the strength of the misogyny embedded in the Athenian patriarchal order. What remains in the play is only Clytemnestra's murder of Agamemnon and her complete vilification. At the end, the chorus mourns Agamemnon as one who had to fight a war for a woman and then be killed by one (lines 1453–1454).

The third play, *The Eumenides*, decides the winner of the battle of the sexes within the play, within Athens, and within the genealogy of the gods. From a feminist perspective, it is ironic that this play dramatizes the so-called beginnings of democracy. Moreover, within theatre history, *The Eumenides* is often marked as the play of the new order of civilization which created our western tradition of reason and fair play. This may be an accurate description, for it does make the deciding gender judgments of Athenian culture and condemns women to their subservient role in Western civilization. The play rests upon a new genealogy of the gods. It opens with the old order, the vile goddesses, the Eumenides. They create an ugly, frightening characterization of the earlier Cthonic female religions. The masks created for them were famous for their disgusting appearance. An extant remark about them states that "Aeschylus' Eumenides horrified women into miscarriages"[14] — an interesting anecdote for its gender and sexual connotations. The Eumenides have arrived in Athens, while pursuing Orestes to revenge his murder of his mother. They describe their role as the punishment of matricide (line 210). Orestes appeals to Apollo for help and Athena appears to solve the problem. She

---

[11] Hartsock, p. 192.

[12] Hartsock, p. 198.

[13] All citations of *The Oresteia* are from Aeschylus, *The Oresteia in Complete Greek Tragedies, Aeschylus*, eds. David Grene, Richmond Lattimore (Chicago: Chicago University Press, 1960).

[14] Sir Arthur Pickard-Cambridge, *The Dramatic Festivals of Athens* (Oxford: Clarendon Press, 1968), p. 265.

institutes a trial, exhibiting Athenian methods of justice, to try Orestes for his murder. The decision is to set Orestes free. This conclusion is damning evidence for the public rationalization of misogyny, for it rests upon establishing the parental line as male. The mother is not the parent, but the nurse of the child. The parent is defined as he who mounts (lines 658–661). Athena is the supreme proof of this fact because she had no mother and was begat by the male god Zeus (lines 734–738). The Eumenides are confined to a cave and their function is no longer to revenge matricide, but to preside over marriages. Thus, the trilogy which began with the end of the Trojan war and proceeded through the house of Agamemnon ends with the institution of democracy deciding the role of gender and the definition of procreation. This ending can be seen as paradigmatic of future plot structures in the Western playwriting tradition. A majority of plays will conclude various kinds of civic, historical, and psychological problems with the institution of marriage. The proper gender role for women is inscribed in this conclusion.

The feminist reader of *The Oresteia* discovers that she must read against the text, resisting not only its internal sense of pathos and conclusion, but also the historical and cultural codes which surround it, including its treatment within theatre history. The pathos the feminist reader feels may be for Iphigenia and Clytemnestra rather than for Agamemnon. She may perceive Athena as a male-identified woman in alliance with the male network of power rather than as a hero of Athens. She definitely feels excluded from the conventions of the stage, bewildered by the convention of cross-gender casting which is only practiced in terms of female characters. Mimesis is not possible for her. Perhaps the feminist reader will decide that the female roles have nothing to do with women, that these roles should be played by men, as fantasies of "Woman" as "Other" than men, disruptions of a patriarchal society which illustrates its fear and loathing of the female parts. In fact, the feminist reader might become persuaded that the Athenian roles of Medea, Clytemnestra, Cassandra or Phaedra are properly played as drag roles. The feminist reader might conclude that women need not relate to these roles or even attempt to identify with them. Moreover, the feminist historian might conclude that these roles contain no information about the experience of real women in the classical world. Nevertheless, the feminist scholar must recognize that theatre originated in this kind of cultural climate and that the Athenian experience will continue to provide a certain paradigm of theatrical practice for the rest of Western theatrical/cultural history. By linking practice, text, and cultural practice in this new way, she may enhance her understanding of how the hegemonic structure of patriarchal practice was instituted in Athens. . . .

II

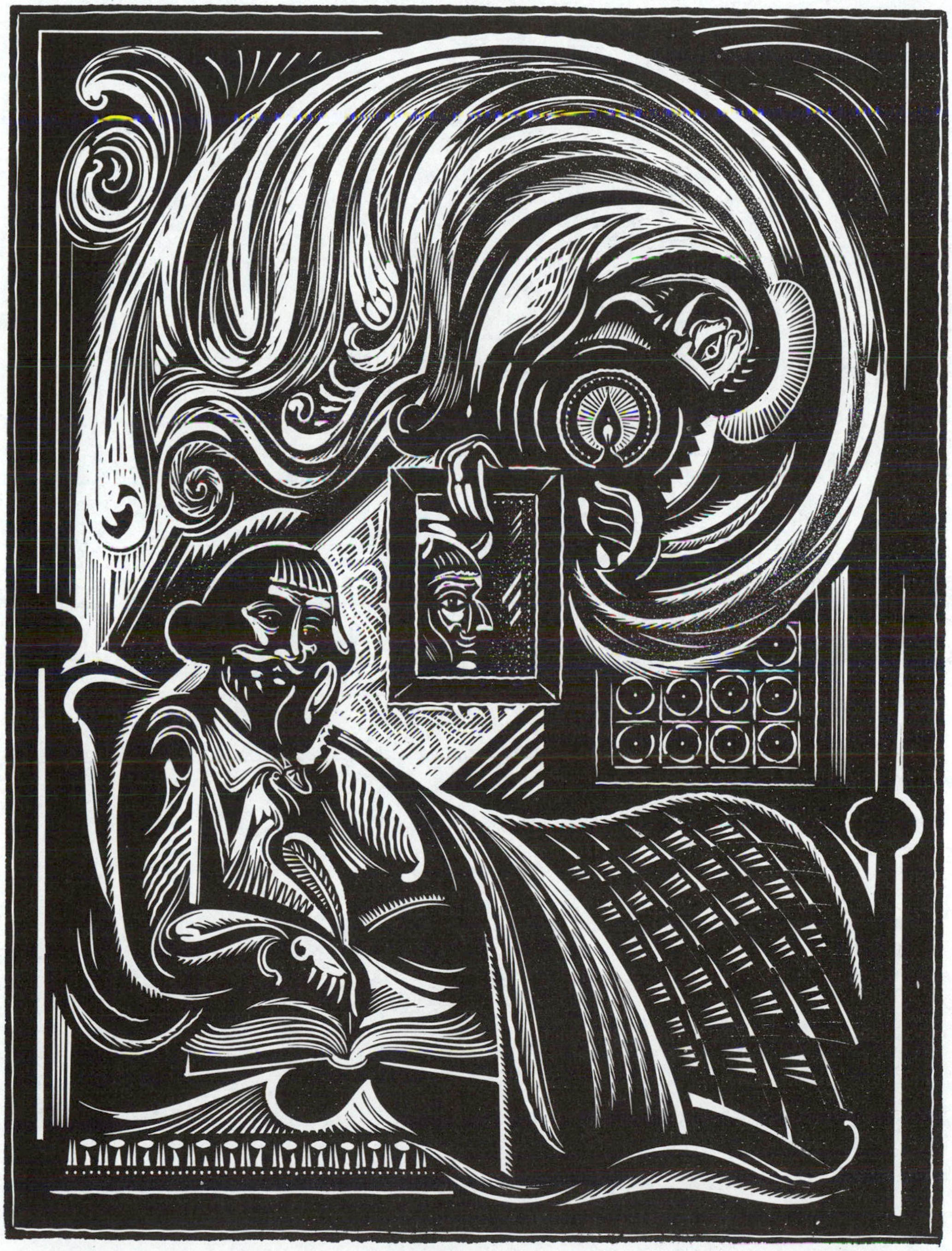

Drama and Theater in Medieval and Renaissance England

THE FIFTEENTH, SIXTEENTH, and seventeenth centuries saw Europe transformed by the extraordinary cultural revolution we now call the European Renaissance. Fueled by new technology, like printing, and by new scientific, political, and religious ideas, explosive change transformed European culture. The known world expanded beyond the sea to embrace the New World; the recovery of Greek and Latin literature spurred a sweeping intellectual revolution; strong centralized monarchies in Spain, Portugal, France, and England created new empires abroad and fought to control an increasingly restive populace at home; the Protestant Reformation undermined the religious and political authority of the Catholic Church, beginning a period of violent religious conflict; the "new philosophy" — modern science — of Copernicus, Bacon, and Galileo seemed to put even the physical world of heaven and earth in doubt. "'Tis all in pieces, all coherence gone," the poet John Donne wrote in 1611, voicing the profound anxiety and exhilaration of many of his contemporaries: "Prince, subject, father, son are things forgot. / For every man alone thinks that he hath got / To be a Phoenix." The changing tides of thought swept away the crumbling edifice of the medieval world — the feudal state, the universal Church, scholastic philosophy, an ordered heaven, and revealed truth — and opened the way for the modern world.

This revolution also infused the theater; the Renaissance — especially in Italy, France, Spain, and England — is one of the great ages of theatrical and dramatic achievement. In England, the professional theater as we know it originated at this time: the history of the secular, profit-making, commercial theater is conventionally dated from the opening of the first theater building, The Theatre, in London in 1576. Licensed and protected as an aristocratic entertainment, the theater was also a popular institution, in which commoners such as William Shakespeare, Richard Burbage, Edward Alleyn, Inigo Jones, and others, could indeed rise like the phoenix. However, to understand the revolutionary impact of theater and drama in Shakespeare's era, we need to understand their conservative inheritance, their deep indebtedness to the medieval stage that preceded them.

Dramatic performance in medieval Europe was thoroughly conditioned by the Catholic Church's central role in the life of the community. Having closed the Roman theaters in the sixth century, the Church maintained a vigilant opposition to the secular theater and the vices associated with it. Yet the revival of theater in Europe, beginning in the tenth century, was inspired and sponsored by the Church itself. The four major dramatic forms in the late Middle Ages were connected with the Church, its rituals, and its calendar of religious observances: **LITURGICAL DRAMA**, enacted as part of the liturgy of the Catholic Mass; **CYCLE PLAYS**, illustrating scriptural history and performed by craft guilds on the feast of Corpus Christi; **MORALITY DRAMA**, enacting the symbolic structure of Christian life; and plays written and performed in schools and universities, sometimes imitating classical plays. In England, cycle and morality plays particularly influenced the later, secular drama of the sixteenth century.

The earliest dramatic records, dating from the ninth century, are musical **TROPES**, brief elaborations of the authorized liturgy, written to amplify the scriptural text and enhance its impact and appeal. These compositions were set to music and sung in **ANTIPHONAL PERFORMANCE** (back and forth, in dialogue) between monks or boy choristers to accompany the liturgy of the Mass. In England, Ethelwold, Bishop of Winchester, wrote a series of lessons concerning the conduct of the Mass, the *Regularis Concordia* (965–975), including instructions for such performances. These are his instructions to the priests for representing the visit of the three Marys to the tomb of Christ after the Crucifixion (translated from Latin):

> While the third lesson is being chanted, let four brethren vest themselves; of whom, let one, vested in an alb, enter as if to take part in the service, and let him without being observed approach the place of the sepulchre [i.e., near the altar], and there, holding a palm in his hand, let him sit down quietly. While the third responsory is being sung, let the remaining three follow, all of them vested in copes, and carrying in their hands censers filled with incense; and slowly, in the manner of seeking something, let them come before the place of the sepulchre. These things are done in imitation of the angel seated in the monument, and of the women coming with spices to anoint the body of Jesus. When therefore that one seated shall see the three, as if straying about and seeking something, approach him, let him begin in a dulcet voice of medium pitch to sing:

> *Whom seek ye in the sepulchre, O followers of Christ?*

When he has sung this to the end, let the three respond in unison:

> *Jesus of Nazareth, which was crucified, O celestial one.*

To whom that one:

> *He is not here; he is risen; just as he foretold.*
> *Go, announce that he is risen from the dead.*

At the word of this command let those three turn themselves to the choir, saying:

> *Alleluia! The Lord is risen to-day.*
> *The strong lion, the Christ, the Son of God. Give thanks to God.*

This said, let the former, again seating himself, as if recalling them, sing the anthem:

> *Come, and see the place where the Lord was laid. Alleluia! Alleluia!*

And saying this, let him rise and let him lift the veil and show them the place bare of the cross, but only the cloths laid there with which the cross was wrapped. Seeing which, let them set down the censers which they carried into the same sepulchre, and let them take up the cloth and spread it out before the eyes of the clergy; and as if making known that the Lord had risen and was not now therein wrapped, let them sing this anthem:

> *The Lord is risen from the sepulchre.*
> *Who for us hung upon the cross.*

And let them place the cloth upon the altar. The anthem being ended, let the Prior, rejoicing with them at the triumph of our King, in that, having conquered death, he arose, begin the hymn:

> *We praise thee, O God.*

This begun, all the bells chime out together.[1]

Despite its brevity, and the limitations imposed by the liturgy itself, this trope has the elements of drama: a progressive plot, the involvement of specific characters, conflict and

---

[1] *Regularis Concordia*, in *Chief Pre-Shakespearean Dramas*, ed. Joseph Quincy Adams (Boston: Houghton Mifflin, 1924), 9–10.

resolution. Ethelwold's "stage directions" convey a subtle sense of how character can be created by performance and a fine sense of visual spectacle as well, all within the narrow scope allowed by the Mass.

Throughout the Middle Ages and beyond, liturgical plays of this kind became increasingly common and complex. Enacted in different locations—called **MANSIONS**—within the church, liturgical drama provided a model for the forms of religious drama that came to be performed outside the church and outside the framework of the liturgy. In the tenth and eleventh centuries, the church sponsored dramatized scenes from the life of Christ or the lives of the saints, staged on important Christian holidays. A town, for example, might commemorate the entrance of Christ into Jerusalem on Palm Sunday with a procession to the cathedral in which townspeople enacted various roles. In addition, the church oversaw the production of cycles of plays, which became a principal mode of theatrical and dramatic innovation. These cycles were performed sixty days after Easter as part of the Feast of Corpus Christi, a holiday inaugurated in the fourteenth century to celebrate the doctrine of the Eucharist. The Corpus Christi festival frequently featured the performance of a series of plays dramatizing scriptural history—the Creation, Old Testament events (Noah and the Flood, Abraham and Isaac), scenes from the New Testament (the Annunciation, Herod and the Slaughter of the Innocents), and prophetic plays concerning the Harrowing of Hell and the Last Judgment. The production of these plays could last several days or weeks and called on the services of the entire town. Each craft guild (or *mystery*, as the guilds were called; the cycles are sometimes called **MYSTERY CYCLES**) financed and produced a different play, often on a subject appropriate to the guild. The shipwrights' guild might undertake the Noah play, the Three Kings play might be assigned to the goldsmiths, and so on. The plays were the property of the guilds and passed through generations of guild members. In major towns with many craft guilds, the cycles often included a large number of plays. Of the English cycles, the York cycle is the longest, containing forty-eight plays, the Wakefield cycle has thirty-two, and the Chester cycle has twenty-four.

Although they were produced for a popular, largely illiterate audience, the cycle dramas are extremely sophisticated and involved the talents of trained performers. One of the cycles' most powerful and typical features is their use of **ANACHRONISM**—the blending of the historical past with contemporary events and characters. Many of the characters who appear in the plays are medieval English peasants, who often display an ironic, even theatrical sense of their involvement in the scriptural events of the past. One of the most telling uses of this technique occurs in the York *Crucifixion*, for one of the ways that the York playwright conveys the Roman soldiers' hardness to the message of Christ is by making them jest with him about the cruxifixion they are performing:

> 1 SOLDIER: (to Christ) Say, Sir, how likes you now
> This work that we have wrought?
> 2 SOLDIER: We pray you say us how
> Ye feel, or faint ye aught.
> JESUS: . . . My Father, that all bales [evils] may beet [abate].
> Forgive these men that do me pine [pain].
> What they work wot [know] they nought;
> Therefore, my Father, I crave,
> Let never their sins be sought,
> But see their souls to save.
> 1 SOLDIER: We! Hark! he jangles like a jay.[2]

---

[2]The York *Crucifixion*, in *Everyman and Other Medieval Miracle Plays*, ed. A. C. Cawley (New York: Dutton, 1959), 153–54.

MEDIEVAL PAGEANT WAGON

One actor is playing in the street in front of the wagon.

By characterizing the jesting Roman soldiers as, in effect, contemporaries of the medieval audience, the play implies that biblical events are part of the audience's contemporary history. Seeing their neighbors enacting the biblical scenes, and seeing contemporary characters share the stage with biblical figures, must have emphasized the immediacy of the ongoing Christian story.

Like the cycle plays, morality plays dramatized elements of Christian life. Instead of staging events from scriptural history, morality drama stages a symbolic **ALLEGORY** of the Christian's spiritual journey through life. Increasingly popular throughout the fourteenth and fifteenth centuries, plays like *The Castle of Perseverance* (c. 1425), *Mankind* (c. 1470), and *Everyman* (c. 1500) emphasized the individual's struggle with sin, while the cycle plays emphasized the larger patterns of Christian history. Later playwrights, including Shakespeare, found both models useful. The cycles provided a pattern for staging the epic sweep of secular English history, and morality drama provided a supple device for representing psychological and moral conflict. Morality plays often provided the structure for the secular plays written at schools and universities, as well, and for the **INTERLUDES** performed at court as a break from holiday feasting. They also provided a staple technique for characterization in the later secular drama. Christopher Marlowe's *Doctor Faustus* (1590) uses the Good and Evil Angels to externalize Faustus's moral conflict, and other playwrights frequently used the devices of morality drama to dramatize the difficulties of political choice. In John Skelton's interlude, *Magnificence* (1516)—written for Henry VIII—or Thomas Sackville and Thomas Norton's *Gorboduc* (1561), the monarch is shown to make his decisions framed by a host of allegorized counsellors, good and bad advisers who approximate the role played in morality drama by angels and demons.

STAGING MEDIEVAL DRAMA

Medieval plays were often acted on or near **PAGEANT WAGONS**. In some towns, it appears that the audience remained stationary at various locations, while the wagons and their plays proceeded past them; at others, the wagons were drawn in a procession of **TABLEAUX VIVANTS** (posed scenes) through the town and then arranged in an open area for the performance, allowing the audience to move from play to play. The plays combined historical and contemporary elements; in performance, the staging produced a close and powerful relationship between the dramatic characters and the audience. In the Coventry play of the Magi, for example, Herod raves when he discovers that the three kings have escaped him:

> I Stamp! I Stare! I look all about!
> Might I them take, I should them burn at a glede [fire]!
> I rant! I run! and now run I wode [mad]
> A! That these villain traitors hath marred this my mood!
> They shall be hanged, if I may come them to!
> *Here Herod rages in the pagond* [pageant wagon] *and in the street also.*[3]

Herod's rage was certainly one of the highlights of the medieval cycles. Shakespeare, at least, seems to refer to it in *Hamlet* (1600), when he has Hamlet remind his actors that they should be restrained and natural in their performance, for overacting "out-Herods Herod." The stage direction also suggests that Herod's frenzy carried him from the wagon and into the street, into a closer and more effective relationship to his audience. This interaction between actor and audience is characteristic of popular theater and is a feature of medieval performance carried into Renaissance acting. It also suggests that the "place" of medieval

---

[3] The Coventry *Magi, Herod, and the Slaughter of the Innocents,* in *Chief Pre-Shakespearean Dramas,* ed. Joseph Quincy Adams (Boston: Houghton Mifflin, 1924), 163.

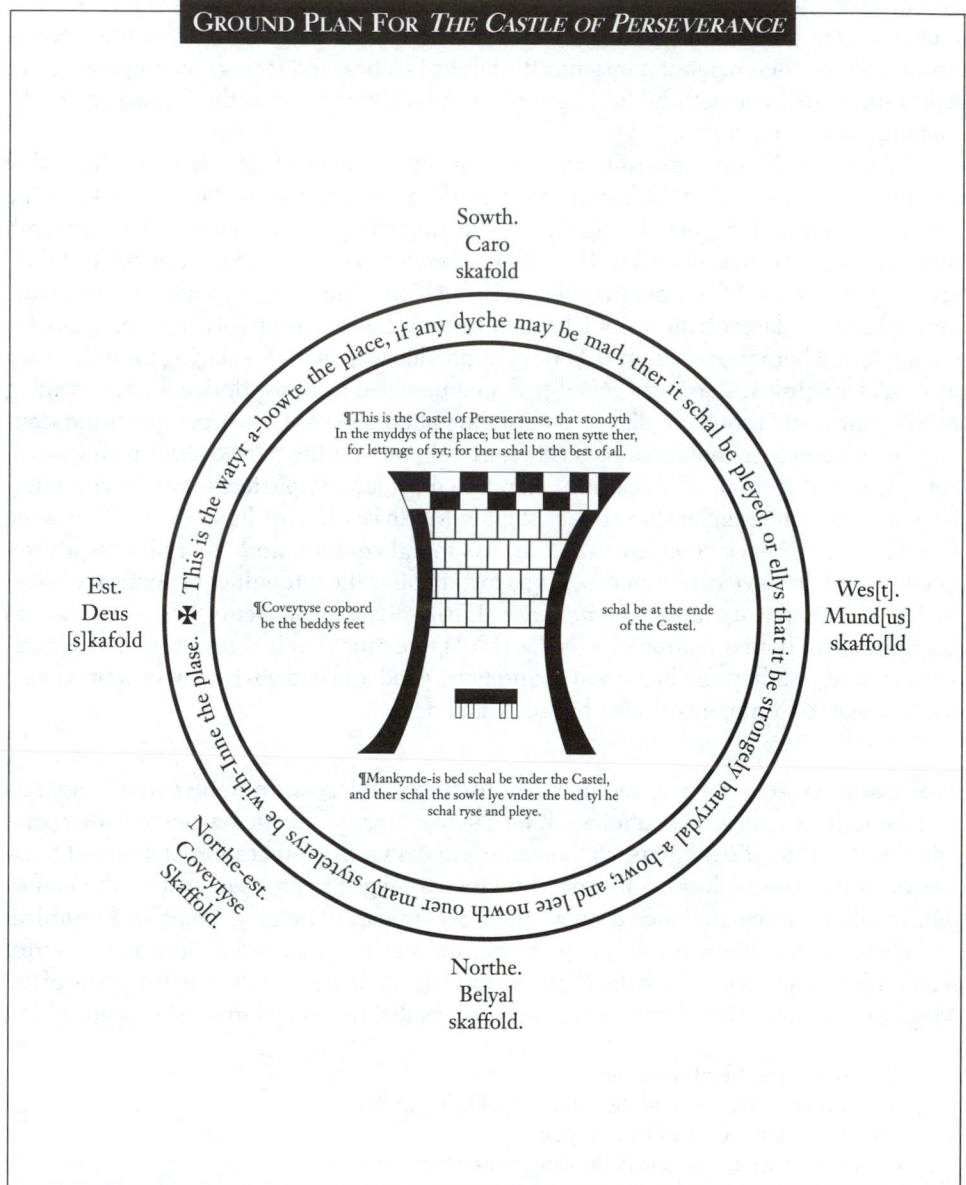

GROUND PLAN FOR *THE CASTLE OF PERSEVERANCE*

Sowth.
Caro
skafold

This is the watyr a-bowte the place, if any dyche may be mad, ther it schal be pleyed, or ellys that it be strongely barryd al a-bowt; and lete nowth ouer many syteleerys be with-Inne the plase.

¶This is the Castel of Perseueraunse, that stondyth
In the myddys of the place; but lete no men sytte ther,
for lettynge of syt; for ther schal be the best of all.

Est.
Deus
[s]kafold

¶Coveytyse copbord
be the beddys feet

schal be at the ende
of the Castel.

Wes[t].
Mund[us]
skaffo[ld

¶Mankynde-is bed schal be vnder the Castel,
and ther schal the sowle lye vnder the bed tyl he
schal ryse and pleye.

Northe-est.
Coveytyse
Skaffold.

Northe.
Belyal
skaffold.

Ground-plot for the medieval morality play The Castle of Perseverance.
*The drawing shows five scaffolds (North, Northeast, South, East, and
West) arranged around a playing area, with the castle in the center. A
ditch encircled the castle, to keep the spectators at a distance. In the
manuscript, a note beneath the drawing describes the costumes and
special effects: "He that shall play Belial [a devil], look that he have
gunpowder burning in pipes in his hands and in his ears, and in his
arse, when he goes to battle. The four daughters should be clad in
mantles; Mercy in white, Ruthwiseness in red, all together, Truth in sad
green, and Peace all in black; and they shall play in the place all
together until they bring up the soul."*

drama, the fictitious locale of the play, was not firmly localized onstage; the actors/ characters could move easily back and forth between Herod's Jerusalem and the medieval audience, and even onstage places could be rapidly and easily transformed. This flexibility also allowed medieval playwrights to treat stage space symbolically. The ground plot for *The Castle of Perseverance*, for instance—with its scaffolds for various evils, its moat, and its central castle—clearly offers us a symbolic locale rather than an actual geography. The various demons on their scaffolds stand at a symbolic distance, not an actual distance, from the central castle.

This complex of dramatic conventions, staging practices, and audience attitudes is a legacy of the medieval theater passed on to later theater. Although the medieval stage was only one of many influences on it, the drama of the sixteenth and seventeenth centuries is reminiscent of medieval drama in many ways. Renaissance drama frequently treats secular history according to a providential design similar to that of the cycles; it often treats its characters in the symbolic terms of the medieval moralities; and it uses both acting and stage space to create an immediacy between the fictive play and its audience. These habits take on very different meanings in Renaissance London, in a city and in a state in which the Anglican Protestant church is the state religion and where signs of Catholicism—or, in fact, of any religious subject matter—in the theater could be read as an act of sedition. The medieval theater provided the forms of drama and the practices of theater that were refashioned by the political, social, and theatrical pressures of the new era.

DRAMA AND THEATER IN RENAISSANCE LONDON

The explosion of theatrical and dramatic activity in London can be marked by two dates: 1576, when James Burbage erected The Theatre, London's first permanent theater building; and 1642, when plays were suspended and theaters were closed at the outbreak of the Civil War. The theater underwent profound changes from the reign of Elizabeth I (ruled 1558–1603) to the reigns of her successors James I (1603–1625) and Charles I (1625–1642, executed 1649) and yet at the same time it endured the intense social and cultural upheavals of the period with remarkable consistency. As an institution, the new professional theater witnessed the emergence of England as a modern state; the rise of England as an important mercantile and naval power, aided by the defeat of the Spanish Armada in 1588; the expansion of English interests in the New World; the growth of the city of London to roughly 250,000 inhabitants; and the ascendance of the Puritan faction that closed the theaters and deposed and executed the king.

The professional theater—a new institution in England, though already established on the continent—necessarily reflected the political and social strains of the time. These strains are most readily visible in the many laws regulating theatrical performance. The location of theater buildings, the structure and organization of theater companies, and the entire scene of theatrical activity in Renaissance London epitomized the fundamental tensions of English society as it moved from the medieval to the modern world.

THE PROFESSIONAL THEATER AND ITS SOCIETY

The sixteenth century witnessed intense religious and civil controversy, dating in part from Henry VIII's divorce from Catherine of Aragon in 1532 and his consequent excommunication from the Catholic church in 1533. Once Henry established the Protestant Church of England as the religion of the realm in 1535, English politics were often dictated by England's vulnerability to the massive, hostile powers of the Catholic church in Rome and Catholic states such as France and Spain. Within England, a variety of Protestant sects competed with each other, with the government, and with the Church of England for power. This was also a period of profound changes in the ordering of society, a period of growing mercantile power, of aristocratic discontent with the power of the Crown, and of the rise of new merchants and other social groups into prominence and power. As a result, the Crown was eternally on guard to suppress civil unrest or religious nonconformity.

Given this volatile political climate, it is not surprising that the Crown sought to limit and control public assembly, including theatrical performances. Laws were frequently directed against the theater, particularly against productions identified with England's Catholic past. In 1548, for example, the English church cancelled the Feast of Corpus Christi, and the production of the cycle plays was systematically suppressed. In 1569, the York cycle was performed for the last time, and in 1575, the Mayor of Chester was arrested for allowing cycle plays to be performed. Morality plays may have seemed less sectarian in the kind of instruction they offered; features of morality drama were more readily absorbed by the secular theater.

Yet while the Crown limited and censored the stage, it also maintained its traditional patronage of the theater as well. The famous "Act for the punishment of Vagabonds" of 1572 is a case in point. The law prohibited itinerant players and entertainers from wandering throughout the realm, but its ultimate effect was to establish permanent theatrical companies under the protection of noble patrons. The law ordered that "all Fencers, Bearwards, Common Players in Interludes, and Minstrels, not belonging to any Baron of this Realm, or towards any other honorable Personage of greater Degree . . . [who] wander abroad and have not License of two Justices of the Peace at the least . . . shall be taken adjudged and deemed Rogues Vagabonds and Sturdy Beggars." Unless they belonged to the retinue of a nobleman, players were classed with common vagrants and could be arrested and fined. Protected as servants, a company of players could receive a license to perform in public.

The statute points to the strong bond between the theater and the aristrocracy, and patents granted by Elizabeth entitled noblemen to retain companies of actors as servants. These patents—granted for the Lord Chamberlain's Men (Shakespeare's company), the Lord Admiral's Men (who produced Marlowe's plays), and others—shaped the professional theater of Renaissance London. Elizabeth authorized such companies to perform "Comedies, Tragedies, Interludes, and stage plays" in public, both in London and elsewhere. Yet, in granting these privileges, the Crown made significant qualifications. Elizabeth required the companies to submit their plays to her Master of Revels for approval. She also stipulated that plays "be not published or shown in the time of common prayer, or in the time of great and common plague in our said City of London." Religious and civic officials exerted considerable authority over when and where plays could actually be performed and where theaters could legally be built, and they often closed theaters for months at a time due to plague or civil strife.

The City of London, like many towns, had its own ordinances prohibiting plays within the city limits, and for this reason James Burbage—a member of the Earl of Leicester's company—built The Theatre to the north of the city. Within a decade theaters had been built both to the north of the city and to the south, across the Thames River.

Although they were technically "servants," the major acting companies—the most famous being the Lord Chamberlain's Men, patented in 1593 and then given royal sponsorship as the King's Men when King James I succeeded Elizabeth in 1603—were organized as stockholding, profit-making corporations, that is, as business enterprises in the modern sense. Their economic survival depended on their public performances, for their patron might command and finance only a few productions per year. Several investors, or SHARERS, put up the capital to finance the company and took a percentage of its profits. The sharers were not just investors, they were involved in all aspects of the theater. The sharers of the King's Men, for example, included Shakespeare (playwright and actor), Richard Burbage (James Burbage's son and the company's principal actor, who was the first to

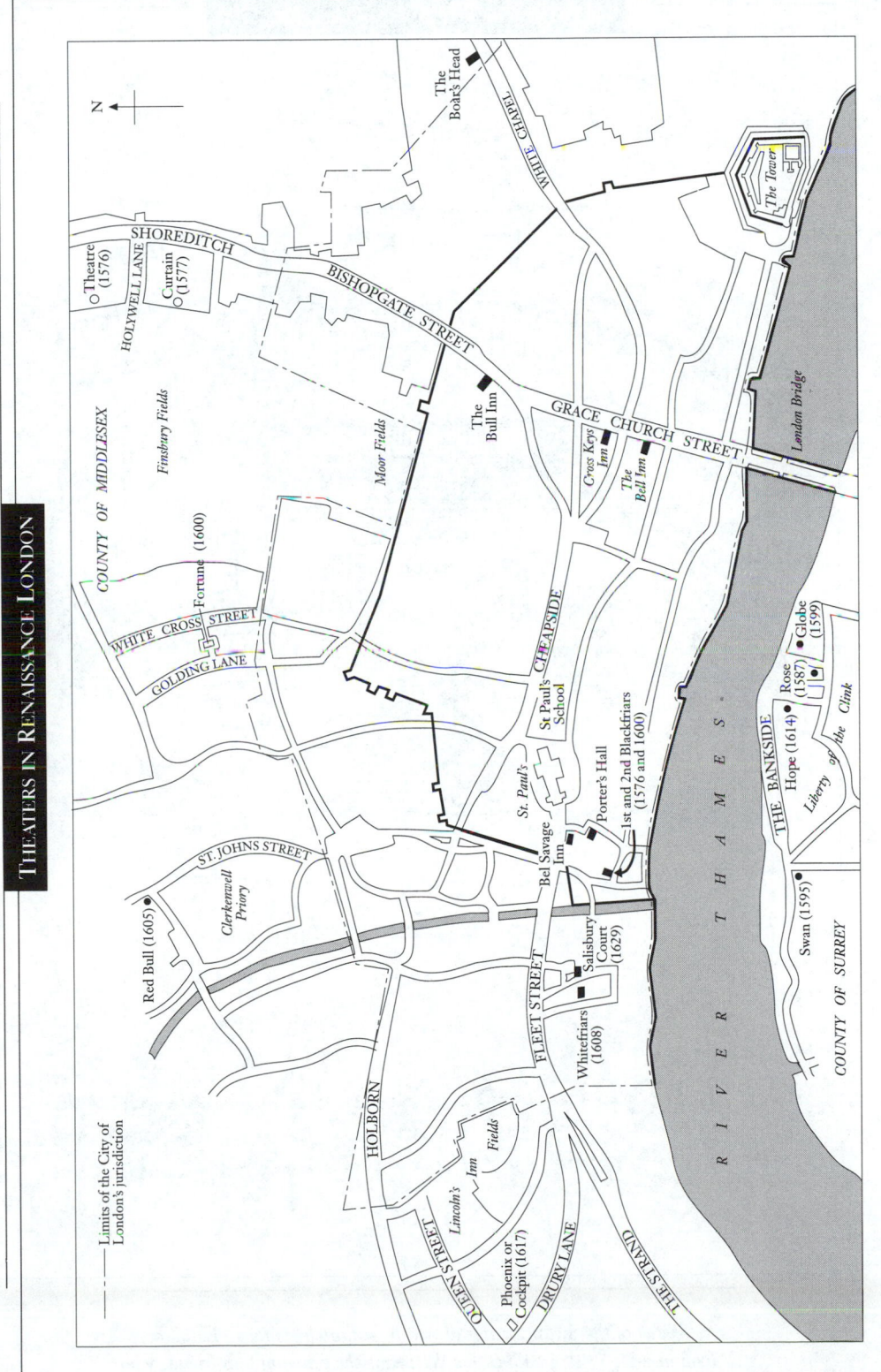

London, around 1630, showing theaters constructed after 1574. The dark line extending from The Tower (lower right) to Blackfriars in the west is the city wall; note that with the exception of the first and second Blackfriars theaters, the theaters are either to the north of the city (the Fortune, the Theatre, the Curtain) or are located across the Thames in Southwark (the Swan, the Hope, the Rose, the Globe).

DRAWING OF THE SWAN THEATER, 1596

*Sketch of the Swan theater drawn by a Dutch visitor to London,
Johannes De Witt, in 1596. De Witt sent the drawing to a friend, who
made this copy. The drawing shows the tiring-house with its two stage
doors, a three-tiered gallery, the platform stage, and the standing pit.*

MODERN RECONSTRUCTION OF THE SWAN THEATER

Reconstruction of the Swan theater based on the De Witt drawing, by C. Walter Hodges.

play Shakespeare's King Lear, Hamlet, and Macbeth), the actors John Heminges and Henry Condell (who later published Shakespeare's plays), and several others. The sharers were responsible for building or leasing a theater, for purchasing plays, for taking on boy actors as apprentices, and for hiring other actors for each production. They also were liable when legal proceedings were brought against the company.

Although several companies flourished during the theater's heyday, life for actors and playwrights was hard. Any company could be forced (by theatrical fashion, plague, or fear of unrest) to leave the relative profit and security of London to take up the dangerous life of an itinerant troupe. Playwrights, who were paid a flat fee by the company for the script of a play, hustled to scrape together a living, and even a famous dramatist like Ben Jonson could die in penury. On the other hand, the theater also provided an opportunity for advancement as well. Several actors, including Richard Burbage and Edward Alleyn, were able to amass considerable fortunes. Shakespeare used the money he received as sharer to invest in property both in London and in his home, Stratford-upon-Avon, where he purchased a large house and land. Such careers were the exception rather than the rule, however, in an era when the theater was widely regarded as illicit and was frequently declared illegal.

THE THEATERS   English companies performed on three kinds of stage—large, open, outdoor buildings called **PUBLIC THEATERS** that held as many as 3,000 people; smaller, indoor, more elite **PRIVATE THEATERS** holding perhaps 700; and private performances at court or at the home of the patron. Public theaters, inspired both by the innyard booths where itinerant companies performed and by the circular arenas used for animal baiting, were outdoor buildings accommodating a large and diverse audience for afternoon performances. Although one theater, the Fortune, was rectangular, most public theaters were eight- to twelve-sided structures. The roughly circular, three-storey gallery surrounded an open pit for standing audiences, into which a stage extended at about the height of five feet. The stage was partly roofed, and two doors used for entrances were set into the rear wall, or **TIRING HOUSE**. On the gallery level above the stage, small rooms were used for aristocratic seating, for music, and for scenes requiring action above the stage—as in the balcony scene in *Romeo and Juliet*, or when Prospero appears "aloft" in *The Tempest*. The stage had a central trapdoor (or **GRAVE TRAP**), and its roofed area held a pulley for raising or lowering actors or properties. The public theaters catered to a paying audience, charging one penny to enter the pit and an additional penny to enter each of the galleries, where seating was provided on benches. Estimates on the size of the theaters vary, but the largest—like the Globe or the Fortune—were about 99 feet in external diameter, with a standing pit about 70 feet across, and a stage 45 feet wide and 27 feet deep; they could hold audiences of 2,000 to 3,000 people. Some theaters were considerably smaller. The Rose theater (whose foundation was discovered in 1988) was a twelve-sided building about 70 feet across, with a pit 50 feet in diameter and a stage roughly 25 by 15 feet. Most of the plays we associate with the Renaissance theater—those of Marlowe, Shakespeare, Jonson, John Webster, John Fletcher, and others—were produced in public theaters like the Globe, the Rose, the Hope, the Swan, or the Fortune.

Although a number of theaters were built in the period, the prestige of the public theaters seems to have declined in the 1620s and 1630s as companies shifted much of their attention to the more lucrative private theaters. These theaters stood within the City of London, on lands called "liberties"—property which had once belonged to monasteries and which had remained outside the city's legal jurisdiction, even though it was within the city limit. Best-known of these theaters is the Blackfriars playhouse (the property originally belonged to the Dominican friars, who wore black gowns). Blackfriars was used intermittently throughout the 1590s by boys' companies, troupes of boy chapel choristers who on occasion formed companies for acting plays. Blackfriars was acquired by the King's Men and used by them for performances after 1608. These theaters were modeled along the lines of a great-house banqueting room: long indoor rooms illuminated by candles, with a low stage at one end, faced by benches for seating and flanked by additional seats along side galleries. The private theaters generally charged upwards of sixpence for basic admission, with additional charges for special seating. Companies performed at private theaters in winter and at public theaters in summer and generally brought the same repertory to both venues. The private theaters did develop the reputation, however, for originating a more satirical and erudite body of drama.

One of the principal obligations of the professional companies was to perform at court or for their patron. Performances at court often took place during holidays and were commanded with increasing frequency by James I and Charles I. The companies performed many of their staple plays at court, but they also performed special entertainments called **MASQUES**, elaborate set pieces that were written in verse, usually on mythological subjects. Masques also involved dancing, fanciful costumes, music, and special scenic machinery and effects; and sometimes included members of the aristocracy or the royal family as performers. The little play that Prospero puts on for Ferdinand and Miranda in Shakespeare's *The Tempest* resembles court masques in many ways, with its cast of goddesses, its formal singing and dancing, and the ceremonial quality of the occasion it celebrates. The masques were unusually expensive — one of King James's masques cost over £4,000. Much of this money was spent on the elaborate changeable scenery that accompanied the masques, the first changeable scenery in the English theater. The masques were largely designed by the architect Inigo Jones, who used staggered **WINGS AND BACKDROP** staging to convey a sense of perspective; his designs became more complex after he visited Italy, where perspective scenery was already in use. This kind of scenery was used originally for court productions, but when the theaters reopened in 1660, the English companies brought this aristocratic inheritance with them: Jones's scenic designs became the basic model for changeable scenery throughout the eighteenth century.

Performing plays in **REPERTORY** over perhaps as many as 200 days a year, the London companies competed with each other for their audiences and generated an enormous demand for new plays. The plays that they bought and performed are among the greatest works of English literature. In the main, English drama in this period comprises plays on English history (such as Shakespeare's *Henry V* and *Richard III*, or Marlowe's *Edward II*); on classical history (Shakespeare's *Julius Caesar* and *Coriolanus*, Ben Jonson's *Sejanus*); of romantic comedies (like Shakespeare's *A Midsummer Night's Dream*); city comedies (Shakespeare's *Measure for Measure*, Jonson's *Volpone*); heroic tragedies (Shakespeare's *Hamlet* and *King Lear*, John Webster's *The Duchess of Malfi*); or plays of intrigue or satire (John Marston's *The Malcontent*, Thomas Middleton's *The Changeling*). Later in the period, audiences seemed to develop a taste for plays they called **TRAGICOMEDIES**, usually romantic plays that begin in the tragic vein but proceed to a happy resolution. Several of John Fletcher's plays are tragicomedies of this kind, and Shakespeare's *Cymbeline* and *The Tempest* resemble tragicomedy as well.

This list of genres suggests both the fertile range of innovation in the Renaissance theater and the drama's dependence on models drawn from the classical and medieval theaters. Roman drama — the comedies of Plautus and Terence, and the tragedies of Seneca — was widely used in schools and universities as part of the teaching of Latin, and university students often staged these plays in Latin. It is not surprising, then, that some features of classical drama made their way into the Renaissance theater. The model of Shakespearean romantic comedy — mistaken identities, separated lovers, an irascible old man or father, a wily servant — derives directly from Plautus' plays; indeed, Shakespeare's *Comedy of Errors* directly adapts Plautus' *Menaechmi*. In a similar fashion, the violence of Seneca's tragedies makes its way directly into the action of Elizabethan drama. Formally and thematically, however, Renaissance drama also differs sharply from its classical ancestors. Renaissance plays tend to be more diffuse, involving a greater variety of characters and multiple plots; in tragedy, the action is often not quite as closely focused on the fortunes of a single hero as it is in classical tragedy. In these and other ways — in the Christian providence that seems to stand behind the action of many plays, in its variety of contemporary characters, in its use of symbolic anachronism, and in the complex relationship between the dramatic world and the world of the audience — Renaissance drama bears the signs of its medieval inheritance.

Playwrights generally wrote in **BLANK VERSE**, an unrhymed **IAMBIC PENTAMETER** line (ten syllables with alternating stress), and occasionally used other verse forms as well. They often used prose, sometimes for emphasis, sometimes to develop the qualities of a particular character. Although modern editors divided the plays into five acts, in most cases Renaissance playwrights probably did not compose their plays in this form. Performance on the public theater stage was rapid and continuous. The theaters used an open stage, few large properties, and had little or no scenery onstage, so that scenes could follow one another without interruption.

DRAMA AND PERFORMANCE

Despite the absence of elaborate stage sets, performance in the Renaissance theater was nonetheless spectacular. Actors used costumes, properties, and language to transform the midafternoon stage into a dramatic locale — Prospero's desert island, Lear's heath, Faustus's study. Some larger properties could be wheeled out from the rear doors, or perhaps raised from the trap: a throne, for instance, or a bed for Desdemona in *Othello*, or the hell-mouth used at the end of *Doctor Faustus*. A cannon fired during a production of Shakespeare's *Henry VIII* in 1613 unfortunately set fire to the Globe and burned it to the ground.

The unlocalized stage of medieval drama can be seen as the forerunner of the Renaissance theater's fluid use of stage space. The open stage made for a kind of cinematic flexibility in performance, as the play could range rapidly from scene to scene, place to place. Costuming was eclectic and anachronistic: the actors wore mainly Elizabethan clothing, adding armor, royal finery, motley, or some "classical" style of gowns when needed. The actors — Burbage, Alleyn, Will Kemp, among many others — were widely praised for their power and effectiveness. Their acting style was oratorical in tragedy and extemporaneous in comedy, but there is no doubt that many were consummate performers, in command of dozens of roles that could be put into play at short notice.

WOMEN IN DRAMA AND PERFORMANCE

Boy actors played a significant part in the experience of English theater, for boy actors played the parts of women and girls onstage, including major roles like Lady Macbeth, Ophelia, and Cleopatra. Much as they did in classical Athens, "women" emerged onstage in Renaissance London only as a side-effect of masculine attitudes and performances. In the English theater, this CROSS-DRESSING came into special prominence, though, because the romantic, sexual, and political intrigue so popular in Renaissance plays was often focused on female characters and therefore on the performance of the boy actors. Indeed, the drama frequently uses cross-dressing as a way of interrogating the power and perquisites of gender, in ways that sometimes confirm and sometimes question the role of gender in English society. English society was an overtly hierarchical one, and despite the power of the "Virgin Queen," women had little access to education, most could not hold property, and they were generally subject to discrimination of many kinds. In this social economy — and in a theater in which Puritan opposition to the stage frequently criticized the theater's "effeminacy" — the absence of women from the stage became a powerful sign of their absence from other scenes of power. Much as sumptuary laws prevented individuals from wearing jewels and clothing above their social station, so, too, was cross-dressing a legal offense in sixteenth-century England, punishable by whipping and a prison sentence. The license of the theater, the freedom to create magical new worlds on the stage, was, like other forms of power in the period, the prerogative of men, and the images that men created for the stage are in important ways imprinted with the signs of a specifically masculine imagination. As with all stage conventions, cross-dressing was deeply implicated in the values of the culture outside the theater, so much so that when women did perform onstage in England — a French company used actresses at Blackfriars in 1629 — they met with hostility, ridicule, and rejection.

The theater had an extraordinary hold on the English imagination. In their many progresses, pageants, and allegorical entertainments, the English monarchs revealed a keen sense of the power of fictive images to represent reality, or a version of it, and so to shape their subjects' understanding of royal power. Playwrights and audiences also found in the theater a magical image of human possibility. Think of Prospero summoning the storm, Ariel, and other spirits with his stagey magic; or of the playwright John Webster's description of "an excellent actor": "All men have been of his occupation, and indeed what he doth feignedly, that do others essentially: this day one plays a Monarch, the next a private

COSTUMES FOR SHAKESPEARE'S *TITUS ANDRONICUS*

This drawing, dating from about 1595, appears to show a scene from Shakespeare's play Titus Andronicus. *Note that two of the actors wear pseudoclassical Roman costumes, while the others are dressed in Elizabethan clothing.*

person. Here one acts a Tyrant, on the morrow an Exile; a Parasite [tricky servant] this man tonight, tomorrow a Precisian [Puritan], and so of divers others." Acting and the theater provided a liberating image of human — or, at least, masculine — power: the power to transform oneself and the world. However, the rich, strange, transforming freedom of the theater could also seem empty and terrifying, even demonic. Rather than an image of human potential, the theater could seem to offer an image of the poverty of human action, the sterile and deceptive emptiness of the world we make and inhabit. As King Lear preaches to blinded Gloucester: "When we are born, we cry that we are come / To this great stage of fools." Puritan critics of the theater insistently reminded audiences that the stage's methods — to seduce with the vain and showy image of a false reality — were also Satan's, and that the theater subversively invited audiences to "unman, unChristian, uncreate themselves." Yet it is precisely this transforming power that lies at the heart of the Renaissance theater's fascination for its audience. For while the theater sometimes seemed to depict a world threatened with constant change and loss, it also presented the power of illusion to recreate the real.

EVERYMAN

Everyman was written late in the fifteenth century and strongly resembles a Flemish play, *Elckerlijc* ("Everyman"), which was printed in 1495. It seems likely that one of the two plays is a translation of the other, but scholars are uncertain about which is the original. Given the play's subtle treatment of the Catholic doctrine of salvation, it has sometimes been argued that *Everyman* was written by a monk or cleric. Yet *Everyman* is hardly a theological treatise; it brims with a vitality that brings the reality of impending death vividly to the stage.

In the play, God orders Death to seek out Everyman and prepare him to die. Like most people, though, Everyman is not ready to meet his end. He first tries to bribe Death and then pleads unsuccessfully for mercy. When Death does not relent, Everyman begins a kind of spiritual journey, confronting several allegorical figures and asking them to accompany him to the grave. Medieval allegory often involved the personification of moral or psychological abstractions, much like the characters that Everyman meets: Fellowship, Kindred, Goods, Good Deeds, Knowledge, and so on. In performance, however, these abstractions become vividly fleshed-out, for the playwright gives these characters traits and behaviors that make them powerfully "real" and recognizable as individuals on the stage rather than as abstract moral emblems. As Everyman proceeds toward death, he is deserted by most of his worldly attributes, but Good Deeds remains faithful to him, especially once he has repented. Although the playwright concludes *Everyman* with a moralizing sermon by the Doctor, we may well feel that the theatrical lesson of the play has at least as much to do with the humanizing of Everyman and his poignant confrontation with our common mortality.

EVERYMAN

Anonymous

EDITED BY A. C. CAWLEY

— CHARACTERS —

GOD	KNOWLEDGE
MESSENGER	CONFESSION
DEATH	BEAUTY
EVERYMAN	STRENGTH
FELLOWSHIP	DISCRETION
KINDRED	FIVE WITS
COUSIN	ANGEL
GOODS	DOCTOR
GOOD DEEDS	

Here beginneth a treatise how the High Father of Heaven sendeth death to summon every creature to come and give account of their lives in this world, and is in manner of a moral play.

MESSENGER: I pray you all give your audience,
  And hear this matter with reverence,
  By figure a moral play:
  The *Summoning of Everyman* called it is,
5 That of our lives and ending shows
  How transitory we be all day.
  This matter is wondrous precious,
  But the intent of it is more gracious,
  And sweet to bear away.
10 The story saith: Man, in the beginning
  Look well, and take good heed to the ending,
  Be you never so gay!
  Ye think sin in the beginning full sweet,
  Which in the end causeth the soul to weep,
15 When the body lieth in clay.
  Here shall you see how Fellowship and Jollity,
  Both Strength, Pleasure, and Beauty,
  Will fade from thee as flower in May;
  For ye shall hear how our Heaven King
20 Calleth Everyman to a general reckoning:
  Give audience, and hear what he doth say.   (*Exit.*)

(GOD *speaketh:*)

GOD: I perceive, here in my majesty,
  How that all creatures be to me unkind,
  Living without dread in worldly prosperity:
25 Of ghostly sight the people be so blind,
  Drowned in sin, they know me not for their God;
  In worldly riches is all their mind,
  They fear not my righteousness, the sharp rod.
  My law that I showed, when I for them died,
30 They forget clean, and shedding of my blood red;
  I hanged between two, it cannot be denied;
  To get them life I suffered to be dead;
  I healed their feet, with thorns hurt was my head.
  I could do no more than I did, truly;
35 And now I see the people do clean forsake me:
  They use the seven deadly sins damnable,

As pride, covetise, wrath, and lechery
  Now in the world be made commendable;
  And thus they leave of angels the heavenly company.
  Every man liveth so after his own pleasure,   40
  And yet of their life they be nothing sure:
  I see the more that I them forbear
  The worse they be from year to year.
  All that liveth appaireth fast;
  Therefore I will, in all the haste,   45
  Have a reckoning of every man's person;
  For, and I leave the people thus alone
  In their life and wicked tempests,
  Verily they will become much worse than beasts;
  For now one would by envy another up eat;   50
  Charity they do all clean forget.
  I hoped well that every man
  In my glory should make his mansion,
  And thereto I had them all elect;
  But now I see, like traitors deject,   55
  They thank me not for the pleasure that I to them meant,
  Nor yet for their being that I them have lent,
  I proffered the people great multitude of mercy,
  And few there be that asketh it heartily.
  They be so cumbered with worldly riches   60
  That needs on them I must do justice,
  On every man living without fear.
  Where art thou, Death, thou mighty messenger?

(*Enter* DEATH)

DEATH: Almighty God, I am here at your will,
  Your commandment to fulfill.   65
GOD: Go thou to Everyman,
  And show him, in my name,
  A pilgrimage he must on him take,
  Which he in no wise may escape;
  And that he bring with him a sure reckoning   70
  Without delay or any tarrying.   (GOD *withdraws*)

---

3 **By figure** in form   6 **all day** always   8 **But . . . gracious** but the purpose of it is more devout   23 **unkind** ungrateful   25 **Of ghostly sight** in spiritual vision   32 **I . . . dead** I consented to die

37 **covetise** covetousness   41 **and . . . sure** and yet their lives are by no means obscure   44 **appaireth** degenerates   47 **and** if   48 **tempests** tumults   55 **deject** abject   59 **heartily** earnestly

DEATH: Lord, I will in the world go run overall,
    And cruelly outsearch both great and small;
    Every man will I beset that liveth beastly
75 Out of God's laws, and dreadeth not folly.
    He that loveth riches I will strike with my dart,
    His sight to blind, and from heaven to depart—
    Except that alms be his good friend—
    In hell for to dwell, world without end.
80 Lo, yonder I see Everyman walking.
    Full little he thinketh on my coming;
    His mind is on fleshly lusts and his treasure,
    And great pain it shall cause him to endure
    Before the Lord, Heaven King.

(Enter EVERYMAN)

85 Everyman, stand still! Whither art thou going
    Thus gaily? Hast thou thy Maker forget?
    EVERYMAN: Why askest thou?
    Wouldest thou wit?
    DEATH: Yea, sir; I will show you:
90 In great haste I am sent to thee
    From God out of his majesty.
    EVERYMAN: What, sent to me?
    DEATH: Yea, certainly.
    Though thou have forget him here,
95 He thinketh on thee in the heavenly sphere,
    As, ere we depart, thou shalt know.
    EVERYMAN: What desireth God of me?
    DEATH: That shall I show thee:
    A reckoning he will needs have
100 Without any longer respite.
    EVERYMAN: To give a reckoning longer leisure I crave;
    This blind matter troubleth my wit.
    DEATH: On thee thou must take a long journey;
    Therefore thy book of count with thee thou bring,
105 For turn again thou cannot by no way.
    And look thou be sure of thy reckoning,
    For before God thou shalt answer, and show
    Thy many bad deeds, and good but a few;
    How thou hast spent thy life, and in what wise,
110 Before the chief Lord of paradise.
    Have ado that we were in that way,
    For, wit thou well, thou shalt make none
        attorney.
    EVERYMAN: Full unready I am such reckoning to give.
    I know thee not. What messenger art thou?
115 DEATH: I am Death, that no man dreadeth,
    For every man I rest, and no man spareth;
    For it is God's commandment
    That all to me should be obedient.
    EVERYMAN: O Death, thou comest when I had thee
        least in mind!
120 In thy power it lieth me to save;
    Yet of my good will I give thee, if thou will be kind:
    Yea, a thousand pound shalt thou have,
    And defer this matter till another day.

DEATH: Everyman, it may not be, by no way.
    I set not by gold, silver, nor riches,   125
    Ne by pope, emperor, king, duke, ne princes;
    For, and I would receive gifts great,
    All the world I might get;
    But my custom is clean contrary.
    I give thee no respite. Come hence, and not tarry.   130
EVERYMAN: Alas, shall I have no longer respite?
    I may say Death giveth no warning!
    To think on thee, it maketh my heart sick,
    For all unready is my book of reckoning.
    But twelve year and I might have abiding,   135
    My counting-book I would make so clear
    That my reckoning I should not need to fear.
    Wherefore, Death, I pray thee, for God's mercy,
    Spare me till I be provided of remedy.
DEATH: Thee availeth not to cry, weep, and pray;   140
    But haste thee lightly that thou were gone that journey,
    And prove thy friends if thou can;
    For, wit thou well, the tide abideth no man,
    And in the world each living creature
    For Adam's sin must die of nature.   145
EVERYMAN: Death, if I should this pilgrimage take,
    And my reckoning surely make,
    Show me, for saint charity,
    Should I not come again shortly?
DEATH: No, Everyman; and thou be once there,   150
    Thou mayst never more come here,
    Trust me verily.
EVERYMAN: O gracious God in the high seat celestial,
    Have mercy on me in this most need!
    Shall I have no company from this vale terrestrial   155
    Of mine acquaintance, that way me to lead?
DEATH: Yea, if any be so hardy
    That would go with thee and bear thee company.
    Hie thee that thou were gone to God's magnificence,
    Thy reckoning to give before his presence.   160
    What, weenest thou thy life is given thee,
    And thy worldly goods also?
EVERYMAN: I had wend so, verily.
DEATH: Nay, nay; it was but lent thee;
    For as soon as thou art go,   165
    Another a while shall have it, and then go therefro,
    Even as thou hast done.
    Everyman, thou art mad! Thou hast thy wits five,
    And here on earth will not amend thy life;
    For suddenly I do come.   170
EVERYMAN: O wretched caitiff, whither shall I flee,
    That I might scape this endless sorrow?
    Now, gentle Death, spare me till to-morrow,
    That I may amend me
    With good advisement.   175
DEATH: Nay, thereto I will not consent,
    Nor no man will I respite;
    But to the heart suddenly I shall smite
    Without any advisement.
    And now out of thy sight I will me hie;   180

72 **overall** everywhere   77 **depart** separate   88 **wit** know   102 **blind**
obscure   104 **count** account   105 **turn again** return   111 **Have . . .**
way i.e., let's see about making that journey   112 **none attorney** no one
[your] advocate   115 **that . . . dreadeth** who fears no man   116 **rest**
arrest   121 **good** goods   123 **And defer** if you defer

125 **set not by** care not for   143 **tide** time   161 **weenest** suppose   163
wend supposed   165 **go** gone   166 **therefro** from it   175 **advisement**
reflection

See thou make thee ready shortly,
For thou mayst say this is the day
That no man living may scape away.   (*Exit* DEATH.)
EVERYMAN: Alas, I may well weep with sighs deep!

185 Now have I no manner of company
To help me in my journey, and me to keep;
And also my writing is full unready.
How shall I do now for to excuse me?
I would to God I had never be get!

190 To my soul a full great profit it had be;
For now I fear pains huge and great.
The time passeth. Lord, help, that all wrought!
For though I mourn it availeth nought.
The day passeth, and is almost ago;

195 I wot not well what for to do.
To whom were I best my complaint to make?
What and I to Fellowship thereof spake,
And showed him of this sudden chance?
For in him is all mine affiance;

200 We have in the world so many a day
Be good friends in sport and play.
I see him yonder, certainly.
I trust that he will bear me company;
Therefore to him will I speak to ease my sorrow.

205 Well met, good Fellowship, and good morrow!

(FELLOWSHIP *speaketh:*)

FELLOWSHIP: Everyman, good morrow, by this day!
Sir, why lookest thou so piteously?
If any thing be amiss, I pray thee me say,
That I may help to remedy.

210 EVERYMAN: Yea, good Fellowship, yea;
I am in great jeopardy.
FELLOWSHIP: My true friend, show to me your mind;
I will not forsake thee to my life's end,
In the way of good company.

215 EVERYMAN: That was well spoken, and lovingly.
FELLOWSHIP: Sir, I must needs know your heaviness;
I have pity to see you in any distress.
If any have you wronged, ye shall revenged be,
Though I on the ground be slain for thee—

220 Though that I know before that I should die.
EVERYMAN: Verily, Fellowship, gramercy.
FELLOWSHIP: Tush! by thy thanks I set not a straw.
Show me your grief, and say no more.
EVERYMAN: If I my heart should to you break,

225 And then you to turn your mind from me,
And would not me comfort when ye hear me speak,
Then should I ten times sorrier be.
FELLOWSHIP: Sir, I say as I will do indeed.
EVERYMAN: Then be you a good friend at need:

230 I have found you true herebefore.
FELLOWSHIP: And so ye shall evermore;
For, in faith, and thou go to hell,
I will not forsake thee by the way.
EVERYMAN: Ye speak like a good friend; I believe you well.

235 I shall deserve it, and I may.

FELLOWSHIP: I speak of no deserving, by this day!
For he that will say, and nothing do,
Is not worthy with good company to go;
Therefore show me the grief of your mind,
As to your friend most loving and kind.   240

EVERYMAN: I shall show you how it is:
Commanded I am to go a journey,
A long way, hard and dangerous,
And give a strait count, without delay,
Before the high Judge, Adonai.   245
Wherefore, I pray you, bear me company,
As ye have promised, in this journey.
FELLOWSHIP: That is matter indeed. Promise is duty;
But, and I should take such a voyage on me,
I know it well, it should be to my pain;   250
Also it maketh me afeard, certain.
But let us take counsel here as well as we can,
For your words would fear a strong man.
EVERYMAN: Why, ye said if I had need
Ye would me never forsake, quick ne dead,   255
Though it were to hell, truly.
FELLOWSHIP: So I said, certainly,
But such pleasures be set aside, the sooth to say;
And also, if we took such a journey,
When should we come again?   260
EVERYMAN: Nay, never again, till the day of doom.
FELLOWSHIP: In faith, then will not I come there!
Who hath you these tidings brought?
EVERYMAN: Indeed, Death was with me here.
FELLOWSHIP: Now, by God that all hath bought,   265
If Death were the messenger,
For no man that is living to-day
I will not go that loath journey—
Not for the father that begat me!
EVERYMAN: Ye promised, otherwise, pardie.   270
FELLOWSHIP: I wot well I said so, truly;
And yet if thou wilt eat, and drink, and make good cheer,
Or haunt to women the lusty company,
I would not forsake you while the day is clear,
Trust me verily.   275
EVERYMAN: Yea, thereto ye would be ready!
To go to mirth, solace, and play,
Your mind will sooner apply,
Than to bear me company in my long journey.
FELLOWSHIP: Now, in good faith, I will not that way.   280
But and thou will murder, or any man kill,
In that I will help thee with a good will.
EVERYMAN: O, that is a simple advice indeed.
Gentle fellow, help me in my necessity!
We have loved long, and now I need;   285
And now, gentle Fellowship, remember me.
FELLOWSHIP: Whether ye have loved me or no,
By Saint John, I will not with thee go.
EVERYMAN: Yet, I pray thee, take the labour, and do so much
for me

---

186 **keep** guard   187 **writing** the writing of Everyman's accounts   189
be get been born   194 **ago** gone   197 **and if**   199 **affiance** trust   206
by this day an asseveration   216 **heaviness** sorrow   224 **break** open
235 **deserve** repay

244 **strait count** strict account   245 **Adonai** a Hebrew name for God
248 **That . . . indeed** that is a good reason indeed [for asking me]   253
fear frighten   265 **bought** redeemed   268 **loath** loathsome   270
pardie by God   273 **Or . . . company** or frequent the pleasant company
of women   274 **while . . . clear** until daybreak   278 **apply** attend

290   To bring me forward, for saint charity,
      And comfort me till I come without the town.
    FELLOWSHIP: Nay, and thou would give me a new gown,
      I will not a foot with thee go;
      But, and thou had tarried, I would not have left thee so.
295   And as now God speed thee in thy journey,
      For from thee I will depart as fast as I may.
    EVERYMAN: Whither away, Fellowship? Will thou forsake me?
    FELLOWSHIP: Yea, by my fay! To God I betake thee.
    EVERYMAN: Farewell, good Fellowship; for thee my heart is
      sore.
300   Adieu for ever! I shall see thee no more.
    FELLOWSHIP: In faith, Everyman, farewell now at the ending;
      For you I will remember that parting is mourning.

(Exit FELLOWSHIP.)

    EVERYMAN: Alack! shall we thus depart indeed—
      Ah, Lady, help!—without any more comfort?
305   Lo, Fellowship forsaketh me in my most need.
      For help in this world whither shall I resort?
      Fellowship herebefore with me would merry make,
      And now little sorrow for me doth he take.
      It is said, 'In prosperity men friends may find,
310   Which in adversity be full unkind.'
      Now whither for succour shall I flee,
      Sith that Fellowship hath forsaken me?
      To my kinsmen I will, truly,
      Praying them to help me in my necessity;
315   I believe that they will do so,
      For kind will creep where it may not go.
      I will go say, for yonder I see them.
      Where be ye now, my friends and kinsmen?

(Enter KINDRED and COUSIN)

    KINDRED: Here be we now at your commandment.
320   Cousin, I pray you show us your intent
      In any wise, and do not spare.
    COUSIN: Yea, Everyman, and to us declare
      If ye be disposed to go anywhither;
      For, wit you well, we will live and die together.
325   KINDRED: In wealth and woe we will with you hold,
      For over his kin a man may be bold.
    EVERYMAN: Gramercy, my friends and kinsmen kind.
      Now shall I show you the grief of my mind:
      I was commanded by a messenger,
330   That is a high king's chief officer;
      He bade me go a pilgrimage, to my pain,
      And I know well I shall never come again;
      Also I must give a reckoning strait,
      For I have a great enemy that hath me in wait,
335   Which intendeth me for to hinder.
    KINDRED: What account is that which ye must render?
      That would I know.

    EVERYMAN: Of all my works I must show
      How I have lived and my days spent;
      Also of ill deeds that I have used   340
      In my time, sith life was me lent;
      And of all virtues that I have refused.
      Therefore, I pray you, go thither with me
      To help to make mine account, for saint charity.
    COUSIN: What, to go thither? Is that the matter?   345
      Nay, Everyman, I had liefer fast bread and water
      All this five year and more.
    EVERYMAN: Alas, that ever I was bore!
      For now shall I never be merry,
      If that you forsake me.   350
    KINDRED: Ah, sir, what ye be a merry man!
      Take good heart to you, and make no moan.
      But one thing I warn you, by Saint Anne—
      As for me, ye shall go alone.
    EVERYMAN: My Cousin, will you not with me go?   355
    COUSIN: No, by our Lady! I have the cramp in my toe.
      Trust not to me, for, so God me speed,
      I will deceive you in your most need.
    KINDRED: It availeth not us to tice.
      Ye shall have my maid with all my heart;   360
      She loveth to go to feasts, there to be nice,
      And to dance, and abroad to start:
      I will give her leave to help you in that journey,
      If that you and she may agree.
    EVERYMAN: Now show me the very effect of your mind: 365
      Will you go with me, or abide behind?
    KINDRED: Abide behind? Yea, that will I, and I may!
      Therefore farewell till another day.   *(Exit KINDRED.)*
    EVERYMAN: How should I be merry or glad?
      For fair promises men to me make,   370
      But when I have most need they me forsake.
      I am deceived; that maketh me sad.
    COUSIN: Cousin Everyman, farewell now,
      For verily I will not go with you.
      Also of mine own an unready reckoning   375
      I have to account; therefore I make tarrying.
      Now God keep thee, for now I go.   *(Exit COUSIN.)*
    EVERYMAN: Ah, Jesus, is all come hereto?
      Lo, fair words maketh fools fain;
      They promise, and nothing will do, certain.   380
      My kinsmen promised me faithfully
      For to abide with me steadfastly,
      And now fast away do they flee:
      Even so Fellowship promised me.
      What friend were best me of to provide?   385
      I lose my time here longer to abide.
      Yet in my mind a thing there is:
      All my life I have loved riches;
      If that my Good now help me might,
      He would make my heart full light.   390
      I will speak to him in this distress—
      Where art thou, my Goods and riches?

---

290 **bring me forward** escort me   298 **fay** faith **betake** commend   303
depart part   312 **Sith** since   316 **For . . . go** For kinship will creep
where it cannot walk, that is, blood is thicker than water   317 **go say**
essay, try   321 **In . . . spare** without fail, and do not hold back   323
anywhither anywhere   325 **hold** side   326 **For . . . bold** for a man
may be sure of his kinsfolk   334 **For . . . wait** a great enemy (the devil)
who has me under observation

340 **used** practised   346 **I . . . water** I had rather fast on bread and
water   348 **bore** born   351 **what . . . man** what a merry man you are
359 **It . . . tice** it is no use trying to entice us   361 **nice** wanton   362
abroad to start go out and about   365 **effect** tenor   385 **me . . . provide** to provide myself with   389 **Good** goods

(GOODS *speaks from a corner*)

GOODS: Who calleth me? Everyman? What! hast thou haste?
    I lie here in corners, trussed and piled so high,
395   And in chests I am locked so fast,
    Also sacked in bags. Thou mayst see with thine eye
    I cannot stir; in packs low I lie.
    What would ye have? Lightly me say.
EVERYMAN: Come hither, Goods, in all the haste thou may,
400   For of counsel I must desire thee.
GOODS: Sir, and ye in the world have sorrow or adversity,
    That can I help you to remedy shortly.
EVERYMAN: It is another disease that grieveth me;
    In this world it is not, I tell thee so.
405   I am sent for, another way to go,
    To give a strait count general
    Before the highest Jupiter of all;
    And all my life I have had joy and pleasure in thee,
    Therefore, I pray thee, go with me;
410   For, peradventure, thou mayst before God Almighty
    My reckoning help to clean and purify;
    For it is said ever among
    That money maketh all right that is wrong.
GOODS: Nay, Everyman, I sing another song.
415   I follow no man in such voyages;
    For, and I went with thee,
    Thou shouldst fare much the worse for me;
    For because on me thou did set thy mind,
    Thy reckoning I have made blotted and blind,
420   That thine account thou cannot make truly;
    And that hast thou for the love of me.
EVERYMAN: That would grieve me full sore,
    When I should come to that fearful answer.
    Up, let us go thither together.
425 GOODS: Nay, not so! I am too brittle, I may not endure;
    I will follow no man one foot, be ye sure.
EVERYMAN: Alas, I have thee loved, and had great pleasure
    All my life-days on good and treasure.
GOODS: That is to thy damnation, without leasing,
430   For my love is contrary to the love everlasting;
    But if thou had me loved moderately during,
    As to the poor to give part of me,
    Then shouldst thou not in this dolour be,
    Nor in this great sorrow and care.
435 EVERYMAN: Lo, now was I deceived ere I was ware,
    And all I may wite misspending of time.
GOODS: What, weenest thou that I am thine?
EVERYMAN: I had wend so.
GOODS: Nay, Everyman, I say no.
440   As for a while I was lent thee;
    A season thou hast had me in prosperity.
    My condition is man's soul to kill;
    If I save one, a thousand I do spill.

Weenest thou that I will follow thee?
    Nay, not from this world, verily.   445
EVERYMAN: I had wend otherwise.
GOODS: Therefore to thy soul Goods is a thief;
    For when thou art dead, this is my guise—
    Another to deceive in this same wise
    As I have done thee, and all to his soul's reprief.   450
EVERYMAN: O false Goods, cursed may thou be,
    Thou traitor to God, that hast deceived me
    And caught me in thy snare!
GOODS: Marry, thou brought thyself in care,
    Whereof I am glad;   455
    I must needs laugh, I cannot be sad.
EVERYMAN: Ah, Goods, thou hast had long my heartly love;
    I gave thee that which should be the Lord's above.
    But wilt thou not go with me indeed?
    I pray thee truth to say.   460
GOODS: No, so God me speed!
    Therefore farewell, and have good day.

(*Exit* GOODS)

EVERYMAN: O, to whom shall I make my moan
    For to go with me in that heavy journey?
    First Fellowship said he would with me gone;   465
    His words were very pleasant and gay,
    But afterward he left me alone.
    Then spake I to my kinsmen, all in despair,
    And also they gave me words fair;
    They lacked no fair speaking,   470
    But all forsook me in the ending.
    Then went I to my Goods, that I loved best,
    In hope to have comfort, but there had I least;
    For my Goods sharply did me tell
    That he bringeth many into hell.   475
    Then of myself I was ashamed,
    And so I am worthy to be blamed;
    Thus may I well myself hate.
    Of whom shall I now counsel take?
    I think that I shall never speed   480
    Till that I go to my Good Deed.
    But, alas, she is so weak
    That she can neither go nor speak;
    Yet will I venture on her now.
    My Good Deeds, where be you?   485

(GOOD DEEDS *speaks from the ground*)

GOOD DEEDS: Here I lie, cold in the ground;
    Thy sins hath me sore bound,
    That I cannot stir.
EVERYMAN: O Good Deeds, I stand in fear!
    I must you pray of counsel,   490
    For help now should come right well.
GOOD DEEDS: Everyman, I have understanding
    That ye be summoned account to make
    Before Messias, of Jerusalem King;
    And you do by me, that journey with you will I take.   495
EVERYMAN: Therefore I come to you, my moan to make;
    I pray you that ye will go with me.

398 **Lightly** quickly   400 **For . . . thee** for I must entreat your advice
403 **disease** trouble   412 **For . . . among** for it is sometimes said   419
blind obscure   429 **without leasing** without a lie, that is, truly   431-2
But . . . me but if you had loved me moderately during your lifetime, so
as to give part of me to the poor   433 **dolour** distress   435 **ware**
aware   436 **And . . . time** and I may blame it all on the bad use I have
made of time   438 **wend** supposed   442 **condition** nature   443 **spill**
ruin

448 **guise** practice   450 **reprief** shame   457 **heartly** heartfelt   483 **go**
walk   484 **venture** gamble   491 **For . . . well** For help would now be
very welcome   495 **And . . . me** if you do as I advise

GOOD DEEDS: I would full fain, but I cannot stand, verily.
EVERYMAN: Why, is there anything on you fall?
500 GOOD DEEDS: Yea, sir, I may thank you of all;
If ye had perfectly cheered me,
Your book of count full ready had be.
Look, the books of your works and deeds eke!
Behold how they lie under the feet,
505 To your soul's heaviness.
EVERYMAN: Our Lord Jesus help me!
For one letter here I cannot see.
GOOD DEEDS: There is a blind reckoning in time of distress.
EVERYMAN: Good Deeds, I pray you help me in this need,
510 Or else I am for ever damned indeed;
Therefore help me to make reckoning
Before the Redeemer of all thing,
That King is, and was, and ever shall.
GOOD DEEDS: Everyman, I am sorry of your fall,
515 And fain would I help you, and I were able.
EVERYMAN: Good Deeds, your counsel I pray you give me.
GOOD DEEDS: That shall I do verily;
Though that on my feet I may not go,
I have a sister that shall with you also,
520 Called Knowledge, which shall with you abide,
To help you to make that dreadful reckoning.

(Enter KNOWLEDGE)

KNOWLEDGE: Everyman, I will go with thee, and be thy
guide,
In thy most need to go by thy side.
EVERYMAN: In good condition I am now in every thing,
525 And am wholly content with this good thing,
Thanked be God my creator.
GOOD DEEDS: And when she hath brought you there
Where thou shalt heal thee of thy smart,
Then go you with your reckoning and your Good Deeds
together,
530 For to make you joyful at heart
Before the blessed Trinity.
EVERYMAN: My Good Deeds, gramercy!
I am well content, certainly,
With your words sweet.
535 KNOWLEDGE: Now go we together lovingly
To Confession, that cleansing river.
EVERYMAN: For joy I weep; I would we were there!
But, I pray you, give me cognition
Where dwelleth that holy man, Confession.
540 KNOWLEDGE: In the house of salvation:
We shall find him in that place,
That shall us comfort, by God's grace.

(KNOWLEDGE takes EVERYMAN to CONFESSION)

Lo, this is Confession. Kneel down and ask mercy,
For he is in good conceit with God Almighty.

EVERYMAN: O glorious fountain, that all uncleanness doth   545
clarify,
Wash from me the spots of vice unclean,
That on me no sin may be seen.
I come with Knowledge for my redemption,
Redempt with heart and full contrition;
For I am commanded a pilgrimage to take,   550
And great accounts before God to make.
Now I pray you, Shrift, mother of salvation,
Help my Good Deeds for my piteous exclamation.
CONFESSION: I know your sorrow well, Everyman.
Because with Knowledge ye come to me,   555
I will you comfort as well as I can,
And a precious jewel I will give thee,
Called penance, voider of adversity;
Therewith shall your body chastised be,
With abstinence and perseverance in God's service.   560
Here shall you receive that scourge of me,
Which is penance strong that ye must endure,
To remember thy Saviour was scourged for thee
With sharp scourges, and suffered it patiently;
So must thou, ere thou scape that painful pilgrimage.   565
Knowledge, keep him in this voyage,
And by that time Good Deeds will be with thee.
But in any wise be siker of mercy,
For your time draweth fast; and ye will saved be,
Ask God mercy, and he will grant truly.   570
When with the scourge of penance man doth him bind,
The oil of forgiveness then shall he find.
EVERYMAN: Thanked be God for his gracious work!
For now I will my penance begin;
This hath rejoiced and lighted my heart,   575
Though the knots be painful and hard within.
KNOWLEDGE: Everyman, look your penance that ye fulfil,
What pain that ever it to you be;
And Knowledge shall give you counsel at will
How your account ye shall make clearly.   580
EVERYMAN: O eternal God, O heavenly figure,
O way of righteousness, O goodly vision,
Which descended down in a virgin pure
Because he would every man redeem,
Which Adam forfeited by his disobedience: 585
O blessed Godhead, elect and high divine,
Forgive my grievous offence;
Here I cry thee mercy in this presence.
O ghostly treasure, O ransomer and redeemer,
Of all the world hope and conductor,   590
Mirror of joy, and founder of mercy,
Which enlumineth heaven and earth thereby,
Hear my clamorous complaint, though it late be;
Receive my prayers, of thy benignity;
Though I be a sinner most abominable,   595

---

499 **fall** befallen   500 **of** for   501 **If . . . me** If you had encouraged me fully   503 **eke** also   508 **There . . . distress** a sinful person in this hour of need finds that the account of his good deeds is dimly written and difficult to read   520 **Knowledge** the meaning of Knowledge here is acknowledgment or recognition of sins   528 **smart** pain   538 **cognition** knowledge   540 **In . . . salvation** in the church   544 **conceit** esteem

549 **Redempt . . . contrition** redeemed by heartfelt and full contrition   552 **Shrift** confession   553 **for . . . exclamation** in answer to my piteous cry   558 **voider** expeller   568 **siker** sure   569 **draweth fast** draws quickly to an end **and** if   571 **him** himself   575 **lighted** lightened   576 **Though . . . within** though the knots [of the scourge] be painful and hard to my body   586 **divine** divinity   588 **in this presence** in the presence of this company   592 **thereby** besides

Yet let my name be written in Moses' table.
O Mary, pray to the Maker of all thing,
Me for to help at my ending;
And save me from the power of my enemy,
600 For Death assaileth me strongly.
And, Lady, that I may by mean of thy prayer
Of your Son's glory to be partner,
By the means of his passion, I it crave;
I beseech you help my soul to save.
605 Knowledge, give me the scourge of penance;
My flesh therewith shall give acquittance:
I will now begin, if God give me grace.
KNOWLEDGE: Everyman, God give you time and space!
Thus I bequeath you in the hands of our Saviour;
610 Now may you make your reckoning sure.
EVERYMAN: In the name of the Holy Trinity,
My body sore punished shall be:
Take this, body, for the sin of the flesh!

(Scourges himself.)

Also thou delightest to go gay and fresh,
615 And in the way of damnation thou did me bring,
Therefore suffer now strokes and punishing.
Now of penance I will wade the water clear,
To save me from purgatory, that sharp fire.

(GOOD DEEDS rises from the ground)

GOOD DEEDS: I thank God, now I can walk and go,
620 And am delivered of my sickness and woe.
Therefore with Everyman I will go, and not spare;
His good works I will help him to declare.
KNOWLEDGE: Now, Everyman, be merry and glad!
Your Good Deeds cometh now; ye may not be sad.
625 Now is your Good Deeds whole and sound,
Going upright upon the ground.
EVERYMAN: My heart is light, and shall be evermore;
Now will I smite faster than I did before.
GOOD DEEDS: Everyman, pilgrim, my special friend,
630 Blessed be thou without end;
For thee is preparate the eternal glory.
Ye have me made whole and sound,
Therefore I will bide by thee in every stound.
EVERYMAN: Welcome, my Good Deeds; now I hear thy voice,
635 I weep for very sweetness of love.
KNOWLEDGE: Be no more sad, but ever rejoice;
God seeth thy living in his throne above.
Put on this garment to thy behoof,
Which is wet with your tears,
640 Or else before God you may it miss,
When ye to your journey's end come shall.
EVERYMAN: Gentle Knowledge, what do ye it call?

KNOWLEDGE: It is a garment of sorrow:
From pain it will you borrow;
Contrition it is,   645
That geteth forgiveness;
It pleaseth God passing well.
GOOD DEEDS: Everyman, will you wear it for your heal?
EVERYMAN: Now blessed be Jesu, Mary's Son,
For now have I on true contrition.   650
And let us go now without tarrying;
Good Deeds, have we clear our reckoning?
GOOD DEEDS: Yea, indeed, I have it here.
EVERYMAN: Then I trust we need not fear;
Now, friends, let us not part in twain.   655
KNOWLEDGE: Nay, Everyman, that will we not, certain.
GOOD DEEDS: Yet must thou lead with thee
Three persons of great might.
EVERYMAN: Who should they be?
GOOD DEEDS: Discretion and Strength they hight,   660
And thy Beauty may not abide behind.
KNOWLEDGE: Also ye must call to mind
Your Five Wits as for your counsellors.
GOOD DEEDS: You must have them ready at all hours.
EVERYMAN: How shall I get them hither?   665
KNOWLEDGE: You must call them all together,
And they will hear you incontinent.
EVERYMAN: My friends, come hither and be present,
Discretion, Strength, my Five Wits, and Beauty.

(Enter BEAUTY, STRENGTH, DISCRETION, and FIVE WITS)

BEAUTY: Here at your will we be all ready.   670
What will ye that we should do?
GOOD DEEDS: That ye would with Everyman go,
And help him in his pilgrimage.
Advise you, will ye with him or not in that voyage?
STRENGTH: We will bring him all thither,   675
To his help and comfort, ye may believe me.
DISCRETION: So will we go with him all together.
EVERYMAN: Almighty God, lofed may thou be!
I give thee laud that I have hither brought
Strength, Discretion, Beauty, and Five Wits. Lack   680
    I nought.
And my Good Deeds, with Knowledge clear,
All be in my company at my will here;
I desire no more to my business.
STRENGTH: And I, Strength, will by you stand in distress,
Though thou would be in battle fight on the ground.   685
FIVE WITS: And though it were through the world round,
We will not depart for sweet ne sour.
BEAUTY: No more will I unto death's hour
Whatsoever thereof befall.
DISCRETION: Everyman, advise you first of all;   690
Go with a good advisement and deliberation.
We all give you virtuous monition
That all shall be well.

596 **Yet . . . table** medieval theologians regarded the two tables given on Sinai as symbols of baptism and penance, respectively. Thus Everyman is asking to be numbered among those who have escaped damnation by doing penance for their sins.   599 **my enemy** the devil   601–603 **And . . . crave** and, Lady, I beg that through the mediation of thy prayer I may share in your Son's glory, in consequence of His passion   606 **acquittance** satisfaction (as a part of the sacrament of penance)   608 **space** opportunity   631 **preparate** prepared   633 **stound** trial   638 **behoof** advantage

644 **borrow** release   647 **passing** exceedingly   648 **heal** salvation   660 **hight** are called   663 **wits** senses   667 **incontinent** immediately   674 **Advise** consider   678 **lofed** praised   683 **to** for   687 **for . . . sour** that is, in happiness or adversity   688 **unto** until   691 **advisement** reflection   692 **monition** forewarning

EVERYMAN: My friends, harken what I will tell:
695 I pray God reward you in his heavenly sphere.
Now harken, all that be here,
For I will make my testament
Here before you all present:
In alms half my good I will give with my hands twain
700 In the way of charity, with good intent,
And the other half still shall remain
In queth, to be returned there it ought to be.
This I do in despite of the fiend of hell,
To go quit out of his peril
705 Ever after and this day.
KNOWLEDGE: Everyman, harken what I say:
Go to priesthood, I you advise,
And receive of him in any wise
The holy sacrament and ointment together.
710 Then shortly see ye turn again hither;
We will all abide you here.
FIVE WITS: Yea, Everyman, hie you that ye ready were.
There is no emperor, king, duke, ne baron,
That of God hath commission
715 As hath the least priest in the world being;
For of the blessed sacraments pure and benign
He beareth the keys, and thereof hath the cure
For man's redemption — it is ever sure —
Which God for our soul's medicine
720 Gave us out of his heart with great pine.
Here in this transitory life, for thee and me,
The blessed sacraments seven there be:
Baptism, confirmation, with priesthood good,
And the sacrament of God's precious flesh and blood,
725 Marriage, the holy extreme unction, and penance;
These seven be good to have in remembrance,
Gracious sacraments of high divinity.
EVERYMAN: Fain would I receive that holy body,
And meekly to my ghostly father I will go.
730 FIVE WITS: Everyman, that is the best that ye can do.
God will you to salvation bring,
For priesthood exceedeth all other thing:
To us Holy Scripture they do teach,
And converteth man from sin heaven to reach;
735 God hath to them more power given
Than to any angel that is in heaven.
With five words he may consecrate,
God's body in flesh and blood to make,
And handleth his Maker between his hands.
740 The priest bindeth and unbindeth all bands,
Both in earth and in heaven.
Thou ministers all the sacraments seven;
Though we kissed thy feet, thou were worthy;
Thou art surgeon that cureth sin deadly:
745 No remedy we find under God

But all only priesthood.
Everyman, God gave priests that dignity,
And setteth them in his stead among us to be;
Thus be they above angels in degree.

(EVERYMAN *goes to the priest to receive the last sacraments*)

KNOWLEDGE: If priests be good, it is so, surely.   750
But when Jesus hanged on the cross with great smart,
There he gave out of his blessed heart
The same sacrament in great torment:
He sold them not to us, that Lord omnipotent.
Therefore Saint Peter the apostle doth say   755
That Jesu's curse hath all they
Which God their Saviour do buy or sell,
Or they for any money do take or tell.
Sinful priests giveth the sinners example bad;
Their children sitteth by other men's fires, I have heard;   760
And some haunteth women's company
With unclean life, as lusts of lechery:
These be with sin made blind.
FIVE WITS: I trust to God no such may we find;
Therefore let us priesthood honour,   765
And follow their doctrine for our souls' succour.
We be their sheep, and they shepherds be
By whom we all be kept in surety.
Peace, for yonder I see Everyman come,
Which hath made true satisfaction.   770
GOOD DEEDS: Methink it is he indeed.

(*Re-enter* EVERYMAN)

EVERYMAN: Now Jesu be your alder speed!
I have received the sacrament for my redemption,
And then mine extreme unction:
Blessed be all they that counselled me to take it!   775
And now, friends, let us go without longer respite;
I thank God that ye have tarried so long.
Now set each of you on this rood your hand,
And shortly follow me:
I go before there I would be; God be our guide!   780
STRENGTH: Everyman, we will not from you go
Till ye have done this voyage long.
DISCRETION: I, Discretion, will bide by you also.
KNOWLEDGE: And though this pilgrimage be never so strong,
I will never part you fro.   785
STRENGTH: Everyman, I will be as sure by thee
As ever I did by Judas Maccabee.

(EVERYMAN *comes to his grave*)

EVERYMAN: Alas, I am so faint I may not stand;
My limbs under me doth fold.
Friends, let us not turn again to this land,   790
Not for all the world's gold;

701–702 **And . . . be** the meaning seems to be that Everyman's immovable property (his body) will lie at rest in the earth   704–705 **To . . . day** to go free out of his power today and ever after   708 **in any wise** without fail   712 **hie . . . were** hurry and prepare yourself   714 **commission** authority   715 **being** living   720 **pine** suffering   728 **that holy body** the sacrament   729 **ghostly** spiritual   737 **five words** *Hoc est enim corpus meum* ("This is my body")   742 **ministers** administer

746 **But . . . priesthood** except only from the priesthood   750 **it is so** that they are above the angels   755–757 **Therefore . . . sell** the reference here is to the sin of simony (Acts viii.18 ff.)   760 **Their . . . fires** their children are illegitimate   772 **be . . . speed** be the helper of you all   778 **rood** cross   784 **strong** grievous   785 **you fro** from you   786–787 **Everyman . . . Maccabee** I will stand by you as steadfastly as ever I did by Judas Maccabaeus (I Macc. iii)

For into this cave must I creep
And turn to earth, and there to sleep.
BEAUTY: What, into this grave? Alas!
795 EVERYMAN: Yea, there shall ye consume, more and less.
BEAUTY: And what, should I smother here?
EVERYMAN: Yea, by my faith, and never more appear.
In this world live no more we shall,
But in heaven before the highest Lord of all.
800 BEAUTY: I cross out all this; adieu, by Saint John!
I take my cap in my lap, and am gone.
EVERYMAN: What, Beauty, whither will ye?
BEAUTY: Peace, I am deaf; I look not behind me,
Not and thou wouldest give me all the gold in thy chest.

(*Exit* BEAUTY.)

805 EVERYMAN: Alas, whereto may I trust?
Beauty goeth fast away from me;
She promised with me to live and die.
STRENGTH: Everyman, I will thee also forsake and deny;
Thy game liketh me not at all.
810 EVERYMAN: Why, then, ye will forsake me all?
Sweet Strength, tarry a little space.
STRENGTH: Nay, sir, by the rood of grace!
I will hie me from thee fast,
Though thou weep till thy heart to-brast.
815 EVERYMAN: Ye would ever bide by me, ye said.
STRENGTH: Yea, I have you far enough conveyed.
Ye be old enough, I understand,
Your pilgrimage to take on hand;
I repent me that I hither came.
820 EVERYMAN: Strength, you to displease I am to blame;
Yet promise is debt, this ye well wot.
STRENGTH: In faith, I care not.
Thou art but a fool to complain;
You spend your speech and waste your brain.
825 Go thrust thee into the ground!

(*Exit* STRENGTH.)

EVERYMAN: I had wend surer I should you have found.
He that trusteth in his Strength
She him deceiveth at the length.
Both Strength and Beauty forsaketh me;
830 Yet they promised me fair and lovingly.
DISCRETION: Everyman, I will after Strength be gone;
As for me, I will leave you alone.
EVERYMAN: Why, Discretion, will you forsake me?
DISCRETION: Yea, in faith, I will go from thee,
835 For when Strength goeth before
I follow after evermore.
EVERYMAN: Yet, I pray thee, for the love of the Trinity,
Look in my grave once piteously.
DISCRETION: Nay, so nigh will I not come;
840 Farewell, every one!

(*Exit* DISCRETION.)

EVERYMAN: O, all thing faileth, save God alone—
Beauty, Strength, and Discretion;
For when Death bloweth his blast,
They all run from me full fast.
FIVE WITS: Everyman, my leave now of thee I take;   845
I will follow the other, for here I thee forsake.
EVERYMAN: Alas, then may I wail and weep,
For I took you for my best friend.
FIVE WITS: I will no longer thee keep;
Now farewell, and there an end.   850

(*Exit* FIVE WITS.)

EVERYMAN: O Jesu, help! All hath forsaken me.
GOOD DEEDS: Nay, Everyman; I will bide with thee.
I will not forsake thee indeed;
Thou shalt find me a good friend at need.
EVERYMAN: Gramercy, Good Deeds! Now may I true friends   855
see.
They have forsaken me, every one;
I loved them better than my Good Deeds alone.
Knowledge, will ye forsake me also?
KNOWLEDGE: Yea, Everyman, when ye to Death shall go;
But not yet, for no manner of danger.   860
EVERYMAN: Gramercy, Knowledge, with all my heart.
KNOWLEDGE: Nay, yet I will not from hence depart
Till I see where ye shall become.
EVERYMAN: Methink, alas, that I must be gone
To make my reckoning and my debts pay,   865
For I see my time is nigh spent away.
Take example, all ye that this do hear or see,
How they that I loved best do forsake me,
Except my Good Deeds that bideth truly.
GOOD DEEDS: All earthly things is but vanity: 870
Beauty, Strength, and Discretion do man forsake,
Foolish friends, and kinsmen, that fair spake—
All fleeth save Good Deeds, and that am I.
EVERYMAN: Have mercy on me, God most mighty;
And stand by me, thou mother and maid, holy Mary.   875
GOOD DEEDS: Fear not; I will speak for thee.
EVERYMAN: Here I cry God mercy.
GOOD DEEDS: Short our end, and minish our pain;
Let us go and never come again.
EVERYMAN: Into thy hands, Lord, my soul I commend;   880
Receive it, Lord, that it be not lost,
As thou me boughtest, so me defend,
And save me from the fiend's boast,
That I may appear with that blessed host
That shall be saved at the day of doom.   885
In manus tuas, of mights most
For ever, *commendo spiritum meum.*

(*He sinks into his grave.*)

KNOWLEDGE: Now hath he suffered that we all shall endure;
The Good Deeds shall make all sure.
Now hath he made ending;   890
Methinketh that I hear angels sing,

---

795 **consume . . . less** decay, all of you   800 **I . . . this** I cancel all this, that is, my promise to stay with you   801 **I . . . lap** I doff my cap (so low that it comes) into my lap   809 **liketh** pleases   811 **space** while   814 **to-brast** break   820 **you . . . blame** I am to blame for displeasing you

863 **where . . . become** what shall become of you   878 **Short . . . pain** shorten our end, and diminish our pain   886–887 **In . . . meum** Into thy hands, most mighty One for ever, I commend my spirit

And make great joy and melody
Where Everyman's soul received shall be.
ANGEL: Come, excellent elect spouse, to Jesu!
895   Hereabove thou shalt go
Because of thy singular virtue.
Now the soul is taken the body fro,
Thy reckoning is crystal-clear.
Now shalt thou into the heavenly sphere,
900   Unto the which all ye shall come
That liveth well before the day of doom.

(Enter DOCTOR)

DOCTOR: This moral men may have in mind.
Ye hearers, take it of worth, old and young,
And forsake Pride, for he deceiveth you in the end;
905   And remember Beauty, Five Wits, Strength, and
Discretion,

They all at the last do every man forsake,
Save his Good Deeds there doth he take.
But beware, for and they be small
Before God, he hath no help at all;
None excuse may be there for every man.   910
Alas, how shall he do then?
For after death amends may no man make,
For then mercy and pity doth him forsake.
If his reckoning be not clear when he doth come,
God will say: 'Ite, maledicti, in ignem eternum.'   915
And he that hath his account whole and sound,
High in heaven he shall be crowned;
Unto which place God bring us all thither,
That we may live body and soul together.
Thereto help the Trinity!   920
Amen, say ye, for saint charity.

894 **spouse** bride of Jesus [a common medieval metaphor to express the idea of the soul's union with God]   903 **take . . . worth** value it

907 **Save** unless   915 **Ite . . . eternum** depart, ye cursed, into everlasting fire (Matt. xxv. 41)

✦ THUS ENDETH THIS MORAL PLAY OF EVERYMAN ✦

CHRISTOPHER MARLOWE

Born in the same year as Shakespeare, Christopher Marlowe (1564–1593) pursued a very different kind of life than his famous contemporary. Unlike Shakespeare, Marlowe had a university education; schooled at the King's School in Canterbury, Marlowe then attended Corpus Christi college, Cambridge. Marlowe left Cambridge in 1587, and his first play — *Tamburlaine*, in two full-length parts — was produced later that year. He wrote several important plays in the course of the next six years: *Doctor Faustus* (c. 1589), *The Jew of Malta* (c. 1590), *Edward II* (c. 1591). Marlowe also wrote *Dido, Queen of Carthage*, possibly while still at Cambridge, and a play about the St. Bartholomew massacre of Huguenots in Paris, *The Massacre at Paris* (1593). Marlowe was an accomplished poet and wrote the narrative poem *Hero and Leander* (published in 1598), among many others. He was known at court and to influential advisers to Queen Elizabeth, such as Sir Walter Raleigh and Sir Francis Walsingham. It is not surprising that Marlowe's life has been much-romanticized, especially given his reputation for iconoclasm, his association with occultists, and his service as one of Elizabeth's spies in Europe. Marlowe was arrested on several occasions for fighting and died from injuries he received in a tavern fight in 1593. He was 28 years old.

Despite the brevity of his career, Marlowe is deservedly ranked among the greatest of English playwrights. The rhetorical flourish of what Ben Jonson called his "mighty line" and the brilliance of his language are unsurpassed in their majesty and power. His plays were popular in part no doubt because they starred Edward Alleyn, the major actor of the 1580s and early 1590s. Alleyn was the son-in-law of Philip Henslowe, a theatrical entrepreneur who built several theaters in London; their efforts, and Marlowe's plays, made them rich men. Indeed, Marlowe's plays remain alive today through the depth and force of their principal roles. In Faustus and Tamburlaine, Marlowe created roles of a rich and involved subjectivity, characters of the psychological complexity that would become one of the hallmarks of English drama.

Doctor Faustus

Marlowe based his play on a popular German narrative, the *History of Doctor Johann Faust*, published in 1587. Audiences might also have seen in Faustus some resemblance to John Dee, Queen Elizabeth's royal astrologer. *Doctor Faustus* was celebrated in its day and would certainly have made a spectacular impression on audiences in the public theater. We know from Henslowe's accounts that his theater had a "hell mouth for Doctor Faustus" — some kind of grotesque opening from which the devils could leap to snare Faustus and haul him off to damnation. The devils themselves were covered with flames, fireworks, and firecrackers; tradition has it that Alleyn — clearly a real showman — wore a cross prominently displayed around his neck, as a way of "defending" himself should real devils be summoned by his performance of Faustus.

The magic of the play, however, arises from the attraction exerted by Faustus himself. Like many of Marlowe's heroes, Faustus is an "overreacher," a man who magnificently and self-destructively tries to go beyond his own limitations, perhaps even beyond the limits of human nature itself. We can see this magnificent energy at the play's opening, when Faustus turns away from Aristotle and philosophy, from medicine, from the law, and from theology to the seductive arts of magic, striking the bargain with the devil that gives him the power to gratify his insatiable curiosity in exchange for his mortal soul.

Modern readers are sometimes confused by *Doctor Faustus*'s morality-play elements, the pageant of the Seven Deadly Sins, and the Good and Evil angels who frame Faustus's temptation. Marlowe brings a medieval vision of the tragic "fall of those who stood in high degree" into collision with the more psychologically oriented vision of tragedy that is characteristic of the modern secular world. Certainly the Good and Evil angels point to what is right and wrong about Faustus's temptation. What is fascinating about the play is the way that Faustus's desire to be ravished by new experiences not only overcomes *his* scruples, but *ours* in the audience as well. Marlowe's play relies on the fact that despite the angels' warnings, we will want to see where Faustus's overreaching will take him.

Faustus — like Prospero in Shakespeare's *The Tempest* — could be taken as a figure for the Renaissance sense of human potential, here realized in its negative or self-destructive dimension. Faustus also seems to provide a figure for the morality of the theater itself, for the power that Faustus exercises in the play increasingly seems to be illusory, merely theatrical. The spectacles that Faustus conjures are finally *only* shows—Mephostophilis and Helen are just devils in disguise—and the power he wields has increasingly trivial results: tricking the Pope degenerates into hoodwinking the horse-courser and setting antlers on Benvolio's head. Faustus is damned for bargaining away his soul, but what finally seems to turn the play toward tragedy is what he sells his soul for: not for the world, but for the illusion of a world, a kind of endless and impoverished theater. We might well recall that the illusions that damn Faustus are, in many ways, the same illusions we have come to the theater to see. The theater makes Faustus's temptation real to its audience by tempting it with many of the same arts.

DOCTOR FAUSTUS

Christopher Marlowe

EDITED BY SYLVAN BARNET

— CHARACTERS —

CHORUS
DOCTOR FAUSTUS
WAGNER, *his student and servant*
GOOD ANGEL
BAD ANGEL
VALDES ⎤
CORNELIUS ⎦ *magicians*
THREE SCHOLARS
LUCIFER, *prince of devils*
MEPHOSTOPHILIS, *a devil*
ROBIN, *a clown*
BELZEBUB, *a devil*
PRIDE ⎤
COVETOUSNESS │
ENVY │
WRATH ⎬ *the Seven Deadly Sins*
GLUTTONY │
SLOTH │
LECHERY ⎦
DICK, *a clown*
POPE ADRIAN

RAYMOND, *King of Hungary*
BRUNO, *rival Pope appointed by the Emperor*
TWO CARDINALS
ARCHBISHOP OF RHEIMS
FRIARS
VINTNER
MARTINO ⎤
gentlemen at the Emperor's court FREDERICK
BENVOLIO ⎦
THE GERMAN EMPEROR, CHARLES THE FIFTH
DUKE OF SAXONY
TWO SOLDIERS
HORSE-COURSER, *a clown*
CARTER, *a clown*
HOSTESS OF A TAVERN
DUKE OF VANHOLT
DUCHESS OF VANHOLT
SERVANT
OLD MAN
DARIUS OF PERSIA, ALEXANDER THE GREAT, ALEXANDER'S PARAMOUR,
HELEN OF TROY, DEVILS, PIPER, CARDINALS, MONKS, FRIARS,
ATTENDANTS, SOLDIERS, SERVANTS, TWO CUPIDS

— PROLOGUE —

(*Enter* CHORUS.)

Not marching in the fields of Trasimene
Where Mars did mate the warlike Carthagens,
Nor sporting in the dalliance of love
In courts of kings where state is overturned,
5   Nor in the pomp of proud audacious deeds
Intends our muse to vaunt his heavenly verse.
Only this, gentles—We must now perform
The form of Faustus' fortunes, good or bad:
And now to patient judgments we appeal
10   And speak for Faustus in his infancy.
Now is he born of parents base of stock
In Germany within a town called Rhode;
At riper years to Wittenberg he went
Whereas his kinsmen chiefly brought him up.
15   So much he profits in divinity
That shortly he was graced with doctor's name,
Excelling all, and sweetly can dispute
In th' heavenly matters of theology;
Till swoll'n with cunning, of a self-conceit,

His waxen wings did mount above his reach   20
And melting, heavens conspired his overthrow!
For falling to a devilish exercise
And glutted now with learning's golden gifts
He surfeits upon cursèd necromancy:
Nothing so sweet as magic is to him   25
Which he prefers before his chiefest bliss—
And this the man that in his study sits.

(*Exit.*)

— ACT ONE —

SCENE I

FAUSTUS *in his study.*

FAUSTUS: Settle thy studies Faustus, and begin
   To sound the depth of that thou wilt profess.
   Having commenced, be a divine in show—

Yet level at the end of every art
5   And live and die in Aristotle's works.
Sweet *Analytics*, 'tis thou hast ravished me.
Bene disserere est finis logices.
Is to dispute well logic's chiefest end?
Affords this art no greater miracle?
10   Then read no more, thou has attained that end.
A greater subject fitteth Faustus' wit:
Bid *on kai me on* farewell, and Galen come:
Be a physician Faustus, heap up gold,
And be eternized for some wondrous cure.
15   *Summum bonum medicinae sanitas,*
The end of physic is our body's health.
Why Faustus hast thou not attained that end?
Are not thy bills hung up as monuments
Whereby whole cities have escaped the plague
20   And thousand desperate maladies been cured?
Yet art thou still but Faustus and a man.
Could'st thou make men to live eternally
Or being dead raise them to life again,
Then this profession were to be esteemed.
25   Physic farewell! Where is Justinian?
Si una eademque res legatur duobus, alter rem, alter
    valorem rei, et cetera.
A petty case of paltry legacies.
Exhereditare filium non potest pater, nisi—
30   Such is the subject of the *Institute*
And universal body of the law!
This study fits a mercenary drudge
Who aims at nothing but external trash,
Too servile and illiberal for me.
35   When all is done, divinity is best.
Jerome's Bible, Faustus, view it well.
Stipendium peccati mors est. Ha! *Stipendium et cetera.* The
reward of sin is death? That's hard: *Si peccasse negamus, falli-*
mur, et nulla est in nobis veritas. If we say that we have no sin,
40   we deceive ourselves, and there is no truth in us. Why, then
belike, we must sin, and so consequently die.
Ay, we must die an everlasting death.
What doctrine call you this? *Che serà, serà:*
What will be, shall be! Divinity, adieu!

---

4 **level** aim   6 **Analytics** title of two treatises by Aristotle on logic   7
Bene . . . logices the end (i.e., purpose) of logic is to argue well
(Latin)   11 **wit** intelligence   12 **on kai me on** being and not being
(Greek)   12 **Galen** Greek authority on medicine, 2nd century A.D.
15 **Summum . . . sanitas** health is the greatest good of medicine (Latin,
translated from Aristotle's *Nichomachean Ethics*)   16 **physic**
medicine   18 **bills** prescriptions   25 **Justinian** Roman emperor and
authority on law (483–565) who ordered the compilation of the *Insti-*
tutes   26–27 **Si . . . et cetera** if one thing is willed to two persons, one
of them shall have the thing itself, the other the value of the thing, and
so forth (Latin)   29 **Exhereditare . . . nisi** a father cannot disinherit his
son unless (Latin)   36 **Jerome's Bible** the Latin translation made by St.
Jerome (c.340–420)   37 **Stipendium . . . est** the wages of sin is death
(Romans 6:23; if Faustus had gone on to read the rest of the verse, he
would have found that "the gift of God is eternal life through Jesus
Christ our Lord")   38–39 **Si . . . veritas** from I John 1:8, translated in
the next two lines; Faustus neglects the following verse: "If we confess
our sins, He is faithful and just to forgive us our sins, and to cleanse us
from all unrighteousness"   43 **Che serà, serà** (Italian, translated in the
first half of the next line)

These metaphysics of magicians   45
And negromantic books are heavenly;
Lines, circles, letters, characters—
Ay, these are those that Faustus most desires.
O, what a world of profit and delight,
Of power, of honor, and omnipotence   50
Is promised to the studious artisan!
All things that move between the quiet poles
Shall be at my command: emperors and kings
Are but obeyed in their several provinces
But his dominion that exceeds in this   55
Stretcheth as far as doth the mind of man:
A sound magician is a demi-god!
Here tire my brains to get a deity!

(Enter WAGNER.*)*

Wagner, commend me to my dearest friends.
The German Valdes and Cornelius.   60
Request them earnestly to visit me.
WAGNER: I will, sir.   *(Exit.)*
FAUSTUS: Their conference will be a greater help to me
Than all my labors, plod I ne'er so fast.

(Enter the [GOOD] ANGEL *and* [the EVIL] SPIRIT.*)*

GOOD ANGEL: O Faustus, lay that damnèd book aside   65
And gaze not on it lest it tempt thy soul
And heap God's heavy wrath upon thy head!
Read, read the Scriptures—that is blasphemy!
BAD ANGEL: Go forward Faustus, in that famous art
Wherein all nature's treasure is contained.   70
Be thou on earth as Jove is in the sky,
Lord and commander of these elements!

(Exeunt ANGELS.*)*

FAUSTUS: How am I glutted with conceit of this!
Shall I make spirits fetch me what I please?
Resolve me of all ambiguities?   75
Perform what desperate enterprise I will?
I'll have them fly to India for gold,
Ransack the ocean for orient pearl,
And search all corners of the new-found world
For pleasant fruits and princely delicates;   80
I'll have them read me strange philosophy
And tell the secrets of all foreign kings;
I'll have them wall all Germany with brass
And make swift Rhine circle fair Wittenberg;
I'll have them fill the public schools with silk   85
Wherewith the students shall be bravely clad.
I'll levy soldiers with the coin they bring

---

45 **metaphysics** subjects lying beyond (or studied after) physics   46
negromantic black magical (though probably here also associated with
"necromantic," i.e., concerned with raising the spirits of the dead)   51
artisan i.e., expert   52 **quiet** motionless   55 **this** i.e., magic   58 **get**
beget   63 **conference** conversation.   s.d. **Spirit** Bad Angel, devil (the
two angels probably enter the stage from separate doors)   68 **that** i.e.,
the book of magic   73 **conceit of this** i.e., the conception of being a
magician   75 **Resolve me of** explain to me   77 **India** either the West
Indies (America) or the East Indies   78 **orient** lustrous and precious
85 **public schools** universities   86 **bravely** splendidly

And chase the Prince of Parma from our land
And reign sole king of all the provinces!
90   Yea, stranger engines for the brunt of war
Than was the fiery keel at Antwerp bridge
I'll make my servile spirits to invent.

(*Enter* VALDES *and* CORNELIUS.)

Come German Valdes and Cornelius
And make me blest with your sage conference.
95   Valdes, sweet Valdes, and Cornelius,
Know that your words have won me at the last
To practice magic and concealèd arts.
Philosophy is odious and obscure,
Both law and physic are for petty wits,
100   Divinity is basest of the three —
Unpleasant, harsh, contemptible, and vile.
'Tis magic, magic, that hath ravished me!
Then, gentle friends, aid me in this attempt
And I, that have with subtle syllogisms
105   Graveled the pastors of the German church
And made the flow'ring pride of Wittenberg
Swarm to my problems as th' infernal spirits
On sweet Musaeus when he came to hell,
Will be as cunning as Agrippa was,
110   Whose shadows made all Europe honor him.
VALDES: Faustus, these books, thy wit, and our experience
Shall make all nations to canonize us.
As Indian Moors obey their Spanish lords,
So shall the spirits of every element
115   Be always serviceable to us three:
Like lions shall they guard us when we please,
Like Almain rutters with their horsemen's staves
Or Lapland giants trotting by our sides;
Sometimes like women or unwedded maids
120   Shadowing more beauty in their airy brows
Than has the white breasts of the queen of love;
From Venice shall they drag huge argosies
And from America the golden fleece
That yearly stuffs old Philip's treasury,
125   If learnèd Faustus will be resolute.
FAUSTUS: Valdes, as resolute am I in this
As thou to live; therefore object it not.
CORNELIUS: The miracles that magic will perform
Will make thee vow to study nothing else.
130   He that is grounded in astrology,
Enriched with tongues, well seen in minerals,
Hath all the principles magic doth require.
Then doubt not Faustus but to be renowned

And more frequented for this mystery
Than heretofore the Delphian oracle.   135
The spirits tell me they can dry the sea
And fetch the treasure of all foreign wracks,
Yea, all the wealth that our forefathers hid
Within the massy entrails of the earth.
Then tell me Faustus, what shall we three want?   140
FAUSTUS: Nothing, Cornelius O, this cheers my soul!
Come, show me some demonstrations magical
That I may conjure in some bushy grove
And have these joys in full possession.
VALDES: Then haste thee to some solitary grove,   145
And bear wise Bacon's and Albanus' works,
The Hebrew Psalter, and New Testament;
And whatsoever else is requisite
We will inform thee ere our conference cease.
CORNELIUS: Valdes, first let him know the words of art,   150
And then, all other ceremonies learned,
Faustus may try his cunning by himself.
VALDES: First I'll instruct thee in the rudiments,
And then wilt thou be perfecter than I.
FAUSTUS: Then come and dine with me, and after meat   155
We'll canvass every quiddity thereof,
For ere I sleep I'll try what I can do:
This night I'll conjure though I die therefor!

(*Exeunt omnes.*)

SCENE II

Enter two SCHOLARS.

1 SCHOLAR: I wonder what's become of Faustus that was wont to
make our schools ring with *sic probo*.

(*Enter* WAGNER.)

2 SCHOLAR: That shall we presently know. Here comes his boy.
1 SCHOLAR: How now sirrah, where's thy master?
WAGNER: God in heaven knows.   5
1 SCHOLAR: Why, dost not thou know then?
WAGNER: Yes, I know, but that follows not.
1 SCHOLAR: Go to sirrah, leave your jesting and tell us where he
is.
WAGNER: That follows not by force of argument, which you,   10
being licentiates, should stand upon; therefore, acknowledge
your error and be attentive.
2 SCHOLAR: Then you will not tell us?
WAGNER: You are deceived, for I will tell you. Yet if you were not
dunces, you would never ask me such a question. For is he   15

---

88 **Prince of Parma** Spanish governor-general of the Low Countries
during 1579–1592   90 **brunt** assault   91 **fiery keel** burning ship sent
by the Netherlanders in 1585 against a bridge erected by Parma to block-
ade Antwerp (Antwerp here is adjectival, not genitive)   105 **Graveled**
confounded   107 **problems** questions proposed for disputation   108
Musaeus legendary Greek poet   109 **Agrippa** Cornelius Agrippa of
Nettesheim (1486–1535), German author of *De occulta philosophia*, a
survey of Renaissance magic; Agrippa was believed to have raised spirits
("shadows") from the dead   113 **Indian Moors** American Indians   117
Almain rutters German cavalrymen   120 **Shadowing** sheltering   124
Philip King Philip II of Spain (1527–1598)   131 **well seen** skilled

134 **frequented for this mystery** resorted to for this art   135 **Delphian
oracle** oracle of Apollo at Delphi   139 **massy** massive   140 **want**
lack   143 **conjure** raise spirits   146 **Bacon** Roger Bacon, medieval friar
and scientist   146 **Albanus** perhaps Pietro d'Abano, medieval writer on
medicine and philosophy   156 **canvass every quiddity** discuss every essential detail.   s.d. **omnes** all (Latin)   I.ii.2 **sic probo** thus I prove it
(Latin)   3 **presently** at once   3 **boy** servant (an impoverished student)   4 **sirrah** (term of address used to an inferior)   8 **Go to**
(exclamation of impatience)   11 **licentiates** possessors of a degree preceding the master's degree   11 **stand upon** make much of   15 **dunces**
(1) fools (2) hairsplitters

not *corpus naturale*? And is not that *mobile*? Then wherefore should you ask me such a question? But that I am by nature phlegmatic, slow to wrath, and prone to lechery—to love, I would say—it were not for you to come within forty foot of the place of execution—although I do not doubt but to see you both hanged the next sessions. Thus, having triumphed over you, I will set my countenance like a precisian and begin to speak thus: Truly, my dear brethren, my master is within at dinner, with Valdes and Cornelius, as this wine, if it could speak, would inform your worships; and so, the Lord bless you, preserve you, and keep you, my dear brethren.

(Exit.)

1 SCHOLAR: O Faustus, then I fear that which I have long
   suspected,
   That thou art fall'n into that damnèd art
   For which they two are infamous through the world.
2 SCHOLAR: Were he a stranger, not allied to me,
   The danger of his soul would make me mourn.
   But come, let us go and inform the rector.
   It may be his grave counsel may reclaim him.
1 SCHOLAR: I fear me nothing will reclaim him now.
2 SCHOLAR: Yet let us see what we can do.

(Exeunt.)

SCENE III

Thunder. Enter LUCIFER *and four* DEVILS. FAUSTUS *to them with this speech.*

FAUSTUS: Now that the gloomy shadow of the night,
   Longing to view Orion's drizzling look,
   Leaps from th' antarctic world unto the sky
   And dims the welkin with her pitchy breath,
   Faustus, begin thine incantations
   And try if devils will obey thy hest,
   Seeing thou hast prayed and sacrificed to them.
   Within this circle is Jehovah's name
   Forward and backward anagrammatized,
   Th' abbreviated names of holy saints,
   Figures of every adjunct to the heavens,
   And characters of signs and erring stars,
   By which the spirits are enforced to rise:
   Then fear not, Faustus, to be resolute
   And try the utmost magic can perform.

(Thunder.)

Sint mihi dei Acherontis propitii! Valeat numen triplex Iehovae! Ignei, aerii, aquatici, spiritus, salvete! Orientis princeps, Belzebub inferni ardentis monarcha, et Demogorgon, propitiamus vos ut appareat et surgat Mephostophilis! Quid tu moraris? Per Iehovam, Gehennam, et consecratam aquam quam nunc spargo, signumque crucis quod nunc facio, et per vota nostra, ipse nunc surgat nobis dicatus Mephostophilis!

(Enter a DEVIL.*)*

I charge thee to return and change thy shape,
Thou art too ugly to attend on me.
Go, and return an old Franciscan friar:
That hold shape becomes a devil best.

(Exit DEVIL.*)*

I see there's virtue in my heavenly words.
Who would not be proficient in this art?
How pliant is this Mephostophilis,
Full of obedience and humility,
Such is the force of magic and my spells.

(Enter MEPHOSTOPHILIS.*)*

MEPHOSTOPHILIS: Now Faustus, what wouldst thou have me
   do?
FAUSTUS: I charge thee wait upon me whilst I live
   To do whatever Faustus shall command,
   Be it to make the moon drop from her sphere
   Or the ocean to overwhelm the world.
MEPHOSTOPHILIS: I am a servant to great Lucifer
   And may not follow thee without his leave.
   No more than he commands must we perform.
FAUSTUS: Did not he charge thee to appear to me?
MEPHOSTOPHILIS: No, I came now hither of mine own
   accord.
FAUSTUS: Did not my conjuring raise thee? Speak.
MEPHOSTOPHILIS: That was the cause, but yet *per accidens:*
   For when we hear one rack the name of God,
   Abjure the Scriptures and his savior Christ,
   We fly in hope to get his glorious soul.
   Nor will we come unless he use such means
   Whereby he is in danger to be damned.
   Therefore the shortest cut for conjuring
   Is stoutly to abjure the Trinity
   And pray devoutly to the prince of hell.

16 **corpus naturale . . . mobile** natural matter . . . movable (Latin, scholastic definition of the subject-matter of physics) 18 **phlegmatic** sluggish 20 **the place of execution** the place of action, i.e., the dining room (with quibble on gallows) 21 **sessions** sittings of a court 22 **precisian** Puritan (Wagner goes on to parody the style of the Puritans) 32 **rector** head of the university I.iii. s.d. **Enter . . . Devils** (they are invisible to Faustus; perhaps they enter through a trapdoor and climb to the upper playing area, as implied in V.ii. s.d.) 2 **Orion** constellation appearing at the beginning of winter, associated with rain 4 **welkin** sky 8 **circle** circle the conjuror draws around him on the ground, to call the spirits and to protect himself from them 11 **adjunct to** heavenly body fixed to 12 **signs and erring stars** signs of the Zodiac and planets

16–23 **Sint . . . Mephostophilis** may the gods of the lower region be favorable to me. Away with the trinity of Jehovah. Hail, spirits of fire, air, water. Prince of the east, Bezlebub monarch of burning hell, and Demogorgon, we pray to you that Mephostophilis may appear and rise. Why do you delay? By Jehovah, Gehenna, and the holy water which now I sprinkle, and the sign of the cross which now I make, and by our vows, may Mephostophilis himself now rise to serve us (Latin). s.d. **Devil** (the word "dragon" oddly appears, after "surgat Mephostophilis," in the preceding conjuration. It makes no sense in the sentence, and it has therefore been omitted from the present text, but perhaps it indicates that a dragon briefly appears at that point, or perhaps the devil referred to in the present stage direction is disguised as a dragon) 44 **per accidens** the immediate (but not ultimate) cause (Latin) 45 **rack** torture 47 **glorious** (1) splendid (2) presumptuous

FAUSTUS: So Faustus hath already done, and holds this
    principle,
    There is no chief but only Belzebub:
55   To whom Faustus doth dedicate himself.
    This word "damnation" terrifies not me
    For I confound hell in Elysium:
    My ghost be with the old philosophers!
    But leaving these vain trifles of men's souls,
60   Tell me, what is that Lucifer thy Lord?
MEPHOSTOPHILIS: Arch-regent and commander of all spirits.
FAUSTUS: Was not that Lucifer an angel once?
MEPHOSTOPHILIS: Yes Faustus, and most dearly loved of God.
FAUSTUS: How comes it then that he is prince of devils?
65 MEPHOSTOPHILIS: O, by aspiring pride and insolence,
    For which God threw him from the face of heaven.
FAUSTUS: And what are you that live with Lucifer?
MEPHOSTOPHILIS: Unhappy spirits that fell with Lucifer,
    Conspired against our God with Lucifer,
70   And are forever damned with Lucifer.
FAUSTUS: Where are you damned?
MEPHOSTOPHILIS: In hell.
FAUSTUS: How comes it then that thou art out of hell?
MEPHOSTOPHILIS: Why this is hell, nor am I out of it.
75   Think'st thou that I who saw the face of God
    And tasted the eternal joys of heaven
    Am not tormented with ten thousand hells
    In being deprived of everlasting bliss?
    O Faustus, leave these frivolous demands
80   Which strikes a terror to my fainting soul!
FAUSTUS: What, is great Mephostophilis so passionate
    For being deprivèd of the joys of heaven?
    Learn thou of Faustus manly fortitude
    And scorn those joys thou never shalt possess.
85   Go bear these tidings to great Lucifer:
    Seeing Faustus hath incurred eternal death
    By desperate thoughts against Jove's deity,
    Say he surrenders up to him his soul
    So he will spare him four and twenty years,
90   Letting him live in all voluptuousness,
    Having thee ever to attend on me,
    To give me whatsoever I shall ask,
    To tell me whatsoever I demand,
    To slay mine enemies and to aid my friends
95   And always be obedient to my will.
    Go and return to mighty Lucifer
    And meet me in my study at midnight,
    And then resolve me of thy master's mind.
MEPHOSTOPHILIS: I will, Faustus.
100 FAUSTUS: Had I as many souls as there be stars
    I'd give them all for Mephostophilis.
    By him I'll be great emperor of the world,
    And make a bridge through the moving air
    To pass the ocean with a band of men;
105   I'll join the hills that bind the Afric shore

    And make that country continent to Spain,
    And both contributary to my crown;
    The Emperor shall not live but by my leave,
    Nor any potentate of Germany.
    Now that I have obtained what I desired   110
    I'll live in speculation of this art
    Till Mephostophilis return again.

(Exit.)

(Exeunt LUCIFER *and* DEVILS.*)*

SCENE IV

Enter WAGNER *and* [ROBIN] *the clown.*

WAGNER: Come hither, sirrah boy.
ROBIN: Boy! O, disgrace to my person! Zounds, boy in your face!
    You have seen many boys with such pickadevants, I am sure.
WAGNER: Sirrah, hast thou no comings in?
ROBIN: Yes, and goings out too, you may see sir.   5
WAGNER: Alas, poor slave! See how poverty jests in his naked-
    ness. I know the villain's out of service, and so hungry that I
    know he would give his soul to the devil for a shoulder of
    mutton, though it were blood-raw.
ROBIN: Not so, neither! I had need to have it well roasted, and   10
    good sauce to it, if I pay so dear, I can tell you.
WAGNER: Sirrah, wilt thou be my man and wait on me? And I
    will make thee go like *Qui mihi discipulus.*
ROBIN: What, in verse?
WAGNER: No, slave, in beaten silk and stavesacre.   15
ROBIN: Stavesacre? That's good to kill vermin! Then, belike, if I
    serve you I shall be lousy.
WAGNER: Why, so thou shalt be, whether thou dost it or no; for
    sirrah, if thou dost not presently bind thyself to me for seven
    years, I'll turn all the lice about thee into familiars and make   20
    them tear thee in pieces.
ROBIN: Nay sir, you may save yourself a labor, for they are as
    familiar with me as if they paid for their meat and drink, I can
    tell you.
WAGNER: Well sirrah, leave your jesting and take these guilders.   25
ROBIN: Yes marry sir, and I thank you too.
WAGNER: So, now thou art to be at an hour's warning when-
    soever and wheresoever the devil shall fetch thee.
ROBIN: Here, take your guilders, I'll none of 'em!
WAGNER: Not I, thou art pressed. Prepare thyself, for I will pres-   30
    ently raise up two devils to carry thee away. Banio! Belcher!
ROBIN: Belcher! And Belcher come here I'll belch him. I am not
    afraid of a devil!

106 **continent to** continuous with   111 **speculation** contemplation
I.iv. s.d. **Clown** buffoon   2 **Zounds** by God's wounds   3 **pickadevants**
pointed beards   4 **comings in** income (the Clown then quibbles on
"goings out," i.e., expenses and also holes in his clothes thorough which
his body pokes   13 ***Qui mihi discipulus*** one who is my disciple, i.e.,
like the servant of a learned man (the Latin is the beginning of a poem,
familiar to Renaissance schoolboys on proper behavior)   15 **beaten**
embroidered (leading to the quibble on the sense "hit")   15 **stavesacre**
preparation from seeds of delphinium, used to kill vermin   20 **familiars**
attendant demons   25 **guilders** Dutch coins   26 **marry** indeed (a mild
oath, from "by the Virgin Mary")   30 **pressed** enlisted into service   32
And if

57 **confound hell in Elysium** do not distinguish between hell and
Elysium   58 **ghost** spirit   58 **old** i.e., pre-Christian   61 **spirits**
devils   80 **strikes** (it is not unusual to have a plural subject — especially
when it has a collective force — take a verb ending in -s)   81 **passionate**
emotional   98 **resolve** inform   103 **through** (pronounced "thorough")

(Enter two DEVILS.*)*

WAGNER: How now sir, will you serve me now?

35 ROBIN: Ay, good Wagner, take away the devil then.

WAGNER: Spirits, away! *(Exeunt* DEVILS.*)* Now sirrah, follow me.

ROBIN: I will sir! But hark you master, will you teach me this
    conjuring occupation?

WAGNER: Ay sirrah, I'll teach thee to turn thyself to a dog or a cat

40   or a mouse or a rat or anything.

ROBIN: A dog or a cat or a mouse or a rat? O brave Wagner!

WAGNER: Villain, call me Master Wagner. And see that you
    walk attentively, and let your right eye be always diametrally
    fixed upon my left heel, that thou mayst *quasi vestigiis nostris*

45   *insistere.*

ROBIN: Well sir, I warrant you.

(Exeunt.)

— ACT TWO —

SCENE I

Enter FAUSTUS *in his study.*

FAUSTUS: Now, Faustus, must thou needs be damned;
    Canst thou not be saved!
    What boots it then to think on God or heaven?
    Away with such vain fancies, and despair—

5   Despair in God and trust in Belzebub!
    Now go not backward, Faustus, be resolute!
    Why waver'st thou? O something soundeth in mine ear,
    "Abjure this magic, turn to God again."
    Ay, and Faustus will turn to God again.

10   To God? He loves thee not;
    The god thou serv'st is thine own appetite
    Wherein is fixed the love of Belzebub!
    To him I'll build an altar and a church
    And offer lukewarm blood of newborn babies!

(Enter the two ANGELS.*)*

15 BAD ANGEL: Go forward, Faustus, in that famous art.

GOOD ANGEL: Sweet Faustus, leave that execrable art.

FAUSTUS: Contrition, prayer, repentance, what of these?

GOOD ANGEL: O, they are means to bring thee unto heaven.

BAD ANGEL: Rather illusions, fruits of lunacy,

20   That make men foolish that do use them most.

GOOD ANGEL: Sweet Faustus, think of heaven and heavenly
    things.

BAD ANGEL: No Faustus, think of honor and of wealth.

(Exeunt ANGELS.*)*

FAUSTUS: Wealth!
    Why, the signory of Emden shall be mine!

25   When Mephostophilis shall stand by me
    What power can hurt me? Faustus, thou art safe.
    Cast no more doubts! Mephostophilis, come,

    And bring glad tidings from great Lucifer.
    Is't not midnight? Come Mephostophilis,
    Veni, veni, Mephostophile!   30

(Enter MEPHOSTOPHILIS.*)*

    Now tell me, what saith Lucifer thy Lord?

MEPHOSTOPHILIS: That I shall wait on Faustus whilst he lives,
    So he will buy my service with his soul.

FAUSTUS: Already Faustus hath hazarded that for thee.

MEPHOSTOPHILIS: But now thou must bequeath it solemnly   35
    And write a deed of gift with thine own blood,
    For that security craves Lucifer.
    If thou deny it I must back to hell.

FAUSTUS: Stay Mephostophilis and tell me
    What good will my soul do thy lord?   40

MEPHOSTOPHILIS: Enlarge his kingdom.

FAUSTUS: Is that the reason why he tempts us thus?

MEPHOSTOPHILIS: *Solamen miseris socios habuisse doloris.*

FAUSTUS: Why, have you any pain that torture other?

MEPHOSTOPHILIS: As great as have the human souls of men.   45
    But tell me, Faustus, shall I have thy soul—
    And I will be thy slave and wait on thee
    And give thee more than thou hast wit to ask?

FAUSTUS: Ay Mephostophilis, I'll give it him.

MEPHOSTOPHILIS: Then, Faustus, stab thy arm courageously   50
    And bind thy soul that at some certain day
    Great Lucifer may claim it as his own.
    And then be thou as great as Lucifer!

FAUSTUS: Lo, Mephostophilis, for love of thee
    Faustus hath cut his arm and with his proper blood   55
    Assures his soul to be great Lucifer's,
    Chief lord and regent of perpetual night.
    View here this blood that trickles from mine arm
    And let it be propitious for my wish.

MEPHOSTOPHILIS: But Faustus,   60
    Write it in manner of a deed of gift.

FAUSTUS: Ay so I do—But Mephostophilis,
    My blood congeals and I can write no more.

MEPHOSTOPHILIS: I'll fetch thee fire to dissolve it straight.

(Exit.)

FAUSTUS: What might the staying of my blood portend?   65
    Is it unwilling I should write this bill?
    Why streams it not that I may write afresh:
    "Faustus gives to thee his soul"? O there it stayed.
    Why shouldst thou not? Is not thy soul thine own?
    Then write again: "Faustus gives to thee his soul."   70

(Enter MEPHOSTOPHILIS *with the chafer of fire.)*

MEPHOSTOPHILIS: See Faustus, here is fire. Set it on.

FAUSTUS: So, now the blood begins to clear again.
    Now will I make an end immediately.

MEPHOSTOPHILIS: *(aside)* What will not I do to obtain his
    soul!

---

41 **brave** splendid 43 **diametrally** directly 44 **quasi vestigiis nostris
insistere** as if to step in our footsteps II.i.3 **boots** avails 24 **signory of
Emden** lordship of the rich German port at the mouth of the Ems

30 **Veni, veni, Mephostophile** come, come, Mephostophilis (Latin)
43 **Solamen . . . doloris** misery loves company (Latin) 44 **other**
others 49 **him** i.e., to Lucifer 55 **proper** own 56 **Assures** conveys
by contract 66 **bill** contract 70 s.d. **chafer** portable grate 71 **it** i.e.,
the receptacle containing the congealed blood

75 FAUSTUS: *Consummatum est!* This bill is ended:
   And Faustus hath bequeathed his soul to Lucifer.
   —But what is this inscription on mine arm?
   Homo fuge! Whither should I fly?
   If unto God, He'll throw me down to hell.
80 My senses are deceived, here's nothing writ.
   O yes, I see it plain! Even here is writ.
   Homo fuge! Yet shall not Faustus fly!
   MEPHOSTOPHILIS: *(aside)* I'll fetch him somewhat to delight
      his mind.

   (Exit.)

   (Enter DEVILS *giving crowns and rich apparel to* FAUSTUS. *They
   dance and then depart.)*

   (Enter MEPHOSTOPHILIS.*)*

   FAUSTUS: What means this show? Speak, Mephostophilis.
85 MEPHOSTOPHILIS: Nothing Faustus, but to delight thy mind
      And let thee see what magic can perform.
   FAUSTUS: But may I raise such spirits when I please?
   MEPHOSTOPHILIS: Ay Faustus, and do greater things than
      these.
   FAUSTUS: Then, Mephostophilis, receive this scroll,
90 A deed of gift of body and of soul:
   But yet conditionally that thou perform
   All covenants and articles between us both.
   MEPHOSTOPHILIS: Faustus, I swear by hell and Lucifer
      To effect all promises between us both.
95 FAUSTUS: Then hear me read it, Mephostophilis:
   "On these conditions following:
   First, that Faustus may be a spirit in form and substance.
   Secondly, that Mephostophilis shall be his servant and be by
   him commanded.
100 Thirdly, that Mephostophilis shall do for him and bring him
   whatsoever.
   Fourthly, that he shall be in his chamber or house invisible.
   Lastly, that he shall appear to the said John Faustus at all
   times in what form or shape soever he please:
105 I, John Faustus of Wittenberg, Doctor, by these presents, do
   give both body and soul to Lucifer, prince of the east, and his
   minister Mephostophilis, and furthermore grant unto them
   that, four and twenty years being expired, and these articles
   above written being inviolate, full power to fetch or carry the
110 said John Faustus, body and soul, flesh, blood, or goods, into
   their habitation wheresoever.
                           By me John Faustus."
   MEPHOSTOPHILIS: Speak Faustus, do you deliver this as your
      deed?
   FAUSTUS: Ay, take it, and the devil give thee good of it!
115 MEPHOSTOPHILIS: So now Faustus, ask me what thou wilt.
   FAUSTUS: First will I question with thee about hell.
      Tell me, where is the place that men call hell?
   MEPHOSTOPHILIS: Under the heavens.
   FAUSTUS: Ay, so are all things else, but whereabouts?

MEPHOSTOPHILIS: Within the bowels of these elements   120
   Where we are tortured and remain forever.
   Hell hath no limits nor is circumscribed
   In one self place, but where we are is hell,
   And where hell is there must we ever be.
   And to be short, when all the world dissolves   125
   And every creature shall be purified
   All places shall be hell that is not heaven!
FAUSTUS: I think hell's a fable.
MEPHOSTOPHILIS: Ay, think so still—till experience change
   thy mind!
FAUSTUS: Why, dost thou think that Faustus shall be damned?   130
MEPHOSTOPHILIS: Ay, of necessity, for here's the scroll
   In which thou hast given thy soul to Lucifer.
FAUSTUS: Ay, and body too; but what of that?
   Think'st thou that Faustus is so fond to imagine
   That after this life there is any pain?   135
   No, these are trifles and mere old wives' tales.
MEPHOSTOPHILIS: But I am an instance to prove the contrary,
   For I tell thee I am damned and now in hell!
FAUSTUS: Nay, and this be hell, I'll willingly be damned—
   What, sleeping, eating, walking, and disputing?   140
   But leaving this, let me have a wife, the fairest maid in
      Germany, for I am wanton and lascivious and cannot
      live without a wife.
MEPHOSTOPHILIS: Well Faustus, thou shalt have a wife.

(He fetches in a woman DEVIL *[with fireworks].)*

FAUSTUS: What sight is this?   145
MEPHOSTOPHILIS: Now Faustus, wilt thou have a wife?
FAUSTUS: Here's a hot whore indeed! No, I'll no wife.
MEPHOSTOPHILIS: Marriage is but a ceremonial toy,

(Exit SHE-DEVIL.*)*

   And if thou lovest me, think no more of it.
   I'll cull thee out the fairest courtesans   150
   And bring them every morning to thy bed.
   She whom thine eye shall like thy heart shall have,
   Were she as chaste as was Penelope,
   As wise as Saba, or as beautiful
   As was bright Lucifer before his fall.   155
   Here, take this book and peruse it well.
   The iterating of these lines brings gold;
   The framing of this circle on the ground
   Brings thunder, whirlwinds, storm, and lightning;
   Pronounce this thrice devoutly to thyself,   160
   And men in harness shall appear to thee,
   Ready to execute what thou command'st.
FAUSTUS: Thanks Mephostophilis for this sweet book.
   This will I keep as chary as my life.   *(Exeunt.)*

134 **fond** foolish   148 **toy** trifle   150 **cull thee out** select for you   153
Penelope wife of Ulysses, famed for her fidelity   154 **Saba** the Queen of
Sheba   157 **iterating** repetition   158 **framing** drawing   161 **harness**
armor   164 s.d. **Exeunt** (a scene following this stage direction has probably been lost. Earlier Wagner hired the Clown; later the Clown is an
ostler possessed of one of Faustus' conjuring books. Possibly, then, the
lost scene was a comic one, showing the Clown stealing a book and
departing)

75 **Consummatum est** it is finished (Latin; a blasphemous repetition of
Christ's words on the cross; see John 19:30)   78 **Homo fuge** fly, man
(Latin)   97 **spirit** evil spirit, devil (but to see Faustus as transformed
now into a devil deprived of freedom to repent is to deprive the remainder of the play of much of its meaning)   109 **inviolate** unviolated

SCENE II

Enter FAUSTUS *in his study and* MEPHOSTOPHILIS.

FAUSTUS: When I behold the heavens, then I repent
    And curse thee, wicked Mephostophilis,
    Because thou has deprived me of those joys.
MEPHOSTOPHILIS: 'Twas thine own seeking Faustus, thank
    thyself.
5   But think'st thou heaven is such a glorious thing?
    I tell thee, Faustus, it is not half so fair
    As thou or any man that breathe on earth.
FAUSTUS: How prov'st thou that?
MEPHOSTOPHILIS: 'Twas made for man; then he's more
    excellent.
10 FAUSTUS: If heaven was made for man, 'twas made for me!
    I will renounce this magic and repent.

(Enter the two ANGELS.)

GOOD ANGEL: Faustus, repent: yet God will pity thee!
BAD ANGEL: Thou art a spirit: God cannot pity thee!
FAUSTUS: Who buzzeth in mine ears I am a spirit?
15 Be I a devil, yet God may pity me—
    Yea, God will pity me if I repent.
BAD ANGEL: Ay, but Faustus never shall repent.

(Exit ANGELS.)

FAUSTUS: My heart is hardened, I cannot repent.
    Scarce can I name salvation, faith, or heaven,
20 Swords, poison, halters, and envenomed steel
    Are laid before me to dispatch myself.
    And long ere this I should have done the deed
    Had not sweet pleasure conquered deep despair.
    Have not I made blind Homer sing to me
25 Of Alexander's love and Oenon's death?
    And hath not he that built the walls of Thebes
    With ravishing sound of his melodious harp
    Made music with my Mephostophilis?
    Why should I die then or basely despair?
30 I am resolved, Faustus shall not repent!
    Come Mephostophilis, let us dispute again
    And reason of divine astrology
    Speak, are there many spheres above the moon?
    Are all celestial bodies but one globe
35 As is the substance of this centric earth?
MEPHOSTOPHILIS: As are the elements, such are the heavens,
    Even from the moon unto the empyreal orb
    Mutually folded in each others' spheres,
    And jointly move upon one axle-tree,
40 Whose terminè is termed the world's wide pole.
    Nor are the names of Saturn, Mars, or Jupiter
    Feigned but are erring stars.

FAUSTUS: But have they all one motion,
    Both *situ et tempore*?
MEPHOSTOPHILIS: All move from east to west in four and twenty   45
    hours upon the poles of the world but differ in their motions
    upon the poles of the zodiac.
FAUSTUS: These slender questions Wagner can decide.
    Hath Mephostophilis no greater skill?
    Who knows not the double motion of the planets?   50
    That the first is finished in a natural day.
    The second thus: Saturn in thirty years;
    Jupiter in twelve; Mars in four; the sun, Venus, and Mercury
    in a year; the moon in twenty-eight days. These are fresh-
    men's suppositions. But tell me, hath every sphere a domin-   55
    ion or *intelligentia*?
MEPHOSTOPHILIS: Ay.
FAUSTUS: How many heavens or spheres are there?
MEPHOSTOPHILIS: Nine: the seven planets, the firmament, and
    the empyreal heaven.   60
FAUSTUS: But is there not *coelum igneum et crystallinum*?
MEPHOSTOPHILIS: No Faustus, they be but fables.
FAUSTUS: Resolve me then in this one question. Why are not
    conjunctions, oppositions, aspects, eclipses all at one time,
    but in some years we have more, in some less?   65
MEPHOSTOPHILIS: *Per inaqualem motum respectu totius.*
FAUSTUS: Well, I am answered. Now tell me, who made the
    world?
MEPHOSTOPHILIS: I will not.
FAUSTUS: Sweet Mephostophilis, tell me.   70
MEPHOSTOPHILIS: Move me not, Faustus!
FAUSTUS: Villain, have not I bound thee to tell me anything?
MEPHOSTOPHILIS: Ay, that is not against our kingdom. This is.
    Thou art damned. Think thou of hell!
FAUSTUS: Think, Faustus, upon God, that made the world.   75
MEPHOSTOPHILIS: Remember this!

(Exit.)

FAUSTUS: Ay, go accursèd spirit to ugly hell!
    'Tis thou hast damned distressèd Faustus' soul—
    Is't not too late?

(Enter the two ANGELS.)

BAD ANGEL: Too late.   80
GOOD ANGEL: Never too late, if Faustus will repent.
BAD ANGEL: If thou repent, devils will tear thee in pieces.
GOOD ANGEL: Repent, and they shall never raze thy skin.

(Exeunt ANGELS.)

FAUSTUS: O Christ, my savior, my savior!
    Help to save distressèd Faustus' soul.   85

(Enter LUCIFER, BELZEBUB, *and* MEPHOSTOPHILIS.)

LUCIFER: Christ cannot save thy soul, for He is just.
    There's none but I have interest in the same.

II.ii.12 **yet** still, even now   25 **Alexander . . . Oenone** Paris, also called
Alexander, was Oenone's lover, but he later deserted her for Helen of
Troy, causing the Trojan War, the subject of Homer's *Iliad*   26 **he**
Amphion, whose music charmed stones to form the walls of Thebes
35 **centric** central   36 **such** i.e., separate but combined; the idea is that
the heavenly bodies are separate but their spheres are concentric
("folded"), and all—from the nearest (the moon) to the farthest ("the
empyreal orb" or empyrean)—move on one axletree   40 **terminè** end,
extremity   42 **erring stars** planets

44 **situ et tempore** in place and in time   51 **natural day** twenty-four
hours   55 **suppositions** premises   56 **dominion or intelligentia**
governing angel or intelligence (believed to impart motion to the
sphere)   61 **coelum igneum et crystallinum** a heaven of fire and a crys-
taline sphere (Latin)   64 **at one time** i.e., at regular intervals   66 **Per . . .
totius** because of unequal speed within the system (Latin)   71 **Move**
anger   82 **raze** scratch   87 **interest in** legal claim on

FAUSTUS: O, what art thou that look'st so terribly?

LUCIFER: I am Lucifer

90   And this is my companion prince in hell.

FAUSTUS: O Faustus, they are come to fetch thy soul!

BELZEBUB: We are come to tell thee thou dost injure us.

LUCIFER: Thou call'st on Christ contrary to thy promise.

BELZEBUB: Thou should'st not think on God.

LUCIFER: Think on the Devil.

95   BELZEBUB: And his dam too.

FAUSTUS: Nor will Faustus henceforth. Pardon him for this,

   And Faustus vows never to look to heaven!

   Never to name God or to pray to Him,

   To burn His Scriptures, slay His ministers,

100   And make my spirits pull His churches down.

LUCIFER: So shalt thou show thyself an obedient servant,

   And we will highly gratify thee for it.

BELZEBUB: Faustus, we are come from hell in person to show

   thee some pastime. Sit down and thou shalt behold the Seven

105   Deadly Sins appear to thee in their own proper shapes and

   likeness.

FAUSTUS: That sight will be as pleasant to me as Paradise was to

   Adam the first day of his creation.

LUCIFER: Talk not of Paradise or creation but mark the show. Go

110   Mephostophilis, fetch them in.

(*Enter the* SEVEN DEADLY SINS [*led by a* PIPER].)

BELZEBUB: Now Faustus, question them of their names and

   dispositions.

FAUSTUS: That shall I soon. What art thou, the first?

PRIDE: I am Pride. I disdain to have any parents. I am like to

115   Ovid's flea, I can creep into every corner of a wench: some-

   times, like a periwig I sit upon her brow; next, like a necklace

   I hang about her neck; then, like a fan of feathers I kiss her;

   and then, turning myself to a wrought smock, do what I list—

   But fie, what a smell is here! I'll not speak a word more for a

120   king's ransom unless the ground be perfumed and covered

   with cloth of arras.

FAUSTUS: Thou art a proud knave indeed. What art thou, the

   second?

COVETOUSNESS: I am Covetousness, begotten of an old churl in

125   a leather bag; and might I now obtain my wish, this house,

   you and all, should turn to gold that I might lock you safe into

   my chest. O my sweet gold!

FAUSTUS: And what art thou, the third?

ENVY: I am Envy, begotten of a chimney-sweeper and an oyster-

130   wife. I cannot read and therefore wish all books burned. I am

   lean with seeing others eat. O, that there would come a fam-

   ine over all the world that all might die and I live alone! Then

   thou shouldst see how fat I'd be. But must thou sit and I

   stand? Come down, with a vengeance!

135   FAUSTUS: Out, envious wretch! But what art thou, the fourth?

WRATH: I am Wrath. I had neither father nor mother. I leapt out

   of a lion's mouth when I was scarce an hour old and ever since

have run up and down the world with these case of rapiers,

wounding myself when I could get none to fight withal. I was

born in hell! And look to it, for some of you shall be my   140

father.

FAUSTUS: And what art thou, the fifth?

GLUTTONY: I am Gluttony. My parents are all dead, and the

devil a penny they have left me, but a small pension: and that

buys me thirty meals a day and ten bevers, a small trifle to   145

suffice nature. I come of a royal pedigree. My father was a

gammon of bacon, and my mother was a hogshead of claret

wine. My godfathers were these: Peter Pickled-herring and

Martin Martlemas-beef. But my godmother, O, she was an

ancient gentlewoman: her name was Margery March-beer.   150

Now Faustus, thou hast heard all my progeny, wilt thou bid

me to supper?

FAUSTUS: Not I.

GLUTTONY: Then the devil choke thee!

FAUSTUS: Choke thyself, glutton! What art thou, the sixth?   155

SLOTH: Heigh-ho! I am Sloth. I was begotten on a sunny bank.

Heigh-ho, I'll not speak a word more for a king's ransom.

FAUSTUS: And what are you, Mistress Minx, the seventh and

last?

LECHERY: Who, I, I sir? I am one that loves an inch of raw   160

mutton better than an ell of fried stockfish, and the first letter

of my name begins with Lechery.

LUCIFER: Away to hell, away! On, piper!

(*Exeunt the* SEVEN SINS.)

FAUSTUS: O, how this sight doth delight my soul!

LUCIFER: But Faustus, in hell is all manner of delight.   165

FAUSTUS: O, might I see hell and return again safe, how

happy were I then!

LUCIFER: Faustus, thou shalt. At midnight I will send for

   thee.

   Meanwhile peruse this book and view it thoroughly,

   And thou shalt turn thyself into what shape thou wilt.   170

FAUSTUS: Thanks mighty Lucifer.

   This will I keep as chary as my life.

LUCIFER: Now Faustus, farewell.

FAUSTUS: Farewell great Lucifer. Come Mephostophilis.

(*Exeunt omnes several ways.*)

SCENE III

Enter [ROBIN] *the clown.*

ROBIN: What, Dick, look to the horses there till I come again! I

have gotten one of Doctor Faustus' conjuring books, and now

we'll have such knavery as't passes.

(*Enter* DICK.)

DICK: What, Robin, you must come away and walk the horses.

---

95 **dam** mother   104–105 **Seven Deadly Sins** (so called because they cause spiritual death; they are Pride, Covetousness, Envy, Wrath, Gluttony, Sloth, Lechery)   115 **Ovid's flea** flea in *Carmen de pulce,* a lewd poem mistakenly attributed to Ovid   118 **wrought smock** decorated petticoat   121 **cloth of arras** Flemish cloth used for tapestries   125 **leather bag** moneybag (?)   129–130 **chimney-sweeper . . . oyster-wife** i.e., dirty and smelly

138 **these case** this pair   145 **bevers** snacks (literally drinks)   147 **gammon** haunch   149 **Martlemas-beef** cattle slaughtered at Martinmas (11 November) and salted for winter consumption   150 **March-beer** strong beer brewed in March   151 **progeny** ancestry   156 **Heigh-ho** (a yawn or tired greeting)   160–161 **inch of raw mutton** i.e., penis ("mutton" in a bawdy sense commonly alludes to a prostitute, but since here the speaker is a woman, the allusion must be to a male)   161 **an ell of . . . stockfish** forty-five inches of dried cod   172 **chary** carefully   175 s.d. **several** various

5   ROBIN: I walk the horses? I scorn't, 'faith. I have other matters in
hand. Let the horses walk themselves an they will. [*Reading*]
A *per se*—a; t, h, e—the; o *per se*—o; deny orgon—gorgon.
Keep further from me, O thou illiterate and unlearned
hostler!

10   DICK: 'Snails, what hast thou got there, a book? Why, thou canst
not tell ne'er a word on't.

ROBIN: That thou shalt see presently. Keep out of the circle, I
say, lest I send you into the hostry with a vengeance.

DICK: That's like, 'faith! You had best leave your foolery, for an

15   my master come, he'll conjure you, 'faith.

ROBIN: My master conjure me? I'll tell thee what. An my master
come here, I'll clap as fair a pair of horns on's head as e'er
thou sawest in thy life.

DICK: Thou need'st not do that, for my mistress hath done it.

20   ROBIN: Ay, there be of us here that have waded as deep into
matters as other men—if they were disposed to talk.

DICK: A plague take you! I thought you did not sneak up and
down after her for nothing. But I prithee tell me in good sadness Robin, is that a conjuring book?

25   ROBIN: Do but speak what thou't have me to do, and I'll do't. If
thou't dance naked, put off thy clothes, and I'll conjure thee
about presently. Or if thou't go but to the tavern with me, I'll
give thee white wine, red wine, claret wine, sack, muscadine,
malmsey, and whippincrust—hold-belly-hold. And we'll not

30   pay one penny for it.

DICK: O brave! Prithee let's to it presently, for I am as dry as a
dog.

ROBIN: Come then, let's away.

(*Exeunt.*)

— ACT THREE —

Enter the CHORUS.

Learnèd Faustus,
To find the secrets of astronomy
Graven in the book of Jove's high firmament,
Did mount him up to scale Olympus' top:
5   Where, sitting in a chariot burning bright
Drawn by the strength of yokèd dragons' necks,
He views the clouds, the planets, and the stars,
The tropics, zones, and quarters of the sky,
From the bright circle of the hornèd moon
10   Even to the height of *primum mobile*:
And whirling round with this circumference
Within the concave compass of the pole,
From east to west his dragons swiftly glide
And in eight days did bring him home again.

Not long he stayed within his quiet house   15
To rest his bones after his weary toil
But new exploits do hale him out again.
And mounted then upon a dragon's back,
That with his wings did part the subtle air,
He now is gone to prove cosmography,   20
That measures coasts and kingdoms of the earth,
And as I guess will first arrive at Rome
To see the Pope and manner of his court
And take some part of holy Peter's feast,
The which this day is highly solemnized.   25

(*Exit.*)

SCENE I

Enter FAUSTUS *and* MEPHOSTOPHILIS.

FAUSTUS: Having now, my good Mephostophilis,
Passed with delight the stately town of Trier,
Environed round with airy mountain tops,
With walls of flint, and deep-entrenchèd lakes,
Not to be won by any conquering prince: 5
From Paris next, coasting the realm of France,
We saw the river Main fall into Rhine,
Whose banks are set with groves of fruitful vines:
Then up to Naples, rich Campania,
Whose buildings fair and gorgeous to the eye,   10
The streets straight forth and paved with finest brick,
Quarters the town in four equivalents.
There saw we learnèd Maro's golden tomb,
The way he cut an English mile in length
Through a rock of stone in one night's space.   15
From thence to Venice, Padua, and the rest,
In one of which a sumptuous temple stands
That threats the stars with her aspiring top,
Whose frame is paved with sundry colored stones
And roofed aloft with curious work in gold.   20
Thus hitherto hath Faustus spent his time.
But tell me now, what resting-palace is this?
Hast thou, as erst I did command,
Conducted me within the walls of Rome?

MEPHOSTOPHILIS: I have, my Faustus, and for proof thereof   25
This is the goodly palace of the Pope,
And 'cause we are no common guests
I choose his privy chamber for our use.

FAUSTUS: I hope his Holiness will bid us welcome.

MEPHOSTOPHILIS: All's one, for we'll be bold with his venison. 30
But now my Faustus, that thou may'st perceive
What Rome contains for to delight thine eyes,
Know that this city stands upon seven hills
That underprop the groundwork of the same:
Just through the midst runs flowing Tiber's stream   35
With winding banks that cut it in two parts,
Over the which four stately bridges lean
That make safe passage to each part of Rome.
Upon the bridge called Ponte Angelo

II.iii. 6 **an** if   7 **per se** by itself (Latin; the idea is, "A by itself spells
A")   7 **deny orgon—gorgon** (Robin is trying to read the name "Demogorgon")   10 **'Snails** by God's nails   13 **hostry** hostelry inn   17
horns (as the next speech indicates, horns were said to adorn the head of
a man whose wife was unfaithful)   23 **in good sadness** seriously   28
sack sherry   29 **whippincrust** illiterate pronunciation of "hippocras," a
spiced wine   III Chorus   8 **zones** segments of the sky   9 **circle** orbit
10 **primun mobile** the outermost sphere, the empryean   20 **prove cosmography** test maps, i.e., explore the universe   III.i.2 **Trier** German
city on the Moselle, also known as Trèves   4 **deep-entrenchèd lakes**
moats   13 **Maro** Vergil (Publius Vergilius Maro, 70–19 B.C.)

15 **Through** (pronounced "thorough")   37 **lean** bend   45 **pyramides**
obelisk (pronounced py-ràm-i-des)   48–49 **Styx, Acheron, Phlegethon**
rivers of the underworld

40 Erected is a castle passing strong
    Where thou shalt see such store of ordinance
    As that the double cannons forged of brass
    Do match the number of the days contained
    Within the compass of one complete year,
45 Beside the gates and high pryamides
    That Julius Caesar brought from Africa.
    FAUSTUS: Now, by the kingdoms of infernal rule,
    Of Styx, of Acheron, and the fiery lake
    Of ever-burning Phlegethon, I swear
50 That I do long to see the monuments
    And situation of bright-splendent Rome.
    Come therefore, let's away.
    MEPHOSTOPHILIS: Nay stay my Faustus. I know you'd see the
        Pope
    And take some part of holy Peter's feast,
55 The which this day with high solemnity,
    This day, is held through Rome and Italy
    In honor of the Pope's triumphant victory.
    FAUSTUS: Sweet Mephostophilis, thou pleasest me.
    Whilst I am here on earth let me be cloyed
60 With all things that delight the heart of man.
    My four and twenty years of liberty
    I'll spend in pleasure and in dalliance,
    That Faustus' name, whilst this bright frame doth stand,
    May be admirèd through the furthest land.
65 MEPHOSTOPHILIS: 'Tis well said, Faustus, come then, stand
        by me
    And thou shalt see them come immediately.
    FAUSTUS: Nay stay, my gentle Mephostophilis,
    And grant me my request, and then I go.
    Thou know'st, within the compass of eight days
70 We viewed the face of heaven, of earth, and hell.
    So high our dragons soared into the air
    That looking down the earth appeared to me
    No bigger than my hand in quantity —
    There did we view the kingdoms of the world,
75 And what might please mine eye I there beheld.
    Then in this show let me an actor be
    That this proud Pope may Faustus' cunning see!
    MEPHOSTOPHILIS: Let it be so, my Faustus, but first stay
    And view their triumphs as they pass this way.
80 And then devise what best contents thy mind
    By cunning in thine art to cross the Pope
    Or dash the pride of this solemnity —
    To make his monks and abbots stand like apes
    And point like antics at his triple crown,
85 To beat the beads about the friars' pates,
    Or clap huge horns upon the cardinals' heads,
    Or any villainy thou canst devise —
    And I'll perform it, Faustus. Hark, they come!
    This day shall make thee be admired in Rome!

(Enter the CARDINALS and BISHOPS, some bearing crosiers, some
the pillars; MONKS and FRIARS singing their procession; then the
POPE and RAYMOND King of Hungary, with BRUNO led in
chains.)

POPE: Cast down our footstool.
RAYMOND: Saxon Bruno, stoop,   90
    Whilst on thy back his Holiness ascends
    Saint Peter's chair and state pontifical.
BRUNO: Proud Lucifer, that state belongs to me —
    But thus I fall to Peter, not to thee.
POPE: To me and Peter shalt thou grov'lling lie   95
    And crouch before the papal dignity!
    Sound triumpets then, for thus Saint Peter's heir
    From Bruno's back ascends Saint Peter's chair!

(A flourish while he ascends.)

    Thus as the gods creep on with feet of wool
    Long ere with iron hands they punish men,   100
    So shall our sleeping vengeance now arise
    And smite with death thy hated enterprise.
    Lord Cardinals of France and Padua,
    Go forthwith to our holy consistory
    And read amongst the statutes decretal   105
    What by the holy council held at Trent
    The sacred synod hath decreed for him
    That doth assume the papal government
    Without election and a true consent.
    Away, and bring us word with speed!   110
1 CARDINAL: We go my lord.

(Exeunt [two] CARDINALS.)

POPE: Lord Raymond —

(Talks to him apart.)

FAUSTUS: Go haste thee, gentle Mephostophilis,
    Follow the cardinals to the consistory
    And as they turn their superstitious books   115
    Strike them with sloth and drowsy idleness
    And make them sleep so sound that in their shapes
    Thyself and I may parley with this Pope,
    This proud confronter of the Emperor!
    —And in despite of all his holiness   120
    Restore this Bruno to his liberty
    And bear him to the states of Germany!
MEPHOSTOPHILIS: Faustus, I go.
FAUSTUS: Dispatch it soon.
    The Pope shall curse that Faustus came to Rome.   125

(Exit FAUSTUS and MEPHOSTOPHILIS.)

BRUNO: Pope Adrian, let me have some right of law:
    I was elected by the Emperor.
POPE: We will depose the Emperor for that deed
    And curse the people that submit to him.
    Both he and thou shalt stand excommunicate   130
    And interdict from church's privilege
    And all society of holy men.
    He grows too proud in his authority,
    Lifting his lofty head above the clouds,
    And like a steeple overpeers the church.   135
    But we'll pull down his haughty insolence.

---

79 **triumphs** spectacular displays   84 **antics** grotesque figures, buffoons   89 **admired** wondered at   89s.d. **Raymond King of Hungary . . .
Bruno** (unhistorical figures; Bruno is the emperor's nominee for the
papal throne)

92 **state** throne   98s.d. **flourish** trumpet fanfare   104 **consistory** i.e.,
meeting-place of the papal consistory or senate   105 **statues decretal**
i.e., ecclesiastical laws   106 **council held at Trent** (intermittently from
1545 to 1563)   107 **synod** council

And as Pope Alexander, our progenitor,
Trod on the neck of German Frederick,
Adding this golden sentence to our praise:
140   "That Peter's heirs should tread on emperors
And walk upon the dreadful adder's back,
Treading the lion and the dragon down,
And fearless spurn the killing basilisk" —
So will we quell that haughty schismatic
145   And by authority apostolical
Depose him from his regal government.
  BRUNO: Pope Julius swore to princely Sigismond,
For him and the succeeding Popes of Rome,
To hold the emperors their lawful lords.
150   POPE: Pope Julius did abuse the church's rites
And therefore none of his decrees can stand.
Is not all power on earth bestowed on us?
And therefore though we would, we cannot err.
Behold this silver belt whereto is fixed
155   Seven golden keys fast sealed with seven seals
In token of our sevenfold power from heaven
To bind or loose, lock fast, condemn, or judge,
Resign or seal, or whatso pleaseth us.
Then he and thou and all the world shall stoop —
160   Or be assurèd of our dreadful curse
To light as heavy as the pains of hell.

(Enter FAUSTUS *and* MEPHOSTOPHILIS *like the* CARDINALS.*)*

MEPHOSTOPHILIS: *(aside)* Now tell me Faustus, are we not
    fitted well?
FAUSTUS: *(aside)* Yes Mephostophilis, and two such cardinals
Ne'er served a holy Pope as we shall do.
165   But whilst they sleep within the consistory
Let us salute his reverend Fatherhood.
RAYMOND: Behold my lord, the cardinals are returned.
POPE: Welcome grave fathers, answer presently,
What have our holy council there decreed
170   Concerning Bruno and the Emperor
In quittance of their late conspiracy
Against our state and papal dignity?
FAUSTUS: Most sacred patron of the church of Rome,
By full consent of all the synod
175   Of priests and prelates it is thus decreed:
That Bruno and the German Emperor
Be held as lollards and bold schismatics
And proud disturbers of the church's peace.
And if that Bruno by his own assent,
180   Without enforcement of the German peers,
Did seek to wear the triple diadem
And by your death to climb Saint Peter's chair,
The statutes decretal have thus decreed:
He shall be straight condemned of heresy
185   And on a pile of fagots burnt to death.
POPE: It is enough. Here, take him to your charge
And bear him straight to Ponte Angelo
And in the strongest tower enclose him fast.

Tomorrow, sitting in our consistory
With all our college of grave cardinals   190
We will determine of his life or death.
Here, take his triple crown along with you
And leave it in the church's treasury.
Make haste again, my good lord cardinals,
And take our blessing apostolical.   195
MEPHOSTOPHILIS: *(aside)* So, so! Was never devil thus blessed
  before.
FAUSTUS: *(aside)* Away sweet Mephostophilis, be gone!
The cardinals will be plagued for this anon.

(Exeunt FAUSTUS *and* MEPHOSTOPHILIS *[with* BRUNO*].)*

POPE: Go presently and bring a banquet forth,
That we may solemnize Saint Peter's feast   200
And with Lord Raymond, King of Hungary,
Drink to our late and happy victory.

(Exeunt.)

SCENE II

A *sennet while the banquet is brought in, and then enter* FAU-
STUS *and* MEPHOSTOPHILIS *in their own shapes.*

MEPHOSTOPHILIS: Now Faustus, come prepare thyself for
  mirth.
The sleepy cardinals are hard at hand
To censure Bruno, that is posted hence,
And on a proud-paced steed as swift as thought
Flies o'er the Alps to fruitful Germany,   5
There to salute the woeful Emperor.
FAUSTUS: The Pope will curse them for their sloth today
That slept both Bruno and his crown away.
But now, that Faustus may delight his mind
And by their folly make some merriment,   10
Sweet Mephostophilis, so charm me here
That I may walk invisible to all
And do whate'er I please unseen of any.
MEPHOSTOPHILIS: Faustus, thou shalt. Then kneel down
  presently,
  Whilst on thy head I lay my hand   15
  And charm thee with this magic wand.
  First wear this girdle, then appear
  Invisible to all are here:
  The planets seven, the gloomy air,
  Hell, and the Furies' forkèd hair,   20
  Pluto's blue fire, and Hecat's tree
  With magic spells so compass thee
  That no eye may thy body see.
So Faustus, now for all their holiness,
Do what thou wilt, thou shalt not be discerned.   25
FAUSTUS: Thanks Mephostophilis. Now friars, take heed
Lest Faustus make your shaven crowns to bleed.
MEPHOSTOPHILIS: Faustus, no more. See where the cardinals
  come.

---

137 **Pope Alexander** Pope Alexander III (d. 1181) compelled the Emperor Frederick Barbarossa to kneel before him   137 **progenitor**
predecessor   143 **basilisk** fabulous monster said to kill with a glance
158 **Resign** unseal   168 **presently** immediately   171 **quittance of**
requital for   177 **lollards** heretics

154 **again** i.e., to return   III.ii. s.d. **sennet** set of notes played on a
trumpet signaling an approach or a departure   20 **Furies' forkèd hair**
(the hair of the Furies consisted of snakes, whose forked tongues may be
implied here)   21 **Hecat** Hecate, goddess of magic (possibly her "tree"
is the gallows-tree, but possibly "tree" is a slip for "three," Hecate being
the triple goddess of heaven, earth, and hell)

(Enter POPE *[and* FRIARS] *and all the* LORDS *[with* KING RAY-
MOND *and the* ARCHBISHOP OF RHEIMS]. *Enter the [two]* CAR-
DINALS *with a book.)*

POPE: Welcome lord cardinals. Come, sit down.
30   Lord Raymond, take your seat. Friars, attend,
      And see that all things be in readiness
      As best beseems this solemn festival.
1 CARDINAL: First may it please your sacred Holiness
      To view the sentence of the reverend synod
35   Concerning Bruno and the Emperor.
POPE: What needs this question? Did I not tell you
      Tomorrow we would sit i' th' consistory
      And there determine of his punishment?
      You brought us word, even now, it was decreed
40   That Bruno and the cursèd Emperor
      Were by the holy council both condemned
      For loathèd lollards and base schismatics.
      Then wherefore would you have me view that book?
1 CARDINAL: Your Grace mistakes. You gave us no such
      charge.
45 RAYMOND: Deny it not; we all are witnesses
      That Bruno here was late delivered you
      With his rich triple crown to be reserved
      And put into the church's treasury.
BOTH CARDINALS: By holy Paul we saw them not.
50 POPE: By Peter you shall die
      Unless you bring them forth immediately.
      Hale them to prison, lade their limbs with gyves.
      False prelates, for this hateful treachery
      Cursed be your souls to hellish misery.

(Exeunt ATTENDANTS *with two* CARDINALS.*)*

55 FAUSTUS: So, they are safe. Now Faustus, to the feast.
      The Pope had never such a frolic guest.
POPE: Lord Archbishop of Rheims, sit down with us.
ARCHBISHOP: I thank your Holiness.
FAUSTUS: Fall to, the devil choke you an you spare!
60 POPE: Who's that spoke? Friars, look about.
      Lord Raymond, pray fall to. I am beholding
      To the Bishop of Milan for this so rare a present.
FAUSTUS: *(aside)* I thank you, sir!

(Snatches the dish.)

POPE: How now! Who snatched the meat from me?
65   Villains, why speak you not?
      My good Lord Archbishop, here's a most dainty dish
      Was sent me from a cardinal in France.
FAUSTUS: *(aside)* I'll have that too!

(Snatches the dish.)

POPE: What lollards do attend our Holiness
70   That we receive such great indignity!
      Fetch me some wine.
FAUSTUS: *(aside)* Ay, pray do, for Faustus is adry.
POPE: Lord Raymond, I drink unto your Grace.
FAUSTUS: *(aside)* I pledge your Grace.

(Snatches the goblet.)

POPE: My wine gone too? Ye lubbers, look about   75
      And find the man that doth this villainy,
      Or by our sanctitude you all shall die.
      I pray, my lords, have patience at this troublesome
          banquet.
ARCHBISHOP: Please it your Holiness, I think it be some ghost
      crept out of purgatory, and now is come unto your Holiness   80
      for his pardon.
POPE: It may be so:
      Go then, command our priests to sing a dirge
      To lay the fury of this same troublesome ghost.

(Exit ATTENDANT.*)*

(The POPE *crosses himself before eating.)*

FAUSTUS: How now! Must every bit be spicèd with a cross?   85
      Nay then, take that!

(Strikes the POPE.*)*

POPE: O, I am slain! Help me my lords!
      O come and help to bear my body hence.
      Damned be this soul forever for this deed.

(Exeunt the POPE *and his train.)*

MEPHOSTOPHILIS: Now Faustus, what will you do now?   90
      For I can tell you, you'll be cursed with bell, book, and
      candle.
FAUSTUS: Bell, book, and candle. Candle, book, and bell.
      Forward and backward, to curse Faustus to hell!

(Enter the FRIARS, *with bell, book, and candle for the dirge.)*

1 FRIAR: Come brethren, let's about our business with good   95
      devotion.
      Cursèd be he that stole his Holiness' meat from the table.
          Maledicat Dominus!
      Cursèd be he that struck his Holiness a blow on the face.
          Maledicat Dominus!

*(*FAUSTUS *strikes a* FRIAR.*)*

      Cursèd be he that took Friar Sandelo a blow on the pate.   100
          Maledicat Dominus!
      Cursèd be he that disturbeth our holy dirge.
          Maledicat Dominus!
      Cursèd be he that took away his Holiness' wine.
          Maledicat Dominus!   105

*([*FAUSTUS *and* MEPHOSTOPHILIS] *beat the* FRIARS, *fling fireworks among them and exeunt.)*

SCENE III

*Enter [*ROBIN] *the clown and* DICK *with a cup.*

DICK: Sirrah Robin, we were best look that your devil can answer
      the stealing of this same cup, for the vintner's boy follows us at
      the hard heels.
ROBIN: 'Tis no matter, let him come! An he follow us I'll so
      conjure him as he was never conjured in his life, I warrant   5
      him. Let me see the cup.

52 **gyves** fetters   59 **Fall to** set to work (here, as commonly, "start
eating")

91–92 **bell, book, and candle** implements used in excommunicating
(the bell was tolled, the book closed, the candle extinguished)   98
Maledicat Dominus may the Lord curse him (Latin)   III.iii. 3 **at the
hard heels** hard at heel, closely

(Enter VINTNER.*)*

DICK: Here 'tis. Yonder he comes. Now Robin, now or never
show thy cunning.
VINTNER: O, are you here? I am glad I have found you. You are
10   a couple of fine companions! Pray, where's the cup you stole
from the tavern?
ROBIN: How, how! We steal a cup? Take heed what you say. We
look not like cup-stealers, I can tell you.
VINTNER: Never deny't, for I know you have it, and I'll search
15   you.
ROBIN: Search me? Ay, and spare not! *(Aside)* Hold the cup,
Dick. —Come, come. Search me, search me.

*(*VINTNER *searches him.)*

VINTNER: Come on sirrah, let me search you now.
DICK: Ay ay, do do. *(Aside)* Hold the cup, Robin. —I fear not
20   your searching. We scorn to steal your cups, I can tell you.

*(*VINTNER *searches him.)*

VINTNER: Never outface me for the matter, for sure the cup is
between you two.
ROBIN: Nay, there you lie! 'Tis beyond us both.
VINTNER: A plague take you. I thought 'twas your knavery to
25   take it away. Come, give it me again.
ROBIN: Ay, much! When, can you tell? *(Aside)* Dick, make me a
circle and stand close at my back and stir not for thy life.
Vintner, you shall have your cup anon. *(Aside)* Say nothing,
Dick! O *per se,* o; Demogorgon, Belcher, and Mephos-
30   tophilis!

(Enter MEPHOSTOPHILIS. *Exit* VINTNER.*)*

MEPHOSTOPHILIS: You princely legions of infernal rule,
How am I vexèd by these villains' charms!
From Constantinople have they brought me now
Only for pleasure of these damnèd slaves.
35 ROBIN: By lady sir, you have had a shrewd journey of it. Will it
please you to take a shoulder of mutton to supper and a tester
in your purse and go back again?
DICK: Ay, I pray you heartily, sir. For we called you but in jest, I
promise you.
40 MEPHOSTOPHILIS: To purge the rashness of this cursèd deed,
First be thou turnèd to this ugly shape,
For apish deeds transformèd to an ape.
ROBIN: O brave! An ape! I pray sir, let me have the carrying of
him about to show some tricks.
45 MEPHOSTOPHILIS: And so thou shalt. Be thou transformed to a
dog and carry him upon thy back. Away, be gone!
ROBIN: A dog! That's excellent. Let the maids look well to their
porridge-pots, for I'll into the kitchen presently. Come Dick,
come.

(Exeunt the two CLOWNS.*)*

50 MEPHOSTOPHILIS: Now with the flames of ever-burning fire
I'll wing myself and forthwith fly amain
Unto my Faustus, to the Great Turk's court.

(Exit.)

10 **companions** fellows (contemptuous)   23 **beyond us both**
(apparently Robin has managed to place the cup at some distance from
where he now stands)   26 **When, can you tell** (a scornful reply)   35
shrewd bad   36 **tester** sixpence.   41 **apish** (1) foolish (2) imitative

— ACT FOUR —

Enter CHORUS.

When Faustus had with pleasure ta'en the view
Of rarest things and royal courts of kings,
He stayed his course and so returnèd home,
Where such as bare his absence but with grief,
I mean his friends and nearest companions,   5
Did gratulate his safety with kind words.
And in their conference of what befell
Touching his journey through the world and air
They put forth questions of astrology
Which Faustus answered with such learnèd skill   10
As they admired and wondered at his wit
Now is his fame spread forth in every land.
Amongst the rest the Emperor is one,
Carolus the Fifth, at whose palace now
Faustus is feasted 'mongst his noblemen.   15
What there he did in trial of his art
I leave untold, your eyes shall see performed.

(Exit.)

SCENE I

Enter MARTINO *and* FREDERICK *at several doors.*

MARTINO: What ho, officers, gentlemen!
Hie to the presence to attend the Emperor.
Good Frederick, see the rooms be voided straight,
His Majesty is coming to the hall.
Go back and see the state in readiness.   5
FREDERICK: But where is Bruno, our elected Pope,
That on a fury's back came post from Rome?
Will not his Grace consort the Emperor?
MARTINO: O yes, and with him comes the German conjurer,
The learnèd Faustus, fame of Wittenberg,   10
The wonder of the world for magic art:
And he intends to show great Carolus
The race of all his stout progenitors
And bring in presence of his Majesty
The royal shapes and warlike semblances   15
Of Alexander and his beauteous paramour.
FREDERICK: Where is Benvolio?
MARTINO: Fast asleep, I warrant you.
He took his rouse with stoups of Rhenish wine
So kindly yesternight to Bruno's health
That all this day the sluggard keeps his bed.   20
FREDERICK: See, see, his window's ope. We'll call to him.
MARTINO: What ho, Benvolio!

(Enter BENVOLIO *above at a window, in his nightcap, but-*
toning.)

BENVOLIO: What a devil ail you two?
MARTINO: Speak softly sir, lest the devil hear you,
For Faustus at the court is late arrived   25

IV Chorus   6 **gratulate** express joy in   7 **conference** discussion   14
Carolus the Fifth Charles V (1500–58), Holy Roman Emperor   IV.i.
s.d. **several** separate   2 **presence** presence-chamber   3 **voided straight**
emptied immediately   5 **state** chair of state, throne   8 **consort**
attend   16 **Alexander and his beauteous paramour** Alexander the
Great and his mistress Thaïs   18 **took his rouse with stoups** had drinking bouts with full goblets

At his heels a thousand furies wait
To accomplish whatsoever the doctor please.
BENVOLIO: What of this?
MARTINO: Come, leave thy chamber first, and thou shalt see
30   This conjurer perform such rare exploits
Before the Pope and royal Emperor
As never yet was seen in Germany.
BENVOLIO: Has not the Pope enough of conjuring yet?
He was upon the devil's back late enough!
35   And if he be so far in love with him
I would he would post with him to Rome again.
FREDERICK: Speak, wilt thou come and see this sport?
BENVOLIO: Not I.
MARTINO: Wilt thou stand in thy window and see it then?
BENVOLIO: Ay, and I fall not asleep i' th' meantime.
40 MARTINO: The Emperor is at hand, who comes to see
What wonders by black spells may compassed be.
BENVOLIO: Well, go you attend the Emperor. I am content for
this once to thrust my head out at a window, for they say if a
man be drunk overnight the devil cannot hurt him in the
45   morning. If that be true, I have a charm in my head shall
control him as well as the conjurer, I warrant you.

(Exit [MARTINO with FREDERICK. BENVOLIO remains at win-
dow].)

SCENE II

A *sennet*. CHARLES *the German Emperor*, BRUNO, [DUKE *of*]
SAXONY, FAUSTUS, MEPHOSTOPHILIS, FREDERICK, MARTINO,
and ATTENDANTS.

EMPEROR: Wonder of men, renowned magician,
Thrice-learnèd Faustus, welcome to our court,
This deed of thine in setting Bruno free
From his and our professèd enemy,
5   Shall add more excellence unto thine art
Than if by powerful necromantic spells
Thou could'st command the world's obedience.
For ever be beloved of Carolus!
And if this Bruno thou hast late redeemed
10   In peace possess the triple diadem
And sit in Peter's chair despite of chance,
Thou shalt be famous through all Italy
And honored of the German Emperor.
FAUSTUS: These gracious words, most royal Carolus
15   Shall make poor Faustus to his utmost power
Both love and serve the German Emperor
And lay his life at holy Bruno's feet.
For proof whereof, if so your Grace be pleased,
The doctor stands prepared by power of art
20   To cast his magic charms that shall pierce through
The ebon gates of ever-burning hell,

And hale the stubborn furies from their caves
To compass whatsoe'er your Grace commands.
BENVOLIO: Blood! He speaks terribly. But for all that I do not
greatly believe him. He looks as like a conjurer as the Pope to   25
a costermonger.
EMPEROR: Then Faustus, as thou late didst promise us,
We would behold that famous conqueror
Great Alexander and his paramour
In their true shapes and state majestical,   30
That we may wonder at their excellence.
FAUSTUS: Your Majesty shall see them presently. —
Mephostophilis away,
And with a solemn noise of trumpets' sound
Present before this royal Emperor   35
Great Alexander and his beauteous paramour.
MEPHOSTOPHILIS: Faustus, I will.

(*Exit.*)

BENVOLIO: Well master doctor, an your devils come not away
quickly, you shall have me asleep presently. Zounds, I could
eat myself for anger to think I have been such an ass all this   40
while to stand gaping after the devils' governor and can see
nothing.
FAUSTUS: I'll make you feel something anon if my art fail me
not!
My lord, I must forewarn your Majesty
That when my spirits present the royal shapes   45
Of Alexander and his paramour,
Your Grace demand no questions of the King
But in dumb silence let them come and go.
EMPEROR: Be it as Faustus please; we are content.
BENVOLIO: Ay ay, and I am content too. And thou bring Alex-   50
ander and his paramour before the Emperor, I'll be Actaeon
and turn myself to a stag.
FAUSTUS: (*aside*) And I'll play Diana and send you the horns
presently.

(*Sennet. Enter at one [door] the* EMPEROR ALEXANDER, *at the
other* DARIUS. *They meet.* DARIUS *is thrown down.* ALEXANDER
kills him, takes off his crown, and offering to go out, his PARA-
MOUR *meets him. He embraceth her and sets* DARIUS' *crown
upon her head, and coming back both salute the* EMPEROR; *who
leaving his state offers to embrace them, which* FAUSTUS *seeing
suddenly stays him. Then trumpets cease and music sounds.*)

My gracious lord, you do forget yourself.   55
These are but shadows, not substantial.
EMPEROR: O pardon me, my thoughts are so ravished
With sight of this renownèd Emperor,
That in mine arms I would have compassed him.
But Faustus, since I may not speak to them,   60
To satisfy my longing thoughts at full,
Let me this tell thee: I have heard it said
That this fair lady whilst she lived on earth,
Had on her neck a little wart or mole.
How may I prove that saying to be true?   65

FAUSTUS: Your Majesty may boldly go and see.
EMPEROR: Faustus, I see it plain!
  And in this sight thou better pleasest me
  Than if I gained another monarchy.
70 FAUSTUS: Away, be gone!

(Exit show.)

  See, see my gracious lord, what strange beast is yon that
  thrusts his head out at the window!
EMPEROR: O wondrous sight! See, Duke of Saxony,
  Two spreading horns most strangely fastened
75 Upon the head of young Benvolio.
SAXONY: What, is he asleep or dead?
FAUSTUS: He sleeps my lord, but dreams not of his horns.
EMPEROR: This sport is excellent. We'll call and wake him.
  What ho, Benvolio!
80 BENVOLIO: A plague upon you! Let me sleep awhile.
EMPEROR: I blame thee not to sleep much, having such a head
  of thine own.
SAXONY: Look up Benvolio! 'Tis the Emperor calls.
BENVOLIO: The Emperor! Where? O zounds, my head!
85 EMPEROR: Nay, and thy horns hold, 'tis no matter for thy head,
  for that's armed sufficiently.
FAUSTUS: Why, how now Sir Knight? What, hanged by the
  horns? This is most horrible! Fie fie, pull in your head for
  shame! Let not all the world wonder at you.
90 BENVOLIO: Zounds doctor, is this your villainy?
FAUSTUS: Oh, say not so sir: The doctor has no skill,
  No art, no cunning to present these lords
  Or bring before this royal Emperor
  The mighty monarch, warlike Alexander.
95 If Faustus do it, you are straight resolved
  In bold Actaeon's shape to turn a stag.
  And therefore my lord, so please your Majesty,
  I'll raise a kennel of hounds shall hunt him so
  As all his footmanship shall scarce prevail
100 To keep his carcass from their bloody fangs.
  Ho, Belimote, Argiron, Asterote!
BENVOLIO: Hold, hold! Zounds, he'll raise up a kennel of devils
  I think, anon. Good my lord, entreat for me. 'Sblood, I am
  never able to endure these torments.
105 EMPEROR: Then good master doctor,
  Let me entreat you to remove his horns.
  He has done penance now sufficiently.
FAUSTUS: My gracious lord, not so much for injury done to me,
  as to delight your Majesty with some mirth, hath Faustus
110 justly requited this injurious knight; which being all I desire, I
  am content to remove his horns. Mephostophilis, transform
  him. And hereafter sir, look you speak well of scholars.
BENVOLIO: *(aside)* Speak well of ye! 'Sblood, and scholars be
  such cuckold-makers to clap horns of honest men's heads o'
115 this order, I'll ne'er trust smooth faces and small ruffs more.
  But an I be not revenged for this, would I might be turned to a
  gaping oyster and drink nothing but salt water.

(Exit.)

87–88 **hanged by the horns** (the spreading horns prevent Benvolio from
pulling his head inside of the window) 104 **'Sblood** by God's blood
110 **injurious** insulting 115 **small ruffs** (worn by scholars, in contrast to
the large ruffs worn by courtiers)

EMPEROR: Come Faustus, while the Emperor lives,
  In recompense of this thy high desert,
  Thou shalt command the state of Germany 120
  And live beloved of mighty Carolus.

(Exeunt omnes.)

SCENE III

Enter BENVOLIO, MARTINO, FREDERICK, *and* SOLDIERS.

MARTINO: Nay, sweet Benvolio, let us sway thy thoughts
  From this attempt against the conjurer.
BENVOLIO: Away! You love me not to urge me thus.
  Shall I let slip so great an injury
  When every servile groom jests at my wrongs 5
  And in their rustic gambols proudly say,
  "Benvolio's head was graced with horns today"?
  O, may these eyelids never close again
  Till with my sword I have that conjurer slain!
  If you will aid me in this enterprise, 10
  Then draw your weapons and be resolute;
  If not, depart. Here will Benvolio die
  But Faustus' death shall quit my infamy.
FREDERICK: Nay, we will stay with thee, betide what may,
  And kill that doctor if he come this way. 15
BENVOLIO: Then, gentle Frederick, hie thee to the grove
  And place our servants and our followers
  Close in an ambush there behind the trees.
  By this, I know, the conjurer is near.
  I saw him kneel and kiss the Emperor's hand 20
  And take his leave laden with rich rewards.
  Then soldiers, boldly fight. If Faustus die,
  Take you the wealth, leave us the victory.
FREDERICK: Come soldiers, follow me unto the grove.
  Who kills him shall have gold and endless love. 25

(Exit FREDERICK *with the* SOLDIERS.)*

BENVOLIO: My head is lighter than it was by th' horns—
  But yet my heart more ponderous than my head,
  And pants until I see that conjurer dead.
MARTINO: Where shall we place ourselves, Benvolio?
BENVOLIO: Here will we stay to bide the first assault. 30
  O, were that damnèd hell-hound but in place
  Thou soon should'st see me quit my foul disgrace.

(Enter FREDERICK.)*

FREDERICK: Close, close! The conjurer is at hand
  And all alone comes walking in his gown.
  Be ready then and strike the peasant down! 35
BENVOLIO: Mine be that honor then! Now sword, strike
  home!
  For horns he gave I'll have his head anon.

(Enter FAUSTUS *with the false head.)*

MARTINO: See see, he comes.
BENVOLIO: No words. This blow ends all!

(Strikes FAUSTUS.)*

IV.iii.4 **let slip** ignore 13 **But** unless 13 **quit** avenge 35 **peasant**
low fellow

FAUSTUS: O!

40 FREDERICK: Groan you, master doctor?

BENVOLIO: Break may his heart with groans! Dear Frederick, see,
    Thus will I end his griefs immediately.

(Cuts off FAUSTUS' *false head.)*

MARTINO: Strike with a willing hand! His head is off.

BENVOLIO: The devil's dead, the furies now may laugh.

45 FREDERICK: Was this that stern aspect, that awful frown,
    Made the grim monarch of infernal spirits
    Tremble and quake at his commanding charms?

MARTINO: Was this that damnèd head whose heart conspired
    Benvolio's shame before the Emperor?

50 BENVOLIO: Ay, that's the head, and here the body lies
    Justly rewarded for his villainies.

FREDERICK: Come let's devise how we may add more shame
    To the black scandal of his hated name.

BENVOLIO: First, on his head in quittance of my wrongs

55 I'll nail huge forkèd horns and let them hang
    Within the window where he yoked me first
    That all the world may see my just revenge.

MARTINO: What use shall we put his beard to?

BENVOLIO: We'll sell it to a chimney-sweeper. It will wear out

60 ten birchen brooms, I warrant you.

FREDERICK: What shall eyes do?

BENVOLIO: We'll put out his eyes, and they shall serve for but-
    tons to his lips to keep his tongue from catching cold.

MARTINO: An excellent policy! And now sirs, having divided

65 him, what shall the body do?

*(*FAUSTUS *rises.)*

BENVOLIO: Zounds, the devil's alive again!

FREDERICK: Give him his head for God's sake!

FAUSTUS: Nay keep it. Faustus will have heads and hands,
    Ay, all your hearts, to recompense this deed.

70 Knew you not, traitors, I was limited
    For four and twenty years to breathe on earth?
    And had you cut my body with your swords
    Or hewed this flesh and bones as small as sand,
    Yet in a minute had my spirit returned

75 And I had breathed a man made free from harm.
    But wherefore do I dally my revenge?
    Asteroth, Belimoth, Mephostophilis!

(Enter MEPHOSTOPHILIS *and other* DEVILS.)*

Go horse these traitors on your fiery backs
And mount aloft with them as high as heaven,

80 Thence pitch them headlong to the lowest hell.
Yet stay, the world shall see their misery,
And hell shall after plague their treachery.
Go Belimoth, and take this caitiff hence
And hurl him in some lake of mud and dirt:

85 Take thou this other, drag him through the woods
Amongst the pricking thorns and sharpest briars:
Whilst with my gentle Mephostophilis
This traitor flies unto some steepy rock
That rolling down may break the villain's bones

83 **caitiff** wretch

As he intended to dismember me.   90
Fly hence, dispatch my charge immediately!

FREDERICK: Pity us, gentle Faustus, save our lives!

FAUSTUS: Away!

FREDERICK: He must needs go that the devil drives.

(Exeunt SPIRITS *with the* KNIGHTS.)*

(Enter the ambushed SOLDIERS.)*

1 SOLDIER: Come sirs, prepare yourselves in readiness.
    Make haste to help these noble gentlemen.   95
    I heard them parley with the conjurer.

2 SOLDIER: See where he comes, dispatch, and kill the slave!

FAUSTUS: What's here, an ambush to betray my life?
    Then Faustus, try thy skill. Base peasants, stand!
    For lo, these trees remove at my command   100
    And stand as bulwarks 'twixt yourselves and me
    To shield me from your hated treachery!
    Yet to encounter this your weak attempt
    Behold an army comes incontinent.

*(*FAUSTUS *strikes the door, and enter a* DEVIL *playing on a drum, after him another bearing an ensign, and divers with weapons:* MEPHOSTOPHILIS *with fireworks: they set upon the* SOLDIERS *and drive them out. [Exeunt all.])*

SCENE IV

Enter at several doors BENVOLIO, FREDERICK, *and* MARTINO, *their heads and faces bloody and besmeared with mud and dirt, all having horns on their heads.*

MARTINO: What ho, Benvolio!

BENVOLIO: Here! What, Frederick, ho!

FREDERICK: O, help me gentle friend. Where is Martino?

MARTINO: Dear Frederick, here,
    Half smothered in a lake of mud and dirt,
    Through which the furies dragged me by the heels.   5

FREDERICK: Martino, see, Benvolio's horns again.

MARTINO: O misery! How now Benvolio?

BENVOLIO: Defend me, heaven! Shall I be haunted still?

MARTINO: Nay fear not man, we have no power to kill.

BENVOLIO: My friends transformèd thus! O hellish spite,   10
    Your heads are all set with horns.

FREDERICK: You hit it right:
    It is your own you mean. Feel on your head.

BENVOLIO: Zounds, horns again!

MARTINO: Nay chafe not man, we all are sped.

BENVOLIO: What devil attends this damned magician,
    That spite of spite our wrongs are doubled?   15

FREDERICK: What may we do that we may hide our shames?

BENVOLIO: If we should follow him to work revenge
    He'd join long asses' ears to these huge horns
    And make us laughing-stocks to all the world.

MARTINO: What shall we then do, dear Benvolio?   20

---

100 **remove** move   104 **incontinent** immediately   IV.iv.8 **haunted** (the following line suggests that there is a quibble on "hunted," Benvolio now resembling a stag)   13 **chafe** fret   13 **sped** done for, ruined (because of the horns)

BENVOLIO: I have a castle joining near these woods,
    And thither we'll repair and live obscure
    Till time shall alter this our brutish shapes.
    Sith black disgrace hath thus eclipsed our fame,
25   We'll rather die with grief than live with shame.

(Exeunt omnes.)

SCENE V

Enter FAUSTUS *and the* HORSE-COURSER.

HORSE-COURSER: I beseech your worship, accept of these forty
    dollars.
FAUSTUS: Friend, thou canst not buy so good a horse for so small
    a price. I have no great need to sell him, but if thou likest him
5   for ten dollars more, take him, because I see thou hast a good
    mind to him.
HORSE-COURSER: I beseech you sir, accept of this. I am a very
    poor man and have lost very much of late by horse-flesh, and
    this bargain will set me up again.
10 FAUSTUS: Well, I will not stand with thee. Give me the money.
    Now sirrah, I must tell you that you may ride him o'er hedge
    and ditch and spare him not. But, do you hear, in any case
    ride him not into the water.
HORSE-COURSER: How sir, not into the water! Why, will he not
15   drink of all waters?
FAUSTUS: Yes, he will drink of all waters, but ride him not into
    the water: o'er hedge and ditch or where thou wilt, but not
    into the water. Go bid the hostler deliver him unto you, and
    remember what I say.
20 HORSE-COURSER: I warrant you sir. O joyful day! Now am I a
    made man forever.

(Exit.)

FAUSTUS: What art thou, Faustus, but a man condemned to
    die?
    Thy fatal time draws to a final end;
    Despair doth drive distrust into my thoughts.
25   Confound these passions with a quiet sleep.
    Tush, Christ did call the thief upon the cross!
    Then rest thee Faustus, quiet in conceit.

(He sits to sleep.)

(Enter the HORSE-COURSER *wet.)*

HORSE-COURSER: O what a cozening doctor was this! I riding
    my horse into the water, thinking some hidden mystery had
30   been in the horse, I had nothing under me but a little straw
    and had much ado to escape drowning. Well, I'll go rouse
    him and make him give me my forty dollars again. Ho, sirrah
    doctor, you cozening scab! Master doctor, awake and rise,
    and give me my money again, for your horse is turned to a
35   bottle of hay. Master doctor!

24 **Sith** since   IV.v. s.d. **Horse-courser** horse trader 2 **dollars** German
coins 8 **horse-flesh** (the possibility of a quibble on "whores' flesh" is
increased by "set me up" and "stand" in the ensuing dialogue) 10
stand haggle 16 **drink of all waters** i.e., go anywhere 23 **fatal time**
life span 26 **Christ . . . cross** (in Luke 23:39–43 Christ promised one
of the thieves that he would be with Christ in paradise) 27 **quiet in
conceit** with a quiet mind 28 **cozening** deceiving 35 **bottle**
bundle

(He pulls off his leg.)

    Alas, I am undone! What shall I do? I have pulled off his leg.
FAUSTUS: O help, help! The villain hath murdered me!
HORSE-COURSER: Murder or not murder, now he has but one
    leg I'll outrun him, and cast this leg into some ditch or other.
FAUSTUS: Stop him, stop him, stop him! — Ha, ha, ha! Faustus 40
    hath his leg again, and the horse-courser a bundle of hay for
    his forty dollars.

(Enter WAGNER.)

    How now, Wagner? What news with thee?
WAGNER: If it please you, the Duke of Vanholt doth earnestly
    entreat your company, and hath sent some of his men to at- 45
    tend you with provision fit for your journey.
FAUSTUS: The Duke of Vanholt's an honorable gentleman, and
    one to whom I must be no niggard of my cunning. Come,
    away!

(Exeunt.)

SCENE VI

Enter [ROBIN] *the clown,* DICK, HORSE-COURSER, *and a*
CARTER.

CARTER: Come my masters, I'll bring you to the best beer in
    Europe. What ho, hostess! Where be these whores?

(Enter HOSTESS.)

HOSTESS: How now? What lack you? What, my old guests,
    welcome.
ROBIN: *(aside)* Sirrah Dick, dost thou know why I stand so mute? 5
DICK: *(aside)* No Robin, why is't?
ROBIN: *(aside)* I am eighteen pence on the score. But say noth-
    ing. See if she have forgotten me.
HOSTESS: Who's this that stands so solemnly by himself? What,
    my old guest! 10
ROBIN: O, hostess, how do you? I hope my score stands still.
HOSTESS: Ay, there's no doubt of that, for methinks you make no
    haste to wipe it out.
DICK: Why hostess, I say, fetch us some beer!
HOSTESS: You shall, presently. — Look up into th' hall there, 15
    ho!

(Exit.)

DICK: Come sirs, what shall we do now till mine hostess comes?
CARTER: Marry sir, I'll tell you the bravest tale how a conjurer
    served me. You know Doctor Faustus?
HORSE-COURSER: Ay, a plague take him! Here's some on's have 20
    cause to know him. Did he conjure thee too?
CARTER: I'll tell you how he served me. As I was going to Wit-
    tenberg t'other day with a load of hay, he met me and asked
    me what he should give me for as much hay as he could eat.
    Now sir, I, thinking that a little would serve his turn, bad him 25
    take as much as he would for three farthings. So he presently
    gave me my money and fell to eating; and as I am a cursen
    man, he never left eating till he had eat up all my load of hay.
ALL: O monstrous, eat a whole load of hay!

IV.vi.7 **on the score** in debt 27 **cursen** i.e., Christian (dialect form)

30 ROBIN: Yes yes, that may be, for I have heard of one that has eat a load of logs.

HORSE-COURSER: Now sirs, you shall hear how villainously he served me. I went to him yesterday to buy a horse of him, and he would by no means sell him under forty dollars. So sir,
35 because I knew him to be such a horse as would run over hedge and ditch and never tire, I gave him his money. So, when I had my horse, Doctor Faustus bade me ride him night and day and spare him no time. "But," quoth he, "in any case ride him not into the water." Now sir, I thinking the horse had
40 had some quality that he would not have me know of, what did I but rid him into a great river — and when I came just in the midst, my horse vanished away and I sate straddling upon a bottle of hay.

ALL: O brave doctor!

45 HORSE-COURSER: But you shall hear how bravely I served him for it. I went me home to his house, and there I found him asleep. I kept ahallowing and whooping in his ears, but all could not wake him. I seeing that, took him by the leg and never rested pulling till I had pulled me his leg quite off, and
50 now 'tis at home in mine hostry.

DICK: And has the doctor but one leg then? That's excellent, for one of his devils turned me into the likeness of an ape's face.

CARTER: Some more drink, hostess!

ROBIN: Hark you, we'll into another room and drink awhile, and
55 then we'll go seek out the doctor.

(Exeunt omnes.)

SCENE VII

Enter the DUKE OF VANHOLT, *his [*SERVANTS,*]* DUCHESS, FAUSTUS, *and* MEPHOSTOPHILIS.

DUKE: Thanks master doctor, for these pleasant sights. Nor know I how sufficiently to recompense your great deserts in erecting that enchanted castle in the air, the sight whereof so delighted me,
5 As nothing in the world could please me more.

FAUSTUS: I do think myself, my good lord, highly recompensed in that it pleaseth your Grace to think but well of that which Faustus hath performed. — But gracious lady, it may be that you have taken no pleasure in those sights. Therefore I pray
10 you tell me what is the thing you most desire to have: be it in the world it shall be yours. I have heard that great-bellied women do long for things are rare and dainty.

DUCHESS: True master doctor, and since I find you so kind, I will make known unto you what my heart desires to have: and
15 were it now summer, as it is January, a dead time of the winter, I would request no better meat than a dish of ripe grapes.

FAUSTUS: This is but a small matter. Go Mephostophilis, away!

(Exit MEPHOSTOPHILIS.*)*

Madam, I will do more than this for your content.

(Enter MEPHOSTOPHILIS *again with the grapes.)*

Here, now taste ye these. They should be good,
20 For they come from a far country, I can tell you.

DUKE: This makes me wonder more than all the rest, that at this time of the year when every tree is barren of his fruit, from whence you had these ripe grapes.

FAUSTUS: Please it your Grace, the year is divided into two cir-
25 cles over the whole world, so that when it is winter with us, in the contrary circle it is likewise summer with them, as in India, Saba, and such countries that lie far east, where they have fruit twice a year. From whence, by means of a swift spirit that I have, I had these grapes brought as you see.

DUCHESS: And trust me, they are the sweetest grapes that e'er I
30 tasted.

(The CLOWNS [ROBIN, DICK, CARTER, *and* HORSE-COURSER] *bounce at the gate within.)*

DUKE: What rude disturbers have we at the gate?
Go pacify their fury, set it ope,
And then demand of them what they would have.

(They knock again and call out to talk with FAUSTUS.*)*

A SERVANT: Why, how now masters, what a coil is there! 35
What is the reason you disturb the Duke?

DICK: We have no reason for it, therefore a fig for him!

SERVANT: Why saucy varlets, dare you be so bold!

HORSE-COURSER: I hope sir, we have wit enough to be more bold than welcome. 40

SERVANT: It appears so. Pray be bold elsewhere
And trouble not the Duke.

DUKE: What would they have?

SERVANT: They all cry out to speak with Doctor Faustus.

CARTER: Ay, and we will speak with him. 45

DUKE: Will you sir? Commit the rascals.

DICK: Commit with us! He were as good commit with his father as commit with us!

FAUSTUS: I do beseech your Grace, let them come in.
They are good subject for a merriment. 50

DUKE: Do as thou wilt, Faustus, I give thee leave.

FAUSTUS: I thank your Grace.

(Enter [ROBIN] *the clown,* DICK, CARTER, *and* HORSE-COURSER.*)*

Why, how now my good friends?
'Faith, you are too outrageous; but come near,
I have procured your pardons. Welcome all.

ROBIN: Nay sir, we will be welcome for our money, and we will 55
pay for what we take. What ho, give's half a dozen of beer here, and be hanged!

FAUSTUS: Nay, hark you, can you tell me where you are?

CARTER: Ay, marry can I, we are under heaven.

SERVANT: Ay, but Sir Sauce-box, know you in what place? 60

HORSE-COURSER: Ay ay, the house is good enough to drink in.
Zounds, fill us some beer, or we'll break all the barrels in the house and dash out all your brains with your bottles.

30–31 **eat a load of logs** been drunk 50 **hostry** inn IV.vii.11 **great-bellied** i.e., pregnant 16 **meat** food

24 **two circles** i.e., the northern and the southern hemispheres (though later in the speech he talks of east and west rather than of north and south) 31s.d. **bounce** knock 35 **coil** turmoil 36 **reason** (pronounced like "raisin," leading to the quibble on "fig"; a "fig" here is an obscene contemptuous gesture in which the hand is clenched and the thumb is thrust between the first and second fingers, making the thumb resemble the stem of a fig, or a penis) 45 **Commit** imprison (Dick proceeds to quibble on the idea of committing adultery)

FAUSTUS: Be not so furious. Come, you shall have beer.
65   My lord, beseech you give me leave awhile;
    I'll gage my credit 'twill content your Grace.
DUKE: With all my heart, kind doctor, please thyself.
    Our servants and our court's at thy command.
FAUSTUS: I humbly thank your Grace. — Then fetch some beer.
70 HORSE-COURSER: Ay marry, there spake a doctor indeed! And
    'faith, I'll drink a health to thy wooden leg for that word.
FAUSTUS: My wooden leg? What dost thou mean by that?
CARTER: Ha, ha, ha, dost hear him Dick? He has forgot his leg.
HORSE-COURSER: Ay ay, he does not stand much upon that.
75 FAUSTUS: No, 'faith, not much upon a wooden leg.
CARTER: Good lord, that flesh and blood should be so frail
    with your worship! Do not you remember a horse-courser
    you sold a horse to?
FAUSTUS: Yes, I remember I sold one a horse.
80 CARTER: And do you remember you bid he should not ride into
    the water?
FAUSTUS: Yes, I do very well remember that.
CARTER: And do you remember nothing of your leg?
FAUSTUS: No, in good sooth.
85 CARTER: Then I pray remember your curtsy.
FAUSTUS: I thank you sir.
CARTER: 'Tis not so much worth. I pray you tell me one
    thing.
FAUSTUS: What's that?
90 CARTER: Be both your legs bedfellows every night together?
FAUSTUS: Would'st thou make a colossus of me that thou askest
    me such questions?
CARTER: No, truly sir, I would make nothing of you, but I would
    fain know that.

(Enter HOSTESS with drink.)

95 FAUSTUS: Then I assure thee certainly they are.
CARTER: I thank you, I am fully satisfied.
FAUSTUS: But wherefore dost thou ask?
CARTER: For nothing, sir, but methinks you should have a
    wooden bedfellow of one of 'em.
100 HORSE-COURSER: Why, do you hear sir, did not I pull off one of
    your legs when you were asleep?
FAUSTUS: But I have it again now I am awake. Look you here sir.
ALL: O horrible! Had the doctor three legs?
CARTER: Do you remember sir, how you cozened me and eat up
105   my load of —

(FAUSTUS charms him dumb.)

DICK: Do you remember how you made me wear an ape's —

(FAUSTUS charms him.)

HORSE-COURSER: You whoreson conjuring scab! Do you re-
    member how you cozened me with a ho —

(FAUSTUS charms him.)

ROBIN: Ha' you forgotten me? You think to carry it away with
110   your "hey-pass" and "re-pass"? Do you remember the dog's
    fa —

([FAUSTUS charms him.] Exeunt CLOWNS.)

HOSTESS: Who pays for the ale? Hear you master doctor, now
    you have sent away my guests, I pray who shall pay me for
    my a —

([FAUSTUS charms her.] Exit HOSTESS.)

DUCHESS: My Lord,   115
    We are much beholding to this learnèd man.
DUKE: So are we madam, which we will recompense
    With all the love and kindness that we may:
    His artful sport drives all sad thoughts away.

(Exeunt.)

— ACT FIVE —

SCENE I

Thunder and lightning. Enter DEVILS with covered dishes:
MEPHOSTOPHILIS leads them into FAUSTUS' study. Then enter
WAGNER.

WAGNER: I think my master means to die shortly. He has made
    his will and given me his wealth: his house, his goods, and
    store of golden plate — besides two thousand ducats ready
    coined. I wonder what he means. If death were nigh, he
    would not frolic thus. He's now at supper with the scholars, 5
    where there's such belly-cheer as Wagner in his life ne'er saw
    the like! And see where they come. Belike the feast is done.

(Exit.)

(Enter FAUSTUS, MEPHOSTOPHILIS, and two or three
SCHOLARS.)

1 SCHOLAR: Master Doctor Faustus, since our conference
    about fair ladies, which was the beautifulest in all the world,
    we have determined with ourselves that Helen of Greece was 10
    the admirablest lady that ever lived. Therefore master doctor,
    if you will do us so much favor as to let us see that peerless
    dame of Greece, whom all the world admires for majesty, we
    should think ourselves much beholding unto you.
FAUSTUS: Gentlemen,   15
    For that I know your friendship is unfeigned,
    It is not Faustus' custom to deny
    The just request of those that wish him well:
    You shall behold that peerless dame of Greece
    No otherwise for pomp or majesty   20
    Than when Sir Paris crossed the seas with her
    And brought the spoils to rich Dardania.
    Be silent then, for danger is in words.

(Music sounds. MEPHOSTOPHILIS brings in HELEN: she passeth
over the stage.)

2 SCHOLAR: Was this fair Helen, whose admired worth
    Made Greece with ten years' wars afflict poor Troy?   25

---

66 **gage** pledge   74 **stand much upon** (quibble on "attach much impor-
tanct to")   85 **curtsy** (also called "a leg," hence there is a quibble on the
Carter's previous speech)   91 **colossus** huge statue in the harbor at
Rhodes, between whose legs ships were said to have sailed   110 **hey-
pass, re-pass** conjuring expressions

V.i.7 **Belike** most likely   1–7 **I think . . . done** (though printed as prose
in the quarto, as here, perhaps this speech should be verse, the lines
ending *shortly, wealth, plate, coined, nigh, supper, belly-cheer, like,
done*)   22 **spoils** booty (including Helen)   22 **Dardania** Troy

3 SCHOLAR: Too simple is my wit to tell her worth,
　　Whom all the world admires for majesty.
1 SCHOLAR: Now we have seen the pride of nature's work,
　　We'll take our leaves, and for this blessèd sight
30　Happy and blest be Faustus evermore.
FAUSTUS: Gentlemen, farewell, the same wish I to you.

(Exeunt SCHOLARS.*)*

(Enter an OLD MAN.*)*

OLD MAN: O gentle Faustus, leave this damnèd art,
　　This magic that will charm thy soul to hell
　　And quite bereave thee of salvation.
35　Though thou hast now offended like man,
　　Do not persever in it like a devil.
　　Yet, yet, thou hast an amiable soul
　　If sin by custom grow not into nature.
　　Then, Faustus, will repentance come too late!
40　Then, thou are banished from the sight of heaven!
　　No mortal can express the pains of hell!
　　It may be this my exhortation
　　Seems harsh and all unpleasant. Let it not.
　　For gentle son, I speak it not in wrath
45　Or envy of thee but in tender love
　　And pity of thy future misery:
　　And so have hope that this my kind rebuke,
　　Checking thy body, may amend thy soul.
FAUSTUS: Where art thou, Faustus? Wretch, what hast thou
　　done!

*(*MEPHOSTOPHILIS *gives him a dagger.)*

50　Hell claims his right and with a roaring voice
　　Says "Faustus, come, thine hour is almost come!"
　　And Faustus now will come to do thee right!
OLD MAN: O stay, good Faustus, stay thy desperate steps!
　　I see an angel hover o'er thy head,
55　And with a vial full of precious grace
　　Offers to pour the same into thy soul:
　　Then call for mercy and avoid despair.
FAUSTUS: O friend,
　　I feel thy words to comfort my distressèd soul:
60　Leave me awhile to ponder on my sins.
OLD MAN: Faustus, I leave thee, but with grief of heart,
　　Fearing the enemy of thy hapless soul.

(Exit.)

FAUSTUS: Accursèd Faustus! Wretch, what hast thou done!
　　I do repent, and yet I do despair:
65　Hell strives with grace for conquest in my breast!
　　What shall I do to shun the snares of death?
MEPHOSTOPHILIS: Thou traitor Faustus, I arrest thy soul
　　For disobedience to my sovereign lord.
　　Revolt, or I'll in piecemeal tear thy flesh.
70　FAUSTUS: I do repent I e'er offended him.
　　Sweet Mephostophilis, entreat thy lord
　　To pardon my unjust presumption,

And with my blood again I will confirm
　　The former vow I made to Lucifer.
MEPHOSTOPHILIS: Do it then, Faustus, with unfeignèd heart　75
　　Lest greater dangers do attend thy drift.
FAUSTUS: Torment, sweet friend, that base and agèd man
　　That durst dissuade me from thy Lucifer,
　　With greatest torment that our hell affords.
MEPHOSTOPHILIS: His faith is great. I cannot touch his soul.　80
　　But what I may afflict his body with
　　I will attempt, which is but little worth.
FAUSTUS: One thing, good servant, let me crave of thee
　　To glut the longing of my heart's desire:
　　That I may have unto my paramour　　　　　　85
　　That heavenly Helen which I saw of late,
　　Whose sweet embraces may extinguish clear
　　Those thoughts that do dissuade me from my vow,
　　And keep mine oath I made to Lucifer.
MEPHOSTOPHILIS: This or what else my Faustus shall desire　90
　　Shall be performed in twinkling of an eye.

(Enter HELEN *again, passing over between two* CUPIDS.*)*

FAUSTUS: Was this the face that launched a thousand ships
　　And burnt the topless towers of Ilium?
　　Sweet Helen, make me immortal with a kiss.
　　Her lips suck forth my soul. See where it flies!　　95
　　Come Helen, come, give me my soul again.
　　Here will I dwell, for heaven is in these lips
　　And all is dross that is not Helena.
　　I will be Paris, and for love of thee
　　Instead of Troy shall Wittenberg be sacked;　　100
　　And I will combat with weak Menelaus
　　And wear thy colors on my plumèd crest.
　　Yea, I will wound Achilles in the heel
　　And then return to Helen for a kiss.
　　O, thou art fairer than the evening's air　　　105
　　Clad in the beauty of a thousand stars,
　　Brighter art thou than flaming Jupiter
　　When he appeared to hapless Semele,
　　More lovely than the monarch of the sky
　　In wanton Arethusa's azure arms,　　　　　110
　　And none but thou shalt be my paramour.　　　*(Exeunt.)*

SCENE II

Thunder. Enter LUCIFER, BELZEBUB, *and* MEPHOSTOPHILIS.

LUCIFER: Thus from infernal Dis do we ascend
　　To view the subjects of our monarchy,
　　Those souls which sin seals the black sons of hell.
　　'Mong which as chief, Faustus, we come to thee,
　　Bringing with us lasting damnation　　　　　5

---

93 **topless** i.e., so tall their tops are beyond sight　93 **Ilium** Troy　101 **Menelaus** Greek king, deserted by Helen for Paris　103 **Achilles** greatest of the Greek warriors　108 **Semele** beloved by Jupiter, who promised to do whatever she wished; she asked to see him in his full splendor, and the sight incinerated her　110 **Arethusa** a nymph, here apparently loved by Jupiter, "the monarch of the sky"　V.ii. s.d. **Enter Lucifer, Belzebub, and Mephostophilis** (probably they rise out of a trapdoor and ascend to the upper stage, Mephostophilis descending to the main stage at line 85)　1 **infernal Dis** the underworld (named for its ruler)

34 **bereave** deprive　36 **persever** (accent on second syllable)　37 **an amiable soul** a soul worthy of love　48 **Checking** rebuking　69 **Revolt** return (to your allegiance)

To wait upon thy soul. The time is come
Which makes it forfeit.
MEPHOSTOPHILIS: And this gloomy night
Here in this room will wretched Faustus be.
BELZEBUB: And here we'll stay
10   To mark him how he doth demean himself.
MEPHOSTOPHILIS: How should he but in desperate lunacy?
Fond worldling, now his heart blood dries with grief.
His conscience kills it, and his laboring brain
Begets a world of idle fantasies
15   To overreach the devil; but all in vain:
His store of pleasures must be sauced with pain!
He and his servant Wagner are at hand.
Both come from drawing Faustus' lastest will.
See where they come.

(Enter FAUSTUS and WAGNER.)

20   FAUSTUS: Say Wagner, thou hast perused my will;
How dost thou like it?
WAGNER: Sir, so wondrous well
As in all humble duty I do yield
My life and lasting service for your love.

(Enter the SCHOLARS.)

FAUSTUS: Gramercies, Wagner—Welcome gentlemen.

(Exit WAGNER.)

25   1 SCHOLAR: Now worthy Faustus, methinks your looks are
changed.
FAUSTUS: O gentlemen!
2 SCHOLAR: What ails Faustus?
FAUSTUS: Ah my sweet chamber-fellow, had I lived with thee,
then had I lived still!—But now must die eternally. Look sirs,
30   comes he not, comes he not?
1 SCHOLAR: O my dear Faustus, what imports this fear?
2 SCHOLAR: Is all our pleasure turned to melancholy?
3 SCHOLAR: He is not well with being over-solitary.
2 SCHOLAR: If it be so, we'll have physicians and Faustus shall
35   be cured.
3 SCHOLAR: 'Tis but a surfeit sir, fear nothing.
FAUSTUS: A surfeit of deadly sin that hath damned both body
and soul!
2 SCHOLAR: Yet Faustus, look up to heaven and remember
40   mercy is infinite.
FAUSTUS: But Faustus' offense can ne'er be pardoned. The serpent that tempted Eve may be saved, but not Faustus! O gentlemen, hear with patience and tremble not at my speeches.
Though my heart pant and quiver to remember that I have
45   been a student here these thirty years, O, would I had never
seen Wittenberg, never read book.—And what wonders I
have done all Germany can witness, yea all the world, for
which Faustus hath lost both Germany and the world, yea
heaven itself—heaven, the seat of God, the throne of the
50   blessèd, the kingdom of joy—and must remain in hell forever! hell, O hell forever! Sweet friends, what shall become of
Faustus being in hell forever?
2 SCHOLAR: Yet Faustus, call on God.
FAUSTUS: On God, whom Faustus hath abjured? On God,
55   whom Faustus hath blasphemed? O my God, I would weep,

but the devil draws in my tears! Gush forth blood instead of
tears, yea life and soul! O, he stays my tongue! I would lift up
my hands, but see, they hold 'em, they hold 'em!
ALL: Who, Faustus?
FAUSTUS: Why, Lucifer and Mephostophilis. O gentlemen, I   60
gave them my soul for my cunning.
ALL: O, God forbid!
FAUSTUS: God forbade it indeed, but Faustus hath done it. For the
vain pleasure of four and twenty years hath Faustus lost eternal joy and felicity. I writ them a bill with mine own blood.   65
The date is expired. This is the time. And he will fetch me.
1 SCHOLAR: Why did not Faustus tell us of this before, that di-
vines might have prayed for thee?
FAUSTUS: Oft have I thought to have done so, but the devil
threatened to tear me in pieces if I named God—to fetch me   70
body and soul if I once gave ear to divinity; and now 'tis too
late! Gentlemen, away, lest you perish with me.
2 SCHOLAR: O, what may we do to save Faustus?
FAUSTUS: Talk not of me but save yourselves and depart.
3 SCHOLAR: God will strengthen me. I will stay with Faustus.   75
1 SCHOLAR: Tempt not God, sweet friend, but let us into the
next room and pray for him.
FAUSTUS: Ay, pray for me, pray for me. And what noise soever
you hear, come not unto me, for nothing can rescue me.
2 SCHOLAR: Pray thou, and we will pray that God may have   80
mercy upon thee.
FAUSTUS: Gentlemen, farewell! If I live till morning, I'll visit
you. If not, Faustus is gone to hell.
ALL: Faustus, farewell.

(Exeunt SCHOLARS.)

MEPHOSTOPHILIS: Ay, Faustus, now thou hast no hope of   85
heaven.
Therefore, despair! Think only upon hell,
For that must be thy mansion, there to dwell.
FAUSTUS: O thou bewitching fiend, 'twas thy temptation
Hath robbed me of eternal happiness.
MEPHOSTOPHILIS: I do confess it Faustus, and rejoice.   90
'Twas I, that when thou wert i' the way to heaven
Damned up thy passage. When thou took'st the book
To view the Scriptures, then I turned the leaves
And led thine eye.
What, weep'st thou? 'Tis too late, despair, farewell!   95
Fools that will laugh on earth, most weep in hell.

(Exit.)

(Enter the GOOD ANGEL and the BAD ANGEL at several doors.)

GOOD ANGEL: O Faustus, if thou hadst given ear to me
Innumerable joys had followèd thee.
But thou did'st love the world.
BAD ANGEL: Gave ear to me,
And now must taste hell's pains perpetually.   100
GOOD ANGEL: O, what will all thy riches, pleasures, pomps
Avail thee now?
BAD ANGEL: Nothing but vex thee more,
To want in hell, that had on earth such store.

(Music while the throne descends.)

---

12 **Fond** foolish   24 **Gramercies** thank you   36 **a surfeit** indigestion   103s.d. **throne** (symbolic of heaven)   110 **affected** preferred

GOOD ANGEL: O, thou hast lost celestial happiness,
105   Pleasures unspeakable, bliss without end.
    Had'st thou affected sweet divinity,
    Hell or the devil had had no power on thee.
    Had'st thou kept on that way, Faustus behold
    In what resplendent glory thou had'st sat
110   In yonder throne, like those bright shining saints,
    And triumphed over hell! That hast thou lost.

(Throne ascends.)

    And now, poor soul, must thy good angel leave thee,
    The jaws of hell are open to receive thee.

(Exit.)

(Hell is discovered.)

BAD ANGEL: Now Faustus, let thine eyes with horror stare
115   Into that vast perpetual torture-house.
    There are the furies, tossing damnèd souls
    On burning forks. Their bodies boil in lead.
    There are live quarters broiling on the coals,
    That ne'er can die: this ever-burning chair
120   Is for o'er-tortured souls to rest them in.
    These that are fed with sops of flaming fire
    Were gluttons and loved only delicates
    And laughed to see the poor starve at their gates.
    But yet all these are nothing. Thou shalt see
125   Ten thousand tortures that more horrid be.
FAUSTUS: O, I have seen enough to torture me.
BAD ANGEL: Nay, thou must feel them, taste the smart of all:
    He that loves pleasure must for pleasure fall.
    And so I leave thee Faustus, till anon:
130   Then wilt thou tumble in confusion.   *(Exit.)*

(The clock strikes eleven.)

FAUSTUS: O Faustus!
    Now hast thou but one bare hour to live
    And then thou must be damned perpetually.
    Stand still, you ever-moving spheres of Heaven
135   That time may cease and midnight never come:
    Fair nature's eye, rise, rise again and make
    Perpetual day, or let this hour be but a year,
    A month, a week, a natural day—
    That Faustus may repent and save his soul.
140   *O lente lente currite noctis equi!*
    The stars move still, time runs, the clock will strike:
    The devil will come, and Faustus must be damned!
    O, I'll leap up to my God! Who pulls me down?
    See, see where Christ's blood streams in the firmament!
145   One drop of blood will save me. O my Christ!—
    Rend not my heart for naming of my Christ!
    Yet will I call on Him! O spare me, Lucifer!—
    Where is it now? 'Tis gone: and see where God
    Stretcheth out His arm and bends His ireful brows!
150   Mountains and hills, come, come and fall on me
    And hide me from the heavy wrath of God!
    No?

    Then will I headlong run into the earth.
    Gape earth! O no, it will not harbor me.
    You stars that reigned at my nativity,   155
    Whose influence hath allotted death and hell,
    Now draw up Faustus like a foggy mist
    Into the entrails of yon laboring cloud
    That when you vomit forth into the air,
    My limbs may issue from your smoky mouths—   160
    But let my soul mount and ascend to heaven!

(The watch strikes.)

    O half the hour is passed! 'Twill all be passed anon!
    O God,
    If thou wilt not have mercy on my soul
    Yet for Christ's sake, whose blood hath ransomed me,   165
    Impose some end to my incessant pain!
    Let Faustus live in hell a thousand years,
    A hundred thousand, and at last be saved!
    No end is limited to damnèd souls!
    Why wert thou not a creature wanting soul?   170
    Or why is this immortal that thou hast?
    O, Pythagoras' metempsychosis, were that true
    This soul should fly from me and I be changed
    Into some brutish beast.
    All beasts are happy, for when they die   175
    Their souls are soon dissolved in elements.
    But mine must live still to be plagued in hell!
    Cursed be the parents that engendered me!
    No Faustus, curse thyself, curse Lucifer
    That hath deprived thee of the joys of heaven.   180

(The clock strikes twelve.)

    It strikes, it strikes! Now body, turn to air,
    Or Lucifer will bear thee quick to hell!:
    O soul, be changed into small water-drops
    And fall into the ocean, ne'er be found.

(Thunder, and enter the DEVILS.)

    My God, my God! Look not so fierce on me!   185
    Adders and serpents, let me breathe awhile!
    Ugly Hell, gape not! Come not Lucifer!
    I'll burn my books!—O Mephostophilis!

(Exeunt [DEVILS with FAUSTUS].)

SCENE III

(Enter the SCHOLARS.)

1 SCHOLAR: Come gentlemen, let us go visit Faustus,
    For such a dreadful night was never seen
    Since first the world's creation did begin!
    Such fearful shrieks and cries were never heard!
    Pray heaven, the doctor have escaped the danger.   5

---

118 **quarters** bodies   130 **confusion** destruction   140 **O . . . equi** slowly, slowly run, O horses of the night (Latin, adapted from Ovid's *Amores*, I.xiii,40, where a lover regretfully thinks of the coming of the dawn)

169 **limited to** set for   172 **metempsychosis** transmigration of souls (a doctrine held by Pythagoras, philosopher of the sixth century B.C.) 177 **still** always   182 **quick** alive   188s.d. **Exeunt [Devils with Faustus]** (possibly the devils drag Faustus into the "hell" that was "discovered" at V.ii.113, and then toss his limbs onto the stage, or possibly the limbs are revealed in V.iii.6 by withdrawing a curtain at the rear of the stage)

2 SCHOLAR: O, help us heaven, see, here are Faustus' limbs
    All torn asunder by the hand of death!
3 SCHOLAR: The devils whom Faustus served have torn him
      thus:
    For 'twixt the hours of twelve and one, methought
10   I heard him shriek and call aloud for help,
    At which self time the house seemed all on fire
    With dreadful horror of these damnèd fiends.
2 SCHOLAR: Well gentlemen, though Faustus' end be such
    As every Christian heart laments to think on,
15   Yet for he was a scholar once admired
    For wondrous knowledge in our German schools,
    We'll give his mangled limbs due burial;
    And all the students, clothed in mourning black,
    Shall wait upon his heavy funeral.

(Exeunt.)

V.iii.11 **self** same   19 **wait upon** attend   19 **heavy** sad

(Enter CHORUS.*)*

    Cut is the branch that might have grown full straight   20
    And burnèd is Apollo's laurel bough
    That sometime grew within this learnèd man.
    Faustus is gone: regard his hellish fall,
    Whose fiendful fortune may exhort the wise
    Only to wonder at unlawful things,   25
    Whose deepness doth entice such forward wits
    To practice more than heavenly power permits.

(Exit.)

(Terminat hora diem; terminat Author opus.)

Chorus 21 **laurel bough** symbol of wisdom, here associated with Apollo, god of divination   25 **Only to wonder at** i.e., merely to observe at a distance, with awe   27s.d. **Terminat . . . opus** the hour ends the day; the author ends his work (this Latin tag probably is not Marlowe's but the printer's, though it is engaging to believe Marlowe wrote it, ending his play at midnight, the hour of Faustus' death)

WILLIAM SHAKESPEARE

Given the fact that William Shakespeare (1564–1616) was a commoner and that he worked in the ephemeral trades of the theater, what we know about his life is extraordinarily rich and revealing, especially in comparison to the lives of other playwrights of the period like Christopher Marlowe or John Webster. William Shakespeare was born in Stratford-upon-Avon, a town to the northwest of London in Warwickshire. He was baptized on April 26, 1564, and was probably born a few days earlier — his birth date is conventionally given as April 23, the feast day of St. George, the patron saint of England, and the day on which Shakespeare died fifty-two years later in 1616, again at his home in Stratford. One of eight children, Shakespeare was the son of a glover — a tradesman who worked with a variety of leather goods. It is not known whether Shakespeare attended the local school, the King's New School, but like other schools of the period it would have provided him with an extensive grounding in Latin grammar, rhetoric, and literature. Later in his career, Shakespeare often drew on works he could have read at such a school: plays by Terence and Plautus, the poetry of Vergil and Ovid, the writings of Caesar.

He married Anne Hathaway in November of 1582; she was twenty-six and he was eighteen. In May of 1583 they had their first daughter, Susannah, followed by twins, Hamnet and Judith, born in 1585. Although his wife and children remained in Stratford throughout his career, Shakespeare went to London sometime in the late 1580s, possibly joining one of the theater companies that passed through Stratford.

By the 1590s, Shakespeare was established in London as an up-and-coming playwright; he was associated with the Lord Chamberlain's Men; he had written several plays on English history; and he was at work on several comedies and tragedies. When plague closed the theaters in London from the summer of 1592 through the spring of 1594, Shakespeare wrote two narrative poems, *Venus and Adonis* and *The Rape of Lucrece*, which he dedicated to Henry Wriothesley, the third Earl of Southampton, in a bid for patronage. He later wrote *The Phoenix and the Turtle* and circulated a brilliant and ambitious sequence of sonnets in manuscript before publishing it in 1609. As a shareholder of the Lord Chamberlain's Men, Shakespeare would have had many duties; no doubt he acted many parts, and we know he appeared in two plays by his contemporary Ben Jonson — *Every Man In His Humour* and *Sejanus*. In 1598, the Lord Chamberlain's men tore down The Theatre, brought the timbers south of the city and used them to build a new theater, the Globe. The Globe would remain the principal public-theater venue for the rest of Shakespeare's career, complemented by court and private-theater performances.

Shakespeare became the most popular playwright in London. He profited handsomely from his efforts at the Globe and from the patronage of the court, particularly after James I came to the throne in 1603 and took on the Lord Chamberlain's company as his own King's Men. Shakespeare used his income to buy a large house — called New Place — in Stratford, and throughout his career added to his property there; he retired and returned to Stratford in 1613. He drew up a will shortly before he died in 1616, leaving property to his family and mentioning gifts for several of his friends, including members of the King's Men: Richard Burbage, John Heminges, and Henry Condell. Heminges and Condell proved true to Shakespeare, for in 1623 they took Shakespeare's plays and published them in a single large volume. In an era when plays were not regarded as "literature," this was an important event. Although many of Shakespeare's plays had been published individually during his lifetime, roughly half of Shakespeare's plays (*Macbeth*, *Antony and Cleopatra*, and *The Tempest*, for instance) existed only in manuscript form at Shakespeare's death and certainly would not have survived without the efforts of Heminges and Condell. This complete volume is now usually called the "First Folio" because it is printed in a large, FOLIO-sized format (about twice the dimensions of this book). The First Folio contains 36 of Shakespeare's plays; two more plays published in his lifetime (*Pericles* and *The Two Noble Kinsmen*) were left out of the Folio, and it is generally thought that Shakespeare contributed to a thirty-ninth play, *Sir Thomas More*. Finally, although many people have advanced the thesis that someone else actually wrote the "Shakespeare" plays — Sir Francis Bacon, Francis Walsingham, the Earl of Oxford, among others — these claims belong to the realm of myth, not to the realm of history.

The range of Shakespeare's accomplishment as a playwright is astonishing. Early in his career, Shakespeare wrote two cycles of plays on English history — *Henry VI* (*Parts 1, 2,* and *3*), and *Richard*

III; and *Richard II*, *Henry IV* (*Parts 1* and *2*), and *Henry V*—that not only established a vogue for history plays but gave the English audience an epic version of the struggles that founded the Tudor and Stuart dynasties. Shakespeare's early comedies—*The Comedy of Errors, Two Gentlemen of Verona*—are very much in the vein of Plautus. Later comedies—*A Midsummer Night's Dream, As You Like It, Twelfth Night, The Merchant of Venice*—explore a variety of complex relations between love, sexuality, adulthood, ethnic discrimination, power, politics, and money. To many audiences today, Shakespeare is most remembered for *Hamlet* and the magisterial series of tragedies that followed—including *Othello, King Lear*, and *Macbeth*. Shakespeare's achievement often began with experimentation. The major tragedies benefitted from his earlier efforts in the mode of the Roman playwright Seneca in *Titus Andronicus*, in morality drama in *Richard III*, in romantic tragedy in *Romeo and Juliet*, and political intrigue-drama in *Julius Caesar*. In his final years as a playwright, Shakespeare seems to have collaborated with John Fletcher on a few occasions and to have turned his hand to plays in the vein of "tragicomedy," now generally called ROMANCE: *Pericles, Cymbeline, The Winter's Tale*, and *The Tempest*.

King Lear

In the twentieth century, *King Lear* has become one of Shakespeare's most celebrated and admired plays. It has tested the finest English actors (John Gielgud, Laurence Olivier, Paul Scofield) and has inspired powerful essays by Jan Kott, Maynard Mack, and Stanley Cavell, and Akira Kurosawa's magnificent film *Ran*, as well. As Jan Kott suggests in his famous essay, "*King Lear* or *Endgame*," one of the reasons for this popularity may have to do with the striking resemblance its bleak and impoverished world has to our own.

As he did in other plays, Shakespeare worked from a variety of sources in writing *King Lear*. The legend of King Lear and his daughters exists in many versions: as a folk tale; as part of Geoffrey of Monmouth's twelfth-century *History of Britain*; in Raphael Holinshed's *Chronicles of England, Scotland, and Ireland* (1587), one of Shakespeare's most-used sourcebooks; and in Edmund Spenser's epic poem, *The Faerie Queene* (1590). The Gloucester story is adapted from Sir Philip Sidney's prose romance, *Arcadia* (1590). Shakespeare also seems to have followed the plot of a relatively recent play, the anonymous *True Chronicle History of King Leir*, which was first staged in the 1590s and published (and perhaps staged again) around the time that Shakespeare wrote his play. The old play has many of *King Lear's* elements, particularly its underlying structure of moral parable. In the *True Chronicle History*, King Leir resumes the throne, recognizes the wrongs he has done to Cordelia and is reunited with her. In Shakespeare's play, however, innocent Cordelia dies despite her virtue, Lear expires howling in grief, and the characters are left onstage in stunned silence: "Speak what we feel, not what we ought to say:/The oldest hath borne most; we that are young/Shall never see so much, nor live so long." If the *True Chronicle History* provided its audience with the solace of a morally ordered world, where virtue is rewarded and evil punished, *King Lear* seems much less confident in such order. In Shakespeare's play, suffering begets only suffering.

Shakespeare's recasting of the older play also points to one of *King Lear's* most challenging features, the tension between a desire for moral justice and the painful sense that justice may not prevail on "this great stage of fools." We see this tension developed in several ways in the play. Running parallel to the main narrative of *King Lear* is a neat subplot, the story of Gloucester and his two sons. Edgar, the good, legitimate son, is unrecognized by his father, Gloucester, who perilously entrusts himself to the care of his bastard (or "natural") son, Edmund. If we are looking for a parable of justice in the play, we find it most clearly in the subplot, and only in the subplot. Here, Gloucester's blinding literalizes his failure of moral vision and leads to a recognition scene reminiscent of morality drama: "O my follies!" he shouts, after Cornwell blinds him, "Then Edgar was abused!" In the subplot, it is easy to recognize good and evil; it is possible to right wrongs, to recognize guilt and repent, to acknowledge one's errors—all of the acts that are accomplished only provisionally, if at all, in the main narrative.

King Lear's power lies in its unmitigated investigation of "the thing itself," of human suffering in some immediate and essential form. From the opening scene, where Lear explodes at his daughter for failing to acknowledge him as he wills, the play develops a terrible arithmetic of suffering, depriva-tion, and loss. Lear believes he will retain "the name and all addition of a king," but the action of the play relentlessly strips him of all such accommodations: of royal authority, of paternal care, of his retinue, of his shabby garments, even of his reason. Although Lear and Cordelia are united and Lear comes to understand his betrayal by Goneril and Regan, these recognitions seem unable to offset or explain the terrible wrongs we are finally forced to witness: the merciless punishment given to Lear and Gloucester in the play, the execution of Cordelia, the exhausted expiration of the old king. In the uncompromising vision of *King Lear,* to be alive is to suffer, without the solace of some mysterious providential design.

King Lear was performed at court on December 26, 1606, and had presumably been in produc-tion for some time. Some version of this text of the play was published in QUARTO form in 1608—a cheap, one-volume version of the play, along the lines of a paperback today. The play was published again twice after Shakespeare had died, in 1619 and again in the First Folio of 1623. The quarto and folio versions are quite different; although the folio seems more accurate, it omits about 300 lines from the quarto and also adds many lines not in the quarto. Editors generally have conflated both texts of the play, in an effort to preserve every word of Shakespeare's, a practice followed in this edition of *King Lear* as well. Today, however, editors sometimes regard the two versions of the play as inde-pendent, thinking that Shakespeare revised the play later in his career.

THE TRAGEDY OF KING LEAR

William Shakespeare

EDITED BY DAVID BEVINGTON

— CHARACTERS —

LEAR, *King of Britain*
KING OF FRANCE
DUKE OF BURGUNDY
DUKE OF CORNWALL, *husband to Regan*
DUKE OF ALBANY, *husband to Goneril*
EARL OF KENT
EARL OF GLOUCESTER
EDGAR, *son to Gloucester*
EDMUND, *bastard son to Gloucester*
CURAN, *a courtier*
OLD MAN, *tenant to Gloucester*
DOCTOR

FOOL
OSWALD, *steward to Goneril*
CAPTAIN *employed by Edmund*
GENTLEMAN
HERALD
SERVANTS *to Cornwall*
GONERIL
daughters to Lear — REGAN
CORDELIA
KNIGHTS *of Lear's train*, CAPTAINS, MESSENGERS, SOLDIERS, *and* ATTENDANTS

— ACT ONE —

SCENE I

Britain.

(*Enter* KENT, GLOUCESTER, *and* EDMUND.)

KENT: I thought the King had more affected the Duke of Albany than Cornwall.
GLOUCESTER: It did always seem so to us; but now, in the division of the kingdom, it appears not which of the dukes he
5 values most, for equalities are so weigh'd that curiosity in neither can make choice of either's moi'ty.
KENT: Is not this your son, my lord?
GLOUCESTER: His breeding, sir, hath been at my charge. I have so often blush'd to acknowledge him, that now I am braz'd to 't.
10 KENT: I cannot conceive you.
GLOUCESTER: Sir, this young fellow's mother could; whereupon she grew round-womb'd, and had, indeed, sir, a son for her cradle ere she had a husband for her bed. Do you smell a fault?
15 KENT: I cannot wish the fault undone, the issue of it being so proper.
GLOUCESTER: But I have a son, sir, by order of law, some year elder than this, who yet is no dearer in my account. Though this knave came something saucily to the world before he was
20 sent for, yet was his mother fair; there was good sport at his making, and the whoreson must be acknowledg'd. Do you know this noble gentleman, Edmund?

I.i. **Location: King Lear's palace.**
1 **more affected** better liked.   **Albany** i.e., Scotland   5–6 **equalities . . . moi'ty** the shares balance so equally that close scrutiny cannot find advantage in either's portion   8 **breeding** raising, care.   **charge** expense   9 **braz'd** hardened   10 **conceive** understand.   (But Gloucester puns in the sense of *become pregnant*.)   16 **proper** handsome   18 **account** estimation   19 **something** somewhat   21 **whoreson** low fellow; suggesting bastardy, but (like *knave* above) used with affectionate condescension

EDMUND: No, my lord.
GLOUCESTER: My lord of Kent. Remember him hereafter as my honorable friend.   25
EDMUND: My services to your lordship.
KENT: I must love you, and sue to know you better.
EDMUND: Sir, I shall study deserving.
GLOUCESTER: He hath been out nine years, and away he shall again. The King is coming.   30

(*Sennet. Enter* KING LEAR, CORNWALL, ALBANY, GONERIL, REGAN, CORDELIA, *and* ATTENDANTS.)

LEAR: Attend the lords of France and Burgundy, Gloucester.
GLOUCESTER: I shall, my lord.

(*Exit* [*with* EDMUND].)

LEAR: Meantime we shall express our darker purpose.
Give me the map there. (*Takes a map.*) Know that we have divided
In three our kingdom; and 'tis our fast intent   35
To shake all cares and business from our age,
Conferring them on younger strengths, while we
Unburden'd crawl toward death. Our son of Cornwall,
And you, our no less loving son of Albany,
We have this hour a constant will to publish   40
Our daughters' several dowers, that future strife
May be prevented now. The princes, France and Burgundy,
Great rivals in our youngest daughter's love,
Long in our court have made their amorous sojourn,
And here are to be answer'd. Tell me, my daughters—   45
Since now we will divest us both of rule,

29 **out** i.e., abroad, absent   30 **s.d. Sennet** trumpet signal heralding a procession   33 **darker purpose** undeclared intention   35 **fast** firm   40 **constant . . . publish** firm resolve to proclaim   41 **several** individual

174

Interest of territory, cares of state —
Which of you shall we say doth love us most,
That we our largest bounty may extend
50 Where nature doth with merit challenge? Goneril,
Our eldest-born, speak first.

GONERIL: Sir, I love you more than word can wield the
matter;
Dearer than eyesight, space, and liberty,
Beyond what can be valued, rich or rare,
55 No less than life, with grace, health, beauty, honor;
As much as child e'er lov'd, or father found;
A love that makes breath poor, and speech unable.
Beyond all manner of so much I love you.

CORDELIA: (Aside) What shall Cordelia speak? Love, and be
silent.

60 LEAR: (Indicating on map) Of all these bounds, even from this
line to this,
With shadowy forests and with champains rich'd,
With plenteous rivers and wide-skirted meads,
We make thee lady. To thine and Albany's issue
Be this perpetual. — What says our second daughter,
65 Our dearest Regan, wife of Cornwall? Speak.

REGAN: I am made of that self mettle as my sister,
And prize me at her worth. In my true heart
I find she names my very deed of love;
Only she comes too short, that I profess
70 Myself an enemy to all other joys
Which the most precious square of sense possesses,
And find I am alone felicitate
In your dear Highness' love.

CORDELIA: (Aside)   Then poor Cordelia!
And yet not so, since I am sure my love's
75 More ponderous than my tongue.

LEAR: To thee and thine hereditary ever
Remain this ample third of our fair kingdom,
No less in space, validity, and pleasure
Than that conferr'd on Goneril. — Now, our joy,
80 Although our last and least, to whose young love
The vines of France and milk of Burgundy
Strive to be interess'd, what can you say to draw
A third more opulent than your sisters'? Speak.

CORDELIA: Nothing, my lord.

85 LEAR: Nothing?

CORDELIA: Nothing.

LEAR: Nothing will come of nothing. Speak again.

CORDELIA: Unhappy that I am, I cannot heave
My heart into my mouth. I love your Majesty
90 According to my bond, no more nor less.

LEAR: How, how, Cordelia? Mend your speech a little,
Lest you may mar your fortunes.

CORDELIA: Good my lord,
You have begot me, bred me, lov'd me. I
Return those duties back as are right fit,
Obey you, love you, and most honor you.   95
Why have my sisters husbands, if they say
They love you all? Happily, when I shall wed,
That lord whose hand must take my plight shall carry
Half my love with him, half my care and duty.
Sure I shall never marry like my sisters,   100
[To love my father all.]

LEAR: But goes thy heart with this?

CORDELIA: Ay, my good lord.

LEAR: So young, and so untender?

CORDELIA: So young, my lord, and true.

LEAR: Let it be so; thy truth, then, be thy dow'r!   105
For, by the sacred radiance of the sun,
The mysteries of Hecate and the night,
By all the operation of the orbs
From whom we do exist and cease to be,
Here I disclaim all my paternal care,   110
Propinquity and property of blood,
And as a stranger to my heart and me
Hold thee, from this, forever. The barbarous Scythian,
Or he that makes his generation messes
To gorge his appetite, shall to my bosom   115
Be as well neighbor'd, pitied, and reliev'd,
As thou my sometime daughter.

KENT: Good my liege —

LEAR: Peace, Kent!
Come not between the dragon and his wrath.
I lov'd her most, and thought to set my rest   120
On her kind nursery. (To CORDELIA.) Hence, and avoid my
sight! —
So be my grave my peace, as here I give
Her father's heart from her! Call France. Who stirs?
Call Burgundy. Cornwall and Albany,
With my two daughters' dow'rs digest the third;   125
Let pride, which she calls plainness, marry her.
I do invest you jointly with my power,
Preeminence, and all the large effects
That troop with majesty. Ourself, by monthly course,
With reservation of an hundred knights,   130
By you to be sustain'd, shall our abode
Make with you by due turns. Only we shall retain
The name, and all th' addition to a king.
The sway, revenue, execution of the rest,
Beloved sons, be yours; which to confirm,   135
This coronet part between you.

47 **Interest** possession   50 **Where . . . challenge** where both natural affection and merit claim it as due   57 **breath . . . unable** language cheap and speech inadequate   61 **champains rich'd** fertile plains   66 **self** same   67 **prize . . . worth** value myself as her equal (in love for you)   68 **names . . . love** describes my love in very deed   69 **that** in that   71 **most . . . possesses** most sensitive measurement is capable of recording   72 **felicitate** made happy   75 **ponderous** weighty   78 **validity** value   80 **least** youngest   81 **vines** vineyards.   **milk** pastures (?)   82 **interess'd** affiliated   90 **bond** filial obligation

94 **right fit** proper and fitting   97 **Happily** haply, perhaps   98 **plight** pledge   107 **Hecate** goddess of witchcraft   108 **operation** influence.   **orbs** heavenly bodies   111 **Propinquity . . . blood** intimacy and close kinship   113 **this** this time forth.   **Scythian** (Scythians were famous in antiquity for savagery.)   114 **makes . . . messes** makes meals of his children   117 **sometime** former   120 **set my rest** repose myself. (A phrase from a game of cards meaning "to stake all.")   121 **nursery** nursing, care   122 **So . . . peace, as** let me rest peacefully in my grave, only as   128 **effects** outward shows   129 **Ourself** I. (The royal "we.")   133 **addition** honors and prerogatives   136 **coronet** i.e., the symbol of regal authority, perhaps a chaplet or garland

KENT: Royal Lear,
   Whom I have ever honor'd as my king
   Lov'd as my father, as my master follow'd,
   As my great patron thought on in my prayers —
140 LEAR: The bow is bent and drawn, make from the shaft.
   KENT: Let it fall rather, though the fork invade
   The region of my heart. Be Kent unmannerly,
   When Lear is mad. What wouldst thou do, old man?
   Think'st thou that duty shall have dread to speak
145 When power to flattery bows?
   To plainness honor's bound,
   When majesty falls to folly. Reserve thy state,
   And in thy best consideration check
   This hideous rashness. Answer my life my judgment,
150 Thy youngest daughter does not love thee least,
   Nor are those empty-hearted whose low sounds
   Reverb no hollowness.
   LEAR: Kent, on thy life, no more.
   KENT: My life I never held but as a pawn
   To wage against thine enemies; nor fear to lose it,
   Thy safety being motive.
155 LEAR: Out of my sight!
   KENT: See better, Lear, and let me still remain
   The true blank of thine eye.
   LEAR: Now, by Apollo —
   KENT: Now, by Apollo, King,
   Thou swear'st thy gods in vain.
   LEAR: O, vassal! Miscreant!

(Laying his hand on his sword.)

160 ALBANY, CORNWALL: Dear sir, forbear.
   KENT: Kill thy physician, and thy fee bestow
   Upon the foul disease. Revoke thy gift,
   Or, whilst I can vent clamor from my throat,
   I'll tell thee thou dost evil.
165 LEAR: Hear me, recreant, on thine allegiance, hear me!
   That thou hast sought to make us break our vows,
   Which we durst never yet, and with strain'd pride
   To come betwixt our sentence and our power,
   Which nor our nature nor our place can bear,
170 Our potency made good, take thy reward.
   Five days we do allot thee, for provision
   To shield thee from disasters of the world,
   And on the sixth to turn thy hated back
   Upon our kingdom. If, on the tenth day following,
175 Thy banish'd trunk be found in our dominions,
   The moment is thy death. Away! By Jupiter,
   This shall not be revok'd.

KENT: Fare thee well, King. Sith thus thou wilt appear,
   Freedom lives hence, and banishment is here.
   (To CORDELIA.*)* The gods to their dear shelter take thee,   180
      maid,
   That justly think'st and hast most rightly said!
   (To REGAN *and* GONERIL.*)* And your large speeches may
      your deeds approve,
   That good effects may spring from words of love.
   Thus Kent, O princes, bids you all adieu.
   He'll shape his old course in a country new.   185

(Exit.)

(Flourish. Enter GLOUCESTER, *with* FRANCE *and* BURGUNDY;
ATTENDANTS.*)*

GLOUCESTER: Here's France and Burgundy, my noble lord.
LEAR: My lord of Burgundy,
   We first address toward you, who with this king
   Hath rival'd for our daughter. What, in the least,
   Will you require in present dower with her,   190
   Or cease your quest of love?
BURGUNDY: Most royal Majesty,
   I crave no more than hath your Highness offer'd,
   Nor will you tender less.
LEAR: Right noble Burgundy,
   When she was dear to us, we did hold her so;
   But now her price is fallen. Sir, there she stands.   195
   If aught within that little seeming substance,
   Or all of it, with our displeasure piec'd,
   And nothing more, may fitly like your Grace,
   She's there, and she is yours.
BURGUNDY: I know no answer.
LEAR: Will you, with those infirmities she owes,   200
   Unfriended, new-adopted to our hate,
   Dow'r'd with our curse, and stranger'd with our oath,
   Take her, or leave her?
BURGUNDY: Pardon me, royal sir;
   Election makes not up in such conditions.
LEAR: Then leave her, sir; for, by the pow'r that made me, 205
   I tell you all her wealth. *(To* FRANCE.*)* For you, great King,
   I would not from your love make such a stray
   To match you where I hate; therefore beseech you
   T' avert your liking a more worthier way
   Than on a wretch whom nature is asham'd   210
   Almost t' acknowledge hers.
FRANCE: This is most strange,
   That she, whom even but now was your best object,
   The argument of your praise, balm of your age,
   The best, the dearest, should in this trice of time
   Commit a thing so monstrous, to dismantle   215
   So many folds of favor. Sure, her offense
   Must be of such unnatural degree

140 **make from** get out of the way of   141 **fall** strike.   **fork** barbed head of an arrow   146 **To . . . bound** allegiance demands frankness   147 **Reserve thy state** retain your royal authority   149 **Answer . . . judgment** I wager my life on my judgment that   152 **Reverb no hollowness** i.e., do not reverberate like a hollow drum, insincerely   153 **pawn** stake, chess piece   154 **wage** wager, hazard in warfare   157 **blank** white center of the target   159 **vassel** i.e., wretch.   **Miscreant** (Literally, infidel; hence, villain, rascal.)   165 **recreant** traitor   166 **That** in that, since   167 **strain'd** excessive   168 **To . . . power** i.e., to block my power to give sentence   169 **Which . . . place** which neither my personal inclination nor my office as king   170 **Our . . . good** my potency now being validated   175 **trunk** body

178 **Sith** since   182 **your . . . approve** may your deeds confirm your speeches with their vast claims   185 **shape . . . course** follow his traditional ways   193 **tender** offer   196 **seeming** specious, insincere   197 **piec'd** added, joined   198 **like** please   200 **owes** owns   202 **stranger'd with** made a stranger by   204 **Election . . . conditions** no choice is possible under such conditions   207 **make such a stray** stray so far   209 **avert your liking** turn your affections   213 **argument** theme

That monsters it, or your fore-vouch'd affection
Fall into taint, which to believe of her
220 Must be a faith that reason without miracle
Should never plant in me.
CORDELIA: I yet beseech your Majesty—
If for I want that glib and oily art
To speak and purpose not, since what I well intend,
225 I'll do 't before I speak—that you make known
It is no vicious blot, murder, or foulness,
No unchaste action, or dishonored step,
That hath depriv'd me of your grace and favor,
But even for want of that for which I am richer—
230 A still-soliciting eye, and such a tongue
That I am glad I have not, though not to have it
Hath lost me in your liking.
LEAR: Better thou hadst
Not been born than not t' have pleas'd me better.
FRANCE: Is it but this—a tardiness in nature
235 Which often leaves the history unspoke
That it intends to do? My lord of Burgundy,
What say you to the lady? Love's not love
When it is mingled with regards that stands
Aloof from th' entire point. Will you have her?
She is herself a dowry.
240 BURGUNDY: Royal King,
Give but that portion which yourself propos'd,
And here I take Cordelia by the hand,
Duchess of Burgundy.
LEAR: Nothing. I have sworn; I am firm.
245 BURGUNDY: I am sorry, then, you have so lost a father
That you must lose a husband.
CORDELIA: Peace be with Burgundy!
Since that respects of fortune are his love,
I shall not be his wife.
FRANCE: Fairest Cordelia, that art most rich being poor,
250 Most choice forsaken, and most lov'd despis'd,
Thee and thy virtues here I seize upon,
Be it lawful I take up what's cast away.

(Takes her hand.)

Gods, gods! 'Tis strange that from their cold'st neglect
My love should kindle to inflam'd respect.
255 Thy dow'rless daughter, King, thrown to my chance,
Is queen of us, of ours, and our fair France.
Not all the dukes of wat'rish Burgundy
Can buy this unpriz'd precious maid of me.
Bid them farewell, Cordelia, though unkind.
260 Thou losest here, a better where to find.
LEAR: Thou hast her, France. Let her be thine, for we
Have no such daughter, nor shall ever see
That face of hers again. (To CORDELIA.) Therefore be gone

Without our grace, our love, our benison.
Come, noble Burgundy.   265

(Flourish. Exeunt [all but FRANCE, GONERIL, REGAN, and
CORDELIA].)

FRANCE: Bid farewell to your sisters.
CORDELIA: The jewels of our father, with wash'd eyes
Cordelia leaves you. I know you what you are,
And like a sister am most loath to call
Your faults as they are nam'd. Love well our father. 270
To your professed bosoms I commit him.
But yet, alas, stood I within his grace,
I would prefer him to a better place.
So, farewell to you both.
REGAN: Prescribe not us our duty.
GONERIL: Let your study   275
Be to content your lord, who hath receiv'd you
At fortune's alms. You have obedience scanted,
And well are worth the want that you have wanted.
CORDELIA: Time shall unfold what plighted cunning hides,
Who covers faults, at last shame them derides.   280
Well may you prosper!
FRANCE: Come, my fair Cordelia.

(Exeunt FRANCE and CORDELIA.)

GONERIL: Sister, it is not little I have to say of what most nearly
appertains to us both. I think our father will hence tonight.
REGAN: That's most certain, and with you; next month with us.
GONERIL: You see how full of changes his age is; the observation 285
we have made of it hath not been little. He always lov'd our
sister most; and with what poor judgment he hath now cast
her off appears too grossly.
REGAN: 'Tis the infirmity of his age, yet he hath ever but slen-
derly known himself.   290
GONERIL: The best and soundest of his time hath been but rash;
then must we look from his age to receive not alone the im-
perfections of long-ingraff'd condition, but therewithal the
unruly waywardness that infirm and choleric years bring with
them.   295
REGAN: Such unconstant starts are we like to have from him as
this of Kent's banishment.
GONERIL: There is further compliment of leave-taking between
France and him. Pray you, let us hit together; if our father
carry authority with such disposition as he bears, this last sur- 300
render of his will but offend us.
REGAN: We shall further think of it.
GONERIL: We must do something, and i' th' heat.

(Exeunt.)

264 **benison** blessing   267 **wash'd** tear-washed   269 **like a sister** i.e.,
because I am your sister   270 **as . . . nam'd** by their true names   271
professed bosoms publicly avowed love   273 **prefer** raise, promote   277 **At . . . alms** as a pittance or dole from fortune   278 **well . . .
wanted** well deserve the lack of affection which you yourself have
shown. (*Want* may also refer to her dowry.)   279 **plighted** pleated, en-
folded   280 **Who . . . derides** i.e., time may conceal faults for a while,
but at last they are shamefully exposed and derided   288 **grossly** obviously   291 **The best . . . rash** i.e., even in the prime of his life, he was
stormy and unpredictable   293 **long-engraff'd condition** long-im-
planted habit.   **therewithal** added thereto   296 **unconstant starts** impulsive acts.   **like** likely   298 **compliment** ceremony   299 **hit**
agree   300 **last surrender** latest abdication   301 **offend** harm, injure   303 **i' th' heat** i.e., while the iron is hot

218 **monsters** makes monstrous.   **or ere**, before.   **fore-vouch'd** hitherto affirmed   219 **taint** decay   221 **Should** could   223 **for I want**
because I lack   224 **purpose not** not intend to do what I say   230 **still-
soliciting** ever-begging   238–239 **regards . . . point** irrelevant considerations   247 **respects of fortune** concern for wealth and position   254
inflam'd respect ardent affection   257 **wat'rish** (1) well-watered with
rivers (2) feeble, fickle   258 **unpriz'd** not appreciated (with perhaps a
sense also of *priceless*)   260 **here** this place.   **where** place elsewhere

SCENE II

(Enter bastard [EDMUND, *with a letter*].*)*

EDMUND: Thou, nature, art my goddess; to thy law
My services are bound. Wherefore should I
Stand in the plague of custom, and permit
The curiosity of nations to deprive me,
5   For that I am some twelve or fourteen moonshines
Lag of a brother? Why bastard? Wherefore base?
When my dimensions are as well compact,
My mind as generous, and my shape as true,
As honest madam's issue? Why brand they us
10   With base? With baseness? Bastardy? Base, base?
Who, in the lusty stealth of nature, take
More composition and fierce quality
Than doth within a dull, stale, tired bed
Go to th' creating a whole tribe of fops
15   Got 'tween asleep and wake? Well, then,
Legitimate Edgar, I must have your land.
Our father's love is to the bastard Edmund
As to th' legitimate. Fine word, "legitimate"!
Well, my legitimate, if this letter speed
20   And my invention thrive, Edmund the base
Shall top th' legitimate. I grow, I prosper.
Now, gods, stand up for bastards!

(Enter GLOUCESTER.*)*

GLOUCESTER: Kent banish'd thus? And France in choler
parted?
And the King gone tonight? Prescrib'd his pow'r,
25   Confin'd to exhibition? All this done
Upon the gad! Edmund, how now? What news?
EDMUND: *(Putting up the letter)* So please your lordship,
none.
GLOUCESTER: Why so earnestly seek you to put up that letter?
EDMUND: I know no news, my lord.
30   GLOUCESTER: What paper were you reading?
EDMUND: Nothing, my lord.
GLOUCESTER: No? What needed, then, that terrible dispatch of
it into your pocket? The quality of nothing hath not such
need to hide itself. Let's see. Come, if it be nothing, I shall
35   not need spectacles.
EDMUND: I beseech you, sir, pardon me. It is a letter from my
brother, that I have not all o'er-read; and for so much as I have
perus'd, I find it not fit for your o'erlooking.
GLOUCESTER: Give me the letter, sir.
40   EDMUND: I shall offend, either to detain or give it. The contents, as in part I understand them, are to blame.
GLOUCESTER: Let's see, let's see.   *(EDMUND gives letter.)*

EDMUND: I hope, for my brother's justification, he wrote this
but as an essay or taste of my virtue.
GLOUCESTER: *(Reads)* "This policy and reverence of age makes   45
the world bitter to the best of our times; keeps our fortunes
from us till our oldness cannot relish them. I begin to find an
idle and fond bondage in the oppression of aged tyranny, who
sways, not as it hath power, but as it is suffer'd. Come to me,
that of this I may speak more. If our father would sleep till I   50
wak'd him, you should enjoy half his revenue forever, and live
the belov'd of your brother,

Edgar."
Hum! Conspiracy! — "Sleep till I wak'd him, you should en-
joy half his revenue." My son Edgar! Had he a hand to write
this? A heart and brain to breed it in? — When came you to   55
this? Who brought it?
EDMUND: It was not brought me, my lord; there's the cunning of
it. I found it thrown in at the casement of my closet.
GLOUCESTER: You know the character to be your brother's?
EDMUND: If the matter were good, my lord, I durst swear it were   60
his; but, in respect of that, I would fain think it were not.
GLOUCESTER: It is his.
EDMUND: It is his hand, my lord; but I hope his heart is not in
the contents.
GLOUCESTER: Has he never before sounded you in this busi-   65
ness?
EDMUND: Never, my lord. But I have heard him oft maintain it
to be fit that, sons at perfect age and fathers declin'd, the father should be as ward to the son, and the son manage his
revenue.   70
GLOUCESTER: O villain, villain! His very opinion in the letter!
Abhorred villain! Unnatural, detested, brutish villain! Worse
than brutish! Go, sirrah, seek him; I'll apprehend him.
Abominable villain! Where is he?
EDMUND: I do not well know, my lord. If it shall please you to   75
suspend your indignation against my brother till you can derive from him better testimony of his intent, you should run a
certain course; where, if you violently proceed against him,
mistaking his purpose, it would make a great gap in your own
honor, and shake in pieces the heart of his obedience. I dare   80
pawn down my life for him that he hath writ this to feel my
affection to your honor, and to no other pretense of danger.
GLOUCESTER: Think you so?
EDMUND: If your honor judge it meet, I will place you where
you shall hear us confer of this, and by an auricular assurance   85
have your satisfaction, and that without any further delay
than this very evening.
GLOUCESTER: He cannot be such a monster —
[EDMUND: Nor is not, sure.

I.ii. **Location: The Earl of Gloucester's house.**
1 **nature** i.e., the material world, governed solely by mechanistic
amoral forces   3 **Stand . . . custom** submit to the vexatious injustice of
convention   4 **curiosity** fastidious distinctions.   **nations** societies   5
For that because.   **moonshines** months   6 **Lag of** younger than   7
compact knit together, fitted   8 **generous** noble, refined   9 **honest**
chaste   11–12 **take . . . quality** acquire greater completeness and energetic force   15 **Got** begotten   19 **speed** succeed   20 **invention thrive**
scheme prosper   24 **Prescrib'd** limited   25 **exhibition** an allowance,
pension   26 **Upon the gad** suddenly, as if pricked by a gad or spur   32
terrible terrified   38 **o'erlooking** perusal   41 **to blame** blameworthy

44 **essay or taste** i.e., assay, test   45 **policy and reverence of** i.e., policy
of reverencing   46 **the best . . . times** the best years of our lives, i.e.,
our youth   48 **idle** useless.   **fond** foolish   48–49 **who sways** which
rules   49 **suffer'd** permitted (by the young, who could seize power if
they wished)   55–56 **to this** upon this (letter)   58 **casement** window.   **closet** private room   59 **character** handwriting   60 **matter** contents   61 **in . . . that** considering what the contents are.   **fain**
gladly   68 **perfect age** full maturity.   **declin'd** having become feeble   71 **villain** i.e., vile wretch, diabolical schemer   72 **Abhorred** ab-
horrent.   **detested** detestable   78 **certain** safe.   **where** whereas   81
feel feel out   82 **pretense of danger** dangerous purpose

90 GLOUCESTER: To his father, that so tenderly and entirely loves
    him. Heaven and earth!] Edmund, seek him out; wind me
    into him, I pray you. Frame the business after your own wis-
    dom. I would unstate myself, to be in a due resolution.
    EDMUND: I will seek him, sir, presently, convey the business as I
95 shall find means, and acquaint you withal.
    GLOUCESTER: These late eclipses in the sun and moon portend
    no good to us. Though the wisdom of nature can reason it
    thus and thus, yet nature finds itself scourg'd by the sequent
    effects. Love cools, friendship falls off, brothers divide; in
100 cities, mutinies; in countries, discord; in palaces, treason; and
    the bond crack'd 'twixt son and father. This villain of mine
    comes under the prediction; there's son against father. The
    King falls from bias of nature; there's father against child. We
    have seen the best of our time. Machinations, hollowness,
105 treachery, and all ruinous disorders follow us disquietly to our
    graves. Find out this villain, Edmund. It shall lose thee noth-
    ing; do it carefully. And the noble and true-hearted Kent ban-
    ish'd! His offense, honesty! 'Tis strange.   (Exit.)
    EDMUND: This is the excellent foppery of the world, that when we
110 are sick in fortune — often the surfeits of our own behavior —
    we make guilty of our disasters the sun, the moon, and stars,
    as if we were villains on necessity, fools by heavenly compul-
    sion, knaves, thieves, and treachers by spherical predomi-
    nance, drunkards, liars, and adulterers by an enforc'd
115 obedience of planetary influence, and all that we are evil in,
    by a divine thrusting on. An admirable evasion of whoremas-
    ter man, to lay his goatish disposition on the charge of a star!
    My father compounded with my mother under the Dragon's
    Tail, and my nativity was under Ursa Major, so that it follows
120 I am rough and lecherous. Fut, I should have been that I am,
    had the maidenliest star in the firmament twinkled on my
    bastardizing. Edgar —

    (Enter EDGAR.)

    and pat he comes like the catastrophe of the old comedy.
    My cue is villainous melancholy, with a sigh like Tom o'
125 Bedlam. — O, these eclipses do portend these divisions! Fa,
    sol, la, mi.
    EDGAR: How now, brother Edmund, what serious contempla-
    tion are you in?
    EDMUND: I am thinking, brother, of a prediction I read this
130 other day, what should follow these eclipses.
    EDGAR: Do you busy yourself with that?
    EDMUND: I promise you, the effects he writes of succeed unhap-
    pily, [as of unnaturalness between the child and the parent,
    death, dearth, dissolutions of ancient amities, divisions in
135 state, menaces and maledictions against king and nobles,

needless diffidences, banishment of friends, dissipation of co-
horts, nuptial breaches, and I know not what.
EDGAR: How long have you been a sectary astronomical?
EDMUND: Come, come,] when saw you my father last?
EDGAR: The night gone by.   140
EDMUND: Spake you with him?
EDGAR: Ay, two hours together.
EDMUND: Parted you in good terms? Found you no displeasure
    in him by word nor countenance?
EDGAR: None at all.   145
EDMUND: Bethink yourself wherein you may have offended
    him; and at my entreaty forbear his presence until some little
    time hath qualified the heat of his displeasure, which at this
    instant so rageth in him that with the mischief of your person
    it would scarcely allay.   150
EDGAR: Some villain hath done me wrong.
EDMUND: That's my fear. I pray you, have a continent for-
    bearance till the speed of his rage goes slower; and, as I say,
    retire with me to my lodging, from whence I will fitly bring
    you to hear my lord speak. Pray ye, go; there's my key. (Gives 155
    key.) If you do stir abroad, go arm'd.
EDGAR: Arm'd, brother?
EDMUND: Brother, I advise you to the best. I am no honest man
    if there be any good meaning toward you. I have told you
    what I have seen and heard; but faintly, nothing like the im-   160
    age and horror of it. Pray you, away.
EDGAR: Shall I hear from you anon?
EDMUND: I do serve you in this business.

(Exit [EDGAR].)

A credulous father and a brother noble,
Whose nature is so far from doing harms   165
That he suspects none; on whose foolish honesty
My practices ride easy. I see the business.
Let me, if not by birth, have lands by wit.
All with me's meet that I can fashion fit.

(Exit.)

SCENE III

(Enter GONERIL, and [OSWALD, her] steward.)

GONERIL: Did my father strike my gentleman for chiding of his
    fool?
OSWALD: Ay, madam.
GONERIL: By day and night he wrongs me! Every hour
    He flashes into one gross crime or other,   5
    That sets us all at odds. I'll not endure it.
    His knights grow riotous, and himself upbraids us
    On every trifle. When he returns from hunting,
    I will not speak with him; say I am sick.

91–92 **wind me into him** insinuate yourself into his confidence. (*Me* is
the ethical dative.) **Frame** arrange   93 **unstate . . . resolution** suffer
loss of all to know the truth   94 **presently** immediately.   **convey** manage   96 **late** recent   97 **wisdom of nature** natural science   98–99
sequent effects i.e., devastating consequences   103 **bias of nature** natural inclination   109 **foppery** foolishness   113 **treachers** traitors.
113–114 **spherical predominance** astrological determinism   117 **goat-
ish** lecherous   118–119 **compounded . . . Dragon's Tail** had sex with
my mother under the constellation Draco.   **Ursa Major** the big
bear   123 **castrastophe** conclusion, resolution (of a play)   124–125
Tom o' Bedlam a lunatic patient of Bethlehem Hospital in London turned
out to beg for his bread   132–133 **succeed unhappily** follow unluckily
136 **needless diffidences** groundless distrust of others.

136–137 **dissipation of cohorts** falling away of supporters   138 **sectary
astronomical** believer in astrology   148 **qualified** moderated   149
mischief . . . person harmful effect of your presence   150 **allay** be al-
layed   152–153 **have . . . forbearance** keep a wary distance   154 **fitly** at
a fit time   160–161 **image and horror** horrid reality   167 **practices**
plots   168 **wit** intelligence   169 **meet** justifiable. **fit** i.e., to my
purpose

I.iii. **Location: The Duke of Albany's palace.**
5 **crime** offense

10   If you come slack of former services,
      You shall do well; the fault of it I'll answer.

(Horns within.)

OSWALD: He's coming, madam; I hear him.
GONERIL: Put on what weary negligence you please,
15   You and your fellows. I'd have it come to question.
      If he distaste it, let him to my sister,
      Whose mind and mine, I know, in that are one,
      [Not to be overrul'd. Idle old man,
      That still would manage those authorities
20   That he hath given away! Now, by my life,
      Old fools are babes again, and must be us'd
      With checks as flatteries, when they are seen abus'd.]
      Remember what I have said.
OSWALD: Well, madam.
GONERIL: And let his knights have colder looks among you.
25   What grows of it, no matter. Advise your fellows so.
      [I would breed from hence occasions, and I shall,
      That I may speak.] I'll write straight to my sister
      To hold my course. Prepare for dinner.

(Exeunt.)

SCENE IV

(Enter KENT *[disguised].)*

KENT: If but as well I other accents borrow,
      That can my speech defuse, my good intent
      May carry through itself to that full issue
      For which I raz'd my likeness. Now, banish'd Kent,
5   If thou canst serve where thou dost stand condemn'd,
      So may it come, thy master, whom thou lov'st,
      Shall find thee full of labors.

(Horns within. Enter LEAR, *[KNIGHTS,] and* ATTENDANTS.*)*

LEAR: Let me not stay a jot for dinner; go get it ready. *(Exit an Attendant.)* How now, what art thou?
10   KENT: A man, sir.
LEAR: What dost thou profess? What wouldst thou with us?
KENT: I do profess to be no less than I seem, to serve him truly that will put me in trust, to love him that is honest, to converse with him that is wise and says little, to fear judgment, to
15   fight when I cannot choose, and to eat no fish.
LEAR: What art thou?
KENT: A very honest-hearted fellow, and as poor as the King.

LEAR: If thou be'st as poor for a subject as he's for a king, thou art poor enough. What wouldst thou?
KENT: Service.   20
LEAR: Who wouldst thou serve?
KENT: You.
LEAR: Dost thou know me, fellow?
KENT: No, sir; but you have that in your countenance which I would fain call master.   25
LEAR: What's that?
KENT: Authority.
LEAR: What services canst thou do?
KENT: I can keep honest counsel, ride, run, mar a curious tale in telling it, and deliver a plain message bluntly. That which   30
      ordinary men are fit for, I am qualified in, and the best of me is diligence.
LEAR: How old art thou?
KENT: Not so young, sir, to love a woman for singing, nor so old to dote on her for any thing. I have years on my back forty eight. 35
LEAR: Follow me; thou shalt serve me. If I like thee no worse after dinner, I will not part from thee yet. Dinner, ho, dinner! Where's my knave? My fool? Go you and call my fool hither.

(Exit an ATTENDANT.*)*

(Enter steward [OSWALD]*.)*

      You, you, sirrah, where's my daughter?
OSWALD: So please you —   40

(Exit.)

LEAR: What says the fellow there? Call the clotpoll back. *(Exit a* KNIGHT.*)* Where's my fool, ho? I think the world's asleep.

(Enter KNIGHT.*)*

      How now? Where's that mongrel?
KNIGHT: He says, my lord, your daughter is not well.
LEAR: Why came not the slave back to me when I call'd him?   45
KNIGHT: Sir, he answer'd me in the roundest manner, he would not.
LEAR: He would not?
KNIGHT: My lord, I know not what the matter is, but, to my judgment, your Highness is not entertain'd with that ceremo-   50
      nious affection as you were wont. There's a great abatement of kindness appears as well in the general dependents as in the Duke himself also and your daughter.
LEAR: Ha? Say'st thou so?
KNIGHT: I beseech you, pardon me, my lord, if I be mistaken, for   55
      my duty cannot be silent when I think your Highness wrong'd.
LEAR: Thou but rememb'rest me of mine own conception. I have perceiv'd a most faint neglect of late, which I have rather blam'd as mine own jealous curiosity than as a very pretense
      and purpose of unkindness. I will look further into 't. But   60
      where's my fool? I have not seen him this two days.
KNIGHT: Since my young lady's going into France, sir, the fool hath much pin'd away.
LEAR: No more of that; I have noted it well. Go you and tell my daughter I would speak with her. *(Exit an* ATTENDANT.*)* Go   65
      you call hither my fool.

---

10 **come slack** fall short   15 **distaste** dislike   17 **Idle** foolish   18 **manage those authorities** i.e., assert those prerogatives   21 **With . . . abus'd** with rebukes instead of flattery, when they (old men) act unselfknowingly (as Lear does)   26–27 **I would . . . speak** I wish to create from these incidents the opportunity to speak out

I.iv. Location: The Duke of Albany's palace still. The sense of time is virtually continuous.
1 **as well** i.e., as well as I have disguised myself by means of costume   2 **defuse** disguise   3 **carry . . . issue** succeed to that perfect result   4 **raz'd my likeness** erased my outward appearance (perhaps shaving beard?)   8 **stay** wait   11 **What . . . profess** what is your special calling. (But Kent puns in his answer on *profess* meaning to *claim*.)   13–14 **converse** associate   14 **judgment** i.e., God's judgment   15 **choose** i.e., choose but to fight.   **eat no fish** i.e., eat a manly diet (?)

29 **keep honest counsel** respect confidences.   **curious** ornate, elaborate   41 **clotpoll** blockhead   46 **roundest** bluntest   57 **rememb'rest** remind   58 **faint** half-hearted   59 **jealous curiosity** overscrupulous regard for minutiae.   **very pretense** true intention

(Exit an ATTENDANT.*)*

(Enter steward [OSWALD].*)*

O, you, sir, you, come you hither, sir. Who am I, sir?
OSWALD: My lady's father.
LEAR: "My lady's father"? My lord's knave! You whoreson dog,
70 you slave, you cur!
OSWALD: I am none of these, my lord, I beseech your pardon.
LEAR: Do you bandy looks with me, you rascal?

(Striking him.)

OSWALD: I'll not be strucken, my lord.
KENT: Nor tripp'd neither, you base football player.

(Tripping up his heels.)

75 LEAR: I thank thee, fellow. Thou serv'st me, and I'll love thee.
KENT: Come, sir, arise, away! I'll teach you differences. Away,
away! If you will measure your lubber's length again, tarry;
but away! Go to. Have you wisdom? So.

(Pushes OSWALD *out.)*

LEAR: Now, my friendly knave, I thank thee. There's earnest of
80 thy service.

(Gives KENT *money.)*

(Enter FOOL.*)*

FOOL: Let me hire him too. Here's my coxcomb.

(Offering KENT *his cap.)*

LEAR: How now, my pretty knave, how dost thou?
FOOL: Sirrah, you were best take my coxcomb.
KENT: Why, fool?
85 FOOL: Why? For taking one's part that's out of favor. Nay, an
thou canst not smile as the wind sits, thou 'lt catch cold
shortly. There, take my coxcomb. Why, this fellow has banish'd two on 's daughters, and did the third a blessing against
his will; if thou follow him, thou must needs wear my
90 coxcomb. —How now, nuncle? Would I had two coxcombs
and two daughters.
LEAR: Why, my boy?
FOOL: If I gave them all my living, I'd keep my coxcombs myself. There's mine; beg another of thy daughters.
95 LEAR: Take heed, sirrah; the whip.
FOOL: Truth's a dog must to kennel; he must be whipp'd out,
when the Lady Brach may stand by th' fire and stink.
LEAR: A pestilent gall to me!
FOOL: Sirrah, I'll teach thee a speech.
100 LEAR: Do.
FOOL: Mark it, nuncle:
Have more than thou showest,

Speak less than thou knowest,
Lend less than thou owest,
Ride more than thou goest,   105
Learn more than thou trowest,
Set less than thou throwest;
Leave thy drink and thy whore,
And keep in-a-door,
And thou shalt have more   110
Than two tens to a score.
KENT: This is nothing, fool.
FOOL: Then 'tis like the breath of an unfee'd lawyer; you gave me
nothing for 't. Can you make no use of nothing, nuncle?
LEAR: Why, no, boy; nothing can be made out of nothing.   115
FOOL: *(To* KENT*)* Prithee, tell him, so much the rent of his land
comes to. He will not believe a fool.
LEAR: A bitter fool!
FOOL: Dost thou know the difference, my boy, between a bitter
fool and a sweet one?   120
LEAR: No, lad; teach me.
FOOL: [That lord that counsel'd thee
To give away thy land,
Come place him here by me,
Do thou for him stand.   125
The sweet and bitter fool
Will presently appear;
The one in motley here,
The other found out there.
LEAR: Dost thou call me fool, boy?   130
FOOL: All thy other titles thou hast given away; that thou wast
born with.
KENT: This is not altogether fool, my lord.
FOOL: No, faith, lords and great men will not let me; if I had a
monopoly out, they would have part on 't. And ladies too, 135
they will not let me have all the fool to myself; they'll be
snatching.] Nuncle, give me an egg, and I'll give thee two
crowns.
LEAR: What two crowns shall they be?
FOOL: Why, after I have cut the egg i' th' middle and eat up the 140
meat, the two crowns of the egg. When thou clovest thy
crown i' th' middle and gav'st away both parts, thou bor'st
thine ass on thy back o'er the dirt. Thou hadst little wit in thy
bald crown when thou gav'st thy golden one away. If I speak
like myself in this, let him be whipp'd that first finds it so. 145

---

72 **bandy** volley, exchange (as in tennis) 74 **football** (A raucous street game played by the lower classes.) 76 **differences** distinctions in rank 79 **earnest** partial advance payment 81 **coxcomb** fool's cap, crested with a red comb 86 **smile . . . sits** i.e., play along with those in power 87–88 **banish'd** (i.e., paradoxically, by giving Goneril and Regan his kingdom, Lear has lost them, given them power over him.) 88 **blessing** i.e., bestowing Cordelia on France 90 **nuncle** (Contraction of "mine uncle.") 92 **living** property 97 **Brach** hound bitch (here suggesting flattery) 98 **gall** irritation

104 **owest** own 105 **goest** i.e., on foot 106 **Learn** i.e., listen to. **trowest** believe 107 **Set . . . throwest** stake less at dice than you have a chance to throw, i.e., don't bet all you can 109 **in-a-door** indoors, at home 110–111 **shalt . . . score** i.e., will do better than break even (since a *score* equals two tens, or 20) 113 **breath** speech, counsel 116 **rent** (Lear has no land, hence no rent.) 118 **bitter** satirical 128 **motley** the particolored dress of the professional fool. (The Fool identifies himself as the sweet fool, Lear as the bitter fool who counseled himself to give away his kingdom.) 134 **No . . . let me** i.e., great persons at court will not let me monopolize folly; I am not *altogether fool* in the sense of being *all the fool there is* 135 **a monopoly out** a corner on the market. (The granting of monopolies was a common abuse under King James and Queen Elizabeth.) **on 't** of it 142–143 **bor'st . . . dirt** i.e., bore the ass instead of letting the ass bear you 145 **like myself** i.e., like a fool. **whipp'd** i.e., as a fool. **finds it so** discovers from his experience that it is true (as Lear is now discovering)

(Sings.)   "Fools had ne'er less grace in a year,
    For wise men are grown foppish,
    And know not how their wits to wear,
    Their manners are so apish."

150 LEAR: When were you wont to be so full of songs, sirrah?
FOOL: I have us'd it, nuncle, e'er since thou mad'st thy daughters thy mothers; for when thou gav'st them the rod, and put'st down thine own breeches,

(Sings.)

    "Then they for sudden joy did weep,
155   And I for sorrow sung,
    That such a king should play bo-peep,
    And go the fools among."

Prithee, nuncle, keep a schoolmaster that can teach thy fool to lie. I would fain learn to lie.
160 LEAR: An you lie, sirrah, we'll have you whipp'd.
FOOL: I marvel what kin thou and thy daughters are. They'll have me whipp'd for speaking true, thou 'lt have me whipp'd for lying; and sometimes I am whipp'd for holding my peace. I had rather be any kind o' thing than a fool, and yet I would
165 not be thee, nuncle; thou hast par'd thy wit o' both sides, and left nothing i' th' middle. Here comes one o' the parings.

(Enter GONERIL)

LEAR: How now, daughter? What makes that frontlet on?
    You are too much of late i' th' frown.
FOOL: Thou wast a pretty fellow when thou hadst no need to
170 care for her frowning; now thou art an O without a figure. I am better than thou art now; I am a fool, thou art nothing. *(To GONERIL.)* Yes, forsooth, I will hold my tongue; so your face bids me, though you say nothing.
    Mum, mum,
175   He that keeps nor crust nor crumb,
    Weary of all, shall want some.
(Pointing to LEAR.) That's a sheal'd peascod.
GONERIL: Not only, sir, this your all-licens'd fool,
    But other of your insolent retinue
180 Do hourly carp and quarrel, breaking forth
In rank and not-to-be-endured riots. Sir,
I had thought, by making this well known unto you,
To have found a safe redress, but now grow fearful,
By what yourself too late have spoke and done,
185 That you protect this course and put it on
By your allowance; which if you should, the fault
Would not scape censure, nor the redresses sleep,
Which, in the tender of a wholesome weal,
Might in their working do you that offense

Which else were shame, that then necessity   190
Will call discreet proceeding.
FOOL: For, you know, nuncle,
    "The hedge-sparrow fed the cuckoo so long
    That it had it head bit off by it young."
So, out went the candle, and we were left darkling.
LEAR: Are you our daughter?   195
GONERIL: I would you would make use of your good wisdom,
Whereof I know you are fraught, and put away
These dispositions which of late transport you
From what you rightly are.
FOOL: May not an ass know when the cart draws the horse?   200
    Whoop, Jug! I love thee.
LEAR: Does any here know me? This is not Lear.
Does Lear walk thus? Speak thus? Where are his eyes?
Either his notion weakens, his discernings
Are lethargied—Ha! Waking? 'Tis not so.   205
Who is it that can tell me who I am?
FOOL: Lear's shadow.
[LEAR: I would learn that; for, by the marks of sovereignty,
Knowledge, and reason, I should be false persuaded
I had daughters.   210
FOOL: Which they will make an obedient father.]
LEAR: Your name, fair gentlewoman?
GONERIL: This admiration, sir, is much o' th' savor
Of other your new pranks. I do beseech you
To understand my purposes aright.   215
As you are old and reverend, should be wise.
Here do you keep a hundred knights and squires,
Men so disorder'd, so debosh'd and bold,
That this our court, infected with their manners,
Shows like a riotous inn. Epicurism and lust   220
Makes it more like a tavern or a brothel
Than a grac'd palace. The shame itself doth speak
For instant remedy. Be then desir'd
By her, that else will take the thing she begs,
A little to disquantity your train,   225
And the remainders that shall still depend
To be such men as may besort your age,
Which know themselves and you.
LEAR: Darkness and devils!
Saddle my horses; call my train together.
Degenerate bastard! I'll not trouble thee.   230
Yet have I left a daughter.
GONERIL: You strike my people, and your disorder'd rabble
Make servants of their betters.

(Enter ALBANY.)

146 **Fools . . . year** fools have never enjoyed less favor; i.e., they are made obsolete by the folly of supposed wise men   147 **foppish** foolish, vain   148 **wear** use   151 **us'd** practiced   156 **bo-peep** a child's game   167 **frontlet** a band worn on the forehead; here, frown   170 **O without a figure** cipher of no value unless preceded by a digit   175 **crumb** the bread inside the crust   176 **want** lack   177 **sheal'd peascod** shelled pea pod   178 **all-licens'd** authorized to speak or act freely   183 **safe** certain   184 **too late** all too recently   185 **put it on** encourage it   186 **allowance** approval   187 **redresses sleep** punishments (for the riotous conduct of Lear's attendants) lie dormant   188 **tender . . . weal** care for preservation of the peace of the state   190 **else were** in other circumstances would be regarded as.   **then necessity** the necessity of the times   191 **discreet** prudent   192 **cuckoo** a bird which lays its eggs in other birds' nests   193 **it head** its head.   **it young** i.e., the young cuckoo   194 **darkling** in the dark   197 **fraught** freighted, laden   201 **Jug** i.e., Joan. (The origin of this phrase is uncertain.)   204 **notion** intellectual power   204–205 **discernings Are lethargied** faculties are asleep   205 **Waking** i.e., am I really awake   208 **marks of sovereignty** outward and visible evidence that I am king   211 **Which** whom   213 **admiration** (guise of) wonderment   216 **should** i.e., you should   218 **debosh'd** debauched   220 **Epicurism** luxury   222 **grac'd** honorable   225 **disquantity your train** diminish the number of your attendants   226 **the remainders . . . depend** those who remain to attend you   227 **besort** befit

LEAR: Woe, that too late repents! [O, sir, are you come?]
235 Is it your will? Speak, sir. — Prepare my horses. —
     Ingratitude, thou marble-hearted fiend,
     More hideous when thou show'st thee in a child
     Than the sea-monster!
ALBANY: Pray, sir, be patient.
LEAR: *(To* GONERIL*)*   Detested kite, thou liest!
240 My train are men of choice and rarest parts,
     That all particulars of duty know,
     And in the most exact regard support
     The worships of their name. O most small fault,
     How ugly didst thou in Cordelia show!
245 Which, like an engine, wrench'd my frame of nature
     From the fix'd place; drew from my heart all love,
     And added to the gall. O Lear, Lear, Lear!
     Beat at this gate, that let thy folly in *(Striking his head)*
     And thy dear judgment out! Go, go, my people.

     (Exeunt KNIGHTS *and* KENT.*)*

250 ALBANY: My lord, I am guiltless as I am ignorant
     Of what hath moved you.
LEAR: It may be so, my lord.
     Hear, Nature, hear; dear goddess, hear!
     Suspend thy purpose, if thou didst intend
     To make this creature fruitful!
255 Into her womb convey sterility;
     Dry up in her the organs of increase,
     And from her derogate body never spring
     A babe to honor her! If she must teem,
     Create her child of spleen, that it may live
260 And be a thwart disnatur'd torment to her!
     Let it stamp wrinkles in her brow of youth,
     With cadent tears fret channels in her cheeks,
     Turn all her mother's pains and benefits
     To laughter and contempt, that she may feel
265 How sharper than a serpent's tooth it is
     To have a thankless child! Away, away!   *(Exit.)*
ALBANY: Now, gods that we adore, whereof comes this?
GONERIL: Never afflict yourself to know more of it,
     But let his disposition have that scope
270 As dotage gives it.

     (Enter LEAR.*)*

LEAR: What, fifty of my followers at a clap?
     Within a fortnight?
ALBANY: What's the matter, sir?
LEAR: I'll tell thee. *(To* GONERIL.*)* Life and death! I am
     asham'd
     That thou hast power to shake my manhood thus,
275 That these hot tears, which break from me perforce,
     Should make thee worth them. Blasts and fogs upon thee!

Th' untented woundings of a father's curse
Pierce every sense about thee! Old fond eyes,
Beweep this cause again, I'll pluck ye out,
And cast you, with the waters that you loose,   280
To temper clay. [Yea, is 't come to this?]
Ha! Let it be so. I have another daughter,
Who, I am sure, is kind and comfortable.
When she shall hear this of thee, with her nails
She'll flay thy wolvish visage. Thou shalt find   285
That I'll resume the shape which thou dost think
I have cast off for ever.

(Exit [LEAR, *with* KENT, *and* ATTENDANTS].*)*

GONERIL: Do you mark that?
ALBANY: I cannot be so partial, Goneril,
     To the great love I bear you —
GONERIL: Pray you, content. — What, Oswald, ho!   290
     (To the FOOL.*)* You, sir, more knave than fool, after
     your master.
FOOL: Nuncle Lear, nuncle Lear, tarry, take the fool with thee.
     A fox, when one has caught her,
     And such a daughter,
     Should sure to the slaughter,   295
     If my cap would buy a halter.
     So the fool follows after.

(Exit.)

GONERIL: This man hath had good counsel — a hundred
     knights!
     'Tis politic and safe to let him keep
     At point a hundred knights — yes, that on every dream,   300
     Each buzz, each fancy, each complaint, dislike,
     He may enguard his dotage with their pow'rs
     And hold our lives in mercy. — Oswald, I say!
ALBANY: Well, you may fear too far.
GONERIL: Safer than trust too far.   305
     Let me still take away the harms I fear,
     Not fear still to be taken. I know his heart.
     What he hath utter'd I have writ my sister.
     If she sustain him and his hundred knights,
     When I have show'd th' unfitness —

(Enter steward [OSWALD].*)*

                         How now, Oswald?   310
     What, have you writ that letter to my sister?
OSWALD: Ay, madam.
GONERIL: Take you some company, and away to horse.
     Inform her full of my particular fear,
     and thereto add such reasons of your own   315
     As may compact it more. Get you gone,
     And hasten your return. *(Exit* OSWALD.*)* No, no, my lord,
     This milky gentleness and course of yours

---

234 **Woe, that** woe to the person who   239 **kite** bird of prey   240 **parts** qualities   242 **in . . . regard** with extreme care   243 **worships** honors, reputations   245 **engine** powerful mechanical contrivance, able to wrench Lear's *frame of nature* or natural self from his *fix'd place* or foundation like a building being torn from its foundation   257 **derogate** debased   258 **teem** increase the species   260 **thwart disnatur'd** obstinate perverse   262 **cadent** falling   263 **mother's** motherly.   **benefits** kind offerings   270 **As** which

277 **untented**   too deep to be probed and cleansed   278 **fond** foolish   279 **Beweep** if you weep for   280 **loose** let loose   281 **temper** soften   283 **comfortable** willing to comfort   299 **politic** prudent (Said ironically.)   300 **At point** under arms   301 **buzz** idle rumor   303 **in mercy** at his mercy   304 **fear too far** overestimate the danger   306 **take away** remove   306, 307 **still** always   307 **taken** overtaken (by the *harms*)   316 **compact** confirm   318 **milky . . . course** humane and gentle way

320 Though I condemn not, yet, under pardon,
You are much more attask'd for want of wisdom
Than prais'd for harmful mildness.
ALBANY: How far your eyes may pierce I cannot tell.
Striving to better, oft we mar what's well.
GONERIL: Nay, then —
325 ALBANY: Well, well; th' event.   [*Exeunt.*]

SCENE V

Enter LEAR, KENT [*disguised as Caius*], *and* FOOL.

LEAR: Go you before to Gloucester with these letters. (*Gives let-*
ter.) Acquaint my daughter no further with anything you
know than comes from her demand out of the letter. If your
diligence be not speedy, I shall be there afore you.
5 KENT: I will not sleep, my lord, till I have deliver'd your letter.

(*Exit.*)

FOOL: If a man's brains were in 's heels, were 't not in danger
of kibes?
LEAR: Ay, boy.
FOOL: Then, I prithee, be merry; thy wit shall not go slip-shod.
10 LEAR: Ha, ha, ha!
FOOL: Shalt see thy other daughter will use thee kindly; for
though she's as like this as a crab's like an apple, yet I can tell
what I can tell.
LEAR: What canst tell, boy?
15 FOOL: She will taste as like this as a crab does to a crab. Thou
canst tell why one's nose stands i' th' middle on 's face?
LEAR: No.
FOOL: Why, to keep one's eyes of either side 's nose, that what a
man cannot smell out he may spy into.
20 LEAR: I did her wrong.
FOOL: Canst tell how an oyster makes his shell?
LEAR: No.
FOOL: Nor I neither; but I can tell why a snail has a house.
LEAR: Why?
25 FOOL: Why, to put 's head in; not to give it away to his daughters,
and leave his horns without a case.
LEAR: I will forget my nature. So kind a father! — Be my horses
ready?
FOOL: Thy asses are gone about 'em. The reason why the seven
30 stars are no moe than seven is a pretty reason.
LEAR: Because they are not eight.
FOOL: Yes, indeed. Thou wouldst make a good fool.
LEAR: To take 't again perforce! Monster ingratitude!

319 **under pardon** if you'll excuse my saying so   320 **attask'd** taken to
task for, blamed   321 **harmful mildness** mildness that causes
harm   322 **pierce** i.e., see into matters   325 **th' event** i.e., time will
show

I.v. Location: Before Albany's palace.
1 **Gloucester** i.e., the palace in Gloucestershire.   **these letters** this letter   7 **kibes** chilblains   9 **slip-shod** in slippers, worn because of chilblains. (There are no brains, thinks the Fool, in Lear's heels when they
are on their way to visit Regan.)   11 **Shalt** thou shalt.   **kindly** (1) according to filial nature. (Said ironically.) (2) according to her own nature   12 **crab** crab apple   16 **on 's** of his   20 **her** i.e., Cordelia   26
horns (Suggests cuckold's horns, as though Lear were figuratively not
the father of Goneril and Regan.)   29 **Thy . . . 'em** i.e., your servants
(who labor like asses) have gone about readying the horses   29–30
seven stars Pleiades   33 **again** back again

FOOL: If thou wert my fool, nuncle, I'd have thee beaten for
being old before thy time.   35
LEAR: How's that?
FOOL: Thou shouldst not have been old till thou hadst been wise.
LEAR: O, let me not be mad, not mad, sweet heaven!
Keep me in temper; I would not be mad!

(*Enter* GENTLEMAN.)

How now, are the horses ready?   40
GENTLEMAN: Ready, my lord.
LEAR: Come, boy.
FOOL: She that's a maid now, and laughs at my departure,
Shall not be a maid long, unless things be cut shorter.

(*Exeunt.*)

— ACT TWO —

SCENE I

Enter bastard [EDMUND] *and* CURAN, *severally.*

EDMUND: Save thee, Curan.
CURAN: And you, sir. I have been with your father, and given
him notice that the Duke of Cornwall and Regan his duchess
will be here with him this night.
EDMUND: How comes that?   5
CURAN: Nay, I know not. You have heard of the news abroad — I
mean the whisper'd ones, for they are yet but ear-kissing
arguments?
EDMUND: Not I. Pray you, what are they?
CURAN: Have you heard of no likely wars toward, 'twixt the   10
Dukes of Cornwall and Albany?
EDMUND: Not a word.
CURAN: You may do, then, in time. Fare you well, sir.

(*Exit.*)

EDMUND: The Duke be here tonight? The better! Best!
This weaves itself perforce into my business.   15
My father hath set guard to take my brother,
And I have one thing, of a queasy question,
Which I must act. Briefness and fortune, work!
Brother, a word. Descend. Brother, I say!

(*Enter* EDGAR.)

My father watches. O sir, fly this place!   20
Intelligence is given where you are hid.
You have now the good advantage of the night.
Have you not spoken 'gainst the Duke of Cornwall?
He's coming hither, now, i' th' night, i' th' haste,
And Regan with him. Have you nothing said   25

44 **things** i.e., penises.   **cut shorter** (A bawdy joke addressed to the
audience.)

II.i. Location: The Earl of Gloucester's house.
s.d. **severally** separately   1 **Save** God save   7–8 **ear-kissing arguments**
lightly whispered topics   10 **toward** impending   17 **queasy question**
hazardous or ticklish nature   18 **Briefness and fortune** expeditious dispatch and good luck

Upon his party 'gainst the Duke of Albany?
Advise yourself.
EDGAR: I am sure on 't, not a word.
EDMUND: I hear my father coming. Pardon me;
In cunning I must draw my sword upon you.
30   Draw, seem to defend yourself; now quit you well. —

(They draw.)

Yield! Come before my father! — Light, ho, here! —
Fly, brother. — Torches, torches! — So, farewell.

(Exit EDGAR.*)*

Some blood drawn on me would beget opinion

(Wounds his arm.)

Of my more fierce endeavor. I have seen drunkards
35   Do more than this in sport. — Father, father!
Stop, stop! No help?

(Enter GLOUCESTER, *and* SERVANTS *with torches.)*

GLOUCESTER: Now, Edmund, where's the villain?
EDMUND: Here stood he in the dark, his sharp sword out,
Mumbling of wicked charms, conjuring the moon
To stand auspicious mistress.
40   GLOUCESTER: But where is he?
EDMUND: Look, sir, I bleed.
GLOUCESTER: Where is the villain, Edmund?
EDMUND: Fled this way, sir. When by no means he could —
GLOUCESTER: Pursue him, ho! Go after. *(Exeunt some*
SERVANTS.*)* By no means what?
EDMUND: Persuade me to the murder of your lordship,
45   But that I told him the revenging gods
'Gainst parricides did all the thunder bend,
Spoke with how manifold and strong a bond
The child was bound to th' father; sir, in fine,
Seeing how loathly opposite I stood
50   To his unnatural purpose, in fell motion
With his prepared sword he charges home
My unprovided body, latch'd mine arm;
And when he saw my best alarum'd spirits,
Bold in the quarrel's right, rous'd to th' encounter,
55   Or whether gasted by the noise I made,
Full suddenly he fled.
GLOUCESTER: Let him fly far.
Not in this land shall he remain uncaught;
And found — dispatch. The noble Duke my master,
My worthy arch and patron, comes tonight.
60   By his authority I will proclaim it
That he which finds him shall deserve our thanks,
Bringing the murderous coward to the stake;
He that conceals him, death.
EDMUND: When I dissuaded him from his intent,
65   And found him pight to do it, with curst speech

I threaten'd to discover him. He replied,
"Thou unpossessing bastard, dost thou think,
If I would stand against thee, would the reposal
Of any trust, virtue, or worth in thee
Make thy words faith'd? No. What I should deny —   70
As this I would, ay, though thou didst produce
My very character — I'd turn it all
To thy suggestion, plot, and damned practice;
And thou must make a dullard of the world,
If they not thought the profits of my death   75
Were very pregnant and potential spirits
To make thee seek it."
GLOUCESTER: O strange and fast'ned villain!
Would he deny his letter, said he?
[I never got him.]

(Tucket within.)

Hark, the Duke's trumpets! I know not why he comes.   80
All ports I'll bar; the villain shall not scape;
The Duke must grant me that. Besides, his picture
I will send far and near, that all the kingdom
May have due note of him; and of my land,
Loyal and natural boy, I'll work the means   85
To make thee capable.

(Enter CORNWALL, REGAN, *and* ATTENDANTS*)*

CORNWALL: How now, my noble friend? Since I came hither,
Which I can call but now, I have heard strange news.
REGAN: If it be true, all vengeance comes too short
Which can pursue th' offender. How dost, my lord?   90
GLOUCESTER: O, madam, my old heart is crack'd, it's crack'd!
REGAN: What, did my father's godson seek your life?
He whom my father nam'd? Your Edgar?
GLOUCESTER: O, lady, lady, shame would have it hid!
REGAN: Was he not companion with the riotous knights   95
That tended upon my father?
GLOUCESTER: I know not, madam. 'Tis too bad, too bad.
EDMUND: Yes, madam, he was of that consort.
REGAN: No marvel, then, though he were ill affected.
'Tis they have put him on the old man's death,   100
To have th' expense and waste of his revenues.
I have this present evening from my sister
Been well inform'd of them, and with such cautions,
That if they come to sojourn at my house,
I'll not be there.
CORNWALL: Nor I, assure thee, Regan.   105
Edmund, I hear that you have shown your father
A child-like office.

26 Upon his party 'gainst i.e., reflecting on his feud with   **27 Advise yourself** think it over carefully   **30 quit you** acquit yourself   **46 bend** aim   **48 in fine** in conclusion   **49 loathly opposite** loathingly opposed   **50 fell motion** deadly thrust   **52 unprovided** unarmed.   **latch'd** nicked, lanced   **53 best alarum'd** thoroughly aroused to action as by a trumpet   **54 quarrel's right** justice of the cause   **55 gasted** frightened   **58 dispatch** i.e., that will be the end for him   **59 arch** chief   **65 pight** determined.   **curst** angry

66 discover expose   **67 unpossessing** unable to inherit, beggarly   **68 reposal** placing   **70 faith'd** believed   **72 character** written testimony   **73 suggestion** instigation.   **practice** plot   **74 make . . . world** think everyone idiotic   **75 not thought** did not think.   **of my death** i.e., that Edmund would gain through Edgar's death   **76 pregnant . . . spirits** fertile and potent tempters   **77 fast'ned** confirmed   **79 got** begot   s.d. **Tucket** series of notes on the trumpet, here indicating Cornwall's arrival   **81 ports** gateways   **86 capable** legally able to become the inheritor   **98 consort** set, company   **100 put him on** incited him to   **101 expense and waste** squandering   **107 child-like** filial

EDMUND: It was my duty, sir.
GLOUCESTER: He did bewray his practice, and receiv'd
    This hurt you see, striving to apprehend him.
110 CORNWALL: Is he pursued?
GLOUCESTER: Ay, my good lord.
CORNWALL: If he be taken, he shall never more
    Be fear'd of doing harm. Make your own purpose,
    How in my strength you please. For you, Edmund,
115 Whose virtue and obedience doth this instant
    So much commend itself, you shall be ours.
    Natures of such deep trust we shall much need;
    You we first seize on.
EDMUND: I shall serve you, sir,
    Truly, however else.
120 GLOUCESTER: For him I thank your Grace.
CORNWALL: You know not why we came to visit you—
REGAN: Thus out of season, threading dark-ey'd night.
    Occasions, noble Gloucester, of some prize,
    Wherein we must have use of your advice.
125 Our father he hath writ, so hath our sister,
    Of differences, which I best thought it fit
    To answer from our home; the several messengers
    From hence attend dispatch. Our good old friend,
    Lay comforts to your bosom, and bestow
130 Your needful counsel to our businesses,
    Which craves the instant use.
GLOUCESTER: I serve you, madam.
    Your Graces are right welcome.

(Exeunt. Flourish.)

SCENE II

(Enter KENT [disguised as Caius] and steward [OSWALD], severally.)

OSWALD: Good dawning to thee, friend. Art of this house?
KENT: Ay.
OSWALD: Where may we set our horses?
KENT: I' th' mire.
5 OSWALD: Prithee, if thou lov'st me, tell me.
KENT: I love thee not.
OSWALD: Why, then, I care not for thee.
KENT: If I had thee in Lipsbury pinfold, I would make thee
    care for me.
10 OSWALD: Why dost thou use me thus? I know thee not.
KENT: Fellow, I know thee.
OSWALD: What dost thou know me for?

KENT: A knave, a rascal, an eater of broken meats; a base, proud,
    shallow, beggarly, three-suited, hundred-pound, filthy,
    worsted-stocking knave; a lily-liver'd, action-taking, whore- 15
    son, glass-gazing, superservicable, finical rogue; one-trunk-
    inheriting slave; one that wouldst be a bawd in way of good
    service, and art nothing but the composition of a knave, beg-
    gar, coward, pander, and the son and heir of a mongrel bitch;
    one whom I will beat into clamorous whining, if thou deny'st 20
    the least syllable of thy addition.
OSWALD: Why, what a monstrous fellow art thou, thus to rail on
    one that is neither known of thee nor knows thee!
KENT: What a brazen-fac'd varlet art thou, to deny thou knowest
    me! Is it two days since I tripp'd up thy heels and beat thee 25
    before the King? Draw, you rogue, for, though it be night, yet
    the moon shines. I'll make a sop o' th' moonshine of you. You
    whoreson cullionly barber-monger, draw!

(Draws his sword.)

OSWALD Away! I have nothing to do with thee.
KENT: Draw, you rascal! You come with letters against the King, 30
    and take Vanity the puppet's part against the royalty of her
    father. Draw, you rogue, or I'll so carbonado your shanks.
    Draw, you rascal! Come your ways.
OSWALD: Help, ho! Murder! Help!
KENT: Strike, you slave! Stand, rogue, stand, you neat slave, 35
    strike!

(Beats him.)

OSWALD: Help, ho! Murder! Murder!

(Enter bastard [EDMUND, with his rapier drawn], CORNWALL, REGAN, GLOUCESTER, SERVANTS.)

EDMUND: How now, what's the matter? Part!
KENT: With you, goodman boy, if you please! Come, I'll flesh
    ye. Come on, young master.   40
GLOUCESTER: Weapons? Arms? What's the matter here?
CORNWALL: Keep peace, upon your lives! (KENT *and* OSWALD
    are parted). He dies that strikes again. What is the matter?
REGAN: The messengers from our sister and the King.
CORNWALL: What is your difference? Speak.   45
OSWALD: I am scarce in breath, my lord.
KENT: No marvel, you have so bestirr'd your valor. You cowardly
    rascal, nature disclaims in thee. A tailor made thee.

---

13 **broken meats** scraps of food   14 **three-suited** (Three suits a year were allowed to servants.)   **hundred-pound** (Possible allusion to the minimum property qualification for the status of gentleman.)   15 **worsted-stocking** i.e., too poor and menial to wear silk stockings   15 **action-taking** settling quarrels by resort to law instead of arms, cowardly   16 **glass-gazing** fond of looking in the mirror   **superservicable** officious.   **finical** foppish, fastidious.   16–17 **one-trunk-inheriting** possessing effects sufficient for one trunk only   17–18 **bawd . . . service** i.e., pimp or pander as a way of providing good service   18 **composition** composite   21 **addition** titles   27 **sop o' th' moonshine** something so perforated that it will soak up moonshine as a sop (floating piece of toast) soaks up liquor   28 **cullionly barber-monger** base frequenter of barber shops, fop. (*Cullion* originally meant *testicle*.)   31 **Vanity . . . part** i.e., the part of Goneril (here personified as a character in a morality play)   32 **carbonado** cut crosswise like meat for broiling   33 **Come your ways** come on   35 **neat** (1) foppish (2) calf-like. (*Neat* means "horned cattle.")   38 **matter** i.e., trouble. (But Kent takes the meaning *cause for quarrel*.)   39 **goodman boy** (A contemptuous epithet.)   39 **flesh** initiate into combat   48 **disclaims in** disowns

---

108 **bewray his practice** expose his (Edgar's) plot   113–114 **Make . . . please** form your plans, making free use of my authority   114 **For** as for   123 **prize** significance   126 **differences** quarrels   127 **from** away from   128 **attend dispatch** wait to be dispatched   130 **needful** necessary   131 **instant use** immediate attention

II.ii. Location: Before Gloucester's house.
1 **dawning** (It is not yet day.)   5 **if thou lov'st me** i.e., if you bear good will toward me. (But Kent deliberately takes the phrase in its literal, not courtly, sense.)   8 **Lipsbury pinfold** i.e., within the pinfold of the lips, between my teeth. (A *pinfold* is a pound for stray animals.)

CORNWALL: Thou art a strange fellow. A tailor make a man?

50 KENT: A tailor, sir. A stone-cutter or a painter could not have made him so ill, though they had been but two years o' th' trade.

CORNWALL: Speak yet, how grew your quarrel?

OSWALD: This ancient ruffian, sir, whose life I have spar'd at suit

55 of his gray beard —

KENT: Thou whoreson zed! Thou unnecessary letter! My lord, if you will give me leave, I will tread this unbolted villain into mortar, and daub the wall of a jakes with him. Spare my gray beard, you wagtail?

60 CORNWALL: Peace, sirrah!

You beastly knave, know you no reverence?

KENT: Yes, sir; but anger hath a privilege.

CORNWALL: Why art thou angry?

KENT: That such a slave as this should wear a sword,

65 Who wears no honesty. Such smiling rogues as these,

Like rats, oft bite the holy cords a-twain

Which are too intrinse t' unloose; smooth every passion

That in the natures of their lords rebel,

Bring oil to fire, snow to their colder moods;

70 Renege, affirm, and turn their halcyon beaks

With every gale and vary of their masters,

Knowing nought, like dogs, but following.

A plague upon your epileptic visage!

Smile you my speeches, as I were a fool?

75 Goose, if I had you upon Sarum plain,

I'd drive ye cackling home to Camelot.

CORNWALL: What, art thou mad, old fellow?

GLOUCESTER: How fell you out? Say that.

KENT: No contraries hold more antipathy

80 Than I and such a knave.

CORNWALL: Why dost thou call him knave? What is his fault?

KENT: His countenance likes me not.

CORNWALL: No more, perchance, does mine, nor his, nor hers.

KENT: Sir, 'tis my occupation to be plain:

85 I have seen better faces in my time

Than stands on any shoulder that I see

Before me at this instant.

CORNWALL: This is some fellow

Who, having been prais'd for bluntness, doth affect

A saucy roughness, and constrains the garb

90 Quite from his nature. He cannot flatter, he,

An honest mind and plain, he must speak truth!

An they will take it, so; if not, he's plain.

These kind of knaves I know, which in this plainness

Harbor more craft and more corrupter ends

Than twenty silly ducking observants   95

That stretch their duties nicely.

KENT: Sir, in good faith, in sincere verity,

Under th' allowance of your great aspect,

Whose influence, like the wreath of radiant fire

On flick'ring Phoebus' front —

CORNWALL: What mean'st by this?   100

KENT: To go out of my dialect, which you discommend so much. I know, sir, I am no flatterer. He that beguil'd you in a plain accent was a plain knave, which for my part I will not be, though I should win your displeasure to entreat me to 't.

CORNWALL: What was th' offense you gave him?   105

OSWALD: I never gave him any.

It pleas'd the King his master very late

To strike at me, upon his misconstruction;

When he, compact, and flattering his displeasure,

Tripp'd me behind; being down, insulted, rail'd,   110

And put upon him such a deal of man

That worthied him, got praises of the King

For him attempting who was self-subdu'd,

And, in the fleshment of this dread exploit,

Drew on me here again.   115

KENT: None of these rogues and cowards

But Ajax is their fool.

CORNWALL: Fetch forth the stocks!

You stubborn ancient knave, you reverent braggart,

We'll teach you —

KENT: Sir, I am too old to learn.

Call not your stocks for me. I serve the King,   120

On whose employment I was sent to you.

You shall do small respect, show too bold malice

Against the grace and person of my master,

Stocking his messenger.

CORNWALL: Fetch forth the stocks! As I have life and honor,   125

There shall he sit till noon.

REGAN: Till noon? Till night, my lord; and all night too.

KENT: Why, madam, if I were your father's dog,

You should not use me so.

REGAN: Sir, being his knave, I will.   130

---

56 **zed** the letter z, regarded as unnecessary and often not included in dictionaries   57 **unbolted** unsifted; hence, coarse   58 **daub** plaster. **jakes** privy   59 **wagtail** i.e., bird wagging its tailfeathers in pert obsequiousness   66 **holy cords** sacred bonds of affection and order   67 **intrinse** intricate, tightly knotted.   **smooth** flatter, humor   70 **Renege** deny.   **halcyon beaks** (The halcyon of kingfisher, if hung up, would supposedly turn its beak against the wind.)   71 **gale and vary** variation in the wind   73 **epileptic** i.e., pale with fright and distorted with a grin (?)   74 **Smile you** do you smile at.   **as** as if   75 **Sarum** Salisbury   76 **Camelot** legendary seat of King Arthur and his Round Table, said to have been at Cadbury and at Winchester and hence in the general vicinity of Salisbury and Gloucester   82 **likes** pleases   89–90 **constrains . . . nature** i.e., distorts plainness to the point of caricature, away from its true purpose

95 **ducking observants** bowing, obsequious courtiers   96 **nicely** punctiliously   97 **Sir, in good faith,** etc. (Kent assumes the wordy mannerisms of courtly flattery.)   98 **allowance** approval.   **aspect** (1) countenance (2) astrological position   99 **influence** astrological might   100 **Phoebus' front** i.e., the sun's forehead   102 – 103 **He . . . accent** i.e., the man who used plain speech to you craftily (see ll. 93–96) and thereby taught you to suspect plain speakers of deceit   103–104 **which . . . me to 't** i.e., I will no longer use plain speech, despite the incentive of incurring your displeasure by doing so. (Kent prefers to displease Cornwall, since Cornwall is pleased only by flatterers, and Kent has assumed until now that plain speech was the best way to offend; but he now argues mockingly that he can no longer speak plainly since his honest utterance will be interpreted as duplicity.)   107 **late** recently   108 **misconstruction** misunderstanding (me)   109 **he** i.e., Kent.   **compact** joined, united with the King   111 **put . . . man** acted like such a hero   114 **worthied** won reputation for   113 **For . . . self-subdu'd** for assailing one (i.e., myself) who chose not to resist   114 **fleshment** excitement resulting from a first success   116–117 **None . . . fool** i.e., you never find any rogues and cowards of this sort who do not outdo the blustering Ajax in their boasting   118 **reverent** reverend (because old)   123 **grace** sovereignty

CORNWALL: This is a fellow of the self-same color
  Our sister speaks of. Come, bring away the stocks!

(Stocks brought out.)

GLOUCESTER: Let me beseech your Grace not to do so.
  [His fault is much, and the good King his master
135   Will check him for 't. Your purpos'd low correction
  Is such as basest and contemned'st wretches
  For pilf'rings and most common trespasses
  Are punish'd with.] The King must take it ill
  That he, so slightly valued in his messenger,
  Should have him thus restrain'd.
140 CORNWALL: I'll answer that.
REGAN: My sister may receive it much more worse
  To have her gentleman abus'd, assaulted,
  [For following her affairs. Put in his legs.]

(KENT is put in the stocks.)

  Come, my lord, away.

(Exit [with all but GLOUCESTER and KENT].)

145 GLOUCESTER: I am sorry for thee, friend. 'Tis the Duke's
    pleasure,
  Whose disposition, all the world well knows,
  Will not be rubb'd nor stopp'd. I'll entreat for thee.
KENT: Pray, do not, sir. I have watch'd and travel'd hard.
  Some time I shall sleep out, the rest I'll whistle.
150 A good man's fortune may grow out at heels.
  Give you good morrow!
GLOUCESTER: The Duke's to blame in this. 'Twill be ill taken.

(Exit.)

KENT: Good King, that must approve the common saw,
  Thou out of heaven's benediction com'st
155 To the warm sun!
  Approach, thou beacon to this under globe,
  That by thy comfortable beams I may
  Peruse this letter. Nothing almost sees miracles
  But misery. *(Examines letter.)* I know 'tis from Cordelia,
160 Who hath most fortunately been inform'd
  Of my obscured course; and shall find time
  From this enormous state, seeking to give
  Losses their remedies. All weary and o'erwatch'd,
  Take vantage, heavy eyes, not to behold
165 This shameful lodging.
  Fortune, good night. Smile once more; turn thy wheel!

(Sleeps.)

132 **away** along   135 **check** rebuke, correct   147 **rubb'd** hindered, obstructed. (A term from bowls.)   148 **watch'd** gone sleepless   150 **A . . . heels** i.e., even good men suffer decline in fortune at times   151 **Give you** i.e., God give you   153 **approve** prove true.   **saw** proverb (i.e., "To run out of God's blessing into the warm sun," meaning "to go from better to worse")   156 **beacon . . . globe** the moon (see ll. 26—27 and 166)   157 **comfortable** useful, aiding   158–159 **Nothing . . . misery** i.e., scarcely anything can make one appreciate miracles like being in a state of misery   161 **obscured** disguised.   **shall** she shall   161—163 **and . . . remedies** (This incoherent passage is either textually corrupt or fragments from the letter Kent is reading.)   162 **From** i.e., to provide relief from (?)   **enormous state** monstrous state of affairs, enormity   163 **Losses** reversals of fortune.   **o'erwatch'd** exhausted with staying awake   164 **vantage** advantage (of sleep)   165 **lodging** i.e., the stocks   166 **wheel** (Since Kent is at the bottom of Fortune's wheel, any turning will improve his situation.)

[SCENE III]

Enter EDGAR.

EDGAR: I heard myself proclaim'd,
  And by the happy hollow of a tree
  Escap'd the hunt. No port is free, no place
  That guard and most unusual vigilance
  Does not attend my taking. Whiles I may scape,   5
  I will preserve myself, and am bethought
  To take the basest and most poorest shape
  That ever penury, in contempt of man,
  Brought near to beast. My face I'll grime with filth,
  Blanket my loins, elf all my hairs in knots,   10
  And with presented nakedness outface
  The winds and persecutions of the sky.
  The country gives me proof and precedent
  Of Bedlam beggars, who, with roaring voices,
  Strike in their numb'd and mortified arms   15
  Pins, wooden pricks, nails, sprigs of rosemary;
  And with this horrible object, from low farms,
  Poor pelting villages, sheep-cotes, and mills,
  Sometimes with lunatic bans, sometime with prayers,
  Enforce their charity. Poor Turlygod! Poor Tom!   20
  That's something yet. Edgar I nothing am.

(Exit.)

[SCENE IV]

Enter LEAR, FOOL, and GENTLEMAN.

LEAR: 'Tis strange that they should so depart from home,
  And not send back my messenger.
GENTLEMAN: As I learn'd,
  The night before there was no purpose in them
  Of this remove.
KENT: Hail to thee, noble master!
LEAR: Ha?   5
  Mak'st thou this shame thy pastime?
KENT: No, my lord.
FOOL: Ha, ha, he wears cruel garters. Horses are tied by the
  heads, dogs and bears by th' neck, monkeys by th' loins, and
  men by th' legs. When a man's over-lusty at legs, then he
  wears wooden nether-stocks.   10
LEAR: What's he that hath so much thy place mistook
  To set thee here?
KENT: It is both he and she;
  Your son and daughter.
LEAR: No.
KENT: Yes.   15
LEAR: No, I say.

II.iii. Location: Scene continues. Kent is dozing in the stocks.
2 **happy** luckily found   5 **attend** watch, wait for   6 **bethought** resolved   10 **elf** tangle into elf-locks   11 **presented** i.e., this display of   13 **proof** example   14 **Bedlam** (See note to I.ii. 124–125.)   15 **Strike** stick.   **mortified** deadened   16 **wooden pricks** skewers   17 **object** spectacle.   **low** lowly   18 **pelting** paltry   19 **bans** curses   20 **Turlygod** (Meaning unknown.)   21 **Edgar** i.e., as Edgar

II.iv. Location: Scene continues before Gloucester's house. Kent still dozing in the stocks.
4 **remove** change of residence   7 **cruel** (Q: *crewell*, a double meaning [1] unkind [2] crewel, a thin yarn of which garters were made.)   9 **over-lusty at legs** given to running away   10 **nether-stocks** stockings

KENT: I say, yea.
[LEAR: No, no, they would not.
KENT: Yes, they have.]
20 LEAR: By Jupiter, I swear no.
KENT: By Juno, I swear ay.
LEAR: They durst not do 't!
  They could not, would not do 't. 'Tis worse than murder
  To do upon respect such violent outrage.
  Resolve me, with all modest haste, which way
25 Thou mightst deserve, or they impose, this usage,
  Coming from us.
    KENT: My lord, when at their home
  I did commend your Highness' letters to them,
  Ere I was risen from the place that show'd
  My duty kneeling, came there a reeking post,
30 Stew'd in his haste, half breathless, panting forth
  From Goneril his mistress salutations;
  Deliver'd letters, spite of intermission,
  Which presently they read; on whose contents
  They summon'd up their meiny, straight took horse,
35 Commanded me to follow and attend
  The leisure of their answer, gave me cold looks;
  And meeting here the other messenger,
  Whose welcome, I perceiv'd, had poison'd mine—
  Being the very fellow which of late
40 Display'd so saucily against your Highness—
  Having more man than wit about me, drew.
  He rais'd the house with loud and coward cries.
  Your son and daughter found this trespass worth
  The shame which here it suffers.
45 FOOL: Winter's not gone yet, if the wild-geese fly that way.
      Fathers that wear rags
        Do make their children blind,
      But fathers that bear bags
        Shall see their children kind.
50   Fortune, that arrant whore,
      Ne'er turns the key to th' poor.
  But, for all this, thou shalt have as many dolors for thy daugh-
  ters as thou canst tell in a year.
  LEAR: O, how this mother swells up toward my heart!
55 Hysterica passio, down, thou climbing sorrow,
  Thy element's below!—Where is this daughter?
  KENT: With the Earl, sir, here within.
  LEAR: Follow me not; stay here.   (Exit.)
  GENTLEMAN: Made you no more offense but what you speak of?
60 KENT: None.
  How chance the King comes with so small a number?

FOOL: An thou hadst been set i' th' stocks for that question,
  thou'dst well deserv'd it.
KENT: Why, fool?
FOOL: We'll set thee to school to an ant, to teach thee there's no   65
  laboring i' th' winter. All that follow their noses are led by
  their eyes but blind men, and there's not a nose among twenty
  but can smell him that's stinking. Let go thy hold when a great
  wheel runs down a hill, lest it break thy neck with following;
  but the great one that goes upward, let him draw thee after.   70
  When a wise man gives thee better counsel, give me mine
  again. I would have none but knaves follow it, since a fool
  gives it.
      That sir which serves and seeks for gain,
        And follows but for form,   75
      Will pack when it begins to rain,
        And leave thee in the storm.
      But I will tarry; the fool will stay,
        And let the wise man fly.
      The knave turns fool that runs away;   80
        The fool no knave, perdy.

(Enter LEAR and GLOUCESTER.)

KENT: Where learn'd you this, fool?
FOOL: Not i' th' stocks, fool.
LEAR: Deny to speak with me? They are sick? They are weary?
  They have travel'd all the night? Mere fetches,   85
  The images of revolt and flying off.
  Fetch me a better answer.
GLOUCESTER: My dear lord,
  You know the fiery quality of the Duke,
  How unremovable and fix'd he is
  In his own course.   90
LEAR: Vengeance! Plague! Death! Confusion!
  Fiery? What quality? Why, Gloucester, Gloucester,
  I 'd speak with the Duke of Cornwall and his wife.
GLOUCESTER: Well, my good lord, I have inform'd them so.
LEAR: Inform'd them? Dost thou understand me, man?   95
GLOUCESTER: Ay, my good lord.
LEAR: The King would speak with Cornwall. The dear father
  Would with his daughter speak, commands, tends, service.
  Are they inform'd of this? My breath and blood!
  Fiery? The fiery Duke? Tell the hot Duke that—   100
  No, but not yet. May be he is not well.
  Infirmity doth still neglect all office
  Whereto our health is bound; we are not ourselves
  When nature, being oppress'd, commands the mind
  To suffer with the body. I'll forbear,   105
  And am fallen out with my more headier will,
  To take the indispos'd and sickly fit
  For the sound man. (Looks at KENT.) Death on my state!
    Wherefore

23 **upon respect** i.e., against my delegates (who deserve respect) 24
Resolve enlighten. **modest** moderate 26 **their home** (Kent and Oswald went first to Cornwall's palace after leaving Albany's palace.) 27
commend deliver 29 **reeking** steaming (with heat of travel) 30 **Stew'd**
i.e., thoroughly heated 32 **spite of intermission** in disregard of interrupting me 33 **presently** instantly 34 **meiny** retinue of servants, household
40 **Display'd so saucily** behaved so insolently 41 **man** manhood 45
Winter . . . way i.e., the signs will point to continued and worsening
fortune 47 **blind** i.e., indifferent to their father's needs 48 **bags** i.e., of
gold 51 **turns the key** i.e., opens the door 52 **dolors** griefs (with pun on
dollars, English word for an Austrian or Spanish coin) 53 **tell** (1) relate (2)
count 54, 55 **mother, Hysterica passio** i.e., hysteria, giving the sensation
of choking or suffocating 56 **element's** proper place is. (Hysteria was
thought to be produced by vapors ascending from the abdomen.)

61 **chance** chances it 65–66 **We'll . . . winter** i.e., just as the ant knows
not to labor in the winter, the wise man knows not to labor for one whose
fortunes are fallen 66–68 **All . . . stinking** i.e., one who is out of favor
can be easily detected (he smells of misfortune), and so is easily avoided by
timeservers 76 **pack** be off 80 **The knave . . . away** i.e., deserting one's
master is the greatest folly 81 **perdy** *par Dieu* (French), by God 85
fetches pretexts, dodges 86 **images** signs. **flying off** desertion 98 **tends**
attends, waits for 102–103 **all . . . bound** duties which in good health we
are bound to perform 106–107 **am . . . take** now disapprove of my more
impetuous will in taking 108 **state** royal authority

Should he sit here? This act persuades me
110 That this remotion of the Duke and her
Is practice only. Give me my servant forth.
Go tell the Duke and 's wife I'd speak with them,
Now, presently. Bid them come forth and hear me,
Or at their chamber-door I'll beat the drum
115 Till it cry sleep to death.
GLOUCESTER: I would have all well betwixt you.

(Exit.)

LEAR: O me, my heart, my rising heart! But down!
FOOL: Cry to it, nuncle, as the cockney did to the eels when she
put 'em i' th' paste alive. She knapp'd 'em o' th' coxcombs
120 with a stick, and cried "Down, wantons, down!" 'Twas her
brother that, in pure kindness to his horse, butter'd his hay.

(Enter CORNWALL, REGAN, GLOUCESTER, [and] SERVANTS.)

LEAR: Good morrow to you both.
CORNWALL: Hail to your Grace!

(KENT here set at liberty.)

REGAN: I am glad to see your Highness.
LEAR: Regan, I think you are. I know what reason
125 I have to think so. If thou shouldst not be glad,
I would divorce me from thy mother's tomb,
Sepulchring an adultress. (To KENT.) O, are you free?
Some other time for that. — Beloved Regan,
Thy sister's naught. O Regan, she hath tied
130 Sharp-tooth'd unkindness, like a vulture, here.

(Points to his heart.)

I can scarce speak to thee. Thou 'lt not believe
With how deprav'd a quality — O Regan!
REGAN: I pray you, sir, take patience. I have hope
You less know how to value her desert
Than she to scant her duty.
135 LEAR: Say, how is that?
REGAN: I cannot think my sister in the least
Would fail her obligation. If, sir, perchance
She have restrain'd the riots of your followers,
'Tis o' such ground, and to such wholesome end,
140 As clears her from all blame.
LEAR: My curses on her!
REGAN: O, sir, you are old;
Nature in you stands on the very verge
Of his confine. You should be rul'd and led
By some discretion that discerns your state
145 Better than you yourself. Therefore, I pray you
That to our sister you do make return;
Say you have wrong'd her.

LEAR: Ask her forgiveness?
Do you but mark how this becomes the house:
"Dear daughter, I confess that I am old;

(Kneels.)

Age is unnecessary. On my knees I beg   150
That you'll vouchsafe me raiment, bed, and food."
REGAN: Good sir, no more. These are unsightly tricks.
Return you to my sister.
LEAR: (Rising)   Never, Regan.
She hath abated me of half my train,
Look'd black upon me, struck me with her tongue,   155
Most serpent-like, upon the very heart.
All the stor'd vengeances of heaven fall
On her ingrateful top! Strike her young bones,
You taking airs, with lameness!
CORNWALL: Fie, sir, fie!
LEAR: You nimble lightnings, dart your blinding flames   160
Into her scornful eyes! Infect her beauty,
You fen-suck'd fogs, drawn by the pow'rful sun,
To fall and blister!
REGAN: O the blest gods! So will you wish on me,
When the rash mood is on.   165
LEAR: No, Regan, thou shalt never have my curse.
Thy tender-hefted nature shall not give
Thee o'er to harshness. Her eyes are fierce, but thine
Do comfort and not burn. 'Tis not in thee
To grudge my pleasures, to cut off my train,   170
To bandy hasty words, to scant my sizes,
And in conclusion to oppose the bolt
Against my coming in. Thou better know'st
The offices of nature, bond of childhood,
Effects of courtesy, dues of gratitude.   175
Thy half o' th' kingdom hast thou not forgot,
Wherein I thee endow'd.
REGAN: Good sir, to th' purpose.
LEAR: Who put my man i' th' stocks?

(Tucket within.)

CORNWALL: What trumpet's that?
REGAN: I know 't, my sister's. This approves her letter,
That she would soon be here.

(Enter steward [OSWALD].)

                                    Is your lady come?   180
LEAR: This is a slave, whose easy-borrowed pride
Dwells in the fickle grace of her he follows.
Out, varlet, from my sight!
CORNWALL: What means your Grace?
LEAR: Who stock'd my servant? Regan, I have good hope
Thou didst not know on 't.

110 **remotion** removal, inaccessibility 111 **practice** deception 115 **cry sleep to death** i.e., hound sleep to death 118 **cockney** i.e., Londoner, ignorant of ways of cooking eels 119 **paste** pastry pie. **knapp'd** rapped. **coxcombs** heads 120 **wantons** playful creatures, promiscuous things 120–121 **'Twas . . . hay** (Another city ignorance; the act is well-intended, but horses do not like greasy hay.) 126 **divorce me** i.e., refuse to be buried beside 127 **Sepulchring** i.e., since it would surely contain the dead body of 129 **naught** wicked 132 **quality** disposition 142–143 **Nature . . . confine** i.e., your life has almost completed its allotted scope 144 **discretion** discreet person. **discerns your state** understands your situation

148 **becomes the house** suits domestic decorum 158 **ingrateful top** ungrateful head 159 **taking** infectious 162 **fen-suck'd** (It was supposed that the sun sucked up poisons from fens or marshes.) 163 **fall** strike 167 **tender-hefted** gently disposed 171 **scant my sizes** diminish my allowances 172 **oppose the bolt** lock the door 174 **offices of nature** natural duties 175 **Effects** actions 177 **purpose** point 179 **approves** confirms 181 **easy-borrowed** i.e., acquired with little collateral, weak commitment 182 **grace** favor 183 **varlet** worthless fellow

(Enter GONERIL.*)*

185
                     Who comes here? O heavens,
If you do love old men, if your sweet sway
Allow obedience, if you yourselves are old,
Make it your cause; send down, and take my part!
(To GONERIL.*)* Art not asham'd to look upon this beard?

*(*GONERIL *and* REGAN *join hands.)*

190
   O Regan, will you take her by the hand?
GONERIL: Why not by th' hand, sir? How have I offended?
   All's not offense that indiscretion finds
   And dotage terms so.
LEAR: O sides, you are too tough!
   Will you yet hold? How came my man i' th' stocks?
195
CORNWALL: I set him there, sir; but his own disorders
   Deserv'd much less advancement.
LEAR: You? Did you?
REGAN: I pray you, father, being weak, seem so.
   If, till the expiration of your month,
   You will return and sojourn with my sister,
200
   Dismissing half your train, come then to me.
   I am now from home, and out of that provision
   Which shall be needful for your entertainment.
LEAR: Return to her, and fifty men dismiss'd?
   No! Rather I abjure all roofs, and choose
205
   To wage against the enmity o' th' air,
   To be a comrade with the wolf and owl—
   Necessity's sharp pinch. Return with her?
   Why, the hot-blooded France, that dowerless took
   Our youngest born, I could as well be brought
210
   To knee his throne, and squire-like, pension beg
   To keep base life afoot. Return with her?
   Persuade me rather to be slave and sumpter
   To this detested groom.

(Points to OSWALD.*)*

GONERIL: At your choice, sir.
LEAR: I prithee, daughter, do not make me mad.
215
   I will not trouble thee, my child; farewell.
   We'll no more meet, no more see one another.
   But yet thou art my flesh, my blood, my daughter;
   Or rather a disease that's in my flesh,
   Which I must needs call mine. Thou art a boil,
220
   A plague-sore, or embossed carbuncle
   In my corrupted blood. But I'll not chide thee;
   Let shame come when it will, I do not call it.
   I do not bid the thunder-bearer shoot,
   Nor tell tales of thee to high-judging Jove.
225
   Mend when thou canst, be better at thy leisure;
   I can be patient. I can stay with Regan,
   I and my hundred knights.
REGAN: Not altogether so.
   I look'd not for you yet, nor am provided
230
   For your fit welcome. Give ear, sir, to my sister;

For those that mingle reason with your passion
Must be content to think you old, and so—
But she knows what she does.
LEAR: Is this well spoken?
REGAN: I dare avouch it, sir. What, fifty followers?
   Is it not well? What should you need of more?   235
   Yea, or so many, sith that both charge and danger
   Speak 'gainst so great a number? How, in one house,
   Should many people under two commands
   Hold amity? 'Tis hard, almost impossible.
GONERIL: Why might not you, my lord, receive attendance   240
   From those that she calls servants or from mine?
REGAN: Why not, my lord? If then they chanc'd to slack ye,
   We could control them. If you will come to me—
   For now I spy a danger—I entreat you
   To bring but five and twenty. To no more   245
   Will I give place or notice.
LEAR: I gave you all—
REGAN: And in good time you gave it.
LEAR: Made you my guardians, my depositaries,
   But kept a reservation to be followed
   With such a number. What, must I come to you   250
   With five and twenty? Regan, said you so?
REGAN: And speak 't again, my lord; no more with me.
LEAR: Those wicked creatures yet do look well-favor'd
   When others are more wicked; not being the worst
   Stands in some rank of praise. *(To* GONERIL.*)* I'll go with 255
     thee.
   Thy fifty yet doth double five-and-twenty,
   And thou art twice her love.
GONERIL: Hear me, my lord:
   What need you five and twenty, ten, or five,
   To follow in a house where twice so many
   Have a command to tend you?
REGAN: What need one?   260
LEAR: O, reason not the need! Our basest beggars
   Are in the poorest thing superfluous.
   Allow not nature more than nature needs,
   Man's life is cheap as beast's. Thou art a lady;
   If only to go warm were gorgeous,   265
   Why, nature needs not what thou gorgeous wear'st,
   Which scarcely keeps thee warm. But, for true need—
   You heavens, give me that patience, patience I need!
   You see me here, you gods, a poor old man,
   As full of grief as age, wretched in both.   270
   If it be you that stirs these daughters' hearts
   Against their father, fool me not so much
   To bear it tamely; touch me with noble anger,

---

231 **mingle . . . passion** consider your passionate behavior reasonably   234 **avouch** vouch for   236 **sith that** since.   **charge** expense   242 **slack** neglect   246 **notice** recognition, acknowledgment   248 **depositaries** trustees   249 **kept a reservation** reserved a right   255 **Stands . . . praise** achieves, by necessity, some relative deserving of praise   261 **reason not** do not dispassionately analyze   262 **Are . . . superfluous** have some wretched possession they can dispense with   263 **Allow not** if you do not allow.   **needs** i.e., to survive   265–267 **If . . . warm** ie., if fashions in clothes were determined only by the need for warmth, this natural standard wouldn't justify the rich robes you wear to be gorgeous—which don't serve well for warmth in any case   272–273 **fool . . . To** do not make me so foolish as to

---

187 **Allow** approve, sanction   205 **wage** wage war   208 **hot-blooded** choleric (Cf. I.ii. 23.)   210 **knee** fall on my knees before   212 **sumpter** pack horse; hence, drudge   220 **embossed** swollen, tumid   222 **call** summon   223 **thunder-bearer** i.e., Jove   224 **high-judging** judging from on high

And let not women's weapons, water-drops,
275   Stain my man's cheeks! No, you unnatural hags,
I will have such revenges on you both,
That all the world shall—I will do such things—
What they are, yet I know not, but they shall be
The terrors of the earth. You think I'll weep;
280   No, I'll not weep.

(Storm and tempest.)

I have full cause of weeping; but this heart
Shall break into a hundred thousand flaws
Or ere I'll weep. O fool, I shall go mad!

(Exeunt [LEAR, GLOUCESTER, KENT, and FOOL].)

CORNWALL: Let us withdraw; 'twill be a storm.
285   REGAN: This house is little. The old man and 's people
Cannot be well bestow'd.
GONERIL: 'Tis his own blame hath put himself from rest,
And must needs taste his folly.
REGAN: For his particular, I'll receive him gladly,
290   But not one follower.
GONERIL: So am I purpos'd. Where is my Lord of Gloucester?
CORNWALL: Follow'd the old man forth.

(Enter GLOUCESTER.)

                                    He is return'd.
GLOUCESTER: The King is in high rage.
CORNWALL: Whither is he going?
GLOUCESTER: He calls to horse, but will I know not whither.
295   CORNWALL: 'Tis best to give him way; he leads himself.
GONERIL: My lord, entreat him by no means to stay.
GLOUCESTER: Alack, the night comes on, and the high winds
Do sorely ruffle; for many miles about
There's scarce a bush.
REGAN: O, sir, to willful men
300   The injuries that they themselves procure
Must be their schoolmasters. Shut up your doors.
He is attended with a desperate train,
And what they may incense him to, being apt
To have his ear abus'd, wisdom bids fear.
305   CORNWALL: Shut up your doors, my lord; 'tis a wild night.
My Regan counsels well. Come out o' th' storm.

(Exeunt.)

— ACT THREE —

SCENE I

Storm still. Enter KENT [*disguised as Caius*] *and a* GENTLE-
MAN, *severally.*

KENT: Who's there, besides foul weather?
GENTLEMAN: One minded like the weather, most unquietly.

282 **flaws** fragments   283 **Or ere** before   286 **bestow'd** lodged   287 **blame** fault.   **from rest** i.e., out of the house; also, lacking peace of mind   288 **taste** experience   289 **For his particular** as for him individually   298 **ruffle** bluster   303–304 **being . . . abus'd** (he) being inclined to hearken to wild counsel

III.i. Location: An open place in Gloucestershire.

KENT: I know you. Where's the King?
GENTLEMAN: Contending with the fretful elements;
Bids the wind blow the earth into the sea,   5
Or swell the curled waters 'bove the main,
That things might change or cease; [tears his white hair,
Which the impetuous blasts, with eyeless rage,
Catch in their fury, and make nothing of;
Strives in his little world of man to outscorn   10
The to-and-fro-conflicting wind and rain.
This night, wherein the cub-drawn bear would couch,
The lion and the belly-pinched wolf
Keep their fur dry, unbonneted he runs,
And bids what will take all.]
KENT: But who is with him?   15
GENTLEMAN: None but the fool, who labors to outjest
His heart-struck injuries.
KENT: Sir, I do know you,
And dare, upon the warrant of my note,
Commend a dear thing to you. There is division,
Although as yet the face of it is cover'd   20
With mutual cunning, 'twixt Albany and Cornwall;
Who have—as who have not, that their great stars
Thron'd and set high?—servants, who seem no less,
Which are to France the spies and speculations
Intelligent of our state. What hath been seen,   25
Either in snuffs and packings of the Dukes,
Or the hard rein which both of them hath borne
Against the old kind King, or something deeper,
Whereof perchance these are but furnishings—
[But, true it is, from France there comes a power   30
Into this scattered kingdom, who already,
Wise in our negligence, have secret feet
In some of our best ports, and are at point
To show their open banner. Now to you:
If on my credit you dare build so far   35
To make your speed to Dover, you shall find
Some that will thank you, making just report
Of how unnatural and bemadding sorrow
The King hath cause to plain.
I am a gentleman of blood and breeding,   40
And, from some knowledge and assurance, offer
This office to you.]
GENTLEMAN: I will talk further with you.
KENT: No, do not.
For confirmation that I am much more
Than my out-wall, open this purse, and take   45
What it contains. *(Gives purse and ring.)* If you shall see
Cordelia—

6 **main** mainland   9 **make nothing of** treat disrespectfully   10 **little world of man** i.e., the microcosm, which is an epitome of the macrocosm or universe   12 **cub-drawn** famished, with udders sucked dry (and hence ravenous).   **couch** lie close in its den   15 **take all** (A cry of desperate defiance, said by a gambler in staking his last.)   18 **upon . . . note** on the strength of what I know (about you)   19 **Commend . . . thing** entrust a precious undertaking   22 **that** whom.   **stars** destinies   23 **no less** i.e., no other than servants   24 **speculations** scouts, spies   25 **Intelligent of** supplying intelligence pertinent to   26 **snuffs** quarrels.   **packings** intrigues   29 **furnishings** outward shows   30 **power** armed force   31 **scattered** divided   32 **Wise in** taking advantage of.   **feet** i.e., troops   33 **at point** ready   35 **credit** trustworthiness   39 **plain** complain   42 **office** service   45 **out-wall** exterior appearance

As fear not but you shall—show her this ring,
And she will tell you who that fellow is
That yet you do not know. Fie on this storm!
50 I will go seek the King.
GENTLEMAN: Give me your hand. Have you no more to say?
KENT: Few words, but, to effect, more than all yet:
That when we have found the King—in which your pain
That way, I'll this—he that first lights on him
55 Holla the other.

(*Exeunt [severally].*)

SCENE II

Storm still. Enter LEAR *and* FOOL.

LEAR: Blow, winds, and crack your cheeks! Rage, blow!
You cataracts and hurricanoes, spout
Till you have drench'd our steeples, drown'd the cocks!
You sulph'rous and thought-executing fires,
5 Vaunt-couriers of oak-cleaving thunderbolts,
Singe my white head! And thou, all-shaking thunder,
Strike flat the thick rotundity o' th' world!
Crack nature's molds, all germains spill at once,
That makes ingrateful man!
10 FOOL: O nuncle, court holy-water in a dry house is better than
this rain-water out o' door. Good nuncle, in, ask thy daugh-
ters' blessing. Here's a night pities neither wise men nor fools.
LEAR: Rumble thy bellyful! Spit, fire! Spout, rain!
Nor rain, wind, thunder, fire, are my daughters.
15 I tax not you, you elements, with unkindness;
I never gave you kingdom, call'd you children,
You owe me no subscription. Then let fall
Your horrible pleasure. Here I stand, your slave,
A poor, infirm, weak, and despis'd old man.
20 But yet I call you servile ministers,
That will with two pernicious daughters join
Your high-engender'd battles 'gainst a head
So old and white as this. O, ho! 'Tis foul!
FOOL: He that has a house to put 's head in has a good head-
25 piece.
    The codpiece that will house
        Before the head has any,
    The head and he shall louse;
        So beggars marry many.
30   The man that makes his toe
        What he his heart should make
    Shall of a corn cry woe,
        And turn his sleep to wake.

For there was never yet fair woman but she made mouths in a
glass.   35
LEAR: No, I will be the pattern of all patience;
I will say nothing.

(*Enter* KENT [*disguised as Caius*].)

KENT: Who's there?
FOOL: Marry, here's grace and a codpiece; that's a wise man
and a fool.   40
KENT: Alas, sir, are you here? Things that love night
Love not such nights as these. The wrathful skies
Gallow the very wanderers of the dark,
And make them keep their caves. Since I was man,
Such sheets of fire, such bursts of horrid thunder,   45
Such groans of roaring wind and rain, I never
Remember to have heard. Man's nature cannot carry
Th' affliction nor the fear.
LEAR: Let the great gods,
That keep this dreadful pudder o'er our heads,
Find out their enemies now. Tremble, thou wretch,   50
That hast within thee undivulged crimes,
Unwhipp'd of justice! Hide thee, thou bloody hand,
Thou perjur'd, and thou simular of virtue
That art incestuous! Caitiff, to pieces shake,
That under covert and convenient seeming   55
Has practic'd on man's life! Close pent-up guilts,
Rive your concealing continents, and cry
These dreadful summoners grace! I am a man
More sinn'd against than sinning.
KENT: Alack, bare-headed?
Gracious my lord, hard by here is a hovel;   60
Some friendship will it lend you 'gainst the tempest.
Repose you there, while I to this hard house—
More harder than the stones whereof 'tis rais'd,
Which even but now, demanding after you,
Denied me to come in—return, and force   65
Their scanted courtesy.
LEAR: My wits begin to turn.
Come on, my boy. How dost, my boy? Art cold?
I am cold myself. Where is this straw, my fellow?
The art of our necessities is strange,
That can make vile things precious. Come, your hovel.   70
Poor fool and knave, I have one part in my heart
That's sorry yet for thee.
FOOL: (*Sings.*)
    "He that has and a little tiny wit—
        With heigh-ho, the wind and the rain—
    Must make content with his fortunes fit,   75
        Though the rain it raineth every day."
LEAR: True, boy. Come, bring us to this hovel.

(*Exit [with* KENT].)

48 **fellow** i.e., Kent   52 **to effect** to the purpose   53–54 **pain That way**
laborious quest (take you) that way

III.ii. Location: An open place, as before.
2 **hurricanoes** waterspouts   3 **drench'd** drowned.   **cocks** weather-
cocks   4 **thought-executing** acting with the quickness of thought   5
Vaunt-couriers forerunners   8 **nature's molds** the molds in which Nature makes men.   **germains** germs, seeds.   **spill** destroy   10 **court
holy-water** flattery   15 **tax** accuse   17 **subscription** allegiance   22
high-engender'd battles battalions created by the heavens   26–33 **The
codpiece . . . wake** i.e., a man who cohabits sexually but improviden-
tially can expect penury; and one who elevates what is base above what is
noble (as Lear has done with his daughters) can expect misery and wake-
ful tossing also

34–35 **made . . . glass** practiced making attractive faces in a mirror   43
Gallow frighten   44 **keep** occupy, remain inside   47 **carry** endure   49 **pudder** pother, turmoil   50 **Find . . . now** i.e., expose criminals (by their display of fear)   53 **simular** pretender   54 **Caitiff** wretch
55 **seeming** hypocrisy   56 **practic'd on** plotted against.   **Close** secret   57 **Rive** split.   **continents** covering, containers   57–58 **cry . . .
grace** pray for mercy at the hands of the officers of divine justice. (A
summoner was the police officer of an ecclesiastical court.)   64 **Which**
i.e., the occupants of the house.   **demanding** inquiring   66 **scanted**
stinted   78 **brave** fine

FOOL: This is a brave night to cool a courtezan. I'll speak a
prophecy ere I go:

80   When priests are more in word than matter;
        When brewers mar their malt with water;
        When nobles are their tailors' tutors;
        No heretics burn'd, but wenches' suitors;
        Then shall the realm of Albion
85   Come to great confusion.
        When every case in law is right;
        No squire in debt, nor no poor knight;
        When slanders do not live in tongues;
        Nor cutpurses come not to throngs;
90   When usurers tell their gold i' th' field,
        And bawds and whores do churches build;
        Then comes the time, who lives to see 't,
        That going shall be us'd with feet.
      This prophecy Merlin shall make, for I live before his time.

(Exit.)

SCENE III

Enter GLOUCESTER and EDMUND [with lights].

GLOUCESTER: Alack, alack, Edmund, I like not this unnatural
dealing. When I desir'd their leave that I might pity him, they
took from me the use of mine own house, charg'd me on pain
of perpetual displeasure neither to speak of him, entreat for
5   him, or any way sustain him.
EDMUND: Most savage and unnatural!
GLOUCESTER: Go to; say you nothing. There is division between the Dukes, and a worse matter than that. I have receiv'd a letter this night; 'tis dangerous to be spoken; I have
10 lock'd the letter in my closet. These injuries the King now
bears will be reveng'd home; there is part of a power already
footed. We must incline to the King. I will look him and
privily relieve him. Go you and maintain talk with the Duke,
that my charity be not of him perceiv'd. If he ask for me, I am
15 ill and gone to bed. If I die for it, as no less is threat'ned me,
the King my old master must be reliev'd. There is strange
things toward, Edmund; pray you be careful.

(Exit.)

EDMUND: This courtesy forbid thee shall the Duke
Instantly know, and of that letter too.

This seems a fair deserving, and must draw me   20
That which my father loses — no less than all.
The younger rises when the old doth fall.

(Exit.)

SCENE IV

Enter LEAR, KENT [disguised as Caius] and FOOL.

KENT: Here is the place, my lord. Good my lord, enter.
    The tyranny of the open night's too rough
    For nature to endure.

(Storm still.)

LEAR: Let me alone.
KENT: Good my lord, enter here.
LEAR: Wilt break my heart?
KENT: I had rather break mine own. Good my lord, enter.   5
LEAR: Thou think'st 'tis much that this contentious storm
    Invades us to the skin. So 'tis to thee,
    But where the greater malady is fix'd,
    The lesser is scarce felt. Thou'dst shun a bear,
    But if thy flight lay toward the roaring sea,   10
    Thou'dst meet the bear i' th' mouth. When the mind's free,
    The body's delicate. The tempest in my mind
    Doth from my senses take all feeling else
    Save what beats there. Filial ingratitude!
    Is it not as this mouth should tear this hand   15
    For lifting food to 't? But I will punish home.
    No, I will weep no more. In such a night
    To shut me out? Pour on; I will endure.
    In such a night as this? O Regan, Goneril,
    Your old kind father, whose frank heart gave all —   20
    O, that way madness lies; let me shun that!
    No more of that.
KENT: Good my lord, enter here.
LEAR: Prithee, go in thyself; seek thine own ease.
    This tempest will not give me leave to ponder
    On things would hurt me more. But I'll go in.   25
    (To the FOOL.) In, boy; go first. You houseless poverty —
    Nay, get thee in. I'll pray, and then I'll sleep.

(Exit [FOOL into the hovel].)

    Poor naked wretches, wheresoe'er you are,
    That bide the pelting of this pitiless storm,
    How shall your houseless heads and unfed sides,   30
    Your loop'd and window'd raggedness, defend you
    From seasons such as these? O, I have ta'en
    Too little care of this! Take physic, pomp;
    Expose thyself to feel what wretches feel,

---

80 **more . . . matter** better in speech than in substance or Gospel truth.
(This and the next three lines satirize the present state of affairs.) 81
mar adulterate 82 **are . . . tutors** i.e., know more than their tailors
about fashion 83 **burn'd** (i.e., heretics in love catch venereal disease.) 84 **realm of Albion** kingdom of England 86 **right** just. (This
and the next five lines offer a utopian vision of justice and charity that
will never be realized in this corrupted world.) 90 **tell** count. **i' th'
field** i.e., openly, without fear 93 **going . . . feet** walking will be done
on foot 94 **Merlin** (A great wizard of the court of King Arthur, who
came before Lear.)

III. iii. Location: Gloucester's house.
2 **pity** have mercy on 10 **closet** private chamber 11 **home** thoroughly. **power** armed force 12 **footed** landed. **incline to** side
with. **look** look for 17 **toward** impending 18 **courtesy forbid thee**
kindness (to Lear) which you were forbidden to show

---

20 **fair deserving** meritorious action

III. iv. Location: An open place. Before a hovel.
4 **break my heart** i.e., cause me anguish by relieving my physical wants
and thus forcing me to confront again my *greater malady* (l. 8) 8 **fix'd**
lodged, implanted 11 **i' th' mouth** i.e., head-on. **free** free of anxiety 15 **as** as if 16 **home** fully 20 **frank** liberal 29 **bide** endure 31
loop'd and window'd full of openings like windows and loopholes 33
Take physic, pomp cure yourself, O distempered great ones

35   That thou mayst shake the superflux to them,
      And show the heavens more just.
EDGAR: (Within) Fathom and half, fathom and half! Poor
      Tom!

(Enter FOOL [from the hovel].)

FOOL: Come not in here, nuncle, here's a spirit. Help me,
40   help me!
KENT: Give me thy hand. Who's there?
FOOL: A spirit, a spirit! He says his name's poor Tom.
KENT: What art thou that dost grumble there i' th' straw?
      Come forth.

(Enter EDGAR [disguised as a madman].)

45   EDGAR: Away! The foul fiend follows me! Through the sharp
      hawthorn blows the cold wind. Hum! Go to thy bed, and
      warm thee.
LEAR: Didst thou give all to thy daughters?
      And art thou come to this?
50   EDGAR: Who gives anything to poor Tom? Whom the foul fiend
      hath led through fire and through flame, through ford and
      whirlpool, o'er bog and quagmire; that hath laid knives under
      his pillow, and halters in his pew, set ratsbane by his porridge,
      made him proud of heart, to ride on a bay trotting-horse over
55   four-inch'd bridges, to course his own shadow for a traitor.
      Bless thy five wits! Tom's a-cold—O, do de, do de, do de.
      Bless thee from whirlwinds, star-blasting, and taking!
      Do poor Tom some charity, whom the foul fiend vexes.
      There could I have him now—and there—and there again,
60   and there.

(Storm still.)

LEAR: Has his daughters brought him to this pass?
      Couldst thou save nothing? Wouldst thou give 'em all?
FOOL: Nay, he reserv'd a blanket, else we had been all sham'd.
LEAR: Now, all the plagues that in the pendulous air
65   Hang fated o'er men's faults light on thy daughters!
KENT: He hath no daughters, sir.
LEAR: Death, traitor! Nothing could have subdu'd nature
      To such a lowness but his unkind daughters.
      Is it the fashion, that discarded fathers
70   Should have thus little mercy on their flesh?
      Judicious punishment! 'Twas the flesh begot
      Those pelican daughters.
EDGAR: Pillicock sat on Pillicock-hill. Alow, alow, loo, loo!
FOOL: This cold night will turn us all to fools and madmen.

EDGAR: Take heed o' th' foul fiend. Obey thy parents; keep thy   75
      word's justice; swear not; commit not with man's sworn
      spouse; set not thy sweet heart on proud array. Tom's a-cold.
LEAR: What hast thou been?
EDGAR: A servingman, proud in heart and mind; that curl'd my
      hair; wore gloves in my cap; serv'd the lust of my mistress'   80
      heart, and did the act of darkness with her; swore as many
      oaths as I spake words, and broke them in the sweet face of
      heaven. One that slept in the contriving of lust, and wak'd to
      do it. Wine lov'd I deeply, dice dearly; and in woman out-
      paramour'd the Turk. False of heart, light of ear, bloody of   85
      hand; hog in sloth, fox in stealth, wolf in greediness, dog in
      madness, lion in prey. Let not the creaking of shoes nor the
      rustling of silks betray thy poor heart to woman. Keep thy foot
      out of brothels, thy hand out of plackets, thy pen from
      lenders' books, and defy the foul fiend. Still through the   90
      hawthorn blows the cold wind; says suum, mun, nonny. Dol-
      phin my boy, boy, sessa! Let him trot by.

(Storm still.)

LEAR: Thou wert better in a grave than to answer with thy un-
      cover'd body this extremity of the skies. Is man no more than
      this? Consider him well. Thou ow'st the worm no silk, the   95
      beast no hide, the sheep no wool, the cat no perfume. Ha!
      Here's three on 's are sophisticated. Thou art the thing itself;
      unaccommodated man is no more but such a poor, bare,
      forked animal as thou art. Off, off, you lendings! Come, un-
      button here.   100

(Tearing off his clothes.)

FOOL: Prithee, nuncle, be contented; 'tis a naughty night to
      swim in. Now a little fire in a wild field were like an old
      lecher's heart—a small spark, all the rest on 's body cold.

(Enter GLOUCESTER, with a torch.)

      Look, here comes a walking fire.
EDGAR: This is the foul Flibbertigibbet! He begins at curfew,   105
      and walks till the first cock; he gives the web and the pin,
      squints the eye, and makes the hare-lip; mildews the white
      wheat, and hurts the poor creature of earth.
            Swithold footed thrice the 'old;
            He met the night-mare, and her nine-fold;   110
               Bit her alight,
               And her troth plight,
            And, aroint thee, witch, aroint thee!

35 **superflux** superfluity (with suggestion of *flux, bodily discharge,* introduced by *physic, purgative,* in l. 33)   37 **Fathom and half** (A sailor's cry
while taking soundings, hence appropriate to a deluge.)   45–46
Through . . . wind (A line from a ballad.)   52–53 **knives, halters,
ratsbane** (Tempting means to commit suicide and hence be damned.)
54–55 **over four-inch'd bridges** i.e., taking mad risks on narrow bridges
with the devil's assistance   55 **course** chase.   **for** as   57 **star-blasting**
being blighted by influence of the stars.   **taking** pestilence; or witchcraft   61 **pass** miserable plight   63 **reserv'd a blanket** kept a wrap (for
his nakedness)   64 **pendulous** suspended   70 **have . . . flesh** i.e., punish themselves, as Edgar has done   72 **pelican** greedy. (Young pelicans
supposedly fed on the blood of their mothers' breasts.)   73 **Pillicock**
(From an old rhyme, suggested by the sound of *pelican. Pillicock* in
nursery rhyme seems to have been a euphemism for penis, *Pillicock-hill*
for the Mount of Venus.)

76 **commit not** i.e., do not commit adultery   80 **gloves** i.e., his mistress' favors   84–85 **out-paramour'd the Turk** outdid the Sultan in
keeping mistresses   85 **light of ear** foolishly credulous; frivolous   87
prey preying   89 **plackets** slits in skirts or petticoats   89–90 **thy pen . . .
books** i.e., do not sign a contract for a loan   91 **suum . . . nonny**
(Imitative of the wind?)   91–92 **Dolphin my boy** (A slang phrase, or bit
of song?)   95 **ow'st** have borrowed from   96 **cat** civet cat   97 **sophisticated** clad in the trappings of civilized life; adulterated   102 **wild** barren, uncultivated   105 **Flibbertigibbet** (A devil from Elizabethan folklore whose name appears in Samuel Harsnett's *Declaration* of 1603 and
elsewhere.)   106 **first cock** midnight.   **web and the pin** cataract of the
eye   107 **white** ripening   109 **Swithold** St. Withold, a famous Anglo-
Saxon exorcist.   **footed . . . 'old** thrice traversed the wold (tract of hilly
upland)   110 **night-mare** demon.   **nine-fold** nine offspring (with possible pun on *fold, foal*)   112 **her troth plight** give her promise (to do no
harm)   113 **aroint thee** begone

KENT: How fares your Grace?

115 LEAR: What's he?

KENT: Who's there? What is 't you seek?

GLOUCESTER: What are you there? Your names?

EDGAR: Poor Tom, that eats the swimming frog, the toad, the
tadpole, the wall-newt and the water; that in the fury of his
120 heart, when the foul fiend rages, eats cow-dung for sallets;
swallows the old rat and the ditch-dog; drinks the green mantle of the standing pool; who is whipp'd from tithing to tithing,
and stock-punish'd and imprison'd; who hath had three suits
to his back, six shirts to his body,
125   Horse to ride, and weapons to wear;
    But mice and rats, and such small deer,
    Have been Tom's food for seven long year.
Beware my follower. Peace, Smulkin, peace, thou fiend!

GLOUCESTER: What, hath your Grace no better company?

130 EDGAR: The prince of darkness is a gentleman. Modo he's call'd,
and Mahu.

GLOUCESTER: Our flesh and blood, my lord, is grown so vile
That it doth hate what gets it.

EDGAR: Poor Tom's a-cold.

135 GLOUCESTER: Go in with me. My duty cannot suffer
T' obey in all your daughters' hard commands.
Though their injunction be to bar my doors
And let this tyrannous night take hold upon you,
Yet have I ventured to come seek you out,
140   And bring you where both fire and food is ready.

LEAR: First let me talk with this philosopher.
What is the cause of thunder?

KENT: Good my lord, take his offer; go into th' house.

LEAR: I'll talk a word with this same learned Theban.
145   What is your study?

EDGAR: How to prevent the fiend, and to kill vermin.

LEAR: Let me ask you one word in private.

KENT: (To GLOUCESTER) Importune him once more to go,
my lord.
His wits begin t' unsettle.

GLOUCESTER: Canst thou blame him?

(Storm still.)

150   His daughters seek his death. Ah, that good Kent!
He said it would be thus, poor banish'd man.
Thou sayest the King grows mad; I'll tell thee, friend,
I am almost mad myself. I had a son,
Now outlaw'd from my blood; he sought my life,
155   But lately, very late. I lov'd him, friend,
No father his son dearer. True to tell thee,
The grief hath craz'd my wits. What a night 's this!—
I do beseech your Grace—

LEAR: O, cry you mercy, sir.
Noble philosopher, your company.   160

EDGAR: Tom's a-cold.

GLOUCESTER: (To EDGAR) In, fellow, there, into th' hovel.
Keep thee warm.

LEAR: (Starting toward the hovel) Come, let's in all.

KENT: This way, my lord.

LEAR: With him!
I will keep still with my philosopher.

KENT: (To GLOUCESTER) Good my lord, soothe him; let take   165
the fellow.

GLOUCESTER: (To KENT) Take him you on.

KENT: (To EDGAR) Sirrah, come on; go along with us.

LEAR: Come, good Athenian.

GLOUCESTER: No words, no words! Hush.

EDGAR: Child Rowland to the dark tower came;   170
His word was still, "Fie, foh, and fum,
I smell the blood of a British man."

(Exeunt.)

SCENE V

Enter CORNWALL *and* EDMUND [*with a letter*].

CORNWALL: I will have my revenge ere I depart his house.

EDMUND: How, my lord, I may be censur'd, that nature thus
gives way to loyalty, something fears me to think 'of.

CORNWALL: I now perceive it was not altogether your brother's
evil disposition made him seek his death, but a provoking   5
merit, set a-work by a reproveable badness in himself.

EDMUND: How malicious is my fortune, that I must repent to be
just! This is the letter which he spoke of, which approves him
an intelligent party to the advantages of France. O heavens!
That this treason were not, or not I the detector!   10

CORNWALL: Go with me to the Duchess.

EDMUND: If the matter of this paper be certain, you have mighty
business in hand.

CORNWALL: True or false, it hath made thee Earl of Gloucester.
Seek out where thy father is, that he may be ready for our   15
apprehension.

EDMUND: (Aside) If I find him comforting the King, it will stuff
his suspicion more fully.—I will persevere in my course
of loyalty, though the conflict be sore between that and
my blood.   20

CORNWALL: I will lay trust upon thee; and thou shalt find a
dearer father in my love.

(Exeunt.)

---

119 **water** i.e., water-newt   120 **sallets** salads   121 **ditch-dog** i.e., dead
dog in a ditch   121–122 **mantle** scum   122 **tithing to tithing** i.e., one
ward or parish to another   123 **stock-punish'd** placed in the
stocks   126 **deer** animals   128, 130–131 **Smulkin, Modo, Mahu**
(Shakespeare found these Elizabethan devils in Samuel Harsnett's *Declaration*.)   133 **gets** begets   135 **suffer** permit me   144 **Theban** i.e.,
one deeply versed in "philosophy" or natural science   145 **study** special
competence   146 **prevent** thwart   154 **outlaw'd . . . blood** exiled from
kinship with me

159 **cry you mercy** I beg your pardon   166 **Take . . . on** i.e., take Edgar
along with you   168 **Athenian** i.e., philosopher   170 **Child Rowland**,
etc. (Fragments of a ballad about the hero of the Charlemagne legends.
A *child* is a candidate for knighthood.)   171 **still** always

III.v. Location: Gloucester's house.
3 **something fears** somewhat frightens   5 **his** i.e., his father's   5–6 **a
provoking . . . himself** i.e., an evil propensity in Edgar himself, incited
also by the badness of Gloucester which deserved punishment   8 **approves** proves   9 **an intelligent . . . advantages** a spy in the service   17
him i.e., Gloucester   18 **his** i.e., Cornwall's   20 **blood** family loyalty,
filial instincts

SCENE VI

Enter KENT [*disguised as Caius*] *and* GLOUCESTER.

GLOUCESTER: Here is better than the open air; take it thank
fully. I will piece out the comfort with what addition I can. I
will not be long from you.
KENT: All the pow'r of his wits have given way to his impatience.
5   The gods reward your kindness!

(*Exit* [GLOUCESTER].)

Enter LEAR, EDGAR [*as Mad Tom*], *and* FOOL.)

EDGAR: Fraretto calls me, and tells me Nero is an angler in the
lake of darkness. Pray, innocent, and beware the foul fiend.
FOOL: Prithee, nuncle, tell me whether a madman be a gentleman or a yeoman?
10   LEAR: A King, a king!
FOOL: No, he's a yeoman that has a gentleman to his son; for he's
a mad yeoman that sees his son a gentleman before him.
LEAR: To have a thousand with red burning spits
Come hizzing in upon 'em —
15   [EDGAR: The foul fiend bites my back.
FOOL: He's mad that trusts in the tameness of a wolf, a horse's
health, a boy's love, or a whore's oath.
LEAR: It shall be done; I will arraign them straight.
(*To* EDGAR.) Come, sit thou here, most learned justice;
20   (*To the* FOOL.) Thou, sapient sir, sit here. Now, you she-
foxes!
EDGAR: Look where he stands and glares! Want'st thou eyes at
trial, madam?
(*Sings.*) Come o'er the bourn, Bessy, to me —
FOOL: (*Sings.*)

25   Her boat hath a leak,
            And she must not speak
        Why she dares not come over to thee.

EDGAR: The foul fiend haunts poor Tom in the voice of a night-
ingale. Hoppedance cries in Tom's belly for two white her-
ring. Croak not, black angel; I have no food for thee.
30   KENT: How do you, sir? Stand you not so amaz'd.
Will you lie down and rest upon the cushions?
LEAR: I'll see their trial first. Bring in their evidence.
(*To* EDGAR.) Thou robed man of justice, take thy place;
(*To the* FOOL.) And thou, his yoke-fellow of equity,
35   Bench by his side. (*To* KENT.) You are o' th' commission,
Sit you too.

(*They sit.*)

EDGAR: Let us deal justly.

(*Sings.*)

        Sleepest or wakest thou, jolly shepherd?
            Thy sheep be in the corn;
        And for one blast of thy minikin mouth,   40
            Thy sheep shall take no harm.

    Purr the cat is gray.
LEAR: Arraign her first; 'tis Goneril, I here take my oath before
this honorable assembly, kick'd the poor King her father.
FOOL: Come hither, mistress. Is your name Goneril?   45
LEAR: She cannot deny it.
FOOL: Cry you mercy, I took you for a joint-stool.
LEAR: And here's another, whose warp'd looks proclaim
What store her heart is made on. Stop her there!
Arms, arms, sword, fire! Corruption in the place!   50
False justicer, why hast thou let her scape?]
EDGAR: Bless thy five wits!
KENT: O pity! Sir, where is the patience now
That you so oft have boasted to retain?
EDGAR: (*Aside*) My tears begin to take his part so much   55
They mar my counterfeiting.
LEAR: The little dogs and all,
Tray, Blanch, and Sweet-heart, see, they bark at me.
EDGAR: Tom will throw his head at them. Avaunt, you curs!
        Be thy mouth or black or white,   60
        Tooth that poisons if it bite;
        Mastiff, greyhound, mongrel grim,
        Hound or spaniel, brach or lym,
        Or bobtail tike or trundle-tail,
        Tom will make him weep and wail;   65
        For, with throwing thus my head,
        Dogs leapt the hatch, and all are fled.
    Do de, de, de. Sessa! Come, march to wakes and fairs and
    market-towns. Poor Tom, thy horn is dry.
LEAR: Then let them anatomize Regan; see what breeds about   70
her heart. Is there any cause in nature that make these hard
hearts? (*To* EDGAR.) You, sir, I entertain for one of my hundred; only I do not like the fashion of your garments. You will
say they are Persian; but let them be chang'd.
KENT: Now, good my lord, lie here and rest awhile.   75
LEAR: (*Lying on cushions*) Make no noise, make no noise; draw
the curtains. So, so. We'll go to supper i' th' morning.

(*Sleeps.*)

FOOL: And I'll go to bed at noon.

(*Enter* GLOUCESTER.)

III.vi. Location: Within a building on Gloucester's estate, near or adjoining his house; or part of the house itself. See III.iv. 135–143. Cushions are provided, and a stool.
4 impatience rage   6 Fraretto (Another of the fiends from Harsnett.)   Nero is an angler (See Chaucer's "Monk's Tale," ll. 485–486; in
Rabelais, ii. 30, Nero is described as a fiddler and Trajan an angler in
the underworld.)   7 innocent simpleton, fool (i.e., the Fool)   14
hizzing hissing   21 he (Probably one of Edgar's devils.)   21–22
Want'st . . . trial do you lack spectators at your trial (?)   23 Come . . .
me (First line of a ballad by William Birche, 1558. A *bourn* is a *burn* or
brook. The Fool makes a ribald reply, in which the *leaky boat* suggests
her easy virtue.)   28 Hoppedance (Harsnett mentions "Hobberdi-
dance.")   white unsmoked (contrasted with *black devil*)   29 Croak
(Refers to the rumbling in Edgar's stomach denoting hunger.)   30
amaz'd bewildered   32 their evidence the witnesses against them   34
yoke-fellow of equity partner in the law   35 o' th' commission one
commissioned to be a justice

39 corn grain field   40 minikin dainty, pretty   42 Purr the cat (A devil
from Harsnett; see III.iv. 105, note.)   47 joint-stool low stool made by
a *joiner*, or maker of furniture with joined parts. (Proverbially this phrase
meant "I beg your pardon for failing to notice you." The reference is also
presumably to a real stool on stage.)   49 store material   50 Corruption
in the place i.e., there is iniquity or bribery in this court   59 throw his
head at i.e., threaten   63 brach hound bitch.   lym bloodhound   64
bobtail short-tailed small dog, cur.   trundle-tail long-tailed dog   67
hatch lower half of a divided door   68 Sessa i.e., away.   wakes (Here,
parish festivals.)   69 horn i.e., horn bottle used by beggars to beg for
drinks.   74 Persian i.e., gorgeous intricate attire   77 curtains bed-
curtains. (They presumably exist only in Lear's mad imagination.)

GLOUCESTER: Come hither, friend. Where is the King
my master?

80 KENT: Here, sir; but trouble him not, his wits are gone.
GLOUCESTER: Good friend, I prithee, take him in thy arms.
I have o'erheard a plot of death upon him.
There is a little ready; lay him in 't,
And drive toward Dover, friend, where thou shalt meet
85 Both welcome and protection. Take up thy master.
If thou shouldst dally half an hour, his life,
With thine and all that offer to defend him,
Stand in assured loss. Take up, take up,
And follow me, that will to some provision
Give thee quick conduct.

90 [KENT: Oppressed nature sleeps.
This rest might yet have balm'd thy broken sinews,
Which, if convenience will not allow,
Stand in hard cure. *(To the* FOOL.*)* Come, help to bear thy
master;
Thou must not stay behind.]

(They pick up LEAR.*)*

GLOUCESTER: Come, come, away.

(Exeunt [all but EDGAR].*)*

95 [EDGAR: When we our betters see bearing our woes,
We scarcely think our miseries our foes.
Who alone suffers suffers most i' th' mind,
Leaving free things and happy shows behind;
But then the mind much sufferance doth o'erskip,
100 When grief hath mates, and bearing fellowship.
How light and portable my pain seems now,
When that which makes me bend makes the King bow.
He childed as I fathered! Tom, away!
Mark the high noises, and thyself bewray
105 When false opinion, whose wrong thoughts defile thee,
In thy just proof repeals and reconciles thee.
What will hap more tonight, safe scape the King!
Lurk, lurk.]

(Exit.)

SCENE VII

Enter CORNWALL, REGAN, GONERIL, *bastard* [EDMUND], *and*
SERVANTS.

CORNWALL: *(To* GONERIL*)* Post speedily to my lord your husband; show him this letter. *(Gives letter.)* The army of France
is landed. —Seek out the traitor Gloucester.

88 **Stand . . . loss** will assuredly be lost   89 **provision** supplies; or,
means of providing for safety   90 **conduct** guidance   91 **balm'd**
cured, healed.   **sinews** nerves   92 **convenience** fortunate circumstances   93 **Stand . . . cure** will be hard to cure   95 **our woes** woes like
ours   96 **our foes** i.e., hostile toward us alone (since we see how human
suffering afflicts even the great)   97 **Who . . . mind** i.e., he who suffers
alone suffers mental agonies greater than those who perceive they have
companions in misery   98 **free** carefree.   **shows** scenes   99 **suf-**
ferance suffering   100 **bearing fellowship** tribulation (has) company   101 **portable** bearable, endurable   104 **Mark . . . noises** i.e.,
observe what is being said about those in high places, or about great
events.   **bewray** reveal   106 **In . . . thee** upon your being proved innocent recalls you and restores you to favor   107 **What . . . King** whatever
else happens tonight, may the King escape safely

III.vii. Location: Gloucester's house.

(Exeunt some of the SERVANTS.*)*

REGAN: Hang him instantly.
GONERIL: Pluck out his eyes.   5
CORNWALL: Leave him to my displeasure. Edmund, keep you
our sister company; the revenges we are bound to take upon
your traitorous father are not fit for your beholding. Advise
the Duke, where you are going, to a most festinate preparation; we are bound to the like. Our posts shall be swift and   10
intelligent betwixt us. Farewell, dear sister; farewell, my Lord
of Gloucester.

(Enter steward [OSWALD].*)*

How now? Where's the King?
OSWALD: My Lord of Gloucester hath convey'd him hence.
Some five or six and thirty of his knights,   15
Hot questrists after him, met him at gate,
Who, with some other of the lord's dependants,
Are gone with him toward Dover, where they boast
To have well-armed friends.
CORNWALL: Get horses for your mistress.   20

(Exit OSWALD.*)*

GONERIL: Farewell, sweet lord, and sister.
CORNWALL: Edmund, farewell.

*(Exit [*GONERIL *with* EDMUND].*)*

                                 Go seek the traitor Gloucester,
Pinion him like a thief, bring him before us.

(Exeunt other SERVANTS.*)*

Though well we may not pass upon his life
Without the form of justice, yet our power   25
Shall do a court'sy to our wrath, which men
May blame, but not control.

(Enter GLOUCESTER *and* SERVANTS *[leading him].)*

                                 Who's there? The traitor?
REGAN: Ingrateful fox! 'Tis he.
CORNWALL: Bind fast his corky arms.
GLOUCESTER: What means your Graces? Good my friends,   30
consider
You are my guests. Do me no foul play, friends.
CORNWALL: Bind him, I say.

*(*SERVANTS *bind him.)*

REGAN: Hard, hard. O filthy traitor!
GLOUCESTER: Unmerciful lady as you are, I'm none.
CORNWALL: To this chair bind him. Villain, thou shalt find—

*(*REGAN *plucks his beard.)*

GLOUCESTER: By the kind gods, 'tis most ignobly done   35
To pluck me by the beard.

7 **sister** i.e., sister-in-law, Goneril   9 **the Duke** i.e., Albany.   **festinate**
hasty   10 **posts** messengers   11 **intelligent** serviceable in bearing information, knowledgeable   11–12 **my . . . Gloucester** i.e., Edmund, the
recipient now of his father's forfeited estate and title. (Two lines later,
Oswald uses the same title to refer to Edmund's father.)   15–16 **his,**
him i.e., Lear's, Lear   16 **questrists** searchers   17 **the lord's** i.e.,
Gloucester's   24 **pass upon** pass sentence upon   29 **corky** withered
with age

REGAN: So white, and such a traitor?
GLOUCESTER: Naughty lady,
  These hairs which thou dost ravish from my chin
  Will quicken, and accuse thee. I am your host.
40 With robbers' hands my hospitable favors
  You should not ruffle thus. What will you do?
CORNWALL: Come, sir, what letters had you late from France?
REGAN: Be simple-answer'd, for we know the truth.
CORNWALL: And what confederacy have you with the traitors
  Late footed in the kingdom?
45 REGAN: To whose hands
  You have sent the lunatic King. Speak.
GLOUCESTER: I have a letter guessingly set down,
  Which came from one that's of a neutral heart,
  And not from one oppos'd.
CORNWALL: Cunning.
REGAN: And false.
50 CORNWALL: Where hast thou sent the King?
GLOUCESTER: To Dover.
REGAN: Wherefore to Dover? Wast thou not charg'd at peril —
CORNWALL: Wherefore to Dover? Let him answer that.
GLOUCESTER: I am tied to th' stake, and I must stand the
  course.
55 REGAN: Wherefore to Dover?
GLOUCESTER: Because I would not see thy cruel nails
  Pluck out his poor old eyes; nor thy fierce sister
  In his anointed flesh stick boarish fangs.
  The sea, with such a storm as his bare head
60 In hell-black night endur'd, would have buoy'd up
  And quench'd the stelled fires;
  Yet, poor old heart, he help the heavens to rain.
  If wolves had at thy gate howl'd that stern time,
  Thou shouldst have said, "Good porter, turn the key."
65 All cruels else subscribe. But I shall see
  The winged vengeance overtake such children.
CORNWALL: See 't shalt thou never. Fellows, hold the chair.
  Upon these eyes of thine I'll set my foot.
GLOUCESTER: He that will think to live till he be old,
70 Give me some help! O cruel! O you gods!

(SERVANTS *hold the chair as* CORNWALL *grinds out one of*
GLOUCESTER'S *eyes with his boot.*)

REGAN: One side will mock another; th' other too.
CORNWALL: If you see vengeance —
FIRST SERVANT: Hold your hand, my lord!
  I have serv'd you ever since I was a child;
  But better service have I never done you
  Than now to bid you hold.
75 REGAN: How now, you dog?

FIRST SERVANT: If you did wear a beard upon your chin,
  I'd shake it on this quarrel. What do you mean?
CORNWALL: My villain?

(*They draw and fight.*)

FIRST SERVANT: Nay, then, come on, and take the chance
  of anger.

(CORNWALL *is wounded.*)

REGAN: Give me thy sword. A peasant stand up thus?   80

([*Takes a sword, and runs at him behind.*] *Kills him.*)

FIRST SERVANT: O, I am slain! My lord, you have one eye left
  To see some mischief on him. O!

(*Dies.*)

CORNWALL: Lest it see more, prevent it. Out, vile jelly!

(*He puts out* GLOUCESTER'S *other eye.*)

  Where is thy luster now?
GLOUCESTER: All dark and comfortless. Where's my son   85
  Edmund?
  Edmund, enkindle all the sparks of nature,
  To quit this horrid act.
REGAN: Out, treacherous villain!
  Thou call'st on him that hates thee. It was he
  That made the overture of thy treasons to us;
  Who is too good to pity thee.   90
GLOUCESTER: O my follies! Then Edgar was abus'd.
  Kind gods, forgive me that, and prosper him!
REGAN: Go thrust him out at gates, and let him smell
  His way to Dover. (*Exit [one] with* GLOUCESTER.) How is
  't, my lord? How look you?
CORNWALL: I have receiv'd a hurt. Follow me, lady. —   95
  Turn out that eyeless villain; throw this slave
  Upon the dunghill. — Regan, I bleed apace.
  Untimely comes this hurt. Give my your arm.

(*Exeunt* [CORNWALL, *led by* REGAN].)

[SECOND SERVANT: I'll never care what wickedness I do,
  If this man come to good.
THIRD SERVANT: If she live long,   100
  And in the end meet the old course of death,
  Women will all turn monsters.
SECOND SERVANT: Let's follow the old Earl, and get the
  Bedlam
  To lead him where he would. His roguish madness
  Allows itself to anything.   105
THIRD SERVANT: Go thou. I'll fetch some flax and whites
  of eggs
  To apply to his bleeding face. Now, heaven help him!]

(*Exeunt* [*severally*].)

— ACT FOUR —

SCENE I

Enter EDGAR *[disguised as Mad Tom].*

EDGAR: Yet better thus, and known to be contemn'd,
　　Than still contemn'd and flatter'd. To be worst,
　　The lowest and most dejected thing of fortune,
　　Stands still in esperance, lives not in fear.
5　　The lamentable change is from the best;
　　The worst returns to laughter. Welcome, then,
　　Thou unsubstantial air that I embrace!
　　The wretch that thou hast blown unto the worst
　　Owes nothing to thy blasts.

(Enter GLOUCESTER, *and an* OLD MAN *[leading him].)*

　　　　　　　　　　　But who comes here?
10　My father, poorly led? World, world, O world!
　　But that thy strange mutations make us hate thee,
　　Life would not yield to age.
OLD MAN: O, my good lord, I have been your tenant,
　　And your father's tenant, these fourscore years.
15 GLOUCESTER: Away, get thee away! Good friend, be gone.
　　Thy comforts can do me no good at all;
　　Thee they may hurt.
OLD MAN:　　　　　You cannot see your way.
GLOUCESTER: I have no way, and therefore want no eyes;
　　I stumbled when I saw. Full oft 'tis seen
20　Our means secure us, and our mere defects
　　Prove our commodities. O dear son Edgar,
　　The food of thy abused father's wrath!
　　Might I but live to see thee in my touch,
　　I'd say I had eyes again!
OLD MAN:　　　　　How now? Who's there?
25 EDGAR: *(Aside)* O gods! Who is 't can say "I am at the worst"?
　　I am worse than e'er I was.
OLD MAN:　　　　　'Tis poor mad Tom.
EDGAR: *(Aside)* And worse I may be yet. The worst is not
　　So long as we can say "This is the worst."
OLD MAN: Fellow, where goest?
GLOUCESTER:　　　　Is it a beggar-man?
30 OLD MAN: Madman and beggar too.
GLOUCESTER: He has some reason, else he could not beg.
　　I' th' last night's storm I such a fellow saw,
　　Which made me think a man a worm. My son
　　Came then into my mind, and yet my mind
35　Was then scarce friends with him. I have heard more since.
　　As flies to wanton boys are we to th' gods,
　　They kill us for their sport.
EDGAR: *(Aside)*　　　How should this be?

Bad is the trade that must play fool to sorrow,
Ang'ring itself and others. —Bless thee, master!
GLOUCESTER: Is that the naked fellow?
OLD MAN:　　　　　　Ay, my lord.　　　　　40
GLOUCESTER: Then prithee get thee gone. If for my sake
　　Thou wilt o'ertake us hence a mile or twain
　　I' th' way toward Dover, do it for ancient love,
　　And bring some covering for this naked soul,
　　Which I'll entreat to lead me.
OLD MAN:　　　　　Alack, sir, he is mad.　　45
GLOUCESTER: 'Tis the times' plague, when madmen lead
　　the blind.
　　Do as I bid thee, or rather do thy pleasure;
　　Above the rest, be gone.
OLD MAN: I'll bring him the best 'parel that I have,
　　Come on 't what will.　　　　　　　　　50

(Exit.)

GLOUCESTER: Sirrah, naked fellow—
EDGAR: Poor Tom's a-cold. *(Aside.)* I cannot daub it further.
GLOUCESTER: Come hither, fellow.
EDGAR: *(Aside)* And yet I must. —Bless thy sweet eyes, they
　　bleed.
GLOUCESTER: Know'st thou the way to Dover?　　55
EDGAR: Both stile and gate, horse-way and foot-path. Poor Tom
　　hath been scar'd out of his good wits. Bless thee, good man's
　　son, from the foul fiend! [Five fiends have been in poor Tom
　　at once: of lust, as Obidicut; Hobbididance, prince of dumb-
　　ness; Mahu, of stealing; Modo, of murder; Flibbertigibbet, of　60
　　mopping and mowing, who since possesses chambermaids
　　and waiting-women. So, bless thee, master!]
GLOUCESTER: Here, take this purse, thou whom the heavens'
　　plagues

(Gives purse.)

Have humbled to all strokes. That I am wretched
Makes thee the happier. Heavens, deal so still!　　65
Let the superfluous and lust-dieted man,
That slaves your ordinance, that will not see
Because he does not feel, feel your pow'r quickly;
So distribution should undo excess,
And each man have enough. Dost thou know Dover?　70
EDGAR: Ay, master.
GLOUCESTER: There is a cliff, whose high and bending head
　　Looks fearfully in the confined deep.
　　Bring me but to the very brim of it,
　　And I'll repair the misery thou dost bear　　75
　　With something rich about me. From that place
　　I shall no leading need.

IV.i. Location: **An open place.**
1 **contemn'd** despised 3 **dejected . . . of** debased or humbled by 4 **esperance** hope 5–6 **The lamentable . . . laughter** i.e., any change from the best is grievous, just as any change from the worst is an occasion for joy 9 **Owes nothing** can pay no more 11–12 **But . . . age** i.e., if it were not for your hateful inconstancy, we would never be reconciled to old age and death 16 **comforts** kindness 20 **Our means secure us** our prosperity makes us overconfident. **mere defects** sheer afflictions 21 **commodities** benefits 22 **abused** deceived 23 **in** i.e., by means of 31 **reason** power of reason 36 **wanton** playful

39 **Ang'ring** offending, distressing 42 **o'ertake us** catch up to us (after you have found clothing for Tom o' Bedlam) 43 **ancient love** i.e., the mutually trusting relationship of tenant and master that Gloucester and the Old Man have long enjoyed 46 **times' plague** i.e., spreading sickness of our present state 52 **daub it further** i.e., keep up this pretense 59–60 **Obidicut . . . Flibbertigibbet** (Fiends borrowed, as before in III.iv.128–131, from Harsnett.) 61 **mopping and mowing** making grimaces and mouths 66 **superfluous** having a superfluity. **lust-dieted** feeding luxuriously 67 **slaves your ordinance** i.e., makes the laws of heaven his slaves 72 **bending** overhanging 73 **in . . . deep** i.e., to the sea below, where it is confined by its shores

EDGAR: Give me thy arm.
   Poor Tom shall lead thee.

(Exeunt.)

SCENE II

Enter GONERIL *[and] bastard* [EDMUND].

GONERIL: Welcome, my lord. I marvel our mild husband
   Not met us on the way.

([Enter] steward [OSWALD].*)*

              Now, where's your master?
OSWALD: Madam, within, but never man so chang'd.
   I told him of the army that was landed;
5 He smil'd at it. I told him you were coming;
   His answer was "The worse." Of Gloucester's treachery,
   And of the loyal service of his son,
   When I inform'd him, then he call'd me sot,
   And told me I had turn'd the wrong side out.
10 What most he should dislike seems pleasant to him;
   What like, offensive.
GONERIL: *(To* EDMUND*)* Then shall you go no further.
   It is the cowish terror of his spirit,
   That dares not undertake. He'll not feel wrongs
15 Which tie him to an answer. Our wishes on the way
   May prove effects. Back, Edmund, to my brother;
   Hasten his musters and conduct his pow'rs.
   I must change names at home, and give the distaff
   Into my husband's hands. This trusty servant
20 Shall pass between us. Ere long you are like to hear,
   If you dare venture in your own behalf,
   A mistress's command. Wear this; spare speech.

(Gives a favor.)

   Decline your head. *(Kisses him.)* This kiss, if it durst speak,
   Would stretch thy spirits up into the air.
25 Conceive, and fare thee well.
EDMUND: Yours in the ranks of death.

(Exit.)

GONERIL: My most dear Gloucester!
   O, the difference of man and man!
   To thee a woman's services are due;
   My fool usurps my body.
30 OSWALD: Madam, here comes my lord.

(Exit.)

IV.ii. Location: Before the Duke of Albany's palace.
1 **Welcome** (Goneril, who has just arrived home from Gloucestershire
escorted by Edmund, bids him brief welcome before he must return.) 2 **Not met** has not met 8 **sot** fool 13 **cowish** cowardly 14
undertake venture 15 **tie . . . answer** oblige him to respond, to
fight. **Our . . . way** i.e., our wishes expressed by me to you on the way
that you might supplant Albany 16 **prove effects** come to
pass. **brother** i.e., brother-in-law, Cornwall 17 **musters** assembling
of troops. **pow'rs** armed forces 18 **change names** i.e., exchange the
roles of master and mistress of the household. **distaff** spinning-staff,
symbolizing the wife's role 25 **Conceive** understand, take my meaning
(with sexual double entendre, continuing from *stretch thy spirits* in the
previous line) 29 **My fool . . . body** i.e., my husband forcibly occupies
my body

(Enter ALBANY.*)*
GONERIL: I have been worth the whistle.
ALBANY: O Goneril,
   You are not worth the dust which the rude wind
   Blows in your face. [I fear your disposition;
   That nature which contemns its origin
   Cannot be bordered certain in itself.   35
   She that herself will sliver and disbranch
   From her material sap, perforce must wither
   And come to deadly use.
GONERIL: No more; the text is foolish.
ALBANY: Wisdom and goodness to the vile seem vile; 40
   Filths savor but themselves. What have you done?
   Tigers, not daughters, what have you perform'd?
   A father, and a gracious aged man,
   Whose reverence even the head-lugg'd bear would lick,
   Most barbarous, most degenerate, have you madded. 45
   Could my good brother suffer you to do it?
   A man, a prince, by him so benefited!
   If that the heavens do not their visible spirits
   Send quickly down to tame these vile offenses,
   It will come,   50
   Humanity must perforce prey on itself,
   Like monsters of the deep.]
GONERIL: Milk-liver'd man,
   That bear'st a cheek for blows, a head for wrongs,
   Who hast not in thy brows an eye discerning
   Thine honor from thy suffering, [that not know'st 55
   Fools do those villains pity who are punish'd
   Ere they have done their mischief. Where's thy drum?
   France spreads his banners in our noiseless land,
   With plumed helm thy state begins to threat,
   Whilst thou, a moral fool, sits still and cries 60
   "Alack, why does he so?"]
ALBANY: See thyself, devil!
   Proper deformity seems not in the fiend
   So horrid as in woman.
GONERIL: O vain fool!
[ALBANY: Thou changed and self-cover'd thing, for shame,
   Be-monster not thy feature. Were 't my fitness 65

31 **worth the whistle** i.e., worth the attentions of men. (Alludes to the
proverb, "It is a poor dog that is not worth the whistling.") 33 **fear your
disposition** mistrust your nature 35 **bordered certain** safely restrained,
kept within bounds 36 **sliver** tear off 37 **material sap** nourishing substance 41 **savor but themselves** i.e., hunger only for that which is
filthy 44 **head-lugg'd** dragged by the head and infuriated 45 **madded** driven mad 48 **visible** made visible 52 **Milk-liver'd** i.e., cowardly 54–55 **discerning . . . suffering** able to tell the difference between an insult to your honor and something you should tolerate 56
Fools i.e., only fools. (Goneril goes on to say that only fools are so
tenderhearted as to worry about injustices to potential troublemakers,
like Lear and Gloucester, instead of applauding measures taken to in-
sure order.) 57 **thy drum** i.e., your military preparations 58 **noiseless** peaceful, having none of the bustle of war 59 **thy state . . . threat**
i.e., France begins to threaten your kingdom 60 **moral** moralizing 61 **why does he so** i.e., why does the King of France invade England 62 **Proper deformity** i.e., the deformity appropriate to the
fiend 64 **changed** transformed. **self-cover'd** having the true nature
concealed 65 **Be-monster . . . feature** i.e., do not, however evil you
are, take on the outward form of a monster or fiend. **my fitness** suitable for me

To let these hands obey my blood,
They are apt enough to dislocate and tear
Thy flesh and bones. Howe'er thou art a fiend,
A woman's shape doth shield thee.
70 GONERIL: Marry, your manhood, mew!]

(*Enter a* MESSENGER.)

[ALBANY: What news?]
MESSENGER: O, my good lord, the Duke of Cornwall's dead,
Slain by his servant, going to put out
The other eye of Gloucester.
ALBANY: Gloucester's eyes!
75 MESSENGER: A servant that he bred, thrill'd with remorse,
Oppos'd against the act, bending his sword
To his great master, who, thereat enrag'd,
Flew on him, and amongst them fell'd him dead,
But not without that harmful stroke which since
Hath pluck'd him after.
80 ALBANY: This shows you are above,
You justicers, that these our nether crimes
So speedily can venge! But, O poor Gloucester!
Lost he his other eye?
MESSENGER: Both, both, my lord. —
This letter, madam, craves a speedy answer;
'Tis from your sister.

(*Gives her a letter.*)

85 GONERIL: (*Aside*)   One way I like this well;
But being widow, and my Gloucester with her,
May all the building in my fancy pluck
Upon my hateful life. Another way,
The news is not so tart. —I'll read, and answer.

(*Exit.*)

90 ALBANY: Where was his son when they did take his eyes?
MESSENGER: Come with my lady hither.
ALBANY: He is not here.
MESSENGER: No, my good lord; I met him back again.
ALBANY: Knows he the wickedness?
MESSENGER: Ay, my good lord. 'Twas he inform'd against
    him,
95 And quit the house on purpose that their punishment
Might have the freer course.
ALBANY: Gloucester, I live
To thank thee for the love thou show'dst the King,
And to revenge thine eyes. Come hither, friend.
Tell me what more thou know'st.

(*Exeunt.*)

SCENE [III]

Enter KENT *and a* GENTLEMAN.

KENT: Why the King of France is so suddenly gone back know
    you no reason?
GENTLEMAN: Something he left imperfect in the state, which
    since his coming forth is thought of, which imports to the
    kingdom so much fear and danger that his personal return   5
    was most requir'd and necessary.
KENT: Who hath he left behind him general?
GENTLEMAN: The Marshal of France, Monsieur La Far.
KENT: Did your letters pierce the Queen to any demonstration
    of grief?   10
GENTLEMAN: Ay, sir. She took them, read them in my
        presence,
    And now and then an ample tear trill'd down
    Her delicate cheek. It seem'd she was a queen
    Over her passion, who, most rebel-like,
    Sought to be king o'er her.
KENT: O, then it moved her?   15
GENTLEMAN: Not to a rage. Patience and sorrow strove
    Who should express her goodliest. You have seen
    Sunshine and rain at once. Her smiles and tears
    Were like a better way; those happy smilets
    That play'd on her ripe lip seem'd not to know   20
    What guests were in her eyes, which parted thence
    As pearls from diamonds dropp'd. In brief,
    Sorrow would be a rarity most beloved,
    If all could so become it.
KENT: Made she no verbal question?   25
GENTLEMAN: Faith, once or twice she heav'd the name
        of "father"
    Pantingly forth, as if it press'd her heart;
    Cried "Sisters, sisters! Shame of ladies, sisters!
    Kent! Father! Sisters! What, i' th' storm, i' th' night?
    Let pity not be believ'd!" There she shook   30
    The holy water from her heavenly eyes,
    And, clamor-moistened, then away she started
    To deal with grief alone.
KENT: It is the stars,
    The stars above us, govern our conditions,
    Else one self mate and make could not beget   35
    Such different issues. You spoke not with her since?
GENTLEMAN: No.
KENT: Was this before the King return'd?
GENTLEMAN: No, since.
KENT: Well, sir, the poor distressed Lear 's i' th' town,
    Who sometime, in his better tune, remembers   40
    What we are come about, and by no means
    Will yield to see his daughter.

---

66 **blood** passion   70 **mew** (An exclamation of disgust; or, *mew up*,
restrain as one restrains a falcon.)   75 **bred** nurtured, trained.   **thrill'd
with remorse** deeply moved with pity   76–77 **bending . . . To** directing
his sword against   78 **amongst them** together with the others (?) in their
midst (?) out of their number (?)   80 **after** along (to death)   81 **nether**
i.e., committed here below, on earth   85 **One way** i.e., because Edmund is now Duke of Gloucester and Cornwall, a dangerous rival for
the throne, is dead   88–89 **May . . . life** i.e., may pull down my imagined happiness (of possessing the entire kingdom with Edmund) and
make hateful my life   89 **tart** bitter, sour   92 **back** going back

IV.iii. Location: The French camp near Dover.
3 **imperfect in the state** unsettled in state affairs   4 **imports** por-
tends   12 **trill'd** trickled   19 **like a better way** better than that, though
similar   24 **If . . . it** i.e., if all persons were as attractive in sorrow as she
26 **heav'd** breathed out   30 **believ'd** i.e., believed to be extant
32 **clamor-moistened** i.e., her outcry of grief assuaged by
tears.   **started** i.e., went   34 **conditions** characters   35 **Else . . .
make** otherwise, one couple (husband and wife)   36 **issues** offspring   40 **better tune** more composed state

GENTLEMAN: Why, good sir?
KENT: A sovereign shame so elbows him—his own
    unkindness,
    That stripp'd her from his benediction, turn'd her
45 To foreign casualties, gave her dear rights
    To his dog-hearted daughters—these things sting
    His mind so venomously, that burning shame
    Detains him from Cordelia.
GENTLEMAN: Alack, poor gentleman!
50 KENT: Of Albany's and Cornwall's powers you heard not?
GENTLEMAN: 'Tis so, they are afoot.
KENT: Well, sir, I'll bring you to our master Lear,
    And leave you to attend him. Some dear cause
    Will in concealment wrap me up awhile;
55 When I am known aright, you shall not grieve
    Lending me this acquaintance. I pray you go
    Along with me.

(Exeunt.)

SCENE [IV]

Enter, with drum and colors, CORDELIA, DOCTOR, *and*
SOLDIERS.

CORDELIA: Alack, 'tis he! Why, he was met even now
    As mad as the vex'd sea, singing aloud,
    Crown'd with rank fumiter and furrow-weeds,
    With hardocks, hemlock, nettles, cuckoo-flow'rs,
5   Darnel, and all the idle weeds that grow
    In our sustaining corn. A century send forth!
    Search every acre in the high-grown field,
    And bring him to our eye. *(Exit an Officer.)* What can
        man's wisdom
    In the restoring his bereaved sense?
10 He that helps him take all my outward worth.
DOCTOR: There is means, madam.
    Our foster-nurse of nature is repose,
    The which he lacks. That to provoke in him
    Are many simples operative, whose power
    Will close the eye of anguish.
15 CORDELIA: All blest secrets,
    All you unpublish'd virtues of the earth,
    Spring with my tears! Be aidant and remediate
    In the good man's distress! Seek, seek for him,
    Lest his ungovern'd rage dissolve the life
    That wants the means to lead it.

(Enter MESSENGER.)

MESSENGER: News, madam.   20
    The British pow'rs are marching hitherward.
CORDELIA: 'Tis known before. Our preparation stands
    In expectation of them. O dear father,
    It is thy business that I go about;
    Therefore great France   25
    My mourning and importun'd tears hath pitied.
    No blown ambition doth our arms incite,
    But love, dear love, and our ag'd father's right.
    Soon may I hear and see him!

(Exeunt.)

SCENE [V]

Enter REGAN *and steward* [OSWALD].

REGAN: But my brother's pow'rs set forth?
OSWALD: Ay, madam.
REGAN: Himself in person there?
OSWALD: Madam, with much ado.
    Your sister is the better soldier.   5
REGAN: Lord Edmund spake not with your lord at home?
OSWALD: No, madam.
REGAN: What might import my sister's letter to him?
OSWALD: I know not, lady.
REGAN: Faith, he is posted hence on serious matter. 10
    It was great ignorance, Gloucester's eyes being out,
    To let him live. Where he arrives he moves
    All hearts against us. Edmund, I think, is gone,
    In pity of his misery, to dispatch
    His nighted life; moreover, to descry   15
    The strength o' th' enemy.
OSWALD: I must needs after him, madam, with my letter.
REGAN: Our troops set forth tomorrow. Stay with us;
    The ways are dangerous.
OSWALD: I may not, madam.
    My lady charg'd my duty in this business.   20
REGAN: Why should she write to Edmund? Might not you
    Transport her purposes by word? Belike
    Something—I know not what. I'll love thee much,
    Let me unseal the letter.
OSWALD: Madam, I had rather—
REGAN: I know your lady does not love her husband,   25
    I am sure of that; and at her late being here
    She gave strange oeillades and most speaking looks
    To noble Edmund. I know you are of her bosom.
OSWALD: I, madam?
REGAN: I speak in understanding; y' are, I know 't.   30
    Therefore I do advise you, take this note:
    My lord is dead; Edmund and I have talk'd,
    And more convenient is he for my hand

43 **sovereign** overruling. **elbows** i.e., prods his memory   45 **foreign casualties** chances of fortune abroad   53 **dear cause** important purpose

IV.iv. Location: The French camp.
3 **fumiter** i.e., fumitory, a weed or herb   4 **hardocks** i.e., burdocks or hoardocks, white-leaved   5 **Darnel** (A weed of the grass kind.) **idle** worthless   6 **sustaining** giving sustenance. **corn** grain. **century** troop of 100 men   8 **What . . . wisdom** whatever can man's knowledge accomplish   10 **outward** material   13 **That to provoke** to induce that   14 **simples** medicinal plants. **operative** effective   16 **unpublish'd virtues** little-known benign herbs   17 **Spring** grow. **aidant and remediate** helpful and remedial

20 **wants** lacks. **means** i.e., his reason   26 **importun'd** importunate   27 **blown** puffed up with pride

IV.v. Location: Gloucester's house.
8 **import** bear as its purport, express   10 **is posted** has hurried   11 **ignorance** error   15 **nighted** benighted, blinded   20 **charg'd** ordered strictly   22 **Belike** it may be   26 **late** recently   27 **oeillades** amorous glances   28 **of her bosom** in her confidence   31 **take this note** i.e., mark this advice

Than for your lady's. You may gather more.
35 If you do find him, pray you, give him this;
And when your mistress hears thus much from you,
I pray, desire her call her wisdom to her.
So, fare you well.
If you do chance to hear of that blind traitor,
40 Preferment falls on him that cuts him off.
OSWALD: Would I could meet him, madam! I should show
What party I do follow.
REGAN: Fare thee well.

(Exeunt [severally].)

SCENE [VI]

Enter GLOUCESTER *[being led], and* EDGAR *[dressed like a peasant].*

GLOUCESTER: When shall I come to th' top of that same hill?
EDGAR: You do climb up it now. Look how we labor.
GLOUCESTER: Methinks the ground is even.
EDGAR: Horrible steep.
Hark, do you hear the sea?
GLOUCESTER: No, truly.
5 EDGAR: Why, then, your other senses grow imperfect
By your eyes' anguish.
GLOUCESTER: So may it be, indeed.
Methinks thy voice is alter'd, and thou speak'st
In better phrase and matter than thou didst.
EDGAR: Y' are much deceiv'd. In nothing am I chang'd
But in my garments.
10 GLOUCESTER: Methinks y' are better spoken.
EDGAR: Come on, sir, here's the place. Stand still.
How fearful
And dizzy 'tis, to cast one's eyes so low!
The crows and choughs that wing the midway air
Show scarce so gross as beetles. Half way down
15 Hangs one that gathers samphire, dreadful trade!
Methinks he seems no bigger than his head.
The fishermen that walk upon the beach
Appear like mice; and yond tall anchoring bark,
Diminish'd to her cock; her cock, a buoy
20 Almost too small for sight. The murmuring surge,
That on th' unnumb'red idle pebbles chafes,
Cannot be heard so high. I'll look no more,
Lest my brain turn, and the deficient sight
Topple down headlong.
GLOUCESTER: Set me where you stand.
25 EDGAR: Give me your hand. You are now within a foot
Of th' extreme verge. For all beneath the moon
Would I not leap upright.
GLOUCESTER: Let go my hand.
Here, friend, 's another purse; in it a jewel

Well worth a poor man's taking. Fairies and gods
Prosper it with thee! *(Gives purse.)* Go thou further off.   30
Bid me farewell, and let me hear thee going.
EDGAR: *(Moving away)*
Now fare ye well, good sir.
GLOUCESTER: With all my heart.
EDGAR: *(Aside)* Why I do trifle thus with his despair
Is done to cure it.
GLOUCESTER: *(Kneeling)* O you mighty gods!   35
This world I do renounce, and in your sights
Shake patiently my great affliction off.
If I could bear it longer, and not fall
To quarrel with your great opposeless wills,
My snuff and loathed part of nature should   40
Burn itself out. If Edgar live, O, bless him!
Now, fellow, fare thee well.

(He falls forward.)

EDGAR: Gone, sir. Farewell—
And yet I know not how conceit may rob
The treasury of life, when life itself
Yields to the theft. Had he been where he thought,   45
By this, had thought been past. Alive or dead?—
Ho, you sir! Friend! Hear you, sir! Speak!—
Thus might he pass indeed; yet he revives—
What are you, sir?
GLOUCESTER: Away, and let me die.
EDGAR: Hadst thou been aught but gossamer, feathers, air,   50
So many fathom down precipitating,
Thou 'dst shiver'd like an egg; but thou dost breathe,
Hast heavy substance, bleed'st not, speak'st, art sound.
Ten masts at each make not the altitude
Which thou hast perpendicularly fell.   55
Thy life's a miracle. Speak yet again.
GLOUCESTER: But have I fall'n, or no?
EDGAR: From the dread summit of this chalky bourn.
Look up a-height; the shrill-gorg'd lark so far
Cannot be seen or heard. Do but look up.   60
GLOUCESTER: Alack, I have no eyes.
Is wretchedness depriv'd that benefit
To end itself by death? 'Twas yet some comfort
When misery could beguile the tyrant's rage,
And frustrate his proud will.
EDGAR: Give me your arm.   65

(Lifts him up.)

Up—so. How is 't? Feel you your legs? You stand.
GLOUCESTER: Too well, too well.
EDGAR: This is above all strangeness.
Upon the crown o' th' cliff, what thing was that
Which parted from you?
GLOUCESTER: A poor unfortunate beggar.

---

34 **gather more,** i.e., infer what I am trying to suggest   35 **this** i.e., this information   37 **call . . . to her** recall her to her senses   40 **Preferment** advancement

IV.vi. Location: Open place near Dover.
13 **choughs** jackdaws. **midway** halfway down   14 **gross** large   15 **samphire** (A herb used for pickles.)   19 **Diminish'd . . . cock** reduced to the size of her cockboat, small ship's boat   21 **unnumb'red** innumerable   23–24 **the deficient sight Topple** my failing sight topple me   27 **upright** i.e., up and down, much less forward

39 **To quarrel with** into rebellion against. **opposeless** irresistible   40 **snuff** i.e., useless residue. (Literally, the smoking wick of a candle.) **of nature** i.e., of my life   43 **conceit** imagination   45 **Yields** consents   48 **pass** die   49 **What** who. (Edgar now speaks in a new voice, differing from that of "poor Tom" and also from the "alter'd" voice he used at the start of this scene; see ll. 5–9.)   54 **at each** end to end   58 **bourn** limit, boundary   59 **a-height** on high. **shrill-gorg'd** shrill-throated   64 **beguile** outwit

70 EDGAR: As I stood here below, methought his eyes
Were two full moons; he had a thousand noses,
Horns whelk'd and waved like the enridged sea.
It was some fiend. Therefore, thou happy father,
Think that the clearest gods, who make them honors
75 Of men's impossibilities, have preserved thee.
GLOUCESTER: I do remember now. Henceforth I'll bear
Affliction till it do cry out itself
"Enough, enough," and die. That thing you speak of,
I took it for a man; often 'twould say
80 "The fiend, the fiend." He led me to that place.
EDGAR: Bear free and patient thoughts.

(Enter LEAR *[mad, bedecked with weeds].)*

But who comes here?
The safer sense will ne'er accommodate
His master thus.
LEAR: No, they cannot touch me for coining; I am the King
85 himself.
EDGAR: O thou side-piercing sight!
LEAR: Nature's above art in that respect. There's your press-
money. That fellow handles his bow like a crowkeeper; draw
me a clothier's yard. Look, look, a mouse! Peace, peace; this
90 piece of toasted cheese will do 't. There's my gauntlet; I'll
prove it on a giant. Bring up the brown bills. O, well flown,
bird! I' th' clout, i' th' clout—hewgh! Give the word.
EDGAR: Sweet marjoram.
LEAR: Pass.
95 GLOUCESTER: I know that voice.
LEAR: Ha! Goneril, with a white beard? They flatter'd me like a
dog, and told me I had white hairs in my beard ere the black
ones were there. To say "ay" and "no" to everything that I
said! "Ay," and "no" too, was no good divinity. When the rain
100 came to wet me once, and the wind to make me chatter,
when the thunder would not peace at my bidding, there I
found 'em, there I smelt 'em out. Go to, they are not men o'
their words. They told me I was everything. 'Tis a lie, I am
not ague-proof.
105 GLOUCESTER: The trick of that voice I do well remember.
Is 't not the King?

LEAR: Ay, every inch a king.
When I do stare, see how the subject quakes.
I pardon that man's life. What was thy cause?
Adultery?
Thou shalt not die. Die for adultery? No. 110
The wren goes to 't, and the small gilded fly
Does lecher in my sight.
Let copulation thrive; for Gloucester's bastard son
Was kinder to his father than my daughters
Got 'tween the lawful sheets. 115
To 't, luxury, pell-mell, for I lack soldiers.
Behold yond simp'ring dame,
Whose face between her forks presages snow,
That minces virtue, and does shake the head
To hear of pleasure's name; 120
The fitchew, nor the soiled horse, goes to 't
With a more riotous appetite.
Down from the waist they are Centaurs,
Though women all above.
But to the girdle do the gods inherit, 125
Beneath is all the fiends'.
There's hell, there's darkness, there is the sulphurous pit,
Burning, scalding, stench, consumption. Fie, fie, fie!
Pah, pah! Give me an ounce of civet, good apothecary,
sweeten my imagination. There's money for thee. 130
GLOUCESTER: O, let me kiss that hand!
LEAR: Let me wipe it first; it smells of mortality.
GLOUCESTER: O ruin'd piece of nature! This great world
Shall so wear out to nought. Dost thou know me?
LEAR: I remember thine eyes well enough. Dost thou squiny at 135
me? No, do thy worst, blind Cupid; I'll not love. Read thou
this challenge; mark but the penning of it.
GLOUCESTER: Were all thy letters suns, I could not see.
EDGAR: *(Aside)* I would not take this from report; it is,
And my heart breaks at it. 140
LEAR: Read.
GLOUCESTER: What, with the case of eyes?
LEAR: O, ho, are you there with me? No eyes in your head, nor
no money in your purse? Your eyes are in a heavy case, your
purse in a light; yet you see how this world goes. 145
GLOUCESTER: I see it feelingly.
LEAR: What, art mad? A man may see how this world goes with
no eyes. Look with thine ears. See how yond justice rails
upon yond simple thief. Hark in thine ear: change places,
and, handy-dandy, which is the justice, which is the thief? 150
Thou hast seen a farmer's dog bark at a beggar?
GLOUCESTER: Ay, sir.

---

72 whelk'd twisted, convoluted.   **enridged** furrowed (by the wind)   73
happy father lucky old man   74 **clearest** purest, most righteous   74–
75 **who . . . impossibilities** who win our awe and reverence by doing
things impossible to men   81 **free** i.e., free from despair   82 **The safer
sense** a sane mind.   **accommodate** furnish, dress   84 **touch** arrest,
prosecute.   **coining** minting coins. (A royal prerogative; the King wants
money for his imaginary soldiers, ll. 87–88)   87 **Nature's . . . respect**
i.e., a king, graced with divine right like Nature herself, is above the
forger who learns his craft by art or skill (?)   87–88 **press-money** enlistment bonus   88 **crow-keeper** laborer hired to scare away the crows   89
me for me.   **clothier's yard** arrow the length of a cloth yard   90 **do 't**
i.e., capture the mouse, an imagined enemy.   **gauntlet** armored glove
thrown down as a challenge   91 **prove it on** maintain it against.
brown bills soldiers carrying pikes (painted brown), or the pikes themselves   91–92 **well flown, bird** (Lear uses the language of hawking to
describe the flight of an arrow.)   92 **clout** target, bull's eye.   **word** password   93 **Sweet marjoram** (A herb used to cure madness.)   96–97 **like
a dog** i.e., as a dog fawns   97 **had . . . beard** i.e., had wisdom   98 **To . . .
"no"** i.e., to agree   99 **no good divinity** not good theology, contrary to
biblical teaching. (See II Cor. 1:18 and James 5:12.)   102 **found 'em**
found them out

105 trick peculiar characteristic   **108 cause** offense   **116 luxury** lechery   **118 Whose . . . snow** whose frosty countenance seems to suggest
frigidity between her legs   **119 minces** affects, mimics   **120 pleasure's
name** i.e., any talk of sexual pleasure   **121 fitchew** polecat.   **soiled
horse** horse turned out to grass   **123 Centaurs** incontinent monsters,
half man, half horse   **125 But** only.   **girdle** waist.   **inherit** possess   **129 civet** musk perfume   **133 piece** masterpiece.   **This great
world** i.e., the macrocosm, of which man, the masterpiece of nature, is
the microcosm   **134 so** similarly   **135 squiny** squint   **139 take** believe, credit   **142 case** mere sockets   **143 are . . . me** is that your situation   **144 heavy case** sad plight (with pun on *case* in l. 142)   **146 feelingly** (1) by touch (2) keenly, painfully   **150 handy-dandy** take your
choice of hands (as in a well-known child's game)

LEAR: And the creature run from the cur? There thou mightst
   behold the great image of authority; a dog's obey'd in office.
155 Thou rascal beadle, hold thy bloody hand!
   Why dost thou lash that whore? Strip thy own back;
   Thou hotly lusts to use her in that kind
   For which thou whipp'st her. The usurer hangs the
     cozener.
   Through tatter'd clothes small vices do appear;
160 Robes and furr'd gowns hide all. Plate sin with gold,
   And the strong lance of justice hurtless breaks;
   Arm it in rags, a pigmy's straw does pierce it.
   None does offend, none, I say, none! I'll able 'em.
   Take that of me, my friend, who have the power
165 To seal th' accuser's lips. Get thee glass eyes,
   And, like a scurvy politician, seem
   To see the things thou dost not. Now, now, now, now!
   Pull off my boots. Harder, harder! So.
EDGAR: (Aside) O, matter and impertinency mix'd!
170 Reason in madness!
LEAR: If thou wilt weep my fortunes, take my eyes.
   I know thee well enough; thy name is Gloucester.
   Thou must be patient. We came crying hither.
   Thou know'st, the first time that we smell the air
175 We wawl and cry. I will preach to thee. Mark.
GLOUCESTER: Alack, alack the day!
LEAR: When we are born, we cry that we are come
   To this great stage of fools. — This' a good block.
   It were a delicate stratagem to shoe
180 A troop of horse with felt. I'll put 't in proof,
   And when I have stol'n upon these son-in-laws,
   Then, kill, kill, kill, kill, kill, kill!

(Enter a GENTLEMAN [with ATTENDANTS].)

GENTLEMAN: O, here he is. Lay hand upon him. — Sir,
   Your most dear daughter —
185 LEAR: No rescue? What, a prisoner? I am even
   The natural fool of fortune. Use me well;
   You shall have ransom. Let me have surgeons;
   I am cut to th' brains.
GENTLEMAN: You shall have anything.
LEAR: No seconds? All myself?
190 Why, this would make a man a man of salt
   To use his eyes for garden water-pots,
   [Ay, and laying autumn's dust.
GENTLEMAN: Good sir —]
LEAR: I will die bravely, like a smug bridegroom. What?
   I will be jovial. Come, come, I am a king,
195 Masters, know you that?

GENTLEMAN: You are a royal one, and we obey you.
LEAR: Then there's life in 't. Come, an you get it, you shall get it
   by running. Sa, sa, sa, sa.

(Exit [running; ATTENDANTS follow].)

GENTLEMAN: A sight most pitiful in the meanest wretch,
   Past speaking of in a king! Thou hast one daughter   200
   Who redeems nature from the general curse
   Which twain have brought her to.
EDGAR: Hail, gentle sir.
GENTLEMAN: Sir, speed you. What's your will?
EDGAR: Do you hear aught, sir, of a battle toward?
GENTLEMAN: Most sure and vulgar. Everyone hears that   205
   Which can distinguish sound.
EDGAR: But, by your favor,
   How near's the other army?
GENTLEMAN: Near and on speedy foot. The main descry
   Stands on the hourly thought.
EDGAR: I thank you, sir; that's all.   210
GENTLEMAN: Though that the Queen on special cause
   is here,
   Her army is mov'd on.
EDGAR: I thank you, sir.

(Exit [GENTLEMAN].)

GLOUCESTER: You ever-gentle gods, take my breath from me;
   Let not my worser spirit tempt me again
   To die before you please!
EDGAR: Well pray you, father.   215
GLOUCESTER: Now, good sir, what are you?
EDGAR: A most poor man, made tame to fortune's blows,
   Who, by the art of known and feeling sorrows,
   Am pregnant to good pity. Give me your hand,
   I'll lead you to some biding.

(Offers his arm.)

GLOUCESTER: Hearty thanks.   220
   The bounty and the benison of heaven
   To boot, and boot!

(Enter steward [OSWALD].)

OSWALD: A proclaim'd prize! Most happy!

(Draws sword.)

   That eyeless head of thine was first fram'd flesh
   To raise my fortunes. Thou old unhappy traitor,
   Briefly thyself remember. The sword is out   225
   That must destroy thee.
GLOUCESTER: Now let thy friendly hand
   Put strength enough to 't.

---

153 **creature** poor fellow   154 **a dog's . . . office** i.e., even currish power commands submission   155 **beadle** parish officer, responsible for giving whippings   157 **kind** way   158 **The usurer** i.e., a judge guilty of lending money at usurious rates.   **cozener** petty cheater   161 **hurtless breaks** splinters harmlessly   163 **able** give warrant to   164 **that** i.e., a guarantee of immunity   165 **glass eyes** spectacles (?)   166 **politician** opportunist   169 **matter and impertinency** sense and nonsense   178 **This'** this is.   **block** felt hat (?) (Lear may refer to the weeds strewn in his hair, which he removes as though doffing a hat before preaching a sermon.)   179 **delicate** subtle   180 **in proof** to the test   186 **natural fool** born plaything   188 **cut** wounded   189 **seconds** supporters   190 **of salt** of salt tears   193 **smug** trimly dressed. (*Bridegroom* continues the punning sexual suggestion of *die bravely*, have sex successfully.)

197 **life** i.e., hope still   198 **Sa . . . sa** (A hunting cry.)   201 **general curse** universal damnation   203 **speed** God speed   204 **toward** imminent   205 **vulgar** in everyone's mouth, generally known   206 **Which** who   208–209 **The main . . . thought** the full view of the main body is expected every hour   211 **on special cause** for a special reason, i.e., to minister to Lear   214 **worser spirit** bad angel   216 **what** who. (Again, Edgar alters his voice to personate a new stranger assisting Gloucester.)   218 **feeling** heartfelt, deep   219 **pregnant** prone   220 **biding** abiding place   221–222 **The bounty . . . and boot** i.e., in addition to my thanks, I wish you the bounty of heaven   222 **proclaim'd prize** one with a price on his head.   **happy** fortunate   223 **fram'd flesh** born   225 **thyself remember** i.e., confess your sins

(EDGAR *interposes*.)

OSWALD: Wherefore, bold peasant,
  Dar'st thou support a publish'd traitor? Hence,
  Lest that th' infection of his fortune take
230 Like hold on thee. Let go his arm.
EDGAR: 'Chill not let go, zir, without vurther 'casion.
OSWALD: Let go, slave, or thou diest!
EDGAR: Good gentleman, go your gait, and let poor volk pass.
  An 'chud ha' bin zwagger'd out of my life, 'twould not ha' bin
235 zo long as 'tis by a vortnight. Nay, come not near th' old man;
  keep out, 'che vor ye, or Ise try whether your costard or my
  ballow be the harder. 'Chill be plain with you.
OSWALD: Out, dunghill!

(*They fight*.)

EDGAR: 'Chill pick your teeth, zir. Come, no matter vor your
240 foins.

(EDGAR *fells him with his cudgel*.)

OSWALD: Slave, thou hast slain me. Villain, take my purse.
  If ever thou wilt thrive, bury my body,
  And give the letters which thou find'st about me
  To Edmund Earl of Gloucester; seek him out
245 Upon the English party. O, untimely death!
  Death!

(*Dies*.)

EDGAR: I know thee well: a serviceable villain,
  As duteous to the vices of thy mistress
  As badness would desire.
GLOUCESTER: What, is he dead?
250 EDGAR: Sit you down, father; rest you.

(GLOUCESTER *sits*.)

  Let's see these pockets; the letters that he speaks of
  May be my friends. He's dead; I am only sorry
  He had no other deathsman. Let us see.

(*Finds letter, and opens it*.)

  Leave, gentle wax, and, manners, blame us not.
255 To know our enemies' minds, we rip their hearts;
  Their papers is more lawful.

(*Reads the letter*.)

  "Let our reciprocal vows be remem'bred. You have many
  opportunities to cut him off; if your will want not, time and
  place will be fruitfully offer'd. There is nothing done, if he
260 return the conqueror. Then am I the prisoner, and his bed my
  jail, from the loath'd warmth whereof deliver me, and supply
  the place for your labor.
  "Your—wife, so I would say—
                    "Affectionate servant,   Goneril."

O indistinguish'd space of woman's will!   265
A plot upon her virtuous husband's life,
And the exchange my brother! Here, in the sands,
Thee I'll rake up, the post unsanctified
Of murderous lechers; and in the mature time
With this ungracious paper strike the sight   270
Of the death-practic'd Duke. For him 'tis well
That of thy death and business I can tell.
GLOUCESTER: The King is mad. How stiff is my vile sense,
  That I stand up, and have ingenious feeling
  Of my huge sorrows! Better I were distract;   275
  So should my thoughts be sever'd from my griefs,
  And woes by wrong imaginations lose
  The knowledge of themselves.

(*Drum afar off*.)

EDGAR: Give me your hand.
  Far off, methinks I hear the beaten drum.
  Come, father, I'll bestow you with a friend.   280

(*Exeunt*.)

SCENE VII

Enter CORDELIA, KENT [*dressed still in his disguise costume,*
DOCTOR] *and* GENTLEMAN.

CORDELIA: O thou good Kent, how shall I live and work
  To match thy goodness? My life will be too short,
  And every measure fail me.
KENT: To be acknowledg'd, madam, is o'erpaid.
  All my reports go with the modest truth,   5
  Nor more nor clipp'd, but so.
CORDELIA: Be better suited.
  These weeds are memories of those worser hours;
  I prithee, put them off.
KENT: Pardon, dear madam;
  Yet to be known shortens my made intent.
  My boon I make it that you know me not   10
  Till time and I think meet.
CORDELIA: Then be 't so, my good lord. (*To the* DOCTOR.)
    How does the King?
DOCTOR: Madam, sleeps still.
CORDELIA: O you kind gods,
  Cure this great breach in his abused nature!
  Th' untun'd and jarring senses, O, wind up   15
  Of this child-changed father!

228 **publish'd** proclaimed   231 **'Chill** I will. (Literally, a contraction of
Ich will. Edgar adopts Somerset dialect, a stage convention regularly
used for peasants.)   233 **go your gait** go your own way   234 **An 'chud** if
I could.   **zwagger'd** swaggered, bluffed   236 **'che vor ye** I warrant
you.   **Ise** I shall.   **costard** head (Literally, an apple.)   237 **ballow**
cudgel   240 **foins** thrusts   243 **letters** letter.   **about me** upon my person   245 **party** side   247 **serviceable** officious   253 **deathsman** exe-
cutioner   254 **Leave** by your leave.   **wax** wax seal on the letter   258
want not is not lacking

265 **indistinguish'd . . . will** incalculable range of woman's appetite
268 **rake up** cover up.   **post unsanctified** unholy messenger   269 **in . . .
time** when the time is ripe   270 **ungracious** wicked.   **strike** blast   271
death-practic'd whose death is plotted   273 **stiff** obstinate.   **sense**
consciousness, sanity   274 **ingenious** conscious   275 **distract** distracted, crazy   277 **wrong imaginations** delusions   280 **bestow** lodge.
(At the scene's end, Edgar leads off Gloucester; presumably he also disposes of Oswald's body, which must be removed from the stage or somehow concealed.)

IV.vii. Location: A tent in the French camp.
5 **go** conform   6 **Nor . . . clipp'd** i.e., neither more nor less   6 **suited**
dressed   7 **weeds** garments.   **memories** remembrances   9 **Yet . . . intent** i.e., to reveal my true identity now would alter my carefully made
plan   10 **My . . . it** the reward I seek is   11 **meet** appropriate   16 **wind
up** tune (as by winding the slackened string of an instrument)   17
child-changed changed (in mind) by children's cruelty

DOCTOR: So please your Majesty
    That we may wake the King? He hath slept long.
20 CORDELIA: Be govern'd by your knowledge, and proceed
    I' th' sway of your own will. Is he array'd?

(*Enter* LEAR *in a chair carried by* SERVANTS.)

GENTLEMAN: Ay, madam; in the heaviness of sleep
    We put fresh garments on him.
DOCTOR: Be by, good madam, when we do awake him.
    I doubt not of his temperance.
25 [CORDELIA: Very well.

(*Music.*)

DOCTOR: Please you, draw near. — Louder the music there!]
CORDELIA: O my dear father! Restoration hang
    Thy medicine on my lips, and let this kiss
    Repair those violent harms that my two sisters
    Have in thy reverence made!

(*Kisses him.*)

30 KENT: Kind and dear princess!
CORDELIA: Had you not been their father, these white flakes
    Did challenge pity of them. Was this a face
    To be oppos'd against the warring winds?
    [To stand against the deep dread-bolted thunder?
35   In the most terrible and nimble stroke
    Of quick cross lightning? To watch — poor perdu! —
    With this thin helm?] Mine enemy's dog,
    Though he had bit me, should have stood that night
    Against my fire; and wast thou fain, poor father,
40   To hovel thee with swine, and rogues forlorn,
    In short and musty straw? Alack, alack!
    'Tis wonder that thy life and wits at once
    Had not concluded all. — He wakes; speak to him.
DOCTOR: Madam, do you; 'tis fittest.
45 CORDELIA: How does my royal lord? How fares your Majesty?
LEAR: You do me wrong to take me out o' th' grave.
    Thou art a soul in bliss; but I am bound
    Upon a wheel of fire, that mine own tears
    Do scald like molten lead.
CORDELIA: Sir, do you know me?
50 LEAR: You are a spirit, I know. When did you die?
CORDELIA: Still, still, far wide!
DOCTOR: He's scarce awake. Let him alone awhile.
LEAR: Where have I been? Where am I? Fair daylight?
    I am mightily abus'd. I should e'en die with pity
55   To see another thus. I know not what to say.
    I will not swear these are my hands. Let's see;
    I feel this pin prick. Would I were assur'd
    Of my condition!
CORDELIA: O, look upon me, sir,
    And hold your hand in benediction o'er me.

(*He attempts to kneel.*)

    You must not kneel.   60
LEAR: Pray, do not mock me.
    I am a very foolish fond old man,
    Fourscore and upward, not an hour more nor less;
    And, to deal plainly,
    I fear I am not in my perfect mind.   65
    Methinks I should know you, and know this man,
    Yet I am doubtful; for I am mainly ignorant
    What place this is, and all the skill I have
    Remembers not these garments, nor I know not
    Where I did lodge last night. Do not laugh at me;   70
    For, as I am a man, I think this lady
    To be my child Cordelia.
CORDELIA: (*Weeping*)   And so I am, I am.
LEAR: Be your tears wet? Yes, faith. I pray weep not.
    If you have poison for me, I will drink it.
    I know you do not love me; for your sisters   75
    Have, as I do remember, done me wrong.
    You have some cause, they have not.
CORDELIA: No cause, no cause.
LEAR: Am I in France?
KENT: In your own kingdom, sir.
LEAR: Do not abuse me.
DOCTOR: Be comforted, good madam. The great rage,   80
    You see, is kill'd in him, [and yet it is danger
    To make him even o'er the time he has lost.]
    Desire him to go in. Trouble him no more
    Till further settling.
CORDELIA: Will 't please your Highness walk?   85
LEAR: You must bear with me.
    Pray you now, forget and forgive.
    I am old and foolish.

(*Exeunt* [*all but* KENT *and* GENTLEMAN].)

[GENTLEMAN: Holds it true, sir, that the Duke of Cornwall was
    so slain?   90
KENT: Most certain, sir.
GENTLEMAN: Who is conductor of his people?
KENT: As 'tis said, the bastard son of Gloucester.
GENTLEMAN: They say Edgar, his banish'd son, is with the
    Earl of Kent in Germany.   95
KENT: Report is changeable. 'Tis time to look about; the
    powers of the kingdom approach apace.
GENTLEMAN: The arbitrement is like to be bloody. Fare you
    well, sir.

(*Exit.*)

KENT: My point and period will be throughly wrought,   100
    Or well or ill, as this day's battle's fought.

(*Exit.*)

---

21 **I' th' sway** under the direction   31 **Had you** even if you had. **flakes** locks of hair   32 **Did challenge** would have demanded   34 **dread-bolted** furnished with the dreadful thunderstone   36 **perdu** soldier placed in a position of peculiar danger   37 **helm** helmet, i.e., his scanty hair   43 **concluded all** come to an end altogether   48 **wheel of fire** (A hellish torment for the eternally damned.)   54 **abus'd** confused

67 **mainly** perfectly   79 **abuse** deceive   82 **even o'er** fill in, go over in his mind   84 **settling** composing of his mind   97 **powers** armies   98 **arbitrement** decision by arms   100 **My . . . wrought** i.e., the conclusion of my destiny will be thoroughly brought about   101 Or either. **as** according as

— ACT FIVE —

SCENE I

Enter, with drum and colors, EDMUND, REGAN, GENTLEMAN, *and* SOLDIERS.

EDMUND: Know of the Duke if his last purpose hold,
　Or whether since he is advis'd by aught
　To change the course. He's full of alteration
　And self-reproving. Bring his constant pleasure.

(To a GENTLEMAN, *who goes out.)*

5　REGAN: Our sister's man is certainly miscarried.
EDMUND: 'Tis to be doubted, madam.
REGAN:　　　　　　　　　　　　Now, sweet lord,
　You know the goodness I intend upon you.
　Tell me, but truly — but then speak the truth —
　Do you not love my sister?
EDMUND:　　　　　　　　In honor'd love.
10　REGAN: But have you never found my brother's way
　To the forfended place?
[EDMUND: That thought abuses you.
REGAN: I am doubtful that you have been conjunct
　And bosom'd with her, as far as we call hers.]
15　EDMUND: No, by mine honor, madam.
REGAN: I never shall endure her. Dear my lord,
　Be not familiar with her.
EDMUND: Fear me not. — She and the Duke her husband!

(Enter, with drum and colors, ALBANY, GONERIL, [and]
SOLDIERS.)

[GONERIL: *(Aside)* I had rather lose the battle than that sister
20　Should loosen him and me.]
ALBANY: Our very loving sister, well be-met.
　Sir, this I heard: the King is come to his daughter,
　With others whom the rigor of our state
　Forc'd to cry out. [Where I could not be honest,
25　I never yet was valiant. For this business,
　It touches us as France invades our land,
　Not bolds the King, with others whom, I fear,
　Most just and heavy causes make oppose.
EDMUND: Sir, you speak nobly.]
REGAN:　　　　　　　　　Why is this reason'd?
30　GONERIL: Combine together 'gainst the enemy;
　For these domestic and particular broils
　Are not the question here.
ALBANY:　　　　　　　Let's then determine
　With th' ancient of war on our proceeding.

V.i. Location: The British camp near Dover.
1 **Know** inquire.　**last purpose hold** most recent intention (to fight)
remain firm　2 **since** since then.　**advis'd** persuaded　4 **constant
pleasure** settled decision　5 **miscarried** lost, perished　6 **doubted**
feared　7 **intend** intend to confer　9 **honor'd** honorable　11 **forfended** forbidden　12 **abuses** degrades, wrongs　13–14 **I am . . . hers** I
suspect that you have been joined together in the fullest manner　17
familiar intimate　24 **honest** honorable　26 **touches us as** concerns us
insofar as　27 **Not . . . others** not because France encourages the King
and others　28 **heavy causes** weighty reasons.　**make oppose** compel
to fight (against us)　29 **reason'd** argued　31 **particular broils** private
quarrels　33 **ancient of war** veteran officers

[EDMUND: I shall attend you presently at your tent.]
REGAN: Sister, you'll go with us?　　　　　　　35
GONERIL: No.
REGAN: 'Tis most convenient. Pray go with us.
GONERIL: *(Aside)* O, ho, I know the riddle. — I will go.

([As they are going out,] enter EDGAR *[disguised].)*

EDGAR: *(To Albany)* If e'er your Grace had speech with man
　so poor,
　Hear me one word.　　　　　　　　　　40
ALBANY: *(To his troops)* I'll overtake you. — Speak.

(Exeunt both the armies.)

EDGAR: Before you fight the battle, ope this letter.

(Gives letter.)

　If you have victory, let the trumpet sound
　For him that brought it. Wretched though I seem,
　I can produce a champion that will prove　　45
　What is avouched there. If you miscarry,
　Your business of the world hath so an end,
　And machination ceases. Fortune love you!
ALBANY: Stay till I have read the letter.
EDGAR: I was forbid it.　　　　　　　　　50
　When time shall serve, let but the herald cry,
　And I'll appear again.
ALBANY: Why, fare thee well. I will o'erlook thy paper.

*(Exit [*EDGAR*].)*

(Enter EDMUND.)

EDMUND: The enemy's in view; draw up your powers.
　Here is the guess of their true strength and forces　55
　By diligent discovery; but your haste
　Is now urg'd on you.
ALBANY:　　　　　　We will greet the time.

(Exit.)

EDMUND: To both these sisters have I sworn my love;
　Each jealous of the other, as the stung
　Are of the adder. Which of them shall I take?　60
　Both? One? Or neither? Neither can be enjoy'd,
　If both remain alive. To take the widow
　Exasperates, makes mad her sister Goneril;
　And hardly shall I carry out my side,
　Her husband being alive. Now then, we'll use　65
　His countenance for the battle, which being done,
　Let her who would be rid of him devise
　His speedy taking off. As for the mercy
　Which he intends to Lear and to Cordelia,

---

37 **convenient** proper, befitting　38 **know the riddle** i.e., understand
Regan's enigmatic demand that Goneril accompany her, which is that
Regan wants to keep Goneril from Edmund　43 **sound** sound a summons　46 **miscarry** perish, come to destruction　48 **machination** plotting (against your life)　53 **o'erlook** peruse　55 **guess** estimate　56 **discovery** reconnoitering　57 **greet the time** meet the occasion　59
jealous suspicious　64 **carry out my side** fulfill my ambition, and satisfy
her (Goneril)　66 **countenance** backing, authority of his name

70   The battle done, and they within our power,
        Shall never see his pardon; for my state
        Stands on me to defend, not to debate.

(Exit.)

SCENE II

Alarum within. Enter, with drum and colors, LEAR, CORDELIA,
and SOLDIERS, *over the stage; and exeunt.*

(Enter EDGAR *and* GLOUCESTER.)

EDGAR: Here, father, take the shadow of this tree
        For your good host; pray that the right may thrive.
        If ever I return to you again,
        I'll bring you comfort.
GLOUCESTER: Grace go with you, sir!

(Exit [EDGAR].)

(Alarum and retreat within. Enter EDGAR.)

5   EDGAR: Away, old man, give me thy hand, away!
        King Lear hath lost, he and his daughter ta'en.
        Give me thy hand; come on.
    GLOUCESTER: No further, sir; a man may rot even here.
    EDGAR: What, in ill thoughts again? Men must endure
10   Their going hence, even as their coming hither;
        Ripeness is all. Come on.
    GLOUCESTER: And that's true too.

(Exeunt.)

SCENE III

Enter, in conquest, with drum and colors, EDMUND; LEAR *and*
CORDELIA, *as prisoners;* SOLDIERS, CAPTAIN, *[etc.].*

EDMUND: Some officers take them away. Good guard,
        Until their greater pleasures first be known
        That are to censure them.
CORDELIA: We are not the first
        Who, with best meaning, have incurr'd the worst.
5   For thee, oppressed king, I am cast down;
        Myself could else out-frown false fortune's frown.
        Shall we not see these daughters and these sisters?
LEAR: No, no, no, no! Come, let's away to prison.
        We two alone will sing like birds i' th' cage.
10   When thou dost ask me blessing, I'll kneel down,
        And ask of thee forgiveness. So we'll live,
        And pray, and sing, and tell old tales, and laugh
        At gilded butterflies, and hear poor rogues

---

71 **Shall** they shall   71–72 **my state . . . debate** my position depends
upon maintenance by force, not by talk

V.ii. Location: A field between the two camps.
11 **Ripeness** i.e., fulfillment of one's allotted years and readiness for
death when it comes

V.iii. Location: The British camp.
2 **their greater pleasures** i.e., the wishes of those in command   3 **censure** judge   4 **meaning** intentions   13 **gilded butterflies** i.e., gaily
dressed courtiers and other ephemeral types

        Talk of court news; and we'll talk with them too—
        Who loses and who wins; who's in, who's out—   15
        And take upon 's the mystery of things,
        As if we were God's spies; and we'll wear out,
        In a wall'd prison, packs and sects of great ones,
        That ebb and flow by th' moon.
EDMUND: Take them away.
LEAR: Upon such sacrifices, my Cordelia,   20
        The gods themselves throw incense. Have I caught thee?
        He that parts us shall bring a brand from heaven,
        And fire us hence like foxes. Wipe thine eyes;
        The good-years shall devour them, flesh and fell,
        Ere they shall make us weep! We'll see 'em starv'd first. 25
        Come.

(Exit [with CORDELIA, *guarded].)*

EDMUND: Come hither, captain; hark.
        Take thou this note *(Gives a paper)*; go follow them to
                prison,
        One step I have advanc'd thee; if thou dost
        As this instructs thee, thou dost make thy way   30
        To noble fortunes. Know thou this, that men
        Are as the time is. To be tender-minded
        Does not become a sword. Thy great employment
        Will not bear question; either say thou 'lt do 't,
        Or thrive by other means.
CAPTAIN: I'll do 't, my lord.   35
EDMUND: About it; and write happy when th' hast done.
        Mark, I say, instantly, and carry it so
        As I have set it down.
[CAPTAIN: I cannot draw a cart, nor eat dried oats;
        If it be man's work, I'll do 't.]   40

(Exit CAPTAIN.)

(Flourish. Enter ALBANY, GONERIL, REGAN, *[another* CAPTAIN,
and] SOLDIERS.)

ALBANY: Sir, you have show'd today your valiant strain,
        And fortune led you well. You have the captives
        Who were the opposites of this day's strife;
        I do require them of you, so to use them
        As we shall find their merits and our safety   45
        May equally determine.
EDMUND: Sir, I thought it fit
        To send the old and miserable King
        To some retention [and appointed guard],
        Whose age had charms in it, whose title more,   50
        To pluck the common bosom on his side,

---

17 **God's spies** i.e., detached observers surveying the deeds of mankind
from an eternal vantage point.   **wear out** outlast   18–19 **packs . . .
moon** i.e., followers and cliques attached to persons of high station,
whose fortunes change erratically and constantly   21 **throw incense**
participate as celebrants   22–23 **He . . . foxes** i.e., anyone seeking to
part us will have to employ a heavenly firebrand to drive us out of our
prison refuge as foxes are driven out of their holes by fire and smoke.
(Suggests that only death will part them.)   23 **good-years** (Apparently a
word connoting evil or conceivably the passage of time.)   **flesh and fell**
flesh and skin, completely   33 **become a sword** i.e., suit a warrior   34
bear question admit of discussion   36 **write happy** call yourself fortunate   43 **opposites** enemies   49 **retention** confinement   51 **common
bosom** affection of the multitude

And turn our impress'd lances in our eyes
Which do command them. With him I sent the Queen,
My reason all the same; and they are ready
55 Tomorrow, or at further space, t' appear
Where you shall hold your session. [At this time
We sweat and bleed; the friend hath lost his friend;
And the best quarrels, in the heart, are curs'd
By those that feel their sharpness.
60 The question of Cordelia and her father
Requires a fitter place.]
ALBANY: Sir, by your patience,
I hold you but a subject of this war,
Not as a brother.
REGAN: That's as we list to grace him.
Methinks our pleasure might have been demanded
65 Ere you had spoke so far. He led our powers,
Bore the commission of my place and person;
The which immediacy may well stand up
And call itself your brother.
GONERIL: Not so hot.
In his own grace he doth exalt himself
More than in your addition.
70 REGAN: In my rights,
By me invested, he compeers the best.
GONERIL: That were the most if he should husband you.
REGAN: Jesters do oft prove prophets.
GONERIL: Holla, holla!
That eye that told you so look'd but a-squint.
75 REGAN: Lady, I am not well, else I should answer
From a full-flowing stomach. General,
Take thou my soldiers, prisoners, patrimony;
Dispose of them, of me; the walls is thine.
Witness the world that I create thee here
My lord and master.
80 GONERIL: Mean you to enjoy him?
ALBANY: The let-alone lies not in your good will.
EDMUND: Nor in thine, lord.
ALBANY: Half-blooded fellow, yes.
REGAN: (To EDMUND) Let the drum strike, and prove my
title thine.
ALBANY: Stay yet; hear reason. Edmund, I arrest thee
85 On capital treason; and, in thy attaint,
This gilded serpent. (Points to GONERIL.) For your claim,
fair sister,
I bar it in the interest of my wife;
'Tis she is sub-contracted to this lord,

And I, her husband, contradict your banns.
If you will marry, make your loves to me,   90
My lady is bespoke.
GONERIL: An interlude!
ALBANY: Thou art arm'd, Gloucester. Let the trumpet sound.
If none appear to prove upon thy person
Thy heinous, manifest, and many treasons,
There is my pledge. (Throws down a glove.) I'll make it on   95
thy heart,
Ere I taste bread, thou art in nothing less
Than I have here proclaim'd thee.
REGAN: Sick, O, sick!
GONERIL: (Aside) If not, I'll ne'er trust medicine.
EDMUND: There's my exchange. (Throws down a glove.) What
in the world he is
That names me traitor, villain-like he lies.   100
Call by the trumpet. He that dares approach,
On him, on you—who not?—I will maintain
My truth and honor firmly.
ALBANY: A herald, ho!
[EDMUND: A herald, ho, a herald!]
ALBANY: Trust to thy single virtue; for thy soldiers,   105
All levied in my name, have in my name
Took their discharge.
REGAN: My sickness grows upon me.
ALBANY: She is not well. Convey her to my tent.

(Exit REGAN, led.)

(Enter a HERALD.)

Come hither, herald. Let the trumpet sound,
And read out this.   110

(Gives paper.)

[CAPTAIN: Sound, trumpet!]

(A trumpet sounds.)

HERALD: (Reads) "If any man of quality or degree within the lists
of the army will maintain upon Edmund, supposed Earl of
Gloucester, that he is a manifold traitor, let him appear by the
third sound of the trumpet. He is bold in his defense."   115
[EDMUND: Sound!]

(First trumpet.)

HERALD: Again!

(Second trumpet.)

HERALD: Again!

(Third trumpet.)

(Trumpet answers within.)

(Enter EDGAR [at the third sound], armed [with a trumpeter
before him].)

ALBANY: Ask him his purposes, why he appears
Upon this call o' th' trumpet.

---

52 turn . . . eyes i.e., turn against us the weapons of those very troops
whom we impressed into service   53 Which we who   55 space interval of time   58 quarrels causes   59 sharpness keenness, painful consequences   62 subject of subordinate in   63 list please   64 pleasure
wish.   demanded asked about   67 immediacy nearness of connection   70 your addition the titles you confer   71 compeers is equal
with   72 That . . . most that investiture would be most complete   76
full-flowing stomach full tide of angry rejoinder   77 patrimony inheritance   78 the walls is thine i.e., the citadel of my heart surrenders
completely to you   81 let-alone preventing, denying   82 Half-
blooded only partly of noble blood   83 Let . . . strike i.e., let there be a
public announcement (?) a battle (?)   85 in thy attaint i.e., as partner
in your corruption

89 banns public announcement of a proposed marriage   91 interlude
play; i.e., you are being melodramatic   95 make prove   96 in nothing
less in no respect less guilty   98 medicine i.e., poison   99 What whoever   105 single virtue unaided prowess   112 degree rank

120 HERALD: What are you?
     Your name, your quality? And why you answer
     This present summons?
     EDGAR: Know my name is lost,
     By treason's tooth bare-gnawn and canker-bit.
     Yet am I noble as the adversary
     I come to cope.
125 ALBANY: Which is that adversary?
     EDGAR: What's he that speaks for Edmund Earl
          of Gloucester?
     EDMUND: Himself. What say'st thou to him?
     EDGAR: Draw thy sword,
     That, if my speech offend a noble heart,
     Thy arm may do thee justice. Here is mine.

     (Draws.)

130 Behold, it is my privilege,
     The privilege of mine honors,
     My oath, and my profession. I protest,
     Maugre thy strength, place, youth, and eminence,
     Despite thy victor sword and fire-new fortune,
135 Thy valor, and thy heart, thou art a traitor—
     False to thy gods, thy brother, and thy father,
     Conspirant 'gainst this high-illustrious prince,
     And, from th' extremest upward of thy head
     To the descent and dust below thy foot
140 A most toad-spotted traitor. Say thou "No,"
     This sword, this arm, and my best spirits, are bent
     To prove upon thy heart, whereto I speak,
     Thou liest.
     EDMUND: In wisdom I should ask thy name;
     But, since thy outside looks so fair and warlike,
145 And that thy tongue some say of breeding breathes,
     What safe and nicely I might well delay
     By rule of knighthood I disdain and spurn.
     Back do I toss these treasons to thy head,
     With the hell-hated lie o'erwhelm thy heart,
150 Which—for they yet glance by and scarcely bruise—
     This sword of mine shall give them instant way,
     Where they shall rest forever. Trumpets, speak!

     ([He draws.] Alarums. Fight. [EDMUND falls.])

     ALBANY: Save him, save him!
     GONERIL: This is practice, Gloucester.
     By th' law of war thou wast not bound to answer
155 An unknown opposite. Thou art not vanquish'd,
     But cozen'd and beguil'd.
     ALBANY: Shut your mouth, dame,
     Or with this paper shall I stop it.—Hold, sir.—

     (To GONERIL.) Thou worse than any name, read thine
          own evil.

     (Shows her the letter.)

     No tearing, lady; I perceive you know it.
     GONERIL: Say if I do, the laws are mine, not thine.   160
     Who can arraign me for 't?
     ALBANY: Most monstrous! O!
     Know'st thou this paper?
     GONERIL: Ask me not what I know.

     (Exit.)

     ALBANY: Go after her. She's desperate; govern her.

     (Exit an OFFICER.)

     EDMUND: What you have charg'd me with, that have I done,
     And more, much more. The time will bring it out.   165
     'Tis past, and so am I. But what art thou
     That hast this fortune on me? If thou 'rt noble,
     I do forgive thee.
     EDGAR: Let's exchange charity.
     I am no less in blood than thou art, Edmund;
     If more, the more th' hast wrong'd me.   170
     My name is Edgar, and thy father's son.
     The gods are just, and of our pleasant vices
     Make instruments to plague us.
     The dark and vicious place where thee he got
     Cost him his eyes.   175
     EDMUND: Th' hast spoken right, 'tis true.
     The wheel is come full circle; I am here.
     ALBANY: Methought thy very gait did prophesy
     A royal nobleness. I must embrace thee.

     (They embrace.)

     Let sorrow split my heart, if ever I   180
     Did hate thee or thy father!
     EDGAR: Worthy prince, I know 't.
     ALBANY: Where have you hid yourself?
     How have you known the miseries of your father?
     EDGAR: By nursing them, my lord. List a brief tale, 185
     And when 'tis told, O, that my heart would burst!
     The bloody proclamation to escape
     That follow'd me so near—O, our lives' sweetness,
     That we the pain of death would hourly die
     Rather than die at once!—taught me to shift   190
     Into a madman's rags, t' assume a semblance
     That very dogs disdain'd; and in this habit
     Met I my father with his bleeding rings,
     Their precious stones new lost; became his guide,
     Led him, begg'd for him, sav'd him from despair;   195
     Never—O fault!—reveal'd myself unto him
     Until some half-hour past, when I was arm'd.
     Not sure, though hoping, of this good success,
     I ask'd his blessing, and from first to last
     Told him our pilgrimage. But his flaw'd heart—   200
     Alack, too weak the conflict to support—

120 **What** who   123 **canker-bit** eaten as by the caterpillar   125 **cope** encounter   137 **of mine honors** i.e., of my knighthood   132 **profession** i.e., knighthood   133 **Maugre** in spite of   134 **fire-new** newly minted   135 **heart** courage   138 **upward** top   139 **descent** lowest extreme   140 **toad-spotted** venomous, or having spots of infamy   143 **wisdom** prudence   145 **say** flavor, indication   146 **safe and nicely** prudently and punctiliously   148 **treasons . . . head** i.e., accusations of treason in your teeth   149 **hell-hated** hated as hell is hated   150 **for** since.   **yet** as yet   151 **give . . . way** i.e., provide them an immediate pathway to your heart   153 **Save** spare   153 **practice** trickery; or (said sardonically) astute management   156 **cozen'd** tricked

163 **govern** restrain   167 **fortune on** victory over   172 **pleasant** pleasurable   174 **got** begot   177 **wheel** i.e., wheel of fortune.   **here** i.e., at its bottom   187 **The . . . escape** in order to escape the death-threatening proclamation   193 **rings** sockets   200 **flaw'd** cracked

'Twixt two extremes of passion, joy and grief,
Burst smilingly.
EDMUND: This speech of yours hath mov'd me,
And shall perchance do good. But speak you on;
205   You look as you had something more to say.
ALBANY: If there be more, more woeful, hold it in,
For I am almost ready to dissolve,
Hearing of this.
[EDGAR: This would have seem'd a period
To such as love not sorrow; but another,
210   To amplify too much, would make much more,
And top extremity. Whilst I
Was big in clamor, came there in a man
Who, having seen me in my worst estate,
Shunn'd my abhorr'd society; but then, finding
215   Who 'twas that so endur'd, with his strong arms
He fastened on my neck, and bellowed out
As he'd burst heaven; threw him on my father;
Told the most piteous tale of Lear and him
That ever ear receiv'd, which in recounting
220   His grief grew puissant, and the strings of life
Began to crack. Twice then the trumpets sounded,
And there I left him tranc'd.
ALBANY: But who was this?
EDGAR: Kent, sir, the banish'd Kent, who in disguise
Follow'd his enemy king, and did him service
225   Improper for a slave.]

(Enter a GENTLEMAN [with a bloody knife].)

GENTLEMAN: Help, help, O, help!
EDGAR: What kind of help?
ALBANY: Speak, man.
EDGAR: What means this bloody knife?
GENTLEMAN: 'Tis hot, it smokes.
It came even from the heart of—O, she's dead!
ALBANY: Who's dead? Speak, man.
230   GENTLEMAN: Your lady, sir, your lady; and her sister
By her is poison'd; she confesses it.
EDMUND: I was contracted to them both. All three
Now marry in an instant.
EDGAR: Here comes Kent.

(Enter KENT.)

ALBANY: Produce the bodies, be they alive or dead.

(Exit GENTLEMAN.)

235   This judgment of the heavens, that makes us tremble,
Touches us not with pity. —O, is this he?
The time will not allow the compliment
Which very manners urges.
KENT: I am come
To bid my king and master aye good night.
Is he not here?
240   ALBANY: Great thing of us forgot!
Speak, Edmund, where's the King? And where's Cordelia?

(GONERIL's and REGAN's bodies [are] brought out.)

See'st thou this object, Kent?
KENT: Alack, why thus?
EDMUND: Yet Edmund was belov'd.
The one the other poison'd for my sake,
And after slew herself.   245
ALBANY: Even so. Cover their faces.
EDMUND: I pant for life. Some good I mean to do,
Despite of mine own nature. Quickly send,
Be brief in it, to th' castle, for my writ
Is on the life of Lear and on Cordelia.   250
Nay, send in time.
ALBANY: Run, run, O, run!
EDGAR: To who, my lord? Who has the office? Send
Thy token of reprieve.
EDMUND: Well thought on. Take my sword,
Give it the captain.
EDGAR: Haste thee, for thy life.   255

(Exit OFFICER with EDMUND's sword.)

EDMUND: He hath commission from thy wife and me
To hang Cordelia in the prison, and
To lay the blame upon her own despair,
That she fordid herself.
ALBANY: The gods defend her! Bear him hence awhile.   260

(EDMUND is borne off.)

(Enter LEAR, with CORDELIA in his arms; [GENTLEMAN, CAP-
TAIN, and others following].)

LEAR: Howl, howl, howl! O, you are men of stones!
Had I your tongues and eyes, I 'd use them so
That heaven's vault should crack. She's gone for ever!
I know when one is dead, and when one lives;
She's dead as earth. Lend me a looking-glass;   265
If that her breath will mist or stain the stone,
Why, then she lives.
KENT: Is this the promis'd end?
EDGAR: Or image of that horror?
ALBANY: Fall, and cease!
LEAR: This feather stirs; she lives! If it be so,
It is a chance which does redeem all sorrows   270
That ever I have felt.
KENT: (Kneeling)   O my good master!
LEAR: Prithee, away.
EDGAR: 'Tis noble Kent, your friend.
LEAR: A plague upon you, murderers, traitors all!
I might have sav'd her; now she's gone forever!
Cordelia, Cordelia! Stay a little. Ha!   275
What is 't thou say'st? Her voice was ever soft,
Gentle, and low, an excellent thing in woman.
I kill'd the slave that was a-hanging thee.
CAPTAIN: 'Tis true, my lords, he did.
LEAR: Did I not, fellow?
I have seen the day, with my good biting falchion   280

---

208 **a period** the limit   209–211 **but . . . extremity** i.e., another sorrowful circumstance, adding to what is already too much, would increase it and exceed the limit   212 **big in clamor** loud in my lament-
ing   220 **puissant** powerful   222 **tranc'd** entranced, senseless   227
smokes steams   237 **compliment** ceremony   238 **very manners urges**
mere decency requires

242 **object** sight   243 **Yet** despite everything   252 **office** commission   259 **fordid** destroyed   266 **stone** crystal or polished stone of
which the mirror is made   267 **promis'd end** i.e., Last Judgment   268
image duplicate.   268 **Fall, and cease** i.e., let heavens fall and all
things cease   280 **falchion** light sword

I would have made them skip. I am old now,
And these same crosses spoil me. Who are you?
Mine eyes are not o' th' best; I'll tell you straight.
KENT: If Fortune brag of two she lov'd and hated,
285   One of them we behold.
LEAR: This is a dull sight. Are you not Kent?
KENT: The same,
    Your servant Kent. Where is your servant Caius?
LEAR: He's a good fellow, I can tell you that;
    He'll strike, and quickly too. He's dead and rotten.
290 KENT: No, my good lord, I am the very man—
LEAR: I'll see that straight.
KENT: That from your first of difference and decay
    Have follow'd your sad steps—
LEAR: You are welcome hither.
KENT: Nor no man else. All's cheerless, dark, and deadly.
295   Your eldest daughters have fordone themselves,
    And desperately are dead.
LEAR: Ay, so I think.
ALBANY: He knows not what he says, and vain is it
    That we present us to him.
EDGAR: Very bootless.

(Enter a MESSENGER.)

MESSENGER: Edmund is dead, my lord.
300 ALBANY: That's but a trifle here.
    You lords and noble friends, know our intent.
    What comfort to this great decay may come
    Shall be applied. For us, we will resign,
    During the life of this old majesty,

To him our absolute power. (To EDGAR and KENT.) You, to   305
    your rights,
With boot, and such addition as your honors
Have more than merited. All friends shall taste
The wages of their virtue, and all foes
The cup of their deservings. O, see, see!
LEAR: And my poor fool is hang'd! No, no, no life?   310
    Why should a dog, a horse, a rat, have life,
    And thou no breath at all? Thou'lt come no more,
    Never, never, never, never, never!
    Pray you, undo this button. Thank you, sir.
    Do you see this? Look on her, look, her lips,   315
    Look there, look there!

(He dies.)

EDGAR: He faints. My lord, my lord!
KENT: Break, heart, I prithee, break!
EDGAR: Look up, my lord.
KENT: Vex not his ghost. O, let him pass! He hates him
    That would upon the rack of this tough world
    Stretch him out longer.
EDGAR: He is gone, indeed.   320
KENT: The wonder is he hath endur'd so long.
    He but usurp'd his life.
ALBANY: Bear them from hence. Our present business
    Is general woe. (To KENT and EDGAR.) Friends of my soul,
    you twain
    Rule in this realm, and the gor'd state sustain.   325
KENT: I have a journey, sir, shortly to go;
    My master calls me, I must not say no.
EDGAR: The weight of this sad time we must obey,
    Speak what we feel, not what we ought to say.
    The oldest hath borne most; we that are young   330
    Shall never see so much, nor live so long.

(Exeunt, with a dead march.)

---

282 **crosses spoil me** adversities take away my strength   283 **I'll . . . straight** I'll recognize you in a moment   284 **two** i.e., Lear, and a hypothetical individual whose misfortunes are without parallel.   **lov'd and hated** i.e., first raised and then lowered   286 **This . . . sight** i.e., my vision is clouding   287 **Caius** (Kent's disguise name.)   291 **see that straight** attend to that soon; or, comprehend that soon   292 **first of difference** beginning of your change for the worst   294 **Nor . . . else** no, not I nor anyone else   295 **fordone** destroyed   296 **desperately** in despair   302 **What . . . come** i.e., whatever means of comforting this ruined king may present themselves

306 **boot** advantage, good measure.   **addition** titles, further distinctions   310 **poor fool** i.e., Cordelia. (*Fool* is here a term of endearment.)   319 **rack** torture rack (with suggestion, in F and Q spelling *wracke*, of shipwreck, disaster)   331 **s.d. Exeunt** (Presumably the dead bodies are borne out in procession.)

WILLIAM SHAKESPEARE

The Tempest

The Tempest was staged at court in 1611. It is probably the last play that Shakespeare wrote without a collaborator, and generations of readers and audiences have taken Prospero as an image of Shakespeare himself: when Prospero puts aside his powerful, theatrical magic, Shakespeare may in a sense be making his farewell to the stage.

Renaissance audiences might have taken *The Tempest* as an example of a new kind of play becoming increasingly popular in the early seventeenth century: **TRAGICOMEDY**. Renaissance tragicomedy generally opens in the severe, disturbing mood of tragedy and builds to a moment of crisis; it then resolves into a comic finale of festivity, marriage, and harmony. That is, this version of "tragicomedy" concerns the play's plot structure, rather than its tone or mood. Shakespeare's company, the King's Men, had staged several plays by John Fletcher, one of the premier writers of tragicomedy, and it is inviting to see Shakespeare trying out his hand at the new genre late in his career in plays such as *Pericles, Cymbeline, The Winter's Tale,* and *The Tempest. The Tempest* begins as something like a revenge tragedy: Prospero plots to revenge himself on his usurping brother Antonio, and Sebastian's plot to murder Alonso also smacks of tragic intrigue. However, *The Tempest,* while raising the problems of tragedy, resolves them in the mode of comedy. Instead of murdering his brother, Prospero marries his daughter, Miranda, to Alonso's son, Ferdinand. For the spirit Ariel prompts Prospero to discover that "The rarer action is/In virtue than in vengeance."

In other respects, *The Tempest* shares the forms and moods of Shakespearean comedy. In a plot reminiscent of many of Shakespeare's earlier comedies, Prospero's daughter Miranda falls instantly in love with Alonso's son Ferdinand, for in *The Tempest,* virtue "naturally" recognizes virtue in others. The marriage also promises to heal the political rifts between Milan and Naples, and Prospero devises an elegant entertainment to lend the engagement an aura of sanctity. In its mythological characters, verse, song, and dance, Prospero's play resembles the masques frequently performed at court on such occasions. The romantic comedy of Ferdinand and Miranda is balanced by the play's more ironic treatment of Caliban, Stephano, and Trinculo. If the magical meeting of the lovers urges us to believe that the virtuous are drawn naturally together, the fact that Caliban takes the boozy Stephano and Trinculo for gods, and that the three of them try to overthrow Prospero from his second kingdom, suggests a paraellel recognition — that bad nature also seeks itself out in others.

Although Prospero and Doctor Faustus may practice different kinds of magic, both are figures of the common desire to transcend nature through art. But much as Faustus is finally damned for his bargain with Mephostophilis, so Prospero learns that his own nature, and human nature generally, cannot be overcome. Prospero must learn to forgive in order to return to the world from his magic island-prison. Indeed, if the power of Prospero's artful magic is symbolized by the capable spirit Ariel, its limitations are suggested by Caliban. In some ways, Caliban represents a European imagination of human nature in its elemental form, an image of human nature that in the sixteenth and seventeenth centuries was often reinforced by European contacts with the indigenous peoples of the Americas and Africa. For although Prospero's island is located in the Mediterranean, many of its features — and the shipwreck motif — seem to be drawn from pamphlets describing the exploration of the New World. In 1609, a fleet of English ships bound for Virginia was wrecked by a storm in the Bermudas; and while many of the ships eventually reached Jamestown, one, the *Sea Adventure,* remained lost for nearly a year. When the ship finally reached Virginia in May of 1610, the Englishmen's story of survival and their encounters with the natives of the "still-vexed Bermoothes" was widely published in pamphlets that Shakespeare seems to have read while writing the play.

The play's setting and sources have led critics to see *The Tempest* as a play not only about the state of human nature, but also about the conquest and subjection of the native peoples represented by Caliban. Caliban is clearly seen from the point of view of the European settlers: Prospero calls him a devil and a slave and uses him as a beast of burden; his language is simple; and instead of using the arts of romance on Miranda, as Ferdinand does, he tries to rape Miranda in an effort to people the island with Calibans. Caliban was the master of the island's nature, its "fresh springs, brine pits, barren place and fertile," but in attempting to civilize Caliban, Prospero has succeeded only in deforming him. Caliban is now neither "natural" nor civilized, but a parody of European "humanity": "You taught me language, and my profit on't/Is, I know how to curse."

Prospero's stagey magic, his ability to conjure storms and spectacles, is a glorious image of Renaissance "overreaching." As in A *Midsummer Night's Dream* or *Hamlet*, Shakespeare uses *The Tempest* to frame his final, most subtle imaging of the extraordinary powers of art — the arts of magic, of civilization, of the theater. At the same time, *The Tempest* also expresses the limitations of that art: neither Sebastian nor Antonio seem fundamentally changed by Prospero's magic. And much as Caliban has been changed, the play finally can find no voice, no language for Caliban to speak.

THE TEMPEST

William Shakespeare

EDITED BY DAVID BEVINGTON

— CHARACTERS —

ALONSO, *King of Naples*
SEBASTIAN, *his brother*
PROSPERO, *the right Duke of Milan*
ANTONIO, *his brother, the usurping Duke of Milan*
FERDINAND, *son to the King of Naples*
GONZALO, *an honest old Counselor*
ADRIAN *and*
FRANCISCO, } *Lords*
CALIBAN, *a savage and deformed Slave*
TRINCULO, *a Jester*
STEPHANO, *a drunken Butler*

MASTER *of a Ship*
BOATSWAIN
MARINERS
MIRANDA, *daughter to Prospero*
ARIEL, *an airy Spirit*

[presented by] SPIRITS {
IRIS,
CERES,
JUNO,
NYMPHS,
REAPERS,

[Other SPIRITS *attending on Prospero.]*

— ACT ONE —

SCENE I

An uninhabited island.

(A tempestuous noise of thunder and lightning heard. Enter a SHIP-MASTER *and a* BOATSWAIN.*)*

MASTER: Boatswain!

BOATSWAIN: Here, master. What cheer?

MASTER: Good speak to th' mariners. Fall to 't, yarely, or we run ourselves aground. Bestir, bestir.

(Exit.)

(Enter MARINERS.*)*

5 BOATSWAIN: Heigh, my hearts! Cheerly, cheerly, my hearts! Yare, yare! Take in the topsail. Tend to th' master's whistle. — Blow till thou burst thy wind, if room enough!

(Enter ALONSO, SEBASTIAN, ANTONIO, FERDINAND, GONZALO, *and others.)*

ALONSO: Good boatswain, have care. Where's the master? Play the men.

10 BOATSWAIN: I pray now, keep below.

ANTONIO: Where is the master, bos'n?

BOATSWAIN: Do you not hear him? You mar our labor. Keep your cabins; you do assist the storm.

GONZALO: Nay, good, be patient.

15 BOATSWAIN: When the sea is. Hence! What cares these roarers for the name of king? To cabin! Silence! Trouble us not.

GONZALO: Good, yet remember whom thou hast aboard.

BOATSWAIN: None that I more love than myself. You are a counselor; if you can command these elements to silence, and work the peace of the present, we will not hand a rope more.

20 Use your authority. If you cannot, give thanks you have liv'd

so long, and make yourself ready in your cabin for the mischance of the hour, if it so hap. —Cheerly, good hearts! — Out of our way, I say.

(Exit.)

GONZALO: I have great comfort from this fellow. Methinks he   25
hath no drowning mark upon him; his complexion is perfect gallows. Stand fast, good Fate, to his hanging! Make the rope of his destiny our cable, for our own doth little advantage. If he be not born to be hang'd, our case is miserable.

(Exeunt.)

(Enter BOATSWAIN.*)*

BOATSWAIN: Down with the topmast! Yare! Lower, lower! Bring   30
her to try with main-course. *(A cry within.)* A plague upon this howling! They are louder than the weather or our office.

(Enter SEBASTIAN, ANTONIO, *and* GONZALO.*)*

Yet again? What do you here? Shall we give o'er and drown? Have you a mind to sink?

SEBASTIAN: A pox o' your throat, you bawling, blasphemous,   35
incharitable dog!

BOATSWAIN: Work you then.

ANTONIO: Hang, cur! Hang, you whoreson, insolent noisemaker! We are less afraid to be drown'd than thou art.

GONZALO: I'll warrant him for drowning, though the ship were no   40
stronger than a nutshell and as leaky as an unstanch'd wench.

BOATSWAIN: Lay her a-hold, a-hold! Set her two courses off to sea again! Lay her off!

(Enter MARINERS *wet.)*

I.i. Location: On a ship at sea.
3 **Good** i.e., it's good you've come; or, my good fellow.   **yarely** nimbly   6 **Tend** attend   7 **Blow** (Addressed to the wind.)   7 **if room enough** as long as we have sea-room enough   8–9 **Play the men** act like men (?) ply, urge the men to exert themselves (?)   15 **roarers** waves or winds, or both; spoken to as though they were "bullies" or "blusterers"   20 **hand** handle

26–27 **complexion . . . gallows** appearance shows he was born to be hanged (and therefore, according to the proverb, in no danger of drowning)   28 **our . . . advantage** i.e., our own cable is of little benefit   30–31 **Bring . . . course** sail her close to the wind by means of the mainsail   32 **our office** i.e., the noise we make at our work   40 **warrant him for drowning** guarantee that he will never be drowned   41 **unstanch'd** insatiable, loose, unrestrained   42 **a-hold** a-hull, close to the wind.   **courses** sails, i.e., foresail as well as mainsail, set in an attempt to get the ship back out into open water

217

MARINERS: All lost! To prayers, to prayers! All lost!

(Exeunt.)

45 BOATSWAIN: What, must our mouths be cold?
GONZALO: The King and Prince at prayers! Let's assist them,
    For our case is as theirs.
SEBASTIAN: I am out of patience.
ANTONIO: We are merely cheated of our lives by drunkards.
    This wide-chopp'd rascal! Would thou mightst lie drowning
    The washing of ten tides!
50 GONZALO: He'll be hang'd yet,
    Though every drop of water swear against it
    And gape at wid'st to glut him.
    (A confused noise within:)
                              "Mercy on us!" —
    "We split, we split!" — "Farewell my wife and children!" —
    "Farewell, brother!" — "We split, we split, we split!"

(Exit BOATSWAIN.)

55 ANTONIO: Let's all sink wi' th' King.
SEBASTIAN: Let's take leave of him.

(Exit [with ANTONIO].)

GONZALO: Now would I give a thousand furlongs of sea for an
    acre of barren ground, long heath, brown furze, anything.
    The wills above be done! But I would fain die a dry death.

(Exit.)

SCENE II

Enter PROSPERO [in his magic robes] and MIRANDA.

MIRANDA: If by your art, my dearest father, you have
    Put the wild waters in this roar, allay them.
    The sky, it seems, would pour down stinking pitch,
    But that the sea, mounting to th' welkin's cheek,
5   Dashes the fire out. O, I have suffered
    With those that I saw suffer! A brave vessel,
    Who had, no doubt, some noble creature in her,
    Dash'd all to pieces. O, the cry did knock
    Against my very heart! Poor souls, they perish'd.
10 Had I been any god of power, I would
    Have sunk the sea within the earth or ere
    It should the good ship so have swallow'd and
    The fraughting souls within her.
PROSPERO: Be collected.
    No more amazement. Tell your piteous heart
    There's no harm done.
MIRANDA: O, woe the day!
15 PROSPERO: No harm.
    I have done nothing but in care of thee,
    Of thee, my dear one, thee, my daughter, who

45 must . . . cold i.e., let us heat up our mouths with liquor 48 merely
quite 49 wide-chopp'd with mouth wide open 49–50 lie . . . tides
(Pirates were hanged on the shore and left until three tides had come
in.) 52 glut swallow 58 heath uncultivated ground; heather. furze
a weed growing on waste land

I.ii. Location: The island. Before Prospero's cell.
4 welkin's cheek sky's face 6 brave gallant, splendid 11 or ere before 13 fraughting forming the cargo. collected calm, composed
14 amazement consternation

Art ignorant of what thou art, nought knowing
Of whence I am, nor that I am more better
Than Prospero, master of a full poor cell,   20
And thy no greater father.
MIRANDA: More to know
    Did never meddle with my thoughts.
PROSPERO: 'Tis time
    I should inform thee farther. Lend thy hand,
    And pluck my magic garment from me. So,

(Lays down his magic robe and staff.)

    Lie there, my art. Wipe thou thine eyes; have comfort.   25
    The direful spectacle of the wrack, which touch'd
    The very virtue of compassion in thee,
    I have with such provision in mine art
    So safely ordered that there is no soul —
    No, not so much perdition as an hair   30
    Betid to any creature in the vessel
    Which thou heard'st cry, which thou saw'st sink. Sit down;
    For thou must now know farther.
MIRANDA: You have often
    Begun to tell me what I am, but stopp'd
    And left me to a bootless inquisition,   35
    Concluding, "Stay, not yet."
PROSPERO: The hour's now come;
    The very minute bids thee ope thine ear.
    Obey and be attentive. Canst thou remember
    A time before we came unto this cell?
    I do not think thou canst, for then thou wast not   40
    Out three years old.
MIRANDA: Certainly, sir, I can.
PROSPERO: By what? By any other house or person?
    Of anything the image, tell me, that
    Hath kept with thy remembrance.
MIRANDA: 'Tis far off,
    And rather like a dream than an assurance   45
    That my remembrance warrants. Had I not
    Four or five women once that tended me?
PROSPERO: Thou hadst, and more, Miranda. But how is it
    That this lives in thy mind? What seest thou else
    In the dark backward and abysm of time?   50
    If thou remem'rest aught ere thou cam'st here,
    How thou cam'st here thou mayst.
MIRANDA: But that I do not.
PROSPERO: Twelve year since, Miranda, twelve year since,
    Thy father was the Duke of Milan and
    A prince of power.
MIRANDA: Sir, are not you my father?   55
PROSPERO: Thy mother was a piece of virtue, and
    She said thou wast my daughter; and thy father
    Was Duke of Milan; and thou his only heir
    And princess no worse issued.
MIRANDA: O the heavens!
    What foul play had we, that we came from thence?   60
    Or blessed was 't we did?

20 full very 30 perdition loss 31 Betid happened 35 bootless inquisition profitless inquiry 41 Out fully 45–46 assurance . . . warrants certainty that my memory guarantees 56 piece masterpiece, ex-
emplar 59 issued born, descended

PROSPERO: Both, both, my girl.
By foul play, as thou say'st, were we heav'd thence,
But blessedly holp hither.
MIRANDA: O, my heart bleeds
To think o' th' teen that I have turn'd you to,
65   Which is from my remembrance! Please you, farther.
PROSPERO: My brother and thy uncle, call'd Antonio—
I pray thee mark me—that a brother should
Be so perfidious!—he whom next thyself
Of all the world I lov'd, and to him put
70   The manage of my state, as at that time
Through all the signories it was the first
And Prospero the prime duke, being so reputed
In dignity, and for the liberal arts
Without a parallel; those being all my study,
75   The government I cast upon my brother
And to my state grew stranger, being transported
And rapt in secret studies. Thy false uncle—
Dost thou attend me?
MIRANDA: Sir, most heedfully.
PROSPERO: Being once perfected how to grant suits,
80   How to deny them, who t' advance and who
To trash for overtopping, new created
The creatures that were mine, I say, or chang'd 'em,
Or else new form'd 'em; having both the key
Of officer and office, set all hearts i' th' state
85   To what tune pleas'd his ear, that now he was
The ivy which had hid my princely trunk,
And suck'd my verdure out on 't. Thou attend'st not.
MIRANDA: O, good sir, I do.
PROSPERO: I pray thee mark me.
I, thus neglecting worldly ends, all dedicated
90   To closeness and the bettering of my mind
With that which, but by being so retir'd,
O'er-priz'd all popular rate, in my false brother
Awak'd an evil nature; and my trust,
Like a good parent, did beget of him
95   A falsehood in its contrary as great
As my trust was, which had indeed no limit,
A confidence sans bound. He being thus lorded,
Not only with what my revenue yielded,
But what my power might else exact—like one
100   Who having into truth, by telling of it,
Made such a sinner of his memory
To credit his own lie—he did believe
He was indeed the Duke, out o' th' substitution,

And executing th' outward face of royalty,
With all prerogative. Hence his ambition growing—   105
Dost thou hear?
MIRANDA: Your tale, sir, would cure deafness.
PROSPERO: To have no screen between this part he play'd
And him he play'd it for, he needs will be
Absolute Milan. Me, poor man, my library
Was dukedom large enough. Of temporal royalties   110
He thinks me now incapable; confederates—
So dry he was for sway—wi' th' King of Naples
To give him annual tribute, do him homage,
Subject his coronet to his crown, and bend
The dukedom yet unbow'd—alas, poor Milan!—   115
To most ignoble stooping.
MIRANDA: O the heavens!
PROSPERO: Mark his condition and th' event, then tell me
If this might be a brother.
MIRANDA: I should sin
To think but nobly of my grandmother.
Good wombs have borne bad sons.
PROSPERO: Now the condition.   120
This King of Naples, being an enemy
To me inveterate, hearkens my brother's suit,
Which was that he, in lieu o' th' premises
Of homage and I know not how much tribute,
Should presently extirpate me and mine   125
Out of the dukedom and confer fair Milan
With all the honors on my brother. Whereon,
A treacherous army levied, one midnight
Fated to th' purpose, did Antonio open
The gates of Milan, and, i' th' dead of darkness,   130
The ministers for th' purpose hurried thence
Me and thy crying self.
MIRANDA: Alack, for pity!
I, not rememb'ring how I cried out then,
Will cry it o'er again. It is a hint
That wrings mine eyes to 't.
PROSPERO: Hear a little further,   135
And then I'll bring thee to the present business
Which now's upon 's, without the which this story
Were most impertinent.
MIRANDA: Wherefore did they not
That hour destroy us?
PROSPERO: Well demanded, wench.
My tale provokes that question. Dear, they durst not,   140
So dear the love my people bore me, nor set
A mark so bloody on the business, but
With colors fairer painted their foul ends.
In few, they hurried us aboard a bark,
Bore us some leagues to sea, where they prepar'd   145

63 **holp** helped   64 **teen . . . to** trouble I've caused you to remember, or put you to   65 **from** out of   71 **signories** i.e., city-states of northern Italy   79 **perfected** grown skillful   81 **trash** check a hound by tying a weight to its neck.   **overtopping** running too far ahead of the pack; or, growing too tall   82 **creatures** dependents.   **or** either   83 **key** (1) key for unlocking (2) tool for tuning stringed instruments   90 **closeness** retirement, seclusion   91–92 **but . . . rate** except that it was done in retirement, (would have) surpassed in value all popular estimate   94 **good parent** (Alludes to the proverb that good parents often bear bad children; see also l. 120.)   97 **sans** without.   **lorded** raised to lordship, with power and wealth   100–102 **Who . . . lie** i.e., who, by repeatedly telling the lie (that he was indeed Duke of Milan), made his memory such a confirmed sinner against truth that he began to believe his own lie   103 **out o'** as a result of

104 **And . . . royalty** and (as a result) his carrying out all the ceremonial functions of royalty   108 **him** i.e., himself   109 **Absolute Milan** unconditional Duke of Milan   110 **temporal royalties** practical prerogatives and responsibilities of a sovereign   111 **confederates** conspires, allies himself   112 **dry** thirsty   113 **him** i.e., the King of Naples   114 **his . . . his** Antonio's . . . the King of Naples'   117 **condition** pact.   **event** outcome   123 **in . . . premises** in return for the stipulation   125 **presently extirpate** at once remove   134 **hint** occasion   138 **impertinent** irrelevant   144 **few** few words

A rotten carcass of a butt, not rigg'd,
Nor tackle, sail, nor mast; the very rats
Instinctively have quit it. There they hoist us,
To cry to th' sea that roar'd to us, to sigh
150 To th' winds whose pity, sighing back again,
Did us but loving wrong.
MIRANDA: Alack, what trouble
Was I then to you!
PROSPERO: O, a cherubin
Thou wast that did preserve me. Thou didst smile,
Infused with a fortitude from heaven,
155 When I have deck'd the sea with drops full salt,
Under my burden groan'd, which rais'd in me
An undergoing stomach, to bear up
Against what should ensue.
MIRANDA: How came we ashore?
PROSPERO: By Providence divine.
160 Some food we had, and some fresh water, that
A noble Neapolitan, Gonzalo,
Out of his charity, who being then appointed
Master of this design, did give us, with
Rich garments, linens, stuffs, and necessaries,
165 Which since have steaded much. So, of his gentleness,
Knowing I lov'd my books, he furnish'd me
From mine own library with volumes that
I prize above my dukedom.
MIRANDA: Would I might
But ever see that man!
PROSPERO: Now I arise.

(Resumes his magic robes.)

170 Sit still, and hear the last of our sea-sorrow.
Here in this island we arriv'd; and here
Have I, thy schoolmaster, made thee more profit
Than other princess' can that have more time
For vainer hours and tutors not so careful.
175 MIRANDA: Heavens thank you for 't! And now, I pray you, sir,
For still 'tis beating in my mind, your reason
For raising this sea-storm?
PROSPERO: Know thus far forth.
By accident most strange, bountiful Fortune,
Now my dear lady, hath mine enemies
180 Brought to this shore; and by my prescience
I find my zenith doth depend upon
A most auspicious star, whose influence
If now I court not but omit, my fortunes
Will ever after droop. Here cease more questions.
185 Thou art inclin'd to sleep; 'tis a good dullness,
And give it way. I know thou canst not choose.

(MIRANDA sleeps.)

Come away, servant, come! I am ready now.
Approach, my Ariel, come.

(Enter ARIEL.)

ARIEL: All hail, great master! Grave sir, hail! I come
To answer thy best pleasure; be 't to fly,   190
To swim, to dive into the fire, to ride
On the curl'd clouds. To thy strong bidding, task
Ariel and all his quality.
PROSPERO: Hast thou, spirit,
Perform'd to point the tempest that I bade thee?
ARIEL: To every article.   195
I boarded the King's ship; now on the beak,
Now in the waist, the deck, in every cabin,
I flam'd amazement. Sometime I'd divide,
And burn in many places; on the topmast,
The yards, and boresprit, would I flame distinctly,   200
Then meet and join. Jove's lightnings, the precursors
O' th' dreadful thunder-claps, more momentary
And sight-outrunning were not; the fire and cracks
Of sulphurous roaring the most mighty Neptune
Seem to besiege and make his bold waves tremble,   205
Yea, his dread trident shake.
PROSPERO: My brave spirit!
Who was so firm, so constant, that this coil
Would not infect his reason?
ARIEL: Not a soul
But felt a fever of the mad and play'd
Some tricks of desperation. All but mariners   210
Plung'd in the foaming brine and quit the vessel;
Then all afire with me, the King's son, Ferdinand,
With hair up-staring—then like reeds, not hair—
Was the first man that leapt; cried, "Hell is empty,
And all the devils are here."
PROSPERO: Why, that's my spirit!   215
But was not this nigh shore?
ARIEL: Close by, my master.
PROSPERO: But are they, Ariel, safe?
ARIEL: Not a hair perish'd.
On their sustaining garments not a blemish,
But fresher than before; and, as thou bad'st me,
In troops I have dispers'd them 'bout the isle.   220
The King's son have I landed by himself,
Whom I left cooling of the air with sighs
In an odd angle of the isle and sitting,
His arms in this sad knot.

(Folds his arms.)

PROSPERO: Of the King's ship,
The mariners, say how thou hast dispos'd,   225
And all the rest o' th' fleet.
ARIEL: Safely in harbor
Is the King's ship; in the deep nook, where once
Thou call'dst me up at midnight to fetch dew

146 **butt** cask, tub   151 **loving wrong** (i.e., the winds pitied Prospero and Miranda though of necessity they blew them from shore.)   155 **deck'd** covered (with salt tears); adorned   156 **which** i.e., the smile   157 **undergoing stomach** courage to go on   165 **steaded much** been of much use   172 **more profit** profit more   173 **princess'** princesses   181 **zenith** height of fortune. (Astrological term.)   182 **influence** astrological power   187 **Come away** come

192 **task** make demands upon   193 **quality** (1) fellow-spirits (2) abilities   194 **to point** to the smallest detail   196 **beak** prow   197 **waist** midships.   **deck** poopdeck at the stern   198 **flam'd amazement** struck terror in the guise of fire, i.e., St. Elmo's fire   200 **boresprit** bowsprit.   **distinctly** in different places   207 **coil** tumult   209 **of the mad** i.e., such as madmen feel   213 **up-staring** standing on end   218 **sustaining garments** garments that buoyed them up in the sea   223 **angle** corner   224 **sad knot** (Folded arms are indicative of melancholy.)   227 **nook** bay

From the still-vex'd Bermoothes, there she's hid;
230 The mariners all under hatches stow'd,
Who, with a charm join'd to their suff'red labor,
I have left asleep; and for the rest o' th' fleet,
Which I dispers'd, they all have met again
And are upon the Mediterranean flote
235 Bound sadly home for Naples,
Supposing that they saw the King's ship wrack'd
And his great person perish.
PROSPERO: Ariel, thy charge
Exactly is perform'd. But there's more work.
What is the time o' th' day?
ARIEL: Past the mid season.
240 PROSPERO: At least two glasses. The time 'twixt six and now
Must by us both be spent most preciously.
ARIEL: Is there more toil? Since thou dost give me pains,
Let me remember thee what thou hast promis'd,
Which is not yet perform'd me.
PROSPERO: How now? Moody?
What is 't thou canst demand?
245 ARIEL: My liberty.
PROSPERO: Before the time be out? No more!
ARIEL: I prithee,
Remember I have done thee worthy service,
Told thee no lies, made thee no mistakings, serv'd
Without or grudge or grumblings. Thou didst promise
To bate me a full year.
250 PROSPERO: Dost thou forget
From what a torment I did free thee?
ARIEL: No.
PROSPERO: Thou dost, and think'st it much to tread the ooze
Of the salt deep,
To run upon the sharp wind of the north,
255 To do me business in the veins o' th' earth
When it is bak'd with frost.
ARIEL: I do not, sir.
PROSPERO: Thou liest, malignant thing! Hast thou forgot
The foul witch Sycorax, who with age and envy
Was grown into a hoop? Hast thou forgot her?
260 ARIEL: No, sir.
PROSPERO: Thou hast. Where was she born? Speak. Tell me.
ARIEL: Sir, in Argier.
PROSPERO: O, was she so? I must
Once in a month recount what thou hast been,
Which thou forget'st. This damn'd witch Sycorax,
265 For mischiefs manifold and sorceries terrible
To enter human hearing, from Argier,
Thou know'st, was banish'd; for one thing she did
They would not take her life. Is not this true?
ARIEL: Ay, sir.
270 PROSPERO: This blue-ey'd hag was hither brought with child
And here was left by th' sailors. Thou, my slave,

As thou report'st thyself, was then her servant;
And, for thou wast a spirit too delicate
To act her earthy and abhorr'd commands,
Refusing her grand hests, she did confine thee,   275
By help of her more potent ministers,
And in her most unmitigable rage,
Into a cloven pine, within which rift
Imprison'd thou didst painfully remain
A dozen years; within which space she died   280
And left thee there, where thou did'st vent thy groans
As fast as mill-wheels strike. Then was this island —
Save for the son that she did litter here,
A freckled whelp hag-born — not horor'd with
A human shape.
ARIEL: Yes, Caliban her son.   285
PROSPERO: Dull thing, I say so; he, that Caliban
Whom now I keep in service. Thou best know'st
What torment I did find thee in; thy groans
Did make wolves howl and penetrate the breasts
Of ever angry bears. It was a torment   290
To lay upon the damn'd, which Sycorax
Could not again undo. It was mine art,
When I arriv'd and heard thee, that made gape
The pine and let thee out.
ARIEL: I thank thee, master.
PROSPERO: If thou more murmur'st, I will rend an oak   295
And peg thee in his knotty entrails till
Thou hast howl'd away twelve winters.
ARIEL: Pardon, master;
I will be correspondent to command
And do my spriting gently.
PROSPERO: Do so, and after two days   300
I will discharge thee.
ARIEL: That's my noble master!
What shall I do? Say what? What shall I do?
PROSPERO: Go make thyself like a nymph o' th' sea.
Be subject
To no sight but thine and mine, invisible
To every eyeball else. Go take this shape   305
And hither come in 't. Go, hence with diligence!

(*Exit* [ARIEL]).

Awake, dear heart, awake! Thou hast slept well;
Awake!
MIRANDA: The strangeness of your story put
Heaviness in me.
PROSPERO: Shake it off. Come on;   310
We'll visit Caliban my slave, who never
Yields us kind answer.
MIRANDA: 'Tis a villain, sir,
I do not love to look on.
PROSPERO: But, as 'tis,
We cannot miss him. He does make our fire,
Fetch in our wood, and serves in offices   315
That profit us. What, ho! Slave! Caliban!
Thou earth, thou! Speak.
CALIBAN: (*Within*)   There's wood enough within.

229 **still-vex'd Bermoothes** ever stormy Bermudas. (Perhaps refers to the then-recent Bermuda shipwreck; see Play Introduction.)   231 **with . . . labor** by means of a spell added to all the labor they have undergone   234 **flote** sea   239 **mid season** noon   240 **glasses** i.e., hourglasses   243 **remember** remind   250 **bate** remit, deduct   258 **envy** malice   262 **Argier** Algiers   267 **one . . . did** (Perhaps a reference to her pregnancy, for which her life would be spared.)   270 **blue-ey'd** with dark circles under the eyes

273 **for** because   275 **hests** commands   296 **his** its   298 **correspondent** responsive, submissive   314 **miss** do without

PROSPERO: Come forth, I say! There's other business for thee.
Come, thou tortoise! When?

(Enter ARIEL *like a water-nymph.)*

320   Fine apparition! My quaint Ariel,
Hark in thine ear.

(Whispers.)

ARIEL: My lord, it shall be done.

(Exit.)

PROSPERO: Thou poisonous slave, got by the devil himself
Upon thy wicked dam, come forth!

(Enter CALIBAN.)

CALIBAN: As wicked dew as e'er my mother brush'd
325   With raven's feather from unwholesome fen
Drop on you both! A south-west blow on ye
And blister you all o'er!

PROSPERO: For this, be sure, tonight thou shalt have cramps,
Side-stitches that shall pen thy breath up; urchins
330   Shall, for that vast of night that they may work,
All exercise on thee. Thou shalt be pinch'd
As thick as honeycomb, each pinch more stinging
Than bees that made 'em.

CALIBAN: I must eat my dinner.
This island's mine, by Sycroax my mother,
335   Which thou tak'st from me. When thou cam'st first,
Thou strok'st me and made much of me, wouldst
give me
Water with berries in 't, and teach me how
To name the bigger light, and how the less,
That burn by day and night; and then I lov'd thee
340   And show'd thee all the qualities o' th' isle,
The fresh springs, brine-pits, barren place and fertile.
Curs'd be I that did so! All the charms
Of Sycorax, toads, beetles, bats, light on you!
For I am all the subjects that you have,
345   Which first was mine own king; and here you sty me
In this hard rock, whiles you do keep from me
The rest o' th' island.

PROSPERO: Thou most lying slave,
Whom stripes may move, not kindness! I have us'd
thee,
Filth as thou art, with humane care, and lodg'd
thee
350   In mine own cell, till thou didst seek violate
The honor of my child.

CALIBAN: O ho, O ho! Would't had been done!
Thou didst prevent me; I had peopled else
This isle with Calibans.

MIRANDA: Abhorred slave,
355   Which any print of goodness wilt not take,
Being capable of all ill! I pitied thee,
Took pains to make thee speak, taught thee each
hour

One thing or other. When thou didst not, savage,
Know thine own meaning, but wouldst gabble like
A thing most brutish, I endow'd thy purposes   360
With words that made them known. But thy vile
race,
Though thou didst learn, had that in 't which
good natures
Could not abide to be with; therefore wast thou
Deservedly confin'd into this rock,
Who hadst deserv'd more than a prison.   365

CALIBAN: You taught me language, and my profit on 't
Is, I know how to curse. The red plague rid you
For learning me your language!

PROSPERO: Hag-seed, hence!
Fetch us in fuel; and be quick, thou 'rt best,
To answer other business. Shrug'st thou, malice?   370
If thou neglect'st or dost unwillingly
What I command, I'll rack thee with old cramps,
Fill all thy bones with aches, make thee roar
That beasts shall tremble at thy din.

CALIBAN: No, pray thee.
(Aside.) I must obey. His art is of such pow'r,   375
It would control my dam's god, Setebos,
And make a vassal of him.

PROSPERO: So, slave, hence!

(Exit CALIBAN.)

(Enter FERDINAND; *and* ARIEL, *invisible, playing and singing.*
[FERDINAND *does not see* PROSPERO *and* MIRANDA.])

(ARIEL's song.)
Come unto these yellow sands,
     And then take hands.
Curtsied when you have and kiss'd,   380
     The wild waves whist,
Foot it featly here and there;
And, sweet sprites, the burden bear.
     Hark, hark!

(Burden, dispersedly [within].)

     Bow-wow.   385
     The watch-dogs bark.

(Burden, dispersedly [within].)

     Bow-wow.
Hark, hark! I hear
The strain of strutting chanticleer
Cry, Cock-a-diddle-dow.   390

FERDINAND: Where should this music be? I' th' air or
th' earth?
It sounds no more; and, sure, it waits upon
Some god o' th' island. Sitting on a bank,
Weeping again the King my father's wrack,
This music crept by me upon the waters,   395

---

320 **quaint** ingenious   323 **wicked** mischievous, harmful   326 **south-west** i.e., wind thought to bring disease   329 **urchins** hedgehogs; here, suggesting goblins in the guise of hedgehogs   330 **vast** lengthy, desolate time.   **that . . . work** (Malignant spirits were thought to be restricted to the hours of darkness.)   348 **stripes** lashes   354–365 **Abhorred . . . prison** (Sometimes assigned by editors to Prospero.)

360 **purposes** meanings, desires   361 **race** natural disposition; species, nature   367 **red plague** bubonic plague.   **rid** destroy   368 **learning** teaching.   **Hag-seed** offspring of a female demon   369 **thou'rt best** you'd be well advised   372 **old** such as old people suffer; or, plenty of   373 **aches** (Pronounced "aitches.")   381 **whist** being hushed   382 **featly** nimbly   383 **burden** refrain, undersong   383 s.d. **dispersedly** i.e., from all directions

Allaying both their fury and my passion
With its sweet air. Thence I have follow'd it,
Or it hath drawn me rather. But 'tis gone.
No, it begins again.

(ARIEL'S *song*.)

400   Full fathom five thy father lies;
  Of his bones are coral made;
 Those are pearls that were his eyes.
  Nothing of him that doth fade
405   But doth suffer a sea-change
 Into something rich and strange.
 Sea-nymphs hourly ring his knell:

(*Burden* [*within*].)

 Ding-dong.
 Hark, now I hear them — Ding-dong,
  bell.

FERDINAND: The ditty does remember my drown'd father.
410 This is no mortal business, nor no sound
 That the earth owes. I hear it now above me.
PROSPERO: The fringed curtains of thine eye advance
 And say what thou seest yond.
MIRANDA: What is 't! A spirit!
 Lord, how it looks about! Believe me, sir,
415 It carries a brave form. But 'tis a spirit.
PROSPERO: No, wench, it eats and sleeps and hath such senses
 As we have, such. This gallant which thou seest
 Was in the wrack; and, but he's something stain'd
 With grief, that's beauty's canker, thou mightst call him
420 A goodly person. He hath lost his fellows
 And strays about to find 'em.
MIRANDA: I might call him
 A thing divine, for nothing natural
 I ever saw so noble.
PROSPERO: (*Aside*) It goes on, I see,
 As my soul prompts it. Spirit, fine spirit, I'll free thee
 Within two days for this.
425   FERDINAND: (*Seeing* MIRANDA) Most sure, the goddess
 On whom these airs attend! — Vouchsafe my pray'r
 May know if you remain upon this island,
 And that you will some good instruction give
 How I may bear me here. My prime request,
430 Which I do last pronounce, is, O you wonder!
 If you be maid or no?
MIRANDA: No wonder, sir,
 But certainly a maid.
FERDINAND: My language? Heavens!
 I am the best of them that speak this speech,
 Were I but where 'tis spoken.
PROSPERO: (*Coming forward*) How? The best?
435 What wert thou, if the King of Naples heard thee?
FERDINAND: A single thing, as I am now, that wonders

To hear thee speak of Naples. He does hear me;
And that he does I weep. Myself am Naples,
Who with mine eyes, never since at ebb, beheld
The King my father wrack'd.
MIRANDA: Alack, for mercy! 440
FERDINAND: Yes, faith, and all his lords, the Duke of Milan
And his brave son being twain.
PROSPERO: (*Aside*)   The Duke of Milan
And his more braver daughter could control thee,
If now 'twere fit to do 't. At the first sight
They have chang'd eyes. Delicate Ariel, 445
I'll set thee free for this. (*To* FERDINAND.) A word, good sir,
I fear you have done yourself some wrong. A word!
MIRANDA: (*Aside*) Why speaks my father so ungently? This
Is the third man that e'er I saw, the first
That e'er I sigh'd for. Pity move my father 450
To be inclin'd my way!
FERDINAND: O, if a virgin,
And your affection not gone forth, I'll make you
The Queen of Naples.
PROSPERO: Soft, sir! One word more.
(*Aside*) They are both in either's pow'rs; but this swift
 business
I must uneasy make, lest too light winning 455
Make the prize light. (*To* FERDINAND.) One word more: I
 charge thee
That thou attend me. Thou dost here usurp
The name thou ow'st not, and hast put thyself
Upon this island as a spy, to win it
From me, the lord on 't.
FERDINAND: No, as I am a man. 460
MIRANDA: There's nothing ill can dwell in such a temple.
If the ill spirit have so fair a house,
Good things will strive to dwell with 't.
PROSPERO: Follow me. —
Speak not you for him; he's a traitor. — Come,
I'll manacle thy neck and feet together. 465
Sea-water shalt thou drink; thy food shall be
The fresh-brook mussels, wither'd roots, and husks
Wherein the acorn cradled. Follow.
FERDINAND: No.
I will resist such entertainment till
Mine enemy has more pow'r.

(*He draws, and is charmed from moving.*)

MIRANDA: O dear father, 470
Make not too rash a trial of him, for
He's gentle, and not fearful.
PROSPERO: What, I say,
My foot my tutor? — Put thy sword up, traitor,
Who mak'st a show but dar'st not strike, thy conscience

---

409 **remember** commemorate 411 **owes** owns 412 **advance** raise 415 **brave** excellent 418 **but** except that. **something stain'd** somewhat disfigured 419 **canker** cankerworm (feeding on buds and leaves) 423 **It goes on** i.e., my plan works 427 **remain** dwell 429 **bear me** conduct myself. **prime** chief 433 **best** i.e., in birth

436 **single** (1) solitary (2) feeble 437–438 **He . . . weep** i.e., this man to whom I speak (Prospero) hears me as I hear him, proving to me I am indeed alive, not dreaming, and am in the sad plight I imagined (?) 438 **Naples** the King of Naples (also in l. 437) 442 **son** (The only reference in the play to a son of Antonio.) 443 **control** confute 445 **chang'd eyes** exchanged amorous glances 447 **done . . . wrong** i.e., spoken falsely 455 **uneasy** difficult 455–456 **light . . . light** easy . . . cheap 458 **ow'st** ownest 469 **entertainment** treatment 472 **gentle** wellborn. **fearful** cowardly 473 **foot** subordinate (Miranda, the foot, presumes to instruct Prospero, the head.)

475 Is so possess'd with guilt. Come, from thy ward,
For I can here disarm thee with this stick
And make thy weapon drop.

(Brandishes his staff.)

MIRANDA: *(Trying to hinder him.)*   Beseech you, father.
PROSPERO: Hence! Hang not on my garments.
MIRANDA: Sir, have pity!
I'll be his surety.
PROSPERO: Silence! One word more
480 Shall make me chide thee, if not hate thee. What,
An advocate for an imposter? Hush!
Thou think'st there is no more such shapes as he,
Having seen but him and Caliban. Foolish wench,
To th' most of men this is a Caliban
And they to him are angels.
485 MIRANDA: My affections
Are then most humble; I have no ambition
To see a goodlier man.
PROSPERO: *(To FERDINAND.)* Come on, obey.
Thy nerves are in their infancy again
And have no vigor in them.
FERDINAND: So they are.
490 My spirits, as in a dream, are all bound up.
My father's loss, the weakness which I feel,
The wrack of all my friends, nor this man's threats
To whom I am subdu'd, are but light to me,
Might I put through my prison once a day
495 Behold this maid. All corners else o' th' earth
Let libery make use of; space enough
Have I in such a prison.
PROSPERO: *(Aside)* It works. *(To FERDINAND.)* Come on. —
Thou hast done well, fine Ariel! *(To FERDINAND.)* Follow
me.
(To ARIEL.) Hark what thou else shalt do me.
MIRANDA: *(To FERDINAND.)*   Be of comfort.
500 My father's of a better nature, sir,
Than he appears by speech. This is unwonted
Which now came from him.
PROSPERO: *(To ARIEL.)*   Thou shalt be as free
As mountain winds, but then exactly do
All points of my command.
ARIEL: To th' syllable.
505 PROSPERO: *(To FERDINAND.)* Come, follow. *(To MIRANDA.)*
Speak not for him.

(Exeunt.)

— ACT TWO —

SCENE I

Enter ALONSO, SEBASTIAN, ANTONIO, GONZALO, ADRIAN,
FRANCISCO, *and others.*

GONZALO: Beseech you, sir, be merry. You have cause,
So have we all, of joy, for our escape

Is much beyond our loss. Our hint of woe
Is common; every day some sailor's wife,
The masters of some merchant, and the merchant,   5
Have just our theme of woe; but for the miracle,
I mean our preservation, few in millions
Can speak like us. Then wisely, good sir, weigh
Our sorrow with our comfort.
ALONSO: Prithee, peace.
SEBASTIAN: *(To ANTONIO.)* He receives comfort like cold   10
porridge.
ANTONIO: *(To SEBASTIAN.)* The visitor will not give him o'er so.
SEBASTIAN: Look, he's winding up the watch of his wit; by and by
it will strike.
GONZALO: Sir —
SEBASTIAN: *(To ANTONIO.)* One. Tell.   15
GONZALO: When every grief is entertain'd that's offer'd,
Comes to th' entertainer —
SEBASTIAN: A dollar.
GONZALO: Dolor comes to him, indeed. You have spoken truer
than you purpos'd.   20
SEBASTIAN: You have taken it wiselier than I meant you should.
GONZALO: Therefore, my lord —
ANTONIO: Fie, what a spendthrift is he of his tongue!
ALONSO: I prithee, spare.
GONZALO: Well, I have done. But yet —   25
SEBASTIAN: He will be talking.
ANTONIO: Which, of he or Adrian, for a good wager, first begins
to crow?
SEBASTIAN: The old cock.
ANTONIO: The cock'rel.   30
SEBASTIAN: Done. The wager?
ANTONIO: A laughter.
SEBASTIAN: A match!
ADRIAN: Though this island seem to be desert —
SEBASTIAN: Ha, ha, ha!   35
ANTONIO: So, you're paid.
ADRIAN: Uninhabitable and almost inaccessible —
SEBASTIAN: Yet —
ADRIAN: Yet —
ANTONIO: He could not miss 't.   40
ADRIAN: It must needs be of subtle, tender, and delicate
temperance.

3 **hint of** occasion for   5 **masters . . . the merchant** officers of some
merchant vessel and the merchant himself, the owner   10 **porridge**
(with a pun on *peace* and *pease*, a usual ingredient of porridge)   11
visitor one taking nourishment and comfort to the sick, i.e.,
Gonzalo   12 **give him o'er** abandon him   15 **Tell** keep count   16–17
When . . . entertainer when every sorrow that presents itself is accepted
without resistance, there comes to the recipient   18 **dollar** widely-cir-
culated coin, the German *Thaler* and the Spanish *piece of eight.* (Sebastian puns on *entertainer* in the sense of *innkeeper;* to Gonzalo, *dollar*
suggests *dolor,* grief.)   27–28 **Which . . . crow** which of the two,
Gonzalo or Adrian, do you bet will speak (crow) first   29 **old cock** i.e.,
Gonzalo   30 **cock'rel** i.e., Adrian   32 **laughter** (1) burst of laughter (2)
sitting of eggs. (When Adrian, the *cock'rel,* begins to speak two lines
later, Sebastian loses the bet. Some editors alter the speech prefixes in ll.
35–36 so that Antonio enjoys his laugh as the prize for winning, but
possibly Sebastian pays for losing with a laugh.)   33 **A match** a bargain;
agreed   40 **miss 't** (1) avoid saying "Yet" (2) miss the island   42 **temperance** climate

475 **ward** defensive posture (in fencing)   484 **To** compared to   488
nerves sinews   499 **me** for me

II.i. Location: Another part of the island.

ANTONIO: Temperance was a delicate wench.

SEBASTIAN: Ay, and a subtle, as he most learnedly deliver'd.

45 ADRIAN: The air breathes upon us here most sweetly.

SEBASTIAN: As if it had lungs, and rotten ones.

ANTONIO: Or as 'twere perfum'd by a fen.

GONZALO: Here is everything advantageous to life.

ANTONIO: True, save means to live.

50 SEBASTIAN: Of that there's none, or little.

GONZALO: How lush and lusty the grass looks! How green!

ANTONIO: The ground indeed is tawny.

SEBASTIAN: With an eye of green in 't.

ANTONIO: He misses not much.

55 SEBASTIAN: No; he doth but mistake the truth totally.

GONZALO: But the rarity of it is—which is indeed almost beyond credit—

SEBASTIAN: As many vouch'd rarities are.

GONZALO: That our garments, being, as they were, drench'd in
60 the sea, hold notwithstanding their freshness and glosses, being rather new-dyed than stain'd with salt water.

ANTONIO: If but one of his pockets could speak, would it not say
he lies?

SEBASTIAN: Ay, or very falsely pocket up his report.

65 GONZALO: Methinks our garments are now as fresh as when we
put them on first in Afric, at the marriage of the King's fair
daughter Claribel to the King of Tunis.

SEBASTIAN: 'Twas a sweet marriage, and we prosper well in our
return.

70 ADRIAN: Tunis was never grac'd before with such a paragon to
their queen.

GONZALO: Not since widow Dido's time.

ANTONIO: Widow! A pox o' that! How came that widow in?
Widow Dido!

75 SEBASTIAN: What if he had said "widower Aeneas" too? Good
Lord, how you take it!

ADRIAN: "Widow Dido" said you? You make me study of that.
She was of Carthage, not of Tunis.

GONZALO: This Tunis, sir, was Carthage.

80 ADRIAN: Carthage?

GONZALO: A assure you, Carthage.

ANTONIO: His word is more than the miraculous harp.

SEBASTIAN: He hath rais'd the wall and houses too.

ANTONIO: What impossible matter will he make easy next?

SEBASTIAN: I think he will carry this island home in his pocket   85
and give it his son for an apple.

ANTONIO: And, sowing the kernels of it in the sea, bring forth
more islands.

GONZALO: Ay.

ANTONIO: Why, in good time.   90

GONZALO: (To ALONSO.) Sir, we were talking that our garments
seem now as fresh as when we were at Tunis at the marriage of
your daughter, who is now queen.

ANTONIO: And the rarest that e'er came there.

SEBASTIAN: Bate, I beseech you, widow Dido.   95

ANTONIO: O, widow Dido? Ay, widow Dido.

GONZALO: Is not, sir, my doublet as fresh as the first day I wore
it? I mean, in a sort.

ANTONIO: That "sort" was well fish'd for.

GONZALO: When I wore it at your daughter's marriage?   100

ALONSO: You cram these words into mine ears against
The stomach of my sense. Would I had never
Married my daughter there! For, coming thence,
My son is lost and, in my rate, she too,   105
Who is so far from Italy removed
I ne'er again shall see her. O thou mine heir
Of Naples and of Milan, what strange fish
Hath made his meal on thee?

FRANCISCO: Sir, he may live.
I saw him beat the surges under him,
And ride upon their backs. He trod the water,   110
Whose enmity he flung aside, and breasted
The surge most swoll'n that met him. His bold head
'Bove the contentious waves he kept, and oared
Himself with his good arms in lusty stroke
To th' shore, that o'er his wave-worn basis bowed,   115
As stooping to relieve him. I not doubt
He came alive to land.

ALONSO: No, no, he's gone.

SEBASTIAN: Sir, you may thank yourself for this great loss,
That would not bless our Europe with your daughter,
But rather loose her to an African,   120
Where she at least is banish'd from your eye,
Who hath cause to wet the grief on 't.

ALONSO: Prithee, peace.

SEBASTIAN: You were kneel'd to and importun'd otherwise
By all of us, and the fair soul herself
Weigh'd between loathness and obedience, at   125
Which end o' th' beam should bow. We have lost your son,
I fear, for ever. Milan and Naples have
Moe widows in them of their business' making
Than we bring men to comfort them.
The fault's your own.   130

---

43 **Temperance** a girl's name.   **delicate** (Here it means *given to plea-sure, voluptuous*; in l.41, *pleasant*. Antonio is evidently suggesting that "tender, and delicate temperance" sounds like a Puritan phrase, which Antonio then mocks by applying the words to a woman rather than an island. He began this bawdy comparison with a double entendre on *inaccessible*, l. 37.)   44 **subtle** (Here it means *tricky*; in l. 41, *delicate*.)   44 **deliver'd** uttered. (Sebastian joins in the Puritan baiting of Antonio with his use of the pious cant phrase "learnedly deliver'd.")   51 **lusty** healthy   52 **tawny** dull brown, yellowish   53 **eye** tinge, or spot (perhaps with reference to Gonzalo's eye or judgment)   58 **vouch'd** certified   62 **pockets** i.e., because they are muddy   64 **pocket up** receive unprotestingly, fail to respond to a challenge   70 **to** for   72 **widow Dido** Queen of Carthage, deserted by Aeneas. (She was in fact a widow when Aeneas, a widower, met her, but Antonio may be amused at the term "widow" to describe a woman deserted by her lover.)   82 **miraculous harp** (Alludes to Amphion's harp with which he raised the walls of Thebes; Gonzalo has exceeded that deed by creating a modern Carthage—walls *and* houses—mistakenly on the site of Tunis.)

89 **Ay** (Gonzalo may be reasserting his point about Carthage, or he may be responding ironically to Antonio who in turn answers sar-castically.)   90 **in good time** (An expression of ironical acquiescence or amazement; i.e., *sure, right away*.)   94 **rarest** most remarkable, beautiful   95 **Bate** abate, except, leave out. (i.e., don't forget Dido; or, let's have no more talk of Dido.)   98 **in a sort** in a way   102 **stomach** appetite   103 **Married** given in marriage   104 **rate** estimation, considera-tion   114 **lusty** vigorous   115 **that . . . bowed** that hung out over its wave-worn foot   116 **As** as if   122 **Who** which, i.e., the eye   124–126 **the fair . . . bow** i.e., Claribel herself was poised uncertain between unwillingness to marry and obedience to her father as to which end of the scale should sink, which should prevail   128 **Moe** more

ALONSO: So is the dear'st o' th' loss.

GONZALO: My lord Sebastian,
The truth you speak doth lack some gentleness,
And time to speak it in. You rub the sore,
When you should bring the plaster.

SEBASTIAN: Very well.

135 ANTONIO: And most chirurgeonly.

GONZALO: It is foul weather in us all, good sir,
When you are cloudy.

SEBASTIAN: (To ANTONIO.) Foul weather?

ANTONIO: (To SEBASTIAN.)   Very foul.

GONZALO: Had I plantation of this isle, my lord —

ANTONIO: He'd sow 't with nettle-seed.

SEBASTIAN: Or docks, or mallows.

140 GONZALO: And were the king on 't, what would I do?

SEBASTIAN: Scape being drunk for want of wine.

GONZALO: I' th' commonwealth I would by contraries
Execute all things; for no kind of traffic
Would I admit; no name of magistrate;

145 Letters should not be known; riches, poverty,
And use of service, none; contract, succession,
Bourn, bound of land, tilth, vineyard, none;
No use of metal, corn, or wine, or oil;
No occupation; all men idle, all,

150 And women too, but innocent and pure;
No sovereignty —

SEBASTIAN: Yet he would be king on 't.

ANTONIO: The latter end of his commonwealth forgets the
beginning.

GONZALO: All things in common nature should produce

155 Without sweat or endeavor. Treason, felony,
Sword, pike, knife, gun, or need of any engine,
Would I not have; but nature should bring forth,
Of it own kind, all foison, all abundance,
To feed my innocent people.

160 SEBASTIAN: No marrying 'mong his subjects?

ANTONIO: None, man; all idle — whores and knaves.

GONZALO: I would with such perfection govern, sir,
T' excel the golden age.

SEBASTIAN: Save his Majesty!

ANTONIO: Long live Gonzalo!

GONZALO: And — do you mark me, sir?

165 ALONSO: Prithee, no more. Thou dost talk nothing to me.

GONZALO: I do well believe your Highness, and did it to minister occasion to these gentlemen, who are of such sensible and
nimble lungs that they always use to laugh at nothing.

ANTONIO: 'Twas you we laugh'd at.

170 GONZALO: Who in this kind of merry fooling am nothing to you;
so you may continue and laugh at nothing still.

---

131 **dear'st** heaviest, most costly   133 **time** appropriate time   135 **chi-rurgeonly** like a skilled surgeon. (Antonio mocks Gonzalo's medical analogy of a *plaster* applied curatively to a wound.)   138 **plantation** colonization (with subsequent wordplay on the literal meaning)   139 **docks, mallows** (Various weeds.)   142 **by contraries** by what is directly opposite to usual custom   143 **traffic** trade   145 **Letters** learning   146 **use of service** custom of employing servants.   **succession** holding of property by right of inheritance   147 **Bourn** boundaries.   **bound of land** landmarks.   **tilth** tillage of soil   148 **corn** grain   156 **engine** in-strument of warfare   158 **it** its.   **foison** plenty   163 **Save** God save   166–167 **minister occasion** furnish opportunity   167 **sensible** sensitive

ANTONIO: What a blow was there given!

SEBASTIAN: An it had not fall'n flat-long.

GONZALO: You are gentlemen of brave mettle; you would lift the
moon out of her sphere, if she would continue in it five weeks   175
without changing.

(Enter ARIEL [invisible] playing solemn music.)

SEBASTIAN: We would so, and then go a-batfowling.

ANTONIO: Nay, good my lord, be not angry.

GONZALO: No, I warrant, you, I will not adventure my discretion so weakly. Will you laugh me asleep? For I am very   180
heavy.

ANTONIO: Go sleep, and hear us.

(All sleep except ALONSO, SEBASTIAN, and ANTONIO.)

ALONSO: What, all so soon asleep? I wish mine eyes
Would, with themselves, shut up my thoughts. I find
They are inclin'd to do so.

SEBASTIAN: Please you, sir,   185
Do not omit the heavy offer of it.
It seldom visits sorrow; when it doth,
It is a comforter.

ANTONIO: We two, my lord,
Will guard your person while you take your rest,
And watch your safety.

ALONSO: Thank you. Wondrous heavy.   190

(ALONSO sleeps. Exit ARIEL.)

SEBASTIAN: What a strange drowsiness possesses them!

ANTONIO: It is the quality o' th' climate.

SEBASTIAN: Why
Doth it not then our eyelids sink? I find not
Myself dispos'd to sleep.

ANTONIO: Nor I; my spirits are nimble.
They fell together all, as by consent;   195
They dropp'd, as by a thunder-stroke. What might,
Worthy Sebastian? O, what might — ? No more —
And yet methinks I see it in thy face,
What thou shouldst be. Th' occasion speaks thee, and
My strong imagination sees a crown   200
Dropping upon thy head.

SEBASTIAN: What, art thou waking?

ANTONIO: Do you not hear me speak?

SEBASTIAN: I do; and surely
It is a sleepy language and thou speak'st
Out of thy sleep. What is it thou didst say?
This is a strange repose, to be asleep   205
With eyes wide open — standing, speaking, moving —
And yet so fast asleep.

ANTONIO: Noble Sebastian,
Thou let'st thy fortune sleep — die, rather; wink'st
Whiles thou art waking.

---

173 **An** if.   **flat-long** with the flat of the sword, i.e., ineffectually. (Cf. *fallen flat.*)   177 **a-batfowling** hunting birds at night with lantern and stick; also, gulling a simpleton. (Gonzalo is the simpleton, or fowl, and Sebastian will use the moon as his lantern.)   179–180 **adventure . . . weakly** risk my reputation for discretion for so trivial a cause (by getting angry at these sarcastic fellows)   181 **heavy** sleep   182 **Go . . . us** let our laughing send you to sleep, or, go to sleep and hear us laugh at you   186 **omit** neglect.   **heavy** drowsy   199 **speaks** calls upon; or, pronounces, proclaims (Sebastian as usurper of Alonso's crown)   208 **wink'st** shut your eyes

SEBASTIAN: Thou dost snore distinctly;
210   There's meaning in thy snores.
ANTONIO: I am more serious than my custom. You
    Must be so too, if heed me; which to do
    Trebles thee o'er.
SEBASTIAN: Well, I am standing water.
ANTONIO: I'll teach you how to flow.
SEBASTIAN: Do so. To ebb
    Hereditary sloth instructs me.
215   ANTONIO: O,
    If you but knew how you the purpose cherish
    Whiles thus you mock it! How, in stripping it,
    You more invest it! Ebbing men, indeed,
    Most often do so near the bottom run
    By their own fear or sloth.
220   SEBASTIAN: Prithee say on.
    The setting of thine eye and cheek proclaim
    A matter from thee, and a birth indeed
    Which throes thee much to yield.
    ANTONIO: Thus, sir:
    Although this lord of weak remembrance, this,
225   Who shall be of as little memory
    When he is earth'd, hath here almost persuaded—
    For he's a spirit of persuasion, only
    Professes to persuade—the King his son's alive,
    'Tis as impossible that he's undrown'd
    As he that sleeps here swims.
230   SEBASTIAN: I have no hope
    That he's undrown'd.
    ANTONIO: O, out of that "no hope"
    What great hope have you! No hope that way is
    Another way so high a hope that even
    Ambition cannot pierce a wink beyond,
235   But doubt discovery there. Will you grant with me
    That Ferdinand is drown'd?
    SEBASTIAN: He's gone.
    ANTONIO: Then, tell me,
    Who's the next heir of Naples?
    SEBASTIAN: Claribel.
    ANTONIO: She that is Queen of Tunis; she that dwells
    Ten leagues beyond man's life; she that from Naples
240   Can have no note, unless the sun were post—
    The man i' th' moon's too slow—till new-born chins

Be rough and razorable; she that from whom
We all were sea-swallow'd, though some cast again,
And by that destiny to perform an act
Whereof what's past is prologue, what to come   245
In yours and my discharge.
SEBASTIAN: What stuff is this? How say you?
    'Tis true, my brother's daughter's Queen of Tunis;
    So is she heir of Naples; 'twixt which regions
    There is some space.
ANTONIO: A space whose ev'ry cubit   250
    Seems to cry out, "How shall that Claribel
    Measure us back to Naples? Keep in Tunis,
    And let Sebastian wake." Say this were death
    That now hath seiz'd them; why, they were no worse
    Than now they are. There be that can rule Naples   255
    As well as he that sleeps; lords that can prate
    As amply and unnecessarily
    As this Gonzalo; I myself could make
    A chough of as deep chat. O, that you bore
    The mind that I do! What a sleep were this   260
    For your advancement! Do you understand me?
SEBASTIAN: Methinks I do.
ANTONIO: And how does your content
    Tender your own good fortune?
SEBASTIAN: I remember
    You did supplant your brother Prospero.
ANTONIO: True.
    And look how well my garments sit upon me,   265
    Much feater than before. My brother's servants
    Were then my fellows; now they are my men.
SEBASTIAN: But, for your conscience?
ANTONIO: Ay, sir, where lies that? If 'twere a kibe,
    'Twould put me to my slipper; but I feel not   270
    This deity in my bosom. Twenty consciences,
    That stand 'twixt me and Milan, candied be they
    And melt ere they molest! Here lies your brother,
    No better than the earth he lies upon,
    If he were that which now he's like—that's dead,   275
    Whom I, with this obedient steel, three inches of it,
    Can lay to bed forever; whiles you, doing thus,
    To the perpetual wink for aye might put
    This ancient morsel, this Sir Prudence, who
    Should not upbraid our course. For all the rest,   280
    They'll take suggestion as a cat laps milk;
    They'll tell the clock to any business that
    We say befits the hour.
SEBASTIAN: Thy case, dear friend,
    Shall be my precedent. As thou got'st Milan,
    I'll come by Naples. Draw thy sword. One stroke   285
    Shall free thee from the tribute which thou payest,
    And I the king shall love thee.

213 **Trebles thee o'er** makes you three times as great and rich.   **standing water** water which neither ebbs nor flows, at a standstill, indecisive   215 **Hereditary sloth** natural laziness   216 **purpose** i.e., of being king.   **cherish** i.e., make dear, enrich   218 **invest** clothe. (Antonio's paradox is that by sceptically stripping away illusions Sebastian can see the essence of a situation and the opportunity it presents, or that by disclaiming and deriding his purpose Sebastian shows how he values it.)   219 **the bottom** i.e., on which unadventurous men may go aground and miss the tide of fortune   221 **setting** set expression (of earnestness)   222 **matter** matter of importance   223 **throes** causes pain, as in giving birth   224 **this lord** i.e., Gonzalo.   **remembrance** (1) power of remembering (2) being remembered after his death   226 **earth'd** buried   227–228 **only . . . persuade** i.e., whose whole function (as a privy councilor) is to persuade   232 **that way** i.e., in regard to Ferdinand's being saved   234–235 **Ambition . . . there** ambition itself cannot see any further than that hope (of the crown), but is unsure of itself in seeing even so far, is dazzled by daring to think so high   239 **Ten . . . life** i.e., it would take more than a lifetime to get there   240 **note** news, imtimation.   **post** messenger

242 **from** on our voyage from   243 **cast** were disgorged (with a pun on *casting* of parts for a play)   246 **discharge** performance   252 **Measure us** i.e., traverse the cubits, find her way   253 **wake** i.e., to his good fortune   258–259 **I . . . chat** I could teach a jackdaw to talk as wisely, or, be such a garrulous talker myself   262 **content** desire, inclination   263 **Tender** regard, look after   266 **feater** more becomingly, fittingly   269 **kibe** chilblain, sore on the heel   270 **put me to** oblige me to wear   272 **Milan** the dukedom of Milan.   **candied** frozen, congealed in crystalline form   278 **wink** sleep, closing of eyes   282 **tell the clock** i.e., answer appropriately, chime   286 **tribute** (See I.ii. 113–124)

ANTONIO: Draw together;
And when I rear my hand, do you the like,
To fall it on Gonzalo.

(They draw.)

SEBASTIAN: O, but one word.

(They talk apart.)

(Enter ARIEL *[invisible], with music and song.)*

290 ARIEL: My master through his art foresees the danger
That you, his friend, are in, and sends me forth —
For else his project dies — to keep them living.

(Sings in GONZALO'S *ear.)*

While you here do snoring lie,
Open-ey'd conspiracy
295   His time doth take.
If of life you keep a care,
Shake off slumber, and beware.
Awake, awake!

ANTONIO: Then let us both be sudden.
300 GONZALO: *(Waking)* Now, good angels preserve the King!

(The others wake.)

ALONSO: Why, how now, ho, awake? Why are you drawn?
Wherefore this ghastly looking?
GONZALO: What's the matter?
SEBASTIAN: Whiles we stood here securing your repose,
Even now, we heard a hollow burst of bellowing
305 Like bulls, or rather lions. Did 't not wake you?
It struck mine ear most terribly.
ALONSO: I heard nothing.
ANTONIO: O, 'twas a din to fright a monster's ear,
To make an earthquake! Sure it was the roar
Of a whole herd of lions.
310 ALONSO: Heard you this, Gonzalo?
GONZALO: Upon mine honor, sir, I heard a humming,
And that a strange one too, which did awake me.
I shak'd you, sir, and cried. As mine eyes open'd,
I saw their weapons drawn. There was a noise,
315 That's verily. 'Tis best we stand upon our guard,
Or that we quit this place. Let's draw our weapons.
ALONSO: Lead off this ground, and let's make further search
For my poor son.
GONZALO: Heavens keep him from these beasts!
For he is, sure, i' th' island.
ALONSO: Lead away.
320 ARIEL: *(Aside)* Prospero my lord shall know what I have done.
So, King, go safely on to seek thy son.

(Exeunt [severally].)

SCENE II

Enter CALIBAN *with a burden of wood. A noise of thunder heard.*

CALIBAN: All the infections that the sun sucks up
From bogs, fens, flats, on Prosper fall and make him

---

295 **time** opportunity   303 **securing** standing guard over
II.ii. Location: **Another part of the island.**

By inch-meal a disease! His spirits hear me,
And yet I needs must curse. But they'll nor pinch,
Fright me with urchin-shows, pitch me i' th' mire,   5
Nor lead me, like a firebrand, in the dark
Out of my way, unless he bid 'em; but
For every trifle are they set upon me;
Sometime like apes that mow and chatter at me
And after bite me, then like hedgehogs which   10
Lie tumbling in my barefoot way and mount
Their pricks at my footfall; sometime am I
All wound with adders who with cloven tongues
Do hiss me into madness.

(Enter TRINCULO.*)*

                    Lo, now, lo!
Here comes a spirit of his, and to torment me   15
For bringing wood in slowly. I'll fall flat;
Perchance he will not mind me.

(Lies down.)

TRINCULO: Here's neither bush nor shrub, to bear off any
weather at all, and another storm brewing; I hear it sing i' th'
wind. Yond same black cloud, yond huge one, looks like a   20
foul bombard that would shed his liquor. If it should thunder
as it did before, I know not where to hide my head. Yond
same cloud cannot choose but fall by pailfuls. *(Sees* CALIBAN.*)*
What have we here? A man or a fish? Dead or alive? A fish, he
smells like a fish; a very ancient and fish-like smell; a kind of   25
not of the newest Poor-John. A strange fish! Were I in England now, as once I was, and had but this fish painted, not a
holiday fool there but would give a piece of silver. There
would this monster make a man; any strange beast there
makes a man. When they will not give a doit to relieve a lame   30
beggar, they will lay out ten to see a dead Indian. Legg'd like a
man! And his fins like arms! Warm, o' my troth! I do now let
loose my opinion, hold it no longer: this is no fish, but an
islander, that hath lately suffer'd by a thunderbolt. *(Thunder.)*
Alas, the storm is come again! My best way is to creep under   35
his gaberdine; there is no other shelter hereabout. Misery acquaints a man with strange bedfellows. I will here shroud till
the dregs of the storm be past.

(Creeps under CALIBAN's *garment.)*

(Enter STEPHANO, *singing, [a bottle in his hand].)*

STEPHANO: "I shall no more to sea, to sea,
Here shall I die ashore —"   40

This is a very scurvy tune to sing at a man's funeral.
Well, here's my comfort.

(Drinks.)
(Sings.)

"The master, the swabber, the boatswain and I,
The gunner and his mate

---

3 **By inch-meal** inch by inch   4 **nor** neither   5 **urchin-shows** apparitions shaped like hedgehogs   6 **like a firebrand** in the guise of a will-o'-
the-wisp   9 **mow** make faces   17 **mind** notice   18 **bear off** keep
off   21 **foul bombard** dirty leathern bottle.   **his** its   26 **Poor-John**
salted hake, type of poor fare   27 **painted** i.e., painted on a sign set up
outside a booth or tent at a fair   29 **make a man** make one's fortune   30 **doit** small coin   36 **gaberdine** cloak, loose upper garment   37 **shroud** take shelter   38 **dregs** i.e., last remains

45   Lov'd Mall, Meg, and Marian, and Margery,
      But none of us car'd for Kate;
      For she had a tongue with a tang,
      Would cry to a sailor, 'Go hang!'
    She lov'd not the savor of tar nor of pitch,
50   Yet a tailor might scratch her where'er she did
      itch.
      Then to sea, boys, and let her go hang!"

This is a scurvy tune too; but here's my comfort.

(Drinks.)

CALIBAN: Do not torment me! Oh!

STEPHANO: What's the matter? Have we devils here? Do you put
55   tricks upon 's with savages and men of Ind, ha? I have not
    scap'd drowning to be afeard now of your four legs; for it hath
    been said, "As proper a man as ever went on four legs cannot
    make him give ground"; and it shall be said so again while
    Stephano breathes at' nostrils.
60 CALIBAN: This spirit torments me! Oh!

STEPHANO: This is some monster of the isle with four legs, who
    hath got, as I take it, an ague. Where the devil should he
    learn our language? I will give him some relief, if it be but for
    that. If I can recover him and keep him tame and get to Na-
65   ples with him, he's a present for any emperor that ever trod on
    neat's-leather.

CALIBAN: Do not torment me, prithee. I'll bring my wood home
    faster.

STEPHANO: He's in his fit now and does not talk after the wisest.
70   He shall taste of my bottle; if he have never drunk wine afore,
    it will go near to remove his fit. If I can recover him and keep
    him tame, I will not take too much for him; he shall pay for
    him that hath him, and that soundly.

CALIBAN: Thou dost me yet but little hurt;
75   Thou wilt anon, I know it by thy trembling.
    Now Prosper works upon thee.

STEPHANO: Come on your ways; open your mouth; here is that
    which will give language to you, cat. Open your mouth; this
    will shake your shaking, I can tell you, and that soundly.
80   *(Gives* CALIBAN *drink.)* You cannot tell who's your friend.
    Open your chaps again.

TRINCULO: I should know that voice. It should be — but he is
    drown'd; and these are devils. O defend me!

STEPHANO: Four legs and two voices; a most delicate monster!
85   His forward voice now is to speak well of his friend; his back-
    ward voice is to utter foul speeches and to detract. If all the
    wine in my bottle will recover him, I will help his ague.
    Come. *(Gives drink.)* Amen! I will pour some in thy other
    mouth.
90 TRINCULO: Stephano!

STEPHANO: Doth thy other mouth call me? Mercy, mercy! This
    is a devil, and no monster. I will leave him; I have no long
    spoon.

TRINCULO: Stephano! If thou beest Stephano, touch me and
    speak to me; for I am Trinculo — be not afeard — thy good   95
    friend Trinculo.

STEPHANO: If thou beest Trinculo, come forth. I'll pull thee by
    the lesser legs. If any be Trinculo's legs, these are they. *(Pulls
    him out.)* Thou art very Trinculo indeed! How cam'st thou to
    be the siege of this moon-calf? Can he vent Trinculos?   100

TRINCULO: I took him to be kill'd with a thunder-stroke. But art
    thou not drown'd, Stephano? I hope now thou art not
    drown'd. Is the storm overblown? I hid me under the dead
    moon-calf's gaberdine for fear of the storm. And art thou liv-
    ing, Stephano? O Stephano, two Neapolitans scap'd!   105

STEPHANO: Prithee, do not turn me about; my stomach is not
    constant.

CALIBAN: These be fine things, an if they be not sprites.
    That's a brave god and bears celestial liquor.
    I will kneel to him.   110

STEPHANO: How didst thou scape? How cam'st thou hither?
    Swear by this bottle how thou cam'st hither. I escap'd upon a
    butt of sack which the sailors heav'd o'erboard — by this bot-
    tle, which I made of the bark of a tree with mine own hands
    since I was cast ashore.   115

CALIBAN: *(Kneeling)* I'll swear upon that bottle to be thy true
    subject, for the liquor is not earthly.

STEPHANO: Here; swear then how thou escap'dst.

TRINCULO: Swum ashore, man, like a duck. I can swim like a
    duck, I'll be sworn.   120

STEPHANO: Here, kiss the book. Though thou canst swim like a
    duck, thou art made like a goose.

(Gives drink.)

TRINCULO: O Stephano, hast any more of this?

STEPHANO: The whole butt, man. My cellar is in a rock by the
    sea-side where my wine is hid. How now, moon-calf? How   125
    does thine ague?

CALIBAN: Hast thou not dropp'd from heaven?

STEPHANO: Out o' th' moon, I do assure thee. I was the man i'
    th' moon when time was.

CALIBAN: I have seen thee in her and I do adore thee.   130
    My mistress show'd me thee and thy dog and thy bush.

STEPHANO: Come, swear to that; kiss the book. I will furnish it
    anon with new contents. Swear.

(Gives drink.)

TRINCULO: By this good light, this is a very shallow monster! I
    afeard of him? A very weak monster! The man i' th' moon? A   135
    most poor credulous monster! Well drawn, monster, in good
    sooth!

CALIBAN: I'll show thee every fertile inch o' th' island;
    And I will kiss thy foot. I prithee, by my god.

TRINCULO: By this light, a most perfidious and drunken mons-   140
    ter! When 's god's asleep, he'll rob his bottle.

CALIBAN: I'll kiss thy foot. I'll swear myself thy subject.

---

55 **Ind** India   57 **proper** handsome   57 **four legs** (The conventional phrase would supply *two legs*.)   59 **at'** at the   63–64 **for that** i.e., for knowing our language.   **recover** restore   66 **neat's-leather** cowhide   72 **I will . . . much** i.e., no sum can be too much   73 **hath** possesses, receives   78 **cat . . . mouth** (Allusion to the proverb, "Good liquor will make a cat speak.")   81 **chaps** jaws   92–93 **long spoon** (Allusion to the proverb, "He that sups with the devil has need of a long spoon.")

100 **siege** excrement   **moon-calf** monster, abortion. (Supposed to be caused by the influence of the moon.)   **vent** emit   106–107 **not constant** unsteady   108 **an if** if   109 **brave** fine, magnificent   113 **butt of sack** barrel of Canary wine   121 **book** i.e., bottle   129 **when time was** once upon a time   131 **dog . . . bush** (The man in the moon was popularly imagined to have with him a dog and a bush of thorn.)   134 **By . . . light** by God's light, by this good light from heaven   136 **Well drawn** well pulled (on the bottle)

STEPHANO: Come on then; down, and swear.

(CALIBAN *swears*.)

TRINCULO: I shall laugh myself to death at this puppy-headed
145   monster. A most scurvy monster! I could find in my heart to
    beat him —
STEPHANO: Come, kiss.
TRINCULO: But that the poor monster's in drink. An abominable
    monster!
150 CALIBAN: I'll show thee the best springs; I'll pluck thee berries;
    I'll fish for thee and get thee wood enough.
    A plague upon the tyrant that I serve!
    I'll bear him no more sticks, but follow thee,
    Thou wondrous man.
155 TRINCULO: A most ridiculous monster, to make a wonder of a
    poor drunkard!
CALIBAN: I prithee, let me bring thee where crabs grow;
    And I with my long nails will dig thee pig-nuts,
    Show thee a jay's nest, and instruct thee how
160   To snare the nimble marmoset. I'll bring thee
    To clust'ring filberts, and sometimes I'll get thee
    Young scamels from the rock. Wilt thou go with me?
STEPHANO: I prithee now, lead the way without any more talk-
    ing. Trinculo, the King and all our company else being
165   drown'd, we will inherit here. Here! Bear my bottle. Fellow
    Trinculo, we'll fill him by and by again.
CALIBAN: (*Sings drunkenly*.)
        Farewell, master; farewell, farewell!
TRINCULO: A howling monster; a drunken monster!
CALIBAN:

    No more dams I'll make for fish,
170   Nor fetch in firing
      At requiring,
    Nor scrape trenchering, nor wash dish.
     'Ban, 'Ban, Ca–Caliban
     Has a new master, get a new man.
175   Freedom, high-day! High-day, freedom! Freedom,
    high-day, freedom!

STEPHANO: O brave monster! Lead the way.

(*Exeunt*.)

— ACT THREE —

SCENE I

Enter FERDINAND, *bearing a log*.

FERDINAND: There be some sports are painful, and their labor
    Delight in them sets off; some kinds of baseness
    Are nobly undergone; and most poor matters

157 **crabs** crab apples 158 **pig-nuts** peanuts 160 **marmoset** small
monkey 162 **scamels** (Possibly "seamews," mentioned in Strachey's
letter, or shellfish; or perhaps from *squamelle*, furnished with little
scales. (Contemporary French and Italian travel accounts report that the
natives of Patagonia in South America ate small fish described as *fort
scameux* and *squame*.) 165 **inherit** take possession 172 **trenchering**
trenchers, wooden plates 175 **high-day** holiday (?)
III.i. Location: Before Prospero's cell.
2 **sets off** makes seem greater by contrast

Point to rich ends. This my mean task
Would be as heavy to me as odious, but   5
The mistress which I serve quickens what's dead
And makes my labors pleasures. O, she is
Ten times more gentle than her father's crabbed,
And he's compos'd of harshness. I must remove
Some thousands of these logs and pile them up,   10
Upon a sore injunction. My sweet mistress
Weeps when she sees me work, and says such baseness
Had never like executor. I forget;
But these sweet thoughts do even refresh my labors,
Most busy lest, when I do it.

(*Enter* MIRANDA; *and* PROSPERO [*at a distance, unseen*].)

MIRANDA: Alas, now, pray you,   15
    Work not so hard. I would the lightning had
    Burnt up those logs that you are enjoin'd to pile!
    Pray, set it down and rest you. When this burns,
    'Twill weep for having wearied you. My father
    Is hard at study; pray now, rest yourself.   20
    He's safe for these three hours.
FERDINAND: O most dear mistress,
    The sun will set before I shall discharge
    What I must strive to do.
MIRANDA: If you'll sit down,
    I'll bear your logs the while. Pray give me that.
    I'll carry it to the pile.
FERDINAND: No, precious creature,   25
    I had rather crack my sinews, break my back,
    Than you should such dishonor undergo
    While I sit lazy by.
MIRANDA: It would become me
    As well as it does you; and I should do it
    With much more ease, for my good will is to it,   30
    And yours it is against.
PROSPERO: (*Aside*)   Poor worm, thou art infected!
    This visitation shows it.
MIRANDA: You look wearily.
FERDINAND: No, noble mistress, 'tis fresh morning with me
    When you are by at night. I do beseech you —
    Chiefly that I might set it in my prayers —   35
    What is your name?
MIRANDA: Miranda. — O my father,
    I have broke your hest to say so.
FERDINAND: Admir'd Miranda!
    Indeed the top of admiration! Worth
    What's dearest to the world! Full many a lady
    I have ey'd with best regard, and many a time   40
    Th' harmony of their tongues hath into bondage
    Brought my too diligent ear. For several virtues
    Have I lik'd several women, never any
    With so full soul but some defect in her
    Did quarrel with the noblest grace she ow'd   45
    And put it to the foil. But you, O you,

6 **quickens** gives life to 11 **sore injunction** severe command 15 **Most
. . . it** i.e., least troubled by my labor when I think of her (?). (The line
may be in need of emendation.) 32 **visitation** (1) visit (2) visitation of
the plague, i.e., infection of love 37 **hest** command 45 **ow'd**
owned 46 **put . . . foil** (1) overthrew it (as in wrestling) (2) served as a
"foil" or contrast to set it off

So perfect and so peerless, are created
Of every creature's best!
MIRANDA: I do not know
One of my sex; no woman's face remember,
50 Save, from my glass, mine own. Nor have I seen
More that I may call men than you, good friend,
And my dear father. How features are abroad,
I am skilless of; but, by my modesty,
The jewel in my dower, I would not wish
55 Any companion in the world but you,
Nor can imagination form a shape,
Besides yourself, to like of. But I prattle
Something too wildly, and my father's precepts
I therein do forget.
FERDINAND: I am in my condition
60 A prince, Miranda; I do think, a king—
I would, not so!—and would no more endure
This wooden slavery than to suffer
The flesh-fly blow my mouth. Hear my soul speak:
The very instant that I saw you, did
65 My heart fly to your service; there resides,
To make me slave to it; and for your sake
Am I this patient log-man.
MIRANDA: Do you love me?
FERDINAND: O heaven, O earth, bear witness to this sound,
And crown what I profess with kind event
70 If I speak true! If hollowly, invert
What best is boded me to mischief! I
Beyond all limit of what else i' th' world
Do love, prize, honor you.
MIRANDA: (Weeping)   I am a fool
To weep at what I am glad of.
PROSPERO: (Aside)   Fair encounter
75 Of two most rare affections! Heavens rain grace
On that which breeds between 'em!
FERDINAND: Wherefore weep you?
MIRANDA: At mine unworthiness, that dare offer
What I desire to give, and much less take
What I shall die to want. But this is trifling,
80 And all the more it seeks to hide itself
The bigger bulk it shows. Hence, bashful cunning,
And prompt me, plain and holy innocence!
I am your wife, if you will marry me;
If not, I'll die your maid. To be your fellow
85 You may deny me, but I'll be your servant,
Whether you will or no.
FERDINAND: My mistress, dearest,
And I thus humble ever.
MIRANDA: My husband, then?
FERDINAND: Ay, with a heart as willing
As bondage e'er of freedom. Here's my hand.
90 MIRANDA: And mine, with my heart in 't. And now farewell
Till half an hour hence.
FERDINAND: A thousand thousand!

(Exeunt [FERDINAND and MIRANDA severally].)

PROSPERO: So glad of this as they I cannot be,
Who are surpris'd with all; but my rejoicing
At nothing can be more. I'll to my book,
For yet ere supper-time must I perform   95
Much business appertaining.

SCENE II

Enter CALIBAN, STEPHANO, *and* TRINCULO.

STEPHANO: Tell not me. When the butt is out, we will drink
water, not a drop before. Therefore bear up, and board 'em.
Servant-monster, drink to me.
TRINCULO: Servant-monster? The folly of this island! They say
there's but five upon this isle; we are three of them. If th' other 5
two be brain'd like us, the state totters.
STEPHANO: Drink, servant-monster, when I bid thee. Thy eyes
are almost set in thy head.

(Gives drink.)

TRINCULO: Where should they be set else? He were a brave
monster indeed if they were set in his tail.   10
STEPHANO: My man-monster hath drown'd his tongue in sack.
For my part, the sea cannot drown me; I swam, ere I could
recover the shore, five and thirty leagues off and on. By this
light, thou shalt be my lieutenant, monster, or my standard.
TRINCULO: Your lieutenant, if you list; he's no standard.   15
STEPHANO: We'll not run, Monsieur Monster.
TRINCULO: Nor go neither, but you'll lie like dogs and yet say
nothing neither.
STEPHANO: Moon-calf, speak once in thy life, if thou beest a
good moon-calf.   20
CALIBAN: How does thy honor? Let me lick thy shoe.
I'll not serve him; he is not valiant.
TRINCULO: Thou liest, most ignorant monster, I am in case to
justle a constable. Why, thou debosh'd fish thou, was there
ever man a coward that hath drunk so much sack as I today?   25
Wilt thou tell a monstrous lie, being but half a fish and half a
monster?
CALIBAN: Lo, how he mocks me! Wilt thou let him, my lord?
TRINCULO: "Lord," quoth he? That a monster should be such a
natural!   30
CALIBAN: Lo, lo, again! Bite him to death, I prithee.
STEPHANO: Trinculo, keep a good tongue in your head. If you
prove a mutineer—the next tree! The poor monster's my sub-
ject and he shall not suffer indignity.
CALIBAN: I thank my noble lord. Wilt thou be pleas'd   35
To hearken once again to the suit I made to thee?

III.ii. Location: Another part of the island.
1 **out** empty   2 **bear . . . 'em** (Stephano uses the terminology of ma-
neuvering at sea and boarding a vessel under attack as a way of urging an
assault on the liquor supply.)   8 **set** fixed in a drunken stare; or sunk,
like the sun   9 **brave** fine, splendid   13 **recover** arrive at   14 **standard**
standard-bearer, ancient, i.e., ensign (as distinguished from *lieutenant*,
l. 15)   15 **list** prefer.   **no standard** i.e., not able to stand up   16 **run**
(1) retreat (2) urinate (taking Trinculo's *standard* l. 15, in the old sense of
conduit)   17 **go** walk.   **lie** (1) tell lies (2) lie prostrate (3) excrete   23–
24 **case . . . constable** i.e., in fit condition, made valiant by drink, to
taunt or challenge the police.   **debosh'd** i.e., debauched   30 **natural**
(1) idiot (2) natural as opposed to unnatural, monster-like   33 **the next
tree** i.e., you'll hang

53 **skilless** ignorant   63 **blow** befoul with fly-eggs   69 **kind event** favorable outcome   70 **hollowly** insincerely, falsely   71 **boded** destined
for   79 **want** lack   84 **fellow** mate, equal

STEPHANO: Marry, will I. Kneel and repeat it; I will stand,
    and so shall Trinculo.

(CALIBAN *kneels.*)

(Enter ARIEL, *invisible.*)

CALIBAN: As I told thee before, I am subject to a tyrant,
40   A sorcerer, that by his cunning hath
    Cheated me of the island.
ARIEL: Thou liest.
CALIBAN: Thou liest, thou jesting monkey, thou!
    I would my valiant master would destroy thee.
    I do not lie.
45 STEPHANO: Trinculo, if you trouble him any more in 's tale, by
    this hand, I will supplant some of your teeth.
TRINCULO: Why, I said nothing.
STEPHANO: Mum, then, and no more. — Proceed.
CALIBAN: I say, by sorcery he got this isle;
50   From me he got it. If thy greatness will
    Revenge it on him — for I know thou dar'st,
    But this thing dare not —
STEPHANO: That's most certain.
CALIBAN: Thou shalt by lord of it, and I'll serve thee.
55 STEPHANO: How now shall this be compass'd? Canst thou being
    me to the party?
CALIBAN: Yea, yea, my lord. I'll yield him thee asleep,
    Where thou mayst knock a nail into his head.
ARIEL: Thou liest; thou canst not.
60 CALIBAN: What a pied ninny's this! Thou scurvy patch!
    I do beseech thy greatness, give him blows
    And take his bottle from him. When that's gone
    He shall drink nought but brine, for I'll now show him
    Where the quick freshes are.
65 STEPHANO: Trinculo, run into no further danger. Interrupt the
    monster one word further, and, by this hand, I'll turn my
    mercy out o' doors and make a stock-fish of thee.
TRINCULO: Why, what did? I did nothing. I'll go farther off.
STEPHANO: Didst thou not say he lied?
70 ARIEL: Thou liest.
STEPHANO: Do I so? Take thou that. (Beats TRINCULO.) As
    you like this, give me the lie another time.
TRINCULO: I did not give the lie. Out o' your wits and hearing
    too? A pox o' your bottle! This can sack and drinking do. A
75   murrain on your monster, and the devil take your fingers!
CALIBAN: Ha, ha, ha!
STEPHANO: Now, forward with your tale.

(To TRINCULO.)

    Prithee, stand further off.
CALIBAN: Beat him enough. After a little time
80   I'll beat him too.
STEPHANO: Stand farther. — Come, proceed.
CALIBAN: Why, as I told thee, 'tis a custom with him
    I' th' afternoon to sleep. There thou mayst brain him,
    Having first seiz'd his books, or with a log

Batter his skull, or paunch him with a stake,   85
Or cut his wezand with thy knife. Remember
First to possess his books; for without them
He's but a sot, as I am, nor hath not
One spirit to command. They all do hate him
As rootedly as I. Burn but his books.   90
He has brave utensils — for so he calls them —
Which, when he has a house, he'll deck withal.
And that most deeply to consider is
The beauty of his daughter. He himself
Calls her a nonpareil. I never saw a woman,   95
But only Sycorax my dam and she;
But she as far surpasseth Sycorax
As great'st does least.
STEPHANO: Is it so brave a lass?
CALIBAN: Ay, lord; she will become thy bed, I warrant,   100
    And bring thee forth brave brood.
STEPHANO: Monster, I will kill this man. His daughter and I will
    be king and queen — save our Graces! — and Trinculo and
    thyself shall be viceroys. Dost thou like the plot, Trinculo?
TRINCULO: Excellent.   105
STEPHANO: Give me thy hand. I am sorry I beat thee; but,
    while thou liv'st, keep a good tongue in thy head.
CALIBAN: Within this half hour will he be asleep.
    Wilt thou destroy him then?
STEPHANO: Ay, on mine honor.   110
ARIEL: (Aside) This will I tell my master.
CALIBAN: Thou mak'st me merry; I am full of pleasure.
    Let us be jocund. Will you troll the catch
    You taught me but while-ere?
STEPHANO: At thy request, monster, I will do reason, any rea- 115
    son. Come on, Trinculo, let us sing.

(Sings.)

        "Flout 'em and scout 'em
        And scout 'em and flout 'em!
            Thought is free."

CALIBAN: That's not the tune.   120

(ARIEL *plays the tune on a tabor and pipe.*)

STEPHANO: What is this same?
TRINCULO: This is the tune of our catch, play'd by the picture of
    Nobody.
STEPHANO: If thou beest a man, show thyself in thy likeness. If
    thou beest a devil, take 't as thou list.   125
TRINCULO: O, forgive me my sins!
STEPHANO: He that dies pays all debts. I defy thee. Mercy upon us!
CALIBAN: Art thou afeard?
STEPHANO: No, monster, not I.
CALIBAN: Be not afeard. This isle is full of noises,   130
    Sounds and sweet airs, that give delight and hurt not.
    Sometimes a thousand twangling instruments
    Will hum about mine ears, and sometimes voices

37 **Marry** i.e., indeed. (Originally an oath by the Virgin Mary.) 52
this thing i.e., Trinculo 60 **pied ninny** fool in motley. **patch**
fool 64 **quick freshes** running springs 67 **stock-fish** dried cod beaten
before cooking 72 **give me the lie** call me a liar to my face 75 **mur-rain** plague. (Literally, a cattle disease.)

85 **paunch** stab in the belly 86 **wezand** windpipe 88 **sot** fool 91
brave utensils fine furnishings 112 **troll the catch** sing the round 113
while-ere a short time ago 118 **scout** deride 121 **s.d. tabor** small
drum 122–123 **picture of Nobody** (Refers to a familiar figure with
head, arms, and legs, but no trunk.) 125 **take 't . . . list** i.e., take my
defiance as you please, as best you can

That, if I then had wak'd after long sleep,
135 Will make me sleep again; and then, in dreaming,
The clouds methought would open and show riches
Ready to drop upon me, that, when I wak'd,
I cried to dream again.
STEPHANO: This will prove a brave kingdom to me, where I shall
140 have my music for nothing.
CALIBAN: When Prospero is destroy'd.
STEPHANO: That shall be by and by. I remember the story.
TRINCULO: The sound is going away. Let's follow it, and after do
our work.
145 STEPHANO: Lead, monster; we'll follow. I would I could see this
taborer; he lays it on.
TRINCULO: Wilt come? I'll follow, Stephano.

(*Exeunt* [*following* ARIEL's *music*].)

SCENE III

Enter ALONSO, SEBASTIAN, ANTONIO, GONZALO, ADRIAN,
FRANCISCO, *etc.*

GONZALO: By 'r lakin, I can go no further, sir;
My old bones aches. Here's a maze trod indeed
Through forth-rights and meanders! By your patience,
I needs must rest me.
ALONSO: Old lord, I cannot blame thee,
5 Who am myself attach'd with weariness,
To th' dulling of my spirits. Sit down, and rest.
Even here I will put off my hope and keep it
No longer for my flatterer. He is drown'd
Whom thus we stray to find, and the sea mocks
10 Our frustrate search on land. Well, let him go.

(ALONSO *and* GONZALO *sit.*)

ANTONIO: (*Aside to* SEBASTIAN.) I am right glad that he's so out
of hope.
Do not, for one repulse, forego the purpose
That you resolv'd t' effect.
SEBASTIAN: (*To* ANTONIO.)   The next advantage
Will we take throughly.
ANTONIO: (*To* SEBASTIAN.)   Let it be tonight,
15 For, now they are oppress'd with travail, they
Will not, nor cannot, use such vigilance
As when they are fresh.
SEBASTIAN: (*To* ANTONIO.)   I say tonight. No more.

(*Solemn and strange music; and* PROSPERO *on the top,
invisible.*)

ALONSO: What harmony is this? My good friends, hark!
GONZALO: Marvelous sweet music!

(*Enter several strange* SHAPES, *bringing in a banquet, and dance
about it with gentle actions of salutations; and, inviting the
KING, etc., to eat, they depart.*)

20 ALONSO: Give us kind keepers, heavens! What were these?

III.iii. Location: Another part of the island.
1 **By'r lakin** by our Ladykin, by our Lady   3 **forth-rights and meanders**
paths straight and crooked   5 **attach'd** seized   12 **for** because of   14
throughly thoroughly   17 **s.d. on the top** at some high point of the
tiring-house or the theatre   20 **kind keepers** guardian angels

---

SEBASTIAN: A living drollery. Now I will believe
That there are unicorns, that in Arabia
There is one tree, the phoenix' throne, one phoenix
At this hour reigning there.
ANTONIO: I'll believe both;
And what does else want credit, come to me,   25
And I'll be sworn 'tis true. Travelers ne'er did lie,
Though fools at home condemn 'em.
GONZALO: If in Naples
I should report this now, would they believe me
If I should say I saw such islanders?
For, certes, these are people of the island,   30
Who, though they are of monstrous shape, yet, note,
Their manners are more gentle, kind, than of
Our human generation you shall find
Many, nay, almost any.
PROSPERO: (*Aside*)   Honest lord,
Thou hast said well; for some of you there present   35
Are worse than devils.
ALONSO: I cannot too much muse
Such shapes, such gesture, and such sound, expressing,
Although they want the use of tongue, a kind
Of excellent dumb discourse.
PROSPERO: (*Aside*)   Praise in departing.
FRANCISCO: They vanish'd strangely.
SEBASTIAN: No matter, since   40
They have left their viands behind; for we have stomachs.
Will 't please you taste of what is here?
ALONSO: Not I.
GONZALO: Faith, sir, you need not fear. When we were boys,
Who would believe that there were mountaineers
Dew-lapp'd like bulls, whose throats had hanging at 'em   45
Wallets of flesh? Or that there were such men
Whose heads stood in their breasts? Which now we find
Each putter-out of five for one will bring us
Good warrant of.
ALONSO: I will stand to and feed,
Although my last—no matter, since I feel   50
The best is past. Brother, my lord the Duke,
Stand to and do as we.

(*They approach the table.*)

(*Thunder and lightning. Enter* ARIEL, *like a harpy; claps his
wings upon the table; and, with a quaint device, the banquet
vanishes.*)

ARIEL: You are three men of sin, whom Destiny,
That hath to instrument this lower world
And what is in 't, the never-surfeited sea   55

---

21 **drollery** puppet show   25 **want credit** lack credence   30 **certes** certainly   36 **muse** wonder at   39 **Praise in departing** i.e., save your
praise until the end of the performance   45 **Dew-lapp'd** having a dew-
lap, or fold of skin hanging from the neck, like cattle   47 **in their
breasts** (i.e., like the Anthropophagi described in *Othello.*)   48 **putter-
out . . . one** one who invests money, or gambles on the risks of travel on
the condition that, if he returns safely, he is to receive five times the
amount deposited; hence, any traveler   49 **stand to** fall to; take the
risk   52 **s.d. harpy** a fabulous monster with a woman's face and vulture's body, supposed to be a minister of divine vengeance. **quaint
device** ingenious stage contrivance. **banquet vanishes** i.e., the food
vanishes; the table remains until l.82

Hath caus'd to belch up you, and on this island
Where man doth not inhabit—you 'mongst men
Being most unfit to live. I have made you mad;
And even with such-like valor men hang and drown
Their proper selves.

(ALONSO, SEBASTIAN, *and* ANTONIO *draw their swords.*)

60   You fools! I and my fellows
Are ministers of Fate. The elements,
Of whom your swords are temper'd, may as well
Wound the loud winds, or with bemock'd-at stabs
Kill the still-closing waters, as diminish
65   One dowle that's in my plume. My fellow-ministers
Are like invulnerable. If you could hurt,
Your swords are now too massy for your strengths
And will not be uplifted. But remember—
For that's my business to you—that you three
70   From Milan did supplant good Prospero;
Expos'd unto the sea, which hath requit it,
Him and his innocent child; for which foul deed
The pow'rs, delaying, not forgetting, have
Incens'd the seas and shores, yea, all the creatures,
75   Against your peace. Thee of thy son, Alonso,
They have bereft; and do pronounce by me
Ling'ring perdition, worse than any death
Can be at once, shall step by step attend
You and your ways; whose wraths to guard you from—
80   Which here, in this most desolate isle, else falls
Upon your heads—is nothing but heart's sorrow
And a clear life ensuing.

(*He vanishes in thunder; then, to soft music, enter the* SHAPES
*again, and dance, with mocks and mows, and carrying out the
table.*)

PROSPERO: Bravely the figure of this harpy hast thou
    Perform'd, my Ariel; a grace it had devouring.
85   Of my instruction hast thou nothing bated
In what thou hadst to say. So, with good life
And observation strange, my meaner ministers
Their several kinds have done. My high charms work,
And these mine enemies are all knit up
90   In their distractions. They now are in my pow'r;
And in these fits I leave them, while I visit
Young Ferdinand, whom they suppose is drown'd,
And his and mine lov'd darling.

(*Exit above.*)

GONZALO: I' th' name of something holy, sir, why stand you
    In this strange stare?
ALONSO: O, it is monstrous, monstrous!   95
Methought the billows spoke and told me of it;
The winds did sing it to me, and the thunder,
That deep and dreadful organ-pipe, pronounc'd
The name of Prosper; it did bass my trespass.
Therefore my son i' th' ooze is bedded, and   100
I'll seek him deeper than e'er plummet sounded
And with him there lie mudded.

(*Exit.*)

SEBASTIAN: But one fiend at a time,
    I'll fight their legions o'er.
ANTONIO: I'll be thy second.

(*Exeunt* [SEBASTIAN *and* ANTONIO].)

GONZALO: All three of them are desperate. Their great guilt,   105
    Like poison given to work a great time after,
Now 'gins to bite the spirits. I do beseech you,
That are of suppler joints, follow them swiftly
And hinder them from what this ecstasy
May now provoke them to.
ADRIAN: Follow, I pray you.   110

(*Exeunt omnes.*)

— ACT FOUR —

SCENE I

Enter PROSPERO, FERDINAND, *and* MIRANDA.

PROSPERO: If I have too austerely punish'd you,
    Your compensation makes amends, for I
Have given you here a third of mine own life,
Or that for which I live; who once again
I tender to thy hand. All thy vexations   5
Were but my trials of thy love, and thou
Hast strangely stood the test. Here, afore Heaven,
I ratify this my rich gift. O Ferdinand,
Do not smile at me that I boast her off,
For thou shalt find she will outstrip all praise   10
And make it halt behind her.
FERDINAND: I do believe it
    Against an oracle.
PROSPERO: Then, as my gift and thine own acquisition
    Worthily purchas'd, take my daughter. But
If thou dost break her virgin-knot before   15
All sanctimonious ceremonies may

With full and holy rite be minist'red,
No sweet aspersion shall the heavens let fall
To make this contract grow; but barren hate,
20 Sour-ey'd disdain, and discord shall bestrew
The union of your bed with weeds so loathly
That you shall hate it both. Therefore take heed,
As Hymen's lamps shall light you.

FERDINAND: As I hope
For quiet days, fair issue, and long life,
25 With such love as 'tis now, the murkiest den,
The most opportune place, the strong'st suggestion
Our worser genius can, shall never melt
Mine honor into lust, to take away
The edge of that day's celebration
30 When I shall think or Phoebus' steeds are founder'd
Or Night kept chain'd below.

PROSPERO: Fairly spoke.
Sit then and talk with her; she is thine own.

(FERDINAND *and* MIRANDA *sit.*)

What, Ariel! My industrious servant, Ariel!

(*Enter* ARIEL.)

ARIEL: What would my potent master? Here I am.
35 PROSPERO: Thou and thy meaner fellows your last service
Did worthily perform; and I must use you
In such another trick. Go bring the rabble,
O'er whom I give thee pow'r, here to this place.
Incite them to quick motion, for I must
40 Bestow upon the eyes of this young couple
Some vanity of mine art. It is my promise,
And they expect it from me.

ARIEL: Presently?
PROSPERO: Ay, with a twink.
ARIEL: Before you can say "come" and "go,"
45 And breathe twice and cry "so, so,"
Each one, tripping on his toe,
Will be here with mop and mow.
Do you love me, master? No?
PROSPERO: Dearly, my delicate Ariel. Do not approach
Till thou dost hear me call.
50 ARIEL: Well, I conceive.

(*Exit.*)

PROSPERO: Look thou be true; do not give dalliance
Too much the rein. The strongest oaths are straw
To th' fire i' th' blood. Be more abstemious,
Or else good night your vow!
FERDINAND: I warrant you, sir;
55 The white cold virgin snow upon my heart
Abates the ardor of my liver.
PROSPERO: Well.
Now come, my Ariel! Bring a corollary,

Rather than want a spirit. Appear, and pertly!
No tongue! All eyes! Be silent.

(*Soft music.*)

(*Enter* IRIS.)

IRIS: Ceres, most bounteous lady, thy rich leas   60
Of wheat, rye, barley, vetches, oats, and pease;
Thy turfy mountains, where live nibbling sheep,
And flat meads thatch'd with stover, them to keep;
Thy banks with pioned and twilled brims,
Which spongy April at thy hest betrims,   65
To make cold nymphs chaste crowns; and thy
    broom-groves,
Whose shadow the dismissed bachelor loves,
Being lass-lorn; thy pole-clipt vineyard;
And thy sea-marge, sterile and rocky-hard,
Where thou thyself dost air—the queen o' th' sky,   70
Whose wat'ry arch and messenger am I,
Bids thee leave these, and with her sovereign grace.

(JUNO *descends [slowly in her car].*)

Here on this grass-plot, in this very place,
To come and sport. Her peacocks fly amain.
Approach, rich Ceres, her to entertain.   75

(*Enter* CERES.)

CERES: Hail, many-color'd messenger, that ne'er
Dost disobey the wife of Jupiter,
Who with thy saffron wings upon my flow'rs
Diffusest honey-drops, refreshing show'rs,
And with each end of thy blue bow dost crown   80
My bosky acres and my unshrubb'd down,
Rich scarf to my proud earth; why hath thy Queen
Summon'd me hither, to this short-grass'd green?
IRIS: A contract of true love to celebrate,
And some donation freely to estate   85
On the bless'd lovers.
CERES: Tell me, heavenly bow,
If Venus or her son, as thou dost know,
Do now attend the Queen? Since they did plot
The means that dusky Dis my daughter got,
Her and her blind boy's scandal'd company   90
I have forsworn.
IRIS: Of her society
Be not afraid. I met her deity

---

18 **aspersion** dew, shower   23 **Hymen's** (Hymen was the Greek and Roman god of marriage.)   27 **worser genius** evil genius, or evil attendant spirit   30 **or** either.   **founder'd** broken down, made lame. (i.e., Ferdinand will wait impatiently for the bridal night.)   37 **rabble** band, i.e., the *meaner fellows* of l. 35   41 **vanity** illusion   47 **mop and mow** gestures and grimaces   50 **conceive** understand   56 **liver** (as the presumed seat of the passions)   57 **corollary** surplus, extra supply

58 **want** lack.   **pertly** briskly   59 **s.d. Iris** goddess of the rainbow, and Juno's messenger   60 **Ceres** goddess of the generative power of nature.   **leas** meadows   61 **vetches** plants for forage, fodder   63 **stover** winter fodder for cattle   64 **pioned and twilled** undercut by the swift current and protected by roots and branches woven into a mat (?)   66 **broom-groves** clumps of broom, gorse, yellow-flowered shrub   67 **dismissed bachelor** rejected male lover   68 **pole-clipt** hedged in with poles; or pruned   70 **queen o' th' sky** i.e., Juno   71 **wat'ry arch** rainbow   72 **s.d. Juno descends** i.e., starts her descent from the "heavens" above the stage (?)   74 **peacocks** birds sacred to Juno, and used to pull her chariot.   **amain** with full speed   75 **entertain** receive   81 **bosky** wooded.   **down** upland   85 **estate** bestow   87 **son** i.e., Cupid   89 **Dis . . . got** (Pluto, or Dis, god of the infernal regions, carried off Persephone, daughter of Ceres, to be his bride in Hades.)   90 **Her** i.e., Venus   **scandal'd** scandalous   92 **her deity** i.e., her highness

Cutting the clouds towards Paphos, and her son
Dove-drawn with her. Here thought they to have done
95 Some wanton charm upon this man and maid,
Whose vows are, that no bed-right shall be paid
Till Hymen's torch be lighted; but in vain;
Mars's hot minion is return'd again;
Her waspish-headed son has broke his arrows,
100 Swears he will shoot no more, but play with sparrows
And be a boy right out.

(JUNO alights.)

CERES: Highest Queen of state,
Great Juno, comes; I know her by her gait.
JUNO: How does my bounteous sister? Go with me
To bless this twain, that they may prosperous be
105 And honor'd in their issue.

(They sing.)

JUNO:

Honor, riches, marriage-blessing,
Long continuance, and increasing,
Hourly joys be still upon you!
Juno sings her blessings on you.

CERES:

110 Earth's increase, foison plenty,
Barns and garners never empty,
Vines with clust'ring bunches growing,
Plants with goodly burden bowing;

Spring come to you at the farthest
115 In the very end of harvest!
Scarcity and want shall shun you;
Ceres' blessing so is on you.

FERDINAND: This is a most majestic vision, and
Harmonious charmingly. May I be bold
To think these spirits?
120 PROSPERO: Spirits, which by mine art
I have from their confines call'd to enact
My present fancies.
FERDINAND: Let me live here ever;
So rare a wond'red father and a wife
Makes this place Paradise.

(JUNO and CERES whisper, and send IRIS on employment.)

PROSPERO: Sweet now, silence!
125 Juno and Ceres whisper seriously;
There's something else to do. Hush and be mute,
Or else our spell is marr'd.
IRIS: You nymphs, call'd Naiads, of the windring brooks,
With your sedg'd crowns and ever-harmless looks,
130 Leave your crisp channels, and on this green land
Answer your summons; Juno does command.
Come, temperate nymphs, and help to celebrate
A contract of true love; be not too late.

(Enter certain NYMPHS.)

You sunburnt sicklemen, of August weary,
Come hither from the furrow and be merry.
135 Make holiday; your rye-straw hats put on
And these fresh nymphs encounter every one
In country footing.

(Enter certain REAPERS, properly habited. They join with the NYMPHS in a graceful dance, towards the end whereof PROSPERO starts suddenly, and speaks; after which, to a strange, hollow, and confused noise, they heavily vanish.)

PROSPERO: *(Aside)* I had forgot that foul conspiracy
Of the beast Caliban and his confederates
140 Against my life. The minute of their plot
Is almost come. *(To the SPIRITS.)* Well done! Avoid;
no more!
FERDINAND: This is strange. Your father's is some passion
That works him strongly.
MIRANDA: Never till this day
Saw I him touch'd with anger so distemper'd.
145 PROSPERO: You do look, my son, in a mov'd sort,
As if you were dismay'd. Be cheerful, sir.
Our revels now are ended. These our actors,
As I foretold you, were all spirits and
Are melted into air, into thin air;
150 And, like the baseless fabric of this vision,
The cloud-capp'd tow'rs, the gorgeous palaces,
The solemn temples, the great globe itself,
Yea, all which it inherit, shall dissolve
And, like this insubstantial pageant faded,
155 Leave not a rack behind. We are such stuff
As dreams are made on, and our little life
Is rounded with a sleep. Sir, I am vex'd.
Bear with my weakness; my old brain is troubled.
Be not disturb'd with my infirmity.
160 If you be pleas'd, retire into my cell
And there repose. A turn or two I'll walk
To still my beating mind.
FERDINAND, MIRANDA: We wish your peace.

(Exeunt.)

PROSPERO: Come with a thought! I thank thee, Ariel. Come.

(Enter ARIEL.)

ARIEL: Thy thoughts I cleave to. What's thy pleasure?
165 PROSPERO: Spirit,
We must prepare to meet with Caliban.
ARIEL: Ay, my commander. When I presented Ceres,
I thought to have told thee of it, but I fear'd
Lest I might anger thee.
170 PROSPERO: Say again, where didst thou leave these varlets?
ARIEL: I told you, sir, they were red-hot with drinking,
So full of valor that they smote the air

---

93 **Paphos** place on the island of Cyprus, sacred to Venus   98 **Mars' hot minion** i.e., Venus, the beloved of Mars   99 **waspish-headed** fiery, hotheaded, peevish   100 **sparrows** (Supposed lustful, and sacred to Venus.)   101 **right out** outright   110 **foison plenty** plentiful harvest   111 **garners** granaries   123 **wond'red** wonder-performing, wondrous.   **wife** (Sometimes emended to *wise*.)   128 **windring** wandering, winding (?)   130 **crisp** curled, rippled   132 **temperate** chaste

138 **country footing** country dancing   138 **s.d. heavily** slowly, dejectedly   142 **Avoid** depart, withdraw   146 **mov'd sort** troubled state, condition   148 **revels** entertainments, pageants   151 **baseless** without substance   154 **which it inherit** who occupy it   156 **rack** wisp of cloud   157 **on** of   164 **with a thought** i.e., on the instant, or summoned by my thought, no sooner thought on than here   167 **presented** acted the part of, or introduced

For breathing in their faces; beat the ground
For kissing of their feet; yet always bending
175   Towards their project. Then I beat my tabor,
At which, like unback'd colts, they prick'd their ears,
Advanc'd their eyelids, lifted up their noses
As they smelt music. So I charm'd their ears
That calf-like they my lowing follow'd through
180   Tooth'd briers, sharp furzes, pricking goss, and thorns,
Which ent'red their frail shins. At last I left them
I' th' filthy-mantled pool beyond your cell,
There dancing up to th' chins, that the foul lake
O'erstunk their feet.
PROSPERO: This was well done, my bird.
185   Thy shape invisible retain thou still.
The trumpery in my house, go bring it hither,
For stale to catch these thieves.
ARIEL: I go, I go.

(Exit.)

PROSPERO: A devil, a born devil, on whose nature
Nurture can never stick; on whom my pains,
190   Humanely taken, all, all lost, quite lost!
And as with age his body uglier grows,
So his mind cankers. I will plague them all,
Even to roaring.

(Enter ARIEL, *loaden with glistering apparel, etc.)*

        Come, hang them on this line.

*([*ARIEL *hangs up the showy finery;* PROSPERO *and* ARIEL *remain, invisible.] Enter* CALIBAN, STEPHANO, *and* TRINCULO, *all wet.)*

CALIBAN: Pray you, tread softly, that the blind mole may not
195   Hear a foot fall. We now are near his cell.
STEPHANO: Monster, your fairy, which you say is a harmless
fairy, has done little better than play'd the Jack with us.
TRINCULO: Monster, I do smell all horse-piss, at which my nose
is in great indignation.
200 STEPHANO: So is mine. Do you hear, monster? If I should take a
displeasure against you, look you—
TRINCULO: Thou wert but a lost monster.
CALIBAN: Good my lord, give me thy favor still.
Be patient, for the prize I'll bring thee to
205   Shall hoodwink this mischance. Therefore speak softly.
All's hush'd as midnight yet.
TRINCULO: Ay, but to lose our bottles in the pool—
STEPHANO: There is not only disgrace and dishonor in that,
monster, but an infinite loss.
210 TRINCULO: That's more to me than my wetting. Yet this is
your harmless fairy, monster!
STEPHANO: I will fetch off my bottle, though I be o'er ears for my
labor.

CALIBAN: Prithee, my King, be quiet. See'st thou here,
This is the mouth o' th' cell. No noise, and enter.   215
Do that good mischief which may make this island
Thine own for ever, and I, thy Caliban,
For aye thy foot-licker.
STEPHANO: Give me thy hand. I do begin to have bloody
thoughts.   220
TRINCULO: *(Seeing the finery)* O King Stephano! O peer! O worthy Stephano! Look what a wardrobe here is for thee!
CALIBAN: Let it alone, thou fool! It is but trash.
TRINCULO: O, ho, monster! We know what belongs to a frippery. O King Stephano!   *(Takes a gown.)*   225
STEPHANO: Put off that gown, Trinculo. By this hand, I'll have
that gown.
TRINCULO: Thy Grace shall have it.
CALIBAN: The dropsy drown this fool! What do you mean
To dote thus on such luggage? Let's alone   230
And do the murder first. If he awake,
From toe to crown he'll fill our skins with pinches,
Make us strange stuff.
STEPHANO: Be you quiet, monster. Mistress line, is not this my
jerkin? *(Takes it down.)* Now is the jerkin under the line.   235
Now, jerkin, you are like to lose your hair and prove a bald
jerkin.
TRINCULO: Do, do! We steal by line and level, an 't like your
Grace.
STEPHANO: I thank thee for that jest. Here's a garment for 't.   240
(Gives a garment.) Wit shall not go unrewarded while I am
king of this country. "Steal by line and level" is an excellent
pass of pate. There's another garment for 't.
TRINCULO: Monster, come, put some lime upon your fingers,
and away with the rest.   245
CALIBAN: I have none on 't. We shall lose our time,
And all be turn'd to barnacles, or to apes
With foreheads villainous low.
STEPHANO: Monster, lay to your fingers. Help to bear this away
where my hogshead of wine is, or I'll turn you out of my   250
kingdom. Go to, carry this.
TRINCULO: And this.
STEPHANO: Ay, and this.

(They collect more and more garments.)

(A noise of hunters heard. Enter divers SPIRITS, *in shape of dogs and hounds, hunting them about,* PROSPERO *and* ARIEL *setting them on.)*

---

176 **unback'd** unbroken, unridden   177 **Advanc'd** lifted up   180 **goss** gorse, a prickly shrub   182 **filthy-mantled** covered with a slimy coating   186 **trumpery** cheap goods, the *glistering apparel* mentioned in the following stage direction   187 **stale** (1) decoy (2) out of fashion garments (with possible further suggestions of *fit for a stale* or prostitute, *stale* meaning "horse-piss," l. 198, and *steal*, pronounced like *stale*)   192 **cankers** festers, grows malignant   193 **line** lime tree or linden   197 **Jack** (1) Knave (2) will-o-the wisp   205 **hoodwink** cover up, make you not see (A hawking term.)

221 **King . . . peer** (Alludes to the old ballad beginning, "King Stephen was a worthy peer.")   224 **frippery** place where cast-off clothes are sold   230 **luggage** cumbersome trash   235 **jerkin** jacket make of leather **under the line** under the lime tree (with punning sense of being south of the equinoctial line or equator; sailors to the southern regions were popularly supposed to lose their hair from scurvy or other diseases. Stephano also quibbles bawdily on losing hair through syphilis, and in *Mistress* and *jerkin.*)   238 **by line and level** i.e., by means of plumb-line and carpenter's level, methodically (with pun on *line*, "lime tree," l. 235, and *steal* pronounced *stale*, i.e., prostitute, continuing Stephano's bawdy quibble). **an 't like** if it please   243 **pass of pate** sally of wit   244 **lime** birdlime, sticky substance (to give Caliban sticky fingers)   247 **barnacles** barnacle geese, formerly supposed to be hatched from seashells attached to trees and to fall thence into the water; here evidently used, like *apes*, as types of simpletons   248 **villainous** miserably

PROSPERO: Hey, Mountain, hey!
255   ARIEL: Silver! There it goes, Silver!
PROSPERO: Fury, Fury! There, Tyrant, there! Hark! Hark!

(CALIBAN, STEPHANO, *and* TRINCULO *are driven out.*)

Go charge my goblins that they grind their joints
With dry convulsions, shorten up their sinews
With aged cramps, and more pitch-spotted make them
Than pard or cat o' mountain.
260   ARIEL: Hark, they roar!
PROSPERO: Let them be hunted soundly. At this hour
Lies at my mercy all mine enemies.
Shortly shall all my labors end, and thou
Shalt have the air at freedom. For a little
265   Follow, and do me service.

(*Exeunt.*)

— ACT FIVE —

SCENE I

Enter PROSPERO *in his magic robes, [with his staff,] and* ARIEL.

PROSPERO: Now does my project gather to a head.
My charms crack not, my spirits obey, and Time
Goes upright with his carriage. How's the day?
ARIEL: On the sixth hour; at which time, my lord,
You said our work should cease.
5   PROSPERO: I did say so,
When first I rais'd the tempest. Say, my spirit,
How fares the King and 's followers?
ARIEL: Confin'd together
In the same fashion as you gave in charge,
Just as you left them; all prisoners, sir,
10   In the line-grove which weather-fends your cell.
They cannot budge till your release. The King,
His brother, and yours, abide all three distracted,
And the remainder mourning over them,
Brimful of sorrow and dismay; but chiefly
15   Him that you term'd, sir, "The good old lord, Gonzalo."
His tears runs down his beard like winter's drops
From eaves of reeds. Your charm so strongly works 'em
That if you now beheld them, your affections
Would become tender.
PROSPERO: Dost thou think so, spirit?
ARIEL: Mine would, sir, were I human.
20   PROSPERO: And mine shall.
Hast thou, which art but air, a touch, a feeling
Of their afflictions, and shall not myself,
One of their kind, that relish all as sharply,

Passion as they, be kindlier mov'd than thou art?
Though with their high wrongs I am struck to th' quick,   25
Yet with my nobler reason 'gainst my fury
Do I take part. The rarer action is
In virtue than in vengeance. They being penitent,
The sole drift of my purpose doth extend
Not a frown further. Go release them, Ariel.   30
My charms I'll break, their senses I'll restore,
And they shall be themselves.
ARIEL: I'll fetch them, sir.

(*Exit.*)

(PROSPERO *traces a charmed circle with his staff.*)

PROSPERO: Ye elves of hills, brooks, standing lakes, and groves,
And ye that on the sands with printless foot
Do chase the ebbing Neptune, and do fly him   35
When he comes back; you demi-puppets that
By moonshine do the green sour ringlets make,
Whereof the ewe not bites; and you whose pastime
Is to make midnight mushrooms, that rejoice
To hear the solemn curfew; by whose aid,   40
Weak masters though ye be, I have bedimm'd
The noontide sun, call'd forth the mutinous winds,
And 'twixt the green sea and the azur'd vault
Set roaring war; to the dread rattling thunder
Have I given fire, and rifted Jove's stout oak   45
With his own bolt; the strong-bas'd promontory
Have I made shake, and by the spurs pluck'd up
The pine and cedar; graves at my command
Have wak'd their sleepers, op'd, and let 'em forth
By my so potent art. But this rough magic   50
I here abjure, and, when I have requir'd
Some heavenly music, which even now I do,
To work mine end upon their senses that
This airy charm is for, I'll break my staff,
Bury it certain fathoms in the earth,   55
And deeper than did ever plummet sound
I'll drown my book.

(*Solemn music.*)

(*Here enters* ARIEL *before; then* ALONSO, *with a frantic gesture,
attended by* GONZALO; SEBASTIAN *and* ANTONIO *in like manner, attended by* ADRIAN *and* FRANCISCO. *They all enter the
circle which* PROSPERO *had made, and there stand charm'd;
which* PROSPERO *observing, speaks:*)

A solemn air, and the best comforter
To an unsettled fancy, cure thy brains,
Now useless, boil'd within thy skull! There stand,   60
For you are spell-stopp'd.
Holy Gonzalo, honorable man,
Mine eyes, ev'n sociable to the show of thine,

258 **dry** associated with age, arthritic (?). **convulsions** cramps   259
aged characteristic of old age   260 **pard** panther or leopard.   **cat o'
mountain** wildcat
V.i. Location: Before Prospero's cell.
3 **his carriage** its burden (i.e., Time is unstopped, runs smoothly.)   10
line-grove grove of lime trees.   **weather-fends** protects from the
weather   11 **your release** you release them   17 **eaves of reeds** thatched
roofs   23 **relish all** experience quite

24 **Passion** experience deep feeling   27 **rarer** nobler   33–50 **Ye . . . art**
(Ths famous passage is an embellished paraphrase of Golding's translation of Ovid's *Metamorphoses*, vii. 197–219.)   36 **demi-puppets** puppets of half-size, i.e., elves and fairies   37 **green sour ringlets** fairy
rings, circles in grass (actually produced by mushrooms)   44–45 **to . . .
fire** I have discharged the dread rattling thunderbolt   45 **rifted** riven,
split   47 **spurs** roots   51 **requir'd** requested   58 **and** i.e., which
is   63 **sociable** sympathetic.   **show** appearance

Fall fellowly drops. The charm dissolves apace,
65 And as the morning steals upon the night,
Melting the darkness, so their rising senses
Begin to chase the ignorant fumes that mantle
Their clearer reason. O good Gonzalo,
My true preserver, and a loyal sir
70 To him thou follow'st! I will pay thy graces
Home both in word and deed. Most cruelly
Didst thou, Alonso, use me and my daughter.
Thy brother was a furtherer in the act.
Thou art pinch'd for 't now, Sebastian. Flesh and blood,
75 You, brother mine, that entertain'd ambition,
Expell'd remorse and nature, who, with Sebastian,
Whose inward pinches therefore are most strong,
Would here have kill'd your king, I do forgive thee,
Unnatural though thou art. —Their understanding
80 Begins to swell, and the approaching tide
Will shortly fill the reasonable shore
That now lies foul and muddy. Not one of them
That yet looks on me, or would know me. Ariel,
Fetch me the hat and rapier in my cell.

(ARIEL *goes to the cell and returns immediately.*)

85 I will discase me, and myself present
As I was sometime Milan. Quickly, spirit;
Thou shalt ere long be free.

(ARIEL *sings and helps to attire him.*)

ARIEL: Where the bee sucks, there suck I;
               In a cowslip's bell I lie;
90   There I couch when owls do cry.
               On the bat's back I do fly
               After summer merrily.
             Merrily, merrily shall I live now
             Under the blossom that hangs on the bough.
95 PROSPERO: Why, that's my dainty Ariel! I shall miss thee;
But yet thou shalt have freedom. So, so, so.
To the King's ship, invisible as thou art!
There shalt thou find the mariners asleep
Under the hatches. The master and the boatswain
100 Being awake, enforce them to this place,
And presently, I prithee.
ARIEL: I drink the air before me, and return
Or ere your pulse twice beat.   (*Exit.*)
GONZALO: All torment, trouble, wonder, and amazement
105 Inhabits here. Some heavenly power guide us
Out of this fearful country!
PROSPERO: Behold, sir King,
The wronged Duke of Milan, Prospero.
For more assurance that a living prince
Does now speak to thee, I embrace thy body;
110 And to thee and thy company I bid
A hearty welcome.

(*Embraces him.*)

ALONSO: Whe'er thou be'st he or no,
Or some enchanted trifle to abuse me,
As late I have been, I not know. Thy pulse
Beats as of flesh and blood; and, since I saw thee,
Th' affliction of my mind amends, with which,   115
I fear, a madness held me. This must crave,
An if this be at all, a most strange story.
Thy dukedom I resign, and do entreat
Thou pardon me my wrongs. But how should Prospero
Be living and be here?
PROSPERO: (*To* GONZALO)   First, noble friend,   120
Let me embrace thine age, whose honor cannot
Be measur'd or confin'd.

(*Embraces him.*)

GONZALO: Whether this be
Or be not, I'll not swear.
PROSPERO: Yet do yet taste
Some subtleties o' th' isle, that will not let you
Believe things certain. Welcome, my friends all!   125
(*Aside to* SEBASTIAN *and* ANTONIO.) But you, my brace of
     lords,
I here could pluck his Highness' frown upon you
And justify you traitors. At this time
I will tell no tales.
SEBASTIAN: The devil speaks in him.
PROSPERO: No.
For you, most wicked sir, whom to call brother   130
Would even infect my mouth, I do forgive
Thy rankest fault—all of them; and require
My dukedom of thee, which perforce I know
Thou must restore.
ALONSO: If thou be'st Prospero,
Give us particulars of thy preservation,   135
How thou hast met us here, who three hours since
Were wrack'd upon this shore; where I have lost—
How sharp the point of this remembrance is!—
My dear son Ferdinand.
PROSPERO: I am woe for 't, sir.
ALONSO: Irreparable is the loss, and Patience   140
Says it is past her cure.
PROSPERO: I rather think
You have not sought her help, of whose soft grace
For the like loss I have her sovereign aid
And rest myself content.
ALONSO: You the like loss?
PROSPERO: As great to me as late; and, supportable   145
To make the dear loss, have I means much weaker
Than you may call to comfort you, for I
Have lost my daughter.
ALONSO: A daughter?
O heavens, that they were living both in Naples,   150
The king and queen there! That they were, I wish

---

64 **Fall** let fall 70 **pay thy graces** reward your favors 71 **Home**
fully 76 **remorse** pity. **nature** natural feeling 85 **discase** dis-
robe 86 **As ... Milan** in my former appearance as Duke of Milan 96
So, so, so (Expresses approval of Ariel's help as valet.)

112 **trifle** trick of magic. **abuse** deceive 116 **crave** require 117 **An ...
all** if this is actually happening 118 **Thy ... resign** (Alonso made
arrangement with Antonio at the time of Prospero's banishment for
Milan to pay tribute to Naples; see I.ii. 113–127.) 124 **subtleties** illusions, magical powers 128 **justify you** prove you to be 139 **woe**
sorry 145 **late** recent

Myself were mudded in that oozy bed
Where my son lies. When did you lose your daughter?

PROSPERO: In this last tempest. I perceive these lords
155   At this encounter do so much admire
That they devour their reason and scarce think
Their eyes do offices of truth, their words
Are natural breath. But, howsoev'r you have
Been justled from your senses, know for certain
160   That I am Prospero and that very duke
Which was thrust forth of Milan, who most strangely
Upon this shore, where you were wrack'd, was landed,
To be the lord on 't. No more yet of this,
For 'tis a chronicle of day by day,
165   Not a relation for a breakfast nor
Befitting this first meeting. Welcome, sir;
This cell's my court. Here have I few attendants
And subjects none abroad. Pray you look in.
My dukedom since you have given me again,
170   I will requite you with as good a thing,
At least bring forth a wonder, to content ye
As much as me my dukedom.

(Here PROSPERO *discovers* FERDINAND *and* MIRANDA, *playing at chess.)*

MIRANDA: Sweet lord, you play me false.
FERDINAND: No, my dearest love,
175   I would not for the world.
MIRANDA: Yes, for a score of kingdoms you should wrangle,
And I would call it fair play.
ALONSO: If this prove
A vision of the island, one dear son
Shall I twice lose.
SEBASTIAN: A most high miracle!
180   FERDINAND: Though the seas threaten, they are merciful;
I have curs'd them without cause.   *(Kneels.)*
ALONSO: Now all the blessings
Of a glad father compass thee about!
Arise, and say how thou cam'st here.
MIRANDA: O, wonder!
How many goodly creatures are there here!
185   How beauteous mankind is! O brave new world,
That has such people in 't!
PROSPERO: 'Tis new to thee.
ALONSO: What is this maid with whom thou wast at play?
Your eld'st acquaintance cannot be three hours.
Is she the goddess that hath sever'd us,
And brought us thus together?
190   FERDINAND: Sir, she is mortal;
But by immortal Providence she's mine.
I chose her when I could not ask my father

For his advice, nor thought I had one. She
Is daughter to this famous Duke of Milan,
Of whom so often I have heard renown,   195
But never saw before; of whom I have
Receiv'd a second life; and second father
This lady makes him to me.
ALONSO: I am hers.
But, O, how oddly will it sound that I
Must ask my child forgiveness!
PROSPERO: There, sir, stop.   200
Let us not burden our remembrances with
A heaviness that's gone.
GONZALO: I have inly wept
Or should have spoke ere this. Look down, you gods,
And on this couple drop a blessed crown!
For it is you that have chalk'd forth the way   205
Which brought us hither.
ALONSO: I say Amen, Gonzalo!
GONZALO: Was Milan thrust from Milan, that his issue
Should become kings of Naples? O, rejoice
Beyond a common joy, and set it down
With gold on lasting pillars: In one voyage   210
Did Claribel her husband find at Tunis,
And Ferdinand, her brother, found a wife
Where he himself was lost; Prospero his dukedom
In a poor isle; and all of us ourselves
When no man was his own.
ALONSO: *(To* FERDINAND *and* MIRANDA.*)* Give me your hands.   215
Let grief and sorrow still embrace his heart
That doth not wish you joy!
GONZALO: Be it so! Amen!

(Enter ARIEL, *with the* MASTER *and* BOATSWAIN *amazedly following.)*

O, look, sir, look, sir! Here is more of us.
I prophesied, if a gallows were on land,
This fellow could not drown. Now, blasphemy,   220
That swear'st grace o'erboard, not an oath on shore?
Hast thou no mouth by land? What is the news?
BOATSWAIN: The best news is that we have safely found
Our King and company; the next, our ship —
Which, but three glasses since, we gave out split —   225
Is tight and yare and bravely rigg'd as when
We first put out to sea.
ARIEL: *(Aside to* PROSPERO.*)* Sir, all this service
Have I done since I went.
PROSPERO: *(Aside to* ARIEL.*)* My tricksy spirit!
ALONSO: These are not natural events; they strengthen
From strange to stranger. Say, how came you hither?   230
BOATSWAIN: If I did think, sir, I were well awake,
I'd strive to tell you. We were dead of sleep,
And — how we know not — all clapp'd under hatches;
Where but even now with strange and several noises
Of roaring, shrieking, howling, jingling chains,   235
And moe diversity of sounds, all horrible,
We were awak'd; straightway, at liberty;

155 **admire** wonder   156–158 **scarce . . . breath** scarcely believe that their eyes inform them accurately what they see or that their words are naturally spoken   172 **s.d. discovers** i.e., by opening a curtain, presumably rear-stage   176–177 **Yes . . . play** i.e., yes, even if we were playing for twenty kingdoms, something less than the whole world, you would still contend mightily against me and play me false, and I would let you do it as though it were fair play; or, if you were to play not just for stakes but literally for kingdoms, my accusation of false play would be out of order in that your "wrangling" would be proper   185 **brave** splendid, gorgeously appareled, handsome   188 **eld'st** longest

207 **Was Milan** was the Duke of Milan   216 **still** always.   **his** that man's   217 **That** who   225 **glasses** i.e., hours.   **gave out** reported   226 **yare** ready

Where we, in all her trim, freshly beheld
Our royal, good, and gallant ship, our master
240   Cap'ring to eye her. On a trice, so please you,
Even in a dream, were we divided from them
And were brought moping hither.
ARIEL: *(Aside to* PROSPERO.*)*   Was 't well done?
PROSPERO: *(Aside to* ARIEL.*)* Bravely, my diligence. Thou shalt
be free.
ALONSO: This is as strange a maze as e'er men trod,
245   And there is in this business more than nature
Was ever conduct of. Some oracle
Must rectify our knowledge.
PROSPERO: Sir, my liege,
Do not infest your mind with beating on
The strangeness of this business. At pick'd leisure,
250   Which shall be shortly, single I'll resolve you,
Which to you shall seem probable, of every
These happen'd accidents; till when, be cheerful
And think of each thing well. *(Aside to* ARIEL.*)* Come
hither, spirit.
Set Caliban and his companions free;
255   Untie the spell. *(Exit* ARIEL.*)* How fares my gracious sir?
There are yet missing of your company
Some few odd lads that you remember not.

Enter ARIEL, *driving in* CALIBAN, STEPHANO, *and* TRINCULO,
in their stol'n apparel.)

STEPHANO: Every man shift for all the rest, and let no man take
care of himself; for all is but fortune. Coragio, bully-monster,
260   coragio!
TRINCULO: If these be true spies which I wear in my head, here's
a goodly sight.
CALIBAN: O Setebos, these be brave spirits indeed!
How fine my master is! I am afraid
265   He will chastise me.
SEBASTIAN: Ha, ha!
What things are these, my lord, Antonio?
Will money buy 'em?
ANTONIO: Very like. One of them
Is a plain fish, and no doubt marketable.
270   PROSPERO: Mark but the badges of these men, my lords,
Then say if they be true. This misshapen knave,
His mother was a witch, and one so strong
That could control the moon, make flows and ebbs,
And deal in her command without her power.
275   These three have robb'd me; and this demi-devil —
For he's a bastard one — had plotted with them
To take my life. Two of these fellows you
Must know and own; this thing of darkness I
Acknowledge mine.

CALIBAN: I shall be pinch'd to death.
ALONSO: Is not this Stephano, my drunken butler?   280
SEBASTIAN: He is drunk now. Where had he wine?
ALONSO: And Trinculo is reeling ripe. Where should they
Find this grand liquor that hath gilded 'em?
How cam'st thou in this pickle?
TRINCULO: I have been in such a pickle since I saw you last that,   285
I fear me, will never out of my bones. I shall not fear fly-
blowing.
SEBASTIAN: Why, how now, Stephano?
STEPHANO: O, touch me not! I am not Stephano, but a
cramp.   290
PROSPERO: You'd be king o' the isle, sirrah?
STEPHANO: I should have been a sore one then.
ALONSO: *(Pointing to* CALIBAN.*)* This is a strange thing as e'er I
look'd on.
PROSPERO: He is as disproportion'd in his manners
As in his shape. Go, sirrah, to my cell;   295
Take with you your companions. As you look
To have my pardon, trim it handsomely.
CALIBAN: Ay, that I will; and I'll be wise hereafter
And seek for grace. What a thrice-double ass
Was I to take this drunkard for a god   300
And worship this dull fool!
PROSPERO: Go to; away!
ALONSO: Hence, and bestow your luggage where you found it.
SEBASTIAN: Or stole it, rather.

(Exeunt CALIBAN, STEPHANO, *and* TRINCULO.*)*

PROSPERO: Sir, I invite your Highness and your train
To my poor cell, where you shall take your rest   305
For this one night; which, part of it, I'll waste
With such discourse as, I not doubt, shall make it
Go quick away — the story of my life,
And the particular accidents gone by
Since I came to this isle. And in the morn   310
I'll bring you to your ship, and so to Naples,
Where I have hope to see the nuptial
Of these our dear-belov'd solemnized;
And thence retire me to my Milan, where
Every third thought shall be my grave.
ALONSO: I long   315
To hear the story of your life, which must
Take the ear strangely.
PROSPERO: I'll deliver all;
And promise you calm seas, auspicious gales,
And sail so expeditious that shall catch
Your royal fleet far off. *(Aside to* ARIEL.*)* My Ariel, chick,   320
That is thy charge. Then to the elements
Be free, and fare thou well! — Please you, draw near.

(Exeunt omnes.)

---

240 **Cap'ring to eye** dancing for joy to see   242 **moping** in a daze   246 **conduct** guide, leader   248 **infest** harass, disturb   249 **pick'd** chosen, convenient   250 **single** i.e., by my own human powers   252 **accidents** occurrences   259 **Coragio** courage   259 **bully-monster** gallant monster. (Ironical.)   264 **fine** splendidly attired   270 **badges** emblems of cloth or silver worn on the arms of retainers. (Prospero refers here to the stolen clothes as emblems of their villainy.)   271 **true** honest   274 **deal . . . power** wield the moon's power, either without her authority or beyond her influence   278 **own** recognize, admit as belonging to you

283 **gilded** (1) flushed, made drunk (2) covered with gilt (suggesting the horse-urine)   284 **pickle** (1) fix, predicament (2) pickling brine (in this case, horse urine)   286–287 **fly-blowing** i.e., being fouled by fly-eggs (from which he is saved by being pickled)   291 **sirrah** (Standard form of address to an inferior.)   292 **sore** (1) tyrannical (2) wracked by pain   306 **waste** spend   309 **accidents** occurrences   317 **Take** take effect upon, enchant.   **deliver** declare, relate   322 **draw near** i.e., enter my cell

— EPILOGUE —

Spoken by PROSPERO.

Now my charms are all o'erthrown,
And what strength I have 's mine own,
Which is most faint. Now, 'tis true,
I must be here confin'd by you,
5   Or sent to Naples. Let me not,
Since I have my dukedom got
And pardon'd the deceiver, dwell
In this bare island by your spell,
But release me from my bands
10 With the help of your good hands.

Gentle breath of yours my sails
Must fill, or else my project fails,
Which was to please. Now I want
Spirits to enforce, art to enchant,
And my ending is despair,   15
Unless I be reliev'd by prayer,
Which pierces so that it assaults
Mercy itself and frees all faults.
As you from crimes would pardon'd be,
Let your indulgence set me free.   20

(Exit.)

Epilogue.
9 **bands** bonds   10 **hands** i.e., applause (the noise of which would break the spell of silence)

13 **want** lack   16 **prayer** i.e., Prospero's petition to the audience   17 **assaults** rightfully gains the attention of   18 **frees** obtains forgiveness of   19 **crimes** sins

PHILIP SIDNEY WAS ONE of the preeminent courtiers of his day. He was a familiar figure at the court of Queen Elizabeth I, led an ill-fated military expedition to the Netherlands (where he was fatally wounded), wrote an important sonnet sequence, Astrophil *and* Stella, *and a prose romance,* Arcadia. *His* Apology for Poetry *develops a defense of poets and poetry based on their ability to offer a fictive "golden world," an idealized image of reality that can edify, entertain, and instruct.*

SIR PHILIP SIDNEY
(1554–1586)

FROM ***Apology for Poetry***
(1598)

EDITED BY
FORREST G. ROBINSON

. . . There is no art delivered to mankind that hath not the works of nature for his principal object, without which they could not consist, and on which they so depend, as they become actors and players, as it were, of what nature will have set forth. So doth the astronomer look upon the stars, and by that he seeth, setteth down what order nature hath taken therein. So do the geometrician and arithmetician in their diverse sorts of quantities. So doth the musician in times tell you which by nature agree, which not. The natural philosopher thereon hath his name, and the moral philosopher standeth upon the natural virtues, vices, and passions of man; and follow nature (saith he) therein, and thou shalt not err. The lawyer saith what men have determined; the historian what men have done. The grammarian speaketh only of the rules of speech, and the rhetorician and logician, considering what in nature will soonest prove and persuade, thereon give artificial[1] rules, which still are compassed within the circle of a question, according to the proposed matter. The physician weigheth the nature of a man's body, and the nature of things helpful or hurtful unto it. And the metaphysic, though it be in the second and abstract notions, and therefore be counted supernatural, yet doth he indeed build upon the depth of nature. Only the poet, disdaining to be tied to any such subjection, lifted up with the vigor of his own invention, doth grow in effect another nature, in making things either better than nature bringeth forth, or quite anew, forms such as never were in nature, as the Heroes, Demigods, Cyclops, Chimeras, Furies, and such like; so as he goeth hand in hand with nature, not enclosed within the narrow warrant of her gifts, but freely ranging only within the zodiac of his own wit.

Nature never set forth the earth in so rich tapestry as divers poets have done, neither with pleasant rivers, fruitful trees, sweet smelling flowers, nor whatsoever else may make the too much loved earth more lovely. Her world is brazen, the poets only deliver a golden. . . .

Our tragedies and comedies (not without cause cried out against), observing rules neither of honest civility nor of skillful poetry, excepting *Gorboduc*[2] (again I say, of those that I have seen), which notwithstanding, as it is full of stately speeches and well sounding phrases, climbing to the height of Seneca his[3] style, and as full of notable morality, which it doth most delightfully teach, and so obtain the very end of poesy; yet in troth it is very defectious in the circumstances, which grieveth me, because it might not remain as an exact model of all tragedies. For it is faulty both in place and time, the two necessary companions of all corporal actions. For where the stage should always represent but one place, and the uttermost time presupposed in it should be, both by Aristotle's precept and common reason, but one day, there is both many days and many places inartificially[4] imagined.

But if it be so in *Gorboduc*, how much more in all the rest? where you shall have Asia of the one side, and Afric of the other, and so many other under-kingdoms, that the player, when he cometh in, must ever begin with telling where he is, or else the tale will not be conceived. Now ye shall have three ladies walk to gather flowers, and then we must believe the stage to be a garden. By and by we hear news of shipwreck in the same place, and then we are to blame if we accept it not for a rock. Upon the back of that comes out a hideous monster with fire and smoke, and then the miserable

---

[1]**artificial** humanly contrived, rather than natural
[2]***Gorboduc*** an early English play (first performed in 1562), modelled on the tragedies of Seneca
[3]**Seneca his** Seneca's
[4]**inartificially** artlessly

beholders are bound to take it for a cave. While in the meantime two armies fly in, represented with four swords and bucklers, and then what hard heart will not receive it for a pitched field?

Now of time they are much more liberal, for ordinary it is that two young princes fall in love. After many traverses, she is got with child, delivered of a fair boy, he is lost, groweth a man, falls in love, and is ready to get another child, and all this in two hours' space: which, how absurd it is in sense, even sense may imagine, and art hath taught, and all ancient examples justified, and at this day, the ordinary players in Italy will not err in. Yet will some bring in an example of *Eunuchus* in Terence, that containeth matter of two days, yet far short of twenty years. True it is, and so was it to be played in two days, and so fitted to the time it set forth. And though Plautus hath in one place done amiss, let us hit with him, and not miss with him. But they will say, how then shall we set forth a story which containeth both many places and many times? And do they not know that a tragedy is tied to the laws of poesy, and not of history, not bound to follow the story, but having liberty, either to feign a quite new matter, or to frame the history to the most tragical conveniency? Again, many things may be told which cannot be showed, if they know the difference betwixt reporting and representing. . . .

MIKHAIL BAKHTIN

(1895–1975)

FROM *Rabelais and His World*

(1965)

TRANSLATED BY

HÉLÈNE ISWOLSKY

MIKHAIL BAKHTIN, A MAJOR RUSSIAN PHILOSOPHER, LINGUIST, AND LITERARY THEORIST, SPENT much of his career attempting to subvert the Stalinist oppression of intellectuals in the Soviet Union of the 1930s. His book on Rabelais, written in the 1930s, was published only in 1965. This selection, on the "grotesque body," develops an influential reading of how the body can be used to represent the social order, its dominant classes and its points of resistance. Although Bakhtin developed this reading of the body in connection with Rabelais's novels, it is applicable to the grotesque bodies appearing on the English stage as well—blinded Gloucester, mad Lear, poor Tom, Caliban.

. . . We find at the basis of grotesque imagery a special concept of the body as a whole and of the limits of this whole. The confines between the body and the world and between separate bodies are drawn in the grotesque genre quite differently than in the classic and naturalist images. We have already seen this difference in a number of Rabelaisian images. In the present chapter we must broaden our observations, systematize them, and disclose the sources of Rabelais' grotesque concept of the body.

But let us first have a look at another example cited by Schneegans: the caricature of Napoleon and the exaggeration of the size of his nose. According to Schneegans, the grotesque starts when the exaggeration reaches fantastic dimensions, the human nose being transformed into a snout or beak. We shall not discuss the nature of these caricatures per se; it is but superficial satire, deprived of true grotesque character. We are interested in the theme of the nose itself, which occurs throughout world literature in nearly every language, as well as in abusive and degrading gesticulations. Schneegans correctly points out the grotesque character of the transformation of the human element into an animal one; the combination of human and animal traits is, as we know, one of the most ancient grotesque forms. But the author does not grasp the meaning of the grotesque image of the nose: that it always symbolizes the phallus. Laurent Joubert, the famous sixteenth-century physician and a contemporary of Rabelais, whose theory of laughter we have already mentioned, wrote a book on popular superstitions in medicine.[1] In Part 5, Chapter 6 of this book he speaks of the popular belief that the size and potency of the genital organs can be inferred from the dimensions and form of the nose. Friar John also expresses this belief in his monastic jargon. Such is the usual interpretation of this image in the literature of the Middle Ages and the Renaissance, linked with the popular-festive system. The most widely known example of this symbolism is the famous carnival "Dance of the Noses" of Hans Sachs (*Nasentanz*).

Of all the features of the human face, the nose and mouth play the most important part in the grotesque image of the body; the head, ears, and nose also acquire a grotesque character when they adopt the animal form or that of inanimate objects. The eyes have no part in these comic images; they express an individual, so to speak, self-sufficient human life, which is not essential to the grotesque.

---

[1] Laurent Joubert, *Erreurs populaires et propos vulgaires touchant la médecine et le régime de santé.* Bordeaux, 1579.

The grotesque is interested only in protruding eyes, like the eyes of the stutterer in the scene described earlier. It is looking for that which protrudes from the body, all that seeks to go out beyond the body's confines. Special attention is given to the shoots and branches, to all that prolongs the body and links it to other bodies or to the world outside. Moreover, the bulging eyes manifest a purely bodily tension. But the most important of all human features for the grotesque is the mouth. It dominates all else. The grotesque face is actually reduced to the gaping mouth; the other features are only a frame encasing this wide-open bodily abyss.

The grotesque body, as we have often stressed, is a body in the act of becoming. It is never finished, never completed; it is continually built, created, and builds and creates another body. Moreover, the body swallows the world and is itself swallowed by the world (let us recall the grotesque image in the episode of Gargantua's birth on the feast of cattle-slaughtering). This is why the essential role belongs to those parts of the grotesque body in which it outgrows its own self, transgressing its own body, in which it conceives a new, second body: the bowels and the phallus. These two areas play the leading role in the grotesque image, and it is precisely for this reason that they are predominantly subject to positive exaggeration, to hyperbolization; they can even detach themselves from the body and lead an independent life, for they hide the rest of the body, as something secondary (The nose can also in a way detach itself from the body.) Next to the bowels and the genital organs is the mouth, through which enters the world to be swallowed up. And next is the anus. All these convexities and orifices have a common characteristic; it is within them that the confines between bodies and between the body and the world are overcome: there is an interchange and an interorientation. This is why the main events in the life of the grotesque body, the acts of the bodily drama, take place in this sphere. Eating, drinking, defecation and other elimination (sweating, blowing of the nose, sneezing), as well as copulation, pregnancy, dismemberment, swallowing up by another body — all these acts are performed on the confines of the body and the outer world, or on the confines of the old and new body. In all these events the beginning and end of life are closely linked and interwoven.

Thus the artistic logic of the grotesque image ignores the closed, smooth, and impenetrable surface of the body and retains only its excrescences (sprouts, buds) and orifices, only that which leads beyond the body's limited space or into the body's depths.[2] Mountains and abysses, such is the relief of the grotesque body; or speaking in architectural terms, towers and subterranean passages.

Grotesque images may, of course, present other members, organs and parts of the body (especially dismembered parts), but they play a minor role in the drama. They are never stressed unless they replace a leading image.

Actually, if we consider the grotesque image in its extreme aspect, it never presents an individual body; the image consists of orifices and convexities that present another, newly conceived body. It is a point of transition in a life eternally renewed, the inexhaustible vessel of death and conception.

As we have said, the grotesque ignores the impenetrable surface that closes and limits the body as a separate and completed phenomenon. The grotesque image displays not only the outward but also the inner features of the body: blood, bowels, heart and other organs. The outward and inward features are often merged into one.

We have already sufficiently stressed the fact that grotesque imagery constructs what we might call a double body. In the endless chain of bodily life it retains the parts in which one link joins the other, in which the life of one body is born from the death of the preceding, older one.

Finally, let us point out that the grotesque body is cosmic and universal. It stresses elements common to the entire cosmos: earth, water, fire, air; it is directly related to the sun, to the stars. It contains the signs of the zodiac. It reflects the cosmic hierarchy. This body can merge with various natural phenomena, with mountains, rivers, seas, islands, and continents. It can fill the entire universe.

The grotesque mode of representing the body and bodily life prevailed in art and creative forms of speech over thousands of years. From the point of view of extensive use, this mode of representation still exists today; grotesque forms of the body not only predominate in the art of European peoples but

---

[2]This grotesque logic is also extended to images of nature and of objects in which depths (holes) and convexities are emphasized.

also in their folklore, especially in the comic genre. Moreover, these images predominate in the extra-official life of the people. For example, the theme of mockery and abuse is almost entirely bodily and grotesque. The body that figures in all the expressions of the unofficial speech of the people is the body that fecundates and is fecundated, that gives birth and is born, devours and is devoured, drinks, defecates, is sick and dying. In all languages there is a great number of expressions related to the genital organs, the anus and buttocks, the belly, the mouth and nose. But there are few expressions for the other parts of the body: arms and legs, face, and eyes. Even these comparatively few forms of speech have, in most cases, a narrow, practical character; they are related to the nearby area, determine distance, dimensions, or number. They have no broader, symbolic meaning, nor are they especially expressive. They do not participate in abuse and mockery.

Wherever men laugh and curse, particularly in a familiar environment, their speech is filled with bodily images. The body copulates, defecates, overeats, and men's speech is flooded with genitals, bellies, defecations, urine, disease, noses, mouths, and dismembered parts. Even when the flood is contained by norms of speech, there is still an eruption of these images into literature, especially if the literature is gay or abusive in character. The common human fund of familiar and abusive gesticulations is also based on these sharply defined images.

This boundless ocean of grotesque bodily imagery within time and space extends to all languages, all literatures, and the entire system of gesticulation; in the midst of it the bodily canon of art, belles lettres, and polite conversation of modern times is a tiny island. This limited canon never prevailed in antique literature. In the official literature of European peoples it has existed only for the last four hundred years.

We shall give a brief characterization of the new canon, concerning ourselves less with the pictorial arts than with literature. We shall build this characterization by comparing it to the grotesque conception and bringing out the differences.

The new bodily canon, in all its historic variations and different genres, presents an entirely finished, completed, strictly limited body, which is shown from the outside as something individual. That which protrudes, bulges, sprouts, or branches off (when a body transgresses its limits and a new one begins) is eliminated, hidden, or moderated. All orifices of the body are closed. The basis of the image is the individual, strictly limited mass, the impenetrable façade. The opaque surface and the body's "valleys" acquire an essential meaning as the border of a closed individuality that does not merge with other bodies and with the world. All attributes of the unfinished world are carefully removed, as well as all the signs of its inner life. The verbal norms of official and literary language, determined by the canon, prohibit all that is linked with fecundation, pregnancy, childbirth. There is a sharp line of division between familiar speech and "correct" language. . . .

In the new canon, such parts of the body as the genital organs, the buttocks, belly, nose and mouth cease to play the leading role. Moreover, instead of their original meaning they acquire an exclusiveness; in other words, they convey a merely individual meaning of the life of one single, limited body. The belly, nose, and mouth, are of course retained in the image and cannot be hidden, but in an individual, completed body they either fulfill purely expressive functions (this is true of the mouth only) or the functions of characterization and individualization. There is no symbolic, broad meaning whatever in the organs of this body. If they are not interpreted as a characterization and an expressive feature, they are referred to on the merely practical level in brief explanatory comments. Generally speaking, all that does not contain an element of characterization in the literary image is reduced to a simple bodily remark added to speech or action.

In the modern image of the individual body, sexual life, eating, drinking, and defecation have radically changed their meaning: they have been transferred to the private and psychological level where their connotation becomes narrow and specific, torn away from the direct relation to the life of society and to the cosmic whole. In this new connotation they can no longer carry on their former philosophical functions.

In the new bodily canon the leading role is attributed to the individually characteristic and expressive parts of the body: the head, face, eyes, lips, to the muscular system, and to the place of the body in the external world. The exact position and movements of this finished body in the finished outside world are brought out, so that the limits between them are not weakened.

The body of the new canon is merely one body; no signs of duality have been left. It is self-sufficient and speaks in its name alone. All that happens within it concerns it alone, that is, only the individual, closed sphere. Therefore, all the events taking place within it acquire one single meaning: death is only death, it never coincides with birth; old age is torn away from youth; blows merely hurt, without assisting an act of birth. All actions and events are interpreted on the level of a single, individual life. They are enclosed within the limits of the same body, limits that are the absolute beginning and end and can never meet.

In the grotesque body, on the contrary, death brings nothing to an end, for it does not concern the ancestral body, which is renewed in the next generation. The events of the grotesque sphere are always developed on the boundary dividing one body from the other and, as it were, at their points of intersection. One body offers its death, the other its birth, but they are merged in a two-bodied image.

In the new canon the duality of the body is preserved only in one theme, a pale reflection of its former dual nature. This is the theme of nursing a child.[3] But the image of the mother and the child is strictly individualized and closed, the line of demarcation cannot be removed. This is a completely new phase of the artistic conception of bodily interaction.

Finally, the new canon is completely alien to hyperbolization. The individualized image has no place for it. All that is permitted is a certain accentuation of expressive and characterized features. The severance of the organs from the body or their independent existence is no longer permitted.

We have roughly sketched the basic outlines of the modern canon, as they generally appear in the norms of literature and speech.[4] . . .

---

[3] Let us recall Goethe's remarks as reported by Eckermann in "Conversations with Goethe" concerning Correggio's painting "The Weaning of a Child." Goethe is attracted by the duality of the image, preserved in an attenuated form.

[4] Similar classical concepts of the body form the basis of the new canon of behavior. Good education demands: not to place the elbows on the table, to walk without protruding the shoulder blades or swinging the hips, to hold in the abdomen, to eat without loud chewing, not to snort and pant, to keep the mouth shut, etc.; in other words, to close up and limit the body's confines and to smooth the bulges. It is interesting to trace the struggle of the grotesque and classical concept in the history of dress and fashion. Even more interesting is this struggle in the history of dance.

The scholar and critic Alvin B. Kernan has written widely on literature and society from Shakespeare's era to the present time. His many books include The Cankered Muse, The Imaginary Library, *and* The Death of Literature. *In* The Playwright as Magician, *Kernan examines how Shakespeare's plays reflect on the nature and limitations of drama and theater.*

ALVIN B. KERNAN
FROM *The Playwright as Magician*
(1979)

. . . It is a measure of Shakespeare's practical and theoretical commitment to the theater, and the full-scale involvement with the world at every level that it represented, that he did not simply resolve the artistic tension his plays manifest either by scornfully abandoning the public theater as an impossible setting for true art, as Jonson did to some degree, or by forgetting any artistic concerns and cynically providing, as Beaumont and Fletcher did, the entertainment commodity for which the theater of the day seemed most easily suited.

Shakespeare seems not to have conceived of himself as a romantic artist caught in and betrayed by his medium, but as an artist working in the theatrical medium; and while the theater was the source of severe difficulties, he never treated it as mere nuisance but as the necessary condition of his art and the revelation of genuine and important aesthetic issues. The Dark Lady of the *Sonnets* remains to the end a true image of his own complex view throughout his career of the muse of the theater, at once attractive and repellent, sensuous, changeable, mysterious, morally ambivalent, illicit, exciting, and trivial. But like one of the many great figures who followed in the Dark Lady's entourage, age did not wither nor custom stale her infinite variety, and the poet is hers utterly, until he steps forward and begs his audience for their mercy to release him from the "bare island" of the stage.

The image of the poet in the theater who at last emerges as the magician Prospero reflects the same divided and distinguished attitudes toward the theater as the Dark Lady. Earlier Renaissance images of the poet as a religious and secular savior, or as a courtier in the palace of a great prince, are relatively straightforward in the claims they make for the poet and his social function, as befits artists who are supported by society and express its values. But an exiled duke, practicing an illicit art on an isolated and barren island, expresses the ironic situation of the professional playwright working in the public theater. A magician is at once a mere trickster or sleight-of-hand artist and a philosopher who communicates with and commands spirits who control the universe.

The irony would have been somewhat sharper in Shakespeare's time than in our own, for while, as Keith Thomas's magisterial book, *Religion and the Decline of Magic*, makes clear, there was considerable skepticism about magic, there was also enough belief in it to justify statutes against magical practices and discussions about its efficacy on the part of theologians and kings. Shakespeare was careful, as many studies of *The Tempest* have shown,[1] to associate his magician with the most powerful and intellectually respectable tradition of magic, the Hermetic or Neoplatonic system of white magic, in which the name of Ariel appears as a powerful spirit. Prospero is no village wizard, no Mother Bombie, nor is he a mere "cunning man" like Doctor Subtle, the alchemist and astrologer in Jonson's *Alchemist*—probably played in the same theatrical season as *The Tempest* by Shakespeare's company—who also contrives and manages a large number of theatrical pretenses and illusions, all designed to delude and swindle his audience.[2] Nor does Prospero have to sell his soul as Faustus does in order to lure devils to him in order to acquire the powers of black magic.

Prospero is, rather, the practitioner of a "sacerdotal science," as Curry calls it, with a long and respectable tradition deriving from such philosophers as Iamblichus and Proclus, Ficino and Agrippa, which enabled magicians to deal with spirits by way of command, not by supplication or the barter of souls. Prospero's powers are derived from his deep reading and his experience, and they are exercised partly for revenge but primarily for the beneficent purpose of marrying off his daughter and bringing his enemies to repentance for their earlier crimes. His magic, as Robert West points out, "is not natural magic, or mathematical magic or the magic of fascination, but predominantly spirit magic,"[3] and the spirits he commands are actors. Instead of casting figures, reciting incantations, or uttering spells, he commands his spirit-actors to sing songs, stage tempests, and perform masques which reveal the mysteries of what West, with appropriate caution, calls "outerness."

Shakespeare is following Marlowe in using the magician to prefigure the playwright, but Marlowe makes of the theater a form of black magic, instrumented by devils over whom the playwright has limited control and to whom he must sell his soul in return for a few shabby and unsatisfactory illusions. It is a measure of Shakespeare's greater confidence in the theater that his playwright-magician, like that earlier magical producer Oberon, commands "spirits of another sort" and uses his power to create majestic visions and to effect moral reformation within the magic circle he draws where all "stand charmed." Yet the Marlovian irony about the theater is still operative in *The Tempest*, where Prospero refers to his spirit-actors as "rabble," speaks of his leading actor, Ariel, as a "malignant thing," calls his great masque only "some vanity of mine art," and in the end, like Faustus, repents, drowns his book, and buries his staff in order to go, not to hell, but back to Milan.

Prospero's spirit magic, while not criminal, was still an unlawful art, and so designated in the statutes; and it was generally understood to be ultimately limited as well:

> No magician, however "white," however masterful, could be supposed to rule in the hierarchy of being all the way to its top. At some stage he had to supplicate, and unless he was a "holy magician" like the Apostles, this supplication was directed well short of Christian Godhead.[4]

So short, in fact, in the theater, that in Prospero's epilogue the supplication is directed to the audience, on whose mercy and indulgence the playwright-magician, wanting "Spirits to enforce, art to enchant," is entirely dependent for his release from the "bare island" of the stage.

---

[1] The most thorough and learned treatment of this subject appears in an essay on *The Tempest* by Walter Clyde Curry in his *Shakespeare's Philosophical Patterns* (Baton Rouge: Louisiana State University Press, 1937.)

[2] The similarities and differences of the two plays and the two magicians are explored in detail by Harry Levin, "Two Magian Comedies: *The Tempest* and *The Alchemist*," in *Shakespeare and the Revolution of the Times* (New York: Oxford University Press, 1976), pp. 210–31.

[3] *Shakespeare and the Outer Mystery* (Lexington: University of Kentucky Press, 1968), p. 84.

[4] *Ibid.*, p. 86.

The power to command spirits and complete dependence on the indulgence of an audience, the "potent art" which can open graves and yet is no more than a mere "vanity," the creation of harmonious visions of the gods themselves and a mere desire to please — these are the contradictions which Shakespeare's image of the playwright-magician holds in tension. In the end the theater seems to have been paradoxical for him: at one and the same time, only a transitory illusion and an image of transcendent reality, a trick and a vision, mere entertainment and a means of directing life to meaningful ends.

The paradox, represented by the image of the poet as magician, of art as mere illusion and high vision, was forced upon Shakespeare by an irresolvable conflict between this Renaissance conception of poetry as a superior kind of truth and his material situation as a professional playwright working in the public theater where plays were only transitory shows. Every aspect of that theater, from his own professional status as a provider of entertainment for pay to the structure of the playhouse itself, reminded him of the contingency of his own art within a reality more problematic and more durable than itself. He might outflank it, as he does in *Hamlet* and *The Tempest*, by showing the theater latent in all life prior to any of its forms or rationalizations, but the very plays which reveal the "Myth of the Cosmic Drama" are subject to the reality of the theater and the world and depend for their effects on actors like Bottom, audiences like Claudius and his court, and a few properties like a cushion for a crown and a jointstool for a throne. In the end, even Prospero must turn to this audience and petition them to free him to return to the real world of Milan (or Stratford). "The best in this kind are but shadows; and the worst are no worse, if imagination amend them," but the playwright, master magician though he may be, cannot finally command but must supplicate the world for that imaginative response on which his art depends.

While the particular conditions of the Elizabethan and Jacobean theater were unique to that particular time and place, they anticipate and define the circumstances in which the many subsequent writers who earned their livings as professionals writing for the public have had to work. The Elizabethan playwrights were the first modern writers for whom the circumstances of a public art dependent in various ways on complex forces outside itself made the status of the poet problematic and the relationship of his fictions to reality questionable. Since Shakespeare, many different images of the poet have appeared which have attempted to resolve the art-reality conflict inherent in a public art by eliminating one of the terms of the conflict. If Milton and the long line of romantic poets emphasized art and vision over a mundane reality, then the Doctor Johnson, the King of Grub Street created by Samuel Johnson and Boswell, who declared that "he could write the Life of a Broomstick" if necessary, emphasized the involvement of the poet with the marketplace and the given social world.

But the image of the poet as magician, which Shakespeare did not invent but fixed and stabilized, holds in tension both the belief of the poets that their art commands spirits, and the view of a rationalistic and scientific society that art is mere trivial make-believe and an entertainment commodity manufactured for pay. The magician has therefore remained one of the dominant images of the poet in the modern world, appearing in such various displaced, and sometimes debased, forms as Goethe's Faust, Melville's confidence man, Joyce's fabulous artificer, Yeats's Irish bards and Byzantine craftsmen, Wilde's liar, Kafka's sideshow freak, Mann's magicians, Borges's contrivers of labyrinths, and Hesse's child who felt that "everything was full of reality and everything was full of magic, the two grew confidently side by side, both of them belonged to me."[5]

---

[5]Hermann Hesse, "Childhood of the Magician," in *Autobiographical Writings*, ed. Theodore Ziolkowski, trans. Denver Lindley (New York: Farrar, Straus and Giroux, 1972), p. 7.

CONTEMPORARY PERSPECTIVES

IN THIS ARTICLE, THE feminist scholar Lynda Boose examines the relationship between gender and power in the Elizabethan family and the rituals that govern the transfer of women in Shakespeare's plays. Drawing on the methods of social anthropology, Boose provides a way of describing how masculine power is enacted in society through the disposition of women as a kind of property.

LYNDA E. BOOSE

FROM *"The Father and the Bride in Shakespeare"* (1982)

The aristocratic family of Shakespeare's England was, according to social historian Lawrence Stone, "patrilinear, primogenitural, and patriarchal." Parent-child relations were in general remote and formal, singularly lacking in affective bonds and governed solely by a paternal authoritarianism through which the "husband and father lorded it over his wife and children with the quasi-authority of a despot" (*Crisis* 271). Stone characterizes the society of the sixteenth and early seventeenth centuries as one in which "a majority of individuals . . . found it very difficult to establish close emotional ties to any other person" (*Family* 99)[1] and views the nuclear family as a burdensome social unit, valued only for its ability to provide the means of patrilineal descent. Second and third sons counted for little and daughters for even less. A younger son could, it is true, be kept around as a "walking sperm bank in case the elder son died childless," but daughters "were often unwanted and might be regarded as no more than a tiresome drain on the economic resources of the family" (Stone, *Family* 88, 112).[2]

Various Elizabethan documents, official and unofficial, that comment on family relations support Stone's hypothesis of the absence of affect.[3] Yet were we to turn from Stone's conclusions to those we might draw from Shakespeare's plays, the disparity of implication — especially if we assume that the plays to some extent mirror the life around them — must strike us as significant. Shakespeare's dramas consistently explore affective family dynamics with an intensity that justifies the growing inference among Shakespearean scholars that the plays may be primarily "about" family relations and only secondarily about the macrocosm of the body politic.[4] Not the absence of affect but the possessive overabundance of it is the force that both defines and threatens the family in Shakespeare. When we measure Stone's assertions against the Shakespeare canon, the plays must seem startlingly ahistorical in focusing on what would seem to have been the least valued relationship of all: that between father and daughter.

While father and son appear slightly more often in the canon, figuring in twenty-three plays, father and daughter appear in twenty-one dramas and in one narrative poem. As different as these father-daughter plays are, they have one thing in common: almost without exception the relationships they depict depend on significant underlying substructures of ritual. Shakespeare apparently created his dramatic mirrors not solely from the economic and social realities that historians infer as having dictated family behavior but from archetypal models, psychological in import and ritual in expression. And the particular ritual model on which Shakespeare most frequently drew for the father-daughter relationship was the marriage ceremony.[5]

In an influential study of the sequential order or "relative positions within ceremonial wholes," Arnold van Gennep isolated three phases in ritual enactment that always recur in the same underlying arrangement and that form, in concert, "the pattern of the rites of passage": separation, transition, and reincorporation.[6] The church marriage service — as familiar to a modern audience as it was to Shakespeare's — contains all three phases. When considered by itself, it is basically a separation rite preceding the transitional phase of consummation and culminating in the incorporation of a new family unit. In Hegelian terms, the ceremonial activities associated with marriage move from thesis through antithesis to synthesis; the anarchic release to fertility is positioned between two phases of relative stasis. The ritual enables society to allow for a limited transgression of its otherwise universal taboo against human eroticism. Its middle movement is the dangerous phase of transition and transgression; its conclusion, the controlled reincorporation into the stability of family. But before the licensed transgression can take place — the transgression that generates the stability and continuity of society itself — the ritual must separate the sanctified celebrants from the sterile forces of social interdiction. The marriage ritual is thus a pattern of and for the community that surrounds it, as well as a rite of passage of and for the individuals who enact it. It serves as an especially effective substructure for the father-daughter relation because within its pattern lies the paradigm of all the conflicts that define this bond at its liminal moment of severance. The ceremony ritualizes two particularly significant events: a daughter and a son are being incorporated into a new family unit, an act that explicitly breaks down the boundaries of two previously existing families; yet, at the same time, the bonds being dissolved, particularly those between father and daughter, are being memorialized and thus, paradoxically, reasserted. In early comedies like *The Taming of the Shrew*, Shakespeare followed the Roman design of using the father of the young male lover as the *senex iratus*, a blocking figure to be circumvented. The mature comedies, tragedies, and romances reconstruct the problems of family bonds, filial obedience, and paternal possessiveness around the father and daughter, the relation put into focus by the marriage ceremony. When marriage activities are viewed from the perspective of their ritual implications, the bride and groom are not joined until the transitional phase of the wedding-night consummation; before that, a marriage may be annulled. What the church service is actually all about is the separation of the daughter from the interdicting father.

The wedding ceremony of Western tradition has always recognized the preeminence of the father-daughter bond. Until the thirteenth century, when the church at last managed to gain control of marriage law, marriage was considered primarily a private contract between two families concerning property exchange. The validity and legality of matrimony rested on the *consensus nuptialis* and the property contract, a situation that set up a potential for conflict by posing the mutual consent of the two children, who owed absolute obedience to their parents, against the desires of their families, who must agree beforehand to the contract governing property exchange. However true it was that the couple's willing consent was necessary for valid matrimony and however vociferously the official conduct books urged parents to consider the compatibility of the match, fathers like Cymbeline, Egeus, and Baptista feel perfectly free to disregard these requirements. Although lack of parental consent did not affect the validity of a marriage and, after 1604, affected the legality only when a minor was involved,[7] the family control over the dowry was a powerful psychological as well as economic weapon. Fathers like Capulet, Lear, and Brabantio depend on threats of disinheritance to coerce their children. When their daughters nonetheless wed without the paternal blessing, the marriages are adversely affected not because any legal statutes have been breached but because the ritual base of marriage has been circumvented and the psychological separation of daughter from father thus rendered incomplete. For in Shakespeare's time—as in our own—the ceremony acknowledged the special bond between father and daughter and the need for the power of ritual to release the daughter from its hold.

As specified in the 1559 *Book of Common Prayer*, the marriage ritual enjoins that the father (or, in his absence, the legal guardian)[8] deliver his daughter to the altar, stand by her in mute testimony that there are no impediments to her marriage, and then witness her pledge henceforth to forsake all others and "obey and serve, love honor and keep" the man who stands at her other side. To the priest's question, "Who giveth this woman to be married unto this man?"—a question that dates in English tradition back to the York manual (*Book of Common Prayer* 290–99; 408, n.)—the father must silently respond by physically relinquishing his daughter, only to watch the priest place her right hand into the possession of another man. Following this expressly physical symbolic transfer, the father's role in his daughter's life is ended; custom dictates that he now leave the stage, resign his active part in the rite, and become a mere observer. After he has withdrawn, the couple plight their troths, and the groom receives the ring, again from the priest. Taking the bride's hand into his, the groom places the ring on her finger with the words, "With this ring I thee wed, with my body I thee worship, and with all my worldly goods I thee endow," thus solemnizing the transfer in its legal, physical and material aspects.[9]

Before us we have a tableau paradigmatic of the problematic father-daughter relation: decked in the symbols of virginity, the bride stands at the altar between her father and husband, pulled as it were between the two important male figures in her life. To resolve the implied dilemma, the force of the priest and the community presides over and compels the transfer of an untouched daughter into the physical possession of a male whom the ceremony authorizes both as the invested successor to the father's authority and as the sanctified transgressor of prohibitions that the father has been compelled to observe. [10] By making the father transfer his intact daughter to the priest in testimony that he knows of no impediments to her lawful union, the service not only reaffirms the taboo against incest but implicitly levels the full weight of that taboo on the relationship between father and daughter. The groom's family does not enter into the archetypal dynamics going on at this altar except through the priest's reference to marriage as the cause why a man "shall leave father and mother and shall be joined unto his wife." The mother of the bride is a wholly excluded figure — as indeed she is throughout almost the entire Shakespeare canon. Only the father must act out, must dramatize his loss before the audience of the community. Within the ritual circumscription, the father is compelled to give his daughter to a rival male; and as Georges Bataille comments:

> The gift itself is a renunciation . . . Marriage is a matter less for the partners than for the man who gives the woman away, the man whether father or brother who might have freely enjoyed the woman, daughter or sister, yet who bestows her on someone else. This gift is perhaps a substitute for the sexual act; for the exuberance of giving has a significance akin to that of the act itself; it is also a spending of resources. [11]

By playing out his role in the wedding ceremony, the father implicitly gives the blessing that licenses the daughter's deliverance from family bonds that might otherwise become a kind of bondage. Hence in A Midsummer Night's Dream, a play centered on marriage, the intransigent father Egeus, supported by the king-father figure Theseus, poses a threat that must be converted to a blessing to ensure the comic solution. In Love's Labor's Lost, the sudden death of the Princess' father, who is likewise the king-father figure for all the French ladies, prevents the necessary blessing, thus cutting sharply across the movement toward comic resolution and postponing the happy ending. In plots constructed around a daughter without a father, the absent father frequently assumes special dramatic prominence. This absence felt almost as a presence may well contribute to the general unease and unresolved tensions emanating from the three "problem plays," for Helena, Isabella, and Cressida are all daughters severed from their fathers. . . .

In tragedies like Lear, Othello, and Romeo and Juliet, the father's failure to act out his required role has a special significance, one that we can best apprehend by looking not at the logic of causal narrative progression but at the threat implied by the violation of ritual. . . .

Through the use of ceremonial substructures, Shakespeare invokes a sacramentality, a context of sacredness, for a certain moment and space within the play. Such structures temporally and spatially set the ritualized moments away from the undifferentiated profane events of the drama. But once a ritual has been invoked, has in effect drawn a circle of archetypal reference around the moment and space, any events from the nonsacramental surrounding world that interrupt or counter its prescribed direction take on special, portentous significance. [12] By interrupting or converting the invoked ritual to parody, such profane invasions rupture its sacramental context. . . .

The opening scene of King Lear, however, is infused with the additional tension of colliding, incompatible ritual structures: the attempt of the man who is both king and father to substitute the illegitimate transfer of his kingdom for the legitimate one of his daughter.

In King Lear, the father's grudging recognition of the need to confer his daughter on younger strengths while he unburdened crawls toward death should be understood as the basal structure underlying his divestiture of his kingdom. Lear has called his court together in the opening scene because he must at last face the postponed reckoning with Cordelia's two princely suitors, who "Long in our court have made their amorous sojourn, / And here are to be answer'd" (1.1.47–48). But instead of justly relinquishing his daughter, Lear tries to effect a substitution of paternal divestitures: he portions out his kingdom as his "daughters' several dowers," attaching to Cordelia's share a stipulation designed to thwart her separation. In substituting his public paternity for his private one, the inherently indivisible entity for the one that biologically must divide and recombine, Lear violates both his kingly role in the hierarchical universe and his domestic one in the family. Nor is it accident — as it was in Hamlet 5.1 — that brings these two incompatible rituals into collision in Lear 1.1. It is the willful action of the king and father, the lawgiver and protector of both domain and family, that is fully responsible for this explosion of chaos.

Yet of course Lear's bequest of his realm is in no way an unconditional transfer of the kingdom from one rulership to another. Instead, Lear wants to retain the dominion he theoretically casts off and to "manage those authorities/That he hath given away" (1.3.17–18). Likewise, the bequest of his daughter is actually an attempt to keep her, a motive betrayed by the very words he uses. When he *dis*claims "all my paternal care" and orders Cordelia "as a stranger to my heart and me/Hold thee from this for ever" (113, 115–16), his verb holds to his heart rather than expels from it the daughter he says is "adopted to our hate" (203), another verbal usage that betrays his retentive motives. His disastrous attempts to keep the two dominions he sheds are structurally linked through the parodic divestiture of his kingdom as dowry. In recognition of the family's economic interest in marriage, the terms of sixteenth-century dowries were required to be fully fixed before the wedding, thus making the property settlement a precondition for the wedding.[13] But Lear the father will not freely give his daughter her endowment unless she purchases it with pledges that would nullify those required by the wedding ceremony. If she will not love him all, she will mar her fortunes, lose her dowry, and thus forfeit the symbolic separation. And yet, as she asserts, she cannot marry if she loves her father all. The circularity of Lear's proposition frustrates the ritual phase of separation: by disinheriting Cordelia, Lear casts her away not to let her go but to prevent her from going. In Lévi-Strauss' terms, Lear has to give up Cordelia because the father must obey the basic social rule of reciprocity, which has a necessarily communal effect, functioning as a "distribution to undo excess." Lear's refusal is likewise communal in its effect, and it helps create the universe that he has "ta'en too little care of."

Insofar as Burgundy's suit is concerned, Lear's quantitatively constructed presumption works. Playing the mime priest and intentionally desecrating the sacramental ritual question he imitates, Lear asks the first bridegroom-candidate:

> Will you, with those infirmities she owes,
> Unfriended, new adopted to our hate,
> Dow'r'd with our curse, and stranger'd with our oath,
> Take her, or leave her?   (1.1.202–05)

Burgundy's hedged response is what Lear anticipates—this suitor will gladly "take Cordelia by the hand" only if Lear will give "but that portion which yourself propos'd" (243, 242). Shrewdly intuiting that France cannot be dissuaded by so quantitative a reason as "her price is fallen," Lear then adopts a strategy based on qualitative assumptions in his attempt to discourage the rival he most greatly fears. Insisting to France that

> For you, great King
> I would not from your love make such a stray
> To match you where I hate; therefore beseech you
> T'avert your liking a more worthier way   (208–11)

Lear tries to avoid even making the required ritual offer. By calling his own daughter "a wretch whom Nature is asham'd/Almost t'acknowledge hers" (212–13), Lear implies by innuendo the existence of some unnatural impediment in Cordelia that would make her unfit to marry and would thus prevent her separation. Effectively, the scene presents an altar tableau much like that in *Much Ado*, with a bride being publicly pronounced unfit for marriage. In *Lear*, however, it is the father rather than the groom who defames the character of the bride, and his motives are to retain her rather than to reject her. In this violated ceremony, the slandered daughter—instead of fainting—staunchly denies the alleged impediments by demanding that her accuser "make known/It is no vicious blot . . . No unchaste action, or dishonored step,/That hath deprived me of your grace and favor" (226–29). And here the groom himself takes up the role implicit in his vows, defending Cordelia's suborned virtue by his statement that to believe Lear's slanders would require "a faith that reason without mira-cle/Should never plant in me" (222–23). The physical separation of the daughter from the father is finally achieved only by France's perception that "this unpriz'd precious maid . . . is herself a dowry" (259, 241); France recognizes the qualitative meaning of the dowry that Burgundy could only under-stand quantitatively.

EDITOR'S NOTE: Boose's citations are to a different edition of Shakespeare plays than is used in this anthology; act, scene, and line references will differ from those here.

In Cordelia's almost archetypal definition of a daughter's proper loyalties (1.1.95–104), Shakespeare uses a pun to link the fundamental predicament of the daughter—held under the aegis of the father—to its only possible resolution in the marriage troth: "That lord whose hand must take my plight shall carry/Half my love with him" (101–02), says Cordelia. When France later addresses his bride as "Fairest Cordelia, that art most rich being poor,/Most choice forsaken, and most lov'd despis'd" (250–51), he echoes the husband's traditional pledge to love "for richer, for poorer" the daughter who has "forsaken all others." And France himself then endows Lear's "dow'rless daughter" with all his worldly goods by making her "queen of us, of ours, and our fair France" (256–57). His statement "Be it lawful I take up what's cast away" (253) even suggests a buried stage direction through its implied allusion to the traditional conclusion of the *consensus nuptialis* as explained in the Sarum and York manuals: the moment when the bride, in token of receiving a dowry of land from her husband, prostrates herself at her husband's feet and he responds by lifting her up again (*Rathen* 36, Legg 190, Howard 306–07).

The visual and verbal texts of this important opening scene allude to the separation phase of the marriage ritual; the ritual features are emphasized because here, unlike the similar scene in *Othello*, the daughter's right to choose a husband she loves is not at issue. Because the ritual is sacred, Cordelia dispassionately refuses to follow her sisters in prostituting it. Lear, in contrast, passionately destroys his kingdom in order to thwart the fixed movement of the ritual pattern and to convert the pattern's linear progression away from the father into a circular return to him.[14] The discord his violation engenders continues to be projected through accumulating ritual substructures: in a parody of giving his daughter's hand, Lear instead gives her "father's heart from her" (126); in a parody of the ring rite, Lear takes the golden round uniting king and country and parts it, an act that both dramatizes the consequences of dividing his realm and demonstrates the anguish he feels at losing his daughter to a husband.

Once Lear has shattered the invoked sacred space by collapsing two incompatible rituals into it, he shatters also all claims to paternal authority. From this scene onward, the question of Lear's paternal relation to his daughters and his kingdom pervades the drama through the King's ceremonial invocations of sterility against the daughters he has generated and the land he has ruled. In the prototype of a harmonious wedding that concludes *As You Like It*, Hymen—who "peoples every town"—defines Duke Senior's correct paternal role as that of the exogamous giver of the daughter created in heaven:

> Hymen from heaven brought her,
>   Yea, brought her hither,
> That thou mightst join her hand with his
> Whose heart within his bosom is.   (5.4.112–15)[15]

Hymen characterizes the generating of children as a gift from heaven, an essential spending of the self designed to increase the world. By contrast, Lear's image of the father is the "barbarous Scythian,/Or he that makes his generation messes/To gorge his appetite" (1.1.116–18). The definition is opposite to the very character of ritual. It precludes the possibility of transformation, for the father devours the flesh he begets. Here, generation becomes primarily an autogamous act, a retention and recycling of the procreative energies, which become mere extensions of private appetite feeding on its own production. The unnatural appetite of the father devouring his paternity is implicit even in the motive Lear reveals behind his plan to set his rest on Cordelia's "kind nursery" (124), an image in which the father pictures himself as an infant nursing from his daughter. The implied relationship is unnatural because it allows the father to deflect his original incestuous passions into Oedipal ones, thus effecting a newly incestuous proximity to the daughter, from whom the marriage ritual is designed to detach him. And when this form of appetite is thwarted by France's intervention, Lear effects yet another substitution of state for daughter: having ordered Cornwall and Albany to "digest the third" part of his kingdom, he and his gluttonous knights proceed to feed off it and through their "Epicurism and lust/Make . . . it more like a tavern or a brothel/Than a grac'd palace" (1.4.244–46). Compelled by nature to give up his daughter, he unnaturally gives up his kingdom; when his appetites cannot feed on her, they instead devour the paternity of his land.

The father devouring his own flesh is the monstrous extension of the circular terms of Lear's dowry proposal. The image belongs not only to the play's pervasive cluster of monsters from the deep but also to its dominant spatial pattern of circularity. Within both the narrative movement and the repeated spatial structure inside the drama, the father's retentive passions deny the child's rite of passage. When Cordelia departs from the father's realm for a new life in her husband's, ostensibly fulfilling the ritual separation, the journey is condemned to futility at its outset, for Cordelia departs dowered with Lear's curse: "Without our grace, our love, our benison" (1.1.265). Although the bride and groom have exchanged vows, the denial of the father's blessing renders the separation incomplete and the daughter's future blighted. Cordelia, like Rosalind, must therefore return to be reincorporated with her father before she can undergo the ritual severance that will enable her to progress. She thus chooses father over husband, returning to Lear to ask his blessing: "look upon me, sir, / And hold your hand in benediction o'er me" (4.7.56–57). In lines that indicate how futile the attempt at incorporation has been when the precedent rites of passage have been perverted, Cordelia asserts, "O dear father, / It is thy business that I go about" (4.4.23–24), and characterizes her life with France as having been one of constant mourning for the father to whom she is still bound.

Shakespeare rewrote the source play *Leir* to make Cordelia remain in England alone (rather than with France at her side) to fight, lose, and die with her father, a revision that vividly illustrates the tragic failure of the family unit to divide, recombine, and regenerate. The only respite from pain the tragedy offers is the beauty of Lear's reunion with Cordelia, but that reunion takes place at the cost of both the daughter's life and the future life of the family. And for all the poignancy of this reunion, the father's intransigence—which in this play both initiates and conditions the tragedy—remains unchanged: it is still writ large in his fantasy that he and his daughter will be forever imprisoned together like birds in a cage. [16] At the end of the play, excluding any thought of Cordelia's new life with France, Lear focuses solely on the father-daughter merger, which he joyfully envisions enclosed in a perpetuity where no interlopers—short of a divine messenger—can threaten it: "He that parts us shall bring a brand from heaven, / And fire us hence like foxes" (5.3.22–23). The rejoining is the precise opposite of that in *As You Like It*. To Rosalind's question, "if I bring in your Rosalind, / You will bestow her on Orlando here?" Duke Senior responds, "That would I, had I kingdoms to give with her" (*AYL* 5.4.6–7, 8). In the Duke's characterization of Orlando's newly received endowment as "a potent Dukedom" (5.4.169), the implied fertility of both kingdom and family is ensured through the father's submission to the necessary movement of ritual. In *King Lear*, the father who imagined that he "gave his daughters all" extracts from his daughter at the end of the play the same price he demanded in the opening scene—that she love her father all. The play's tragic circles find their counterpart in its ritual movements. Cordelia returns to her father, and the final scene stages the most sterile of altar tableaux: a dead father with his three dead daughters, the wheel having come full circle back to the opening scene of the play. Initially barren of mothers, the play concludes with the death of all the fathers and all the daughters; the only figures who survive to emphasize the sterility of the final tableau are Albany, a widower, and Edgar, an unmarried son. . . .

. . . [F]requently throughout the canon, Shakespeare draws on ritual substructures for the conclusions of his plays. Within these patterns, tragedy ends with an emphasis on broken or inverted ritual designs; comedy ends with the scattered elements of ritual regrouped and correctly enacted. And in the four late romances—plays in which oracular prophecies and the sudden descent of divine beings constantly reshape the linear narrative—the shattered human world, through obsessive reenactments of broken rituals, strives to recapture what has been lost and thus to reconnect itself with the sacred world of its origins. The design closely approximates Mircea Eliade's description of the ritual process as humanity's attempt to effect the "myth of the eternal return." Within these late plays, the declining world of inflexible paternal authority rediscovers a redemptive teleology through the ritualized reclamation of that particular bond which could only be viewed as a liability to the family's prospects for economic and patrilineal prosperity. In *The Winter's Tale*, the murderous wrath Leontes directs against his innocent wife and daughter is punished by the immediately conjunctive death of the son he imagines will carry his lineal posterity. Only when he comes to value "that which has been lost"—the daughter Perdita, who is a matrilineal rather than a patrilineal extension—is Leontes allowed the partial restitution implicit in his adoption of Florizel. And even this compensation is made possible only through the return and affirmation of the hitherto unvalued daughter. . . .

The father-daughter relation in *The Tempest*, the last of the romances, is somewhat similar, in that Miranda, like Perdita [in *The Winter's Tale*] and Marina [in *Pericles*], is the force that preserves her father. Here, however, there is no mother for Prospero to rediscover when he at last gives up his daughter and abandons his island. Instead of the miraculous reunion with a lost daughter as the force that suddenly resuscitates life, *The Tempest* shows us a father who has never lost his child and whose concern for her welfare has always given him his will to live. And of all the Shakespearean fathers of daughters, Prospero is undoubtedly the most successful in enacting his proper role. His purpose, much like that defined by Hymen in *As You Like It*, has always been to educate, discipline, and nurture Miranda so that he can set her free, as he does Ariel. Prospero understands the need to play the father's mock role as the barrier to young love, the need to make Ferdinand realize the value of his daughter through laboring to earn her lest "too light winning/Make the prize light" (1.2.452–53). He also understands the need for the daughter to choose her husband over her father, a choice that Desdemona and Cordelia could not make their fathers accept. When he commands Miranda not to talk with his prisoner or reveal her name, he is purposely acting to fulfill both roles. While Lear casts Cordelia away so that he can keep her, Prospero ties Miranda to him so that she will disobey his commands and initiate the required transition of loyalties from father to husband. Yet, for all his awareness, Prospero turns aside from watching Miranda and Ferdinand play out the parts he himself has written for them and makes the pained commend "So glad of this as they I cannot be" (3.1.92).

Shakespeare shows us that it is no easier for Prospero to give up Miranda, even to a husband he himself has chosen, than it was for poor Brabantio to relinquish Desdemona. Throughout the play Prospero remains disproportionately preoccupied with tormenting thoughts of his daughter sexually possessed by another male, an obsession that has its analogue in Brabantio's dream. Hence the father lectures Ferdinand — the future son-in-law whom old Prospero never manages to like very much — that

> If thou dost break her virgin-knot before
> All sanctimonious ceremonies may . . . be minist'red,
> . . . barren hate . . . and discord shall bestrew
> The union of your bed with weeds so loathly
> That you shall hate it both.   (4.1.15–22)

And hence he sets Ferdinand to work hauling logs, doing the labor that Caliban refused to do, thereby domesticating Ferdinand's energies in a way that could never reform the uneducable lust of Caliban. In his betrothal gift to Miranda and Ferdinand, the dowry masque he evokes out of the powers of his mind, Prospero includes the rainbow goddess Iris, the emblematic fertility of Ceres, and the archetypal wife-consort Juno. Significantly, from this vision the father banishes Venus and her son, turning them back on their way to the celebration, where he fears they would have done "some wanton charm upon this man and maid/Whose vows are, that no bedright shall be paid/Till Hymen's torch be lighted" (4.1.95–97).

The forces of erotic chaos that Prospero hoped to banish from his daughter's prothalamion are, however, not so easily vanquished. For before the masque has ended, Prospero realizes that Caliban and his confederates are on their way, and the very thought of the would-be rapist abruptly dissolves the insubstantial pageant into thin air.

In *The Tempest*, Prospero essentially overcomes his incestuous desire to retain his daughter imprisoned on his island. He recognizes his own repressed but monstrous wishes in confessing that Caliban, who would people the island with Calibans, is a "thing of darkness I/[must] Acknowledge mine" (5.1.275–76). Caliban, the monster of *The Tempest*, whose name suggests an anagram for "cannibal," refigures the incestuous, self-consumptive desires imaged in Lear's "barbarous Scythian" and in the "monstrous lust" between Antiochus and his daughter in *Pericles*. He is also a force on whose nature nurture will not stick. And so while daughter and father are simultaneously released from the enchantment of living together forever isolated on an island controlled by the father's shaping fancies, Caliban must remain enslaved on it. Their release and their ability to return to the natural order of civilization are made possible only by the arrival of Ferdinand, who comes — like the prince of the fairy tale — to take the bride away from her father's fortress and lead her out into generative space and time.

The end of *The Tempest* leaves us with a father who has learned what nature requires of him: the father must take part with his nobler reason against his fury and let his admired Mirando go. Yet doing so leaves Prospero with the lonely emptiness apparent in his confession to Alonzo: "I/Have lost my daughter . . . In this last tempest" (5.1.147–48, 153). As in *Pericles* and *The Winter's Tale*, the ritual dissolution of the father-daughter bond is dramatically realized; but in this final play the relationship gains added depth through the exploration of the central paradox always inherent in its resolution. Here, we are not left entirely with the "brave new world" imagined by Miranda and in some respects promised to the reclaimed families of the two earlier romances. For Shakespeare goes beyond the happy ending to show us the pain and loss bequeathed to the isolated father who has acted out the required rite of separation. For while at first glance the church ceremony might seem only to dramatize the transfer of a passive female object from one male to another, in reality it ritualizes the community's coercion, not of the bride, but of her father. Ultimately, it is he who must pay the true "bride price" at the altar and, by doing so, become the displaced and dispossessed actor. As the celebratory reunification that concludes Shakespeare's comedy begins in the final scene, it is therefore left up to Prospero to complete the demands dictated by his role and — like every father of every bride — retire from the scene to seek out his seat in the congregation. Thus Prospero concludes the ritual and the play with his only remaining expectation:

> to see the nuptial
> Of these our dear-belov'd solemnized,
> And thence retire me to my Milan, where
> Every third thought shall be my grave.   (5.1.309–12)

Notes

[1]Stone accounts for the drama and poetry of the sixteenth and early seventeenth centuries by modifying his "rather pessimistic view of a society with little love and generally low affect" to allow for "romantic love and sexual intrigue . . . in one very restricted social group . . . that is the households of princes and great nobles" (*Family* 103–04). This qualification does not extend to his view of parent-child relationships.

[2]Stone also points out that the high infant-mortality rate, "which made it folly to invest too much emotional capital in such ephemeral beings," was as much responsible for this lack of affective family ties as were any economic motives (*Family* 105). For Stone, paternal authority — not affection — was the almost exclusive source of the family's coherence. Furthermore, the domestic patriarchy of the sixteenth century was not merely a replica of family structures inherited from the past but a social pattern consciously exploited and reinforced by the state to emphasize the injunctions of obedience and authority; nor was it replaced until absolute monarchy was overthrown (see *Family* 151–218). Meanwhile, because of the prevalent child-rearing practices, the maternal impact was relatively insignificant, hence not nearly so important to the psychological process of maturation; in Stone's estimate, our familiar "maternal, child-oriented, affectionate and permissive mode" of child rearing did not emerge till about 1800 (*Family* 405). During the Elizabethan era, the upper-class practice of transferring a newborn infant immediately to a village wet nurse, who nurtured the child for two years, substantially muted any maternal influence on child development and no doubt created an inestimable psychological distance between mother and child. Stone cites the strained and formal relationship between Juliet and Lady Capulet as vivid testimony of the absence of affective mother-child bonds that results from such an arrangement (106); in the Capulet household, it is even left up to the nurse, not the mother, to remember Juliet's birthday. Yet Stone does not measure the relationship between Juliet and her father against his hypothesis of the absence of affect. Old Capulet is indeed the authoritarian dictator of Stone's model, but he is also a "careful father" who deeply loves his child. Instead of being eager to have her off his

hands, Capulet is notably reluctant to give up the daughter he calls "the hopeful lady of my earth" (1.2.15; all Shakespeare quotations are from the Evans ed.); his bull-headed determination to marry her to Paris following Tybalt's death is born, paradoxically enough, from the deeply rooted affection that Stone's hypothesis excludes.

[3]As Christopher Hill suggests in his review of Stone's *Family*, much of the evidence used could well imply its opposite: "The vigour of the preachers' propaganda on behalf . . . of breaking children's wills, suggests that such attitudes were by no means so universally accepted as they would have wished" (461). Hill and others have criticized Stone for asserting that love and affection were negligible social phenomena before 1700 and for presuming throughout "that values percolate downwards from the upper to the lower classes" (Hill 462). Because of the scope and importance of Stone's subject, his book has been widely reviewed. As David Berkowitz comments, "the possibility of endless symposia on Stone's vision and performance looms as a fashionable activity for the next half-dozen years" (396). Hill's review and the reviews by Keith Thomas and John Demos seem particularly well balanced.

[4]One could chart the new emphasis on the family by reviewing the Shakespeare topics at recent MLA conventions. The 1979 convention featured Marriage and the Family in Shakespeare, Shirley Nelson Garner chairing, as its Shakespeare Division topic and also included a related special session, The Love between Shakespeare's Fathers and Daughters, Paul A. Jorgensen chairing. Before becoming the division topic, the subject had been examined in special sessions for three consecutive years: 1976, Marianne Novy chairing; 1977, John Bean and Coppélia Kahn chairing; and 1978, Carol Thomas Neely chairing. Special sessions continued in 1980 and 1981, with Shirley Nelson Garner and Madelon S. Gohlke as chairs. A parallel phenomenon has meanwhile been taking place in sixteenth-, seventeenth-, and eighteenth-century historical scholarship, which Hill explains by saying that ". . . the family as an institution rather suddenly became fashionable, perhaps as a by-product of the women's liberation movement" (450).

Most of the work on fathers and daughters in Shakespeare has been done, as might be expected, on the romances. See the essays by Cyrus Hoy, D. W. Harding, and Charles Frey. Of particular interest is the Schwartz and Kahn collection, which was published after I had written this paper but which includes several essays related to my own. See esp. David Sundelson's "So Rare a Wonder'd Father: Prospero's *Tempest*," C. L. Barber's "The Family in Shakespeare's Development: Tragedy and Sacredness," and Coppélia Kahn's "The Providential Tempest and the Shakespearean Family."

[5]Margaret Loftus Ranald has done substantial work on the legal background of marriage in Shakespeare plays. I have found no marriages (or funerals) staged literally in the plays of Shakespeare or of his contemporaries. Although, for instance, the marriage of Kate and Petruchio would seem to offer a rich opportunity for an indecorously comic scene appropriate for *The Taming of the Shrew*, the action occurs offstage and we only hear of it secondhand. Nor do we witness the Olivia-Sebastian marriage in *Twelfth Night*. Even the fragment of the botched ceremony in *Much Ado* does not follow the liturgy with any precision but presents a dramatized version of it. This omission — apparently consistent in Elizabethan and Jacobean drama — may have resulted from the 1559 Act of Uniformity of Common Prayer and Divine Service in the Church, which stipulates sanctions against "any persone or persones whatsoever . . . [who] shall in anye Entreludes Playes Songes, Rymes or by other open Woordes, declare or speake anye thing in the derogation depraving or despising of the same Booke, or of any thing therein conteyned" (1 Elizabeth I, c. 2, in *Statutes* 4:355–58). Given the rising tempo of the Puritan attack on the theaters at this time, we may reasonably infer that the omission of liturgy reflects the dramatists' conscientious wish to avoid conflict. Richmond Noble's study corroborates this assumption (82). Of the services to which Shakespeare does refer, Noble notes that the allusions to "distinctive features, words, and phrases of Holy Matrimony are extremely numerous" (83).

[6]Van Gennep built his study on the work of Hartland, Frazer, Ciszewski, Hertz, Crowley, and others who had noted resemblances among the components of various disparate rites. His tripartite diachronic structure provides the basis for Victor W. Turner's discussions in the essay "Liminality and Communitas" (*Ritual Process* 94–203).

[7]The church canons of 1604 seem to have confused the situation further by continuing to recognize the validity of the nuptial pledge but forbidding persons under twenty-one to marry without parental consent; this ruling would make the marriage of minors illegal but nonetheless binding for life and hence valid (Stone, *Family* 32). Until the passage of Lord Hardwicke's Marriage Act in 1753, confusion was rife over what constituted a legal marriage and what a valid one. In addition to bringing coherence to the marriage laws, this act was designed to protect increasingly threatened parental interests by denying the validity as well as the legality of a religious ceremony performed without certain conditions, including parental consent for parties under twenty-one (Stone, *Family* 35–36).

The concern for parental approval has always focused on, and in fact ritualized, the consent of the bride's father. In 1858, the Reverend Charles Wheatly, a noted authority on church law, attributed the father's giving away his daughter as signifying the care that must be taken of the female sex, "who are always

supposed to be under the tuition of a father or guardian, whose consent is necessary to make their acts valid" (496). For supportive authority Wheatly looks back to Richard Hooker, whose phrasing is substantially harsher. Hooker felt that the retention of the custom "hath still this vse that it putteth vs men in mind of a dutie whereunto the verie imbecillitie of their [women's] nature and sex doth binde them, namely to be alwaies directed, guided and ordered by others . . ." (215).

Even though the validity of a marriage was not vested in parental consent, "the Protestants, including the Anglicans, considered the consent of the parents to be as essential to the marriage as the consent of the bride and bridegroom" (Flandrin 131). Paradoxically, "both Church and State claimed to be supporting, at one and the same time, freedom of marriage and the authority of parents" (Flandrin 132). The ambiguity arose because the child was obliged, under pain of mortal sin, to obey the parent. Technically, the child was free to choose a marriage partner, but since the church never took steps against the prerogatives of the father, the notion of choice was problematic.

[8]Given the high parent mortality rate, a number of brides necessarily went to the altar on the arms of their legal guardians. Peter Laslett notes that in Manchester between 1553–1657 over half of the girls marrying for the first time were fatherless (103), but some historians have criticized his reliance on parish registers as the principal demographic barometer.

[9]The groom's pledge suggests the wedding ring's dual sexual and material symbolism. Historically, the ring symbolizes the dowry payment that the woman will receive from her husband by the entitlement of marriage; it apparently superseded the custom of placing tokens of espousal on the prayer book (see *Book of Common Prayer* 408). It also signifies the physical consummation, a point frequently exploited in Renaissance drama and also implied by the rubrics in the older Roman Catholic manuals, which direct the placing of the ring. The Martène manual specifies that the bride is to wear it on the left hand to signify "a difference between the estate and the episcopal order, by whom the ring is publicly worn on the right hand as a symbol of full and entire chastity" (Legg 207). *The Rathen Manual*, which follows the Use of Sarum, contains a rather charming piece of folklore widely believed through the eighteenth century. It, too, allusively suggests the sexual significance of the ring: "For in the fourth finger there is a certain vein proceeding to the heart and by the chime of silver there is represented the internal affection which ought always to be fresh between them" (35–36; see also Wheatly 503). Even after the priest took over the ceremonial role of transferring the bride's hand from her father's to her husband's, he did not also become the intermediary in transferring the ring from the groom's keeping to the bride's finger. Such an incorporation of duties might seem logical were it not that this part of the ritual simultaneously imitates and licenses the sexual act.

The English reformers retained both the symbol of the ring and the groom's accompanying pledge to "worship" his wife's body, a retention that generated considerable attack from the more radical reformers. The controversy over this wording occupies the major portion of Hooker's defense of the Anglican marriage rite (see also Stone, *Family* 522, on the attempts in 1641 and 1661 to alter the wording of the vow from "worship" to "honor"). Hooker justifies the husband's "worship" as a means of transferring to the wife the "dignitie" incipient in her husband's legitimizing of the children he now allows her to bear. She furthermore receives, by this annexation of his worship, a right to participate in his material possessions. The movement of the vow, from sexual to material pledge, thus sequences a formal rite of passage, a pattern alluded to in Hooker's phrase, "the former branch hauing granted the principall, the latter graunteth that which is annexed thereunto" (216).

¹⁰The ceremonial transfer of the father's authority to the husband is acknowledged by the Reverend John Shepherd in his historical commentary accompanying the 1853 Family Prayer Book: ". . . the ceremony shows the father's consent; and that the authority, which he before possessed, he now resigns to the husband" (Brownell 465). By implication, however, the ceremony resolves the incestuous attraction between father and daughter by ritualizing his "gift" of her hand, a signification unlikely to be discussed in the commentary of church historians. When first the congregation and next the couple are asked to name any impediments to the marriage, there are, Wheatly says, three specific impediments the church is charging all knowledgeable parties to declare: a preceding marriage or contract, consanguinity or affinity, and want of consent (483). The final act of Ben Jonson's *Epicoene* enumerates all the possible legal impediments that might be subsumed under these three.

The bride's father, by virtue of his special prominence in the ritual, functions as a select witness whose presence attests to the validity of the contract. The Friar in *Much Ado* asks Hero and Claudio whether they "know any inward impediment why you should not be cojoin'd" (4.1.12–13). Leonato dares to respond for Claudio, "I dare make his answer, none," because, as father of the bride, he presumes to have full knowledge that no impediment exists. When he learns of Hero's supposed taint, the rage he vents over the loss of his own honor is the more comprehensible when we understand his special position in the ceremony as a sworn witness to the transfer of an intact daughter.

¹¹The sections on the celebration of "Festiuall daies" and times of fast that precede Hooker's defense of the English "Celebration of Matrimonie" are especially helpful in understanding Elizabethan ritual, for in these sections Hooker expands his defense of the Anglican rites into an explanation of, and rationale for, the whole notion of ritual. Having first isolated three sequential elements necessary for festival—praise, bounty, and rest—he goes on to justify "bountie" in terms remarkably compatible with the theories of both Bataille and Lévi-Strauss on the essential "spending-gift" nature of marriage. To Hooker, the "bountie" essential to celebration represents the expression of a "charitable largenesse of somewhat more then common bountie. . . . Plentifull and liberall expense is required in them that abounde, partly as a signe of their owne joy in the goodnesse of God toward them" (292, 293). Bounty is important to all festival rites, but within the marriage rite this "spending" quality incorporates the specific idea of sexual orgasm as the ultimate and precious expenditure given the bride by her husband, a notion alluded to in Bataille and one that functioned as a standard Elizabethan metaphor apparent in phrases like "Th' expense of spirit" (sonnet 129) or Othello's comment to Desdemona, "The purchase made, the fruits are to ensue;/That profit's yet to come 'tween me and you" (2.3.9–10). The wedding ceremony ritualizes this notion of bounty as the gift of life by having the father give the groom the family treasure, which the father cannot "use" but can only bequeath or hoard. The groom, who ritually

places coins or a gold ring on the prayer book as a token "bride price," then fully "purchases" the father's treasure through his own physical expenditure, an act that guarantees the father's "interest" through future generations. This money-sex image complex is pervasive and important in many of Shakespeare's plays. The pattern and its relation to festival are especially evident in Juliet's ecstatic and impatient speech urging night to come and bring her husband:

> O, I have bought the mansion of a love,
> But not possess'd it, and though I am sold,
> Not yet enjoy'd. So tedious is this day
> As is the night before some festival.   (3.2.26–29)

In another context, this pattern enables us fully to understand Shylock's miserly refusal to give or spend and the implications of his simultaneous loss of daughter and hoarded fortune. His confusion of daughter and ducats is foreshadowed when he recounts the story of Jacob and equates the increase of the flock through the "work of generation" to the increase of money through retentive "use." To Antonio's question, "Or is your gold and silver ewes and rams?" Shylock responds, "I cannot tell, I make it breed as fast" (*MV* 1.3.95–96).

¹²Hooker also makes the point that the sacramentality invoked by ritual is profaned when festival celebration overflows the measure or when the form of ceremony becomes parodic. Hooker asserts that the festivals of the "Israelites and heathens," though they contained the necessary elements, "failed in the ende it self, so neither could they discerne rightly what forme and measure Religion therein should obserue. . . . they are in every degree noted to haue done amisse, their Hymnes or songs of praise were idolatrie, their bountie excesse, and their rest wantonnesse" (294). On the use of ritual as the human means to recover the sacred dimension of existence, see Eliade: "Driven from religious life in the strict sense, the *celestial sacred* remains active through symbolism. A religious symbol conveys its message even if it is no longer consciously understood in every part. For a symbol speaks to the whole human being and not only to the intelligence. . . . Hence the supreme function of the myth is to "fix" the paradigmatic models for all rites and all significant human activities. . . . By the continuous reactualization of paradigmatic divine gestures, the world is sanctified." (129, 98–99). Unquestionably, the late C. L. Barber's study is the best book to date on the relation of Shakespeare's plays to underlying patterns of ritual.

¹³*Measure for Measure* provides the most dramatic testimony to the importance of fixing the dowry provisions before the wedding. Although Juliet is nearly nine months pregnant and although she and Claudio believe themselves spiritually married, they have not legalized the wedding in church because of still unresolved dowry provisions.

¹⁴Alan Dundes points out the psychological dimensions of various folktale types underlying a number of Shakespeare's plays; significantly, the central figure in the folktale is usually the daughter-heroine. The theme of incest, which Freud himself recognized as a powerful undercurrent in *King Lear*, is manifest in the folktale father who demands that his daughter marry him; Shakespeare transforms the overt demand into a love test requiring that she love her father all (358). In Dundes' interpretation, the more obvious father-daughter incest wish is

actually an Electral daughter-father desire that has been transformed through projection. Dundes also lists other discussions of the father-daughter incest theme in *King Lear* (359).

[15]Hymen's verses emphasize the religious sense of the marriage ritual. In this context the genetic father is only a surrogate parent, appointed by the heavenly parent to act out the specific role of bequeathing the daughter to a new union; Hymen himself functions as the mythic priest, the agent authorized by heaven to oversee the transfer. Wheatly's notes reflect this same sense of the religious meaning of the roles played by father and priest: ". . . the woman is to be given not to the man, but to the Minister; for the rubric orders, that the minister shall receive her *at her father's or friend's hands*; which signifies, to be sure, that the father resigns her up to God, and that it is God, who, by His Priest, now gives her in marriage . . ." (497).

[16]See Barber's essay in Schwartz and Kahn, esp. pp. 198–221. Barber additionally provides a striking iconographic association, noting the image of Lear with Cordelia in his arms as being effectively "a *pietá* with the roles reversed, not Holy Mother with her Dead Son, but father with his dead daughter" (200).

Works Cited

Barber, C. L. *Shakespeare's Festive Comedy*. Princeton: Princeton Univ. Press, 1959.

Bataille, Georges. *Death and Sensuality: A Study of Eroticism and the Taboo*. 1962; rpt. New York: Arno, 1977.

Berkowitz, David. *Renaissance Quarterly* 32 (1979): 396–403.

The Book of Common Prayer, 1559 Ed. John E. Booty. Charlottesville: Univ. of Virginia Press, 1967.

Brownell, Thomas Church, ed. *The Family Prayer Book; or, The Book of Common Prayer according to the Use of the Protestant Episcopal Church*. New York: Stanford and Swords, 1853.

Demos, John. *New York Times Book Review*, 25 Dec. 1977, 1.

Dundes, Alan. "'To Love My Father All': A Psychoanalytic Study of the Folktale Source of *King Lear*." *Southern Folklore Quarterly* 40 (1976): 353–66.

Eliade, Mircea. *The Sacred and the Profane*. Trans. Willard R. Trask. New York: Harcourt, 1959.

Evans, G. Blakemore, ed. *The Riverside Shakespeare*. Boston: Houghton, 1974.

Flandrin, Jean-Louis. *Families in Former Times: Kinship, Household and Sexuality*. Trans. Richard Southern. Cambridge: Cambridge Univ. Press, 1979.

Frey, Charles. "'O sacred, shadowy, cold, and constant queen': Shakespeare's Imperiled and Chastening Daughters of Romance." *South Atlantic Bulletin* 43 (1978):125–40.

Harding, D. W. "Father and Daughter in Shakespeare's Last Plays." *TLS*, 30 Nov. 1979, 59–61.

Hill, Christopher. "Sex, Marriage and the Family in England." *Economic History Review*, 2nd ser., 31 (1978):450–63.

Hooker, Richard. *Of the Lawes of Ecclesiasticall Politie*. 1594; facsim. rpt. Amsterdam: Theatrum Orbis Terrarum, 1971.

Hoy, Cyrus. "Fathers and Daughters in Shakespeare's Romances." In *Shakespeare's Romances Reconsidered*. Ed. Carol McGinnis Kay and Henry E. Jacobs. Lincoln: Univ. of Nebraska Press, 1978, 77–90.

Laslett, Peter. *The World We Have Lost*. 2nd ed. 1965; rpt. London: Methuen, 1971.

Legg, J. Wickham. *Ecclesiological Essays*. London: De La More Press, 1905.

Lévi-Strauss, Claude. *The Elementary Structures of Kinship*. Trans. James Harle Bell. Ed. John Richard von Sturmer and Rodney Needham. Paris, 1949; rpt. Boston: Beacon, 1969.

Noble, Richmond. *Shakespeare's Use of the Bible and* The Book of Common Prayer. London: Society for the Promotion of Biblical Knowledge, 1935.

Ranald, Margaret Loftus. "'As Marriage Binds, and Blood Breaks': English Marriage and Shakespeare." *Shakespeare Quarterly* 30 (1979):68–81.

Schwartz, Murray M., and Coppélia Kahn, eds. *Representing Shakespeare: New Psychoanalytic Essays*. Baltimore: Johns Hopkins Univ. Press, 1980.

The Statutes of the Realm. London: Record Commissions, 1820–28; facsim. ed. 1968.

Stone, Lawrence. *The Crisis of the Aristrocracy: 1558–1660*. Abridged ed. London: Oxford Univ. Press, 1971.

————. *The Family, Sex and Marriage in England: 1500–1800*. New York: Harper, 1977.

Thomas, Keith. *TLS*, 21 Oct. 1977, 1226.

Turner, Victor W. *The Ritual Process: Structure and Anti-Structure*. Chicago: Aldine, 1969.

Van Gennep, Arnold. *The Rites of Passage*. Trans. Monika B. Vizedom and Gabrielle L. Caffee. 1908; rpt. London: Routledge and Kegan Paul, 1960.

Wheatly, Charles. A *Rational Illustration of* The Book of Common Prayer *According to the Use of the Church of England*. Cambridge: Cambridge Univ. Press, 1858.

III

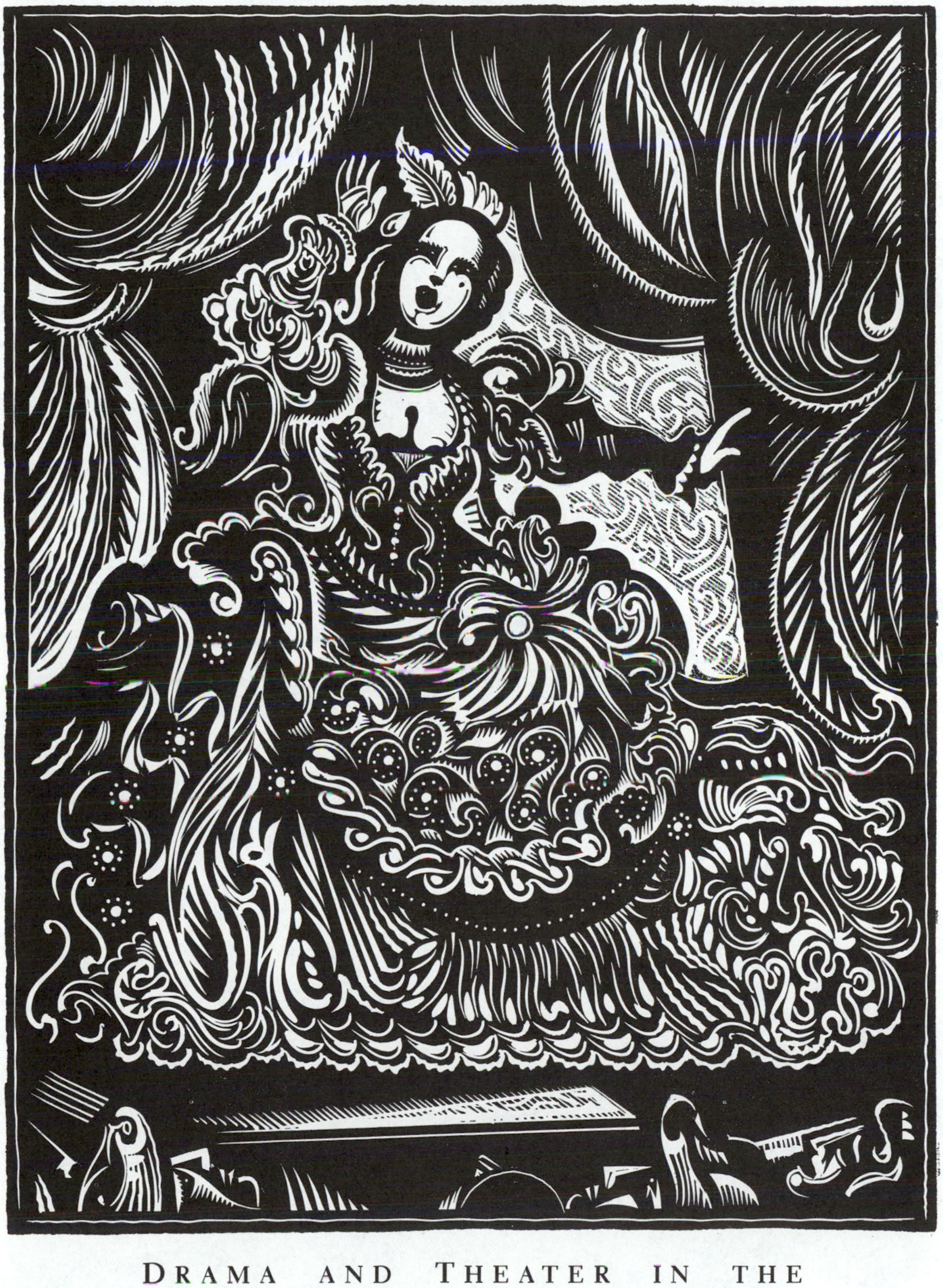

Drama and Theater in the Late Seventeenth Century: Restoration England and Louis XIV's France

RAMA AND THEATER IN
both London and Paris experienced a second "renaissance" in the late seventeenth century. In both cities, the theater came under the influence and protection of the king and his court, and the theaters of both London and Paris adapted Italian staging practices. In both cities, theater buildings achieved the form they would hold well into the nineteenth century, and the work of new playwrights and new dramatic designs invigorated the dramatic repertory.

Yet for all their similarities, the theaters of Restoration England and of Louis XIV's France were sustained by two very different social and political climates. In France, Louis XIV declared *"L'état, c'est moi"* — "I am the state" — in 1660, confidently drawing all state authority into the person of the king and his magnificent court. The later seventeenth century in France was a period of royal absolutism, as the throne worked to consolidate its power. In England, conditions were very different, for 1660 brought the restoration of the monarchy. The Restoration period saw an ongoing negotiation between newly installed Charles II and Parliament for power, in which Parliament gradually gained control of many royal prerogatives. In both countries, the theater became associated with the throne and reflected the tensions animating social and political life.

In France, a character in Molière's play *Tartuffe* drew the official portrait of the absolute monarch: "A Prince who sees into our inmost hearts,/And can't be fooled by any trickster's arts." Yet the authoritarian policies of the French government, the internecine competition among members of the court, and even the fortunes of the theater suggest that the king's claim of absolute power was challenged in a variety of ways. Under Louis XIII (reigned 1610–1643) and Louis XIV (reigned 1643–1715), the Crown strove to centralize its power by crushing the claims of the landed nobility and by expanding French rule in a series of costly wars. Since Louis XIII came to the throne at the age of nine, when his father — Henry IV — was assassinated, much of this expansion was carried on by his chief minister, Cardinal Richelieu (1585–1642), and Richelieu's successor, Cardinal Mazarin (1602–1661). The suppression of the traditional nobility was achieved largely through Richelieu's formation of a new bureaucracy loyal to the Crown, partly composed of politically active clergy and partly of commoners promoted over the heads of the nobility to critical positions in the government. Allowing these "new men" to buy aristocratic titles, the Crown raised money and further diluted the power of the nobility. The Crown's ravenous appetite for cash to pay for the lavish life of the court and for expensive building projects, such as the palace of Versailles (built by Louis XIV in 1673), further weakened the nobility and alienated the peasantry. Using tax-farmers, who paid a fixed sum to the government in exchange for the authority to collect taxes and pocket the excess as profit, the Crown squeezed the nobles' wealth directly into the royal coffers, impoverishing their lands and making the peasantry increasingly rebellious.

A poor and disaffected peasantry, a jealous aristocracy, an upstart bourgeoisie, and an increasingly authoritarian and isolated monarchy: this became the recipe for revolution. Although the French Revolution did not erupt until 1789, France suffered civil convulsions throughout the seventeenth century that dramatize the tension between Louis's absolutist rhetoric and the political realities of his reign. The nobles led a series of rebellions called the Fronde throughout the 1640s and 1650s, in an effort to unseat Louis and his powerful ministers. Louis defeated these uprisings and finally sealed the fate of his enemies when he required the nobility to attend him at Versailles, so he could keep his eye on their activities. However, the Fronde was part of a more pervasive unrest. Relentless taxation, economic stagnation, and repeated famines throughout the seventeenth century made the peasants angry, as well, and peasant riots and rebellions took place in nearly every province of France in nearly every decade of the century. Finally, Louis XIV also had difficulty with the most volatile issue of seventeenth-century Europe — religious dissent. The close ties between the Crown and the church often resulted in the suppression of Protestant sects, particularly the Calvinist French Huguenots. Protestant rebellion had forced the enactment of the Edict of Nantes in 1598, granting the Huguenots considerable religious freedom. Louis XIV revoked the Edict in 1685, giving the government wider latitude to suppress increasingly energetic religious protest. Louis XIV carefully crafted the image of the "Le Roi Soleil" — the Sun King — whose absolute authority seemed almost a force of nature, not a fact of politics. Throughout his reign, though, Louis had to contend with recalcitrant factions who refused to accept completely his characterization of the king's power.

In England, resistance to royal authority had been much more successful. Between 1603 and 1642, the Stuart kings James I (reigned 1603–1625) and his son, Charles I (reigned 1625–1649), increasingly worked to limit the power of Parliament and to enforce increasingly strict religious laws that suppressed the Protestant Puritan sects and demanded conformity with the Church of England. In 1642, Parliament passed legislation limiting the powers of the throne, and Civil War between Parliamentary and Royalist forces erupted. Charles I was executed in 1649, while his wife and children (including the future king, Charles II) escaped to France. From 1653 to 1658, Oliver Cromwell served as Lord Protector of the realm, but Royalist sentiments eventually prevailed and established Charles II (reigned 1660–1685) on the throne.

Although the monarchy was restored — the term *Restoration* refers generally to the period of Charles II's reign and the remainder of the seventeenth century — Charles II was in no position to command the nation, and English politics in the later seventeenth century mainly concerned the negotiation of power between the Crown and Parliament. Charles's death in 1685 spurred a crisis in that his son James II (reigned 1685–1688) was Catholic and threatened to compromise English religious and civil autonomy from the Catholic church and the Catholic states of Europe. In 1689, Parliament effectively deposed James, inviting his Protestant daughter Mary (reigned as Mary II, 1689–1694) and her husband William of Orange (reigned as William III, 1689–1702) to return to England and assume the throne. While Louis XIV increasingly insisted on the autonomous power of the throne in France, the Parliament in England finally achieved a lasting compromise with the Crown in the form of a constitutional monarchy. For in bringing William and Mary into power, Parliament gained the authority of consent over royal succession, a power it confirmed in 1702 in naming James II's daughter Anne as successor (reigned as Queen Anne, 1702–1714).

THEATER IN FRANCE, 1660–1700

Louis XIV's familiar sobriquet, "Le Roi Soleil," derives from a role he played in a court ballet devised for him in 1653. He was in fact a fine dancer and sponsored and took part in a wide variety of entertainments. Moreover, the centralization of power in the king and the court paralleled the increasing institutionalization of the arts under Louis XIV, as a means of advancing his own prestige and of keeping control over potentially seditious activities. The most famous of these institutions — the ACADÉMIE FRANÇAISE — was chartered in 1637, and used by Cardinal Richelieu to evaluate a critical controversy surrounding Pierre Corneille's play *The Cid*. Corneille's detractors had sharply attacked the play, and Richelieu urged the Académie to resolve whether *The Cid* could legitimately be described as effective tragedy in neoclassical terms (on *neoclassicism*, see page 270). In return, Richelieu promoted the Académie and its aims, the purification of French language and literature, and the advancement of official French culture. Louis XIV assumed the role of official protector of the Académie Française in 1672 and sponsored other institutions as ornaments to his reign: the Académie Royale de Musique (1672), the Académie Royale de Peinture et de Sculpture (1648), the Académie des Inscriptions (1663), the Académie des Sciences (1666), and the Académie de l'Architecture (1671). The institution of the stage was no exception. Theatrical companies had always needed the king's license to play in Paris, and Louis licensed several companies and named Molière's company as the *Troupe du roi*. After Molière's death in 1673, the leading tragic actress in Paris, Mademoiselle Champmeslé, joined with Molière's troupe and gained the king's patronage. The new company—the **COMÉDIE FRANÇAISE**—opened in August of 1680. It held a **MONOPOLY** on the production of all spoken drama in French, and although this monopoly has long since vanished, the Comédie Française remains the principal company performing the French classical repertoire.

In Louis XIV's Paris, the institutions of art—including the theater—were identified with the prerogatives of the king and his court, though the structure of the theater had its roots in practices dating back to the Middle Ages. Throughout the later Middle Ages and into the sixteenth century, stage production in Paris was controlled by the Confrérie de la Passion, a guild-like corporation initially formed to stage religious drama. In 1545 the Confrérie purchased land in Paris from the Duke of Burgundy and erected the Hôtel de Bourgogne, at the time probably the only permanent theater building in Europe (*hôtel* in this case means "hall" or "large building"). Extensively remodelled in 1647, the Hôtel de Bourgogne served as the model for other theaters built in the seventeenth century: the Théâtre du Marais (built in a tennis court in 1629, rebuilt in 1644); the Palais-Cardinal (built by Richelieu in 1640; later renamed the Palais-Royal); the Salle des Machines (1642), and the Comédie Française (1689).

The shape of these theaters owes something to the Hôtel de Bourgogne, and something to tennis courts as well, for tennis courts were often used as theaters. (In the sixteenth and seventeenth centuries, tennis courts were long indoor rooms with side galleries.) These theaters generally had deep, **RAKED STAGES** (40 feet deep, 45 feet wide at the Hôtel de Bourgogne) that faced an open **PIT** called the *PARTERRE* (literally, "on the ground") which was used for standing spectators. The auditorium had **BOXES** on three sides; **GALLERY** seating rose above the boxes opposite the stage; some patrons were also seated on the stage itself. The theaters were large—the Hôtel de Bourgogne initially held 1,600 spectators, the Comédie Française held 2,000—and many theaters made extensive use of stage scenery, sometimes concocting extraordinary spectacles. In a fantasy celebrating Louis XIV's wedding in 1662, the entire royal family and its entourage were "flown" by machines in the Salle des Machines; in a production in 1671, 300 deities were lifted aloft. The dramatic theaters—the Hôtel de Bourgogne, the Palais-Royal, the Comédie Française—tended to avoid such effects, using instead a single setting for each play, depending on the genre of the play. The theaters generally used a series of staggered **WINGS AND BACKDROP** to create the effect of perspective, adapting both scenic practices and scene-changing technology from Italian theaters.

Acting companies in Paris were organized as investment corporations requiring the patronage of the Crown and had long included women in their ranks. Louis XIV's reign saw a series of great actresses take the stage, Mademoiselle DuParc and Mademoiselle Champmeslé among them. Companies were comprised of twelve members (eight men, four women), who shared the company's profits. The company hired additional actors when necessary. The Comédie Française standardized this practice: its twelve main actors—called *SOCIÉTAIRES*—ran the company for twenty years, and new sociétaires could be recruited only after the retirement of current members. Actors in the Comédie Française received an annual subsidy from the Crown and a retirement pension if they completed their twenty years with the company. The company purchased plays, which were cast by the author. Throughout the 1650s and 1660s the major companies kept about 70 plays in repertory and generally played three or four times per week. After the 1680s, the Comédie Française began daily performances, beginning at 5 P.M.

We should recall that life at court was itself a kind of performance, and that attending the theater provided ample opportunity for aristocrats, courtiers, and aspiring courtiers to display and preen themselves. In a milieu so dependent on the king's preference, we can easily imagine how stage seating and side boxes emphasized that the evening's entertainment included the audience's performances as well as the actors'. This sense of the reciprocity between court and stage is signalled more concretely by the fortunes of the Parisian theaters after Louis XIV moved the court to Versailles. Although five companies flourished in Paris while Louis kept court in the city, by 1700 only two remained.

THEATER IN ENGLAND, 1660–1700

At the outbreak of the Civil War in 1642, Parliament closed the London theaters, putting a stop to dramatic performance. Some companies managed to mount secret productions between 1642 and 1660, but Parliament and city officials moved quickly to suppress them, sometimes by destroying the theater buildings. In the 1650s, however, William Davenant (1606–1668), a Royalist supporter of Charles I and successor to Ben Jonson as writer of court masques, attempted to mount operas. In 1656 he succeeded in staging a production of *The Seige of Rhodes* at Rutland House, performing it again in 1658 and 1659 at the Cockpit theater and elsewhere in London.

The restoration of Charles II to the throne in 1660 inaugurated a period of renewed theatrical vitality. As in France — where Charles developed a taste for theater during his exile — the theater was closely associated with royal prerogatives. Upon his return, Charles rewarded PATENTS to William Davenant and Thomas Killegrew (1612–1683) to open theaters under royal authority. These PATENT THEATERS (also called "theaters royal") — Davenant's Duke's company, and Killigrew's King's company — thus held a royal monopoly on the production of spoken English drama. Although they underwent huge modifications, the patent theaters dominated the legitimate theater until the mid-nineteenth century, when legislation was passed that finally broke their monopoly. Yet monopoly could not guarantee support. The two companies were unable to turn a profit and were united into a single company from 1682 to 1695.

When the theaters reopened in 1660, theatrical taste had changed significantly. Although a few of the older, pre-1642 theater buildings were still standing, they could not handle the new theater technology. For, as in the French theater, the English theater rapidly encouraged the development of scenic practices already well-known in Italy — a PROSCENIUM stage and moveable painted wings and backdrop used to create a visual setting for the play. Onstage, theaters used stock sets — one for classical tragedy, one for romantic comedy, and so on — that conformed to the dramatic genre of the play. In 1661, Davenant converted Lisle's Tennis Court to the Lincoln's Inn Fields Theater, which measured 30 by 70 feet; he replaced this theater with the Dorset Garden Theater in 1671. Killegrew erected his Theatre Royal in Bridges Street in 1663. When it burned in 1672, he built a new Theatre Royal in Drury Lane, which opened in 1674; a theater has occupied this site down to the present time.

The new English theaters were much smaller than the French theaters. The Drury Lane theater, for example, held 650–700 people, though it was expanded throughout the late seventeenth and eighteenth centuries and eventually held over 2,000. Nonetheless,

GROUND PLAN OF THE COMÉDIE FRANÇAISE THEATER

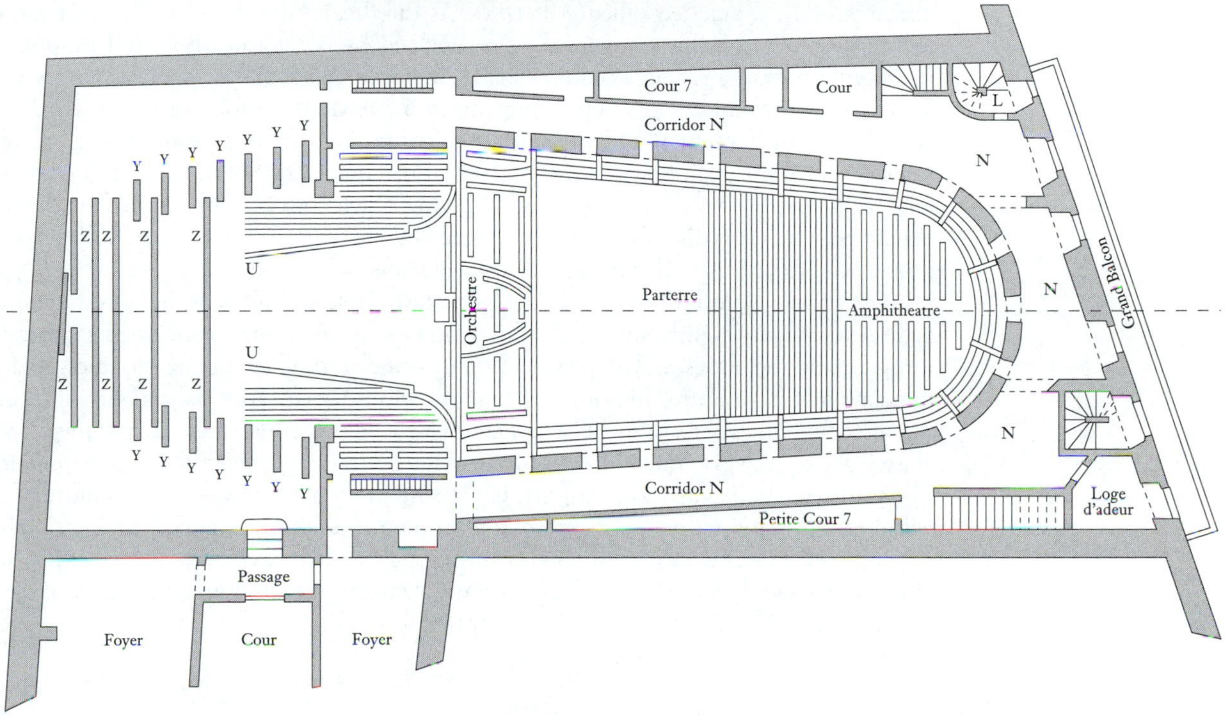

The Comédie Française had this basic design from 1689 to 1770. Note the open parterre, *the wings (marked* Y) *and backdrops (marked* Z). *The benches on the stage were added during the eighteenth century.*

like the French theaters, the English houses also introduced new design and staging practices: a proscenium stage flanked by a large **APRON**, footlights to illuminate the stage, a raked pit with benches (the French *parterre* was flat and had no seats), side and rear box seats, and a rear gallery. This division of the house accorded with social and class distinctions in the audience, which was in any event a narrow selection of the English public, in part because the theater was recognized as the ornament of the privileged, and — not incidentally — because plays were produced in the afternoon, when working people could not easily attend. The entire auditorium was lighted by chandeliers, making the audience itself very much a part of the show: in an important sense the performance did not stop at the edge of the stage. Although the theaters were not at the court itself, they were frequently patronized by courtiers and the nobility, who preened and displayed themselves to the audience — sometimes from seats onstage. Charles II — who numbered the well-known actress Nell Gwynne (1650–1687) among his many mistresses — was also frequently in the audience.

Companies were generally managed by one of the actors, and avoided the need for lengthy casting and rehearsal by developing **LINES OF BUSINESS**, in which each actor would specialize in a particular type of character: heroic lead, comic lead, male heavy, female heavy, utility player, and so on. Acting style was relatively formal, and actors often played downstage on the apron directly to the audience; a famous speech — one of Hamlet's soliloquies, for example — would be delivered directly to the audience, something like an operatic aria today, a practice called POINTING. As the theater developed in the later seventeenth century, sharing companies were replaced by companies financed by outside investors, who paid the actors salaries and took a percentage of the profits. Companies were large and salaries low; actors were compensated by BENEFIT performances, in which the actor (on his or her benefit night) received the entire profit from a given evening's performance, minus the operating expenses of the house. The practice of supplementing salaries with benefit performances continued well into the nineteenth century, and although most benefit nights — after the house expenses were deducted — left the actors with little additional pay, benefits provided an excuse to keep actors' salaries low.

By far the greatest innovation in the English theater, though, was the introduction of actresses onstage. English comedies in this period were often frankly concerned with sexual intrigue, and the actresses who played in them — and in the new heroic tragedies, and in the plays by Shakespeare, Jonson, Fletcher, and other Renaissance playwrights who continued to hold the stage — also had a reputation for sexual licentiousness. Yet, while several actresses, like Nell Gwynne, were mistresses of the famous and powerful, the phenomenon of regarding actresses as sexual objects, of classing them with prostitutes, has more to do with the status and vulnerability of working women in a highly stratified and patriarchal society than it does with the immorality of the stage or its performers. Indeed, actresses' ongoing struggle to assert themselves as legitimate performers is born at this time as well, epitomized in the careers of Elizabeth Barry (1658–1713), Anne Bracegirdle (1663–1748), and many others.

DRAMATIC INNOVATION IN FRANCE AND ENGLAND

Although theatrical production extended into a number of other forms — ballet, opera, royal pageants, and the special-effects extravaganzas called MACHINE PLAYS — prevailing attitudes prohibited the mixing of dramatic genres: tragedy and comedy were firmly discriminated from one another and from other kinds of entertainment. In France, comedy — and, indeed, the organization of theatrical companies — was particularly influenced by the techniques of the Italian COMMEDIA DELL' ARTE. The term means the "comedy of the professional players," and *commedia* became popular throughout Europe in the sixteenth century. *Commedia* companies were itinerant (though one was established in Paris for part of Louis XIV's reign), organized around ten or twelve actors, men and women, each of whom played a stock character who could be easily recognized by typical and routine behavior. Although the characters were fixed, the plots that *commedia* companies played were generally improvised. The actor relied on the traits of his or her character and a core of stage business from which to invent action and dialogue. The cast usually included one or two pairs of young lovers (the INNAMORATO and INNAMORATA), good-looking, aristocratic or fashionable characters played without masks. The rest of the cast was masked and played more stereotypical roles: the CAPITANO, a military braggart and coward, played with sword and cape; the PANTALONE, an elderly dupe, often in love, played in stockings, breeches and slippers; the DOTTORE, sometimes actually a doctor, but otherwise a pedantic friend of Pantalone's; and a variety of comic parts called ZANNI, usually sly servants. The most familiar of these parts is *Arlecchino*, or HARLEQUIN, a cunning character who is usually an acrobat, wearing a patched costume (later refined to a diamond-shaped pattern), a black cap, and carrying his slapstick — the origin of our term "slapstick," which gives some idea of what *commedia* humor was like. *Commedia* was also popular in England, but its long-term effects were less on the comic drama than on the rise of English PANTOMIME. In England, plays were often followed by a short AFTERPIECE, which frequently led Harlequin into

CHRISTOPHER WREN'S THEATRE ROYAL, DRURY LANE

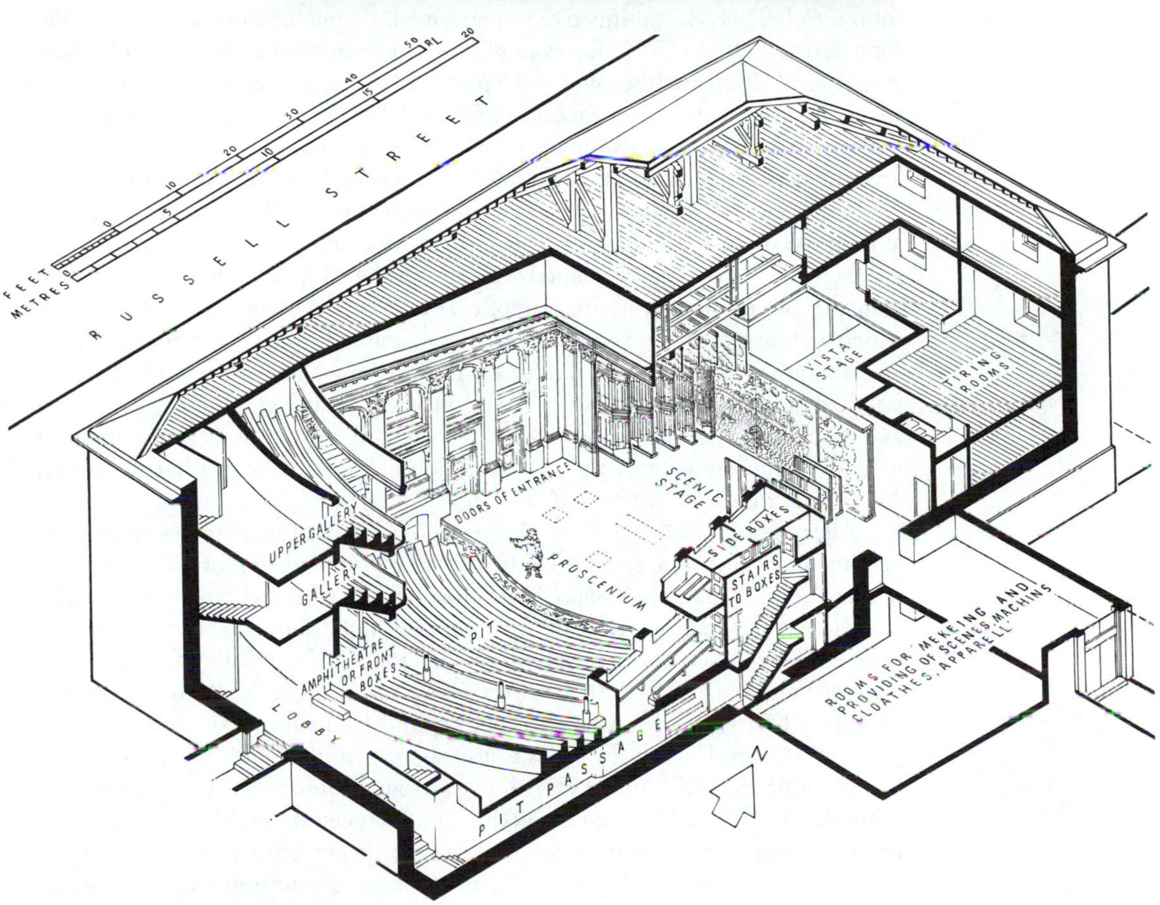

In 1674, the architect Christopher Wren designed a new Theatre Royal, Drury Lane. Note that the acting area extends to the apron, in front of the wing and backdrop stage scenery. Pit seating, side boxes, and two galleries also are visible.

adventures with mythological characters. John Rich (1692–1761), taking the name Lun, was the most famous Harlequin of the early eighteenth-century English stage.

French tragic drama inherited a taste for classical subject matter from the schools and universities, which had led Europe in translating Greek and Roman playwrights into French. Throughout the sixteenth century, the court sponsored a variety of efforts to classicize the theater, supporting several important playwrights, including Robert Garnier and Étienne Jodelle, who created highly wrought and refined tragedies based on the model of classical drama. The heroic tragedies of Pierre Corneille (1606–1684) and Jean Racine (1639–1699) epitomize this tradition while also turning it in a new direction, refracting contemporary moral, political, and philosophical issues through the lens of a classical style.

English drama in the Restoration was also affected by the **HEROIC TRAGEDIES** of France and Spain, as well as by the tragedies of Shakespeare, and of Francis Beaumont and John Fletcher, which continued to be performed, though often in revised or adapted form. John Dryden (1631–1700), for example, not only adapted versions of *The Tempest* and *Antony and Cleopatra* (the latter as *All for Love*, 1677), but also wrote plays in the mode of heroic tragedy, such as *Aureng-Zebe* (1675) and *The Conquest of Granada* (1669). Heroic tragedy generally represents the idealized passions of characters forced to choose between love and personal honor. Comic drama took its inspiration both from European models — Molière's plays, for example — and from the earlier plays of Ben Jonson, but in the plays of William Wycherley (1640–1716), Sir George Etherege (1635–1692), and William Congreve (1670–1729), English comedy rapidly developed its own original style. Restoration comedies are most often in the vein of **COMEDY OF MANNERS**, contemporary dramas in which witty aristocrats, city dupes and dandies, and dull country gentlemen are engaged in an elaborate adventure of sexual intrigue. Restoration comedy is often elegant and verbally polished, and obsessed with issues of class, privilege, manners, and sex. In addition, much as the Restoration theater witnessed the rise of actresses onstage, it also saw the first women to achieve success as playwrights: Aphra Behn (1640–1689), Catharine Trotter (1679–1749), and Susanna Centlivre (1670–1723).

After the turn of the century, the risqué character of many plays spurred one of the perennial movements to restrain the theater as an immoral institution. Partly as a result of Jeremy Collier's diatribe *A Short View of the Immorality and Profaneness of the English Stage* (1698), and partly as a result of changing attitudes and social mores, English comedy after 1700 — the plays of Sir Richard Steele (1672–1729), Colley Cibber (1671–1757), George Farquhar (1678–1707), Oliver Goldsmith (1728–1774), and Richard Brinsley Sheridan (1751–1816), for instance — became more romantic and sentimental. Moreover, political satire in English theater was also sharply limited, with the passing of the Stage Licensing Act of 1737. After 1737, all plays produced for public entertainment had to be submitted for censorship prior to production. The censor could require changes, delete words, passages, or scenes, or refuse to grant permission entirely. Confronting the Act by producing a nonlicensed play was to risk the fining and imprisonment of everyone involved in the production. While theaters found a variety of ways to subvert or sidestep the law, the censorship remained in effect — with some modifications — until 1968, inhibiting the possibility of dramatic innovation.

NEOCLASSICISM, DRAMA, AND THEATER

In both France and England, the arts in general and drama in particular were closely regulated by the state, a state of affairs sustained by the rise of **NEOCLASSICISM**. Neoclassicism is, in the simplest sense, the revival of what was taken to be a "classical" ordering of the arts. The literature of classical Greece and Rome began to be recovered in the fourteenth and fifteenth centuries, first through the dissemination of texts preserved in monasteries and later through expanded contact with the Islamic world in the sixteenth and seventeenth centuries. Translating, imitating, and adapting classical texts, European writers in the later seventeenth century appeared to "revive" the principles of classical art. In practice, however, neoclassicism offered an *interpretation* of the classics, emphasizing order, control, decorum, reason, and harmony.

In many respects, neoclassicism relied on the authority of Aristotle's *Poetics*, published first in Latin translation in 1498 and then in Italian in 1549, and from the series of critical commentaries written on Aristotle throughout the sixteenth century. Aristotle's *Poetics* is something of a naturalist's description of the several species of poetry and their characteristics, but readers in the sixteenth and seventeenth centuries fell under the influence of Aristotle's enormous authority (see *Doctor Faustus*, Act 1) and quickly transformed the

PANTALONE AND HARLEQUIN

A Pantalone *(left) in* commedia dell' arte *from one of Jacques Callot's famous series of seventeenth-century etchings. Note mask and breeches. Also, a* commedia dell' arte *Harlequin (right). This anonymous seventeenth-century etching shows Harlequin's mask, his slapstick, and his diamond-shaped patches.*

Poetics into a prescription, a series of rules, for producing the most perfect and effective tragedies. Two central precepts of the *Poetics* regard the tragic hero's actions: those acts must seem both necessary and probable, and they should not entirely violate moral expectations. Neoclassical critics and playwrights schematized Aristotle's descriptions as necessary features of dramatic composition, arguing that a tragedy should be rigorously and causally plotted and should reveal the workings of providential justice through the actions of universalized or typical characters. These goals were transformed into the famous "unities" of neoclassicism: a play should take place within a single day (unity of time), in one location (unity of place), and consist of a single line of action, a single plot (unity of action). The action of neoclassical tragedy, therefore, is concentrated, maintaining a uniformity of tone and style called DECORUM. Plays in this mode maintain a single, narrow range of language and behavior; the action is either idealized (rather than realistic) in tragedy, or commonplace in comedy: tragic characters are classic and heroic, while comic characters are contemporary, even bourgeois; tragedy undertakes the conflict between the ideal passions of love and honor, while comedy takes its cue from more earthly desires — lust, greed, hypocrisy, and so on. Following the recovery of Vitruvius' *De Architectura* (15 B.C.) in 1414, this neoclassical sensibility urged the modern stage to imitate Vitruvius' distinction between the proper stage settings of tragedy and comedy: classical architecture for tragedy, urban architecture for comedy. Especially in seventeenth-century Paris, theaters adjusted their stagecraft to these ideals of regularity and decorum, assigning a generalized palace setting to the elevated world of tragedy, and the *chambre à quatre portes* — the room with four doors — to the lower, contemporary world of comedy.

Writing later in the eighteenth century, the Englishman Thomas Davies characterized the differences between French and English audiences, and suggests that neoclassical ideals did not take root as deeply in the English theater as they did in France:

> The Frenchman, when he goes to a play, seems to make his entertainment a matter of importance. The long speeches in the plays of Corneille, Racine, Crebillon, and Voltaire, which would disgust an English ear, are extremely pleasing to our light neighbours: they sit in silence, and enjoy the beauty of sentiment, and energy of language; and are taught habitually to cry at scenes of distress. The Englishman looks upon the theatre as a place of amusement; he does not expect to be alarmed with terror, or wrought upon by scenes of commiseration; but he is surprised into the feeling of those passions, and sheds tears because he cannot avoid it. The theatre, to most Englishmen, becomes a place of instruction by chance.

Davies, of course, betrays a common chauvinism of the English toward the French: while the French are pedantic and calculating, the English are spontaneous. But this distinction between English and French theaters — one for "art," one for "entertainment;" one tragic, one comic — conceals the fundamental likenesses between the two institutions and the plays they put on the stage. As the plays of Corneille, Racine, and Dryden suggest, neoclassical tragedy imposes severe and artificial forms on the irrepressible forces of the passions, which inevitably break through the formal speech and decorous behavior of the characters to destroy them and sometimes the state as well. Comedy of the period in England and in France reveals a cognate tension, as the formal acting styles and stereotyped characters common in Restoration comedy seem barely able to contain the bottomless appetites of the plays' heroes. To this extent, neoclassical decorum embodies a barely contained anxiety about the power of forms — forms of conduct, forms of art, forms of state — to prevent a revolution of unreason and disorder.

MOLIÈRE

Jean-Baptiste Poquelin (1622–1673) was born into a prosperous mercantile family with connections at court; his father, Jean Poquelin, secured the honor of *tapissier ordinaire du roi*, the upholsterer to the court, which carried an annual pension. Jean Poquelin also educated his son in the traditional disciplines of the humanities, philosophy, and the classics and must have intended a life at court for him. In 1643, Jean-Baptiste joined with the Illustre Théâtre, a theatrical company run by the Béjart family, took the stage name Molière, and after a brief period performing in Parisian tennis courts, left with the company to play in the provinces. In 1658, after several hard and impoverished years of touring, when Molière is thought to have mastered the techniques of *commedia dell' arte*, the company was invited to perform in Paris.

Molière's career was closely tied to the court. When his brother died in 1660, he received the position of court upholsterer and the income it provided. More important, Molière became an important playwright and both wrote and acted in a splendid series of plays that satirized the manners and morals of elegant society: *Les Précieuses Ridicules* (1659), *Sganarelle* (1660), *School for Husbands* (1661), *School for Wives* (1662), *Don Juan* (1665), *The Misanthrope* (1666), *The Doctor in Spite of Himself* (1666), *The Miser* (1668), *The Learned Ladies* (1672), and *The Imaginary Invalid* (1673). Molière also prepared other entertainments at court, including many royal pageants, ballets, and machine plays devised by and for Louis. In addition to being a great dramatist, Molière was a fine comic actor as well and performed in his own plays; he died shortly after playing the title role in the fourth performance of *The Imaginary Invalid*.

The fortunes of *Tartuffe* suggest Molière's importance at court. When Molière initially produced the first three acts of the play in 1664, the clergy protested and banned the play from production in Paris. Many of Molière's plays had excited controversy, and in this case Molière appealed to the king and proceeded to revise the play. Louis's attitude is perhaps revealed by the fact that he made Molière's company the *Troupe du roi* ("King's Company") in 1665, but even the throne could not prevent the clergy from censoring Molière's second version of the play in 1667, newly titled *The Impostor*. Molière finally produced the play to acclaim in 1669, and the record of his efforts is preserved in the series of letters and prefaces included here.

Molière's theatrical company was the most influential of its day. After his death, his young wife Amanda Béjart and the actress Mademoiselle Champmeslé — newly defected from the rival company at the Hôtel de Bourgogne — established a new company, the Comédie Française. Yet although Molière achieved extraordinary status at court, because he was an actor he remained stigmatized in ways that playwrights like Racine and Corneille were not. Following its standard practice, and perhaps because of *Tartuffe*'s notoriety, the church refused to bury Molière in sacred ground. Louis XIV intervened, but was only able to persuade the Archbishop of Paris to bury Molière in a parish cemetery. The burial was conducted at night, by two priests, with no funeral ceremony.

Tartuffe

The Catholic church criticized *Tartuffe* for its portrait of hypocritical piety, but the fact that Molière played the part of Orgon may suggest that the play is as much about Tartuffe's effect on that benighted householder as it is about the title character. For if Tartuffe is hypocritical, Orgon is obsessed, less with piety than with his own desire to achieve a kind of total power and authority in his household, a kind of domestic absolutism; he is, in a sense, a comic, bourgeois Louis XIV in miniature. Moreover, Tartuffe dupes Orgon not by tricking him, but by inviting Orgon to fulfill his own fantasy of autonomy and authority. As he brags to the sensible Cléante, under Tartuffe's teaching, "my soul's been freed/From earthly loves, and every human tie:/My mother, children, brother, and wife could die,/And I'd not feel a single moment's pain." Helping Orgon to realize this fantasy, Tartuffe transforms him into a kind of monster: Orgon comes near to selling his daughter, disinheriting his son, allowing his wife to be raped, and losing his family's property and fortune.

Tartuffe is very much a play of the world, a satiric comedy. Set in an urban landscape, the play insistently translates the idealized passions of tragedy and romantic comedy — love, honor, loyalty —

into their ironic counterparts — lust, hypocrisy, betrayal. Molière peoples the play with individualized versions of the unchanging types of *commedia dell' arte* and the Roman comedy that inspired it: the reasonable and attractive heroes; an old, pedantic, self-absorbed dupe; a wily and conniving villain; a clever and witty servant. Yet Molière reinvents this range of stock characters, brilliantly turning his play toward an exploration of the folly of self-deception. For while we might take the neoclassical conflict between reason and the passions to be the hallmark of tragedy, it surges through this play as well. Orgon's passionate solipsism is, for all its ridiculousness, no less profound, troubling, or destructive than the obsessed affections of Racine's Phaedra and Hippolytus. Also, Orgon's redemption, by fiat of the king, seems no less arbitrary than the vengeful caprice of Venus or Neptune in Racine's tragedy.

Since the characters cannot change in Molière's comedy, then change must happen to them. Molière's most brilliant device here arises in the person of the king's officer, who appears to apprehend Tartuffe and to restore Orgon and his family to their property: property is what establishes the position, the place, the social and individual identity of these characters. Although Molière's *DEUS EX MACHINA* might be regarded as an elegant (though somewhat clumsy) compliment to the king — and, perhaps, as a sly jab at the clerical critics who attacked *Tartuffe* — this device plays a subtle role in dramatizing the nature of royal authority. For in *Tartuffe*, the king has the power to assign every person to his or her proper place, to see into our inmost hearts, to structure the moral and social order of the world as the reflection of his own will and judgment: *"L'état, c'est moi."* In this sense, even though *Tartuffe* unleashes the uncontrollable power of self-delusion, and the power and destructive fantasies of absolute authority, it concludes by asserting the legitimacy of that absolute power. Molière's *deus ex machina* testifies both to the power and to the arbitrariness of the king's authority.

— PREFACE[1] —

Here is a comedy that has excited a good deal of discussion and that has been under attack for a long time; and the persons who are mocked by it have made it plain that they are more powerful in France than all whom my plays have satirized up to this time. Noblemen, ladies of fashion, cuckolds, and doctors all kindly consented to their presentation, which they themselves seemed to enjoy along with everyone else; but hypocrites do not understand banter: they became angry at once, and found it strange that I was bold enough to represent their actions and to care to describe a profession shared by so many good men. This is a crime for which they cannot forgive me, and they have taken up arms against my comedy in a terrible rage. They were careful not to attack it at the point that had wounded them: they are too crafty for that and too clever to reveal their true character. In keeping with their lofty custom, they have used the cause of God to mask their private interests; and *Tartuffe*, they say, is a play that offends piety: it is filled with abominations from beginning to end, and nowhere is there a line that does not deserve to be burned. Every syllable is wicked, the very gestures are criminal, and the slightest glance, turn of the head, or step from right to left conceals mysteries that they are able to explain to my disadvantage. In vain did I submit the play to the criticism of my friends and the scrutiny of the public: all the corrections I could make, the judgment of the king and queen who saw the play,[2] the approval of great princes and ministers of state who honored it with their presence, the opinion of good men who found it worthwhile, all this did not help. They will not let go of their prey, and every day of the week they have pious zealots abusing me in public and damning me out of charity.

I would care very little about all they might say except that their devices make enemies of men whom I respect and gain the support of genuinely good men, whose faith they know and who, because of the warmth of their piety, readily accept the impressions that others present to them. And it is this which forces me to defend myself. Especially to the truly devout do I wish to vindicate my play,

---

[1] Molière added his three petitions to Louis XIV; they follow the preface.
[2] Louis XIV was married to Marie Thérèse of Austria.

and I beg of them with all my heart not to condemn it before seeing it, to rid themselves of preconceptions, and not aid the cause of men dishonored by their actions.

If one takes the trouble to examine my comedy in good faith, he will surely see that my intentions are innocent throughout, and tend in no way to make fun of what men revere; that I have presented the subject with all the precautions that its delicacy imposes; and that I have used all the art and skill that I could to distinguish clearly the character of the hypocrite from that of the truly devout man. For that purpose I used two whole acts to prepare the appearance of my scoundrel. Never is there a moment's doubt about his character; he is known at once from the qualities I have given him; and from one end of the play to the other, he does not say a word, he does not perform an action which does not depict to the audience the character of a wicked man, and which does not bring out in sharp relief the character of the truly good man which I oppose to it.

I know full well that by way of reply, these gentlemen try to insinuate that it is not the role of the theater to speak of these matters; but with their permission, I ask them on what do they base this fine doctrine. It is a proposition they advance as no more than a supposition, for which they offer not a shred of proof; and surely it would not be difficult to show them that comedy, for the ancients, had its origin in religion and constituted a part of its ceremonies; that our neighbors, the Spaniards, have hardly a single holiday celebration in which a comedy is not a part; and that even here in France, it owes its birth to the efforts of a religious brotherhood who still own the Hôtel de Bourgogne, where the most important mystery plays of our faith were presented;[3] that you can still find comedies printed in gothic letters under the name of a learned doctor of the Sorbonne;[4] and without going so far, in our own day the religious dramas of Pierre Corneille[5] have been performed to the admiration of all France.

If the function of comedy is to correct men's vices, I do not see why any should be exempt. Such a condition in our society would be much more dangerous than the thing itself; and we have seen that the theater is admirably suited to provide correction. The most forceful lines of a serious moral statement are usually less powerful than those of satire; and nothing will reform most men better than the depiction of their faults. It is a vigorous blow to vices to expose them to public laughter. Criticism is taken lightly, but men will not tolerate satire. They are quite willing to be mean, but they never like to be ridiculed.

I have been attacked for having placed words of piety in the mouth of my impostor. Could I avoid doing so in order to represent properly the character of a hypocrite? It seemed to me sufficient to reveal the criminal motives which make him speak as he does, and I have eliminated all ceremonial phrases, which nonetheless he would not have been found using incorrectly. Yet some say that in the fourth act he sets forth a vicious morality; but is not this a morality which everyone has heard again and again? Does my comedy say anything new here? And is there any fear that ideas so thoroughly detested by everyone can make an impression on men's minds; that I make them dangerous by presenting them in the theater; that they acquire authority from the lips of a scoundrel? There is not the slightest suggestion of any of this; and one must either approve the comedy of *Tartuffe* or condemn all comedies in general.

This has indeed been done in a furious way for some time now, and never was the theater so much abused.[6] I cannot deny that there were Church Fathers who condemned comedy; but neither will it be denied me that there were some who looked on it somewhat more favorably. Thus authority, on which censure is supposed to depend, is destroyed by this disagreement; and the only conclusion that can be drawn from this difference of opinion among men enlightened by the same wisdom is that they viewed comedy in different ways, and that some considered it in its purity, while others regarded

---

[3] A reference to the *Confrérie de la Passion et Résurrection de Notre-Seigneur* (the Fraternity of the Passion and Resurrection of Our Saviour), founded in 1402. The Hôtel de Bourgogne was a rival theater of Molière.

[4] Probably Maitre Jehán Michel, a medical doctor who wrote mystery plays.

[5] Pierre Corneille (1606–1684) and Racine were France's two greatest writers of classic tragedy. The two dramas Molière doubtlessly had in mind were *Polyeucte* (1643) and *Théodore, vierge et martyre* (1645).

[6] Molière had in mind Nicole's two attacks on the theater: *Visionnaries* (1666) and *Traité de Comédie*, the Prince de Conti's *Traité de Comédie* (1666).

it in its corruption and confused it with all those wretched performances which have been rightly called performances of filth.

And in fact, since we should talk about things rather than words, and since most misunderstanding comes from including contrary notions in the same word, we need only to remove the veil of ambiguity and look at comedy in itself to see if it warrants condemnation. It will surely be recognized that as it is nothing more than a clever poem which corrects men's faults by means of agreeable lessons, it cannot be condemned without injustice. And if we listened to the voice of ancient times on this matter, it would tell us that its most famous philosophers have praised comedy—they who professed so austere a wisdom and who ceaselessly denounced the vices of their times. It would tell us that Aristotle spent his evenings at the theater[7] and took the trouble to reduce the art of making comedies to rules. It would tell us that some of its greatest and most honored men took pride in writing comedies themselves,[8] and that others did not disdain to recite them in public; that Greece expressed its admiration for this art by means of handsome prizes and magnificent theaters to honor it; and finally, that in Rome this same art also received extraordinary honors; I do not speak of Rome run riot under the license of the emperors, but of disciplined Rome, governed by the wisdom of the consuls, and in the age of the full vigor of Roman dignity.

I admit that there have been times when comedy became corrupt. And what do men not corrupt every day? There is nothing so innocent that men cannot turn it to crime; nothing so beneficial that its values cannot be reversed; nothing so good in itself that it cannot be put to bad uses. Medical knowledge benefits mankind and is revered as one of our most wonderful possessions; and yet there was a time when it fell into discredit, and was often used to poison men. Philosophy is a gift of Heaven; it has been given to us to bring us to the knowledge of a God by contemplating the wonders of nature; and yet we know that often it has been turned away from its function and has been used openly in support of impiety. Even the holiest of things are not immune from human corruption, and every day we see scoundrels who use and abuse piety, and wickedly make it serve the greatest of crimes. But this does not prevent one from making the necessary distinctions. We do not confuse in the same false inference the goodness of things that are corrupted with the wickedness of the corrupt. The function of an art is always distinguished from its misuse; and as medicine is not forbidden because it was banned in Rome,[9] nor philosophy because it was publicly condemned in Athens,[10] we should not suppress comedy simply because it has been condemned at certain times. This censure was justified then for reasons which no longer apply today; it was limited to what was then seen; and we should not seize on these limits, apply them more rigidly than is necessary, and include in our condemnation the innocent along with the guilty. The comedy that this censure attacked is in no way the comedy that we want to defend. We must be careful not to confuse the one with the other. There may be two persons whose morals may be completely different. They may have no resemblance to one another except in their names, and it would be a terrible injustice to want to condemn Olympia, who is a good woman, because there is also an Olympia who is lewd. Such procedures would make for great confusion everywhere. Everything under the sun would be condemned; now since this rigor is not applied to the countless instances of abuse we see every day, the same should hold for comedy, and those plays should be approved in which instruction and virtue reign supreme.

I know there are some so delicate that they cannot tolerate a comedy, who say that the most decent are the most dangerous, that the passions they present are all the more moving because they are virtuous, and that men's feelings are stirred by these presentations. I do not see what great crime it is to be affected by the sight of a generous passion; and this utter insensitivity to which they would lead us is indeed a high degree of virtue! I wonder if so great a perfection resides within the strength of human nature, and I wonder if it is not better to try to correct and moderate men's passions than to try to suppress them altogether. I grant that there are places better to visit than the theater; and if we want to condemn every single thing that does not bear directly on God and our salvation, it is right that

---

[7]A reference to Aristotle's *Poetics* (composed between 335 and 322 B.C., the year of his death).

[8]The Roman consul and general responsible for the final destruction of Carthage in 146 B.C., Scipio Africanus Minor (*ca.* 185–129 B.C.), collaborated with the writer of comedies, Terence (Publius Terentius Afer, *ca.* 195 or 185 -*ca.* 159 B.C.).

[9]Pliny the Elder says that the Romans expelled their doctors at the same time that the Greeks did theirs.

[10]An allusion to Socrates' condemnation to death.

comedy be included, and I should willingly grant that it be condemned along with everything else. But if we admit, as is in fact true, that the exercise of piety will permit interruptions, and that men need amusement, I maintain that there is none more innocent than comedy. I have dwelled too long on this matter. Let me finish with the words of a great prince on the comedy, *Tartuffe*.[11]

Eight days after it had been banned, a play called *Scaramouche the Hermit*[12] was performed before the court; and the king, on his way out, said to this great prince: "I should really like to know why the persons who make so much noise about Molière's comedy do not say a word about *Scaramouche*." To which the prince replied, "It is because the comedy of *Scaramouche* makes fun of Heaven and religion, which these gentlemen do not care about at all, but that of Molière makes fun of *them*, and that is what they cannot bear."

Molière

FIRST PETITION[13]
(PRESENTED TO THE KING ON THE COMEDY OF TARTUFFE)

Sire,

As the duty of comedy is to correct men by amusing them, I believed that in my occupation I could do nothing better than attack the vices of my age by making them ridiculous; and as hypocrisy is undoubtedly one of the most common, most improper, and most dangerous, I thought, Sire, that I would perform a service for all good men of your kingdom if I wrote a comedy which denounced hypocrites and placed in proper view all of the contrived poses of these incredibly virtuous men, all of the concealed villainies of these counterfeit believers who would trap others with a fraudulent piety and a pretended virtue.

I have written this comedy, Sire, with all the care and caution that the delicacy of the subject demands; and so as to maintain all the more properly the admiration and respect due to truly devout men, I have delineated my character as sharply as I could; I have left no room for doubt; I have removed all that might confuse good with evil, and have used for this painting only the specific colors and essential lines that make one instantly recognize a true and brazen hypocrite.

Nevertheless, all my precautions have been to no avail. Others have taken advantage of the delicacy of your feelings on religious matters, and they have been able to deceive you on the only side of your character which lies open to deception: your respect for holy things. By underhanded means, the Tartuffes have skillfully gained Your Majesty's favor, and the models have succeeded in eliminating the copy, no matter how innocent it may have been and no matter what resemblance was found between them.

Although the suppression of this work was a serious blow for me, my misfortune was nonetheless softened by the way in which Your Majesty explained his attitude on the matter; and I believed, Sire, that Your Majesty removed any cause I had for complaint, as you were kind enough to declare that you found nothing in this comedy that you would forbid me to present in public.

Yet, despite this glorious declaration of the greatest and most enlightened king in the world, despite the approval of the Papal Legate[14] and of most of our churchmen, all of whom, at private readings of my work, agreed with the views of Your Majesty, despite all this, a book has appeared by a certain priest[15] which boldly contradicts all of these noble judgments. Your Majesty expressed himself

---

[11]One of Molière's benefactors who liked the play was the Prince de Condé; de Condé had *Tartuffe* read to him and also privately performed for him.

[12]A troupe of Italian comedians had just performed the licentious farce, where a hermit dressed as a monk makes love to a married woman, announcing that *questo e per mortificar la carne* ("this is to mortify the flesh").

[13]The first of the three *petitions* or *placets* to Louis XIV concerning the play. On May 12, 1664, *Tartuffe*—or at least the first three acts roughly as they now stand—was performed at Versailles. A cabal unfavorable to Molière, including the Archbishop of Paris, Hardouin de Péréfixe, Queen-Mother Anne of Austria, certain influential courtiers, and the Brotherhood or Company of the Holy Sacrament (formed in 1627 to enforce morality), arranged that the play be banned and Molière censured.

[14]Cardinal Legate Chigi, nephew to Pope Alexander VII, heard a reading of *Tartuffe* at Fontainebleau on August 4, 1664.

[15]Pierre Roullé, the curate of St. Barthélémy, who wrote a scathing attack on the play and sent his book to the king.

in vain, and the Papal Legate and churchmen gave their opinion to no avail: sight unseen, my comedy is diabolical, and so is my brain; I am a devil garbed in flesh and disguised as a man,[16] a libertine, a disbeliever who deserves a punishment that will set an example. It is not enough that fire expiate my crime in public, for that would be letting me off too easily: the generous piety of this good man will not stop there; he will not allow me to find any mercy in the sight of God; he demands that I be damned, and that will settle the matter.

This book, Sire, was presented to Your Majesty; and I am sure that you see for yourself how unpleasant it is for me to be exposed daily to the insults of these gentlemen, what harm these abuses will do my reputation if they must be tolerated, and finally, how important it is for me to clear myself of these false charges and let the public know that my comedy is nothing more than what they want it to be. I will not ask, Sire, for what I need for the sake of my reputation and the innocence of my work: enlightened kings such as you do not need to be told what is wished of them; like God, they see what we need and know better than we what they should give us. It is enough for me to place my interests in Your Majesty's hands, and I respectfully await whatever you may care to command.

(*August*, *1664*)

SECOND PETITION[17]

(PRESENTED TO THE KING IN HIS CAMP BEFORE THE CITY OF LILLE, IN FLANDERS)

Sire,

It is bold indeed for me to ask a favor of a great monarch in the midst of his glorious victories; but in my present situation, Sire, where will I find protection anywhere but where I seek it, and to whom can I appeal against the authority of the power that crushes me,[18] if not to the source of power and authority, the just dispenser of absolute law, the sovereign judge and master of all?

My comedy, Sire, has not enjoyed the kindnesses of Your Majesty. All to no avail, I produced it under the title of *The Hypocrite* and disguised the principal character as a man of the world; in vain I gave him a little hat, long hair, a wide collar, a sword, and lace clothing,[19] softened the action and carefully eliminated all that I thought might provide even the shadow of grounds for discontent on the part of the famous models of the portrait I wished to present; nothing did any good. The conspiracy of opposition revived even at mere conjecture of what the play would be like. They found a way of persuading those who in all other matters plainly insist that they are not to be deceived. No sooner did my comedy appear than it was struck down by the very power which should impose respect; and all that I could do to save myself from the fury of this tempest was to say that Your Majesty had given me permission to present the play and I did not think it was necessary to ask this permission of others, since only Your Majesty could have refused it.

I have no doubt, Sire, that the men whom I depict in my comedy will employ every means possible to influence Your Majesty, and will use, as they have used already, those truly good men who are all the more easily deceived because they judge of others by themselves.[20] They know how to display all of their aims in the most favorable light; yet, no matter how pious they may seem, it is surely not the interests of God which stir them; they have proven this often enough in the comedies they have allowed to be performed hundreds of times without making the least objection. Those plays

---

[16]Molière took some of these phrases from Roullé.

[17]On August 5, 1667, *Tartuffe* was performed at the Palais-Royal. The opposition — headed by the First President of Parliament — brought in the police, and the play was stopped. Since Louis was campaigning in Flanders, friends of Molière brought the second *placet* to Lille. Louis had always been favorable toward the playwright; in August 1665, Molière's company, the *Troupe de Monsieur* (nominally sponsored by Louis's brother Philippe, Duc d'Orléans) had become the *Troupe du Roi*.

[18]President de Lanvignon, in charge of the Paris police.

[19]There is evidence that in 1664 Tartuffe played his role dressed in a cassock, thus allying him more directly to the clergy.

[20]Molière apparently did not know that de Lanvignon had been affiliated with the Company of the Holy Sacrament for the previous ten years.

attacked only piety and religion, for which they care very little; but this play attacks and makes fun of them, and that is what they cannot bear. They will never forgive me for unmasking their hypocrisy in the eyes of everyone. And I am sure that they will not neglect to tell Your Majesty that people are shocked by my comedy. But the simple truth, Sire, is that all Paris is shocked only by its ban, that the most scrupulous persons have found its presentation worthwhile, and men are astounded that individuals of such known integrity should show so great a deference to people whom everyone should abominate and who are so clearly opposed to the true piety which they profess.

I respectfully await the judgment that Your Majesty will deign to pronounce: but it's certain, Sire, that I need not think of writing comedies if the Tartuffes are triumphant, if they thereby seize the right to persecute me more than ever, and find fault with even the most innocent lines that flow from my pen.

Let your goodness, Sire, give me protection against their envenomed rage, and allow me, at your return from so glorious a campaign, to relieve Your Majesty from the fatigue of his conquests, give him innocent pleasures after such noble accomplishments, and make the monarch laugh who makes all Europe tremble!

(August, 1667)

THIRD PETITION

(PRESENTED TO THE KING)

Sire,

A very honest doctor[21] whose patient I have the honor to be, promises and will legally contract to make me live another thirty years if I can obtain a favor for him from Your Majesty. I told him of his promise that I do not deserve so much, and that I should be glad to help him if he will merely agree not to kill me. This favor, Sire, is a post of canon at your royal chapel of Vincennes, made vacant by death.

May I dare to ask for this favor from Your Majesty on the very day of the glorious resurrection of *Tartuffe*, brought back to life by your goodness? By this first favor I have been reconciled with the devout, and the second will reconcile me with the doctors.[22] Undoubtedly this would be too much grace for me at one time, but perhaps it would not be too much for Your Majesty, and I await your answer to my petition with respectful hope.

(February, 1669)

---

[21]A physician friend, M. de Mauvillain, who helped Molière with some of the medical details of *Le Malada imaginaire*.

[22]Doctors are ridiculed to varying degrees in earlier plays of Molière: *Dom Juan*, *L'Amour médecin*, and *Le Médecin malgré lui*.

T A R T U F F E

Molière

TRANSLATED BY RICHARD WILBUR

— CHARACTERS —

MADAME PERNELLE, *Orgon's mother*
ORGON, *Elmire's husband*
ELMIRE, *Orgon's wife*
DAMIS, *Orgon's son, Elmire's stepson*
MARIANE, *Orgon's daughter, Elmire's stepdaughter, in love with Valère*
VALÈRE, *in love with Mariane*
CLÉANTE, *Orgon's brother-in-law*

TARTUFFE, *a hypocrite*
DORINE, *Mariane's lady's-maid*
M. LOYAL, *a bailiff*
A POLICE OFFICER
FLIPOTE, *Mme Pernelle's maid*

The scene throughout: Orgon's house in Paris

— ACT ONE —

SCENE I

MADAME PERNELLE *and* FLIPOTE, *her maid*, ELMIRE, MAR-
IANE, DORINE, DAMIS, CLÉANTE

MADAME PERNELLE: Come, come, Flipote; it's time I left this
    place.
ELMIRE: I can't keep up, you walk at such a pace.
MADAME PERNELLE: Don't trouble, child; no need to show
    me out.
    It's not your manners I'm concerned about.
5 ELMIRE: We merely pay you the respect we owe.
    But, Mother, why this hurry? Must you go?
MADAME PERNELLE: I must. This house appals me. No one
    in it
    Will pay attention for a single minute.
    Children, I take my leave much vexed in spirit.
10 I offer good advice, but you won't hear it.
    You all break in and chatter on and on.
    It's like a madhouse with the keeper gone.
DORINE: If . . .
MADAME PERNELLE: Girl, you talk too much, and I'm afraid
    You're far too saucy for a lady's-maid.
15 You push in everywhere and have your say.
DAMIS: But . . .
MADAME PERNELLE: You, boy, grow more foolish every day.
    To think my grandson should be such a dunce!
    I've said a hundred times, if I've said it once,
    That if you keep the course on which you've started,
20 You'll leave your worthy father broken-hearted.
MARIANE: I think . . .
MADAME PERNELLE: And you, his sister, seem so pure,
    So shy, so innocent, and so demure.
    But you know what they say about still waters.
    I pity parents with secretive daughters.
ELMIRE: Now, Mother . . .
25 MADAME PERNELLE: And as for you, child, let me add
    That your behavior is extremely bad,
    And a poor example for these children, too.
    Their dear, dead mother did far better than you.
    You're much too free with money, and I'm distressed
30 To see you so elaborately dressed.

When it's one's husband that one aims to please,
One has no need of costly fripperies.
CLÉANTE: Oh, Madam, really . . .
MADAME PERNELLE: You are her brother, Sir,
    And I respect and love you; yet if I were
    My son, this lady's good and pious spouse,   35
    I wouldn't make you welcome in my house.
    You're full of worldly counsels which, I fear,
    Aren't suitable for decent folk to hear.
    I've spoken bluntly, Sir; but it behooves us
    Not to mince words when righteous fervor moves us.   40
DAMIS: Your man Tartuffe is full of holy speeches . . .
MADAME PERNELLE: And practises precisely what he
    preaches.
    He's a fine man, and should be listened to.
    I will not hear him mocked by fools like you.
DAMIS: Good God! Do you expect me to submit   45
    To the tyranny of that carping hypocrite?
    Must we forgo all joys and satisfactions
    Because that bigot censures all our actions?
DORINE: To hear him talk—and he talks all the time—
    There's nothing one can do that's not a crime.   50
    He rails at everything, your dear Tartuffe.
MADAME PERNELLE: Whatever he reproves deserves reproof.
    He's out to save your souls, and all of you
    Must love him, as my son would have you do.
DAMIS: Ah no, Grandmother, I could never take   55
    To such a rascal, even for my father's sake.
    That's how I feel, and I shall not dissemble.
    His every action makes me seethe and tremble
    With helpless anger, and I have no doubt
    That he and I will shortly have it out.   60
DORINE: Surely it is a shame and a disgrace
    To see this man usurp the master's place—
    To see this beggar who, when first he came,
    Had not a shoe or shoestring to his name
    So far forget himself that he behaves   65
    As if the house were his, and we his slaves.
MADAME PERNELLE: Well, mark my words, your souls would
    fare far better
    If you obeyed his precepts to the letter.

DORINE: You see him as a saint. I'm far less awed;
70   In fact, I see right through him. He's a fraud.
MADAME PERNELLE: Nonsense!
DORINE: His man Laurent's the same, or worse;
      I'd not trust either with a penny purse.
MADAME PERNELLE: I can't say what his servant's morals may
          be;
      His own great goodness I can guarantee.
75   You all regard him with distaste and fear
      Because he tells you what you're loath to hear,
      Condemns your sins, points out your moral flaws,
      And humbly strives to further Heaven's cause.
DORINE: If sin is all that bothers him, why is it
80   He's so upset when folk drop in to visit?
      Is Heaven so outraged by a social call
      That he must prophesy against us all?
      I'll tell you what I think: if you ask me,
      He's jealous of my mistress' company.
85 MADAME PERNELLE: Rubbish! (To ELMIRE.) He's not alone,
          child, in complaining
      Of all of your promiscuous entertaining.
      Why, the whole neighborhood's upset, I know,
      By all these carriages that come and go,
      With crowds of guests parading in and out
90   And noisy servants loitering about.
      In all of this, I'm sure there's nothing vicious;
      But why give people cause to be suspicious?
CLÉANTE: They need no cause; they'll talk in any case.
      Madam, this world would be a joyless place
95   If, fearing what malicious tongues might say,
      We locked our doors and turned our friends away.
      And even if one did so dreary a thing,
      D'you think those tongues would cease their chattering?
      One can't fight slander; it's a losing battle;
100   Let us instead ignore their tittle-tattle.
      Let's strive to live by conscience' clear decrees,
      And let the gossips gossip as they please.
DORINE: If there is talk against us, I know the source:
      It's Daphne and her little husband, of course.
105   Those who have greatest cause for guilt and shame
      Are quickest to besmirch a neighbor's name.
      When there's a chance for libel, they never miss it;
      When something can be made to seem illicit
      They're off at once to spread the joyous news,
110   Adding to fact what fantasies they choose.
      By talking up their neighbor's indiscretions
      They seek to camouflage their own transgressions,
      Hoping that others' innocent affairs
      Will lend a hue of innocence to theirs,
115   Or that their own black guilt will come to seem
      Part of a general shady color-scheme.
MADAME PERNELLE: All that is quite irrelevant. I doubt
      That anyone's more virtuous and devout
      Than dear Orante; and I'm informed that she
120   Condemns your mode of life most vehemently.
DORINE: Oh, yes, she's strict, devout, and has no taint
      Of worldliness; in short, she seems a saint.
      But it was time which taught her that disguise;
      She's thus because she can't be otherwise.
125   So long as her attractions could enthrall,

      She flounced and flirted and enjoyed it all,
      But now that they're no longer what they were
      She quits a world which fast is quitting her,
      And wears a veil of virtue to conceal
      Her bankrupt beauty and her lost appeal.   130
      That's what becomes of old coquettes today:
      Distressed when all their lovers fall away,
      They see no recourse but to play the prude,
      And so confer a style on solitude.
      Thereafter, they're severe with everyone,   135
      Condemning all our actions, pardoning none,
      And claiming to be pure, austere, and zealous
      When, if the truth were known, they're merely jealous,
      And cannot bear to see another know
      The pleasures time has forced them to forgo.   140
MADAME PERNELLE: (Initially to ELMIRE) That sort of talk is
          what you like to hear;
      Therefore you'd have us all keep still, my dear,
      While Madam rattles on the livelong day.
      Nevertheless, I mean to have my say.
      I tell you that you're blest to have Tartuffe   145
      Dwelling, as my son's guest, beneath this roof;
      That Heaven has sent him to forestall its wrath
      By leading you, once more, to the true path;
      That all he reprehends is reprehensible,
      And that you'd better heed him, and be sensible.   150
      These visits, balls, and parties in which you revel
      Are nothing but inventions of the Devil.
      One never hears a word that's edifying:
      Nothing but chaff and foolishness and lying,
      As well as vicious gossip in which one's neighbor   155
      Is cut to bits with epee, foil, and saber.
      People of sense are driven half-insane
      At such affairs, where noise and folly reign
      And reputations perish thick and fast.
      As a wise preacher said on Sunday last,   160
      Parties are Towers of Babylon, because
      The guests all babble on with never a pause;
      And then he told a story which, I think . . .

(To CLÉANTE.)

      I heard that laugh, Sir, and I saw that wink!
      Go find your silly friends and laugh some more!   165
      Enough; I'm going; don't show me to the door.
      I leave this household much dismayed and vexed;
      I cannot say when I shall see you next.

(Slapping FLIPOTE.)

      Wake up, don't stand there gaping into space!
      I'll slap some sense into that stupid face.   170
      Move, move, you slut.

SCENE II

CLÉANTE, DORINE

CLÉANTE: I think I'll stay behind;
      I want no further pieces of her mind.
      How that old lady . . .
DORINE: Oh, what wouldn't she say
      If she could hear you speak of her that way!

5   She'd thank you for the *lady*, but I'm sure
      She'd find the *old* a little premature.
CLÉANTE: My, what a scene she made, and what a din!
      And how this man Tartuffe has taken her in!
DORINE: Yes, but her son is even worse deceived;
10   His folly must be seen to be believed.
      In the late troubles, he played an able part
      And served his king with wise and loyal heart,
      But he's quite lost his senses since he fell
      Beneath Tartuffe's infatuating spell.
15   He calls him brother, and loves him as his life,
      Preferring him to mother, child, or wife.
      In him and him alone will he confide;
      He's made him his confessor and his guide;
      He pets and pampers him with love more tender
20   Than any pretty mistress could engender,
      Gives him the place of honor when they dine,
      Delights to see him gorging like a swine,
      Stuffs him with dainties till his guts distend,
      And when he belches, cries "God bless you, friend!"
25   In short, he's mad; he worships him; he dotes;
      His deeds he marvels at, his words he quotes,
      Thinking each act a miracle, each word
      Oracular as those that Moses heard.
      Tartuffe, much pleased to find so easy a victim,
30   Has in a hundred ways beguiled and tricked him,
      Milked him of money, and with his permission
      Established here a sort of Inquisition.
      Even Laurent, his lackey, dares to give
      Us arrogant advice on how to live;
35   He sermonizes us in thundering tones
      And confiscates our ribbons and colognes.
      Last week he tore a kerchief into pieces
      Because he found it pressed in a *Life of Jesus*:
      He said it was a sin to juxtapose
40   Unholy vanities and holy prose.

SCENE III

ELMIRE, MARIANE, DAMIS, CLÉANTE, DORINE

ELMIRE: *(To* CLÉANTE*)* You did well not to follow; she stood
      in the door
      And said *verbatim* all she'd said before.
      I saw my husband coming. I think I'd best
      Go upstairs now, and take a little rest.
5 CLÉANTE: I'll wait and greet him here; then I must go.
      I've really only time to say hello.
DAMIS: Sound him about my sister's wedding, please.
      I think Tartuffe's against it, and that he's
      Been urging Father to withdraw his blessing.
10   As you well know, I'd find that most distressing.
      Unless my sister and Valère can marry,
      My hopes to wed *his* sister will miscarry,
      And I'm determined . . .
DORINE: He's coming.

SCENE IV

ORGON, CLÉANTE, DORINE

ORGON: Ah, Brother, good-day.

CLÉANTE: Well, welcome back. I'm sorry I can't stay.
      How was the country? Blooming, I trust, and green?
ORGON: Excuse me, Brother; just one moment.

(To DORINE*.)*

                                        Dorine . . .

(To CLÉANTE*.)*

      To put my mind at rest, I always learn   5
      The household news the moment I return.

(To DORINE*)*

      Has all been well, these two days I've been gone?
      How are the family? What's been going on?
DORINE: Your wife, two days ago, had a bad fever,
      And a fierce headache which refused to leave her.   10
ORGON: Ah. And Tartuffe?
DORINE: Tartuffe? Why, he's round and red,
      Bursting with health, and excellently fed.
ORGON: Poor fellow!
DORINE: That night, the mistress was unable
      To take a single bite at the dinner-table.
      Her headache-pains, she said, were simply hellish.   15
ORGON: Ah. And Tartuffe?
DORINE: He ate his meal with relish,
      And zealously devoured in her presence
      A leg of mutton and a brace of pheasants.
ORGON: Poor fellow!
DORINE: Well, the pains continued strong,
      And so she tossed and tossed the whole night long,   20
      Now icy-cold, now burning like a flame.
      We sat beside her bed till morning came.
ORGON: Ah. And Tartuffe?
DORINE: Why, having eaten, he rose
      And sought his room, already in a doze,
      Got into his warm bed, and snored away   25
      In perfect peace until the break of day.
ORGON: Poor fellow!
DORINE: After much ado, we talked her
      Into dispatching someone for the doctor.
      He bled her, and the fever quickly fell.
ORGON: Ah. And Tartuffe?
DORINE: He bore it very well.   30
      To keep his cheerfulness at any cost,
      And make up for the blood *Madame* had lost,
      He drank, at lunch, four beakers full of port.
ORGON: Poor fellow!
DORINE: Both are doing well, in short.
      I'll go and tell *Madame* that you've expressed   35
      Keen sympathy and anxious interest.

SCENE V

ORGON, CLÉANTE

CLÉANTE: That girl was laughing in your face, and though
      I've no wish to offend you, even so
      I'm bound to say that she had some excuse.
      How can you possibly be such a goose?
      Are you so dazed by this man's hocus-pocus   5
      That all the world, save him, is out of focus?

You've given him clothing, shelter, food, and care;
Why must you also . . .
ORGON: Brother, stop right there.
You do not know the man of whom you speak.
10   CLÉANTE: I grant you that. But my judgment's not so weak
That I can't tell, by his effect on others . . .
ORGON: Ah, when you meet him, you two will be like
      brothers!
There's been no loftier soul since time began.
He is a man who . . . a man who . . . an excellent man.
15   To keep his precepts is to be reborn,
And view this dunghill of a world with scorn.
Yes, thanks to him I'm a changed man indeed.
Under his tutelage my soul's been freed
From earthly loves, and every human tie:
20   My mother, children, brother, and wife could die,
And I'd not feel a single moment's pain.
CLÉANTE: That's a fine sentiment, Brother; most humane.
ORGON: Oh, had you seen Tartuffe as I first knew him,
Your heart, like mine, would have surrendered to him.
25   He used to come into our church each day
And humbly kneel nearby, and start to pray.
He'd draw the eyes of everybody there
By the deep fervor of his heartfelt prayer;
He'd sigh and weep, and sometimes with a sound
30   Of rapture he would bend and kiss the ground;
And when I rose to go, he'd run before
To offer me holy-water at the door.
His serving-man, no less devout than he,
Informed me of his master's poverty;
35   I gave him gifts, but in his humbleness
He'd beg me every time to give him less.
"Oh, that's too much," he'd cry, "too much by twice!
I don't deserve it. The half, Sir, would suffice."
And when I wouldn't take it back, he'd share
40   Half of it with the poor, right then and there.
At length, Heaven prompted me to take him in
To dwell with us, and free our souls from sin.
He guides our lives, and to protect my honor
Stays by my wife, and keeps an eye upon her;
45   He tells me whom she sees, and all she does,
And seems more jealous than I ever was!
And how austere he is! Why, he can detect
A mortal sin where you would least suspect;
In smallest trifles, he's extremely strict.
50   Last week, his conscience was severely pricked
Because, while praying, he had caught a flea
And killed it, so he felt, too wrathfuly.
CLÉANTE: Good God, man! Have you lost your common
      sense—
Or is this all some joke at my expense?
55   How can you stand there and in all sobriety . . .
ORGON: Brother, your language savors of impiety.
Too much free-thinking's made your faith unsteady,
And as I've warned you many times already,
'Twill get you into trouble before you're through.
60   CLÉANTE: So I've been told before by dupes like you:
Being blind, you'd have all others blind as well;
The clear-eyed man you call an infidel,
And he who sees through humbug and pretense

Is charged, by you, with want of reverence.
Spare me your warnings, Brother; I have no fear   65
Of speaking out, for you and Heaven to hear,
Against affected zeal and pious knavery.
There's true and false in piety, as in bravery,
And just as those whose courage shines the most
In battle, are the least inclined to boast,   70
So those whose hearts are truly pure and lowly
Don't make a flashy show of being holy.
There's a vast difference, so it seems to me,
Between true piety and hypocrisy:
How do you fail to see it, may I ask?   75
Is not a face quite different from a mask?
Cannot sincerity and cunning art,
Reality and semblance, be told apart?
Are scarecrows just like men, and do you hold
That a false coin is just as good as gold?   80
Ah, Brother, man's a strangely fashioned creature
Who seldom is content to follow Nature,
But recklessly pursues his inclination
Beyond the narrow bounds of moderation,
And often, by transgressing Reason's laws,   85
Perverts a lofty aim or noble cause.
A passing observation, but it applies.
ORGON: I see, dear Brother, that you're profoundly wise;
You harbor all the insight of the age.
You are our one clear mind, our only sage,   90
The era's oracle, its Cato too,
And all mankind are fools compared to you.
CLÉANTE: Brother, I don't pretend to be a sage,
Nor have I all the wisdom of the age.
There's just one insight I would dare to claim: 95
I know that true and false are not the same;
And just as there is nothing I more revere
Than a soul whose faith is steadfast and sincere,
Nothing that I more cherish and admire
Than honest zeal and true religious fire,   100
So there is nothing that I find more base
Than specious piety's dishonest face—
Than these bold mountebanks, these histrios
Whose impious mummeries and hollow shows
Exploit our love of Heaven, and make a jest   105
Of all that men think holiest and best;
These calculating souls who offer prayers
Not to their Maker, but as public wares,
And seek to buy respect and reputation
With lifted eyes and sighs of exaltation;   110
These charlatans, I say, whose pilgrim souls
Proceed, by way of Heaven, toward earthly goals,
Who weep and pray and swindle and extort,
Who preach the monkish life, but haunt the court,
Who make their zeal the partner of their vice—   115
Such men are vengeful, sly, and cold as ice,
And when there is an enemy to defame
They cloak their spite in fair religion's name,
Their private spleen and malice being made
To seem a high and virtuous crusade,   120
Until, to mankind's reverent applause,
They crucify their foe in Heaven's cause.
Such knaves are all too common; yet, for the wise,

True piety isn't hard to recognize,
125 And, happily, these present times provide us
With bright examples to instruct and guide us.
Consider Ariston and Périandre;
Look at Oronte, Alcidamas, Clitandre;
Their virtue is acknowledged; who could doubt it?
130 But you won't hear them beat the drum about it.
They're never ostentatious, never vain,
And their religion's moderate and humane;
It's not their way to criticize and chide:
They think censoriousness a mark of pride,
135 And therefore, letting others preach and rave,
They show, by deeds, how Christians should behave.
They think no evil of their fellow man,
But judge of him as kindly as they can.
They don't intrigue and wangle and conspire;
140 To lead a good life is their one desire;
The sinner wakes no rancorous hate in them;
It is the sin alone which they condemn;
Nor do they try to show a fiercer zeal
For Heaven's cause than Heaven itself could feel.
145 These men I honor, these men I advocate
As models for us all to emulate.
Your man is not their sort at all, I fear;
And, while your praise of him is quite sincere,
I think that you've been dreadfully deluded.
150 ORGON: Now then, dear Brother, is your speech concluded?
CLÉANTE: Why, yes.
ORGON: Your servant, Sir.

(He turns to go.)

CLÉANTE: No, Brother; wait.
There's one more matter. You agreed of late
That young Valère might have your daughter's hand.
ORGON: I did.
CLÉANTE: And set the date, I understand.
ORGON: Quite so.
155 CLÉANTE: You've now postponed it; is that true?
ORGON: No doubt.
CLÉANTE: The match no longer pleases you?
ORGON: Who knows?
CLÉANTE: D'you mean to go back on your word?
ORGON: I won't say that.
CLÉANTE: Has anything occurred
Which might entitle you to break your pledge?
ORGON: Perhaps.
160 CLÉANTE: Why must you hem, and haw, and hedge?
The boy asked me to sound you in this affair . . .
ORGON: It's been a pleasure.
CLÉANTE: But what shall I tell Valère?
ORGON: Whatever you like.
CLÉANTE: But what have you decided?
What are your plans?
ORGON: I plan, Sir, to be guided
By Heaven's will.
165 CLÉANTE: Come, Brother, don't talk rot.
You've given Valère your word; will you keep it, or not?
ORGON: Good day.
CLÉANTE: This looks like poor Valère's undoing;
I'll go and warn him that there's trouble brewing.

— ACT TWO —

SCENE I

ORGON, MARIANE

ORGON: Mariane.
MARIANE: Yes, Father?
ORGON: A word with you; come here.
MARIANE: What are you looking for?
ORGON:

(Peering into a small closet.)

                                    Eavesdroppers, dear.
I'm making sure we shan't be overheard.
Someone in there could catch our every word.
Ah, good, we're safe. Now, Mariane, my child,   5
You're a sweet girl who's tractable and mild,
Whom I hold dear, and think most highly of.
MARIANE: I'm deeply grateful, Father, for your love.
ORGON: That's well said, Daughter; and you can repay me
If, in all things, you'll cheerfully obey me.   10
MARIANE: To please you, Sir, is what delights me best.
ORGON: Good, good. Now, what d'you think of Tartuffe, our
    guest?
MARIANE: I, Sir?
ORGON: Yes. Weigh your answer; think it through.
MARIANE: Oh, dear. I'll say whatever you wish me to.
ORGON: That's wisely said, my Daughter. Say of him, then, 15
That he's the very worthiest of men,
And that you're fond of him, and would rejoice
In being his wife, if that should be my choice.
Well?
MARIANE: What?
ORGON: What's that?
MARIANE: I . . .
ORGON: Well?
MARIANE: Forgive me, pray.
ORGON: Did you not hear me?
MARIANE: Of *whom*, Sir, must I say   20
That I am fond of him, and would rejoice
In being his wife, if that should be your choice?
ORGON: Why, of Tartuffe.
MARIANE: But, Father, that's false, you know.
Why would you have me say what isn't so?
ORGON: Because I am resolved it shall be true.   25
That it's my wish should be enough for you.
MARIANE: You can't mean, Father . . .
ORGON: Yes, Tartuffe shall be
Allied by marriage to this family,
And he's to be your husband, is that clear?
It's a father's privilege . . .   30

SCENE II

DORINE, ORGON, MARIANE

ORGON:

(To DORINE.)

                                What are you doing in here?

Is curiosity so fierce a passion
With you, that you must eavesdrop in this fashion?
DORINE: There's lately been a rumor going about—
5 Based on some hunch or chance remark, no doubt—
That you mean Mariane to wed Tartuffe.
I've laughed it off, of course, as just a spoof.
ORGON: You find it so incredible?
DORINE: Yes, I do.
I won't accept that story, even from you.
10 ORGON: Well, you'll believe it when the thing is done.
DORINE: Yes, yes, of course. Go on and have your fun.
ORGON: I've never been more serious in my life.
DORINE: Ha!
ORGON: Daughter, I mean it; you're to be his wife.
DORINE: No, don't believe your father; it's all a hoax.
ORGON: See here, young woman . . .
15 DORINE: Come, Sir, no more
jokes;
You can't fool us.
ORGON: How dare you talk that way?
DORINE: All right, then: we believe you, sad to say.
But how a man like you, who looks so wise
And wears a moustache of such splendid size,
Can be so foolish as to . . .
20 ORGON: Silence, please!
My girl, you take too many liberties.
I'm master here, as you must not forget.
DORINE: Do let's discuss this calmly; don't be upset.
You can't be serious, Sir, about this plan.
25 What should that bigot want with Mariane?
Praying and fasting ought to keep him busy.
And then, in terms of wealth and rank, what is he?
Why should a man of property like you
Pick out a beggar son-in-law?
ORGON: That will do.
30 Speak of his poverty with reverence.
His is a pure and saintly indigence
Which far transcends all worldly pride and pelf.
He lost his fortune, as he says himself,
Because he cared for Heaven alone, and so
35 Was careless of his interests here below.
I mean to get him out of his present straits
And help him to recover his estates—
Which, in his part of the world, have no small fame.
Poor though he is, he's a gentleman just the same.
40 DORINE: Yes, so he tells us; and, Sir, it seems to me
Such pride goes very ill with piety.
A man whose spirit spurns this dungy earth
Ought not to brag of lands and noble birth;
Such worldly arrogance will hardly square
45 With meek devotion and the life of prayer.
. . . But this approach, I see, has drawn a blank;
Let's speak, then, of his person, not his rank.
Doesn't it seem to you a trifle grim
To give a girl like her to a man like him?
50 When two are so ill-suited, can't you see
What the sad consequences is bound to be?
A young girl's virtue is imperilled, Sir,
When such a marriage is imposed on her;
For if one's bridegroom isn't to one's taste,

It's hardly an inducement to be chaste,   55
And many a man with horns upon his brow
Has made his wife the thing that she is now.
It's hard to be a faithful wife, in short,
To certain husbands of a certain sort,
And he who gives his daughter to a man she hates   60
Must answer for her sins at Heaven's gates.
Think, Sir, before you play so risky a role.
ORGON: This servant-girl presumes to save my soul!
DORINE: You would do well to ponder what I've said.
ORGON: Daughter, we'll disregard this dunderhead.   65
Just trust your father's judgment. Oh, I'm aware
That I once promised you to young Valère;
But now I hear he gambles, which greatly shocks me;
What's more, I've doubts about his orthodoxy.
His visits to church, I note, are very few.   70
DORINE: Would you have him go at the same hours as you,
And kneel nearby, to be sure of being seen?
ORGON: I can dispense with such remarks, Dorine.

(*To* MARIANE.)

Tartuffe, however, is sure of Heaven's blessing,
And that's the only treasure worth possessing.   75
This match will bring you joys beyond all measure;
Your cup will overflow with every pleasure;
You two will interchange your faithful loves
Like two sweet cherubs, or two turtle-doves.
No harsh word shall be heard, no frown be seen,   80
And he shall make you happy as a queen.
DORINE: And she'll make him a cuckold, just wait and see.
ORGON: What language!
DORINE: Oh, he's a man of destiny;
He's *made* for horns, and what the stars demand
Your daughter's virtue surely can't withstand.   85
ORGON: Don't interrupt me further. Why can't you learn
That certain things are none of your concern?
DORINE: It's for your own sake that I interfere.

(*She repeatedly interrupts* ORGON *just as he is turning to speak to his daughter.*)

ORGON: Most kind of you. Now, hold your tongue, d'you
hear?
DORINE: If I didn't love you . . .
ORGON: Spare me your affection.   90
DORINE: I'll love you, Sir, in spite of your objection.
ORGON: Blast!
DORINE: I can't bear, Sir, for your honor's sake,
To let you make this ludicrous mistake.
ORGON: You mean to go on talking?
DORINE: If I didn't protest
This sinful marriage, my conscience couldn't rest.   95
ORGON: If you don't hold your tongue, you little shrew . . .
DORINE: What, lost your temper? A pious man like you?
ORGON: Yes! Yes! You talk and talk. I'm maddened by it.
Once and for all, I tell you to be quiet.
DORINE: Well, I'll be quiet. But I'll be thinking hard.   100
ORGON: Think all you like, but you had better guard
That saucy tongue of yours, or I'll . . .

(*Turning back to* MARIANE.)

Now, child,
I've weighed this matter fully.

DORINE:

(Aside.)

It drives me wild
That I can't speak.

(ORGON turns his head, and she is silent.)

ORGON: Tartuffe is no young dandy,
But, still, his person . . .

DORINE:

(Aside.)

105   Is as sweet as candy.
ORGON: Is such that, even if you shouldn't care
For his other merits . . .

(He turns and stands facing DORINE, arms crossed.)

DORINE:

(Aside.)

They'll make a lovely pair.
If I were she, no man would marry me
Against my inclination, and go scot-free.
110   He'd learn, before the wedding-day was over,
How readily a wife can find a lover.

ORGON:

(To DORINE.)

It seems you treat my orders as a joke.
DORINE: Why, what's the matter? 'Twas not to you I spoke.
ORGON: What *were* you doing?
DORINE: Talking to myself, that's all.
115 ORGON: Ah! *(Aside.)* One more bit of impudence and gall,
And I shall give her a good slap in the face.

(He puts himself in position to slap her; DORINE, whenever he glances at her, stands immobile and silent.)

Daughter, you shall accept, and with good grace,
The husband I've selected . . . Your wedding-day . . .

(To DORINE.)

Why don't you talk to yourself?
DORINE: I've nothing to say.
ORGON: Come, just one word.
120 DORINE: No thank you, Sir. I pass.
ORGON: Come, speak; I'm waiting.
DORINE: I'd not be such an ass.
ORGON:

(Turning to MARIANE.)

In short, dear Daughter, I mean to be obeyed,
And you must bow to the sound choice I've made.
DORINE:

(Moving away.)

I'd not wed such a monster, even in jest.

(ORGON attempts to slap her, but misses.)

125 ORGON: Daughter, that maid of yours is a thorough pest;
She makes me sinfully annoyed and nettled.

I can't speak further; my nerves are too unsettled.
She's so upset me by her insolent talk,
I'll calm myself by going for a walk.

SCENE III

DORINE, MARIANE

DORINE:

(Returning.)

Well, have you lost your tongue, girl? Must I play
Your part, and say the lines you ought to say?
Faced with a fate so hideous and absurd,
Can you not utter one dissenting word?
MARIANE: What good would it do? A father's power is great.   5
DORINE: Resist him now, or it will be too late.
MARIANE: But . . .
DORINE: Tell him one cannot love at a father's
whim;
That you shall marry for yourself, not him;
That since it's you who are to be the bride,
It's you, not he, who must be satisfied;   10
And that if his Tartuffe is so sublime,
He's free to marry him at any time.
MARIANE: I've bowed so long to Father's strict control,
I couldn't oppose him now, to save my soul.
DORINE: Come, come, Mariane. Do listen to reason, won't   15
you?
Valère has asked your hand. Do you love him, or don't
you?
MARIANE: Oh, how unjust of you! What can you mean
By asking such a question, dear Dorine?
You know the depth of my affection for him;
I've told you a hundred times how I adore him.   20
DORINE: I don't believe in everything I hear;
Who knows if your professions were sincere?
MARIANE: They were, Dorine, and you do me wrong to doubt
it;
Heaven knows that I've been all too frank about it.
DORINE: You love him, then?
MARIANE: Oh, more than I can express.   25
DORINE: And he, I take it, cares for you no less?
MARIANE: I think so.
DORINE: And you both, with equal fire,
Burn to be married?
MARIANE: That is our one desire.
DORINE: What of Tartuffe, then? What of your father's plan?
MARIANE: I'll kill myself, if I'm forced to wed that man.   30
DORINE: I hadn't thought of that recourse. How splendid!
Just die, and all your troubles will be ended!
A fine solution. Oh, it maddens me
To hear you talk in that self-pitying key.
MARIANE: Dorine, how harsh you are! It's most unfair.   35
You have no sympathy for my despair.
DORINE: I've none at all for people who talk drivel
And, faced with difficulties, whine and snivel.
MARIANE: No doubt I'm timid, but it would be wrong . . .
DORINE: True love requires a heart that's firm and strong. 40
MARIANE: I'm strong in my affection for Valère,
But coping with my father is his affair.

DORINE: But if your father's brain has grown so cracked
    Over his dear Tartuffe that he can retract
45   His blessing, though your wedding-day was named,
    It's surely not Valère who's to be blamed.
MARIANE: If I defied my father, as you suggest,
    Would it not seem unmaidenly, at best?
    Shall I defend my love at the expense
50   Of brazenness and disobedience?
    Shall I parade my heart's desires, and flaunt . . .
DORINE: No, I ask nothing of you. Clearly you want
    To be Madame Tartuffe, and I feel bound
    Not to oppose a wish so very sound.
55   What right have I to criticize the match?
    Indeed, my dear, the man's a brilliant catch.
    Monsieur Tartuffe! Now, there's a man of weight!
    Yet, yes, Monsieur Tartuffe, I'm bound to state,
    Is quite a person; that's not to be denied;
60   'Twill be no little thing to be his bride.
    The world already rings with his renown;
    He's a great noble—in his native town;
    His ears are red, he has a pink complexion,
    And all in all, he'll suit you to perfection.
MARIANE: Dear God!
65 DORINE: Oh, how triumphant you will feel
    At having caught a husband so ideal!
MARIANE: Oh, do stop teasing, and use your cleverness
    To get me out of this appalling mess.
    Advise me, and I'll do whatever you say.
70 DORINE: Ah no, a dutiful daughter must obey
    Her father, even if he weds her to an ape.
    You've a bright future; why struggle to escape?
    Tartuffe will take you back where his family lives,
    To a small town aswarm with relatives—
75   Uncles and cousins whom you'll be charmed to meet.
    You'll be received at once by the elite,
    Calling upon the bailiff's wife, no less—
    Even, perhaps, upon the mayoress,
    Who'll sit you down in the *best* kitchen chair.
80   Then, once a year, you'll dance at the village fair
    To the drone of bagpipes—two of them, in fact—
    And see a puppet-show, or an animal act.
    Your husband . . .
MARIANE: Oh, you turn my blood to ice!
    Stop torturing me, and give me your advice.
DORINE:

(Threatening to go.)

    Your servant, Madam.
85 MARIANE: Dorine, I beg of you . . .
DORINE: No, you deserve it; this marriage must go through.
MARIANE: Dorine!
DORINE: No.
MARIANE: Not Tartuffe! You know I think him . . .
DORINE: Tartuffe's your cup of tea, and you shall drink him.
MARIANE: I've always told you everything, and relied . . .
90 DORINE: No. You deserve to be tartuffified.
MARIANE: Well, since you mock me and refuse to care,
    I'll henceforth seek my solace in despair:
    Despair shall be my counsellor and friend,
    And help me bring my sorrows to an end.

(She starts to leave.)

DORINE: There now, come back; my anger has subsided.   95
    You do deserve some pity, I've decided.
MARIANE: Dorine, if Father makes me undergo
    This dreadful martyrdom, I'll die, I know.
DORINE: Don't fret; it won't be difficult to discover
    Some plan of action . . . But here's Valère, your lover.   100

SCENE IV

VALÈRE, MARIANE, DORINE

VALÈRE: Madam, I've just received some wondrous news
    Regarding which I'd like to hear your views.
MARIANE: What news?
VALÈRE: You're marrying Tartuffe.
MARIANE: I find
    That Father does have such a match in mind.
VALÈRE: Your father, Madam . . .
MARIANE: . . . has just this minute   5
  said
    That it's Tartuffe he wishes me to wed.
VALÈRE: Can he be serious?
MARIANE: Oh, indeed he can;
    He's clearly set his heart upon the plan.
VALÈRE: And what position do you propose to take,
    Madam?
MARIANE: Why—I don't know.?
VALÈRE: For heaven's sake—   10
    You don't know?
MARIANE: No.
VALÈRE: Well, well!
MARIANE: Advise me, do.
VALÈRE: Marry the man. That's my advice to you.
MARIANE: That's your advice?
VALÈRE: Yes.
MARIANE: Truly?
VALÈRE: Oh, absolutely.
    You couldn't choose more wisely, more astutely.
MARIANE: Thanks for this counsel; I'll follow it, of course.   15
VALÈRE: Do, do; I'm sure 'twill cost you no remorse.
MARIANE: To give it didn't cause your heart to break.
VALÈRE: I gave it, Madam, only for your sake.
MARIANE: And it's for your sake that I take it, Sir.
DORINE:

(Withdrawing to the rear of the stage.)

    Let's see which fool will prove the stubborner.   20
VALÈRE: So! I am nothing to you, and it was flat
    Deception when you . . .
MARIANE: Please, enough of that.
    You've told me plainly that I should agree
    To wed the man my father's chosen for me,
    And since you've deigned to counsel me so wisely,   25
    I promise, Sir, to do as you advise me.
VALÈRE: Ah, no, 'twas not by me that you were swayed.
    No, your decision was already made;
    Though now, to save appearances, you protest
    That you're betraying me at my behest.   30
MARIANE: Just as you say.

VALÈRE: Quite so. And I now see
That you were never truly in love with me.
MARIANE: Alas, you're free to think so if you choose.
VALÈRE: I choose to think so, and here's a bit of news:
35   You've spurned my hand, but I know where to turn
For kinder treatment, as you shall quickly learn.
MARIANE: I'm sure you do. Your noble qualities
Inspire affection . . .
VALÈRE: Forget my qualities, please.
They don't inspire you overmuch, I find.
40   But there's another lady I have in mind
Whose sweet and generous nature will not scorn
To compensate me for the loss I've borne.
MARIANE: I'm no great loss, and I'm sure that you'll transfer
Your heart quite painlessly from me to her.
45   VALÈRE: I'll do my best to take it in my stride.
The pain I feel at being cast aside
Time and forgetfulness may put an end to.
Or if I can't forget, I shall pretend to.
No self-respecting person is expected
50   To go on loving once he's been rejected.
MARIANE: Now, that's a fine, high-minded sentiment.
VALÈRE: One to which any sane man would assent.
Would you prefer it if I pined away
In hopeless passion till my dying day?
55   Am I to yield you to a rival's arms
And not console myself with other charms?
MARIANE: Go then: console yourself; don't hesitate.
I wish you to; indeed, I cannot wait.
VALÈRE: You wish me to?
MARIANE: Yes.
VALÈRE: That's the final straw.
60   Madam, farewell. Your wish shall be my law.

(He starts to leave, and then returns: this repeatedly.)

MARIANE: Splendid.
VALÈRE:

(Coming back again.)

                 This breach, remember, is of your making;
It's you who've driven me to the step I'm taking.
MARIANE: Of course.
VALÈRE:

(Coming back again.)

                 Remember, too, that I am merely
Following your example.
MARIANE: I see that clearly.
65   VALÈRE: Enough. I'll go and do your bidding, then.
MARIANE: Good.
VALÈRE:

(Coming back again.)

                 You shall never see my face again.
MARIANE: Excellent.
VALÈRE:

(Walking to the door, then turning about.)

                 Yes?
MARIANE: What?
VALÈRE: What's that? What did you
say?

MARIANE: Nothing. You're dreaming.
VALÈRE: Ah. Well, I'm on my
way.
Farewell, *Madame.*

(He moves slowly away.)

MARIANE: Farewell.
DORINE:

(To MARIANE.)

                              If you ask me,
Both of you are as mad as mad can be.   70
Do stop this nonsense, now. I've only let you
Squabble so long to see where it would get you.
Whoa there, Monsieure Valère!

(She goes and seizes VALÈRE by the arm; he makes a great show of resistance.)

VALÈRE: What's this, Dorine?
DORINE: Come here.
VALÈRE: No, no, my heart's too full of spleen.
Don't hold me back; her wish must be obeyed.   75
DORINE: Stop!
VALÈRE: It's too late now; my decision's made.
DORINE: Oh, pooh!
MARIANE:

(Aside.)

                 He hates the sight of me, that's plain.
I'll go, and so deliver him from pain.
DORINE:

(Leaving VALÈRE, running after MARIANE.)

And now *you* run away! Come back.
MARIANE: No, no.
Nothing you say will keep me here. Let go!   80
VALÈRE:

(Aside.)

She cannot bear my presence, I perceive.
To spare her further torment, I shall leave.
DORINE:

(Leaving MARIANE, running after VALÈRE.)

Again! You'll not escape, Sir; don't you try it.
Come here, you two. Stop fussing, and be quiet.

(She takes VALÈRE by the hand, then MARIANE, and draws them together.)

VALÈRE:

(To DORINE.)

What do you want of me?
MARIANE:

(To DORINE.)

                              What is the point of this?   85
DORINE: We're going to a have little armistice.

(To VALÈRE.)

Now, weren't you silly to get so overheated?
VALÈRE: Didn't you see how badly I was treated?

DORINE:

(To MARIANE.)

Aren't you a simpleton, to have lost your head?
90 MARIANE: Didn't you hear the hateful things he said?
DORINE:

(To VALÈRE.)

You're both great fools. Her sole desire, Valère,
Is to be yours in marriage. To that I'll swear.

(To MARIANE.)

He loves you only, and he wants no wife
But you, Mariane. On that I'll stake my life.
MARIANE:

(To VALÈRE.)

95   Then why you advised me so, I cannot see.
VALÈRE:

(To MARIANE.)

On such a question, why ask advice of *me*?
DORINE: Oh, you're impossible. Give me your hands, you
    two.

(To VALÈRE.)

Yours first.
VALÈRE:

(Giving DORINE his hand.)

            But why?
DORINE:

(To MARIANE.)

            And now a hand from you.

MARIANE:

(Also giving DORINE her hand.)

What are you doing?
DORINE: There: a perfect fit.
100   You suit each other better than you'll admit.

(VALÈRE and MARIANE hold hands for some time without looking
at each other.)

VALÈRE:

(Turning toward MARIANE.)

Ah, come, don't be so haughty. Give a man
A look of kindness, won't you, Mariane?

(MARIANE turns toward VALÈRE and smiles.)

DORINE: I tell you, lovers are completely mad!
VALÈRE:

(To MARIANE.)

Now come, confess that you were very bad
105   To hurt my feelings as you did just now.
I have a just complaint, you must allow.
MARIANE: *You* must allow that you were most unpleasant . . .
DORINE: Let's table that discussion for the present;
    Your father has a plan which must be stopped.
110 MARIANE: Advise us, then; what means must we adopt?
DORINE: We'll use all manner of means, and all at once.

(To MARIANE.)

Your father's addled; he's acting like a dunce.
Therefore you'd better humor the old fossil.
Pretend to yield to him, be sweet and docile,
And then postpone, as often as necessary,   115
The day on which you have agreed to marry.
You'll thus gain time, and time will turn the trick.
Sometimes, for instance, you'll be taken sick,
And that will seem good reason for delay;
Or some bad omen will make you change the day —   120
You'll dream of muddy water, or you'll pass
A dead man's hearse, or break a looking-glass.
If all else fails, no man can marry you
Unless you take his ring and say "I do."
But now, let's separate. If they should find   125
Us talking here, our plot might be divined.

(To VALÈRE.)

Go to your friends, and tell them what's occurred,
And have them urge her father to keep his word.
Meanwhile, we'll stir her brother into action,
And get Elmire, as well, to join our faction.   130
Good-bye.
VALÈRE:

(To MARIANE.)

            Though each of us will do his best,
It's your true heart on which my hopes shall rest.
MARIANE:

(To VALÈRE.)

Regardless of what Father may decide,
None but Valère shall claim me as his bride.
VALÈRE: Oh, how those words content me! Come what will . . .   135
DORINE: Oh, lover, lovers! Their tongues are never still.
    Be off, now.
VALÈRE:

(Turning to go, then turning back.)

            One last word . . .
DORINE: No time to chat:
    You leave by this door; and *you* leave by that.

(DORINE pushes them, by the shoulders, toward opposing doors.)

— ACT THREE —

SCENE I

DAMIS, DORINE

DAMIS: May lightning strike me even as I speak,
    May all men call me cowardly and weak,
    If any fear or scruple holds me back
    From settling things, at once, with that great quack!
DORINE: Now, don't give way to violent emotion.   5
    Your father's merely talked about this notion,
    And words and deeds are far from being one.
    Much that is talked about is left undone.
DAMIS: No, I must stop that scoundrel's machinations;
    I'll go and tell him off; I'm out of patience.   10
DORINE: Do calm down and be practical. I had rather
    My mistress dealt with him — and with your father.

She has some influence with Tartuffe, I've noted.
He hangs upon her words, seems most devoted,
15   And may, indeed, be smitten by her charm.
Pray Heaven it's true! 'Twould do our cause no harm.
She sent for him, just now, to sound him out
On this affair you're so incensed about;
She'll find out where he stands, and tell him, too,
20   What dreadful strife and trouble will ensue
If he lends countenance to your father's plan.
I couldn't get in to see him, but his man
Says that he's almost finished with his prayers.
Go, now. I'll catch him when he comes downstairs.
25   DAMIS: I want to hear this conference, and I will.
DORINE: No, they must be alone.
DAMIS: Oh, I'll keep still.
DORINE: Not you. I know your temper. You'd start a brawl,
And shout and stamp your foot and spoil it all.
Go on.
DAMIS: I won't; I have a perfect right . . .
30   DORINE: Lord, you're a nuisance! He's coming; get out of
        sight.

(DAMIS *conceals himself in a closet at the rear of the stage.*)

SCENE II

TARTUFFE, DORINE

TARTUFFE:

(*Observing* DORINE, *and calling to his manservant offstage.*)

Hang up my hair-shirt, put my scourge in place,
And pray, Laurent, for Heaven's perpetual grace.
I'm going to the prison now, to share
My last few coins with the poor wretches there.
DORINE:

(*Aside.*)

5   Dear God, what affectation! What a fake!
TARTUFFE: You wished to see me?
DORINE: Yes . . .
TARTUFFE:

(*Taking a handkerchief from his pocket.*)

                                For mercy's sake,
Please take this handkerchief, before you speak.
DORINE: What?
TARTUFFE: Cover that bosom, girl. The flesh is weak,
And unclean thoughts are difficult to control.
10   Such sights as that can undermine the soul.
DORINE: Your soul, it seems, has very poor defenses,
And flesh makes quite an impact on your senses.
It's strange that you're so easily excited;
My own desires are not so soon ignited,
15   And if I saw you naked as a beast,
Not all your hide would tempt me in the least.
TARTUFFE: Girl, speak more modestly; unless you do,
I shall be forced to take my leave of you.
DORINE: Oh, no, it's I who must be on my way;
20   I've just one little message to convey.
Madame is coming down, and begs you, Sir,
To wait and have a word or two with her.

TARTUFFE: Gladly.
DORINE:

(*Aside.*)

                That had a softening effect!
I think my guess about him was correct.
TARTUFFE: Will she be long?
DORINE: No: that's her step I hear.   25
Ah, here she is, and I shall disappear.

SCENE III

ELMIRE, TARTUFFE

TARTUFFE: May Heaven, whose infinite goodness we adore,
Preserve your body and soul forevermore,
And bless your days, and answer thus the plea
Of one who is its humblest votary.
ELMIRE: I thank you for that pious wish. But please,   5
Do take a chair and let's be more at ease.

(*They sit down.*)

TARTUFFE: I trust that you are once more well and strong?
ELMIRE: Oh, yes: the fever didn't last for long.
TARTUFFE: My prayers are too unworthy, I am sure,
To have gained from Heaven this most gracious   10
        cure;
But lately, Madam, my every supplication
Has had for object your recuperation.
ELMIRE: You shouldn't have troubled so. I don't deserve it.
TARTUFFE: Your health is priceless, Madam, and to preserve it
I'd gladly give my own, in all sincerity.   15
ELMIRE: Sir, you outdo us all in Christian charity.
You've been most kind. I count myself your debtor.
TARTUFFE: 'Twas nothing, Madam. I long to serve you better.
ELMIRE: There's a private matter I'm anxious to discuss.
I'm glad there's no one here to hinder us.   20
TARTUFFE: I too am glad; it floods my heart with bliss
To find myself alone with you like this.
For just this chance I've prayed with all my power—
But prayed in vain, until this happy hour.
ELMIRE: This won't take long, Sir, and I hope you'll be   25
Entirely frank and unconstrained with me.
TARTUFFE: Indeed, there's nothing I had rather do
Than bare my inmost heart and soul to you.
First, let me say that what remarks I've made
About the constant visits you are paid   30
Were prompted not by any mean emotion,
But rather by a pure and deep devotion,
A fervent zeal . . .
ELMIRE: No need for explanation.
Your sole concern, I'm sure, was my salvation.
TARTUFFE:

(*Taking* ELMIRE'S *hand and pressing her fingertips.*)

Quite so; and such great fervor do I feel . . .   35
ELMIRE: Ooh! Please! You're pinching!
TARTUFFE: 'Twas from excess of
        zeal.
I never meant to cause you pain, I swear.
I'd rather . . .

(*He places his hand on* ELMIRE'S *knee.*)

ELMIRE: What can your hand be doing there?
TARTUFFE: Feeling your gown; what soft, fine-woven stuff!
40 ELMIRE: Please, I'm extremely ticklish. That's enough.

(She draws her chair away; TARTUFFE *pulls his after her.)*

TARTUFFE:

(Fondling the lace collar of her gown.)

    My, my, what lovely lacework on your dress!
    The workmanship's miraculous, no less.
    I've not seen anything to equal it.
ELMIRE: Yes, quite. But let's talk business for a bit.
45   They say my husband means to break his word
    And give his daughter to you, Sir. Had you heard?
TARTUFFE: He did once mention it. But I confess
    I dream of quite a different happiness.
    It's elsewhere, Madam, that my eyes discern
50   The promise of that bliss for which I yearn.
ELMIRE: I see: you care for nothing here below.
TARTUFFE: Ah, well—my heart's not made of stone, you
    know.
ELMIRE: All your desires mount heavenward, I'm sure,
    In scorn of all that's earthly and impure.
55 TARTUFFE: A love of heavenly beauty does not preclude
    A proper love for earthly pulchritude;
    Our senses are quite rightly captivated
    By perfect works our Maker has created.
    Some glory clings to all that Heaven has made;
60   In you, all Heaven's marvels are displayed.
    On that fair face, such beauties have been lavished,
    The eyes are dazzled and the heart is ravished;
    How could I look on you, O flawless creature,
    And not adore the Author of all Nature,
65   Feeling a love both passionate and pure
    For you, his triumph of self-portraiture?
    At first, I trembled lest that love should be
    A subtle snare that Hell had laid for me;
    I vowed to flee the sight of you, eschewing
70   A rapture that might prove my soul's undoing;
    But soon, fair being, I became aware
    That my deep passion could be made to square
    With rectitude, and with my bounden duty.
    I thereupon surrendered to your beauty.
75   It is, I know, presumptuous on my part
    To bring you this poor offering of my heart,
    And it is not my merit, Heaven knows,
    But your compassion on which my hopes repose.
    You are my peace, my solace, my salvation;
80   On you depends my bliss—or desolation;
    I bide your judgment and, as you think best,
    I shall be either miserable or blest.
ELMIRE: Your declaration is most gallant, Sir,
    But don't you think it's out of character?
85   You'd have done better to restrain your passion
    And think before you spoke in such a fashion.
    It ill becomes a pious man like you . . .
TARTUFFE: I may be pious, but I'm human too:
    With your celestial charms before his eyes,
90   A man has not the power to be wise.
    I know such words sound strangely, coming from me,
    But I'm no angel, nor was meant to be,

    And if you blame my passion, you must needs
    Reproach as well the charms on which it feeds.
    Your loveliness I had no sooner seen   95
    Than you became my soul's unrivalled queen;
    Before your seraph glance, divinely sweet,
    My heart's defenses crumbled in defeat,
    And nothing fasting, prayer, or tears might do
    Could stay my spirit from adoring you.   100
    My eyes, my sighs have told you in the past
    What now my lips make bold to say at last,
    And if, in your great goodness, you will deign
    To look upon your slave, and ease his pain, —
    If, in compassion for my soul's distress,   105
    You'll stoop to comfort my unworthiness,
    I'll raise to you, in thanks for that sweet manna,
    An endless hymn, an infinite hosanna.
    With me, of course, there need be no anxiety.
    No fear of scandal or of notoriety.   110
    These young court gallants, whom all the ladies fancy,
    Are vain in speech, in action rash and chancy;
    When they succeed in love, the world soon knows it;
    No favor's granted them but they disclose it
    And by the looseness of their tongues profane   115
    The very altar where their hearts have lain.
    Men of my sort, however, love discreetly,
    And one may trust our reticence completely.
    My keen concern for my good name insures
    The absolute security of yours;   120
    In short, I offer you, my dear Elmire,
    Love without scandal, pleasure without fear.
ELMIRE: I've heard your well-turned speeches to the end,
    And what you urge I clearly apprehend.
    Aren't you afraid that I may take a notion   125
    To tell my husband of your warm devotion,
    And that, supposing he were duly told,
    His feelings toward you might grow rather cold?
TARTUFFE: I know, dear lady, that your exceeding charity
    Will lead your heart to pardon my temerity; 130
    That you'll excuse my violent affection
    As human weakness, human imperfection;
    And that—O fairest!—you will bear in mind
    That I'm but flesh and blood, and am not blind.
ELMIRE: Some women might do otherwise, perhaps, 135
    But I shall be discreet about your lapse;
    I'll tell my husband nothing of what's occurred
    If, in return, you'll give your solemn word
    To advocate as forcefully as you can
    The marriage of Valère and Mariane,   140
    Renouncing all desire to dispossess
    Another of his rightful happiness,
    And . .

SCENE IV

DAMIS, ELMIRE, TARTUFFE

DAMIS:

(Emerging from the closet where he has been hiding.)

    No! We'll not hush up this vile affair;
    I heard it all inside that closet there,
    Where Heaven, in order to confound the pride

Of this great rascal, prompted me to hide.
5 Ah, now I have my long-awaited chance
To punish his deceit and arrogance,
And give my father clear and shocking proof
Of the black character of his dear Tartuffe.
ELMIRE: Ah no, Damis; I'll be content if he
10 Will study to deserve my leniency.
I've promised silence—don't make me break my word;
To make a scandal would be too absurd.
Good wives laugh off such trifles, and forget them;
Why should they tell their husbands, and upset them?
15 DAMIS: You have your reasons for taking such a course,
And I have reasons, too, of equal force.
To spare him now would be insanely wrong.
I've swallowed my just wrath for far too long
And watched this insolent bigot bringing strife
20 And bitterness into our family life.
Too long he's meddled in my father's affairs,
Thwarting my marriage-hopes, and poor Valère's.
It's high time that my father was undeceived,
And now I've proof that can't be disbelieved—
25 Proof that was furnished me by Heaven above.
It's too good not to take advantage of.
This is my chance, and I deserve to lose it
If, for one moment, I hesitate to use it.
ELMIRE: Damis . . .
DAMIS: No, I must do what I think right.
30 Madam, my heart is bursting with delight,
And, say whatever you will, I'll not consent
To lose the sweet revenge on which I'm bent.
I'll settle matters without more ado;
And here, most opportunely, is my cue.

SCENE V

ORGON, DAMIS, TARTUFFE, ELMIRE

DAMIS: Father, I'm glad you've joined us. Let us advise you
Of some fresh news which doubtless will surprise you.
You've just now been repaid with interest
For all your loving-kindness to our guest.
5 He's proved his warm and grateful feelings toward you;
It's with a pair of horns he would reward you.
Yes, I surprised him with your wife, and heard
His whole adulterous offer, every word.
She, with her all too gentle disposition,
10 Would not have told you of his proposition;
But I shall not make terms with brazen lechery,
And feel that not to tell you would be treachery.
ELMIRE: And I hold that one's husband's peace of mind
Should not be spoilt by tattle of this kind.
15 One's honor doesn't require it: to be proficient
In keeping men at bay is quite sufficient.
These are my sentiments, and I wish, Damis,
That you had heeded me and held your peace.

SCENE VI

ORGON, DAMIS, TARTUFFE

ORGON: Can it be true, this dreadful thing I hear?
TARTUFFE: Yes, Brother, I'm a wicked man, I fear:

A wretched sinner, all depraved and twisted,
The greatest villain that has ever existed.
My life's one heap of crimes, which grows each minute; 5
There's naught but foulness and corruption in it;
And I perceive that Heaven, outraged by me,
Has chosen this occasion to mortify me.
Charge me with any deed you wish to name;
I'll not defend myself, but take the blame. 10
Believe what you are told, and drive Tartuffe
Like some base criminal from beneath your roof;
Yes, drive me hence, and with a parting curse:
I shan't protest, for I deserve far worse.
ORGON:

(To DAMIS.)

Ah, you deceitful boy, how dare you try 15
To stain his purity with so foul a lie?
DAMIS: What! Are you taken in by such a bluff?
Did you not hear . . . ?
ORGON: Enough, you rogue, enough!
TARTUFFE: Ah, Brother, let him speak: you're being unjust.
Believe his story; the boy deserves your trust. 20
Why, after all, should you have faith in me?
How can you know what I might do, or be?
Is it on my good actions that you base
Your favor? Do you trust my pious face?
Ah, no, don't be deceived by hollow shows; 25
I'm far, alas, from being what men suppose;
Though the world takes me for a man of worth,
I'm truly the most worthless man on earth.

(To DAMIS.)

Yes, my dear son, speak out now: call me the chief
Of sinners, a wretch, a murderer, a thief; 30
Load me with all the names men most abhor;
I'll not complain; I've earned them all, and more;
I'll kneel here while you pour them on my head
As a just punishment for the life I've led.
ORGON:

(To TARTUFFE.)

This is too much, dear Brother.

(To DAMIS.)

       Have you no heart? 35
DAMIS: Are you so hoodwinked by this rascal's art. . . ?
ORGON: Be still, you monster.

(To TARTUFFE.)

      Brother, I pray you, rise.

(To DAMIS.)

Villain!
DAMIS: But . . .
ORGON: Silence!
DAMIS: Can't you realize. . . ?
ORGON: Just one word more, and I'll tear you limb from limb.
TARTUFFE: In God's name, Brother, don't be harsh with him. 40
I'd rather far be tortured at the stake
Than see him bear one scratch for my poor sake.

ORGON:

(To DAMIS.)

Ingrate!

TARTUFFE: If I must beg you, on bended knee,
To pardon him . . .

ORGON:

(Falling to his knees, addressing TARTUFFE.)

                    Such goodness cannot be!

(To DAMIS.)

Now, *there's* true charity!

DAMIS: What, you. . . ?

45 ORGON: Villain, be still!
I know your motives; I know you wish him ill:
Yes, all of you—wife, children, servants, all—
Conspire against him and desire his fall,
Employing every shameful trick you can
50 To alienate me from this saintly man.
Ah, but the more you seek to drive him away,
The more I'll do to keep him. Without delay,
I'll spite this household and confound its pride
By giving him my daughter as his bride.
55 DAMIS: You're going to force her to accept his hand?
ORGON: Yes, and this very night, d'you understand?
I shall defy you all, and make it clear
That I'm the one who gives the orders here.
Come, wretch, kneel down and clasp his blessed feet,
60 And ask his pardon for your black deceit.
DAMIS: I ask that swindler's pardon? Why, I'd rather . . .
ORGON: So! You insult him, and defy your father!
A stick! A stick! (To TARTUFFE.) No, no—release me, do.

(To DAMIS.)

Out of my house this minute! Be off with you,
65 And never dare set foot in it again.
DAMIS: Well, I shall go, but . . .
ORGON: Well, go quickly, then.
I disinherit you; an empty purse
Is all you'll get from me—except my curse!

SCENE VII

ORGON, TARTUFFE

ORGON: How he blasphemed your goodness! What a son!
TARTUFFE: Forgive him, Lord, as I've already done.

(To ORGON.)

You can't know how it hurts when someone tries
To blacken me in my dear Brother's eyes.
ORGON: Ahh!
5 TARTUFFE: The mere thought of such ingratitude
Plunges my soul into so dark a mood . . .
Such horror grips my heart . . . I gasp for breath,
And cannot speak, and feel myself near death.
ORGON:

(He runs, in tears, to the door through which he has just driven his son.)

You blackguard! Why did I spare you? Why did I not
10 Break you in little pieces on the spot?
Compose yourself, and don't be hurt, dear friend.

TARTUFFE: These scenes, these dreadful quarrels, have got to end.
I've much upset your household, and I perceive
That the best thing will be for me to leave.
ORGON: What are you saying!
TARTUFFE: They're all against me here;   15
They'd have you think me false and insincere.
ORGON: Ah, what of that? Have I ceased believing in you?
TARTUFFE: Their adverse talk will certainly continue,
And charges which you now repudiate
You may find credible at a later date.   20
ORGON: No, Brother, never.
TARTUFFE: Brother, a wife can sway
Her husband's mind in many a subtle way.
ORGON: No, no.
TARTUFFE: To leave at once is the solution;
Thus only can I end their persecution.
ORGON: No, no, I'll not allow it; you shall remain.   25
TARTUFFE: Ah, well; 'twill mean much martyrdom and pain,
But if you wish it . . .
ORGON: Ah!
TARTUFFE: Enough; so be it.
But one thing must be settled, as I see it.
For your dear honor, and for our friendship's sake,
There's one precaution I feel bound to take.   30
I shall avoid your wife, and keep away . . .
ORGON: No, you shall not, whatever they may say.
It pleases me to vex them, and for spite
I'd have them see you with her day and night.
What's more, I'm going to drive them to despair   35
By making you my only son and heir;
This very day, I'll give to you alone
Clear deed and title to everything I own.
A dear, good friend and son-in-law-to-be
Is more than wife, or child, or kin to me.   40
Will you accept my offer, dearest son?
TARTUFFE: In all things, let the will of Heaven be done.
ORGON: Poor fellow! Come, we'll go draw up the deed.
Then let them burst with disappointed greed!

— ACT FOUR —

SCENE I

CLÉANTE, TARTUFFE

CLÉANTE: Yes, all the town's discussing it, and truly,
Their comments do not flatter you unduly.
I'm glad we've met, Sir, and I'll give my view
Of this sad matter in a word or two.
As for who's guilty, that I shan't discuss;   5
Let's say it was Damis who caused the fuss;
Assuming, then, that you have been ill-used
By young Damis, and groundlessly accused,
Ought not a Christian to forgive, and ought
He not to stifle every vengeful thought?   10
Should you stand by and watch a father make
His only son an exile for your sake?
Again I tell you frankly, be advised:
The whole town, high and low, is scandalized;
This quarrel must be mended, and my advice is   15

Not to push matters to a further crisis.
No, sacrifice your wrath to God above,
And help Damis regain his father's love.
TARTUFFE: Alas, for my part I should take great joy
20   In doing so. I've nothing against the boy.
I pardon all, I harbor no resentment;
To serve him would afford me much contentment.
But Heaven's interest will not have it so:
If he comes back, then I shall have to go.
25   After his conduct—so extreme, so vicious—
Our further intercourse would look suspicious.
God knows what people would think! Why, they'd describe
My goodness to him as a sort of bribe;
They'd say that out of guilt I made pretense
30   Of loving-kindness and benevolence—
That, fearing my accuser's tongue, I strove
To buy his silence with a show of love.
CLÉANTE: Your reasoning is badly warped and stretched,
And these excuses, Sir, are most far-fetched.
35   Why put yourself in charge of Heaven's cause?
Does Heaven need our help to enforce its laws?
Leave vengeance to the Lord, Sir; while we live,
Our duty's not to punish, but forgive;
And what the Lord commands, we should obey
40   Without regard to what the world may say.
What! Shall the fear of being misunderstood
Prevent our doing what is right and good?
No, no; let's simply do what Heaven ordains,
And let no other thoughts perplex our brains.
45   TARTUFFE: Again, Sir, let me say that I've forgiven
Damis, and thus obeyed the laws of Heaven;
But I am not commanded by the Bible
To live with one who smears my name with libel.
CLÉANTE: Were you commanded, Sir, to indulge the whim
50   Of poor Orgon, and to encourage him
In suddenly transferring to your name
A large estate to which you have no claim?
TARTUFFE: 'Twould never occur to those who know me best
To think I acted from self-interest.
55   The treasures of this world I quite despise;
Their specious glitter does not charm my eyes;
And if I have resigned myself to taking
The gift which my dear Brother insists on making,
I do so only, as he well understands,
60   Lest so much wealth fall into wicked hands,
Lest those to whom it might descend in time
Turn it to purposes of sin and crime,
And not, as I shall do, make use of it.
For Heaven's glory and mankind's benefit.
65   CLÉANTE: Forget these trumped-up fears. Your argument
Is one the rightful heir might well resent;
It *is* a moral burden to inherit
Such wealth, but give Damis a chance to bear it.
And would it not be worse to be accused
70   Of swindling, than to see that wealth misused?
I'm shocked that you allowed Orgon to broach
This matter, and that you feel no self-reproach;
Does true religion teach that lawful heirs
May freely be deprived of what is theirs?
75   And if the Lord has told you in your heart
That you and young Damis must dwell apart,

Would it not be the decent thing to beat
A generous and honorable retreat,
Rather than let the son of the house be sent,
For your convenience, into banishment?   80
Sir, if you wish to prove the honesty
Of your intentions . . .
TARTUFFE: Sir, it is half-past three.
I've certain pious duties to attend to,
And hope my prompt departure won't offend you.
CLÉANTE:

(*Alone.*)

Damn.   85

SCENE II

ELMIRE, MARIANE, CLÉANTE, DORINE

DORINE: Stay, Sir, and help Mariane, for Heaven's sake!
She's suffering so, I fear her heart will break.
Her father's plan to marry her off tonight
Has put the poor child in a desperate plight.
I hear him coming. Let's stand together, now,   5
And see if we can't change his mind, somehow,
About this match we all deplore and fear.

SCENE III

ORGON, ELMIRE, MARIANE, CLÉANTE, DORINE

ORGON: Hah! Glad to find you all assembled here.

(*To* MARIANE.)

This contract, child, contains your happiness,
And what it says I think your heart can guess.
MARIANE:

(*Falling to her knees.*)

Sir, by that Heaven which sees me here distressed,
And by whatever else can move your breast,   5
Do not employ a father's power, I pray you,
To crush my heart and force it to obey you,
Nor by your harsh commands oppress me so
That I'll begrudge the duty which I owe—
And do not so embitter and enslave me   10
That I shall hate the very life you gave me.
If my sweet hopes must perish, if you refuse
To give me to the one I've dared to choose,
Spare me at least—I beg you, I implore—
The pain of wedding one whom I abhor;   15
And do not, by a heartless use of force,
Drive me to contemplate some desperate course.
ORGON:

(*Feeling himself touched by her.*)

Be firm, my soul. No human weakness, now.
MARIANE: I don't resent your love for him. Allow
Your heart free rein, Sir; give him your property,   20
And if that's not enough, take mine from me;
He's welcome to my money; take it, do,
But don't, I pray, include my person too.
Spare me, I beg you; and let me end the tale
Of my sad days behind a convent veil.   25

ORGON: A convent! Hah! When crossed in their amours,
    All lovesick girls have the same thought as yours.
    Get up! The more you loathe the man, and dread
      him,
    The more ennobling it will be to wed him.
30   Marry Tartuffe, and mortify your flesh!
    Enough; don't start that whimpering afresh.
DORINE: But why. . . ?
ORGON: Be still, there. Speak when you're
    spoken to.
    Not one more bit of impudence out of you.
CLÉANTE: If I may offer a word of counsel here . . .
35 ORGON: Brother, in counseling you have no peer;
    All your advice is forceful, sound, and clever;
    I don't propose to follow it, however.
ELMIRE:

(To ORGON.*)*

    I am amazed, and don't know what to say;
    Your blindness simply takes my breath away.
40   You are indeed bewitched, to take no warning
    From our account of what occurred this morning.
ORGON: Madam, I know a few plain facts, and one
    Is that you're partial to my rascal son;
    Hence, when he sought to make Tartuffe the victim
45   Of a base lie, you dared not contradict him.
    Ah, but you underplayed your part, my pet;
    You should have looked more angry, more upset.
ELMIRE: When men make overtures, must we reply
    With righteous anger and a battle-cry?
50   Must we turn back their amorous advances
    With sharp reproaches and with fiery glances?
    Myself, I find such offers merely amusing,
    And make no scenes and fusses in refusing;
    My taste is for good-natured rectitude,
55   And I dislike the savage sort of prude
    Who guards her virtue with her teeth and claws,
    And tears men's eyes out for the slightest cause;
    The Lord preserve me from such honor as that,
    Which bites and scratches like an alley-cat!
60   I've found that a polite and cool rebuff
    Discourages a lover quite enough.
ORGON: I know the facts, and I shall not be shaken.
ELMIRE: I marvel at your power to be mistaken.
    Would it, I wonder, carry weight with you
65   If I could *show* you that our tale was true?
ORGON: Show me?
ELMIRE: Yes.
ORGON: Rot.
ELMIRE: Come, what if I found a way
    To make you see the facts as plain as day?
ORGON: Nonsense.
ELMIRE: Do answer me; don't be absurd.
    I'm not now asking you to trust our word.
70   Suppose that from some hiding-place in here
    You learned the whole sad truth by eye and ear—
    What would you say of your good friend, after that?
ORGON: Why, I'd say . . . nothing, by Jehoshaphat!
    It can't be true.
ELMIRE: You've been too long deceived,
75   And I'm quite tired of being disbelieved.

    Come now: let's put my statements to the test,
    And you shall see the truth made manifest.
ORGON: I'll take that challenge. Now do your uttermost.
    We'll see how you make good your empty boast.
ELMIRE:

(To DORINE.*)*

    Send him to me.
DORINE: He's crafty; it may be hard   80
    To catch the cunning scoundrel off his guard.
ELMIRE: No, amorous men are gullible. Their conceit
    So blinds them that they're never hard to cheat.
    Have him come down *(To* CLÉANTE *and* MARIANE) Please
    leave us, for a bit.

SCENE IV

ELMIRE, ORGON

ELMIRE: Pull up this table, and get under it.
ORGON: What?
ELMIRE: It's essential that you be well-hidden.
ORGON: Why there?
ELMIRE: Oh, Heavens! Just do as you are bidden
    I have my plans; we'll soon see how they fare.
    Under the table, now; and once you're there,   5
    Take care that you are neither seen nor heard.
ORGON: Well, I'll indulge you, since I gave my word
    To see you through this infantile charade.
ELMIRE: Once it is over, you'll be glad we played.

(To her husband, who is now under the table.)

    I'm going to act quite strangely, now, and you   10
    Must not be shocked at anything I do.
    Whatever I may say, you must excuse
    As part of that deceit I'm forced to use.
    I shall employ sweet speeches in the task
    Of making that impostor drop his mask;   15
    I'll give encouragement to his bold desires,
    And furnish fuel to his amorous fires.
    Since it's for your sake, and for his destruction,
    That I shall seem to yield to his seduction,
    I'll gladly stop whenever you decide   20
    That all your doubts are fully satisfied.
    I'll count on you, as soon as you have seen
    What sort of man he is, to intervene,
    And not expose me to his odious lust
    One moment longer than you feel you must.   25
    Remember: you're to save me from my plight
    Whenever . . . He's coming! Hush! Keep out of sight!

SCENE V

TARTUFFE, ELMIRE, ORGON

TARTUFFE: You wish to have a word with me, I'm told.
ELMIRE: Yes. I've a little secret to unfold.
    Before I speak, however, it would be wise
    To close that door, and look about for spies.

*(*TARTUFFE *goes to the door, closes it, and returns.)*

    The very last thing that must happen now   5
    Is a repetition of this morning's row.

I've never been so badly caught off guard.
Oh, how I feared for you! You saw how hard
I tried to make that troublesome Damis
10   Control his dreadful temper, and hold his peace.
In my confusion, I didn't have the sense
Simply to contradict his evidence;
But as it happened, that was for the best,
And all has worked out in our interest.
15   This storm has only bettered your position;
My husband doesn't have the least suspicion,
And now, in mockery of those who do,
He bids me be continually with you.
And that is why, quite fearless of reproof,
20   I now can be alone with my Tartuffe,
And why my heart—perhaps too quick to yield—
Feels free to let its passion be revealed.
TARTUFFE: Madam, your words confuse me. Not long ago,
You spoke in quite a different style, you know.
25   ELMIRE: Ah, Sir, if that refusal made you smart,
It's little that you know of woman's heart,
Or what that heart is trying to convey
When it resists in such a feeble way!
Always, at first, our modesy prevents
30   The frank avowal of tender sentiments;
However high the passion which inflames us,
Still, to confess its power somehow shames us.
Thus we reluct, at first, yet in a tone
Which tells you that our heart is overthrown,
35   That what our lips deny, our pulse confesses,
And that, in time, all noes will turn to yesses.
I fear my words are all too frank and free,
And a poor proof of woman's modesty;
But since I'm started, tell me, if you will—
40   Would I have tried to make Damis be still,
Would I have listened, calm and unoffended,
Until your lengthy offer of love was ended,
And been so very mild in my reaction,
Had your sweet words not given me satisfaction?
45   And when I tried to force you to undo
The marriage-plans my husband has in view,
What did my urgent pleading signify
If not that I admired you, and that I
Deplored the thought that someone else might own
50   Part of a heart I wished for mine alone?
TARTUFFE: Madam, no happiness is so complete
As when, from lips we love, come words so sweet;
Their nectar floods my every sense, and drains
In honeyed rivulets through all my veins.
55   To please you is my joy, my only goal;
Your love is the restorer of my soul;
And yet I must beg leave, now, to confess
Some lingering doubts as to my happiness
Might this not be a trick? Might not the catch
60   Be that you wish me to break off the match
With Mariane, and so have feigned to love me?
I shan't quite trust your fond opinion of me
Until the feelings you've expressed so sweetly
Are demonstrated somewhat more concretely,
65   And you have shown, by certain kind concessions,
That I may put my faith in your professions.

ELMIRE:

(She coughs, to warn her husband.)

Why be in such a hurry? Must my heart
Exhaust its bounty at the very start?
To make that sweet admission cost me dear,
But you'll not be content, it would appear,   70
Unless my store of favors is disbursed
To the last farthing, and at the very first.
TARTUFFE: The less we merit, the less we dare to hope,
And with our doubts, mere words can never cope.
We trust no promised bliss till we receive it;   75
Not till a joy is ours can we believe it.
I, who so little merit your esteem,
Can't credit this fulfillment of my dream,
And shan't believe it, Madam, until I savor
Some palpable assurance of your favor.   80
ELMIRE: My, how tyrannical your love can be,
And how it flusters and perplexes me!
How furiously you take one's heart in hand,
And make your every wish a fierce command!
Come, must you hound and harry me to death?   85
Will you not give me time to catch my breath?
Can it be right to press me with such force,
Give me no quarter, show me no remorse,
And take advantage, by your stern insistence,
Of the fond feelings which weaken my resistance?   90
TARTUFFE: Well, if you look with favor upon my love,
Why, then, begrudge me some clear proof thereof?
ELMIRE: But how can I consent without offense
To Heaven, toward which you feel such reverence?
TARTUFFE: If Heaven is all that holds you back, don't worry.   95
I can remove that hindrance in a hurry.
Nothing of that sort need obstruct our path.
ELMIRE: Must one not be afraid of Heaven's wrath?
TARTUFFE: Madam, forget such fears, and be my pupil,
And I shall teach you how to conquer scruple.   100
Some joys, it's true, are wrong in Heaven's eyes;
Yet Heaven is not averse to compromise;
There is a science, lately formulated,
Whereby one's conscience may be liberated,
And any wrongful act you care to mention   105
May be redeemed by purity of intention.
I'll teach you, Madam, the secrets of that science;
Meanwhile, just place on me your full reliance.
Assuage my keen desires, and feel no dread:
The sin, if any, shall be on my head.   110

(ELMIRE coughs, this time more loudly.)

You've a bad cough.
ELMIRE: Yes, yes. It's bad indeed.
TARTUFFE:

(Producing a little paper bag.)

A bit of licorice may be what you need.
ELMIRE: No, I've a stubborn cold, it seems. I'm sure it
Will take much more than licorice to cure it.
TARTUFFE: How aggravating.
ELMIRE: Oh, more than I can say.   115

TARTUFFE: If you're still troubled, think of things this way:
  No one shall know our joys, save us alone,
  And there's no evil till the act is known;
  It's scandal, Madam, which makes it an offense,
120 And it's no sin to sin in confidence.
  ELMIRE:

(Having coughed once more.)

  Well, clearly I must do as you require,
  And yield to your importunate desire.
  It is apparent, now, that nothing less
  Will satisfy you, and so I acquiesce.
125 To go so far is much against my will;
  I'm vexed that it should come to this; but still,
  Since you are so determined on it, since you
  Will not allow mere language to convince you,
  And since you ask for concrete evidence, I
130 See nothing for it, now, but to comply.
  If this is sinful, if I'm wrong to do it,
  So much the worse for him who drove me to it.
  The fault can surely not be charged to me.
  TARTUFFE: Madam, the fault is mine, if fault there be,
  And . . .
135 ELMIRE: Open the door a little, and peek out;
  I wouldn't want my husband poking about.
  TARTUFFE: Why worry about the man? Each day he grows
  More gullible; one can lead him by the nose.
  To find us here would fill him with delight,
140 And if he saw the worst, he'd doubt his sight.
  ELMIRE: Nevertheless, do step out for a minute
  Into the hall, and see that no one's in it.

SCENE VI

ORGON, ELMIRE

ORGON:

(Coming out from under the table.)

  That man's a perfect monster, I must admit!
  I'm simply stunned. I can't get over it.
  ELMIRE: What, coming out so soon? How premature!
  Get back in hiding, and wait until you're sure.
5 Stay till the end, and be convinced completely;
  We mustn't stop till things are proved concretely.
  ORGON: Hell never harbored anything so vicious!
  ELMIRE: Tut, don't be hasty. Try to be judicious.
  Wait, and be certain that there's no mistake.
10 No jumping to conclusions, for Heaven's sake!

(She places ORGON *behind her, as* TARTUFFE *re-enters.)*

SCENE VII

TARTUFFE, ELMIRE, ORGON

TARTUFFE:

(Not seeing ORGON.*)*

  Madam, all things have worked out to perfection;
  I've given the neighboring rooms a full inspection;
  No one's about; and now I may at last . . .

ORGON:

(Intercepting him.)

  Hold on, my passionate fellow, not so fast!
  I should advise a little more restraint.   5
  Well, so you thought you'd fool me, my dear saint!
  How soon you wearied of the saintly life—
  Wedding my daughter, and coveting my wife!
  I've long suspected you, and had a feeling
  That soon I'd catch you at your double-dealing.   10
  Just now, you've given me evidence galore;
  It's quite enough; I have no wish for more.
ELMIRE:

(To TARTUFFE.*)*

  I'm sorry to have treated you so slyly.
  But circumstances forced me to be wily.
  TARTUFFE: Brother, you can't think . . .
  ORGON: No more talk from   15
    you;
  Just leave this household, without more ado.
  TARTUFFE: What I intended . . .
  ORGON: That seems fairly clear.
  Spare me your falsehoods and get out of here.
  TARTUFFE: No, I'm the master, and you're the one to go!
  This house belongs to me, I'll have you know,   20
  And I shall show you that you can't hurt *me*
  By this contemptible conspiracy,
  That those who cross me know not what they do,
  And that I've means to expose and punish you,
  Avenge offended Heaven, and make you grieve   25
  That ever you dared order me to leave.

SCENE VIII

ELMIRE, ORGON

ELMIRE: What was the point of all that angry chatter?
ORGON: Dear God, I'm worried. This is no laughing matter.
ELMIRE: How so?
ORGON: I fear I understood his drift.
  I'm much disturbed about that deed of gift.
ELMIRE: You gave him. . . ?
ORGON: Yes, it's all been drawn and   5
    signed.
  But one thing more is weighing on my mind.
ELMIRE: What's that?
ORGON: I'll tell you; but first let's see if there's
  A certain strong-box in his room upstairs.

— ACT FIVE —

SCENE I

ORGON, CLÉANTE

CLÉANTE: Where are you going so fast?
ORGON: God knows!
CLÉANTE: Then wait;
  Let's have a conference, and deliberate
  On how this situation's to be met.

ORGON: That strong-box has me utterly upset;
5   This is the worst of many, many shocks.
CLÉANTE: Is there some fearful mystery in that box?
ORGON: My poor friend Argas brought that box to me
    With his own hands, in utmost secrecy;
    'Twas on the very morning of his flight.
10   It's full of papers which, if they came to light,
    Would ruin him—or such is my impression.
CLÉANTE: Then why did you let it out of your possession?
ORGON: Those papers vexed my conscience, and it seemed
        best
    To ask the counsel of my pious guest.
15   The cunning scoundrel got me to agree
    To leave the strong-box in his custody,
    So that, in case of an investigation,
    I could employ a slight equivocation
    And swear I didn't have it, and thereby,
20   At no expense to conscience, tell a lie.
CLÉANTE: It looks to me as if you're out on a limb.
    Trusting him with that box, and offering him
    That deed of gift, were actions of a kind
    Which scarcely indicate a prudent mind.
25   With two such weapons, he has the upper hand,
    And since you're vulnerable, as matters stand,
    You erred once more in bringing him to bay.
    You should have acted in some subtler way.
ORGON: Just think of it: behind that fervent face,
30   A heart so wicked, and a soul so base!
    I took him in, a hungry beggar, and then . . .
    Enough, by God! I'm through with pious men:
    Henceforth I'll hate the whole false brotherhood.
    And persecute them worse than Satan could.
35 CLÉANTE: Ah, there you go—extravagant as ever.
    Why can you not be rational? You never
    Manage to take the middle course, it seems,
    But jump, instead, between absurd extremes
    You've recognized your recent grave mistake
40   In falling victim to a pious fake;
    Now, to correct that error, must you embrace
    An even greater error in its place,
    And judge our worthy neighbors as a whole
    By what you've learned of one corrupted soul?
45   Come, just because one rascal made you swallow
    A show of zeal which turned out to be hollow,
    Shall you conclude that all men are deceivers,
    And that, today, there are no true believers?
    Let atheists make that foolish inference;
50   Learn to distinguish virtue from pretense,
    Be cautious in bestowing admiration,
    And cultivate a sober moderation.
    Don't humor fraud, but also don't asperse
    True piety; the latter fault is worse,
55   And it is best to err, if err one must,
    As you have done, upon the side of trust.

SCENE II

DAMIS, ORGON, CLÉANTE

DAMIS: Father, I hear that scoundrel's uttered threats
    Against you; that he pridefully forgets

How, in his need, he was befriended by you,
    And means to use your gifts to crucify you.
ORGON: It's true, my boy. I'm too distressed for tears.   5
DAMIS: Leave it to me, Sir; let me trim his ears.
    Faced with such insolence, we must not waver.
    I shall rejoice in doing you the favor
    Of cutting short his life, and your distress.
CLÉANTE: What a display of young hotheadedness!   10
    Do learn to moderate your fits of rage.
    In this just kingdom, this enlightened age,
    One does not settle things by violence.

SCENE III

MADAME PERNELLE, MARIANE, ELMIRE, DORINE, DAMIS, OR-
GON, CLÉANTE

MADAME PERNELLE: I hear strange tales of very strange events.
ORGON: Yes, strange events which these two eyes beheld.
    The man's ingratitude is unparalleled.
    I save a wretched pauper from starvation.
    House him, and treat him like a blood relation,   5
    Shower him every day with my largesse,
    Give him my daughter, and all that I possess;
    And meanwhile the unconscionable knave
    Tries to induce my wife to misbehave;
    And not content with such extreme rascality,   10
    Now threatens me with my own liberality,
    And aims, by taking base advantage of
    The gifts I gave him out of Christian love,
    To drive me from my house, a ruined man,
    And make me end a pauper, as he began.   15
DORINE: Poor fellow!
MADAME PERNELLE: No, my son, I'll never bring
    Myself to think him guilty of such a thing.
ORGON: How's that?
MADAME PERNELLE: The righteous always were maligned.
ORGON: Speak clearly, Mother. Say what's on your mind.
MADAME PERNELLE: I mean that I can smell a rat, my dear.   20
    You know how everybody hates him, here.
ORGON: That has no bearing on the case at all.
MADAME PERNELLE: I told you a hundred times, when you
        were small,
    That virtue is this world is hated ever;
    Malicious men may die, but malice never.   25
ORGON: No doubt that's true, but how does it apply?
MADAME PERNELLE: They've turned you against him by a
        clever lie.
ORGON: I've told you, I was there and saw it done.
MADAME PERNELLE: Ah, slanderers will stop at nothing, Son.
ORGON: Mother, I'll lose my temper . . . For the last time, 30
    I tell you I was witness to the crime.
MADAME PERNELLE: The tongues of spite are busy night and
        noon
    And to their venom no man is immune.
ORGON: You're talking nonsense. Can't you realize
    I saw it; saw it; saw it with my eyes?   35
    Saw, do you understand me? Must I shout it
    Into your ears before you'll cease to doubt it?
MADAME PERNELLE: Appearances can deceive, my son. Dear me,
    We cannot always judge by what we see.

ORGON: Drat! Drat!

40 MADAME PERNELLE: One often interprets things awry;
　　Good can seem evil to a suspicious eye.
ORGON: Was I to see his pawing at Elmire
　　As an act of charity?
MADAME PERNELLE: Till his guilt is clear,
　　A man deserves the benefit of the doubt.
45 You should have waited, to see how things turned out.
ORGON: Great God in Heaven, what more proof did I need?
　　Was I to sit there, watching, until he'd . . .
　　You drive me to the brink of impropriety.
MADAME PERNELLE: No, no, a man of such surpassing piety
50 Could not do such a thing. You cannot shake me.
　　I don't believe it, and you shall not make me.
ORGON: You vex me so that, if you weren't my mother,
　　I'd say to you . . . some dreadful thing or other.
DORINE: It's your turn now, Sir, not to be listened to;
55 You'd not trust us, and now she won't trust you.
CLÉANTE: My friends, we're wasting time which should be
　　spent
　　In facing up to our predicament.
　　I fear that scoundrel's threats weren't made in sport.
DAMIS: Do you think he'd have the nerve to go to court?
60 ELMIRE: I'm sure he won't: they'd find it all too crude
　　A case of swindling and ingratitude.
CLÉANTE: Don't be too sure. He won't be at a loss
　　To give his claims a high and righteous gloss;
　　And clever rogues with far less valid cause
65 Have trapped their victims in a web of laws.
　　I say again that to antagonize
　　A man so strongly armed was most unwise.
ORGON: I know it; but the man's appalling cheek
　　Outraged me so, I couldn't control my pique.
70 CLÉANTE: I wish to Heaven that we could devise
　　Some truce between you, or some compromise.
ELMIRE: If I had known what cards he held, I'd not
　　Have roused his anger by my little plot.
ORGON:

(*To* DORINE, *as* M. LOYAL *enters.*)

　　What is that fellow looking for? Who is he?
75 Go talk to him—and tell him that I'm busy.

SCENE IV

MONSIEUR LOYAL, MADAME PERNELLE, ORGON, DAMIS, MAR-
IANE, DORINE, ELMIRE, CLÉANTE

MONSIEUR LOYAL: Good day, dear sister. Kindly let me see
　　Your master.
DORINE: He's involved with company,
　　And cannot be disturbed just now, I fear.
MONSIEUR LOYAL: I hate to intrude; but what has brought me
　　here
5 Will not disturb your master, in any event.
　　Indeed, my news will make him most content.
DORINE: Your name?
MONSIEUR LOYAL: Just say that I bring greetings from
　　Monsieur Tartuffe, on whose behalf I've come.
DORINE:

(*To* ORGON.)

Sir, he's a very gracious man, and bears
A message from Tartuffe, which, he declares,   10
　　Will make you most content.
CLÉANTE: Upon my word,
　　I think this man had best be seen, and heard.
ORGON: Perhaps he has some settlement to suggest.
　　How shall I treat him? What manner would be best?
CLÉANTE: Control your anger, and if he should mention   15
　　Some fair adjustment, give him your full attention.
MONSIEUR LOYAL: Good health to you, good Sir. May
　　Heaven confound
　　Your enemies, and may your joys abound.
ORGON:

(*Aside*, *to* CLÉANTE.)

　　A gentle salutation: it confirms
　　My guess that he is here to offer terms.   20
MONSIEUR LOYAL: I've always held your family most dear;
　　I served your father, Sir, for many a year.
ORGON: Sir, I must ask your pardon; to my shame,
　　I cannot now recall your face or name.
MONSIEUR LOYAL: Loyal's my name; I come from Normandy,   25
　　And I'm a bailiff, in all modesty.
　　For forty years, praise God, it's been my boast
　　To serve with honor in that vital post,
　　And I am here, Sir, if you will permit
　　The liberty, to serve you with this writ . . .   30
ORGON: To—*what?*
MONSIEUR LOYAL: Now, please, Sir, let us have no friction:
　　It's nothing but an order of eviction.
　　You are to move your goods and family out
　　And make way for new occupants, without
　　Deferment or delay, and give the keys . . .   35
ORGON: I? Leave this house?
MONSIEUR LOYAL: Why yes, Sir, if you please.
　　This house, Sir, from the cellar to the roof,
　　Belongs now to the good Monsieur Tartuffe,
　　And he is lord and master of your estate
　　By virtue of a deed of present date,   40
　　Drawn in due form, with clearest legal phrasing . . .
DAMIS: Your insolence is utterly amazing!
MONSIEUR LOYAL: Young man, my business here is not with
　　you,
　　But with your wise and temperate father, who,
　　Like every worthy citizen, stands in awe   45
　　Of justice, and would never obstruct the law.
ORGON: But . . .
MONSIEUR LOYAL: Not for a million, Sir, would you rebel
　　Against authority; I know that well.
　　You'll not make trouble, Sir, or interfere
　　With the execution of my duties here.   50
DAMIS: Someone may execute a smart tattoo
　　On that black jacket of yours, before you're through.
MONSIEUR LOYAL: Sir, bid your son be silent. I'd much regret
　　Having to mention such a nasty threat
　　Of violence, in writing my report.   55
DORINE:

(*Aside.*)

　　This man Loyal's a most disloyal sort!

MONSIEUR LOYAL: I love all men of upright character,
  And when I agreed to serve these papers, Sir,
  It was your feelings that I had in mind.
60 I couldn't bear to see the case assigned
  To someone else, who might esteem you less
  And so subject you to unpleasantness.
ORGON: What's more unpleasant than telling a man to leave
  His house and home?
MONSIEUR LOYAL: You'd like a short reprieve?
65 If you desire, Sir, I shall not press you,
  But wait until tomorrow to dispossess you.
  Splendid. I'll come and spend the night here, then,
  Most quietly, with half a score of men.
  For form's sake, you might bring me, just before
70 You go to bed, the keys to the front door.
  My men, I promise, will be on their best
  Behavior, and will not disturb your rest.
  But bright and early, Sir, you must be quick
  And move out all your furniture, every stick;
75 The men I've chosen are both young and strong,
  And with their help it shouldn't take you long.
  In short, I'll make things pleasant and convenient,
  And since I'm being so extremely lenient,
  Please show me, Sir, a like consideration,
80 And give me your entire cooperation.
ORGON:

(Aside.)

  I may be all but bankrupt, but I vow
  I'd give a hundred louis, here and now,
  Just for the pleasure of landing one good clout
  Right on the end of that complacent snout.
CLÉANTE: Careful; don't make things worse.
85 DAMIS: My bootsole
    itches
  To give that beggar a good kick in the breeches.
DORINE: Monsieur Loyal, I'd love to hear the whack
  Of a stout stick across your fine broad back.
MONSIEUR LOYAL: Take care: a woman too may go to jail if
90 She uses threatening language to a bailiff.
CLÉANTE: Enough, enough, Sir. This must not go on.
  Give me that paper, please, and then begone.
MONSIEUR LOYAL: Well, *au revoir*. God give you all good
    cheer!
ORGON: May God confound you, and him who sent you here!

SCENE V

ORGON, CLÉANTE, MARIANE, ELMIRE, MADAME PERNELLE,
DORINE, DAMIS

ORGON: Now, Mother, was I right or not? This writ
  Should change your notion of Tartuffe a bit.
  Do you perceive his villainy at last?
MADAME PERNELLE: I'm thunderstruck. I'm utterly aghast.
5 DORINE: Oh, come, be fair. You mustn't take offense
  At this new proof of his benevolence.
  He's acting out of selfless love, I know.
  Material things enslave the soul, and so
  He kindly has arranged your liberation
10 From all that might endanger your salvation.

ORGON: Will you not ever hold your tongue, you dunce?
CLÉANTE: Come, you must take some action, and at once.
ELMIRE: Go tell the world of the low trick he's tried.
  The deed of gift is surely nullified
  By such behavior, and public rage will not   15
  Permit the wretch to carry out his plot.

SCENE VI

VALÈRE, ORGON, CLÉANTE, ELMIRE, MARIANE, MADAME
PERNELLE, DAMIS, DORINE

VALÈRE: Sir, though I hate to bring you more bad news,
  Such is the danger that I cannot choose.
  A friend who is extremely close to me
  And knows my interest in your family
  Has, for my sake, presumed to violate   5
  The secrecy that's due to things of state,
  And sends me word that you are in a plight
  From which your one salvation lies in flight.
  That scoundrel who's imposed upon you so
  Denounced you to the King an hour ago   10
  And, as supporting evidence, displayed
  The strong-box of a certain renegade
  Whose secret papers, so he testified,
  You had disloyally agreed to hide.
  I don't know just what charges may be pressed,   15
  But there's a warrant out for your arrest;
  Tartuffe has been instructed, furthermore,
  To guide the arresting officer to your door.
CLÉANTE: He's clearly done this to facilitate
  His seizure of your house and your estate.   20
ORGON: That man, I must say, is a vicious beast!
VALÈRE: Quick, Sir; you mustn't tarry in the least.
  My carriage is outside, to take you hence;
  This thousand louis should cover all expense.
  Let's lose no time, or you shall be undone;   25
  The sole defense, in this case, is to run.
  I shall go with you all the way, and place you
  In a safe refuge to which they'll never trace you.
ORGON: Alas, dear boy, I wish that I could show you
  My gratitude for everything I owe you.   30
  But now is not the time; I pray the Lord
  That I may live to give you your reward.
  Farewell, my dears; be careful . . .
CLÉANTE: Brother, hurry.
  We shall take care of things; you needn't worry.

SCENE VII

The OFFICER, TARTUFFE, VALÈRE, ORGON, ELMIRE, MARIANE,
MADAME PERNELLE, DORINE, CLÉANTE, DAMIS

TARTUFFE: Gently, Sir, gently; stay right where you are.
  No need for haste; your lodging isn't far.
  You're off to prison, by order of the Prince.
ORGON: This is the crowning blow, you wretch; and since
  It means my total ruin and defeat,   5
  Your villainy is now at last complete.
TARTUFFE: You needn't try to provoke me; it's no use.
  Those who serve Heaven must expect abuse.

CLÉANTE: You are indeed most patient, sweet, and blameless.
10 DORINE: How he exploits the name of Heaven! It's shameless.
TARTUFFE: Your taunts and mockeries are all for naught;
   To do my duty is my only thought.
MARIANE: Your love of duty is more meritorious,
   And what you've done is little short of glorious.
15 TARTUFFE: All deeds are glorious, Madam, which obey
   The sovereign prince who sent me here today.
ORGON: I rescued you when you were destitute,
   Have you forgotten that, you thankless brute?
TARTUFFE: No, no, I well remember everything;
20   But my first duty is to serve my King.
   That obligation is so paramount
   That other claims, beside it, do not count;
   And for it I would sacrifice my wife,
   My family, my friend, or my own life.
ELMIRE: Hypocrite!
25 DORINE: All that we most revere, he uses
   To cloak his plots and camouflage his ruses.
CLÉANTE: If it is true that you are animated
   By pure and loyal zeal, as you have stated,
   Why was this zeal not roused until you'd sought
30   To make Orgon a cuckold, and been caught?
   Why weren't you moved to give your evidence
   Until your outraged host had driven you hence?
   I shan't say that the gift of all his treasure
   Ought to have damped your zeal in any measure;
35   But if he is a traitor, as you declare,
   How could you condescend to be his heir?
TARTUFFE:

(To the OFFICER.*)*

   Sir, spare me all this clamor; it's growing shrill.
   Please carry out your orders, if you will.
OFFICER: Yes, I've delayed too long, Sir. Thank you kindly.
40   You're just the proper person to remind me.
   Come, you are off to join the other boarders
   In the King's prison, according to his orders.
TARTUFFE: Who? I, Sir?
OFFICER: Yes.
TARTUFFE: To prison? This can't be true!
OFFICER: I owe an explanation, but not to you.

(To ORGON.*)*

45   Sir, all is well; rest easy, and be grateful.
   We serve a Prince to whom all sham is hateful,
   A Prince who sees into our inmost hearts,
   And can't be fooled by any trickster's arts.
   His royal soul, though generous and human,
50   Views all things with discernment and acumen;
   His sovereign reason is not lightly swayed,
   And all his judgments are discreetly weighed.
   He honors righteous men of every kind,
   And yet his zeal for virtue is not blind,

Nor does his love of piety numb his wits 55
And make him tolerant of hypocrites.
'Twas hardly likely that this man could cozen
A King who's foiled such liars by the dozen.
With one keen glance, the King perceived the whole
Perverseness and corruption of his soul, 60
And thus high Heaven's justice was displayed:
Betraying you, the rogue stood self-betrayed.
The King soon recognized Tartuffe as one
Notorious by another name, who'd done
So many vicious crimes that one could fill 65
Ten volumes with them, and be writing still.
But to be brief: our sovereign was appalled
By this man's treachery toward you, which he called
The last, worst villainy of a vile career,
And bade me follow the impostor here 70
To see how gross his impudence could be,
And force him to restore your property.
Your private papers, by the King's command,
I hereby seize and give into your hand.
The King, by royal order, invalidates 75
The deed which gave this rascal your estates,
And pardons, furthermore, your grave offense
In harboring an exile's documents.
By these decrees, our Prince rewards you for
Your loyal deeds in the late civil war, 80
And shows how heartfelt is his satisfaction
In recompensing any worthy action,
How much he prizes merit, and how he makes
More of men's virtues than of their mistakes.
DORINE: Heaven be praised!
MADAME PERNELLE: I breathe again, at last. 85
ELMIRE: We're safe.
MARIANE: I can't believe the danger's past.
ORGON:

(To TARTUFFE.*)*

   Well, traitor, now you see . . .
CLÉANTE: Ah, Brother, please,
   Let's not descend to such indignities.
   Leave the poor wretch to his unhappy fate,
   And don't say anything to aggravate 90
   His present woes; but rather hope that he
   Will soon embrace an honest piety,
   And mend his ways, and by a true repentance
   Move our just King to moderate his sentence.
   Meanwhile, go kneel before your sovereign's throne 95
   And thank him for the mercies he has shown.
ORGON: Well said: let's go at once and, gladly kneeling,
   Express the gratitude which all are feeling.
   Then, when that first great duty has been done,
   We'll turn with pleasure to a second one, 100
   And give Valère, whose love has proven so true,
   The wedded happiness which is his due.

JEAN RACINE

Jean Racine (1639–1699) pursued a career closely connected with the dominant institutions of Parisian culture: the court, the church, and the stage. Racine's parents both died in his early childhood, and he was raised by his grandfather and enrolled at the school of the famous and controversial abbey at Port-Royal. Port-Royal was associated with an emphatically unworldly Catholic sect — the Jansenists — that was brutally suppressed in the seventeenth century. Racine's education at Port-Royal played a decisive role in his intellectual life and in the course of his career as a dramatist.

At Port-Royal, Racine perfected his study of Greek and Latin, considered a career in the church, and became ambitious for public success and for a life at court. By the early 1660s he had written several courtly poems — on Louis XIV's marriage, on his illness — that brought him to the attention of the established writers at court: Jean La Fontaine, Nicholas Boileau-Despréaux, and Molière. His first surviving play, *La Thebaïde* was performed by Molière's company in 1664. In 1665, he gave *Alexandre* to Molière's company, as well, but was dissatisfied with Molière's production. He then gave the play to the rival company at the Hôtel de Bourgogne, where it played opposite Molière's production. Molière withdrew the play, and the hostilities between the two playwrights intensified in 1667 when Mademoiselle DuParc, Molière's leading lady — and possibly Racine's mistress — defected from Molière's company to create the title role in Racine's *Andromaque*. This play initiates the stunning series of Racine's major plays, *Britannicus* (1669), *Bérénice* (1670), *Bajazet* (1672), *Mithradate* (1673), *Iphigénie* (1674), and *Phaedra* (1677). *Phaedra* is Racine's most celebrated play, and his most controversial. The play, originally entitled *Phaedra and Hippolytus*, opened in January 1677 at the Hôtel de Bourgogne, but Racine's enemies at court persuaded Jacques Pradon (1632–1698), a minor playwright, to open his own play about Phaedra at the Palais-Royal theater. The plays ran against one another, inviting comparison and criticism. After *Phaedra*, Racine married and retired from Paris to Port-Royal. He was also appointed to the coveted position of court historiographer and wrote a history of Louis XIV's wars in 1684. Racine's two last plays, *Esther* (1688) and *Athalie* (1690), are religious dramas, written at the request of Louis's second wife, Madame de Maintenon, to be performed privately at St. Cyr, a girls' academy. Racine was buried at Port-Royal in 1699, and his remains were moved when the abbey was subsequently destroyed.

Throughout his career, Racine maintained contact with Port-Royal, responding to its criticism of his work in the theater, defending Port-Royal in ecclesiastical matters, and writing a history of the abbey. However, Port-Royal's most pervasive influence on Racine's drama has to do with the Jansenist sense of sin, of the impossibility of redeeming human action. Inspired by the writing of Cornelius Otto Jansen (1558–1638), the Jansenists held that mankind lives in a state of essential sin and corruption, and summoned their followers to retire from the world in order to contemplate the moral abyss dividing mankind from God's mercy. What made Jansenism particularly threatening to the church in the seventeenth century was its resistance to the authority of Rome, and its call for a solitary and contemplative clergy, which challenged the massive public and political role played by the church in the affairs of the French state. Racine's plays touch only metaphorically on the strictly religious issues surrounding the Jansenist debate, but they are directly concerned with the philosophical themes of Jansenist belief: the sense of unavoidable guilt, the tortuous process of introspection, the desire to escape the world of action.

Phaedra

If Descartes' famous *cogito ergo sum* ("I think, therefore I am") can be taken to represent a neoclassical concern for rational order, *Phaedra* might be said to illustrate a similar principle in terms of tragedy: "I feel, therefore I suffer." The play's main characters, particularly Hippolytus and Phaedra, feel and suffer precisely because reason fails to control the massive passions welling up within them, passions that deepen the rift between the corruption they feel and the uncorrupted ideals they never can achieve.

Racine's Jansenist beliefs have an indirect but profound impact in *Phaedra*. The world of the play is a world of unavoidable sin, in which action leads inevitably to wrongdoing and catastrophe, and in which flight is impossible. The characters define themselves according to fixed and unattainable ideals that are subverted by their irresistible, even criminal passions. Hippolytus pursues an ideal of heroic innocence and self-containment, violated in his own eyes by his love for Aricia. Theseus is consumed by his passion for power, conquest, and authority, and feels betrayed when he believes that he has been usurped by his son. Phaedra's honor, and even her humanity, is shattered by her adulterous, incestuous desire for her stepson. The play's elegant compression concentrates the action exclusively on these characters; their confidants—Theramenes, Oenone—function largely as screens on which Racine projects the tempestuous passions of the main characters. Although the characters blame the gods for the desire they suffer, the destructive force of the characters' passions really rises from within. In the world of *Phaedra*, action is impossible and sin is inevitable. The characters are each destroyed by the monsters they become.

— PREFACE —

TRANSLATED BY R. C. KNIGHT

Here is another tragedy on a subject taken from Euripides. The action follows a somewhat different course, but I have enriched my play with everything in his that I considered most strikingly beautiful. Had I borrowed no more than the conception of Phaedra's character, I might say I owe him the most reasonable thing, perhaps, that I have given to the theatre. I am not surprised that this character was so successful in Euripides' time, and now again in our own, considering that it has every quality required by Aristotle in the tragic hero, and proper to arouse compassion and terror. For Phaedra is not altogether guilty, and not altogether innocent. She is drawn by her destiny, and the anger of the Gods, into an unlawful passion which she is the first to hold in horror. She makes every endeavour to overcome it. She chooses death rather than disclose it to anyone. And when forced to reveal it, she speaks of it with such shame and confusion as leave no doubt that her crime is rather a punishment from the Gods, than an impulse of her own will.

I have even taken pains to make her a little less odious than she is in the tragedies of antiquity, where she brings herself, unprompted, to accuse Hippolytus. I felt that a false testimony was something too base, too black, to put into the mouth of a Princess possessed otherwise of sentiments so noble and virtuous. Such baseness seemed to me more fitting to a Nurse, who might have more slave-like propensities; though even she only enters upon the lying accusation to save the life and honour of her mistress. If Phaedra acquiesces, it is because she is beside herself in the agitation of her thoughts, and the next moment she comes on with the intention of vindicating the guiltless and publishing the truth.

Hippolytus is accused, in Euripides and in Seneca, of actually raping his step-mother—*vim corpus tulit*; here, of no more than the intention. I desired to spare Theseus a sense of shame which might have made him less acceptable to my audience.

As for the figure of Hippolytus, I had read in ancient authors that Euripides was blamed for depicting him as a philosopher free of all imperfection—so that the death of the youthful Prince gave rise to far more indignation than pity. I felt I should give him a failing that might render him somewhat guilty towards his father, without detracting at all from that magnanimity which makes him spare Phaedra's honour and go to his doom without accusing her. By failing I mean his involuntary passion for Aricia, the daughter and the sister of his father's mortal enemies.

This Aricia is not a child of my invention. Virgil relates that Hippolytus married her, and she bore him a son, after Aesculapius had brought him back to life. And I have read too, in certain authors, that Hippolytus had married and brought into Italy an Athenian maiden of high birth, named Aricia, who had given her name to an Italian township.

I adduce these authorities, because I have most scrupulously endeavoured to keep close to the legend. I have even taken the history of Theseus just as it is in Plutarch.

It is this historian who mentions that the belief in Theseus' descent to the underworld to abduct Proserpine, was occasioned by a journey he made into Epirus towards the source of the Acheron, where a King, whose wife Pirithous sought to carry off, held Theseus prisoner after putting Pirithous to death. Thus I have tried to retain the verisimilitude of history, and yet to lose none of the embellishments of fable, so rich in the stuff of poetry. And the rumour of Theseus' death, based on the legendary journey, gives rise to that declaration of Phaedra's love which proves one of the principal causes of her unhappy plight, and which she would never have dared utter while she believed her husband to be alive.

For the rest, I dare not yet assert this play to be in truth the best of my tragedies. I leave my readers, and time, to set its rightful price upon it. What I can assert is that I have composed none where virtue is shown to more advantage than here. The slightest faults are severely punished. The bare thought of crime is regarded with no less horror than crime itself. The failings of love are treated as real failings. The passions are offered to view only to show all the ravage they create. And vice is everywhere painted in such hues, that its hideous face may be recognised and loathed. Here is the proper aim for every man to keep in sight who works for the public. And this, above all, was the purpose of the earliest tragic poets. Their stage was a school where virtue was taught no less well than in the schools of the philosophers. Thus Aristotle consented to draw up the rules of the dramatic poem; Socrates, the sagest of the philosophers, thought it no shame to set his hand to the tragedies of Euripides. It were much to be desired that our works should be found as serious and as full of useful instruction as the pages of those poets. It might bring about a reconciliation between the tragic art and a number of persons, noted for their religion and learning, who have denounced it of late, but might well look upon it with less disfavour if authors cared as much to instruct as to entertain their audience, and carried out thereby the true purpose of tragedy.

Jean Racine
(1677)

PHAEDRA

Jean Racine

TRANSLATED BY R. C. KNIGHT

— CHARACTERS —

THESEUS, *son of Aegeus, King of Athens*
PHAEDRA, *wife of Theseus, daughter of Minos and Pasiphaë*
HIPPOLYTUS, *son of Theseus by Antiope Queen of the Amazons*
ARICIA, *daughter of Pallas, descended from the ancient kings of Athens*
OENONE, *nurse and confidant of Phaedra*

THERAMENES, *governor of Hippolytus*
ISMENE, *confidant to Aricia*
PANOPE, *one of Phaedra's women*
GUARDS

The scene is in Trozen, a town in the Peloponnese.

— ACT ONE —

HIPPOLYTUS, THERAMENES

HIPPOLYTUS: My mind's made up: I sail, Theramenes.
  No more for me the tranquil days of Trozen,
  For in the mortal tempest of my doubts
  I am dishonoured if I linger here.
5 Six months ago my father sailed and left me
  Ignorant what befalls a head so cherished,
  Ignorant even where he may be hidden —
THERAMENES: So where will you go to look for him, my lord?
  Already, to relieve a fear I shared,
10 I have scoured the two seas that Corinth holds asunder.
  Demanded Theseus of the tribes that live
  Where Acheron drives down headlong into Hell,
  Searched Elis, skirted Taenarum, and even
  Traversed the waves where Icarus fell and perished.
15 What hope new-risen or what happier skies
  Will light you to his footsteps? Why, perhaps,
  Who knows, perhaps the King your father wishes
  Not to unveil the mystery of his venture,
  And while his peril fills your thought and ours,
20 Serene, weaving the latest of his loves,
  The hero waits to seize the unguarded moment —
HIPPOLYTUS: Stop, good Theramenes. You slander Theseus;
  There is a nobler cause for these delays;
  After the follies of forgotten youth
25 The wanderings of his inconstant heart
  Are fixed at length, and Phaedra fears no rival.
  So once more — I shall go where duty points
  And fly a land I cannot bear to see.
THERAMENES: But my lord, how long have you despised the presence
30 Of these calm fields, the pleasure of your childhood
  Whose solitude was dearer to you than
  The splendid stir of Athens and the court?
  What fear has banished you, or else what heartache?
HIPPOLYTUS: Those days are past. Pleasure and peace have vanished
35 Since first the Gods directed to our shore
  The child of Minos and Pasiphaë.
THERAMENES: I see: there is the cause, the hated presence —
  Phaedra, who came, your father's dangerous bride,
  Looked on you once, and by your prompt exile
40 Gave the first measure of her new-won power.

But all that dogged hate and old aversion
Has passed with time, passed or at least abated;
And after all what danger lies in her,
A woman dying, crying out for death?
Stricken by ills that none can make her utter,   45
Tired of her life, tired of the day that lights her,
What can she do to you?
HIPPOLYTUS: I do not fear
  Anything her aversion could devise.
  I sail to fly another enemy,
  I do admit: I fly Aricia,   50
  The youngest and the last of all that house
  In fatal league against ours.
THERAMENES: You, my lord,
  Are turned against her too? But Pallas' daughter
  Surely had no part in her brothers' treason,
  And must you hate that unoffending grace?   55
HIPPOLYTUS: I would not fly her if I hated her.
THERAMENES: My lord, have I permission to interpret
  Your flight? Must I suppose that you are not
  The old implacable Hippolytus,
  The outlaw of Love's empire, he that vowed   60
  Never to wear the yoke his father wore?
  Can it be that a slighted and a smarting Goddess
  Will press you to the service of her shrine,
  Reduce you to the rank of common men
  And vindicate that father by your fate?   65
  Can it be love, my lord?
HIPPOLYTUS: How can you say it,
  My friend, that knew the childhood of my heart
  And all its growth in pride and fierce resolve?
  Shall I dishonour it, disown myself?
  First, as a babe, at an Amazonian breast   70
  I drank the resolution that astounds you,
  But once of age to look upon myself
  I wished to be no other than I was.
  Then, in the faithful service of your kindness
  As you rehearsed for me my father's story,   75
  Do you remember how my soul blazed up
  At each particular in the noble toils
  Of the intrepid hero, as we showed him
  Turning the world from thoughts of lost Alcides
  By monsters strangled and by brigands slain —   80
  Procrustes, Sinnis, Sciro, Cercyon

And Epidaurus scattered with the limbs
Of her gigantic tyrant, and the gore
Reeking from all Crete, of the Minotaur?
85 But when you told other ignobler feats —
A faith so cheaply pledged, and ever new,
Helen torn from a mother's arms in Sparta,
In Salamis the sighs of Periboea,
So many more than he can even name,
90 Victims too credulous of a lover's tongue;
What barren rocks heard Ariadne's sorrows;
How Phaedra, last and under happier auspice,
Followed him — then I wished the tale untold;
Often I urged you hasten and be done;
95 And would my wishes had redeemed from fame
That darker half of such a fair renown!
And now, by the spite of Heaven, shall I be
Degraded to the same indignity?
— Baseness beyond excuse, for those were frailties
100 Unseen amid a multitude of honours,
While not one trophy of a monster slain
Entitles me to fail as he has failed.
Even if I lost my freedom and my pride
How could I yield them to Aricia?
105 How could my disobedient sense forget
That which divides us irremovably?
The King denies her, denies her fallen brothers,
By violent laws, continuance of their line;
Their name must die for ever in her death,
110 Their guilty branch must bear no other fruit,
And till the tomb, submissive and sequestered,
The torch of wedlock must not burn for her.
Am I to oppose my father and his wrath?
Embrace her claims? and give a precedent
To treason? and embark my youth —
115 THERAMENES: My lord,
If the marked hour draws on, our arguments
Escape the notice of the incurious Heavens.
No. Theseus wished you blind, and gave you eyes;
His hate inflames the passion he forbids you,
120 And adds enchantment to his prisoner's charms.
But come, why look askance at honest love?
Why not make trial where its sweetness lies?
Why be enchained by vain and foolish scruples?
Who fears to stray that follows Hercules?
125 Many a stubborn heart has Venus bent —
Where would you be yourself and your defiance
Had chaste Antiope been as chaste as you
And never warmed to Theseus' flame? But why
Face out a falsehood with the pride of words?
130 Confess how things have changed: not now as once,
Aloof, intractable, we see you guide
A skimming chariot along the beaches
Or, adept in the mystery Neptune taught,
Break an unmastered courser to the curb;
135 Less often our halloos awake the forests;
Your eyes droop, weighted with a secret fire . . .
The case is clear — you are in love, in flame,
In torment, and you will not show your wound.
Is it Aricia?
HIPPOLYTUS: Theramenes,
140 I sail today, and go to find my father.

THERAMENES: Without an audience of Phaedra?
HIPPOLYTUS: No.
I will see her; I cannot well do less.
You may send word. — But what is the fresh misfortune
Disturbs her favorite Oenone so?

(Enter OENONE)

OENONE: Alas, my lord, what grief can equal mine?   145
The Queen is near her utmost bourne of fate;
She that I watch by night and day unsleeping
Dies in my arms, and will not tell her sickness.
Her thought is all at variance with itself;
Her sick disquiet drives her from her bed   150
To see the light of day. But by her orders
No eye of man may see her suffering.
— Here she is.
HIPPOLYTUS: Very well; then I retire
Not to offend with this unwelcome face.

(Exeunt HIPPOLYTUS and THERAMENES)

(Enter PHAEDRA)

PHAEDRA: No more, for I can move no more, Oenone.   155
Let me rest; I am faint, my strength has left me.
My darkened eyes are dazzled by the light,
My wavering knees are weak beneath my weight.
Ah me!

(Sits)

OENONE: High Gods, relent and see our tears!
PHAEDRA: These fripperies, these veils, they hang so heavy!   160
Whose was the unkind hand that piled and bound
These clustering locks that weigh upon my brow?
So feeble and so weary, all these things
Grieve me and weary me.
OENONE: How can we please you?
Yourself, repentant of your wicked thoughts,   165
You called in haste for clothes and ornaments;
Yourself you rallied your forgotten vigour,
You wanted to be out and see the sunlight.
Now you are here, my lady, and it seems
You loathe the very light that you desired.   170
PHAEDRA: Splendid begetter of a seed afflicted,
Father from whom my mother claimed her birth,
O blushing Sun ashamed of my despair,
Now, for the last time, I salute thy face.
OENONE: What, still possessed of such a fearful purpose?   175
Shall I for ever see you, turned from life,
Enact the mournful ritual of your death?
PHAEDRA: Oh give me the shadow of the forest glades!
Or let my eye piercing the glorious dust
Follow the wheeling chariot in the course!   180
OENONE: My lady?
PHAEDRA: Oh, I am mad. What have I said?
Where am I, where are my thoughts, my wandering mind?
Lost, for the Gods have taken it away.
My face is hot, Oenone, with my shame;
I cannot hide my guilty sufferings   185
And tears descend that I cannot restrain.

OENONE: Blush if you must, but blush to keep a silence
That doubles all the misery you suffer.
Rebellious to all tending, deaf to all pleas,
190 Will you unpitying allow your life
To flow away? What madness cuts it short?
What spell, what poison stanches up its course?
Thrice has the sky been muffled up in shade
And still is sleep a stranger to your eyes;
195 Thrice has the day displaced the gloom of night
And still you fast, and still your body wastes.
What dark temptation leads you on? What right
Invests you with the power to take your life —
Wronging the Gods from whom you draw your being,
200 Failing the husband who received your promise,
Failing still more your helpless children, doomed
To bitter lives of bondage; for reflect,
The very day that takes their mother from them
Rebuilds the hope of that Barbarian's child,
205 That arrogant enemy of you and yours,
The boy the Amazonian stranger bore,
Hippolytus —
PHAEDRA: O Gods!
OENONE: That charge strikes home!
PHAEDRA: Woman, how dare you name that name to me?
OENONE: Why, now your anger is most justly roused.
210 It heartens me that you should shrink to hear
That fatal name. Then live. For love, for duty,
Live; if you would not have the Scythian's son,
Bending your children to his hated yoke,
Lord it over the fairest blood of Greece
215 And of the Gods. But do not wait, each moment
You die. Rally, betimes, your prostrate vigour
While yet your almost spent and guttering life
Still glows, and may be kindled once again.
PHAEDRA: I have outlived the right to live already.
220 OENONE: Why, is there some remorse that feeds upon you?
What have you done that drives you so distraught?
Your hands have never dipped in guiltless blood?
PHAEDRA: I thank the Gods my hands are free of evil.
Would that my heart were innocent as they!
225 OENONE: What resolution, then, have you conceived
To terrify your heart before the time?
PHAEDRA: I have said enough. Ask me no more, have pity;
For if I die it is to keep within me
This dreadful secret.
OENONE: Keep it then, and die;
230 But other hands, not mine, will close your eyes.
Yours is a weak and flickering fire, but I
Will lose my spirit first among the dead;
There are many avenues and all unbarred;
An injured heart will soon perceive the best. —
235 Ungrateful mistress, when did I betray you?
Have you forgotten that these hands received you
When you were born? My children and my home,
I have left all for you: and all for this.
PHAEDRA: What do you think to gain by this beseeching?
240 You will shrink with horror if I break my silence.
OENONE: What can you tell me then more horrible
Than thus to see you die before my face?
PHAEDRA: And when you know my destiny and my weakness
Still I shall die, and only die more guilty.

OENONE: My lady, by the tears I shed for you,   245
By these your trembling knees I hold entwined,
Deliver me from deadly fear and doubt.
PHAEDRA: You wish it. Rise.
OENONE: Speak on, and I will listen.
PHAEDRA: How shall I tell, ye Gods, or where begin?
OENONE: Your fears are insults to my loyalty.   250
PHAEDRA: O deathless hate of Venus, fatal vengeance!
O heavy doom of love upon my mother!
OENONE: Forget, my lady. Hide that memory
And keep it from the ears of later times.
PHAEDRA: Love left thee dying, sweet sister Ariadne,   255
Lying forsaken by the alien waters.
OENONE: Let by, my lady. Must your mortal grief
Be vented on the dearest of your blood?
PHAEDRA: Of this doomed blood, I, by the will of Venus,
I perish now the last and most accursed.   260
OENONE: You love!
PHAEDRA: To madness and to ecstasy.
OENONE: Who?
PHAEDRA: There's the horror that surpasses horror:
I love . . . at the fatal name I blench and tremble —
I love . . .
OENONE: But who?
PHAEDRA: You know the Amazon's son,
The young Prince who endured so much, through me . . . 265
OENONE: O Gods! Hippolytus!
PHAEDRA: You spoke the name!
OENONE: Sweet Heavens! You have chilled my very blood.
O race polluted, hopeless, lamentable!
Woe worth the day that brought us to these shores!
Why did we venture?
PHAEDRA: It was long ago   270
And far from here. When first the rite of Hymen
Bound my obedience to the son of Aegeus —
My happiness, my peace then seemed so plain —
Careless in Athens stood my conqueror.
I saw and gazed, I blushed and paled again,   275
A blind amazement rose and blurred my mind;
My eyes were dim, my lips forgot to speak,
This, I knew, was the awful flame of Venus,
The fated torment of her chosen victims.
I tried to ward it off with prayers, with vows   280
And offerings, a temple built and decked,
And in the midst of endless sacrifices
I searched the entrails for my erring wisdom.
Weak drugs for irremediable love!
Even as my hand spilt incense at the shrine,   285
Even as my lips invoked the name of Venus
I prayed Hippolytus, my eyes beheld
Hippolytus, and while the altars steamed
I offered all to him I dared not name.
I fled him everywhere. O bitterness,   290
He looked upon me in his father's features.
At last, I turned upon myself. I forced
Myself to play the torturer against
The dreaded enemy I loved too well,
Put on the bride's abhorrence of the stepson,   295
Pleaded and pressed until I banished him
Out of his father's arms, his father's heart.
Once more I breathed; and after this, Oenone,

My life, serener, flowed in blameless ways,
300 Pleasing my husband, covering my pain,
Tending the fruits of his unhappy bed:
Foolish expedients! and inexorable
Hardness of destiny! — My lord himself
Brought me to Trozen and my banished foe.
305 The ancient wound gaped deep, and bled again.
No longer is it a secret flame that flickers
About my veins: headlong in onset Venus
Hangs on her quarry! I abhorred my guilt,
Life was a curse, my love a misery;
310 I looked for death to save my name, and bury
Far from the day the darkness of these fires.
I could not face your strivings and your tears.
Now you know all; and it is well, if you
Stand but aside from my advancing death.
315 Abstain at last from undeserved reproaches,
And leave your useless effort to revive
The embers of a fast-expiring fire.

(Enter PANOPE)

PANOPE: I wish that I could hide the news, my lady,
That I am forced to bring you. Death has taken
320 Your lord, our most indomitable King;
And you alone are ignorant of your loss.
OENONE: What is this, Panope?
                              My lady's prayers
Will never now bring Theseus back to Athens,
And mariners that landed here today
325 Have told Hippolytus that he is dead.
PHAEDRA: Gods!
PANOPE: Athens wavers in the choice of masters.
One boasts allegiance to the Prince your son;
One, reckless of the statutes of the land,
Presumes to favour the Barbarian's child,
330 My lady; and they say a rank sedition
Proclaims Aricia and the blood of Pallas.
I knew it was my duty to report
Such perils. Hippolytus is ready now
To sail, and many fear if he arrives
335 In this tempestuous season, he will sway
A fickle multitide.
OENONE: Panope, thank you:
Your news was precious, and the Queen has heard.

(Exit PANOPE)

OENONE: My lady, I had thrown away all pleadings,
All hope to move you, and my only thought
340 Was to attend you past the gates of the tomb,
But new disaster points new purposes,
An altered fortune, and an altered duty.
    Theseus is dead, and you are his successor,
My lady, with a son that looks to you —
345 A slave alone, and if you live a king.
No other will uphold his friendless quarrel,
No other wipe away his orphan tears;
Only in Heaven will his hearers be
The Gods, your judges and his ancestors.
350 Live then, in liberty from all misgiving;
Your love is now as unremarkable
As any love, for death disjoins the bond

That made its foulness and its infamy.
Henceforth the image of Hippolytus
Is not so terrible, and you may see him   355
With perfect guiltlessness. But what if now,
Despairing of a better understanding,
He takes command of these rebellious throngs?
Open his eyes, soften that stubborn heart.
Prince of these smiling coasts, his patrimony   360
Is here in Trozen, but he knows the laws;
He knows that they deliver to your son
The queenly ramparts that Minerva reared.
Your rightful enemy is also his:
Unite your forces to defeat Aricia.   365
PHAEDRA: So be it. I commit my way to you.
I will live, if I still have strength to live
And if a mother's love can even now
Revive in my wasted flesh the seeds of life.

— ACT TWO —

ARICIA, ISMENE

ARICIA: He asked to see me here? Hippolytus
Wanted to see me and to say farewell?
Are you quite certain? Is this true, Ismene?
ISMENE: Much more than this, now that the King is dead.
Prepare yourself, my lady; all the hearts   5
He kept at bay will cluster at your feet.
All Greece will bring its tributes to Aricia,
Enfranchised now and sovereign of her fortunes.
ARICIA: So then, Ismene, it is no idle talk.
And I have no oppressor and no foe?   10
ISMENE: My lady, none. The Heavens have relented
And Theseus walks among your fathers' shades.
ARICIA: What enterprise has brought him to his death?
Do they say?
ISMENE: Rumours wild and past belief;
Some say that in a lover's last adventure   15
The seas have claimed this ever-wandering husband;
Some say, and everywhere the news is sown,
That with Pirithous he went down to Hell,
Saw the Cocytus and the coasts of darkness
And stood alive amid a world of shadows,   20
But could not scale the gloomy track again
Nor pass the bourne men never pass but once.
ARICIA: Shall mortal men, before the last leave-taking,
Fathom those sullen deeps of the Departed?
What sorcery lured him to their awful shore?   25
ISMENE: My lady, he is dead, and you alone
Doubt it. All Athens grieves for him, all Trozen
Knows, and salutes Hippolytus for Prince.
And in these walls, despairing for her son,
Phaedra takes counsel of her trembling friends.   30
ARICIA: And you suppose that, kinder than his father,
Hippolytus will make my bondage sweeter
And pity me?
ISMENE: My lady, yes, I do.
ARICIA: But do you know the hard Hippolytus?
What makes you fancy he could feel compassion   35

For me alone, who never felt for woman?
He never joins our customary paths
And hides himself wherever we are not.
ISMENE: Oh, I know all the legend of his coldness;
40 But when you met the proud Hippolytus
I own the strangeness of his reputation
Sharpened the edge of my curiosity.
I saw a face at variance with the fable;
At once your eyes disturbed that hard assurance
45 And his, avoiding you but all in vain,
Melted at once, and could not turn away.
His pride may yet refuse the name of lover
But I'll believe his looks, and not his tongue.
ARICIA: Ah, sweet Ismene, how my heart devours
50 The unhoped-for comfort of a mere perhaps!
You that have known me, did you once imagine
This heart, the plaything of unpitying Fortune,
Starved of all sustenance except despair,
Would learn of love and the wild woes of love?
55 Child of Earth's child, last of a royal lineage,
Sole remnant spared by battlefield and hatred,
I lost the last proud blossoms of our tree,
Six brothers, in the springtime of their year.
The steel reaped all, and Earth's unwilling furrows
60 Drank her own blood, the blood of her Erechtheus.
Since then you know what rigorous decree
Defies all Greeks to lift their eyes to mine —
For a mutinous ardour in the sister's breast
Might wake the embers in her brothers' urns —
65 And you remember how I laughed to scorn
Those calculations of the victor's fear;
I held that love itself was slavery
And even thanked the King for a constraint
So fit and favourable to my distaste —
70 Then, yes; but then I had not seen his son.
Not that subservient to the eye's seduction
I love him for that beauty, that demeanour,
Graces of partial Nature, gifts that he
Ignores, if ever he has noticed them;
75 I see richer and dearer treasures in him —
His father's parts, and not his father's failings;
For I confess I love the manly pride
That never bent under the yoke of Love.
Phaedra was flattered by the doubtful glory
80 Of Theseus' courtly sighs: but I am prouder
And will not stoop to share an easy prize
Or occupy an undefended heart.
No, but to shape a will as yet unbending,
To waken pain in a proof-armoured bosom,
85 To lead a slave that never thought to serve,
Vainly at war against the pleasing chain —
There's a reward worthy of my ambition;
Hercules was an easier adversary
Who readily disarmed and quick to yield
90 Lent no such lustre to his overthrow.
But dear Ismene, these are reckless dreams:
Resistance there will be, and all too stubborn,
And you shall hear me soon in humbler strain
Lament the coldness that I praise today.
95 He love, Hippolytus? What heights of fortune
Could ever bring him —

ISMENE: Only let him speak;
He is coming now.

(Enter HIPPOLYTUS)

HIPPOLYTUS: My lady, before I sail
I owe you some account of my intentions.
My father's dead: and well enough my fears
Foretold the causes of his late homecoming —   100
Death only, and the closure of his toils
Could hold him from the world so long. The Gods
At last abandon to the fatal Spinners
Alcides' friend, his fellow, his successor.
—I know your enmity will not forbid   105
His son to assert these titles he has earned. —
One hope alleviates my deepest sorrow,
For I can end a harsh and long subjection:
I here revoke laws that have caused me grief —
The full bestowal of your life and hand   110
Is yours alone, and in my patrimony,
This Trozen, seat of Pittheus my grandfather,
Which willingly defers his crown to me
I leave you free and freer than its Prince.
ARICIA: Show me less kindness, I could bear it better.   115
So much regard for me in my abjection
Binds me, my lord, more even than you know,
To that constraint you would have put away.
HIPPOLYTUS: Doubtful who stands the next in title, Athens
Canvasses you, and me, and Phaedra's son.   120
ARICIA: Me, my lord?
HIPPOLYTUS: I have never shut my eyes
To arrogant laws that seem to bar my claim:
The Greeks reject me for my mother's race.
But if my brother were my only rival
I could appeal to certain natural laws   125
And make them good against the law's caprice.
I have a better reason to refrain:
To you I yield, say rather I restore
The seat, the sceptre, that your fathers held
Of the illustrious mortal, son of Earth.   130
It only passed to Aegeus by adoption;
And next my father, Athens' second founder,
Was hailed and crowned for all his benefits
While your unhappy brothers lay forgotten.
Now, Athens calls you home within her ramparts,   135
Too long the ancient quarrel lives in pain,
Too long your blood, that flowed along her fields,
Reeks from the furrows where it found its birth. —
Trozen I hold. As for the son of Phaedra
The Cretan acres yield him rich retirement.   140
Attica falls to you. I sail, to join
My partisans with yours, in your support.
ARICIA: At every word more troubled and bewildered,
Can I, or dare I, think I heard you rightly?
Have I my senses, is this your intent?   145
What God, my lord, what God inspired your mind?
Rightly your glory sounds in every climate
But reputation falls behind the truth.
What, will you cheat yourself on my behalf?
It was enough indeed to think that you   150
Hated me not, and held a mind untainted
By this long enmity —

HIPPOLYTUS: How could I hate you?
 Men may deride this proud unconquered heart
 But do they think a monster gave me birth?
155 What brutishness or what inveterate malice
 Could see your face and not forget its fury?
 And how should I withstand this subtle spell—
ARICIA: My lord! . . .
HIPPOLYTUS: My tongue has carried me too far;
 But wisdom fails and yields to the compulsion . . .
160 Now that my silence has been partly broken,
 My lady, I must needs go on, and speak
 The secret that my soul cannot contain. —
 Here stands a Prince of all men most unhappy,
 A monument of overthrown presumption;
165 I, long a truant from the law of love
 And long a mocker of its votaries,
 That stayed ashore watching the luckless sailor
 And never thought myself to fight the tempest,
 Levelled at last beneath the common fate
170 By strange tides I am borne far from myself.
 My wanton liberty has learnt to yield
 And in an instant this bold heart was tamed.
 Six months or nearly, in despair and shame,
 I've borne the arrow burning in my side;
175 Vainly I pit my strength against myself
 And you. I fly you where you are, and find you
 Where you are not; deep in the forest glade
 Your picture chases me; sunlight and shade
 Alike retrace your features and alike
180 Betray the fugitive that would be free,
 And I, for all my fruitless pains, look round
 To find Hippolytus, and know him not.
 My bow, my bounds, my spear, my chariot,
 Weary me. Neptune's lessons are forgotten;
185 Only my lamentations fill the groves,
 My stabled coursers know my voice no more.
  Perhaps this tale I tell of uncouth passion
 Will make you blush to own your handiwork:
 Wild terms, indeed, to offer up a heart!
190 And chains too fair for such a slave to claim!
 And yet my tribute therefore ranks the higher;
 Consider that I speak an unknown language
 And do not spurn these faltered words of love
 That you alone could teach Hippolytus.

(Enter THERAMENES)

195 THERAMENES: Close on my heels, my lord, the Queen
  approaches
 Asking for you.
HIPPOLYTUS: For me?
THERAMENES: In what intention
 I do not know, but messengers have come
 Bidding you wait on her before you sail.
HIPPOLYTUS: The Queen? What should I say to her? Or she . . .
200 ARICIA: You cannot disappoint her wish, my lord.
 Even to such an enemy is due
 Some sign of formal pity for her grief.
HIPPOLYTUS: So you go. And I sail. And still I know not
 Whether my worship has incensed my goddess,
205 Whether this heart I leave in your two hands . . .

ARICIA: Sail, Prince. Pursue your noble purposes;
 Bring me the realm of Athens for dominion;
 Whatever gift you make shall be accepted,
 But that imperial, that unhoped-for state
 Is not the dearest of your offerings.   210

(Exeunt ARICIA and ISMENE)

HIPPOLYTUS: Good friend, are all things ready?—But I hear
 The Queen.—Have all things ordered for our sailing.
 Send out the signal. Haste, command, return
 And free me from the burden of this meeting.

(Exit THERAMENES)

(Enter PHAEDRA and OENONE)

PHAEDRA: He is here. My blood retreats toward my heart.   215
 I see him, and forget what I should speak.
OENONE: Be mindful of the son that trusts in you!
PHAEDRA: They say that you are taking ship at once,
 My lord. I came to join my grief with yours,
 And with the story of a mother's terrors—   220
 My child is fatherless, and soon the day
 Will dawn that brings him to another deathbed;
 So fiercely even now assailed and threatened,
 Your strength alone can champion his weakness. —
 But deep within me throbs the preying thought   225
 That his complaint will never reach your ear,
 That through my child your angry justice soon
 Will strike a hated memory.
HIPPOLYTUS: My lady,
 So infamous a wish was never mine.
PHAEDRA: But you have seen me unremittingly   230
 Pursue your hate, my lord; and how could you
 Explore the bottom of my soul and read
 My secret there? I threw myself upon
 Your just resentment; I would not suffer you
 Within the self-same frontiers; privily   235
 And openly I waged my war, and set
 The width of seas between your path and mine.
 I even gave explicit orders not
 To breathe your name before my presence. Yet,
 If by the wrong the penalty were measured,   240
 If only hatred could achieve your hatred,
 Never did woman more deserve your tears,
 My lord, and less your enmity.
HIPPOLYTUS: No mother
 That watches for her children's interest
 Forgives the other children of her house;   245
 I know, my lady. Untoward mistrust
 Is always near when men have married twice.
 Another in your place would have conceived
 No less suspicion, and I might have suffered
 Deeper indignities.
PHAEDRA: Ah but, my lord,   250
 The Gods—as now they stand my witnesses—
 Deigned to release me from this general law.
 How different are the thoughts that ravage me!
HIPPOLYTUS: It is too soon, my lady, for such thoughts;
 The sunshine may still light your husband's eye,   255
 And Heaven still may yield him to our prayers;

Neptune's his friend, and that high patronage
Will not in vain be canvassed by my father.

PHAEDRA: No man has twice explored the coasts of Death,
260   My lord. If Theseus touched the sullen shores
Vainly we look for Gods to send him home:
Harsh Acheron is grasping and holds fast
His prey. But did I say that he is dead?
He breathes again in you; I see the King,
265   See him, speak to him, thrill . . . My mind is wandering,
My lord, my madness speaks the thing it should not.

HIPPOLYTUS: This is a prodigy of loyal love:
Theseus is gone, yet lives within your mind
And fires the ardour of your loving heart.

270   PHAEDRA: Yes, Prince, for him indeed I yearn, I languish;
I love him — not the man that Hell has claimed,
The butterfly that every beauty lured,
The adulterous ravisher that would have stained
The God of Hell's own bed; but faithful, fine,
275   Sometimes aloof, and pure, gallant and gay,
Young, stealing every heart upon his road —
So do they character our Gods, and so
I see you now; those eyes, that voice, were his,
That generous red of virtue in your cheek,
280   When first he drove across the Cretan foam,
Meet meditation for the virgin dreams
Of Minos' daughters. You, where were you then
Among the flower and chivalry of Greece?
Where was Hippolytus — alas, too young —
285   The day his vessel grounded on our shore?
You would have slain the terror of the island,
The monster lapped in labyrinthine wiles;
Into your hand my sister would have thrust,
To unweave those riddling and deceitful ways,
290   The thread of life and death. But no, she would not —
Love would have found a readier wit in me,
And I, Prince, I, devoted and assured,
Could have resolved the devious Labyrinth;
What would I not have done for that sweet head?
295   How should a thread content your fearful lover?
Half-claimant in the peril that you claimed
I would have walked before you in the way,
And Phaedra, steadfast in the Labyrinth,
Would have returned again with you, or else
With you remained.

300   HIPPOLYTUS: Great Gods, what have you said?
My lady, can it be that you forget
That Theseus is my father, and your husband?

PHAEDRA: And why do you suppose I had forgotten,
Prince? Do I appear so careless of my honour?

305   HIPPOLYTUS: Forgive, my lady. I own, I blush to own
How blameless are the words that I reproved.
My shame can face it out no more before you,
So let me go . . .

PHAEDRA: Ah, leave your heartless lying.
You understand and you have heard enough.
310   Very well then, you shall learn what Phaedra is
And all her frenzy. Yes; I am in love.
But never think that even while I love you
I can absolve myself, or hide my face
From my own guiltiness. And never think

The wanton love that blurs my better mind   315
Grew with the treachery of my consent.
I, singled out for a celestial vengeance,
Unpitied victim, I abhor myself
More than you hate me. Let the Gods bear witness,
Those Gods that set the fire within my breast,   320
The fatal fire of my accursed line;
Those Gods whose majesty and might exulted
In the beguiling of a mortal's weakness.
Turn back the past yourself; how I have laboured
To seem malignant, savage, how I fostered   325
Your hatred as my ally in the fight.
Did I escape you? No, I banished you.
What fruit repaid these unavailing cares?
You loathed me more, I could not love you less;
Your suffering doubled the spell that binds me,   330
The withering ravage of my flames, my tears.
Your eyes can testify that this is true —
If for one moment they could bear my sight.
Why, this confession of my bitter secret,
My shameful secret, do you think that I   335
Have made it willingly? I came in fear
For one defenceless that I dare not fail:
I came to pray you not to hate my child.
Precarious resolution of a mind
Too full of what it loves! I came, and spoke   340
Of nothing else but you. So now, do justice.
Punish me for this execrable passion.
Approve yourself a hero's son indeed
And sweep this monster from the universe.
Dare Theseus' widow love Hippolytus?   345
Truly so vile a monster must not live.
My heart is here, and here is where you strike.
Eager to make atonement for its fault
I feel it swell and bound to meet your hand:
Strike. Or am I unworthy of your steel,   350
Or will your hate refuse to sweet a doom,
Or would ignoble blood sully your fingers?
Then hold your hand and let me have your sword.
Give it me.

OENONE: Stop, my lady. Heavenly powers!
What would you do? But somebody is coming: 355
Escape their sight, be quick, come back, or face
Inevitable shame.

(*Exeunt* PHAEDRA *and* OENONE. *Enter* THERAMENES)

THERAMENES: Was that the Queen
Half dragged, half rushing out? What, my lord, what
Are all these marks of grief? You stand disarmed,
Dumb, pale . . .

HIPPOLYTUS: Come, let us go, Theramenes.   360
I cannot think of what I have heard and witnessed;
I cannot see myself without disgust.
Phaedra . . . No more, great Gods! Oblivion
Must shroud away the secret and the shame.

THERAMENES: If you would leave, my lord, the sail hangs   365
ready;
But Athens is beforehand with her answer:
Her chiefs have counted votes among the tribes;
Your brother has their suffrage, Phaedra wins.

HIPPOLYTUS: Phaedra!
THERAMENES: A herald of the will of Athens
370   Will bring the reins of state into her hands.
      Her son is King.
HIPPOLYTUS: Ye Gods that know her heart,
      Is it her righteousness you would repay?
THERAMENES: And now dark rumours speak again of Theseus:
      Some tell that men have seen him in Epirus
375   Alive; though, I, who went to seek him there,
      I know full well, my lord . . .
HIPPOLYTUS: It may be so.
      But I would hear whatever rumour tells,
      Consult this public cry, divine its sources.
      If it be worthless to delay our journey
380   We sail; and cost the venture what it will
      I'll save the sceptre for a worthy hand.

— ACT THREE —

PHAEDRA, OENONE

PHAEDRA: Send them away, these heralds and these honours.
      Have they a balm to ease a tortured mind?
      Unkind, is Phaedra fit for public show?
      Rather conceal me, for my secret's out:
5   Intemperate desire has seen the light,
      And what these lips had never thought to utter
      He heard. Immortal Gods! and how he listened,
      How long he parried, how deviously he turned
      To baffle the approaches of my speech!
10   How visibly he yearned to leave my presence!
      How painfully his blush revived my shame!
      Why did you disappoint me of my death?
      Ah, when his weapon pointed at my breast
      Did he blench? Did he stir to snatch it back?
15   Enough for him my fingers at the hilt
      And in his heartless reckoning it was vile,
      Profaned, a blade that would defile his hand.
OENONE: And so complaining, dwelling on your sorrow,
      You feed a fire that wisdom would have quenched.
20   Should not a worthy child of Minos' blood
      Look for serenity in nobler tasks,
      Fly from a stuggle that you cannot win,
      Learn to assume the guidance of a kingdom
      And be a Queen?
PHAEDRA: Queen, I? And hold command,
25   While my own senses rage in mutiny,
      While in my soul wisdom has lost dominion,
      While shame and slavery has bowed my head,
      And death is waiting?
OENONE: Fly.
PHAEDRA: I cannot leave him.
OENONE: You drove him away, and cannot go from him?
30   PHAEDRA: I cannot now. He has seen my raging soul,
      Seen me transgress the rigid pale of virtue;
      Before those stony eyes I have poured out
      My shame, and now, unbidden, secret hope
      Has slipped into my breast. Ay, you yourself,
35   Rallying the wasted forces of my life,
      The parting spirit ready on my lips,

Wooed me from death with false and soothing words;
      You half persuaded me that I might love.
OENONE: Ah, call me guilty, or call me innocent,
      I would do worse if anything could save you.   40
      But, if resentment ever stung your mind,
      Can you forget the blow of his rebuff,
      The insolence, the icy cruelty
      That eyed you all but prostrate at his feet,
      The arrogant disdain? — how odious   45
      Had Phaedra only seen him as I saw!
PHAEDRA: What if he lost this arrogance, Oenone?
      He has the harshness of his forest ways,
      And in his arduous life Hippolytus
      Has never heard of love until today.   50
      What if surprise had robbed him of his speech?
      What if we blamed him more than he deserved?
OENONE: He was conceived in a Barbarian's womb.
PHAEDRA: Barbarian, Scythian, still she learned to love.
OENONE: He hates our sex with firm and deadly hate.   55
PHAEDRA: So I shall never fear another woman.
      Enough: such counsels had their season once;
      My passion now commands you, and not my reason.
      Though hard and inaccessible to love,
      Another side lies weaker to attack —   60
      The sweets of empire tempted him, I think;
      Athens allured him more than he could hide.
      His ships already turned their prows to sea
      With canvas rigged and offered to the breeze.
      Find him, Oenone, find the ambitious boy,   65
      Show him the glitter of the Athenian crown,
      Bid him assume the diadem and the glory;
      I only ask to lay it on his brow,
      Into his hand descends authority
      I cannot grasp, and he shall teach my son   70
      The science of command — even he might
      Look as a father on him. In his power
      I now resign the orphan and the mother.
      Incline his heart by any means you know,
      Use — do not blush — the voice of supplication,   75
      I sanction all. I have no other hope;
      Go, till you come again I cannot tell
      What else I have to do.

(Exit OENONE)

PHAEDRA: (Alone)   O Thou, that knowest
      How deep in shame my soul is overwhelmed,
      Venus, O Venus unappeasable,   80
      This is the consummation of thy hatred.
      These must be the limits of thy cruelty.
      Thy triumph is entire, each shot has told.
      Art thou not sated yet with victory?
      Find tougher quarry then: Hippolytus   85
      Rejects thy deity, derides thy wrath,
      He never bent the knee before thy altar;
      Thy name seems hideous in his stubborn ears,
      Goddess, avenge; our grievances are one!
      Teach him to love . . . Oenone, here so soon?   90
      I am rejected then, you were not heard.

(Enter OENONE)

OENONE: Stifle the memory of a hopeless passion,
My lady; summon up your earlier virtue.
The King's not dead, and you will see him soon.
95   Theseus has landed. He is coming here.
The populace are rushing to salute him,
And as I passed obedient to your mission
Unending cheers rose up on every hand—
PHAEDRA: He is not dead. Nothing else signifies,
100   Oenone. I revealed a lawless love
That wounds him in his honour. And he lives.
What needs there more?
OENONE: But yet—
PHAEDRA: I told you so;
And you would not. Foreboding and remorse
Have yielded to your tears. Only this morning
105   My death was not unworthy to be pitied:
I took your counsel, and I die disgraced.
OENONE: Die?
PHAEDRA: Righteous Gods! The things this day has seen!
And now, as I meet my husband and his son
110   I know this witness of adulterous passion
Studies my countenance before his father—
My heart heavy with sighs he would not hear,
My eyelids drenched with tears that he despised.
Do you think his tenderness for Theseus' honour
115   Would hide away the memory of my falsehood,
My treason to a father and a King?
Will he repress the loathing I inspire?
What if he did? I know my treachery,
Oenone. And if there are intrepid women
120   Who taste a flawless quietude in crime
And force their countenance to show no shame,
I am not such. My misdeeds rise before me;
And even now these over-arching walls
Seem full of tongues, impatient to accuse me
125   Before my husband, and proclaim his wrong.
Oh for a death, and surcease from this anguish!
Is life so precious and so hard to leave?
Need the tormented hesitate to die?
Only I fear the name I leave behind—
130   The legacy of horror for my children,
Whose blood, the very blood of Jupiter,
Should swell their hearts with pride: now they must lift
The burden of a mother's infamy.
My soul foretells that malice, soon or late,
135   Will throw my black reproach into their faces,
And crushed so cruelly they may never dare
To look with level eyes upon their kind.
OENONE: It is most true. They both are to be pitied,
And never sorrow was foretold more surely.
140   But why abandon them to the ordeal?
Why be the witness that betrays your cause?
For all is lost; and all the world will judge
That Phaedra knows her guilt, and dare not wait
The awful presence of an outraged husband.
145   Hippolytus should thank you for a deed
Stronger than all his words on his behalf;
And what can I respond to your accuser?
Confounded, tongue-tied, I must live to see
Him taste a hideous triumph undisturbed

And chronicle your shame to all mankind.   150
May fire from Heaven fall upon me sooner!
But tell me this, and tell without dissembling:
Do you still love him, this presumptuous Prince?
How does he now appear. . . ?
PHAEDRA: I see him now
Grim as a monster and as terrible.   155
OENONE: Then why concede him victory unresisted?
Do you fear him? Attack before he strikes
And use the imputation he prepares
For you. What can refute you? Every sign
Informs against him—first his sword that Fortune   160
Leaves in your hands, and then this day's distress,
And those disconsolate months of misery,
And long ago his father's mind prepared
When long ago you claimed his banishment.
PHAEDRA: Shall I defame and murder innocence?   165
OENONE: Lend me but silence and my zeal suffices.
Like you I shudder at my remedy
And dread it deeper than a thousand deaths.
But either this, or else I lose my mistress,
And in your loss all other values fade.   170
So I will speak. Theseus will rage, but still
He'll take no more revenge than banishment.
A father punishing is still a father
Whose love is louder than the voice of justice;
But guiltless blood is nothing in the scales   175
Against the imperilled honour of your name.
That is a jewel far too dear to hazard;
It is a law we dare not disobey;
And when our honour stands at such a cost
Virtue itself must go for sacrifice.   180
—Here they are. I see Theseus.
PHAEDRA: And I see
Hippolytus, and his unflinching eyes
Spell my dishonour. Do what you will, Oenone.
I am in your hands. In this tormented hour
To save myself is more than I can do.   185

(Enter THESEUS, HIPPOLYTUS, and THERAMENES)

THESEUS: Fortune has smiled again, my dearest lady,
And now your sweet embrace—
PHAEDRA: No, Theseus; stop,
Do not pollute this love and this delight.
No longer I deserve this tenderness.
You have been wronged. The jealousy of Fortune   190
Has not respected her you left behind you;
And now, unworthy to approach your love,
My sole desire must be for solitude.

(Exit PHAEDRA)

THESEUS: What is this cheerless welcome that I find here,
My son?
HIPPOLYTUS: A riddle Phaedra must interpret,   195
No one else can. But now if prayers can move
I ask but this, my lord, never to see
Her face again, but to live out my life
Safe, far away, forgotten by the Queen.
THESEUS: Now you, my son, forsake me!

HIPPOLYTUS: For you know
    I never sought her, but you brought her here   200
    At your departure; and the coasts of Trozen
    Became the dwelling of Aricia
    And of the Queen. I was to be their guardian.
    But now what duty keeps me from my life?   205
    Inglorious victories among the forests
    Weary my idle youth, my wasted skill.
    I long to waken from obscurity
    And tip my hunter's spear in a nobler red.
    Before you had spent the years that I have counted 210
    What robbers, what oppressors, and what monsters
    Had known the weight of that revengeful arm,
    Victor and scourge of wanton insolence!
    While on the quiet shore of either sea
    The traveller learnt to take his road in peace;   215
    Hercules heard your prowess and drew breath,
    Leaving his triumphs and his toils to you—
    And I, the unknown son of such a father,
    Have much to do to reach my mother's footsteps.
    Now let my unfledged valour learn to dare;   220
    Let me, if anywhere some monster yet
    Escapes you, drag its trophy to your feet,
    Or by the record of a glorious failure
    Find life for ever in a fitting death
    And show posterity I was your son.   225
THESEUS: What is it, what invading blast of fear
    Empties my very home at my approach?
    Why, O ye Gods, to face these shrinking looks,
    This lack of love, did ye deliver me?
    I had one friend. His unregarding passion   230
    Conspired to carry back from far Epirus
    The tyrant's Queen. I helped, against my will,
    But Fate was pitiless, and we were blind.
    The villain caught me all unarmed, unwatching,
    And these two eyes—that weep him yet—beheld   235
    Pirithous under the fangs of beasts
    Fatted on human slaughter; and I spent
    Deep in the sightless silence of his dungeons
    Down near the horrible empire of the Dead,
    Six months. Then Heaven thought on me again.   240
    I tricked the watchful eyes. I purged creation
    Of one perfidious enemy, and his blood
    Glutted his own fell monsters. Now at length
    Free, and restored to all that's left to love,
    Now that my soul aspires to nothing more   245
    Than the enjoyment of their blessed sight,
    Grief and lament is all my salutation,
    None will abide to suffer my embraces;
    And, chilled by the contagion of the fears
    That breathe about my path, I'd rather be   250
    A prisoner again and in Epirus.
        Speak out. Phaedra declares I've been betrayed.
    Who wronged me? Why is not the wrong avenged?
    Has Greece, so long beholden to this arm,
    Offered a refuge to the criminal?   255
    —You will not answer? Is my son, my son,
    A shield and ally of my enemies?
    I will go in, for this suspense unmans me.
    I will find out the culprit and the offence.
    Phaedra must tell me what her sorrow is.   260

(Exit THESEUS)

HIPPOLYTUS: What did her words portend? They froze my
        blood:
    Would Phaedra in her ecstasy of frenzy
    Denounce her guilt and give her case away?
    Gods, when the King is told! Death-dealing Love,
    What blighting mists thou hast wrapped around his house!   265
    And I with my secret of disloyal passion,
    What was I once, what will he think me now!
    My mind is dark with unaccomplished shapes
    Of evil: but need innocence be afraid?
    I must look for better times and better ways   270
    To move my father's heart, and then reveal
    Love he may doom to parting and to tears
    But fixed beyond his force to overthrow.

— ACT FOUR —

THESEUS, OENONE

THESEUS: Ah! What have you said? The rebel, the betrayer
    Conceived this outrage on his father's honour?
    How unrelenting is thy hand upon me,
    O Destiny! I know not where I go,
    I know not what I do. All my long kindness   5
    Wasted, paid with this hideous wanton plot!
    And with the argument and threat of steel
    To enforce his dark design! I know that sword,
    I gave it him, I strapped it to his side—
    For nobler work than this. Not all the bonds   10
    Of blood itself could hold him back; and she
    Could hesitate to punish, and her silence
    Showed mercy to the wrongdoer!
OENONE: Say rather
    Showed mercy to a father's suffering.
    Shamed by a lover's frenzy, and ashamed   15
    That her chaste eyes could kindle such a fire,
    She would have died, my lord, and dimmed for ever
    Herself the innocent lustre of those eyes.
    The arm was raised. I hastened, I preserved
    Her life for the embraces of her lord,   20
    And pitying your fears and her confusion
    Became the unwilling spokesman of her tears.
THESEUS: The perfidy! Yes, for all his craft, he paled;
    He quaked with fear, I saw it as he came;
    I marvelled then to feel his joylessness   25
    And froze against the chill of his embrace.
    —Did you not say, the love that burns in him
    Had shown itself in Athens long before?
OENONE: My lord, remember how the Queen abhorred him;
    It was unhallowed love that caused her hatred.   30
THESEUS: And now, in Trozen, it has flared again?
OENONE: I have told you all, my lord; but I have left
    My lady too long now with her deadly sorrow,
    And, by your leave, my place is at her side.

(Exit OENONE. *Enter* HIPPOLYTUS)

THESEUS: So, here he comes. Great Gods, that noble carriage   35
    Would it not blind another's eye, as mine?
    Then sacrilegious and adulterous heads
    May flaunt the sacred emblem of the pure?

40 Why is there no infallible badge to blazon
    The minds of our dissembling race of men?
    HIPPOLYTUS: May I not know, my lord, why such a weight
    Of cloud darkens the majesty of your brow?
    Must this be secret from my loyalty?
    THESEUS: Dissembler! Dare you come so near to me?
45 Monster the thunderbolts reprieve too long,
    Corrupted straggler of the brigand race
    I cleansed the earth of once, how dare you still
    Parade that odious face, here where your frenzy
    Clutched at a father's bed? How dare you pace
50 These halls where all things tell of your dishonour?
    Why are you not far hence, where skies unknown
    Illumine coasts that never knew my name?
    Away, you traitor. Do not stand and tempt
    A hate, an anger hardly to be stayed.
55 Enough for me the indelible reproach
    Of fathering you, without the soil of murder
    To smother my bright deeds from memory.
    —Away. And if you would not share the sentence
    Of all the villains that this hand has felled
60 Take care that never again the sun that lights us
    Finds your rebellious feet upon this shore.
    Away, I tell you, out of my dominions
    And cleanse them for ever of your loathsome presence.
    And now hear, Neptune, hear. If once my courage
65 Scoured off a scum of bandits from thy coasts
    Remember thou hast sworn in recompense
    To grant one prayer. In long and stern confinement
    I called not thy undying power; I saved thee
    Thrifty of all the aid I hoped for, till
70 A greater need. Today I pray: avenge
    A mourning father. To thy wrath I leave
    This profligate. Still his lust is his blood.
    Let Theseus read thy kindness in thy rage.
    HIPPOLYTUS: With such a love Hippolytus is charged
75 By Phaedra! Weight of horror crushes me;
    So many assaults unlooked-for, stroke on stroke,
    Leave me no words.
    THESEUS: And so you judged that Phaedra's
    Compliant silence would have muffled up
    Your savage insolence. You might have waited
80 To gather up the sword that now, in her hands,
    Helps to convict you. Or why not, better still,
    Heap up the measure of your infamy
    With one good blow to finish breath and life?
    HIPPOLYTUS: After a calumny so infamous
85 I should let truth be heard—but for a secret
    That touches you, my lord. I beg you sanction
    Respect that silences what I might say;
    Labour no more to probe into your pain,
    Look on my life, consider what I am:
90 The greatest crimes have lesser crimes before them;
    The rest is easy when the way is known;
    Like virtue, vice is gradual. No one day
    Made any good man vile, murderous, incestuous,
    And innocence is slow to dare, and slow
95 To push beyond the boundaries of law.
    I had a mother, as chaste as she was valiant,
    Nor have I derogated from my blood;
    Pittheus, wise among men, took up my nurture

    After her hands. I would not praise myself,
    But, if one virtue was allotted mine,   100
    May I not claim, my lord, to loathe that act
    My enemies presume to speak of? This
    Has made Hippolytus his name in Greece—
    Unstudied honour rude in its excess,
    Rugged, intractable austerity.   105
    The daylight is no cleaner than the deeps
    Of this my heart. What, sacrilegious lust
    Could stain Hippolytus?
    THESEUS: And this condemns you:
    That was the foul source fed your vaunted coldness—
    No one but Phaedra could bewitch your eyes;   110
    No other woman's love was worth your interest
    Unless it offered pleasures more than lawful.
    HIPPOLYTUS: No, father, you shall hear the truth. This heart
    Has not refused an honourable yoke.
    Here at your feet I will confess—I love,   115
    And love in disobedience to your will.
    Aricia's beauty holds my heart enslaved
    And Pallas' daughter has subdued your son.
    I worship her, forgetful of my duty
    And have no room to feel another passion.   120
    THESEUS: You love her! No—a pitiful pretence;
    You feign that crime to clear yourself of this.
    HIPPOLYTUS: These six months I have hid from love, and
        loved,
    My lord; I came here to confess to you
    In trembling. But is it so? Will nothing move you?   125
    What fearful oath will you win to believe?
    Witness the Earth, the Heavens, and all Nature . . .
    THESEUS: What felon ever feared a perjury?
    Peace, peace. Waste no more time on idle stories
    If that fine virtue rests on aids like these.   130
    HIPPOLYTUS: You see it as a mockery, a lie:
    But Phaedra in her heart of hearts knows better.
    THESEUS: Shall I endure so much effrontery?
    HIPPOLYTUS: What place of exile, and how long a time
    Do you appoint?
    THESEUS: Past the Pillars of Hercules   135
    A traitor's presence is too close for me.
    HIPPOLYTUS: What friendship shall I find to comfort me
    When you have cast me out, dishonoured thus?
    THESEUS: Find yourself friends whose dangerous regard
    Goes to adultery and honours incest,   140
    Deceivers, ingrates, free of law and shame,
    Fit to protect a criminal like you.
    HIPPOLYTUS: And still you taunt me with adultery
    And incest. How can I reply? But Phaedra
    Came of a mother, Phaedra's is a blood,   145
    My lord, you do not need me to recall it,
    More laden with their awful taint than mine.
    THESEUS: How dare you go so far before my face?
    For the last time, villain, avoid my sight,
    Leave me; or force a father in his rage   150
    To have you flung with infamy from the place.

    (*Exit* HIPPOLYTUS)

    And now you go towards your waiting doom
    Irrevocably. For by that River's name
    Terrible even to the immortal Gods,

155 Neptune has sworn his oath, and will perform it.
Yes, and I loved you, and in spite of all,
Before the hour is come, my bowels yearn
For pity of you. But I have too much cause—
Did ever a deeper injury wound a father?
160 Ye righteous Gods, that see me thus prostrated,
Did I give being to a son like this?

(Enter PHAEDRA)

PHAEDRA: My lord, you see me here impelled by terror:
Just now, when that terrible voice assailed my ears,
I thought the threat might come to a fulfilment.
165 Let me beg you, if there still is time, have pity
On your own race, your own blood; do not force me,
My lord, to hear it crying from the earth.
Spare me the endless misery of laying
That fearful stain on a paternal hand.
170 THESEUS: My lady, I have kept my hand unstained
And still the unnatural boy has not escaped;
Immortal hands will undertake his doom,
Neptune's my debtor; you shall be avenged.
PHAEDRA: Your debtor, Neptune! Then your prayer of hate . . .
175 THESEUS: Are you afraid it might be heard too soon?
No, join your own entreaty with my curses,
Paint me his crimes once more in all their blackness
Inflame my faint and still-too-sluggish rage—
He has added guilt more than the guilt you knew;
180 His frenzy spends itself in railing on you,
He swears that all your words are perjuries,
He says Aricia claims his heart, his love,
His loyalty.
PHAEDRA: No, my lord!
THESEUS: That is what he told me;
Not that a flimsy lie could impose on me.
185 I hope to hear that Neptune's justice falls
Swiftly, and till that hour I'll ply his altars
And keep him mindful of his undying word.

(Exit THESEUS)

PHAEDRA: He leaves me, with this dreadful news, alone.
Ah Gods, the fire that I dreamed was safely stifled
190 To wake no more! Dreadful, unlooked-for news!
All trepidation and remorse, all speed
Out of Oenone's clinging arms of fear
I came to save his son. And who can tell
What might have been had conscience had its way?
195 Whether I might have spoken of my guilt,
Might have let slip, had he but left me time,
The entire and awful truth?—He has felt love,
Hippolytus, who never felt for me;
Aricia claims his loyalty, his heart . . .
200 Gods! while I pleaded, while my prayer beat
On those rigid eyes, that unrelenting brow,
I thought he bore impenetrable armour
Always the same and closed to all alike.
And now another has overthrown his pride,
205 Another finds favour in the tyrant's eyes;
Perhaps his heart is easy to entreat
And condescends to any plea but mine.
And I am fool enough to be his friend!

(Enter OENONE)

—Oenone, do you know what I have heard?
OENONE: No; I have tried to find you in alarm,   210
Wondering what sudden impulse drove you here
And how it may imperil you . . .
PHAEDRA: Oenone,
Who would have thought there was another woman?
OENONE: You say—
PHAEDRA: Hippolytus, I tell you, loves—
The adversary I could never shake,   215
Vexed by submission, impatient of complaining,
The ogre that I never could encounter
Undaunted; he is tamed and brought to heel,
Aricia has forced the access to his heart.
OENONE: Aricia!
PHAEDRA: Oh, I never thought of these,   220
These newest tortures that I live to taste:
All the old despairs, the ecstasies, the broodings,
Raging of flame, and horror of remorse,
And that slight of unendurable denial
Were barely foretastes of my torment here.   225
They, lovers! Did they bewitch these watchful eyes?
What time did they find to meet? Since when? What place?
What furtive means? You knew. Why was I left
To treasure foolish dreams? You might have told me
Of their stolen pleasure. Were they often seen   230
Speaking, or lingering? Was it the forest shades
That sheltered them? Ah, but they had liberty
To see the face they sought. The Heavens smiled
On the innocence of their embrace, no fear
Restrained their eager steps, and each fair day   235
Rose clear and candid on their love. And I
Disowned, dishonoured in the whole creation
I fled the sun, I could not face the daylight,
Death was the only godhead I could pray;
Gall on my tongue, and tears my only drink;   240
Happy, if any privacy of grief
Had left me this one pitiable solace,
To taste a last precarious luxury;
But the forced travesty of a smiling face
Deprived me even of the right to weep.   245
OENONE: They reap no harvest of their vain desires:
They'll meet no more.
PHAEDRA: They'll love for evermore.
Now as I speak—the poison of the thought!—
Mocking the fury of a rival wronged,
Forgetful of the exile that divides them,   250
They swear a thousand times never to part.
No, I will not yield to the insult of their joy,
Oenone. Help me, pity my jealousy.
Aricia must be crushed. I must stir up
My husband's wrath against that hated house—   255
No feeble sentence serves, the sister's crime
Is more than all her brothers'. I'll entreat him
In rage and jealousy.
                       What am I doing?
Where is reason in my wandering mind? I, jealous?
I, entreat Theseus? He, my husband, lives   260
And still I burn—for whom? Still yearn—for whom?
At every word each separate hair lifts up

Upon my head. My guilt has filled the measure —
I crave for incest, dream of calumny,
265 My murderous hands, avid of vengeance, burn
To bathe in the blood of innocence. Misery!
And dare I live, and dare I face the sight
Of that sacred Sun, the giver of my life,
I, grandchild of the high Father of the Gods,
270 My forebears crowding Heaven and all creation?
Where may I hide? Flee to the night of Hell?
No, no, not there; for there my father's hands
Inexorable lift the doomsday urn,
They say, and Minos stands in deathly justice
275 Over the pallid multitudes of men.
Will that great shade not start in ghastly anger
When I in shame before his awful gaze,
His daughter, plead my guilt, and deeds perhaps
Unheard in all the calendar of Hell?
280 Father, what will you say to these? I see
The tremendous urn roll thundering at your feet;
I see you ponder unknown penalties
To execute yourself upon your own . . .
Forgive. A cruel God detests your seed,
285 A heavenly vengeance breathed in me the frenzy
You see. Alas, and still of all the guilt
And all the shame that never will release me
My fearful heart has never reaped the sweets.
Pursued while yet I breathe by ceaseless evils
290 I wait to yield a bruised and broken life.
OENONE: My lady, come, dismiss a causeless terror,
Be more indulgent to a venial failing —
You love; but driven by a fatal charm.
It is not ours to challenge Destiny.
295 Was this a wonder never seen till now?
Were you the first that Love has overthrown?
Weakness was ever part of man's condition;
So, mortal, bow to a mortal's destiny.
You struggle against an immemorial yoke:
300 Even the Gods that live in high Olympus
Whose judgements hold a guilty world in dread
Have loved, and sometimes loved against the law.
PHAEDRA: Still you dare speak? And this is your advice,
And till the end you mean to drug my mind?
305 I hate you. All your help has been my downfall.
You dragged me back to the unbearable sunshine;
Your prayers were louder than the voice of right;
The man that I shunned, you made me see.
Was it your business? And now have all the lies
310 Of those false lips dared blacken such a life?
You may have killed him. His father's impious vows
And blind revenge perhaps are gratified
Already. I'll hear no more. Leave me alone,
Loathly inhuman monster; leave my sight,
315 Leave me alone to shape my bitter future.
On you I pray the justice of the Gods;
And may they make you the eternal warning
Of all cringing cunning sycophants that nourish
Their masters' dearest weakness, urge the way
320 Their cravings tend, and smooth the slope of crime;
Accursed flatterers, deadliest gift of all
That angry Heaven inflicts upon a King!

(Exit)

OENONE: (Alone) O ye Gods! To have borne so much for
her, forgone
So much! — This is my pay. And it is just.

— ACT FIVE —

HIPPOLYTUS, ARICIA, ISMENE

ARICIA: And in this extremity you will not speak
And will not undeceive a loving father?
Cruel, if you can disregard my tears
And lightly say goodbye to me for ever,
Then sail, and leave Aricia with her grief;   5
But do not go in certainty of death.
Fight the foul imputation on your honour,
Constrain your father to unsay his curses.
There is time yet. What reason, or what folly
Makes you leave all the advantage to the accuser?   10
Tell Theseus what you know.
HIPPOLYTUS: Have I not told
What may be told? Would you have me reveal
To light the shameful mystery of his bed
Or by too scrupulous report bring down
Confusion on a father's honoured head?   15
Alone you know this horror. You, and the Gods,
Alone receive the outpouring of my heart.
See if I love you: I have shown to you
What I would fain have veiled from my own thoughts.
But under what a seal, you know. Forget,   20
My lady, if you can, that I have spoken;
Let me believe this hideous affair
Will never be breathed between those blameless lips.
We set our trust upon the righteous Heavens.
My cause is theirs; and Phaedra, whether soon   25
Or in the slow procedure of their justice,
Will not escape disgrace. This deference
I ask of you; and all the rest I sweep
Before the liberty of my wrath. I bid you
No longer be a slave. I bid you dare   30
To come with me, dare to be banned with me.
Break from a poisoned house where Virtue breathes
A deathly and a desecrated air;
Turn into profit for a headlong flight
All the disorder following on my fall.   35
The means I offer: you have still no guard
But my own men. Most powerful patrons wait us —
Argos extends her arms, and Sparta welcomes;
Let common friends receive our just laments,
Otherwise Phaedra rakes our wreckage up,   40
Evicts us both from a throne our fathers left us,
And strips us both for spoils to deck her son.
The moment beckons, grasp it. But what fear
Restrains you? What suspends your doubtful mind?
Only for your sake have I dared so far.   45
When I am all on fire, why are you ice?
Are you unwilling to adventure on
An outlaw's path?
ARICIA: Oh, but how happily,
My lord, I'd taste of exile so; how eagerly
Embrace a life forgotten of all beside   50

And linked with yours! But lacking that sweet bond
Can I in honour join your wanderings?
I know the sternest laws do not forbid me
To fly your father's power: he is not mine,
55 I owe him no obedience; and to fly
From an oppressor is the right of all.
But you, my lord, love me. And anxious honour . . .
HIPPOLYTUS: And can you think I rate that honour cheaply?
No, no. I came with worthier designs—
60 Escape your foes, and follow as my bride.
Free in adversity, since Heaven has freed us,
Our pledges need no words but ours, and Hymen
Robbed of his torchlit rites is Hymen still.
    By Trozen's gates, among those sepulchres,
65 Antique memorials of my father's pride,
A wayside temple holy and renowned
Stands grim protector of the plighted word;
There falsehood dare not raise her voice, or falls
Blasted at once, and certitude of death
70 Lays chains invincible on perjury.
May we not there with solemn mutual oath
Give and receive our hearts' enduring faith
Before the shrine, and pray the Deity
For his protection and paternal love?
75 I will invoke each mighty God to hear me—
Maiden Diana, Juno's majesty,
And every name whose present patronage
Shall seal and sanctify my true intent.
ARICIA: The King is here. Fly, Prince, depart at once.
80 I shall remain awhile to hide my purpose.
Away—but send me back a trusty servant
To guide my footsteps safely to your side.

(Exit HIPPOLYTUS)

(Enter THESEUS)

THESEUS: Lighten the mists, ye Gods, and show my eyes
The truth they seek for here!
                            Now, sweet Ismene,
85 See everything is done. Be ready quickly.

(Exit ISMENE)

THESEUS: You seem disturbed, your colour fails, my lady.
What was Hippolytus doing in this place?
ARICIA: Taking an everlasting leave, my lord.
THESEUS: And so your eyes have tamed that rebel heart
90 And brought him to his earliest thoughts of love.
ARICIA: I must not hide the truth from you, my lord.
He has not learnt your unjust hate from you;
He did not treat me like a criminal.
THESEUS: You mean he vowed you everlasting passion.
95 I should not build on that unsettled heart.
He swore as deep to others.
ARICIA: He, my lord?
THESEUS: I wish you could have taught him constancy.
How could you bear that loathsome competition?
ARICIA: And how can you bear loathsome calumnies
100 To blacken all the lustre of his fame?
Have you so little knowledge of his nature?
Can you not tell the guiltless from the guilty?
Only your eyes are darkened by a cloud

That lets his goodness gleam on all the world.
Oh stop, relent. He must not be the victim   105
Of false accusers. Repent your murderous curses.
Tremble, my lord, tremble, lest frowning Heaven
Hate you enough to take you at your word—
Gods may accept our offerings in anger
And punish with the presents we entreated.   110
THESEUS: No, blind as you are with ill-requited love
You will not blind me to his villainy;
For I have witnesses, beyond reproach,
Beyond suspicion—I have seen tears flow,
Tears that were true.
ARICIA: Look to yourself, my lord: 115
Your matchless weight of arm redeemed mankind
From monsters past all counting—but not all,
The breed is not destroyed, and you have saved
One . . . I must say no more; your son forbids me.
Knowing what deference his heart still holds   120
I should increase his suffering too much
Dared I continue. Let me imitate
His generous scruple, and excuse myself
While nothing forces me to break my silence.

(Exit ARICIA)

THESEUS: (Alone) But what is in her mind? What lurks below 125
A tale so often broached, and never told?
Is it a stratagem without a meaning?
Is it conspiracy to bind me on
A rack of doubt? And secret in my heart
Steeled to be cruel, what is the small voice   130
That pleads for mercy, and unmans my wrath,
Perplexes me and tears me?—I must see
Her woman once again; I know too little.
—Guard! Fetch Oenone, and send her in alone.

(Enter PANOPE)

PANOPE: I cannot say what thoughts are in her heart,   135
But the distraction motions of the Queen
Fill me with fear, my lord. Death and despair
Are painted on her face, and the deathly tint
Sits even now upon her cheeks. Already
Pursued with scorn and chiding from her side,   140
Oenone has plunged to death among the waves.
None knows what wild will drove her, and her voice
Is covered in the murmur of the tide.
THESEUS: What have you said?
PANOPE: Her going gave no peace;
Confusion gains in the Queen's divided soul: 145
One moment, soothing her mysterious grief,
She takes her children, bathes them in her tears;
And suddenly, her motherhood dismissed,
She drives them from her with a look of loathing.
Her restless steps come and go purposeless   150
And we are strangers in her fevered eyes.
Thrice she was written, only to repent,
And thrice destroyed the message uncompleted.
My lord, be gracious: see her, comfort her.
THESEUS: Is it so? Oenone's dead, and Phaedra waits   155
For death? Call for my son, let him plead his cause,
Let him speak to me, and I will listen.

(Exit PANOPE*)*

Neptune,
Delay thy deadly gift, be not too sudden,
Rather refuse it utterly. What if
160   I was seduced too soon by worthless words?
What if my cruel hands were raised too rashly?
What wretchedness would follow from that vow!

(Enter THERAMENES*)*

THESEUS: Is it you, Theramenes? Where is my son?
What have you done with him? His careful tending
165   Has been your change from earliest infancy.
But why the tears I see upon your cheeks?
What of my son?
THERAMENES: O late, O vain regret,
O useless love! Hippolytus is no more.
THESEUS: Oh Gods!
THERAMENES: I saw him die, the best and sweetest
170   Of human kind—and, let me say, my lord,
The purest also.
THESEUS: Is my son dead? Now,
Now that these arms reached out for him, the Gods
Impatient urged his execution on?
How did I lose him? What immortal stroke. . . ?
175   THERAMENES: Still close behind us lay the gates of Trozen.
He drove his chariot, his grieving guard
Matching his silence, marched on either hand.
Sunk in his thought, the loose reins lying free,
He brought us on the causeway to Mycenae;
180   And the noble beasts, so eager once to leap
At the least inflexion of a master's voice,
Now bent dull eyes to earth and drooping crests
As if communing with his bitter mood.
—Suddenly from the sea an awful cry
185   Shattered the silence of the air. And then
A second voice wailed answer from the landward.
Our blood was frozen in our inmost hearts.
Stiffly rose up the listening horses' manes.
And now from the level deep immense there heaves
190   A boiling mount of brine, and still it swells,
Rears wavelike foaming down on us and breaks
To belch a ravening monster at our feet
Whose threatening brow is broadened with huge horns,
Whose body, cased in golden glint of scales,
195   Thrashes a train of sinuous writhing whorls.
Indomitable bull, malignant dragon,
Its long-drawn bellows rumble down the shore;
Heaven quails, earth shudders at the portent, air
Reeks with its pestilential breath. The wave
200   Withdraws again, aghast at what it bore.
We fly to the nearby temple; not one lingers
Or wraps himself in unavailing valour.
Hippolytus, honouring his hero blood,
Hippolytus alone checks, wheels his team,
205   Snatches the spears, charges upon the creature,
Aims, and unerring flings. A gaping slash
Fair in the monster's flank drives it in bounds
Of pain and fury to the horses' feet
To roar and wallow and from flaming jaws
210   To spatter them with blood and cloud and fire.

Reckless, they plunge aside. They hear no more,
Answer no more to bridle or to voice.
The charioteer spends all his strength in vain
While they redden the bits with spume that is bright with
    blood.
Even, men say, some more than mortal shape   215
Borne on the horrible confusion plied
Their dusty flanks with goads. Where terror leads them
Stand rocks. The axle screeches, snaps. The car
Crashes in fragments; and my fearless master
Drops tangled in the reins. . .—Forgive my weakness.   220
In that tormenting image lives a source
Of quenchless tears.—I watched, my lord, I watched
Your helpless son dragging behind the steeds
His hands had fed. He tried to call to them:
Instead, his cries startle them. So they gallop   225
And make one wound of all his living flesh.
    Now as the plain is pealing with our grief
The violent fit is spent. They slacken speed,
And stop, where close at hand his father's tombs
And ancient sculptures hold the chill remains   230
And memories of Kings. I run, behind me
Run all his guard, reading the traces painted
By his gallant blood, past the empurpled crags,
Past dripping brambles hung about with spoils
Of bloody hair. I reach him, I speak; he gives me   235
A hand and greets me with a dying gaze
That quickly closes. And I hear these words:
    'My guiltless days are forfeit to the Gods.
Do you after my death be watchful over
The sad Aricia; and, sweet friend, if ever   240
My father undeceived should come to mourn
The misadventure of a slandered son,
To lay in peace my blood and wailing shade
Bid him be gentle to the captive maiden,
Render her . . .' On the word the lifeless youth   245
Fell back into my arms a ravaged corpse,
The dreadful triumph of an angry Heaven,
Where not a father's eye could undertake
To know his child.
THESEUS: O child! O dearest hope
I cast away! Gods, ye unswerving Gods,   250
Too faithfully ye served me! Now must life
Henceforward be a death of long-drawn sorrow.
THERAMENES: And now in fear and haste Aricia,
Stealing, my lord, from your captivity
To hear his nuptial vow before the Gods,   255
Approached. There are the red and steaming grasses,
And there—what welcome for a bride's regard!—
There is Hippolytus, but motionless,
Featureless, bloodless. First she seeks to question
Her misery, and, seeing, still demands   260
Hippolytus. Then, too pitifully assured,
After one glance reproachful to the skies
Cold, with one cry, lifeless upon the dead
She falls. Ismene, weeping, is beside her
And draws her back to life and life's despair;   265
And I, still subject to the hostile daylight,
Return to speak a hero's last desires
And so fulfil the grievous ministry

His dying heart committed to my love.
270   —But here I see the deadliest of his foes.

(Enter PHAEDRA, PANOPE *and* GUARDS*)*

THESEUS: Well, victory is yours: my son is gone. Much, much
        I could suspect; deep rankling doubt
        Acquits him in my heart and troubled mind—
        But he is dead: your sacrifice, my lady;
275   Take it, find satisfaction in the forfeit
        Unmerited or just. It matters little
        That evermore my eyes be blindfolded;
        Let him be criminal if you accuse.
        His loss alone is theme enough for sorrow,
280   No need to look for new and fearful knowledge
        That, impotent to bring the dead again,
        Could pile at most new suffering on the old.
        Let me escape, leave you and leave these shores,
        Flying the bloody image of a son
285   Mangled—before that harrying memory
        I could long for exile from the world of men.
        All things upbraid me, all increase my anguish—
        My very name (for nameless, I could hide),
        The very honours that the Gods bestowed,
290   Whose murderous grace I'll mourn, and not again
        Importune them with fruitless prayers of mine;
        Do what they might, their fatal condescension
        Could not console for what they took away.
PHAEDRA: Theseus, I have repented of my silence.
295   Your son requires his innocence from my lips;
        Yes, he was guiltless.
THESEUS: This to me, his father!
        And on your solemn faith I sentenced him.
        Can any pretext for an act so vile—
PHAEDRA: My time is measured. Listen to me, Theseus.

I, on your dutiful and temperate son,   300
Looked with profaning and incestuous eyes—
The flame of Heaven lighted in my bosom
A fatal fire. Oenone did the rest;
She feared Hippolytus, my passion known,
Would publish all the madness that he loathed;   305
Presuming on my feebleness, she came
With that base story of my victim's guilt.
Self-chosen, easy death among the waves
Punished her perfidy and foiled my anger,
And by now the knife would have cleft my destiny,   310
But goodness still cried out for vindication.
I chose the slower path. I chose to pour
Into your ears before I joined the dead
The chronicle of my remorse. I have drained
And mingled with my burning blood a draught   315
Medea left in Athens. Now already
Her poison makes it progress toward my heart
Striking that heart with cold it never knew;
Faintly already I perceive the daylight
And you I wrong by my unworthy presence;   320
And death, blurring the sunbeams from these eyes
Whose glance polluted them, restores the light
To perfect purity.
PANOPE: My lord, she is dying.
THESEUS: And would the dark remembrance too might die
Of what she has done! Come, all is now too plain.   325
I must enfold what still remains to touch
Of my dear son, and expiate in tears
The blind curse I shall evermore bewail
With dear-bought honours rendered at his tomb;
And, better to placate his injured spirit,   330
I will forget the voice of ancient vengeance
And look upon his lover as my child.

APHRA BEHN

Little is known about the early life of England's first female professional playwright, Aphra Behn (1640–1689). As a child, she moved to Surinam with her parents, where she lived until returning to England in the late 1650s. In 1658, she married a merchant named Behn and served Charles II as a spy in Antwerp in the mid-1660s. When she returned to England penniless in 1667, she was sent to debtors' prison and appealed to the government for her wages. Between 1670 and her death in 1689, Behn wrote fifteen plays, beginning with *The Forced Marriage: or, The Jealous Bridegroom*, a tragicomedy produced by Thomas Betterton at Lincoln's Inn Fields. Behn's major plays are mainly in the mode of Restoration comedy, including *The Rover* (1677), *The Feigned Courtesans* (1679), *The Second Part of The Rover* (1681), and *The City Heiress* (1682). In 1688, Behn published a novel, *Oronooko: or, The Royal Slave*, set in the West Indies. The novel was dramatized by Thomas Southerne in 1695 and was popular onstage throughout the eighteenth century. Aphra Behn is buried in Westminster Abbey.

The Rover

The Rover is a comedy of intrigue, set in Naples during the Carnival. The play concerns the sexual adventures of a band of Englishmen — Belvile, Willmore (the Rover), and Blunt — and their efforts to seduce the heroine Florinda and her sister Hellena. Like many Restoration comedies, *The Rover* takes a frank attitude toward sexual and financial negotiation, which are often paired in the play. The play opens with Hellena's rejection of a life in the convent, and her decision to "provide myself this Carnival, if there be e'er a handsome proper fellow." In the course of the play, Hellena flirts with Willmore; Willmore wins the services (and, unfortunately, the love) of the courtesan Angelica, who eventually tries to murder him; Willmore and Blunt nearly rape Florinda on several occasions; and Blunt is tricked by a prostitute and turned out into the street in his shirt and underwear, "before consummation."

Yet despite the licentiousness of its action, the play clearly depends on a deeply ingrained sense of propriety, much of which operates through class distinctions. While it "would anger us vilely to be trussed up for a rape upon a maid of quality," one of the gentlemen declares, it seems otherwise acceptable to "ruffle a harlot." Morality, in *The Rover*, is in many ways determined by class and wealth. These distinctions are both troubled and confirmed by the important function of disguise and masking in the play. Since the action of *The Rover* takes place during Carnival, the main characters meet only in disguise. Masking enables the characters both to flirt without dishonoring themselves and to discover the truth about one another. In fact, masking in the play empowers the women, in that the temporary masking of the Carnival allows the women to escape their enforced lives at home and to meet men in public. Florinda and Hellena, for instance, can marry only with their brother Pedro's permission. He wants to marry his sisters to the wealthiest — and oldest — suitors, who will be able to settle large fortunes on them. However, the young Englishmen who attract the two sisters are Royalist supporters of Charles II, currently exiled from Cromwell's Protectorate because they support the Crown. As a result, although they are well-born, they are currently without funds and so are a poor match for Florinda and Hellena, at least in Pedro's eyes.

Masking also enables the women to escape Pedro's control, to act on their own behalf. Indeed, although the women are more modest than the Rover, they are equally devious in their pursuit of a lover — though the women insist on marriage as the price of their virginity. In Behn's brilliant comedy, the women emerge as the agents — as well as the objects — of the play's erotic intrigue.

THE ROVER
OR THE BANISH'D CAVALIERS
Aphra Behn
EDITED BY MONTAGUE SUMMERS

— CHARACTERS —

Don ANTONIO, *the Vice-Roy's Son*
Don PEDRO, *a Noble Spaniard, his Friend*
BELVILE, *an English Colonel in love with Florinda*
WILLMORE, *the Rover*
FREDERICK, *an English Gentleman, and Friend to
   Belvile and Blunt*
BLUNT, *an English Country Gentleman*
STEPHANO, *Servant to Don Pedro*
PHILIPPO, *Lucetta's Gallant*
SANCHO, *Pimp to Lucetta*
BISKEY *and* SEBASTIAN, *two Bravoes to Angelica*
DIEGO, *Page to Don Antonio*
PAGE *to Hellena*
BOY, *Page to Belvile*
Blunt's MAN
OFFICERS *and* SOLDIERS

FLORINDA, *Sister to Don Pedro*
HELLENA, *a gay young Woman design'd for a Nun,
   and Sister to Florinda*
VALERIA, *a Kinswoman to Florinda*
ANGELICA BIANCA, *a famous Curtezan*
MORETTA, *her Woman*
CALLIS, *Governess to Florinda and Hellena*
LUCETTA, *a jilting Wench*
SERVANTS, *other* MASQUERADERS, MEN *and* WOMEN

SCENE: *Naples,* in Carnival-time.

— PROLOGUE —
WRITTEN BY A PERSON OF QUALITY

WITS, like Physicians, never can agree,
When of a different Society;
And Rabel's Drops were never more cry'd down
By all the Learned Doctors of the Town,
5   Than a new Play, whose Author is unknown:
Nor can those Doctors with more Malice sue
(And powerful Purses) the dissenting Few,
Than those with an insulting Pride do rail
At all who are not of their own Cabal.
10   If a Young Poet hit your Humour right,
You judge him then out of Revenge and Spite;
So amongst Men there are ridiculous Elves,
Who Monkeys hate for being too like themselves:
So that the Reason of the Grand Debate,
15   Why Wit so oft is damn'd, when good Plays take,
Is, that you censure as you love or hate.
Thus, like a learned Conclave, Poets sit
Catholick Judges both of Sense and Wit,
And damn or save, as they themselves think fit.
20   Yet those who to others Faults are so severe,
Are not so perfect, but themselves may err.
Some write correct indeed, but then the whole
(Bating their own dull Stuff i'th' Play) is stole:
As Bees do suck from Flowers their Honey-dew,
25   So they rob others, striving to please you.
   Some write their Characters genteel and fine,
But then they do so toil for every Line,
That what to you does easy seem, and plain,
Is the hard issue of their labouring Brain.
30   And some th' Effects of all their Pains we see,

Is but to mimick good Extempore.
Others by long Converse about the Town,
Have Wit enough to write a leud Lampoon,
But their chief Skill lies in a Baudy Song.
In short, the only Wit that's now in Fashion   35
Is but the Gleanings of good Conversation.
As for the Author of this coming Play,
I ask'd him what he thought fit I should say,
In thanks for your good Company to day:
He call'd me Fool, and said it was well known,   40
You came not here for our sakes, but your own.
New Plays are stuff'd with Wits, and with Debauches,
That croud and sweat like Cits in *May*-day Coaches.

— ACT ONE —

SCENE I

A chamber.

(*Enter* FLORINDA *and* HELLENA.)

FLORINDA: What an impertient thing is a young Girl bred in a
   Nunnery! How full of Questions! Prithee no more, Hellena; I
   have told thee more than thou understand'st already.

HELLENA: The more's my Grief; I wou'd fain know as much as
   you, which makes me so inquisitive; nor is't enough to know   5
   you're a Lover, unless you tell me too, who 'tis you sigh for.

FLORINDA: When you are a Lover, I'll think you fit for a Secret
   of that nature.

HELLENA: 'Tis true, I was never a Lover yet — but I begin to have
   a shreud Guess, what 'tis to be so, and fancy it very pretty to   10
   sigh, and sing, and blush and wish, and dream and wish, and
   long and wish to see the Man; and when I do, look pale and

tremble; just as you did when my Brother brought home the
fine *English* Colonel to see you — what do you call him? Don
Belvile.

FLORINDA: Fie, *Hellena*.

HELLENA: That Blush betrays you — I am sure 'tis so — or is it
Don *Antonio* the Vice-Roy's Son? — or perhaps the rich old
Don *Vincentio*, whom my father designs for your Hus-
band? — Why do you blush again?

FLORINDA: With Indignation; and how near soever my Father
thinks I am to marrying that hated Object, I shall let him see I
understand better what's due to my Beauty, Birth and Fortune, and more to my Soul, than to obey those unjust
Commands.

HELLENA: Now hang me, if I don't love thee for that dear Disobedience. I love Mischief strangely, as most of our Sex do,
who are come to love nothing else — But tell me, dear *Florinda*, don't you love that fine *Anglese*? — for I vow next to
loving him my self, 'twill please me most that you do so, for
he is so gay and so handsom.

FLORINDA: *Hellena*, a Maid design'd for a Nun ought not to be
so curious in a Discourse of Love.

HELLENA: And dost thou think that ever I'll be a Nun? Or at least
till I'm so old, I'm fit for nothing else. Faith no, Sister; and
that which makes me long to know whether you love *Belvile*,
is because I hope he has some mad Companion or other, that
will spoil my Devotion; nay I'm resolv'd to provide my self this
Carnival, if there be e'er a handsom Fellow of my Humour
above Ground, tho I ask first.

FLORINDA: Prithee be not so wild.

HELLENA: Now you have provided your self with a Man, you
take no Care for poor me — Prithee tell me, what dost thou
see about me that is unfit for Love — have not I a world of
Youth? a Humour gay? a Beauty passable? a Vigour desirable?
well shap'd? clean limb'd? sweet breath'd? and Sense enough
to know how all these ought to be employ'd to the best Advantage: yes, I do and will. Therefore lay aside your Hopes of my
Fortune, by my being a Devotee, and tell me how you came
acquainted with this *Belvile*; for I perceive you knew him before he came to *Naples*.

FLORINDA: Yes, I knew him at the Siege of *Pampelona*, he was
then a Colonel of *French* Horse, who when the Town was
ransack'd, nobly treated my Brother and my self, preserving
us from all Insolencies; and I must own, (besides great Obligations) I have I know not what, that pleads kindly for him
about my Heart, and will suffer no other to enter — But see
my Brother.

(*Enter* DON PEDRO, STEPHANO, *with a Masquing Habit, and*
CALLIS.)

PEDRO: Good morrow, Sister. Pray, when saw you your Lover
Don *Vincentio*?

FLORINDA: I know not, Sir — *Callis*, when was he here? for I
consider it so little, I know not when it was.

PEDRO: I have a Command from my Father here to tell you, you
ought to despise him, a Man of so vast a Fortune, and such a
Passion for you — *Stephano*, my things —

(*Puts on his Masquing Habit.*)

FLORINDA: A Passion for me! 'tis more than e'er I saw, or had a
desire should be known — I hate *Vincentio*, and I would not
have a Man so dear to me as my Brother follow the ill Customs of our Country, and make a Slave of his Sister — And
Sir, my Father's Will, I'm sure, you may divert.

PEDRO: I know not how dear I am to you, but I wish only to be
rank'd in your Esteem, equal with the *English* Colonel *Belvile* — Why do you frown and blush? Is there any Guilt belongs to the Name of that Cavalier?

FLORINDA: I'll not deny I value *Belvile*: when I was expos'd to
such Dangers as the licens'd Lust of common Soldiers threat-
ned, when Rage and Conquest flew thro the City — then *Belvile*, this Criminal for my sake, threw himself into all Dangers
to save my Honour, and will you not allow him my
Esteem?

PEDRO: Yes, pay him what you will in Honour — but you must
consider Don *Vincentio's* Fortune, and the Jointure he'll
make you.

FLORINDA: Let him consider my Youth, Beauty and Fortune;
which ought not to be thrown away on his Age and Jointure.

PEDRO: 'Tis true, he's not so young and fine a Gentleman as that
Belvile — but what Jewels will that Cavalier present you with?
those of his Eyes and Heart?

HELLENA: And are not those better than any Don *Vincentio* has
brought from the *Indies*?

PEDRO: Why how now! Has your Nunnery-breeding taught you
to understand the Value of Hearts and Eyes?

HELLENA: Better than to believe *Vincentio* deserves Value from
any woman — He may perhaps encrease her Bags, but not her
Family.

PEDRO: This is fine — Go up to your Devotion, you are not design'd for the Conversation of Lovers.

HELLENA: (*Aside.*) Nor Saints yet a while I hope.
Is't not enough you make a Nun of me, but you must cast my
Sister away too, exposing her to a worse confinement than a
religious Life?

PEDRO: The Girl's mad — Is it a Confinement to be carry'd into
the Country, to an antient Villa belonging to the Family of
the *Vincentio's* these five hundred Years, and have no other
Prospect than that pleasing one of seeing all her own that
meets her Eyes — a fine Air, large Fields and Gardens, where
she may walk and gather Flowers?

HELLENA: When? By Moon-Light? For I'm sure she dares not
encounter with the heat of the Sun; that were a Task only for
Don *Vincentio* and his *Indian* Breeding, who loves it in the
Dog-days — And if these be her daily Divertisements, what
are those of the Night? to lie in a wide Moth-eaten Bed-
Chamber with Furniture in Fashion in the Reign of King
Sancho the First; the Bed that which his Forefathers liv'd and
dy'd in.

PEDRO: Very well.

HELLENA: This Apartment (new furbisht and fitted out for the
young Wife) he (out of Freedom) makes his Dressing-room;
and being a frugal and a jealous Coxcomb, instead of a Valet

---

52 **Siege of Pampelona** Pampluna, the strongly fortified capital of Na-
varra and very frequently a center of military operations

114 **King Sancho the First** Sancho I, 'the Fat,' of Castile and Leon,
reigned 955–67: Sancho I of Aragon 1067–94. But the phrase is here
only in a vague general sense to denote some musty and immemorial
antiquity without any exact reference

120 to uncase his feeble Carcase, he desires you to do that Office—Signs of Favour, I'll assure you, and such as you must
not hope for, unless your Woman be out of the way.

PEDRO: Have you done yet?

HELLENA: That Honour being past, the Giant stretches it self,
125 yawns and sighs a Belch or two as loud as a Musket, throws
himself into Bed, and expects you in his foul Sheets, and e'er
you can get your self undrest, calls you with a Snore or two—
And are not these fine Blessings to a young Lady?

PEDRO: Have you done yet?

130 HELLENA: And this man you must kiss, nay, you must kiss none
but him too—and nuzle thro his Beard to find his Lips—and
this you must submit to for threescore Years, and all for a
Jointure.

PEDRO: For all your Character of Don Vincentio, she is as like to
135 marry him as she was before.

HELLENA: Marry Don Vincentio! hang me, such a Wedlock
would be worst than Adultery with another Man: I had rather
see her in the Hostel de Dieu, to waste her Youth there in
Vows, and be a Handmaid to Lazers and Cripples, than to
140 lose it in such a Marriage.

PEDRO: You have consider'd, Sister, that Belvile has no Fortune
to bring you to, is banisht his Country, despis'd at home, and
pity'd abroad.

HELLENA: What then? the Vice-Roy's Son is better than that
145 Old Sir Fisty. Don Vincentio! Don Indian! he thinks he's
trading to Gambo still, and wou'd barter himself (that Bell
and Bawble) for your Youth and Fortune.

PEDRO: Callis, take her hence, and lock her up all this Carnival,
and at Lent she shall begin her everlasting Penance in a
150 Monastery.

HELLENA: I care not, I had rather be a Nun, than be oblig'd to
marry as you wou'd have me, if I were design'd for't.

PEDRO: Do not fear the Blessing of that Choice—you shall be a
Nun.

155 HELLENA: Shall I so? you may chance to be mistaken in my way
of Devotion—(Aside.) A Nun! yes I am like to make a fine
Nun! I have an excellent Humour for a Grate: No, I'll have a
Saint of my own to pray to shortly, if I like any that dares
venture on me.

160 PEDRO: Callis, make it your Business to watch this wild Cat. As
for you, Florinda, I've only try'd you all this while, and urg'd
my Father's Will; but mine is, that you would love Antonio,
he is brave and young, and all that can compleat the Happiness of a gallant Maid—This Absence of my Father will give
165 us opportunity to free you from Vincentio, by marrying here,
which you must do to morrow.

FLORINDA: To morrow!

PEDRO: To morrow, or 'twill be too late—'tis not my Friendship
to Antonio, which makes me urge this, but Love to thee, and
170 Hatred to Vincentio—therefore resolve upon't to morrow.

FLORINDA: Sir, I shall strive to do, as shall become your Sister.

PEDRO: I'll both believe and trust you—Adieu.

(Exeunt PEDRO and STEPHANO.)

138 **Hostel de Dieu** The first Spanish hospital was erected at Granada by
St. Juan de Dios before 1550   146 **Gambo** The Gambia in West Africa
has been a British Colony since 1664, when a fort, now Fort James, was
founded at the mouth of the river

HELLENA: As become his Sister!—That is, to be as resolved your
way, as he is his—

(HELLENA goes to CALLIS.)

FLORINDA: I ne'er till now perceiv'd my Ruin near,   175
I've no Defence against Antonio's Love,
For he has all the Advantages of Nature,
The moving Arguments of Youth and Fortune.

HELLENA: But hark you, Callis, you will not be so cruel to lock
me up indeed: will you?   180

CALLIS: I must obey the Commands I hate—besides, do you
consider what a Life you are going to lead?

HELLENA: Yes, Callis, that of a Nun: and till then I'll be indebted a World of Prayers to you, if you let me now see, what I
never did, the Divertisements of a Carnival.   185

CALLIS: What, go in Masquerade? 'twill be a fine farewell to the
World I take it—pray what wou'd you do there?

HELLENA: That which all the World does, as I am told, be as
mad as the rest, and take all innocent Freedom—Sister,
you'll go too, will you not? come prithee be not sad—We'll   190
out-wit twenty Brothers, if you'll be rul'd by me—Come put
off this dull Humour with your Clothes, and assume one as
gay, and as fantastick as the Dress my Cousin Valeria and I
have provided, and let's ramble.

FLORINDA: Callis, will you give us leave to go?   195

CALLIS: I have a youthful Itch of going my self.

(Aside.)

—Madam, if I thought your Brother might not know it, and I
might wait on you, for by my troth I'll not trust young Girls
alone.

FLORINDA: Thou see'st my Brother's gone already, and thou   200
shalt attend and watch us.

(Enter STEPHANO.)

STEPHANO: Madam, the Habits are come, and your Cousin Valeria is drest, and stays for you.

FLORINDA: 'Tis well—I'll write a Note, and if I chance to see
Belvile, and want an opportunity to speak to him, that shall let 205
him know what I've resolv'd in favour of him.

HELLENA: Come, let's in and dress us.

(Exeunt.)

SCENE II

A Long Street.

(Enter BELVILE, melancholy, BLUNT and FREDERICK.)

FREDERICK: Why, what the Devil ails the Colonel, in a time
when all the World is gay, to look like mere Lent thus? Hadst
thou been long enough in Naples to have been in love, I
should have sworn some such Judgment had befall'n thee.

BELVILE: No, I have made no new Amours since I came to   5
Naples.

FREDERICK: You have left none behind you in Paris.

BELVILE: Neither.

FREDERICK: I can't divine the Cause then; unless the old Cause,
the want of Mony.   10

BLUNT: And another old Cause, the want of a Wench—Wou'd
not that revive you?

BELVILE: You're mistaken, *Ned*.

BLUNT: Nay, 'Sheartlikins, then thou art past Cure.

15 FREDERICK: I have found it out; thou hast renew'd thy Acquaintance with the Lady that cost thee so many Sighs at the Siege
of *Pampelona* — pox on't, what d'ye call her — her Brother's a
noble *Spaniard* — Nephew to the dead General — *Florinda* —
ay, *Florinda* — And will nothing serve thy turn but that
20 damn'd virtuous Woman, whom on my Consicience thou
lov'st in spite too, because thou seest little or no possibility of
gaining her?

BELVILE: Thou art mistaken, I have Interest enough in that
lovely Virgin's Heart, to make me proud and vain, were it
25 not abated by the Severity of a Brother, who perceiving my
Happiness —

FREDERICK: Has civilly forbid thee the House?

BELVILE: 'Tis so, to make way for a powerful Rival, the Vice-
Roy's Son, who has the advantage of me, in being a Man of
30 Fortune, a *Spaniard*, and her Brother's Friend; which gives
him liberty to make his Court, whilst I have recourse only to
Letters, and distant Looks from her Window, which are as
soft and kind as those which Heav'n sends down on Penitents.

BLUNT: Hey day! 'Sheartlikins, Simile! by this Light the Man is
35 quite spoil'd — *Frederick*, what the Devil are we made of, that
we cannot be thus concern'd for a Wench? — 'Sheartlikins,
our *Cupids* are like the Cooks of the Camp, they can roast or
boil a Woman, but they have none of the fine Tricks to set 'em
off, no Hogoes to make the Sauce pleasant, and the Stomach
40 sharp.

FREDERICK: I dare swear I have had a hundred as young, kind
and handsom as this *Florinda*; and Dogs eat me, if they were
not as troublesom to me i'th' Morning as they were welcome
o'er night.

45 BLUNT: And yet, I warrant, he wou'd not touch another
Woman, if he might have her for nothing.

BELVILE: That's thy Joy, a cheap Whore.

BLUNT: Why, 'dsheartlikins, I Love a frank Soul — When did
you ever hear of an honest Woman that took a Man's Mony? I
50 warrant 'em good ones — But, Gentlemen, you may be free,
you have been kept so poor with Parliaments and Protectors,
that the little Stock you have is not worth preserving — but I
thank my Stars, I have more Grace than to forfeit my Estate
by Cavaliering.

55 BELVILE: Methinks only following the Court should be sufficient to entitle 'em to that.

BLUNT: 'Sheartlikins, they know I follow it to do it no good,
unless they pick a hole in my Coat for lending you Mony now
and then; which is a greater Crime to my Conscience, Gen-
60 tlemen, than to the Common-wealth.

(*Enter* WILLMORE.)

WILLMORE: Ha! dear *Belvile*! noble Colonel!

BELVILE: *Willmore*! welcome ashore, my dear Rover! — what
happy Wind blew us this good Fortune?

WILLMORE: Let me salute you my dear *Fred*, and then com-
65 mand me — How is't honest Lad?

FREDERICK: Faith, Sir, the old Complement, infinitely the better to see my dear mad *Willmore* again — Prithee why camest
thou ashore? and where's the Prince?

WILLMORE: He's well, and reigns still Lord of the watery Ele-
ment — I must aboard again within a Day or two, and my 70
Business ashore was only to enjoy my self a little this
Carnival.

BELVILE: Pray know our new Friend, Sir, he's but bashful, a raw
Traveller, but honest, stout, and one of us.

(*Embraces* BLUNT.)

WILLMORE: That you esteem him, gives him an Interest here. 75

BLUNT: Your Servant, Sir.

WILLMORE: But well — Faith I'm glad to meet you again in a
warm Climate, where the kind Sun has its god-like Power still
over the Wine and Woman. — Love and Mirth are my Business in *Naples*; and if I mistake not the Place, here's an excel- 80
lent Market for Chapmen of my Humour.

BELVILE: See here be those kind Merchants of Love you look for.

(*Enter several* MEN *in masquing Habits, some playing on Mu-
sick, others dancing after;* WOMEN *drest like Curtezans, with
Papers pinn'd to their Breasts, and Baskets of Flowers in their
Hands.*)

BLUNT: 'Sheartlikins, what have we here!

FREDERICK: Now the Game begins.

WILLMORE: Fine pretty Creatures! may a stranger have leave to 85
look and love? — What's here — (*Reads the Paper.*) Roses for
every Month!

BLUNT: Roses for every Month! what means that?

BELVILE: They are, or wou'd have you think they're Curtezans,
who here in *Naples* are to be hir'd by the Month. 90

WILLMORE: Kind and obliging to inform us — Pray where do
these Roses grow? I would fain plant some of 'em in a Bed of
mine.

WOMAN: Beware such Roses, Sir.

WILLMORE: A Pox of fear: I'll be bak'd with thee between a pair 95
of Sheets, and that's thy proper Still, so I might but strow such
Roses over me and under me — Fair one, wou'd you wou'd
give me leave to gather at your Bush this idle Month, I wou'd
go near to make some Body smell of it all the Year after.

BELVILE: And thou hast need of such a Remedy, for thou stinkest 100
of Tar and Rope-ends, like a Dock or Pesthouse.

(*The* WOMAN *puts her self into the Hands of a* MAN, *and Exit.*)

WILLMORE: Nay, nay, you shall not leave me so.

BELVILE: By all means use no Violence here.

WILLMORE: Death! just as I was going to be damnably in love, to
have her led off! I could pluck that Rose out of his Hand, and 105
even kiss the Bed, the Bush it grew in.

FREDERICK: No Friend to Love like a long Voyage at Sea.

BLUNT: Except a Nunnery, *Frederick*.

WILLMORE: Death! but will they not be kind, quickly be kind?
Thou know'st I'm no tame Sigher, but a rampant Lion of the 110
Forest.

(*Two* MEN *drest all over the Horns of several sorts, making Grimaces at one another, with Papers pinn'd on their Backs, advance
from the farther end of the Scene.*)

BELVILE: Oh the fantastical Rogues, how they are dress'd! 'tis a
Satir against the whole Sex.

WILLMORE: Is this a Fruit that grows in this warm Country?

BELVILE: Yes: 'Tis pretty to see these *Italian* start, swell, and stab 115
at the Word *Cuckold*, and yet stumble at Horns on every
Threshold.

14 **'sheartlikins.** by God's heart   39 **Hogoes** Haut-goût, a relish

WILLMORE: See what's on their Back—(Reads.) Flowers for every Night. — Ah Rogue! And more sweet than Roses of ev'ry
120 Month! This is a Gardiner of Adam's own breeding.

(They dance.)

BELVILE: What think you of those grave People? — is a Wake in
Essex half so mad or extravagant?

WILLMORE: I like their sober grave way, 'tis a kind of legal au-
125 thoriz'd Fornication, where the Men are not chid for 't, nor
the Women despis'd, as amongst our dull English; even the
Monsieurs want that part of good Manners.

BELVILE: But here in Italy a Monsieur is the humblest best-bred
Gentleman—Duels are so baffled by Bravo's that an age
130 shews not one, but between a Frenchman and a Hang-man,
who is as much too hard for him on the Piazza, as they are for
a Dutchman on the new Bridge—But see another Crew.

(Enter FLORINDA, HELLENA, and VALERIA, drest like Gipsies;
CALLIS and STEPHANO, LUCETTA, PHILIPPO and SANCHO in
Masquerade.)

HELLENA: Sister, there's your Englishman, and with him a
handsome proper Fellow—I'll to him, and instead of telling
him his Fortune, try my own.

135 WILLMORE: Gipsies, on my Life—Sure these will prattle if a
Man cross their Hands. (Goes to Hellena)—Dear pretty (and
I hope) young Devil, will you tell an amorous Stranger what
Luck he's like to have?

HELLENA: Have a care how you venture with me, Sir, lest I pick
140 your Pocket, which will more vex your English Humour,
than an Italian Fortune will please you.

WILLMORE: How the Devil cam'st thou to show my Country and
Humour?

HELLENA: The first I guess by a certain forward Impudence,
145 which does not displease me at this time; and the Loss of your
Money will vex you, because I hope you have but very little to
lose.

WILLMORE: Egad Child, thou'rt i'th' right; it is so little, I dare
not offer it thee for a Kindness—But cannot you divine what
150 other things of more value I have about me, that I would
more willingly part with?

HELLENA: Indeed no, that's the Business of a Witch, and I am
but a Gipsy yet—Yet, without looking in your Hand, I have a
parlous Guess, 'tis some foolish Heart you mean, an incon-
155 stant English Heart, as little worth stealing as your Purse.

WILLMORE: Nay, then thou dost deal with the Devil, that's certain—Thou hast guess'd as right as if thou hadst been one of
that Number it has languisht for—I find you'll be better acquainted with it; nor can you take it in a better time, for I am
160 come from Sea, Child; and Venus not being propitious to me
in her own Element, I have a world of Love in store—Wou'd
you would be good-natur'd, and take some on't off my Hands.

HELLENA: Why—I could be inclin'd that way—but for a foolish
Vow I am going to make—to die a Maid.

165 WILLMORE: Then thou art damn'd without Redemption; and as
I am a good Christian, I ought to charity to divert so wicked a
Design—therefore prithee, dear Creature, let me know
quickly when and where I shall begin to set a helping hand to
so good a Work.

170 HELLENA: If you should prevail with my tender Heart (as I begin
to fear you will, for you have horrible loving Eyes) there will
be difficulty in't that you'll hardly undergo for my sake.

WILLMORE: Faith, Child, I have been bred in Dangers, and
wear a Sword that has been employ'd in a worse Cause, than
for a handsom kind Woman—Name the Danger—let it be 175
any thing but a long Siege, and I'll undertake it.

HELLENA: Can you storm?

WILLMORE: Oh, most furiously.

HELLENA: What think you of a Nunnery-wall? for he that wins
me, must gain that first. 180

WILLMORE: A Nun! Oh how I love thee for't! there's no Sinner
like a young Saint—Nay, now there's no denying me: the old
Law had no Curse (to a Woman) like dying a Maid; witness
Jephtha's Daughter.

HELLENA: A very good Text this, if well handled; and I perceive, 185
Father Captain, you would impose no severe Penance on her
who was inclin'd to console her self before she took Orders.

WILLMORE: If she be young and handsom.

HELLENA: Ay, there's it—but if she be not—

WILLMORE: By this Hand, Child, I have an implicit Faith, and 190
dare venture on thee with all Faults—besides, 'tis more meritorious to leave the World when thou hast tasted and prov'd
the Pleasure on't; then 'twill be a Virtue in thee, which now
will be pure Ignorance.

HELLENA: I perceive, good Father Captain, you design only to 195
make me fit for Heaven—but if on the contrary you should
quite divert me from it, and bring me back to the World
again, I should have a new Man to seek I find; and what a grief
that will be—for when I begin, I fancy I shall love like any
thing: I never try'd yet. 200

WILLMORE: Egad, and that's kind—Prithee, dear Creature, give
me Credit for a Heart, for faith, I'm a very honest Fellow—
Oh, I long to come first to the Banquet of Love; and such a
swinging Appetite I bring—Oh, I'm impatient. Thy Lodging, Sweetheart, thy Lodging, or I'm a dead man. 205

HELLENA: Why must we be either guilty of Fornication or Murder, if we converse with you Men?—And is there no difference between leave to love me, and leave to lie with me?

WILLMORE: Faith, Child, they were made to go together.

LUCETTA: (Pointing to BLUNT.) Are you sure this is the Man? 210

SANCHO: When did I mistake your Game?

LUCETTA: This is a stranger, I know by his gazing; if he be brisk
he'll venture to follow me; and then, if I understand my
Trade, he's mine: he's English too, and they say that's a sort of
good natur'd loving People, and have generally so kind an 215
opinion of themselves, that a Woman with any Wit may flatter 'em into any sort of Fool she pleases.

BLUNT: 'Tis so—she is taken—I have Beauties which my false
Glass at home did not discover.

(She often passes by BLUNT and gazes on him; he struts, and
cocks, and walks, and gazes on her.)

FLORINDA: This Woman watches me so, I shall get no Oppor- 220
tunity to discover my self to him, and so miss the intent of my
coming—But as I was saying, Sir—(Looking in his Hand.) by
this Line you should be a Lover.

BELVILE: I thought how right you guess'd, all Men are in love, or
pretend to be so—Come, let me go, I'm weary of this fooling. 225

(Walks away.)

FLORINDA: I will not, till you have confess'd whether the Passion
that you have vow'd Florinda be true or false.

(She holds him, he strives to get from her.)

BELVILE: *Florinda!*

(*Turns quick towards her.*)

FLORINDA: Softly.

230   BELVILE: Thou hast nam'd one will fix me here for ever.
FLORINDA: She'll be disappointed then, who expects you this
        Night at the Garden-gate, and if you'll fail not—as let me see
        the other Hand—you will go near to do—she vows to die or
        make you happy.

(*Looks on* CALLIS, *who observes 'em.*)

235   BELVILE: What canst thou mean?
FLORINDA: That which I say—Farewel.

(*Offers to go.*)

BELVILE: Oh charming Sybil, stay, complete that Joy, which, as
        it is, will turn into Distraction!—Where must I be? at the
        Garden-gate? I know it—at night you say—I'll sooner forfeit
240   Heaven than disobey.

(*Enter* DON PEDRO *and other Masquers, and pass over the
Stage.*)

CALLIS: Madam, your Brother's here.
FLORINDA: Take this to instruct you farther.

(*Gives him a Letter, and goes off.*)

FREDERICK: Have a care, Sir, what you promise; this may be a
        Trap laid by her Brother to ruin you.
245   BELVILE: Do not disturb my Happiness with Doubts.

(*Opens the Letter.*)

WILLMORE: My dear pretty Creature, a Thousand Blessings on
        thee; still in this Habit, you say, and after Dinner at this Place.
HELLENA: Yes, if you will swear to keep your Heart, and not
        bestow it between this time and that.
250   WILLMORE: By all the little Gods of Love I swear, I'll leave it
        with you; and if you run away with it, those Deities of Justice
        will revenge me.

(*Exeunt all the Women except* LUCETTA.)

FREDERICK: Do you know the Hand?
BELVILE: 'Tis *Florinda's.*
255   All Blessings fall upon the virtuous Maid.
FREDERICK: Nay, no Idolatry, a sober Sacrifice I'll allow you.
BELVILE: Oh Friends! the welcom'st News, the softest Letter!—
        nay, you shall see it; and could you now be serious, I might be
        made the happiest Man the Sun shines on.
260   WILLMORE: The Reason of this mighty Joy.
BELVILE: See how kindly she invites me to deliver her from the
        threaten'd Violence of her Brother—will you not assist me?
WILLMORE: I know not what thou mean'st, but I'll make one at
        any Mischief where a Woman's concern'd—but she'll be
265   grateful to us for the Favour, will she not?
BELVILE: How mean you?
WILLMORE: How should I mean? Thou know'st there's but one
        way for a Woman to oblige me.
BELVILE: Don't prophane—the Maid is nicely virtuous.
270   WILLMORE: Who pox, then she's fit for nothing but a Husband;
        let her e'en go, Colonel.
FREDERICK: Peace, she's the Colonel's Mistress, Sir.
WILLMORE: Let her be the Devil; if she be thy Mistress, I'll serve
        her—name the way.

BELVILE: Read here this Postcript.   275

(*Gives him a Letter.*)

WILLMORE: (*Reads.*) *At Ten at night—at the Garden-Gate—of
        which, if I cannot get the Key, I will contrive a way over the
        Wall*—come attended with a Friend or two.—Kind heart, if
        we three cannot weave a String to let her down a Garden-
        Wall, 'twere pity but the Hangman wove one for us all.   280
FREDERICK: Let her alone for that: your Woman's Wit, your fair
        kind Woman, will not out-trick a Brother or a Jew, and con-
        trive like a Jesuit in Chains—but see, *Ned Blunt* is stoln out
        after the Lure of a Damsel.

(*Exit* BLUNT *and* LUCETTA.)

BELVILE: So he'll scarce find his way home again, unless we get   285
        him cry'd by the Bell-man in the Market-place, and 'twou'd
        sound prettily—a lost *English* Boy of Thirty.
FREDERICK: I hope 'tis some common crafty Sinner, one that
        will fit him; it may be she'll sell him for *Peru*, the Rogue's
        sturdy and would work well in a Mine; at least I hope she'll   290
        dress him our our Mirth; cheat him of all, then have him
        well-favour'dly bang'd, and turn'd out naked at Midnight.
WILLMORE: Prithee what Humour is he of, that you wish him so
        well?
BELVILE: Why, of an *English* Elder Brother's Humour, educated   295
        in a Nursery, with a Maid to tend him till Fifteen, and lies
        with his Grand-mother till he's of Age; one that knows no
        Pleasure beyond riding to the next Fair, or going up to *Lon-
        don* with his right Worshipful Father in Parliament-time;
        wearing gay Clothes, or making honourable Love to his Lady   300
        Mother's Landry-Maid; gets drunk at a Hunting-Match, and
        ten to one then gives some Proofs of his Prowess—A pox upon
        him, he's our Banker, and has all our Cash about him, and if
        he fail we are all broke.
FREDERICK: Oh let him alone for that matter, he's of a damn'd   305
        stingy Quality, that will secure our Stock. I know not in what
        Danger it were indeed, if the Jilt should pretend she's in love
        with him, for 'tis a kind believing Coxcomb; otherwise if he
        part with more than a Piece of Eight—geld him: for which
        offer he may chance to be beaten, if she be a Whore of the   310
        first Rank.
BELVILE: Nay the Rogue will not be easily beaten, he's stout
        enough; perhaps if they talk beyond his Capacity, he may
        chance to exercise his Courage upon some of them; else I'm
        sure they'll find it as difficult to beat as to please him.   315
WILLMORE: 'Tis a lucky Devil to light upon so kind a Wench!
FREDERICK: Thou hadst a great deal of talk with thy little Gipsy,
        coud'st thou do no good upon her? for mine was hard-
        hearted.
WILLMORE: Hang her, she was some damn'd honest Person of   320
        Quality, I'm sure, she was so very free and witty. If her Face
        be but answerable to her Wit and Humour, I would be bound
        to Constancy this Month to gain her. In the mean time, have
        you made no kind Acquaintance since you came to Town?—
        You do not use to be honest so long, Gentlemen.   325
FREDERICK: Faith Love has kept us honest, we have been all fir'd
        with a Beauty newly come to Town, the famous *Paduana
        Angelica Bianca.*

---

309 **a Piece of Eight** A piastre, a coin of varying values in different
countries

WILLMORE: What, the Mistress of the dead *Spanish* General?

330 BELVILE: Yes, she's now the only ador'd Beauty of all the Youth
in *Naples*, who put on all their charms to appear lovely in her
sight, their Coaches, Liveries, and themselves, all gay, as on a
Monarch's Birth-Day, to attract the Eyes of this fair Charmer,
while she has the Pleasure to behold all languish for her that

335 see her.

FREDERICK: 'Tis pretty to see with how much Love the Men
regard her, and how much Envy the Women.

WILLMORE: What Gallant has she?

BELVILE: None, she's exposed to Sale, and four Days in the

340 Week she's yours — for so much a Month.

WILLMORE: The very Thought of it quenches all manner of Fire
in me — yet prithee let's see her.

BELVILE: Let's first to Dinner, and after that we'll pass the Day as
you please — but at Night ye must all be at my Devotion.

345 WILLMORE: I will not fail you.

(Exeunt.)

— ACT TWO —

SCENE I

The Long Street.

(Enter BELVILE *and* FREDERICK *in Masquing-Habits, and*
WILLMORE *in his own Clothes, with a Vizard in his Hand.)*

WILLMORE: But why thus disguis'd and muzzl'd?

BELVILE: Because whatever Extravagances we commit in these
Faces, our own may not be oblig'd to answer 'em.

WILLMORE: I should have chang'd my Eternal Buff too: but no

5 matter, my little Gipsy wou'd not have found me out then: for
if she should change hers, it is impossible I should know her,
unless I should hear her prattle — A Pox on't, I cannot get her
out of my Head: Pray Heaven, if ever I do see her again, she
prove damnable ugly, that I may fortify my self against her

10 Tongue.

BELVILE: Have a care of Love, for o' my conscience she was not
of a Quality to give thee any hopes.

WILLMORE: Pox on 'em, why do they draw a Man in then? She
has play'd with my Heart so, that 'twill never lie still till I have

15 met with some kind Wench, that will play the Game out with
me — Oh for my Arms full of soft, white, kind — Woman!
such as I fancy *Angelica.*

BELVILE: This is her House, if you were but in stock to get admittance; they have not din'd yet; I perceive the Picture is not out.

(Enter BLUNT.*)*

20 WILLMORE: I long to see the Shadow of the fair Substance, a
Man may gaze on that for nothing.

BLUNT: Colonel, thy Hand — and thine, *Frederick.* I have been
an Ass, a deluded Fool, a very Coxcomb from my Birth till
this Hour, and heartily repent my little Faith.

25 BELVILE: What the Devil's the matter with thee *Ned?*

BLUNT: Oh such a Mistress, *Frederick,* such a Girl!

WILLMORE: Ha! where? *Frederick.* Ay where!

BLUNT: So fond, so amorous, so toying and fine! and all for
sheer Love, ye Rogue! Oh how she lookt and kiss'd! and

30 sooth'd my Heart from my Bosom. I cannot think I was

awake, and yet methinks I see and feel her Charms still —
Frederick. — Try if she have not left the Taste of her balmy
Kisses upon my Lips —

(Kisses him.)

BELVILE: Ha, ha, ha! *Willmore.* Death Man, where is she?

35 BLUNT: What a Dog was I to stay in dull *England* so long — How
have I laught at the Colonel when he sigh'd for Love! but now
the little Archer has reveng'd him, and by his own Dart, I can
guess at all his Joys, which then I took for Fancies, mere
Dreams and Fables — Well, I'm resolved to sell all in *Essex,*
and plant here for ever. 40

BELVILE: What a Blessing 'tis, thou hast a Mistress thou dar'st
boast of; for I know thy Humour is rather to have a proclaim'd
Clap, than a secret Amour.

WILLMORE: Dost know her Name?

BLUNT: Her Name? No, 'sheartlikins: what care I for Names? — 45
She's fair, young, brisk and kind, even to ravishment: and
what a Pox care I for knowing her by another Title?

WILLMORE: Didst give her anything?

BLUNT: Give her! — Ha, ha, ha! why, she's a Person of Quality —
That's a good one, give her! 'sheartlikins dost think such Crea- 50
tures are to be bought? Or are we provided for such a Purchase? Give her, quoth ye? Why she presented me with this
Bracelet, for the Toy of a Diamond I us'd to wear: No, Gentlemen, *Ned Blunt* is not every Body — She expects me
again to night. 55

WILLMORE: Egad that's well; we'll all go.

BLUNT: Not a Soul: No, Gentlemen, you are Wits; I am a dull
Country Rogue, I.

FREDERICK: Well, Sir, for all your Person of Quality, I shall be
very glad to understand your Purse be secure; 'tis our whole 60
Estate at present, which we are loth to hazard in one Bottom:
come, Sir, unload.

BLUNT: Take the necessary Trifle, useless now to me, that am
belov'd by such a Gentlewoman — 'sheartlikins Money! Here
take mine too. 65

FREDERICK: No, keep that to be cozen'd, that we may laugh.

WILLMORE: Cozen'd! — Death! wou'd I cou'd meet with one,
that wou'd cozen me of all the Love I cou'd spare to night.

FREDERICK: Pox 'tis some common Whore upon my Life.

BLUNT: A Whore! yes with such Clothes! such Jewels! such a 70
House! such Furniture, and so attended! a Whore!

BELVILE: Why yes, Sir, they are Whores, tho they'll neither entertain you with Drinking, Swearing, or Baudy; are Whores
in all those gay Clothes, and right Jewels; are Whores with
great Houses richly furnisht with Velvet Beds, Store of Plate, 75
handsome Attendance, and fine Coaches, are Whores and
errant ones.

WILLMORE: Pox on't, where do these fine Whores live?

BELVILE: Where no Rogue in Office yclep'd Constables dare
give 'em laws, nor the Wine-inspired Bullies of the Town 80
break their Windows; yet they are Whores, tho this *Essex* Calf
believe them Persons of Quality.

BLUNT: 'Sheartlikins, y'are all Fools, there are things about this
Essex Calf, that shall take with the Ladies, beyond all your
Wits and Parts — This Shape and Size, Gentlemen, are not to 85
be despis'd; my Waste tolerably long, with other inviting
Signs, that shall be nameless.

WILLMORE: Egad I believe he may have met with some Person
of Quality that may be kind to him.

90 BELVILE: Dost thou perceive any such tempting things about him, should make a fine Woman, and of Quality, pick him out from all Mankind, to throw away her Youth and Beauty upon, nay, and her dear Heart too?—no, no, *Angelica* has rais'd the Price too high.

95 WILLMORE: May she languish for Mankind till she die, and be damn'd for that one Sin alone.

(*Enter two* BRAVOES, *and hang up a great Picture of* AN-GELICA'S, *against the Balcony, and two little ones at each side of the Door.*)

BELVILE: See there the fair Sign to the Inn, where a Man may lodge that's Fool enough to give her Price.

(WILLMORE *gazes on the Picture.*)

BLUNT: 'Sheartlikins, Gentlemen, what's this?

100 BELVILE: A famous Curtezan that's to be sold.

BLUNT: How! to be sold! nay then I have nothing to say to her—sold! what Impudence is practis'd in this Country?—With Order and Decency Whoring's established here by virtue of the Inquisition—Come let's be gone, I'm sure we're no

105 Chapmen for this Commodity.

FREDERICK: Thou art none, I'm sure, unless thou could'st have her in thy Bed at the Price of a Coach in the Street.

WILLMORE: How wondrous fair she is—a Thousand Crowns a Month—by Heaven as many Kingdoms were too little. A

110 plague of this Poverty—of which I ne'er complain, but when it hinders my Approach to Beauty, which Virtue ne'er could purchase.

(*Turns from the Picture.*)

BLUNT: What's this?—(*Reads.*) A *Thousand Crowns a Month!* —'Sheartlikins, here's a Sum! sure 'tis a mistake.

115 —Hark you, Friend, does she take or give so much by the Month!

FREDERICK: A Thousand Crowns! Why, 'tis a Portion for the *Infanta.*

BLUNT: Hark ye, Friends, won't she trust?

120 BRAVO: This is a Trade, Sir, that cannot live by Credit.

(*Enter* DON PEDRO *in Masquerade, follow'd by* STEPHANO.)

BELVILE: See, here's more Company, let's walk off a while.

(PEDRO *reads. Exeunt* ENGLISH. *Enter* ANGELICA *and* MO-RETTA *in the Balcony, and draw a Silk Curtain.*)

PEDRO: Fetch me a Thousand Crowns, I never wish to buy this Beauty at an easier Rate.

(*Passes off.*)

ANGELICA: Prithee what said those Fellows to thee?

125 BRAVO: Madam, the first were Admirers of Beauty only, but no purchasers; they were merry with your Price and Picture, laught at the Sum, and so past off.

ANGELICA: No matter, I'm not displeas'd with their rallying; their Wonder feeds my Vanity, and he that wishes to buy,

130 gives me more Pride, than he that gives my Price can make me Pleasure.

BRAVO: Madam, the last I knew thro all his disguises to be Don *Pedro,* Nephew to the General, and who was with him in *Pampelona.*

135 ANGELICA: Don *Pedro*! my old Gallant's Nephew! When his Uncle dy'd, he left him a vast Sum of Money; it is he who was

so in love with me at *Padua,* and who us'd to make the General so jealous.

MORETTA: Is this he that us'd to prance before our Window and take such care to shew himself an amorous Ass? if I am not 140 mistaken, he is the likeliest Man to give your Price.

ANGELICA: The Man is brave and generous, but of an Humour so uneasy and inconstant, that the victory over his Heart is as soon lost as won; a Slave that can add little to the Triumph of the Conqueror; but inconstancy's the Sin of all Mankind, 145 therefore I'm resolv'd that nothing but Gold shall charm my Heart.

MORETTA: I'm glad on't; 'tis only interest that Women of our Profession ought to consider: tho I wonder what has kept you from that general Disease of our Sex so long, I mean that of 150 being in love.

ANGELICA: A kind, but sullen Star, under which I had the Happiness to be born; yet I have had no time for Love; the bravest and noblest of Mankind have purchas'd my Favours at so dear a Rate, as if no Coin but Gold were current with our Trade— 155 But here's Don *Pedro* again, fetch me my Lute—for 'tis for him or Don *Antonio* the Vice-Roy's Son, that I have spread my Nets.

(*Enter at one Door Don* PEDRO, *and* STEPHANO; *Don* ANTONIO *and* DIEGO [*his page*], *at the other Door, with* PEOPLE *following him in Masquerade, antickly attir'd, some with Musick: they both go up to the Picture.*)

ANTONIO: A thousand Crowns! had not the Painter flatter'd her, I should not think it dear. 160

PEDRO: Flatter'd her! by Heaven he cannot. I have seen the Original, nor is there one Charm here more than adorns her Face and Eyes; all this soft and sweet, with a certain languishing Air, that no Artist can represent.

ANTONIO: What I heard of her Beauty before had fir'd my Soul, 165 but this confirmation of it has blown it into a flame.

PEDRO: Ha!

PAGE: Sir, I have known you throw away a Thousand Crowns on a worse Face, and tho y' are near your Marriage, you may venture a little Love here; *Florinda*—will not miss it. 170

PEDRO: Ha! *Florinda*! Sure 'tis *Antonio*.

(*Aside.*)

ANTONIO: *Florinda*! name not those distant Joys, there's not one thought of her will check my Passion here.

PEDRO: *Florinda* scorn'd! and all my Hopes defeated of the Possession of *Angelica*! (*A noise of a Lute above. Antonio gazes* 175 *up*) Her Injuries by Heaven he shall not boast of.

(*Song to a Lute above.*)

SONG

When Damon *first began to love,*
He languisht in a soft Desire,
And knew not how the Gods to move,
To lessen or increase his Fire,
For Caelia *in her charming Eyes* 180
Wore all Love's Sweet, and all his Cruelties.

II

But as beneath a Shade he lay,
Weaving of Flow'rs for Caelia's *Hair,*
She chanc'd to lead her Flock that way, 185

And saw the am'rous Shepherd there.
She gaz'd around upon the Place,
And saw the Grove (resembling Night)
To all the Joys of Love invite,
190   *Whilst guilty Smiles and Blushes drest her Face..*
At this the bashful Youth all Transport grew,
And with kind Force he taught the Virgin how
To yield what all his Sighs cou'd never do.

ANTONIO: By Heav'n she's charming fair!

(ANGELICA *throws open the Curtains, and bows to* ANTONIO, *who pulls off his Vizard, and bows and blows up Kisses.* PEDRO *unseen looks in his Face.*)

195 PEDRO: 'Tis he, the false *Antonio!*
ANTONIO: Friend, where must I pay my offering of Love?

(*To the* BRAVO.)

   My Thousand Crowns I mean.
PEDRO: That offering I have design'd to make,
   And yours will come too late.
200 ANTONIO: Prithee be gone, I shall grow angry else,
   And then thou art not safe.
PEDRO: My Anger may be fatal, Sir, as yours;
   And he that enters here may prove this Truth.
ANTONIO: I know not who thou art, but I am sure thou'rt worth
205   my killing, and aiming at *Angelica.*

(*They draw and fight.*)

(*Enter* WILLMORE *and* BLUNT, *who draw and part 'em.*)

BLUNT: 'Sheartlikins, here's fine doings.
WILLMORE: Tilting for the Wench I'm sure—nay gad, if that
   wou'd win her, I have as good a Sword as the best of ye—Put
   up—put up, and take another time and place, for this is de-
210   sign'd for Lovers only.

(*They all put up.*)

PEDRO: We are prevented; dare you meet me to morrow on the
   Molo?
   For I've a Title to a better quarrel,
   That of *Florinda,* in whose credulous Heart
215   Thou'st make an Int'rest, and destroy'd my Hopes.
ANTONIO: Dare?
   I'll meet thee there as early as the Day.
PEDRO: We will come thus disguis'd, that whosoever chance to
   get the better, he may escape unknown.
220 ANTONIO: It shall be so.

(*Exit* PEDRO *and* STEPHANO.)

   Who shou'd this Rival be? unless the *English* Colonel, of
   whom I've often heard Don *Pedro* speak; it must be he, and
   time he were removed, who lays a Claim to all my Happiness.

(WILLMORE *having gaz'd all this while on the Picture, pulls down a little one.*)

WILLMORE: This posture's loose and negligent,
225   The sight on't wou'd beget a warm desire
   In Souls, whom Impotence and Age had chill'd.
   —This must along with me.
BRAVO: What means this rudeness, Sir?—restore the Picture.
ANTONIO: Ha! Rudeness committed to the fair *Angelica!*—
230   Restore the Picture, Sir.

WILLMORE: Indeed I will not, Sir.
ANTONIO: By Heav'n but you shall.
WILLMORE: Nay, do not shew your Sword; if you do, by this dear
   Beauty—I will shew mine too.
235 ANTONIO: What right can you pretend to't?
WILLMORE: That of Possession which I will maintain—you
   perhaps have 1000 Crowns to give for the Original.
ANTONIO: No matter, Sir, you shall restore the Picture.
ANGELICA: Oh, *Moretta!* what's the matter?

(ANGELICA *and* MORETTA *above.*)

ANTONIO: Or leave your Life behind.
240
WILLMORE: Death! you lye—I will do neither.
ANGELICA: Hold, I command you, if for me you fight.

(*They fight, the Spaniards join with* ANTONIO, BLUNT *laying on like mad. They leave off and bow.*)

WILLMORE: How heavenly fair she is!—ah Plague of her Price.
ANGELICA: You Sir in Buff, you that appear a Soldier, that first
   began this Insolence.
245
WILLMORE: 'Tis true, I did so, if you call it Insolence for a Man
   to preserve himself; I saw your charming Picture, and was
   wounded: quite thro my Soul each pointed Beauty ran; and
   wanting a Thousand Crowns to procure my Remedy, I laid
   this little Picture to my Bosom—which if you cannot allow
250
   me, I'll resign.
ANGELICA: No, you may keep the Trifle.
ANTONIO: You shall first ask my leave, and this.

(*Fight again as before.*)

(*Enter* BELVILE *and* FREDERICK *who join with the* ENGLISH.)

ANGELICA: Hold; will you ruin me?—*Biskey, Sebastian,* part
   them.
255

(*The* SPANIARDS *are beaten off.*)

MORETTA: Oh Madam, we're undone, a pox upon that rude
   Fellow, he's set on to ruin us: we shall never see good days, till
   all these fighting poor Rogues are sent to the Gallies.

(*Enter* BELVILE, BLUNT *and* WILLMORE, *with his shirt bloody.*)

BLUNT: 'Sheartlikins, beat me at this Sport, and I'll ne'er wear
   Sword more.
260
BELVILE: The Devil's in thee for a mad Fellow, thou art always
   one at an unlucky Adventure.—Come, let's be gone whilst
   we're safe, and remember these are *Spaniards,* a sort of People that know how to revenge an Affront.
FREDERICK: You bleed; I hope you are not wounded.
265

(*To* WILLMORE.)

WILLMORE: Not much:—a plague upon your Dons, if they fight
   no better they'll ne'er recover *Flanders.*—What the Devil
   was't to them that I took down the Picture?
BLUNT: Took it! 'Sheartlikins, we'll have the great one too; 'tis
   ours by Conquest.—Prithee, help me up, and I'll pull it
270
   down.—
ANGELICA: Stay, Sir, and e'er you affront me further, let me
   know how you durst commit this Outrage—To you I speak,
   Sir, for you appear like a Gentleman.
WILLMORE: To me, Madam?—Gentlemen, your Servant.
275

(BELVILE *stays him.*)

BELVILE: Is the Devil in thee? Do'st know the danger of entring the house of an incens'd Curtezan?

WILLMORE: I thank you for your care — but there are other matters in hand, there are, tho we have no great Temptation. —
280 Death! let me go.

FREDERICK: Yes, to your Lodging, if you will, but not in here. —
Damn these gay Harlots — by this Hand I'll have as sound and
handsome a Whore for a Patacoone. — Death, Man, she'll
murder thee.

285 WILLMORE: Oh! fear me not, shall I not venture where a Beauty
calls? a lovely charming Beauty? for fear of danger! when by
Heaven there's none so great as to long for her, whilst I want
Money to purchase her.

FREDERICK: Therefore 'tis loss of time, unless you had the thou-
290 sand Crowns to pay.

WILLMORE: It may be she may give a Favour, at least I shall have
the pleasure of saluting her when I enter, and when I depart.

BELVILE: Pox, she'll as soon lie with thee, as kiss thee, and
sooner stab than do either — you shall not go.

295 ANGELICA: Fear not, Sir, all I have to wound with, is my Eyes.

BLUNT: Let him go, 'Sheartlikins, I believe the Gentlewoman
means well.

BELVILE: Well, take thy Fortune, we'll expect you in the next
Street. — Farewell Fool, — farewell —

300 WILLMORE: B'ye Colonel —

(*Goes in.*)

FREDERICK: The Rogue's stark mad for a Wench.

(*Exeunt.*)

SCENE II

A Fine Chamber.

(*Enter* WILLMORE, ANGELICA, *and* MORETTA.)

ANGELICA: Insolent, Sir, how durst you pull down my Picture?

WILLMORE: Rather, how durst you set it up, to tempt poor amorous Mortals with so much Excellence? which I find you have
but too well consulted by the unmerciful price you set
5 upon't. — Is all this Heaven of Beauty shewn to move Despair
in those that cannot buy? and can you think the effects of that
Despair shou'd be less extravagant than I have shewn?

ANGELICA: I sent for you to ask my Pardon, Sir, not to aggravate
your Crime. — I thought I shou'd have seen you at my Feet
10 imploring it.

WILLMORE: You are deceived, I came to rail at you, and talk
such Truths, too, as shall let you see the Vanity of that Pride,
which taught you how to set such a Price on Sin. For such it
is, whilst that which is Love's due is meanly barter'd for.

15 ANGELICA: Ha, ha, ha, alas, good Captain, what pity 'tis your
edifying Doctrine will do no good upon me — *Moretta,* fetch
the Gentleman a Glass, and let him survey himself, to see
what Charms he has, — (*Aside in a soft tone.*) and guess my
Business.

20 MORETTA: He knows himself of old, I believe those Breeches
and he have been acquainted ever since he was beaten at
Worcester.

ANGELICA: Nay, do not abuse the poor Creature. —

MORETTA: Good Weather-beaten Corporal, will you march off?
we have no need of your Doctrine, tho you have of our Char- 25
ity; but at present we have no Scraps, we can afford no kindness for God's sake; in fine, Sirrah, the Price is too high i'th'
Mouth for you, therefore troop I say.

WILLMORE: Here, good Fore-Woman of the Shop, serve me,
and I'll be gone. 30

MORETTA: Keep it to pay your Landress, your Linen stinks of the
Gun-Room; for here's no selling by Retail.

WILLMORE: Thou hast sold plenty of thy stale Ware at a cheap
Rate.

MORETTA: Ay, the more silly kind Heart I, but this is an Age 35
wherein Beauty is at higher Rates. — In fine, you know the
price of this.

WILLMORE: I grant you 'tis here set down a thousand Crowns a
Month — Baud, take your black Lead and sum it up, that I
may have a Pistole-worth of these vain gay things, and I'll 40
trouble you no more.

MORETTA: Pox on him, he'll fret me to Death: — abominable
Fellow, I tell thee, we only sell by the whole Piece.

WILLMORE: 'Tis very hard, the whole Cargo or nothing — Faith,
Madam, my Stock will not reach it, I cannot be your Chap- 45
man. — Yet I have Countrymen in Town, Merchants of Love,
like me; I'll see if they'll put for a share, we cannot lose much
by it, and what we have no use for, we'll sell upon the *Friday's*
Mart, at — *Who gives more?* I am studying, Madam, how to
purchase you, tho at present I am unprovided of Money. 50

ANGELICA: Sure, this from any other Man would anger me —
nor shall he know the Conquest he has made — Poor angry
Man, how I despise this railing.

WILLMORE: Yes, I am poor — but I'm a Gentleman,
And one that scorns this Baseness which you practise. 55
Poor as I am, I would not sell my self,
No, not to gain your charming high-priz'd Person.
Tho I admire you strangely for your Beauty,
Yet I contemn your Mind.
— And yet I wou'd at any rate enjoy you; 60
At your own rate — but cannot — See here
The only Sum I can command on Earth;
I know not where to eat when this is gone:
Yet such a Slave I am to Love and Beauty,
This last reserve I'll sacrifice to enjoy you. 65
— Nay, do not frown, I know you are to be bought,
And wou'd be bought by me, by me,
For a mean trifling Sum, if I could pay it down.
Which happy knowledge I will still repeat,
And lay it to my Heart, it has a Virtue in't, 70
And soon will cure those Wounds your Eyes have made.
— And yet — there's something so divinely powerful there —
Nay, I will gaze — to let you see my Strength.

(*Holds her, looks on her, and pauses and sighs.*)

By Heaven, bright Creature — I would not for the World
Thy Fame were half so fair as thy Face. 75

(*Turns her away from him.*)

ANGELICA: (*Aside.*) His words go thro me to the very Soul.
— If you have nothing else to say to me.

WILLMORE: Yes, you shall hear how infamous you are —
  For which I do not hate thee:
80 But that secures my Heart, and all the Flames it feels
  Are but so many Lusts,
  I know it by their sudden bold intrusion.
  The Fire's impatient and betrays, 'tis false —
  For had it been the purer Flame of Love,
85 I should have pin'd and languish'd at your Feet,
  E'er found the Impudence to have discover'd it.
  I now dare stand your Scorn, and your Denial.

MORETTA: Sure she's bewitcht, that you can stand thus tamely,
  and hear his saucy railing. — Sirrah, will you be gone?

90 ANGELICA: (To MORETTA.) How dare you take this liberty? —
  Withdraw. — Pray, tell me, Sir, are not you guilty of the same
  mercenary Crime? When a Lady is proposed to you for a
  Wife, you never ask, how fair, discreet, or virtuous she is; but
  what's her Fortune — which if but small, you cry — She will
95 not do my business — and basely leave her, tho she languish
  for you. — Say, is not this as poor?

WILLMORE: It is a barbarous Custom, which I will scorn to defend in our Sex, and do despise in yours.

ANGELICA: Thou art a brave Fellow! put up thy Gold, and
100 know,
  That were thy Fortune large, as is thy Soul,
  Thou shouldst not buy my Love,
  Couldst thou forget those mean Effects of Vanity,
  Which set me out to sale; and as a Lover, prize
105 My yielding Joys.
  Canst thou believe they'l be entirely thine,
  Without considering they were mercenary?

WILLMORE: (Aside.) I cannot tell, I must bethink me first —
  ha, Death, I'm going to believe her.

110 ANGELICA: Prithee, confirm that Faith — or if thou canst
  not — flatter me a little, 'twill please me from thy Mouth.

WILLMORE: Curse on thy charming Tongue! dost thou return
  My feign'd Contempt with so much subtilty?

(Aside.)

  Thou'st found the easiest way into my Heart,
115 Tho I yet know that all thou say'st is false.

(Turning from her in a Rage.)

ANGELICA: By all that's good 'tis real,
  I never lov'd before, tho oft a Mistress.
  — Shall my first Vows be slighted?

WILLMORE: (Aside.) What can she mean?
120 ANGELICA: (In an angry tone.) I find you cannot credit me.
WILLMORE: I know you take me for an errant Ass,
  An Ass that may be sooth'd into Belief,
  And then be us'd at pleasure.
  — But, Madam, I have been so often cheated
125 By perjur'd, soft, deluding Hypocrites,
  That I've no Faith left for the cozening Sex,
  Especially for Women of your Trade.

ANGELICA: The low esteem you have of me, perhaps
  May bring my Heart again:
130 For I have Pride that yet surmounts my Love.

(She turns with Pride, he holds her.)

WILLMORE: Throw off this Pride, this Enemy to Bliss,
  And shew the Power of Love: 'tis with those Arms
  I can be only vanquist, made a Slave.

ANGELICA: Is all my mighty Expectation vanisht?
  — No, I will not hear thee talk, — thou hast a Charm   135
  In every word, that draws my Heart away.
  And all the thousand Trophies I design'd,
  Thou hast undone — Why are thou soft?
  Thy Looks are bravely rough, and meant for War.
  Could thou not storm on still?   140
  I then perhaps had been as free as thou.

WILLMORE: (Aside.) Death! how she throws her Fire about my
  Soul!
  — Take heed, fair Creature, how you raise my Hopes,
  Which once assum'd pretend to all Dominion.
  There's not a Joy thou hast in store   145
  I shall not then command:
  For which I'll pay thee back my Soul, my Life.
  Come, let's begin th' account this happy minute.

ANGELICA: And will you pay me then the Price I ask?
WILLMORE: Oh, why dost thou draw me from an awful   150
  Worship,
  By shewing thou art no Divinity?
  Conceal the Fiend, and shew me all the Angel;
  Keep me but ignorant, and I'll be devout,
  And pay my Vows for ever at this Shrine.

(Kneels, and kisses her Hand.)

ANGELICA: The Pay I mean is but thy Love for mine. — Can you   155
  give that?

WILLMORE: Intirely — come, let's withdraw: where I'll renew my
  vows, — and breathe 'em with such Ardour, thou shalt not
  doubt my Zeal.

ANGELICA: Thou hast a Power too strong to be resisted.   160

(Exit WILLMORE and ANGELICA.)

MORETTA: Now my Curse go with you — Is all our Project fallen
  to this? to love the only Enemy to our Trade? Nay, to love
  such a Shameroon, a very Beggar; nay, a Pirate-Beggar,
  whose Business is to rifle and be gone, a No-Purchase, No-
  Pay tatterdemalion, an English Piccaroon; a Rogue that fights   165
  for daily Drink, and takes a Pride in being loyally lousy — Oh,
  I could curse now, if I durst — This is the Fate of most
  Whores.

Trophies, which from believing Fops we win,
Are Spoils to those who cozen us again.   170

— ACT THREE —

SCENE I

A Street.

(*Enter* FLORINDA, VALERIA, HELLENA, *in Antick different Dresses from what they were in before,* CALLIS *attending.*)

FLORINDA: I wonder what should make my Brother in so ill a
  Humour: I hope he has not found out our Ramble this
  Morning.

HELLENA: No, if he had, we should have heard on't at both
  Ears, and have been mew'd up this Afternoon; which I would   5

---

163 **shameroon** A trickster, a cozening rascal

not for the World should have happen'd — Hey ho! I'm sad as a Lover's Lute.

VALERIA: Well, methinks we have learnt this Trade of Gipsies as readily as if we had been bred upon the Road to *Loretto*: and yes I did so fumble, when I told the Stranger his Fortune, that I was afraid I should have told my own and yours by mistake — But methinks *Hellena* has been very serious ever since.

FLORINDA: I would give my Garters she were in love, to be reveng'd upon her, for abusing me — How is't, *Hellena*?

HELLENA: Ah! — would I had never seen my mad Monsieur — and yet for all your laughing I am not in love — and yet this small Acquaintance, o'my Conscience, will never out of my Head.

VALERIA: Ha, ha, ha — I laugh to think how thou art fitted with a Lover, a Fellow that, I warrant, loves every new Face he sees.

HELLENA: Hum — he has not kept his Word with me here — and may be taken up — that thought is not very pleasant to me — what the Duce should this be now that I feel?

VALERIA: What is't like?

HELLENA: Nay, the Lord knows — but if I should be hanged, I cannot chuse but be angry and afraid, when I think that mad Fellow should be in love with any Body but me — What to think of my self I know not — Would I could meet with some true damn'd Gipsy, that I might know my Fortune.

VALERIA: Know it! why there's nothing so easy; thou wilt love this wandering Inconstant till thou find'st thy self hanged about his Neck, and then be as mad to get free again.

FLORINDA: Yes, *Valeria*; we shall see her bestride his Baggage-horse, and follow him to the Campaign.

HELLENA: So, so; now you are provided for, there's no care taken of poor me — But since you have set my Heart a wishing, I am resolv'd to know for what. I will not die of the Pip, so I will not.

FLORINDA: Art thou mad to talk so? Who will like thee well enough to have thee, that hears what a mad Wench thou art?

HELLENA: Like me! I don't intend every he that likes me shall have me, but he that I like: I shou'd have staid in the Nunnery still, if I had lik'd my Lady Abbess as well as she lik'd me. No, I came thence, not (as my wise Brother imagines) to take an eternal Farewel of the World, but to love and to be belov'd; and I will be belov'd, or I'll get one of your Men, so I will.

VALERIA: Am I put into the Number of Lovers?

HELLENA: You! my Couz, I know thou art too good natur'd to leave us in any Design: Thou wou't venture a Cast, tho thou comest off a Loser, especially with such a Gamester — I observ'd your Man, and your willing ears incline that way; and if you are not a Lover, 'tis an Art soon learnt — that I find.

(*Sighs.*)

FLORINDA: I wonder how you learnt to love so easily, I had a thousand Charms to meet my Eyes and Ears, e'er I cou'd yield; and 'twas the knowledge of *Belvile's* Merit, not the surprising Person, took my Soul — Thou art too rash to give a Heart at first sight.

HELLENA: Hang your considering Lover; I ne'er thought beyond the Fancy, that 'twas a very pretty, idle, silly kind of Pleasure to pass ones time with, to write little, soft, nonsensical Billets, and with great difficulty and danger receive Answers; in which I shall have my Beauty prais'd, my Wit admir'd (tho little or none) and have the Vanity and Power to know I am desirable; then I have the more Inclination that way, because

I am to be a Nun, and so shall not be suspected to have any such earthly Thoughts about me — But when I walk thus — and sigh thus — they'll think my Mind's upon my Monastery, and cry, how happy 'tis she's so resolv'd! — But not a Word of Man.

FLORINDA: What a mad Creature's this!

HELLENA: I'll warrant, if my Brother hears either of you sigh, he cries (gravely) — I fear you have the Indiscretion to be in love, but take heed of the Honour of our House, and your own unspotted Fame; and so he conjures on till he has laid the soft-wing'd God in your Hearts, or broke the Birds-nest — But see here comes your Lover: but where's my inconstant? let's stop aside, and we may learn something.

(*Go aside.*)

(*Enter* BELVILE, FREDERICK *and* BLUNT.)

BELVILE: What mean this? the Picture's taken in.

BLUNT: It may be the Wench is good-natur'd, and will be kind *gratis*. Your Friend's a proper handsom Fellow.

BELVILE: I rather think she has cut his Throat and is fled: I am mad he should throw himself into Dangers — Pox on't, I shall want him to night — let's knock and ask for him.

HELLENA: My heart goes a-pit a-pat, for fear 'tis my Man they talk of.

(*Knock*, MORETTA *above.*)

What would you have?

BELVILE: Tell the Stranger that enter'd here about two Hours ago, that his Friends stay here for him.

MORETTA: A Curse upon him for *Moretta*, would he were at the Devil — but he's coming to you.

(*Enter* WILLMORE.)

HELLENA: I, I, 'tis he. Oh how this vexes me.

BELVILE: And how, and how, dear Lad, has Fortune smil'd? Are we to break her Windows, or raise up Altars to her! hah!

WILLMORE: Does not my Fortune sit triumphant on my Brow? dost not see the little wanton God there all gay and smiling? have I not an Air about my Face and Eyes, that distinguish me from the Croud of common Lovers? By Heav'n, *Cupid's* Quiver has not half so many Darts as her Eyes — Oh such a *Bona Roba*, to sleep in her Arms is lying in Fresco, all perfum'd Air about me.

HELLENA: (*Aside.*) Here's fine encouragement for me to fool on.

WILLMORE: Hark ye, where didst thou purchase that rich Canary we drank to-day? Tell me, that I may adore the Spigot, and sacrifice to the Butt: the Juice was divine, into which I must dip my Rosary, and then bless all things that I would have bold or fortunate.

BELVILE: Well, Sir, let's go take a Bottle, and hear the Story of your Success.

FREDERICK: Would not *French* Wine do better?

WILLMORE: Damn the hungry Balderdash; cheerful Sack has a generous Virtue in't, inspiring a successful Confidence, gives Eloquence to the Tongue, and Vigour to the Soul; and has in a few Hours compleated all my Hopes and Wishes. There's nothing left to raise a new Desire in me — Come let's be gay and wanton — and, Gentlemen, study, study what you want, for here are Friends, — that will supply, Gentlemen, — hark! what a charming sound they make — 'tis he and she Gold whilst here, shall beget new Pleasures every moment.

BLUNT: But hark ye, Sir, you are not married, are you?

120 WILLMORE: All the Honey of Matrimony, but none of the Sting, Friend.

BLUNT: 'Sheartlikins, thou'rt a fortunate Rogue.

WILLMORE: I am so, Sir, let these inform you. —Ha, how sweetly they chime! Pox of Poverty, it makes a Man a Slave,
125 makes Wit and Honour sneak, my Soul grew lean and rusty for want of Credit.

BLUNT: 'Sheartlikins, this I like well, it looks like my lucky Bargain! Oh how I long for the Approach of my Squire, that is to conduct me to her House again. Why! here's two provided
130 for.

FREDERICK: By this light y're happy Men.

BLUNT: Fortune is pleased to smile on us, Gentlemen, —to smile on us.

(Enter SANCHO, and pulls BLUNT by the Sleeve. They go aside.)

SANCHO: Sir, my Lady expects you —she has remov'd all that
135 might oppose your Will and Pleasure —and is impatient till you come.

BLUNT: Sir, I'll attend you —Oh the happiest Rogue! I'll take no leave, lest they either dog me, or stay me.

(Exit with SANCHO.)

BELVILE: But then the little Gipsy is forgot?

140 WILLMORE: A Mischief on thee for putting her into my thoughts; I had quite forgot her else, and this Night's Debauch had drunk her quite down.

HELLENA: Had it so, good Captain?

(Claps him on the Back.)

WILLMORE: Ha! I hope she did not hear.

145 HELLENA: What, afraid of such a Champion!

WILLMORE: Oh! you're a fine Lady of your word, are you not? to make a Man languish a whole day —

HELLENA: In tedious search of me.

WILLMORE: Egad, Child, thou'rt in the right, hadst thou seen
150 what a melancholy Dog I have been ever since I was a Lover, how I have walkt the Streets like a *Capuchin*, with my Hands in my Sleeves —Faith, Sweetheart, thou wouldst pity me.

HELLENA: Now, if I should be hang'd, I can't be angry with him, he dissembles so heartily —Alas, good Captain, what pains
155 you have taken —Now were I ungrateful not to reward so true a Servant.

WILLMORE: Poor Soul! that's kindly said, I see thou bearest a Conscience —come then for a beginning shew me thy dear Face.

160 HELLENA: I'm afraid, my small Acquaintance, you have been staying that swinging stomach you boasted of this morning; I remember then my little Collation would have gone down with you, without the Sauce of a handsom Face —Is your Stomach so quesy now?

165 WILLMORE: Faith long fasting, Child, spoils a Man's Appetite — yet if you durst treat, I could so lay about me still.

HELLENA: And would you fall to, before a Priest says Grace?

WILLMORE: Oh fie, fie, what an old out-of-fashion'd thing hast thou nam'd? Thou could'st not dash me more out of Counte-
170 nance, shouldst thou shew me an ugly Face.

(Whilst he is seemingly courting HELLENA, enter ANGELICA, MORETTA, BISKEY, and SEBASTIAN, all in Masquerade: AN-GELICA sees WILLMORE and starts.)

ANGELICA: Heavens, is't he? and passionately fond to see another Woman?

MORETTA: What cou'd you expect less from such a Swaggerer?

ANGELICA: Expect! as much as I paid him, a Heart intire,
Which I had pride enough to think when e'er I gave   175
It would have rais'd the Man above the Vulgar,
Made him all Soul, and that all soft and constant.

HELLENA: You see, Captain, how willing I am to be Friends with you, till Time and Ill-luck make us Lovers; and ask you the Question first, rather than put your Modesty to the blush,   180
by asking me: for alas, I know you Captains are such strict Men, severe Observers of your Vows to Chastity, that 'twill be hard to prevail with your tender Conscience to marry a young willing Maid.

WILLMORE: Do not abuse me, for fear I should take thee at thy   185
word, and marry thee indeed, which I'm sure will be Revenge sufficient.

HELLENA: O' my Conscience, that will be our Destiny, because we are both of one humour; I am as inconstant as you, for I have considered, Captain, that a handsom Woman has a   190
great deal to do whilst her Face is good, for then is our Harvest-time to gather Friends; and should I in these days of my Youth, catch a fit of foolish Constancy, I were undone; 'tis loitering by day-light in our great Journey: therefore declare, I'll allow but one year for Love, one year for Indifference, and   195
one year for Hate —and then —go hang your self —for I professe myself the gay, the kind, and the inconstant —the Devil's in't if this won't please you.

WILLMORE: Oh most damnably! —I have a Heart with a hole quite thro it too, no Prison like mine to keep a Mistress in.   200

ANGELICA: *(Aside.)* Purjur'd Man! how I believe thee now!

HELLENA: Well, I see our Business as well as Humours are alike, yours to cozen as many Maids as will trust you, and I as many Men as have Faith —See if I have not as desperate a lying look, as you can have for the heart of you.   205

(Pulls off her Vizard; he starts.)

—How do you like it, Captain?

WILLMORE: Like it! by Heav'n, I never saw so much Beauty. Oh the Charms of those sprightly black Eyes, that strangely fair Face, full of Smiles and Dimples! those soft round melting cherry Lips! and small even white Teeth! not to be exprest, but   210
silently adored! —Oh one Look more, and strike me dumb, or I shall repeat nothing else till I am mad.

(He seems to court her to pull off her Vizard: she refuses.)

ANGELICA: I can endure no more —nor is it fit to interrupt him; for if I do, my Jealousy has so destroy'd my Reason, —I shall undo him —Therefore I'll retire. And you *Sebastian (To one*   215
of her BRAVOES) follow that Woman, and learn who 'tis; while you tell the Fugitive, I would speak to him instantly.

(To the other BRAVO. Exit.)

(This while FLORINDA is talking to BELVILE, who stands sullenly. FREDERICK courting VALERIA.)

VALERIA: Prithee, dear Stranger, be not so sullen; for tho you have lost your Love, you see my Friend frankly offers you hers, to play with in the mean time.   220

BELVILE: Faith, Madam, I am sorry I can't play at her Game.

FREDERICK: Pray leave your Intercession, and mind your own

Affair, they'll better agree apart; he's a model Sigher in Company, but alone no Woman escapes him.

225 FLORINDA: Sure he does but rally — yet if it should be true — I'll tempt him farther — Believe me, noble Stranger, I'm no common Mistress — and for a little proof on't — wear this Jewel — nay, take it, Sir, 'tis right, and Bills of Exchange may sometimes miscarry.

230 BELVILE: Madam, why am I chose out of all Mankind to be the Object of your Bounty?

VALERIA: There's another civil Question askt.

FREDERICK: Pox of's Modesty, it spoils his own Markets, and hinders mine.

235 FLORINDA: Sir, from my Window I have often seen you; and Women of Quality have so few opportunities for Love, that we ought to lose none.

FREDERICK: Ay, this is something! here's a Woman! — When shall I be blest with so much kindness from your fair Mouth?

240 (Aside to BELVILE.) Take the Jewel, Fool.

BELVILE: You tempt me strangely, Madam, every way.

FLORINDA: (Aside.) So, if I find him false, my whole Repose is gone.

BELVILE: And but for a Vow I've made to a very fine Lady, this

245 Goodness had subdu'd me.

FREDERICK: Pox on't be kind, in pity to me be kind, for I am to thrive here but as you treat her Friend.

HELLENA: Tell me what did you in yonder House, and I'll unmasque.

250 WILLMORE: Yonder House — oh — I went to — a — to — why, there's a Friend of mine lives there.

HELLENA: What a she, or a he Friend?

WILLMORE: A Man upon my Honour! a Man — A she Friend! no, no, Madam, you have done my Business, I thank you.

255 HELLENA: And was't your Man Friend, that had more Darts in's Eyes than *Cupid* carries in a whole Budget of Arrows?

WILLMORE: So —

HELLENA: Ah such a *Bona Roba*: to be in her Arms is lying in *Fresco*, all perfumed Air about me — Was this your Man

260 Friend too?

WILLMORE: So —

HELLENA: That gave you the He, and the She — Gold, that begets young Pleasures.

WILLMORE: Well, well, Madam, then you see there are Ladies

265 in the World, that will not be cruel — there are, Madam, there are —

HELLENA: And there be Men too as fine, wild, inconstant Fellows as your self, there be, Captain, there be, if you go to that now — therefore I'm resolv'd —

270 WILLMORE: Oh!

HELLENA: To see your Face no more —

WILLMORE: Oh!

HELLENA: Till to morrow.

WILLMORE: Egad you frighted me.

275 HELLENA: Nor then neither, unless you'l swear never to see that Lady more.

WILLMORE: See her! — why! never to think of Womankind again?

HELLENA: Kneel, and swear.

(Kneels, she gives him her hand.)

280 WILLMORE: I do, never to think — to see — to love — nor lie with any but thy self.

HELLENA: Kiss the Book.

WILLMORE: Oh, most religiously.

(Kisses her Hand.)

HELLENA: Now what a wicked Creature am I, to damn a proper

285 Fellow.

CALLIS: (To FLORINDA.) Madam, I'll stay no longer, 'tis e'en dark.

FLORINDA: However, Sir, I'll leave this with you — that when I'm gone, you may repent the opportunity you have lost by

290 your modesty.

(Gives him the Jewel, which is her Picture, and Exits. He gazes after her.)

WILLMORE: 'Twill be an Age till to morrow, — and till then I will most impatiently expect you — Adieu, my dear pretty Angel.

(Exeunt all the WOMEN.)

BELVILE: Ha! *Florinda's* Picture! 'twas she her self — what a dull Dog was I? I would have given the World for one minute's discourse with her. —

295

FREDERICK: This comes of your Modesty, — ah pox on your Vow, 'twas ten to one but we had lost the Jewel by't.

BELVILE: *Willmore!* the blessed'st Opportunity lost! — *Florinda*, Friends, *Florinda*!

WILLMORE: Ah Rogue! such black Eyes, such a Face, such a 300 Mouth, such Teeth, — and so much Wit!

BELVILE: All, all, and a thousand Charms besides.

WILLMORE: Why, dost thou know her?

BELVILE: Know her! ay, ay, and a Pox take me with all my Heart for being modest.

305

WILLMORE: But hark ye, Friend of mine, are you my Rival? and have I been only beating the Bush all this while?

BELVILE: I understand thee not — I'm mad — see here —

(Shews the Picture.)

WILLMORE: Ha! whose Picture is this? — 'tis a fine Wench.

FREDERICK: The Colonel's Mistress, Sir. 310

WILLMORE: Oh, oh, here — I thought it had been another Prize — come, come, a Bottle will set thee right again.

(Gives the Picture back.)

BELVILE: I am content to try, and by that time 'twill be late enough for our Design.

WILLMORE: Agreed. 315

Love does all day the Soul's great Empire keep,
But Wine at night lulls the soft God asleep.

(Exeunt.)

SCENE II

LUCETTA's *House.*

(Enter BLUNT *and* LUCETTA *with a Light.*)

LUCETTA: Now we are safe and free, no fears of the coming home of my old jealous Husband, which made me a little thoughtful when you came in first — but now Love is all the business of my Soul.

BLUNT: (Aside.) I am transported — Pox on't, that I had but some 5 fine things to say to her, such as Lovers use — I was a Fool not to learn of *Frederick* a little by Heart before I came — something I must say. —

'Sheartlikins, sweet Soul, I am not us'd to complement, but
10   I'm an honest Gentleman, and thy humble Servant.

LUCETTA: I have nothing to pay for so great a Favour, but such a Love as cannot but be great, since at first sight of that sweet Face and Shape it made me your absolute Captive.

BLUNT: *(Aside.)* Kind heart, how prettily she talks! Egad I'll
15   show her Husband a *Spanish* Trick; send him out of the World, and marry her: she's damnably in love with me, and will ne'er mind Settlements, and so there's that sav'd.

LUCETTA: Well, Sir, I'll go and undress me, and be with you instantly.

20   BLUNT: Make haste then, for 'dsheartlikins, dear Soul, thou canst not guess at the pain of a longing Lover, when his Joys are drawn within the compass of a few minutes.

LUCETTA: You speak my Sense, and I'll make haste to provide it.

(Exit.)

BLUNT: 'Tis a rare Girl, and this one night's enjoyment with her
25   will be worth all the days I ever past in Essex. — Would she'd go with me into *England*, tho to say truth, there's plenty of Whores there already. — But a pox on 'em they are such mercenary prodigal Whores, that they want such a one as this, that's free and generous, to give 'em good Examples: — Why,
30   what a House she has! how rich and fine!

(Enter SANCHO.*)*

SANCHO: Sir, my Lady has sent me to conduct you to her Chamber.

BLUNT: Sir, I shall be proud to follow — Here's one of her Servants too: 'dsheartlikins, by his Garb and Gravity he might be
35   a Justice of Peace in *Essex*, and is but a Pimp here.

(Exeunt.)

(The Scene changes to a Chamber with an Alcove-Bed in it, a Table, &c. LUCETTA *in Bed. Enter* SANCHO *and* BLUNT, *who takes the Candle of* SANCHO *at the Door.)*

SANCHO: Sir, my Commission reaches no farther.

BLUNT: Sir, I'll excuse your Complement: — what, in Bed, my sweet Mistress?

LUCETTA: You see, I still out-do you in kindness.

40   BLUNT: And thou shalt see what haste I'll make to quit scores — oh the luckiest Rogue!

(Undresses himself.)

LUCETTA: Shou'd you be false or cruel now!

BLUNT: False, 'Sheartlikins, what dost thou take me for a *Jew*? an insensible Heathen, — A Pox of thy old jealous Husband:
45   and he were dead, egad, sweet Soul, it shou'd be none of my fault, if I did not marry thee.

LUCETTA: It never shou'd be mine.

BLUNT: Good Soul, I'm the fortunatest Dog!

LUCETTA: Are you not undrest yet?

50   BLUNT: As much as my Impatience will permit.

(Goes towards the Bed in his Shirt and Drawers.)

LUCETTA: Hold, Sir, put out the Light, it may betray us else.

BLUNT: Any thing, I need no other Light but that of thine Eyes! — *(Aside.)* 'sheartlikins, there I think I had it.

(Puts out the Candle, the Bed descends, he gropes about to find it.)

— Why — why — where am I got? what, not yet? — where are
55   your sweetest? — ah, the Rogue's silent now — a pretty Love-trick this — how she'll laugh at me anon! — you need not, my dear Rogue! you need not! I'm all on a fire already — come, come, now call me in for pity — Sure I'm enchanted! I have been round the Chamber, and can find neither Woman, nor
60   Bed — I lockt the Door, I'm sure she cannot go that way; or if she cou'd, the Bed cou'd not — Enough, enough, my pretty Wanton, do not carry the Jest too far — Ha, betray'd! Dogs! Rogues! Pimps! help! help!

(Lights on a Trap, and is let down. Enter LUCETTA, PHILIPPO, *and* SANCHO *with a Light.)*

PHILIPPO: Ha, ha, ha, he's dispatcht finely.

LUCETTA: Now, Sir, had I been coy, we had mist of this Booty.   65

PHILIPPO: Nay when I saw 'twas a substantial Fool, I was mollified; but when you doat upon a Serenading Coxcomb, upon a Face, fine Clothes, and a Lute, it makes me rage.

LUCETTA: You know I never was guilty of that Folly, my dear *Philippo*, but with your self — But come let's see what we have   70
got by this.

PHILIPPO: A rich Coat! — Sword and Hat! — these Breeches too — are well lin'd! — see here a Gold Watch! — a Purse — ha! Gold! — at least two hundred Pistoles! a bunch of Diamond Rings; and one with the Family Arms! — a Gold Box! — with a   75
Medal of his King! and his Lady Mother's Picture! — these were sacred Reliques, believe me! — see, the Wasteband of his Breeches have a Mine of Gold! — Old Queen *Bess's*. We have a Quarrel to her ever since *Eighty Eight*, and may therefore justify the Theft, the Inquisition might have committed it.   80

LUCETTA: See, a Bracelet of bow'd Gold, these his Sister ty'd about his Arm at parting — but well — for all this, I fear his being a Stranger may make a noise, and hinder our Trade with them hereafter.

PHILIPPO: That's our security; he is not only a Stranger to us, but   85
to the Country too — the Common-Shore into which he is descended, thou know'st, conducts him into another Street, which this Light will hinder him from ever finding again — he knows neither your Name, nor the Street where your House is, nay, nor the way to his own Lodgings.   90

LUCETTA: And art not thou an unmerciful Rogue, not to afford him one Night for all this? — I should not have been such a *Jew*.

PHILIPPO: Blame me not, *Lucetta*, to keep as much of thee as I can to my self — come, that thought makes me wanton, —   95
let's to Bed, — *Sancho*, lock up these.

This is the Fleece which Fools do bear,
Design'd for witty Man to sheer.

(Exeunt.)

(The Scene changes, and discovers BLUNT, *creeping out of a Common Shore, his Face, &c., all dirty.)*

BLUNT: Oh Lord!

(Climbing up.)

81 **bow'd Gold** Bowed is still used in the North of England for bent: 'A bowed pin'

100 I am got out at last, and (which is a Miracle) without a Clue—
and now to Damning and Cursing—but if that would ease
me, where shall I begin? with my Fortune, my self, or the
Queen that cozen'd me—What a dog was I to believe in
Women! Oh Coxcomb—ignorant conceited Coxcomb! to
105 fancy she cou'd be enamour'd with my Person, at the first
sight enamour'd—Oh, I'm a cursed Puppy, 'tis plain, Fool
was writ upon my Forehead, she perceiv'd it,—saw the *Essex*
Calf there—for what Allurements could there be in this
Countenance? which I can indure, because I'm acquainted
110 with it—Oh, dull silly Dog! to be thus sooth'd into a Cozening! Had I been drunk, I might fondly have credited the
young Quean! but as I was in my right Wits, to be thus
cheated, confirms I am a dull believing *English* Country
Fop.—But my Comrades! Death and the Devil, there's the
115 worst of all—then a Ballad will be sung to Morrow on the
Prado, to a lousy Tune of the enchanted Squire, and the anni-
hilated Damsel—But *Frederick* that Rogue, and the Colonel,
will abuse me beyond all Christian patience—had she left me
my Clothes, I have a Bill of Exchange at home wou'd have
120 sav'd my Credit—but now all hope is taken from me—Well,
I'll home (if I can find the way) with this Consolation, that I
am not the first kind believing Coxcomb; but there are, Gallants, many such good Natures amongst ye.

And tho you've better Arts to hide your Follies,
125 *Adsheartlikins y'are all as errant Cullies.*

SCENE III

The Garden, in the Night.

(Enter FLORINDA, *undress'd, with a Key, and a little Box.)*

FLORINDA: Well, thus far I'm in my way to Happiness; I have got
my self free from *Callis*; my Brother too, I find by yonder
light, is gone into his Cabinet, and thinks not of me: I have by
good Fortune got the Key of the Garden Back-door,—I'll
5 open it, to prevent *Belvile's* knocking,—a little noise will now
alarm my Brother. Now am I as fearful as a young Thief.
(Unlocks the Door)—Hark,—what noise is that?—Oh, 'twas
the Wind that plaid amongst the Boughs.—*Belvile* stays long,
methinks—it's time—stay—for fear of a surprize, I'll hide
10 these Jewels in yonder Jessamin.

(She goes to lay down the Box.)

(Enter WILLMORE *drunk.)*

WILLMORE: What the Devil is become of these Fellows, *Belvile*
and *Frederick*? They promis'd to stay at the next corner for
me, but who the Devil knows the corner of a full Moon?—
Now—whereabouts am I?—hah—what have we here? a
15 Garden!—a very convenient place to sleep in—hah—what
has God sent us here?—a Female—by this light, a Woman;
I'm a Dog if it be not a very Wench.—
FLORINDA: He's come!—hah—who's there?
WILLMORE: Sweet Soul, let me salute thy Shoe-string.
20 FLORINDA: 'Tis not my *Belvile*—good Heavens, I know him
not.—Who are you, and from whence come you!
WILLMORE: Prithee—prithee, Child—not so many hard Ques-
tions—let it suffice I am here, Child—Come, come kiss me.
FLORINDA: Good Gods! what luck is mine?

WILLMORE: Only good luck, Child, parlous good luck.—Come 25
hither,—'tis a delicate shining Wench,—by this Hand she's
perfum'd, and smells like any Nosegay.—Prithee, dear Soul,
let's not play the Fool, and lose time,—precious time—for as
Gad shall save me, I'm as honest a Fellow as breathes, tho I
am a little disguis'd at present.—Come, I say,—why, thou 30
may'st be free with me, I'll be very secret. I'll not boast who
'twas oblig'd me, not I—for hang me if I know thy Name.
FLORINDA: Heavens! what a filthy beast is this!
WILLMORE: I am so, and thou oughtst the sooner to lie with me
for that reason,—for look you, Child, there will be no Sin 35
in't, because 'twas neither design'd nor premeditated; 'tis pure
Accident on both sides—that's a certain thing now—Indeed
should I make love to you, and you vow Fidelity—and swear
and lye till you believ'd and yielded—Thou art therefore (as
thou art a good Christian) oblig'd in Conscience to deny me 40
nothing. Now—come, be kind, without any more idle
prating.
FLORINDA: Oh, I am ruin'd—wicked Man, unhand me.
WILLMORE: Wicked! Egad, Child, a Judge, were he young and
vigorous, and saw those Eyes of thine, would know 'twas they 45
gave the first blow—the first provocation.—Come, prithee
let's lose no time, I say—this is a fine convenient place.
FLORINDA: Sir, let me go, I conjure you, or I'll call out.
WILLMORE: Ay, ay, you were best to call Witness to see how
finely you treat me—do.— 50
FLORINDA: I'll cry Murder, Rape, or any thing, if you do not
instantly let me go.
WILLMORE: A Rape! Come, come, you lye, you Baggage, you
lye: What, I'll warrant you would fain have the World believe
now that you are not so forward as I. No, not you,—why at 55
this time of Night was your Cobweb-door set open, dear Spider—but to catch Flies?—Hah come—or I shall be damnably angry.—Why what a Coil is here.—
FLORINDA: Sir, can you think—
WILLMORE: That you'd do it for nothing? oh, oh, I find what 60
you'd be at—look here, here's a Pistole for you—here's a work
indeed—here—take it, I say.—
FLORINDA: For Heaven's sake, Sir, as you're a Gentleman—
WILLMORE: So—now—she would be wheedling me for
more—what, you will not take it then—you're resolv'd you 65
will not.—Come, come, take it, or I'll put it up again; for,
look ye, I never give more.—Why, how now, Mistress, are
you so high i'th' Mouth, a Pistole won't down with you?—
hah—why, what a work's here—in good time—come, no
struggling, be gone—But an y'are good at a dumb Wrestle, 70
I'm for ye,—look ye,—I'm for ye.—

(She struggles with him.)

(Enter BELVILE *and* FREDERICK.)

BELVILE: The Door is open, a Pox of this mad Fellow, I'm angry
that we've lost him, I durst have sworn he had follow'd us.
FREDERICK: But you were so hasty, Colonel, to be gone.
FLORINDA: Help, help,—Murder!—help—oh, I'm ruin'd. 75
BELVILE: Ha, sure that's *Florinda's* Voice.

(Comes up to them.)

—A Man! Villain, let go that Lady.

30 **disguis'd** A common phrase for drunk

(*A noise.*)

(WILLMORE *turns and draws*, FREDERICK *interposes*.)

FLORINDA: *Belvile!* Heavens! my Brother too is coming, and 'twill be impossible to escape. — *Belvile*, I conjure you to walk
80 under my Chamber-window, from whence I'll give you some instructions what to do — This rude Man has undone us.

(*Exit.*)

WILLMORE: *Belvile!*

(*Enter* PEDRO, STEPHANO, *and other Servants with Lights*.)

PEDRO: I'm betray'd; run, *Stephano*, and see if *Florinda* be safe.

(*Exit* STEPHANO.)

So who'er they be, all is not well, I'll to *Florinda's* Chamber.

(*They fight, and* PEDRO's *Party beats 'em out; going out, meets* STEPHANO.)

85 STEPHANO: You need not, Sir, the poor Lady's fast asleep, and thinks no harm: I wou'd not wake her, Sir, for fear of frightning her with your danger.
PEDRO: I'm glad she's there — Rascals, how came the Garden-Door open?
90 STEPHANO: That Question comes too late, Sir: some of my Fellow-Servants Masquerading I'll warrant.
PEDRO: Masquerading! a leud Custom to debauch our Youth — there's something more in this than I imagine.

(*Exeunt.*)

SCENE IV

Changes to the Street.

(*Enter* BELVILE *in Rage*, FREDERICK *holding him, and* WILLMORE *melancholy*.)

WILLMORE: Why, how the Devil shou'd I know *Florinda?*
BELVILE: Ah plague of your ignorance! if it had not been *Florinda*, must you be a Beast? — a Brute, a senseless Swine?
WILLMORE: Well, Sir, you see I am endu'd with Patience — I can
5 bear — the egad y're very free with me methinks, — I was in good hopes the Quarrel wou'd have been on my side, for so uncivilly interrupting me.
BELVILE: Peace, Brute, whilst thou'rt safe — oh, I'm distracted.
WILLMORE: Nay, nay, I'm an unlucky Dog, that's certain.
10 BELVILE: Ah curse upon the Star that rul'd my Birth! or whatsoever other Influence that makes me still so wretched.
WILLMORE: Thou break'st my Heart with these Complaints; there is no Star in fault, no Influence but Sack, the cursed Sack I drank.
15 FREDERICK: Why, how the Devil came you so drunk?
WILLMORE: Why, how the Devil came you so sober?
BELVILE: A curse upon his thin Skull, he was always before-hand that way.
FREDERICK: Prithee, dear Colonel, forgive him, he's sorry for
20 his fault.
BELVILE: He's always so after he has done a mischief — a plague on all such Brutes.
WILLMORE: By this Light I took her for an errant Harlot.
BELVILE: Damn your debaucht Opinion: tell me, Sot, hadst

thou so much sense and light about thee to distinguish her to 25
be a Woman, and could'st not see something about her Face and Person, to strike an awful Reverence into thy Soul?
WILLMORE: Faith no, I consider'd her as mere a Woman as I could wish.
BELVILE: 'Sdeath I have no patience — draw, or I'll kill you. 30
WILLMORE: Let that alone till to morrow, and if I set not all right again, use your Pleasure.
BELVILE: To morrow, damn it.
The spiteful Light will lead me to no happiness.
To morrow is *Antonio's*, and perhaps 35
Guides him to my undoing; — oh that I could meet
This Rival, this powerful Fortunate.
WILLMORE: What then?
BELVILE: Let thy own Reason, or my Rage instruct thee.
WILLMORE: I shall be finely inform'd then, no doubt; hear me, 40
Colonel — hear me — shew me the Man and I'll do his Business.
BELVILE: I know him no more than thou, or if I did, I should not need thy aid.
WILLMORE: This you say is *Angelica's* House, I promis'd the 45
kind Baggage to lie with her to Night.

(*Offers to go in.*)

(*Enter* ANTONIO *and his Page*. ANTONIO *knocks on the Hilt of his Sword*.)

ANTONIO: You paid the thousand Crowns I directed?
PAGE: To the Lady's old Woman, Sir, I did.
WILLMORE: Who the Devil have we here?
BELVILE: I'll now plant my self under *Florinda's* Window, and if 50
I find no comfort there, I'll die.

(*Exit* BELVILE *and* FREDERICK. *Enter* MORETTA.)

MORETTA: Page!
PAGE: Here's my Lord.
WILLMORE: How is this, a Piccaroon going to board my Frigate! here's one Chase-Gun for you. 55

(*Drawing his Sword, justles* ANTONIO *who turns and draws. They fight,* ANTONIO *falls*.)

MORETTA: Oh, bless us, we are all undone!

(*Runs in, and shuts the Door.*)

PAGE: Help, Murder!

(BELVILE *returns at the noise of fighting*.)

BELVILE: Ha, the mad Rogue's engag'd in some unlucky Adventure again.

(*Enter two or three* MASQUERADERS.)

MASQUERADER: Ha, a Man kill'd! 60
WILLMORE: How! a Man kill'd! then I'll go home to sleep.

(*Puts up, and reels out. Exeunt* MASQUERADERS *another way*.)

BELVILE: Who shou'd it be! pray Heaven the Rogue is safe, for all my Quarrel to him.

(*As* BELVILE *is groping about, enter an* OFFICER *and six* SOLDIERS.)

SOLDIER: Who's there?
OFFICER: So, here's one dispatcht — secure the Murderer. 65

BELVILE: Do not mistake my Charity for Murder: I came to his Assistance.

(SOLDIERS *sieze on* BELVILE.)

OFFICER: That shall be tried, Sir. — St. *Jago*, Swords drawn in the Carnival time!

(*Goes to* ANTONIO.)

70 ANTONIO: Thy Hand prithee.

OFFICER: Ha, Don *Antonio*! look well to the Villain there. — How is't, Sir?

ANTONIO: I'm hurt.

BELVILE: Has my Humanity made me a Criminal?

75 OFFICER: Away with him.

BELVILE: What a curst Chance is this!

(*Exeunt* SOLDIERS *with* BELVILE.)

ANTONIO: (*To the* OFFICER.) This is the Man that has set upon me twice — carry him to my Apartment till you have further Orders from me.

(*Exit.* ANTONIO *led.*)

— ACT FOUR —

SCENE I

A fine Room.

(*Discovers* BELVILE, *as by Dark alone.*)

BELVILE: When shall I be weary of railing on Fortune, who is resolv'd never to turn with Smiles upon me? — Two such Defeats in one Night — none but the Devil and that mad Rogue could have contriv'd to have plagued me with — I am here a

5 Prisoner — but where? — Heaven knows — and if there be Murder done, I can soon decide the Fate of a Stranger in a Nation without Mercy — Yet this is nothing to the Torture my Soul bows with, when I think of losing my fair, my dear *Florinda*. — Hark — my Door opens — a Light — a Man — and

10 seems of Quality — arm'd too. — Now shall I die like a Dog without defence.

(*Enter* ANTONIO *in a Night-Gown, with a Light; his Arm in a Scarf, and a Sword under his Arm: He sets the Candle on the Table.*)

ANTONIO: Sir, I come to know what Injuries I have done you, that could provoke you to so mean an Action, as to attack me basely, without allowing time for my Defence.

15 BELVILE: Sir, for a Man in my Circumstances to plead Innocence, would look like Fear — but view me well, and you will find no marks of a Coward on me, nor any thing that betrays that Brutality you accuse me of.

ANTONIO: In vain, Sir, you impose upon my Sense,

20 You are not only he who drew on me last Night,
But yesterday before the same House, that of *Angelica*.
Yet there is something in your Face and Mein —

BELVILE: I own I fought to day in the defence of a Friend of mine, with whom you (if you're the same) and your

25 Party were first engag'd.
Perhaps you think this Crime enough to kill me,
But if you do, I cannot fear you'll do it basely.

ANTONIO: No, Sir, I'll make you fit for a Defence with this.

(*Gives him the Sword.*)

BELVILE: This Gallantry surprizes me — nor know I how to use this Present, Sir, against a Man so brave.   30

ANTONIO: You shall not need;
For know, I come to snatch you from a Danger
That is decreed against you;
Perhaps your Life, or long Imprisonment:
And 'twas with so much Courage you offended,   35
I cannot see you punisht.

BELVILE: How shall I pay this Generosity?

ANTONIO: It had been safer to have kill'd another,
Than have attempted me:
To shew your Danger, Sir, I'll let you know my Quality;   40
And 'tis the Vice-Roy's Son whom you have wounded.

BELVILE: (*Aside.*) The Vice-Roy's Son!
Death and Confusion! was this Plague reserved
To compleat all the rest? — oblig'd by him!
The Man of all the World I would destroy.   45

ANTONIO: You seem disorder'd, Sir.

BELVILE: Yes, trust me, Sir, I am, and 'tis with pain
That Man receives such Bounties,
Who wants the pow'r to pay 'em back again.

ANTONIO: To gallant Spirits 'tis indeed uneasy;   50
— But you may quickly over-pay me, Sir.

BELVILE: Then I am well — (*Aside.*) kind Heaven! but set us even,
That I may fight with him, and keep my Honour safe.
— Oh, I'm impatient, Sir, to be discounting
The mighty Debt I owe you; command me quickly —   55

ANTONIO: I have a Quarrel with a Rival, Sir,
About the Maid we love.

BELVILE: (*Aside.*) Death, 'tis *Florinda* he means —
That Thought destroys my Reason, and I shall kill him —

ANTONIO: My Rival, Sir.   60
Is one has all the Virtues Man can boast of.

BELVILE: Death! who shou'd this be?

ANTONIO: He challeng'd me to meet him on the *Molo*,
As soon as Day appear'd; but last Night's quarrel
Has made my Arm unfit to guide a Sword.   65

BELVILE: I apprehend you, Sir, you'd have me kill the Man
That lays a claim to the Maid you speak of.
— I'll do't — I'll fly to do it.

ANTONIO: Sir, do you know her?

BELVILE: — No, Sir, but 'tis enough she is admired by you.   70

ANTONIO: Sir, I shall rob you of the Glory on't,
For you must fight under my Name and Dress.

BELVILE: That Opinion must be strangely obliging that makes
You think I can personate the brave *Antonio*,
Whom I can but strive to imitate.   75

ANTONIO: You say too much to my Advantage.
Come, Sir, the Day appears that calls you forth.
Within, Sir, is the Habit.

(*Exit* ANTONIO.)

BELVILE: Fantastick Fortune, thou deceitful Light,
That cheats the wearied Traveller by Night,   80
Tho on a Precipice each step you tread,
I am resolv'd to follow where you lead.

(*Exit.*)

SCENE II

The Molo.

(Enter FLORINDA *and* CALLIS *in Masques, with* STEPHANO.)

FLORINDA: *(Aside.)* I'm dying with my fears; *Belvile's* not
    coming,
    As I expected, underneath my Window,
    Makes me believe that all those Fears are true.
    —Canst thou not tell with whom my Brother fights?

5 STEPHANO: No, Madam, they were both in Masquerade, I was
    by when they challeng'd one another, and they had decided
    the Quarrel then, but were prevented by some Cavaliers;
    which made 'em put it off till now—but I am sure 'tis about
    you they fight.

10 FLORINDA: *(Aside.)* Nay then 'tis with *Belvile,* for what other
    Lover have I that dares fight for me, except *Antonio?* and he is
    too much in favour with my Brother—If it be he, for whom
    shall I direct my Prayers to Heaven?

    STEPHANO: Madam, I must leave you; for if my Master see me, I

15   shall be hang'd for being your Conductor.—I escap'd nar-
    rowly for the Excuse I made for you last night i'th' Garden.

    FLORINDA: And I'll reward thee for't—prithee no more.

(Exit STEPHANO.)

(Enter Don PEDRO *in his Masquing Habit.)*

PEDRO: *Antonio's* late to day, the place will fill, and we may
    be prevented.

(Walks about.)

20 FLORINDA: *(Aside.) Antonio!* sure I heard amiss.
    PEDRO: But who would not excuse a happy Lover.
    When soft fair Arms comfine the yielding Neck;
    And the kind Whisper languishingly breathes,
    Must you be gone so soon?

25   Sure I had dwelt for ever on her Bosom.
    —But stay, he's here.

(Enter BELVILE *drest in* ANTONIO's *Clothes.)*

FLORINDA: 'Tis not *Belvile,* half my Fears are vanish't.
    PEDRO: *Antonio!*—
    BELVILE: *(Aside.)* This must be he.

30   You're early, Sir,—I do not use to be out-done this way.
    PEDRO: The wretched, Sir, are watchful, and 'tis enough
    You have the advantage of me in *Angelica.*
    BELVILE: *(Aside.) Angelica!*
    Or I've mistook my Man! Or else *Antonio,*

35   Can he forget his Interest in *Florinda,*
    And fight for common Prize?
    PEDRO: Come, Sir, you know our terms—
    BELVILE: *(Aside.)* Be Heaven, not I.
    —No talking, I am ready, Sir.

(Offers to fight. FLORINDA *runs in.)*

40 FLORINDA: *(To* BELVILE.) Oh, hold! who'er you be, I do con-
    jure you hold. If you strike here—I die—
    PEDRO: *Florinda!*
    BELVILE: *Florinda* imploring for my Rival!
    PEDRO: Away, this Kindness is unseasonable.

(Puts her by, they fight; she runs in just as BELVILE *disarms*
PEDRO.)

FLORINDA: Who are you, Sir, that dare deny my Prayers?   45
BELVILE: Thy Prayers destroy him; if thou wouldst preserve
    him.
    Do that thou'rt unacquainted with, and curse him.

(She holds him.)

FLORINDA: By all you hold most dear, by her you love,
    I do conjure you, touch him not.
BELVILE: By her I love!   50
    See—I obey—and at your Feet resign
    The useless Trophy of my Victory.

(Lays his sword at her Feet.)

PEDRO: *Antonio,* you've done enough to prove you love
    Florinda.
BELVILE: Love *Florinda!*   55
    Does Heaven love Adoration, Pray'r, or Penitence?
    Love her! here Sir,—your Sword again.

(Snatches up the Sword, and gives it him.)

    Upon this Truth I'll fight my Life away.
PEDRO: No, you've redeem'd my Sister, and my Friendship.
BELVILE: Don *Pedro!*   60

(He gives him FLORINDA *and pulls off his Vizard to shew his
Face, and puts it on again.)*

PEDRO: Can you resign your Claims to other Women,
    And give your Heart intirely to *Florinda?*
BELVILE: Intire, as dying Saints Confessions are.
    I can delay my happiness no longer.
    This minute let me make *Florinda* mine: 65
PEDRO: This minute let it be—no time so proper,
    This Night my Father will arrive from *Rome,*
    And possibly may hinder what we propose.
FLORINDA: Oh Heavens! this Minute!

(Enter MASQUERADERS, *and pass over.)*

BELVILE: Oh, do not ruin me!   70
PEDRO: The place begins to fill; and that we may not be observ'd,
    do you walk off to St. *Peter's* Church, where I will meet you,
    and conclude your Happiness.
BELVILE: I'll meet you there—*(Aside.)* if there be no more
    Saints Churches in *Naples.*   75
FLORINDA: Oh stay, Sir, and recall your hasty Doom:
    Alas I have not yet prepar'd my Heart
    To entertain so strange a Guest.
PEDRO: Away, this silly Modesty is assum'd too late.
BELVILE: Heaven, Madam! what do you do?   80
FLORINDA: Do! despise the Man that lays a Tyrant's Claim
    To what he ought to conquer by Submission.
BELVILE: You do not know me—move a little this way.

(Draws her aside.)

FLORINDA: Yes, you may even force me to the Altar,
    But not the holy Man that offers there   85
    Shall force me to be thine.

*(*PEDRO *talks to* CALLIS *this while.)*

BELVILE: Oh do not lose so blest an opportunity!
    See—'tis your *Belvile*—not *Antonio,*
    Whom your mistaken Scorn and Anger ruins.

(Pulls off his Vizard.)

90   FLORINDA: *Belvile!*
Where was my Soul it cou'd not meet thy Voice,
And take this knowledge in?

(As they are talking, enter WILLMORE *finely drest, and* FREDERICK.)

WILLMORE: No Intelligence! no News of *Belvile* yet — well I am
95   the most unlucky Rascal in Nature — ha! — am I deceiv'd — or
is it he — look, *Frederick* — 'tis he — my dear *Belvile.*

(Runs and embraces him. BELVILE's *Vizard falls out on's Hand.)*

BELVILE: Hell and Confusion seize thee!
PEDRO: Ha! *Belvile!* I beg your Pardon, Sir.

(Takes FLORINDA *from him.)*

BELVILE: Nay, touch her not, she's mine by Conquest, Sir.
I won her by my Sword.
100 WILLMORE: Did'st thou so — and egad, Child, we'll keep her by
the Sword.

(Draws on PEDRO, BELVILE *goes between.)*

BELVILE: Stand off.
Thou'rt so profanely leud, so curst by Heaven,
All Quarrels thou espousest must be fatal.
105 WILLMORE: Nay, an you be so hot, my Valour's coy,
And shall be courted when you want it next.

(Puts up his Sword.)

BELVILE: You know I ought to claim a Victor's Right,

(To PEDRO.)

But you're the Brother to divine *Florinda,*
To whom I'm such a Slave — to purchase her,
110 I durst not hurt the Man she holds so dear.
PEDRO: 'Twas by *Antonio's,* not by *Belvile's* Sword,
This Question should have been decided, Sir:
I must confess much to your Bravery's due,
Both now, and when I met you last in Arms.
115 But I am nicely punctual in my word,
As Men of Honour ought, and beg your Pardon.
(Aside to FLORINDA *as they are going out.)*
— For this Mistake another Time shall clear.
— This was some Plot between you and *Belvile:*
But I'll prevent you.

*(*BELVILE *looks after her, and begins to walk up and down in a Rage.)*

120 WILLMORE: Do not be modest now, and lose the Woman: but if
we shall fetch her back, so —
BELVILE: Do not speak to me.
WILLMORE: Not speak to you! — Egad, I'll speak to you, and will
be answered too.
125 BELVILE: Will you, Sir?
WILLMORE: I know I've done some mischief, but I'm so dull a
Puppy, that I am the Son of a Whore, if I know how, or
where — prithee inform my Understanding. —
BELVILE: Leave me I say, and leave me instantly.
130 WILLMORE: I will not leave you in this humour, nor till I
know my Crime.
BELVILE: Death, I'll tell you, Sir —

(Draws and runs at WILLMORE; *he runs out;* BELVILE *after him,* FREDERICK *interposes.)*

(Enter ANGELICA, MORETTA, *and* SEBASTIAN.)

ANGELICA: Ha — *Sebastian* — Is not that *Willmore?* haste, haste,
and bring him back.
FREDERICK: The Colonel's mad — I never saw him thus before;   135
I'll after 'em, lest he do some mischief, for I am sure *Willmore*
will not draw on him.

(Exit.)

ANGELICA: I am all Rage! my first desires defeated
For one, for ought he knows, that has no
Other Merit than her Quality, —   140
Her being Don *Pedro's* Sister — He loves her:
I know 'tis so — dull, dull, insensible —
He will not see me now tho oft invited;
And broke his Word last night — false perjur'd Man!
— He that but yesterday fought for my Favours,   145
And would have made his Life a Sacrifice
To've gain'd one Night with me,
Must now be hired and courted to my Arms.
MORETTA: I told you what wou'd come on't, but *Moretta's* an
old doating Fool — Why did you give him five hundred   150
Crowns, but to set himself out for other Lovers? You shou'd
have kept him poor, if you had meant to have had any good
from him.
ANGELICA: On, name not such mean Trifles. — Had I given
         him all
My Youth has earn'd from Sin,   155
I had not lost a Thought nor Sigh upon't.
But I have given him my eternal Rest,
My whole Repose, my future Joys, my Heart;
My Virgin Heart. *Moretta!* oh' tis gone!
MORETTA: Curse on him, here he comes;   160
How fine she has made him too!

(Enter WILLMORE *and* SEBASTIAN. ANGELICA *turns and walks away.)*

WILLMORE: How now, turn'd Shadow?
Fly when I pursue, and follow when I fly!

(Sings.)

Stay gentle Shadow of my Dove,
And tell me e'er I go,   165
Whether the Substance may not prove
A fleeting Thing like you.

There's a soft kind Look remaining yet.

(As she turns she looks on him.)

ANGELICA: Well, Sir, you may be gay; all Happiness, all Joys
pursue you still, Fortune's your Slave, and gives you every   170
hour choice of new Hearts and Beauties, till you are cloy'd
with the repeated Bliss, which others vainly languish for —
But know, false Man, that I shall be reveng'd.

(Turns away in a Rage.)

WILLMORE: So, 'gad, there are of those faint-hearted Lovers,
whom such a sharp Lesson next their Hearts would make as   175
impotent as Fourscore — pox o' this whining — my Bus'ness is

to laugh and love—a pox on't; I hate your sullen Lover, a
Man shall lose as much time to put you in Humour now, as
would serve to gain a new Woman.

180 ANGELICA: I scorn to cool that Fire I cannot raise,
     Or do the Drudgery of your virtuous Mistress.

WILLMORE: A virtuous Mistress! Death, what a thing thou hast
found out for me! why what the Devil should I do with a
virtuous Woman?—a fort of ill'natur'd Creatures, that take a
185 Pride to torment a Lover. Virtue is but an Infirmity in
Women, a Disease that renders even the handsom ungrateful;
whilst the ill-favour'd, for want of Sollicitations and Address,
only fancy themselves so.—I have lain with a Woman of
Quality, who has all the while been railing at Whores.

190 ANGELICA: I will not answer for your Mistress's Virtue,
     Tho she be young enough to know no Guilt:
     And I could wish you would persuade my Heart,
     'Twas the two hundred thousand Crowns you courted.

WILLMORE: Two hundred thousand Crowns! what Story's
195 this?—what Trick?—what Woman?—ha.

ANGELICA: How strange you make it! have you forgot the Creature you entertain'd on the Piazza last night?

WILLMORE: Ha, my Gipsy worth two hundred thousand
Crowns!—oh how I long to be with her—pox, I knew she was
200 of Quality.

ANGELICA: False Man, I see my Ruin in thy Face.
     How many vows you breath'd upon my Bosom,
     Never to be unjust—have you forgot so soon?

WILLMORE: Faith no, I was just coming to repeat 'em—but
205 here's a Humour indeed—would make a Man a Saint—
     (Aside.) Wou'd she'd be angry enough to leave me, and com-
     mand me not to wait on her.

(Enter HELLENA, drest in Man's Clothes.)

HELLENA: This must be Angelica, I know it by her mumping
Matron here—Ay, ay, 'tis she: my mad Captain's with her
210 too, for all his swearing—how this unconstant Humour
makes me love him:—pray, good grave Gentlewoman, is not
this Angelica?

MORETTA: My too young Sir, it is—I hope 'tis one from Don
Antonio.

(Goes to ANGELICA.)

215 HELLENA: (Aside.) Well, something I'll do to vex him for this.

ANGELICA: I will not speak with him; am I in humour to receive
a Lover?

WILLMORE: Not speak with him! why I'll be gone—and wait
your idler minutes—Can I shew less Obedience to the thing I
220 love so fondly?

(Offers to go.)

ANGELICA: A fine Excuse this—stay—

WILLMORE: And hinder your Advantage: should I repay your
Bounties so ungratefully?

ANGELICA: Come, hither, Boy,—that I may let you see
225 How much above the Advantages you name
     I prize one Minute's Joy with you.

WILLMORE: Oh, you destroy me with this Endearment.

(Impatient to be gone.)

     —Death, how shall I get away!—Madam, 'twill not be fit I
     should be seen with you—besides, it will not be conve-
230 nient—and I've a Friend—that's dangerously sick.

ANGELICA: I see you're impatient—yet you shall stay.   235

WILLMORE: And miss my Assignation with my Gipsy.

(Aside, and walks about impatiently. MORETTA brings HEL-
LENA, who addresses her self to ANGELICA.)

HELLENA: Madam, You'l hardly pardon my Intrusion,
     When you shall know my Business;
     And I'm too young to tell my Tale with Art: 235
     But there must be a wondrous store of Goodness
     Where so much Beauty dwells.

ANGELICA: A pretty Advocate, whoever sent thee,
     —Prithee proceed—Nay, Sir, you shall not go.

(To WILLMORE who is stealing off.)

WILLMORE: Then shall I lose my dear Gipsy for ever.   240
     (Aside.) —Pox on't, she stays me out of spite.

HELLENA: I am related to a Lady, Madam,
     Young, rich, and nobly born, but has the fate
     To be in love with a young English Gentleman.
     Strangely she loves him, at first sight she lov'd him,   245
     But did adore him when she heard him speak;
     For he, she said, had Charms in every word,
     That fail'd not to surprize, to wound, and conquer—

WILLMORE: (Aside.) Ha, Egad I hope this concerns me.

ANGELICA: 'Tis my false Man, he means—wou'd he were   250
     gone.
     This Praise will raise his Pride and ruin me—(To
     WILLMORE.) Well,
     Since you are so impatient to be gone.
     I will release you, Sir.

WILLMORE: (Aside.) Nay, then I'm sure 'twas me he spoke of,
     this cannot be the Effects of Kindness in her.   255
     —No, Madam, I've consider'd better on't,
     And will not give you cause of Jealousy.

ANGELICA: But, Sir, I've—business, that—

WILLMORE: This shall not do, I know 'tis but to try me.

ANGELICA: (Aside.) Well, to your Story, Boy,—tho 'twill undo   260
     me.

HELLENA: With this Addition to his other Beauties,
     He won her unresisting tender Heart,
     He vow'd and sigh'd, and swore he lov'd her dearly;
     And she believ'd the cunning Flatterer,
     And thought her self the happiest Maid alive: 265
     To day was the appointed time by both,
     To consummate their Bliss;
     The Virgin, Altar, and the Priest were drest,
     And whilst she languisht for the expected Bridegroom,
     She heard, he paid his broken Vows to you.   270

WILLMORE: (Aside.) So, this is some dear Rogue that's in love
     with me, and this way lets me know it; or if it be not me, she
     means some one whose place I may supply.

ANGELICA: Now I perceive
     The cause of thy Impatience to be gone,   275
     And all the business of this glorious Dress.

WILLMORE: Damn the young Prater, I know not what he means.

HELLENA: Madam,
     In your fair Eyes I read too much concern
     To tell my farther Business.   280

ANGELICA: Prithee, sweet Youth, talk on, thou may'st perhaps
     Raise here a Storm that may undo my Passion,
     And then I'll grant thee any thing.

HELLENA: Madam, 'tis to intreat you, (oh unreasonable!)
285   You wou'd not see this Stranger;
For if you do, she vows you are undone,
Tho Nature never made a Man so excellent;
And sure he'ad been a God, but for Inconstancy.
WILLMORE: (Aside.) Ah, Rogue, how finely he's instructed!
290   —'Tis plain some Woman that has seen me en passant.
ANGELICA: Oh, I shall burst with Jealousy! do you know the
Man you speak of? —
HELLENA: Yes, Madam, he us'd to be in Buff and Scarlet.
ANGELICA: (To WILLMORE.) Thou, false as Hell, what canst
295   thou say to this?
WILLMORE: By Heaven —
ANGELICA: Hold, do not damn thy self —
HELLENA: Nor hope to be believ'd.

(He walks about, they follow.)

ANGELICA: Oh, perjur'd Man!
300   Is't thus you pay my generous Passion back?
HELLENA: Why wou'd you, Sir, abuse my Lady's Faith?
ANGELICA: And use me so unhumanly?
HELLENA: A Maid so young, so innocent —
WILLMORE: Ah, young Devil!
305 ANGELICA: Dost thou not know thy Life is in my Power?
HELLENA: Or think my Lady cannot be reveng'd?
WILLMORE: (Aside.) So, so, the Storm comes finely on.
ANGELICA: Now thou art silent, Guilt has struck thee dumb.
Oh, hadst thou still been so, I'd liv'd in safety.

(She turns away and weeps.)

310 WILLMORE: (Aside to HELLENA, looks towards ANGELICA to
watch her turning; and as she comes towards them, he meets
her.) Sweetheart, the Lady's Name and House — quickly: I'm
impatient to be with her. —
HELLENA: (Aside.) So now is he for another Woman.
315 WILLMORE: The impudent'st young thing in Nature!
I cannot persuade him out of his Error, Madam.
ANGELICA: I know he's in the right, — yet thou'st a Tongue
That wou'd persuade him to deny his Faith.

(In Rage walks away.)

WILLMORE: (Said softly to HELLENA.) Her Name, her Name,
320   dear Boy —
HELLENA: Have you forgot it, Sir?
WILLMORE: (Aside.) Oh, I perceive he's not to know I am a
Stranger to his Lady.
—Yes, yes, I do know — but — I have forgot the —

(ANGELICA turns.)

325   —By Heaven, such early confidence I never saw.
ANGELICA: Did I not charge you with this Mistress, Sir?
Which you denied, tho I beheld your Perjury.
This little Generosity of thine has render'd back my Heart.

(Walks away.)

WILLMORE: So, you have made sweet work here, my little
mischief;
330   Look your Lady be kind and good-natur'd now, or
I shall have but a cursed Bargain on't.

(ANGELICA turns towards them.)

—The Rogue's bred up to Mischief,
Art thou so great a Fool to credit him?
ANGELICA: Yes, I do; and you in vain impose upon me.
—Come hither, Boy — Is not this he you speak of?   335
HELLENA: (HELLENA looks in his Face, he gazes on her.) I
think — it is; I cannot swear, but I vow he has just such an-
other lying Lover's look.
WILLMORE: (Aside.) Hah! do not I know that Face? —
By Heaven, my little Gipsy! what a dull Dog was I?   340
Had I but lookt that way, I'd known her.
Are all my hopes of a new Woman banisht?
—Egad, if I don't fit thee for this, hang me.
—Madam, I have found out the Plot.
HELLENA: Oh Lord, what does he say? am I discover'd now?   345
WILLMORE: Do you see this young Spark here?
HELLENA: He'll tell her who I am.
WILLMORE: Who do you think this is?
HELLENA: Ay, ay, he does know me. — Nay, dear Captain, I'm
undone if you discover me.   350
WILLMORE: Nay, nay, no cogging; she shall know what a pre-
cious Mistress I have.
HELLENA: Will you be such a Devil?
WILLMORE: Nay, nay, I'll teach you to spoil sport you will not
make. — This small Ambassador comes not from a Person of   355
Quality, as you imagine, and he says; but from a very errant
Gipsy, the talkingst, pratingst, cantingst little Animal thou
ever saw'st.
ANGELICA: What news you tell me! that's the thing I mean.
HELLENA: (Aside.) Wou'd I were well off the place. — If ever I go   360
a Captain-hunting again. —
WILLMORE: Mean that thing? that Gipsy thing? thou may'st as
well be jealous of thy Monkey, or Parrot as her: a German
Motion were worth a dozen of her, and a Dream were a better
Enjoyment, a Creature of Constitution fitter for Heaven than   365
Man.
HELLENA: (Aside.) Tho I'm sure he lyes, yet this vexes me.
ANGELICA: You are mistaken, she's a Spanish Woman
Made up of no such dull Materials.
WILLMORE: Materials! Egad, and she be made of any that will   370
either dispense, or admit of Love, I'll be bound to
continence.
HELLENA: (Aside to him.) Unreasonable Man, do you think so?
WILLMORE: You may Return, my little Brazen Head, and tell
your Lady, that till she be handsom enough to be belov'd, or I   375
dull enough to be religious, there will be small hopes of me.
ANGELICA: Did you not promise then to marry her?
WILLMORE: Not I, by Heaven.
ANGELICA: You cannot undeceive my fears and torments, till
you have vow'd you will not marry her.   380
HELLENA: If he swears that, he'll be reveng'd on me indeed for
all my Rogueries.
ANGELICA: I know what Arguments you'll bring against me,
Fortune and Honour.
WILLMORE: Honour! I tell you, I hate it in your Sex; and those   385
that fancy themselves possest of that Foppery, are the most
impertinently troublesom of all Woman-kind, and will trans-
gress nine Commandments to keep one: and to satisfy your
Jealousy I swear —

---

351 **cogging** To cog = to trick, wheedle or cajole

390 HELLENA: (*Aside to him.*) Oh, no swearing, dear Captain—
WILLMORE: If it were possible I should ever be inclin'd to marry,
it should be some kind young Sinner, one that has Generosity
enough to give a favour handsomely to one that can ask it
discreetly, one that has Wit enough to manage an Intrigue of
395 Love—oh, how civil such a Wench is, to a Man than does
her the Honour to marry her.
ANGELICA: By Heaven, there's no Faith in any thing he says.

(*Enter* SEBASTIAN.)

SEBASTIAN: Madam, *Don Antonio*—
ANGELICA: Come hither.
400 HELLENA: Ha, *Antonio*! he may be coming hither, and he'll certainly discover me, I'll therefore retire without a Ceremony.

(*Exit* HELLENA.)

ANGELICA: I'll see him, get my Coach ready.
SEBASTIAN: It waits you, Madam.
WILLMORE: This is lucky: what, Madam, now I may be gone
405 and leave you to the enjoyment of my Rival?
ANGELICA: Dull Man, that canst not see how ill, how poor
That false dissimulation looks—Be gone,
And never let me see thy cozening Face again,
Lest I relapse and kill thee.
410 WILLMORE: Yes, you can spare me now,—farewell till you are
in a better Humour—I'm glad of this release—
Now for my Gipsy:
For tho to worse we change, yet still we find
New Joys, New Charms, in a new Miss that's kind.

(*Exit* WILLMORE.)

415 ANGELICA: He's gone, and in this Ague of My Soul
The shivering Fit returns;
Oh with what willing haste he took his leave,
As if the long'd for Minute were arriv'd,
Of some blest Assignation.
420 In vain I have consulted all my Charms,
In vain this Beauty priz'd, in vain believ'd
My eyes cou'd kindle any lasting Fires.
I had forgot my Name, my Infamy,
And the Reproach that Honour lays on those
425 That dare pretend a sober passion here.
Nice Reputation, tho it leave behind
More Virtues than inhabit where that dwells,
Yet that once gone, those virtues shine no more.
—Then since I am not fit to belov'd,
430 I am resolv'd to think on a Revenge
On him that sooth'd me thus to my undoing.

(*Exeunt.*)

SCENE III

A *Street*.

(*Enter* FLORINDA *and* VALERIA *in Habits different from what
they have been seen in.*)

FLORINDA: We're happily escap'd, yet I tremble still.
VALERIA: A Lover and fear! why, I am but half a one, and yet I
have Courage for any Attempt. Would *Hellena* were here. I
wou'd fain have had her as deep in this Mischief as we, she'll
5 fare but ill else I doubt.

FLORINDA: She pretended a Visit to the *Augustine* Nuns, but I
believe some other design carried her out, pray Heavens we
light on her.
VALERIA: When I saw no reason wou'd go good on her, I follow'd
her into the Wardrobe, and as she was looking for something 10
in a great Chest, I tumbled her in by the Heels, snatcht the
Key of the Apartment where you were confin'd, lockt her in,
and left her bauling for help.
FLORINDA: 'Tis well you resolve to follow my Fortunes, for thou
darest never appear at home again after such an Action. 15
VALERIA: That's according as the young Stranger and I shall
agree—But to our business—I deliver'd your Letter, your
Note to *Belvile*, when I got out under pretence of going to
Mass, I found him at his Lodging, and believe me it came
seasonably; for never was Man in so desperate a Condition. I 20
told him of your Resolution of making your escape to day, if
your Brother would be absent long enough to permit you; if
not, die rather than be *Antonio's*.
FLORINDA: Thou shou'dst hav told him I was confin'd to my
Chamber upon my Brother's suspicion, that the Business on 25
the *Molo* was a Plot laid between him and I.
VALERIA: I said all this, and told him your Brother was now gone
to his Devotion, and he resolves to visit every Church till he
find him; and not only undeceive him in that, but caress him
so as shall delay his return home. 30
FLORINDA: Oh Heavens! he's here, and *Belvile* with him too.

(*They put on their Vizards.*)

(*Enter Don* PEDRO, BELVILE, WILLMORE; BELVILE *and Don*
PEDRO *seeming in serious Discourse.*)

VALERIA: Walk boldly by them, I'll come at a distance, lest he
suspect us.

(*She walks by them, and looks back on them.*)

WILLMORE: Ha! A Woman! and of an excellent Mien!
PEDRO: She throws a kind look back on you. 35
WILLMORE: Death, tis a likely Wench, and that kind look shall
not be cast away—I'll follow her.
BELVILE: Prithee do not.
WILLMORE: Do not! By Heavens to the Antipodes, with such an
Invitation. 40

(*She goes out, and* WILLMORE *follows her.*)

BELVILE: 'Tis a mad Fellow for a Wench.

(*Enter* FREDERICK.)

FREDERICK: Oh Colonel, such News.
BELVILE: Prithee what?
FREDERICK: News that will make you laugh in spite of Fortune.
BELVILE: What, *Blunt* has had some damn'd Trick put upon 45
him, cheated, bang'd, or clapt?
FREDERICK: Cheated, Sir, rarely cheated of all but his Shirt and
Drawers; the unconscionable Whore too turn'd him out be-
fore Consummation, so that traversing the Streets at Mid-
night, the Watch found him in this *Fresco*, and conducted 50
him home: By Heaven 'tis such a slight, and yet I durst as well
have been hang'd as laugh at him, or pity him; he beats all
that do but ask him a Question, and is in such a Humour—
PEDRO: Who is't has met with this ill usage, Sir?
BELVILE: (*Aside.*) A Friend of ours, whom you must see for 55
Mirth's sake. I'll imploy him to give *Florinda* time for an escape.

PEDRO: Who is he?

BELVILE: A young Countryman of ours, one that has been educated at so plentiful a rate, he yet ne'er knew the want of
60   Money, and 'twill be a great Jest to see how simply he'll look
without it. For my part I'll lend him none, and the Rogue
knows not how to put on a borrowing Face, and ask first. I'll
let him see how good 'tis to play our parts whilst I play his —
Prithee, *Frederick* do go home and keep him in that posture
65   till we come.

(*Exeunt.*)

(*Enter* FLORINDA *from the farther end of the Scene, looking behind her.*)

FLORINDA: I am follow'd still — hah — my Brother too advancing
this way, good Heavens defend me from being seen by him.

(*She goes off.*)

(*Enter* WILLMORE, *and after him* VALERIA, *at a little distance.*)

WILLMORE: Ah! There she sails, she looks back as she were willing to be boarded, I'll warrant her Prize.

(*He goes out,* VALERIA *following.*)

(*Enter* HELLENA, *just as he goes out, with a* PAGE.)

70   HELLENA: Hah, is not that my Captain that has a Woman in
chase? — 'tis not *Angelica*. Boy, follow those People at a distance, and bring me an Account where they go in. — I'll find
his Haunts, and plague him every where. — ha — my Brother!

(*Exit* PAGE. BELVILE, WILLMORE, *and* PEDRO *cross the Stage:*
HELLENA *runs off.*)

(*Scene changes to another Street. Enter* FLORINDA.)

FLORINDA: What shall I do, my Brother now pursues me. Will
75   no kind Power protect me from his Tyranny? — Hah, here's a
Door open, I'll venture in, since nothing can be worse than to
fall into his Hands, my Life and Honour are at stake, and my
Necessity has no choice.

(*She goes in. Enter* VALERIA, *and* HELLENA'S PAGE *peeping after*
FLORINDA.)

PAGE: Here she went in, I shall remember this House.

(*Exit* BOY.)

80   VALERIA: This is *Belvile's* Lodgings; she's gone in as readily as if
she knew it — hah — here's that mad Fellow again, I dare not
venture in — I'll watch my Opportunity.

(*Goes aside. Enter* WILLMORE, *gazing about him.*)

WILLMORE: I have lost her hereabouts — Pox on't she must not
scape me so.

(*Goes out.*)

(*Scene changes to* BLUNT'S *chamber, discovers him sitting on a
couch in his shirt and drawers, reading.*)

85   BLUNT: So, now my Mind's a little at Peace, since I have resolv'd
Revenge — A Pox on this Taylor tho, for not bringing home
the Clothes I bespoke; and a Pox of all poor Cavaliers, a Man
can never keep a spare Suit for 'em; and I shall have these
Rogues come in and find me naked; and then I'm undone;
90   but I'm resolv'd to arm my self — the Rascals shall not insult
over me too much.

(*Puts on an old rusty Sword and Buff-Belt.*)

—Now, how like a Morrice-Dancer I am equipt — a fine
Lady-like Whore to cheat me thus, without affording me a
Kindness for my Money, a Pox light on her, I shall never be
reconciled to the Sex more, she has made me as faithless as a   95
Physician, as uncharitable as a Churchman, and as ill-
natur'd as a Poet. O how I'll use all Womenkind hereafter!
what wou'd I give to have one of 'em within my reach now!
any Mortal thing in Petticoats, kind Fortune, send me; and
I'll forgive thy last Night's Malice — Here's a cursed Book too,   100
(a Warning to all young Travellers) that can instruct me how
to prevent such Mischiefs now 'tis too late. Well 'tis a rare
convenient thing to read a little now and then, as well as hawk
and hunt.

(*Sits down again and reads.*)

(*Enter to him* FLORINDA.)

FLORINDA: This House is haunted sure, 'tis well furnisht and no   105
living thing inhabits it — hah — a Man! Heavens how he's attir'd! sure 'tis some Rope-dancer, or Fencing-Master; I tremble now for fear, and yet I must venture now to speak to
him — Sir, if I may not interrupt your Meditations —

(*He starts up and gazes.*)

BLUNT: Hah — what's here? Are my wishes granted? and is not   110
that a she Creature? Adsheartlikins 'tis! what wretched thing
art thou — hah!

FLORINDA: Charitable Sir, you've told your self already what I
am; a very wretched Maid, forc'd by a strange unlucky Accident, to seek a safety here, and must be ruin'd, if you do not   115
grant it.

BLUNT: Ruin'd! Is there any Ruin so inevitable as that which
now threatens thee? Dost thou know, miserable Woman, into
what Den of Mischiefs thou art fall'n? what a Bliss of Confusion? — hah — dost not see something in my looks that frights   120
thy guilty Soul, and makes thee wish to change that Shape of
Woman for any humble Animal, or Devil? for those were
safer for thee, and less mischievous.

FLORINDA: Alas, what mean you, Sir? I must confess your Looks
have something in 'em makes me fear; but I beseech you, as   125
you seem a Gentleman, pity a harmless Virgin, that takes
your House for Sanctuary.

BLUNT: Talk on, talk on, and weep too, till my faith return. Do,
flatter me out of my Senses again — a harmless Virgin with a
Pox, as much one as t'other, adsheartlikins. Why, what the   130
Devil can I not be safe in my House for you? not in my
Chamber? nay, even being naked too cannot secure me. This
is an Impudence greater than has invaded me yet. — Come,
no Resistance.

(*Pulls her rudely.*)

FLORINDA: Dare you be so cruel?   135

BLUNT: Cruel, adsheartlikins as a Gally-slave, or a *Spanish*
Whore: Cruel, yes, I will kiss and beat them all over; kiss, and
see thee all over; thou shalt lie with me too, not that I care for
the Injoyment, but to let you see I have ta'en deliberated Malice to thee, and will be revenged on one Whore for the Sins of   140
another; I will smile and deceive thee, flatter thee, and beat
thee, kiss and swear, and lye to thee, imbrace thee and rob
thee, as she did me, fawn on thee, and strip thee stark naked,
then hang thee out at my Window by the Heels, with a Paper

145 of scurvey Verses fasten'd to thy Breast, in praise of damnable
     Women—Come, come along.
FLORINDA: Alas, Sir, must I be sacrific'd for the Crimes of the
     most infamous of my Sex? I never understood the Sins you
     name.
150 BLUNT: Do, persuade the Fool you love him, or that one of you
     can be just or honest; tell me I was not an easy Coxcomb, or
     any strange impossible Tale: it will be believ'd sooner than thy
     false Showers or Protestations. A Generation of damn'd Hyp-
     ocrites, to flatter my very Clothes from my back! dissembling
155 Witches! are these the Returns you make an honest Gentle-
     man that trusts, believes, and loves you?—But if I be not even
     with you—Come along, or I shall—

(Pulls her again.)

(Enter FREDERICK.)

FREDERICK: Hah, what's here to do?
BLUNT: Adsheartlikins, *Frederick* I am glad thou art come, to be
160   a Witness of my dire Revenge.
FREDERICK: What's this, a Person of Quality too, who is upon
     the Ramble to supply the Defects of some grave impotent
     Husband?
BLUNT: No, this has another Pretence, some very unfortunate
165   Accident brought her hither, to save a Life pursued by I know
     not who, or why, and forc'd to take Sanctuary here at Fools
     Haven. Adsheartlikins to me of all Mankind for Protection? Is
     the Ass to be cajol'd again, think ye? No, young one, no
     Prayers or Tears shall mitigate my Rage; therefore prepare for
170   both my Pleasure of Enjoyment and Revenge, for I am re-
     solved to make up my Loss here on thy Body, I'll take it out in
     kindness and in beating.
FREDERICK: Now, Mistress of mine, what do you think of this?
FLORINDA: I think he will not—dares not be so barbarous.
175 FREDERICK: Have a care, *Blunt*, she fetch'd a deep Sigh, she is
     inamour'd with thy Shirt and Drawers, she'll strip thee even of
     that. There are of her Calling such unconscionable Bag-
     gages, and such dexterous Thieves, they'll flea a Man, and he
     shall ne'er miss his Skin, till he feels the Cold. There was a
180   Country-man of ours robb'd of a Row of Teeth whilst he was
     sleeping, which the Jilt made him buy again when he
     wak'd—You see, Lady, how little Reason we have to trust
     you.
BLUNT: 'Dsheartlikins, why, this is most abominable.
185 FLORINDA: Some such Devils there may be, but by all that's holy
     I am none such, I entered here to save a Life in danger.
BLUNT: For no goodness I'll warrant her.
FREDERICK: Faith, Damsel, you had e'en confess the plain
     Truth, for we are Fellows not to be caught twice in the same
190   Trap: Look on that Wreck, a tight Vessel when he set out of
     Haven, well trim'd and laden, and see how a Female Pic-
     caroon of this Island of Rogues has shatter'd him, and canst
     thou hope for any Mercy?
BLUNT: No, no, Gentlewoman, come along, adsheartlikins we
195   must be better acquainted—we'll both lie with her, and then
     let me alone to bang her.
FREDERICK: I am ready to serve you in matters of Revenge, that
     has a double Pleasure in't.
BLUNT: Well said. You hear, little one, how you are condemn'd
200   by publick Vote to the Bed within, there's no resisting your
     Destiny, Sweetheart.

(Pulls her.)

FLORINDA: Stay, Sir, I have seen you with *Belvile*, an *English*
     Cavalier, for his sake use me kindly; you know how, Sir.
BLUNT: *Belvile!* why, yes, Sweeting, we do know *Belvile*, and
     wish he were with us now, he's a Cormorant at Whore and   205
     Bacon, he'd have a Limb or two of thee, my Virgin Pullet: but
     'tis no matter, we'll leave him the Bones to pick.
FLORINDA: Sir, if you have any Esteem for that *Belvile*, I conjure
     you to treat me with more Gentleness; he'll thank you for the
     Justice.   210
FREDERICK: Hark ye, *Blunt*, I doubt we are mistaken in this
     matter.
FLORINDA: Sir, If you find me not worth *Belvile's* Care, use me
     as you please; and that you may think I merit better treatment
     than you threaten—pray take this Present—   215

(Gives him a Ring: He looks on it.)

BLUNT: Hum—A Diamond! why, 'tis a wonderful Virtue now
     that lies in this Ring, a mollifying Virtue; adsheartlikins
     there's more persuasive Rhetorick in't, than all her Sex can
     utter.
FREDERICK: I begin to suspect something; and 'twou'd anger us   220
     vilely to be truss'd up for a Rape upon a Maid of Quality,
     when we only believe we ruffle a Harlot.
BLUNT: Thou art a credulous Fellow, but adsheartlikins I have
     no Faith yet; why, my Saint prattled as parlously as this does,
     she gave me a Bracelet too, a Devil on her: but I sent my Man 225
     to sell it to day for Necessaries, and it prov'd as counterfeit as
     her Vows of Love.
FREDERICK: However let it reprieve her till we see *Belvile*.
BLUNT: That's hard, yet I will grant it.

(Enter a SERVANT.)

SERVANT: Oh, Sir, the Colonel is just come with his new Friend 230
     and a *Spaniard* of Quality, and talks of having you to Dinner
     with 'em.
BLUNT: 'Dsheartlikins, I'm undone—I would not see 'em for the
     World: Harkye, *Frederick* lock up the Wench in your
     Chamber.   235
FREDERICK: Fear nothing, Madam, whate'er he threatens,
     you're safe whilst in my Hands.

(Exit FREDERICK *and* FLORINDA.)

BLUNT: And, Sirrah—upon your Life, say—I am not at
     home—or that I am asleep—or—or any thing—away—I'll
     prevent them coming this way.   240

(Locks the Door and Exeunt.)

— ACT FIVE —

SCENE I

BLUNT'S *Chamber.*

(After a great knocking as at his Chamber-door, enter BLUNT
softly, crossing the Stage in his Shirt and Drawers, as before.)

(Call within.) Ned, Ned Blunt, Ned Blunt.
BLUNT: The Rogues are up in Arms, 'dsheartlikins, this vil-

lainous *Frederick* has betray'd me, they have heard of my
blessed Fortune.

5 (*And knocking within.*) *Ned Blunt, Ned, Ned*—

BELVILE: Why, he's dead, sir, without dispute dead, he has not
been seen to day; let's break open the Door—here—Boy—

BLUNT: Ha, break open the Door! 'dsheartlikins that mad Fellow
will be as good as his word.

10 BELVILE: Boy, bring something to force the Door.

(*A great noise within at the Door again.*)

BLUNT: So, now must I speak in my own Defence, I'll try what
Rhetorick will do—hold—hold, what do you mean, Gentlemen, what do you mean?

BELVILE: Oh Rogue, art alive? prithee open the Door, and con-
15 vince us.

BLUNT: Yes, I am alive, Gentlemen—but at present a little busy.

BELVILE: (*Within.*) How! *Blunt* grown a man of Business!
come, come, open, and let's see this Miracle.

BLUNT: No, no, no, no, Gentlemen, 'tis no great Business—
20 but—I am—at—my Devotion,—'dsheartlikins, will you not
allow a man time to pray?

BELVILE: (*Within.*) Turn'd religious! a greater Wonder than the
first, therefore open quickly, or we shall unhinge, we shall.

BLUNT: This won't do—Why, hark ye, Colonel; to tell you the
25 plain Truth, I am about a necessary Affair of Life.—I have a
Wench with me—you apprehend me? the Devil's in't they
be so uncivil as to disturb me now.

WILLMORE: How, a Wench! Nay, then we must enter and par-
take; no Resistance,—unless it be your Lady of Quality, and
30 then we'll keep our distance.

BLUNT: So, the Business is out.

WILLMORE: Come, come, lend more hands to the Door,—now
heave altogether—so, well done, my Boys—

(*Breaks open the Door. Enter* BELVILE, WILLMORE, FREDERICK,
PEDRO *and* BELVILE'S PAGE: BLUNT *looks simply, they all laugh
at him, he lays his hand on his Sword, and comes up to*
WILLMORE.)

BLUNT: Hark ye, Sir, laugh out your laugh quickly, d'ye hear,
35 and be gone, I shall spoil your sport else; 'dsheartlikins, Sir,
I shall—the Jest has been carried on too long,—(*Aside.*) a
Plague upon my Taylor—

WILLMORE: 'Sdeath, how the Whore has drest him! Faith, Sir,
I'm sorry.

40 BLUNT: Are you so, Sir? keep't to your self then, Sir, I advise
you, d'ye hear? for I can as little endure your Pity as his Mirth.

(*Lays his Hand on's Sword.*)

BELVILE: Indeed, *Willmore*, thou wert a little too rough with
Ned Blunt's Mistress; call a Person of Quality Whore, and
one so young, so handsome, and so eloquent!—ha, ha, ha.

45 BLUNT: Hark ye, Sir, you know me, and know I can be angry;
have a care—for 'dsheartlikins I can fight too—I can, Sir,—
do you mark me—no more.

BELVILE: Why so peevish, good *Ned*? some Disappointments,
I'll warrant—What! did the jealous Count her Husband re-
50 turn just in the nick?

(*They laugh.*)

BLUNT: Or the Devil, Sir,—d'ye laugh?
Look ye, settle me a good sober Countenance, and that
quickly too, or you shall know *Ned Blunt* is not—

BELVILE: Not every Body, we know that.

55 BLUNT: Not an Ass, to be laught at, Sir.

WILLMORE: Unconscionable Sinner, to bring a Lover so near
his Happiness, a vigorous passionate Lover, and then not only
cheat him of his Moveables, but his Desires too.

BELVILE: Ah, Sir, a Mistress is a Trifle with *Blunt*, he'll have a
60 dozen the next time he looks abroad; his Eyes have Charms
not to be resisted: There needs no more than to expose that
taking Person to the view of the Fair, and he leads 'em all in
Triumph.

PEDRO: Sir, tho I'm a stranger to you, I'm ashamed at the rude-
65 ness of my Nation; and could you learn who did it, would
assist you to make an Example of 'em.

BLUNT: Why, ay, there's one speaks sense now, and handsomly;
and let me tell you Gentlemen, I should not have shew'd my
self like a Jack-Pudding, thus to have made you Mirth, but
70 that I have revenge within my power; for know, I have got into
my possession a Female, who had better have fallen under
any Curse, than the Ruin I design her: 'dsheartlikins, she assaulted me here in my own Lodgings, and had doubtless
committed a Rape upon me, had not this Sword defended
75 me.

FREDERICK: I knew not that, but o' my Conscience thou hadst
ravisht her, had she not redeem'd her self with a Ring—let's
see't, *Blunt*.

(BLUNT *shews the Ring.*)

BELVILE: (*Goes to whisper to him.*) Hah!—the Ring I gave *Florinda* when we exchang'd our Vows!—hark ye, *Blunt*—

80 WILLMORE: No whispering, good Colonel, there's a Woman in
the case, no whispering.

BELVILE: Hark ye, Fool, be advis'd, and conceal both the Ring
and the Story, for your Reputation's sake; don't let People
know what despis'd Cullies we *English* are: to be cheated and
85 abus'd by one Whore, and another rather bribe thee than be
kind to thee, is an Infamy to our Nation.

WILLMORE: Come, come, where's the Wench! we'll see her, let
her be what she will, we'll see her.

PEDRO: Ay, ay, let us see her, I can soon discover whether she be
90 of Quality, or for your Diversion.

BLUNT: She's in *Frederick's* Custody.

WILLMORE: Come, come, the Key.

(*To* FREDERICK *who gives him the Key, they are going.*)

BELVILE: Death! what shall I do?—stay, Gentlemen—yet if I
95 hinder 'em, I shall discover all—hold, let's go one at once—
give me the Key.

WILLMORE: Nay, hold there, Colonel, I'll go first.

FREDERICK: Nay, no Dispute, *Ned* and I have the property of
her.

100 WILLMORE: Damn Property—then we'll draw Cuts.

(BELVILE *goes to whisper* WILLMORE.)

Nay, no Corruption, good Colonel: come, the longest Sword
carries her.—

(*They all draw, forgetting Don* PEDRO, *being a Spaniard, had
the longest.*)

BLUNT: I yield up my Interest to you Gentlemen, and that will
be Revenge sufficient.

WILLMORE: The Wench is yours—(*To* PEDRO) Pox of his
105 *Toledo*, I had forgot that.

FREDERICK: Come, Sir, I'll conduct you to the Lady.

(*Exit* FREDERICK *and* PEDRO.)

BELVILE: (*Aside.*) To hinder him will certainly discover—
Dost know, dull Beast, what Mischief thou hast done?

(WILLMORE *walking up and down out of Humour.*)

110 WILLMORE: Ay, ay, to trust our Fortune to Lots, a Devil on't,
'twas madness, that's the Truth on't.
BELVILE: Oh intolerable Sot!

(*Enter* FLORINDA, *running masqu'd,* PEDRO *after her,* WILL-
MORE *gazing round her.*)

FLORINDA: (*Aside.*) Good Heaven, defend me from discovery.
PEDRO: 'Tis but in vain to fly me, you are fallen to my Lot.
115 BELVILE: Sure she is undiscover'd yet, but now I fear there is no
way to bring her off.
WILLMORE: Why, what a Pox is not this my Woman, the same I
follow'd but now?

(PEDRO *talking to* FLORINDA, *who walks up and down.*)

PEDRO: As if I did not know ye, and your Business here.
120 FLORINDA: (*Aside.*) Good Heaven! I fear he does indeed—
PEDRO: Come, pray be kind, I know you meant to be so when
you enter'd here, for these are proper Gentlemen.
WILLMORE: But, Sir—perhaps the Lady will not be impos'd
upon, she'll chuse her Man.
125 PEDRO: I am better bred, than not to leave her Choice free.

(*Enter* VALERIA, *and is surpriz'd at the Sight of Don* PEDRO.)

VALERIA: (*Aside.*) Don *Pedro* here! there's no avoiding him.
FLORINDA: (*Aside.*) *Valeria!* then I'm undone—
VALERIA: (*To* PEDRO, *running to him.*) Oh! have I found you,
Sir—
130 —The strangest Accident—if I had breath—to tell it.
PEDRO: Speak—is *Florinda* safe? *Hellena* well?
VALERIA: Ay, ay, Sir—*Florinda*—is safe—from any fears of
you.
PEDRO: Why, where's *Florinda?*—speak.
135 VALERIA: Ay, where indeed, Sir? I wish I could inform you,—
But to hold you no longer in doubt—
FLORINDA: (*Aside.*) Oh, what will she say!
VALERIA: She's fled away in the Habit of one of her Pages, Sir—
but *Callis* thinks you may retrieve her yet, if you make haste
140 away; she'll tell you, Sir, the rest—(*Aside.*) if you can find her
out.
PEDRO: Dishonourable Girl, she has undone my Aim—Sir—
you see my necessity of leaving you, and I hope you'll pardon
it: my Sister, I know, will make her flight to you; and if she do,
145 I shall expect she should be render'd back.
BELVILE: I shall consult my Love and Honour, Sir.

(*Exit* PEDRO.)

FLORINDA: (*To* VALERIA.) My dear Preserver, let me imbrace thee.
WILLMORE: What the Devil's all this?
BLUNT: Mystery by this Light.
150 VALERIA: Come, come, make haste and get your selves married
quickly, for your Brother will return again.
BELVILE: I am so surpriz'd with Fears and Joys, so amaz'd to find
you here in safety, I can scarce persuade my Heart into a
Faith of what I see—

WILLMORE: Harkye, Colonel, is this that Mistress who has cost   155
you so many Sighs, and me so many Quarrels with you?
BELVILE: (*To* FLORINDA.) It is—Pray give him the Honour of
your Hand.
WILLMORE: Thus it must be receiv'd then.

(*Kneels and kisses her Hand.*)

And with it give your Pardon too.   160
FLORINDA: The Friend to *Belvile* may command me anything.
WILLMORE: (*Aside.*) Death, wou'd I might, 'tis a surprizing
Beauty.
BELVILE: Boy, run and fetch a Father instantly.

(*Exit* BOY.)

FREDERICK: So, now do I stand like a Dog, and have not a Sylla-   165
ble to plead my own Cause with: by this Hand, Madam, I was
never thorowly confounded before, nor shall I ever more dare
look up with Confidence, till you are pleased to pardon me.
FLORINDA: Sir, I'll be reconcil'd to you on one Condition, that
you'll follow the Example of your Friend, in marrying a Maid   170
that does not hate you, and whose Fortune (I believe) will not
be unwelcome to you.
FREDERICK: Madam, had I no Inclinations that way, I shou'd
obey your kind Commands.
BELVILE: Who, *Frederick* marry; he has so few Inclinations for   175
Womankind, that had he been possest of Paradise, he might
have continu'd there to this Day, if no Crime but Love cou'd
have disinherited him.
FREDERICK: Oh, I do not use to boast of my Intrigues.
BELVILE: Boast! why thou do'st nothing but boast; and I dare   180
swear, wer't thou as innocent from the Sin of the Grape, as
thou art from the Apple, thou might'st yet claim that right in
Eden which our first Parents lost by too much loving.
FREDERICK: I wish this Lady would think me so modest a Man.
VALERIA: She shou'd be sorry then, and not like you half so well,   185
and I shou'd be loth to break my Word with you; which was,
That if your Friend and mine are agreed, it shou'd be a Match
between you and I.

(*She gives him her Hand.*)

FREDERICK: Bear witness, Colonel, 'tis a Bargain.

(*Kisses her Hand.*)

BLUNT: (*To* FLORINDA.) I have a Pardon to beg too; but   190
adsheartlikins I am so out of Countenance, that I am a Dog if
I can say any thing to purpose.
FLORINDA: Sir, I heartily forgive you all.
BLUNT: That's nobly said, sweet Lady—*Belvile*, prithee present
her her Ring again, for I find I have not Courage to approach   195
her my self.

(*Gives him the Ring, he gives it to* FLORINDA. *Enter* BOY.)

BOY: Sir, I have brought the Father that you sent for.
BELVILE: 'Tis well, and now my dear *Florinda*, let's fly to com-
pleat that mighty Joy we have so long wish'd and sigh'd for. —
Come, *Frederick* you'll follow?   200
FREDERICK: Your Example, Sir, 'twas ever my Ambition in War,
and must be so in Love.
WILLMORE: And must not I see this juggling Knot ty'd?
BELVILE: No, thou shalt do us better Service, and be our Guard,
lest Don *Pedro's* sudden Return interrupt the Ceremony.   205

WILLMORE: Content; I'll secure this Pass.

(*Exit* BELVILE, FLORINDA, FREDERICK, *and* VALERIA. *Enter* BOY.)

BOY: (*To* WILLMORE.) Sir, there's a Lady without wou'd speak to you.

WILLMORE: Conduct her in, I dare not quit my Post.

210 BOY: And, Sir, your Taylor waits you in your Chamber.

BLUNT: Some comfort yet, I shall not dance naked at the Wedding.

(*Exit* BLUNT *and* BOY.)

(*Enter again the* BOY, *conducting in* ANGELICA *in a masquing Habit and a Vizard,* WILLMORE *runs to her.*)

WILLMORE: This can be none but my pretty Gipsy—Oh, I see you can follow as well as fly—Come, confess thy self the most
215 malicious Devil in Nature, you think you have done my Bus'ness with *Angelica*—

ANGELICA: Stand off, base Villain—

(*She draws a Pistol and holds to his Breast.*)

WILLMORE: Hah, 'tis not she: who art thou? and what's thy Business?

220 ANGELICA: One thou hast injur'd, and who comes to kill thee for't.

WILLMORE: What the Devil canst thou mean?

ANGELICA: By all my Hopes to kill thee—

(*Holds still the Pistol to his Breast,* he going back, *she following still.*)

WILLMORE: Prithee on what Acquaintance? for I know thee not.
225 ANGELICA: Behold this Face!—so lost to thy Remembrance! And then call all thy Sins about thy Soul,

(*Pulls off her Vizard.*)

And let them die with thee.

WILLMORE: *Angelica!*

ANGELICA: Yes, Traitor.
230 Does not thy guilty Blood run shivering thro thy Veins? Hast thou no Horrour at this Sight, that tells thee, Thou hast not long to boast thy shameful Conquest?

WILLMORE: Faith, no Child, my Blood keeps it old Ebbs and Flows still, and that usual Heat too, that cou'd oblige thee
235 with a Kindness, had I but opportunity.

ANGELICA: Devil! dost wanton with my Pain—have at thy Heart.

WILLMORE: Hold, dear Virago! hold thy Hand a little, I am not now at leisure to be kill'd—hold and hear me—
240 (*Aside.*) Death, I think she's in earnest.

ANGELICA: (*Aside, turning from him.*) Oh if I take not heed, My coward Heart will leave me to his Mercy.
—What have you, Sir, to say?—but should I hear thee, Thou'dst talk away all that is brave about me:

(*Follows him with the Pistol to his Breast.*)

245 And I have vow'd thy Death, by all that's sacred.

WILLMORE: Why, then, there's an end of a proper handsom Fellow, that might have liv'd to have done good Service yet: —That's all I can say to't.

ANGELICA: (*Pausingly.*) Yet—I wou'd give thee—time for
250 Penitence.

WILLMORE: Faith, Child, I thank God, I have ever took care to lead a good, sober, hopeful Life, and am of a Religion that teaches me to believe, I shall depart in Peace.

ANGELICA: So will the Devil: tell me
How many poor believing Fools thou hast undone; 255
How many Hearts thou hast betray'd to ruin!
—Yet, these are little Mischiefs to the Ills
Thou'st taught mine to commit: thou'st taught it Love.

WILLMORE: Egad, 'twas shreudly hurt the while.

ANGELICA: —Love, that has robb'd if of its Unconcern, 260
Of all that Pride that taught me how to value it,
And in its room a mean submissive Passion was convey'd,
That made me humbly bow, which I ne'er did
To any thing but Heaven.
—Thou, perjur'd Man, didst this, and with thy Oaths, 265
Which on thy Knees thou didst devoutly make,
Soften'd my yielding Heart—And then, I was a Slave—
Yet still had been content to've worn my Chains,
Worn 'em with Vanity and Joy for ever,
Hadst thou not broke those Vows that put them on. 270
—'Twas then I was undone.

(*All this while follows him with a Pistol to his Breast.*)

WILLMORE: Broke my Vows! why, where hast thou lived?
Amongst the Gods! For I never heard of mortal Man,
That has not broke a thousand Vows.

ANGELICA: Oh, Impudence! 275

WILLMORE: *Angelica!* that Beauty has been too long tempting,
Not to have made a thousand Lovers languish,
Who in the amorous Favour, no doubt have sworn
Like me; did they all die in that Faith? still adoring?
I do not think they did. 280

ANGELICA: No, faithless Man: had I repaid their Vows, as I did thine, I wou'd have kill'd the ungrateful that had abandon'd me.

WILLMORE: This old General has quite spoil'd thee, nothing makes a Woman so vain, as being flatter'd; your old Lover ever supplies the Defects of Age, with intolerable Dotage, vast 285
Charge, and that which you call Constancy; and attributing all this to your own Merits, you domineer, and throw your Favours in's Teeth, upbraiding him still with the Defects of Age, and cuckold him as often as he deceives your Expectations. But the gay, young, brisk Lover, that brings his equal 290
Fires, and can give you Dart for Dart, he'll be as nice as you sometimes.

ANGELICA: All this thou'st made me know, for which I hate thee.
Had I remain'd in innocent Security,
I shou'd have thought all Men were born my Slaves; 295
And worn my Pow'r like Lightning in my Eyes,
To have destroy'd at Pleasure when offended.
—But when Love held the Mirror, the undeceiving Glass
Reflected all the Weakness of my Soul, and made me know,
My richest Treasure being lost, my Honour, 300
All the remaining Spoil cou'd not be worth
The Conqueror's Care or Value.
—Oh how I fell like a long worship'd Idol,
Discovering all the Cheat!
Wou'd not the Incense and rich Sacrifice, 305
Which blind Devotion offer'd at my Altars,

Have fall'n to thee?
Why woud'st thou then destroy my fancy'd Power?
WILLMORE: By Heaven thou art brave, and I admire thee
    strangely.
310 I wish I were that dull, that constant thing,
Which thou woud'st have, and Nature never meant me:
I must, like chearful Birds, sing in all Groves,
And perch on every Bough,
Billing the next kind She that flies to meet me;
315 Yet after all cou'd build my Nest with thee,
Thither repairing when I'd lov'd my round,
And still reserve a tributary Flame.
(Offers her a Purse of Gold.)
—To gain your Credit, I'll pay you back your Charity,
And be oblig'd for nothing but for Love.
320 ANGELICA: Oh that thou wert in earnest!
So mean a Thought of me,
Wou'd turn my Rage to Scorn, and I shou'd pity thee,
And give thee leave to live;
Which for the publick Safety of our Sex,
325 And my own private Injuries, I dare not do.
Prepare—

(Follows still, as before.)

—I will no more be tempted with Replies.
WILLMORE: Sure—
ANGELICA: Another Word will damn thee! I've heard thee talk
    too long.

*(She follows him with a Pistol ready to shoot: he retires still
amaz'd.)*

(Enter Don ANTONIO, *his Arm in a Scarf, and lays hold on the
Pistol.)*

330 ANTONIO: Hah! *Angelica!*
ANGELICA: *Antonio!* What Devil brought thee hither?
ANTONIO: Love and Curiosity, seeing your Coach at Door.
    Let me disarm you of this unbecoming Instrument of
    Death. —

(Takes away the Pistol.)

335 Amongst the Number of your Slaves, was there not one worthy
    the Honour to have fought your Quarrel?
    —Who are you, Sir, that are so very wretched
    To merit Death from her?
WILLMORE: One, sir, that cou'd have made a better End of an
340 amorous Quarrel without you, than with you.
ANTONIO: Sure 'tis some Rival—hah—the very Man took down
    her Picture yesterday—the very same that set on me last
    night—Blest opportunity—

(Offers to shoot him.)

ANGELICA: Hold, you're mistaken, Sir.
345 ANTONIO: By Heaven the very same!
    —Sir, what pretensions have you to this Lady?
WILLMORE: Sir, I don't use to be examin'd, and am ill at all
    Disputes but this—

(Draws, ANTONIO *offers to shoot.)*

ANGELICA: *(To* WILLMORE.) Oh, hold! you see he's arm'd with
    certain Death:

—And you, *Antonio,* I command you hold,   350
By all the Passion you've so lately vow'd me.

(Enter Don PEDRO, *sees* ANTONIO, *and stays.)*

PEDRO: *(Aside.)* Hah, *Antonio!* and *Angelica!*
ANTONIO: When I refuse Obedience to your Will,
May you destroy me with your mortal Hate.
By all that's Holy I adore you so,   355
That even my Rival, who has Charms enough
To make him fall a Victim to my Jealousy,
Shall live, nay, and have leave to love on still.
PEDRO: *(Aside.)* What's this I hear?
ANGELICA: *(Pointing to* WILLMORE.) Ah thus, 'twas thus he   360
    talk'd, and I believ'd.
    —*Antonio,* yesterday,
I'd not have sold my Interest in his Heart,
For all the Sword has won and lost in Battle.
—But now to show my utmost of Contempt,
I give thee Life—which if thou would'st preserve,   365
Live where my Eyes may never see thee more,
Live to undo some one, whose Soul may prove
So bravely constant to revenge my Love.

(Goes out, ANGELICA *follows, but* PEDRO *pulls him back.)*

PEDRO: *Antonio*—stay.
ANTONIO: Don *Pedro*—   370
PEDRO: What Coward Fear was that prevented thee
    From meeting me this Morning on the *Molo?*
ANTONIO: Meet thee?
PEDRO: Yes me; I was the Man that dar'd thee to't.
ANTONIO: Hast thou so often seen me fight in War,   375
    To find no better Cause to excuse my Absence?
    —I sent my Sword and one to do thee Right,
Finding my self uncapable to use a Sword.
PEDRO: But 'twas *Florinda's* Quarrel that we fought,
    And you to shew how little you esteem'd her,   380
Sent me your Rival, giving him your Interest.
—But I have found the Cause of this Affront,
But when I meet you fit for the Dispute,
—I'll tell you my Resentment.
ANTONIO: I shall be ready, Sir, e'er long to do your Reason.   385

(Exit ANTONIO.)

PEDRO: If I cou'd find *Florinda,* now whilst my Anger's high, I
    think I shou'd be kind, and give her to *Belvile* in Revenge.
WILLMORE: Faith, Sir, I know not what you wou'd do, but I
    believe the Priest within has been so kind.
PEDRO: How! my Sister married?   390
WILLMORE: I hope by this time she is, and bedded too, or he has
    not my longings about him.
PEDRO: Dares he do thus? Does he not fear my Pow'r?
WILLMORE: Faith not at all. If you will go in, and thank him for
    the Favour he has done your Sister, so; if not, Sir, my Power's   395
    greater in this House than yours; I have a damn'd surly Crew
    here, that will keep you till the next Tide, and then clap you
    an board my Prize; my Ship lies but a League off the *Molo,*
    and we shall show your Donship a damn'd *Tramontana*
    Rover's Trick.   400

399 **Tramontana** Italian and Spanish *tramontano* = from beyond the
mountains

(Enter BELVILE.)

BELVILE: This Rogue's in some new Mischief—hah, *Pedro* return'd!

PEDRO: Colonel *Belvile*, I hear you have married my Sister.

BELVILE: You have heard truth then, Sir.

405 PEDRO: Have I so? then, Sir, I wish you Joy.

BELVILE: How!

PEDRO: By this Embrace I do, and I glad on't.

BELVILE: Are you in earnest?

PEDRO: By our long Friendship and my Obligations to thee, I
410 am. The sudden Change I'll give you Reasons for anon. Come lead me into my Sister, that she may know I now approve her Choice.

(Exit BELVILE with PEDRO. WILLMORE goes to follow them. Enter HELLENA as before in Boy's Clothes, and pulls him back.)

WILLMORE: Ha! my Gipsy—Now a thousand Blessings on thee for this Kindness. Egad, Child, I was e'en in despair of ever
415 seeing thee again; my Friends are all provided for within, each Man his kind Woman.

HELLENA: Hah! I thought they had serv'd me some such Trick.

WILLMORE: And I was e'en resolv'd to go aboard, condemn my self to my lone Cabin, and the Thoughts of thee.

420 HELLENA: And cou'd you have left me behind? wou'd you have been so ill-natur'd?

WILLMORE: Why, 'twou'd have broke my Heart, Child—but since we are met again, I defy foul Weather to part us.

HELLENA: And wou'd you be a faithful Friend now, if a Maid
425 shou'd trust you?

WILLMORE: For a Friend I cannot promise, thou art of a Form so excellent, a Face and Humour too good for cold dull Friendship; I am parlously afraid of being in love, Child, and you have not forgot how severely you have us'd me.

430 HELLENA: That's all one, such Usage you must still look for, to find out all your Haunts, to rail at you to all that love you, till I have made you love only me in your own Defence, because no body else will love.

WILLMORE: But hast thou no better Quality to recommend thy
435 self by?

HELLENA: Faith none, Captain—Why, 'twill be the greater Charity to take me for thy Mistress, I am a lone Child, a kind of Orphan Love; and why I shou'd die a Maid, and in a Captain's Hands too, I do not understand.

440 WILLMORE: Egad, I was never claw'd away with Broad-Sides from any Female before, thou hast one Virtue I adore, good-Nature; I hate a coy demure Mistress, she's as troublesom as a Colt, I'll break none; no, give me a mad Mistress when mew'd, and in flying on[e] I dare trust upon the Wing, that
445 whilst she's kind will come to the Lure.

HELLENA: Nay, as kind as you will, good Captain, whilst it lasts, but let's lose no time.

WILLMORE: My time's as precious to me, as thine can be; therefore, dear Creature, since we are so well agreed, let's retire to
450 my Chamber, and if ever thou were treated with such savory Love—Come—My Bed's prepar'd for such a Guest, all clean and sweet as thy fair self; I love to steal a Dish and a Bottle with a Friend, and hate long Graces—Come, let's retire and fall to.

HELLENA: 'Tis but getting my Consent, and the Business is soon
455 done; let but old Gaffer *Hymen* and his Priest say Amen to't,

and I dare lay my Mother's Daughter by as proper a Fellow as your Father's Son, without fear or blushing.

WILLMORE: Hold, hold, no Bugg Words, Child, Priest and *Hymen*: prithee add Hangman to 'em to make up the Consort—
460 No, no, we'll have no Vows but Love, Child, nor Witness but the Lover; the kind Diety injoins naught but love and enjoy. *Hymen* and Priest wait still upon Portion, and Joynture; Love and Beauty have their own Ceremonies. Marriage is as certain a Bane to Love, as lending Money is to Friendship: I'll
465 neither ask nor give a Vow, tho I could be content to turn Gipsy, and become a Left-hand Bridegroom, to have the Pleasure of working that great Miracle of making a Maid a Mother, if you durst venture; 'tis upse Gipsy that, and if I miss, I'll lose my Labour.

470 HELLENA: And if you do not lose, what shall I get? A Cradle full of Noise and Mischief, with a Pack of Repentance at my Back? Can you teach me to weave Incle to pass my time with? 'Tis upse Gipsy that too.

WILLMORE: I can teach thee to weave a true Love's Knot better.

475 HELLENA: So can my Dog.

WILLMORE: Well, I see we are both upon our Guard, and I see there's no way to conquer good Nature, but by yielding—here—give me thy Hand—one Kiss and I am thine—

HELLENA: One Kiss! How like my Page he speaks; I am resolv'd
480 you shall have none, for asking such a sneaking Sum—He that will be satisfied with one Kiss, will never die of that Longing; good Friend single-Kiss, is all your talking come to this? A Kiss, a Caudle! farewel, Captain single-Kiss.

(Going out he stays her.)

WILLMORE: Nay, if we part so, let me die like a Bird upon a
485 Bough, at the Sheriff's Charge. By Heaven, both the *Indies* shall not buy thee from me. I adore thy Humour and will marry thee, and we are so of one Humour, it must be a Bargain—give me thy Hand—

(Kisses her hand.)

And now let the blind ones (Love and Fortune) do their worst.

490 HELLENA: Why, God-a-mercy, Captain!

WILLMORE: But harkye—The Bargain is now made; but is it not fit we should know each other's Names? That when we have Reason to curse one another hereafter, and People ask me who 'tis I give to the Devil, I may at least be able to tell what
495 Family you came of.

HELLENA: Good reason, Captain; and where I have cause, (as I doubt not but I shall have plentiful) that I may know at whom to throw my—Blessings—I beseech ye your Name.

WILLMORE: I am call'd *Robert the Constant*.

500 HELLENA: A very fine Name! pray was it your Faulkner or Butler that christen'd you? Do they not use to whistle when then call you?

WILLMORE: I hope you have a better, that a Man may name without crossing himself, you are so merry with mine.

505 HELLENA: I am call'd *Hellena the Inconstant*.

(Enter PEDRO, BELVILE, FLORINDA, FREDERICK, and VALERIA.)

---

468 **upse** Op zijn = in the fashion or manner of, *Upse Gipsy* = like a gipsy   472 **Incle** Linen thread or yarn which was woven into a tape once very much in use

PEDRO: Hah! *Hellena!*

FLORINDA: *Hellena!*

HELLENA: The very same—hah my Brother! now, Captain,
shew your Love and Courage; stand to your Arms, and defend
510 me bravely, or I am lost for ever.

PEDRO: What's this I hear? false Girl, how came you hither, and
what's your Business? Speak.

(Goes roughly to her.)

WILLMORE: Hold off, Sir, you have leave to parly only.

(Puts himself between.)

HELLENA: I had e'en as good tell it, as you guess it. Faith,
515 Brother, my Business is the same with all living Creatures of
my Age, to love, and be loved, and here's the Man.

PEDRO: Perfidious Maid, hast thou deceiv'd me too, deceiv'd thy
self and Heaven?

HELLENA: 'Tis time enough to make my Peace with that: Be you
520 but kind, let me alone with Heaven.

PEDRO: *Belvile,* I did not expect this false Play from you; was't
not enough you'd gain *Florinda* (which I pardon'd) but your
leud Friends too must be inrich'd with the Spoils of a noble
Family?

525 BELVILE: Faith, Sir, I am as much surpriz'd at this as you can be:
Yet, Sir, my Friends are Gentlemen, and ought to be esteem'd for their Misfortunes, since they have the Glory to
suffer with the best of Men and Kings; 'tis true, he's a Rover of
Fortune, yet a Prince aboard his little wooden World.

530 PEDRO: What's this to the maintenance of a Woman or her Birth
and Quality?

WILLMORE: Faith, Sir, I can boast of nothing but a Sword which
does me Right where-e'er I come, and has defended a worse
Cause than a Woman's: and since I lov'd her before I either
535 knew her Birth or Name, I must pursue my Resolution, and
marry her.

PEDRO: And is all your holy Intent of becoming a Nun debauch'd into a Desire of Man?

HELLENA: Why—I have consider'd the matter, Brother, and
540 find the Three hundred thousand Crowns my Uncle left me
(and you cannot keep from me) will be better laid out in Love
than in Religion, and turn to as good an Account—let most
Voices carry it, for Heaven or the Captain?

ALL CRY: a Captain, a Captain.

545 HELLENA: Look ye, Sir, 'tis a clear Case.

PEDRO: *(Aside.)* Oh I am mad—if I refuse, my Life's in Danger—
—Come—There's one motive induces me—take her—I
shall now be free from the fear of her Honour; guard it you
now, if you can, I have been a Slave to't long enough.

(Gives her to him.)

550 WILLMORE: Faith, Sir, I am of a Nation, that are of opinion a
Woman's Honour is not worth guarding when she has a mind
to part with it.

HELLENA: Well said, Captain.

PEDRO: *(To* VALERIA.*)* This was your Plot, Mistress, but I hope
555 you have married one that will revenge my Quarrel to you—

VALERIA: There's no altering Destiny, Sir.

PEDRO: Sooner than a Woman's Will, therefore I forgive you
all—and wish you may get my Father's Pardon as easily;
which I fear.

(Enter BLUNT *drest in a Spanish Habit, looking very ridiculously; his* MAN *adjusting his Band.)*

MAN: 'Tis very well, Sir. 560

BLUNT: Well, Sir, 'dsheartlikins I tell you 'tis damnable ill, Sir—
a Spanish Habit, good Lord! cou'd the Devil and my Taylor
devise no other Punishment for me, but the Mode of a Nation
I abominate?

BELVILE: What's the matter, *Ned?* 565

BLUNT: Pray view me round, and judge—

(Turns round.)

BELVILE: I must confess thou art a kind of an odd Figure.

BLUNT: In a Spanish Habit with a Vengeance! I had rather be in
the Inquisition for Judaism, than in this Doublet and
Breeches; a Pillory were an easy Collar to this, three Handfuls 570
high; and these Shoes too are worse than the Stocks, with the
Sole an Inch shorter than my Foot: In fine, Gentlemen,
methinks I look altogether like a Bag of Bays stuff'd full of
Fools Flesh.

BELVILE: Methinks 'tis well, and makes the look *en Cavalier:* 575
Come, Sir, settle your Face, and salute our Friends, Lady—

BLUNT: Hah! Say'st thou so, my little Rover?

(To HELLENA.*)*

Lady—(if you be one) give me leave to kiss your Hand, and
tell you, adsheartlikins, for all I look so, I am your humble
Servant—A Pox of my *Spanish* Habit. 580

WILLMORE: Hark—what's this?

(Musick is heard to Play. Enter BOY.*)*

BOY: Sir, as the Custom is, the gay People in Masquerade, who
make every Man's House their own, are coming up.

(Enter several MEN *and* WOMEN *in masquing Habits, with Musick, they put themselves in order and dance.)*

BLUNT: Adsheartlikins, wou'd 'twere lawful to pull off their false
Faces, that I might see if my Doxy were not amongst 'em. 585

BELVILE: Ladies and Gentlemen, since you are come so *a
propos,* you must take a small Collation with us.

(To the MASQUERADERS.*)*

WILLMORE: Whilst we'll to the Good Man within, who stays to
give us a Cast of his Office.

(To HELLENA.*)*

—Have you no trembling at the near approach? 590

HELLENA: No more than you have in an Engagement or a
Tempest.

WILLMORE: Egad, thou'rt a brave Girl, and I admire thy Love
and Courage.

Lead on, no other Dangers they can dread, 595
Who venture in the Storms o'th' Marriage-Bed.

(Exeunt.)

— EPILOGUE —

THE *banisht Cavaliers! a Roving Blade!*
A *popish Carnival! a Masquerade!*
The *Devil's in't if this will please the Nation,*

In these our blessed Times of Reformation,
5 When Conventicling is so much in Fashion.
And yet—
That mutinous Tribe less Factions do beget,
Than your continual differing in Wit;
Your Judgment's (as your Passions) a Disease:
10 Nor Muse nor Miss your Appetite can please;
You're grown as nice as queasy Consciences,
Whose each Convulsion, when the Spirit moves,
Damns every thing that Maggot disapproves.
    With canting Rule you wou'd the Stage refine,
15 And to dull Method all our Sense confine.
With th' Insolence of Common-wealths you rule,
Where each gay Fop, and politick brave Fool
On Monarch Wit impose without controul.
As for the last who seldom sees a Play,
20 Unless it be the old Black-Fryers way,
Shaking his empty Noddle o'er Bamboo,
He crys—Good Faith, these Plays will never do.
—Ah, Sir, in my young days, what lofty Wit,
What high-strain'd Scenes of Fighting there were writ:
25 These are slight airy Toys. But tell me, pray,

What has the House of Commons done to day?
Then shews his Politicks, to let you see
Of State Affairs he'll judge as notably,
As he can do of Wit and Poetry.
    The younger Sparks, who hither do resort,   30
Cry—
Pox o' your gentle things, give us more Sport;
—Damn me, I'm sure 'twill never please the Court.
    Such Fops are never pleas'd, unless the Play
Be stuff'd with Fools, as brisk and dull as they: 35
Such might the Half-Crown spare, and in a Glass
At home behold a more accomplisht Ass,
Where they may set their Cravats, Wigs and Faces,
And practice all their Buffoonry Grimaces;
See how this—Huff becomes—this Dammy—flare—   40
Which they at home may act, because they dare,
But—must with prudent Caution do elsewhere.
Oh that our Nokes, or Tony Lee could show
A Fop but half so much to th' Life as you.

43 **Nokes, or Tony Lee** James Nokes and Antony Leigh, the two famous actors, were the leading low comedians of the day

✦ CRITICAL CONTEXTS ✦

JEAN CHAPELAIN
(1595–1674)

Summary of a Poetics of the Drama
(published posthumously)

TRANSLATED BY
BARRETT H. CLARK

JEAN CHAPELAIN WAS *one of the founding members of the Académie Française. He also wrote* the Académie's famous Judgment of the Académie on The Cid (1638) *on whether* Corneille's *play* The Cid (1636) *sufficiently expressed the neoclassical "rules" of drama. The Académie argued that* The Cid *violated the Aristotelian "unities" and that its action was often improbable and occasionally morally offensive. Cardinal Richelieu urged the Académie to make an example of Corneille, and its censure of* The Cid *established the limits of neoclassical dramatic practice. In his* Summary of a Poetics of the Drama, *Chapelain digests some of the principles embodied in the detailed discussion of* The Cid *and provides a more succinct outline to the forms and values of neoclassicism.*

The object of representative as well as of narrative poetry is the imitation of human action; their necessary condition is truth to life [*le vraysemblable*]; in its perfection it strives for the marvelous.

From the judicious union of the verisimilar and the marvelous springs the excellence of works of this sort. Both these elements belong to invention.

In Tragedy, which is the noblest form of drama, the poet imitates the actions of the great; in Comedy, those of people in middle or low condition. The ending of Comedy is happy.

Tragi-comedy was known to the Ancients only as tragedy with a happy ending. Witness the *Iphigenia in Tauris*. The modern French have made the form very popular, and as a result of the characters and the action have put it into a class nearer to tragedy than to comedy.

The Pastoral was invented and introduced by the Italians less than a hundred years after the Eclogue; it is a sort of Tragi-comedy, imitating the actions of shepherds, but in a more elevated manner and with higher sentiments than can be employed in the Eclogue.

In plays, poets depict, besides action, the various manners, customs, and passions of human beings.

They take particular care to make each personage speak according to his condition, age, and sex; and by propriety, they mean not only that which is decent, but what is fitting and appropriate to the characters—be they good or evil—as they are at first set forth in the play.

In their tragedies and comedies a good plot never had more than one principal action to which the others are related. This is what is termed Unity of Action.

They have allowed to the development of the action of a play the space of a single natural day. This is what is termed the Twenty-four-hour rule.

They have set the physical limit of their action to a single place. This is what is termed the Unity of Place.

All this is a necesssary corollary to the verisimilar, without which the mind is neither moved nor persuaded.

The action of the play consists in exposition of the story, its complication [*embrouillement*] and its development.

The most worthy and agreeable effect that can be produced by a play, is that as a result of the artful conduct of the story the spectator is left suspended and puzzled to know the outcome, and cannot decide what the end of the adventure will be.

The Latins divided plays into five acts, while the Greeks divided them only into scenes.

Each act has several scenes. It will seem too short if it have only four, and too long if more than seven.

In the first act the principal points of the story are made clear; in the second, complications arise; in the third, the trouble deepens; in the fourth, matters look desperate; in the fifth, the knot is loosed—in a natural way, however, but in an unforeseen manner—and from this results the Marvelous.

There are some who insist that no more than three characters should appear on the stage at the same time in the same scene, in order to avoid confusion. I approve of this, except when it applies to the last scenes of the last act, where everything ought to point toward the end and where confusion only renders the unraveling more noble and more beautiful.

Others insist that each scene be intimately bound to the other. This, it is true, produces a more agreeable effect; but the practice of the Ancients proves how unnecessary it is.

What seems most necessary to me is that no character should enter or leave without apparent reason.

NORTHROP FRYE
(1912–1991)
FROM *Anatomy of Criticism*
(1957)

NORTHROP FRYE WAS THE AUTHOR OF MANY INFLUENTIAL WORKS OF LITERARY AND CULTURAL criticism, and his Anatomy of Criticism *is one of the most important works of literary theory written in the twentieth century. In it, Frye attempts a systematic overview of the ordering structures and themes of Western literature. In this selection, he discusses character-types commonly found in literature and suggests how they have been drawn from comic types first used in the comedies of Plautus and Terence. The specificity of a work of literature, Frye argues, arises from its adaptation of, and confrontation with, basic elements such as these.*

Dramatic comedy, from which fictional comedy is mainly descended, has been remarkably tenacious of its structural principles and character types. Bernard Shaw remarked that a comic dramatist could get a reputation for daring originality by stealing his method from Molière and his characters from Dickens: if we were to read Menander and Aristophanes for Molière and Dickens the statement would be hardly less true, at least as a general principle. The earliest extant European comedy, Aristophanes' *The Acharnians*, contains the *miles gloriosus* or military braggart who is still going strong in Chaplin's *Great Dictator*; the Joxer Daly of O'Casey's *Juno and the Paycock* has the same character and dramatic function as the parasites of twenty-five hundred years ago, and the audiences of vaudeville, comic strips, and television programs still laugh at the jokes that were declared to be outworn at the opening of *The Frogs*.

The plot structure of Greek New Comedy, as transmitted by Plautus and Terence, in itself less a form than a formula, has become the basis for most comedy, especially in its more highly conventionalized dramatic form, down to our own day. It will be most convenient to work out the theory of comic construction from drama, using illustrations from fiction only incidentally. What normally happens is that a young man wants a young woman, that his desire is resisted by some opposition, usually paternal, and that near the end of the play some twist in the plot enables the hero to have his will. In this simple pattern there are several complex elements. In the first place, the movement of comedy is usually a movement from one kind of society to another. At the beginning of the play the obstructing characters are in charge of the play's society, and the audience recognizes that they are usurpers. At the end of the play the device in the plot that brings hero and heroine together causes a new society to crystallize around the hero, and the moment when this crystallization occurs is the point of resolution in the action, the comic discovery, *anagnorisis* or *cognitio*.

The appearance of this new society is frequently signalized by some kind of party or festive ritual, which either appears at the end of the play or is assumed to take place immediately afterward. Weddings are most common, and sometimes so many of them occur, as in the quadruple wedding at the end of *As You Like It*, that they suggest also the wholesale pairing off that takes place in a dance, which is another common conclusion, and the normal one for the masque. The banquet at the end of *The Taming of the Shrew* has an ancestry that goes back to Greek Middle Comedy; in Plautus the audience is sometimes jocosely invited to an imaginary banquet afterwards; Old Comedy, like the modern Christmas pantomime, was more generous, and occasionally threw bits of food to the audience. As the final society reached by comedy is the one that the audience has recognized all along to be the proper and desirable state of affairs, an act of communion with the audience is in order. Tragic actors expect to be applauded as well as comic ones, but nevertheless the word "plaudite" at the end of a Roman comedy, the invitation to the audience to form part of the comic society, would seem rather out of place at the end of a tragedy. The resolution of comedy comes, so to speak, from the audience's side of the stage; in a tragedy it comes from some mysterious world on the opposite side. In the movie, where darkness permits a more erotically oriented audience, the plot usually moves toward an act which, like death in Greek tragedy, takes place offstage, and is symbolized by a closing embrace.

The obstacles to the hero's desire, then, form the action of the comedy, and the overcoming of them the comic resolution. The obstacles are usually parental, hence comedy often turns on a clash between a son's and a father's will. Thus the comic dramatist as a rule writes for the younger men in his audience, and the older members of almost any society are apt to feel that comedy has something subversive about it. This is certainly one element in the social persecution of drama, which is not peculiar to Puritans or even Christians, as Terence in pagan Rome met much the same kind of social opposition that Ben Jonson did. There is one scene in Plautus where a son and father are making love to the same courtesan, and the son asks his father pointedly if he really does love mother. One has to see this scene against the background of Roman family life to understand its importance as psychological release. Even in Shakespeare there are startling outbreaks of baiting older men, and in contemporary movies the triumph of youth is so relentless that the moviemakers find some difficulty in getting anyone over the age of seventeen into their audiences.

The opponent to the hero's wishes, when not the father, is generally someone who partakes of the father's closer relation to established society: that is, a rival with less youth and more money. In Plautus and Terence he is usually either the pimp who owns the girl, or a wandering soldier with a supply of ready cash. The fury with which these characters are baited and exploded from the stage shows that they are father-surrogates, and even if they were not, they would still be usurpers, and their claim to possess the girl must be shown up as somehow fraudulent. They are, in short, impostors, and the extent to which they have real power implies some criticism of the society that allows them their power. In Plautus and Terence this criticism seldom goes beyond the immorality of brothels and professional harlots, but in Renaissance dramatists, including Jonson, there is some sharp observation of the rising power of money and the sort of ruling class it is building up.

The tendency of comedy is to include as many people as possible in its final society: the blocking characters are more often reconciled or converted than simply repudiated. Comedy often includes a scapegoat ritual of expulsion which gets rid of some irreconcilable character, but exposure and disgrace make for pathos, or even tragedy. *The Merchant of Venice* seems almost an experiment in coming as close as possible to upsetting the comic balance. If the dramatic role of Shylock is ever so slightly exaggerated, as it generally is when the leading actor of the company takes the part, it is upset, and the play becomes the tragedy of the Jew of Venice with a comic epilogue. *Volpone* ends with a great bustle of sentences to penal servitude and the galleys, and one feels that the deliverance of society hardly needs so much hard labor; but then *Volpone* is exceptional in being a kind of comic imitation of a tragedy, with the point of Volpone's hybris carefully marked.

The principle of conversion becomes clearer with characters whose chief function is the amusing of the audience. The original *miles gloriosus* in Plautus is a son of Jove and Venus who has killed an elephant with his fist and seven thousand men in one day's fighting. In other words, he is trying to put on a good show: the exuberance of his boasting helps to put the play over. The convention says that the braggart must be exposed, ridiculed, swindled, and beaten. But why should a professional dramatist, of all people, want so to harry a character who is putting on a good show—*his* show at that? When we find Falstaff invited to the final feast in *The Merry Wives*, Caliban reprieved, attempts made to mollify Malvolio, and Angelo and Parolles allowed to live down their disgrace, we are seeing a fundamental principle of comedy at work. The tendency of the comic society to include rather than exclude is the reason for the traditional importance of the parasite, who has no business to be at the final festival but is nevertheless there. The word "grace," with all its Renaissance overtones from the graceful courtier of Castiglione to the gracious God of Christianity, is a most important thematic word in Shakespearean comedy.

The action of comedy in moving from one social center to another is not unlike the action of a lawsuit, in which plaintiff and defendant construct different versions of the same situation, one finally being judged as real and the other as illusory. This resemblance of the rhetoric of comedy to the rhetoric of jurisprudence has been recognized from earliest times. A little pamphlet called the *Tractatus Coislinianus*, closely related to Aristotle's *Poetics*, which sets down all the essential facts about comedy in about a page and a half, divides the *dianoia* of comedy into two parts, opinion (*pistis*) and proof (*gnosis*). These correspond roughly to the usurping and the desirable societies respectively. Proofs (i.e., the means of bringing about the happier society) are subdivided into oaths, compacts, witnesses, ordeals (or tortures), and laws—in other words the five forms of material proof in law cases listed in the *Rhetoric*. We notice how often the action of a Shakespearean comedy begins with some absurd, cruel, or irrational law: the law of killing Syracusans in the *Comedy of Errors*, the law of compulsory marriage in A *Midsummer Night's Dream*, the law that confirms Shylock's bond, the attempts of Angelo to legislate people into righteousness, and the like, which the action of the comedy then evades or breaks. Compacts are as a rule the conspiracies formed by the hero's society; witnesses, such as overhearers of conversations or people with special knowledge (like the hero's old nurse with her retentive memory for birthmarks), are the commonest devices for bringing about the comic discovery. Ordeals (*basanoi*) are usually tests or touchstones of the hero's character: the Greek word also means touchstones, and seems to be echoed in Shakespeare's Bassanio whose ordeal it is to make a judgment on the worth of metals.

There are two ways of developing the form of comedy: one is to throw the main emphasis on the blocking characters; the other is the throw it forward on the scenes of discovery and reconciliation. One is the general tendency of comic irony, satire, realism, and studies of manners; the other is the tendency of Shakespearean and other types of romantic comedy. In the comedy of manners the main ethical interest falls as a rule on the blocking characters. The technical hero and heroine are not often very interesting people: the *adulescentes* of Plautus and Terence are all alike, as hard to tell apart in the dark as Demetrius and Lysander, who may be parodies of them. Generally the hero's character has the neutrality that enables him to represent a wish-fulfilment. It is very different with the miserly or ferocious parent, the boastful or foppish rival, or the other characters who stand in the way of the action. In Molière we have a simple but fully tested formula in which the ethical interest is focussed on a single blocking character, a heavy father, a miser, a misanthrope, a hypocrite, or a hypochondriac. These are the figures that we remember, and the plays are usually named after them, but we can seldom remember all the Valentins and Angeliques who wriggle out of their clutches. In *The Merry Wives* the technical hero, a man named Fenton, has only a bit part, and this play has picked up a hint or two from Plautus's *Casina*, where the hero and heroine are not even brought on the stage at all. Fictional comedy, especially Dickens, often follows the same practice of grouping its interesting characters around a somewhat dullish pair of technical leads. Even Tom Jones, though far more fully realized, is still deliberately associated, as his commonplace name indicates, with the conventional and typical.

Comedy usually moves toward a happy ending, and the normal response of the audience to a happy ending is "this should be," which sounds like a moral judgement. So it is, except that it is not moral in the restricted sense, but social. Its opposite is not the villainous but the absurd, and comedy finds the virtues of Malvolio as absurd as the vices of Angelo. Molière's misanthrope, being committed to sincerity, which is a virtue, is morally in a strong position, but the audience soon realizes that his friend Philinte, who is ready to lie quite cheerfully in order to enable other people to preserve their self-respect, is the more genuinely sincere of the two. It is of course quite possible to have a moral comedy, but the result is often the kind of melodrama that we have described as comedy without humor, and which achieves its happy ending with a self-righteous tone that most comedy avoids. It is hardly possible to imagine a drama without conflict, and it is hardly possible to imagine a conflict without some kind of enmity. But just as love, including sexual love, is a very different thing from lust, so enmity is a very different thing from hatred. In tragedy, of course, enmity almost always includes hatred; comedy is different, and one feels that the social judgement against the absurd is closer to the comic norm than the moral judgement against the wicked.

The question then arises of what makes the blocking character absurd. Ben Jonson explained this by his theory of the "humor," the character dominated by what Pope calls a ruling passion. The humor's dramatic function is to express a state of what might be called ritual bondage. He is obsessed by his humor, and his function in the play is primarily to repeat his obsession. A sick man is not a humor, but a hypochondriac is, because, *qua* hypochondriac, he can never admit to good health, and can never do anything inconsistent with the role that he has prescribed for himself. A miser can do and say nothing that is not connected with the hiding of gold or saving of money. In *The Silent Woman*, Jonson's nearest approach to Molière's type of construction, the whole action recedes from the humor of Morose, whose determination to eliminate noise from his life produces so loquacious a comic action.

The principle of the humor is the principle that unincremental repetition, the literary imitation of ritual bondage, is funny. In a tragedy — *Oedipus Tyrannus* is the stock example — repetition leads logically to catastrophe. Repetition overdone or not going anywhere belongs to comedy, for laughter is partly a reflex, and like other reflexes it can be conditioned by a simple repeated pattern. In Synge's *Riders to the Sea* a mother, after losing her husband and five sons at sea, finally loses her last son, and the result is a very beautiful and moving play. But if it had been a full-length tragedy plodding glumly through the seven drownings one after another, the audience would have been helpless with unsympathetic laughter long before it was over. The principle of repetition as the basis of humor both in Jonson's sense and in ours is well known to the creators of comic strips, in which a character is established as a parasite, a glutton (often confined to one dish), or a shrew, and who begins to be funny after the point has been made every day for several months. Continuous comic radio programs, too, are much more amusing to habitués than to neophytes. The girth of Falstaff and the hallucinations of Quixote are based on much the same comic laws. Mr. E. M. Forster speaks with disdain of Dickens's Mrs. Micawber, who never says anything except that she will never desert Mr. Micawber: a strong contrast is marked here between the refined writer too finicky for popular formulas, and the major one who exploits them ruthlessly.

The humor in comedy is usually someone with a good deal of social prestige and power, who is able to force much of the play's society into line with his obsession. Thus the humor is intimately connected with the theme of the absurd or irrational law that the action of comedy moves toward breaking. It is significant that the central character of our earliest humor comedy, *The Wasps*, is obsessed by law cases: Shylock, too, unites a craving for the law with the humor of revenge. Often the absurd law appears as a whim of a bemused tyrant whose will is law, like Leontes or the humorous Duke Frederick in Shakespeare, who makes some arbitrary decision or rash promise: here law is replaced by "oath," also mentioned in the *Tractatus*. Or it may take the form of a sham Utopia, a society of ritual bondage constructed by an act of humorous or pedantic will, like the academic retreat in *Love's Labor's Lost*. This theme is also as old as Aristophanes, whose parodies of Platonic social schemes in *The Birds* and *Ecclesiazusae* deal with it.

The society emerging at the conclusion of comedy represents, by contrast, a kind of moral norm, or pragmatically free society. Its ideals are seldom defined or formulated: definition and formulation belong to the humors, who want predictable activity. We are simply given to understand that the newly-married couple will live happily ever after, or that at any rate they will get along in a relatively unhumorous and clear-sighted manner. That is one reason why the character of the successful hero is so often left undeveloped: his real life begins at the end of the play, and we have to believe him to be potentially a more interesting character than he apepars to be. In Terence's *Adelphoi*, Demea, a harsh father, is contrasted with his brother Micio, who is indulgent. Micio being more liberal, he leads the way to the comic resolution, and converts Demea, but then Demea points out the indolence inspiring a good deal of Micio's liberality, and releases him from a complementary humorous bondage.

Thus the movement from *pistis* to *gnosis*, from a society controlled by habit, ritual bondage, arbitrary law and the older characters to a society controlled by youth and pragmatic freedom is fundamentally, as the Greek words suggest, a movement from illusion to reality. Illusion is whatever is fixed or definable, and reality is best understood as its negation: whatever reality is, it's not *that*. Hence the importance of the theme of creating and dispelling illusion in comedy: the illusions caused by disguise, obsession, hypocrisy, or unknown parentage.

The comic ending is generally manipulated by a twist in the plot. In Roman comedy the heroine, who is usually a slave or courtesan, turns out to be the daughter of somebody respectable, so that the hero can marry her without loss of face. The *cognitio* in comedy, in which the characters find out who their relatives are, and who is left of the opposite sex not a relative, and hence available for marriage, is one of the features of comedy that have never changed much: *The Confidential Clerk* indicates that it still holds the attention of dramatists. There is a brilliant parody of a *cognitio* at the end of *Major Barbara* (the fact that the hero of this play is a professor of Greek perhaps indicates an unusual affinity to the conventions of Euripides and Menander), where Undershaft is enabled to break the rule that he cannot appoint his son-in-law as successor by the fact that the son-in-law's own father married his deceased wife's sister in Australia, so that the son-in-law is his own first cousin as well as himself. It sounds complicated, but the plots of comedy often are complicated because there is something inherently absurd about complications. As the main character interest in comedy is so often focussed on the defeated characters, comedy regularly illustrates a victory of arbitrary plot over consistency of character. Thus, in striving contrast to tragedy, there can hardly be such a thing as inevitable comedy, as far as the action of the individual play is concerned. That is, we may know that the convention of comedy will make some kind of happy ending inevitable, but still for each play the dramatist must produce a distinctive "gimmick" or "weenie," to use two disrespectful Hollywood synonyms for *anagnorisis*. Happy endings do not impress us as true, but as desirable, and they are brought about by manipulation. The watcher of death and tragedy has nothing to do but sit and wait for the inevitable end; but something gets born at the end of comedy, and the watcher of birth is a member of a busy society.

The manipulation of plot does not always involve metamorphosis of character, but there is no violation of comic decorum when it does. Unlikely conversions, miraculous transformations, and providential assistance are inseparable from comedy. Further, whatever emerges is supposed to be there for good: if the curmudgeon becomes lovable, we understand that he will not immediately relapse again into his ritual habit. Civilizations which stress the desirable rather than the real, and the religious as opposed to the scientific perspective, think of drama almost entirely in terms of comedy. In the classical drama of India, we are told, the tragic ending was regarded as bad taste, much as the manipulated endings of comedy are regarded as bad taste by novelists interested in ironic realism.

The total *mythos* of comedy, only a small part of which is ordinarily presented, has regularly what in music is called a ternary form: the hero's society rebels against the society of the *senex* and triumphs, but the hero's society is a Saturnalia, a reversal of social standards which recalls a golden age in the past before the main action of the play begins. Thus we have a stable and harmonious order disrupted by folly, obsession, forgetfulness, "pride and prejudice," or events not understood by the characters themselves, and then restored. Often there is a benevolent grandfather, so to speak, who overrules the action set up by the blocking humor and so links the first and third parts. An example is Mr. Burchell, the disguised uncle of the wicked squire, in *The Vicar of Wakefield*. A very long play, such as the Indian *Sakuntala*, may present all three phases; a very intricate one, such as many of Menander's evidently were, may indicate their outlines. But of course very often the first phase is not given at all: the audience simply understands an ideal state of affairs which it knows to be better than what is revealed in the play, and which it recognizes as like that to which the action leads. This ternary action is, ritually, like a contest of summer and winter in which winter occupies the middle action; psychologically, it is like the removal of a neurosis or blocking point and the restoring of an unbroken current of energy and memory. The Jonsonian masque, with the antimasque in the middle, gives a highly conventionalized or "abstract" version of it.

We pass now to the typical characters of comedy. In drama, characterization depends on function; what a character is follows from what he has to do in the play. Dramatic function in its turn depends on the structure of the play; the character has certain things to do because the play has such and such a shape. The structure of the play in its turn depends on the category of the play; if it is a comedy, its structure will require a comic resolution and a prevailing comic mood. Hence when we speak of typical characters, we are not trying to reduce lifelike characters to stock types, though we certainly are suggesting that the sentimental notion of an antithesis between the lifelike character and the stock type is a vulgar error. All lifelike characters, whether in drama or fiction, owe their consistency to the appropriateness of the stock type which belongs to their dramatic function. That stock type is not the character but it is as necessary to the character as a skeleton is to the actor who plays it.

With regard to the characterization of comedy, the *Tractatus* lists three types of comic characters: the *alazons* or impostors, the *eirons* or self-deprecators, and the buffoons (*bomolochoi*). This list is closely related to a passage in the *Ethics* which contrasts the first two, and then goes on to contrast the buffoon with a character whom Aristotle calls *agroikos* or churlish, literally rustic. We may reasonably accept the churl as a fourth character type, and so we have two opposed pairs. The contest of *eiron* and *alazon* forms the basis of the comic action, and the buffoon and the churl polarize the comic mood.

We have previously dealt with the terms *eiron* and *alazon*. The humorous blocking characters of comedy are nearly always impostors, though it is more frequently a lack of self-knowledge than simple hypocrisy that characterizes them. The multitudes of comic scenes in which one character complacently soliloquizes while another makes sarcastic asides to the audience show the contest of *eiron* and *alazon* in its purest form, and show too that the audience is sympathetic to the *eiron* side. Central to the *alazon* group is the *senex iratus* or heavy father, who with his rages and threats, his obsessions and his gullibility, seems closely related to some of the demonic characters of romance, such as Polyphemus. Occasionally a character may have the dramatic function of such a figure without his characteristics: an example is Squire Allworthy in *Tom Jones*, who as far as the plot is concerned behaves almost as stupidly as Squire Western. Of heavy-father surrogates, the *miles gloriosus* has been mentioned: his popularity is largely due to the fact that he is a man of words rather than deeds, and is consequently far more useful to a practising dramatist than any tight-lipped hero could ever be. The pedant, in Renaissance comedy often a student of the occult sciences, the fop or coxcomb, and similar humors, require no comment. The female *alazon* is rare: Katharina the shrew represents to some extent a female *miles gloriosus,* and the *précieuse ridicule* a female pedant, but the "menace" or siren who gets in the way of the true heroine is more often found as a sinister figure of melodrama or romance than as a ridiculous figure in comedy.

The *eiron* figures need a little more attention. Central to this group is the hero, who is an *eiron* figure because, as explained, the dramatist tends to play him down and make him rather neutral and unformed in character. Next in importance is the heroine, also often played down: in Old Comedy, when a girl accompanies a male hero in his triumph, she is generally a stage prop, a *muta persona* not previously introduced. A more difficult form of *cognitio* is achieved when the heroine disguises herself or through some other device brings about the comic resolution, so that the person whom the hero is seeking turns out to be the person who has sought him. The fondness of Shakespeare for this "she stoops to conquer" theme needs only to be mentioned here, as it belongs more naturally to the *mythos* of romance.

Another central *eiron* figure is the type entrusted with hatching the schemes which bring about the hero's victory. This character in Roman comedy is almost always a tricky slave (*dolosus servus*), and in Renaissance comedy he becomes the scheming valet who is so frequent in Continental plays, and in Spanish drama is called the *gracioso*. Modern audiences are most familiar with him in Figaro and in the Leporello of *Don Giovanni*. Through such intermediate nineteenth-century figures as Micawber and the Touchwood of Scott's *St. Ronan's Well*, who, like the gracioso, have buffoon affiliations, he evolves into the amateur detective of modern fiction. The Jeeves of P. G. Wodehouse is a more direct descendant. Female confidantes of the same general family are often brought in to oil the machinery of the well-made play. Elizabethan comedy had another type of trickster, represented by the Matthew Merrygreek of *Ralph Roister Doister*, who is generally said to be developed from the vice or iniquity of the morality plays: as usual, the analogy is sound enough, whatever historians decide about origins. The vice, to give him that name, is very useful to a comic dramatist because he acts from pure love of mischief, and can set a comic action going with the minimum of motivation. The vice may be as light-hearted as Puck or as malignant as Don John in *Much Ado,* but as a rule the vice's activity is, in spite of his name, benevolent. One of the tricky slaves in Plautus, in a soliloquy, boasts that he is the *architectus* of the comic action: such a character carries out the will of the author to reach a happy ending. He is in fact the spirit of comedy, and the two clearest examples of the type in Shakespeare, Puck and Ariel, are both spiritual beings. The tricky slave often has his own freedom in mind as the reward of his exertions: Ariel's longing for release is in the same tradition.

The role of the vice includes a great deal of disguising, and the type may often be recognized by disguise. A good example is the Brainworm of Jonson's *Every Man in His Humour,* who calls the action of the play the day of his metamorphoses. Similarly Ariel has to surmount the difficult stage direction of "Enter invisible." The vice is combined with the hero whenever the latter is a cheeky, improvident young man who hatches his own schemes and cheats his rich father or uncle into giving him his patrimony along with the girl.

Another *eiron* type has not been much noticed. This is a character, generally an older man, who begins the action of the play by withdrawing from it, and ends the play by returning. He is often a father with the motive of seeing what his son will do. The action of *Every Man in His Humour* is set going in this way by Knowell Senior. The disappearance and return of Lovewit, the owner of the house which is the scene of *The Alchemist*, has the same dramatic function, though the characterization is different. The clearest Shakespearean example is the Duke in *Measure for Measure,* but Shakespeare is more addicted to the type that might appear at first glance. In Shakespeare the vice is rarely the real *architectus*: Puck and Ariel both act under orders from an older man, if one may call Oberon a man for the moment. In *The Tempest* Shakespeare returns to a comic action established by Aristophanes, in which an older man, instead of retiring from the action, builds it up on the stage. When the heroine takes the vice role in Shakespeare, she is often significantly related to her father, even when the father is not in the play at all, like the father of Helena, who gives her his medical knowledge, or the father of Portia, who arranges the scheme of the caskets. A more conventionally treated example of the same benevolent Prospero figure turned up recently in the psychiatrist of *The Cocktail Party*, and one may compare the mysterious alchemist who is the father of the heroine of *The Lady's Not for Burning*. The formula is not confined to comedy: Polonius, who knows so many of the disadvantages of a literary education, attempts the role of a retreating paternal *eiron* three times, once too often. *Hamlet* and *King Lear* contain subplots which are ironic versions of stock comic themes, Gloucester's story being the regular comedy theme of the gullible *senex* swindled by a clever and unprincipled son.

We pass now to the buffoon types, those whose function it is to increase the mood of festivity rather than to contribute to the plot. Renaissance comedy, unlike Roman comedy, had a great variety of such characters, professional fools, clowns, pages, singers, and incidental characters with established comic habits like malapropism or foreign accents. The oldest buffoon of this incidental nature is the parasite, who may be given something to do, as Jonson gives Mosca the role of a vice in *Volpone*, but who, *qua* parasite, does nothing but entertain the audience by talking about his appetite. He derives chiefly from Greek Middle Comedy, which appears to have been very full of food, and where he was, not unnaturally, closely associated with another established buffoon type, the cook, a conventional figure who breaks into comedies to bustle and order about and make long speeches about the mysteries of cooking. In the role of cook the buffoon or entertainer appears, not simply as a gratuitous addition like the parasite, but as something more like a master of ceremonies, a center for the comic mood. There is no cook in Shakespeare, though there is a superb description of one in the *Comedy of Errors*, but a similar role is often attached to a jovial and loquacious host, like the "mad host" of *The Merry Wives* or the Simon Eyre of *The Shoemakers Holiday*. In Middleton's *A Trick to Catch the Old One* the mad host type is combined with the vice. In Falstaff and Sir Toby Belch we can see the affinities of the buffoon or entertainer type both with the parasite and with the master of revels. If we study this entertainer or host role carefully we shall soon realize that it is a development of what in Aristophanic comedy is represented by the chorus, and which in its turn goes back to the *komos* or revel from which comedy is said to be descended.

Finally, there is a fourth group to which we have assigned the word *agroikos*, and which usually means either churlish or rustic, depending on the context. This type may also be extended to cover the Elizabethan gull and what in vaudeville used to be called the straight man, the solemn or inarticulate character who allows the humor to bounce off him, so to speak. We find churls in the miserly, snobbish, or priggish characters whose role is that of the refuser of festivity, the killjoy who tries to stop the fun, or, like Malvolio, locks up the food and drink instead of dispensing it. The melancholy Jaques of *As You Like It*, who walks out on the final festivities, is closely related. In the sulky and self-centered Bertram of *All's Well* there is a most unusual and ingenious combination of this type with the hero. More often, however, the churl belongs to the *alazon* group, all miserly old men in comedies, including Shylock, being churls. In *The Tempest* Caliban has much the same relation to the churlish type that Ariel has to the vice or tricky slave. But often, where the mood is more light-hearted, we may translate *agroikos* simply by rustic, as with the innumerable country squires and similar characters who provide amusement in the urban setting of drama. Such types do not refuse the mood of festivity, but they mark the extent of its range. In a pastoral comedy the idealized virtues of rural life may be represented by a simple man who speaks for the pastoral ideal, like Corin in *As You Like It*. Corin has the same *agroikos* role as the "rube" or "hayseed" of more citified comedies, but the moral attitude to the role is reversed. Again we notice the principle that dramatic structure is a permanent and moral attitude a variable factor in literature.

In a very ironic comedy a different type of character may play the role of the refuser of festivity. The more ironic the comedy, the more absurd the society, and an absurd society may be condemned by, or at least contrasted with, a character that we may call the plain dealer, an outspoken advocate of a kind of moral norm who has the sympathy of the audience. Wycherley's Manly, though he provides the name for the type, is not a particularly good example of it: a much better one is the Cléante of *Tartuffe*. Such a character is appropriate when the tone is ironic enough to get the audience confused about its sense of the social norm: he corresponds roughly to the chorus in a tragedy, which is there for a similar reason. When the tone deepens from the ironic to the bitter, the plain dealer may become a malcontent or railer, who may be morally superior to his society, as he is to some extent in Marston's play of that name, but who may also be too motivated by envy to be much more than another aspect of his society's evil, like Thersites, or to some extent Apemantus. . . .

**CONTEMPORARY
PERSPECTIVES**

KATHARINE
EISAMAN MAUS

FROM *"'Playhouse
Flesh and Blood':
Sexual Ideology and
the Restoration
Actress"*
(1979)

*KATHARINE EISAMAN
Maus has written widely
about seventeenth-century
literature, including a
book on the playwright Ben Jonson. In this essay, Maus explores the relationship between Restoration
actresses, their reputation for sexual promiscuity, and the politics of gender in the Restoration theater
and society.*

Sometime in the fall of 1660—no one is quite sure when or at which theater—the first professional
English actress made her debut on the public stage. Her appearance was not entirely without prece-
dents. In the first half of the seventeenth century, Queen Henrietta Maria and her ladies performed
extensively in the English court theater. During the interregnum, when the theaters were officially
closed, William D'Avenant used at least one woman—a Mrs. Edward Coleman—in his opera *The
Siege of Rhodes*. On the Continent, women had been employed on the stage since the sixteenth
century, and many royalists became familiar with the French custom when they followed Prince
Charles into exile. However, women had never been used on the English stage in any regular or
systematic way.

Before the war, adolescent boys had performed the women's parts in the public theater. In
November, 1629, when a French company with actresses came to London, Thomas Brand informed
Archbishop Laud that "those women . . . giving just offense to all virtuous and well-disposed persons
in this town . . . were hissed, hooted, and pippin-pelted from the stage."[1] By the Restoration, though,
attitudes toward women on the stage seem to have changed radically. The new actresses were accepted
almost immediately into the life of the theater, and there was surprisingly little controversy over their
suitability for the stage.

What caused this striking reversal of audience attitudes? Was it merely a case of English theatergoers belatedly relinquishing a set of absurd scruples? Discussions of seventeenth-century actresses
have assumed that they succeeded on the stage because they could provide a more plausible portrayal
of women characters than transvestite actors could.[2] There are two objections to this kind of explanation. For one thing, there is no evidence which implies that the female impersonators were incompetent. Female parts written by Shakespeare, Webster, Ford, Middleton, and others suggest no mean
estimate by the playwrights of the boys' abilities; Elizabethan and Jacobean audiences applauded
male Juliets, Rosalinds, and Cleopatras. The usual explanation of the actresses' success further assumes that naturalism is an obvious and desireable goal in theatrical representation—an assumption
which is questionable to say the least. E. H. Gombrich has shown that standards of naturalism—
what will seem "true to life" in a drawing or painting—vary from generation to generation depending
upon the conventions which inform and have informed artistic production. What seems natural or
conventional is not universal across time and space, but is historically and culturally conditioned.[3]
There is no reason to suppose that naturalism in the theater is any less problematic than naturalism in
the visual arts. Why should male impersonation of women seem more intolerable than other kinds of
artificiality—extravagantly exotic sets, or a highly rhetorical acting style? The Restoration audience
expected, and enjoyed, stage conventions which grievously ignore the demands of realism as understood by, say, Ibsen or Chekhov.

The orthodox explanation of the actresses' new acceptability is, if not entirely wrong, at least
seriously insufficient. What is required is an examination of the issues in terms of the attitudes
prevailing in Restoration culture. This examination logically begins with the contemporary accounts
of the actresses, and inevitably widens to include analysis of Restoration attitudes toward women and
the theater in general.

Unfortunately, there is very little comment upon the actresses in the years when they are first introduced, when the quality of contemporary response might best help illuminate the reasons for their
professional success. Since no one seriously questioned women's fitness for the stage, the few attempts
to account for the innovation involve no very elaborate process of justification. In 1660, the players
and owners of theatrical companies were complaining that the hiatus in the theatrical tradition had

created a dearth of well-trained female inpersonators. The available actors were all too masculine-looking, they claimed, to excel in women's parts. As Thomas Jordan lamented in his preface to a revival of *Othello*:

> Our women are defective, and so siz'd
> You'ld think they were some of the guard disguis'd
> For to speak truth, men act that are between
> Forty and fifty, wenches of fifteen
> With bone so large and nerve so incompliant
> When you call *Desdemona*, enter *Geant*.[4]

According to this line of argument, the peculiar circumstances of the Restoration theater necessitated the employment of women. The closing of the theaters during the interregnum had interrupted the old system of apprenticeship, which had supplied the Elizabethan and Jacobean companies with adequately-trained female impersonators.

This explanation, even if true, would only reveal by what chance women arrived on the stage, and not how and why they were successful once they got there. Furthermore, the plight of the producers was not nearly so severe as Jordan represents it. According to John Downes in *Roscius Anglicanus*, the King's Company at its inception included four actors "Bred up from Boys, under the Master ACTORS."[5] The Duke's Company included six actors, who "commonly Acted Women's Parts"—notably Edward Kynaston, who "being young made a complete Femal Stage Beauty, performing his part so well . . . that it hath since been disputable among the Judicious, whether any Woman that succeeded him so sensibly touched the audience as he."[6] Pepys and Cibber, as well as Downes, comment upon the excellence of Kynaston's impersonations, as well as upon the more than passable abilities of the lesser actors.[7] Surely if the Restoration audience had greeted the women players with the hisses and orange pips of an earlier generation, the companies would have made do for a while with ungainly performances by untrained adolescent boys. The perceived unsuitability of male actors for female roles is really more a symptom than an explanation of changing attitudes.

As the theaters reopened, actors and producers urged yet another argument for the introduction of actresses, which seems at least in retrospect equally unsatisfactory as a real explanation. Initially some people hoped that the presence of women on the stage would eliminate the obscene and corrupt aspects of English drama, and encourage the adoption of purer standards for theatrical spectacle. The patents issued to William D'Avenant and Thomas Killigrew in 1660, and reissued in 1662, contain the following clause:

> forasmuch as many plays formerly acted, do conteine severall prophane, obscene, and scurrilous passages, and the women's parts therein have been acted by men in the habit of women, at which some have taken offense; for the preventing of these abuses for the future, we doe straitly charge, command, and enjoyn that henceforth no . . . play shall be acted by either of the said companies conteining any passages offensive to piety or good manners . . . And we doe likewise permit and give leave that all the women's parts to be acted in either of the said two companies may be performed by women so long as these recreations, which by reason of the abuses aforesaid were scandalous and offensive, may by such reformation be esteemed not only harmlesse delight but useful instruction.[8]

By this account the actresses were introduced in order to help the dramatic arts exert a beneficial effect upon the community. Whether or not this apparently pious hope was initially a sincere one, it remained unrealized on the Restoration stage. Restoration drama, especially comedy, tends to be sexually more explicit and morally more subversive than the drama of earlier decades—and the sexual explicitness, at least, largely depends upon the physical presence of genuine women on the stage. "We can only conclude," writes a twentieth century critic, "that [the actresses'] chief effect on dramatic literature was to push it steadily in the direction of sex and sensuality."[9] The threat implied in the language of the patents—that the women's continued employment depended upon their moral efficacy—was of course never carried out. If women were now considered appropriate on the public stage, it was not for their purifying influence, any more than it was due to a shortage of teenage boys.

Since the overt attempts at contemporary justification seem inadequate, it is reasonable to suspect that the new acceptability of actresses is associated with ideological changes more fundamental or far-reaching than a mere modification of theatrical custom might indicate. The first such change which needs to be examined is the transformation in audience attitudes toward players in the latter part of the seventeenth century—a change which makes the success of the Restoration actress even more striking. Before the war, even the most appreciative playgoers seem not have been particularly interested in the offstage lives of Burbage, Kempe, or Alleyn. In the more intimate Restoration theater, though, the personalities of both male and female players intrigued the comparatively small and loyal audience. Actresses as well as actors were praised not for their ability to depict any character with equal skill, but for the ability to inform their dramatic portrayals with the force of their personal talent and idiosyncratic vision. In James Wright's *Historia Histrionica* (London, 1699), Truewit assumes that even in reading an old play one is curious about the personalities of the original actors:

> I wish they had printed in the last age (so I call the times before the rebellion) the actors names over against the parts they acted, as they have done since the restoration: and thus one might have guess'd at the action of the men, by the parts which we now read in the old plays.   (p. 3)

Restoration theater did not really challenge the actor to submit himself to the demands of a fictional role; rather it provided, at least for the leading players, manifold opportunities for self-expression. In the case of women like Nell Gwynn, Elizabeth Barry, or Ann Bracegirdle, this kind of attention constituted a virtually unprecedented celebration of female personality—at least of middle- and lower-class female personality.

As Restoration playwrights worked very closely with the theatrical companies, they inevitably wrote with particular performers in mind. They were thus able to play upon the spectators' sense of the relationship between an actor's pesonality and the roles he was required to enact. Nell Gwynn and Charles Hart, lovers behind the scenes, played witty, amoral "mad couples" together—Florimel and Celadon in Dryden's *Secret Love*, Miridia and Philidor in Howard's *All Mistaken*, Jacintha and Wildblood in Dryden's *Evening's Love*, Olivia and Wildish in Sedley's *Mulberry Garden*. Ann Bracegirdle, who resisted the advances of enamored aristocrats throughout her career, and who was the object of a melodramatic rape attempt, became famous for her portrayal of chaste women in distress. She was applauded when, as Cordelia in the revised *Lear*, she described herself as "Arm'd in my Virgin Innocence"—although the promiscuous Mrs. Barry, "in the same part, more fam'd for her Stage Performance than the other, at the words, *Virgin Innocence*, has created a Horse-laugh . . . and the scene of generous Pity and Compassion at the close turn'd to Ridicule."[10]

Prologues and epilogues, with their ambiguous position between the fictional and the real, provided ideal opportunities to exploit the relation between the player and the part. The most extreme, and probably the funniest, example occurs at the end of Dryden's *Tyrannic Love*. Nell Gwynn, playing a doomed princess despite her generally recognized ineptitude in tragic roles, finally expires. Servants load her corpse onto a litter and are carrying it out when she suddenly sits bolt upright and exclaims, "Hold, you are mad? You damn'd confounded Dog! I am to rise, and speak the Epilogue!" She leaps off the bier and begins the final speech:

> I come, kind Gentlemen, strange news to tell ye
> I am the ghost of poor departed Nelly . . .
> To tell you truth, I walk because I die
> Out of my calling, in a Tragedy.
> O Poet, dam'd dull Poet, who could prove
> So senseless to make Nelly die for love! . . .
> As for my epitaph when I am gone,
> I'll trust no poet, but will write my own:
> "Here Nelly lies, who, though she liv'd a Slattern
> Yet dy'd a princess, acting in Saint Cathar'n."[11]

In *An Essay of Dramatic Poetry*, and *The Grounds of Criticism in Tragedy*, Dryden's qualified admiration for the French tradition testifies to his interest in and sensitivity to the requirements of theatrical decorum. But the demands of the tragic situation, even for Dryden, are overridden by the demands of Nell's personality.

It is tempting to think of the new acceptance of female assertiveness on the stage as part of a general revaluation of women's status—a reassessment that would eventually allow them to participate more fully in all aspects of public life. Certainly all the evidence suggests that although the actresses were never as numerous or as well-paid as their male colleagues, they participated extensively in the life of the companies to which they belonged. They were granted the same special privileges as the actors — most significantly a relative immunity from prosecution for debt. And with the formation of the Lincoln's Inn Fields Company in 1695, two actresses — Ann Bracegirdle and Mary Saunderson Betterton — became shareholders, with a right to a certain percentage of the company's profits.

The employment of actresses does not, however, coincide with a more general broadening of female participation in public life. In fact, during the second half of the seventeenth century women seem to have been losing rather than acquiring opportunities for gainful employment. Men were encroaching upon such traditionally female occupations as brewing, textile manufacture, dressmaking, and midwifery. Women were less and less likely to run businesses or enter trades independently of their husbands, to help their husbands in a family venture, or to continue such a venture when they were widowed. By the beginning of the eighteenth century, there were few alternatives for undowered, unmarried women — or married women whose husbands could not support them — other than domestic service or prostitution.[12] The success of the actress has to be explained in ways which take into account the drastically different experience of women in other professions.

Actresses, in other words, seem to be anomalous rather than typical; the task is to isolate the factors that make their case so special. It is reasonable to look more closely to the audience's actual response to the women on the stage, in order to establish revealing patterns of assumptions. One such pattern is so obvious as to be unavoidable. Everyone from Dryden on has remarked upon the audience's extraordinarily lively, even obsessive, concern with the actresses' sexuality. John Downes, in *Roscius Anglicanus*, regales the reader with sly anecdotes:

> And all the Women's Parts admirably Acted: chiefly *Celia* [Moll Davis], a Shepherdess being Mad for Love; especially in Singing several Wild and Mad Songs. *My Lodging is on the Cold Ground*, etc. She perform'd that so Charmingly, that not long after, it Rais'd her from her Bed on the Cold Ground, to a Bed Royal.

> Note, Mrs. Johnson is this Comedy, Dancing a Jigg so Charming Well, *Love's power in a little time after Coerc'd her to Dance more Charming else where.*[13]

Others were less delicate. The anonymous author of "Satyr on Players" (London, ca. 1685), declares that actresses are "so lewd in every kind/You'd swear that Rogue and Whore had both combin'd," and goes on to support his claim in explicit detail:

> Sue Percival so long as known the Stage
> She grows in Lewdness faster, than in Age:
> From Eight to Nine she there has swiving been;
> So calls that Nature, which is truly Sin.   (page 2)

Despite the difference in tone, Downes and the author of the "Satyr" both assume that the sexual exploits of the actress are an extension of his histrionic function rather than an irrelevant side-issue. Moll Davis's change of beds is described as the direct result of her fine performance; Mrs. Johnson gets invited to dance elsewhere because she has danced so well on the stage; Sue Percival's theatrical and sexual exploits coincide. Modern critics like John Harold Wilson and Allardyce Nicoll conclude that the presence of the actresses debased the theater, by lending it the atmosphere of a brothel.[14] . . .

No doubt the fuss is partly due to the fact that the actresses' sex lives really were fairly unorthodox. As Allardyce Nicoll primly declares, "very few of these women led chaste lives."[15] Elizabeth Barry was the mistress of John, Earl of Rochester; Elizabeth Hall the mistress of Sir Philip Howard; the Mrs. Johnson of Downe's anecdote the mistress of Henry, Earl of Peterborough. Margaret Hughes was the mistress of Prince Rupert, Susannah Hall the mistress of Sir Robert Howard, Ann Reeves the mistress of Dryden, Elizabeth Barry (again) of Otway, and Ann Bracegirdle (perhaps) of Congreve. Hester Davenport was irregularly married to the Earl of Oxford — when she refused to become his mistress he dressed up one of his servants as a parson, and had an invalid marriage ceremony performed. Nell Gwynn and Moll Davis went all the way to the top, and became mistresses of Charles II. Others, like Elizabeth Boutell and Rebecca Marshall, played the field.

Nonetheless, there were alternative models, like Mary Saunderson Betterton, who was the leading tragic actress before Mrs. Barry, and who seems to have led a faithful married life throughout her long career. An actress like Nell Gwynn, however, whose stage career lasted only five years, and whose histrionic talents were probably much smaller, seemed a much more exemplary specimen. When Ann Bracegirdle proved unexpectedly chaste, the audience did not divert its attention from her sexuality, but focused upon it all the more sharply.

RAMBLE: And Mrs. Bracegridle . . .
CRITIC: Is a haughty conceited Woman, that has got more Money by dissembling her Lewdness, than others by professing it.
SULLEN: But does that Romantick Virgin still keep up her great reputation?
CRITIC: D'ye mean her Reputation for Acting?
SULLEN: I mean her Reputation for not acting; you understand me — .[16]

By contrast, audience interest in the male players tended not to involve such an avid concern with their sex lives. Actors like Charles Hart, Edward Kynaston, and Cardell Goodman were "kept" by aristocratic ladies — in Goodman's case his connection with Lady Castlemaine obtained him a pardon after he had been convicted of highway robbery, a capital crime. But contemporary comment on their situation is muted; their sexuality is not considered part and parcel with their histrionic vocation. . . .

If hierarchical assumptions dominate conceptions of gender difference, boys and women occupy a similar position — they are inferior versions of mature men, *hommes manqués*. From one point of view, as *As You Like It*'s Rosalind-Ganymede knows, boys and women are cattle of the same color. The convention of the boy-actresses has a certain logic; at any rate it does not pose a profound or necessary challenge to the audience's ideological convictions. If sexual difference is understood in terms of opposition, however, transvestite role-playing involves a much greater rupture of decorum — a rupture which may be ludicrous, implausible, or titillating depending upon the context. Boys no longer seem appropriate in women's tragic roles; a Cleopatra who shaves is the occasion for a jest.[17] The Restoration audience was more eager to see women in male disguise, but arguably this eagerness is rooted in the same attitudes which make the boy impersonators seem obsolete. John Harold Wilson has remarked upon the surprisingly "indelicate" methods by which women players in male disguise were unmasked in Restoration comedy.[18] Surely all the loosened hair, all the naked breasts in the fifth acts are meant to heighten an incongruity of which the audience was already aware; the unmasking reinforces a histrionic appeal which depends upon the seductive appeal of female difference.

From this perspective one can see why the actresses appeared on the public stage for the first time at the Restoration; why their success could coincide with a more general withdrawal of women from public life; and also why their achievement took the specific forms that it did. It is not merely new attitudes toward women and the theater, but the persistence of old ones, which make possible the novel phenomenon of the Restoration actress, and which condition the highly selective enthusiasm of her audience.

Notes

[1]John Payne Collier, *History of Dramatic Poetry to the Time of Shakespeare: And Annals of the Stage to the Restoration* (London: John Murray, 1831), II, pp. 23–24.

[2]e.g., Colley Cibber, *An Apology of the Life of Colley Cibber* (London, 1740), p. 55: "The characters of Women, on former Theatres, were perform'd by Boys, or young Men of the most effeminate Aspect. And what Grace, or Master-Stroke of Action, can we conceive such ungain Hoydens to have been capable of?"

Allardyce Nicoll, *The History of Restoration Drama 1660–1700* (Cambridge: Cambridge Univ. Press, 1928), p. 71: "the actresses certainly made possible a more charming presentation of Shakespearean tragedy and comedy, shedding a fresh light on the Desdemonas and Ophelias of the past."

Rosamund Gilder, *Enter the Actresses* (London: George C. Harrup, 1931), pp. 134–35: "In England the curtain of legal prohibition drops in 1642 on a stage peopled by squeaking Cleopatras, and rises eighteen years later on a rout of beautiful, witty, and accomplished actresses."

John Harold Wilson, *All the King's Ladies: Actresses of the Restoration* (Chicago: Univ. of Chicago Press, 1958), p. 90: "As creators of character there can be little doubt that the new actresses were superior to their juvenile predecessors . . . the stage life of the female impersonator was usually short, and his interpretation of a character could never be more than superficially correct."

[3]E. H. Gombrich, *Art and Illusion* (New York: Pantheon, 1960), esp. pp. 181–287.

[4]Thomas Jordan, "A Prologue, to introduce the first Woman that came to act on the Stage, in the tragedy called The Moor of Venice," in *A Royal Arbour of Loyal Poesie* (London, 1664), p. 22.

[5]John Downes, *Roscius Anglicanus, or An Historical View of the Stage* (London, 1708), p. 2.

[6]*Ibid.*, p. 19.

[7]Samuel Pepys, *The Diary of Samuel Pepys*, ed. R. Latham and W. Matthews (London: G. Bell, 1970), I, 224 (August 18, 1660) and II, 7 (January 7, 1660–61). Cibber, p. 71.

[8]Nicoll, pp. 285–86n.

[9]Wilson, p. 107.

[10]William Chetwood, *A General History of the Stage* (London, 1749), p. 28.

[11]John Dryden, *The Dramatic Works*, ed. Montague Summers (London: Nonesuch, 1931), II, p. 395.

[12]The standard work on the subject is still Alice Clark's *Working Life of Women in the Seventeenth Century* (London: Routledge and Sons, 1919). Her conclusion—that women were progressively excluded from the job market during the seventeenth century—though not her Marxist analysis, has recently been supported by Roger Thompson, *Women In Stuart England and America* (London: Routledge and Kegan Paul, 1974), pp. 74–75.

[13]Downes, pp. 23–24, p. 33.

[14]Wilson, *passim.*; Nicoll, p. 72.

[15]Nicoll, p. 72.

[16]Anon. (sometimes ascribed to Charles Gildon), *A Comparison Between The Two Stages* (London, 1702), p. 17.

[17]Cibber, p. 71.

[18]Wilson, p. 85.

Sophocles' play OEDIPUS AT COLONUS is produced in the classical amphitheater at Epidaurus. Although this modern production is probably quite different from performances in the classical period, it does illustrate some important features of performance in the ancient Greek theater: note the outdoor setting, the SKENE to the rear, the round ORCHESTRA with its central altar stone, and the synchronized movements of the masked chorus.

This production of KING LEAR shows some of the advantages of open staging, the kind of staging that was used in Shakespeare's theater. Although there is no fixed set, the actors are able to create Lear's throne room with a few props and objects.

This recent production of TARTUFFE at the Huntington Theatre Company uses a stage design much different from the staging that would have been used by Molière's company in the late seventeenth century. Yet the designers of this production have used both the costuming and the physical gesture of the performers to suggest something of the elegance of neoclassical performance.

This photograph shows the Moscow Art Theater's original production of Chekhov's THE CHERRY ORCHARD, and provides an excellent example of naturalistic staging at the turn of the century. Note how the proscenium arch acts as an invisible "fourth wall," allowing the audience to peer into a fully-realized domestic "environment." In this production, the actor and director Constantin Stanislavsky played the role of Gayev; he is standing on the extreme left of the photography, gesturing at the bookcase.

This scene from Sam Shepard's TRUE WEST suggests how realistic theatrical style has developed since the turn of the century. Instead of forming an "environment" that frames the characters, the objects onstage — the golf clubs, the toasters — are unmoored from their use in everyday reality outside the theater. The objects become weapons in the dual between Austin and Lee — played by Gary Sinise and John Malkovich — who decide what their function will be, and what they will mean.

This scene from Jean Genet's THE BLACKS — with James Earl Jones and Cicely Tyson — shows how the modern theater can use metadramatic techniques for political purposes. Here, the black actors perform for the masked "white" audience.

In this scene from M. BUTTERFLY, the stage has moved completely away from modern realism and represents at once Gallimard's prison — the rectangular area in the center — and the past of his memory, here his first meeting with Song Liling. The brilliant runway that encircles Gallimard seems to suggest the spiraling deceptions of the play's action.

These photographs
of different produc-
tions of Shakespeare's
THE TEMPEST *suggest*
how production style and
adaptation can affect our
understanding of the play
as theatrical spectators.
The first photographs show
how different productions
have established a rela-
tionship between Prospero
and his fairy spirit, Ariel.

Each production shows
Prospero with his magic
staff, and yet the cos-
tuming, gesture, and be-
havior of the actors in
each production creates a
very different relationship
between Ariel and
Prospero.

The final photo, below
from Peter Greenaway's
film PROSPERO'S BOOKS,
suggests how the material
from Shakespearean
drama can be adapted to
new narratives and new
media. (The stage produc-
tions come from The Old
Globe Theater, American
Shakespeare Theater in
Connecticut, and Jean
Cocteau Repertory Co.)

Adolphus Cusins prepares to receive the spirit of Dionysus Undershaft, at the end of Act 2 of MAJOR BARBARA, *in the 1980 production at the Circle in the Square Theatre in New York.*

As Pirandello suggests in his stage directions to SIX CHARACTERS IN SEARCH OF AN AUTHOR, *the Characters here (the Little Boy, the Mother, the Little Girl, and the Father) are clothed simply, to give them a statuesque and mystical unreality.*

This staging of the trial scene in Arthur Miller's THE CRUCIBLE *was the climax of the 1991 National Actors Theater production.*

Irene Worth plays Winnie in the first act of Samuel Beckett's HAPPY DAYS. *Note Willie is to the rear of the mound while Winnie's bag and parasol are within her reach.*

When the cast first comes on stage in Ntozake Shange's SPELL #7, the actors, who are all black, wear blackface and appear beneath a gigantic black-face mask.

Justine Bateman, Treat Williams, and Wayne Rogers appear in the 1991 Williamstown Theater Festival production of David Mamet's SPEED-THE-PLOW.

IV

DRAMA AND THEATER
IN MODERN EUROPE

N MANY WAYS THE WORLD
we live in today was forged between 1850 and 1950. Since the mid-nineteenth century, enormous political changes have redrawn the map of the planet: two world wars; the rise of the United States and the Union of Soviet Socialist Republics as world superpowers; revolutions in Russia and China; worldwide liberation from European colonial rule in Mexico, the Philippines, Latin America, Africa, India, and Southeast Asia. Political change was spurred by a series of industrial and technological revolutions. This is the century of the telephone, radio, film, and television; of the automobile and the highway; of the airplane and the rocket; of penicillin, anesthetics, vaccination, and artificial organs; of the assembly line and mass production; of multinational corporations extending their markets and influence around the globe. The acceleration of technological change altered the fabric of daily life, creating new forms of living, working, and relating to one another, and new ways of measuring our lives: suburbs and housing developments, trade unions and public corporations, the time clock and the wristwatch, public education and compulsory retirement. It witnessed huge changes in the landscape of life: the growth of the modern cityscape, of modern slums, skyscrapers, subways, and even city streets; of massive public projects like the Panama and Suez canals, the Empire State Building, the Eiffel Tower, and their grim cousins, the gas chambers of Auschwitz, the nuclear bombing of Hiroshima and Nagasaki.

Political and social changes were rivaled by the intellectual and cultural revolutions that gave—or attempted to give—meaning to modern experience. This is the century of Darwin and the theory of evolution; of Marx and Lenin; of Gandhi's nonviolent resistance; of Einstein, Oppenheimer, and Teller, and a revolution in our understanding of the physical cosmos; of Freud's discovery of the unconscious; of Proust, Joyce, Stein, Eliot, and Woolf; of the Impressionist painters, and of Picasso, and Pollock; of Diaghilev and Nijinsky, of Fred Astaire and Ginger Rogers, of Isadora Duncan and Martha Graham; of Wagner, of Stravinsky and Schoenberg, of ragtime and jazz.

This complex of revolutions extends to the modern theater. Technological innovation, political developments, and two major wars encouraged an increasing internationalism across the arts of Europe, evident in the "international" style of architecture popularized by Le Corbusier, the Bauhaus, and their followers; in Cubist painting and sculpture; and in modernist writing and music. This internationalism, however, hardly fostered a single, monolithic sense of "modernism" in the arts. Instead, it gave rise to a series of fragmentary AVANT-GARDE movements—imagism, cubism, vorticism, futurism, symbolism, surrealism, dada, and so on—each with its own ideals, esthetics, and audience, and usually with its own resistant posture toward society as well. The fragment—the poetic image, Joyce's "epiphanies," Schoenberg's twelve-tone row, montage in film—came to be valued as a means of expression in itself.

Modernist art also developed a distinction between "high art" and the esthetics of mass culture that parallels the modern division of labor and implies a division between highbrow and lowbrow, the elite and the popular. In many respects, the modernist theater became definitive of "high art" as it was edged from the center of cultural life by other performance media—film, radio, and later television—which claimed greater immediacy and wider distribution. After the turn of the century, the modern theater and drama was increasingly pressed to define what is germane, special, essential to live dramatic performance.

This unit (and unit 6) surveys the theater more widely than previous units, focusing not on a single city or site of performance, but instead on the broader developments of this international movement. For although the theaters of Chekhov's Moscow, Shaw's London, and Brecht's Berlin reflected very different social dynamics, they were engaged in a common, distinctly modernist project: bringing the stage into a critical relation to the forms of modern life by taking an experimental attitude toward theatrical production.

THE MODERN THEATER

Theatrical innovation always takes place on three fronts: as technology, as esthetics, and as ideology. The history of the modern theater is in one sense a history of new strategies and techniques for stage production: electric lighting, revolving stages, increasingly spectacular and illusionistic stage machinery, and new techniques of stage design, acting, and direction. What makes these changes meaningful is how they are used to represent and explain the world around us.

Reviewing the history of nineteenth-century drama, Brander Matthews — the first professor of dramatic literature in the United States — remarked in 1910 that modern drama owed its innovation more to Edison than to Ibsen, that the new drama was "the inevitable consequence of the incandescent bulb." The technological revolutions that brought engines and electricity to the public transformed theater throughout Europe and America: the replacement of candle lighting and gas lighting with more flexible electric lighting; the installation of the PROSCENIUM frame, emphasizing the pictorial coherence of the stage; the gradual disappearance of galleries and boxes in favor of seating the audience in darkened, fan-shaped theaters, emphasizing a perspective view of the proscenium; elevators to raise and lower sets; revolving stages on which several settings could be placed at one time. This technology could be put to a variety of uses, and the nineteenth-century theaters of Europe and America had an extraordinarily spectacular dimension, fostering a taste for EXTRAVAGANZAS, MELODRAMAS, NAUTICAL SHOWS, PANTOMIMES, and TABLEAUX. However, the apparatus of the modern theater came increasingly to be dominated by the notion of SCENIC UNITY, the idea that the stage set, the costumes, the behavior of the actors, and the dramatic action all should correspond to a single historical era and social milieu. Shakespeare's actors had mixed contemporary Elizabethan dress with "antique" costumes in the production of plays with classical settings. Throughout the eighteenth century, actors wore contemporary clothing regardless of the historical era of the play. By the late nineteenth century, however, following the example of Charles Kean and Henry Irving in England, the company of George II, the Duke of Saxe-Meiningen in Germany, and others, productions increasingly strove to establish a unified style on the stage, in which the dialogue, acting style, costumes, setting, and dramatic action all conformed to a single point-of-view.

The use of a unified theatrical style to assert a thorough VERISIMILITUDE, a photographic "slice of life" onstage, became the cornerstone of modern REALISM in drama and theater and of the movement called NATURALISM in which it began. In a series of essays calling for a "naturalism in the theater," published in the 1870s, the French novelist and playwright Émile Zola argued that the technology of the late nineteenth-century theater could be used to represent a more clinical or scientific attitude toward the world. He urged the stage to adopt a more lifelike and "naturalistic" style by adopting the "objective" methods and perspective of the natural sciences. By filling the stage with objects — real doors, real walls, pictures, furniture, fireplaces — the theater could place men and women in their "environment" rather than in the idealized "setting" of the classical theater, and the characters could then be seen as influenced by that material environment. In contrast to the ideal heroes of earlier drama, the characters of modern plays would become part of that stage milieu, influenced by the forces of history, society, economy, and psychology. Naturalism, that is, uses the technology of the stage to claim a "scientific" attitude toward social problems, usually emphasizing the determining role that the social environment plays in the characters' actions. It organized the theater's new technology and the idea of scenic unity it made possible, and provided it with a characteristic kind of meaning: the achievement of verisimilitude.

Naturalism and realism are notoriously difficult to distinguish; here we can describe them as two phases in the history of modern theater and drama. In this sense, naturalism provides the thematic inspiration and many of the dramatic techniques we now associate with modern realistic drama. Realism in the theater is also committed to verisimilitude, but usually develops a wider range of style and a more problematic sense of the relationship of character and environment. While naturalistic plays tend to be preoccupied with the duplication of material reality onstage, realistic plays sometimes distort the verisimilitude of the stage picture in order to dramatize an inner, psychological truth. Tom, in Tennessee Williams's *The Glass Menagerie* (see unit 5), for example, moves in and out of the realistic setting onstage, between the world of memory, the world of the audience, and the objective social reality of the drama. Realism extends and refines the techniques first explored by Zola's generation of playwrights, directors, and actors: a simple and direct speaking style that usually masks a SUBTEXT of subtle, unspoken motives; middle- or lower-class characters; action that revolves around the discovery of some past crime or indiscretion; a three-dimensional stage set, usually a domestic interior. Rather than using the play as a vehicle for a single "star" actor, realistic performance emphasizes the ensemble playing of the cast, so that each character becomes important in the overall action. Onstage, realism often treats the boundary of the proscenium as an invisible FOURTH WALL dividing the environment onstage from the audience. The fourth wall prevents the actors from playing to the audience and so from destroying the unity of illusion onstage.

Realism has become the dominant mode of dramatic performance today, so pervasive that it may be difficult for us to recapture its special excitement and danger when first introduced in the 1880s and 1890s. For in the first blush of the modern era, the ability to picture an untheatrical, apparently "real" world on the stage was in itself a kind of spectacle, akin to the magic of the new, competing art of photography. Moreover, the first generation of realistic playwrights often adopted a critical posture toward the pieties of the middle-class audience whose attitudes were embodied in the "realistic" vision of the world. Plays like Ibsen's *Ghosts* and *A Doll House*, Strindberg's *Miss Julie*, and even Glaspell's *Trifles* raised the scandalous topics of sexual betrayal, marital discord, class conflict, sexual freedom, and gender politics in ways that challenged the conventional morality of the bourgeois audience.

The realistic theater developed many of the practices we are familiar with today: new sets for each production, rather than the same furniture recycled from show to show, in order to create the play's specific environment; the fourth wall; the darkened auditorium. Although realistic drama became pervasive, it first flourished in the small avant-garde theaters of the INDEPENDENT THEATER MOVEMENT at the turn of the century. Throughout Europe and the United States, playwrights and directors worked to carve a place for themselves outside the commercial mainstream, which often resisted and sometimes censored the controversial plays of the new realism. André Antoine founded the Théâtre Libre ("Free Theater") in Paris as a subscription theater in 1887; since the shows were open only to subscribers and not to the general public, he was able to avoid censorship and to produce plays like Ibsen's *Ghosts* and Strindberg's *The Father*. Antoine's work was paralleled by the German Freie Bühne ("Free Stage") in 1889. In England, the actress Janet Achurch mounted a production of Ibsen's *A Doll House* in 1889; J. T. Grein's Independent Theater opened in 1891 with a production of *Ghosts* and went on to produce plays by Ibsen, Shaw, and other contemporary playwrights. In Russia, Constantin Stanislavsky and Vladimir Nemirovich-Danchenko founded the Moscow Art Theater in 1898, launching one of the

A PROSCENIUM STAGE: THE SHAKESPEARE MEMORIAL THEATRE

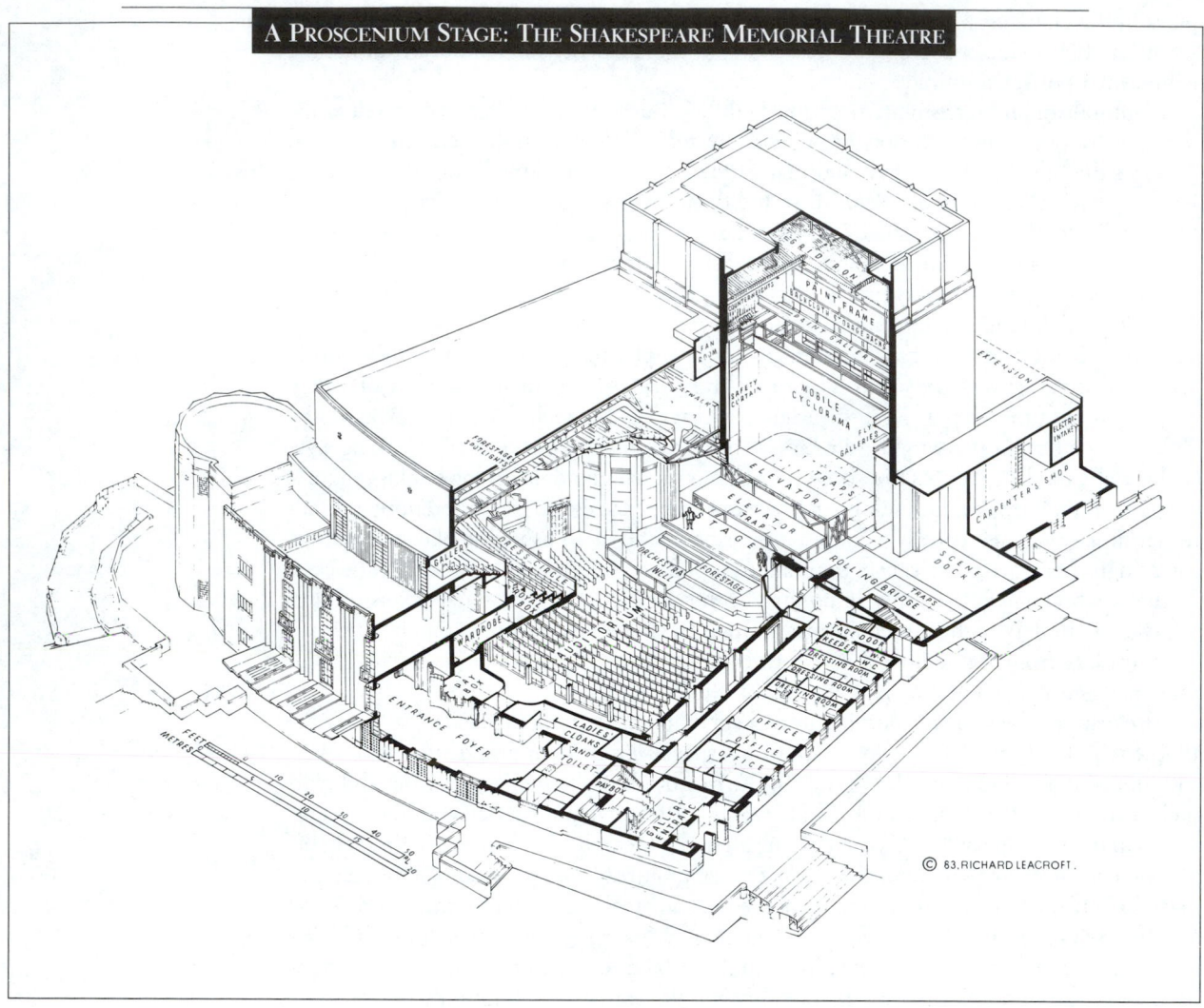

The Shakespeare Memorial Theatre, Stratford-upon-Avon, 1932, displays an extensive backstage area used for scenic machinery.

most influential of modern theaters with their production of Chekhov's *The Seagull*. Independent theaters were often part of nationalist movements as well, especially in Norway, Sweden, Italy, and Ireland. In Ireland, W. B. Yeats, Lady Augusta Gregory, John Millington Synge, and a solid cast of amateur actors established a nationalist theater company in 1902 and opened The Abbey Theater in 1904. Here, the artistic resistance of the independent theater was allied to political resistance and national self-definition. The influence of these theaters was felt in the United States throughout the first decades of the twentieth century. David Belasco's minute fidelity to detail had firmly established a realistic idiom in the American theater, but it took the **LITTLE THEATER MOVEMENT**, inaugurated by Eugene O'Neill, Susan Glaspell, and the Provincetown Playhouse in 1915, to establish a repertoire of modern drama in the United States, and they were soon followed by other companies.

SHAKESPEARE MEMORIAL THEATRE INTERIOR VIEW

Although the Shakespeare Memorial Theatre has a forestage apron extending toward the audience, it is in many respects typical of the proscenium theaters of the early twentieth century. The audience is seated in a fan-shaped auditorium, in fixed seats, facing the illuminated stage.

FORMS OF MODERN DRAMA

The rise of the independent theaters also points to the theater's fragmentation and its marginalization in modern society. The theater no longer commands the cultural centrality that it had in classical Athens or in London and Paris in the sixteenth and seventeenth centuries. Instead, it has become the site for a diverse, sometimes confusing array of artistic experiments. Naturalism and realism were the first dramatic modes to consider themselves not as expressing the dominant political and ideological order, but as criticizing the values and institutions of middle-class society. The major plays of the realistic canon often tend to criticize modern life, particularly its dehumanizing, exploitative routine. The major heroes of the realistic mode — Nora Helmer, Major Barbara, Laura Wingfield — are all characters whose desire for freedom, vitality, and life is threatened by the deadening, deceptive world in which they live. Because realistic drama usually sees that world as an all-embracing "environment," though, its social themes don't finally lead to a call for social change. Modern society may be a prison, but the liberation urged by realistic drama is imagined on the individual level; the characters' search for freedom, value, and meaning leaves the world unchanged. Despite its critical stance toward modern society, realistic drama tacitly accepts the world and its values as an unchanging, and unchangeable, environment in which the characters live out their lives.

For this reason, realistic drama has often seemed an inadequate vehicle for a sustained critique of the forces of modern life, and almost from the moment of its inception in the 1880s and 1890s, realism inspired antagonistic forms of drama and theater. The history of modern drama is a series of reactions against bourgeois society and its values, and against the realistic drama that seemed to represent it and its vision of the world.

Although it was finally concerned with many of the same issues, the EXPRESSIONIST THEATER popular from the turn of the century through the 1930s marked an exciting stylistic departure from the realistic mode. Expressionist plays like Strindberg's *A Dream Play*, or American plays like Elmer Rice's *The Adding Machine*, Sophie Treadwell's *Machinal*, or Eugene O'Neill's *The Emperor Jones*, transformed the terms of realistic theater and drama. Rather than showing a character whose inner vitality is crushed by the bourgeois environment, expressionist plays try to show the mind and heart of the character visually, to express it directly in the objects and actions of the stage. The stage set becomes distorted, nearly dreamlike, and it is often peopled by characters who are exaggerated, mechanized, or fantastic, as a way of conveying the emotional coloring of the central character's experience. In O'Neill's play, for instance, the Emperor Jones is haunted by his "Little Formless Fears" when he flees into the forest; his flight is accompanied by the sound of a drum, which beats faster and louder as the play proceeds (see unit 5). More often, characters in expressionist drama are unnamed, like the Young Woman of *Machinal* or Mr. Zero of *The Adding Machine*, emphasizing that they have become cogs in the modern social and industrial machine. The action of expressionist drama is episodic and much like morality drama. Ernst Toller even named the scenes of his play *Transfiguration* "stations" to stress the play's likeness to a Christian passion play.

Thematically, expressionist theater resembles realism in its attention to character psychology and in its portrayal — however distorted or exaggerated — of the dehumanizing process of modern life. However, the style of expressionism also subverts realism in important ways, challenging both the logical, causal ordering of realistic dramatic action and the visual verisimilitude of the realistic theater. The SYMBOLIST THEATER also developed antirealistic attitudes toward drama and staging and extended the expressionist theater's repudiation of the drama of modern life. Written in prose or in verse, symbolic drama created a dim and mysterious other world, sometimes drawn from mythology or simply from the poet's imagination. The Belgian playwright Maurice Maeterlinck created a vogue for this kind of drama at the turn of the century, a drama which finds analogies in the work of Stéphane Mallarmé, August Strindberg, T. S. Eliot, W. B. Yeats, and Samuel Beckett. Yeats's mythological plays — such as *On Baile's Strand* — are typical of this special and influential mode. Relatively static in action, the plays rely on a densely figurative language to enlarge and energize the "poetic" meaning of events onstage.

Finally, an explicitly Marxist theory of the ideologically coercive dimension of realism — the sense that realism claims that its special perspective of the world is *natural*, that is, unavoidable and *real* — stands at the center of modern EPIC THEATER. Though usually associated with Bertolt Brecht, many of the techniques of epic theater were developed by Erwin Piscator in Berlin during the 1920s and early 1930s and by Vsevolod Meyerhold in his brilliant experiments with CONSTRUCTIVIST THEATER after the Russian Revolution of 1917. Brecht assimilated these techniques to a political purpose that he called epic theater. Rather than claiming to represent reality directly onstage by concealing the workings of the theater, epic theater alerts the audience to the ideological dimension of theater practice by constantly keeping the stage's "means of production" in view. Brecht developed the ALIENATION EFFECT as a way of alerting the audience to the constructed nature of stage events. While the realistic theater claims that the theater and drama, actor and character, stage and dramatic locale are the same, epic theater shows how they are different. In so doing, Brecht argued, the epic theater enables the audience to ask how—with what purpose, to what effect—stage practice is making this dramatic effect come about, and so leads the audience to take a more critical view of the process of the theater. Epic acting, then, comments on itself as "acting." The stage is not unified as a single dramatic locale, but always remains visibly a stage. Brecht also argued that epic drama should be structured differently than realistic plays. Instead of the apparently organic, "causal" action of realistic drama, Brecht's plays are written in a series of episodes. This technique, Brecht argued, allows the actors and the audience to reconsider the character's possibilities for action and change afresh in each scene. By calling the audience's attention to how the play comes into being onstage, epic theater encourages the audience to develop a dialectical sense of how social reality— in the theater and in the world at large—comes into being, how it is made through the interaction of individual and social forces and the interaction of material reality and **IDEOLOGY**. Epic theater has had an enormous influence on drama and theater around the world, particularly in the 1960s, 1970s, 1980s, and 1990s.

Stage practice has developed its own rich history, too—again often in reaction to realistic verisimilitude. Throughout the twentieth century, for instance, designers and architects have experimented with different ways of orienting the audience to the stage, in **THEATER-IN-THE-ROUND** and in **ENVIRONMENTAL THEATER**, for instance. To see the dramatic action surrounded by spectators or to have the play take place among the audience alters the audience's relationship to both the drama and its performance and changes how the audience can read the production. The Constructivist experiments of Vsevolod Meyerhold following the Russian Revolution placed a nonrepresentational "construction" onstage, a structure that the actors used as a "machine for acting" rather than as a realistic set. Similarly, experimental performance altered notions of what dramatic and theatrical representation could be like. Following World War I, writers like Tristan Tzara called for an art that was formless and irrational, a process rather than a product; such "Dada"—a nonsense term—poems, plays, and monologues were often given **CABARET PERFORMANCE** in Zurich, Berlin, and Paris. **DADA** and **SURREALIST THEATER** developed a kind of hallucinatory intimacy between stage and audience, laying the foundations for Artaud's **THEATER OF CRUELTY** (see unit 6). In all of these experiments, the theater worked to disperse the visual unity characteristic of the realistic stage in ways that led to new configurations of the relationship between the audience and the performers and to new interpretive perspectives on drama and on the possibilities of theater.

Realism, expressionism, symbolist theater, and *epic theater*—these useful labels necessarily limit and categorize the rich variety of the stage in ways that are artificial and untrue to the dynamics of change in the modern theater, for new innovations tend to draw their techniques from several of these modes. Modern plays, for instance, often blend representational techniques as a way of challenging the audience's understanding of the drama and its implication in the world. Despite their "realistic" anchoring in a material, lifelike setting, for example, Chekhov's plays sometimes disturb the stability of that illusion with odd, almost "symbolic" effects—the breaking string in *The Cherry Orchard*, for instance. The action of Strindberg's *Miss Julie*, too, for all the play's emphasis on class and social environment, seems to lurch and accelerate in ways more characteristic of an "expressionist" linking of the dramatic form to the characters' psychological experience. In Pirandello's *Six Characters in Search of an Author*—a play indebted in many ways to the "symbolist" theater—the Characters want the Actors to produce a play much in the manner of Ibsen's drama, a realistic drama of hidden crime and its discovery. These labels are useful in helping us to describe some of the outlines of a given play, but we should remember that many modern playwrights wrote in a variety of modes, and that each play is itself a kind of experiment.

ACTING AND PERFORMANCE

The modern theater's radical redefinitions of the style and purpose of drama required similar redefinitions of acting and performance. At the turn of the century, a theatrical company would have been organized according to each actor's typical LINE OF BUSINESS. Something like the company in Pirandello's *Six Characters*, companies had a leading comic actor, a villain or "heavy," a leading man, a leading lady, a comic old man, a comic woman, and a variety of other parts. Unlike *commedia dell' arte*, actors each played a variety of different characters; nonetheless, each actor would have elaborated some relatively conventional "business" for acting the kind of character he or she usually played. The unity of illusion demanded by the realistic theater, however, required each character to be more finely individualized. Much as the stage designer provided a new set for each production and the costume designer provided clothing appropriate to the character and his or her setting, so the actors were forced to particularize their performances in new ways.

A second stimulus for this innovation was the drama itself. Playwrights like Ibsen and Chekhov typically created characters against the grain of theatrical stereotypes. Nora Helmer, for example, seems like a typical SOUBRETTE at the opening of *A Doll House*, the pert and clever young woman of light comedy. However, as the play develops, Ibsen challenges this convention and forces the actress to discover new ways of producing the character. Realistic plays frequently ask actors to work against the apparent "type" of the role, to discover the psychological subtext of will and desire beneath the spoken words that motivates the character's actions. Actors and actresses at the turn of the century frequently had difficulty reading the new realistic plays, precisely because they couldn't see how to represent the more indirect action and individualized characters through the kinds of stage behavior they had been trained to use.

A new kind of drama requires a new kind of acting, and companies throughout Europe developed ways of acting more behavioristically onstage. The most systematic approach to acting was undertaken by the actor and director Constantin Stanislavsky at the Moscow Art Theater around the turn of the century. Although Stanislavsky thought that his techniques could be applied to any play, he discovered the need for such acting largely in his work on Chekhov's plays. Chekhov's plays were frustrating to actors of the old school because the characters did not conform to traditional types and the action seemed so indirect and inconsequential, lacking familiar dramatic rhythms and climaxes. Stanislavsky developed techniques for approaching each character as an individual, techniques that were later systematized as a "method" of actor-training. Stanislavsky trained the actor to associate his or her personal history with the invented actions of the dramatic character so that the actor could tap that emotional spontaneity, a "life in art," as part of the performance. By using the MAGIC IF — imagining themselves *as* the character, rather than applying a stock line of business — and using their own EMOTION MEMORY to vivify the character's inner life, Stanislavsky's actors were taught to bring authentic emotional experience into their performances. Of course, Stanislavsky also emphasized the many other abilities that an actor must develop — physical training, vocal control, grace, concentration — but his real contribution to the modern stage is the emphasis on the actor's emotional reality in performance. The realistic theater uses real objects to create a persuasive material environment, and its characters come alive through the actor's real feeling. Stanislavsky's work has been extremely influential, particularly in the United States, where it was adapted as the school of METHOD ACTING in the 1930s, and it remains — in very different and modified forms — at the center of much actor-training today.

Antirealistic drama also called for the development of new styles of performance. Meyerhold developed BIOMECHANICS as a way to make the actor's performance more physical, less directly concerned with the behavioral and psychological verisimilitude typical of

Stanislavskian realistic acting. His work has analogies in the use of dance and ritualized performance in symbolist theater and in the nonrepresentational physicality of Antonin Artaud's Theater of Cruelty (see unit 6). Symbolist theater also repudiated the lifelike quality of realistic acting. It required a highly artificial and statuesque stillness from performers, allowing the actors to strike powerful but ethereal poses in order to deliver the densely poetic language of the play without interference. Yeats — whose antipathy to realism was profound — thought of training his actors in barrels, to keep them from moving and gesturing as they would do in everyday life: the art of the symbolist theater should be emphatically artificial, thoroughly apart from the conduct of life beyond the stage.

Brecht, again, voiced the most thorough critique of realistic acting. To Brecht, the problem of realistic acting was that it showed the "character" as a finished product, a commodity, rather than revealing *how* the character had come into being, both through the social forces described in the drama and through the decisions taken by the actor as part of the performance. Brecht argued that the actor should acknowledge that he or she both empathizes with the character and demonstrates the character to the audience, that acting is both feeling and showing at the same time. This dialectical approach invites the audience to see how the actor is making the "character" and allows the public to interpret both the process and the product of theater art, the dramatic "character" and the actor's labor.

WOMEN IN MODERN DRAMA AND THEATER

Most readers of modern drama immediately note the prominence of women characters in the plays — Nora Helmer in *A Doll House*, Julie in *Miss Julie*, Barbara in *Major Barbara*, Courage in *Mother Courage*. Playwrights frequently associated the political and social limitations of middle-class life with male characters and used female characters to pose subversive questions about that social order. However, in the drama, as in society, this subversive freedom sometimes emerges as illusory or problematic. Ibsen, for instance, enables Nora to recognize how she has been defined by the men in her life, but the world outside her home hardly seems inviting; is there really anywhere for her to go? Many of the women — Miss Julie, Major Barbara — are also assigned an erotic power opposed to the "reason" of their male antagonists. While this power, too, can be disruptive, it sometimes also reinforces traditional gender stereotypes. Feminine erotic power in the drama carries with it other ascribed values, defining women as more emotional, as more subject to the influence of the body, as closer to "nature." Men retain a pragmatic, "rational" authority that places them at the center of society, and that defines the arena of culture and civilization as an implicitly male domain. The apparent freedom of these stage women, that is, often signals their deeper captivity to the gendered economy of modern society, a captivity shared by actresses in the period as well. Although this is also a period in which actresses — Sarah Bernhardt, Eleonora Duse, or Ellen Terry, for example — could earn an international reputation, they worked in a theater in which men greatly outnumbered women in the audience and in which nearly all of the managers and producers were men. In a male-dominated industry like the modern theater, it is not surprising that women onstage — both dramatic characters and performers — should reflect fundamentally masculine attitudes about the place of women in society.

To think of the history of theater and drama since Ibsen is to think of an increasingly large and problematic array of dramatic styles, modes of theatrical production, and conceptions of the audience and its world. Many of these innovations were local at first, responding to the social and theatrical conditions of a specific time and place: Brecht's Marxist theater arose in the cabaret culture of Berlin in the late 1920s; Pirandello's **METATHEATER** was part of the lively Italian avant-garde following World War I; Shaw's drama was informed by the progressive politics of the British Fabian society and by dramatic conventions drawn from the popular plays of the late Victorian stage. The drama of modern Europe develops a posture of resistant inquiry toward the pieties of contemporary social life. It works both to represent that world and to change it, to affect our ideas about character and personality, about the political realities of our world, and even about the metaphysical certainties we have come to believe.

HENRIK IBSEN

At the turn of the century, Henrik Ibsen (1828–1906) was synonymous with modernity in the European theater; much of the territory of modern drama was first explored in Ibsen's work. Born into a mercantile family in provincial Norway, Ibsen had planned to study medicine; however, after failing to matriculate at the university, he turned to a career as a writer. From 1850 through 1864, Ibsen worked for the nationalist Norwegian Theater in Bergen and then for the Mollergate Theater in Christiania (now Oslo). As literary manager, stage manager, and assistant to the director, Ibsen learned the craft of practical theater firsthand. He also wrote a series of romantic history plays, some in prose and some in verse. Although his fame now rests on the realistic plays he wrote later in his career, in his own lifetime these history plays—such as *The Vikings at Helgeland* (1858)—were quite popular, especially in Norway.

In 1864, Ibsen left Norway and settled in Rome, where he wrote two pivotal plays, *Brand* (1866) and *Peer Gynt* (1867). The story of an idealistic minister, *Brand* established Ibsen as an important European writer and announced one of his central themes: the cost of moral idealism in the modern world. *Peer Gynt* is often taken as a companion-piece to *Brand*, for Peer's picaresque journey throughout Europe is undertaken simply for the purpose of his own self-satisfaction: while Brand's motto is "Be wholly what you are," Peer Gynt's is "To thine own self be . . . enough." In 1877, after extensive work on the Hegelian history drama *Emperor and Galilean*, Ibsen wrote *Pillars of Society*, a prose drama of modern life, inaugurating the stunning series of plays that made him famous and established the contours of modern realistic drama. In *A Doll House (1879)*, *Ghosts* (1881), and *An Enemy of the People* (1882), Ibsen explored the conflict between the social and moral restrictions of bourgeois society and the psychological, often unconscious demands of individual freedom. Ibsen adapted the suspenseful, rigorously plotted form of the **WELL-MADE PLAY** (or *pièce bien faite*) popularized throughout Europe by French playwrights Eugène Scribe and Victorien Sardou and used it in plays of modern life critical of bourgeois morality and society. The well-made play is notoriously difficult to define, even though its features are familiar: a rigorously "causal" plot, a secret gradually revealed to the audience, a "necessary scene" (the *scène-à-faire*) in which the secret is revealed to the characters, a character (the *raisonneur*) who explains and moralizes the action to the others, and a predominance of coincidental events. In his earlier plays, Ibsen takes these formal conventions and makes them function as forces in the dramatic world. The world of the play comes to seem mechanistic, determined by a secret that will out, full of busybodies explaining and interpreting the action. The mechanics of the well-made play, that is, are identified with the deadening force of social convention, which painfully threatens to extinguish the vitality of the central characters. This conflict between deadening social convention and a mysterious inner vitality pervades Ibsen's mature plays as well, which increasingly moved away from the "well-made" form: *The Wild Duck* (1885), *Rosmersholm* (1887), *The Lady from the Sea* (1888), and *Hedda Gabler* (1890). Ibsen's last plays seem more poetic or symbolic, though they take place in the familiar milieu of the realistic stage: *The Master Builder* (1892), *Little Eyolf* (1894), *John Gabriel Borkman* (1896), and the unfinished *When We Dead Awaken* (1900). Ibsen suffered a paralyzing series of strokes in 1900 that left him unable to write. He died in 1906.

Ibsen's effect on his contemporaries and his influence on the course of modern drama were immediate and profound. His plays were rapidly translated into the major European languages, and stage productions—which often inaugurated the new "independent" theaters—frequently became the subject of sensation and controversy. Indeed, "Ibsenism" came to be a catchword for a variety of social causes, though Ibsen himself generally avoided politics. Although Ibsen's plays brought new issues to the stage, it was his practice as a playwright that proved truly revolutionary. Many playwrights had adopted the realistic theater's use of a material stage environment, its emphasis on the burden of the past, and its sense of a mechanized and constricting society. Ibsen not only used this material with powerful subtlety and resonance, he gave the stage its first distinctively modern characters: complex, contradictory individuals driven by a desire for something—the "joy of life," a sense of themselves—that they can barely recognize or name.

A Doll House

A *Doll House* was inspired by a series of incidents that came to Ibsen's attention in 1878 when a woman named Laura Kieler contacted him. Kieler had signed a secret—and illegal—loan to raise money for a cure for her tubercular husband. She wrote to Ibsen asking him to recommend the novel she had written to his publisher, in hopes that the profits from its sale would allow her to repay the loan. Ibsen refused. Kieler forged a check and was caught. Her husband committed her to an asylum, had her charged as an unfit mother, and demanded a legal separation. When she was released from the asylum, however, the family remained together.

We can see the shaping power of Ibsen's imagination in his transformation of Laura Kieler's tragedy into the ironic masterpiece, *A Doll House*. For the play—which by the turn of the century was a rallying point for international feminist demands for the vote and for other legal rights and protections for women—organizes the conflict between Nora and Helmer around a subtle set of contrasts: the childlike and protected Nora and the world-weary Mrs. Linde; the upright and protective Helmer and the unscrupulous loan shark, Krogstad; the privations of the past and the financial freedom Nora sees on the horizon. However, as the play proceeds, the stable, bourgeois world that Helmer represents is revealed as a tissue of deception—the institutions of marriage, respectability, and social justice turn out to be fictions that the privileged use to manipulate their world. Nora comes to seem effective, efficient, worldly wise, and finally independent, while Helmer readily compromises his principles to save his reputation. The world of financial freedom Nora glimpses at the play's outset turns out to be a kind of prison and is replaced by another kind of freedom at the end of the play: the frightening freedom to cut herself loose from the bonds of marriage, family, and society.

Helmer had more authority with audiences in the 1880s and 1890s than he does today, and Nora was conventionally criticized as an "unwomanly woman" for taking the loan, deceiving her husband, and leaving her family. Indeed, the first English actress to be offered the part turned it down, because she didn't want audiences to think of her as the kind of woman who would desert her children. Yet the play tends to validate Nora's personal growth and her final decision to leave her family, and cannily uses the material environment of the stage setting to convey the suffocating situation in which Nora finds herself. The play takes place in one room: the drawing room where the upwardly mobile Helmers (deluxe books on the shelf, piano against the wall, framed art prints) receive their guests and conduct their lives. The room itself represents the Helmers' concern for social status and assumes a symbolic importance as well: it stands between the unseen privacy of the kitchen and bedroom—the domestic world of marriage and children—and the threatening public world beyond the front door, the world of Krogstad, of the dark and icy river, of Nora's final escape. The room becomes a kind of prison, a room in which Rank's declaration of love for Nora seems inappropriate, in which Helmer criticizes her dizzying tarantella—a Sicilian dance thought to imitate the death throes of someone bitten by a tarantula—as too abandoned, and in which Nora's final discussion with Helmer makes her submission to him impossible. That is, the room makes concrete the play's concern for the social constraints on a woman's life, becoming a visual image of how Helmer's masculine, bourgeois moral authority imprisons Nora. It is not entirely clear that Nora can survive in the harsh social and economic climate outside the comfortable parlor, but it is clear that escape from the parlor is her final alternative.

A DOLL HOUSE

Henrik Ibsen

TRANSLATED BY ROLF FJELDE

— CHARACTERS —

TORVALD HELMER, *a lawyer*	THE HELMERS' THREE	*The action takes place in* HELMER's *residence.*
NORA, *his wife*	SMALL CHILDREN	
DR. RANK	ANNE-MARIE, *their nurse*	
MRS. LINDE	HELENE, *a maid*	
NILS KROGSTAD, *a bank clerk*	A DELIVERY BOY	

— ACT ONE —

A comfortable room, tastefully but not expensively furnished. A door to the right in the back wall leads to the entryway; another to the left leads to HELMER's *study. Between these doors, a piano. Midway in the left-hand wall a door, and further back a window. Near the window a round table with an armchair and a small sofa. In the right-hand wall, toward the rear, a door, and nearer the foreground a porcelain stove with two armchairs and a rocking chair beside it. Between the stove and the side door, a small table. Engravings on the walls. An etagère with china figures and other small art objects; a small bookcase with richly bound books; the floor carpeted; a fire burning in the stove. It is a winter day.*

A bell rings in the entryway; shortly after we hear the door being unlocked. NORA *comes into the room, humming happily to herself; she is wearing street clothes and carries an armload of packages, which she puts down on the table to the right. She has left the hall door open; and through it a* DELIVERY BOY *is seen, holding a Christmas tree and a basket, which he gives to the* MAID *who let them in.*

NORA: Hide the tree well, Helene. The children mustn't get a glimpse of it till this evening, after it's trimmed. (*To the* DE-LIVERY BOY, *taking out her purse.*) How much?

DELIVERY BOY: Fifty, ma'am.

5 NORA: There's a crown. No, keep the change. (*The* BOY *thanks her and leaves.* NORA *shuts the door. She laughs softly to herself while taking off her street things. Drawing a bag of macaroons from her pocket, she eats a couple, then steals over and listens at her husband's study door.*) Yes, he's home. (*Hums*

10 *again as she moves to the table right.*)

HELMER: (*from the study.*) Is that my little lark twittering out there?

NORA: (*busy opening some packages.*) Yes, it is.

HELMER: Is that my squirrel rummaging around?

15 NORA: Yes!

HELMER: When did my squirrel get in?

NORA: Just now. (*Putting the macaroon bag in her pocket and wiping her mouth.*) Do come in, Torvald, and see what I've bought.

20 HELMER: Can't be disturbed. (*After a moment he opens the door and peers in, pen in hand.*) Bought, you say? All that there? Has the little spendthrift been out throwing money around again?

NORA: Oh, but Torvald, this year we really should let ourselves

25 go a bit. It's the first Christmas we haven't had to economize.

HELMER: But you know we can't go squandering.

NORA: Oh yes, Torvald, we can squander a little now. Can't we? Just a tiny, wee bit. Now that you've got a big salary and are going to make piles and piles of money.

HELMER: Yes — starting New Year's. But then it's a full three 30 months till the raise comes through.

NORA: Pooh! We can borrow that long.

HELMER: Nora! (*Goes over and playfully takes her by the ear.*) Are your scatterbrains off again? What if today I borrowed a thousand crowns, and you squandered them over Christmas 35 week, and then on New Year's Eve a roof tile fell on my head, and I lay there —

NORA: (*putting her hand on his mouth.*) Oh! Don't say such things!

HELMER: Yes, but what if it happened — then what? 40

NORA: If anything so awful happened, then it just wouldn't matter if I had debts or not.

HELMER: Well, but the people I'd borrowed from?

NORA: Them? Who cares about them! They're strangers.

HELMER: Nora, Nora, how like a woman! No, but seriously, 45 Nora, you know what I think about that. No debts! Never borrow! Something of freedom's lost — and something of beauty, too — from a home that's founded on borrowing and debt. We've made a brave stand up to now, the two of us; and we'll go right on like that the little while we have to. 50

NORA: (*going toward the stove.*) Yes, whatever you say, Torvald.

HELMER: (*following her.*) Now, now, the little lark's wings mustn't droop. Come on, don't be a sulky squirrel. (*Taking out his wallet.*) Nora, guess what I have here.

NORA: (*turning quickly.*) Money! 55

HELMER: There, see. (*Hands her some notes.*) Good grief, I know how costs go up in a house at Christmastime.

NORA: Ten — twenty — thirty — forty. Oh, thank you, Torvald; I can manage no end on this.

HELMER: You really will have to. 60

NORA: Oh yes, I promise I will! But come here so I can show you everything I bought. And so cheap! Look, new clothes for Ivar here — and a sword. Here a horse and a trumpet for Bob. And a doll and a doll's bed here for Emmy; they're nothing much, but she'll tear them to bits in no time anyway. And here I have 65 dress material and handkerchiefs for the maids. Old Anne-Marie really deserves something more.

HELMER: And what's in that package there?

NORA: (*with a cry.*) Torvald, no! You can't see that till tonight!

HELMER: I see. But tell me now, you little prodigal, what have 70 you thought of for yourself?

NORA: For myself? Oh, I don't want anything at all.

HELMER: Of course you do. Tell me just what — within reason — you'd most like to have.

75 NORA: I honestly don't know. Oh, listen, Torvald —

HELMER: Well?

NORA: *(fumbling at his coat buttons, without looking at him.)* If you want to give me something, then maybe you could — you could —

80 HELMER: Come on, out with it.

NORA: *(hurriedly.)* You could give me money, Torvald. No more than you think you can spare; then one of these days I'll buy something with it.

HELMER: But Nora —

85 NORA: Oh, please, Torvald darling, do that! I beg you, please. Then I could hang the bills in pretty gilt paper on the Christmas tree. Wouldn't that be fun?

HELMER: What are those little birds called that always fly through their fortunes?

90 NORA: Oh yes, spendthrifts; I know all that. But let's do as I say, Torvald; then I'll have time to decide what I really need most. That's very sensible, isn't it?

HELMER: *(smiling.)* Yes, very — that is, if you actually hung onto the money I give you, and you actually used it to buy yourself

95 something. But it goes for the house and for all sorts of foolish things, and then I only have to lay out some more.

NORA: Oh, but Torvald —

HELMER: Don't deny it, my dear little Nora. *(Putting his arm around her waist.)* Spendthrifts are sweet, but they use up a

100 frightful amount of money. It's incredible what it costs a man to feed such birds.

NORA: Oh, how can you say that! Really, I save everything I can.

HELMER: *(laughing.)* Yes, that's the truth. Everything you can. But that's nothing at all.

105 NORA: *(humming, with a smile of quiet satisfaction.)* Hm, if you only knew what expenses we larks and squirrels have, Torvald.

HELMER: You're an odd little one. Exactly the way your father was. You're never at a loss for scaring up money; but the mo-

110 ment you have it, it runs right out through your fingers; you never know what you've done with it. Well, one takes you as you are. It's deep in your blood. Yes, these things are hereditary, Nora.

NORA: Ah, I could wish I'd inherited many of Papa's qualities.

115 HELMER: And I couldn't wish you anything but just what you are, my sweet little lark. But wait; it seems to me you have a very — what should I call it? — a very suspicious look today —

NORA: I do?

HELMER: You certainly do. Look me straight in the eye.

120 NORA: *(looking at him.)* Well?

HELMER: *(shaking an admonitory finger.)* Surely my sweet tooth hasn't been running riot in town today, has she?

NORA: No. Why do you imagine that?

HELMER: My sweet tooth really didn't make a little detour

125 through the confectioner's?

NORA: No, I assure you, Torvald —

HELMER: Hasn't nibbled some pastry?

NORA: No, not at all.

HELMER: Not even munched a macaroon or two?

130 NORA: No, Torvald, I assure you, really —

HELMER: There, there now. Of course I'm only joking.

NORA: *(going to the table, right.)* You know I could never think of going against you.

HELMER: No, I understand that; and you *have* given me your word. *(Going over to her.)* Well, you keep your little 135 Christmas secrets to yourself, Nora darling. I expect they'll come to light this evening, when the tree is lit.

NORA: Did you remember to ask Dr. Rank?

HELMER: No. But there's no need for that; it's assumed he'll be dining with us. All the same, I'll ask him when he stops by 140 here this morning. I've ordered some fine wine. Nora, you can't imagine how I'm looking forward to this evening.

NORA: So am I. And what fun for the children, Torvald!

HELMER: Ah, it's so gratifying to know that one's gotten a safe, secure job, and with a comfortable salary. It's a great satisfac- 145 tion, isn't it?

NORA: Oh, it's wonderful!

HELMER: Remember last Christmas? Three whole weeks before, you shut yourself in every evening till long after midnight, making flowers for the Christmas tree, and all the other deco- 150 rations to surprise us. Ugh, that was the dullest time I've ever lived through.

NORA: It wasn't at all dull for me.

HELMER: *(smiling.)* But the outcome *was* pretty sorry, Nora.

NORA: Oh, don't tease me with that again. How could I help it 155 that the cat came in and tore everything to shreds.

HELMER: No, poor thing, you certainly couldn't. You wanted so much to please us all, and that's what counts. But it's just as well that the hard times are past.

NORA: Yes, it's really wonderful. 160

HELMER: Now I don't have to sit here alone, boring myself, and you don't have to tire your precious eyes and your fair little delicate hands —

NORA: *(clapping her hands.)* No, is it really true, Torvald, I don't have to? Oh, how wonderfully lovely to hear! *(Taking his* 165 *arm.)* Now I'll tell you just how I've thought we should plan things. Right after Christmas — *(The doorbell rings.)* Oh, the bell. *(Straightening the room up a bit.)* Somebody would have to come. What a bore!

HELMER: I'm not at home to visitors, don't forget. 170

MAID: *(from the hall doorway.)* Ma'am, a lady to see you —

NORA: All right, let her come in.

MAID: *(to* HELMER.*)* And the doctor's just come too.

HELMER: Did he go right to my study?

MAID: Yes, he did. 175

(HELMER goes into his room. The MAID shows in MRS. LINDE, dressed in traveling clothes, and shuts the door after her.)

MRS. LINDE: *(in a dispirited and somewhat hesitant voice.)* Hello, Nora.

NORA: *(uncertain.)* Hello —

MRS. LINDE: You don't recognize me.

NORA: No, I don't know — but wait, I think — *(Exclaiming.)* 180 What! Kristine! Is it really you?

MRS. LINDE: Yes, it's me.

NORA: Kristine! To think I didn't recognize you. But then, how could I? *(More quietly.)* How you've changed, Kristine!

MRS. LINDE: Yes, no doubt I have. In nine — ten long years. 185

NORA: Is it so long since we met! Yes, it's all of that. Oh, these last eight years have been a happy time, believe me. And so

now you've come in to town, too. Made the long trip in the winter. That took courage.

190 MRS. LINDE: I just got here by ship this morning.

NORA: To enjoy yourself over Christmas, of course. Oh, how lovely! Yes, enjoy ourselves, we'll do that. But take your coat off. You're not still cold? (*Helping her.*) There now, let's get cozy here by the stove. No, the easy chair there! I'll take the

195 rocker here. (*Seizing her hands.*) Yes, now you have your old look again; it was only in that first moment. You're a bit more pale, Kristine — and maybe a bit thinner.

MRS. LINDE: And much, much older, Nora.

NORA: Yes, perhaps a bit older; a tiny, tiny bit; not much at all.

200 (*Stopping short; suddenly serious.*) Oh, but thoughtless me, to sit here, chattering away. Sweet, good Kristine, can you forgive me?

MRS. LINDE: What do you mean, Nora?

NORA: (*softly.*) Poor Kristine, you've become a widow.

205 MRS. LINDE: Yes, three years ago.

NORA: Oh, I knew it, of course; I read it in the papers. Oh, Kristine, you must believe me; I often thought of writing you then, but I kept postponing it, and something always interfered.

210 MRS. LINDE: Nora dear, I understand completely.

NORA: No, it was awful of me, Kristine. You poor thing, how much you must have gone through. And he left you nothing?

MRS. LINDE: No.

NORA: And no children?

215 MRS. LINDE: No.

NORA: Nothing at all, then?

MRS. LINDE: Not even a sense of loss to feed on.

NORA: (*looking incredulously at her.*) But Kristine, how could that be?

220 MRS. LINDE: (*smiling wearily and smoothing her hair.*) Oh, sometimes it happens, Nora.

NORA: So completely alone. How terribly hard that must be for you. I have three lovely children. You can't see them now; they're out with the maid. But now you must tell me

225 everything —

MRS. LINDE: No, no, no, tell me about yourself.

NORA: No, you begin. Today I don't want to be selfish. I want to think only of you today. But there *is* something I must tell you. Did you hear of the wonderful luck we had recently?

230 MRS. LINDE: No, what's that?

NORA: My husband's been made manager in the bank, just think!

MRS. LINDE: Your husband? How marvelous!

NORA: Isn't it? Being a lawyer is such an uncertain living, you

235 know, especially if one won't touch any cases that aren't clean and decent. And of course Torvald would never do that, and I'm with him completely there. Oh, we're simply delighted, believe me! He'll join the bank right after New Year's and start getting a huge salary and lots of commissions. From now on

240 we can live quite differently — just as we want. Oh, Kristine, I feel so light and happy! Won't it be lovely to have stacks of money and not a care in the world?

MRS. LINDE: Well, anyway, it would be lovely to have enough for necessities.

245 NORA: No, not just for necessities, but stacks and stacks of money!

MRS. LINDE: (*smiling.*) Nora, Nora, aren't you sensible yet? Back in school you were such a free spender.

NORA: (*with a quiet laugh.*) Yes, that's what Torvald still says.

250 (*Shaking her finger.*) But "Nora, Nora" isn't as silly as you all think. Really, we've been in no position for me to go squandering. We've had to work, both of us.

MRS. LINDE: You too?

NORA: Yes, at odd jobs — needlework, crocheting, embroidery,

255 and such — (*Casually.*) and other things too. You remember that Torvald left the department when we were married? There was no chance of promotion in his office, and of course he needed to earn more money. But that first year he drove himself terribly. He took on all kinds of extra work that kept

260 him going morning and night. It wore him down, and then he fell deathly ill. The doctors said it was essential for him to travel south.

MRS. LINDE: Yes, didn't you spend a whole year in Italy?

NORA: That's right. It wasn't easy to get away, you know. Ivar had

265 just been born. But of course we had to go. Oh, that was a beautiful trip, and it saved Torvald's life. But it cost a frightful sum, Kristine.

MRS. LINDE: I can well imagine.

NORA: Four thousand, eight hundred crowns it cost. That's re-

270 ally a lot of money.

MRS. LINDE: But it's lucky you had it when you needed it.

NORA: Well, as it was, we got it from Papa.

MRS. LINDE: I see. It was just about the time your father died.

NORA: Yes, just about then. And, you know, I couldn't make

275 that trip out to nurse him. I had to stay here, expecting Ivar any moment, and with my poor sick Torvald to care for. Dearest Papa, I never saw him again, Kristine. Oh, that was the worst time I've known in all my marriage.

MRS. LINDE: I know how you loved him. And then you went off

280 to Italy?

NORA: Yes. We had the means now, and the doctors urged us. So we left a month after.

MRS. LINDE: And your husband came back completely cured?

NORA: Sound as a drum!

285 MRS. LINDE: But — the doctor?

NORA: Who?

MRS. LINDE: I thought the maid said he was a doctor, the man who came in with me.

NORA: Yes, that was Dr. Rank — but he's not making a sick call.

290 He's our closest friend, and he stops by at least once a day. No, Torvald hasn't had a sick moment since, and the children are fit and strong, and I am, too. (*Jumping up and clapping her hands.*) Oh, dear God, Kristine, what a lovely thing to live and be happy! But how disgusting of me — I'm talking of nothing but my own affairs. (*Sits on a stool close by* KRISTINE,

295 *arms resting across her knees.*) Oh, don't be angry with me! Tell me, is it really true that you weren't in love with your husband? Why did you marry him, then?

MRS. LINDE: My mother was still alive, but bedridden and helpless — and I had my two younger brothers to look after. In all

300 conscience, I didn't think I could turn him down.

NORA: No, you were right there. But was he rich at the time?

MRS. LINDE: He was very well off, I'd say. But the business was shaky, Nora. When he died, it all fell apart, and nothing was left.

305 NORA: And then — ?

MRS. LINDE: Yes, so I had to scrape up a living with a little shop and a little teaching and whatever else I could find. The last three years have been like one endless workday without a rest

310 for me. Now it's over, Nora. My poor mother doesn't need me, for she's passed on. Nor the boys, either; they're working now and can take care of themselves.

NORA: How free you must feel —

MRS. LINDE: No — only unspeakably empty. Nothing to live for 315 now. (Standing up anxiously.) That's why I couldn't take it any longer out in that desolate hole. Maybe here it'll be easier to find something to do and keep my mind occupied. If I could only be lucky enough to get a steady job, some office work —

320 NORA: Oh, but Kristine, that's so dreadfully tiring, and you already look so tired. It would be much better for you if you could go off to a bathing resort.

MRS. LINDE: (going toward the window.) I have no father to give me travel money, Nora.

325 NORA: (rising.) Oh, don't be angry with me.

MRS. LINDE: (going to her.) Nora dear, don't you be angry with me. The worst of my kind of situation is all the bitterness that's stored away. No one to work for, and yet you're always having to snap up your opportunities. You have to live; and so 330 you grow selfish. When you told me the happy change in your lot, do you know I was delighted less for your sakes than for mine?

NORA: How so? Oh, I see. You think maybe Torvald could do something for you.

335 MRS. LINDE: Yes, that's what I thought.

NORA: And he will, Kristine! Just leave it to me; I'll bring it up so delicately — find something attractive to humor him with. Oh, I'm so eager to help you.

MRS. LINDE: How very kind of you, Nora, to be so concerned 340 over me — doubly kind, considering you really know so little of life's burdens yourself.

NORA: I — ? I know so little — ?

MRS. LINDE: (smiling.) Well, my heavens — a little needlework and such — Nora, you're just a child.

345 NORA: (tossing her head and pacing the floor.) You don't have to act so superior.

MRS. LINDE: Oh?

NORA: You're just like the others. You all think I'm incapable of anything serious —

350 MRS. LINDE: Come now —

NORA: That I've never had to face the raw world.

MRS. LINDE: Nora dear, you've just been telling me all your troubles.

NORA: Hm! Trivia! (Quietly.) I haven't told you the big thing.

355 MRS. LINDE: Big thing? What do you mean?

NORA: You look down on me so, Kristine, but you shouldn't. You're proud that you worked so long and hard for your mother.

MRS. LINDE: I don't look down on a soul. But it is true: I'm 360 proud — and happy, too — to think it was given to me to make my mother's last days almost free of care.

NORA: And you're also proud thinking of what you've done for your brothers.

MRS. LINDE: I feel I've a right to be.

365 NORA: I agree. But listen to this, Kristine — I've also got something to be proud and happy for.

MRS. LINDE: I don't doubt it. But whatever do you mean?

NORA: Not so loud. What if Torvald heard! He mustn't, not for anything in the world. Nobody must know, Kristine. No one 370 but you.

MRS. LINDE: But what is it, then?

NORA: Come here. (Drawing her down beside her on the sofa.) It's true — I've also got something to be proud and happy for. I'm the one who saved Torvald's life.

MRS. LINDE: Saved — ? Saved how? 375

NORA: I told you about the trip to Italy. Torvald never would have lived if he hadn't gone south —

MRS. LINDE: Of course; your father gave you the means —

NORA: (smiling.) That's what Torvald and all the rest think, but —

MRS. LINDE: But — ? 380

NORA: Papa didn't give us a pin. I was the one who raised the money.

MRS. LINDE: You? That whole amount?

NORA: Four thousand, eight hundred crowns. What do you say to that? 385

MRS. LINDE: But Nora, how was it possible? Did you win the lottery?

NORA: (disdainfully.) The lottery? Pooh! No art to that.

MRS. LINDE: But where did you get it from then?

NORA: (humming, with a mysterious smile.) Hmm, tra-la-la-la. 390

MRS. LINDE: Because you couldn't have borrowed it.

NORA: No? Why not?

MRS. LINDE: A wife can't borrow without her husband's consent.

NORA: (tossing her head.) Oh, but a wife with a little business sense, a wife who knows how to manage — 395

MRS. LINDE: Nora, I simply don't understand —

NORA: You don't have to. Whoever said I borrowed the money? I could have gotten it other ways. (Throwing herself back on the sofa.) I could have gotten it from some admirer or other. After all, a girl with my ravishing appeal — 400

MRS. LINDE: You lunatic.

NORA: I'll bet you're eaten up with curiosity, Kristine.

MRS. LINDE: Now listen here, Nora — you haven't done something indiscreet?

NORA: (sitting up again.) Is it indiscreet to save your husband's 405 life?

MRS. LINDE: I think it's indiscreet that without his knowledge you —

NORA: But that's the point: he mustn't know! My Lord, can't you understand? He mustn't ever know the close call he had. It 410 was to me the doctors came to say his life was in danger — that nothing could save him but a stay in the south. Didn't I try strategy then! I began talking about how lovely it would be for me to travel abroad like other young wives; I begged and I cried; I told him please to remember my condition, to be kind 415 and indulge me; and then I dropped a hint that he could easily take out a loan. But at that, Kristine, he nearly exploded. He said I was frivolous, and it was his duty as man of the house not to indulge me in whims and fancies — as I think he called them. Aha, I thought, now you'll just have to be 420 saved — and that's when I saw my chance.

MRS. LINDE: And your father never told Torvald the money wasn't from him?

NORA: No, never. Papa died right about then. I'd considered bringing him into my secret and begging him never to tell. 425 But he was too sick at the time — and then, sadly, it didn't matter.

MRS. LINDE: And you've never confided in your husband since?

NORA: For heaven's sake, no! Are you serious? He's so strict on that subject. Besides — Torvald, with all his mascu- 430 line pride — how painfully humiliating for him if he ever found out he was in debt to me. That would just ruin our relationship. Our beautiful, happy home would never be the same.

435 MRS. LINDE: Won't you ever tell him?

NORA: (*thoughtfully, half smiling.*) Yes—maybe sometime, years from now, when I'm no longer so attractive. Don't laugh! I only mean when Torvald loves me less than now, when he stops enjoying my dancing and dressing up and re-
440 citing for him. Then it might be wise to have something in reserve—(*Breaking off.*) How ridiculous! That'll never happen— Well, Kristine, what do you think of my big secret? I'm capable of something too, hm? You can imagine, of course, how this thing hangs over me. It really hasn't been easy meet-
445 ing the payments on time. In the business world there's what they call quarterly interest and what they call amortization, and these are always so terribly hard to manage. I've had to skimp a little here and there, wherever I could, you know. I could hardly spare anything from my house allowance, be-
450 cause Torvald has to live well. I couldn't let the children go poorly dressed; whatever I got for them, I felt I had to use up completely—the darlings!

MRS. LINDE: Poor Nora, so it had to come out of your own budget, then?

455 NORA: Yes, of course. But I was the one most responsible, too. Every time Torvald gave me money for new clothes and such, I never used more than half; always bought the simplest, cheapest outfits. It was a godsend that everything looks so well on me that Torvald never noticed. But it did weigh me down
460 at times, Kristine. It *is* such a joy to wear fine things. You understand.

MRS. LINDE: Oh, of course.

NORA: And then I found other ways of making money. Last winter I was lucky enough to get a lot of copying to do. I locked
465 myself in and sat writing every evening till late in the night. Ah, I was tired so often, dead tired. But still it was wonderful fun, sitting and working like that, earning money. It was almost like being a man.

MRS. LINDE: But how much have you paid off this way so far?

470 NORA: That's hard to say, exactly. These accounts, you know, aren't easy to figure. I only know that I've paid out all I could scrape together. Time and again I haven't known where to turn. (*Smiling.*) Then I'd sit here dreaming of a rich old gentleman who had fallen in love with me—

475 MRS. LINDE: What! Who is he?

NORA: Oh, really! And that he'd died, and when his will was opened, there in big letters it said, "All my fortune shall be paid over in cash, immediately, to that enchanting Mrs. Nora Helmer."

480 MRS. LINDE: But Nora dear—who *was* this gentleman?

NORA: Good grief, can't you understand? The old man never existed; that was only something I'd dream up time and again whenever I was at my wits' end for money. But it makes no difference now; the old fossil can go where he pleases for all I
485 care; I don't need him or his will—because now I'm free. (*Jumping up.*) Oh, how lovely to think of that, Kristine! Carefree! To know you're carefree, utterly carefree; to be able to romp and play with the children, and to keep up a beautiful, charming home—everything just the way Torvald likes it!
490 And think, spring is coming, with big blue skies. Maybe we can travel a little then. Maybe I'll see the ocean again. Oh yes, it *is* so marvelous to live and be happy!

(*The front doorbell rings.*)

MRS. LINDE: (*rising.*) There's the bell. It's probably best that I go.

NORA: No, stay. No one's expected. It must be for Torvald.

MAID: (*from the hall doorway.*) Excuse me, ma'am—there's a 495 gentleman here to see Mr. Helmer, but I didn't know—since the doctor's with him—

NORA: Who is the gentleman?

KROGSTAD: (*from the doorway.*) It's me, Mrs. Helmer.

(MRS. LINDE *starts and turns away toward the window.*)

NORA: (*stepping toward him, tense, her voice a whisper.*) You? 500 What is it? Why do you want to speak to my husband?

KROGSTAD: Bank business—after a fashion. I have a small job in the investment bank, and I hear now your husband is going to be our chief—

NORA: In other words, it's— 505

KROGSTAD: Just dry business, Mrs. Helmer. Nothing but that.

NORA: Yes, then please be good enough to step into the study. (*She nods indifferently as she sees him out by the hall door, then returns and begins stirring up the stove.*)

MRS. LINDE: Nora—who was that man? 510

NORA: That was a Mr. Krogstad—a lawyer.

MRS. LINDE: Then it really was him.

NORA: Do you know that person?

MRS. LINDE: I did once—many years ago. For a time he was a law clerk in our town. 515

NORA: Yes, he's been that.

MRS. LINDE: How he's changed.

NORA: I understand he had a very unhappy marriage.

MRS. LINDE: He's a widower now.

NORA: With a number of children. There now, it's burning. 520 (*She closes the stove door and moves the rocker a bit to one side.*)

MRS. LINDE: They say he has a hand in all kinds of business.

NORA: Oh? That may be true; I wouldn't know. But let's not think about business. It's so dull.

(DR. RANK *enters from* HELMER's *study.*)

RANK: (*still in the doorway.*) No, no, really—I don't want to 525 intrude, I'd just as soon talk a little while with your wife. (*Shuts the door, then notices* MRS. LINDE.) Oh, beg pardon. I'm intruding here too.

NORA: No, not at all. (*Introducing him.*) Dr. Rank, Mrs. Linde.

RANK: Well now, that's a name much heard in this house. I be- 530 lieve I passed the lady on the stairs as I came.

MRS. LINDE: Yes, I take the stairs very slowly. They're rather hard on me.

RANK: Uh-hm, some touch of internal weakness?

MRS. LINDE: More overexertion, I'd say. 535

RANK: Nothing else? Then you're probably here in town to rest up in a round of parties?

MRS. LINDE: I'm here to look for work.

RANK: Is that the best cure for overexertion?

MRS. LINDE: One has to live, Doctor. 540

RANK: Yes, there's a common prejudice to that effect.

NORA: Oh, come on, Dr. Rank—you really do want to live yourself.

RANK: Yes, I really do. Wretched as I am, I'll gladly prolong my torment indefinitely. All my patients feel like that. And 545 it's quite the same, too, with the morally sick. Right at this moment there's one of those moral invalids in there with Helmer—

MRS. LINDE: *(softly.)* Ah!

550 NORA: Who do you mean?

RANK: Oh, it's a lawyer, Krogstad, a type you wouldn't know. His character is rotten to the root—but even he began chattering all-importantly about how he had to *live.*

NORA: Oh? What did he want to talk to Torvald about?

555 RANK: I really don't know. I only heard something about the bank.

NORA: I didn't know that Krog—that this man Krogstad had anything to do with the bank.

RANK: Yes, he's gotten some kind of berth down there. *(To* MRS. LINDE.*)* I don't know if you also have, in your neck of the

560 woods, a type of person who scuttles about breathlessly, sniffing out hints of moral corruption, and then maneuvers his victim into some sort of key position where he can keep an eye on him. It's the healthy these days that are out in the cold.

MRS. LINDE: All the same, it's the sick who most need to be

565 taken in.

RANK: *(with a shrug.)* Yes, there we have it. That's the concept that's turning society into a sanatorium.

(NORA, lost in her thoughts, breaks out into quiet laughter and claps her hands.)

RANK: Why do you laugh at that? Do you have any real idea of what society is?

570 NORA: What do I care about dreary old society? I was laughing at something quite different—something terribly funny. Tell me, Doctor—is everyone who works in the bank dependent now on Torvald?

RANK: Is that what you find so terribly funny?

575 NORA: *(smiling and humming.)* Never mind, never mind! *(Pacing the floor.)* Yes, that's really immensely amusing: that we— that Torvald has so much power now over all those people. *(Taking the bag out of her pocket.)* Dr. Rank, a little macaroon on that?

580 RANK: See here, macaroons! I thought they were contraband here.

NORA: Yes, but these are some that Kristine gave me.

MRS. LINDE: What? I—?

NORA: Now, now, don't be afraid. You couldn't possibly know that Torvald had forbidden them. You see, he's worried they'll

585 ruin my teeth. But hmp! Just this once! Isn't that so, Dr. Rank? Help yourself! *(Puts a macaroon in his mouth.)* And you too, Kristine. And I'll also have one, only a little one—or two, at the most. *(Walking about again.)* Now I'm really tremendously happy. Now there's just one last thing in the world

590 that I have an enormous desire to do.

RANK: Well! And what's that?

NORA: It's something I have such a consuming desire to say so Torvald could hear.

RANK: And why can't you say it?

595 NORA: I don't dare. It's quite shocking.

MRS. LINDE: Shocking?

RANK: Well, then it isn't advisable. But in front of us you certainly can. What do you have such a desire to say so Torvald could hear?

600 NORA: I have such a huge desire to say—to hell and be damned!

RANK: Are you crazy?

MRS. LINDE: My goodness, Nora!

RANK: Go on, say it. Here he is.

NORA: *(hiding the macaroon bag.)* Shh, shh, shh!

(HELMER comes in from his study, hat in hand, overcoat over his arm.)

NORA: *(going toward him.)* Well, Torvald dear, are you through   605
with him?

HELMER: Yes, he just left.

NORA: Let me introduce you—this is Kristine, who's arrived here in town.

HELMER: Kristine—? I'm sorry, but I don't know—   610

NORA: Mrs. Linde, Torvald dear. Mrs. Kristine Linde.

HELMER: Of course. A childhood friend of my wife's, no doubt?

MRS. LINDE: Yes, we knew each other in those days.

NORA: And just think, she made the long trip down here in order to talk with you.   615

HELMER: What's this?

MRS. LINDE: Well, not exactly—

NORA: You see, Kristine is remarkably clever in office work, and so she's terribly eager to come under a capable man's supervision and add more to what she already knows—   620

HELMER: Very wise, Mrs. Linde.

NORA: And then when she heard that you'd become a bank manager—the story was wired out to the papers—then she came in as fast as she could and—Really, Torvald, for my sake you can do a little something for Kristine, can't you?   625

HELMER: Yes, it's not at all impossible. Mrs. Linde, I suppose you're a widow?

MRS. LINDE: Yes.

HELMER: Any experience in office work?

MRS. LINDE: Yes, a good deal.   630

HELMER: Well, it's quite likely that I can make an opening for you—

NORA: *(clapping her hands.)* You see, you see!

HELMER: You've come at a lucky moment, Mrs. Linde.

MRS. LINDE: Oh, how can I thank you?   635

HELMER: Not necessary. *(Putting his overcoat on.)* But today you'll have to excuse me—

RANK: Wait, I'll go with you. *(He fetches his coat from the hall and warms it at the stove.)*

NORA: Don't stay out long, dear.   640

HELMER: An hour; no more.

NORA: Are you going too, Kristine?

MRS. LINDE: *(putting on her winter garments.)* Yes, I have to see about a room now.

HELMER: Then perhaps we can all walk together.   645

NORA: *(helping her.)* What a shame we're so cramped here, but it's quite impossible for us to—

MRS. LINDE: Oh, don't even think of it! Good-bye, Nora dear, and thanks for everything.

NORA: Good-bye for now. Of course you'll be back this evening.   650
And you too, Dr. Rank. What? If you're well enough? Oh, you've got to be! Wrap up tight now.

(In a ripple of small talk the company moves out into the hall; children's voices are heard outside on the steps.)

NORA: There they are! There they are! *(She runs to open the door. The children come in with their nurse,* ANNE-MARIE.*)* Come in, come in! *(Bends down and kisses them.)* Oh, you darlings—! Look at them, Kristine. Aren't they lovely!   655

RANK: No loitering in the draft here.

HELMER: Come, Mrs. Linde—this place is unbearable now for anyone but mothers.

(DR. RANK, HELMER, and MRS. LINDE *go down the stairs.* ANNE-MARIE *goes into the living room with the children.* NORA *follows, after closing the hall door.)*

660 NORA: How fresh and strong you look. Oh, such red cheeks you
have! Like apples and roses. *(The children interrupt her
throughout the following.)* And it was so much fun? That's
wonderful. Really? You pulled both Emmy and Bob on the
sled? Imagine, all together! Yes, you're a clever boy, Ivar. Oh,
665 let me hold her a bit, Anne-Marie. My sweet little doll baby!
(Takes the smallest from the nurse and dances with her.) Yes,
yes, Mama will dance with Bob as well. What? Did you throw
snowballs? Oh, if I'd only been there! No, don't bother,
Anne-Marie—I'll undress them myself. Oh yes, let me. It's
670 such fun. Go in and rest; you look half frozen. There's hot
coffee waiting for you on the stove. *(The nurse goes into the
room to the left.* NORA *takes the children's winter things off,
throwing them about, while the children talk to her all at
once.)* Is that so? A big dog chased you? But it didn't bite? No,
675 dogs never bite little, lovely doll babies. Don't peek in the
packages, Ivar! What is it? Yes, wouldn't you like to know.
No, no, it's an ugly something. Well? Shall we play? What
shall we play? Hide-and-seek? Yes, let's play hide-and-seek.
Bob must hide first. I must? Yes, let me hide first. *(Laughing
680 and shouting, she and the children play in and out of the
living room and the adjoining room to the right. At last* NORA
*hides under the table. The children come storming in, search,
but cannot find her, then hear her muffled laughter, dash over
to the table, lift the cloth up and find her. Wild shouting. She
685 creeps forward as if to scare them. More shouts. Meanwhile, a
knock at the hall door; no one has noticed it. Now the door half
opens, and* KROGSTAD *appears. He waits a moment; the game
goes on.)*
KROGSTAD: Beg pardon, Mrs. Helmer—
690 NORA: *(with a strangled cry, turning and scrambling to her
knees.)* Oh! What do you want?
KROGSTAD: Excuse me. The outer door was ajar; it must be
someone forgot to shut it—
NORA: *(rising.)* My husband isn't home, Mr. Krogstad.
695 KROGSTAD: I know that.
NORA: Yes—then what do you want here?
KROGSTAD: A word with you.
NORA: With—? *(To the children, quietly.)* Go in to Anne-
Marie. What? No, the strange man won't hurt Mama. When
700 he's gone, we'll play some more. *(She leads the children into
the room to the left and shuts the door after them. Then, tense
and nervous:)* You want to speak to me?
KROGSTAD: Yes, I want to.
NORA: Today? But it's not yet the first of the month—
705 KROGSTAD: No, it's Christmas Eve. It's going to be up to you
how merry a Christmas you have.
NORA: What is it you want? Today I absolutely can't—
KROGSTAD: We won't talk about that till later. This is something
else. You do have a moment to spare, I suppose?
710 NORA: Oh yes, of course—I do, except—
KROGSTAD: Good. I was sitting over at Olsen's Restaurant when
I saw your husband go down the street—
NORA: Yes?
KROGSTAD: With a lady.
715 NORA: Yes. So?
KROGSTAD: If you'll pardon my asking: wasn't that lady a Mrs.
Linde?
NORA: Yes.
KROGSTAD: Just now come into town?
720 NORA: Yes, today.

KROGSTAD: She's a good friend of yours?
NORA: Yes, she is. But I don't see—
KROGSTAD: I also knew her once.
NORA: I'm aware of that.
725 KROGSTAD: Oh? You know all about it. I thought so. Well, then
let me ask you short and sweet: is Mrs. Linde getting a job in
the bank?
NORA: What makes you think you can cross-examine me, Mr.
Krogstad—you, one of my husband's employees? But since
730 you ask, you might as well know—yes, Mrs. Linde's going to
be taken on at the bank. And I'm the one who spoke for her,
Mr. Krogstad. Now you know.
KROGSTAD: So I guessed right.
NORA: *(pacing up and down.)* Oh, one does have a tiny bit of
735 influence, I should hope. Just because I am a woman, don't
think it means that— When one has a subordinate position,
Mr. Krogstad, one really ought to be careful about pushing
somebody who—hm—
KROGSTAD: Who has influence?
740 NORA: That's right.
KROGSTAD: *(in a different tone.)* Mrs. Helmer, would you be
good enough to use your influence on my behalf?
NORA: What? What do you mean?
KROGSTAD: Would you please make sure that I keep my subordi-
745 nate position in the bank?
NORA: What does that mean? Who's thinking of taking away
your position?
KROGSTAD: Oh, don't play the innocent with me. I'm quite
aware that your friend would hardly relish the chance of run-
750 ning into me again; and I'm also aware now whom I can
thank for being turned out.
NORA: But I promise you—
KROGSTAD: Yes, yes, yes, to the point: there's still time, and I'm
advising you to use your influence to prevent it.
755 NORA: But Mr. Krogstad, I have absolutely no influence.
KROGSTAD: You haven't? I thought you were just saying—
NORA: You shouldn't take me so literally. I! How can you believe
that I have any such influence over my husband?
KROGSTAD: Oh, I've known your husband from our student
760 days. I don't think the great bank manager's more steadfast
than any other married man.
NORA: You speak insolently about my husband, and I'll show
you the door.
KROGSTAD: The lady has spirit.
765 NORA: I'm not afraid of you any longer. After New Year's, I'll
soon be done with the whole business.
KROGSTAD: *(restraining himself.)* Now listen to me, Mrs. Helmer. If necessary, I'll fight for my little job in the bank as if it
were life itself.
770 NORA: Yes, so it seems.
KROGSTAD: It's not just a matter of income; that's the least of it.
It's something else— All right, out with it! Look, this is the
thing. You know, just like all the others, of course, that once,
a good many years ago, I did something rather rash.
775 NORA: I've heard rumors to that effect.
KROGSTAD: The case never got into court; but all the same, every
door was closed in my face from then on. So I took up those
various activities you know about. I had to grab hold somewhere; and I dare say I haven't been among the worst. But
780 now I want to drop all that. My boys are growing up. For their
sakes, I'll have to win back as much respect as possible here in

town. That job in the bank was like the first rung in my ladder. And now your husband wants to kick me right back down in the mud again.

785 NORA: But for heaven's sake, Mr. Krogstad, it's simply not in my power to help you.

KROGSTAD: That's because you haven't the will to — but I have the means to make you.

NORA: You certainly won't tell my husband that I owe you

790 money?

KROGSTAD: Hm — what if I told him that?

NORA: That would be shameful of you. (Nearly in tears.) This secret — my joy and my pride — that he should learn it in such a crude and disgusting way — learn it from you. You'd expose

795 me to the most horrible unpleasantness —

KROGSTAD: Only unpleasantness?

NORA: (vehemently.) But go on and try. It'll turn out the worse for you, because then my husband will really see what a crook you are, and then you'll never be able to hold your job.

800 KROGSTAD: I asked if it was just domestic unpleasantness you were afraid of?

NORA: If my husband finds out, then of course he'll pay what I owe at once, and then we'd be through with you for good.

KROGSTAD: (a step closer.) Listen, Mrs. Helmer — you've either

805 got a very bad memory, or else no head at all for business. I'd better put you a little more in touch with the facts.

NORA: What do you mean?

KROGSTAD: When your husband was sick, you came to me for a loan of four thousand, eight hundred crowns.

810 NORA: Where else could I go?

KROGSTAD: I promised to get you that sum —

NORA: And you got it.

KROGSTAD: I promised to get you that sum, on certain conditions. You were so involved in your husband's illness, and so

815 eager to finance your trip, that I guess you didn't think out all the details. It might just be a good idea to remind you. I promised you the money on the strength of a note I drew up.

NORA: Yes, and that I signed.

KROGSTAD: Right. But at the bottom I added some lines for your

820 father to guarantee the loan. He was supposed to sign down there.

NORA: Supposed to? He did sign.

KROGSTAD: I left the date blank. In other words, your father would have dated his signature himself. Do you remember

825 that?

NORA: Yes, I think —

KROGSTAD: Then I gave you the note for you to mail to your father. Isn't that so?

NORA: Yes.

830 KROGSTAD: And naturally you sent it at once — because only some five, six days later you brought me the note, properly signed. And with that, the money was yours.

NORA: Well, then; I've made my payments regularly, haven't I?

KROGSTAD: More or less. But — getting back to the point — those

835 were hard times for you then, Mrs. Helmer.

NORA: Yes, they were.

KROGSTAD: Your father was very ill, I believe.

NORA: He was near the end.

KROGSTAD: He died soon after?

840 NORA: Yes.

KROGSTAD: Tell me, Mrs. Helmer, do you happen to recall the date of your father's death? The day of the month, I mean.

NORA: Papa died the twenty-ninth of September.

KROGSTAD: That's quite correct; I've already looked into that. And now we come to a curious thing — (Taking out a paper.) 845 which I simply cannot comprehend.

NORA: Curious thing? I don't know —

KROGSTAD: This is the curious thing: that your father co-signed the note for your loan three days after his death.

NORA: How —? I don't understand. 850

KROGSTAD: Your father died the twenty-ninth of September. But look. Here your father dated his signature October second. Isn't that curious, Mrs. Helmer? (NORA is silent.) Can you explain it to me? (NORA remains silent.) It's also remarkable that the words "October second" and the year aren't written in 855 your father's hand, but rather in one that I think I know. Well, it's easy to understand. Your father forgot perhaps to date his signature, and then someone or other added it, a bit sloppily, before anyone knew of his death. There's nothing wrong in that. It all comes down to the signature. And there's no question about that, Mrs. Helmer. It really was your father who 860 signed his own name here, wasn't it?

NORA: (after a short silence, throwing her head back and looking squarely at him.) No, it wasn't. I signed Papa's name.

KROGSTAD: Wait, now — are you fully aware that this is a dangerous confession? 865

NORA: Why? You'll soon get your money.

KROGSTAD: Let me ask you a question — why didn't you send the paper to your father?

NORA: That was impossible. Papa was so sick. If I'd asked him for 870 his signature, I also would have had to tell him what the money was for. But I couldn't tell him, sick as he was, that my husband's life was in danger. That was just impossible.

KROGSTAD: Then it would have been better if you'd given up the trip abroad. 875

NORA: I couldn't possibly. The trip was to save my husband's life. I couldn't give that up.

KROGSTAD: But didn't you ever consider that this was a fraud against me?

NORA: I couldn't let myself be bothered by that. You weren't any 880 concern of mine. I couldn't stand you, with all those cold complications you made, even though you knew how badly off my husband was.

KROGSTAD: Mrs. Helmer, obviously you haven't the vaguest idea of what you've involved yourself in. But I can tell you 885 this: it was nothing more and nothing worse that I once did — and it wrecked my whole reputation.

NORA: You? Do you expect me to believe that you ever acted bravely to save your wife's life?

KROGSTAD: Laws don't inquire into motives. 890

NORA: Then they must be very poor laws.

KROGSTAD: Poor or not — if I introduce this paper in court, you'll be judged according to law.

NORA: This I refuse to believe. A daughter hasn't a right to protect her dying father from anxiety and care? A wife hasn't a 895 right to save her husband's life? I don't know much about laws, but I'm sure that somewhere in the books these things are allowed. And you don't know anything about it — you who practice the law? You must be an awful lawyer, Mr. Krogstad. 900

KROGSTAD: Could be. But business — the kind of business we two are mixed up in — don't you think I know about that? All right. Do what you want now. But I'm telling you this: if I get

905 shoved down a second time, you're going to keep me company. (*He bows and goes out through the hall.*)

NORA: (*pensive for a moment, then tossing her head.*) Oh, really! Trying to frighten me! I'm not so silly as all that. (*Begins gathering up the children's clothes, but soon stops.*) But—? No, but that's impossible! I did it out of love.

910 THE CHILDREN: (*in the doorway, left.*) Mama, that strange man's gone out the door.

NORA: Yes, yes, I know it. But don't tell anyone about the strange man. Do you hear? Not even Papa!

THE CHILDREN: No, Mama. But now will you play again?

915 NORA: No, not now.

THE CHILDREN: Oh, but Mama, you promised.

NORA: Yes, but I can't now. Go inside; I have too much to do. Go in, go in, my sweet darlings. (*She herds them gently back in the room and shuts the door after them. Settling on the sofa,*

920 *she takes up a piece of embroidery and makes some stitches, but soon stops abruptly.*) No! (*Throws the work aside, rises, goes to the hall door and calls out.*) Helene! Let me have the tree in here. (*Goes to the table, left, opens the table drawer, and stops again.*) No, but that's utterly impossible!

925 MAID: (*with the Christmas tree.*) Where should I put it, ma'am?

NORA: There. The middle of the floor.

MAID: Should I bring anything else?

NORA: No, thanks. I have what I need.

(*The* MAID, *who has set the tree down, goes out.*)

NORA: (*absorbed in trimming the tree.*) Candles here—and

930 flowers here. That terrible creature! Talk, talk, talk! There's nothing to it at all. The tree's going to be lovely. I'll do anything to please you, Torvald. I'll sing for you, dance for you—

(HELMER *comes in from the hall, with a sheaf of papers under his arm.*)

NORA: Oh! You're back so soon?

HELMER: Yes. Has anyone been here?

935 NORA: Here? No.

HELMER: That's odd. I saw Krogstad leaving the front door.

NORA: So? Oh yes, that's true. Krogstad was here a moment.

HELMER: Nora, I can see by your face that he's been here, begging you to put in a good word for him.

940 NORA: Yes.

HELMER: And it was supposed to seem like your own idea? You were to hide it from me that he'd been here. He asked you that, too, didn't he?

NORA: Yes, Torvald, but—

945 HELMER: Nora, Nora, and you could fall for that? Talk with that sort of person and promise him anything? And then in the bargain, tell me an untruth.

NORA: An untruth—?

HELMER: Didn't you say that no one had been here? (*Wagging*

950 *his finger.*) My little songbird must never do that again. A songbird needs a clean beak to warble with. No false notes. (*Putting his arm about her waist.*) That's the way it should be, isn't it? Yes, I'm sure of it. (*Releasing her.*) And so, enough of that. (*Sitting by the stove.*) Ah, how snug and cozy it is here.

955 (*Leafing among his papers.*)

NORA: (*busy with the tree, after a short pause.*) Torvald!

HELMER: Yes.

NORA: I'm so much looking forward to the Stenborgs' costume party, day after tomorrow.

960 HELMER: And I can't wait to see what you'll surprise me with.

NORA: Oh, that stupid business!

HELMER: What?

NORA: I can't find anything that's right. Everything seems so ridiculous, so inane.

965 HELMER: So my little Nora's come to *that* recognition?

NORA: (*going behind his chair, her arms resting on its back.*) Are you very busy, Torvald?

HELMER: Oh—

NORA: What papers are those?

970 HELMER: Bank matters.

NORA: Already?

HELMER: I've gotten full authority from the retiring management to make all necessary changes in personnel and procedure. I'll need Christmas week for that. I want to have ev-

975 erything in order by New Year's.

NORA: So that was the reason this poor Krogstad—

HELMER: Hm.

NORA: (*still leaning on the chair and slowly stroking the nape of his neck.*) If you weren't so very busy, I would have asked you an enormous favor, Torvald.

980 HELMER: Let's hear. What is it?

NORA: You know, there isn't anyone who has your good taste— and I want so much to look well at the costume party. Torvald, couldn't you take over and decide what I should be and plan my costume?

985 HELMER: Ah, is my stubborn little creature calling for a lifeguard?

NORA: Yes, Torvald, I can't get anywhere without your help.

HELMER: All right—I'll think it over. We'll hit on something.

NORA: Oh, how sweet of you. (*Goes to the tree again. Pause.*)

990 Aren't the red flowers pretty—? But tell me, was it really such a crime that this Krogstad committed?

HELMER: Forgery. Do you have any idea what that means?

NORA: Couldn't he have done it out of need?

HELMER: Yes, or thoughtlessness, like so many others. I'm not

995 so heartless that I'd condemn a man categorically for just one mistake.

NORA: No, of course not, Torvald!

HELMER: Plenty of men have redeemed themselves by openly confessing their crimes and taking their punishment.

1000 NORA: Punishment—?

HELMER: But now Krogstad didn't go that way. He got himself out by sharp practices, and that's the real cause of his moral breakdown.

NORA: Do you really think that would—?

1005 HELMER: Just imagine how a man with that sort of guilt in him has to lie and cheat and deceive on all sides, has to wear a mask even with the nearest and dearest he has, even with his own wife and children. And with the children, Nora—that's where it's most horrible.

1010 NORA: Why?

HELMER: Because that kind of atmosphere of lies infects the whole life of a home. Every breath the children take in is filled with the germs of something degenerate.

NORA: (*coming closer behind him.*) Are you sure of that?

1015 HELMER: Oh, I've seen it often enough as a lawyer. Almost everyone who goes bad early in life has a mother who's a chronic liar.

NORA: Why just—the mother?

HELMER: It's usually the mother's influence that's dominant,
1020 but the father's works in the same way, of course. Every lawyer is quite familiar with it. And still this Krogstad's been
going home year in, year out, poisoning his own children
with lies and pretense; that's why I call him morally lost.
(Reaching his hands out toward her.) So my sweet little Nora
1025 must promise me never to plead his cause. Your hand on it.
Come, come, what's this? Give me your hand. There, now.
All settled. I can tell you it'd be impossible for me to work
alongside of him. I literally feel physically revolted when I'm
anywhere near such a person.
1030 NORA: *(withdraws her hand and goes to the other side of the
Christmas tree.)* How hot it is here! And I've got so much to do.
HELMER: *(getting up and gathering his papers.)* Yes, and I have
to think about getting some of these read through before dinner. I'll think about your costume, too. And something to
1035 hang on the tree in gilt paper, I may even see about that.
(Putting his hand on her head.) Oh you, my darling little
songbird. *(He goes into his study and closes the door after him.)*
NORA: *(softly, after a silence.)* Oh, really! it isn't so. It's impossible. It must be impossible.
1040 ANNE-MARIE: *(in the doorway, left.)* The children are begging so
hard to come in to Mama.
NORA: No, no, no, don't let them in to me! You stay with them,
Anne-Marie.
ANNE-MARIE: Of course, ma'am. *(Closes the door.)*
1045 NORA: *(pale with terror.)* Hurt my children —! Poison my home?
(A moment's pause; then she tosses her head.) That's not true.
Never. Never in all the world.

— ACT TWO —

*Same room. Beside the piano the Christmas tree now stands
stripped of ornament, burned-down candle stubs on its ragged
branches. NORA's street clothes lie on the sofa. NORA, alone in the
room, moves restlessly about; at last she stops at the sofa and
picks up her coat.*

NORA: *(dropping the coat again.)* Someone's coming! *(Goes toward the door, listens.)* No—there's no one. Of course—nobody's coming today, Christmas Day—or tomorrow, either.
But maybe— *(Opens the door and looks out.)* No, nothing in
5 the mailbox. Quite empty. *(Coming forward.)* What nonsense! He won't do anything serious. Nothing terrible could
happen. It's impossible. Why, I have three small children.

*(ANNE-MARIE, with a large carton, comes in from the room to the
left.)*

ANNE-MARIE: Well, at last I found the box with the masquerade
clothes.
10 NORA: Thanks. Put it on the table.
ANNE-MARIE: *(does so.)* But they're all pretty much of a mess.
NORA: Ahh! I'd love to rip them in a million pieces!
ANNE-MARIE: Oh, mercy, they can be fixed right up. Just a little
patience.
15 NORA: Yes, I'll go get Mrs. Linde to help me.

ANNE-MARIE: Out again now? In this nasty weather? Miss Nora
will catch cold—get sick.
NORA: Oh, worse things could happen—How are the children?
ANNE-MARIE: The poor mites are playing with their Christmas
presents, but— 20
NORA: Do they ask for me much?
ANNE-MARIE: They're so used to having Mama around, you
know.
NORA: Yes, but Anne-Marie, I *can't* be together with them as
much as I was. 25
ANNE-MARIE: Well, small children get used to anything.
NORA: You think so? Do you think they'd forget their mother if
she was gone for good?
ANNE-MARIE: Oh, mercy—gone for good!
NORA: Wait, tell me, Anne-Marie—I've wondered so often— 30
how could you ever have the heart to give your child over to
strangers?
ANNE-MARIE: But I had to, you know, to become little Nora's
nurse.
NORA: Yes, but how could you *do* it? 35
ANNE-MARIE: When I could get such a good place? A girl who's
poor and who's gotten in trouble is glad enough for that. Be-
cause that slippery fish, he didn't do a thing for me, you
know.
NORA: But your daughter's surely forgotten you. 40
ANNE-MARIE: Oh, she certainly has not. She's written to me,
both when she was confirmed and when she was married.
NORA: *(clasping her about the neck.)* You old Anne-Marie, you
were a good mother for me when I was little.
ANNE-MARIE: Poor little Nora, with no other mother but me. 45
NORA: And if the babies didn't have one, then I know that
you'd— What silly talk! *(Opening the carton.)* Go in to them.
Now I'll have to— Tomorrow you can see how lovely I'll look.
ANNE-MARIE: Oh, there won't be anyone at the party as lovely as
Miss Nora. *(She goes off into the room, left.)* 50
NORA: *(begins unpacking the box, but soon throws it aside.)* Oh,
if I dared to go out. If only nobody would come. If only nothing would happen here while I'm out. What craziness—nobody's coming. Just don't think. This muff—needs a brushing. Beautiful gloves, beautiful gloves. Let it go. Let it go! 55
One, two, three, four, five, six— *(With a cry.)* Oh, there they
are! *(Poises to move toward the door, but remains irresolutely
standing. MRS. LINDE enters from the hall, where she has removed her street clothes.)*
NORA: Oh, it's you, Kristine. There's no one else out there? How 60
good that you've come.
MRS. LINDE: I hear you were up asking for me.
NORA: Yes, I just stopped by. There's something you really can
help me with. Let's get settled on the sofa. Look, there's going
to be a costume party tomorrow evening at the Stenborgs' 65
right above us, and now Torvald wants me to go as a Neapolitan peasant girl and dance the tarantella that I learned in
Capri.
MRS. LINDE: Really, are you giving a whole performance?
NORA: Torvald says yes, I should. See, here's the dress. Torvald 70
had it made for me down there; but now it's all so tattered that
I just don't know—
MRS. LINDE: Oh, we'll fix that up in no time. It's nothing more
than the trimmings—they're a bit loose here and there. Needle and thread? Good, now we have what we need. 75

NORA: Oh, how sweet of you!

MRS. LINDE: *(sewing.)* So you'll be in disguise tomorrow, Nora. You know what? I'll stop by then for a moment and have a look at you all dressed up. But listen, I've absolutely forgotten
80 to thank you for that pleasant evening yesterday.

NORA: *(getting up and walking about.)* I don't think it was as pleasant as usual yesterday. You should have come to town a bit sooner, Kristine— Yes, Torvald really knows how to give a home elegance and charm.

85 MRS. LINDE: And you do, too, if you ask me. You're not your father's daughter for nothing. But tell me, is Dr. Rank always so down in the mouth as yesterday?

NORA: No, that was quite an exception. But he goes around critically ill all the time—tuberculosis of the spine, poor man.
90 You know, his father was a disgusting thing who kept mistresses and so on—and that's why the son's been sickly from birth.

MRS. LINDE: *(lets her sewing fall to her lap.)* But my dearest Nora, how do you know about such things?

95 NORA: *(walking more jauntily.)* Hmp! When you've had three children, then you've had a few visits from—from women who know something of medicine, and they tell you this and that.

MRS. LINDE: *(resumes sewing; a short pause.)* Does Dr. Rank
100 come here every day?

NORA: Every blessed day. He's Torvald's best friend from childhood, and *my* good friend, too. Dr. Rank almost belongs to this house.

MRS. LINDE: But tell me—is he quite sincere? I mean, doesn't
105 he rather enjoy flattering people?

NORA: Just the opposite. Why do you think that?

MRS. LINDE: When you introduced us yesterday, he was proclaiming that he'd often heard my name in this house; but later I noticed that your husband hadn't the slightest idea who
110 I really was. So how could Dr. Rank—?

NORA: But it's all true, Kristine. You see, Torvald loves me beyond words, and, as he puts it, he'd like to keep me all to himself. For a long time he'd almost be jealous if I even mentioned any of my old friends back home. So of course I
115 dropped that. But with Dr. Rank I talk a lot about such things, because he likes hearing about them.

MRS. LINDE: Now listen, Nora; in many ways you're still like a child. I'm a good deal older than you, with a little more experience. I'll tell you something: you ought to put an end to all
120 this with Dr. Rank.

NORA: What should I put an end to?

MRS. LINDE: Both parts of it, I think. Yesterday you said something about a rich admirer who'd provide you with money—

NORA: Yes, one who doesn't exist—worse luck. So?

125 MRS. LINDE: Is Dr. Rank well off?

NORA: Yes, he is.

MRS. LINDE: With no dependents?

NORA: No, no one. But—

MRS. LINDE: And he's over here every day?

130 NORA: Yes, I told you that.

MRS. LINDE: How can a man of such refinement be so grasping?

NORA: I don't follow you at all.

MRS. LINDE: Now don't try to hide it, Nora. You think I can't guess who loaned you the forty-eight hundred crowns?

135 NORA: Are you out of your mind? How could you think such a

thing! A friend of ours, who comes here every single day. What an intolerable situation that would have been!

MRS. LINDE: Then it really wasn't him.

NORA: No, absolutely not. It never even crossed my mind for a moment— And he had nothing to lend in those days; his 140 inheritance came later.

MRS. LINDE: Well, I think that was a stroke of luck for you, Nora dear.

NORA: No, it never would have occurred to me to ask Dr. Rank— Still, I'm quite sure that if I had asked him— 145

MRS. LINDE: Which you won't, of course.

NORA: No, of course not. I can't see that I'd ever need to. But I'm quite positive that if I talked to Dr. Rank—

MRS. LINDE: Behind your husband's back?

NORA: I've got to clear up this other thing; *that's* also behind his 150 back. I've *got* to clear it all up.

MRS. LINDE: Yes, I was saying that yesterday, but—

NORA: *(pacing up and down.)* A man handles these problems so much better than a woman—

MRS. LINDE: One's husband does, yes. 155

NORA: Nonsense. *(Stopping.)* When you pay everything you owe, then you get your note back, right?

MRS. LINDE: Yes, naturally.

NORA: And can rip it into a million pieces and burn it up—that filthy scrap of paper! 160

MRS. LINDE: *(looking hard at her, laying her sewing aside, and rising slowly.)* Nora, you're hiding something from me.

NORA: You can see it in my face?

MRS. LINDE: Something's happened to you since yesterday morning. Nora, what is it? 165

NORA: *(hurrying toward her.)* Kristine! *(Listening.)* Shh! Torvald's home. Look, go in with the children a while. Torvald can't bear all this snipping and stitching. Let Anne-Marie help you.

MRS. LINDE: *(gathering up some of the things.)* All right, but I'm 170 not leaving here until we've talked this out. *(She disappears into the room, left, as* TORVALD *enters from the hall.)*

NORA: Oh, how I've been waiting for you, Torvald dear.

HELMER: Was that the dressmaker?

NORA: No, that was Kristine. She's helping me fix up my cos- 175 tume. You know, it's going to be quite attractive.

HELMER: Yes, wasn't that a bright idea I had?

NORA: Brilliant! But then wasn't I good as well to give in to you?

HELMER: Good—because you give in to your husband's judgment? All right, you little goose, I know you didn't mean it 180 like that. But I won't disturb you. You'll want to have a fitting, I suppose.

NORA: And you'll be working?

HELMER: Yes. *(Indicating a bundle of papers.)* See, I've been down to the bank. *(Starts toward his study.)* 185

NORA: Torvald.

HELMER: *(stops.)* Yes.

NORA: If your little squirrel begged you, with all her heart and soul, for something—?

HELMER: What's that? 190

NORA: Then would you do it?

HELMER: First, naturally, I'd have to know what it was.

NORA: Your squirrel would scamper about and do tricks, if you'd only be sweet and give in.

HELMER: Out with it. 195

NORA: Your lark would be singing high and low in every room—

HELMER: Come on, she does that anyway.

NORA: I'd be a wood nymph and dance for you in the moonlight.

200 HELMER: Nora—don't tell me it's that same business from this morning?

NORA: *(coming closer.)* Yes, Torvald, I beg you, please!

HELMER: And you actually have the nerve to drag that up again?

NORA: Yes, yes, you've got to give in to me; you *have* to let Krogstad keep his job in the bank.

205 HELMER: My dear Nora, I've slated his job for Mrs. Linde.

NORA: That's awfully kind of you. But you could just fire another clerk instead of Krogstad.

HELMER: This is the most incredible stubbornness! Because you go and give an impulsive promise to speak up for him, I'm

210 expected to—

NORA: That's not the reason, Torvald. It's for your own sake. That man does writing for the worst papers; you said it yourself. He could do you any amount of harm. I'm scared to death of him—

215 HELMER: Ah, I understand. It's the old memories haunting you.

NORA: What do you mean by that?

HELMER: Of course, you're thinking about your father.

NORA: Yes, all right. Just remember how those nasty gossips wrote in the papers about Papa and slandered him so cruelly. I

220 think they'd have had him dismissed if the department hadn't sent you up to investigate, and if you hadn't been so kind and open-minded toward him.

HELMER: My dear Nora, there's a notable difference between your father and me. Your father's official career was hardly

225 above reproach. But mine is; and I hope it'll stay that way as long as I hold my position.

NORA: Oh, who can ever tell what vicious minds can invent? We could be so snug and happy now in our quiet, carefree home—you and I and the children, Torvald! That's why I'm

230 pleading with you so—

HELMER: And just by pleading for him you make it impossible for me to keep him on. It's already known at the bank that I'm firing Krogstad. What if it's rumored around now that the new bank manager was vetoed by his wife—

235 NORA: Yes, what then—?

HELMER: Oh yes—as long as our little bundle of stubbornness gets her way—! I should go and make myself ridiculous in front of the whole office—give people the idea I can be swayed by all kinds of outside pressure. Oh, you can bet I'd

240 feel the effects of that soon enough! Besides—there's something that rules Krogstad right out at the bank as long as I'm the manager.

NORA: What's that?

HELMER: His moral failings I could maybe overlook if I had to—

245 NORA: Yes, Torvald, why not?

HELMER: And I hear he's quite efficient on the job. But he was a crony of mine back in my teens—one of those rash friendships that crop up again and again to embarrass you later in life. Well, I might as well say it straight out: we're on a first-

250 name basis. And that tactless fool makes no effort at all to hide it in front of others. Quite the contrary—he thinks that entitles him to take a familiar air around me, and so every other second he comes booming out with his "Yes, Torvald!" and "Sure thing, Torvald!" I tell you, it's been excruciating for

255 me. He's out to make my place in the bank unbearable.

NORA: Torvald, you can't be serious about all this.

HELMER: Oh no? Why not?

NORA: Because these are such petty considerations.

HELMER: What are you saying? Petty? You think I'm petty!

260 NORA: No, just the opposite, Torvald dear. That's exactly why—

HELMER: Never mind. You call my motives petty; then I might as well be just that. Petty! All right! We'll put a stop to this for good. *(Goes to the hall door and calls.)* Helene!

NORA: What do you want?

265 HELMER: *(searching among his papers.)* A decision. *(The* MAID *comes in.)* Look here; take this letter; go out with it at once. Get hold of a messenger and have him deliver it. Quick now. It's already addressed. Wait, here's some money.

MAID: Yes, sir. *(She leaves with the letter.)*

270 HELMER: *(straightening his papers.)* There, now, little Miss Willful.

NORA: *(breathlessly.)* Torvald, what was that letter?

HELMER: Krogstad's notice.

NORA: Call it back, Torvald! There's still time. Oh, Torvald, call

275 it back! Do it for my sake—for your sake, for the children's sake! Do you hear, Torvald; do it! You don't know how this can harm us.

HELMER: Too late.

NORA: Yes, too late.

280 HELMER: Nora dear, I can forgive you this panic, even though basically you're insulting me. Yes, you are! Or isn't it an insult to think that *I* should be afraid of a courtroom hack's revenge? But I forgive you anyway, because this shows so beautifully how much you love me. *(Takes her in his arms.)*

285 This is the way it should be, my darling Nora. Whatever comes, you'll see: when it really counts, I have strength and courage enough as a man to take on the whole weight myself.

NORA: *(terrified.)* What do you mean by that?

HELMER: The whole weight, I said.

290 NORA: *(resolutely.)* No, never in all the world.

HELMER: Good. So we'll share it, Nora, as man and wife. That's as it should be. *(Fondling her.)* Are you happy now? There, there, there—not these frightened dove's eyes. It's nothing at all but empty fantasies— Now you should run through your

295 tarantella and practice your tambourine. I'll go to the inner office and shut both doors, so I won't hear a thing; you can make all the noise you like. *(Turning in the doorway.)* And when Rank comes, just tell him where he can find me. *(He nods to her and goes with his papers into the study, closing the*

300 *door.)*

NORA: *(standing as though rooted, dazed with fright, in a whisper.)* He really could do it. He will do it. He'll do it in spite of everything. No, not that, never, never! Anything but that! Escape! A way out— *(The doorbell rings.)* Dr. Rank! Any-

305 thing but that! *Anything,* whatever it is! *(Her hands pass over her face, smoothing it; she pulls herself together, goes over and opens the hall door.* DR. RANK *stands outside, hanging his fur coat up. During the following scene, it begins getting dark.)*

NORA: Hello, Dr. Rank. I recognized your ring. But you mustn't

310 go in to Torvald yet; I believe he's working.

RANK: And you?

NORA: For you, I always have an hour to spare—you know that. *(He has entered, and she shuts the door after him.)*

RANK: Many thanks. I'll make use of these hours while I can.

315 NORA: What do you mean by that? While you can?

RANK: Does that disturb you?

NORA: Well, it's such an odd phrase. Is anything going to happen?

RANK: What's going to happen is what I've been expecting so long—but I honestly didn't think it would come so soon.

320 NORA: (gripping his arm.) What is it you've found out? Dr. Rank, you have to tell me!

RANK: (sitting by the stove.) It's all over with me. There's nothing to be done about it.

NORA: (breathing easier.) Is it you—then—?

325 RANK: Who else? There's no point in lying to one's self. I'm the most miserable of all my patients, Mrs. Helmer. These past few days I've been auditing my internal accounts. Bankrupt! Within a month I'll probably be laid out and rotting in the churchyard.

330 NORA: Oh, what a horrible thing to say.

RANK: The thing itself is horrible. But the worst of it is all the other horror before it's over. There's only one final examination left; when I'm finished with that, I'll know about when my disintegration will begin. There's something I want to say.

335 Helmer with his sensitivity has such a sharp distaste for anything ugly. I don't want him near my sickroom.

NORA: Oh, but Dr. Rank—

RANK: I won't have him in there. Under no condition. I'll lock my door to him— As soon as I'm completely sure of the

340 worst, I'll send you my calling card marked with a black cross, and you'll know then the wreck has started to come apart.

NORA: No, today you're completely unreasonable. And I wanted you so much to be in a really good humor.

RANK: With death up my sleeve? And then to suffer this way for

345 somebody else's sins. Is there any justice in that? And in every single family, in some way or another, this inevitable retribution of nature goes on—

NORA: (her hands pressed over her ears.) Oh, stuff! Cheer up! Please—be gay!

350 RANK: Yes, I'd just as soon laugh at it all. My poor, innocent spine, serving time for my father's gay army days.

NORA: (by the table, left.) He was so infatuated with asparagus tips and pâté de foie gras, wasn't that it?

RANK: Yes—and with truffles.

355 NORA: Truffles, yes. And then with oysters, I suppose?

RANK: Yes, tons of oysters, naturally.

NORA: And then the port and champagne to go with it. It's so sad that all these delectable things have to strike at our bones.

RANK: Especially when they strike at the unhappy bones that

360 never shared in the fun.

NORA: Ah, that's the saddest of all.

RANK: (looks searchingly at her.) Hm.

NORA: (after a moment.) Why did you smile?

RANK: No, it was you who laughed.

365 NORA: No, it was you who smiled, Dr. Rank!

RANK: (getting up.) You're even a bigger tease than I'd thought.

NORA: I'm full of wild ideas today.

RANK: That's obvious.

NORA: (putting both hands on his shoulders.) Dear, dear Dr.

370 Rank, you'll never die for Torvald and me.

RANK: Oh, that loss you'll easily get over. Those who go away are soon forgotten.

NORA: (looks fearfully at him.) You believe that?

RANK: One makes new connections, and then—

375 NORA: Who makes new connections?

RANK: Both you and Torvald will when I'm gone. I'd say you're well under way already. What was that Mrs. Linde doing here last evening?

NORA: Oh, come—you can't be jealous of poor Kristine?

380 RANK: Oh yes, I am. She'll be my successor here in the house. When I'm down under, that woman will probably—

NORA: Shh! Not so loud. She's right in there.

RANK: Today as well. So you see.

NORA: Only to sew on my dress. Good gracious, how unreason-

385 able you are. (Sitting on the sofa.) Be nice now, Dr. Rank. Tomorrow you'll see how beautifully I'll dance; and you can imagine then that I'm dancing only for you—yes, and of course for Torvald, too—that's understood. (Takes various items out of the carton.) Dr. Rank, sit over here and I'll show

390 you something.

RANK: (sitting.) What's that?

NORA: Look here. Look.

RANK: Silk stockings.

NORA: Flesh-colored. Aren't they lovely? Now it's so dark here, but tomorrow— No, no, no, just look at the feet. Oh well,

395 you might as well look at the rest.

RANK: Hm—

NORA: Why do you look so critical? Don't you believe they'll fit?

RANK: I've never had any chance to form an opinion on that.

NORA: (glancing at him a moment.) Shame on you. (Hits him

400 lightly on the ear with the stockings.) That's for you. (Puts them away again.)

RANK: And what other splendors am I going to see now?

NORA: Not the least bit more, because you've been naughty. (She hums a little and rummages among her things.)

405 RANK: (after a short silence.) When I sit here together with you like this, completely easy and open, then I don't know—I simply can't imagine—whatever would have become of me if I'd never come into this house.

NORA: (smiling.) Yes, I really think you feel completely at ease

410 with us.

RANK: (more quietly, staring straight ahead.) And then to have to go away from it all—

NORA: Nonsense, you're not going away.

RANK: (his voice unchanged.)—and not even be able to leave

415 some poor show of gratitude behind, scarcely a fleeting regret—no more than a vacant place that anyone can fill.

NORA: And if I asked you now for—? No—

RANK: For what?

NORA: For a great proof of your friendship—

420 RANK: Yes, yes?

NORA: No, I mean—for an exceptionally big favor—

RANK: Would you really, for once, make me so happy?

NORA: Oh, you haven't the vaguest idea what it is.

RANK: All right, then tell me.

425 NORA: No, but I can't, Dr. Rank—it's all out of reason. It's advice and help, too—and a favor—

RANK: So much the better. I can't fathom what you're hinting at. Just speak out. Don't you trust me?

NORA: Of course. More than anyone else. You're my best and

430 truest friend, I'm sure. That's why I want to talk to you. All right, then, Dr. Rank: there's something you can help me prevent. You know how deeply, how inexpressibly dearly Torvald loves me; he'd never hesitate a second to give up his life for me.

435

RANK: *(leaning close to her.)* Nora—do you think he's the only one—

NORA: *(with a slight start.)* Who—?

RANK: Who'd gladly give up his life for you.

440   NORA: *(heavily.)* I see.

RANK: I swore to myself you should know this before I'm gone. I'll never find a better chance. Yes, Nora, now you know. And also you know now that you can trust me beyond anyone else.

NORA: *(rising, natural and calm.)* Let me by.

445   RANK: *(making room for her, but still sitting.)* Nora—

NORA: *(in the hall doorway.)* Helene, bring the lamp in. *(Goes over to the stove.)* Ah, dear Dr. Rank, that was really mean of you.

RANK: *(getting up.)* That I've loved you just as deeply as some-

450   body else? Was *that* mean?

NORA: No, but that you came out and told me. That was quite unnecessary—

RANK: What do you mean? Have you known—?

(The MAID comes in with the lamp, sets it on the table, and goes out again.)

RANK: Nora—Mrs. Helmer—I'm asking you: have you known

455   about it?

NORA: Oh, how can I tell what I know or don't know? Really, I don't know what to say— Why did you have to be so clumsy, Dr. Rank! Everything was so good.

RANK: Well, in any case, you now have the knowledge that my

460   body and soul are at your command. So won't you speak out?

NORA: *(looking at him.)* After that?

RANK: Please, just let me know what it is.

NORA: You can't know anything now.

RANK: I have to. You mustn't punish me like this. Give me the

465   chance to do whatever is humanly possible for you.

NORA: Now there's nothing you can do for me. Besides, actually, I don't need any help. You'll see—it's only my fantasies. That's what it is. Of course! *(Sits in the rocker, looks at him, and smiles.)* What a nice one you are, Dr. Rank. Aren't you a

470   little bit ashamed, now that the lamp is here?

RANK: No, not exactly. But perhaps I'd better go—for good?

NORA: No, you certainly can't do that. You must come here just as you always have. You know Torvald can't do without you.

RANK: Yes, but *you?*

475   NORA: You know how much I enjoy it when you're here.

RANK: That's precisely what threw me off. You're a mystery to me. So many times I've felt you'd almost rather be with me than with Helmer.

NORA: Yes—you see, there are some people that one loves most

480   and other people that one would almost prefer being with.

RANK: Yes, there's something to that.

NORA: When I was back home, of course I loved Papa most. But I always thought it was so much fun when I could sneak down to the maids' quarters, because they never tried to improve

485   me, and it was always so amusing, the way they talked to each other.

RANK: Aha, so it's *their* place that I've filled.

NORA: *(jumping up and going to him.)* Oh, dear, sweet Dr. Rank, that's not what I meant at all. But you can understand

490   that with Torvald it's just the same as with Papa—

(The MAID enters from the hall.)

MAID: Ma'am—please! *(She whispers to NORA and hands her a calling card.)*

NORA: *(glancing at the card.)* Ah! *(Slips it into her pocket.)*

RANK: Anything wrong?

NORA: No, no, not at all. It's only some—it's my new dress—   495

RANK: Really? But—there's your dress.

NORA: Oh, that. But this is another one—I ordered it—Torvald mustn't know—

RANK: Ah, now we have the big secret.

NORA: That's right. Just go in with him—he's back in the inner   500

study. Keep him there as long as—

RANK: Don't worry. He won't get away. *(Goes into the study.)*

NORA: *(to the MAID.)* And he's standing waiting in the kitchen?

MAID: Yes, he came up by the back stairs.

NORA: But didn't you tell him somebody was here?   505

MAID: Yes, but that didn't do any good.

NORA: He won't leave?

MAID: No, he won't go till he's talked with you, ma'am.

NORA: Let him come in, then—but quietly. Helene, don't breathe a word about this. It's a surprise for my husband.   510

MAID: Yes, yes, I understand— *(Goes out.)*

NORA: This horror—it's going to happen. No, no, no, it can't happen, it mustn't. *(She goes and bolts HELMER's door. The MAID opens the hall door for KROGSTAD and shuts it behind him. He is dressed for travel in a fur coat, boots, and a fur cap.)*   515

NORA: *(going toward him.)* Talk softly. My husband's home.

KROGSTAD: Well, good for him.

NORA: What do you want?

KROGSTAD: Some information.

NORA: Hurry up, then. What is it?   520

KROGSTAD: You know, of course, that I got my notice.

NORA: I couldn't prevent it, Mr. Krogstad. I fought for you to the bitter end, but nothing worked.

KROGSTAD: Does your husband's love for you run so thin? He knows everything I can expose you to, and all the same he   525

dares to—

NORA: How can you imagine he knows anything about this?

KROGSTAD: Ah, no—I can't imagine it either, now. It's not at all like my fine Torvald Helmer to have so much guts—

NORA: Mr. Krogstad, I demand respect for my husband!   530

KROGSTAD: Why, of course—all due respect. But since the lady's keeping it so carefully hidden, may I presume to ask if you're also a bit better informed than yesterday about what you've actually done?

NORA: More than you ever could teach me.   535

KROGSTAD: Yes, I *am* such an awful lawyer.

NORA: What is it you want from me?

KROGSTAD: Just a glimpse of how you are, Mrs. Helmer. I've been thinking about you all day long. A cashier, a night-court scribbler, a—well, a type like me also has a little of what they   540

call a heart, you know.

NORA: Then show it. Think of my children.

KROGSTAD: Did you or your husband ever think of mine? But never mind. I simply wanted to tell you that you don't need to take this thing too seriously. For the present, I'm not proceed-   545

ing with any action.

NORA: Oh no, really! Well—I knew that.

KROGSTAD: Everything can be settled in a friendly spirit. It doesn't have to get around town at all; it can stay just among us three.   550

NORA: My husband must never know anything of this.

KROGSTAD: How can you manage that? Perhaps you can pay me the balance?

NORA: No, not right now.

555 KROGSTAD: Or you know some way of raising the money in a day or two?

NORA: No way that I'm willing to use.

KROGSTAD: Well, it wouldn't have done you any good, anyway. If you stood in front of me with a fistful of bills, you still

560 couldn't buy your signature back.

NORA: Then tell me what you're going to do with it.

KROGSTAD: I'll just hold onto it—keep it on file. There's no outsider who'll even get wind of it. So if you've been thinking of taking some desperate step—

565 NORA: I have.

KROGSTAD: Been thinking of running away from home—

NORA: I have!

KROGSTAD: Or even of something worse—

NORA: How could you guess that?

570 KROGSTAD: You can drop those thoughts.

NORA: How could you guess I was thinking of *that*?

KROGSTAD: Most of us think about *that* at first. I thought about it too, but I discovered I hadn't the courage—

NORA: (*lifelessly.*) I don't either.

575 KROGSTAD: (*relieved.*) That's true, you haven't the courage? You too?

NORA: I don't have it—I don't have it.

KROGSTAD: It would be terribly stupid, anyway. After that first storm at home blows out, why, then— I have here in my

580 pocket a letter for your husband—

NORA: Telling everything?

KROGSTAD: As charitably as possible.

NORA: (*quickly.*) He mustn't ever get that letter. Tear it up. I'll find some way to get money.

585 KROGSTAD: Beg pardon, Mrs. Helmer, but I think I just told you—

NORA: Oh, I don't mean the money I owe you. Let me know how much you want from my husband, and I'll manage it.

KROGSTAD: I don't want any money from your husband.

590 NORA: What do you want, then?

KROGSTAD: I'll tell you what. I want to recoup, Mrs. Helmer; I want to get on in the world—and there's where your husband can help me. For a year and a half I've kept myself clean of anything disreputable—all that time struggling with the worst

595 conditions; but I was satisfied, working my way up step by step. Now I've been written right off, and I'm just not in the mood to come crawling back. I tell you, I want to move on. I want to get back in the bank—in a better position. Your husband can set up a job for me—

600 NORA: He'll never do that!

KROGSTAD: He'll do it. I know him. He won't dare breathe a word of protest. And once I'm in there together with him, you just wait and see! Inside of a year, I'll be the manager's right-hand man. It'll be Nils Krogstad, not Torvald Helmer, who

605 runs the bank.

NORA: You'll never see the day!

KROGSTAD: Maybe you think you can—

NORA: I have the courage now—for *that*.

KROGSTAD: Oh, you don't scare me. A smart, spoiled lady like

610 you—

NORA: You'll see; you'll see!

KROGSTAD: Under the ice, maybe? Down in the freezing, coal-black water? There, till you float up in the spring, ugly, unrecognizable, with your hair falling out—

NORA: You don't frighten me. 615

KROGSTAD: Nor do you frighten me. One doesn't do these things, Mrs. Helmer. Besides, what good would it be? I'd still have him safe in my pocket.

NORA: Afterwards? When I'm no longer—?

KROGSTAD: Are you forgetting that *I'll* be in control then over 620 your final reputation? (NORA *stands speechless, staring at him.*) Good; now I've warned you. Don't do anything stupid. When Helmer's read my letter, I'll be waiting for his reply. And bear in mind that it's your husband himself who's forced me back to my old ways. I'll never forgive him for that. Good- 625 bye, Mrs. Helmer. (*He goes out through the hall.*)

NORA: (*goes to the hall door, opens it a crack, and listens.*) He's gone. Didn't leave the letter. Oh no, no, that's impossible too! (*Opening the door more and more.*) What's that? He's standing outside—not going downstairs. He's thinking it over? Maybe 630 he'll—? (*A letter falls in the mailbox; then* KROGSTAD'S *footsteps are heard, dying away down a flight of stairs.* NORA *gives a muffled cry and runs over toward the sofa table. A short pause.*) In the mailbox. (*Slips warily over to the hall door.*) It's lying there. Torvald, Torvald—now we're lost! 635

MRS. LINDE: (*entering with the costume from the room, left.*) There now, I can't see anything else to mend. Perhaps you'd like to try—

NORA: (*in a hoarse whisper.*) Kristine, come here.

MRS. LINDE: (*tossing the dress on the sofa.*) What's wrong? You 640 look upset.

NORA: Come here. See that letter? *There!* Look—through the glass in the mailbox.

MRS. LINDE: Yes, yes, I see it.

NORA: That letter's from Krogstad— 645

MRS. LINDE: Nora—it's Krogstad who loaned you the money!

NORA: Yes, and now Torvald will find out everything.

MRS. LINDE: Believe me, Nora, it's best for both of you.

NORA: There's more you don't know. I forged a name.

MRS. LINDE: But for heaven's sake—? 650

NORA: I only want to tell you that, Kristine, so that you can be my witness.

MRS. LINDE: Witness? Why should I—?

NORA: If I should go out of my mind—it could easily happen—

MRS. LINDE: Nora! 655

NORA: Or anything else occurred—so I couldn't be present here—

MRS. LINDE: Nora, Nora, you aren't yourself at all!

NORA: And someone should try to take on the whole weight, all of the guilt, you follow me—

MRS. LINDE: Yes, of course, but why do you think—? 660

NORA: Then you're the witness that it isn't true, Kristine. I'm very much myself; my mind right now is perfectly clear; and I'm telling you: nobody else has known about this; I alone did everything. Remember that.

MRS. LINDE: I will. But I don't understand all this. 665

NORA: Oh, how could you ever understand it? It's the miracle now that's going to take place.

MRS. LINDE: The miracle?

NORA: Yes, the miracle. But it's so awful, Kristine. It mustn't take place, not for anything in the world. 670

MRS. LINDE: I'm going right over and talk with Krogstad.

NORA: Don't go near him; he'll do you some terrible harm!

MRS. LINDE: There was a time once when he'd gladly have done anything for me.

675 NORA: He?

MRS. LINDE: Where does he live?

NORA: Oh, how do I know? Yes. (Searches in her pocket.) Here's his card. But the letter, the letter—!

HELMER: (from the study, knocking on the door.) Nora!

680 NORA: (with a cry of fear.) Oh! What is it? What do you want?

HELMER: Now, now, don't be so frightened. We're not coming in. You locked the door—are you trying on the dress?

NORA: Yes, I'm trying it. I'll look just beautiful, Torvald.

MRS. LINDE: (who has read the card.) He's living right around 685 the corner.

NORA: Yes, but what's the use? We're lost. The letter's in the box.

MRS. LINDE: And your husband has the key?

NORA: Yes, always.

MRS. LINDE: Krogstad can ask for his letter back unread; he can 690 find some excuse—

NORA: But it's just this time that Torvald usually—

MRS. LINDE: Stall him. Keep him in there. I'll be back as quick as I can. (She hurries out through the hall entrance.)

NORA: (goes to HELMER's door, opens it, and peers in.) Torvald!

695 HELMER: (from the inner study.) Well—does one dare set foot in one's own living room at last? Come on, Rank, now we'll get a look— (In the doorway.) But what's this?

NORA: What, Torvald dear?

HELMER: Rank had me expecting some grand masquerade.

700 RANK: (in the doorway.) That was my impression, but I must have been wrong.

NORA: No one can admire me in my splendor—not till tomorrow.

HELMER: But Nora dear, you look so exhausted. Have you practiced too hard?

705 NORA: No, I haven't practiced at all yet.

HELMER: You know, it's necessary—

NORA: Oh, it's absolutely necessary, Torvald. But I can't get anywhere without your help. I've forgotten the whole thing completely.

710 HELMER: Ah, we'll soon take care of that.

NORA: Yes, take care of me, Torvald, please! Promise me that? Oh, I'm so nervous. That big party— You must give up everything this evening for me. No business—don't even touch your pen. Yes? Dear Torvald, promise?

715 HELMER: It's a promise. Tonight I'm totally at your service—you little helpless thing. Hm—but first there's one thing I want to— (Goes toward the hall door.)

NORA: What are you looking for?

HELMER: Just to see if there's any mail.

720 NORA: No, no, don't do that, Torvald!

HELMER: Now what?

NORA: Torvald, please. There isn't any.

HELMER: Let me look, though. (Starts out. NORA, at the piano, strikes the first notes of the tarentella. HELMER, at the door, 725 stops.) Aha!

NORA: I can't dance tomorrow if I don't practice with you.

HELMER: (going over to her.) Nora dear, are you really so frightened?

NORA: Yes, so terribly frightened. Let me practice right now; 730 there's still time before dinner. Oh, sit down and play for me, Torvald. Direct me. Teach me, the way you always have.

HELMER: Gladly, if it's what you want. (Sits at the piano.)

NORA: (snatches the tambourine up from the box, then a long, varicolored shawl, which she throws around herself, whereupon she springs forward and cries out:) Play for me now! Now 735 I'll dance!

(HELMER plays and NORA dances. RANK stands behind HELMER at the piano and looks on.)

HELMER: (as he plays.) Slower. Slow down.

NORA: Can't change it.

HELMER: Not so violent, Nora!

NORA: Has to be just like this. 740

HELMER: (stopping.) No, no, that won't do at all.

NORA: (laughing and swinging her tambourine.) Isn't that what I told you?

RANK: Let me play for her.

HELMER: (getting up.) Yes, go on. I can teach her more easily 745 then.

(RANK sits at the piano and plays; NORA dances more and more wildly. HELMER has stationed himself by the stove and repeatedly gives her directions; she seems not to hear them; her hair loosens and falls over her shoulders; she does not notice, but goes on dancing. MRS. LINDE enters.)

MRS. LINDE: (standing dumbfounded at the door.) Ah—!

NORA: (still dancing.) See what fun, Kristine!

HELMER: But Nora darling, you dance as if your life were at stake.

NORA: And it is. 750

HELMER: Rank, stop! This is pure madness. Stop it, I say!

(RANK breaks off playing, and NORA halts abruptly).

HELMER: (going over to her.) I never would have believed it. You've forgotten everything I taught you.

NORA: (throwing away the tambourine.) You see for yourself.

HELMER: Well, there's certainly room for instruction here. 755

NORA: Yes, you see how important it is. You've got to teach me to the very last minute. Promise me that, Torvald?

HELMER: You can bet on it.

NORA: You mustn't, either today or tomorrow, think about anything else but me; you mustn't open any letters—or the mail- 760 box—

HELMER: Ah, it's still the fear of that man—

NORA: Oh yes, yes, that too.

HELMER: Nora, it's written all over you—there's already a letter from him out there. 765

NORA: I don't know. I guess so. But you mustn't read such things now; there mustn't be anything ugly between us before it's all over.

RANK: (quietly to HELMER.) You shouldn't deny her.

HELMER: (putting his arm around her.) The child can have her 770 way. But tomorrow night, after you've danced—

NORA: Then you'll be free.

MAID: (in the doorway, right.) Ma'am, dinner is served.

NORA: We'll be wanting champagne, Helene.

MAID: Very good, ma'am. (Goes out.) 775

HELMER: So—a regular banquet, hm?

NORA: Yes, a banquet—champagne till daybreak! (Calling out.) And some macaroons, Helene. Heaps of them—just this once.

HELMER: (taking her hands.) Now, now, now—no hysterics. Be my own little lark again. 780

NORA: Oh, I will soon enough. But go on in—and you, Dr. Rank. Kristine, help me put up my hair.

RANK: *(whispering, as they go.)* There's nothing wrong—really wrong, is there?

785 HELMER: Oh, of course not. It's nothing more than this childish anxiety I was telling you about. *(They go out, right.)*

NORA: Well?

MRS. LINDE: Left town.

NORA: I could see by your face.

790 MRS. LINDE: He'll be home tomorrow evening. I wrote him a note.

NORA: You shouldn't have. Don't try to stop anything now. After all, it's a wonderful joy, this waiting here for the miracle.

MRS. LINDE: What is it you're waiting for?

795 NORA: Oh, you can't understand that. Go in to them; I'll be along in a moment.

(MRS. LINDE goes into the dining room. NORA stands a short while as if composing herself; then she looks at her watch.)

NORA: Five. Seven hours to midnight. Twenty-four hours to the midnight after, and then the tarantella's done. Seven and twenty-four? Thirty-one hours to live.

800 HELMER: *(in the doorway, right.)* What's become of the little lark?

NORA: *(going toward him with open arms.)* Here's your lark!

— ACT THREE —

Same scene. The table, with chairs around it, has been moved to the center of the room. A lamp on the table is lit. The hall door stands open. Dance music drifts down from the floor above. MRS. LINDE *sits at the table, absently paging through a book, trying to read, but apparently unable to focus her thoughts. Once or twice she pauses, tensely listening for a sound at the outer entrance.*

MRS. LINDE: *(glancing at her watch.)* Not yet—and there's hardly any time left. If only he's not—*(Listening again.)* Ah, there he is. *(She goes out in the hall and cautiously opens the outer door. Quiet footsteps are heard on the stairs. She whis-*

5 *pers:)* Come in. Nobody's here.

KROGSTAD: *(in the doorway.)* I found a note from you at home. What's back of all this?

MRS. LINDE: I just *had* to talk to you.

KROGSTAD: Oh? And it just *had* to be here in this house?

10 MRS. LINDE: At my place it was impossible; my room hasn't a private entrance. Come in; we're all alone. The maid's asleep, and the Helmers are at the dance upstairs.

KROGSTAD: *(entering the room.)* Well, well, the Helmers are dancing tonight? Really?

15 MRS. LINDE: Yes, why not?

KROGSTAD: How true—why not?

MRS. LINDE: All right, Krogstad, let's talk.

KROGSTAD: Do we two have anything more to talk about?

MRS. LINDE: We have a great deal to talk about.

20 KROGSTAD: I wouldn't have thought so.

MRS. LINDE: No, because you've never understood me, really.

KROGSTAD: Was there anything more to understand—except what's all too common in life? A calculating woman throws over a man the moment a better catch comes by.

25 MRS. LINDE: You think I'm so thoroughly calculating? You think I broke it off lightly?

KROGSTAD: Didn't you?

MRS. LINDE: Nils—is that what you really thought?

KROGSTAD: If you cared, then why did you write me the way you

30 did?

MRS. LINDE: What else could I do? If I had to break off with you, then it was my job as well to root out everything you felt for me.

KROGSTAD: *(wringing his hands.)* So that was it. And this—all

35 this, simply for money!

MRS. LINDE: Don't forget I had a helpless mother and two small brothers. We couldn't wait for you, Nils; you had such a long road ahead of you then.

KROGSTAD: That may be; but you still hadn't the right to aban-

40 don me for somebody else's sake.

MRS. LINDE: Yes—I don't know. So many, many times I've asked myself if I did have that right.

KROGSTAD: *(more softly.)* When I lost you, it was as if all the solid ground dissolved from under my feet. Look at me; I'm a half-drowned man now, hanging onto a wreck.

45

MRS. LINDE: Help may be near.

KROGSTAD: It was near—but then you came and blocked it off.

MRS. LINDE: Without my knowing it, Nils. Today for the first time I learned that it's you I'm replacing at the bank.

KROGSTAD: All right—I believe you. But now that you know,

50 will you step aside?

MRS. LINDE: No, because that wouldn't benefit you in the slightest.

KROGSTAD: Not "benefit" me, hm! I'd step aside anyway.

MRS. LINDE: I've learned to be realistic. Life and hard, bitter

55 necessity have taught me that.

KROGSTAD: And life's taught me never to trust fine phrases.

MRS. LINDE: Then life's taught you a very sound thing. But you do have to trust in actions, don't you?

KROGSTAD: What does that mean?

60

MRS. LINDE: You said you were hanging on like a half-drowned man to a wreck.

KROGSTAD: I've good reason to say that.

MRS. LINDE: I'm also like a half-drowned woman on a wreck. No one to suffer with; no one to care for.

65

KROGSTAD: You made your choice.

MRS. LINDE: There wasn't any choice then.

KROGSTAD: So—what of it?

MRS. LINDE: Nils, if only we two shipwrecked people could reach across to each other.

70

KROGSTAD: What are you saying?

MRS. LINDE: Two on one wreck are at least better off than each on his own.

KROGSTAD: Kristine!

MRS. LINDE: Why do you think I came into town?

75

KROGSTAD: Did you really have some thought of me?

MRS. LINDE: I have to work to go on living. All my born days, as long as I can remember, I've worked, and it's been my best and my only joy. But now I'm completely alone in the world; it frightens me to be so empty and lost. To work for yourself—

80 there's no joy in that. Nils, give me something—someone to work for.

KROGSTAD: I don't believe all this. It's just some hysterical feminine urge to go out and make a noble sacrifice.

MRS. LINDE: Have you ever found me to be hysterical?

85

KROGSTAD: Can you honestly mean this? Tell me—do you know everything about my past?

MRS. LINDE: Yes.

90 KROGSTAD: And you know what they think I'm worth around here.

MRS. LINDE: From what you were saying before, it would seem that with me you could have been another person.

KROGSTAD: I'm positive of that.

MRS. LINDE: Couldn't it happen still?

95 KROGSTAD: Kristine—you're saying this in all seriousness? Yes, you are! I can see it in you. And do you really have the courage, then—?

MRS. LINDE: I need to have someone to care for; and your children need a mother. We both need each other. Nils, I have

100 faith that you're good at heart—I'll risk everything together with you.

KROGSTAD: (gripping her hands.) Kristine, thank you, thank you—Now I know I can win back a place in their eyes. Yes—but I forgot—

105 MRS. LINDE: (listening.) Shh! The tarantella. Go now! Go on!

KROGSTAD: Why? What is it?

MRS. LINDE: Hear the dance up there? When that's over, they'll be coming down.

KROGSTAD: Oh, then I'll go. But—it's all pointless. Of course,

110 you don't know the move I made against the Helmers.

MRS. LINDE: Yes, Nils, I know.

KROGSTAD: And all the same, you have the courage to—?

MRS. LINDE: I know how far despair can drive a man like you.

KROGSTAD: Oh, if I only could take it all back.

115 MRS. LINDE: You easily could—your letter's still lying in the mailbox.

KROGSTAD: Are you sure of that?

MRS. LINDE: Positive. But—

KROGSTAD: (looks at her searchingly.) Is that the meaning of it,

120 then? You'll save your friend at any price. Tell me straight out. Is that it?

MRS. LINDE: Nils—anyone who's sold herself for somebody else once isn't going to do it again.

KROGSTAD: I'll demand my letter back.

125 MRS. LINDE: No, no.

KROGSTAD: Yes, of course. I'll stay here till Helmer comes down; I'll tell him to give me my letter again—that it only involves my dismissal—that he shouldn't read it—

MRS. LINDE: No, Nils, don't call the letter back.

130 KROGSTAD: But wasn't that exactly why you wrote me to come here?

MRS. LINDE: Yes, in that first panic. But it's been a whole day and night since then, and in that time I've seen such incredible things in this house. Helmer's got to learn everything; this

135 dreadful secret has to be aired; those two have to come to a full understanding; all these lies and evasions can't go on.

KROGSTAD: Well, then, if you want to chance it. But at least there's one thing I can do, and do right away—

MRS. LINDE: (listening.) Go now, go, quick! The dance is over.

140 We're not safe another second.

KROGSTAD: I'll wait for you downstairs.

MRS. LINDE: Yes, please do; take me home.

KROGSTAD: I can't believe it; I've never been so happy. (He leaves by way of the outer door; the door between the room and

145 the hall stays open.)

MRS. LINDE: (straightening up a bit and getting together her street clothes.) How different now! How different! Someone to work for, to live for—a home to build. Well, it is worth the

try! Oh, if they'd only come! (Listening.) Ah, there they are. Bundle up. (She picks up her hat and coat. NORA's and HEL-

150 MER's voices can be heard outside; a key turns in the lock, and HELMER brings NORA into the hall almost by force. She is wearing the Italian costume with a large black shawl about her; he has on evening dress, with a black domino open over it.)

NORA: (struggling in the doorway.) No, no, no, not inside! I'm

155 going up again. I don't want to leave so soon.

HELMER: But Nora dear—

NORA: Oh, I beg you, please, Torvald. From the bottom of my heart, please—only an hour more!

HELMER: Not a single minute, Nora darling. You know our

160 agreement. Come on, in we go; you'll catch cold out here. (In spite of her resistance, he gently draws her into the room.)

MRS. LINDE: Good evening.

NORA: Kristine!

HELMER: Why, Mrs. Linde—are you here so late?

165 MRS. LINDE: Yes, I'm sorry, but I did want to see Nora in costume.

NORA: Have you been sitting here, waiting for me?

MRS. LINDE: Yes. I didn't come early enough; you were all up-

170 stairs; and then I thought I really couldn't leave without see-ing you.

HELMER: (removing NORA's shawl.) Yes, take a good look. She's worth looking at, I can tell you that, Mrs. Linde. Isn't she lovely?

175 MRS. LINDE: Yes, I should say—

HELMER: A dream of loveliness, isn't she? That's what everyone thought at the party, too. But she's horribly stubborn—this sweet little thing. What's to be done with her? Can you imag-ine, I almost had to use force to pry her away.

180 NORA: Oh, Torvald, you're going to regret you didn't indulge me, even for just a half hour more.

HELMER: There, you see. She danced her tarantella and got a tumultuous hand—which was well earned, although the per-formance may have been a bit too naturalistic—I mean it

185 rather overstepped the proprieties of art. But never mind—what's important is, she made a success, an overwhelming success. You think I could let her stay on after that and spoil the effect? Oh no; I took my lovely little Capri girl—my capri-cious little Capri girl, I should say—took her under my arm;

190 one quick tour of the ballroom, a curtsy to every side, and then—as they say in novels—the beautiful vision disap-peared. An exit should always be effective, Mrs. Linde, but that's what I can't get Nora to grasp. Phew, it's hot in here. (Flings the domino on a chair and opens the door to his room.)

195 Why's it dark in here? Oh yes, of course. Excuse me. (He goes in and lights a couple of candles.)

NORA: (in a sharp, breathless whisper.) So?

MRS. LINDE: (quietly.) I talked with him.

NORA: And—?

200 MRS. LINDE: Nora—you must tell your husband everything.

NORA: (dully.) I knew it.

MRS. LINDE: You've got nothing to fear from Krogstad, but you have to speak out.

NORA: I won't tell.

205 MRS. LINDE: Then the letter will.

NORA: Thanks, Kristine. I know now what's to be done. Shh!

HELMER: (reentering.) Well, then, Mrs. Linde—have you ad-mired her?

MRS. LINDE: Yes, and now I'll say good night.

210 HELMER: Oh, come, so soon? Is this yours, this knitting?

MRS. LINDE: Yes, thanks. I nearly forgot it.

HELMER: Do you knit, then?

MRS. LINDE: Oh yes.

HELMER: You know what? You should embroider instead.

215 MRS. LINDE: Really? Why?

HELMER: Yes, because it's a lot prettier. See here, one holds the embroidery so, in the left hand, and then one guides the needle with the right — so — in an easy, sweeping curve — right?

MRS. LINDE: Yes, I guess that's —

220 HELMER: But, on the other hand, knitting — it can never be anything but ugly. Look, see here, the arms tucked in, the knitting needles going up and down — there's something Chinese about it. Ah, that was really a glorious champagne they served.

225 MRS. LINDE: Yes, good night, Nora, and don't be stubborn anymore.

HELMER: Well put, Mrs. Linde!

MRS. LINDE: Good night, Mr. Helmer.

HELMER: (accompanying her to the door.) Good night, good

230 night. I hope you get home all right. I'd be very happy to — but you don't have far to go. Good night, good night. (She leaves. He shuts the door after her and returns.) There, now, at last we got her out the door. She's a deadly bore, that creature.

235 NORA: Aren't you pretty tired, Torvald?

HELMER: No, not a bit.

NORA: You're not sleepy?

HELMER: Not at all. On the contrary, I'm feeling quite exhilarated. But you? Yes, you really look tired and sleepy.

240 NORA: Yes, I'm very tired. Soon now I'll sleep.

HELMER: See! You see! I was right all along that we shouldn't stay longer.

NORA: Whatever you do is always right.

HELMER: (kissing her brow.) Now my little lark talks sense. Say,

245 did you notice what a time Rank was having tonight?

NORA: Oh, was he? I didn't get to speak with him.

HELMER: I scarcely did either, but it's a long time since I've seen him in such high spirits. (Gazes at her a moment, then comes nearer her.) Hm — it's marvelous, though, to be back home

250 again — to be completely alone with you. Oh, you bewitchingly lovely young woman!

NORA: Torvald, don't look at me like that!

HELMER: Can't I look at my richest treasure? At all that beauty that's mine, mine alone — completely and utterly.

255 NORA: (moving around to the other side of the table.) You mustn't talk to me that way tonight.

HELMER: (following her.) The tarantella is still in your blood, I can see — and it makes you even more enticing. Listen. The guests are beginning to go. (Dropping his voice.) Nora — it'll

260 soon be quiet through this whole house.

NORA: Yes, I hope so.

HELMER: You do, don't you, my love? Do you realize — when I'm out at a party like this with you — do you know why I talk to you so little, and keep such a distance away; just send you a

265 stolen look now and then — you know why I do it? It's because I'm imagining then that you're my secret darling, my secret young bride-to-be, and that no one suspects there's anything between us.

NORA: Yes, yes; oh, yes, I know you're always thinking of me.

270 HELMER: And then when we leave and I place the shawl over those fine young rounded shoulders — over that wonderful curving neck — then I pretend that you're my young bride, that we're just coming from the wedding, that for the first time I'm bringing you into my house — that for the first time I'm

275 alone with you — completely alone with you, your trembling young beauty! All this evening I've longed for nothing but you. When I saw you turn and sway in the tarantella — my blood was pounding till I couldn't stand it — that's why I brought you down here so early —

280 NORA: Go away, Torvald! Leave me alone. I don't want all this.

HELMER: What do you mean? Nora, you're teasing me. You will, won't you? Aren't I your husband — ?

(A knock at the outside door.)

NORA: (startled.) What's that?

HELMER: (going toward the hall.) Who is it?

285 RANK: (outside.) It's me. May I come in a moment?

HELMER: (with quiet irritation.) Oh, what does he want now? (Aloud.) Hold on. (Goes and opens the door.) Oh, how nice that you didn't just pass us by!

RANK: I thought I heard your voice, and then I wanted so badly

290 to have a look in. (Lightly glancing about.) Ah, me, these old familiar haunts. You have it snug and cozy in here, you two.

HELMER: You seemed to be having it pretty cozy upstairs, too.

RANK: Absolutely. Why shouldn't I? Why not take in everything in life? As much as you can, anyway, and as long as you can.

295 The wine was superb —

HELMER: The champagne especially.

RANK: You noticed that too? It's amazing how much I could guzzle down.

NORA: Torvald also drank a lot of champagne this evening.

300 RANK: Oh?

NORA: Yes, and that always makes him so entertaining.

RANK: Well, why shouldn't one have a pleasant evening after a well-spent day?

HELMER: Well spent? I'm afraid I can't claim that.

305 RANK: (slapping him on the back.) But I can, you see!

NORA: Dr. Rank, you must have done some scientific research today.

RANK: Quite so.

HELMER: Come now — little Nora talking about scientific

310 research!

NORA: And can I congratulate you on the results?

RANK: Indeed you may.

NORA: Then they were good?

RANK: The best possible for both doctor and patient — certainty.

315 NORA: (quickly and searchingly.) Certainty?

RANK: Complete certainty. So don't I owe myself a gay evening afterwards?

NORA: Yes, you're right, Dr. Rank.

HELMER: I'm with you — just so long as you don't have to suffer

320 for it in the morning.

RANK: Well, one never gets something for nothing in life.

NORA: Dr. Rank — are you very fond of masquerade parties?

RANK: Yes, if there's a good array of odd disguises —

NORA: Tell me, what should we two go as at the next masquerade?

HELMER: You little featherhead — already thinking of the next!

325 RANK: We two? I'll tell you what: you must go as Charmed Life —

HELMER: Yes, but find a costume for *that!*

RANK: Your wife can appear just as she looks every day.

HELMER: That was nicely put. But don't you know what you're
330   going to be?

RANK: Yes, Helmer, I've made up my mind.

HELMER: Well?

RANK: At the next masquerade I'm going to be invisible.

HELMER: That's a funny idea.

335 RANK: They say there's a hat—black, huge—have you never
heard of the hat that makes you invisible? You put it on, and
then no one on earth can see you.

HELMER: (*suppressing a smile.*) Ah, of course.

RANK: But I'm quite forgetting what I came for. Helmer, give me
340   a cigar, one of the dark Havanas.

HELMER: With the greatest pleasure. (*Holds out his case.*)

RANK: Thanks. (*Takes one and cuts off the tip.*)

NORA: (*striking a match.*) Let me give you a light.

RANK: Thank you. (*She holds the match for him; he lights the
345   cigar.*) And now good-bye.

HELMER: Good-bye, good-bye, old friend.

NORA: Sleep well, Doctor.

RANK: Thanks for that wish.

NORA: Wish me the same.

350 RANK: You? All right, if you like— Sleep well. And thanks for
the light. (*He nods to them both and leaves.*)

HELMER: (*his voice subdued.*) He's been drinking heavily.

NORA: (*absently.*) Could be. (HELMER *takes his keys from his
pocket and goes out in the hall.*) Torvald—what are you after?

355 HELMER: Got to empty the mailbox; it's nearly full. There won't
be room for the morning papers.

NORA: Are you working tonight?

HELMER: You know I'm not. Why—what's this? Someone's
been at the lock.

360 NORA: At the lock—?

HELMER: Yes, I'm positive. What do you suppose—? I can't
imagine one of the maids—? Here's a broken hairpin. Nora,
it's yours—

NORA: (*quickly.*) Then it must be the children—

365 HELMER: You'd better break them of that. Hm, hm—well,
opened it after all. (*Takes the contents out and calls into the
kitchen.*) Helene! Helene, would you put out the lamp in the
hall. (*He returns to the room, shutting the hall door, then
displays the handful of mail.*) Look how it's piled up. (*Sorting
370   through them.*) Now what's this?

NORA: (*at the window.*) The letter! Oh, Torvald, no!

HELMER: Two calling cards—from Rank.

NORA: From Dr. Rank?

HELMER: (*examining them.*) "Dr. Rank, Consulting Physician."
375   They were on top. He must have dropped them in as he left.

NORA: Is there anything on them?

HELMER: There's a black cross over the name. See? That's a
gruesome notion. He could almost be announcing his own
death.

380 NORA: That's just what he's doing.

HELMER: What! You've heard something? Something he's told
you?

NORA: Yes. That when those cards came, he'd be taking his leave
of us. He'll shut himself in now and die.

385 HELMER: Ah, my poor friend! Of course I knew he wouldn't be
here much longer. But so soon— And then to hide himself
away like a wounded animal.

NORA: If it has to happen, then it's best it happens in silence—
don't you think so, Torvald?

HELMER: (*pacing up and down.*) He'd grown right into our lives. 390
I simply can't imagine him gone. He with his suffering and
loneliness—like a dark cloud setting off our sunlit happiness.
Well, maybe it's best this way. For him, at least. (*Standing
still.*) And maybe for us too, Nora. Now we're thrown back on
each other, completely. (*Embracing her.*) Oh you, my darling 395
wife, how can I hold you close enough? You know what,
Nora—time and again I've wished you were in some terrible
danger, just so I could stake my life and soul and everything,
for your sake.

NORA: (*tearing herself away, her voice firm and decisive.*) Now 400
you must read your mail, Torvald.

HELMER: No, no, not tonight. I want to stay with you, dearest.

NORA: With a dying friend on your mind?

HELMER: You're right. We've both had a shock. There's ugliness
between us—these thoughts of death and corruption. We'll 405
have to get free of them first. Until then—we'll stay apart.

NORA: (*clinging about his neck.*) Torvald—good night! Good
night!

HELMER: (*kissing her on the cheek.*) Good night, little songbird.
Sleep well, Nora. I'll be reading my mail now. (*He takes the 410
letters into his room and shuts the door after him.*)

NORA: (*with bewildered glances, groping about, seizing* HEL-
MER's *domino, throwing it around her, and speaking in short,
hoarse, broken whispers.*) Never see him again. Never, never.
(*Putting her shawl over her head.*) Never see the children ei- 415
ther—them, too. Never, never. Oh, the freezing black water!
The depths—down— Oh, I wish it were over— He has it
now; he's reading it—now. Oh no, no, not yet. Torvald,
good-bye, you and the children— (*She starts for the hall; as
she does,* HELMER *throws open his door and stands with an 420
open letter in his hand.*)

HELMER: Nora!

NORA: (*screams.*) Oh—!

HELMER: What is this? You know what's in this letter?

NORA: Yes, I know. Let me go! Let me out! 425

HELMER: (*holding her back.*) Where are you going?

NORA: (*struggling to break loose.*) You can't save me, Torvald!

HELMER: (*slumping back.*) True! Then it's true what he writes?
How horrible! No, no, it's impossible—it can't be true.

NORA: It *is* true. I've loved you more than all this world. 430

HELMER: Ah, none of your slippery tricks.

NORA: (*taking one step toward him.*) Torvald—!

HELMER: What *is* this you've blundered into!

NORA: Just let me loose. You're not going to suffer for my sake.
You're not going to take on my guilt. 435

HELMER: No more playacting. (*Locks the hall door.*) You stay
right here and give me a reckoning. You understand what
you've done? Answer! You understand?

NORA: (*looking squarely at him, her face hardening.*) Yes. I'm
beginning to understand everything now. 440

HELMER: (*striding about.*) Oh, what an awful awakening! In all
these eight years—she who was my pride and joy—a hypocrite, a liar—worse, worse—a criminal! How infinitely disgusting it all is! The shame! (NORA *says nothing and goes on
looking straight at him. He stops in front of her.*) I should have 445
suspected something of the kind. I should have known. All
your father's flimsy values— Be still! All your father's flimsy
values have come out in you. No religion, no morals, no

450 sense of duty— Oh, how I'm punished for letting him off! I did it for your sake, and you repay me like this.

NORA: Yes, like this.

HELMER: Now you've wrecked all my happiness—ruined my whole future. Oh, it's awful to think of. I'm in a cheap little grafter's hands; he can do anything he wants with me, ask for
455 anything, play with me like a puppet—and I can't breathe a word. I'll be swept down miserably into the depths on account of a featherbrained woman.

NORA: When I'm gone from this world, you'll be free.

HELMER: Oh, quit posing. Your father had a mess of those
460 speeches too. What good would that ever do me if you were gone from this world, as you say? Not the slightest. He can still make the whole thing known; and if he does, I could be falsely suspected as your accomplice. They might even think that I was behind it—that I put you up to it. And all that I can
465 thank you for—you that I've coddled the whole of our marriage. Can you see now what you've done to me?

NORA: (icily calm.) Yes.

HELMER: It's so incredible, I just can't grasp it. But we'll have to patch up whatever we can. Take off the shawl. I said, take it
470 off! I've got to appease him somehow or other. The thing has to be hushed up at any cost. And as for you and me, it's got to seem like everything between us is just as it was—to the outside world, that is. You'll go right on living in this house, of course. But you can't be allowed to bring up the children; I
475 don't dare trust you with them—Oh, to have to say this to someone I've loved so much, and that I still—! Well, that's done with. From now on happiness doesn't matter; all that matters is saving the bits and pieces, the appearance— (The doorbell rings. HELMER starts.) What's that? And so late.
480 Maybe the worst—? You think he'd—? Hide, Nora! Say you're sick. (NORA remains standing motionless. HELMER goes and opens the door.)

MAID: (half dressed, in the hall.) A letter for Mrs. Helmer.

HELMER: I'll take it. (Snatches the letter and shuts the door.) Yes,
485 it's from him. You don't get it; I'm reading it myself.

NORA: Then read it.

HELMER: (by the lamp.) I hardly dare. We may be ruined, you and I. But—I've got to know. (Rips open the letter, skims through a few lines, glances at an enclosure, then cries out
490 joyfully.) Nora! (NORA looks inquiringly at him.) Nora! Wait—better check it again— Yes, yes, it's true. I'm saved. Nora, I'm saved!

NORA: And I?

HELMER: You too, of course. We're both saved, both of us.
495 Look. He's sent back your note. He says he's sorry and ashamed—that a happy development in his life—oh, who cares what he says! Nora, we're saved! No one can hurt you. Oh, Nora, Nora—but first, this ugliness all has to go. Let me see— (Takes a look at the note.) No, I don't want to see it; I
500 want the whole thing to fade like a dream. (Tears the note and both letters to pieces, throws them into the stove and watches them burn.) There—now there's nothing left— He wrote that since Christmas Eve you—Oh, they must have been three terrible days for you, Nora.
505 NORA: I fought a hard fight.

HELMER: And suffered pain and saw no escape but—No, we're not going to dwell on anything unpleasant. We'll just be grateful and keep on repeating: it's over now, it's over! You hear me, Nora? You don't seem to realize—it's over. What's it

510 mean—that frozen look? Oh, poor little Nora, I understand. You can't believe I've forgiven you. But I have, Nora; I swear I have. I know that what you did, you did out of love for me.

NORA: That's true.

HELMER: You loved me the way a wife ought to love her hus-
515 band. It's simply the means that you couldn't judge. But you think I love you any the less for not knowing how to handle your affairs? No, no—just lean on me; I'll guide you and teach you. I wouldn't be a man if this feminine helplessness didn't make you twice as attractive to me. You mustn't mind
520 those sharp words I said—that was all in the first confusion of thinking my world had collapsed. I've forgiven you, Nora; I swear I've forgiven you.

NORA: My thanks for your forgiveness. (She goes out through the door, right.)

HELMER: No, wait— (Peers in.) What are you doing in there?
525 NORA: (inside.) Getting out of my costume.

HELMER: (by the open door.) Yes, do that. Try to calm yourself and collect your thoughts again, my frightened little song-bird. You can rest easy now; I've got wide wings to shelter you
530 with. (Walking about close by the door.) How snug and nice our home is, Nora. You're safe here; I'll keep you like a hunted dove I've rescued out of a hawk's claws. I'll bring peace to your poor, shuddering heart. Gradually it'll happen, Nora; you'll see. Tomorrow all this will look different to you;
535 then everything will be as it was. I won't have to go on repeating I forgive you; you'll feel it for yourself. How can you imag-ine I'd ever conceivably want to disown you—or even blame you in any way? Ah, you don't know a man's heart, Nora. For a man there's something indescribably sweet and satisfying in
540 knowing he's forgiven his wife—and forgiven her out of a full and open heart. It's as if she belongs to him in two ways now: in a sense he's given her fresh into the world again, and she's become his wife and his child as well. From now on that's what you'll be to me—you little, bewildered, helpless thing.
545 Don't be afraid of anything, Nora; just open your heart to me, and I'll be conscience and will to you both— (NORA enters in her regular clothes.) What's this? Not in bed? You've changed your dress?

NORA: Yes, Torvald, I've changed my dress.

HELMER: But why now, so late?
550 NORA: Tonight I'm not sleeping.

HELMER: But Nora dear—

NORA: (looking at her watch.) It's still not so very late. Sit down, Torvald; we have a lot to talk over. (She sits at one side of the table.)
555 HELMER: Nora—what is this? That hard expression—

NORA: Sit down. This'll take some time. I have a lot to say.

HELMER: (sitting at the table directly opposite her.) You worry me, Nora. And I don't understand you.

NORA: No, that's exactly it. You don't understand me. And I've
560 never understood you either—until tonight. No, don't inter-rupt. You can just listen to what I say. We're closing out ac-counts, Torvald.

HELMER: How do you mean that?

NORA: (after a short pause.) Doesn't anything strike you about
565 our sitting here like this?

HELMER: What's that?

NORA: We've been married now eight years. Doesn't it occur to you that this is the first time we two, you and I, man and wife, have ever talked seriously together?
570

HELMER: What do you mean — seriously?

NORA: In eight whole years — longer even — right from our first acquaintance, we've never exchanged a serious word on any serious thing.

575 HELMER: You mean I should constantly go and involve you in problems you couldn't possibly help me with?

NORA: I'm not talking of problems. I'm saying that we've never sat down seriously together and tried to get to the bottom of anything.

580 HELMER: But dearest, what good would that ever do you?

NORA: That's the point right there: you've never understood me. I've been wronged greatly, Torvald — first by Papa, and then by you.

HELMER: What! By us — the two people who've loved you more

585 than anyone else?

NORA: (shaking her head.) You never loved me. You've thought it fun to be in love with me, that's all.

HELMER: Nora, what a thing to say!

NORA: Yes, it's true now, Torvald. When I lived at home with

590 Papa, he told me all his opinions, so I had the same ones too; or if they were different I hid them, since he wouldn't have cared for that. He used to call me his doll-child, and he played with me the way I played with my dolls. Then I came into your house —

595 HELMER: How can you speak of our marriage like that?

NORA: (unperturbed.) I mean, then I went from Papa's hands into yours. You arranged everything to your own taste, and so I got the same taste as you — or I pretended to; I can't remember. I guess a little of both, first one, then the other. Now

600 when I look back, it seems as if I'd lived here like a beggar — just from hand to mouth. I've lived by doing tricks for you, Torvald. But that's the way you wanted it. It's a great sin what you and Papa did to me. You're to blame that nothing's become of me.

605 HELMER: Nora, how unfair and ungrateful you are! Haven't you been happy here?

NORA: No, never. I thought so — but I never have.

HELMER: Not — not happy!

NORA: No, only lighthearted. And you've always been so kind

610 to me. But our home's been nothing but a playpen. I've been your doll-wife here, just as at home I was Papa's doll-child. And in turn the children have been my dolls. I thought it was fun when you played with me, just as they thought it fun when I played with them. That's been our marriage,

615 Torvald.

HELMER: There's some truth in what you're saying — under all the raving exaggeration. But it'll all be different after this. Playtime's over; now for the schooling.

NORA: Whose schooling — mine or the children's?

620 HELMER: Both yours and the children's, dearest.

NORA: Oh, Torvald, you're not the man to teach me to be a good wife to you.

HELMER: And you can say that?

NORA: And I — how am I equipped to bring up children?

625 HELMER: Nora!

NORA: Didn't you say a moment ago that that was no job to trust me with?

HELMER: In a flare of temper! Why fasten on that?

NORA: Yes, but you were so very right. I'm not up to the job.

630 There's another job I have to do first. I have to try to educate

myself. You can't help me with that. I've got to do it alone. And that's why I'm leaving you now.

HELMER: (jumping up.) What's that?

NORA: I have to stand completely alone, if I'm ever going to discover myself and the world out there. So I can't go on 635 living with you.

HELMER: Nora, Nora!

NORA: I want to leave right away. Kristine should put me up for the night —

HELMER: You're insane! You've no right! I forbid you! 640

NORA: From here on, there's no use forbidding me anything. I'll take with me whatever is mine. I don't want a thing from you, either now or later.

HELMER: What kind of madness is this!

NORA: Tomorrow I'm going home — I mean, home where I 645 came from. It'll be easier up there to find something to do.

HELMER: Oh, you blind, incompetent child!

NORA: I must learn to be competent, Torvald.

HELMER: Abandon your home, your husband, your children! And you're not even thinking what people will say. 650

NORA: I can't be concerned about that. I only know how essential this is.

HELMER: Oh, it's outrageous. So you'll run out like this on your most sacred vows.

NORA: What do you think are my most sacred vows? 655

HELMER: And I have to tell you that! Aren't they your duties to your husband and children?

NORA: I have other duties equally sacred.

HELMER: That isn't true. What duties are they?

NORA: Duties to myself. 660

HELMER: Before all else, you're a wife and a mother.

NORA: I don't believe in that anymore. I believe that, before all else, I'm a human being, no less than you — or anyway, I ought to try to become one. I know the majority thinks you're right, Torvald, and plenty of books agree with you, too. But I 665 can't go on believing what the majority says, or what's written in books. I have to think over these things myself and try to understand them.

HELMER: Why can't you understand your place in your own home? On a point like that, isn't there one everlasting guide 670 you can turn to? Where's your religion?

NORA: Oh, Torvald, I'm really not sure what religion is.

HELMER: What — ?

NORA: I only know what the minister said when I was confirmed. He told me religion was this thing and that. When I 675 get clear and away by myself, I'll go into that problem too. I'll see if what the minister said was right, or, in any case, if it's right for me.

HELMER: A young woman your age shouldn't talk like that. If religion can't move you, I can try to rouse your conscience. 680 You do have some moral feeling? Or, tell me — has that gone too?

NORA: It's not easy to answer that, Torvald. I simply don't know. I'm all confused about these things. I just know I see them so differently from you. I find out, for one thing, that the law's 685 not at all what I'd thought — but I can't get it through my head that the law is fair. A woman hasn't a right to protect her dying father or save her husband's life! I can't believe that.

HELMER: You talk like a child. You don't know anything of the world you live in. 690

NORA: No, I don't. But now I'll begin to learn for myself. I'll try to discover who's right, the world or I.

HELMER: Nora, you're sick; you've got a fever. I almost think you're out of your head.

695 NORA: I've never felt more clearheaded and sure in my life.

HELMER: And—clearheaded and sure—you're leaving your husband and children?

NORA: Yes.

HELMER: Then there's only one possible reason.

700 NORA: What?

HELMER: You no longer love me.

NORA: No. That's exactly it.

HELMER: Nora! You can't be serious!

NORA: Oh, this is so hard, Torvald—you've been so kind to me 705 always. But I can't help it. I don't love you anymore.

HELMER: (struggling for composure.) Are you also clearheaded and sure about that?

NORA: Yes, completely. That's why I can't go on staying here.

HELMER: Can you tell me what I did to lose your love?

710 NORA: Yes, I can tell you. It was this evening when the miraculous thing didn't come—then I knew you weren't the man I'd imagined.

HELMER: Be more explicit; I don't follow you.

NORA: I've waited now so patiently eight long years—for, my 715 Lord, I know miracles don't come every day. Then this crisis broke over me, and such a certainty filled me: now the miraculous event would occur. While Krogstad's letter was lying out there, I never for an instant dreamed that you could give in to his terms. I was so utterly sure you'd say to him: go on, 720 tell your tale to the whole wide world. And when he'd done that—

HELMER: Yes, what then? When I'd delivered my own wife into shame and disgrace—!

NORA: When he'd done that, I was so utterly sure that you'd step 725 forward, take the blame on yourself and say: I am the guilty one.

HELMER: Nora—!

NORA: You're thinking I'd never accept such a sacrifice from you? No, of course not. But what good would my protests be against you? That was the miracle I was waiting for, in terror 730 and hope. And to stave that off, I would have taken my life.

HELMER: I'd gladly work for you day and night, Nora—and take on pain and deprivation. But there's no one who gives up honor for love.

NORA: Millions of women have done just that.

735 HELMER: Oh, you think and talk like a silly child.

NORA: Perhaps. But you neither think nor talk like the man I could join myself to. When your big fright was over—and it wasn't from any threat against me, only for what might damage you—when all the danger was past, for you it was just as if 740 nothing had happened. I was exactly the same, your little lark, your doll, that you'd have to handle with double care now that I'd turned out so brittle and frail. (Gets up.) Torvald—in that instant it dawned on me that for eight years I've been living here with a stranger, and that I'd even conceived 745 three children—oh, I can't stand the thought of it! I could tear myself to bits.

HELMER: (heavily.) I see. There's a gulf that's opened between us—that's clear. Oh, but Nora, can't we bridge it somehow?

NORA: The way I am now, I'm no wife for you.

HELMER: I have the strength to make myself over. 750

NORA: Maybe—if your doll gets taken away.

HELMER: But to part! To part from you! No, Nora, no—I can't imagine it.

NORA: (going out, right.) All the more reason why it has to be. (She reenters with her coat and a small overnight bag, which 755 she puts on a chair by the table.)

HELMER: Nora, Nora, not now! Wait till tomorrow.

NORA: I can't spend the night in a strange man's room.

HELMER: But couldn't we live here like brother and sister—

NORA: You know very well how long that would last. (Throws her 760 shawl about her.) Good-bye, Torvald. I won't look in on the children. I know they're in better hands than mine. The way I am now, I'm no use to them.

HELMER: But someday, Nora—someday—?

NORA: How can I tell? I haven't the least idea what'll become 765 of me.

HELMER: But you're my wife, now and wherever you go.

NORA: Listen, Torvald—I've heard that when a wife deserts her husband's house just as I'm doing, then the law frees him from all responsibility. In any case, I'm freeing you from be- 770 ing responsible. Don't feel yourself bound, any more than I will. There has to be absolute freedom for us both. Here, take your ring back. Give me mine.

HELMER: That too?

NORA: That too. 775

HELMER: There it is.

NORA: Good. Well, now it's all over. I'm putting the keys here. The maids know all about keeping up the house—better than I do. Tomorrow, after I've left town, Kristine will stop by to pack up everything that's mine from home. I'd like those 780 things shipped up to me.

HELMER: Over! All over! Nora, won't you ever think about me?

NORA: I'm sure I'll think of you often, and about the children and the house here.

HELMER: May I write you? 785

NORA: No—never. You're not to do that.

HELMER: Oh, but let me send you—

NORA: Nothing. Nothing.

HELMER: Or help you if you need it.

NORA: No. I accept nothing from strangers. 790

HELMER: Nora—can I never be more than a stranger to you?

NORA: (picking up the overnight bag.) Ah, Torvald—it would take the greatest miracle of all—

HELMER: Tell me the greatest miracle!

NORA: You and I both would have to transform ourselves to the 795 point that— Oh, Torvald, I've stopped believing in miracles.

HELMER: But I'll believe. Tell me! Transform ourselves to the point that—?

NORA: That our living together could be a true marriage. (She goes out down the hall.) 800

HELMER: (sinks down on a chair by the door, face buried in his hands.) Nora! Nora! (Looking about and rising.) Empty. She's gone. (A sudden hope leaps in him.) The greatest miracle—?

(From below, the sound of a door slamming shut.)

AUGUST STRINDBERG

The Swedish playwright August Strindberg (1849–1912) was a modern Renaissance man — he wrote some fifty plays, several autobiographical novels, and a variety of scientific and occult works as well. A series of tempestuous marriages marked Strindberg's life and are reflected in his corrosively misogynistic attitudes and in his hostility toward Ibsen, who seemed to Strindberg to advocate a new order of feminine domination. Calling *A Doll House* "sick like its father," Strindberg wrote *The Father* (1887) in reply to Ibsen, a play in which a calculating woman drives her husband into madness. Although Strindberg considered the play to be an experiment in the new "naturalism," it is really a kind of psychological thriller: the characters are so consumed by their sexual combat with one another that the worldly environment hardly seems important. Strindberg sent the play to Zola, who found it absorbing and curious, but lacking in the material social reality he demanded of the new drama. Strindberg then wrote *Miss Julie* (1888) and considered the play's use of naturalism in his famous preface to the play. The battle of the sexes is one of Strindberg's preoccupations, examined in a series of plays including *Creditors* (1888) and *The Dance of Death, Parts 1 and 2* (1901).

The battle of the sexes was also the battle that occupied Strindberg's life outside the theater. His three marriages all involved periods of psychological breakdown and creative fertility. His breakdown of the mid-1890s after marrying his second wife is documented in *The Inferno* (1897) and is symptomatic of Strindberg's volatile and unstable frame of mind. Much of Strindberg's manic energy was focused on women — he believed that his wife was attempting to drive him mad by sending rays through the walls. Strindberg also developed a passion for the occult and for alchemy, and in addition to his plays, poems, and novels, he wrote a number of scientific and pseudoscientific treatises. Unlike Ibsen, Strindberg experimented in a variety of dramatic genres throughout his career. Calling himself the "Zola of the occult," Strindberg wrote an influential series of expressionist and symbolic plays; the best known today are *To Damascus* (in three parts, 1898–1901) and *A Dream Play* (1901). He also wrote several important plays on Swedish history, including *Erik XIV* (1899), *Gustav Adolph* (1900), and *Gustav III* (1902). In 1907 he founded a small theater — the Intimate Theater — which brought the independent theater movement to Sweden and produced his intense and often symbolic series of "chamber plays," including *The Ghost Sonata* (1907) and *The Pelican* (1907). When Strindberg died in 1912, he had become not only the most significant literary and theatrical figure in Swedish history, but also a major influence on the course of modern drama.

Miss Julie

Despite its setting, *Miss Julie* is a good example of Strindberg's subversive attitude toward the conventions of realistic theater. The play concerns the intense, erotic struggle between Jean and Julie, a struggle that takes place at once in the material world they inhabit and in the shadowy realm of fantasy and desire as well. This oblique angle on realism is suggested in Strindberg's opening stage directions. Instead of a setting oriented frontally, toward the audience, creating the impression of a full and objective disclosure, Strindberg sets the stage at an angle, acknowledging that our vision of the characters will be imbalanced, skewed. The setting creates a real environment for the characters, but Strindberg also includes the symbolic Cupid upstage and the signs of Julie's father, the Count. Throughout the play his absent presence weighs on the scene, a disembodied reminder of the social realities governing the scene, personified by the speaking tube and the elegant, polished riding boots and spurs.

The play is set on Midsummer's Night, traditionally a holiday of festive release, but here the occasion for a duel to the death, as Jean fights to possess and destroy Julie. *Miss Julie* is at once a complex psychological drama and an examination of the dynamics of power governing the relations between classes and between men and women. Much as Julie represents the forbidden pleasures of the upper classes to Jean, she also represents the process of his own degradation; the story of his escape from her garden through the outhouse provides an emblem of his experience in relation to the privileged upper classes of the play. Yet if Jean is trapped in servitude, Julie is no less trapped by the conventional society that hems her in and by the ferocious erotic combat that Strindberg sees as definitive of mature sexuality.

— PREFACE —

TRANSLATED BY EVERT SPRINCHORN

Like the arts in general, the theater has for a long time seemed to me a *Biblia Pauperum*, a picture Bible for those who cannot read, and the playwright merely a lay preacher who hawks the latest ideals in popular form, so popular that the middle classes—the bulk of the audiences—can grasp them without racking their brains too much. That explains why the theater has always been an elementary school for youngsters and the half-educated, and for women, who still retain a primitive capacity for deceiving themselves and for letting themselves be deceived, that is, for succumbing to illusions and responding hypnotically to the suggestions of the author. Consequently, now that the rudimentary and undeveloped mental processes that operate in the realm of fantasy appear to be evolving to the level of reflection, research, and experimentation, I believe that the theater, like religion, is about to be replaced as a dying institution for whose enjoyment we lack the necessary qualifications. Support for my view is provided by the theater crisis through which all of Europe is now passing, and still more by the fact that in those highly cultured lands which have produced the finest minds of our time— England and Germany—the drama is dead, as for the most part are the other fine arts.

Other countries, however, have thought to create a new drama by filling the old forms with new contents. But since there has not been enough time to popularize the new ideas, the public cannot understand them. And in the second place, controversy has so stirred up the public that they can no longer look on with a pure and dispassionate interest, especially when they see their most cherished ideals assailed or hear an applauding or booing majority openly exercise its tyrannical power, as can happen in the theater. And in the third place, since the new forms for the new ideas have not been created, the new wine has burst the old bottles.

In the play that follows I have not tried to accomplish anything new—that is impossible. I have only tried to modernize the form to satisfy what I believe up-to-date people expect and demand of this art. And with that in mind I have seized upon—or let myself be seized by—a theme that may be said to lie outside current party strife, since the question of being on the way up or on the way down the social ladder, of being on the top or on the bottom, superior or inferior, man or woman, is, has been, and will be of perennial interest. When I took this theme from real life—I heard about it a few years ago and it made a deep impression on me—I thought it would be a suitable subject for a tragedy, since it still strikes us as tragic to see a happily favored individual go down in defeat, and even more so to see an entire family line die out. But perhaps a time will come when we shall be so highly developed and so enlightened that we can look with indifference upon the brutal, cynical, and heartless spectacle that life offers us, a time when we shall have laid aside those inferior and unreliable mechanical apparatuses called emotions, which will become superfluous and even harmful as our mental organs develop. The fact that my heroine wins sympathy is due entirely to the fact that we are still too weak to overcome the fear that the same fate might overtake us. The extremely sensitive viewer will of course not be satisfied with mere expressions of sympathy, and the man who believes in progress will demand that certain positive actions be taken for getting rid of the evil, a kind of program, in other words. But in the first place absolute evil does not exist. The decline of one family is the making of another, which now gets its chance to rise. This alternate rising and falling provides one of life's greatest pleasures, for happiness is, after all, relative. As for the man who has a program for changing the disagreeable circumstance that the hawk eats the chicken and that lice eat up the hawk, I should like to ask him why it should be changed. Life is not prearranged with such idiotic mathematical precision that only the larger gets to eat the smaller. Just as frequently the bee destroys the lion (in Aesop's fable)—or at least drives him wild.

If my tragedy makes most people feel sad, that is their fault. When we get to be as strong as the first French Revolutionists were, we shall be perfectly content and happy to watch the forests being cleared of rotting, superannuated trees that have stood too long in the way of others with just as much right to grow and flourish for a while—as content as we are when we see an incurably ill man finally die.

Recently my tragedy *The Father* was censured for being too unpleasant—as if one wanted merry tragedies. "The joy of life" is now the slogan of the day. Theater managers send out orders for nothing but farces, as if the joy of living lay in behaving like a clown and in depicting people as if they were afflicted with St. Vitus's dance or congenital idiocy. I find the joy of living in the fierce and ruthless battles of life, and my pleasure comes from learning something, from being taught something. That is why I have chosen for my play an unusual but instructive case, an exception, in other words—but an important exception of the kind that proves the rule—a choice of subject that I know will offend all lovers of the conventional. The next thing that will bother simple minds is that the motivation for the action is not simple and that the point of view is not single. Usually an event in life—and this is a fairly new discovery—is the result of a whole series of more or less deep-rooted causes. The spectator, however, generally chooses the one that puts the least strain on his mind or reflects most credit on his insight. Consider a case of suicide. "Business failure," says the merchant. "Unhappy love," say the women. "Physical illness," says the sick man. "Lost hopes," says the down-and-out. But it may be that the reason lay in all of these or in none of them, and that the suicide hid his real reason behind a completely different one that would reflect greater glory on his memory.

I have motivated the tragic fate of Miss Julie with an abundance of circumstances: her mother's basic instincts, her father's improper bringing-up of the girl, her own inborn nature, and her fiancé's sway over her weak and degenerate mind. Further and more immediately: the festive atmosphere of Midsummer Eve, her father's absence, her period, her preoccupation with animals, the erotic excitement of the dance, the long summer twilight, the highly aphrodisiac influence of flowers, and finally chance itself, which drives two people together in an out-of-the-way room, plus the boldness of the aroused man.

As one can see, I have not been entirely the physiologist, not been obsessively psychological, not traced everything to her mother's heredity, not found the sole cause in her period, not attributed everything to our "immoral times," and not simply preached a moral lesson. Lacking a priest, I have let the cook handle that.

I am proud to say that this complicated way of looking at things is in tune with the times. And if others have anticipated me in this, I am proud that I am not alone in my paradoxes, as all new discoveries are called. And no one can say this time that I am being one-sided.

As far as the drawing of characters is concerned, I have made the people in my play fairly "characterless" for the following reasons. In the course of time the word *character* has acquired many meanings. Originally it probably meant the dominant and fundamental trait in the soul complex and was confused with temperament. Later the middle class used it to mean an automaton. An individual who once for all had found his own true nature or adapted himself to a certain role in life, who in fact had ceased to grow, was called a man of character, while the man who was constantly developing, who, like a skillful sailor on the currents of life, did not sail with close-tied sheets but who fell off before the wind in order to luff again, was called a man of no character—derogatorily of course, since he was so difficult to keep track of, to pin down and pigeonhole. This middle-class conception of a fixed character was transferred to the stage, where the middle class has always ruled. A character there came to mean someone who was always one and the same, always drunk, always joking, always melancholy, and who needed to be characterized only by some physical defect such as a club foot, a wooden leg, or a red nose, or by the repetition of some such phrase as, "That's capital," or "Barkis is willin'." This uncomplicated way of viewing people is still to be found in the great Molière. Harpagon is nothing but a miser, although Harpagon could have been both a miser and an exceptional financier, a fine father, and a good citizen. Worse still, his "defect" is extremely advantageous to his son-in-law and his daughter who will be his heirs and who therefore should not find fault with him, even if they do have to wait a while to jump into bed together. So I do not believe in simple stage characters. And the summary judgments that writers pass on people—he is stupid, this one is brutal, that one is jealous, this one is stingy, and so on—should not pass unchallenged by the naturalists who know how complicated the soul is and who realize that vice has a reverse side very much like virtue.

Since the persons in my play are modern characters, living in a transitional era more hectic and hysterical than the previous one at least, I have depicted them as more unstable, as torn and divided, a mixture of the old and the new. Nor does it seem improbable to me that modern ideas might also have seeped down through newspapers and kitchen talk to the level of the servants. Consequently the valet may belch forth from his inherited slave soul certain modern ideas. And if there are those who find it wrong to allow people in a modern drama to talk Darwin and who recommend the practice of Shakespeare to our attention, may I remind them that the gravedigger in *Hamlet* talks the then fashionable philosophy of Giordano Bruno (Bacon's philosophy), which is even more improbable, seeing that the means of spreading ideas were fewer then than now. And besides, the fact of the matter is that Darwinism has always existed, ever since Moses' history of creation from the lower animals up to man, but it was not until recently that we discovered it and formulized it.

My souls — or characters — are conglomerations from various stages of culture, past and present, walking scrapbooks, shreds of human lives, tatters torn from old rags that were once Sunday best — hodgepodges just like the human soul. I have even supplied a little source history into the bargain by letting the weaker steal and repeat words of the stronger, letting them get ideas (suggestions as they are called) from one another, from the environment (the songbird's blood), and from objects (the razor). I have also arranged for *Gedankenübertragung*[1] through an inanimate medium to take place (the count's boots, the servant's bell). And I have even made use of "waking suggestions" (a variation of hypnotic suggestion), which have by now been so popularized that they cannot arouse ridicule or skepticism as they would have done in Mesmer's time.

I say Miss Julie is a modern character not because the man-hating half-woman has not always existed but because she has now been brought out into the open, has taken the stage, and is making a noise about herself. Victim of a superstition (one that has seized even stronger minds) that woman, that stunted form of human being, standing with man, the lord of creation, the creator of culture, is meant to be the equal of man or could ever possibly be, she involves herself in an absurd struggle with him in which she falls. Absurd because a stunted form, subject to the laws of propagation, will always be born stunted and can never catch up with the one who has the lead. As follows: A (the man) and B (the woman) start from the same point C, A with a speed of let us say 100 and B with a speed of 60. When will B overtake A? Answer: never. Neither with the help of equal education or equal voting rights — nor by universal disarmament and temperance societies — any more than two parallel lines can ever meet. The half-woman is a type that forces itself on others, selling itself for power, medals, recognition, diplomas, as formerly it sold itself for money. It represents degeneration. It is not a strong species for it does not maintain itself, but unfortunately it propagates its misery in the following generation. Degenerate men unconsciously select their mates from among these half-women, so that they breed and spread, producing creatures of indeterminate sex to whom life is a torture, but who fortunately are overcome eventually either by a hostile reality, or by the uncontrolled breaking loose of their repressed instincts, or else by their frustration in not being able to compete with the male sex. It is a tragic type, offering us the spectacle of a desperate fight against nature; a tragic legacy of romanticism, which is now being dissipated by naturalism — a movement that seeks only happiness, and for that strong and healthy species are required.

Miss Julie, however, is also a vestige of the old warrior nobility that is now being superseded by a new nobility of nerve and brain. She is a victim of the disorder produced within a family by a mother's "crime," of the mistakes of a whole generation gone wrong, of circumstances, of her own defective constitution — all of which put together is equivalent to the fate or universal law of the ancients. The naturalists have banished guilt along with God, but the consequences of an act — punishment, imprisonment, or the fear of it — cannot be banished for the simple reason that they remain whether or not the naturalist dismisses the case from his court. Those sitting on the sidelines can easily afford to be lenient; but what of the injured parties? And even if her father were compelled to forgo taking his revenge, Miss Julie would take vengeance on herself, as she does in the play, because of that inherited or acquired sense of honor that has been transmitted to the upper classes from — well, where does it come from? From the age of barbarism, from the first Aryans, from the chivalry of the Middle Ages. And a very fine code it was, but now inimical to the survival of the race. It is the aristocrat's form of hara-kiri, a law of conscience that bids the Japanese to slice his own stomach when someone else dishonors him. The same sort of thing survives, slightly modified, in that exclusive prerogative of the aristocracy, the duel. (Example: the husband challenges his wife's lover to a duel; the lover shoots the husband and runs off with the wife. Result: the husband has saved his *honor* but lost his wife.) Hence the servant Jean lives on; but not Miss Julie, who cannot live without honor. The advantage that the slave has over his master is that he has not committed himself to this defeatist principle. In all of us Aryans there is enough of the nobleman, or of the Don Quixote, to make us sympathize with the man who takes his own life after having dishonored himself by shameful deeds. And we are all of us

---

[1] Telepathy

aristocrats enough to be distressed at the sight of a great man lying like a dead hulk ready for the scrap pile, even, I suppose, if he were to raise himself up again and redeem himself by honorable deeds.

The servant Jean is the beginning of a new species in which noticeable differentiation has already taken place. He began as a child of a poor worker and is now evolving through self-education into a future gentleman of the upper classes. He is quick to learn, has highly developed senses (smell, taste, sight), and a keen appreciation of beauty. He has already come up in the world, for he is strong enough not to hesitate to make use of other people. He is already a stranger to his old friends, whom he despises as reminders of past stages in his development, and whom he fears and avoids because they know his secrets, guess his intentions, look with envy on his rise and with joyful expectation toward his fall. Hence his character is unformed and divided. He wavers between an admiration of high positions and a hatred of the men who occupy them. He is an aristocrat—he says so himself—familiar with the ins and outs of good society. He is polished on the outside, but coarse underneath. He wears his frock coat with elegance but offers no guarantee that he keeps his body clean.

Although he respects Miss Julie, he is afraid of Christine, because she knows his innermost secrets. Yet he is sufficiently hard-hearted not to let the events of the night upset his plans for the future. Possessing both the coarseness of the slave and the toughmindedness of the born ruler, he can look at blood without fainting, shake off bad luck like water, and take calamity by the horns. Consequently he will escape from the battle unwounded, probably ending up as proprietor of a hotel. And if he himself does not get to be a Rumanian count, his son will doubtless go to college and possibly end up as a government official.

Now his observations about life as the lower classes see it, from below, are well worth listening to—that is, they are whenever he is telling the truth, which is not too often, because he is more likely to say what is advantageous to him than what is true. When Miss Julie supposes that everyone in the lower classes must feel greatly oppressed by the weight of the classes above, Jean naturally agrees with her since he wants to win her sympathy. But he promptly takes it all back when he finds it expedient to separate himself from the mob.

Apart from the fact that Jean is coming up in the world, he is also superior to Miss Julie in that he is a man. In the sexual sphere, he is the aristocrat. He has the strength of the male, more highly developed senses, and the ability to take the initiative. His inferiority is merely the result of his social environment, which is only temporary and which he will probably slough off along with his livery.

His slave nature expresses itself in his awe of the count (the boots) and his religious superstitions. But he is awed by the count mainly because the count occupies the place he wants most in life; and this awe is still there even after he has won the daughter of the house and seen how empty that beautiful shell was.

I do not believe that any love in the "higher" sense can be born from the union of two such different souls; so I have let Miss Julie's love be refashioned in her imagination as a love that protects and purifies, and I have let Jean imagine that even his love might have a chance to grow under other social circumstances. For I suppose love is very much like the hyacinth that must strike roots deep in the dark earth *before* it can produce a vigorous blossom. Here it shoots up, bursts into bloom, and turns to seed all at once. Such plants can only be short-lived.

Christine—finally to get to her—is a female slave, spineless and phlegmatic after years spent at the kitchen stove, bovinely unconscious of her own hypocrisy, and with a full quota of moral and religious notions that serve as scapegoats and cloaks for her sins—which a stronger soul does not require since he is able either to carry the burden of his own sins or to rationalize them out of existence. She attends church regularly where she deftly unloads unto Jesus her household thefts and picks up from him another load of innocence. She is only a secondary character, and I have deliberately done no more than sketch her in—just as I treated the country doctor and parish priest in *The Father* where I only wanted to draw ordinary everyday people such as most country doctors and parsons are. That some have found my minor characters one-dimensional is due to the fact that ordinary people while at work are to a certain extent one-dimensional and do lack an independent existence, showing only one side of themselves in the performance of their duties. And as long as the audience does not feel it needs to see them from different angles, my abstract sketches will pass muster.

Now as far as the dialogue is concerned, I have broken somewhat with tradition in refusing to make my characters into interlocutors who ask stupid questions to elicit witty answers. I have avoided the symmetrical and mathematical design of the artfully constructed French dialogue and have let minds work as irregularly as they do in real life, where no subject is quite exhausted before another mind engages at random some cog in the conversation and governs it for a while. My dialogue wanders here and there, gathers material in the first scenes which is later picked up, repeated, reworked, developed, and expanded like the theme in a piece of music.

The action of the play poses no problem. Since it really involves only two people, I have limited myself to these two, introducing only one minor character, the cook, and keeping the unhappy spirit of the father brooding over the action as a whole. I have chosen this course because I have noticed that what interests people most nowadays is the psychological action. Our inveterately curious souls are no longer content to see a thing happen; we want to see how it happens. We want to see the strings, look at the machinery, examine the double-bottom drawer, put on the magic ring to find the hidden seam, look in the deck for the marked cards.

In treating the subject this way I have had in mind the case-history novels of the Goncourt brothers, which appeal to me more than anything else in modern literature.

As far as play construction is concerned, I have made a stab at getting rid of act divisions. I was afraid that the spectator's declining susceptibility to illusion might not carry him through the intermission, when he would have time to think about what he has seen and to escape the suggestive influence of the author-hypnotist. I figure my play lasts about ninety minutes. Since one can listen to a lecture, a sermon, or a political debate for that long or even longer, I have convinced myself that a play should not exhaust an audience in that length of time. As early as 1872 in one of my first attempts at the drama, *The Outlaw*, I tried out this concentrated form, although with little success. I had finished the work in five acts when I noticed the disjointed and disturbing effect it produced. I burned it, and from the ashes there arose a single, complete reworked act of fifty pages that would run for less than an hour. Although this play form is not completely new, it seems to be my special property and has a good chance of gaining favor with the public when tastes change. My hope is to educate a public to sit through a full evening's show in one act. But this whole question must first be probed more deeply. In the meantime, in order to establish resting places for the audience and the actors without destroying the illusion, I have made use of three arts that belong to the drama: the monologue, the pantomime, and the ballet, all of which were part of classic tragedy, the monody having become the monologue and the choral dance, the ballet.

The realists have banished the monologue from the stage as implausible. But if I can motivate it, I make it plausible, and I can then use it to my advantage. Now it is certainly plausible for a speaker to pace the floor and read his speech aloud to himself. It is plausible for an actor to practice his part aloud, for a child to talk to her cat, a mother to babble to her baby, an old lady to chatter to her parrot, and a sleeping man to talk in his sleep. And in order to give the actor a chance to work on his own for once and for a moment not be obliged to follow the author's directions, I have not written out the monologues in detail but simply outlined them. Since it makes very little difference what is said while asleep, or to the parrot or the cat, inasmuch as it does not affect the main action, a gifted player who is in the midst of the situation and mood of the play can probably improvise the monologue better than the author, who cannot estimate ahead of time how much may be said and for how long before the illusion is broken.

Some theaters in Italy have, as we know, returned to the art of improvisation and have thereby trained actors who are truly inventive — without, however, violating the intentions of the author. This seems to be a step in the right direction and possibly the beginning of a new, fertile form of art that will be genuinely *creative*.

In places where the monologue cannot be properly motivated, I have resorted to pantomime. Here I have given the actor even more freedom to be creative and win honor on his own. Nevertheless, not to try the audience beyond its limits, I have relied on music — well motivated by the Midsummer Eve dance — to exercise its hypnotic powers during the pantomime scene. I beg the music director to select his tunes with great care, so that associations foreign to the mood of the play will not be produced by reminders of popular operettas or current dance numbers or by folk music of interest only to ethnologists.

The ballet that I have introduced cannot be replaced by a so-called crowd scene. Such scenes are always badly acted, with a pack of babbling fools taking advantage of the occasion to "gag it up," thereby destroying the illusion. Inasmuch as country people do not improvise their taunts but make use of material already to hand by giving it a double meaning, I have not composed an original lampoon but have made use of a little known round dance that I noted down in the Stockholm district. The words do not fit the situation exactly, which is what I intended, since the slave in his cunning (that is, weakness) never attacks directly. At any rate, let us have no comedians in this serious story and no obscene smirking over an affair that nails the lid on a family coffin.

As far as the scenery is concerned, I have borrowed from impressionistic painting the idea of asymmetrical and open composition, and I believe that I have thereby gained something in the way of greater illusion. Because the audience cannot see the whole room and all the furniture, they will have to surmise what's missing; that is, their imagination will be stimulated to fill in the rest of the picture. I have gained something else by this: I have avoided those tiresome exits through doors. Stage doors are made of canvas and rock at the slightest touch. They cannot even be used to indicate the wrath of an angry father who storms out of the house after a bad dinner, slamming the door behind him "so that the whole house shakes." (In the theater it sways and billows.) Furthermore, I have confined the action to one set, both to give the characters a chance to become part and parcel of their environment and to cut down on scenic extravagance. If there is only one set, one has a right to expect it to be as realistic as possible. Yet nothing is more difficult than to make a room look like a room, however easy it may be for the scene painter to create waterfalls and erupting volcanos. I suppose we shall have to put up with walls made of canvas, but isn't it about time that we stopped painting shelves and pots and pans on the canvas? There are so many other conventions in the theater that we are told to accept in good faith that we should be spared the strain of believing in painted saucepans.

I have placed the backdrop and the table at an angle to force the actors to play face to face or in half profile when they are seated opposite each other at the table. In a production of *Aida* I saw a flat placed at such an angle, which led the eye out in an unfamiliar perspective. Nor did it look as if it had been set that way simply to be different to avoid those monotonous right angles.

Another desirable innovation would be the removal of the footlights. I understand that the purpose of lighting from below is to make the actors look more full in the face. But may I ask why all actors should have full faces? Doesn't this kind of lighting wipe out many of the finer features in the lower part of the face, especially around the jaws? Doesn't it distort the shape of the nose and throw false shadows above the eyes? If not, it certainly does something else: it hurts the actor's eyes. The footlights hit the retina at an angle from which it is usually shielded (except in sailors who must look at the sunlight reflected in the water), and the result is the loss of any effective play of the eyes. All one ever sees on stage are goggle-eyed glances sideways at the boxes or upward at the balcony, with only the whites of the eyes being visible in the latter case. And this probably also accounts for that tiresome fluttering of the eyelashes that the female performers are particularly guilty of. If an actor nowadays wants to express something with his eyes, he can only do it looking right at the audience, in which case he makes direct contact with someone outside the proscenium arch—a bad habit known, justifiably or not, as "saying hello to friends."[2]

I should think that the use of sufficiently strong side lights (through the use of reflectors or something like them) would provide the actor with a new asset: an increased range of expression made possible by the play of the eyes, the most expressive part of the face.

I have scarcely any illusions about getting actors to play for the audience and not directly at them, although this should be the goal. Nor do I dream of ever seeing an actor play through all of an important scene with his back to the audience. But is it too much to hope that crucial scenes could be played where the author indicated and not in front of the prompter's box as if they were duets demanding applause? I am not calling for a revolution, only for some small changes. I am well aware that transforming the stage into a real room with the fourth wall missing and with some of the furniture placed with backs to the auditorium would only upset the audience, at least for the present.

If I bring up the subject of make-up, it is not because I dare hope to be heeded by the ladies, who would rather be beautiful than truthful. But the male actor might do well to consider if it is an advantage to paint his face with character lines that remain there like a mask. Let us imagine an actor who pencils in with soot a few lines between his eyes to indicate great anger, and let us suppose that in

---

[2]"Counting the house" would be the equivalent in American theater slang. —Trans.

that permanently enraged state he finds he has to smile on a certain line. Imagine the horrible grimace! And how can the old character actor wrinkle his brows in anger when his false bald pate is as smooth as a billiard ball?

In a modern psychological drama, in which every tremor of the soul should be reflected more by facial expressions than by gestures and grunts, it would probably be most sensible to experiment with strong side lighting on a small stage, using actors without any make-up or a minimum of it.

And then, if we could get rid of the visible orchestra with its disturbing lights and the faces turned toward the public; if the auditorium floor could be raised so that the spectator's eyes are not level with the actor's knees; if we could get rid of the proscenium boxes and their occupants, arriving giggling and drunk from their dinners; and if we could have it dark in the auditorium during the performance; and if, above everything else, we could have a *small* stage and an *intimate* auditorium — then possibly a new drama might arise and at least one theater become a refuge for cultured audiences. While we are waiting for such a theater, we shall have to write for the dramatic stockpile and prepare the repertory that one day shall come.

Here is my attempt. If I have failed, there is still time to try again!

August Strindberg
(1888)

MISS JULIE

August Strindberg

TRANSLATED BY EVERT SPRINCHORN

— CHARACTERS —

MISS JULIE,[3] *twenty-five years old*
JEAN, *valet, thirty years old*
CHRISTINE, *cook, thirty-five years old*
THE CHORUS, *a party of country folk*

The scene is a country estate in Sweden.

The time: A Midsummer Night in the 1880s. The hours after midnight, June 24, St. John the Baptist's Day.

The scene is the kitchen of the estate belonging to the count, MISS JULIE'*s father. It is a large kitchen, situated along with the servants' quarters in the basement of the manor house. The side walls and the ceiling of the kitchen are masked by the tormentors and borders of the set. The rear wall runs obliquely upstage from the left. On this wall to the left are two shelves with pots and pans of copper, iron, and pewter. The shelves are decorated with goffered paper. A little to the right can be seen three-fourths of a deep arched entry with two glass doors, and through them can be seen a fountain with a statue of a cupid, lilac bushes in bloom, and the tops of some Lombardy poplars.*

From the left of the stage the corner of a large, Dutch-tile kitchen stove protrudes with part of the hood showing.

Projecting from the right side of the stage is one end of the servants' dining table of white pine, with a few chairs around it.

The stove is decorated with branches of birch leaves; the floor is strewn with juniper twigs.

On the end of the table is a large Japanese spice jar filled with lilacs.

An icebox, a sink, a washbasin.

Over the door a big old-fashioned bell; and to the left of the door the gaping mouth of a speaking tube.

✢   ✢   ✢

CHRISTINE *is standing at the stove, frying something in a pan. She is wearing a light-colored cotton dress and an apron.*

JEAN *enters, dressed in livery and carrying a pair of high-top boots with spurs. He sets them where they are clearly visible.*

JEAN: What a night! She's wild again! Miss Julie's absolutely wild!

CHRISTINE: You sure took your time getting back!

JEAN: I took the count down to the station, and on my way back, I passed the barn and went in for a dance. And there was Miss Julie leading the dance with the game warden. Then she noticed me. And she ran right into my arms and chose me for the ladies' waltz. And she's been dancing ever since like — like I don't know what. Wild, I tell you, absolutely wild!

CHRISTINE: That's nothing new. But she's been worse than ever during the last two weeks, ever since her engagement was broken off.   10

JEAN: Yes. I never did hear all there was to that. He was a good man, too, even if he wasn't rich. Well, they've got such crazy ideas. *(He sits down at the end of the table.)* Tell me, isn't it strange that a young girl like her — all right, young woman —   15 prefers to stay home here with the servants rather than go with her father to visit her relatives?

CHRISTINE: I suppose she's ashamed to face them after that fiasco with her young man.

JEAN: No doubt. He wouldn't take any nonsense from her. Do   20 you know what happened, Christine? I saw the whole thing. Of course, I didn't let on.

CHRISTINE: You were there? I don't believe it.

JEAN: Well, I was. They were in the stable yard one evening — and she was training him, that's what she called it. Do you   25 know what? She was making him jump over her riding whip — training him like a dog. He jumped over twice, and she whipped him both times. But the third time, he grabbed the whip from her, [scratched her face with it — long scratch on her left cheek;] then broke it in a thousand pieces — and   30 walked off.

CHRISTINE: I don't believe it! What do you know!

JEAN: Yes, that put an end to that affair. — What have you got for me that's really good, Christine?

CHRISTINE: *(serving him from the frying pan)* Just a little bit of   35 kidney. Cut it from the veal roast.

JEAN: *(smelling it)* Wonderful! One of my special *délices!* *(Feeling the plate.)* Hey, you didn't warm the plate!

CHRISTINE: You're more fussy than the count himself when you set your mind to it. *(She rumples his hair affectionately.)*   40

JEAN: *(irritated)* Cut it out! Don't muss up my hair. You know how particular I am!

CHRISTINE: Oh, don't get mad. Can I help it if I like you?

(JEAN eats. CHRISTINE *gets out a bottle of beer.)*

JEAN: Beer on Midsummer Eve! No thank you! I've got something much better than that. *(He opens a drawer in the table*   45 *and takes out a bottle of red wine with a gold seal.)* Do you see that? Gold Seal. Now give me a glass.

29–30 **scratched . . . left cheek** the passage in brackets was deleted in Strindberg's manuscript, probably by Strindberg himself

---

[3]Julie is not a countess; she is the daughter of a count. Her title "fröken" corresponds to the German "Fräulein" and the French "mademoiselle."

(She hands him a tumbler.)

—No, a wineglass of course. This has to be drunk properly. No water.

50 CHRISTINE: *(goes back to the stove and puts on a small saucepan)* Lord help the woman who gets you for a husband. You're an old fussbudget!

JEAN: Talk, talk! You'd consider yourself lucky if you got yourself a man as good as me. It hasn't done you any harm to have

55 people think I'm your fiancé. *(He tastes the wine.)* Very good. Excellent. But warmed just a little too little. *(Warming the glass in his hands.)* We bought this in Dijon. Four francs a liter, unbottled—and the tax on top of that. . . . What on earth are you cooking? It stinks like hell!

60 CHRISTINE: Some damn mess that Miss Julie wants for her Diana, that damn dog of hers.

JEAN: You should watch your language, Christine. . . . Why do you have to stand in front of the stove on a holiday, cooking for that mutt? Is it sick?

65 CHRISTINE: Oh, she's sick, all right! She sneaked out to the gatekeeper's pug and—got herself in a fix. And you know Miss Julie, she can't stand anything like that.

JEAN: She's too stuck-up in some ways and not proud enough in others. Just like her mother. The countess felt right at home

70 in the kitchen or down in the barn with the cows, but when she went driving, one horse wasn't enough for her, she had to have a pair. Her sleeves were always dirty, but her buttons had the royal crown on them. As for Miss Julie, she doesn't give a hoot in hell how she looks and acts. I mean, she's not really

75 refined, not really. Just now, down at the barn, she grabbed the game warden right from under Anna's eyes and asked him to dance. You wouldn't see anybody in our class behaving like that. But that's what happens when the gentry try to act like the common people—they become common! . . . However,

80 I'll say one thing for her: she *is* beautiful! Statuesque! Ah, those shoulders—those—and so forth, and so forth!

CHRISTINE: Oh, don't exaggerate. Clara tells me all about her, and Clara dresses her.

JEAN: Clara, pooh! You women are always jealous of each other.

85 I've been out riding with her. . . . And how she can dance . . . !

CHRISTINE: Listen, Jean, you *are* going to dance with me, aren't you, when I'm finished here?

JEAN: Certainly! Of course I am.

CHRISTINE: Promise?

90 JEAN: Promise! Listen if I say I'm going to do a thing, I do it. . . . Christine, I thank you for a delicious meal. Superb! *(He shoves the cork back into the bottle.)*

(MISS JULIE appears in the entry, talking to someone outside.)

MISS JULIE: I'll be right back. Don't wait for me.

(JEAN slips the bottle into the table drawer quickly and rises respectfully. MISS JULIE comes in and crosses over to CHRISTINE, who is at the stove.)

MISS JULIE: Did you get it ready?

(CHRISTINE signals that JEAN is present.)

95 JEAN: *(polite and charming)* Are you ladies sharing secrets?

MISS JULIE: *(flipping her handkerchief in his face)* Don't be nosy!

JEAN: Oh, that smells good! Violets.

MISS JULIE: *(flirting with him)* Don't be impudent! And don't

tell me you're an expert on perfumes, too. I love the way you dance!—No, mustn't look! Go away! 100

JEAN: *(cocky but pleasant)* What are the ladies cooking up? A witches' brew for Midsummer Eve? So they can tell the future? Read what's in the cards for them, and see who they'll marry?

MISS JULIE: *(curtly)* You'd have to have good eyes to see that. *(To* 105 CHRISTINE.*)* Pour it into a small bottle, and seal it tight. . . . Jean, come and dance a schottische with me.

JEAN: *(hesitating)* I hope you don't think I'm being rude, but I've already promised this dance to Christine.

MISS JULIE: She can always find someone. Isn't that so, Chris- 110 tine? You don't mind if I borrow Jean for a minute, do you?

CHRISTINE: It ain't up to me. If Miss Julie is gracious enough to invite you, it ain't right for you to say no, Jean. You go on, and thank her for the honor.

JEAN: Frankly, Miss Julie, I don't want to hurt your feelings, but 115 I wonder if it's wise—I mean for you to dance twice in a row with the same partner. Especially since the people around here love to talk.

MISS JULIE: *(bridling)* What do you mean? What kind of talk? What are you trying to say? 120

JEAN: *(retreating)* I wish you wouldn't misunderstand me, Miss Julie. It just doesn't look right for you to prefer one of your servants to the others who are hoping for the same unusual honor.

MISS JULIE: Prefer! What an idea! I'm really surprised. I, the 125 mistress of the house, am good enough to come to their dance, and when I feel like dancing, I want to dance with someone who knows how to lead. After all I don't want to look ridiculous.

JEAN: As you wish, Miss Julie. I am at your orders. 130

MISS JULIE: *(gently)* Don't take it as an order. Tonight we're all just having a good time. There's no question of rank. Now give me your arm.—Don't worry, Christine. I won't run off with your boyfriend.

(JEAN gives her his arm and leads her out.)

✳   ✳   ✳

PANTOMIME SCENE

This should be played as if the actress were actually alone. She turns her back on the audience when she feels like it; she does not look out into the auditorium; she does not rush through the scene as if afraid the audience will grow impatient.

CHRISTINE *alone. In the distance the sound of the violins playing the schottische.* CHRISTINE, *humming in time with the music, cleans up after* JEAN, *washes the dishes, dries them, and puts them away in a cupboard. Then she takes off her apron, takes a little mirror from one of the table drawers, and leans it against the jar of lilacs on the table. She lights a tallow candle, heats a curling iron, and curls the bangs on her forehead. Then she goes to the doorway and stands listening to the music. She comes back to the table and finds the handkerchief that* MISS JULIE *left behind. She smells it, spreads it out, and then, as if lost in thought, stretches it, smooths it out, and folds it in four.*

✳   ✳   ✳

(JEAN *enters alone.*)

JEAN: Wild! I told you she was wild! You should have seen the way she was dancing. Everyone was peeking at her from behind the doors and laughing at her. What's the matter with her, Christine?

5   CHRISTINE: You might know it's her monthlies, Jean. She always acts peculiar then. . . . Well, are you going to dance with me?

JEAN: You're not mad at me because I broke my promise?

CHRISTINE: Of course not. Not for a little thing like that, you 10   know that. I know my place.

JEAN: (*grabs her around the waist*) You're a sensible girl, Christine. You're going to make somebody a good wife —

(MISS JULIE, *coming in, sees them together. She is unpleasantly surprised.*)

MISS JULIE: (*with forced gaiety*) Well, aren't you the gallant beau — running away from your partner!

15   JEAN: On the contrary, Miss Julie. As you can see, I've hurried back to the partner I deserted.

MISS JULIE: (*changing tack*) You know, you're the best dancer I've met. — Why are you wearing livery on a holiday? Take it off at once.

20   JEAN: I'd have to ask you to leave for a minute. My black coat is hanging right here — (*He moves to the right and points.*)

MISS JULIE: You're not embarrassed because I'm here, are you? Just to change your coat? Go in your room and come right back again. Or else stay here and I'll turn my back.

25   JEAN: If you'll excuse me, Miss Julie. (*He goes off to the right. His arm can be seen as he changes his coat.*)

MISS JULIE: (*to* CHRISTINE) Tell me something, Christine. Is Jean your fiancé? He acts so familiar with you.

CHRISTINE: Fiancé? I suppose so. At least we say we are.

30   MISS JULIE: What do you mean?

CHRISTINE: Well, Miss Julie, you have had fiancés yourself, and you know —

MISS JULIE: But we were properly engaged — !

CHRISTINE: I know, but did anything come of it?

(JEAN *comes back, wearing a black cutaway coat and derby.*)

35   MISS JULIE: *Très gentil, monsieur Jean! Très gentil!*

JEAN: *Vous voulez plaisanter, madame.*

MISS JULIE: *Et vous voulez parler français!* Where did you learn to speak French?

JEAN: In Switzerland. I was *sommelier* in one of the biggest 40   hotels in Lucerne.

MISS JULIE: My! but you look quite the gentleman in that coat! *Charmant!* (*She sits down at the table.*)

JEAN: Flatterer!

MISS JULIE: (*stiffening*) Who said I was flattering you?

45   JEAN: My natural modesty would not allow me to presume that you were paying sincere compliments to someone like me, and therefore I could only assume that you were exaggerating, which, in this case, means flattering me.

MISS JULIE: You certainly have a way with words. Where did 50   you learn to talk like that? Seeing plays?

JEAN: And other places. You don't think I stayed in the house for six years when I was a valet in Stockholm, do you?

MISS JULIE: I thought you were born in this district. Weren't you?

JEAN: My father worked as a farmhand on the district attorney's estate, next door to yours. I used to see you when you were 55   little. Of course you didn't notice me.

MISS JULIE: Did you really?

JEAN: Yes. I remember one time in particular —. But I can't tell you about that!

MISS JULIE: Of course you can. . . . Oh, come on. Just this 60   once — for me.

JEAN: No. No, I really couldn't. Not now. Some other time maybe.

MISS JULIE: Some other time? That means never. What's the harm in telling me now? 65

JEAN: There's no harm. I just don't feel like it. — Look at her.

(*He nods at* CHRISTINE, *who has fallen asleep in a chair by the stove.*)

MISS JULIE: Won't she make somebody a pretty wife! I'll bet she snores, too.

JEAN: No, she doesn't. But she talks in her sleep.

MISS JULIE: (*archly*) Now how could you know she talks in her 70   sleep?

JEAN: (*coolly*) I've heard her . . .

(*Pause. They look at each other.*)

MISS JULIE: Why don't you sit down?

JEAN: I wouldn't take the liberty in your presence.

MISS JULIE: Not even if I ordered you? 75

JEAN: Of course I'd obey.

MISS JULIE: Well then: sit down. — Wait a minute. Could you get me something to drink?

JEAN: I don't know what there is in the icebox. Only beer, I suppose. 80

MISS JULIE: Only beer?! I have simple tastes. I prefer beer to wine.

(JEAN *takes a bottle of beer from the icebox and opens it. He looks in the cupboard for a glass and a plate, and serves her.*)

JEAN: At your service, *mademoiselle.*

MISS JULIE: Thank you. What about you?

JEAN: I'm not much of a beer-drinker, thank you, but if it's your wish — 85

MISS JULIE: My wish! I should think a gentleman would want to keep his lady company.

JEAN: A point well taken! (*He opens another bottle and takes a glass.*)

MISS JULIE: Now drink a toast to me! 90

(JEAN *hesitates.*)

You're not shy, are you? A big, strong man like you?

(*Playfully,* JEAN *kneels and raises his glass in mock gallantry.*)

JEAN: To my lady's health!

MISS JULIE: Bravo! Now you have to kiss my shoe, too. Then you will have hit it off perfectly.

(JEAN *hesitates, then boldly grasps her foot and touches it lightly with his lips.*)

Superb! You should have been an actor. 95

JEAN: (*rising*) This has got to stop, Miss Julie! Someone might come in and see us.

MISS JULIE: So what?

JEAN: People would talk, that's what! If you knew how their tongues were wagging out there just a few minutes ago! 100

MISS JULIE: What did they say? Tell me. Sit down and tell me.

JEAN: I don't want to hurt your feelings. . . . They used expressions that—that hinted at certain—you know what I mean. You're not a child. And when they see a woman drinking, alone with a man—and a servant at that—in the middle of the night—well . . .

MISS JULIE: Well what?! Besides, we're not alone. Christine is here.

JEAN: Sleeping!

MISS JULIE: I'll wake her up. (She goes over to CHRISTINE.) Christine! Are you asleep? (CHRISTINE babbles in her sleep.) Christine! —My, how sound she sleeps!

CHRISTINE: (talking in her sleep) Count's boots are brushed . . . put on the coffee . . . right away, right away, right . . . mm— mm . . . poofff . . .

(MISS JULIE shakes CHRISTINE.)

MISS JULIE: Wake up, will you!

JEAN: (sternly) Let her alone! Let her sleep!

MISS JULIE: (sharply) What?

JEAN: She's been standing over the stove all day. She's worn out when night comes. Anyone asleep is entitled to some consideration.

MISS JULIE: (changing her tone) That's a very kind thought. It does you credit, Jean. You're right, of course. (She offers JEAN her hand.) Now come on out and pick some lilacs for me.

(During the following, CHRISTINE wakes up and, drunk with sleep, shuffles off to the right to go to bed. A polka can be heard in the distance.)

JEAN: With you, Miss Julie?

MISS JULIE: Yes, with me.

JEAN: That's no good. Absolutely not.

MISS JULIE: I don't know what you're thinking. Aren't you letting your imagination run away with you?

JEAN: No. Other people are.

MISS JULIE: How? Imagining that I'm—verliebt with a servant?

JEAN: I'm not conceited, but it's been known to happen. And to these people nothing's sacred.

MISS JULIE: "These people!" Why, I do believe you're an aristocrat!

JEAN: Yes, I am.

MISS JULIE: I'm climbing down—

JEAN: Don't climb down, Miss Julie! Take my advice. No one will believe that you climbed down deliberately. They'll say you fell.

MISS JULIE: I have a higher opinion of these people than you do. Let's see who's right! Come on! (She gives him a long, steady look.)

JEAN: You know, you're very strange.

MISS JULIE: Perhaps. But then so are you. . . . Besides, everything is strange. Life, people, everything. It's all scum, drifting and drifting on the water until it sinks—drowns. There's a dream I have every now and then. It's coming back to me now. I'm sitting on top of a pillar. I've climbed up it somehow and I don't know how to get back down. When I look down I get dizzy. I have to get down but I don't have the courage to jump. I can't hold on much longer and I want to fall; but I don't fall. I know I won't have any peace until I get down; no rest until I get down, down on the ground. And if I ever got down on the ground, I'd want to go farther down, right down into the earth. . . . Have you ever felt anything like that?

JEAN: Never! I used to dream that I'm lying under a tall tree in a dark woods. I want to get up, up to the very top, to look out over the bright landscape with the sun shining on it, to rob the bird's nest up there with the golden eggs in it. And I climb and I climb, but the trunk is so thick, and so smooth, and it's such a long way to that first branch. But I know that if I could just reach that first branch, I'd go right to the top as if on a ladder. I've never reached it yet, but someday I will—even if only in my dreams.

MISS JULIE: Here I am talking about dreams with you. Come out with me. Only into the park a way. (She offers him her arm, and they start to go.)

JEAN: Let's sleep on nine midsummer flowers, Miss Julie, and then our dreams will come true!

(MISS JULIE and JEAN suddenly turn around in the doorway. JEAN is holding his hand over one eye.)

MISS JULIE: You've caught something in your eye. Let me see.

JEAN: It's nothing. Just a bit of dust. It'll go away.

MISS JULIE: The sleeve of my dress must have grazed your eye. Sit down and I'll help you. (She takes him by the arm and sits him down. She takes his head and leans it back. With the corner of her handkerchief she tries to get out the bit of dust.) Now sit still, absolutely still. (She slaps his hand.) Do as you're told. Why, I believe you're trembling—a big, strong man like you. (She feels his biceps.) With such big arms!

JEAN: (warningly) Miss Julie!

MISS JULIE: Yes, Monsieur Jean?

JEAN: Attention! Je ne suis qu'un homme!

MISS JULIE: Sit still, I tell you! . . . There now! It's out. Kiss my hand and thank me!

JEAN: (rising to his feet) Listen to me, Miss Julie—Christine has gone to bed! —Listen to me, I tell you!

MISS JULIE: Kiss my hand first!

JEAN: Listen to me!

MISS JULIE: Kiss my hand first!

JEAN: All right. But you'll have no one to blame but yourself.

MISS JULIE: For what?

JEAN: For what! Are you twenty-five years old and still a child? Don't you know it's dangerous to play with fire?

MISS JULIE: Not for me, I'm insured!

JEAN: (boldly) Oh, no, you're not! And even if you are, there's inflammable stuff next door.

MISS JULIE: Meaning you?

JEAN: Yes. Not just because it's me, but because I'm young and—

MISS JULIE: And irresistibly handsome? What incredible conceit! A Don Juan, maybe! Or a Joseph! Yes, bless my soul, that's it: you're a Joseph!

JEAN: You think so?!

MISS JULIE: I'm almost afraid so!

(JEAN boldly steps up to her, grabs her around the waist, tries to kiss her. She slaps his face.)

None of that!

169 **midsummer flowers** a girl would pick in silence on Midsummer Eve nine different sorts of flowers, make a bouquet of them, and place them under her pillow. The man who appeared in her dreams would be the man she would marry.

205 JEAN: More games? Or are you serious?

MISS JULIE: I'm serious.

JEAN: Then you must have been serious a moment ago, too! You take your games too seriously; that's dangerous. Well, I'm tired of your games, and if you'll excuse me, I'll return to my
210 work. *(Takes up the boots and starts to brush them.)* The count will be wanting his boots on time, and it's long past midnight.

MISS JULIE: Put those boots down.

JEAN: No! This is my job. It's what I'm here for. I never under-
215 took to be your playmate. That's something I could never be. I consider myself too good for that.

MISS JULIE: You are proud.

JEAN: In some ways. Not in others.

MISS JULIE: Have you ever been in love?

220 JEAN: We don't use that word around here. But I've hankered after some girls, if that's what you mean. . . . I even got sick once because I couldn't have the one I wanted—really sick, like the princes in the Arabian Nights—who couldn't eat or drink for love.

225 MISS JULIE: Who was she?

(JEAN does not reply.)

Who was the girl?

JEAN: You can't get that out of me.

MISS JULIE: Even if I ask you as an equal—ask you—as a friend? . . . Who was she?

230 JEAN: You.

MISS JULIE: *(sitting down)* How—amusing . . .

JEAN: Yes, maybe so. Ridiculous. . . . That's why I didn't want to tell you about it before. Want to hear the whole story? . . . Have you any idea what you and your people look like from
235 down below? Of course not. Like hawks or eagles, that's what: you hardly ever see their backs because they're always soaring so high up. I lived with seven brothers and sisters—and a pig—out on the wasteland where there wasn't even a tree growing. But from my window I could see the wall of the count's gar-
240 den with the apple trees sticking up over it. That was the Garden of Eden for me, and there were many angry angels with flaming swords standing guard over it. But in spite of them, I and the other boys found a way to the Tree of Life. . . . How contemptible, that's what you're thinking.

245 MISS JULIE: For stealing apples? All boys do that.

JEAN: That's what you say now. All the same, you think me contemptible. Never mind. One day I went with my mother into this paradise to weed the onion beds. Next to the vegetable garden stood a Turkish pavilion, shaded by jasmine and hung
250 all over with honeysuckle. I couldn't imagine what it was used for; I only knew I had never seen such a beautiful building. People went in, and came out again. And then one day the door was left open. I sneaked in. The walls were covered with portraits of kings and emperors, and the windows had red
255 curtains with tassels on them. —Recognize it? Yes, the count's private privy. . . . I—*(He breaks off a lilac and holds it under MISS JULIE's nose.)* I had never been inside a castle, never seen anything besides the church. This was more beautiful. And no matter what I tried to think about, my thoughts
260 always came back—to that little pavilion. And little by little there arose in me a desire to experience just for once the whole pleasure of—. *Enfin*, I sneaked in, looked about, and

marveled. And just then I heard someone coming! There was only one way out—for the upper-class people. But for me there was one more—a lower one. And I had no other choice
265 but to take it. *(MISS JULIE, who has taken the lilac from JEAN, lets it fall to the table.)* Then I began to run like mad, plunging through the raspberry bushes, ploughing through the strawberry patches, and came up on the rose terrace. And there I caught sight of a pink dress and a pair of white stock-
270 ings. You! I crawled under—well, you can imagine what it was like—under thistles that pricked me and wet dirt that stank to high heaven. And all the while I could see you walking among the roses. I said to myself, "If it's true that a thief can enter heaven and be with the angels, isn't it strange that a
275 poor man's child here on God's green earth can't enter the count's park and play with the count's daughter."

MISS JULIE: *(sentimentally)* Do you think all poor children have felt that way?

JEAN: *(hesitatingly at first, then with mounting conviction)* If all
280 poor ch—? Yes—yes, naturally. Of course!

MISS JULIE: It must be terrible to be poor.

JEAN: *(with exaggerated intensity)* Oh, Miss Julie! You don't know! A dog can lie on the sofa with its mistress; a horse can have its nose stroked by the hand of a countess; but a ser-
285 vant—! *(Changing his tone.)* Of course, now and then you meet somebody with guts enough to work his way up in the world, but how often?—Anyway, you know what I did afterward? I threw myself into the millstream with all my clothes on. Got fished out and spanked. But the following Sunday,
290 when Pa and everybody else in the house went to visit Grandma, I arranged things so I'd be left behind. Then I washed myself all over with soap and warm water, put on my best clothes, and went off to church—just to see you there once more. I saw you, and then I went home determined to
295 die. But I wanted to die beautifully and comfortably, without pain. I remembered some stories I had heard about how fatal it was to sleep under an elderberry bush. And we had a big one that had just blossomed out. I stripped it of every leaf and blossom it had and made a bed of them in a bin of oats. Have
300 you ever noticed how smooth oats are? As smooth to the touch as human skin. . . . So I pulled the lid of the bin shut and closed my eyes. Fell asleep. And when they woke me I was really very sick. However, I didn't die, as you can see. —What was I trying to prove? I don't know. There was no hope
305 of winning you. It was just that you were a symbol of the absolute hopelessness of my ever getting out of the class I was born in.

MISS JULIE: You know, you have a real gift for telling stories. Did you go to school?
310

JEAN: A little. But I've read a lot of novels and gone to the theater. And I've also listened to educated people talk. That way I learned the most.

MISS JULIE: You mean to tell me you stand around listening to what we're saying!
315

JEAN: Certainly! And I've heard an awful lot, I can tell you—sitting on the coachman's seat or rowing the boat. One time I heard you and a girlfriend talking—

MISS JULIE: Really? . . . And just what did you hear?

JEAN: Well, now, I don't know if I can repeat it. I can tell you I
320 was a little amazed. I couldn't imagine where you had learned such words. Maybe at bottom there isn't such a big difference as you might think, between people and people.

MISS JULIE: How vulgar! At least people in my class don't be-
325   have like you when we're engaged.

JEAN: *(looking her in the eye)* Are you sure? —Come on now, it's
no use playing the innocent with me.

MISS JULIE: He was a beast. The man I offered my love was a
beast.

330 JEAN: That's what you all say—afterward.

MISS JULIE: All?

JEAN: I'd say so. I've heard the same expression used several
times before in similar circumstances.

MISS JULIE: What kind of circumstances?

335 JEAN: The kind we're talking about. I remember the last time I—

MISS JULIE: *(rising)* That's enough! I don't want to hear any more.

JEAN: How strange! Neither did she! . . . Well, now if you'll
excuse me, I'll go to bed.

MISS JULIE: *(softly)* Go to bed on Midsummer Eve?

340 JEAN: That's right. Dancing with that crowd up there really
doesn't amuse me.

MISS JULIE: Jean, get the key to the boathouse and row me out
on the lake. I want to see the sun come up.

JEAN: Do you think that's wise?

345 MISS JULIE: You sound as if you were worried about your
reputation.

JEAN: Why not? I don't particularly care to be made ridiculous,
or to be kicked out without a recommendation just when I'm
trying to establish myself. Besides, I have a certain obligation
350   to Christine.

MISS JULIE: Oh, I see. It's Christine now.

JEAN: Yes, but I'm thinking of you, too. Take my advise, Miss
Julie. Go up to your room.

MISS JULIE: When did you start giving me orders?

355 JEAN: Just this once. For your own sake! Please! It's very late.
You're so tired, you're drunk; you don't know what you're
doing. Go to bed, Miss Julie. —Besides, if my ears aren't
deceiving me, they're coming this way, looking for me. If they
find us here together, you're done for!

360 THE CHORUS: *(is heard coming nearer, singing)*

        Said Jill to Jack, "Soil needs a tilling."
        Tri-di-ri-di-ralla, tri-di-ri-di-ra.
        Said Jack to Jill, "Time's a-spilling."
        Tri-di-ri-di-ralla-la.
365   Said Jill to Jack, "Gold's a-hoarding."
        Tri-di-ri-di-ralla, tri-di-ri-di-ra.
        Said Jack to Jill, "Tell not my lording."
        Tri-di-ri-di-ralla-la.
        Said Jill to Jack, "Hair is for plaiting."
370   Tri-di-ri-di-ralla, tri-di-ri-di-ra.
        "But Jill for Jack is not waiting."
        Tri-di-ri-di-ralla-la!

MISS JULIE: I know these people. I love them just as they love
me. Let them come. You'll see.

360 **chorus** the Swedish original of this song follows l. 380.

JEAN: Oh, no, Miss Julie, they don't love you! They take the 375
food you give them, but they spit on it as soon as your back is
turned. Believe me! Just listen to them. Listen to what they're
singing. —No, you'd better not listen.

MISS JULIE: *(listening)* What are they singing?

JEAN: A nasty song—about you and me! 380

BANDFOLKETS DANSVISA

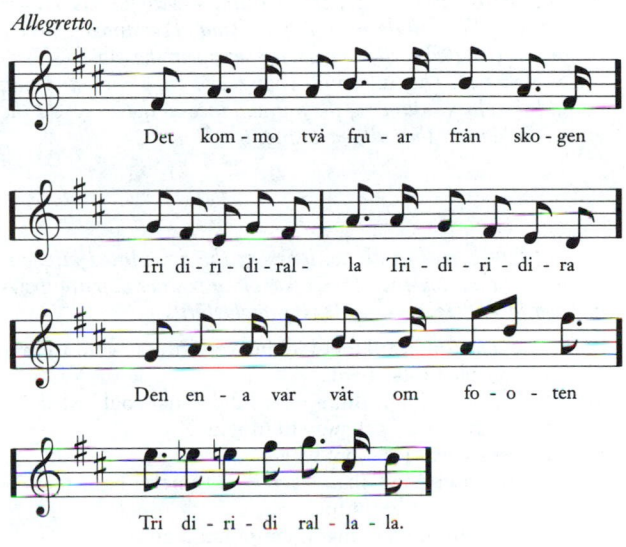

Allegretto.

Det kom-mo två fru-ar från sko-gen

Tri di-ri-di-ral- la Tri-di-ri-di-ra

Den en-a var våt om fo-o-ten

Tri di-ri-di ral-la-la.

De talte om hundra riksdaler
  Tri (etc.)

Men ägde knappast en daler
  Tri (etc.)

Och kransen jag dig skänker
  Tri (etc.)

En annan jag påtänker
  Tri (etc.)

MISS JULIE: How disgusting! Oh, what cowardly, sneaking—

JEAN: That's what the mob always is—cowards! You can't fight
them; you can only run away.

MISS JULIE: Run away? Where? There's no way out of here. And
we can't go in to Christine. 385

JEAN: What about my room? What do you say? Rules don't
count in a situation like this. You can trust me. —You said,
let's be friends. Remember? Well, I'm your friend—your
true, devoted, respectful friend.

MISS JULIE: But suppose—suppose they looked for you there? 390

JEAN: I'll bolt the door. If they try to break it down, I'll shoot.
Come, Miss Julie! *(On his knees.)* Please, Miss Julie!

The melody of the peasants' song was not printed in the first Swedish edition, but it did appear in Charles de
Casanove's French translation of the play in 1893.

MISS JULIE: *(meaningfully)* You promise me that you won't—
JEAN: I swear to you!

(MISS JULIE goes out quickly to the right. JEAN follows her impetuously.)

* * *

THE BALLET

The country people enter in festive costumes, with flowers in their hats. The fiddler is in the lead. A keg of small beer and a little keg of liquor, decorated with greenery, are set up on the table. Glasses are brought out. They all drink. Then they form a circle and sing "Said Jill to Jack," dancing the round dance as they sing. At the end of the dance, they all leave singing.

* * *

(MISS JULIE comes in alone; looks at the devastated kitchen; clasps her hands together; then takes out a powder puff and powders her face. JEAN enters. He is in high spirits.)

JEAN: You see! You heard them, didn't you? You've got to admit it's impossible to stay here.
MISS JULIE: No, I don't. But even if I did, what could we do?
JEAN: Go away, travel, get away from here!
5   MISS JULIE: Travel? Yes—but where?
JEAN: Switzerland, the Italian lakes. You've never been there?
MISS JULIE: No. Is it beautiful?
JEAN: Eternal summer, oranges, laurel trees, ah . . . !
MISS JULIE: What do we do when we get there?
10   JEAN: I'll set up a hotel—a first-class hotel with a first-class clientele.
MISS JULIE: Hotel?
JEAN: I tell you that's the life! Always new faces, new languages. Not a minute to think about yourself or worry about your
15   nerves. No looking for something to do. The work keeps you busy. Day and night the bells ring, the trains whistle, the buses come and go. And all the while the money comes rolling in. I tell you it's the life!
MISS JULIE: Yes, that's the life. But what about me?
20   JEAN: The mistress of the whole place, the star of the establishment! With your looks—and your personality—it can't fail. It's perfect! You'll sit in the office like a queen, setting your slaves in motion by pressing an electric button. The guests will file before your throne and timidly lay their treasures on
25   your table. You can't imagine how people tremble when you shove a bill in their face! I'll salt the bills and you'll sugar them with your prettiest smile. Come on, let's get away from here— *(He takes a timetable from his pocket.)* —right away— the next train! We'll be in Malmö at six-thirty, Hamburg
30   eight-forty in the morning; Frankfurt to Basle in one day, and to Como by way of the Gotthard tunnel in—let me see— three days! Three days!
MISS JULIE: You make it sound so wonderful. But, Jean, you have to give me strength. Tell me you love me. Come and put
35   your arms around me.
JEAN: *(hesitates)* I want to . . . but I don't dare. Not anymore, not in this house. I do love you—without a shadow of a doubt. How can you doubt that, Miss Julie?

MISS JULIE: *(shyly, very becomingly)* You don't have to be formal with me, Jean. You can call me Julie. There aren't any bar-   40
riers between us now. Call me Julie.
JEAN: *(agonized)* I can't! There are still barriers between us, Miss Julie, as long as we stay in this house! There's the past, there's the count. I've never met anyone I feel so much respect for. I've only got to see his gloves lying on a table and I shrivel up.   45
I only have to hear that bell ring and I shy like a frightened horse. I only have to look at his boots standing there so stiff and proud and I feel my spine bending. *(He kicks the boots.)* Superstitions, prejudices that they've drilled into us since we were children! But they can be forgotten just as easily! Just we   50
get to another country where they have a republic! They'll crawl on their hands and knees when they see my uniform. On their hands and knees, I tell you! But not me! Oh, no. I'm not made for crawling. I've got guts, backbone. And once I grab that first branch, you just watch me climb. I may be a   55
valet now, but next year I'll be owning property; in ten years, I'll be living off my investments. Then I'll go to Rumania, get myself some decorations, and maybe—notice I only say maybe—end up as a count!
MISS JULIE: How wonderful, wonderful.   60
JEAN: Listen, in Rumania you can buy titles. You'll be a count- ess after all. My countess.
MISS JULIE: But I'm not interested in that. I'm leaving all that behind. Tell me you love me, Jean, or else—or else what difference does it make what I am?   65
JEAN: I'll tell you a thousand times—but later! Not now. And not here. Above all, let's keep our feelings out of this or we'll make a mess of everything. We have to look at this thing calmly and coolly, like sensible people. *(He takes out a cigar, clips the end, and lights it.)* Now you sit there and I'll sit here,   70
and we'll talk as if nothing had happened.
MISS JULIE: *(in anguish)* My God, what are you? Don't you have any feelings?
JEAN: Feelings? Nobody's got more feelings than I have. But I've learned to control them.   75
MISS JULIE: A few minutes ago you were kissing my shoe—and now—!
JEAN: *(harshly)* That was a few minutes ago. We've got other things to think about now!
MISS JULIE: Don't speak to me like that, Jean!   80
JEAN: I'm just trying to be sensible. We've been stupid once; let's not be stupid again. Your father might be back at any mo- ment, and we've got to decide our future before then. —Now what do you think about my plans? Do you approve or don't you?   85
MISS JULIE: I don't see anything wrong with them. Except one thing. For a big undertaking like that, you'd need a lot of capital. Have you got it?
JEAN: *(chewing on his cigar)* Have I got it? Of course I have. I've got my knowledge of the business, my vast experience, my   90
familiarity with languages. That's capital that counts for something, let me tell you.
MISS JULIE: You can't even buy the railway tickets with it.
JEAN: That's true. That's why I need a backer—someone to put up the money.   95
MISS JULIE: Where can you find him on a moment's notice?
JEAN: You'll find him—if you want to be my partner.
MISS JULIE: I can't. And I don't have a penny to my name.

(Pause.)

JEAN: Then you can forget the whole thing.

100 MISS JULIE: Forget—?

JEAN: And things will stay just the way they are.

MISS JULIE: Do you think I'm going to live under the same roof with you as your mistress? Do you think I'm going to have people sneering at me behind my back? How do you think I'll
105 ever be able to look my father in the face after this? No, no! Take me away from here, Jean—the shame, the humiliation. . . . What have I done? Oh, my God, my God! What have I done! *(She bursts into tears.)*

JEAN: Now don't start singing that tune. It won't work. What
110 have you done that's so awful? You're not the first.

MISS JULIE: *(crying hysterically)* Now you think me contemptible—I'm falling, falling!

JEAN: Fall down to me, and I'll lift you up again!

MISS JULIE: What awful hold did you have over me? What drove
115 me to you? The weak to the strong? The falling to the rising! Or maybe it was love? Love? This? You don't know what love is!

JEAN: Want to bet? Did you think I was a virgin?

MISS JULIE: You're coarse—vulgar! The things you say, the things you think!

120 JEAN: That's the way I was brought up. It's the way I am! Now don't get hysterical. And don't play the fine lady with me. We're eating off the same platter now. . . . That's better. Come over here and be a good girl and I'll treat you to something special. *(He opens the table drawer and takes out the
125 wine bottle. He pours the wine into two used glasses.)*

MISS JULIE: Where did you get that wine?

JEAN: From the wine cellar.

MISS JULIE: My father's burgundy!

JEAN: Should be good enough for his son-in-law.

130 MISS JULIE: I was drinking beer and you—!

JEAN: Shows I have better taste than you.

MISS JULIE: Thief!

JEAN: You going to squeal on me?

MISS JULIE: Oh, God! Partner in crime with a petty house thief!
135 I must have been drunk; I must have been walking in my sleep. Midsummer Night! Night of innocent games—

JEAN: Yes, very innocent!

MISS JULIE: *(pacing up and down)* Is there anyone here on earth as miserable as I am?

140 JEAN: Why be miserable? Look at the conquest you've made! Think of poor Christine in there. Don't you think she's got any feelings?

MISS JULIE: I thought so a while ago; I don't now. A servant's a servant—

145 JEAN: And a whore's a whore!

MISS JULIE: *(falls to her knees and clasps her hands together)* Oh, God in heaven, put an end to my worthless life! Lift me out of this awful filth I'm sinking in! Save me! Save me!

JEAN: I feel sorry for you, I have to admit it. When I was lying in
150 the onion beds, looking up at you on the rose terrace, I—I'm telling you the truth now—I had the same dirty thoughts that all boys have.

MISS JULIE: And you said you wanted to die for me!

JEAN: In the oat bin? That was only a story.

155 MISS JULIE: A lie, you mean.

JEAN: *(getting sleepy)* Practically. I think I read it in a paper about a chimney sweep who curled up in a wood-bin with some lilacs because they were going to arrest him for nonsupport of his child.

160 MISS JULIE: Now I see you as you really are.

JEAN: What did you expect me to do? It's always the fancy talk that gets the women.

MISS JULIE: You dog!

JEAN: You bitch!

165 MISS JULIE: Well, now you've seen the eagle's back—

JEAN: Wasn't exactly its back—!

MISS JULIE: I was going to be the window dressing for your hotel—!

JEAN: And I the hotel—!

170 MISS JULIE: Sitting at the desk, attracting your customers, padding your bills—!

JEAN: I could manage that myself—!

MISS JULIE: How can a human soul be so dirty and filthy?

JEAN: Then why don't you clean it up?

175 MISS JULIE: You lackey! You shoeshine boy! Stand up when I talk to you!

JEAN: You lackey lover! You bootblack's tramp! Shut your mouth and get out of here! Who do you think you are telling me I'm coarse? I've never seen anybody in my class behave as crudely
180 as you did tonight. Have you ever seen any of the girls around here grab at a man like you did? Do you think any of the girls of my class would throw themselves at a man like that? I've never seen the like of it except in animals and prostitutes!

MISS JULIE: *(crushed)* That's right! Hit me! Walk all over me! It's
185 all I deserve. I'm rotten. But help me! Help me to get out of this—if there is any way out for me!

JEAN: *(less harsh)* I'd be doing myself an injustice if I didn't admit that part of the credit for this seduction belongs to me. But do you think a person in my position would have dared to look
190 twice at you if you hadn't asked for it? I'm still amazed—

MISS JULIE: And still proud.

JEAN: Why not? But I've got to confess the victory was a little too easy to give me any real thrill.

MISS JULIE: Go on, hit me again!

195 JEAN: *(standing up)* No. . . . I'm sorry I said that. I never hit a person who's down, especially a woman. I can't deny that, in one way, it was good to find out that what I saw glittering up above was only fool's gold, to see that the eagle's back was as gray as its belly, that the smooth cheek was just powder, and
200 that there could be dirt under the manicured nails, that the handkerchief was soiled even though it smelled of perfume. But, in another way, it hurts to find that everything I was striving for wasn't very high above me after all, wasn't even real. It hurts me to see you sink far lower than your own cook.
205 Hurts, like seeing the last flowers cut to pieces by the autumn rains and turned to muck.

MISS JULIE: You talk as if you already stood high above me.

JEAN: Well, don't I? Don't forget I could make you a countess but you can never make me a count.

210 MISS JULIE: I have a father for a count. You can never have that!

JEAN: True. But I might father my own counts—that is, if—

MISS JULIE: You're a thief! I'm not!

JEAN: There are worse things than being a thief. A lot worse. And besides, when I take a position in a house, I consider
215 myself a member of the family—in a way, like a child in the house. It's no crime for a child to steal a few ripe cherries

when they're falling off the trees, is it? *(He begins to feel passionate again.)* Miss Julie, you're a beautiful woman, much too good for the likes of me. You got carried away by your emotions and now you want to cover up your mistake by telling yourself that you love me. You don't love me. Maybe you were attracted by my looks — in which case your kind of love is no better than mine. But I could never be satisfied to be just an animal for you, and I could never make you love me.

MISS JULIE: How do you know that for sure?

JEAN: You mean there's a chance? I could love you, there's no doubt about that. You're beautiful, you're refined — *(He goes up to her and takes her hand.)* — educated, lovable when you want to be, and once you set a man's heart on fire, I'll bet it burns forever. *(He puts his arm around her waist.)* You're like hot wine with strong spices. One of your kisses is enough to —

(He attempts to lead her out, but she rather reluctantly breaks away from him.)

MISS JULIE: Let me go. You don't get me that way.

JEAN: Then how? Not by petting you and not with pretty words, not by planning for the future, not by saving you from humiliation! Then how, tell me how?

MISS JULIE: How? How? I don't know how! I don't know at all! — I hate you like I hate rats, but I can't get away from you.

JEAN: Then come away with me!

MISS JULIE: *(pulling herself together)* Away? Yes, we'll go away! — But I'm so tired. Pour me a glass of wine, will you?

(JEAN pours the wine, MISS JULIE *looks at her watch.)*

Let's talk first. We still have a little time. *(She empties the glass of wine and holds it out for more.)*

JEAN: Don't overdo it. You'll get drunk.

MISS JULIE: What difference does it make?

JEAN: What difference? It looks cheap. — What did you want to say to me?

MISS JULIE: We're going to run away together, right? But we'll talk first — that is, I'll talk. So far you've done all the talking. You've told me your life, now I'll tell you mine. That way we'll know each other through and through before we become . . . traveling companions.

JEAN: Wait a minute. Are you sure you won't regret this afterward — surrendering your secrets to me?

MISS JULIE: I thought you were my friend.

JEAN: I am — sometimes. Just don't count on it.

MISS JULIE: You don't mean that. Anyway, everybody knows my secrets. — My mother's parents were very ordinary people, just commoners. She was brought up, according to the theories of her time, to believe in equality, the independence of women, and all that. And she had a strong aversion to marriage. When my father proposed to her, she swore she would never become his wife but that she might possibly consent to become his mistress. So he told her he didn't want to see the woman he loved enjoy less respect than he did. But she said she didn't care what the world thought — and he, believing that he couldn't live without her, accepted her conditions. That did it. From then on he was cut off from his old circle of friends and left without anything to do in the house, which couldn't have kept him occupied anyway. Then I came into the world — against my mother's wishes, as far as I can make

out. My mother decided to bring me up as a nature child. And on top of that I had to learn everything a boy learns, so I could be living proof that women were just as good as men. I had to wear boy's clothes, learn to handle horses — but not to milk the cows! Girls did that! I was made to groom the horses and harness them, and learn farming and go hunting — I even had to learn how to slaughter the animals. It was disgusting. Awful! And on the estate all the men were set to doing women's chores, and the women to doing men's work — with the result that the whole place fell to pieces, and we became the local laughing-stock. Finally, my father must have come out of his trance. He rebelled, and everything was changed according to his wishes. They got married — very quietly. Then my mother got sick. I don't know what kind of sickness it was, but she often had convulsions, and she would hide herself in the attic or in the garden, and sometimes she would stay out all night. Then there occurred that big fire you've heard about. The house, the stables, the cowsheds, all burned down — and under very peculiar circumstances that led one to suspect arson. You see, the accident occurred the day after the insurance expired, and the premiums on the new policy, which my father had sent in, were delayed through the messenger's carelessness, and didn't arrive in time.

(She refills her glass and drinks.)

JEAN: You've had enough.

MISS JULIE: Who cares! — We were left without a penny to our name. We had to sleep in the carriages. My father didn't know where to turn for money to rebuild the house. Then Mother suggested to him that he might try to borrow money from an old friend of hers, who owned a brick factory not far from here. Father took out a loan, but there wasn't any interest charged, which surprised him. So the place was rebuilt. *(She drinks some more.)* Do you know who set fire to the place?

JEAN: Your honorable mother!

MISS JULIE: Do you know who the brick manufacturer was?

JEAN: Your mother's lover?

MISS JULIE: Do you know whose money it was?

JEAN: Let me think a minute. . . . No, I give up.

MISS JULIE: It was my mother's!

JEAN: The count's, you mean. Or was there a marriage settlement?

MISS JULIE: There wasn't a settlement. My mother had a little money of her own which she didn't want under my father's control, so she invested it with her — friend.

JEAN: Who pinched it!

MISS JULIE: Right! He kept it for himself. Well, my father found out what happened. But he couldn't go to court, couldn't pay his wife's lover, couldn't prove that it was his wife's money. That was how my mother got her revenge because he had taken control of the house. He was on the verge of shooting himself. There was even a rumor that he tried and failed. But somehow he took a new lease on life and he forced my mother to pay for her mistakes. Can you imagine what those five years were like for me? I loved my father, but I took my mother's side because I didn't know the whole story. She had taught me to hate all men — I'm sure you've heard how she hated men — and I swore to her that I'd never be slave to any man.

JEAN: You got engaged to the attorney, didn't you?

MISS JULIE: Only to make him my slave.

JEAN: I guess he didn't go for that, did he?

MISS JULIE: Oh, he wanted to well enough. I didn't give him the
330   chance. I got bored with him.

JEAN: Yes, so I noticed — in the stable yard.

MISS JULIE: What did you notice?

JEAN: I saw how he —. [Still see it on your cheek.

MISS JULIE: What!

335 JEAN: The stripe on your cheek.] He broke it off.

MISS JULIE: It's a lie! I broke it off! Did he tell you that? He's
   beneath contempt!

JEAN: Come on now, as bad as that? So you hate men, hm?

MISS JULIE: Yes, I do. . . . Most of the time. But sometimes,
340   when I can't help myself — oh . . . *(She shudders in disgust.)*

JEAN: Then you hate me, too?

MISS JULIE: You have no idea how much! I'd like to see you
   killed like an animal —

JEAN: Like when you're caught having sex with an animal: you
345   get two years at hard labor and the animal is killed. Right?

MISS JULIE: Right.

JEAN: But there's no one to catch us — and *no animal!* — So what
   are we going to do?

MISS JULIE: Go away from here.

350 JEAN: To torture ourselves to death?

MISS JULIE: No. To enjoy ourselves for a day or two, or a week,
   for as long as can — and then — to die —

JEAN: Die? That's stupid! I've got a better idea: start a hotel!

MISS JULIE: *(continuing without hearing* JEAN*)* — on the shores
355   of Lake Como, where the sun is always shining, where the
   laurels bloom at Christmas, and the golden oranges glow on
   the trees.

JEAN: Lake Como is a stinking wet hole, and the only oranges I
   saw there were on the fruit stands. But it's a good tourist spot
360   with a lot of villas and cottages that are rented out to lovers.
   Now there's a profitable business. You know why? They rent
   the villa for the whole season, but they leave after three weeks.

MISS JULIE: *(naively)* Why after only three weeks?

JEAN: Because that's about as long as they can stand each other.
365   Why else? But they still have to pay the rent. You see? Then
   you rent it out again to another couple, and so on. There's no
   shortage of love — even if it doesn't last very long.

MISS JULIE: Then you don't want to die with me?

JEAN: I don't want to die at all! I enjoy life too much. And more-
370   over, I consider taking your own life a sin against the Providence that gave us life.

MISS JULIE: You believe in God? You?

JEAN: Yes, certainly I do! I go to church every other Sunday —.
   Honestly, I've had enough of this talk. I'm going to bed.

375 MISS JULIE: Really? You think you're going to get off that easy?
   Don't you know that a man owes something to the woman
   he's dishonored?

JEAN: *(takes out his purse and throws a silver coin on the table)*
   There you are. I don't want to owe anybody anything.

380 MISS JULIE: *(pretending not to notice)* Do you know what the
   law says —?

JEAN: Lucky for you the law says nothing about women who
   seduce men!

MISS JULIE: *(as before)* What else can we do but go away from
385   here, get married, and get divorced?

333–335 **Still . . . cheek** the passage in brackets was deleted in
Strindberg's manuscript, probably by Strindberg himself

JEAN: Suppose I refuse to enter into this *mésalliance?*

MISS JULIE: *Mésalliance?*

JEAN: For me! I've got better ancestors than you. I don't have a
   female arsonist in my family.

MISS JULIE: You can't prove that.   390

JEAN: You can't prove the opposite — because we don't have any
   family records — except in the police files. But I've read the
   whole history of your family in that peerage book in the drawing room. Do you know who the founder of your family line
   was? A miller — who let his wife sleep with the king one night   395
   during the Danish war. I don't have any ancestors like that. I
   don't have any ancestors at all! But I can become an ancestor
   myself.

MISS JULIE: This is what I get for baring my heart and soul to
   someone too low to understand, for sacrificing the honor of   400
   my family —

JEAN: Dishonor! — I warned you, remember? Drinking makes
   one talk, and talking's bad.

MISS JULIE: Oh, how sorry I am! . . . If only it had never happened! . . . If only you at least loved me!   405

JEAN: For the last time — what do you want me to do? Cry? Jump
   over your whip? Kiss you? Lure you to Lake Como for three
   weeks and then —? What am I supposed to do? What do you
   want? I've had more than I can take. This is what I get for
   involving myself with women. . . . Miss Julie, I can see that   410
   you're unhappy; I know that you're suffering; but I simply
   cannot understand you. My people don't behave like this. We
   don't hate each other. We make love for the fun of it, when we
   can get any time off from our work. But we don't have time for
   it all day and all night like you do. If you ask me, you're sick,   415
   Miss Julie. Your mother's mind was affected, you know.
   There are whole counties affected with pietism. That was
   your mother's trouble — pietism. It's spreading like the plague.

MISS JULIE: You can be understanding, Jean. You're talking to
   me like a human being now.   420

JEAN: Well, be human yourself. You spit on me, but you don't
   let me wipe it off — on you.

MISS JULIE: Help me, Jean. Help me. Tell me what I should do,
   that's all — which way to go.

JEAN: For Christ's sake, if only I knew myself!   425

MISS JULIE: I've been crazy — I've been out of my mind — but
   does that mean there's no way out for me?

JEAN: Stay here as if nothing had happened. Nobody knows
   anything.

MISS JULIE: Impossible! Everybody who works here knows.   430
   Christine knows.

JEAN: They don't know a thing. Anyhow they'd never believe it.

MISS JULIE: *(slowly, significantly)* But . . . it might happen again.

JEAN: That's true!

MISS JULIE: And one time there might be . . . consequences.   435

JEAN: *(stunned)* Consequences!! What on earth have I been
   thinking of? You're right. There's only one thing to do: get
   away from here! Immediately! I can't go with you — that
   would give the whole game away. You'll have to go by yourself. Somewhere — I don't care where!   440

MISS JULIE: By myself? Where? — Oh, no, Jean, I can't. I can't!

JEAN: You've got to! Before the count comes back. You know as
   well as I do what will happen if you stay here. After one
   mistake, you figure you might as well go on — the damage is
   already done. Then you get more and more careless until —   445

finally you're exposed. I tell you, you've got to get out of the country. Afterward you can write to the count and tell him everything—leaving me out, of course. He'd never figure it was me. He wouldn't even let himself think it was me.

450 MISS JULIE: I'll go—if you'll come with me!

JEAN: Lady, are you out of your mind? "Miss Julie elopes with her footman." The day after tomorrow it would be in all the papers. The count would never live it down.

MISS JULIE: I can't go away. I can't stay. Help me. I'm so tired, 455 so awfully tired. . . . Tell me what to do. Order me. Start me going. I can't think anymore, can't move anymore . . .

JEAN: Now do you realize how weak you all are? What gives you the right to go strutting around with your noses in the air as if you owned the world? All right, I'll give you your orders. Go 460 up and get dressed. Get some traveling money. And come back down here.

MISS JULIE: (almost in a whisper) Come up with me!

JEAN: To your room? . . . You're going crazy again! (He hesitates a moment.) No! No! Go! Right now! (He takes her hand and 465 leads her out.)

MISS JULIE: (as she is leaving) Don't be so harsh, Jean.

JEAN: Orders always sound harsh. You've never had to take them.

(JEAN, left alone, heaves a sigh of relief and sits down at the table. He takes out a notebook and a pencil and begins to calculate, counting aloud now and then. The pantomime continues until CHRISTINE enters, dressed for church, and carrying JEAN's white tie and shirtfront in her hand.)

CHRISTINE: Lord in Heaven, what a mess! What on earth have you been doing?

470 JEAN: It was Miss Julie. She dragged the whole crowd in here. You must have been sleeping awfully sound if you didn't hear anything.

CHRISTINE: I slept like a log.

JEAN: You already dressed for church?

475 CHRISTINE: Yes, indeed. Don't you remember you promised to go to communion with me today?

JEAN: Oh, yes. Of course, I remember. I see you've brought my things. All right. Come on, put it on me. (He sits down, and CHRISTINE starts to put the white tie and shirtfront on him. 480 Pause.)

JEAN: (yawning) What's the lesson for today?

CHRISTINE: The beheading of John the Baptist, what else? It's Midsummer. It's his feast day.

JEAN: My God, that will go on forever. —Hey, you're choking 485 me! . . . Oh, I'm so sleepy, so sleepy.

CHRISTINE: What were you doing up all night? You look green in the face.

JEAN: I've been sitting here talking with Miss Julie.

CHRISTINE: That girl! She doesn't know how to behave herself!

(Pause.)

490 JEAN: Tell me something, Christine . . .

CHRISTINE: Well, what?

JEAN: Isn't it strange when you think about it? Her, I mean.

CHRISTINE: What's so strange?

JEAN: Everything!

(Pause. CHRISTINE looks at the half-empty glasses on the table.)

CHRISTINE: Have you been drinking with her?   495

JEAN: Yes!

CHRISTINE: Shame on you! —Look me in the eyes! You haven't. . .?

JEAN: Yes!

CHRISTINE: Is it possible? Is it really possible?

JEAN: (thinking about it) Yes. It is.   500

CHRISTINE: Oh, how disgusting! I could never have believed anything like this would happen! No. No. This is too much!

JEAN: Don't tell me you're jealous of her?

CHRISTINE: No, not of her. If it had been Clara—or Sophie—I would have scratched your eyes out! But her—? That's differ- 505 ent. I don't know why. . . . But it's still disgusting!

JEAN: You're not mad at her?

CHRISTINE: No. Mad at you. You were mean and cruel to do a thing like that, very mean. The poor girl! . . . Let me tell you, I'm not going to stay in this house a moment longer, not 510 when I can't have any respect for my employers.

JEAN: Why do you want to respect them?

CHRISTINE: Don't try to be smart. You don't want to work for people who behave like pigs, do you? Well, do you? If you ask me, you'd be lowering yourself by doing that.   515

JEAN: Oh, I don't know. I think it's rather comforting to find out that they're not one damn bit better than we are.

CHRISTINE: Well, I don't. If they're not any better, there's no point in us trying to be like them. —And think of the count. Think of all the sorrows he's been through in his time. My 520 God! I won't stay in this house any longer. . . . Imagine! You, of all people! If it had been the attorney fellow; if it had been somebody respectable—

JEAN: Now just a minute—!

CHRISTINE: Oh, you're all right in your own way. But there's a 525 big difference between one class and another. You can't deny that. —No, this is something I can never get over. She was so proud, and so sarcastic about men, you'd never believe she'd go and throw herself at one. And at somebody like you! And she was going to have Diana shot because the poor thing ran 530 after the gatekeeper's mongrel! —Well, I tell you, I've had enough! I'm not going to stay here any longer. When my term's up, I'm leaving.

JEAN: Then what'll you do?

CHRISTINE: Well, since you brought it up, it's about time that 535 you got yourself a decent place, if we're going to get married.

JEAN: Why should I go looking for another place? I could never get a job like this if I'm married.

CHRISTINE: Well, I know that! But you could get a job as a por- ter, or maybe try to get a government job as a caretaker some- 540 where. A square deal and a square meal, that's what you get from the government—and a pension for the wife and children.

JEAN: (wryly) Fine, fine! But I'm not the kind of guy who thinks about dying for his wife and children this early in the game. Let me tell you, I've got slightly bigger plans than that.   545

CHRISTINE: Plans! Ha! What about your obligations? You'd bet- ter start giving them a little thought!

JEAN: Don't start nagging me about obligations! I know what I have to do without you telling me. (He hears a sound up- stairs.) Anyhow, we'll have plenty of chance to talk about this 550 later. You just go and get yourself ready, and we'll be off to church.

CHRISTINE: Who is that walking around up there?

JEAN: I don't know. Clara, I suppose. Who else?

555 CHRISTINE: (*starting to leave*) It can't be the count, can it? Could he have come back without anybody hearing him?

JEAN: (*frightened*) The count? No, it can't be. He would have rung.

CHRISTINE: (*leaving*) God help us! I've never heard the like of this.

(*The sun has now risen and strikes the tops of the trees in the park. As the scene progresses, the light shifts gradually until it is shining very obliquely through the windows.* JEAN *goes to the door and signals.* MISS JULIE *enters, dressed for travel, and carrying a small birdcage, covered with a towel. She sets the cage down on a chair.*)

560 MISS JULIE: I'm ready now.

JEAN: Shh! Christine's awake.

MISS JULIE: (*extremely tense and nervous during the following*) Did she suspect anything?

JEAN: She doesn't know a thing. — My God, what happened to

565 you?

MISS JULIE: What do you mean? Do I look so strange?

JEAN: You're white as a ghost, and you've — excuse me — you've got dirt on your face.

MISS JULIE: Let me wash it off. (*She goes over to the washbasin

570 and washes her face and hands.*) There! Do you have a towel? . . . Oh, look, the sun's coming up!

JEAN: That breaks the magic spell!

MISS JULIE: Yes, we were spellbound last night, weren't we? Midsummer madness . . . Jean, listen to me! Come with me.

575 I've got the money!

JEAN: (*suspiciously*) Enough?

MISS JULIE: Enough for a start. Come with me, Jean. I can't travel alone today. Midsummer Day on a stifling hot train, packed in with crowds of people, all staring at me — stopping

580 at every station when I want to be flying. I can't, Jean, I can't! . . . And everything will remind me of the past. Midsummer Day when I was a child and the church was decorated with leaves — birch leaves and lilacs . . . the table spread for dinner with friends and relatives . . . and after dinner, dancing in the

585 park, with flowers and games. Oh, no matter how far you travel, the memories tag right along in the baggage car . . . and the regrets and the remorse.

JEAN: All right, I'll go with you! But it's got to be now — before it's too late! This very instant!

590 MISS JULIE: Hurry and get dressed! (*She picks up the birdcage.*)

JEAN: No baggage! It would give us away.

MISS JULIE: Nothing. Only what we can take to our seats.

JEAN: (*as he gets his hat*) What in the devil have you got there? What is that?

595 MISS JULIE: It's only my canary. I can't leave it behind.

JEAN: A canary! My God, do you expect us to carry a birdcage around with us? You're crazy. Put that cage down!

MISS JULIE: It's the only thing I'm taking with me from my home — the only living thing who loves me since Diana was

600 unfaithful to me! Don't be cruel, Jean. Let me take it with me!

JEAN: I told you to put that cage down! — And don't talk so loud. Christine can hear us.

MISS JULIE: No, I won't leave it with a stranger. I won't. I'd rather have you kill it.

605 JEAN: Give it here, the little pest. I'll wring its neck.

MISS JULIE: Oh, don't hurt it. Don't —. No, I can't do it!

JEAN: Don't worry, I can. Give it here.

(MISS JULIE *takes the bird out of the cage and kisses it.*)

MISS JULIE: Oh, my little Serena, must you die and leave your mistress?

JEAN: You don't have to make a scene of it. It's a question of your

610 whole life and future. You're wasting time!

(JEAN *grabs the canary from her, carries it to the chopping block, and picks up a meat cleaver.* MISS JULIE *turns away.*)

You should have learned how to kill chickens instead of shooting revolvers — (*He brings the cleaver down.*) — then a drop of blood wouldn't make you faint.

615 MISS JULIE: (*screaming*) Kill me too! Kill me! You can kill an innocent creature without turning a hair — then kill me. Oh, how I hate you! I loathe you! There's blood between us. I curse the moment I first laid eyes on you! I curse the moment I was conceived in my mother's womb.

620 JEAN: What good does your cursing do? Let's get out of here!

MISS JULIE: (*approaches the chopping block, drawn to it against her will*) No, I don't want to go yet. I can't. — I have to see. — Shh! (*She listens but keeps her eyes fastened on the chopping block and cleaver.*) You don't think I can stand the sight of blood, do you? You think I'm so weak, don't you? Oh, how I'd

625 love to see your blood, your brains on that chopping block. I'd love to see the whole of your sex swimming in a sea of blood just like that. I could drink blood out of your skull. Use your chest as a foot bath, dip my toes in your guts! I could eat your heart roasted whole! — You think I'm weak! You think I loved

630 you because my womb hungered for your semen. You think I want to carry your brood under my heart and feed it with my blood? Bear your child and take your name? — Come to think of it, what is your name? I've never even heard your last name. I'll bet you don't have one. I'd be Mrs. Doorman or

635 Madame Garbageman. You dog with *my* name on your collar — you lackey with *my* initials on your buttons! Do you think I'm going to share you with my cook and fight over you with my maid?! Ohh! — You think I'm a coward who's going to run away! No, I'm going to stay — come hell or high water.

640 My father will come home — find his desk broken into — his money gone. He'll ring — on that bell — two rings for the valet. And then he'll send for the sheriff — and I'll tell him everything. Everything! Oh, what a relief it'll be to have it all over . . . over and done with . . . if only it will be over. . . .

645 He'll have a stroke and die . . . and there'll be an end to all of us. There'll be peace . . . and quiet . . . forever. . . . The coat of arms will be broken on his coffin; the count's line will be extinct — while the valet's breed will continue in an orphanage, win triumphs in the gutter, and end in jail!

650

(CHRISTINE *enters, dressed for church and with a hymn-book in her hand.* MISS JULIE *rushes over to her and throws herself into her arms as if seeking protection.*)

MISS JULIE: Help me, Christine! Protect me against this man!

CHRISTINE: (*cold and unmoved*) This is a fine way to behave on a holy day! (*She sees the chopping block.*) Just look at the mess

655 you've made there! How do you explain that? And what's all this shouting and screaming about?

MISS JULIE: Christine, you're a woman, you're my friend! I warn you, watch out for this — this monster!

JEAN: (feeling awkward) If you ladies are going to talk, you won't want me around. I think I'll go and shave. (He slips out to the
660 right.)

MISS JULIE: You've got to understand, Christine! You've got to listen to me!

CHRISTINE: No, I don't. I don't understand this kind of shenanigans at all. Where do you think you're going dressed like
665 that? And Jean with his hat on? — Well? — Well?

MISS JULIE: Listen to me, Christine! If you'll just listen to me, I'll tell you everything.

CHRISTINE: I don't want to know anything.

MISS JULIE: You've got to listen to me — !

670 CHRISTINE: What about? About your stupid behavior with Jean? I tell you that doesn't bother me at all, because it's none of my business. But if you have any silly idea about talking him into skipping out with you, I'll soon put a stop to that.

MISS JULIE: (extremely tense) Christine, please don't get upset.
675 Listen to me. I can't stay here, and Jean can't stay here. So you see, we have to go away.

CHRISTINE: Hm, hm, hm.

MISS JULIE: (suddenly brightening up) Wait! I've got an idea! Why couldn't all three of us go away together? — out of the coun-
680 try — to Switzerland — and start a hotel? I've got the money, you see. Jean and I would be responsible for the whole affair — and Christine, you could run the kitchen, I thought. Doesn't that sound wonderful! Say you'll come, Christine, then everything will be settled. Say you will! Please! (She
685 throws her arms around CHRISTINE and pats her.)

CHRISTINE: (remaining aloof and unmoved) Hm. Hm.

MISS JULIE: (presto tempo) You've never been traveling, Christine. You have to get out and see the world. You can't imagine how wonderful it is to travel by train — constantly new faces,
690 new countries. We'll go to Hamburg, and stop over to look at the zoo — it's famous, has everything — you'll love that. And we'll go to the theater and the opera. And then when we get to Munich, we'll go to the museums, Christine. They have Rubenses and Raphaels there — those great painters, you
695 know. Of course you've heard about Munich where King Ludwig lived — you know, the king who went mad. And then we can go and see his castles — they're just like the ones you read about in fairy tales. And from there it's just a short trip to Switzerland — with the Alps. Think of the Alps, Christine,
700 covered with snow in the middle of summer. And oranges grow there, and laurel trees that are green the whole year round —

(JEAN can be seen in the wings at the right, sharpening his straight razor on a strop held between his teeth and his left hand. He listens to MISS JULIE with a satisfied expression on his face, now and then nodding approvingly. MISS JULIE continues tempo prestissimo.)

— and that's where we'll get a hotel. I'll sit at the desk while Jean stands at the door and receives the guests, goes out shop-
705 ping, writes the letters. What a life that will be! The train whistle blowing, then the bus arriving, then a bell ringing

upstairs, then the bell in the restaurant rings — and I'll be making out the bills — and I know just how much to salt them — you can't imagine how timid tourists are when you shove a bill in their face! — And you, Christine, you'll run the
710 whole kitchen — there'll be not standing at the stove for you — of course not. If you're going to talk to the people, you'll have to dress. And with your looks — I'm not trying to flatter you, Christine — you'll run off with some man one fine day — a rich Englishman, that's who it'll be, they're so easy to —
715 (Slowing down) — to catch. — Then we'll all be rich. — We'll build a villa on Lake Como. — Maybe it does rain there sometimes, but — (More and more lifelessly.) — the sun has to shine sometimes, too — even if it looks cloudy. — And — then . . . or else we can always travel some more — and come back
720 . . . (Pause.) — here . . . or somewhere else . . .

CHRISTINE: Do you really believe a word of that yourself, Miss Julie?

MISS JULIE: (completely beaten) Do I believe a word of it myself?

CHRISTINE: Do you?
725

MISS JULIE: (exhausted) I don't know. I don't believe anything anymore. (She sinks down on the bench and lays her head between her arms on the table.) Nothing. Nothing at all.

CHRISTINE: (turns to the right and faces JEAN) So! You were planning to run away, were you?
730

JEAN: (taken aback, lays his razor down on the table) We weren't exactly going to run away! Don't exaggerate. You heard Miss Julie's plans. Even if she's tired now after being up all night, her plans are perfectly practical.

CHRISTINE: Well, just listen to you! Did you really think you
735 could get me to cook for that little — !

JEAN: (sharply) You keep a respectful tongue in your mouth when you talk to your mistress! Understand?

CHRISTINE: Mistress!

JEAN: Yes, mistress!
740

CHRISTINE: Well of all the — ! I don't have to listen —

JEAN: Yes, you do! You need to listen more and blabber less. Miss Julie is your mistress. Don't you forget that! And if you're going to despise her for what she did, you ought to despise yourself for the same reason.
745

CHRISTINE: I've always held myself high enough to —

JEAN: High enough to make you look down on others!

CHRISTINE: — enough to keep from lowering myself beneath my station. Don't you dare say that the count's cook has ever had anything to do with the stable groom or the swineherd. Don't
750 you dare!

JEAN: Yes, you got yourself a decent man. Lucky you!

CHRISTINE: What kind of a decent man is it who sells the oats from the count's stables?

JEAN: Listen to who's talking! You get the gravy on the groceries
755 and take bribes from the butcher!

CHRISTINE: How dare you say a thing like that!

JEAN: And you say you can't respect your employers. You of all people! You!

CHRISTINE: Are you going to church or aren't you? You need a
760 good sermon after your great exploits.

JEAN: No, I'm not going to church! Go yourself. Go tell God how bad you are.

CHRISTINE: Yes, I'll do just that. And I'll come back with enough forgiveness for your sins, too. Our Redeemer suffered
765 and died on the cross for all our sins, and if we come to Him

in faith and with a penitent heart, He will take all our sins upon Himself.

JEAN: Rake-offs included?

MISS JULIE: Do you really believe that, Christine?

CHRISTINE: With all my heart, as sure as I'm standing here. It was the faith I was born into, and I've held on to it since I was a little girl, Miss Julie. Where sin aboundeth, there grace aboundeth also.

MISS JULIE: If I had your faith, Christine, if only —

CHRISTINE: But you see, that's something you can't have without God's special grace. And it is not granted to everyone to receive it.

MISS JULIE: Then who receives it?

CHRISTINE: That's the secret of the workings of grace, Miss Julie, and God is no respecter of persons. With Him the last shall be first —

MISS JULIE: In that case, he does have respect for the last, doesn't he?

CHRISTINE: (continuing) — and it is easier for a camel to go through the eye of a needle than for a rich man to enter the kingdom of God. That's how things are, Miss Julie. I'm going to leave now — alone. And on my way out I'm going to tell the stable boy not to let any horses out, in case anyone has any ideas about leaving before the count comes home. Goodbye. (She leaves.)

JEAN: She's a devil in skirts! — All because of a canary!

MISS JULIE: (listlessly) Never mind the canary. . . . Do you see any way out of this, any end to it?

JEAN: (after thinking for a moment) No.

MISS JULIE: What would you do if you were in my place?

JEAN: In your place? Let me think. . . . An aristocrat, a woman, and — fallen. . . . I don't know. — Or maybe I do.

MISS JULIE: (picks up the razor and makes a gesture with it) Like this?

JEAN: Yes. But I wouldn't do it, you understand. That's the difference between us.

MISS JULIE: Because you're a man and I'm a woman? What difference does that make?

JEAN: Just the difference that there is — between a man and a woman.

MISS JULIE: (holding the razor in her hand) I want to! But I can't do it. My father couldn't do it either, that time when he should have.

JEAN: No, he was right not to. He had to get his revenge first.

MISS JULIE: And now my mother is getting her revenge again through me.

JEAN: Didn't you ever love your father, Miss Julie?

MISS JULIE: Yes, enormously. But I must have hated him too. I must have hated him without knowing it. It was he who brought me up to despise my own sex, to be half woman and half man. Who's to blame for what has happened? My father, my mother, myself? Myself? I don't have a self that's my own. I don't have a single thought I didn't get from my father, not an emotion I didn't get from my mother. And that last idea — about all people being equal — I got that from him, my fiancé. That's why I say he's beneath contempt. How can it be my own fault? Put the blame on Jesus, like Christine does? I'm too proud to do that — and too intelligent, thanks to what my father taught me. . . . A rich man can't get into heaven? That's a lie. But at least Christine, who's got money in the savings bank, won't get in. . . . Who's to blame? What difference does it make who's to blame? I'm still the one who has to bear the guilt, suffer the consequences —

JEAN: Yes, but —

(The bell rings sharply twice. MISS JULIE jumps up. JEAN changes his coat.)

JEAN: The count's back! What if Christine — (He goes to the speaking tube, taps on it, and listens.)

MISS JULIE: Has he looked in his desk yet?

JEAN: This is Jean, sir! (Listens. The audience cannot hear what the count says.) Yes, sir! (Listens.) Yes, sir! Yes, as soon as I can. (Listens.) Yes, at once, sir! (Listens.) Very good, sir! In half an hour.

MISS JULIE: (trembling with anxiety) What did he say? For God's sake, what did he say?

JEAN: He ordered his boots and his coffee in half an hour.

MISS JULIE: Half an hour then! . . . Oh, I'm so tired. I can't bring myself to do anything. Can't repent, can't run away, can't stay, can't live . . . can't die. Help me, Jean. Command me, and I'll obey like a dog. Do me this last favor. Save my honor, save his name. You know what I ought to do but can't force myself to do. Let me use your willpower. You command me and I'll obey.

JEAN: I don't know —. I can't either, not now. I don't know why. It's as if this coat made me — I can't give you orders in this. And now, after the count has spoken to me, I — I can't really explain it — but — I've got the backbone of a damned lackey! If the count came down here now and ordered me to cut my throat, I'd do it on the spot.

MISS JULIE: Then pretend you're him. Pretend I'm you. You were such a good actor just a while ago, when you were kneeling before me. You were the aristocrat then. Or else — have you been to the theater and seen a hypnotist?

(JEAN nods.)

He says to his subject, "Take this broom!" and he takes it. He says, "Now sweep!" and he sweeps.

JEAN: The person has to be asleep!

MISS JULIE: (ecstatic, transported) I'm already asleep. The whole room has turned to smoke. You seem like an iron stove, a stove that looks like a man in black with a high hat. Your eyes are glowing like fading coals in a dying fire. Your face is a white smudge, like ashes.

(The sun is now shining in on the floor and falls on JEAN.)

It's so good and warm — (She rubs her hands together as if warming them at a fire.) — and so bright — and so peaceful.

JEAN: (takes the razor and puts it in her hand) There's the broom. Go now, when the sun is up — out into the barn — and — (He whispers in her ear.)

MISS JULIE: (waking up) Thanks! I'm going to get my rest. But tell me one thing. Tell me that the first can also receive the gift of grace. Tell me that, even if you don't believe it.

JEAN: The first? I can't tell you that. Wait a moment, Miss Julie. I know what I can tell you. You're no longer one of the first. You're one of — the last.

MISS JULIE: That's true! I'm one of the last. I am the very last! — Oh! — Now I can't go! Tell me just once more, tell me to go!

JEAN: Now I can't either. I can't!

880 MISS JULIE: And the first shall be the last . . .

JEAN: Don't think — don't think! You're taking all my strength from me. You're making me a coward. . . . What?! I thought I saw the bell move. No. . . . Let me stuff some paper in it. — Afraid of a bell! But it isn't just a bell. There's somebody be-
885 hind it. A hand that makes it move. And there's something that makes the hand move. — Stop your ears, that's it, stop your ears! But it only rings louder. Rings louder and louder until you answer it. And then it's too late. Then the sheriff comes — and then — *(There are two sharp rings on the bell.* JEAN *gives a start, then straightens himself up.)* It's horrible! 890 But there's no other way for it to end. — Go!

(MISS JULIE *walks resolutely out through the door.)*

ANTON CHEKHOV

The work of Anton Chekhov (1860–1904) is noted for its objectivity, its sympathetic yet almost clinical examination of turn-of-the-century Russian life. Born in the provincial town of Taganrog, Chekhov trained for a career in medicine and began practicing as a physician in the mid-1880s. At that time he also began to write his first short stories. In his fiction, as in his later plays, Chekhov adopted a mildly ironic attitude toward his subjects, one that resisted sensation and melodrama in favor of a more neutral stance; as he wrote in a letter, "It is necessary that on stage everything should be as complex and as simple as in life. People are having dinner, and while they're having it, their future happiness may be decided or their lives may be about to be shattered." Chekhov's life was shattered in just this way, simply, suddenly, and casually. In 1884 he coughed up blood, the sure sign that he had contracted tuberculosis. The disease could not be cured and required repeated periods of convalescence; an early death was a certainty.

Chekhov began writing plays in the 1880s as well, mainly short comic sketches he called "vaudevilles," among them *The Bear* (1888), *The Proposal* (1889), and *The Wedding* (1890). In 1896, the Alexandrinsky Theater in St. Petersburg performed his full-length drama *The Seagull*. The play's indirect plotting and its avoidance of the conventional climaxes of melodrama confused actors and audiences alike, and it failed. Chekhov was persuaded by Constantin Stanislavsky and Vladimir Nemirovich-Danchenko to mount the play in their newly founded Moscow Art Theater (MAT) in 1898. Stanislavsky's commitment to a restrained style of performance, emphasizing psychological complexity and balanced playing by the entire ensemble is generally credited with making the MAT production a success; a seagull became the company's signature. Chekhov produced three more major plays with the MAT. He revised *The Wood Demon* (1889) as *Uncle Vanya* in 1899 and then produced *Three Sisters* (1901) and *The Cherry Orchard* (1904). Chekhov married the actress Olga Knipper — who played leading roles in his plays, including Madame Ranevskaya in *The Cherry Orchard* — in 1901 and spent the final years of his life convalescing in Yalta.

The Cherry Orchard

The action of Chekhov's plays is usually indirect, not progressive and consequential in the manner of Ibsen's work. Instead, a Chekhov play generally opens with the arrival of some well-to-do characters in the provincial scene of the play and closes with their departure: Yelena and Serbryakov in *Uncle Vanya*, the regiment and its romantic Lieutenant Colonel Vershinin in *Three Sisters*, Madame Ranevskaya and her entourage in *The Cherry Orchard*. In between, we see how the lives of the characters are changed, and yet somehow remain the same, as though their interaction worked to reveal the fundamentally static condition of their lives.

More than Chekhov's earlier plays, perhaps, *The Cherry Orchard* also seems to prefigure the fall of a class: the leisured, ineffectual, yet attractive Madame Ranevskaya and her brother, who own the estate but are incapable of bringing it into the twentieth century. We are left with the final vision of the ancient servant Firs, himself a relic of the emancipation of the serfs half a century before, locked in the house while the orchard falls to the axes. The future seems to promise a brutal and sudden change which the main characters of the play are unable to face. The play takes, at best, an ironic attitude toward the fortunes of Lyubov and Gayev. Tragedies in Chekhov's plays occur in the momentary actions of daily life; they are casual and haphazard, almost accidental, and yet alter the course of life irrevocably. Varya and Lopakhin, for example, bumble their way through the long-expected scene of their engagement, but the scene doesn't come off. Lopakhin remains uncommitted and Varya remains a poor relation dependent on the charity of her family, soon to be sent away to work as a governess. For Varya, the misplayed scene has a bitter and tragic finality.

Chekhov calls the play a "comedy," and despite its mournful tone we might consider what he might have had in mind. Chekhov seems sympathetic to the tragedies of daily life, but often trains a skeptical eye on characters who assume the self-regarding accents of high tragedy, or whose sense of themselves verges on self-delusion, the solipsistic inability to see the world around them. Throughout *The Cherry Orchard*, some characters seem lost in a world of dreams: think of Gayev and his sister arriving in their childhood nursery, of Trofimov's vague and clumsy plans for the future, of kindly old Firs. Chekhov forces us to regard his characters with a certain distance, largely by weaving a texture of comedy into the fabric of the play. Everyone ridicules Gayev's sentimental apostrophe to the bookcase in Act 1, and Chekhov adds a list of vaudeville tricks to his characters' performances: Lopakhin's "Moo-o-o" at the opening of the play, Yepikhodov crushing the hatbox with the suitcase in Act 4, Trofimov tumbling down the stairs, Charlotta's music-hall turns, Firs's feeble efforts to keep everyone warm. The famous, inexplicable sound effect of Act 2 — the breaking string — may work in this way as well. It both underscores the mournful tone of the scene and interrupts the illusionistic surface of the action, forcing the audience out of a fully sympathetic engagement with Chekhov's sentimental characters. The play, in this light, seems "tragic" only if we accept the main characters' view of their predicament and accept their idle, self-absorbed fantasies as the stuff of tragedy.

Chekhov went to some lengths to keep the play's tone unsettled, in part because he knew that Stanislavsky tended to regard his work as high tragedy. Chekhov suggested to Stanislavsky that he play the part of Lopakhin: "When I was writing Lopakhin," he wrote in a letter to the actor, "I thought of it as a part for you. . . . Lopakhin is a merchant, of course, but he is a very decent person in every sense. He must behave with perfect decorum, like an educated man, with no petty ways or tricks of any sort, and it seemed to me that this part, the central one of the play, would come out brilliantly in your hands. . . . you must remember that Varya, a serious and religious girl, is in love with Lopakhin; she wouldn't be in love with a mere money-grubber." Describing Lopakhin in terms of Varya is typical of Chekhov's tendency to think of the ensemble as a whole, rather than in terms of individual characters; but we might also think that Chekhov has strategic designs on Stanislavsky as well. Fearing that Stanislavsky would want to play the part of Gayev, and would play the part too sympathetically, Chekhov tried to persuade him to train his talents on the comic part of Lopakhin. Imagining Stanislavsky as Lopakhin, we begin to see the kind of drama Chekhov had imagined: had he taken the part (Stanislavsky played Gayev after all), Stanislavsky would have played against the grain of broad humor that underlies Lopakhin, humanizing the role, creating neither a fully sympathetic character nor a vulgar comedian, but something in between. Similarly, *The Cherry Orchard* as a whole strikes a balance somewhere between comedy and tragedy, in which comic and tragic possibilities strain against one another as ways of interpreting the play and the experience of our lives.

As it turned out, Stanislavsky's direction emphasized the play's somber tone, the sense of a generation falling before modern progress as the orchard falls to the axes. After the Russian Revolution in 1917, *The Cherry Orchard* came to be regarded as nearly a prophetic allegory of the progress of history, the displacing of the feudal past by the modern, industrial present.

THE CHERRY ORCHARD

Anton Chekhov

TRANSLATED BY ANN DUNNIGAN

— CHARACTERS —

RANEVSKAYA, LYUBOV ANDREYEVNA, *a landowner*
ANYA, *her daughter, seventeen years old*
VARYA, *her adopted daughter, twenty-four years old*
GAYEV, *Leonid Andreyevich, Madame Ranevskaya's brother*
LOPAKHIN, *Yermolai Alekseyevich, a merchant*
TROFIMOV, *Pyotr Sergeyevich, a student*
SEMYONOV-PISHCHIK, *Boris Borisovich, a landowner*
CHARLOTTA IVANOVNA, *a governess*

YEPIKHODOV, *Semyon Panteleyevich, a clerk*
DUNYASHA, *a maid*
FIRS, *an old valet, eighty seven years old*
YASHA, *a young footman*
A STRANGER
THE STATIONMASTER
A POST-OFFICE CLERK
GUESTS, SERVANTS

The action takes place on MADAME RANEVSKAYA's *estate.*

— ACT ONE —

(A room that is still called the nursery. One of the doors leads into ANYA's *room. Dawn; the sun will soon rise. It is May, the cherry trees are in bloom, but it is cold in the orchard; there is a morning frost. The windows in the room are closed. Enter* DUNYASHA *with a candle, and* LOPAKHIN *with a book in his hand.)*

LOPAKHIN: The train is in, thank God. What time is it?

DUNYASHA: Nearly two. *(Blows out the candle.)* It's already light.

LOPAKHIN: How late is the train, anyway? A couple of hours at
5 least. *(Yawns and stretches.)* I'm a fine one! What a fool I've made of myself! Came here on purpose to meet them at the station, and then overslept. . . . Fell asleep in the chair. It's annoying. . . . You might have waked me.

DUNYASHA: I thought you had gone. *(Listens.)* They're coming
10 now, I think!

LOPAKHIN: *(listens)* No . . . they've got to get the luggage and one thing and another. *(Pause)* Lyubov Andreyevna has lived abroad for five years. I don't know what she's like now. . . . She's a fine person. Sweet-tempered, simple. I remember
15 when I was a boy of fifteen, my late father — he had a shop in the village then — gave me a punch in the face and made my nose bleed. . . . We had come into the yard here for some reason or other, and he'd had a drop too much. Lyubov Andreyevna — I remember as if it were yesterday — still young,
20 and so slender, led me to the washstand in this very room, the nursery. "Don't cry, little peasant," she said, "it will heal in time for your wedding. . . ." *(Pause)* Little peasant . . . my father was a peasant, it's true, and here I am in a white waist-coat and tan shoes. Like a pig in a pastry shop. . . . I may be
25 rich, I've made a lot of money, but if you think about it, analyze it, I'm a peasant through and through. *(Turning pages of the book)* Here I've been reading this book, and I didn't understand a thing. Fell asleep over it. *(Pause)*

DUNYASHA: The dogs didn't sleep all night: they can tell that
30 their masters are coming.

LOPAKHIN: What's the matter with you, Dunyasha, you're so . . .

DUNYASHA: My hands are trembling. I'm going to faint.

LOPAKHIN: You're much too delicate, Dunyasha. You dress like
a lady, and do your hair like one, too. It's not right. You should know your place. 35

(Enter YEPIKHODOV *with a bouquet; he wears a jacket and highly polished boots that squeak loudly. He drops the flowers as he comes in.)*

YEPIKHODOV: *(picking up the flowers)* Here, the gardener sent these. He says you're to put them in the dining room. *(Hands the bouquet to* DUNYASHA.)*

LOPAKHIN: And bring me some kvas.

DUNYASHA: Yes, sir. *(Goes out.)* 40

YEPIKHODOV: There's a frost this morning — three degrees — and the cherry trees are in bloom. I cannot approve of our climate. *(Sighs.)* I cannot. Our climate is not exactly conducive. And now, Yermolai Alekseyevich, permit me to append: the day before yesterday I bought myself a pair of boots, 45 which, I venture to assure you, squeak so that it's quite infeasible. What should I grease them with?

LOPAKHIN: Leave me alone. You make me tired.

YEPIKHODOV: Every day some misfortune happens to me. But I don't complain, I'm used to it, I even smile. 50

*(*DUNYASHA *enters, serves* LOPAKHIN *the kvas.)*

YEPIKHODOV: I'm going. *(Stumbles over a chair and upsets it.)* There! *(As if in triumph.)* Now you see, excuse the expression . . . the sort of circumstance, incidentally. . . . It's really quite remarkable! *(Goes out.)*

DUNYASHA: You know, Yermolai Alekseyevich, I have to confess 55 that Yepikhodov has proposed to me.

LOPAKHIN: Ah!

DUNYASHA: And I simply don't know. . . . He's a quiet man, but sometimes, when he starts talking, you can't understand a thing he says. It's nice, and full of feeling, only it doesn't 60 make sense. I sort of like him. He's madly in love with me. But he's an unlucky fellow: every day something happens to him. They tease him about it around here; they call him Two-and-twenty Troubles.

LOPAKHIN: *(listening)* I think I hear them coming . . . 65

DUNYASHA: They're coming! What's the matter with me? I'm cold all over.

LOPAKHIN: They're really coming. Let's go and meet them. Will she recognize me? It's five years since we've seen each other.

70 DUNYASHA: (agitated) I'll faint this very minute . . . oh, I'm going to faint!

(Two carriages are heard driving up to the house. LOPAKHIN and DUNYASHA go out quickly. The stage is empty. There is a hubbub in the adjoining rooms. FIRS hurriedly crosses the stage leaning on a stick. He has been to meet LYUBOV ANDREYEVNA and wears old-fashioned livery and a high hat. He mutters something to himself, not a word of which can be understood. The noise off-stage grows louder and louder. A voice: "Let's go through here. . . ." Enter LYUBOV ANDREYEVNA, ANYA, CHARLOTTA IVANOVNA with a little dog on a chain, all in traveling dress; VARYA wearing a coat and kerchief; GAYEV, SEMYONOV-PISHCHIK, LOPAKHIN, DUNYASHA with a bundle and parasol; servants with luggage—all walk through the room.)

ANYA: Let's go this way. Do you remember, Mama, what room this is?

LYUBOV ANDREYEVNA: (joyfully, through tears) The nursery!

75 VARYA: How cold it is! My hands are numb. (To LYUBOV AN-DREYEVNA) Your rooms, both the white one and the violet one, are just as you left them, Mama.

LYUBOV ANDREYEVNA: The nursery . . . my dear, lovely nursery. . . . I used to sleep here when I was little. . . . (Weeps.)

80 And now, like a child, I . . . (Kisses her brother, VARYA, then her brother again.) Varya hasn't changed; she still looks like a nun. And I recognized Dunyasha. . . . (Kisses DUNYASHA.)

GAYEV: The train was two hours late. How's that? What kind of management is that?

85 CHARLOTTA: (to PISHCHIK) My dog even eats nuts.

PISHCHIK: (amazed) Think of that now!

(They all go out except ANYA and DUNYASHA.)

DUNYASHA: We've been waiting and waiting for you. . . . (Takes off ANYA's coat and hat.)

ANYA: I didn't sleep for four nights on the road . . . now I feel cold.

90 DUNYASHA: It was Lent when you went away, there was snow and frost then, but now? My darling! (Laughs and kisses her.) I've waited so long for you, my joy, my precious . . . I must tell you at once, I can't wait another minute. . . .

ANYA: (listlessly) What now?

95 DUNYASHA: The clerk, Yepikhodov, proposed to me just after Easter.

ANYA: You always talk about the same thing. . . . (Straightening her hair) I've lost all my hairpins. . . . (She is so exhausted she can hardly stand.)

100 DUNYASHA: I really don't know what to think. He loves me—he loves me so!

ANYA: (looking through the door into her room, tenderly) My room, my windows . . . it's just as though I'd never been away. I am home! Tomorrow morning I'll get up and run into the

105 orchard. . . . Oh, if I could only sleep! I didn't sleep during the entire journey, I was so tormented by anxiety.

DUNYASHA: Pyotr Sergeich arrived the day before yesterday.

ANYA: (joyfully) Petya!

DUNYASHA: He's asleep in the bathhouse, he's staying there.

110 "I'm afraid of being in the way," he said. (Looks at her pocket

watch.) I ought to wake him up, but Varvara Mikhailovna told me not to. "Don't you wake him," she said.

(Enter VARYA with a bunch of keys at her waist.)

VARYA: Dunyasha, coffee, quickly . . . Mama's asking for coffee.

DUNYASHA: This very minute. (Goes out.)

VARYA: Thank God, you've come! You're home again. (Caressing 115 her.) My little darling has come back! My pretty one is here!

ANYA: I've been through so much.

VARYA: I can imagine!

ANYA: I left in Holy Week, it was cold then. Charlotta never stopped talking and doing her conjuring tricks the entire jour- 120 ney. Why did you saddle me with Charlotta?

VARYA: You couldn't have traveled alone, darling. At seventeen!

ANYA: When we arrived in Paris, it was cold, snowing. My French is awful. . . . Mama was living on the fifth floor, and when I got there, she had all sorts of Frenchmen and ladies 125 with her, and an old priest with a little book, and it was full of smoke, dismal. Suddenly I felt sorry for Mama, so sorry. I took her head in my arms and held her close and couldn't let her go. Afterward she kept hugging me and crying. . . .

VARYA: (through her tears) Don't talk about it, don't talk about 130 it. . . .

ANYA: She had already sold her villa near Mentone, and she had nothing left, nothing. And I hadn't so much as a kopeck left, we barely managed to get there. But Mama doesn't under-stand! When we had dinner in a station restaurant, she always 135 ordered the most expensive dishes and tipped each of the waiters a ruble. Charlotta is the same. And Yasha also ordered a dinner, it was simply awful. You know, Yasha is Mama's footman; we brought him with us.

VARYA: I saw the rogue. 140

ANYA: Well, how are things? Have you paid the interest?

VARYA: How could we?

ANYA: Oh, my God, my God!

VARYA: In August the estate will be put up for sale.

ANYA: My God! 145

(LOPAKHIN peeps in at the door and moos like a cow.)

LOPAKHIN: Moo-o-o! (Disappears.)

VARYA: (through her tears) What I couldn't do to him! (Shakes her fist.)

ANYA: (embracing VARYA, softly) Varya, has he proposed to you? (VARYA shakes her head.) But he loves you. . . . Why don't you 150 come to an understanding, what are you waiting for?

VARYA: I don't think anything will ever come of it. He's too busy, he has no time for me . . . he doesn't even notice me. I've washed my hands of him, it makes me miserable to see him. . . . Everyone talks of our wedding, they all congratulate me, and 155 actually there's nothing to it—it's all like a dream. . . . (In a different tone.) You have a brooch like a bee.

ANYA: (sadly) Mama bought it. (Goes into her own room; speaks gaily, like a child.) In Paris I went up in a balloon!

VARYA: My darling is home! My pretty one has come back! 160

(DUNYASHA has come in with the coffeepot and prepares coffee.)

VARYA: (stands at the door of ANYA's room) You know, darling, all day long I'm busy looking after the house, but I keep dream-ing. If we could marry you to a rich man I'd be at peace. I could go into a hermitage, then to Kiev, to Moscow, and from

165 one holy place to another. . . . I'd go on and on. What a blessing!

ANYA: The birds are singing in the orchard. What time is it?

VARYA: It must be after two. Time you were asleep, darling. (Goes into ANYA's room.) What a blessing!

(YASHA enters with a lap robe and a traveling bag.)

170 YASHA: (crosses the stage mincingly) May one go through here?

DUNYASHA: A person would hardly recognize you, Yasha. Your stay abroad has done wonders for you.

YASHA: Hm. . . . And who are you?

DUNYASHA: When you left here I was only that high — (indicat-

175 ing with her hand). I'm Dunyasha, Fyodor Kozoyedov's daughter. You don't remember!

YASHA: Hm. . . . A little cucumber! (Looks around, then embraces her; she cries out and drops a saucer. He quickly goes out.)

VARYA: (in a tone of annoyance, from the doorway) What's going

180 on here?

DUNYASHA: (tearfully) I broke a saucer.

VARYA: That's good luck.

ANYA: We ought to prepare Mama: Petya is here. . . .

VARYA: I gave orders not to wake him.

185 ANYA: (pensively) Six years ago Father died, and a month later brother Grisha drowned in the river . . . a pretty little seven-year-old boy. Mama couldn't bear it and went away . . . went without looking back. . . . (Shudders.) How I understand her, if she only knew! (Pause) And Petya Trofimov was Grisha's

190 tutor, he may remind her. . . .

(Enter FIRS wearing a jacket and a white waistcoat.)

FIRS: (goes to the coffeepot, anxiously) The mistress will have her coffee here. (Puts on white gloves.) Is the coffee ready? (To DUNYASHA, sternly.) You! Where's the cream?

DUNYASHA: Oh, my goodness! (Quickly goes out.)

195 FIRS: (fussing over the coffeepot) Ah, what an addlepate! (Mutters to himself.) They've come back from Paris. . . . The master used to go to Paris . . . by carriage. . . . (Laughs.)

VARYA: What is it, Firs?

FIRS: If you please? (Joyfully) My mistress has come home! At

200 last! Now I can die. . . . (Weeps with joy.)

(Enter LYUBOV ANDREYEVNA, GAYEV, and SEMYONOV-PISHCHIK, the last wearing a sleeveless peasant coat of fine cloth and full trousers. GAYEV, as he comes in, goes through the motions of playing billiards.)

LYUBOV ANDREYEVNA: How does it go? Let's see if I can remember . . . cue ball into the corner! Double the rail to center table.

GAYEV: Cut shot into the corner! There was a time, sister, when

205 you and I used to sleep here in this very room, and now I'm fifty-one, strange as it may seem. . . .

LOPAKHIN: Yes, time passes.

GAYEV: How's that?

LOPAKHIN: Time, I say, passes.

210 GAYEV: It smells of patchouli here.

ANYA: I'm going to bed. Good night, Mama. (Kisses her mother.)

LYUBOV ANDREYEVNA: My precious child. (Kisses her hands.) Are you glad to be home? I still feel dazed.

ANYA: Good night, Uncle.

215 GAYEV: (kisses her face and hands) God bless you. How like your mother you are! (To his sister) At her age you were exactly like her, Lyuba.

(ANYA shakes hands with LOPAKHIN and PISHCHIK and goes out, closing the door after her.)

LYUBOV ANDREYEVNA: She's exhausted.

PISHCHIK: Must have been a long journey.

220 VARYA: Well, gentlemen? It's after two, high time you were going.

LYUBOV ANDREYEVNA: (laughs) You haven't changed, Varya. (Draws VARYA to her and kisses her.) I'll just drink my coffee and then we'll all go. (FIRS places a cushion under her feet.) Thank you, my dear. I've got used to coffee. I drink it day and

225 night. Thanks, dear old man. (Kisses him.)

VARYA: I'd better see if all the luggage has been brought in.

LYUBOV ANDREYEVNA: Is this really me sitting here? (Laughs.) I feel like jumping about and waving my arms. (Buries her face in her hands.) What if it's only a dream! God knows I love

230 my country, love it dearly. I couldn't look out the train window, I was crying so! (Through tears) But I must drink my coffee. Thank you, Firs, thank you, my dear old friend. I'm so glad you're still alive.

FIRS: The day before yesterday.

235 GAYEV: He's hard of hearing.

LOPAKHIN: I must go now, I'm leaving for Kharkov about five o'clock. It's so annoying! I wanted to have a good look at you, and have a talk. You're as splendid as ever.

PISHCHIK: (breathing heavily) Even more beautiful. . . . Dressed

240 like a Parisienne. . . . There goes my wagon, all four wheels!

LOPAKHIN: Your brother here, Leonid Andreich, says I'm a boor, a moneygrubber, but I don't mind. Let him talk. All I want is that you should trust me as you used to, and that your wonderful, touching eyes should look at me as they did then.

245 Merciful God! My father was one of your father's serfs, and your grandfather's, but you yourself did so much for me once, that I've forgotten all that and love you as if you were my own kin — more than my kin.

LYUBOV ANDREYEVNA: I can't sit still, I simply cannot. (Jumps

250 up and walks about the room in great excitement.) I cannot bear this joy. . . . Laugh at me, I'm silly. . . . My dear little bookcase . . . (Kisses bookcase.) my little table . . .

GAYEV: Nurse died while you were away.

LYUBOV ANDREYEVNA: (sits down and drinks coffee) Yes, God

255 rest her soul. They wrote me.

GAYEV: And Anastasy is dead. Petrushka Kosoi left me and is now with the police inspector in town. (Takes a box of hard candies from his pocket and begins to suck one.)

PISHCHIK: My daughter, Dashenka . . . sends her regards . . .

260 LOPAKHIN: I wish I could tell you something very pleasant and cheering. (Glances at his watch.) I must go directly, there's no time to talk, but . . . well, I'll say it in a couple of words. As you know, the cherry orchard is to be sold to pay your debts. The auction is set for August twenty-second, but you need

265 not worry, my dear, you can sleep in peace, there is a way out. This is my plan. Now, please listen! Your estate is only twenty versts from town, the railway runs close by, and if the cherry orchard and the land along the river were cut up into lots and leased for summer cottages, you'd have, at the very least, an

270 income of twenty-five thousand a year.

GAYEV: Excuse me, what nonsense!

LYUBOV ANDREYEVNA: I don't quite understand you, Yermolai Alekseich.

LOPAKHIN: You will get, at the very least, twenty-five rubles a year for a two-and-a-half-acre lot, and if you advertise now, I guarantee you won't have a single plot of ground left by autumn, everything will be snapped up. In short, I congratulate you, you are saved. The site is splendid, the river is deep. Only, of course, the ground must be cleared . . . you must tear down all the old outbuildings, for instance, and this house, which is worthless, cut down the old cherry orchard—

LYUBOV ANDREYEVNA: Cut it down? Forgive me, my dear, but you don't know what you are talking about. If there is one thing in the whole province that is interesting, not to say remarkable, it's our cherry orchard.

LOPAKHIN: The only remarkable thing about this orchard is that it is very big. There's a crop of cherries every other year, and then you can't get rid of them, nobody buys them.

GAYEV: This orchard is even mentioned in the *Encyclopedia.*

LOPAKHIN: *(glancing at his watch)* If we don't think of something and come to a decision, on the twenty-second of August the cherry orchard, and the entire estate, will be sold at auction. Make up your minds! There is no other way out, I swear to you. None whatsoever.

FIRS: In the old days, forty or fifty years ago, the cherries were dried, soaked, marinated, and made into jam, and they used to—

GAYEV: Be quiet, Firs.

FIRS: And they used to send cartloads of dried cherries to Moscow and Kharkov. And that brought in money! The dried cherries were soft and juicy in those days, sweet, fragrant. . . . They had a method then . . .

LYUBOV ANDREYEVNA: And what has become of that method now?

FIRS: Forgotten. Nobody remembers. . . .

PISHCHIK: How was it in Paris? What's it like there? Did you eat frogs?

LYUBOV ANDREYEVNA: I ate crocodiles.

PISHCHIK: Think of that now!

LOPAKHIN: There used to be only the gentry and the peasants living in the country, but now these summer people have appeared. All the towns, even the smallest ones, are surrounded by summer cottages. And it is safe to say that in another twenty years these people will multiply enormously. Now the summer resident only drinks tea on his porch, but it may well be that he'll take to cultivating his acre, and then your cherry orchard will be a happy, rich, luxuriant—

GAYEV: *(indignantly)* What nonsense!

(Enter VARYA and YASHA.)

VARYA: There are two telegrams for you, Mama. *(Picks out a key and with a jingling sound opens an old-fashioned bookcase.)* Here they are.

LYUBOV ANDREYEVNA: From Paris. *(Tears up the telegrams without reading them.)* That's all over. . . .

GAYEV: Do you know, Lyuba, how old this bookcase is? A week ago I pulled out the bottom drawer, and what do I see? Some figures burnt into it. The bookcase was made exactly a hundred years ago. What do you think of that? Eh? We could have celebrated its jubilee. It's an inanimate object, but nevertheless, for all that, it's a bookcase.

PISHCHIK: A hundred years . . . think of that now!

GAYEV: Yes . . . that is something. . . . *(Feeling the bookcase)* Dear, honored bookcase, I salute thy existence, which for over one hundred years has served the glorious ideals of goodness and justice; thy silent appeal to fruitful endeavor, unflagging in the course of a hundred years, tearfully sustaining through generations of our family, courage and faith in a better future, and fostering in us ideals of goodness and social consciousness. . . .

(A pause)

LOPAKHIN: Yes . . .

LYUBOV ANDREYEVNA: You are the same as ever, Lyonya.

GAYEV: *(somewhat embarrassed)* Carom into the corner, cut shot to center table.

LOPAKHIN: *(looks at his watch)* Well, time for me to go.

YASHA: *(hands medicine to LYUBOV ANDREYEVNA)* Perhaps you will take your pills now.

PISHCHIK: Don't take medicaments, dearest lady, they do neither harm nor good. Let me have them, honored lady. *(Takes the pill box, shakes the pills into his hand, blows on them, puts them into his mouth, and washes them down with kvas.)* There!

LYUBOV ANDREYEVNA: *(alarmed)* Why, you must be mad!

PISHCHIK: I've taken all the pills.

LOPAKHIN: What a glutton!

(Everyone laughs.)

FIRS: The gentleman stayed with us during Holy Week . . . ate half a bucket of pickles. . . . *(Mumbles.)*

LYUBOV ANDREYEVNA: What is he saying?

VARYA: He's been muttering like that for three years now. We've grown used to it.

YASHA: He's in his dotage.

(CHARLOTTA IVANOVNA, very thin, tightly laced, in a white dress with a lorgnette at her belt, crosses the stage.)

LOPAKHIN: Forgive me, Charlotta Ivanovna, I haven't had a chance to say how do you do to you. *(Tries to kiss her hand.)*

CHARLOTTA: *(pulls her hand away)* If I permit you to kiss my hand you'll be wanting to kiss my elbow next, then my shoulder.

LOPAKHIN: I have no luck today. *(Everyone laughs.)* Charlotta Ivanovna, show us a trick!

LYUBOV ANDREYEVNA: Charlotta, show us a trick!

CHARLOTTA: No. I want to sleep. *(Goes out.)*

LOPAKHIN: In three weeks we'll meet again. *(Kisses LYUBOV ANDREYEVNA's hand.)* Good-bye till then. Time to go. *(To GAYEV.)* Good-bye. *(Kisses PISHCHIK.)* Good-bye. *(Shakes hands with VARYA, then with FIRS and YASHA.)* I don't feel like going. *(To LYUBOV ANDREYEVNA)* If you make up your mind about the summer cottages and come to a decision, let me know; I'll get you a loan of fifty thousand or so. Think it over seriously.

VARYA: *(angrily)* Oh, why don't you go!

LOPAKHIN: I'm going, I'm going. *(Goes out.)*

GAYEV: Boor. Oh, pardon. Varya's going to marry him, he's Varya's young man.

VARYA: Uncle dear, you talk too much.

LYUBOV ANDREYEVNA: Well, Varya, I shall be very glad. He's a good man.

PISHCHIK: A man, I must truly say . . . most worthy. . . . And my

385 Dashenka . . . says, too, that . . . says all sorts of things. (*Snores but wakes up at once.*) In any case, honored lady, oblige me . . . a loan of two hundred and forty rubles . . . tomorrow the interest on my mortgage is due. . . .

VARYA: (*in alarm*) We have nothing, nothing at all!

390 LYUBOV ANDREYEVNA: I really haven't any money.

PISHCHIK: It'll turn up. (*Laughs.*) I never lose hope. Just when I thought everything was lost, that I was done for, lo and be-hold—the railway line ran through my land . . . and they paid me for it. And before you know it, something else will

395 turn up, if not today—tomorrow. . . . Dashenka will win two hundred thousand . . . she's got a lottery ticket.

LYUBOV ANDREYEVNA: The coffee is finished, we can go to bed.

FIRS: (*brushing* GAYEV's *clothes, admonishingly*) You've put on the wrong trousers again. What am I to do with you?

400 VARYA: (*softly*) Anya's asleep. (*Quietly opens the window.*) The sun has risen, it's no longer cold. Look, Mama dear, what wonderful trees! Oh, Lord, the air! The starlings are singing!

GAYEV: (*opens another window*) The orchard is all white. You haven't forgotten, Lyuba? That long avenue there that runs

405 straight—straight as a stretched-out strap; it gleams on moonlight nights. Remember? You've not forgotten?

LYUBOV ANDREYEVNA: (*looking out the window at the orchard*) Oh, my childhood, my innocence! I used to sleep in this nursery, I looked out from here into the orchard, happiness

410 awoke with me each morning, it was just as it is now, nothing has changed. (*Laughing with joy*) All, all white! Oh, my orchard! After the dark, rainy autumn and the cold winter, you are young again, full of happiness, the heavenly angels have not forsaken you. . . . If I could cast off this heavy stone

415 weighing on my breast and shoulders, if I could forget my past!

GAYEV: Yes, and the orchard will be sold for our debts, strange as it may seem. . . .

LYUBOV ANDREYEVNA: Look, our dead mother walks in the orchard . . . in a white dress! (*Laughs with joy.*) It is she!

420 GAYEV: Where?

VARYA: God be with you, Mama dear.

LYUBOV ANDREYEVNA: There's no one there, I just imagined it. To the right, as you turn to the summerhouse, a slender white sapling is bent over . . . it looks like a woman.

(*Enter* TROFIMOV *wearing a shabby student's uniform and spectacles.*)

425 LYUBOV ANDREYEVNA: What a wonderful orchard! The white masses of blossoms, the blue sky—

TROFIMOV: Lyubov Andreyevna! (*She looks around at him.*) I only want to pay my respects, then I'll go at once. (*Kisses her hand ardently.*) I was told to wait until morning, but I hadn't

430 the patience.

(LYUBOV ANDREYEVNA *looks at him, puzzled.*)

VARYA: (*through tears*) This is Petya Trofimov.

TROFIMOV: Petya Trofimov, I was Grisha's tutor. . . . Can I have changed so much?

(LYUBOV ANDREYEVNA *embraces him, quietly weeping.*)

GAYEV: (*embarrassed*) There, there, Lyuba.

435 VARYA: (*crying*) Didn't I tell you, Petya, to wait till tomorrow?

LYUBOV ANDREYEVNA: My Grisha . . . my little boy . . . Grisha . . . my son. . . .

VARYA: What can we do, Mama dear? It's God's will.

TROFIMOV: (*gently, through tears*) Don't, don't. . . .

440 LYUBOV ANDREYEVNA: (*quietly weeping*) My little boy dead, drowned. . . . Why? Why, my friend? (*In a lower voice.*) Anya is sleeping in there, and I'm talking loudly . . . making all this noise. . . . But Petya, why do you look so bad? Why have you grown so old?

445 TROFIMOV: A peasant woman in the train called me a mangy gentleman.

LYUBOV ANDREYEVNA: You were just a boy then, a charming little student, and now your hair is thin—and spectacles! Is it possible you are still a student? (*Goes toward the door.*)

450 TROFIMOV: I shall probably be an eternal student.

LYUBOV ANDREYEVNA: (*kisses her brother, then* VARYA) Now, go to bed. . . . You've grown older too, Leonid.

PISHCHIK: (*follows her*) Well, seems to be time to sleep. . . . Oh, my gout! I'm staying the night. Lyubov Andreyevna, my soul, tomorrow morning . . . two hundred and forty rubles. . . .

455 GAYEV: He keeps at it.

PISHCHIK: Two hundred and forty rubles . . . to pay the interest on my mortgage.

LYUBOV ANDREYEVNA: I have no money, my friend.

PISHCHIK: My dear, I'll pay it back. . . . It's a trifling sum.

460 LYUBOV ANDREYEVNA: Well, all right, Leonid will give it to you. . . . Give it to him, Leonid.

GAYEV: Me give it to him! . . . Hold out your pocket!

LYUBOV ANDREYEVNA: It can't be helped, give it to him. . . . He needs it. . . . He'll pay it back.

465 (LYUBOV ANDREYEVNA, TROFIMOV, PISHCHIK, *and* FIRS *go out.* GAYEV, VARYA, *and* YASHA *remain.*)

GAYEV: My sister hasn't yet lost her habit of squandering money. (*To* YASHA.) Go away, my good fellow, you smell of the henhouse.

470 YASHA: (*with a smirk*) And you, Leonid Andreyevich, are just the same as ever.

GAYEV: How's that? (*To* VARYA) What did he say?

VARYA: Your mother has come from the village; she's been sitting in the servants' room since yesterday, waiting to see you. . . .

YASHA: Let her wait, for God's sake!

475 VARYA: Aren't you ashamed?

YASHA: A lot I need her! She could have come tomorrow. (*Goes out.*)

VARYA: Mama's the same as ever, she hasn't changed a bit. She'd give away everything, if she could.

480 GAYEV: Yes. . . . (*A pause*) If a great many remedies are suggested for a disease, it means that the disease is incurable. I keep thinking, racking my brains, I have many remedies, a great many, and that means, in effect, that I have none. It would be good to receive a legacy from someone, good to

485 marry our Anya to a very rich man, good to go to Yaroslav and try our luck with our aunt, the Countess. She is very, very rich, you know.

VARYA: (*crying*) If only God would help us!

GAYEV: Stop bawling. Auntie's very rich, but she doesn't like us.

490 In the first place, sister married a lawyer, not a nobleman . . . (ANYA *appears in the doorway.*) She married beneath her, and it cannot be said that she has conducted herself very virtuously. She is good, kind, charming, and I love her dearly, but no matter how much you allow for extenuating circum-

495 stances, you must admit she leads a sinful life. You feel it in her slightest movement.

VARYA: *(in a whisper)* Anya is standing in the doorway.

GAYEV: What? *(Pause)* Funny, something got into my right eye . . . I can't see very well. And Thursday, when I was in the
500   district court . . .

(ANYA enters.)

VARYA: Why aren't you asleep, Anya?

ANYA: I can't get to sleep. I just can't.

GAYEV: My little one! *(Kisses ANYA's face and hands.)* My child. . . . *(Through tears)* You are not my niece, you are my angel,
505   you are everything to me. Believe me, believe . . .

ANYA: I believe you, Uncle. Everyone loves you and respects you, but, Uncle dear, you must keep quiet, just keep quiet. What were you saying just now about my mother, about your own sister? What made you say that?

510 GAYEV: Yes, yes. . . . *(Covers his face with her hand.)* Really, it's awful! My God! God help me! And today I made a speech to the bookcase . . . so stupid! And it was only when I had finished that I realized it was stupid.

VARYA: It's true, Uncle dear, you ought to keep quiet. Just don't
515   talk, that's all.

ANYA: If you could keep from talking, it would make things easier for you, too.

GAYEV: I'll be quiet. *(Kisses ANYA's and VARYA's hands.)* I'll be quiet. Only this is about business. On Thursday I was in the
520   district court, well, a group of us gathered together and began talking about one thing and another, this and that, and it seems it might be possible to arrange a loan on a promissory note to pay the interest at the bank.

VARYA: If only God would help us!

525 GAYEV: On Tuesday I'll go and talk it over again. *(To VARYA)* Stop bawling. *(To ANYA)* Your mama will talk to Lopakhin; he, of course, will not refuse her. . . . And as soon as you've rested, you will go to Yaroslav to the Countess, your great-aunt. In that way we shall be working from three directions —
530   and our business is in the hat. We'll pay the interest, I'm certain of it. . . . *(Puts a candy in his mouth.)* On my honor, I'll swear by anything you like, the estate shall not be sold. *(Excitedly.)* By my happiness, I swear it! Here's my hand on it, call me a worthless, dishonorable man if I let it come to
535   auction! I swear by my whole being!

ANYA: *(a calm mood returns to her, she is happy.)* How good you are, Uncle, how clever! *(Embraces him.)* Now I am at peace! I'm at peace! I'm happy!

(Enter FIRS.)

FIRS: *(reproachfully)* Leonid Andreich, have you no fear of God?
540   When are you going to bed?

GAYEV: Presently, presently. Go away, Firs. I'll . . . all right, I'll undress myself. Well, children, bye-bye. . . . Details tomorrow, and now go to sleep. *(Kisses ANYA and VARYA.)* I am a man of the eighties. . . . They don't think much of that period
545   today, nevertheless, I can say that in the course of my life I have suffered not a little for my convictions. It is not for nothing that the peasant loves me. You have to know the peasant! You have to know from what —

ANYA: There you go again, Uncle!

550 VARYA: Uncle dear, do be quiet.

FIRS: *(angrily)* Leonid Andreich!

GAYEV: I'm coming, I'm coming. . . . Go to bed. A clean double rail shot to center table. . . . *(Goes out; FIRS hobbles after him.)*

ANYA: I'm at peace now. I would rather not go to Yaroslav, I 555 don't like my great-aunt, but still, I'm at peace, thanks to Uncle. *(She sits down.)*

VARYA: We must get some sleep. I'm going now. Oh, something unpleasant happened while you were away. In the old servants' quarters, as you know, there are only the old people: 560 Yefimushka, Polya, Yevstignei, and, of course, Karp. They began letting in all sorts of rogues to spend the night — I didn't say anything. But then I heard they'd been spreading a rumor that I'd given an order for them to be fed nothing but dried peas. Out of stinginess, you see. . . . It was all Yevstignei's 565 doing. . . . Very well, I think, if that's how it is, you just wait. I send for Yevstignei . . . *(yawning)* he comes. . . . "How is it, Yevstignei," I say, "that you could be such a fool. . . ." *(Looks at ANYA.)* She's fallen asleep. *(Takes her by the arm.)* Come to your little bed. . . . Come along. *(Leading her)* My little dar- 570 ling fell asleep. Come. . . . *(They go.)*

(In the distance, beyond the orchard, a shepherd is playing on a reed pipe. TROFIMOV crosses the stage and, seeing VARYA and ANYA, stops.)

VARYA: Sh! She's asleep . . . asleep. . . . Come along, darling.

ANYA: *(softly, half-asleep)* I'm so tired. . . . Those bells . . . Uncle . . . dear . . . Mama and Uncle . . .

VARYA: Come, darling, come along. *(They go into ANYA's room.)* 575

TROFIMOV: *(deeply moved)* My sunshine! My spring!

— ACT TWO —

(A meadow. An old, lopsided, long-abandoned little chapel; near it a well, large stones that apparently were once tombstones, and an old bench. A road to the GAYEV manor house can be seen. On one side, where the cherry orchard begins, tall poplars loom. In the distance a row of telegraph poles, and far, far away, on the horizon, the faint outline of a large town, which is visible only in very fine, clear weather. The sun will soon set. CHARLOTTA, YASHA, and DUNYASHA are sitting on the bench; YEPIKHODOV stands near playing something sad on the guitar. They are all lost in thought. CHARLOTTA wears an old forage cap; she has taken a gun from her shoulder and is adjusting the buckle on the sling.)

CHARLOTTA: *(reflectively)* I haven't got a real passport, I don't know how old I am, but it always seems to me that I'm quite young. When I was a little girl, my father and mother used to travel from one fair to another giving performances — very good ones. And I did the *salto mortale* and all sorts of tricks. 5 Then when Papa and Mama died, a German lady took me to live with her and began teaching me. Good. I grew up and became a governess. But where I come from and who I am — I do not know. . . . Who my parents were — perhaps they weren't even married — I don't know. *(Takes a cucumber out 10 of her pocket and eats it.)* I don't know anything. *(Pause)* One wants so much to talk, but there isn't anyone to talk to . . . I have no one.

YEPIKHODOV: *(plays the guitar and sings)*

> What care I for the clamorous world, 15
> what's friend or foe to me? . . .

How pleasant it is to play a mandolin!

DUNYASHA: That's a guitar, not a mandolin. (*Looks at herself in a hand mirror and powders her face.*)

20 YEPIKHODOV: To a madman, in love, it is a mandolin. . . . (*Sings.*)

> Would that the heart were warmed
> by the flame of requited love . . .

(YASHA *joins in.*)

CHARLOTTA: How horribly these people sing! . . . Pfui! Like
25   jackals!

DUNYASHA: (*to* YASHA) Really, how fortunate to have been abroad!

YASHA: Yes, to be sure. I cannot but agree with you there. (*Yawns, then lights a cigar.*)

YEPIKHODOV: It stands to reason. Abroad everything has long
30   since been fully constituted.

YASHA: Obviously.

YEPIKHODOV: I am a cultivated man, I read all sorts of remarkable books, but I am in no way able to make out my own inclinations, what it is I really want, whether, strictly speak-
35   ing, to live or to shoot myself; nevertheless, I always carry a revolver on me. Here it is. (*Shows revolver.*)

CHARLOTTA: Finished. Now I'm going. (*Slings the gun over her shoulder.*) You're a very clever man, Yepikhodov, and quite terrifying; women must be mad about you. Brrr! (*Starts to
40   go.*) These clever people are all so stupid, there's no one for me to talk to. . . . Alone, always alone, I have no one . . . and who I am, and why I am, nobody knows. . . . (*Goes out unhurriedly.*)

YEPIKHODOV: Strictly speaking, all else aside, I must state re-
45   garding myself, that fate treats me unmercifully, as a storm does a small ship. If, let us assume, I am mistaken, then why, to mention a single instance, do I wake up this morning, and there on my chest see a spider of terrifying magnitude? . . . Like that. (*Indicates with both hands.*) And likewise, I take up
50   some kvas to quench my thirst, and there see something in the highest degree unseemly, like a cockroach. (*Pause.*) Have you read Buckle? (*Pause.*) If I may trouble you, Avdotya Fedorovna, I should like to have a word or two with you.

DUNYASHA: Go ahead.

55 YEPIKHODOV: I prefer to speak with you alone. . . . (*Sighs.*)

DUNYASHA: (*embarrassed*) Very well . . . only first bring me my little cape . . . you'll find it by the cupboard. . . . It's rather damp here. . . .

YEPIKHODOV: Certainly, ma'am . . . I'll fetch it, ma'am. . . .
60   Now I know what to do with my revolver. . . . (*Takes the guitar and goes off playing it.*)

YASHA: Two-and-twenty Troubles! Between ourselves, a stupid fellow. (*Yawns.*)

DUNYASHA: God forbid that he should shoot himself. (*Pause.*)
65   I've grown so anxious, I'm always worried. I was only a little girl when I was taken into the master's house, and now I'm quite unused to the simple life, and my hands are white as can be, just like a lady's. I've become so delicate, so tender and ladylike, I'm afraid of everything. . . . Frightfully so.
70   And, Yasha, if you deceive me, I just don't know what will become of my nerves.

YASHA: (*kisses her*) You little cucumber! Of course, a girl should never forget herself. What I dislike above everything is when a girl doesn't conduct herself properly.

75 DUNYASHA: I'm passionately in love with you; you're educated, you can discuss anything. (*Pause*)

YASHA: (*yawns*) Yes. . . . As I see it, it's like this: if a girl loves somebody, that means she's immoral. (*Pause*) Very pleasant smoking a cigar in the open air. . . . (*Listens.*) Someone's coming this way. . . . It's the masters. (DUNYASHA *impulsively   80
embraces him.*) You go home, as if you'd been to the river to bathe; take that path, otherwise they'll see you and suspect me of having a rendezvous with you. I can't endure that sort of thing.

DUNYASHA: (*with a little cough*) My head is beginning to ache   85
from your cigar. . . . (*Goes out.*)

(YASHA *remains, sitting near the chapel.* LYUBOV ANDREYEVNA, GAYEV, *and* LOPAKHIN *enter.*)

LOPAKHIN: You must make up your mind once and for all — time won't stand still. The question, after all, is quite simple. Do you agree to lease the land for summer cottages or not? Answer in one word: yes or no? Only one word!   90

LYUBOV ANDREYEVNA: Who is it that smokes those disgusting cigars out here? (*Sits down.*)

GAYEV: Now that the railway line is so near, it's made things convenient. (*Sits down.*) We went to town and had lunch . . . cue ball to the center! I feel like going to the house first and   95
playing a game.

LYUBOV ANDREYEVNA: Later.

LOPAKHIN: Just one word! (*Imploringly*) Do give me an answer!

GAYEV: (*yawning*) How's that?

LYUBOV ANDREYEVNA: (*looks into her purse*) Yesterday I had a   100
lot of money, and today there's hardly any left. My poor Varya tries to economize by feeding everyone milk soup, and in the kitchen the old people get nothing but dried peas, while I squander money foolishly. . . . (*Drops the purse, scattering gold coins.*) There they go. . . . (*Vexed*)   105

YASHA: Allow me, I'll pick them up in an instant. (*Picks up the money.*)

LYUBOV ANDREYEVNA: Please do, Yasha. And why did I go to town for lunch? . . . That miserable restaurant of yours with its music, and tablecloths smelling of soap. . . . Why drink so   110
much, Lyonya? Why eat so much? Why talk so much? Today in the restaurant again you talked too much, and it was all so pointless. About the seventies, about the decadents. And to whom? Talking to waiters about the decadents!

LOPAKHIN: Yes.   115

GAYEV: (*waving his hand*) I'm incorrigible, that's evident. . . . (*Irritably to* YASHA) Why do you keep twirling about in front of me?

YASHA: (*laughs*) I can't help laughing when I hear your voice.

GAYEV: (*to his sister*) Either he or I —   120

LYUBOV ANDREYEVNA: Go away, Yasha, run along.

YASHA: (*hands* LYUBOV ANDREYEVNA *her purse*) I'm going, right away. (*Hardly able to contain his laughter.*) This very instant. . . . (*Goes out.*)

LOPAKHIN: That rich man, Deriganov, is prepared to buy the   125
estate. They say he's coming to the auction himself.

LYUBOV ANDREYEVNA: Where did you hear that?

LOPAKHIN: That's what they're saying in town.

LYUBOV ANDREYEVNA: Our aunt in Yaroslavl promised to send us something, but when and how much, no one knows.   130

LOPAKHIN: How much do you think she'll send? A hundred thousand? Two hundred?

LYUBOV ANDREYEVNA: Oh . . . ten or fifteen thousand, and we'll be thankful for that.

135 LYOPAKHIN: Forgive me, but I have never seen such frivolous, such queer, unbusinesslike people as you, my friends. You are told in plain language that your estate is to be sold, and it's as though you don't understand it.

LYUBOV ANDREYEVNA: But what are we to do? Tell us what to do.

140 LOPAKHIN: I tell you every day. Every day I say the same thing. Both the cherry orchard and the land must be leased for summer cottages, and it must be done now, as quickly as possible—the auction is close at hand. Try to understand! Once you definitely decide on the cottages, you can raise as much 145 money as you like, and then you are saved.

LYUBOV ANDREYEVNA: Cottages, summer people—forgive me, but it's so vulgar.

GAYEV: I agree with you, absolutely.

LOPAKHIN: I'll either burst into tears, start shouting, or fall into a 150 faint! I can't stand it! You've worn me out! (*To* GAYEV) You're an old woman!

GAYEV: How's that?

LOPAKHIN: An old woman! (*Starts to go.*)

LYUBOV ANDREYEVNA: (*alarmed*) No, don't go, stay, my dear. I 155 beg you. Perhaps we'll think of something!

LOPAKHIN: What is there to think of?

LYUBOV ANDREYEVNA: Don't go away, please. With you here it's more cheerful somehow. . . . (*Pause.*) I keep expecting something to happen, like the house caving in on us.

160 GAYEV: (*in deep thought*) Double rail shot into the corner. . . . Cross table to the center. . . .

LYUBOV ANDREYEVNA: We have sinned so much. . . .

LOPAKHIN: What sins could you have—

GAYEV: (*puts a candy into his mouth*) They say I've eaten up my 165 entire fortune in candies. . . . (*Laughs.*)

LYUBOV ANDREYEVNA: Oh, my sins. . . . I've always squandered money recklessly, like a madwoman, and I married a man who did nothing but amass debts. My husband died from champagne—he drank terribly—then, to my sorrow, I 170 fell in love with another man, lived with him, and just at that time—that was my first punishment, a blow on the head— my little boy was drowned . . . here in the river. And I went abroad, went away for good, never to return, never to see this river. . . . I closed my eyes and ran, beside myself, and *he* after 175 me . . . callously, without pity. I bought a villa near Mentone, because he fell ill there, and for three years I had no rest, day or night. The sick man wore me out, my soul dried up. Then last year, when the villa was sold to pay my debts, I went to Paris, and there he stripped me of everything, and left 180 me for another woman; I tried to poison myself. . . . So stupid, so shameful. . . . And suddenly I felt a longing for Russia, for my own country, for my little girl. . . . (*Wipes away her tears.*) Lord, Lord, be merciful, forgive my sins! Don't punish me any more! (*Takes a telegram out of her* 185 *pocket.*) This came today from Paris. . . . He asks my forgiveness, begs me to return. . . . (*Tears up telegram.*) Do I hear music? (*Listens.*)

GAYEV: That's our famous Jewish band. You remember, four violins, a flute and double bass.

190 LYUBOV ANDREYEVNA: It's still in existence? We ought to send for them some time and give a party.

LOPAKHIN: (*listens*) I don't hear anything. . . . (*Sings softly.*) "The Germans, for pay, will turn Russians into Frenchmen, they say." (*Laughs.*) What a play I saw yesterday at the thea-195 ter—very funny!

LYUBOV ANDREYEVNA: There was probably nothing funny about it. Instead of going to see plays you ought to look at yourselves a little more often. How drab your lives are, how full of futile talk!

LOPAKHIN: That's true. I must say, this life of ours is stupid. . . . 200 (*Pause*) My father was a peasant, an idiot; he understood nothing, taught me nothing; all he did was beat me when he was drunk, and always with a stick. As a matter of fact, I'm as big a blockhead and idiot as he was. I never learned anything, my handwriting's disgusting, I write like a pig—I'm ashamed 205 to have people see it.

LYUBOV ANDREYEVNA: You ought to get married, my friend.

LOPAKHIN: Yes . . . that's true.

LYUBOV ANDREYEVNA: To our Varya. She's a nice girl.

LOPAKHIN: Yes. 210

LYUBOV ANDREYEVNA: She's a girl who comes from simple people, works all day long, but the main thing is she loves you. Besides, you've liked her for a long time now.

LOPAKHIN: Well? I've nothing against it. . . . She's a good girl. (*Pause*) 215

GAYEV: I've been offered a place in the bank. Six thousand a year. . . . Have you heard?

LYUBOV ANDREYEVNA: How could you! You stay where you are. . . .

(FIRS *enters carrying an overcoat.*)

FIRS: (*To* GAYEV) If you please, sir, put this on, it's damp. 220

GAYEV: (*puts on the overcoat*) You're a pest, old man.

FIRS: Never mind. . . . You went off this morning without telling me. (*Looks him over.*)

LYUBOV ANDREYEVNA: How you have aged, Firs!

FIRS: What do you wish, madam? 225

LOPAKHIN: She says you've grown very old!

FIRS: I've lived a long time. They were arranging a marriage for me before your papa was born. . . . (*Laughs.*) I was already head footman when the Emancipation came. At that time I wouldn't consent to my freedom, I stayed with the masters. . . . 230 (*Pause*) I remember, everyone was happy, but what they were happy about, they themselves didn't know.

LOPAKHIN: It was better in the old days. At least they flogged them.

FIRS: (*not hearing*) Of course. The peasants kept to the masters, 235 the masters kept to the peasants; but now they have all gone their own ways, you can't tell about anything.

GAYEV: Be quiet, Firs. Tomorrow I must go to town. I've been promised an introduction to a certain general who might let us have a loan. 240

LOPAKHIN: Nothing will come of it. And you can rest assured, you won't even pay the interest.

LYUBOV ANDREYEVNA: He's raving. There is no such general.

(Enter TROFIMOV, ANYA, *and* VARYA.)

GAYEV: Here come our young people.

ANYA: There's Mama.

LYUBOV ANDREYEVNA: (*tenderly*) Come, come along, my darlings. (*Embraces* ANYA *and* VARYA.) If you only knew how I love you both! Sit here beside me—there, like that. 245

(*They all sit down.*)

LOPAKHIN: Our eternal student is always with the young ladies.

TROFIMOV: That's none of your business. 250

LOPAKHIN: He'll soon be fifty, but he's still a student.

TROFIMOV: Drop your stupid jokes.

LOPAKHIN: What are you so angry about, you queer fellow?

TROFIMOV: Just leave me alone.

255 LOPAKHIN: (laughs) Let me ask you something: what do you make of me?

TROFIMOV: My idea of you, Yermolai Alekseich, is this: you're a rich man, you will soon be a millionaire. Just as the beast of prey, which devours everything that crosses its path, is neces-
260 sary in the metabolic process, so are you necessary.

(Everyone laughs.)

VARYA: Petya, you'd better tell us something about the planets.

LYUBOV ANDREYEVNA: No, let's go on with yesterday's conversation.

TROFIMOV: What was it about?

265 GAYEV: About the proud man.

TROFIMOV: We talked a long time yesterday, but we didn't get anywhere. In the proud man, in your sense of the word, there's something mystical. And you may be right from your point of view, but if you look at it simply, without being ab-
270 struse, why even talk about pride? Is there any sense in it if, physiologically, man is poorly constructed, if, in the vast majority of cases, he is coarse, ignorant, and profoundly unhappy? We should stop admiring ourselves. We should just work, and that's all.

275 GAYEV: You die, anyway.

TROFIMOV: Who knows? And what does it mean—to die? It may be that man has a hundred senses, and at his death only the five that are known to us perish, and the other ninety-five go on living.

280 LYUBOV ANDREYEVNA: How clever you are, Petya!

LOPAKHIN: (ironically) Terribly clever!

TROFIMOV: Mankind goes forward, perfecting its powers. Everything that is now unattainable will some day be comprehensible and within our grasp, only we must work, and help with
285 all our might those who are seeking the truth. So far, among us here in Russia, only a very few work. The great majority of the intelligentsia that I know seek nothing, do nothing, and as yet are incapable of work. They call themselves the intelligentsia, yet they belittle their servants, treat the peasants like
290 animals, are wretched students, never read anything serious, and do absolutely nothing; they only talk about science and know very little about art. They all look serious, have grim expressions, speak of weighty matters, and philosophize; and meanwhile anyone can see that the workers eat abominably,
295 sleep without pillows, thirty or forty to a room, and everywhere there are bedbugs, stench, dampness, and immorality. . . . It's obvious that all our fine talk is merely to delude ourselves and others. Show me the day nurseries they are always talking about—and where are the reading rooms? They only
300 write about them in novels, but in reality they don't exist. There is nothing but filth, vulgarity, asiaticism. . . . I'm afraid of those very serious countenances, I don't like them, I'm afraid of serious conversations. We'd do better to remain silent.

LOPAKHIN: You know, I get up before five in the morning, and I
305 work from morning to night; now, I'm always handling money, my own and other people's, and I see what people around me are like. You have only to start doing something to find out how few honest, decent people there are. Sometimes, when I can't sleep, I think: "Lord, Thou gavest us vast

forests, boundless fields, broad horizons, and living in their 310 midst we ourselves ought truly to be giants. . . ."

LYUBOV ANDREYEVNA: Now you want giants! They're good only in fairy tales, otherwise they're frightening.

(YEPIKHODOV crosses at the rear of the stage, playing the guitar.)

LYUBOV ANDREYEVNA: (pensively) There goes Yepikhodov . . .

ANYA: (pensively) There goes Yepikhodov . . . 315

GAYEV: The sun has set, ladies and gentlemen.

TROFIMOV: Yes.

GAYEV: (in a low voice, as though reciting) Oh, Nature, wondrous Nature, you shine with eternal radiance, beautiful and indifferent; you, whom we call mother, unite within yourself 320 both life and death, giving life and taking it away. . . .

VARYA: (beseechingly) Uncle dear!

ANYA: Uncle, you're doing it again!

TROFIMOV: You'd better cue ball into the center.

GAYEV: I'll be silent, silent. 325

(All sit lost in thought. The silence is broken only by the subdued muttering of FIRS. Suddenly a distant sound is heard, as if from the sky, like the sound of a snapped string mournfully dying away.)

LYUBOV ANDREYEVNA: What was that?

LOPAKHIN: I don't know. Somewhere far off in a mine shaft a bucket's broken loose. But somewhere very far away.

GAYEV: It might be a bird of some sort . . . like a heron.

TROFIMOV: Or an owl . . . 330

LYUBOV ANDREYEVNA: (shudders) It's unpleasant somehow. . . . (Pause)

FIRS: The same thing happened before the troubles: an owl hooted and the samovar hissed continually.

GAYEV: Before what troubles? 335

FIRS: Before the Emancipation.

LYUBOV ANDREYEVNA: Come along, my friends, let us go, evening is falling. (To ANYA) There are tears in your eyes—what is it, my little one?

(Embraces her.)

ANYA: It's all right, Mama. It's nothing. 340

TROFIMOV: Someone is coming.

(A STRANGER appears wearing a shabby white forage cap and an overcoat. He is slightly drunk.)

STRANGER: Permit me to inquire, can I go straight through here to the station?

GAYEV: You can. Follow the road.

STRANGER: I am deeply grateful to you. (Coughs.) Splendid 345 weather. . . . (Reciting) "My brother, my suffering brother . . . come to the Volga, whose groans" . . . (To VARYA) Mademoiselle, will you oblige a hungry Russian with thirty kopecks?

(VARYA, frightened, cries out.)

LOPAKHIN: (angrily) There's a limit to everything.

LYUBOV ANDREYEVNA: (panic-stricken) Here you are—take 350 this. . . . (Fumbles in her purse.) I have no silver. . . . Never mind, here's a gold piece for you . . .

STRANGER: I am deeply grateful to you. (Goes off.)

(Laughter)

VARYA: (frightened) I'm leaving . . . I'm leaving. . . . Oh,

355 Mama, dear, there's nothing in the house for the servants to eat, and you give him a gold piece!

LYUBOV ANDREYEVNA: What's to be done with such a silly creature? When we get home I'll give you all I've got. Yermolai Alekseyevich, you'll lend me some more!

360 LOPAKHIN: At your service.

LYUBOV ANDREYEVNA: Come, my friends, it's time to go. Oh, Varya, we have definitely made a match for you. Congratulations!

VARYA: (through tears) Mama, that's not something to joke about.

365 LOPAKHIN: "Aurelia, get thee to a nunnery . . ."

GAYEV: Look, my hands are trembling: it's a long time since I've played a game of billiards.

LOPAKHIN: "Aurelia, O Nymph, in thy orisons, be all my sins remember'd!"

370 LYUBOV ANDREYEVNA: Let us go, my friends, it will soon be suppertime.

VARYA: He frightened me. My heart is simply pounding.

LOPAKHIN: Let me remind you, ladies and gentlemen: on the twenty-second of August the cherry orchard is to be sold.

375 Think about that! — Think!

(All go out except TROFIMOV and ANYA.)

ANYA: (laughs) My thanks to the stranger for frightening Varya, now we are alone.

TROFIMOV: Varya is so afraid we might suddenly fall in love with each other that she hasn't left us alone for days. With her

380 narrow mind she can't understand that we are above love. To avoid the petty and the illusory, which prevent our being free and happy — that is the aim and meaning of life. Forward! We are moving irresistibly toward the bright star that burns in the distance! Forward! Do not fall behind, friends!

385 ANYA: (clasping her hands) How well you talk! (Pause) It's marvelous here today!

TROFIMOV: Yes, the weather is wonderful.

ANYA: What have you done to me, Petya, that I no longer love the cherry orchard as I used to? I loved it so tenderly, it

390 seemed to me there was no better place on earth than our orchard.

TROFIMOV: All Russia is our orchard. It is a great and beautiful land, and there are many wonderful places in it. (Pause) Just think, Anya: your grandfather, your great-grandfather, and all

395 your ancestors were serf-owners, possessors of living souls. Don't you see that from every cherry tree, from every leaf and trunk, human beings are peering out at you? Don't you hear their voices? To possess living souls — that has corrupted all of you, those who lived before and you who are living now, so

400 that your mother, you, your uncle, no longer perceive that you are living in debt, at someone else's expense, at the expense of those whom you wouldn't allow to cross your threshold. . . . We are at least two hundred years behind the times, we have as yet absolutely nothing, we have no definite atti-

405 tude toward the past, we only philosophize, complain of boredom, or drink vodka. Yet it's quite clear that to begin to live we must first atone for the past, be done with it, and we can atone for it only by suffering, only by extraordinary, unceasing labor. Understand this, Anya.

410 ANYA: The house we live in hasn't really been ours for a long time, and I shall leave it, I give you my word.

TROFIMOV: If you have the keys of the household, throw them into the well and go. Be as free as the wind.

ANYA: (in ecstasy) How well you put that!

TROFIMOV: Believe me, Anya, believe me! I am not yet thirty, I 415 am young, still a student, but I have already been through so much! As soon as winter comes, I am hungry, sick, worried, poor as a beggar, and — where has not fate driven me! Where have I not been? And yet always, every minute of the day and night, my soul was filled with inexplicable premonitions. I 420 have a premonition of happiness, Anya, I can see it . . .

ANYA: The moon is rising.

(YEPIKHODOV is heard playing the same melancholy song on the guitar. The moon rises. Somewhere near the poplars VARYA is looking for ANYA and calling: "Anya, where are you?")

TROFIMOV: Yes, the moon is rising. (Pause) There it is — happiness . . . it's coming, nearer and nearer, I can hear its footsteps. And if we do not see it, if we do not recognize it, what 425 does it matter? Others will see it.

VARYA'S VOICE: Anya! Where are you?

TROFIMOV: That Varya again! (Angrily) It's revolting!

ANYA: Well? Let's go down to the river. It's lovely there.

TROFIMOV: Come on. (They go.) 430

VARYA'S VOICE: Anya! Anya!

— ACT THREE —

(The drawing room, separated by an arch from the ballroom. The chandelier is lighted. The Jewish band that was mentioned in Act Two is heard playing in the hall. It is evening. In the ballroom they are dancing a grand rond. The voice of SEMYONOV-PISHCHIK: "Promenade à une paire!" They all enter the drawing room: PISHCHIK and CHARLOTTA IVANOVNA are the first couple, TROFIMOV and LYUBOV ANDREYEVNA the second, ANYA and the POST-OFFICE CLERK the third, VARYA and the STATIONMASTER the fourth, etc. VARYA, quietly weeping, dries her tears as she dances. DUNYASHA is in the last couple. As they cross the drawing room PISHCHIK calls: "Grand rond, balancez!" and "Les cavaliers à genoux et remercier vos dames!" FIRS, wearing a dress coat, brings in a tray with seltzer water. PISHCHIK and TROFIMOV come into the drawing room.)

PISHCHIK: I'm a full-blooded man, I've already had two strokes, and dancing's hard work for me, but as they say, "If you run with the pack, you can bark or not, but at least wag your tail." At that, I'm as strong as a horse. My late father — quite a joker he was, God rest his soul — used to say, talking about our 5 origins, that the ancient line of Semyonov-Pishchik was descended from the very horse that Caligula had seated in the Senate. . . . (Sits down.) But the trouble is — no money! A hungry dog believes in nothing but meat. . . . (Snores but wakes up at once.) It's the same with me — I can think of 10 nothing but money. . . .

TROFIMOV: You know, there really is something equine about your figure.

PISHCHIK: Well, a horse is a fine animal. . . . You can sell a horse.

(There is the sound of a billiard game in the next room. VARYA appears in the archway.)

TROFIMOV: (teasing her) Madame Lopakhina! Madame 15 Lopakhina!

VARYA: (angrily) Mangy gentleman!

TROFIMOV: Yes, I am a mangy gentleman, and proud of it!

VARYA: (reflecting bitterly) Here we've hired musicians, and what are we going to pay them with? (Goes out.)

TROFIMOV: (To PISHCHIK) If the energy you have expended in the course of your life trying to find money to pay interest had gone into something else, ultimately, you might very well have turned the world upside down.

PISHCHIK: Nietzsche . . . the philosopher . . . the greatest, most renowned . . . a man of tremendous intellect . . . says in his works that it is possible to forge banknotes.

TROFIMOV: And have you read Nietzsche?

PISHCHIK: Well . . . Dashenka told me. I'm in such a state now that I'm just about ready for forging. . . . The day after tomorrow I have to pay three hundred and ten rubles . . . I've got a hundred and thirty. . . . (Feels in his pocket, grows alarmed.) The money is gone! I've lost the money! (Tearfully) Where is my money? (Joyfully) Here it is, inside the lining. . . . I'm all in a sweat . . .

(LYUBOV ANDREYEVNA and CHARLOTTA IVANOVNA come in.)

LYUBOV ANDREYEVNA: (humming a Lezginka) Why does Leonid take so long? What is he doing in town? (To DUNYASHA) Dunyasha, offer the musicians some tea.

TROFIMOV: In all probability, the auction didn't take place.

LYUBOV ANDREYEVNA: It was the wrong time to have the musicians, the wrong time to give a dance. . . . Well, never mind. . . . (Sits down and hums softly.)

CHARLOTTA: (gives PISHCHIK a deck of cards) Here's a deck of cards for you. Think of a card.

PISHCHIK: I've thought of one.

CHARLOTTA: Now shuffle the pack. Very good. And now, my dear Mr. Pishchik, hand it to me. Ein, zwei, drei! Now look for it—it's in your side pocket.

PISHCHIK: (takes the card out of his side pocket) The eight of spades—absolutely right! (Amazed) Think of that, now!

CHARLOTTA: (holding the deck of cards in the palm of her hand, to TROFIMOV) Quickly, tell me, which card is on top?

TROFIMOV: What? Well, the queen of spades.

CHARLOTTA: Right! (To PISHCHIK) Now which card is on top?

PISHCHIK: The ace of hearts.

CHARLOTTA: Right! (Claps her hands and the deck of cards disappears.) What lovely weather we're having today! (A mysterious feminine voice, which seems to come from under the floor, answers her: "Oh, yes, splendid weather, madam.") You are so nice, you're my ideal. . . . (The voice: "And I'm very fond of you, too, madam.")

STATIONMASTER: (applauding) Bravo, Madame Ventriloquist!

PISHCHIK: (amazed) Think of that, now! Most enchanting Charlotta Ivanovna . . . I am simply in love with you. . . .

CHARLOTTA: In love? (Shrugs her shoulders.) Is it possible that you can love? Guter Mensch, aber schlechter Musikant.

TROFIMOV: (claps PISHCHIK on the shoulder) You old horse, you!

CHARLOTTA: Attention, please! One more trick. (Takes a lap robe from a chair.) Here's a very fine lap robe; I should like to sell it. (Shakes it out.) Doesn't anyone want to buy it?

PISHCHIK: (amazed) Think of that, now!

CHARLOTTA: Ein, zwei, drei! (Quickly raises the lap robe; behind it stands Anya, who curtseys, runs to her mother, embraces her, and runs back into the ballroom amid the general enthusiasm.)

LYUBOV ANDREYEVNA: (applauding) Bravo, bravo!

CHARLOTTA: Once again! Ein, zwei, drei. (Raises the lap robe; behind it stands VARYA, who bows.)

PISHCHIK: (amazed) Think of that, now!

CHARLOTTA: The end! (Throws the robe at PISHCHIK, makes a curtsey, and runs out of the room.)

PISHCHIK: (hurries after her) The minx! . . . What a woman! What a woman! (Goes out.)

LYUBOV ANDREYEVNA: And Leonid still not here. What he is doing in town so long, I do not understand! It must be all over by now. Either the estate is sold, or the auction didn't take place—but why keep us in suspense so long!

VARYA: (trying to comfort her) Uncle has bought it, I am certain of that.

TROFIMOV: (mockingly) Yes.

VARYA: Great-aunt sent him power of attorney to buy it in her name and transfer the debt. She's doing it for Anya's sake. And I am sure, with God's help, Uncle will buy it.

LYUBOV ANDREYEVNA: Our great-aunt in Yaroslavl sent fifteen thousand to buy the estate in her name—she doesn't trust us—but that's not even enough to pay the interest. (Covers her face with her hands.) Today my fate will be decided, my fate . . .

TROFIMOV: (teasing VARYA) Madame Lopakhina!

VARYA: (angrily) Eternal student! Twice already you've been expelled from the university.

LYUBOV ANDREYEVNA: Why are you so cross, Varya? If he teases you about Lopakhin, what of it? Go ahead and marry Lopakhin if you want to. He's a nice man, he's interesting. And if you don't want to, don't. Nobody's forcing you, my pet.

VARYA: To be frank, Mama dear, I regard this matter seriously. He is a good man, I like him.

LYUBOV ANDREYEVNA: Then marry him. I don't know what you're waiting for!

VARYA: Mama, I can't propose to him myself. For the last two years everyone's been talking to me about him; everyone talks, but he is either silent or he jokes. I understand. He's getting rich, he's absorbed in business, he has no time for me. If I had some money, no matter how little, if it were only a hundred rubles, I'd drop everything and go far away. I'd go into a nunnery.

TROFIMOV: A blessing!

VARYA: (to TROFIMOV) A student ought to be intelligent! (In a gentle tone, tearfully) How homely you have grown, Petya, how old! (To LYUBOV ANDREYEVNA, no longer crying) It's just that I cannot live without work, Mama. I must be doing something every minute.

(YASHA enters.)

YASHA: (barely able to suppress his laughter) Yepikhodov has broken a billiard cue! (Goes out.)

VARYA: But why is Yepikhodov here? Who gave him permission to play billiards? I don't understand these people. . . . (Goes out.)

LYUBOV ANDREYEVNA: Don't tease her, Petya. You can see she's unhappy enough without that.

TROFIMOV: She's much too zealous, always meddling in other people's affairs. All summer long she's given Anya and me no peace—afraid a romance might develop. What business is it of hers? Besides, I've given no occasion for it, I am far removed from such banality. We are above love!

135 LYUBOV ANDREYEVNA: And I suppose I am beneath love. *(In great agitation)* Why isn't Leonid here? If only I knew whether the estate had been sold or not! The disaster seems to me so incredible that I don't even know what to think, I'm lost. . . . I could scream this very instant . . . I could do

140 something foolish. Save me, Petya. Talk to me, say something. . . .

TROFIMOV: Whether or not the estate is sold today—does it really matter? That's all done with long ago; there's no turning back, the path is overgrown. Be calm, my dear. One must not

145 deceive oneself; at least once in one's life one ought to look the truth straight in the eye.

LYUBOV ANDREYEVNA: What truth? You can see where there is truth and where there isn't, but I seem to have lost my sight, I see nothing. You boldly settle all the important problems, but

150 tell me, my dear boy, isn't it because you are young and have not yet had to suffer for a single one of your problems? You boldly look ahead, but isn't it because you neither see nor expect anything dreadful, since life is still hidden from your young eyes? You're bolder, more honest, deeper than we are,

155 but think about it, be just a little bit magnanimous, and spare me. You see, I was born here, my mother and father lived here, and my grandfather. I love this house, without the cherry orchard my life has no meaning for me, and if it must be sold, then sell me with the orchard. . . . *(Embraces*

160 TROFIMOV *and kisses him on the forehead.)* And my son was drowned here. . . . *(Weeps.)* Have pity on me, you good, kind man.

TROFIMOV: You know I feel for you with all my heart.

LYUBOV ANDREYEVNA: But that should have been said differ-

165 ently, quite differently. . . . *(Takes out her handkerchief and a telegram falls to the floor.)* My heart is heavy today, you can't imagine. It's so noisy here, my soul quivers at every sound, I tremble all over, and yet I can't go to my room. When I am alone the silence frightens me. Don't condemn me, Petya . . .

170 I love you as if you were my own. I would gladly let you marry Anya, I swear it, only you must study, my dear, you must get your degree. You do nothing, fate simply tosses you from place to place—it's so strange. . . . Isn't that true? Isn't it? And you must do something about your beard, to make it grow

175 somehow. . . . *(Laughs.)* You're so funny!

TROFIMOV: *(picks up the telegram)* I have no desire to be an Adonis.

LYUBOV ANDREYEVNA: That's a telegram from Paris. I get them every day. One yesterday, one today. That wild man has fallen

180 ill again, he's in trouble again. . . . He begs my forgiveness, implores me to come, and really, I ought to go to Paris to be near him. Your face is stern, Petya, but what can one do, my dear? What am I to do? He is ill, he's alone and unhappy, and who will look after him there, who will keep him from mak-

185 ing mistakes, who will give him his medicine on time? And why hide it or keep silent, I love him, that's clear. I love him, love him. . . . It's a millstone round my neck, I'm sinking to the bottom with it, but I love that stone, I cannot live without it. *(Presses* TROFIMOV's *hand.)* Don't think badly of me,

190 Petya, and don't say anything to me, don't say anything. . . .

TROFIMOV: *(through tears)* For God's sake, forgive my frankness: you know that he robbed you!

LYUBOV ANDREYEVNA: No, no, no, you mustn't say such things! *(Covers her ears.)*

TROFIMOV: But he's a scoundrel! You're the only one who 195 doesn't know it! He's a petty scoundrel, a nonentity—

LYUBOV ANDREYEVNA: *(angry, but controlling herself)* You are twenty-six or twenty-seven years old, but you're still a schoolboy!

TROFIMOV: That may be! 200

LYUBOV ANDREYEVNA: You should be a man, at your age you ought to understand those who love. And you ought to be in love yourself. *(Angrily)* Yes, yes! It's not purity with you, it's simply prudery, you're a ridiculous crank, a freak—

TROFIMOV: *(horrified)* What is she saying! 205

LYUBOV ANDREYEVNA: "I am above love!" You're not above love, you're just an addlepate, as Firs would say. Not to have a mistress at your age!

TROFIMOV: *(in horror)* This is awful! What is she saying! . . . *(Goes quickly toward the ballroom.)* This is awful . . . I can't 210 . . . I won't stay here. . . . *(Goes out, but immediately returns.)* All is over between us! *(Goes out to the hall.)*

LYUBOV ANDREYEVNA: *(calls after him)* Petya, wait! You absurd creature, I was joking! Petya!

(In the hall there is the sound of someone running quickly downstairs and suddenly falling with a crash. ANYA *and* VARYA *scream, but a moment later laughter is heard.)*

LYUBOV ANDREYEVNA: What was that? 215

*(*ANYA *runs in.)*

ANYA: *(laughing)* Petya fell down the stairs! *(Runs out.)*

LYUBOV ANDREYEVNA: What a funny boy that Petya is!

(The STATIONMASTER *stands in the middle of the ballroom and recites A. Tolstoy's "The Sinner." Everyone listens to him, but he has no sooner spoken a few lines than the sound of a waltz is heard from the hall and the recitation is broken off. They all dance.* TROFIMOV, ANYA, VARYA, *and* LYUBOV ANDREYEVNA *come in from the hall.)*

LYUBOV ANDREYEVNA: Come, Petya . . . come, you pure soul . . . please, forgive me. . . . Let's dance. . . . *(They dance.)*

*(*ANYA *and* VARYA *dance.* FIRS *comes in, puts his stick by the side door.* YASHA *also comes into the drawing room and watches the dancers.)*

YASHA: What is it, grandpa? 220

FIRS: I don't feel well. In the old days we used to have generals, barons, admirals, dancing at our balls, but now we send for the post-office clerk and the stationmaster, and even they are none too eager to come. Somehow I've grown weak. The late master, their grandfather, dosed everyone with sealing wax, 225 no matter what ailed them. I've been taking sealing wax every day for twenty years or more; maybe that's what's kept me alive.

YASHA: You bore me, grandpa. *(Yawns.)* High time you croaked.

FIRS: Ah, you . . . addlepate! *(Mumbles.)* 230

*(*TROFIMOV *and* LYUBOV ANDREYEVNA *dance from the ballroom into the drawing room.)*

LYUBOV ANDREYEVNA: *Merci.* I'll sit down a while. *(Sits.)* I'm tired.

*(*ANYA *comes in.)*

ANYA: (excitedly) There was a man in the kitchen just now saying that the cherry orchard was sold today.

235 LYUBOV ANDREYEVNA: Sold to whom?

ANYA: He didn't say. He's gone. (Dances with TROFIMOV; they
go into the ballroom.)

YASHA: That was just some old man babbling. A stranger.

FIRS: Leonid Andreich is not back yet, still hasn't come. And

240 he's wearing the light, between-seasons overcoat; like enough
he'll catch cold. Ah, when they're young they're green.

LYUBOV ANDREYEVNA: This is killing me. Yasha, go and find
out who it was sold to.

YASHA: But that old man left long ago. (Laughs.)

245 LYUBOV ANDREYEVNA: (slightly annoyed) Well, what are you
laughing at? What are you so happy about?

YASHA: That Yepikhodov is very funny! Hopeless! Two-and-
twenty Troubles.

LYUBOV ANDREYEVNA: Firs, if the estate is sold, where will you go?

250 FIRS: Wherever you tell me to go, I'll go.

LYUBOV ANDREYEVNA: Why do you look like that? Aren't you
well? You ought to go to bed.

FIRS: Yes. . . . (With a smirk.) Go to bed, and without me who
will serve, who will see to things? I'm the only one in the

255 whole house.

YASHA: (to LYUBOV ANDREYEVNA) Lyubov Andreyevna! Permit
me to make a request, be so kind! If you go back to Paris again,
do me the favor of taking me with you. It is positively impossible for me to stay here. (Looking around, then in a low voice)

260 There's no need to say it, you can see for yourself, it's an
uncivilized country, the people have no morals, and the boredom! The food they give us in the kitchen is unmentionable,
and besides, there's this Firs who keeps walking about mumbling all sorts of inappropriate things. Take me with you, be so

265 kind!

(Enter PISHCHIK.)

PISHCHIK: May I have the pleasure of a waltz with you, fairest
lady? (LYUBOV ANDREYEVNA goes with him.) I really must
borrow a hundred and eighty rubles from you, my charmer . . .
I really must. . . . (Dancing.) Just a hundred and eighty

270 rubles. . . . (They pass into the ballroom.)

YASHA: (softly sings) "Wilt thou know my soul's unrest . . ."

(In the ballroom a figure in a gray top hat and checked trousers is
jumping about, waving its arms; there are shouts of "Bravo,
Charlotta Ivanovna!")

DUNYASHA: (stopping to powder her face) The young mistress
told me to dance—there are lots of gentlemen and not
enough ladies—but dancing makes me dizzy, and my heart

275 begins to thump. Firs Nikolayevich, the post-office clerk just
said something to me that took my breath away.

(The music grows more subdued.)

FIRS: What did he say to you?

DUNYASHA: "You," he said, "are like a flower."

YASHA: (yawns) What ignorance. . . . (Goes out.)

280 DUNYASHA: Like a flower. . . . I'm such a delicate girl, I just
adore tender words.

FIRS: You'll get your head turned.

(Enter YEPIKHODOV.)

YEPIKHODOV: Avdotya Fyodorovna, you are not desirous of seeing me . . . I might almost be some sort of insect. (Sighs.) Ah,
life!   285

DUNYASHA: What is you want?

YEPIKHODOV: Indubitably, you may be right. (Sighs.) But, of
course, if one looks at it from a point of view, then, if I may so
express myself, and you will forgive my frankness, you have
completely reduced me to a state of mind. I know my fate,   290
every day some misfortune befalls me, but I have long since
grown accustomed to that; I look upon my fate with a smile.
But you gave me your word, and although I—

DUNYASHA: Please, we'll talk about it later, but leave me in
peace now. Just now I'm dreaming. . . . (Plays with her fan.)   295

YEPIKHODOV: Every day a misfortune, and yet, if I may so express myself, I merely smile, I even laugh.

(VARYA enters from the ballroom.)

VARYA: Are you still here, Semyon? What a disrespectful man
you are, really! (To DUNYASHA) Run along, Dunyasha. (To
YEPIKHODOV) First you play billiards and break a cue, then   300
you wander about the drawing room as though you were a
guest.

YEPIKHODOV: You cannot, if I may so express myself, penalize
me.

VARYA: I am not penalizing you, I'm telling you. You do nothing 305
but wander from one place to another, and you don't do your
work. We keep a clerk, but for what, I don't know.

YEPIKHODOV: (offended) Whether I work, or wander about, or
eat, or play billiards, these are matters to be discussed only by
persons of discernment, and my elders.   310

VARYA: You dare say that to me! (Flaring up) You dare? You
mean to say I have no discernment? Get out of here! This
instant!

YEPIKHODOV: (intimidated) I beg you to express yourself in a
more delicate manner.   315

VARYA: (beside herself) Get out, this very instant! Get out! (He
goes to the door, she follows him.) Two-and-twenty Troubles!
Don't let me set eyes on you again!

YEPIKHODOV: (goes out, his voice is heard behind the door) I shall
lodge a complaint against you!   320

VARYA: Oh, you're coming back? (Seizes the stick left near the
door by FIRS.) Come, come on. . . . Come, I'll show you. . . .
Ah, so you're coming, are you? Then take that— (Swings the
stick just as LOPAKHIN enters.)

LOPAKHIN: Thank you kindly.   325

VARYA: (angrily and mockingly) I beg your pardon.

LOPAKHIN: Not at all. I humbly thank you for your charming
reception.

VARYA: Don't mention it. (Walks away, then looks back and gently asks.) I didn't hurt you, did I?   330

LOPAKHIN: No, it's nothing. A huge bump coming up, that's all.

(Voices in the ballroom: "Lopakhin has come! Yermolai Alekseich!" PISHCHIK enters.)

PISHCHIK: As I live and breathe! (Kisses LOPAKHIN.) There is a
whiff of cognac about you, dear soul. And we've been making
merry here, too.

(Enter LYUBOV ANDREYEVNA.)

335 LYUBOV ANDREYEVNA: Is that you, Yermolai Alekseich? What kept you so long? Where's Leonid?

LOPAKHIN: Leonid Andreich arrived with me, he's coming . . .

LYUBOV ANDREYEVNA: (agitated) Well, what happened? Did the sale take place? Tell me!

340 LOPAKHIN: (embarrassed, fearing to reveal his joy) The auction was over by four o'clock. . . . We missed the train, had to wait till half past nine. (Sighing heavily) Ugh! My head is swimming. . . .

(Enter GAYEV; he carries his purchases in one hand and wipes away his tears with the other.)

LYUBOV ANDREYEVNA: Lyonya, what happened? Well, Lyonya?
345 (Impatiently, through tears.) Be quick, for God's sake!

GAYEV: (not answering her, simply waves his hand. To FIRS, weeping) Here, take these. . . . There's anchovies, Kerch herrings. . . . I haven't eaten anything all day. . . . What I have been through! (The click of billiard balls is heard through the
350 open door to the billiard room, and YASHA's voice: "Seven and eighteen!" GAYEV's expression changes, he is no longer weeping.) I'm terribly tired. Firs, help me change. (Goes through the ballroom to his own room, followed by FIRS.)

PISHCHIK: What happened at the auction? Come on, tell us!

355 LYUBOV ANDREYEVNA: Is the cherry orchard sold?

LOPAKHIN: It's sold.

LYUBOV ANDREYEVNA: Who bought it?

LOPAKHIN: I bought it. (Pause)

(LYUBOV ANDREYEVNA is overcome; she would fall to the floor if it were not for the chair and table near which she stands. VARYA takes the keys from her belt and throws them on the floor in the middle of the drawing room and goes out.)

LOPAKHIN: I bought it! Kindly wait a moment, ladies and gentle-
360 men, my head is swimming, I can't talk. . . . (Laughs.) We arrived at the auction, Deriganov was already there. Leonid Andreich had only fifteen thousand, and straight off Deriganov bid thirty thousand over and above the mortgage. I saw how the land lay, so I got into the fight and bid forty. He
365 bid forty-five. I bid fifty-five. In other words, he kept raising it by five thousand, and I by ten. Well, it finally came to an end. I bid ninety thousand above the mortgage, and it was knocked down to me. The cherry orchard is now mine! Mine! (Laughs uproariously.) Lord! God in heaven! The cherry orchard
370 is mine! Tell me I'm drunk, out of my mind, that I imagine it. . . . (Stamps his feet.) Don't laugh at me! If my father and my grandfather could only rise from their graves and see all that has happened, how their Yermolai, their beaten, half-literate Yermolai, who used to run about barefoot in winter,
375 how that same Yermolai has bought an estate, the most beautiful estate in the whole world! I bought the estate where my father and grandfather were slaves, where they weren't even allowed in the kitchen. I'm asleep, this is just some dream of mine, it only seems to be. . . . It's the fruit of your imagina-
380 tion, hidden in the darkness of uncertainty. . . . (Picks up the keys, smiling tenderly.) She threw down the keys, wants to show that she's not mistress here any more. . . . (Jingles the keys.) Well, no matter. (The orchestra is heard tuning up.) Hey, musicians, play, I want to hear you! Come on, every-
385 body, and see how Yermolai Lopakhin will lay the ax to the cherry orchard, how the trees will fall to the ground! We're going to build summer cottages, and our grandsons and great-grandsons will see a new life here. . . . Music! Strike up!

(The orchestra plays. LYUBOV ANDREYEVNA sinks into a chair and weeps bitterly.)

LOPAKHIN: (reproachfully) Why didn't you listen to me, why? My poor friend, there's no turning back now. (With tears)
390 Oh, if only all this could be over quickly, if somehow our discordant, unhappy life could be changed!

PISHCHIK: (takes him by the arm; speaks in an undertone) She's crying. Let's go into the ballroom, let her be alone. . . . Come on. . . . (Leads him into the ballroom.)
395 LOPAKHIN: What's happened? Musicians, play so I can hear you! Let everything be as I want it! (Ironically) Here comes the new master, owner of the cherry orchard! (Accidentally bumps into a little table, almost upsetting the candelabrum.) I can pay for everything! (Goes out with PISHCHIK.)
400

(There is no one left in either the drawing room or the ballroom except LYUBOV ANDREYEVNA, who sits huddled up and weeping bitterly. The music plays softly. ANYA and TROFIMOV enter hurriedly. ANYA goes to her mother and kneels before her. TROFIMOV remains in the doorway of the ballroom.)

ANYA: Mama! . . . Mama, you're crying! Dear, kind, good Mama, my beautiful one, I love you . . . I bless you. The cherry orchard is sold, it's gone, that's true, true, but don't cry, Mama, life is still before you, you still have your good, pure soul. . . . Come with me, come, darling, we'll go away
405 from here! . . . We'll plant a new orchard, more luxuriant than this one. You will see it and understand; and joy, quiet, deep joy, will sink into your soul, like the evening sun, and you will smile, Mama! Come, darling, let us go. . . .

— ACT FOUR —

(The scene is the same as Act One. There are neither curtains on the windows nor pictures on the walls, and only a little furniture piled up in one corner, as if for sale. There is a sense of emptiness. Near the outer door, at the rear of the stage, suitcases, traveling bags, etc., are piled up. Through the open door on the left the voices of VARYA and ANYA can be heard. LOPAKHIN stands waiting. YASHA is holding a tray with little glasses of champagne. In the hall, YEPIKHODOV is tying up a box. Off stage, at the rear, there is a hum of voices. It is the peasants who have come to say good-bye. GAYEV's voice: "Thanks, brothers, thank you.")

YASHA: The peasants have come to say good-bye. In my opinion, Yermolai Alekseich, peasants are good-natured, but they don't know much.

(The hum subsides. LYUBOV ANDREYEVNA enters from the hall with GAYEV. She is not crying, but she is pale, her face twitches, and she cannot speak.)

GAYEV: You gave them your purse, Lyuba. That won't do! That won't do!
5
LYUBOV ANDREYEVNA: I couldn't help it! I couldn't help it! (They both go out.)

LOPAKHIN: (in the doorway, calls after them) Please, do me the honor of having a little glass at parting. I didn't think of bringing champagne from town, and at the station I found only
10

one bottle. Please! What's the matter, friends, don't you want any? *(Walks away from the door.)* If I'd known that, I wouldn't have bought it. Well, then I won't drink any either. *(YASHA carefully sets the tray down on a chair.)* At least you have a glass, Yasha.

YASHA: To those who are departing! Good luck! *(Drinks.)* This champagne is not the real stuff, I can assure you.

LOPAKHIN: Eight rubles a bottle. *(Pause)* It's devilish cold in here.

YASHA: They didn't light the stoves today; it doesn't matter, since we're leaving. *(Laughs.)*

LOPAKHIN: Why are you laughing?

YASHA: Because I'm pleased.

LOPAKHIN: It's October, yet it's sunny and still outside, like summer. Good for building. *(Looks at his watch, then calls through the door.)* Bear in mind, ladies and gentlemen, only forty-six minutes till train time! That means leaving for the station in twenty minutes. Better hurry up!

(TROFIMOV enters from outside wearing an overcoat.)

TROFIMOV: Seems to me it's time to start. The carriages are at the door. What the devil has become of my rubbers? They're lost. *(Calls through the door.)* Anya, my rubbers are not here. I can't find them.

LOPAKHIN: I've got to go to Kharkov. I'm taking the same train you are. I'm going to spend the winter in Kharkov. I've been hanging around here with you, and I'm sick and tired of loafing. I can't live without work, I don't know what to do with my hands; they dangle in some strange way, as if they didn't belong to me.

TROFIMOV: We'll soon be gone, then you can take up your useful labors again.

LOPAKHIN: Here, have a little drink.

TROFIMOV: No, I don't want any.

LOPAKHIN: So you're off for Moscow?

TROFIMOV: Yes, I'll see them into town, and tomorrow I'll go to Moscow.

LOPAKHIN: Yes. . . . Well, I expect the professors haven't been giving any lectures: they're waiting for you to come!

TROFIMOV: That's none of your business.

LOPAKHIN: How many years is it you've been studying at the university?

TROFIMOV: Can't you think of something new? That's stale and flat. *(Looks for his rubbers.)* You know, we'll probably never see each other again, so allow me to give you one piece of advice at parting: don't wave your arms about! Get out of that habit—of arm-waving. And another thing, building cottages and counting on the summer residents in time becoming independent farmers—that's just another form of arm-waving. Well, when all's said and done, I'm fond of you anyway. You have fine, delicate fingers, like an artist; you have a fine delicate soul.

LOPAKHIN: *(embraces him)* Good-bye, my dear fellow. Thank you for everything. Let me give you some money for the journey, if you need it.

TROFIMOV: What for? I don't need it.

LOPAKHIN: But you haven't any!

TROFIMOV: I have. Thank you. I got some money for a translation. Here it is in my pocket. *(Anxiously)* But where are my rubbers?

VARYA: *(from the next room)* Here, take the nasty things! *(Flings a pair of rubbers onto the stage.)*

TROFIMOV: What are you so cross about, Varya? Hm. . . . But these are not my rubbers.

LOPAKHIN: In the spring I sowed three thousand acres of poppies, and now I've made forty thousand rubles clear. And when my poppies were in bloom, what a picture it was! So, I'm telling you, I've made forty thousand, which means I'm offering you a loan because I can afford to. Why turn up your nose? I'm a peasant—I speak bluntly.

TROFIMOV: Your father was a peasant, mine was a pharmacist—which proves absolutely nothing. *(LOPAKHIN takes out his wallet.)* No, don't—even if you gave me two hundred thousand I wouldn't take it. I'm a free man. And everything that is valued so highly and held so dear by all of you, rich and poor alike, has not the slightest power over me—it's like a feather floating in the air. I can get along without you, I can pass you by, I'm strong and proud. Mankind is advancing toward the highest truth, the highest happiness attainable on earth, and I am in the front ranks!

LOPAKHIN: Will you get there?

TROFIMOV: I'll get there. *(Pause)* I'll either get there or I'll show others the way to get there.

(The sound of axes chopping down trees is heard in the distance.)

LOPAKHIN: Well, good-bye, my dear fellow. It's time to go. We turn up our noses at one another, but life goes on just the same. When I work for a long time without stopping, my mind is easier, and it seems to me that I, too, know why I exist. But how many there are in Russia, brother, who exist nobody knows why. Well, it doesn't matter, that's not what makes the wheels go round. They say Leonid Andreich has taken a position in the bank, six thousand a year. . . . Only, of course, he won't stick it out, he's too lazy. . . .

ANYA: *(in the doorway)* Mama asks you not to start cutting down the cherry orchard until she's gone.

TROFIMOV: Yes, really, not to have had the tact . . . *(Goes out through the hall.)*

LOPAKHIN: Right away, right away. . . . Ach, what people. . . . *(Follows TROFIMOV out.)*

ANYA: Has Firs been taken to the hospital?

YASHA: I told them this morning. They must have taken him.

ANYA: *(to YEPIKHODOV, who is crossing the room)* Semyon Panteleich, please find out if Firs has been taken to the hospital.

YASHA: *(offended)* I told Yegor this morning. Why ask a dozen times?

YEPIKHODOV: It is my conclusive opinion that the venerable Firs is beyond repair; it's time he was gathered to his fathers. And I can only envy him. *(Puts a suitcase down on a hatbox and crushes it.)* There you are! Of course! I knew it! *(Goes out.)*

YASHA: *(mockingly)* Two-and-twenty Troubles!

VARYA: *(through the door)* Has Firs been taken to the hospital?

ANYA: Yes, he has.

VARYA: Then why didn't they take the letter to the doctor?

ANYA: We must send it on after them. . . . *(Goes out.)*

VARYA: *(from the adjoining room)* Where is Yasha? Tell him his mother has come to say good-bye to him.

YASHA: *(waves his hand)* They really try my patience.

(DUNYASHA has been fussing with the luggage; now that YASHA is alone she goes up to him.)

125 DUNYASHA: You might give me one little look, Yasha. You're going away . . . leaving me. . . . (*Cries and throws herself on his neck.*)

YASHA: What's there to cry about? (*Drinks champagne.*) In six days I'll be in Paris again. Tomorrow we'll take the express, off

130 we go, and that's the last you'll see of us. I can hardly believe it. *Vive la France!* This place is not for me, I can't live here. . . . It can't be helped. I've had enough of this ignorance—I'm fed up with it. (*Drinks champagne.*) What are you crying for? Behave yourself properly, then you won't cry.

135 DUNYASHA: (*looks into a small mirror and powders her face*) Send me a letter from Paris. You know, I loved you, Yasha, how I loved you! I'm such a tender creature, Yasha!

YASHA: Here they come. (*Busies himself with the luggage, humming softly.*)

(*Enter* LYUBOV ANDREYEVNA, GAYEV, CHARLOTTA IVANOVNA.)

140 GAYEV: We ought to be leaving. There's not much time now. (*Looks at* YASHA.) Who smells of herring?

LYUBOV ANDREYEVNA: In about ten minutes we should be getting into the carriages. (*Glances around the room.*) Good-

145 bye, dear house, old grandfather. Winter will pass, spring will come, and you will no longer be here, they will tear you down. How much these walls have seen! (*Kisses her daughter warmly.*) My treasure, you are radiant, your eyes are sparkling like two diamonds. Are you glad? Very?

ANYA: Very! A new life is beginning, Mama!

150 GAYEV: (*cheerfully*) Yes, indeed, everything is all right now. Before the cherry orchard was sold we were all worried and miserable, but afterward, when the question was finally settled once and for all, everybody calmed down and felt quite cheerful. . . . I'm in a bank now, a financier . . . cue ball into the

155 center . . . and you, Lyuba, say what you like, you look better, no doubt about it.

LYUBOV ANDREYEVNA: Yes. My nerves are better, that's true. (*Her hat and coat are handed to her.*) I sleep well. Carry out my things, Yasha, it's time. (*To* ANYA) My little girl, we shall

160 see each other soon. . . . I shall go to Paris and live there on the money your great-aunt sent to buy the estate—long live Auntie!—but that money won't last long.

ANYA: You'll come back soon, Mama, soon . . . won't you? I'll study hard and pass my high-school examinations, and then I

165 can work and help you. We'll read all sorts of books together, Mama. . . . Won't we? (*Kisses her mother's hand.*) We'll read in the autumn evenings, we'll read lots of books, and a new and wonderful world will open up before us. . . . (*Dreaming*) Mama, come back. . . .

170 LYUBOV ANDREYEVNA: I'll come, my precious. (*Embraces her.*)

(*Enter* LOPAKHIN. CHARLOTTA IVANOVNA *is softly humming a song.*)

GAYEV: Happy Charlotta: she's singing!

CHARLOTTA: (*picks up a bundle and holds it like a baby in swaddling clothes*) Bye, baby, bye. . . . (*A baby's crying is heard,* "Wah! Wah!") Be quiet, my darling, my dear little boy.

175 ("Wah! Wah!") I'm so sorry for you! (*Throws the bundle down.*) You will find me a position, won't you? I can't go on like this.

LOPAKHIN: We'll find something, Charlotta Ivanovna, don't worry.

GAYEV: Everyone is leaving us, Varya's going away . . . all of a 180 sudden nobody needs us.

CHARLOTTA: I have nowhere to go in town. I must go away. (*Hums.*) It doesn't matter . . .

(*Enter* PISHCHIK.)

LOPAKHIN: Nature's wonder!

PISHCHIK: (*panting*) Ugh! Let me catch my breath. . . . I'm 185 exhausted. . . . My esteemed friends. . . . Give me some water. . . .

GAYEV: After money, I suppose? Excuse me, I'm fleeing from temptation. . . . (*Goes out.*)

PISHCHIK: It's a long time since I've been to see you . . . fairest 190 lady. . . . (*To* LOPAKHIN) So you're here. . . . Glad to see you, you intellectual giant. . . . Here . . . take it . . . four hundred rubles . . . I still owe you eight hundred and forty . . .

LOPAKHIN: (*shrugs his shoulders in bewilderment*) I must be dreaming. . . . Where did you get it? 195

PISHCHIK: Wait . . . I'm hot. . . . A most extraordinary event. Some Englishmen came to my place and discovered some kind of white clay on my land. (*To* LYUBOV ANDREYEVNA) And four hundred for you . . . fairest, most wonderful lady. . . . (*Hands her the money.*) The rest later. (*Takes a drink of wa-* 200 *ter.*) Just now a young man in the train was saying that a certain . . . great philosopher recommends jumping off roofs. . . . "Jump!" he says, and therein lies the whole problem. (*In amazement*) Think of that, now! . . . Water!

LOPAKHIN: Who were those Englishmen? 205

PISHCHIK: I leased them the tract of land with the clay on it for twenty-four years. . . . And now, excuse me, I have no time . . . I must be trotting along . . . I'm going to Znoikov's . . . to Kardamanov's . . . I owe everybody. (*Drinks.*) Keep well . . . I'll drop in on Thursday . . . 210

LYUBOV ANDREYEVNA: We're just moving into town, and tomorrow I go abroad . . .

PISHCHIK: What? (*Alarmed*) Why into town? That's why I see the furniture . . . suitcases. . . . Well, never mind. (*Through tears*) Never mind. . . . Men of the greatest intel- 215 lect, those Englishmen. . . . Never mind. . . . Be happy . . . God will help you. . . . Never mind. . . . Everything in this world comes to an end. . . . (*Kisses* LYUBOV ANDREYEVNA'*s hand.*) And should the news reach you that my end has come, just remember this old horse, and say: "There once 220 lived a certain Semyonov-Pishchik, God rest his soul." . . . Splendid weather. . . . Yes. . . . (*Goes out greatly disconcerted, but immediately returns and speaks from the doorway.*) Dashenka sends her regards. (*Goes out.*)

LYUBOV ANDREYEVNA: Now we can go. I am leaving with two 225 things on my mind. First—that Firs is sick. (*Looks at her watch.*) We still have about five minutes. . . .

ANYA: Mama, Firs has already been taken to the hospital. Yasha sent him there this morning.

LYUBOV ANDREYEVNA: My second concern is Varya. She's used 230 to getting up early and working, and now, with no work to do, she's like a fish out of water. She's grown pale and thin, and cries all the time, poor girl. . . . (*Pause*) You know very well, Yermolai Alekseich, that I dreamed of marrying her to you, and everything pointed to your getting married. (*Whispers to* 235

ANYA, *who nods to* CHARLOTTA, *and they both go out.*) She loves you, you are fond of her, and I don't know—I don't know why it is you seem to avoid each other. I can't understand it!

240 LOPAKHIN: To tell you the truth, I don't understand it myself. The whole thing is strange, somehow. . . . If there's still time, I'm ready right now. . . . Let's finish it up—and *basta*, but without you I feel I'll never be able to propose to her.

LYUBOV ANDREYEVNA: Splendid! After all, it only takes a min-
245 ute. I'll call her in at once. . . .

LOPAKHIN: And we even have the champagne. (*Looks at the glasses.*) Empty! Somebody's already drunk it. (YASHA *coughs.*) That's what you call lapping it up.

LYUBOV ANDREYEVNA: (*animatedly*) Splendid! We'll leave you.
250 . . . Yasha, *allez!* I'll call her. . . . (*At the door*) Varya, leave everything and come here. Come! (*Goes out with* YASHA.)

LOPAKHIN: (*looking at his watch*) Yes. . . . (*Pause*)

(*Behind the door there is smothered laughter and whispering; finally* VARYA *enters.*)

VARYA: (*looking over the luggage for a long time*) Strange, I can't seem to find it . . .

255 LOPAKHIN: What are you looking for?

VARYA: I packed it myself, and I can't remember . . . (*Pause*)

LOPAKHIN: Where are you going now, Varya Mikhailovna?

VARYA: I? To the Ragulins'. . . . I've agreed to go there to look after the house . . . as a sort of housekeeper.

260 LOPAKHIN: At Yashnevo? That would be about seventy versts from here. (*Pause*) Well, life in this house has come to an end. . . .

VARYA: (*examining the luggage*) Where can it be? . . . Perhaps I put it in the trunk. . . . Yes, life in this house has come to an
265 end . . . there'll be no more . . .

LOPAKHIN: And I'm off for Kharkov . . . by the next train. I have a lot to do. I'm leaving Yepikhodov here . . . I've taken him on.

VARYA: Really!

270 LOPAKHIN: Last year at this time it was already snowing, if you remember, but now it's still and sunny. It's cold though. . . . About three degrees of frost.

VARYA: I haven't looked. (*Pause*) And besides, our thermometer's broken. (*Pause*)

(*A voice from the yard calls:* "Yermolai Alekseich!")

275 LOPAKHIN: (*as if he had been waiting for a long time for the call.*) Coming! (*Goes out quickly.*)

(VARYA *sits on the floor, lays her head on a bundle of clothes, and quietly sobs. The door opens and* LYUBOV ANDREYEVNA *enters cautiously.*)

LYUBOV ANDREYEVNA: Well? (*Pause*) We must be going.

VARYA: (*no longer crying, dries her eyes*) Yes, it's time, Mama dear. I can get to the Ragulins' today, if only we don't miss the
280 train.

LYUBOV ANDREYEVNA: (*in the doorway*) Anya, put your things on!

(*Enter* ANYA, *then* GAYEV *and* CHARLOTTA IVANOVNA. GAYEV *wears a warm overcoat with a hood. The servants and coachmen come in.* YEPIKHODOV *bustles about the luggage.*)

LYUBOV ANDREYEVNA: Now we can be on our way.

ANYA: (*joyfully*) On our way!

285 GAYEV: My friends, my dear, cherished friends! Leaving this house forever, can I pass over in silence, can I refrain from giving utterance, as we say farewell, to those feelings that now fill my whole being—

ANYA: (*imploringly*) Uncle!

290 VARYA: Uncle dear, don't!

GAYEV: (*forlornly*) Double the rail off the white to center table . . . yellow into the side pocket. . . . I'll be quiet. . . .

(*Enter* TROFIMOV, *then* LOPAKHIN.)

TROFIMOV: Well, ladies and gentlemen, it's time to go!

LOPAKHIN: Yepikhodov, my coat!

295 LYUBOV ANDREYEVNA: I'll sit here just one more minute. It's as though I had never before seen what the walls of this house were like, what the ceilings were like, and now I look at them hungrily, with such tender love . . .

300 GAYEV: I remember when I was six years old, sitting on this window sill on Whitsunday, watching my father going to church . . .

LYUBOV ANDREYEVNA: Have they taken all the things?

LOPAKHIN: Everything, I think. (*Puts on his overcoat.*) Yepikhodov, see that everything is in order.

305 YEPIKHODOV: (*in a hoarse voice*) Rest assured, Yermolai Alekseich!

LOPAKHIN: What's the matter with your voice?

YEPIKHODOV: Just drank some water . . . must have swallowed something.

310 YASHA: (*contemptuously*) What ignorance!

LYUBOV ANDREYEVNA: When we go—there won't be a soul left here. . . .

LOPAKHIN: Till spring.

VARYA: (*pulls an umbrella out of a bundle as though she were
315 going to hit someone;* LOPAKHIN *pretends to be frightened*) Why are you—I never thought of such a thing!

TROFIMOV: Ladies and gentlemen, let's get into the carriages— it's time now! The train will soon be in!

VARYA: Petya, there they are—your rubbers, by the suitcase.
320 (*Tearfully*) And what dirty old things they are!

TROFIMOV: (*putting on his rubbers*) Let's go, ladies and gentlemen!

GAYEV: (*extremely upset, afraid of bursting into tears*) The train . . . the station. . . . Cross table to the center, double the rail
325 . . . on the white into the corner.

LYUBOV ANDREYEVNA: Let us go!

GAYEV: Are we all here? No one in there? (*Locks the side door on the left.*) There are some things stored in there, we must lock up. Let's go!

330 ANYA: Good-bye, house! Good-bye, old life!

TROFIMOV: Hail to the new life! (*Goes out with* ANYA.)

(VARYA *looks around the room and slowly goes out.* YASHA *and* CHARLOTTA *with her dog go out.*)

LOPAKHIN: And so, till spring. Come along, my friends. . . . Till we meet! (*Goes out.*)

(LYUBOV ANDREYEVNA *and* GAYEV *are left alone. As though they had been waiting for this, they fall onto each other's necks and break into quiet, restrained sobs, afraid of being heard.*)

GAYEV: (in despair) My sister, my sister. . . .

335   LYUBOV ANDREYEVNA: Oh, my dear, sweet, lovely orchard! . . .
   My life, my youth, my happiness, good-bye! . . . Good-bye!

ANYA'S VOICE: (gaily calling) Mama!

TROFIMOV'S VOICE: (gay and excited) Aa-oo!

LYUBOV ANDREYEVNA: One last look at these walls, these win-
340   dows. . . . Mother loved to walk about in this room. . . .

GAYEV: My sister, my sister!

ANYA'S VOICE: Mama!

TROFIMOV'S VOICE: Aa-oo!

LYUBOV ANDREYEVNA: We're coming! (They go out.)

(The stage is empty. There is the sound of doors being locked, then
of the carriages driving away. It grows quiet. In the stillness there
is the dull thud of an ax on a tree, a forlorn, melancholy sound.
Footsteps are heard. From the door on the right FIRS appears. He
is dressed as always in a jacket and white waistcoat, and wears
slippers. He is ill.)

FIRS: (goes to the door and tries the handle) Locked. They have   345
   gone. . . . (Sits down on the sofa.) They've forgotten me. . . .
   Never mind . . . I'll sit here awhile. . . . I expect Leonid
   Andreich hasn't put on his fur coat and has gone off in his
   overcoat. (Sighs anxiously.) And I didn't see to it. . . . When
   they're young, they're green! (Mumbles something which can-   350
   not be understood.) I'll lie down awhile. . . . There's no
   strength left in you, nothing's left, nothing. . . . Ach, you . . .
   addlepate! (Lies motionless.)

(A distant sound is heard that seems to come from the sky, the
sound of a snapped string mournfully dying away. A stillness
falls, and nothing is heard but the thud of the ax on a tree far
away in the orchard.)

WILLIAM BUTLER YEATS

William Butler Yeats (1865–1939) is the preeminent modern poet of the English language. Born in Ireland, Yeats was an early and ardent supporter of Irish independence from England. He wrote brilliantly in support of the independence movement in poems like "Easter 1916," "The Tower," "Meditation in Time of Civil War," in plays like *Cathleen Ni Houlihan*, and in his cycle of plays on the mythological hero Cuchulain. Throughout his long career, Yeats worked to establish a national theater in Ireland, one that would support and legitimize a truly native Irish culture. For although Dublin had supported theaters since the seventeenth century, these theaters expressed an English, colonial attitude toward Ireland and the Irish. Yeats, who was of Anglo-Irish Protestant descent, was an established poet by the turn of the century, when he joined forces with Lady Augusta Gregory (an accomplished playwright who had also gathered a collection of Irish myths and legends), the playwright John Millington Synge, and the inspired amateur actors Frank and W. G. Fay. Organized under a variety of names, and playing in a variety of venues from 1899–1902, the Irish National Theater Society was first established by Yeats and his associates in 1902. They opened at their new house—the Abbey Theater—in December 1904 with a program featuring Yeats's *On Baile's Strand* and Lady Gregory's *Spreading the News*.

The Abbey Theater more than fulfilled its mission. In the plays of Yeats, Lady Gregory, Synge, Sean O'Casey, Lennox Robinson, Brendan Behan, Micheál Mac Liammoir and many others, the Abbey sponsored a truly national drama. Also, like independent theaters in England, on the Continent, and in the United States, the Abbey brought the new drama of Europe and America to Dublin, staging plays by Hauptmann, Strindberg, O'Neill, Glaspell, and—among many others—two ex-patriate Irishmen: Bernard Shaw and Samuel Beckett. In the early decades of the twentieth century, the Abbey's repertoire of Irish drama was divided mainly into two genres. One was based on the material of Irish legend and history—Yeats's *Cathleen Ni Houlihan* (1902) and *On Baile's Strand* (1904), Synge's unfinished *Deirdre of the Sorrows* (1910)—and worked to foster a national identity by forging a shared national and political mythology. The Abbey also became known for plays about the Irish peasantry, such as Synge's *Riders to the Sea* (1904) and *The Playboy of the Western World* (1907). To these, Sean O'Casey later added a third genre, plays depicting the hard life of the Dublin slums and the political oppression by the English before independence was gained in 1922—plays like *The Shadow of a Gunman* (1923), *Juno and the Paycock* (1924), and *The Plough and the Stars* (1926). The Abbey's support of the nationalist cause was recognized in 1925, when it received a subsidy from the Irish Free State government, and the theater was reconstructed in 1966. The Abbey also has been influential as a model of nationalist theater in Northern Ireland, still part of the United Kingdom, inspiring companies like Brian Friel's Field Day Theater Company (on Friel, see unit 6).

Yeats worked assiduously and successfully in a narrow yet powerful vein, writing mainly verse plays in the symbolic mode. *On Baile's Strand* is one of a series of plays Yeats wrote on the subject of Cuchulain, the legendary warrior and a symbol of Irish nationalism. In 1914, Yeats began to work in a new mode, deeply influenced by his study of Japanese NOH DRAMA, a highly symbolic and literary dramatic form. The first of his "plays for dancers," *At the Hawk's Well* (1914), was written to be performed in an aristocratic drawing room by two actors and a dancer, with three musicians who outline the action in song. This fusion of verse, music, and dance in a highly refined and elite form of theater attracted Yeats throughout the rest of his life and is evident in *The Only Jealousy of Emer* (1919), *The Dreaming of the Bones* (1919), and *The Death of Cuchulain* (1939). Although Yeats never found a wide public for his drama, his control of the stage became increasingly confident and his plays vibrate with a special gem-like beauty and grace. He was awarded the Nobel Prize in 1923, but wrote much of his greatest work thereafter: the volumes *The Tower* (1928), *The Winding Stair* (1933), and *Last Poems* (1939); and the plays *Purgatory* (1939) and *The Death of Cuchulain*.

On Baile's Strand

On Baile's Strand is a good example of Yeats's technique in the theater. The play concerns the hero Cuchulain, who is forced to submit his will to the rule of King Conchubar at the opening of the play. Cuchulain symbolizes a passionate freedom, an unselfconscious intensity of feeling and expression that Yeats defined as "subjective." Conchubar represents the imposition of an external, "objective" order and restraint, the rule of the hearth, a civilizing principle that is finally opposed to the heroic self-defining identity of Cuchulain. The nature of heroic identity is a theme of much of Yeats's work, and it surfaces here in Cuchulain's relationship with the Young Man. Both are wild and free, and Cuchulain recognizes this kinship of spirit when he refuses to fight the redheaded stranger. Irritated by Conchubar's urging, and reminded that he has pledged to obey the king, Cuchulain strikes Conchubar — a wild deed that seems to possess everyone with the notion that they have been bewitched. Cuchulain turns on the Young Man, they leave by the upstage door and fight outside on the beach, where Cuchulain kills the young challenger. When it is revealed to him that the Young Man was his son, Cuchulain recognizes that in taking the oath of obedience he has betrayed himself and his future: he runs mad and fights the waves.

The heroic drama of delusion, obedience, and freedom is paralleled by a Shakespearean subplot, the story of the wandering Blind Man and the Fool, narrower versions of Conchubar and Cuchulain. More important, however, the Blind Man and the Fool suggest how identity is formed through a dialectical opposition between the self and its opposite, the anti-self that Yeats called the "mask" and that he explored in his extended philosophical and mythological meditation *A Vision* (1925). Characters in Yeats's mythology become themselves only by pursuing their "mask" — that opposite, anti-self — as Cuchulain discovers his self-destructive destiny when he opposes his own identity and agrees to be ruled by Conchubar. *On Baile's Strand* also suggests the indirect nature of Yeats's nationalist theater. The play advocates no immediate course of action to its audience. Instead, it shows the Irish hero both betraying himself and a powerful and attractive future, represented by the Young Man, when he accepts Conchubar's rule.

ON BAILE'S STRAND

William Butler Yeats

EDITED BY A. NORMAN JEFFARES

— CHARACTERS —

A FOOL
A BLIND MAN
CUCHULAIN, *King of Muirthemne*
CONCHUBAR, *High King of Uladh*
A YOUNG MAN, *son of Cuchulain*
KINGS AND SINGING WOMEN

A great hall at Dundealgan, not "Cuchulain's great ancient house" but an assembly-house nearer to the sea. A big door at the back, and through the door misty light as of sea-mist. There are many chairs and one long bench. One of these chairs, which is towards the front of the stage, is bigger than the others. Somewhere at the back there is a table with flagons of ale upon it and drinking-horns. There is a small door at one side of the hall. A FOOL *and* BLIND MAN, *both ragged, and their features made grotesque and extravagant by masks, come in through the door at the back. The* BLIND MAN *leans upon a staff.*

FOOL: What a clever man you are though you are blind! There's nobody with two eyes in his head that is as clever as you are. Who but you could have thought that the hen-wife sleeps every day a little at noon? I would never be able to steal any-
5 thing if you didn't tell me where to look for it. And what a good cook you are! You take the fowl out of my hands after I have stolen it and plucked it, and you put it into the big pot at the fire there, and I can go out and run races with the witches at the edge of the waves and get an appetite, and when I've got
10 it, there's the hen waiting inside for me, done to the turn.
BLIND MAN: *(who is feeling about with his stick.)* Done to the turn.
FOOL: *(putting his arm round* BLIND MAN's *neck.)* Come now, I'll have a leg and you'll have a leg, and we'll draw lots for the
15 wish-bone. I'll be praising you, I'll be praising you while we're eating it, for your good plans and for your good cooking. There's nobody in the world like you, Blind Man. Come, come. Wait a minute. I shouldn't have closed the door. There are some that look for me, and I wouldn't like them not to find
20 me. Don't tell it to anybody, Blind Man. There are some that follow me. Boann herself out of the river and Fand out of the deep sea. Witches they are, and they come by in the wind, and they cry, "Give a kiss, Fool, give a kiss," that's what they cry. That's wide enough. All the witches can come in now. I
25 wouldn't have them beat at the door and say, "Where is the Fool? Why has he put a lock on the door?" Maybe they'll hear the bubbling of the pot and come in and sit on the ground. But we won't give them any of the fowl. Let them go back to the sea, let them go back to the sea.
30 BLIND MAN: *(feeling legs of big chair with his hands.)* Ah! *(Then, in a louder voice as he feels the back of it.)* Ah — ah —
FOOL: Why do you say "Ah-ah"?
BLIND MAN: I know the big chair. It is to-day the High King Conchubar is coming. They have brought out his chair. He is
35 going to be Cuchulain's master in earnest from this day out. It is that he's coming for.
FOOL: He must be a great man to be Cuchulain's master.
BLIND MAN: So he is. He is a great man. He is over all the rest of the kings of Ireland.
40 FOOL: Cuchulain's master! I thought Cuchulain could do any-thing he liked.
BLIND MAN: So he did, so he did. But he ran too wild, and

Conchubar is coming to-day to put an oath upon him that will stop his rambling and make him as biddable as a house-dog and keep him always at his hand. He will sit in this chair 45 and put the oath upon him.
FOOL: How will he do that?
BLIND MAN: You have no wits to understand such things. *(The* BLIND MAN *has got into the chair.)* He will sit up in this chair and he'll say: "Take the oath, Cuchulain. I bid you take the 50 oath. Do as I tell you. What are your wits compared with mine, and what are your riches compared with mine? And what sons have you to pay your debts and to put a stone over you when you die? Take the oath, I tell you. Take a strong oath." 55
FOOL: *(crumpling himself up and whining.)* I will not. I'll take no oath. I want my dinner.
BLIND MAN: Hush, hush! It is not done yet.
FOOL: You said it was done to a turn.
BLIND MAN: Did I, now? Well, it might be done, and not done. 60 The wings might be white, but the legs might be red. The flesh might stick hard to the bones and not come away in the teeth. But, believe me, Fool, it will be well done before you put your teeth in it.
FOOL: My teeth are growing long with the hunger. 65
BLIND MAN: I'll tell you a story — the kings have story-tellers while they are waiting for their dinner — I will tell you a story with a fight in it, a story with a champion in it, and a ship and a queen's son that has his mind set on killing somebody that you and I know. 70
FOOL: Who is that? Who is he coming to kill?
BLIND MAN: Wait, now, till you hear. When you were stealing the fowl, I was lying in a hole in the sand, and I heard three men coming with a shuffling sort of noise. They were wound-ed and groaning. 75
FOOL: Go on. Tell me about the fight.
BLIND MAN: There had been a fight, a great fight, a tremendous great fight. A young man had landed on the shore, the guard-ians of the shore had asked his name, and he had refused to tell it, and he had killed one, and others had run away. 80
FOOL: That's enough. Come on now to the fowl. I wish it was bigger. I wish it was as big as a goose.
BLIND MAN: Hush! I haven't told you all. I know who that young man is. I heard the men who were running away say he

451

85   had red hair, that he had come from Aoife's country, that he
     was coming to kill Cuchulain.
FOOL: Nobody can do that.

(To a tune)

            Cuchulain has killed kings,
            Kings and sons of kings,
90   Dragons out of the water,
            And witches out of the air,
     Banachas and Bonachas and people of the woods.

BLIND MAN: Hush! hush!
FOOL: *(still singing.)*

            Witches that steal the milk,
95   Fomor that steal the children,
            Hags that have heads like hares,
            Hares that have claws like witches,
            All riding a-cock-horse

(Spoken)

     Out of the very bottom of the bitter black North.
100 BLIND MAN: Hush, I say!
FOOL: Does Cuchulain know that he is coming to kill him?
BLIND MAN: How would he know that with his head in the
     clouds? He doesn't care for common fighting. Why would he
     put himself out, and nobody in it but that young man? Now
105 if it were a white fawn that might turn into a queen before
     morning —
FOOL: Come to the fowl. I wish it was as big as a pig; a fowl with
     goose grease and pig's crackling.
BLIND MAN: No hurry, no hurry. I know whose son it is. I
110 wouldn't tell anybody else, but I will tell you, — a secret is
     better to you than your dinner. You like being told secrets.
FOOL: Tell me the secret.
BLIND MAN: That young man is Aoife's son. I am sure it is
     Aoife's son, it flows in upon me that it is Aoife's son. You have
115 often heard me talking of Aoife, the great woman-fighter Cu-
     chulain got the mastery over in the North.
FOOL: I know, I know. She is one of those cross queens that live
     in hungry Scotland.
BLIND MAN: I am sure it is her son. I was in Aoife's country for a
120 long time.
FOOL: That was before you were blinded for putting a curse
     upon the wind.
BLIND MAN: There was a boy in her house that had her own red
     colour on him, and everybody said he was to be brought up to
125 kill Cuchulain, that she hated Cuchulain. She used to put a
     helmet on a pillar-stone and call it Cuchulain and set him
     casting at it. There is a step outside — Cuchulain's step.

(CUCHULAIN passes by in the mist outside the big door.)

FOOL: Where is Cuchulain going?
BLIND MAN: He is going to meet Conchubar that has bidden
130 him to take the oath.
FOOL: Ah, an oath, Blind Man. How can I remember so many
     things at once? Who is going to take an oath?
BLIND MAN: Cuchulain is going to take an oath to Conchubar
     who is High King.
135 FOOL: What a mix-up you make of everything, Blind Man! You
     were telling me one story, and now you are telling me another

story. . . . How can I get the hang of it at the end if you mix
everything at the beginning? Wait till I settle it out. There
now, there's Cuchulain *(he points to one foot)*, and there is the
young man *(he points to the other foot)* that is coming to kill   140
him, and Cuchulain doesn't know. But where's Conchubar?
(Takes bag from side.) That's Conchubar with all his riches —
Cuchulain, young man, Conchubar. — And where's Aoife?
(Throws up cap.) There is Aoife, high up on the mountains in
high hungry Scotland. Maybe it is not true after all. Maybe it   145
was your own making up. It's many a time you cheated me
before with your lies. Come to the cooking-pot, my stomach
is pinched and rusty. Would you have it to be creaking like a
gate?
BLIND MAN: I tell you it's true. And more than that is true. If you   150
     listen to what I say, you'll forget your stomach.
FOOL: I won't.
BLIND MAN: Listen. I know who the young man's father is, but I
     won't say. I would be afraid to say. Ah, Fool, you would forget
     everything if you could know who the young man's father is.   155
FOOL: Who is it? Tell me now quick, or I'll shake you. Come,
     out with it, or I'll shake you.

(A murmur of voices in the distance.)

BLIND MAN: Wait, wait. There's somebody coming. . . . It is
     Cuchulain is coming. He's coming back with the High
     King. Go and ask Cuchulain. He'll tell you. It's little you'll   160
     care about the cooking-pot when you have asked Cuchulain,
     that . . .

(BLIND MAN goes out by side door.)

FOOL: I'll ask him. Cuchulain will know. He was in Aoife's
     country. *(Goes up stage.)* I'll ask him. *(Turns and goes down
     stage.)* But, no, I won't ask him, I would be afraid. *(Going up*   165
     again.) Yes, I will ask him. What harm in asking? The Blind
     Man said I was to ask him. *(Going down.)* No, no. I'll not ask
     him. He might kill me. I have but killed hens and geese and
     pigs. He has killed kings. *(Goes up again almost to big door.)*
     Who says I'm afraid? I'm not afraid. I'm no coward. I'll ask   170
     him. No, no, Cuchulain, I'm not going to ask you.

            He has killed kings,
            Kings and the sons of kings,
            Dragons out of the water,
            And witches out of the air,   175
     Banachas and Bonachas and people of the woods.

*(FOOL goes out by side door, the last words being heard outside.
CUCHULAIN and CONCHUBAR enter through the big door at the
back. While they are still outside, CUCHULAIN's voice is heard
raised in anger. He is a dark man, something over forty years of
age. CONCHUBAR is much older and carries a long staff, elaborately carved or with an elaborate gold handle.)*

CUCHULAIN: Because I have killed men without your bidding
     And have rewarded others at my own pleasure,
     Because of half a score of trifling things,
     You'd lay this oath upon me, and now — and now   180
     You add another pebble to the heap,
     And I must be your man, well-nigh your bondsman,
     Because a youngster out of Aoife's country
     Has found the shore ill-guarded.

CONCHUBAR: He came to land
185   While you were somewhere out of sight and hearing,
       Hunting or dancing with your wild companions.
CUCHULAIN: He can be driven out. I'll not be bound.
       I'll dance or hunt, or quarrel or make love,
       Wherever and whenever I've a mind to.
190   If time had not put water in your blood,
       You never would have thought it.
CONCHUBAR: I would leave
       A strong and settled country to my children.
CUCHULAIN: And I must be obedient in all things;
       Give up my will to yours; go where you please;
195   Come when you call; sit at the council-board
       Among the unshapely bodies of old men;
       I whose mere name has kept this country safe,
       I that in early days have driven out
       Maeve of Cruachan and the northern pirates,
200   The hundred kings of Sorcha, and the kings
       Out of the Garden in the East of the World.
       Must I, that held you on the throne when all
       Had pulled you from it, swear obedience
       As if I were some cattle-raising king?
205   Are my shins speckled with the heat of the fire,
       Or have my hands no skill but to make figures
       Upon the ashes with a stick? Am I
       So slack and idle that I need a whip
       Before I serve you?
CONCHUBAR: No, no whip, Cuchulain,
210   But every day my children come and say:
       "This man is growing harder to endure.
       How can we be at safety with this man
       That nobody can buy or bid or bind?
       We shall be at his mercy when you are gone;
215   He burns the earth as if he were a fire,
       And time can never touch him."
CUCHULAIN: And so the tale
       Grows finer yet; and I am to obey
       Whatever child you set upon the throne,
       As if it were yourself!
CONCHUBAR: Most certainly.
220   I am High King, my son shall be High King;
       And you for all the wildness of your blood,
       And though your father came out of the sun,
       Are but a little king and weigh but light
       In anything that touches government,
225   If put into the balance with my children.
CUCHULAIN: It's well that we should speak our minds out
           plainly,
       For when we die we shall be spoken of
       In many countries. We in our young days
       Have seen the heavens like a burning cloud
230   Brooding upon the world, and being more
       Than men can be now that cloud's lifted up,
       We should be the more truthful. Conchubar,
       I do not like your children — they have no pith,
       No marrow in their bones, and will lie soft
       Where you and I lie hard.
235   CONCHUBAR: You rail at them
       Because you have no children of your own.
CUCHULAIN: I think myself most lucky that I leave
       No pallid ghost or mockery of a man
       To drift and mutter in the corridors
       Where I have laughed and sung.
CONCHUBAR: That is not true,   240
       For all your boasting of the truth between us;
       For there is no man having house and lands,
       That have been in the one family, called
       By that one family's name for centuries,
       But is made miserable if he know   245
       They are to pass into a stranger's keeping,
       As yours will pass.
CUCHULAIN: The most of men feel that,
       But you and I leave names upon the harp.
CONCHUBAR: You play with arguments as lawyers do,
       And put no heart in them. I know your thoughts,   250
       For we have slept under the one cloak and drunk
       From the one wine-cup. I know you to the bone,
       I have heard you cry, aye, in your very sleep,
       "I have no son," and with such bitterness
       That I have gone upon my knees and prayed   255
       That it might be amended.
CUCHULAIN: For you thought
       That I should be as biddable as others
       Had I their reason for it; but that's not true;
       For I would need a weightier argument
       Than one that marred me in the copying,   260
       As I have that clean hawk out of the air
       That, as men say, begot this body of mine
       Upon a mortal woman.
CONCHUBAR: Now as ever
       You mock at every reasonable hope,
       And would have nothing, or impossible things.   265
       What eye has ever looked upon the child
       Would satisfy a mind like that?
CUCHULAIN: I would leave
       My house and name to none that would not face
       Even myself in battle.
CONCHUBAR: Being swift of foot,
       And making light of every common chance,   270
       You should have overtaken on the hills
       Some daughter of the air, or on the shore
       A daughter of the Country-under-Wave.
CUCHULAIN: I am not blasphemous.
CONCHUBAR: Yet you despise
       Our queens, and would not call a child your own,   275
       If one of them had borne him.
CUCHULAIN: I have not said it.
CONCHUBAR: Ah! I remember I have heard you boast,
       When the ale was in your blood, that there was one
       In Scotland, where you had learnt the trade of war,
       That had a stone-pale cheek and red-brown hair;   280
       And that although you had loved other women,
       You'd sooner that fierce woman of the camp
       Bore you a son than any queen among them.
CUCHULAIN: You call her a "fierce woman of the camp,"
       For, having lived among the spinning-wheels,   285
       You'd have no woman near that would not say,
       "Ah! how wise!" "What will you have for supper?"
       "What shall I wear that I may please you, sir?"
       And keep that humming through the day and night
       For ever. A fierce woman of the camp!   290
       But I am getting angry about nothing.

You have never seen her. Ah! Conchubar, had you seen her
With that high, laughing, turbulent head of hers
Thrown backward, and the bowstring at her ear,
295 Or sitting at the fire with those grave eyes
Full of good counsel as it were with wine,
Or when love ran through all the lineaments
Of her wild body—although she had no child,
None other had all beauty, queen or lover,
300 Or was so fitted to give birth to kings.
   CONCHUBAR: There's nothing I can say but drifts you farther
From the one weighty matter. That very woman—
For I know well that you are praising Aoife—
Now hates you and will leave no subtlety
305 Unknotted that might run into a noose
About your throat, no army in idleness
That might bring ruin on this land you serve.
   CUCHULAIN: No wonder in that, no wonder at all in that.
I never have known love but as a kiss
310 In the mid-battle, and a difficult truce
Of oil and water, candles and dark night,
Hillside and hollow, the hot-footed sun
And the cold, sliding, slippery-footed moon—
A brief forgiveness between opposites
315 That have been hatreds for three times the age
Of this long-'stablished ground.
   CONCHUBAR: Listen to me.
Aoife makes war on us, and every day
Our enemies grow greater and beat the walls
More bitterly, and you within the walls
320 Are every day more turbulent; and yet,
When I would speak about these things, your fancy
Runs as it were a swallow on the wind.

(Outside the door in the blue light of the sea-mist are many old
and young KINGS; among them are three WOMEN, two of whom
carry a bowl of fire. The third, in what follows, puts from time to
time fragrant herbs into the fire so that it flickers up into brighter
flame.)

Look at the door and what men gather there—
Old counsellors that steer the land with me,
325 And younger kings, the dancers and harp-players
That follow in your tumults, and all these
Are held there by the one anxiety.
Will you be bound into obedience
And so make this land safe for them and theirs?
330 You are but half a king and I but half;
I need your might of hand and burning heart,
And you my wisdom.
   CUCHULAIN: (going near to door.) Nestlings of a high nest,
Hawks that have followed me into the air
And looked upon the sun, we'll out of this
335 And sail upon the wind once more. This king
Would have me take an oath to do his will,
And having listened to his tune from morning,
I will no more of it. Run to the stable
And set the horses to the chariot-pole,
340 And send a messenger to the harp-players.
We'll find a level place among the woods,
And dance awhile.
   A YOUNG KING: Cuchulain, take the oath.
There is none here that would not have you take it.

CUCHULAIN: You'd have me take it? Are you of one mind?
THE KINGS: All, all, all, all!
A YOUNG KING: Do what the High King bids you.   345
CONCHUBAR: There is not one but dreads this turbulence
   Now that they're settled men.
CUCHULAIN: Are you so changed,
Or have I grown more dangerous of late?
But that's not it. I understand it all.
It's you that have changed. You've wives and children now,   350
And for that reason cannot follow one
That lives like a bird's flight from tree to tree. —
It's time the years put water in my blood
And drowned the wildness of it, for all's changed,
But that unchanged. —I'll take what oath you will: 355
The moon, the sun, the water, light, or air,
I do not care how binding.
CONCHUBAR: On this fire
That has been lighted from your hearth and mine;
The older men shall be my witnesses,
The younger, yours. The holders of the fire   360
Shall purify the thresholds of the house
With waving fire, and shut the outer door,
According to the custom; and sing rhyme.
That has come down from the old law-makers
To blow the witches out. Considering   365
That the wild will of man could be oath-bound,
But that a woman's could not, they bid us sing
Against the will of woman at its wildest
In the Shape-Changers that run upon the wind.

(CONCHUBAR has gone on to his throne.)

THE WOMEN: (They sing in a very low voice after the first few
   words so that the others all but drown their words.)

May this fire have driven out   370
The Shape-Changers that can put
Ruin on a great king's house
Until all be ruinous.
Names whereby a man has known
The threshold and the hearthstone,   375
Gather on the wind and drive
The women none can kiss and thrive,
For they are but whirling wind,
Out of memory and mind.
They would make a prince decay   380
With light images of clay
Planted in the running wave;
Or, for many shapes they have,
They would change them into hounds
Until he had died of his wounds,   385
Though the change were but a whim;
Or they'd hurl a spell at him,
That he follow with desire
Bodies that can never tire
Or grow kind, for they anoint   390
All their bodies, joint by joint,
With a miracle-working juice
That is made out of the grease
Of the ungoverned unicorn.
But the man is thrice forlorn,   395
Emptied, ruined, wracked, and lost,
That they follow, for at most

400 They will give him kiss for kiss
While they murmur, "After this
Hatred may be sweet to the taste."
Those wild hands that have embraced
All his body can but shove
At the burning wheel of love
Till the side of hate comes up.
405 Therefore in this ancient cup
May the sword-blades drink their fill
Of the home-brew there, until
They will have for masters none
But the threshold and hearthstone.

410 CUCHULAIN: (speaking, while they are singing.) I'll take and
      keep this oath, and from this day
I shall be what you please, my chicks, my nestlings.
Yet I had thought you were of those that praised
Whatever life could make the pulse run quickly,
Even though it were brief, and that you held
415 That a free gift was better than a forced. —
But that's all over. — I will keep it, too;
I never gave a gift and took it again.
If the wild horse should break the chariot-pole,
It would be punished. Should that be in the oath?

(Two of the WOMEN, still singing, crouch in front of him holding
the bowl over their heads. He spreads his hands over the flame.)

420 I swear to be obedient in all things
To Conchubar, and to uphold his children.
CONCHUBAR: We are one being, as these flames are one:
I give my wisdom, and I take your strength.
Now thrust the swords into the flame, and pray
425 That they may serve the threshold and the hearthstone
With faithful service.

(THE KINGS kneel in a semicircle before the two WOMEN and
CUCHULAIN, who thrusts his sword into the flame. They all put
the points of their swords into the flame. The third WOMAN is at
the back near the big door.)

CUCHULAIN: O pure, glittering ones
That should be more than wife or friend or mistress,
Give us the enduring will, the unquenchable hope,
The friendliness of the sword! —

(The song grows louder, and the last words ring out clearly. There
is a loud knocking at the door, and a cry of "Open! open!")

430 CONCHUBAR: Some king that has been loitering on the way.
Open the door, for I would have all know
That the oath's finished and Cuchulain bound,
And that the swords are drinking up the flame.

(The door is opened by the third WOMAN, and a YOUNG MAN
with a drawn sword enters.)

YOUNG MAN: I am of Aoife's country.

(The KINGS rush towards him. CUCHULAIN throws himself
between.)

CUCHULAIN: Put up your swords.
435 He is but one. Aoife is far away.
YOUNG MAN: I have come alone into the midst of you
To weigh this sword against Cuchulain's sword.

CONCHUBAR: And are you noble? for if of common seed,
You cannot weigh your sword against his sword
But in mixed battle.
YOUNG MAN: I am under bonds   440
To tell my name to no man; but it's noble.
CONCHUBAR: But I would know your name and not your
   bonds.
You cannot speak in the Assembly House,
If you are not noble.
FIRST OLD KING: Answer the High King!
YOUNG MAN: I will give no other proof than the hawk gives   445
That it's no sparrow!

(He is silent for a moment, then speaks to all.)

                    Yet look upon me, kings.
I, too, am of that ancient seed, and carry
The signs about this body and in these bones.
CUCHULAIN: To have shown the hawk's grey feather is
   enough,
And you speak highly, too. Give me that helmet.   450
I'd thought they had grown weary sending champions.
That sword and belt will do. This fighting's welcome.
The High King there has promised me his wisdom;
But the hawk's sleepy till its well-beloved
Cries out amid the acorns, or it has seen   455
Its enemy like a speck upon the sun.
What's wisdom to the hawk, when that clear eye
Is burning nearer up in the high air?

(Looks hard at YOUNG MAN; then comes down steps and grasps
YOUNG MAN by shoulder.)

Hither into the light.
(To CONCHUBAR.)   The very tint
Of her that I was speaking of but now.   460
Not a pin's difference.
(To YOUNG MAN.)   You are from the North,
Where there are many that have that tint of hair —
Red-brown, the light red-brown. Come nearer, boy,
For I would have another look at you.
There's more likeness — a pale, a stone-pale cheek.   465
What brought you, boy? Have you no fear of death?
YOUNG MAN: Whether I live or die is in the gods' hands.
CUCHULAIN: That is all words, all words; a young man's talk.
I am their plough, their harrow, their very strength;
For he that's in the sun begot this body   470
Upon a mortal woman, and I have heard tell
It seemed as if he had outrun the moon
That he must follow always through waste heaven,
He loved so happily. He'll be but slow
To break a tree that was so sweetly planted.   475
Let's see that arm. I'll see it if I choose.
That arm had a good father and a good mother,
But it is not like this.
YOUNG MAN: You are mocking me;
You think I am not worthy to be fought.
But I'll not wrangle but with this talkative knife.   480
CUCHULAIN: Put up your sword; I am not mocking you.
I'd have you for my friend, but if it's not
Because you have a hot heart and a cold eye,
I cannot tell the reason.
(To CONCHUBAR.)   He has got her fierceness,

485 And nobody is as fierce as those pale women.
     But I will keep him with me, Conchubar,
     That he may set my memory upon her
     When the day's fading. — You will stop with us,
     And we will hunt the deer and the wild bulls;
490 And, when we have grown weary, light our fires
     Between the wood and water, or on some mountain
     Where the Shape-Changers of the morning come.
     The High King there would make a mock of me
     Because I did not take a wife among them.
495 Why do you hang your head? It's a good life:
     The head grows prouder in the light of the dawn,
     And friendship thickens in the murmuring dark
     Where the spare hazels meet the wool-white foam.
     But I can see there's no more need for words
500 And that you'll be my friend from this day out.
     CONCHUBAR: He has come hither not in his own name
     But in Queen Aoife's, and has challenged us
     In challenging the foremost man of us all.
     CUCHULAIN: Well, well, what matter?
     CONCHUBAR: You think it does not matter,
505 And that a fancy lighter than the air,
     A whim of the moment, has more matter in it.
     For, having none that shall reign after you,
     You cannot think as I do, who would leave
     A throne too high for insult.
     CUCHULAIN: Let your children
510 Re-mortar their inheritance, as we have,
     And put more muscle on. — I'll give you gifts,
     But I'd have something too — that arm-ring, boy.
     We'll have this quarrel out when you are older.
     YOUNG MAN: There is no man I'd sooner have my friend
515 Than you, whose name has gone about the world
     As if it had been the wind; but Aoife'd say
     I had turned coward.
     CUCHULAIN: I will give you gifts
     That Aoife'll know, and all her people know,
     To have come from me.

     (Showing cloak.)

                         My father gave me this.
520 He came to try me, rising up at dawn
     Out of the cold dark of the rich sea.
     He challenged me to battle, but before
     My sword had touched his sword, told me his name,
     Gave me this cloak, and vanished. It was woven
525 By women of the Country-under-Wave
     Out of the fleeces of the sea. O! tell her
     I was afraid, or tell her what you will.
     No; tell her that I heard a raven croak
     On the north side of the house, and was afraid.
530 CONCHUBAR: Some witch of the air has troubled Cuchulain's
        mind.
     CUCHULAIN: No witchcraft. His head is like a woman's head
     I had a fancy for.
     CONCHUBAR: A witch of the air
     Can make a leaf confound us with memories.
     They run upon the wind and hurl the spells
535 That make us nothing, out of the invisible wind.
     They have gone to school to learn the trick of it.

     CUCHULAIN: No, no — there's nothing out of common here;
     The winds are innocent. — That arm-ring, boy.
     A KING: If I've your leave I'll take this challenge up.
     ANOTHER KING: No, give it me, High King, for this wild   540
        Aoife
     Has carried off my slaves.
     ANOTHER KING: No, give it me,
     For she has harried me in house and herd.
     ANOTHER KING: I claim this fight.
     OTHER KINGS: *(together.)*   And I! And I! And I!
     CUCHULAIN: Back! back! Put up your swords! Put up your
        swords!
     There's none alive that shall accept a challenge   545
     I have refused. Laegaire, put up your sword!
     YOUNG MAN: No, let them come. If they've a mind for it,
     I'll try it out with any two together.
     CUCHULAIN: That's spoken as I'd have spoken it at your age.
     But you are in my house. Whatever man   550
     Would fight with you shall fight it out with me.
     They're dumb, they're dumb. How many of you would
        meet

     (Draws sword.)

     This mutterer, this old whistler, this sand-piper,
     This edge that's greyer than the tide, this mouse
     That's gnawing at the timbers of the world,   555
     This, this — Boy, I would meet them all in arms
     If I'd a son like you. He would avenge me
     When I have withstood for the last time the men
     Whose fathers, brothers, sons, and friends I have killed
     Upholding Conchubar, when the four provinces   560
     Have gathered with the ravens over them.
     But I'd need no avenger. You and I
     Would scatter them like water from a dish.
     YOUNG MAN: We'll stand by one another from this out.
     Here is the ring.
     CUCHULAIN: No, turn and turn about.   565
     But my turn's first because I am the older.

     (Spreading out cloak.)

     Nine queens out of the Country-under-Wave
     Have woven it with the fleeces of the sea
     And they were long embroidering at it. — Boy,
     If I had fought my father, he'd have killed me,   570
     As certainly as if I had a son.
     And fought with him, I should be deadly to him;
     For the old fiery fountains are far off
     And every day there is less heat o' the blood.
     CONCHUBAR: *(in a loud voice.)* No more of this. I will not   575
        have this friendship.
     Cuchulain is my man, and I forbid it.
     He shall not go unfought, for I myself —
     CUCHULAIN: I will not have it.
     CONCHUBAR: You lay commands on me?
     CUCHULAIN: *(seizing* CONCHUBAR.*)* You shall not stir, High
        King.
     I'll hold you there.   580
     CONCHUBAR: Witchcraft has maddened you.
     THE KINGS: *(shouting.)*   Yes, witchcraft! witchcraft!
     FIRST OLD KING: Some witch has worked upon your mind,
        Cuchulain.

The head of that young man seemed like a woman's
You'd had a fancy for. Then of a sudden
585 You laid your hands on the High King himself!
CUCHULAIN: And laid my hands on the High King himself?
CONCHUBAR: Some witch is floating in the air above us.
CUCHULAIN: Yes, witchcraft! witchcraft! Witches of the air!
     (*To* YOUNG MAN.) Why did you? Who was it set you to this
     work?
590 Out, out! I say, for now it's sword on sword!
YOUNG MAN: But . . . but I did not.
CUCHULAIN: Out, I say, out, out!

(YOUNG MAN *goes out followed by* CUCHULAIN. THE KINGS *follow them out with confused cries, and words one can hardly hear because of the noise. Some cry,* "Quicker, quicker!" "Why are you so long at the door?" "We'll be too late!" "Have they begun to fight?" "Can you see if they are fighting?" *and so on. Their voices drown each other. The three* WOMEN *are left alone.*)

FIRST WOMAN: I have seen, I have seen!
SECOND WOMAN: What do you cry aloud?
FIRST WOMAN: The Ever-living have shown me what's to
     come.
THIRD WOMAN: How? Where?
FIRST WOMAN: In the ashes of the bowl.
595 SECOND WOMAN: While you were holding it between your
     hands?
THIRD WOMAN: Speak quickly!
FIRST WOMAN: I have seen Cuchulain's roof-tree
     Leap into fire, and the walls split and blacken.
SECOND WOMAN: Cuchulain has gone out to die.
THIRD WOMAN: O! O!
SECOND WOMAN: Who could have thought that one so great
     as he
600 Should meet his end at this unnoted sword!
FIRST WOMAN: Life drifts between a fool and a blind man
     To the end, and nobody can know his end.
SECOND WOMAN: Come, look upon the quenching of this
     greatness.

(*The other two go to the door, but they stop for a moment upon the threshold and wail.*)

FIRST WOMAN: No crying out, for there'll be need of cries
605 And rending of the hair when it's all finished.

(*The* WOMEN *go out. There is the sound of clashing swords from time to time during what follows. Enter the* FOOL, *dragging the* BLIND MAN.)

FOOL: You have eaten it, you have eaten it! You have left me nothing but the bones.

(*He throws* BLIND MAN *down by big chair.*)

BLIND MAN: O, that I should have to endure such a plague! O, I ache all over! O, I am pulled to pieces! This is the way you pay
610 me all the good I have done you.
FOOL: You have eaten it! You have told me lies. I might have known you had eaten it when I saw your slow, sleepy walk. Lie there till the kings come. O, I will tell Conchubar and Cuchulain and all the kings about you!
615 BLIND MAN: What would have happened to you but for me, and you without your wits? If I did not take care of you, what would you do for food and warmth?

FOOL: You take care of me? You stay safe, and send me into every kind of danger. You sent me down the cliff for gulls' eggs
620 while you warmed your blind eyes in the sun; and then you ate all that were good for food. You left me the eggs that were neither egg nor bird. (BLIND MAN *tries to rise;* FOOL *makes him lie down again.*) Keep quiet now, till I shut the door. There is some noise outside—a high vexing noise, so that I
625 can't be listening to myself. (*Shuts the big door.*) Why can't they be quiet? Why can't they be quiet? (BLIND MAN *tries to get away.*) Ah! you would get away, would you? (*Follows* BLIND MAN *and brings him back.*) Lie there! lie there! No, you won't get away! Lie there till the kings come. I'll tell them
630 all about you. I will tell it all. How you sit warming yourself, when you have made me light a fire of sticks, while I sit blowing it with my mouth. Do you not always make me take the windy side of the bush when it blows, and the rainy side when it rains?
635 BLIND MAN: O, good Fool! listen to me. Think of the care I have taken of you. I have brought you to many a warm hearth, where there was a good welcome for you, but you would not stay there; you were always wandering about.
FOOL: The last time you brought me in, it was not I who wan-
640 dered away, but you that got put out because you took the crubeen out of the pot when nobody was looking. Keep quiet, now!
CUCHULAIN: (*rushing in.*) Witchcraft! There is no witchcraft on the earth, or among the witches of the air, that these hands
645 cannot break.
FOOL: Listen to me, Cuchulain. I left him turning the fowl at the fire. He ate it all, though I had stolen it. He left me nothing but the feathers.
CUCHULAIN: Fill me a horn of ale!
650 BLIND MAN: I gave him what he likes best. You do not know how vain this Fool is. He likes nothing so well as a feather.
FOOL: He left me nothing but the bones and feathers. Nothing but the feathers, though I had stolen it.
CUCHULAIN: Give me that horn. Quarrels here, too! (*Drinks.*)
     What is there between you two that is worth a quarrel? Out
655 with it!
BLIND MAN: Where would he be but for me? I must be always thinking—thinking to get food for the two of us, and when we've got it, if the moon is at the full or the tide on the turn, he'll leave the rabbit in the snare till it is full of maggots, or let
660 the trout slip back through his hands into the stream.

(*The* FOOL *has begun singing while the* BLIND MAN *is speaking.*)

FOOL: (*singing*)

     When you were an acorn on the tree-top,
         Then was I an eagle-cock;
     Now that you are a withered old block,
         Still am I an eagle-cock.
665

BLIND MAN: Listen to him, now. That's the sort of talk I have to put up with day out, day in.

(*The* FOOL *is putting the feathers into his hair.* CUCHULAIN *takes a handful of feathers out of a heap the* FOOL *has on the bench beside him, and out of the* FOOL's *hair, and begins to wipe the blood from his sword with them.*)

FOOL: He has taken my feathers to wipe his sword. It is blood that he is wiping from his sword.

670   CUCHULAIN: *(goes up to door at back and throws away feathers.)*
      They are standing about his body. They will not awaken him
      for all his witchcraft.
      BLIND MAN: It is that young champion that he has killed. He
      that came out of Aoife's country.
675   CUCHULAIN: He thought to have saved himself with witchcraft.
      FOOL: That Blind Man there said he would kill you. He came
      from Aoife's country to kill you. That Blind Man said they
      had taught him every kind of weapon that he might do it. But
      I always knew that you would kill him.
680   CUCHULAIN: *(to the* BLIND MAN.) You knew him, then?
      BLIND MAN: I saw him, when I had my eyes, in Aoife's country.
      CUCHULAIN: You were in Aoife's country?
      BLIND MAN: I knew him and his mother there.
      CUCHULAIN: He was about to speak of her when he died.
685   BLIND MAN: He was a queen's son.
      CUCHULAIN: What queen? what queen? *(Seizes* BLIND MAN,
      who is now sitting upon the bench.) Was it Scathach? There
      were many queens. All the rulers there were queens.
      BLIND MAN: No, not Scathach.
690   CUCHULAIN: It was Uathach, then? Speak! speak!
      BLIND MAN: I cannot speak; you are clutching me too tightly.
      *(*CUCHULAIN *lets him go.)* I cannot remember who it was. I
      am not certain. It was some queen.
      FOOL: He said a while ago that the young man was Aoife's son.
695   CUCHULAIN: She? No, no! She had no son when I was there.
      FOOL: That Blind Man there said that she owned him for her
      son.
      CUCHULAIN: I had rather he had been some other woman's son.
      What father had he? A soldier out of Alba? She was an amo-
700   rous woman — a proud, pale, amorous woman.
      BLIND MAN: None knew whose son he was.
      CUCHULAIN: None knew! Did you know, old listener at doors?
      BLIND MAN: No, no; I knew nothing.
      FOOL: He said a while ago that he heard Aoife boast that she'd
705   never but the one lover, and he the only man that had over-
      come her in battle.   *(Pause.)*
      BLIND MAN: Somebody is trembling. Fool! The bench is shak-
      ing. Why are you trembling? Is Cuchulain going to hurt us? It
      was not I who told you, Cuchulain.
710   FOOL: It is Cuchulain who is trembling. It is Cuchulain who is
      shaking the bench.
      BLIND MAN: It is his own son he has slain.
      CUCHULAIN: 'Twas they that did it, the pale windy people.
      Where? where? where? My sword against the thunder!
715   But no, for they have always been my friends;
      And though they love to blow a smoking coal
      Till it's all flame, the wars they blow aflame
      Are full of glory, and heart-uplifting pride,
      And not like this. The wars they love awaken
720   Old fingers and the sleepy strings of harps.
      Who did it then? Are you afraid? Speak out!
      For I have put you under my protection,

And will reward you well. Dubthach the Chafer?
He'd an old grudge. No, for he is with Maeve.
Laegaire did it! Why do you not speak?   725
What is this house? *(Pause.)* Now I remember all.

(Comes before CONCHUBAR's *chair, and strikes out with his
sword, as if* CONCHUBAR *was sitting upon it.)*

'Twas you who did it — you who sat up there
With your old rod of kingship, like a magpie
Nursing a stolen spoon. No, not a magpie,
A maggot that is eating up the earth!   730
Yes, but a magpie, for he's flown away.
Where did he fly to?
BLIND MAN: He is outside the door.
CUCHULAIN: Outside the door?
BLIND MAN: Between the door and the sea.
CUCHULAIN: Conchubar, Conchubar! the sword into your
    heart!

(He rushes out. Pause. FOOL *creeps up to the big door and looks
after him.)*

FOOL: He is going up to King Conchubar. They are all about the   735
    young man. No, no, he is standing still. There is a great wave
    going to break, and he is looking at it. Ah! now he is running
    down to the sea, but he is holding up his sword as if he were
    going into a fight. *(Pause.)* Well struck! well struck!
BLIND MAN: What is he doing now?   740
FOOL: O! he is fighting the waves!
BLIND MAN: He sees King Conchubar's crown on every one of
    them.
FOOL: There, he has struck at a big one! He has struck the crown
    off it; he has made the foam fly. There again, another big one!   745
BLIND MAN: Where are the kings? What are the kings doing?
FOOL: They are shouting and running down to the shore, and
    the people are running out of the houses. They are all
    running.
BLIND MAN: You say they are running out of the houses? There   750
    will be nobody left in the houses. Listen, Fool!
FOOL: There, he is down! He is up again. He is going out in the
    deep water. There is a big wave. It has gone over him. I can-
    not see him now. He has killed kings and giants, but the waves
    have mastered him, the waves have mastered him!   755
BLIND MAN: Come here, Fool!
FOOL: The waves have mastered him.
BLIND MAN: Come here!
FOOL: The waves have mastered him.
BLIND MAN: Come here, I say.   760
FOOL: *(coming towards him, but looking backwards towards the
    door.)* What is it?
BLIND MAN: There will be nobody in the houses. Come this
    way; come quickly! The ovens will be full. We will put our
    hands into the ovens.   *(They go out.)*   765

BERNARD SHAW

George Bernard Shaw (1856–1950) — Shaw disliked the name "George" and never used it, preferring the initials G. B. S. — was a man of wide-ranging passions and huge abilities. By his fortieth birthday he had written five novels, three volumes of classic music criticism, and three volumes of incendiary theater reviews; he had become visible in the influential socialist political organization, the FABIAN SOCIETY; he had written the first books in English on Wagner's operas and on Ibsen's plays; and he had just started his career as a dramatist, a career that would eventually include over fifty plays.

Shaw was born in Dublin. Like Jonathan Swift and Richard Brinsley Sheridan before him, Shaw retained the satiric perspective of the Irish outsider in England. His mother was a music teacher and his sister was a promising singer when they left for London while Shaw was in his teens. He followed them to London in 1876. A shy and self-effacing young man, Shaw took a variety of jobs that brought him into contact with the public, and he used the opportunity of lecturing for the Fabian Society to develop the brilliantly articulate persona we recognize today as "G. B. S." Throughout the 1880s, Shaw worked with the Fabians, adopting their plan of gradual social reform in place of a more rigorously Marxist call for social revolution. The Fabians strove to change society through a strategy of permeation, working to get their members elected into prominent offices, where their educational and social reforms might be put into effect. Shaw was deeply influenced by the Fabians' gradualist scheme for social improvement, a scheme that underlies the utopian project of his greatest plays. For Fabian gradualism synchronized with Shaw's other passion, Creative Evolution. Appalled by what he regarded as the mindless mechanism of Darwinian natural selection, Shaw resisted the notion that human evolution followed a random and inevitable process. He urged instead that humanity take command of its future by willing itself to evolve in certain humane directions, and he advocated eugenics, capital punishment, and other ideas in the interest of the development of the species. Shaw attempted an uneasy synthesis of the Fabian socialist project of gradual social evolution with the individualist metaphysics of Creative Evolution: the improvement of society through the improvement of each of its members.

Shaw's friend William Archer once described seeing Shaw in the British Museum reading room simultaneously reading Marx's *Das Kapital* and the score of Wagner's *Ring of the Niebelung* cycle. The blending of political substance with a rich and deeply harmonized verbal music became a constant feature of Shaw's drama. Writing as a theater critic in the 1890s, Shaw became the champion of Ibsen in England. Vowing to lay siege to the conventions of the nineteenth-century theater, he touted Ibsen's plays and lambasted the corny tearjerkers, simplistic melodramas, and overstuffed Shakespearean productions that were the theater's common fare. Not incidentally, he worked to create a taste for his own plays, an operatic drama of the intellectual passions.

Shaw's career as a playwright falls into three main phases. Shaw's earliest plays — *Widowers' Houses* (1892) and *Mrs. Warren's Profession* (1893) — attacked specific social problems, like slum landlords and international prostitution. But Shaw more often linked social ills to the smug pieties of conventional morality. His plays generally work to disillusion his main characters — and his audience — from the ready acceptance of bourgeois ideology as a natural "reality." This process of disillusionment informs Shaw's lighter comedies of the 1890s, plays like *Arms and the Man* (1894), *Candida* (1894), and *Caesar and Cleopatra* (1898). After the turn of the century, however, Shaw entered on his maturity as a playwright, undertaking a series of major comedies that place this process of disillusionment directly in conflict with society's most important institutions: marriage and sexuality in *Man and Superman* (1903); British imperialism in Ireland in *John Bull's Other Island* (1904); salvation, damnation, and raw power in *Major Barbara* (1905); medicine in *The Doctor's Dilemma* (1906); language and class in *Pygmalion* (1912). Several of these plays were first produced at the Court Theater, under the management of Shaw's close friend Harley Granville Barker, who originated the part of Cusins in *Major Barbara* and other Shavian roles. Under Barker and his partner J. E. Vedrenne, the Court Theater in 1904–1907 became the most influential theater in London before World War I. Through its efforts, and Shaw's own energy as playwright, director, and advisor, the Court made Shaw's reputation as a major dramatist. With the coming of World War I, and the violent waste of civilization it brought with it, Shaw's confidence in the eventual perfection of humanity was deeply shaken, and the plays of his final half-century are much bleaker, more uncertain in tone: his magnificent "fantasia in the Russian manner on English themes," *Heartbreak House* (1919), modeled on Chekhov's *The Cherry Orchard; Saint Joan* (1923), perhaps his best-loved play; his five-play quintet on the origin and future of the species, *Back to Methuselah* (1921); and many others. In contrast to the confidence of Shaw's earlier plays, the later dramas generally seem to ask the question that Shaw gave to his Saint Joan, "O God that madest this beautiful earth, when will it be ready to receive Thy saints? How long, O Lord, how long?"

Major Barbara

Shaw was born before the publication of Darwin's *Origin of Species* in 1859, and he died after the dropping of the atomic bomb on Hiroshima. His major plays, like *Major Barbara*, treat the problems of the twentieth century in the dramatic vocabulary of Edwardian COMEDY OF MANNERS. *Major Barbara* is typical of the dialectical process of Shaw's plays. From the outset—when Stephen learns that his income is derived from his father's munitions empire—Shaw forces the audience and his characters to question the nature of their values, particularly the sense that good and evil, morality and economics, the power to save and the power to destroy can be easily or conveniently distinguished from one another. As a result, the play forces a deeply ironic experience on its characters and on the audience. For Shaw is interested in salvation, not simply the moralizing salvation promised by the Salvation Army, but a Nietzschean transvaluation of values, a salvation beyond the conventional abstractions of good and evil that he regards as necessary to the transformation of English society.

The play is structured dialectically, progressing from thesis, to antithesis, to a problematic synthesis. The "thesis" of Act 1 concerns the values of Wilton Crescent: the comfortable morality of the English upper classes. As the scene proceeds, though, Shaw suggests that conventional morality, the innate knowledge of right and wrong, is in fact supported by Undershaft's money and gunpowder. The "antithesis" of Act 2 offers the unconventional morality of the Salvation Army; Barbara's shelter in West Ham claims to provide true salvation by requiring a more sincere form of religious conviction. However, as it turns out, both Wilton Crescent and West Ham are equally in the grip of Bodger and Undershaft. The distiller and the munitions-maker determine the material realities on which society erects its illusory social "ideals" and calls them "reality." The Dionysian sacrifice of Barbara at the end of Act 2—with its echoes of Christ's crucifixion as well—prepares us for her resurrection in the "synthesis" offered by Act 3; in Perivale St Andrews, the spiritual Barbara and the intellectual Cusins are married with the blessing of the explosive Undershaft. We might be troubled, though, by the "synthesis" offered by the utopian factory town, for Undershaft's utopia hardly seems revolutionary. In many ways, Perivale St Andrews largely duplicates turn-of-the-century English class society and industrial capitalism, with the poverty and dirt cleaned up. The play's last act is often said to be unconvincing, and we might wonder whether that is in fact part of Shaw's purpose in *Major Barbara*. Once Shaw instructs us in the process of dialectical criticism, perhaps he invites us to scrutinize even Undershaft's bourgeois utopia, to see Perivale St Andrews as itself in need of further (r)evolution.

Shaw made Andrew Undershaft a magnificently melodramatic, attractive, amoral munitions-maker, whose creative ability is harnessed to the power to destroy. Moreover, Shaw drew a parallel between Undershaft and a crucial dramatic precursor, the Dionysus of Euripides' *The Bacchae*. The character of Cusins was modeled on Shaw's friend, the well-known classical scholar Gilbert Murray, and in the original production, Cusins was even played to resemble Murray. In Act 2, Cusins quotes a brief passage adapted from Murray's translation of *The Bacchae*, part of the choral speech delivered just before Pentheus is led out to spy on the Bacchae and be killed. We might take this invocation of Dionysus as a final clue to the play's attitude. Much like Euripides, Shaw prevents his audience from sympathizing entirely with his hero, from readily accepting the terrible power necessary to change the world. Although the play ends with a ceremonial marriage characteristic of ROMANTIC COMEDY—symbolizing the union of intellect, spirit, and power—the fact that Dionysus Undershaft presides over this union should give us pause. Can the power he wields really be harnessed for our salvation?

MAJOR BARBARA

Bernard Shaw

— CHARACTERS —

STEPHEN UNDERSHAFT

LADY BRITOMART

BARBARA UNDERSHAFT

SARAH UNDERSHAFT

ANDREW UNDERSHAFT

JENNY HILL

BILL WALKER

MORRISON

ADOLPHUS CUSINS

CHARLES LOMAX

RUMMY MITCHENS

SNOBBY PRICE

PETER SHIRLEY

BILTON

MRS BAINES

— ACT ONE —

It is after dinner in January 1906, in the library in LADY BRITOMART UNDERSHAFT's *house in Wilton Crescent. A large and comfortable settee is in the middle of the room, upholstered in dark leather. A person sitting on it (it is vacant at present) would have, on his right,* LADY BRITOMART's *writing table, with the lady herself busy at it; a smaller writing table behind him on his left; the door behind him on* LADY BRITOMART's *side; and a window with a window seat directly on his left. Near the window is an armchair.*

LADY BRITOMART *is a woman of fifty or thereabouts, well dressed and yet careless of her dress, well bred and quite reckless of her breeding, well mannered and yet appallingly outspoken and indifferent to the opinion of her interlocutors, amiable and yet peremptory, arbitrary, and high-tempered to the last bearable degree, and withal a very typical managing matron of the upper class, treated as a naughty child until she grew into a scolding mother, and finally settling down with plenty of practical ability and worldly experience, limited in the oddest way with domestic and class limitations, conceiving the universe exactly as if it were a large house in Wilton Crescent, though handling her corner of it very effectively on that assumption, and being quite enlightened and liberal as to the books in the library, the pictures on the walls, the music in the portfolios, and the articles in the papers.*

Her son, STEPHEN, *comes in. He is a gravely correct young man under 25, taking himself very seriously, but still in some awe of his mother, from childish habit and bachelor shyness rather than from any weakness of character.*

STEPHEN: Whats the matter?

LADY BRITOMART: Presently, Stephen.

*(*STEPHEN *submissively walks to the settee and sits down. He takes up a Liberal weekly called The Speaker.)*

LADY BRITOMART: Dont begin to read, Stephen. I shall require all your attention.

5 STEPHEN: It was only while I was waiting—

LADY BRITOMART: Dont make excuses, Stephen. *(He puts down The Speaker.)* Now! *(She finishes her writing; rises; and comes to the settee.)* I have not kept you waiting very long, I think.

10 STEPHEN: Not at all, mother.

LADY BRITOMART: Bring me my cushion. *(He takes the cushion from the chair at the desk and arranges it for her as she sits down on the settee.)* Sit down. *(He sits down and fingers his tie nervously.)* Dont fiddle with your tie, Stephen: there is nothing the matter with it. 15

STEPHEN: I beg your pardon. *(He fiddles with his watch chain instead.)*

LADY BRITOMART: Now are you attending to me, Stephen?

STEPHEN: Of course, mother.

LADY BRITOMART: No: it's not of course. I want something 20 much more than your everyday matter-of-course attention. I am going to speak to you very seriously, Stephen. I wish you would let that chain alone.

STEPHEN: *(hastily relinquishing the chain)* Have I done anything to annoy you, mother? If so, it was quite unintentional. 25

LADY BRITOMART: *(astonished)* Nonsense! *(With some remorse)* My poor boy, did you think I was angry with you?

STEPHEN: What is it, then, mother? You are making me very uneasy.

LADY BRITOMART: *(squaring herself at him rather aggressively)* 30 Stephen: may I ask how soon you intend to realize that you are a grown-up man, and that I am only a woman?

STEPHEN: *(amazed)* Only a—

LADY BRITOMART: Dont repeat my words, please: it is a most aggravating habit. You must learn to face life seriously, Ste- 35 phen. I really cannot bear the whole burden of our family affairs any longer. You must advise me: you must assume the responsibility.

STEPHEN: I!

LADY BRITOMART: Yes, you, of course. You were 24 last June. 40 Youve been at Harrow and Cambridge. Youve been to India and Japan. You must know a lot of things, now; unless you have wasted your time most scandalously. Well, advise me.

STEPHEN: *(much perplexed)* You know I have never interfered in the household— 45

LADY BRITOMART: No: I should think not. I dont want you to order the dinner.

STEPHEN: I mean in our family affairs.

LADY BRITOMART: Well, you must interfere now; for they are getting quite beyond me. 50

STEPHEN: *(troubled)* I have thought sometimes that perhaps I ought; but really, mother, I know so little about them; and what I do know is so painful! it is so impossible to mention some things to you — *(he stops, ashamed.)*

55 LADY BRITOMART: I suppose you mean your father.

STEPHEN: *(almost inaudibly)* Yes.

LADY BRITOMART: My dear: we cant go on all our lives not mentioning him. Of course you were quite right not to open the subject until I asked you to; but you are old enough now to be 60 taken into my confidence, and to help me to deal with him about the girls.

STEPHEN: But the girls are all right. They are engaged.

LADY BRITOMART: *(complacently)* Yes: I have made a very good match for Sarah. Charles Lomax will be a millionaire at 35. 65 But that is ten years ahead; and in the meantime his trustees cannot under the terms of his father's will allow him more than £800 a year.

STEPHEN: But the will says also that if he increases his income by his own exertions, they may double the increase.

70 LADY BRITOMART: Charles Lomax's exertions are much more likely to decrease his income than to increase it. Sarah will have to find at least another £800 a year for the next ten years; and even then they will be as poor as church mice. And what about Barbara? I thought Barbara was going to make the most 75 brilliant career of all of you. And what does she do? Joins the Salvation Army; discharges her maid; lives on a pound a week and walks in one evening with a professor of Greek whom she has picked up in the street, and who pretends to be a Salvationist, and actually plays the big drum for her in public be- 80 cause he has fallen head over ears in love with her.

STEPHEN: I was certainly rather taken aback when I heard they were engaged. Cusins is a very nice fellow, certainly: nobody would ever guess that he was born in Australia; but —

LADY BRITOMART: Oh, Adolphus Cusins will make a very good 85 husband. After all, nobody can say a word against Greek: it stamps a man at once as an educated gentleman. And my family, thank Heaven, is not a pig-headed Tory one. We are Whigs, and believe in liberty. Let snobbish people say what they please: Barbara shall marry, not the man they like, but 90 the man *I* like.

STEPHEN: Of course I was thinking only of his income. However, he is not likely to be extravagant.

LADY BRITOMART: Dont be too sure of that, Stephen. I know your quiet, simple, refined, poetic people like Adolphus: 95 quite content with the best of everything! They cost more than your extravagant people, who are always as mean as they are second rate. No: Barbara will need at least £2000 a year. You see it means two additional households. Besides, my dear, you must marry soon. I dont approve of the present 100 fashion of philandering bachelors and late marriages; and I am trying to arrange something for you.

STEPHEN: It's very good of you, mother; but perhaps I had better arrange that for myself.

LADY BRITOMART: Nonsense! you are much too young to begin 105 matchmaking: you would be taken in by some pretty little nobody. Of course I dont mean that you are not to be consulted: you know that as well as I do. (STEPHEN *closes his lips and is silent.)* Now dont sulk, Stephen.

STEPHEN: I am not sulking, mother. What has all this got to do 110 with — with — with my father?

LADY BRITOMART: My dear Stephen: where is the money to come from? It is easy enough for you and the other children to live on my income as long as we are in the same house; but I cant keep four families in four separate houses. You know how poor my father is: he has barely seven thousand a year 115 now; and really, if he were not the Earl of Stevenage, he would have to give up society. He can do nothing for us. He says, naturally enough, that it is absurd that he should be asked to provide for the children of a man who is rolling in money. You see, Stephen, your father must be fabulously 120 wealthy, because there is always a war going on somewhere.

STEPHEN: You need not remind me of that, mother. I have hardly ever opened a newspaper in my life without seeing our name in it. The Undershaft torpedo! The Undershaft quick firers! The Undershaft ten inch! the Undershaft disappearing 125 rampart gun! the Undershaft submarine! and now the Undershaft aerial battleship! At Harrow they called me the Woolwich Infant. At Cambridge it was the same. A little brute at King's who was always trying to get up revivals, spoilt my Bible — your first birthday present to me — by writing under my 130 name, "Son and heir to Undershaft and Lazarus, Death and Destruction Dealers: address Christendom and Judea." But that was not so bad as the way I was kowtowed to everywhere because my father was making millions by selling cannons.

LADY BRITOMART: It is not only the cannons, but the war loans 135 that Lazarus arranges under cover of giving credit for the cannons. You know, Stephen, it's perfectly scandalous. Those two men, Andrew Undershaft and Lazarus, positively have Europe under their thumbs. That is why your father is able to behave as he does. He is above the law. Do you think Bis- 140 marck or Gladstone or Disraeli could have openly defied every social and moral obligation all their lives as your father has? They simply wouldnt have dared. I asked Gladstone to take it up. I asked The Times to take it up. I asked the Lord Chamberlain to take it up. But it was just like asking them to 145 declare war on the Sultan. They wouldnt. They said they couldnt touch him. I believe they were afraid.

STEPHEN: What could they do? He does not actually break the law.

LADY BRITOMART: Not break the law! He is always breaking the 150 law. He broke the law when he was born: his parents were not married.

STEPHEN: Mother! Is that true?

LADY BRITOMART: Of course it's true: that was why we separated. 155

STEPHEN: He married without letting you know that!

LADY BRITOMART: *(rather taken aback by this inference)* Oh no. To do Andrew justice, that was not the sort of thing he did. Besides, you know the Undershaft motto: Unashamed. Everybody knew. 160

STEPHEN: But you said that was why you separated.

LADY BRITOMART: Yes, because he was not content with being a foundling himself: he wanted to disinherit you for another foundling. That was what I couldnt stand.

STEPHEN: *(ashamed)* Do you mean for — for — for — 165

LADY BRITOMART: Dont stammer, Stephen. Speak distinctly.

STEPHEN: But this is so frightful to me, mother. To have to speak to you about such things!

LADY BRITOMART: It's not pleasant for me, either, especially if you are still so childish that you must make it worse by a 170 display of embarrassment. It is only in the middle classes, Stephen, that people get into a state of dumb helpless horror when they find that there are wicked people in the world. In our class, we have to decide what is to be done with wicked people; and nothing should disturb our self-possession. Now ask your question properly.

STEPHEN: Mother: have you no consideration for me? For Heaven's sake either treat me as a child, as you always do, and tell me nothing at all or tell me everything and let me take it as best I can.

LADY BRITOMART: Treat you as a child! What do you mean? It is most unkind and ungrateful of you to say such a thing. You know I have never treated any of you as children. I have always made you my companions and friends, and allowed you perfect freedom to do and say whatever you like, so long as you liked what I could approve of.

STEPHEN: (desperately) I daresay we have been the very imperfect children of a very perfect mother; but I do beg you to let me alone for once, and tell me about this horrible business of my father wanting to set me aside for another son.

LADY BRITOMART: (amazed) Another son! I never said anything of the kind. I never dreamt of such a thing. This is what comes of interrupting me.

STEPHEN: But you said—

LADY BRITOMART: (cutting him short) Now be a good boy, Stephen, and listen to me patiently. The Undershafts are descended from a foundling in the parish of St Andrew Undershaft in the city. That was long ago, in the reign of James the First. Well, this foundling was adopted by an armorer and gun-maker. In the course of time the foundling succeeded to the business; and from some notion of gratitude, or some vow or something, he adopted another foundling, and left the business to him. And that foundling did the same. Ever since that, the cannon business has always been left to an adopted foundling named Andrew Undershaft.

STEPHEN: But did they never marry? Were there no legitimate sons?

LADY BRITOMART: Oh yes: they married just as your father did; and they were rich enough to buy land for their own children and leave them well provided for. But they always adopted and trained some foundling to succeed them in the business; and of course they always quarrelled with their wives furiously over it. Your father was adopted in that way; and he pretends to consider himself bound to keep up the tradition and adopt somebody to leave the business to. Of course I was not going to stand that. There may have been some reason for it when the Undershafts could only marry women in their own class, whose sons were not fit to govern great estates. But there could be no excuse for passing over my son.

STEPHEN: (dubiously) I am afraid I should make a poor hand of managing a cannon foundry.

LADY BRITOMART: Nonsense! you could easily get a manager and pay him a salary.

STEPHEN: My father evidently had no great opinion of my capacity.

LADY BRITOMART: Stuff, child! you were only a baby: it had nothing to do with your capacity. Andrew did it on principle, just as he did every perverse and wicked thing on principle. When my father remonstrated, Andrew actually told him to his face that history tells us of only two successful institutions: one the Undershaft firm, and the other the Roman Empire under the Antonines. That was because the Antonine em-

perors all adopted their successors. Such rubbish! The Stevenages are as good as the Antonines, I hope; and you are a Stevenage. But that was Andrew all over. There you have the man! Always clever and unanswerable when he was defending nonsense and wickedness: always awkward and sullen when he had to behave sensibly and decently!

STEPHEN: Then it was on my account that your home life was broken up, mother. I am sorry.

LADY BRITOMART: Well, dear, there were other differences. I really cannot bear an immoral man. I am not a Pharisee, I hope; and I should not have minded his merely doing wrong things: we are none of us perfect. But your father didnt exactly do wrong things: he said them and thought them: that was what was so dreadful. He really had a sort of religion of wrongness. Just as one doesnt mind men practising immorality so long as they own that they are in the wrong by preaching morality; so I couldnt forgive Andrew for preaching immorality while he practised morality. You would all have grown up without principles, without any knowledge of right and wrong, if he had been in the house. You know, my dear, your father was a very attractive man in some ways. Children did not dislike him; and he took advantage of it to put the wickedest ideas into their heads, and make them quite unmanageable. I did not dislike him myself: very far from it; but nothing can bridge over moral disagreement.

STEPHEN: All this simply bewilders me, mother. People may differ about matters of opinion, or even about religion; but how can they differ about right and wrong? Right is right; and wrong is wrong; and if a man cannot distinguish them properly, he is either a fool or a rascal: thats all.

LADY BRITOMART: (touched) Thats my own boy (she pats his cheek)! Your father never could answer that: he used to laugh and get out of it under cover of some affectionate nonsense. And now that you understand the situation, what do you advise me to do?

STEPHEN: Well, what can you do?

LADY BRITOMART: I must get the money somehow.

STEPHEN: We cannot take money from him. I had rather go and live in some cheap place like Bedford Square or even Hampstead than take a farthing of his money.

LADY BRITOMART: But after all, Stephen, our present income comes from Andrew.

STEPHEN: (shocked) I never knew that.

LADY BRITOMART: Well, you surely didnt suppose your grandfather had anything to give me. The Stevenages could not do everything for you. We gave you social position. Andrew had to contribute something. He had a very good bargain, I think.

STEPHEN: (bitterly) We are utterly dependent on him and his cannons, then?

LADY BRITOMART: Certainly not: the money is settled. But he provided it. So you see it is not a question of taking money from him or not: it is simply a question of how much. I dont want any more for myself.

STEPHEN: Nor do I.

LADY BRITOMART: But Sarah does; and Barbara does. That is, Charles Lomax and Adolphus Cusins will cost them more. So I must put my pride in my pocket and ask for it, I suppose. That is your advice, Stephen, is it not?

STEPHEN: No.

LADY BRITOMART: (sharply) Stephen!

STEPHEN: Of course if you are determined—

295 LADY BRITOMART: I am not determined: I ask your advice; and I am waiting for it. I will not have all the responsibility thrown on my shoulders.

STEPHEN: (obstinately) I would die sooner than ask him for another penny.

300 LADY BRITOMART: (resignedly) You mean that I must ask him. Very well, Stephen: it shall be as you wish. You will be glad to know that your grandfather concurs. But he thinks I ought to ask Andrew to come here and see the girls. After all, he must have some natural affection for them.

STEPHEN: Ask him here!!!

305 LADY BRITOMART: Do not repeat my words, Stephen. Where else can I ask him?

STEPHEN: I never expected you to ask him at all.

LADY BRITOMART: Now dont tease, Stephen. Come! you see that it is necessary that he should pay us a visit, dont you?

310 STEPHEN: (reluctantly) I suppose so, if the girls cannot do without his money.

LADY BRITOMART: Thank you, Stephen: I knew you would give me the right advice when it was properly explained to you. I have asked your father to come this evening. (Stephen bounds

315 from his seat.) Dont jump, Stephen: it fidgets me.

STEPHEN: (in utter consternation) Do you mean to say that my father is coming here tonight—that he may be here at any moment?

LADY BRITOMART: (looking at her watch) I said nine. (He gasps.

320 She rises.) Ring the bell, please. (STEPHEN goes to the smaller writing table; presses a button on it; and sits at it with his elbows on the table and his head in his hands, outwitted and overwhelmed.) It is ten minutes to nine yet; and I have to prepare the girls. I asked Charles Lomax and Adolphus to

325 dinner on purpose that they might be here. Andrew had better see them in case he should cherish any delusions as to their being capable of supporting their wives. (The butler enters: LADY BRITOMART goes behind the settee to speak to him.) Morrison: go up to the drawing room and tell everybody to

330 come down here at once. (MORRISON withdraws. LADY BRITOMART turns to STEPHEN.) Now remember, Stephen: I shall need all your countenance and authority. (He rises and tries to recover some vestige of these attributes.) Give me a chair, dear. (He pushes a chair forward from the wall to where

335 she stands, near the smaller writing table. She sits down; and he goes to the armchair, into which he throws himself.) I dont know how Barbara will take it. Ever since they made her a major in the Salvation Army she has developed a propensity to have her own way and order people about which quite cows

340 me sometimes. It's not ladylike: I'm sure I dont know where she picked it up. Anyhow, Barbara shant bully me; but still it's just as well that your father should be here before she has time to refuse to meet him or make a fuss. Dont look nervous, Stephen: it will only encourage Barbara to make difficulties. I

345 am nervous enough, goodness knows; but I dont shew it.

(SARAH and BARBARA come in with their respective young men, CHARLES LOMAX and ADOLPHUS CUSINS. SARAH is slender, bored, and mundane. BARBARA is robuster, jollier, much more energetic. SARAH is fashionably dressed: BARBARA is in Salvation Army uniform. LOMAX, a young man about town, is like many other young men about town. He is afflicted with a frivolous sense of humor which plunges him at the most inopportune moments into paroxysms of imperfectly suppressed laughter. CUSINS is a spectacled student, slight, thin haired, and sweet voiced, with a more complex form of LOMAX's complaint. His sense of humor is intellectual and subtle, and is complicated by an appalling temper. The lifelong struggle of a benevolent temperament and a high conscience against impulses of inhuman ridicule and fierce impatience has set up a chronic strain which has visibly wrecked his constitution. He is a most implacable, determined, tenacious, intolerant person who by mere force of character presents himself as—and indeed actually is—considerate, gentle, explanatory, even mild and apologetic, capable possibly of murder, but not of cruelty or coarseness. By the operation of some instinct which is not merciful enough to blind him with the illusions of love, he is obstinately bent on marrying BARBARA. LOMAX likes SARAH and thinks it will be rather a lark to marry her. Consequently he has not attempted to resist LADY BRITOMART's arrangements to that end.

All four look as if they had been having a good deal of fun in the drawing room. The girls enter first, leaving the swains outside. SARAH comes to the settee. BARBARA comes in after her and stops at the door.)

BARBARA: Are Cholly and Dolly to come in?

LADY BRITOMART: (forcibly) Barbara: I will not have Charles called Cholly: the vulgarity of it positively makes me ill.

BARBARA: It's all right, mother: Cholly is quite correct nowadays. Are they to come in?   350

LADY BRITOMART: Yes, if they will behave themselves.

BARBARA: (through the door) Come in, Dolly; and behave yourself.

(BARBARA comes to her mother's writing table. CUSINS enters smiling, and wanders towards LADY BRITOMART.)

SARAH: (calling) Come in, Cholly. (LOMAX enters, controlling his features very imperfectly, and places himself vaguely between SARAH and BARBARA.)   355

LADY BRITOMART: (peremptorily) Sit down, all of you. (They sit. CUSINS crosses to the window and seats himself there. LOMAX takes a chair. BARBARA sits at the writing table and SARAH on the settee.) I dont in the least know what you are   360 laughing at, Adolphus. I am surprised at you, though I expected nothing better from Charles Lomax.

CUSINS: (in a remarkably gentle voice) Barbara has been trying to teach me the West Ham Salvation March.

LADY BRITOMART: I see nothing to laugh at in that; nor should   365 you if you are really converted.

CUSINS: (sweetly) You were not present. It was really funny, I believe.

LOMAX: Ripping.

LADY BRITOMART: Be quiet, Charles. Now listen to me, children. Your father is coming here this evening.   370

(General stupefaction. LOMAX, SARAH, and BARBARA rise: SARAH scared, and BARBARA amused and expectant.)

LOMAX: (remonstrating) Oh I say!

LADY BRITOMART: You are not called on to say anything, Charles.

SARAH: Are you serious, mother?   375

LADY BRITOMART: Of course I am serious. It is on your account, Sarah, and also on Charles's. (*Silence.* SARAH *sits, with a shrug.* CHARLES *looks painfully unworthy.*) I hope you are not going to object, Barbara.

380 BARBARA: I! why should I? My father has a soul to be saved like anybody else. He's quite welcome as far as I am concerned. (*She sits on the table, and softly whistles 'Onward, Christian Soldiers'.*)

LOMAX: (*still remonstrant*) But really, dont you know! Oh I say!

385 LADY BRITOMART: (*frigidly*) What do you wish to convey, Charles?

LOMAX: Well, you must admit that this is a bit thick.

LADY BRITOMART: (*turning with ominous suavity to* CUSINS) Adolphus: you are a professor of Greek. Can you translate

390 Charles Lomax's remarks into reputable English for us?

CUSINS: (*cautiously*) If I may say so, Lady Brit, I think Charles has rather happily expressed what we all feel. Homer, speaking of Autolycus, uses the same phrase. πυκινὸν δόμον ἐλθεῖν means a bit thick.

395 LOMAX: (*handsomely*) Not that I mind, you know, if Sarah dont. (*He sits.*)

LADY BRITOMART: (*crushingly*) Thank you. Have I your permission, Adolphus, to invite my own husband to my own house?

CUSINS: (*gallantly*) You have my unhesitating support in every-

400 thing you do.

LADY BRITOMART: Tush! Sarah: have you nothing to say?

SARAH: Do you mean that he is coming regularly to live here?

LADY BRITOMART: Certainly not. The spare room is ready for him if he likes to stay for a day or two and see a little more of

405 you; but there are limits.

SARAH: Well, he cant eat us, I suppose. I dont mind.

LOMAX: (*chuckling*) I wonder how the old man will take it.

LADY BRITOMART: Much as the old woman will, no doubt, Charles.

410 LOMAX: (*abashed*) I didnt mean—at least—

LADY BRITOMART: You didnt think, Charles. You never do; and the result is, you never mean anything. And now please attend to me, children. Your father will be quite a stranger to us.

415 LOMAX: I suppose he hasnt seen Sarah since she was a little kid.

LADY BRITOMART: Not since she was a little kid, Charles, as you express it with that elegance of diction and refinement of thought that seem never to desert you. Accordingly—er— (*impatiently*) Now I have forgotten what I was going to say.

420 That comes of your provoking me to be sarcastic, Charles. Adolphus: will you kindly tell me where I was.

CUSINS: (*sweetly*) You were saying that as Mr Undershaft has not seen his children since they were babies, he will form his opinion of the way you have brought them up from their be-

425 havior tonight, and that therefore you wish us all to be particularly careful to conduct ourselves well, especially Charles.

LADY BRITOMART: (*with emphatic approval*) Precisely.

LOMAX: Look here, Dolly: Lady Brit didnt say that.

LADY BRITOMART: (*vehemently*) I did, Charles. Adolphus's rec-

430 ollection is perfectly correct. It is most important that you should be good; and I do beg you for once not to pair off into opposite corners and giggle and whisper while I am speaking to your father.

BARBARA: All right, mother. We'll do you credit. (*She comes off*

435 *the table, and sits in her chair with ladylike elegance.*)

LADY BRITOMART: Remember, Charles, that Sarah will want to feel proud of you instead of ashamed of you.

LOMAX: Oh I say! theres nothing to be exactly proud of, dont you know.

440 LADY BRITOMART: Well, try and look as if there was.

(MORRISON, *pale and dismayed, breaks into the room in unconcealed disorder.*)

MORRISON: Might I speak a word to you, my lady?

LADY BRITOMART: Nonsense! Shew him up.

MORRISON: Yes, my lady. (*He goes.*)

LOMAX: Does Morrison know who it is?

445 LADY BRITOMART: Of course. Morrison has always been with us.

LOMAX: It must be a regular corker for him, dont you know.

LADY BRITOMART: Is this a moment to get on my nerves, Charles, with your outrageous expressions?

450 LOMAX: But this is something out of the ordinary, really—

MORRISON: (*at the door*) The—er—Mr Undershaft. (*He retreats in confusion.*)

(ANDREW UNDERSHAFT *comes in. All rise.* LADY BRITOMART *meets him in the middle of the room behind the settee.*

ANDREW *is, on the surface, a stoutish, easygoing elderly man, with kindly patient manners, and an engaging simplicity of character. But he has a watchful, deliberate, waiting, listening face, and formidable reserves of power, both bodily and mental, in his capacious chest and long head. His gentleness is partly that of a strong man who has learnt by experience that his natural grip hurts ordinary people unless he handles them very carefully, and partly the mellowness of age and success. He is also a little shy in his present very delicate situation.*)

LADY BRITOMART: Good evening, Andrew.

UNDERSHAFT: How d'ye do, my dear.

LADY BRITOMART: You look a good deal older.

455 UNDERSHAFT: (*apologetically*) I am somewhat older. (*Taking her hand with a touch of courtship*) Time has stood still with you.

LADY BRITOMART: (*throwing away his hand*) Rubbish! This is

460 your family.

UNDERSHAFT: (*surprised*) Is it so large? I am sorry to say my memory is failing very badly in some things. (*He offers his hand with paternal kindness to* LOMAX.)

LOMAX: (*jerkily shaking his hand*) Ahdedoo.

465 UNDERSHAFT: I can see you are my eldest. I am very glad to meet you again, my boy.

LOMAX: (*remonstrating*) No, but look here dont you know— (*Overcome*) Oh I say!

LADY BRITOMART: (*recovering from momentary speechlessness*)

470 Andrew: do you mean to say that you dont remember how many children you have?

UNDERSHAFT: Well, I am afraid I—. They have grown so much—er. Am I making any ridiculous mistake? I may as well confess: I recollect only one son. But so many things

475 have happened since, of course—er—

LADY BRITOMART: (*decisively*) Andrew: you are talking nonsense. Of course you have only one son.

UNDERSHAFT: Perhaps you will be good enough to introduce me, my dear.

480 LADY BRITOMART: That is Charles Lomax, who is engaged to Sarah.

UNDERSHAFT: My dear sir, I beg your pardon.

LOMAX: Notatall. Delighted, I assure you.

LADY BRITOMART: This is Stephen.

485 UNDERSHAFT: (bowing) Happy to make your acquaintance, Mr Stephen. Then (going to CUSINS) you must be my son. (Taking CUSINS' hands in his) How are you, my young friend? (To LADY BRITOMART) He is very like you, my love.

CUSINS: You flatter me, Mr Undershaft. My name is Cusins: engaged to Barbara. (Very explicitly) That is Major Barbara

490 Undershaft, of the Salvation Army. That is Sarah, your second daughter. This is Stephen Undershaft, your son.

UNDERSHAFT: My dear Stephen, I beg your pardon.

STEPHEN: Not at all.

495 UNDERSHAFT: Mr Cusins: I am much indebted to you for explaining so precisely. (Turning to SARAH) Barbara, my dear—

SARAH: (prompting him) Sarah.

UNDERSHAFT: Sarah, of course. (They shake hands. He goes over to BARBARA) Barbara—I am right this time, I hope?

500 BARBARA: Quite right. (They shake hands.)

LADY BRITOMART: (resuming command) Sit down, all of you. Sit down, Andrew. (She comes forward and sits on the settee. CUSINS also brings his chair forward on her left. BARBARA and STEPHEN resume their seats. LOMAX gives his chair to SARAH

505 and goes for another.)

UNDERSHAFT: Thank you, my love.

LOMAX: (conversationally, as he brings a chair forward between the writing table and the settee, and offers it to UNDERSHAFT) Takes you some time to find out exactly where you are, dont it?

510 UNDERSHAFT: (accepting the chair, but remaining standing) That is not what embarrasses me, Mr Lomax. My difficulty is that if I play the part of a father, I shall produce the effect of an intrusive stranger; and if I play the part of a discreet stranger, I may appear a callous father.

515 LADY BRITOMART: There is no need for you to play any part at all, Andrew. You had much better be sincere and natural.

UNDERSHAFT: (submissively) Yes, my dear: I daresay that will be best. (He sits down comfortably.) Well, here I am. Now what can I do for you all?

520 LADY BRITOMART: You need not do anything, Andrew. You are one of the family. You can sit with us and enjoy yourself.

(A painfully conscious pause. BARBARA makes a face at LOMAX, whose too long suppressed mirth immediately explodes in agonized neighings.)

LADY BRITOMART: (outraged) Charles Lomax: if you can behave yourself, behave yourself. If not, leave the room.

LOMAX: I'm awfully sorry, Lady Brit; but really you know, upon

525 my soul! (He sits on the settee between LADY BRITOMART and UNDERSHAFT, quite overcome.)

BARBARA: Why dont you laugh if you want to, Cholly? It's good for your inside.

LADY BRITOMART: Barbara: you have had the education of a

530 lady. Please let your father see that; and dont talk like a street girl.

UNDERSHAFT: Never mind me, my dear. As you know, I am not a gentleman; and I was never educated.

LOMAX: (encouragingly) Nobody'd know it, I assure you. You

535 look all right, you know.

CUSINS: Let me advise you to study Greek, Mr Undershaft. Greek scholars are privileged men. Few of them know Greek; and none of them know anything else; but their position is unchallengeable. Other languages are the qualifications of waiters and commercial travellers: Greek is to a man of posi- 540 tion what the hallmark is to silver.

BARBARA: Dolly: dont be insincere. Cholly: fetch your concertina and play something for us.

LOMAX: (jumps up eagerly, but checks himself to remark doubtfully to UNDERSHAFT) Perhaps that sort of thing isnt in 545 your line, eh?

UNDERSHAFT: I am particularly fond of music.

LOMAX: (delighted) Are you? Then I'll get it. (He goes upstairs for the instrument.)

UNDERSHAFT: Do you play, Barbara? 550

BARBARA: Only the tambourine. But Cholly's teaching me the concertina.

UNDERSHAFT: Is Cholly also a member of the Salvation Army?

BARBARA: No: he says it's bad form to be a dissenter. But I dont despair of Cholly. I made him come yesterday to a meeting at 555 the dock gates, and take the collection in his hat.

UNDERSHAFT: (looks whimsically at his wife)!!

LADY BRITOMART: It is not my doing, Andrew. Barbara is old enough to take her own way. She has no father to advise her.

BARBARA: Oh yes she has. There are no orphans in the Salvation 560 Army.

UNDERSHAFT: Your father there has a great many children and plenty of experience, eh?

BARBARA: (looking at him with quick interest and nodding) Just so. How did you come to understand that? (LOMAX is heard at 565 the door trying the concertina.)

LADY BRITOMART: Come in, Charles. Play us something at once.

LOMAX: Righto! (He sits down in his former place, and preludes.)

UNDERSHAFT: One moment, Mr Lomax. I am rather interested 570 in the Salvation Army. Its motto might be my own: Blood and Fire.

LOMAX: (shocked) But not your sort of blood and fire, you know.

UNDERSHAFT: My sort of blood cleanses: my sort of fire purifies.

BARBARA: So do ours. Come down tomorrow to my shelter—the 575 West Ham shelter—and see what we're doing. We're going to march to a great meeting in the Assembly Hall at Mile End. Come and see the shelter and then march with us: it will do you a lot of good. Can you play anything?

UNDERSHAFT: In my youth I earned pennies, and even shillings 580 occasionally, in the streets and in public house parlors by my natural talent for stepdancing. Later on, I became a member of the Undershaft orchestral society, and performed passably on the tenor trombone.

LOMAX: (scandalized—putting down the concertina) Oh I say! 585

BARBARA: Many a sinner has played himself into heaven on the trombone, thanks to the Army.

LOMAX: (to BARBARA, still rather shocked) Yes; but what about the cannon business, dont you know? (To UNDERSHAFT) Getting into heaven is not exactly in your line, is it? 590

LADY BRITOMART: Charles!!!

LOMAX: Well; but it stands to reason, dont it? The cannon business may be necessary and all that: we cant get on without cannons; but it isnt right, you know. On the other hand, there may be a certain amount of tosh about the Salvation Army— 595

I belong to the Established Church myself — but still you cant deny that it's religion; and you cant go against religion, can you? At least unless youre downright immoral, dont you know.

600 UNDERSHAFT: You hardly appreciate my position, Mr Lomax —

LOMAX: *(hastily)* I'm not saying anything against you personally —

UNDERSHAFT: Quite so, quite so. But consider for a moment. Here I am, a profiteer in mutilation and murder. I find myself

605 in a specially amiable humor just now because, this morning, down at the foundry, we blew twenty-seven dummy soldiers into fragments with a gun which formerly destroyed only thirteen.

LOMAX: *(leniently)* Well, the more destructive war becomes, the

610 sooner it will be abolished, eh?

UNDERSHAFT: Not at all. The more destructive war becomes the more fascinating we find it. No, Mr Lomax: I am obliged to you for making the usual excuse for my trade; but I am not ashamed of it. I am not one of those men who keep their

615 morals and their business in watertight compartments. All the spare money my trade rivals spend on hospitals, cathedrals, and other receptacles for conscience money, I devote to experiments and researches in improved methods of destroying life and property. I have always done so; and I always shall.

620 Therefore your Christmas card moralities of peace on earth and goodwill among men are of no use to me. Your Christianity, which enjoins you to resist not evil, and to turn the other cheek, would make me a bankrupt. My morality — my religion — must have a place for cannons and torpedoes in it.

625 STEPHEN: *(coldly — almost sullenly)* You speak as if there were half a dozen moralities and religions to choose from, instead of one true morality and one true religion.

UNDERSHAFT: For me there is only one true morality; but it might not fit you, as you do not manufacture aerial battle-

630 ships. There is only one true morality for every man; but every man has not the same true morality.

LOMAX: *(overtaxed)* Would you mind saying that again? I didnt quite follow it.

CUSINS: It's quite simple. As Euripides says, one man's meat is

635 another man's poison morally as well as physically.

UNDERSHAFT: Precisely.

LOMAX: Oh, that! Yes, yes, yes. True. True.

STEPHEN: In other words, some men are honest and some are scoundrels.

640 BARBARA: Bosh! There are no scoundrels.

UNDERSHAFT: Indeed? Are there any good men?

BARBARA: No. Not one. There are neither good men nor scoundrels: there are just children of one Father; and the sooner they stop calling one another names the better. You neednt

645 talk to me: I know them. I've had scores of them through my hands: scoundrels, criminals, infidels, philanthropists, missionaries, county councillors, all sorts. Theyre all just the same sort of sinner; and theres the same salvation ready for them all.

650 UNDERSHAFT: May I ask have you ever saved a maker of cannons?

BARBARA: No. Will you let me try?

UNDERSHAFT: Well, I will make a bargain with you. If I go to see you tomorrow in your Salvation Shelter, will you come the

655 day after to see me in my cannon works?

BARBARA: Take care. It may end in your giving up the cannons for the sake of the Salvation Army.

UNDERSHAFT: Are you sure it will not end in your giving up the Salvation Army for the sake of the cannons?

660 BARBARA: I will take my chance of that.

UNDERSHAFT: And I will take my chance of the other. *(They shake hands on it.)* Where is your shelter?

BARBARA: In West Ham. At the sign of the cross. Ask anybody in Canning Town. Where are your works?

665 UNDERSHAFT: In Perivale St Andrews. At the sign of the sword. Ask anybody in Europe.

LOMAX: Hadnt I better play something?

BARBARA: Yes. Give us 'Onward, Christian Soldiers.'

LOMAX: Well, thats rather a strong order to begin with, dont you

670 know. Suppose I sing Thou't passing hence, my brother. It's much the same tune.

BARBARA: It's too melancholy. You get saved, Cholly; and youll pass hence, my brother, without making such a fuss about it.

LADY BRITOMART: Really, Barbara, you go on as if religion were

675 a pleasant subject. Do have some sense of propriety.

UNDERSHAFT: I do not find it an unpleasant subject, my dear. It is the only one that capable people really care for.

LADY BRITOMART: *(looking at her watch)* Well, if you are determined to have it, I insist on having it in a proper and respect

680 able way. Charles: ring for prayers.

(General amazement. STEPHEN *rises in dismay.)*

LOMAX: *(rising)* Oh I say!

UNDERSHAFT: *(rising)* I am afraid I must be going.

LADY BRITOMART: You cannot go now, Andrew: it would be most improper. Sit down. What will the servants think?

685 UNDERSHAFT: My dear: I have conscientious scruples. May I suggest a compromise? If Barbara will conduct a little service in the drawing room, with Mr Lomax as organist, I will attend it willingly. I will even take part, if a trombone can be procured.

690 LADY BRITOMART: Dont mock, Andrew.

UNDERSHAFT: *(shocked — to* BARBARA*)* You dont think I am mocking, my love, I hope.

BARBARA: No, of course not; and it wouldnt matter if you were: half the Army came to their first meeting for a lark. *(Rising)*

695 Come along. *(She throws her arm round her father and sweeps him out, calling to the others from the threshold)* Come, Dolly. Come, Cholly.

*(CUSINS *rises.)*

LADY BRITOMART: I will not be disobeyed by everybody. Adolphus: sit down. *(He does not.)* Charles: you may go. You are

700 not fit for prayers: you cannot keep your countenance.

LOMAX: Oh I say! *(He goes out.)*

LADY BRITOMART: *(continuing)* But you, Adolphus, can behave yourself if you choose to. I insist on your staying.

CUSINS: My dear Lady Brit: there are things in the family prayer

705 book that I couldnt bear to hear you say.

LADY BRITOMART: What things, pray?

CUSINS: Well, you would have to say before all the servants that we have done things we ought not to have done, and left undone things we ought to have done, and that there is no

710 health in us. I cannot bear to hear you doing yourself such an injustice, and Barbara such an injustice. As for myself, I flatly

deny it: I have done my best. I shouldnt dare to marry Barbara—I couldnt look you in the face—if it were true. So I
must go to the drawing room.

715 LADY BRITOMART: (offended) Well, go. (He starts for the door.)
And remember this, Adolphus (he turns to listen): I have a
very strong suspicion that you went to the Salvation Army to
worship Barbara and nothing else. And I quite appreciate the
very clever way in which you systematically humbug me. I
720 have found you out. Take care Barbara doesnt. Thats all.

CUSINS: (with unruffled sweetness) Dont tell on me. (He steals
out.)

LADY BRITOMART: Sarah: if you want to go, go. Anything's better than to sit there as if you wished you were a thousand miles
725 away.

SARAH: (languidly) Very well, mamma. (She goes.)

(LADY BRITOMART, with a sudden flounce, gives way to a little
gust of tears.)

STEPHEN: (going to her) Mother: whats the matter?

LADY BRITOMART: (swishing away her tears with her handkerchief) Nothing. Foolishness. You can go with him, too, if
730 you like, and leave me with the servants.

STEPHEN: Oh, you mustnt think that, mother. I—I dont like
him.

LADY BRITOMART: The others do. That is the injustice of a
woman's lot. A woman has to bring up her children; and that
735 means to restrain them, to deny them things they want, to set
them tasks, to punish them when they do wrong, to do all the
unpleasant things. And then the father, who has nothing to
do but pet them and spoil them, comes in when all her work
is done and steals their affection from her.

740 STEPHEN: He has not stolen our affection from you. It is only
curiosity.

LADY BRITOMART: (violently) I wont be consoled, Stephen.
There is nothing the matter with me. (She rises and goes towards the door.)

745 STEPHEN: Where are you going, mother?

LADY BRITOMART: To the drawing room, of course. (She goes
out. 'Onward, Christian Soldiers,' on the concertina, with
tambourine accompaniment, is heard when the door opens.)
Are you coming, Stephen?

750 STEPHEN: No. Certainly not. (She goes. He sits down on the
settee, with compressed lips and an expression of strong
dislike.)

— ACT TWO —

The yard of the West Ham shelter of the Salvation Army is a cold
place on a January morning. The building itself, an old warehouse, is newly whitewashed. Its gabled end projects into the yard
in the middle, with a door on the ground floor, and another in the
loft above it without any balcony or ladder, but with a pulley
rigged over it for hoisting sacks. Those who come from this central
gable end into the yard have the gateway leading to the street on
their left, with a stone horse-trough just beyond it, and, on the
right, a penthouse shielding a table from the weather. There are
forms at the table; and on them are seated a man and a woman,
both much down on their luck, finishing a meal of bread (one
thick slice each, with margarine and golden syrup) and diluted
milk.

The man, a workman out of employment, is young, agile, a
talker, a poser, sharp enough to be capable of anything in reason
except honesty or altruistic considerations of any kind. The
woman is a commonplace old bundle of poverty and hard-worn
humanity. She looks sixty and probably is forty-five. If they were
rich people, gloved and muffed and well wrapped up in furs and
overcoats, they would be numbed and miserable; for it is a grind-
ingly cold raw January day; and a glance at the background of
grimy warehouses and leaden sky visible over the whitewashed
walls of the yard would drive any idle rich person straight to the
Mediterranean. But these two, being no more troubled with visions of the Mediterranean than of the moon, and being compelled to keep more of their clothes in the pawnshop, and less on
their persons, in winter than in summer, are not depressed by the
cold: rather are they stung into vivacity, to which their meal has
just now given an almost jolly turn. The man takes a pull at his
mug, and then gets up and moves about the yard with his hands
deep in his pockets, occasionally breaking into a stepdance.

THE WOMAN: Feel better arter your meal, sir?

THE MAN: No. Call that a meal! Good enough for you, praps;
but wot is it to me, an intelligent workin man.

THE WOMAN: Workin man! Wot are you?

THE MAN: Painter.   5

THE WOMAN: (sceptically) Yus, I dessay.

THE MAN: Yus, you dessay! I know. Every loafer that cant do
nothink calls isself a painter. Well, I'm a real painter: grainer,
finisher, thirty-eight bob a week when I can get it.

THE WOMAN: Then why dont you go and get it?   10

THE MAN: I'll tell you why. Fust: I'm intelligent—fffff! it's rotten
cold here (he dances a step or two)—yes: intelligent beyond
the station o life into which it has pleased the capitalists to call
me; and they dont like a man that sees through em. Second,
an intelligent bein needs a doo share of appiness; so I drink   15
somethink cruel when I get the chawnce. Third, I stand by
my class and do as little as I can so's to leave arf the job for me
fellow workers. Fourth, I'm fly enough to know wots inside
the law and wots outside it; and inside it I do as the capitalists
do: pinch wot I can lay me ands on. In a proper state of society   20
I am sober, industrious and honest: in Rome, so to speak, I do
as the Romans do. Wots the consequence? When trade is
bad—and it's rotten bad just now—and the employers az to
sack arf their men, they generally start on me.

THE WOMAN: Whats your name?   25

THE MAN: Price. Bronterre O'Brien Price. Usually called Snobby Price, for short.

THE WOMAN: Snobby's a carpenter, aint it? You said you was a
painter.

PRICE: Not that kind of snob, but the genteel sort. I'm too up-   30
pish, owing to my intelligence, and my father being a Char-
tist and a reading, thinking man: a stationer, too. I'm none of
your common hewers of wood and drawers of water; and dont
you forget it. (He returns to his seat at the table, and takes up
his mug.) Wots your name?   35

THE WOMAN: Rummy Mitchens, sir.

PRICE: (quaffing the remains of his milk to her) Your elth, Miss
Mitchens.

RUMMY: (correcting him) Missis Mitchens.

PRICE: Wot! Oh Rummy, Rummy! Respectable married wom-   40
an, Rummy, gittin rescued by the Salvation Army by pretendin to be a bad un. Same old game!

RUMMY: What am I to do? I cant starve. Them Salvation lasses is dear good girls; but the better you are, the worse they likes to
45 think you were before they rescued you. Why shouldnt they av a bit o credit, poor loves? theyre worn to rags by their work. And where would they get the money to rescue us if we was to let on we're no worse than other people? You know what ladies and gentlemen are.

50 PRICE: Thievin swine! Wish I ad their job, Rummy, all the same. Wot does Rummy stand for? Pet name praps?

RUMMY: Short for Romola.

PRICE: For wot!?

RUMMY: Romola. It was out of a new book. Somebody me
55 mother wanted me to grow up like.

PRICE: We're companions in misfortune, Rummy. Both on us got names that nobody cawnt pronounce. Consequently I'm Snobby and youre Rummy because Bill and Sally wasnt good enough for our parents. Such is life!

60 RUMMY: Who saved you, Mr Price? Was it Major Barbara?

PRICE: No: I come here on my own. I'm going to be Bronterre O'Brien Price, the converted painter. I know wot they like. I'll tell em how I blasphemed and gambled and wopped my poor old mother—

65 RUMMY: (shocked) Used you to beat your mother?

PRICE: Not likely. She used to beat me. No matter: you come and listen to the converted painter, and youll hear how she was a pious woman that taught me me prayers at er knee, an how I used to come home drunk and drag her out o bed be er
70 snow white airs, an lam into er with the poker.

RUMMY: Thats whats so unfair to us women. Your confessions is just as big lies as ours: you dont tell what you really done no more than us; but you men can tell your lies right out at the meetins and be made much of for it; while the sort o confes-
75 sions we az to make az to be wispered to one lady at a time. It aint right, spite of all their piety.

PRICE: Right! Do you spose the Army'd be allowed if it went and did right? Not much. It combs our air and makes us good little blokes to be robbed and put upon. But I'll play the game
80 as good as any of em. I'll see somebody struck by lightnin, or hear a voice sayin 'Snobby Price: where will you spend eternity?' I'll av a time of it, I tell you.

RUMMY: You wont be let drink, though.

PRICE: I'll take it out in gorspellin, then. I dont want to drink if I
85 can get fun enough any other way.

(JENNY HILL, a pale, overwrought, pretty Salvation lass of 18, comes in through the yard gate, leading PETER SHIRLEY, a half hardened, half worn-out elderly man, weak with hunger.)

JENNY: (supporting him) Come! pluck up. I'll get you something to eat. Youll be all right then.

PRICE: (rising and hurrying officiously to take the old man off Jenny's hands) Poor old man! Cheer up, brother: youll find
90 rest and peace and appiness ere. Hurry up with the food, miss: e's fair done. (Jenny hurries into the shelter.) Ere, buck up, daddy! she's fetchin y'a thick slice o breadn treacle, an a mug o skyblue. (He seats him at the corner of the table.)

RUMMY: (gaily) Keep up your old art! Never say die!

95 SHIRLEY: I'm not an old man. I'm only 46. I'm as good as ever I was. The grey patch come in my hair before I was thirty. All it wants is three pennorth o hair dye: am I to be turned on the streets to starve for it? Holy God! I've worked ten to twelve hours a day since I was thirteen, and paid my way all through;

and now am I to be thrown into the gutter and my job given to 100
a young man that can do it no better than me because Ive black hair that goes white at the first change?

PRICE: (cheerfully) No good jawrin about it. Youre only a jumped-up, jerked-off, orspittle-turned-out incurable of an ole workin man: who cares about you? Eh? Make the thievin 105
swine give you a meal: theyve stole many a one from you. Get a bit o your own back. (Jenny returns with the usual meal.) There you are, brother. Awsk a blessin an tuck that into you.

SHIRLEY: (looking at it ravenously but not touching it, and crying like a child) I never took anything before. 110

JENNY: (petting him) Come, come! the Lord sends it to you: he wasnt above taking bread from his friends; and why should you be? Besides, when we find you a job you can pay us for it if you like.

SHIRLEY: (eagerly) Yes, yes: thats true. I can pay you back: it's 115
only a loan. (Shivering) O Lord! oh Lord! (He turns to the table and attacks the meal ravenously.)

JENNY: Well, Rummy, are you more comfortable now?

RUMMY: God bless you, lovey! youve fed my body and saved my soul, havnt you? (Jenny, touched, kisses her.) Sit down and 120
rest a bit: you must be ready to drop.

JENNY: Ive been going hard since morning. But theres more work than we can do. I mustnt stop.

RUMMY: Try a prayer for just two minutes. Youll work all the better after. 125

JENNY: (her eyes lighting up) Oh isnt it wonderful how a few minutes prayer revives you! I was quite lightheaded at twelve o'clock, I was so tired; but Major Barbara just sent me to pray for five minutes; and I was able to go on as if I had only just begun. (To Price) Did you have a piece of bread? 130

PRICE: (with unction) Yes, miss; but Ive got the piece that I value more; and thats the peace that passeth hall hannerstennin.

RUMMY: (fervently) Glory Hallelujah!

(BILL WALKER, a rough customer of about 25, appears at the yard gate and looks malevolently at JENNY.)

JENNY: That makes me so happy. When you say that, I feel wicked for loitering here. I must get to work again. 135

(She is hurrying to the shelter, when the new-comer moves quickly up to the door and intercepts her. His manner is so threatening that she retreats as he comes at her truculently, driving her down the yard.)

BILL: Aw knaow you. Youre the one that took away maw girl. Youre the one that set er agen me. Well, I'm gowin to ev er aht. Not that Aw care a carse for er or you: see? Bat Aw'll let er knaow; and Aw'll let you knaow. Aw'm gowing to give her a doin thatll teach er to cat away from me. Nah in wiv you and 140
tell er to cam aht afore Aw cam in and kick er aht. Tell er Bill Walker wants er. She'll knaow wot thet means; and if she keeps me witin itll be worse. You stop to jawr beck at me; and Aw'll stawt on you: d'ye eah? Theres your wy. In you gow. (He takes her by the arm and slings her towards the door of the 145
shelter. She falls on her hand and knee. RUMMY helps her up again.)

PRICE: (rising, and venturing irresolutely towards BILL) Easy there, mate. She aint doin you no arm.

BILL: Oo are you callin mite? (Standing over him threateningly) 150
Youre gowin to stend ap for er, aw yer? Put ap your ends.

RUMMY: (*running indignantly to him to scold him*) Oh, you great brute — (*He instantly swings his left hand back against her face. She screams and reels back to the trough, where she sits down, covering her bruised face with her hands and rocking herself and moaning with pain.*)

JENNY: (*going to her*) Oh, God forgive you! How could you strike an old woman like that?

BILL: (*seizing her by the hair so violently that she also screams, and tearing her away from the old woman*) You Gawd forgimme again an Aw'll Gawk forgive you one on the jawr thetll stop you pryin for a week. (*Holding her and turning fiercely on* PRICE) Ev you ennything to sy agen it?

PRICE: (*intimidated*) No, matey: she aint anything to do with me.

BILL: Good job for you! Aw'd pat two meals into you and fawt you with one finger arter, you stawved cur. (*To* JENNY) Nah are you gowin to fetch aht Mog Ebbijem; or em Aw to knock your fice off you and fetch her meself?

JENNY: (*writhing in his grasp*) Oh please someone go in and tell Major Barbara — (*she screams again as he wrenches her head down; and* PRICE *and* RUMMY *flee into the shelter.*)

BILL: You want to gow in and tell your Mijor of me, do you?

JENNY: Oh please dont drag my hair. Let me go.

BILL: Do you or downt you? (*She stifles a scream.*) Yus or nao?

JENNY: God give me strength —

BILL: (*striking her with his fist in the face*) Gow an shaow her thet, and tell her if she wants one lawk it to cam and interfere with me. (JENNY, *crying with pain, goes into the shed. He goes to the form and addresses the old man.*) Eah: finish your mess; an git aht o maw wy.

SHIRLEY: (*springing up and facing him fiercely, with the mug in his hand*) You take a liberty with me, and I'll smash you over the face with the mug and cut your eye out. Aint you satisfied — young whelps like you — with takin the bread out o the mouths of your elders that have brought you up and slaved for you, but you must come shovin and cheekin and bullyin in here, where the bread o charity is sickenin in our stummicks?

BILL: (*contemptuously, but backing a little*) Wot good are you, you aold palsy mag? Wot good are you?

SHIRLEY: As good as you and better. I'll do a day's work agen you or any fat young soaker of your age. Go and take my job at Horrockses, where I worked for ten year. They want young men there: they cant afford to keep men over forty-five. Theyre very sorry — give you a character and happy to help you to get anything suited to your years — sure a steady man wont be long out of a job. Well, let em try you. Theyll find the differ. What do you know? Not as much as how to beeyave yourself — layin your dirty fist across the mouth of a respectable woman!

BILL: Downt provowk me to ly it acrost yours: d'ye eah?

SHIRLEY: (*with blighting contempt*) Yes: you like an old man to hit, dont you, when youve finished with the women. I aint seen you hit a young one yet.

BILL: (*stung*) You loy, you aold soupkitchener, you. There was a yang menn eah. Did Aw offer to itt him or did Aw not?

SHIRLEY: Was he starvin or was he not? Was he a man or only a crosseyed thief an a loafer? Would you hit my son-in-law's brother?

BILL: Oo's ee?

SHIRLEY: Todger Fairmile o Balls Pond. Him that won £20 off the Japanese wrastler at the music hall by standin out 17 minutes 4 seconds agen him.

BILL: (*sullenly*) Aw'm nao music awl wrastler. Ken he box?

SHIRLEY: Yes: an you cant.

BILL: Wot! Aw cawnt, cawnt Aw? Wots thet you sy (*threatening him*)?

SHIRLEY: (*not budging an inch*) Will you box Todger Fairmile if I put him on to you? Say the word.

BILL: (*subsiding with a slouch*) Aw'll stend ap to enny menn alawv, if he was ten Todger Fairmawls. But Aw dont set ap to be a perfeshnal.

SHIRLEY: (*looking down on him with unfathomable disdain*) You box! Slap an old woman with the back o your hand! You hadnt even the sense to hit her where a magistrate couldnt see the mark of it, you silly young lump of conceit and ignorance. Hit a girl in the jaw and ony make her cry! If Todger Fairmile'd done it, she wouldnt a got up inside o ten minutes, no more than you would if he got on to you. Yah! I'd set about you myself if I had a week's feedin in me instead o two months' starvation. (*He turns his back on him and sits down moodily at the table.*)

BILL: (*following him and stooping over him to drive the taunt in*) You loy! youve the bread and treacle in you that you cam eah to beg.

SHIRLEY: (*bursting into tears*) Oh God! it's true: I'm only an old pauper on the scrap heap. (*Furiously*) But youll come to it yourself; and then youll know. Youll come to it sooner than a teetotaller like me, fillin yourself with gin at this hour o the mornin!

BILL: Aw'm nao gin drinker, you oald lawr; bat wen Aw want to give my girl a bloomin good awdin Aw lawk to ev a bit o devil in me: see? An eah Aw emm, talkin to a rotten aold blawter like you sted o givin her wot for. (*Working himself into a rage*) Aw'm gowin in there to fetch her aht. (*He makes vengefully for the shelter door.*)

SHIRLEY: Youre going to the station on a stretcher, more likely; and theyll take the gin and the devil out of you there when they get you inside. You mind what youre about: the major here is the Earl o Stevenage's granddaughter.

BILL: (*checked*) Garn!

SHIRLEY: Youll see.

BILL: (*his resolution oozing*) Well, Aw aint dan nathin to er.

SHIRLEY: Spose she said you did! who'd believe you?

BILL: (*very uneasy, skulking back to the corner of the penthouse*) Gawd! theres no jastice in this cantry. To think wot them people can do! Aw'm as good as er.

SHIRLEY: Tell her so. It's just what a fool like you would do.

(BARBARA, *brisk and businesslike, comes from the shelter with a note book, and addresses herself to* SHIRLEY. BILL, *cowed, sits down in the corner on a form, and turns his back on them.*)

BARBARA: Good morning.

SHIRLEY: (*standing up and taking off his hat*) Good morning, miss.

BARBARA: Sit down: make yourself at home. (*He hesitates; but she puts a friendly hand on his shoulder and makes him obey.*) Now then! since youve made friends with us, we want to know all about you. Names and addresses and trades.

SHIRLEY: Peter Shirley. Fitter. Chucked out two months ago because I was too old.

BARBARA: *(not at all surprised)* Youd pass still. Why didnt you dye your hair?

270 SHIRLEY: I did. Me age come out at a coroner's inquest on me daughter.

BARBARA: Steady?

SHIRLEY: Teetotaller. Never out of a job before. Good worker. And sent to the knackers like an old horse!

275 BARBARA: No matter: if you did your part God will do his.

SHIRLEY: *(suddenly stubborn)* My religion's no concern of anybody but myself.

BARBARA: *(guessing)* I know. Secularist?

SHIRLEY: *(hotly)* Did I offer to deny it?

280 BARBARA: Why should you? My own father's a Secularist, I think. Our Father—yours and mine—fulfils himself in many ways; and I daresay he knew what he was about when he made a Secularist of you. So buck up, Peter! we can always find a job for a steady man like you. (SHIRLEY, *disarmed and*

285 *a little bewildered, touches his hat. She turns from him to* BILL.) Whats your name?

BILL: *(insolently)* Wots thet to you?

BARBARA: *(calmly making a note)* Afraid to give his name. Any trade?

290 BILL: Oo's afride to give is nime? *(Doggedly, with a sense of heroically defying the House of Lords in the person of Lord Stevenage)* If you want to bring a chawge agen me, bring it. *(She waits, unruffled.)* Moy nime's Bill Walker.

BARBARA: *(as if the name were familiar: trying to remember how)*

295 Bill Walker? *(Recollecting)* Oh, I know: youre the man that Jenny Hill was praying for inside just now. *(She enters his name in her note book.)*

BILL: Oo's Jenny Ill? And wot call as she to pry for me?

BARBARA: I dont know. Perhaps it was you that cut her lip.

300 BILL: *(defiantly)* Yus, it was me that cat her lip. Aw aint afride o you.

BARBARA: How could you be, since youre not afraid of God? Youre a brave man, Mr Walker. It takes some pluck to do our work here; but none of us dare lift our hand against a girl like

305 that, for fear of her father in heaven.

BILL: *(sullenly)* I want nan o your kentin jawr. I spowse you think Aw cam eah to beg from you, like this demmiged lot eah. Not me. Aw downt want your bread and scripe and ketlep. Aw dont blieve in your Gawd, no more than you do yourself.

310 BARBARA: *(sunnily apologetic and ladylike, as on a new footing with him)* Oh, I beg your pardon for putting your name down, Mr Walker. I didnt understand. I'll strike it out.

BILL: *(taking this as a slight, and deeply wounded by it)* Eah! you let maw nime alown. Aint it good enaff to be in your book?

315 BARBARA: *(considering)* Well, you see, theres no use putting down your name unless I can do something for you, is there? Whats your trade?

BILL: *(still smarting)* Thets nao concern o yours.

BARBARA: Just so. *(Very businesslike)* I'll put you down as *(writ-*

320 *ing)* the man who—struck—poor little Jenny Hill—in the mouth.

BILL: *(rising threateningly)* See eah. Awve ed enaff o this.

BARBARA: *(quite sunny and fearless)* What did you come to us for?

325 BILL: Aw cam for maw gel, see? Aw cam to tike her aht o this and to brike er jawr fur er.

BARBARA: *(complacently)* You see I was right about your trade.

(BILL, on the point of retorting furiously, finds himself, to his great shame and terror, in danger of crying instead. He sits down again suddenly.) Whats her name? 330

BILL: *(dogged)* Er nime's Mog Ebbijem: thets wot her nime is.

BARBARA: Mog Habbijam! Oh, she's gone to Canning Town, to our barracks there.

BILL: *(fortified by his resentment of Mog's perfidy)* Is she? *(Vindictively)* Then Aw'm gowin to Kennintahn arter her. *(He* 335 *crosses to the gate; hesitates; finally comes back at Barbara.)* Are you loyin to me to git shat o me?

BARBARA: I dont want to get shut of you. I want to keep you here and save your soul. Youd better stay: youre going to have a bad time today, Bill. 340

BILL: Oo's gowin to give it to me? You, preps?

BARBARA: Someone you dont believe in. But youll be glad afterwards.

BILL: *(slinking off)* Aw'll gow to Kennintahn to be aht o reach o your tangue. *(Suddenly turning on her with intense malice)* 345 And if Aw downt fawnd Mog there, Aw'll cam beck and do two years for you, selp me Gawd if Aw downt!

BARBARA: *(a shade kindlier, if possible)* It's no use, Bill. She's got another bloke.

BILL: Wot! 350

BARBARA: One of her own converts. He fell in love with her when he saw her with her soul saved, and her face clean, and her hair washed.

BILL: *(surprised)* Wottud she wash it for, the carroty slat? It's red.

BARBARA: It's quite lovely now, because she wears a new look in 355 her eyes with it. It's a pity youre too late. The new bloke has put your nose out of joint, Bill.

BILL: Aw'll put his nowse aht o joint for him. Not that Aw care a carse for er, mawnd thet. But Aw'll teach her to drop me as if Aw was dirt. And Aw'll teach him to meddle with maw judy. 360 Wots iz bleedin nime?

BARBARA: Sergeant Todger Fairmile.

SHIRLEY: *(rising with grim joy)* I'll go with him, miss. I want to see them two meet. I'll take him to the infirmary when it's over.

BILL: *(to SHIRLEY, with undissembled misgiving)* Is thet im you 365 was speakin on?

SHIRLEY: Thats him.

BILL: Im that wrastled in the music awl?

SHIRLEY: The competitions at the National Sportin Club was worth nigh a hundred a year to him. He's gev em up now for 370 religion; so he's a bit fresh for want of the exercise he was accustomed to. He'll be glad to see you. Come along.

BILL: Wots is wight?

SHIRLEY: Thirteen four. (BILL's *last hope expires.*)

BARBARA: Go and talk to him, Bill. He'll convert you. 375

SHIRLEY: He'll convert your head into a mashed potato.

BILL: *(sullenly)* Aw aint afride of im. Aw aint afride of ennybody. Bat e can lick me. She's dan me. *(He sits down moodily on the edge of the horse trough.)*

SHIRLEY: You aint going. I thought not. *(He resumes his seat.)* 380

BARBARA: *(calling)* Jenny!

JENNY: *(appearing at the shelter door with a plaster on the corner of her mouth)* Yes, Major.

BARBARA: Send Rummy Mitchens out to clear away here.

JENNY: I think she's afraid 385

BARBARA: *(her resemblance to her mother flashing out for a moment)* Nonsense! she must do as she's told.

JENNY: (calling into the shelter) Rummy: the Major says you must come.

(JENNY comes to BARBARA, purposely keeping on the side next to BILL, lest he should suppose that she shrank from him or bore malice.)

390 BARBARA: Poor little Jenny! Are you tired? (Looking at the wounded cheek) Does it hurt?

JENNY: No: it's all right now. It was nothing.

BARBARA: (critically) It was as hard as he could hit, I expect. Poor Bill! You dont feel angry with him, do you?

395 JENNY: Oh no, no, no: indeed I dont, Major, bless his poor heart! (BARBARA kisses her; and she runs away merrily into the shelter. BILL writhes with an agonizing return of his new and alarming symptoms, but says nothing. RUMMY MITCHENS comes from the shelter.)

400 BARBARA: (going to meet RUMMY) Now Rummy, bustle. Take in those mugs and plates to be washed; and throw the crumbs about for the birds.

(RUMMY takes the three plates and mugs; but SHIRLEY takes back his mug from her, as there is still some milk left in it.)

RUMMY: There aint any crumbs. This aint a time to waste good bread on birds.

405 PRICE: (appearing at the shelter door) Gentleman come to see the shelter, Major. Says he's your father.

BARBARA: All right. Coming. (SNOBBY goes back into the shelter, followed by BARBARA.)

RUMMY: (stealing across to BILL and addressing him in a subdued voice, but with intense conviction) I'd av the lor of you,
410 you flat eared pignosed potwalloper, if she'd let me. Youre no gentleman, to hit a lady in the face. (BILL, with greater things moving in him, takes no notice.)

SHIRLEY: (following her) Here! in with you and dont get yourself
415 into more trouble by talking.

RUMMY: (with hauteur) I aint ad the pleasure o being hintroduced to you, as I can remember. (She goes into the shelter with the plates.)

SHIRLEY: Thats the—

420 BILL: (savagely) Downt you talk to me, d'ye eah? You lea me alown, or Aw'll do you a mischief. Aw'm not dirt under your feet, ennywy.

SHIRLEY: (calmly) Dont you be afeerd. You aint such prime company that you need expect to be sought after. (He is about
425 to go into the shelter when BARBARA comes out, with UNDERSHAFT on her right.)

BARBARA: Oh, there you are, Mr Shirley! (Between them) This is my father: I told you he was a Secularist, didnt I? Perhaps youll be able to comfort one another.

430 UNDERSHAFT: (startled) A Secularist! Not the least in the world: on the contrary, a confirmed mystic.

BARBARA: Sorry, I'm sure. By the way, papa, what is your religion? in case I have to introduce you again.

UNDERSHAFT: My religion? Well, my dear, I am a Millionaire.
435 That is my religion.

BARBARA: Then I'm afraid you and Mr Shirley wont be able to comfort one another after all. Youre not a Millionaire, are you, Peter?

SHIRLEY: No; and proud of it.

UNDERSHAFT: (gravely) Poverty, my friend, is not a thing to be 440 proud of.

SHIRLEY: (angrily) Who made your millions for you? Me and my like. Whats kep us poor? Keepin you rich. I wouldnt have your conscience, not for all your income.

UNDERSHAFT: I wouldnt have your income, not for all your 445 conscience, Mr Shirley. (He goes to the penthouse and sits down on a form.)

BARBARA: (stopping SHIRLEY adroitly as he is about to retort) You wouldnt think he was my father, would you, Peter? Will you go into the shelter and lend the lasses a hand for a while; 450 we're worked off our feet.

SHIRLEY: (bitterly) Yes: I'm in their debt for a meal, aint I?

BARBARA: Oh, not because youre in their debt, but for love of them, Peter, for love of them. (He cannot understand, and is rather scandalized) There! dont stare at me. In with you; and 455 give that conscience of yours a holiday (bustling him into the shelter.)

SHIRLEY: (as he goes in) Ah! it's a pity you never was trained to use your reason, miss. Youd have been a very taking lecturer on Secularism. 460

(BARBARA turns to her father.)

UNDERSHAFT: Never mind me, my dear. Go about your work; and let me watch it for a while.

BARBARA: All right.

UNDERSHAFT: For instance, whats the matter with that outpatient over there? 465

BARBARA: (looking at BILL, whose attitude has never changed, and whose expression of brooding wrath has deepened) Oh, we shall cure him in no time. Just watch. (She goes over to BILL and waits. He glances up at her and casts his eyes down again, uneasy, but grimmer than ever.) It would be nice to just stamp 470 on Mog Habbijam's face, wouldnt it, Bill?

BILL: (starting up from the trough in consternation) It's a loy: Aw never said so. (She shakes her head.) Oo taold you wot was in moy mawnd?

BARBARA: Only your new friend. 475

BILL: Wot new friend?

BARBARA: The devil, Bill. When he gets round people they get miserable, just like you.

BILL: (with a heartbreaking attempt at devil-may-care cheerfulness) Aw aint miserable. (He sits down again, and stretches 480 his legs in an attempt to seem indifferent.)

BARBARA: Well, if youre happy, why dont you look happy, as we do?

BILL: (his legs curling back in spite of him) Aw'm eppy enaff, Aw tell you. Woy cawnt you lea me alown? Wot ev I dan to you? 485 Aw aint smashed your fice, ev Aw?

BARBARA: (softly: wooing his soul) It's not me thats getting at you, Bill.

BILL: Oo else is it?

BARBARA: Somebody that doesnt intend you to smash women's 490 faces, I suppose. Somebody or something that wants to make a man of you.

BILL: (blustering) Mike a menn o me! Aint Aw a menn? eh? Oo sez Aw'm not a menn?

BARBARA: Theres a man in you somewhere, I suppose. But why 495 did he let you hit poor little Jenny Hill? That wasnt very manly of him, was it?

BILL: (tormented) Ev dan wiv it, Aw tell you. Chack it. Aw'm sick o your Jenny Ill and er silly little fice.

500 BARBARA: Then why do you keep thinking about it? Why does it keep coming up against you in your mind? Youre not getting converted, are you?

BILL: (with conviction) Not ME. Not lawkly.

BARBARA: Thats right, Bill. Hold out against it. Put out your
505 strength. Dont lets get you cheap. Todger Fairmile said he wrestled for three nights against his salvation harder than he ever wrestled with the Jap at the music hall. He gave in to the Jap when his arm was going to break. But he didnt give in to his salvation until his heart was going to break. Perhaps youll
510 escape that. You havnt any heart, have you?

BILL: Wot d'ye mean? Woy aint Aw got a awt the sime as ennybody else?

BARBARA: A man with a heart wouldnt have bashed poor little Jenny's face, would he?

515 BILL: (almost crying) Ow, will you lea me alown? Ev Aw ever offered to meddle with you, that you cam neggin and provowkin me lawk this? (He writhes convulsively from his eyes to his toes.)

BARBARA: (with a steady soothing hand on his arm and a gentle
520 voice that never lets him go) It's your soul thats hurting you, Bill, and not me. Weve been through it all ourselves. Come with us, Bill. (He looks wildly round.) To brave manhood on earth and eternal glory in heaven. (He is on the point of breaking down.) Come. (A drum is heard in the shelter; and BILL,
525 with a gasp, escapes from the spell as BARBARA turns quickly. ADOLPHUS enters from the shelter with a big drum.) Oh! there you are, Dolly. Let me introduce a new friend of mine, Mr Bill Walker. This is my bloke, Bill: Mr Cusins. (CUSINS salutes with his drumstick.)

530 BILL: Gowin to merry im?

BARBARA: Yes.

BILL: (fervently) Gawd elp im! Gaw-aw-aw-awd elp im!

BARBARA: Why? Do you think he wont be happy with me?

BILL: Awve aony ed to stend it for a mawnin: e'll ev to stend it for
535 a lawftawm.

CUSINS: That is a frightful reflection, Mr Walker. But I cant tear myself away from her.

BILL: Well, Aw ken. (To BARBARA) Eah! do you knaow where Aw'm gowin to, and wot Aw'm gowin to do?

540 BARBARA: Yes: youre going to heaven; and youre coming back here before the week's out to tell me so.

BILL: You loy. Aw'm gowin to Kennintahn, to spit in Todger Fairmawl's eye. Aw beshed Jenny Ill's fice; an nar Aw'll git me aown fice beshed and cam beck and shaow it to er. Ee'll itt me
545 ardern Aw itt her. Thatll mike us square. (To ADOLPHUS) Is thet fair or is it not? Youre a genlmn: you oughter knaow.

BARBARA: Two black eyes wont make one white one, Bill.

BILL: Aw didnt awst you. Cawnt you never keep your mahth shat? Oy awst the genlmn.

550 CUSINS: (reflectively) Yes: I think youre right, Mr Walker. Yes: I should do it. It's curious: it's exactly what an ancient Greek would have done.

BARBARA: But what good will it do?

CUSINS: Well, it will give Mr Fairmile some exercise; and it will
555 satisfy Mr Walker's soul.

BILL: Rot! there aint nao such a thing as a saoul. Ah kin you tell wevver Awve a saoul or not? You never seen it.

BARBARA: Ive seen it hurting you when you went against it.

BILL: (with compressed aggravation) If you was maw gel and took
560 the word aht o me mahth lawk thet, Aw'd give you sathink youd feel urtin, Aw would. (To ADOLPHUS) You tike maw tip, mite. Stop er jawr; or youll doy afoah your tawm (With intense expression) Wore aht: thets wot youll be: wore aht. (He goes away through the gate.)

565 CUSINS: (looking after him) I wonder!

BARBARA: Dolly! (indignant, in her mother's manner.)

CUSINS: Yes, my dear, it's very wearing to be in love with you. If it lasts, I quite think I shall die young.

BARBARA: Should you mind?

570 CUSINS: Not at all. (He is suddenly softened, and kisses her over the drum, evidently not for the first time, as people cannot kiss over a big drum without practice. UNDERSHAFT coughs.)

BARBARA: It's all right, papa, weve not forgotten you. Dolly: explain the place to papa: I havnt time. (She goes busily into the
575 shelter.)

(UNDERSHAFT and ADOLPHUS now have the yard to themselves. UNDERSHAFT, seated on a form, and still keenly attentive, looks hard at ADOLPHUS. ADOLPHUS looks hard at him.)

UNDERSHAFT: I fancy you guess something of what is in my mind, Mr Cusins. (CUSINS flourishes his drumsticks as if in the act of beating a lively rataplan, but makes no sound.) Exactly so. But suppose Barbara finds you out!

580 CUSINS: You know, I do not admit that I am imposing on Barbara. I am quite genuinely interested in the views of the Salvation Army. The fact is, I am a sort of collector of religions; and the curious thing is that I find I can believe them all. By the way, have you any religion?

585 UNDERSHAFT: Yes.

CUSINS: Anything out of the common?

UNDERSHAFT: Only that there are two things necessary to Salvation.

CUSINS: (disappointed, but polite) Ah, the Church Catechism.
590 Charles Lomax also belongs to the Established Church.

UNDERSHAFT: The two things are—

CUSINS: Baptism and—

UNDERSHAFT: No. Money and gunpowder.

CUSINS: (surprised, but interested) That is the general opinion of
595 our governing classes. The novelty is in hearing any man confess it.

UNDERSHAFT: Just so.

CUSINS: Excuse me: is there any place in your religion for honor, justice, truth, love, mercy and so forth?

600 UNDERSHAFT: Yes: they are the graces and luxuries of a rich, strong, and safe life.

CUSINS: Suppose one is forced to choose between them and money or gunpowder?

UNDERSHAFT: Choose money and gunpowder; for without
605 enough of both you cannot afford the others.

CUSINS: That is your religion?

UNDERSHAFT: Yes.

(The cadence of this reply makes a full close in the conversation, CUSINS twists his face dubiously and contemplates UNDERSHAFT. UNDERSHAFT contemplates him.)

CUSINS: Barbara wont stand that. You will have to choose between your religion and Barbara.

610 UNDERSHAFT: So will you, my friend. She will find out that that drum of yours is hollow.

CUSINS: Father Undershaft: you are mistaken: I am a sincere Salvationist. You do not understand the Salvation Army. It is the army of joy, of love, of courage: it has banished the fear

615 and remorse and despair of the old hell-ridden evangelical sects: it marches to fight the devil with trumpet and drum, with music and dancing, with banner and palm, as becomes a sally from heaven by its happy garrison. It picks the waster out of the public house and makes a man of him: it finds a worm

620 wriggling in a back kitchen, and lo! a woman! Men and women of rank too, sons and daughters of the Highest. It takes the poor professor of Greek, the most artificial and self-suppressed of human creatures, from his meal of roots, and lets loose the rhapsodist in him; reveals the true worship of

625 Dionysos to him; sends him down the public street drumming dithyrambs (he plays a thundering flourish on the drum.)

UNDERSHAFT: You will alarm the shelter.

CUSINS: Oh, they are accustomed to these sudden ecstasies. However, if the drum worries you—(he pockets the drum-

630 sticks; unhooks the drum; and stands it on the ground opposite the gateway.)

UNDERSHAFT: Thank you.

CUSINS: You remember what Euripides says about your money and gunpowder?

635 UNDERSHAFT: No.

CUSINS: (declaiming)

> One and another
> In money and guns may outpass his brother;
> And men in their millions float and flow
640 > And seethe with a million hopes as leaven;
> And they win their will; or they miss their will;
> And their hopes are dead or are pined for still;
> But who'er can know
> As the long days go
645 > That to live is happy, has found his heaven.

My translation: what do you think of it?

UNDERSHAFT: I think, my friend, that if you wish to know, as the long days go, that to live is happy, you must first acquire money enough for a decent life, and power enough to be your

650 own master.

CUSINS: You are damnably discouraging. (He resumes his declamation.)

> Is it so hard a thing to see
> That the spirit of God—whate'er it be—
655 > The law that abides and changes not, ages long,
> The Eternal and Nature-born: these things be strong?
> What else is Wisdom? What of Man's endeavor,
> Or God's high grace so lovely and so great?
> To stand from fear set free? to breathe and wait?
660 > To hold a hand uplifted over Fate?
> And shall not Barbara be loved for ever?

UNDERSHAFT: Euripides mentions Barbara, does he?

CUSINS: It is a fair translation. The word means Loveliness.

UNDERSHAFT: May I ask—as Barbara's father—how much a

665 year she is to be loved for ever on?

CUSINS: As for Barbara's father, that is more your affair than mine. I can feed her by teaching Greek: that is about all.

UNDERSHAFT: Do you consider it a good match for her?

CUSINS: (with polite obstinacy) Mr Undershaft: I am in many

670 ways a weak, timid, ineffectual person; and my health is far from satisfactory. But whenever I feel that I must have anything, I get it, sooner or later. I feel that way about Barbara. I dont like marriage: I feel intensely afraid of it; and I dont know what I shall do with Barbara or what she will do with me. But

675 I feel that I and nobody else must marry her. Please regard that as settled.—Not that I wish to be arbitrary; but why should I waste your time in discussing what is inevitable?

UNDERSHAFT: You mean that you will stick at nothing: not even the conversion of the Salvation Army to the worship of

680 Dionysos.

CUSINS: The business of the Salvation Army is to save, not to wrangle about the name of the pathfinder. Dionysos or another: what does it matter?

UNDERSHAFT: (rising and approaching him) Professor Cusins:

685 you are a young man after my own heart.

CUSINS: Mr Undershaft: you are, as far as I am able to gather, a most infernal old rascal; but you appeal very strongly to my sense of ironic humor.

(UNDERSHAFT mutely offers his hand. They shake.)

UNDERSHAFT: (suddenly concentrating himself) And now to

690 business.

CUSINS: Pardon me. We are discussing religion. Why go back to such an uninteresting and unimportant subject as business?

UNDERSHAFT: Religion is our business at present, because it is through religion alone that we can win Barbara.

695 CUSINS: Have you, too, fallen in love with Barbara?

UNDERSHAFT: Yes, with a father's love.

CUSINS: A father's love for a grown-up daughter is the most dangerous of all infatuations. I apologize for mentioning my own pale, coy, mistrustful fancy in the same breath with it.

700 UNDERSHAFT: Keep to the point. We have to win her; and we are neither of us Methodists.

CUSINS: That doesnt matter. The power Barbara wields here—the power that wields Barbara herself—is not Calvinism, not Presbyterianism, not Methodism—

705 UNDERSHAFT: Not Greek Paganism either, eh?

CUSINS: I admit that. Barbara is quite original in her religion.

UNDERSHAFT: (triumphantly) Aha! Barbara Undershaft would be. Her inspiration comes from within herself.

CUSINS: How do you suppose it got there?

710 UNDERSHAFT: (in towering excitement) It is the Undershaft inheritance. I shall hand on my torch to my daughter. She shall make my converts and preach my gospel—

CUSINS: What! Money and gunpowder!

UNDERSHAFT: Yes, money and gunpowder. Freedom and

715 power. Command of life and command of death.

CUSINS: (urbanely: trying to bring him down to earth) This is extremely interesting, Mr Undershaft. Of course you know that you are mad.

UNDERSHAFT: (with redoubled force) And you?

720 CUSINS: Oh, mad as a hatter. You are welcome to my secret since I have discovered yours. But I am astonished. Can a madman make cannons?

UNDERSHAFT: Would anyone else than a madman make them? And now (with surging energy) question for question. Can a sane man translate Euripides?

725 CUSINS: No.

UNDERSHAFT: (*seizing him by the shoulder*) Can a sane woman make a man of a waster or a woman of a worm?

730 CUSINS: (*reeling before the storm*) Father Colossus — Mammoth Millionaire —

UNDERSHAFT: (*pressing him*) Are there two mad people or three in this Salvation shelter today?

CUSINS: You mean Barbara is as mad as we are?

735 UNDERSHAFT: (*pushing him lightly off and resuming his equanimity suddenly and completely*) Pooh, Professor! let us call things by their proper names. I am a millionaire; you are a poet: Barbara is a savior of souls. What have we three to do with the common mob of slaves and idolators? (*He sits down again with a shrug of contempt for the mob.*)

740 CUSINS: Take care! Barbara is in love with the common people. So am I. Have you never felt the romance of that love?

UNDERSHAFT: (*cold and sardonic*) Have you ever been in love with Poverty, like St Francis? Have you ever been in love with Dirt, like St Simeon! Have you ever been in love with disease
745 and suffering, like our nurses and philanthropists? Such passions are not virtues, but the most unnatural of all the vices. This love of the common people may please an earl's granddaughter and a university professor; but I have been a common man and a poor man; and it has no romance for me.
750 Leave it to the poor to pretend that poverty is a blessing: leave it to the coward to make a religion of his cowardice by preaching humility: we know better than that. We three must stand together above the common people: how else can we help their children to climb up beside us? Barbara must belong to
755 us, not to the Salvation Army.

CUSINS: Well, I can only say that if you think you will get her away from the Salvation Army by talking to her as you have been talking to me, you dont know Barbara.

UNDERSHAFT: My friend: I never ask for what I can buy.

760 CUSINS: (*in a white fury*) Do I understand you to imply that you can buy Barbara?

UNDERSHAFT: No; but I can buy the Salvation Army.

CUSINS: Quite impossible.

UNDERSHAFT: You shall see. All religious organizations exist by
765 selling themselves to the rich.

CUSINS: Not the Army. That is the Church of the poor.

UNDERSHAFT: All the more reason for buying it.

CUSINS: I dont think you quite know what the Army does for the poor.

770 UNDERSHAFT: Oh yes I do. It draws their teeth: that is enough for me as a man of business.

CUSINS: Nonsense! It makes them sober —

UNDERSHAFT: I prefer sober workmen. The profits are larger.

CUSINS: — honest —

775 UNDERSHAFT: Honest workmen are the most economical.

CUSINS: — attached to their homes —

UNDERSHAFT: So much the better: they will put up with anything sooner than change their shop.

CUSINS: — happy —

780 UNDERSHAFT: An invaluable safeguard against revolution.

CUSINS: — unselfish —

UNDERSHAFT: Indifferent to their own interests, which suits me exactly.

CUSINS: — with their thoughts on heavenly things —

785 UNDERSHAFT: (*rising*) And not on Trade Unionism nor Socialism. Excellent.

CUSINS: (*revolted*) You really are an infernal old rascal.

UNDERSHAFT: (*indicating* PETER SHIRLEY, *who has just come from the shelter and strolled dejectedly down the yard between them*) And this is an honest man! 790

SHIRLEY: Yes; and what av I got by it? (*he passes on bitterly and sits on the form, in the corner of the penthouse.*)

(SNOBBY PRICE, *beaming sanctimoniously, and* JENNY HILL, *with a tambourine full of coppers, come from the shelter and go to the drum, on which* JENNY *begins to count the money.*)

UNDERSHAFT: (*replying to* SHIRLEY) Oh, your employers must have got a good deal by it from first to last. (*He sits on the table, with one foot on the side form,* CUSINS, *overwhelmed,* 795 *sits down on the same form nearer the shelter.* BARBARA *comes from the shelter to the middle of the yard. She is excited and a little overwrought.*)

BARBARA: Weve just had a splendid experience meeting at the other gate in Cripps's lane. Ive hardly ever seen them so much 800 moved as they were by your confession, Mr Price.

PRICE: I could almost be glad of my past wickedness if I could believe that it would elp to keep hathers straight.

BARBARA: So it will, Snobby. How much, Jenny?

JENNY: Four and tenpence, Major. 805

BARBARA: Oh Snobby, if you had given your poor mother just one more kick, we should have got the whole five shillings!

PRICE: If she heard you say that, miss, she'd be sorry I didnt. But I'm glad. Oh what a joy it will be to her when she hears I'm saved! 810

UNDERSHAFT: Shall I contribute the odd twopence, Barbara? The millionaire's mite, eh? (*He takes a couple of pennies from his pocket.*)

BARBARA: How did you make that twopence?

UNDERSHAFT: As usual. By selling cannons, torpedoes, submarines, and my new patent Grand Duke hand grenade. 815

BARBARA: Put it back in your pocket. You cant buy your salvation here for twopence: you must work it out.

UNDERSHAFT: Is twopence not enough? I can afford a little more, if you press me. 820

BARBARA: Two million millions would not be enough. There is bad blood on your hands; and nothing but good blood can cleanse them. Money is no use. Take it away. (*She turns to* CUSINS.) Dolly: you must write another letter for me to the papers. (*He makes a wry face.*) Yes: I know you dont like it; but 825 it must be done. The starvation this winter is beating us: everybody is unemployed. The General says we must close this shelter if we cant get more money. I force the collections at the meetings until I am ashamed: dont I, Snobby?

PRICE: It's a fair treat to see you work it, miss. The way you got 830 them up from three-and-six to four-and-ten with that hymn, penny by penny and verse by verse, was a caution. Not a Cheap Jack on Mile End Waste could touch you at it.

BARBARA: Yes; but I wish we could do without it. I am getting at last to think more of the collection than of the people's souls. 835 And what are those hatfuls of pence and halfpence? We want thousands! tens of thousands! hundreds of thousands! I want to convert people, not to be always begging for the Army in a way I'd die sooner than beg for myself.

UNDERSHAFT: (*in profound irony*) Genuine unselfishness is capable of anything, my dear. 840

BARBARA: (*unsuspectingly, as she turns away to take the money from the drum and put it in a cash bag she carries*) Yes, isnt it? (UNDERSHAFT *looks sardonically at* CUSINS.)

845 CUSINS: (aside to UNDERSHAFT) Mephistopheles! Machiavelli!

BARBARA: (tears coming into her eyes as she ties the bag and pockets it) How are we to feed them? I cant talk religion to a man with bodily hunger in his eyes. (Almost breaking down) It's frightful.

850 JENNY: (running to her) Major, dear —

BARBARA: (rebounding) No: dont comfort me. It will be all right. We shall get the money.

UNDERSHAFT: How?

JENNY: By praying for it, of course. Mrs Baines says she prayed

855 for it last night; and she has never prayed for it in vain: never once. (She goes to the gate and looks out into the street.)

BARBARA: (who has dried her eyes and regained her composure) By the way, dad, Mrs Baines has come to march with us to our big meeting this afternoon; and she is very anxious to

860 meet you, for some reason or other. Perhaps she'll convert you.

UNDERSHAFT: I shall be delighted, my dear.

JENNY: (at the gate: excitedly) Major! Major! heres that man back again.

865 BARBARA: What man?

JENNY: The man that hit me. Oh, I hope he's coming back to join us.

(BILL WALKER, with frost on his jacket, comes through the gate, his hands deep in his pockets and his chin sunk between his shoulders, like a cleaned-out gambler. He halts between BARBARA and the drum.)

BARBARA: Hullo, Bill! Back already!

BILL: (nagging at her) Bin talkin ever sence, ev you?

870 BARBARA: Pretty nearly. Well, has Todger paid you out for poor Jenny's jaw?

BILL: Nao e aint.

BARBARA: I thought your jacket looked a bit snowy.

BILL: Sao it is snaowy. You want to knaow where the snaow cam

875 from, downt you?

BARBARA: Yes.

BILL: Well, it cam from orf the grahnd in Pawkinses Corner in Kennintahn. It got rabbed orf be maw shaoulders: see?

BARBARA: Pity you didnt rub some off with your knees, Bill! That

880 would have done you a lot of good.

BILL: (with sour mirthless humor) Aw was sivin another menn's knees at the tawm. E was kneelin on moy ed, e was.

JENNY: Who was kneeling on your head?

BILL: Todger was. E was pryin for me: pryin camfortable wiv me

885 as a cawpet. Sow was Mog. Sao was the aol bloomin meetin. Mog she sez 'Ow Lawd brike is stabborn sperrit; bat downt urt is dear art.' Thet was wot she said. 'Downt urt is dear art'! An er blowk—thirteen stun four!—kneelin wiv all is wight on me. Fanny, aint it?

890 JENNY: Oh no. We're so sorry, Mr Walker.

BARBARA: (enjoying it frankly) Nonsense! of course it's funny. Served you right, Bill! You must have done something to him first.

BILL: (doggedly) Aw did wot Aw said Aw'd do. Aw spit in is eye. E

895 looks ap at the skoy and sez, 'Ow that Aw should be fahnd worthy to be spit upon for the gospel's sike!' e sez; an Mog sez 'Glaory Allelloolier!'; an then e called me Braddher, an dahned me as if Aw was a kid and e was me mather worshin me a Setterda nawt. Aw ednt jast nao shaow wiv im at all. Arf

the street pryed; an the tather arf larfed fit to split theirselves. 900 (To BARBARA) There! are you settisfawd nah?

BARBARA: (her eyes dancing) Wish I'd been there, Bill.

BILL: Yus: youd a got in a hextra bit o talk on me, wouldnt you?

JENNY: I'm so sorry, Mr Walker.

BILL: (fiercely) Downt you gow being sorry for me: youve no call. 905 Listen eah. Aw browk your jawr.

JENNY: No, it didn't hurt me: indeed it didnt, except for a moment. It was only that I was frightened.

BILL: Aw downt want to be forgive be you, or be ennybody. Wot Aw did Aw'll py for. Aw trawd to gat me aown jawr browk to 910 settisfaw you —

JENNY: (distressed) Oh no —

BILL: (impatiently) Tell y' Aw did: cawnt you listen to wots bein taold you? All Aw got be it was bein mide a sawt of in the pablic street for me pines. Well, if Aw cawnt settisfaw you one 915 wy, Aw ken anather. Listen eah! Aw ed two quid sived agen the frost; an Awve a pahnd of it left. A mite o mawn last week ed words with the judy e's gowing to merry. E give er wot-for; an e's bin fawnd fifteen bob. E ed a rawt to itt er cause they was gowin to be merrid; but Aw ednt nao rawt to itt you; sao put 920 another fawv bob on an call it a pahnd's worth. (He produces a sovereign.) Eahs the manney. Tike it; and lets ev no more o your forgivin an pryin and your Mijor jawrin me. Let wot Aw dan be dan an pide for; and let there be a end of it.

JENNY: Oh, I couldnt take it, Mr Walker. But if you would give a 925 shilling or two to poor Rummy Mitchens! you really did hurt her; and she's old.

BILL: (contemptuously) Not lawkly. Aw'd give her anather as soon as look at er. Let her ev the lawr o me as she threatened! She aint forgiven me: not mach. Wot Aw dan to er is not on 930 me mawnd—wot she (indicating BARBARA) mawt call on me conscience—no more than stickin a pig. It's this Christian gime o yours that Aw wownt ev plyed agen me: this bloomin forgivin an neggin an jawrin that mikes a menn thet sore that iz lawf's a burdn to im. Aw wownt ev it, Aw tell you; sao tike 935 your manney and stop thraowin your silly beshed fice hap agen me.

JENNY: Major: may I take a little of it for the Army?

BARBARA: No: the Army is not to be bought. We want your soul, Bill; and we'll take nothing less. 940

BILL: (bitterly) Aw knaow. Me an maw few shillins is not good enaff for you. Youre a earl's grendorter, you are. Nathink less than a andered pahnd for you.

UNDERSHAFT: Come, Barbara! you could do a great deal of good with a hundred pounds. If you will set this gentleman's mind 945 at east by taking his pound, I will give the other ninety-nine.

(BILL, dazed by such opulence, instinctively touches his cap.)

BARBARA: Oh, youre too extravagant, papa. Bill offers twenty pieces of silver. All you need offer is the other ten. That will make the standard price to buy anybody who's for sale. I'm not; and the Army's not. (To BILL) Youll never have another 950 quiet moment, Bill, until you come round to us. You cant stand out against your salvation.

BILL: (sullenly) Aw cawnt stend aht agen music awl wrastlers and awful tangued women. Awve offered to py. Aw can do no more. Tike it or leave it. There it is. (He throws the sovereign 955 on the drum, and sits down on the horse-trough. The coin fascinates SNOBBY PRICE, who takes an early opportunity of dropping his cap on it.)

(MRS BAINES *comes from the shelter. She is dressed as a Salvation Army Commissioner. She is an earnest looking woman of about 40, with a caressing, urgent voice, and an appealing manner.*)

960 BARBARA: This is my father, Mrs Baines. (UNDERSHAFT *comes from the table, taking his hat off with marked civility.*) Try what you can do with him. He wont listen to me, because he remembers what a fool I was when I was a baby. (*She leaves them together and chats with* JENNY.)

965 MRS BAINES: Have you been shewn over the shelter, Mr Undershaft? You know the work we're doing, of course.

UNDERSHAFT: (*very civilly*) The whole nation knows it, Mrs Baines.

MRS BAINES: No, sir: the whole nation does not know it, or we should not be crippled as we are for want of money to carry 970 our work through the length and breadth of the land. Let me tell you that there would have been rioting this winter in London but for us.

UNDERSHAFT: You really think so?

MRS BAINES: I know it. I remember 1886, when you rich gentle-975 men hardened your hearts against the cry of the poor. They broke the windows of your clubs in Pall Mall.

UNDERSHAFT: (*gleaming with approval of their method*) And the Mansion House Fund went up next day from thirty thousand pounds to seventy-nine thousand! I remember quite well.

980 MRS BAINES: Well, wont you help me to get at the people? They wont break windows then. Come here, Price. Let me shew you to this gentleman (PRICE *comes to be inspected.*) Do you remember the window breaking?

PRICE: My ole father thought it was the revolution, maam.

985 MRS BAINES: Would you break windows now?

PRICE: Oh no, maam. The windows of eaven av bin opened to me. I know now that the rich man is a sinner like myself.

RUMMY: (*appearing above at the loft door*) Snobby Price!

SNOBBY: Wot is it?

990 RUMMY: Your mother's askin for you at the other gate in Cripps's Lane. She's heard about your confession (PRICE *turns pale.*)

MRS BAINES: Go, Mr Price; and pray with her.

JENNY: You can go through the shelter, Snobby.

PRICE: (*to* MRS BAINES) I couldnt face her now, maam, with all 995 the weight of my sins fresh on me. Tell her she'll find her son at ome, waitin for her in prayer. (*He skulks off through the gate, incidentally stealing the sovereign on his way out by picking up his cap from the drum.*)

MRS BAINES: (*with swimming eyes*) You see how we take the an-1000 ger and the bitterness against you out of their hearts, Mr Undershaft.

UNDERSHAFT: It is certainly most convenient and gratifying to all large employers of labor, Mrs Baines.

MRS BAINES: Barbara: Jenny: I have good news: most wonderful 1005 news. (JENNY *runs to her.*) My prayers have been answered. I told you they would, Jenny, didnt I?

JENNY: Yes, yes.

BARBARA: (*moving nearer to the drum*) Have we got money enough to keep the shelter open?

1010 MRS BAINES: I hope we shall have enough to keep all the shelters open. Lord Saxmundham has promised us five thousand pounds—

BARBARA: Hooray!

JENNY: Glory!

1015 MRS BAINES: —if—

BARBARA: 'If!' If what?

MRS BAINES: —if five other gentlemen will give a thousand each to make it up to ten thousand.

BARBARA: Who is Lord Saxmundham? I never heard of him.

1020 UNDERSHAFT: (*who has pricked up his ears at the peer's name, and is now watching* BARBARA *curiously*) A new creation, my dear. You have heard of Sir Horace Bodger?

BARBARA: Bodger! Do you mean the distiller? Bodger's whisky!

UNDERSHAFT: That is the man. He is one of the greatest of our 1025 public benefactors. He restored the cathedral at Hakington. They made him a baronet for that. He gave half a million to the funds of his party: they made him a baron for that.

SHIRLEY: What will they give him for the five thousand?

UNDERSHAFT: There is nothing left to give him. So the five 1030 thousand, I should think, is to save his soul.

MRS BAINES: Heaven grant it may! Oh Mr Undershaft, you have some very rich friends. Cant you help us towards the other five thousand? We are going to hold a great meeting this afternoon at the Assembly Hall in the Mile End Road. If I could 1035 only announce that one gentleman had come forward to support Lord Saxmundham, others would follow. Dont you know somebody? couldnt you? wouldnt you? (*her eyes fill with tears*) oh, think of those poor people, Mr Undershaft: think of how much it means to them, and how little to a great 1040 man like you.

UNDERSHAFT: (*sardonically gallant*) Mrs Baines: you are irresistible. I cant disappoint you; and I cant deny myself the satisfaction of making Bodger pay up. You shall have your five thousand pounds.

1045 MRS BAINES: Thank God!

UNDERSHAFT: You dont thank me?

MRS BAINES: Oh sir, dont try to be cynical: dont be ashamed of being a good man. The Lord will bless you abundantly; and our prayers will be like a strong fortification round you all the 1050 days of your life. (*With a touch of caution*) You will let me have the cheque to shew at the meeting, wont you? Jenny: go in and fetch a pen and ink. (JENNY *runs to the shelter door.*)

UNDERSHAFT: Do not disturb Miss Hill: I have a fountain pen (JENNY *halts. He sits at the table and writes the cheque.* CU-1055 SINS *rises to make room for him. They all watch him silently.*)

BILL: (*cynically, aside to* BARBARA, *his voice and accent horribly debased*) Wot prawce selvytion nah?

BARBARA: Stop. (UNDERSHAFT *stops writing: they all turn to her in surprise.*) Mrs Baines: are you really going to take this 1060 money?

MRS BAINES: (*astonished*) Why not, dear?

BARBARA: Why not! Do you know what my father is? Have you forgotten that Lord Saxmundham is Bodger the whisky man? Do you remember how we implored the County Council to 1065 stop him from writing Bodger's Whisky in letters of fire against the sky; so that the poor drink-ruined creatures on the Embankment could not wake up from their snatches of sleep without being reminded of their deadly thirst by that wicked sky sign? Do you know that the worst thing I have had to fight 1070 here is not the devil, but Bodger, Bodger, Bodger, with his whisky, his distilleries, and his tied houses? Are you going to make our shelter another tied house for him, and ask me to keep it?

BILL: Rotten dranken whisky it is too.

1075 MRS BAINES: Dear Barbara: Lord Saxmundham has a soul to be saved like any of us. If heaven has found the way to make a good use of his money, are we to set ourselves up against the answer to our prayers?

1080 BARBARA: I know he has a soul to be saved. Let him come down here; and I'll do my best to help him to his salvation. But he wants to send his cheque down to buy us, and go on being as wicked as ever.

UNDERSHAFT: (*with a reasonableness which* CUSINS *alone perceives to be ironical*) My dear Barbara: alcohol is a very neces-
1085 sary article. It heals the sick—

BARBARA: It does nothing of the sort.

UNDERSHAFT: Well, it assists the doctor: that is perhaps a less questionable way of putting it. It makes life bearable to millions of people who could not endure their existence if they
1090 were quite sober. It enables Parliament to do things at eleven at night that no sane person would do at eleven in the morning. Is it Bodger's fault that this inestimable gift is deplorably abused by less than one per cent of the poor? (*He turns again to the table; signs the cheque; and crosses it.*)

1095 MRS BAINES: Barbara: will there be less drinking or more if all those poor souls we are saving come tomorrow and find the doors of our shelters shut in their faces? Lord Saxmundham gives us the money to stop drinking—to take his own business from him.

1100 CUSINS: (*impishly*) Pure self-sacrifice on Bodger's part, clearly! Bless dear Bodger! (BARBARA *almost breaks down as* ADOLPHUS, *too, fails her.*)

UNDERSHAFT: (*tearing out the cheque and pocketing the book as he rises and goes past* CUSINS *to* MRS BAINES) I also, Mrs
1105 Baines, may claim a little disinterestedness. Think of my business! think of the widows and orphans! the men and lads torn to pieces with shrapnel and poisoned with lyddite! (MRS BAINES *shrinks; but he goes on remorselessly*) the oceans of blood, not one drop of which is shed in a really just cause! the
1110 ravaged crops! the peaceful peasants forced, women and men, to till their fields under the fire of opposing armies on pain of starvation! the bad blood of the fierce little cowards at home who egg on others to fight for the gratification of their national vanity! All this makes money for me: I am never
1115 richer, never busier than when the papers are full of it. Well, it is your work to preach peace on earth and good will to men. (MRS BAINES'S *face lights up again.*) Every convert you make is a vote against war. (*Her lips move in prayer.*) Yet I give you this money to help you to hasten my own commercial ruin.
1120 (*He gives her the cheque.*)

CUSINS: (*mounting the form in an ecstasy of mischief*) The millennium will be inaugurated by the unselfishness of Undershaft and Bodger. Oh be joyful! (*He takes the drum-sticks from his pocket and flourishes them.*)

1125 MRS BAINES: (*taking the cheque*) The longer I live the more proof I see that there is an Infinite Goodness that turns everything to the work of salvation sooner or later. Who would have thought that any good could have come out of war and drink? And yet their profits are brought today to the feet of
1130 salvation to do its blessed work. (*She is affected to tears.*)

JENNY: (*running to* MRS BAINES *and throwing her arms round her*) Oh dear! how blessed, how glorious it all is!

CUSINS: (*in a convulsion of irony*) Let us seize this unspeakable moment. Let us march to the great meeting at once. Excuse
1135 me just an instant. (*He rushes into the shelter.* JENNY *takes her tambourine from the drum head.*)

MRS BAINES: Mr Undershaft: have you ever seen a thousand people fall on their knees with one impulse and pray? Come with us to the meeting. Barbara shall tell them that the Army is saved, and saved through you.

1140 CUSINS: (*returning impetuously from the shelter with a flag and a trombone, and coming between* MRS BAINES *and* UNDERSHAFT) You shall carry the flag down the first street, Mrs Baines (*he gives her the flag.*) Mr Undershaft is a gifted trombonist: he shall intone an Olympian diapason to the West
1145 Ham Salvation March. (*Aside to* UNDERSHAFT, *as he forces the trombone on him*) Blow, Machiavelli, blow.

UNDERSHAFT: (*aside to him, as he takes the trombone*) The trumpet in Zion! (CUSINS *rushes to the drum, which he takes up and puts on.* UNDERSHAFT *continues, aloud*) I will do my
1150 best. I could vamp a bass if I knew the tune.

CUSINS: It is a wedding chorus from one of Donizetti's operas; but we have converted it. We convert everything to good here, including Bodger. You remember the chorus. 'For thee immense rejoicing—immenso giubilo—immenso giubilo.'
1155 (*With drum obbligato*) Rum tum ti tum tum, tum tum ti ta—

BARBARA: Dolly: you are breaking my heart.

CUSINS: What is a broken heart more or less here? Dionysos Undershaft has descended. I am possessed.

MRS BAINES: Come, Barbara: I must have my dear Major to
1160 carry the flag with me.

JENNY: Yes, yes, Major darling.

(CUSINS *snatches the tambourine out of* JENNY's *hand and mutely offers it to* BARBARA.)

BARBARA: (*coming forward a little as she puts the offer behind her with a shudder, whilst* CUSINS *recklessly tosses the tambourine
1165 back to* JENNY *and goes to the gate*) I cant come.

JENNY: Not come!

MRS BAINES: (*with tears in her eyes*) Barbara: do you think I am wrong to take the money?

BARBARA: (*impulsively going to her and kissing her*) No, no: God
1170 help you, dear, you must: you are saving the Army. Go; and may you have a great meeting!

JENNY: But arnt you coming?

BARBARA: No. (*She begins taking off the silver S brooch from her collar.*)

1175 MRS BAINES: Barbara: what are you doing?

JENNY: Why are you taking your badge off? You cant be going to leave us, Major.

BARBARA: (*quietly*) Father: come here.

UNDERSHAFT: (*coming to her*) My dear! (*Seeing that she is going
1180 to pin the badge on his collar, he retreats to the penthouse in some alarm.*)

BARBARA: (*following him*) Dont be frightened. (*She pins the badge on and steps back towards the table, shewing him to the others*) There! It's not much for £5000, is it?

1185 MRS BAINES: Barbara: if you wont come and pray with us, promise me you will pray for us.

BARBARA: I cant pray now. Perhaps I shall never pray again.

MRS BAINES: Barbara!

JENNY: Major!

1190 BARBARA: (*almost delirious*) I cant bear any more. Quick march!

CUSINS: (*calling to the procession in the street outside*) Off we go. Play up, there! Immenso giubilo. (*He gives the time with his drum; and the band strikes up the march, which rapidly becomes more distant as the procession moves briskly away.*)

1195 MRS BAINES: I must go, dear. Youre overworked: you will be all
right tomorrow. We'll never lose you. Now Jenny: step out
with the old flag. Blood and Fire! (*She marches out through
the gate with her flag.*)

JENNY: Glory Hallelujah! (*flourishing her tambourine and*
1200 *marching.*)

UNDERSHAFT: (*to* CUSINS, *as he marches out past him easing the
slide of his trombone*) 'My ducats and my daughter'!

CUSINS: (*following him out*) Money and gunpowder!

BARBARA: Drunkenness and Murder! My God: why hast thou
1205 forsaken me?

(*She sinks on the form with her face buried in her hands. The
march passes away into silence.* BILL WALKER *steals across to
her.*)

BILL: (*taunting*) Wot prawce selvytion nah?

SHIRLEY: Dont you hit her when she's down.

BILL: She itt me wen aw wiz dahn. Waw shouldnt Aw git a bit o
me aown beck?

1210 BARBARA: (*raising her head*) I didnt take your money, Bill. (*She
crosses the yard to the gate and turns her back on the two men
to hide her face from them.*)

BILL: (*sneering after her*) Naow, it warnt enaff for you. (*Turning
to the drum, he misses the money*) Ellow! If you aint took it
1215 sammun else ez. Weres it gorn? Bly me if Jenny Ill didnt tike
it after all!

RUMMY: (*screaming at him from the loft*) You lie, you dirty
blackguard! Snobby Price pinched it off the drum when he
took up his cap. I was up here all the time an see im do it.

1220 BILL: Wot! Stowl maw manney! Waw didnt you call thief on
him, you silly aold macker you?

RUMMY: To serve you aht for ittin me across the fice. It's cost
y'pahnd, that az. (*Raising a pœan of squalid triumph*) I done
you. I'm even with you. Uve ad it aht o y — (BILL *snatches up*
1225 SHIRLEY's *mug and hurls it at her. She slams the loft door and
vanishes. The mug smashes against the door and falls in
fragments.*)

BILL: (*beginning to chuckle*) Tell us, aol menn, wot o'clock this
mawnin was it wen im as they call Snobby Prawce was sived?

1230 BARBARA: (*turning to him more composedly, and with unspoiled
sweetness*) About half past twelve, Bill. And he pinched your
pound at a quarter to two. I know. Well, you cant afford to
lose it. I'll send it to you.

BILL: (*his voice and accent suddenly improving*) Not if Aw wiz to
1235 stawve for it. Aw aint to be bought.

SHIRLEY: Aint you? Youd sell yourself to the devil for a pint o
beer; only there aint no devil to make the offer.

BILL: (*unashamed*) Sao Aw would, mite, and often ev, cheerful.
But she cawnt baw me. (*Approaching* BARBARA) You wanted
1240 maw saoul, did you? Well, you aint got it.

BARBARA: I nearly got it, Bill. But weve sold it back to you for ten
thousand pounds.

SHIRLEY: And dear at the money!

BARBARA: No, Peter: it was worth more than money.

1245 BILL: (*salvationproof*) It's nao good: you cawnt get rahnd me
nah. Aw downt blieve in it; and Awve seen tody that Aw was
rawt. (*Going*) Sao long, aol soupkitchener! Ta, ta, Mijor
Earl's Grendorter! (*Turning at the gate*) Wot prawce selvytion
nah? Snobby Prawce! Ha! ha!

1250 BARBARA: (*offering her hand*) Goodbye, Bill.

BILL: (*taken aback, half plucks his cap off; then shoves it on again

defiantly) Git aht. (BARBARA *drops her hand, discouraged. He
has a twinge of remorse.*) But thets aw rawt, you knaow.
Nathink pasnl. Naow mellice. Sao long, Judy. (*He goes.*)

1255 BARBARA: No malice. So long, Bill.

SHIRLEY: (*shaking his head*) You make too much of him, miss,
in your innocence.

BARBARA: (*going to him*) Peter: I'm like you now. Cleaned out,
and lost my job.

1260 SHIRLEY: Youve youth an hope. Thats two better than me.

BARBARA: I'll get you a job, Peter. Thats hope for you: the youth
will have to be enough for me. (*She counts her money.*) I have
just enough left for two teas at Lockharts, a Rowton doss for
you, and my tram and bus home. (*He frowns and rises with
1265 offended pride. She takes his arm.*) Dont be proud, Peter: it's
sharing between friends. And promise me youll talk to me
and not let me cry. (*She draws him towards the gate.*)

SHIRLEY: Well, I'm not accustomed to talk to the like of you —

BARBARA: (*urgently*) Yes, yes: you must talk to me. Tell me about
1270 Tom Paine's books and Bradlaugh's lectures. Come along.

SHIRLEY: Ah, if you would only read Tom Paine in the proper
spirit, miss! (*They go out through the gate together*)

— ACT THREE —

Next day after lunch LADY BRITOMART *is writing in the library
in Wilton Crescent.* SARAH *is reading in the armchair near the
window.* BARBARA, *in ordinary fashionable dress, pale and
brooding, is on the settee.* CHARLES LOMAX *enters. He starts on
seeing* BARBARA *fashionably attired and in low spirits.*

LOMAX: Youve left off your uniform!

(BARBARA *says nothing; but an expression of pain passes over her
face.*)

LADY BRITOMART: (*warning him in low tones to be careful*)
Charles!

LOMAX: (*much concerned, coming behind the settee and bending
sympathetically over* BARBARA) I'm awfully sorry, Barbara.   5
You know I helped you all I could with the concertina and so
forth. (*Momentously*) Still, I have never shut my eyes to the
fact that there is a certain amount of tosh about the Salvation
Army. Now the claims of the Church of England —

LADY BRITOMART: Thats enough, Charles. Speak of something   10
suited to your mental capacity.

LOMAX: But surely the Church of England is suited to all our
capacities.

BARBARA: (*pressing his hand*) Thank you for your sympathy,
Cholly. Now go and spoon with Sarah.   15

LOMAX: (*dragging a chair from the writing table and seating
himself affectionately by* SARAH's *side*) How is my ownest
today?

SARAH: I wish you wouldnt tell Cholly to do things, Barbara. He
always comes straight and does them. Cholly: we're going to   20
the works this afternoon.

LOMAX: What works?

SARAH: The cannon works.

LOMAX: What? your governor's shop!

SARAH: Yes.   25

LOMAX: Oh I say!

(CUSINS *enters in poor condition. He also starts visibly when he
sees* BARBARA *without her uniform.*)

BARBARA: I expected you this morning, Dolly. Didnt you guess that?

CUSINS: (*sitting down beside her*) I'm sorry. I have only just breakfasted.

SARAH: But weve just finished lunch.

BARBARA: Have you had one of your bad nights?

CUSINS: No: I had rather a good night: in fact, one of the most remarkable nights I have ever passed.

BARBARA: The meeting?

CUSINS: No: after the meeting.

LADY BRITOMART: You should have gone to bed after the meeting. What were you doing?

CUSINS: Drinking.

LADY BRITOMART:	Adolphus!
SARAH:	Dolly!
BARBARA:	Dolly!
LOMAX:	Oh I say!

LADY BRITOMART: What were you drinking, may I ask?

CUSINS: A most devilish kind of Spanish burgundy, warranted free from added alcohol: a Temperance burgundy in fact. Its richness in natural alcohol made any addition superfluous.

BARBARA: Are you joking, Dolly?

CUSINS: (*patiently*) No. I have been making a night of it with the nominal head of this household: that is all.

LADY BRITOMART: Andrew made you drunk!

CUSINS: No: he only provided the wine. I think it was Dionysos who made me drunk. (*To* BARBARA) I told you I was possessed.

LADY BRITOMART: Youre not sober yet. Go home to bed at once.

CUSINS: I have never before ventured to reproach you, Lady Brit; but how could you marry the Prince of Darkness?

LADY BRITOMART: It was much more excusable to marry him than to get drunk with him. That is a new accomplishment of Andrew's, by the way. He usent to drink.

CUSINS: He doesnt now. He only sat there and completed the wreck of my moral basis, the rout of my convictions, the purchase of my soul. He cares for you, Barbara. That is what makes him so dangerous to me.

BARBARA: That has nothing to do with it, Dolly. There are larger loves and diviner dreams than the fireside ones. You know that, dont you?

CUSINS: Yes: that is our understanding. I know it. I hold to it. Unless he can win me on that holier ground he may amuse me for a while; but he can get no deeper hold, strong as he is.

BARBARA: Keep to that; and the end will be right. Now tell me what happened at the meeting?

CUSINS: It was an amazing meeting. Mrs Baines almost died of emotion. Jenny Hill simply gibbered with hysteria. The Prince of Darkness played his trombone like a madman: its brazen roarings were like the laughter of the damned. 117 conversions took place then and there. They prayed with the most touching sincerity and gratitude for Bodger, and for the anonymous donor of the £5000. Your father would not let his name be given.

LOMAX: That was rather fine of the old man, you know. Most chaps would have wanted the advertisement.

CUSINS: He said all the charitable institutions would be down on him like kites on a battle-field if he gave his name.

LADY BRITOMART: Thats Andrew all over. He never does a proper thing without giving an improper reason for it.

CUSINS: He convinced me that I have all my life been doing improper things for proper reasons.

LADY BRITOMART: Adolphus: now that Barbara has left the Salvation Army, you had better leave it too. I will not have you playing that drum in the streets.

CUSINS: Your orders are already obeyed, Lady Brit.

BARBARA: Dolly: were you ever really in earnest about it? Would you have joined if you had never seen me?

CUSINS: (*disingenuously*) Well — er — well, possibly, as a collector of religions —

LOMAX: (*cunningly*) Not as a drummer, though, you know. You are a very clearheaded brainy chap, Dolly; and it must have been apparent to you that there is a certain amount of tosh about —

LADY BRITOMART: Charles: if you must drivel, drivel like a grown-up man and not like a schoolboy.

LOMAX: (*out of countenance*) Well, drivel is drivel, dont you know, whatever a man's age.

LADY BRITOMART: In good society in England, Charles, men drivel at all ages by repeating silly formulas with an air of wisdom. Schoolboys make their own formulas out of slang, like you. When they reach your age, and get political private secretaryships and things of that sort, they drop slang and get their formulas out of the Spectator or The Times. You had better confine yourself to The Times. You will find that there is a certain amount of tosh about The Times; but at least its language is reputable.

LOMAX: (*overwhelmed*) You are so awfully strong-minded, Lady Brit —

LADY BRITOMART: Rubbish! (MORRISON *comes in.*) What is it?

MORRISON: If you please, my lady, Mr Undershaft has just drove up to the door.

LADY BRITOMART: Well, let him in. (MORRISON *hesitates.*) Whats the matter with you?

MORRISON: Shall I announce him, my lady; or is he at home here, so to speak, my lady?

LADY BRITOMART: Announce him.

MORRISON: Thank you, my lady. You wont mind my asking, I hope. The occasion is in a manner of speaking new to me.

LADY BRITOMART: Quite right. Go and let him in.

MORRISON: Thank you, my lady. (*He withdraws.*)

LADY BRITOMART: Children: go and get ready. (SARAH *and* BARBARA *go upstairs for their out-of-door wraps.*) Charles: go and tell Stephen to come down here in five minutes: you will find him in the drawing room. (CHARLES *goes.*) Adolphus: tell them to send round the carriage in about fifteen minutes. (ADOLPHUS *goes.*)

MORRISON: (*at the door*) Mr Undershaft.

(UNDERSHAFT *comes in.* MORRISON *goes out.*)

UNDERSHAFT: Alone! How fortunate!

LADY BRITOMART: (*rising*) Dont be sentimental, Andrew. Sit down. (*She sits on the settee: he sits beside her, on her left. She comes to the point before he has time to breathe.*) Sarah must have £800 a year until Charles Lomax comes into his property. Barbara will need more, and need it permanently, because Adolphus hasnt any property.

UNDERSHAFT: (*resignedly*) Yes, my dear: I will see to it. Anything else? for yourself, for instance?

LADY BRITOMART: I want to talk to you about Stephen.

145 UNDERSHAFT: (*rather wearily*) Dont, my dear. Stephen doesnt interest me.

LADY BRITOMART: He does interest me. He is our son.

UNDERSHAFT: Do you really think so? He has induced us to bring him into the world; but he chose his parents very incon-
150 gruously, I think. I see nothing of myself in him, and less of you.

LADY BRITOMART: Andrew: Stephen is an excellent son, and a most steady, capable, highminded young man. You are simply trying to find an excuse for disinheriting him.

155 UNDERSHAFT: My dear Biddy: the Undershaft tradition disinherits him. It would be dishonest of me to leave the cannon foundry to my son.

LADY BRITOMART: It would be most unnatural and improper of you to leave it to anyone else, Andrew. Do you suppose this
160 wicked and immoral tradition can be kept up for ever? Do you pretend that Stephen could not carry on the foundry just as well as all the other sons of the big business houses?

UNDERSHAFT: Yes: he could learn the office routine without understanding the business, like all the other sons; and the firm
165 would go on by its own momentum until the real Undershaft—probably an Italian or a German—would invent a new method and cut him out.

LADY BRITOMART: There is nothing that any Italian or German could do that Stephen could not do. And Stephen at least has
170 breeding.

UNDERSHAFT: The son of a foundling! Nonsense!

LADY BRITOMART: My son, Andrew! And even you may have good blood in your veins for all you know.

UNDERSHAFT: True. Probably I have. That is another argument
175 in favour of a foundling.

LADY BRITOMART: Andrew: dont be aggravating. And dont be wicked. At present you are both.

UNDERSHAFT: This conversation is part of the Undershaft tradition, Biddy. Every Undershaft's wife has treated him to it ever
180 since the house was founded. It is mere waste of breath. If the tradition be ever broken it will be for an abler man than Stephen.

LADY BRITOMART: (*pouting*) Then go away.

UNDERSHAFT: (*deprecatory*) Go away!

185 LADY BRITOMART: Yes: go away. If you will do nothing for Stephen, you are not wanted here. Go to your foundling, whoever he is; and look after him.

UNDERSHAFT: The fact is, Biddy—

LADY BRITOMART: Dont call me Biddy. I dont call you Andy.

190 UNDERSHAFT: I will not call my wife Britomart: it is not good sense. Seriously, my love, the Undershaft tradition has landed me in a difficulty. I am getting on in years; and my partner Lazarus has at last made a stand and insisted that the succession must be settled one way or the other; and of course he is
195 quite right. You see, I havent found a fit successor yet.

LADY BRITOMART: (*obstinately*) There is Stephen.

UNDERSHAFT: Thats just it: all the foundlings I can find are exactly like Stephen.

LADY BRITOMART: Andrew!!

200 UNDERSHAFT: I want a man with no relations and no schooling: that is, a man who would be out of the running altogether if he were not a strong man. And I cant find him. Every blessed foundling nowadays is snapped up in his infancy by Barnardo

homes, or School Board officers, or Boards of Guardians; and if he shews the least ability he is fastened on by schoolmasters; 205 trained to win scholarships like a racehorse; crammed with secondhand ideas; drilled and disciplined in docility and what they call good taste; and lamed for life so that he is fit for nothing but teaching. If you want to keep the foundry in the family, you had better find an eligible foundling and marry 210 him to Barbara.

LADY BRITOMART: Ah! Barbara! Your pet! You would sacrifice Stephen to Barbara.

UNDERSHAFT: Cheerfully. And you, my dear, would boil Barbara to make soup for Stephen. 215

LADY BRITOMART: Andrew: this is not a question of our likings and dislikings: it is a question of duty. It is your duty to make Stephen your successor.

UNDERSHAFT: Just as much as it is your duty to submit to your husband. Come, Biddy! these tricks of the governing class are 220 of no use with me. I am one of the governing class myself; and it is waste of time giving tracts to a missionary. I have the power in this matter; and I am not to be humbugged into using it for your purposes.

LADY BRITOMART: Andrew: you can talk my head off; but you 225 cant change wrong into right. And your tie is all on one side. Put it straight.

UNDERSHAFT: (*disconcerted*) It wont stay unless it's pinned (*he fumbles at it with childish grimaces*)—

(STEPHEN *comes in.*)

STEPHEN: (*at the door*) I beg your pardon (*about to retire.*) 230

LADY BRITOMART: No: come in, Stephen. (STEPHEN *comes forward to his mother's writing table.*)

UNDERSHAFT: (*not very cordially*) Good afternoon.

STEPHEN: (*coldly*) Good afternoon.

UNDERSHAFT: (*to* LADY BRITOMART) He knows all about the 235 tradition, I suppose?

LADY BRITOMART: Yes. (*To* STEPHEN) It is what I told you last night, Stephen.

UNDERSHAFT: (*sulkily*) I understand you want to come into the cannon business. 240

STEPHEN: I go into trade! Certainly not.

UNDERSHAFT: (*opening his eyes, greatly eased in mind and manner*) Oh! in that case—

LADY BRITOMART: Cannons are not trade, Stephen. They are enterprise. 245

STEPHEN: I have no intention of becoming a man of business in any sense. I have no capacity for business and no taste for it. I intend to devote myself to politics.

UNDERSHAFT: (*rising*) My dear boy: this is an immense relief to me. And I trust it may prove an equally good thing for the 250 country. I was afraid you would consider yourself disparaged and slighted. (*He moves towards* STEPHEN *as if to shake hands with him.*)

LADY BRITOMART: (*rising and interposing*) Stephen: I cannot allow you to throw away an enormous property like this. 255

STEPHEN: (*stiffly*) Mother: there must be an end of treating me as a child, if you please. (LADY BRITOMART *recoils, deeply wounded by his tone.*) Until last night I did not take your attitude seriously, because I did not think you meant it seriously. But I find now that you left me in the dark as to matters 260 which you should have explained to me years ago. I am extremely hurt and offended. Any further discussion of my intentions had better take place with my father, as between one man and another.

265 LADY BRITOMART: Stephen! *(She sits down again, her eyes filling with tears.)*

UNDERSHAFT: *(with grave compassion)* You see, my dear, it is only the big men who can be treated as children.

STEPHEN: I am sorry, mother, that you have forced me —

270 UNDERSHAFT: *(stopping him)* Yes, yes, yes, yes: thats all right, Stephen. She wont interfere with you any more: your independence is achieved: you have won your latchkey. Dont rub it in; and above all, dont apologize. *(He resumes his seat.)* Now what about your future, as between one man and an-

275 other — I beg your pardon, Biddy: as between two men and a woman.

LADY BRITOMART: *(who has pulled herself together strongly)* I quite understand, Stephen. By all means go your own way if you feel strong enough. (STEPHEN *sits down magisterially in*

280 *the chair at the writing table with an air of affirming his majority.)*

UNDERSHAFT: It is settled that you do not ask for the succession to the cannon business.

STEPHEN: I hope it is settled that I repudiate the cannon

285 business.

UNDERSHAFT: Come, come! dont be so devilishly sulky: it's boyish. Freedom should be generous. Besides, I owe you a fair start in life in exchange for disinheriting you. You cant become prime minister all at once. Havnt you a turn for some-

290 thing? What about literature, art, and so forth?

STEPHEN: I have nothing of the artist about me, either in faculty or character, thank Heaven!

UNDERSHAFT: A philosopher, perhaps? Eh?

STEPHEN: I make no such ridiculous pretension.

295 UNDERSHAFT: Just so. Well, there is the army, the navy, the Church, the Bar. The Bar requires some ability. What about the Bar?

STEPHEN: I have not studied law. And I am afraid I have not the necessary push — I believe that is the name barristers give to

300 their vulgarity — for success in pleading.

UNDERSHAFT: Rather a difficult case, Stephen. Hardly anything left but the stage, is there? (STEPHEN *makes an impatient movement.)* Well, come! is there anything you know or care for?

305 STEPHEN: *(rising and looking at him steadily)* I know the difference between right and wrong.

UNDERSHAFT: *(hugely tickled)* You dont say so! What! no capacity for business, no knowledge of law, no sympathy with art, no pretension to philosophy; only a simple knowledge of the

310 secret that has puzzled all the philosophers, baffled all the lawyers, muddled all the men of business, and ruined most of the artists: the secret of right and wrong. Why, man, youre a genius, a master of masters, a god! At twentyfour, too!

STEPHEN: *(keeping his temper with difficulty)* You are pleased to

315 be facetious. I pretend to nothing more than any honorable English gentleman claims as his birthright *(he sits down angrily.)*

UNDERSHAFT: Oh, thats everybody's birthright. Look at poor little Jenny Hill, the Salvation lassie! she would think you were

320 laughing at her if you asked her to stand up in the street and

teach grammar or geography or mathematics or even drawing room dancing; but it never occurs to her to doubt that she can teach morals and religion. You are all alike, you respectable people. You cant tell me the bursting strain of a ten-inch gun, which is a very simple matter; but you all think you can tell   325 me the bursting strain of a man under temptation. You darent handle high explosives; but youre all ready to handle honesty and truth and justice and the whole duty of man, and kill one another at that game. What a country! What a world!

LADY BRITOMART: *(uneasily)* What do you think he had better   330 do, Andrew?

UNDERSHAFT: Oh, just what he wants to do. He knows nothing and he thinks he knows everything. That points clearly to a political career. Get him a private secretaryship to someone who can get him an Under Secretaryship; and then leave him   335 alone. He will find his natural and proper place in the end on the Treasury Bench.

STEPHEN: *(springing up again)* I am sorry, sir, that you force me to forget the respect due to you as my father. I am an Englishman and I will not hear the Government of my country in-   340 sulted. *(He thrusts his hands in his pockets, and walks angrily across to the window.)*

UNDERSHAFT: *(with a touch of brutality)* The government of your country! *I* am the government of your country: I, and Lazarus. Do you suppose that you and half a dozen amateurs   345 like you, sitting in a row in that foolish gabble shop, can govern Undershaft and Lazarus? No, my friend: you will do what pays us. You will make war when it suits us, and keep peace when it doesnt. You will find out that trade requires certain measures when we have decided on those measures. When I   350 want anything to keep my dividends up, you will discover that my want is a national need. When other people want something to keep my dividends down, you will call out the police and military. And in return you shall have the support and applause of my newspapers, and the delight of imagining that   355 you are a great statesman. Government of your country! Be off with you, my boy, and play with your caucuses and leading articles and historic parties and great leaders and burning questions and the rest of your toys. *I* am going back to my counting-house to pay the piper and call the tune.   360

STEPHEN: *(actually smiling, and putting his hand on his father's shoulder with indulgent patronage)* Really, my dear father, it is impossible to be angry with you. You dont know how absurd all this sounds to me. You are very properly proud of having been industrious enough to make money; and it is   365 greatly to your credit that you have made so much of it. But it has kept you in circles where you are valued for your money and deferred to for it, instead of in the doubtless very old-fashioned and behind-the-times public school and university where I formed my habits of mind. It is natural for you to   370 think that money governs England; but you must allow me to think I know better.

UNDERSHAFT: And what does govern England, pray?

STEPHEN: Character, father, character.

UNDERSHAFT: Whose character? Yours or mine?   375

STEPHEN: Neither yours nor mine, father, but the best elements in the English national character.

UNDERSHAFT: Stephen: Ive found your profession for you. Youre a born journalist. I'll start you with a high-toned weekly review. There!   380

(*Before* STEPHEN *can reply,* SARAH, BARBARA, LOMAX, *and* CUSINS *come in ready for walking.* BARBARA *crosses the room to the window and looks out.* CUSINS *drifts amiably to the arm-chair.* LOMAX *remains near the door, whilst* SARAH *comes to her mother.*)

(STEPHEN *goes to the smaller writing table and busies himself with his letters.*)

SARAH: Go and get ready, mamma: the carriage is waiting. (LADY BRITOMART *leaves the room.*)

UNDERSHAFT: (*to* SARAH) Good day, my dear. Good afternoon, Mr Lomax.

385 LOMAX: (*vaguely*) Ahdedoo.

UNDERSHAFT: (*to* CUSINS) Quite well after last night, Euripides, eh?

CUSINS: As well as can be expected.

UNDERSHAFT: Thats right. (*To* BARBARA) So you are coming to
390 see my death and devastation factory, Barbara?

BARBARA: (*at the window*) You came yesterday to see my salvation factory. I promised you a return visit.

LOMAX: (*coming forward between* SARAH *and* UNDERSHAFT) Youll find it awfully interesting. Ive been through the Wool-
395 wich Arsenal; and it gives you a ripping feeling of security, you know, to think of the lot of beggars we could kill if it came to fighting. (*To* UNDERSHAFT, *with sudden solemnity*) Still, it must be rather an awful reflection for you, from the religious point of view as it were. Youre getting on, you know, and all that.

400 SARAH: You dont mind Cholly's imbecility, papa, do you?

LOMAX: (*much taken aback*) Oh I say!

UNDERSHAFT: Mr Lomax looks at the matter in a very proper spirit, my dear.

LOMAX: Just so. Thats all I meant, I assure you.

405 SARAH: Are you coming, Stephen?

STEPHEN: Well, I am rather busy—er—(*Magnanimously*) Oh well, yes: I'll come. That is, if there is room for me.

UNDERSHAFT: I can take two with me in a little motor I am experimenting with for field use. You wont mind its being
410 rather unfashionable. It's not painted yet; but it's bullet proof.

LOMAX: (*appalled at the prospect of confronting Wilton Crescent in an unpainted motor*) Oh I say!

SARAH: The carriage for me, thank you. Barbara doesnt mind what she's seen in.

415 LOMAX: I say, Dolly, old chap: do you really mind the car being a guy? Because of course if you do I'll go in it. Still—

CUSINS: I prefer it.

LOMAX: Thanks awfully, old man. Come, my ownest. (*He hurries out to secure his seat in the carriage.* SARAH *follows him.*)

420 CUSINS: (*moodily walking across to* LADY BRITOMART's *writing table*) Why are we two coming to this Works Department of Hell? that is what I ask myself.

BARBARA: I have always thought of it as a sort of pit where lost creatures with blackened faces stirred up smoky fires and were
425 driven and tormented by my father? Is it like that, dad?

UNDERSHAFT: (*scandalized*) My dear! It is a spotlessly clean and beautiful hillside town.

CUSINS: With a Methodist chapel? Oh do say theres a Methodist chapel.

430 UNDERSHAFT: There are two: a Primitive one and a sophisticated one. There is even an Ethical Society; but it is not much patronized, as my men are all strongly religious. In the High Explosives Sheds they object to the presence of Agnostics as unsafe.

435 CUSINS: And yet they dont object to you!

BARBARA: Do they obey all your orders?

UNDERSHAFT: I never give them any orders. When I speak to one of them it is 'Well, Jones, is the baby doing well? and has Mrs Jones made a good recovery?' 'Nicely, thank you, sir.'
440 And thats all.

CUSINS: But Jones has to be kept in order. How do you maintain discipline among your men?

UNDERSHAFT: I dont. They do. You see, the one thing Jones wont stand is any rebellion from the man under him, or any
445 assertion of social equality between the wife of the man with 4 shillings a week less than himself, and Mrs Jones! Of course they all rebel against me, theoretically. Practically, every man of them keeps the man just below him in his place. I never meddle with them. I never bully them. I dont even bully
450 Lazarus. I say that certain things are to be done; but I dont order anybody to do them. I dont say, mind you, that there is no ordering about and snubbing and even bullying. The men snub the boys and order them about; the carmen snub the sweepers; the artisans snub the unskilled laborers; the fore-
455 men drive and bully both the laborers and artisans; the assistant engineers find fault with the foremen; the chief engineers drop on the assistants; the departmental managers worry the chiefs; and the clerks have tall hats and hymnbooks and keep up the social tone by refusing to associate on equal terms with
460 anybody. The result is a colossal profit, which comes to me.

CUSINS: (*revolted*) You really are a—well, what I was saying yesterday.

BARBARA: What was he saying yesterday?

UNDERSHAFT: Never mind, my dear. He thinks I have made you
465 unhappy. Have I?

BARBARA: Do you think I can be happy in this vulgar silly dress? I! who have worn the uniform. Do you understand what you have done to me? Yesterday I had a man's soul in my hand. I set him in the way of life with his face to salvation. But when
470 we took your money he turned back to drunkenness and derision. (*With intense conviction*) I will never forgive you that. If I had a child, and you destroyed its body with your explosives—if you murdered Dolly with your horrible guns—I could forgive you if my forgiveness would open the gates of
475 heaven to you. But to take a human soul from me, and turn it into the soul of a wolf! that is worse than any murder.

UNDERSHAFT: Does my daughter despair so easily? Can you strike a man to the heart and leave no mark on him?

BARBARA: (*her face lighting up*) Oh, you are right: he can never
480 be lost now: where was my faith?

CUSINS: Oh, clever clever devil!

BARBARA: You may be a devil; but God speaks through you sometimes. (*She takes her father's hands and kisses them.*) You have given me back my happiness: I feel it deep down
485 now, though my spirit is troubled.

UNDERSHAFT: You have learnt something. That always feels at first as if you had lost something.

BARBARA: Well, take me to the factory of death; and let me learn something more. There must be some truth or other behind
490 all this frightful irony. Come, Dolly. (*She goes out.*)

CUSINS: My guardian angel! (*To* UNDERSHAFT) Avaunt! (*He follows* BARBARA.)

STEPHEN: (*quietly, at the writing table*) You must not mind
Cusins, father. He is a very amiable good fellow; but he is a
495 Greek scholar and naturally a little eccentric.
UNDERSHAFT: Ah, quite so. Thank you, Stephen. Thank you.
(*He goes out.*)

(STEPHEN *smiles patronizingly; buttons his coat responsibly;
and crosses the room to the door.* LADY BRITOMART, *dressed for
out-of-doors, opens it before he reaches it. She looks round for
others; looks at* STEPHEN; *and turns to go without a word.*)

STEPHEN: (*embarrassed*) Mother—
LADY BRITOMART: Dont be apologetic, Stephen. And dont for-
500 get that you have outgrown your mother. (*She goes out.*)

(*Perivale St Andrews lies between two Middlesex hills, half
climbing the northern one. It is an almost smokeless town of
white walls, roofs of narrow green slates or red tiles, tall trees,
domes, campaniles, and slender chimney shafts, beautifully situated and beautiful in itself. The best view of it is obtained from
the crest of a slope about half a mile to the east, where the high
explosives are dealt with. The foundry lies hidden in the depths
between, the tops of its chimneys sprouting like huge skittles into
the middle distance. Across the crest runs an emplacement of
concrete, with a firestep, and a parapet which suggests a fortification, because there is a huge cannon of the obsolete Woolwich
Infant pattern peering across it at the town. The cannon is
mounted on an experimental gun carriage: possibly the original
model of the Undershaft disappearing rampart gun alluded to by
STEPHEN. The firestep, being a convenient place to sit, is furnished here and there with straw disc cushions; and at one place
there is the additional luxury of a fur rug.*

BARBARA *is standing on the firestep, looking over the parapet
towards the town. On her right is the cannon; on her left the end
of a shed raised on piles, with a ladder of three or four steps up to
the door, which opens outwards and has a little wooden landing
at the threshold, with a fire bucket in the corner of the landing.
Several dummy soldiers more or less mutilated, with straw protruding from their gashes, have been shoved out of the way under
the landing. A few others are nearly upright against the shed;
and one has fallen forward and lies, like a grotesque corpse, on
the emplacement. The parapet stops short of the shed, leaving a
gap which is the beginning of the path down the hill through the
foundry to the town. The rug is on the firestep near this gap.
Down on the emplacement behind the cannon is a trolley carrying a huge conical bombshell with a red band painted on it.
Further to the right is the door of an office, which, like the sheds,
is of the lightest possible construction.*

CUSINS *arrives by the path from the town.*)

BARBARA: Well?
CUSINS: Not a ray of hope. Everything perfect! wonderful! real!
It only needs a cathedral to be a heavenly city instead of a
hellish one.
505 BARBARA: Have you found out whether they have done anything
for old Peter Shirley?
CUSINS: They have found him a job as gatekeeper and time-
keeper. He's frightfully miserable. He calls the time-keeping
brainwork, and says he isnt used to it; and his gate lodge is so
510 splendid that he's ashamed to use the rooms, and skulks in the
scullery.
BARBARA: Poor Peter!

(STEPHEN *arrives from the town. He carries a fieldglass.*)

STEPHEN: (*enthusiastically*) Have you two seen the place? Why
did you leave us?
CUSINS: I wanted to see everything I was not intended to see; and 515
Barbara wanted to make the men talk.
STEPHEN: Have you found anything discreditable?
CUSINS: No. They call him Dandy Andy and are proud of his
being a cunning old rascal; but it's all horribly, frightfully,
immorally, unanswerably perfect. 520

(SARAH *arrives.*)

SARAH: Heavens! what a place! (*She crosses to the trolley.*) Did
you see the nursing home!? (*She sits down on the shell.*)
STEPHEN: Did you see the libraries and schools!?
SARAH: Did you see the ball room and the banqueting chamber
in the Town Hall!? 525
STEPHEN: Have you gone into the insurance fund, the pension
fund, the building society, the various applications of
cooperation!?

(UNDERSHAFT *comes from the office, with a sheaf of telegrams in
his hand.*)

UNDERSHAFT: Well, have you seen everything? I'm sorry I was
called away. (*Indicating the telegrams*) Good news from 530
Manchuria.
STEPHEN: Another Japanese victory?
UNDERSHAFT: Oh, I dont know. Which side wins does not concern us here. No: the good news is that the aerial battleship is
a tremendous success. At the first trial it has wiped out a fort 535
with three hundred soldiers in it.
CUSINS: (*from the platform*) Dummy soldiers?
UNDERSHAFT: (*striding across to* STEPHEN *and kicking the prostrate dummy brutally out of his way*) No: the real thing.

(CUSINS *and* BARBARA *exchange glances. Then* CUSINS *sits on
the step and buries his face in his hands.* BARBARA *gravely lays
her hand on his shoulder. He looks up at her in whimsical
desperation.*)

UNDERSHAFT: Well, Stephen, what do you think of the place? 540
STEPHEN: Oh, magnificent. A perfect triumph of modern industry. Frankly, my dear father, I have been a fool: I had no
idea of what it all meant: of the wonderful forethought, the
power of organization, the administrative capacity, the financial genius, the colossal capital it represents. I have been re- 545
peating to myself as I came through your streets 'Peace hath
her victories no less renowned than War.' I have only one
misgiving about it all.
UNDERSHAFT: Out with it.
STEPHEN: Well, I cannot help thinking that all this provision for 550
every want of your workmen may sap their independence and
weaken their sense of responsibility. And greatly as we enjoyed our tea at that splendid restaurant—how they gave us
all that luxury and cake and jam and cream for threepence I
really cannot imagine!—still you must remember that restau- 555
rants break up home life. Look at the continent, for instance!
Are you sure so much pampering is really good for the men's
characters?
UNDERSHAFT: Well you see, my dear boy, when you are organizing civilization you have to make up your mind whether 560
trouble and anxiety are good things or not. If you decide that
they are, then, I take it, you simply dont organize civilization;

and there you are, with trouble and anxiety enough to make us all angels! But if you decide the other way, you may as well go through with it. However, Stephen, our characters are safe here. A sufficient dose of anxiety is always provided by the fact that we may be blown to smithereens at any moment.

SARAH: By the way, papa, where do you make the explosives?

UNDERSHAFT: In separate little sheds, like that one. When one of them blows up, it costs very little; and only the people quite close to it are killed.

(STEPHEN, *who is quite close to it, looks at it rather scaredly, and moves away quickly to the cannon. At the same moment the door of the shed is thrown abruptly open; and a foreman in overalls and list slippers comes out on the little landing and holds the door for* LOMAX, *who appears in the doorway.*)

LOMAX: (*with studied coolness*) My good fellow: you neednt get into a state of nerves. Nothing's going to happen to you; and I suppose it wouldnt be the end of the world if anything did. A little bit of British pluck is what you want, old chap. (*He descends and strolls across to* SARAH.)

UNDERSHAFT: (*to the foreman*) Anything wrong, Bilton?

BILTON: (*with ironic calm*) Gentleman walked into the high explosives shed and lit a cigaret, sir: thats all.

UNDERSHAFT: Ah, quite so. (*Going over to* LOMAX) Do you happen to remember what you did with the match?

LOMAX: Oh come! I'm not a fool. I took jolly good care to blow it out before I chucked it away.

BILTON: The top of it was red hot inside, sir.

LOMAX: Well, suppose it was! I didnt chuck it into any of your messes.

UNDERSHAFT: Think no more of it, Mr Lomax. By the way, would you mind lending me your matches.

LOMAX: (*offering his box*) Certainly.

UNDERSHAFT: Thanks. (*He pockets the matches*).

LOMAX: (*lecturing to the company generally*) You know, these high explosives dont go off like gunpowder, except when theyre in a gun. When theyre spread loose, you can put a match to them without the least risk: they just burn quietly like a bit of paper. (*Warming to the scientific interest of the subject*) Did you know that, Undershaft? Have you ever tried?

UNDERSHAFT: Not on a large scale, Mr Lomax. Bilton will give you a sample of gun cotton when you are leaving if you ask him. You can experiment with it at home. (BILTON *looks puzzled.*)

SARAH: Bilton will do nothing of the sort, papa. I suppose it's your business to blow up the Russians and Japs; but you might really stop short of blowing up poor Cholly. (BILTON *gives it up and retires into the shed.*)

LOMAX: My ownest, there is no danger. (*He sits beside her on the shell.*)

(LADY BRITOMART *arrives from the town with a bouquet.*)

LADY BRITOMART: (*impetuously*) Andrew: you shouldnt have let me see this place.

UNDERSHAFT: Why, my dear?

LADY BRITOMART: Never mind why: you shouldnt have: thats all. To think of all that (*indicating the town*) being yours! and that you have kept it to yourself all these years!

UNDERSHAFT: It does not belong to me. I belong to it. It is the Undershaft inheritance.

LADY BRITOMART: It is not. Your ridiculous cannons and that noisy banging foundry may be the Undershaft inheritance; but all that plate and linen, all that furniture and those houses and orchards and gardens belong to us. They belong to me: they are not a man's business. I wont give them up. You must be out of your senses to throw them all away; and if you persist in such folly, I will call in a doctor.

UNDERSHAFT: (*stooping to smell the bouquet*) Where did you get the flowers, my dear?

LADY BRITOMART: Your men presented them to me in your William Morris Labor Church.

CUSINS: Oh! It needed only that. A Labor Church! (*he mounts the firestep distractedly, and leans with his elbows on the parapet, turning his back to them.*)

LADY BRITOMART: Yes, with Morris's words in mosaic letters ten feet high round the dome. NO MAN IS GOOD ENOUGH TO BE ANOTHER MAN'S MASTER. The cynicism of it!

UNDERSHAFT: It shocked the men at first, I am afraid. But now they take no more notice of it than of the ten commandments in church.

LADY BRITOMART: Andrew: you are trying to put me off the subject of the inheritance by profane jokes. Well, you shant. I dont ask it any longer for Stephen: he has inherited far too much of your perversity to be fit for it. But Barbara has rights as well as Stephen. Why should not Adolphus succeed to the inheritance? I could manage the town for him; and he can look after the cannons, if they are really necessary.

UNDERSHAFT: I should ask nothing better if Adolphus were a foundling. He is exactly the sort of new blood that is wanted in English business. But he's not a foundling; and theres an end of it. (*He makes for the office door.*)

CUSINS: (*turning to them*) Not quite. (*They all turn and stare at him.*) I think — Mind! I am not committing myself in any way as to my future course —— but I think the foundling difficulty can be got over. (*He jumps down to the emplacement.*)

UNDERSHAFT: (*coming back to him*) What do you mean?

CUSINS: Well, I have something to say which is in the nature of a confession.

SARAH:
LADY BRITOMART:
BARBARA: } Confession!
STEPHEN:

LOMAX: Oh I say!

CUSINS: Yes, a confession. Listen, all. Until I met Barbara I thought myself in the main an honorable, truthful man, because I wanted the approval of my conscience more than I wanted anything else. But the moment I saw Barbara, I wanted her far more than the approval of my conscience.

LADY BRITOMART: Adolphus!

CUSINS: It is true. You accused me yourself, Lady Brit, of joining the Army to worship Barbara; and so I did. She bought my soul like a flower at a street corner; but she bought it for herself.

UNDERSHAFT: What! Not for Dionysos or another?

CUSINS: Dionysos and all the others are in herself. I adored what was divine in her, and was therefore a true worshipper. But I was romantic about her too. I thought she was a woman of the people, and that a marriage with a professor of Greek would be far beyond the wildest social ambitions of her rank.

LADY BRITOMART: Adolphus!!

LOMAX: Oh I say!!!

CUSINS: When I learnt the horrible truth —

LADY BRITOMART: What do you mean by the horrible truth, pray?

CUSINS: That she was enormously rich; that her grandfather was an earl; that her father was the Prince of Darkness — 680

UNDERSHAFT: Chut!

CUSINS: — and that I was only an adventurer trying to catch a rich wife, then I stooped to deceive her about my birth.

BARBARA: (rising) Dolly!

LADY BRITOMART: Your birth! Now Adolphus, dont dare to 685 make up a wicked story for the sake of these wretched cannons. Remember: I have seen photographs of your parents; and the Agent General for South Western Australia knows them personally and has assured me that they are most re-690 spectable married people.

CUSINS: So they are in Australia; but here they are outcasts. Their marriage is legal in Australia, but not in England. My mother is my father's deceased wife's sister; and in this island I am consequently a foundling. (Sensation.)

BARBARA: Silly! (She climbs to the cannon, and leans, listening, 695 in the angle it makes with the parapet.)

CUSINS: Is the subterfuge good enough, Machiavelli?

UNDERSHAFT: (thoughtfully) Biddy: this may be a way out of the difficulty.

LADY BRITOMART: Stuff! A man cant make cannons any the 700 better for being his own cousin instead of his proper self (she sits down on the rug with a bounce that expresses her downright contempt for their casuistry.)

UNDERSHAFT: (to CUSINS) You are an educated man. That is 705 against the tradition.

CUSINS: Once in ten thousand times it happens that the schoolboy is a born master of what they try to teach him. Greek has not destroyed my mind: it has nourished it. Besides, I did not learn it at an English public school.

UNDERSHAFT: Hm! Well, I cannot afford to be too particular: 710 you have cornered the foundling market. Let it pass. You are eligible, Euripides: you are eligible.

BARBARA: Dolly: yesterday morning, when Stephen told us all about the tradition, you became very silent; and you have 715 been strange and excited ever since. Were you thinking of your birth then?

CUSINS: When the finger of Destiny suddenly points at a man in the middle of his breakfast, it makes him thoughtful.

UNDERSHAFT: Aha! You have had your eye on the business, my 720 young friend, have you?

CUSINS: Take care! There is an abyss of moral horror between me and your accursed aerial battleships.

UNDERSHAFT: Never mind the abyss for the present. Let us settle the practical details and leave your final decision open. 725 You know that you will have to change your name. Do you object to that?

CUSINS: Would any man named Adolphus — any man called Dolly! — object to be called something else?

UNDERSHAFT: Good. Now, as to money! I propose to treat you 730 handsomely from the beginning. You shall start at a thousand a year.

CUSINS: (with sudden heat, his spectacles twinkling with mischief) A thousand! You dare offer a miserable thousand to the son-in-law of a millionaire! No, by Heavens, Machiavelli! 735 you shall not cheat me. You cannot do without me; and I can do without you. I must have two thousand five hundred a year

for two years. At the end of that time, if I am a failure, I go. But if I am a success, and stay on, you must give me the other five thousand.

UNDERSHAFT: What other five thousand? 740

CUSINS: To make the two years up to five thousand a year. The two thousand five hundred is only half pay in case I should turn out a failure. The third year I must have ten per cent on the profits.

UNDERSHAFT: (taken aback) Ten per cent! Why, man, do you 745 know what my profits are?

CUSINS: Enormous, I hope: otherwise I shall require twenty-five per cent.

UNDERSHAFT: But, Mr Cusins, this is a serious matter of business. You are not bringing any capital into the concern. 750

CUSINS: What! no capital! Is my mastery of Greek no capital? Is my access to the subtlest thought, the loftiest poetry yet attained by humanity, no capital? My character! my intellect! my life! my career! what Barbara calls my soul! are these no capital? Say another word; and I double my salary. 755

UNDERSHAFT: Be reasonable —

CUSINS: (peremptorily) Mr Undershaft: you have my terms. Take them or leave them.

UNDERSHAFT: (recovering himself) Very well. I note your terms; and I offer you half. 760

CUSINS: (disgusted) Half!

UNDERSHAFT: (firmly) Half.

CUSINS: You call yourself a gentleman; and you offer me half!!

UNDERSHAFT: I do not call myself a gentleman; but I offer you half. 765

CUSINS: This to your future partner! your successor! your son-in-law!

BARBARA: You are selling your own soul, Dolly, not mine. Leave me out of the bargain, please.

UNDERSHAFT: Come! I will go a step further for Barbara's sake. I 770 will give you three fifths; but that is my last word.

CUSINS: Done!

LOMAX: Done in the eye! Why, I get only eight hundred, you know.

CUSINS: By the way, Mac, I am a classical scholar, not an arith- 775 metical one. Is three fifths more than half or less?

UNDERSHAFT: More, of course.

CUSINS: I would have taken two hundred and fifty. How you can succeed in business when you are willing to pay all that money to a University don who is obviously not worth a ju- 780 nior clerk's wages! — well! What will Lazarus say?

UNDERSHAFT: Lazarus is a gentle romantic Jew who cares for nothing but string quartets and stalls at fashionable theatres. He will be blamed for your rapacity in money matters, poor fellow! as he has hitherto been blamed for mine. You are a 785 shark of the first order, Euripides. So much the better for the firm!

BARBARA: Is the bargain closed, Dolly? Does your soul belong to him now?

CUSINS: No: the price is settled: that is all. The real tug of war is 790 still to come. What about the moral question?

LADY BRITOMART: There is no moral question in the matter at all, Adolphus. You must simply sell cannons and weapons to people whose cause is right and just, and refuse them to foreigners and criminals. 795

UNDERSHAFT: (determinedly) No: none of that. You must keep the true faith of an Armorer, or you dont come in here.

CUSINS: What on earth is the true faith of an Armorer?

UNDERSHAFT: To give arms to all men who offer an honest price for them, without respect of persons or principles: to aristocrat and republican, to Nihilist and Tsar, to Capitalist and Socialist, to Protestant and Catholic, to burglar and policeman, to black man, white man and yellow man, to all sorts and conditions, all nationalities, all faiths, all follies, all causes and all crimes. The first Undershaft wrote up in his shop IF GOD GAVE THE HAND, LET NOT MAN WITHHOLD THE SWORD. The second wrote up ALL HAVE THE RIGHT TO FIGHT: NONE HAVE THE RIGHT TO JUDGE. The third wrote up TO MAN THE WEAPON: TO HEAVEN THE VICTORY. The fourth had no literary turn; so he did not write up anything; but he sold cannons to Napoleon under the nose of George the Third. The fifth wrote up PEACE SHALL NOT PREVAIL SAVE WITH A SWORD IN HER HAND. The sixth, my master, was the best of all. He wrote up NOTHING IS EVER DONE IN THIS WORLD UNTIL MEN ARE PREPARED TO KILL ONE ANOTHER IF IT IS NOT DONE. After that, there was nothing left for the seventh to say. So he wrote up, simply, UNASHAMED.

CUSINS: My good Machiavelli, I shall certainly write something up on the wall; only, as I shall write it in Greek, you wont be able to read it. But as to your Armorer's faith, if I take my neck out of the noose of my own morality I am not going to put it into the noose of yours. I shall sell cannons to whom I please and refuse them to whom I please. So there!

UNDERSHAFT: From the moment when you become Andrew Undershaft, you will never do as you please again. Dont come here lusting for power, young man.

CUSINS: If power were my aim I should not come here for it. You have no power.

UNDERSHAFT: None of my own, certainly.

CUSINS: I have more power than you, more will. You do not drive this place: it drives you. And what drives the place?

UNDERSHAFT: (enigmatically) A will of which I am a part.

BARBARA: (startled) Father! Do you know what you are saying; or are you laying a snare for my soul?

CUSINS: Dont listen to his metaphysics, Barbara. The place is driven by the most rascally part of society, the money hunters, the pleasure hunters, the military promotion hunters; and he is their slave.

UNDERSHAFT: Not necessarily. Remember the Armorer's Faith. I will take an order from a good man as cheerfully as from a bad one. If you good people prefer preaching and shirking to buying my weapons and fighting the rascals, dont blame me. I can make cannons: I cannot make courage and conviction. Bah! you tire me, Euripides, with your morality mongering. Ask Barbara: she understands. (He suddenly reaches up and takes BARBARA's hands, looking powerfully into her eyes) Tell him, my love, what power really means.

BARBARA: (hypnotized) Before I joined the Salvation Army, I was in my own power; and the consequence was that I never knew what to do with myself. When I joined it, I had not time enough for all the things I had to do.

UNDERSHAFT: (approvingly) Just so. And why was that, do you suppose?

BARBARA: Yesterday I should have said, because I was in the power of God. (She resumes her self-possession, withdrawing her hands from his with a power equal to his own.) But you came and shewed me that I was in the power of Bodger and Undershaft. Today I feel — oh! how can I put it into words?

Sarah: do you remember the earthquake at Cannes, when we were little children? — how little the surprise of the first shock mattered compared to the dread and horror of waiting for the second? That is how I feel in this place today. I stood on the rock I thought eternal; and without a word of warning it reeled and crumbled under me. I was safe with an infinite wisdom watching me, an army marching to Salvation with me; and in a moment, at a stroke of your pen in a cheque book, I stood alone; and the heavens were empty. That was the first shock of the earthquake: I am waiting for the second.

UNDERSHAFT: Come, come, my daughter! dont make too much of your little tinpot tragedy. What do we do here when we spend years of work and thought and thousands of pounds of solid cash on a new gun or an aerial battleship that turns out just a hairsbreadth wrong after all? Scrap it. Scrap it without wasting another hour or another pound on it. Well, you have made for yourself something that you call a morality or a religion or what not. It doesnt fit the facts. Well, scrap it. Scrap it and get one that does fit. That is what is wrong with the world at present. It scraps its obsolete steam engines and dynamos; but it wont scrap its old prejudices and its old moralities and its old religions and its old political constitutions. Whats the result? In machinery it does very well; but in morals and religion and politics it is working at a loss that brings it nearer bankruptcy every year. Dont persist in that folly. If your old religion broke down yesterday, get a newer and a better one for tomorrow.

BARBARA: Oh how gladly I would take a better one to my soul! But you offer me a worse one. (Turning on him with sudden vehemence.) Justify yourself: shew me some light through the darkness of this dreadful place, with its beautifully clean workshops, and respectable workmen, and model homes.

UNDERSHAFT: Cleanliness and respectability do not need justification, Barbara: they justify themselves. I see no darkness here, no dreadfulness. In your Salvation shelter I saw poverty, misery, cold and hunger. You gave them bread and treacle and dreams of heaven. I give from thirty shillings a week to twelve thousand a year. They find their own dreams; but I look after the drainage.

BARBARA: And their souls?

UNDERSHAFT: I save their souls just as I saved yours.

BARBARA: (revolted) You saved my soul! What do you mean?

UNDERSHAFT: I fed you and clothed you and housed you. I took care that you should have money enough to live handsomely — more than enough; so that you could be wasteful, careless, generous. That saved your soul from the seven deadly sins.

BARBARA: (bewildered) The seven deadly sins!

UNDERSHAFT: Yes, the deadly seven. (Counting on his fingers) Food, clothing, firing, rent, taxes, respectability and children. Nothing can lift those seven millstones from Man's neck but money; and the spirit cannot soar until the millstones are lifted. I lifted them from your spirit. I enabled Barbara to become Major Barbara; and I saved her from the crime of poverty.

CUSINS: Do you call poverty a crime?

UNDERSHAFT: The worst of crimes. All the other crimes are virtues beside it: all the other dishonors are chivalry itself by comparison. Poverty blights whole cities; spreads horrible pestilences; strikes dead the very souls of all who come within sight, sound, or smell of it. What you call crime is nothing: a

920 murder here and a theft there, a blow now and a curse then: what do they matter? they are only the accidents and illnesses of life: there are not fifty genuine professional criminals in London. But there are millions of poor people, abject people, dirty people, ill fed, ill clothed people. They poison us mor-
925 ally and physically: they kill the happiness of society: they force us to do away with our own liberties and to organize unnatural cruelties for fear they should rise against us and drag us down into their abyss. Only fools fear crime: we all fear poverty. Pah! (*turning on* BARBARA) you talk of your half-
930 saved ruffian in West Ham: you accuse me of dragging his soul back to perdition. Well, bring him to me here; and I will drag his soul back again to salvation for you. Not by words and dreams; but by thirtyeight shillings a week, a sound house in a handsome street, and a permanent job. In three weeks he will
935 have a fancy waistcoat; in three months a tall hat and a chapel sitting; before the end of the year he will shake hands with a duchess at a Primrose League meeting, and join the Conservative Party.

BARBARA: And will he be the better for that?

940 UNDERSHAFT: You know he will. Dont be a hypocrite, Barbara. He will be better fed, better housed, better clothed, better behaved; and his children will be pounds heavier and bigger. That will be better than an American cloth mattress in a shelter, chopping firewood, eating bread and treacle, and being
945 forced to kneel down from time to time to thank heaven for it: knee drill, I think you call it. It is cheap work converting starving men with a Bible in one hand and a slice of bread in the other. I will undertake to convert West Ham to Mahometanism on the same terms. Try your hand on my men:
950 their souls are hungry because their bodies are full.

BARBARA: And leave the east end to starve?

UNDERSHAFT: (*his energetic tone dropping into one of bitter and brooding remembrance*) I was an east ender. I moralized and starved until one day I swore that I would be a full-fed free
955 man at all costs; that nothing should stop me except a bullet, neither reason nor morals nor the lives of other men. I said 'Thou shalt starve ere I starve'; and with that word I became free and great. I was a dangerous man until I had my will: now I am a useful, beneficent, kindly person. That is the history of
960 most self-made millionaires, I fancy. When it is the history of every Englishman we shall have an England worth living in.

LADY BRITOMART: Stop making speeches, Andrew. This is not the place for them.

UNDERSHAFT: (*punctured*) My dear: I have no other means of
965 conveying my ideas.

LADY BRITOMART: Your ideas are nonsense. You got on because you were selfish and unscrupulous.

UNDERSHAFT: Not at all. I had the strongest scruples about poverty and starvation. Your moralists are quite unscrupulous
970 about both: they make virtues of them. I had rather be a thief than a pauper. I had rather be a murderer than a slave. I dont want to be either; but if you force the alternative on me, then, by Heaven, I'll choose the braver and more moral one. I hate poverty and slavery worse than any other crimes whatsoever.
975 And let me tell you this. Poverty and slavery have stood up for centuries to your sermons and leading articles: they will not stand up to my machine guns. Dont preach at them: dont reason with them. Kill them.

BARBARA: Killing. Is that your remedy for everything?

UNDERSHAFT: It is the final test of conviction, the only lever 980 strong enough to overturn a social system, the only way of saying Must. Let six hundred and seventy fools loose in the streets; and three policemen can scatter them. But huddle them together in a certain house in Westminster; and let them go through certain ceremonies and call themselves certain 985 names until at last they get the courage to kill; and your six hundred and seventy fools become a government. Your pious mob fills up ballot papers and imagines it is governing its masters; but the ballot paper that really governs is the paper that has a bullet wrapped up in it. 990

CUSINS: That is perhaps why, like most intelligent people, I never vote.

UNDERSHAFT: Vote! Bah! When you vote, you only change the names of the cabinet. When you shoot, you pull down governments, inaugurate new epochs, abolish old orders and set 995 up new. Is that historically true, Mr Learned Man, or is it not?

CUSINS: It is historically true. I loathe having to admit it. I repudiate your sentiments. I abhor your nature. I defy you in every possible way. Still, it is true. But it ought not to be true. 1000

UNDERSHAFT: Ought! ought! ought! ought! ought! Are you going to spend your life saying ought, like the rest of our moralists? Turn your oughts into shalls, man. Come and make explosives with me. Whatever can blow men up can blow society up. The history of the world is the history of those who 1005 had courage enough to embrace this truth. Have you the courage to embrace it, Barbara?

LADY BRITOMART: Barbara: I positively forbid you to listen to your father's abominable wickedness. And you, Adolphus, ought to know better than to go about saying that wrong 1010 things are true. What does it matter whether they are true if they are wrong?

UNDERSHAFT: What does it matter whether they are wrong if they are true?

LADY BRITOMART: (*rising*) Children: come home instantly. An- 1015 drew: I am exceedingly sorry I allowed you to call on us. You are wickeder than ever. Come at once.

BARBARA: (*shaking her head*) It's no use running away from wicked people, mamma.

LADY BRITOMART: It is every use. It shews your disapprobation 1020 of them.

BARBARA: It does not save them.

LADY BRITOMART: I can see that you are going to disobey me. Sarah: are you coming home or are you not?

SARAH: I daresay it's very wicked of papa to make cannons; but I 1025 dont think I shall cut him on that account.

LOMAX: (*pouring oil on the troubled waters*) The fact is, you know, there is a certain amount of tosh about this notion of wickedness. It doesnt work. You must look at facts. Not that I would say a word in favor of anything wrong; but then, you 1030 see, all sorts of chaps are always doing all sorts of things; and we have to fit them in somehow, dont you know. What I mean is that you cant go cutting everybody; and thats about what it comes to. (*Their rapt attention to his eloquence makes him nervous.*) Perhaps I dont make myself clear. 1035

LADY BRITOMART: You are lucidity itself, Charles. Because Andrew is successful and has plenty of money to give to Sarah, you will flatter him and encourage him in his wickedness.

LOMAX: (*unruffled*) Well, where the carcase is, there will the

1040   eagles be gathered, dont you know. *(To* UNDERSHAFT*)* Eh? What?

UNDERSHAFT: Precisely. By the way, may I call you Charles?

LOMAX: Delighted. Cholly is the usual ticket.

UNDERSHAFT: *(to* LADY BRITOMART*)* Biddy—

1045   LADY BRITOMART: *(violently)* Dont dare call me Biddy. Charles Lomax: you are a fool. Adolphus Cusins: you are a Jesuit. Stephen: you are a prig. Barbara: you are a lunatic. Andrew: you are a vulgar tradesman. Now you all know my opinion; and my conscience is clear, at all events *(she sits down with a*
1050   *vehemence that the rug fortunately softens.)*

UNDERSHAFT: My dear: you are the incarnation of morality. *(She snorts.)* Your conscience is clear and your duty done when you have called everybody names. Come, Euripides! it is getting late; and we all want to go home. Make up your
1055   mind.

CUSINS: Understand this, you old demon—

LADY BRITOMART: Adolphus!

UNDERSHAFT: Let him alone, Biddy. Proceed, Euripides.

CUSINS: You have me in a horrible dilemma. I want Barbara.

1060   UNDERSHAFT: Like all young men, you greatly exaggerate the difference between one young woman and another.

BARBARA: Quite true, Dolly.

CUSINS: I also want to avoid being a rascal.

UNDERSHAFT: *(with biting contempt)* You lust for personal righ-
1065   teousness, for self-approval, for what you call a good con-science, for what Barbara calls salvation, for what I call pa-tronizing people who are not so lucky as yourself.

CUSINS: I do not: all the poet in me recoils from being a good man. But there are things in me that I must reckon with.
1070   Pity—

UNDERSHAFT: Pity! The scavenger of misery.

CUSINS: Well, love.

UNDERSHAFT: I know. You love the needy and the outcast: you love the oppressed races, the negro, the Indian ryot, the un-
1075   derdog everywhere. Do you love the Japanese? Do you love the French? Do you love the English?

CUSINS: No. Every true Englishman detests the English. We are the wickedest nation on earth; and our success is a moral horror.

1080   UNDERSHAFT: That is what comes of your gospel of love, is it?

CUSINS: May I not love even my father-in-law?

UNDERSHAFT: Who wants your love, man? By what right do you take the liberty of offering it to me? I will have your due heed and respect, or I will kill you. But your love! Damn your
1085   impertinence!

CUSINS: *(grinning)* I may not be able to control my affections, Mac.

UNDERSHAFT: You are fencing, Euripides. You are weakening: your grip is slipping. Come! try your last weapon. Pity and
1090   love have broken in your hand: forgiveness is still left.

CUSINS: No: forgiveness is a beggar's refuge. I am with you there: we must pay our debts.

UNDERSHAFT: Well said. Come! you will suit me. Remember the words of Plato.

1095   CUSINS: *(starting)* Plato! You dare quote Plato to me!

UNDERSHAFT: Plato says, my friend, that society cannot be saved until either the Professors of Greek take to making gun-powder, or else the makers of gunpowder become Professors of Greek.

CUSINS: Oh, tempter, cunning tempter!   1100

UNDERSHAFT: Come! choose, man, choose.

CUSINS: But perhaps Barbara will not marry me if I make the wrong choice.

BARBARA: Perhaps not.

CUSINS: *(desperately perplexed)* You hear!   1105

BARBARA: Father: do you love nobody?

UNDERSHAFT: I love my best friend.

LADY BRITOMART: And who is that, pray?

UNDERSHAFT: My bravest enemy. That is the man who keeps me up to the mark.   1110

CUSINS: You know, the creature is really a sort of poet in his way. Suppose he is a great man, after all!

UNDERSHAFT: Suppose you stop talking and make up your mind, my young friend.

CUSINS: But you are driving me against my nature. I hate war.   1115

UNDERSHAFT: Hatred is the coward's revenge for being intimi-dated. Dare you make war on war? Here are the means: my friend Mr Lomax is sitting on them.

LOMAX: *(springing up)* Oh I say! You dont mean that this thing is loaded, do you? My ownest: come off it.   1120

SARAH: *(sitting placidly on the shell)* If I am to be blown up, the more thoroughly it is done the better. Dont fuss, Cholly.

LOMAX: *(to* UNDERSHAFT, *strongly remonstrant)* Your own daughter, you know!

UNDERSHAFT: So I see! *(To* CUSINS*)* Well, my friend, may we   1125
expect you here at six tomorrow morning?

CUSINS: *(firmly)* Not on any account. I will see the whole estab-lishment blown up with its own dynamite before I will get up at five. My hours are healthy, rational hours: eleven to five.

UNDERSHAFT: Come when you please: before a week you will   1130
come at six and stay until I turn you out for the sake of your health. *(Calling)* Bilton! *(He turns to* LADY BRITOMART, *who rises.)* My dear: let us leave these two young people to them-selves for a moment. *(*BILTON *comes from the shed.)* I am going to take you through the gun cotton shed.   1135

BILTON: *(barring the way)* You cant take anything explosive in here, sir.

LADY BRITOMART: What do you mean? Are you alluding to me?

BILTON: *(unmoved)* No, maam. Mr Undershaft has the other gentleman's matches in his pocket.   1140

LADY BRITOMART: *(abruptly)* Oh! I beg your pardon. *(She goes into the shed.)*

UNDERSHAFT: Quite right, Bilton, quite right: here you are. *(He gives* BILTON *the box of matches.)* Come, Stephen. Come, Charles. Bring Sarah. *(He passes into the shed.)*   1145

*(*BILTON *opens the box and deliberately drops the matches into the fire-bucket.)*

LOMAX: Oh! I say *(*BILTON *stolidly hands him the empty box.)* Infernal nonsense! Pure scientific ignorance! *(He goes in.)*

SARAH: Am I all right, Bilton?

BILTON: Youll have to put on list slippers, miss: thats all. Weve got em inside. *(She goes in.)*   1150

STEPHEN: *(very seriously to* CUSINS*)* Dolly, old fellow, think. Think before you decide. Do you feel that you are a suffi-ciently practical man? It is a huge undertaking, an enormous responsibility. All this mass of business will be Greek to you.

CUSINS: Oh, I think it will be much less difficult than Greek.   1155

STEPHEN: Well, I just want to say this before I leave you to your-selves. Dont let anything I have said about right and wrong prejudice you against this great chance in life. I have satisfied myself that the business is one of the highest character and a credit to our country. (*Emotionally*) I am very proud of my father. I — (*Unable to proceed, he presses* CUSINS' *hand and goes hastily into the shed, followed by* BILTON.)

(BARBARA *and* CUSINS, *left alone together, look at one another silently.*)

CUSINS: Barbara: I am going to accept this offer.

BARBARA: I thought you would.

CUSINS: You understand, dont you, that I had to decide without consulting you. If I had thrown the burden of the choice on you, you would sooner or later have despised me for it.

BARBARA: Yes: I did not want you to sell your soul for me any more than for this inheritance.

CUSINS: It is not the sale of my soul that troubles me: I have sold it too often to care about that. I have sold it for a professorship. I have sold it for an income. I have sold it to escape being imprisoned for refusing to pay taxes for hangmen's ropes and unjust wars and things that I abhor. What is all human con-duct but the daily and hourly sale of our souls for trifles? What I am now selling it for is neither money nor position nor comfort, but for reality and for power.

BARBARA: You know that you will have no power, and that he has none.

CUSINS: I know. It is not for myself alone. I want to make power for the world.

BARBARA: I want to make power for the world too; but it must be spiritual power.

CUSINS: I think all power is spiritual: these cannons will not go off by themselves. I have tried to make spiritual power by teaching Greek. But the world can never be really touched by a dead language and a dead civilization. The people must have power; and the people cannot have Greek. Now the power that is made here can be wielded by all men.

BARBARA: Power to burn women's houses down and kill their sons and tear their husbands to pieces.

CUSINS: You cannot have power for good without having power for evil too. Even mother's milk nourishes murderers as well as heroes. This power which only tears men's bodies to pieces has never been so horribly abused as the intellectual power, the imaginative power, the poetic, religious power that can enslave men's souls. As a teacher of Greek I gave the intellec-tual man weapons against the common man. I now want to give the common man weapons against the intellectual man. I love the common people. I want to arm them against the lawyers, the doctors, the priests, the literary men, the pro-fessors, the artists, and the politicians, who, once in author-ity, are more disastrous and tyrannical than all the fools, ras-cals, and impostors. I want a power simple enough for common men to use, yet strong enough to force the intellec-tual oligarchy to use its genius for the general good.

BARBARA: Is there no higher power than that (*pointing to the shell*)?

CUSINS: Yes; but that power can destroy the higher powers just as a tiger can destroy a man: therefore Man must master that power first. I admitted this when the Turks and Greeks were last at war. My best pupil went out to fight for Hellas. My parting gift to him was not a copy of Plato's Republic, but a revolver and a hundred Undershaft cartridges. The blood of every Turk he shot — if he shot any — is on my head as well as on Undershaft's. That act committed me to this place for ever. Your father's challenge has beaten me. Dare I make war on war? I must. I will. And now, is it all over between us?

BARBARA: (*touched by his evident dread of her answer*) Silly baby Dolly! How could it be!

CUSINS: (*overjoyed*) Then you — you — you — Oh for my drum! (*He flourishes imaginary drumsticks.*)

BARBARA: (*angered by his levity*) Take care, Dolly, take care. Oh, if only I could get away from you and from father and from it all! if I could have the wings of a dove and fly away to heaven!

CUSINS: And leave me!

BARBARA: Yes, you, and all the other naughty mischievous chil-dren of men. But I cant. I was happy in the Salvation Army for a moment. I escaped from the world into a paradise of enthusiasm and prayer and soul saving; but the moment our money ran short, it all came back to Bodger: it was he who saved our people: he, and the Prince of Darkness, my papa. Undershaft and Bodger: their hands stretch everywhere: when we feed a starving fellow creature, it is with their bread, be-cause there is no other bread; when we tend the sick, it is in the hospitals they endow; if we turn from the churches they build, we must kneel on the stones of the streets they pave. As long as that lasts, there is no getting away from them. Turning our backs on Bodger and Undershaft is turning our backs on life.

CUSINS: I thought you were determined to turn your back on the wicked side of life.

BARBARA: There is no wicked side: life is all one. And I never wanted to shirk my share in whatever evil must be endured, whether it be sin or suffering. I wish I could cure you of middle-class ideas, Dolly.

CUSINS: (*gasping*) Middle cl — ! A snub! A social snub to me! from the daughter of a foundling!

BARBARA: That is why I have no class, Dolly: I come straight out of the heart of the whole people. If I were middle-class I should turn my back on my father's business; and we should both live in an artistic drawing room, with you reading the reviews in one corner, and I in the other at the piano, playing Schumann: both very superior persons, and neither of us a bit of use. Sooner than that, I would sweep out the guncotton shed, or be one of Bodger's barmaids. Do you know what would have happened if you had refused papa's offer?

CUSINS: I wonder!

BARBARA: I should have given you up and married the man who accepted it. After all, my dear old mother has more sense than any of you. I felt like her when I saw this place — felt that I must have it — that never, never, never could I let it go; only she thought it was the houses and the kitchen ranges and the linen and china, when it was really all the human souls to be saved: not weak souls in starved bodies, sobbing with gratitude for a scrap of bread and treacle, but fullfed, quarrelsome, snobbish, uppish creatures, all standing on their little rights and dignities, and thinking that my father ought to be greatly obliged to them for making so much money for him — and so he ought. That is where salvation is really wanted. My father shall never throw it in my teeth again that my converts were bribed with bread. (*She is transfigured.*) I have got rid of the bribe of bread. I have got rid of the bribe of heaven. Let God's work be done for its own sake: the work he had to create us to do because it cannot be done except by living men and women. When I die, let him be in my debt, not I in his; and let me forgive him as becomes a woman of my rank.

CUSINS: Then the way of life lies through the factory of death?

BARBARA: Yes, through the raising of hell to heaven and of man to God, through the unveiling of an eternal light in the Valley of The Shadow. *(Seizing him with both hands)* Oh, did you think my courage would never come back? did you believe that I was a deserter? that I, who have stood in the streets, and taken my people to my heart, and talked of the holiest and greatest things with them, could ever turn back and chatter foolishly to fashionable people about nothing in a drawing room? Never, never, never, never: Major Barbara will die with the colors. Oh! and I have my dear little Dolly boy still; and he has found me my place and my work. Glory Hallelujah! *(She kisses him.)*

CUSINS: My dearest: consider my delicate health. I cannot stand as much happiness as you can.

BARBARA: Yes: it is not easy work being in love with me, is it? But it's good for you. *(She runs to the shed, and calls, childlike)* Mamma! Mamma! (BILTON *comes out of the shed, followed by* UNDERSHAFT.) I want Mamma.

UNDERSHAFT: She is taking off her list slippers, dear. *(He passes on to* CUSINS.*)* Well? What does she say?

CUSINS: She has gone right up into the skies.

LADY BRITOMART: *(coming from the shed and stopping on the steps, obstructing* SARAH, *who follows with* LOMAX. BARBARA *clutches like a baby at her mother's skirt)* Barbara: when will you learn to be independent and to act and think for yourself? I know as well as possible what that cry of 'Mamma, Mamma,' means. Always running to me!

SARAH: *(touching* LADY BRITOMART's *ribs with her finger tips and imitating a bicycle horn)* Pip! pip!

LADY BRITOMART: *(highly indignant)* How dare you say Pip! pip! to me, Sarah? You are both very naughty children. What do you want, Barbara?

BARBARA: I want a house in the village to live in with Dolly. *(Dragging at the skirt)* Come and tell me which one to take.

UNDERSHAFT: *(to* CUSINS*)* Six o'clock tomorrow morning, Euripides.

LUIGI PIRANDELLO

Luigi Pirandello (1867–1936) created a diverse and influential body of plays, but his work is now most often associated with the preoccupations of his *Six Characters in Search of an Author*. Like *Six Characters*, Pirandello's plays use METATHEATER — roleplaying, plays-within-plays, and a flexible sense of the limits of stage illusion — to examine a highly theatricalized vision of identity. Can any of us be certain of our identity when others hold radically different perspectives on our actions, on who we are?

Pirandello was born in Sicily. He studied language and literature and received his doctoral degree in 1891 from the University of Rome. He then married the daughter of his father's business partner, but the collapse of the business forced him into a career as a writer. He wrote hundreds of stories in the 1890s and in the first decades of the twentieth century, as well as critical and scholarly articles. Pirandello's dramatic interest in the uncertainty of identity can be traced partly to his troubled marriage. His wife suffered a long mental illness and constantly accused him of adultery, despite his careful and constant attention to her health. In a sense, Pirandello was caught between his own sense of himself and the role he was given in this domestic tragedy.

Pirandello's use of the theater as a metaphor for representing this conflict pervades his mature plays: *Six Characters in Search of an Author* (1921; extensively revised 1925), *Enrico IV* (1922), *Each in His Own Way* (1924), and *Tonight We Improvise* (1930). In these plays, the struggle to discover and maintain identity is subjected to the pressure of performance in the world, performance that renders the "self" a kind of fiction. Yet while all behavior seems to verge on mere "acting," undermining our confidence in the authority or reality of a "self," Pirandello's plays do not seem nostalgic for the fixed and determined characters of realistic drama. For in Pirandello's drama, the "self" can also become a kind of prison, a role that traps the individual in a single and confining performance. This is the tragedy that the nameless hero of *Enrico IV* discovers at the close of that play, much as the hero — a famous author like Pirandello himself — of *When One Is Somebody* (1933) is gradually transformed from a man into a statue by the force of his admirers' adulation.

Pirandello became the director of his own company, the Art Theater of Rome, in 1924, and his major plays entered the world repertoire almost immediately. Pirandello's company toured throughout Europe and the Americas, influencing a generation of playwrights with the power of his theatrical conception of modern life. In addition to his short stories and criticism, Pirandello wrote over forty plays. He was awarded the Nobel Prize in 1934 in recognition of his achievement in the modern theater.

Six Characters in Search of an Author

Six Characters seems at first to elaborate a simple and striking idea. What would happen if a cast of dramatic "characters" confronted the actors who gave them life on the stage? Pirandello had toyed with the idea for some time and had sketched it out as a short story. Onstage, though, the story develops a new and challenging dimension, for the confrontation between the Characters and Actors explores the nature of theatrical representation itself. As the play proceeds, it becomes clear that the Actors and Characters represent opposed versions of reality and of the theater, and their contest calls our understanding of the difference between them into question. The Characters need completion. Their melodramatic incest drama has defined each of them in an imprisoning role, as though the climactic moment of their unfinished play — when the Father nearly (or does he?) procures the Stepdaughter in Madame Pace's brothel — was definitive of the identity of each character. That is, Pirandello questions our fundamental notions of how dramatic characters represent the lives of real people, how they represent the rich complexity of a "life" through a short series of a few typical deeds. As the Father asks at one point, who of us would want his or her life summed up in one moment, one act?

The Actors, on the other hand, seem even less real than the Characters. Although the Characters are "fixed" by the design of their common story, that very consistency gives them a coherence and weight that the flighty Actors seem to lack. The Actors are entirely absorbed in the conventions of their lines of business and the petty jealousies of working together; the Leading Actor must always be "acting" the "Leading Actor," whether he is onstage or not, and so on through the rest of the cast. Oddly enough, then, *Six Characters* does not seem to allow us to choose between the Actors or Characters, to decide which kind of representation — narrative or stage performance — provides a more accurate depiction of "reality." The drama of *Six Characters* arises from the unresolved collision between these two perspectives. In the theater, the process of *Six Characters* insistently disorients its audience from the stable categories of "reality" and "illusion," which is perhaps why audiences rioted when the play was first produced. The Characters are, of course, played by actors, while the Actors are clearly "characters" to the audience. Are we, in the audience, any more "real?" Are we outside the play looking in, or has Pirandello managed to place *us* onstage, showing the audience also to be playing a role in the endless roleplaying of the theater? For this reason, when reading the play we should resist locating its "meanings" in the Father's philosophical monologues, those moments of *pirandellismo* that seem to sum up the play's confrontation between illusion and reality. The play's meaning arises through the entire process of its action, the baffling, inconclusive, and frustrating confrontation between Characters, Actors, and audience, a confrontation that finally prevents the Characters' drama from ever taking the stage.

SIX CHARACTERS
IN SEARCH OF AN AUTHOR

Luigi Pirandello

TRANSLATED BY ANTHONY CAPUTI

— CHARACTERS —

The Characters of the Play-within-the Play

THE FATHER
THE MOTHER
THE STEPDAUGHTER
THE SON
THE BOY
THE LITTLE GIRL   } *they do not speak*
MADAME PACE, *who appears when invoked*

The Members of the Company

THE DIRECTOR
THE LEADING ACTRESS
THE LEADING ACTOR
THE SUPPORTING ACTRESS
THE INGENUE
THE YOUNG LEADING MAN
OTHER ACTORS AND ACTRESSES
THE STAGE MANAGER
THE PROMPTER
THE PROPERTY MAN
THE STAGE TECHNICIAN
THE DIRECTOR'S SECRETARY
THE DOORMAN
BACKSTAGE WORKERS

It is daytime; the scene is the stage of a theater.

(N.B. *The play has no acts or scenes. The performance will be interrupted a first time, without the curtain's being lowered, when the* DIRECTOR *and the* FATHER *retire to work out the scenario and the* ACTORS *leave the stage, and a second time when by mistake the* STAGE TECHNICIAN *lowers the curtain.*)

— ACT ONE —

(*As the spectators come in, they will find the curtain raised and the stage as it is during the day, without flats or scenery, empty and rather dark. From the beginning they should have the impression of a performance that has not been prepared.*

Two small stairways, one at the right and the other at the left, facilitate going from the stage to the auditorium.

On the stage the small, dome-shaped hood that screens the PROMPTER *has been moved to the side of his well in the stage floor.*

At the side, on the apron, there is a small table and an armchair, the back toward the audience, for the DIRECTOR.

Two further tables, one larger than the other, with several chairs, are set at random on the apron to be ready as they are needed for the rehearsal. Still other chairs are scattered about for the AC-TORS, *and at the back of the stage, to one side, almost out of sight, there is a piano.*

When the lights in the auditorium are down, the STAGE TECHNI-CIAN, *in blue coveralls and with a satchel hanging from his belt,* enters from the wings and takes a few boards from a corner at the rear. These he arranges on the apron, and, kneeling, he begins to nail them. At the sounds of the hammer the* STAGE MANAGER *comes from the door leading to the dressing rooms.*)

STAGE MANAGER: What are you doing?

STAGE TECHNICIAN: Doing? I'm nailing.

STAGE MANAGER: Now? (*He looks at his watch.*) It's 10:30 already. The Director will be here any minute for the rehearsal.

STAGE TECHNICIAN: Hey, look, I've got to have time for my work too!   5

STAGE MANAGER: You'll have it. But not now.

STAGE TECHNICIAN: When then?

STAGE MANAGER: When we're not rehearsing. Come on, now, get all this out of here so I can arrange the scene for the second act of *The Game of Parts*.   10

(*The* STAGE TECHNICIAN, *grumbling under his breath, gathers up the boards and goes off. In the meantime the* ACTORS, *both men and women, begin to come in from the wings, first one, then another, then two together, altogether nine or ten, as many as are needed for the rehearsal of Pirandello's play* The Game of Parts *scheduled for this day. They greet the* STAGE MANAGER *and each other as they enter. Some go to their dressing rooms; others, including the* PROMPTER, *who has the play text in a roll under his arm, wait on the stage for the* DIRECTOR *to arrive and start the rehearsal. While waiting, some sitting with their legs crossed and others standing, they exchange a few words. One lights a cigarette; one complains about the role he has been assigned; one reads quite loudly for the benefit of the others a news item from a theatrical newspaper. It will be fitting if both the* ACTRESSES *and the* ACTORS *are dressed in rather bright, cheerful clothes and if this first improvised scene is very lively while being entirely natural. At some point one of the* ACTORS *might sit at the piano and begin playing a dance tune, and the youngest among them might dance.)*

STAGE MANAGER: *(clapping his hands to call them to order.)* Come now, come on! Stop that! Here's the Director.

(The music and dancing cease on the spot, and the ACTORS *turn and look toward the auditorium where the* DIRECTOR *appears. Wearing a derby hat and with a cane under his arm and a large cigar in his mouth, he passes down the aisle and, to greetings from the* ACTORS, *comes up one of the small stairways to the stage. His* SECRETARY *hands him his mail: a couple of newspapers and a playtext in a wrapper.)*

DIRECTOR: Any letters?

15   SECRETARY: None. This is all there is.

DIRECTOR: *(handing him the playtext.)* Take it to my dressing room. *(Then, looking around and turning to the* STAGE MANAGER.*)* You can't see anything here. Please, give us a little light.

20   STAGE MANAGER: Right away.

(He goes to give the order. A few moments later the right side of the stage, where the ACTORS *are, is flooded in brilliant white light. In the meantime the* PROMPTER *has taken his place in the well, lit the lamp, and spread out the text in front of him.)*

DIRECTOR: *(clapping his hands.)* Come on, come on, let's begin. *(To the* STAGE MANAGER.*)* Is anyone missing?

STAGE MANAGER: Our Leading Lady.

DIRECTOR: As usual. *(He looks at his watch.)* We're ten minutes

25   late already. Make a note of it, please. We've got to teach her to be on time for rehearsals.

(He has not finished saying this when from the rear of the auditorium the voice of the LEADING ACTRESS *is heard.)*

LEADING ACTRESS: No. No. Please. Here I am! Here I am!

(Dressed all in white, she wears a large, flamboyant hat and has a pretty little dog in her arms. She runs down the aisle and hurries up one of the small stairways.)

DIRECTOR: You make a point of making us wait.

LEADING ACTRESS: I'm sorry. I looked everywhere for a taxi.

30   But now I see you haven't even begun. And I don't come on right away. *(Then, calling the* STAGE MANAGER *by name and handing him the dog.)* Please, put him in my dressing room.

DIRECTOR: *(grumbling.)* That's all we needed. As if there weren't enough dogs around here. *(He claps his hands again*

35   *and turns to the* PROMPTER.*)* Come on now, come on—the second act of *The Game of Parts. (Sitting in his chair.)* Pay attention, everybody. Who's on stage?

(The ACTORS *and* ACTRESSES *clear the apron and go to sit at the side except for the three who are about to start the rehearsal and the* LEADING ACTRESS, *who, without paying any attention to the* DIRECTOR'*s question, seats herself at one of the two tables.)*

DIRECTOR: *(to the* LEADING ACTRESS.*)* You're on stage now?

LEADING ACTRESS: Me? No.

40   DIRECTOR: *(annoyed.)* Well, get up then, for God's sake!

(The LEADING ACTRESS *gets up and goes to sit with the other* ACTORS, *who have already distanced themselves.)*

DIRECTOR: *(to the* PROMPTER.*)* Begin. Begin.

PROMPTER: *(reading from the text.)* "In the house of Leone Gala. A strange combination of both living room and study."

DIRECTOR: *(turning to the* STAGE MANAGER.*)* Set up the red room.

45

STAGE MANAGER: *(taking notes on a sheet of paper.)* The red one. Fine.

PROMPTER: *(continuing to read from the text.)* "A table set for dining and a desk with books and papers. Shelves full of books and glass-doored cupboards containing fine china and utensils. An exit on the left to the kitchen. The main entrance is to the right."

50

DIRECTOR: *(getting up and pointing.)* O.K., pay attention now. The main entrance is that way. The kitchen that way. *(Turning to the actor who plays the part of Socrates.)* You'll come in and go out this way. *(To the* STAGE MANAGER.*)* Put the interior door at the rear there, and put up some curtains. *(He sits again.)*

55

STAGE MANAGER: *(taking notes.)* Got it.

PROMPTER: *(reading, as above.)* "First scene. Leone Gala, Guido Venanzi, Filippo known as Socrates." *(To the* DIRECTOR.*)* Should I read the stage directions too?

60

DIRECTOR: Yes. Yes. I've told you a hundred times!

PROMPTER: *(reading, as above.)* "As the curtain goes up, Leone Gala, in a chef's hat and apron, is intently whipping an egg with a wooden mixing spoon. Filippo, also dressed like a cook, is doing the same. Guido Venanzi, seated, watches and listens."

65

LEADING ACTOR: *(to the* DIRECTOR.*)* Excuse me. Do I have to wear this chef's hat?

DIRECTOR: *(irritated.)* Of course! If that's what the text says! *(He points to the text.)*

70

LEADING ACTOR: But it's ridiculous.

DIRECTOR: *(leaping to his feet, angry.)* "Ridiculous," you say. What do you want from me if France isn't sending us anything good just now and we have to do plays by Pirandello? Three cheers for whoever understands them! They're made expressly to irritate everyone—actors, critics, and the public!

75

(The ACTORS *laugh. Then he, getting up and going close to the* LEADING ACTOR, *bellows.)*

The chef's hat, you'll wear it! And you'll beat the eggs! And don't think that beating these eggs is all you have to think about. Don't kid yourself. You've still got to act the shell of the eggs you're beating.

80

(The ACTORS *start laughing again and begin making jesting comments to each other.)*

Quiet! And pay attention when I explain! *(Turning again to the* LEADING ACTOR.*)* That's right, the shell: or, as we ought to say, the empty form of reason, without the fullness of instinct, which is blind. You are reason and your wife is instinct in a game of assigned roles in which whoever plays his part is intentionally a puppet of himself. Understand?

85

LEADING ACTOR: *(opening his arms.)* No.

DIRECTOR: *(going back to his place.)* And neither do I! But let's get on with it, then you can congratulate me when it's over. *(Confidentially.)* Please, face three quarters front. If you don't, what with the abstruseness of the dialogue and your not

90

being heard, everything will be lost. (*Clapping his hands again.*) All right now. Look sharp now. Let's go.

95 PROMPTER: Excuse me, but is it all right if I pull the hood over me? There's a bit of a draught here.

DIRECTOR: Yes, yes. Go ahead.

(*In the meantime the* DOORMAN *has come into the auditorium and he comes down the aisle. As he nears the stage, he announces to the* DIRECTOR *the arrival of six characters, who, by now in the auditorium as well, begin to follow him looking lost and perplexed.*

Whoever wishes to undertake a production of this play should use every device available to set the six characters off from the actors of the company. The placement of the two groups when the characters go up onto the stage, as already indicated in the stage directions, will of course help, as will different colorations by way of special lights. But the most suitable and effective device will be the use of special masks for the characters, masks made of materials that will not wilt from perspiration and yet be light-weight for the performers who wear them. They should be cut and shaped so as to leave the eyes, the nostrils, and the mouth free.

All this should sharpen the underlying meaning of the play. The characters should not in fact seem like phantasms, but like created realities, unchanging constructions of the imagination and therefore more substantial and real than the unstable naturalness of the actors. The masks should help give the impression of faces fashioned by art, each fixed in the expression of its fundamental emotion, whether it be remorse for the FATHER, *vindictiveness for the* STEPDAUGHTER, *disdain for the* SON, *or acute grief for the* MOTHER. *She should have fixed wax tears in the swellings around her eyes and down her cheeks such as we see in sculptured and painted images of the* Mater Dolorosa *in churches. And let their clothes, too, be of a special material and style, without extravagance, with stiff pleats and of an almost statuary mass, altogether of a kind not made of material that could be purchased or cut and sewn in a tailor shop.*

The FATHER *is in his fifties, going bald but not yet so, with light brown hair and thick mustaches that curl around his still young mouth, a mouth that often breaks into an uncertain and empty smile. He is pale—notably his ample forehead, and his eyes are blue, very bright and keen. He is dressed in light trousers and a dark jacket. At times he speaks almost mellifluously; at others he is given to bitter, severe outbursts.*

The MOTHER *seems broken and crushed by an intolerable weight of shame and dejection. Wearing a heavy widow's veil, she is dressed humbly in black, and when she raises her veil, she reveals not a face torn by suffering, but one that looks set in wax. She always keeps her eyes down.*

The STEPDAUGHTER, *eighteen years old, is bold, almost impudent. Beautiful, she too is dressed in mourning, but with a showy elegance. She is contemptuous of the air of timidity, distress, and lostness of her younger brother, a dreary child of fourteen, also dressed in black; but she shows a lively tenderness for her little sister, a child of about four dressed in white with a black sash at her waist.*

The SON, *twenty-two years old and tall, seems by turns almost frozen in a studied contempt for the* FATHER *and a sullen indifference for the* MOTHER; *he wears a light blue overcoat and a long green scarf around his neck.*

DOORMAN: (*his hat in his hand.*) Excuse me, sir.

DIRECTOR: (*explosively and rudely.*) What is it now?

DOORMAN: (*timidly.*) Some people are asking to see you. 100

(*The* DIRECTOR *and the* ACTORS *turn in astonishment to look into the auditorium.*)

DIRECTOR: (*furious again.*) But I'm rehearsing! You know perfectly well that during rehearsal no one is allowed in here. (*Turning himself around.*) Who are you people? What do you want?

FATHER: (*coming forward to one of the two stairways, followed by* 105 *the others.*) We're here in search of an author.

DIRECTOR: (*angry and amazed.*) For an author? What author?

FATHER: For any author, sir.

DIRECTOR: But there's no author here; we're not rehearsing a new play. 110

STEPDAUGHTER: (*with cheerful vivacity as she quickly comes up the stairs.*) So much the better, then. So much the better. We can be your new play.

AN ACTOR: (*amid comments and laughter from the others.*) Did you hear that? 115

FATHER: (*following the* STEPDAUGHTER *to the stage.*) Yes, but if there's no author . . . (*To the* DIRECTOR.) Unless you'd be willing to be him . . .

(*The* BOY *and the* MOTHER, *holding the* CHILD *by the hand, come up the first steps of the stairway and stop. The* SON *remains below, peevish.*)

DIRECTOR: Are you trying to be funny?

FATHER: Not at all, sir. On the contrary. We are bringing you a 120 powerful drama.

STEPDAUGHTER: We could make this your lucky day.

DIRECTOR: Will you please do me a favor and go away; we don't have time to lose with crazies.

FATHER: (*hurt but elegantly in hand.*) Sir, you know perfectly 125 well that life is infinitely crazy; its absurdities don't even need to seem plausible because they're true.

DIRECTOR: What the devil are you talking about?

FATHER: I'm saying that there is something crazy about doing what life does not do, that is, making its absurdities seem 130 plausible so that they then appear to be true. And if that's crazy, let me point out, it's what you do all the time.

(*The* ACTORS *stir, annoyed.*)

DIRECTOR: (*rising and looking him up and down.*) So you think that ours is a profession of madmen?

FATHER: Well, to make appear true what isn't—on no compul- 135 sion, as a game . . . Isn't it your business to give life to characters who've been dreamed up?

DIRECTOR: (*quickly, becoming the spokesman for the rising indignation of his* ACTORS.) I do hope you understand, my dear sir, that acting is a noble profession. If nowadays our play- 140 wrights give us stupid plays and puppets to act instead of men, be aware that we also take pride in having given life—here, on these very boards—to immortal works!

(The ACTORS, *satisfied, applaud him.)*

FATHER: *(bursting into this, heatedly.)* That's right! Very good! You've given life to living beings, beings more alive than those who breathe and wear clothes! Less real, perhaps, but truer! We agree with each other perfectly.

(The ACTORS *look at each other, dumbfounded.)*

DIRECTOR: But how? If you were just saying . . .

FATHER: But no, please. I said that because you said you didn't have time for crazies. In fact no one knows better than you that nature makes use of the imagination to carry its creative work — this work that could be called crazy — forward, ever higher.

DIRECTOR: All right. All right. But what are you trying to conclude from all this?

FATHER: Nothing. Merely to show that one can be born into life in many forms, as a tree or a stone, as water or a butterfly . . . or a woman. And one can even be born as a character in a play.

DIRECTOR: *(with feigned ironic astonishment.)* And you, as well as these people with you, were born characters?

FATHER: Precisely. And alive, as you see.

(The DIRECTOR *and the* ACTORS *burst out laughing.)*

FATHER: *(hurt.)* I'm sorry you find this funny because, as I've said, we carry within us a painful drama, as you might guess from this woman veiled in black.

(Saying this, he extends his hand to the MOTHER *to help her up the last steps and, continuing to hold her hand, leads her with a kind of tragic solemnity to the other side of the stage where suddenly an unearthly light comes on. The* CHILD *and the* BOY *follow the* MOTHER, *then the* SON, *who will keep to himself, in the rear, then the* STEPDAUGHTER, *who also sets herself off, on the apron, leaning against the proscenium. The* ACTORS, *at first stunned then moved to admiration at this development, break into applause, as if for an entertainment offered to them.)*

DIRECTOR: *(at first lost for words, then angry.)* Enough of this now! Be quiet! *(Then, turning to the* CHARACTERS*)* And you, go! Clear out of here! *(To the* STAGE MANAGER.*)* For God's sake, get them out of here!

STAGE MANAGER: *(coming forward, but then stopping as if held by a strange fear.)* Please leave now. Let's go.

FATHER: *(to the* DIRECTOR.*)* But no, look here, we . . .

DIRECTOR: After all, we've got work to do!

LEADING ACTOR: It's not right to make fools of . . .

FATHER: *(coming forward, determined.)* I'm astonished! Why don't you believe me? Aren't you by now accustomed to seeing characters in a script spring to life, face to face? Is it because he *(he points to the* PROMPTER.*)* has no text for us?

STEPDAUGHTER: *(approaching the* DIRECTOR, *smiling and ingratiating.)* You'll see, we are six really terribly interesting characters. Even if we have been side-tracked.

FATHER: *(brushing her aside.)* Yes, "side-tracked." That's good. *(To the* DIRECTOR, *in a rush.)* In the sense that the author who brought us into being, alive in his mind, wouldn't or couldn't put us materially into a work of art. And that was a crime, sir, because whoever has the good luck to be born a living character is superior even to death. He cannot die. The man, the writer, the instrument of creation — he will die; but his creation does not die. And to live forever this creation doesn't even need extraordinary gifts or need to do wonderful things. Who was Sancho Panza? Who was Don Abbondio? And yet they live forever because they were living seeds that had the good luck to find a fertile soil, an imagination that knew how to raise and nourish them, to make them live forever.

DIRECTOR: All this is fine. But what do you people want here?

FATHER: We want to live!

DIRECTOR: *(ironically.)* Forever?

FATHER: No, sir; but at least for a moment, in them.

AN ACTOR: Just listen to that, will you?

LEADING ACTRESS: They want to live in us.

YOUNG LEADING MAN: *(indicating the* STEPDAUGHTER.*)* That's all right with me, if this one comes to me.

FATHER: But look here! The play has to be made. *(To the* DIRECTOR.*)* Yet if you are willing, and your actors are willing, we can arrange it quickly among ourselves.

DIRECTOR: *(annoyed.)* What is this "arrange"? We don't give concerts here, with arrangements. We perform dramas and comedies!

FATHER: All right. We've come here precisely for that, to you.

DIRECTOR: And where's the text?

FATHER: It's in us.

(The ACTORS *laugh.)*

The drama is in us; it is us. And we're impatient to play it; a passion drives us to it.

STEPDAUGHTER: *(sneering, impudent, with treacherous charm.)* My passion . . . for him.

(She indicates the FATHER *and makes a pretense of embracing him, but then breaks into coarse laughter.)*

FATHER: *(with sudden anger.)* You stay where you are, for now. And please don't laugh like that!

STEPDAUGHTER: No? In that case permit me, *mesdames et messieurs:* although I've been an orphan barely two months, please observe how I sing and dance. *(She begins to sing with wicked playfulness the first stanza of "Prends garde à Tchou-Thin-Tchou" by Dave Stamper, arranged as a fox-trot or slow one-step by Francis Salabert. She dances as she sings.)*

Les chinois sont un peuple malin,
De Shangai à Pekin,
Ils ont mis des écriteaux partout:
Prenez-garde à Tchou-Thin-Tchou!

(While she sings and dances, the ACTORS, *and especially the young ones, move toward her, as if drawn by a strange fascination, and raise their hands just enough to seem about to take hold of her. She eludes them; when they applaud and the* DIRECTOR *reproves her, she becomes distant and prepossessed.)*

THE ACTORS AND ACTRESSES: *(laughing and applauding.)* Bravo! Well done! Very good!

190 **Sancho Panza** Don Quixote's servant in Miguel de Cervantes's classic *The History of Don Quixote de la Mancha* (1605–15)   **Don Abbondio** A comic priest in Alessandro Manzoni's novel *The Betrothed* (1825–26)   223–226 **Les chinois**   **Tchou** "The Chinese are a cunning lot, / From Shanghai to Peking, / They've put up placards everywhere: / Beware of Tchou-Thin-Tchou"

DIRECTOR: *(angry.)* Quiet! What is this, a cabaret-concert?

(Taking the FATHER *a little apart, dismayed.)*

230   Tell me, is she mad?

FATHER: Mad? No. It's worse than that.

STEPDAUGHTER: *(going quickly to the* DIRECTOR.*)* Worse! Yes, worse! And still worse than that! Listen, please. Let us put this play on, right away, so that you can see that at a certain mo-
235   ment I—when this darling here

(She takes the CHILD, *who has been next to the* MOTHER, *by the hand and leads her to the* DIRECTOR.*)*

—you see how pretty she is?

(She picks her up and kisses her.)

Darling. Darling.

(She puts the CHILD *down, moved, almost against her will.)*

Well, when this darling here, when God takes her, suddenly, from this poor mother, and this little idiot

(Taking hold of the BOY *by the sleeve, she jerks him forward.)*

240   does the worst of the worst things imaginable, like the half-wit he is

(she pushes him back toward the MOTHER.*)*

—then you'll see me take off. Yes, my dear sir, I'll be off! Gone! And I can't wait, believe me, I can't wait! Because after what happened between him and me—oh, very intimate—
245   *(she indicates the* FATHER *with a horrible wink.)* I can't stay with them, to watch this mother's suffering at the hands of that clown there. *(She indicates the* SON.*)* Look at him! Just look at him! Indifferent and cold, because he's the legitimate son, him; full of contempt for me, and for him, *(she indicates*
250   *the* BOY.*)* and for the baby, because we're bastards. Do you understand? Bastards. *(She goes to the* MOTHER *and embraces her.)* And this poor mother, the mother of us all, he refuses to recognize as his mother. He looks down on her—him!—as the mother of bastards. Vile! *(She says all this rapidly, with*
255   *great agitation, and when she gets to "vile," having raised her voice sharply on "bastards," she speaks the word quietly, al-most spitting it out.)*

MOTHER: *(with great anguish, to the* DIRECTOR.*)* In the name of these two children, I beg of you . . . *(She grows faint and*
260   *seems about to fall.)* Oh, my God.

FATHER: *(moving quickly to support her, as do almost all the* AC-TORS, *stunned and bewildered.)* Please, a chair, a chair for this poor widow.

THE ACTORS: *(hurrying.)* But it's really true then? She's really
265   fainting.

DIRECTOR: A chair here, quickly!

(One of the ACTORS *gets a chair; the others gather around, con-cerned. The* MOTHER, *seated, tries to stop the* FATHER *as he raises the veil covering her face.)*

FATHER: Look at her, ladies and gentlemen, look at her!

MOTHER: No, in the name of God, stop it!

FATHER: Let them see you. *(He raises the veil.)*

270   MOTHER: *(getting up and covering her face with her hands, de-spondent.)* Sir, I beg you to stop him. Don't let him do this. For me it's horrible.

DIRECTOR: *(perplexed.)* I don't understand any of you. What is the situation here? *(To the* FATHER.*)* Is this woman your wife?

FATHER: Yes, sir, my wife.   275

DIRECTOR: Then how come she's a widow if you're alive?

(The ACTORS *relieve their astonishment by breaking into loud laughter.)*

FATHER: *(hurt and irritated.)* Don't laugh! Don't laugh like that, for God's sake! Her drama turns precisely on that point. She had another man, a lover who ought to be here.

MOTHER: *(with a cry.)* No! No!   280

STEPDAUGHTER: He's the lucky one: he's dead. Two months ago, as I told you. We're still in mourning, as you can see.

FATHER: But, look, though he's dead, that's not the reason he's not here. He's not here because . . . Well, look at her, sir, please, it's all there. Her drama could not turn on her having   285
two lovers: she's not made that way; she hardly felt anything for them beyond, perhaps, a little gratitude (and that not for me, but for the other one). No, she's not that kind of woman. She's a mother. And her drama—powerful, very powerful— consists entirely in these four children by the two men she's had.   290

MOTHER: Me? That I've had? Do you dare to say I had them, as if I had wanted them? He did it. He pushed me on the other one. He forced me to go away with him.

STEPDAUGHTER: *(in a burst, indignant.)* That's not true!

MOTHER: *(stunned.)* What do you mean it's not true?   295

STEPDAUGHTER: It's not true! *(to the* DIRECTOR.*)* Don't believe it. Do you know why she says it? For that one there. *(She points to the* SON.*)* She wastes away, she tortures herself for neglecting him, and she tries to make him understand that if she abandoned him when he was two, it was because he *(she*   300
indicates the FATHER.*)* made her.

MOTHER: *(heatedly.)* He forced me. He forced me. As God is my witness! *(To the* DIRECTOR.*)* Ask him about it. *(She indi-cates her husband.)* Ask him if it's not true. Make him say it! She *(she indicates the* STEPDAUGHTER.*)* couldn't know any-   305
thing about it.

STEPDAUGHTER: I know that with my father, as long as he lived, you were always at peace and happy. You can't deny it.

MOTHER: I don't deny it. No . . .

STEPDAUGHTER: Always affectionate and attentive to you. *(To*   310
the BOY, *angrily.)* It's true, isn't it! Tell them! Why don't you speak, you little fool?

MOTHER: Leave the poor boy alone. Why do you want to make me seem ungrateful, child? I don't want to offend your father. I'm simply saying it wasn't my fault and it wasn't for my plea-   315
sure that I left his house and my son.

FATHER: It's true. It was me.

(Pause.)

LEADING ACTOR: *(to the company.)* What a spectacle!

LEADING ACTRESS: And we're the audience this time.

YOUNG LEADING MAN: For a change.   320

DIRECTOR: *(who is beginning to be interested.)* We're listening. We're listening. *(Saying this, he goes down one of the stair-ways into the auditorium and stands facing the stage as if to get a spectator's view of the scene.)*

SON: *(without moving, cold, unruffled, ironic.)* Right. And now   325
you'll hear a pretty piece of philosophy. Now he'll tell you about the demon of experiment.

FATHER: You're a stupid cynic, and I've said so a hundred times. *(To the* DIRECTOR *in the auditorium.)* He makes fun of me because of this expression I use to defend myself.

SON: Expressions!

FATHER: Yes, expressions! Words! Aren't they a solace for all of us? When we're face to face with a fact that can't be explained, or an evil that eats us up, isn't it a help to find a word that may say nothing but that brings relief?

STEPDAUGHTER: They even help remorse. In fact, especially remorse.

FATHER: Remorse? That's not true. I've never relieved remorse with words alone.

STEPDAUGHTER: Of course a little money helps too. Oh, yes, you can get relief with a little money. Like the hundred lire he was going to pay me, ladies and gentlemen!

(A wave of horror among the ACTORS.*)*

SON: *(with contempt for the* STEPDAUGHTER.*)* This is vile!

STEPDAUGHTER: Vile? There they were in a light blue envelope on a little mahogany table at the back of Madame Pace's shop. You know Madame Pace, sir. She's one of those madames who behind the sham of selling *robes et manteaux* attracts poor girls of good family to her workshop.

SON: And with that money she has bought the right to tyrannize over all of us, with the hundred lire he was going to pay but that—and note this carefully—he fortunately had no reason to pay.

STEPDAUGHTER: But it was a near thing. *(She bursts into laughter.)*

MOTHER: *(protesting.)* Shame, child! Shame!

STEPDAUGHTER: Shame? This is my revenge! I'm trembling, sir, trembling to live it, that scene. The room . . . here the showcase with the capes, there the daybed, the mirror, a screen, and by the window that mahogany table with the light blue envelope and the hundred lire. I see it. I could almost pick it up. But you gentlemen are going to have to turn away, because I'm practically nude. I don't blush anymore. I leave the blushing to him. *(She indicates the* FATHER.*)* Ah he was pale, very pale indeed, just then. *(To the* DIRECTOR.*)* Believe me, sir.

DIRECTOR: I can't make this out at all!

FATHER: Of course. Set upon from all sides like this. Insist on a little order, sir. Let me tell you how it was, and pay no attention to all the abuse she's trying to heap on me. With such ferocity. Without any attempt to explain.

STEPDAUGHTER: This is no place to tell stories. Here they don't tell stories.

FATHER: But I'm not telling a story. I want to explain.

STEPDAUGHTER: Sure. Wonderful. In your own way.

(At this point the DIRECTOR *comes back to the stage to re-establish order.)*

FATHER: But all the trouble is there, in words. We all have within us a world of things, each of us our own special world made of these things. Now how can we understand each other if I use words for these things that have meanings and values particular to my special world, while whoever hears my words relates them to meanings and values particular to his special world? We think we understand each other, but we never do. Look: my pity, all my pity for this woman, *(he indicates the* MOTHER.*)* she sees as the most ferocious cruelty.

MOTHER: You drove me away!

FATHER: Do you hear? "Drove" her. She really believes I drove her away.

MOTHER: You have the words. I don't. But believe me, sir, after he married me—who knows why (I was a poor, simple woman) . . .

FATHER: But that was precisely it: I married you for your simplicity, which I loved, believing . . .

(He stops when she gestures her disbelief, then seeing that he'll never get her to understand him, he opens his arms and turns again to the DIRECTOR.*)*

No. You see? She says no. Terrifying, my dear sir, it's terrifying, believe me, this mental deafness. *(He taps his forehead.)* Feeling she has, yes, for her children. But a deafness, a deafness of mind that will drive you crazy.

STEPDAUGHTER: Yes. Now make him tell you what a lot of good his intelligence has done for us.

FATHER: If we could only foresee the harm that can come from the good we think we're doing!

(At this point the LEADING ACTRESS, *who has been growing furious watching the* LEADING ACTOR *flirt with the* STEPDAUGHTER, *comes forward and asks the* DIRECTOR.*)*

LEADING ACTRESS: Excuse me, but are we going to continue the rehearsal?

DIRECTOR: Of course. Of course. But let me listen now.

YOUNG LEADING MAN: This is quite original.

INGENUE: Fascinating.

LEADING ACTRESS: For people interested in this sort of thing. *(She looks meaningfully at the* LEADING ACTOR.*)*

DIRECTOR: *(to the* FATHER.*)* But you must explain yourself clearly. *(He sits.)*

FATHER: Very well. It was like this: I had a man working for me, a secretary, a poor man who was wholly devoted, and he found a soulmate in her *(he indicates the* MOTHER.*)* and she in him. There wasn't a hint of wrongdoing, mind you—good, simple, like her, incapable not only of doing wrong, but of thinking it.

STEPDAUGHTER: So *he* thought it for them, and *he* did it.

FATHER: That's not true. I meant to do them good, and, yes, I admit it, to do myself good too. I had reached a point where I couldn't say a word to either of them without seeing them exchange knowing looks and one search the expression of the other for help on how to interpret me and to keep me from getting angry. You can imagine that that was enough to keep me in a constant rage, an intolerable state of exasperation.

DIRECTOR: And why didn't you send him away, this secretary?

FATHER: Very good! In fact, I did send him away. But then I had to watch this poor woman drag around the house as if she were lost, like some stray animal you take home out of pity.

MOTHER: Eh! Naturally.

FATHER: *(turning on her suddenly, in anticipation.)* The son, right?

MOTHER: He had already taken my son from me!

FATHER: But not out of cruelty! So he could grow up healthy and strong, in contact with the earth!

---

347 robes et manteaux "Dresses and coats"

STEPDAUGHTER: (*pointing to the* SON, *ironically.*) So we see.

FATHER: (*quickly.*) And that's my fault too, I suppose, that he's
435 turned out like this? I sent him to a wet nurse in the country, a
peasant woman, because his mother didn't seem strong
enough, even if she was of simple stock. I did it for the same
reason I had married her. A foolish reason, perhaps, but there
you are. I've always had a cursed yearning for a certain solid
440 moral sanity.

(*The* STEPDAUGHTER *again breaks into a noisy laugh.*)

Make her stop! This is unbearable!

DIRECTOR: Stop it! Let me hear him out, for God's sake!

(*In a flash, once again, at the* DIRECTOR*'s rebuke she seems under a spell, distanced, the laughter still half-formed on her lips.
Again the* DIRECTOR *goes down from the stage to gather an impression of the scene.*)

FATHER: I couldn't keep her with me any longer. (*He indicates
the* MOTHER.) But, believe me, not so much out of irritation,
445 or boredom — the suffocating boredom — as out of the suffering, the painful anguish I felt for her.

MOTHER: And he sent me away!

FATHER: Well provided with everything, to the other man, ladies
and gentlemen, so she could be free of me.

450 MOTHER: And he could be free too!

FATHER: Yes. Me too. I admit it. And from that a great wrong
has come. I meant well when I did it . . . and I did it more for
her than for me. I swear it. (*He folds his arms and turns again
to the* MOTHER.) Did I ever lose sight of you? — tell them —
455 did I ever let you out of my sight? Until all at once he took you
to another town, without my knowing it, because he became
foolishly alarmed by my interest, a pure interest, believe me,
sir, without the least ulterior motive. I watched her raise her
new family with the tenderest concern. Even she'll tell you.
460 (*He indicates the* STEPDAUGHTER.)

STEPDAUGHTER: Oh yes, and more! I was a little doll, you realize, with pigtails down my shoulders and underwear longer
than my skirt, a doll, and I used to see him waiting at the
entrance when I came out of school. He came to see how I
465 was coming along.

FATHER: This is perverse! Abominable!

STEPDAUGHTER: Really? And why?

FATHER: Abominable! Abominable! (*With great excitement, to
the* DIRECTOR, *explaining.*) With her gone, sir, my house
470 seemed empty. She was my torment, but her presence filled it
for me. Alone, I wandered through the rooms like a trapped
fly. This one here, (*he indicates the* SON.) raised elsewhere — I
don't know — when he came home, he didn't seem mine any
more. Without a mother there to bring us together, he grew
475 up without any connection with me, either intellectual or
emotional, on his own. And then (it's strange but true). I
became curious about her little family. And little by little I
was drawn to them, this issue of what I had done. The very
thought of her began to fill the emptiness around me. I
480 needed, really needed, to believe she was at peace, happy,
busy with the simple duties of living, fortunate to be at a safe
distance from the complicated torments of my spirit. And to
assure myself that this was so, I used to go to see the child
coming out of school.

485 STEPDAUGHTER: That's right. He used to follow me, and smile
at me, and, when I got home, he'd wave to me, like this.

I used to stare at him, annoyed. I didn't know who he was. I
told my mother about him, and she must have guessed right
off it was him.

(*The* MOTHER *nods yes.*)

At first she didn't want to send me to school any more, for 490
several days. And when I went again, there he was at the door
again — ridiculous — with a big package. He came up to me,
he caressed me, and he took from the package a lovely large
straw hat with a little garland of tiny May roses. For me.

DIRECTOR: But all this is only a loose narrative, dear people. 495

SON: (*disdainful.*) Of course. Literature! Literature!

FATHER: What do you mean "literature"? This is life, sir! Passion!

DIRECTOR: That may be. But it isn't theatrical.

FATHER: I agree, sir. All this is background. I'm not suggesting
that this be staged. As you see, in fact, she (*indicating the* 500
STEPDAUGHTER.) is no longer that little girl with pigtails
down her shoulders —

STEPDAUGHTER: — and underwear showing below her skirt.

FATHER: The drama comes now, sir. New, complex.

STEPDAUGHTER: (*coming forward somberly, fierce.*) As soon as 505
my father was dead . . .

FATHER: (*quickly, to drown her out.*) . . . They were destitute.
And so they came back here, without letting me know. All her
foolishness. (*He indicates the* MOTHER.) It's true she hardly
knows how to write. But she could have had her daughter, or 510
that boy, write to me that they were hard up.

MOTHER: Tell me, sir, how was I supposed to guess he felt this way?

FATHER: That's precisely your failing: you've never understood
my feelings.

MOTHER: After so many years of separation, and all that had 515
happened . . .

FATHER: And is it my fault if that wonderful man took you away?
(*He turns again to the* DIRECTOR.) As I told you, it happened
overnight . . . because he had found some kind of job or
other. It was impossible to trace them, and then, over some 520
years, my interest inevitably waned. The drama erupted, unexpected and violent, on their return, when I, unfortunately,
driven by the needs of my flesh, still keen . . . Ah, the wretchedness, the wretchedness, truly, of a man alone who despises
squalid liaisons, not yet old enough to do without women, 525
and not young enough to be able, normally and without embarrassment, to look for one. Did I say "wretchedness"? It's
worse than that. A horror! A horror! Because no woman will
give him love. And when you've understood that . . . I suppose you ought to do without. But no. Each of us, for the eyes 530
of others, dresses himself in a certain dignity, while at the
same time we all know perfectly well what's going on in our
intimate selves. Unspeakable. And we yield, we give in to
temptation, and then immediately afterwards straighten up
again — God help us — to recompose as quickly as possible 535
this dignity of ours, complete and undamaged, like a monument over a pit, burying and hiding even from our eyes every
sign and memory of our shame. It's the same with everybody.
But it takes courage to admit these things.

STEPDAUGHTER: But the courage to do them, everybody's got that. 540

FATHER: Everybody. Though always in secret. And for that reason it takes still more courage to admit them. Let just one
person admit these things, and bang, he's tarred with the
brush of cynic. Yet it's not true: he's like everyone else, better
in fact, better because he's not afraid to use his mind and to 545

expose the red rawness of shame, there, in his human bestiality, where the eyes never look so as not to see it. Look at women—how does a woman behave? She looks at us, provocative and inviting. You take her in your arms. Then as soon as she's held, she closes her eyes. In that gesture she symbolizes her mission; it says to the man: "Be blind like me!"

STEPDAUGHTER: And when she stops closing them? When she no longer needs to conceal the rawness of her shame, and instead sees, now dry-eyed and indifferent, the shame of the man who, as devoid of love as she, has refused to see it. Eh, how disgusting, then, all this philosophy that discovers the beast and then tries to redeem it . . . I can't listen to it. When anyone tries to simplify life—by reducing it to the level of beasts, for example—and he throws out all the human encumbrances of aspiration, innocence, all sense of the ideal, duty, decency, and shame, nothing is more contemptible and nauseous than his remorse. Crocodile tears!

DIRECTOR: Let's get to the point, my friends, let's get to the point! This is just a lot of talk.

FATHER: All right. But a fact is like a sack: when it's empty, it won't stand up. To make it stand up, we've got to put reason and feeling into it to give it body. I couldn't possibly know about the death of that man, or their return here in poverty, or that she, to provide for her children, (he indicates the MOTHER.) would find work as a seamstress, or that she'd find it with Madame Pace!

STEPDAUGHTER: A modiste of the most elegant sort, if you really want to know, gentlemen. On the surface she serves the best clientele, but she has arranged things that these fashionable ladies serve her in turn, and without prejudice to the other ladies, who also serve her and who are not so special.

MOTHER: Believe me, sir, it never entered my mind that that witch gave me work because she had her eyes on my daughter . . .

STEPDAUGHTER: Poor Mama. Do you know what she used to do, that one, when I brought back the work Mama had finished? She'd show me how Mama had ruined it, and then she'd reduce the pay. And she did that again and again. In the end I was the one who paid while this poor dear believed she was sacrificing herself for me and those two there, sewing into the night for Madame Pace.

(Movement and exclamations of dismay among the ACTORS.)

DIRECTOR: (quickly.) And there, one day, you met . . .

STEPDAUGHTER: (indicating the FATHER.) Him. Yes sir, him. An old customer. You'll see what a scene that will make! Superb!

FATHER: With her coming in, the Mother—

STEPDAUGHTER: (quickly, maliciously.) —almost in time—

FATHER: (screaming.) No, in time! In time! Because, luckily, I recognized her in time. And then I take them all home with me. Try to imagine the situation, mine and hers, now that we know each other: she as you see her now and me unable to look her in the face.

STEPDAUGHTER: Ridiculous! How is it possible for me to pretend, after all this, to be a proper young lady, virtuous and well brought up, in sympathy with his cursed yearning for "a solid moral sanity"?

FATHER: For me the drama is precisely in that, in my consciousness that I, that each of us, in fact, believes himself to be one person, when that's not true. Each of us is many persons, many, depending on all the possibilities for being within us.

For this man we're one person, for that one another. We're multiple. Yet we live with the illusion that we're the same for everyone—always the same person in everything we do. It's not true! We see this very clearly in those desperately unfortunate things we sometimes do. All at once we feel caught and hauled aloft, suspended. What I'm trying to say is that we see then that that one act is not all of us, that only a part of us is present in it, and that therefore it's a dreadful injustice to judge us by that act alone, to keep us hanging there, in pillory, for a whole lifetime, as if our life were summed up in that act. Now can you understand the treachery of this girl? She surprised me in a place—in an act—where we ought never to have existed for each other. And now she wants to impose that reality on me—a reality that I would never have dreamed of assuming toward her—because of this fleeting, shameful moment in my life. This I feel above all. And as you'll see, from this the drama derives tremendous value. Then there's the situation of the others. There's his . . . (He indicates the SON.)

SON: (shrugging contemptuously.) Leave me alone! I have nothing to do with this.

FATHER: What do you mean you have nothing to do with it?

SON: Just that. And I don't want to have anything to do with it. You know perfectly well I don't belong with the rest of you.

STEPDAUGHTER: We're vulgar. He's refined. You may have noticed, sir, how whenever I look at him—with the contempt he deserves, of course—he lowers his eyes. Because he knows the wrong he's done me.

SON: (barely glancing at her.) Me?

STEPDAUGHTER: You! You! I owe to you, dear boy, that I went on the streets!

(Movement and expressions of horror among the ACTORS.)

You denied us—admit it!—I won't say the intimacy of your home, but that courtesy that makes guests feel welcome. We were intruders who invaded your "legitimacy." Sir, I would like you to see certain little scenes we played, he and I. He says I ran roughshod over everyone. But, don't you see, it was really because of his attitude that I took advantage of what had happened to gain access to his house, with my mother, who is also his mother. He calls that "vile," but I came in as the lady of the house!

SON: (slowly coming forward.) It's easy for them to make me look bad. But imagine what it's like for a son who one fine day, as he sits quietly at home, sees a young woman show up, arrogant, her head high. She asks for his father, whom she has to tell God knows what, and then he sees her come back, still with the same manner, this time with the child there. And finally he sees her treat his father—who knows why—in a strange, brusque way, asking for money in a tone suggesting he had to give it to her because it was his duty.

FATHER: But in fact it is my duty, because of your mother.

SON: And how should I know that? When have I ever seen her? When have I ever heard you speak of her? I saw her appear, one day, with her (he indicates the STEPDAUGHTER.) and that boy and the child. They tell me, "By the way, she's your mother too, you know." Gradually, I gather from her behavior (again he indicates the STEPDAUGHTER.) why, suddenly like that, they've moved in. Frankly, sir, I'd rather not try to express what I feel and think. I might just possibly whisper it, and I won't even do that, not even to myself. That's why, as

665 you see, I can't lend myself to any of this. I tell you, sir, I'm an unrealized character dramatically. I'm ill at ease in their company. Let them leave me alone!

FATHER: But wait a minute. It's just because you're like this . . .

SON: (infuriated.) And what would you know about how I am? When did you ever pay any attention to me?

670 FATHER: I admit it. I admit it. And isn't that a situation too? This aloofness of yours, so cruel for me and for your mother, who, once in the house, sees you almost for the first time, grown up as you are, and she doesn't know you though she knows you're her son . . . (Indicating the MOTHER to the DIRECTOR.)
675 There she is! Look at her! She's crying!

STEPDAUGHTER: (angry, stamping her foot.) Like an idiot!

FATHER: (pointing to the STEPDAUGHTER.) And she can't stand him, you know (Turning and referring to the SON.) He says he has nothing to do with it, yet he's practically the hub of the
680 whole action. Look at that little boy, always next to his mother, bewildered and ashamed . . . He's like that because of him! It's possible his situation is the most painful of all: he feels left out, more than the others; he feels a painful humiliation, poor boy, for having been taken in like this, out of char-
685 ity. (Confidentially.) He's like his father. Humble. He doesn't speak.

DIRECTOR: He's not especially goodlooking. You can't imagine what a nuisance boys are on the stage.

FATHER: Oh, he eliminates that nuisance quickly. The child,
690 too—in fact she's the first to go.

DIRECTOR: Wonderful. Yes. I tell you, all this interests me, it interests me a lot. I can feel, I feel there's material here for a good play.

STEPDAUGHTER: (trying to insinuate herself.) With a character
695 like me!

FATHER: (pushing her away, concerned about the DIRECTOR's decision.) Be quiet, you!

DIRECTOR: (continuing without paying attention to the interruption.) New, yes . . .

700 FATHER: Absolutely new, sir.

DIRECTOR: It took a lot of nerve, nonetheless, to throw it at me like that . . .

FATHER: It's understandable, sir, born as we are for the stage . . .

DIRECTOR: Are you amateur actors?

705 FATHER: No. I said "born for the stage" in that . . .

DIRECTOR: Come on, you must have acted!

FATHER: But no. Only the role in life that each of us assigns himself or that's assigned to us by others. In me, as it happens, passion always becomes, all by itself when I'm excited—as in
710 everyone—a little theatrical . . .

DIRECTOR: Oh, come on, come on! You do understand that without an author . . . Of course I could send you to someone . . .

FATHER: But no. Look, you be the author.

DIRECTOR: Me? What do you mean?

715 FATHER: You. Yes, you. Why not?

DIRECTOR: Because I've never been an author.

FATHER: Well, why couldn't you be one now? There's nothing to it. Everybody does it. And your job will be made much simpler by the fact that we're here, all of us, living, before your eyes.

720 DIRECTOR: But that's not enough.

FATHER: Why not? Seeing us live our drama . . .

DIRECTOR: Maybe so. But someone still has to write it.

FATHER: No. Someone has only to write it down, if even that, having us right here, living it, scene by scene. It will be

725 enough to sketch it out in advance, quickly, just an outline, and then rehearse.

DIRECTOR: (going back up on the stage.) Hm. I'm almost, almost tempted. For the hell of it. I could actually try . . .

FATHER: Of course. You'll see what scenes will emerge! I can
730 note them down for you right now.

DIRECTOR: It tempts me, it tempts me. All right, let's try it. Come with me to my office. (Turning to the ACTORS.) You take a break for a few minutes, but don't wander away. In fifteen, twenty minutes, be back here. (To the FATHER.) Let's
735 go. Let's try. Maybe something extraordinary will come out of it . . .

FATHER: I'm sure of it. They'd better come too, don't you think? (He indicates the CHARACTERS.)

DIRECTOR: Yes. Come on. Come on. (He starts off, but then
740 turns again to the ACTORS.) Please! Be punctual. In a quarter of an hour.

(The DIRECTOR and the six CHARACTERS cross the stage and go off. The ACTORS remain, stunned, looking at each other.)

LEADING ACTOR: Is he serious? What does he want to do?

YOUNG LEADING MAN: It's lunacy pure and simple.

A THIRD ACTOR: Does he want us to improvise a play, on the
745 spur of the moment?

YOUNG LEADING MAN: That's right. Like the actors in commedia dell' arte.

LEADING ACTRESS: If he thinks I'm going to lend myself to that kind of joke . . .

750 INGENUE: And neither will I!

A FOURTH ACTOR: I'd like to know who those people are. (He alludes to the CHARACTERS.)

THIRD ACTOR: Who do you imagine? They're either crazy or up to some scheme.

755 YOUNG LEADING MAN: And he takes them seriously!

INGENUE: Vanity. Now he sees himself as an author . . .

LEADING ACTOR: But this is unheard of. If the theater has come to this . . .

A FIFTH ACTOR: I find it amusing.

760 THIRD ACTOR: Well, after all, we've yet to see what comes out of it.

(Then, talking among themselves, the ACTORS leave the stage, some going by the door at the rear, some through the wings to their dressing rooms.

The curtain remains up. The performance will be suspended for twenty minutes.)

— ACT TWO —

(The theater buzzer announces that the performance is about to continue.

The ACTORS, the STAGE MANAGER, the STAGE TECHNICIAN, the PROMPTER, and the PROPERTY MAN come from the wings, the

---

746–747 commedia dell' arte The phrase describes professional theatrical troupes of the late sixteenth, seventeenth, and eighteenth centuries in Italy in which each of the actors specialized in one of a largely fixed set of characters; the troupe then improvised the plays it performed from mere outlines of the action, or scenarios

door at the rear, and the auditorium as the DIRECTOR *and the six* CHARACTERS *come from his office.*

The lights in the auditorium go out, and the stage lights come on as before.)

DIRECTOR: Come, come, ladies and gentlemen. Are we all here? Pay attention now. Let's begin. Technician!
STAGE TECHNICIAN: Here.
DIRECTOR: Set up the scene in the private room. Two flats for
5   the sides and another with a door for the rear. Quickly, please!

(The STAGE TECHNICIAN *hurries about these tasks, and, while the* DIRECTOR *is conferring with the* STAGE MANAGER, *the* PROPERTY MAN, *the* PROMPTER, *and the* ACTORS, *he arranges a simulation of the scene called for: two side flats and a rear flat with a door, all with wallpaper in pink and gold stripes.)*

DIRECTOR: *(to the* PROPERTY MAN.*)* You might see if there's a sofa-bed in the storeroom.
PROPERTY MAN: There is, there's that green one.
STEPDAUGHTER: No. Green won't do. It was yellow, flowered,
10   plush, very large. And very accommodating.
PROPERTY MAN: Hmm. There's nothing like that.
DIRECTOR: It doesn't matter. Bring out what you have.
STEPDAUGHTER: What do you mean it doesn't matter? This is the notorious couch of Madame Pace!
15   DIRECTOR: We're only rehearsing now. Please, don't interfere. *(To the* STAGE MANAGER.*)* See if there isn't a glass show-case, something long and low.
STEPDAUGHTER: And the little table, the little mahogany table for the pale blue envelope!
20   STAGE MANAGER: *(to the* DIRECTOR.*)* There's that little one, with gold trim.
DIRECTOR: Good. Use it.
FATHER: And a mirror.
STEPDAUGHTER: And a screen. By all means a screen. Other-
25   wise how can I manage?
STAGE MANAGER: All right. We've got a lot of screens. Don't worry about it.
DIRECTOR: *(to the* STEPDAUGHTER.*)* Then some clothes trees, isn't that right?
30   STEPDAUGHTER: Yes, lots of them, lots of them.
DIRECTOR: *(to the* STAGE MANAGER.*)* See how many there are and have them brought in.
STAGE MANAGER: I'll take care of it.

(The STAGE MANAGER *also hurries to carry out these orders, and, while the* DIRECTOR *continues to speak with the* PROMPTER *and then with the* CHARACTERS *and the* ACTORS, *he will have the items brought in and will arrange them as seems to him most suitable.)*

DIRECTOR: *(to the* PROMPTER.*)* You, meantime, take your
35   place. Look, this is the outline of the scenes, act by act. *(He hands him some sheets of paper.)* But now I'm going to have to ask you to do something rather extraordinary.
PROMPTER: Take it down in shorthand?
DIRECTOR: *(pleasantly surprised.)* Ah, wonderful! Do you know
40   shorthand?
PROMPTER: I may not know how to prompt, but shorthand . . .
DIRECTOR: Better and better. *(Turning to a* STAGEHAND.*)* Go fetch some paper from my office, a lot of it, all you can find.

(The STAGEHAND *hurries off and returns shortly with a large sheaf of paper which he hands to the* PROMPTER.*)*

DIRECTOR: *(continuing to the* PROMPTER.*)* You follow the scenes as they're presented and try to get the lines down, at   45 least the most important. *(Then, turning to the* ACTORS.*)* Let's clear the stage, ladies and gentlemen. Here, you go over there. *(He points to a location at the side.)* And be very attentive!
LEADING ACTRESS: But, excuse me, we . . .   50
DIRECTOR: *(anticipating her.)* You won't have to improvise. Don't worry.
LEADING ACTOR: What *are* we to do?
DIRECTOR: Nothing. For the moment just listen and watch. Later everyone will have a written part. For now, as best we   55 can, we'll have a rehearsal. They're going to do it. *(He indicates the* CHARACTERS.*)*
FATHER: *(bewildered amid the confusion on stage.)* We? Excuse me, but what do you mean a rehearsal?
DIRECTOR: A rehearsal. A rehearsal for them. *(He indicates the   60 ACTORS.*)*
FATHER: But if we are the characters . . .
DIRECTOR: All right, you're the characters, if you say so. But here, my dear sir, characters don't perform. Here actors perform. The characters are there, in the text *(he points to the   65 PROMPTER's well.)* — when there is a text.
FATHER: Exactly. And since there isn't one and you have the good luck to have the characters here in front of you, alive . . .
DIRECTOR: Oh splendid! You want to do it all yourselves? To act, to appear before the public?   70
FATHER: Yes, just as we are.
DIRECTOR: I guarantee you'd make a stunning spectacle!
LEADING ACTOR: And what's the point of our being here then?
DIRECTOR: I hope you don't delude yourself that you know anything at all about acting. You'll make me laugh.   75

(The ACTORS *begin to laugh.)*

There, you see, they're all laughing. *(Recalling what he was about.)* But, yes, to my business. I've got to assign the parts, but that should be easy because they practically assign themselves. *(To the* SUPPORTING ACTRESS.*)* You, Madame, the Mother. *(To the* FATHER.*)* We'll have to find a name for her.   80
FATHER: Amalia.
DIRECTOR: But that's your wife's name. We wouldn't want to use her real name.
FATHER: And why not, since it *is* her real name . . . ? Ah, yes, if this woman is going to be . . . *(With a small gesture he indi-   85 cates the* SUPPORTING ACTRESS.*)* I see her *(he indicates the* MOTHER.*)* as Amalia. But do as you like . . . *(Becoming more confused.)* I don't know what to tell you. Already my own words — I don't know — begin to sound false. They have a different ring altogether.   90
DIRECTOR: Don't worry about it, don't worry. We'll be responsible for getting the right ring. And as for her name, if you want, let it be "Amalia" — she's Amalia. Or we'll find another. For now we'll assign the characters like this: *(To the* YOUNG LEADING MAN.*)* You the Son. *(To the* LEADING ACTRESS.*)*   95 You, of course, the Stepdaughter.
STEPDAUGHTER: *(amused.)* What? Me? That woman? *(She bursts into laughter.)*
DIRECTOR: *(irritated.)* And what's so funny?

100 LEADING ACTRESS: (indignant.) No one has ever dared laugh at me! I insist on being treated with respect or I'm leaving.

STEPDAUGHTER: No, please, I'm not laughing at you.

DIRECTOR: You ought to feel honored to be played by . . .

LEADING ACTRESS: (interrupting, with disdain.) "That woman!"

105 STEPDAUGHTER: But I wasn't thinking of you. Believe me. I meant myself, because I can't see anything of myself in you. That's all. I don't know, you aren't—you don't resemble me at all.

FATHER: Exactly! That's right! Look, sir, our way of expressing

110 ourselves . . .

DIRECTOR: What are you talking about, your way of expressing yourselves? Do you think you have your way of expressing yourselves locked inside you? Not at all!

FATHER: What are you saying? That we don't have our own way

115 of expressing ourselves?

DIRECTOR: Not at all! Here your way of expressing yourselves becomes material which the actors give new body and shape, voice and gesture to. These same actors, I might point out to you, have very effectively given expression to much more ex-

120 alted material than yours. If your little drama makes it on the stage, the credit, believe me, will go entirely to my actors.

FATHER: I wouldn't dream of contradicting you, sir. But you must understand that seeing them is very hard on us since we are as you see us, with our bodies and our faces . . .

125 DIRECTOR: (interrupting, impatient.) But we'll take care of that with make-up—with make-up, dear sir, as far as the face is concerned.

FATHER: All right. But the voice, the gestures . . .

DIRECTOR: Look now, after all! Here, on stage, as yourselves,

130 you can't exist! Here an actor represents you and that's all there is to it!

FATHER: I understand. And now perhaps I also see why our author, who saw us alive, as we are, didn't want to put us on the stage. I don't want to offend your actors, heaven help me. But I

135 think that to see myself acted now . . . by whom I don't know . . .

LEADING ACTOR: (rising with lofty dignity and coming toward him, followed by the giddy young ACTRESSES.) By me, if you've no objection.

FATHER: (humbly, very evenly.) Most honored, dear sir. (He

140 bows.) Still, I think that however much this gentleman tries, with the best will in the world and all his art, to take me into himself . . . (He is momentarily at a loss for words.)

LEADING ACTOR: Finish. Say what you want to say.

(Laughter from the ACTRESSES.)

FATHER: Well, I must say, his performance will be—even if he

145 does his best with make-up to look like me—I must say, given his height . . .

(all the ACTORS laugh.)

it will hardly be a representation of me, as I really am. Instead, he'll be as he interprets me, as he finds me—if he finds me—and not as I feel myself to be within myself. And it

150 seems to me that anyone who is called upon to form an opinion about us should take this into account.

DIRECTOR: Now you're worrying about the critics! While I'm still waiting to get started! Let them say what they like. And let's us think about putting on this play—if that's possible!

155 (Standing apart and looking around.) Come on, now. Is the stage set? (To the ACTORS and the CHARACTERS.) Stand back

there! Stand back! Let me see! (He goes down into the auditorium.) Let's not lose any more time! (To the STEPDAUGHTER.) Does the set seem all right to you?

STEPDAUGHTER: Not really. I can't say I find myself here. 160

DIRECTOR: Oh, come now! You can't imagine we're going to build the room you knew, as it was, at the back of Madame Pace's shop! (To the FATHER.) You told me a little room with flowered wallpaper.

FATHER: That's right. White. 165

DIRECTOR: Well, this isn't white; it's got stripes. But it doesn't matter. As for the furniture, more or less, it seems to me we're all right. That little table, move it a little forward here.

(The STAGEHANDS move the table.)

(To the PROPERTY MAN.) You try to find an envelope, light blue if possible, and give it to this gentleman. (He indicates 170 the FATHER.)

PROPERTY MAN: An envelope for letters?

DIRECTOR and FATHER: For letters! For letters!

PROPERTY MAN: Right away. (He goes out.)

DIRECTOR: Let's go. Let's go. The first scene is with the young lady. 175

(The LEADING ACTRESS comes forward.)

No, wait. Her. I said the young lady. (He indicates the STEPDAUGHTER.) You stand and watch . . .

STEPDAUGHTER: (overlapping, quickly.) . . . how I'll live it!

LEADING ACTRESS: (annoyed.) And don't think I won't know how to live it! Once I get into it! 180

DIRECTOR: (his hands at his head.) Ladies and gentlemen, please! No more talk! All right. The first scene is the young lady's with Madame Pace. Oh! (Lost, he looks around and goes back up on the stage.) And this Madame Pace? Where is she?

FATHER: She's not with us. 185

DIRECTOR: Well, what do we do now?

FATHER: But she's alive; she's alive too.

DIRECTOR: That's fine. But where?

FATHER: Well . . . Look, let me explain. (Turning to the ACTRESSES.) If these ladies will be so kind as to lend me their 190 hats for a moment.

THE ACTRESSES: (half-surprised and half-laughing in chorus.) What?
Our hats?
What did he say? 195
Why?
Listen to this!

DIRECTOR: What do you want with their hats?

(The ACTORS laugh.)

FATHER: Nothing, really. To hang them on these clothes trees for a moment. And if someone would be so good as to take off 200 her coat?

THE ACTORS: (still laughing.) A coat too.
And what then?
He must be mad.

A FEW OF THE ACTRESSES: (still bemused.) But why? 205
Only the coat?

FATHER: To hang it here for a moment . . . Please. As a favor to me. Will you?

THE ACTRESSES: (as they take off their hats and one of them supplies a coat, they continue to laugh and hang their contribu- 210 tions on the clothes trees.) Well, why not?

There you are.

But, seriously, what a joke!

Are we putting them up for sale?

FATHER: Precisely, Miss, like that, as if for sale.

DIRECTOR: Would you please tell me what you're trying to do?

FATHER: It's like this: perhaps, with the stage set a little more suitably for her, maybe, drawn by her stock in trade — who knows — maybe she'll come among us . . . *(He directs their gaze to the door at the rear of the stage.)* Look now! Look!

(The door at the rear opens and MADAME PACE *enters, takes a few steps, and stops. She's a grim old battleaxe, very fat, with a garish, carrot-colored wig and a bright red rose at her ear, Spanish style. Heavily made-up, she is dressed with the ludicrous elegance of a showy red silk dress; she holds a feather fan in one hand and a lit cigarette in the other, slightly raised. At her appearance the* ACTORS *and the* DIRECTOR *bolt from the stage with terrified cries, scurrying down the stairways and giving every sign of fleeing up the aisle. The* STEPDAUGHTER, *meanwhile, hurries to her, humble, as one might to an employer.)*

STEPDAUGHTER: *(moving rapidly.)* Here she is! Here she is!

FATHER: *(pleased with himself.)* It's her! What did I tell you? There she is!

DIRECTOR: *(overcoming his initial shock and indignant.)* What kind of trick is this?

LEADING ACTOR: *(This speech and the following come one on top of each other.)* What is this, after all?

YOUNG LEADING MAN: Where did she come from?

INGENUE: They've been holding her in reserve!

LEADING ACTRESS: This is a trick from some magic act!

FATHER: *(overriding the protests.)* Please! Why do you want to spoil this marvel in the name of a vulgar, factual truth? Here we see a reality that's teased, shaped, and called into life by the scene itself, and that has a better right to live here than you do because it's very much truer than you are. Now which of you actresses will play Madame Pace? Well, this *is* Madame Pace! Surely you have to admit that the actress who plays her will be less true than she is. There she is in person! See how my daughter recognized her and went straight to her! Now watch, now you'll see the scene.

(Hesitantly, the DIRECTOR *and the* ACTORS *come back onto the stage.*

But the scene between the STEPDAUGHTER *and* MADAME PACE *has already begun during the protests by the* ACTORS *and the* FATHER's *explanation. They're speaking in whispers, in a way that's natural enough but impossible on the stage. And when the* ACTORS, *called to attention by the* FATHER, *turn to watch, they see that* MADAME PACE *has just put her hand under the* STEP-DAUGHTER's *chin to make her look up, but they cannot hear what is said. They listen intently for a moment, then they give up.)*

DIRECTOR: Well?

LEADING ACTOR: What's she saying?

LEADING ACTRESS: You can't hear anything.

YOUNG LEADING MAN: Louder! Louder!

STEPDAUGHTER: *(leaving* MADAME PACE, *who breaks into a priceless smile, she comes down to the group of actors.)* "Louder?" Oh, sure. What do you mean "louder?" These aren't things you can speak about loudly! I spoke out about them a moment ago to shame him *(she indicates the* FATHER.)*

and have my revenge. But with Madame Pace it's another matter, ladies and gentlemen. There's the danger of prison.

DIRECTOR: That's great! So that's it! Well here, my dear, you have to make yourself heard! Yet even we can't hear you, up on the stage! Think of the problem for an audience in the theater! You have to make the scene carry. Besides, we won't be here as we are now: you can speak right up. You simply pretend you're alone, in the room at the back of the shop, and no one can hear you.

(Smiling impishly, the STEPDAUGHTER *very prettily gestures no with her finger.)*

DIRECTOR: What do you mean no?

STEPDAUGHTER: *(sottovoce, mysterious.)* Someone else will hear if she *(she indicates* MADAME PACE.) *speaks up.

DIRECTOR: *(nervously.)* You mean someone else is going to pop out?

(The ACTORS *get ready to run from the stage again.)*

FATHER: No, sir. She's referring to me. I have to be here, there behind the door, waiting. And Madame knows it. So, with your permission, I'll go so I'll be ready.

DIRECTOR: *(stopping him.)* No. Wait. We have to respect the demands of the theater here. Before you get set for your part . . .

STEPDAUGHTER: *(interrupting him.)* Oh come on now! Get on with it! I'm dying to live it, I tell you, to live this scene! If he wants to go ahead with it, I'm more than ready.

DIRECTOR: *(forcefully.)* But first we've got to show the scene between you and her, *(he indicates* MADAME PACE.) *so it can be understood. Do you understand?

STEPDAUGHTER: Good Lord! She merely told me what you already know: that Mama's sewing has been badly done again and the material's ruined. If she's going to continue to help us in our difficulties, I have to bear with her.

MADAME PACE: *(coming forward with an air of importance.)* Eh, bien, señor. I no desiderar profitto. Yo no profitto from the señorita . . .

DIRECTOR: *(alarmed.)* What? Is that the way she speaks?

(All the ACTORS *break into loud laughter.)*

STEPDAUGHTER: *(laughing as well.)* Yes, sir, that's the way she speaks: half Spanish, half Italian, in a funny hodge-podge.

MADAME PACE: Ah, no mi seem cortesia make comico da me when I speak Italiano, señor.

DIRECTOR: But of course! You're right. Speak like that, just like that, Madame. It couldn't be better if only to give a little comic relief to the coarseness of the situation. Speak like that! It'll be marvellous!

STEPDAUGHTER: Marvellous! And why not? Hearing certain proposals made in a language like that, well, how can you resist? It sounds like a joke. You have to laugh when you hear there's a "señor anziano" who wants to amuse himself "con mi." Isn't that so, Madame?

MADAME PACE: A little anziano, sì, un poco, bella mia. But better per te porque even if no please you, ha mucha prudencia.

MOTHER: *(rushing forward amid the shock and consternation of the* ACTORS, *who have not been paying attention to her, she throws herself on* MADAME PACE *as the* ACTORS *try with smiles to restrain her, tears off her wig, and throws it to the floor.)* Witch! Witch! My little girl!

STEPDAUGHTER: (rushing to hold her back.) No Mama, no! Please!

305 FATHER: (rushing to her as well.) Be calm! Be calm, now! Come sit down.

MOTHER: Take her out of my sight!

STEPDAUGHTER: (to the DIRECTOR, who has also come over.) My mother can't possibly stay here.

310 FATHER: (to the DIRECTOR as well.) They can't be in the same place. That's why, you see, when we came in, that one wasn't with us. When they're together, you understand, everything's revealed at once, inevitably.

DIRECTOR: It doesn't matter. It doesn't matter. For the moment
315 it's only a first sketch. Every little bit helps, so that I can pull together, even like this, all the various elements. (Turning again to the MOTHER and leading her back to her place.) Come now, Madame. Be calm. Just be calm. Sit down again.

(Meanwhile the STEPDAUGHTER goes again to center stage and addresses MADAME PACE.)

STEPDAUGHTER: Go on with it, Madame, go on.

320 MADAME PACE: (offended.) Ah no, muchas gracias. Aquì I no do nada con tu madre presente.

STEPDAUGHTER: Oh, come on. Bring on this "señor anziano" so he can amuse himself "con mi." (Turning on the others imperiously.) At last, we can play it, this scene! Let's get on
325 with it! (To MADAME PACE.) You can go.

MADAME PACE: Certo, me voy, me voy — seguramente!

(She goes out, furious, snatching up her wig and glaring fiercely at the ACTORS, who, laughing mockingly, applaud her.)

STEPDAUGHTER: (to the FATHER.) Now you make your entrance. No, there's no reason for you to go out and come back. Come here. Imagine you've already come in. Now I'm
330 standing here with my eyes down, modestly. Come on, speak up! Say "Good afternoon, Miss" in that special tone of voice, as if you've just come in from outside.

DIRECTOR: (he has gone down into the auditorium again.) Listen to her, will you! Hey, who's the Director here, you or me?
335 (To the FATHER, who looks on lost and perplexed.) Yes, go on, do it. Go upstage but don't go off, and then come back.

(The FATHER does this, bewildered. He is very pale, but he quickly enters into the reality of his created life, smiling as he approaches the rear of the stage like someone wholly unaware of the drama about to sweep over him. The ACTORS are instantly attentive as the scene begins.)

DIRECTOR: (whispering rapidly to the prompter in his well.) And you, on your toes, ready to write now!

THE SCENE

FATHER: (coming forward, in a new tone of voice.) "Good afternoon, Miss."

STEPDAUGHTER: (her head down, she speaks as if trying to conceal her disgust.) "Good afternoon."

5 FATHER: (he glances beneath the brim of her hat, which almost hides her face, and sees that she is very young. Partly out of fear, partly out of fear that he will compromise himself in a risky adventure, he stammers, almost to himself.) "Ah! . . . — But . . . look, this wouldn't be your first time . . . that you're
10 here? Would it?"

STEPDAUGHTER: (as before.) "No, sir."

FATHER: "You've been here before?"

(The STEPDAUGHTER nods yes.)

"More than once?" (He waits a moment for her reply, and again studies her face beneath the brim of her hat. He smiles and then goes on.) "Well, then . . . there's no need to be so . . . 15 Permit me to take your hat."

STEPDAUGHTER: (quickly, to stop him, unable to conceal her disgust.) "No, I'll take it off myself."

(She does so, shaking with emotion. Meanwhile, the MOTHER, the SON, and the two smaller children pressed against her form a group across from the ACTORS. She follows the scene on tenterhooks, registering in turn pain, disdain, anxiety, and horror at the words and gestures of the FATHER and STEPDAUGHTER. Part of the time she covers her face with her hands, at other times she sobs.)

MOTHER: Oh my God! My God!

FATHER: (he does not move for a moment, as if turned to stone; 20 then he resumes his former tone.) "Here, give it to me. I'll put it down for you." (He takes the hat.) "But a charming, pretty little head like yours should really have a more stylish hat. Would you like to help me choose one from among those that Madame is offering? No?" 25

INGENUE: (interrupting.) Be careful there. Those are our hats.

DIRECTOR: (flying into a fury.) For God's sake, shut up! Spare us your wit! We're working on this scene! (Turning again to the STEPDAUGHTER.) Begin again please, Miss.

STEPDAUGHTER: (continuing.) "No thank you, sir." 30

FATHER: "Come on, don't say no. You must accept it. I'll take it amiss . . . Look, there are some lovely ones. And this way we'll make Madame happy. She puts them out here on purpose."

STEPDAUGHTER: "No, sir. Look, I couldn't possibly wear it." 35

FATHER: "You mean because of what they'd say at home, if you came in with a new hat? Really! Don't you know how to handle that? Shall I tell you what to say?"

STEPDAUGHTER: (highly agitated, about to explode.) "That's not the reason! I wouldn't be able to wear it because I'm . . . as 40 you see. By now you should have noticed!" (Indicating the black dress.)

FATHER: "You're in mourning. Of course. Yes, I see now. Please forgive me. Believe me, I'm terribly sorry."

STEPDAUGHTER: (pulling herself together in an attempt to over- 45 come her contempt and revulsion.) "Stop, please. Don't say any more. It's my place to thank you and not yours to feel ashamed or upset. Please pay no attention to what I said. For me too, you understand — I really should forget" (she forces herself to smile and then goes on.) "that I'm dressed like this." 50

DIRECTOR: (interrupting, he speaks to the PROMPTER as he comes back up on stage.) Hold it. Just a minute. Don't take down that last line. Leave it. (Turning to the FATHER and the STEPDAUGHTER.) It's going very, very well. (Then to the FATHER alone.) Then she'll go on as we worked it out. (To the 55 ACTORS.) Pretty good that scene with the hat, don't you think?

STEPDAUGHTER: But the best part is coming now. Why aren't we going on?

DIRECTOR: Be patient a moment. (Turning to the ACTORS.) Of course it will have to be handled with a lighter touch — 60

LEADING ACTOR: — yes, with nimbleness —

LEADING ACTRESS: Of course. It won't be difficult. *(To the* LEADING ACTOR.) Shall we try it now?

LEADING ACTOR: It's all right with me. I'll get ready for my
65   entrance.

(He goes out to be ready to re-enter from the door at the rear.)

DIRECTOR: *(to the* LEADING ACTRESS.) All right, then. Listen. The scene between you and Madame Pace has finished — I'll see about writing it. You are standing . . . No, where are you going?

70 LEADING ACTRESS: Wait a minute. I'll put my hat on. *(She crosses to take her hat from a clothes tree.)*

DIRECTOR: Ah, yes. Very good. Now you're standing here, with your head down.

STEPDAUGHTER: *(amused.)* But she's not dressed in black.

75 LEADING ACTRESS: I *will* be dressed in black, and much more tellingly than you!

DIRECTOR: *(to the* STEPDAUGHTER.) Be quiet, please. Just stand and watch. You may learn something. *(Clapping his hands.)* Let's go now. Let's go. With his entrance.

(He goes down from the stage again to get perspective on the scene. The door at the rear opens, and the LEADING ACTOR *comes forward with the breezy, roguish air of an aging gallant. From his first words the scene as the* ACTORS *play it seems another thing, yet without the least suggestion of burlesque. It seems, somehow, simplified and cleansed of grit. Of course the* STEPDAUGHTER *and* FATHER *cannot recognize themselves in the* LEADING ACTRESS *and* ACTOR, *and as they hear them speak their words, they register their surprise, astonishment, anguish, etc., in a variety of gestures, smiles, protests, etc., as will be seen presently. From the* PROMPTER's *box the* PROMPTER's *voice can be clearly heard prompting each line.)*

80 LEADING ACTOR: "Good afternoon, Miss."

FATHER: *(immediately, unable to restrain himself.)* Oh, no!

(Seeing the LEADING ACTOR *enter as he does, the* STEPDAUGHTER *breaks into laughter.)*

DIRECTOR: *(angry.)* Be quiet! And you, once and for all, stop laughing! We'll never get anywhere this way!

STEPDAUGHTER: *(coming to the apron.)* Excuse me, but it's only
85   natural. This lady *(she indicates the* LEADING ACTRESS.) is taking my part, right enough; but since she's supposed to be me, I can assure her that if I heard someone say "Good afternoon" like that, in that tone, I'd burst out laughing — just as I did.

FATHER: That's right . . . The manner, the tone . . .

90 DIRECTOR: That's enough about manner and tone! Will you please get out of the way and let me watch the rehearsal?

LEADING ACTOR: *(coming forward.)* Look, if I'm supposed to play an old man who comes to a house of ill-fame . . .

DIRECTOR: Of course, pay no attention, for God's sake! Please
95   go on. It's going splendidly. *(Waiting for the* ACTOR *to go on.)* Well?

LEADING ACTOR: "Good afternoon, Miss."

LEADING ACTRESS: "Good afternoon."

LEADING ACTOR: *(imitating the* FATHER's *business of glancing*
100   *under the brim of her hat and then registering, very distinctly, first his kindness and then his fear.)* "Ah! . . . — But . . . look, this wouldn't be your first time . . . that you're here? Is it?"

FATHER: *(correcting him automatically.)* Not "Is it." "Would it." "Would it."

DIRECTOR: Say "Would it" — as a question. 105

LEADING ACTOR: *(pointing to the* PROMPTER.) I heard "Is it."

DIRECTOR: All right. They're both the same, "would it" or "is it." Go on now. Go on. *(He goes back up on the stage, and himself runs quickly through the business up to the* FATHER's *entrance.)* "Good afternoon, Miss." 110

LEADING ACTRESS: "Good afternoon."

DIRECTOR: "Ah! . . . — But . . . look," *(turning to the* LEADING ACTOR *to show him how he glimpses the* LEADING ACTRESS *under the brim of her hat.)* Surprise . . . fear and kindness . . . *(Then, starting again, he turns to the* LEADING ACTRESS.) 115 "This wouldn't be your first time . . . that you're here? Would it?" *(Again he turns to the* LEADING ACTOR, *now with a questioning look.)* Do I make myself clear? *(To the* LEADING ACTRESS.) And then you say: "No, sir." *(Again to the* LEADING ACTOR.) How can I be clearer than that? It wants supple- 120 ness. *(Again he goes down into the auditorium.)*

LEADING ACTRESS: "No, sir . . ."

LEADING ACTOR: "You've been here before? More than once?"

DIRECTOR: Good Lord, no. Hold the second line until she *(he indicates the* LEADING ACTRESS.) nods yes. "You've been 125 here before?"

(The LEADING ACTRESS *raises her head a little, half-closing her eyes as if out of pain and disgust, and then when the* DIRECTOR *says "Down," she lets her head sink twice.)*

STEPDAUGHTER: *(involuntarily.)* My God! *(She quickly puts her hand over her mouth to stifle her laughter.)*

DIRECTOR: *(turning.)* What's wrong?

STEPDAUGHTER: *(quickly.)* Nothing, nothing. 130

DIRECTOR: *(to the* LEADING ACTOR.) It's your cue. Go on.

LEADING ACTOR: "More than once? Well, then . . . there's no need to be so . . . Permit me to take your hat."

(He says this last line with a tone and gesture that force the STEPDAUGHTER, *her hands still over her mouth, to burst into laughter despite her efforts. She laughs noisily through her fingers.)*

LEADING ACTRESS: *(turning, indignant.)* No! I'm not going to stay here to be laughed at by that creature! 135

LEADING ACTOR: And neither am I! Let's call the whole thing off!

DIRECTOR: *(to the* STEPDAUGHTER, *screaming.)* Once and for all, will you stop it? Keep quiet!

STEPDAUGHTER: Yes. I'm very sorry. Very sorry.

DIRECTOR: You're rude and ill-bred, that's what you are. You go 140 too far.

FATHER: *(trying to intervene.)* Yes, it's true. It's true. But be generous.

DIRECTOR: *(coming back up on the stage.)* What do you want me to be generous about? Her behavior is indecent! 145

FATHER: That's right. But believe me, all this does seem strange —

DIRECTOR: . . . Strange? What do you mean "strange"? How strange?

FATHER: Dear sir, I admire your actors. That gentleman there 150 *(he indicates the* LEADING ACTOR.) and the young lady, *(he indicates the* LEADING ACTRESS.) but certainly . . . well, they're not us.

DIRECTOR: Of course! How could they be you? They're actors!

FATHER: Exactly. They're actors. And they play our parts well, 155 both of them. But for us, believe me, we hardly recognize what they're doing. It tries to be like us, but it isn't.

DIRECTOR: What do you mean it isn't? What is it like then?

FATHER: Something that . . . it becomes theirs. It's not ours any
160   longer.

DIRECTOR: But that's inevitable! I've already told you that!

FATHER: Yes, I know. I understand . . . —

DIRECTOR: — Well, then, that's all there is to it! *(He turns again to the* ACTORS.*)* That means that *we'll* handle the rehearsals,
165   as it should be. I've always found it a curse to rehearse with the author present. They're never satisfied! *(Turning again to the* FATHER *and the* STEPDAUGHTER.*)* Come on, let's begin again. And let's see if you can keep from laughing.

STEPDAUGHTER: I won't laugh any more. I promise. My best
170   part is just coming up. You'll see.

DIRECTOR: Now, when you say: "Please pay no attention to what I said. For me too, you understand—" *(turning to the* FATHER.*)* you should break in quickly: "I understand, yes, I understand . . ." and then immediately ask—

175 STEPDAUGHTER: *(interrupting.)* Wait a minute. What does he ask?

DIRECTOR: — the reason for your mourning.

STEPDAUGHTER: Oh, no. Not at all. Look, when I tell him that I shouldn't fret about being dressed like this, do you know
180   what he says? "All right, then, let's take it off, let's take this dress off right now!"

DIRECTOR: Great! Better and better! That *would* bring the house down!

STEPDAUGHTER: But it's the truth.

185 DIRECTOR: Oh, come off it—what truth? Spare me! This is theater! The truth, yes, but up to a certain point!

STEPDAUGHTER: What do you want, then, if you don't mind?

DIRECTOR: You'll see. You'll see. Leave it to me now!

STEPDAUGHTER: No, I won't. I know what you want to do.
190   From my nausea, from everything that makes me what I am, like this, one reason more brutal and more vile than the other, you want to serve up a little sentimental cream puff, with him asking me why I'm in mourning and me answering, in tears, that my father died two months ago. Oh, no. That
195   won't do! He must say what he really said: "All right, then, let's take it off, let's take this dress off right now!" And I with my heart still full of two month's mourning, I went over there—do you see?—behind that screen, and with these fingers trembling with shame and disgust I unhooked the dress
200   and the brassiere . . .

DIRECTOR: *(digging his fingers into his hair.)* For God's sake! What are you saying?

STEPDAUGHTER: The truth! The truth!

DIRECTOR: Of course. I don't deny it. It probably is the truth . . .
205   and I understand, believe me, all your horror, Miss. But you must understand, too, that all this is impossible on the stage!

STEPDAUGHTER: Impossible? Well, then, thanks for everything, I'm leaving.

DIRECTOR: But wait. Listen . . .

210 STEPDAUGHTER: I'm leaving! I'll have nothing more to do with it! The two of you, when you were in there, worked out what is possible on the stage. I see that now, and thanks. He's eager to get to the part *(affecting the* FATHER's *manner.)* where he plays his spiritual torments. But I want to play my drama!
215   Mine!

DIRECTOR: *(annoyed, shrugging his shoulders impatiently.)* Ah, there we have it, don't we? *Your* drama! But there's not only yours, you know. There's also the drama of the others. His drama, *(he indicates the* FATHER.*)* your mother's drama. We
220   can't have one character dominating everything, overwhelming the others, taking over the stage. We have to balance everything in a harmonious picture and then represent what is representable. I know perfectly well that everyone has an interior life and that he wants to give expression to it. But what's
225   difficult is precisely that: to know how to bring out only that part of it that's necessary, in relation to the others, and yet by means of that small part to convey a sense of all the life that remains within. Oh, wouldn't it be lovely if each character in a nice little monologue, or—with no apologies at all—in a
230   lecture, could serve up to the audience all that's boiling within him? *(In a good-humored, conciliatory tone.)* You must discipline yourself, Miss. Believe me, in your own best interests. Because you can easily make a bad impression, I warn you, with all this fury torn to shreds, this exasperated
235   disgust, especially when you yourself, I'm sorry, have admitted that you had been with others, before him, at Madame Pace's, more than once.

STEPDAUGHTER: *(lowering her head; after a pause in which she pulls herself together, in a new, deeper tone.)* It's true. But you
240   know all those others, for me, were him.

DIRECTOR: *(not understanding.)* How do you mean, the others? What are you saying?

STEPDAUGHTER: For anyone who has gone wrong, isn't the person who caused the first lapse responsible for everything. For
245   me he's that person, and it all goes back to even before I was born. Look at him; see if it's not true.

DIRECTOR: All right. And does this burden of remorse seem nothing to you. Give him a chance to show it!

STEPDAUGHTER: But how, if you don't mind my asking? How
250   can he show all his "noble" remorse, all his "moral" torment, if you're going to spare him the horror of one fine day finding in his arms, after having invited her to take off her mourning clothes, the little girl he used to watch coming out of school, that same little girl who's now a whore?

(She says these last words with a voice quivering with emotion. Hearing her speak like this, the MOTHER, *overcome by a rush of anguish which she expresses first in stifled sobs, at last breaks into unrestrained weeping. Everyone is deeply moved. A long pause.)*

255 STEPDAUGHTER: *(as soon as the* MOTHER *shows signs of coming under control, speaking gravely and firmly.)* We're here among ourselves now, and the public knows nothing of us. Tomorrow you'll present this play about us, which you'll believe in, having arranged it in your own way. But do you want
260   to see the real drama? To see it explode into life, as it really happened?

DIRECTOR: Of course, I'd like nothing better, so that I can use from it as much as possible.

STEPDAUGHTER: Then make my mother leave.

265 MOTHER: *(rising from her chair, her soft weeping becoming a cry.)* No, no! Don't allow it, sir! Don't allow it!

DIRECTOR: But it's only so I can see how it was.

MOTHER: I can't bear it! I can't bear it!

DIRECTOR: But if it's all happened before? After all. I don't
270   understand.

MOTHER: No. It's happening now! It's happening all the time! I'm not pretending this anguish. I'm alive here and now, always, feeling every moment of my suffering, constantly, and it keeps renewing itself, in the present. These two children
275 here, you haven't heard them speak, have you? That's because they can't speak anymore! They keep hanging on me, all the time, to keep the pain alive in me. For themselves they no longer exist—no longer exist! And this one (*she indicates the* STEPDAUGHTER), *she fled, she ran away from me and got*
280 lost! Lost! If she's here now, it's for the same reason, for that alone, to renew in me constantly, constantly, constantly, to keep alive and present the pain I've suffered on her account.
FATHER: (*solemnly.*) The eternal moment. As I tried to tell you, sir. She (*he indicates the* STEPDAUGHTER) she's here to hold
285 me, to fix me, to keep me hooked and suspended, forever in pillory, in that one fugitive, shameful moment of my life. She can't let go, and you, sir, you can't save me from it.
DIRECTOR: Yes. But I'm not saying we won't present it. On the contrary, it will form the core of the whole first act, up to the
290 point where she arrives and surprises you—(*He indicates the* MOTHER.)
FATHER: That's good. Because that's my punishment, sir; all our passion must culminate in her final scream. (*Again indicating the* MOTHER.)
295 STEPDAUGHTER: It's still ringing in my ears. It drove me mad, that scream!—You can have me acted as you wish, sir—it doesn't matter. Even dressed. As long as my arms—only my arms—are bare. So that, look, standing like this,

(*She goes to the* FATHER *and puts her head on his chest.*)

with my head resting like this, and my arms like this around
300 his neck, I see here, in my arm, a vein throbbing. And then as if only that living vein disgusts me, I shut my eyes, like this, and bury my head in his chest. (*Turning to the* MOTHER.) Scream! Scream, Mama! (*She buries her head in the* FATHER's *chest and with her shoulders hunched as if to fend off the*
305 *scream, she goes on in a voice of stifled pain.*) Scream the way you screamed then!
MOTHER: (*hurling herself on them to separate them.*) No, my darling! My darling daughter! (*And after having separated her from him*) You brute! Brute! She's my daughter! Don't you see
310 she's my daughter?
DIRECTOR: (*retreating at the scream, down to the footlights, amid the dismay of the* ACTORS.) Wonderful! Yes, wonderful! And then the curtain.
FATHER: (*hurrying to him, convulsed.*) That's it, because it ac-
315 tually happened like that!
DIRECTOR: (*full of admiration, conclusively.*) Yes, right here. No doubt about it. Curtain. Curtain.

(*At the* DIRECTOR's *calls for curtain, the* STAGE TECHNICIAN *lowers it, catching the* DIRECTOR *and the* FATHER *standing in front of it.*)

DIRECTOR: (*looking to heaven, his arms raised.*) The fools! I say curtain meaning that the act should finish here, and he ac-
320 tually lowers the curtain! (*To the* FATHER, *raising the hem of the curtain to pass upstage.*) But that's wonderful! Wonderful! A marvellous effect! It must finish like that. I guarantee it, I guarantee the power of this first act. (*He goes in with the* FATHER.)

— ACT THREE —

(*When the curtain goes up, we see that the* STAGEHANDS *have taken down the scenery used in the previous act and in its place brought out a small garden fountain.*

On one side of the stage the ACTORS *are seated in a row, on the other the* CHARACTERS. *The* DIRECTOR *stands in the middle of the stage with his fist clenched over his mouth, thinking.*)

DIRECTOR: (*after a brief pause, shrugging his shoulders.*) All right, then, let's go ahead with the second act. If you'll leave everything to me, as we agreed, it'll be fine.
STEPDAUGHTER: We go to live in his house. (*She indicates the* FATHER.) Despite his objections. (*She indicates the* SON.)   5
DIRECTOR: (*impatient.*) That's right, but let me take care of it, will you?
STEPDAUGHTER: Just so his opposition is clear.
MOTHER: (*shaking her head in her corner.*) For all the good that's come of it . . .   10
STEPDAUGHTER: (*turning on her quickly.*) That doesn't matter! The more we're hurt, the more he can feel remorse!
DIRECTOR: (*impatient.*) I know. I know. And all this will be taken into account, after all. Don't worry!
MOTHER: (*pleading.*) But treat it so that it's clear, please, to set   15
my mind at rest, that I tried everything to—
STEPDAUGHTER: (*interrupting spitefully, and completing her sentence.*) —to pacify me, to persuade me not to take this wretch down a peg. (*To the* DIRECTOR.) Go on, do as she asks, make her happy, because it's true, she did try hard. While I   20
took the greatest pleasure in what I was doing. Even now you can see: the more submissive she is, the more he's aloof—absent! I can't imagine what she gets out of it!
DIRECTOR: Do you think we can start the second act now?
STEPDAUGHTER: I won't say another word. But you'll see that   25
you can't play all of it in the garden, as you'd like to.
DIRECTOR: Why not?
STEPDAUGHTER: Because he (*she indicates the* SON *again.*) always stays shut up in his room, by himself! And then all the parts concerning that bewildered devil of a boy there happen   30
in the house. As I told you.
DIRECTOR: All right. At the same time you realize we can't keep putting up signs indicating the locale, or change the set three or four times in one act.
LEADING ACTOR: They used to do it, once upon a time . . .   35
DIRECTOR: Sure! When the public was as simple as that baby over there!
LEADING ACTRESS: And illusions were easier to create!
FATHER: (*getting up quickly.*) Illusions? For God's sake, don't talk about illusions! Please don't even mention the word: it's   40
particularly painful for us.
DIRECTOR: (*stunned.*) And why is that, if you please?
FATHER: It's just painful! Painful! You should understand that!
DIRECTOR: And what should we call it, then? This illusion that we create here, for the audience—   45
LEADING ACTOR: —with our acting—
DIRECTOR: —this illusion of a reality?
FATHER: I understand you, sir. But perhaps you can't understand us. Forgive me. Because—here, you see—here for you and your actors—all this is only—and rightly so—it's only a   50
game.

LEADING ACTRESS: *(interrupting, indignant.)* What do you mean a game? We're scarcely children, after all. Our work is serious.

55 FATHER: I'm not saying it isn't. And, in fact, what I mean is the game of your art, which should convey—as he says—a perfect illusion of reality.

DIRECTOR: Exactly.

FATHER: Now, try to keep in mind that we, as we are here, *(he 60 indicates summarily the other five* CHARACTERS.*)* we have no reality outside this illusion.

DIRECTOR: *(stunned, then looking at his* ACTORS, *who are also helpless with amazement.)* And what does that mean?

FATHER: *(with a faint smile, after having looked at them briefly.)* 65 But of course, ladies and gentlemen. What other reality exists for us? What for you is an illusion, something to be fabricated, is for us, instead, our only reality. *(Brief pause. He comes forward a few steps toward the* DIRECTOR *and then goes on.)* And that's true not only for us, you know. Think about it 70 carefully. *(He looks in the* DIRECTOR's *eyes.)* Can you tell me who you are? *(He keeps his finger pointed at the* DIRECTOR.*)*

DIRECTOR: *(upset, but with half a smile.)* What do you mean, who am I?—I'm me!

FATHER: And what if I said that isn't true, because you're me?

75 DIRECTOR: I'd tell you you're crazy.

(The ACTORS *laugh.)*

FATHER: They're quite right to laugh, because here everything's a game. *(To the* DIRECTOR.*)* That's why you can point out to me that as part of the game that gentleman there, *(he indicates the* LEADING ACTOR.*)* who is himself, has to be me, 80 while, at the same time, I am myself, the man you see here. You see, I've caught you.

(The ACTORS *begin to laugh again.)*

DIRECTOR: *(annoyed.)* But we heard all this a little while ago! Are we going to go through it all again?

FATHER: No. In fact, that isn't what I wanted to say. Actually, 85 I'm trying to offer you a way out of this game *(looking at the* LEADING ACTRESS, *as if anticipating her.)* of art! Yes, art! The game you regularly play here with your actors. And again I ask you seriously, who are you?

DIRECTOR: *(turning to the* ACTORS *with amazement and irritation.)* 90 You've got a lot of nerve! Someone who tells us he's a character asks me who I am!

FATHER: *(with dignity but no trace of annoyance.)* A character, dear sir, can always ask a man who he is. Because a character truly has a life of his own, one stamped by his own specific 95 traits, traits which always declare he's "somebody." While a man—I'm not speaking of you now—a man, so-to-speak in general, can be "nobody."

DIRECTOR: All right. But now you're asking me, the head man! I'm the Director! Do you understand that?

100 FATHER: *(very softly, with something like honeyed humility.)* I ask, sir, only to learn if you see yourself now, really, to be the same as you were once, if, given the perspective of time, with all you know now about the illusions of that time, all the things within you and around you, as they seemed then—and 105 as they were, yes, real for you? Well, thinking back on those illusions, long since discarded, all those things which no longer seem what in fact they *were* then, don't you think that

tomorrow, not merely the floorboards of this stage, but what you are feeling now as well, your reality for today, in fact the very earth beneath your feet, might also seem an illusion? 110

DIRECTOR: *(having difficulty following him, a bit dazed by the elusive argument.)* So? And what do you conclude from that?

FATHER: Nothing, dear sir. Only to make you see that if we *(he indicates again the* CHARACTERS *and himself.)* have no reality outside illusion, then you too have reason to mistrust your 115 reality. Because what you are breathing and touching today—like yesterday's reality—is sure to seem an illusion tomorrow.

DIRECTOR: *(deciding to make fun of him.)* Very good! But you're saying too that in this play you're putting on you're more real than I am. 120

FATHER: *(intensely serious.)* That is certainly true.

DIRECTOR: Really?

FATHER: I was sure you realized that from the beginning.

DIRECTOR: More real than I am?

FATHER: If your reality can change from today to tomorrow . . . 125

DIRECTOR: But we all know it can change, for God's sake! It's always changing, like everybody else's!

FATHER: *(emphatically.)* But ours doesn't change! Don't you see? That's the difference between us. Ours doesn't change. It can't change, it can't be something else, never, because it's 130 fixed—like this—this is it!—forever. It's terrible, this unchanging reality. It should make you shudder to come near us.

DIRECTOR: *(struck by a thought, he quickly moves squarely in front of the* FATHER.*)* Yet I'd like to know this: whoever saw a character step out of his role and start lecturing about it, and 135 make suggestions about it, and explain it, the way you're doing? When? Can you tell me? I've never seen it happen!

FATHER: You've not seen it because authors usually conceal the labor that goes into their creations. When characters are alive, actually living in the presence of their author, he faith- 140 fully reproduces their words and actions. The characters suggest them to him, and it's important that he wants them to be as the characters say they should be—there's trouble if he doesn't! When a character is born, he instantly acquires a being so independent—even from his creator—that it's easy 145 to see him in a great many situations that the author never even thought of. He can even take on, sometimes, a meaning that the author never dreamed of giving him.

DIRECTOR: I know that!

FATHER: Well, then, why are you so amazed at us? Consider 150 what a disaster it is for a character to be created by an author's imagination and then to be denied life. Then tell me that this same character, abandoned like this, alive but without a life, isn't right to do what we're doing now, here, in your presence, after having spent ages, ages, believe me, with him, persuad- 155 ing him, pushing him, first me, then her, *(he indicates the* STEPDAUGHTER.*)* then her poor mother . . .

STEPDAUGHTER: *(coming forward, lost in a reverie.)* It's true. Me too, to prevail on him, so many times, in the gloom of his study, just at dusk. He'd be sitting there, sunk in his armchair, 160 with the light off. The shadows filled the room; the darkness seethed with our presence. We had come to try to persuade him . . . *(As if she sees herself in the study. She's annoyed at the presence of the* ACTORS.*)* All of you clear out! Please leave us alone! Mama here with her son—me with the little girl— 165 that boy there always alone—and then me with him *(she indicates the* FATHER.*)* —and then me alone, alone . . . —in the shadows. (*All of a sudden she turns as if in her vision of herself, gleaming in the shadows and alive, she wants to seize herself.*)

170 Oh, what a life! What scenes, what scenes we proposed to him! I tried to persuade him—even more than the others!

FATHER: That's so! And maybe it was because of you he did nothing, because you were so insistent, because of your ridiculous lack of control!

175 STEPDAUGHTER: Not at all! Didn't he himself make me that way? (*She goes to the* DIRECTOR *to speak to him in confidence.*) I think it's more likely that he was depressed about the theater, even despised it as the public saw it and wanted it . . .

DIRECTOR: Let's get on with it, let's get going, for God's sake! 180 Let's get to the point, my friends!

STEPDAUGHTER: I'm sorry, but it seems to me that, with our moving into his house (*she indicates the* FATHER.) there's already too much action. You said we couldn't put up signs announcing new locales or change sets every five minutes.

185 DIRECTOR: Of course! That's true! We have to combine things, group them together in a tight unified action. What you want to do is out of the question—to first see your little brother coming home from school and then wandering through the house like a shadow, hiding behind doors and hatching a 190 scheme. What did you say this did to him?

STEPDAUGHTER: Drained him. Dried him up.

DIRECTOR: Have it your way. You said you could only tell that from his eyes, right?

STEPDAUGHTER: That's right! Look at him! (*She points to him* 195 *next to the* MOTHER.)

DIRECTOR: You're terrific! And then at the same time you would like the little girl to be playing in her little world, in the garden. One in the house, the other in the garden! Come on now!

STEPDAUGHTER: Yes, in the sun, happy! That's my only plea-200 sure, her joy, her delight, in that garden, far from the misery and squalor of the miserable room where the four of us slept—her with me. With me—just think of it!—me with my vile body next to hers, and with her hugging me tight in her little arms, so tender and innocent. As soon as she saw 205 me, in the garden, she'd run and take me by the hand. She didn't care for the big flowers; she ran around looking for the tee-tiny ones, because she wanted to show them to me. So happy! So happy!

(*Saying this, wracked by the memory, she gives a long, despairing cry and beats her head on her arms lying limply on the table. Everyone is deeply moved. The* DIRECTOR *goes to her with almost fatherly concern and speaks gently to her.*)

DIRECTOR: We'll do the garden scene, we'll do the garden scene. 210 Don't fret about it. And you'll see, you'll be pleased. We'll group the scenes around that. (*He calls a* STAGEHAND.) Look, lower a few branches of tree for me! Two small cypresses just here, in front of the fountain.

(*We see two cypresses descend from the flies. The* STAGE TECHNICIAN *hurries up to nail their bases in place.*)

(*To the* STEPDAUGHTER.) This will do for now, just to give 215 you the idea. (*He again calls the* STAGEHAND.) Now give me a little something for sky!

STAGEHAND: (*from above.*) What do you want?

DIRECTOR: A little sky. A backcloth that comes down here, behind the fountain.

(*We see a white cloth descend from the flies.*)

Not white. I said sky. This doesn't give us anything. But leave 220 it, I'll take care of it. (*Calling.*) Hey, electrician! Take down the lights and give me a little atmosphere . . . a kind of lunar atmosphere . . . blue from the instruments and blue on the cloth—and use the reflector! That's it! That'll do.

(*In keeping with these orders, a mysterious lunar light floods the scene, a light so distinctive that it induces the* ACTORS *to speak and move as if it were a moonlit evening in a garden.*)

(*To the* STEPDAUGHTER.) There. You see? And now instead 225 of the boy's hiding behind doors in the house, he can move about the garden and hide behind these trees. But you do realize it'll be hard to find a little girl that young to play the scene with you, where she shows you the flowers. (*Turning to the* BOY.) Come here you, come here. Let's see how this works. 230

(*But the* BOY *doesn't move.*)

Come on, come over here!

(*Then, pulling him forward and trying to make him hold his head up, to no avail.*)

Ah, really! This is a nuisance, the boy too . . . But what's wrong? Good God, he's going to have to say something, after all . . .

(*He moves close to him and puts a hand on his shoulder, then leads him behind one of the trees.*)

Come on, come. A bit more. Let me see! Hide here . . . 235 That's it . . . Try showing your head just a little, to spy . . .

(*He moves to one side to see the effect. As the* BOY *executes this action, the* ACTORS *are transfixed.*)

Ah, very good . . . excellent . . . (*Turning to the* STEPDAUGHTER.) As I was about to say, if the little girl, now, were to catch him spying like that and would run over to him: he could say something. 240

STEPDAUGHTER: (*getting to her feet.*) Don't expect him to speak as long as that one's here. (*She indicates the* SON.) You'll have to send him away first.

SON: (*heading toward one of the small stairways.*) At your service! Delighted! Nothing will please me more! 245

DIRECTOR: (*quickly holding him back.*) No! Where are you going? Wait!

(*The* MOTHER *gets up, distraught, upset at the thought that he's actually leaving, and instinctively she raises her arms as if to restrain him, though she doesn't move from her place.*)

SON: (*at the footlights, to the* DIRECTOR, *who is holding him.*) In fact, I have really nothing to do here. Let me go, please! Let me go! 250

DIRECTOR: What do you mean you have nothing to do?

STEPDAUGHTER: (*serenely, ironically.*) But you don't have to hold him. He's not going anywhere.

FATHER: He has to play the terrible scene in the garden, with his mother. 255

SON: (*quickly, determined and angry.*) I'm not going to play anything! I've said so from the beginning! (*To the* DIRECTOR.) Let me go!

STEPDAUGHTER: (*going to the* DIRECTOR.) If you don't mind, sir.

(She makes him release his hold on the SON.*)*

260   Let him go. *(Then, turning on the* SON *as quickly as the* DI-
RECTOR *has let him go.)* All right now, get out!

(The SON *stays where he is, straining for the stairs, but, as if held
by an occult force, unable to move. Then, amid the stupor and
dismay of the* ACTORS, *he moves slowly along the edge of the
apron toward the second stairway, yet there too he stops and
strains but cannot descend. The* STEPDAUGHTER, *who has followed him with her eyes, as if daring him, breaks into laughter.)*

—He can't, see? He can't do it! He's got to stay here, chained
to us! There's no escape! And since I'm the one who finally
takes off, after what must happen has happened, and I do it
265   because I hate him and can't stand the sight of him—well, if
I'm still here now and somehow I'm managing to put up with
him—why in heaven should he go? After all, he has to stay,
afterwards, with his precious father, and his mother there,
who then has no children except him . . . *(Turning to the*
270   MOTHER.*)* Come on, Mama. Come. *(Turning back to the*
DIRECTOR *and pointing to her.)* You see? She got up, she got
up to hold him back . . . *(To the* MOTHER, *moving her as if by
magic.)* Come on. Come on. *(Then, to the* DIRECTOR.*)*
Imagine what it must be like for her to reveal to your actors
275   what she's feeling. But the pressure to be near him is so great
that—look at her—you see? Now she's ready to live her scene!

(The MOTHER *has in fact approached the* SON, *and, as soon as
the* STEPDAUGHTER *finishes, she opens her arms as a gesture that
she's ready.)*

SON: *(quickly.)* But not me! No! Not me! If I can't go, then I'll
stay here. But I repeat: I won't perform anything!
FATHER: *(to the* DIRECTOR, *trembling.)* You can make him!
280   SON: No one can make me!
FATHER: I'll make you!
STEPDAUGHTER: Wait! Wait! First the baby has to go to the
fountain!

(She hurries to the LITTLE GIRL, *kneels down in front of her, and
takes her face in her hands.)*

My poor darling, you look so lost, with those beautiful eyes.
285   Who knows what all this seems like to you? We're on a stage,
sweetheart. And what's a stage? Well, don't you see? It's a
place where they play and are serious about it. Here they put
on plays. And right now we're putting on a play. Really and
truly. You too . . .

*(She embraces her, pulling her to her breast and rocking her
gently.)*

290   Oh my darling, my darling, what a horrible part you have to
play! What terrible things they've thought up for you! The
garden, the fountain . . . Oh, it's a make-believe fountain, of
course. The trouble is, sweetheart, it's all make-believe here.
But maybe for you, a little girl, a make-believe fountain is
295   better than a real one, so you can play in it, eh? No: for the
others it's a game, but not for you, unfortunately. You're real,
darling, and you play for real in a real fountain, beautiful,
large, green, with bamboo palms casting shadows over it. You
watch your reflection in the water, and lots of baby ducks are
300   swimming there, breaking up the shadows. You want to catch

one of the baby ducks . . . *(With a cry that frightens everyone.)*
No, Rosetta, no! Mama's not watching you! Because of that
pig of a son! I'm going mad . . . And that one there . . .

(She leaves the LITTLE GIRL, *and grabs the* BOY.*)*

What are you doing here, always mooning around like a beggar? It'll be your fault too if the baby drowns, with this stupid   305
way of yours. As if I didn't pay for all of us when I got us in here!

(She seizes his arm to force his hand out of his pocket.)

What have you got there? What are you hiding? Out with it!
Show me that hand!

*(She pulls his hand from the pocket, and to everyone's horror he's
holding a revolver. She looks at him for a moment, as if she has
satisfied herself about something, then says darkly.)*

Huh! Where, how did you get it?

(And when the BOY, *frightened, his eyes still bewildered and vacant, does not reply.)*

Idiot! If I were you, instead of killing myself I'd kill one of   310
them, or both of them, both father and son!

*(She pushes him behind the cypress where he had been hiding,
then she takes the* LITTLE GIRL *and lowers her into the fountain,
laying her down so that she cannot be seen. At last she sinks down
there, her face in her arms against the edge of the fountain.)*

DIRECTOR: Very good! *(Turning to the* SON.*)* And at the same
time . . .
SON: *(contemptuously.)* What do you mean "at the same time"?
That can't be! There was no scene here between her and me!   315
(He indicates the MOTHER.*)* Let her tell you herself how it was.

(Meanwhile, the SUPPORTING ACTRESS *and the* YOUNG LEAD-
ING MAN *have stepped away from the group of* ACTORS. *She has
gone up to the* MOTHER *and she's studying her carefully, and he
to the* SON, *as if in preparation for acting their roles.)*

MOTHER: It's true, sir. I went to his room.
SON: To my room! Understand? Not in the garden!
DIRECTOR: But that's not important. We have to re-group the
scenes, as I said.   320
SON: *(becoming aware of the* YOUNG LEADING MAN.*)* What do
you want?
YOUNG LEADING MAN: Nothing. I'm just watching.
SON: *(turning away; then to the* SUPPORTING ACTRESS.*)* Ah,
and here *you* are! Getting ready to play her part? *(He indicates   325
the* MOTHER.*)*
DIRECTOR: Precisely. Precisely. And you should be grateful, it
seems to me, for their application.
SON: Naturally! Thanks. But you still don't understand that you
can't do this play. You haven't the faintest idea of what we are;   330
the best your actors can do is to study us, from outside. Do
you really think it's possible for someone to live in a mirror
image of himself? Especially when the image is frozen, or,
even worse, a grotesque distortion in which we can't recognize ourselves?   335
FATHER: That's right. That's right. I agree about that.
DIRECTOR: *(to the* YOUNG LEADING MAN *and the* SUPPORTING
ACTRESS.*)* All right. Go back with the others.
SON: It's no use. I won't do a thing.

340   DIRECTOR: Be quiet now and let me hear what your mother has
      to say. (To the MOTHER.) All right. You went to his room.

      MOTHER: Yes, to his room. I couldn't bear it any longer. I
      wanted to tell him everything, to pour out my heart to him,
      all my torment. But as soon as he saw me—

345   SON: —There was no scene. I left. I left to avoid a scene. Be-
      cause I don't make scenes! Understand?

      MOTHER: That's true. That's the way it was. Like that.

      DIRECTOR: But now we have to create that scene between you.
      It's indispensable.

350   MOTHER: As for me, I'm ready. It might even give me the chance
      to speak to him for a moment, to tell him what's in my heart.

      FATHER: (moving close to the SON, intense.) You'll do it! For
      your mother! For your mother!

      SON: (more determined than ever.) I won't do anything!

355   FATHER: (taking hold of his jacket and shaking him.) By God, do
      as I say! Do as I say! Don't you hear how she's speaking to you?
      What kind of son are you?

      SON: (seizing him in turn.) No. No. That's enough, once and
      for all!

      (General confusion. The MOTHER, terrified, tries to intervene
      and separate them.)

360   MOTHER: For the love of God! Please!

      FATHER: (without letting go.) Listen to me! Listen!

      SON: (he continues to struggle with him until at last, to every-
      one's horror, he throws him to the floor near the stairway.)
      What's come over you? Have you gone mad? Have you lost all

365   self-respect that you want to show everyone your disgrace, and
      ours? I'll have nothing to do with it! Nothing! And that's what
      our author wanted: he didn't want to put us on the stage!

      DIRECTOR: But after all is said and done you've come here.

      SON: (pointing to the FATHER.) Him! Not me!

370   DIRECTOR: And aren't you here too?

      SON: He wanted to come, dragging all of us with him! Then he
      went in there with you to patch together not only what really
      happened but, as if that weren't enough, what never
      happened!

375   DIRECTOR: Well, you tell me then, at least tell me what really
      happened. Tell it to me. You left your room. Without saying
      anything?

      SON: (after a moment's hesitation.) Without saying anything.
      Because I didn't want to make a scene.

380   DIRECTOR: (urging him on.) Well, and then? What did you do?

      SON: (amid spellbound anguish on all sides he takes a few steps
      across the stage.) Nothing . . . Crossing the garden . . . (He
      stops, absorbed and depressed.)

      DIRECTOR: (still urging him on, impressed by his reluctance.)

385   Well? Crossing the garden?

      SON: (exasperated, hiding his face in his arms.) Why do you want
      to make me say it? It's horrible.

      (The MOTHER is visibly shaking with stifled sobs; she's looking
      toward the fountain.)

      DIRECTOR: (catching sight of her look, he turns to the SON and
      with growing apprehension, softly.) The little girl?

390   SON: (looking straight ahead, into the auditorium.) There, in
      the fountain . . .

      FATHER: (still on the floor, pointing to the MOTHER, pityingly.)
      And she was following him!

      DIRECTOR: (anxiously, to the SON.) And then what did you do?

      SON: (slowly, continuing to look straight ahead.) I ran, I hurried   395
      to pull her out . . . But then I stopped, dead in my tracks,
      because behind that tree I saw something that froze me: the
      boy was standing there, stock still, with the eyes of a mad
      creature, looking at his little sister drowned in the fountain.

      (The STEPDAUGHTER, still bent over the fountain so as to con-
      ceal the LITTLE GIRL, sobs out of control, like an echo from the
      deep.)

      (A pause.)

      I started to go nearer, and then . . .   400

      (Behind the tree where the SON has been hiding there's the sound
      of a shot.)

      MOTHER: (with a piercing cry she and the SON and the ACTORS
      amid complete confusion run to the place.) My son! Oh, my
      son! (And then against the turmoil and disconnected cries of
      the others.) Help! Help!

      DIRECTOR: (amidst the screams, trying to make his way through   405
      the others, as the SON is raised up and carried behind the white
      backcloth.) Is he wounded? Is he really wounded?

      (Everyone, except the DIRECTOR and the FATHER, still on the
      floor near the stairway, has by now disappeared behind the back-
      cloth for the sky, and we hear them there talking anxiously for a
      few moments. Then the ACTORS come back around both sides of
      the cloth.)

      LEADING ACTRESS: (coming from the right, deeply moved.) He's
      dead! The poor boy! He's dead! How horrible!

      LEADING ACTOR: (coming from the left, laughing.) What do you   410
      mean "dead"? It's all a fiction. Make-believe. Don't you be-
      lieve it!

      OTHER ACTORS FROM THE RIGHT: Fiction? It's real! Real! He's
      dead!

      FATHER: (getting up and shouting at them.) A fiction? Don't   415
      deceive yourselves! It's real! Reality, ladies and gentlemen!
      Reality! (He too goes off behind the white backdrop,
      disconsolate.)

      DIRECTOR: (at the end of his rope.) Fiction! Reality! Go to hell
      all of you! Lights! Lights! Lights!   420

      (All at once the entire stage and the auditorium are flooded with
      brilliant light. The DIRECTOR heaves a sigh as if rid of an in-
      cubus, while all the others look at each other, stunned and lost.)

      Damn! Nothing like this has ever happened to me before!
      They've made me lose a whole day! (He looks at his watch.)
      You can all go now. There's nothing we can do now. It's too
      late to pick up the rehearsal again. I'll see you all this evening.

      (The ACTORS take their leave. As soon as they're gone.)

      Hey, electrician, turn off the lights!   425

      (As soon as he has said this, the theater is plunged in complete
      darkness.)

      Hey, for God's sake, leave at least a little light so I can see
      where I'm walking.

      (Suddenly, behind the backcloth, as if because of a bad connec-
      tion, a green light comes on which projects, large and sharply

outlined, *the shadows of the* CHARACTERS, *except for the* BOY *and the* LITTLE GIRL. *Seeing them, the* DIRECTOR *scurries from the stage, terrified. At that instant this light goes off and on the stage the blue night light mentioned earlier comes on. Slowly the* SON *comes from the right side of the curtain, followed by the* MOTHER *with her arms extended toward him. Then from the left side the* FATHER. *They stop half way onto the stage and stand as if bemused. Lastly, the* STEPDAUGHTER *comes from the left and runs toward one of the stairways. On the first step she stops to look at the other three for a moment and breaks into a coarse laugh. Then she hurries down the stairs and runs up an aisle, stopping once more to laugh at the other three still standing there. At last she rushes out of the auditorium. Even from the lobby her laughter can be heard.*

Shortly after this the curtain falls.)

BERTOLT BRECHT

Bertolt Brecht (1898–1956) changed the course of the modern European theater — and theater around the world — more than any playwright since Ibsen. However, Brecht's sphere of influence extends beyond his career as a playwright. As a dramatist, he wrote an unsurpassed body of plays; as a theoretician, Brecht's conception of "alienation" in the epic theater opened the way for sweeping innovation in our understanding of the possibilities of the stage; as a director, Brecht's work with his company, the Berliner Ensemble, made it the most influential and important theater in postwar Europe. The challenge of understanding Brecht is to understand the dialectical interplay between theory and practice that informs his assault on stage realism, and on the bourgeois theater itself.

Eugen Berthold Brecht (he later changed his name to Bertolt) was born in Augsburg, Bavaria, in 1898 to a prosperous family. In 1917, he enrolled at Munich University in the natural sciences and worked as a drama critic on the side. He also began work on several plays, including *Baal* (1917). In 1918 he was conscripted into military service for the remainder of World War I and worked in a military hospital. He returned briefly to the university after the war, but soon turned his attention full time to the theater. He moved to Berlin — Germany's theatrical capital at the time — and had the good fortune to work with two influential directors, Max Reinhardt and Erwin Piscator. Piscator advocated the use of new technologies in the theater, as a way of developing a kind of performance more responsive to the mechanized and accelerated routines of modern life. Brecht acknowledged that many of his own staging techniques were derived from his work with Piscator in the 1920s. Throughout the 1920s and early 1930s, Brecht wrote a series of plays that brought him notoriety, largely for their satire of the bourgeois establishment: *Drums in the Night* (1919), *In the Jungle of Cities* (1921), *Man Is Man* (1926), and the musical plays he wrote in collaboration with the composer Kurt Weill, *The Threepenny Opera* (1928) and *The Rise and Fall of the City of Mahagonny* (1930).

Brecht also began his serious reading of Marx in the 1920s, and it was his application of Marxist dialectic to the process of theater that gave rise to his most powerful and original ideas for the stage. From Marx, Brecht adopted a revolutionary posture, not only toward the class struggle, but toward the stage of bourgeois "realism." To Brecht, the realistic theater was not an unbiased window on social reality. Instead, Brecht argued that realistic theater presented a particular political vision, a view of society as inevitably determined by history and evolution, and therefore not susceptible to change. In order to displace "realism," and to demonstrate these hidden politics, Brecht redefined Marx's conception of "alienation" as a theatrical practice. In *Das Kapital*, Marx argues that the division of labor in modern industrial production has altered the relationship between mankind and the world. In modern industry, workers sell their labor in order to produce commodities. These commodities, Marx contends, then seem "alien" in that they appear to have arisen magically. Capitalist production conceals the signs of how they were produced, so that commodities come to have a "natural" life of their own. Yet, even as commodities seem to come alive, the workers become dehumanized, incorporated into the machinery of production. In the world of capital, where everything is for sale, all human relations, lives, and desires become commodified. The prevailing view of the world — in which commodities confront workers as something natural and entirely separate from their makers — is, to Marx, a *false* view, perpetuated within the bourgeois social order to the political advantage of the ruling classes.

Brecht's theater works to provide its audience with ways of regarding bourgeois reality — including realistic theater and drama — as "unnatural," as a political vision, as an ideological view of the world produced in the interest of profit. Brecht's theater, that is, works to "alienate" or "estrange" the audience from the commonplace "realities" of daily life — which we have unreflectively come to regard as "natural" and "inevitable" — in order to train us to question the world made by modern capitalism and the society it sustains. As he wrote in "The Modern Theater is the Epic Theater," his theater is based on a "radical separation of the elements" of production, rather than on the scenic unity typical of realism. The seamless illusion of the realistic stage is that theater's most seductive commodity, for it constantly and subliminally urges the audience to accept its "picture" of reality as a natural, apolitical image of the world as it is. Brecht's theater, in contrast, always shows both the dramatic illusion (the character, the setting, the action) and the process of its making (the work of the actor, the machinery of the theater, the activities of the stage). Brecht works to show the "means of production" in his theater, as a way of suggesting that stage realism, like social reality outside the theater, is *made*, not given.

Brecht called this theater by a variety of names, including EPIC THEATER, the term now generally used for Brecht's body of theory and technique. Brecht's plays tend to be episodic, a disconnected, open-ended MONTAGE of scenes: The audience must arrive at its own understanding of how the events are linked together, rather than being given an apparently inevitable narrative. Brecht generally left the stage bare in his productions, as a way of preventing the audience from seeing a complete illusion of some fictional dramatic locale. He exposed the lights above the stage, so the audience could see how lights influence the mood of the scene and so influence the audience's judgment. Brecht fragmented the "realistic" unity of the setting in other ways, too. Films could be projected on screens above the stage, forcing the audience to hold the drama in counterpoint to more recent events; placards onstage described the action to take place before the scene began. Finally, Brecht also urged his actors not to empathize entirely with the characters they played, but to strike a balance between a Stanislavskian identification with the character (being "in character," acting the character entirely from his or her point of view) and a more demonstrative attitude, one that enables the actor to represent the character from a variety of perspectives. Through these means, Brecht worked to involve the audience in the process of the play's production. Rather than being seduced by a commodified illusion of reality, the audience of epic theater is invited to consider, and enjoy, how the theater makes its fictions—as a way of teaching the audience to adopt a more critical, "alienated" way of seeing life outside the theater.

Brecht used many of these devices in *The Threepenny Opera* and in the series of plays he wrote in exile. Forced to flee Germany by Nazi purges of left-wing writers in 1933, Brecht spent the greater part of his creative life on the run, living briefly in Sweden, in Finland, and finally in Santa Monica, California, from 1941 to 1947. He worked extensively on *Life of Galileo* in California, collaborating on an English version with the actor Charles Laughton. He was also questioned by the House Un-American Activities Committee in 1947, as part of its infamous investigation of communism in the entertainment industry. Brecht was not charged and left the United States the following day to return to Europe and Germany. Living in exile, with no theater and little support, Brecht wrote his major plays: *Life of Galileo* (1938), *The Good Person of Szechwan* (1939), *Mother Courage and Her Children* (1939), *The Caucasian Chalk Circle* (1944). He also wrote his most important theoretical essays, including *A Short Organum for the Theater* (1948).

Brecht returned to East Berlin in 1947 and established his company, the Berliner Ensemble. Brecht's antirealist plays had long been the source of conflict with the SOCIAL REALISM advocated by the Communist Party, and even after the war Brecht had to work with a wary eye on the East German authorities. Nonetheless, the Berliner Ensemble—under Brecht's guidance and with the talents of his wife, Helene Weigel—became the leading European production company of the 1950s, sowing the seeds of innovation in every country they visited. Brecht died in August of 1956, just before the Berliner Ensemble's stunning visit to London, but the influence of his conception of theater has become worldwide, visible in plays from Jean Genet's *The Blacks* to Luis Valdez's *Los Vendidos* to Caryl Churchill's *Vinegar Tom*.

Mother Courage and Her Children

Mother Courage and Her Children is typical of Brecht's innovative approach to theater and to "political theater" as well. Rather than presenting a thesis, the play works to question the audience's attitudes about a variety of social institutions: warfare, business, motherhood, morality. In a parable-like series of scenes reminiscent both of expressionist theater and of morality drama, *Mother Courage and Her Children* invites the audience to estrange, and so reconsider, its ways of mapping the world.

In his model-book of the play, Brecht wrote that he wanted to show that "war, which is a continuation of business by other means, makes the human virtues fatal to their possessors." The play considers this problem in a variety of challenging ways. Although it is perhaps tempting to see Courage—Why is she called Courage? Was she courageous?—as a tragic heroine, the play relentlessly questions her "heroic" survival, and our own attitudes about the distinctions between war, business, and morality. As Scene I demonstrates, war and business create an all-embracing market in which everything is commodified, for sale. Mother Courage sells a belt buckle and loses a son as part of the same transaction.

Much of the play's power onstage arises through its use of physical space and a few significant properties. The wagon — Courage's home, her means of survival, her mode of production — becomes in a sense the play's central "character." Placing it on a turntable, most productions convey the sense that the wagon is almost always in motion, yet never actually getting anywhere, much as Courage herself enters the play and leaves it singing the same song. Courage's fortunes are emblematized by the wagon as well. Loaded with goods and pulled by her two strong sons in the first scene, it is battered, barren, and empty in the last, pulled by Mother Courage herself as she struggles to catch up with the army. Brecht was attracted to the idea of using the wagon, the play's economic and material "base," so to speak, to elucidate some of the play's symbolic or moral themes. He used Courage's wash-line to link the wagon to the cannon at the opening of Scene III, tying warfare, the economy, and the domestic sphere together. He raised the harness-poles to form a kind of crucifix after the death of Swiss Cheese. Many of the most ironic moments of the Berliner Ensemble production of the play were Weigel's invention: as Mother Courage, she bit the coin in Scene I and slowly measured her pennies out of her purse when she paid the peasants to bury Kattrin at the end of the play. This is the kind of moment that Brecht worked — in theory, as a playwright, in directing productions — to make happen in the theater, a moment when a single gesture forces the audience to consider the scene in a new light, to question the relationship between its ideas of identity and morality and the society that gives them shape and meaning.

MOTHER COURAGE
AND HER CHILDREN
A CHRONICLE OF THE THIRTY YEARS' WAR

Bertolt Brecht

TRANSLATED BY RALPH MANHEIM

— CHARACTERS —

MOTHER COURAGE
KATTRIN, *her mute daughter*
EILIF, *her elder son*
SWISS CHEESE, *her younger son*
THE RECRUITER
THE SERGEANT
THE COOK
THE GENERAL
THE CHAPLAIN
THE ORDNANCE OFFICER
YVETTE POTTIER
THE MAN WITH THE PATCH OVER HIS EYE
THE OTHER SERGEANT

THE OLD COLONEL
A CLERK
A YOUNG SOLDIER
AN OLDER SOLDIER
A PEASANT
THE PEASANT'S WIFE
THE YOUNG MAN
THE OLD WOMAN
ANOTHER PEASANT
THE PEASANT WOMAN
A YOUNG PEASANT
THE LIEUTENANT
SOLDIERS
A VOICE

SCENE I

> Spring, 1624. General Oxenstjerna recruits troops in Dalarna for the Polish campaign. The canteen woman, Anna Fierling, known as Mother Courage, loses a son.

Highway near a city.

A sergeant and a recruiter stand shivering.

THE RECRUITER: How can anybody get a company together in a place like this? Sergeant, sometimes I feel like committing suicide. The general wants me to recruit four platoons by the twelfth, and the people around here are so depraved I can't
5 sleep at night. I finally get hold of a man, I close my eyes and pretend not to see that he's chicken-breasted and he's got varicose veins, I get him good and drunk and he signs up. While I'm paying for the drinks, he steps out, I follow him to the door because I smell a rat: Sure enough, he's gone, like a fart
10 out of a goose. A man's word doesn't mean a thing, there's no honor, no loyalty. This place has undermined my faith in humanity, sergeant.

THE SERGEANT: It's easy to see these people have gone too long without a war. How can you have morality without a war,
15 I ask you? Peace is a mess, it takes a war to put things in order. In peacetime the human race goes to the dogs. Man and beast are treated like so much dirt. Everybody eats what they like, a big piece of cheese on white bread, with a slice of meat on top of the cheese. Nobody knows how many young men or good
20 horses there are in that town up ahead, they've never been counted. I've been in places where they hadn't had a war in as much as seventy years, the people had no names, they didn't even know who they were. It takes a war before you get decent lists and records; then your boots are done up in bales and
25 your grain in sacks, man and beast are properly counted and marched away, because people realize that without order they can't have a war.

THE RECRUITER: How right you are!

THE SERGEANT: Like all good things, a war is hard to get started.
30 But once it takes root, it's vigorous; then people are as scared of peace as dice players are of laying off, because they'll have to reckon up their losses. But at first they're scared of war. It's the novelty.

THE RECRUITER: Say, there comes a wagon. Two women and
35 two young fellows. Keep the old woman busy, sergeant. If this is another flop, you won't catch me standing out in this April wind any more.

(A Jew's harp is heard. Drawn by two young men, a covered wagon approaches. In the wagon sit MOTHER COURAGE *and her mute daughter* KATTRIN.)

MOTHER COURAGE: Good morning, sergeant.

THE SERGEANT: *(barring the way)* Good morning, friends.
40 Who are you?

MOTHER COURAGE: Business people. *(Sings)*

Hey, Captains, make the drum stop drumming
And let your soldiers take a seat.
Here's Mother Courage, with boots she's coming
45 To help along their aching feet.
How can they march off to the slaughter
With baggage, cannon, lice and fleas
Across the rocks and through the water
Unless their boots are in one piece?
   The spring is come. Christian, revive!
50   The snowdrifts melt. The dead lie dead.
   And if by chance you're still alive
   It's time to rise and shake a leg.

55 O Captains, don't expect to send them
    To death with nothing in their crops.
    First you must let Mother Courage mend them
    In mind and body with her schnapps.
    On empty bellies it's distressing
    To stand up under shot and shell.
60 But once they're full, you have my blessing
    To lead them to the jaws of hell.
        The spring is come. Christian, revive!
        The snowdrifts melt, the dead lie dead.
        And if by chance you're still alive
65   It's time to rise and shake a leg.

THE SERGEANT: Halt, you scum. Where do you belong?
THE ELDER SON: Second Finnish Regiment.
THE SERGEANT: Where are your papers?
MOTHER COURAGE: Papers?
70 THE YOUNGER SON: But she's Mother Courage!
THE SERGEANT: Never heard of her. Why Courage?
MOTHER COURAGE: They call me Courage, sergeant, because
    when I saw ruin staring me in the face I drove out of Riga
    through cannon fire with fifty loaves of bread in my wagon.
75 They were getting moldy, it was high time, I had no choice.
THE SERGEANT: No wisecracks. Where are your papers?
MOTHER COURAGE: (fishing a pile of papers out of a tin box and
    climbing down) Here are my papers, sergeant. There's a
    whole missal, picked it up in Alt-Ötting to wrap cucumbers
80 in, and a map of Moravia, God knows if I'll ever get there, if I
    don't it's a total loss. And this here certifies that my horse
    hasn't got foot-and-mouth disease, too bad, he croaked on us,
    he cost fifteen guilders, but not out of my pocket, glory be. Is
    that enough paper?
85 THE SERGEANT: Are you trying to pull my leg? I'll teach you to
    get smart. You know you need a license.
MOTHER COURAGE: You mind your manners and don't go tell-
    ing my innocent children that I'd go anywhere near your leg,
    it's indecent. I want no truck with you. My license in the
90 Second Regiment is my honest face, and if you can't read it,
    that's not my fault. I'm not letting anybody put his seal on it.
THE RECRUITER: Sergeant, I detect a spirit of insubordination
    in this woman. In our camp we need respect for authority.
MOTHER COURAGE: Wouldn't sausage be better?
95 THE SERGEANT: Name.
MOTHER COURAGE: Anna Fierling.
THE SERGEANT: Then you're all Fierlings?
MOTHER COURAGE: What do you mean? Fierling is my name.
    Not theirs.
100 THE SERGEANT: Aren't they all your children?
MOTHER COURAGE: That they are, but why should they all have
    the same name? (Pointing at the elder son) This one, for in-
    stance. His name is Eilif Nojocki. How come? Because his
    father always claimed to be called Kojocki or Mojocki. The
105 boy remembers him well, except the one he remembers was
    somebody else, a Frenchman with a goatee. But aside from
    that, he inherited his father's intelligence; that man could
    strip the pants off a peasant's ass without his knowing it. So,
    you see, we've each got our own name.
110 THE SERGEANT: Each different, you mean?
MOTHER COURAGE: Don't act so innocent.
THE SERGEANT: I suppose that one's a Chinaman? (Indicating
    the younger son)

MOTHER COURAGE: Wrong. He's Swiss.
THE SERGEANT: After the Frenchman?   115
MOTHER COURAGE: What Frenchman? I never heard of any
    Frenchman. Don't get everything balled up or we'll be here
    all day. He's Swiss, but his name is Fejos, the name has noth-
    ing to do with his father. He had an entirely different name,
    he was an engineer, built fortifications, but he drank.   120

(SWISS CHEESE nods, beaming; the mute KATTRIN is also tickled.)

THE SERGEANT: Then how can his name be Fejos?
MOTHER COURAGE: I wouldn't want to offend you, but you
    haven't got much imagination. Naturally his name is Fejos
    because when he came I was with a Hungarian, it was all the
    same to him, he was dying of kidney trouble though he never 125
    touched a drop, a very decent man. The boy takes after him.
THE SERGEANT: But you said he wasn't his father?
MOTHER COURAGE: He takes after him all the same. I call him
    Swiss Cheese, how come, because he's good at pulling the
    wagon. (Pointing at her daughter) Her name is Kattrin   130
    Haupt, she's half German.
THE SERGEANT: A fine family, I must say.
MOTHER COURAGE: Yes, I've been all over the world with my
    wagon.
THE SERGEANT: It's all being taken down. (He takes it down)   135
    You're from Bamberg, Bavaria. What brings you here?
MOTHER COURAGE: I couldn't wait for the war to kindly come
    to Bamberg.
THE RECRUITER: You wagon pullers ought to be called Jacob
    Ox and Esau Ox. Do you ever get out of harness?   140
EILIF: Mother, can I clout him one on the kisser? I'd like to.
MOTHER COURAGE: And I forbid you. You stay put. And now,
    gentlemen, wouldn't you need a nice pistol, or a belt buckle,
    yours is all worn out, sergeant.
THE SERGEANT: I need something else. I'm not blind. Those   145
    young fellows are built like tree trunks, big broad chests,
    sturdy legs. Why aren't they in the army? That's what I'd like
    to know.
MOTHER COURAGE: (quickly) Nothing doing, sergeant. My
    children aren't cut out for soldiers.   150
THE RECRUITER: Why not? There's profit in it, and glory. Ped-
    dling shoes is woman's work. (To EILIF) Step up; let's feel if
    you've got muscles or if you're a sissy.
MOTHER COURAGE: He's a sissy. Give him a mean look and
    he'll fall flat on his face.   155
THE RECRUITER: And kill a calf if it happens to be standing in
    the way. (Tries to lead him away)
MOTHER COURAGE: Leave him alone. He's not for you.
THE RECRUITER: He insulted me. He referred to my face as a
    kisser. Him and me will now step out in the field and discuss 160
    this thing as man to man.
EILIF: Don't worry, mother. I'll take care of him.
MOTHER COURAGE: You stay put. You no-good! I know you,
    always fighting. He's got a knife in his boot, he's a knifer.
THE RECRUITER: I'll pull it out of him like a milk tooth. Come 165
    on, boy.
MOTHER COURAGE: Sergeant, I'll report you to the colonel.
    He'll throw you in the lock-up. The lieutenant is courting my
    daughter.
THE SERGEANT: No rough stuff, brother. (To MOTHER COUR- 170
    AGE) What have you got against the army? Wasn't his father a
    soldier? Didn't he die fair and square? You said so yourself.

MOTHER COURAGE: He's only a child. You want to lead him off to slaughter, I know you. You'll get five guilders for him.

175 THE RECRUITER: He'll get a beautiful cap and top boots.

EILIF: Not from you.

MOTHER COURAGE: Oh, won't you come fishing with me? said the fisherman to the worm. (To SWISS CHEESE) Run and yell that they're trying to steal your brother. (She pulls a knife) Just

180 try and steal him. I'll cut you down, you dogs. I'll teach you to put him in your war! We do an honest business in ham and shirts, we're peaceful folk.

THE SERGEANT: I can see by the knife how peaceful you are. You ought to be ashamed of yourself, put that knife away, you

185 bitch. A minute ago you admitted you lived off war, how else would you live, on what? How can you have a war without soldiers?

MOTHER COURAGE: It doesn't have to be my children.

THE SERGEANT: I see. You'd like the war to eat the core and spit

190 out the apple. You want your brood to batten on war, tax-free. The war can look out for itself, is that it? You call yourself Courage, eh? And you're afraid of the war that feeds you. Your sons aren't afraid of it, I can see that.

EILIF: I'm not afraid of any war.

195 THE SERGEANT: Why should you be? Look at me: Has the soldier's life disagreed with me? I was seventeen when I joined up.

MOTHER COURAGE: You're not seventy yet.

THE SERGEANT: I can wait.

MOTHER COURAGE: Sure. Under ground.

200 THE SERGEANT: Are you trying to insult me? Telling me I'm going to die?

MOTHER COURAGE: But suppose it's the truth? I can see the mark on you. You look like a corpse on leave.

SWISS CHEESE: She's got second sight. Everybody says so. She

205 can tell the future.

THE RECRUITER: Then tell the sergeant his future. It might amuse him.

THE SERGEANT: I don't believe in that stuff.

MOTHER COURAGE: Give me your helmet. (He gives it to her)

210 THE SERGEANT: It doesn't mean any more than taking a shit in the grass. But go ahead for the laugh.

MOTHER COURAGE: (takes a sheet of parchment and tears it in two) Eilif, Swiss Cheese, Kattrin: That's how we'd all be torn apart if we got mixed up too deep in the war. (To THE SER-

215 GEANT) Seeing it's you, I'll do it for nothing. I make a black cross on this piece. Black is death.

SWISS CHEESE: She leaves the other one blank. Get it?

MOTHER COURAGE: Now I fold them, and now I shake them up together. Same as we're all mixed up together from the cradle

220 to the grave. And now you draw, and you'll know the answer. (THE SERGEANT hesitates)

THE RECRUITER: (to EILIF) I don't take everybody, I'm known to be picky and choosy, but you've got spirit, I like that.

THE SERGEANT: (fishing in the helmet) Damn foolishness! Hocus-

225 pocus!

SWISS CHEESE: He's pulled a black cross. He's through.

THE RECRUITER: Don't let them scare you, there's not enough bullets for everybody.

THE SERGEANT: (hoarsely) You've fouled me up.

230 MOTHER COURAGE: You fouled yourself up the day you joined the army. And now we'll be going, there isn't a war every day, I've got to take advantage.

THE SERGEANT: Hell and damnation! Don't try to hornswoggle me. We're taking your bastard to be a soldier.

EILIF: I'd like to be a soldier, mother. 235

MOTHER COURAGE: You shut your trap, you Finnish devil.

EILIF: Swiss Cheese wants to be a soldier too.

MOTHER COURAGE: That's news to me. I'd better let you draw too, all three of you. (She goes to the rear to mark crosses on slips of parchment) 240

THE RECRUITER: (to EILIF) It's been said to our discredit that a lot of religion goes on in the Swedish camp, but that's slander to blacken our reputation. Hymn singing only on Sunday, one verse! And only if you've got a voice.

MOTHER COURAGE: (comes back with the slips in the sergeant's 245 helmet) Want to sneak away from their mother, the devils, and run off to war like calves to a salt lick. But we'll draw lots on it, then they'll see that the world is no vale of smiles with a "Come along, son, we're short on generals." Sergeant, I'm very much afraid they won't come through the war. They've 250 got terrible characters, all three of them. (She holds out the helmet to EILIF) There. Pick a slip. (He picks one and unfolds it. She snatches it away from him) There you have it. A cross! Oh, unhappy mother that I am, oh, mother of sorrows. Has he got to die? Doomed to perish in the springtime of his life? 255 If he joins the army, he'll bite the dust, that's sure. He's too brave, just like his father. If he's not smart, he'll go the way of all flesh, the slip proves it. (She roars at him) Are you going to be smart?

EILIF: Why not? 260

MOTHER COURAGE: The smart thing to do is to stay with your mother, and if they make fun of you and call you a sissy, just laugh.

THE RECRUITER: If you're shitting in your pants, we'll take your brother. 265

MOTHER COURAGE: I told you to laugh. Laugh! And now you pick, Swiss Cheese. I'm not so worried about you, you're honest. (He picks a slip) Oh! Why, have you got that strange look? It's got to be blank. There can't be a cross on it. No, I can't lose you. (She takes the slip) A cross? Him too? Maybe 270 it's because he's so stupid. Oh, Swiss Cheese, you'll die too, unless you're very honest the whole time, the way I've taught you since you were a baby, always bringing back the change when I sent you to buy bread. That's the only way you can save yourself. Look, sergeant, isn't that a black cross? 275

THE SERGEANT: It's a cross all right. I don't see how I could have pulled one. I always stay in the rear. (To THE RECRUITER) It's on the up and up. Her own get it too.

SWISS CHEESE: I get it too. But I can take a hint.

MOTHER COURAGE: (to KATTRIN) Now you're the only one I'm 280 sure of, you're a cross yourself because you've got a good heart. (She holds up the helmet to KATTRIN in the wagon, but she herself takes out the slip) It's driving me to despair. It can't be right, maybe I mixed them wrong. Don't be too good-natured, Kattrin, don't, there's a cross on your path too. Al- 285 ways keep very quiet, that ought to be easy seeing you're dumb. Well, now you know. Be careful, all of you, you'll need to be. And now we'll climb up and drive on. (She returns THE SERGEANT's helmet and climbs up into the wagon)

THE RECRUITER: (to THE SERGEANT) Do something! 290

THE SERGEANT: I'm not feeling so good.

THE RECRUITER: Maybe you caught cold when you took your

helmet off in the wind. Tell her you want to buy something. Keep her busy. *(Aloud)* You could at least take a look at that
295 buckle, sergeant. After all, selling things is these good people's living. Hey, you, the sergeant wants to buy that belt buckle.

MOTHER COURAGE: Half a guilder. A buckle like that is worth two guilders. *(She climbs down)*

300 THE SERGEANT: It's not new. This wind! I can't examine it here. Let's go where it's quiet. *(He goes behind the wagon with the buckle)*

MOTHER COURAGE: I haven't noticed any wind.

THE SERGEANT: Maybe it is worth half a guilder. It's silver.

305 MOTHER COURAGE: *(joins him behind the wagon)* Six solid ounces.

THE RECRUITER: *(to EILIF)* And then we'll have a drink, just you and me. I've got your enlistment bonus right here. Come on. *(EILIF stands undecided)*

310 MOTHER COURAGE: All right. Half a guilder.

THE SERGEANT: I don't get it. I always stay in the rear. There's no safer place for a sergeant. You can send the men up forward to win glory. You've spoiled my dinner. It won't go down, I know it, not a bite.

315 MOTHER COURAGE: Don't take it to heart. Don't let it spoil your appetite. Just keep behind the lines. Here, take a drink of schnapps, man. *(She hands him the bottle)*

THE RECRUITER: *(has taken EILIF's arm and is pulling him away toward the rear)* A bonus of ten guilders, and you'll be a brave
320 man and you'll fight for the king, and the women will tear each other's hair out over you. And you can clout me one on the kisser for insulting you. *(Both go out)*

(Mute KATTRIN jumps down from the wagon and emits raucous sounds.)

MOTHER COURAGE: Just a minute, Kattrin, just a minute. The sergeant's paying up. *(Bites the half guilder)* I'm always sus-
325 picious of money. I'm a burnt child, sergeant. But your coin is good. And now we'll be going. Where's Eilif?

SWISS CHEESE: He's gone with the recruiter.

MOTHER COURAGE: *(stands motionless, then)* You simple soul. *(To KATTRIN)* I know. You can't talk, you couldn't help it.

330 THE SERGEANT: You could do with a drink yourself, mother. That's the way it goes. Soldiering isn't the worst thing in the world. You want to live off the war, but you want to keep you and yours out of it. Is that it?

MOTHER COURAGE: Now you'll have to pull with your brother,
335 Kattrin.

(Brother and sister harness themselves to the wagon and start pulling. MOTHER COURAGE walks beside them. The wagon rolls off.)

THE SERGEANT: *(looking after them)*
If you want the war to work for you
You've got to give the war its due.

SCENE II

In 1625 and 1626 Mother Courage crosses Poland in the train of the Swedish armies. Outside the fortress of Wallhof she meets her son again. — A capon is successfully sold, the brave son's fortunes are at their zenith.

The general's tent.

Beside it the kitchen. The thunder of cannon. The cook is arguing with MOTHER COURAGE, *who is trying to sell him a capon.*

THE COOK: Sixty hellers for that pathetic bird?

MOTHER COURAGE: Pathetic bird? You mean this plump beauty? Are you trying to tell me that a general who's the biggest eater for miles around—God help you if you haven't got anything for his dinner—can't afford a measly sixty hellers? 5

THE COOK: I can get a dozen like it for ten hellers right around the corner.

MOTHER COURAGE: What, you'll find a capon like this right around the corner? With a siege on and everybody so starved you can see right through them. Maybe you'll scare up a rat, 10 maybe, I say, 'cause they've all been eaten, I've seen five men chasing a starved rat for hours. Fifty hellers for a giant capon in the middle of a siege.

THE COOK: We're not besieged; they are. We're the besiegers, can't you get that through your head? 15

MOTHER COURAGE: But we haven't got anything to eat either, in fact we've got less than the people in the city. They've hauled it all inside. I hear their life is one big orgy. And look at us. I've been around to the peasants, they haven't got a thing.

THE COOK: They've got plenty. They hide it. 20

MOTHER COURAGE: *(triumphantly)* Oh, no! They're ruined, that's what they are. They're starving. I've seen them. They're so hungry they're digging up roots. They lick their fingers when they've eaten a boiled strap. That's the situation. And here I've got a capon and I'm supposed to let it go for forty 25 hellers.

THE COOK: Thirty, not forty. Thirty, I said.

MOTHER COURAGE: It's no common capon. They tell me this bird was so talented that he wouldn't eat unless they played music, he had his own favorite march. He could add and 30 subtract, that's how intelligent he was. And you're trying to tell me forty hellers is too much. The general will bite your head off if there's nothing to eat.

THE COOK: You know what I'm going to do? *(He takes a piece of beef and sets his knife to it)* Here I've got a piece of beef. I'll 35 roast it. Think it over. This is your last chance.

MOTHER COURAGE: Roast and be damned. It's a year old.

THE COOK: A day old. That ox was running around only yesterday afternoon, I saw him with my own eyes.

MOTHER COURAGE: Then he must have stunk on the hoof. 40

THE COOK: I'll cook it five hours if I have to. We'll see if it's still tough. *(He cuts into it)*

MOTHER COURAGE: Use plenty of pepper, maybe the general won't notice the stink.

(THE GENERAL, a CHAPLAIN and EILIF enter the tent.)

THE GENERAL: *(slapping EILIF on the back)* All right, son, into 45 your general's tent you go, you'll sit at my right hand. You've done a heroic deed and you're a pious trooper, because this is a war of religion and what you did was done for God, that's what counts with me. I'll reward you with a gold bracelet when I take the city. We come here to save their souls and 50 what do those filthy, shameless peasants do? They drive their cattle away. And they stuff their priests with meat, front and back. But you taught them a lesson. Here's a tankard of red wine for you. *(He pours)* We'll down it in one gulp. *(They do so)* None for the chaplain, he's got his religion. What would 55 you like for dinner, sweetheart?

EILIF: A scrap of meat. Why not?

THE GENERAL: Cook! Meat!

THE COOK: And now he brings company when there's nothing
to eat.

(Wanting to listen, MOTHER COURAGE *makes him stop talking.)*

EILIF: Cutting down peasants whets the appetite.

MOTHER COURAGE: God, it's my Eilif.

THE COOK: Who?

MOTHER COURAGE: My eldest. I haven't seen hide nor hair of
him in two years, he was stolen from me on the highway. He
must be in good if the general invites him to dinner, and what
have you got to offer? Nothing. Did you hear what the general's guest wants for dinner? Meat! Take my advice, snap up
this capon. The price is one guilder.

THE GENERAL: *(has sat down with* EILIF. *Bellows)* Food, Lamb,
you lousy, no-good cook, or I'll kill you.

THE COOK: All right, hand it over. This is extortion.

MOTHER COURAGE: I thought it was a pathetic bird.

THE COOK: Pathetic is the word. Hand it over. Fifty hellers! It's
highway robbery.

MOTHER COURAGE: One guilder, I say. For my eldest son, the
general's honored guest, I spare no expense.

THE COOK: *(gives her the money)* Then pluck it at least while I
make the fire.

MOTHER COURAGE: *(sits down to pluck the capon)* Won't he be
glad to see me! He's my brave, intelligent son. I've got a stupid
one too, but he's honest. The girl's a total loss. But at least she
doesn't talk, that's something.

THE GENERAL: Take another drink, son, it's my best Falerno,
I've only got another barrel or two at the most, but it's worth it
to see that there's still some true faith in my army. The good
shepherd here just looks on, all he knows how to do is preach.
Can he do anything? No. And now, Eilif my son, tell us all
about it, how cleverly you hoodwinked those peasants and
captured those twenty head of cattle. I hope they'll be here soon.

EILIF: Tomorrow. Maybe the day after.

MOTHER COURAGE: Isn't my Eilif considerate, not bringing
those oxen in until tomorrow, or you wouldn't have even said
hello to my capon.

EILIF: Well, it was like this: I heard the peasants were secretly —
mostly at night — rounding up the oxen they'd hidden in a
certain forest. The city people had arranged to come and get
them. I let them round the oxen up, I figured they'd find
them easier than I would. I made my men ravenous for meat,
put them on short rations for two days until their mouths
watered if they even heard a word beginning with *me* . . . like
measles.

THE GENERAL: That was clever of you.

EILIF: Maybe. The rest was a pushover. Except the peasants had
clubs and there were three times more of them and they fell
on us like bloody murder. Four of them drove me into a
clump of bushes, they knocked my sword out of my hand and
yelled: Surrender! Now what'll I do, I says to myself, they'll
make hash out of me.

THE GENERAL: What did you do?

EILIF: I laughed.

THE GENERAL: You laughed?

EILIF: I laughed. Which led to a conversation. The first thing
you know, I'm bargaining. Twenty guilders is too much for
that ox, I say, how about fifteen? Like I'm meaning to pay.

They're flummoxed, they scratch their heads. Quick, I reach
for my sword and mow them down. Necessity knows no law.
See what I mean?

THE GENERAL: What do you say to that, shepherd?

CHAPLAIN: Strictly speaking, that maxim is not in the Bible. But
our Lord was able to turn five loaves into five hundred. So
there was no question of poverty; he could tell people to love
their neighbors because their bellies were full. Nowadays it's
different.

THE GENERAL: *(laughs)* Very different. All right, you Pharisee,
take a swig. *(To* EILIF) You mowed them down, splendid, so
my fine troops could have a decent bite to eat. Doesn't the
Good Book say: "Whatsoever thou doest for the least of my
brethren, thou doest for me"? And what have you done for
them? You've got them a good chunk of beef for their dinner.
They're not used to moldy crusts; in the old days they had a
helmetful of white bread and wine before they went out to
fight for God.

EILIF: Yes, I reached for my sword and I mowed them down.

THE GENERAL: You're a young Caesar. You deserve to see the
king.

EILIF: I have, in the distance. He shines like a light. He's my ideal.

THE GENERAL: You're something like him already, Eilif. I know
the worth of a brave soldier like you. When I find one, I treat
him like my own son. *(He leads him to the map)* Take a look at
the situation, Eilif; we've still got a long way to go.

MOTHER COURAGE: *(who has been listening starts plucking her
capon furiously)* He must be a rotten general.

THE COOK: Eats like a pig, but why rotten?

MOTHER COURAGE: Because he needs brave soldiers, that's
why. If he planned his campaigns right, what would he need
brave soldiers for? The run-of-the-mill would do. Take it from
me, whenever you find a lot of virtues, it shows that something's wrong.

THE COOK: I'd say it proves that something is all right.

MOTHER COURAGE: No, that something's wrong. See, when a
general or a king is real stupid and leads his men up shit creek,
his troops need courage, that's a virtue. If he's stingy and
doesn't hire enough soldiers, they've all got to be Herculeses.
And if he's a slob and lets everything go to pot, they've got to
be as sly as serpents or they're done for. And if he's always
expecting too much of them, they need an extra dose of loyalty. A country that's run right, or a good king or a good general, doesn't need any of these virtues. You don't need virtues
in a decent country, the people can all be perfectly ordinary,
medium-bright, and cowards too for my money.

THE GENERAL: I bet your father was a soldier.

EILIF: A great soldier, I'm told. My mother warned me about it.
Makes me think of a song.

THE GENERAL: Sing it! *(Bellowing)* Where's that food!

EILIF: It's called: The Song of the Old Wife and the Soldier.

(He sings, doing a war dance with his saber.)

A gun or a pike, they can kill who they like
And the torrent will swallow a wader
You had better think twice before battling with ice
Said the old wife to the soldier.
Cocking his rifle he leapt to his feet
Laughing for joy as he heard the drum beat
The wars cannot hurt me, he told her.
He shouldered his gun and he picked up his knife

175 To see the wide world. That's the soldier's life.
Those were the words of the soldier.
Ah, deep will they lie who wise counsel defy
Learn wisdom from those that are older
Oh, don't venture too high or you'll fall from the sky
180 Said the old wife to the soldier.
But the young soldier with knife and with gun
Only laughed a cold laugh and stepped into the run.
The water can't hurt me, he told her.
And when the moon on the rooftop shines white
185 We'll be coming back. You can pray for that night.
Those were the words of the soldier.

MOTHER COURAGE: (in the kitchen, continues the song, beating
a pot with a spoon)

Like the smoke you'll be gone and no warmth linger on
190 And your deeds only leave me the colder!
Oh, see the smoke race. Oh, dear God keep him safe!
That's what she said of the soldier.

EILIF: What's that?
MOTHER COURAGE: (goes on singing)

195 And the young soldier with knife and with gun
Was swept from his feet till he sank in the run
And the torrent swallowed the waders.
Cold shone the moon on the rooftop white
But the soldier was carried away with the ice
200 And what was it she heard from the soldiers?
Like the smoke he was gone and no warmth lingered on
And his deeds only left her the colder.
Ah, deep will they lie who wise counsel defy!
That's what she said to the soldiers.

205 THE GENERAL: What do they think they're doing in my kitchen?
EILIF: (has gone into the kitchen. He embraces his mother)
Mother! It's you! Where are the others?
MOTHER COURAGE: (in his arms) Snug as a bug in a rug. Swiss
Cheese is paymaster of the Second Regiment; at least he won't
210 be fighting, I couldn't keep him out altogether.
EILIF: And how about your feet?
MOTHER COURAGE: Well, it's hard getting my shoes on in the
morning.
THE GENERAL: (has joined them) Ah, so you're his mother. I
215 hope you've got more sons for me like this fellow here.
EILIF: Am I lucky! There you're sitting in the kitchen hearing
your son being praised.
MOTHER COURAGE: I heard it all right! (She gives him a slap in
the face)
220 EILIF: (holding his cheek) For capturing the oxen?
MOTHER COURAGE: No. For not surrendering when the four of
them were threatening to make hash out of you! Didn't I
teach you to take care of yourself? You Finnish devil!

(THE GENERAL and the chaplain laugh.)

SCENE III

⎡ Three years later Mother Courage and parts of a Finnish
  regiment are taken prisoner. She is able to save her
⎣ daughter and her wagon, but her honest son dies.

Army camp.

Afternoon. On a pole the regimental flag. MOTHER COURAGE
has stretched a clothesline between her wagon, on which all sorts
of merchandise is hung in display, and a large cannon. She and
KATTRIN are folding washing and piling it on the cannon. At the
same time she is negotiating with an ordnance officer over a sack
of bullets. SWISS CHEESE, now in the uniform of a paymaster, is
looking on. A pretty woman, YVETTE POTTIER, is sitting with a
glass of brandy in front of her, sewing a gaudy-colored hat. She is
in her stocking feet, her red high-heeled shoes are on the ground
beside her.

THE ORDNANCE OFFICER: I'll let you have these bullets for two
guilders. It's cheap, I need the money, because the colonel's
been drinking with the officers for two days and we're out of
liquor.
MOTHER COURAGE: That's ammunition for the troops. If it's   5
found here, I'll be court-martialed. You punks sell their bullets and the men have nothing to shoot at the enemy.
THE ORDNANCE OFFICER: Don't be hard-hearted, you scratch
my back, I'll scratch yours.
MOTHER COURAGE: I'm not taking any army property. Not at   10
that price.
THE ORDNANCE OFFICER: You can sell it for five guilders,
maybe eight, to the ordnance officer of the Fourth before the
day is out, if you're quiet about it and give him a receipt for
twelve. He hasn't an ounce of ammunition left.   15
MOTHER COURAGE: Why don't you do it yourself?
THE ORDNANCE OFFICER: Because I don't trust him, he's a
friend of mine.
MOTHER COURAGE: (takes the sack) Hand it over. (To KATTRIN)
Take it back there and pay him one and a half guilders. (In   20
response to THE ORDNANCE OFFICER's protest) One and a half
guilders, I say. (KATTRIN drags the sack behind the wagon,
THE ORDNANCE OFFICER follows her. MOTHER COURAGE to
SWISS CHEESE) Here's your underdrawers, take good care of
them, this is October, might be coming on fall, I don't say it   25
will be, because I've learned that nothing is sure to happen
the way we think, not even the seasons. But whatever happens, your regimental funds have to be in order. Are your
funds in order?
SWISS CHEESE: Yes, mother.   30
MOTHER COURAGE: Never forget that they made you paymaster
because you're honest and not brave like your brother, and
especially because you're too simple-minded to get the idea of
making off with the money. That's a comfort to me. And
don't go mislaying your drawers.   35
SWISS CHEESE: No, mother. I'll put them under my mattress.
(Starts to go)
THE ORDNANCE OFFICER: I'll go with you, paymaster.
MOTHER COURAGE: Just don't teach him any of your tricks.

(Without saying good-bye THE ORDNANCE OFFICER goes out
with SWISS CHEESE.)

YVETTE: (waves her hand after THE ORDNANCE OFFICER) You   40
might say good-bye, officer.
MOTHER COURAGE: (to YVETTE) I don't like to see those two
together. He's not the right kind of company for my Swiss
Cheese. But the war's getting along pretty well. More countries are joining in all the time, it can go on for another four,   45
five years, easy. With a little planning ahead, I can do good
business if I'm careful. Don't you know you shouldn't drink
in the morning with your sickness?

YVETTE: Who says I'm sick, it slander.

50 MOTHER COURAGE: Everybody says so.

YVETTE: Because they're all liars. Mother Courage, I'm desperate. They all keep out of my way like I'm a rotten fish on account of those lies. What's the good of fixing my hat? (*She throws it down*) That's why I drink in the morning. I never

55 used to, I'm getting crow's-feet, but it doesn't matter now. In the Second Finnish Regiment they all know me. I should have stayed home when my first love walked out on me. Pride isn't for the likes of us. If we can't put up with shit, we're through.

60 MOTHER COURAGE: Just don't start in on your Pieter and how it all happened in front of my innocent daughter.

YVETTE: She's just the one to hear it, it'll harden her against love.

MOTHER COURAGE: Nothing can harden them.

YVETTE: Then I'll talk about it because it makes me feel better.

65 It begins with my growing up in fair Flanders, because if I hadn't I'd never have laid eyes on him and I wouldn't be here in Poland now, because he was an army cook, blond, a Dutchman, but skinny. Kattrin, watch out for the skinny ones, but I didn't know that then, and another thing I didn't

70 know is that he had another girl even then, and they all called him Pete the Pipe, because he didn't even take his pipe out of his mouth when he was doing it, that's all it meant to him. (*She sings the Song of Fraternization.*)

When I was only sixteen
75 The foe came into our land.
He laid aside his sabre
And with a smile he took my hand.
    After the May parade
    The May light starts to fade.
80   The regiment dressed by the right
    Then drums were beaten, that's the drill.
    The foe took us behind the hill
    And fraternized all night.

There were so many foes came
85 And mine worked in the mess.
I loathed him in the daytime.
At night I loved him none the less.
    After the May parade
    The May light starts to fade.
90   The regiment dressed by the right
    Then drums were beaten, that's the drill.
    The foe took us behind the hill
    And fraternized all night.

The love which came upon me
95 Was wished on me by fate.
My friends could never grasp why
I found it hard to share their hate.
    The fields were wet with dew
    When sorrow first I knew.
100   The regiment dressed by the right
    Then drums were beaten, that's the drill
    And then the foe, my lover still
    Went marching from our sight.

Well, I followed him, but I never found him. That was five
105 years ago. (*She goes behind the wagon with an unsteady gait.*)

MOTHER COURAGE: You've left your hat.

YVETTE: Anybody that wants it can have it.

MOTHER COURAGE: Let that be a lesson to you, Kattrin. Have no truck with soldiers. It's love that makes the world go round, so you'd better watch out. Even with a civilian it's no picnic. 110 He says he'd kiss the ground you put your little feet on, talking of feet, did you wash yours yesterday, and then you're his slave. Be glad you're dumb, that way you'll never contradict yourself or want to bite your tongue off because you've told the truth, it's a gift of God to be dumb. Here comes the general's cook, I wonder what he wants. 115

(THE COOK *and* THE CHAPLAIN *enter*.)

THE CHAPLAIN: I've got a message for you from your son Eilif. The cook here thought he'd come along, he's taken a shine to you.

THE COOK: I only came to get a breath of air. 120

MOTHER COURAGE: You can always do that here if you behave, and if you don't, I can handle you. Well, what does he want? I've got no money to spare.

THE CHAPLAIN: Actually he wanted me to see his brother, the paymaster. 125

MOTHER COURAGE: He's not here any more, or anywhere else either. He's not his brother's paymaster. I don't want him leading him into temptation and being smart at his expense. (*Gives him money from the bag slung around her waist*) Give him this, it's a sin, he's speculating on mother love and he 130 ought to be ashamed.

THE COOK: He won't do it much longer, then he'll be marching off with his regiment, maybe to his death, you never can tell. Better make it a little more, you'll be sorry later. You women are hard-hearted, but afterwards you're sorry. A drop of 135 brandy wouldn't have cost much when it was wanted, but it wasn't given, and later, for all you know, he'll be lying in the cold ground and you can't dig him up again.

THE CHAPLAIN: Don't be sentimental, cook. There's nothing wrong with dying in battle, it's a blessing, and I'll tell you 140 why. This is a war of religion. Not a common war, but a war for the faith, and therefore pleasing to God.

THE COOK: That's a fact. In a way you could call it a war, because of the extortion and killing and looting, not to mention a bit of rape, but it's a war of religion, which makes it different 145 from all other wars, that's obvious. But it makes a man thirsty all the same, you've got to admit that.

THE CHAPLAIN: (*To* MOTHER COURAGE, *pointing at* THE COOK) I tried to discourage him, but he says you've turned his head, he sees you in his dreams. 150

THE COOK: (*lights a short-stemmed pipe*) All I want is a glass of brandy from your fair hand, nothing more sinful. I'm already so shocked by the jokes the chaplain's been telling me, I bet I'm still red in the face.

MOTHER COURAGE: And him a clergyman! I'd better give you 155 fellows something to drink or you'll be making me immoral propositions just to pass the time.

THE CHAPLAIN: This is temptation, said the deacon, and succumbed to it. (*Turning toward* KATTRIN *as he leaves*) And who is this delightful young lady? 160

MOTHER COURAGE: She's not delightful, she's a respectable young lady.

(THE CHAPLAIN *and* THE COOK *go behind the wagon with* MOTHER COURAGE. KATTRIN *looks after them, then she walks away from the washing and approaches the hat. She picks it up, sits down and puts on the red shoes. From the rear* MOTHER COURAGE *is heard talking politics with* THE CHAPLAIN *and* THE COOK.)

MOTHER COURAGE: The Poles here in Poland shouldn't have butted in. All right, our king marched his army into their country. But instead of keeping the peace, the Poles start butting into their own affairs and attack the king while he's marching quietly through the landscape. That was a breach of the peace and the blood is on their head.

THE CHAPLAIN: Our king had only one thing in mind: freedom. The emperor had everybody under his yoke, the Poles as much as the Germans; the king had to set them free.

THE COOK: I see it this way, your brandy's first-rate, I can see why I liked your face, but we were talking about the king. This freedom he was trying to introduce into Germany cost him a fortune, he had to levy a salt tax in Sweden, which, as I said, cost the poor people a fortune. Then he had to put the Germans in jail and break them on the rack because they liked being the emperor's slaves. Oh yes, the king made short shrift of anybody that didn't want to be free. In the beginning he only wanted to protect Poland against wicked people, especially the emperor, but the more he ate the more he wanted, and pretty soon he was protecting all of Germany. But the Germans didn't take it lying down and the king got nothing but trouble for all his kindness and expense, which he naturally had to defray from taxes, which made for bad blood, but that didn't discourage him. He had one thing in his favor, the word of God, which was lucky, because otherwise people would have said he was doing it all for himself and what he hoped to get out of it. As it was, he always had a clear conscience and that was all he really cared about.

MOTHER COURAGE: It's easy to see you're not a Swede, or you wouldn't talk like that about the Hero-King.

THE CHAPLAIN: You're eating his bread, aren't you?

THE COOK: I don't eat his bread, I bake it.

MOTHER COURAGE: He can't be defeated because his men believe in him. *(Earnestly)* When you listen to the big wheels talk, they're making war for reasons of piety, in the name of everything that's fine and noble. But when you take another look, you see that they're not so dumb; they're making war for profit. If they weren't, the small fry like me wouldn't have anything to do with it.

THE COOK: That's a fact.

THE CHAPLAIN: And it wouldn't hurt you as a Dutchman to take a look at that flag up there before you express opinions in Poland.

MOTHER COURAGE: We're all good Protestants here! Prosit!

(KATTRIN *has started strutting about with* YVETTE's *hat on, imitating* YVETTE's *gait.*)

(*Suddenly cannon fire and shots are heard. Drums.* MOTHER COURAGE, THE COOK *and* THE CHAPLAIN *run out from behind the wagon, the two men still with glasses in hand.* THE ORDNANCE OFFICER *and a* SOLDIER *rush up to the cannon and try to push it away.*)

MOTHER COURAGE: What's going on? Let me get my washing first, you lugs. (*She tries to rescue her washing*)

THE ORDNANCE OFFICER: The Catholics. They're attacking. I don't know as we'll get away. (*To the* SOLDIER) Get rid of the gun! (*Runs off*)

THE COOK: Christ, I've got to find the general. Courage, I'll be back for a little chat in a day or two. (*Rushes out*)

MOTHER COURAGE: Stop, you've forgotten your pipe.

THE COOK: (*from a distance*) Keep it for me! I'll need it.

MOTHER COURAGE: Just when we were making a little money!

THE CHAPLAIN: Well, I guess I'll be going too. It might be dangerous though, with the enemy so close. Blessed are the peaceful is the best motto in wartime. If only I had a cloak to cover up with.

MOTHER COURAGE: I'm not lending any cloaks, not on your life. I've had bitter experience in that line.

THE CHAPLAIN: But my religion puts me in special danger.

MOTHER COURAGE: (*bringing him a cloak*) It's against my better conscience. And now run along.

THE CHAPLAIN: Thank you kindly, you've got a good heart. But maybe I'd better sit here a while. The enemy might get suspicious if they see me running.

MOTHER COURAGE: (*to* THE SOLDIER) Leave it lay, you fool, you won't get paid extra. I'll take care of it for you, you'd only get killed.

THE SOLDIER: (*running away*) I tried. You're my witness.

MOTHER COURAGE: I'll swear it on the Bible. (*Sees her daughter with the hat*) What are you doing with that floozy hat? Take it off, have you gone out of your mind? Now of all times, with the enemy on top of us? (*She tears the hat off* KATTRIN's *head*) You want them to find you and make a whore out of you? And those shoes! Take them off, you woman of Babylon! (*She tries to pull them off*) Jesus Christ, chaplain, make her take those shoes off! I'll be right back. (*She runs to the wagon*)

YVETTE: (*enters, powdering her face*) What's this I hear? The Catholics are coming? Where's my hat? Who's been stamping on it? I can't be seen like this if the Catholics are coming. What'll they think of me? I haven't even got a mirror. (*To* THE CHAPLAIN) How do I look? Too much powder?

THE CHAPLAIN: Just right.

YVETTE: And where are my red shoes? (*She doesn't see them because* KATTRIN *hides her feet under her skirt*) I left them here. I've got to get back to my tent. In my bare feet. It's disgraceful! (*Goes out*)

(SWISS CHEESE *runs in carrying a small box.*)

MOTHER COURAGE: (*Comes out with her hands full of ashes. To* KATTRIN) Ashes. (*To* SWISS CHEESE) What you got there?

SWISS CHEESE: The regimental funds.

MOTHER COURAGE: Throw it away! No more paymastering for you.

SWISS CHEESE: I'm responsible for it. (*He goes rear*)

MOTHER COURAGE: (*to* THE CHAPLAIN) Take your clergyman's coat off, chaplain, or they'll recognize you, cloak or no cloak. (*She rubs* KATTRIN's *face with ashes*) Hold still! There. With a little dirt you'll be safe. What a mess! The sentries were drunk. Hide your light under a bushel, as the Good Book says. When a soldier, especially a Catholic, sees a clean face, she's a whore before she knows it. Nobody feeds them for weeks. When they finally loot some provisions, the next thing they want is women. That'll do it. Let me look at you. Not bad. Like you'd been wallowing in a pigsty. Stop shaking.

You're safe now. *(To* SWISS CHEESE*)* What did you do with the cashbox?

SWISS CHEESE: I thought I'd put it in the wagon.

270 MOTHER COURAGE: *(horrified)* What! In my wagon? Of all the sinful stupidity! If my back is turned for half a second! They'll hang us all!

SWISS CHEESE: Then I'll put it somewhere else, or I'll run away with it.

275 MOTHER COURAGE: You'll stay right here. It's too late.

THE CHAPLAIN: *(still changing, comes forward)* Heavens, the flag!

MOTHER COURAGE: *(takes down the regimental flag)* Bozhe moi! I'm so used to it I don't see it. Twenty-five years I've had it.

(The cannon fire grows louder.)

(Morning, three days later. The cannon is gone. MOTHER COUR-AGE, KATTRIN, THE CHAPLAIN *and* SWISS CHEESE *are sitting dejectedly over a meal.)*

SWISS CHEESE: This is the third day I've been sitting here doing 280 nothing; the sergeant has always been easy on me, but now he must be starting to wonder: where can Swiss Cheese be with the cashbox?

MOTHER COURAGE: Be glad they haven't tracked you down.

THE CHAPLAIN: What about me? I can't hold a service here either. 285 The Good Book says: "Whosoever hath a full heart, his tongue runneth over." Heaven help me if mine runneth over.

MOTHER COURAGE: That's the way it is. Look what I've got on my hands: one with a religion and one with a cashbox. I don't know which is worse.

290 THE CHAPLAIN: Tell yourself that we're in the hands of God.

MOTHER COURAGE: I don't think we're that bad off, but all the same I can't sleep at night. If it weren't for you, Swiss Cheese, it'd be easier. I think I've put myself in the clear. I told them I was against the antichrist; he's a Swede with horns, I told 295 them, and I'd noticed the left horn was kind of worn down. I interrupted the questioning to ask where I could buy holy candles cheap. I knew what to say because Swiss Cheese's father was a Catholic and he used to make jokes about it. They didn't really believe me, but their regiment had no pro-300 visioner, so they looked the other way. Maybe we stand to gain. We're prisoners, but so are lice on a dog.

THE CHAPLAIN: This milk is good. Though there's not very much of it or of anything else. Maybe we'll have to cut down on our Swedish appetites. But such is the lot of the vanquished.

305 MOTHER COURAGE: Who's vanquished? Victory and defeat don't always mean the same thing to the big wheels up top and the small fry underneath. Not by a long shot. In some cases defeat is a blessing to the small fry. Honor's lost, but nothing else. One time in Livonia our general got such a 310 shellacking from the enemy that in the confusion I laid hands on a beautiful white horse from the baggage train. That horse pulled my wagon for seven months, until we had a victory and they checked up. On the whole, you can say that victory and defeat cost us plain people plenty. The best thing for us is 315 when politics gets bogged down. *(To* SWISS CHEESE*)* Eat!

SWISS CHEESE: I've lost my appetite. How's the sergeant going to pay the men?

MOTHER COURAGE: Troops never get paid when they're running away.

320 SWISS CHEESE: But they've got it coming to them. If they're not paid, they don't need to run. Not a step.

MOTHER COURAGE: Swiss Cheese, you're too conscientious, it almost frightens me. I brought you up to be honest, because you're not bright, but somewhere it's got to stop. And now me and the chaplain are going to buy a Catholic flag and some 325 meat. Nobody can buy meat like the chaplain, he goes into a trance and heads straight for the best piece, I guess it makes his mouth water and that shows him the way. At least they let me carry on my business. Nobody cares about a shopkeeper's religion, all they want to know is the price. Protestant pants 330 are as warm as any other kind.

THE CHAPLAIN: Like the friar said when somebody told him the Lutherans were going to stand the whole country on its head. They'll always need beggars, he says. (MOTHER COURAGE *disappears into the wagon*) But she's worried about that cash-335 box. They've taken no notice of us so far, they think we're all part of the wagon. But how long can that go on?

SWISS CHEESE: I can take it away.

THE CHAPLAIN: That would be almost more dangerous. What if somebody sees you? They've got spies. Yesterday morning, 340 just as I'm relieving myself, one of them jumps out of the ditch. I was so scared I almost let out a prayer. That would have given me away. I suppose they think they can tell a Pro-testant by the smell of his shit. He was a little runt with a patch over one eye. 345

MOTHER COURAGE: *(climbing down from the wagon with a bas-ket)* Look what I've found. You shameless slut! *(She holds up the red shoes triumphantly)* Yvette's red shoes! She's swiped them in cold blood. It's your fault. Who told her she was a delightful young lady? *(She puts them into the basket)* I'm 350 giving them back. Stealing Yvette's shoes! She ruins herself for money, that I can understand. But you'd like to do it free of charge, for pleasure. I've told you, you'll have to wait for peace. No soldiers! Just wait for peace with your worldly ways.

THE CHAPLAIN: She doesn't seem very worldly to me. 355

MOTHER COURAGE: Too worldly for me. In Dalarna she was like a stone, which is all they've got around there. The people used to say: We don't see the cripple. That's the way I like it. That way she's safe. *(To* SWISS CHEESE*)* You leave that box where it is, hear? And keep an eye on your sister, she needs it. 360 The two of you will be the death of me. I'd sooner take care of a bag of fleas. *(She goes off with* THE CHAPLAIN. KATTRIN *starts clearing away the dishes.)*

SWISS CHEESE: Won't be many more days when I can sit in the sun in my shirtsleeves. (KATTRIN *points to a tree*) Yes, the 365 leaves are all yellow. (KATTRIN *asks him, by means of gestures, whether he wants a drink*) Not now. I'm thinking. *(Pause)* She says she can't sleep. I'd better get the cashbox out of here, I've found a hiding place. All right, get me a drink. (KATTRIN *goes behind the wagon*) I'll hide it in the rabbit hole down by the 370 river until I can take it away. Maybe late tonight. I'll go get it and take it to the regiment. I wonder how far they've run in three days? Won't the sergeant be surprised! Well, Swiss Cheese, this is a pleasant disappointment, that's what he'll say. I trust you with the regimental cashbox and you bring it 375 back.

(As KATTRIN *comes out from behind the wagon with a glass of brandy, she comes face to face with two men. One is a* SER-GEANT. *The other removes his hat and swings it through the air in a ceremonious greeting. He has a patch over one eye.)*

THE MAN WITH THE PATCH: Good morning, my dear. Have you by any chance seen a man from the headquarters of the Second Finnish Regiment?

(*Scared out of her wits*, KATTRIN *runs front, spilling the brandy. The two exchange looks and withdraw after seeing* SWISS CHEESE *sitting there.*)

380 SWISS CHEESE: (*starting up from his thoughts*) You've spilled half of it. What's the fuss about? Poke yourself in the eye? I don't understand you. I'm getting out of here, I've made up my mind, it's best. (*He stands up. She does everything she can think of to call his attention to the danger. He only evades her.*)
385 I wish I could understand you. Poor thing, I know you're trying to tell me something, you just can't say it. Don't worry about spilling the brandy, I'll be drinking plenty more. What's one glass? (*He takes the cashbox out of the wagon and hides it under his jacket*) I'll be right back. Let me go, you're
390 making me angry. I know you mean well. If only you could talk.

(*When she tries to hold him back, he kisses her and tears himself away. He goes out. She is desperate, she races back and forth, uttering short inarticulate sounds.* THE CHAPLAIN *and* MOTHER COURAGE *come back.* KATTRIN *gesticulates wildly at her mother.*)

MOTHER COURAGE: What's the matter? You're all upset. Has somebody hurt you? Where's Swiss Cheese? Tell it to me in order, Kattrin. Your mother understands you. What, the no-good's taken the cashbox? I'll hit him over the head with it,
395 the sneak. Take your time, don't talk nonsense, use your hands, I don't like it when you howl like a dog, what will the chaplain think? It gives him the creeps. A one-eyed man?
THE CHAPLAIN: The one-eyed man is a spy. Did they arrest Swiss Cheese? (KATTRIN *shakes her head and shrugs her shoul-*
400 *ders*) We're done for.
MOTHER COURAGE: (*takes a Catholic flag out of her basket.* THE CHAPLAIN *fastens it to the flagpole*) Hoist the new flag!
THE CHAPLAIN: (*bitterly*) All good Catholics here.

(*Voices are heard from the rear. The two men bring in* SWISS CHEESE.)

SWISS CHEESE: Let me go, I haven't got anything. Stop twisting
405 my shoulder, I'm innocent.
THE SERGEANT: He belongs here. You know each other.
MOTHER COURAGE: What makes you think that?
SWISS CHEESE: I don't know them. I don't even know who they are. I had a meal here, it cost me ten hellers. Maybe you saw
410 me sitting here, it was too salty.
THE SERGEANT: Who are you anyway?
MOTHER COURAGE: We're respectable people. And it's true. He had a meal here. He said it was too salty.
THE SERGEANT: Are you trying to tell me you don't know each
415 other?
MOTHER COURAGE: Why should I know him? I don't know everybody. I don't ask people what their name is or if they're heathens; if they pay, they're not heathens. Are you a heathen?
SWISS CHEESE: Of course not.
420 THE CHAPLAIN: He ate his meal and he behaved himself. He didn't open his mouth except when he was eating. Then you have to.
THE SERGEANT: And who are you?

MOTHER COURAGE: He's only my bartender. You gentlemen must be thirsty, I'll get you a drink of brandy, you must be hot 425
and tired.
THE SERGEANT: We don't drink on duty. (*To* SWISS CHEESE) You were carrying something. You must have hidden it by the river. You had something under your jacket when you left here.
MOTHER COURAGE: Was it really him? 430
SWISS CHEESE: I think you must have seen somebody else. I saw a man running with something under his jacket. You've got the wrong man.
MOTHER COURAGE: That's what I think too, it's a misunderstanding. These things happen. I'm a good judge of people, 435
I'm Mother Courage, you've heard of me, everybody knows me. Take it from me, this man has an honest face.
THE SERGEANT: We're looking for the cashbox of the Second Finnish Regiment. We know what the man in charge of it looks like. We've been after him for two days. You're him. 440
SWISS CHEESE: I'm not.
THE SERGEANT: Hand it over. If you don't you're a goner, you know that. Where is it?
MOTHER COURAGE: (*with urgency*) He'd hand it over, wouldn't he, knowing he was a goner if he didn't? I've got it, he'd say, 445
take it, you're stronger. He's not that stupid. Speak up, you stupid idiot, the sergeant's giving you a chance.
SWISS CHEESE: But I haven't got it.
THE SERGEANT: In that case come along. We'll get it out of you.

(*They lead him away.*)

MOTHER COURAGE: (*shouts after him*) He'd tell you. He's not 450
that stupid. And don't twist his shoulder off! (*Runs after them*)

(*The same evening.* THE CHAPLAIN *and mute* KATTRIN *are washing dishes and scouring knives.*)

THE CHAPLAIN: That boy's in trouble. There are cases like that in the Bible. Take the Passion of our Lord and Saviour. There's an old song about it. (*He sings the Song of the Hours*)

> In the first hour Jesus mild 455
> Who had prayed since even
> Was betrayed and led before
> Pontius the heathen.
>
> Pilate found him innocent
> Free from fault and error. 460
> Therefore, having washed his hands
> Sent him to King Herod.
>
> In the third hour he was scourged
> Stripped and clad in scarlet
> And a plaited crown of thorns 465
> Set upon his forehead.
>
> On the Son of Man they spat
> Mocked him and made merry.
> Then the cross of death was brought
> Given him to carry. 470
>
> At the sixth hour with two thieves
> To the cross they nailed him
> And the people and the thieves
> Mocked him and reviled him.
>
> This is Jesus King of Jews 475
> Cried they in derision

Till the sun withdrew its light
From that awful vision.
480 At the ninth hour Jesus wailed
Why hast thou me forsaken?
Soldiers brought him vinegar
Which he left untaken.

Then he yielded up the ghost
And the earth was shaken.
485 Rended was the temple's veil
And the saints were wakened.

Soldiers broke the two thieves' legs
As the night descended
Thrust a spear in Jesus' side
490 When his life had ended.

Still they mocked, as from his wound
Flowed the blood and water
Thus blasphemed the Son of Man
With their cruel laughter.

495 MOTHER COURAGE: (enters in a state of agitation) His life's at
stake. But they say the sergeant will listen to reason. Only it
mustn't come out that he's our Swiss Cheese, or they'll say
we've been giving him aid and comfort. All they want is
money. But where will we get the money? Hasn't Yvette been
500 here? I met her just now, she's latched onto a colonel, he's
thinking of buying her a provisioner's business.

THE CHAPLAIN: Are you really thinking of selling?

MOTHER COURAGE: How else can I get the money for the
sergeant?

505 THE CHAPLAIN: But what will you live on?

MOTHER COURAGE: That's the hitch.

(YVETTE POTTIER comes in with a doddering colonel.)

YVETTE: (embracing MOTHER COURAGE) My dear Mother
Courage. Here we are again! (Whispering) He's willing.
(Aloud) This is my dear friend who advises me on business
510 matters. I just chanced to hear that you wish to sell your
wagon, due to circumstances. I might be interested.

MOTHER COURAGE: Mortgage it, not sell it, let's not be hasty.
It's not so easy to buy a wagon like this in wartime.

YVETTE: (disappointed) Only mortgage it? I thought you wanted
515 to sell it. In that case, I don't know if I'm interested. (To THE
COLONEL) What do you think?

THE COLONEL: Just as you say, my dear.

MOTHER COURAGE: It's only being mortgaged.

YVETTE: I thought you needed money.

520 MOTHER COURAGE: (firmly) I need the money, but I'd rather
run myself ragged looking for an offer than sell now. The
wagon is our livelihood. It's an opportunity for you, Yvette,
God knows when you'll find another like it and have such a
good friend to advise you. See what I mean?

525 YVETTE: My friend thinks I should snap it up, but I don't know.
If it's only being mortgaged . . . Don't you agree that we ought
to buy?

THE COLONEL: Yes, my dear.

MOTHER COURAGE: Then you'll have to look for something
530 that's for sale, maybe you'll find something if you take your
time and your friend goes around with you. Maybe in a week
or two you'll find the right thing.

YVETTE: Then we'll go looking, I love to go looking for things,
and I love to go around with you, Poldi, it's a real pleasure.
Even if it takes two weeks. When would you pay the money 535
back if you get it?

MOTHER COURAGE: I can pay it back in two weeks, maybe one.

YVETTE: I can't make up my mind, Poldi, chéri, tell me what to
do. (She takes THE COLONEL aside) I know she's got to sell,
that's definite. The lieutenant, you know who I mean, the 540
blond one, he'd be glad to lend me the money. He's mad
about me, he says I remind him of somebody. What do you
think?

THE COLONEL: Keep away from that lieutenant. He's no good.
He'll take advantage. Haven't I told you I'd buy you some- 545
thing, pussykins?

YVETTE: I can't accept it from you. But then if you think the
lieutenant might take advantage . . . Poldi, I'll accept it from
you.

THE COLONEL: I hope so. 550

YVETTE: Your advice is to take it?

THE COLONEL: That's my advice.

YVETTE: (goes back to MOTHER COURAGE) My friend advises
me to do it. Write me out a receipt, say the wagon belongs to
me complete with stock and furnishings when the two weeks 555
are up. We'll take inventory right now, then I'll bring you the
two hundred guilders. (To THE COLONEL) You go back to
camp, I'll join you in a little while, I've got to take inventory, I
don't want anything missing from my wagon. (She kisses him.
He leaves. She climbs up in the wagon) I don't see very many 560
boots.

MOTHER COURAGE: Yvette. This is no time to inspect your
wagon if it is yours. You promised to see the sergeant about
my Swiss Cheese, you've got to hurry. They say he's to be
court-martialed in an hour. 565

YVETTE: Just let me count the shirts.

MOTHER COURAGE: (pulls her down by the skirt) You hyena, it's
Swiss Cheese, his life's at stake. And don't tell anybody where
the offer comes from, in heaven's name say it's your gentleman friend, or we'll all get it, they'll say we helped him. 570

YVETTE: I've arranged to meet One-Eye in the woods, he must
be there already.

THE CHAPLAIN: And there's no need to start out with the whole
two hundred, offer a hundred and fifty, that's plenty.

MOTHER COURAGE: Is it your money? You just keep out of this. 575
Don't worry, you'll get your bread and soup. Go on now and
don't haggle. It's his life. (She gives YVETTE a push to start her
on her way)

THE CHAPLAIN: I didn't mean to butt in, but what are we going
to live on? You've got an unemployable daughter on your 580
hands.

MOTHER COURAGE: You muddlehead, I'm counting on the regimental cashbox. They'll allow for his expenses, won't they?

THE CHAPLAIN: But will she handle it right?

MOTHER COURAGE: It's in her own interest. If I spend her two 585
hundred, she gets the wagon. She's mighty keen on it, how
long can she expect to hold on to her colonel? Kattrin, you
scour the knives, use pumice. And you, don't stand around
like Jesus on the Mount of Olives, bestir yourself, wash those
glasses, we're expecting at least fifty for dinner, and then it'll 590
be the same old story: "Oh my feet, I'm not used to running
around, I don't run around in the pulpit." I think they'll set

him free. Thank God they're open to bribery. They're not wolves, they're human and out for money. Bribe-taking in humans is the same as mercy in God. It's our only hope. As long as people take bribes, you'll have mild sentences and even the innocent will get off once in a while.

YVETTE: (comes in panting) They want two hundred. And we've got to be quick. Or it'll be out of their hands. I'd better take One-Eye to see my colonel right away. He confessed that he'd had the cashbox, they put the thumb screws on him. But he threw it in the river when he saw they were after him. The box is gone. Should I run and get the money from my colonel?

MOTHER COURAGE: The box is gone? How will I get my two hundred back?

YVETTE: Ah, so you thought you could take it out of the cashbox? You thought you'd put one over on me. Forget it. If you want to save Swiss Cheese, you'll just have to pay, or maybe you'd like me to drop the whole thing and let you keep your wagon?

MOTHER COURAGE: This is something I hadn't reckoned with. But don't rush me, you'll get the wagon, I know it's down the drain, I've had it for seventeen years. Just let me think a second, it's all so sudden. What'll I do, I can't give them two hundred, I guess you should have bargained. If I haven't got a few guilders to fall back on, I'll be at the mercy of the first Tom, Dick, or Harry. Say I'll give them a hundred and twenty, I'll lose my wagon anyway.

YVETTE: They won't go along. One-Eye's in a hurry, he's so keyed-up he keeps looking behind him. Hadn't I better give them the whole two hundred?

MOTHER COURAGE: (in despair) I can't do it. Thirty years I've worked. She's twenty-five and no husband. I've got her to keep too. Don't needle me, I know what I'm doing. Say a hundred and twenty or nothing doing.

YVETTE: It's up to you. (Goes out quickly)

(MOTHER COURAGE looks neither at THE CHAPLAIN nor at her daughter. She sits down to help KATTRIN scour the knives.)

MOTHER COURAGE: Watch what you're doing, you'll cut yourself. Swiss Cheese will be back, I'll pay two hundred if I have to. You'll have your brother. With eighty guilders we can buy a peddler's pack and start all over. Worse things have happened.

THE CHAPLAIN: The Lord will provide.

MOTHER COURAGE: Rub them dry. (They scour the knives in silence. Suddenly KATTRIN runs sobbing behind the wagon)

YVETTE: (comes running) They won't go along. I warned you. One-Eye wanted to run out on me, he said it was no use. He said we'd hear the drums any minute, meaning he'd been sentenced. I offered a hundred and fifty. He didn't even bother to shrug his shoulders. When I begged and pleaded, he promised to wait till I'd spoken to you again.

MOTHER COURAGE: Say I'll give him the two hundred. Run. (YVETTE runs off. They sit in silence. THE CHAPLAIN has stopped washing the glasses) Maybe I bargained too long. (Drums are heard in the distance. THE CHAPLAIN stands up and goes to the rear. MOTHER COURAGE remains seated. It grows dark. The drums stop. It grows light again. MOTHER COURAGE has not moved.)

YVETTE: (enters, very pale) Now you've done it with your haggling and wanting to keep your wagon. Eleven bullets he got,

that's all. I don't know why I bother with you any more, you don't deserve it. But I've picked up a little information. They don't believe the cashbox is really in the river. They suspect it's here and they think you were connected with him. They're going to bring him here, they think maybe you'll give yourself away when you see him. I'm warning you: You don't know him, or you're all dead ducks. I may as well tell you, they're right behind me. Should I keep Kattrin out of the way? (MOTHER COURAGE shakes her head) Does she know? Maybe she didn't hear the drums or maybe she didn't understand.

MOTHER COURAGE: She knows. Get her.

(YVETTE brings KATTRIN, who goes to her mother and stands beside her. MOTHER COURAGE takes her by the hand. Two SOLDIERS come in with a stretcher on which something is lying under a sheet. THE SERGEANT walks beside them. They set the stretcher down.)

THE SERGEANT: We've got a man here and we don't know his name. We need it for the records. He had a meal with you. Take a look, see if you know him. (He removes the sheet) Do you know him? (MOTHER COURAGE shakes her head) What? You'd never seen him before he came here for a meal? (MOTHER COURAGE shakes her head) Pick him up. Throw him on the dump. Nobody knows him. (They carry him away)

SCENE IV

⌐ Mother Courage sings the Song of the Great Capitulation. ⌐

Outside an officer's tent.

MOTHER COURAGE *is waiting. A clerk looks out of the tent.*

THE CLERK: I know you. You had a Protestant paymaster at your place, he was hiding. I wouldn't put in any complaints if I were you.

MOTHER COURAGE: I'm putting in a complaint. I'm innocent. If I take this lying down, it'll look as if I had a guilty conscience. First they ripped up my whole wagon with their sabers, then they wanted me to pay a fine of five talers for no reason at all.

THE CLERK: I'm advising you for your own good: Keep your trap shut. We haven't got many provisioners and we'll let you keep on with your business, especially if you've got a guilty conscience and pay a fine now and then.

MOTHER COURAGE: I'm putting in a complaint.

THE CLERK: Have it your way. But you'll have to wait till the captain can see you. (Disappears into the tent)

A YOUNG SOLDIER: (enters in a rage) Bouque la Madonne! Where's that stinking captain? He's embezzled my reward and now he's drinking it up with his whores. I'm going to get him!

AN OLDER SOLDIER: (comes running after him) Shut up. They'll put you in the stocks!

THE YOUNG SOLDIER: Come on out, you crook! I'll make chops out of you. Embezzling my reward! Who jumps in the river? Not another man in the whole squad, only me. And I can't even buy myself a beer. I won't stand for it. Come on out and let me cut you to pieces!

THE OLDER SOLDIER: Holy Mary! He'll ruin himself.

MOTHER COURAGE: They didn't give him a reward?

THE YOUNG SOLDIER: Let me go. I'll run you through too, the more the merrier.

30 THE OLDER SOLDIER: He saved the colonel's horse and they didn't give him a reward. He's young, he hasn't been around long.

MOTHER COURAGE: Let him go, he's not a dog, you don't have to tie him up. Wanting a reward is perfectly reasonable. Why
35 else would he distinguish himself?

THE YOUNG SOLDIER: And him drinking in there! You're all a lot of yellowbellies. I distinguished myself and I want my reward.

MOTHER COURAGE: Young man, don't shout at me. I've got my
40 own worries and besides, go easy on your voice, you may need it. You'll be hoarse when the captain comes out, you won't be able to say boo and he won't be able to put you in the stocks till you're blue in the face. People that yell like that don't last long, maybe half an hour, then they're so exhausted you have
45 to sing them to sleep.

THE YOUNG SOLDIER: I'm not exhausted and who wants to sleep? I'm hungry. They make our bread out of acorns and hemp seed, and they skimp on that. He's whoring away my reward and I'm hungry. I'll murder him.

50 MOTHER COURAGE: I see. You're hungry. Last year your general made you cut across the fields to trample down the grain. I could have sold a pair of boots for ten guilders if anybody's had ten guilders and if I'd had any boots. He thought he'd be someplace else this year, but now he's still here and every-
55 body's starving. I can see that you might be good and mad.

THE YOUNG SOLDIER: He can't do this to me, save your breath, I won't put up with injustice.

MOTHER COURAGE: You're right, but for how long? How long won't you put up with injustice? An hour? Two hours? You
60 see, you never thought of that, though it's very important, because it's miserable in the stocks when it suddenly dawns on you that you *can* put up with injustice.

THE YOUNG SOLDIER: I don't know why I listen to you. Bouque la Madonne! Where's the captain?

65 MOTHER COURAGE: You listen to me because I'm not telling you anything new. You know your temper has gone up in smoke, it was a short temper and you need a long one, but that's a hard thing to come by.

THE YOUNG SOLDIER: Are you trying to say I've no right to
70 claim my reward?

MOTHER COURAGE: Not at all. I'm only saying your temper isn't long enough, it won't get you anywhere. Too bad. If you had a long temper, I'd even egg you on. Chop the bastard up, that's what I'd say, but suppose you don't chop him up, be-
75 cause your tail's drooping and you know it. I'm left standing there like a fool and the captain takes it out on me.

THE OLDER SOLDIER: You're right. He's only blowing off steam.

THE YOUNG SOLDIER: We'll see about that. I'll cut him to pieces. (*He draws his sword*) When he comes out, I'll cut him
80 to pieces.

THE CLERK: (*looks out*) The captain will be here in a moment. Sit down.

(THE YOUNG SOLDIER *sits down.*)

MOTHER COURAGE: There he sits. What did I tell you? Sitting, aren't you? Oh, they know us like a book, they know how to
85 handle us. Sit down! And down we sit. You can't start a riot sitting down. Better not stand up again, you won't be able to stand the way you were standing before. Don't be embarrassed on my account, I'm no better, not a bit of it. We were full of piss and vinegar, but they've bought it off. Look at me. No back talk, it's bad for business. Let me tell you about the great 90 capitulation. (*She sings the Song of the Great Capitulation*)

When I was young, no more than a spring chicken
I too thought that I was really quite the cheese
(No common peddler's daughter, not I with my
    looks and my talent and striving for higher things!)
One little hair in the soup would make me sicken 95
And at me no man would dare to sneeze.
(It's all or nothing, no second best for me. I've got
    what it takes, the rules are for somebody else!)
But a chickadee
Sang wait and see!
    And you go marching with the show 100
    In step, however fast or slow
    And rattle off your little song:
    It won't be long.
    And then the whole thing slides.
    You think God provides — 105
    But you've got it wrong.

And before one single year had wasted
I had learned to swallow down the bitter brew
(Two kids on my hands and the price of bread and
    who do they take me for anyway!)
May, the double-edged shellacking that I tasted 110
On my ass and knees I was when they were through.
(You've got to get along with people, one good turn
    deserves another, no use trying to ram your head
    through the wall!)
And the chickadee
Sang wait and see!
    And she goes marching with the show 115
    In step, however fast or slow
    And rattles off her little song:
    It won't be long.
    And then the whole thing slides
    You think God provides — 120
    But you've got it wrong.

I've seen many fired by high ambition
No star's big or high enough to reach out for.
(It's ability that counts, where there's a will there's a
    way, one way or another we'll swing it!)
Then while moving mountains they get a suspicion 125
That to wear a straw hat is too big a chore.
(No use being too big for your britches!)
And the chickadee
Sings wait and see!
    And they go marching with the show 130
    In step, however fast or slow
    And rattle off their little song:
    It won't be long.
    And then the whole thing slides!
    You think God provides — 135
    But you've got it wrong!

MOTHER COURAGE: (to THE YOUNG SOLDIER) So here's what I think: Stay here with your sword if your anger's big enough, I know you have good reason, but if it's a short quick anger,
140   better make tracks!

THE YOUNG SOLDIER: Kiss my ass! (He staggers off, THE OLDER SOLDIER after him)

THE CLERK: (sticking his head out) The captain is here. You can put in your complaint now.

145 MOTHER COURAGE: I've changed my mind. No complaint.
      (She goes out)

SCENE V

> Two years have passed. The war has spread far and wide.
> With scarcely a pause Mother Courage's little wagon rolls
> through Poland, Moravia, Bavaria, Italy, and back again
> to Bavaria. 1631. Tilly's victory at Magdeburg costs
> Mother Courage four officers' shirts.

MOTHER COURAGE's wagon has stopped in a devastated village.

Thin military music is heard from the distance. Two soldiers at the bar are being waited on by KATTRIN and MOTHER COURAGE. One of them is wearing a lady's fur coat over his shoulders.

MOTHER COURAGE: What's that? You can't pay? No money, no schnapps. Plenty of victory marches for the Lord but no pay for the men.

THE SOLDIER: I want my schnapps. I come too late for the loot-
5   ing. The general skunked us: permission to loot the city for exactly one hour. Says he's not a monster; the mayor must have paid him.

THE CHAPLAIN: (staggers in) There's still some wounded in the house. The peasant and his family. Help me, somebody, I
10   need linen.

(THE SECOND SOLDIER goes out with him. KATTRIN gets very excited and tries to persuade her mother to hand out linen.)

MOTHER COURAGE: I haven't got any. The regiment's bought up all my bandages. You think I'm going to rip up my officers' shirts for the likes of them?

THE CHAPLAIN: (calling back) I need linen, I tell you.

15 MOTHER COURAGE: (sitting down on the wagon steps to keep KATTRIN out) Nothing doing. They don't pay, they got noth-ing to pay with.

THE CHAPLAIN: (bending over a woman whom he has carried out) Why did you stay here in all that gunfire?

20 THE PEASANT WOMAN: (feebly) Farm.

MOTHER COURAGE: You won't catch them leaving their prop-erty. And I'm expected to foot the bill. I won't do it.

THE FIRST SOLDIER: They're Protestants. Why do they have to be Protestants?

25 MOTHER COURAGE: Religion is the least of their worries.
      They've lost their farm.

THE SECOND SOLDIER: They're no Protestants. They're Catho-lics like us.

THE FIRST SOLDIER: How do we know who we're shooting at?

30 A PEASANT: (whom THE CHAPLAIN brings in) They got my arm.

THE CHAPLAIN: Where's the linen?

(All look at MOTHER COURAGE, who does not move.)

MOTHER COURAGE: I can't give you a thing. What with all my taxes, duties, fees and bribes! (Making guttural sounds, KAT-TRIN picks up a board and threatens her mother with it) Are
35   you crazy? Put that board down, you slut, or I'll smack you. I'm not giving anything, you can't make me, I've got to think of myself. (THE CHAPLAIN picks her up from the step and puts her down on the ground. Then he fishes out some shirts and tears them into strips) My shirts! Half a guilder apiece! I'm
40   ruined!

(The anguished cry of a baby is heard from the house.)

THE PEASANT: The baby's still in there!

(KATTRIN runs in.)

THE CHAPLAIN: (to the woman) Don't move. They're bringing him out.

MOTHER COURAGE: Get her out of there. The roof'll cave in.

THE CHAPLAIN: I'm not going in there again.

45 MOTHER COURAGE: (torn) Don't run hog-wild with my expen-sive linen.

(KATTRIN emerges from the ruins carrying an infant.)

MOTHER COURAGE: Oh, so you've found another baby to carry around with you? Give that baby back to its mother this min-ute, or it'll take me all day to get it away from you. Do you
50   hear me? (to THE SECOND SOLDIER) Don't stand there gap-ing, go back and tell them to stop that music, I can see right here that they've won a victory. Your victory's costing me a pretty penny.

(KATTRIN rocks the baby in her arms, humming a lullaby.)

55 MOTHER COURAGE: There she sits, happy in all this misery; give it back this minute, the mother's coming to. (She pounces on THE FIRST SOLDIER who has been helping himself to the drinks and is now making off with the bottle) Pshagreff! Beast! Haven't you had enough victories for today? Pay up.

60 THE FIRST SOLDIER: I'm broke.

MOTHER COURAGE: (tears the fur coat off him) Then leave the coat here, it's stolen anyway.

THE CHAPLAIN: There's still somebody in there.

SCENE VI

> Outside Ingolstadt in Bavaria Mother Courage attends
> the funeral of Tilly, the imperial field marshal. Conver-
> sations about heroes and the longevity of the war. The
> chaplain deplores the waste of his talents. Mute Kattrin
> gets the red shoes. 1632.

Inside MOTHER COURAGE's tent.

A bar open to the rear. Rain. In the distance drum rolls and funeral music. THE CHAPLAIN and the regimental clerk are play-ing a board game. MOTHER COURAGE and her daughter are tak-ing inventory.

THE CHAPLAIN: The procession's starting.

MOTHER COURAGE: It's a shame about the general—socks: twenty-two pairs—I hear he was killed by accident. On ac-count of the fog in the fields. He's up front encouraging the troops. "Fight to the death, boys," he sings out. Then he rides 5 back, but he gets lost in the fog and rides back forward. Before you know it he's in the middle of the battle and stops a bullet—lanterns: we're down to four. (A *whistle from the rear. She goes to the bar*) You men ought to be ashamed, running out on your late general's funeral! (*She pours drinks*)

THE CLERK: They shouldn't have been paid before the funeral. Now they're getting drunk instead.

THE CHAPLAIN: (*to* THE CLERK) Shouldn't you be at the funeral?

THE CLERK: In this rain?

MOTHER COURAGE: With you it's different, the rain might spoil your uniform. It seems they wanted to ring the bells, naturally, but it turned out the churches had all been shot to pieces by his orders, so the poor general won't hear any bells when they lower him into his grave. They're going to fire a three-gun salute instead, so it won't be too dull—seventeen sword belts.

CRIES: (*from the bar*) Hey! Brandy!

MOTHER COURAGE: Money first! No, you can't come into my tent with your muddy boots! You can drink outside, rain or no rain. (*To* THE CLERK) I'm only letting officers in. It seems the general had been having his troubles. Mutiny in the Second Regiment because he hadn't paid them. It's a war of religion, he says, should they profit by their faith?

(*Funeral march. All look to the rear.*)

THE CHAPLAIN: Now they're marching past the body.

MOTHER COURAGE: I feel sorry when a general or an emperor passes away like this, maybe he thought he'd do something big, that posterity would still be talking about and maybe put up a statue in his honor, conquer the world, for instance, that's a nice ambition for a general, he doesn't know any better. So he knocks himself out, and then the common people come and spoil it all, because what do they care about greatness, all they care about is a mug of beer and maybe a little company. The most beautiful plans have been wrecked by the smallness of the people that are supposed to carry them out. Even an emperor can't do anything by himself, he needs the support of his soldiers and his people. Am I right?

THE CHAPLAIN: (*laughing*) Courage, you're right, except about the soldiers. They do their best. With those fellows out there, for instance, drinking their brandy in the rain, I'll undertake to carry on one war after another for a hundred years, two at once if I have to, and I'm not a general by trade.

MOTHER COURAGE: Then you don't think the war might stop?

THE CHAPLAIN: Because the general's dead? Don't be childish. They grow by the dozen, there'll always be plenty of heroes.

MOTHER COURAGE: Look here, I'm not asking you for the hell of it. I've been wondering whether to lay in supplies while they're cheap, but if the war stops, I can throw them out the window.

THE CHAPLAIN: I understand. You want a serious answer. There have always been people who say: "The war will be over some day." I say there's no guarantee the war will ever be over. Naturally a brief intermission is conceivable. Maybe the war needs a breather, a war can even break its neck, so to speak. There's always a chance of that, nothing is perfect here below. Maybe there never will be a perfect war, one that lives up to all our expectations. Suddenly, for some unforeseen reason, a war can bog down, you can't think of everything. Some little oversight and your war's in trouble. And then you've got to

pull it out of the mud. But the kings and emperors, not to mention the pope, will always come to its help in adversity. On the whole, I'd say this war has very little to worry about, it'll live to a ripe old age.

A SOLDIER: (*sings at the bar*)

> A drink, and don't be slow!
> A soldier's got to go
> And fight for his religion.
>
> Make it double, this is a holiday.

MOTHER COURAGE: If I could only be sure . . .

THE CHAPLAIN: Figure it out for yourself. What's to stop the war?

THE SOLDIER: (*sings*)

> Your breasts, girl, don't be slow!
> A soldier's got to go
> And ride away to Pilsen.

THE CLERK: (*suddenly*) But why can't we have peace? I'm from Bohemia, I'd like to go home when the time comes.

THE CHAPLAIN: Oh, you'd like to go home? Ah, peace! What becomes of the hole when the cheese has been eaten?

THE SOLDIER: (*sings*)

> Play cards, friends, don't be slow!
> A soldier's got to go
> No matter if it's Sunday.
>
> A prayer, priest, don't be slow!
> A soldier's got to go
> And die for king and country.

THE CLERK: In the long run nobody can live without peace.

THE CHAPLAIN: The way I see it, war gives you plenty of peace. It has its peaceful moments. War meets every need, including the peaceful ones, everything's taken care of, or your war couldn't hold its own. In a war you can shit the same as in the dead of peace, you can stop for a beer between battles, and even on the march you can always lie down on your elbows and take a little nap by the roadside. You can't play cards when you're fighting; but then you can't when you're plowing in the dead of peace either, but after a victory the sky's the limit. Maybe you've had a leg shot off, at first you raise a howl, you make a big thing of it. But then you calm down or they give you schnapps, and in the end you're hopping around again and the war's no worse off than before. And what's to prevent you from multiplying in the thick of the slaughter, behind a barn or someplace, in the long run how can they stop you, and then the war has your progeny to help it along. Take it from me, the war will always find an answer. Why would it have to stop?

(KATTRIN *has stopped working and is staring at* THE CHAPLAIN.)

MOTHER COURAGE: Then I'll buy the merchandise. You've convinced me. (KATTRIN *suddenly throws down a basket full of bottles and runs out*) Kattrin! (*Laughs*) My goodness, the poor thing's been hoping for peace. I promised her she'd get a husband when peace comes. (*She runs after her*)

THE CLERK: (*getting up*) I win, you've been too busy talking. Pay up.

MOTHER COURAGE: (*comes back with* KATTRIN) Be reasonable, the war'll go on a little longer and we'll make a little more money, then peace will be even better. Run along to town now, it won't take you ten minutes, and get the stuff from the

Golden Lion, only the expensive things, we'll pick up the rest in the wagon later, it's all arranged, the regimental clerk here will go with you. They've almost all gone to the general's funeral, nothing can happen to you. Look sharp, don't let them take anything away from you, think of your dowry.

(KATTRIN *puts a kerchief over her head and goes with* THE CLERK.)

THE CHAPLAIN: Is it all right letting her go with the clerk?

MOTHER COURAGE: Who'd want to ruin her? She's not pretty enough.

THE CHAPLAIN: I've come to admire the way you handle your business and pull through every time. I can see why they call you Mother Courage.

MOTHER COURAGE: Poor people need courage. Why? Because they're sunk. In their situation it takes gumption just to get up in the morning. Or to plow a field in the middle of a war. They even show courage by bringing children into the world, because look at the prospects. The way they butcher and execute each other, think of the courage they need to look each other in the face. And putting up with an emperor and a pope takes a whale of a lot of courage, because those two are the death of the poor. (*She sits down, takes a small pipe from her pocket and smokes*) You could be making some kindling.

THE CHAPLAIN: (*reluctantly takes his jacket off and prepares to chop*) Chopping wood isn't really my trade, you know, I'm a shepherd of souls.

MOTHER COURAGE: Sure. But I have no soul and I need firewood.

THE CHAPLAIN: What's that pipe?

MOTHER COURAGE: Just a pipe.

THE CHAPLAIN: No, it's not "just a pipe," it's a very particular pipe.

MOTHER COURAGE: Really?

THE CHAPLAIN: It's the cook's pipe from the Oxenstjerna regiment.

MOTHER COURAGE: If you know it all, why the mealy-mouthed questions?

THE CHAPLAIN: I didn't know if *you* knew. You could have been rummaging through your belongings and laid hands on some pipe and picked it up without thinking.

MOTHER COURAGE: Yes. Maybe that's how it was.

THE CHAPLAIN: Except it wasn't. You knew who that pipe belongs to.

MOTHER COURAGE: What of it?

THE CHAPLAIN: Courage, I'm warning you. It's my duty. I doubt if you ever lay eyes on the man again, but that's no calamity, in fact you're lucky. If you ask me, he wasn't steady. Not at all.

MOTHER COURAGE: What makes you say that? He was a nice man.

THE CHAPLAIN: Oh, you think he was nice? I differ. Far be it from me to wish him any harm, but I can't say he was nice. I'd say he was a scheming Don Juan. If you don't believe me, take a look at his pipe. You'll have to admit that it shows up his character.

MOTHER COURAGE: I don't see anything. It's beat up.

THE CHAPLAIN: It's half bitten through. A violent man. That is the pipe of a ruthless, violent man, you must see that if you still got an ounce of good sense.

MOTHER COURAGE: Don't wreck my chopping block.

THE CHAPLAIN: I've told you I wasn't trained to chop wood. I studied theology. My gifts and abilities are being wasted on muscular effort. The talents that God gave me are lying fallow. That's a sin. You've never heard me preach. With one sermon I can whip a regiment into such a state that they take the enemy for a flock of sheep. Then men care no more about their lives than they would about a smelly old sock that they're ready to throw away in hopes of final victory. God has made me eloquent. You'll swoon when you hear me preach.

MOTHER COURAGE: I don't want to swoon. What good would that do me?

THE CHAPLAIN: Courage, I've often wondered if maybe you didn't conceal a warm heart under that hard-bitten talk of yours. You too are human, you need warmth.

MOTHER COURAGE: The best way to keep this tent warm is with plenty of firewood.

THE CHAPLAIN: Don't try to put me off. Seriously, Courage, I sometimes wonder if we couldn't make our relationship a little closer. I mean, seeing that the whirlwind of war has whirled us so strangely together.

MOTHER COURAGE: Seems to me it's close enough. I cook your meals and you do chores, such as chopping wood, for instance.

THE CHAPLAIN: (*goes toward her*) You know what I mean by "closer"; it has nothing to do with meals and chopping wood and such mundane needs. Don't harden your heart, let it speak.

MOTHER COURAGE: Don't come at me with that ax. That's too close a relationship.

THE CHAPLAIN: Don't turn it to ridicule. I'm serious, I've given it careful thought.

MOTHER COURAGE: Chaplain, don't be silly. I like you, I don't want to have to scold you. My aim in life is to get through, me and my children and my wagon. I don't think of it as mine and besides I'm not in the mood for private affairs. Right now I'm taking a big risk, buying up merchandise with the general dead and everybody talking peace. What'll you do if I'm ruined? See? You don't know. Chop that wood, then we'll be warm in the evening, which is a good thing in times like these. Now what? (*She stands up*)

(*Enter* KATTRIN *out of breath, with a wound across her forehead and over one eye. She is carrying all sorts of things, packages, leather goods, a drum, etc.*)

MOTHER COURAGE: What's that? Assaulted? On the way back? She was assaulted on the way back. Must have been that soldier that got drunk here! I shouldn't have let you go! Throw the stuff down! It's not bad, only a flesh wound. I'll bandage it, it'll heal in a week. They're worse than wild beasts. (*She bandages the wound*)

THE CHAPLAIN: I can't find fault with them. At home they never raped anybody. I blame the people that start wars, they're the ones that dredge up man's lowest instincts.

MOTHER COURAGE: Didn't the clerk bring you back? That's because you're respectable, they don't give a damn. It's not a deep wound, it won't leave a mark. There, all bandaged. Don't fret, I've got something for you. I've been keeping it for you on the sly, it'll be a surprise. (*She fishes* YVETTE's *red shoes out of a sack*) See? You've always wanted them. Now you've got them. Put them on quick before I regret it. It won't leave a mark, though I wouldn't mind if it did. The girls that attract them get the worst of it. They drag them around till there's nothing left of them. If you don't appeal to them, they won't harm you. I've seen girls with pretty faces, a few years later they'd have given a wolf the creeps. They can't step behind a bush without fearing the worst. It's like trees. The straight tall ones get chopped down for ridgepoles, the crooked ones enjoy life. In other words, it's a lucky break. The shoes are still in good condition, I've kept them nicely polished.

240

(KATTRIN *leaves the shoes where they are and crawls into the wagon.*)

THE CHAPLAIN: I hope she won't be disfigured.
MOTHER COURAGE: There'll be a scar. She can stop waiting for peace.
245   THE CHAPLAIN: She didn't let them take anything.
MOTHER COURAGE: Maybe I shouldn't have drummed it into her. If I only knew what went on in her head. One night she stayed out, the only time in all these years. Afterwards she traipsed around as usual, except she worked harder. I never
250   could find out what happened. I racked may brains for quite some time. (*She picks up the articles brought by* KATTRIN *and sorts them angrily*) That's war for you! A fine way to make a living!

(*Cannon salutes are heard.*)

THE CHAPLAIN: Now they're burying the general. This is a his-
255   toric moment.
MOTHER COURAGE: To me it's a historic moment when they hit my daughter over the eye. She's a wreck, she'll never get a husband now, and she's so crazy about children. It's the war that made her dumb too, a soldier stuffed something in her
260   mouth when she was little. I'll never see Swiss Cheese again and where Eilif is, God knows. God damn the war.

SCENE VII

⌈ Mother Courage at the height of her business career. ⌉
Highway.

THE CHAPLAIN, MOTHER COURAGE *and her daughter* KATTRIN *are pulling the wagon. New wares are banging on it.* MOTHER COURAGE *is wearing a necklace of silver talers.*

MOTHER COURAGE: Stop running down the war. I won't have it. I know it destroys the weak, but the weak haven't a chance in peacetime either. And war is a better provider. (*Sings*)

5   If you're not strong enough to take it
       The victory will find you dead.
       A war is only what you make it.
       It's business, not with cheese but lead.

And what good is it staying in one place? The stay-at-homes are the first to get it. (*Sings*)

10   Some people think they'd like to ride out
       The war, leave danger to the brave
       And dig themselves a cozy hideout —
       They'll dig themselves an early grave.
       I've seen them running from the thunder
15   To find a refuge from the war
       But once they're resting six feet under
       They wonder what they hurried for.

(*They plod on.*)

SCENE VIII

⌈ In the same year Gustavus Adolphus, King of Sweden, is
  killed at the battle of Lützen. Peace threatens to ruin
  Mother Courage's business. Her brave son performs one
  heroic deed too many and dies an ignominious death. ⌉

A camp.

A summer morning. An old woman and her son are standing by the wagon. The son is carrying a large sack of bedding.

MOTHER COURAGE'S VOICE: (*from the wagon*) Does it have to be at this unearthly hour?
THE YOUNG MAN: We've walked all night, twenty miles, and we've got to go back today.
MOTHER COURAGE'S VOICE: What can I do with bedding? The   5
people haven't any houses.
THE YOUNG MAN: Wait till you've seen it.
THE OLD WOMAN: She won't take it either. Come on.
THE YOUNG MAN: They'll sell the roof from over our heads for taxes. Maybe she'll give us three guilders if you throw in the   10
cross. (*Bells start ringing*) Listen, mother!
VOICES: (*from the rear*) Peace! The king of Sweden is dead!
MOTHER COURAGE: (*sticks her head out of the wagon. She has not yet done her hair*) Why are the bells ringing in the middle of the week?   15
THE CHAPLAIN: (*crawls out from under the wagon*) What are they shouting?
MOTHER COURAGE: Don't tell me peace has broken out when I've just taken in more supplies.
THE CHAPLAIN: (*shouting toward the rear*) Is it true? Peace?   20
VOICE: Three weeks ago, they say. But we just found out.
THE CHAPLAIN: (*to* MOTHER COURAGE) What else would they ring the bells for?
VOICE: There's a whole crowd of Lutherans, they've driven their carts into town. They brought the news.   25
THE YOUNG MAN: Mother, it's peace. What's the matter?

(THE OLD WOMAN *has collapsed.*)

MOTHER COURAGE: (*going back into the wagon*) Heavenly saints! Kattrin, peace! Put your black dress on! We're going to church. We owe it to Swiss Cheese. Can it be true?
THE YOUNG MAN: The people here say the same thing. They've   30
made peace. Can you get up? (THE OLD WOMAN *stands up, still stunned*) I'll get the saddle shop started again. I promise. Everything will be all right. Father will get his bed back. Can you walk? (*To* THE CHAPLAIN) She fainted. It was the news. She thought peace would never come again. Father said it   35
would. We'll go straight home. (*Both go out*)
MOTHER COURAGE'S VOICE: Give her some brandy.
THE CHAPLAIN: They're gone.
MOTHER COURAGE'S VOICE: What's going on in camp?
THE CHAPLAIN: A big crowd. I'll go see. Shouldn't I put on my   40
clericals?
MOTHER COURAGE'S VOICE: Better make sure before you step out in your antichrist costume. I'm glad to see peace, even if I'm ruined. At least I've brought two of my children through the war. Now I'll see my Eilif again.   45
THE CHAPLAIN: Look who's coming down the road. If it isn't the general's cook!

THE COOK: (*rather bedraggled, carrying a bundle*) Can I believe my eyes? The chaplain!

50 THE CHAPLAIN: Courage! A visitor!

(MOTHER COURAGE *climbs down.*)

THE COOK: Didn't I promise to come over for a little chat as soon as I had time? I've never forgotten your brandy, Mrs. Fierling.

MOTHER COURAGE: Mercy, the general's cook! After all these
55 years! Where's Eilif, my eldest?

THE COOK: Isn't he here yet? He left ahead of me, he was coming to see you too.

THE CHAPLAIN: I'll put on my clericals, wait for me. (*Goes out behind the wagon*)

60 MOTHER COURAGE: Then he'll be here any minute. (*Calls into the wagon*) Kattrin, Eilif's coming! Bring the cook a glass of brandy! (KATTRIN *does not appear*) Put a lock of hair over it, and forget it! Mr. Lamb is no stranger. (*Gets the brandy herself*) She won't come out. Peace doesn't mean a thing to her,
65 it's come too late. They hit her over the eye, there's hardly any mark, but she thinks people are staring at her.

THE COOK: Ech, war! (*He and* MOTHER COURAGE *sit down*)

MOTHER COURAGE: Cook, you find me in trouble. I'm ruined.

THE COOK: What? Say, that's a shame.

70 MOTHER COURAGE: Peace has done me in. Only the other day I stocked up. The chaplain's advice. And now they'll all demobilize and leave me sitting on my merchandise.

THE COOK: How could you listen to the chaplain? If I'd had time, I'd have warned you against him, but the Catholics
75 came too soon. He's a fly-by-night. So now he's the boss here?

MOTHER COURAGE: He washed my dishes and helped me pull the wagon.

THE COOK: Him? Pulling? I guess he's told you a few of his jokes too, I wouldn't put it past him, he has an unsavory attitude
80 toward women, I tried to reform him, it was hopeless. He's not steady.

MOTHER COURAGE: Are you steady?

THE COOK: If nothing else, I'm steady. Prosit!

MOTHER COURAGE: Steady is no good. I've only lived with one
85 steady man, thank the Lord. I never had to work so hard, he sold the children's blankets when spring came, and he thought my harmonica was unchristian. In my opinion you're not doing yourself any good by admitting you're steady.

THE COOK: You've still got your old bite, but I respect you for it.

90 MOTHER COURAGE: Don't tell me you've been dreaming about my old bite.

THE COOK: Well, here we sit, with the bells of peace and your world-famous brandy, that hasn't its equal.

MOTHER COURAGE: The bells of peace don't strike my fancy
95 right now. I don't see them paying the men, they're behindhand already. Where does that leave me with my famous brandy? Have you been paid?

THE COOK: (*hesitantly*) Not really. That's why we demobilized ourselves. Under the circumstances, I says to myself, why
100 should I stay on? I'll go see my friends in the meantime. So here we are.

MOTHER COURAGE: You mean you're out of funds?

THE COOK: If only they'd stop those damn bells! I'd be glad to go into some kind of business. I'm sick of being a cook. They
105 give me roots and shoe leather to work with, and then they throw the hot soup in my face. A cook's got a dog's life these days. I'd rather be in combat, but now we've got peace. (THE CHAPLAIN *appears in his original dress*) We'll discuss it later.

THE CHAPLAIN: It's still in good condition. There were only a
110 few moths in it.

THE COOK: I don't see why you bother. They won't take you back. Who are you going to inspire now to be an honest soldier and earn his pay at the risk of his life? Besides, I've got a bone to pick with you. Advising this lady to buy useless mer-
115 chandise on the ground that the war would last forever.

THE CHAPLAIN: (*heatedly*) And why, I'd like to know, is it any of your business?

THE COOK: Because it's unscrupulous. How can you meddle in other people's business and give unsolicited advice?

120 THE CHAPLAIN: Who's meddling? (*To* MOTHER COURAGE) I didn't know you were accountable to this gentleman, I didn't know you were so intimate with him.

MOTHER COURAGE: Don't get excited, the cook is only giving his private opinion. And you can't deny that your war was a dud.

125 THE CHAPLAIN: Courage, don't blaspheme against peace. You're a battlefield hyena.

MOTHER COURAGE: What am I?

THE COOK: If you insult this lady, you'll hear from me.

THE CHAPLAIN: I'm not talking to you. Your intentions are too
130 obvious. (*To* MOTHER COURAGE) But when I see you picking up peace with thumb and forefinger like a snotty handkerchief, it revolts my humanity; you don't want peace, you want war, because you profit by it, but don't forget the old saying: "He hath need of a long spoon that eateth with the
135 devil."

MOTHER COURAGE: I've no use for war and war hasn't much use for me. Anyway, I'm not letting anybody call me a hyena, you and me are through.

THE CHAPLAIN: How can you complain about peace when it's
140 such a relief to everybody else? On account of the old rags in your wagon?

MOTHER COURAGE: My merchandise isn't old rags, it's what I live off, and so did you.

THE CHAPLAIN: Off war, you mean. Aha!

145 THE COOK: (*to* THE CHAPLAIN) You're a grown man, you ought to know there's no sense in giving advice. (*To* MOTHER COURAGE) The best thing you can do now is to sell off certain articles quick, before the prices hit the floor. Dress yourself and get started, there's no time to lose.

150 MOTHER COURAGE: That's very sensible advice. I think I'll do it.

THE CHAPLAIN: Because the cook says so!

MOTHER COURAGE: Why didn't *you* say so? He's right, I'd better run over to the market. (*She goes to the wagon*)

THE COOK: My round, chaplain. No presence of mind. Here's
155 what you should have said: me give you advice? All I ever did was talk politics! Don't try to take me on. Cockfighting is undignified in a clergyman.

THE CHAPLAIN: If you don't shut up, I'll murder you, undignified or not.

160 THE COOK: (*taking off his shoe and unwinding the wrappings from his feet*) If the war hadn't made a godless bum out of you, you could easily come by a parsonage now that peace is here. They won't need cooks, there's nothing to cook, but people still do a lot of believing, that hasn't changed.

165 THE CHAPLAIN: See here, Mr. Lamb. Don't try to squeeze me

out. Being a bum has made me a better man. I couldn't
preach to them any more.

(YVETTE POTTIER *enters, elaborately dressed in black, with a*
cane. She is much older and fatter and heavily powdered. Behind
her a servant.)

YVETTE: Hello there! Is this the residence of Mother Courage?
THE CHAPLAIN: Right you are. With whom have we the
170   pleasure?
YVETTE: The Countess Starhemberg, my good people. Where
is Mother Courage?
THE CHAPLAIN: (*calls into the wagon*) Countess Starhemberg
wishes to speak to you!
175   MOTHER COURAGE: I'm coming.
YVETTE: It's Yvette!
MOTHER COURAGE'S VOICE: My goodness! It's Yvette!
YVETTE: Just dropped in to see how you're doing. (THE COOK
has turned around in horror) Pieter!
180   THE COOK: Yvette!
YVETTE: Blow me down! How did you get here?
THE COOK: In a cart.
THE CHAPLAIN: Oh, you know each other? Intimately?
YVETTE: I should think so. (*She looks* THE COOK *over*) Fat!
185   THE COOK: You're not exactly willowy yourself.
YVETTE: All the same I'm glad I ran into you, you bum. Now I
can tell you what I think of you.
THE CHAPLAIN: Go right ahead, spare no details, but wait until
Courage comes out.
190   MOTHER COURAGE: (*comes out with all sorts of merchandise.*)
Yvette! (*They embrace*) But what are you in mourning for?
YVETTE: Isn't it becoming? My husband the colonel died a few
years ago.
MOTHER COURAGE: The old geezer that almost bought my
195   wagon?
YVETTE: His eldest brother.
MOTHER COURAGE: You must be pretty well fixed. It's nice to
find somebody that's made a good thing out of the war.
YVETTE: Oh well, it's been up and down and back up again.
200   MOTHER COURAGE: Let's not say anything bad about colonels.
They make money by the bushel.
THE CHAPLAIN: If I were you, I'd put my shoes back on again.
(*To* YVETTE) Countess Starhemberg, you promised to tell us
what you think of this gentleman.
205   THE COOK: Don't make a scene here.
MOTHER COURAGE: He's a friend of mine, Yvette.
YVETTE: He's Pete the Pipe, that's who he is.
THE COOK: Forget the nicknames, my name is Lamb.
MOTHER COURAGE: (*laughs*) Pete the Pipe! That drove the
210   women crazy! Say, I've saved your pipe.
THE CHAPLAIN: And smoked it.
YVETTE: It's lucky I'm here to warn you. He's the worst rotter
that ever infested the coast of Flanders. He ruined more girls
than he's got fingers.
215   THE COOK: That was a long time ago. I've changed.
YVETTE: Stand up when a lady draws you into a conversation!
How I loved this man! And all the while he was seeing a little
bandylegged brunette, ruined her too, naturally.
THE COOK: Seems to me I started you off on a prosperous career.
220   YVETTE: Shut up, you depressing wreck! Watch your step with
him, his kind are dangerous even when they've gone to seed.

MOTHER COURAGE: (*to* YVETTE) Come along, I've got to sell
my stuff before the prices drop. Maybe you can help me, with
your army connections. (*Calls into the wagon*) Kattrin, forget
about church, I'm running over to the market. When Eilif   225
comes, give him a drink. (*Goes out with* YVETTE)
YVETTE: (*in leaving*) To think that such a man could lead me
astray! I can thank my lucky stars that I was able to rise in the
world after that. I've put a spoke in your wheel, Pete the Pipe,
and they'll give me credit for it in heaven when my time   230
comes.
THE CHAPLAIN: Our conversation seems to illustrate the old
adage: The mills of God grind slowly. What do you think of
my jokes now?
THE COOK: I'm just unlucky. I'll come clean: I was hoping for a   235
hot meal. I'm starving. And now they're talking about me,
and she'll get the wrong idea. I think I'll beat it before she
comes back.
THE CHAPLAIN: I think so too.
THE COOK: Chaplain, I'm fed up on peace already. Men are   240
sinners from the cradle, fire and sword are their natural lot. I
wish I were cooking for the general again, God knows where
he is, I'd roast a fine fat capon, with mustard sauce and a few
carrots.
THE CHAPLAIN: Red cabbage. Red cabbage with capon.   245
THE COOK: That's right, but he wanted carrots.
THE CHAPLAIN: He was ignorant.
THE COOK: That didn't prevent you from gorging yourself.
THE CHAPLAIN: With repugnance.
THE COOK: Anyway you'll have to admit those were good times.   250
THE CHAPLAIN: I might admit that.
THE COOK: Now you've called her a hyena, your good times
here are over. What are you staring at?
THE CHAPLAIN: Eilif! (EILIF *enters, followed by* SOLDIERS *with*
pikes. His hands are fettered. He is deathly pale) What's   255
wrong?
EILIF: Where's mother?
THE CHAPLAIN: Gone to town.
EILIF: I heard she was here. They let me come and see her.
THE COOK: (*to the* SOLDIERS) Where are you taking him?   260
A SOLDIER: No good place.
THE CHAPLAIN: What has he done?
THE SOLDIER: Broke into a farm. The peasant's wife is dead.
THE CHAPLAIN: How could you do such a thing?
EILIF: It's what I've been doing all along.   265
THE COOK: But in peacetime!
EILIF: Shut your trap. Can I sit down till she comes?
THE SOLDIER: We haven't time.
THE CHAPLAIN: During the war they honored him for it, he sat
at the general's right hand. Then it was bravery. Couldn't we   270
speak to the officer?
THE SOLDIER: No use. What's brave about taking a peasant's
cattle?
THE COOK: It was stupid.
EILIF: If I'd been stupid, I'd have starved, wise guy.   275
THE COOK: And for being smart your head comes off.
THE CHAPLAIN: Let's get Kattrin at least.
EILIF: Leave her be. Get me a drink of schnapps.
THE SOLDIER: No time. Let's go!
THE CHAPLAIN: And what should we tell your mother?   280
EILIF: Tell her it wasn't any different, tell her it was the same. Or
don't tell her anything.

(The SOLDIERS drive him away.)

THE CHAPLAIN: I'll go with you on your hard journey.

EILIF: I don't need any sky pilot.

285   THE CHAPLAIN: You don't know yet. (He follows him)

THE COOK: (calls after them) I'll have to tell her, she'll want to see him.

THE CHAPLAIN: Better not tell her anything. Or say he was here and he'll come again, maybe tomorrow. I'll break it to her

290   when I get back. (Hurries out)

(THE COOK looks after them, shaking his head, then he walks anxiously about. Finally he approaches the wagon.)

THE COOK: Hey! Come on out! I can see why you'd hide from peace. I wish I could do it myself. I'm the general's cook, remember? Wouldn't you have a bite to eat, to do me till your mother gets back? A slice of ham or just a piece of bread while

295   I'm waiting. (He looks in) She's buried her head in a blanket. (The sound of gunfire in the rear)

MOTHER COURAGE: (runs in. She is out of breath and still has her merchandise) Cook, the peace is over, the war started up again three days ago. I hadn't sold my stuff yet when I found

300   out. Heaven be praised! They're shooting each other up in town, the Catholics and Lutherans. We've got to get out of here. Kattrin, start packing. What have you got such a long face about? What's wrong?

THE COOK: Nothing.

305   MOTHER COURAGE: Something's wrong, I can tell by your expression.

THE COOK: Maybe it's the war starting up again. Now I probably won't get anything hot to eat before tomorrow night.

MOTHER COURAGE: That's a lie, cook.

310   THE COOK: Eilif was here. He couldn't stay.

MOTHER COURAGE: He was here? Then we'll see him on the march. I'm going with our troops this time. How does he look?

THE COOK: The same.

MOTHER COURAGE: He'll never change. The war couldn't take

315   him away from me. He's smart. Could you help me pack? (She starts packing) Did he tell you anything? Is he in good with the general? Did he say anything about his heroic deeds?

THE COOK: (gloomily) They say he's been at one of them again.

MOTHER COURAGE: Tell me later, we've got to be going. (KAT-

320   TRIN emerges) Kattrin, peace is over. We're moving. (To THE COOK) What's the matter with you?

THE COOK: I'm going to enlist.

MOTHER COURAGE: I've got a suggestion. Why don't . . . ? Where's the chaplain?

325   THE COOK: Gone to town with Eilif.

MOTHER COURAGE: Then come a little way with me, Lamb. I need help.

THE COOK: That incident with Yvette . . .

MOTHER COURAGE: It hasn't lowered you in my estimation. Far

330   from it. Where there's smoke there's fire. Coming?

THE COOK: I won't say no.

MOTHER COURAGE: The Twelfth Regiment has shoved off. Take the shaft. Here's a chunk of bread. We'll have to circle around to meet the Lutherans. Maybe I'll see Eilif tonight.

335   He's my favorite. It's been a short peace. And we're on the move again. (She sings, while THE COOK and KATTRIN harness themselves to the wagon)

From Ulm to Metz, from Metz to Pilsen
Courage is right there in the van.

The war both in and out of season   340
With shot and shell will feed its man.
But lead alone is not sufficient
The war needs soldiers to subsist!
Its diet elseways is deficient.
The war is hungry! So enlist!   345

SCENE IX

The great war of religion has been going on for sixteen years. Germany has lost more than half its population. Those whom the slaughter has spared have been laid low by epidemics. Once-flourishing countrysides are ravaged by famine. Wolves prowl through the charred ruins of the cities. In the fall of 1634 we find Mother Courage in Germany, in the Fichtelgebirge, at some distance from the road followed by the Swedish armies. Winter comes early and is exceptionally severe. Business is bad, begging is the only resort. The cook receives a letter from Utrecht and is dismissed.

Outside a half-demolished presbytery.

Gray morning in early winter. Gusts of wind. MOTHER COURAGE and THE COOK in shabby sheepskins by the wagon.

THE COOK: No light. Nobody's up yet.

MOTHER COURAGE: But it's a priest. He'll have to crawl out of bed to ring the bells. Then he'll get himself a nice bowl of hot soup.

THE COOK: Go on, you saw the village, everything's been   5
burned to a crisp.

MOTHER COURAGE: But somebody's here, I heard a dog bark.

THE COOK: If the priest's got anything, he won't give it away.

MOTHER COURAGE: Maybe if we sing . . .

THE COOK: I've had it up to here. (Suddenly) I got a letter from   10
Utrecht. My mother's died of cholera and the tavern belongs to me. Here's the letter if you don't believe me. It's no business of yours what my aunt says about my evil ways, but never mind, read it.

MOTHER COURAGE: (reads the letter) Lamb, I'm sick of roam-   15
ing around, myself. I feel like a butcher's dog that pulls the meat cart but doesn't get any for himself. I've nothing left to sell and the people have no money to pay for it. In Saxony a man in rags tried to foist a cord of books on me for two eggs, and in Württemberg they'd have let their plow go for a little   20
bag of salt. What's the good of plowing? Nothing grows but brambles. In Pomerania they say the villagers have eaten up all the babies, and that nuns have been caught at highway robbery.

THE COOK: It's the end of the world.   25

MOTHER COURAGE: Sometimes I have visions of myself driving through hell, selling sulphur and brimstone, or through heaven peddling refreshments to the roaming souls. If me and the children I've got left could find a place where there's no shooting, I wouldn't mind a few years of peace and quiet.   30

THE COOK: We could open up the tavern again. Think it over, Anna. I made up my mind last night; with or without you, I'm going back to Utrecht. In fact I'm leaving today.

MOTHER COURAGE: I'll have to talk to Kattrin. It's kind of sud-   35
den, and I don't like to make decisions in the cold with noth-ing in my stomach. Kattrin! (KATTRIN climbs out of the

wagon) Kattrin, I've got something to tell you. The cook and me are thinking of going to Utrecht. They've left him a tavern there. You'd be living in one place, you'd meet people. A lot
40 of men would be glad to get a nice, well-behaved girl, looks aren't everything. I'm all for it. I get along fine with the cook. I've got to hand it to him: He's got a head for business. We'd eat regular meals, wouldn't that be nice? And you'd have your own bed, wouldn't you like that? It's no life on the road, year
45 in year out. You'll go to rack and ruin. You're crawling with lice already. We've got to decide, you see, we could go north with the Swedes, they must be over there. *(She points to the left)* I think we'll do it, Kattrin.

THE COOK: Anna, could I have a word with you alone?
50 MOTHER COURAGE: Get back in the wagon, Kattrin.

(KATTRIN climbs back in.)

THE COOK: I interrupted you because I see there's been a misunderstanding. I thought it was too obvious to need saying. But if it isn't, I'll just have to say it. You can't take her, it's out of the question. Is that plain enough for you?

(KATTRIN sticks her head out of the wagon and listens.)

55 MOTHER COURAGE: You want me to leave Kattrin?
THE COOK: Look at it this way. There's no room in the tavern. It's not one of those places with three taprooms. If the two of us put our shoulder to the wheel, we can make a living, but not three, it can't be done. Kattrin can keep the wagon.
60 MOTHER COURAGE: I'd been thinking she could find a husband in Utrecht.
THE COOK: Don't make me laugh! How's she going to find a husband? At her age? And dumb! And with that scar!
MOTHER COURAGE: Not so loud.
65 THE COOK: Shout or whisper, the truth's the truth. And that's another reason why I can't have her in the tavern. The customers won't want a sight like that staring them in the face. Can you blame them?
MOTHER COURAGE: Shut up. Not so loud, I say.
70 THE COOK: There's a light in the presbytery. Let's sing.
MOTHER COURAGE: How could she pull the wagon by herself? She's afraid of the war. She couldn't stand it. The dreams she must have! I hear her groaning at night. Especially after battles. What she sees in her dreams, God knows. It's pity that
75 makes her suffer so. The other day the wagon hit a hedgehog, I found it hidden in her blanket.
THE COOK: The tavern's too small. *(He calls)* Worthy gentleman and members of the household! We shall now sing the Song of Solomon, Julius Caesar, and other great men, whose
80 greatness didn't help them any. Just to show you that we're God-fearing people ourselves, which makes it hard for us, especially in the winter. *(They sing)*

You saw the wise King Solomon
You know what came of him.
85 To him all hidden things were plain.
He cursed the hour gave birth to him
And saw that everything was vain.
How great and wise was Solomon!
Now think about his case. Alas
90 A useful lesson can be won.
It's wisdom that had brought him to that pass!
How happy is the man with none!

Our beautiful song proves that virtues are dangerous things, better steer clear of them, enjoy life, eat a good breakfast, a bowl of hot soup, for instance. Take me, I haven't got any 95 soup and wish I had, I'm a soldier, but what has my bravery in all those battles got me, nothing, I'm starving, I'd be better off if I'd stayed home like a yellowbelly. And I'll tell you why.

You saw the daring Caesar next
You know what he became. 100
They deified him in his life
But then they killed him just the same.
And as they raised the fatal knife
How loud he cried: "You too, my son!"
Now think about his case. Alas 105
A useful lesson can be won.
It's daring that had brought him to that pass!
How happy is the man with none!

(In an undertone) They're not even looking out. Worthy gentleman and members of the household! Maybe you'll say, all 110 right, if bravery won't keep body and soul together, try honesty. That may fill your belly or at least get you a drop to drink. Let's look into it.

You've heard of honest Socrates
Who never told a lie. 115
They weren't so grateful as you'd think
Instead they sentenced him to die
And handed him the poisoned drink.
How honest was the people's noble son!
Now think about his case. Alas 120
A useful lesson can be won.
His honesty had brought him to that pass.
How happy is the man with none!

Yes, they tell us to be charitable and to share what we have, but what if we haven't got anything? Maybe philanthropists 125 have a rough time of it too, it stands to reason, they need a little something for themselves. Yes, charity is a rare virtue, because it doesn't pay.

St. Martin couldn't bear to see
His fellows in distress. 130
He saw a poor man in the snow.
"Take half my cloak!" He did, and lo!
They both of them froze none the less.
He thought his heavenly reward was won.
Now think about his case. Alas 135
A useful lesson can be won.
Unselfishness had brought him to that pass.
How happy is the man with none!

That's our situation. We're God-fearing folk, we stick together, we don't steal, we don't murder, we don't set fire to 140 anything! You could say that we set an example which bears out the song, we sink lower and lower, we seldom see any soup, but if we were different, if we were thieves and murderers, maybe our bellies would be full. Because virtue isn't rewarded, only wickedness, the world needn't be like this, 145 but it is.

And here you see God-fearing folk
Observing God's ten laws.
So far He hasn't taken heed.

150
　　You people sitting warm indoors
　　Help to relieve our bitter need!
　　Our virtue can be counted on.
　　Now think about our case. Alas
155　A useful lesson can be won.
　　The fear of God has brought us to this pass.
　　How happy is the man with none!

VOICE: (*from above*) Hey, down there! Come on up! We've got
　　some good thick soup.

MOTHER COURAGE: Lamb, I couldn't get anything down. I
160　know what you say makes sense, but is it your last word? We've
　　always been good friends.

THE COOK: My last word. Think it over.

MOTHER COURAGE: I don't need to think it over. I won't leave her.

THE COOK: It wouldn't be wise, but there's nothing I can do. I'm
165　not inhuman, but it's a small tavern. We'd better go in now, or
　　there won't be anything left, we'll have been singing in the
　　cold for nothing.

MOTHER COURAGE: I'll get Kattrin.

THE COOK: Better bring it down for her. They'll get a fright if the
170　three of us barge in. (*They go out*)

(KATTRIN *climbs out of the wagon. She is carrying a bundle. She
looks around to make sure the others are gone. Then she spreads
out an old pair of the cook's trousers and a skirt belonging to her
mother side by side on a wheel of the wagon so they can easily be
seen. She is about to leave with her bundle when* MOTHER COUR-
AGE *comes out of the house.*)

MOTHER COURAGE: (*with a dish of soup*) Kattrin! Stop! Kattrin!
　　Where do you think you're going with that bundle? Have you
　　taken leave of your wits? (*She examines the bundle*) She's
　　packed her things. Were you listening? I've told him it's no go
175　with Utrecht and his lousy tavern, what would we do there? A
　　tavern's no place for you and me. The war still has a thing or
　　two up its sleeve for us. (*She sees the trousers and skirt*) You're
　　stupid. Suppose I'd seen that and you'd been gone? (KATTRIN
　　tries to leave, MOTHER COURAGE *holds her back*) And don't go
180　thinking I've given him the gate on your account. It's the
　　wagon. I won't part with the wagon, I'm used to it, it's not
　　you, it's the wagon. We'll go in the other direction, we'll put
　　the cook's stuff out here where he'll find it, the fool. (*She
　　climbs up and throws down a few odds and ends to join the
185　trousers*) There. Now we're shut of him, you won't see me
　　taking anyone else into the business. From now on it's you
　　and me. This winter will go by like all the rest. Harness up, it
　　looks like snow.

(*They harness themselves to the wagon, turn it around and pull it
away. When* THE COOK *comes out he sees his things and stands
dumbfounded.*)

SCENE X

> Throughout 1635 Mother Courage and her daughter
> Kattrin pull the wagon over the roads of central Germany
> in the wake of the increasingly bedraggled armies.

Highway.

MOTHER COURAGE *and* KATTRIN *are pulling the wagon. They
come to a peasant's house. A voice is heard singing from within.*

THE VOICE:

　　The rose bush in our garden
　　Rejoiced our hearts in spring
　　It bore such lovely flowers.
　　We planted it last season　　　　　　　　　5
　　Before the April showers.
　　A garden is a blessèd thing
　　It bore such lovely flowers.

　　When winter comes a-stalking
　　And gales great snow storms bring　　　　10
　　They trouble us but little.
　　We've lately finished caulking
　　The roof with moss and wattle.
　　A sheltering roof's a blessèd thing
　　When winter comes a-stalking.　　　　　　15

(MOTHER COURAGE *and* KATTRIN *have stopped to listen. Then
they move on.*)

SCENE XI

> January 1636. The imperial troops threaten the Pro-
> testant city of Halle. The stone speaks. Mother Courage
> loses her daughter and goes on alone. The end of the war
> is not in sight.

*The wagon, much the worse for wear, is standing beside a peasant
house with an enormous thatch roof. The house is built against
the side of a stony hill. Night.*

A LIEUTENANT *and three* SOLDIERS *in heavy armor step out of
the woods.*

THE LIEUTENANT: I don't want any noise. If anybody yells, run
　　him through with your pikes.

FIRST SOLDIER: But we need a guide. We'll have to knock if we
　　want them to come out.

THE LIEUTENANT: Knocking sounds natural. It could be a cow　　5
　　bumping against the barn wall.

(*The* SOLDIERS *knock on the door. A* PEASANT WOMAN *opens.
They hold their hands over her mouth. Two* SOLDIERS *go in.*)

A MAN'S VOICE: (*inside*) Who's there?

(*The* SOLDIERS *bring out a* PEASANT *and his son.*)

THE LIEUTENANT: (*points to the wagon, in which* KATTRIN *has
　　appeared*) There's another one. (*A* SOLDIER *pulls her out*)
　　Anybody else live here?　　　　　　　　　　　　　　　　　　10

THE PEASANT COUPLE: This is our son. —That's a dumb
　　girl. —Her mother's gone into the town on business. —Buy-
　　ing up people's belongings, they're selling cheap because
　　they're getting out. —They're provisioners.

THE LIEUTENANT: I'm warning you to keep quiet, one squawk　　15
　　and you'll get a pike over the head. All right. I need somebody
　　who can show us the path into the city. (*Points to* THE YOUNG
　　PEASANT) You. Come here!

THE YOUNG PEASANT: I don't know no path.

THE SECOND SOLDIER: (*grinning*) He don't know no path.　　　20

THE YOUNG PEASANT: I'm not helping the Catholics.

THE LIEUTENANT: (*to* THE SECOND SOLDIER) Give him a feel
　　of your pike!

THE YOUNG PEASANT: *(forced down on his knees and threatened with the pike)* You can kill me. I won't do it.

THE FIRST SOLDIER: I know what'll make him think twice. *(He goes over to the barn)* Two cows and an ox. Get this: If you don't help us, I'll cut them down.

THE YOUNG PEASANT: Not the animals!

THE PEASANT WOMAN: *(in tears)* Captain, spare our animals or we'll starve.

THE LIEUTENANT: If he insists on being stubborn, they're done for.

THE FIRST SOLDIER: I'll start with the ox.

THE YOUNG PEASANT: *(to THE OLD MAN)* Do I have to? *(THE OLD WOMAN nods)* I'll do it.

THE PEASANT WOMAN: And thank you kindly for your forbearance, Captain, for ever and ever, amen.

(THE PEASANT stops her from giving further thanks.)

THE FIRST SOLDIER: Didn't I tell you? With them it's the animals that come first.

(Led by THE YOUNG PEASANT, THE LIEUTENANT and the SOLDIERS continue on their way.)

THE PEASANT: I wish I knew what they're up to. Nothing good.

THE PEASANT WOMAN: Maybe they're only scouts. —What are you doing?

THE PEASANT: *(putting a ladder against the roof and climbing up)* See if they're alone. *(On the roof)* Men moving in the woods. All the way to the quarry. Armor in the clearing. And a cannon. It's more than a regiment. God have mercy on the city and everybody in it.

THE PEASANT WOMAN: See any light in the city?

THE PEASANT: No. They're asleep. *(He climbs down)* If they get in, they'll kill everybody.

THE PEASANT WOMAN: The sentry will see them in time.

THE PEASANT: They must have killed the sentry in the tower on the hill, or he'd have blown his horn.

THE PEASANT WOMAN: If there were more of us . . .

THE PEASANT: All by ourselves up here with a cripple . . .

THE PEASANT WOMAN: We can't do a thing. Do you think . . .

THE PEASANT: Not a thing.

THE PEASANT WOMAN: We couldn't get down there in the dark.

THE PEASANT: The whole hillside is full of them. We can't even give a signal.

THE PEASANT WOMAN: They'd kill us.

THE PEASANT: No, we can't do a thing.

THE PEASANT WOMAN: *(to KATTRIN)* Pray, poor thing, pray! We can't stop the bloodshed. If you can't talk, at least you can pray. He'll hear you if nobody else does. I'll help you. *(All kneel, KATTRIN behind the PEASANTS)* Our Father which art in heaven, hear our prayer. Don't let the town perish with everybody in it, all asleep and unsuspecting. Wake them, make them get up and climb the walls and see the enemy coming through the night with cannon and pikes, through the fields and down the hillside. *(Back to KATTRIN)* Protect our mother and don't let the watchman sleep, wake him before it's too late. And succor our brother-in-law, he's in there with his four children, let them not perish, they're innocent and don't know a thing. *(To KATTRIN, who groans)* The littlest is less than two, the oldest is seven. *(Horrified, KATTRIN stands up)* Our Father, hear us, for Thou alone canst help, we'll all be killed, we're weak, we haven't any pikes or anything, we are powerless and in Thine hands, we and our animals and the whole farm, and the city too, it's in Thine hands, and the enemy is under the walls with great might.

(KATTRIN has crept unnoticed to the wagon, taken something out of it, put it under her apron and climbed up the ladder to the roof of the barn.)

THE PEASANT WOMAN: Think upon the children in peril, especially the babes in arms and the old people that can't help themselves and all God's creatures.

THE PEASANT: And forgive us our trespasses as we forgive them that trespass against us. Amen.

(KATTRIN, sitting on the roof, starts beating the drum that she has taken out from under her apron.)

THE PEASANT WOMAN: Jesus! What's she doing?

THE PEASANT: She's gone crazy.

THE PEASANT WOMAN: Get her down, quick!

(THE PEASANT runs toward the ladder, but KATTRIN pulls it up on the roof.)

THE PEASANT WOMAN: She'll be the death of us all.

THE PEASANT: Stop that, you cripple!

THE PEASANT WOMAN: She'll have the Catholics down on us.

THE PEASANT: *(looking around for stones)* I'll throw rocks at you.

THE PEASANT WOMAN: Have you no pity? Have you no heart? We're dead if they find out it's us! They'll run us through!

(KATTRIN stares in the direction of the city, and goes on drumming.)

THE PEASANT WOMAN: *(to THE PEASANT)* I told you not to let those tramps stop here. What do they care if the soldiers drive our last animals away?

THE LIEUTENANT: *(rushes in with his SOLDIERS and THE YOUNG PEASANT)* I'll cut you to pieces!

THE PEASANT WOMAN: We're innocent, captain. We couldn't help it. She sneaked up there. We don't know her.

THE LIEUTENANT: Where's the ladder?

THE PEASANT: Up top.

THE LIEUTENANT: *(to KATTRIN)* Throw down that drum. It's an order!

(KATTRIN goes on drumming.)

THE LIEUTENANT: You're all in this together! This'll be the end of you!

THE PEASANT: They've felled some pine trees in the woods over there. We could get one and knock her down . . .

THE FIRST SOLDIER: *(to THE LIEUTENANT)* Request permission to make a suggestion. *(He whispers something in THE LIEUTENANT's ear. He nods)* Listen. We've got a friendly proposition. Come down, we'll take you into town with us. Show us your mother and we won't touch a hair of her head.

(KATTRIN goes on drumming.)

THE LIEUTENANT: *(pushes him roughly aside)* She doesn't trust you. No wonder with your mug. *(He calls up)* If I give you my word? I'm an officer, you can trust my word of honor.

(She drums still louder.)

THE LIEUTENANT: Nothing is sacred to her.

THE YOUNG PEASANT: It's not just her mother, lieutenant!

THE FIRST SOLDIER: We can't let this go on. They'll hear it in the city.

125 THE LIEUTENANT: We'll have to make some kind of noise that's louder than the drums. What could we make noise with?

THE FIRST SOLDIER: But we're not supposed to make noise.

THE LIEUTENANT: An innocent noise, stupid. A peaceable noise.

THE PEASANT: I could chop wood.

130 THE LIEUTENANT: That's it, chop! (THE PEASANT *gets an ax and chops at a log*) Harder! Harder! You're chopping for your life.

(*Listening,* KATTRIN *has been drumming more softly. Now she looks anxiously around and goes on drumming as before.*)

THE LIEUTENANT: (*to* THE PEASANT) Not loud enough. (*To* THE FIRST SOLDIER) You chop too.

THE PEASANT: There's only one ax. (*Stops chopping*)

135 THE LIEUTENANT: We'll have to set the house on fire. Smoke her out.

THE PEASANT: That won't do any good, captain. If the city people see fire up here, they'll know what's afoot.

(*Still drumming,* KATTRIN *has been listening again. Now she laughs.*)

THE LIEUTENANT: Look, she's laughing at us. I'll shoot her

140 down, regardless. Get the musket!

(*Two* SOLDIERS *run out.* KATTRIN *goes on drumming.*)

THE PEASANT WOMAN: I've got it, captain. That's their wagon over there. If we start smashing it up, she'll stop. The wagon's all they've got.

THE LIEUTENANT: (*to* THE YOUNG PEASANT) Smash away. (*To*

145 KATTRIN) We'll smash your wagon if you don't stop.

(THE YOUNG PEASANT *strikes a few feeble blows at the wagon.*)

THE PEASANT WOMAN: Stop it, you beast!

(KATTRIN *stares despairingly at the wagon and emits pitiful sounds. But she goes on drumming.*)

THE LIEUTENANT: Where are those stinkers with the musket?

THE FIRST SOLDIER: They haven't heard anything in the city yet, or we'd hear their guns.

150 THE LIEUTENANT: (*to* KATTRIN) They don't hear you. And now we're going to shoot you down. For the last time: Drop that drum!

THE YOUNG PEASANT: (*suddenly throws the plank away*) Keep on drumming! Or they'll all be killed! Keep on drumming,

155 keep on drumming . . .

(*The* SOLDIER *throws him down and hits him with his pike.* KATTRIN *starts crying, but goes on drumming.*)

THE PEASANT WOMAN: Don't hit him in the back! My God, you're killing him.

(*The* SOLDIERS *run in with the musket.*)

THE SECOND SOLDIER: The colonel's foaming at the mouth. We'll be court-martialed.

160 THE LIEUTENANT: Set it up! Set it up! (*To* KATTRIN, *while the musket is being set up on its stand*) For the last time: Stop that drumming! (KATTRIN *in tears drums as loud as she can*) Fire!

(*The* SOLDIERS *fire.* KATTRIN *is hit. She beats the drum a few times more and then slowly collapses.*)

THE LIEUTENANT: Now we'll have some quiet.

(*But* KATTRIN'S *last drumbeats are answered by the city's cannon. A confused hubbub of alarm bells and cannon is heard in the distance.*)

FIRST SOLDIER: She's done it.

SCENE XII

Night, toward morning. The fifes and drums of troops marching away.

Outside the wagon MOTHER COURAGE *sits huddled over her daughter. The peasant couple are standing beside them.*

THE PEASANT: (*hostile*) You'll have to be going, woman. There's only one more regiment to come. You can't go alone.

MOTHER COURAGE: Maybe I can get her to sleep. (*She sings*)

> Lullaby baby
> What stirs in the hay?   5
> The neighbor brats whimper
> Mine are happy and gay.
> They go in tatters
> And you in silk down
> Cut from an angel's   10
> Best party gown.
>
> They've nothing to munch on
> And you will have pie
> Just tell your mother
> In case it's too dry.   15
> Lullaby baby
> What stirs in the hay?
> The one lies in Poland
> The other — who can say?

Now she's asleep. You shouldn't have told her about your   20
brother-in-law's children.

THE PEASANT: Maybe it wouldn't have happened if you hadn't gone to town to swindle people.

MOTHER COURAGE: I'm glad she's sleeping now.

THE PEASANT WOMAN: She's not sleeping, you'll have to face it,   25
she's dead.

THE PEASANT: And it's time you got started. There are wolves around here, and what's worse, marauders.

MOTHER COURAGE: Yes. (*She goes to the wagon and takes out a sheet of canvas to cover the body with*)   30

THE PEASANT WOMAN: Haven't you anybody else? Somebody you can go to?

MOTHER COURAGE: Yes, there's one of them left. Eilif.

THE PEASANT: (*while* MOTHER COURAGE *covers the body*) Go find him. We'll attend to this one, give her a decent burial.   35
Set your mind at rest.

MOTHER COURAGE: Here's money for your expenses. (*She gives* THE PEASANT *money*)

(THE PEASANT *and his son shake hands with her and carry* KATTRIN *away.*)

THE PEASANT WOMAN: (*on the way out*) Hurry up!

MOTHER COURAGE: (*harnesses herself to the wagon*) I hope I   40
can pull the wagon alone. I'll manage, there isn't much in it.
I've got to get back in business.

(Another regiment marches by with fifes and drums in the rear.)

MOTHER COURAGE: Hey, take me with you! *(She starts to pull)*

(Singing is heard in the rear:)

45   With all the killing and recruiting
          The war will worry on a while.
          In ninety years they'll still be shooting.
          It's hardest on the rank-and-file.

Our food is swill, our pants all patches
The higher-ups steal half our pay
And still we dream of God-sent riches.   50
Tomorrow is another day!
    The spring is come! Christian, revive!
    The snowdrifts melt, the dead lie dead!
    And if by chance you're still alive
    It's time to rise and shake a leg.   55

AN INFLUENTIAL NOVEL-
ist, playwright, and literary theorist, Zola became
the spokesman for natu-
ralism in the theater in a series of articles he wrote in the 1870s, collected as Naturalism in the Theatre
in 1878. In these essays, Zola urged the theater to adopt an attitude of scientific objectivity, an attitude
reflected in the development of a new dramatic style. The naturalistic theater asserted such objectivity
through its choice of subject matter (middle-class life), its treatment of characters (driven by "physiological" motives, not by "metaphysical" passions), its use of a prosaic, antiliterary language, and by
the importance attached to the material environment.

ÉMILE ZOLA
(1840–1902)

FROM *Naturalism in
the Theatre*
(1878)

TRANSLATED BY
ALBERT BERMEL

It seems impossible that the movement of inquiry and analysis, which is precisely the movement
of the nineteenth century, can have revolutionized all the sciences and arts and left dramatic art to
one side, as if isolated. The natural sciences date from the end of the last century; chemistry and
physics are less than a hundred years old; history and criticism have been renovated, virtually recreated since the Revolution; an entire world has arisen; it has sent us back to the study of documents,
to experience, made us realize that to start afresh we must first take things back to the beginning,
become familiar with man and nature, verify what is. Thenceforward, the great naturalistic school,
which has spread secretly, irrevocably, often making its way in darkness but always advancing, can
finally come out triumphantly into the light of day. To trace the history of this movement, with the
misunderstandings that might have impeded it and the multiple causes that have thrust it forward or
slowed it down, would be to trace the history of the century itself. An irresistible current carries our
society towards the study of reality. In the novel Balzac has been the bold and mighty innovator who
has replaced the observation of the scholar with the imagination of the poet. But in the theatre the
evolution seems slower. No eminent writer has yet formulated the new idea with any clarity.

I certainly do not say that some excellent works have not been produced, with characters in them
who are ingeniously examined and bold truths taken right on to the stage. Let me, for instance, cite
certain plays by M. Dumas *fils*, whose talent I scarcely admire, and M. Émile Augier, the most
humane and powerful of all. Still, they are midgets beside Balzac; they lack the genius to lay down the
formula. It must be said that one can never tell quite when a movement is getting under way;
generally its source is remote and lost in the earlier movement from which it emerged. In a manner of
speaking, the naturalistic current has always existed. It brings with it nothing absolutely novel. But it
has finally flowed into a period favourable to it; it is succeeding and expanding because the human
mind has attained the necessary maturity. I do not, therefore, deny the past; I affirm the present. The
strength of naturalism is precisely that it has deep roots in our national literature which contains
plenty of wisdom. It comes from the very entrails of humanity; it is that much the stronger because it
has taken longer to grow and is found in a greater number of our masterpieces.

Certain things have come to pass and I point them out. Can we believe that *L'Ami Fritz* would
have been applauded at the Comédie-Française twenty years ago? Definitely not! This play, in which
people eat all the time and the lover talks in such homely language, would have disgusted both the
classicists and the romantics. To explain its success we must concede that as the years have gone by a
secret fermentation has been at work. Lifelike paintings, which used to repel the public, today attract
them. The majority has been won over and the stage is open to every experiment. This is the only
conclusion to draw.

So that is where we stand. To explain my point better—I am not afraid of repeating myself—I
will sum up what I have said. Looking closely at the history of our dramatic literature, one can detect
several clearly separated periods. First, there was the infancy of the art, farces and the mystery plays of
the Middle Ages, the reciting of simple dialogues which developed as part of a naïve convention, with
primitive staging and sets. Gradually, the plays became more complex but in a crude fashion. When
Corneille appeared he was acclaimed most of all for his status as an innovator, for refining the
dramatic formula of the time, and for hallowing it by means of his genius. It would be very interesting
to study the pertinent documents and discover how our classical formula came to be created. It
corresponded to the social spirit of the period. Nothing is solid that is not built on necessity. Tragedy

reigned for two centuries because it satisfied the exact requirements of those centuries. Geniuses of differing temperaments had buttressed it with their masterpieces. And it continued to impose itself long afterwards, even when second-rate talents were producing inferior work. It acquired a momentum. It persisted also as the literary expression of that society, and nothing would have overthrown it if the society had not itself disappeared. After the Revolution, after that profound disturbance that was meant to transform everything and give birth to a new world, tragedy struggled to stay alive for a few more years. Then the formula cracked and romanticism broke through. A new formula asserted itself. We must look back at the first half of the century to understand the meaning of this cry for liberty. The young society was in the tremor of its infancy. The excited, bewildered, violently unleashed people were still racked by a dangerous fever; and in the first flush of their new liberty they yearned for prodigious adventures and superhuman love affairs. They gaped at the stars; some committed suicide, a very curious reaction to the social enfranchisement which had just been declared at the cost of so much blood. Turning specifically to dramatic literature, I maintain that romanticism in the theatre was an uncomplicated revolt, the invasion by a victorious group who took over the stage violently with drums beating and flags flying. In these early moments the combatants dreamed of making their imprint with a new form; to one rhetoric they opposed another: the Middle Ages to Antiquity, the exalting of passion to the exalting of duty. And that was all, for only the scenic conventions were altered. The characters remained marionettes in new clothing. Only the exterior aspect and the language were modified. But for the period that was enough. Romanticism had taken possession of the theatre in the name of literary freedom and it carried out its revolutionary task with incomparable bravura. But who does not see today that its role could extend no farther than that? Does romanticism have anything whatever to say about our present society? Does it meet one of our requirements? Obviously not. It is as outmoded as a jargon we no longer follow. It confidently expected to replace classical literature which had lasted for two centuries because it was based on social conditions. But romanticism was based on nothing but the fantasy of a few poets or, if you will, on the passing malady of minds overwhelmed by historical events; it was bound to disappear with the malady. It provided the occasion for a magnificent flowering of lyricism; that will be its eternal glory. Today, however, with the evolution accomplished, it is plain that romanticism was no more than the necessary link between classicism and naturalism. The struggle is over; now we must found a secure state. Naturalism flows out of classical art, just as our present society has arisen from the wreckage of the old society. Naturalism alone corresponds to our social needs; it alone has deep roots in the spirit of our times; and it alone can provide a living, durable formula for our art, because this formula will express the nature of our contemporary intelligence. There may be fashions and passing fantasies that exist outside naturalism but they will not survive for long. I say again, naturalism is the expression of our century and it will not die until a new upheaval transforms our democratic world.

Only one thing is needed now: men of genius who can fix the naturalistic formula. Balzac has done it for the novel and the novel is established. When will our Corneilles, Molières and Racines appear to establish our new theatre? We must hope and wait.

✱   ✱   ✱

The period when romantic drama ruled now seems distant. In Paris five or six of its playhouses prospered. The demolition of the old theatres along the Boulevard du Temple was a catastrophe of the first order. The theatres became separated from one another, the public changed, different fashions arose. But the discredit into which the drama has fallen proceeds mostly from the exhaustion of the genre — ridiculous, boring plays have gradually taken over from the potent works of 1830.

To this enfeeblement we must add the absolute lack of new actors who understand and can interpret these kinds of plays, for every dramatic formula that vanishes carries away its interpreters with it. Today the drama, hunted from stage to stage, has only two houses that really belong to it, the Ambigu and the Théâtre-Historique. Even at the Saint-Martin the drama is lucky to win a brief showing for itself, between one great spectacle and the next.

An occasional success may renew its courage. But its decline is inevitable; romantic drama is sliding into oblivion, and if it seems sometimes to check its descent, it does so only to roll even lower afterwards. Naturally, there are loud complaints. The tail-end romanticists are desperately unhappy.

They swear that except in the drama — meaning their kind of drama — there is no salvation for dramatic literature. I believe, on the contrary, that we must find a new formula that will transform the drama, just as the writers in the first half of the century transformed tragedy. That is the essence of the matter. Today the battle is between romantic drama and naturalistic drama. By romantic drama I mean every play that mocks truthfulness in its incidents and characterization, that struts about in its puppet-box, stuffed to the belly with noises that flounder, for some idealistic reason or other, in pastiches of Shakespeare and Hugo. Every period has its formula; ours is certainly not that of 1830. We are an age of method, of experimental science; our primary need is for precise analysis. We hardly understand the liberty we have won if we use it only to imprison ourselves in a new tradition. The way is open: we can now return to man and nature.

Finally, there have been great efforts to revive the historical drama. Nothing could be better. A critic cannot roundly condemn the choice of historical subjects, even if his own preferences are entirely for subjects that are modern. It is simply that I am full of distrust. The manager one gives this sort of play to frightens me in advance. It is a question of how history is treated, what unusual characters are presented bearing the names of kings, great captains or great artists, and what awful sauce they are served up in to make the history palatable. As soon as the authors of these concoctions move into the past they think everything is permitted: improbabilities, cardboard dolls, monumental idiocies, the hysterical scribblings that falsely represent local colour. And what strange dialogue — François I talking like a haberdasher straight out of the Rue Saint-Denis, Richelieu using the words of a criminal from the Boulevard du Crime, Charlotte Corday with the weeping sentimentalities of a factory girl.

What astounds me is that our playwrights do not seem to suspect for a moment that the historical genre is unavoidably the least rewarding, the one that calls most strongly for research, integrity, a consummate gift of intuition, a talent for reconstruction. I am all for historical drama when it is in the hands of poets of genius or men of exceptional knowledge who are capable of making the public see an epoch come alive with its special quality, its manners, its civilization. In that case we have a work of prophecy or of profoundly interesting criticism.

But unfortunately I know what it is these partisans of historical drama want to revive: the swaggering and swordplay, the big spectacle with big words, the play of lies that shows off in front of the crowd, the gross exhibition that saddens honest minds. Hence my distrust. I think that all this antiquated business is better left in our museum of dramatic history under a pious layer of dust.

There are, undeniably, great obstacles to original experiments: we run up against the hypocrisies of criticism and the long education in idiocies that has been foisted on the public. This public, which titters at every childishness in melodramas, nevertheless lets itself be carried away by outbursts of fine sentiment. But the public is changing. Shakespeare's public and Molière's are no longer ours. We must reckon with shifts in outlook, with the need for reality which is everywhere getting more insistent. The last few romantics vainly repeat that the public wants this and the public wants that; the day is coming when the public will want the truth.

✤   ✤   ✤

The old formulas, classical and romantic, were based on the rearrangement and systematic amputation of the truth. They determined on principle that the truth is not good enough; they tried to draw out of it an essence, a 'poetry', on the pretext that nature must be expurgated and magnified. Up to the present the different literary schools disputed only over the question of the best way to disguise the truth so that it might not look too brazen to the public. The classicists adopted the toga; the romantics fought a revolution to impose the coat of mail and the doublet. Essentially the change of dress made little difference; the counterfeiting of nature went on. But today the naturalistic thinkers are telling us that the truth does not need clothing; it can walk naked. That, I repeat, is the quarrel.

Writers with any sense understand perfectly that tragedy and romantic drama are dead. The majority, though, are badly troubled when they turn their minds to the as-yet-unclear formula of tomorrow. Does the truth seriously ask them to give up the grandeur, the poetry, the traditional epic effects that their ambition tells them to put into their plays? Does naturalism demand that they shrink their horizons and risk not one flight into fantasy?

I will try to reply. But first we must determine the methods used by the idealists to lift their works into poetry. They begin by placing their chosen subject in a distant time. That provides them with costumes and makes the framework of the story vague enough to give them full scope for lying. Next, they generalize instead of particularizing; their characters are no longer living people but sentiments, arguments, passions that have been induced by reasoning. This false framework calls for heroes of marble or cardboard. A man of flesh and bone with his own originality would jar in such a legendary setting. Moreover, when we see the characters in romantic drama or tragedy walking about they are stiffened into an attitude, one representing duty, another patriotism, a third superstition, a fourth maternal love; thus, all the abstract ideas file by. Never the thorough analysis of an organism, never a character whose muscles and brain function as in nature.

These, then, are the mannerisms that writers with epic inclinations do not want to give up. For them poetry resides in the past and in abstraction, in the idealizing of facts and characters. As soon as one confronts them with daily life, with the people who fill our streets, they blink, they stammer, they are afraid; they no longer see clearly; they find everything ugly and not good enough for art. According to them, a subject must enter the lies of legend, men must harden and turn to stone like statues before the artist can accept them and make them fit the disguises he has prepared.

Now, it is at this point that the naturalistic movement comes along and says squarely that poetry is everywhere, in everything, even more in the present and the real than in the past and the abstract. Each event at each moment has its poetic, superb aspect. We brush up against heroes who are great and powerful in different respects from the puppets of the epic-makers. Not one playwright in this century has brought to life figures as lofty as Baron Hulot, Old Grandet, César Birotteau, and all the other characters of Balzac, who are so individual and so alive. Beside these real, giant creations Greek and Roman heroes quake; the heroes of the Middle Ages fall flat on their faces like lead soldiers.

With the superior works being produced in these times by the naturalistic school — works of high endeavour, pulsing with life — it is ridiculous and false to park our poetry in some antiquated temple and bury it in cobwebs. Poetry flows at its full force through everything that exists; the truer to life, the greater it becomes. And I mean to give the word poetry its widest definition, not to pin it down exclusively to the cadence of two rhymes, nor to burn it in a narrow coterie of dreamers, but to restore its real human significance which concerns the expansion and encouragement of every kind of truth.

Take our present environment, then, and try to make men live in it: you will write great works. It will undoubtedly call for some effort; it means sifting out of the confusion of life the simple formula of naturalism. Therein lies the difficulty: to do great things with the subjects and characters that our eyes, accustomed to the spectacle of the daily round, have come to see as small. I am aware that it is more convenient to present a marionette to the public and name it Charlemagne and puff it up with such tirades that the public believes it is watching a colossus; it is more convenient than taking a bourgeois of our time, a grotesque, unsightly man, and drawing sublime poetry out of him, making him, for example, Père Goriot, the father who gives his guts for his daughters, a figure so gigantic with truth and love that no other literature can offer his equal.

Nothing is as easy as persuading the managers with known formulas; and heroes in the classical or romantic taste cost so little labour that they are manufactured by the dozen, and have become standardized articles that clutter up our literature. But it takes hard work to create a real hero, intelligently analysed, alive and performing. That is probably why naturalism terrifies those authors who are used to fishing up great men from the troubled waters of history. They would have to burrow too deeply into humanity, learn about life, go straight for the greatness of reality and make it function with all their power. And let nobody gainsay this true poetry of humanity; it has been sifted out in the novel and can be in the theatre; only the method of adaptation remains to be found.

I am troubled by a comparison; it has been haunting me and I will now free myself of it. For two long months a play called *Les Danicheff* has been running at the Odéon. It takes place in Russia. It has been very successful here, but is apparently so dishonest, so packed with gross improbabilities, that the author, a Russian, has not even dared to show it in his country. What can you think of this work which is applauded in Paris and would be booed in St Petersburg? Well, imagine for a moment that the Romans could come back to life and see a performance of *Rome vaincue*. Can you hear their roars of laughter? Do you think the play would complete one performance? It would strike them as a parody; it would sink under the weight of mockery. And is there one historical play that could be performed before the society it claims to portray? A strange theatre, this, which is plausible only among foreigners, is based on the disappearance of the generations it deals with, and is made up of so much misinformation that it is good only for the ignorant!

The future is with naturalism. The formula will be found; it will be proved that there is more poetry in the little apartment of a bourgeois than in all the empty, worm-eaten palaces of history; in the end we will see that everything meets in the real: lovely fantasies that are free of capriciousness and whimsy, and idylls, and comedies, and dramas. Once the soil has been turned over, the task that seems alarming and unfeasible today will become easy.

I am not qualified to pronounce on the form that tomorrow's drama will take; that must be left to the voice of some genius to come. But I will allow myself to indicate the path I consider our theatre will follow.

First, the romantic drama must be abandoned. It would be disastrous for us to take over its outrageous acting, its rhetoric, its inherent thesis of action at the expense of character analysis. The finest models of the genre are, as has been said, mere operas with big effects. I believe, then, that we must go back to tragedy — not, heaven forbid, to borrow more of its rhetoric, its system of confidants, its declaiming, its endless speeches, but to return to its simplicity of action and its unique psychological and physiological study of the characters. Thus understood, the tragic framework is excellent; one deed unwinds in all its reality, and moves the characters to passions and feelings, the exact analysis of which constitutes the sole interest of the play — and in a contemporary environment, with the people who surround us.

My constant concern, my anxious vigil, has made me wonder which of us will have the strength to raise himself to the pitch of genius. If the naturalistic drama must come into being, only a genius can give birth to it. Corneille and Racine made tragedy. Victor Hugo made romantic drama. Where is the as-yet-unknown author who must make the naturalistic drama? In recent years experiments have not been wanting. But either because the public was not ready or because none of the beginners had the necessary staying-power, not one of these attempts has had decisive results.

In battles of this kind, small victories mean nothing; we need triumphs that overwhelm the adversary and win the public to the cause. Audiences would give way before the onslaught of a really strong man. This man would come with the expected word, the solution to the problem, the formula for a real life on stage, combining it with the illusions necessary in the theatre. He would have what the newcomers have as yet lacked: the cleverness or the might to impose himself and to remain so close to truth that his cleverness could not lead him into lies.

And what an immense place this innovator would occupy in our dramatic literature! He would be at the peak. He would build his monument in the middle of the desert of mediocrity that we are crossing, among the jerry-built houses strewn about our most illustrious stages. He would put everything in question and remake everything, scour the boards, create a world whose elements he would lift from life, from outside our traditions. Surely there is no more ambitious dream that a writer of our time could fulfil. The domain of the novel is crowded; the domain of the theatre is free. At this time in France an imperishable glory awaits the man of genius who takes up the work of Molière and finds in the reality of living comedy the full, true drama of modern society.

✤   ✤   ✤

Physiological Man

. . . In effect, the great naturalistic evolution, which comes down directly from the fifteenth century to ours has everything to do with the gradual substitution of physiological man for metaphysical man. In tragedy metaphysical man, man according to dogma and logic, reigned absolutely. The body did not count; the soul was regarded as the only interesting piece of human machinery; drama took place in the air, in pure mind. Consequently, what use was the tangible world? Why worry about the place where the action was located? Why be surprised at a baroque costume or false declaiming? Why notice that Queen Dido was a boy whose budding beard forced him to wear a mask? None of that mattered; these trifles were not worth stooping to; the play was heard out as if it were a school essay or a law case; it was on a higher plane than man, in the world of ideas, so far away from real man that any intrusion of reality would have spoiled the show.

Such is the point of departure — in Mystery plays, the religious point; the philosophical point in tragedy. And from that beginning natural man, stifling under the rhetoric and dogma, struggled secretly, tried to break free, made lengthy, futile efforts, and in the end asserted himself, limb by limb.

The whole history of our theatre is in this conquest by the physiological man, who emerged more clearly in each period from behind the dummy of religious and philosophical idealism. Corneille, Molière, Racine, Voltaire, Beaumarchais and, in our day, Victor Hugo, Émile Augier, Alexandre Dumas *fils*, even Sardou, have had only one task, even when they were not completely aware of it: to increase the reality of our corpus of drama, to progress towards truth, to sift out more and more of the natural man and impose him on the public. And inevitably, the evolution will not end with them. It continues; it will continue forever. Mankind is very young. . . .

Costume, Stage Design, Speech

Modern clothes make a poor spectacle. If we depart from bourgeois tragedy, shut in between its four walls, and wish to use the breadth of larger stages for crowd scenes we are embarrassed and constrained by the monotony and the uniformly funereal look of the extras. In this case, I think, we should take advantage of the variety of garb offered by the different classes and occupations. To elaborate: I can imagine an author setting one act in the main marketplace of les Halles in Paris. The setting would be superb, with its bustling life and bold possibilities. In this immense setting we could have a very picturesque ensemble by displaying the porters wearing their large hats, the saleswomen with their white aprons and vividly-coloured scarves, the customers dressed in silk or wool or cotton prints, from the ladies accompanied by their maids to the female beggars on the prowl for anything they can pick up off the street. For inspiration it would be enough to go to les Halles and look about. Nothing is gaudier or more interesting. All of Paris would enjoy seeing this set if it were realized with the necessary accuracy and amplitude.

And how many other settings for popular drama there are for the taking! Inside a factory, the interior of a mine, the gingerbread market, a railway station, flower stalls, a racetrack, and so on. All the activities of modern life can take place in them. It will be said that such sets have already been tried. Unquestionably we have seen factories and railway stations in fantasy plays; but these were fantasy stations and factories. I mean, these sets were thrown together to create an illusion that was at best incomplete. What we need is detailed reproduction: costumes supplied by tradespeople, not sumptuous but adequate for the purposes of truth and for the interest of the scenes. Since everybody mourns the death of the drama our playwrights certainly ought to make a try at this type of popular, contemporary drama. At one stroke they could satisfy the public hunger for spectacle and the need for exact studies which grows more pressing every day. Let us hope, though, that the playwrights will show us real people and not those whining members of the working class who play such strange roles in boulevard melodrama.

As M. Adolphe Jullien has said — and I will never be tired of repeating it — everything is interdependent in the theatre. Lifelike costumes look wrong if the sets, the diction, the plays themselves are not lifelike. They must all march in step along the naturalistic road. When costume becomes more accurate, so do sets; actors free themselves from bombastic declaiming; plays study reality more closely and their characters are more true to life. I could make the same observations about sets I have just made about costume. With them too, we may seem to have reached the highest possible degree of truth, but we still have long strides to take. Most of all we would need to intensify the illusion in reconstructing the environments, less for their picturesque quality than for dramatic utility. The environment must determine the character. When a set is planned so as to give the lively impression of a description by Balzac; when, as the curtain rises, one catches the first glimpse of the characters, their personalities and behaviour, if only to see the actual locale in which they move, the importance of exact reproduction in the decor will be appreciated. Obviously, that is the way we are going. Environment, the study of which has transformed science and literature, will have to take a large role in the theatre. And here I may mention again the question of metaphysical man, the abstraction who had to be satisfied with his three walls in tragedy — whereas the physiological man in our modern works is asking more and more compellingly to be determined by his setting, by the environment that produced him. We see then that the road to progress is still long, for sets as well as costume. We are coming upon the truth but we can hardly stammer it out.

Another very serious matter is diction. True, we have got away from the chanting, the plainsong, of the seventeenth century. But we now have a 'theatre voice', a false recitation that is very obtrusive and very annoying. Everything that is wrong with it comes from the fixed traditional code set up by the majority of critics. They found the theatre in a certain state and, instead of looking to the future, and judging the progress we are making and the progress we shall make by the progress we have already made, they stubbornly defend the relics of the old conventions, swearing that these relics must be preserved. Ask them why, make them see how far we have travelled; they will give you no logical reason. They will reply with assertions based on a set of conditions that are disappearing.

In diction the errors come from what the critics call 'theatre language'. Their theory is that on stage you must not speak as you do in everyday life. To support this viewpoint they pick examples from traditional practices, from what was happening yesterday — and is happening still — without taking account of the naturalistic movement, the phases of which have been established for us by M. Jullien's book.[1] Let us realize that there is no such thing as 'theatre language'. There has been a rhetoric which grew more and more feeble and is now dying out. Those are the facts. If you compare the declaiming of actors under Louis XIV with that of Lekain, and if you compare Lekain's with that of our own artists today, you will clearly distinguish the phases, from tragic chanting down to our search for the natural, precise tone, the cry of truth. It follows that 'theatre language', that language of booming sonority, is vanishing. We are moving towards simplicity, the exact word spoken without emphasis, quite naturally. How many examples I could give if I had unlimited space! Consider the powerful effect that Geoffroy has on the public; all his talent comes from his natural personality. He holds the public because he speaks on stage as he does at home. When a sentence sounds outlandish he cannot pronounce it; the author has to find another one. That is the fundamental criticism of so-called 'theatre language'. Again, follow the diction of a talented actor and at the same time watch the public; the cheers go up, the house is in raptures when a truthful accent gives the words the exact value they must have. All the great successes of the stage are triumphs over convention.

Alas, yes, there is a 'theatre language'. It is the clichés, the resounding platitudes, the hollow words that roll about like empty barrels, all that intolerable rhetoric of our vaudevilles and dramas, which is beginning to make us smile. It would be very interesting to study the style of such talented authors as MM. Augier, Dumas and Sardou. I could find much to criticize, especially in the last two with their conventional language, a language of their own that they put into the mouths of all their characters, men, women, children, old folk, both sexes and all ages. This irritates me, for each character has his own language, and to create living people you must give them to the public not merely in accurate dress and in the environments that have made them what they are, but with their individual ways of thinking and expressing themselves. I repeat that that is the obvious aim of our theatre. There is no theatre language regulated by such a code as 'cadenced sentences' or sonority. There is simply a kind of dialogue that is growing more precise and is following — or rather, leading — sets and costumes towards naturalistic progress. When plays are more truthful, the actors' diction will gain enormously in simplicity and naturalness.

To conclude, I will repeat that the battle of the conventions is far from being finished, and that it will no doubt last forever. Today we are beginning to see clearly where we are going, but our steps are still impeded by the melting slush of rhetoric and metaphysics.

---

[1] Adolphe Jullien 1845–1932, writer on music and the theatre. The book Zola cites is *Histoire du costume au théâtre*, 1880.

IN THIS ESSAY, BRECHT ATTACKS THE BOURGEOIS NOTION THAT THE THEATER CAN BE DIVIDED *into two kinds of art, as though drama were* either *instructive or* entertaining. *As he does in his plays, Brecht dialecticizes these categories, showing that they define one another and therefore exist within one another. Realistic plays, after all, not only entertain their audiences, but also offer an image of the world, a kind of instruction. On the other hand, intellectual or critical activity is not only pleasurable in itself, but it also can lead to a lively kind of theater as well, as Brecht's plays illustrate. This essay was unpublished in Brecht's lifetime: John Willett dates it from 1935 or 1936. He notes that Brecht uses the word* Entfremdung *here for "alienation," the same word used by Marx and Hegel. Brecht later coined his own word* Verfremdungseffekt *for "alienation effect."*

BERTOLT BRECHT

(1898–1956)

"Theater for Pleasure or Theater for Instruction"

(1935–1936)

TRANSLATED BY

JOHN WILLETT

A few years back, anybody talking about the modern theatre meant the theatre in Moscow, New York and Berlin. He might have thrown in a mention of one of Jouvet's productions in Paris or Cochran's in London, or *The Dybbuk* as given by the Habima (which is to all intents and purposes part of the Russian theatre, since Vakhtangov was its director). But broadly speaking there were only three capitals so far as modern theatre was concerned.

Russian, American and German theatres differed widely from one another, but were alike in being modern, that is to say in introducing technical and artistic innovations. In a sense they even achieved a certain stylistic resemblance, probably because technology is international (not just that part which is directly applied to the stage but also that which influences it, the film for instance), and because large progressive cities in large industrial countries are involved. Among the older capitalist countries it is the Berlin theatre that seemed of late to be in the lead. For a period all that is common to the modern theatre received its strongest and (so far) maturest expression there.

The Berlin theatre's last phase was the so-called epic theatre, and it showed the modern theatre's trend of development in its purest form. Whatever was labelled *'Zeitstück'* or *'Piscatorbühne'* or *'Lehrstück'* belongs to the epic theatre.

The Epic Theatre

Many people imagine that the term 'epic theatre' is self-contradictory, as the epic and dramatic ways of narrating a story are held, following Aristotle, to be basically distinct. The difference between the two forms was never thought simply to lie in the fact that the one is performed by living beings while the other operates via the written word; epic works such as those of Homer and the medieval singers were at the same time theatrical performances, while dramas like Goethe's *Faust* and Byron's *Manfred* are agreed to have been more effective as books. Thus even by Aristotle's definition the difference between the dramatic and epic forms was attributed to their different methods of construction, whose laws were dealt with by two different branches of aesthetics. The method of construction depended on the different way of presenting the work to the public, sometimes via the stage, sometimes through a book; and independently of that there was the 'dramatic element' in epic works and the 'epic element' in dramatic. The bourgeois novel in the last century developed much that was 'dramatic,' by which was meant the strong centralization of the story, a momentum that drew the separate parts into a common relationship. A particular passion of utterance, a certain emphasis on the clash of forces are hallmarks of the 'dramatic'. The epic writer Döblin provided an excellent criterion when he said that with an epic work, as opposed to a dramatic, one can as it were take a pair of scissors and cut it into individual pieces, which remain fully capable of life.

This is no place to explain how the opposition of epic and dramatic lost its rigidity after having long been held to be irreconcilable. Let us just point out that the technical advances alone were enough to permit the stage to incorporate an element of narrative in its dramatic productions. The possibility of projections, the greater adaptability of the stage due to mechanization, the film, all completed the theatre's equipment, and did so at a point where the most important transactions between people could no longer be shown simply by personifying the motive forces or subjecting the characters to invisible metaphysical powers.

To make these transactions intelligible the environment in which the people lived had to be brought to bear in a big and 'significant' way.

This environment had of course been shown in the existing drama, but only as seen from the central figure's point of view, and not as an independent element. It was defined by the hero's reactions to it. It was seen as a storm can be seen when one sees the ships on a sheet of water unfolding their sails, and the sails filling out. In the epic theatre it was to appear standing on its own.

The stage began to tell a story. The narrator was no longer missing, along with the fourth wall. Not only did the background adopt an attitude to the events on the stage — by big screens recalling other simultaneous events elsewhere, by projecting documents which confirmed or contradicted what the characters said, by concrete and intelligible figures to accompany abstract conversations, by figures and sentences to support mimed transactions whose sense was unclear — but the actors too refrained from going over wholly into their role, remaining detached from the character they were playing and clearly inviting criticism of him.

The spectator was no longer in any way allowed to submit to an experience uncritically (and without practical consequences) by means of simple empathy with the characters in a play. The production took the subject-matter and the incidents shown and put them through a process of alienation: the alienation that is necessary to all understanding. When something seems 'the most obvious thing in the world' it means that any attempt to understand the world has been given up.

What is 'natural' must have the force of what is startling. This is the only way to expose the laws of cause and effect. People's activity must simultaneously be so and be capable of being different.

It was all a great change.

The dramatic theatre's spectator says: Yes, I have felt like that too—Just like me—It's only natural—It'll never change—The sufferings of this man appal me, because they are inescapable—That's great art; it all seems the most obvious thing in the world—I weep when they weep, I laugh when they laugh.

The epic theatre's spectator says: I'd never have thought it—That's not the way—That's extraordinary, hardly believable—It's got to stop—The sufferings of this man appal me, because they are unnecessary—That's great art: nothing obvious in it—I laugh when they weep, I weep when they laugh.

The stage began to be instructive.

The Instructive Theatre

Oil, inflation, war, social struggles, the family, religion, wheat, the meat market, all became subjects for theatrical representation. Choruses enlightened the spectator about facts unknown to him. Films showed a montage of events from all over the world. Projections added statistical material. And as the 'background' came to the front of the stage so people's activity was subjected to criticism. Right and wrong courses of action were shown. People were shown who knew what they were doing, and others who did not. The theatre became an affair for philosophers, but only for such philosophers as wished not just to explain the world but also to change it. So we had philosophy, and we had instruction. And where was the amusement in all that? Were they sending us back to school, teaching us to read and write? Were we supposed to pass exams, work for diplomas?

Generally there is felt to be a very sharp distinction between learning and amusing oneself. The first may be useful, but only the second is pleasant. So we have to defend the epic theatre against the suspicion that it is a highly disagreeable, humourless, indeed strenuous affair.

Well: all that can be said is that the contrast between learning and amusing oneself is not laid down by divine rule; it is not one that has always been and must continue to be.

Undoubtedly there is much that is tedious about the kind of learning familiar to us from school, from our professional training, etc. But it must be remembered under what conditions and to what end that takes place.

It is really a commercial transaction. Knowledge is just a commodity. It is acquired in order to be resold. All those who have grown out of going to school have to do their learning virtually in secret, for anyone who admits that he still has something to learn devalues himself as a man whose knowledge is inadequate. Moreover the usefulness of learning is very much limited by factors outside the learner's control. There is unemployment, for instance, against which no knowledge can protect one. There is the division of labour, which makes generalized knowledge unnecessary and impossible. Learning is often among the concerns of those whom no amount of concern will get any forwarder. There is not much knowledge that leads to power, but plenty of knowledge to which only power can lead.

Learning has a very different function for different social strata. There are strata who cannot imagine any improvement in conditions: they find the conditions good enough for them. Whatever happens to oil they will benefit from it. And: they feel the years beginning to tell. There can't be all that many years more. What is the point of learning a lot now? They have said their final word: a grunt. But there are also strata 'waiting their turn' who are discontented with conditions, have a vast interest in the practical side of learning, want at all costs to find out where they stand, and know that they are lost without learning; these are the best and keenest learners. Similar differences apply to countries and peoples. Thus the pleasure of learning depends on all sorts of things; but none the less there is such a thing as pleasurable learning, cheerful and militant learning.

If there were not such amusement to be had from learning the theatre's whole structure would unfit it for teaching.

Theatre remains theatre even when it is instructive theatre, and in so far as it is good theatre it will amuse.

Theatre and Knowledge

But what has knowledge got to do with art? We know that knowledge can be amusing, but not everything that is amusing belongs in the theatre.

I have often been told, when pointing out the invaluable services that modern knowledge and science, if properly applied, can perform for art and specially for the theatre, that art and knowledge are two estimable but wholly distinct fields of human activity. This is a fearful truism, of course, and it is as well to agree quickly that, like most truisms, it is perfectly true. Art and science work in quite different ways: agreed. But, bad as it may sound, I have to admit that I cannot get along as an artist without the use of one or two sciences. This may well arouse serious doubts as to my artistic capacities. People are used to seeing poets as unique and slightly unnatural beings who reveal with a truly godlike assurance things that other people can only recognize after much sweat and toil. It is naturally distasteful to have to admit that one does not belong to this select band. All the same, it must be admitted. It must at the same time be made clear that the scientific occupations just confessed to are not pardonable side interests, pursued on days off after a good week's work. We all know how Goethe was interested in natural history, Schiller in history: as a kind of hobby, it is charitable to assume. I have no wish promptly to accuse these two of having needed these sciences for their poetic activity; I am not trying to shelter behind them; but I must say that I do need the sciences. I have to admit, however, that I look askance at all sorts of people who I know do not operate on the level of scientific understanding: that is to say, who sing as the birds sing, or as people imagine the birds to sing. I don't mean by that that I would reject a charming poem about the taste of fried fish or the delights of a boating party just because the writer had not studied gastronomy or navigation. But in my view the great and complicated things that go on in the world cannot be adequately recognized by people who do not use every possible aid to understanding.

Let us suppose that great passions or great events have to be shown which influence the fate of nations. The lust for power is nowadays held to be such a passion. Given that a poet 'feels' this lust and wants to have someone strive for power, how is he to show the exceedingly complicated machinery within which the struggle for power nowadays takes place? If his hero is a politician, how do politics work? If he is a business man, how does business work? And yet there are writers who find business and politics nothing like so passionately interesting as the individual's lust for power. How are they to acquire the necessary knowledge? They are scarcely likely to learn enough by going round and keeping their eyes open, though even then it is more than they would get by just rolling their eyes in an exalted frenzy. The foundation of a paper like the *Völkischer Beobachter* or a business like Standard Oil is a pretty complicated affair, and such things cannot be conveyed just like that. One important field for the playwright is psychology. It is taken for granted that a poet, if not an ordinary man, must be able without further instruction to discover the motives that lead a man to commit murder; he must be able to give a picture of a murderer's mental state 'from within himself.' It is taken for granted that one only has to look inside oneself in such a case; and then there's always one's imagination. . . . There are various reasons why I can no longer surrender to this agreeable hope of getting a result quite so simply. I can no longer find in myself all those motives which the press or scientific reports show to have been observed in people. Like the average judge when pronouncing sentence, I cannot without further ado conjure up an adequate picture of a murderer's mental state. Modern psychology, from psychoanalysis to behaviourism, acquaints me with facts that lead me to judge the case quite differently, especially if I bear in mind the findings of sociology and do not overlook economics and history. You will say: but that's getting complicated. I have to answer that it *is* complicated. Even if you let yourself be convinced, and agree with me that a large slice of literature is exceedingly primitive, you may still ask with profound concern: won't an evening in such a theatre be a most alarming affair? The answer to that is: no.

Whatever knowledge is embodied in a piece of poetic writing has to be wholly transmuted into poetry. Its utilization fulfils the very pleasure that the poetic element provokes. If it does not at the same time fulfil that which is fulfilled by the scientific element, none the less in an age of great discoveries and inventions one must have a certain inclination to penetrate deeper into things — a desire to make the world controllable — if one is to be sure of enjoying its poetry.

Is the Epic Theatre Some Kind of 'Moral Institution'?

According to Friedrich Schiller the theatre is supposed to be a moral institution. In making this demand it hardly occurred to Schiller that by moralizing from the stage he might drive the audience out of the theatre. Audiences had no objection to moralizing in his day. It was only later that Friedrich Nietzsche attacked him for blowing a moral trumpet. To Nietzsche any concern with morality was a depressing affair; to Schiller it seemed thoroughly enjoyable. He knew of nothing that could give greater amusement and satisfaction than the propagation of ideas. The bourgeoisie was setting about forming the ideas of the nation.

Putting one's house in order, patting oneself on the back, submitting one's account, is something highly agreeable. But describing the collapse of one's house, having pains in the back, paying one's account, is indeed a depressing affair, and that was how Friedrich Nietzsche saw things a century later. He was poorly disposed towards morality, and thus towards the previous Friedrich too.

The epic theatre was likewise often objected to as moralizing too much. Yet in the epic theatre moral arguments only took second place. Its aim was less to moralize than to observe. That is to say it observed, and then the thick end of the wedge followed: the story's moral. Of course we cannot pretend that we started our observations out of a pure passion for observing and without any more practical motive, only to be completely staggered by their results. Undoubtedly there were some painful discrepancies in our environment, circumstances that were barely tolerable, and this not merely on account of moral considerations. It is not only moral considerations that make hunger, cold and oppression hard to bear. Similarly the object of our inquiries was not just to arouse moral objections to such circumstances (even though they could easily be felt—though not by all the audience alike; such objections were seldom for instance felt by those who profited by the circumstances in question) but to discover means for their elimination. We were not in fact speaking in the name of morality but in that of the victims. These truly are two distinct matters, for the victims are often told that they ought to be contented with their lot, for moral reasons. Moralists of this sort see man as existing for morality, not morality for man. At least it should be possible to gather from the above to what degree and in what sense the epic theatre is a moral institution.

Stylistically speaking, there is nothing all that new about the epic theatre. Its expository character and its emphasis on virtuosity bring it close to the old Asiatic theatre. Didactic tendencies are to be found in the medieval mystery plays and the classical Spanish theatre, and also in the theatre of the Jesuits.

These theatrical forms corresponded to particular trends of their time, and vanished with them. Similarly the modern epic theatre is linked with certain trends. It cannot by any means be practised universally. Most of the great nations today are not disposed to use the theatre for ventilating their problems. London, Paris, Tokyo and Rome maintain their theatres for quite different purposes. Up to now favourable circumstances for an epic and didactic theatre have only been found in a few places and for a short period of time. In Berlin Fascism put a very definite stop to the development of such a theatre.

It demands not only a certain technological level but a powerful movement in society which is interested to see vital questions freely aired with a view to their solution, and can defend this interest against every contrary trend.

The epic theatre is the broadest and most far-reaching attempt at large-scale modern theatre, and it has all those immense difficulties to overcome that always confront the vital forces in the sphere of politics, philosophy, science and art.

Can Epic Theatre Be Played Anywhere?

ROLAND BARTHES STUDIED FRENCH LITERATURE AT THE UNIVERSITY OF PARIS AND TAUGHT *French in Egypt and Romania before joining the Centre National de la Recherche Scientifique in Paris. Working in the fields of linguistics and sociology, Barthes was instrumental in articulating the relationship between the structure of language and the structures of other systems of signification. This "structuralist" approach to how meanings are produced was adapted to study in a variety of fields— anthropology, literary criticism, psychoanalysis—in the 1950s, 1960s, and 1970s. Throughout his brilliant and eclectic career, Barthes examined the nature of signification in literature, film, photography, and popular culture. His many books include* Writing Degree Zero (1953), Mythologies (1957), Sade/Fourier/Loyola (1971), The Pleasure of the Text (1973), *and* Camera Lucida (1980).

In 1956, Barthes wrote a series of essays in response to the visit of the Berliner Ensemble to Paris. Here, he records the effect of the Berliner Ensemble's production, marking a fundamental shift in how we think about theater, society, and stage representation.

ROLAND BARTHES
(1915–1980)

"The Tasks of Brechtian Criticism"
(1956)

TRANSLATED BY
RICHARD HOWARD

It is safe to predict that Brecht's work will become increasingly important for us; not only because it is great, but because it is exemplary as well; it shines, today at least, with an exceptional luster amid two deserts: the desert of our contemporary theater, where aside from his there are no great names to cite; and the desert of revolutionary art, sterile since the beginnings of the Zhdanovian impasse. Any reflection on theater and on revolution must come to terms with Brecht, who brought about this situation himself: the entire force of his work opposes the reactionary myth of unconscious genius; its greatness is the kind which best suits our period, the greatness of responsibility; it is a work which is in a state of "complicity" with the world, with our world: a knowledge of Brecht, a reflection on Brecht, in a word, Brechtian criticism is by definition extensive with the problematics of our time. We must tirelessly repeat this truth: knowing Brecht is of a different order of importance from knowing Shakespeare or Gogol; because it is for us, precisely, that Brecht has written his plays, and not for eternity. Brechtian criticism will therefore be written by the spectator, the reader, the consumer, and not the exegete: it is a criticism of a *concerned* man. And if I myself were to write the criticism whose context I am sketching here, I should not fail to suggest, at the risk of appearing indiscreet, how this work touches me and helps me, personally, as an individual. But to confine myself here to the essentials of a program of Brechtian criticism, I shall merely suggest the levels of analysis which such criticism should successively investigate.

(1) Sociology

Generally speaking, we do not yet have adequate means of investigation to define the theater's public, or publics. Furthermore, in France at least, Brecht has not yet emerged from the experimental theaters (except for the TNP's *Mother Courage*, a production so misconceived that the case is anything but instructive). For the moment, therefore, we can study only the press reactions.

There are four types to distinguish. By the extreme right, Brecht's work is totally discredited because of its political commitment: Brecht's theater is mediocre *because* it is communist. By the right (a more complicated right, which can extend to the "modernist" bourgeoisie of *L'Express*), Brecht is subjected to the usual political denaturation: the man is dissociated from the work, the former consigned to politics (emphasizing successively and contradictorily his independence and his servility with regard to the Party), and the latter enlisted under the banners of an eternal theater: Brecht's work, we are told, is great in spite of Brecht, against Brecht.

On the left, there is first of all a humanist reading: Brecht is made into one of those giant creative figures committed to a humanitarian promotion of man, like Romain Rolland or Barbusse. This sympathetic view unfortunately disguises an anti-intellectualist prejudice frequent in certain far-left circles: in order to "humanize" Brecht, the theoretical part of his work is discredited or at least minimized: the plays are great *despite* Brecht's systematic views on epic theater, the actor, alienation, etc.: here we encounter one of the basic theorems of *petit-bourgeois* culture, the romantic contrast between heart and head, between intuition and reflection, between the ineffable and the rational — an opposition which ultimately masks a magical conception of art. Finally, the communists themselves express certain reservations (in France, at least) with regard to Brecht's opposition to the positive hero, his epic conception of theater, and the "formalist" orientation of his dramaturgy. Apart from the contestation of Roger Vailland, based on a defense of French tragedy as a dialectical art of crisis, these criticisms proceed from a Zhdanovian conception of art.

I am citing a dossier from memory; it should be examined in detail. The point, moreover, is not to refute Brecht's critics, but rather to approach Brecht by the means our society spontaneously employs to digest him. Brecht reveals whoever speaks about him, and this revelation naturally concerns Brecht to the highest degree.

(2) Ideology

Must we oppose the "digestions" of the Brechtian canon by a canonical truth of Brecht? In a sense and within certain limits, yes. There is a specific ideological content, coherent, consistent, and remarkably organized, in Brecht's theater, one which protests against abusive distortions. This content must be described.

In order to do this, we possess two kinds of texts: first of all, the theoretical texts, of an acute intelligence (it is no matter of indifference to encounter a man of the theater who is intelligent), of a great ideological lucidity, and which it would be childish to underrate on the pretext that they are only an intellectual appendage to an essentially *creative* body of work. Of course Brecht's theater is made to be performed. But before performing it or seeing it performed, there is no ban on its being understood: this intelligence is organically linked to its constitutive function, which is to transform a public even as it is being entertained. In a Marxist like Brecht, the relations between theory and practice must not be underestimated or distorted. To separate the Brechtian theater from its theoretical foundations would be as erroneous as to try to understand Marx's action without reading *The Communist*

Manifesto or Lenin's politics without reading *The State and the Revolution*. There is no official decree or supernatural intervention which graciously dispenses the theater from the demands of theoretical reflection. Against an entire tendency of our criticism, we must assert the capital importance of Brecht's systematic writings: it does not weaken the creative value of this theater to regard it as a reasoned theater.

Moreover, the plays themselves afford the chief elements of Brechtian ideology. I can indicate here only the principal ones: the historical and not "natural" character of human misfortunes; the spiritual contagion of economic alienation, whose final effect is to blind the very men it oppresses as to the causes of their servitude; the correctible status of Nature, the tractability of the world; the necessary adequation of means and situations (for instance, in a bad society, the law can be reestablished only by a reprobate judge); the transformation of ancient psychological "conflicts" into historical contradictions, subject as such to the corrective power of men.

We must note here that these truths are never set forth except as the consequence of concrete situations, and these situations are infinitely plastic. Contrary to the rightist prejudice, Brecht's theater is not a thesis theater, not a propaganda theater. What Brecht takes from Marxism are not slogans, an articulation of arguments, but a general method of explanation. It follows that in Brecht's theater the Marxist elements always seem to be recreated. Basically, Brecht's greatness, and his solitude, is that he keeps inventing Marxism. The ideological theme, in Brecht, could be precisely defined as a dynamic of events which combines observation and explanation, ethics and politics: according to the profoundest Marxist teaching, each theme is at once the expression of what men want to be and of what things are, at once a protest (because it unmasks) and a reconciliation (because it explains).

Semiology is the study of signs and significations. I do not want to engage here in a discussion of this science, which was postulated some forty years ago by the linguist Saussure and which is generally accused of formalism. Without letting ourselves be intimidated by the words, we might say that Brechtian dramaturgy, the theory of *Episierung*, of alienation, and the entire practice of the Berliner Ensemble with regard to sets and costumes, propose an explicit semiological problem. For what Brechtian dramaturgy postulates is that today at least, the responsibility of a dramatic art is not so much to express reality as to signify it. Hence there must be a certain distance between signified and signifier: revolutionary art must admit a certain arbitrary nature of signs, it must acknowledge a certain "formalism," in the sense that it must treat form according to an appropriate method, which is the semiological method. All Brechtian art protests against the Zhdanovian confusion between ideology and semiology, which has led to such an esthetic impasse.

We realize, moreover, why this aspect of Brechtian thought is most antipathetic to bourgeois and Zhdanovian criticism: both are attached to an esthetic of the "natural" expression of reality: art for them is a false Nature, a *pseudo-Physis*. For Brecht, on the contrary, art today—i.e., at the heart of a historical conflict whose stake in human disalienation—art today must be an *anti-Physis*. Brecht's formalism is a radical protest against the confusions of the bourgeois and *petit-bourgeois* false Nature: in a still-alienated society, art must be critical, it must cut off all illusions, even that of "Nature": the sign must be partially arbitrary, otherwise we fall back on an art of expression, an art of essentialist illusion.

(3) Semiology

Brechtian theater is a moral theater, that is, a theater which asks, with the spectator: what is to be done in such a situation? At this point we should classify and describe the archetypical situations of the Brechtian theater; they may be reduced, I think, to a single question: how to be good in a bad society? It seems to me very important to articulate the moral structure of Brecht's theater: granted that Marxism has had other more urgent tasks than to concern itself with problems of individual conduct; nonetheless capitalist society endures, and communism itself is being transformed: revolutionary action must increasingly cohabit, and in an almost institutional fashion, with the norms of bourgeois and *petit-bourgeois* morality: problems of conduct, and no longer of action, arise. Here is where Brecht can have a great cleansing power, a pedagogical power.

Especially since his morality has nothing catechistic about it, being for the most part strictly interrogative. Indeed, some of his plays conclude with a literal interrogation of the public, to whom the author leaves the responsibility of finding its own solution to the problem raised. Brecht's moral

(4) Morality

role is to infiltrate a question into what seems self-evident (this is the theme of the exception and the rule). For what is involved here is essentially a morality of invention. Brechtian invention is a tactical process to unite with revolutionary correction. In other words, for Brecht the outcome of every moral impasse depends on a more accurate analysis of the concrete situation in which the subject finds himself: the issue is joined by representing in explicit terms the historical particularity of this situation, its artificial, purely conformist nature. Essentially, Brecht's morality consists of a correct reading of history, and the plasticity of the morality *(to change Custom when necessary)* derives from the very plasticity of history.

CONTEMPORARY
PERSPECTIVES

MICHAEL GOLDMAN IS the author of several influential books tracing the relationship between acting and drama: Shakespeare and the Energies of Drama *(1972),* Acting and Action in Shakespearean Tragedy *(1985), and* The Actor's Freedom *(1975). In this essay, Goldman suggests that many of the features of modern realistic theater are indebted to an earlier, disruptively Romantic sensibility.*

MICHAEL GOLDMAN

"The Ghost of Joy: Romanticism and the Forms of Modern Drama"
(1977)

An actor appears on a stage. The moment is innately interesting; all plays begin well. This fact is crucial for understanding the "form" or "structure" of drama, whatever general name, that is, we give to the principle of maintained interest that seems to hold a play together—the whatever-it-is that lets excitement lead to excitement, that makes us feel moment calling to moment in a satisfying and significant way. For the promise of interest, and hence the source of any particular principle of interest, is already present in that first moment. Imagine the following exercise: write the *shortest possible* opening sequence of a play that would succeed in boring an audience. What would the minimum time be, I wonder? Thirty seconds? Twenty? Not much less, at any rate. The point is, it takes time for drama to bore us. The first word of a poem—as we first receive it—cannot be interesting in itself; the first moment of a play is; and thus we may seek in that first moment a quality which speaks to the uniqueness of drama as an art.

A man who is acting stands in a place set aside for acting. The innate interest springs from the appeal of acting itself, from·the promise that the special kind of behavior we call "acting" will continue, transmitting to us its special kind of pleasure and energy. We may think of this energy as a kind of hauntedness. Primitive drama is almost exclusively concerned with the activity of ghosts and the impersonation of the dead. This has less to do with any religious "origin" of drama than with an essential feature of acting—the actor is inevitably a person who appears to be both himself and not himself, a figure specially liberated and set apart because he inhabits or is inhabited by another's identity. In this respect an actor is like a ghost, and it is no wonder that society has turned to acting and drama in its effort to grapple with the brooding presence of its dead. Conversely, if the appeal of acting has to do with the quality of hauntedness, then the continuing interest of a play has to do with the ways in which we feel this hauntedness exercised and transmitted, with who or what is haunting whom. Ghosts spook us—they transmit an unsettling and volatile energy to us and encourage us to haunt as we are haunted. Like Orestes or Hamlet or Oswald Alving, the haunted man becomes something of a ghost himself. When method actors look for the "spine" of a play, and, indeed, when we employ any method to identify what unifies a play's action as dramatic experience (and not, say, as theme), what we are seeking is a source of haunting for the play as a whole, the principle or premise which keeps the histrionic energy alive through a whole performance by providing an echo throughout the play of that strange displacement of the actor's being that is involved in acting a part.

Characters in modern drama are typically haunted by a feeling of being cut off from the joy of life, or indeed from life itself, a feeling of being dead. This is a Romantic feeling, and in this essay I wish to put forward the notion that the history of modern drama is essentially that of adapting this feeling to dramatic representation. The adaptation is a difficult one, and modern drama becomes successful only when it learns to treat the difficulty itself as an expressive device. I should add that I make my claims in an undogmatic and exploratory spirit, and that my plan here is not to offer a comprehensive and detailed analysis, but a series of reflections that I hope will stimulate further discussion. I aim simply to explain what I mean as clearly as I can, and then to point to certain connections and patterns in the modern repertory that support my notion and that are, I think, illuminated by it.

First we must return to the feeling I have described, of being cut off from the joy of life. The feeling is romantic because it is the negative reflex or unfulfilled aspect of the romantic project of self-fulfillment. Like the feeling of being dead, the quest for self-fulfillment is hardly original with the

From *Romantic and Modern: Revaluations of Literary Tradition*, ed. George Bornstein (University of Pittsburgh Press 1977), pp. 54–67.

Romantic era, but certain terms of the quest become paramount as the era dawns, above all a particular notion of where fulfillment lies, of how the self defines itself and how the joy of life is recognized.

A major defining impulse of Romanticism is the drive to conquer inner space, to possess internally a transcendent quality of being. This is often sought through action in the external world: revolt, travel, the pursuit of sublimity or freedom; but the ultimate reference of such activity is internal. The Romantic quest is validated by an expansion, possession, or transfiguration of the self. Inner space is no Romantic discovery, of course, but the shift of emphasis, the new notion of what the space is for, and perhaps of the effort required to explore it, is radical and seems to gain momentum as the Romantic era approaches. From our point of view, the shift is elusive, for two reasons. First, the traditional Western emphasis on inner discovery—as we find it, say, in Plato, or St. Augustine, or Shakespeare—is easily assimilated to our post-Romantic (or still-Romantic) reading of the world. Second, we are apt to project the Romantic reading backward onto self-absorbed literary heroes from the past—Homer's Achilles, say. In consequence, it is easy for us to miss the revolutionary character of the Romantic emphasis. Western thought has always been concerned with the individual and his private vision, but in the Romantic period private experience takes on a new articulation, a new primacy, which it retains today. When Janis Joplin's face fills the screen and describes the experience of singing, "You get inside yourself—and that becomes the entirety," she makes a statement that, with a little effort and translation, would have been perfectly intelligible (if not acceptable) to Shelley, say, as a description of a kind of satisfaction, a kind of awareness of self. But I suspect that it would be nearly unintelligible to anyone before Rousseau. Joplin is talking about the artistic process and the value of art. Both, she is certain, flow from the search for a pleasure to be found and won inside the self, a life within, realer and truer than anything outside.

This must be contrasted with the search for pleasure and achievement as it is understood in earlier periods. A stress on the life within appears, for instance, in Elizabethan literature, but the relation between inner and outer realms is quite different; and this applies to both the secular and religious perspectives. When Tamburlaine caps his great encomium to the restless human soul by defining its highest achievement as "the sweet fruition of an earthly crown," the phrase is apt to strike a modern reader oddly, as falling curiously short of the powers and ambitions evoked. We are likely to think of the sweet fruition of the artist or guru or philosopher as being greater because more inward, hence more profound. Tamburlaine's conclusion sounds odd to us because we no longer believe in the ultimate significance of outer kingdoms. Now, it is true that Tamburlaine's phrase might have struck some members of the Elizabethan audience as deficient, too—but only because they would have been thinking of the *heavenly* crown which was the soul's true goal. For the Elizabethan, there could be no doubt that the splendor and activity of the individual's inner world only pointed to the glory of some outer kingdom, whether earthly or heavenly. Shakespeare's heroes venture deep into the inner world and bring back news of the ripeness to be gained there, but, for even the most inward of them, that ripeness exists only in coordination with the outer world, usually the world of political achievement, in which the hero also lives in a primary way. Hamlet complains about having to set right the particularly ugly situation in Denmark; it is only Romantic criticism that imagines him to be complaining about having to act at all. We are accustomed to finding the external world deprecated in traditional Christian literature, but this is always and only in favor of a better world, which is distinguishable from the merely internal world of the individual. The kingdom of God is within us, to be sure, but it is larger and other than we are. Only in our era do we find the outer world deprecated in all its forms, the kingdom of God itself but a metaphor for the properly self-delighted soul. And in this sense at least, our era begins with the Romantics.

The heroes of Wordsworth and Keats, of Shelley, Byron, Goethe, Stendhal, Ibsen, and Chekhov are seeking sweet fruition in the Romantic sense. They may seem to find it in world traveling, or a life spent in nature, or the fight for freedom, or a high position in the church, or financial power, or building homes for human beings, or in sexual adventures, or even ecological adventures (like Dr. Astrov or Faust). These all may be vehicles for sweet fruition. But it is the sweet fruition itself, the expansion of the self into its internal kingdom, that they are after, and not whatever earthly or unearthly crown may help them to it.

What is new, then, is that the conquest of an inner realm is seen as an end in itself and not as a sign of having conquered an external one. For drama, the consequences are immense, though they take several decades to become apparent. The most obvious result is that characters are provided with a new type of intention. Consider, for example, the spine of *Ghosts*, as Francis Fergusson describes it: "to control the Alving heritage for my own life."[1] The last phrase is crucial. Some of the minor characters, like Engstrand, seem to be satisfied with putting the inheritance to good use in the external world, but this is a sign of their limited vision; it is why they are minor. What the heroine, Mrs. Alving, wants from the inheritance is "the joy of life," and this can only be verified internally. The orchard in *The Cherry Orchard* works well as a dramatic symbol because its flowering loveliness—like that of the forests Astrov loves in *Uncle Vanya*—stands for an inner achievement that seems to elude all the characters. To possess the orchard itself, as Lopakhin discovers, guarantees nothing. Like the Lyubovs, he cannot keep what is his. The central concern of the heroes of Ibsen, Strindberg, and Chekhov is always romantic in this sense. They aim, finally, to make something happen inside, to clear or refurnish a place in their secular souls.

This shift in focus changes the nature of drama because it changes the meaning of the stage. One quality of the acting area which stems directly from the peculiar hauntedness of acting, is that the area has always been felt to be a place where inner and outer worlds are powerfully superimposed. In all societies, the stage is perceived as a highly charged condensation of the outside world. It is like places the audience knows, or is marked by important features of place in the known world (the bull's-eye altar-center of the Greek theater, the hierarchical pageant-facade of the Elizabethan). At the same time, by the very nature of the dramatic occasion, the stage is charged with the special significance of the heightened life of acting. It is a place where crucial events will happen, a scene where the life of a few people can be projected into actions and statements that are clear and whole. In classical Greece and Elizabethan England, the structure of the scene glowed with the potential excitement of acting, with the felt receptivity of the stage to the thrusting inner world of acted characters. Now, for contrast, think of Romantic drama, the theater of Schiller and Hugo—and of its successor, modern realistic drama, the theater of Ibsen and Hauptmann. On the first of these stages, we see Romantic heroes in antique, pseudo-Shakespearean settings. On the next, Romantic heroes in tasteless parlors. In both cases, the outer worlds cannot glow with the possibilities of the inner, because the inner cannot fulfill its possibilities upon them.

The characters of high Romantic drama charge round a quasi-Elizabethan stage, stumbling upon opportunities for Romantic poetry, but not at all at home in the world of dramatic action the Elizabethan stage requires. Some great isoladoes, like Kleist and Büchner, manage to make of this failure to connect a compelling, if spasmodic stage poetry of absence, of ancient gestures like a dive into the void. But the Romantic drama proper is a spectacle of poets thrashing about in costume on an exhumed stage, speaking all the more loudly—and at times beautifully—for the silence of the painted world around them. Büchner's and Kleist's heroes seem to stagger or dream their way through busy theatrical worlds, like the Shakespearean-historical clamors of *Danton's Death* or *The Prince of Homburg*. What distinguishes their achievement from any of their contemporaries is that they are thus able to express—and to make dramatic meaning out of—the incompatibility of the Romantic hero's concerns with the external traffic of the stage.

We must bear this in mind when we come to consider Ibsen's "realistic" dramaturgy. Part of the sensation of forward movement we get from an Ibsen play comes from the steady solution of problems of plausibility, of matching the haunting thrust of the main characters to some notion of familiar social behavior and to a probable sequence of events. But the solution is never quite perfect; it never leaves the reader entirely comfortable. And for Ibsen, I would suggest, this is just the point. It was not only the awareness of a new external reality that governed his realism. It was not simply that people now lived in flats and used the telegraph and the railway, as opposed to living in palaces and riding on horseback. What mattered most was that this new reality could function as an irritant within the work of art itself. As a resistance to action and expression, it could suggest a tragic defect in the very impulse toward joy and self-fulfillment by which Ibsen's heroes were defined.

Here we may have a clue to the apparent unsatisfactoriness of the artist characters in Ibsen's later plays. There is always something grotesque and unlikely about their projects and achievements. Solness' "home for human beings" with a funny tower on top, Rubek's "Resurrection" with animal figures in the foreground, even Lovborg's *History of the Future*, have always struck critics as curiously awkward, defective as realism and heavy-handed as symbolism. It is as if Ibsen's weight of meaning could not quite be borne by any plausible book or statue or architectural design. My suggestion is that, in all these cases, the oddness in the portrait expresses the inadequacy of any contact between the romantic individual and the matter of the world. The ordinary home with the tower on it, the statue of the nude surrounded (and somehow "pushed to the background") by animals — a statue moreover that has been exhibited "all over the world" — these make us feel something unsatisfactory, a sense of disproportion or absurdity in what we are asked to think of as the highest possibilities of individual expression. Like Borkman's empty, grandiose dreams, or Mrs. Alving's great campaign for the joy of life (which consists, finally, in trying to convince her son's half-sister to become his mistress in order to take his mind off his syphilitic decline) they have the effect of yanking the stage out from under the hero.

In one form or another, this is the major pattern in Ibsen, and it stands at the heart of his realism. From the earliest prose plays, the climactic moments are those in which the individual's outlet to the world goes up in smoke. The orphanage burns down and reveals that Mrs. Alving cannot make an orphan of her son. The monument to Capt. Alving that was supposed to exorcise his baleful influence is destroyed; his influence is more virulent than ever. In *A Doll's House*, the letter from Krogstad plunks into the letter box but fails to produce the "wonderful thing" that Nora has hoped for. Both these climaxes deliberately remind us of the well-made play, of a dramaturgy that lets issues resolve themselves in neatly patterned change in the external world, but if (as reviewers from time to time complain) these contrivances "creak," in Ibsen it is the deliberate creak of a machine that has made nothing happen. Mrs. Alving and Nora turn to the world, to others, for an action that will expand their souls, and the world does not respond. *A Doll's House* remains unique among Ibsen's plays because it contrives to suggest that the world might respond; Nora runs off (with Ibsen, one might say) into a night of hope. But we have only to compare that final scene with the rest of Ibsen's plays to see what the hope amounts to. Onstage, in fact, all we can see is Helmer, and his hope for a wonderful resurrection is answered by the slam of the door; there is nothing creaking here.

The spectacular sunrise on the mountains at the end of *Ghosts*, the fire in the orphanage, the ominous letter box of *A Doll's House*, Ekdal's "hunting" garret in *The Wild Duck*, the snow-covered hillside in *Borkman* — these are all scenic devices whose literal character renders them at odds with the psychological expansiveness of the characters on stage. They express the characters' situation, to be sure, and sometimes very profoundly, but they do not join with them, they do not receive and extend the characters' actions as, say, the crowns in *Tamburlaine* or the carpet in the *Agamemnon* do. There is a seam in Ibsen that always shows between the inner life of his characters and their condition. James notices it in his famous review of *John Gabriel Borkman*. "If the spirit is a lamp within us," he observes, "glowing through what the world and flesh make of us as through a ground-glass shade, then such pictures as *Little Eyolf* and *John Gabriel* are each a *chassez-croisez* of lamps burning, as in tasteless parlors, with the flame practically exposed.[2] But the seam — the incompatibility of lamp and shade, of haunted hero and tasteless parlor — is not a sign of defective workmanship. It is the essential mark of Ibsen's tragic dramaturgy, the point where the romantic project fails to connect with the outer scene. It expresses the drama of the romantic self in its necessarily unsatisfactory commerce with the world.

Near the end of Pirandello's *Enrico IV*, the hero has a speech which offers a fine example of both the dramatic problem posed by the romantic project and the type of solution modern drama has found. The speech combines a profoundly ambiguous notion of reality with what appears to be a powerfully expansive and emphatic statement of individual transcendence. By doing so, it makes us feel both the haunting romantic drive toward a joy which escapes the formal constraints of life in society and a puzzling blockage which renders the drive unrealizable. Enrico has turned on his guests with scorn and contempt. In a series of big speeches, he seems bent on demonstrating the superiority of his conscious masquerade to the general falseness of the lives around him. Then, ostensibly in the same vein, he introduces an unexpected reminiscence:

> I remember a priest, certainly Irish, a nice-looking priest, who was sleeping in the sun one November day, with his arm on the corner of the bench of a public garden. He was lost in the golden delight of the mild sunny air which must have seemed for him almost summery. One may be sure that in that moment he did not know any more that he was a priest, or even where he was.

He was dreaming. . . . A little boy passed with a flower in his hand. He touched the priest with it here on the neck. I saw him open his laughing eyes, while all his mouth smiled with the beauty of his dream. He was forgetful of everything. [3]

The little boy with a flower: it is a romantic intervention *par excellence,* a touch of nature breaking through the rigidities of convention, the body shocked and freed by immediate, sensual contact with life. Enrico continues:

He was forgetful of everything. . . . But all at once, he pulled himself together, and stretched out his priest's cassock; and there came back to his eyes the same seriousness which you have seen in mine; because the Irish priests defend the seriousness of their Catholic faith with the same zeal with which I defend the sacred rights of hereditary monarchy!

The sequence is surprising. At the touch of the flower, the priest goes from the golden delight of his dream to the grim seriousness of his priestly role—from freedom, life, and pleasure to repression and rigidity. The effect is not far from the terrible climaxes of Ibsen—the moment of intensest contact with the longed-for, dreamed-of joy of life guttering, because of the contact, into absolute inhibition.

Indeed, I would call this the model sequence of modern drama. Here is the paradigm: First, we are caught up in the campaign of the individual soul to break through to reality in what the soul perceives to be an unreal world, a campaign on the side of joy, of an inner flowering, a campaign that seems to be leading to a breakthrough. And then comes the moment of breakthrough, in which the campaigning soul plunges into—an absence of some sort. In the nineteenth century, this is usually represented as an absence of joy, of fulfilled life. Later dramatists tend to treat it as an absence of reality. But whether it be Mrs. Alving discovering that the joy of life is impossible, or the revolutionaries in *The Balcony* learning that their war against illusion can only be sustained by illusion, or Brecht's Shen Te finding that she can only be a good woman by masquerading as a bad man, the final revelation opens a fissure between the individual drive that makes for the play's action—that "haunts" the main actor—and the world in which he tries to act.

Pirandello is perhaps the first dramatist to make this sequence explicitly question the nature of reality. In the speech just discussed, Enrico's train of thought undercuts his claim to have made a superior contact with the real. He argues that he is free, but he concludes in images of entrapment. He resembles the priest not in the brief moment of release, but in the long career of rigidity. Though he strikes the pose of the triumphant revenger, the liberated hero exposing the madness of a society he disdains, the play regularly shows him as trapped in his posture of liberation. All his life, Enrico has longed for human contact and been terrified of exclusion from life. His solution to the problem has been the masquerade, which has excluded him even more absolutely. Behind his performance as emperor lies a restless search for freedom. Speaking as emperor at the end of the first act, he has seen himself as dead and begged for resurrection:

It isn't enough that [the Pope] should receive me! You know he can do *everything*—*everything* I tell you! He can even call up the dead. [*Touches his chest.*] Behold me! Do you see me? There is no magic art unknown to him. Well, Monsignor, my Lady, my torment is really this: that whether here or there [*Pointing to his portrait almost in fear.*] I can't free myself from this magic. I am a penitent now, you see; and I swear to you I shall remain so until he receives me. But you two, when the excommunication is taken off, must ask the Pope to do this thing he can so easily do: to take me away from that; [*Indicating the portrait again.*] and let me live wholly and freely my miserable life.   (p. 172)

Two acts later, the climax of the play, like the story of the dreaming priest that precedes it, shows that Enrico cannot be reawakened. His impulse to grasp life issues in emptiness suggesting the real function of the theatrical metaphor in *Enrico IV.* In the course of the play, role-playing comes to stand for an inhibition, a limit on the real life which, we are led to feel, lies behind the masquerade. But the action is contrived so that we feel—just as the impulse breaks through—that there is nothing but the masquerade available to the actor. Enrico, as is often pointed out, has no "real" name; we know him only by the name of the eleventh-century emperor he pretends to be. The point is not that all life is a masquerade. This is the type of "Pirandellism" that Pirandello is always trailing before us as a sort of philosophical red herring. The point is not a point at all, but an experience — the experience of breaking through to an emptiness that is charged with our longing for fullness. Enrico's masquerade is a device for exploring, in theatrical terms, the romantic impulse to private fulfillment.

The moment before he kills Belcredi, Enrico has roughly grasped Frida in his arms, and so we see him at the end not as a romantic hero defying society, but as an aging man grotesquely embracing a woman young enough to be his daughter, the daughter by another man of the woman he once loved. This sudden and disturbing version of the primal scene brutally mates reality and fantasy. The sad reality behind the masquerade and the pathetic fantasy behind the real embrace are both made visible. This is Enrico's reentry into real life — a painfully actual version of his grand desire. It may remind us of the similar scene that stands at the center of *Six Characters*, when the father approaches the step-daughter in Mme. Pace's brothel. *Six Characters*, too, is about the desire for "life," as the Characters keep telling us. In his preface to the play, Pirandello explicitly associates this desire with romanticism. More than that, he associates his presentation of the characters' desires, his success in making a play out of the *failure* of a play to be made, with the failure of romantic desire to make contact with reality:

> I have presented [a drama] . . . in which . . . there is a discreet satire on romantic procedures: in the six characters thus excited to the point where they stifle themselves in the roles which each of them plays in a certain drama while I present them as characters in another play which they don't know and don't suspect the existence of, so that this inflammation of their passion — which belongs to the realm of romantic procedures — is humorously "placed," located in the void.
>
> (pp. 373–74)

Modern drama's greatest successes are largely of this kind. They show the failure of romanticism through theatrical forms in which one kind of dramatic procedure fails and is contained in another. The effect is to "locate" the self in the void.

Whenever we wish to inquire about the career of drama in a given period, we will always do well to inquire after the fate of *Hamlet* in that period. For in writing *Hamlet*, Shakespeare managed to hold a mirror up to the nature of drama. In the Romantic era, Hamlet, naturally enough, became a Romantic. But in transforming Hamlet into that extremely influential Hamlet-like image of itself, the era gave away a number of its secrets.

The Romantic Hamlet is a man set down in a world not of his own making and, perhaps even more significantly, a man who is ponderously disturbed, if not bewildered by this fact. Whether he be described as a delicate vase into which an oak tree has inadvertently been inserted (Goethe) or a procrastinating philosopher brutally constrained to practical action (Coleridge), Hamlet is seen by the Romantic imagination as a man at odds with the very conditions of existence in a real world. Indeed we might say that the Romantic imagination regards Hamlet as a poet unfairly and tragically forced to make an appearance in a play.

Hamlet is at his most Romantic when he claims that he has that within him which passes show. With this statement he places "real life" beyond the reach of theater. It is a position Shakespeare's Hamlet quickly learns he must abandon — for four-and-a-half acts of intricate action and play-acting — but the Hamlet of the Romantic imagination clings to it. If all that matters most to Hamlet is inaccessibly *within*, then he can never get beyond the withdrawal of his first appearance at Claudius' court. And this is the attitude in which Romantic criticism freezes Shakespeare's prince — the soulful adolescent brooding at the feast. Once more, the portrait points to the difficult relation between Romanticism and drama.

This is not to say, of course, that Romantic critics did not believe in action. In his discussion of *Hamlet*, Coleridge insists that "action is the chief end of existence," and Goethe's Faust finds happiness redeeming swampland. This will remind us, if we need reminding, that the nineteenth century was an age of projectors and revolutionaries, of adventurers with an itch for changing the order of the world. It will remind us of Borkman and Solness. In every case, however, the romantic itch for action expresses a yearning for inner fulfillment. The sweet fruition, even for Faust, is internal, an event inside the spirit. Ibsen differs from Goethe and Coleridge here only in that he firmly grasps the absurdity of the itch for action, the incompatibility between homes for human beings and the restless inner expansionism of the romantic project. It is not, I think, that Ibsen saw more clearly than Coleridge or Goethe, or that he came later and knew more. He *had* to see the incompatibility because his genius was dramatic. On any living stage, the Romantic Hamlet is an absurdity, a whirlwind of passion disconnected from the world around him, a bad poet in an inflated closet drama, beating his sensibilities in vain.

Goethe's characterization of Hamlet as "a costly vase" provides a key to the defects of the Romantic stage, to the inability of its great poets to produce real drama. Hamlet, in Goethe's metaphor, is a beautiful container, shattered by misuse. The image implies a conception of dramatic character as something to be displayed or exclaimed over, something that remarkably indicates the rarity of its composition — Hamlet as a delicate vase, not the oak tree it contains, certainly not a Renaissance prince.

Like Coleridge, Goethe too saw Hamlet's inability to act as a sign of failure. Hamlet lacked "the strength of nerve which makes the hero," but my point is that the hero desiderated here is just another kind of vase, sturdier than the Hamlet variety, displaying, shall we say, the strength-of-nerve pattern. On the early nineteenth-century stage, such heroes are inevitably less interesting than a Prince of Homburg or a Danton — than characters who fall back deliberately and dangerously into the void, who puzzle over their discontinuity with the stage world they move in. The romantic project was neither a mistake nor an aberration, and I hope that nothing I have said suggests that it was. On the contrary, it was a necessary step into the labyrinth of being — and one result of it was a new and rich critical sensitivity to the inwardness of Shakespeare's heroes. Its gift to the drama was a new source for haunting, the imperious hunger for inner space, a flight from spiritual deadness which ultimately transformed every object on the realistic stage into a ghost, a persecuting agent of the dead external world. But it took some time to discover the forms by which this haunting could be released in dramatic action.

Romantic man invented a secret place, the ego, and then set out to explore it. It was like a cavern or a heaven or a beautiful day or a sublime landscape, but it was different from all these in that it was inaccessible, or accessible only to its inventor, "I." And "I" seemed simultaneously imprisoned in his secret place and excluded from it. The Romantic egoist was doomed to explore his secret place in secret, though not in silence. Any traffic with the ego was subject to a fundamental interruption. Nothing could be brought into the cavern in its own state, as grace, say, could be brought to the Christian soul, victories to the hero, realms to the king, friends to the social man. All such had now to be translated into the currency of the secret place, which was by its nature private, coined and counted only by the Romantic individual in his private cave.

The art of Romantic man was a public form of this currency, a scrip one might say, a way of communicating value, of speaking to other privacies about the private cave. Today, we are accustomed to translating all art into such terms, and very likely it *is* an aspect of all art, at least all sophisticated Western art, but, in truth, there is little we can do to avoid thinking this way. We cannot escape the Romantic translation because we cannot escape our past. For the purposes of this essay, however, it is only necessary to note how the public forms of art became firmly related to the inaccessible privacy of the artist. The full purport of the privacy and the problems it raised were perhaps not immediately clear. Wordsworth could think of the poet as a man speaking to men, and thus, quite honestly, offer his unprecedented exploration of private experience in terms that linked it to a kind of Horatian conversation. But the solitaries who inhabit Wordsworth's landscapes like features in it, and the conversations in which Wordsworth and his interlocutor are clearly speaking different languages, tell a different story. The Wordsworthian conversation is extraordinary, like nothing before it in English poetry, but he talks with men as he might with a flower or a rock. It is not that their speech is less meaningful or less respected than his own; it is simply other. And it speaks finally of the otherness of his private place. The poet who talks of a man speaking to men is the same as the boy who had to cling to a tree to keep the world from disappearing.

The contradictions already implicit in Wordsworth become crucial in the work of succeeding generations. The ambiguous privacy of the poet and his driven, unsatisfactory commerce with a dissolving world — these are themes the art of the period 1780–1830 bequeathed to the modern era. In one fashion or another, they make themselves felt in all the experiments of modern drama. We feel them at play in Enrico Quattro's struggle to make contact with the world, and in the struggles of

Borkman, or Miss Julie, or Peter Handke's Kaspar. Much more explicitly, they form the basis for one of the great innovative dramas of the modern repertory — Brecht's first play, *Baal. Baal* is about a poet, a most un-Wordsworthian one in personal style, to be sure, but he too seems both locked in the depths of private experience and haunted by a desire to embrace the ungraspable world. It is fitting to close with a look at this prodigal, refractory work, which has always proved so resistant to analysis. *Baal* was conceived as a counter-play to Hanns Johst's *Der Einsame*, an Expressionist paean to the Romantic playwright, Grabbe. As such, it gives us a figure whose absorption in the personal is so complete as to be monstrous. At the beginning of the play, we see Baal surrounded by a throng of bourgeois poetry-lovers. They react to him as might an audience at some more conventional play — like Johst's — about the glories and sorrows of a stereotyped Romantic artist. But Baal neither responds nor performs as they wish. He takes what he wants from them — food, drink, the promise of an assignation. Quickly, he alienates them all. They leave, angry and troubled. At the end of the scene, the stage is empty except for Baal, who "goes on drinking."[4]

Baal haunts his play — and holds it together — by this endless capacity for ingestion. Like any Romantic artist, he values himself for what he contains, and he wishes to contain not only multitudes, but all — trees, sky, rain, death. There is some suggestion in the play that this desire amounts to a wish, on the poet's part, to incorporate the mother — if so, it is a brilliant insight into the romantic project with its dissatisfied yearning after death, apocalypse, self-generation, the womb. In any case, the movement toward ingestion is also a movement to dissolution. Scenically and structurally, the play seems to dissolve. There are no resistances; everything flows into Baal, and the more he dominates, the more he decays. His haunting power comes from the way he goes beyond whatever is extreme, whatever is romantic in those who surround him. He estranges them, and the audience, ever further by rejecting any of the pieties or limits by which we ordinarily accommodate the limitless romantic absorption in self to acceptable behavior in the world.

At the end of the play, Baal crawls out of a shabby workman's hut, dying, calling not on God, but on "dear Baal." For Brecht, this marks the fate of the private ego, grown absolute and terrifying in its asociality. Does Baal want to live more than he wants to die? It is not clear, but the absolute absorption in self that he represents is inseparable from his restless drive toward dissolution. Brecht's own artistic career is a brilliant, hopeless struggle to be free of the Romantic legacy. Throughout it, he remains profoundly ambivalent toward *Baal*, constantly trying to redefine the play in notes which serve only to emphasize the unsettling tensions it embodies. And Baal's destructive, restless, stirring, self-absorbed personality keeps recurring in his plays, never quite tamed by the distancing devices that surround it.

Writing near the end of his life, Brecht tries to assimilate *Baal* to the Marxist usefulness of epic theater. He finds it difficult, and prefaces his remarks with a wry warning: "*Baal* is a play which could present all kinds of difficulties to those who have not learned to think dialectically." Denying that the play is "a glorification of unrelieved egotism," he pictures Baal as "standing out against the demands and discouragements of a world whose form of production is designed for exploitation rather than usefulness." It is an unpersuasive argument, and Brecht himself seems unsatisfied with it. Finally, he asks us simply to accept *Baal* as a kind of weak spot in his oeuvre: "I have left the play as it was, not having the strength to alter it. I admit (and advise you): this play is lacking in wisdom."[5]

The conclusion is dismissive, but in the course of his remarks, Brecht makes an observation that is of great importance to our discussion. By emphasizing the unredeemed capitalism of the world Baal moves in, Brecht manages to hint at a significant and troubling relation between *Baal* and modern social thought, which also bears upon its relation to Romanticism. As a revolutionary play, Brecht suggests, *Baal* may be taken to have the following moral: "Humanity's urge for happiness can never be entirely killed."

This is a perplexing commentary on a play whose self-obsessed hero seems infinitely remote from the fraternal optimism of a phrase like "Humanity's urge for happiness." But is the distance so great? Just as the figure of Baal carries to extremes and thus subverts the cheerful glorification of the Romantic artist, so Baal's monstrous asocial appetite is an extreme expression of the Romantic notion of happiness as a purely internal achievement. The urge for happiness in this sense is ultimately subversive of any society or even of any coherent life in the world. In this, *Baal* is also very much in the mainstream of the modern theatrical investigation of romantic possibilities. In the twentieth century, drama has pursued to the source — more doggedly and deeply perhaps than any other form — the great promise of an internal kingdom that the revolutionary desires of the eighteenth and nineteenth centuries opened for our imagination. The link between the political and personal is crucial here — and not a little disturbing. "Bliss was it in that dawn to be alive," writes Wordsworth, and surely a great reason why it was bliss for a young Romantic to be alive as the French Revolution began was that the fraternal dreams of the Revolution and the more private dreams of the Romantic ego on the verge of new self-discovery seemed for a moment to be one. Freedom, for both self and society, was the promise in the air. Modern tragedy, based as it is on the failure of the Romantic project, strikes at the hopeful social vision that informed the blissful dawn of the modern idea of liberty, the political version of Mrs. Alving's "joy of life." As O'Neill's Larry Slade says, surveying the ragged, drunken wrecks about him in the first act of *The Iceman Cometh*, "It's a great game, the pursuit of happiness."

Notes

[1]*The Idea of a Theater* (Princeton: Princeton University Press, 1949), p. 150.

[2]Henry James, *The Scenic Art: Notes on Acting and the Drama*, ed. Allan Wade (New York: Hill and Wang, 1957), p. 293.

[3]*Naked Masks*, ed. Eric Bentley (New York: Dutton, 1952), p. 205. Hereafter cited in the text.

[4]There are many versions of *Baal*. Some of the difficulties in deciding on a preferred text are discussed by Ralph Manheim and John Willett in the introduction and notes to the first volume of their edition of Brecht's *Collected Plays* (New York: Vintage Books, 1971). I follow Brecht's first published version of 1922, which has been translated by Eric Bentley and Martin Esslin (New York: Grove Press, 1964).

[5]Manheim and Willett, pp. 345–46.

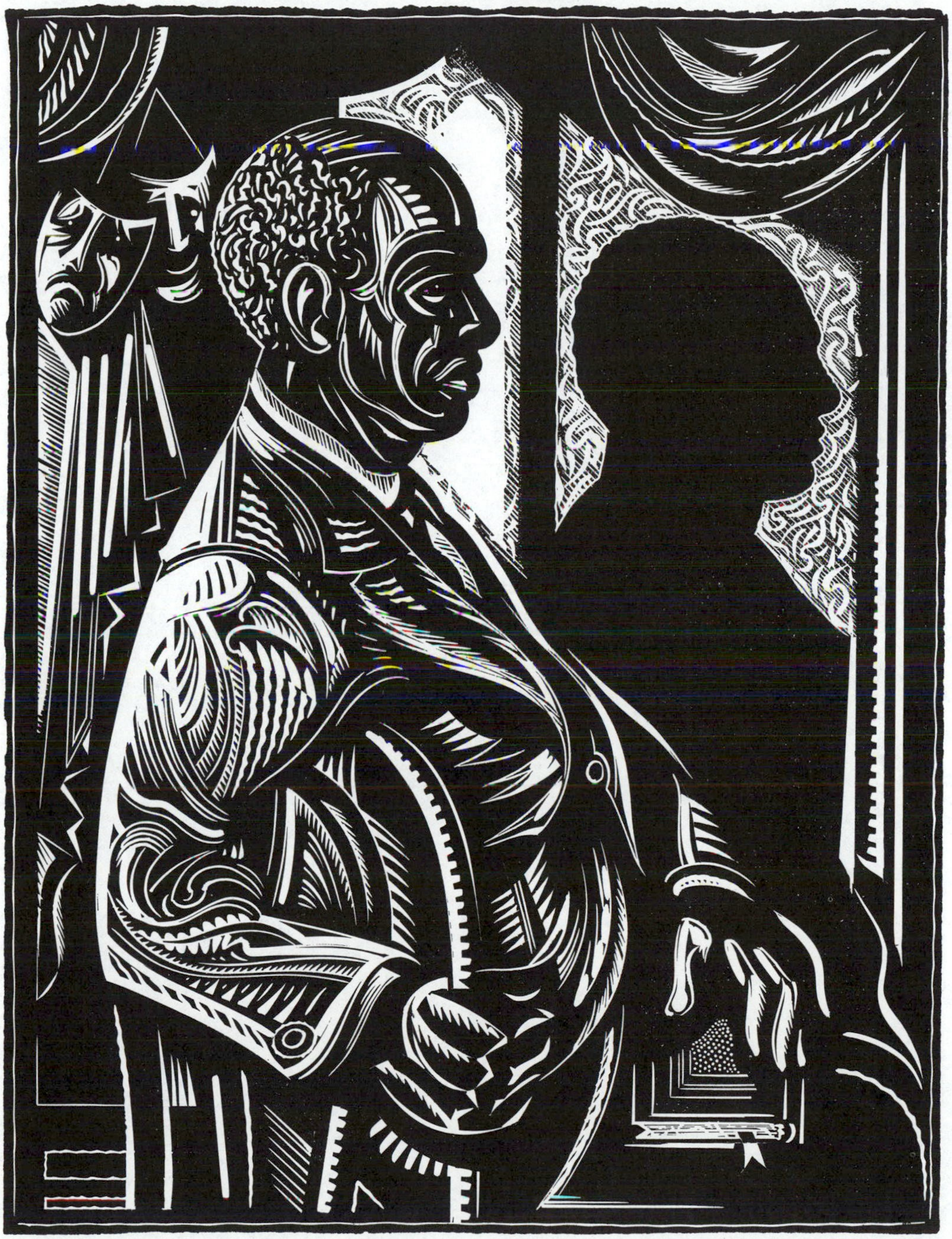

DRAMA AND THEATER
IN THE UNITED STATES

SOCIAL AND TECHNOLOGICAL change transformed the world in the late nineteenth and early twentieth centuries. Between 1860 and 1980, the United States emerged from a crippling civil war and then two world wars to become a dominant global power. However, despite the nation's emergence as a major player on the world stage, the arts in the United States were shaped by divided and contradictory impulses. The desire to imitate European models competed with a desire to bring distinctively American arts into being. Even as the Civil War threatened to destroy the nation itself, writers such as Walt Whitman, Ralph Waldo Emerson, Henry David Thoreau, and others gave voice to a national literature that both incorporated and redefined European traditions. With the global expansion of U.S. influence, especially after World War I, the question of an "American culture" became a pressing one; after World War II, certain forms of culture became one of the United States' most significant exports.

In the theater, the modern era has brought with it the search for a quintessentially "American" drama, in which theme, setting, and characterization explore American experience, often by invoking and then discarding styles and attitudes derived from the European stage. In a sense, American drama in the twentieth century translates the idea of American political freedom into more abstract, metaphorical, even Romantic terms, as a conflict between individual freedom and the pressures of confining social realities such as economic hardship, social class, gender, and race. The search for an American idiom in the theater absorbs the stylistic experiments of European modernism and reshapes them, bending the formal innovation of the European theater to American issues and concerns.

"THE" AMERICAN THEATER?

The democratic experience and populist rhetoric of American public life has generally resisted the idea of a national culture emanating from a single center like New York City or Washington, D.C. For this reason, perhaps, the dream of a national theater has repeatedly failed. In the nineteenth century, westward expansion brought theater from New York, Philadelphia, and Boston to the midwestern cities of Chicago, St. Louis, and Kansas City, and then to Los Angeles and San Francisco, and to scores of smaller towns between the Mississippi and the Pacific. The theater was a widely dispersed, local affair. Towns often boasted theaters that could be used for opera, drama, or vaudeville, and that supported local companies while also catering to touring shows with stars drawn from New York and Europe. Although a lively local theater thrived throughout the country, offering melodrama, classical plays, comedies, and other entertainments, the appetite for touring shows created a demand for organizations capable of handling scheduling problems for local theaters and regional booking agencies.

In 1896 a group of theatrical entrepreneurs headed by Charles Frohman formed a nationwide organization of booking agents called the **SYNDICATE**. In a sense, they created the first model of how a national theater might work in the United States. The Syndicate offered theater managers a full season of touring shows—provided that the manager contracted to deal only with the Syndicate. By gaining exclusive control over theaters on key travel routes, the Syndicate thwarted competition from other touring producers and often even denied local companies the use of local theaters. At its height, the Syndicate had exclusive rights to over 700 theaters. It could blackball non-Syndicate performers from working by threatening producers who hired them, and it could withdraw Syndicate support from any manager who booked non-Syndicate shows or performers.

The effects of the Syndicate were profound and shaped the American theater for the next half-century. The Syndicate's grip on the theater effectively extinguished major professional theater outside New York as a source of new plays and productions; it also influenced playwriting, since the Syndicate developed plays only as commercial properties that could be successfully marketed to a general audience coast-to-coast. Although the Syndicate's power was resisted by a few famous actors and powerful producers, its approach was imitated by other groups. The parochial interests of the New York stage — where the shows of such organizations originated — became in practice the interests of the American theater, and New York became the center of theatrical production and theatrical investment. The revival of significant, professional "regional" theaters as centers of new productions — Margo Jones's Theater 47 in Dallas, the Alley Theater of Houston, the Arena Stage in Washington, D.C., the Actors Workshop of San Francisco, the Guthrie Theater in Minneapolis — had to wait until the 1940s and 1950s. The Syndicate's fortunes also point out the fallacy inherent in the notion of *an* American theater. Throughout its history, the American theater has embraced a range of dynamic and contradictory attitudes toward the stage and its place in society: New York *vs.* the "provinces," mainstream *vs.* elite, conventional *vs.* experimental, commercial *vs.* artistic. Theatrical innovation has been spurred primarily by theaters outside the commercial mainstream, especially by small, amateur "little theaters," by university and college theaters, by community theaters, and by ethnic theaters.

EUROPEAN INFLUENCE AND AMERICAN INNOVATION

The growth of American drama and theater was decisively shaped by the commercial climate of the stage, and also by the United States' isolation from the energetic traditions of European theater. Although turn-of-the-century Broadway developed a homegrown version of theatrical realism — epitomized by writer/producer David Belasco's *The Governor's Lady* (1912), which reproduced the interior of a familiar theater-district restaurant onstage — European experimentation made its impact on America in more indirect ways, usually only after those experiments had crystallized into a body of theatrical practices and conventions. Many major companies toured the United States. The Abbey Theater came with John Millington Synge's *The Playboy of the Western World* in 1911–1912, and the German producer Max Reinhardt brought his spectacular productions to the U.S. in 1912, 1914, 1924, and 1927–1928. The British director Harley Granville Barker, who sponsored Shaw's plays and had gained fame as an innovative director of Shakespeare, directed in New York in 1915; the Ballets Russes toured in 1916; and the Moscow Art Theater — whose disciples Richard Boleslavsky and Maria Ouspenskaya founded the American Laboratory Theater in 1923 — performed in 1923–1924.

Many of these companies — the Abbey and the Moscow Art Theater in particular — had begun as small, independent, amateur theaters, and their work was most immediately implemented in the United States by similar groups. Some innovation came from the new college and university programs in drama, George Pierce Baker's famous playwriting course at Harvard University in the first decades of the century (taken by Eugene O'Neill, among many others) and George T. Montgomery's program for black writers and performers at Howard University in the 1920s were only the beginning of a concerted effort to bring theater and drama into the university curriculum and to develop a greater awareness of progressive theater. However, it largely fell to the **LITTLE THEATER MOVEMENT** to assimilate this new work and redirect it toward particularly American concerns. Innovation in the American theater came largely from these small companies, committed to mounting new and uncommercial work. The Chicago Little Theater, the Toy Theater of Boston, the Neighborhood Playhouse and the Washington Square Playhouse of New York, and Detroit's Arts and Crafts Theater were all in operation by 1917, and the Little Negro Theater Movement was producing plays in Harlem and Washington, D.C., as well.

The Provincetown Playhouse provides a model of the "little theaters" and their fortunes in the early twentieth century. Founded in 1915 in Provincetown, Massachusetts — an artists' retreat at the tip of Cape Cod — the company was initially a group of young amateurs intent on theater, including the playwright Susan Glaspell; her husband, George Cram Cook; and, later, Eugene O'Neill. In the first year, the players produced plays in their summer homes. In 1916 they converted an old wharf building into a small theater and produced, among other plays, O'Neill's *Bound East for Cardiff*. In the autumn, the players returned to New York and opened a small theater in Greenwich Village. The company could hardly afford complex and expensive sets and turned its efforts instead toward a simple and realistic kind of performance. Eugene O'Neill's early plays were produced by the Provincetown company, and after he became a successful Broadway playwright, he continued to open many of his plays there. Like all of the "little theaters," the Provincetown had difficulty managing the transition from a small amateur company to the larger demands of a self-sustaining professional company. It went through a series of transformations before closing in 1929, having introduced O'Neill to the stage and having staged plays by John Reed, Edna St. Vincent Millay, Susan Glaspell, Djuna Barnes, Edmund Wilson, Paul Green, Wallace Stevens, Theodore Dreiser, August Strindberg, and many others.

In the United States, the freedom to make theater has always been qualified by the need to make it pay. The trials of sustaining artistic ambition in the commercial environment of the theater is the central narrative of the most innovative theatrical companies of the modern era. The ideal of an American theater remained tantalizing yet elusive and was often pursued in several ways, usually by developing a distinctive repertory of plays, or by trying to define a typically American performance idiom. "Little theaters" like the Provincetown emphasized the production of American drama. Other theaters tried to produce American drama, the new European drama, and the classics for a larger audience than the "little theaters" could reach. The Theater Guild, for example, was organized in 1919 in New York as a subscription company specifically for the purpose of producing noncommercial plays. In the course of the next decade, the Guild staged plays by Shaw, Pirandello, Ibsen, and Strindberg, as well as plays by Americans like O'Neill and Elmer Rice. The Guild succeeded in incorporating American plays like O'Neill's *Strange Interlude* (1928) and Rice's *The Adding Machine* (1923) into the repertory of serious modern drama and in bringing it to a significant public. However, following the stock market crash of 1929 and the economic depression that ensued, the Guild invested in a less adventuresome repertory in the hopes of drawing a larger audience and so lost its original mission.

Although it sponsored an innovative selection of plays, the Theater Guild did not develop an original style of production. In 1931, several Guild members began a spin-off company — called simply the Group — for the purpose of investigating different kinds of drama and different approaches to performance. Eventually including Harold Clurman, Cheryl Crawford, Lee Strasberg, Elia Kazan, Sanford Meisner, and many others, the Group at first worked on plays examining the social ferment of the 1930s and the hardship of the Great Depression. Much as Chekhov became the centerpiece of Stanislavsky's Moscow Art Theater, so the plays of Clifford Odets became the Group's standards: *Awake and Sing!*, *Waiting for Lefty*, and *Golden Boy*. However, the Group's most extensive contribution to the American theater was its systematic importation of Stanislavskian acting techniques. In the Group, and later in the Actors Studio, actors were trained in Stanislavsky's approach to EMOTION MEMORY and GIVEN CIRCUMSTANCES, laying the groundwork for what became a distinctly "American" style of acting, acting that was emotionally spontaneous, grounded in subtext, psychologically realistic and nuanced. Nonetheless, the

Group, the Studio, and the training they devised produced a generation of actors ready to meet the challenges of the burgeoning American drama of the 1940s and 1950s: Marlon Brando, Ben Gazzara, Karl Malden, Geraldine Page, Kim Stanley, Maureen Stapleton, and many others.

The impact of this acting can be seen in the great stage productions of the post-war period. The 1940s and early 1950s saw the development of a distinctively American approach to stage realism, balancing nuanced characterization with a concern for the social environment. Arthur Miller's *Death of a Salesman* and *The Crucible*, Tennessee Williams's *A Streetcar Named Desire* and *The Glass Menagerie*, and Eugene O'Neill's *The Iceman Cometh* and *Long Day's Journey into Night* demanded the subtle realism that became the hallmark of American acting and of American drama in the world repertoire. These plays — and their descendants, like the plays of Beth Henley, David Mamet, or Sam Shepard — succeeded by criticizing American ideals and institutions while at the same time exploring the psyche of the American character. Indeed, in these plays the American character often seems to be thwarted precisely by the process of American society. The concern for political purity destroys John Proctor in *The Crucible*; the fragile beauty of Tennessee Williams's Southern belles is usually crushed by the sordid realities of modern urban life; in Shepard's *True West*, the American West becomes a mythic battleground, where a yuppie and a drifter shoot it out for control of the image.

If the Group and the Studio created an identifiably "American" approach to acting, the Federal Theater Project succeeded — briefly — in creating a truly national theater. An act of Congress established the Federal Theater Project in 1935 under the Works Projects Administration. Like other WPA projects, the Federal Theater was designed both to employ workers idled by the depression and to provide service to the community. Given the mission of providing employment by hiring large casts and supporting personnel, and a commitment to dramatizing contemporary social issues, the Federal Theater developed its most notable genre, the Living Newspaper. Through a series of vignettes, readings, films, and other techniques — many drawn from European experiments — each Newspaper examined a problem in current national and world affairs: the farm crisis in *Triple A Plowed Under* (1936), housing in *One-Third of a Nation* (1938). At its height, the Federal Theater had branches in forty states. These branches staged productions devised by the project's directors, using their own local resources, and often developed their own material. In 1936, for instance, a stage adaptation of Sinclair Lewis's *It Can't Happen Here* opened simultaneously in twenty-one theaters around the country, including black-cast and Yiddish productions. The Federal Theater ran for four full seasons. It financed twelve hundred productions of 830 major works, at times employing over 10,000 people, most of whom had been unemployed. In New York alone, over 12 million people saw its productions. In an era of labor unrest and the pervasive fear of outside agitation, however, the Newspapers were seen by the Project's enemies as too left-wing for government support: Congress terminated the Federal Theater in 1939. Nonetheless, the Federal Theater enabled a generation of actors, designers, directors, and playwrights to survive, and it brought the theater powerfully into the national scene.

POSTWAR EXPERIMENTS

After World War II, the most significant innovations in American theater have come from small "experimental" theater companies. In part through the influence of Antonin Artaud's conception of a **THEATER OF CRUELTY** (see unit 6), and the several tours of Jerzy Grotowski's Lab Theater of Poland, experimental theater in the 1960s and 1970s tended to reject the esthetic of stage realism in favor of producing an immediate, quintessentially *theatrical* experience for its audiences. As a result, many productions in the 1960s and

1970s—the Living Theater's *Paradise Now*, the Performance Group's *Dionysus in 69*, the Open Theater's *The Serpent*, the work of the Bread and Puppet theater, of Mabou Mines, and many others—incorporated the audience as participants in the action. Many of these experiments also led to new forms of playwriting, in which classical notions of representation were also broken down. In Ntozake Shange's *spell #7* actors assume a variety of roles and represent them through a powerful and original blending of drama, music, and poetry.

Moreover, American drama continued to strike a compromise with the innovations of the European theater after the war. Eric Bentley—a brilliant scholar, director, playwright, and translator—worked indefatigably to bring Bertolt Brecht to the attention of the American theater. Brecht became particularly important in the United States as the Vietnam War and widespread civil and social discontent spurred the theater in more agitational, political directions. Feminist theater, ethnic theater, and gay and lesbian theater have all at times availed themselves of Brecht's theater theory and practice. The work of Luis Valdez and El Teatro Campesino in California in the 1960s and 1970s is a direct extension of Brecht's sense of theater. Bringing a flatbed truck to farmworkers' strikes, Teatro Campesino produced its short, political dramas to an active, involved audience and became part of the process of social change. "Absurdist" playwrights like Samuel Beckett, Harold Pinter, and Eugène Ionesco were also both produced and imitated in the United States, influencing the work of American playwrights like Edward Albee, Maria Irene Fornes, Jack Gelber, Adrienne Kennedy, David Mamet, and Sam Shepard. Indeed, in plays like Amiri Baraka's *Dutchman*, Sam Shepard's *True West*, and Maria Irene Fornes's *Mud*, we can see the inflections of theater of the absurd in plays that are recognizably "American" in style and subject matter.

AFRICAN-AMERICAN DRAMA AND THEATER

The Federal Theater Project also sponsored a Negro Unit, directed by John Houseman and Orson Welles, which operated in ten cities around the U.S.; two of its productions, an all-black *Macbeth* and *The Swing Mikado*, were among the Federal Theater's most successful productions. The fact of a separate Negro Unit points to a different crisis in the idea of an American theater. How could a theater largely in the hands of the white, Anglo, male, middle class adequately represent the diversity of the nation's experience, particularly the experience of the oppressed? As the poet and playwright Langston Hughes noted in "Notes on Commercial Theater," published in 1940, the stage had in many ways appropriated African-American culture, systematically absorbing it into its own dominant values:

> Yep, you done taken my blues and gone.
> You also took my spirituals and gone.
> You put me in Macbeth and Carmen Jones
> And all kinds of Swing Mikados
> And in everything but what's about me—
> But someday somebody'll
> Stand up and talk about me,
> And write about me—
> Black and beautiful—

Far from representing authentic black experience in America, such theater more often confirmed the discriminatory fantasies already prominent on the stage and in society. Such stereotypes as the boozy Irishman, the dull Swede, the sunny and/or murderous Italian, and the greedy Jew—appearing even in "realistic" plays like Rice's *Street Scene* (1929)—work to reinforce the "normative" perspective of dominant culture, reflecting the attitudes, behavior, and social practices that oppress such groups in the world outside the theater. It is

not surprising, then, that throughout the history of the United States, ethnic theaters have played a prominent part in maintaining the cultural identity of America's minority populations: the Yiddish theater of New York, Polish theaters in Chicago, Scandinavian theaters throughout the Midwest, a thriving circuit of Spanish-language theaters shared by Mexico and Southwestern states from Texas to California, Cuban-influenced theater in Florida, and Puerto Rican theater in New York. Some of these theaters produced versions of classic European plays in their own accents, but most developed their own dramatic forms, as ways of maintaining themselves in the face of a brutally exclusive "American" culture.

The experience of slavery places African Americans in a different position vis-à-vis the culture of the United States, and the black theater has had a profound impact on the course of the American stage. Although an African Theater Company was founded in New York in 1821 — sponsoring, among others, the brilliant Shakespearean actor Ira Aldridge (1807–1867) who left the United States for a distinguished career in Europe — in the main, African Americans had little direct access to the theater before the twentieth century. Black characters had long figured as stage villains and comic buffoons in American drama. Played by white actors in blackface makeup, these abusive types literally enacted white attitudes toward racial difference. "Jim Crow" was first popularized by the white song-and-dance man T. D. Rice in the 1830s, and more "sympathetic" characters, like Tom in the hugely popular stage adaptations of Harriet Beecher Stowe's *Uncle Tom's Cabin* (1832), were devised by white authors and played by white actors. The minstrel troupes that became popular after the Civil War for depicting romanticized vignettes of plantation life were also first performed by white actors. Later, black performers — in minstrel troupes, or in the newly popular "Negro musicals" — often had little choice other than to enact these stereotypes themselves, for such roles were the only openings available on the stage (even black theaters were usually financed and operated by white entrepreneurs). Despite small inroads like the Lafayette Theater (founded in Harlem in 1915), representing black experience to America at large was almost exclusively the prerogative of white actors, producers, playwrights, and performers. In this regard, the theater — like the institutions of literature, the press, the legal system, and state and federal government — denied African Americans their own voice.

Spurred in part by successful plays by white dramatists that self-consciously attempted to "humanize" black characters for white audiences — O'Neill's *The Emperor Jones* (1920) and *All God's Chillun Got Wings* (1924), Marc Connelly's *The Green Pastures* (1930), Paul Green's *In Abraham's Bosom* (1926), and Dubose and Dorothy Heyward's *Porgy* (1920; transformed into the Gershwin musical *Porgy and Bess* in 1935) — black actors and writers became galvanized to "stand up and talk" about themselves. Throughout the 1920s the LITTLE NEGRO THEATER MOVEMENT sponsored plays of black life largely for black audiences. The Lafayette Theater, for example, opened Willis Richardson's *The Chipwoman's Fortune* in 1923; it later became the first play by a black playwright to reach Broadway. In the 1920s and 1930s, black drama increasingly addressed the politics of racism in the United States, while also depicting the effect of racism in daily life. Several organizations worked to sponsor African-American drama and theater. W. E. B. DuBois, a founder of the National Association for the Advancement of Colored People (NAACP), used his *Crisis* magazine — in collaboration with the National Urban League's *Opportunity* — to give a series of prizes to promising black playwrights; winners included Eulalie Spence's *Foreign Mail* (1926), Zora Neale Hurston's *Colorstruck* and *Spears* (1925), and Georgia Douglas Johnson's *Blue Blood* (1926). The NAACP also sponsored the production of plays, including Angelina Weld Grimke's influential drama of a young woman's reaction to the lynching of her father and brother, *Rachel* (1916). *Rachel* was one of the first of a series of plays about lynching. How this important genre of black theater — and a crucial element of black

experience in the United States—was both overlooked and distorted by white theater is the subject of Alice Childress's brilliant play *Trouble in Mind*, which opened off-Broadway in 1955. Finally, black colleges, universities, and even high schools also became centers for a new dramatic repertory. In 1921, Montgomery T. Gregory formed a department of Dramatic Arts at Howard University in Washington, D.C., and with Alain Locke developed an influential program in acting, playwriting, and theatrical production, offering the first institutionalized training for black writers and performers in the United States.

In a 1926 playbill for Harlem's Krigwa Players, W. E. B. DuBois described the goals of a black theater:

> The plays of a real Negro theater must be: *One: About us.* That is, they must have plots which reveal Negro life as it is. *Two: By us.* That is, they must be written by Negro authors who understand from birth and continual association just what it means to be a Negro today. *Three: For us.* That is, the theater must cater primarily to Negro audiences and be supported and sustained by their entertainment and approval. *Fourth: Near us.* The theater must be in a Negro neighborhood near the mass of ordinary Negro people.

Throughout the 1930s and 1940s, African-American playwrights and actors came into increasing national prominence, both by developing DuBois's agenda and by working to bring an authentic black drama to a wider audience. Langston Hughes wrote a number of plays in the 1930s, including the well-known *Mulatto* (1935); the Federal Theater Project produced W. E. B. DuBois's *Haiti* at the Lafayette Theater; and playwrights trained at Howard were produced in New York and elsewhere. The founding of the companies like the American Negro Theater in 1939, the Negro Playwrights Company in 1940, and the Negro Ensemble Company in 1957 began to meet DuBois's charge, developing the actors, the production experience, and the financing that would sustain the explosive growth of black American drama after World War II. When Lorraine Hansberry's *A Raisin in the Sun* opened in 1959, it was the first play written by a black woman to reach Broadway, the first directed by a black director (Lloyd Richards), and the first financed predominantly by African Americans. The success of *Raisin* foretold the success of black theater in the coming decades, as black playwrights—Amiri Baraka, Adrienne Kennedy, Charles Gordone, Ed Bullins, Charles Fuller, Ntozake Shange, August Wilson, and many others—came to shape the American theater.

POPULAR THEATER AND MASS CULTURE

The tension between commercial viability and dramatic achievement is perhaps best symbolized by Broadway itself, the American theater's "magnificent invalid," where even the greatest American plays can hardly compare in terms of commercial and popular success with Broadway's most uniquely American genre: the musical. Musical theater has a long history in the United States, and in many respects its fortunes parallel those of the dramatic theater. Musical theater also witnessed the tyranny of national producing syndicates, the impact of European innovation, and the powerful contributions of black and ethnic cultures. However, the integration of song and dance, orchestral music, and (usually) a romantic plot characteristic of the Broadway musical really dates to the period of World War II, probably to Richard Rodgers and Oscar Hammerstein's *Oklahoma!* (1943), which ran for 2248 performances (*Death of a Salesman*, in contrast, ran for 742). *Oklahoma!* provided the model not only for other Rodgers and Hammerstein hits—*Carousel* (1945), *South Pacific* (1949), *The King and I* (1951)—but for other musicals as well: Alan Jay Lerner and Frederick Loewe's updating of Shaw's *Pygmalion* in *My Fair Lady* (1956), Frank Loesser's *Guys and Dolls* (1950), and Leonard Bernstein, Stephen Sondheim, and Arthur Laurents's *West Side Story* (1957). Although the form of the Broadway musical underwent significant

changes in the 1970s and 1980s, its popularity points to one of the ways that the theater has sought to recapture an audience from film and television: by emphasizing the unique excitement of a dazzling live spectacle. The musical theater also points to the fundamental conditions of the Broadway theatrical economy as well. Musicals remain popular with producers because the huge financial investment required to mount a musical can repay much larger returns for investors than any "straight" play.

Throughout the history of the stage in the West, important theaters have succeeded both in creating innovative drama and in creating a public. However, the American theater—if there is *an* American theater—is a different entity altogether from the citizens' theater of classical Athens, the courtly theater of Racine and Molière, or even the educated circle of subscribers to Shaw's Court Theater. In a sense, this difference can be traced to the fact that the American theater first came into force only in the twentieth century, at just the moment when other dramatic media—film and television—began to compete with it. The American theater has had to define itself in the environment of modern mass culture. Not only are film and television more accessible to most people, but the technology and distribution of such mass media have fundamentally altered our understanding both of drama and performance, and of what an audience *is*. "The American theater" has always been a critical fiction, homogenizing the diversity of stage activity in the United States, writing some forms of drama—chiefly American realistic plays—into history, and writing others out of it. Today, it may be equally artificial to separate live theater from other forms of dramatic production, forms that have massively changed the terrain where dramatic performance takes place.

SUSAN GLASPELL

Susan Glaspell (1882–1948) was born in Iowa, studied at Drake University in Des Moines and at the University of Chicago, and then briefly pursued a career as a journalist. With her husband, George Cram Cook, she founded the Provincetown Playhouse and wrote many of the plays it produced: *Suppressed Desires* (1914, written with Cook), a spoof of the vogue for psychoanalysis among New York's intellectual elite; *Trifles* (1916); *Close the Book* (1917); *A Woman's Honor* (1918), and *Tickless Time* (1918, again written with Cook). After the reorganization of the Provincetown in 1921, Glaspell wrote a series of full-length, often experimental, plays: *Inheritors* (1920), *The Verge* (1921), and *Alison's House* (1930). *Alison's House*, based loosely on Emily Dickinson and her family, won Glaspell the Pulitzer Prize in 1930. Glaspell then retired from playwriting and largely from the theater as well, returning briefly to serve as the director of the Mid-West Play Bureau for the Federal Theater Project.

Trifles

Trifles is an important play in the development of American realism. It poses a distinct contrast to Eugene O'Neill's early plays, with which it shared the Provincetown stage. O'Neill's realistic plays attempt to filter an abstract, metaphysical longing into the drab world of his down-and-out drifters and sailors. Glaspell's drama more directly examines the values and behavior of the society she brings to the stage. In *Trifles*—and in the short story "A Jury of Her Peers," which she adapted from the play the following year—Glaspell considers the relationship between truth, power, and gender. The play is a murder mystery. A local man, John Wright, has been found dead, and his wife, Minnie, is suspected of killing him. Called to investigate, County Attorney George Henderson, Henry Peters, and Lewis Hale readily assume a masculine prerogative to discover the truth of John Wright's murder, telling their wives to remain in the kitchen out of the way. However, the truth of the crime is in fact concealed *in* the kitchen, and only the women are able to discover it. For Glaspell shows the audience that the "trifles" of the women's world are the signs of a reality wholly unreadable to the men, precisely because it is a world they regard as feminine, and therefore unimportant and uninteresting. *Trifles*, that is, works to subvert our notions of reality and truth by suggesting how such ideas are constructed within a specific social order—the masculine order of modern society.

TRIFLES
A PLAY IN ONE ACT
Susan Glaspell

— CHARACTERS —

GEORGE HENDERSON, *County Attorney*
HENRY PETERS, *Sheriff*
LEWIS HALE, *A Neighboring Farmer*
MRS. PETERS
MRS. HALE

THE SETTING: *The kitchen in the now abandoned farmhouse of* JOHN WRIGHT

SCENE: *The kitchen in the now abandoned farmhouse of John Wright, a gloomy kitchen, and left without having been put in order — unwashed pans under the sink, a loaf of bread outside the breadbox, a dish towel on the table — other signs of incompleted work. At the rear the outer door opens and the* SHERIFF *comes in followed by the* COUNTY ATTORNEY *and* HALE. *The* SHERIFF *and* HALE *are men in middle life, the* COUNTY ATTORNEY *is a young man; all are much bundled up and go at once to the stove. They are followed by the two women — the* SHERIFF'S *wife first; she is a slight wiry woman, a thin nervous face.* MRS. HALE *is larger and would ordinarily be called more comfortable looking, but she is disturbed now and looks fearfully about as she enters. The women have come in slowly, and stand close together near the door.*

COUNTY ATTORNEY: (*Rubbing his hands*) This feels good. Come up to the fire, ladies.
MRS. PETERS: (*After taking a step forward*) I'm not — cold.
SHERIFF: (*Unbuttoning his overcoat and stepping away from the*
5   *stove as if to mark the beginning of official business*) Now, Mr. Hale, before we move things about, you explain to Mr. Henderson just what you saw when you came here yesterday morning.
COUNTY ATTORNEY: By the way, has anything been moved? Are
10   things just as you left them yesterday?
SHERIFF: (*Looking about*) It's just the same. When it dropped below zero last night I thought I'd better send Frank out this morning to make a fire for us — no use getting pneumonia with a big case on, but I told him not to touch anything except
15   the stove — and you know Frank.
COUNTY ATTORNEY: Somebody should have been left here yesterday.
SHERIFF: Oh — yesterday. When I had to send Frank to Morris Center for that man who went crazy — I want you to know I
20   had my hands full yesterday, I knew you could get back from Omaha by today and as long as I went over everything here myself —
COUNTY ATTORNEY: Well, Mr. Hale, tell just what happened when you came here yesterday morning.
25   HALE: Harry and I had started to town with a load of potatoes. We came along the road from my place and as I got here I said, "I'm going to see if I can't get John Wright to go in with me on a party telephone." I spoke to Wright about it once before and he put me off, saying folks talked too much any-
30   way, and all he asked was peace and quiet — I guess you know about how much he talked himself; but I thought maybe if I went to the house and talked about it before his wife, though I

said to Harry that I didn't know as what his wife wanted made much difference to John —
COUNTY ATTORNEY: Let's talk about that later, Mr. Hale. I do   35
want to talk about that, but tell now just what happened when you got to the house.
HALE: I didn't hear or see anything; I knocked at the door, and still it was all quiet inside. I knew they must be up, it was past eight o'clock. So I knocked again, and I thought I heard   40
somebody say, "Come in." I wasn't sure, I'm not sure yet, but I opened the door — this door (*indicating the door by which the two women are still standing*) and there in that rocker — (*pointing to it*) sat Mrs. Wright.

(*They all look at the rocker.*)

COUNTY ATTORNEY: What — was she doing?   45
HALE: She was rockin' back and forth. She had her apron in her hand and was kind of — pleating it.
COUNTY ATTORNEY: And how did she — look?
HALE: Well, she looked queer.
COUNTY ATTORNEY: How do you mean — queer?   50
HALE: Well, as if she didn't know what she was going to do next. And kind of done up.
COUNTY ATTORNEY: How did she seem to feel about your coming?
HALE: Why, I don't think she minded — one way or other. She   55
didn't pay much attention. I said, "How do, Mrs. Wright, it's cold, ain't it?" And she said, "Is it?" — and went on kind of pleating at her apron. Well, I was surprised; she didn't ask me to come up to the stove, or to set down, but just sat there, not even looking at me, so I said, "I want to see John." And then   60
she — laughed. I guess you would call it a laugh. I thought of Harry and the team outside, so I said a little sharp: "Can't I see John?" "No," she says, kind o' dull like. "Ain't he home?" says I. "Yes," says she, "he's home." "Then why can't I see him?" I asked her, out of patience. "'Cause he's dead," says she.   65
"*Dead?*" says I. She just nodded her head, not getting a bit excited, but rockin' back and forth. "Why — where is he?" says I, not knowing what to say. She just pointed upstairs — like that (*Himself pointing to the room above.*) I got up, with the idea of going up there. I walked from there to here — then   70
I says, "Why, what did he die of?" "He died of a rope round his neck," says she, and just went on pleatin' at her apron. Well, I went out and called Harry. I thought I might — need help. We went upstairs and there he was lyin' —
COUNTY ATTORNEY: I think I'd rather have you go into that up-   75
stairs, where you can point it all out. Just go on now with the rest of the story.

578

HALE: Well, my first thought was to get that rope off. It looked . . . (*Stops, his face twitches*) . . . but Harry, he went up to him, and he said, "No, he's dead all right, and we'd better not touch anything." So we went back down stairs. She was still sitting that same way. "Has anybody been notified?" I asked. "No," says she, unconcerned. "Who did this, Mrs. Wright?" said Harry. He said it businesslike—and she stopped pleatin' of her apron. "I don't know," she says. "You don't *know*?" says Harry. "No," says she. "Weren't you sleepin' in the bed with him?" says Harry. "Yes," says she, "but I was on the inside." "Somebody slipped a rope round his neck and strangled him and you didn't wake up?" says Harry. "I didn't wake up," she said after him. We must 'a looked as if we didn't see how that could be, for after a minute she said. "I sleep sound." Harry was going to ask her more questions but I said maybe we ought to let her tell her story first to the coroner, or the sheriff, so Harry went fast as he could to Rivers' place, where there's a telephone.

COUNTY ATTORNEY: And what did Mrs. Wright do when she knew that you had gone for the coroner?

HALE: She moved from that chair to this one over here (*Pointing to a small chair in the corner*) and just sat there with her hands held together and looking down. I got a feeling that I ought to make some conversation, so I said I had come in to see if John wanted to put in a telephone, and at that she started to laugh, and then she stopped and looked at me—scared. (*The* COUNTY ATTORNEY, *who has had his notebook out, makes a note.*) I dunno, maybe it wasn't scared. I wouldn't like to say it was. Soon Harry got back, and then Dr. Lloyd came, and you, Mr. Peters, and so I guess that's all I know that you don't.

COUNTY ATTORNEY: (*Looking around*) I guess we'll go upstairs first—and then out to the barn and around there. (*To the* SHERIFF) You're convinced that there was nothing important here—nothing that would point to any motive.

SHERIFF: Nothing here but kitchen things.

(*The* COUNTY ATTORNEY *after again looking around the kitchen, opens the door of a cupboard closet. He gets up on a chair and looks on a shelf. Pulls his hand away, sticky.*)

COUNTY ATTORNEY: Here's a nice mess.

(*The women draw nearer.*)

MRS. PETERS: (*To the other woman*) Oh, her fruit; it did freeze. (*To the* COUNTY ATTORNEY) She worried about that when it turned so cold. She said the fire'd go out and her jars would break.

SHERIFF: Well, can you beat the women! Held for murder and worryin' about her preserves.

COUNTY ATTORNEY: I guess before we're through she may have something more serious than preserves to worry about.

HALE: Well, women are used to worrying over trifles.

(*The two women move a little closer together.*)

COUNTY ATTORNEY: (*With the gallantry of a young politician*) And yet, for all their worries, what would we do without the ladies? (*The women do not unbend. He goes to the sink, takes a dipperful of water from the pail and pouring it into a basin, washes his hands. Starts to wipe them on the roller towel, turns it for a cleaner place*) Dirty towels! (*Kicks his foot against the pans under the sink*) Not much of a housekeeper, would you say, ladies?

MRS. HALE: (*Stiffly*) There's a great deal of work to be done on a farm.

COUNTY ATTORNEY: To be sure. And yet (*With a little bow to her*) I know there are some Dickson county farmhouses which do not have such roller towels.

(*He gives it a pull to expose its full length again.*)

MRS. HALE: Those towels get dirty awful quick. Men's hands aren't always as clean as they might be.

COUNTY ATTORNEY: Ah, loyal to your sex, I see. But you and Mrs. Wright were neighbors. I suppose you were friends, too.

MRS. HALE: (*Shaking her head*) I've not seen much of her of late years. I've not been in this house—it's more than a year.

COUNTY ATTORNEY: And why was that? You didn't like her?

MRS. HALE: I liked her all well enough. Farmers' wives have their hands full, Mr. Henderson. And then—

COUNTY ATTORNEY: Yes—?

MRS. HALE: (*Looking about*) It never seemed a very cheerful place.

COUNTY ATTORNEY: No—it's not cheerful. I shouldn't say she had the homemaking instinct.

MRS. HALE: Well, I don't know as Wright had, either.

COUNTY ATTORNEY: You mean that they didn't get on very well?

MRS. HALE: No, I don't mean anything. But I don't think a place'd be any cheerfuller for John Wright's being in it.

COUNTY ATTORNEY: I'd like to talk more of that a little later. I want to get the lay of things upstairs now.

(*He goes to the left, where three steps lead to a stair door.*)

SHERIFF: I suppose anything Mrs. Peters does'll be all right. She was to take in some clothes for her, you know, and a few little things. We left in such a hurry yesterday.

COUNTY ATTORNEY: Yes, but I would like to see what you take, Mrs. Peters, and keep an eye out for anything that might be of use to us.

MRS. PETERS: Yes, Mr. Henderson.

(*The women listen to the men's steps on the stairs, then look about the kitchen.*)

MRS. HALE: I'd hate to have men coming into my kitchen, snooping around and criticising.

(*She arranges the pans under sink which the* COUNTY ATTORNEY *had shoved out of place.*)

MRS. PETERS: Of course it's no more than their duty.

MRS. HALE: Duty's all right, but I guess that deputy sheriff that came out to make the fire might have got a little of this on. (*Gives the roller towel a pull*) Wish I'd thought of that sooner. Seems mean to talk about her for not having things slicked up when she had to come away in such a hurry.

MRS. PETERS: (*Who has gone to a small table in the left rear corner of the room, and lifted one end of a towel that covers a pan*) She had bread set.

(*Stands still*)

MRS. HALE: (*Eyes fixed on a loaf of bread beside the breadbox, which is on a low shelf at the other side of the room. Moves slowly toward it*) She was going to put this in there. (*Picks up loaf, then abruptly drops it. In a manner of returning to familiar things*) It's a shame about her fruit. I wonder if it's all gone.

180 (Gets up on the chair and looks) I think there's some here that's all right, Mrs. Peters. Yes — here; (Holding it toward the window) this is cherries, too. (Looking again) I declare I believe that's the only one. (Gets down, bottle in her hand. Goes to the sink and wipes it off on the outside) She'll feel awful bad
185 after all her hard work in the hot weather. I remember the afternoon I put up my cherries last summer.

(She puts the bottle on the big kitchen table, center of the room. With a sigh, is about to sit down in the rocking-chair. Before she is seated realizes what chair it is; with a slow look at it, steps back. The chair which she has touched rocks back and forth.)

MRS. PETERS: Well, I must get those things from the front room closet. (She goes to the door at the right, but after looking into the other room, steps back.) You coming with me, Mrs. Hale?
190 You could help me carry them.

(They go in the other room; reappear, MRS. PETERS carrying a dress and skirt, MRS. HALE following with a pair of shoes.)

MRS. PETERS: My, it's cold in there.

(She puts the clothes on the big table, and hurries to the stove.)

MRS. HALE: (Examining the skirt) Wright was close. I think maybe that's why she kept so much to herself. She didn't even belong to the Ladies Aid. I suppose she felt she couldn't do
195 her part, and then you don't enjoy things when you feel shabby. She used to wear pretty clothes and be lively, when she was Minnie Foster, one of the town girls singing in the choir. But that — oh, that was thirty years ago. This all you was to take in?
200 MRS. PETERS: She said she wanted an apron. Funny thing to want, for there isn't much to get you dirty in jail, goodness knows. But I suppose just to make her feel more natural. She said they was in the top drawer in this cupboard. Yes, here. And then her little shawl that always hung behind the door.
205 (Opens stair door and looks) Yes, here it is.

(Quickly shuts door leading upstairs)

MRS. HALE: (Abruptly moving toward her) Mrs. Peters?
MRS. PETERS: Yes, Mrs. Hale?
MRS. HALE: Do you think she did it?
MRS. PETERS: (In a frightened voice) Oh, I don't know.
210 MRS. HALE: Well, I don't think she did. Asking for an apron and her little shawl. Worrying about her fruit.
MRS. PETERS: (Starts to speak, glances up, where footsteps are heard in the room above. In a low voice) Mr. Peters says it looks bad for her. Mr. Henderson is awful sarcastic in a speech and
215 he'll make fun of her sayin' she didn't wake up.
MRS. HALE: Well, I guess John Wright didn't wake when they was slipping that rope under his neck.
MRS. PETERS: No, it's strange. It must have been done awful crafty and still. They say it was such a — funny way to kill a
220 man, rigging it all up like that.
MRS. HALE: That's just what Mr. Hale said. There was a gun in the house. He says that's what he can't understand.
MRS. PETERS: Mr. Henderson said coming out that what was needed for the case was a motive; something to show anger,
225 or — sudden feeling.
MRS. HALE: (Who is standing by the table) Well, I don't see any signs of anger around here. (She puts her hand on the dish

towel which lies on the table, stands looking down at table, one half of which is clean, the other half messy.) It's wiped to here. (Makes a move as if to finish work, then turns and looks
230 at loaf of bread outside the breadbox. Drops towel. In that voice of coming back to familiar things) Wonder how they are finding things upstairs. I hope she had it a little more red-up up there. You know, it seems kind of sneaking. Locking her up in town and then coming out here and trying to get her
235 own house to turn against her!
MRS. PETERS: But Mrs. Hale, the law is the law.
MRS. HALE: I s'pose 'tis. (Unbuttoning her coat) Better loosen up your things, Mrs. Peters. You won't feel them when you go out.
240

(MRS. PETERS takes off her fur tippet, goes to hang it on hook at back of room, stands looking at the under part of the small corner table.)

MRS. PETERS: She was piecing a quilt.

(She brings the large sewing basket and they look at the bright pieces.)

MRS. HALE: It's log cabin pattern. Pretty, isn't it? I wonder if she was goin' to quilt it or just knot it?

(Footsteps have been heard coming down the stairs. The SHERIFF enters followed by HALE and the COUNTY ATTORNEY.)

SHERIFF: They wonder if she was going to quilt it or just knot it!

(The men laugh; the women look abashed.)

COUNTY ATTORNEY: (Rubbing his hands over the stove) Frank's
245 fire didn't do much up there, did it? Well, let's go out to the barn and get that cleared up.

(The men go outside.)

MRS. HALE: (Resentfully) I don't know as there's anything so strange, our takin' up our time with little things while we're waiting for them to get the evidence. (She sits down at the big
250 table smoothing out a block with decision.) I don't see as it's anything to laugh about.
MRS. PETERS: (Apologetically) Of course they've got awful important things on their minds.

(Pulls up a chair and joins MRS. HALE at the table)

MRS. HALE: (Examining another block) Mrs. Peters, look at this
255 one. Here, this is the one she was working on, and look at that sewing! All the rest of it has been so nice and even. And look at this! It's all over the place! Why, it looks as if she didn't know what she was about!

(After she has said this they look at each other, then start to glance back at the door. After an instant MRS. HALE has pulled at a knot and ripped the sewing.)

MRS. PETERS: Oh, what are you doing, Mrs. Hale?
260 MRS. HALE: (Mildly) Just pulling out a stitch or two that's not sewed very good. (Threading a needle) Bad sewing always made me fidgety.
MRS. PETERS: (Nervously) I don't think we ought to touch things.
265 MRS. HALE: I'll just finish up this end. (Suddenly stopping and leaning forward) Mrs. Peters?
MRS. PETERS: Yes, Mrs. Hale?

MRS. HALE: What do you suppose she was so nervous about?

270 MRS. PETERS: Oh—I don't know. I don't know as she was nervous. I sometimes sew awful queer when I'm just tired. (MRS.
HALE *starts to say something, looks at* MRS. PETERS, *then goes
on sewing.*) Well, I must get these things wrapped up. They
may be through sooner than we think. (*Putting apron and
275 other things together*) I wonder where I can find a piece of
paper, and string.

MRS. HALE: In that cupboard, maybe.

MRS. PETERS: (*Looking in cupboard*) Why, here's a birdcage.
(*Holds it up*) Did she have a bird, Mrs. Hale?

280 MRS. HALE: Why, I don't know whether she did or not—I've
not been here for so long. There was a man around last year
selling canaries cheap, but I don't know as she took one;
maybe she did. She used to sing real pretty herself.

MRS. PETERS: (*Glancing around*) Seems funny to think of a bird
285 here. But she must have had one, or why would she have a
cage? I wonder what happened to it.

MRS. HALE: I s'pose maybe the cat got it.

MRS. PETERS: No, she didn't have a cat. She's got that feeling
some people have about cats—being afraid of them. My cat
290 got in her room and she was real upset and asked me to take
it out.

MRS. HALE: My sister Bessie was like that. Queer, ain't it?

MRS. PETERS: (*Examining the cage*) Why, look at this door. It's
broke. One hinge is pulled apart.

295 MRS. HALE: (*Looking too*) Looks as if someone must have been
rough with it.

MRS. PETERS: Why, yes.

(*She brings the cage forward and puts it on the table.*)

MRS. HALE: I wish if they're going to find any evidence they'd be
about it. I don't like this place.

300 MRS. PETERS: But I'm awful glad you came with me, Mrs.
Hale. It would be lonesome for me sitting here alone.

MRS. HALE: It would, wouldn't it? (*Dropping her sewing*) But I
tell you what I do wish, Mrs. Peters. I wish I had come over
sometimes when *she* was here. I—(*Looking around the
305 room*)—wish I had.

MRS. PETERS: But of course you were awful busy, Mrs. Hale—
your house and your children.

MRS. HALE: I could've come. I stayed away because it weren't
cheerful—and that's why I ought to have come. I—I've never
310 liked this place. Maybe because it's down in a hollow and you
don't see the road. I dunno what it is, but it's a lonesome place
and always was. I wish I had come over to see Minnie Foster
sometimes. I can see now—

(*Shakes her head*)

MRS. PETERS: Well you mustn't reproach yourself, Mrs. Hale.
315 Somehow we just don't see how it is with other folks until—
something comes up.

MRS. HALE: Not having children makes less work—but it makes
a quiet house, and Wright out to work all day, and no company when he did come in. Did you know John Wright, Mrs.
320 Peters?

MRS. PETERS: Not to know him; I've seen him in town. They
say he was a good man.

MRS. HALE: Yes—good; he didn't drink, and kept his word as
well as most, I guess, and paid his debts. But he was a hard

man, Mrs. Peters. Just to pass the time of day with him— 325
(*Shivers*) Like a raw wind that gets to the bone. (*Pauses, her
eye falling on the cage*) I should think she would 'a wanted a
bird. But what do you suppose went with it?

MRS. PETERS: I don't know, unless it got sick and died.

(*She reaches over and swings the broken door, swings it again.
Both women watch it.*)

MRS. HALE: You weren't raised round here, were you? (MRS. 330
PETERS *shakes her head.*) You didn't know—her?

MRS. PETERS: Not till they brought her yesterday.

MRS. HALE: She—come to think of it, she was kind of like a bird
herself—real sweet and pretty, but kind of timid and—flut-
tery. How—she—did—change. (*Silence; then as if struck by 335
a happy thought and relieved to get back to every day things*)
Tell you what, Mrs. Peters, why don't you take the quilt in
with you? It might take up her mind.

MRS. PETERS: Why, I think that's a real nice idea, Mrs. Hale.
There couldn't possibly be any objection to it, could there? 340
Now, just what would I take? I wonder if her patches are in
here—and her things.

(*They look in the sewing basket.*)

MRS. HALE: Here's some red. I expect this has got sewing things
in it. (*Brings out a fancy box*) What a pretty box. Looks like
something somebody would give you. Maybe her scissors are 345
in here. (*Opens box. Suddenly puts her hand to her nose*)
Why—(MRS. PETERS *bends nearer, then turns her face
away.*) There's something wrapped up in this piece of silk.

MRS. PETERS: Why, this isn't her scissors.

MRS. HALE: (*Lifting the silk*) Oh, Mrs. Peters—its— 350

(MRS. PETERS *bends closer.*)

MRS. PETERS: It's the bird.

MRS. HALE: (*Jumping up*) But, Mrs. Peters—look at it! Its neck!
Look at its neck! It's all—other side *to.*

MRS. PETERS: Somebody—wrung—its—neck.

(*Their eyes meet. A look of growing comprehension, of horror.
Steps are heard outside.* MRS. HALE *slips box under quilt pieces,
and sinks into her chair. Enter* SHERIFF *and* COUNTY ATTOR-
NEY. MRS. PETERS *rises.*)

COUNTY ATTORNEY: (*As one turning from serious things to little 355
pleasantries*) Well, ladies, have you decided whether she was
going to quilt it or knot it?

MRS. PETERS: We think she was going to —knot it.

COUNTY ATTORNEY: Well, that's interesting, I'm sure. (*Seeing
the birdcage*) Has the bird flown? 360

MRS. HALE: (*Putting more quilt pieces over the box*) We think
the—cat got it.

COUNTY ATTORNEY: (*Preoccupied*) Is there a cat?

(MRS. HALE *glances in a quick covert way at* MRS. PETERS.)

MRS. PETERS: Well, not *now.* They're superstitious, you know.
They leave. 365

COUNTY ATTORNEY: (*To* SHERIFF PETERS *continuing an interrupted conversation*) No sign at all of anyone having come
from the outside. Their own rope. Now let's go up again and
go over it piece by piece. (*They start upstairs.*) It would have
to have been someone who knew just the— 370

(MRS. PETERS *sits down. The two women sit there not looking at one another, but as if peering into something and at the same time holding back. When they talk now it is in the manner of feeling their way over strange ground, as if afraid of what they are saying, but as if they cannot help saying it.*)

MRS. HALE: She liked the bird. She was going to bury it in that pretty box.

MRS. PETERS: (*In a whisper*) When I was a girl — my kitten — there was a boy took a hatchet, and before my eyes — and
375　before I could get there — (*Covers her face an instant*) If they hadn't held me back I would have — (*Catches herself, looks upstairs where steps are heard, falters weakly*) — hurt him.

MRS. HALE: (*With a slow look around her*) I wonder how it would seem never to have had any children around. (*Pause*)
380　No, Wright wouldn't like the bird — a thing that sang. She used to sing. He killed that, too.

MRS. PETERS: (*Moving uneasily*) We don't know who killed the bird.

MRS. HALE: I knew John Wright.

385　MRS. PETERS: It was an awful thing was done in this house that night, Mrs. Hale. Killing a man while he slept, slipping a rope around his neck that choked the life out of him.

MRS. HALE: His neck. Choked the life out of him.

(*Her hand goes out and rests on the birdcage.*)

MRS. PETERS: (*With rising voice*) We don't know who killed
390　him. We don't know.

MRS. HALE: (*Her own feeling not interrupted*) If there'd been years and years of nothing, then a bird to sing to you, it would be awful — still, after the bird was still.

MRS. PETERS: (*Something within her speaking*) I know what
395　stillness is. When we homesteaded in Dakota, and my first baby died — after he was two years old, and me with no other then —

MRS. HALE: (*Moving*) How soon do you suppose they'll be through, looking for the evidence?

400　MRS. PETERS: I know what stillness is. (*Pulling herself back*) The law has got to punish crime, Mrs. Hale.

MRS. HALE: (*Not as if answering that*) I wish you'd seen Minnie Foster when she wore a white dress with blue ribbons and stood up there in the choir and sang. (*A look around the room*)
405　Oh, I *wish* I'd come over here once in a while! That was a crime! That was a crime! Who's going to punish that?

MRS. PETERS: (*Looking upstairs*) We mustn't — take on.

MRS. HALE: I might have known she needed help! I know how things can be — for women. I tell you, it's queer, Mrs. Peters.
410　We live close together and we live far apart. We all go through the same things — it's all just a different kind of the same thing. (*Brushes her eyes; noticing the bottle of fruit, reaches out for it*) If I was you I wouldn't tell her her fruit was gone. Tell her it *ain't*. Tell her it's all right. Take this in to prove it to
415　her. She — she may never know whether it was broke or not.

MRS. PETERS: (*Takes the bottle, looks about for something to wrap it in, takes petticoat from the clothes brought from the*

other room, *very nervously begins winding this around the bottle. In a false voice*) My, it's a good thing the men couldn't hear us. Wouldn't they just laugh! Getting all stirred up over a
420　little thing like a — dead canary. As if that could have anything to do with — with — wouldn't they *laugh*!

(*The men are heard coming down stairs.*)

MRS. HALE: (*Under her breath*) Maybe they would — maybe they wouldn't.

COUNTY ATTORNEY: No, Peters, it's all perfectly clear except a
425　reason for doing it. But you know juries when it comes to women. If there was some definite thing. Something to show — something to make a story about — a thing that would connect up with this strange way of doing it —

(*The women's eyes meet for an instant. Enter* HALE *from outer door.*)

HALE: Well, I've got the team around. Pretty cold out there.　430

COUNTY ATTORNEY: I'm going to stay here a while by myself. (*To the* SHERIFF) You can send Frank out for me, can't you? I want to go over everything. I'm not satisfied that we can't do better.

SHERIFF: Do you want to see what Mrs. Peters is going to take in?　435

(*The* COUNTY ATTORNEY *goes to the table, picks up the apron, laughs.*)

COUNTY ATTORNEY: Oh, I guess they're not very dangerous things the ladies have picked out. (*Moves a few things about, disturbing the quilt pieces which cover the box. Steps back*) No, Mrs. Peters doesn't need supervising. For that matter, a sheriff's wife is married to the law. Ever think of it that way,　440
Mrs. Peters?

MRS. PETERS: Not — just that way.

SHERIFF: (*Chuckling*) Married to the law. (*Moves toward the other room*) I just want you to come in here a minute, George. We ought to take a look at these windows.　445

COUNTY ATTORNEY: (*Scoffingly*) Oh, windows!

SHERIFF: We'll be right out, Mr. Hale.

(HALE *goes outside. The* SHERIFF *follows the* COUNTY ATTORNEY *into the other room. Then* MRS. HALE *rises, hands tight together, looking intensely at* MRS. PETERS, *whose eyes make a slow turn, finally meeting* MRS. HALE's. *A moment* MRS. HALE *holds her, then her own eyes point the way to where the box is concealed. Suddenly* MRS. PETERS *throws back quilt pieces and tries to put the box in the bag she is wearing. It is too big. She opens box, starts to take bird out, cannot touch it, goes to pieces, stands there helpless. Sound of a knob turning in the other room.* MRS. HALE *snatches the box and puts it in the pocket of her big coat. Enter* COUNTY ATTORNEY *and* SHERIFF.)

COUNTY ATTORNEY: (*Facetiously*) Well, Henry, at least we found out that she was not going to quilt it. She was going to — what is it you call it, ladies?　450

MRS. HALE: (*her hand against her pocket*) We call it — knot it, Mr. Henderson.

EUGENE O'NEILL

Born the son of the famous turn-of-the-century actor, James O'Neill, Eugene O'Neill (1888 – 1953) became America's greatest dramatist. Much of O'Neill's younger life is described in his late play, *Long Day's Journey Into Night*: how he spent his first several years touring with his family following his father's career on the stage; his stints in boarding school and at Princeton; some time spent working on ships sailing to South America and Africa, and bumming around in Buenos Aires and New York; a serious bout with tuberculosis. In the play, O'Neill leaves the future of his young poet-hero uncertain, but in fact illness provided O'Neill with the time to begin writing seriously. When he recovered, O'Neill attended George Pierce Baker's playwriting classes at Harvard. He worked briefly in Greenwich Village and then joined the Provincetown Playhouse company on Cape Cod in 1916, where his first plays were produced.

O'Neill had a long and tumultous career in the theater. An admirer of Strindberg's drama, and widely read in Nietzsche, Freud, and Jung, O'Neill experimented in a variety of different theatrical styles, always searching for new ways to reveal the complex working of a character's psychology. He wrote a series of short realistic plays that were produced at the Provincetown and other "little theaters," the best of which concern life at sea: *Bound East for Cardiff* (1916), *Fog* (1917), *In the Zone* (1917), *The Long Voyage Home* (1917), and *The Moon of the Caribbees* (1918). His first Broadway production, *Beyond the Horizon* (1920) won him the first of four Pulitzer Prizes; he later won for *Anna Christie* (1921), *Strange Interlude* (1928), and *Long Day's Journey Into Night* (awarded posthumously in 1956). Throughout the 1920s, the period of his greatest success in the theater, O'Neill both wrote realistic plays like *Desire Under the Elms* (1924) and experimented in a variety of other modes. He tried expressionistic techniques in *The Hairy Ape* (1922) and *The Emperor Jones* (1920); masks in *The Great God Brown* (1926); and revealing "asides" in *Strange Interlude*, in which characters speak their unspoken "thoughts" directly to the audience. He also took a chance with comedy in *Ah, Wilderness!* (1932), something of a study for *Long Day's Journey*.

O'Neill's decade of success was followed by a series of impressive failures. Some of these plays are nonetheless fascinating. Although it played well in 1928, the asides and length (over eight hours) of *Strange Interlude* have militated against many revivals; the parallels between Aeschylus' *Oresteia* and O'Neill's *Mourning Becomes Electra* (1931) still attract comment and discussion. Much of O'Neill's work from the late 1920s and 1930s is inflated and bombastic, and plays like *Lazarus Laughed* (1928), *Marco Millions* (1929), *Dynamo* (1929), and *Days Without End* (1934) seemed to mark his flagging powers as a writer. When O'Neill won the Nobel Prize in 1936, his career was widely regarded as finished. His plays had become empty and grandiose, and he suffered from Parkinson's disease, which made it increasingly difficult for him to write. Throughout the 1930s and 1940s, though, O'Neill planned a massive cycle of plays concerning the fortunes of an American family, called *A Tale of Possessors Self-dispossessed*; of these he completed only *A Touch of the Poet* (written 1935–1942) and a draft of *More Stately Mansions* (1935–1940). However, in the 1940s, O'Neill also wrote his greatest plays, realistic dramas based for the most part on his family's history and on his own life. These hard-won plays may have been out of keeping with the national mood in the aftermath of World War II: when *The Iceman Cometh* opened in 1946, it ran for only 136 performances, and *A Moon for the Misbegotten* (1947) closed in Ohio before reaching New York. Yet when *Iceman* was revived in 1956, directed by Jose Quintero, it was a huge success and prompted a widespread reevaluation of O'Neill's drama.

Since O'Neill was raised on his father's melodramatic portrayal of *The Count of Monte Cristo*, it is not surprising that he was at times also infected with the spirit of melodrama. O'Neill's plays often recall melodrama's emphasis on the passions of the characters, its striking moments of stage action, its penchant for the romantic and the sentimental. O'Neill's experimentation and sure sense of the stage enabled him to achieve an unparalleled body of work and to define the course of drama in the United States in the first half of the twentieth century.

The Emperor Jones

The Emperor Jones was one of O'Neill's earliest successes, and one of the first plays with a black hero to be produced with a mixed-race cast in the United States. O'Neill cast Charles Gilpin — a successful actor in the Harlem theater — in the role of the Emperor Jones, and when the play moved from the bohemian milieu of Greenwich Village to the "legitimate" precincts of Broadway, he insisted that Gilpin remain in the part. During the play's revival in 1926, O'Neill cast Paul Robeson as Jones, a role Robeson played in the film version as well.

The Emperor Jones epitomizes the difficulties of staging black Americans in the white theater. O'Neill's use of expressionistic techniques—the drums, the formless fears, the dreamlike scenes of his past—as a way of collapsing Jones's individual and racial history makes for powerful and effective theater. Yet, despite O'Neill's fascination with his main character, the play raises the question of the use of racial stereotypes. Jones's speech, for instance, is firmly in the dialect tradition of stage-blacks dating back to the minstrel shows and beyond. Charles Gilpin angered O'Neill by cutting the word "nigger" from his performances and substituting other less pejorative epithets. Gilpin seems to have recognized the extent to which *The Emperor Jones* potentially confirmed the racist attitudes of the audience, attitudes perhaps implicit in the structure of the play itself. For by tracing Jones's flight back through his personal history to a racial memory of Africa, the play may imply that Jones is somehow closer to "nature," more "primitive" in some essential way than the white characters or the largely white audience of the play. From a contemporary perspective, Jones may seem to emerge as an exoticized "other," whose powerful humanity nonetheless remains outside the privileged values of white culture.

The Emperor Jones, that is, raises different issues for contemporary audiences than it did in the 1920s. To the play's first Broadway audiences, *The Emperor Jones* brought what seemed an authentic black experience to the stage. Not only did O'Neill succeed in bringing important African-American actors into the Broadway theater, he forced his audience to confront black experience in new ways, to confront the institutions of slavery and discrimination through the experience of a powerful, psychologically complex African-American man.

THE EMPEROR JONES

Eugene O'Neill

— CHARACTERS —

BRUTUS JONES, *Emperor*
HENRY SMITHERS, *A Cockney Trader*
AN OLD NATIVE WOMAN
LEM, *A Native Chief*
SOLDIERS, *Adherents of Lem*
The LITTLE FORMLESS FEARS; JEFF; *The* NEGRO CONVICTS;
  The PRISON GUARD; *The* PLANTERS; *The* AUCTIONEER;
  The SLAVES; *The* CONGO WITCH-DOCTOR; *The*
  CROCODILE GOD

The action of the play takes place on an island in the West Indies as yet not self-determined by white Marines. The form of native government is, for the time being, an empire.

— SCENE ONE —

SCENE: *The audience chamber in the palace of the Emperor—a spacious, high-ceilinged room with bare, white-washed walls. The floor is of white tiles. In the rear, to the left of center, a wide archway giving out on a portico with white pillars. The palace is evidently situated on high ground, for beyond the portico nothing can be seen but a vista of distant hills, their summits crowned with thick groves of palm trees. In the right wall, center, a smaller arched doorway leading to the living quarters of the palace. The room is bare of furniture with the exception of one huge chair made of uncut wood which stands at center, its back to rear. This is very apparently the Emperor's throne. It is painted a dazzling, eye-smiting scarlet. There is a brilliant orange cushion on the seat and another smaller one is placed on the floor to serve as a footstool. Strips of matting, dyed scarlet, lead from the foot of the throne to the two entrances.*

It is late afternoon but the sunlight still blazes yellowly beyond the portico and there is an oppressive burden of exhausting heat in the air.

As the curtain rises, a native Negro WOMAN *sneaks in cautiously from the entrance on the right. She is very old, dressed in cheap calico, bare-footed, a red bandana handkerchief covering all but a few stray wisps of white hair. A bundle bound in colored cloth is carried over her shoulder on the end of a stick. She hesitates beside the doorway, peering back as if in extreme dread of being discovered. Then she begins to glide noiselessly a step at a time, toward the doorway in the rear. At this moment,* SMITHERS *appears beneath the portico.*

SMITHERS *is a tall, stoop-shouldered man about forty. His bald head, perched on a long neck with an enormous Adam's apple, looks like an egg. The tropics have tanned his naturally pasty face with its small, sharp features to a sickly yellow, and native rum has painted his pointed nose to a startling red. His little, washy-blue eyes are red-rimmed and dart about him like a ferret's. His expression is one of unscrupulous meanness, cowardly and dangerous. He is dressed in a worn riding suit of dirty white drill, puttees, spurs, and wears a white cork helmet. A cartridge belt with an automatic revolver is around his waist. He carries a riding whip in his hand. He sees the* WOMAN *and stops to watch her suspiciously. Then, making up his mind, he steps quickly on tiptoe into the room. The* WOMAN, *looking back over her shoulder continually, does not see him until it is too late. When she does* SMITHERS *springs forward and grabs her firmly by the shoulder. She struggles to get away, fiercely but silently.*

SMITHERS: *(Tightening his grasp—roughly)* Easy! None o' that, me birdie. You can't wriggle out now. I got me 'ooks on yer.

WOMAN: *(Seeing the uselessness of struggling, gives way to frantic terror, and sinks to the ground, embracing his knees supplicatingly)* No tell him! No tell him, Mister!   5

SMITHERS: *(With great curiosity)* Tell 'im? *(Then scornfully.)* Oh, you mean 'is bloomin' Majesty. What's the gaime, any 'ow? What are you sneakin' away for? Been stealin' a bit, I s'pose. *(He taps her bundle with his riding whip significantly.)*

WOMAN: *(Shaking her head vehemently)* No, me no steal.   10

SMITHERS: Bloody liar! But tell me what's up. There's somethin' funny goin' on. I smelled it in the air first thing I got up this mornin'. You blacks are up to some devilment. This palace of 'is is like a bleedin' tomb. Where's all the 'ands? *(The* WOMAN *keeps sullenly silent.* SMITHERS *raises his whip threateningly.)*   15
Ow, yer won't, won't yer? I'll show yer what's what.

WOMAN: *(Coweringly)* I tell, Mister. You no hit. They go—all go. *(She makes a sweeping gesture toward the hills in the distance.)*

SMITHERS: Run away—to the 'ills?   20

WOMAN: Yes, Mister. Him Emperor—Great Father. *(She touches her forehead to the floor with a quick mechanical jerk.)* Him sleep after eat. Then they go—all go. Me old woman. Me left only. Now me go too.

SMITHERS: *(His astonishment giving way to an immense, mean satisfaction)* Ow! So that's the ticket! Well, I know bloody well wot's in the air—when they runs orf to the 'ills. The tom-tom 'll be thumping out there bloomin' soon. *(With extreme vindictiveness.)* And I'm bloody glad of it, for one! Serve 'im right! Puttin' on airs, the stinkin' nigger! 'Is Majesty! Gawd blimey! I only 'opes I'm there when they takes 'im out to shoot 'im. *(Suddenly)* 'E's still 'ere all right, ain't 'e?   25   30

WOMAN: Yes. Him sleep.

SMITHERS: 'E's bound to find out soon as 'e wakes up. 'E's cunnin' enough to know when 'is time's come. *(He goes to the doorway on right and whistles shrilly with his fingers in his mouth. The old* WOMAN *springs to her feet and runs out of the doorway, rear.* SMITHERS *goes after her, reaching for his revolver.)* Stop or I'll shoot! *(Then stopping—indifferently)* Pop orf then, if yer like, yer black cow. *(He stands in the doorway, looking after her.)*   35   40

(JONES *enters from the right. He is a tall, powerfully-built, full-blooded Negro of middle age. His features are typically negroid, yet there is something decidedly distinctive about his face—an underlying strength of will, a hardy, self-reliant confidence in himself that inspires respect. His eyes are alive with a keen, cunning intelligence. In manner he is shrewd, suspicious, evasive. He wears a light blue uniform coat, sprayed with brass buttons, heavy gold chevrons on his shoulders, gold braid on the collar, cuffs, etc. His pants are bright red with a light blue stripe down the side. Patent-leather laced boots with brass spurs, and a belt with a long-barreled, pearl-handled revolver in a holster complete his make up. Yet there is something not altogether ridiculous about his grandeur. He has a way of carrying it off.*)

JONES: *(Not seeing anyone—greatly irritated and blinking sleepily—shouts)* Who dare whistle dat way in my palace? Who dare wake up de Emperor? I'll git de hide fravled off some o'
45   you niggers sho'!
SMITHERS: *(Showing himself—in a manner half-afraid and half-defiant)* It was me whistled to yer. *(As* JONES *frowns angrily)* I got news for yer.
JONES: *(Putting on his suavest manner, which fails to cover up
50   his contempt for the white man)* Oh it's you, Mister Smithers. *(He sits down on his throne with easy dignity.)* What news you got to tell me?
SMITHERS: *(Coming close to enjoy his discomfiture)* Don't yer notice nothin' funny today?
55 JONES: *(Coldly)* Funny? No, I ain't perceived nothin' of de kind!
SMITHERS: Then yer ain't so foxy as I thought yer was. Where's all your court? *(Sarcastically)* The Generals and the Cabinet Ministers and all?
JONES: *(Imperturbably)* Where dey mostly runs de minute I
60   close my eyes—drinkin' rum and talkin' big down in de town. *(Sarcastically)* How come you don't know dat? Ain't you sousin' with 'em most every day?
SMITHERS: *(Stung but pretending indifference—with a wink)* That's part of the day's work. I got ter—ain't I—in my
65   business?
JONES: *(Contemptuously)* Yo' business!
SMITHERS: *(Imprudently enraged)* Gawd blimey, you was glad enough for me ter take yer in on it when you landed here first. You didn' 'ave no 'igh and mighty airs in them days!
70 JONES: *(His hand going to his revolver like a flash—menacingly)* Talk polite, white man! Talk polite, you heah me! I'm boss heah now, is you fergittin'? *(The Cockney seems about to challenge this last statement with the facts but something in the other's eyes holds and cows him.)*
75 SMITHERS: *(In a cowardly whine)* No 'arm meant, old top.
JONES: *(Condescendingly)* I accept yo' apology. *(Lets his hand fall from his revolver.)* No use'n you rakin' up ole times. What I was den is one thing. What I is now 's another. You didn't let me in on yo' crooked work out o' no kind feelin's dat time. I
80   done de dirty work fo' you—and most o' de brain work, too, fo' dat matter—and I was wu'th money to you, dat's de reason.
SMITHERS: Well, blimey, I give yer a start, didn't I—when no one else would. I wasn't afraid to 'ire yer like the rest was—
85   'count of the story about your breakin' jail back in the States.
JONES: No, you didn't have no s'cuse to look down on me fo' dat. You been in jail you'self more'n once.

SMITHERS: *(Furiously)* It's a lie! *(Then trying to pass it off by an attempt at scorn)* Garn! Who told yer that fairy tale?
JONES: Dey's some tings I ain't got to be tole. I kin see 'em in   90
folk's eyes. *(Then after a pause—meditatively)* Yes, you sho' give me a start. And it didn't take long from dat time to get dese fool, woods' niggers right where I wanted dem. *(With pride)* From stowaway to Emperor in two years! Dat's goin' some!   95
SMITHERS: *(With curiosity)* And I bet you got yer pile o' money 'id safe some place.
JONES: *(With satisfaction)* I sho' has! And it's in a foreign bank where no pusson don't ever git it out but me no matter what come. You didn't s'pose I was holdin' down dis Emperor job   100
for de glory in it, did you? Sho'! De fuss and glory part of it, dat's only to turn de heads o' de low-flung, bush niggers dat's here. Dey wants de big circus show for deir money. I gives it to 'em an' I gits de money. *(With a grin)* De long green, dat's me every time! *(Then rebukingly)* But you ain't got no kick agin   105
me, Smithers. I'se paid you back all you done for me many times. Ain't I pertected you and winked at all de crooked tradin' you been doin' right out in de broad day? Sho' I has— and me makin' laws to stop it at de same time! *(He chuckles.)*
SMITHERS: *(Grinning)* But, meanin' no 'arm, you been grabbin'   110
right and left yourself, ain't yer? Look at the taxes you've put on 'em! Blimey! You've squeezed 'em dry!
JONES: *(Chuckling)* No, dey ain't *all* dry yet. I'se still heah, ain't I?
SMITHERS: *(Smiling at his secret thought)* They're dry right now, you'll find out. *(Changing the subject abruptly.)* And as for   115
me breakin' laws, you've broke 'em all yerself just as fast as yer made 'em.
JONES: Ain't I de Emperor? De laws don't go for him. *(Judicially)* You heah what I tells you, Smithers. Dere's little stealin' like you does, and dere's big stealin' like I does. For de   120
little stealin' dey gits you in jail soon or late. For de big stealin' dey makes you Emperor and puts you in de Hall o' Fame when you croaks. *(Reminiscently)* If dey's one thing I learns in ten years on de Pullman ca's listenin' to de white quality talk, it's dat same fact. And when I gits a chance to use it I   125
winds up Emperor in two years.
SMITHERS: *(Unable to repress the genuine admiration of the small fry for the large)* Yes, yer turned the bleedin' trick, all right. Blimey, I never seen a bloke 'as 'ad the bloomin' luck you 'as.   130
JONES: *(Severely)* Luck? What you mean—luck?
SMITHERS: I suppose you'll say as that swank about the silver bullet ain't luck—and that was what first got the fool blacks on yer side the time of the revolution, wasn't it?
JONES: *(With a laugh)* Oh, dat silver bullet! Sho' was luck! But I   135
makes dat luck, you heah? I loads de dice! Yessuh! When dat murderin' nigger ole Lem hired to kill me takes aim ten feet away and his gun misses fire and I shoots him dead, what you heah me say?
SMITHERS: You said yer'd got a charm so's no lead bullet'd kill   140
yer. You was so strong only a silver bullet could kill yer, you told 'em. Blimey, wasn't that swank for yer—and plain, fat-'eaded luck?
JONES: *(Proudly)* I got brains and I uses 'em quick. Dat ain't luck.   145
SMITHERS: Yer know they wasn't 'ardly liable to get no silver bullets. And it was luck 'e didn't 'it you that time.

JONES: (*Laughing*) And dere all dem fool, bush niggers was kneelin' down and bumpin' deir heads on de ground like I was a miracle out o' de Bible. Oh Lawd, from dat time on I had dem all eatin' out of my hand. I cracks de whip and dey jumps through.

SMITHERS: (*With a sniff*) Yankee bluff done it.

JONES: Ain't a man's talkin' big what makes him big—long as he makes folks believe it? Sho', I talks large when I ain't got nothin' to back it up, but I ain't talkin' wild just de same. I knows I kin fool 'em—I *knows* it—and dat's backin' enough fo' my game. And ain't I got to learn deir lingo and teach some of dem English befo' I kin to talk to 'em? Ain't dat wuk? You ain't never learned ary word er it, Smithers, in de ten years you been heah, dough yo' knows it's money in yo' pocket tradin' wid 'em if you does. But you'se too shiftless to take de trouble.

SMITHERS: (*Flushing*) Never mind about me. What's this I've 'eard about yer really 'avin' a silver bullet moulded for yourself?

JONES: It's playin' out my bluff. I has de silver bullet moulded and I tells 'em when de time comes I kills myself wid it. I tells 'em dat's 'cause I'm de on'y man in de world big enough to git me. No use'n deir tryin'. And dey falls down and bumps deir heads. (*He laughs.*) I does so's I kin take a walk in peace widout no jealous nigger gunnin' at me from behind de trees.

SMITHERS: (*Astonished*) Then you 'ad it made— 'onest?

JONES: Sho' did. Heah she be. (*He takes out his revolver, breaks it, and takes the silver bullet out of one chamber.*) Five lead an' dis silver baby at de last. Don't she shine pretty? (*He holds it in his hand, looking at it admiringly, as if strangely fascinated.*)

SMITHERS: Let me see. (*Reaches out his hand for it.*)

JONES: (*Harshly*) Keep yo' hands whar dey b'long, white man. (*He replaces it in the chamber and puts the revolver back on his hip.*)

SMITHERS: (*Snarling*) Gawd blimey! Think I'm a bleedin' thief, you would.

JONES: No, 'tain't dat. I knows you'se scared to steal from me. On'y I ain't 'lowin' nary body to touch dis baby. She's my rabbit's foot.

SMITHERS: (*Sneering*) A bloomin' charm, wot? (*Venomously*) Well, you'll need all the bloody charms you 'as before long, s' 'elp me!

JONES: (*Judicially*) Oh, I'se good for six months yit 'fore dey gits sick o' my game. Den, when I sees trouble comin', I makes my getaway.

SMITHERS: Ho! You got it all planned, ain't yer?

JONES: I ain't no fool. I knows dis Emperor's time is sho't. Dat why I make hay when de sun shine. Was you thinkin' I'se aimin' to hold down dis job for life? No, suh! What good is gittin' money if you stays back in dis raggedy country? I wants action when I spends. And when I sees dese niggers gittin' up deir nerve to tu'n me out, and I'se got all de money in sight, I resigns on de spot and beats it quick.

SMITHERS: Where to?

JONES: None o' yo' business.

SMITHERS: Not back to the bloody States, I'll lay my oath.

JONES: (*Suspiciously*) Why don't I? (*Then with an easy laugh*) You mean 'count of dat story 'bout me breakin' from jail back dere? Dat's all talk.

SMITHERS: (*Skeptically*) Ho, yes!

JONES: (*Sharply*) You ain't 'sinuatin' I'se a liar, is you?

SMITHERS: (*Hastily*) No, Gawd strike me! I was only thinkin' o' the bloody lies you told the blacks 'ere about killin' white men in the States.

JONES: (*Angered*) How come dey're lies?

SMITHERS: You'd 'ave been in jail if you 'ad, wouldn't yer then? (*With venom*) And from what I've 'eard, it ain't 'ealthy for a black to kill a white man in the States. They burns 'em in oil, don't they?

JONES: (*With cool deadliness*) You mean lynchin' 'd scare me? Well, I tells you, Smithers, maybe I does kill one white man back dere. Maybe I does. And maybe I kills another right heah 'fore long if he don't look out.

SMITHERS: (*Trying to force a laugh*) I was on'y spoofin' yer. Can't yer take a joke? And you was just sayin' you'd never been in jail.

JONES: (*In the same tone—slightly boastful*) Maybe I goes to jail dere for gettin' in an argument wid razors ovah a crap game. Maybe I gits twenty years when dat colored man die. Maybe I gits in 'nother argument wid de prison guard was overseer ovah us when we're wukin' de roads. Maybe he hits me wid a whip and I splits his head wid a shovel and runs away and files de chain off my leg and gits away safe. Maybe I does all dat an' maybe I don't. It's a story I tells you so's you knows I'se de kind of man dat if you evah repeats one word of it, I ends yo' stealin' on dis yearth mighty damn quick!

SMITHERS: (*Terrified*) Think I'd peach on yer? Not me! Ain't I always been yer friend?

JONES: (*Suddenly relaxing*) Sho' you has—and you better be.

SMITHERS: (*Recovering his composure—and with it his malice*) And just to show yer I'm yer friend, I'll tell yer that bit o' news I was goin' to.

JONES: Go ahead! Shoot de piece. Must be bad news from de happy way you look.

SMITHERS: (*Warningly*) Maybe it's gettin' time for you to re-sign—with that bloomin' silver bullet, wot? (*He finishes with a mocking grin.*)

JONES: (*Puzzled*) What's dat you say? Talk plain.

SMITHERS: Ain't noticed any of the guards or servants about the place today, I 'aven't.

JONES: (*Carelessly*) Dey're all out in de garden sleepin' under de trees. When I sleeps, dey sneaks a sleep, too, and I pretends I never suspicions it. All I got to do is to ring de bell and dey come flyin', makin' a bluff dey was wukin' all de time.

SMITHERS: (*In the same mocking tone*) Ring the bell now an' you'll bloody well see what I means.

JONES: (*Startled to alertness, but preserving the same careless tone*) Sho' I rings. (*He reaches below the throne and pulls out a big, common dinner bell which is painted the same vivid scarlet as the throne. He rings this vigorously—then stops to listen. Then he goes to both doors, rings again, and looks out.*)

SMITHERS: (*Watching him with malicious satisfaction, after a pause—mockingly*) The bloody ship is sinkin' an' the bleedin' rats 'as slung their 'ooks.

JONES: (*In a sudden fit of anger flings the bell clattering into a corner*) Low-flung, woods' niggers! (*Then catching Smithers' eye on him, he controls himself and suddenly bursts into a low chuckling laugh.*) Reckon I overplays my hand dis once! A man can't take de pot on a bob-tailed flush all de time. Was I

sayin' I'd sit in six months mo'? Well, I'se changed my mind den, I cashes in and resigns de job of Emperor right dis
270 minute.

SMITHERS: (With real admiration) Blimey, but you're a cool bird, and no mistake.

JONES: No use'n fussin'. When I knows de game's up I kisses it good-bye widout no long waits. Dey've all run off to de hills, ain't
275 dey?

SMITHERS: Yes — every bleedin' man jack of 'em.

JONES: Den de revolution is at de post. And de Emperor better git his feet smokin' up de trail. (He starts for the door in rear.)

SMITHERS: Goin' out to look for your 'orse? Yer won't find any.
280 They steals the 'orses first thing. Mine was gone when I went for 'im this mornin'. That's wot first give me a suspicion of wot was up.

JONES: (Alarmed for a second, scratches his head, then philosophically) Well, den I hoofs it. Feet, do yo' duty! (He pulls out a
285 gold watch and looks at it.) Three-thuty. Sundown's at six-thuty or dere-abouts. (Puts his watch back — with cool confidence.) I got plenty o' time to make it easy.

SMITHERS: Don't be so bloomin' sure of it. They'll be after you 'ot and 'eavy. Ole Lem is at the bottom o' this business an' 'e
290 'ates you like 'ell. 'E'd rather do for you than eat 'is dinner, 'e would!

JONES: (Scornfully) Dat fool no-count nigger! Does you think I'se scared o' him? I stands him on his thick head mor'n once befo' dis, and I does it again if he come in my way . . .
295 (Fiercely) and dis time I leave him a dead nigger fo' sho'!

SMITHERS: You'll 'ave to cut through the big forest — an' these blacks 'ere can sniff and follow a trail in the dark like 'ounds. You'd 'ave to 'ustle to get through that forest in twelve hours even if you knew all the bloomin' trails like a native.
300 JONES: (With indignant scorn) Look-a-heah, white man! Does you think I'se a natural bo'n fool? Give me credit fo' havin' some sense, fo' Lawd's sake! Don't you s'pose I'se looked ahead and made sho' of all de chances? I'se gone out in dat big forest, pretendin' to hunt, so many times dat I knows it high
305 an' low like a book. I could go through on dem trails wid my eyes shut. (With great contempt) Think dese ign'rent bush niggers dat ain't got brains enuff to know deir own names even can catch Brutus Jones? Huh, I s'pects not! Not on yo' life! Why, man, de white men went after me wid bloodhounds
310 where I come from an I jes' laughs at 'em. It's a shame to fool dese black trash around heah, dey're so easy. You watch me, man! I'll make dem look sick, I will. I'll be 'cross de plain to de edge of de forest by time dark comes. Once in de woods in de night, dey got a swell chance o' findin' dis baby! Dawn tomor-
315 row I'll be out at de oder side and on de coast whar dat French gunboat is stayin'. She picks me up, take me to Martinique when she go dar, and dere I is safe wid a mighty big bankroll in my jeans. It's easy as rollin' off a log.

SMITHERS: (Maliciously) But s'posin' somethin' 'appens wrong
320 an' they do nab yer?

JONES: (Decisively) Dey don't — dat's de answer.

SMITHERS: But, just for argyment's sake — what'd you do?

JONES: (Frowning) I'se got five lead bullets in dis gun good enuff fo' common bush niggers — and after dat I got de silver bullet
325 left to cheat 'em out o' gittin' me.

SMITHERS: (Jeeringly) Ho, I was fergettin' that silver bullet. You'll bump yourself orf in style, won't yer? Blimey!

JONES: (Gloomily) You kin bet yo whole roll on one thing, white man. Dis baby plays out his string to de end and when he quits, he quits wid a bang de way he ought. Silver bullet ain't
330 none too good for him when he go, dat's a fac'! (Then shaking off his nervousness — with a confident laugh) Sho'! What is I talkin' about? Ain't come to dat yit and I never will — not wid trash niggers like dese yere. (Boastfully) Silver bullet bring me luck anyway. I kin outguess, outrun, outfight, an' outplay de
335 whole lot o' dem all ovah de board any time o' de day er night! You watch me! (From the distant hills comes the faint, steady thump of a tom-tom, low and vibrating. It starts at a rate exactly corresponding to normal pulse beat — 72 to the min-ute — and continues at a gradually accelerating rate from this
340 point uninterruptedly to the very end of the play.)

(JONES starts at the sound. A strange look of apprehension creeps into his face for a moment as he listens. Then he asks, with an attempt to regain his most casual manner) What's dat drum beatin' fo'?
345
SMITHERS: (With a mean grin) For you. That means the bleedin' ceremony 'as started. I've 'eard it before and I knows.

JONES: Cer'mony? What cer'mony?

SMITHERS: The blacks is 'oldin' a bloody meetin', 'avin' a war dance, gettin' their courage worked up b'fore they starts after
350 you.

JONES: Let dem! Dey'll sho' need it!

SMITHERS: And they're there 'oldin their 'eathen religious ser-vice — makin' no end of devil spells and charms to 'elp 'em against your silver bullet. (He guffaws loudly.) Blimey, but
355 they're balmy as 'ell!

JONES: (A tiny bit awed and shaken in spite of himself) Huh! Takes more'n dat to scare dis chicken!

SMITHERS: (Scenting the other's feeling — maliciously) Ternight when it's pitch black in the forest, they'll 'ave their pet devils
360 and ghosts 'oundin' after you. You'll find yer bloody 'air 'll be standin' on end before termorrow mornin'. (Seriously) It's a bleedin' queer place, that stinkin' forest, even in daylight. Yer don't know what might 'appen in there, it's that rotten still. Always sends the cold shivers down my back minute I gets in it.
365
JONES: (With a contemptuous sniff) I ain't no chicken-liver like you is. Trees an' me, we'se friends, and dar's a full moon comin' bring me light. And let dem po' niggers make all de fool spells dey'se a min' to. Does yo' s'pect I'se silly enuff to b'lieve in ghosts an' ha'ants an' all dat ole woman's talk?
370 G'long, white man! You ain't talkin' to me. (With a chuckle) Doesn't you know dey's got to do wid a man was member in good standin' o' de Baptist Church? Sho' I was dat when I was porter on de Pullmans, befo' I gits into my little trouble. Let dem try deir heathen tricks. De Baptist Church done pertect
375 me and land dem all in hell. (Then with more confident satis-faction) And I'se got little silver bullet o' my own, don't forgit.

SMITHERS: Ho! You 'aven't give much 'eed to your Baptist Church since you been down 'ere. I've 'eard myself you 'ad turned yer coat an' was takin' up with their blarsted witch-
380 doctors, or whatever the 'ell yer calls the swine.

JONES: (Vehemently) I pretends to! Sho' I pretends! Dat's part o' my game from de fust. If I finds out dem niggers believes dat black is white, den I yells it out louder 'n deir loudest. It don't git me nothin' to do missionary work for de Baptist Church.
385 I'se after de coin, an' I lays my Jesus on de shelf for de time bein'. (Stops abruptly to look at his watch — alertly.) But I

ain't got de time to waste no more fool talk wid you. I'se gwine away from heah dis secon'. (*He reaches in under the throne and pulls out an expensive Panama hat with a bright multi-colored band and sets it jauntily on his head.*) So long, white man! (*With a grin*) See you in jail sometime, maybe!

SMITHERS: Not me, you won't. Well, I wouldn't be in your bloody boots for no bloomin' money, but 'ere's wishin' yer luck just the same.

JONES: (*Contemptuously*) You're de frightenedest man evah I see! I tells you I'se safe's 'f I was in New York City. It takes dem niggers from now to dark to git up de nerve to start somethin'. By dat time, I'se got a head start dey never kotch up wid.

SMITHERS: (*Maliciously*) Give my regards to any ghosts yer meets up with.

JONES: (*Grinning*) If dat ghost got money, I'll tell him never ha'nt you less'n he wants to lose it.

SMITHERS: (*Flattered*) Garn! (*Then curiously*) Ain't yer takin' no luggage with yer?

JONES: I travels light when I want to move fast. and I got tinned grub buried on de edge o' de forest. (*Boastfully*) Now say that I don't look ahead an' use my brains! (*With a wide, liberal gesture*) I will all dat's left in de palace to you — and you better grab all you kin sneak away wid befo' dey gits here.

SMITHERS: (*Gratefully*) Righto — and thanks ter yer. (*As* JONES *walks toward the door in rear — cautioningly*) Say! Look 'ere, you ain't goin' out that way, are yer?

JONES: Does you think I'd slink out de back door like a common nigger? I'se Emperor yit, ain't I? And de Emperor Jones leaves de way he comes, and dat black trash don't dare stop him — not yit, leastways. (*He stops for a moment in the doorway, listening to the far-off but insistent beat of the tom-tom.*) Listen to dat roll-call, will you? Must be mighty big drum carry dat far. (*Then with a laugh*) Well, if dey ain't no whole brass band to see me off, I sho' got de drum part of it. So long, white man. (*He puts his hands in his pockets and with studied carelessness, whistling a tune, he saunters out of the doorway and off to the left.*)

SMITHERS: (*Looks after him with a puzzled admiration*) 'E's got 'ise bloomin' nerve with 'im, s'elp me! (*Then angrily*) Ho — the bleedin' nigger — puttin' on 'is bloody airs! I 'opes they nabs 'im an' gives 'im what's what! (*Then putting business before the pleasure of this thought, looking around him with cupidity*) A bloke ought to find a 'ole lot in this palace that'd go for a bit of cash. Let's take a look, 'Arry, me lad. (*He starts for the doorway on right as the curtain falls.*)

— SCENE TWO —

SCENE: *Nightfall. The end of the plain where the Great Forest begins. The foreground is sandy, level ground dotted by a few stones and clumps of stunted bushes cowering close against the earth to escape the buffeting of the trade wind. In the rear the forest is a wall of darkness dividing the world. Only when the eye becomes accustomed to the gloom can the outlines of separate trunks of the nearest trees be made out, enormous pillars of deeper blackness. A somber monotone of wind lost in the leaves moans in the air. Yet this sound serves but to intensify the impression of the forest's relentless immobility, to form a background throwing into relief its brooding, implacable silence.*

(JONES *enters from the left, walking rapidly. He stops as he nears the edge of the forest, looks around him quickly, peering into the dark as if searching for some familiar landmark. Then, apparently satisfied that he is where he ought to be, he throws himself on the ground, dog-tired.*)

Well, heah I is. In de nick o' time, too! Little mo' an' it'd be blacker'n de ace of spades heah-abouts. (*He pulls a bandana handkerchief from his hip pocket and mops off his perspiring face.*) Sho'! Gimme air! I'se tuckered out sho' nuff. Dat soft Emperor job ain't no trainin' fo' a long hike ovah dat plain in de brilin' sun. (*Then with a chuckle*) Cheah up, nigger, de worst is yet to come. (*He lifts his head and stares at the forest. His chuckle peters out abruptly. In a tone of awe*) My goodness, look at dem woods, will you? Dat no-count Smithers said day'd be black an' he sho' called de turn. (*Turning away from them quickly and looking down at his feet, he snatches at a chance to change the subject — solicitously*) Feet, you is holdin' up yo' end fine an' I sutinly hopes you ain't blisterin' none. It's time you git a rest. (*He takes off his shoes, his eyes studiously avoiding the forest. He feels of the soles of his feet gingerly.*) You is still in de pink — on'y a little mite feverish. Cool yo'selfs. Remember you done got a long journey yit befo' you. (*He sits in a weary attitude, listening to the rhythmic beating of the tom-tom. He grumbles in a loud tone to cover up a growing uneasiness.*) Bush niggers! Wonder dey wouldn't git sick o' beatin' dat drum. Sound louder, seem like. I wonder if dey's startin' after me? (*He scrambles to his feet, looking back across the plain.*) Couldn't see dem now, nohow, if dey was hundred feet away. (*Then shaking himself like a wet dog to get rid of these depressing thoughts*) Sho', dey's miles an' miles behind. What you gittin' fidgety about? (*But he sits down and begins to lace up his shoes in great haste, all the time muttering reassuringly.*) You know what? Yo' belly is empty, dat's what's de matter wid you. Come time to eat! Wid nothin' but wind on yo' stumach, o' course you feels jiggedy. Well, we eats right heah an' now soon's I gits dese pesky shoes laced up! (*He finishes lacing up his shoes.*) Dere! le's see. (*Gets on his hands and knees and searches the ground around him with his eyes.*) White stone, white stone, where is you? (*He sees the first white stone and crawls to it — with satisfaction.*) Heah you is! I knowed dis was de right place. Box of grub, come to me. (*He turns over the stone and feels under it — in a tone of dismay.*) Ain't heah! Gorry, is I in de right place or isn't I? Dere's 'nother stone. Guess dat's it. (*He scrambles to the next stone and turns it over.*) Ain't heah, neither! Grub, whar is you? Ain't heah. Gorry, has I got to go hungry into dem woods — all de night? (*While he is talking he scrambles from one stone to another, turning them over in frantic haste. Finally, he jumps to his feet excitedly.*) Is I lost de place? Must have! But how dat happen when I was followin' de trail across de plain in broad daylight? (*Almost plaintively*) I'se hungry, I is! I gotta git my feed. Whar's my strength gonna come from if I doesn't? Gorry, I gotta find dat grub high an' low somehow! Why it come dark so quick like dat? Can't see nothin' (*He scratches a match on his trousers and peers about him. The rate of the beat of the far-off tom-tom increases perceptibly as he does so. He mutters in a bewildered voice.*) How come all dese white stones come heah when I only remembers one? (*Suddenly, with a frightened grasp, he flings the match on the*

55 *ground and stamps on it.)* Nigger, is you gone crazy mad? Is you lightin' matches to show dem whar you is? Fo' Lawd's sake, use yo' haid. Gorry, I'se got to be careful. *(He stares at the plain behind him apprehensively, his hand on his revolver.)* But how come all dese white stones? And whar's dat tin box o' 60 grub I had all wrapped up in oil cloth?

(While his back is turned, the LITTLE FORMLESS FEARS *creep out from the deeper blackness of the forest. They are black, shapeless, only their glittering little eyes can be seen. If they have any describable form at all it is that of a grubworm about the size of a creeping child. They move noiselessly, but with deliberate, painful effort, striving to raise themselves on end, failing and sinking prone again.* JONES *turns about to face the forest. He stares up at the tops of the trees, seeking vainly to discover his whereabouts by their conformation.)*

Can't tell nothing' from dem trees! Gorry, nothin' 'round heah look like I evah seed it befo'. I'se done lost de place sho' 'nuff! *(With mournful foreboding)* It's mighty queer! It's mighty queer! *(With sudden forced defiance — in an angry* 65 *tone)* Woods, is you tryin' to put somethin' ovah on me?

(From the formless creatures on the ground in front of him comes a tiny gale of low mocking laughter like a rustling of leaves. They squirm upward toward him in twisted attitudes. JONES *looks down, leaps backward with a yell of terror, yanking* 70 *out his revolver as he does so — in a quavering voice)* What's dat? Who's dar? What is you? Git away from me befo' I shoots you up! You don't? . . .

(He fires. There is a flash, a loud report, then silence broken only by the far-off, quickened throb of the tom-tom. The formless creatures have scurried back into the forest. JONES *remains fixed in his position, listening intently. The sound of the shot, the reassuring feel of the revolver in his hand, have somewhat restored his shaken nerve. He addresses himself with renewed confidence.)*

Dey're gone. Dat shot fix 'em. Dey was only little animals — little wild pigs, I reckon. Dey've maybe rooted out yo' grub an' 75 eat it. Sho', you fool nigger, what you think dey is — ha'nts? *(Excitedly)* Gorry, you give de game away when you fire dat shot. Dem niggers heah dat fo' su'tin! *(He starts for the forest — hesitates before the plunge — then urging himself in with manful resolution)* Git in, nigger! What you skeered at? Ain't 80 nothin' dere but de trees! Git in! *(He plunges boldly into the forest.)*

— SCENE THREE —

SCENE: *Nine o'clock. In the forest. The moon has just risen. It beams, drifting through the canopy of leaves, makes a barely perceptible, suffused, eerie glow. A dense low wall of underbrush and creepers is in the nearer foreground, fencing in a small triangular clearing. Beyond this is the massed blackness of the forest like an encompassing barrier. A path is dimly discerned leading down to the clearing from the left, rear, and winding away from it again toward the right. As the scene opens nothing can be distinctly made out. Except for the beating of the tom-tom,*

which is a trifle louder and quicker than in the previous scene, there is silence, broken every few seconds by a queer, clicking sound. Then gradually the figure of the Negro, JEFF, *can be discerned crouching on his haunches at the rear of the triangle. He is middle-aged, thin, brown in color, is dressed in a Pullman porter's uniform, cap, etc. He is throwing a pair of dice on the ground before him, picking them up, shaking them, casting them out with the regular, rigid, mechanical movements of an automaton. The heavy, plodding footsteps of someone approaching along the trail from the left are heard and* JONES' *voice, pitched in a slightly higher key and strained in a cheering effort to overcome its own tremors.*

De moon's rizen. Does you heah dat, nigger? You gits more light from dis out. No mo' buttin' yo' fool head agin' de trunks an' scratchin' de hide off yo' legs in de bushes. Now you sees whar yo'se gwine. So cheer up! From now on you has a snap. *(He steps just to the rear of the triangular clearing and mops* 5 *off his face on his sleeve. He has lost his Panama hat. His face is scratched, his brilliant uniform shows several large rents.)* What time's it gittin' to be, I wonder? I dassent light no match to find out. Phoo'. It's wa'm an' dat's a fac'! *(Wearily)* How long I been makin' tracks in dese woods? Must be hours an' 10 hours. Seems like fo'evah! Yit can't be, when de moon's jes' riz. Dis am a long night fo' yo', yo' Majesty! *(With a mournful chuckle)* Majesty! Der ain't much majesty 'bout dis baby now. *(With attempted cheerfulness)* Never min'. It's all part o' de game. Dis night come to an end like everything else. And 15 when you gits dar safe and has dat bankroll in yo' hands you laughs at all dis. *(He starts to whistle but checks himself abruptly.)* What yo' whistlin' for, you po' dope! Want all de worl' to heah you? *(He stops talking to listen.)* Heah dat ole drum! Sho' gits nearer from de sound. Dey're packin' it along 20 wid 'em. Time fo' me to move. *(He takes a step forward, then stops — worriedly.)* What's dat odder queer clickety sound I heah? Dere it is! Sound close! Sound like — sound like — Fo' God sake, sound like some nigger was shootin' crap! *(Frightenedly)* I better beat it quick when I gits dem notions. *(He* 25 *walks quickly into the clear space — then stands transfixed as he sees* JEFF — *in a terrified gasp)* Who dar? Who dat? It dat you, Jeff? *(Starting toward the other, forgetful for a moment of his surroundings and really believing it is a living man that he sees — in a tone of happy relief.)* Jeff! I'se sho' mighty glad to 30 see you! Dey tol' me you done died from dat razor cut I gives you. *(Stopping suddenly, bewilderedly)* But how you come to be heah, nigger? *(He stares fascinatedly at the other who continues his mechanical play with the dice.* JONES' *eyes begin to roll wildly. He stutters.)* Ain't you gwine — look up — can't 35 you speaks to me? Is you — is you — a ha'nt? *(He jerks out his revolver in a frenzy of terrified rage.)* Nigger, I kills you dead once. Has I got to kill you again? You take it den. *(He fires. When the smoke clears away* JEFF *has disappeared.* JONES *stands trembling — then with a certain reassurance)* He's 40 gone, anyway. Ha'nt or no ha'nt, dat shot fix him. *(The beat of the far-off tom-tom is perceptibly louder and more rapid.* JONES *becomes conscious of it — with a start, looking back over his shoulder.)* Dey's gittin' near! Dey's comin' fast! And heah I is shootin' shots to let 'em knows jes' whar I is. Oh, Gorry, I'se 45 got to run. *(Forgetting the path he plunges wildly into the underbrush in the rear and disappears in the shadow.)*

— SCENE FOUR —

SCENE: *Eleven o'clock. In the forest. A wide dirt road runs diagonally from right, front, to left, rear. Rising sheer on both sides the forest walls it in. The moon is now up. Under its light the road glimmers ghastly and unreal. It is if the forest had stood aside momentarily to let the road pass through and accomplish its veiled purpose. This done, the forest will fold in upon itself again and the road will be no more.* JONES *stumbles in from the forest on the right. His uniform is ragged and torn. He looks about him with numbed surprise when he sees the road, his eyes blinking in the bright moonlight. He flops down exhaustedly and pants heavily for a while. Then with sudden anger*

I'm meltin' wid heat! Runnin' an' runnin' an' runnin'! Damn dis heah coat! Like a strait-jacket! *(He tears off his coat and flings it away from him, revealing himself stripped to the waist.)* Dere! Dat's better! Now I kin breathe! *(Looking down*
5 *at his feet, the spurs catch his eye.)* And to hell wid dese high-fangled spurs. Dey're what's been a-trippin' me up an' breakin' my neck. *(He unstraps them and flings them away disgustedly.)* Dere! I gits rid o' dem frippety Emperor trappin's an' I travels lighter. Lawd! I'se tired! *(After a pause, listening*
10 *to the insistent beat of the tom-tom in the distance)* I must 'a put some distance between myself an' dem — runnin' like dat — and yit — dat damn drum sounds jes' de same — nearer, even. Well, I guess I a'most holds my lead anyhow. Dey won't never catch up. *(With a sigh)* If on'y my fool legs stands up.
15 Oh, I'se sorry I evah went in for dis. Dat Emperor's job is sho' hard to shake. *(He looks around him suspiciously.)* How'd this road evah git heah? Good level road, too. I never remembers seein' it befo'. *(Shaking his head apprehensively)* Dese woods is sho' full o' de queerest things at night. *(With a sudden ter-*
20 *ror)* Lawd God, don't let me see no more o' dem ha'nts! Dey gits my goat! *(Then trying to talk himself into confidence)* Ha'nts! You fool nigger, dey ain't no such things! Don't de Baptist parson tell you dat many times? Is you civilized, or is you like dese ign'rent black niggers heah? Sho'! Dat was all in
25 yo' own head. Wasn't nothin' dere. Wasn't no Jeff! Know what? You jus' get seein' dem things' 'cause yo' belly's empty and you's sick wid hunger inside. Hunger 'fects yo' head and yo' eyes. Any fool know dat. *(Then pleading fervently)* But bless God, I don't come across no more o' dem, whatever dey
30 is! *(Then cautiously)* Rest! Don't talk! Rest! You needs it. Den you gits on yo' way again. *(Looking at the moon)* Night's half gone a'most. You hits de coast in de mawning! Den you'se all safe.

(From the right forward a small gang of NEGROES *enter. They are dressed in striped convict suits, their heads are shaven, one leg drags limpingly, shackled to a heavy ball and chain. Some carry picks, the others shovels. They are followed by a white man dressed in the uniform of a prison guard. A Winchester rifle is slung across his shoulders and he carries a heavy whip. At a signal from the* GUARD *they stop on the road opposite where* JONES *is sitting.* JONES, *who has been staring up at the sky, unmindful of their noiseless approach, suddenly looks down and sees them. His eyes pop out, he tries to get to his feet and fly, but sinks back, too numbed by fright to move. His voice catches in a choking prayer)*

Lawd Jesus!

(The PRISON GUARD *cracks his whip — noiselessly — and at that signal all the convicts start to work on the road. They swing their picks, they shovel, but not a sound comes from their labor. Their movements, like those of* JEFF *in the preceding scene, are those of automatons — rigid, slow, and mechanical. The* PRISON GUARD *points sternly at* JONES *with his whip, motions him to take his place among the other shovelers.* JONES *gets to his feet in a hypnotized stupor. He mumbles subserviently.)*

Yes, suh! Yes, suh! I'se comin'.   35

(As he shuffles, dragging one foot, over to his place, he curses under his breath with rage and hatred.)

God damn yo' soul, I gits even wid you yit, sometime.

(As if there were a shovel in his hands he goes through weary, mechanical gestures of digging up dirt, and throwing it to the roadside. Suddenly the GUARD *approaches him angrily, threateningly. He raises his whip and lashes* JONES *viciously across the shoulders with it.* JONES *winces with pain and cowers abjectly. The* GUARD *turns his back on him and walks away contemptuously. Instantly* JONES *straightens up. With arms upraised as if his shovel were a club in his hands he springs murderously at the unsuspecting* GUARD. *In the act of crashing down his shovel on the white man's skull,* JONES *suddenly becomes aware that his hands are empty. He cries despairingly)*

Whar's my shovel? Gimme my shovel till I splits his damn head! *(Appealing to his fellow convicts)* Gimme a shovel, one o' you, fo' God's sake!

(They stand fixed in motionless attitudes, their eyes on the ground. The GUARD *seems to wait expectantly, his back turned to the attacker.* JONES *bellows with baffled, terrified rage, tugging frantically at his revolver)*

I kills you, you white debil, if it's de last thing I evah does!   40 Ghost or debil, I kill you again!

(He frees the revolver and fires point blank at the GUARD'S *back. Instantly the walls of the forest close in from both sides, the road and the figures of the convict gang are blotted out in an enshrouding darkness. The only sounds are a crashing in the underbrush as* JONES *leaps away in mad flight and the throbbing of the tom-tom, still distant, but increased in volume of sound and rapidity of beat.)*

— SCENE FIVE —

SCENE: *One o'clock. A large circular clearing, enclosed by the serried ranks of gigantic trunks of tall trees whose tops are lost to view. In the center is a big dead stump worn by time into a curious resemblance to an auction block. The moon floods the clearing with a clear light.* JONES *forces his way in through the forest on the left. He looks wildly about the clearing with hunted, fearful glances. His pants are in tatters, his shoes cut and mishapen, flapping about his feet. He slinks cautiously to the stump in the center and sits down in a tense position, ready for instant flight. Then he holds his head in his hands and rocks back and forth, moaning to himself miserably.*

Oh Lawd, Lawd! Oh Lawd, Lawd! *(Suddenly he throws himself on his knees and raises his clasped hands to the sky — in a voice*

of agonized pleading.) Lawd Jesus, heah my prayer! I'se a po'
sinner, a po' sinner! I knows I done wrong, I knows it! When I
cotches Jeff cheatin' wid loaded dice my anger overcomes me
and I kills him dead! Lawd, I done wrong! When dat guard
hits me wid de whip, my anger overcomes me, and I kills him
dead. Lawd, I done wrong! And down heah whar dese fool
bush niggers raises me up to de seat o' de mighty, I steals all I
could grab. Lawd, I done wrong! I knows it! I'se sorry! Forgive
me, Lawd! Forgive dis po' sinner! *(Then beseeching terri-
fiedly)* And keep dem away, Lawd! Keep dem away from me!
And stop dat drum soundin' in my ears! Dat begin to sound
ha'nted, too. *(He gets to his feet, evidently slightly reassured
by his prayer—with attempted confidence)* De Lawd'll preserve me from dem ha'nts after dis. *(Sits down on the stump
again.)* I ain't skeered o' real men. Let dem come. But dem
odders . . . *(He shudders—then looks down at his feet, working his toes inside the shoes—with a groan.)* Oh, my po' feet!
Dem shoes ain't no use no more 'ceptin' to hurt. I'se better off
widout dem. *(He unlaces them and pulls them off—holds the
wrecks of the shoes in his hands and regards them mournfully.)*
You was real, A-one patin' leather, too. Look at you now.
Emperor, you'se gittin' mighty low!

*(He sits dejectedly and remains with bowed shoulders, staring
down at the shoes in his hands as if reluctant to throw them
away. While his attention is thus occupied, a crowd of figures
silently enters the clearing from all sides. All are dressed in
Southern costumes of the period of the fifties of the last century.
There are middle-aged men who are evidently well-to-do
planters. There is one spruce, authoritative individual—the*
AUCTIONEER. *There is a crowd of curious spectators, chiefly
young belles and dandies who have come to the slave-market for
diversion. All exchange courtly greetings in dumb show and chat
silently together. There is something stiff, rigid, unreal, mar-
ionettish about their movements. They group themselves about
the stump. Finally a batch of* SLAVES *are led in from the left by
an attendant—three men of different ages, two women, one with
a baby in her arms, nursing. They are placed to the left of the
stump, beside* JONES.

The white PLANTERS *look them over appraisingly as if they were
cattle, and exchange judgments on each. The dandies point with
their fingers and make witty remarks. The belles titter bewitchingly. All this in silence save for the ominous throb of the tom-
tom. The* AUCTIONEER *holds up his hand, taking his place at the
stump. The group strains forward attentively. He touches* JONES
*on the shoulder peremptorily, motioning for him to stand on the
stump—the auction block.*

JONES *looks up, sees the figures on all sides, looks wildly for some
opening to escape, sees none, screams and leaps madly to the top
of the stump to get as far away from them as possible. He stands
there, cowering, paralyzed with horror. The* AUCTIONEER *begins
his silent spiel. He points to* JONES, *appeals to the* PLANTERS *to
see for themselves. Here is a good field hand, sound in wind and
limb as they can see. Very strong still in spite of his being middle-
aged. Look at that back. Look at those shoulders. Look at the
muscles in his arms and his sturdy legs. Capable of any amount
of hard labor. Moreover, of a good disposition, intelligent and
tractable. Will any gentleman start the bidding? The* PLANTERS
*raise their fingers, make their bids. They are apparently all eager
to possess* JONES. *The bidding is lively, the crowd interested.*

While this has been going on, JONES *has been seized by the courage of desperation. He dares to look down and around him. Over
his face abject terror gives way to mystification, to gradual realization—stutteringly)*

What you all doin', white folks? What's all dis? What you all
lookin' at me fo'? What you doin' wid me, anyhow? *(Suddenly convulsed with raging hatred and fear)* Is dis a auction?
Is you sellin' me like dey uster befo' de war? *(Jerking out his
revolver just as the* AUCTIONEER *knocks him down to one of the*
PLANTERS—*glaring from him to the purchaser.)* And you sells
me? And *you* buys me? I shows you I'se a free nigger, damn yo'
souls! *(He fires at the* AUCTIONEER *and at the* PLANTER *with
such rapidity that the two shots are almost simultaneous. As if
this were a signal the walls of the forest fold in. Only blackness remains and silence broken by* JONES *as he rushes off,
crying with fear—and by the quickened, ever louder beat of the
tom-tom.)*

— SCENE SIX —

SCENE: *Three o'clock. A cleared space in the forest. The limbs of
the trees meet over it forming a low ceiling about five feet from the
ground. The interlocked ropes of creepers reaching upward to en-
twine the tree trunks give an arched appearance to the sides. The
space thus enclosed is like the dark, noisome hold of some ancient
vessel. The moonlight is almost completely shut out and only a
vague, wan light filters through. There is the noise of someone
approaching from the left, stumbling and crawling through the
undergrowth.* JONES' *voice is heard between chattering moans.*

Oh, Lawd, what I gwine do now? Ain't got no bullet left on'y de
silver one. If mo' o' dem ha'nts come after me, how I gwine
skeer dem away? Oh, Lawd, on'y de silver one left—an' I
gotta save dat fo' luck. If I shoots dat one I'm a goner sho'!
Lawd, it's black heah! Whar's de moon? Oh, Lawd, don't dis
night evah come to an end? *(By the sounds, he is feeling his
way cautiously forward.)* Dere! Dis feels like a clear space. I
gotta lie down an' rest. I don't care if dem niggers does cotch
me. I gotta rest.

*(He is well forward now where his figure can be dimly made out.
His pants have been so torn away that what is left of them is no
better than a breech cloth. He flings himself full length, face
downward on the ground, panting with exhaustion. Gradually it
seems to grow lighter in the enclosed space and two rows of seated
figures can be seen behind* JONES. *They are sitting in crumbled,
despairing attitudes, hunched, facing one another with their
backs touching the forest walls as if they were shackled to them.
All are Negroes, naked save for loin cloths. At first they are silent
and motionless. Then they begin to sway slowly forward toward
each other and back again in unison, as if they were laxly letting
themselves follow the long roll of a ship at sea. At the same time,
a low, melancholy murmur rises among them, increasing gradually by rhythmic degrees which seem to be directed and controlled
by the throb of the tom-tom in the distance, to a long, tremulous
wail of despair that reaches a certain pitch, unbearably acute,
then falls by slow gradations of tone into silence and is taken up
again.* JONES *starts, looks up, sees the figures, and throws himself
down again to shut out the sight. A shudder of terror shakes his
whole body as the wail rises up about him again. But the next*

time, his voice, as if under some uncanny compulsion, starts with the others. As their chorus lifts he rises to a sitting posture similar to the others, swaying back and forth. His voice reaches the highest pitch of sorrow, of desolation. The light fades out, the other voices cease, and only darkness is left. JONES *can be heard scrambling to his feet and running off, his voice sinking down the scale and receding as he moves farther and farther away in the forest. The tom-tom beats louder, quicker, with a more insistent, triumphant pulsation.)*

— SCENE SEVEN —

SCENE: *Five o'clock. The foot of a gigantic tree by the edge of a great river. A rough structure of boulders, like an altar, is by the tree. The raised river bank is in the nearer background. Beyond this the surface of the river spreads out, brilliant and unruffled in the moonlight, blotted out and merged into a veil of bluish mist in the distance.* JONES' *voice is heard from the left rising and falling in the long, despairing wail of the chained slaves, to the rhythmic beat of the tom-tom. As his voice sinks into silence, he enters the open space. The expression of his face is fixed and stony, his eyes have an obsessed glare, he moves with a strange deliberation like a sleepwalker or one in a trance. He looks around at the tree, the rough stone altar, the moonlit surface of the river beyond, and passes his hand over his head with a vague gesture of puzzled bewilderment. Then, as if in obedience to some obscure impulse, he sinks into a kneeling, devotional posture before the altar. Then he seems to come to himself partly, to have an uncertain realization of what he is doing, for he straightens up and stares about him horrifiedly—in an incoherent mumble)*

What—what is I doin'? What is—dis place? Seems like—seems like I know dat tree—an' dem stones—an' de river. I remember—seems like I ben heah befo'. *(Tremblingly)* Oh, Gorry, I'se skeered in dis place! I'se skeered! Oh, Lawd, pertect dis sinner!

5

(Crawling away from the altar, he cowers close to the ground, his face hidden, his shoulders heaving with sobs of hysterical fright. From behind the trunk of the tree, as if he had sprung out of it, the figure of the CONGO WITCH-DOCTOR *appears. He is wizened and old, naked except for the fur of some small animal tied about his waist, its bushy tail hanging down in front. His body is stained all over a bright red. Antelope horns are on each side of his head, branching upward. In one hand he carries a bone rattle, in the other a charm stick with a bunch of white cockatoo feathers tied to the end. A great number of glass beads and bone ornaments are about his neck, ears, wrists, and ankles. He struts noiselessly with a queer prancing step to a position in the clear ground between* JONES *and the altar. Then with a preliminary, summoning stamp of his foot on the earth, he begins to dance and to chant. As if in response to his summons the beating of the tom-tom grows to a fierce, exultant boom whose throbs seem to fill the air with vibrating rhythm.* JONES *looks up, starts to spring to his feet, reaches a half-kneeling, half-squatting position and remains rigidly fixed there, paralyzed with awed fascination by his new apparition. The* WITCH-DOCTOR *sways, stamping with his foot, his bone rattle clicking the time. His voice rises and falls in a weird, monotonous croon, without articulate word divisions. Gradually his dance becomes clearly one of a narrative in*

pantomime, his croon is an incantation, a charm to allay the fierceness of some implacable deity demanding sacrifice. He flees, he is pursued by devils, he hides, he flees again. Ever wilder and wilder becomes his flight, nearer and nearer draws the pursuing evil, more and more the spirit of terror gains possession of him. His croon, rising to intensity, is punctuated by shrill cries. JONES *has become completely hypnotized. His voice joins in the incantation, in the cries, he beats time with his hands and sways his body to and fro from the waist. The whole spirit and meaning of the dance has entered into him, has become his spirit. Finally the theme of the pantomime halts on a howl of despair, and is taken up again in a note of savage hope. There is a salvation. The forces of evil demand sacrifice. They must be appeased. The* WITCH-DOCTOR *points with his wand to the sacred tree, to the river beyond, to the altar, and finally to* JONES *with a ferocious command.* JONES *seems to sense the meaning of this. It is he who must offer himself for sacrifice. He beats his forehead abjectly to the ground, moaning hysterically.)*

Mercy, Oh Lawd! Mercy! Mercy on dis po' sinner.

(The WITCH-DOCTOR *springs to the river bank. He stretches out his arms and calls to some god within its depths. Then he starts backward slowly, his arms remaining out. A huge head of a* CROCODILE *appears over the bank and its eyes, glittering greenly, fasten upon* JONES. *He stares into them fascinatedly. The* WITCH-DOCTOR *prances up to him, touches him with his wand, motions with hideous command toward the waiting monster.* JONES *squirms on his belly nearer and nearer, moaning continually.)*

Mercy, Lawd! Mercy!

(The CROCODILE *heaves more of his enormous hulk onto the land.* JONES *squirms toward him. The* WITCH-DOCTOR's *voice shrills out in furious exultation, the tom-tom beats madly.* JONES *cries out in a fierce, exhausted spasm of anguished pleading.)*

Lawd, save me! Lawd Jesus, heah my prayer!

(Immediately, in answer to his prayer, comes the thought of the one bullet left him. He snatches at his hip, shouting defiantly.)

De silver bullet! You don't git me yit!

(He fires at the green eyes in front of him. The head of the crocodile sinks back behind the river bank, the WITCH-DOCTOR *springs behind the sacred tree and disappears.* JONES *lies with his face to the ground, his arms outstretched, whimpering with fear as the throb of the tom-tom fills the silence about him with a somber pulsation, a baffled but revengeful power.)*

— SCENE EIGHT —

SCENE: *Dawn. Same as Scene Two, the dividing line of forest and plain. The nearest tree trunks are dimly revealed but the forest behind them is still a mass of glooming shadows. The tom-tom seems on the very spot, so loud and continuously vibrating are its beats.* LEM *enters from the left, followed by a small squad of his soldiers, and by the Cockney trader,* SMITHERS. LEM *is a heavy-set, ape-faced old savage of the extreme African type, dressed only in loin cloth. A revolver and cartridge belt are about his waist. His soldiers are in different degrees of rag-concealed nakedness. All wear broad palm-leaf hats. Each one carries a rifle.* SMITHERS *is the same as in Scene One. One of the soldiers, evidently a tracker, is peering about keenly on the ground. He grunts and points at the spot where Jones entered the forest.* LEM *and* SMITHERS *come to look.*

SMITHERS: *(After a glance, turns away in disgust)* That's where 'e went in right enough. Much good it'll do yer. 'E's miles orf by this an' safe to the Coast, damn 'is 'ide! I tole yer yer'd lose 'im, didn't I?—wastin' the 'ole bloomin' night beatin' yer bloody drum and castin' yer silly spells! Gawd blimey, wot a pack!

5

LEM: *(Gutturally)* We cotch him. You see. *(He makes a motion to his soldiers who squat down on their haunches in a semicircle.)*

10 SMITHERS: *(Exasperatedly)* Well, ain't yer goin' in an' 'unt 'im in the woods? What the 'ell's the good of waitin'?

LEM: *(Imperturbably—squatting down himself)* We cotch him.

SMITHERS: *(Turning away from him contemptuously)* Aw! Garn! 'E's a better man than the lot o' you put together. I 'ates the sight of 'im but I'll say that for 'im. *(A sound of snapping twigs comes from the forest. The* SOLDIERS *jump to their feet, cocking their rifles alertly.* LEM *remains sitting with an imperturbable expression, but listening intently. The sound from the woods is repeated.* LEM *makes a quick signal with his hand. His followers creep quickly but noiselessly into the forest, scattering so that each enters at a different spot.)*

15

20

SMITHERS: *(In the silence that follows—in a contemptuous whisper)* You ain't thinkin' that would be 'im, I 'ope?

LEM: *(Calmly)* We cotch him.

25 SMITHERS: Blarsted fat 'eads! *(Then after a second's thought—wonderingly)* Still an' all, it might 'appen. If 'e lost 'is bloody way in these stinkin' woods 'e'd likely turn in a circle without 'is knowin' it. They all does.

LEM: *(Peremptorily)* Sssh! *(The reports of several rifles sound from the forest, followed a second later by savage, exultant yells.)*

30

The beating of the tom-tom abruptly ceases. LEM *looks up at the white man with a grin of satisfaction.)* We cotch him. Him dead.

SMITHERS: *(With a snarl)* 'Ow d'yer know it's 'im an' 'ow d'yer know 'e's dead?   35

LEM: My mens dey got 'um silver bullets. Dey kill him shore.

SMITHERS: *(Astonished)* They got silver bullets?

LEM: Lead bullet no kill him. He got um strong charm. I cook um money, make um silver bullet, make um strong charm, too.   40

SMITHERS: *(Light breaking upon him)* So that's wot you was up to all night, wot? You was scared to put after 'im till you'd moulded silver bullets, eh?

LEM: *(Simply stating a fact)* Yes. Him got strong charm. Lead no good.   45

SMITHERS: *(Slapping his thigh and guffawing)* Haw-haw! If yer don't beat all 'ell! *(Then recovering himself—scornfully)* I'll bet yer it ain't 'im they shot at all, yer bleedin' looney!

LEM: *(Calmly)* Dey come bring him now. *(The* SOLDIERS *come out of the forest, carrying* JONES' *limp body. There is a little   50 reddish-purple hole under his left breast. He is dead. They carry him to* LEM, *who examines his body with great satisfaction.* SMITHERS *leans over his shoulder—in a tone of frightened awe.)* Well, they did for yer right enough, Jonsey, me lad! Dead as a 'erring! *(Mockingly)* Where's yer 'igh an'   55 mighty airs now, yer bloomin' Majesty? *(Then with a grin)* Silver bullets! Gawd blimey, but yer died in the 'eight o' style, any'ow! *(LEM *makes a motion to the* SOLDIERS *to carry the body out left.* SMITHERS *speaks to him sneeringly.)*

SMITHERS: And I s'pose you think it's yer bleedin' charms and   60 yer silly beatin' the drum that made 'im run in a circle when 'e'd lost 'imself, don't yer? *(But* LEM *makes no reply, does not seem to hear the question, walks out left after his men.* SMITHERS *looks after him with contemptuous scorn.)* Stupid as 'ogs, the lot of 'em! Blarsted niggers!   65

TENNESSEE WILLIAMS

Like Amanda Wingfield in *The Glass Menagerie*, Tennessee Williams (1911-1983) regarded himself as a product of the Old South and its genteel, rural, and — finally — obsolete traditions. Born Thomas Lanier Williams to a traveling shoe salesman and his wife, Williams was raised in Mississippi before moving to the tenements of St. Louis. As a child, Williams contracted diphtheria, which briefly paralyzed his legs and left him frail and homebound for some time. During his convalescence, Williams read and wrote avidly and published his first story at the age of sixteen. After high school, he briefly attended the University of Missouri, but withdrew when his poor health prevented him from passing the ROTC course. He then worked for three years in a shoe factory, then tried Washington University in St. Louis, but again dropped out. He finally took his degree in playwriting from the University of Iowa in 1938, when he changed his name to "Tennessee." In the 1930s, Williams's embattled relation to the world was deepened by the "loss" of his beloved sister Rose. Rose became chronically depressed, and Williams's mother, unable to cope with her erratic and wild behavior, consented to having a lobotomy performed. Rose was left docile but inert and became the prototype of several of Williams's most memorable dramatic characters, women whose inner beauty is too delicate to be disclosed to the world. At this time Williams also recognized his own homosexuality, a recognition that deepened his sense of the threatening conformity imposed by mainstream American society.

Coming of age in the Great Depression was formative for Williams's drama, particularly the range of themes associated with his mature work: a sexual tension surging beneath the surface of the characters' lives, the collapse of a sustaining family and social order, the attraction of misfits destroyed by a world that will not accept them. Williams wrote several now-lost plays in the late 1930s, and *Battle of Angels* (1940; later revised as *Orpheus Descending* in 1957) was produced by the Theater Guild in Boston, where it failed. Williams scored a major success with his next play, *The Glass Menagerie* (1944). He continued his success with a series of important dramas: *Summer and Smoke* (1947), *A Streetcar Named Desire* (1947), *The Rose Tattoo* (1951), *Camino Real* (1953), *Cat on a Hot Tin Roof* (1955), *Sweet Bird of Youth* (1959), *Night of the Iguana* (1961). In his later years, Williams's drama became increasingly gothic and sensational, and his personal life suffered as well; Williams became an alcoholic and was institutionalized on several occasions. He continued to write plays to the end of his life, developing his characteristic strengths: a feel for the nuances of character, and a flair for dramatizing the victims of an unfeeling world.

The Glass Menagerie

First performed in 1944, *The Glass Menagerie* looks back to the 1930s. Its characters are reminiscent of Williams and his family, and their grinding poverty recalls the depression-era plays of Elmer Rice and Clifford Odets. In many ways, *The Glass Menagerie* is a play in the realistic tradition. Laura's menagerie recalls how Ibsen, Chekhov, and Strindberg used stage objects (Nora's Christmas tree in *A Doll House*, the cherry orchard, Miss Julie's bird) to evoke and symbolize the characters' motives and sensibilities. However, Williams also uses the device of the "memory play" to disrupt the linearity of realistic drama. Tom constructs the scene and the characters for the audience, and slide projections of phrases and images often illustrate the action as it takes place. These devices lend *The Glass Menagerie* the flavor of symbolist theater. Moreover, Tom's anticipation of the Spanish Civil War and World War II sets the play in a larger social and political context that looms forebodingly over the fragile and self-absorbed characters. Amanda and Laura seem doomed never to escape the drab apartment, and even Tom, wandering the world, finally cannot escape it either. Deeply personal, *The Glass Menagerie* also provides a kind of study for Williams's later plays, for it includes a typical panoply of Williams's characters: the blunt, sexually aggressive, emotionally stunted Jim; Amanda, the faded Southern belle; Laura, more crippled emotionally than physically; and Tom, who falls in love with long distance yet never succeeds in escaping his past or in finding his future.

— PRODUCTION NOTES —

Being a "memory play," *The Glass Menagerie* can be presented with unusual freedom of convention. Because of its considerably delicate or tenuous material, atmospheric touches and subtleties of direction play a particularly important part. Expressionism and all other unconventional techniques in drama have only one valid aim, and that is a closer approach to truth. When a play employs unconventional techniques, it is not, or certainly shouldn't be, trying to escape its responsibility of dealing with reality, or interpreting experience, but is actually or should be attempting to find a closer approach, a more penetrating and vivid expression of things as they are. The straight realistic play with its genuine Frigidaire and authentic ice-cubes, its characters who speak exactly as its audience speaks, corresponds to the academic landscape and has the same virtue of a photographic likeness. Everyone should know nowadays the unimportance of the photographic in art: that truth, life, or reality is an organic thing which the poetic imagination can represent or suggest, in essence, only through transformation, through changing into other forms than those which were merely present in appearance.

These remarks are not meant as a preface only to this particular play. They have to do with a conception of a new, plastic theatre which must take the place of the exhausted theatre of realistic conventions if the theatre is to resume vitality as a part of our culture.

THE SCREEN DEVICE: There is *only one important difference between the original and the acting version of the play* and that is the *omission* in the latter of the device that I tentatively included in my *original* script. This device was the use of a screen on which were projected magic-lantern slides bearing images or titles. I do not regret the omission of this device from the original Broadway production. The extraordinary power of Miss Taylor's performance made it suitable to have the utmost simplicity in the physical production. But I think it may be interesting to some readers to see how this device was conceived. So I am putting it into the published manuscript. These images and legends, projected from behind, were cast on a section of wall between the front-room and dining-room areas, which should be indistinguishable from the rest when not in use.

The purpose of this will probably be apparent. It is to give accent to certain values in each scene. Each scene contains a particular point (or several) which is structurally the most important. In an episodic play, such as this, the basic structure or narrative line may be obscured from the audience; the effect may seem fragmentary rather than architectural. This may not be the fault of the play so much as a lack of attention in the audience. The legend or image upon the screen will strengthen the effect of what is merely allusion in the writing and allow the primary point to be made more simply and lightly than if the entire responsibility were on the spoken lines. Aside from this structural value, I think the screen will have a definite emotional appeal, less definable but just as important. An imaginative producer or director may invent many other uses for this device than those indicated in the present script. In fact the possibilities of the device seem much larger to me than the instance of this play can possibly utilize.

THE MUSIC: Another extra-literary accent in this play is provided by the use of music. A single recurring tune, "The Glass Menagerie," is used to give emotional emphasis to suitable passages. This tune is like circus music, not when you are on the grounds or in the immediate vicinity of the parade, but when you are at some distance and very likely thinking of something else. It seems under those circumstances to continue almost interminably and it weaves in and out of your preoccupied consciousness; then it is the lightest, most delicate music in the world and perhaps the saddest. It expresses the surface vivacity of life with the underlying strain of immutable and inexpressible sorrow. When you look at a piece of delicately spun glass you think of two things: how beautiful it is and how easily it can be broken. Both of those ideas should be woven into the recurring tune, which dips in and out of the play as if it were carried on a wind that changes. It serves as a thread of connection and allusion between the narrator with his separate point in time and space and the subject of his story. Between each episode it returns as reference to the emotion, nostalgia, which is the first condition of the play. It is primarily Laura's music and therefore comes out most clearly when the play focuses upon her and the lovely fragility of glass which is her image.

THE LIGHTING: The lighting in the play is not realistic. In keeping with the atmosphere of memory, the stage is dim. Shafts of light are focused on selected areas or actors, sometimes in contradistinction to what is the apparent center. For instance, in the quarrel scene between Tom and Amanda, in which Laura has no active part, the clearest pool of light is on her figure. This is also true of the supper scene, when her silent figure on the sofa should remain the visual center. The light upon Laura should be distinct from the others, having a peculiar pristine clarity such as light used in early religious portraits of female saints or madonnas. A certain correspondence to light in religious paintings, such as El Greco's, where the figures are radiant in atmosphere that is relatively dusky, could be effectively used throughout the play. (It will also permit a more effective use of the screen.) A free, imaginative use of light can be of enormous value in giving a mobile, plastic quality to plays of a more or less static nature.

Tennessee Williams

THE GLASS MENAGERIE
Tennessee Williams

— CHARACTERS —

AMANDA WINGFIELD (*the mother*), *a little woman of great but confused vitality clinging frantically to another time and place. Her characterization must be carefully created, not copied from type. She is not paranoiac, but her life is paranoia. There is much to admire in Amanda, and as much to love and pity as there is to laugh at. Certainly she has endurance and a kind of heroism, and though her foolishness makes her unwittingly cruel at times, there is tenderness in her slight person.*

LAURA WINGFIELD (*her daughter*), *Amanda, having failed to establish contact with reality, continues to live vitally in her illusions, but Laura's situation is even graver. A childhood illness has left her crippled, one leg slightly shorter than the other, and held in a brace. This defect need not be more than suggested on the stage. Stemming from this, Laura's separation increases till she is like a piece of her own glass collection, too exquisitely fragile to move from the shelf.*

TOM WINGFIELD (*her son*), *and the narrator of the play. A poet with a job in a warehouse. His nature is not remorseless, but to escape from a trap he has to act without pity.*

JIM O'CONNOR (*the gentleman caller*), *a nice, ordinary, young man.*

SCENE: *An Alley in St. Louis*

   Part I. Preparation for a Gentleman Caller.
   Part II. The Gentlemen calls.

TIME: *Now and the Past.*

— SCENE ONE —

The Wingfield apartment is in the rear of the building, one of those vast hive-like conglomerations of the cellular living-units that flower as warty growths in overcrowded urban centers of lower middle-class population and are symptomatic of the impulse of this largest and fundamentally enslaved section of American society to avoid fluidity and differentiation and to exist and function as one interfused mass of automatism.

The apartment faces an alley and is entered by a fire escape, a structure whose name is a touch of accidental poetic truth, for all of these huge buildings are always burning with the slow and implacable fires of human desperation. The fire escape is part of what we see—that is, the landing of it and steps descending from it.

The scene is memory and is therefore nonrealistic. Memory takes a lot of poetic license. It omits some details; others are exaggerated, according to the emotional value of the articles it touches, for memory is seated predominantly in the heart. The interior is therefore rather dim and poetic.

At the rise of the curtain, the audience is faced with the dark, grim rear wall of the Wingfield tenement. This building is flanked on both sides by dark, narrow alleys which run into murky canyons of tangled clotheslines, garbage cans, and the sinister latticework of neighboring fire escapes. It is up and down these side alleys that exterior entrances and exits are made during the play. At the end of TOM's opening commentary, the dark tenement wall slowly becomes transparent and reveals the interior of the ground-floor Wingfield apartment.

Nearest the audience is the living room, which also serves as a sleeping room for LAURA, the sofa unfolding to make her bed. Just beyond, separated from the living room by a wide arch or second proscenium with transparent faded portieres (or second curtain), is the dining room. In an old-fashioned whatnot in the living room are seen scores of transparent glass animals. A blown-up photograph of the father hangs on the wall of the living room, to the left of the archway. It is the face of a very handsome young man in a doughboy's First World War cap. He is gallantly smiling, ineluctably smiling, as if to say "I will be smiling forever."

Also hanging on the wall, near the photograph, are a typewriter keyboard chart and a Gregg shorthand diagram. An upright typewriter on a small table stands beneath the charts.

The audience hears and sees the opening scene in the dining room through both the transparent fourth wall of the building and the transparent gauze portieres of the dining-room arch. It is during this revealing scene that the fourth wall slowly ascends, out of sight. This transparent exterior wall is not brought down again until the very end of the play, during TOM's final speech.

The narrator is an undisguised convention of the play. He takes whatever license with dramatic convention is convenient to his purposes.

TOM *enters, dressed as a merchant sailor, and strolls across to the fire escape. There he stops and lights a cigarette. He addresses the audience.*

TOM: Yes, I have tricks in my pocket, I have things up my sleeve. But I am the opposite of a stage magician. He gives you illusion that has the appearance of truth. I give you truth in the pleasant disguise of illusion.

   To begin with, I turn back time. I reverse it to that quaint 5 period, the thirties, when the huge middle class of America was matriculating in a school for the blind. Their eyes had failed them, or they had failed their eyes, and so they were having their fingers pressed forcibly down on the fiery Braille alphabet of a dissolving economy. 10

   In Spain there was revolution. Here there was only shouting and confusion. In Spain there was Guernica. Here there were disturbances of labor, sometimes pretty violent, in otherwise peaceful cities such as Chicago, Cleveland, Saint Louis . . . This is the social background of the play. 15

(*Music begins to play.*)

The play is memory. Being a memory play, it is dimly lighted, it is sentimental, it is not realistic. In memory everything seems to happen to music. That explains the fiddle in the wings.

I am the narrator of the play, and also a character in it. The other characters are my mother, Amanda, my sister, Laura, and a gentleman caller who appears in the final scenes. He is the most realistic character in the play, being an emissary from a world of reality that we were somehow set apart from. But since I have a poet's weakness for symbols, I am using this character also as a symbol; he is the long-delayed but always expected something that we live for.

There is a fifth character in the play who doesn't appear except in this larger-than-life-size photograph over the mantel. This is our father who left us a long time ago. He was a telephone man who fell in love with long distances; he gave up his job with the telephone company and skipped the light fantastic out of town . . .

The last we heard of him was a picture postcard from Mazatlan, on the Pacific coast of Mexico, containing a message of two words: "Hello—Goodbye!" and no address.

I think the rest of the play will explain itself. . . .

(AMANDA's *voice becomes audible through the portieres.*)

(*Legend on screen:* "Ou sont les neiges.")

(TOM *divides the portieres and enters the dining room.* AMANDA *and* LAURA *are seated at a drop-leaf table. Eating is indicated by gestures without food or utensils.* AMANDA *faces the audience.* TOM *and* LAURA *are seated in profile. The interior has lit up softly and through the scrim we see* AMANDA *and* LAURA *seated at the table.*)

AMANDA: (*calling*) Tom?
TOM: Yes, Mother.
AMANDA: We can't say grace until you come to the table!
TOM: Coming, Mother. (*He bows slightly and withdraws, reappearing a few moments later in his place at the table.*)
AMANDA: (*to her son*) Honey, don't *push* with your *fingers*. If you have to push with something, the thing to push with is a crust of bread. And chew—chew! Animals have secretions in their stomachs which enable them to digest food without mastication, but human beings are supposed to chew their food before they swallow it down. Eat food leisurely, son, and really enjoy it. A well-cooked meal has lots of delicate flavors that have to be held in the mouth for appreciation. So chew your food and give your salivary glands a chance to function!

(TOM *deliberately lays his imaginary fork down and pushes his chair back from the table.*)

TOM: I haven't enjoyed one bite of this dinner because of your constant directions on how to eat it. It's you that make me rush through meals with your hawklike attention to every bite I take. Sickening—spoils my appetite—all this discussion of—animals' secretion—salivary glands—mastication!
AMANDA: (*lightly*) Temperament like a Metropolitan star!

(TOM *rises and walks toward the living room.*)

You're not excused from the table.
TOM: I'm getting a cigarette.
AMANDA: You smoke too much.

(LAURA *rises.*)

LAURA: I'll bring in the blanc mange.

(TOM *remains standing with his cigarette by the portieres.*)

AMANDA: (*rising*) No, sister, no, sister—you be the lady this time and I'll be the darky.
LAURA: I'm already up.
AMANDA: Resume your seat, little sister—I want you to stay fresh and pretty—for gentlemen callers!
LAURA: (*sitting down*) I'm not expecting any gentlemen callers.
AMANDA: (*crossing out to the kitchenette, airily*) Sometimes they come when they are least expected! Why, I remember one Sunday afternoon in Blue Mountain—

(*She enters the kitchenette.*)

TOM: I know what's coming!
LAURA: Yes. But let her tell it.
TOM: Again?
LAURA: She loves to tell it.

(AMANDA *returns with a bowl of dessert.*)

AMANDA: One Sunday afternoon in Blue Mountain—your mother received—*seventeen!*—gentlemen callers! Why, sometimes there weren't chairs enough to accommodate them all. We had to send the nigger over to bring in folding chairs from the parish house.
TOM: (*remaining at the portieres*) How did you entertain those gentlemen callers?
AMANDA: I understood the art of conversation!
TOM: I bet you could talk.
AMANDA: Girls in those days *knew* how to talk, I can tell you.
TOM: Yes?

(*Image on screen:* AMANDA *as a girl on a porch, greeting callers.*)

AMANDA: They knew how to entertain their gentlemen callers. It wasn't enough for a girl to be possessed of a pretty face and a graceful figure—although I wasn't slighted in either respect. She also needed to have a nimble wit and a tongue to meet all occasions.
TOM: What did you talk about?
AMANDA: Things of importance going on in the world! Never anything coarse or common or vulgar.

(*She addresses* TOM *as though he were seated in the vacant chair at the table though he remains by the portieres. He plays this scene as though reading from a script.*)

My callers were gentlemen—all! Among my callers were some of the most prominent young planters of the Mississippi Delta—planters and sons of planters!

(TOM *motions for music and a spot of light on* AMANDA. *Her eyes lift, her face glows, her voice becomes rich and elegiac.*)

(*Screen legend:* "Ou sont les neiges d'antan?")

There was young Champ Laughlin who later became vice-president of the Delta Planters Bank. Hadley Stevenson who was drowned in Moon Lake and left his widow one hundred and fifty thousand in Government bonds. There were the Cutrere brothers, Wesley and Bates. Bates was one of my bright particular beaux! He got in a quarrel with that wild Wainwright boy. They shot it out on the floor of Moon Lake Casino. Bates was shot through the stomach. Died in the

105 ambulance on his way to Memphis. His widow was also well
     provided-for, came into eight or ten thousand acres, that's all.
     She married him on the rebound—never loved her—carried
     my picture on him the night he died! And there was that boy
     that every girl in the Delta had set her cap for! That beautiful,
     brilliant young Fitzhugh boy from Greene County!

110 TOM: What did he leave his widow?

AMANDA: He never married! Gracious, you talk as though all of
     my old admirers had turned up their toes to the daisies!

TOM: Isn't this the first you've mentioned that still survives?

AMANDA: That Fitzhugh boy went North and made a fortune—
115 came to be known as the Wolf of Wall Street! He had the
     Midas touch, whatever he touched turned to gold! And I
     could have been Mrs. Duncan J. Fitzhugh, mind you! But—
     I picked your *father!*

LAURA: *(rising)* Mother, let me clear the table.

120 AMANDA: No, dear, you go in front and study your typewriter
     chart. Or practice your shorthand a little. Stay fresh and
     pretty!—It's almost time for our gentlemen callers to start ar-
     riving. *(She flounces girlishly toward the kitchenette)* How
     many do you suppose we're going to entertain this afternoon?

(TOM throws down the paper and jumps up with a groan.)

125 LAURA: *(alone in the dining room)* I don't believe we're going to
     receive any, Mother.

AMANDA: *(reappearing, airily)* What? No one—not one? You
     must be joking!

*(LAURA nervously echoes her laugh. She slips in a fugitive man-
ner through the half-open portieres and draws them gently behind her. A shaft of very clear light is thrown on her face against
the faded tapestry of the curtains. Faintly the music of "The
Glass Menagerie" is heard as she continues, lightly:)*

     Not one gentleman caller? It can't be true! There must be a
130 flood, there must have been a tornado!

LAURA: It isn't a flood, it's not a tornado, Mother. I'm just not
     popular like you were in Blue Mountain. . . .

*(TOM utters another groan. LAURA glances at him with a faint,
apologetic smile. Her voice catches a little:)*

     Mother's afraid I'm going to be an old maid.

(The scene dims out with the "Glass Menagerie" music.)

— SCENE TWO —

*On the dark stage the screen is lighted with the image of blue
roses. Gradually LAURA's figure becomes apparent and the screen
goes out. The music subsides.*

*LAURA is seated in the delicate ivory chair at the small claw-foot
table. She wears a dress of soft violet material for a kimono—her
hair is tied back from her forehead with a ribbon. She is washing
and polishing her collection of glass. AMANDA appears on the fire
escape steps. At the sound of her ascent, LAURA catches her
breath, thrusts the bowl of ornaments away, and seats herself
stiffly before the diagram of the typewriter keyboard as though it
held her spellbound. Something has happened to AMANDA. It is
written in her face as she climbs to the landing: a look that is grim
and hopeless and a little absurd. She has on one of those cheap or*

*imitation velvety-looking cloth coats with imitation fur collar.
Her hat is five or six years old, one of those dreadful cloche hats
that were worn in the late Twenties, and she is clutching an enormous black patent-leather pocketbook with nickel clasps and initials. This is her full-dress outfit, the one she usually wears to the
D.A.R. Before entering she looks through the door. She purses her
lips, opens her eyes very wide, rolls them upward and shakes her
head. Then she slowly lets herself in the door. Seeing her mother's
expression LAURA touches her lips with a nervous gesture.*

LAURA: Hello, Mother, I was— *(She makes a nervous gesture to-
     ward the chart on the wall.* AMANDA *leans against the shut
     door and stares at* LAURA *with a martyred look.)*

AMANDA: Deception? Deception? *(She slowly removes her hat
     and gloves, continuing the sweet suffering stare. She lets the*   5
     hat and gloves fall on the floor—a bit of acting.)

LAURA: *(shakily)* How was the D.A.R. meeting?

*(AMANDA slowly opens her purse and removes a dainty white
handkerchief which she shakes out delicately and delicately
touches to her lips and nostrils.)*

     Didn't you go to the D.A.R. meeting, Mother?

AMANDA: *(faintly, almost inaudibly)* —No.—No. *(then more
     forcibly:)* I did not have the strength—to go to the D.A.R. In   10
     fact, I did not have the courage! I wanted to find a hole in the
     ground and hide myself in it forever! *(She crosses slowly to the
     wall and removes the diagram of the typewriter keyboard. She
     holds it in front of her for a second, staring at it sweetly and
     sorrowfully—then bites her lips and tears it into two pieces.)*   15

LAURA: *(faintly)* Why did you do that, Mother?

*(AMANDA repeats the same procedure with the chart of the Gregg
Alphabet.)*

     Why are you—

AMANDA: Why? Why? How old are you, Laura?

LAURA: Mother, you know my age.

AMANDA: I thought that you were an adult; it seems that I was   20
     mistaken. *(She crosses slowly to the sofa and sinks down and
     stares at Laura.)*

LAURA: Please don't stare at me, Mother.

*(AMANDA closes her eyes and lowers her head. There is a ten-
second pause.)*

AMANDA: What are we going to do, what is going to become of
     us, what is the future?   25

(There is another pause.)

LAURA: Has something happened, Mother?

*(AMANDA draws a long breath, takes out the handkerchief again,
goes through the dabbing process.)*

     Mother, has—something happened?

AMANDA: I'll be all right in a minute, I'm just bewildered— *(She
     hesitates.)* —by life. . . .

LAURA: Mother, I wish that you would tell me what's happened!   30

AMANDA: As you know, I was supposed to be inducted into my
     office at the D.A.R. this afternoon.

(Screen image: A swarm of typewriters.)

     But I stopped off at Rubicam's Business College to speak to
     your teachers about your having a cold and ask them what
     progress they thought you were making down there.   35

LAURA: Oh. . . .

AMANDA: I went to the typing instructor and introduced myself as your mother. She didn't know who you were. "Wingfield," she said, "We don't have any such student enrolled at the school!"

I assured her she did, that you had been going to classes since early in January.

"I wonder," she said, "If you could be talking about that terribly shy little girl who dropped out of school after only a few days' attendance?"

"No," I said, "Laura, my daughter, has been going to school every day for the past six weeks!"

"Excuse me," she said. She took the attendance book out and there was your name, unmistakably printed, and all the dates you were absent until they decided that you had dropped out of school.

I still said, "No, there must have been some mistake! There must have been some mix-up in the records!"

And she said, "No — I remember her perfectly now. Her hands shook so that she couldn't hit the right keys! The first time we gave a speed test, she broke down completely — was sick at the stomach and almost had to be carried into the wash room! After that morning she never showed up any more. We phoned the house but never got any answer" — While I was working at Famous–Barr, I suppose, demonstrating those —

(She indicates a brassiere with her hands.)

Oh! I felt so weak I could barely keep on my feet! I had to sit down while they got me a glass of water! Fifty dollars' tuition, all of our plans — my hopes and ambitions for you — just gone up the spout, just gone up the spout like that.

(LAURA draws a long breath and gets awkwardly to her feet. She crosses to the Victrola and winds it up.)

What are you doing?

LAURA: Oh! (She releases the handle and returns to her seat.)

AMANDA: Laura, where have you been going when you've gone out pretending that you were going to business college?

LAURA: I've just been going out walking.

AMANDA: That's not true.

LAURA: It is. I just went walking.

AMANDA: Walking? Walking? In winter? Deliberately courting pneumonia in that light coat? Where did you walk to, Laura?

LAURA: All sorts of places — mostly in the park.

AMANDA: Even after you'd started catching that cold?

LAURA: It was the lesser of two evils, Mother.

(Screen image: Winter scene in a park.)

I couldn't go back there. I — threw up — on the floor!

AMANDA: From half past seven till after five every day you mean to tell me you walked around in the park, because you wanted to make me think that you were still going to Rubicam's Business College?

LAURA: It wasn't as bad as it sounds. I went inside places to get warmed up.

AMANDA: Inside where?

LAURA: I went in the art museum and the bird houses at the Zoo. I visited the penguins every day! Sometimes I did without lunch and went to the movies. Lately I've been spending most of my afternoons in the Jewel Box, that big glass house where they raise the tropical flowers.

AMANDA: You did all this to deceive me, just for deception? (LAURA looks down.) Why?

LAURA: Mother, when you're disappointed, you get that awful suffering look on your face, like the picture of Jesus' mother in the museum!

AMANDA: Hush!

LAURA: I couldn't face it.

(There is a pause. A whisper of strings is heard. Legend on screen: "The Crust of Humility.")

AMANDA: (hopelessly fingering the huge pocketbook) So what are we going to do the rest of our lives? Stay home and watch the parades go by? Amuse ourselves with the glass menagerie, darling? Eternally play those worn-out phonograph records your father left as a painful reminder of him? We won't have a business career — we've given that up because it gave us nervous indigestion! (She laughs wearily.) What is there left but dependency all our lives? I know so well what becomes of unmarried women who aren't prepared to occupy a position. I've seen such pitiful cases in the South — barely tolerated spinsters living upon the grudging patronage of sister's husband or brother's wife! — stuck away in some little mousetrap of a room — encouraged by one in-law to visit another — little birdlike women without any nest — eating the crust of humility all their life!

Is that the future that we've mapped out for ourselves? I swear it's the only alternative I can think of! (She pauses.) It isn't a very pleasant alternative, is it? (She pauses again.) Of course — some girls do marry.

(LAURA twists her hands nervously.)

Haven't you ever liked some boy?

LAURA: Yes. I liked one once. (She rises.) I came across his picture a while ago.

AMANDA: (with some interest) He gave you his picture?

LAURA: No, it's in the yearbook.

AMANDA: (disappointed) Oh — a high school boy.

(Screen image: JIM as the high school hero bearing a silver cup.)

LAURA: Yes. His name was Jim. (She lifts the heavy annual from the claw-foot table.) Here he is in The Pirates of Penzance.

AMANDA: (absently) The what?

LAURA: The operetta the senior class put on. He had a wonderful voice and we sat across the aisle from each other Mondays, Wednesdays and Fridays in the Aud. Here he is with the silver cup for debating! See his grin?

AMANDA: (absently) He must have had a jolly disposition.

LAURA: He used to call me — Blue Roses.

(Screen image: Blue roses.)

AMANDA: Why did he call you such a name as that?

LAURA: When I had that attack of pleurosis — he asked me what was the matter when I came back. I said pleurosis — he thought that I said Blue Roses! So that's what he always called me after that. Whenever he saw me, he'd holler, "Hello, Blue Roses!" I didn't care for the girl that he went out with. Emily Meisenbach. Emily was the best-dressed girl at Soldan. She never struck me, though, as being sincere . . . It says in the Personal Section — they're engaged. That's — six years ago! They must be married by now.

AMANDA: Girls that aren't cut out for business careers usually wind up married to some nice man. (*She gets up with a spark of revival.*) Sister, that's what you'll do!

(LAURA *utters a startled, doubtful laugh. She reaches quickly for a piece of glass.*)

LAURA: But, Mother—

145   AMANDA: Yes? (*She goes over to the photograph.*)

LAURA: (*in a tone of frightened apology*) I'm—crippled!

AMANDA: Nonsense! Laura, I've told you never, never to use that word. Why, you're not crippled, you just have a little defect—hardly noticeable, even! When people have some

150   slight disadvantage like that, they cultivate other things to make up for it—develop charm—and vivacity—and—charm! That's all you have to do! (*She turns again to the photograph.*) One thing your father had *plenty of*—was charm!

(*The scene fades out with music.*)

— SCENE THREE —

Legend on screen: "After the fiasco—"

TOM *speaks from the fire escape landing.*

TOM: After the fiasco at Rubicam's Business College, the idea of getting a gentleman caller for Laura began to play a more and more important part in Mother's calculations. It became an obsession. Like some archetype of the universal uncon-

5   scious, the image of the gentleman caller haunted our small apartment. . . .

(*Screen image: A young man at the door of a house with flowers.*)

An evening at home rarely passed without some allusion to this image, this specter, this hope. . . . Even when he wasn't mentioned, his presence hung in Mother's preoccupied look

10   and in my sister's frightened, apologetic manner—hung like a sentence passed upon the Wingfields!

Mother was a woman of action as well as words. She began to take logical steps in the planned direction. Late that winter and in the early spring—realizing that extra money would be

15   needed to properly feather the nest and plume the bird—she conducted a vigorous campaign on the telephone, roping in subscribers to one of those magazines for matrons called *The Homemaker's Companion*, the type of journal that features the serialized sublimations of ladies of letters who think in

20   terms of delicate cuplike breasts, slim, tapering waists, rich, creamy thighs, eyes like wood smoke in autumn, fingers that soothe and caress like strains of music, bodies as powerful as Etruscan sculpture.

(*Screen image: The cover of a glamor magazine.*)

(AMANDA *enters with the telephone on a long extension cord. She is spotlighted in the dim stage.*)

AMANDA: Ida Scott? This is Amanda Wingfield! We *missed* you at

25   the D.A.R. last Monday! I said to myself: She's probably suffering with that sinus condition! How is that sinus condition?

Horrors! Heaven have mercy!—You're a Christian martyr, yes, that's what you are, a Christian martyr!

Well, I just now happened to notice that your subscription to

30   the *Companion*'s about to expire! Yes, it expires with the next

issue, honey!—just when that wonderful new serial by Bessie Mae Hopper is getting off to such an exciting start. Oh, honey, it's something that you can't miss! You remember how *Gone with the Wind* took everybody by storm! You simply couldn't go out if you hadn't read it. All everybody *talked* was   35 Scarlett O'Hara. Well, this is a book that critics already compare to *Gone with the Wind*. It's the *Gone with the Wind* of the post-World-War generation!—What?—Burning?—Oh, honey, don't let them burn, go take a look in the oven and I'll hold the wire! Heavens—I think she's hung up!   40

(*The scene dims out.*)

(*Legend on screen: "You think I'm in love with Continental Shoemakers?"*)

(*Before the lights come up again, the violent voices of* TOM *and* AMANDA *are heard. They are quarreling behind the portieres. In front of them stands* LAURA *with clenched hands and panicky expression. A clear pool of light is on her figure throughout this scene.*)

TOM: What in Christ's name am I—

AMANDA: (*shrilly*) Don't you use that—

TOM: —supposed to do!

AMANDA: —expression! Not in my—

TOM: Ohhh!   45

AMANDA: —presence! Have you gone out of your senses?

TOM: I have, that's true, *driven* out!

AMANDA: What is the matter with you, you—big—big—IDIOT!

TOM: Look!—I've got *no* thing, no single thing—   50

AMANDA: Lower your voice!

TOM: —in my life here that I can call my OWN! Everything is—

AMANDA: Stop that shouting!

TOM: Yesterday you confiscated my books! You had the nerve to—

AMANDA: I took that horrible novel back to the library—yes!   55 That hideous book by that insane Mr. Lawrence.

(TOM *laughs wildly.*)

I cannot control the output of diseased minds or people who cater to them—

(TOM *laughs still more wildly.*)

BUT I WON'T ALLOW SUCH FILTH BROUGHT INTO MY HOUSE! No, no, no, no, no!   60

TOM: House, house! Who pays rent on it, who makes a slave of himself to—

AMANDA: (*fairly screeching*) Don't you DARE to—

TOM: No, no, I mustn't say things! *I've* got to just—

AMANDA: Let me tell you—   65

TOM: I don't want to hear any more!

(*He tears the portieres open. The dining-room area is lit with a turgid smoky red glow. Now we see* AMANDA; *her hair is in metal curlers and she is wearing a very old bathrobe, much too large for her slight figure, a relic of the faithless Mr. Wingfield. The upright typewriter now stands on the drop-leaf table, along with a wild disarray of manuscripts. The quarrel was probably precipitated by* AMANDA's *interruption of* TOM's *creative labor. A chair lies overthrown on the floor. Their gesticulating shadows are cast on the ceiling by the fiery glow.*)

AMANDA: You *will* hear more, you—

TOM: No, I won't hear more, I'm going out!

AMANDA: You come right back in—

70 TOM: Out, out, out! Because I'm—

AMANDA: Come back here, Tom Wingfield! I'm not through talking to you!

TOM: Oh, go—

LAURA: (desperately)—Tom!

75 AMANDA: You're going to listen, and no more insolence from you! I'm at the end of my patience!

(He comes back toward her.)

TOM: What do you think I'm at? Aren't I supposed to have any patience to reach the end of, Mother? I know, I know. It seems unimportant to you, what I'm doing—what I want to
80 do—having a little difference between them! You don't think that—

AMANDA: I think you've been doing things that you're ashamed of. That's why you act like this. I don't believe that you go every night to the movies. Nobody goes to the movies night
85 after night. Nobody in their right minds goes to the movies as often as you pretend to. People don't go to the movies at nearly midnight, and movies don't let out at two A.M. Come in stumbling. Muttering to yourself like a maniac! You get three hours' sleep and then go to work. Oh, I can picture the
90 way you're doing down there. Moping, doping, because you're in no condition.

TOM: (wildly) No, I'm in no condition!

AMANDA: What right have you got to jeopardize your job? Jeopardize the security of us all? How do you think we'd manage if you
95 were—

TOM: Listen! You think I'm crazy about the warehouse? (He bends fiercely toward her slight figure.) You think I'm in love with the Continental Shoemakers? You think I want to spend fifty-five years down there in that—celotex interior! with—fluorescent—
100 tubes! Look! I'd rather somebody picked up a crowbar and battered out my brains—than go back mornings! I go! Every time you come in yelling that Goddamn "Rise and Shine!" "Rise and Shine!" I say to myself, "How lucky dead people are!" But I get up. I go! For sixty-five dollars a month I give up all that I dream
105 of doing and being ever! And you say self—self's all I ever think of. Why, listen, if self is what I thought of, Mother, I'd be where he is—GONE! (He points to his father's picture.) As far as the system of transportation reaches! (He starts past her. She grabs his arm.) Don't grab at me, Mother!

110 AMANDA: Where are you going?

TOM: I'm going to the movies!

AMANDA: I don't believe that lie!

(TOM crouches toward her, overtowering her tiny figure. She backs away, gasping.)

TOM: I'm going to opium dens! Yes, opium dens, dens of vice and criminals' hangouts, Mother. I've joined the Hogan
115 Gang, I'm a hired assassin, I carry a tommy gun in a violin case! I run a string of cat houses in the Valley! They call me Killer, Killer Wingfield, I'm leading a double-life, a simple, honest warehouse worker by day, by night a dynamic czar of the underworld, Mother. I go to gambling casinos, I spin away
120 fortunes on the roulette table! I wear a patch over one eye and a false mustache, sometimes I put on green whiskers. On those occasions they call me—El Diablo! Oh, I could tell you

many things to make you sleepless! My enemies plan to dynamite this place. They're going to blow us all sky-high some
125 night! I'll be glad, very happy, and so will you! You'll go up, up on a broomstick, over Blue Mountain with seventeen gentlemen callers! You ugly—babbling old—witch. . . . (He goes through a series of violent, clumsy movements, seizing his overcoat, lunging to the door, pulling it fiercely open. The
130 women watch him, aghast. His arm catches in the sleeve of the coat as he struggles to pull it on. For a moment he is pinioned by the bulky garment. With an outraged groan he tears the coat off again, splitting the shoulder of it, and hurls it across the room. It strikes against the shelf of LAURA's glass collection,
135 and there is a tinkle of shattering glass. LAURA cries out as if wounded.)

(Music.)

(Screen legend: "The Glass Menagerie.")

LAURA: (shrilly) My glass!—menagerie. . . . (She covers her face and turns away.)

(But AMANDA is still stunned and stupefied by the "ugly witch" so that she barely notices this occurrence. Now she recovers her speech.)

AMANDA: (in an awful voice) I won't speak to you—until you
140 apologize!

(She crosses through the portieres and draws them together behind her. TOM is left with LAURA. LAURA clings weakly to the mantel with her face averted. TOM stares at her stupidly for a moment. Then he crosses to the shelf. He drops awkwardly on his knees to collect the fallen glass, glancing at LAURA as if he would speak but couldn't.)

("The Glass Menagerie" music steals in as the scene dims out.)

— SCENE FOUR —

The interior of the apartment is dark. There is a faint light in the alley. A deep-voiced bell in a church is tolling the hour of five.

TOM appears at the top of the alley. After each solemn boom of the bell in the tower, he shakes a little noisemaker or rattle as if to express the tiny spasm of man in contrast to the sustained power and dignity of the Almighty. This and the unsteadiness of his advance make it evident that he has been drinking. As he climbs the few steps to the fire escape landing light steals up inside. LAURA appears in the front room in a nightdress. She notices that TOM's bed is empty. TOM fishes in his pockets for his door key, removing a motley assortment of articles in the search, including a shower of movie ticket stubs and an empty bottle. At last he finds the key, but just as he is about to insert it, it slips from his fingers. He strikes a match and crouches below the door.

TOM: (bitterly) One crack—and it falls through!

(LAURA opens the door.)

LAURA: Tom! Tom, what are you doing?

TOM: Looking for a door key.

LAURA: Where have you been all this time?

TOM: I have been to the movies.

LAURA: All this time at the movies?

TOM: There was a very long program. There was a Garbo picture and a Mickey Mouse and a travelogue and a newsreel and a preview of coming attractions. And there was an organ solo
10 and a collection for the Milk Fund—simultaneously—which ended up in a terrible fight between a fat lady and an usher!

LAURA: (*innocently*) Did you have to stay through everything?

TOM: Of course! And, oh, I forgot! There was a big stage show!
15 The headliner on this stage show was Malvolio the Magician. He performed wonderful tricks, many of them, such as pouring water back and forth between pitchers. First it turned to wine and then it turned to beer and then it turned to whisky. I know it was whisky it finally turned into because he needed
20 somebody to come up out of the audience to help him, and I came up—both shows! It was Kentucky Straight Bourbon. A very generous fellow, he gave souvenirs. (*He pulls from his back pocket a shimmering rainbow-colored scarf.*) He gave me this. This is his magic scarf. You can have it, Laura. You wave
25 it over a canary cage and you get a bowl of goldfish. You wave it over the goldfish bowl and they fly away canaries. . . . But the wonderfullest trick of all was the coffin trick. We nailed him into a coffin and he got out of the coffin without removing one nail. (*He has come inside.*) There is a trick that would
30 come in handy for me—get me out of this two-by-four situation! (*He flops onto the bed and starts removing his shoes.*)

LAURA: Tom—shhh!

TOM: What're you shushing me for?

LAURA: You'll wake up Mother.

35 TOM: Goody, goody! Pay 'er back for all those "Rise an' Shines." (*He lies down, groaning.*) You know it don't take much intelligence to get yourself into a nailed-up coffin, Laura. But who in hell ever got himself out of one without removing one nail?

(*As if in answer, the father's grinning photograph lights up. The scene dims out.*)

(*Immediately following, the church bell is heard striking six. At the sixth stroke the alarm clock goes off in AMANDA's room, and after a few moments we hear her calling: "Rise and Shine! Rise and Shine! LAURA, go tell your brother to rise and shine!"*)

TOM: (*sitting up slowly*) I'll rise—but I won't shine.

(*The light increases.*)

40 AMANDA: Laura, tell your brother his coffee is ready.

(*LAURA slips into the front room.*)

LAURA: Tom!—It's nearly seven. Don't make Mother nervous.

(*He stares at her stupidly.*)

(*beseechingly:*) Tom, speak to Mother this morning. Make up with her, apologize, speak to her!

TOM: She won't to me. It's her that started not speaking.

45 LAURA: If you just say you're sorry she'll start speaking.

TOM: Her not speaking—is that such a tragedy?

LAURA: Please—please!

AMANDA: (*calling from the kitchenette*) Laura, are you going to do what I asked you to do, or do I have to get dressed and go
50 out myself?

LAURA: Going, going—soon as I get on my coat!

(*She pulls on a shapeless felt hat with a nervous, jerky movement, pleadingly glancing at TOM. She rushes awkwardly for her coat.*)

The coat is one of AMANDA's, inaccurately made-over, the sleeves too short for LAURA.)

Butter and what else?

AMANDA: (*entering from the kitchenette*) Just butter. Tell them to charge it.

LAURA: Mother, they make such faces when I do that.   55

AMANDA: Sticks and stones can break our bones, but the expression on Mr. Garfinkel's face won't harm us! Tell your brother his coffee is getting cold.

LAURA: (*at the door*) Do what I asked you, will you, will you, Tom?

(*He looks sullenly away.*)

AMANDA: Laura, go now or just don't go at all!   60

LAURA: (*rushing out*) Going—going!

(*A second later she cries out. TOM springs up and crosses to the door. TOM opens the door.*)

TOM: Laura?

LAURA: I'm all right. I slipped, but I'm all right.

AMANDA: (*peering anxiously after her*) If anyone breaks a leg on those fire-escape steps, the landlord ought to be sued for every   65
cent he possesses! (*She shuts the door. Now she remembers she isn't speaking to TOM and returns to the other room.*)

(*As TOM comes listlessly for his coffee, she turns her back to him and stands rigidly facing the window on the gloomy gray vault of the areaway. Its light on her face with its aged but childish features is cruelly sharp, satirical as a Daumier print.*)

(*The music of "Ave Maria" is heard softly.*)

(*TOM glances sheepishly but sullenly at her averted figure and slumps at the table. The coffee is scalding hot; he sips it and gasps and spits it back in the cup. At his gasp, AMANDA catches her breath and half turns. Then she catches herself and turns back to the window. TOM blows on his coffee, glancing sidewise at his mother. She clears her throat. TOM clears his. He starts to rise, sinks back down again, scratches his head, clears his throat again. AMANDA coughs. TOM raises his cup in both hands to blow on it, his eyes staring over the rim of it at his mother for several moments. Then he slowly sets the cup down and awkwardly and hesitantly rises from the chair.*)

TOM: (*hoarsely*) Mother. I—I apologize, Mother.

(*AMANDA draws a quick, shuddering breath. Her face works grotesquely. She breaks into childlike tears.*)

I'm sorry for what I said, for everything that I said, I didn't mean it.   70

AMANDA: (*sobbingly*) My devotion has made me a witch and so I make myself hateful to my children!

TOM: No, you *don't*.

AMANDA: I worry so much, don't sleep, it makes me nervous!

TOM: (*gently*) I understand that.   75

AMANDA: I've had to put up a solitary battle all these years. But you're my right-hand bower! Don't fall down, don't fail!

TOM: (*gently*) I try, Mother.

AMANDA: (*with great enthusiasm*) Try and you will *succeed!* (*The notion makes her breathless.*) Why, you—you're just *full* of   80
natural endowments! Both of my children—they're *unusual* children! Don't you think I know it? I'm so—*proud!* Happy and—feel I've—so much to be thankful for but—promise me one thing, son!

85 TOM: What, Mother?

AMANDA: Promise, son, you'll—never be a drunkard!

TOM: (turns to her grinning) I will never be a drunkard, Mother.

AMANDA: That's what frightened me so, that you'd be drinking! Eat a bowl of Purina!

90 TOM: Just coffee, Mother.

AMANDA: Shredded wheat biscuit?

TOM: No. No, Mother, just coffee.

AMANDA: You can't put in a day's work on an empty stomach. You've got ten minutes—don't gulp! Drinking too-hot liquids

95 makes cancer of the stomach. . . . Put cream in.

TOM: No, thank you.

AMANDA: To cool it.

TOM: No! No, thank you, I want it black.

AMANDA: I know, but it's not good for you. We have to do all that

100 we can to build ourselves up. In these trying times we live in, all that we have to cling to is—each other. . . . That's why it's so important to—Tom, I—sent out your sister so I could discuss something with you. If you hadn't spoken I would have spoken to you. (She sits down.)

105 TOM: (gently) What is it, Mother, that you want to discuss?

AMANDA: Laura!

(TOM puts his cup down slowly.)

(Legend on screen: "Laura." Music: "The Glass Menagerie.")

TOM: —Oh. —Laura . . .

AMANDA: (touching his sleeve) You know how Laura is. So quiet but—still water runs deep! She notices things and I think

110 she—broods about them.

(TOM looks up.)

A few days ago I came in and she was crying.

TOM: What about?

AMANDA: You.

TOM: Me?

115 AMANDA: She has an idea that you're not happy here.

TOM: What gave her that idea?

AMANDA: What gives her any idea? However, you do act strangely. I—I'm not criticizing, understand that! I know your ambitions do not lie in the warehouse, that like everybody in the

120 whole wide world—you've had to—make sacrifices, but—Tom—Tom—life's not easy, it calls for—Spartan endurance! There's so many things in my heart that I cannot describe to you! I've never told you but I—loved your father. . . .

TOM: (gently) I know that, Mother.

125 AMANDA: And you—when I see you taking after his ways! Staying out late—and—well, you had been drinking the night you were in that—terrifying condition! Laura says that you hate the apartment and that you go out nights to get away from it! Is that true, Tom?

130 TOM: No. You say there's so much in your heart that you can't describe to me. That's true of me, too. There's so much in my heart that I can't describe to you! So let's respect each other's—

AMANDA: But, why—why, Tom—are you always so restless? Where do you go to, nights?

135 TOM: I—go to the movies.

AMANDA: Why do you go to the movies so much, Tom?

TOM: I go to the movies because—I like adventure. Adventure is something I don't have much of at work, so I go to the movies.

AMANDA: But, Tom, you go to the movies entirely too much!

140 TOM: I like a lot of adventure.

(AMANDA looks baffled, then hurt. As the familiar inquisition resumes, TOM becomes hard and impatient again. AMANDA slips back into her querulous attitude toward him.)

(Image on screen: A sailing vessel with Jolly Roger.)

AMANDA: Most young men find adventure in their careers.

TOM: Then most young men are not employed in a warehouse.

AMANDA: The world is full of young men employed in warehouses and offices and factories.

145 TOM: Do all of them find adventure in their careers?

AMANDA: They do or they do without it! Not everybody has a craze for adventure.

TOM: Man is by instinct a lover, a hunter, a fighter, and none of those instincts are given much play at the warehouse!

150 AMANDA: Man is by instinct! Don't quote instinct to me! Instinct is something that people have got away from! It belongs to animals! Christian adults don't want it!

TOM: What do Christian adults want, then, Mother?

AMANDA: Superior things! Things of the mind and the spirit!

155 Only animals have to satisfy instincts! Surely your aims are somewhat higher than theirs! Than monkeys—pigs—

TOM: I reckon they're not.

AMANDA: You're joking. However, that isn't what I wanted to discuss.

160 TOM: (rising) I haven't much time.

AMANDA: (pushing his shoulders) Sit down.

TOM: You want me to punch in red at the warehouse, Mother?

AMANDA: You have five minutes. I want to talk about Laura.

(Screen legend: "Plans and Provisions.")

TOM: All right! What about Laura?

165 AMANDA: We have to be making some plans and provisions for her. She's older than you, two years, and nothing has happened. She just drifts along doing nothing. It frightens me terribly how she just drifts along.

TOM: I guess she's the type that people call home girls.

170 AMANDA: There's no such type, and if there is, it's a pity! That is unless the home is hers, with a husband!

TOM: What?

AMANDA: Oh, I can see the handwriting on the wall as plain as I see the nose in front of my face! It's terrifying! More and more

175 you remind me of your father! He was out all hours without explanation!—Then left! Goodbye! And me with the bag to hold. I saw that letter you got from the Merchant Marine. I know what you're dreaming of. I'm not standing here blindfolded. (She pauses.) Very well, then. Then do it! But not till there's somebody to take your place.

180 TOM: What do you mean?

AMANDA: I mean that as soon as Laura has got somebody to take care of her, married, a home of her own, independent—why, then you'll be free to go wherever you please, on land, on sea, whichever way the wind blows you! But until that time you've

185 got to look out for your sister. I don't say me because I'm old and don't matter! I say for your sister because she's young and dependent.

I put her in business college—a dismal failure! Frightened her so it made her sick at the stomach. I took her over to the

190 Young People's League at the church. Another fiasco. She spoke to nobody, nobody spoke to her. Now all she does is fool with those pieces of glass and play those worn-out records. What kind of a life is that for a girl to lead?

195   TOM: What can I do about it?
AMANDA: Overcome selfishness! Self, self, self is all that you
    ever think of!

(TOM *springs up and crosses to get his coat. It is ugly and bulky.
He pulls on a cap with earmuffs.*)

    Where is your muffler? Put your wool muffler on!

(*He snatches it angrily from the closet, tosses it around his neck
and pulls both ends tight.*)

    Tom! I haven't said what I had in mind to ask you.
200   TOM: I'm too late to—
AMANDA: (*catching his arm—very importunately; then shyly*)
    Down at the warehouse, aren't there some—nice young men?
TOM: No!
AMANDA: There *must* be—*some* . . .
205   TOM: Mother—(*He gestures.*)
AMANDA: Find out one that's clean-living—doesn't drink and
    ask him out for sister!
TOM: What?
AMANDA: For *sister!* To *meet! Get acquainted!*
210   TOM: (*stamping to the door*) Oh, my *go-osh!*
AMANDA: Will you?

(*He opens the door. She says, imploringly:*)

    Will you?

(*He starts down the fire escape.*)

    Will you? *Will* you, dear?
TOM: (*calling back*) Yes!

(AMANDA *closes the door hesitantly and with a troubled but
faintly hopeful expression.*)

(*Screen image:* The cover of a glamor magazine.)

(*The spotlight picks up* AMANDA *at the phone.*)

215   AMANDA: Ella Cartwright? This is Amanda Wingfield!
    How are you, honey?
    How is that kidney condition?

(*There is a five-second pause.*)

    Horrors!

(*There is another pause.*)

    You're a Christian martyr, yes, honey, that's what you are, a
220   Christian martyr! Well, I just now happened to notice in my
    little red book that your subscription to the *Companion* has
    just run out! I knew that you wouldn't want to miss out on the
    wonderful serial starting in this new issue. It's by Bessie Mae
    Hopper, the first thing she's written since *Honeymoon for*
225   *Three.* Wasn't that a strange and interesting story? Well, this
    one is even lovelier, I believe. It has a sophisticated, society
    background. It's all about the horsey set on Long Island!

(*The light fades out.*)

— SCENE FIVE —

Legend on the screen: "Annunciation."

Music is heard as the light slowly comes on.

*It is early dusk of a spring evening. Supper has just been finished
in the Wingfield apartment.* AMANDA *and* LAURA, *in light-colored dresses, are removing dishes from the table in the dining
room, which is shadowy, their movements formalized almost as a
dance or ritual, their moving forms as pale and silent as moths.*
TOM, *in white shirt and trousers, rises from the table and crosses
toward the fire escape.*

AMANDA: (*as he passes her*) Son, will you do me a favor?
TOM: What?
AMANDA: Comb your hair! You look so pretty when your hair is
    combed!

(TOM *slouches on the sofa with the evening paper. Its enormous
headline reads:* "Franco Triumphs.")

    There is only one respect in which I would like you to emu-   5
    late your father.
TOM: What respect is that?
AMANDA: The care he always took of his appearance. He never
    allowed himself to look untidy.

(*He throws down the paper and crosses to the fire escape.*)

    Where are you going?   10
TOM: I'm going out to smoke.
AMANDA: You smoke too much. A pack a day at fifteen cents a
    pack. How much would that amount to in a month? Thirty
    times fifteen is how much, Tom? Figure it out and you will be
    astounded at what you could save. Enough to give you a   15
    night-school course in accounting at Washington U! Just
    think what a wonderful thing that would be for you, son!

(TOM *is unmoved by the thought.*)

TOM: I'd rather smoke. (*He steps out on the landing, letting the
    screen door slam.*)
AMANDA: (*sharply*) I know! That's the tragedy of it. . . . (*Alone,   20
    she turns to look at her husband's picture.*)

(*Dance music:* "The World Is Waiting for the Sunrise!")

TOM: (*to the audience*) Across the alley from us was the Paradise
    Dance Hall. On evenings in spring the windows and doors
    were open and the music came outdoors. Sometimes the
    lights were turned out except for a large glass sphere that hung   25
    from the ceiling. It would turn slowly about and filter the
    dusk with delicate rainbow colors. Then the orchestra played
    a waltz or a tango, something that had a slow and sensuous
    rhythm. Couples would come outside, to the relative privacy
    of the alley. You could see them kissing behind ash pits and   30
    telephone poles. This was the compensation for lives that
    passed like mine, without any change or adventure. Adven-
    ture and change were imminent in this year. They were wait-
    ing around the corner for all these kids. Suspended in the mist
    over Berchtesgaden, caught in the folds of Chamberlain's   35
    umbrella. In Spain there was Guernica! But here there was
    only hot swing music and liquor, dance halls, bars, and
    movies, and sex that hung in the gloom like a chandelier and
    flooded the world with brief, deceptive rainbows. . . . All the
    world was waiting for bombardments!   40

(AMANDA *turns from the picture and comes outside.*)

AMANDA: (*sighing*) A fire escape landing's a poor excuse for a
    porch. (*She spreads a newspaper on a step and sits down,*

gracefully and demurely as if she were settling into a swing on a Mississippi veranda.) What are you looking at?

45 TOM: The moon.

AMANDA: Is there a moon this evening?

TOM: It's rising over Garfinkel's Delicatessen.

AMANDA: So it is! A little silver slipper of a moon. Have you made a wish on it yet?

50 TOM: Um-hum.

AMANDA: What did you wish for?

TOM: That's a secret.

AMANDA: A secret, huh? Well, I won't tell mine either. I will be just as mysterious as you.

55 TOM: I bet I can guess what yours is.

AMANDA: Is my head so transparent?

TOM: You're not a sphinx.

AMANDA: No, I don't have secrets. I'll tell you what I wished for on the moon. Success and happiness for my precious chil-

60 dren! I wish for that whenever there's a moon, and when there isn't a moon, I wish for it, too.

TOM: I thought perhaps you wished for a gentleman caller.

AMANDA: Why do you say that?

TOM: Don't you remember asking me to fetch one?

65 AMANDA: I remember suggesting that it would be nice for your sister if you brought home some nice young man from the warehouse. I think that I've made that suggestion more than once.

TOM: Yes, you have made it repeatedly.

70 AMANDA: Well?

TOM: We are going to have one.

AMANDA: *What?*

TOM: A gentleman caller!

(The annunciation is celebrated with music.)

(AMANDA rises.)

(Image on screen: A caller with a bouquet.)

AMANDA: You mean you have asked some nice young man to

75 come over?

TOM: Yep. I've asked him to dinner.

AMANDA: You really did?

TOM: I did!

AMANDA: You did, and did he — *accept?*

80 TOM: He did!

AMANDA: Well, well — well, well! That's — lovely!

TOM: I thought that you would be pleased.

AMANDA: It's definite then?

TOM: Very definite.

85 AMANDA: Soon?

TOM: Very soon.

AMANDA: For heaven's sake, stop putting on and tell me some things, will you?

TOM: What things do you want me to tell you?

90 AMANDA: *Naturally* I would like to know when he's *coming!*

TOM: He's coming tomorrow.

AMANDA: *Tomorrow?*

TOM: Yep. Tomorrow.

AMANDA: But, Tom!

95 TOM: Yes, Mother?

AMANDA: Tomrrow gives me no time!

TOM: Time for what?

AMANDA: Preparations! Why didn't you phone me at once, as soon as you asked him, the minute that he accepted? Then don't you see, I could have been getting ready!   100

TOM: You don't have to make any fuss.

AMANDA: Oh, Tom, Tom, Tom, of course I have to make a fuss! I want things nice, not sloppy! Not thrown together. I'll certainly have to do some fast thinking, won't I?

TOM: I don't see why you have to think at all.   105

AMANDA: You just don't know. We can't have a gentleman caller in a pigsty! All my wedding silver has to be polished, the monogrammed table linen ought to be laundered! The windows have to be washed and fresh curtains put up. And how about clothes? We have to *wear* something, don't we?   110

TOM: Mother, this boy is no one to make a fuss over!

AMANDA: Do you realize he's the first young man we've introduced to your sister? It's terrible, dreadful, disgraceful that poor little sister has never received a single gentleman caller! Tom, come inside! *(She opens the screen door.)*   115

TOM: What for?

AMANDA: I want to ask you some things.

TOM: If you're going to make such a fuss, I'll call it off, I'll tell him not to come!

AMANDA: You certainly won't do anything of the kind. Nothing   120
offends people worse than broken engagements. It simply means I'll have to work like a Turk! We won't be brilliant, but we will pass inspection. Come on inside.

(TOM follows her inside, groaning.)

Sit down.

TOM: Any particular place you would like me to sit?   125

AMANDA: Thank heavens I've got that new sofa! I'm also making payments on a floor lamp I'll have sent out! And put the chintz covers on, they'll brighten things up! Of course I'd hoped to have these walls re-papered. . . . What is the young man's name?   130

TOM: His name is O'Connor.

AMANDA: That, of course, means fish — tomorrow is Friday! I'll have that salmon loaf — with Durkee's dressing! What does he do? He works at the warehouse?

TOM: Of course! How else would I —   135

AMANDA: Tom, he — doesn't drink?

TOM: Why do you ask me that?

AMANDA: Your father *did!*

TOM: Don't get started on that!

AMANDA: He *does* drink, then?   140

TOM: Not that I know of!

AMANDA: Make sure, be certain! The last thing I want for my daughter's a boy who drinks!

TOM: Aren't you being a little bit premature? Mr. O'Connor has not yet appeared on the scene!   145

AMANDA: But will tomorrow. To meet your sister, and what do I know about his character? Nothing! Old maids are better off than wives of drunkards!

TOM: Oh, my God!

AMANDA: Be still!   150

TOM: *(leaning forward to whisper)* Lots of fellows meet girls whom they don't marry!

AMANDA: Oh, talk sensibly, Tom — and don't be sarcastic! *(She has gotten a hairbrush.)*

TOM: What are you doing?   155

AMANDA: I'm brushing that cowlick down! (*She attacks his hair with the brush.*) What is this young man's position at the warehouse?

TOM: (*submitting grimly to the brush and the interrogation*) This young man's position is that of a shipping clerk, Mother.

AMANDA: Sounds to me like a fairly responsible job, the sort of a job *you* would be in if you just had more *get-up.* What is his salary? Have you any idea?

TOM: I would judge it to be approximately eighty-five dollars a month.

AMANDA: Well — not princely, but —

TOM: Twenty more than I make.

AMANDA: Yes, how well I know! But for a family man, eighty-five dollars a month is not much more than you can just get by on. . . .

TOM: Yes, but Mr. O'Connor is not a family man.

AMANDA: He might be, mightn't he? Some time in the future?

TOM: I see. Plans and provisions.

AMANDA: You are the only young man that I know of who ignores the fact that the future becomes the present, the present the past, and the past turns into everlasting regret if you don't plan for it!

TOM: I will think that over and see what I can make of it.

AMANDA: Don't be supercilious with your mother! Tell me some more about this — what do you call him?

TOM: James D. O'Connor. The D. is for Delaney.

AMANDA: Irish on *both* sides! *Gracious!* And doesn't drink?

TOM: Shall I call him up and ask him right this minute?

AMANDA: The only way to find out about those things is to make discreet inquiries at the proper moment. When I was a girl in Blue Mountain and it was suspected that a young man drank, the girl whose attentions he had been receiving, if any girl *was,* would sometimes speak to the minister of his church, or rather her father would if her father was living, and sort of feel him out on the young man's character. That is the way such things are discreetly handled to keep a young woman from making a tragic mistake!

TOM: Then how did you happen to make a tragic mistake?

AMANDA: That innocent look of your father's had everyone fooled! He *smiled* — the world was *enchanted!* No girl can do worse than put herself at the mercy of a handsome appearance! I hope that Mr. O'Connor is not too good-looking.

TOM: No, he's not too good-looking. He's covered with freckles and hasn't too much of a nose.

AMANDA: He's not right-down homely, though?

TOM: Not right-down homely. Just medium homely, I'd say.

AMANDA: Character's what to look for in a man.

TOM: That's what I've always said, Mother.

AMANDA: You've never said anything of the kind and I suspect you would never give it a thought.

TOM: Don't be so suspicious of me.

AMANDA: At least I hope he's the type that's up and coming.

TOM: I think he really goes in for self-improvement.

AMANDA: What reason have you to think so?

TOM: He goes to night school.

AMANDA: (*beaming*) Splendid! What does he do, I mean study?

TOM: Radio engineering and public speaking!

AMANDA: Then he has visions of being advanced in the world! Any young man who studies public speaking is aiming to have an executive job some day! And radio engineering? A thing for the future! Both of these facts are very illuminating. Those

are the sort of things that a mother should know concerning any young man who comes to call on her daughter. Seriously or — not.

TOM: One little warning. He doesn't know about Laura. I didn't let on that we had dark ulterior motives. I just said, why don't you come and have dinner with us? He said okay and that was the whole conversation.

AMANDA: I bet it was! You're eloquent as an oyster. However, he'll know about Laura when he gets here. When he sees how lovely and sweet and pretty she is, he'll thank his lucky stars he was asked to dinner.

TOM: Mother, you mustn't expect too much of Laura.

AMANDA: What do you mean?

TOM: Laura seems all those things to you and me because she's ours and we love her. We don't even notice she's crippled any more.

AMANDA: Don't say crippled! You know that I never allow that word to be used!

TOM: But face facts, Mother. She is and — that's not all —

AMANDA: What do you mean "not all"?

TOM: Laura is very different from other girls.

AMANDA: I think the difference is all to her advantage.

TOM: Not quite all — in the eyes of others — strangers — she's terribly shy and lives in a world of her own and those things make her seem a little peculiar to people outside the house.

AMANDA: Don't say peculiar.

TOM: Face the facts. She is.

(*The dance hall music changes to a tango that has a minor and somewhat ominous tone.*)

AMANDA: In what way is she peculiar — may I ask?

TOM: (*gently*) She lives in a world of her own — a world of little glass ornaments, Mother. . . .

(*He gets up.* AMANDA *remains holding the brush, looking at him, troubled.*)

She plays old phonograph records and — that's about all — (*He glances at himself in the mirror and crosses to the door.*)

AMANDA: (*sharply*) Where are you going?

TOM: I'm going to the movies. (*He goes out the screen door.*)

AMANDA: Not to the movies, every night to the movies! (*She follows quickly to the screen door.*) I don't believe you always go to the movies!

(*He is gone.* AMANDA *looks worriedly after him for a moment. Then vitality and optimism return and she turns from the door, crossing to the portieres.*)

Laura! Laura!

(LAURA *answers from the kitchenette.*)

LAURA: Yes, Mother.

AMANDA: Let those dishes go and come in front!

(LAURA *appears with a dish towel.* AMANDA *speaks to her gaily.*)

Laura, come here and make a wish on the moon!

(*Screen image:* The Moon.)

LAURA: (*entering*) Moon — moon?

AMANDA: A little silver slipper of a moon. Look over your left shoulder, Laura, and make a wish!

(LAURA *looks faintly puzzled as if called out of sleep.* AMANDA *seizes her shoulders and turns her at an angle by the door.*)

Now! Now, darling, *wish!*

LAURA: What shall I wish for, Mother?

AMANDA: *(her voice trembling and her eyes suddenly filling with tears)* Happiness! Good fortune!

(*The sound of the violin rises and the stage dims out.*)

— SCENE SIX —

The light comes up on the fire escape landing. TOM *is leaning against the grill, smoking.*

(Screen image: The high school hero.)

TOM: And so the following evening I brought Jim home to dinner. I had known Jim slightly in high school. In high school
Jim was a hero. He had tremendous Irish good nature and
vitality with the scrubbed and polished look of white china-
5   ware. He seemed to move in a continual spotlight. He was a
star in basketball, captain of the debating club, president of
the senior class and the glee club and he sang the male lead in
the annual light operas. He was always running or bounding,
never just walking. He seemed always at the point of defeating
10   the law of gravity. He was shooting with such velocity through
his adolescence that you would logically expect him to arrive
at nothing short of the White House by the time he was thirty.
But Jim apparently ran into more interference after his gradu-
ation from Soldan. His speed had definitely slowed. Six years
15   after he left high school he was holding a job that wasn't
much better than mine.

(Screen image: The Clerk.)

He was the only one at the warehouse with whom I was on
friendly terms. I was valuable to him as someone who could
remember his former glory, who had seen him win basketball
20   games and the silver cup in debating. He knew of my secret
practice of retiring to a cabinet of the washroom to work on
poems when business was slack in the warehouse. He called
me Shakespeare. And while the other boys in the warehouse
regarded me with suspicious hostility, Jim took a humorous
25   attitude toward me. Gradually his attitude affected the others,
their hostility wore off and they also began to smile at me as
people smile at an oddly fashioned dog who trots across their
path at some distance.
    I knew that Jim and Laura had known each other at Sol-
30   dan, and I had heard Laura speak admiringly of his voice. I
didn't know if Jim remembered her or not. In high school
Laura had been as unobtrusive as Jim had been astonishing.
If he did remember Laura, it was not as my sister, for when I
asked him to dinner, he grinned and said, "You know, Shake-
35   speare, I never thought of you as having folks!"
    He was about to discover that I did. . . .

(Legend on screen: "The accent of a coming foot.")

(*The light dims out on* TOM *and comes up in the* Wingfield *living room — a delicate lemony light. It is about five on a Friday eve-ning of late spring which comes "scattering poems in the sky."*)

(AMANDA *has worked like a Turk in preparation for the gentle-man caller. The results are astonishing. The new floor lamp with its rose silk shade is in place, a colored paper lantern conceals the broken light fixture in the ceiling, new billowing white curtains are at the windows, chintz covers are on the chairs and sofa, a pair of new sofa pillows make their initial appearance. Open boxes and tissue paper are scattered on the floor.*)

(LAURA *stands in the middle of the room with lifted arms while* AMANDA *crouches before her, adjusting the hem of a new dress, devout and ritualistic. The dress is colored and designed by mem-ory. The arrangement of* LAURA's *hair is changed; it is softer and more becoming. A fragile, unearthly prettiness has come out in* LAURA: *she is like a piece of translucent glass touched by light, given a momentary radiance, not actual, not lasting.*)

AMANDA: *(impatiently)* Why are you trembling?

LAURA: Mother, you've made me so nervous!

AMANDA: How have I made you nervous?

LAURA: By all this fuss! You make it seem so important!   40

AMANDA: I don't understand you, Laura. You couldn't be satisfied with just sitting home, and yet whenever I try to arrange
something for you, you seem to resist it. *(She gets up.)* Now
take a look at yourself. No, wait! Wait just a moment — I have
an idea!   45

LAURA: What is it now?

(AMANDA *produces two powder puffs which she wraps in hand-kerchiefs and stuffs in* LAURA's *bosom.*)

LAURA: Mother, what are you doing?

AMANDA: They call them "Gay Deceivers"!

LAURA: I won't wear them!

AMANDA: You will!   50

LAURA: Why should I?

AMANDA: Because, to be painfully honest, your chest is flat.

LAURA: You make it seem like we were setting a trap.

AMANDA: All pretty girls are a trap, a pretty trap, and men expect
them to be.   55

(Legend on screen: "A pretty trap.")

Now look at yourself, young lady. This is the prettiest you will
ever be! *(She stands back to admire* LAURA.*)* I've got to fix
myself now! You're going to be surprised by your mother's
appearance!

(AMANDA *crosses through the portieres, humming gaily.* LAURA *moves slowly to the long mirror and stares solemnly at herself. A wind blows the white curtains inward in a slow, graceful motion and with a faint, sorrowful sighing.*)

AMANDA: *(from somewhere behind the portieres)* It isn't dark   60
enough yet.

(LAURA *turns slowly before the mirror with a troubled look.*)

(Legend on screen: "This is my sister: Celebrate her with strings!" *Music plays.*)

AMANDA: *(laughing, still not visible)* I'm going to show you
something. I'm going to make a spectacular appearance!

LAURA: What is it, Mother?

AMANDA: Possess your soul in patience — you will see! Some-   65
thing I've resurrected from that old trunk! Styles haven't
changed so terribly much after all. . . . *(She parts the por-tieres.)* Now just look at your mother! *(She wears a girlish*

frock of yellowed voile with a blue silk sash. She carries a bunch
70 *of jonquils — the legend of her youth is nearly revived. Now she*
speaks feverishly:) This is the dress in which I led the cotillion.
Won the cakewalk twice at Sunset Hill, wore one Spring to
the Governor's Ball in Jackson! See how I sashayed around
the ballroom, Laura? *(She raises her skirt and does a mincing*
75 *step around the room.)* I wore it on Sundays for my gentlemen
callers! I had it on the day I met your father. . . . I had malaria
fever all that Spring. The change of climate from East Tennessee to the Delta — weakened resistance. I had a little temperature all the time — not enough to be serious — just enough
80 to make me restless and giddy! Invitations poured in — parties
all over the Delta! "Stay in bed," said Mother, "you have a
fever!" — but I just wouldn't. I took quinine but kept on
going, going! Evenings, dances! Afternoons, long, long rides!
Picnics — lovely! So lovely, that country in May — all lacy
85 with dogwood, literally flooded with jonquils! That was the
spring I had the craze for jonquils. Jonquils became an absolute obsession. Mother said, "Honey, there's no more room
for jonquils." And still I kept on bringing in more jonquils.
Whenever, wherever I saw them, I'd say "Stop! Stop! I see
90 jonquils!" I made the young men help me gather the jonquils! It was a joke, Amanda and her jonquils. Finally there
were no more vases to hold them, every available space was
filled with jonquils. No vases to hold them? All right, I'll hold
them myself! And then I — *(She stops in front of the picture.*
95 *Music plays.)* met your father! Malaria fever and jonquils and
then — this — boy. . . . *(She switches on the rose-colored*
lamp.) I hope they get here before it starts to rain. *(She crosses*
the room and places the jonquils in a bowl on the table.) I gave
your brother a little extra change so he and Mr. O'Connor
100 could take the service car home.
LAURA: *(with an altered look)* What did you say his name was?
AMANDA: O'Connor.
LAURA: What is his first name?
AMANDA: I don't remember. Oh, yes, I do. It was — Jim!

(LAURA sways slightly and catches hold of a chair.)

(Legend on screen: "Not Jim!")

105 LAURA: *(faintly)* Not — Jim!
AMANDA: Yes, that was it, it was Jim! I've never known a Jim that
wasn't nice!

(The music becomes ominous.)

LAURA: Are you sure his name is Jim O'Connor?
AMANDA: Yes. Why?
110 LAURA: Is he the one that Tom used to know in high school?
AMANDA: He didn't say so. I think he just got to know him at the
warehouse.
LAURA: There was a Jim O'Connor we both knew in high school
— *(then, with effort)* If that is the one that Tom is bringing to
115 dinner — you'll have to excuse me, I won't come to the table.
AMANDA: What sort of nonsense is this?
LAURA: You asked me once if I'd ever liked a boy. Don't you
remember I showed you this boy's picture?
AMANDA: You mean the boy you showed me in the yearbook?
120 LAURA: Yes, that boy.
AMANDA: Laura, Laura, were you in love with that boy?
LAURA: I don't know, Mother. All I know is I couldn't sit at the
table if it was him!

AMANDA: It won't be him! It isn't the least bit likely. But whether
it is or not, you will come to the table. You will not be excused.   125
LAURA: I'll have to be, Mother.
AMANDA: I don't intend to humor your silliness, Laura. I've had
too much from you and your brother, both! So just sit down
and compose yourself till they come. Tom has forgotten his
key so you'll have to let them in, when they arrive.   130
LAURA: *(panicky)* Oh, Mother — *you* answer the door!
AMANDA: *(lightly)* I'll be in the kitchen — busy!
LAURA: Oh, Mother, please answer the door, don't make me do it!
AMANDA: *(crossing into the kitchenette)* I've got to fix the dressing for the salmon. Fuss, fuss — silliness! — over a gentleman   135
caller!

(The door swings shut. LAURA is left alone.)

(Legend on screen: "Terror!")

(She utters a low moan and turns off the lamp — sits stiffly on the
edge of the sofa, knotting her fingers together.)

(Legend on screen: "The Opening of a Door!")

(TOM and JIM appear on the fire escape steps and climb to the
landing. Hearing their approach, LAURA rises with a panicky
gesture. She retreats to the portieres. The doorbell rings. LAURA
catches her breath and touches her throat. Low drums sound.)

AMANDA: *(calling)* Laura, sweetheart! The door!

(LAURA stares at it without moving.)

JIM: I think we just beat the rain.
TOM: Uh-huh. *(He rings again, nervously. JIM whistles and*
fishes for a cigarette.)   140
AMANDA: *(very, very gaily)* Laura, that is your brother and Mr.
O'Connor! Will you let them in, darling?

(LAURA crosses toward the kitchenette door.)

LAURA: *(breathlessly)* Mother — you go to the door!

(AMANDA steps out of the kitchenette and stares furiously at
LAURA. She points imperiously at the door.)

LAURA: Please, please!
AMANDA: *(in a fierce whisper)* What is the matter with you, you   145
silly thing?
LAURA: *(desperately)* Please, you answer it, *please!*
AMANDA: I told you I wasn't going to humor you, Laura. Why
have you chosen this moment to lose your mind?
LAURA: Please, please, please, you go!   150
AMANDA: You'll have to go to the door because I can't!
LAURA: *(despairingly)* I can't either!
AMANDA: *Why?*
LAURA: I'm *sick!*
AMANDA: I'm sick, too — of your nonsense! Why can't you and   155
your brother be normal people? Fantastic whims and behavior!

(TOM gives a long ring.)

Preposterous goings on! Can you give me one reason — *(She*
calls out lyrically.) Coming! Just one second! — why you
should be afraid to open a door? Now you answer it, Laura!
LAURA: Oh, oh, oh . . . *(She returns through the portieres, darts*   160
to the Victrola, winds it frantically and turns it on.)
AMANDA: Laura Wingfield, you march right to that door!
LAURA: Yes — yes, Mother!

(A faraway, scratchy rendition of "Dardanella" softens the air and gives her strength to move through it. She slips to the door and draws it cautiously open. TOM *enters with the caller,* JIM O'CONNOR.*)*

TOM: Laura, this is Jim. Jim, this is my sister, Laura.

165 JIM: *(stepping inside)* I didn't know that Shakespeare had a sister!

LAURA: *(retreating, stiff and trembling, from the door)* How—how do you do?

JIM: *(heartily, extending his hand)* Okay!

*(*LAURA *touches it hesitantly with hers.)*

JIM: Your hand's cold, Laura!

170 LAURA: Yes, well—I've been playing the Victrola. . . .

JIM: Must have been playing classical music on it! You ought to play a little hot swing music to warm you up!

LAURA: Excuse me—I haven't finished playing the Victrola. . . . *(She turns awkwardly and hurries into the front room. She*

175 *pauses a second by the Victrola. Then she catches her breath and darts through the portieres like a frightened deer.)*

JIM: *(grinning)* What was the matter?

TOM: Oh—with Laura? Laura is—terribly shy.

JIM: Shy, huh? It's unusual to meet a shy girl nowadays. I don't

180 believe you ever mentioned you had a sister.

TOM: Well, now you know. I have one. Here is the *Post Dispatch*. You want a piece of it?

JIM: Uh-huh.

TOM: What piece? The comics?

185 JIM: Sports! *(He glances at it.)* Ole Dizzy Dean is on his bad behavior.

TOM: *(uninterested)* Yeah? *(He lights a cigarette and goes over to the fire-escape door.)*

JIM: Where are *you* going?

190 TOM: I'm going out on the terrace.

JIM: *(going after him)* You know, Shakespeare—I'm going to sell you a bill of goods!

TOM: What goods?

JIM: A course I'm taking.

195 TOM: Huh?

JIM: In public speaking! You and me, we're not the warehouse type.

TOM: Thanks—that's good news. But what has public speaking got to do with it?

200 JIM: It fits you for—executive positions!

TOM: Awww.

JIM: I tell you it's done a helluva lot for me.

(Image on screen: Executive at his desk.)

TOM: In what respect?

JIM: In every! Ask yourself what is the difference between you

205 an' me and men in the office down front? Brains?—No!—Ability?—No! Then what? Just one little thing—

TOM: What is that one little thing?

JIM: Primarily it amounts to—social poise! Being able to square up to people and hold your own on any social level!

210 AMANDA *(from the kitchenette)* Tom?

TOM: Yes, Mother.

AMANDA: Is that you and Mr. O'Connor?

TOM: Yes, Mother.

AMANDA: Well, you just make yourselves comfortable in there.

215 TOM: Yes, Mother.

AMANDA: Ask Mr. O'Connor if he would like to wash his hands.

JIM: Aw, no—no—thank you—I took care of that at the warehouse. Tom—

TOM: Yes?

JIM: Mr. Mendoza was speaking to me about you.   220

TOM: Favorably?

JIM: What do you think?

TOM: Well—

JIM: You're going to be out of a job if you don't wake up.

TOM: I am waking up—   225

JIM: You show no signs.

TOM: The signs are interior.

(Image on screen: The sailing vessel with the Jolly Roger again.)

TOM: I'm planning to change. *(He leans over the fire-escape rail, speaking with quiet exhilaration. The incandescent marquees and signs of the first-run movie houses light his face from across*   230
the alley. He looks like a voyager.) I'm right at the point of committing myself to a future that doesn't include the warehouse and Mr. Mendoza or even a night-school course in public speaking.

JIM: What are you gassing about?   235

TOM: I'm tired of the movies.

JIM: Movies!

TOM: Yes, movies! Look at them— *(a wave toward the marvels of Grand Avenue)* All of those glamorous people—having adventures—hogging it all, gobbling the whole thing up! You   240
know what happens? People go to the *movies* instead of *moving*! Hollywood characters are supposed to have all the adventures for everybody in America, while everybody in America sits in a dark room and watches them have them! Yes, until there's a war. That's when adventure becomes available to the   245
masses! *Everyone's* dish, not only Gable's! Then the people in the dark room come out of the dark room to have some adventures themselves—goody, goody! It's our turn now, to go to the South Sea Island—to make a safari—to be exotic, far-off! But I'm not patient. I don't want to wait till then. I'm tired of   250
the *movies* and I am *about* to *move*!

JIM: *(incredulously)* Move?

TOM: Yes.

JIM: When?

TOM: Soon!   255

JIM: Where? Where?

(The music seems to answer the question, while TOM *thinks it over. He searches in his pockets.)*

TOM: I'm starting to boil inside. I know I seem dreamy, but inside—well, I'm boiling! Whenever I pick up a shoe, I shudder a little thinking how short life is and what I am doing!—Whatever that means, I know it doesn't mean shoes—except   260
as something to wear on a traveler's feet! *(He finds what he has been searching for in his pockets and holds out a paper to Jim.)* Look—

JIM: What?

TOM: I'm a member.   265

JIM: *(reading)* The Union of Merchant Seamen.

TOM: I paid my dues this month, instead of the light bill.

JIM: You will regret it when they turn the lights off.

TOM: I won't be here.

JIM: How about your mother?   270

TOM: I'm like my father. The bastard son of a bastard! Did you notice how he's grinning in his picture in there? And he's been absent going on sixteen years!

JIM: You're just talking, you drip. How does your mother feel about it?

TOM: Shhh! Here comes Mother! Mother is not acquainted with my plans!

AMANDA: (coming through the portieres) Where are you all?

TOM: On the terrace, Mother.

(They start inside. She advances to them. TOM is distinctly shocked at her appearance. Even JIM blinks a little. He is making his first contact with girlish Southern vivacity and in spite of the night-school course in public speaking is somewhat thrown off the beam by the unexpected outlay of social charm. Certain responses are attempted by JIM but are swept aside by AMANDA's gay laughter and chatter. TOM is embarrassed but after the first shock JIM reacts very warmly. He grins and chuckles, is altogether won over.)

(Image on screen: AMANDA as a girl.)

AMANDA: (coyly smiling, shaking her girlish ringlets) Well, well, well, so this is Mr. O'Connor. Introductions entirely unnecessary. I've heard so much about you from my boy. I finally said to him, Tom—good gracious!—why don't you bring this paragon to supper? I'd like to meet this nice young man at the warehouse!—instead of just hearing him sing your praises so much! I don't know why my son is so stand-offish—that's not Southern behavior!

Let's sit down and—I think we could stand a little more air in here! Tom, leave the door open. I felt a nice fresh breeze a moment ago. Where has it gone to? Mmm, so warm already! And not quite summer, even. We're going to burn up when summer really gets started. However, we're having—we're having a very light supper. I think light things are better fo' this time of year. The same as light clothes are. Light clothes an' light food are what warm weather calls fo'. You know our blood gets so thick during th' winter—it takes a while fo' us to adjust ou'selves!—when the season changes . . . It's come so quick this year. I wasn't prepared. All of a sudden—heavens! Already summer! I ran to the trunk an' pulled out this light dress—terribly old! Historical almost! But feels so good—so good an' co-ol, y' know. . . .

TOM: Mother—

AMANDA: Yes, honey?

TOM: How about—supper?

AMANDA: Honey, you go ask Sister if supper is ready! You know that Sister is in full charge of supper! Tell her you hungry boys are waiting for it. (to JIM) Have you met Laura?

JIM: She—

AMANDA: Let you in? Oh, good, you've met already! It's rare for a girl as sweet an' pretty as Laura to be domestic! But Laura is, thank heavens, not only pretty but also very domestic. I'm not at all. I never was a bit. I never could make a thing but angel-food cake. Well, in the South we had so many servants. Gone, gone, gone. All vestige of gracious living! Gone completely! I wasn't prepared for what the future brought me. All of my gentlemen callers were sons of planters and so of course I assumed that I would be married to one and raise my family on a large piece of land with plenty of servants. But man

proposes—and woman accepts the proposal! To vary that old, old saying a little bit—I married no planter! I married a man who worked for the telephone company! That gallantly smiling gentleman over there! (She points to the picture.) A telephone man who—fell in love with long-distance! Now he travels and I don't even know where! But what am I going on for about my—tribulations? Tell me yours—I hope you don't have any! Tom?

TOM: (returning) Yes, Mother?

AMANDA: Is supper nearly ready?

TOM: It looks to me like supper is on the table.

AMANDA: Let me look—(She rises prettily and looks through the portieres.) Oh, lovely! But where is Sister?

TOM: Laura is not feeling well and she says that she thinks she'd better not come to the table.

AMANDA: What? Nonsense! Laura? Oh, Laura!

LAURA: (from the kitchenette, faintly) Yes, Mother.

AMANDA: You really must come to the table. We won't be seated until you come to the table! Come in, Mr. O'Connor. You sit over there, and I'll. . . . Laura? Laura Wingfield! You're keeping us waiting, honey! We can't say grace until you come to the table!

(The kitchenette door is pushed weakly open and LAURA comes in. She is obviously quite faint, her lips trembling, her eyes wide and staring. She moves unsteadily toward the table.)

(Screen legend: "Terror!")

(Outside a summer storm is coming on abruptly. The white curtains billow inward at the windows and there is a sorrowful murmur from the deep blue dusk.)

(LAURA suddenly stumbles; she catches at a chair with a faint moan.)

TOM: Laura!

AMANDA: Laura!

(There is a clap of thunder.)

(Screen legend: "Ah!")

(despairingly) Why, Laura, you are ill, darling! Tom, help your sister into the living room, dear! Sit in the living room, Laura—rest on the sofa. Well! (to JIM as TOM helps his sister to the sofa in the living room) Standing over the hot stove made her ill! I told her that it was just too warm this evening, but—

(TOM comes back to the table.)

Is Laura all right now?

TOM: Yes.

AMANDA: What is that? Rain? A nice cool rain has come up! (She gives JIM a frightened look.) I think we may—have grace—now . . .

(TOM looks at her stupidly.) Tom, honey—you say grace!

TOM: Oh . . . "For these and all thy mercies—"

(They bow their heads, AMANDA stealing a nervous glance at JIM. In the living room LAURA, stretched on the sofa, clenches her hand to her lips, to hold back a shuddering sob.)

God's Holy Name be praised—

(The scene dims out.)

— SCENE SEVEN —

It is half an hour later. Dinner is just being finished in the dining room, LAURA *is still huddled upon the sofa, her feet drawn under her, her head resting on a pale blue pillow, her eyes wide and mysteriously watchful. The new floor lamp with its shade of rose-colored silk gives a soft, becoming light to her face, bringing out the fragile, unearthly prettiness which usually escapes attention. From outside there is a steady murmur of rain, but it is slackening and soon stops; the air outside becomes pale and luminous as the moon breaks through the clouds. A moment after the curtain rises, the lights in both rooms flicker and go out.*

JIM: Hey, there, Mr. Light Bulb!

*(*AMANDA *laughs nervously.)*

(Legend on screen: "Suspension of a public service.")

AMANDA: Where was Moses when the lights went out? Ha-ha. Do you know the answer to that one, Mr. O'Connor?

LAURA: No, Ma'am, what's the answer?

5 AMANDA: In the dark!

*(*JIM *laughs appreciatively.)*

Everybody sit still. I'll light the candles. Isn't it lucky we have them on the table? Where's a match? Which of you gentlemen can provide a match?

JIM: Here.

10 AMANDA: Thank you, Sir.

JIM: Not at all, Ma'am!

AMANDA: *(as she lights the candles)* I guess the fuse has burnt out. Mr. O'Connor, can you tell a burnt-out fuse? I know I can't and Tom is a total loss when it comes to mechanics.

(They rise from the table and go into the kitchenette, from where their voices are heard.)

15 Oh, be careful you don't bump into something. We don't want our gentleman caller to break his neck. Now wouldn't that be a fine howdy-do?

JIM: Ha-ha! Where is the fuse-box?

AMANDA: Right here next to the stove. Can you see anything?

20 JIM: Just a minute.

AMANDA: Isn't electricity a mysterious thing? Wasn't it Benjamin Franklin who tied a key to a kite? We live in such a mysterious universe, don't we? Some people say that science clears up all the mysteries for us. In my opinion it only creates

25 more! Have you found it yet?

JIM: No, Ma'am. All these fuses look okay to me.

AMANDA: Tom!

TOM: Yes, Mother?

AMANDA: That light bill I gave you several days ago. The one I

30 told you we got the notices about?

(Legend on screen: "Ha!")

TOM: Oh—yeah.

AMANDA: You didn't neglect to pay it by any chance?

TOM: Why, I—

AMANDA: Didn't! I might have known it!

35 JIM: Shakespeare probably wrote a poem on that light bill, Mrs. Wingfield.

AMANDA: I might have known better than to trust him with it! There's such a high price for negligence in this world!

JIM: Maybe the poem will win a ten-dollar prize.

40 AMANDA: We'll just have to spend the remainder of the evening in the nineteenth century, before Mr. Edison made the Mazda lamp!

JIM: Candlelight is my favorite kind of light.

AMANDA: That shows you're romantic! But that's no excuse for

45 Tom. Well, we got through dinner. Very considerate of them to let us get through dinner before they plunged us into everlasting darkness, wasn't it, Mr. O'Connor?

JIM: Ha-ha!

AMANDA: Tom, as a penalty for your carelessness you can help

50 me with the dishes.

JIM: Let me give you a hand.

AMANDA: Indeed you will not!

JIM: I ought to be good for something.

AMANDA: Good for something? *(Her tone is rhapsodic.)* You?

55 Why, Mr. O'Connor, nobody, *nobody's* given me this much entertainment in years—as you have!

JIM: Aw, now, Mrs. Wingfield!

AMANDA: I'm not exaggerating, not one bit! But Sister is all by her lonesome. You go keep her company in the parlor! I'll

60 give you this lovely old candelabrum that used to be on the altar at the Church of the Heavenly Rest. It was melted a little out of shape when the church burnt down. Lightning struck it one spring. Gypsy Jones was holding a revival at the time and he intimated that the church was destroyed because the Epis-

65 copalians gave card parties.

JIM: Ha-ha.

AMANDA: And how about you coaxing Sister to drink a little wine? I think it would be good for her! Can you carry both at once?

70 JIM: Sure. I'm Superman!

AMANDA: Now, Thomas, get into this apron!

*(*JIM *comes into the dining room, carrying the candelabrum, its candles lighted, in one hand and a glass of wine in the other. The door of the kitchenette swings closed on* AMANDA's *gay laughter; the flickering light approaches the portieres.* LAURA *sits up nervously as* JIM *enters. She can hardly speak from the almost intolerable strain of being alone with a stranger.)*

(Screen legend: "I don't suppose you remember me at all!")

(At first, before JIM's *warmth overcomes her paralyzing shyness,* LAURA's *voice is thin and breathless, as though she had just run up a steep flight of stairs.* JIM's *attitude is gently humorous. While the incident is apparently unimportant, it is to* LAURA *the climax of her secret life.)*

JIM: Hello there, Laura.

LAURA: *(faintly)* Hello.

(She clears her throat.)

JIM: How are you feeling now? Better?

75 LAURA: Yes. Yes, thank you.

JIM: This is for you. A little dandelion wine. *(He extends the glass toward her with extravagant gallantry.)*

LAURA: Thank you.

JIM: Drink it—but don't get drunk!

(He laughs heartily. LAURA *takes the glass uncertainly; she laughs shyly.)*

Where shall I set the candles?   80

LAURA: Oh—oh, anywhere . . .

JIM: How about here on the floor? Any objections?

LAURA: No.

JIM: I'll spread a newspaper under to catch the drippings. I like to
85 sit on the floor. Mind if I do?

LAURA: Oh, no.

JIM: Give me a pillow?

LAURA: What?

JIM: A pillow!

90 LAURA: Oh . . . (*She hands him one quickly.*)

JIM: How about you? Don't you like to sit on the floor?

LAURA: Oh—yes.

JIM: Why don't you, then?

LAURA: I—will.

95 JIM: Take a pillow!

   (LAURA *does. She sits on the floor on the other side of the candelabrum.* JIM *crosses his legs and smiles engagingly at her.*) I
   can't hardly see you sitting way over there.

LAURA: I can—see you.

100 JIM: I know, but that's not fair, I'm in the limelight.

(LAURA *moves her pillow closer.*)

   Good! Now I can see you! Comfortable?

LAURA: Yes.

JIM: So am I. Comfortable as a cow! Will you have some gum?

LAURA: No, thank you.

105 JIM: I think that I will indulge, with your permission. (*He mus-
   ingly unwraps a stick of gum and holds it up.*) Think of the
   fortune made by the guy that invented the first piece of chewing gum. Amazing, huh? The Wrigley Building is one of the
   sights of Chicago—I saw it when I went up to the Century of
110 Progress. Did you take in the Century of Progress?

LAURA: No, I didn't.

JIM: Well, it was quite a wonderful exposition. What impressed
   me most was the Hall of Science. Gives you an idea of what
   the future will be in America, even more wonderful than the
115 present time is! (*There is a pause. Jim smiles at her.*) Your
   brother tells me you're shy. Is that right, Laura?

LAURA: I—don't know.

JIM: I judge you to be an old-fashioned type of girl. Well, I think
   that's a pretty good type to be. Hope you don't think I'm being
120 too personal—do you?

LAURA: (*hastily, out of embarrassment*) I believe I *will* take a
   piece of gum, if you—don't mind. (*clearing her throat*) Mr.
   O'Connor, have you—kept up with your singing?

JIM: Singing? Me?

125 LAURA: Yes. I remember what a beautiful voice you had.

JIM: When did you hear me sing?

(LAURA *does not answer, and in the long pause which follows a
man's voice is heard singing offstage.*)

VOICE:
   O blow, ye winds, heigh-ho,
   A-roving I will go!
130 I'm off to my love
   With a boxing glove—
   Ten thousand miles away!

JIM: You say you've heard me sing?

LAURA: Oh, yes! Yes, very often . . . I—don't suppose—you
135 remember me—at all?

JIM: (*smiling doubtfully*) You know I have an idea I've seen you
   before. I had that idea soon as you opened the door. It seemed
   almost like I was about to remember your name. But the
   name that I started to call you—wasn't a name! And so I
   stopped myself before I said it.   140

LAURA: Wasn't it—Blue Roses?

JIM: (*springing up, grinning*) Blue Roses! My gosh, yes—Blue
   Roses! That's what I had on my tongue when you opened the
   door! Isn't it funny what tricks your memory plays? I didn't
   connect you with high school somehow or other. But that's   145
   where it was; it was high school. I didn't even know you were
   Shakespeare's sister! Gosh, I'm sorry.

LAURA: I didn't expect you to. You—barely knew me!

JIM: But we did have a speaking acquaintance, huh?

LAURA: Yes, we—spoke to each other.   150

JIM: When did you recognize me?

LAURA: Oh, right away!

JIM: Soon as I came in the door?

LAURA: When I heard your name I thought it was probably you.
   I knew that Tom used to know you a little in high school. So   155
   when you came in the door—well, then I was—sure.

JIM: Why didn't you *say* something, then?

LAURA: (*breathlessly*) I didn't know what to say, I was—too
   surprised!

JIM: For goodness' sakes! You know, this sure is funny!   160

LAURA: Yes! Yes, isn't it, though . . .

JIM: Didn't we have a class in something together?

LAURA: Yes, we did.

JIM: What class was that?

LAURA: It was—singing—chorus!   165

JIM: Aw!

LAURA: I sat across the aisle from you in the Aud.

JIM: Aw.

LAURA: Mondays, Wednesdays, and Fridays.

JIM: Now I remember—you always came in late.   170

LAURA: Yes, it was so hard for me, getting upstairs. I had that
   brace on my leg—it clumped so loud!

JIM: I never heard any clumping.

LAURA: (*wincing at the recollection*) To me it sounded like—
   thunder!   175

JIM: Well, well, well, I never even noticed.

LAURA: And everybody was seated before I came in. I had to walk
   in front of all those people. My seat was in the back row. I had
   to go clumping all the way up the aisle with everyone watching!

JIM: You shouldn't have been self-conscious.   180

LAURA: I know, but I was. It was always such a relief when the
   singing started.

JIM: Aw, yes, I've placed you now! I used to call you Blue Roses.
   How was it that I got started calling you that?

LAURA: I was out of school a little while with pleurosis. When I   185
   came back you asked me what was the matter. I said I had
   pleurosis—you thought I said *Blue Roses.* That's what you
   always called me after that!

JIM: I hope you didn't mind.

LAURA: Oh, no—I liked it. You see, I wasn't acquainted with   190
   many—people. . . .

JIM: As I remember you sort of stuck by yourself.

LAURA: I—I—never have had much luck at—making friends.

JIM: I don't see why you wouldn't.

LAURA: Well, I—started out badly.   195

JIM: You mean being—
LAURA: Yes, it sort of—stood between me—
JIM: You shouldn't have let it!
LAURA: I know, but it did, and—
200 JIM: You were shy with people!
LAURA: I tried not to be but never could—
JIM: Overcome it?
LAURA: No, I—I never could!
JIM: I guess being shy is something you have to work out of kind
205   of gradually.
LAURA: *(sorrowfully)* Yes—I guess it—
JIM: Takes time!
LAURA: Yes—
JIM: People are not so dreadful when you know them. That's
210   what you have to remember! And everybody has problems,
       not just you, but practically everybody has got some prob-
       lems. You think of yourself as having the only problems, as
       being the only one who is disappointed. But just look around
       you and you will see lots of people as disappointed as you are.
215   For instance, I hoped when I was going to high school that I
       would be further along at this time, six years later, than I am
       now. You remember that wonderful write-up I had in *The
       Torch?*
LAURA: Yes! *(She rises and crosses to the table.)*
220 JIM: It said I was bound to succeed in anything I went into!

(LAURA returns with the high school yearbook.)

   Holy Jeez! *The Torch!*

*(He accepts it reverently. They smile across the book with mutual
wonder. LAURA crouches beside him and they begin to turn the
pages. LAURA's shyness is dissolving in his warmth.)*

LAURA: Here you are in *The Pirates of Penzance!*
JIM: *(wistfully)* I sang the baritone lead in that operetta.
LAURA: *(raptly)* So—*beautifully!*
225 JIM: *(protesting)* Aw—
LAURA: Yes, yes—beautifully—beautifully!
JIM: You heard me?
LAURA: All three times!
JIM: No!
230 LAURA: Yes!
JIM: All three performances?
LAURA: *(looking down)* Yes.
JIM: Why?
LAURA: I—wanted to ask you to—autograph my program. *(She
235   takes the program from the back of the yearbook and shows it
       to him.)*
JIM: Why didn't you ask me to?
LAURA: You were always surrounded by your own friends so
       much that I never had a chance to.
240 JIM: You should have just—
LAURA: Well, I—thought you might think I was—
JIM: Thought I might think you was—what?
LAURA: Oh—
JIM: *(with reflective relish)* I was beleaguered by females in those
245   days.
LAURA: You were terribly popular!
JIM: Yeah—
LAURA: You had such a—friendly way—
JIM: I was spoiled in high school.

LAURA: Everybody—liked you!   250
JIM: Including you?
LAURA: I—yes, I—did, too—*(She gently closes the book in her
       lap.)*
JIM: Well, well, well! Give me that program, Laura.

(She hands it to him. He signs it with a flourish.)

   There you are—better late than never!   255
LAURA: Oh, I—want a—surprise!
JIM: My signature isn't worth very much right now. But some
       day—maybe—it will increase in value! Being disappointed is
       one thing and being discouraged is something else. I am dis-
       appointed but I am not discouraged. I'm twenty-three years   260
       old. How old are you?
LAURA: I'll be twenty-four in June.
JIM: That's not old age!
LAURA: No, but—
JIM: You finished high school?   265
LAURA: *(with difficulty)* I didn't go back.
JIM: You mean you dropped out?
LAURA: I made bad grades in my final examinations. *(She rises
       and replaces the book and the program on the table. Her voice
       is strained.)* How is—Emily Meisenbach getting along?   270
JIM: Oh, that kraut-head!
LAURA: Why do you call her that?
JIM: That's what she was.
LAURA: You're not still—going with her?
JIM: I never see her.   275
LAURA: It said in the "Personal" section that you were—engaged!
JIM: I know, but I wasn't impressed by that—propaganda!
LAURA: It wasn't—the truth?
JIM: Only in Emily's optimistic opinion!
LAURA: Oh—   280

(Legend: "What have you done since high school?")

*(JIM lights a cigarette and leans indolently back on his elbows
smiling at LAURA with a warmth and charm which lights her
inwardly with altar candles. She remains by the table, picks up a
piece from the glass menagerie collection, and turns it in her
hands to cover her tumult.)*

JIM: *(after several reflective puffs on his cigarette)* What have you
       done since high school?

(She seems not to hear him.)

   Huh?

(LAURA looks up.)

   I said what have you done since high school, Laura?
LAURA: Nothing much.   285
JIM: You must have been doing something these six long years.
LAURA: Yes.
JIM: Well, then, such as what?
LAURA: I took a business course at business college—
JIM: How did that work out?   290
LAURA: Well, not very—well—I had to drop out, it gave me—
       indigestion—

(JIM laughs gently.)

JIM: What are you doing now?

LAURA: I don't do anything—much. Oh, please don't think I sit
295   around doing nothing! My glass collection takes up a good
deal of time. Glass is something you have to take good care of.

JIM: What did you say—about glass?

LAURA: Collection I said—I have one—(*She clears her throat
and turns away again, acutely shy.*)

300   JIM: (*abruptly*) You know what I judge to be the trouble with
you? Inferiority complex! Know what that is? That's what they
call it when someone low-rates himself! I understand it because I had it, too. Although my case was not so aggravated as
yours seems to be. I had it until I took up public speaking,
305   developed my voice, and learned that I had an aptitude for
science. Before that time I never thought of myself as being
outstanding in any way whatsoever! Now I've never made a
regular study of it, but I have a friend who says I can analyze
people better than doctors that make a profession of it. I don't
310   claim that to be necessarily true, but I can sure guess a person's psychology, Laura! (*He takes out his gum.*) Excuse me,
Laura. I always take it out when the flavor is gone. I'll use this
scrap of paper to wrap it in. I know how it is to get it stuck on a
shoe. (*He wraps the gum in paper and puts it in his pocket.*)
315   Yep—that's what I judge to be your principal trouble. A lack
of confidence in yourself as a person. You don't have the
proper amount of faith in yourself. I'm basing that fact on a
number of your remarks and also on certain observations I've
made. For instance that clumping you thought was so awful
320   in high school. You say that you even dreaded to walk into
class. You see what you did? You dropped out of school, you
gave up an education because of a clump, which as far as I
know was practically non-existent! A little physical defect is
what you have. Hardly noticeable even! Magnified thousands
325   of times by imagination! You know what my strong advice to
you is? Think of yourself as *superior* in some way!

LAURA: In what way would I think?

JIM: Why, man alive, Laura! Just look about you a little. What
do you see? A world full of common people! All of 'em born
330   and all of 'em going to die! Which of them has one-tenth of
your good points! Or mine! Or anyone else's, as far as that
goes—gosh! Everybody excels in some one thing. Some in
many! (*He unconsciously glances at himself in the mirror.*) All
you've got to do is discover in *what*! Take me, for instance.
335   (*He adjusts his tie at the mirror.*) My interest happens to lie in
electro-dynamics. I'm taking a course in radio engineering at
night school, Laura, on top of a fairly responsible job at the
warehouse. I'm taking that course and studying public
speaking.

340   LAURA: Ohhhh.

JIM: Because I believe in the future of television! (*turning his
back to her.*) I wish to be ready to go up right along with it.
Therefore I'm planning to get in on the ground floor. In fact
I've already made the right connections and all that remains is
345   for the industry itself to get under way! Full steam—(*His eyes
are starry.*) Knowledge—Zzzzzp! Money—Zzzzzp!—Power!
That's the cycle democracy is built on!

(*His attitude is convincingly dynamic.* LAURA *stares at him,
even her shyness eclipsed in her absolute wonder. He suddenly
grins.*)

I guess you think I think a lot of myself!

LAURA: No—o-o-o, I—

JIM: Now how about you? Isn't there something you take more   350
interest in than anything else?

LAURA: Well, I do—as I said—have my—glass collection—

(*A peal of girlish laughter rings from the kitchenette.*)

JIM: I'm not right sure I know what you're talking about. What
kind of glass is it?

LAURA: Little articles of it, they're ornaments mostly! Most of   355
them are little animals made out of glass, the tiniest little
animals in the world. Mother calls them a glass menagerie!
Here's an example of one, if you'd like to see it! This one is
one of the oldest. It's nearly thirteen.

(*Music: "The Glass Menagerie."*)

(*He stretches out his hand.*)

Oh, be careful—if you breathe, it breaks!   360

JIM: I'd better not take it. I'm pretty clumsy with things.

LAURA: Go on, I trust you with him! (*She places the piece in his
palm.*) There now—you're holding him gently! Hold him
over the light, he loves the light! You see how the light shines
through him?   365

JIM: It sure does shine!

LAURA: I shouldn't be partial, but he is my favorite one.

JIM: What kind of a thing is this one supposed to be?

LAURA: Haven't you noticed the single horn on his forehead?

JIM: A unicorn, huh?   370

LAURA: Mmmm-hmmm!

JIM: Unicorns—aren't they extinct in the modern world?

LAURA: I know!

JIM: Poor little fellow, he must feel sort of lonesome.

LAURA: (*smiling*) Well, if he does, he doesn't complain about it.   375
He stays on a shelf with some horses that don't have horns and
all of them seem to get along nicely together.

JIM: How do you know?

LAURA: (*lightly*) I haven't heard any arguments among them!

JIM: (*grinning*) No arguments, huh? Well, that's a pretty good   380
sign! Where shall I set him?

LAURA: Put him on the table. They all like a change of scenery
once in a while!

JIM: Well, well, well, well—(*He places the glass piece on the
table, then raises his arms and stretches.*) Look how big my   385
shadow is when I stretch!

LAURA: Oh, oh, yes—it stretches across the ceiling!

JIM: (*crossing to the door*) I think it's stopped raining. (*He opens
the fire-escape door and the background music changes to a
dance tune.*) Where does the music come from?   390

LAURA: From the Paradise Dance Hall across the alley.

JIM: How about cutting the rug a little, Miss Wingfield?

LAURA: Oh, I—

JIM: Or is your program filled up? Let me have a look at it. (*He
grasps an imaginary card.*) Why, every dance is taken! I'll just   395
have to scratch some out.

(*Waltz music: "La Golondrina."*)

Ahhh, a waltz! (*He executes some sweeping turns by himself,
then holds his arms toward Laura.*)

LAURA: (*breathlessly*) I—can't dance!

JIM: There you go, that inferiority stuff!   400

LAURA: I've never danced in my life!

JIM: Come on, try!

LAURA: Oh, but I'd step on you!

JIM: I'm not made out of glass.

405 LAURA: How—how—how do we start?

JIM: Just leave it to me. You hold your arms out a little.

LAURA: Like this?

JIM: (taking her in his arms) A little bit higher. Right. Now don't tighten up, that's the main thing about it—relax.

410 LAURA: (laughing breathlessly) It's hard not to.

JIM: Okay.

LAURA: I'm afraid you can't budge me.

JIM: What do you bet I can't? (He swings her into motion.)

LAURA: Goodness, yes, you can!

415 JIM: Let yourself go, now, Laura, just let yourself go.

LAURA: I'm—

JIM: Come on!

LAURA: —trying!

JIM: Not so stiff—easy does it!

420 LAURA: I know but I'm—

JIM: Loosen th' backbone! There now, that's a lot better.

LAURA: Am I?

JIM: Lots, lots better! (He moves her about the room in a clumsy waltz.)

425 LAURA: Oh, my!

JIM: Ha-ha!

LAURA: Oh, my goodness!

JIM: Ha-ha-ha!

(They suddenly bump into the table, and the glass piece on it falls to the floor. JIM stops the dance.)

What did we hit on?

430 LAURA: Table.

JIM: Did something fall off it? I think—

LAURA: Yes.

JIM: I hope that it wasn't the little glass horse with the horn!

LAURA: Yes. (She stoops to pick it up.)

435 JIM: Aw, aw, aw. Is it broken?

LAURA: Now it is just like all the other horses.

JIM: It's lost its—

LAURA: Horn! It doesn't matter. Maybe it's a blessing in disguise.

JIM: You'll never forgive me. I bet that that was your favorite

440 piece of glass.

LAURA: I don't have favorites much. It's no tragedy, Freckles. Glass breaks so easily. No matter how careful you are. The traffic jars the shelves and things fall off them.

JIM: Still I'm awfully sorry that I was the cause.

445 LAURA: (smiling) I'll just imagine he had an operation. The horn was removed to make him feel less—freakish!

(They both laugh.)

Now he will feel more at home with the other horses, the ones that don't have horns. . . .

JIM: Ha-ha, that's very funny! (Suddenly he is serious.) I'm glad

450 to see that you have a sense of humor. You know—you're—well—very different! Surprisingly different from anyone else I know! (His voice becomes soft and hesitant with a genuine feeling.) Do you mind me telling you that?

(LAURA is abashed beyond speech.)

I mean it in a nice way—

(LAURA nods shyly, looking away.)

You make me feel sort of—I don't know how to put it! I'm   455
usually pretty good at expressing things, but—this is something that I don't know how to say!

(LAURA touches her throat and clears it—turns the broken unicorn in her hands. His voice becomes softer.)

Has anyone ever told you that you were pretty?

(There is a pause, and the music rises slightly. LAURA looks up slowly, with wonder, and shakes her head.)

Well, you are! In a very different way from anyone else. And all the nicer because of the difference, too.   460

(His voice becomes low and husky. LAURA turns away, nearly faint with the novelty of her emotions.)

I wish that you were my sister. I'd teach you to have some confidence in yourself. The different people are not like other people, but being different is nothing to be ashamed of. Because other people are not such wonderful people. They're one hundred times one thousand. You're one times one!   465
They walk all over the earth. You just stay here. They're common as—weeds, but—you—well, you're—Blue Roses!

(Image on screen: Blue Roses.)

(The music changes.)

LAURA: But blue is wrong for—roses. . . .

JIM: It's right for you! You're—pretty!

LAURA: In what respect am I pretty?   470

JIM: In all respects—believe me! Your eyes—your hair—are pretty! (He catches hold of her hand.) You think I'm making this up because I'm invited to dinner and have to be nice. Oh, I could do that! I could put on an act for you, Laura, and say lots of things without being very sin-   475
cere. But this time I am. I'm talking to you sincerely. I happened to notice you had this inferiority complex that keeps you from feeling comfortable with people. Somebody needs to build your confidence up and make you proud instead of shy and turning away and—blushing. Somebody—ought   480
to—kiss you, Laura!

(His hand slips slowly up her arm to her shoulder as the music swells tumultuously. He suddenly turns her about and kisses her on the lips. When he releases her, LAURA sinks on the sofa with a bright, dazed look. JIM backs away and fishes in his pocket for a cigarette.)

(Legend on screen: "A souvenir.")

Stumblejohn!

(He lights the cigarette, avoiding her look. There is a peal of girlish laughter from AMANDA in the kitchenette. LAURA slowly raises and opens her hand. It still contains the little broken glass animal. She looks at it with a tender, bewildered expression.)

Stumblejohn! I shouldn't have done that—that was way off the beam. You don't smoke, do you?

(She looks up, smiling, not hearing the question. He sits beside her rather gingerly. She looks at him speechlessly—waiting. He coughs decorously and moves a little farther aside as he considers *the situation and senses her feelings, dimly, with perturbation. He speaks gently.)*

485   Would you — care for a — mint?

(She doesn't seem to hear him but her look grows brighter even.)

Peppermint? Life Saver? My pocket's a regular drugstore — wherever I go. . . . *(He pops a mint in his mouth. Then he gulps and decides to make a clean breast of it. He speaks slowly and gingerly.)* Laura, you know, if I had a sister like you, I'd do the same thing as Tom. I'd bring out fellows and — introduce her to them. The right type of boys — of a type to — appreciate her. Only — well — he made a mistake about me. Maybe I've got no call to be saying this. That may not have been the idea in having me over. But what if it was? There's nothing wrong about that. The only trouble is that in my case — I'm not in a situation to — do the right thing. I can't take down your number and say I'll phone. I can't call up next week and — ask for a date. I thought I had better explain the situation in case you — misunderstood it and — I hurt your feelings. . . .

(There is a pause. Slowly, very slowly, LAURA's look changes, her eyes returning slowly from his to the glass figure in her palm. AMANDA utters another gay laugh in the kitchenette.)

LAURA: *(faintly)* You — won't — call again?

JIM: No, Laura. I can't. *(He rises from the sofa.)* As I was just explaining, I've — got strings on me. Laura, I've — been going steady! I go out all the time with a girl named Betty. She's a home-girl like you, and Catholic, and Irish, and in a great many ways we — get along fine. I met her last summer on a moonlight boat trip up the river to Alton, on the *Majestic.* Well — right away from the start it was — love!

(Legend: Love!)

(LAURA sways slightly forward and grips the arm of the sofa. He fails to notice, now enrapt in his own comfortable being.)

The power of love is really pretty tremendous! Love is something that — changes the whole world, Laura!

(The storm abates a little and LAURA leans back. He notices her again.)

It happened that Betty's aunt took sick, she got a wire and had to go to Centralia. So Tom — when he asked me to dinner — I naturally just accepted the invitation, not knowing that you — that he — that I — *(He stops awkwardly.)* Huh — I'm a stumblejohn!

(He flops back on the sofa. The holy candles on the altar of LAURA's face have been snuffed out. There is a look of almost infinite desolation. JIM glances at her uneasily.)

I wish that you would — say something.

(She bites her lip which was trembling and then bravely smiles. She opens her hand again on the broken glass figure. Then she gently takes his hand and raises it level with her own. She care-

fully places the unicorn in the palm of his hand, then pushes his fingers closed upon it.)

What are you — doing that for? You want me to have him? Laura?

(She nods.)

What for?   515

LAURA: A — souvenir. . . .

(She rises unsteadily and crouches beside the Victrola to wind it up.)

(Legend on screen: "Things have a way of turning out so badly!" Or image: "Gentleman caller waving goodbye — gaily.")

(At this moment AMANDA rushes brightly back into the living room. She bears a pitcher of fruit punch in an old-fashioned cut-glass pitcher, and a plate of macaroons. The plate has a gold border and poppies painted on it.)

AMANDA: Well, well, well! Isn't the air delightful after the shower? I've made you children a little liquid refreshment.

(She turns gaily to JIM.) Jim, do you know that song about lemonade?   520

"Lemonade, lemonade
Made in the shade and stirred with a spade —
Good enough for any old maid!"

JIM: *(uneasily)* Ha-ha! No — I never heard it.

AMANDA: Why, Laura! You look so serious!   525

JIM: We were having a serious conversation.

AMANDA: Good! Now you're better acquainted!

JIM: *(uncertainly)* Ha-ha! Yes.

AMANDA: You modern young people are much more serious-minded than my generation. I was so gay as a girl!   530

JIM: You haven't changed, Mrs. Wingfield.

AMANDA: Tonight I'm rejuvenated! The gaiety of the occasion, Mr. O'Connor! *(She tosses her head with a peal of laughter, spilling some lemonade.)* Oooo! I'm baptizing myself!

JIM: Here — let me —   535

AMANDA: *(setting the pitcher down)* There now. I discovered we had some maraschino cherries. I dumped them in, juice and all!

JIM: You shouldn't have gone to that trouble, Mrs. Wingfield.

AMANDA: Trouble, trouble? Why, it was loads of fun! Didn't you   540
hear me cutting up in the kitchen? I bet your ears were burning! I told Tom how outdone with him I was for keeping you to himself so long a time! He should have brought you over much, much sooner! Well, now that you've found your way, I want you to be a very frequent caller! Not just occasional but   545
all the time. Oh, we're going to have a lot of gay times together! I see them coming! Mmm, just breathe that air! So fresh, and the moon's so pretty! I'll skip back out — I know where my place is when young folks are having a — serious conversation!   550

JIM: Oh, don't go out, Mrs. Wingfield. The fact of the matter is I've got to be going.

AMANDA: Going, now? You're joking! Why, it's only the shank of the evening, Mr. O'Connor!

JIM: Well, you know how it is.   555

AMANDA: You mean you're a young workingman and have to keep workingmen's hours. We'll let you off early tonight. But only on the condition that next time you stay later. What's the best night for you? Isn't Saturday night the best night for you workingmen?

JIM: I have a couple of time-clocks to punch, Mrs. Wingfield. One at morning, another one at night!

AMANDA: My, but you *are* ambitious! You work at night, too?

JIM: No, Ma'am, not work but — Betty!

(He crosses deliberately to pick up his hat. The band at the Paradise Dance Hall goes into a tender waltz.)

AMANDA: Betty? Betty? Who's — Betty!

(There is an ominous cracking sound in the sky.)

JIM: Oh, just a girl. The girl I go steady with!

(He smiles charmingly. The sky falls.)

(Legend: "The Sky Falls.")

AMANDA: *(a long-drawn exhalation)* Ohhhh . . . Is it a serious romance, Mr. O'Connor?

JIM: We're going to be married the second Sunday in June.

AMANDA: Ohhhh — how nice! Tom didn't mention that you were engaged to be married.

JIM: The cat's not out of the bag at the warehouse yet. You know how they are. They call you Romeo and stuff like that. *(He stops at the oval mirror to put on his hat. He carefully shapes the brim and the crown to give a discreetly dashing effect.)* It's been a wonderful evening, Mrs. Wingfield. I guess this is what they mean by Southern hospitality.

AMANDA: It really wasn't anything at all.

JIM: I hope it don't seem like I'm rushing off. But I promised Betty I'd pick her up at the Wabash depot, an' by the time I get my jalopy down there her train'll be in. Some women are pretty upset if you keep 'em waiting.

AMANDA: Yes, I know — the tyranny of women! *(She extends her hand.)* Goodbye, Mr. O'Connor. I wish you luck — and happiness — and success! All three of them, and so does Laura! Don't you, Laura?

LAURA: Yes!

JIM: *(taking LAURA's hand)* Goodbye, Laura. I'm certainly going to treasure that souvenir. And don't you forget the good advice I gave you. *(He raises his voice to a cheery shout.)* So long, Shakespeare! Thanks again, ladies. Good night!

(He grins and ducks jauntily out. Still bravely grimacing, AMANDA closes the door on the gentleman caller. Then she turns back to the room with a puzzled expression. She and LAURA don't dare to face each other. LAURA crouches beside the Victrola to wind it.)

AMANDA: *(faintly)*: Things have a way of turning out so badly. I don't believe that I would play the Victrola. Well, well — well! Our gentleman caller was engaged to be married! *(She raises her voice.)* Tom!

TOM: *(from the kitchenette)* Yes, Mother?

AMANDA: Come in here a minute. I want to tell you something awfully funny.

TOM: *(entering with a macaroon and a glass of the lemonade)* Has the gentleman caller gotten away already?

AMANDA: The gentleman caller has made an early departure. What a wonderful joke you played on us!

TOM: How do you mean?

AMANDA: You didn't mention that he was engaged to be married.

TOM: Jim? Engaged?

AMANDA: That's what he just informed us.

TOM: I'll be jiggered! I didn't know about that.

AMANDA: That seems very peculiar.

TOM: What's peculiar about it?

AMANDA: Didn't you call him your best friend down at the warehouse?

TOM: He is, but how did I know?

AMANDA: It seems extremely peculiar that you wouldn't know your best friend was going to be married!

TOM: The warehouse is where I work, not where I know things about people!

AMANDA: You don't know things anywhere! You live in a dream; you manufacture illusions!

(He crosses to the door.)

Where are you going?

TOM: I'm going to the movies.

AMANDA: That's right, now that you've had us make such fools of ourselves. The effort, the preparations, all the expense! The new floor lamp, the rug, the clothes for Laura! All for what? To entertain some other girl's fiancé! Go to the movies, go! Don't think about us, a mother deserted, an unmarried sister who's crippled and has no job! Don't let anything interfere with your selfish pleasure! Just go, go, go — to the movies!

TOM: All right, I will! The more you shout about my selfishness to me the quicker I'll go, and I won't go to the movies!

AMANDA: Go, then! Go to the moon — you selfish dreamer!

(TOM smashes his glass on the floor. He plunges out on the fire escape, slamming the door. LAURA screams in fright. The dance-hall music becomes louder. TOM stands on the fire escape, gripping the rail. The moon breaks through the storm clouds, illuminating his face.)

(Legend on screen: "And so goodbye . . .")

(TOM's closing speech is timed with what is happening inside the house. We see, as though through soundproof glass, that AMANDA appears to be making a comforting speech to LAURA, who is huddled upon the sofa. Now that we cannot hear the mother's speech, her silliness is gone and she has dignity and tragic beauty. LAURA's hair hides her face until, at the end of the speech, she lifts her head to smile at her mother. AMANDA's gestures are slow and graceful, almost dancelike, as she comforts her daughter. At the end of her speech she glances a moment at the father's picture — then withdraws through the portieres. At the close of TOM's speech, LAURA blows out the candles, ending the play.)

TOM: I didn't go to the moon, I went much further — for time is the longest distance between two places. Not long after that I was fired for writing a poem on the lid of a shoe-box. I left Saint Louis. I descended the steps of this fire escape for a last time and followed, from then on, in my father's footsteps, attempting to find in motion what was lost in space. I traveled around a great deal. The cities swept about me like dead leaves, leaves that were brightly colored but torn away from the branches. I would have stopped, but I was pursued by something. It always came upon me unawares, taking me altogether by surprise. Perhaps it was a familiar bit of music.

Perhaps it was only a piece of transparent glass. Perhaps I am walking along a street at night, in some strange city, before I have found companions. I pass the lighted window of a shop 645 where perfume is sold. The window is filled with pieces of colored glass, tiny transparent bottles in delicate colors, like bits of a shattered rainbow. Then all at once my sister touches my shoulder. I turn around and look into her eyes. Oh, Laura, Laura, I tried to leave you behind me, but I am more 650 faithful than I intended to be! I reach for a cigarette, I cross the street, I run into the movies or a bar, I buy a drink, I speak to the nearest stranger—anything that can blow your candles out!

(LAURA *bends over the candles.*)

For nowadays the world is lit by lightning! Blow out your candles, Laura—and so goodbye. . . .   655

(*She blows the candles out.*)

ARTHUR MILLER

Arthur Miller (b. 1915) was born in Harlem and raised in Brooklyn. The son of Jewish immigrants, Miller often takes the milieu of urban New York as the substance of his drama. Like Tennessee Williams, Miller was formed by the Great Depression. He worked a variety of jobs to help his family make ends meet and eventually gained provisional admission to the University of Michigan, where he studied playwriting and graduated in 1938. He worked briefly for the Federal Theater Project. Although his first play — *The Man Who Had All the Luck* (1944) — failed, Miller went on to write a series of gritty and powerful plays: *All My Sons* (1947), *Death of a Salesman* (1949), an adaptation of Ibsen's *An Enemy of the People* (1950), and *The Crucible* (1953). In 1955, Miller wrote A *View from the Bridge*, a story of honor and betrayal among New York's Italian immigrants. He also married Marilyn Monroe in that year, and his next play, *After the Fall* (1964), is a lightly disguised account of their stormy marriage and its breakup. In 1964 he also produced *Incident at Vichy*, a play concerning the Nazi persecution of the Jews during World War II, and he returned to the subject in his 1981 screenplay *Playing for Time*. Miller has written several other plays, an autobiography, and an account of the production of *Salesman* in the People's Republic of China during the 1980s. He writes and lectures frequently about his career and about American theater.

The Crucible

Miller's is a moral imagination, and his plays typically examine how people are driven to betray themselves and others through the corrupting compromises exacted from them by society. Although *The Crucible* is set in seventeenth-century Massachusetts and takes the witch trials as its subject, it is also a deeply personal protest play. To audiences in 1953, John Proctor's persecution by the witch-hunting tribunal had an immediately present-day resonance. After World War II, the House Un-American Activities Committee (HUAC) was revived to investigate the activities of Soviet spies in the United States. The Soviet Union's consolidation of Eastern Europe, its detonation of an atomic bomb, and the rise of communism in China all ignited a near-hysteria in the United States, galvanizing the "cold war" foreign policy abroad and a "witch hunt" for suspected Communists at home. The committee summoned individuals and pressed them to confess their past activities in radical politics. As the hearings wore on, prominent figures in government and entertainment, fearing guilt by association, were coerced into naming others, whose radical affiliations were sometimes real, but often were tenuous or fabricated.

The effects of the HUAC investigation were profound, as people risked their careers to avoid implicating others, or named names to protect themselves. The playwright Clifford Odets, for instance, both confessed to an association with the Communist party and named friends from the Group Theater of the 1930s as party members as well. Elia Kazan — who directed Miller's *Death of a Salesman* — also named names, opening a rift with Miller. For when Miller was called before the committee in 1956, he admitted attending Communist party meetings in the 1930s — as did many people looking for social change during the depression — but he refused to name others: "I take the responsibility for everything I have ever done, but I cannot take responsibility for another human being," he testified. Miller was fined $500, cited for contempt, and given a thirty-day suspended sentence. Although his potential blacklisting in the entertainment industry — fearful of bad publicity, the industry often refused to hire performers who were interviewed or named in the HUAC hearings — was averted to some extent in 1958 when the courts exonerated him, the incident had a profound effect on Miller's career.

In *The Crucible*, a New England village is similarly whipped into hysteria by Abigail Williams, a young woman who turns the community's fear of invisible wrongdoing against its most prominent citizens. Several girls had played at summoning the devil with a Caribbean servant, Tituba. When one of the girls falls into a trance, Tituba confesses to witchcraft out of fear of being punished, and the girls fall into fits, apparently possessed by a new-found power to detect witches and demons. Fear of witchcraft grips the village, sustained by an aggregation of all-too-human vices: envy, greed, and jealousy. For Abigail is motivated by her desire for Proctor, who has returned to his wife after having

had an adulterous affair with Abigail. By charging Elizabeth Proctor with witchcraft, Abigail forces Proctor into the position of having to reveal his adultery to the tribunal and to confess to witchcraft to save his wife. In the end, however, Proctor refuses to incriminate himself or others. By steadfastly denying the practice of witchcraft, Proctor sentences himself to death.

The play's power arises from the confrontation between the individual and the larger forces at work in society. *The Crucible* is finally interested only in the stand of a single individual, John Proctor, whose guilt at betraying his wife condemns him in his own mind more completely than do the accusations of others. Although Proctor finally has only to confess to witchcraft to avoid hanging, he will not perjure himself. This theme—taking full responsibility for one's actions—is the critical theme of Miller's drama, the central force of his tragic vision.

— A NOTE ON THE HISTORICAL ACCURACY OF THIS PLAY —

This play is not history in the sense in which the word is used by the academic historian. Dramatic purposes have sometimes required many characters to be fused into one; the number of girls involved in the "crying-out" has been reduced; Abigail's age has been raised; while there were several judges of almost equal authority, I have symbolized them all in Hathorne and Danforth. However, I believe that the reader will discover here the essential nature of one of the strangest and most awful chapters in human history. The fate of each character is exactly that of his historical model, and there is no one in the drama who did not play a similar—and in some cases exactly the same—role in history.

As for the characters of the persons, little is known about most of them excepting what may be surmised from a few letters, the trial record, certain broadsides written at the time, and references to their conduct in sources of varying reliability. They may therefore be taken as creations of my own, drawn to the best of my ability in conformity with their known behavior, except as indicated in the commentary I have written for this text.

Arthur Miller

THE CRUCIBLE

Arthur Miller

— CHARACTERS —

REVEREND PARRIS
BETTY PARRIS
TITUBA
ABIGAIL WILLIAMS
SUSANNA WALCOTT
MRS. ANN PUTNAM
THOMAS PUTNAM
MERCY LEWIS
MARY WARREN
JOHN PROCTOR
REBECCA NURSE

GILES COREY
REVEREND JOHN HALE
ELIZABETH PROCTOR
FRANCIS NURSE
EZEKIEL CHEEVER
MARSHAL HERRICK
JUDGE HATHORNE
DEPUTY GOVERNOR DANFORTH
SARAH GOOD
HOPKINS

— ACT ONE —
(AN OVERTURE)

A small upper bedroom in the home of Reverend Samuel Parris, Salem, Massachusetts, in the spring of the year 1692.

There is a narrow window at the left. Through its leaded panes the morning sunlight streams. A candle still burns near the bed, which is at the right. A chest, a chair, and a small table are the other furnishings. At the back a door opens on the landing of the stairway to the ground floor. The room gives off an air of clean spareness. The roof rafters are exposed, and the wood colors are raw and unmellowed.

As the curtain rises, Reverend Parris is discovered kneeling beside the bed, evidently in prayer. His daughter, Betty Parris, aged ten, is lying on the bed, inert.

At the time of these events Parris was in his middle forties. In history he cut a villainous path, and there is very little good to be said for him. He believed he was being persecuted wherever he went, despite his best efforts to win people and God to his side. In meeting, he felt insulted if someone rose to shut the door without first asking his permission. He was a widower with no interest in children, or talent with them. He regarded them as young adults, and until this strange crisis he, like the rest of Salem, never conceived that the children were anything but thankful for being permitted to walk straight, eyes slightly lowered, arms at the sides, and mouths shut until bidden to speak.

His house stood in the "town"—but we today would hardly call it a village. The meeting house was nearby, and from this point outward—toward the bay or inland—there were a few small-windowed, dark houses snuggling against the raw Massachusetts winter. Salem had been established hardly forty years before. To the European world the whole province was a barbaric frontier inhabited by a sect of fanatics who, nevertheless, were shipping out products of slowly increasing quantity and value.

No one can really know what their lives were like. They had no novelists—and would not have permitted anyone to read a novel if one were handy. Their creed forbade anything resembling a theater or "vain enjoyment." They did not celebrate Christmas, and a holiday from work meant only that they must concentrate even more upon prayer.

Which is not to say that nothing broke into this strict and somber way of life. When a new farmhouse was built, friends assembled to "raise the roof," and there would be special foods cooked and probably some potent cider passed around. There was a good supply of ne'er-do-wells in Salem, who dallied at the shovelboard in Bridget Bishop's tavern. Probably more than the creed, hard work kept the morals of the place from spoiling, for the people were forced to fight the land like heroes for every grain of corn, and no man had very much time for fooling around.

That there were some jokers, however, is indicated by the practice of appointing a two-man patrol whose duty was to "walk forth in the time of God's worship to take notice of such as either lye about the meeting house, without attending to the word and ordinances, or that lye at home or in the fields without giving good account thereof, and to take the names of such persons, and to present them to the magistrates, whereby they may be accordingly proceeded against." This predilection for minding other people's business was time-honored among the people of Salem, and it undoubtedly created many of the suspicions which were to feed the coming madness. It was also, in my opinion, one of the things that a John Proctor would rebel against, for the time of the armed camp had almost passed, and since the country was reasonably—although not wholly—safe, the old disciplines were beginning to rankle. But, as in all such matters, the issue was not clear-cut, for danger was still a possibility, and in unity still lay the best promise of safety.

The edge of the wilderness was close by. The American continent stretched endlessly west, and it was full of mystery for them. It stood, dark and threatening, over their shoulders night and day, for out of it Indian tribes marauded from time to time, and Reverend Parris had parishioners who had lost relatives to these heathen.

The parochial snobbery of these people was partly responsible for their failure to convert the Indians. Probably they also preferred to take land from heathens rather than from fellow Christians. At any rate, very few Indians were converted, and the Salem folk believed that the virgin forest was the Devil's last preserve, his home base and the citadel of his final stand. To the best of their knowledge the American forest was the last place on earth that was not paying homage to God.

For these reasons, among others, they carried about an air of innate resistance, even of persecution. Their fathers had, of course, been persecuted in England. So now they and their church found it necessary to deny any other sect its freedom, lest their New Jerusalem be defiled and corrupted by wrong ways and deceitful ideas.

They believed, in short, that they held in their steady hands the candle that would light the world. We have inherited this belief, and it has helped and hurt us. It helped them with the discipline it gave them. They were a dedicated folk, by and large, and they had to be to survive the life they had chosen or been born into in this country.

The proof of their belief's value to them may be taken from the opposite character of the first Jamestown settlement, farther south, in Virginia. The Englishmen who landed there were motivated mainly by a hunt for profit. They had thought to pick off the wealth of the new country and then return rich to England. They were a band of individualists, and a much more ingratiating group than the Massachusetts men. But Virginia destroyed them. Massachusetts tried to kill off the Puritans, but they combined; they set up a communal society which, in the beginning, was little more than an armed camp with an autocratic and very devoted leadership. It was, however, an autocracy by consent, for they were united from top to bottom by a commonly held ideology whose perpetuation was the reason and justification for all their sufferings. So their self-denial, their purposefulness, their suspicion of all vain pursuits, their hardhanded justice, were altogether perfect instruments for the conquest of this space so antagonistic to man.

But the people of Salem in 1692 were not quite the dedicated folk that arrived on the *Mayflower*. A vast differentiation had taken place, and in their own time a revolution had unseated the royal government and substituted a junta which was at this moment in power. The times, to their eyes, must have been out of joint, and to the common folk must have seemed as insoluble and complicated as do ours today. It is not hard to see how easily many could have been led to believe that the time of confusion had been brought upon them by deep and darkling forces. No hint of such speculation appears on the court record, but social order in any age breeds such mystical suspicions, and when, as in Salem, wonders are brought forth from below the social surface, it is too much to expect people to hold back very long from laying on the victims with all the force of their frustrations.

The Salem tragedy, which is about to begin in these pages, developed from a paradox. It is a paradox in whose grip we still live, and there is no prospect yet that we will discover its resolution. Simply, it was this: for good purposes, even high purposes, the people of Salem developed a theocracy, a combine of state and religious power whose function was to keep the community together, and to prevent any kind of disunity that might open it to destruction by material or ideological enemies. It was forged for a necessary purpose and accomplished that purpose. But all organization is and must be grounded on the idea of exclusion and prohibition, just as two objects cannot occupy the same space. Evidently the time came in New England when the repressions of order were heavier than seemed warranted by the dangers against which the order was organized. The witch-hunt was a perverse manifestation of the panic which set in among all classes when the balance began to turn toward greater individual freedom.

When one rises above the individual villainy displayed, one can only pity them all, just as we shall be pitied someday. It is still impossible for man to organize his social life without repressions, and the balance has yet to be struck between order and freedom.

The witch-hunt was not, however, a mere repression. It was also, and as importantly, a long overdue opportunity for everyone so inclined to express publicly his guilt and sins, under the cover of accusations against the victims. It suddenly became possible — and patriotic and holy — for a man to say that Martha Corey had come into his bedroom at night, and that, while his wife was sleeping at his side, Martha laid herself down on his chest and "nearly suffocated him." Of course it was her spirit only, but his satisfaction at confessing himself was no lighter than if it had been Martha herself. One could not ordinarily speak such things in public.

Long-held hatreds of neighbors could now be openly expressed, and vengeance taken, despite the Bible's charitable injunctions. Land-lust which had been expressed before by constant bickering over boundaries and deeds, could now be elevated to the arena of morality; one could cry witch against one's neighbor and feel perfectly justified in the bargain. Old scores could be settled on a plane of heavenly combat between Lucifer and the Lord; suspicions and the envy of the miserable toward the happy could and did burst out in the general revenge.

(REVEREND PARRIS *is praying now, and, though we cannot hear his words, a sense of his confusion hangs about him. He mumbles, then seems about to weep; then he weeps, then prays again; but his daughter does not stir on the bed.*)

The door opens, and his Negro slave enters. TITUBA *is in her forties.* PARRIS *brought her with him from Barbados, where he spent some years as a merchant before entering the ministry. She enters as one does who can no longer bear to be barred from the sight of her beloved, but she is also very frightened because her slave sense has warned her that, as always, trouble in this house eventually lands on her back.*)

TITUBA: (*already taking a step backward*) My Betty be hearty soon?
PARRIS: Out of here!
TITUBA: (*backing to the door*) My Betty not goin' die . . .
PARRIS: (*scrambling to his feet in a fury*) Out of my sight! (*She is gone.*) Out of my — (*He is overcome with sobs. He clamps his*   5

teeth against them and closes the door and leans against it, exhausted.) Oh, my God! God help me! *(Quaking with fear, mumbling to himself through his sobs, he goes to the bed and gently takes* BETTY's *hand.)* Betty. Child. Dear child. Will you
10 wake, will you open up your eyes! Betty, little one . . .

(He is bending to kneel again when his niece, ABIGAIL WIL-LIAMS, *seventeen, enters—a strikingly beautiful girl, an orphan, with an endless capacity for dissembling. Now she is all worry and apprehension and propriety.)*

ABIGAIL: Uncle? *(He looks to her.)* Susanna Walcott's here from Doctor Griggs.
PARRIS: Oh? Let her come, let her come.
ABIGAIL: *(leaning out the door to call to* SUSANNA, *who is down*
15 *the hall a few steps)* Come in, Susanna.

*(*SUSANNA WALCOTT, *a little younger than* ABIGAIL, *a nervous, hurried girl, enters.)*

PARRIS: *(eagerly)* What does the doctor say, child?
SUSANNA: *(craning around* PARRIS *to get a look at* BETTY*)* He bid me come and tell you, reverend sir, that he cannot discover no medicine for it in his books.
20 PARRIS: Then he must search on.
SUSANNA: Aye, sir, he have been searchin' his books since he left you, sir. But he bid me tell you, that you might look to unnatural things for the cause of it.
PARRIS: *(his eyes going wide)* No—no. There be no unnatural
25 cause here. Tell him I have sent for Reverend Hale of Beverly, and Mr. Hale will surely confirm that. Let him look to medicine and put out all thought of unnatural causes here. There be none.
SUSANNA: Aye, sir. He bid me tell you. *(She turns to go.)*
30 ABIGAIL: Speak nothin' of it in the village, Susanna.
PARRIS: Go directly home and speak nothing of unnatural causes.
SUSANNA: Aye, sir. I pray for her. *(She goes out.)*
ABIGAIL: Uncle, the rumor of witchcraft is all about; I think you'd best go down and deny it yourself. The parlor's packed
35 with people, sir. I'll sit with her.
PARRIS: *(pressed, turns on her)* And what shall I say to them? That my daughter and my niece I discovered dancing like heathen in the forest?
ABIGAIL: Uncle, we did dance; let you tell them I confessed it—
40 and I'll be whipped if I must be. But they're speakin' of witchcraft. Betty's not witched.
PARRIS: Abigail, I cannot go before the congregation when I know you have not opened with me. What did you do with her in the forest?
45 ABIGAIL: We did dance, uncle, and when you leaped out of the bush so suddenly, Betty was frightened and then she fainted. And there's the whole of it.
PARRIS: Child. Sit you down.
ABIGAIL: *(quavering, as she sits)* I would never hurt Betty. I love
50 her dearly.
PARRIS: Now look you, child, your punishment will come in its time. But if you trafficked with spirits in the forest I must know it now, for surely my enemies will, and they will ruin me with it.
55 ABIGAIL: But we never conjured spirits.
PARRIS: Then why can she not move herself since midnight? This child is desperate! *(*ABIGAIL *lowers her eyes.)* It must

come out—my enemies will bring it out. Let me know what you done there. Abigail, do you understand that I have many enemies?
60
ABIGAIL: I have heard of it, uncle.
PARRIS: There is a faction that is sworn to drive me from my pulpit. Do you understand that?
ABIGAIL: I think so, sir.
PARRIS: Now then, in the midst of such disruption, my own
65 household is discovered to be the very center of some obscene practice. Abominations are done in the forest—
ABIGAIL: It were sport, uncle!
PARRIS: *(pointing at* BETTY*)* You call this sport? *(She lowers her eyes. He pleads)* Abigail, if you know something that may
70 help the doctor, for God's sake tell it to me. *(She is silent.)* I saw Tituba waving her arms over the fire when I came on you. Why was she doing that? And I heard a screeching and gibberish coming from her mouth. She were swaying like a dumb beast over that fire!
75
ABIGAIL: She always sings her Barbados songs, and we dance.
PARRIS: I cannot blink what I saw, Abigail, for my enemies will not blink it. I saw a dress lying on the grass.
ABIGAIL: *(innocently)* A dress?
PARRIS: *(—it is very hard to say)* Aye, a dress. And I thought I
80 saw—someone naked running through the trees!
ABIGAIL: *(in terror)* No one was naked! You mistake yourself, uncle.
PARRIS: *(with anger)* I saw it! *(He moves from her. Then, resolved)* Now tell me true, Abigail. And I pray you feel the weight of
85 truth upon you, for now my ministry's at stake, my ministry and perhaps your cousin's life. Whatever abomination you have done, give me all of it now, for I dare not be taken unaware when I go before them down there.
ABIGAIL: There is nothin' more. I swear it, uncle.
90
PARRIS: *(studies her, then nods, half convinced)* Abigail, I have fought here three long years to bend these stiff-necked people to me, and now, just now when some good respect is rising for me in the parish, you compromise my very character. I have given you a home, child, I have put clothes upon your back—
95 now give me upright answer. Your name in the town—it is entirely white, is it not?
ABIGAIL: *(with an edge of resentment)* Why, I am sure it is, sir. There be no blush about my name.
PARRIS: *(to the point)* Abigail, is there any other cause than you
100 have told me, for your being discharged from Goody Proctor's service? I have heard it said, and I tell you as I heard it, that she comes so rarely to the church this year for she will not sit so close to something soiled. What signified that remark?
ABIGAIL: She hates me, uncle, she must, for I would not be her
105 slave. It's a bitter woman, a lying, cold, sniveling woman, and I will not work for such a woman!
PARRIS: She may be. And yet it has troubled me that you are now seven month out of their house, and in all this time no other family has ever called for your service.
110
ABIGAIL: They want slaves, not such as I. Let them send to Barbados for that. I will not black my face for any of them! *(With ill-concealed resentment at him)* Do you begrudge my bed, uncle?
PARRIS: No—no.
115
ABIGAIL: *(in a temper)* My name is good in the village! I will not have it said my name is soiled! Goody Proctor is a gossiping liar!

(Enter MRS. ANN PUTNAM. *She is a twisted soul of forty-five, a death-ridden woman, haunted by dreams.)*

PARRIS: *(as soon as the door begins to open)* No—no, I cannot have anyone. *(He sees her, and a certain deference springs into*
120 *him, although his worry remains.)* Why, Goody Putnam, come in.

MRS. PUTNAM: *(full of breath, shiny-eyed)* It is a marvel. It is surely a stroke of hell upon you.

PARRIS: No, Goody Putnam, it is—

125 MRS. PUTNAM: *(glancing at* BETTY) How high did she fly, how high?

PARRIS: No, no, she never flew—

MRS. PUTNAM: *(very pleased with it)* Why, it's sure she did. Mr. Collins saw her goin' over Ingersoll's barn, and come down
130 light as bird, he says!

PARRIS: Now, look you, Goody Putnam, she never—*(Enter* THOMAS PUTNAM, *a well-to-do, hard-handed landowner, near fifty.)* Oh, good morning, Mr. Putnam.

PUTNAM: It is a providence the thing is out now! It is a provi-
135 dence. *(He goes directly to the bed.)*

PARRIS: What's out, sir, what's—?

(MRS. PUTNAM goes to the bed.)

PUTNAM: *(looking down at* BETTY) Why, *her* eyes is closed! Look you, Ann.

MRS. PUTNAM: Why, that's strange. *(To* PARRIS) Ours is open.
140 PARRIS: *(shocked)* Your Ruth is sick.

MRS. PUTNAM: *(with vicious certainty)* I'd not call it sick; the Devil's touch is heavier than sick. It's death, y'know, it's death drivin' into them, forked and hoofed.

PARRIS: Oh, pray not! Why, how does Ruth ail?

145 MRS. PUTNAM: She ails as she must—she never waked this morning, but her eyes open and she walks, and hears naught, sees naught, and cannot eat. Her soul is taken, surely.

(PARRIS is struck.)

PUTNAM: *(as though for further details)* They say you've sent for Reverend Hale of Beverly?

150 PARRIS: *(with dwindling conviction now)* A precaution only. He has much experience in all demonic arts, and I—

MRS. PUTNAM: He has indeed; and found a witch in Beverly last year, and let you remember that.

PARRIS: Now, Goody Ann, they only thought that were a witch,
155 and I am certain there be no element of witchcraft here.

PUTNAM: No witchcraft! Now look you, Mr. Parris—

PARRIS: Thomas, Thomas, I pray you, leap not to witchcraft. I know that you—you least of all, Thomas, would ever wish so disastrous a charge laid upon me. We cannot leap to witch-
160 craft. They will howl me out of Salem for such corruption in my house.

A word about Thomas Putnam. He was a man with many grievances, at least one of which appears justified. Some time before, his wife's brother-in-law, James Bayley, had been turned down as minister of Salem. Bayley had all the qualifications, and a two-thirds vote into the bargain, but a faction stopped his acceptance, for reasons that are not clear.

Thomas Putnam was the eldest son of the richest man in the village. He had fought the Indians at Narragansett, and was deeply interested in parish affairs. He undoubt-

edly felt it poor payment that the village should so blatantly disregard his candidate for one of its more important offices, especially since he regarded himself as the intellectual superior of most of the people around him.

His vindictive nature was demonstrated long before the witchcraft began. Another former Salem minister, George Burroughs, had had to borrow money to pay for his wife's funeral, and, since the parish was remiss in his salary, he was soon bankrupt. Thomas and his brother John had Burroughs jailed for debts the man did not owe. The incident is important only in that Burroughs succeeded in becoming minister where Bayley, Thomas Putnam's brother-in-law, had been rejected; the motif of resentment is clear here. Thomas Putnam felt that his own name and the honor of his family had been smirched by the village, and he meant to right matters however he could.

Another reason to believe him a deeply embittered man was his attempt to break his father's will, which left a disproportionate amount to a stepbrother. As with every other public cause in which he tried to force his way, he failed in this.

So it is not surprising to find that so many accusations against people are in the handwriting of Thomas Putnam, or that his name is so often found as a witness corroborating the supernatural testimony, or that his daughter led the crying-out at the most opportune junctures of the trials, especially when—But we'll speak of that when we come to it.

PUTNAM: *(—at the moment he is intent upon getting* PARRIS, *for whom he has only contempt, to move toward the abyss)* Mr. Parris, I have taken your part in all contention here, and I would continue; but I cannot if you hold back in this. There
165 are hurtful, vengeful spirits layin' hands on these children.

PARRIS: But, Thomas, you cannot—

PUTNAM: Ann! Tell Mr. Parris what you have done.

MRS. PUTNAM: Reverend Parris, I have laid seven babies unbap-
170 tized in the earth. Believe me, sir, you never saw more hearty babies born. And yet, each would wither in my arms the very night of their birth. I have spoke nothin', but my heart has clamored intimations. And now, this year, my Ruth, my only—I see her turning strange. A secret child she has be-
175 come this year, and shrivels like a sucking mouth were pullin' on her life too. And so I thought to send her to your Tituba—

PARRIS: To Tituba! What may Tituba—?

MRS. PUTNAM: Tituba knows how to speak to the dead, Mr. Parris.

PARRIS: Goody Ann, it is a formidable sin to conjure up the
180 dead!

MRS. PUTNAM: I take it on my soul, but who else may surely tell us what person murdered my babies?

PARRIS: *(horrified)* Woman!

MRS. PUTNAM: They were murdered, Mr. Parris! And mark this
185 proof! Mark it! Last night my Ruth were ever so close to their little spirits; I know it, sir. For how else is she struck dumb now except some power of darkness would stop her mouth? It is a marvelous sign, Mr. Parris!

PUTNAM: Don't you understand it, sir? There is a murdering
190 witch among us, bound to keep herself in the dark. *(PARRIS*

turns to BETTY, *a frantic terror rising in him.*) Let your enemies make of it what they will, you cannot blink it more.

PARRIS: (*to* ABIGAIL) Then you were conjuring spirits last night.

195 ABIGAIL: (*whispering*) Not I, sir — Tituba and Ruth.

PARRIS: (*turns now, with new fear, and goes to* BETTY, *looks
down at her, and then, gazing off*) Oh, Abigail, what proper
payment for my charity! Now I am undone.

PUTNAM: You are not undone! Let you take hold here. Wait for
200 no one to charge you — declare it yourself. You have discovered witchcraft —

PARRIS: In my house? In my house, Thomas? They will topple
me with this! They will make of it a —

(*Enter* MERCY LEWIS, *the* PUTNAM'S *servant, a fat, sly, merciless
girl of eighteen.*)

MERCY: Your pardons. I only thought to see how Betty is.

205 PUTNAM: Why aren't you home? Who's with Ruth?

MERCY: Her grandma come. She's improved a little, I think —
she give a powerful sneeze before.

MRS. PUTNAM: Ah, there's a sign of life!

MERCY: I'd fear no more, Goody Putnam. It were a grand sneeze;
210 another like it will shake her wits together, I'm sure. (*She goes
to the bed to look.*)

PARRIS: Will you leave me now, Thomas? I would pray a while
alone.

ABIGAIL: Uncle, you've prayed since midnight. Why do you not
215 go down and —

PARRIS: No-no. (*to* PUTNAM) I have no answer for that crowd.
I'll wait till Mr. Hale arrives. (*To get* MRS. PUTNAM *to leave*) If
you will, Goody Ann . . .

PUTNAM: Now look you, sir. Let you strike out against the Devil,
220 and the village will bless you for it! Come down, speak to
them — pray with them. They're thirsting for your word, Mister! Surely you'll pray with them.

PARRIS: (*swayed*) I'll lead them in a psalm, but let you say nothing of witchcraft yet. I will not discuss it. The cause is yet
225 unknown. I have had enough contention since I came; I want
no more.

MRS. PUTNAM: Mercy, you go home to Ruth, d'y'hear?

MERCY: Aye, mum.

(MRS. PUTNAM *goes out.*)

PARRIS: (*to* ABIGAIL) If she starts for the window, cry for me at
230 once.

ABIGAIL: I will, uncle.

PARRIS: (*to* PUTNAM) There is a terrible power in her arms today.
(*He goes out with* PUTNAM.)

ABIGAIL: (*with hushed trepidation*) How is Ruth sick?

235 MERCY: It's weirdish, I know not — she seems to walk like a dead
one since last night.

ABIGAIL: (*turns at once and goes to* BETTY, *and now, with fear in
her voice*) Betty? (BETTY *doesn't move. She shakes her.*) Now
stop this! Betty! Sit up now!

(BETTY *doesn't stir.* MERCY *comes over.*)

240 MERCY: Have you tried beatin' her? I gave Ruth a good one and
it waked her for a minute. Here, let me have her.

ABIGAIL: (*holding* MERCY *back*) No, he'll be comin' up. Listen
now; if they be questioning us, tell them we danced — I told
him as much already.

245 MERCY: Aye. And what more?

ABIGAIL: He knows Tituba conjured Ruth's sisters to come out of
the grave.

MERCY: And what more?

ABIGAIL: He saw you naked.

250 MERCY: (*clapping her hands together with a frightened laugh*)
Oh, Jesus!

(*Enter* MARY WARREN, *breathless. She is seventeen, a subservient, naive, lonely girl.*)

MARY WARREN: What'll we do? The village is out! I just come
from the farm; the whole country's talkin' witchcraft! They'll
be callin' us witches, Abby!

255 MERCY: (*pointing and looking at* MARY WARREN) She means to
tell, I know it.

MARY WARREN: Abby, we've got to tell. Witchery's a hangin' error, a hangin' like they done in Boston two year ago! We must
tell the truth, Abby! You'll only be whipped for dancin', and
260 the other things!

ABIGAIL: Oh, *we'll* be whipped!

MARY WARREN: I never done none of it, Abby. I only looked!

MERCY: (*moving menacingly toward* MARY) Oh, you're a great
one for lookin', aren't you, Mary Warren? What a grand peep-
265 ing courage you have!

(BETTY, *on the bed, whimpers.* ABIGAIL *turns to her at once.*)

ABIGAIL: Betty? (*She goes to* BETTY.) Now, Betty, dear, wake up
now. It's Abigail. (*She sits* BETTY *up and furiously shakes her.*)
I'll beat you, Betty! (BETTY *whimpers.*) My, you seem improving. I talked to your papa and I told him everything. So
270 there's nothing to —

BETTY: (*darts off the bed, frightened of* ABIGAIL, *and flattens herself against the wall*) I want my mama!

ABIGAIL: (*with alarm, as she cautiously approaches* BETTY)
What ails you, Betty? Your mama's dead and buried.

275 BETTY: I'll fly to Mama. Let me fly! (*She raises her arms as
though to fly, and streaks for the window, gets one leg out.*)

ABIGAIL: (*pulling her away from the window*) I told him everything; he knows now, he knows everything we —

BETTY: You drank blood, Abby! You didn't tell him that!

280 ABIGAIL: Betty, you never say that again! You will never —

BETTY: You did, you did! You drank a charm to kill John Proctor's wife! You drank a charm to kill Goody Proctor!

ABIGAIL: (*smashes her across the face*) Shut it! Now shut it!

BETTY: (*collapsing on the bed*) Mama, Mama! (*She dissolves
into sobs.*)

285 ABIGAIL: Now look you. All of you. We danced. And Tituba
conjured Ruth Putnam's dead sisters. And that is all. And
mark this. Let either of you breathe a word, or the edge of a
word, about the other things, and I will come to you in the
black of some terrible night and I will bring a pointy reck-
290 oning that will shudder you. And you know I can do it; I saw
Indians smash my dear parents' heads on the pillow next to
mine, and I have seen some reddish work done at night, and I
can make you wish you had never seen the sun go down! (*She
goes to* BETTY *and roughly sits her up.*) Now, you — sit up and
295 stop this!

(*But* BETTY *collapses in her hands and lies inert on the bed.*)

MARY WARREN. (*with hysterical fright*) What's got her? (ABIGAIL
stares in fright at BETTY.) Abby, she's going to die! It's a sin to
conjure, and we —

300 ABIGAIL: (*starting for* MARY) I say shut it, Mary Warren!

(*Enter* JOHN PROCTOR. *On seeing him,* MARY WARREN *leaps in fright.*)

Proctor was a farmer in his middle thirties. He need not have been a partisan of any faction in the town, but there is evidence to suggest that he had a sharp and biting way with hypocrites. He was the kind of man — powerful of body, even-tempered, and not easily led — who cannot refuse support to partisans without drawing their deepest resentment. In Proctor's presence a fool felt his foolishness instantly — and a Proctor is always marked for calumny therefore.

But as we shall see, the steady manner he displays does not spring from an untroubled soul. He is a sinner, a sinner not only against the moral fashion of the time, but against his own vision of decent conduct. These people had no ritual for the washing away of sins. It is another trait we inherited from them, and it has helped to discipline us as well as to breed hypocrisy among us. Proctor, respected and even feared in Salem, has come to regard himself as a kind of fraud. But no hint of this has yet appeared on the surface, and as he enters from the crowded parlor below it is a man in his prime we see, with a quiet confidence and an unexpressed, hidden force. Mary Warren, his servant, can barely speak for embarrassment and fear.

MARY WARREN: Oh! I'm just going home, Mr. Proctor.

PROCTOR: Be you foolish, Mary Warren? Be you deaf? I forbid you leave the house, did I not? Why shall I pay you? I am looking for you more often than my cows!

305 MARY WARREN: I only come to see the great doings in the world.

PROCTOR: I'll show you a great doin' on your arse one of these days. Now get you home; my wife is waitin' with your work! (*Trying to retain a shred of dignity, she goes slowly out.*)

310 MERCY LEWIS: (*both afraid of him and strangely titillated*) I'd best be off. I have my Ruth to watch. Good morning, Mr. Proctor.

(MERCY *sidles out. Since* PROCTOR'*s entrance,* ABIGAIL *has stood as though on tiptoe, absorbing his presence, wide-eyed. He glances at her, then goes to* BETTY *on the bed.*)

ABIGAIL: Gah! I'd almost forgot how strong you are, John Proctor!

PROCTOR: (*looking at* ABIGAIL *now, the faintest suggestion of a knowing smile on his face*) What's this mischief here?

315 ABIGAIL: (*with a nervous laugh*) Oh, she's only gone silly somehow.

PROCTOR: The road past my house is a pilgrimage to Salem all morning. The town's mumbling witchcraft.

ABIGAIL: Oh posh! (*Winningly she comes a little closer, with a*
320 *confidential, wicked air.*) We were dancin' in the woods last night, and my uncle leaped in on us. She took fright, is all.

PROCTOR: (*his smile widening*) Ah, you're wicked yet, aren't y'! (*A trill of expectant laughter escapes her, and she dares come closer, feverishly looking into his eyes.*) You'll be clapped in the
325 stocks before you're twenty.

(*He takes a step to go, and she springs into his path.*)

ABIGAIL: Give me a word, John. A soft word. (*Her concentrated desire destroys his smile.*)

PROCTOR: No, no, Abby. That's done with.

ABIGAIL: (*tauntingly*) You come five mile to see a silly girl fly? I know you better. 330

PROCTOR: (*setting her firmly out of his path*) I come to see what mischief your uncle's brewin' now. (*With final emphasis*) Put it out of mind, Abby.

ABIGAIL: (*grasping his hand before he can release her*) John — I am waitin' for you every night. 335

PROCTOR: Abby, I never give you hope to wait for me.

ABIGAIL: (*now beginning to anger — she can't believe it*) I have something better than hope, I think!

PROCTOR: Abby, you'll put it out of mind. I'll not be comin' for you more. 340

ABIGAIL: You're surely sportin' with me.

PROCTOR: You know me better.

ABIGAIL: I know how you clutched my back behind your house and sweated like a stallion whenever I come near! Or did I dream that? It's she put me out, you cannot pretend it were 345 you. I saw your face when she put me out, and you loved me then and you do now!

PROCTOR: Abby, that's a wild thing to say —

ABIGAIL: A wild thing may say wild things. But not so wild, I think. I have seen you since she put me out; I have seen you 350 nights.

PROCTOR: I have hardly stepped off my farm this sevenmonth.

ABIGAIL: I have a sense for heat, John, and yours has drawn me to my window, and I have seen you looking up, burning in your loneliness. Do you tell me you've never looked up at my 355 window?

PROCTOR: I may have looked up.

ABIGAIL: (*now softening*) And you must. You are no wintry man. I know you, John. I *know* you. (*She is weeping.*) I cannot sleep for dreamin'; I cannot dream but I wake and walk about 360 the house as though I'd find you comin' through some door. (*She clutches him desperately.*)

PROCTOR: (*gently pressing her from him, with great sympathy but firmly*) Child —

ABIGAIL: (*with a flash of anger*) How do you call me child! 365

PROCTOR: Abby, I may think of you softly from time to time. But I will cut off my hand before I'll ever reach for you again. Wipe it out of mind. We never touched, Abby.

ABIGAIL: Aye, but we did.

PROCTOR: Aye, but we did not. 370

ABIGAIL: (*with a bitter anger*) Oh, I marvel how such a strong man may let such a sickly wife be —

PROCTOR: (*angered — at himself as well*) You'll speak nothin' of Elizabeth!

ABIGAIL: She is blackening my name in the village! She is telling 375 lies about me! She is a cold, sniveling woman, and you bend to her! Let her turn you like a —

PROCTOR: (*shaking her*) Do you look for whippin'?

(*A psalm is heard being sung below.*)

ABIGAIL: (*in tears*) I look for John Proctor that took me from my sleep and put knowledge in my heart! I never knew what pretense Salem was, I never knew the lying lessons I was taught 380 by all these Christian women and their covenanted men! And now you bid me tear the light out of my eyes? I will not, I cannot! You loved me, John Proctor, and whatever sin it is,

385   you love me yet! (*He turns abruptly to go out. She rushes to him.*) John, pity me, pity me!

(*The words "going up to Jesus" are heard in the psalm, a:•1 BETTY claps her ears suddenly and whines loudly.*)

ABIGAIL: Betty? (*She hurries to BETTY, who is now sitting up and screaming. PROCTOR goes to BETTY as ABIGAIL is trying to pull her hands down, calling "BETTY!"*)

390   PROCTOR: (*growing unnerved*) What's she doing? Girl, what ails you? Stop that wailing!

(*The singing has stopped in the midst of this, and now PARRIS rushes in.*)

PARRIS: What happened? What are you doing to her? Betty! (*He rushes to the bed, crying, "BETTY, BETTY!" MRS. PUTNAM enters, feverish with curiosity, and with her THOMAS PUTNAM*
395   *and MERCY LEWIS. PARRIS, at the bed, keeps lightly slapping BETTY's face, while she moans and tries to get up.*)

ABIGAIL: She heard you singin' and suddenly she's up and screamin'.

MRS. PUTNAM: The psalm! The psalm! She cannot bear to hear
400   the Lord's name!

PARRIS: No, God forbid. Mercy, run to the doctor! Tell him what's happened here! (*MERCY LEWIS rushes out.*)

MRS. PUTNAM: Mark it for a sign, mark it!

(*REBECCA NURSE, seventy-two, enters. She is white-haired, leaning upon her walking-stick.*)

PUTNAM: (*pointing at the whimpering BETTY*) That is a noto-
405   rious sign of witchcraft afoot, Goody Nurse, a prodigious sign!

MRS. PUTNAM: My mother told me that! When they cannot bear to hear the name of—

PARRIS: (*trembling*) Rebecca, Rebecca, go to her, we're lost. She
410   suddenly cannot bear to hear the Lord's—

(*GILES COREY, eighty-three, enters. He is knotted with muscle, canny, inquisitive, and still powerful.*)

REBECCA: There is hard sickness here, Giles Corey, so please to keep the quiet.

GILES: I've not said a word. No one here can testify I've said a word. Is she going to fly again? I hear she flies.

415   PUTNAM: Man, be quiet now!

(*Everything is quiet. REBECCA walks across the room to the bed. Gentleness exudes from her. BETTY is quietly whimpering, eyes shut. REBECCA simply stands over the child, who gradually quiets.*)

And while they are so absorbed, we may put a word in for Rebecca. Rebecca was the wife of Francis Nurse, who, from all accounts, was one of those men for whom both sides of the argument had to have respect. He was called upon to arbitrate disputes as though he were an unofficial judge, and Rebecca also enjoyed the high opinion most people had for him. By the time of the delusion, they had three hundred acres, and their children were settled in separate homesteads within the same estate. However, Francis had originally rented the land, and one theory has it that, as he gradually paid for it and raised his social status, there were those who resented his rise.

Another suggestion to explain the systematic campaign against Rebecca, and inferentially against Francis, is the land war he fought with his neighbors, one of whom was a Putnam. This squabble grew to the proportions of a battle in the woods between partisans of both sides, and it is said to have lasted for two days. As for Rebecca herself, the general opinion of her character was so high that to explain how anyone dared cry her out for a witch—and more, how adults could bring themselves to lay hands on her—we must look to the fields and boundaries of that time.

As we have seen, Thomas Putnam's man for the Salem ministry was Bayley. The Nurse clan had been in the faction that prevented Bayley's taking office. In addition, certain families allied to the Nurses by blood or friendship, and whose farms were contiguous with the Nurse farm or close to it, combined to break away from the Salem town authority and set up Topsfield, a new and independent entity whose existence was resented by old Salemites.

That the guiding hand behind the outcry was Putnam's is indicated by the fact that, as soon as it began, this Topsfield-Nurse faction absented themselves from church in protest and disbelief. It was Edward and Jonathan Putnam who signed the first complaint against Rebecca; and Thomas Putnam's little daughter was the one who fell into a fit at the hearing and pointed to Rebecca as her attacker. To top it all, Mrs. Putnam—who is now staring at the bewitched child on the bed—soon accused Rebecca's spirit of "tempting her to iniquity," a charge that had more truth in it than Mrs. Putnam could know.

MRS. PUTNAM: (*astonished*) What have you done?

(*REBECCA, in thought, now leaves the bedside and sits.*)

PARRIS: (*wondrous and relieved*) What do you make of it, Rebecca?

PUTNAM: (*eagerly*) Goody Nurse, will you go to my Ruth and see if you can wake her?

REBECCA: (*sitting*) I think she'll wake in time. Pray calm your-
420   selves. I have eleven children, and I am twenty-six times a grandma, and I have seen them all through their silly seasons, and when it come on them they will run the Devil bowlegged keeping up with their mischief. I think she'll wake when she tires of it. A child's spirit is like a child, you can never catch it
425   by running after it; you must stand still, and, for love, it will soon itself come back.

PROCTOR: Aye, that's the truth of it, Rebecca.

MRS. PUTNAM: This is no silly season, Rebecca. My Ruth is bewildered, Rebecca; she cannot eat.
430

REBECCA: Perhaps she is not hungered yet. (*To PARRIS*) I hope you are not decided to go in search of loose spirits, Mr. Parris. I've heard promise of that outside.

PARRIS: A wide opinion's running in the parish that the Devil may be among us, and I would satisfy them that they are
435   wrong.

PROCTOR: Then let you come out and call them wrong. Did you consult the wardens before you called this minister to look for devils?

PARRIS: He is not coming to look for devils!
440
PROCTOR: Then what's he coming for?

PUTNAM: There be children dyin' in the village, Mister!

PROCTOR: I seen none dyin'. This society will not be a bag to swing around your head, Mr. Putnam. *(To* PARRIS*)* Did you call a meeting before you—?

PUTNAM: I am sick of meetings; cannot the man turn his head without he have a meeting?

PROCTOR: He may turn his head, but not to Hell!

REBECCA: Pray, John, be calm. *(Pause. He defers to her.)* Mr. Parris, I think you'd best send Reverend Hale back as soon as he come. This will set us all to arguin' again in the society, and we thought to have peace this year. I think we ought rely on the doctor now, and good prayer.

MRS. PUTNAM: Rebecca, the doctor's baffled!

REBECCA: If so he is, then let us go to God for the cause of it. There is prodigious danger in the seeking of loose spirits. I fear it, I fear it. Let us rather blame ourselves and—

PUTNAM: How may we blame ourselves? I am one of nine sons; the Putnam seed have peopled this province. And yet I have but one child left of eight—and now she shrivels!

REBECCA: I cannot fathom that.

MRS. PUTNAM: *(with a growing edge of sarcasm)* But I must! You think it God's work you should never lose a child, nor grandchild either, and I bury all but one? There are wheels within wheels in this village, and fires within fires!

PUTNAM: *(to* PARRIS*)* When Reverend Hale comes, you will proceed to look for signs of witchcraft here.

PROCTOR: *(to* PUTNAM*)* You cannot command Mr. Parris. We vote by name in this society, not by acreage.

PUTNAM: I never heard you worried so on this society, Mr. Proctor. I do not think I saw you at Sabbath meeting since snow flew.

PROCTOR: I have trouble enough without I come five mile to hear him preach only hellfire and bloody damnation. Take it to heart, Mr. Parris. There are many others who stay away from church these days because you hardly ever mention God any more.

PARRIS: *(now aroused)* Why, that's a drastic charge!

REBECCA: It's somewhat true; there are many that quail to bring their children—

PARRIS: I do not preach for children, Rebecca. It is not the children who are unmindful of their obligations toward this ministry.

REBECCA: Are there really those unmindful?

PARRIS: I should say the better half of Salem village—

PUTNAM: And more than that!

PARRIS: Where is my wood? My contract provides I be supplied with all my firewood. I am waiting since November for a stick, and even in November I had to show my frostbitten hands like some London beggar!

GILES: You are allowed six pound a year to buy your wood, Mr. Parris.

PARRIS: I regard that six pound as part of my salary. I am paid little enough without I spend six pound on firewood.

PROCTOR: Sixty, plus six for firewood—

PARRIS: The salary is sixty-six pound, Mr. Proctor! I am not some preaching farmer with a book under my arm; I am a graduate of Harvard College.

GILES: Aye, and well instructed in arithmetic!

PARRIS: Mr. Corey, you will look far for a man of my kind at sixty pound a year! I am not used to this poverty; I left a thrifty business in the Barbados to serve the Lord. I do not fathom it, why am I persecuted here? I cannot offer one proposition but there be a howling riot of argument. I have often wondered if the Devil be in it somewhere; I cannot understand you people otherwise.

PROCTOR: Mr. Parris, you are the first minister ever did demand the deed to this house—

PARRIS: Man! Don't a minister deserve a house to live in?

PROCTOR: To live in, yes. But to ask ownership is like you shall own the meeting house itself; the last meeting I were at you spoke so long on deeds and mortgages I thought it were an auction.

PARRIS: I want a mark of confidence, is all! I am your third preacher in seven years. I do not wish to be put out like the cat whenever some majority feels the whim. You people seem not to comprehend that a minister is the Lord's man in the parish; a minister is not to be so lightly crossed and contradicted—

PUTNAM: Aye!

PARRIS: There is either obedience or the church will burn like Hell is burning!

PROCTOR: Can you speak one minute without we land in Hell again? I am sick of Hell!

PARRIS: It is not for you to say what is good for you to hear!

PROCTOR: I may speak my heart, I think!

PARRIS: *(in a fury)* What, are we Quakers? We are not Quakers here yet, Mr. Proctor. And you may tell that to your followers!

PROCTOR: My followers!

PARRIS: *(—now he's out with it)* There is a party in this church. I am not blind; there is a faction and a party.

PROCTOR: Against you?

PUTNAM: Against him and all authority!

PROCTOR: Why, then I must find it and join it.

(There is shock among the others.)

REBECCA: He does not mean that.

PUTNAM: He confessed it now!

PROCTOR: I mean it solemnly, Rebecca; I like not the smell of this "authority."

REBECCA: No, you cannot break charity with your minister. You are another kind, John. Clasp his hand, make your peace.

PROCTOR: I have a crop to sow and lumber to drag home. *(He goes angrily to the door and turns to* COREY *with a smile.)* What say you, Giles, let's find the party. He says there's a party.

GILES: I've changed my opinion of this man, John. Mr. Parris, I beg your pardon. I never thought you had so much iron in you.

PARRIS: *(surprised)* Why, thank you, Giles!

GILES: It suggests to the mind what the trouble be among us all these years. *(To all)* Think on it. Wherefore is everybody suing everybody else? Think on it now, it's a deep thing, and dark as a pit. I have been six time in court this year—

PROCTOR: *(familiarly, with warmth, although he knows he is approaching the edge of* GILES' *tolerance with this)* Is it the Devil's fault that a man cannot say you good morning without you clap him for defamation? You're old, Giles, and you're not hearin' so well as you did.

GILES: *(—he cannot be crossed)* John Proctor, I have only last month collected four pound damages for you publicly sayin' I burned the roof off your house, and I—

PROCTOR: *(laughing)* I never said no such thing, but I've paid you for it, so I hope I can call you deaf without charge. Now come along, Giles, and help me drag my lumber home.

PUTNAM: A moment, Mr. Proctor. What lumber is that you're draggin', if I may ask you?

PROCTOR: My lumber. From out my forest by the riverside.

PUTNAM: Why, we are surely gone wild this year. What anarchy
565 is this? That tract is in my bounds, it's in my bounds, Mr. Proctor.

PROCTOR: In your bounds! (*Indicating* REBECCA) I bought that tract from Goody Nurse's husband five months ago.

PUTNAM: He had no right to sell it. It stands clear in my grand-
570 father's will that all the land between the river and—

PROCTOR: Your grandfather had a habit of willing land that never belonged to him, if I may say it plain.

GILES: That's God's truth; he nearly willed away my north pasture but he knew I'd break his fingers before he'd set his name
575 to it. Let's get your lumber home, John. I feel a sudden will to work coming on.

PUTNAM: You load one oak of mine and you'll fight to drag it home!

GILES: Aye, and we'll win too, Putnam—this fool and I. Come
580 on! (*He turns to* PROCTOR *and starts out.*)

PUTNAM: I'll have my men on you, Corey! I'll clap a writ on you!

(*Enter* REVEREND JOHN HALE *of Beverly.*)

Mr. Hale is nearing forty, a tight-skinned, eager-eyed intellectual. This is a beloved errand for him; on being called here to ascertain witchcraft he felt the pride of the specialist whose unique knowledge has at last been publicly called for. Like almost all men of learning, he spent a good deal of his time pondering the invisible world, especially since he had himself encountered a witch in his parish not long before. That woman, however, turned into a mere pest under his searching scrutiny, and the child she had allegedly been afflicting recovered her normal behavior after Hale had given her his kindness and a few days of rest in his own house. However, that experience never raised a doubt in his mind as to the reality of the underworld or the existence of Lucifer's many-faced lieutenants. And his belief is not to his discredit. Better minds than Hale's were—and still are—convinced that there is a society of spirits beyond our ken. One cannot help noting that one of his lines has never yet raised a laugh in any audience that has seen this play; it is his assurance that "We cannot look to superstition in this. The Devil is precise." Evidently we are not quite certain even now whether diabolism is holy and not to be scoffed at. And it is no accident that we should be so bemused.

Like Reverend Hale and the others on this stage, we conceive the Devil as a necessary part of a respectable view of cosmology. Ours is a divided empire in which certain ideas and emotions and actions are of God, and their opposites are of Lucifer. It is as impossible for most men to conceive of a morality without sin as of an earth without "sky." Since 1692 a great but superficial change has wiped out God's beard and the Devil's horns, but the world is still gripped between two diametrically opposed absolutes. The concept of unity, in which positive and negative are attributes of the same force, in which good and evil are relative, ever-changing, and always joined to the same phenomenon—such a concept is still reserved to the physical sciences and to the few who have grasped the history of ideas. When it is recalled that until the Christian era the underworld was never regarded as a hostile area, that all gods were useful and essentially friendly to man despite occasional lapses; when we see the steady and methodical inculcation into humanity of the idea of man's worthlessness—until redeemed—the necessity of the Devil may become evident as a weapon, a weapon designed and used time and time again in every age to whip men into a surrender to a particular church or church-state.

Our difficulty in believing the—for want of a better word—political inspiration of the Devil is due in great part to the fact that he is called up and damned not only by our social antagonists but by our own side, whatever it may be. The Catholic Church, through its Inquisition, is famous for cultivating Lucifer as the arch-fiend, but the Church's enemies relied no less upon the Old Boy to keep the human mind enthralled. Luther was himself accused of alliance with Hell, and he in turn accused his enemies. To complicate matters further, he believed that he had had contact with the Devil and had argued theology with him. I am not surprised at this, for at my own university a professor of history—a Lutheran, by the way—used to assemble his graduate students, draw the shades, and commune in the classroom with Erasmus. He was never, to my knowledge, officially scoffed at for this, the reason being that the university officials, like most of us, are the children of a history which still sucks at the Devil's teats. At this writing, only England has held back before the temptations of contemporary diabolism. In the countries of the Communist ideology, all resistance of any import is linked to the totally malign capitalist succubi, and in America any man who is not reactionary in his views is open to the charge of alliance with the Red hell. Political opposition, thereby, is given an inhumane overlay which then justifies the abrogation of all normally applied customs of civilized intercourse. A political policy is equated with moral right, and opposition to it with diabolical malevolence. Once such an equation is effectively made, society becomes a congeries of plots and counterplots, and the main role of government changes from that of the arbiter to that of the scourge of God.

The results of this process are no different now from what they ever were, except sometimes in the degree of cruelty inflicted, and not always even in that department. Normally the actions and deeds of a man were all that society felt comfortable in judging. The secret intent of an action was left to the ministers, priests, and rabbis to deal with. When diabolism rises, however, actions are the least important manifests of the true nature of a man. The Devil, as Reverend Hale said, is a wily one, and, until an hour before he fell, even God thought him beautiful in Heaven.

The analogy, however, seems to falter when one considers that, while there were no witches then, there are Communists and capitalists now, and in each camp there is certain proof that spies of each side are at work undermining the other. But this is a snobbish objection and not at all warranted by the facts. I have no doubt that people *were* communing with, and even worshiping, the Devil in Salem, and if the whole truth could be known in this case, as it is in others, we should discover a regular and

conventionalized propitiation of the dark spirit. One certain evidence of this is the confession of Tituba, the slave of Reverend Parris, and another is the behavior of the children who were known to have indulged in sorceries with her.

There are accounts of similar *klatches* in Europe, where the daughters of the towns would assemble at night and, sometimes with fetishes, sometimes with a selected young man, give themselves to love, with some bastardly results. The Church, sharp-eyed as it must be when gods long dead are brought to life, condemned these orgies as witchcraft and interpreted them, rightly, as a resurgence of the Dionysiac forces it had crushed long before. Sex, sin, and the Devil were early linked, and so they continued to be in Salem, and are today. From all accounts there are no more puritanical mores in the world than those enforced by the Communists in Russia, where women's fashions, for instance, are as prudent and all-covering as any American Baptist would desire. The divorce laws lay a tremendous responsibility on the father for the care of his children. Even the laxity of divorce regulations in the early years of the revolution was undoubtedly a revulsion from the nineteenth-century Victorian immobility of marriage and the consequent hypocrisy that developed from it. If for no other reasons, a state so powerful, so jealous of the uniformity of its citizens, cannot long tolerate the atomization of the family. And yet, in American eyes at least, there remains the conviction that the Russian attitude toward women is lascivious. It is the Devil working again, just as he is working within the Slav who is shocked at the very idea of a woman's disrobing herself in a burlesque show. Our opposites are always robed in sexual sin, and it is from this unconscious conviction that demonology gains both its attractive sensuality and its capacity to infuriate and frighten.

Coming into Salem now, Reverend Hale conceives of himself much as a young doctor on his first call. His painfully acquired armory of symptoms, catchwords, and diagnostic procedures are now to be put to use at last. The road from Beverly is unusually busy this morning, and he has passed a hundred rumors that make him smile at the ignorance of the yeomanry in this most precise science. He feels himself allied with the best minds of Europe—kings, philosophers, scientists, and ecclesiasts of all churches. His goal is light, goodness and its preservation, and he knows the exaltation of the blessed whose intelligence, sharpened by minute examinations of enormous tracts, is finally called upon to face what may be a bloody fight with the Fiend himself.

(He appears loaded down with half a dozen heavy books.)

HALE: Pray you, someone take these!

PARRIS: *(delighted)* Mr. Hale! Oh! it's good to see you again! *(Taking some books)* My, they're heavy!

585 HALE: *(setting down his books)* They must be; they are weighted with authority.

PARRIS: *(a little scared)* Well, you do come prepared!

HALE: We shall need hard study if it comes to tracking down the Old Boy. *(Noticing* REBECCA*)* You cannot be Rebecca Nurse?

590 REBECCA: I am, sir. Do you know me?

HALE: It's strange how I knew you, but I suppose you look as such a good soul should. We have all heard of your great charities in Beverly.

PARRIS: Do you know this gentleman? Mr. Thomas Putnam. And his good wife Ann.   595

HALE: Putnam! I had not expected such distinguished company, sir.

PUTNAM: *(pleased)* It does not seem to help us today, Mr. Hale. We look to you to come to our house and save our child.

HALE: Your child ails too?   600

MRS. PUTNAM: Her soul, her soul seems flown away. She sleeps and yet she walks . . .

PUTNAM: She cannot eat.

HALE: Cannot eat! *(Thinks on it. Then, to* PROCTOR *and* GILES COREY*)* Do you men have afflicted children?   605

PARRIS: No, no, these are farmers. John Proctor—

GILES COREY: He don't believe in witches.

PROCTOR: *(to* HALE*)* I never spoke on witches one way or the other. Will you come, Giles?

GILES: No—no, John, I think not. I have some few queer questions of my own to ask this fellow.   610

PROCTOR: I've heard you to be a sensible man, Mr. Hale. I hope you'll leave some of it in Salem.

*(*PROCTOR *goes.* HALE *stands embarrassed for an instant.)*

PARRIS: *(quickly)* Will you look at my daughter, sir? *(Leads* HALE *to the bed.)* She has tried to leap out the window; we discovered her this morning on the highroad, waving her arms as though she'd fly.   615

HALE: *(narrowing his eyes)* Tries to fly.

PUTNAM: She cannot bear to hear the Lord's name, Mr. Hale; that's a sure sign of witchcraft afloat.   620

HALE: *(holding up his hands)* No, no. Now let me instruct you. We cannot look to superstition in this. The Devil is precise; the marks of his presence are definite as stone, and I must tell you all that I shall not proceed unless you are prepared to believe me if I should find no bruise of hell upon her.   625

PARRIS: It is agreed, sir—it is agreed—we will abide by your judgment.

HALE: Good then. *(He goes to the bed, looks down at* BETTY. *To* PARRIS*)* Now, sir, what were your first warning of this strangeness?   630

PARRIS: Why, sir—I discovered her—*(indicating* ABIGAIL*)* — and my niece and ten or twelve of the other girls, dancing in the forest last night.

HALE: *(surprised)* You permit dancing?

PARRIS: No, no, it were secret—   635

MRS. PUTNAM: *(unable to wait)* Mr. Parris's slave has knowledge of conjurin', sir.

PARRIS: *(to* MRS. PUTNAM*)* We cannot be sure of that, Goody Ann—

MRS. PUTNAM: *(frightened, very softly)* I know it sir. I sent my child—she should learn from Tituba who murdered her sisters.   640

REBECCA: *(horrified)* Goody Ann! You sent a child to conjure up the dead?

MRS. PUTNAM: Let God blame me, not you, not you, Rebecca! I'll not have you judging me any more! *(To* HALE*)* Is it a natural work to lose seven children before they live a day?   645

PARRIS: Sssh!

*(*REBECCA, *with great pain, turns her face away. There is a pause.)*

HALE: Seven dead in childbirth.

MRS. PUTNAM: *(softly)* Aye. *(Her voice breaks; she looks up at*
650   *him. Silence.* HALE *is impressed.* PARRIS *looks to him. He goes*
    to his books, opens one, turns pages, then reads. All wait,
    avidly.)

PARRIS: *(hushed)* What book is that?

MRS. PUTNAM: What's there, sir?

655 HALE: *(with a tasty love of intellectual pursuit)* Here is all the
    invisible world, caught, defined, and calculated. In these
    books the Devil stands stripped of all his brute disguises. Here
    are all your familiar spirits — your incubi and succubi; your
    witches that go by land, by air, and by sea; your wizards of the
660   night and of the day. Have no fear now — we shall find him
    out if he has come among us, and I mean to crush him utterly
    if he has shown his face! *(He starts for the bed.)*

REBECCA: Will it hurt the child, sir?

HALE: I cannot tell. If she is truly in the Devil's grip we may have
665   to rip and tear to get her free.

REBECCA: I think I'll go, then. I am too old for this. *(She rises.)*

PARRIS: *(striving for conviction)* Why, Rebecca, we may open up
    the boil of all our troubles today!

REBECCA: Let us hope for that. I go to God for you, sir.

670 PARRIS: *(with trepidation — and resentment)* I hope you do not
    mean we go to Satan here! *(Slight pause.)*

REBECCA: I wish I knew. *(She goes out; they feel resentful of her*
    note of moral superiority.)

PUTNAM: *(abruptly)* Come, Mr. Hale, let's get on. Sit you here.

675 GILES: Mr. Hale, I have always wanted to ask a learned man —
    what signifies the readin' of strange books?

HALE: What books?

GILES: I cannot tell; she hides them.

HALE: Who does this?

680 GILES: Martha, my wife. I have waked at night many a time and
    found her in a corner, readin' of a book. Now what do you
    make of that?

HALE: Why, that's not necessarily —

GILES: It discomfits me! Last night — mark this — I tried and
685   tried and could not say my prayers. And then she close her
    book and walks out of the house, and suddenly — mark this —
    I could pray again!

> Old Giles must be spoken for, if only because his fate was
> to be so remarkable and so different from that of all the
> others. He was in his early eighties at this time, and was
> the most comical hero in the history. No man has ever
> been blamed for so much. If a cow was missed, the first
> thought was to look for her around Corey's house; a fire
> blazing up at night brought suspicion of arson to his door.
> He didn't give a hoot for public opinion, and only in his
> last years — after he had married Martha — did he bother
> much with the church. That she stopped his prayer is
> very probable, but he forgot to say that he'd only recently
> learned any prayers and it didn't take much to make him
> stumble over them. He was a crank and a nuisance, but
> withal a deeply innocent and brave man. In court once,
> he was asked if it were true that he had been frightened by
> the strange behavior of a hog and had then said he knew it
> to be the Devil in an animal's shape. "What frighted
> you?" he was asked. He forgot everything but the word
> "frighted," and instantly replied, "I do not know that I
> ever spoke that word in my life."

HALE: Ah! The stoppage of prayer — this is strange. I'll speak fur-
    ther on that with you.

GILES: I'm not sayin' she's touched the Devil, now, but I'd ad- 690
    mire to know what books she reads and why she hides them.
    She'll not answer me, y' see.

HALE: Aye, we'll discuss it. *(To all)* Now mark me, if the Devil is
    in her you will witness some frightful wonders in this room,
    so please to keep your wits about you. Mr. Putnam, stand 695
    close in case she flies. Now, Betty, dear, will you sit up? *(PUT-*
    NAM *comes in closer, ready-handed.* HALE *sits* BETTY *up, but*
    she hangs limp in his hands.) Hmmm. *(He observes her care-*
    fully. The others watch breathlessly.) Can you hear me? I am
    John Hale, minister of Beverly. I have come to help you, 700
    dear. Do you remember my two little girls in Beverly? *(She*
    does not stir in his hands.)

PARRIS: *(in fright)* How can it be the Devil? Why would he
    choose my house to strike? We have all manner of licentious
    people in the village! 705

HALE: What victory would the Devil have to win a soul already
    bad? It is the best the Devil wants, and who is better than the
    minister?

GILES: That's deep, Mr. Parris, deep, deep!

PARRIS: *(with resolution now)* Betty! Answer Mr. Hale! Betty! 710

HALE: Does someone afflict you, child? It need not be a woman,
    mind you, or a man. Perhaps some bird invisible to others
    comes to you — perhaps a pig, a mouse, or any beast at all. Is
    there some figure bids you fly? *(The child remains limp in his*
    hands. In silence he lays her back on the pillow. Now, holding 715
    out his hands toward her, he intones) In nomine Domini
    Sabaoth sui filiique ite ad infernos. *(She does not stir. He*
    turns to ABIGAIL, *his eyes narrowing.)* Abigail, what sort of
    dancing were you doing with her in the forest?

ABIGAIL: Why — common dancing is all. 720

PARRIS: I think I ought to say that I — I saw a kettle in the grass
    where they were dancing.

ABIGAIL: That were only soup.

HALE: What sort of soup were in this kettle, Abigail?

ABIGAIL: Why, it were beans — and lentils, I think, and — 725

HALE: Mr. Parris, you did not notice, did you, any living thing
    in the kettle? A mouse, perhaps, a spider, a frog — ?

PARRIS: *(fearfully)* I — do believe there were some movement —
    in the soup.

ABIGAIL: That jumped in, we never put it in! 730

HALE: *(quickly)* What jumped in?

ABIGAIL: Why, a very little frog jumped —

PARRIS: A frog, Abby!

HALE: *(grasping* ABIGAIL) Abigail, it may be your cousin is
    dying. Did you call the Devil last night? 735

ABIGAIL: I never called him! Tituba, Tituba . . .

PARRIS: *(blanched)* She called the Devil?

HALE: I should like to speak with Tituba.

PARRIS: Goody Ann, will you bring her up? *(*MRS. PUTNAM
    exits.) 740

HALE: How did she call him?

ABIGAIL: I know not — she spoke Barbados.

HALE: Did you feel any strangeness when she called him? A sud-
    den cold wind, perhaps? A trembling below the ground?

ABIGAIL: I didn't see no Devil! *(Shaking* BETTY) Betty, wake up. 745
    Betty! Betty!

HALE: You cannot evade me, Abigail. Did your cousin drink any
    of the brew in that kettle?

ABIGAIL: She never drank it!

750 HALE: Did you drink it?

ABIGAIL: No, sir!

HALE: Did Tituba ask you to drink it?

ABIGAIL: She tried, but I refused.

HALE: Why are you concealing? Have you sold yourself to Lucifer?

755 ABIGAIL: I never sold myself! I'm a good girl! I'm a proper girl!

(MRS. PUTNAM *enters with* TITUBA, *and instantly* ABIGAIL *points at* TITUBA.)

ABIGAIL: She made me do it! She made Betty do it!

TITUBA: (*shocked and angry*) Abby!

ABIGAIL: She makes me drink blood!

PARRIS: Blood!!

760 MRS. PUTNAM: My baby's blood?

TITUBA: No, no, chicken blood. I give she chicken blood!

HALE: Woman, have you enlisted these children for the Devil?

TITUBA: No, no, sir, I don't truck with no Devil!

HALE: Why can she not wake? Are you silencing this child?

765 TITUBA: I love me Betty!

HALE: You have sent your spirit out upon this child, have you not? Are you gathering souls for the Devil?

ABIGAIL: She sends her spirit on me in church; she makes me laugh at prayer!

770 PARRIS: She have often laughed at prayer!

ABIGAIL: She comes to me every night to go and drink blood!

TITUBA: You beg *me* to conjure! She beg *me* make charm—

ABIGAIL: Don't lie! (*To* HALE) She comes to me while I sleep; she's always making me dream corruptions!

775 TITUBA: Why you say that, Abby?

ABIGAIL: Sometimes I wake and find myself standing in the open doorway and not a stitch on my body! I always hear her laughing in my sleep. I hear her singing her Barbados songs and tempting me with—

780 TITUBA: Mister Reverend, I never—

HALE: (*resolved now*) Tituba, I want you to wake this child.

TITUBA: I have no power on this child, sir.

HALE: You most certainly do, and you will free her from it now! When did you compact with the Devil?

785 TITUBA: I don't compact with no Devil!

PARRIS: You will confess yourself or I will take you out and whip you to your death, Tituba!

PUTNAM: This woman must be hanged! She must be taken and hanged!

790 TITUBA: (*terrified, falls to her knees*) No, no, don't hang Tituba! I tell him I don't desire to work for him, sir.

PARRIS: The Devil?

HALE: Then you saw him! (TITUBA *weeps.*) Now Tituba, I know that when we bind ourselves to Hell it is very hard to break

795 with it. We are going to help you tear yourself free—

TITUBA: (*frightened by the coming process*) Mister Reverend, I do believe somebody else be witchin' these children.

HALE: Who?

TITUBA: I don't know, sir, but the Devil got him numerous

800 witches.

HALE: Does he! (*It is a clue.*) Tituba, look into my eyes. Come, look into me. (*She raises her eyes to his fearfully.*) You would be a good Christian woman, would you not, Tituba?

TITUBA: Aye, sir, a good Christian woman.

805 HALE: And you love these little children?

TITUBA: Oh, yes, sir, I don't desire to hurt little children.

HALE: And you love God, Tituba?

TITUBA: I love God with all my bein'.

HALE: Now, in God's holy name—

TITUBA: Bless Him. Bless Him. (*She is rocking on her knees,* 810 *sobbing in terror.*)

HALE: And to His glory—

TITUBA: Eternal glory. Bless Him—bless God . . .

HALE: Open yourself, Tituba—open yourself and let God's holy light shine on you. 815

TITUBA: Oh, bless the Lord.

HALE: When the Devil comes to you does he ever come—with another person? (*She stares up into his face.*) Perhaps another person in the village? Someone you know.

PARRIS: Who came with him? 820

PUTNAM: Sarah Good? Did you ever see Sarah Good with him? Or Osburn?

PARRIS: Was it man or woman came with him?

TITUBA: Man or woman. Was—was woman.

PARRIS: What woman? A woman, you said. What woman? 825

TITUBA: It was black dark, and I—

PARRIS: You could see him, why could you not see her?

TITUBA: Well, they was always talking; they was always runnin' round and carryin' on—

PARRIS: You mean out of Salem? Salem witches? 830

TITUBA: I believe so, yes, sir.

(Now HALE *takes her hand. She is surprised.*)

HALE: Tituba. You must have no fear to tell us who they are, do you understand? We will protect you. The Devil can never overcome a minister. You know that, do you not?

TITUBA: (*kisses* HALE's *hand*) Aye, sir, oh, I do. 835

HALE: You have confessed yourself to witchcraft, and that speaks a wish to come to Heaven's side. And we will bless you, Tituba.

TITUBA: (*deeply relieved*) Oh, God bless you, Mr. Hale!

HALE: (*with rising exaltation*) You are God's instrument put in 840 our hands to discover the Devil's agents among us. You are selected, Tituba, you are chosen to help us cleanse our village. So speak utterly, Tituba, turn your back on him and face God—face God, Tituba, and God will protect you.

TITUBA: (*joining with him*) Oh, God, protect Tituba! 845

HALE: (*kindly*) Who came to you with the Devil? Two? Three? Four? How many?

(TITUBA *pants, and begins rocking back and forth again, staring ahead.*)

TITUBA: There was four. There was four.

PARRIS: (*pressing in on her*) Who? Who? Their names, their names! 850

TITUBA: (*suddenly bursting out*) Oh, how many times he bid me kill you, Mr. Parris!

PARRIS: Kill me!

TITUBA: (*in a fury*) He say Mr. Parris must be kill! Mr. Parris no goodly man, Mr. Parris mean man and no gentle man, and 855 he bid me rise out of my bed and cut your throat! (*They gasp.*) But I tell him "No! I don't hate that man. I don't want kill that man." But he say, "You work for me, Tituba, and I make you free! I give you pretty dress to wear, and put you way high up in the air, and you gone fly back to Barbados!" And I say, 860

"You lie, Devil, you lie!" And then he come one stormy night to me, and he say, "Look! I have *white* people belong to me." And I look—and there was Goody Good.

PARRIS: Sarah Good!

865 TITUBA: (*rocking and weeping*) Aye, sir, and Goody Osburn.

MRS. PUTNAM: I knew it! Goody Osburn were midwife to me three times. I begged you, Thomas, did I not? I begged him not to call Osburn because I feared her. My babies always shriveled in her hands!

870 HALE: Take courage, you must give us all their names. How can you bear to see this child suffering? Look at her, Tituba. (*He is indicating* BETTY *on the bed.*) Look at her God-given innocence; her soul is so tender; we must protect her, Tituba; the Devil is out and preying on her like a beast upon the flesh of

875 the pure lamb. God will bless you for your help.

(ABIGAIL *rises, staring as though inspired, and cries out.*)

ABIGAIL: I want to open myself! (*They turn to her, startled. She is enraptured, as though in a pearly light.*) I want the light of God, I want the sweet love of Jesus! I danced for the Devil; I saw him; I wrote in his book; I go back to Jesus; I kiss His

880 hand. I saw Sarah Good with the Devil! I saw Goody Osburn with the Devil! I saw Bridget Bishop with the Devil!

(*As she is speaking,* BETTY *is rising from the bed, a fever in her eyes, and picks up the chant.*)

BETTY: (*staring too*) I saw George Jacobs with the Devil! I saw Goody Howe with the Devil!

PARRIS: She speaks! (*He rushes to embrace* BETTY.) She speaks!

885 HALE: Glory to God! It is broken, they are free!

BETTY: (*calling out hysterically and with great relief*) I saw Martha Bellows with the Devil!

ABIGAIL: I saw Goody Sibber with the Devil! (*It is rising to a great glee.*)

890 PUTNAM: The marshal, I'll call the marshal!

(PARRIS *is shouting a prayer of thanksgiving.*)

BETTY: I saw Alice Barrow with the Devil!

(*The curtain begins to fall.*)

HALE: (*as* PUTNAM *goes out*) Let the marshal bring irons!

ABIGAIL: I saw Goody Hawkins with the Devil!

BETTY: I saw Goody Bibber with the Devil!

895 ABIGAIL: I saw Goody Booth with the Devil!

(*On their ecstatic cries the curtain falls.*)

— ACT TWO —

The common room of PROCTOR's *house, eight days later.*

At the right is a door opening on the fields outside. A fireplace is at the left, and behind it a stairway leading upstairs. It is the low, dark, and rather long living room of the time. As the curtain rises, the room is empty. From above, ELIZABETH *is heard softly singing to the children. Presently the door opens and* JOHN PROCTOR *enters, carrying his gun. He glances about the room as he comes toward the fireplace, then halts for an instant as he hears her singing. He continues on to the fireplace, leans the gun against the wall as he swings a pot out of the fire and smells it.*

Then he lifts out the ladle and tastes. He is not quite pleased. He reaches to a cupboard, takes a pinch of salt, and drops it into the pot. As he is tasting again, her footsteps are heard on the stair. He swings the pot into the fireplace and goes to a basin and washes his hands and face. ELIZABETH *enters.*

ELIZABETH: What keeps you so late? It's almost dark.

PROCTOR: I were planting far out to the forest edge.

ELIZABETH: Oh, you're done then.

PROCTOR: Aye, the farm is seeded. The boys asleep?

ELIZABETH: They will be soon. (*And she goes to the fireplace, proceeds to ladle up stew in a dish.*) 5

PROCTOR: Pray now for a fair summer.

ELIZABETH: Aye.

PROCTOR: Are you well today?

ELIZABETH: I am. (*She brings the plate to the table, and, indicating the food*) It is a rabbit. 10

PROCTOR: (*going to the table*) Oh, is it! In Jonathan's trap?

ELIZABETH: No, she walked into the house this afternoon; I found her sittin' in the corner like she come to visit.

PROCTOR: Oh, that's a good sign walkin' in. 15

ELIZABETH: Pray God. It hurt my heart to strip her, poor rabbit. (*She sits and watches him taste it.*)

PROCTOR: It's well seasoned.

ELIZABETH: (*blushing with pleasure*) I took great care. She's tender? 20

PROCTOR: Aye. (*He eats. She watches him.*) I think we'll see green fields soon. It's warm as blood beneath the clods.

ELIZABETH: That's well.

(PROCTOR *eats, then looks up.*)

PROCTOR: If the crop is good I'll buy George Jacob's heifer. How would that please you? 25

ELIZABETH: Aye, it would.

PROCTOR: (*with a grin*) I mean to please you, Elizabeth.

ELIZABETH: (*—it is hard to say*) I know it, John.

(*He gets up, goes to her, kisses her. She receives it. With a certain disappointment, he returns to the table.*)

PROCTOR: (*as gently as he can*) Cider?

ELIZABETH: (*with a sense of reprimanding herself for having forgot*) Aye! (*She gets up and goes and pours a glass for him. He now arches his back.*) 30

PROCTOR: This farm's a continent when you go foot by foot droppin' seeds in it.

ELIZABETH: (*coming with the cider*) It must be. 35

PROCTOR: (*drinks a long draught, then, putting the glass down*) You ought to bring some flowers in the house.

ELIZABETH: Oh! I forgot! I will tomorrow.

PROCTOR: It's winter in here yet. On Sunday let you come with me, and we'll walk the farm together; I never see such a load of flowers on the earth. (*With good feeling he goes and looks up at the sky through the open doorway.*) Lilacs have a purple smell. Lilac is the smell of nightfall, I think. Massachusetts is a beauty in the spring! 40

ELIZABETH: Aye, it is. 45

(*There is a pause. She is watching him from the table as he stands there absorbing the night. It is as though she would speak but cannot. Instead, now, she takes up his plate and glass and fork and goes with them to the basin. Her back is turned to him. He turns to her and watches her. A sense of their separation rises.)*

PROCTOR: I think you're sad again. Are you?

ELIZABETH: (*— she doesn't want friction, and yet she must*) You come so late I thought you'd gone to Salem this afternoon.

PROCTOR: Why? I have no business in Salem.

50 ELIZABETH: You did speak of going, earlier this week.

PROCTOR: (*— he knows what she means*) I thought better of it since.

ELIZABETH: Mary Warren's there today.

PROCTOR: Why'd you let her? You heard me forbid her go to
55 Salem any more!

ELIZABETH: I couldn't stop her.

PROCTOR: (*holding back a full condemnation of her*) It is a fault, it is a fault, Elizabeth — you're the mistress here, not Mary Warren.

60 ELIZABETH: She frightened all my strength away.

PROCTOR: How may that mouse frighten you, Elizabeth? You —

ELIZABETH: It is a mouse no more. I forbid her go, and she raises up her chin like the daughter of a prince and says to me, "I must go to Salem, Goody Proctor; I am an official of the
65 court!"

PROCTOR: Court! What court?

ELIZABETH: Aye, it is a proper court they have now. They've sent four judges out of Boston, she says, weighty magistrates of the General Court, and at the head sits the Deputy Governor of
70 the Province.

PROCTOR: (*astonished*) Why, she's mad.

ELIZABETH: I would to God she were. There be fourteen people in the jail now, she says. (PROCTOR *simply looks at her, unable to grasp it.*) And they'll be tried, and the court have
75 power to hang them too, she says.

PROCTOR: (*scoffing, but without conviction*) Ah, they'd never hang —

ELIZABETH: The Deputy Governor promise hangin' if they'll not confess, John. The town's gone wild, I think. She speak of
80 Abigail, and I thought she were a saint, to hear her. Abigail brings the other girls into the court, and where she walks the crowd will part like the sea for Israel. And folks are brought before them, and if they scream and howl and fall to the floor — the person's clapped in the jail for bewitchin' them.

85 PROCTOR: (*wide-eyed*) Oh, it is a black mischief.

ELIZABETH: I think you must go to Salem, John. (*He turns to her.*) I think so. You must tell them it is a fraud.

PROCTOR: (*thinking beyond this*) Aye, it is, it is surely.

ELIZABETH: Let you go to Ezekiel Cheever — he knows you well.
90 And tell him what she said to you last week in her uncle's house. She said it had naught to do with witchcraft, did she not?

PROCTOR: (*in thought*) Aye, she did, she did. (*Now, a pause.*)

ELIZABETH: (*quietly, fearing to anger him by prodding*) God forbid you keep that from the court, John. I think they must be
95 told.

PROCTOR: (*quietly, struggling with his thought*) Aye, they must, they must. It is a wonder they do believe her.

ELIZABETH: I would go to Salem now, John — let you go tonight.

PROCTOR: I'll think on it.

100 ELIZABETH: (*with her courage now*) You cannot keep it, John.

PROCTOR: (*angering*) I know I cannot keep it. I say I will think on it!

ELIZABETH: (*hurt, and very coldly*) Good, then, let you think on it. (*She stands and starts to walk out of the room.*)

PROCTOR: I am only wondering how I may prove what she told 105
me, Elizabeth. If the girl's a saint now, I think it is not easy to prove she's fraud, and the town gone so silly. She told it to me in a room alone — I have no proof for it.

ELIZABETH: You were alone with her?

PROCTOR: (*stubbornly*) For a moment alone, aye. 110

ELIZABETH: Why, then, it is not as you told me.

PROCTOR: (*his anger rising*) For a moment, I say. The others come in soon after.

ELIZABETH: (*quietly — she has suddenly lost all faith in him*) Do as you wish, then. (*She starts to turn.*) 115

PROCTOR: Woman. (*She turns to him.*) I'll not have your suspicion any more.

ELIZABETH: (*a little loftily*) I have no —

PROCTOR: I'll not have it!

ELIZABETH: Then let you not earn it. 120

PROCTOR: (*with a violent undertone*) You doubt me yet?

ELIZABETH: (*with a smile, to keep her dignity*) John, if it were not Abigail that you must go to hurt, would you falter now? I think not.

PROCTOR: Now look you — 125

ELIZABETH: I see what I see, John.

PROCTOR: (*with solemn warning*) You will not judge me more, Elizabeth. I have good reason to think before I charge fraud on Abigail, and I will think on it. Let you look to your own improvement before you go to judge your husband any more. 130
I have forgot Abigail, and —

ELIZABETH: And I.

PROCTOR: Spare me! You forget nothin' and forgive nothin'. Learn charity, woman. I have gone tiptoe in this house all seven month since she is gone. I have not moved from there 135
to there without I think to please you, and still an everlasting funeral marches round your heart. I cannot speak but I am doubted, every moment judged for lies, as though I come into a court when I come into this house!

ELIZABETH: John, you are not open with me. You saw her with a 140
crowd, you said. Now you —

PROCTOR: I'll plead my honesty no more, Elizabeth.

ELIZABETH: (*— now she would justify herself*) John, I am only —

PROCTOR: No more! I should have roared you down when first you told me your suspicion. But I wilted, and, like a Chris- 145
tian, I confessed. Confessed! Some dream I had must have mistaken you for God that day. But you're not, you're not, and let you remember it! Let you look sometimes for the goodness in me, and judge me not.

ELIZABETH: I do not judge you. The magistrate sits in your heart 150
that judges you. I never thought you but a good man, John — (*with a smile*) — only somewhat bewildered.

PROCTOR: (*laughing bitterly*) Oh, Elizabeth, your justice would freeze beer! (*He turns suddenly toward a sound outside. He starts for the door as* MARY WARREN *enters. As soon as he sees* 155
her, he goes directly to her and grabs her by her cloak, furious.) How do you go to Salem when I forbid it? Do you mock me? (*Shaking her.*) I'll whip you if you dare leave this house again!

(*Strangely, she doesn't resist him, but hangs limply by his grip.*)

MARY WARREN: I am sick, I am sick, Mr. Proctor. Pray, pray, hurt me not. (*Her strangeness throws him off, and her evident* 160 *pallor and weakness. He frees her.)* My insides are all shuddery; I am in the proceedings all day, sir.

PROCTOR: *(with draining anger—his curiosity is draining it)* And what of these proceedings here? When will you proceed
165 to keep this house, as you are paid nine pound a year to do—and my wife not wholly well?

(As though to compensate, MARY WARREN *goes to* ELIZABETH *with a small rag doll.)*

MARY WARREN: I made a gift for you today, Goody Proctor. I had to sit long hours in a chair, and passed the time with sewing.

ELIZABETH: *(perplexed, looking at the doll)* Why, thank you, it's
170 a fair poppet.

MARY WARREN: *(with a trembling, decayed voice)* We must all love each other now, Goody Proctor.

ELIZABETH: *(amazed at her strangeness)* Aye, indeed we must.

MARY WARREN: *(glancing at the room)* I'll get up early in the
175 morning and clean the house. I must sleep now. *(She turns and starts off.)*

PROCTOR: Mary. *(She halts.)* Is it true? There be fourteen women arrested?

MARY WARREN: No, sir. There be thirty-nine now— *(She sud-*
180 *denly breaks off and sobs and sits down, exhausted.)*

ELIZABETH: Why, she's weepin'! What ails you, child?

MARY WARREN: Goody Osburn—will hang!

(There is a shocked pause, while she sobs.)

PROCTOR: Hang! *(He calls into her face.)* Hang, y'say?

MARY WARREN: *(through her weeping)* Aye.
185 PROCTOR: The Deputy Governor will permit it?

MARY WARREN: He sentenced her. He must. *(To ameliorate it)* But not Sarah Good. For Sarah Good confessed, y'see.

PROCTOR: Confessed! To what?

MARY WARREN: That she—*(in horror at the memory)*—she
190 sometimes made a compact with Lucifer, and wrote her name in his black book—with her blood—and bound herself to torment Christians till God's thrown down—and we all must worship Hell forevermore.

(Pause.)

PROCTOR: But—surely you know what a jabberer she is. Did
195 you tell them that?

MARY WARREN: Mr. Proctor, in open court she near to choked us all to death.

PROCTOR: How, choked you?

MARY WARREN: She sent her spirit out.
200 ELIZABETH: Oh, Mary, Mary, surely you—

MARY WARREN: *(with an indignant edge)* She tried to kill me many times, Goody Proctor!

ELIZABETH: Why, I never heard you mention that before.

MARY WARREN: I never knew it before. I never knew anything
205 before. When she come into the court I say to myself, I must not accuse this woman, for she sleep in ditches, and so very old and poor. But then—then she sit there, denying and denying, and I feel a misty coldness climbin' up my back, and the skin on my skull begin to creep, and I feel a clamp around
210 my neck and I cannot breathe air; and then—*(entranced)*—I hear a voice, a screamin' voice, and it were my voice—and all at once I remembered everything she done to me!

PROCTOR: Why? What did she do to you?

MARY WARREN: *(like one awakened to a marvelous secret in-*
215 *sight)* So many time, Mr. Proctor, she come to this very door, beggin' bread and a cup of cider—and mark this: whenever I turned her away empty, she *mumbled.*

ELIZABETH: Mumbled! She may mumble if she's hungry.

MARY WARREN: But *what* does she mumble? You must remem-
220 ber, Goody Proctor. Last month—a Monday, I think—she walked away, and I thought my guts would burst for two days after. Do you remember it?

ELIZABETH: Why—I do, I think, but—

MARY WARREN: And so I told that to Judge Hathorne, and he
225 asks her so. "Sarah Good," says he, "what curse do you mumble that this girl must fall sick after turning you away?" And then she replies—*(mimicking an old crone)*—"Why, your excellence, no curse at all. I only say my commandments; I hope I may say my commandments," says she!

230 ELIZABETH: And that's an upright answer.

MARY WARREN: Aye, but then Judge Hathorne say, "Recite for us your commandments!"—*(leaning avidly toward them)*—and of all the ten she could not say a single one. She never knew no commandments, and they had her in a flat lie!

235 PROCTOR: And so condemned her?

MARY WARREN: *(now a little strained, seeing his stubborn doubt)* Why, they must when she condemned herself.

PROCTOR: But the proof, the proof!

MARY WARREN: *(with greater impatience with him)* I told you
240 the proof. It's hard proof, hard as rock, the judges said.

PROCTOR: *(pauses an instant, then)* You will not go to court again, Mary Warren.

MARY WARREN: I must tell you, sir, I will be gone every day now. I am amazed you do not see what weighty work we do.

245 PROCTOR: What work you do! It's strange work for a Christian girl to hang old women!

MARY WARREN: But, Mr. Proctor, they will not hang them if they confess. Sarah Good will only sit in jail some time—*(recalling)*—and here's a wonder for you; think on this.
250 Goody Good is pregnant!

ELIZABETH: Pregnant! Are they mad? The woman's near to sixty!

MARY WARREN: They had Doctor Griggs examine her, and she's full to the brim. And smokin' a pipe all these years, and no husband either! But she's safe, thank God, for they'll not hurt
255 the innocent child. But be that not a marvel? You must see it, sir, it's God's work we do. So I'll be gone every day for some time. I'm—I am an official of the court, they say, and I—*(She has been edging toward offstage.)*

PROCTOR: I'll official you! *(He strides to the mantel, takes down
260 the whip hanging there.)*

MARY WARREN: *(terrified, but coming erect, striving for her authority)* I'll not stand whipping any more!

ELIZABETH: *(hurriedly, as* PROCTOR *approaches)* Mary, promise now you'll stay at home—

MARY WARREN: *(backing from him, but keeping her erect pos-*
265 *ture, striving, striving for her way)* The Devil's loose in Salem, Mr. Proctor; we must discover where he's hiding!

PROCTOR: I'll whip the Devil out of you! *(With whip raised he reaches out for her, and she streaks away and yells.)*

MARY WARREN: *(pointing at* ELIZABETH) I saved her life today!
270

(Silence. His whip comes down.)

ELIZABETH: *(softly)* I am accused?

MARY WARREN: (quaking) Somewhat mentioned. But I said I
never see no sign you ever sent your spirit out to hurt no one,
and seeing I do live so closely with you, they dismissed it.

275 ELIZABETH: Who accused me?

MARY WARREN: I am bound by law, I cannot tell it. (To PROC-
TOR) I only hope you'll not be so sarcastical no more. Four
judges and the King's deputy sat to dinner with us but an hour
ago. I—I would have you speak civilly to me, from this out.

280 PROCTOR: (in horror, muttering in disgust at her) Go to bed.

MARY WARREN: (with a stamp of her foot) I'll not be ordered to
bed no more, Mr. Proctor! I am eighteen and a woman, however single!

PROCTOR: Do you wish to sit up? Then sit up.

285 MARY WARREN: I wish to go to bed!

PROCTOR: (in anger) Good night, then!

MARY WARREN: Good night. (Dissatisfied, uncertain of herself,
she goes out. Wide-eyed, both, PROCTOR and ELIZABETH
stand staring.)

290 ELIZABETH: (quietly) Oh, the noose, the noose is up!

PROCTOR: There'll be no noose.

ELIZABETH: She wants me dead. I knew all week it would come
to this!

PROCTOR: (without conviction) They dismissed it. You heard
295 her say—

ELIZABETH: And what of tomorrow? She will cry me out until
they take me!

PROCTOR: Sit you down.

ELIZABETH: She wants me dead, John, you know it!

300 PROCTOR: I say sit down! (She sits, trembling. He speaks quietly,
trying to keep his wits.) Now we must be wise, Elizabeth.

ELIZABETH: (with sarcasm, and a sense of being lost) Oh, indeed, indeed!

PROCTOR: Fear nothing. I'll find Ezekiel Cheever. I'll tell him
305 she said it were all sport.

ELIZABETH: John, with so many in the jail, more than Cheever's
help is needed now, I think. Would you favor me with this?
Go to Abigail.

PROCTOR: (his soul hardening as he senses . . .) What have I to
310 say to Abigail?

ELIZABETH: (delicately) John—grant me this. You have a faulty
understanding of young girls. There is a promise made in any
bed—

PROCTOR: (striving against his anger) What promise!

315 ELIZABETH: Spoke or silent, a promise is surely made. And she
may dote on it now—I am sure she does—and thinks to kill
me, then to take my place.

(PROCTOR's anger is rising: he cannot speak.)

ELIZABETH: It is her dearest hope, John, I know it. There be a
thousand names; why does she call mine? There be a certain
320 danger in calling such a name—I am no Goody Good that
sleeps in ditches, nor Osburn, drunk and half-witted. She'd
dare not call out such a farmer's wife but there be monstrous
profit in it. She thinks to take my place, John.

PROCTOR: She cannot think it! (He knows it is true.)

325 ELIZABETH: ("reasonably") John, have you ever shown her
somewhat of contempt? She cannot pass you in the church
but you will blush—

PROCTOR: I may blush for my sin.

ELIZABETH: I think she sees another meaning in that blush.

PROCTOR: And what see you? What see you, Elizabeth?   330

ELIZABETH: ("conceding") I think you be somewhat ashamed,
for I am there, and she so close.

PROCTOR: When will you know me, woman? Were I stone I
would have cracked for shame this seven month!

ELIZABETH: Then go and tell her she's a whore. Whatever prom-   335
ise she may sense—break it, John, break it.

PROCTOR: (between his teeth) Good, then. I'll go. (He starts for
his rifle.)

ELIZABETH: (trembling, fearfully)— Oh, how unwillingly!

PROCTOR: (turning on her, rifle in hand) I will curse her hotter   340
than the oldest cinder in hell. But pray, begrudge me not my
anger!

ELIZABETH: Your anger! I only ask you—

PROCTOR: Woman, am I so base? Do you truly think me base?

ELIZABETH: I never called you base.   345

PROCTOR: Then how do you charge me with such a promise?
The promise that a stallion gives a mare I gave that girl!

ELIZABETH: Then why do you anger with me when I bid you
break it?

PROCTOR: Because it speaks deceit, and I am honest! But I'll   350
plead no more! I see now your spirit twists around the single
error of my life, and I will never tear it free!

ELIZABETH: (crying out) You'll tear it free—when you come to
know that I will be your only wife, or no wife at all! She has an
arrow in you yet, John Proctor, and you know it well!   355

(Quite suddenly, as though from the air, a figure appears in the
doorway. They start slightly. It is MR. HALE. He is different
now—drawn a little, and there is a quality of deference, even of
guilt, about his manner now.)

HALE: Good evening.

PROCTOR: (still in his shock) Why, Mr. Hale! Good evening to
you, sir. Come in, come in.

HALE: (to ELIZABETH) I hope I do not startle you.

ELIZABETH: No, no, it's only that I heard no horse—   360

HALE: You are Goodwife Proctor.

PROCTOR: Aye; Elizabeth.

HALE: (nods, then) I hope you're not off to bed yet.

PROCTOR: (setting down his gun) No, no. (HALE comes further
into the room. And PROCTOR, to explain his nervousness) We   365
are not used to visitors after dark, but you're welcome here.
Will you sit you down, sir?

HALE: I will. (He sits.) Let you sit, Goodwife Proctor.

(She does, never letting him out of her sight. There is a pause as
HALE looks about the room.)

PROCTOR: (to break the silence) Will you drink cider, Mr. Hale?

HALE: No, it rebels my stomach; I have some further traveling   370
yet tonight. Sit you down, sir. (PROCTOR sits.) I will not keep
you long, but I have some business with you.

PROCTOR: Business of the court?

HALE: No—no, I come of my own, without the court's authority. Hear me. (He wets his lips.) I know not if you are aware,   375
but your wife's name is—mentioned in the court.

PROCTOR: We know it, sir. Our Mary Warren told us. We are
entirely amazed.

HALE: I am a stranger here, as you know. And in my ignorance I
find it hard to draw a clear opinion of them that come accused   380
before the court. And so this afternoon, and now tonight, I go

from house to house—I come now from Rebecca Nurse's house and—

ELIZABETH: *(shocked)* Rebecca's charged!

385 HALE: God forbid such a one be charged. She is, however—mentioned somewhat.

ELIZABETH: *(with an attempt at a laugh)* You will never believe, I hope, that Rebecca trafficked with the Devil.

HALE: Woman, it is possible.

390 PROCTOR: *(taken aback)* Surely you cannot think so.

HALE: This is a strange time, Mister. No man may longer doubt the powers of the dark are gathered in monstrous attack upon this village. There is too much evidence now to deny it. You will agree, sir?

395 PROCTOR: *(evading)* I—have no knowledge in that line. But it's hard to think so pious a woman be secretly a Devil's bitch after seventy year of such good prayer.

HALE: Aye. But the Devil is a wily one, you cannot deny it. However, she is far from accused, and I know she will not be.

400 *(Pause.)* I thought, sir, to put some questions as to the Christian character of this house, if you'll permit me.

PROCTOR: *(coldly, resentful)* Why, we—have no fear of questions sir.

HALE: Good, then. *(He makes himself more comfortable.)* In the

405 book of record that Mr. Parris keeps, I note that you are rarely in the church on Sabbath Day.

PROCTOR: No, sir, you are mistaken.

HALE: Twenty-six time in seventeen month, sir. I must call that rare. Will you tell me why you are so absent?

410 PROCTOR: Mr. Hale, I never knew I must account to that man for I come to church or stay at home. My wife were sick this winter.

HALE: So I am told. But you, Mister, why could you not come alone?

415 PROCTOR: I surely did come when I could, and when I could not I prayed in this house.

HALE: Mr. Proctor, your house is not a church; your theology must tell you that.

PROCTOR: It does, sir, it does; and it tells me that a minister may

420 pray to God without he have golden candlesticks upon the altar.

HALE: What golden candlesticks?

PROCTOR: Since we built the church there were pewter candlesticks upon the altar; Francis Nurse made them, y'know, and a sweeter hand never touched the metal. But Parris came, and

425 for twenty week he preach nothin' but golden candlesticks until he had them. I labor the earth from dawn of day to blink of night, and I tell you true, when I look to heaven and see my money glaring at his elbows—it hurt my prayer, sir, it hurt my prayer. I think, sometimes, the man dreams cathedrals,

430 not clapboard meetin' houses.

HALE: *(thinks, then)* And yet, Mister, a Christian on Sabbath Day must be in church. *(Pause.)* Tell me—you have three children?

PROCTOR: Aye. Boys.

435 HALE: How comes it that only two are baptized?

PROCTOR: *(starts to speak, then stops, then, as though unable to restrain this)* I like it not that Mr. Parris should lay his hand upon my baby. I see no light of God in that man. I'll not conceal it.

440 HALE: I must say it, Mr. Proctor; that is not for you to decide. The man's ordained, therefore the light of God is in him.

PROCTOR: *(flushed with resentment but trying to smile)* What's your suspicion, Mr. Hale?

HALE: No, no, I have no—

PROCTOR: I nailed the roof upon the church, I hung the door—   445

HALE: Oh, did you! That's a good sign, then.

PROCTOR: It may be I have been too quick to bring the man to book, but you cannot think we ever desired the destruction of religion. I think that's in your mind, is it not?

HALE: *(not altogether giving way)* I—have—there is a softness in   450
your record, sir, a softness.

ELIZABETH: I think, maybe, we have been too hard with Mr. Parris. I think so. But sure we never loved the Devil here.

HALE: *(nods, deliberating this. Then, with the voice of one administering a secret test)* Do you know your Commandments,   455
Elizabeth?

ELIZABETH: *(without hesitation, even eagerly)* I surely do. There be no mark of blame upon my life, Mr. Hale. I am a covenanted Christian woman.

HALE: And you, Mister?   460

PROCTOR: *(a trifle unsteadily)* I—am sure I do, sir.

HALE: *(glances at her open face, then at JOHN, then)* Let you repeat them, if you will.

PROCTOR: The Commandments.

HALE: Aye.   465

PROCTOR: *(looking off, beginning to sweat)* Thou shalt not kill.

HALE: Aye.

PROCTOR: *(counting on his fingers)* Thou shalt not steal. Thou shalt not covet thy neighbor's goods, nor make unto thee any graven image. Thou shalt not take the name of the Lord in   470
vain; thou shalt have no other gods before me. *(With some hesitation)* Thou shalt remember the Sabbath Day and keep it holy. *(Pause. Then)* Thou shalt honor thy father and mother. Thou shalt not bear false witness. *(He is stuck. He counts back on his fingers, knowing one is missing.)* Thou   475
shalt not make unto thee any graven image.

HALE: You have said that twice, sir.

PROCTOR: *(lost)* Aye. *(He is flailing for it.)*

ELIZABETH: *(delicately)* Adultery, John.

PROCTOR: *(as though a secret arrow had pained his heart)* Aye.   480
(Trying to grin it away—to HALE) You see, sir, between the two of us we do know them all. *(HALE only looks at PROCTOR, deep in his attempt to define this man. PROCTOR grows more uneasy.)* I think it be a small fault.

HALE: Theology, sir, is a fortress; no crack in a fortress may be   485
accounted small. *(He rises, he seems worried now. He paces a little, in deep thought.)* There be no love for Satan in this house, Mister.

PROCTOR: There be no love for Satan in this house, Mister.

HALE: I pray it, I pray it dearly. *(He looks to both of them, an attempt at a smile on his face, but his misgivings are clear.)*   490
Well, then—I'll bid you good night.

ELIZABETH: *(unable to restrain herself)* Mr. Hale. *(He turns.)* I do think you are suspecting me somewhat? Are you not?

HALE: *(obviously disturbed—and evasive)* Goody Proctor, I do not judge you. My duty is to add what I may to the godly   495
wisdom of the court. I pray you both good health and good fortune. *(To JOHN)* Good night, sir. *(He starts out.)*

ELIZABETH: *(with a note of desperation)* I think you must tell him, John.

HALE: What's that?   500

ELIZABETH: *(restraining a call)* Will you tell him?

(Slight pause. HALE *looks questioningly at* JOHN.*)*

PROCTOR: *(with difficulty)* I—I have no witness and cannot prove it, except my word be taken. But I know the children's sickness had naught to do with witchcraft.

505 HALE: *(stopped, struck)* Naught to do—?

PROCTOR: Mr. Parris discovered them sportin' in the woods. They were startled and took sick.

(Pause.)

HALE: Who told you this?

PROCTOR: *(hesitates, then)* Abigail Williams.

510 HALE: Abigail!

PROCTOR: Aye.

HALE: *(his eyes wide)* Abigail Williams told you it had naught to do with witchcraft!

PROCTOR: She told me the day you came, sir.

515 HALE: *(suspiciously)* Why—why did you keep this?

PROCTOR: I never knew until tonight that the world is gone daft with this nonsense.

HALE: Nonsense! Mister, I have myself examined Tituba, Sarah Good, and numerous others that have confessed to dealing

520 with the Devil. They have *confessed* it.

PROCTOR: And why not, if they must hang for denyin' it? There are them that will swear to anything before they'll hang; have you never thought of that?

HALE: I have. I—I have indeed. *(It is his own suspicion, but he*

525 *resists it. He glances at* ELIZABETH, *then at* JOHN.*)* And you—would you testify to this in court?

PROCTOR: I—had not reckoned with goin' into court. But if I must I will.

HALE: Do you falter here?

530 PROCTOR: I falter nothing, but I may wonder if my story will be credited in such a court. I do wonder on it, when such a steady-minded minister as you will suspicion such a woman that never lied, and cannot, and the world knows she cannot! I may falter somewhat, Mister; I am no fool.

535 HALE: *(quietly—it has impressed him)* Proctor, let you open with me now, for I have a rumor that troubles me. It's said you hold no belief that there may even be witches in the world. Is that true, sir?

PROCTOR: *(—he knows this is critical, and is striving against his*

540 *disgust with* HALE *and with himself for even answering)* I know not what I have said, I may have said it. I have wondered if there be witches in the world—although I cannot believe they come among us now.

HALE: Then you do not believe—

545 PROCTOR: I have no knowledge of it; the Bible speaks of witches, and I will not deny them.

HALE: And you, woman?

ELIZABETH: I—I cannot believe it.

HALE: *(shocked)* You cannot!

550 PROCTOR: Elizabeth, you bewilder him!

ELIZABETH: *(to* HALE*)* I cannot think the Devil may own a woman's soul, Mr. Hale, when she keeps an upright way, as I have. I am a good woman, I know it; and if you believe I may do only good work in the world, and yet be secretly bound to

555 Satan, then I must tell you, sir, I do not believe it.

HALE: But, woman, you do believe there are witches in—

ELIZABETH: If you think that I am one, then I say there are none.

HALE: You surely do not fly against the Gospel, the Gospel—

PROCTOR: She believe in the Gospel, every word!

ELIZABETH: Question Abigail Williams about the Gospel, not 560 myself!

(HALE stares at her.)

PROCTOR: She do not mean to doubt the Gospel, sir, you cannot think it. This be a Christian house, sir, a Christian house.

HALE: God keep you both; let the third child be quickly baptized, and go you without fail each Sunday in to Sabbath 565 prayer; and keep a solemn, quiet way among you. I think—

(GILES COREY appears in doorway.)

GILES: John!

PROCTOR: Giles! What's the matter?

GILES: They take my wife.

(FRANCIS NURSE enters.)

GILES: And his Rebecca! 570

PROCTOR: *(to* FRANCIS*)* Rebecca's in the *jail!*

FRANCIS: Aye, Cheever come and take her in his wagon. We've only now come from the jail, and they'll not even let us in to see them.

ELIZABETH: They've surely gone wild now, Mr. Hale! 575

FRANCIS: *(going to* HALE*)* Reverend Hale! Can you not speak to the Deputy Governor? I'm sure he mistakes these people—

HALE: Pray calm yourself, Mr. Nurse.

FRANCIS: My wife is the very brick mortar of the church, Mr. Hale—*(indicating* GILES*)*—and Martha Corey, there cannot 580 be a woman closer yet to God than Martha.

HALE: How is Rebecca charged, Mr. Nurse?

FRANCIS: *(with a mocking, half-hearted laugh)* For murder, she's charged! *(Mockingly quoting the warrant)* "For the marvelous and supernatural murder of Goody Putnam's babies." 585 What am I to do, Mr. Hale?

HALE: *(turns from* FRANCIS, *deeply troubled, then)* Believe me, Mr. Nurse, if Rebecca Nurse be tainted, then nothing's left to stop the whole green world from burning. Let you rest upon the justice of the court; the court will send her home, I know it. 590

FRANCIS: You cannot mean she will be tried in court!

HALE: *(pleading)* Nurse, though our hearts break, we cannot flinch; these are new times, sir. There is a misty plot afoot so subtle we should be criminal to cling to old respects and ancient friendships. I have seen too many frightful proofs in 595 court—the Devil is alive in Salem, and we dare not quail to follow wherever the accusing finger points!

PROCTOR: *(angered)* How may such a woman murder children?

HALE: *(in great pain)* Man, remember, until an hour before the Devil fell, God thought him beautiful in Heaven. 600

GILES: I never said my wife were a witch, Mr. Hale; I only said she were reading books!

HALE: Mr. Corey, exactly what complaint were made on your wife?

GILES: That bloody mongrel Walcott charge her. Y'see, he buy a 605 pig of my wife four or five year ago, and the pig died soon after. So he come dancin' in for his money back. So my Martha, she says to him, "Walcott, if you haven't the wit to feed a pig properly, you'll not live to own many," she says. Now he goes to court and claims that from that day to this he cannot 610 keep a pig alive for more than four weeks because my Martha bewitch them with her books!

(Enter EZEKIEL CHEEVER. *A shocked silence.)*

CHEEVER: Good evening to you, Proctor.

PROCTOR: Why, Mr. Cheever. Good evening.

615 CHEEVER: Good evening, all. Good evening, Mr. Hale.

PROCTOR: I hope you come not on business of the court.

CHEEVER: I do, Proctor, aye. I am clerk of the court now, y'know.

(Enter MARSHAL HERRICK, *a man in his early thirties, who is somewhat shamefaced at the moment.)*

GILES: It's a pity, Ezekiel, that an honest tailor might have gone

620   to Heaven must burn in Hell. You'll burn for this, do you know it?

CHEEVER: You know yourself I must do as I'm told. You surely know that, Giles. And I'd as lief you'd not be sending me to Hell. I like not the sound of it, I tell you; I like not the sound

625   of it. *(He fears* PROCTOR, *but starts to reach inside his coat.)* Now believe me, Proctor, how heavy be the law, all its tonnage I do carry on my back tonight. *(He takes out a warrant.)* I have a warrant for your wife.

PROCTOR: *(to* HALE.*)* You said she were not charged!

630 HALE: I know nothin' of it. *(To* CHEEVER*)* When were she charged?

CHEEVER: I am given sixteen warrant tonight, sir, and she is one.

PROCTOR: Who charged her?

CHEEVER: Why, Abigail Williams charge her.

635 PROCTOR: On what proof, what proof?

CHEEVER: *(looking about the room)* Mr. Proctor, I have little time. The court bid me search your house, but I like not to search a house. So will you hand me any poppets that your wife may keep here?

640 PROCTOR: Poppets?

ELIZABETH: I never kept no poppets, not since I were a girl.

CHEEVER: *(embarrassed, glancing toward the mantel where sits* MARY WARREN's *poppet)* I spy a poppet, Goody Proctor.

ELIZABETH: Oh! *(Going for it)* Why, this is Mary's.

645 CHEEVER: *(shyly)* Would you please to give it to me?

ELIZABETH: *(handing it to him, asks* HALE*)* Has the court discovered a text in poppets now?

CHEEVER: *(carefully holding the poppet)* Do you keep any others in this house?

650 PROCTOR: No, nor this one either till tonight. What signifies a poppet?

CHEEVER: Why, a poppet — *(he gingerly turns the poppet over)* — a poppet may signify — Now, woman, will you please to come with me?

655 PROCTOR: She will not! *(to* ELIZABETH*)* Fetch Mary here.

CHEEVER: *(ineptly reaching toward* ELIZABETH*)* No, no, I am forbid to leave her from my sight.

PROCTOR: *(pushing his arm away)* You'll leave her out of sight and out of mind, Mister. Fetch Mary, Elizabeth. *(*ELIZABETH

660   *goes upstairs.)*

HALE: What signifies a poppet, Mr. Cheever?

CHEEVER: *(turning the poppet over in his hands)* Why, they say it may signify that she — *(He has lifted the poppet's skirt, and his eyes widen in astonished fear.)* Why, this, this —

665 PROCTOR: *(reaching for the poppet)* What's there?

CHEEVER: Why — *(He draws out a long needle from the poppet)* — it is a needle! Herrick, Herrick, it is a needle!

*(*HERRICK *comes toward him.)*

PROCTOR: *(angrily, bewildered)* And what signifies a needle!

CHEEVER: *(his hands shaking)* Why, this go hard with her, Proctor, this — I had my doubts, Proctor, I had my doubts, but   670 here's calamity. *(To* HALE, *showing the needle)* You see it, sir, it is a needle!

HALE: Why? What meanin' has it?

CHEEVER: *(wide-eyed, trembling)* The girl, the Williams girl, Abigail Williams, sir. She sat to dinner in Reverend Parris's   675 house tonight, and without word nor warnin' she falls to the floor. Like a struck beast, he says, and screamed a scream that a bull would weep to hear. And he goes to save her, and, stuck two inches in the flesh of her belly, he draw a needle out. And demandin' of her how she come to be so stabbed, she — *(to*   680 PROCTOR *now)* — testify it were your wife's familiar spirit pushed it in.

PROCTOR: Why, she done it herself! *(To* HALE*)* I hope you're not takin' this for proof, Mister!

*(*HALE, *struck by the proof, is silent.)*

CHEEVER: 'Tis hard proof! *(To* HALE*)* I find here a poppet Goody   685 Proctor keeps. I have found it, sir. And in the belly of the poppet a needle's stuck. I tell you true, Proctor, I never warranted to see such proof of Hell, and I bid you obstruct me not, for I —

(Enter ELIZABETH *with* MARY WARREN. PROCTOR, *seeing* MARY WARREN, *draws her by the arm to* HALE.*)*

PROCTOR: Here now! Mary, how did this poppet come into my   690 house?

MARY WARREN: *(frightened for herself, her voice very small)* What poppet's that, sir?

PROCTOR: *(impatiently, pointing at the doll in* CHEEVER's *hand)* This poppet, this poppet.   695

MARY WARREN: *(evasively, looking at it)* Why, I — I think it is mine.

PROCTOR: It is your poppet, is it not?

MARY WARREN: *(not understanding the direction of this)* It — is, sir.   700

PROCTOR: And how did it come into this house?

MARY WARREN: *(glancing about at the avid faces)* Why — I made it in the court, sir, and — give it to Goody Proctor tonight.

PROCTOR: *(To* HALE*)* Now, sir — do you have it?   705

HALE: Mary Warren, a needle have been found inside this poppet.

MARY WARREN: *(bewildered)* Why, I meant no harm by it, sir.

PROCTOR: *(quickly)* You stuck that needle in yourself?

MARY WARREN: I — I believe I did, sir, I —   710

PROCTOR: *(to* HALE*)* Why say you now?

HALE: *(watching* MARY WARREN *closely)* Child, you are certain this be your natural memory? May it be, perhaps, that someone conjures you even now to say this?

MARY WARREN: Conjures me? Why, no sir, I am entirely my-   715 self, I think. Let you ask Susanna Walcott — she saw me sewin' it in court. Or better still: Ask Abby, Abby sat beside me when I made it.

PROCTOR: *(to* HALE, *of* CHEEVER*)* Bid him begone. Your mind is surely settled now. Bid him out, Mr. Hale.   720

ELIZABETH: What signifies a needle?

HALE: Mary—you charge a cold and cruel murder on Abigail.

MARY WARREN: Murder! I charge no—

HALE: Abigail were stabbed tonight; a needle were found stuck into her belly—
725

ELIZABETH: And she charges me?

HALE: Aye.

ELIZABETH: (her breath knocked out) Why—! The girl is murder! She must be ripped out of the world!

CHEEVER: (pointing at ELIZABETH) You've heard that, sir! Ripped out of the world! Herrick, you heard it!
730

PROCTOR: (suddenly snatching the warrant out of CHEEVER's hands) Out with you.

CHEEVER: Proctor, you dare not touch the warrant.

PROCTOR: (ripping the warrant) Out with you!
735

CHEEVER: You've ripped the Deputy Governor's warrant, man!

PROCTOR: Damn the Deputy Governor! Out of my house!

HALE: Now, Proctor, Proctor!

PROCTOR: Get y'gone with them! You are a broken minister.

HALE: Proctor, if she is innocent, the court—
740

PROCTOR: If she is innocent! Why do you never wonder if Parris be innocent, or Abigail? Is the accuser always holy now? Were they born this morning as clean as God's fingers? I'll tell you what's walking Salem—vengeance is walking Salem. We are what we always were in Salem, but now the little crazy children are jangling the keys of the kingdom, and common vengeance writes the law! This warrant's vengeance! I'll not give my wife to vengeance!
745

ELIZABETH: I'll go, John—

PROCTOR: You will not go!
750

HERRICK: I have nine men outside. You cannot keep her. The law binds me, John, I cannot budge.

PROCTOR: (to HALE, ready to break him) Will you see her taken?

HALE: Proctor, the court is just—

PROCTOR: Pontius Pilate! God will not let you wash your hands of this!
755

ELIZABETH: John—I think I must go with them. (He cannot bear to look at her.) Mary, there is bread enough for the morning; you will bake, in the afternoon. Help Mr. Proctor as you were his daughter—you owe me that, and much more. (She is fighting her weeping. To PROCTOR) When the children wake, speak nothing of witchcraft—it will frighten them. (She cannot go on.)
760

PROCTOR: I will bring you home. I will bring you soon.
765

ELIZABETH: Oh, John, bring me soon!

PROCTOR: I will fall like an ocean on that court! Fear nothing, Elizabeth.

ELIZABETH: (with great fear) I will fear nothing. (She looks about the room, as though to fix it in her mind.) Tell the children I have gone to visit someone sick.
770

(She walks out the door, HERRICK and CHEEVER behind her. For a moment, PROCTOR watches from the doorway. The clank of chain is heard.)

PROCTOR: Herrick! Herrick, don't chain her! (He rushes out the door. From outside) Damn you, man, you will not chain her! Off with them! I'll not have it! I will not have her chained!

(There are other men's voices against his. HALE, in a fever of guilt and uncertainty, turns from the door to avoid the sight; MARY WARREN bursts into tears and sits weeping. GILES COREY calls to HALE.)

GILES: And yet silent, minister? It is fraud, you know it is fraud! What keeps you, man?
775

(PROCTOR is half braced, half pushed into the room by two deputies and HERRICK.)

PROCTOR: I'll pay you, Herrick, I will surely pay you!

HERRICK: (panting) In God's name, John, I cannot help myself. I must chain them all. Now let you keep inside this house till I am gone! (He goes out with his deputies.)

(PROCTOR stands there, gulping air. Horses and a wagon creaking are heard.)

HALE: (in great uncertainty) Mr. Proctor—
780

PROCTOR: Out of my sight!

HALE: Charity, Proctor, charity. What I have heard in her favor, I will not fear to testify in court. God help me, I cannot judge her guilty or innocent—I know not. Only this consider: the world goes mad, and it profit nothing you should lay the cause to the vengeance of a little girl.
785

PROCTOR: You are a coward! Though you be ordained in God's own tears, you are a coward now!

HALE: Proctor, I cannot think God be provoked so grandly by such a petty cause. The jails are packed—our greatest judges sit in Salem now—and hangin's promised. Man, we must look to cause proportionate. Were there murder done, perhaps, and never brought to light? Abomination? Some secret blasphemy that stinks to Heaven? Think on cause, man, and let you help me to discover it. For there's your way, believe it, there is your only way, when such confusion strikes upon the world. (He goes to GILES and FRANCIS.) Let you counsel among yourselves; think on your village and what may have drawn from heaven such thundering wrath upon you all. I shall pray God open up our eyes.
790

795

800

(HALE goes out.)

FRANCIS: (struck by HALE's mood) I never heard no murder done in Salem.

PROCTOR: (—he has been reached by HALE's words) Leave me, Francis, leave me.

GILES: (shaken) John—tell me, are we lost?
805

PROCTOR: Go home now, Giles. We'll speak on it tomorrow.

GILES: Let you think on it. We'll come early, eh?

PROCTOR: Aye. Go now, Giles.

GILES: Good night, then.

(GILES COREY goes out. After a moment)

MARY WARREN: (in a fearful squeak of a voice) Mr. Proctor, very likely they'll let her come home once they've given proper evidence.
810

PROCTOR: You're coming to the court with me, Mary. You will tell it in the court.

MARY WARREN: I cannot charge murder on Abigail.
815

PROCTOR: (moving menacingly toward her) You will tell the court how that poppet come here and who stuck the needle in.

MARY WARREN: She'll kill me for sayin' that! (PROCTOR continues toward her.) Abby'll charge lechery on you, Mr. Proctor!

PROCTOR: (halting) She's told you!
820

MARY WARREN: I have known it, sir. She'll ruin you with it, I know she will.

PROCTOR: (hesitating, and with deep hatred of himself) Good. Then her saintliness is done with. (MARY backs from him.)

825   We will slide together into our pit; you will tell the court what you know.
MARY WARREN: *(in terror)* I cannot, they'll turn on me—

(PROCTOR strides and catches her, and she is repeating, "I cannot, I cannot.")

PROCTOR: My wife will never die for me! I will bring your guts into your mouth but that goodness will not die for me!
830 MARY WARREN: *(struggling to escape him)* I cannot do it, I cannot!
PROCTOR: *(grasping her by the throat as though he would strangle her)* Make your peace with it! Now Hell and Heaven grapple on our backs, and all our old pretense is ripped away—
835 make your peace! *(He throws her to the floor, where she sobs, "I cannot, I cannot . . ." And now, half to himself, staring, and turning to the open door)* Peace. It is a providence, and no great change; we are only what we always were, but naked now. *(He walks as though toward a great horror, facing the*
840 *open sky.)* Aye, naked! And the wind, God's icy wind, will blow!

(And she is over and over again sobbing, "I cannot, I cannot, I cannot," as the curtain falls)

— ACT THREE —

The vestry room of the Salem meeting house, now serving as the anteroom of the General Court.

As the curtain rises, the room is empty, but for sunlight pouring through two high windows in the back wall. The room is solemn, even forbidding. Heavy beams jut out, boards of random widths make up the walls. At the right are two doors leading into the meeting house proper, where the court is being held. At the left another door leads outside.

There is a plain bench at the left, and another at the right. In the center a rather long meeting table, with stools and a considerable armchair snugged up to it.

Through the partitioning wall at the right we hear a prosecutor's voice, JUDGE HATHORNE's, asking a question; then a woman's voice, MARTHA COREY's, replying.

HATHORNE'S VOICE: Now, Martha Corey, there is abundant evidence in our hands to show that you have given yourself to the reading of fortunes. Do you deny it?
MARTHA COREY'S VOICE: I am innocent to a witch. I know not
5   what a witch is.
HATHORNE'S VOICE: How do you know, then, that you are not a witch?
MARTHA COREY'S VOICE: If I were, I would know it.
HATHORNE'S VOICE: Why do you hurt these children?
10 MARTHA COREY'S VOICE: I do not hurt them. I scorn it!
GILES' VOICE: *(roaring)* I have evidence for the court!

(Voices of townspeople rise in excitement.)

DANFORTH'S VOICE: You will keep your seat!
GILES' VOICE: Thomas Putnam is reaching out for land!
DANFORTH'S VOICE: Remove that man, Marshal!
15 GILES' VOICE: You're hearing lies, lies!

(A roaring goes up from the people.)

HATHORNE'S VOICE: Arrest him, excellency!
GILES' VOICE: I have evidence. Why will you not hear my evidence?

(The door opens and GILES is half carried into the vestry room by HERRICK.)

GILES: Hands off, damn you, let me go!
HERRICK: Giles, Giles!   20
GILES: Out of my way, Herrick! I bring evidence—
HERRICK: You cannot go in there, Giles; it's a court!

(Enter HALE from the court.)

HALE: Pray be calm a moment.
GILES: You, Mr. Hale, go in there and demand I speak.
HALE: A moment, sir, a moment.   25
GILES: They'll be hangin' my wife!

(JUDGE HATHORNE enters. He is in his sixties, a bitter, remorseless Salem judge.)

HATHORNE: How do you dare come roarin' into this court! Are you gone daft, Corey?
GILES: You're not a Boston judge yet, Hathorne. You'll not call me daft!   30

(Enter DEPUTY GOVERNOR DANFORTH and, behind him, EZEKIEL CHEEVER and PARRIS. On his appearance, silence falls. DANFORTH is a grave man in his sixties, of some humor and sophistication that does not, however, interfere with an exact loyalty to his position and his cause. He comes down to GILES, who awaits his wrath.)

DANFORTH: *(looking directly at GILES)* Who is this man?
PARRIS: Giles Corey, sir, and a more contentious—
GILES: *(to PARRIS)* I am asked the question, and I am old enough to answer it! *(To DANFORTH, who impresses him and to whom he smiles through his strain)* My name is Corey, sir, Giles   35
Corey. I have six hundred acres, and timber in addition. It is my wife you be condemning now. *(He indicates the courtroom.)*
DANFORTH: And how do you imagine to help her cause with such contemptuous riot? Now be gone. Your old age alone keeps you out of jail for this.   40
GILES: *(beginning to plead)* They be tellin' lies about my wife, sir, I—
DANFORTH: Do you take it upon yourself to determine what this court shall believe and what it shall set aside?
GILES: Your Excellency, we mean no disrespect for—   45
DANFORTH: Disrespect indeed! It is disruption, Mister. This is the highest court of the supreme government of this province, do you know it?
GILES: *(beginning to weep)* Your Excellency, I only said she were readin' books, sir, and they come and take her out of my   50
house for—
DANFORTH: *(mystified)* Books! What books?
GILES: *(through helpless sobs)* It is my third wife, sir; I never had no wife that be so taken with books, and I thought to find the cause of it, d'y'see, but it were no witch I blamed her for. *(He   55
is openly weeping.)* I have broke charity with the woman, I have broke charity with her. *(He covers his face, ashamed. DANFORTH is respectfully silent.)*
HALE: Excellency, he claims hard evidence for his wife's defense. I think that in all justice you must—   60

DANFORTH: Then let him submit his evidence in proper affidavit. You are certainly aware of our procedure here, Mr. Hale. *(To* HERRICK) Clear this room.

HERRICK: Come now, Giles. *(He gently pushes* COREY *out.)*

65 FRANCIS: We are desperate, sir; we come here three days now and cannot be heard.

DANFORTH: Who is this man?

FRANCIS: Francis Nurse, Your Excellency.

HALE: His wife's Rebecca that were condemned this morning.

70 DANFORTH: Indeed! I am amazed to find you in such uproar. I have only good report of your character, Mr. Nurse.

HATHORNE: I think they must both be arrested in contempt, sir.

DANFORTH: *(to* FRANCIS) Let you write your plea, and in due time I will—

75 FRANCIS: Excellency, we have proof for your eyes; God forbid you shut them to it. The girls, sir, the girls are frauds.

DANFORTH: What's that?

FRANCIS: We have proof of it, sir. They are all deceiving you.

(DANFORTH is shocked, but studying FRANCIS.)

HATHORNE: This is contempt, sir, contempt!

80 DANFORTH: Peace, Judge Hathorne. Do you know who I am, Mr. Nurse?

FRANCIS: I surely do, sir, and I think you must be a wise judge to be what you are.

DANFORTH: And do you know that near to four hundred are in

85 the jails from Marblehead to Lynn, and upon my signature?

FRANCIS: I—

DANFORTH: And seventy-two condemned to hang by that signature?

FRANCIS: Excellency, I never thought to say it to such a weighty

90 judge, but you are deceived.

(Enter GILES COREY from left. All turn to see as he beckons in MARY WARREN with PROCTOR. MARY is keeping her eyes to the ground; PROCTOR has her elbow as though she were near collapse.)

PARRIS: *(on seeing her, in shock)* Mary Warren! *(He goes directly to bend close to her face.)* What are you about here?

PROCTOR: *(pressing PARRIS away from her with a gentle but firm motion of protectiveness)* She would speak with the Deputy

95 Governor.

DANFORTH: *(shocked by this, turns to HERRICK)* Did you not tell me Mary Warren were sick in bed?

HERRICK: She were, Your Honor. When I go to fetch her to the court last week, she said she were sick.

100 GILES: She has been strivin' with her soul all week, Your Honor; she comes now to tell the truth of this to you.

DANFORTH: Who is this?

PROCTOR: John Proctor, sir. Elizabeth Proctor is my wife.

PARRIS: Beware this man, Your Excellency, this man is mischief.

105 HALE: *(excitedly)* I think you must hear the girl, sir, she—

DANFORTH: *(who has become very interested in MARY WARREN and only raises a hand toward HALE)* Peace. What would you tell us, Mary Warren?

(PROCTOR looks at her, but she cannot speak.)

PROCTOR: She never saw no spirits, sir.

110 DANFORTH: *(with great alarm and surprise, to MARY)* Never saw no spirits!

GILES: *(eagerly)* Never.

PROCTOR: *(reaching into his jacket)* She has signed a deposition, sir—

DANFORTH: *(instantly)* No, no, I accept no depositions. *(He is* 115 *rapidly calculating this; he turns from her to* PROCTOR.) Tell me, Mr. Proctor, have you given out this story in the village?

PROCTOR: We have not.

PARRIS: They've come to overthrow the court, sir! This man is—

DANFORTH: I pray you, Mr. Parris. Do you know, Mr. Proctor, 120 that the entire contention of the state in these trials is that the voice of Heaven is speaking through the children?

PROCTOR: I know that, sir.

DANFORTH: *(thinks, staring at* PROCTOR, *then turns to* MARY WARREN) And you, Mary Warren, how came you to cry out 125 people for sending their spirits against you?

MARY WARREN: It were pretense, sir.

DANFORTH: I cannot hear you.

PROCTOR: It were pretense, she says.

DANFORTH: Ah? And the other girls? Susanna Walcott, and— 130 the others? They are also pretending?

MARY WARREN: Aye, sir.

DANFORTH: *(wide-eyed)* Indeed. *(Pause. He is baffled by this. He turns to study* PROCTOR'*s face.)*

PARRIS: *(in a sweat)* Excellency, you surely cannot think to let so 135 vile a lie be spread in open court!

DANFORTH: Indeed not, but it strike hard upon me that she will dare come here with such a tale. Now, Mr. Proctor, before I decide whether I shall hear you or not, it is my duty to tell you this. We burn a hot fire here; it melts down all concealment. 140

PROCTOR: I know that, sir.

DANFORTH: Let me continue. I understand well, a husband's tenderness may drive him to extravagance in defense of a wife. Are you certain in your conscience, Mister, that your evidence is the truth? 145

PROCTOR: It is. And you will surely know it.

DANFORTH: And you thought to declare this revelation in the open court before the public?

PROCTOR: I thought I would, aye—with your permission.

DANFORTH: *(his eyes narrowing)* Now, sir, what is your purpose 150 in so doing?

PROCTOR: Why, I—I would free my wife, sir.

DANFORTH: There lurks nowhere in your heart, nor hidden in your spirit, any desire to undermine this court?

PROCTOR: *(with the faintest faltering)* Why, no, sir. 155

CHEEVER: *(clears his throat, awakening)* I—Your Excellency.

DANFORTH: Mr. Cheever.

CHEEVER: I think it be my duty, sir—*(Kindly, to* PROCTOR) You'll not deny it, John. *(To* DANFORTH) When we come to take his wife, he damned the court and ripped your warrant. 160

PARRIS: Now you have it!

DANFORTH: He did that, Mr. Hale?

HALE: *(takes a breath)* Aye, he did.

PROCTOR: It were a temper, sir. I knew not what I did.

DANFORTH: *(studying him)* Mr. Proctor. 165

PROCTOR: Aye, sir.

DANFORTH: *(straight into his eyes)* Have you ever seen the Devil?

PROCTOR: No, sir.

DANFORTH: You are in all respects a Gospel Christian?

PROCTOR: I am, sir. 170

PARRIS: Such a Christian that will not come to church but once in a month!

DANFORTH: *(restrained—he is curious)* Not come to church?

PROCTOR: I—I have no love for Mr. Parris. It is no secret. But
175   God I surely love.
CHEEVER: He plow on Sunday, sir.
DANFORTH: Plow on Sunday!
CHEEVER: (*apologetically*) I think it be evidence, John. I am an
  official of the court, I cannot keep it.
180 PROCTOR: I—I have once or twice plowed on Sunday. I have
  three children, sir, and until last year my land give little.
GILES: You'll find other Christians that do plow on Sunday if the
  truth be known.
HALE: Your Honor, I cannot think you may judge the man on
185   such evidence.
DANFORTH: I judge nothing. (*Pause. He keeps watching* PROC-
  TOR, *who tries to meet his gaze.*) I tell you straight, Mister—I
  have seen marvels in this court. I have seen people choked
  before my eyes by spirits; I have seen them stuck by pins and
190   slashed by daggers. I have until this moment not the slightest
  reason to suspect that the children may be deceiving me. Do
  you understand my meaning?
PROCTOR: Excellency, does it not strike upon you that so many
  of these women have lived so long with such upright reputa-
195   tion, and—
PARRIS: Do you read the Gospel, Mr. Proctor?
PROCTOR: I read the Gospel.
PARRIS: I think not, or you should surely know that Cain were an
  upright man, and yet he did kill Abel.
200 PROCTOR: Aye, God tells us that. (*To* DANFORTH) But who tells
  us Rebecca Nurse murdered seven babies by sending out her
  spirit on them? It is the children only, and this one will swear
  she lied to you.

(DANFORTH *considers, then beckons* HATHORNE *to him.* HATH-
ORNE *leans in, and he speaks in his ear.* HATHORNE *nods.*)

HATHORNE: Aye, she's the one.
205 DANFORTH: Mr. Proctor, this morning, your wife send me a
  claim in which she states that she is pregnant now.
PROCTOR: My wife pregnant!
DANFORTH: There be no sign of it—we have examined her body.
PROCTOR: But if she say she is pregnant, then she must be! That
210   woman will never lie, Mr. Danforth.
DANFORTH: She will not?
PROCTOR: Never, sir, never.
DANFORTH: We have thought it too convenient to be credited.
  However, if I should tell you now that I will let her be kept
215   another month; and if she begin to show her natural signs,
  you shall have her living yet another year until she is deliv-
  ered—what say you to that? (JOHN PROCTOR *is struck silent.*)
  Come now. You say your only purpose is to save your wife.
  Good, then, she is saved at least this year, and a year is long.
220   What say you, sir? It is done now. (*In conflict,* PROCTOR
  glances at FRANCIS *and* GILES.) Will you drop this charge?
PROCTOR: I—I think I cannot.
DANFORTH: (*now an almost imperceptible hardness in his voice*)
  Then your purpose is somewhat larger.
225 PARRIS: He's come to overthrow this court, Your Honor!
PROCTOR: These are my friends. Their wives are also accused—
DANFORTH: (*with a sudden briskness of manner*) I judge you
  not, sir. I am ready to hear your evidence.
PROCTOR: I come not to hurt the court; I only—
230 DANFORTH: (*cutting him off*) Marshal, go into the court and bid
  Judge Stoughton and Judge Sewall declare recess for one

hour. And let them go to the tavern, if they will. All witnesses
and prisoners are to be kept in the building.
HERRICK: Aye, sir. (*Very deferentially*) If I may say it, sir, I know
  this man all my life. It is a good man, sir.
DANFORTH: (*—it is the reflection on himself he resents*) I am sure
  of it, Marshal. (HERRICK *nods, then goes out.*) Now, what
  deposition do you have for us, Mr. Proctor? And I beg you be
  clear, open as the sky, and honest.
PROCTOR: (*as he takes out several papers*) I am no lawyer, so I'll—
DANFORTH: The pure in heart need no lawyers. Proceed as you
  will.
PROCTOR: (*handing* DANFORTH *a paper*) Will you read this first,
  sir? It's a sort of testament. The people signing it declare their
  good opinion of Rebecca, and my wife, and Martha Corey.
  (DANFORTH *looks down at the paper.*)
PARRIS: (*to enlist* DANFORTH's *sarcasm*) Their good opinion!
  (*But* DANFORTH *goes on reading, and* PROCTOR *is heartened.*)
PROCTOR: These are all landholding farmers, members of the
  church. (*Delicately, trying to point out a paragraph*) If you'll
  notice, sir—they've known the women many years and never
  saw no sign they had dealings with the Devil.

(PARRIS *nervously moves over and reads over* DANFORTH's
shoulder.)

DANFORTH: (*glancing down a long list*) How many names are
  here?
FRANCIS: Ninety-one, Your Excellency.
PARRIS: (*sweating*) These people should be summoned. (DAN-
  FORTH *looks up at him questioningly.*) For questioning.
FRANCIS: (*trembling with anger*) Mr. Danforth, I gave them all
  my word no harm would come to them for signing this.
PARRIS: This is a clear attack upon the court!
HALE: (*to* PARRIS, *trying to contain himself*) Is every defense an
  attack upon the court? Can no one—?
PARRIS: All innocent and Christian people are happy for the
  courts in Salem! These people are gloomy for it. (*To* DAN-
  FORTH *directly*) And I think you will want to know, from each
  and every one of them, what discontents them with you!
HATHORNE: I think they ought to be examined, sir.
DANFORTH: It is not necessarily an attack, I think. Yet—
FRANCIS: These are all covenanted Christians, sir.
DANFORTH: Then I am sure they may have nothing to fear.
  (*Hands* CHEEVER *the paper.*) Mr. Cheever, have warrants
  drawn for all of these—arrest for examination. (*To* PROCTOR)
  Now, Mister, what other information do you have for us?
  (FRANCIS *is still standing, horrified.*) You may sit, Mr. Nurse.
FRANCIS: I have brought trouble on these people; I have—
DANFORTH: No, old man, you have not hurt these people if they
  are of good conscience. But you must understand, sir, that a
  person is either with this court or he must be counted against
  it, there be no road between. This is a sharp time, now, a
  precise time—we live no longer in the dusky afternoon when
  evil mixed itself with good and befuddled the world. Now, by
  God's grace, the shining sun is up, and them that fear not
  light will surely praise it. I hope you will be one of those.
  (MARY WARREN *suddenly sobs.*) She's not hearty, I see.
PROCTOR: No, she's not, sir. (*To* MARY, *bending to her, holding
  her hand, quietly*) Now remember what the angel Raphael
  said to the boy Tobias. Remember it.
MARY WARREN: (*hardly audible*) Aye.

290 PROCTOR: "Do that which is good, and no harm shall come to thee."

MARY WARREN: Aye.

DANFORTH: Come, man, we wait you.

(MARSHAL HERRICK *returns, and takes his post at the door.*)

GILES: John, my deposition, give him mine.

295 PROCTOR: Aye. (*He hands* DANFORTH *another paper.*) This is Mr. Corey's deposition.

DANFORTH: Oh? (*He looks down at it. Now* HATHORNE *comes behind him and reads with him.*)

HATHORNE: (*suspiciously*) What lawyer drew this, Corey?

GILES: You know I never hired a lawyer in my life, Hathorne.

300 DANFORTH: (*finishing the reading*) It is very well phrased. My compliments. Mr. Parris, if Mr. Putnam is in the court, will you bring him in? (HATHORNE *takes the deposition, and walks to the window with it.* PARRIS *goes into the court.*) You have no legal training, Mr. Corey?

305 GILES: (*very pleased*) I have the best, sir — I am thirty-three time in court in my life. And always plaintiff, too.

DANFORTH: Oh, then you're much put-upon.

GILES: I am never put-upon; I know my rights, sir, and I will have them. You know, your father tried a case of mine —

310 might be thirty-five year ago, I think.

DANFORTH: Indeed.

GILES: He never spoke to you of it?

DANFORTH: No, I cannot recall it.

GILES: That's strange, he give me nine pound damages. He were

315 a fair judge, your father. Y'see, I had a white mare that time, and this fellow come to borrow the mare — (*Enter* PARRIS *with* THOMAS PUTNAM. *When he sees* PUTNAM, GILES' *ease goes; he is hard.*) Aye, there he is.

DANFORTH: Mr. Putnam, I have here an accusation by Mr. Co-

320 rey against you. He states that you coldly prompted your daughter to cry witchery upon George Jacobs that is now in jail.

PUTNAM: It is a lie.

DANFORTH: (*turning to* GILES) Mr. Putnam states your charge is a lie. What say you to that?

325 GILES: (*furious, his fists clenched*) A fart on Thomas Putnam, that is what I say to that!

DANFORTH: What proof do you submit for your charge, sir?

GILES: My proof is there! (*Pointing to the paper.*) If Jacobs hangs for a witch he forfeit up his property — that's law! And there is

330 none but Putnam with the coin to buy so great a piece. This man is killing his neighbors for their land!

DANFORTH: But proof, sir, proof.

GILES: (*pointing at his deposition*) The proof is there! I have it from an honest man who heard Putnam say it! The day his

335 daughter cried out on Jacobs, he said she'd given him a fair gift of land.

HATHORNE: And the name of this man?

GILES: (*taken aback*) What name?

HATHORNE: The man that give you this information.

340 GILES: (*hesitates, then*) Why, I — I cannot give you his name.

HATHORNE: And why not?

GILES: (*hesitates, then bursts out*) You know well why not! He'll lay in jail if I give his name!

HATHORNE: This is contempt of the court, Mr. Danforth!

345 DANFORTH: (*to avoid that*) You will surely tell us the name.

GILES: I will not give you no name. I mentioned my wife's name once and I'll burn in hell long enough for that. I stand mute.

DANFORTH: In that case, I have no choice but to arrest you for contempt of this court, do you know that?

350 GILES: This is a hearing; you cannot clap me for contempt of a hearing.

DANFORTH: Oh, it is a proper lawyer! Do you wish me to declare the court in full session here? Or will you give me good reply?

GILES: (*faltering*) I cannot give you no name, sir, I cannot.

355 DANFORTH: You are a foolish old man. Mr. Cheever, begin the record. The court is now in session. I ask you, Mr. Corey —

PROCTOR: (*breaking in*) Your Honor — he has the story in confidence, sir, and he —

PARRIS: The Devil lives on such confidences! (*To* DANFORTH)

360 Without confidences there could be no conspiracy, Your Honor!

HATHORNE: I think it must be broken, sir.

DANFORTH: (*to* GILES) Old man, if your informant tells the truth let him come here openly like a decent man. But if he hide in anonymity I must know why. Now sir, the govern-

365 ment and central church demand of you the name of him who reported Mr. Thomas Putnam a common murderer.

HALE: Excellency —

DANFORTH: Mr. Hale.

HALE: We cannot blink it more. There is a prodigious fear of this

370 court in the country —

DANFORTH: Then there is a prodigious guilt in the country. Are *you* afraid to be questioned here?

HALE: I may only fear the Lord, sir, but there is fear in the country nevertheless.

375

DANFORTH: (*angered now*) Reproach me not with the fear in the country; there is fear in the country because there is a moving plot to topple Christ in the country!

HALE: But it does not follow that everyone accused is part of it.

DANFORTH: No uncorrupted man may fear this court, Mr.

380 Hale! None! (*To* GILES) You are under arrest in contempt of this court. Now sit you down and take counsel with yourself, or you will be set in the jail until you decide to answer all questions.

(GILES COREY *makes a rush for* PUTNAM. PROCTOR *lunges and holds him.*)

385 PROCTOR: No, Giles!

GILES: (*over* PROCTOR's *shoulder at* PUTNAM) I'll cut your throat, Putnam, I'll kill you yet!

PROCTOR: (*forcing him into a chair*) Peace, Giles, peace. (*Releasing him.*) We'll prove ourselves. Now we will. (*He starts to turn to* DANFORTH.)

390

GILES: Say nothin' more, John. (*Pointing at* DANFORTH) He's only playin' you! He means to hang us all!

(MARY WARREN *bursts into sobs.*)

DANFORTH: This is a court of law, Mister. I'll have no effrontery here!

PROCTOR: Forgive him, sir, for his old age. Peace, Giles, we'll

395 prove it all now. (*He lifts up* MARY's *chin.*) You cannot weep, Mary. Remember the angel, what he say to the boy. Hold to it now; there is your rock. (MARY *quiets. He takes out a paper, and turns to* DANFORTH.) This is Mary Warren's deposition. I — I would ask you remember, sir, while you read it, that

400 until two week ago she were no different than the other children are today. (*He is speaking reasonably, restraining all his fears, his anger, his anxiety.*) You saw her scream, she

howled, she swore familiar spirits choked her; she even testi-
405 fied that Satan, in the form of women now in jail, tried to win
her soul away, and then when she refused—
DANFORTH: We know all this.
PROCTOR: Aye, sir. She swears now that she never saw Satan; nor
any spirit, vague or clear, that Satan may have sent to hurt
410 her. And she declares her friends are lying now.

(PROCTOR *starts to hand* DANFORTH *the deposition, and* HALE
comes up to DANFORTH *in a trembling state.*)

HALE: Excellency, a moment. I think this goes to the heart of the
matter.
DANFORTH: *(with deep misgivings)* It surely does.
HALE: I cannot say he is an honest man; I know him little. But in
415 all justice, sir, a claim so weighty cannot be argued by a
farmer. In God's name, sir, stop here; send him home and let
him come again with a lawyer—
DANFORTH: *(patiently)* Now look you, Mr. Hale—
HALE: Excellency, I have signed seventy-two death warrants; I
420 am a minister of the Lord, and I dare not take a life without
there be a proof so immaculate no slightest qualm of conscience may doubt it.
DANFORTH: Mr. Hale, you surely do not doubt my justice.
HALE: I have this morning signed away the soul of Rebecca
425 Nurse, Your Honor. I'll not conceal it, my hand shakes yet as
with a wound! I pray you, sir, *this* argument let lawyers present to you.
DANFORTH: Mr. Hale, believe me; for a man of such terrible
learning you are most bewildered—I hope you will forgive
430 me. I have been thirty-two year at the bar, sir, and I should be
confounded were I called upon to defend these people. Let
you consider, now—*(to* PROCTOR *and the others)* And I bid
you all do likewise. In an ordinary crime, how does one defend the accused? One calls up witnesses to prove his inno-
435 cence. But witchcraft is *ipso facto*, on its face and by its nature, an invisible crime, is it not? Therefore, who may possibly be witness to it? The witch and the victim. None other.
Now we cannot hope the witch will accuse herself;
granted? Therefore, we must rely upon her victims—and
440 they do testify, the children certainly do testify. As for the
witches, none will deny that we are most eager for all their
confessions. Therefore, what is left for a lawyer to bring out? I
think I have made my point. Have I not?
HALE: But this child claims the girls are not truthful, and if they
445 are not—
DANFORTH: That is precisely what I am about to consider, sir.
What more may you ask of me? Unless you doubt my probity?
HALE: *(defeated)* I surely do not, sir. Let you consider it, then.
DANFORTH: And let you put your heart to rest. Her deposition,
450 Mr. Proctor.

(PROCTOR *hands it to him.* HATHORNE *rises, goes beside* DAN-
FORTH, *and starts reading.* PARRIS *comes to his other side.* DAN-
FORTH *looks at* JOHN PROCTOR, *then proceeds to read.* HALE *gets
up, finds position near the judge, reads too.* PROCTOR *glances at*
GILES. FRANCIS *prays silently, hands pressed together.* CHEEVER
waits placidly, the sublime official, dutiful. MARY WARREN *sobs
once.* JOHN PROCTOR *touches her head reassuringly. Presently*
DANFORTH *lifts his eyes, stands up, takes out a kerchief and
blows his nose. The others stand aside as he moves in thought
toward the window.*)

PARRIS: *(hardly able to contain his anger and fear)* I should like
to question—
DANFORTH: *(—his first real outburst, in which his contempt for*
PARRIS *is clear)* Mr. Parris, I bid you be silent! *(He stands in
455 silence, looking out the window. Now, having established that
he will set the gait)* Mr. Cheever, will you go into the court
and bring the children here? (CHEEVER *gets up and goes out
upstage.* DANFORTH *now turns to* MARY.) Mary Warren, how
came you to this turnabout? Has Mr. Proctor threatened you
460 for this deposition?
MARY WARREN: No, sir.
DANFORTH: Has he ever threatened you?
MARY WARREN: *(weaker)* No, sir.
DANFORTH: *(sensing a weakening)* Has he threatened you?
465 MARY WARREN: No, sir.
DANFORTH: Then you tell me that you sat in my court, callously
lying, when you knew that people would hang by your evidence? *(She does not answer.)* Answer me!
MARY WARREN: *(almost inaudibly)* I did, sir.
DANFORTH: How were you instructed in your life? Do you not
470 know that God damns all liars? *(She cannot speak.)* Or is it
now that you lie?
MARY WARREN: No, sir—I am with God now.
DANFORTH: You are with God now.
MARY WARREN: Aye, sir.
475 DANFORTH: *(containing himself)* I will tell you this—you are
either lying now, or you were lying in the court, and in either
case you have committed perjury and you will go to jail for it.
You cannot lightly say you lied, Mary. Do you know that?
MARY WARREN: I cannot lie no more. I am with God, I am with
480 God.

(But she breaks into sobs at the thought of it, and the right door
opens, and enter SUSANNA WALCOTT, MERCY LEWIS, BETTY
PARRIS, and finally ABIGAIL. CHEEVER comes to DANFORTH.)

CHEEVER: Ruth Putnam's not in the court, sir, nor the other
children.
DANFORTH: These will be sufficient. Sit down, children. *(Silently they sit.)* Your friend, Mary Warren, has given us a
485 deposition. In which she swears that she never saw familiar
spirits, apparitions, nor any manifest of the Devil. She claims
as well that none of you have seen these things either. *(Slight
pause.)* Now, children, this is a court of law. The law, based
upon the Bible, and the Bible, writ by Almighty God, forbid
490 the practice of witchcraft, and describe death as the penalty
thereof. But likewise, children, the law and Bible damn all
bearers of false witness. *(Slight pause.)* Now then. It does not
escape me that this deposition may be devised to blind us; it
may well be that Mary Warren has been conquered by Satan,
495 who sends her here to distract our sacred purpose. If so, her
neck will break for it. But if she speak true, I bid you now drop
your guile and confess your pretense, for a quick confession
will go easier with you. *(Pause.)* Abigail Williams, rise. *(ABIGAIL slowly rises.)* Is there any truth in this?
500 ABIGAIL: No, sir.
DANFORTH: *(thinks, glances at* MARY, *then back to* ABIGAIL)
Children, a very augur bit will now be turned into your souls
until your honesty is proved. Will either of you change your
positions now, or do you force me to hard questioning?
505 ABIGAIL: I have naught to change, sir. She lies.
DANFORTH: *(to* MARY) You would still go on with this?

MARY WARREN: *(faintly)* Aye, sir.

510 DANFORTH: *(turning to* ABIGAIL*)* A poppet were discovered in Mr. Proctor's house, stabbed by a needle. Mary Warren claims that you sat beside her in the court when she made it, and that you saw her make it and witnessed how she herself stuck her needle into it for safe-keeping. What say you to that?

515 ABIGAIL: *(with a slight note of indignation)* It is a lie, sir.

DANFORTH: *(after a slight pause)* While you worked for Mr. Proctor, did you see poppets in that house?

ABIGAIL: Goody Proctor always kept poppets.

PROCTOR: Your Honor, my wife never kept no poppets. Mary Warren confesses it was her poppet.

520 CHEEVER: Your Excellency.

DANFORTH: Mr. Cheever.

CHEEVER: When I spoke with Goody Proctor in that house, she said she never kept no poppets. But she said she did keep poppets when she were a girl.

525 PROCTOR: She has not been a girl these fifteen years, Your Honor.

HATHORNE: But a poppet will keep fifteen years, will it not?

PROCTOR: It will keep if it is kept, but Mary Warren swears she never saw no poppets in my house, nor anyone else.

530 PARRIS: Why could there not have been poppets hid where no one ever saw them?

PROCTOR: *(furious)* There might also be a dragon with five legs in my house, but no one has ever seen it.

PARRIS: We are here, Your Honor, precisely to discover what no 535 one has ever seen.

PROCTOR: Mr. Danforth, what profit this girl to turn herself about? What may Mary Warren gain but hard questioning and worse?

DANFORTH: You are charging Abigail Williams with a mar-540 velous cool plot to murder, do you understand that?

PROCTOR: I do, sir. I believe she means to murder.

DANFORTH: *(pointing at* ABIGAIL, *incredulously)* This child would murder your wife?

PROCTOR: It is not a child. Now hear me, sir. In the sight of the 545 congregation she were twice this year put out of this meetin' house for laughter during prayer.

DANFORTH: *(shocked, turning to* ABIGAIL*)* What's this? Laughter during—!

PARRIS: Excellency, she were under Tituba's power at that time, 550 but she is solemn now.

GILES: Aye, now she is solemn and goes to hang people!

DANFORTH: Quiet, man.

HATHORNE: Surely it have no bearing on the question, sir. He charges contemplation of murder.

555 DANFORTH: Aye. *(He studies* ABIGAIL *for a moment, then)* Continue, Mr. Proctor.

PROCTOR: Mary. Now tell the Governor how you danced in the woods.

PARRIS: *(instantly)* Excellency, since I come to Salem this man 560 is blackening my name. He—

DANFORTH: In a moment, sir. *(To* MARY WARREN, *sternly, and surprised)* What is this dancing?

MARY WARREN: I—*(She glances at* ABIGAIL, *who is staring down at her remorselessly. Then, appealing to* PROCTOR*)* Mr. 565 Proctor—

PROCTOR: *(taking it right up)* Abigail leads the girls to the woods, Your Honor, and they have danced there naked—

PARRIS: Your Honor, this—

PROCTOR: *(at once)* Mr. Parris discovered them himself in the dead of night! There's the "child" she is! 570

DANFORTH: *(—it is growing into a nightmare, and he turns astonished, to* PARRIS*)* Mr. Parris—

PARRIS: I can only say, sir, that I never found any of them naked, and this man is—

DANFORTH: But you discovered them dancing in the woods? 575 *(Eyes on* PARRIS, *he points at* ABIGAIL*.)* Abigail?

HALE: Excellency, when I first arrived from Beverly, Mr. Parris told me that.

DANFORTH: Do you deny it, Mr. Parris?

PARRIS: I do not sir, but I never saw any of them naked. 580

DANFORTH: But she have *danced*?

PARRIS: *(unwillingly)* Aye, sir.

*(*DANFORTH, *as though with new eyes, looks at* ABIGAIL*.)*

HATHORNE: Excellency, will you permit me? *(He points at* MARY WARREN*.)*

DANFORTH: *(with great worry)* Pray, proceed. 585

HATHORNE: You say you never saw no spirits, Mary, were never threatened or afflicted by any manifest of the Devil or the Devil's agents.

MARY WARREN: *(very faintly)* No, sir.

HATHORNE: *(with a gleam of victory)* And yet, when people ac-590 cused of witchery confronted you in court, you would faint, saying their spirits came out of their bodies and choked you—

MARY WARREN: That were pretense, sir.

DANFORTH: I cannot hear you.

MARY WARREN: Pretense, sir. 595

PARRIS: But you did turn cold, did you not? I myself picked you up many times, and your skin were icy. Mr. Danforth, you—

DANFORTH: I saw that many times.

PROCTOR: She only pretended to faint, Your Excellency. They're all marvelous pretenders. 600

HATHORNE: Then can she pretend to faint now?

PROCTOR: Now?

PARRIS: Why not? Now there are no spirits attacking her, for none in this room is accused of witchcraft. So let her turn herself cold now, let her pretend she is attacked now, let her 605 faint. *(He turns to* MARY WARREN*.)* Faint!

MARY WARREN: Faint?

PARRIS: Aye, faint. Prove to us how you pretended in the court so many times.

MARY WARREN: *(looking to* PROCTOR*)* I—cannot faint now, sir. 610

PROCTOR: *(alarmed, quietly)* Can you not pretend it?

MARY WARREN: I—*(She looks about as though searching for the passion to faint.)* I—have no *sense* of it now, I—

DANFORTH: Why? What is lacking now?

MARY WARREN: I—cannot tell, sir, I— 615

DANFORTH: Might it be that here we have no afflicting spirit loose, but in the court there were some?

MARY WARREN: I never saw no spirits.

PARRIS: Then see no spirits now, and prove to us that you can faint by your own will, as you claim. 620

MARY WARREN: *(stares, searching for the emotion of it, and then shakes her head)* I—cannot do it.

PARRIS: Then you will confess, will you not? It were attacking spirits made you faint!

MARY WARREN: No, sir, I— 625

PARRIS: Your Excellency, this is a trick to blind the court!

MARY WARREN: It's not a trick! *(She stands.)* I — I used to faint because I — I thought I saw spirits.

DANFORTH: *Thought* you saw them!

630 MARY WARREN: But I did not, Your Honor.

HATHORNE: How could you think you saw them unless you saw them?

MARY WARREN: I — I cannot tell how, but I did. I — I heard the other girls screaming, and you, Your Honor, you seemed to

635 believe them, and I — It were only sport in the beginning, sir, but then the whole world cried spirits, spirits, and I — I promise you, Mr. Danforth, I only thought I saw them but I did not.

(DANFORTH peers at her.)

PARRIS: *(smiling, but nervous because DANFORTH seems to be struck by MARY WARREN's story)* Surely Your Excellency is

640 not taken by this simple lie.

DANFORTH: *(turning worriedly to ABIGAIL)* Abigail. I bid you now search your heart and tell me this — and beware of it, child, to God every soul is precious and His vengeance is terrible on them that take life without cause. Is it possible,

645 child, that the spirits you have seen are illusion only, some deception that may cross your mind when —

ABIGAIL: Why, this — this — is a base question, sir.

DANFORTH: Child, I would have you consider it —

ABIGAIL: I have been hurt, Mr. Danforth; I have seen my blood

650 runnin' out! I have been near to murdered every day because I done my duty pointing out the Devil's people — and this is my reward? To be mistrusted, denied, questioned like a —

DANFORTH: *(weakening)* Child, I do not mistrust you —

ABIGAIL: *(in an open threat)* Let *you* beware, Mr. Danforth.

655 Think you to be so mighty that the power of Hell may not turn *your* wits? Beware of it! There is — *(Suddenly, from an accusatory attitude, her face turns, looking into the air above — it is truly frightened.)*

DANFORTH: *(apprehensively)* What is it, child?

660 ABIGAIL: *(looking about in the air, clasping her arms about her as though cold)* I — I know not. A wind, a cold wind, has come. *(Her eyes fall on MARY WARREN.)*

MARY WARREN: *(terrified, pleading)* Abby!

MERCY LEWIS: *(shivering)* Your Honor, I freeze!

665 PROCTOR: They're pretending!

HATHORNE: *(touching ABIGAIL's hand)* She is cold, Your Honor, touch her!

MERCY LEWIS: *(through chattering teeth)* Mary, do you send this shadow on me?

670 MARY WARREN: Lord, save me!

SUSANNA WALCOTT: I freeze, I freeze!

ABIGAIL: *(shivering visibly)* It is a wind, a wind!

MARY WARREN: Abby, don't do that!

DANFORTH: *(himself engaged and entered by ABIGAIL)* Mary

675 Warren, do you witch her? I say to you, do you send your spirit out?

(With a hysterical cry MARY WARREN starts to run. PROCTOR catches her.)

MARY WARREN: *(almost collapsing)* Let me go, Mr. Proctor, I cannot, I cannot —

ABIGAIL: *(crying to Heaven)* Oh, Heavenly Father, take away

680 this shadow!

(Without warning or hesitation, PROCTOR leaps at ABIGAIL and, grabbing her by the hair, pulls her to her feet. She screams in pain. DANFORTH, astonished, cries, "What are you about?" and HATHORNE and PARRIS call, "Take your hands off her!" and out of it all comes PROCTOR's roaring voice.)

PROCTOR: How do you call Heaven! Whore! Whore!

(HERRICK breaks PROCTOR from her.)

HERRICK: John!

DANFORTH: Man! Man, what do you —

PROCTOR: *(breathless and in agony)* It is a whore!

DANFORTH: *(dumfounded)* You charge — ?   685

ABIGAIL: Mr. Danforth, he is lying!

PROCTOR: Mark her! Now she'll suck a scream to stab me with, but —

DANFORTH: You will prove this! This will not pass!

PROCTOR: *(trembling, his life collapsing about him)* I have   690 known her, sir. I have known her.

DANFORTH: You — you are a lecher?

FRANCIS: *(horrified)* John, you cannot say such a —

PROCTOR: Oh, Francis, I wish you had some evil in you that you might know me! *(To DANFORTH)* A man will not cast away his 695 good name. You surely know that.

DANFORTH: *(dumfounded)* In — in what time? In what place?

PROCTOR: *(his voice about to break, and his shame great)* In the proper place — where my beasts are bedded. On the last night of my joy, some eight months past. She used to serve me in 700 my house, sir. *(He has to clamp his jaw to keep from weeping.)* A man may think God sleeps, but God sees everything, I know it now. I beg you, sir, I beg you — see her what she is. My wife, my dear good wife, took this girl soon after, sir, and put her out on the highroad. And being what she is, a lump of 705 vanity, sir — *(He is being overcome.)* Excellency, forgive me, forgive me. *(Angrily against himself, he turns away from the Governor for a moment. Then, as though to cry out is his only means of speech left)* She thinks to dance with me on my wife's grave! And well she might, for I thought of her softly. God   710 help me, I lusted, and there *is* a promise in such sweat. But it is a whore's vengeance, and you must see it; I set myself entirely in your hands. I know you must see it now.

DANFORTH: *(blanched, in horror, turning to ABIGAIL)* You deny every scrap and tittle of this?   715

ABIGAIL: If I must answer that, I will leave and I will not come back again!

(DANFORTH seems unsteady.)

PROCTOR: I have made a bell of my honor! I have rung the doom of my good name — you will believe me, Mr. Danforth! My wife is innocent, except she knew a whore when she saw one!   720

ABIGAIL: *(stepping up to DANFORTH)* What look do you give me? *(DANFORTH cannot speak.)* I'll not have such looks! *(She turns and starts for the door.)*

DANFORTH: You will remain where you are! *(HERRICK steps into her path. She comes up short, fire in her eyes.)* Mr. Parris, go   725 into the court and bring Goodwife Proctor out.

PARRIS: *(objecting)* Your Honor, this is all a —

DANFORTH: *(sharply to PARRIS)* Bring her out! And tell her not one word of what's been spoken here. And let you knock before you enter. *(PARRIS goes out.)* Now we shall touch the   730

bottom of this swamp. (To PROCTOR) Your wife, you say, is an honest woman.

PROCTOR: In her life, sir, she have never lied. There are them that cannot sing, and them that cannot weep — my wife can not lie. I have paid much to learn it, sir.

DANFORTH: And when she put this girl out of your house, she put her out for a harlot?

PROCTOR: Aye, sir.

DANFORTH: And knew her for a harlot?

PROCTOR: Aye, sir, she knew her for a harlot.

DANFORTH: Good then. (To ABIGAIL) And if she tell me, child, it were for harlotry, may God spread His mercy on you! (There is a knock. He calls to the door.) Hold! (To ABIGAIL) Turn your back. Turn your back. (To PROCTOR) Do likewise. (Both turn their backs — ABIGAIL with indignant slowness.) Now let neither of you turn to face Goody Proctor. No one in this room is to speak one word, or raise a gesture aye or nay. (He turns toward the door, calls) Enter! (The door opens. ELIZABETH enters with PARRIS. PARRIS leaves her. She stands alone, her eyes looking for PROCTOR.) Mr. Cheever, report this testimony in all exactness. Are you ready?

CHEEVER: Ready, sir.

DANFORTH: Come here, woman. (ELIZABETH comes to him, glancing at PROCTOR's back.) Look at me only, not at your husband. In my eyes only.

ELIZABETH: (faintly) Good, sir.

DANFORTH: We are given to understand that at one time you dismissed your servant, Abigail Williams.

ELIZABETH: That is true, sir.

DANFORTH: For what cause did you dismiss her? (Slight pause. Then ELIZABETH tries to glance at PROCTOR.) You will look in my eyes only and not at your husband. The answer is in your memory and you need no help to give it to me. Why did you dismiss Abigail Williams?

ELIZABETH: (not knowing what to say, sensing a situation, wetting her lips to stall for time) She — dissatisfied me. (Pause.) And my husband.

DANFORTH: In what way dissatisfied you?

ELIZABETH: She were — (She glances at PROCTOR for a cue.)

DANFORTH: Woman, look at me! (ELIZABETH does.) Were she slovenly? Lazy? What disturbance did she cause?

ELIZABETH: Your Honor, I — in that time I were sick. And I — My husband is a good and righteous man. He is never drunk as some are, nor wastin' his time at the shovelboard, but always at his work. But in my sickness — you see, sir, I were a long time sick after my last baby, and I thought I saw my husband somewhat turning from me. And this girl — (She turns to ABIGAIL.)

DANFORTH: Look at me.

ELIZABETH: Aye, sir. Abigail Williams — (She breaks off.)

DANFORTH: What of Abigail Williams?

ELIZABETH: I came to think he fancied her. And so one night I lost my wits, I think, and put her out on the highroad.

DANFORTH: Your husband — did he indeed turn from you?

ELIZABETH: (in agony) My husband — is a goodly man, sir.

DANFORTH: Then he did not turn from you.

ELIZABETH: (starting to glance at PROCTOR) He —

DANFORTH: (reaches out and holds her face, then) Look at me! To your own knowledge, has John Proctor ever committed the crime of lechery? (In a crisis of indecision she cannot speak.) Answer my question! Is your husband a lecher!

ELIZABETH: (faintly) No, sir.

DANFORTH: Remove her, Marshal.

PROCTOR: Elizabeth, tell the truth!

DANFORTH: She has spoken. Remove her!

PROCTOR: (crying out) Elizabeth, I have confessed it!

ELIZABETH: Oh, God! (The door closes behind her.)

PROCTOR: She only thought to save my name!

HALE: Excellency, it is a natural lie to tell; I beg you, stop now before another is condemned! I may shut my conscience to it no more — private vengeance is working through this testimony! From the beginning this man has struck me true. By my oath to Heaven, I believe him now, and I pray you call back his wife before we —

DANFORTH: She spoke nothing of lechery, and this man has lied!

HALE: I believe him! (pointing at ABIGAIL) This girl has always struck me false! She has —

(ABIGAIL, with a weird, wild, chilling cry, screams up to the ceiling.)

ABIGAIL: You will not! Begone! Begone, I say!

DANFORTH: What is it, child? (But ABIGAIL, pointing with fear, is now raising up her frightened eyes, her awed face, toward the ceiling — the girls are doing the same — and how HATHORNE, HALE, PUTNAM, CHEEVER, HERRICK, and DANFORTH do the same.) What's there? (He lowers his eyes from the ceiling, and now he is frightened; there is real tension in his voice.) Child! (She is transfixed — with all the girls, she is whimpering open-mouthed, agape at the ceiling.) Girls! Why do you — ?

MERCY LEWIS: (pointing) It's on the beam! Behind the rafter!

DANFORTH: (looking up) Where!

ABIGAIL: Why — ? (She gulps.) Why do you come, yellow bird?

PROCTOR: Where's a bird? I see no bird!

ABIGAIL: (to the ceiling) My face? My face?

PROCTOR: Mr. Hale —

DANFORTH: Be quiet!

PROCTOR: (to HALE) Do you see a bird?

DANFORTH: Be quiet!!

ABIGAIL: (to the ceiling, in a genuine conversation with the "bird," as though trying to talk it out of attacking her) But God made my face; you cannot want to tear my face. Envy is a deadly sin, Mary.

MARY WARREN: (on her feet with a spring, and horrified, pleading) Abby!

ABIGAIL: (unperturbed, continuing to the "bird") Oh, Mary, this is a black art to change your shape. No, I cannot, I cannot stop my mouth; it's God's work I do.

MARY WARREN: Abby, I'm here!

PROCTOR: (frantically) They're pretending, Mr. Danforth!

ABIGAIL: (— now she takes a backward step, as though in fear the bird will swoop down momentarily) Oh, please, Mary! Don't come down.

SUSANNA WALCOTT: Her claws, she's stretching her claws!

PROCTOR: Lies, lies.

ABIGAIL: (backing further, eyes still fixed above) Mary, please don't hurt me!

MARY WARREN: (to DANFORTH) I'm not hurting her!

DANFORTH: (to MARY WARREN) Why does she see this vision?

MARY WARREN: She sees nothin'!

ABIGAIL: (now staring full front as though hypnotized, and mimicking the exact tone of MARY WARREN's cry) She sees nothin'!

MARY WARREN: (pleading) Abby, you mustn't!

850   ABIGAIL AND ALL THE GIRLS: (all transfixed) Abby, you mustn't!
MARY WARREN: (to all the GIRLS) I'm here, I'm here!
GIRLS: I'm here, I'm here!
DANFORTH: (horrified) Mary Warren! Draw back your spirit out of them!
855   MARY WARREN: Mr. Danforth!
GIRLS: (cutting her off) Mr. Danforth!
DANFORTH: Have you compacted with the Devil? Have you?
MARY WARREN: Never, never!
GIRLS: Never, never!
860   DANFORTH: (growing hysterical) Why can they only repeat you?
PROCTOR: Give me a whip—I'll stop it!
MARY WARREN: They're sporting. They—!
GIRLS: They're sporting!
MARY WARREN: (turning on them all hysterically and stamping her feet) Abby, stop it!
865   GIRLS: (stamping their feet) Abby, stop it!
MARY WARREN: Stop it!
GIRLS: Stop it!
MARY WARREN: (screaming it out at the top of her lungs, and raising her fists) Stop it!!
870   GIRLS: (raising their fists) Stop it!!

(MARY WARREN, utterly confounded, and becoming overwhelmed by ABIGAIL's—and the GIRLS'—utter conviction, starts to whimper, hands half raised, powerless, and all the GIRLS begin whimpering exactly as she does.)

DANFORTH: A little while ago you were afflicted. Now it seems you afflict others; where did you find this power?
MARY WARREN: (staring at ABIGAIL) I—have no power.
875   GIRLS: I have no power.
PROCTOR: They're gulling you, Mister!
DANFORTH: Why did you turn about this past two weeks? You have seen the Devil, have you not?
HALE: (indicating ABIGAIL and the GIRLS) You cannot believe them!
880   MARY WARREN: I—
PROCTOR: (sensing her weakening) Mary, God damns all liars!
DANFORTH: (pounding it into her) You have seen the Devil, you have made compact with Lucifer, have you not?
885   PROCTOR: God damns liars, Mary!

(MARY utters something unintelligible, staring at ABIGAIL, who keeps watching the "bird" above.)

DANFORTH: I cannot hear you. What do you say? (MARY utters again unintelligibly.) You will confess yourself or you will hang! (He turns her roughly to face him.) Do you know who I am? I say you will hang if you do not open with me!
890   PROCTOR: Mary, remember the angel Raphael—do that which is good and—
ABIGAIL: (pointing upward) The wings! Her wings are spreading! Mary, please, don't, don't—!
HALE: I see nothing, Your Honor!
895   DANFORTH: Do you confess this power! (He is an inch from her face.) Speak!
ABIGAIL: She's going to come down! She's walking the beam!
DANFORTH: Will you speak!
MARY WARREN: (staring in horror) I cannot!
900   GIRLS: I cannot!
PARRIS: Cast the Devil out! Look him in the face! Trample him! We'll save you, Mary, only stand fast against him and—

ABIGAIL: (looking up) Look out! She's coming down!

(She and all the GIRLS run to one wall, shielding their eyes. And now, as though cornered, they let out a gigantic scream, and MARY, as though infected, opens her mouth and screams with them. Gradually ABIGAIL and the GIRLS leave off, until only MARY is left there, staring up at the "bird," screaming madly. All watch her, horrified by this evident fit. PROCTOR strides to her.)

PROCTOR: Mary, tell the Governor what they—(He has hardly got a word out, when, seeing him coming for her, she rushes out of his reach, screaming in horror.)   905
MARY WARREN: Don't touch me—Don't touch me! (At which the GIRLS halt at the door.)
PROCTOR: (astonished) Mary!
MARY WARREN: (pointing at PROCTOR) You're the Devil's man!   910

(He is stopped in his tracks.)

PARRIS: Praise God!
GIRLS: Praise God!
PROCTOR: (numbed) Mary, how—?
MARY WARREN: I'll not hang with you! I love God, I love God.
DANFORTH: (to MARY) He bid you do the Devil's work?   915
MARY WARREN: (hysterically, indicating PROCTOR) He come at me by night and every day to sign, to sign, to—
DANFORTH: Sign what?
PARRIS: The Devil's book? He come with a book?
MARY WARREN: (hysterically, pointing at PROCTOR, fearful of   920
him) My name, he want my name. "I'll murder you," he says, "if my wife hangs! We must go and overthrow the court," he says!

(DANFORTH's head jerks toward PROCTOR, shock and horror in his face.)

PROCTOR: (turning, appealing to HALE) Mr. Hale!
MARY WARREN: (her sobs beginning) He wake me every night, his eyes were like coals and his fingers claw my neck, and I sign, I   925
sign . . .
HALE: Excellency, this child's gone wild!
PROCTOR: (as DANFORTH's wide eyes pour on him) Mary, Mary!
MARY WARREN: (screaming at him) No, I love God; I go your way no more. I love God, I bless God. (Sobbing, she rushes to   930
ABIGAIL.) Abby, Abby, I'll never hurt you more! (They all watch, as ABIGAIL, out of her infinite charity, reaches out and draws the sobbing MARY to her, and then looks up to DANFORTH.)
DANFORTH: (to PROCTOR) What are you? (PROCTOR is beyond   935
speech in his anger.) You are combined with anti-Christ, are you not? I have seen your power; you will not deny it! What say you, Mister?
HALE: Excellency—
DANFORTH: I will have nothing from you, Mr. Hale! (to PROC-   940
TOR) Will you confess yourself befouled with Hell, or do you keep that black allegiance yet? What say you?
PROCTOR: (his mind wild, breathless) I say—I say—God is dead!
PARRIS: Hear it, hear it!
PROCTOR: (laughs insanely, then) A fire, a fire is burning! I hear   945
the boot of Lucifer, I see his filthy face! And it is my face, and yours, Danforth! For them that quail to bring men out of ignorance, as I have quailed, and as you quail now when you know in all your black hearts that this be fraud—God damns our kind especially, and we will burn, we will burn together!   950
DANFORTH: Marshal! Take him and Corey with him to the jail!

HALE: (*starting across to the door*) I denounce these proceedings!

PROCTOR: You are pulling Heaven down and raising up a whore!

955 HALE: I denounce these proceedings, I quit this court! (*He slams the door to the outside behind him.*)

DANFORTH: (*calling to him in a fury*) Mr. Hale! Mr. Hale!

(*The curtain falls*)

— ACT FOUR —

A cell in Salem jail, that fall.

At the back is a high barred window; near it, a great, heavy door. Along the walls are two benches.

The place is in darkness but for the moonlight seeping through the bars. It appears empty. Presently footsteps are heard coming down a corridor beyond the wall, keys rattle, and the door swings open. Marshal HERRICK *enters with a lantern.*

He is nearly drunk, and heavy-footed. He goes to a bench and nudges a bundle of rags lying on it.

HERRICK: Sarah, wake up! Sarah Good! (*He then crosses to the other bench.*)

SARAH GOOD: (*rising in her rags*) Oh, Majesty! Comin', comin'! Tituba, he's here, His Majesty's come!

5 HERRICK: Go to the north cell; this place is wanted now. (*He hangs his lantern on the wall.* TITUBA *sits up.*)

TITUBA: That don't look to me like His Majesty; look to me like the marshal.

HERRICK: (*taking out a flask*) Get along with you now, clear this

10 place. (*He drinks, and* SARAH GOOD *comes and peers up into his face.*)

SARAH GOOD: Oh, is it you, Marshal! I thought sure you be the devil comin' for us. Could I have a sip of cider for me goin'-away?

15 HERRICK: (*handing her the flask*) And where are you off to, Sarah?

TITUBA: (*as* SARAH *drinks*) We goin' to Barbados, soon the Devil gits here with the feathers and the wings.

HERRICK: Oh? A happy voyage to you.

20 SARAH GOOD: A pair of bluebirds wingin' southerly, the two of us! Oh, it be a grand transformation, Marshal! (*She raises the flask to drink again.*)

HERRICK: (*taking the flask from her lips*) You'd best give me that or you'll never rise off the ground. Come along now.

25 TITUBA: I'll speak to him for you, if you desires to come along, Marshal.

HERRICK: I'd not refuse it, Tituba; it's the proper morning to fly into Hell.

TITUBA: Oh, it be no Hell in Barbados. Devil, him be pleasure-

30 man in Barbados, him be singin' and dancin' in Barbados. It's you folks — you riles him up 'round here; it be too cold 'round here for that Old Boy. He freeze his soul in Massachusetts, but in Barbados he just as sweet and — (*A bellowing cow is heard, and* TITUBA *leaps up and calls to the window*) Aye, sir!

35 That's him, Sarah!

SARAH GOOD: I'm here, Majesty! (*They hurriedly pick up their rags as* HOPKINS, *a guard, enters.*)

HOPKINS: The Deputy Governor's arrived.

HERRICK: (*grabbing* TITUBA) Come along, come along.

TITUBA: (*resisting him*) No, he comin' for me. I goin' home! 40

HERRICK: (*pulling her to the door*) That's not Satan, just a poor old cow with a hatful of milk. Come along now, out with you!

TITUBA: (*calling to the window*) Take me home, Devil! Take me home!

SARAH GOOD: (*following the shouting* TITUBA *out*) Tell him I'm 45

goin', Tituba! Now you tell him Sarah Good is goin' too!

(*In the corridor outside* TITUBA *calls on — "Take me home, Devil; Devil take me home!" and* HOPKINS' *voice orders her to move on.* HERRICK *returns and begins to push old rags and straw into a corner. Hearing footsteps, he turns, and enter* DANFORTH *and* JUDGE HATHORNE. *They are in greatcoats and wear hats against the bitter cold. They are followed in by* CHEEVER, *who carries a dispatch case and a flat wooden box containing his writing materials.*)

HERRICK: Good morning, Excellency.

DANFORTH: Where is Mr. Parris?

HERRICK: I'll fetch him. (*He starts for the door.*)

DANFORTH: Marshal. (HERRICK *stops.*) When did Reverend 50

Hale arrive?

HERRICK: It were toward midnight, I think.

DANFORTH: (*suspiciously*) What is he about here?

HERRICK: He goes among them that will hang, sir. And he prays with them. He sits with Goody Nurse now. And Mr. Parris 55

with him.

DANFORTH: Indeed. That man have no authority to enter here, Marshal. Why have you let him in?

HERRICK: Why, Mr. Parris command me, sir. I cannot deny him.

DANFORTH: Are you drunk, Marshal? 60

HERRICK: No, sir; it is a bitter night, and I have no fire here.

DANFORTH: (*containing his anger*) Fetch Mr. Parris.

HERRICK: Aye, sir.

DANFORTH: There is a prodigious stench in this place.

HERRICK: I have only now cleared the people out for you. 65

DANFORTH: Beware hard drink, Marshal.

HERRICK: Aye, sir. (*He waits an instant for further orders. But* DANFORTH, *in dissatisfaction, turns his back on him, and* HERRICK *goes out. There is a pause.* DANFORTH *stands in thought.*) 70

HATHORNE: Let you question Hale, Excellency; I should not be surprised he have been preaching in Andover lately.

DANFORTH: We'll come to that; speak nothing of Andover. Parris prays with him. That's strange. (*He blows on his hands, moves toward the window, and looks out.*) 75

HATHORNE: Excellency, I wonder if it be wise to let Mr. Parris so continuously with the prisoners. (DANFORTH *turns to him, interested.*) I think, sometimes, the man has a mad look these days.

DANFORTH: Mad? 80

HATHORNE: I met him yesterday coming out of his house, and I bid him good morning — and he wept and went his way. I think it is not well the village sees him so unsteady.

DANFORTH: Perhaps he have some sorrow.

CHEEVER: (*stamping his feet against the cold*) I think it be the 85

cows, sir.

DANFORTH: Cows?

CHEEVER: There be so many cows wanderin' the highroads, now their masters are in the jails, and much disagreement

90 who they will belong to now. I know Mr. Parris be arguin' with farmers all yesterday — there is great contention, sir, about the cows. Contention make him weep, sir; it were always a man that weep for contention. *(He turns, as do* HATHORNE *and* DANFORTH, *hearing someone coming up the* corridor. DANFORTH *raises his head as* PARRIS *enters. He is gaunt, frightened, and sweating in his greatcoat.)*

PARRIS: *(to* DANFORTH, *instantly)* Oh, good morning, sir, thank you for coming, I beg your pardon wakin' you so early. Good morning, Judge Hathorne.

100 DANFORTH: Reverend Hale have no right to enter this —

PARRIS: Excellency, a moment. *(He hurries back and shuts the door.)*

HATHORNE: Do you leave him alone with the prisoners?

DANFORTH: What's his business here?

105 PARRIS: *(prayerfully holding up his hands)* Excellency, hear me. It is a providence. Reverend Hale has returned to bring Rebecca Nurse to God.

DANFORTH: *(surprised)* He bids her confess?

PARRIS: *(sitting)* Hear me. Rebecca have not given me a word

110 this three month since she came. Now she sits with him, and her sister and Martha Corey and two or three others, and he pleads with them, confess their crimes and save their lives.

DANFORTH: Why — this is indeed a providence. And they soften, they soften?

115 PARRIS: Not yet, not yet. But I thought to summon you, sir, that we might think on whether it be not wise, to — *(He dares not say it.)* I had thought to put a question, sir, and I hope you will not —

DANFORTH: Mr. Parris, be plain, what troubles you?

120 PARRIS: There is news, sir, that the court — the court must reckon with. My niece, sir, my niece — I believe she has vanished.

DANFORTH: Vanished!

PARRIS: I had thought to advise you of it earlier in the week, but —

DANFORTH: Why? How long is she gone?

125 PARRIS: This be the third night. You see, sir, she told me she would stay a night with Mercy Lewis. And next day, when she does not return, I send to Mr. Lewis to inquire. Mercy told him she would sleep in *my* house for a night.

DANFORTH: They are both gone?!

130 PARRIS: *(in fear of him)* They are, sir.

DANFORTH: *(alarmed)* I will send a party for them. Where may they be?

PARRIS: Excellency, I think they be aboard a ship. *(*DANFORTH *stands agape.)* My daughter tells me how she heard them

135 speaking of ships last week, and tonight I discover my — my strongbox is broke into. *(He presses his fingers against his eyes to keep back tears.)*

HATHORNE: *(astonished)* She have robbed you?

PARRIS: Thirty-one pound is gone. I am penniless. *(He covers his

140 face and sobs.)*

DANFORTH: Mr. Parris, you are a brainless man! *(He walks in thought, deeply worried.)*

PARRIS: Excellency, it profit nothing you should blame me. I cannot think they would run off except they fear to keep in

145 Salem any more. *(He is pleading.)* Mark it, sir, Abigail had close knowledge of the town, and since the news of Andover has broken here —

DANFORTH: Andover is remedied. The court returns there on Friday, and will resume examinations.

150 PARRIS: I am sure of it, sir. But the rumor here speaks rebellion in Andover, and it —

DANFORTH: There is no rebellion in Andover!

PARRIS: I tell you what is said here, sir. Andover have thrown out the court, they say, and will have no part of witchcraft. There

155 be a faction here, feeding on that news, and I tell you true, sir, I fear there will be riot here.

HATHORNE: Riot! Why at every execution I have seen naught but high satisfaction in the town.

PARRIS: Judge Hathorne — it were another sort that hanged till

160 now. Rebecca Nurse is no Bridget that lived three year with Bishop before she married him. John Proctor is not Isaac Ward that drank his family to ruin. *(To* DANFORTH*)* I would to God it were not so, Excellency, but these people have great weight yet in the town. Let Rebecca stand upon the gibbet

165 and send up some righteous prayer, and I fear she'll wake a vengeance on you.

HATHORNE: Excellency, she is condemned a witch. The court have —

DANFORTH: *(in deep concern, raising a hand to* HATHORNE*)*

170 Pray you. *(To* PARRIS*)* How do you propose, then?

PARRIS: Excellency, I would postpone these hangin's for a time.

DANFORTH: There will be no postponement.

PARRIS: Now Mr. Hale's returned, there is hope, I think — for if he bring even one of these to God, that confession surely

175 damns the others in the public eye, and none may doubt more that they are all linked to Hell. This way, unconfessed and claiming innocence, doubts are multiplied, many honest people will weep for them, and our good purpose is lost in their tears.

180 DANFORTH: *(after thinking a moment, then going to* CHEEVER*)* Give me the list.

*(*CHEEVER *opens the dispatch case, searches.)*

PARRIS: It cannot be forgot, sir, that when I summoned the congregation for John Proctor's excommunication there were hardly thirty people come to hear it. That speak a discontent, I think, and —

185 DANFORTH: *(studying the list)* There will be no postponement.

PARRIS: Excellency —

DANFORTH: Now, sir — which of these in your opinion may be brought to God? I will myself strive with him till dawn. *(He hands the list to* PARRIS, *who merely glances at it.)*

190 PARRIS: There is not sufficient time till dawn.

DANFORTH: I shall do my utmost. Which of them do you have hope for?

PARRIS: *(not even glancing at the list now, and in a quavering voice, quietly)* Excellency — a dagger — *(He chokes up.)*

195 DANFORTH: What do you say?

PARRIS: Tonight, when I open my door to leave my house — a dagger clattered to the ground. *(Silence.* DANFORTH *absorbs this. Now* PARRIS *cries out)* You cannot hang this sort. There is danger for me. I dare not step outside at night!

200 *(*REVEREND HALE *enters. They look at him for an instant in silence. He is steeped in sorrow, exhausted, and more direct than he ever was.)*

DANFORTH: Accept my congratulations, Reverend Hale; we are gladdened to see you returned to your good work.

HALE: (*coming to* DANFORTH *now*) You must pardon them. They will not budge.

(HERRICK *enters, waits.*)

205 DANFORTH: (*conciliatory*) You misunderstand, sir; I canot pardon these when twelve are already hanged for the same crime. It is not just.

PARRIS: (*with failing heart*) Rebecca will not confess?

HALE: The sun will rise in a few minutes. Excellency, I must 210 have more time.

DANFORTH: Now hear me, and beguile yourselves no more. I will not receive a single plea for pardon or postponement. Them that will not confess will hang. Twelve are already executed; the names of these seven are given out, and the village 215 expects to see them die this morning. Postponement now speaks a floundering on my part; reprieve or pardon must cast doubt upon the guilt of them that died till now. While I speak God's law, I will not crack its voice with whimpering. If retaliation is your fear, know this—I should hang ten thousand 220 that dared to rise against the law, and an ocean of salt tears could not melt the resolution of the statutes. Now draw yourselves up like men and help me, as you are bound by Heaven to do. Have you spoken with them all, Mr. Hale?

HALE: All but Proctor. He is in the dungeon.

225 DANFORTH: (*to* HERRICK) What's Proctor's way now?

HERRICK: He sits like some great bird; you'd not know he lived except he will take food from time to time.

DANFORTH: (*after thinking a moment*) His wife—his wife must be well on with child now.

230 HERRICK: She is, sir.

DANFORTH: What think you, Mr. Parris? You have closer knowledge of this man; might her presence soften him?

PARRIS: It is possible, sir. He have not laid eyes on her these three months. I should summon her.

235 DANFORTH: (*to* HERRICK) Is he yet adamant? Has he struck at you again?

HERRICK: He cannot, sir, he is chained to the wall now.

DANFORTH: (*after thinking on it*) Fetch Goody Proctor to me. Then let you bring him up.

240 HERRICK: Aye, sir. (HERRICK *goes. There is silence.*)

HALE: Excellency, if you postpone a week and publish to the town that you are striving for their confessions, that speak mercy on your part, not faltering.

DANFORTH: Mr. Hale, as God have not empowered me like 245 Joshua to stop this sun from rising, so I cannot withhold from them the perfection of their punishment.

HALE: (*harder now*) If you think God wills you to raise rebellion, Mr. Danforth, you are mistaken!

DANFORTH: (*instantly*) You have heard rebellion spoken in the 250 town?

HALE: Excellency, there are orphans wandering from house to house; abandoned cattle bellow on the highroads, the stink of rotting crops hangs everywhere, and no man knows when the harlots' cry will end his life—and you wonder yet if rebellion's 255 spoke? Better you should marvel how they do not burn your province!

DANFORTH: Mr. Hale, have you preached in Andover this month?

HALE: Thank God they have no need of me in Andover.

DANFORTH: You baffle me, sir. Why have you returned here?

HALE: Why, it is all simple. I come to do the Devil's work. I 260 come to counsel Christians they should belie themselves. (*His sarcasm collapses.*) There is blood on my head! Can you not see the blood on my head!!

PARRIS: Hush! (*For he has heard footsteps. They all face the door.* HERRICK *enters with* ELIZABETH. *Her wrists are linked by* 265 *heavy chain, which* HERRICK *now removes. Her clothes are dirty; her face is pale and gaunt.* HERRICK *goes out.*)

DANFORTH: (*very politely*) Goody Proctor. (*She is silent.*) I hope you are hearty?

ELIZABETH: (*as a warning reminder*) I am yet six month before 270 my time.

DANFORTH: Pray be at your ease, we come not for your life. We—(*uncertain how to plead, for he is not accustomed to it.*) Mr. Hale, will you speak with the woman?

HALE: Goody Proctor, your husband is marked to hang this 275 morning.

(*Pause.*)

ELIZABETH: (*quietly*) I have heard it.

HALE: You know, do you not, that I have no connection with the court? (*She seems to doubt it.*) I come of my own, Goody Proctor. I would save your husband's life, for if he is taken I 280 count myself his murderer. Do you understand me?

ELIZABETH: What do you want of me?

HALE: Goody Proctor, I have gone this three month like our Lord into the wilderness. I have sought a Christian way, for damnation's doubled on a minister who counsels men to lie. 285

HATHORNE: It is no lie, you cannot speak of lies.

HALE: It is a lie! They are innocent!

DANFORTH: I'll hear no more of that!

HALE: (*continuing to* ELIZABETH) Let you not mistake your duty as I mistook my own. I came into this village like a bride- 290 groom to his beloved, bearing gifts of high religion; the very crowns of holy law I brought, and what I touched with my bright confidence, it died; and where I turned the eye of my great faith, blood flowed up. Beware, Goody Proctor—cleave to no faith when faith brings blood. It is mistaken law that 295 leads you to sacrifice. Life, woman, life is God's most precious gift; no principle, however glorious, may justify the taking of it. I beg you, woman, prevail upon your husband to confess. Let him give his lie. Quail not before God's judgment in this, for it may well be God damns a liar less than he 300 that throws his life away for pride. Will you plead with him? I cannot think he will listen to another.

ELIZABETH: (*quietly*) I think that be the Devil's argument.

HALE: (*with climactic desperation*) Woman, before the laws of God we are as swine! We cannot read His will! 305

ELIZABETH: I cannot dispute with you, sir; I lack learning for it.

DANFORTH: (*going to her*) Goody Proctor, you are not summoned here for disputation. Be there no wifely tenderness within you? He will die with the sunrise. Your husband. Do you understand it? (*She only looks at him.*) What say you? 310 Will you contend with him? (*She is silent.*) Are you stone? I tell you true, woman, had I no other proof of your unnatural life, your dry eyes now would be sufficient evidence that you delivered up your soul to Hell! A very ape would weep at such calamity! Have the devil dried up any tear of pity in you? (*She* 315 *is silent.*) Take her out. It profit nothing she should speak to him!

ELIZABETH: *(quietly)* Let me speak with him, Excellency.
PARRIS: *(with hope)* You'll strive with him? *(She hesitates.)*
320 DANFORTH: Will you plead for his confession or will you not?
ELIZABETH: I promise nothing. Let me speak with him.

(A sound — the sibilance of dragging feet on stone. They turn. A pause. HERRICK *enters with* JOHN PROCTOR. *His wrists are chained. He is another man, bearded, filthy, his eyes misty as though webs had overgrown them. He halts inside the doorway, his eye caught by the sight of* ELIZABETH. *The emotion flowing between them prevents anyone from speaking for an instant. Now* HALE, *visibly affected, goes to* DANFORTH *and speaks quietly.)*

HALE: Pray, leave them, Excellency.
DANFORTH: *(pressing* HALE *impatiently aside)* Mr. Proctor, you have been notified, have you not? *(*PROCTOR *is silent, staring*
325 *at* ELIZABETH.*)* I see light in the sky, Mister; let you counsel with your wife, and may God help you turn your back on Hell. *(*PROCTOR *is silent, staring at* ELIZABETH.*)*
HALE: *(quietly)* Excellency, let —

*(*DANFORTH *brushes past* HALE *and walks out.* HALE *follows.* CHEEVER *stands and follows,* HATHORNE *behind.* HERRICK *goes.* PARRIS, *from a safe distance, offers:)*

PARRIS: If you desire a cup of cider, Mr. Proctor, I am sure I —
330 *(*PROCTOR *turns an icy stare at him, and he breaks off.* PARRIS *raises his palms toward* PROCTOR.*)* God lead you now. *(*PARRIS *goes out.)*

(Alone. PROCTOR *walks to her, halts. It is as though they stood in a spinning world. It is beyond sorrow, above it. He reaches out his hand as though toward an embodiment not quite real, and as he touches her, a strange soft sound, half laughter, half amazement, comes from his throat. He pats her hand. She covers his hand with hers. And then, weak, he sits. Then she sits, facing him.)*

PROCTOR: The child?
ELIZABETH: It grows.
335 PROCTOR: There is no word of the boys?
ELIZABETH: They're well. Rebecca's Samuel keeps them.
PROCTOR: You have not seen them?
ELIZABETH: I have not. *(She catches a weakening in herself and downs it.)*
340 PROCTOR: You are a — marvel, Elizabeth.
ELIZABETH: You — have been tortured?
PROCTOR: Aye. *(Pause. She will not let herself be drowned in the sea that threatens her.)* They come for my life now.
ELIZABETH: I know it.

(Pause.)

345 PROCTOR: None — have yet confessed?
ELIZABETH: There be many confessed.
PROCTOR: Who are they?
ELIZABETH: There be a hundred or more, they say. Goody Ballard is one; Isaiah Goodkind is one. There be many.
350 PROCTOR: Rebecca?
ELIZABETH: Not Rebecca. She is one foot in Heaven now; naught may hurt her more.
PROCTOR: And Giles?
ELIZABETH: You have not heard of it?
355 PROCTOR: I hear nothin', where I am kept.
ELIZABETH: Giles is dead.

(He looks at her incredulously.)

PROCTOR: When were he hanged?
ELIZABETH: *(quietly, factually)* He were not hanged. He would not answer aye or nay to his indictment; for if he denied the charge they'd hang him surely, and auction out his property. 360 So he stand mute, and died Christian under the law. And so his sons will have his farm. It is the law, for he could not be condemned a wizard without he answer the indictment, aye or nay.
PROCTOR: Then how does he die? 365
ELIZABETH: *(gently)* They press him, John.
PROCTOR: Press?
ELIZABETH: Great stones they lay upon his chest until he plead aye or nay. *(With a tender smile for the old man)* They say he give them but two words. "More weight," he says. And died. 370
PROCTOR: *(numbed — a thread to weave into his agony)* "More weight."
ELIZABETH: Aye. It were a fearsome man, Giles Corey.

(Pause.)

PROCTOR: *(with great force of will, but not quite looking at her)* I have been thinking I would confess to them, Elizabeth. *(She 375 shows nothing.)* What say you? If I give them that?
ELIZABETH: I cannot judge you, John.

(Pause.)

PROCTOR: *(simply — a pure question)* What would you have me do?
ELIZABETH: As you will, I would have it. *(Slight pause)* I want 380 you living, John. That's sure.
PROCTOR: *(pauses, then with a flailing of hope)* Giles' wife? Have she confessed?
ELIZABETH: She will not.

(Pause.)

PROCTOR: It is a pretense, Elizabeth. 385
ELIZABETH: What is?
PROCTOR: I cannot mount the gibbet like a saint. It is a fraud. I am not that man. *(She is silent.)* My honesty is broke, Elizabeth; I am no good man. Nothing's spoiled by giving them this lie that were not rotten long before. 390
ELIZABETH: And yet you've not confessed till now. That speak goodness in you.
PROCTOR: Spite only keeps me silent. It is hard to give a lie to dogs. *(Pause, for the first time he turns directly to her.)* I would have your forgiveness, Elizabeth. 395
ELIZABETH: It is not for me to give, John, I am —
PROCTOR: I'd have you see some honesty in it. Let them that never lied die now to keep their souls. It is pretense for me, a vanity that will not blind God nor keep my children out of the wind. *(Pause.)* What say you? 400
ELIZABETH: *(upon a heaving sob that always threatens)* John, it come to naught that I should forgive you, if you'll not forgive yourself. *(Now he turns away a little, in great agony.)* It is not my soul, John, it is yours. *(He stands, as though in physical pain, slowly rising to his feet with a great immortal longing to* 405 *find his answer. It is difficult to say, and she is on the verge of tears.)* Only be sure of this, for I know it now: Whatever you will do, it is a good man does it. *(He turns his doubting, searching gaze upon her.)* I have read my heart this three

410 month, John. (*Pause.*) I have sins of my own to count. It
needs a cold wife to prompt lechery.

PROCTOR: (*in great pain*) Enough, enough—

ELIZABETH: (*now pouring out her heart*) Better you should know
me!

415 PROCTOR: I will not hear it! I know you!

ELIZABETH: You take my sins upon you, John—

PROCTOR: (*in agony*) No, I take my own, my own!

ELIZABETH: John, I counted myself so plain, so poorly made, no
honest love could come to me! Suspicion kissed you when I
420 did; I never knew how I should say my love. It were a cold
house I kept! (*In fright, she swerves, as* HATHORNE *enters.*)

HATHORNE: What say you, Proctor? The sun is soon up.

(PROCTOR, *his chest heaving, stares, turns to* ELIZABETH. *She
comes to him as though to plead, her voice quaking.*)

ELIZABETH: Do what you will. But let none be your judge.
There be no higher judge under Heaven than Proctor is! For-
425 give me, forgive me, John—I never knew such goodness in
the world! (*She covers her face, weeping.*)

(PROCTOR *turns from her to* HATHORNE; *he is off the earth, his
voice hollow.*)

PROCTOR: I want my life.

HATHORNE: (*electrified, surprised*) You'll confess yourself?

PROCTOR: I will have my life.

430 HATHORNE: (*with a mystical tone*) God be praised! It is a providence! (*He rushes out the door, and his voice is heard calling
down the corridor*) He will confess! Proctor will confess!

PROCTOR: (*with a cry, as he strides to the door*) Why do you cry
it? (*In great pain he turns back to her.*) It is evil, is it not? It
435 is evil.

ELIZABETH: (*in terror, weeping*) I cannot judge you, John, I
cannot!

PROCTOR: Then who will judge me? (*Suddenly clasping his
hands*) God in Heaven, what is John Proctor, what is John
440 Proctor? (*He moves as an animal, and a fury is riding in him,
a tantalized search.*) I think it is honest, I think so; I am no
saint. (*As though she had denied this he calls angrily at her*)
Let Rebecca go like a saint: for me it is fraud!

(*Voices are heard in the hall, speaking together in suppressed
excitement.*)

ELIZABETH: I am not your judge, I cannot be. (*as though giving
445 him release*) Do as you will, do as you will!

PROCTOR: Would you give them such a lie? Say it. Would you
ever give them this? (*She cannot answer.*) You would not; if
tongs of fire were singeing you you would not! It is evil. Good,
then—it is evil, and I do it!

(HATHORNE *enters with* DANFORTH, *and, with them,*
CHEEVER, PARRIS, *and* HALE. *It is a businesslike, rapid entrance, as though the ice had been broken.*)

450 DANFORTH: (*with great relief and gratitude*) Praise to God,
man, praise to God; you shall be blessed in Heaven for this.
(CHEEVER *has hurried to the bench with pen, ink, and paper.*
PROCTOR *watches him.*) Now then, let us have it. Are you
ready, Mr. Cheever?

455 PROCTOR: (*with a cold, cold horror at their efficiency*) Why must
it be written?

DANFORTH: Why, for the good instruction of the village, Mister;
this we shall post upon the church door! (*To* PARRIS, *urgently*)
Where is the marshal?

PARRIS: (*runs to the door and calls down the corridor*) Marshal! 460
Hurry!

DANFORTH: Now, then, Mister, will you speak slowly, and directly to the point, for Mr. Cheever's sake. (*He is on record
now, and is really dictating to* CHEEVER, *who writes.*) Mr.
Proctor, have you seen the Devil in your life? (PROCTOR's 465
jaws lock.) Come, man, there is light in the sky; the town
waits at the scaffold; I would give out this news. Did you see
the Devil?

PROCTOR: I did.

PARRIS: Praise God! 470

DANFORTH: And when he come to you, what were his demand?
(PROCTOR *is silent.* DANFORTH *helps.*) Did he bid you to do
his work upon the earth?

PROCTOR: He did.

DANFORTH: And you bound yourself to his service? (DANFORTH 475
turns, as REBECCA NURSE *enters, with* HERRICK *helping to
support her. She is barely able to walk.*) Come in, come in,
woman!

REBECCA (*brightening as she sees* PROCTOR) Ah, John! You are
well, then, eh? 480

(PROCTOR *turns his face to the wall.*)

DANFORTH: Courage, man, courage—let her witness your good
example that she may come to God herself. Now hear it,
Goody Nurse! Say on, Mr. Proctor. Did you bind yourself to
the Devil's service?

REBECCA: (*astonished*) Why, John! 485

PROCTOR: (*through his teeth, his face turned from* REBECCA) I did.

DANFORTH: Now, woman, you surely see it profit nothin' to
keep this conspiracy any further. Will you confess yourself
with him?

REBECCA: Oh, John—God send his mercy on you! 490

DANFORTH: I say, will you confess yourself, Goody Nurse?

REBECCA: Why, it is a lie, it is a lie; how may I damn myself? I
cannot, I cannot.

DANFORTH: Mr. Proctor. When the Devil came to you did you
see Rebecca Nurse in his company? (PROCTOR *is silent.*) 495
Come, man, take courage—did you ever see her with the
Devil?

PROCTOR: (*almost inaudibly*) No.

(DANFORTH, *now sensing trouble, glances at* JOHN *and goes to
the table, and picks up a sheet—the list of condemned.*)

DANFORTH: Did you ever see her sister, Mary Easty, with the
Devil? 500

PROCTOR: No, I did not.

DANFORTH: (*his eyes narrow on* PROCTOR) Did you ever see
Martha Corey with the Devil?

PROCTOR: I did not.

DANFORTH: (*realizing, slowly putting the sheet down*) Did you 505
ever see anyone with the Devil?

PROCTOR: I did not.

DANFORTH: Proctor, you mistake me. I am not empowered to
trade your life for a lie. You have most certainly seen some
person with the Devil. (PROCTOR *is silent.*) Mr. Proctor, a 510

score of people have already testified they saw this woman
with the Devil.

PROCTOR: Then it is proved. Why must I say it?

515 DANFORTH: Why "must" you say it! Why, you should rejoice to
say it if your soul is truly purged of any love for Hell!

PROCTOR: They think to go like saints. I like not to spoil their
names.

DANFORTH: (inquiring, incredulous) Mr. Proctor, do you think
they go like saints?

520 PROCTOR: (evading) This woman never thought she done the
Devil's work.

DANFORTH: Look you, sir. I think you mistake your duty here. It
matters nothing what she thought—she is convicted of the
unnatural murder of children, and you for sending your spirit

525 out upon Mary Warren. Your soul alone is the issue here,
Mister, and you will prove its whiteness or you cannot live in a
Christian country. Will you tell me now what persons con-
spired with you in the Devil's company? (PROCTOR is silent.)
To your knowledge was Rebecca Nurse ever—

530 PROCTOR: I speak my own sins; I cannot judge another. (Crying
out, with hatred) I have no tongue for it.

HALE: (quickly to DANFORTH) Excellency, it is enough he confess himself. Let him sign it, let him sign it.

PARRIS: (feverishly) It is a great service, sir. It is a weighty name; it

535 will strike the village that Proctor confess. I beg you, let him
sign it. The sun is up, Excellency!

DANFORTH: (considers; then with dissatisfaction) Come, then,
sign your testimony. (To CHEEVER) Give it to him. (CHEEVER
goes to PROCTOR, the confession and a pen in hand. PROCTOR

540 does not look at it.) Come, man, sign it.

PROCTOR: (after glancing at the confession) You have all witnessed it—it is enough.

DANFORTH: You will not sign it?

PROCTOR: You have all witnessed it; what more is needed?

545 DANFORTH: Do you sport with me? You will sign your name or it
is no confession, Mister! (His breast heaving with agonized
breathing, PROCTOR now lays the paper down and signs his
name.)

PARRIS: Praise be to the Lord!

(PROCTOR has just finished signing when DANFORTH reaches for
the paper. But PROCTOR snatches it up, and now a wild terror is
rising in him, and a boundless anger.)

550 DANFORTH: (perplexed, but politely extending his hand) If you
please, sir.

PROCTOR: No.

DANFORTH: (as though PROCTOR did not understand) Mr. Proctor, I must have—

555 PROCTOR: No, no. I have signed it. You have seen me. It is
done! You have no need for this.

PARRIS: Proctor, the village must have proof that—

PROCTOR: Damn the village! I confess to God, and God has seen
my name on this! It is enough!

560 DANFORTH: No, sir, it is—

PROCTOR: You came to save my soul, did you not? Here! I have
confessed myself; it is enough!

DANFORTH: You have not con—

PROCTOR: I have confessed myself! Is there no good penitence

565 but it be public? God does not need my name nailed upon the

church! God sees my name; God knows how black my sins
are! It is enough!

DANFORTH: Mr. Proctor—

PROCTOR: You will not use me! I am no Sarah Good or Tituba, I
am John Proctor! You will not use me! It is no part of salvation 570
that you should use me!

DANFORTH: I do not wish to—

PROCTOR: I have three children—how may I teach them to walk
like men in the world, and I sold my friends?

DANFORTH: You have not sold your friends— 575

PROCTOR: Beguile me not! I blacken all of them when this is
nailed to the church the very day they hang for silence!

DANFORTH: Mr. Proctor, I must have good and legal proof that
you—

PROCTOR: You are the high court, your word is good enough! 580
Tell them I confessed myself; say Proctor broke his knees and
wept like a woman; say what you will, but my name cannot—

DANFORTH: (with suspicion) It is the same, is it not? If I report it
or you sign to it?

PROCTOR: (—he knows it is insane) No, it is not the same! What 585
others say and what I sign to is not the same!

DANFORTH: Why? Do you mean to deny this confession when
you are free?

PROCTOR: I mean to deny nothing!

DANFORTH: Then explain to me, Mr. Proctor, why you will not 590
let—

PROCTOR: (with a cry of his whole soul) Because it is my name!
Because I cannot have another in my life! Because I lie and
sign myself to lies! Because I am not worth the dust on the feet
of them that hang! How may I live without my name? I have 595
given you my soul; leave me my name!

DANFORTH: (pointing at the confession in PROCTOR's hand) Is
that document a lie? If it is a lie I will not accept it! What say
you? I will not deal in lies, Mister! (PROCTOR is motionless.)
You will give me your honest confession in my hand, or I 600
cannot keep you from the rope. (PROCTOR does not reply.)
Which way do you go, Mister?

(His breast heaving, his eyes staring, PROCTOR tears the paper
and crumples it, and he is weeping in fury, but erect.)

DANFORTH: Marshal!

PARRIS: (hysterically, as though the tearing paper were his life)
Proctor, Proctor! 605

HALE: Man, you will hang! You cannot!

PROCTOR: (his eyes full of tears) I can. And there's your first marvel, that I can. You have made your magic now, for now I do
think I see some shred of goodness in John Proctor. Not
enough to weave a banner with, but white enough to keep it 610
from such dogs. (ELIZABETH, in a burst of terror, rushes to
him and weeps against his hand.) Give them no tear! Tears
pleasure them! Show honor now, show a stony heart and sink
them with it! (He has lifted her, and kisses her now with great
passion.) 615

REBECCA: Let you fear nothing! Another judgment waits us all!

DANFORTH: Hang them high over the town! Who weeps for
these, weeps for corruption! (He sweeps out past them. HER-
RICK starts to lead REBECCA, who almost collapses, but PROC-
TOR catches her, and she glances up at him apologetically.) 620

REBECCA: I've had no breakfast.

HERRICK: Come, man.

(HERRICK *escorts them out*, HATHORNE *and* CHEEVER *behind them.* ELIZABETH *stands staring at the empty doorway.*)

PARRIS: *(in deadly fear, to* ELIZABETH) Go to him, Goody Proctor! There is yet time!

(From outside a drumroll strikes the air. PARRIS *is startled.* ELIZABETH *jerks about toward the window.*)

625 PARRIS: Go to him! *(He rushes out the door, as though to hold back his fate.)* Proctor! Proctor!

(Again, a short burst of drums.)

HALE: Woman, plead with him! *(He starts to rush out the door, and then goes back to her.)* Woman! It is pride, it is vanity.

(She avoids his eyes, and moves to the window. He drops to his knees.) Be his helper! — What profit him to bleed? Shall the 630 dust praise him? Shall the worms declare his truth? Go to him, take his shame away!

ELIZABETH: *(supporting herself against collapse, grips the bars of the window, and with a cry)* He have his goodness now. God forbid I take it from him! 635

(The final drumroll crashes, then heightens violently. HALE *weeps in frantic prayer, and the new sun is pouring in upon her face, and the drums rattle like bones in the morning air. The curtain falls.)*

— ECHOES DOWN THE CORRIDOR —

Not long after the fever died, Parris was voted from office, walked out on the highroad, and was never heard of again.

The legend has it that Abigail turned up later as a prostitute in Boston.

Twenty years after the last execution, the government awarded compensation to the victims still living, and to the families of the dead. However, it is evident that some people still were unwilling to admit their total guilt, and also that the factionalism was still alive, for some beneficiaries were actually not victims at all, but informers.

Elizabeth Proctor married again, four years after Proctor's death.

In solemn meeting, the congregation rescinded the excommunications — this in March 1712. But they did so upon orders of the government. The jury, however, wrote a statement praying forgiveness of all who had suffered.

Certain farms which had belonged to the victims were left to ruin, and for more than a century no one would buy them or live on them.

To all intents and purposes, the power of theocracy in Massachusetts was broken.

AMIRI BARAKA / LEROI JONES

Born Everett LeRoi Jones in Newark, New Jersey, in 1934, Amiri Baraka has become the most important revolutionary voice in contemporary black theater in the United States. He attended Rutgers University and Howard University, taking his B.A. from Howard in 1954. Baraka later said that his education at Howard was too involved with "learning to be white." He served in the United States Air Force before returning to New York in 1958. Living in Greenwich Village, he studied at Columbia University, married his first wife—an interracial marriage, lightly disguised in his play *The Slave*—and worked to develop his talents as a writer. Jones worked everywhere to develop a black esthetic, in his own poetry (in the mode of the Beat poets, Gregory Corso and Allen Ginsberg), in essays, and in magazines that he founded and edited. In 1960, Jones was part of a delegation of black Americans invited to Cuba to celebrate Fidel Castro's revolution. That visit had a profound impact on Jones, sharpening his sense of the need both for a distinctive black esthetic and culture, and for a social revolution to eradicate the injustices of white-dominated American society. His plays of the 1960s are, in fact, often directly concerned with this issue and with how white liberalism—ostensibly the ally of black power—finally becomes an obstacle to the more fundamental revolution needed to bring black identity, culture, and power into being. In 1964, three of his plays opened in New York: *The Eighth Ditch*, *The Baptism*, and *Dutchman*, which won the Obie award for the best American play of the season. He then wrote a series of plays examining black activism and revolution in American life: *The Slave* and *The Toilet* (1964), *Experimental Death Unit #1* (1965), and *J-e-l-l-o* (1965). The assassination of Malcolm X in 1965 and the Watts riots in Los Angeles also drove Jones toward a more militant position, as articulated in plays like *A Black Mass* (1966), *Slave Ship* (1966), *The Great Goodness of Life (A Coon Show)* (1967), *Home on the Range* (1968), and *The Death of Malcolm X* (1969), and later in *The Motion of History* (1977), and *Money* (1988). In 1964 Jones established the Black Arts Repertory Theater and School in Harlem and began a program of cultural nationalism there, which he has pursued subsequently in several other organizations and described in several collections of essays. He has been deeply involved in developing a theater that would serve the need for cultural and political revolution in the black community.

As part of his commitment to forging a sustaining system of values for the African-American community, Jones became a Kawaidi Muslim minister in 1968, adopting the title Imamu (spiritual leader) and the name Amiri Baraka at that time. Throughout the 1970s and 1980s, Baraka articulated and solidified the claims of cultural nationalism, frequently in a fiercely revolutionary, Marxist rhetoric. Baraka continues to live in Newark, New Jersey, and is involved in a variety of political and social activities in the black community.

Dutchman

Dutchman is one of Baraka's most powerful plays, both in its indictment of racist culture and in its straightforward confrontation between Lula and Clay. The title alludes to the legendary *Flying Dutchman*, the ship of the dead said to haunt the high seas. The subway car of the play is at once a ghost ship—where the young black man Clay is murdered—and a ghostly incarnation of racist fantasies. At the beginning of the play, Lula seems attracted to the middle-class Clay, but as the play develops it becomes clear that, to seduce Clay, Lula must transform him into something else, a fantasy figure of the white imagination. When Clay refuses to play along, delivering instead an impassioned statement of his own black identity, Lula murders him, with the implied consent of the white riders of the subway. *Dutchman* is a powerful parable of the problems of black identity in white culture.

DUTCHMAN

Amiri Baraka

— CHARACTERS —

CLAY, *twenty-year-old Negro*
LULA, *thirty-year-old white woman*
RIDERS OF COACH, *white and black*
YOUNG NEGRO
CONDUCTOR

In the flying underbelly of the city. Steaming hot, and summer on top, outside. Underground. The subway heaped in modern myth.

Opening scene is a man sitting in a subway seat, holding a magazine but looking vacantly just above its wilting pages. Occasionally he looks blankly toward the window on his right. Dim lights and darkness whistling by against the glass. (Or paste the lights, as admitted props, right on the subway windows. Have them move, even dim and flicker. But give the sense of speed. Also stations, whether the train is stopped or the glitter and activity of these stations merely flashes by the windows.)

The man is sitting alone. That is, only his seat is visible, though the rest of the car is outfitted as a complete subway car. But only his seat is shown. There might be, for a time, as the play begins, a loud scream of the actual train. And it can recur throughout the play, or continue on a lower key once the dialogue starts. The train slows after a time, pulling to a brief stop at one of the stations. The man looks idly up, until he sees a woman's face staring at him through the window; when it realizes that the man has noticed the face, it begins very premeditatedly to smile. The man smiles too, for a moment, without a trace of self-consciousness. Almost an instinctive though undesirable response. Then a kind of awkwardness or embarrassment sets in, and the man makes to look away, is further embarrassed, so he brings back his eyes to where the face was, but by now the train is moving again, and the face would seem to be left behind by the way the man turns his head to look back through the other windows at the slowly fading platform. He smiles then; more comfortably confident, hoping perhaps that his memory of this brief encounter will be pleasant. And then he is idle again.

— SCENE ONE —

Train roars. Lights flash outside the windows.

LULA *enters from the rear of the car in bright, skimpy summer clothes and sandals. She carries a net bag full of paper books, fruit, and other anonymous articles. She is wearing sunglasses, which she pushes up on her forehead from time to time. LULA is a tall, slender, beautiful woman with long red hair hanging straight down her back, wearing only loud lipstick in somebody's good taste. She is eating an apple, very daintily. Coming down the car toward CLAY.*

She stops beside CLAY's *seat and hangs languidly from the strap, still managing to eat the apple. It is apparent that she is going to sit in the seat next to* CLAY, *and that she is only waiting for him to notice her before she sits.*

CLAY *sits as before, looking just beyond his magazine, now and again pulling the magazine slowly back and forth in front of his face in a hopeless effort to fan himself. Then he sees the woman hanging there beside him and he looks up into her face, smiling quizzically.*

LULA: Hello.
CLAY: Uh, hi're you?
LULA: I'm going to sit down. . . . O.K.?
CLAY: Sure.
5 LULA:

(Swings down onto the seat, pushing her legs straight out as if she is very weary)

Oooof! Too much weight.
CLAY: Ha, doesn't look like much to me.

(Leaning back against the window, a little surprised and maybe stiff)

LULA: It's so anyway.

(And she moves her toes in the sandals, then pulls her right leg up on the left knee, better to inspect the bottoms of the sandals and the back of her heel. She appears for a second not to notice that CLAY *is sitting next to her or that she has spoken to him just a second before.* CLAY *looks at the mgagazine, then out the black window. As he does this, she turns very quickly toward him)*

Weren't you staring at me through the window?
CLAY: 10

(Wheeling around and very much stiffened)

What?
LULA: Weren't you staring at me through the window? At the last stop?
CLAY: Staring at you? What do you mean?
LULA: Don't you know what staring means?   15
CLAY: I saw you through the window . . . if that's what it means. I don't know if I was staring. Seems to me you were staring through the window at me.
LULA: I was. But only after I'd turned around and saw you staring through that window down in the vicinity of my ass and legs.   20
CLAY: Really?
LULA: Really. I guess you were just taking those idle potshots. Nothing else to do. Run your mind over people's flesh.
CLAY: Oh boy. Wow, now I admit I was looking in your direction. But the rest of that weight is yours.   25
LULA: I suppose.
CLAY: Staring through train windows is weird business. Much weirder than staring very sedately at abstract asses.
LULA: That's why I came looking through the window . . . so you'd have more than that to go on. I even smiled at you.   30

CLAY: That's right.

LULA: I even got into this train, going some other way than mine. Walked down the aisle . . . searching you out.

CLAY: Really? That's pretty funny.

35 LULA: That's pretty funny. . . . God, you're dull.

CLAY: Well, I'm sorry, lady, but I really wasn't prepared for party talk.

LULA: No, you're not. What are you prepared for?

(Wrapping the apple core in a Kleenex and dropping it on the floor)

CLAY:

(Takes her conversation as pure sex talk. He turns to confront her squarely with this idea)

40   I'm prepared for anything. How about you?

LULA:

(Laughing loudly and cutting it off abruptly)

What do you think you're doing?

CLAY: What?

LULA: You think I want to pick you up, get you to take me some-

45 where and screw me, huh?

CLAY: Is that the way I look?

LULA: You look like you been trying to grow a beard. That's exactly what you look like. You look like you live in New Jersey with your parents and are trying to grow a beard. That's what.

50 You look like you've been reading Chinese poetry and drinking lukewarm sugarless tea.

(Laughs, uncrossing and recrossing her legs)

You look like death eating a soda cracker.

CLAY:

(Cocking his head from one side to the other, embarrassed and trying to make some comeback, but also intrigued by what the woman is saying . . . even the sharp city coarseness of her voice, which is still a kind of gentle sidewalk throb.)

Really? I look like all that?

55 LULA: Not all of it.

(She feigns a seriousness to cover an actual somber tone)

I lie a lot.

(Smiling)

It helps me control the world.

CLAY:

(Relieved and laughing louder than the humor)

Yeah, I bet.

60 LULA: But it's true, most of it, right? Jersey? Your bumpy neck?

CLAY: How'd you know all that? Huh? Really. I mean about Jersey . . . and even the beard. I met you before? You know Warren Enright?

LULA: You tried to make it with your sister when you were ten.

(CLAY leans back hard against the back of the seat, his eyes opening now, still trying to look amused)

65   But I succeeded a few weeks ago.

(She starts to laugh again)

CLAY: What're you talking about? Warren tell you that? You're a friend of Georgia's?

LULA: I told you I lie. I don't know your sister. I don't know Warren Enright.

CLAY: You mean you're just picking these things out of the air? 70

LULA: Is Warren Enright a tall skinny black black boy with a phony English accent?

CLAY: I figured you knew him.

LULA: But I don't. I just figured you would know somebody like that. 75

(Laughs)

CLAY: Yeah, yeah.

LULA: You're probably on your way to his house now.

CLAY: That's right.

LULA:

(Putting her hand on CLAY's closer knee, drawing it from the knee up to the thigh's hinge, then removing it, watching his face very closely, and continuing to laugh, perhaps more gently than before)

Dull, dull, dull. I bet you think I'm exciting. 80

CLAY: You're O.K.

LULA: Am I exciting you now?

CLAY: Right. That's not what's supposed to happen?

LULA: How do I know?

(She returns her hand, without moving it, then takes it away and plunges it in her bag to draw out an apple)

You want this? 85

CLAY: Sure.

LULA:

(She gets one out of the bag for herself)

Eating apples together is always the first step. Or walking up uninhabited Seventh Avenue in the twenties on weekends.

(Bites and giggles, glancing at CLAY and speaking in loose singsong)

Can get you involved . . . boy! Get us involved. Um-huh. 90

(Mock seriousness)

Would you like to get involved with me, Mister Man?

CLAY:

(Trying to be a flippant as LULA, whacking happily at the apple)

Sure. Why not? A beautiful woman like you. Huh, I'd be a fool not to.

LULA: And I bet you're sure you know what you're talking about. 95

(Taking him a little roughly by the wrist, so he cannot eat the apple, then shaking the wrist)

I bet you're sure of almost everything anybody ever asked you about . . . right?

(Shakes his wrist harder)

Right?

CLAY: Yeah, right. . . . Wow, you're pretty strong, you know? Whatta you, a lady wrestler or something? 100

LULA: What's wrong with lady wrestlers? And don't answer because you never knew any. Huh.

(Cynically)

That's for sure. They don't have any lady wrestlers in that part of Jersey. That's for sure.

105 CLAY: Hey, you still haven't tole me how you know so much about me.

LULA: I told you I didn't know anything about *you* . . . you're a well-known type.

CLAY: Really?

110 LULA: Or at least I know the type very well. And your skinny English friend too.

CLAY: Anonymously?

LULA:

(Settles back in seat, single-mindedly finishing her apple and humming snatches of rhythm and blues song)

What?

115 CLAY: Without knowing us specifically?

LULA: Oh boy.

(Looking quickly at CLAY)

What a face. You know, you could be a handsome man.

CLAY: I can't argue with you.

LULA:

(Vague, off-center response)

120 What?

CLAY:

(Raising his voice, thinking the train noise has drowned part of his sentence)

I can't argue with you.

LULA: My hair is turning gray. A gray hair for each year and type I've come through.

125 CLAY: Why do you want to sound so old?

LULA: But it's always gentle when it starts.

(Attention drifting)

Hugged against tenements, day or night.

CLAY: What?

LULA:

(Refocusing)

130 Hey, why don't you take me to that party you're going to?

LULA: You must be a friend of Warren's to know about the party.

LULA: Wouldn't you like to take me to the party?

(Imitates clinging vine)

Oh, come on, ask me to your party.

CLAY: Of course I'll ask you to come with me to the party. And

135 I'll bet you're a friend of Warren's.

LULA: Why not be a friend of Warren's? Why not?

(Taking his arm)

Have you asked me yet?

CLAY: How can I ask you when I don't know your name?

LULA: Are you talking to my name?

140 CLAY: What is it, a secret?

LULA: I'm Lena the Hyena.

CLAY: The famous woman poet?

LULA: Poetess! The same!

CLAY: Well, you know so much about me . . . what's my name?

LULA: Morris the Hyena.   145

CLAY: The famous woman poet?

LULA: The same.

(Laughing and going into her bag)

You want another apple?

CLAY: Can't make it, lady. I only have to keep one doctor away a day.   150

LULA: I bet your name is . . . something like . . . uh, Gerald or Walter. Huh?

CLAY: God, no.

LULA: Lloyd, Norman? One of those hopeless colored names creeping out of New Jersey. Leonard? Gag. . . .   155

CLAY: Like Warren?

LULA: Definitely. Just exactly like Warren. Or Everett.

CLAY: Gag. . . .

LULA: Well, for sure, it's not Willie.

CLAY: It's Clay.   160

LULA: Clay? Really? Clay what?

CLAY: Take your pick. Jackson, Johnson, or Williams.

LULA: Oh, really? Good for you. But it's got to be Williams. You're too pretentious to be a Jackson or Johnson.

CLAY: Thass right.   165

LULA: But Clay's O.K.

CLAY: So's Lena.

LULA: It's Lula.

CLAY: Oh?

LULA: Lula the Hyena.   170

CLAY: Very good.

LULA:

(Starts laughing again)

Now you say to me, "Lula, Lula, why don't you go to this party with me tonight?" It's your turn, and let those be your lines.   175

CLAY: Lula, why don't you go to this party with me tonight, Huh?

LULA: Say my name twice before you ask, and no huh's.

CLAY: Lula, Lula, why don't you go to this party with me tonight?   180

LULA: I'd like to go, Clay, but how can you ask me to go when you barely know me?

CLAY: That is strange, isn't it?

LULA: What kind of reaction is that? You're supposed to say, "Aw, come on, we'll get to know each other better at the 185 party."

CLAY: That's pretty corny.

LULA: What are you into anyway?

(Looking at him half sullenly but still amused)

What thing are you playing at, Mister? Mister Clay Williams?

(Grabs his thigh, up near the crotch)

What are *you* thinking about?   190

CLAY: Watch it now, you're gonna excite me for real.

LULA:

(Taking her hand away and throwing her apple core through the window)

I bet.

(She slumps in the seat and is heavily silent)

CLAY: I thought you knew everything about me? What happened?

(LULA *looks at him, then looks slowly away, then over where the other aisle would be. Noise of the train. She reaches in her bag and pulls out one of the paper books. She puts it on her leg and thumbs the pages listlessly.* CLAY *cocks his head to see the title of the book. Noise of the train.* LULA *flips pages and her eyes drift. Both remain silent*)

195   Are you going to the party with me, Lula?

LULA:

(*Bored and not even looking*)

I don't even know you.

CLAY: You said you know my type.

LULA:

(*Strangely irritated*)

200   Don't get smart with me, Buster. I know you like the palm of my hand.

CLAY: The one you eat the apples with?

LULA: Yeh. And the one I open doors late Saturday evening with. That's my door. Up at the top of the stairs. Five flights.
205   Above a lot of Italians and lying Americans. And scrape carrots with. Also . . .

(*looks at him*)

the same hand I unbutton my dress with, or let my skirt fall down. Same hand. Lover.

CLAY: Are you angry about anything? Did I say something wrong?
210 LULA: Everything you say is wrong.

(*Mock smile*)

That's what makes you so attractive. Ha. In that funnybook jacket with all the buttons.

(*More animate, taking hold of his jacket*)

What've you got the jacket and tie on in all this heat for? And why're you wearing a jacket and tie like that? Did your people
215   ever burn witches or start revolutions over the price of tea? Boy, those narrow-shoulder clothes come from a tradition you ought to feel oppressed by. A three-button suit. What right do you have to be wearing a three-button suit and striped tie? Your grandfather was a slave, he didn't go to Harvard.
220 CLAY: My grandfather was a night watchman.

LULA: And you went to a colored college where everybody thought they were Averell Harriman.

CLAY: All except me.

LULA: And who did you think you were? Who do you think you
225   are now?

CLAY:

(*Laughs as if to make light of the whole trend of the conversation*)

Well, in college I thought I was Baudelaire. But I've slowed down since.

LULA: I bet you never once thought you were a black nigger.

(*Mock serious, then she howls with laughter.* CLAY *is stunned but after initial reaction, he quickly tries to appreciate the humor.* LULA *almost shrieks*)

230   A black Baudelaire.

CLAY: That's right.

LULA: Boy, are you corny. I take back what I said before. Every-

thing you say is not wrong. It's perfect. You should be on television.

CLAY: You act like you're on television already.   235

LULA: That's because I'm an actress.

CLAY: I thought so.

LULA: Well, you're wrong. I'm no actress. I told you I always lie. I'm nothing, honey, and don't you ever forget it.

(*Lighter*)

Although my mother was a Communist. The only person in   240
my family ever to amount to anything.

CLAY: My mother was a Republican.

LULA: And your father voted for the man rather than the party.

CLAY: Right!

LULA: Yea for him. Yea, yea for him.   245

CLAY: Yea!

LULA: And yea for America where he is free to vote for the mediocrity of his choice! Yea!

CLAY: Yea!

LULA: And yea for both your parents who even though they differ   250
about so crucial a matter as the body politic still forged a union of love and sacrifice that was destined to flower at the birth of the noble Clay . . . what's your middle name?

CLAY: Clay.

LULA: A union of love and sacrifice that was destined to flower at   255
the birth of the noble Clay Clay Williams. Yea! And most of all yea yea for you. Clay Clay. The Black Baudelaire! Yes!

(*And with knifelike cynicism*)

My Christ. My Christ.

CLAY: Thank you, ma'am.

LULA: May the people accept you as a ghost of the future. And   260
love you, that you might not kill them when you can.

CLAY: What?

LULA: You're a murderer, Clay, and you know it.

(*Her voice darkening with significance*)

You know goddamn well what I mean.

CLAY: I do?   265

LULA: So we'll pretend the air is light and full of perfume.

CLAY:

(*Sniffing at her blouse*)

It is.

LULA: And we'll pretend the people cannot see you. That is, the citizens. And that you are free of your own history. And I am   270
free of my history. We'll pretend that we are both anonymous beauties smashing along through the city's entrails.

(*She yells as loud as she can*)

GROOVE!

(*Black*)

— SCENE TWO —

Scene is the same as before, though now there are other seats visible in the car. And throughout the scene other people get on the subway. There are maybe one or two seated in the car as the scene opens, though neither CLAY nor LULA notices them. CLAY's tie is open. LULA is hugging his arm.

CLAY: The party!

LULA: I know it'll be something good. You can come in with me, looking casual and significant. I'll be strange, haughty, and silent, and walk with long slow strides.

5 CLAY: Right.

LULA: When you get drunk, pat me once, very lovingly on the flanks, and I'll look at you cryptically, licking my lips.

CLAY: It sounds like something we can do.

LULA: You'll go around talking to young men about your mind,
10 and to old men about your plans. If you meet a very close friend who is also with someone like me, we can stand together, sipping our drinks and exchanging codes of lust. The atmosphere will be slithering in love and half-love and very open moral decision.

15 CLAY: Great. Great.

LULA: And everyone will pretend they don't know your name, and then . . .

(She pauses heavily)

later, when they have to, they'll claim a friendship that denies your sterling character.

20 CLAY:

(Kissing her neck and fingers)

And then what?

LULA: Then? Well, then we'll go down the street, late night, eating apples and winding very deliberately toward my house.

CLAY: Deliberately?

25 LULA: I mean, we'll look in all the shopwindows, and make fun of the queers. Maybe we'll meet a Jewish Buddhist and flatten his conceits over some pretentious coffee.

CLAY: In honor of whose God?

LULA: Mine.

30 CLAY: Who is . . .?

LULA: Me . . . and you

CLAY: A corporate Godhead.

LULA: Exactly. Exactly.

(Notices one of the other people entering)

CLAY: Go on with the chronicle. Then what happens to us?

35 LULA:

(A mild depression, but she still makes her description triumphant and increasingly direct)

To my house, of course.

CLAY: Of course.

LULA: And up the narrow steps of the tenement.

CLAY: You live in a tenement?

40 LULA: Wouldn't live anywhere else. Reminds me specifically of my novel form of insanity.

CLAY: Up the tenement stairs.

LULA: And with my apple-eating hand I push open the door and lead you, my tender big-eyed prey, into my . . . God, what
45 can I call it . . . into my hovel.

CLAY: Then what happens?

LULA: After the dancing and games, after the long drinks and long walks, the real fun begins.

CLAY: Ah, the real fun.

(Embarrassed, in spite of himself)

50 Which is . . .?

LULA:

(Laughs at him)

Real fun in the dark house. Hah! Real fun in the dark house, high up above the street and the ignorant cowboys. I lead you in, holding your wet hand gently in my hand . . .

CLAY: Which is not wet? 55

LULA: Which is dry as ashes.

CLAY: And cold?

LULA: Don't think you'll get out of your responsibility that way. It's not cold at all. You Fascist! Into my dark living room. Where we'll sit and talk endlessly, endlessly. 60

CLAY: About what?

LULA: About what? About your manhood, what do you think? What do you think we've been talking about all this time?

CLAY: Well, I didn't know it was that. That's for sure. Every other thing in the world but that. 65

(Notices another person entering, looks quickly, almost involuntarily, up and down the car, seeing the other people in the car)

Hey, I didn't even notice when those people got on.

LULA: Yeah, I know.

CLAY: Man, this subway is slow.

LULA: Yeah, I know.

CLAY: Well, go on. We were talking about my manhood. 70

LULA: We still are. All the time.

CLAY: We were in your living room.

LULA: My dark living room. Talking endlessly.

CLAY: About my manhood.

LULA: I'll make you a map of it. Just as soon as we get to my 75
house.

CLAY: Well, that's great.

LULA: One of the things we do while we talk. And screw.

CLAY:

(Trying to make his smile broader and less shaky)

We finally got there. 80

LULA: And you'll call my rooms black as a grave. You'll say, "This place is like Juliet's tomb."

CLAY:

(Laughs)

I might.

LULA: I know. You've probably said it before. 85

CLAY: And is that all? The whole grand tour?

LULA: Not all. You'll say to me very close to my face, many, many times, you'll say, even whisper, that you love me.

CLAY: Maybe I will.

LULA: And you'll be lying. 90

CLAY: I wouldn't lie about something like that.

LULA: Hah. It's the only kind of thing you will lie about. Especially if you think it'll keep me alive.

CLAY: Keep you alive? I don't understand.

LULA: 95

(Bursting out laughing, but too shrilly)

Don't understand? Well, don't look at me. It's the path I take, that's all. Where both feet take me when I set them down. One in front of the other.

CLAY: Morbid. Morbid. You sure you're not an actress? All that self-aggrandizement. 100

LULA: Well, I told you I wasn't an actress . . . but I also told you I lie all the time. Draw your own conclusions.

CLAY: And is that all of our lives together you've described? There's no more?

105 LULA: I've told you all I know. Or almost all.

CLAY: There's no funny parts?

LULA: I thought it was all funny.

CLAY: But you mean peculiar, not ha-ha.

LULA: You don't know what I mean.

110 CLAY: Well, tell me the almost part then. You said almost all. What else? I want the whole story.

LULA:

(Searching aimlessly through her bag. She begins to talk breathlessly, with a light and silly tone)

All stories are whole stories. All of 'em. Our whole story . . . nothing but change. How could things go on like that forever?

115 Huh?

(Slaps him on the shoulder, begins finding things in her bag, taking them out and throwing them over her shoulder into the aisle)

Except I do go on as I do. Apples and long walks with deathless intelligent lovers. But you mix it up. Look out the window, all the time. Turning pages. Change change change. Till, shit, I don't know you. Wouldn't, for that matter. You're

120 too serious. I bet you're even too serious to be psychoanalyzed. Like all those Jewish poets from Yonkers, who leave their mothers looking for other mothers, or others' mothers, on whose baggy tits they lay their fumbling heads. Their poems are always funny, and all about sex.

125 CLAY: They sound great. Like movies.

LULA: But you change.

(Blankly)

And things work on you till you hate them.

(More people come into the train. They come closer to the couple, some of them not sitting, but swinging drearily on the straps, staring at the two with uncertain interest)

CLAY: Wow. All these people, so suddenly. They must all come from the same place.

130 LULA: Right. That they do.

CLAY: Oh? You know about them too?

LULA: Oh yeah. About them more than I know about you. Do they frighten you?

CLAY: Frighten me? Why should they frighten me?

135 LULA: 'Cause you're an escaped nigger.

CLAY: Yeah?

LULA: 'Cause you crawled through the wire and made tracks to my side.

CLAY: Wire?

140 LULA: Don't they have wire around plantations?

CLAY: You must be Jewish. All you can think about is wire. Plantations didn't have any wire. Plantations were big open whitewashed places like heaven, and everybody on 'em was grooved to be there. Just strummin' and hummin' all day.

145 LULA: Yes, yes.

CLAY: And that's how the blues was born.

LULA: Yes, yes. And that's how the blues was born.

(Begins to make up a song that becomes quickly hysterical. As she sings she rises from her seat, still throwing things out of her bag into the aisle, beginning a rhythmical shudder and twistlike wiggle, which she continues up and down the aisle, bumping into many of the standing people and tripping over the feet of those sitting. Each time she runs into a person she lets out a very vicious piece of profanity, wiggling and stepping all the time)

And that's how the blues was born. Yes. Yes. Son of a bitch, get out of the way. Yes. Quack. Yes. Yes. And that's how the blues was born. Ten little niggers sitting on a limb, but none 150 of them ever looked like him.

(Points to CLAY, returns toward the seat, with her hands extended for him to rise and dance with her)

And that's how blues was born. Yes. Come on. Clay. Let's do the nasty. Rub bellies. Rub bellies.

CLAY:

(Waves his hands to refuse. He is embarrassed, but determined to get a kick out of the proceedings)

Hey, what was in those apples? Mirror, mirror on the wall, 155 who's the fairest one of all? Snow White, baby, and don't you forget it.

LULA:

(Grabbing for his hands, which he draws away)

Come on, Clay. Let's rub bellies on the train. The nasty. The nasty. Do the gritty grind, like your ol' rag-head mammy. 160 Grind till you lose your mind. Shake it, shake it, shake it, shake it! OOOOweeee! Come on, Clay. Let's do the choo-choo train shuffle, the navel scratcher.

CLAY: Hey, you coming on like the lady who smoked up her grass skirt. 165

LULA:

(Becoming annoyed that he will not dance, and becoming more animated as if to embarrass him still further)

Come on, Clay . . . let's do the thing. Uhh! Uhh! Clay! Clay! You middle-class black bastard. Forget your social-working mother for a few seconds and let's knock stomachs. Clay, you liver-lipped white man. You would-be Christian. You ain't no 170 nigger, you're just a dirty white man. Get up, Clay. Dance with me, Clay.

CLAY: Lula! Sit down, now. Be cool.

LULA:

(Mocking him, in wild dance)

Be cool. Be cool. That's all you know . . . shaking the wildroot 175 cream-oil on your knotty head, jackets buttoning up to your chin, so full of white man's words. Christ! God! Get up and scream at these people. Like scream meaningless shit in these hopeless faces.

(She screams at people in train, still dancing)

Red trains cough Jewish underwear for keeps! Expanding 180 smells of silence. Gravy snot whistling like sea birds. Clay. Clay, you got to break out. Don't sit there dying the way they want you to die. Get up.

CLAY: Oh, sit the fuck down.

(He moves to restrain her)

185   Sit down, goddamn it.

LULA:

(Twisting out of his reach)

Screw yourself, Uncle Tom. Thomas Woolly-Head.

(Begins to dance a kind of jig, mocking CLAY *with loud forced humor)*

There is Uncle Tom . . . I mean, Uncle Thomas Woolly-
Head. With old white matted mane. He hobbles on his
190   wooden cane. Old Tom. Old Tom. Let the white man hump
his ol' mama, and he jes' shuffle off in the woods and hide his
gentle gray head. Ol' Thomas Woolly-Head.

*(Some of the other riders are laughing now. A drunk gets up and
joins* LULA *in her dance, singing, as best he can, her "song."* CLAY
*gets up out of his seat and visibly scans the faces of the other
riders)*

CLAY: Lula! Lula!

*(She is dancing and turning, still shouting as loud as she can.
The drunk too is shouting, and waving his hands wildly)*

Lula . . . you dumb bitch. Why don't you stop it?

*(He rushes half stumbling from his seat, and grabs one of her
flailing arms)*

195   LULA: Let me go! You black son of a bitch.

(She struggles against him)

Let me go! Help!

*(*CLAY *is dragging her towards her seat, and the drunk seeks to
interfere. He grabs* CLAY *around the shoulders and begins wrestling with him.* CLAY *clubs the drunk to the floor without releasing* LULA, *who is still screaming.* CLAY *finally gets her to the seat
and throws her into it)*

CLAY: Now you shut the hell up.

(Grabbing her shoulders)

Just shut up. You don't know what you're talking about. You
don't know anything. So just keep your stupid mouth closed.
200   LULA: You're afraid of white people. And your father was. Uncle
Tom Big Lip!

CLAY:

(Slaps her as hard as he can, across the mouth. LULA's *head
bangs against the back of the seat. When she raises it again,*
CLAY *slaps her again)*

Now shut up and let me talk.

*(He turns toward the other riders, some of whom are sitting on the
edge of their seats. The drunk is on one knee, rubbing his head,
and singing softly the same song. He shuts up too when he sees
CLAY watching him. The others go back to newspapers or stare
out the windows)*

Shit, you don't have any sense, Lula, nor feelings either. I
205   could murder you now. Such a tiny ugly throat. I could
squeeze it flat, and watch you turn blue, on a humble. For
dull kicks. And all these weak-faced ofays squatting around
here, staring over their papers at me. Murder them too. Even
if they expected it. That man there . . .

(Points to well-dressed man)

I could rip that *Times* right out of his hand, as skinny and   210
middle-classed as I am, I could rip that paper out of his hand
and just as easily rip out his throat. It takes no great effort. For
what? To kill you soft idiots? You don't understand anything
but luxury.

LULA: You fool!   215

CLAY:

(Pushing her against the seat)

I'm not telling you again, Tallulah Bankhead! Luxury. In
your face and your fingers. You telling me what I ought to do.

(Sudden scream frightening the whole coach)

Well, don't! Don't you tell me anything! If I'm a middle-class
fake white man . . . let me be. And let me be in the way I   220
want.

(Through his teeth)

I'll rip your lousy breasts off! Let me be who I feel like being.
Uncle Tom. Thomas. Whoever. It's none of your business.
You don't know anything except what's there for you to see.
An act. Lies. Device. Not the pure heart, the pumping black   225
heart. You don't ever know that. And I sit here, in this but-
toned-up suit, to keep myself from cutting all your throats. I
mean wantonly. You great liberated whore! You fuck some
black man, and right away you're an expert on black people.
What a lotta shit that is. The only thing you know is that you   230
come if he bangs you hard enough. And that's all. The belly
rub? You wanted to do the belly rub? Shit, you don't even
know how. You don't know how. That ol' dipty-dip shit you
do, rolling your ass like an elephant. That's not my kind of
belly rub. Belly rub is not Queens. Belly rub is dark places,   235
with big hats and overcoats held up with one arm. Belly rub
hates you. Old bald-headed four-eyed ofays popping their fingers . . . and don't know yet what they're doing. They say, "I
love Bessie Smith." And don't even understand that Bessie
Smith is saying, "Kiss my ass, kiss my black unruly ass." Be-   240
fore love, suffering, desire, anything you can explain, she's
saying, and very plainly, "Kiss my black ass." And if you don't
know that, it's you that's doing the kissing.

Charlie Parker? Charlie Parker. All the hip white boys
scream for Bird. And Bird saying, "Up your ass, feeble-   245
minded ofay! Up your ass." And they sit there talking about
the tortured genius of Charlie Parker. Bird would've played
not a note of music if he just walked up to East Sixty-seventh
Street and killed the first ten white people he saw. Not a note!
And I'm the great would-be poet. Yes. That's right! Poet.   250
Some kind of bastard literature . . . all it needs is a simple
knife thrust. Just let me bleed you, you loud whore, and one
poem vanished. A whole people of neurotics, struggling to
keep from being sane. And the only thing that would cure the
neurosis would be your murder. Simple as that. I mean if I   255
murdered you, then other white people would begin to understand me. You understand? No. I guess not. If Bessie
Smith had killed some white people she wouldn't have
needed that music. She could have talked very straight and
plain about the world. No metaphors. No grunts. No wiggles   260
in the dark of her soul. Just straight two and two are four.
Money. Power. Luxury. Like that. All of them. Crazy niggers

turning their backs on sanity. When all it needs is that simple act. Murder. Just murder! Would make us all sane.

(Suddenly weary)

265 Ahhh. Shit. But who needs it? I'd rather be a fool. Insane. Safe with my words, and no deaths, and clean, hard thoughts, urging me to new conquests. My people's madness. Hah! That's a laugh. My people. They don't need me to claim them. They got legs and arms of their own. Personal

270 insanities. Mirrors. They don't need all those words. They don't need any defense. But listen, though, one more thing. And you tell this to your father, who's probably the kind of man who needs to know at once. So he can plan ahead. Tell him not to preach so much rationalism and cold logic to these

275 niggers. Let them alone. Let them sing curses at you in code and see your filth as simple lack of style. Don't make the mistake, through some irresponsible surge of Christian charity, of talking too much about the advantages of Western rationalism, or the great intellectual legacy of the white man, or

280 maybe they'll begin to listen. And then, maybe one day, you'll find they actually do understand exactly what you are talking about, all these fantasy people. All these blues people. And on that day, as sure as shit, when you really believe you can "accept" them into your fold, as half-white trusties late of

285 the subject peoples. With no more blues, except the very old ones, and not a watermelon in sight, the great missionary heart will have triumphed, and all of those ex-coons will be stand-up Western men, with eyes for clean hard useful lives, sober, pious and sane, and they'll murder you. They'll mur-

290 der you, and have very rational explanations. Very much like your own. They'll cut your throats, and drag you out to the edge of your cities so the flesh can fall away from your bones, in sanitary isolation.

LULA:

(Her voice takes on a different, more businesslike quality)

295 I've heard enough.

CLAY:

(Reaching for his books)

I bet you have. I guess I better collect my stuff and get off this train. Looks like we won't be acting out that little pageant you outlined before.

300 LULA: No. We won't. You're right about that, at least.

(She turns to look quickly around the rest of the car)

All right!

(The others respond)

CLAY:

(Bending across the girl to retrieve his belongings)

Sorry, baby, I don't think we could make it.

(As he is bending over her, the girl brings up a small knife and plunges it into CLAY's chest. Twice. He slumps across her knees, his mouth working stupidly)

LULA: Sorry is right.

(Turning to the others in the car who have already gotten up from their seats)

Sorry is the rightest thing you've said. Get this man off me! 305 Hurry, now!

(The others come and drag CLAY's body down the aisle)

Open the door and throw his body out.

(They throw him off)

And all of you get off at the next stop.

(LULA busies herself straightening her things. Getting everything in order. She takes out a notebook and makes a quick scribbling note. Drops it in her bag. The train apparently stops and all the others get off, leaving her alone in the coach. Very soon a young Negro of about twenty comes into the coach, with a couple of books under his arm. He sits a few seats in back of LULA. When he is seated she turns and gives him a long slow look. He looks up from his book and drops the book on his lap. Then an old Negro CONDUCTOR comes into the car, doing a sort of restrained soft shoe, and half mumbling the words of some song. He looks at the young man, briefly, with a quick greeting.)

CONDUCTOR: Hey, brother!
YOUNG MAN: Hey. 310

(The CONDUCTOR continues down the aisle with his little dance and the mumbled song. LULA turns to stare at him and follows his movements down the aisle. The CONDUCTOR tips his hat when he reaches her seat, and continues out the car)

LUIS VALDEZ

Luis Valdez (b. 1940), was born and raised the son of farmworkers in Delano, California. He majored in drama at San Diego State University, taking his B.A. in 1964, and then joined the San Francisco Mime Troupe, an important experimental theater company. In 1965, when farm workers at the Delano grape plantations went on strike, Valdez formed El Teatro Campesino ("The Farmworkers' Theater"). Valdez and Teatro Campesino devised two dramatic forms: ACTOS, short, satirical plays dramatizing the oppression of the fieldworkers, and MITOS, poetic, lyrical plays on Chicano life. Teatro Campesino became one of several important Chicano theater companies that performed throughout the Southwest and in urban areas of the Midwest and Northeast, drawing on both American and European dramatic traditions, as well as traditions of Mexican and Spanish-language theater in the United States that date to the seventeenth century. In the late 1960s and 1970s, Teatro Campesino toured the United States and Europe and gained an international reputation. Valdez's other *actos* with Teatro Campesino include *Las Dos Caras del Patroncito* (1965), *No Saco Nada de la Escuela* (1969), and *Vietnam Campesino* (1970). Valdez produced the stage play *Zoot Suit* in 1978, which was released as a film in 1981. He wrote and directed the film *La Bamba* in 1987. In 1986 he returned to Teatro Campesino to write *I Don't Have to Show You No Stinking Badges*. Valdez has also held academic appointments at the University of California, Berkeley, and at the University of California, Santa Cruz.

Los Vendidos

One of Teatro Campesino's best and most popular *actos*, *Los Vendidos* — "The Sellouts" — is reminiscent both of Brechtian political theater and more generally of popular satire. In its brief sketch of Honest Sancho's Used Mexican Lot, the play dramatizes a range of stereotypes applied by Anglo culture (represented by the Anglicized Mexican-American, Miss JIM-enez) to Chicano experience: farmworkers, Johnny Pachuco, the *revolucionario*, and the "new 1970 Mexican-American" yuppie. In the play's surprising finale, though, the yuppie turns on Miss JIM-enez, and the "used Mexicans" turn out to run the shop: Honest Sancho is *their* front.

The play clearly engages conflicting attitudes toward social experience, as emblematized by its title. For the title can mean both "those who are sold" — like the "used Mexicans" on Sancho's lot — and "the sellouts," presumably Honest Sancho and Miss JIM-enez. This duplicity is also inflected by the play's language, its mixture of Spanish and English, the two languages Chicano culture uses to define itself and to engage the Anglo world. The play works at the border between two cultures, where language is part of the complex social and political negotiation that characterizes Mexican-American life today.

LOS VENDIDOS

Luis Valdez

— CHARACTERS —

HONEST SANCHO
SECRETARY
FARM WORKER
JOHNNY
REVOLUCIONARIO
MEXICAN-AMERICAN

SCENE: HONEST SANCHO's *Used Mexican Lot and Mexican Curio Shop. Three models are on display in* HONEST SANCHO's *shop: to the right, there is a* REVOLUCIONARIO, *complete with sombrero, carrilleras, and carabina 30-30. At center, on the floor, there is the* FARM WORKER, *under a broad straw sombrero. At stage left is the* PACHUCO, *filero in hand.*

(HONEST SANCHO *is moving among his models, dusting them off and preparing for another day of business.*)

SANCHO: Bueno, bueno, mis monos, vamos a ver a quien vendemos ahora, ¿no? (*To audience.*) ¡Quihubo! I'm Honest Sancho and this is my shop. Antes fui contratista pero ahora logré tener mi negocito. All I need now is a customer. (*A bell rings offstage.*) Ay, a customer!

SECRETARY: (*Entering*) Good morning, I'm Miss Jiménez from —

SANCHO: ¡Ah, una chicana! Welcome, welcome Señorita Jiménez.

SECRETARY: (*Anglo pronunciation*) JIM-enez.

SANCHO: ¿Qué?

SECRETARY: My name is Miss JIM-enez. Don't you speak English? What's wrong with you?

SANCHO: Oh, nothing, Señorita JIM-enez. I'm here to help you.

SECRETARY: That's better. As I was starting to say, I'm a secretary from Governor Reagan's office, and we're looking for a Mexican type for the administration.

SANCHO: Well, you come to the right place, lady. This is Honest Sancho's Used Mexican lot, and we got all types here. Any particular type you want?

SECRETARY: Yes, we were looking for somebody suave —

SANCHO: Suave.

SECRETARY: Debonair.

SANCHO: De buen aire.

SECRETARY: Dark.

SANCHO: Prieto.

SECRETARY: But of course not too dark.

SANCHO: No muy prieto.

SECRETARY: Perhaps, beige.

SANCHO: Beige, just the tone. Así como cafecito con leche, ¿no?

SECRETARY: One more thing. He must be hard-working.

SANCHO: That could only be one model. Step right over here to the center of the shop, lady. (*They cross to the* FARM WORKER.) This is our standard farm worker model. As you can see, in the words of our beloved Senator George Murphy, he is "built close to the ground." Also take special notice of his four-ply Goodyear huaraches, made from the rain tire. This wide-brimmed sombrero is an extra added feature — keeps off the sun, rain, and dust.

SECRETARY: Yes, it does look durable.

SANCHO: And our farm worker model is friendly. Muy amable. Watch. (*Snaps his fingers.*)

FARM WORKER: (*Lifts up head*) Buenos días, señorita. (*His head drops.*)

SECRETARY: My, he's friendly.

SANCHO: Didn't I tell you? Loves his patrones! But his most attractive feature is that he's hard-working. Let me show you. (*Snaps fingers.* FARM WORKER *stands.*)

FARM WORKER: ¡El jale! (*He begins to work.*)

SANCHO: As you can see, he is cutting grapes.

SECRETARY: Oh, I wouldn't know.

SANCHO: He also picks cotton. (*Snap.* FARM WORKER *begins to pick cotton.*)

SECRETARY: Versatile isn't he?

SANCHO: He also picks melons. (*Snap.* FARM WORKER *picks melons.*) That's his slow speed for late in the season. Here's his fast speed. (*Snap.* FARM WORKER *picks faster.*)

SECRETARY: ¡Chihuahua! . . . I mean, goodness, he sure is a hard worker.

SANCHO: (*Pulls the* FARM WORKER *to his feet*) And that isn't the half of it. Do you see these little holes on his arms that appear to be pores? During those hot sluggish days in the field, when the vines or the branches get so entangled, it's almost impossible to move; these holes emit a certain grease that allow our model to slip and slide right through the crop with no trouble at all.

SECRETARY: Wonderful. But is he economical?

SANCHO: Economical? Señorita, you are looking at the Volkswagen of Mexicans. Pennies a day is all it takes. One plate of beans and tortillas will keep him going all day. That, and chile. Plenty of chile. Chile jalapenos, chile verde, chile colorado. But, of course, if you do give him chile (*Snap.* FARM WORKER *turns left face. Snap.* FARM WORKER *bends over.*) then you have to change his oil filter once a week.

SECRETARY: What about storage?

SANCHO: No problem. You know these new farm labor camps our Honorable Governor Reagan has built out by Parlier or Raisin City? They were designed with our model in mind. Five, six, seven, even ten in one of those shacks will give you

---

Scene **carrilleras** literally chin straps, but may refer to cartridge belts   Scene **Pachuco** Chicano slang for 1940s zoot suiter *filero* blade   1–2 **Bueno, bueno, . . . Quihubo** "Good, good, my cute ones, let's see who we can sell now, O.K.?"   3–4 **Antes fui . . . negocito** "I used to be a contractor, but now I've succeeded in having my little business."   30 **Así como . . . leche** like coffee with milk

42 **Muy amable** very friendly   50 **El jale** the job

no trouble at all. You can also put him in old barns, old cars, river banks. You can even leave him out in the field overnight with no worry!

SECRETARY: Remarkable.

85 SANCHO: And here's an added feature: Every year at the end of the season, this model goes back to Mexico and doesn't return, automatically, until next Spring.

SECRETARY: How about that. But tell me: does he speak English?

SANCHO: Another outstanding feature is that last year this model

90 was programmed to go out on STRIKE! (*Snap.*)

FARM WORKER: ¡HUELGA! ¡HUELGA! Hermanos, sálganse de esos files. (*Snap. He stops.*)

SECRETARY: No! Oh no, we can't strike in the State Capitol.

SANCHO: Well, he also scabs. (*Snap.*)

95 FARM WORKER: Me vendo barato, ¿y qué? (*Snap.*)

SECRETARY: That's much better, but you didn't answer my question. Does he speak English?

SANCHO: Bueno . . . no pero he has other —

SECRETARY: No.

100 SANCHO: Other features.

SECRETARY: NO! He just won't do!

SANCHO: Okay, okay pues. We have other models.

SECRETARY: I hope so. What we need is something a little more sophisticated.

105 SANCHO: Sophisti — ¿qué?

SECRETARY: An urban model.

SANCHO: Ah, from the city! Step right back. Over here in this corner of the shop is exactly what you're looking for. Introducing our new 1969 JOHNNY PACHUCO model! This is

110 our fast-back model. Streamlined. Built for speed, low-riding, city life. Take a look at some of these features. Mag shoes, dual exhausts, green chartreuse paint-job, dark-tint windshield, a little poof on top. Let me just turn him on. (*Snap. JOHNNY walks to stage center with a pachuco bounce.*)

115 SECRETARY: What was that?

SANCHO: That, señorita, was the Chicano shuffle.

SECRETARY: Okay, what does he do?

SANCHO: Anything and everything necessary for city life. For instance, survival: He knife fights. (*Snap. JOHNNY pulls out*

120 *switch blade and swings at SECRETARY.*)

(SECRETARY *screams.*)

SANCHO: He dances. (*Snap.*)

JOHNNY: (*Singing*) "Angel Baby, my Angel Baby . . ." (*Snap.*)

SANCHO: And here's a feature no city model can be without. He gets arrested, but not without resisting, of course. (*Snap.*)

125 JOHNNY: ¡En la madre, la placa! I didn't do it! I didn't do it! (*JOHNNY turns and stands up against an imaginary wall, legs spread out, arms behind his back.*)

SECRETARY: Oh no, we can't have arrests! We must maintain law and order.

130 SANCHO: But he's bilingual!

SECRETARY: Bilingual?

SANCHO: Simón que yes. He speaks English! Johnny, give us some English. (*Snap.*)

JOHNNY: (*Comes downstage.*) Fuck-you!

SECRETARY: (*Gasps*) Oh! I've never been so insulted in my 135 whole life!

SANCHO: Well, he learned it in your school.

SECRETARY: I don't care where he learned it.

SANCHO: But he's economical!

SECRETARY: Economical? 140

SANCHO: Nickels and dimes. You can keep Johnny running on hamburgers, Taco Bell tacos, Lucky Lager beer, Thunderbird wine, yesca —

SECRETARY: Yesca?

SANCHO: Mota. 145

SECRETARY: Mota?

SANCHO: Leños . . . Marijuana. (*Snap;* JOHNNY *inhales on an imaginary joint.*)

SECRETARY: That's against the law!

JOHNNY: (*Big smile, holding his breath*) Yeah. 150

SANCHO: He also sniffs glue. (*Snap.* JOHNNY *inhales glue, big smile.*)

JOHNNY: Tha's too much man, ése.

SECRETARY: No, Mr. Sancho, I don't think this —

SANCHO: Wait a minute, he has other qualities I know you'll 155 love. For example, an inferiority complex. (*Snap.*)

JOHNNY: (*To* SANCHO) You think you're better than me, huh ése? (*Swings switch blade.*)

SANCHO: He can also be beaten and he bruises, cut him and he bleeds; kick him and he —(*He beats, bruises and kicks* 160 PACHUCO.) would you like to try it?

SECRETARY: Oh, I couldn't.

SANCHO: Be my guest. He's a great scapegoat.

SECRETARY: No, really.

SANCHO: Please. 165

SECRETARY: Well, all right. Just once. (*She kicks* PACHUCO.) Oh, he's so soft.

SANCHO: Wasn't that good? Try again.

SECRETARY: (*Kicks* PACHUCO) Oh, he's so wonderful! (*She kicks him again.*) 170

SANCHO: Okay, that's enough, lady. You ruin the merchandise. Yes, our Johnny Pachuco model can give you many hours of pleasure. Why, the L.A.P.D. just bought twenty of these to train their rookie cops on. And talk about maintenance. Señorita, you are looking at an entirely self-supporting ma- 175 chine. You're never going to find our Johnny Pachuco model on the relief rolls. No, sir, this model knows how to liberate.

SECRETARY: Liberate?

SANCHO: He steals. (*Snap.* JOHNNY *rushes the* SECRETARY *and steals her purse.*) 180

JOHNNY: ¡Dame esa bolsa, vieja! (*He grabs the purse and runs. Snap by* SANCHO. *He stops.*)

(SECRETARY *runs after* JOHNNY *and grabs purse away from him, kicking him as she goes.*)

SECRETARY: No, no, no! We can't have any *more* thieves in the State Administration. Put him back.

SANCHO: Okay, we still got other models. Come on, Johnny, 185 we'll sell you to some old lady. (SANCHO *takes* JOHNNY *back to his place.*)

SECRETARY: Mr. Sancho, I don't think you quite understand what we need. What we need is something that will attract the women voters. Something more traditional, more romantic. 190

91 **HUELGA!HUELGA!** . . . **esos files** "Strike! Strike! Brothers, leave those rows." 95 **Me vendo . . . qué** "I come cheap, so what?" 98 **Bueno . . . no, pero** "Well, no, but . . ." 125 **En la . . . placa** "Wow, the police!" 132 **Simón . . . yes** yeah, sure

147 **Leños** "joints" of marijuana 181 **Dame esa . . . , vieja** "Gimme that bag, old lady!"

SANCHO: Ah, a lover. (*He smiles meaningfully.*) Step right over here, señorita. Introducing our standard Revolucionario and/or Early California Bandit type. As you can see he is well-built, sturdy, durable. This is the International Harvester of Mexicans.

SECRETARY: What does he do?

SANCHO: You name it, he does it. He rides horses, stays in the mountains, crosses deserts, plains, rivers, leads revolutions, follows revolutions, kills, can be killed, serves as a martyr, hero, movie star — did I say movie star? Did you ever see *Viva Zapata? Viva Villa? Villa Rides? Pancho Villa Returns? Pancho Villa Goes Back? Pancho Villa Meets Abbot and Costello*—

SECRETARY: I've never seen any of those.

SANCHO: Well, he was in all of them. Listen to this. (*Snap.*)

REVOLUCIONARIO: (*Scream*) ¡VIVA VILLAAAAA!

SECRETARY: That's awfully loud.

SANCHO: He has a volume control. (*He adjusts volume. Snap.*)

REVOLUCIONARIO: (*Mousey voice*) ¡Viva Villa!

SECRETARY: That's better.

SANCHO: And even if you didn't see him in the movies, perhaps you saw him on TV. He makes commercials. (*Snap.*)

REVOLUCIONARIO: Is there a Frito Bandito in your house?

SECRETARY: Oh yes, I've seen that one!

SANCHO: Another feature about this one is that he is economical. He runs on raw horsemeat and tequila!

SECRETARY: Isn't that rather savage?

SANCHO: Al contrario, it makes him a lover. (*Snap.*)

REVOLUCIONARIO: (*To* SECRETARY) ¡Ay, mamasota, cochota, ven pa'ca! (*He grabs* SECRETARY *and folds her back—Latin-lover style.*)

SANCHO: (*Snap.* REVOLUCIONARIO *goes back upright.*) Now wasn't that nice?

SECRETARY: Well, it was rather nice.

SANCHO: And finally, there is one outstanding feature about this model I KNOW the ladies are going to love: He's a GENUINE antique! He was made in Mexico in 1910!

SECRETARY: Made in Mexico?

SANCHO: That's right. Once in Tijuana, twice in Guadalajara, three times in Cuernavaca.

SECRETARY: Mr. Sancho, I thought he was an American product.

SANCHO: No, but—

SECRETARY: No, I'm sorry. We can't buy anything but American-made products. He just won't do.

SANCHO: But he's an antique!

SECRETARY: I don't care. You still don't understand what we need. It's true we need Mexican models such as these, but it's more important that he be *American.*

SANCHO: American?

SECRETARY: That's right, and judging from what you've shown me, I don't think you have what we want. Well, my lunch hour's almost over; I better—

SANCHO: Wait a minute! Mexican but American?

SECRETARY: That's correct.

SANCHO: Mexican but . . . (*A sudden flash.*) AMERICAN! Yeah, I think we've got exactly what you want. He just came in today! Give me a minute. (*He exits. Talks from backstage.*) Here he is in the shop. Let me just get some papers off. There. Introducing our new 1970 Mexican-American! Ta-ra-ra-ra-ra-ra-RA-RAAA!

217 **Al contrario** on the contrary

(SANCHO *brings out the* MEXICAN-AMERICAN *model, a clean-shaven middle-class type in business suit, with glasses.*)

SECRETARY: (*Impressed*) Where have you been hiding this one?

SANCHO: He just came in this morning. Ain't he a beauty? Feast your eyes on him! Sturdy US STEEL frame, streamlined, modern. As a matter of fact, he is built exactly like our Anglo models except that he comes in a variety of darker shades: naugahyde, leather, or leatherette.

SECRETARY: Naugahyde.

SANCHO: Well, we'll just write that down. Yes, señorita, this model represents the apex of American engineering! He is bilingual, college educated, ambitious! Say the word "acculturate" and he accelerates. He is intelligent, well-mannered, clean—did I say clean? (*Snap.* MEXICAN-AMERICAN *raises his arm.*) Smell.

SECRETARY: (*Smells*) Old Sobaco, my favorite.

SANCHO: (*Snap.* MEXICAN-AMERICAN *turns toward* SANCHO.) Eric! (*To* SECRETARY.) We call him Eric Garcia. (*To* ERIC.) I want you to meet Miss JIM-enez, Eric.

MEXICAN-AMERICAN: Miss JIM-enez, I am delighted to make your acquaintance. (*He kisses her hand.*)

SECRETARY: Oh, my, how charming!

SANCHO: Did you feel the suction? He has seven especially engineered suction cups right behind his lips. He's a charmer all right!

SECRETARY: How about boards? Does he function on boards?

SANCHO: You name them, he is on them. Parole boards, draft boards, school boards, taco quality control boards, surf boards, two-by-fours.

SECRETARY: Does he function in politics?

SANCHO: Señorita, you are looking at a political MACHINE. Have you ever heard of the OEO, EOC, COD, WAR ON POVERTY? That's our model! Not only that, he makes political speeches.

SECRETARY: May I hear one?

SANCHO: With pleasure. (*Snap.*) Eric, give us a speech.

MEXICAN-AMERICAN: Mr. Congressman, Mr. Chairman, members of the board, honored guests, ladies and gentlemen. (SANCHO *and* SECRETARY *applaud.*) Please, please, I come before you as a Mexican-American to tell you about the problems of the Mexican. The problems of the Mexican stem from one thing and one thing alone: He's stupid. He's uneducated. He needs to stay in school. He needs to be ambitious, forward-looking, harder-working. He needs to think American, American, American, AMERICAN, AMERICAN, AMERICAN. GOD BLESS AMERICA! GOD BLESS AMERICA!! (*He goes out of control.*)

(SANCHO *snaps frantically and the* MEXICAN-AMERICAN *finally slumps forward, bending at the waist.*)

SECRETARY: Oh my, he's patriotic too!

SANCHO: Sí, señorita, he loves his country. Let me just make a little adjustment here. (*Stands* MEXICAN-AMERICAN *up.*)

SECRETARY: What about upkeep? Is he economical?

SANCHO: Well, no, I won't lie to you. The Mexican-American costs a little bit more, but you get what you pay for. He's worth every extra cent. You can keep him running on dry martinis, Langendorf bread.

SECRETARY: Apple pie?

SANCHO: Only Mom's. Of course, he's also programmed to eat

305   Mexican food on ceremonial functions, but I must warn you:
an overdose of beans will plug up his exhaust.

SECRETARY: Fine! There's just one more question: HOW
MUCH DO YOU WANT FOR HIM?

SANCHO: Well, I tell you what I'm gonna do. Today and today
310   only, because you've been so sweet, I'm gonna let you steal
this model from me! I'm gonna let you drive him off the lot
for the simple price of—let's see taxes and license included—
$15,000.

SECRETARY: Fifteen thousand DOLLARS? For a MEXICAN!

315   SANCHO: Mexican? What are you talking, lady? This is a Mexican-
AMERICAN! We had to melt down two pachucos, a farm
worker and three gabachos to make this model! You want
quality, but you gotta pay for it! This is no cheap run-about.
He's got class!

320   SECRETARY: Okay, I'll take him.

SANCHO: You will?

SECRETARY: Here's your money.

SANCHO: You mind if I count it?

SECRETARY: Go right ahead.

325   SANCHO: Well, you'll get your pink slip in the mail. Oh, do you
want me to wrap him up for you? We have a box in the back.

SECRETARY: No, thank you. The Governor is having a lun-
cheon this afternoon, and we need a brown face in the crowd.
How do I drive him?

330   SANCHO: Just snap your fingers. He'll do anything you want.

(SECRETARY snaps. MEXICAN-AMERICAN steps forward.)

MEXICAN-AMERICAN: RAZA QUERIDA, ¡VAMOS LEVAN-
TANDO ARMAS PARA LIBERARNOS DE ESTOS DES-
GRACIADOS GABACHOS QUE NOS EXPLOTAN!
VAMOS.

335   SECRETARY: What did he say?

SANCHO: Something about lifting arms, killing white people,
etc.

SECRETARY: But he's not supposed to say that!

SANCHO: Look, lady, don't blame me for bugs from the factory.
340   He's your Mexican-American; you bought him, now drive
him off the lot!

SECRETARY: But he's broken!

SANCHO: Try snapping another finger.

(SECRETARY snaps. MEXICAN-AMERICAN comes to life again.)

MEXICAN-AMERICAN: ¡ESTA GRAN HUMANIDAD HA
345   DICHO BASTA! Y SE HA PUESTO EN MARCHA!
¡BASTA! ¡BASTA! ¡VIVA LA RAZA! ¡VIVA LA CAUSA!
¡VIVA LA HUELGA! ¡VIVAN LOS BROWN BERETS!
¡VIVAN LOS ESTUDIANTES! ¡CHICANO POWER!

331–334 RAZA QUERIDA, . . . VAMOS "Beloved Raza, let's pick up
arms to liberate ourselves from those damned whites that exploit us!
Let's go." **344–348 ESTA GRAN . . . CHICANO POWER** "This
great mass of humanity has said enough! And it begins to march!
Enough! Enough! Long live La Raza! Long live the Cause! Long live
the strike! Long live the Brown Berets! Long live the students! Chicano
Power!"

*(The MEXICAN-AMERICAN turns toward the SECRETARY, who
gasps and backs up. He keeps turning toward the PACHUCO,
FARM WORKER, and REVOLUCIONARIO, snapping his fingers
and turning each of them on, one by one.)*

PACHUCO: *(Snap. To SECRETARY)* I'm going to get you, baby!
¡Viva La Raza!

FARM WORKER: *(Snap. To SECRETARY)* ¡Viva la huelga! ¡Viva la   350
Huelga! ¡VIVA LA HUELGA!

REVOLUCIONARIO: *(Snap. To SECRETARY)* ¡Viva la revolución!
¡VIVA LA REVOLUCIÓN!

REVOLUCIONARIO: *(Snap. To SECRETARY)* ¡Viva la revolución!   355
¡VIVA LA REVOLUCIÓN!

*(The three models join together and advance toward the SECRE-
TARY who backs up and runs out of the shop screaming. SANCHO
is at the other end of the shop holding his money in his hand. All
freeze. After a few seconds of silence, the PACHUCO moves and
stretches, shaking his arms and loosening up. The FARM WORKER
and REVOLUCIONARIO do the same. SANCHO stays where he is,
frozen to his spot.)*

JOHNNY: Man, that was a long one, ése. *(Others agree with him.)*

FARM WORKER: How did we do?

JOHNNY: Perty good, look all that lana, man! *(He goes over to*
SANCHO *and removes the money from his hand.* SANCHO *stays*   360
where he is.)

REVOLUCIONARIO: En la madre, look at all the money.

JOHNNY: We keep this up, we're going to be rich.

FARM WORKER: They think we're machines.

REVOLUCIONARIO: Burros.   365

JOHNNY: Puppets.

MEXICAN-AMERICAN: The only thing I don't like is—how come
I always got to play the goddamn Mexican-American?

JOHNNY: That's what you get for finishing high school.

FARM WORKER: How about our wages, ése?   370

JOHNNY: Here it comes right now. $3,000 for you, $3,000 for
you, $3,000 for you, and $3,000 for me. The rest we put back
into the business.

MEXICAN-AMERICAN: Too much, man. Heh, where you vatos
going tonight?   375

FARM WORKER: I'm going over to Concha's. There's a party.

JOHNNY: Wait a minute, vatos. What about our salesman? I
think he needs an oil job.

REVOLUCIONARIO: Leave him to me.

*(The PACHUCO, FARM WORKER, and MEXICAN-AMERICAN exit,
talking loudly about their plans for the night. The REVOLU-
CIONARIO goes over to SANCHO, removes his derby hat and cigar,
lifts him up and throws him over his shoulder. SANCHO hangs
loose, lifeless.)*

REVOLUCIONARIO: *(To audience)* He's the best model we got!   380
¡Ajua! *(Exit.)*

NTOZAKE SHANGE

Born Paulette Williams in Trenton, New Jersey, in 1948, Ntozake Shange was raised in New Jersey and St. Louis. She attended Barnard College in Manhattan in 1966, suffering a series of profound bouts of depression and attempting suicide on several occasions. She graduated from Barnard with a B.A. in American studies in 1970 and took her M.A. in American studies at the University of Southern California in 1971, when she took an African name, Ntozake Shange. Shange is a poet, and in the early 1970s, she read her poetry throughout the United States. In the summer of 1974, she began a series of seven poems that explored the realities of life among seven different black women. The women were nameless, and in the course of reading the series of poems to audiences, Shange realized its extraordinary theatrical power. Rather than seeing the monologues as material for a stage play, Shange's recognition of their dramatic power was linked to her interest in music and dance. As she suggested at the time, "with dance I discovered my body more intimately than I had imagined possible. With the acceptance of the ethnicity of my thighs and backside, came a clearer understanding of my voice as a woman and as a poet." Throughout the next year, she experimented with a variety of ways of staging the piece, coining the term "choreopoem" to describe its blending of music, dance, and poetry. As she writes in her introduction to the play, by the time *for colored girls who have considered suicide / when the rainbow is enuf* (1975) opened in California, it "waz a theater piece." The play was then brought to Broadway, where it was hugely popular. Shange's more recent plays continue to use music, lighting, dance, and poetry to examine the experience of black women: *a photograph: lovers in motion* (1977), *boogie woogie landscapes* (1978), and *spell #7 / geechee jibara quik magic trance manual for technologically stressed third world people* (1979). Shange has won many prestigious awards and has also written several collections of poetry — including *Nappy Edges* (1978) — and a novella, *Sassafrass* (1977).

spell #7

Unlike her earlier choreopoem *for colored girls who have considered suicide / when the rainbow is enuf*, *spell #7* is subtitled a "theater piece." Although it uses Shange's powerful fusion of poetry and movement, *spell #7* engages in a critique of the politics of race and the politics of racial representation through the essential means of theater: roleplaying.

From its opening moments, when the audience sees a huge blackface mask hanging above the stage, and *"the rest of the company enters in tattered fieldhand garb, blackface, and the countenance of stepan fetchit when he waz frightened,"* it is apparent that *spell #7* will interrogate how African-American experience has been represented in white society, from the nineteenth-century minstrel shows, through the blackface musicals, comedies, and vaudeville of the 1920s, to contemporary stereotypes. Indeed, the play uses the "magic" of theater not only to investigage the social function of black theater traditions, but they way in which analogous stereotypes conceal, displace, and misrepresent African-American experience in social life. lou the magician enters and tells how his father, a magician,

> . . . retired from magic & took
> up another trade cuz this friend a mine
> from the 3rd grade / asked to be made white
> on the spot.

In *spell #7*, lou does not use his magic to turn black people white, but to reveal the black identity behind the white-imposed mask of blackface. Through lou's theatrical magic, the actors are able to remove their blackface masks and engage in a series of confessions, improvisations, and roleplayings that characterize black experience today.

The identities that emerge from behind the blackface are striking and powerful. The scene changes to eli's bar, a hangout for African-American actors, most of whom are unemployed because they are unable to get significant parts to play — "say as lady macbeth or mother courage," as lou suggests — and are forced to work odd jobs, play the tambourine on the street for subway fare, or to

play stereotypically "black" roles. As bettina angrily complains, "no / my show is not closin / but if that director asks me to play it any blacker / i'm gonna have to do it in a mammy dress." Although blackface and the character stereotypes that accompanied it in an earlier era are no longer common in the theater, cultural stereotypes pervade our entertainment forms, and society as well. For this reason, lou's magic and the actors' anger conspire to produce a series of striking improvisations, as the actors remove their blackface masks and perform more authentic versions of contemporary African-American life: maxine plays "fay," out from Brooklyn to have a good time in Manhattan; lily reveals how she dreams of success while brushing her hair; natalie enacts "sue-jean," who gives birth to and then kills a baby boy named "myself." Finally, natalie and maxine play a "white girl" as a way of turning the tables on the blackface convention. Much as blackface represents black identity from the vantage of a privileged white society, natalie and maxine represent white identity from an oppressed black perspective.

As Shange suggests in her foreword to the play, much of the energy of *spell #7* derives from Shange's effort to maintain and celebrate the legacy of African-American arts, the fusion of poetry, music, and dance that should be an inspiring "cultural reality" for the African-American community.

— foreword / unrecovered losses / black theater traditions —

as a poet in american theater/ i find most activity that takes place on our stages overwhelmingly shallow/ stilted & imitative. that is probably one of the reasons i insist on calling myself a poet or writer/ rather than a playwright/ i am interested solely in the poetry of a moment/ the emotional & aesthetic impact of a character or a line. for too long now afro-americans in theater have been duped by the same artificial aesthetics that plague our white counterparts/ "the perfect play," as we know it to be/ a truly european framework for european psychology/ cannot function efficiently for those of us from this hemisphere.

furthermore/ with the advent of at least 6 musicals about the lives of black musicians & singers/ (EUBIE, BUBBLING BROWN SUGAR, AIN'T MISBEHAVIN', MAHALIA, etc.)/ the lives of millions of black people who dont sing & dance for a living/ are left unattended to in our theatrical literature. not that the lives of Eubie Blake or Fats Waller are well served in productions lacking any significant book/ but if the lives of our geniuses arent artfully rendered/ & the lives of our regular & precious are ignored/ we have a double loss to reckon with.

if we are drawn for a number of reasons/ to the lives & times of black people who conquered their environments/ or at least their pain with their art, & if these people are mostly musicians & singers & dancers/ then what is a writer to do to draw the most human & revealing moments from lives spent in nonverbal activity. first of all we should reconsider our choices/ we are centering ourselves around these artists for what reasons/ because their lives were richer than ours/ because they did something white people are still having a hard time duplicating/ because they proved something to the world like Jesse Owens did/ like Billie Holiday did. i think/ all the above contributes to the proliferation of musicals abt our musicians/ without forcing us to confront the real implications of the dynamic itself. we are compelled to examine these giants in order to give ourselves what we think they gave the worlds they lived in/ which is an independently created afro-american aesthetic. but we are going abt this process backwards/ by isolating the art forms & assuming a very narrow perspective vis-á-vis our own history.

if Fats Waller & Eubie Blake & Charlie Parker & Savilla Fort & Katherine Dunham moved the world outta their way/ how did they do it/ certainly not by mimicking the weakest area in american art/ the american theater. we must move our theater into the drama of our lives/ which is what the artists we keep resurrecting (or allowing others to resurrect) did in the first place/ the music & dance of our renowned predecessors appeals to us because it directly related to lives of those then living & the lives of the art forms.

in other words/ we are selling ourselves & our legacy quite cheaply/ since we are trying to make our primary statements with somebody else's life/ and somebody else's idea of what theater is. i wd suggest that: we demolish the notion of straight theater for a decade or so, refuse to allow playwrights to work without dancers & musicians. "coon shows" were somebody else's idea. we have integrated the notion that a drama must be words/ with no music & no dance/ cuz that wd take away the seriousness of the event/ cuz we all remember too well/ the chuckles & scoffs at the notion that all niggers cd sing & dance/ & most of us can sing & dance/ & the reason that so many plays written to silence & stasis fail/ is cuz most black people have some music & movement in our lives. we do sing & dance. this is a cultural reality. this is why I find the most inspiring theater among us to be in the realms of music & dance.

i think of my collaboration with David Murray on A PHOTOGRAPH/ & on WHERE THE MISSISSIPPI MEETS THE AMAZON & on SPELL #7/ in which music functions as another character. Teddy & his Sizzling Romancers (David Murray, sax.; Anthony Davis, piano; Fred Hopkins, bass; Paul Maddox, drums; Michael Gregory Jackson, guitar, harmonica & vocals) were as important as The Satin Sisters/ though the thirties motif served as a vehicle to introduce the dilemmas of our times. in A PHOTOGRAPH the cello (Abdul Wadud) & synthesizer (Michael Gregory Jackson) solos/ allowed Sean to break into parts of himself that wd have been unavailable had he been unable to "hear." one of the bounties of black culture is our ability to "hear"/ if we were to throw this away in search of less (just language) we wd be damning ourselves. in slave narratives there are numerous references to instruments/ specifically violins, fifes & flutes/ "talking" to the folks. when working with Oliver Lake (sax.) or Baikida Carroll (tr.) in FROM OKRA TO GREENS/ or Jay Hoggard (vibes) in FIVE NOSE RINGS & SOWETO SUITE/ i am terribly aware of a conversation. in the company of Dianne McIntyre/ or Dyane Harvey's work with the Eleo Pomare Dance Company/ one is continually aroused by the immediacy of their movements/ "do this movement like yr life depends on it"/ as McIntyre says.

the fact that we are an interdisciplinary culture/ that we understand more than verbal communication/ lays a weight on afro-american writers that few others are lucky enough to have been born into. we can use with some skill virtually all our physical senses/ as writers committed to bringing the world as we remember it/ imagine it/ & know it to be to the stage/ we must use everything we've got. i suggest that everyone shd cue from Julius Hemphill's wonderful persona, Roi Boye/ who ruminates & dances/ sings & plays a saxophone/ shd cue from Cecil Taylor & Dianne McIntyre's collaboration on SHADOWS/ shd cue from Joseph Jarman & Don Moye (of The Art Ensemble of Chicago) who are able to move/ to speak/ to sing & dance & play a myriad of instruments in EGWU-ANWU. look at Malinke who is an actor/ look at Amina Myers/ Paula Moss/ Aku Kadogo/ Michele Shay/ Laurie Carlos/ Ifa Iyaun Baeza & myself in NEGRESS/ a collective piece which allowed singers, dancers, musicians & writers to pass through the barriers & do more than 1 thing. dance to Hemphill or the B.A.G. (Black Artist Group)/ violinist Ramsey Amin lets his instrument make his body dance & my poems shout. i find that our contemporaries who are musicians are exhibiting more courage than we as writers might like to admit.

in the first version of BOOGIE WOOGIE LANDSCAPES i presented myself with the problem of having my person/ body, voice & language/ address the space as if i were a band/ a dance company & a theater group all at once. cuz a poet shd do that/ create an emotional environment/ felt architecture.

to paraphrase Lester Bowie/ on the night of the World Saxophone Quartet's (David Murray, Julius Hemphill, Hamiett Bluiett & Oliver Lake) performance at the Public Theater/ "those guys are the greatest comedy team since the Marx Brothers." in other words/ they are theater. theater which is an all encompassing moment/ a moment of poetry/ the opportunity to make something happen. We shd think of George Clinton/ a.k.a. Dr. Funkenstein/ as he sings/ "here's a chance to dance our way out of our constrictions." as writers we might think more often of the implications of an Ayler solo/ the meaning of a contraction in anybody's body. we are responsible for saying how we feel. we "ourselves" are high art. our world is honesty & primal response.

1/22/79 NYC

although i rarely read reviews of my work/ two comments were repeated to me by "friends" for some reason/ & now that i am writing abt my own work/ i am finally finding some use for the appraisals of strangers. one new york critic had accused me of being too self-conscious of being a writer/ the other from the midwest had asserted that i waz so involved with the destruction of the english language/ that my writing approached verbal gymnastics like unto a reverse minstrel show. in

reality/ there is an element of truth in both ideas/ but the lady who thought i waz self-conscious of being a writer/ apparently waz never a blk child who knew that no black people conducted themselves like amos n andy/ she waz not a blk child who knew that blk children didnt wear tiger skins n chase lions around trees n then eat pancakes/ she waznt a blk child who spoke an english that had evolved naturally/ only to hear a white man's version of blk speech that waz entirely made up & based on no linguistic system besides the language of racism. the man who thought i wrote with intentions of outdoing the white man in the acrobatic distortions of english waz absolutely correct. i can't count the number of times i have viscerally wanted to attack deform n maim the language that i waz taught to hate myself in/ the language that perpetuates the notions that cause pain to every black child as he/she learns to speak of the world & the "self." yes/ being an afro-american writer is something to be self-conscious abt/ & yes/ in order to think n communicate the thoughts n feelings i want to think n communicate/ i haveta fix my tool to my needs/ i have to take it apart to the bone/ so that the malignancies/ fall away/ leaving us space to literally create our own image.

i have not ceased to be amazed when i hear members of an audience whispering to one another in the foyers of theaters/ that they had never imagined they cd feel so much for characters/ even though they were black (or colored/ or niggers, if they don't notice me eavesdropping). on the other hand/ i hear other members of an audience say that there were so many things in the piece that they had felt/ experienced/ but had never found words to express/ even privately/ to themselves. these two phenomena point to the same dilemma/ the straightjacket that the english language slips over the minds of all americans. there are some thoughts that black people just dont have/ according to popular mythology/ so white people never "imagine" we are having them/ & black people "block" vocabularies we perceive to be white folks' ideas.[1] this will never do. for in addition to the obvious stress of racism n poverty/ afro-american culture/ in attempts to carry on/ to move forward/ has minimized its "emotional" vocabulary to the extent that admitting feelings of rage, defeat, frustration is virtually impossible outside a collective voice. so we can add self-inflicted repression to the cultural causes of our cultural disease of high blood pressure.

in everything i have ever written & everything i hope to write/ i have made use of what Frantz Fanon called "combat breath." although Fanon waz referring to francophone colonies, the schema he draws is sadly familiar:

> there is no occupation of territory, on the one hand, and independence of persons on the other. It is the country as a whole, its history, its daily pulsation that are contested, disfigured, in the hope of final destruction. Under this condition, the individual's breathing is an observed, an occupied breathing. It is a combat breathing.[2]

Fanon goes on to say that "combat breathing" is the living response/ the drive to reconcile the irreconcilable/ the black & white of what we live n where. (unfortunately, this language doesnt allow me to broaden "black" & "white" to figurative terms/ which is criminal since the words are so much larger n richer than our culture allows.) i have lived with this for 31 years/ as my people have lived with cut-off lives n limbs. the three pieces in this collection are the throes of pain n sensation experienced by my characters responding to the involuntary constrictions n amputations of their humanity/ in the context of combat breathing.

each of these pieces was excruciating to write/ for i had to confront/ again & again/ those moments that had left me with little more than fury n homicidal desires. in *spell #7* i included a prologue of a minstrel show/ which made me cry the first times i danced in it/ for the same reasons i had included it. the minstrel may be "banned" as racist/ but the minstrel is more powerful in his deformities than our alleged rejection of him/ for every night we wd be grandly applauded. immediately thereafter/ we began to unveil the "minstrels," who turned out to be as fun-loving as fay:

> please/ let me join you/ i come all the way from brooklyn/ to have a good time/ ya dont think i'm high do ya/ cd i please join ya/ i just wanna have a good ol time.

---

[1] Just examine *Drylongso* by John Langston Gwaltney, Random House, 1980.
[2] Frantz Fanon, *A Dying Colonialism*, Grove Press, 1967.

as contorted as sue-jean:

> *& i lay in the corner laughin/ with my drawers/ twisted round my ankles & my hair standin every which way/ i waz laughin/ knowin i wd have this child/ myself/ & no one wd ever claim him/ cept me/ cuz i was a low-down thing/ layin in sawdust & whiskey stains/ i laughed & had a good time masturbatin in the shadows.*

as angry as the actor who confides:

> *i just want to find out why no one has ever been able to sound a gong & all the reporters recite that the gong is ringin/ while we watch all the white people/ immigrants & invaders/ conquistadors & relatives of london debtors from georgia/ kneel & apologize to us/ just for three or four minutes. now/ this is not impossible.*

& after all that/ our true visions & rigors laid bare/ down from the ceiling comes the huge minstrel face/ laughing at all of us for having been so game/ we believed we cd escape his powers/ how naive cd we be/ the magician explains:

> *crackers are born with the right to be alive/i'm making ours up right here in yr face.*

the most frequently overheard comment abt *spell #7* when it first opened at the public theater/ waz that it waz too intense. the cast & i usedta laugh. if this one hour n 45 minutes waz too much/ how in the world did these same people imagine the rest of our lives were/ & wd they ever be able to handle that/ simply being alive & black & feeling in this strange deceitful country. which brings me to *boogie woogie landscapes*/ totally devoted to the emotional topology of a yng woman/ how she got to be the way she is/ how she sees where she is. here/ again/ in the prologue lies the combat breath of layla/ but she's no all-american girl/ or is she?

> *the lil black things/ pulled to her & whimpered lil black whys/ 'why did those white men make red of our house/ why did those white men want to blacken even the white doors of our house/ why make fire of our trees/ & our legs/ why make fire/ why laugh at us/ say go home/ arent we home/ arent we home?'*

she waz raised to know nothing but black & white two-dimensional planes/ which is what racism allots everyone of us unless we fight. she found solace in jesus & the american way/ though jonestown & american bandstand lay no claims to her:

> *shall i go to jonestown or the disco? i cd wear red sequins or a burlap bag. maybe it doesnt matter/ paradise is fulla surprises/ & the floor of the disco changes colors like special species of vipers . . .*

her lover/ her family/ her friends torment her/ calm her with the little they have left over from their own struggles to remain sane. everything in *boogie woogie landscapes* is the voice of layla's unconscious/ her unspeakable realities/ for no self-respecting afro-american girl wd reveal so much of herself of her own will/ there is too much anger to handle assuredly/ too much pain to keep on truckin/ less ya bury it.

both *spell #7* & *boogie woogie landscapes* have elements of magic or leaps of faith/ in typical afro-american fashion/ not only will the lord find a way/ but there is a way outta here. this is the litany from the spirituals to Jimi Hendrix' "there must be some kinda way outta here"/ acceptance of my combat breath hasnt closed the possibilities of hope to me/ the soothing actualities of music n sorcery/ but that's why i'm doubly proud of *a photograph: lovers in motion*/ which has no cures for our "condition" save those we afford ourselves. the characters michael/ sean/ claire/ nevada/ earl/ are afflicted with the kinds of insecurities & delusions only available to those who learned themselves thru the traumas of racism. what is fascinating is the multiplicity of individual responses to this kind of oppression. michael displays her anger to her lovers:

> *i've kept a lover who waznt all-american/ who didn't believe/ wdnt straighten up/ oh i've loved him in my own men/ sometimes hateful sometimes subtle like high fog & sun/ but who i loved is yr not*

*believin. i loved yr bitterness & hankered after that space in you where you are outta control/ where
you cannot touch or you wd kill me/ or somebody else who loved you. i never even saw a picture &
i've loved him all my life he is all my insanity & anyone who loves me wd understand.*

while nevada finds a nurtured protection from the same phenomenon:

*mama/ will he be handsome & strong/ maybe from memphis/ an old family of freedmen/ one of
them reconstruction senators for a great grandfather . . .*

their particular distortions interfere with them receiving one another as full persons:

CLAIRE: no no/ i want nevada to understand that i understand that sean's a niggah/ & that's why
he's never gonna be great or whatever you call it/ cuz he's a niggah & niggahs cant be nothin.
NEVADA: see/ earl/ she's totally claimed by her station/ she cant imagine anyone growing thru the
prison of poverty to become someone like sean
CLAIRE: sean aint nothin but a niggah nevada/ i didnt know you liked niggahs.

such is the havoc created in the souls of people who arent supposed to exist. the malevolence/ the
deceit/ & manipulation exhibited by these five are simply reflections of the larger world they inhabit/
but do not participate in:

SEAN: contours of life unnoticed/
MICHAEL: unrealized & suspect . . . our form is one of a bludgeoned thing/ wrapped in rhinestones & gauze/ blood almost sparklin/ a wildness lurks always . . .

oppression/ makes us love one another badly/ makes our breathing
mangled/ while i am desperately trying to clear the air/
in the absence of extreme elegance/
madness can set right in like
a burnin gauloise on japanese silk.
though highly cultured/
even the silk must ask
how to burn up discreetly.

Ntozake Shange
3/21/80 NYC

spell # 7
geechee jibara quik magic trance manual for technologically stressed third world people

A THEATER PIECE

Ntozake Shange

— CHARACTERS —

LOU, *a practicing magician*
ALEC, *a frustrated, angry actor's actor*
DAHLIA, *young gypsy (singer/dancer)*
ELI, *a bartender who is also a poet*
BETTINA, *DAHLIA's co-worker in a chorus*

LILY, *an unemployed actress working as a barmaid*
NATALIE, *a not too successful performer*
NATALIE, ROSS, *guitarist-singer with*
MAXINE, *an experienced actress*

— ACT ONE —

(there is a huge black-face mask hanging from the ceiling of the theater as the audience enters. in a way the show has already begun, for the members of the audience must integrate this grotesque, larger than life misrepresentation of life into their pre-show chatter. slowly the house lights fade, but the mask looms even larger in the darkness.

once the mask is all that can be seen, LOU, the magician, enters. he is dressed in the traditional costume of Mr. Interlocutor: tuxedo, bow-tie, top hat festooned with all kinds of whatnots that are obviously meant for good luck, he does a few catchy "soft-shoe" steps & begins singing a traditional version of a black play song)

LOU: *(singing)*

    10 lil picaninnies all in bed
    one fell out and the other nine said:
    i sees yr hiney
    all black & shiny
5   i see yr hiney
    all black & shiny/ shiny

(as a greeting)

    yes/ yes/ yes   isnt life wonderful

(confidentially)

    my father is a retired magician
    which accounts for my irregular behavior
10   everything comes outta magic hats
    or bottles wit no bottoms & parakeets
    are as easy to get as a couple a rabbits
    or 3 fifty-cent pieces/ 1958
    my daddy retired from magic & took
15   up another trade cuz this friend a mine
    from the 3rd grade/ asked to be made white
    on the spot

    what cd any self-respectin colored american magician
    do wit such an outlandish request/ cept
20   put all them razzamatazz hocus pocus zippity-doo-dah

thingamajigs away   cuz
colored chirren believin in magic
waz becomin politically dangerous for the race
& wasnt nobody gonna be made white
on the spot just   25
from a clap of my daddy's hands
& the reason i'm so peculiar's
cuz i been studyin up on my daddy's technique
& everything i do is magic these days
& it's very colored/ very now you see it/ now you   30
dont mess wit me

(boastfully)

                         i come from a family of retired
sorcerers/ active houngans & pennyante fortune tellers
with 41 million spirits/ critturs & celestial bodies
on our side   35
                  i'll listen to yr problems
                  help wit yr career/ yr lover/
                    yr wanderin spouse
                  make yr grandma's stay in
                    heaven more   40
                      gratifyin
                  ease yr mother thru menopause
                    & show yr son
                  how to clean his room

(while LOU has been easing the audience into acceptance of his appearance & the mask [his father, the ancestors, our magic], the rest of the company enters in tattered fieldhand garb, blackface, and the countenance of stepan fetchit when he waz frightened. their presence belies the magician's promise that "you'll be colored n love it," just as the minstrel shows were lies, but LOU continues)

    YES YES YES 3 wishes is all you get   45
      scarlet ribbons for yr hair
      a farm in mississippi
      someone to love you madly

all things are possible
50 but aint no colored magician in his right mind
gonna make you   white
i mean
        this is blk magic
you lookin at
55 & i'm fixin you up good/ fixin you up good & colored
& you gonna be colored all yr life
& you gonna love it/ bein colored/ all yr life/ colored &
    love it
love it/ bein colored. SPELL #7!

(LOU *claps his hands, & the company which had been absolutely
still til this moment/ jumps up. with a rhythm set on a wash-
board carried by one of them/ they begin a series of steps that
identify every period of afro-american entertainment: from acro-
bats, comedians, tap-dancers, calindy dancers, cotton club choruses, apollo theatre du-wop groups, til they reach a frenzy in the
midst of "hambone, hambone where ya been"/ & then take a bow
à la bert williams/ the lights bump up abruptly.*

the magician, LOU, *walks thru the black-faced figures in their
kneeling poses, arms outstretched as if they were going to sing
"mammy." he speaks now [as a companion of the mask] to the
same audience who fell so easily into his hands & who were so
aroused by the way the black-faced figures "sang n danced")*

LOU: why dont you go on & integrate a german-american
60   school in st. louis mo./ 1955/ better yet why dont ya go on
    & be a red niggah in a blk school in 1954/ i got it/ try &
    make one friend at camp in the ozarks in 1957/ crawl thru
    one a jesse james' caves wit a class of white kids waitin
    outside to see the whites of yr eyes/ why dontcha invade a
65   clique of working class italians trying to be protestant in a
    jewish community/ & come up a spade/ be a lil too dark/
    lips a lil too full/ hair entirely too nappy/ to be beautiful/ be
    a smart child trying to be dumb/ you go meet somebody
    who wants/ always/ a lil less/ be cool when yr body says hot/
70   & more/ be a mistake in racial integrity/ an error in white
    folks' most absurd fantasies/ be a blk kid in 1954/ who's not
    blk enuf to lovingly ignore/ not beautiful enuf to leave
    alone/ not smart enuf to move outta the way/ not bitter enuf
    to die at an early age/ why dontchu c'mon & live my life for
75   me/ since the dreams aint enuf/ go on & live my life for
    me/ i didnt want certain moments at all/ i'd give em to
    anybody . . . awright. alec.

(*the black-faced* ALEC *gives his minstrel mask to* LOU *when he
hears his name/* ALEC *rises. the rest of the company is intimidated
by this figure daring to talk without the protection of black-face.
they move away from him/ or move in place as if in mourning)*

ALEC: st. louis/ such a colored town/ a whiskey black space of
    history & neighborhood/ forever ours to lawrenceville/
80   where the only road open to me waz cleared by colonial
    slaves/ whose children never moved/ never seems like
    mended the torments of the Depression or the stains of
    demented spittle/ dropped from the lips of crystal women/
    still makin independence flags/
85   st. louis/ on a halloween's eve to the veiled prophet/
    usurpin the mystery of mardi gras/ i made it mine tho the
    queen waz always fair/ that parade of pagan floats &
    tambourines/ commemorates me/ unlike the lonely walks

wit liberal trick or treaters/ back to my front door/ bag
half empty/   90
    my face enuf to scare anyone i passed/ gee/ a colored kid/
whatta gas. here/ a tree/ wanderin the horizon/ dipped
in blues/ untended bones/ usedta hugs drawls rhythm &
decency here a tree/ waitin to be hanged
    sumner high school/ squat & pale on the corner/ like our 95
vision waz to be vague/ our memory of the war/ that made
us free/ to be forgotten/ becomin paler/ linear
movement from sous' carolina to missouri/ freedmen/
landin in jackie wilson's yelp/ daughters of the manumitted
swimmin in tina turner's grinds/ this is chuck berry's town 100
disavowin miscega-nation/ in any situation/ & they let us
be/ electric blues & bo didley/ the rockin pneumonia &
boogie-woogie flu/ the slop & short fried heads/runnin
always to the river chambersburg/ lil italy/ i passed everyday
at the sweet shoppe/ & waz afraid/ the cops raided truants/ 105
regularly/ & after dark i wd not be seen wit any other
colored/ sane & lovin my life

(*shouts n cries that are those of a white mob are heard, very loud . . .
the still black-faced figures try to move away from the menacing
voices & memories*)

VOICES: hey niggah/ over here
ALEC: behind the truck lay five hands claspin chains
VOICES: hey niggah/ over here   110
ALEC: round the trees/ 4 more sucklin steel
VOICES: hey niggah/ over here
ALEC: this is the borderline
VOICES: hey niggah/ over here
ALEC: a territorial dispute   115
VOICES: hey niggah/ over here
ALEC: (*crouched on floor*) cars loaded with families/ fellas from
    the factory/one or two practical nurses/ become our
    trenches/ some dig into cement wit elbows/ under engines/
    do not be seen in yr hometown   120
after sunset/ we suck up our shadows

(*finally moved to tear off their "shadows," all but two of the company leave with their true faces bared to the audience.* DAHLIA
*has, as if by some magical cause, shed not only her mask, but also
her hideous overalls & picaninny-buckwheat wig, to reveal a finely laced unitard/ the body of a modern dancer. she throws her
mask to* ALEC, *who tosses it away.* DAHLIA *begins a lyrical but
pained solo as* ALEC *speaks for them)*

ALEC: we will stand here
    our shoulders embrace an enormous spirit
    my dreams waddle in my lap
    run round to miz bertha's   125
    where lil richard gets his process
    run backward to the rosebushes
    & a drunk man lyin
    down the block to the nuns
    in pink habits/ prayin in a pink chapel   130
    my dreams run to meet aunt marie
    my dreams haunt me like the little geechee river
    our dreams draw blood from old sores
    this is our space
    we are not movin   135

(DAHLIA *finishes her movement/* ALEC *is seen reaching for her/ lights out. in the blackout they exit as* LOU *enters. lights come up on* LOU *who repeats bitterly his challenge to the audience)*

LOU: why dontchu go on & live my life for me
   i didn't want certain moments at all
   i'd give them to anybody

(LOU *waves his hand commanding the minstrel mask to disappear, which it does. he signals to his left & again by magic, the lights come up higher revealing the interior of a lower manhattan bar & its bartender,* ELI, *setting up for the night.* ELI *greets* LOU *as he continues to set up tables, chairs, candles, etc., for the night's activities.* LOU *goes over to the jukebox, & plays "we are family" by sister sledge.* LOU *starts to tell us exactly where we are, but* ELI *takes over as characters are liable to do. throughout* ELI'S *poem, the other members of the company enter the bar in their street clothes, & doing steps reminiscent of their solos during the minstrel sequence. as each enters, the audience is made aware that these ordinary people are the minstrels. the company continues to dance individually as* ELI *speaks)*

   this is . . .

140 ELI: MY kingdom.
   there shall be no trespassers/ no marauders
   no tourists in my land
   your nurture these gardens   or   be shot on sight
   carelessness & other priorities
145   are not permitted within these walls
   i am mantling an array of strength & beauty
   no one shall interfere with this
   the construction of myself
   my city   my theater
150   my bar   come to my poems
   but understand we speak english carefully
   & perfect antillean french
   our toilets are disinfected
   the plants here sing to me each morning
155   come to my kitchen my parlor even my bed
   i sleep on satin   surrounded by hand made
   infants who bring me good luck & warmth
   come even to my door
   the burglar alarm/ armed guards vault from the east side
160   if i am in danger   a siren shouts
   you are welcome
   to my kingdom   my city   my self
   but yr presence must not disturb these inhabitants
   leave nothing out of place/ push no dust under my rugs
165   leave not a crack in my wine glasses
   no finger prints
   clean up after yrself in the bathroom
   there are no maids here   no days off
   for healing   no insurance policies
170   for dislocation of the psyche
   aliens/ foreigners/ are granted resident status
   we give them a little green card
   as they prove themselves non-injurious
   to the joy of my nation
175 i sustain no intrusions/ no double-entendre romance
   no soliciting of sadness   in my life

are those who love me well
the rest are denied their visas . . .
is everyone ready to boogie

(finally, when ELI calls for a boogie, the company does a dance that indicates these people have worked & played together a long time. as dance ends, the company sits & chats at the tables & at the bar. this is now a safe haven for these "minstrels" off from work. here they are free to be themselves, to reveal secrets, fantasies, nightmares, or hope. it is safe because it is segregated & magic reigns

LILI, the waitress, is continually moving abt the bar, taking orders for drinks & generally staying on top of things)

ALEC: gimme a triple bourbon/ & a glass of angel dust   180
   these thursday nite audiences are abt to kill me

(ELI goes behind bar to get drinks)

DAHLIA: why do i drink so much?
BETTINA, LILY, NATALIE: (in unison) who cares?
DAHLIA: but I'm an actress. i have to ask myself these
   questions   185
LILY: that's a good reason to drink
DAHLIA: no/ i mean the character/ alec, you're a director/ give
   me some motivation
ALEC: motivation/ if you didn't drink you wd remember that
   you're not workin   190
LILY: i wish i cd get just one decent part
LOU: say as lady macbeth or mother courage
ELI: how the hell is she gonna play lady macbeth and mac-
   beth's a white dude?
LILY: ross & natalie/ why are you countin pennies like that?   195
NATALIE: we had to wait on our money again
ROSS: and then we didn't get it
BETTINA: maybe they think we still accept beads & ribbons
NATALIE: i had to go around wit my tambourine just to get
   subway fare   200
ELI: dont worry abt it/ have one on me
NATALIE: thank you eli
BETTINA: (falling out of her chair) oh . . .
ALEC: cut her off eli/ dont give her no more
LILY: what's the matter bettina/ is yr show closin?   205
BETTINA: (gets up, resets chair) no/ my show is not closin/ but
   if that director asks me to play it any blacker/ i'm gonna
   have to do it in a mammy dress
LOU: you know/ countin pennies/ lookin for parts/ breakin
   tambourines/ we must be outta our minds for doin this   210
BETTINA: no we're not outta our minds/ we're just sorta outta
   our minds
LILY: no/ we're not outta our minds/ we've been doing this shit
   a long time . . . ross/ captain theophilis conneau/ in a
   slaver's logbook/ says that "youths of both sexes wear rings in   215
   the nose and lower lip and stick porcupine quills thru the
   cartilage of the ear." ross/ when ringlin' bros. comes to
   madison square garden/ dontcha know the white people
   just go
ROSS: in their cb radios   220
DAHLIA: in their mcdonald's hats
ELI: with their save america t-shirts & those chirren who score
   higher on IQ tests for the white chirren who speak english

ALEC: when the hockey games absorb all america's attention
225   in winter/ they go with their fists clenched & their tongues
battering their women who dont know a puck from a 3-yr-
old harness racer
BETTINA: they go & sweat in fierce anger
ROSS: these factories
230   NATALIE: these middle management positions
ROSS: make madison square garden
BETTINA: the temple of the primal scream

(LILY *gets money from cash register & heads toward jukebox*)

LILY: oh how they love blood
NATALIE: & how they dont even dress for the occasion/ all
235   inconspicuous & pink
ELI: now if willie colon come there
BETTINA: if/ we say/ the fania all stars gonna be there
in that nasty fantasy of the city council
ROSS: where the hot dogs are not even hebrew national
240   LILY: and the bread is stale
ROSS: even in such a place where dance is an obscure notion
BETTINA: where one's joy is good cause for a boring chat with
the pinkerton guard
DAHLIA: where the halls lead nowhere
245   ELI: & "back to yr seat/ folks"
LILY: when all one's budget for cruisin
LOU: one's budget for that special dinner with you know who
LILY: the one you wd like to love you
BETTINA: when yr whole reasonable allowance for leisure
250   activity/buys you a seat where what's goin on dont matter
DAHLIA: cuz you so high up/ you might be in seattle
LILY: even in such a tawdry space
ELI: where vorster & his pals wd spit & expect black folks to
lick it up
255   ROSS: *(stands on chair)* in such a place i've seen miracles
ALL: oh yeah/ aw/ ross
ROSS: the miracles

(*"music for the love of it," by butch morris, comes up on the
jukebox/ this is a catchy uptempo rhythm & blues post WW II. as
they speak the company does a dance that highlights their ease
with one another & their familiarity with "all the new dance
steps"*)

LILY: the commodores
DAHLIA: muhammad ali
260   NATALIE: bob marley
ALEC: & these folks who upset alla 7th avenue with their glow/
how the gold in their braids is new in this world of hard
hats & men with the grace of wounded buffalo/ how these
folks in silk & satin/ in bodies reekin of good love comin/
265   these pretty muthafuckahs
DAHLIA: make this barn
LILY: this insult to good taste
BETTINA: a foray into paradise
DAHLIA, LILY, ALEC, NATALIE, & ROSS: *(in unison)* we dress up
270   BETTINA, ELI, & LOU: *(in unison)* we dress up
DAHLIA: cuz we got good manners
ROSS: cd you really ask dr. funkenstein to come all that way &
greet him in the clothes you sweep yr kitchen in?
ALL: NO!

BETTINA: cd you say to muhammad ali/ well/ i just didnt have   275
a chance to change/ you see i have a job/ & then i went
jogging & well, you know its just madison square garden
LOU: my dear/ you know that wont do
NATALIE: we honor our guests/ if it costs us all we got
DAHLIA: when stevie wonder sings/ he don't want us lookin   280
like we ain't got no common sense/ he wants us to be as
lovely as we really are/ so we strut & reggae
ELI: i seen some doing the jump up/ i myself just got happy/
but i'm tellin you one thing for sure
LILY: we fill up where we at   285
BETTINA: no police
NATALIE: no cheap beer
DAHLIA: no nasty smellin bano
ROSS: no hallways fulla derelicts & hustlers
NATALIE: gonna interfere wit alla this beauty   290
ALEC: if it wasnt for us/ in our latino chic/ our rasta-fare our
outer space funk suits & all the rest i have never seen
BETTINA: tho my daddy cd tell you bout them fox furs &
stacked heels/ the diamonds & marie antoinette wigs
ELI: it's not cuz we got money   295
NATALIE: it's not cuz if we had money we wd spend it
on luxury
LILY: it's just when you gotta audience with the pope/ you look
yr best
BETINNA: when you gonna see the queen of england/ you   300
polish yr nails
NATALIE: when you gonna see one of them/ & you know who
i mean
ALEC: they gotta really know
BETTINA: we gotta make em feel   305
ELI: we dont do this for any old body
LOU: we're doin this for you
NATALIE: we dress up
ALEC: is our way of sayin/ you gettin the very best
DAHLIA: we cant do less/ we love too much to be stingy   310
ROSS: they give us too much to be loved ordinary
LILY: we simply have good manners
ROSS: & an addiction to joy
FEMALE CAST MEMBERS: *(in unison)* WHEE . . .
DAHLIA: we dress up   315
MALE CAST MEMBERS: *(in unison)* HEY . . .
BETTINA: we gotta show the world/ we gotta corner on the color
ROSS: happiness just jumped right outta us/ & we are
lookin good

(*everyone in the bar is having so much fun/ that* MAXINE *takes on
an exaggerated character as she enters/ in order to bring them to
attention. the company freezes, half in respect/ half in parody*)

MAXINE: cognac!   320

(*the company relaxes, goes to tables or the bar. in the meantime,*
ROSS *has remained in the spell of the character that* MAXINE *had
introduced when she came in. he goes over to* MAXINE *who is
having a drink/ & begins an improvisation*)

ROSS: she left the front gate open/ not quite knowing she
wanted someone to walk on thru the wrought iron fence/
scrambled in whiskey bottles broken round old bike spokes/
some nice brown man to wind up in her bed/ she really
didnt know/ the sombrero that enveloped her face was a lil   325

too much for an april nite on the bowery/ & the silver
halter dug out from summer cookouts near riis beach/ didnt
sparkle with the intensity of her promise to have one good
time/ before the children came back from carolina.

330   brooklyn cd be such a drag. every street cept flatbush &
nostrand/ reminiscent of europe during the plague/ seems
like nobody but sickness waz out walkin/ drivels & hypes/ a
few youngsters lookin for more than they cd handle/ & then
there waz fay/

(MAXINE rises, begins acting the story out)

335   waitin for a cab. anyone of the cars inchin along the
boulevard cd see fay waznt no whore/ just a good clean
woman out for the nite/ & tho her left titty jumped out
from under her silver halter/ she didn't notice cuz she waz
lookin for a cab. the dank air fondled her long saggin
340   bosom like a possible companion/ she felt good. she stuck
her tin-ringed hand on her waist & watched her own ankles
dance in the nite. she waz gonna have a good time tonight/
she waz awright/ a whole lotta woman/ wit that special
brooklyn bottom strut. knowin she waznt comin in til
345   dawn/ fay covered herself/ sorta/ wit a light kacky jacket that
just kept her titties from rompin in the wind/ & she pulled
it closer to her/ the winds waz comin/ from nowhere jabbin/
& there wasnt no cabs/ the winds waz beatin her behind/
whisperin/ gigglin/ you aint goin noplace/ you an ol bitch/
350   shd be at home wit ur kids. fay beat off the voices/ & an
EBONY-TRUE-TO-YOU cab climbed the curb to get her.
(as cabdriver)
        hope you aint plannin on stayin in brooklyn/ after 8:00
you dead in brooklyn. (as narrator)
355   she let her titty shake like she thot her mouth oughtta
bubble like/ wd she take off her panties/ i'd take
her anywhere.
MAXINE: (as if in cab) i'm into havin a good time/ yr arms/
veins burstin/ like you usedta lift tobacco onto trucks or cut
360   cane/ i want you to be happy/ long as we dont haveta stay
in brooklyn
ROSS: & she made like she waz gypsy rose lee/ or the hotsy
totsy girls in the carnival round from waycross/ when it waz
segregated
365   MAXINE: what's yr name?
ROSS: my name is raphael
MAXINE: oh that's nice
ROSS: & fay moved where i cd see her out the rear view
mirror/ waz tellin me all bout her children & big eddie who
370   waz away/ while we crossed the manhattan bridge/ i kept
smilin. (as cabdriver) where exactly you goin?
MAXINE: i dont really know. i just want to have a good time.
take me where i can see famous people/ & act bizarre like
sinatra at the kennedys/ maybe even go round & beat up
375   folks like jim brown/ throw somebody offa balcony/ you
know/ for a good time
ROSS: the only place I knew/ i took her/ after i kisst the spaces
she'd been layin open to me. fay had alla her $17 cuz i
hadnt charged her nothin/ turned the meter off/ said it waz
380   wonderful to pick up a lady like her on atlantic avenue/ i
saw nobody but those goddamn whores/ & fay

(MAXINE moves in to ROSS & gives him a very long kiss)

now fay waz a gd clean woman/ & she waz burstin with
pride & enthusiasm when she walked into the place where I
swore/ all the actresses & actors hung out

(the company joins in ROSS' story; responding to MAXINE as tho
she waz entering their bar)

oh yes/ there were actresses in braids & lipstick/ wigs &   385
winged tip pumps/ fay assumed the posture of someone
she'd always admired/ etta james/ the waitress asked her to
leave cuz she waz high/ & fay knew better than that
MAXINE: (responding to LILY's indication of throwing her out) i
aint high/ i'm enthusiastic/ and i'm gonna have me a   390
gooooooood/ ol time
ROSS: she waz all dressed up/ she came all the way from
brooklyn/ she must look high cuz i/ the taxi-man/ well i got
her a lil excited/ that waz all/ but she waz gonna cool out/
cuz she waz gonna meet her friends/ at this place/ yes. she   395
knew that/ & she pushed a bunch of rhododendrum/ outta
her way so she cd get over to that table/ & stood over the
man with the biggest niggah eyes & warmest smellin mouth
MAXINE: please/ let me join you/ i come all the way from
brooklyn/ to have a good time/ you dont think i'm high do   400
ya/ cd i please join ya/ i just wanna have a good ol time
ROSS: (as BETTINA turns away) the woman sipped chablis &
looked out the window hopin to see one of the bowery
drunks fall down somewhere/ fay's voice hoverin/ flirtin
wit hope   405
LOU: (turning to face MAXINE) why dont you go downstairs &
put yr titty in yr shirt/ you cant have no good time lookin
like that/ now go on down & then come up & join us

(BETTINA & LOU rise & move to another table)

ROSS: fay tried to shove her flesh anywhere/ she took off her
hat/ bummed a kool/ swallowed somebody's cognac/ & sat   410
down/ waitin/ for a gd time
MAXINE: (rises & hugs ROSS) aw ross/ when am i gonna get a
chance to feel somethin like that/ i got into this business
cuz i wanted to feel things all the time/ & all they want me
to do is put my leg in my face/ smile/ &   415
LILY: you better knock on some wood/ maxine/ at least
yr workin
BETTINA: & at least yr not playin a whore/ if some other
woman comes in here & tells me she's playin a whore/
i think i might kill her   420
ELI: you'd kill her so you cd say/ oh dahlia died & i know all
her lines
BETTINA: aw hush up eli/ dnt you know what i mean?
ELI: no miss/ i dont/ are you in the theater?
BETTINA: mr. bartender/ poet sir/ i am theater   425
DAHLIA: well miss theater/ that's a surprise/ especially since
you fell all over the damn stage in the middle of my solo
LILY: she did
ELI: miss theater herself fell down?
DAHLIA: yeah/ she cant figure out how to get attention without   430
makin somebody else look bad
MAXINE: now dahlia/ it waznt that bad/ i hardly noticed her
DAHLIA: it waz my solo/ you werent sposed to notice her at all!
BETTINA: you know dahlia/ i didn't do it on purpose/ i cda
hurt myself   435
DAHLIA: that wd be unfortunate

BETTINA: well miss thing with those big ass hips you got/ i
    dont know why you think you can do the ballet anyway

(the company breaks; they're expecting a fight)

DAHLIA: *(crossing to* BETTINA*)* i got this

(demonstrates her leg extension)

440   & alla this

*(*DAHLIA *turns her back to* BETTINA/ & slaps her own backside.*
BETTINA grabs DAHLIA, *turns her around & they begin a series of*
finger snaps that are a paraphrase of ailey choreography for very
dangerous fights. ELI *comes to break up the impending*
altercation)

ELI: ladies ladies ladies

*(*ELI *separates the two)*

ELI: people keep tellin me to put my feet on the ground i get
    mad & scream/ there is no ground
    only shit pieces from dogs horses & men who dont live
445   anywhere/ they tell me think straight & make myself
    somethin/ i shout & sigh/ i am a poet/ i write poems
    i make words cartwheel & somersault down pages
    outta my mouth come visions distilled like bootleg
    whiskey/ i am like a radio but i am a channel of my own
450   i keep sayin i write poems/ & people keep askin me
    what do i do/ what in the hell is going on?
    people keep tellin me these are hard times/ what are
    you gonna be doin ten years from now/
    what in the hell do you think/ i am gonna be writin poems
455   i will have poems inchin up the walls of the lincoln tunnel/
    i am gonna feed my children poems on rye bread with
      horseradish/
    i am gonna send my mailman off with a poem for his
      wagon/
    give my doctor a poem for his heart/ i am a poet/
    i am not a part-time poet/ i am not a amateur poet/
460   i dont even know what that person cd be/ whoever that is
    authorizing poetry as an avocation/ is a fraud/
    put yr own feet on the ground
BETTINA: i'm sorry eli/ i just dont want to be a gypsy all my life

(the bar returns to normal humming & sipping. the lights change
to focus on LILY/ *who begins to say what's really been on her*
mind. the rest of the company is not aware of LILY's *private*
thoughts. only BETTINA *responds to* LILY, *but as a partner in*
fantasy, not as a voyeur)

LILY: *(illustrating her words with movement)* i'm gonna simply
465   brush my hair. rapunzel pull yr tresses back into the tower.
    & lady godiva give up horseback riding. i'm gonna alter my
    social & professional life dramatically. i will brush 100
    strokes in the morning/ 100 strokes midday & 100 strokes
    before retiring. i will have a very busy schedule. between
470   the local trains & the express/ i'm gonna brush. i brush
    between telephone calls. at the disco i'm gonna brush on
    the slow songs/ i dont slow dance with strangers. i'ma brush
    my hair before making love & after. i'll brush my hair in
    taxis. while windowshopping. when i have visitors over the
475   kitchen table/ i'ma brush. i brush my hair while thinking
    abt anything. mostly i think abt how it will be when i get
    my full heada hair. like lifting my head in the morning will

become a chore. i'll try to turn my cheek & my hair will
weigh me down

*(*LILY *falls to the floor.* BETTINA *helps lift her to her knees, then*
begins to dance & mime as LILY *speaks)*

i dream of chaka khan/ chocolate from graham central   480
station with all seven wigs/ & medusa. i brush & brush. i
use olive oil hair food/ & posner's vitamin E. but mostly i
brush & brush. i may lose contact with most of my friends.
i cd lose my job/ but i'm on unemployment & brush while
waiting on line for my check. i'm sure i get good   485
recommendations from my social worker: such a fastidious
woman/ that lily/ always brushing her hair. nothing in my
dreams suggests that hair brushing/ per se/ has anything to
do with my particular heada hair. a therapist might say that
the head fulla hair has to do with something else/ like: a   490
symbol of lily's unconscious desires. but i have no therapist

(she takes imaginary pen from BETTINA, *who was pretending to*
be a therapist/ & sits down at table across from her)

& my dreams mean things to me/ like if you dreamed abt
tobias/ then something has happened to tobias/ or he is
gonna show up. if you dream abt yr grandma who's dead/
then you must be doing something she doesnt like/ or she   495
wdnta gone to all the trouble to leave heaven like that. if
you dream something red/ you shd stop. if you dream
something green/ you shd keep doing it. if a blue person
appears in yr dreams/ then that person is yr true friend.
    & that's how i see my dreams. & this head fulla hair i   500
have in my dreams is lavender & nappy as a 3-yr-old's in a
apple tree. i can fry an egg & see the white of the egg
spreadin in the grease like my hair is gonna spread in the air/
but i'm not egg-yolk yellow/ i am brown & the egg white
isnt white at all/ it is my actual hair/ & it wd go on & on   505
forever/ irregular like a rasta-man's hair. irregular/
gargantuan & lavender. nestled on blue satin pillows/
pillows like the sky. & so i fry my eggs. i buy daisies dyed
lavender & laced lavender tablemats & lavender nail polish.
though i never admit it/ i really do believe in magic/ & can   510
do strange things when something comes over me. soon
everything around me will be lavender/ fluffy &
consuming. i will know not a moment of bitterness/ through
all the wrist aching & tennis elbow from brushing/ i'll
smile. no regrets/ "je ne regrette rien" i'll sing like edith   515
piaf. when my friends want me to go see tina turner or
pacheco/ i'll croon "sorry/ i have to brush my hair."
    i'll find ambrosia. my hair'll grow pomegranates & soil/
rich as round the aswan/ i wake in my bed to bananas/
avocados/ collard greens/ the tramps' latest disco hit/ fresh   520
croissant/ pouilly fuissé/ ishmael reed's essays/ charlotte
carter's stories/ all stream from my hair.
    & with the bricks that plop from where a 9-year-old's top
braid wd be/ i will brush myself a house with running water
& a bidet. i'll have a closet full of clean bed linen & the lil   525
girl from the castro convertible commercial will come &
open the bed repeatedly & stay on as a helper to brush my
hair. lily is the only person i know whose every word leaves
a purple haze on the tip of yr tongue. when this happens i
says clouds are forming/ & i has to close the windows.   530
violet rain is hard to remove from blue satin pillows

(LOU, *the magician, gets up. he points to* LILY *sitting very still. he reminds us that it is only thru him that we are able to know these people without the "masks"/ the lies/ & he cautions that all their thoughts are not benign. they are not safe from what they remember or imagine*)

LOU: you have t come with me/ to this place where magic is/
　　to hear my song/ some times i forget & leave my tune
　　in the corner of the closet under all the dirty clothes/
535　in this place/ magic asks me where i've been/ how i've
　　been singin/ lately i leave my self in all the wrong hands/
　　in this place where magic is involved in
　　undoin our masks/ i am able to smile & answer that.
　　in this place where magic always asks for me
540　i discovered a lot of other people who talk without mouths
　　who listen to what you say/ by watchin yr jewelry dance
　　& in this place where magic stays
　　you can let yrself in or out
　　but when you leave yrself at home/ burglars & daylight
　　　thieves
545　pounce on you & sell yr skin/ at cut-rates on tenth avenue

(ROSS *has been playing the acoustic guitar softly as* LOU *spoke.* ALEC *picks up on the train of* LOU's *thoughts & tells a story that in turn captures* NATALIE's *attention. slowly,* NATALIE *becomes the woman* ALEC *describes*)

ALEC: she had always wanted a baby/ never a family/ never a
　　　man/
　　she had always wanted a baby/ who wd suckle & sleep
　　a baby boy who wd wet/ & cry/ & smile
　　suckle & sleep
550　when she sat in bars/ on the stool/ near the door/ & cross
　　from the juke box/ with her legs straddled & revealin red
　　lace pants/ & lil hair smashed under the stockings/ she wd
　　think how she wanted this baby & how she wd call the
　　baby/ "myself" & as she thot/ bout this brown lil thing/ she
555　ordered another bourbon/ double & tilted her head as if to
　　cuddle some infant/ not present/ the men in the bar never
　　imagined her as someone's mother/ she rarely tended her
　　own self carefully/

(NATALIE *rises slowly, sits astride on the floor*)

　　just enough to exude a languid sexuality that teased the
560　men off work/ & the bartender/ ray who waz her only
　　friend/ women didn't take to her/ so she spent her
　　afternoons with ray/ in the bar round the corner from her lil
　　house/ that shook winsomely in a hard wind/ surrounded by
　　three weepin willows
565　NATALIE: my name is sue-jean & i grew here/ a ordinary
　　colored girl with no claims to any thing/ or anyone/ i drink
　　now/ bourbon/ in harder times/ beer/ but i always wanted to
　　have a baby/ a lil boy/ named myself
　　ALEC: one time/ she made it with ray
570　NATALIE: & there waz nothin special there/ only a hot rough
　　bangin/ a brusque barrelin throwin of torso/ legs & sweat/
　　ray wanted to kiss me/ but i screamed/ cuz i didnt like
　　kissin/ only fuckin/ & we rolled round/ i waz a peculiar sorta
　　woman/ wantin no kisses/ no caresses/ just power/ heat &
575　no eaziness of thrust/ ray pulled himself outa me/ with no
　　particular exclamation/ he smacked me on my behind/ i
　　waz grinnin/ & he took that as a indication of his skill/ he

believed he waz a good lover/ & a woman like me/ didnt
never want nothin but a hard dick/ & everyone believed
that/ tho no one in town really knew　　　　　　　　　　580
ALEC: so ray/ went on behind the bar cuz he had got his
NATALIE: & i lay in the corner laughin/ with my drawers/
　　twisted round my ankles & my hair standin every which way/
　　i waz laughin/ knowin i wd have this child/ myself/ & no
　　one wd ever claim him/ cept me cuz i waz a low-down　　585
　　thing/ layin in sawdust & whiskey stains/ i laughed & had a
　　good time masturbatin in the shadows.
ALEC: sue-jean ate starch for good luck
NATALIE: like mama kareena/ tol me
ALEC: & she planted five okras/ five collards/ & five tomatoes　590
NATALIE: for good luck too/ i waz gonna have this baby/ i even
　　went over to the hospital to learn prenatal care/ & i kept
　　myself clean
ALEC: sue-jean's lanky body got ta spreadin & her stomach
　　waz taut & round high in her chest/ a high pregnancy is　　595
　　sure to be a boy/ & she smiled
NATALIE: I stopped goin to the bar
ALEC: started cannin food
NATALIE: knittin lil booties
ALEC: even goin to church wit the late night radio evangelist　600
NATALIE: I gotta prayer cloth for the boy/ myself waz gonna be
　　safe from all that his mama/ waz prey to
ALEC: sure/ sue-jean waz a scandal/ but that waz to be
　　expected/ cuz she waz always a po criterish chile
NATALIE: & wont no man bout step my way/ ever/ just cuz i　　605
　　hadda bad omen on me/ from the very womb/ i waz
　　bewitched is what the ol women usedta say
ALEC: sue-jean waz born on a full moon/ the year of the flood/
　　the night the river raised her skirts & sat over alla the towns
　　& settlements for 30 miles in each direction/ the nite the　　610
　　river waz in labor/ gruntin & groanin/ splittin trees &
　　families/ spillin cupboards over the ground/ waz the nite
　　sue-jean waz born
NATALIE: & my mother died/ drownin/ holdin me up over the
　　mud crawlin in her mouth　　　　　　　　　　　　　　615
ALEC: somebody took her & she lived to be the town's no one/
　　now with the boy achin & dancin in her belly/ sue jean waz
　　a gay & gracious woman/ she made pies/ she baked cakes &
　　left them on the stoop of the church she had never entered
　　just cuz she wanted/ & she grew plants & swept her floors/　620
　　she waz someone she had never known/ she waz herself
　　with child/ & she waz a wonderful bulbous thing
NATALIE: the nite/ myself waz born/ ol mama kareena from
　　the hills came down to see bout me/ i hollered & breathed/
　　i did exactly like mama kareena said/ & i pushed & pushed　625
　　& there was a earthquake up in my womb/ i wanted to sit
　　up & pull the tons of logs trapped in my crotch out/ so i cd
　　sleep/ but it wdnt go way/ i pushed & thot I saw 19 horses
　　runnin in my pussy/ i waz sure there waz a locomotive
　　stalled up in there burnin coal & steamin & pushin gainst　630
　　a mountain
ALEC: finally the child's head waz within reach & mama
　　kareena/ brought the boy into this world
NATALIE: & he waz awright/ with alla his toes & his fingers/
　　his lil dick & eyes/ elbows that bent/ & legs/ straight/ i　　635
　　wanted a big glassa bourbon/ & mama kareena brought it/
　　right away/ we sat drinkin the bourbon/ & lookin at the

child whose name waz myself/ like i had wanted/ & the two
of us ate placenta stew . . . i waznt really sure . . .

640   ALEC: sue-jean you werent really sure you wanted myself to
wake up/ you always wanted him to sleep/ or at most to
nurse/ the nites yr dreams were disturbed by his cryin

NATALIE: i had no one to help me

ALEC: so you were always with him/ & you didnt mind/ you
645   knew this waz yr baby/ myself/ & you cuddled him/ carried
him all over the house with you all day/ no matter/ what

NATALIE: everythin waz goin awright til/ myself wanted
to crawl

ALEC: (moving closer to NATALIE) & discover a world of his
650   own/ then you became despondent/ & yr tits began to dry &
you lost the fullness of yr womb/ where myself/ had lived

NATALIE: i wanted that back

ALEC: you wanted back the milk

NATALIE: & the tight gourd of a stomach i had when myself
655   waz being in me

ALEC: so you slit his wrists

NATALIE: he waz sleepin

ALEC: sucked the blood back into yrself/ & waited/ myself
shriveled up in his crib

660   NATALIE: a dank lil blk think/ i never touched him again

ALEC: you were always holdin yr womb/ feelin him kick &
sing to you bout love/ & you wd hold yr tit in yr hand

NATALIE: like i always did when i fed him

ALEC: & you waited & waited/ for a new myself. tho there
665   were labor pains

NATALIE: & i screamed in my bed

ALEC: yr legs pinnin to the air

NATALIE: spinnin sometimes like a ferris wheel/ i cd get no
child to fall from me

670   ALEC: & she forgot abt the child bein born/ & waz heavy &
full all her life/ with "myself"

NATALIE: who'll be out/ any day now

(ELI moves from behind the bar to help NATALIE/ or to clean tables. he doesnt really know, he stops suddenly)

ELI: aint that a goddamn shame/ aint that a way
to come into the world
675   sometimes i really cant write
sometimes i cant even talk

(the minstrel mask comes down very slowly. blackout, except for
lights on the big minstrel mask which remains visible throughout
intermission)

— ACT TWO —

(all players onstage are frozen, except LOU, who makes a motion
for the big minstrel mask to disappear again. as the mask flies up,
LOU begins)

LOU: in this place where magic stays
you can let yrself in or out

(he makes a magic motion, a samba is heard from the jukebox &
activity is begun in the bar again, DAHLIA, NATALIE & LILY enter, apparently from the ladies room)

NATALIE: i swear we went to that audition in good faith/ & that
man asked us where we learned to speak english so well/ i

swear this foreigner/ asked us/ from the city of new york/   5
where we learned to speak english.

LILY: all i did was say "bom dia/ como vai"/ and the
englishman got red in the face

LOU: (as the englishman) yr from the states/ aren't you?

LILY: "sim"/ i said/ in good portuguese   10

LOU: but you speak portuguese

LILY: "sim" i said/ in good portuguese

LOU: how did you pick that up?

LILY: i hadda answer so simple/ i cdnt say i learned it/ cuz
niggahs cant learn & that wda been too hard on the man/   15
so i said/ in good english: i held my ear to the ground &
listened to the samba from bêlim

DAHLIA: you should have said: i make a lotta phone calls to
casçais, portugao

BETTINA: i gotta bahiano boyfriend   20

NATALIE: how abt: i waz an angolan freedom fighter

MAXINE: no/ lily/ tell him: i'm a great admirer of zeza motto
& leci brandao

LILY: when the japanese red army invaded san juan/ they
poisoned the papaya with portuguese. i eat a lotta papaya. 25
last week/ i developed a strange schizophrenic condition/
with 4 manifest personalities: one spoke english &
understood nothing/ one spoke french & had access to the
world/ one spoke spanish & voted against statehood for
puerto rico/ one spoke portuguese. "eu naõ falo ingles entaõ 30
y voce"/ i don't speak english anymore/ & you?

(all the women in the company have been doing samba steps as
the others spoke/ now they all dance around a table in their own
ritual/ which stirs ALEC & LOU to interrupt this female segrega-
tion. the women scatter to different tables, leaving the two interlopers alone, so, ALEC & LOU begin their conversation)

ALEC: not only waz she without a tan, but she held her purse
close to her hip like a new yorker. someone who rode the
paris métro or listened to mariachis in plaza santa cecilia.
she waz not from here   35

(he sits at table)

LOU: (following suit) but from there

ALEC: some there where coloureds/ mulattoes/ negroes/ blacks
cd make a living big enough to leave there to come here/
where no one went there much any more for all sorts
of reasons   40

LOU: the big reasons being immigration restrictions &
unemployment. nowadays, immigration restrictions of
every kind apply to any non-european persons who want to
go there from here

ALEC: some who want to go there from here risk fetching   45
trouble with the customs authority there

LOU: or later with the police, who can tell who's not from
there cuz the shoes are pointed & laced strange

ALEC: the pants be for august & yet it's january

LOU: the accent is patterned for pétionville, but working in   50
crown heights

ALEC: what makes a person comfortably ordinary here cd
make him dangerously conspicuous there

LOU: so some go to london or amsterdam or paris/ where they
are so abounding no one tries to tell who is from where   55

ALEC: still the far right wing of every there prints lil pamphlets that say everyone from there shd leave & go back where they came from

LOU: this is manifest legally thru immigration restrictions & personally thru unemployment

ALEC: anyway the yng woman waz from there/ & she waz alone. that waz good. cuz if a person had no big brother in gronigen/ no aunt in rouen

LOU: no sponsor in chicago

ALEC: this brown woman from there might be a good idea. everybody in the world/ european & non-european alike/ everybody knows that rich white girls are hard to find. some of them joined the weather underground/ some the baader-meinhof gang.

LOU: a whole bunch of them gave up men entirely

ALEC: so the exotic lover in the sun routine becomes more difficult to swing/ if she wants to talk abt plastic explosives & the resistance of the black masses to socialism/ instead of giving head as the tide slips in or lending money

LOU: just for the next few days

ALEC: is hard to find a rich white girl who is so dumb/ too

LOU: anyway. the whole world knows/ european & non-european alike/ the whole world knows that nobody loves the black woman like they love farrah fawcett-majors. the whole world dont turn out for a dead black woman like they did for marilyn monroe.

ALEC: actually/ the demise of josephine baker waz an international event

LOU: but she waz a war hero

the worldwide un-beloved black woman is a good idea/ if she is from there & one is a young man with gd looks/ piercing eyes/ & knowledge of several romantic languages

(throughout this conversation, ALEC & LOU will make attempts to seduce, cajole, & woo the women of the bar as their narrative indicates. the women play the roles as described, being so moved by romance)

ALEC: the best dancing spots/ the hill where one can see the entire bay at twilight

LOU: the beach where the seals & pelicans run free/ the hidden "local" restaurants

ALEC: "aw babee/ you so pretty" begins often in the lobby of hotels where the bright handsome yng men wd be loiterers

LOU: were they not needed to tend the needs of the black women from there

ALEC: tourists are usually white people or asians who didnt come all this way to meet a black woman who isnt even foreign

LOU: so hotel managers wink an eye at the yng men in the lobby or by the bar who wd be loitering/ but are gonna help her have a gd time

ALEC: maybe help themselves too

LOU: everybody in the world/ european & non-european alike/ everybody knows the black woman from there is not treated as a princess/ as a jewel/ a cherished lover

ALEC: that's not how sapphire got her reputation/ nor how mrs. jefferson perceives the world

LOU: you know/ babee/ you dont act like them. aw babee/ you so pretty

ALEC: the yng man in the hotel watches the yng blk woman sit & sit & sit/ while the european tourists dance with each other/ & the dapper local fellas mambo frenetically with secretaries from arizona/ in search of the missing rich white girl. our girl sits &

FEMALE CAST MEMBERS: (in unison) sits & sits & sits

ALEC: (to DAHLIA & NATALIE, who move to the music) maybe she is courageous & taps her foot. maybe she is bold & enjoys the music/ smiling/ shaking shoulders. let her sit & let her know she is unwanted

LOU: she is not white & she is not from here

ALEC: let her know she is not pretty enuf to dance the next merengue. then appear/ mysteriously/ in the corner of the bar. stare at her. just stare. when stevie wonder's song/ "isnt she lovely"/ blares thru the red-tinted light/ ask her to dance & hold her as tyrone power wda. hold her & stare

(ROSS & ELI sing the chorus to stevie wonder's "isn't she lovely")

LOU: dance yr ass off. she has been discovered by the non-european fred astaire

ALEC: let her know she is a surprise/ an event. by the look on yr face you've never seen anyone like this black woman from there. you say: "aw/ you not from here?"/ totally astonished. she murmurs that she is from there. as if to apologize for her unfortunate place of birth

LOU: you say

ALEC: aw babee/ you so pretty. & it's all over

LOU: a night in a pension near the sorbonne. pick her up from the mattress. throw her gainst the wall in a show of exotic temper & passion: "maintenant/ tu es ma femme. nous nous sommes mariés." unions of this sort are common wherever the yng black women travel alone. a woman traveling alone is an affront to the non-european man who is known the world over/ to european & non-european alike/ for his way with women

ALEC: his sense of romance/ how he can say:

LOU: aw babee/ you so pretty . . . and even a beautiful woman will believe no one else ever recognized her loveliness

ELI: or else/ he comes to a cafe in willemstad in the height of the sunset, an able-bodied/ sinewy yng man who wants to buy one beer for the yng woman. after the first round/ he discovers he has run out of money/ so she must buy the next round/ when he discovers/ what beautiful legs you have/ how yr mouth is like the breath of tiger lilies. we shall make love in the/ how you call it/ yes in the earth/ in the dirt/ i will have you in my/ how you say/ where things grow/ aw/ yes/ i will have you in the soil. probably under the stars & smelling of wine/ an unforgettable international affair can be consummated

(the company sings "tara's theme" as ELI ends his speech. ELI & BETTINA take a tango walk to the bar, while MAXINE mimics a 1930's photographer, shooting them as they sail off into the sunset)

MAXINE: at 11:30 one evening i waz at the port authority/ new york/ united states/ myself. now i waz there & i spoke english & waz holding approximately $7 american currency/ when a yng man from there came up to me from the front of the line of people waiting for the princeton new

jersey united states local bus. i mean to say/ he gave up his
chance for a good seat to come say to me:

ROSS: i never saw a black woman reading nietzsche

165 MAXINE: i waz demure enough/ i said i have to for a
philosophy class. but as the night went on i noticed this yng
man waz so much like the other yng men from here/ who
use their bodies as bait & their smiles as passport
alternatives. anyway the night did go on. we were snuggled
170 together in the rear of the bus going down the jersey
turnpike. he told me in english/ that he had spoken all his
life in st louis/ where he waz raised:

ROSS: i've wanted all my life to meet someone like you. i want
you to meet my family/ who haven't seen me in a long
175 time/ since i left missouri looking for opportunity . . .

(he is lost for words)

LOU: *(stage whisper)* opportunity to sculpt

ROSS: thank you/ opportunity to sculpt

MAXINE: he had been everyplace/ he said

ROSS: you arent like any black woman i've ever met anywhere

180 MAXINE: here or there

ROSS: i had to come back to new york cuz of immigration
restrictions & high unemployment among black american
sculptors abroad

MAXINE: just as we got to princeton/ he picked my face up
185 from his shoulder & said:

ROSS: aw babee/ you so pretty

MAXINE: aw babee/ you so pretty. i believe that night i must
have looked beautiful for a black woman from there/
though i cd be asked at any moment to tour the universe/ to
190 climb a 6-story walkup with a brilliant & starving painter/ to
share kadushi/ to meet mama/ to getta kiss each time the
swing falls toward the willow branch/ to imagine where he
say he from/ & more. i cd/ i cd have all of it/ but i cd not
be taken/ long as i don't let a stranger be the first to say:

195 LOU: aw babee/ you so pretty

MAXINE: after all/ immigration restrictions & unemployment
cd drive a man to drink or to lie

(she breaks away from ROSS*)*

so if you know yr beautiful & bright & cherishable awready/
when he say/ in whatever language:

200 ALEC: *(to* NATALIE*)* aw babee/ you so pretty

MAXINE: you cd say:

NATALIE: i know. thank you

MAXINE: then he'll smile/ & you'll smile. he'll say:

ELI: *(stroking* BETTINA's *thigh)* what nice legs you have

205 MAXINE: you can say:

BETTINA: *(removing his hand)* yes. they run in the family

MAXINE: oh! whatta universe of beautiful & well traveled
women!

MALE CAST MEMBERS: *(in unison)* aw babee/ i've never met
210 anyone like you

FEMALE CAST MEMBERS: *(in unison, pulling away from men
to stage edges)* that's strange/ there are millions of us!

*(men all cluster after unsuccessful attempts to persuade their
women to talk.* ALEC *gets the idea to serenade the women;* ROSS
*takes the first verse, with men singing back-up. song is "ooh
baby," by smokey robinson)*

ROSS: *(singing)* i did you wrong/ my heart went out to play/
but in the game i lost you/ what a price to pay/ i'm cryin . . .

MALE PLAYERS: *(singing)* oo oo oo/ baby baby. . . . oo oo oo/   215
baby baby

(this brings no response from the women; the men elect ELI *to lead
the second verse)*

ELI: mistakes i know i've made a few/ but i'm only human
you've made mistakes too/ i'm cryin . . .
oo oo oo/ baby baby . . . oo oo oo/ baby baby

*(the women slowly forsake their staunch indignation/ returning
to the arms of their partners. all that is except* LILY, *who walks
abt the room of couples awkwardly)*

MALE CAST MEMBERS & LILY: *(singing)*   220

i'm just about at the end of my rope
but i can't stop trying/ i cant give up hope
cause i/ i believe one day/ i'll hold you near
whisper i love you/ until that day is here
i'm crying . . . oo oo oo/ baby baby   225

*(*LILY *begins as the company continues to sing)*

LILY: unfortunately
the most beautiful man in the world
is unavailable
that's what he told me
i saw him wandering abt/ said well this is one of a kind   230
& i might be able to help him out
so alone & pretty in all this ganja & bodies melting
he danced with me & i cd become that
a certain way to be held that's considered in advance
a way a thoughtful man wd kiss a woman who   235
cd be offended easily/ but waznt cuz
of course the most beautiful man in the world
knows exactly what to do
with someone who knows that's who he is/
these dreads fallin thru my dress   240
so my nipples just stood up
these hands playin the guitar on my back
the lips somewhere between my neck
& my forehead
talking bout ocho rios & how i really must go   245
marcus garvey cda come in the door & we/
we wd still be dancin that dance
the motion that has more to do with kinetic energy
than shootin stars/ more to do with the impossibility
of all this/ & how it waz awready bein too much   250
our reason failed
we tried to go away & be just together
aside from the silence that weeped
with greed/ we didnt need/ anything/ but one another
for tonite   255
but he is the most beautiful man in the world
says he's unavailable/
& this man whose eyes made me
half-naked & still & brazen/ was singin with me
since we cd not talk/ we sang   260

(male players end their chorus with a flourish)

LILY: we sang with bob marley
this man/ surely the most beautiful man in the world/ & i
sang/ "i wanna love you & treat you right/

(the couples begin different kinds of reggae dances)

i wanna love you every day & every nite"
265 THE COMPANY: *(dancing & singing)*

we'll be together with the roof right over our heads
we'll share the shelter of my single bed
we'll share the same room/ jah provide the bread

DAHLIA: *(stops dancing during conversaton)* i tell you it's not
270 just the part that makes me love you so much
LOU: what is it/ wait/ i know/ you like my legs
DAHLIA: yes/ uh huh/ yr legs & yr arms/ & . . .
LOU: but that's just my body/ you started off saying you loved
me & now i see it's just my body
275 DAHLIA: oh/ i didn't mean that/ it's just i dont know you/
except as the character i'm sposed to love/ & well i know
rehearsal is over/ but i'm still in love with you

(they go to the bar to get drinks, then sit at a table)

ROSS: but baby/ you have to go on the road. we need the
money
NATALIE: i'm not going on the road so you can fuck all these
aspiring actresses
280 ROSS: aw/ just some of them/ baby
NATALIE: that's why i'm not going
ROSS: if you don't go on the road i'll still be fuckin em/ but
you & me/ we'll be in trouble/ you understand?
NATALIE: *(stops dancing)* no i don't understand
285 ROSS: well let me break it down to you
NATALIE: please/ break it down to me
BETTINA: *(stops dancing)* hey/ natalie/ why dont you make
him go on the road/ they always want us to be so
goddamned conscientious
290 ALEC: *(stops dancing)* dont you think you shd mind yr
own bizness?
NATALIE: yeah bettina/ mind yr own bizness

(she pulls ROSS *to a table with her)*

BETTINA: *(to* ALEC*)* no/ i'm tired of having to take any & every
old job to support us/ & you get to have artistic integrity &
refuse parts that are beneath you
295 ALEC: thats right/ i'm not playing the fool or the black buck
pimp circus/ i'm an actor not a stereotype/ i've been
trained. you know i'm a classically trained actor
BETTINA: & just what do you think we are?
MAXINE: well/ i got offered another whore part downtown
300 ELI: you gonna take it?
MAXINE: yeah
LILY: if you dont/ i know someone who will
ALEC: *(to* BETTINA*)* i told you/ we arent gonna get anyplace/
by doin every bit part for a niggah that someone waves in
305 fronta my face
BETTINA: & we aren't gonna live long on nothin/ either/ cuz
i'm quittin my job
ALEC: be in the real world for once & try to understand me
BETTINA: you mean/ i shd understand that you are the great
310 artist & i'm the trouper

ALEC: i'm not sayin that we cant be gigglin & laughin all the
time dancin around/ but i cant stay in these "hate whitey"
shows/ cuz they arent true
BETTINA: a failure of imagination on yr part/ i take it
ALEC: no/ an insult to my person   315
BETTINA: oh i see/ you wanna give the people some more
make-believe
ALEC: i cd always black up again & do minstrel work/ wd that
make you happy?
BETTINA: there is nothing niggardly abt a decent job. work is   320
honorable/ work!
ALEC: well/ i got a problem. i got lots of problems/ but i got
one i want you to fix & if you can fix it/ i'll do anything you
say. last spring this niggah from the midwest asked for
president carter to say he waz sorry for that forgettable   325
phenomenon/ slavery/ which brought us all together. i
never did get it/ none of us ever got no apology from no
white folks abt not bein considered human beings/ that
makes me mad & tired. someone told me "roots" was the
way white folks worked out their guilt/ the success of "roots" 330
is the way white folks assuaged their consciences/ i dont
know this/ this is what i waz told. i dont get any pleasure
from nobody watchin me trying to be a slave i once waz/
who got away/ when we all know they had an emancipation
proclamation/ that the civil war waz not fought over us. we   335
all know that we/ actually dont exist unless we play football
or basketball or baseball or soccer/ pélé/ see they still import
a strong niggah to earn money. art here/ isnt like in the old
country/ where we had some spare time & did what we
liked to do/ i dont know this either/ this is also something   340
i've been told. i just want to find out why no one has even
been able to sound a gong & all the reporters recite that the
gong is ringin/ while we watch all the white people/
immigrants & invaders/ conquistadors & relatives of london
debtors from georgia/ kneel & apologize to us/ just for three   345
or four minutes. now/ this is not impossible/ & someone
shd make a day where a few minutes of the pain of our lives
is acknowledged. i have never been very interested in what
white people did/ cuz i waz able/ like most of us/ to have
very lil to do with them/ but if i become a success that   350
means i have to talk to white folks more than in high
school/ they are everywhere/ you know how they talk abt a
neighborhood changin/ we suddenly become all over the
place/ they are now all over my life/ & i dont like it. i am
not talkin abt poets & painters/ not abt women & lovers of   355
beauty/ i am talkin abt that proverbial white person who is
usually a man who just/ turns yr body around/ looks at yr
teeth & yr ass/ who feels yr calves & back/ & agrees on a
price. we are/ you see/ now able to sell ourselves/ & i am
still a person who is tired/ a person who is not into his   360
demise/ just three minutes for our lives/ just three minutes
of silence & a gong in st. louis/ oakland/ in los angeles . . .

*(the entire company looks at him as if he's crazy/ he tries to leave
the bar/ but* BETTINA *stops him)*

BETTINA: you're still outta yr mind. ain't no apologies keeping
us alive.
LOU: what are you gonna do with white folks kneeling all over   365
the country anyway/ man

(LOU *signals everyone to kneel*)

LILY: they say i'm too light to work/ but when i asked him
what he meant/ he said i didnt actually look black. but/ i
said/ my mama knows i'm black & my daddy/ damn sure
370 knows i'm black/ & he is the only one who has a problem
thinkin i'm black/ i said so let me play a white girl/ i'm a
classically trained actress & i need the work & i can do it/
he said that wdnt be very ethical of him. can you imagine
that shit/ not ethical

375 NATALIE: as a red-blooded white woman/ i cant allow you all
to go on like that

(NATALIE *starts jocularly*)

cuz today i'm gonna be a white girl/ i'll retroactively
wake myself up/ ah low & behold/ a white girl in my bed/
but first i'll haveta call a white girl i know to have some
380 more accurate information/ what's the first thing white girls
think in the morning/ do they get up being glad they aint
niggahs/ do they remember mama/ or worry abt gettin to
work/ do they work?/ do they play isadora & wrap
themselves in sheets & go tip toeing to the kitchen to make
385 maxwell house coffee/ oh i know/ the first thing a white girl
does in the morning is fling her hair/
    so now i'm done with that/ i'm gonna water my plants/
but am i a po white trash white girl with a old jellyjar/
    or am i a sophisticated & protestant suburbanite with
390 2 valiums slugged awready & a porcelain water carrier
leading me up the stairs strewn with heads of dolls & nasty
smellin white husband person's underwear/ if i was really
protected from the niggahs/ i might go to early morning
mass & pick up a tomato pie on the way home/ so i cd eat it
395 during the young & the restless. in williams arizona as a
white girl/ i cd push the navaho women outta my way in
the supermarket & push my nose in the air so i wdnt haveta
smell them. coming from bay ridge on the train i cd smile
at all the black & puerto rican people/ & hope they cant tell
400 i want them to go back where they came from/ or at least
be invisible
    i'm still in my kitchen/ so i guess i'll just have to fling my
hair again & sit down. i shd pinch my cheeks to bring the
color back/ i wonder why the colored lady hasn't arrived
405 to clean my house yet/ so i cd go to the beauty parlor &
sit under a sunlamp to get some more color back/ it's
terrible how god gave those colored women such clear
complexions/ it take em years to develop wrinkles/ but
beauty can be bought & flattered into the world.
410 as a white girl on the street/ i can assume since i am a
white girl on the streets/ that everyone notices how beautiful
i am/ especially lil black & caribbean boys/ they love to look
at me/ i'm exotic/ no one in their families looks like me/
poor things. if i waz one of those white girls who loves one
415 of those grown black fellas/ i cd say with my eyes wide
open/ totally sincere/ oh i didnt know that/ i cd say i didnt
know/ i cant/ i dont know how/ cuz i'ma white girl & i dont
have to do much of anything.
    all of this is the fault of the white man's sexism/ oh
420 how i loathe tight-assed thin-lipped pink white men/ even
the football players lack a certain relaxed virility. that's why
my heroes are either just like my father/ who while he still

cdnt speak english knew enough to tell me how the niggers
shd go back where they came from/ or my heroes are
psychotic faggots who are white/ or else they are/ oh/ you 425
know/ colored men.
    being a white girl by dint of my will/ is much more
complicated than i thought it wd be/ but i wanted to try it
cuz so many men like white girls/ white men/ black men/
latin men/ jewish men/ asians/ everybody. so i thought if i 430
waz a white girl for a day i might understand this better/
after all gertrude stein wanted to know abt the black
women/ alice adams wrote *thinking abt billie*/ joyce carol
oates has three different black characters all with the same
name/ i guess cuz we are underdeveloped individuals or cuz 435
we are all the same/ at any rate i'm gonna call this thinkin
abt white girls/ cuz helmut newton's awready gotta book
called *white women*/ see what i mean/ that's a best seller/
one store i passed/ hadda sign said/

WHITE WOMEN
SOLD OUT

---

it's this kinda pressure that forces us white girls to be so 440
absolutely pathological abt the other women in the world/
who now that they're not all servants or peasants want to be
considered beautiful too. we simply krinkle our hair/ learn
to dance the woogie dances/ slant our eyes with make-up or
surgery/ learn spanish & claim argentinian background/ or 445
as a real trump card/ show up looking like a real white girl.
you know all western civilization depends
on us/
    i still havent left my house. i think i'll fling my hair
once more/ but this time with a pout/ cuz i think i havent 450
been fair to the sisterhood/ women's movement faction of
white girls/ although/ they always ask what do you people
really want. as if the colored woman of the world were a
strange sort of neutered workhorse/ which isnt too far from
reality/ since i'm still waiting for my cleaning lady & the 455
lady who takes care of my children & the lady who caters
my parties & the lady who accepts quarters at the bathroom
in sardi's. those poor creatures shd be sterilized/ no one shd
have to live such a life. cd you hand me a towel/ thank-you
caroline. i've left all of maxime's last winter clothes in a pile 460
for you by the back door. they have to be cleaned but i hope
yr girls can make gd use of them.
    oh/ i'm still not being fair/ all the white women in the
world dont wake up being glad they aint niggahs/ only some
of them/ the ones who dont/ wake up thinking how can 465
i survive another day of this culturally condoned
incompetence. i know i'll play a tenor horn & tell all the
colored artists i meet/ that now i'm just like them/ i'm
colored i'll say cuz i have a struggle too. or i cd punish this
white beleaguered body of mine with the advances of a 470
thousand ebony bodies/ all built like franco harris or peter
tosh/ a thousand of them may take me & do what they
want/ cuz i'm so sorry/ yes i'm so sorry they were born
niggahs. but then if i cant punish myself to death for being

475 white/ i certainly cant in good conscience keep waiting for the cleaning lady/ & everytime i attempt even the smallest venture into the world someone comes to help me/ like if i do anything/ anything at all i'm extending myself as a white girl/ cuz part of being a white girl is being absent/ like those

480 women who are just with a man but whose names the black people never remember/ they just say oh yeah his white girl waz with him/ or a white girl got beat & killed today/ why someone will say/ cuz some niggah told her to give him her money & she said no/ cuz she thought he realized that she

485 waz a white girl/ & he did know but he didnt care/ so he killed her & took the money/ but the cops knew she waz a white girl & cdnt be killed by a niggah especially/ when she had awready said no. the niggah was sposed to hop round the corner backwards/ you dig/ so the cops/ found the

490 culprit within 24 hours/ cuz just like emmett till/ niggahs do not kill white girls.

i'm still in my house/ having flung my hair-do for the last time/ what with having to take 20 valium a day/ to consider the ERA & all the men in the world/ & my

495 ignorance of the world/ it is overwhelming. i'm so glad i'm colored. boy i cd wake up in the morning & think abt anything. i can remember emmett till & not haveta smile at anybody.

MAXINE: (compelled to speak by NATALIE's pain) whenever

500 these things happened to me/ & i waz young/ i wd eat a lot/ or buy new fancy underwear with rhinestones & lace/ or go to the movies/ maybe call a friend/ talk to made-up boyfriends til dawn. this waz when i waz under my parents' roof/ & trees that grew into my room had to be cut back

505 once a year/ this waz when the birds sometimes flew thru the halls of the house as if the ceilings were sky & i/ simply another winged creature. yet no one around me noticed me especially. no one around saw anything but a precocious brown girl with peculiar ideas. like during the polio

510 epidemic/ i wanted to have a celebration/ which nobody cd understand since iron lungs & not going swimming waznt nothing to celebrate. but i explained that i waz celebrating the bounty of the lord/ which more people didnt understand/ til i went on to say that/ it waz obvious that god

515 had protected the colored folks from polio/ nobody understood that. i did/ if god had made colored people susceptible to polio/ then we wd be on the pictures & the television with the white children. i knew only white folks cd get that particular disease/ & i celebrated. that's how

520 come i always commemorated anything that affected me or the colored people. according to my history of the colored race/ not enough attention was paid to small victories or small personal defeats of the colored. i celebrated the colored trolley driver/ the colored basketball team/ the

525 colored blues singer/ & the colored light heavy weight champion of the world. then too/ i had a baptist child's version of high mass for the slaves in new orleans whom i had read abt/ & i tried to grow watermelons & rice for the dead slaves from the east. as a child i took on the burden of

530 easing the ghost-colored-folks' souls & trying hard to keep up with the affairs of my own colored world.

when i became a woman, my world got smaller. my grandma closed up the windows/ so the birds wdnt fly in the house any more. waz bad luck for a girl so yng & in my

535 condition to have the shadows of flying creatures over my head. i didn't celebrate the trolley driver anymore/ cuz he might know i waz in this condition. i didnt celebrate the basketball team anymore/ cuz they were yng & handsome/ & yng & handsome cd mean trouble. but trouble waz when

540 white kids called you names or beat you up cuz you had no older brother/ trouble waz when someone died/ or the tornado hit yr house/ now trouble meant something abt yng & handsome/ & white or colored. if he waz yng & handsome that meant trouble. seemed like every one who

545 didnt have this condition/ so birds cdnt fly over yr head/ waz trouble. as i understood it/ my mama & my grandma were sending me out to be with trouble/ but not to get into trouble. the yng & handsome cd dance with me & call for sunday supper/ the yng & handsome cd write my name on

550 their notebooks/ cd carry my ribbons on the field for gd luck/ the uncles cd hug me & chat for hours abt my growing up/ so i counted all 492 times this condition wd make me victim to this trouble/ before i wd be immune to it/ the way colored folks were immune to polio.

555 i had discovered innumerable manifestations of trouble: jealousy/ fear/ indignation & recurring fits of vulnerability that lead me right back to the contradiction i had never understood/ even as a child/ how half the world's population cd be bad news/ be yng & handsome/ & later/ eligible &

560 interested/ & trouble.

plus/ according to my own version of the history of the colored people/ only white people hurt little colored girls or grown colored women/ my mama told me only white people had social disease & molested children/ and my

565 grandma told me only white people committed unnatural acts. that's how come i knew only white folks got polio/ muscular dystrophy/ sclerosis/ & mental illness/ this waz all verified by the television. but i found out that the colored folks knew abt the same vicious & disease-ridden passions

570 that the white folks knew.

the pain i succumbed to each time a colored person did something that i believed only white people did waz staggering. my entire life seems to be worthless/ if my own folks arent better than white folks/ then surely the sagas of

575 slavery & the jim crow hadnt convinced anyone that we were better than them. i commenced to buying pieces of gold/ 14 carat/ 24 carat/ 18 carat gold/ every time some black person did something that waz beneath him as a black person & more like a white person. i bought gold cuz it

580 came from the earth/ & more than likely it came from south africa/ where the black people are humiliated & oppressed like in slavery. i wear all these things at once/ to remind the black people that it cost a lot for us to be here/ our value/ can be known instinctively/ but since so many

585 black people are having a hard time not being like white folks/ i wear these gold pieces to protest their ignorance/ their disconnect from history. i buy gold with a vengeance/ each time someone appropriates my space or my time without permission/ each time someone is discourteous or

590 actually cruel to me/ if my mind is not respected/ my body toyed with/ i buy gold/ & weep. i weep as i fix the chains round my neck/ my wrists/ my ankles. i weep cuz all my childhood ceremonies for the ghost-slaves have been in vain. colored people can get polio & mental illness. slavery

595   is not unfamiliar to me. no one on this planet knows/ what
i know abt gold/ abt anything hard to get & beautiful/
anything lasting/ wrought from pain. no one understands
that surviving the impossible is sposed to accentuate the
positive aspects of a people.

(ALEC *is the only member of the company able to come immediately to* MAXINE. *when he reaches her,* LOU, *in his full magician's regalia, freezes the whole company*)

600   LOU: yes yes yes   3 wishes is all you get
scarlet ribbons for yr hair
a farm in mississippi
someone to love you madly
all things are possible
605   but aint no colored magician in his right mind
gonna make you white
cuz this is blk magic you lookin at

& i'm fixin you up good/ fixin you up good & colored
& you gonna be colored all yr life
& you gonna love it/ bein colored/ all yr life   610
colored & love it/ love it/ bein colored

(LOU *beckons the others to join him in the chant,* "colored & love
it." *it becomes a serious celebration, like church/ like home/ but
then* LOU *freezes them suddenly.*)

LOU: crackers are born with the right to be
alive/ i'm making ours up right here
in yr face/ & we gonna be
colored & love it   615

(*the huge minstrel mask comes down as company continues to
sing* "colored & love it/ love it being colored." *blackout/ but the
minstrel mask remains visible. the company is singing* "colored &
love it being colored" *as audience exits*)

SAM SHEPARD

Sam Shepard (b. 1943), is probably the best-known American playwright of his generation. Born Samuel Shepard Rogers to a military family stationed in Illinois, Shepard's youth was spent moving from base to base, until his father retired and settled the family in southern California. Shepard was an indifferent student and left college for New York City in 1963. He took a job busing tables at the Village Gate jazz club and began to write plays for off-broadway, including *Cowboys* (1964), *Red Cross* (1966), *La Turista* (1966), *The Unseen Hand* (1970), *Cowboy Mouth* (1971), and *Tooth of Crime* (1972). In these plays, Shepard invented what became his characteristic idiom: a search for the "West" of myth, an image both fascinating and elusive, somehow undiscoverable amid the consumer trash of suburban society. He also developed a sense of split and fragmented characters, relying on his typically jazzy use of language. This is particularly true of *Tooth of Crime*, in which a kind of shoot-out between the old rock 'n' roll star, Hoss, and the Keith Richards-like Crow is conducted in an invented language of rock music, drugs, cars, gangsters, and old movies. Shepard won six Obie awards between 1964 and 1970, but his work took a great step forward in the major plays of the late 1970s and 1980s: *Curse of the Starving Class* (1978), *Buried Child* (Pulitzer Prize, 1979), *True West* (1980), *Fool for Love* (1982), and *A Lie of the Mind* (1985). Shepard also has written the screenplay for the Wim Wenders film, *Paris, Texas*, and has starred in several films himself, notably as Chuck Yeager in *The Right Stuff* (1983).

True West

True West is the leanest, most elemental of Shepard's plays and brings the question of identity — individual and cultural — into sharp focus. The play concerns two brothers: Austin, a yuppie screen-writer, and his derelict brother, Lee, a petty thief who spends much of his time in the desert. In the course of the play, however, Austin and Lee subtly change roles and identities: Lee swings a deal to write the screenplay for a Western movie, while Austin seems to abandon the desire to be a writer, working to prove himself to Lee by stealing toasters from the suburban neighbors. *True West* is a kind of Western, though the brothers don't fight it out for any actual piece of territory, since there is no Dodge city, no True West to fight over. What the brothers finally duel for is a mythic terrain, the terrain of their father, of the desert, of Westerns: the "West" of the imagination.

TRUE WEST

Sam Shepard

— CHARACTERS —

AUSTIN, *early thirties, light blue sports shirt, light tan cardigan sweater, clean blue jeans, white tennis shoes*

LEE, *his older brother, early forties, filthy white t-shirt, tattered brown overcoat covered with dust, dark blue baggy suit pants from the Salvation Army, pink suede belt, pointed black forties dress shoes scuffed up, holes in the soles, no socks, no hat, long pronounced sideburns, "Gene Vincent" hairdo, two days' growth of beard, bad teeth*

SAUL KIMMER, *late forties, Hollywood producer, pink and white flower print sports shirt, white sports coat with matching polyester slacks, black and white loafers*

MOM, *early sixties, mother of the brothers, small woman, conservative white skirt and matching jacket, red shoulder bag, two pieces of matching red luggage*

SCENE: *All nine scenes take place on the same set; a kitchen and adjoining alcove of an older home in a Southern California suburb, about 40 miles east of Los Angeles. The kitchen takes up most of the playing area to stage left. The kitchen consists of a sink, upstage center, surrounded by counter space, a wall telephone, cupboards, and a small window just above it bordered by neat yellow curtains. Stage left of sink is a stove. Stage right, a refrigerator. The alcove adjoins the kitchen to stage right. There is no wall division or door to the alcove. It is open and easily accessible from the kitchen and defined only by the objects in it: a small round glass breakfast table mounted on white iron legs, two matching white iron chairs set across from each other. The two exterior walls of the alcove which prescribe a corner in the upstage right are composed of many small windows, beginning from a solid wall about three feet high and extending to the ceiling. The windows look out to bushes and citrus trees. The alcove is filled with all sorts of house plants in various pots, mostly Boston ferns hanging in planters at different levels. The floor of the alcove is composed of green synthetic grass.*

All entrances and exits are made stage left from the kitchen. There is no door. The actors simply go off and come onto the playing area.

NOTE ON SET AND COSTUME: *The set should be constructed realistically with no attempt to distort its dimensions, shapes, objects, or colors. No objects should be introduced which might draw special attention to themselves other than the props demanded by the script. If a stylistic "concept" is grafted onto the set design it will only serve to confuse the evolution of the characters' situation, which is the most important focus of the play.*

Likewise, the costumes should be exactly representative of who the characters are and not added onto for the sake of making a point to the audience.

NOTE ON SOUND: *The Coyote of Southern California has a distinct yapping, dog-like bark, similar to a Hyena. This yapping grows more intense and maniacal as the pack grows in numbers, which is usually the case when they lure and kill pets from suburban yards. The sense of growing frenzy in the pack should be felt in the background, particularly in Scenes 7 and 8. In any case, these Coyotes never make the long, mournful, solitary howl of the Hollywood stereotype.*

The sound of Crickets can speak for itself.

These sounds should also be treated realistically even though they sometimes grow in volume and numbers.

— ACT ONE —

SCENE I

Night. Sound of crickets in dark. Candlelight appears in alcove, illuminating AUSTIN, seated at glass table hunched over a writing notebook, pen in hand, cigarette burning in ashtray, cup of coffee, typewriter on table, stacks of paper, candle burning on table.

Soft moonlight fills kitchen illuminating LEE, beer in hand, six-pack on counter behind him. He's leaning against the sink, mildly drunk; takes a slug of beer.

LEE: So, Mom took off for Alaska, huh?
AUSTIN: Yeah.
LEE: Sorta' left you in charge.

AUSTIN: Well, she knew I was coming down here so she offered
5   me the place.
LEE: You keepin' the plants watered?
AUSTIN: Yeah.
LEE: Keepin' the sink clean? She don't like even a single tea leaf
in the sink ya' know.
10 AUSTIN: (*trying to concentrate on writing*) Yeah, I know.

(*pause*)

LEE: She gonna' be up there a long time?
AUSTIN: I don't know.
LEE: Kinda' nice for you, huh? Whole place to yourself.
AUSTIN: Yeah, it's great.
15 LEE: Ya' got crickets anyway. Tons a' crickets out there. (*looks
around kitchen*) Ya' got groceries? Coffee?
AUSTIN: (*looking up from writing*) What?
LEE: You got coffee?
AUSTIN: Yeah.
20 LEE: At's good. (*short pause*) Real coffee? From the bean?
AUSTIN: Yeah. You want some?
LEE: Naw. I brought some uh — (*motions to beer*)
AUSTIN: Help yourself to whatever's — (*motions to refrigerator*)
LEE: I will. Don't worry about me. I'm not the one to worry
25   about. I mean I can uh — (*pause*) You always work by
candlelight?
AUSTIN: No — uh — Not always.
LEE: Just sometimes?
AUSTIN: (*puts pen down, rubs his eyes*) Yeah. Sometimes it's
30   soothing.
LEE: Isn't that what the old guys did?
AUSTIN: What old guys?
LEE: The Forefathers. You know.
AUSTIN: Forefathers?
35 LEE: Isn't that what they did? Candlelight burning into the
night? Cabins in the wilderness.
AUSTIN: (*rubs hand through his hair*) I suppose.
LEE: I'm not botherin' you am I? I mean I don't wanna break
into yer uh — concentration or nothin'.
40 AUSTIN: No, it's all right.
LEE: That's good. I mean I realize that yer line a' work demands
a lota' concentration.
AUSTIN: It's okay.
LEE: You probably think that I'm not fully able to comprehend
45   somethin' like that, huh?
AUSTIN: Like what?
LEE: That stuff yer doin'. That art. You know. Whatever you call it.
AUSTIN: It's just a little research.
LEE: You may not know it but I did a little art myself once.
50 AUSTIN: You did?
LEE: Yeah! I did some a' that. I fooled around with it. No future
in it.
AUSTIN: What'd you do?
LEE: Never mind what I did! Just never mind about that. (*pause*)
55   It was ahead of its time.

(*pause*)

AUSTIN: So, you went out to see the old man, huh?
LEE: Yeah, I seen him.
AUSTIN: How's he doing?
LEE: Same. He's doin' just about the same.

AUSTIN: I was down there too, you know.
LEE: What d'ya' want, an award? You want some kinda' medal?
You were down there. He told me all about you.
AUSTIN: What'd he say?
LEE: He told me. Don't worry.

(*pause*)

AUSTIN: Well —
LEE: You don't have to say nothin'.
AUSTIN: I wasn't.
LEE: Yeah, you were gonna' make somethin' up. Somethin'
brilliant.

(*pause*)

AUSTIN: You going to be down here very long, Lee?
LEE: Might be. Depends on a few things.
AUSTIN: You got some friends down here?
LEE: (*laughs*) I know a few people. Yeah.
AUSTIN: Well, you can stay here as long as I'm here.
LEE: I don't need your permission do I?
AUSTIN: No.
LEE: I mean she's my mother too, right?
AUSTIN: Right.
LEE: She might've just as easily asked me to take care of her
place as you.
AUSTIN: That's right.
LEE: I mean I know how to water plants.

(*long pause*)

AUSTIN: So you don't know how long you'll be staying then?
LEE: Depends mostly on houses, ya' know.
AUSTIN: Houses?
LEE: Yeah. Houses. Electric devices. Stuff like that. I gotta'
make a little tour first.

(*short pause*)

AUSTIN: Lee, why don't you just try another neighborhood, all
right?
LEE: (*laughs*) What'sa' matter with this neighborhood? This is a
great neighborhood. Lush. Good class a' people. Not many
dogs.
AUSTIN: Well, our uh — Our mother just happens to live here.
That's all.
LEE: Nobody's gonna' know. All they know is somethin's missing. That's all. She'll never even hear about it. Nobody's
gonna' know.
AUSTIN: You're going to get picked up if you start walking around
here at night.
LEE: Me? I'm gonna' git picked up? What about you? You stick
out like a sore thumb. Look at you. You think yer regular
lookin'?
AUSTIN: I've got too much to deal with here to be worrying
about —
LEE: Yer not gonna' have to worry about me! I've been doin' all
right without you. I haven't been anywhere near you for five
years! Now isn't that true?
AUSTIN: Yeah.
LEE: So you don't have to worry about me. I'm a free agent.
AUSTIN: All right.
LEE: Now all I wanna' do is borrow yer car.

AUSTIN: No!

LEE: Just fer a day. One day.

AUSTIN: No!

115   LEE: I won't take it outside a twenty mile radius. I promise ya'. You can check the speedometer.

AUSTIN: You're not borrowing my car! That's all there is to it.

(pause)

LEE: Then I'll just take the damn thing.

AUSTIN: Lee, look—I don't want any trouble, all right?

120   LEE: That's a dumb line. That is a dumb fuckin' line. You git paid fer dreamin' up a line like that?

AUSTIN: Look, I can give you some money if you need money.

(LEE suddenly lunges at AUSTIN, grabs him violently by the shirt and shakes him with tremendous power)

LEE: Don't you say that to me! Don't you ever say that to me! *(just as suddenly he turns him loose, pushes him away and*
125   *backs off)* You may be able to git away with that with the Old Man. Git him tanked up for a week! Buy him off with yer Hollywood blood money, but not me! I can git my own money my own way. Big money!

AUSTIN: I was just making an offer.

130   LEE: Yeah, well keep it to yourself!

(long pause)

Those are the most monotonous fuckin' crickets I ever heard in my life.

AUSTIN: I kinda' like the sound.

LEE: Yeah. Supposed to be able to tell the temperature by the
135   number a' pulses. You believe that?

AUSTIN: The temperature?

LEE: Yeah. The air. How hot it is.

AUSTIN: How do you do that?

LEE: I don't know. Some woman told me that. She was a Bota-
140   nist. So I believed her.

AUSTIN: Where'd you meet her?

LEE: What?

AUSTIN: The woman Botanist?

LEE: I met her on the desert. I been spendin' a lota' time on the
145   desert.

AUSTIN: What were you doing out there?

LEE: *(pause, stares in space)* I forgit. Had me a Pit Bull there for a while but I lost him.

AUSTIN: Pit Bull?

150   LEE: Fightin' dog. Damn I made some good money off that little dog. Real good money.

(Pause)

AUSTIN: You could come up north with me, you know.

LEE: What's up there?

AUSTIN: My family.

155   LEE: Oh, that's right, you got the wife and kiddies now don't ya'. The house, the car, the whole slam. That's right.

AUSTIN: You could spend a couple days. See how you like it. I've got an extra room.

LEE: Too cold up there.

(pause)

160   AUSTIN: You want to sleep for a while?

LEE: *(pause, stares at AUSTIN)* I don't sleep.

(lights to black)

SCENE II

Morning. AUSTIN *is watering plants with a vaporizer,* LEE *sits at glass table in alcove drinking beer.*

LEE: I never realized the old lady was so security-minded.

AUSTIN: How do you mean?

LEE: Made a little tour this morning. She's got locks on every-thing. Locks and double-locks and chain locks and—What's she got that's so valuable?   5

AUSTIN: Antiques I guess. I don't know.

LEE: Antiques? Brought everything with her from the old place, huh. Just the same crap we always had around. Plates and spoons.

AUSTIN: I guess they have personal value to her.   10

LEE: Personal value. Yeah. Just a lota' junk. Most of it's phony anyway. Idaho decals. Now who in the hell wants to eat offa' plate with the State of Idaho starin' ya' in the face. Every time ya' take a bite ya' get to see a little bit more.

AUSTIN: Well it must mean something to her or she wouldn't   15 save it.

LEE: Yeah, well personally I don't wann' be invaded by Idaho when I'm eatin'. When I'm eatin' I'm home. Ya' know what I'm sayin? I'm not driftin', I'm home. I don't need my thoughts swept off to Idaho. I don't need that!   20

(pause)

AUSTIN: Did you go out last night?

LEE: Why?

AUSTIN: I thought I heard you go out.

LEE: Yeah, I went out. What about it?

AUSTIN: Just wondered.   25

LEE: Damn coyotes kept me awake.

AUSTIN: Oh yeah, I heard them. They must've killed some-body's dog or something.

LEE: Yappin' their fool heads off. They don't yap like that on the desert. They howl. These are city coyotes here.   30

AUSTIN: Well, you don't sleep anyway do you?

(pause, LEE *stares at him)*

LEE: You're pretty smart aren't ya?

AUSTIN: How do you mean?

LEE: I mean you never had any more on the ball than I did. But here you are gettin' invited into prominent people's houses.   35 Sittin' around talkin' like you know somethin'.

AUSTIN: They're not so prominent.

LEE: They're a helluva' lot more prominent than the houses I get invited into.

AUSTIN: Well you invite yourself.   40

LEE: That's right. I do. In fact I probably got a wider range a' choices than you do, come to think of it.

AUSTIN: I wouldn't doubt it.

LEE: In fact I been inside some pretty classy places in my time. And I never even went to an Ivy League school either.   45

AUSTIN: You want some breakfast or something?

LEE: Breakfast?

AUSTIN: Yeah. Don't you eat breakfast?

LEE: Look, don't worry about me pal. I can take care a' myself. You just go ahead as though I wasn't even here, all right?   50

(AUSTIN goes into kitchen, makes coffee)

AUSTIN: Where'd you walk to last night?

(pause)

LEE: I went up in the foothills there. Up in the San Gabriels. Heat was drivin' me crazy.

AUSTIN: Well, wasn't it hot out on the desert?

55 LEE: Different kinda' heat. Out there it's clean. Cools off at night. There's a nice little breeze.

AUSTIN: Where were you, the Mojave?

LEE: Yeah. The Mojave. That's right.

AUSTIN: I haven't been out there in years.

60 LEE: Out past Needles there.

AUSTIN: Oh yeah.

LEE: Up here it's different. This country's real different.

AUSTIN: Well, it's been built up.

LEE: Built up? Wiped out is more like it. I don't even hardly

65 recognize it.

AUSTIN: Yeah. Foothills are the same though, aren't they?

LEE: Pretty much. It's funny goin' up in there. The smells and everything. Used to catch snakes up there, remember?

AUSTIN: You caught snakes.

70 LEE: Yeah. And you'd pretend you were Geronimo or some damn thing. You used to go right out to lunch.

AUSTIN: I enjoyed my imagination.

LEE: That what you call it? Looks like yer still enjoyin' it.

AUSTIN: So you just wandered around up there, huh?

75 LEE: Yeah. With a purpose.

AUSTIN: See any houses?

(pause)

LEE: Couple. Couple a' real nice ones. One of 'em didn't even have a dog. Walked right up and stuck my head in the window. Not a peep. Just a sweet kinda' suburban silence.

80 AUSTIN: What kind of a place was it?

LEE: Like a paradise. Kinda' place that sorta' kills ya' inside. Warm yellow lights. Mexican tile all around. Copper pots hangin' over the stove. Ya' know like they got in the magazines. Blonde people movin' in and outa' the rooms, talkin' to

85 each other. *(pause)* Kinda' place you wish you sorta' grew up in, ya' know.

AUSTIN: That's the kind of place you wish you'd grown up in?

LEE: Yeah. why not?

AUSTIN: I thought you hated that kind of stuff.

90 LEE: Yeah, well you never knew too much about me did ya'?

(pause)

AUSTIN: Why'd you go out to the desert in the first place?

LEE: I was on my way to see the old man.

AUSTIN: You mean you just passed through there?

LEE: Yeah. That's right. Three months of passin' through.

95 AUSTIN: Three months?

LEE: Somethin' like that. Maybe more. Why?

AUSTIN: You lived on the Mojave for three months?

LEE: Yeah. What'sa' matter with that?

AUSTIN: By yourself?

100 LEE: Mostly. Had a couple a' visitors. Had that dog for a while.

AUSTIN: Didn't you miss people?

LEE: *(laughs)* People?

AUSTIN: Yeah. I mean I go crazy if I have to spend three nights in a motel by myself.

105 LEE: Yer not in a motel now.

AUSTIN: No, I know. But sometimes I have to stay in motels.

LEE: Well, they got people in motels don't they?

AUSTIN: Strangers.

LEE: Yer friendly aren't ya'? Aren't you the friendly type?

(pause)

AUSTIN: I'm going to have somebody coming by here later, Lee.   110

LEE: Ah! Lady friend?

AUSTIN: No, a producer.

LEE: Aha! What's he produce?

AUSTIN: Film. Movies. You know.

LEE: Oh, movies. Motion Pictures! A Big Wig huh?   115

AUSTIN: Yeah.

LEE: What's he comin' by here for?

AUSTIN: We have to talk about a project.

LEE: Whadya' mean, "a project"? What's a "project"?

AUSTIN: A script.   120

LEE: Oh. That's what yer doin' with all these papers?

AUSTIN: Yeah.

LEE: Well, what's the project about?

AUSTIN: We're uh — it's a period piece.

LEE: What's "a period piece"?   125

AUSTIN: Look, it doesn't matter. The main thing is we need to discuss this alone. I mean —

LEE: Oh, I get it. You want me outa' the picture.

AUSTIN: Not exactly. I just need to be alone with him for a couple of hours. So we can talk.   130

LEE: Yer afraid I'll embarrass ya' huh?

AUSTIN: I'm not afraid you'll embarrass me!

LEE: Well, I tell ya' what — Why don't you just gimme the keys to yer car and I'll be back here around six o'clock or so. That give ya' enough time?   135

AUSTIN: I'm not loaning you my car, Lee.

LEE: You want me to just git lost huh? Take a hike? Is that it? Pound the pavement for a few hours while you bullshit yer way into a million bucks.

AUSTIN: Look, it's going to be hard enough for me to face this   140 character on my own without —

LEE: You don't know this guy?

AUSTIN: No I don't know — He's a producer. I mean I've been meeting with him for months but you never get to know a producer.   145

LEE: Yer tryin' to hustle him? Is that it?

AUSTIN: I'm not trying to hustle him! I'm trying to work out a deal! It's not easy.

LEE: What kinda' deal?

AUSTIN: Convince him it's a worthwhile story.   150

LEE: He's not convinced? How come he's comin' over here if he's not convinced? I'll convince him for ya'.

AUSTIN: You don't understand the way things work down here.

LEE: How do things work down here?

(pause)

AUSTIN: Look, if I loan you my car will you have it back here by   155 six?

LEE: On the button. With a full tank a' gas.

AUSTIN: *(digging in his pocket for keys)* Forget about the gas.

LEE: Hey, these days gas is gold, old buddy.

(AUSTIN hands the keys to LEE)

You remember that car I used to loan you?   160

AUSTIN: Yeah.

LEE: Forty Ford. Flathead.

AUSTIN: Yeah.

LEE: Sucker hauled ass didn't it?

165 AUSTIN: Lee, it's not that I don't want to loan you my car—

LEE: You are loanin' me yer car.

(LEE gives AUSTIN a pat on the shoulder, pause)

AUSTIN: I know. I just wish—

LEE: What? You wish what?

AUSTIN: I don't know. I wish I wasn't—I wish I didn't have to be
170 doing business down here. I'd like to just spend some time
with you.

LEE: I thought it was "Art" you were doin'.

(LEE moves across kitchen toward exit, tosses keys in his hand)

AUSTIN: Try to get it back here by six, okay?

LEE: No sweat. Hey, ya' know, if that uh—story of yours doesn't
175 go over with the guy—tell him I got a couple a' "projects" he
might be interested in. Real commercial. Full a' suspense.
True-to-life stuff.

(LEE exits, AUSTIN stares after LEE then turns, goes to papers at
table, leafs through pages, lights fade to black)

SCENE III

Afternoon. Alcove, SAUL KIMMER and AUSTIN seated across from
each other at table.

SAUL: Well, to tell you the truth Austin, I have never felt so
confident about a project in quite a long time.

AUSTIN: Well, that's good to hear, Saul.

SAUL: I am absolutely convinced we can get this thing off the
5 ground. I mean we'll have to make a sale to television and that
means getting a major star. Somebody bankable. But I think
we can do it. I really do.

AUSTIN: Don't you think we need a first draft before we approach
a star?

10 SAUL: No, no, not at all. I don't think it's necessary. Maybe a
brief synopsis. I don't want you to touch the typewriter until
we have some seed money.

AUSTIN: That's fine with me.

SAUL: I mean it's a great story. Just the story alone. You've really
15 managed to capture something this time.

AUSTIN: I'm glad you like it, Saul.

(LEE enters abruptly into kitchen carrying a stolen television set,
short pause)

LEE: Aw shit, I'm sorry about that. I am really sorry Austin.

AUSTIN: (standing) That's all right.

LEE: (moving toward them) I mean I thought it was way past six
20 already. You said to have it back here by six.

AUSTIN: We were just finishing up. (to SAUL) This is my, uh—
brother, Lee.

SAUL: (standing) Oh, I'm very happy to meet you.

(LEE sets T.V. on sink counter, shakes hands with SAUL)

LEE: I can't tell ya' how happy I am to meet you sir.

25 SAUL: Saul Kimmer.

LEE: Mr. Kipper.

SAUL: Kimmer.

AUSTIN: Lee's been living out on the desert and he just uh—

SAUL: Oh, that's terrific! (to LEE) Palm Springs?

LEE: Yeah. Yeah, right. Right around in that area. Near uh— 30
Bob Hope Drive there.

SAUL: Oh I love it out there. I just love it. The air is wonderful.

LEE: Yeah. Sure is. Healthy.

SAUL: And the golf. I don't know if you play golf, but the golf is
just about the best. 35

LEE: I play a lota' golf.

SAUL: Is that right?

LEE: Yeah. In fact I was hoping I'd run into somebody out here
who played a little golf. I've been lookin' for a partner.

SAUL: Well, I uh— 40

AUSTIN: Lee's just down for a visit while our mother's in Alaska.

SAUL: Oh, your mother's in Alaska?

AUSTIN: Yes. She went up there on a little vacation. This is her
place.

SAUL: I see. Well isn't that something. Alaska. 45

LEE: What kinda' handicap do ya' have, Mr. Kimmer?

SAUL: Oh I'm just a Sunday duffer really. You know.

LEE: That's good 'cause I haven't swung a club in months.

SAUL: Well we ought to get together sometime and have a little
game. Austin, do you play? 50

(SAUL mimes a Johnny Carson golf swing for AUSTIN)

AUSTIN: No. I don't uh—I've watched it on T.V.

LEE: (to SAUL) How 'bout tomorrow morning? Bright and early.
We could get out there and put in eighteen holes before
breakfast.

SAUL: Well, I've got uh—I have several appointments— 55

LEE: No, I mean real early. Crack a' dawn. While the dew's still
thick on the fairway.

SAUL: Sounds really great.

LEE: Austin could be our caddie.

SAUL: Now that's an idea. (laughs) 60

AUSTIN: I don't know the first thing about golf.

LEE: There's nothin' to it. Isn't that right, Saul? He'd pick it up in
fifteen minutes.

SAUL: Sure. Doesn't take long. 'Course you have to play for years
to find your true form. (chuckles) 65

LEE: (to AUSTIN) We'll give ya' a quick run-down on the club
faces. The irons, the woods. Show ya' a couple pointers on
the basic swing. Might even let ya' hit the ball a couple times.
Whadya' think, Saul?

SAUL: Why not. I think it'd be great. I haven't had any exercise in 70
weeks.

LEE: 'At's the spirit! We'll have a little orange juice right afterwards.

(pause)

SAUL: Orange juice?

LEE: Yeah! Vitamin C! Nothin' like a shot a' orange juice after a
round a' golf. Hot shower. Snappin' towels at each others' 75
privates. Real sense a' fraternity.

SAUL: (smiles at AUSTIN) Well, you make it sound very inviting,
I must say. It really does sound great.

LEE: Then it's a date.

SAUL: Well, I'll call the country club and see if I can arrange 80
something.

LEE: Great! Boy, I sure am sorry that I busted in on ya' all in the
middle of yer meeting.

SAUL: Oh that's quite all right. We were just about finished
anyway. 85

LEE: I can wait out in the other room if you want.

SAUL: No really —

LEE: Just got Austin's color T.V. back from the shop. I can watch a little amateur boxing now.

(LEE and AUSTIN exchange looks)

90 SAUL: Oh — Yes.

LEE: You don't fool around in Television, do you Saul?

SAUL: Uh — I have in the past. Produced some T.V. Specials. Network stuff. But it's mainly features now.

LEE: That's where the big money is, huh?

95 SAUL: Yes. That's right.

AUSTIN: Why don't I call you tomorrow, Saul and we'll get together. We can have lunch or something.

SAUL: That'd be terrific.

LEE: Right after the golf.

(pause)

100 SAUL: What?

LEE: You can have lunch right after the golf.

SAUL: Oh, right.

LEE: Austin was tellin' me that yer interested in stories.

SAUL: Well, we develop certain projects that we feel have com-

105 mercial potential.

LEE: What kinda' stuff do ya' go in for?

SAUL: Oh, the usual. You know. Good love interest. Lots of action. (chuckles at AUSTIN)

LEE: Westerns?

110 SAUL: Sometimes.

AUSTIN: I'll give you a ring, Saul.

(AUSTIN tries to move SAUL across the kitchen but LEE blocks their way)

LEE: I got a Western that'd knock yer lights out.

SAUL: Oh really?

LEE: Yeah. Contemporary Western. Based on a true story.

115 'Course I'm not a writer like my brother here. I'm not a man of the pen.

SAUL: Well —

LEE: I mean I can tell ya' a story off the tongue but I can't put it down on paper. That don't make any difference though does it?

120 SAUL: No, not really.

LEE: I mean plenty a' guys have stories don't they? True-life stories. Musta' been a lota' movies made from real life.

SAUL: Yes. I suppose so.

LEE: I haven't seen a good Western since "Lonely Are the

125 Brave." You remember that movie?

SAUL: No, I'm afraid I —

LEE: Kirk Douglas. Helluva' movie. You remember that movie, Austin?

AUSTIN: Yes.

130 LEE: (to SAUL) The man dies for the love of a horse.

SAUL: Is that right?

LEE: Yeah. Ya' hear the horse screamin' at the end of it. Rain's comin' down. Horse is screamin'. Then there's a shot. BLAM! Just a single shot like that. Then nothin' but the sound of

135 rain. And Kirk Douglas is ridin' in the ambulance. Ridin' away from the scene of the accident. And when he hears that shot he knows that his horse has died. He knows. And you see his eyes. And his eyes die. Right inside his face. And then his

eyes close. And you know that he's died too. You know that

140 Kirk Douglas has died from the death of his horse.

SAUL: (eyes AUSTIN nervously) Well, it sounds like a great movie. I'm sorry I missed it.

LEE: Yeah, you shouldn't a' missed that one.

SAUL: I'll have to try to catch it some time. Arrange a screening

145 or something. Well, Austin, I'll have to hit the freeway before rush hour.

AUSTIN: (ushers him toward exit) It's good seeing you, Saul.

(AUSTIN and SAUL shake hands)

LEE: So ya' think there's room for a real Western these days? A true-to-life Western?

SAUL: Well, I don't see why not. Why don't you uh — tell the

150 story to Austin and have him write a little outline.

LEE: You'd take a look at it then?

SAUL: Yes. Sure. I'll give it a read-through. Always eager for new material. (smiles at AUSTIN)

LEE: That's great! You'd really read it then huh?

155 SAUL: It would just be my opinion of course.

LEE: That's all I want. Just an opinion. I happen to think it has a lota' possibilities.

SAUL: Well, it was great meeting you and I'll —

(SAUL and LEE shake)

LEE: I'll call you tomorrow about the golf.

160 SAUL: Oh. Yes, right.

LEE: Austin's got your number, right?

SAUL: Yes.

LEE: So long Saul. (gives SAUL a pat on the back)

(SAUL exits, AUSTIN turns to LEE, looks at T.V. then back to LEE)

AUSTIN: Give me the keys.

165

(AUSTIN extends his hand toward LEE, LEE doesn't move, just stares at AUSTIN, smiles, lights to black)

SCENE IV

Night. Coyotes in distance, fade, sound of typewriter in dark, crickets, candlelight in alcove, dim light in kitchen, lights reveal AUSTIN at glass table typing, LEE sits across from him, foot on table, drinking beer and whiskey, the T.V. is still on sink counter, AUSTIN types for a while, then stops.

LEE: All right, now read it back to me.

AUSTIN: I'm not reading it back to you, Lee. You can read it when we're finished. I can't spend all night on this.

LEE: You got better things to do?

AUSTIN: Let's just go ahead. Now what happens when he leaves

5 Texas?

LEE: Is he ready to leave Texas yet? I didn't know we were that far along. He's not ready to leave Texas.

AUSTIN: He's right at the border.

LEE: (sitting up) No, see this is one a' the crucial parts. Right

10 here. (taps paper with beer can) We can't rush through this. He's not right at the border. He's a good fifty miles from the border. A lot can happen in fifty miles.

AUSTIN: It's only an outline. We're not writing an entire script now.

LEE: Well ya' can't leave things out even if it is an outline. It's

15 one a' the most important parts. Ya' can't go leavin' it out.

AUSTIN: Okay, okay. Let's just—get it done.

LEE: All right. Now. He's in the truck and he's got his horse trailer and his horse.

20 AUSTIN: We've already established that.

LEE: And he sees this other guy comin' up behind him in another truck. And that truck is pullin' a gooseneck.

AUSTIN: What's a gooseneck?

LEE: Cattle trailer. You know the kind with a gooseneck, goes
25 right down in the bed a' the pick-up.

AUSTIN: Oh. All right. (*types*)

LEE: It's important.

AUSTIN: Okay. I got it.

LEE: All these details are important.

(AUSTIN *types as they talk*)

30 AUSTIN: I've got it.

LEE: And this other guy's got his horse all saddled up in the back a' the gooseneck.

AUSTIN: Right.

LEE: So both these guys have got their horses right along with
35 'em, see.

AUSTIN: I understand.

LEE: Then this first guy suddenly realizes two things.

AUSTIN: The guy in front?

LEE: Right. The guy in front realizes two things almost at the
40 same time. Simultaneous.

AUSTIN: What were the two things?

LEE: Number one, he realizes that the guy behind him is the husband of the woman he's been—

(LEE *makes gesture of screwing by pumping his arm*)

AUSTIN: (*sees* LEE's *gesture*) Oh, Yeah.

45 LEE: And number two, he realizes he's in the middle of Tornado Country.

AUSTIN: What's "Tornado Country"?

LEE: Panhandle.

AUSTIN: Panhandle?

50 LEE: Sweetwater. Around in that area. Nothin'. Nowhere. And number three—

AUSTIN: I thought there was only two.

LEE: There's three. There's a third unforeseen realization.

AUSTIN: And what's that?

55 LEE: That he's runnin' outa' gas.

AUSTIN: (*stops typing*) Come on, Lee.

(AUSTIN *gets up, moves to kitchen, gets a glass of water*)

LEE: Whadya' mean, "come on"? That's what it is. Write it down! He's runnin' outa' gas.

AUSTIN: It's too—

60 LEE: What? It's too what? It's too real! That's what ya' mean isn't it? It's too much like real life!

AUSTIN: It's not like real life! It's not enough like real life. Things don't happen like that.

LEE: What! Men don't fuck other men's women?

65 AUSTIN: Yes. But they don't end up chasing each other across the Panhandle. Through "Tornado Country."

LEE: They do in this movie!

AUSTIN: And they don't have horses conveniently along with them when they run out of gas! And they don't run out of gas
70 either!

LEE: These guys run outa' gas! This is my story and one a' these guys runs outa' gas!

AUSTIN: It's just a dumb excuse to get them into a chase scene. It's contrived.

75 LEE: It is a chase scene! It's already a chase scene. They been chasin' each other fer days.

AUSTIN: So now they're supposed to abandon their trucks, climb on their horses and chase each other into the mountains?

LEE: (*standing suddenly*) There aren't any mountains in the
80 Panhandle! It's flat!

(LEE *turns violently toward windows in alcove and throws beer can at them*)

LEE: Goddamn these crickets! (*yells at crickets*) Shut up out there! (*pause, turns back toward table*) This place is like a fuckin' rest home here. How're you supposed to think!

AUSTIN: You wanna' take a break?

85 LEE: No, I don't wanna' take a break! I wanna' get this done! This is my last chance to get this done.

AUSTIN: (*moves back into alcove*) All right. Take it easy.

LEE: I'm gonna' be leavin' this area. I don't have time to mess around here.

AUSTIN: Where are you going?

90 LEE: Never mind where I'm goin'! That's got nothin' to do with you. I just gotta' get this done. I'm not like you. Hangin' around bein' a parasite offa' other fools. I gotta' do this thing and get out.

(*pause*)

AUSTIN: A parasite? Me?

95 LEE: Yeah, you!

AUSTIN: After you break into people's houses and take their televisions?

LEE: They don't need their televisions! I'm doin' them a service.

AUSTIN: Give me back my keys, Lee.

100 LEE: Not until you write this thing! You're gonna' write this outline thing for me or that car's gonna' wind up in Arizona with a different paint job.

AUSTIN: You think you can force me to write this? I was doing you a favor.

105 LEE: Git off yer high horse will ya'! Favor! Big favor. Handin' down favors from the mountain top.

AUSTIN: Let's just write it, okay? Let's sit down and not get upset and see if we can just get through this.

(AUSTIN *sits at typewriter*)

(*long pause*)

110 LEE: Yer not gonna' even show it to him, are ya'?

AUSTIN: What?

LEE: This outline. You got no intention of showin' it to him. Yer just doin' this 'cause yer afraid a' me.

AUSTIN: You can show it to him yourself.

115 LEE: I will, boy! I'm gonna' read it to him on the golf course.

AUSTIN: And I'm not afraid of you either.

LEE: Then how come yer doin' it?

AUSTIN: (*pause*) So I can get my keys back.

(*pause as* LEE *takes keys out of his pocket slowly and throws them on table, long pause,* AUSTIN *stares at keys*)

LEE: There. Now you got yer keys back.

(AUSTIN *looks up at* LEE *but doesn't take keys*)

120   LEE: Go ahead. There's yer keys.

(AUSTIN *slowly takes keys off table and puts them back in his own pocket*)

Now what're you gonna' do? Kick me out?
AUSTIN: I'm not going to kick you out, Lee.
LEE: You couldn't kick me out, boy.
AUSTIN: I know.
125   LEE: So you can't even consider that one. (*pause*) You could call the police. That'd be the obvious thing.
AUSTIN: You're my brother.
LEE: That don't mean a thing. You go down to the L.A. Police Department there and ask them what kinda' people kill each
130   other the most. What do you think they'd say?
AUSTIN: Who said anything about killing?
LEE: Family people. Brothers. Brothers-in-law. Cousins. Real American-type people. They kill each other in the heat mostly. In the Smog-Alerts. In the Brush Fire Season. Right
135   about this time a' year.
AUSTIN: This isn't the same.
LEE: Oh no? What makes it different?
AUSTIN: We're not insane. We're not driven to acts of violence like that. Not over a dumb movie script. Now sit down.

(*long pause,* LEE *considers which way to go with it*)

140   LEE: Maybe not. (*he sits back down at table across from* AUSTIN) Maybe you're right. Maybe we're too intelligent, huh? (*pause*) We got our heads on our shoulders. One of us has even got a Ivy League diploma. Now that means somethin' don't it? Doesn't that mean somethin'?
145   AUSTIN: Look, I'll write this thing for you, Lee. I don't mind writing it. I just don't want to get all worked up about it. It's not worth it. Now, come on. Let's just get through it, okay?
LEE: Nah. I think there's easier money. Lotsa' places I could pick up thousands. Maybe millions. I don't need this shit. I could
150   go up to Sacramento Valley and steal me a diesel. Ten thousand a week dismantling one a' those suckers. Ten thousand a week!

(LEE *opens another beer, puts his foot back up on table*)

AUSTIN: No, really, look, I'll write it out for you. I think it's a great idea.
155   LEE: Nah, you got yer own work to do. I don't wanna' interfere with yer life.
AUSTIN: I mean it'd be really fantastic if you could sell this. Turn it into a movie. I mean it.

(*pause*)

LEE: Ya' think so huh?
160   AUSTIN: Absolutely. You could really turn your life around, you know. Change things.
LEE: I could get me a house maybe.
AUSTIN: Sure you could get a house. You could get a whole ranch if you wanted to.
165   LEE: (*laughs*) A ranch? I could get a ranch?
AUSTIN: 'Course you could. You know what a screenplay sells for these days?
LEE: No. What's it sell for?
AUSTIN: A lot. A whole lot of money.

LEE: Thousands?   170
AUSTIN: Yeah. Thousands.
LEE: Millions?
AUSTIN: Well—
LEE: We could get the old man outa' hock then.
AUSTIN: Maybe.   175
LEE: Maybe? Whadya' mean, maybe?
AUSTIN: I mean it might take more than money.
LEE: You were just tellin' me it'd change my whole life around. Why wouldn't it change his?
AUSTIN: He's different.   180
LEE: Oh, he's of a different ilk huh?
AUSTIN: He's not gonna' change. Let's leave the old man out of it.
LEE: That's right. He's not gonna' change but I will. I'll just turn myself right inside out. I could be just like you then, huh? Sittin' around dreamin' stuff up. Gettin' paid to dream. Ridin'   185
back and forth on the freeway just dreamin' my fool head off.
AUSTIN: It's not all that easy.
LEE: It's not, huh?
AUSTIN: No. There's a lot of work involved.
LEE: What's the toughest part? Deciding whether to jog or play   190
tennis?

(*long pause*)

AUSTIN: Well, look. You can stay here—do whatever you want to. Borrow the car. Come in and out. Doesn't matter to me. It's not my house. I'll help you write this thing or—not. Just let me know what you want. You tell me.   195
LEE: Oh. So now suddenly you're at my service. Is that it?
AUSTIN: What do you want to do Lee?

(*long pause,* LEE *stares at him then turns and dreams at windows*)

LEE: I tell ya' what I'd do if I still had that dog. Ya' wanna' know what I'd do?
AUSTIN: What?   200
LEE: Head out to Ventura. Cook up a little match. God that little dog could bear down. Lota' money in dog fightin'. Big money.

(*pause*)

AUSTIN: Why don't we try to see this through, Lee. Just for the hell of it. Maybe you've really got something here. What do you think?   205

(*pause,* LEE *considers*)

LEE: Maybe so. No harm in tryin' I guess. You think it's such a hot idea. Besides, I always wondered what'd be like to be you.
AUSTIN: You did?
LEE: Yeah, sure. I used to picture you walkin' around some campus with yer arms fulla' books. Blondes chasin' after ya'. 210
AUSTIN: Blondes? That's funny.
LEE: What's funny about it?
AUSTIN: Because I always used to picture you somewhere.
LEE: Where'd you picture me?
AUSTIN: Oh, I don't know. Different places. Adventures. You   215
were always on some adventure.
LEE: Yeah.
AUSTIN: And I used to say to myself, "Lee's got the right idea. He's out there in the world and here I am. What am I doing?"
LEE: Well you were settin' yourself up for somethin'.   220
AUSTIN: I guess.

LEE: We better get started on this thing then.

AUSTIN: Okay.

(AUSTIN *sits up at typewriter, puts new paper in*)

LEE: Oh. Can I get the keys back before I forget?

(AUSTIN *hesitates*)

225   You said I could borrow the car if I wanted, right? Isn't that what you said?

AUSTIN: Yeah. Right.

(AUSTIN *takes keys out of his pocket, sets them on table,* LEE *takes keys slowly, plays with them in his hand*)

LEE: I could get a ranch, huh?

AUSTIN: Yeah. We have to write it first though.

230   LEE: Okay. Let's write it.

(*lights start dimming slowly to end as* AUSTIN *types,* LEE *speaks*)

So they take off after each other straight into an endless black prairie. The sun is just comin' down and they can feel the night on their backs. What they don't know is that each one of 'em is afraid, see. Each one separately thinks that he's the
235   only one that's afraid. And they keep ridin' like that straight into the night. Not knowing. And the one who's chasin' doesn't know where the other one is taking him. And the one who's being chased doesn't know where he's going.

(*lights to black, typing stops in the dark, crickets fade*)

— ACT TWO —

SCENE V

Morning. LEE *at the table in alcove with a set of golf clubs in a fancy leather bag,* AUSTIN *at sink washing a few dishes.*

AUSTIN: He really liked it, huh?

LEE: He wouldn't a' gave me these clubs if he didn't like it.

AUSTIN: He gave you the clubs?

LEE: Yeah. I told ya' he gave me the clubs. The bag too.

5   AUSTIN: I thought he just loaned them to you.

LEE: He said it was part a' the advance. A little gift like. Gesture of his good faith.

AUSTIN: He's giving you an advance?

LEE: Now what's so amazing about that? I told ya' it was a good
10   story. You even said it was a good story.

AUSTIN: Well that is really incredible Lee. You know how many guys spend their whole lives down here trying to break into this business? Just trying to get in the door?

LEE: (*pulling clubs out of bag, testing them*) I got no idea. How
15   many?

(*pause*)

AUSTIN: How much of an advance is he giving you?

LEE: Plenty. We were talkin' big money out there. Ninth hole is where I sealed the deal.

AUSTIN: He made a firm commitment?

20   LEE: Absolutely.

AUSTIN: Well, I know Saul and he doesn't fool around when he says he likes something.

LEE: I thought you said you didn't know him.

AUSTIN: Well, I'm familiar with his tastes.

LEE: I let him get two up on me goin' into the back nine. He was   25
sure he had me cold. You shoulda' seen his face when I pulled out the old pitching wedge and plopped it pin-high, two feet from the cup. He 'bout shit his pants. "Where'd a guy like you ever learn how to play golf like that?" he says.

(LEE *laughs,* AUSTIN *stares at him*)

AUSTIN: 'Course there's no contract yet. Nothing's final until it's   30
on paper.

LEE: It's final, all right. There's no way he's gonna' back out of it now. We gambled for it.

AUSTIN: Saul, gambled?

LEE: Yeah, sure. I mean he liked the outline already so he wasn't   35
risking that much. I just guaranteed it with my short game.

(*pause*)

AUSTIN: Well, we should celebrate or something. I think Mom left a bottle of champagne in the refrigerator. We should have a little toast.

(AUSTIN *gets glasses from cupboard, goes to refrigerator, pulls out bottle of champagne*)

LEE: You shouldn't oughta' take her champagne, Austin. She's   40
gonna' miss that.

AUSTIN: Oh, she's not going to mind. She'd be glad we put it to good use. I'll get her another bottle. Besides, it's perfect for the occasion.

(*pause*)

LEE: Yer gonna' get a nice fee fer writin' the script a' course.   45
Straight fee.

(AUSTIN *stops, stares at* LEE, *puts glasses and bottle on table, pause*)

AUSTIN: I'm writing the script?

LEE: That's what he said. Said we couldn't hire a better screen-writer in the whole town.

AUSTIN: But I'm already working on a script. I've got my own   50
project. I don't have time to write two scripts.

LEE: No, he said he was gonna' drop that other one.

(*pause*)

AUSTIN: What? You mean mine? He's going to drop mine and do yours instead?

LEE: (*smiles*) Now look, Austin, it's jest beginner's luck ya' know.   55
I mean I sank a fifty foot putt for this deal. No hard feelings.

(AUSTIN *goes to phone on wall, grabs it, starts dialing*)

He's not gonna' be in, Austin. Told me he wouldn't be in 'till late this afternoon.

AUSTIN: (*stays on phone, dialing, listen*) I can't believe this. I just can't believe it. Are you sure he said that? Why would he   60
drop mine?

LEE: That's what he told me.

AUSTIN: He can't do that without telling me first. Without talk-ing to me at least. He wouldn't just make a decision like that without talking to me!   65

LEE: Well I was kinda' surprised myself. But he was real enthusi-astic about my story.

(AUSTIN *hangs up phone violently, paces*)

AUSTIN: What'd he say! Tell me everything he said!

LEE: I been tellin' ya'! He said he liked the story a whole lot. It
70   was the first authentic Western to come along in a decade.

AUSTIN: He liked that story! Your story?

LEE: Yeah! What's so surprisin' about that?

AUSTIN: It's stupid! It's the dumbest story I ever heard in my life.

LEE: Hey, hold on! That's my story yer talkin' about!

75   AUSTIN: It's a bullshit story! It's idiotic. Two lamebrains chasing
each other across Texas! Are you kidding? Who do you think's
going to go see a film like that?

LEE: It's not a film! It's a movie. There's a big difference. That's
somethin' Saul told me.

80   AUSTIN: Oh he did, huh?

LEE: Yeah, he said, "In this business we make movies, American movies. Leave the films to the French."

AUSTIN: So you got real intimate with old Saul huh? He started
pouring forth his vast knowledge of Cinema.

85   LEE: I think he liked me a lot, to tell ya' the truth. I think he felt I
was somebody he could confide in.

AUSTIN: What'd you do, beat him up or something?

LEE: (*stands fast*) Hey, I've about had it with the insults buddy!
You think yer the only one in the brain department here? Yer
90   the only one that can sit around and cook things up? There's
other people got ideas too, ya' know!

AUSTIN: You must've done something. Threatened him or
something. Now what'd you do Lee?

LEE: I convinced him!

(LEE *makes sudden menacing lunge toward* AUSTIN, *wielding
golf club above his head, stops himself, frozen moment, long
pause,* LEE *lowers club*)

95   AUSTIN: Oh, Jesus. You didn't hurt him did you?

(*long silence,* LEE *sits back down at table*)

Lee! Did you hurt him?

LEE: I didn't do nothin' to him! He liked my story. Pure and
simple. He said it was the best story he's come across in a long,
long time.

100   AUSTIN: That's what he told me about my story! That's the same
thing he said to me.

LEE: Well, he musta' been lyin'. He musta' been lyin' to one of
us anyway.

AUSTIN: You can't come into this town and start pushing people
105   around. They're gonna' put you away!

LEE: I never pushed anybody around! I beat him fair and square.
(*pause*) They can't touch me anyway. They can't put a finger
on me. I'm gone. I can come in through the window and go
out through the door. They never knew what hit 'em. You,
110   yer stuck. Yer the one that's stuck. Not me. So don't be
warnin' me what to do in this town.

(*pause,* AUSTIN *crosses to table, sits at typewriter, rests*)

AUSTIN: Lee, come on, level with me will you? It doesn't make
any sense that suddenly he'd throw my idea out the window.
I've been talking to him for months. I've got too much at
115   stake. Everything's riding on this project.

LEE: What's yer idea?

AUSTIN: It's just a simple love story.

LEE: What kinda' love story?

AUSTIN: (*stands, cross into kitchen*) I'm not telling you!

LEE: Ha! 'Fraid I'll steal it huh? Competition's gettin' kinda'   120
close to home isn't it?

AUSTIN: Where did Saul say he was going?

LEE: He was gonna' take my story to a couple studios.

AUSTIN: That's *my* outline you know! I wrote that outline!
You've got no right to be peddling it around.   125

LEE: You weren't ready to take credit for it last night.

AUSTIN: Give me my keys!

LEE: What?

AUSTIN: The keys! I want my keys back!

LEE: Where you goin'?   130

AUSTIN: Just give me my keys! I gotta' take a drive. I gotta' get out
of here for a while.

LEE: Where you gonna' go, Austin?

AUSTIN: (*pause*) I might just drive out to the desert for a while. I
gotta' think.   135

LEE: You can think here just as good. This is the perfect setup for
thinkin'. We got some writin' to do here, boy. Now let's just
have us a little toast. Relax. We're partners now.

(LEE *pops the cork of the champagne bottle, pours two drinks as
the lights fade to black*)

SCENE VI

Afternoon. LEE *and* SAUL *in kitchen,* AUSTIN *in alcove*

LEE: Now you tell him. You tell him, Mr. Kipper.

SAUL: Kimmer.

LEE: Kimmer. You tell him what you told me. He don't believe
me.

AUSTIN: I don't want to hear it.   5

SAUL: It's really not a big issue, Austin. I was simply amazed by
your brother's story and —

AUSTIN: Amazed? You lost a bet! You gambled with my material!

SAUL: That's really beside the point, Austin. I'm ready to go all
the way with your brother's story. I think it has a great deal of   10
merit.

AUSTIN: I don't want to hear about it, okay? Go tell it to the
executives! Tell it to somebody who's going to turn it into a
package deal or something. A T.V. series. Don't tell it to me.

SAUL: But I want to continue with your project too, Austin. It's   15
not as though we can't do both. We're big enough for that
aren't we?

AUSTIN: "We"? *I* can't do both! I don't know about "we."

LEE: (*to* SAUL) See, what'd I tell ya'. He's totally unsympathetic.

SAUL: Austin, there's no point in our going to another screenwri-   20
ter for this. It just doesn't make sense. You're brothers. You
know each other. There's a familiarity with the material that
just wouldn't be possible otherwise.

AUSTIN: There's no familiarity with the material! None! I don't
know what "Tornado Country" is. I don't know what a   25
"gooseneck" is. And I don't want to know! (*pointing to* LEE)
He's a hustler! He's a bigger hustler than you are! If you can't
see that, then —

LEE: (*to* AUSTIN) Hey, now hold on. I didn't have to bring this
bone back to you, boy. I persuaded Saul here that you were   30
the right man for the job. You don't have to go throwin' up
favors in my face.

AUSTIN: Favors! I'm the one who wrote the fuckin' outline! You can't even spell.

35 SAUL: (to AUSTIN) Your brother told me about the situation with your father.

(pause)

AUSTIN: What? (looks at LEE)

SAUL: That's right. Now we have a clear-cut deal here, Austin. We have big studio money standing behind this thing. Just on
40 the basis of your outline.

AUSTIN: (to SAUL) What'd he tell you about my father?

SAUL: Well—that he's destitute. He needs money.

LEE: That's right. He does.

(AUSTIN shakes his head, stares at them both)

AUSTIN: (to LEE) And this little assignment is supposed to go
45 toward the old man? A charity project? Is that what this is? Did you cook this up on the ninth green too?

SAUL: It's a big slice, Austin.

AUSTIN: (to LEE) I gave him money! I already gave him money. You know that. He drank it all up!

50 LEE: This is a different deal here.

SAUL: We can set up a trust for your father. A large sum of money. It can be doled out to him in parcels so he can't misuse it.

AUSTIN: Yeah, and who's doing the doling?

55 SAUL: Your brother volunteered.

(AUSTIN laughs)

LEE: That's right. I'll make sure he uses it for groceries.

AUSTIN: (to SAUL) I'm not doing this script! I'm not writing this crap for you or anybody else. You can't blackmail me into it. You can't threaten me into it. There's no way I'm doing it. So
60 just give it up. Both of you.

(long pause)

SAUL: Well, that's it then. I mean this is an easy three hundred grand. Just for a first draft. It's incredible, Austin. We've got three different studios all trying to cut each other's throats to get this material. In one morning. That's how hot it is.

65 AUSTIN: Yeah, well you can afford to give me a percentage on the outline then. And you better get the genius here an agent before he gets burned.

LEE: Saul's gonna' be my agent. Isn't that right, Saul?

SAUL: That's right. (to AUSTIN) Your brother has really got some-
70 thing, Austin. I've been around too long not to recognize it. Raw talent.

AUSTIN: He's got a lota' balls is what he's got. He's taking you right down the river.

SAUL: Three hundred thousand, Austin. Just for a first draft.
75 Now you've never been offered that kind of money before.

AUSTIN: I'm not writing it.

(pause)

SAUL: I see. Well—

LEE: We'll just go to another writer then. Right, Saul? Just hire us somebody with some enthusiasm. Somebody who can rec-
80 ognize the value of a good story.

SAUL: I'm sorry about this, Austin.

AUSTIN: Yeah.

SAUL: I mean I was hoping we could continue both things but now I don't see how it's possible.

AUSTIN: So you're dropping my idea altogether. Is that it? Just
85 trade horses in midstream? After all these months of meetings.

SAUL: I wish there was another way.

AUSTIN: I've got everything riding on this, Saul. You know that. It's my only shot. If this falls through—
90

SAUL: I have to go with what my instincts tell me—

AUSTIN: Your instincts!

SAUL: My gut reaction.

AUSTIN: You lost! That's your gut reaction. You lost a gamble. Now you're trying to tell me you like his story? How could you
95 possibly fall for that story? It's as phony as Hoppalong Cassidy. What do you see in it? I'm curious.

SAUL: It has the ring of truth, Austin.

AUSTIN: (laughs) Truth?

LEE: It is true.
100

SAUL: Something about the real West.

AUSTIN: Why? Because it's got horses? Because it's got grown men acting like little boys?

SAUL: Something about the land. Your brother is speaking from experience.
105

AUSTIN: So am I!

SAUL: But nobody's interested in love these days, Austin. Let's face it.

LEE: That's right.

AUSTIN: (to SAUL) He's been camped out on the desert for three
110 months. Talking to cactus. What's he know about what people wanna' see on the screen! I drive on the freeway every day. I swallow the smog. I watch the news in color. I shop in the Safeway. I'm the one who's in touch! Not him!

SAUL: I have to go now, Austin.
115

(SAUL starts to leave)

AUSTIN: There's no such thing as the West anymore! It's a dead issue! It's dried up, Saul, and so are you.

(SAUL stops and turns to AUSTIN)

SAUL: Maybe you're right. But I have to take the gamble, don't I?

AUSTIN: You're a fool to do this, Saul.

SAUL: I've always gone on my hunches. Always. And I've never
120 been wrong. (to LEE) I'll talk to you tomorrow, Lee.

LEE: All right, Mr. Kimmer.

SAUL: Maybe we could have some lunch.

LEE: Fine with me. (smiles at AUSTIN)

SAUL: I'll give you a ring.
125

(SAUL exits, lights to black as brothers look at each other from a distance)

SCENE VII

Night. Coyotes, crickets, sound of typewriter in dark, candlelight up on LEE at typewriter struggling to type with one finger system, AUSTIN sits sprawled out on kitchen floor with whiskey bottle, drunk.

AUSTIN: (singing, from floor)

> "Red sails in the sunset
> Way out on the blue
> Please carry my loved one
> Home safely to me
>
> Red sails in the sunset—"
5

LEE: (slams fist on table) Hey! Knock it off will ya'! I'm tryin' to concentrate here.

AUSTIN: (laughs) You're tryin' to concentrate?

10　LEE: Yeah. That's right.

AUSTIN: Now you're tryin' to concentrate.

LEE: Between you, the coyotes and the crickets a thought don't have much of a chance.

AUSTIN: "Between me, the coyotes and the crickets." What a

15　great title.

LEE: I don't need a title! I need a thought.

AUSTIN: (laughs) A thought! Here's a thought for ya' —

LEE: I'm not askin' fer yer thoughts! I got my own. I can do this thing on my own.

20　AUSTIN: You're going to write an entire script on your own?

LEE: That's right.

(pause)

AUSTIN: Here's a thought. Saul Kimmer —

LEE: Shut up will ya'!

AUSTIN: He thinks we're the same person.

25　LEE: Don't get cute.

AUSTIN: He does! He's lost his mind. Poor old Saul. (giggles) Thinks we're one and the same.

LEE: Why don't you ease up on that champagne.

AUSTIN: (holding up bottle) This isn't champagne anymore. We

30　went through the champagne a long time ago. This is serious stuff. The days of champagne are long gone.

LEE: Well, go outside and drink it.

AUSTIN: I'm enjoying your company, Lee. For the first time since your arrival I am finally enjoying your company. And

35　now you want me to go outside and drink alone?

LEE: That's right.

(LEE reads through paper in typewriter, makes an erasure)

AUSTIN: You think you'll make more progress if you're alone? You might drive yourself crazy.

LEE: I could have this thing done in a night if I had a little

40　silence.

AUSTIN: Well you'd still have the crickets to contend with. The coyotes. The sounds of the Police Helicopters prowling above the neighborhood. Slashing their searchlights down through the streets. Hunting for the likes of you.

45　LEE: I'm a screenwriter now! I'm legitimate.

AUSTIN: (laughing) A screenwriter!

LEE: That's right. I'm on salary. That's more'n I can say for you. I got an advance coming.

AUSTIN: This is true. This is very true. An advance. (pause)

50　Well, maybe I oughta' go out and try my hand at your trade. Since you're doing so good at mine.

LEE: Ha!

(LEE attempts to type some more but gets the ribbon tangled up, starts trying to re-thread it as they continue talking)

AUSTIN: Well why not? You don't think I've got what it takes to sneak into people's houses and steal their T.V.s?

55　LEE: You couldn't steal a toaster without losin' yer lunch.

(AUSTIN stands with a struggle, supports himself by the sink)

AUSTIN: You don't think I could sneak into somebody's house and steal a toaster?

LEE: Go take a shower or somethin' will ya!

(LEE gets more tangled up with the typewriter ribbon, pulling it out of the machine as though it was fishing line)

AUSTIN: You really don't think I could steal a crumby toaster? How much you wanna' bet I can't steal a toaster! How much? 60 Go ahead! You're a gambler aren't you? Tell me how much yer willing to put on the line. Some part of your big advance? Oh, you haven't got that yet have you. I forgot.

LEE: All right. I'll bet you your car that you can't steal a toaster without gettin' busted. 65

AUSTIN: You already got my car!

LEE: Okay, your house then.

AUSTIN: What're you gonna' give me! I'm not talkin' about my house and my car, I'm talkin' about what are you gonna' give me. You don't have nothin' to give me. 70

LEE: I'll give you — shared screen credit. How 'bout that? I'll have it put in the contract that this was written by the both of us.

AUSTIN: I don't want my name on that piece of shit! I want something of value. You got anything of value? You got any tidbits from the desert? Any Rattlesnake bones? I'm not a 75 greedy man. Any little personal treasure will suffice.

LEE: I'm gonna' just kick yer ass out in a minute.

AUSTIN: Oh, so now you're gonna' kick me out! Now I'm the intruder. I'm the one who's invading your precious privacy.

LEE: I'm trying to do some screenwriting here!! 80

(LEE stands, picks up typewriter, slams it down hard on table, pause, silence except for crickets)

AUSTIN: Well, you got everything you need. You got plenty a' coffee? Groceries. You got a car. A contract. (pause) Might need a new typewriter ribbon but other than that you're pretty well fixed. I'll just leave ya' alone for a while.

(AUSTIN tries to steady himself to leave, LEE makes a move toward him)

LEE: Where you goin'? 85

AUSTIN: Don't worry about me. I'm not the one to worry about.

(AUSTIN weaves toward exit, stops)

LEE: What're you gonna' do? Just go wander out into the night?

AUSTIN: I'm gonna' make a little tour.

LEE: Why don't ya' just go to bed for Christ's sake. Yer makin' me sick. 90

AUSTIN: I can take care a' myself. Don't worry about me.

(AUSTIN weaves badly in another attempt to exit, he crashes to the floor, LEE goes to him but remains standing)

LEE: You want me to call your wife for ya' or something?

AUSTIN: (from floor) My wife?

LEE: Yeah. I mean maybe she can help ya' out. Talk to ya' or somethin'. 95

AUSTIN: (struggles to stand again) She's five hundred miles away. North. North of here. Up in the North country where things are calm. I don't need any help. I'm gonna' go outside and I'm gonna' steal a toaster. I'm gonna' steal some other stuff too. I might even commit bigger crimes. Bigger than you 100 ever dreamed of. Crimes beyond the imagination!

(AUSTIN manages to get himself vertical, tries to head for exit again)

LEE: Just hang on a minute, Austin.

AUSTIN: Why? What for? You don't need my help, right? You got a handle on the project. Besides, I'm lookin' forward to

105 the smell of the night. The bushes. Orange blossoms. Dust in
the driveways. Rain bird sprinklers. Lights in people's houses.
You're right about the lights, Lee. Everybody else is livin' the
life. Indoors. Safe. This is a Paradise down here. You know
that? We're livin' in a Paradise. We've forgotten about that.

110 LEE: You sound just like the old man now.

AUSTIN: Yeah, well we all sound alike when we're sloshed. We
just sorta' echo each other.

LEE: Maybe if we could work on this together we could bring
him back out here. Get him settled down some place.

*(AUSTIN turns violently toward LEE, takes a swing at him, misses
and crashes to the floor again, LEE stays standing)*

115 AUSTIN: I don't want him out here! I've had it with him! I went
all the way out there! I went out of my way. I gave him money
and all he did was play Al Jolson records and spit at me! I gave
him money!

(pause)

LEE: Just help me a little with the characters, all right? You know
120 how to do it, Austin.

AUSTIN: *(on floor, laughs)* The characters!

LEE: Yeah. You know. The way they talk and stuff. I can hear it
in my head but I can't get it down on paper.

AUSTIN: What characters?

125 LEE: The guys. The guys in the story.

AUSTIN: Those aren't characters.

LEE: Whatever you call 'em then. I need to write somethin' out.

AUSTIN: Those are illusions of characters.

LEE: I don't give a damn what ya' call 'em! You know what I'm
130 talkin' about!

AUSTIN: Those are fantasies of a long lost boyhood.

LEE: I gotta' write somethin' out on paper!!

(pause)

AUSTIN: What for? Saul's gonna' get you a fancy screenwriter
isn't he?

135 LEE: I wanna' do it myself!

AUSTIN: Then do it! Yer on your own now, old buddy. You bull-
dogged yer way into contention. Now you gotta' carry it
through.

LEE: I will but I need some advice. Just a couple a' things. Come
140 on, Austin. Just help me get 'em talkin' right. It won't take
much.

AUSTIN: Oh, now you're having a little doubt huh? What happened? The pressure's on, boy. This is it. You gotta' come up
with it now. You don't come up with a winner on your first
145 time out they just cut your head off. They don't give you a
second chance ya' know.

LEE: I got a good story! I know it's a good story. I just need a little
help is all.

AUSTIN: Not from me. Not from yer little old brother. I'm retired.

150 LEE: You could save this thing for me, Austin. I'd give ya' half
the money. I would. I only need half anyway. With this kinda'
money I could be a long time down the road. I'd never bother
ya' again. I promise. You'd never even see me again.

AUSTIN: *(still on floor)* You'd disappear?

155 LEE: I would for sure.

AUSTIN: Where would you disappear to?

LEE: That don't matter. I got plenty a' places.

AUSTIN: Nobody can disappear. The old man tried that. Look
where it got him. He lost his teeth.

LEE: He never had any money. 160

AUSTIN: I don't mean that. I mean his teeth! His real teeth. First
he lost his real teeth, then he lost his false teeth. You never
knew that did ya'? He never confided in you.

LEE: Nah, I never knew that.

AUSTIN: You wanna' drink? 165

*(AUSTIN offers bottle to LEE, LEE takes it, sits down on kitchen
floor with AUSTIN, they share the bottle)*

Yeah, he lost his real teeth one at a time. Woke up every
morning with another tooth lying on the mattress. Finally, he
decides he's gotta' get 'em all pulled out but he doesn't have
any money. Middle of Arizona with no money and no insurance and every morning another tooth is lying on the mat- 170
tress. *(takes a drink)* So what does he do?

LEE: I dunno'. I never knew about that.

AUSTIN: He begs the government. G.I. Bill or some damn thing.
Some pension plan he remembers in the back of his head.
And they send him out the money. 175

LEE: They did?

(they keep trading the bottle between them, taking drinks)

AUSTIN: Yeah. They send him the money but it's not enough
money. Costs a lot to have all yer teeth yanked. They charge
by the individual tooth, ya' know. I mean one tooth isn't
equal to another tooth. Some are more expensive. Like the 180
big ones in the back—

LEE: So what happened?

AUSTIN: So he locates a Mexican dentist in Juarez who'll do the
whole thing for a song. And he takes off hitchhiking to the
border. 185

LEE: Hitchhiking?

AUSTIN: Yeah. So how long you think it takes him to get to the
border? A man his age.

LEE: I dunno.

AUSTIN: Eight days it takes him. Eight days in the rain and the 190
sun and every day he's droppin' teeth on the blacktop nobody'll pick him up 'cause his mouth's full a' blood.

(pause, they drink)

So finally he stumbles into the dentist. Dentist takes all his
money and all his teeth. And there he is, in Mexico, with his
gums sewed up and his pockets empty. 195

(long silence, AUSTIN drinks)

LEE: That's it?

AUSTIN: Then I go out to see him, see. I go out there and I take
him out for a nice Chinese dinner. But he doesn't eat. All he
wants to do is drink Martinis outa' plastic cups. And he takes
his teeth out and lays 'em on the table 'cause he can't stand 200
the feel of 'em. And we ask the waitress for one a' those doggie
bags to take the Chop Suey home in. So he drops his teeth in
the doggie bag along with the Chop Suey. And then we go out
to hit all the bars up and down the highway. Says he wants to
introduce me to all his buddies. And in one a' those bars, in 205
one a' those bars up and down the highway, he left that doggie
bag with his teeth laying in the Chop Suey.

LEE: You never found it?

AUSTIN: We went back but we never did find it. *(pause)* Now that's a true story. True to life.

(they drink as lights fade to black)

SCENE VIII

Very early morning, between night and day. No crickets, coyotes yapping feverishly in distance before light comes up, a small fire blazes up in the dark from alcove area, sound of LEE smashing typewriter with a golf club, lights coming up, LEE seen smashing typewriter methodically then dropping pages of his script into a burning bowl set on the floor of alcove, flames leap up, AUSTIN has a whole bunch of stolen toasters lined up on the sink counter along with LEE's stolen T.V., the toasters are of a wide variety of models, mostly chrome, AUSTIN goes up and down the line of toasters, breathing on them and polishing them with a dish towel, both men are drunk, empty whiskey bottles and beer cans litter floor of kitchen, they share a half empty bottle on one of the chairs in the alcove, LEE keeps periodically taking deliberate ax-chops at the typewriter using a nine-iron as AUSTIN speaks, all of their mother's house plants are dead and drooping.

AUSTIN: *(polishing toasters)* There's gonna' be a general lack of toast in the neighborhood this morning. Many, many unhappy, bewildered breakfast faces. I guess it's best not to even think of the victims. Not to even entertain it. Is that the right psychology?

LEE: *(pauses)* What?

AUSTIN: Is that the correct criminal psychology? Not to think of the victims?

LEE: What victims?

(LEE takes another swipe at typewriter with nine-iron, adds pages to the fire)

AUSTIN: The victims of crime. Of breaking and entering. I mean is it a prerequisite for a criminal not to have a conscience?

LEE: Ask a criminal.

(pause, LEE stares at AUSTIN)

What're you gonna' do with all those toasters? That's the dumbest thing I ever saw in my life.

AUSTIN: I've got hundreds of dollars worth of household appliances here. You may not realize that.

LEE: Yeah, and how many hundreds of dollars did you walk right past?

AUSTIN: It was toasters you challenged me to. Only toasters. I ignored every other temptation.

LEE: I never challenged you! That's no challenge. Anybody can steal a toaster.

(LEE smashes typewriter again.)

AUSTIN: You don't have to take it out on my typewriter ya' know. It's not the machine's fault that you can't write. It's a sin to do that to a good machine.

LEE: A sin?

AUSTIN: When you consider all the writers who never even had a machine. Who would have given an eyeball for a good typewriter. Any typewriter.

(LEE smashes typewriter again)

AUSTIN: *(polishing toasters)* All the ones who wrote on matchbook covers. Paper bags. Toilet paper. Who had their writing destroyed by their jailers. Who persisted beyond all odds. Those writers would find it hard to understand your actions.

(LEE comes down on typewriter with one final crushing blow of the nine-iron then collapses in one of the chairs, takes a drink from bottle, pause)

AUSTIN: *(after pause)* Not to mention demolishing a perfectly good golf club. What about all the struggling golfers? What about Lee Trevino? What do you think he would've said when he was batting balls around with broomsticks at the age of nine. Impoverished.

(pause)

LEE: What time is it anyway?

AUSTIN: No idea. Time stands still when you're havin' fun.

LEE: Is it too late to call a woman? You know any women?

AUSTIN: I'm a married man.

LEE: I mean a local woman.

(AUSTIN looks out at light through window above sink)

AUSTIN: It's either too late or too early. You're the nature enthusiast. Can't you tell the time by the light in the sky? Orient yourself around the North Star or something?

LEE: I can't tell anything.

AUSTIN: Maybe you need a little breakfast. Some toast! How 'bout some toast?

(AUSTIN goes to cupboard, pulls out loaf of bread and starts dropping slices into every toaster, LEE stays sitting, drinks, watches AUSTIN)

LEE: I don't need toast. I need a woman.

AUSTIN: A woman isn't the answer. Never was.

LEE: I'm not talkin' about permanent. I'm talkin' about temporary.

AUSTIN: *(putting toast in toasters)* We'll just test the merits of these little demons. See which brands have a tendency to burn. See which one can produce a perfectly golden piece of fluffy toast.

LEE: How much gas you got in yer car?

AUSTIN: I haven't driven my car for days now. So I haven't had an opportunity to look at the gas gauge.

LEE: Take a guess. You think there's enough to get me to Bakersfield?

AUSTIN: Bakersfield? What's in Bakersfield?

LEE: Just never mind what's in Bakersfield! You think there's enough goddamn gas in the car!

AUSTIN: Sure.

LEE: Sure. You could care less, right. Let me run outa' gas on the Grapevine. You could give a shit.

AUSTIN: I'd say there was enough gas to get you just about anywhere, Lee. With your determination and guts.

LEE: What the hell time is it anyway?

(LEE pulls out his wallet, starts going through dozens of small pieces of paper with phone numbers written on them, drops some on the floor, drops others in the fire)

AUSTIN: Very early. This is the time of morning when the coyotes kill people's cocker spaniels. Did you hear them? That's

75 what they were doing out there. Luring innocent pets away from their homes.

LEE: (*searching through his papers*) What's the area code for Bakersfield? You know?

AUSTIN: You could always call the operator.

LEE: I can't stand that voice they give ya'.

80 AUSTIN: What voice?

LEE: That voice that warns you that if you'd only tried harder to find the number in the phone book you wouldn't have to be calling the operator to begin with.

(LEE *gets up, holding a slip of paper from his wallet, stumbles toward phone on wall, yanks receiver, starts dialing*)

AUSTIN: Well I don't understand why you'd want to talk to any-
85 body else anyway. I mean you can talk to me. I'm your brother.

LEE: (*dialing*) I wanna' talk to a woman. I haven't heard a woman's voice in a long time.

AUSTIN: Not since the Botanist?

90 LEE: What?

AUSTIN: Nothing. (*starts singing as he tends toast*)

"Red sails in the sunset
Way out on the blue
Please carry my loved one
95 Home safely to me"

LEE: Hey, knock it off will ya'! This is long distance here.

AUSTIN: Bakersfield?

LEE: Yeah, Bakersfield. It's Kern County.

AUSTIN: Well, what County are *we* in?

100 LEE: You better get yourself a 7-Up, boy.

AUSTIN: One County's as good as another.

(AUSTIN *hums "Red Sails" softly as* LEE *talks on phone*)

LEE: (*to phone*) Yeah, operator look — first off I wanna' know the area code for Bakersfield. Right. Bakersfield! Okay. Good. Now I wanna' know if you can help me track somebody
105 down. (*pause*) No, no I mean a phone number. Just a phone number. Okay. (*holds a piece of paper up and reads it*) Okay, the name is Melly Ferguson. Melly. (*pause*) I dunno'. Melly. Maybe. Yeah. Maybe Melanie. Yeah. Melanie Ferguson. Okay. (*pause*) What? I can't hear ya' so good. Sounds like yer
110 under the ocean. (*pause*) You got ten Melanie Fergusons? How could that be? Ten Melanie Fergusons in Bakersfield? Well gimme all of 'em then. (*pause*) What d'ya mean? Gimme all ten Melanie Fergusons! That's right. Just a second. (*to* AUSTIN) Gimme a pen.

115 AUSTIN: I gon't have a pen.

LEE: Gimme a pencil then!

AUSTIN: I don't have a pencil.

LEE: (*to phone*) Just a second, operator. (*to* AUSTIN) Yer a writer and ya' don't have a pen or a pencil!

120 AUSTIN: I'm not a writer. You're a writer.

LEE: I'm on the phone here! Get me a pen or a pencil.

AUSTIN: I gotta' watch the toast.

LEE: (*to phone*) Hang on a second, operator.

(LEE *lets the phone drop then starts pulling all the drawers in the kitchen out on the floor and dumping the contents, searching for a pencil,* AUSTIN *watches him casually*)

LEE: (*crashing through drawers, throwing contents around kitchen*) This is the last time I try to live with people, boy! I
125 can't believe it. Here I am! Here I am again in a desperate situation! This would never happen out on the desert. I would never be in this kinda' situation out on the desert. Isn't there a pen or a pencil in this house! Who lives in this house anyway!

AUSTIN: Our mother.
130
LEE: How come she don't have a pen or a pencil! She's a social person isn't she? Doesn't she have to make shopping lists? She's gotta' have a pencil. (*finds a pencil*) Aaha! (*he rushes back to phone, picks up receiver*) All right operator. Operator? Hey! Operator! Goddamnit!
135
(LEE *rips the phone off the wall and throws it down, goes back to chair and falls into it, drinks, long pause*)

AUSTIN: She hung up?

LEE: Yeah, she hung up. I knew she was gonna' hang up. I could hear it in her voice.

(LEE *starts going through his slips of paper again*)

AUSTIN: Well, you're probably better off staying here with me anyway. I'll take care of you.
140
LEE: I don't need takin' care of! Not by you anyway.

AUSTIN: Toast is almost ready.

(AUSTIN *starts buttering all the toast as it pops up*)

LEE: I don't want any toast!

(*long pause*)

AUSTIN: You gotta' eat something. Can't just drink. How long have we been drinking, anyway?
145
LEE: (*looking through slips of paper*) Maybe it was Fresno. What's the area code for Fresno? How could I have lost that number! She was beautiful.

(*pause*)

AUSTIN: Why don't you just forget about that, Lee. Forget about the woman.
150
LEE: She had green eyes. You know what green eyes do to me?

AUSTIN: I know but you're not gonna' get it on with her now anyway. It's dawn already. She's in Bakersfield for Christ's sake.

(*long pause,* LEE *considers the situation*)

LEE: Yeah. (*looks at windows*) It's dawn?

AUSTIN: Let's just have some toast and —
155
LEE: What is this bullshit with the toast anyway! You make it sound like salvation or something. I don't want any goddamn toast! How many times I gotta' tell ya'! (LEE *gets up, crosses upstage to windows in alcove, looks out,* AUSTIN *butters toast*)

AUSTIN: Well it is like salvation sort of. I mean the smell. I love
160 the smell of toast. And the sun's coming up. It makes me feel like anything's possible. Ya' know?

LEE: (*back to* AUSTIN, *facing windows upstage*) So go to church why don't ya'

AUSTIN: Like a beginning. I love beginnings.
165
LEE: Oh yeah. I've always been kinda' partial to endings myself.

AUSTIN: What if I come with you, Lee?

LEE: (*pause as* LEE *turns toward* AUSTIN) What?

AUSTIN: What if I come with you out to the desert?

LEE: Are you kiddin'?
170
AUSTIN: No. I'd just like to see what it's like.

LEE: You wouldn't last a day out there pal.

AUSTIN: That's what you said about the toasters. You said I couldn't steal a toaster either.

175 LEE: A toaster's got nothin' to do with the desert.

AUSTIN: I could make it, Lee. I'm not that helpless. I can cook.

LEE: Cook?

AUSTIN: I can.

LEE: So what! You can cook. Toast.

180 AUSTIN: I can make fires. I know how to get fresh water from condensation.

(AUSTIN *stacks buttered toast up in a tall stack on plate*)

(LEE *slams table*)

LEE: It's not somethin' you learn out of a Boy Scout handbook!

AUSTIN: Well how do you learn it then! How're you supposed to learn it!

(*pause*)

185 LEE: Ya' just learn it, that's all. Ya' learn it 'cause ya' have to learn it. You don't *have* to learn it.

AUSTIN: You could teach me.

LEE: (*stands*) What're you, crazy or somethin'? You went to college. Here, you are down here, rollin' in bucks. Floatin' up

190 and down in elevators. And you wanna' learn how to live on the desert!

AUSTIN: I do, Lee. I really do. There's nothin' down here for me. There never was. When we were kids here it was different. There was a life here then. But now—I keep comin' down

195 here thinkin' it's the fifties or somethin'. I keep finding myself getting off the freeway at familiar landmarks that turn out to be unfamiliar. On the way to appointments. Wandering down streets I thought I recognized that turn out to be replicas of streets I remember. Streets I misremember. Streets I can't

200 tell if I lived on or saw in a postcard. Fields that don't even exist anymore.

LEE: There's no point cryin' about that now.

AUSTIN: There's nothin' real down here, Lee! Least of all me!

LEE: Well I can't save you from that!

205 AUSTIN: You can let me come with you.

LEE: No dice, pal.

AUSTIN: You could let me come with you, Lee!

LEE: Hey, do you actually think I chose to live out in the middle a' nowhere? Do ya'? Ya' think it's some kinda' philosophical

210 decision I took or somethin'? I'm livin' out there 'cause I can't make it here! And yer bitchin' to me about all yer success!

AUSTIN: I'd cash it all in in a second. That's the truth.

LEE: (*pause, shakes his head*) I can't believe this.

AUSTIN: Let me go with you.

215 LEE: Stop sayin' that will ya'! Yer worse than a dog.

(AUSTIN *offers out the plate of neatly stacked toast to* LEE)

AUSTIN: You want some toast?

(LEE *suddenly explodes and knocks the plate out of* AUSTIN's *hand, toast goes flying, long frozen moment where it appears* LEE *might go all the way this time when* AUSTIN *breaks it by slowly lowering himself to his knees and begins gathering the scattered toast from the floor and stacking it back on the plate,* LEE *begins to circle* AUSTIN *in a slow, predatory way, crushing pieces of toast in his wake, no words for a while,* AUSTIN *keeps gathering toast, even the crushed pieces*)

LEE: Tell ya' what I'll do, little brother. I might just consider makin' you a deal. Little trade. (AUSTIN *continues gathering toast as* LEE *circles him through this*) You write me up this screenplay thing just like I tell ya'. I mean you can use all yer 220 usual tricks and stuff. Yer fancy language. Yer artistic hocus pocus. But ya' gotta' write everything like I say. Every move. Every time they run outa' gas, they run outa' gas. Every time they wanna' jump on a horse, they do just that. If they wanna' stay in Texas, by God they'll stay in Texas! (*Keeps circling*) 225 And you finish the whole thing up for me. Top to bottom. And you put my name on it. And I own all the rights. And every dime goes in my pocket. You do that and I'll sure enough take ya' with me to the desert. (LEE *stops, pause, looks down at* AUSTIN) How's that sound? 230

(*pause as* AUSTIN *stands slowly holding plate of demolished toast, their faces are very close, pause*)

AUSTIN: It's a deal.

(LEE *stares straight into* AUSTIN's *eyes, then he slowly takes a piece of toast off the plate, raises it to his mouth and takes a huge crushing bite never taking his eyes off* AUSTIN's *as* LEE *crunches into the toast the lights black out*)

SCENE IX

Mid-day. No sound, blazing heat, the stage is ravaged; bottles, toasters, smashed typewriter, ripped out telephone, etc. All the debris from previous scene is now starkly visible in intense yellow light, the effect should be like a desert junkyard at high noon, the coolness of the preceding scenes is totally obliterated. AUSTIN *is seated at table in alcove, shirt open, pouring with sweat, hunched over a writing notebook, scribbling notes desperately with a ballpoint pen.* LEE *with no shirt, beer in hand, sweat pouring down his chest, is walking a slow circle around the table, picking his way through the objects, sometimes kicking them aside.*

LEE: (*as he walks*) All right, read it back to me. Read it back to me!

AUSTIN: (*scribbling at top speed*) Just a second.

LEE: Come on, come on! Just read what ya' got.

AUSTIN: I can't keep up! It's not the same as if I had a typewriter.

LEE: Just read what we got so far. Forget about the rest. 5

AUSTIN: All right. Let's see—okay—(*wipes sweat from his face, reads as* LEE *circles*) Luke says uh—

LEE: Luke!

AUSTIN: Yeah.

LEE: His name's Luke? All right, all right—we can change the 10 names later. What's he say? Come on, come on.

AUSTIN: He says uh—(*reading*) "I told ya' you were a fool to follow me in here. I know this prairie like the back a' my hand."

LEE: No, no, no! That's not what I said. I never said that.

AUSTIN: That's what I wrote. 15

LEE: It's not what I said. I never said "like the back a' my hand." That's stupid. That's one a' those—whadya' call it? Whadya' call that?

AUSTIN: What?

LEE: Whadya' call it when somethin's been said a thousand 20 times before. Whadya' call that?

AUSTIN: Um—a cliché?

LEE: Yeah. That's right. Cliché. That's what that is. A cliché. "The back a' my hand." That's stupid.

25 AUSTIN: That's what you said.

LEE: I never said that! And even if I did, that's where yer supposed to come in. That's where yer supposed to change it to
somethin' better.

AUSTIN: Well how am I supposed to do that and write down what
30 you say at the same time?

LEE: Ya' just do, that's all! You hear a stupid line you change it.
That's yer job.

AUSTIN: All right. (makes more notes)

LEE: What're you changin' it to?

35 AUSTIN: I'm not changing it. I'm just trying to catch up.

LEE: Well change it! We gotta' change that, we can't leave that in
there like that. ". . . the back a' my hand." That's dumb.

AUSTIN: (stops writing, sits back) All right.

LEE: (pacing) So what'll we change it to?

40 AUSTIN: Um—How 'bout—"I'm on intimate terms with this
prairie."

LEE: (to himself considering line as he walks) "I'm on intimate
terms with this prairie." Intimate terms, intimate terms. Intimate—that means like uh—sexual right?

45 AUSTIN: Well—yeah—or—

LEE: He's on sexual terms with the prairie? How dya' figure that?

AUSTIN: Well it doesn't necessarily have to mean sexual.

LEE: What's it mean then?

AUSTIN: It means uh—close—personal—

50 LEE: All right. How's it sound? Put it into the uh—the line
there. Read it back. Let's see how it sounds. (to himself) "Intimate terms."

AUSTIN: (scribbles in notebook) Okay. It'd go something like this:
(reads) "I told ya' you were a fool to follow me in here. I'm on
55 intimate terms with this prairie."

LEE: That's good. I like that. That's real good.

AUSTIN: You do?

LEE: Yeah. Don't you?

AUSTIN: Sure.

60 LEE: Sounds original now. "Intimate terms." That's good. Okay.
Now we're cookin! That has a real ring to it.

(AUSTIN makes more notes, LEE walks around, pours beer on his
arms and rubs it over his chest feeling good about the new progress, as he does this MOM enters unobtrusively down left with her
luggage, she stops and stares at the scene still holding luggage as
the two men continue, unaware of her presence, AUSTIN absorbed in his writing, LEE cooling himself off with beer)

LEE: (continues) "He's on intimate terms with this prairie."
Sounds real mysterious and kinda' threatening at the same
time.

65 AUSTIN: (writing rapidly) Good.

LEE: Now—(LEE turns and suddenly sees MOM, he stares at her
for a while, she stares back, AUSTIN keeps writing feverishly,
not noticing, LEE walks slowly over to MOM and takes a closer
look, long pause)

70 LEE: Mom?

(AUSTIN looks up suddenly from his writing, sees MOM, stands
quickly, long pause, MOM surveys the damage)

AUSTIN: Mom. What're you doing back?

MOM: I'm back.

LEE: Here, lemme take those for ya.

(LEE sets beer on counter then takes both her bags but doesn't
know where to set them down in the sea of junk so he just keeps
holding them)

AUSTIN: I wasn't expecting you back so soon. I thought uh—
How was Alaska?   75

MOM: Fine.

LEE: See any igloos?

MOM: No. Just glaciers.

AUSTIN: Cold huh?

MOM: What?   80

AUSTIN: It must've been cold up there?

MOM: Not really.

LEE: Musta' been colder than this here. I mean we're havin' a
real scorcher here.

MOM: Oh? (she looks at damage)   85

LEE: Yeah. Must be in the hundreds.

AUSTIN: You wanna' take your coat off, Mom?

MOM: No. (pause, she surveys space) What happened in here?

AUSTIN: Oh um—Me and Lee were just sort of celebrating and
uh—   90

MOM: Celebrating?

AUSTIN: Yeah. Uh—Lee sold a screenplay. A story, I mean.

MOM: Lee did?

AUSTIN: Yeah.

MOM: Not you?   95

AUSTIN: No. Him.

MOM: (to LEE) You sold a screenplay?

LEE: Yeah. That's right. We're just sorta' finishing it up right
now. That's what we're doing here.

AUSTIN: Me and Lee are going out to the desert to live.   100

MOM: You and Lee?

AUSTIN: Yeah. I'm taking off with Lee.

MOM: (she looks back and forth at each of them, pause) You
gonna go live with your father?

AUSTIN: No. We're going to a different desert Mom.   105

MOM: I see. Well, you'll probably wind up on the same desert
sooner or later. What're all these toasters doing here?

AUSTIN: Well—we had kind of a contest.

MOM: Contest?

LEE: Yeah.   110

AUSTIN: Lee won.

MOM: Did you win a lot of money, Lee?

LEE: Well not yet. It's comin' in any day now.

MOM: (to LEE) What happened to your shirt?

LEE: Oh. I was sweatin' like a pig and I took it off.   115

(AUSTIN grabs LEE's shirt off the table and tosses it to him, LEE
sets down suitcases and puts his shirt on)

MOM: Well it's one hell of a mess in here isn't it?

AUSTIN: Yeah, I'll clean it up for you, Mom. I just didn't know
you were coming back so soon.

MOM: I didn't either.

AUSTIN: What happened?   120

MOM: Nothing. I just started missing all my plants.

(she notices dead plants)

AUSTIN: Oh.

MOM: Oh, they're all dead aren't they. (she crosses toward them,
examines them closely) You didn't get a chance to water I guess.

AUSTIN: I was doing it and then Lee came and—   125

LEE: Yeah I just distracted him a whole lot here, Mom. It's not his fault.

(pause, as MOM stares at plants)

MOM: Oh well, one less thing to take care of I guess. (turns toward brothers) Oh, that reminds me — You boys will proba-
130   bly never guess who's in town. Try and guess.

(long pause, brothers stare at her)

AUSTIN: Whadya' mean, Mom?
MOM: Take a guess. Somebody very important has come to town. I read it, coming down on the Greyhound.
LEE: Somebody very important?
135   MOM: See if you can guess. You'll never guess.
AUSTIN: Mom — we're trying to uh — (points to writing pad)
MOM: Picasso. (pause) Picasso's in town. Isn't that incredible? Right now.

(pause)

AUSTIN: Picasso's dead, Mom.
140   MOM: No, he's not dead. He's visiting the museum. I read it on the bus. We have to go down there and see him.
AUSTIN: Mom —
MOM: This is the chance of a lifetime. Can you imagine? We could all go down and meet him. All three of us.
145   LEE: Uh — I don't think I'm really up fer meetin' anybody right now. I'm uh — What's his name?
MOM: Picasso! Picasso! You've never heard of Picasso? Austin, you've heard of Picasso.
AUSTIN: Mom, we're not going to have time.
150   MOM: It won't take long. We'll just hop in the car and go down there. An opportunity like this doesn't come along every day.
AUSTIN: We're gonna' be leavin' here, Mom!

(pause)

MOM: Oh.
LEE: Yeah.

(pause)

155   MOM: You're both leaving?
LEE: (looks at AUSTIN) Well we were thinkin' about that before but now I —
AUSTIN: No, we are! We're both leaving. We've got it all planned.
MOM: (to AUSTIN) Well you can't leave. You have a family.
160   AUSTIN: I'm leaving. I'm getting out of here.
LEE: (to MOM) I don't really think Austin's cut out for the desert do you?
MOM: No. He's not.
AUSTIN: I'm going with you, Lee!
165   MOM: He's too thin.
LEE: Yeah, he'd just burn up out there.
AUSTIN: (to LEE) We just gotta' finish this screenplay and then we're gonna' take off. That's the plan. That's what you said. Come on, let's get back to work, Lee.
170   LEE: I can't work under these conditions here. It's too hot.
AUSTIN: Then we'll do it on the desert.
LEE: Don't be tellin' me what we're gonna' do!
MOM: Don't shout in the house.
LEE: We're just gonna' have to postpone the whole deal.
175   AUSTIN: I can't postpone it! It's gone past postponing! I'm doing everything you said. I'm writing down exactly what you tell me.

LEE: Yeah, but you were right all along see. It is a dumb story. "Two lamebrains chasin' each other across Texas." That's what you said, right?
AUSTIN: I never said that.   180

(LEE sneers in AUSTIN's face then turns to MOM)

LEE: I'm gonna' just borrow some a' your antiques, Mom. You don't mind do ya'? Just a few plates and things. Silverware.

(LEE starts going through all the cupboards in kitchen pulling out plates and stacking them on counter as MOM and AUSTIN watch)

MOM: You don't have any utensils on the desert?
LEE: Nah, I'm fresh out.
AUSTIN: (to LEE) What're you doing?   185
MOM: Well some of those are very old. Bone China.
LEE: I'm tired of eatin' outa' my bare hands, ya' know. It's not civilized.
AUSTIN: (to LEE) What're you doing? We made a deal!
MOM: Couldn't you borrow the plastic ones instead? I have   190
plenty of plastic ones.
LEE: (as he stacks plates) It's not the same. Plastic's not the same at all. What I need is somethin' authentic. Somethin' to keep me in touch. It's easy to get outa' touch out there. Don't worry I'll get 'em back to ya'.   195

(AUSTIN rushes up to LEE, grabs him by shoulders)

AUSTIN: You can't just drop the whole thing, Lee!

(LEE turns, pushes AUSTIN in the chest knocking him backwards into the alcove, MOM watches numbly, LEE returns to collecting the plates, silverware, etc.)

MOM: You boys shouldn't fight in the house. Go outside and fight.
LEE: I'm not fightin'. I'm leavin'.
MOM: There's been enough damage done already.
LEE: (his back to AUSTIN and MOM, stacking dishes on counter) 200
I'm clearin' outa' here once and for all. All this town does is drive a man insane. Look what it's done to Austin there. I'm not lettin' that happen to me. Sell myself down the river. No sir. I'd rather be a hundred miles from nowhere than let that happen to me.   205

(during this AUSTIN has picked up the ripped-out phone from the floor and wrapped the cord tightly around both his hands, he lunges at LEE whose back is still to him, wraps the cord around LEE's neck, plants a foot in LEE's back and pulls back on the cord, tightening it, LEE chokes desperately, can't speak and can't reach AUSTIN with his arms, AUSTIN keeps applying pressure on LEE's back with his foot, bending him into the sink, MOM watches)

AUSTIN: (tightening cord) You're not goin' anywhere! You're not takin' anything with you. You're not takin' my car! You're not takin' the dishes! You're not takin' anything! You're stayin' right here!
MOM: You'll have to stop fighting in the house. There's plenty of 210
room outside to fight. You've got the whole outdoors to fight in.

(LEE tries to tear himself away, he crashes across the stage like an enraged bull dragging AUSTIN with him, he snorts and bellows but AUSTIN hangs on and manages to keep clear of LEE's at-tempts to grab him, they crash into the table, to the floor, LEE is *face down thrashing wildly and choking,* AUSTIN *pulls cord tighter, stands with one foot planted on* LEE*'s back and the cord stretched taut)*

AUSTIN: *(holding cord)* Gimme back my keys, Lee! Take the keys out! Take 'em out!

*(*LEE *desperately tries to dig in his pockets, searching for the car keys,* MOM *moves closer)*

MOM: *(calmly to* AUSTIN*)* You're not killing him are you?

215 AUSTIN: I don't know. I don't know if I'm killing him. I'm stopping him. That's all. I'm just stopping him.

*(*LEE *thrashes but* AUSTIN *is relentless)*

MOM: You oughta' let him breathe a little bit.
AUSTIN: Throw the keys out, Lee!

*(*LEE *finally gets keys out and throws them on floor but out of* AUSTIN*'s reach,* AUSTIN *keeps pressure on cord, pulling* LEE*'s neck back,* LEE *gets one hand to the cord but can't relieve the pressure)*

Reach me those keys would ya', Mom.
220 MOM: *(not moving)* Why are you doing this to him?
AUSTIN: Reach me the keys!
MOM: Not until you stop choking him.
AUSTIN: I can't stop choking him! He'll kill me if I stop choking him!
225 MOM: He won't kill you. He's your brother.
AUSTIN: Just get me the keys would ya'!

(pause. MOM *picks keys up off floor, hands them to* AUSTIN*)*

AUSTIN: *(to* MOM*)* Thanks.
MOM: Will you let him go now?
AUSTIN: I don't know. He's not gonna' let me get outa' here.
230 MOM: Well you can't kill him.
AUSTIN: I can kill him! I can easily kill him. Right now. Right here. All I gotta' do is just tighten up. See? *(he tightens cord,* LEE *thrashes wildly.* AUSTIN *releases pressure a little, maintaining control)* Ya' see that?
235 MOM: That's a savage thing to do.
AUSTIN: Yeah well don't tell me I can't kill him because I can. I can just twist. I can just keep twisting. *(*AUSTIN *twists the cord tighter,* LEE *weakens, his breathing changes to a short rasp)*
MOM: Austin!

*(*AUSTIN *relieves pressure,* LEE *breathes easier but* AUSTIN *keeps him under control)*

240 AUSTIN: *(eyes on* LEE*, holding cord)* I'm goin' to the desert. There's nothing stopping me. I'm going by myself to the desert.

*(*MOM *moving toward her luggage)*

MOM: Well, I'm going to go check into a motel. I can't stand this anymore.
AUSTIN: Don't go yet!   245

*(*MOM *pauses)*

MOM: I can't stay here. This is worse than being homeless.
AUSTIN: I'll get everything fixed up for you, Mom. I promise. Just stay for a while.
MOM: *(picking up luggage)* You're going to the desert.
AUSTIN: Just wait!   250

*(*LEE *thrashes,* AUSTIN *subdues him,* MOM *watches holding luggage, pause)*

MOM: It was the worst feeling being up there. In Alaska. Staring out a window. I never felt so desperate before. That's why when I saw that article on Picasso I thought—
AUSTIN: Stay here, Mom. This is where you live.

(she looks around the stage)

MOM: I don't recognize it at all.   255

(she exits with luggage, AUSTIN *makes a move toward her but* LEE *starts to struggle and* AUSTIN *subdues him again with cord, pause)*

AUSTIN: *(holding cord)* Lee? I'll make ya' a deal. You let me get outa' here. Just let me get to my car. All right, Lee? Gimme a little headstart and I'll turn you loose. Just gimme a little headstart. All right?

*(*LEE *makes no response,* AUSTIN *slowly releases tension cord, still nothing from* LEE*)*

AUSTIN: Lee?   260

*(*LEE *is motionless,* AUSTIN *very slowly begins to stand, still keeping a tenuous hold on the cord and his eyes riveted to* LEE *for any sign of movement,* AUSTIN *slowly drops the cord and stands, he stares down at* LEE *who appears to be dead)*

AUSTIN: *(whispers)* Lee?

(pause, AUSTIN *considers, looks toward exit, back to* LEE*, then makes a small movement as if to leave. Instantly* LEE *is on his feet and moves toward exit, blocking* AUSTIN*'s escape. They square off to each other, keeping a distance between them. Pause, a single coyote heard in distance, lights fade softly into moonlight, the figures of the brothers now appear to be caught in a vast desert-like landscape, they are very still but watchful for the next move, lights go slowly to black as the after-image of the brothers pulses in the dark, coyote fades)*

ARTHUR MILLER WROTE *this essay for the* New York Times *shortly after the opening of* Death of a Salesman. *In the essay, Miller develops a reading of the tragic hero that both contests and modifies Aristotle's description of the form and style of tragic drama. He also identifies his own presiding interests in the dynamics of tragic character.*

ARTHUR MILLER,
"Tragedy and the Common Man"
(1949)

In this age few tragedies are written. It has often been held that the lack is due to a paucity of heroes among us, or else that modern man has had the blood drawn out of his organs of belief by the skepticism of science, and the heroic attack on life cannot feed on an attitude of reserve and circumspection. For one reason or another, we are often held to be below tragedy — or tragedy above us. The inevitable conclusion is, of course, that the tragic mode is archaic, fit only for the very highly placed, the kings or the kingly, and where this admission is not made in so many words it is most often implied.

I believe that the common man is as apt a subject for tragedy in its highest sense as kings were. On the face of it this ought to be obvious in the light of modern psychiatry, which bases its analysis upon classic formulations, such as the Oedipus and Orestes complexes, for instances, which were enacted by royal beings, but which apply to everyone in similar emotional situations.

More simply, when the question of tragedy in art is not at issue, we never hesitate to attribute to the well-placed and the exalted the very same mental processes as the lowly. And finally, if the exaltation of tragic action were truly a property of the high-bred character alone, it is inconceivable that the mass of mankind should cherish tragedy above all other forms, let alone be capable of understanding it.

As a general rule, to which there may be exceptions unknown to me, I think the tragic feeling is evoked in us when we are in the presence of a character who is ready to lay down his life, if need be, to secure one thing — his sense of personal dignity. From Orestes to Hamlet, Medea to Macbeth, the underlying struggle is that of the individual attempting to gain his "rightful" position in his society.

Sometimes he is one who has been displaced from it, sometimes one who seeks to attain it for the first time, but the fateful wound from which the inevitable events spiral is the wound of indignity, and its dominant force is indignation. Tragedy, then, is the consequence of a man's total compulsion to evaluate himself justly.

In the sense of having been initiated by the hero himself, the tale always reveals what has been called his "tragic flaw," a failing that is not peculiar to grand or elevated characters. Nor is it necessarily a weakness. The flaw, or crack in the character, is really nothing — and need be nothing — but his inherent unwillingness to remain passive in the face of what he conceives to be a challenge to his dignity, his image of his rightful status. Only the passive, only those who accept their lot without active retaliation, are "flawless." Most of us are in that category.

But there are among us today, as there always have been, those who act against the scheme of things that degrades them, and in the process of action everything we have accepted out of fear or insensitivity or ignorance is shaken before us and examined, and from this total onslaught by an individual against the seemingly stable cosmos surrounding us — from this total examination of the "unchangeable" environment — comes the terror and the fear that is classically associated with tragedy.

More important, from this total questioning of what has previously been unquestioned, we learn. And such a process is not beyond the common man. In revolutions around the world, these past thirty years, he has demonstrated again and again this inner dynamic of all tragedy.

Insistence upon the rank of the tragic hero, or the so-called nobility of his character, is really but a clinging to the outward forms of tragedy. If rank or nobility of character was indispensable, then it would follow that the problems of those with rank were the particular problems of tragedy. But surely the right of one monarch to capture the domain from another no longer raises our passions, nor are our concepts of justice what they were to the mind of an Elizabethan king.

The quality in such plays that does shake us, however, derives from the underlying fear of being displaced, the disaster inherent in being torn away from our chosen image of what and who we are in this world. Among us today this fear is as strong, and perhaps stronger, than it ever was. In fact, it is the common man who knows this fear best.

Now, if it is true that tragedy is the consequence of a man's total compulsion to evaluate himself justly, his destruction in the attempt posits a wrong or an evil in his environment. And this is precisely the morality of tragedy and its lesson. The discovery of the moral law, which is what the enlightenment of tragedy consists of, is not the discovery of some abstract or metaphysical quantity.

The tragic right is a condition of life, a condition in which the human personality is able to flower and realize itself. The wrong is the condition which suppresses man, perverts the flowing out of his love and creative instinct. Tragedy enlightens — and it must, in that it points the heroic finger at the enemy of man's freedom. The thrust for freedom is the quality in tragedy which exalts. The revolutionary questioning of the stable environment is what terrifies. In no way is the common man debarred from such thoughts or such actions.

Seen in this light, our lack of tragedy may be partially accounted for by the turn which modern literature has taken toward the purely psychiatric view of life, or the purely sociological. If all our miseries, our indignities, are born and bred within our minds, then all action, let alone the heroic action, is obviously impossible.

And if society alone is responsible for the cramping of our lives, then the protagonist must needs be so pure and faultless as to force us to deny his validity as a character. From neither of these views can tragedy derive, simply because neither represents a balanced concept of life. Above all else, tragedy requires the finest appreciation by the writer of cause and effect.

No tragedy can therefore come about when its author fears to question absolutely everything, when he regards any institution, habit or custom as being either everlasting, immutable or inevitable. In the tragic view the need of man to wholly realize himself is the only fixed star, and whatever it is that hedges his nature and lowers it is ripe for attack and examination. Which is not to say that tragedy must preach revolution.

The Greeks could probe the very heavenly origin of their ways and return to confirm the rightness of laws. And Job could face God in anger, demanding his right and end in submission. But for a moment everything is in suspension, nothing is accepted, and in this stretching and tearing apart of the cosmos, in the very action of so doing, the character gains "size," the tragic stature which is spuriously attached to the royal or the highborn in our minds. The commonest of men may take on that stature to the extent of his willingness to throw all he has into the contest, the battle to secure his rightful place in his world.

There is a misconception of tragedy with which I have been struck in review after review, and in many conversations with writers and readers alike. It is the idea that tragedy is of necessity allied to pessimism. Even the dictionary says nothing more about the word than that it means a story with a sad or unhappy ending. This impression is so firmly fixed that I almost hesitate to claim that in truth tragedy implies more optimism in its author than does comedy, and that its final result ought to be the reinforcement of the onlooker's brightest opinions of the human animal.

For, if it is true to say that in essence the tragic hero is intent upon claiming his whole due as a personality, and if this struggle must be total and without reservation, then it automatically demonstrates the indestructible will of man to achieve his humanity.

The possibility of victory must be there in tragedy. Where pathos rules, where pathos is finally derived, a character has fought a battle he could not possibly have won. The pathetic is achieved when the protagonist is, by virtue of his witlessness, his insensitivity or the very air he gives off, incapable of grappling with a much superior force.

Pathos truly is the mode for the pessimist. But tragedy requires a nicer balance between what is possible and what is impossible. And it is curious, although edifying, that the plays we revere, century after century, are the tragedies. In them, and in them alone, lies the belief — optimistic, if you will, in the perfectibility of man.

It is time, I think, that we who are without kings, took up this bright thread of our history and followed it to the only place it can possibly lead in our time — the heart and spirit of the average man.

GEORGE STEINER HAS WRITTEN WIDELY ON LITERATURE AND CULTURE IN BOOKS LIKE LANGUAGE and Silence *(1967),* Antigones *(1984), and many others. In* The Death of Tragedy, *Steiner argues that the essential experience of tragedy can come about only when the drama and its audience share a common culture and a common set of values. Given the fragmentation of modern culture and society, Steiner seems skeptical about the possibility of an authentic tragic drama on the modern stage.*

GEORGE STEINER

FROM
The Death of Tragedy
(1961)

. . . As we have seen, the decline of tragedy is inseparably related to the decline of the organic world view and of its attendant context of mythological, symbolic, and ritual reference. It was on this context that Greek drama was founded, and the Elizabethans were still able to give it imaginative adherence. This ordered and stylized vision of life, with its bent toward allegory and emblematic action, was already in decline at the time of Racine. But by strenuous observance of neo-classic conventions, Racine succeeded in giving to the old mythology, now emptied of belief, the vitality of living form. His was a brilliant rear-guard action. But after Racine the ancient habits of awareness and immediate recognition which gave to tragic drama its frame of reference were no longer prevalent. Ibsen, therefore, faced a real vacuum. He had to create for his plays a context of ideological meaning (an effective mythology), and he had to devise the symbols and theatrical conventions whereby to communicate his meaning to an audience corrupted by the easy virtues of the realistic stage. He was in the position of a writer who invents a new language and must then teach it to his readers.

Being a consummate fighter, Ibsen turned his deprivations to advantage. He made the precariousness of modern beliefs and the absence of an imaginative world order his starting point. Man moves naked in a world bereft of explanatory or conciliating myth. Ibsen's dramas presuppose the withdrawal of God from human affairs, and that withdrawal has left the door open to cold gusts blowing in from a malevolent though inanimate creation. But the most dangerous assaults upon reason and life come not from without, as they do in Greek and Elizabethan tragedy. They arise in the unstable soul. Ibsen proceeds from the modern awareness that there is rivalry and unbalance in the individual psyche. The ghosts that haunt his characters are not the palpable heralds of damnation whom we find in *Hamlet* and *Macbeth*. They are forces of disruption that have broken loose from the core of the spirit. Or, more precisely, they are cancers growing in the soul. In Ibsen's vocabulary, the most deadly of these cancers is "idealism," the mask of hypocrisy and self-deception with which men seek to guard against the realities of social and personal life. When "ideals" seize upon an Ibsen character, they drive him to psychological and material ruin as the Weird Sisters drive Macbeth. Once the mask has grown close to the skin, it can be removed only at suicidal cost. When Rosmer and Rebecca West have attained the ability to confront life, they are on the verge of death. When the mask no longer shields her against the light, Hedda Gabler kills herself.

To articulate this vision of a God-abandoned world and of man's splintered and vulnerable consciousness, Ibsen contrived an astounding series of symbols and figurative gestures. Like most creators of a coherent mythology, moreover, he determined early on his objective incarnations. The meanings assumed by the sea, the fjord, the avalanches, and the spectral bird in *Brand* carry over to Ibsen's very last play, *When We Dead Awaken*. The new church in *Brand* brings on the moment of disaster, as does the new steeple in *The Master Builder*. The white stallion of Peer Gynt foreshadows the ghost-chargers at Rosmersholm. From the start, Ibsen uses certain material objects to concentrate symbolic values (the wild duck, General Gabler's pistols, the flagpole standing in front of the house in *The Lady from the Sea*). And it is the association of an explicit, responsible image of life with the material setting and objects best able to denote and dramatize this image that is the source of Ibsen's power. It allows him to organize his plays into shapes of action richer and more expressive than any the theatre had known since Shakespeare. Consider the stress of dramatic feeling and the complexity of meaning conveyed by the tarantella which Nora dances in *A Doll's House*; by Hedda Gabler's proposal to crown Lövborg with vine leaves; or by the venture into high narrow places that occurs in *Rosmersholm*, *The Master Builder*, and *When We Dead Awaken*. Each is in itself a coherent episode in the play, yet it is at the same time a symbolic act which argues a specific vision of life. Ibsen arrived at this vision, and he devised the stylistic and theatrical means that give it dramatic life. This is his rare achievement.

Ibsen's late plays represent the kind of inward motion that we find also in the late plays of Shakespeare. *Cymbeline*, *The Winter's Tale*, and *The Tempest* retain the conventions of Jacobean tragicomedy. But these conventions act as signposts pointing toward interior meanings. The storms, the music, the allegoric masques have implications which belong less to the common imaginative repertoire than they do to a most private understanding of the world. The current theatrical forms are a mere scaffold to the inner shape. That is exactly the case in *The Master Builder*, *Little Eyolf*, *John Gabriel Borkman*, and *When We Dead Awaken*. These dramas give an appearance of belonging to the realistic tradition and of observing the conventions of the three-walled stage. But, in fact, this is not so. The setting is thinned out so as to become bleakly transparent, and it leads into a strange landscape appropriate to Ibsen's mythology of death and resurrection.

It is in these four plays — and they are among the summits of drama — that Ibsen comes nearest tragedy. But it is tragedy of a peculiar, limited order. These are fables of the dead, set in a cold purgatory. Halvard Solness is dead long before he ascends the tower of his new villa. Allmers and Rita are dead to each other in the suffocation of their marriage. Borkman is an enraged ghost pacing up and down in a coffin that has the semblance of a house. In *When We Dead Awaken*, the purgatorial theme is explicit. In the mad egotism of his art, Rubeck has trampled on the quick of life. He has destroyed Irene by refusing to treat her as a living being. But in such destruction there is always a part of suicide, and the great sculptor — the shaper of life — has withered to a grotesque shadow. Yet there remains a chance of miracle; in sharing mortal danger, the dead may awaken. And so Rubeck and Irene press on, up the storm-swept mountain.

There are in these fierce parables occasional resonances from classic and Shakespearean tragedy. We do, I think, experience a related sense of tragic form when Agamemnon strides across the purple carpet and Solness mounts to his tower. But the focus is utterly different. Ibsen starts where earlier tragedies end, and his plots are epilogues to previous disaster. Suppose Shakespeare had written a play showing Macbeth and Lady Macbeth living out their black lives in exile after they had been defeated by their avenging enemies. We might then have the angle of vision that we find in *John Gabriel Borkman*. These are dramas of afterlife, engaging vivid shadows such as animate the lower regions of the *Purgatorio*. But even in these late works, there is a purpose which goes beyond tragedy. Ibsen is telling us that one need not live in premature burial. He is reading the lesson of meaningful life. The Allmers and the Rubecks of the world can waken from their living death if they establish among themselves relations of honesty and sacrifice. There is a way out, even if it leads up to the glaciers. There is no such way for Agamemnon or Hamlet or Phèdre. In the gloom of the late Ibsen the core of militant hope is intact.

Why is it that this magnificent body of drama has not exercised a greater or more liberating influence on the modern theatre? Such playwrights as Arthur Miller stand toward Ibsen rather as Dryden stood toward Shakespeare. They have observed the technical means of the Ibsen play and adopted some of its conventions and defining gestures. But the rich and complex critique of life implicit in Ibsen, and the transparency of his realistic settings to the light of symbolism, are absent. Where Ibsen has been influential, as in the case of Shaw, it is the programmatic plays that have counted, not the harrowing dramas of his maturity. Why should this be? In part, the answer is that Ibsen did his work too well. Many of the hypocrisies that he strove against have loosened their grip on the mind. Many of the spectres of middle-class oppression have been exorcized. The triumph of the reformer has obscured the greatness of the poet. In part, there is the barrier of language. Those who read Norwegian tell one that Ibsen's mature prose is as tightly wrought in cadence and inner poise as is good verse. As in poetry, moreover, the force and direction of meaning often hinge on the particular inflections and array of sounds. These resist translation. And so there is in the versions of Ibsen's plays available to most readers a prosaic flatness entirely inappropriate to the symbolic design and lyricism of the late dramas. In short, that which translates best in Ibsen is perhaps the least notable. Thus we do not yet have the Ibsen playhouse for which Shaw pleaded at the turn of the century.

If Ibsen falls outside the scope of classic or Shakespearean tragedy, the same is true to an even greater extent of Strindberg and Chekhov.

In the plays of Strindberg we find some of the radical conventions of the late Ibsen, without the sustaining fabric of a responsible vision of life. The symbolism has a wild, arresting brilliance, but there is behind it no controlling mythology. The conception of the world implicit in Strindberg's plays is hysterical and fragmentary. No playwright ever made of so public a form as drama a more private expression. Strindberg's characters are emanations from his own tormented psyche and his harrowed life. Gradually, they lose all connection to a governing centre and are like fragments scattered from some great burst of secret energy. In *The Spook Sonata* and *A Dream Play*, the personages seem to collide at random in a kind of empty space. Hence the conventions of irreality and the allegory of the spectre and the dream. These dramas belong to a theatre of the mind and work inside us like remembered music. But what Strindberg achieved in depth, he lost in theatrical coherence. These ghostplays are shadows of drama.

This queer perspective, as if all things were seen through mist and in broken lines, extends even to the historical plays. Strindberg's treatment of Charles XII diminishes the scale of politics to that of a puppet theatre full of strange, nervous marionettes. It is over the short run that Strindberg succeeds. *Miss Julie* and *Creditors* are masterpieces. The high pitch of feeling and nervous susceptibility on which they rely can be enforced over a single, brief action. Miss Julie's final exit is like the receding terror of a nightmare. We wake from it drugged and appalled. But over the longer or more elaborate course, the tension breaks, and we get the kind of flaccid obscurity that disfigures *To Damascus* and even the finest of Strindberg's surrealistic plays, *The Dance of Death*.

Strindberg is neither in the dominant tradition of the tragic theatre nor does he build forward from Ibsen. He stands with Kleist and Wedekind on that eccentric verge where drama is not primarily an imitation of life, but rather a mirror to the private soul. And the expressive means of his art, influential as they have been on certain experimental movements in modern drama, belong less to the playhouse than they do to the distorting and hallucinatory modes of the film.

In Strindberg's late style, the conflicts of ideology and character from which drama normally proceeds are eroded. Instead, we find the creation of a special mood or atmosphere in which the shape of action becomes fluid and musical. Sometimes, Strindberg uses actual music to establish or modulate the tone of feeling. The theatre of Chekhov always tends toward the condition of music. A Chekhov play is not directed primarily toward a representation of conflict or argument. It seeks to exteriorize, to make sensuously perceptible, certain crises of interior life. The characters move in an atmosphere receptive to the slightest shift in intonation. As if passing through a magnetic field, their every word and gesture provokes a complex disturbance and regrouping of psychological forces. This kind of drama is immensely difficult to produce because the means of realization are very close to music. A Chekhovian dialogue is a musical score set for speaking voice. It alternates between acceleration and retardment. Pitch and timbre are often as meaningful as the explicit sense. The design of the plot, moreover, is polyphonic. Several distinct actions and levels of consciousness are developed at the same time. The characteristic gatherings — the theatrical *soirée* in *The Sea-Gull*, the party at the house of the three sisters, the outing in *The Cherry Orchard* — are ensembles in which the various melodies combine or clash in dissonance. In the second Act of *The Cherry Orchard*, the voices of Madame Ranevsky, Lopakhin, Gayev, Trofimov, and Anya perform a quintet. The melodic lines move in isolation and seeming incongruence. Suddenly a mysterious sound is heard in the evening sky, "the sound of a snapped string." It changes the key of the entire play. The brittle weariness in the different voices now swells to a great sombre chord. "Well, good people, let us go," says Madame Ranevsky, "it's getting dark."

But it is as difficult for the language of criticism to deal with the art of Chekhov as it is for any language to deal with music. All I would stress here is the fact that Chekhov lies outside a consideration of tragedy. He himself insisted that his plays were comedies, and so they are regarded on native ground. It is when travelling west that the wine has darkened. To us, these grave, lyric portrayals of the failure of human beings to master their condition or communicate with each other, convey an unutterable sadness. But perhaps we are reading into them too much lastingness. Chekhov's dramas are rooted in a specific historical circumstance and contain a strong element of political irony and social satire. These bruised, exquisite beings in their genteel poverty are doomed, and their pretensions are ridiculous. The axe must ring out in the cherry orchard if there is to be new life in the world. Lopakhin is a vulgar brute; but vulgarity is health, and it will build houses for the living on the fallow estates of the dead. Chekhov was a physician, and medicine knows grief and even despair in the particular instance, but not tragedy.

Or perhaps one should approach these elusive plays by discarding all traditions of dramatic genre. At the close of the *Symposium*, Socrates compelled his listeners to agree that the genius of comedy was the same as that of tragedy. Being drowsy with wine, they were unable to follow his

argument. One after another, they fell asleep around the master; he alone remained serene and lucid till break of dawn. Even Aristophanes could not stay awake to discover in what manner he might be regarded as a tragedian. Thus the Socratic demonstration of the ultimate unity of tragic and comic drama is forever lost. But the proof is in the art of Chekhov.

RAYMOND WILLIAMS
(1921–1988),

FROM
Modern Tragedy
(1966)

THE BRILLIANT MARXIST CULTURAL CRITIC RAYMOND WILLIAMS HAS WRITTEN EXTENSIVELY ON drama. In Modern Tragedy, *Williams undertakes an indirect reply to George Steiner's* The Death of Tragedy. *Williams invites us to see tragedy not as a universal form or experience, but as something local, an experience that must be discovered and defined anew as the historical circumstances of its surrounding society change. Williams is also the author of several groundbreaking books, including* Culture and Society *(1958),* Drama from Ibsen to Brecht *(1968), and* The Country and the City *(1973).*

We have seen, in our own time, the climax and the decline of liberal tragedy. To understand its structure of feeling is now a central problem. For we are all to some extent still governed by it, even now when we can see that it is failing to hold.

At the centre of liberal tragedy is a single situation: that of a man at the height of his powers and the limits of his strength, at once aspiring and being defeated, releasing and destroyed by his own energies. The structure is liberal in its emphasis on the surpassing individual, and tragic in its ultimate recognition of defeat or the limits of victory. We have known, for nearly four centuries, a tension between this thrust of the individual and an absolute resistance, but the tension has passed through many forms, which we must try to distinguish. What we must trace, finally, is the transformation of the tragic hero into the tragic victim.

Tragedy, for us, has been mainly the conflict between an individual and the forces that destroy him. When any feeling is as strong as this, it can shape the mind so closely that the past itself is absorbed and transmuted, and the art of others lives only in its light. Our reading of Greek tragedy is perhaps the clearest example. Until very recently, against the evidence, we have remade Greek tragic drama in this image of our own: the tragic hero, at the centre of the play, magnificently exposed to a crushing external design. We have tried to take psychology, because that is our science, into the heart of an action to which it can never, critically, be relevant. We have looked for a tragic flaw, capable of starting such an action, in the character of an individual man. Yet it is now becoming clear (at a time, significantly, when our own governing structure of feeling is beginning to disintegrate) that the Greek tragic action was not rooted in individuals, or in individual psychology, in any of our senses. It was rooted in history, and not a human history alone. Its thrust came, not from the personality of an individual but from a man's inheritance and relationships, within a world that ultimately transcended him. What we then see is a general action specified, not an individual action generalised. What we learn is not character but the mutability of the world. Human life as such, always and everywhere, is subject to these exigencies. The exemplary case, reminding us, relieving this knowledge, brings pity and fear, in the general human condition.

It is said that Christianity altered this view of the world, putting a new emphasis on the individual. But this seems doubtful, especially in its assumption of a single Christian tradition. There is no important tragedy, within the Christian world, until there is also humanism and indeed individualism. In our own literature, there is no important tragedy before the release of personal energy, the emphasis of personal destiny, which we can see, looking back, in the complex process of Renaissance and Reformation. By the time of Marlowe and Shakespeare, the structure we now know was being actively shaped: an individual man, from his own aspirations, from his own nature, set out on an action that led him to tragedy.

We are bound to recognise this new spirit, even when we have properly remembered how strong a hold a different and traditional interpretation of life still had. Certainly we cannot understand Elizabethan tragedy if we fail to notice the elements that persisted from a mediaeval view of the world. The old conceptions of order and hierarchy, the intricate connections between man and nature, are there not only in active speech but in some of the essential conventions of the dramatic form. It is comparatively easy to demonstrate such continuities, in particular the continuation of the morality tradition, with all this implied for the relationship between individual and type and a common condition. But the continuities were within a very active process of change. We have only to go back a hundred years from Marlowe, to the morality *Everyman*, to see what these fundamental ideas and conventions produced on their own. Death comes to Everyman, in the midst of life, and of course is feared; the attempt made to avert it. But the action, confidently, takes Everyman forward to the edge of that dark room in which he must disappear, and the most remarkable aspect of this confidence is that physically, on a scaffold above the dark room, God himself is waiting for Everyman to come. The hesitation in entering is still strong; the room itself can not be seen into. But to pass through it is not only inevitable; it is also the only way in which Everyman can come to his Father. While that dimension holds, there is aversion and fear, but the later tragic voice cannot come. When it does come, it is unmistakeable: a man alone in his extremity. It is not only, dramatically, that God has gone from the scaffold. It is also that life, before this extremity, is quite differently experienced. Where there had been, in *Everyman*, a gathering of life into common and formal categories, there is now a particularity, a momentariness, an active awareness of process. Much of the new drama, even when its reference points are familiar categories, takes its most active life from a consciousness of the self in a passing moment of experience: a self-consciousness which is now in itself dramatic, and which new dramatic resources are employed to express. The common process of life is seen at its most intense in an individual experience.

The action changes accordingly. Again and again it is rooted in the nature of a particular man. It is true that this man, this hero, ends by finding his limits: tragic limits, including the absolute limit of death. But it is also true that again and again, if not invariably, he has *reached* for these limits: set his whole energy on an aspiring course which yet finally reveals them. Much of the extraordinary richness of this drama, beyond its incomparable celebration of the particularity of life, is precisely in the discovery and exploration of these limits, which can never be only death. Here, indeed, the persistence of orders and hierarchies, the familiar categories of man, exerts its necessary pressures. There is confusion, an exciting confusion, as the pressures are taken and tested, in the living act.

But the limits men reach, in their challenge to order, are not only of this kind. There are also new limits, within man himself. Order can break there, within the personality, as decisively and as tragically. Breakdown and madness, as private experiences, are quite newly realised and explored. The emphasis, as we take the full weight, is not on the naming of limits, but on their intense and confused discovery and exploration. The traditional categories are affirmed, but everything is questioned, in an outburst of energy so great that it seems, at times, to be shaking the whole body of man to pieces. Here, decisively, is one of the origins of the structure of feeling we are tracing: the thrust of living energy, in individual men, against limits which had once been composed into a confident order but which now, though still present and active, are questioned, fragmented, newly known and named, and are also confused by new experiences, new sources, of tragedy. The tragic voice, of our own immediate tradition, is then first heard: the aspiration for a meaning, at the very limits of a man's strength; the known meanings and answers, affirmed and yet also questioned, broken down, by contradictory experience.

The most important persistence, for the subsequent history of drama, was that of a public order, at the centre of what is otherwise personal tragedy. The hero is still, normally, the man of rank, the prince. An order can rise or fall with him, be affirmed or broken by him, even when what is driving him is a personal energy. The tragic hero is still marked by a social status, which defines his general importance, even when, in this new exploration of life, the hero becomes other than his status, or at least can be otherwise seen. Where in Greek tragedy the hero's status, with all it implied of inheritance, kinship and duty, enclosed the personality, which was developed only so far as the general action required, we find now, in Elizabethan tragedy, a personality within and beyond the similarly defining status, and the conflict that can result from this coexistence is often one of the sources of the tragedy. Thus the tension of the general action, between the exploring energies of life and all that is known of order, is repeated in the hero himself, between the individual man and the social role. In these tensions, this particular tragedy was formed.

At this stage of development, we can properly speak of humanist tragedy, but not yet, in a precise way, of liberal tragedy. The next stage was indeed a collapse of the tensions which had produced this remarkable drama. In the early eighteenth century, a determined attempt was made in England to adapt tragedy to the habits of thinking of middle-class life. This necessary and understandable attempt

had little immediate success, though the imitation of its example in France and Germany provided one of the elements for the emergence of serious modern tragedy. It is easy, looking back, to fix attention on the change most often discussed: that of the status of the hero.

> Stripp'd of Regal Pomp, and glaring Show
> His Muse reports a tale of Private Woe
> Works up Distress from Common Scenes in Life
> A Treach'rous Brother, and an Injur'd Wife.

But something else is happening, beyond the change of rank:

> Long has the Fate of Kings and Empires been
> The common business of the Tragick Scene,
> As if Misfortune made the Throne her Seat,
> And none could be unhappy but the Great . . .
> Stories like this with Wonder we may hear,
> But far remote, and in a higher Sphere,
> We ne'er can pity what we ne'er can share.

Or again:

> The Tragic Muse, sublime, delights to show
> Princes distrest and scenes of royal woe;
> In awful pomp, majestic, to relate
> The fall of nations or some hero's fate:
> That sceptered chiefs may by example know
> The strange vicissitude of things below;
> What dangers on security attend,
> How pride and cruelty in ruin end;
> Hence Providence supreme to know, and own
> Humanity adds glory to a throne.
> In ev'ry former age and foreign tongue
> With native grandeur thus the goddess sung.
> Upon our stage indeed with wished success
> You've sometimes seen her in a humbler dress . . .
> The brilliant drops that fall from each bright eye
> The absent pomp with brighter gems supply.
> Forgive us then, if we attempt to show,
> In artless strains, a tale of private woe,
> A London 'prentice ruined, is our theme . . .

And finally:

> From lower Life we draw our Scene's Distress:
> —Let not your Equals move your Pity less.

What we notice here is the new and single emphasis on pity: pity as sympathy. This is the mark of a growing humanitarianism, at least as aspiration. But what is then interesting is the contrast of pity with pomp, and the extent to which previous tragedy is interpreted as if rank as such were the decisive factor. It was inevitable, of course, in an age of bourgeois revolutions, that feudal and post-feudal connections between princely power and the order of the universe should be rejected. But what happens in practice, in this rejection, is an evident loss of dimension, which we can define as the loss of human connection at anything more than a private level. Humanitarianism, as an ideology, is the exact expression of this reduction. It expresses sympathy and pity between private persons, but tacitly excludes any positive conception of society, and thence any clear view of order or justice.

It is of course easy to blame the bourgeois for this, as so many historians of the drama have done. But simple blame conveniently omits the actual intermediate stage, in which the feudal order, as expressed in drama, collapsed from within. The vigorous exploration of the tensions between individuality and order had in fact ended abruptly in the early seventeenth century, so far as the drama was concerned. The decisive social challenge of the English Revolution might have produced new kinds of drama, but did not; the Puritan distrust of the drama was probably decisive. What in fact happened was a separation of drama from the mainstream of the society, and the reduction of the great tensions of Elizabethan tragedy to 'pomp' and 'show' took place within the continuing minority drama itself. The energy of the hero, reaching out to the human limits, was conventionalised and frozen into the fixed postures of 'heroic tragedy'. Pope might describe Addison's Cato as

> A brave man struggling in the storms of fate,
> And greatly falling with a falling State

but the truer description, of what had become tragedy, is Cotes's:

> What pen but yours could draw the doubtful strife
> Of honour struggling with the love of life?

The conflict of fixed and formal passions with the fixed and formal duties of rank and honour had decisively replaced the earlier and more creative tensions. When the bourgeois tragedians rejected 'pomp' they were hitting an already empty shell.

Rank, that is to say, became class, and once it did so a new definition of tragedy was inevitable. Rank implied order and connection; class was only separation, within an amorphous society. The attempt at human connection was then necessarily a matter of humanitarian sympathy, in 'private woe' and 'private distress'. The growth of active pity was accompanied by a belief in what was called redemption: in fact, repentance and the change of heart. It is not only that this structure of feeling made the writing of tragedy difficult; such a loss would be small, if the structure really held. Nor is it only that the attempt to combine disparate structures produced a sentimental tragedy, which is now valueless. The important loss is one of dimension and reference. There is an evident gap between private sympathy and the public order. The bourgeois tragedians, moved by pity and sympathy, and struggling for realism, were in fact betrayed by this gap, where no realism was possible. For the sources of tragedy were not, even in their experience, *only* private. The best known play of the period, Lillo's *The London Merchant*, is even explicitly social. And what we must then notice is that pity and sympathy have little chance, except as gestures, against the actual and affirmed imperatives of the new society. Where property is in question, as in this story of the thieving apprentice, the judgement is sharp and certain. Thieving is connected with murder as systematically, and as mystically, as once rebellion with disturbing the universe. Then the gallows is erected, with its own kind of inevitability, and the humanitarian feelings of pity and sympathy have to stand in its shadow. Distress accompanies execution, and humanitarianism is at its limits.

What we then see, behind the loss of dimension, is a complacent affirmation of the existing social framework. Crime does not pay, and crime is about property. The arbitrariness of power had been experienced in the blood; its pretensions could be dismissed as pomp. But the arbitrariness of property is a human datum, which the bourgeois tragedians lack the nerve to test. Obliquely, confusedly, the recognition is made, that the struggle for money has replaced the struggle for power as a human motive and as a tragic motive. The disruption of the family by greed for money is obliquely present in Lillo's *Fatal Curiosity*. But the imperative is not seriously questioned, and certainly cannot be connected with the whole body of human desire. Bourgeois tragedy has been blamed for being too social, for excluding the universal reference of Renaissance and humanist tragedy. Another way of putting the matter is that it is not social enough, for with its private ethic of pity and sympathy it could not negotiate the real contradictions of its own time, between human desire and the now social limits set on it. Through its double voice, of pity and certainty, we hear the first weak accents of man the victim: the old far-reaching heroism gone, the limits known but not named. When at last, in fact, the limits were known and named, as a false society, the hero could re-emerge, as a rebel against it. But this, effectively, was still a century ahead, in the period of liberal tragedy.

Bourgeois tragedy, as a creative force, faded quickly, in its original forms. In a sense it went underground, was driven there by its own contradictions. The exploring energy re-emerged, in strange ways, in Romantic tragedy. What is quite evident, through all the failures of Romantic drama, is a renewal and a renewed assertion of individual energy. The desires of man are again intense and imperative; they reach out and test the universe itself. Society is identified as convention,

and convention as the enemy of desire. The individual rebellion is humanist, at a conscious level. Prometheus and Faust, characteristically, are its heroes. But the condition of desire, unconsciously, is that it is always forbidden. What then happens is that the forms of desire become devious and often perverse, and what looks like revolt is more properly a desperate defiance of heaven and hell. There is a related preoccupation with remorse: deep, pervasive, and beyond all its nominal causes. For in Romantic tragedy man is guilty of the ultimate and nameless crime of being himself.

The impossibility of finding a home in the world, the condemnation to a guilty wandering, the dissolution of self and others in a desire that is beyond all relationships: these Romantic themes are an important source of nearly all modern tragedy. Aspiration is absolute, but occurs, paradoxically, within a situation of man on the run from himself. Within this paradox, one dramatist of genius was eventually to work. But also, by the time of Ibsen's maturity, the last source of liberal tragedy had appeared: the increasingly confident identification of a false society as man's real enemy; the naming, in social terms, of the formerly nameless alienation. This body of social thinking had many kinds of influence. In one direction, it led to the denial of tragedy. Man had not only made but could remake himself. The Romantic desire for redemption and regeneration was given, in this tendency, a more or less precise social definition: when man was at the limits which ordinarily produced tragedy he became conscious of their nature and could begin to abolish them. When this abolition was seen as a social process, it did not, at least in the nineteenth century, lead to tragedy at all. The idea of tragedy, indeed, was dismissed as mystification and fatalism: an irony that still haunts us now that collective tragedy, and the tragic society, have been widely and deeply experienced. But this was not, in any case, the liberal path. What emerged there, as a controlling image, was not revolution, but the individual liberator. Acting on his own, and for his own reasons, a single man could change the human limits and transform his world. Looking back to Romantic tragedy, and forward to existentialist tragedy, this conception was still in its purest form in the late nineteenth century. By an act of choice, by an act of will, the individual refused the role of victim and became a new kind of hero. The heroism was not in the nobility of suffering, as the limits were reached. It was now, unambiguously, in the aspiration itself. What was demanded was self-fulfilment, and any such process was a general liberation. The singular man, as a matter of speech, became plural and capital: Man.

Liberal tragedy, at its full development, drew from all the sources that have been named, but in a new form and pressure created a new and specific structure of feeling. It is important, at this stage, not to try to fragment it, when it appears in Ibsen. The humanist exploration of the unknown reaches of life; the bourgeois preoccupation with humanitarianism and with money; the romantic intensities of alienation, remorse and perverted desire; the social recognition of dead institutions and limiting beliefs: all these are present in Ibsen, but in active combination, not as separate influences. To try to resolve his work into one of these lines has been a common practice in criticism: Ibsen the social critic; Ibsen the romantic or existentialist: each has been plausibly presented. But the real interest lies, where the work lies, in the struggle of these forces and in their composition into a particular drama.

Ibsen creates again and again in his plays, with an extraordinary richness of detail, false relationships, a false society, a false condition of man. The marks along this scale are often difficult to discern. The immediate lie is almost always present, but there is great variation in its ultimate reference: sometimes to an alterable condition; sometimes to an absolute condition; often, ambiguously, between these. Yet the generalising reference, in whatever kind, is persistent; the lie is never merely local, for it is seen as a symptom of a general condition. Characteristically, for liberal tragedy, the fight against the lie is individual; a man fights for his own life. Brand's vocation is 'All or Nothing', and compromise is personally impossible:

> One thing is yours you may not spend,
> Your very inmost self of all,
> You may not bind it, may not bend,
> Nor stem the river of your call.

Or again:

> Self completely to fulfil,
> That's a valid right of man,
> And no more than that I will.

At the same time, the 'right' is also the 'call':

> A great one gave me charge. I *must*.

The call to wholeness is seen as self-fulfilment, and yet also as necessary. The right and the duty coincide in self-fulfilment, as in the classic liberal statements.

Yet the whole point about self-fulfilment is that it challenges, to the death, the existing compromise order. For here the lie is actual: men are afraid of wholeness and of self-fulfilment. As the Provost argues:

> The surest way to destroy a man
> Is to turn him into an individual.

Men have settled for a fragmentary life, as the easiest way, but this settlement is the sickness of their own personal lives and of their society. Routine is destructive, but so also are the wild breaks from routine, the simple refusals. What is needed is a new and total assent, for

> Our time, our generation, that is sick
> And must be cured.

Thus the individual, fulfiling himself absolutely, becomes, or offers himself as, the liberator. This position is reached again and again in Ibsen, but the resolution varies. In *Pillars of Society, A Doll's House, Enemy of the People,* the refusal of compromise is unambiguously carried through, if not to liberation, at least to positive individual defiance. In *Peer Gynt,* what looks like the quest for self-fulfilment is shown in the end to be simple evasion: the self alone, detached from the reality of world and relationships, withers and is wasted, to be redeemed only by return. More commonly, in varying degrees of emphasis, the individual's struggle is seen as both necessary and tragic. The evasion of fulfilment, by compromise, breeds false relationships and a sick society, but the attempt at fulfilment ends again and again in tragedy: the individual is destroyed in his attempt to climb out of his partial world.

This is the crux of liberal tragedy, and it is in many ways difficult to understand. The simple position is that of the heroic liberator opposed and destroyed by a false society: the liberal martyr. It is clear that Ibsen knew this feeling; it finds memorable expression in Stockmann. But it is not in this pattern that Ibsen takes his heroes to their deaths. Stockmann, faced only by this, is stronger and survives:

> The strongest man in the world is he who stands most alone.

Nor is it merely by accident and complication that the hero dies. The tragedy, in fact, is built into the form of the aspiration, in the significant concept of *debt*.

In the action and imagery of the plays, the nature of debt is persistently explored. Just as aspiration cannot be reduced simply to social reform, to a religious calling, or to self-expression, but remains obstinately general — the liberation of human spirit and energy — so debt cannot be reduced to inherited obligations, to a society burdened by compromises, or to original sin. These are often the forms in which aspiration and debt appear, but the actual works are more often explorations of the conflicting forces than definitions of them. Thus while in *Brand* there is simple fatalism —

> Blood of children must be spilt
> To atone for parents' guilt

— it is also clear that new debts are contracted in the act of refusal of compromise; it is Brand himself, and not merely Brand the son or the human being, who is eventually guilty. The position would be simpler if this guilt were then condemned, if the voice through the final avalanche — 'He is the God of love' — were a verdict. But this is not the case. Brand had to do what he did, and yet had to come to this point. This is not ethical tragedy, where a different choice would have brought safety. The choice and the fate admit no real alternatives.

What happens, again and again in Ibsen, is that the hero defines an opposing world, full of lies and compromises and dead positions, only to find, as he struggles against it, that as a man he belongs to this world, and has its destructive inheritance in himself. Ibsen turned this way and that, looking for a way out of this tragic deadlock, but normally he returned to it, and confessed its terrible power:

> Ghosts! . . . I almost believe we are all ghosts, Pastor Manders. It is not only what we have inherited from our fathers and mothers that walks in us. It is every kind of dead idea, lifeless old beliefs and so on. They are not alive, but they cling to us for all that, and we can never rid ourselves of them. Whenever I read a newspaper I seem to see ghosts stealing between the lines. There must be ghosts the whole country over, as thick as the sands of the sea. And then we are all of us so wretchedly afraid of the light.

This position, so often stated, is not a gloss for surrender to the darkness. The cry for light, the desire to climb out of such a world, is persistent and emphatic:

> Give me air and the blaze of day . . .
> Through darkness to light . . .
> A summer night on the uplands . . .
> The joy of life . . . always, always the joy of life—light and sunshine
> and glorious air . . .
> Mother, give me the sun.

But as the last phrase, the dying cry of Osvald, reminds us, the light is only a breaking aspiration, at the limits of human endurance. The death of Julian the Apostate, not the death of Christ, is the significant ending:

> Beautiful earth, beautiful life . . . O, Helios, Helios, why hast thou betrayed me?

There is no turning away from life to death, no tragic resignation. Ibsen's heroes, characteristically, die fighting and struggling and climbing: the aspiration to light is confirmed, not contradicted, by their deaths. In this sense, they are still heroes, but also they are tragic heroes. The ghosts

> cling to us . . . we can never rid ourselves of them.

Or as the liberal Rosmer puts it:

> We can never escape them, we of this house.

Ibsen seems to depend, as some of his language certainly depends, on a traditional idea of original sin. But the effect of his whole work is in fact a transformation of this. He never gives up the idea of the false society, even when he has realised that its complications eat into the lives of those opposing it. Nor, truly, does he ever mean 'sin' by 'debt'. The debts that count, in bringing his heroes down, are incurred in the struggle for life and light, however wayward this is often shown to be. When we have said 'sin', of Adam's desire, we have discounted human life, in any aspiring sense. But this desire, in Ibsen, is deep and valid. This is most clearly shown in *Emperor and Galilean*, where the false world of power and the false doctrine of resignation are alike rejected, in the struggle for the 'third empire', in which 'the spirit of men shall re-enter on its heritage'. It is the false condition of spirit against flesh that Julian fights, because

> all that is human has become unlawful since the day when the seer of Galilee became ruler of the world. Through him, life has become death.

The desire fails, or is broken, but is never denied. Ibsen's world, from his historical dramas to his domestic plays, is recognisable always by this fact: the struggle of individual desire, in a false and compromising situation, to break free and know itself. This is why we must not render him back to a dramatic tradition which would show the desire as false or unlawful. In the best sense, this is still a liberal world.

It is also, however, the world of liberal tragedy. Implacably, in most of his plays, the affirmed desire is brought to a breaking-point

—a tight place where you stick fast. There is no going forward or backward—

and the hero, if not the desire itself, is broken. Why should this be so? Why, repeatedly, should so powerful a struggle of human desire fail to break through? It is not any force outside man that breaks him. As Rosmer says, going to his death:

There is no judge over us, and therefore we must do justice upon ourselves.

But the justice, still, is death. The conviction of guilt, and of necessary retribution, is as strong as ever it was when imposed by an external design.

And this is the heart of liberal tragedy, for we have moved from the heroic position of the individual liberator, the aspiring self against society, to a tragic position, of the self against the self. Guilt, that is to say, has become internal and personal, just as aspiration was internal and personal. The internal and personal fact is the only general fact, in the end. Liberalism, in its heroic phase, begins to pass into its twentieth-century breakdown: the self-enclosed, guilty and isolated world; the time of man his own victim.

We are still in this world, and it is doubtful if we can clearly name all its pressures. A characteristic ideology has presented it as truth and even as science, until argument against it has come to seem hopeless. A structure of feeling as deep as this enacts a world, as well as interpreting it, so that we learn it from experience as well as from ideology. All we can say, reflecting on Ibsen's tragedy, is that the deadlock reached there, the heroic deadlock in which men die still struggling to climb, was indeed necessary. For there is no way out, there is only an inevitable tragic consciousness, while desire is seen as essentially individual. We have to push past Ibsen's undoubted social consciousness to discover, at its roots, this same individual consciousness. Certainly there is to be reform, the 'sick earth' is to be 'made whole', but this is to happen, always, by an individual act: the liberal conscience, *against* society. Change is never to be *with* people; if others come, they can at most be led. But also change, significantly often, is against people; it is against their wills that the liberator is thrown, and disillusion is then rapid. He speaks for human desire, as a general fact, but he knows this only as individual fulfilment. The self then makes its most terrible discovery: that there is not only a world outside it, resisting it, but other selves, capable of similar suffering and desire. It is possible then for fulfilment to be re-defined: a getting away from the world and from others; the loneliness of the high mountains. But desire had included the joy of life: the life of earth, and of men and women, which the hero is still governed by, even while he drives himself to reject it. The conflict is then indeed internal: a desire for relationship when all that is known of relationship is restricting; desire narrowing to an image in the mind, until it is realised that the search for warmth and light has ended in cold and darkness. Every move towards relationship ends in guilt. It is significant that nowhere in Ibsen is there a loving, active, lasting relationship; the image of it, at the end of *Peer Gynt*, is as much a relapse from effort, a return to the mother, as a discovery of a loving equal. More often, the tie to the parent is not even relapse. There is a kind of terror in natural inheritance itself. As later in Freudian psychology, the parent-child relationship is guilty as such, and the revelation of the face or feeling of father and mother, behind the adult self, is in itself horrifying. That inescapable connection haunts, quite literally, the liberal idea of the self. In this sense, to be born is to be guilty, and inheritance is inevitably 'debt'. For the identity of the 'free' self is limited and impugned by the necessary physical inheritance. That connection to others is involuntary, and is in the blood. To the liberal self this is not connection but tainting.

Then, driven by individual desire, which cannot admit any final connection, Ibsen's adult persons simply involve and damage each other, beyond the possibility of fulfilment. Freedom is defined as getting away from this net, or exposing it, in the name of truth. But there is nowhere to get away to, except by renunciation of the individual life and desire which are still active and compelling. Desire, consistently, betrays desire. The most active search to fulfil the self leads away from the persons in whom fulfilment is desired. It was this that Ibsen recognised, in his last plays; most notably in the Dramatic Epilogue:

> We see the irretrievable only when . . .
> When? . . .
> When we dead awaken.
> What do we really see then?
> We see that we have never lived.

The search for self-fulfilment has ended in the denial of life:

> It was self-murder, a deadly sin against myself. And that sin I can never expiate.

It is the final tragic recognition: that the self, which is all that is known as desire, leads away from fulfilment, and to its own breakdown.

From this recognition, there is no way out, within the liberal consciousness. There is either the movement to common desire, common aspiration, which politically is socialism, or there is the acceptance, reluctant at first but strengthening and darkening, of failure and breakdown as common and inevitable. In one way or the other, a total condition is asserted, and the differentiated self becomes dramatically rare. It is true that Shaw, in *Saint Joan* and elsewhere, could retain the simpler pattern, of the heroic and liberating individual destroyed by a false society. Numerically, many other plays have repeated this, but, at least in European drama, this pattern has commonly failed to include any of the deepest human energies and problems. The heroic individual, as in Shaw, survives only as a romantic portrait, emptied of personality so that the positive role can be played without complications. The act of liberation, correspondingly, is in the narrow sense historical or political; it is not an absolute human demand, but a limited cause here and there. The problem of the frustrated individual is masked by his theatrical transformation into a movement, leaving all the deeper problems, of history and personality, untouched.

The mainstream of tragedy has gone elsewhere: into the self-enclosed, guilty and isolated world of the breakdown of liberalism. We shall need to trace this through its complicated particular phases. But, with Ibsen in mind, it is worth looking briefly at the plays of Arthur Miller, who represents, essentially, a late revival of liberal tragedy, on the edge (but only on the edge) of its transformation into socialism. What distinguishes Miller from the majority contemporary drama of guilt and breakdown is the retained consciousness of a false society, an alterable condition. In *All My Sons* we are in many ways back in the world of Ibsen: a particular lie becomes the demonstration of a general lie. Joe Keller, a small manufacturer, has committed a social crime for which he has escaped responsibility. He acquiesced in the sending of defective parts to the Air Force in wartime, and allowed another man to take the consequences and imprisonment. The action of the play is that the social crime is made personal (by the fact of the death of Keller's own pilot son), and from this realisation made social again, in a new understanding of what society is. This is, in fact, the overcoming of alienation:

> Joe Keller's trouble . . . is not that he cannot tell right from wrong but that his cast of mind cannot admit that he, personally, has any viable connection with his world, his universe, or his society.

This is

> the concept of a man's becoming a function of production or distribution to the point where his personality becomes divorced from the actions it propels.

By seeing a particular case, to which he has a father's connection, he is forced to recognise the general fact of human connection:

> I think to him they were all my sons. And I guess they were, I guess they were.

However, this new positive consciousness cannot go beyond the level of statement; it is a new feeling, of collective responsibility and of collective guilt, personally affirmed, but the tragedy is in the fact that it is retrospective. Keller, and those he has killed, can only be victims.

This sense of the victim is very deep in Miller. *The Crucible* may remind us, dramatically, of *Enemy of the People,* but there is a wholly new sense of the terrible power of collective persecution. Individuals suffer for what they are and naturally desire, rather than for what they try do do, and the innocent are swept up with the guilty, with epidemic force. The social consciousness has now changed, decisively. Society is not merely a false system, which the liberator can challenge. It is actively destructive and evil, claiming its victims merely because they are alive. It is still seen as a false and alterable society, but merely to live in it, now, is enough to become its victim. In *Death of a Salesman* the victim is not the nonconformist, the heroic but defeated liberator; he is, rather, the conformist, the type of the society itself. Willy Loman is a man who from selling things has passed to selling himself, and has become, in effect, a commodity which like other commodities will at a certain point be discarded by the laws of the economy. He brings tragedy down on himself, not by opposing the lie, but by living it. Ironically, the form of his aspiration is again the form of his defeat, but now for no liberating end; simply to get by, to see himself and his sons all right. The connection between parents and children, seen as necessarily contradictory, is again tragically decisive. A new consciousness is then shaped: that of the victim who has no living way out, but who can try, in death, to affirm his lost identity and his lost will.

Proctor, in *The Crucible*, had died as an act of self-preservation: preservation of the truth of himself and of others, in opposition to the lies of the persecuting authority.

How may I live without my name?

This sense of personal verification by death is the last stage of liberal tragedy. In *The Crucible* it is virtually the position of the liberal martyr, though characteristically complicated by Proctor's personal guilt. But in *Death of a Salesman* and *A View from the Bridge* this wider implication is absent. It is not now the martyr but the victim; the disconnected individual. In Willy Loman's death the disconnection confirmed a general fact about the society; in Eddie Carbone's death, Miller has moved further back, and the death of the victim illustrates a total condition. Here, once again, at the end of a development, is the self against the self. Desire is quickened, releasing energies which destroy. As Eddie moves out of routine and into desire, there is rapid disintegration: the known sexual rhythms break down into their perverse variations, which now alone have energy. He rejects his wife, as his desire transfers to the girl they have brought up. And as his most vital energy drives him towards both incest and homosexuality, guilt becomes so much a part of desire that his identity and his normal connections are simply burned out. In the terror of his complicated jealousies, he betrays the human connection by which he has lived, surrenders immigrants of his wife's kin to the inhuman and alien society. When desire and guilt are thus inextricable, there is no way to live, and he provokes his death shouting 'I want my name'.

It is a last tragic cry, in a disintegrating world. Human desire destroys itself, under intolerable pressures, and the figure of the individual hero, who would remake his life and his world, is now quite forgotten, is one of the old stories, while isolated contemporary man, wanting no more than to be himself, fails even in this and transfers significance to his name and his death. To preserve one's life, as things are, is 'to settle for half', as Miller puts it at the end of *A View from the Bridge*. And if this is so, in a false society which the individual alone cannot change, then the original liberal impulse, of complete self-fulfilment, becomes inevitably tragic. The self that wills and desires destroys the self that lives, yet the rejection of will and desire is also tragedy: a corroding insignificance, as the self is cut down.

The final step, made clear in *After the Fall*, is the acceptance and generalisation of just this insignificance: the personally urgent yet finally complacent acknowledgement that desire and guilt are inextricable; the identification of the false society — torture, betrayal — as part of one's own desires, so that it can no longer be meaningfully opposed, or even bitterly challenged by death, but has simply to be confirmed, forgiven, and lived with, in our separate and isolated suffering. And then at this point the deadlock is absolute, and we are all victims: aspiration itself is only a disguise for cruelty. But when this has happened, in the mind of a whole culture, liberal tragedy has ended, in its own deadlock.

CONTEMPORARY PERSPECTIVES

**AMIRI BARAKA /
LEROI JONES**

*"The Revolutionary
Theatre"*
(1966)

*THE PRECEDING ESSAYS
have, in various ways, described a common dra-
matic tradition. In "The
Revolutionary Theatre," Amiri Baraka describes the challenges posed by an emerging African-American theater.*

The Revolutionary Theatre should force change; it should be change. (All their faces turned into the lights and you work on them black nigger magic, and cleanse them at having seen the ugliness. And if the beautiful see themselves, they will love themselves.) We are preaching virtue again, but by that to mean NOW, toward what seems the most constructive use of the world.

The Revolutionary Theatre must EXPOSE! Show up the insides of these humans, look into black skulls. White men will cower before this theatre because it hates them. Because they themselves have been trained to hate. The Revolutionary Theatre must hate them for hating. For presuming with their technology to deny the supremacy of the Spirit. They will all die because of this.

The Revolutionary Theatre must teach them their deaths. It must crack their faces open to the mad cries of the poor. It must teach them about silence and the truths lodged there. It must kill any God anyone names except Common Sense. The Revolutionary Theatre should flush the fags and murders out of Lincoln's face.

It should stagger through our universe correcting, insulting, preaching, spitting craziness — but a craziness taught to us in our most rational moments. People must be taught to trust true scientists (knowers, diggers, oddballs) and that the holiness of life is the constant possibility of widening the consciousness. And they must be incited to strike back against *any* agency that attempts to prevent this widening.

The Revolutionary Theatre must Accuse and Attack anything that can be accused and attacked. It must Accuse and Attack because it is a theatre of Victims. It looks at the sky with the victims' eyes, and moves the victims to look at the strength in their minds and their bodies.

Clay in *Dutchman*, Ray in *The Toilet*, Walker in *The Slave*, are all victims. In the Western sense they could be heroes. But the Revolutionary Theatre, even if it is Western, must be anti-Western. It must show horrible coming attractions of *The Crumbling of the West*. Even as Artaud designed *The Conquest of Mexico*, so we must design *The Conquest of White Eye*, and show the missionaries and wiggly liberals dying under blasts of concrete. For sound effects, wild screams of joy, from all the peoples of the world.

The Revolutionary Theatre must take dreams and give them a reality. It must isolate the ritual and historical cycles of reality. But it must be food for all those who need food, and daring propaganda for the beauty of the Human Mind. It is a political theatre, a weapon to help in the slaughter of these dimwitted fatbellied white guys who somehow believe that the rest of the world is here for them to slobber on.

This should be a theatre of World Spirit. Where the spirit can be shown to be the most compe-tent force in the world. Force. Spirit. Feeling. The language will be anybody's, but tightened by the poet's backbone. And even the language must show what the facts are in this consciousness epic, what's happening. We will talk about the world, and the preciseness with which we are able to summon the world will be our art. Art is method. And art, "like any ashtray or senator," remains in the world. Wittgenstein said ethics and aesthetics are one. I believe this. So the Broadway theatre is a theatre of reaction whose ethics, like its aesthetics, reflect the spiritual values of this unholy society, which sends young crackers all over the world blowing off colored people's heads. (In some of these flippy Southern towns they even shoot up the immigrants' Favorite Son, be it Michael Schwerner or JFKennedy.)

The Revolutionary Theatre is shaped by the world, and moves to reshape the world, using as its force the natural force and perpetual vibrations of the mind in the world. We are history and desire, what we are, and what any experience can make us.

It is a social theatre, but all theatre is social theatre. But we will change the drawing rooms into places where real things can be said about a real world, or into smoky rooms where the destruction of

Washington can be plotted. The Revolutionary Theatre must function like an incendiary pencil planted in Curtis Lemay's cap. So that when the final curtain goes down brains are splattered over the seats and the floor, and bleeding nuns must wire SOS's to Belgians with gold teeth.

Our theatre will show victims so that their brothers in the audience will be better able to understand that they are the brothers of victims, and that they themselves are victims if they are blood brothers. And what we show must cause the blood to rush, so that pre-revolutionary temperaments will be bathed in this blood, and it will cause their deepest souls to move, and they will find themselves tensed and clenched, even ready to die, at what the soul has been taught. We will scream and cry, murder, run through the streets in agony, if it means some soul will be moved, moved to actual life understanding of what the world is, and what it ought to be. We are preaching virtue and feeling, and a natural sense of the self in the world. All men live in the world, and the world ought to be a place for them to live.

What is called the imagination (from image, magi, magic, magician, etc.) is a practical vector from the soul. It stores all data, and can be called on to solve all our "problems." The imagination is the projection of ourselves past our sense of ourselves as "things." Imagination (Image) is all possibility, because from the image, the initial circumscribed energy, any use (idea) is possible. And so begins that image's use in the world. Possibility is what moves us.

The popular white man's theatre like the popular white man's novel shows tired white lives, and the problems of eating white sugar, or else it herds bigcaboosed blondes onto huge stages in rhinestones and makes believe they are dancing or singing. WHITE BUSINESSMEN OF THE WORLD, DO YOU WANT TO SEE PEOPLE REALLY DANCING AND SINGING??? ALL OF YOU GO UP TO HARLEM AND GET YOURSELF KILLED. THERE WILL BE DANCING AND SINGING, THEN, FOR REAL!! (In *The Slave*, Walker Vessels, the black revolutionary, wears an armband, which is the insignia of the attacking army — a big red-lipped minstrel, grinning like crazy.)

The liberal white man's objection to the theatre of the revolution (if he is "hip" enough) will be on aesthetic grounds. Most white Western artists do not need to be "political," since usually, whether they know it or not, they are in complete sympathy with the most repressive social forces in the world today. There are more junior birdmen fascists running around the West today disguised as Artists than there are disguised as fascists. (But then, that word, *Fascist*, and with it, *Fascism*, has been made obsolete by the words *America*, and *Americanism*.) The American Artist usually turns out to be just a super-Bourgeois, because, finally, all he has to show for his sojourn through the world is "better taste" than the Bourgeois — many times not even that.

Americans will hate the Revolutionary Theatre because it will be out to destroy them and whatever they believe is real. American cops will try to close the theatres where such nakedness of the human spirit is paraded. American producers will say the revolutionary plays are filth, usually because they will treat human life as if it were actually happening. American directors will say that the white guys in the plays are too abstract and cowardly ("don't get me wrong . . . I mean aesthetically . . .") and they will be right.

The force we want is of twenty million spooks storming America with furious cries and unstoppable weapons. We want actual explosions and actual brutality: AN EPIC IS CRUMBLING and we must give it the space and hugeness of its actual demise. The Revolutionary Theatre, which is now peopled with victims, will soon begin to be peopled with new kinds of heroes — not the weak Hamlets debating whether or not they are ready to die for what's on their minds, but men and women (and minds) digging out from under a thousand years of "high art" and weak-faced dalliance. We must make an art that will function so as to call down the actual wrath of world spirit. We are witch doctors and assassins, but we will open a place for the true scientists to expand our consciousness. This is a theatre of assault. The play that will split the heavens for us will be called THE DESTRUCTION OF AMERICA. The heroes will be Crazy Horse, Denmark Vesey, Patrice Lumumba, and not history, not memory, not sad sentimental groping for a warmth in our despair; these will be new men, new heroes, and their enemies most of you who are reading this.

VI

DRAMA AND THEATER TODAY:
THE WORLD STAGE

HISTORIC SOCIAL, POLITICAL, and technological changes have reshaped the world since 1950, with a consequential impact on the theater. The aftermath of World War II has seen the remapping of the planet: the independence of India, Pakistan, and many Asian and African nations from colonial rule; the founding of Israel and the displacement of the Palestinians; and wars in Korea, Indochina, the Middle East, Africa, and the Persian Gulf. Those decades also witnessed bitter civil strife in Northern Ireland, Argentina, Chile, the United States, Europe, and elsewhere; the Cuban missile crisis, the death of Francisco Franco in Spain, and the dismantling of the Berlin Wall; independence movements in the former Soviet Union and in Eastern Europe; the civil rights movement in the United States and the waning of apartheid in South Africa.

With the rise of global communications, a global economy, and global political and military interests, such social and political revolutions immediately become the world's business. They reshape the world we live in even as we watch the changes unfold on our television screens. Television, fortunately, has not really transformed the world's diverse cultures into a single "global village," but local cultures all feel the impact of events around the world. Think of the global effects of environmental disasters like the Chernobyl nuclear meltdown and the deforestation of the rain forests of the Amazon; of medical advances like vaccination and of epidemics like AIDS; of the international effects of social movements like nuclear disarmament, human rights, Amnesty International, feminism, and the peace movement, or, more horrifyingly, of anti-Semitism, racism, and homophobia.

Drama requires the collaboration of playwrights, actors, and audiences; the public structure of a theater site or building; and the social and political incentives and protections that make theatergoing attractive—it is an art deeply woven into the social fabric of a given culture and its history. Although we can still speak of the "London theater" or of "American drama," terms like these have become in our era a critical convenience for reducing the dynamic variety of contemporary theater to the fictional boundaries of a single "national" culture. (This convenience is marked in the organization of this anthology, too, which treats contemporary American plays separately in units 5 and 7, in order to clarify the continuities of American theater and to raise specific questions of canonicity. American drama is, of course, part of "world drama," and the remarks in this introduction apply to those plays as well.) Although the theater still requires the support, work, and energy of its local community, today's dramatic repertory is a global one. American playwright Sam Shepard first produced several of his plays in London. British playwright Edward Bond is more widely produced in Germany than in the United Kingdom. Many Eastern European and Latin American playwrights have been forced by censorship and political persecution to smuggle their plays to Europe or the United States to be staged. South African playwright Athol Fugard has premiered several plays in the United States. Nigerian Wole Soyinka is regularly produced throughout the world. These playwrights are deeply implicated in the working of their native cultures, but their plays have rapidly become part of the world repertory.

The impact of film and television has forced the theater to work to define what kinds of performance are specific to the stage, how live dramatic performances can offer something unique, something not already available in other performance media. For this reason, perhaps, theater and drama since 1950 have necessarily been "experimental," working to

THEATER IN THE ROUND

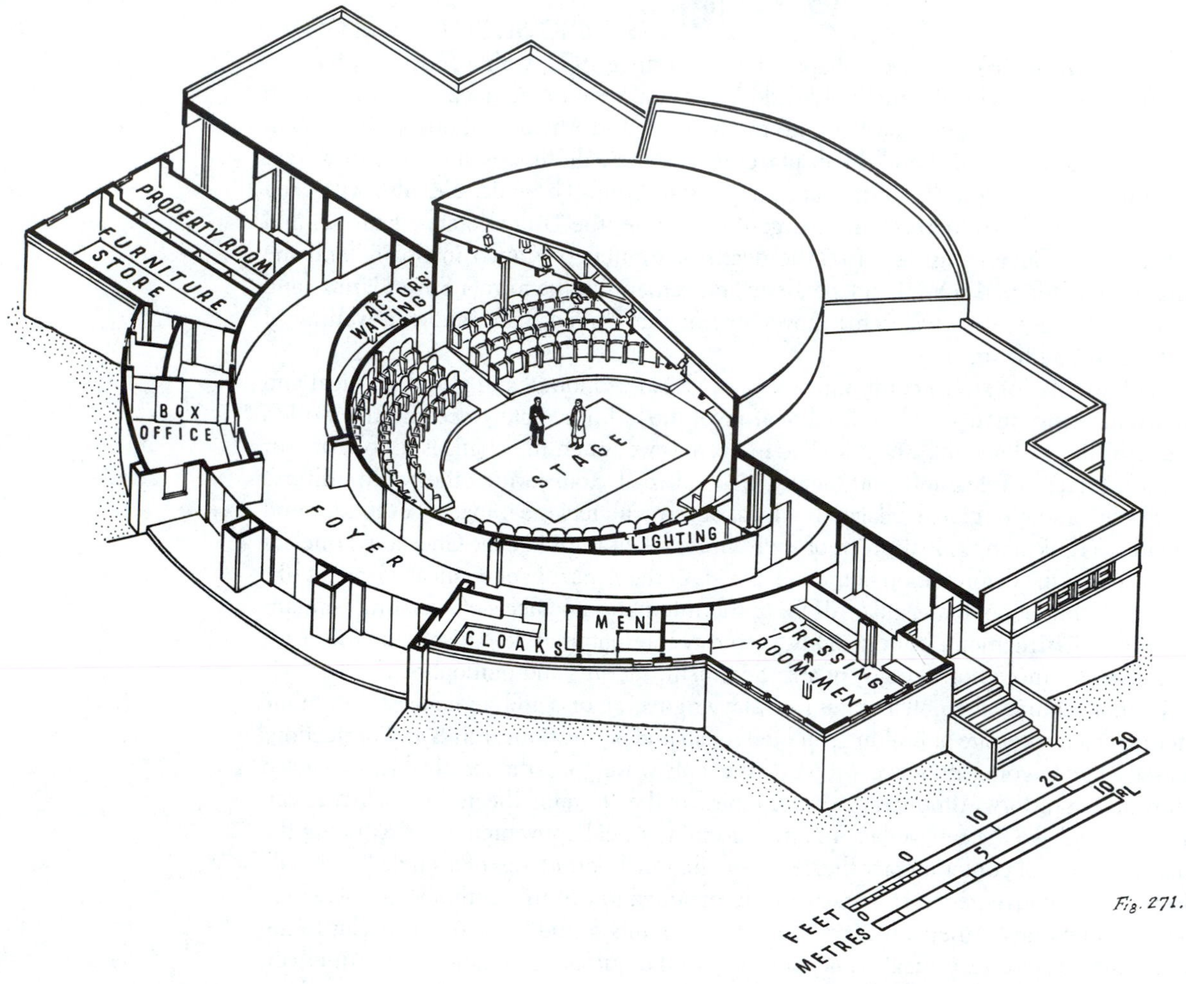

In a theater-in-the-round, the audience no longer faces the stage as in a proscenium theater, but surrounds the action. This kind of theater space lends itself to greater immediacy and contact between the performers and the audience.

develop new kinds of plays, new practices of stage production, and new kinds of theatrical experience for their audiences. Much as the proscenium theaters of the early twentieth century have given way to other, more flexible kinds of theater spaces, so dramatic writing has become much more varied and experimental. Even stage realism — the mode of Ibsen and Chekhov, Miller and Williams — has undergone an important reworking in the plays of Sam Shepard, Harold Pinter, Maria Irene Fornes, and others.

Here, we can identify three patterns of innovation as a way of organizing our thinking about the diversity of the contemporary stage. One strategy — inspired most directly by Antonin Artaud's **THEATER OF CRUELTY** — attacks the notion that the theater is essentially a *representational* medium, emphasizing instead the *experiential* aspect of theater. Rather than staging images of some fictive world to an audience of passive spectators, this kind of theater works to structure the *present experience* of the audience in new ways, as in the participatory and ritualistic theater experiments of the 1960s and 1970s. The influence of Artaud's assault on representation is evident in the contemporary theater in several ways: in absurdist drama, the physicalized "choreopoems" of Ntozake Shange, and the violent visual spectacles of Jean Genet, among others.

The second mode of innovation, **THEATER OF THE ABSURD**, originated as a new form of playwriting rather than as theatrical experimentation. The plays of Samuel Beckett, Slawomir Mrozek, Eugène Ionesco, Boris Vian, Edward Albee, Harold Pinter, and others create a strangely dislocated dramatic world, in which arbitrary or "absurd" events both confront and mystify the characters.

While Artaud inspired an existential or experiential theater, Bertolt Brecht — whose work became widely known and imitated only after World War II — inspired a different kind of assault on the conventions of realistic theater. For contemporary **POLITICAL THEATER** also criticizes the notion of "representation," but in different terms than Artaud or theater of the absurd. For "representation" is a word with two senses; in "representing" a picture of the world, the arts necessarily claim that their images are "representative" in some way. Political theater frequently shows how a social or political order uses its power to "represent" others coercively — for example, by depicting those others through demeaning or limiting stereotypes. For this reason, political theater today is intent on using live performance to change the prejudicial attitudes concealed in conventional ideas of representation.

Of course, no plays fit easily or fully into these three categories, but to think of the drama of the postwar period as raising questions of our existential or our political relation to the theater — and so to the world — provides a useful and powerful way of opening that drama to our understanding. Each of these modes of theater creates a different relationship between the stage and its audience, and we should examine each of them in some detail.

ARTAUD AND THE THEATER OF CRUELTY

The writings of Antonin Artaud, particularly the essays collected in the volume *The Theater and Its Double* (written in the late 1920s and 1930s, published in France in 1938, translated to English in 1958), have had an extraordinary impact on our sense of theater. Like many innovators of his generation — think of Brecht or Pirandello — Artaud worked to undermine the notion that the theater can only show its audiences realistic vignettes of daily life. Instead, Artaud argued that the theater should alter the balance between presentation — the actual, immediate activities of actors and audiences, their *presence* in the theater — and representation, the fictive "drama" that had seemed to define the purpose and scope of theater. Artaud — who used the term *theater of cruelty* for this project — advocated transforming the theater into an all-consuming spectacle, akin both to rituals like the Catholic Mass and to public festivals, in which the boundaries between acting and observing, actor and spectator, fiction and reality, conscious and unconscious would be broken or transgressed. The idea that the theater would "communicate," but not through rational means, is captured in one of Artaud's most powerful metaphors for this nearly unimaginable theater: the plague. Artaud envisioned a theater that would transmit its experiences corporeally, through the body, like disease, like mystical wisdom, alchemically transforming all of its participants. To avoid staging conventional dramas, Artaud called for a theater of "no more masterpieces," one that would use the dramatic text to transform the relations between stage and spectator by making the production a total experience — visual, auditory, gustatory, olfactory, tactile, physical — for the audience.

Stage director Peter Brook once remarked that "Artaud applied is Artaud betrayed," and it is true that Artaud's sense of theater is deeply metaphorical, a kind of theater experience that is almost unimaginable to us, and certainly not imaginable to us as theater. Artaud rarely offers a practical description of how this theater could come into being. Instead, the value and influence of Artaud's writing has been indirect and inspirational, bearing in a variety of tangential ways on kinds of theater that are not in any literal sense "Artaudian." In that Artaud imagines a theater of *presence* — not of representation — involving the audience in an experience rather than showing them a picture, his theater comes into contact with several very different kinds of innovation. Although the American experimental theater of the 1960s and 1970s is the most direct application — and betrayal — of Artaud, Artaud's conception of theater stands distantly behind a variety of more formally constructed plays: the fusion of dance, music, and poetry in Ntozake Shange's work; the dislocating imagery of Beckett and Fornes; perhaps even the ritualized, hallucinatory violence of Pinter's plays. Of course, as *written* plays, "masterpieces," these plays are specifically opposed to the ideals of Artaud's unrealizable theater, while at the same time they explore part of the terrain opened by Artaud's vision.

THEATER OF THE ABSURD

Coined by the theater critic Martin Esslin in 1961, the phrase *theater of the absurd* tries to capture the special irrationality and unpredictability of a certain wave of dramatic writing of the late 1950s and 1960s, including the plays of Samuel Beckett and Harold Pinter, for example. Taking as his keynote Beckett's famous play *Waiting for Godot* (1953) — a play in which two Chaplinesque tramps wait for a mysterious man named Godot, who never arrives — Esslin finds the theater of the absurd to have certain stylistic and thematic characteristics. It rejects the sense of causality found in realistic plays, the sense that it is possible to find the causes for events either in the environment or in the psychological motives of the characters themselves. Instead, theater of the absurd tends to be about a world in which inexplicable, arbitrary, or irrational events happen. Although the events usually seem to be part of some kind of order or scheme, it is an order that the characters and their audience cannot quite grasp. As Hamm says in Beckett's play *Endgame*, "Something is taking its course," but neither the characters nor the audience are ever sure what that "something" is. In Eugène Ionesco's play *Rhinoceros* (1960), the inhabitants of a small French village begin to turn inexplicably into rhinoceroses. In each act of Boris Vian's *The Empire Builders* (1959), a family moves to a smaller room in an apartment building, always accompanied by a mysterious, bandaged figure. In Slawomir Mrozek's *Striptease* (1961), two men are commanded by a huge, silent finger to remove their clothes and don huge conical hats that conceal and blind them. As Esslin suggests, this drama insists that the fictions we use to make sense of our world — ideas of order, causality, rationality — are just that: fictions imposed on an arbitrary and mysterious reality, whose meanings remain fugitive and elusive.

Absurdist drama treats its audience somewhat differently than realistic plays do, rejecting the "dramatic irony" of the traditional theater, in which the audience understands more than the characters onstage. Instead, the theater of the absurd refuses to provide this privilege to its spectators. We are as baffled and frustrated by our attempts to make the events mean something as the characters are; "Mean something!" a character remarks in *Endgame*, "You and I, mean something! (*Brief laugh*)." Our *present* experience as an audience is structured and made significant by absurdist theatrical production. In the theater, we don't just observe the "absurd" drama onstage, we are forced to undergo it, to live it through. For this reason, both the drama onstage and the audience's experience in the theater are sometimes described as *existential*. We have to *decide* the meaning of our being in the theater, without the comfort, solace, or guidance of some transcendent, predetermined worldview.

Much as theater of the absurd works to make the spectators' situation in the theater an extension of the characters' situation on the stage, political theater since Brecht has worked to make the audience's performance in the theater a recognizably political one. By fragmenting the stage space, by showing how the illusion is made rather than concealing its means of production, and by involving the audience more overtly in deciding the meaning of the play's events, the theater is shown to be a political instrument. Like television, newspapers, universities, the courts, and so on, the theater is an institution that produces the ideas and images with which we govern our lives. Both the example of Brecht's plays and his challenging theory of performance have been absorbed and redefined by the world theater. In common with theater of the absurd, political theater works to resist and complicate realistic representation, the "slice of life" of Ibsen, Chekhov, and Miller. Instead of staging an arbitrarily unreal and absurd world, political theater examines "representative" images of reality. Who makes those images? Who benefits from them? Who is injured, governed, or oppressed by them? How do they help to maintain the social *status quo*?

POLITICAL THEATER

For this reason, much political theater connects representation onstage with representation in society, showing how various social groups — women, gay men, lesbians, ethnic and racial groups, the poor — have been staged in society and in the theater. A fundamental assumption of political theater is that these stereotypes are part of the larger system of discrimination that operates in society, and that they reveal the dominant attitudes of those who govern, control, or influence society from positions of power. In plays like Jean Genet's *The Blacks*, Amiri Baraka's *Dutchman*, Ntozake Shange's *spell #7*, and Wole Soyinka's *Death and the King's Horseman*, the racial conflicts informing contemporary society and culture are explored in very different ways: in relation to colonialism, to white myths of black identity, to women's experience. These plays are very different in style, ranging from a kind of realism in *Death and the King's Horseman* to Genet's ritualized spectacle. It is not a single point of view or a single dramatic style that defines political theater, but the use of theatrical representation itself as a way to analyze representation in society at large.

A similar approach to theater informs many of the modern plays gathered in this anthology, for many of them explore the issue of representation: how Asia is represented in the minds of the West in David Henry Hwang's *M. Butterfly*, how the English remapped and so represented the Irish in their own language and political system in Brian Friel's *Translations*, how African tribal traditions are tragically misunderstood by British imperialists in Wole Soyinka's *Death and the King's Horseman*, how the Chicano and Anglo cultures interact in Luis Valdez's *Los Vendidos*, how domesticity degrades its victims in Maria Irene Fornes's *Mud*, how love and honor emerge between men in Manuel Puig's *The Kiss of the Spider Woman*. Political theater sometimes seems highly message oriented, overtly didactic to readers and audiences used to the more subtle instruction offered by realistic plays. Yet the messages of contemporary political theater tend to be fused into the process of theater, so that the politics of the play come into being not in the prepared script of the play but in our experience as an audience. All of these plays disrupt the expectations, attitudes, and preconceptions of the empowered audience and invite the audience to develop different ways of reading their society as part of their involvement in the play.

DRAMA, THEATER, AND THE "POSTMODERN"

On the contemporary stage, though, these modes of theater do not work in isolation from one another, but interact with one another, as part of the dynamic means the theater uses to engage its audiences in an understanding of the world. Indeed, to describe the contemporary theater in terms of its historical inheritance from the modernist theater of Brecht, Artaud, and the absurdists is in an important sense to overlook what is most significant about the stage today: its break from the traditions of modernism. If we look at the range of contemporary performance activity, much of it has little to do with traditional drama. Think of the performance-art monologues of Spalding Gray (one of his best-known, *Swimming to Cambodia*, was made into a film by Jonathan Demme) or Karen Finley (whose work was at the center of the 1990 censorship controversy at the National Endowment for the Arts); of the music of Laurie Anderson; of video art and film; of music television and advertising; of the disorienting stage spectacles of Robert Wilson; even of "plays" like Peter Handke's *Offending the Audience* and *The Ride Across Lake Constance,* or Heiner Müller's *Hamletmachine,* or Samuel Beckett's later work for the theater, *Not I, Footfalls,* and *Ohio Impromptu.*

Theorists of culture and the arts have related these developments to innovations in the visual arts, in architecture, and in writing, characterizing their common features as **POST-MODERN**. The term itself is a difficult one, suggesting that these works often share some of the features of earlier, "modernist" art; the literary and cultural theorist Fredric Jameson suggests that the distinguishing feature of postmodern art is its attitude toward history. Jameson points out that postmodern works frequently invoke or appropriate the style of earlier historical periods, as in the use of neoclassical ornamentation in recent architecture, or the recollection of earlier film styles in more recent movies (**FILM NOIR** in *Chinatown* or *Dead Again*). Jameson labels this technique **PASTICHE**. What is striking about these postmodern quotations of style, though, is not any systematic reinterpretation of tradition or any statement of value, but their tonelessness, their neutrality, the absence of the kind of moral and historical sense we might expect from the act of confronting history. In postmodern pastiche, the recollection of an earlier style does not provide a new understanding of the past, nor does it illuminate our contemporary historical situation. Instead, pastiche denatures that style by removing it from history, and history from it. Style becomes exactly that: simply another option. Winnie's many quotations from English literature in *Happy Days*, the vaudeville performance of Sprenger and Kramer in Churchill's *Vinegar Tom*, and even the American domestic-drama setting of Fornes's *Mud* are perhaps part of this complex problem, for in each case the "past" is presented to the audience in terms of an artistic style that is largely emptied of its force as history.

Moreover, Jameson's discussion of pastiche also emphasizes the importance of the esthetic *surface* in postmodern art. Music video and advertising are sometimes taken as the paradigmatic postmodern forms, forms whose "message" lies almost exclusively in a rapidly changing, brilliantly seductive, series of images. Although this technique relates to the modernist use of **MONTAGE** in film and theater, it is different in several important ways. Modernist montage uses a series of images narratively, to tell a story. Although the camera cuts quickly from image to image, the audience assembles the images in a single complete narrative. Both the narrative and the interpreting spectator achieve a sense of wholeness. In contrast, postmodern images are juxtaposed in striking, sometimes contradictory combinations that resist our ability to impose a single narrative explanation, a single story line. Postmodern performance — on film or video or in the theater — is insistently fragmentary; it asserts the incompletion of the artistic object and the incomplete quality of the spectator's experience as well. Postmodern arts resist imposing a single explanatory interpretation that would both complete the narrative and confirm the audience's sense of wholeness, of self-integration. In this sense, postmodern arts are sometimes described as concerned with the "death of the subject." They question the possibility both of a comprehensible world and of a comprehending individual. By disorienting language, fragmenting narrative, and dispensing with such organizing principles as "plot" and "character," postmodern art claims that we have entered a new age in which the complex disconnections of modern culture have made obsolete many of our beliefs about the world and our ways of representing the world and ourselves.

JEAN GENET

Jean Genet (1910–1986) is perhaps as famous for his life as for his important work as a novelist and playwright. Born the illegitimate son of a Parisian prostitute, he was abandoned at birth and raised by the state. At age 15 he was convicted of theft and sent to a reformatory in Mettray. He served briefly in the French Foreign Legion, then deserted and wandered Europe throughout the 1930s, making a living as a beggar, smuggler, thief, and homosexual prostitute, until his arrest and imprisonment in 1941. In prison, Genet wrote his first poem, "The Condemned to Death," and his first novel, *Our Lady of the Flowers*. He was again sentenced in 1947, but the playwright Jean Cocteau and the philosopher Jean-Paul Sartre launched an appeal to secure his pardon. Genet's career became more closely entwined with Sartre in 1952, when Sartre's biography, *Saint-Genet: Actor and Martyr*, was published as volume 1 of Genet's *Complete Works*. Sartre takes Genet as an example of existential man, forced to enact the role of "criminal" that existence has arbitrarily assigned to him. Genet wrote several other novels, including *Miracle of the Rose* (1946), *Funeral Rites* (1947), and *Querrelle of Brest* (1947), and in 1947 wrote his first play, *The Maids*, followed by *Deathwatch* (1949), *The Balcony* (1951), *The Blacks* (1959), and *The Screens* (1966). Genet's dramatization of Algerian resistance to French rule in *The Screens* caused riots in Paris when it was first produced there. Throughout his flamboyant career as a writer, Genet worked to support a number of oppositional political organizations, including the Black Panthers in the United States and the Palestine Liberation Organization. Genet's memoir of the Middle East and the Palestinians, *A Prisoner of Love*, was published posthumously in 1989.

The Blacks

Genet's plays have an intense, concentrated, flamboyant theatricality, conveyed in part through the erotic dimension of his slangy, yet densely poetic language. In *The Blacks*, Genet trains this sensibility on the representation of race, of "blackness," to a white audience. *The Blacks* reflects white attitudes toward racial "others," attitudes that are criticized from the perspective of those others. The white theater audience is reflected in a distorting mirror by the "white" court occupying the upstage platform. It sees itself now from the point of view of the blacks it oppresses. The play's action is indirect and its language is baroque, but it becomes clear within minutes that both the court upstage and the characters downstage—Village, Bobo, Newport News—are collaborating on another drama, a drama taking place just offstage. For although the play the characters perform onstage concerns the execution of a white woman by the black cast, it becomes clear that this event is a diversion, performed to placate and distract the white audience in the theater from the more subversive drama taking place offstage. It appears—largely from Newport News's reports—that the blacks onstage are part of a resistance group who are executing one of their members offstage, someone who had compromised their real insurrection against the society outside the theater. The "clown show" provided for the theater audience finally becomes the blacks' instrument of resistance. They keep the spectators in their seats, looking at fantasy images of black characters, while they begin to conduct the real revolution just out of sight.

— NOTE —

One evening an actor asked me to write a play for an all-black cast. But what exactly is a black? First of all, what's his color?

This play, written, I repeat, by a white man, is intended for a white audience, but if, which is unlikely, it is ever performed before a black audience, then a white person, male or female, should be invited every evening. The organizer of the show should welcome him formally, dress him in ceremonial costume and lead him to his seat, preferably in the front row of the orchestra. The actors will play for him. A spotlight should be focused upon this symbolic white throughout the performance.

But what if no white person accepted? Then let white masks be distributed to the black spectators as they enter the theater. And if the blacks refuse the masks, then let a dummy be used. —*Jean Genet*

THE BLACKS
A CLOWN SHOW

Jean Genet

TRANSLATED BY BERNARD FRECHTMAN

— CHARACTERS —

ARCHIBALD ABSALOM WELLINGTON

DEODATUS VILLAGE

ADELAIDE BOBO

EDGAR ALAS NEWPORT NEWS

AUGUSTA SNOW

FELICITY TROLLOP PARDON

STEPHANIE VIRTUE SECRET-ROSE DIOP

DIOUF

MISSIONARY

JUDGE

GOVERNOR

QUEEN

VALET

DRUMMER

The curtain is drawn. Not raised — drawn.

THE SET: *Black velvet curtains. Right and left, a few sets of tiers with landings of different heights. One of them, far in the background, toward the right, is higher than the others. Another, rather like a gallery, goes up to the flies and all around the stage. That is where the* COURT *will appear. A green screen is set on a higher landing, just a trifle lower than the one mentioned above. In the middle of the stage, on the floor, a catafalque, covered with a white cloth. On the catafalque, bouquets of flowers: irises, roses, gladiolas, arum lilies. At the foot of the catafalque, a shoe-shine box. The lighting: very garish neon light.*

When the curtain is drawn, four NEGROES *in evening clothes — no, one of them,* NEWPORT NEWS, *who is barefoot, is wearing a woolen sweater — and four negresses in evening gowns are dancing a kind of minuet around the catafalque to an air of Mozart which they whistle and hum. The evening clothes — white ties for the gentlemen — are accompanied by tan shoes. The ladies' costumes — heavily spangled evening gowns — suggest fake elegance, the very height of bad taste. As they dance and whistle, they pluck flowers from their bodices and lapels and lay them on*

the catafalque. Suddenly, on the high platform, left, enters the COURT.

THE COURT: *Each actor playing a member of the* COURT *is a masked* NEGRO *whose mask represents the face of a white person. The mask is worn in such a way that the audience sees a wide black band all around it, and even the actor's kinky hair.*

THE QUEEN: *White, sad mask. Drooping mouth. Royal crown on her head. Sceptre in her hand. Ermine-trimmed cloak with a train. Superb gown. At her right:*

HER VALET: *A puny, mincing little fellow wearing a valet's striped waistcoat. On his arm a towel, with which he toys as if it were a scarf, but with which he will wipe Her Majesty's eyes.*

THE GOVERNOR: *Sublime uniform. Is holding a pair of field glasses.*

THE JUDGE: *Black and red robe. At the* QUEEN's *left.*

THE MISSIONARY: *White robe. Rings. Pectoral cross. At the* JUDGE's *left.*

The members of the COURT, *all standing on the same tier, seem interested in the spectacle of the dancing* NEGROES, *who suddenly stop short, breaking off the minuet. The* NEGROES *approach the footlights, make a ninety degree turn, and bow ceremoniously to the* COURT, *then to the audience. One of them steps forth and speaks, addressing now the audience, now the* COURT:

ARCHIBALD: Ladies and gentlemen . . . (*The* COURT *burst into very shrill, but very well orchestrated laughter. It is not free and easy laughter. This laughter is echoed by the same but even shriller laughter of the* NEGROES *who are standing about*
5   ARCHIBALD. *The* COURT, *bewildered, becomes silent.*) . . . My name is Archibald Absalom Wellington. (*He bows, then moves from one to the other, naming each in turn.*) . . . This is

Mr. Deodatus Village (*he bows*) . . . Miss Adelaide Bobo (*she bows*) . . . Mr. Edgar Alas Newport News (*he bows*) . . . Mrs. Augusta Snow (*she remains upright*) . . . well . . . well . . . 10 madam (*roaring angrily*) bow! (*she remains upright*) . . . I'm asking you, madam, to bow! (*extremely gentle, almost grieved*) I'm asking you, madam, to bow — it's a performance. (SNOW *bows*) . . . Mrs. Felicity Trollop Pardon (*she bows*) . . . and Miss Diop — Stephanie Virtue Secret-rose Diop. 15

DIOUF: And me.

ARCHIBALD: And he. — As you see, ladies and gentlemen, just as you have your lilies and roses, so we — in order to serve you — shall use our beautiful, shiny black make-up. It is Mr. Deodatus Village who gathers the smoke-black and Mrs. Felicity 20 Trollop Pardon who thins it out in our saliva. These ladies help her. We embellish ourselves so as to please you. You are white. And spectators. This evening we shall perform for you . . .

THE QUEEN: (*interrupting the speaker*) Bishop! Bishop-at-large! 25

Scene In Roger Blin's [the director of the premiere] production, the Court entered from the auditorium, after the curtain had been drawn (author's note).

THE MISSIONARY: *(leaning toward her, though without changing place)* Hallelujah!

THE QUEEN: *(plaintively)* Are they going to kill her?

(The NEGROES *below burst into the same shrill and orchestrated laughter as before. But* ARCHIBALD *silences them.)*

ARCHIBALD: Be quiet. If all they have is their nostalgia, let them
30   enjoy it.

SNOW: Grief, sir, is another of their adornments . . .

THE VALET: *(looking about him)* What's happened to my chair?

THE MISSIONARY: *(doing the same)* And to mine? Who took it?

THE VALET: *(to the* MISSIONARY, *querulously)* If my chair
35   hadn't disappeared too, you'd have suspected me. It was my turn to sit down, but I don't know where the hell my chair is. You can count on my good humor and devotion if I have to remain standing all through the show.

THE QUEEN: *(increasingly languid)* I repeat — are they going to
40   kill her?

THE MISSIONARY: *(very somberly)* But Madam . . . *(A pause.)* she's dead!

THE VALET: Is that all you can say to your sovereign? *(as if to himself)* This crowd could stand a good clouting.

45   THE MISSIONARY: The poor unfortunate has been in my prayers since this morning. In the very forefront.

THE QUEEN: *(leaning forward to call* SNOW) Is it true, young lady, that all we have left is our sadness and that it's one of our adornments?

50   ARCHIBALD: And we haven't finished embellishing you. This evening we've come again to round out your grief.

THE GOVERNOR: *(shaking his fist and making as if to descend)* If I let you!

THE VALET: *(holding him back)* Where are you going?

55   THE GOVERNOR: *(with a martial air)* To stamp out the Blacks!

(The NEGROES *below shrug their shoulders in unison.)*

ARCHIBALD: Be quiet. *(to the audience)* This evening we shall perform for you. But, in order that you may remain comfortably settled in your seats in the presence of the drama that is already unfolding here, in order that you be assured that there
60   is no danger of such a drama's worming its way into your precious lives, we shall even have the decency — a decency learned from you — to make communication impossible. We shall increase the distance that separates us — a distance that is basic — by our pomp, our manners, our insolence — for we
65   are also actors. When my speech is over, everything here — *(he stamps his foot in a gesture of rage)* here! — will take place in the delicate world of reprobation. If we sever bonds, may a continent drift off and may Africa sink or fly away . . .

(For some moments, the GOVERNOR, *who had taken a paper from his pocket, has been reading in a low voice.)*

THE QUEEN: May it fly away — was that a metaphor?

70   THE GOVERNOR: *(reading more and more loudly)* ". . . when I fall to earth, scurvily pierced by your spears, look closely, you will behold my ascension. *(in a thundering voice)* My corpse will be on the ground, but my soul and body will rise into the air . . ."

THE VALET: *(shrugging his shoulders)* Learn your role backstage.   75
As for that last sentence, it oughtn't to be rolled off as if it were a proclamation.

THE GOVERNOR: *(turning to the* VALET) I know what I'm doing. *(He resumes his reading.)* "You'll see them and you'll die of fright. First, you'll turn pale, and then you'll fall, and you'll be   80
dead . . ." *(He folds the paper and puts it back into his pocket very conspicuously.)* That was a device to let them know that we know. And we know that we've come to attend our own funeral rites. They think they're compelling us, but it is owing to our good breeding that we shall descend to   85
death. Our suicide . . .

THE QUEEN: *(touching the* GOVERNOR *with her fan)* . . . Preparations for it have begun, but let the Negro speak. Look at that poor, gaping mouth of his, and those columns of flies streaming out of it . . . *(she looks more closely, leaning forward)* . . .   90
or swarming into it. *(to* ARCHIBALD): Continue.

ARCHIBALD: *(after bowing to the* QUEEN) . . . sink or fly away. *(The members of the* COURT *protect their faces, as if a bird were flying at them.)* . . . but let it be off! *(A pause.)* When we leave this stage, we are involved in your life. I am a cook, this lady is   95
a sewing-maid, this gentleman is a medical student, this gentleman is a curate at St. Anne's, this lady . . . skip it. Tonight, our sole concern will be to entertain you. So we have killed this white woman. There she lies. *(He points to the catafalque. The members of the* COURT *wipe away a tear with a*   100
very theatrical gesture and heave a long sob of grief to which the NEGROES *respond with their very shrill and perfectly orchestrated laughter.)* . . . Only *we* could have done it the way we did it — savagely. And now, listen . . . *(he takes a step back)* . . . listen . . . oh, I was forgetting, thieves that we are, we have   105
tried to filch your fine language. Liars that we are, the names I have mentioned to you are false. Listen . . .

(He steps back, but the other actors have stopped listening to him. MRS. FELICITY, *an imposing sixty-year-old negress, has gone up to the top tier, right, where she sits down in an armchair, facing the* COURT.)

BOBO: The flowers, the flowers! Don't touch them!

SNOW: *(taking an iris for her bodice)* Are they yours, or the murdered woman's?   110

BOBO: They're there for the performance. Which doesn't require that you burst into bloom. Put back the iris. Or the rose. Or the tulip.

ARCHIBALD: Bobo's right. You wanted to be more attractive — there's some blacking left.   115

SNOW: All right. Although . . . *(She spits out the flower after biting into it.)*

ARCHIBALD: No needless cruelty, Snow. And no garbage here.

*(*SNOW *picks up the flower and eats it.* ARCHIBALD *runs after* SNOW, *who hides behind the catafalque.* VILLAGE *catches her and brings her back to* ARCHIBALD, *who wants to lecture her.)*

SNOW: *(to* VILLAGE) A regular cop!

ARCHIBALD: *(to* SNOW) The rite doesn't call for your behaving   120
like a spoiled child. *(While all the other* NEGROES *stand still and listen, he turns to* NEWPORT NEWS): And you, sir, you're superfluous. As everything is secret, you've got to get going.

Clear out. Go tell them. Let them know we've started.
125 They're to do their job just as we'll do ours. Everything will go
off in the usual way. I hope so.

(NEWPORT NEWS *bows and is about to leave by the left wing, but*
VILLAGE *stops him.*)

VILLAGE: Not that way, you fool. You were told not to come
back. You're spoiling everything.
NEWPORT NEWS: The trouble . . .
130 ARCHIBALD: (*interrupting him*) Later. Get going.

(*Exit* NEWPORT NEWS, *left.*)

SNOW: (*spitting out the iris*) You always start by picking on me.
BOBO: You let your moods get the better of you. You give way to
your temperament, and you've no right to.
SNOW: I have so! Because of my special outlook on the whole
135 business. If it weren't for me . . .
ARCHIBALD: You've done neither more nor less than the others.
SNOW: And my moods are special too, and so is my temperament, and they suit your purpose. And if it weren't for my
jealousy where you're concerned, Village . . .
140 VILLAGE: (*interrupting her*) We know all about it. You've repeated it often enough. Long before her death (*pointing to the
catafalque*) you hated her bitterly. But her death wasn't meant
to signify merely that she lost her life. With tenderness we all
brooded over it, and not lovingly. (*A long sob from the* COURT.)
145 SNOW: Really? Then let me tell you now — all of you — I've been
burning for so long, burning with such ardent hatred, that
I'm a heap of ashes.
DIOUF: What about us? What are we?
SNOW: It's not the same thing, gentlemen. There was a touch of
150 desire in your hatred of her, which means a touch of love. But
I, and they (*pointing to the other women*), we, the negro
women, we had only our wrath and rage. When she was
killed, we felt no awe, no fear, but no tenderness either. We
were dry, gentlemen. Dry, like the breasts of old Bambara
155 women.

(*The* QUEEN *bursts out laughing. The* MISSIONARY *motions to
her to be quiet. Holding her handkerchief to her mouth, the*
QUEEN *gradually calms down.*)

ARCHIBALD: (*severely*) The tragedy will lie in the color black! It's
that that you'll cherish, *that* that you'll attain, and deserve.
It's *that* that must be earned.
SNOW: (*ecstatically*) My color! Why, you're my very self! But
160 you, Village, what was it you wanted in going after her? (*She
points to the catafalque.*)
VILLAGE: You're starting again with your silly suspicions. Do
you want a detailed description of the humiliations she made
me feel? Do you? Tell me, do you?
165 ALL: (*with a terrible cry*) Yes!
VILLAGE: Negroes, you've yelled too soon and too loud. (*He
takes a deep breath.*) This evening, there'll be something new.
ARCHIBALD: You've no right to change anything in the ceremonial, unless, of course, you hit upon some cruel detail that
170 heightens it.
VILLAGE: In any case, I can keep you on tenterhooks waiting for
the murder.

ARCHIBALD: You're to obey *me*. And the text we've prepared.
VILLAGE: (*banteringly*) But I'm still free to speed up or draw out
my recital and my performance. I can move in slow motion, 175
can't I? I can sigh more often and more deeply.
THE QUEEN: (*amused*) He's charming! Continue, young man!
THE JUDGE: Indeed, your Majesty is forgetting herself!
THE VALET: I rather like him, I must say. (*to* VILLAGE): Do sigh
more often and more deeply, charming blackboy! 180
THE GOVERNOR: (*to the* VALET) That'll do! Instead of that, tell
us how rubber stands on the stock exchange.
THE VALET: (*saluting, and in a single breath*) Goodyear, 4,500.
(*The members of the* COURT *pull a long face.*)
THE GOVERNOR: What about gold? 185
THE VALET: Eastern Ubangi 1,580. Saint Johnny-get-your-gun
1,050. Macupia, 2,002. M'Zaita 20,008.

(*The Members of the* COURT *rub their hands.*)

VILLAGE: (*continuing*) . . . can sigh more often and more
deeply, can relax in the middle of a sentence or word. Besides, I'm tired. You forget that I'm already knocked out from 190
the crime I had to finish off before you arrived, since you need
a fresh corpse for every performance.
THE QUEEN: (*with a cry*) Oh!
THE JUDGE: (*fiercely*) I told you so.
THE VALET: (*very affectedly*) Don't condemn them at the very 195
start. Listen to them. They're exquisitely spontaneous. They
have a strange beauty. Their flesh is weightier . . .
THE GOVERNOR: Be quiet, you whippersnapper! You and your
damned exoticism!
DIOUF: (*to* ARCHIBALD) Actually, we *could* use the same corpse a 200
number of times. Its presence is the thing that counts.
ARCHIBALD: What about the odor, Mr. Vicar General?
BOBO: (*to* ARCHIBALD) Does the stench frighten you now? That's
what rises from my African soil. I, Bobo, want to draw my
train over its thick waves! May I be wafted by an odor of car- 205
rion! And carried off! (*to the* COURT) And you, pale and odor-
less race, race without animal odors, without the pestilence of
our swamps . . .
ARCHIBALD: (*to* BOBO) Let Virtue speak.
VIRTUE: (*prudently*) All the same, we ought to be careful. It gets 210
more dangerous every day. Not only for Village, but for every
hunter.
SNOW: All the better. Since we're working this evening for a
Court of Justice that's been set up especially for us, we'll dedicate our follies to it. 215
ARCHIBALD: That'll do. (*to* VILLAGE): Tell me, Village, there
wasn't any alert this evening either, was there? Everything
went off smoothly, I hope. Where did you find her?
VILLAGE: I told you just before, when I arrived. Right after dinner, Mr. Herod Adventure and I were walking along the 220
docks. The evening was rather mild. A little before the entrance to the bridge, there was an old tramp squatting — or
lying — on a pile of rags. But I've told you all about it . . .
BOBO: The old tramp may consider herself fortunate. She'll have
a first-class funeral. 225
ARCHIBALD: (*to* VILLAGE) But tell us more. Did she scream?
VILLAGE: Not at all. Hadn't time to. Mr. Herod Adventure and I

went straight up to her. She was dozing. She half awoke. The blackness of the night . . .

230   BOBO and SNOW: *(laughing)* Oh! the blackness!

VILLAGE: In the darkness, she must have taken us for policemen. She reeked of wine, like all those they cast out on the docks. She said, "I'm not doing any harm . . ."

ARCHIBALD: And then?

235   VILLAGE: As usual. It was I who bent down. Mr. Herod Adventure held her hands while I strangled her. She stiffened a bit . . . then she had what's called a spasm, and that was that. Mr. Herod Adventure was slightly nauseated by the crone's ugly mug, by the smell of wine and urine, by the filth. He almost

240   puked. But he pulled himself together. We carried her to our Cadillac and brought her here, in a crate.

(A pause.)

SNOW: But that stench, which isn't ours . . .

(VILLAGE takes a cigarette from his pocket.)

BOBO: You're right, let's smoke.

(The NEGROES seem not quite to understand.)

ARCHIBALD: Let's all have a cigarette. Let's smoke her out.

(Each NEGRO takes a cigarette from his pocket. They light matches for each other, bowing ceremoniously as they do, then arrange themselves in a circle and puff smoke around the catafalque. They sing the first line of "Mary had a little lamb" and hum the rest.)

(During the sing-song the COURT grows agitated.)

245   THE GOVERNOR: *(to the VALET)* Now they're smoking her out! It's a hive, it's a nest of hornets, it's a wooden bed swarming with bedbugs, it's a burrow, it's a den of rebels . . . Our corpse! They're going to cook her and eat her! Take their matches away!

(The entire COURT kneels before the QUEEN; the VALET dries her eyes with a towel.)

250   THE MISSIONARY: Let us pray, Madam. *(to the others)*: All of you, on your knees before that august grief.

THE QUEEN: Ahaaha!

THE MISSIONARY: Have confidence, Majesty, God is white.

THE VALET: You seem sure of yourself . . .

255   THE MISSIONARY: Would he have allowed—you young milksop—would he have allowed the Miracle of Greece? For two thousand years God has been white. He eats on a white tablecloth. He wipes his white mouth with a white napkin. He picks at white meat with a white fork. *(A pause.)* He watches

260   the snow fall.

ARCHIBALD: *(to VILLAGE)* Recite the rest to them. Any trouble on the way back?

VILLAGE: None at all. Besides, I had this. *(After working the breech noisily, he shows a revolver, which he lays on the shoe-*

265   *shine box, where it will remain.)*

VIRTUE: *(still very calm)* But after all, do you imagine that this kind of thing can go on much longer, these corpses that are

discovered at dawn—and even in broad daylight—in disgusting places and postures? Sooner or later there'll be a big blow-up. We've also got to beware of possible betrayal.   270

SNOW: What do you mean?

VIRTUE: That a Negro is capable of ratting on another Negro.

SNOW: Speak for yourself, madam.

VIRTUE: It's because of what I see and what goes on in my own soul and what I call the temptation of the Whites . . .   275

THE GOVERNOR: *(triumphantly)* I was sure of it. Sooner or later, they come round. All you have to do is pay the price.

THE QUEEN: I'll offer my jewels! I have cellars full of chests full of pearls fished up by them from their mysterious seas, diamonds, gold, pieces of eight unearthed from their deep   280
mines, I'll give them away, throw them away . . .

THE VALET: What about me?

THE QUEEN: You'll still have your queen, you naughty boy . . . Aged, in rags, but stately. Grand.

ARCHIBALD: *(to the QUEEN)* Allow us to continue.   285

THE JUDGE: *(to ARCHIBALD)* It's you who keep stalling. You promised us a re-enactment of the crime so as to deserve your condemnation. The Queen's waiting. Hurry up.

ARCHIBALD: *(to the JUDGE)* No one's cooperating. Except Virtue.   290

THE JUDGE: Well then, let Virtue lead off, or Village.

VILLAGE: *(panicky)* Negroes, it's not time yet for the part that's to be declaimed. All I have to say now is that the woman was white and that she gave our odor as an excuse for fleeing me. For fleeing me, because she didn't dare chase me away. Ah,   295
the great days when they used to hunt the Negro and the antelope! My father once told me . . .

ARCHIBALD: *(interrupting him)* Your father? Sir, don't use that word again! There was a shade of tenderness in your voice as you uttered it.   300

VILLAGE: And what do you suggest I call the male who knocked up the negress who gave birth to me?

ARCHIBALD: Dammit, do the best you can. Invent—if not words, then phrases that cut you off rather than bind you. Invent, not love, but hatred, and thereby make poetry, since   305
that's the only domain in which we're allowed to operate. For their entertainment? *(pointing to the audience)* We'll see. You referred, quite rightly, to our odor—our scent, which used to lead their hounds to us in the bush—you too were on the right track. Take a whiff and say that "she" *(pointing to the*   310
catafalque) knew that we stink. Proceed delicately. Be clever and choose only reasons for hatred. Keep from magnifying our savageness. Be careful not to seem a wild beast. If you do, you'll tempt their desire without gaining their esteem. So you murdered her. We're going to begin . . .   315

VILLAGE: Just a minute. What can I substitute for the word father?

ARCHIBALD: Your circumlocution is quite satisfactory.

VILLAGE: It's rather long.

ARCHIBALD: By stretching language we'll distort it sufficiently to   320
wrap ourselves in it and hide, whereas the masters contract it.

BOBO: Generally, I'm brief.

ARCHIBALD: You're generally eager to see the others hide behind their words. But, like us, my dear Bobo, you delight the ear with morning-glories that twine round the pillars of the   325
world. We must charm. From their toes to their ears, our pink

tongues—the only part of us that suggests a flower—move artfully and silently round and about our fine, lackadaisical ladies and gentlemen. Will the phrase do?

330 VILLAGE: Yours?

ARCHIBALD: Yours, stupid . . . "the Negro who knocked up" and so on . . . Does everyone approve? Except Snow—still stubborn?

SNOW: (very acrimoniously) If I were sure that Village bumped
335 the woman off in order to heighten the fact that he's a scarred, smelly, thick-lipped, snub-nosed Negro, an eater and guzzler of Whites and all other colors, a drooling, sweating, belching, spitting, coughing, farting goat-fucker, a licker of white boots, a good-for-nothing, sick, oozing oil and sweat, limp
340 and submissive, if I were sure he killed her in order to merge with the night . . . But I know he loved her.

VIRTUE: He didn't.

VILLAGE: I didn't.

SNOW: (to VIRTUE) So you think he loves you, you, the submis-
345 sive black wench?

ARCHIBALD: (severely) Snow!

SNOW: (to VIRTUE) To turn pink, to blush with emotion, with confusion—tender expressions that will never apply to us. Otherwise you'd see Virtue's cheeks turn flaming purple.

350 VIRTUE: Mine?

BOBO: Someone's.

(All the NEGROES are now gathered at the right. They cease to speak. NEWPORT NEWS enters from the wings. He moves forward quietly.)

ARCHIBALD: (going up to him) Well? Has anything happened yet?

NEWPORT NEWS: He's arrived. We've brought him along, hand-
355 cuffed.

(All the NEGROES cluster about NEWPORT NEWS.)

SNOW: What are you going to do?

NEWPORT NEWS: (bending down and picking up the revolver from the shoeshine box) First of all, question him . . .

ARCHIBALD: (interrupting) Say only what you have to. We're be-
360 ing watched.

(They all look up at the COURT.)

THE JUDGE: (crying out) Just because you're disguised as trained dogs you think you know how to talk, and you start inventing riddles . . .

VILLAGE: (to the JUDGE) Some day . . .

365 ARCHIBALD: (interrupting) Cut it. If you lose your temper, you'll betray yourself and betray us. (to NEWPORT NEWS): Did he say anything to justify himself? Anything at all?

NEWPORT NEWS: Nothing. Shall I go?

ARCHIBALD: When the Court of Justice has been set up, come
370 back, and let us know.

(NEWPORT NEWS moves away from the group and is about to leave.)

DIOUF: (timidly) Do you really want to take that object with you? (pointing to the revolver in NEWPORT NEWS' hand)

ARCHIBALD: (to DIOUF, violently) I repeat once again—you're wasting your time. We know your argument. You're going to
375 urge us to be reasonable, to be conciliatory. But we're bent on being unreasonable, on being hostile. You'll speak of love. Go right ahead, since our speeches are set down in the script. (All except DIOUF and NEWPORT NEWS let out an orchestrated laugh.)

NEWPORT NEWS: You really ought to listen to him . . .
380
ARCHIBALD: (imperiously) Clear out! Get back into the wings. Take the revolver and go do your job.

NEWPORT NEWS: But . . .

VILLAGE: (breaking in) No buts about it. Obey Mr. Wellington. (Resignedly, NEWPORT NEWS starts to leave, but VILLAGE
385 stops him.) Not that way, you fool!

(Exit NEWPORT NEWS, left.)

BOBO: You asked for the floor, Mr. Clergyman. Speak up!

DIOUF: (with an effort) Everything about me seems ludicrous to you. I know it does . . .

ARCHIBALD: Bear one thing in mind: we must deserve their rep-
390 robation and get them to deliver the judgment that will condemn us. I repeat, they know about our crime . . .

DIOUF: All the same, let me try to come to an understanding with them, to propose some kind of agreement . . .

ARCHIBALD: (irritably) All right, you may speak, Mr. Diouf. But
395 we'll close our eyes and seal our mouths, and our barren faces will suggest the desert. Let's all shut up . . .

DIOUF: (panicky) Gentlemen, gentlemen, ladies, don't leave!

ARCHIBALD: (implacably) Let's shut up! Let's efface ourselves. Now speak.
400
DIOUF: But who'll hear me? (The COURT bursts out laughing.) You? That's not possible. (He wants to talk to the NEGROES, but they have closed their eyes and mouths and put their hands over their ears.) After all, gentlemen, my good friends, it's not a fresh corpse that we need. I'd like the ceremony to involve
405 us, not in hatred . . .

THE NEGROES: (ironically, and in a dismal voice) . . . but in love!

DIOUF: If it's possible, ladies and gentlemen.

THE MISSIONARY: . . . to involve you, above all, in your love
410 of us.

THE VALET: Are you speaking seriously, Monsignor?

THE JUDGE: Then we shall deign to hear you.

THE GOVERNOR: Although, after this orgy . . .

DIOUF: (with an appeasing gesture of his hand) May I explain? I
415 should indeed like the performance to re-establish in our souls a balance that our plight perpetuates, but I should like it to unfold so harmoniously that they (pointing to the audience) see only the beauty of it, and I would like them to recognize us in that beauty which disposes them to love.
420
(A long silence.)

BOBO: (slowly opening her eyes) The crossing of the desert was long and arduous. Poor Diouf, finding no oasis, you probably opened your veins to drink a little blood!

THE MISSIONARY: (after coughing) Tell me, my dear Vicar,

425 what about the Host? Yes, the Host. Will you invent a black Host? And what will it be made of? Gingerbread, you say? That's brown.

DIOUF: But Monsignor, we have a thousand ingredients. We'll dye it. A gray Host . . .

430 THE GOVERNOR: (*breaking in*) Grant the gray Host and you're sunk. You'll see — he'll demand further concessions, more oddities.

DIOUF: (*plaintively*) White on one side, black on the other.

THE VALET: (*to* DIOUF) Would you be so kind as to inform me —

435 for, after all, I have chosen to be understanding — where the Negro went with his revolver just before?

ARCHIBALD: Backstage. (*to* DIOUF): And stop jabbering. Good God, one would think you were trying to ridicule us.

DIOUF: (*to* ARCHIBALD) Sir, I apologize. I'd like to glorify my

440 color, just as you do. The kindness of the whites settled upon my head, as it did upon yours. Though it rested there lightly, it was unbearable. Their intelligence descended upon my right shoulder, and a whole flock of virtues upon my left. And at times, when I opened my hands, I would find their charity

445 nestling there. In my Negro solitude, I feel the need, just as you do, to glorify my exquisite savageness, but I'm old and I think . . .

BOBO: Who's asking you to? What we need is hatred. Our ideas will spring from hatred.

450 DIOUF: (*ironically*) You're a technician, Bobo, but it's not easy to cast off a guilty meekness that the heart desires. I've suffered too much shame not to want to befoul their beauteous souls, but . . .

ARCHIBALD: No buts about it, or get out! My anger isn't make-

455 believe.

DIOUF: Please, Archy . . .

ARCHIBALD: Don't be so familiar. Not here. Politeness must be raised to such a pitch that it becomes monstrous. It must arouse fear. We're being observed by spectators. Sir, if you

460 have any intention of presenting even the most trivial of their ideas without caricaturing it, then get out! Beat it!

BOBO: He wouldn't mind — it's his day off.

VILLAGE: Let him keep talking. The sound of his voice moves me.

465 SNOW: Bravo! I was expecting something like that from you. Because you, too, fear this moment. Perhaps because the action will separate you and Virtue for a while.

THE GOVERNOR: (*suddenly*) You were told what to do — start off with Village, start off with Virtue.

(*The* NEGROES *are taken aback for a moment and look at each other, then resign themselves.*)

470 VILLAGE: (*bowing to* VIRTUE, *and sighing deeply*) Madam, I bring you nothing comparable to what is called love. What is happening within me is very mysterious and cannot be accounted for by my color. When I beheld you . . .

ARCHIBALD: Be careful, Village, don't start referring to your real

475 life.

VILLAGE: (*with one knee on the floor*) When I beheld you, you were walking in the rain, in high heels. You were wearing a

475 **life** From this point until he says "Careful, Village," Archibald will saw the air with his hands like an orchestra leader, as if he were directing Village's recital.

black silk dress, black stockings, patent leather pumps and were carrying a black umbrella. Oh, if only I hadn't been born into slavery! I'd have been flooded with a strange emo- 480 tion, but we — you and I — were moving along the edges of the world, out of bounds. We were the shadow, or the dark interior, of luminous creatures . . . When I beheld you, suddenly — for perhaps a second — I had the strength to reject everything that wasn't you, and to laugh at the illusion. But 485 my shoulders are very frail. I was unable to bear the weight of the world's condemnation. And I began to hate you when everything about you would have kindled my love and when love would have made men's contempt unbearable, and their contempt would have made my love unbearable. The fact is, 490 I hate you.

(*For some moments, the* COURT *seems to have been growing agitated. The* VALET *seems to be yelling silently into the cupped ear of the* GOVERNOR.)

ARCHIBALD: (*to the* COURT) Please!

THE VALET: (*yelling*) M'Zaita 2,010!

THE GOVERNOR: What about coffee?

THE VALET: (*The entire* COURT *listens very attentively*) Extra- 495 Special Arabica 608–627. Robusta 327–327. Kuilu 313–317.

VILLAGE: (*who had lowered his head, raises it to resume his speech*) . . . I know not whether you are beautiful. I fear you may be. I fear your sparkling darkness. Oh darkness, stately mother of my race, shadow, sheath that swathes me from top 500 to toe, long sleep in which the frailest of your children would love to be shrouded. I know not whether you are beautiful, but you are Africa, oh monumental night, and I hate you. I hate you for filling my black eyes with sweetness. I hate you for making me thrust you from me, for making me hate you. 505 It would take so little for your face, your body, your movements, your heart to thrill me . . .

ARCHIBALD: Careful, Village!

VILLAGE: (*to* VIRTUE) But I hate you! (*to the others*): But let me tell her and tell you about all the pain I have to endure. If love 510 is denied us, I want you to know . . .

BOBO: We know all about it. We're black too. But in order to refer to ourselves, we don't adorn our metaphors with stars. Or grand nocturnal images. But with soot and blacking, with coal and tar. 515

DIOUF: Don't make it so hard for him. If his suffering is too intense, let him use language to ease the strain.

VILLAGE: Ease the strain? I remember how I suffered to see that tall, gleaming body walking the rain. Her feet were getting soaked . . . 520

BOBO: Her black feet. *Black* feet!

VILLAGE: In the rain. Virtue was walking in the rain, looking for White customers, as you know. No, no, there'll be no love for us . . . (*he hesitates*)

VIRTUE: You may speak. Every brothel has its negress. 525

THE GOVERNOR: (*after clearing his throat*) To the whorehouse, dammit! Egad, to the whorehouse! I make my troops tear off a piece every Saturday. Pox and shankers, doesn't matter a damn! Troops should end up lame and limping. To the whorehouse, dammit! 530

(*The entire* COURT *applauds. The* GOVERNOR *puffs himself up.*)

VIRTUE: Then let me tell you that this evening's ceremony will affect me less than the one I perform ten times a day. I'm the only one who experiences shame to the bitter end . . .

ARCHIBALD: Don't allude to your life.

535 VIRTUE: *(ironically)* You've been infected by the squeamishness you've picked up from the Whites. A whore shocks you.

BOBO: She does, if she's one in real life. There's no need for us to know about your personal sufferings and dislikes. That's *your* business . . . in your room.

540 VILLAGE: This ceremony is painful to me.

ARCHIBALD: To us, too. They tell us that we're grown-up children. In that case, what's left for us? The theater! We'll play at being reflected in it, and we'll see ourselves — big black narcissists — slowly disappearing into its waters.

545 VILLAGE: I don't want to disappear.

ARCHIBALD: You're no exception! Nothing will remain of you but the foam of your rage. Since they merge us with an image and drown us in it, let the image set their teeth on edge!

VILLAGE: My body wants to live.

550 ARCHIBALD: You're becoming a specter before their very eyes and you're going to haunt them.

VILLAGE: I love Virtue. She loves me.

ARCHIBALD: Yes, she, perhaps. She has powers that you haven't. There are times when she dominates the Whites — oh, I

555 know, by her magic wiggle. But that's also a way of dominating them. She can therefore bring you what most resembles love: tenderness. In her arms, you'll be her child, not her lover.

VILLAGE: *(obstinately)* I love Virtue.

560 ARCHIBALD: You think you love her. You're a Negro and a performer. Neither of whom will know love. Now, this evening — but this evening only — we cease to be performers, since we are Negroes. On this stage, we're like guilty prisoners who play at being guilty.

565 VILLAGE: We don't want to be guilty of anything any more. Virtue will be my wife.

ARCHIBALD: Then get the hell out! Beat it! Go away. Take her with you. Go join them *(pointing to the audience)* . . . if they'll have you. If they accept you both. And if you succeed

570 in winning their love, come back and let me know. But first discolor yourselves. Get the hell out. Go join them. Go down and be spectators. *We'll be saved by that (pointing to the catafalque).*

THE VALET: *(in an oily tone)* Gentlemen, what if it happened to

575 be a man that you caught in your net one fine summer evening? What would you do about the seduction scene? Have you ever captured a carpenter with his plane? Or a bargeman with his canal-boats and his clothes hanging on a line?

BOBO: *(very insolently)* Yes, we have! We picked up an old down-

580 and-out vaudeville singer: wrapped up and cased. There *(pointing to the catafalque).* Only too happy to dress him up for the ceremony as a governor-general, when he was killed before the eyes of the crowd — last night's, ladies and gentlemen. We deposited him in the attic. Where he still is.

585 *(pointing to the corpse)* Similarly, we did away with a decent, helpless old lady, a milkman, a postman, a seamstress, a government clerk . . . *(The* COURT *shrinks in horror.)*

THE VALET: *(persisting)* And what if there'd been nothing available but a four-year-old lad on his way home from the grocer's

with a bottle of milk? Be careful how you answer and bear in 590 mind the great effort I am making to regard you as human . . .

BOBO: We know only too well what he'll become when he's drunk too much milk. And if we can't find a kid, then an old horse will do, or a dog or a doll.

VILLAGE: So it's always murder that we dream about? 595

ARCHIBALD: Always, and get going!

VILLAGE: *(to* VIRTUE, *though still hesitantly)* Come. Follow me. *(He starts leaving the stage, as if going down to join the audience.)*

ARCHIBALD: *(holding them back)* No, no, that's not necessary. 600 Since we're on the stage, where everything is relative, all I need do is walk backwards in order to create the theatrical illusion of your moving away from me. Off I go. And I'm giving you rope enough to hang yourself, Mr. Wise-guy, by leaving you alone with that woman. You're on your own. The 605 rest of us, let's go.

(ARCHIBALD, BOBO, DIOUF, SNOW and FELICITY turn away and, holding their faces in their hands, move off, when suddenly nine or ten white masks suddenly appear about the COURT.)

VILLAGE: *(to* VIRTUE*)* I love you.

VIRTUE: Let's not rush matters, Village.

VILLAGE: I love you.

VIRTUE: That's an easy thing to say. An easy sentiment to feign, 610 especially if it's limited to desire. You speak of love, but do you think we're alone? *(She points to the* COURT.*)*

VILLAGE: *(alarmed)* As many as that!

VIRTUE: You insisted on being alone.

VILLAGE: *(more and more panicky)* But without them. Archi- 615 bald! *(he cries out:)* Archibald! Bobo! *(They all remain unmoved.)* Snow! *(He rushes over to them, but they do not move. He comes back to* VIRTUE.*)* Virtue? They won't go away, will they?

VIRTUE: Don't be afraid. You wanted to love me. You spoke of 620 leaving everything for . . .

VILLAGE: I don't know whether I'll have the strength to. Now that they're here . . .

VIRTUE: *(she puts her hand on his mouth)* Be still. First, let's love each other, if you have the strength to. 625

(But the members of the COURT *seem to be getting excited, except for the* QUEEN, *who is dozing. They stamp their feet, fidget, clap hands.)*

THE GOVERNOR: Damn it, they're going to gum up the works! Don't let them continue. *(to the* QUEEN*)*: Madam, madam, wake up!

THE JUDGE: The Queen is asleep. *(with a finger to his lips)* She's hatching. Hatching what? Celtic remains and the stained- 630 glass windows of Chartres.

THE GOVERNOR: Damn it, wake her up . . . Give her a dousing, the way they do at the barracks . . .

THE JUDGE: You're out of your mind! Who'll do the hatching? You? 635

THE GOVERNOR: *(sheepishly)* I never knew how.

THE VALET: Neither did I. Especially standing up. For of course no one has seen my chair.

THE MISSIONARY: *(annoyed)* Nor mine. And I have to remain on my feet, although I'm a bishop-at-large. Nevertheless, 640 they've got to be prevented from continuing. Listen . . .

(Below, VILLAGE *and* VIRTUE, *who have been talking voicelessly, now continue aloud.)*

VILLAGE: Our color isn't a wine stain that blotches a face, our face isn't a jackal that devours those it looks at . . . *(shouting)* I'm handsome, you're beautiful, and we love each other! I'm strong! If anyone touches you . . .

645

VIRTUE: *(thrilled)* It would make me happy. *(*VILLAGE *is taken aback.)*

THE GOVERNOR: *(to the* COURT*)* Do you hear them? We've got to stop them. Right away. The Queen ought to speak. Madam,

650   jump out of bed! *(He imitates with his mouth the bugle call of reveille.)*

The JUDGE, *the* MISSIONARY *and the* VALET *are bent over the* QUEEN. *They stand up straight, looking woebegone.)*

THE MISSIONARY: There's no doubt about it, she's snoring.

THE GOVERNOR: What about that great voice of hers? I'm listening.

(A brief silence.)

655   VIRTUE: *(softly, as if in a state of somnambulism)* I am the lily-white Queen of the West. Only centuries and centuries of breeding could achieve such a miracle! Immaculate, pleasing to the eye and to the soul! . . .

(The entire COURT *listens attentively.)*

Whether in excellent health, pink and gleaming, or con-
660   sumed with languor, I am white. If death strikes me, I die in the color of victory. Oh noble pallor, color my temples, my fingers, my belly! Oh eye of mine, delicately shaded iris, bluish iris, iris of the glaciers, violet, hazel, gray-green, evergreen iris, English lawn, Norman lawn, through you, but
665   what do we see . . .

(The QUEEN, *who has finally awakened but is in a dazed state, listens to the poem and then recites along with* VIRTUE*)*

. . . I am white, it's milk that denotes me, it's the lily, the dove, quicklime and the clear conscience, it's Poland with its eagle and snow! Snow . . .

VILLAGE: *(suddenly lyrical)* Snow? If you like. Haunt me, lance
670   bearer. With my long dark strides I roamed the earth. Against that moving mass of darkness the angry but respectful sun flashed its beams. They did not traverse my dusky bulk. I was naked.

VIRTUE and THE QUEEN: *(together)* It's innocence and morn-
675   ing.

VILLAGE: The surfaces of my body were curved mirrors in which all things were reflected: fish, buffaloes, the laughter of tigers, reeds. Naked? Or was my shoulder covered with a leaf? And my member adorned with moss . . .

680   VIRTUE and THE QUEEN: *(together)* . . . except that a bit of shade remained in my armpits . . .

VILLAGE: *(with rising frenzy)* . . . with moss, or seaweed? I was not singing, I was not dancing. Standing insolently — in short, royally — with hand on hip, I was pissing. Oh! Oh! Oh!
685   I crawled through the cotton plants. The dogs sniffed me out. I bit my chains and wrists. Slavery taught me dancing and singing.

VIRTUE: *(alone)* . . . a swarthy violet, almost black, ring is spreading to my cheek. The night . . .

VILLAGE: . . . I died in the hold of the slave ship . . .   690

*(*VIRTUE *approaches him.)*

VIRTUE and THE QUEEN: I love you.

VILLAGE: I'm a long time dying.

THE QUEEN: *(suddenly wide awake)* That'll do! Silence them, they've stolen my voice! Help! . . .

(Suddenly FELICITY *stands up. Everyone looks at her and listens in silence.)*

FELICITY: Dahomey! . . . Dahomey! . . . Negroes from all cor-   695
ners of the earth, to the rescue! Come! Enter into me and only me! Swell me with your tumult! Come barging in! Penetrate where you will: my mouth, my ears — or my nostrils. Nostrils, enormous conches, glory of my race, sunless shafts, tunnels, yawning grottoes where sniffling battalions lie at rest!   700
Giantess with head thrown back, I await you all. Enter into me, ye multitudes, and be, for this evening only, my force and reason.

(She sits down again. The dialogue continues.)

THE QUEEN: *(very solemnly and almost swooning)* "The hind that would be mated by the lion must die for love." —   705
Shakespeare.

THE VALET: Madam is dying!

THE QUEEN: Not yet! To the rescue, angel of the flaming sword, virgins of the Parthenon, stained-glass of Chartres, Lord Byron, Chopin, French cooking, the Unknown Soldier, Ty-   710
rolean songs, Aristotelian principles, heroic couplets, poppies, sunflowers, a touch of coquetry, vicarage gardens . . .

THE ENTIRE COURT: Madam, we're here.

THE QUEEN: Ah, that's a comfort. I thought I'd been abandoned! They would have harmed me!   715

THE JUDGE: There's nothing to worry about. Our laws still hold.

THE MISSIONARY: *(to the* QUEEN, *and facing her)* Have patience. We've only just begun the long death struggle, which gives them such pleasure. Let's put a good face on it. It's in order to please them that we're going to die . . .   720

THE QUEEN: Can't they hurry and get it over with? I'm weary, and their odor is choking me. *(She pretends to be fainting.)*

THE MISSIONARY: Impossible. They've planned it down to the last detail, not in accordance with their own strength, but with our state of exhaustion.   725

THE QUEEN: *(in a dying voice)* And we're still too lively, aren't we? Yet all my blood's ebbing away.

(At that moment, ARCHIBALD, DIOUF, SNOW *and* BOBO *draw themselves up, turn about and move toward* VILLAGE.*)*

ARCHIBALD: Village, for the last time, I beseech you . . .

VILLAGE: For the last time? This evening? *(with sudden decision)* All right. This evening, for the last time. But you'll have   730
to help me. Will you? Will you help me work myself up? Will you work me up?

SNOW: Me first, because I'm sick and tired of your cowardice.

VILLAGE: *(pointing to the catafalque)* It was I who killed her, and yet you accuse me.   735

SNOW: You had to bring yourself to do it.

VILLAGE: How do you know? You were hidden in the garden, you were waiting for me under the locust tree. How could you have possibly seen me hesitating? While you were munching

740 flowers in the twilight, I was bleeding her, without turning a hair.

SNOW: Yes, but you've been speaking about her lovingly ever since.

VILLAGE: Not about her, but about my gesture.

745 SNOW: You're lying!

VILLAGE: You're in love with me!

(From this point on, the entire troupe becomes increasingly frenzied.)

SNOW: You're lying. When you speak of her, such a gentle expression, a look of such poignant sadness, comes over your thick lips and sick eyes that I can see Nostalgia in person peep-
750 ing out. It wasn't your gesture that you were describing when you spoke to me about her lifted blue dress, nor your anger when you described her mouth and teeth, nor the resistance of the flesh to the knife when you mentioned her weary eye-lids, nor your nausea when you told of how her body fell to
755 the rug . . .

VILLAGE: You liar!

SNOW: . . . nor your sorrow when you thought of her pallor, nor your fear of the police when you outlined her ankles. You were talking of a great love. From far off, from Ubangi or
760 Tanganyika, a tremendous love came here to die, to lick white ankles. Negro, you were in love. Like a sergeant in the ma-rines. *(She drops to the floor, exhausted, but* BOBO *and* ARCHI-BALD *lift her up.* BOBO *gives her a slap.)*

BOBO: *(holding up* SNOW's *head, as if she were vomiting)* Con-
765 tinue. Spill it all out. Spill it out! Spill it out!

*(*VILLAGE *gets more and more irritated.)*

SNOW: *(as if trying to find more insults and vomiting them forth, with hiccoughs)* Swear! Just as others change their family or city or country or name, just as they change gods, swear that it never occurred to you to change color in order to attain her.
770 But since you couldn't even dream of royal white, you wished for a green skin . . . You've still got it!

VILLAGE: *(as if on edge)* You misunderstand completely. In or-der to arouse her, to attract her, I had to dance my nuptial flight. I beat my wing sheaths. When it was over, I died,
775 completely exhausted. My body was abandoned, and perhaps she entered while I was resting from my dance—or while I was dancing, who knows?

SNOW: So you admit!

VILLAGE: Not at all! All I know is that I killed her, since there she
780 is *(pointing to the catafalque).* All I know is that one evening, when I went out hunting in the street, hunting the White-woman, I killed the one I brought back to you.

(But they all turn their heads away. MRS. FELICITY *steps down from her throne very majestically. She goes to the catafalque, bends down and slips a few grains under the sheet.)*

BOBO: Already!

FELICITY: I'm not stuffing her, you know. All the same, it's better
785 for her not to dwindle away.

DIOUF: What do you feed her? Rice?

FELICITY: Corn. *(She silently returns to her place.)*

BOBO: Well well, it's a long time since anyone's noticed Mr. Diouf. Look at how he's perked up. My word, he seems quite
790 pleased with himself.

DIOUF: *(alarmed)* Madam . . .

BOBO: What, Madam? Madam yourself. His eyes are gleaming. Does he already see his voluptuous bosom that the Negro lusts after?

DIOUF: *(frightened)* Madam! Bobo! It was wrong of me to have 795 come this evening. Please let me go. Village is the one you ought to be concerned with. He's the one who has to be spurred on!

ARCHIBALD: We'll attend to Village. His crime saves him. If he committed it with hatred . . . 800

VILLAGE: *(screaming)* But it was with hatred! How can you doubt it? Are you all out of your mind? Tell me, ladies and gentlemen, are you crazy? She was standing behind her counter.

(A long silence. The actors seem to be hanging on his words.)

SNOW: You said before: sitting at her sewing-machine. 805

VILLAGE: *(obstinately)* She was standing behind her counter.

BOBO: Well, what did she do?

(They are all attentive.)

VILLAGE: Negroes, I beseech you! She was standing . . .

ARCHIBALD: *(gravely)* I order you to be black to your very veins. Pump black blood through them. Let Africa circulate in 810 them. Let Negroes negrify themselves. Let them persist to the point of madness in what they're condemned to be, in their ebony, in their odor, in their yellow eyes, in their cannibal tastes. Let them not be content with eating Whites, but let them cook each other as well. Let them invent recipes for 815 shin-bones, knee-caps, calves, thick lips, everything. Let them invent unknown sauces. Let them invent hiccoughs, belches, and farts that'll give out a deleterious jazz. Let them invent a criminal painting and dancing. Negroes, if they change toward us, let it not be out of indulgence, but terror. 820 *(to* DIOUF): And you, Mr. Vicar General, for whom Christ died on the cross, you've got to make up your mind. *(to* VIL-LAGE): As for Village, let him continue his spiel. So she was standing behind her counter. And what did she do? What did she say? And you, what did you do for us? 825

VILLAGE: *(pointing to* ARCHIBALD) She was standing there, where you are.

ARCHIBALD: *(stepping back)* No, no, not me.

VILLAGE: *(dancing in front of the coffin)* Then who? *(No one answers.)* Well, who? Now that she's dead, do you want me 830 to open the coffin and repeat what I did with her when she was alive? You realize I'm supposed to re-enact it. I need a straight-man. This evening, I'm going through the whole thing. This evening, I'm giving a farewell performance. Who'll help me? Who? After all, it doesn't much matter who. 835 As everyone knows, the Whites can hardly distinguish one Negro from another.

(They all look at FELICITY. *She hesitates, then draws herself up and speaks.)*

FELICITY: Mr. . . . Samba Graham Diouf! You're it.

DIOUF: *(frightened)* But Madam . . .

FELICITY: This evening, you're the dead woman. Take your places. 840

(Slowly and solemnly, each takes his place. DIOUF *stands in front of the catafalque, facing the audience.)*

FELICITY: (*sitting down again*) Bring in the implements.

(BOBO *brings from behind the right screen a console-table on which are lying a blond wig, a crude cardboard carnival mask representing a laughing white woman with big cheeks, a piece of pink knitting, two balls of wool, a knitting needle and white gloves.*)

FELICITY: Mr. Diouf, make your declaration. You know the formula, I take it.

DIOUF: (*facing the audience*) I, Samba Graham Diouf, born in the swamps of Ubangi Chari, sadly bid you farewell. I am not afraid. Open the door and I shall enter. I shall descend to the death you are preparing for me.

FELICITY: Good. Let's get on with the farewell.

(DIOUF *remains standing in front of the catafalque, while the other actors line up toward the left and walk slowly backward, gently waving small handkerchiefs which the men have drawn from their pockets and the women from their bosoms. Standing in line, they walk backward very slowly about the catafalque, while* DIOUF, *facing the audience, keeps bowing to them in acknowledgement. In an undertone, they sing a kind of lullaby.*)

ALL: (*singing*)

    Whistle gentle blackbirds
    Nimble pickaninnies
    Swimming in the water
    Like any other birdies,
    Birdies of the islands.
    Charming little rascals
    Be careful of the sharks
    There's redness in the sky
    Come back again and sleep
    In shadows on the lawn
    My tears and sobs will comfort me.

(DIOUF *bows and thanks them.*)

DIOUF: Your song was very beautiful, and your sadness does me honor. I'm going to start life in a new world. If ever I return, I'll tell you what it's like there. Great black country, I bid thee farewell. (*He bows.*)

ARCHIBALD: And now, ready for the mask!

DIOUF: (*grumblingly*) Are you sure we couldn't do without it? Look about you—people manage to do without all kinds of things, salt, tobacco, the subway, women, and even salted peanuts for cocktails and eggs for omelettes.

ARCHIBALD: I said let's get on with it. The implements.

(*The actors ceremoniously bring the wig, mask and gloves, with which they bedeck* DIOUF. *Thus adorned, he takes the knitting. While this goes on,* VILLAGE *gets impatient.*)

ARCHIBALD: (*to* VILLAGE) Carry on.

VILLAGE: (*stepping back, as if to judge the effect*) I'd gone to have a drink after work . . .

BOBO: Stop! You're too pale.

(*She runs to the shoeshine box and comes back to blacken* VILLAGE's *face and hands, which she spits on and rubs.*)

S.D. **gloves** In Blin's production—and Blin was right—these props were hooked on a vertical board and were visible to the audience from the very beginning.

BOBO: And if her teeth don't chatter now!

VILLAGE: So there she was . . . (*suddenly he stops and seems to be groping for words*) Are you sure there's any point in going straight through to the end?

SNOW: A little while ago you had no qualms about insulting me, and now you haven't strength enough to kill a white woman who's already dead.

BOBO: Snow's right. She's always right. Your hesitations throw us off. We were beginning to drool with impatience.

ARCHIBALD: (*angrily*) Take back that word, Bobo. No hysteria. This isn't a revival meeting, it's a ceremony.

BOBO: (*to the audience*) I beg your pardon, ladies. I beg your pardon, gentlemen.

VILLAGE: So there she was . . . But, Negroes, you've forgotten the insults.

(*They all look at each other.*)

ARCHIBALD: So we have. He's right. You take it, Virtue. And roll them out, high and clear.

(*Bowing to* DIOUF, VIRTUE *recites a litany the way litanies of the Blessed Virgin are recited in church, in a monotone.*)

VIRTUE:

          LITANY OF THE LIVID

    Livid as a t.b. death rattle,
    Livid as the droppings of a man with jaundice,
    Livid as the belly of a cobra,
    Livid as their convicts,
    Livid as the god they nibble in the morning,
    Livid as a knife in the night,
    Livid . . . except: the English, Germans
    and Belgians, who are red . . . livid as
    jealousy.
    Hail, the livid!

(VIRTUE *steps aside.* SNOW *takes her place and, after bowing to* DIOUF):

SNOW: I, too, greet you, Tower of Ivory, Gate of Heaven flung wide open so that the Negro can enter, majestic and smelly. But how livid you are! What malady consumes you? Will you play Camille this evening? Wondrous, indeed, the malady that makes you ever whiter and that leads you to ultimate whiteness. (*she bursts out laughing*) But what's that I see flowing down your black stockings? So it was true, Lord Jesus, that behind the mask of a cornered White is a poor trembling Negro. (*She steps back and says to* BOBO): Take it.

BOBO: Let's both take it! (*She tucks up her skirt and does an obscene dance.*)

ARCHIBALD: All right. Take it, Village.

VILLAGE: I don't know whether I'll be able . . .

ARCHIBALD: (*furiously*) What? Changing tone again? Whom are you talking to? What are you talking about? This is the theater, not the street. The theater, and drama, and crime.

VILLAGE: (*with sudden fury, he seems about to spring forward, makes a gesture as if to thrust everyone aside*) Stand aside! Here I come! (*He had stepped back, and now moves forward.*) I enter. And I fart. Lumbering along on my thighs, cast iron columns. And I breeze in. I take a look around . . .

BOBO: You're lying. Last night you entered slyly, very cautiously. You're distorting things.

925 VILLAGE: (*continuing*) I enter, and I approach, softly. I take a furtive peep. I look about me. To the right. To the left. "How do you, Madam? (*He bows to* DIOUF, *who, with the knitting in his hand, returns the bow.*) How do you do, Madam? It's not warm. (*They all cock their ears to hear what the* MASK
930 says. *He stops talking, but the actors must have heard him, for they raise their heads and laugh, with their orchestrated laugh.*) It's not warm. I've made so bold as to come in for a moment. Here at least it's nice and comfortable. Are you knitting a helmet? A pink one? The light is very soft. It suits
935 your pretty face. Yes, I'll have a glass of rum. I'll have a nip. (*in a different tone, addressing the* NEGROES): That the right tone?

ALL: (*breathlessly*) Yes!

VILLAGE: The moon—for it was almost night—rose artfully
940 over a landscape inhabited by insects. It's a distant land, madam, but my whole body could sing it. Listen to the singing! Listen! (*Suddenly he breaks off and points to the* MASK, *who is knitting.*) But he's not wearing a skirt! What kind of masquerade is that? I'll stop my speech if you don't put a skirt
945 on him.

ARCHIBALD: Snow, your shawl . . .

SNOW: My net shawl? He'll step on it and tear it.

ARCHIBALD: Well, doesn't anyone have something to give him?

(*They are all silent. Suddenly* FELICITY *stands up. She takes off her skirt and tosses it to* DIOUF.)

FELICITY: Slip it on. It'll hide your shoes.

(DIOUF *stops knitting. He is helped on with the skirt.*)

950 VILLAGE: I'll go back a little . . . "The moon . . ."

BOBO: No, you've already recited that.

VILLAGE: (*resignedly*) All right. I continue. Listen to the singing of my thighs . . . Because . . . (*a rather long pause, during which he pretends to have an important revelation to make*) . . .
955 because my thighs fascinated her. (*fatuously*) Ask her. (*The* NEGROES *go to the* MASK *and whisper in his ear. The* MASK *remains silent, but the* NEGROES *burst out laughing.*) You see! She even has the nerve to boast of it! (*A pause.*) But that's not all, she has to raise a laugh besides! From the attic, where her
960 bed was, I could hear her mother calling for her evening medicine. (*A brief pause; then, to* FELICITY): Well, that's your cue. Play the Mother.

FELICITY: (*imitating a plaintive patient, with her eyes to the ceiling*) Ma-a-rie! Maa-a-arie! Daughter, it's time for my sugared
965 almonds and aspirin! And it's prayer-time.

(*The* MASK *seems to be moving toward the voice. He takes a few short steps in the direction of* FELICITY, *but* VILLAGE *calmly and sternly steps between them.*)

VILLAGE: (*assuming a woman's voice*) Yes, mother dear, right away. The water's heating. I'll iron another couple of sheets and then bring up your sugared almonds. (*to the* MASK): Take it easy, girlie. You don't give a damn about the old hag. Any
970 more than I do. She's had her day. To hell with her and her sugared almonds. If you're heating water, it's for after the fun. What's the matter, what's . . .

FELICITY: Ma-a-arie! My darling little daughter. It's time for my sugared almonds. When your father was still a magistrate, he
975 always used to bring me one at this time of day, in the gloam-

ing. Don't leave me alone in the attic. (*A pause.*) And don't forget, the baker's wife's coming.

ARCHIBALD: (*to* BOBO, *whom he pushes toward the right wing*) Your cue. Enter.

BOBO, *who has stepped back to the wing, enters hesitantly, as if she were in a procession.*)

BOBO: (*acting the neighbor*) Good evening, Marie. Aren't you 980
in? Goodness me, how dark it is. As our constable would say, in that roguish way of his, it's as dark here as up a nigger's ass-hole. Oh! I beg your pardon—I mean a Negro's. One should be polite. (*A pause.*) What, you're checking the day's accounts? All right, then I'll come back tomorrow. I know what 985
that's like. I'm a sensible person. Goodbye, Marie, and goodnight.

(*She mimes all the gestures of departure, but remains on-stage, near the wing, looking off-stage and fixed in an attitude of departure.*)

VILLAGE: (*resuming the formal tone of his recital*) So there I was, nestling in the shadow. And I whispered to her: Listen to the singing of my thighs! Listen! (*he makes his thighs bulge under* 990
his trousers.) That sound is the mewing of panthers and tigers. When they bend, that means leopards are stretching. If I un-button, an eagle of the Great Empire will swoop down from our snowy summits to your Pyrenees. But . . . I'm not dead set on unbuttoning. The fires are being lit. Under our dry fin- 995
gers, the drums . . .

(*They all start dancing in place—even* BOBO, *who is looking into the wings, even the* COURT, *but not the* MASK—*and clapping their hands very softly.*)

Then, in the glade, the dance began! (*turning to the others*) For I had to cast a spell on her, didn't I? My aim, then, was to draw her gently toward her room. The door of the shop opened out into the street, the old bitch was dying upstairs . . . 1000

FELICITY: (*imitating the old mother*) Almonds! A-a-al-monds! Prayers! Pra-a-ayers! It's time for your prayer! Don't forget!

VILLAGE: (*very annoyed*) She's going to spoil everything. (*reassuming the woman's voice*) I have one more layette to finish, mother dear, and then I'll be right up. (*resuming the formal* 1005
tone of his recital): I asked for another glass of rum. The liquor kindled my genius. I was feeling, as they say, a little high. In my eye I trotted out a big parade of our warriors, diseases, alligators, amazons, straw huts, cataracts, hunts, cotton, even leprosy and even a hundred thousand youngsters who 1010
died in the dust. Along my teeth I set adrift our pointiest canoes. With a hand in my pocket, as if I were going to dance the tango, I went up to her and said, "Kind lady, it's nasty outside." She replied:

(*As before, they all listen to the* MASK, *who says nothing. Then they burst out in their orchestrated laugh.*)

. . . Yes, you're quite right. We must be careful. People gossip 1015
in small towns . . .

BOBO: (*pretending to return and to want to enter the shop*) Marie, you still haven't put the light on. You'll spoil your eyes working in the dark. (*A pause.*) I hear someone whistling on the road. It's probably your husband. Good night, Marie. 1020

(*Same pantomime as before. All this time,* VILLAGE *has been looking as if he were very much afraid of being discovered.*)

VILLAGE: (*tone of the recital*) Indeed, one can never be too careful: suns revolve about the earth . . .

FELICITY: (*imitating the old mother*) Ma-a-arie! A-a-al-monds! Beware of the night, child. All cats are black in the dark, and one forgets to give the evening almond to one's old mother. (*A pause.*) Tell your sister Susan to come in.

VILLAGE: (*assuming the voice of a woman*) Susan! Susan! Where are you?

SNOW: (*who has run behind the catafalque, where she is hidden*) Why, I'm here. I'm in the garden.

VILLAGE: (*holding back the* MASK, *who seems to want to go toward the catafalque, and still imitating a woman's voice*) Are you all alone in the garden?

THE MISSIONARY: (*to* ARCHIBALD) Your cue, Archibald.

(ARCHIBALD *runs to the left wing, from which he now seems to be entering very casually, whistling as he walks. However, he merely imitates the movement of walking and actually remains where he is.*)

SNOW: I'm all alone, all by myself. I'm playing knucklebones.

VILLAGE: (*still in a woman's voice*) Be careful, Susan, watch out for prowlers. It hasn't been safe in these parts ever since they began recruiting aviators in Guiana.

VOICE OF SNOW: In Guiana! Aviators!

VILLAGE: (*voice of the recital*) In Guiana, you slut! . . . suns revolve about the earth, eagles swoop down on our battlefields . . . so let's close the window. She acted as if she didn't understand. Gallantly I closed the window. Snow was falling on the town.

VIRTUE: (*rushing toward him in a panic*) Stop it!

BOBO: (*still fixed in a movement of departure, but turning her head to blurt out the following*) Look at how he's carrying on. He's foaming. He's fuming. It's a mirage!

VIRTUE: Village, Village, please, I'm asking you, stop.

VILLAGE: (*looking at* VIRTUE) The limpidity of your blue eyes, that tear gleaming at the corner, your heavenly bosom . . .

VIRTUE: You're raving. Whom are you talking to?

VILLAGE: (*still looking at* VIRTUE) I love you and I can't bear it any longer.

VIRTUE: (*screaming*) Village!

SNOW: (*peeping out from behind the catafalque just long enough to say the following*) But, my dear, it has nothing to do with you, you might have realized it.

VILLAGE: (*turning slowly to the* MASK, *who mechanically goes on with his knitting*) Your feet, the soles of which are the color of periwinkles, your feet, which are varnished on top, walked along the pavement . . .

VIRTUE: You've already said that to me. Stop talking.

ARCHIBALD: (*breaking off his silent whistling and immobile walk and assuming an angry expression*) Negroes, I'm losing my temper. Either we continue the re-enactment or we leave.

VILLAGE: (*imperturbably, now fully facing the* MASK) The gentlest of your movements delineate you so exquisitely that when I'm on your shoulder I feel you're being borne by the wind. The rings under your eyes distress me. Madam, when you go . . . go on. (*to the audience*) For she wasn't coming, she was going. She was going to her bedroom . . .

FELICITY: (*imitating the old woman*) My almond and my prayer!

VOICE OF SNOW: Yes, yes, I'm alone in the garden, astride the jet of water.

BOBO: (*seeming to come back*) Good evening, Marie. Lock your door.

VILLAGE: (*voice of the recital*) . . . to her bedroom, where I followed her in order to strangle her. (*to the* MASK) Get going, slut. And go wash yourself. (*to the audience*) I had to work fast, the cuckold was on his way.

(*The* MASK *is about to start walking.*)

Stop! (*to the audience*): But first let me show you what I was able to get out of my tamed captive . . .

THE JUDGE: But what's Virtue's role in the crime?

(ARCHIBALD *and* BOBO *turn their heads.* SNOW *shows hers. They seem very much interested.*)

VILLAGE: (*after a moment's hesitation*) None. She never ceased to be present, at my side, in her immortal form. (*to the audience*): . . . my tamed captive. For she was clever and highly reputed among those of her race. Come. Stand in a circle. (*He pretends to be speaking both to the audience and to invisible* NEGROES *on the stage.*) Not too close. There. Now I'm going to make her work. (*to the* MASK): Are you ready, kid?

THE JUDGE: No, no. It's better to maintain a formal tone.

VILLAGE: Do you really want me to?

THE JUDGE: Yes, it's better. Don't be afraid to establish distance.

VILLAGE: As you like. (*to the audience*): She can play the piano. Very, very well. Would anyone like to hold her knitting for a moment?

(*He addresses the audience directly, until a* SPECTATOR *comes up and takes the needle from the* MASK's *hands.*)

(*to the* SPECTATOR): Thank you, sir (or "madam"). (*to the* MASK): Now play us a Strauss melody. (*The* MASK *docilely sits down on an invisible stool and, facing the audience, plays on an invisible piano.*) Stop! (*He stops playing. The* COURT *applauds.*)

THE QUEEN: (*simperingly*) Perfect, perfect, she was almost too perfect. Even in adversity, in disaster, our melodies will sing.

THE VALET: (*to* VILLAGE) What else can she do?

VILLAGE: As you've seen, she knits helmets for little chimney-sweeps. On Sunday she sings at the harmonium. She prays. (*to the* MASK): On your knees! (*He kneels.*) With your hands clasped. Eyes upward. Good. Pray! (*The entire* COURT *applauds in elegant fashion.*) She's good at lots of other things. She does water-colors and rinses glasses.

FELICITY: (*voice of the old mother*) Marie! Ma-a-arie! My a-a-almond! Child, it's time for it.

VILLAGE: (*woman's voice*) Right away, mother dear. I've almost finished rinsing the glasses. (*voice of the recital*) One day she even roasted in the flames . . .

THE COURT: (*except the* MISSIONARY) Speed it up, talk faster!

THE MISSIONARY: How dare you allude to that wicked affair.

THE VALET: (*to the* MISSIONARY) Haven't you placed her in heaven since then?

THE QUEEN: But, what do they mean?

VILLAGE: One day they caught her as she was wheeling about on her horse amidst the banners. They put her into prison and burned her at the stake.

SNOW: (*showing her head, and, with a burst of laughter*) Then they ate the pieces.

THE QUEEN: (with a piercing cry) My saint! (Exit, hiding her face and sobbing her heart out; the VALET accompanies her.)

VILLAGE: But, for the most part, she does what she can. When the time comes, she calls the midwife . . . (to BOBO): Take it, Bobo.

(BOBO approaches the MASK and speaks to him gently.)

BOBO: You'd better lie down so that it doesn't hurt too much. (She listens to the MASK, who makes no answer.) Your pride? . . . All right. Remain standing.

(She kneels and puts her hand under the MASK's skirt, from where she takes out a doll about two feet long representing the GOVERNOR.)

THE GOVERNOR: (to the COURT) I'm entering the world! With boots on, decorated . . .

(BOBO keeps searching, and pulls out another doll: the VALET.)

THE VALET: Here comes my mug!

(BOBO searches and takes out the JUDGE.)

THE JUDGE: (in amazement) Me?

THE GOVERNOR: (to the JUDGE) It's the spitting image of you!

(BOBO pulls out the MISSIONARY.)

THE MISSIONARY: The ways of Providence . . .

(BOBO takes out a doll representing the QUEEN.)

THE QUEEN: (re-entering just as the doll emerges) I'd like to see myself come out of there . . . There I come! My mother spawned me standing up! (Exit.)

(The NEGROES have hung up the dolls on the left side of the stage, under the COURT's balcony. They gaze at them and then resume their recital.)

SNOW: (still fixed in an attitude of departure, as if about to enter the right wing; turning her head) In any event, the one who's rotting in the packing case never had such a high old time.

(Exit the GOVERNOR.)

VILLAGE: Let's forget about her. (to the SPECTATOR who is holding the knitting) Give her back her knitting. Thank you, sir. You may go. (The SPECTATOR returns to his seat.) (to the MASK): And now, let's continue. Go on, madam . . .

(The MASK starts walking very slowly toward the right screen.)

Walk! This evening you have the noblest gait in the realm. (to the audience): As you see, the husband arrived too late. He'll find only his wife's corpse, disemboweled but still warm. (to the MASK, who had stopped but who starts walking again): It's no longer a Negro trailing at your skirt; it's a marketful of slaves, all sticking out their tongues. Just because you've kindly given me a drink of rum you think . . . eh, you bitch! Pull me toward your lace . . . (They both move toward the screen, very slowly, the MASK in front of VILLAGE.) . . . Underneath you're surely wearing some sort of black petticoat that's silkier than my gaze . . .

VIRTUE: (falling to her knees) Village!

VILLAGE: (to the MASK) Walk faster, I'm in a hurry. Follow the corridor. Turn right. Good. You know the door of your room. Open it. How gracefully you walk, oh noble and familiar rump!

(They mount the steps and are about to go behind the screen. But before following the MASK there, VILLAGE turns to the audience.)

Are they following me? (to the NEGROES): Are you following me?

(The NEGROES, that is, ARCHIBALD, BOBO and SNOW — VIRTUE remains kneeling — place themselves behind him, in a procession, softly clapping their hands and stamping their feet.)

But if I go too far, stop me.

(Enter the GOVERNOR.)

THE JUDGE: What's the Queen doing?

THE GOVERNOR: She's weeping, sir. Torrents are pouring from her eyes and flowing down to the plains, which, alas, they cannot fertilize, for the water is warm and salty.

THE MISSIONARY: Does she have need of religion?

THE VALET: I'll go and console her. I know how to handle her.

ALL: (except VIRTUE, to VILLAGE) We'll help you. Don't be afraid. Keep walking.

VILLAGE: (imploringly) Tell me, Negroes, what if I couldn't stop?

ALL: (except VIRTUE) Keep going.

BOBO: The Valet has set an example for you. He's already with the Queen.

VILLAGE: (falling to one knee) Negroes, I beg of you . . .

BOBO: (laughing) Inside with you, you lazy lubber!

SNOW: (kneeling) Pour forth torrents. First, showers of sperm and then streams of her blood. (cupping her hands) I'll drink it, Village, I'll wash my chin with it, my belly, my shoulders.

VILLAGE: (A white-gloved hand, that of the MASK, who is behind the screen, comes down on his shoulder and remains there.) Friends, friends, I beg of you . . .

ALL: (still clapping their hands and stamping their feet gently) Go on in. She's already lying down. She's put aside her knitting. She's calling for your big ebony body. She has blown out the candle. She's darkening the room to put you at ease!

VILLAGE: Friends . . .

FELICITY: (suddenly standing up straight) Dahomey! Dahomey! To my rescue, Negroes, all of you! Gentlemen of Timbuctoo, come in, under your white parasols! Stand over there. Tribes covered with gold and mud, rise up from my body, emerge! Tribes of the Rain and Wind, forward! Princes of the Upper Empires, Princes of the bare feet and wooden stirrups, on your caparisoned horses, enter! Enter on horseback. Gallop in! Gallop in! Hop it! Hop it! Hop along! Negroes of the ponds, you who fish with your pointed beaks, enter! Negroes of the docks, of the factories, of the dives, Negroes of the Ford plant, Negroes of General Motors, and you, too, Negroes who braid rushes to encage crickets and roses, enter and remain standing! Conquered soldiers, enter. Conquering soldiers, enter. Crowd in. More. Lay your shields against the walls. You, too, who dig up corpses to suck the brains from skulls, enter unashamedly. You, tangled brother-sister, walking melancholy incest, come in. Barbarians, barbarians, barbarians, come along. I can't describe you all, nor even name you all, nor name your dead, your arms, your ploughs, but enter. Walk gently on your white feet. White? No, black. Black or white? Or blue? Red, green, blue, white, red, green, yellow, who knows, where am I? The colors exhaust me . . . Are you there, Africa with the bulging chest and oblong

thigh? Sulking Africa, wrought of iron, in the fire, Africa of
the millions of royal slaves, deported Africa, drifting continent, are you there? Slowly you vanish, you withdraw into
the past, into the tales of castaways, colonial museums, the
works of scholars, but I call you back this evening to attend a
secret revel. *(pondering)* It's a block of darkness, compact and
evil, that holds its breath, but not its odor. Are you there?
Don't leave the stage unless I tell you to. Let the spectators
behold you. A deep, almost invisible somnolence emanates
from you, spreads all about, hypnotizes them. We shall presently go down amongst them, but before we do . . .

VILLAGE: Madam . . .

FELICITY: . . . but before we do, allow me to present the most
cowardly of all Negroes. Need I name him? *(to VILLAGE):*
Well, get going!

VILLAGE: *(trembling. The white-gloved hand is still resting on his
shoulder.)* Madam . . .

FELICITY: If he's still hesitating, let him take the place of the
dead woman. *(She sits down, exhausted.)*

VILLAGE and VIRTUE: *(together)* No!

ARCHIBALD: *(to VILLAGE)* Go on in.

VILLAGE: *(to the melody of the "Dies Irae")* Madam . . . Madam . . .

SNOW: *(to the "Dies Irae")* Enter, enter . . . deliver us from evil.
Hallelujah . . .

BOBO: *(all the speeches will now be sung to the same melody):* Oh descend, my cataracts!

VILLAGE: Madam . . . Madam . . .

SNOW: I still snow upon your countryside,
            I still snow upon your tombs, and I calm you . . .

VIRTUE: The north winds have been forewarned:
            Let them load it on their shoulders
            All the horses are untethered.

VILLAGE: *(still kneeling; moving backwards, as if drawn by the
white-gloved hand, he disappears behind the screen,
where the MASK is)* Madam . . . Madam . . .

VIRTUE: And thou, evening twilight,
            Weave the cloak that shrouds him.

SNOW: Expire, expire gently,
            Our Lady of the Pelicans,
            Pretty sea gull, politely,
            Gallantly, let yourself be tortured . . .

VIRTUE: Beshroud yourselves, tall forests,
            That he may steal in silently.
            Shod his big feet, oh white dust, with felt slippers.

THE JUDGE: *(to the GOVERNOR, who is looking through his spyglass at what is going on behind the screen)* What do you make
out?

THE GOVERNOR: Nothing out of the ordinary. *(laughing)* The
woman is giving in. You can say what you like about them,
but those fellows are terrific fuckers.

THE MISSIONARY: You're forgetting yourself, my dear governor.

THE GOVERNOR: I'm sorry. I mean that the flesh is weak. It's a
law of nature.

THE JUDGE: But what is it they're doing? Describe it.

THE GOVERNOR: Now he's washing his hands . . . he's drying
them . . . those people are clean. I've always noticed that.
When I was a lieutenant, my orderly . . .

THE JUDGE: What else is he doing?

THE GOVERNOR: He's smiling . . . he's taking out his pack of
Chesterfields . . . puff! He's blown out the candle.

THE JUDGE: Not really?

THE GOVERNOR: Take the spyglass, or the lantern, and have a
look.

(The JUDGE shrugs his shoulders.)

ARCHIBALD: *(suddenly aware of the presence of NEWPORT NEWS,
who entered very slowly while FELICITY was delivering her long
speech)* You! I told you to come back and let us know only
when everything was finished. So it's over? It's done? *(turning
to the COURT, all of whose members have put their hands to
their faces, he screams:)* Keep your masks on!

NEWPORT NEWS: Not quite. He's defending himself as best he
can, but he'll certainly be executed.

ARCHIBALD: *(he has changed his voice; instead of declaiming, he
speaks in his natural tone)* The shot'll make a noise. *(A
pause.)* Are you sure he's guilty? And are you sure he's the one
we've been looking for?

NEWPORT NEWS: *(a little ironically)* Are you suddenly getting
suspicious?

ARCHIBALD: Bear in mind that it's a matter of judging and probably sentencing and executing a Negro. That's a serious affair.
It's no longer a matter of staging a performance. The man
we're holding and for whom we're responsible is a real man.
He moves, he chews, he coughs, he trembles. In a little
while, he'll be killed.

NEWPORT NEWS: That's very tough. But though we can put on
an act in front of them *(pointing to the audience)*, we've got to
stop acting when we're among ourselves. We'll have to get
used to taking responsibility for blood — our own. And the
moral weight . . .

ARCHIBALD: All the same, as I've said, it's a matter of living
blood, hot, supple, reeking blood, of blood that bleeds . . .

NEWPORT NEWS: But then what about the act we put on? Was it
just an entertainment, as far as you were concerned?

ARCHIBALD: *(interrupting him)* Be quiet. *(A pause.)* Is he going
to be executed?

NEWPORT NEWS: He is.

ARCHIBALD: All right. Go back to them.

NEWPORT NEWS: I need to be here. In any case, it's too late. Let
me go through with it. Here.

ARCHIBALD: Well . . . then stay. *(to the NEGRESSES):* And you,
be quiet. Village is working for us. Help him in silence, but
help him.

(Enter the VALET.)

THE GOVERNOR: What about the Queen? What's she doing?

THE VALET: She's still crying. It's the warm rains of September.

THE GOVERNOR: And . . . what did she say?

THE VALET: At least save the child! And see to it that the mother
is received courteously. She has gone astray, but she's a white
woman.

(A very long silence.)

VIRTUE: *(timidly)* He hasn't come back.

BOBO: *(in an undertone)* He hasn't had time to. After all, it's far
away.

VIRTUE: What do you mean far away? It's behind the screen.

BOBO: *(still in an undertone, slightly annoyed)* Of course. But at
the same time they've got to go elsewhere. They have to cross
the room, go through the garden, take a path lined with hazel
trees, turn left, push aside the thorns, throw salt in front of
them, put on boots, enter the woods . . . It's night time. Deep
in the woods . . .

THE GOVERNOR: Gentlemen, we've got to start getting ready. Wake the Queen. We must go and punish them, we must try them, and the journey will be long and arduous.

THE MISSIONARY: I'll need a horse.

1340 THE VALET: Everything has been attended to, Monsignor.

BOBO: (resuming) . . . deep in the woods, look for the gate of the cavern, find the key, go down the steps . . . dig the grave . . . Flee. Will the moon wait? All that takes time. You yourself, when you go upstairs with the gentleman who's on his way 1345 home from his wife's funeral . . .

VIRTUE: (curtly) You're right. I do a conscientious job. But Village ought to have acted it out before our eyes.

BOBO: Greek tragedy, my dear, decorum. The ultimate gesture is performed off-stage.

(ARCHIBALD, irritated, makes a threatening gesture to them and points to VILLAGE, who is about to enter. A rather long silence. Then, enter VILLAGE, quietly. His shirt collar is awry. They all surround him.)

1350 ARCHIBALD: Is it over? Did you have much trouble?

VILLAGE: Same as usual.

SNOW: Nothing happened, did it?

VILLAGE: No, nothing. Or, if you prefer, it all went off as usual, and very smoothly. When Diouf entered behind the screen, 1355 he kindly offered me a seat.

SNOW: And then?

NEWPORT NEWS: Nothing else. They waited on a bench, off stage, and smiled at each other in amusement.

VILLAGE: (catching sight of NEWPORT NEWS) Are you back? You 1360 should still be there, with them . . .

NEWPORT NEWS: I thought that this evening, thanks to you, everything was supposed to change, and that this would be the last night.

VILLAGE: (annoyed) I did what I could. But what about you? 1365 What about them?

NEWPORT NEWS: What they do is no business of yours. It's for them to ask questions. But . . . I'm glad you performed the rite, as you do every evening. It'll be my joy to finish off the performance.

1370 ARCHIBALD: There's nothing new, at least, in the ceremony.

NEWPORT NEWS: (angrily) Do you want to continue it forever and ever? To perpetuate it until the death of the race? As long as the earth revolves about the sun, which is itself carried off in a straight line to the very limits of God, in a secret cham-1375 ber, Negroes will . . .

BOBO: (screaming) Will hate! Yessir!

THE JUDGE: (to the COURT) I think we have no more time to waste.

(A singing is heard—a kind of solemn march, which is sung. Then, the QUEEN appears, leading DIOUF, who is masked and wearing his trappings.)

THE QUEEN: This is the woman whom we must go down and 1380 avenge.

SNOW: Diouf has arrived!

THE QUEEN: (to DIOUF) The journey must have been arduous, poor child. At last you're with your true family. From here, from on high, you'll have a better view of them.

1385 THE MISSIONARY: When we get back, we'll try to beatify her.

THE VALET: A terrific idea! Her Majesty will adopt her. Won't she, child?

THE QUEEN: We'll have to think about that. It's a very delicate matter. After all, she has been defiled. Against her will, I hope, after all, she's liable to be a reminder of our shame. 1390 (after a hesitation) However, the idea is worth considering. (to the JUDGE): What are they doing down there?

THE JUDGE: (looking with the GOVERNOR's fieldglasses) They're wild with anger, with rage, and somewhat confused.

THE QUEEN: What are they saying? 1395

THE JUDGE: They're utterly dumbfounded.

THE QUEEN: But . . . what's going on that's so strange and rare? Is snow falling on their mangroves?

THE JUDGE: Madam . . . it may be that a crime is being committed. 1400

THE QUEEN: No doubt.

THE JUDGE: No, another one. One that's being judged elsewhere.

THE QUEEN: But—what can we do? Prevent it? Or make use of it? 1405

(The members of the COURT all lean forward.)

VILLAGE: (to ARCHIBALD) Are they going to come, sir? Are they coming to judge us, to weigh us? (VILLAGE is trembling.)

ARCHIBALD: (putting his hand on VILLAGE's shoulder) Don't be afraid. It's only play-acting.

VILLAGE: (persisting) To weigh us? With their golden and ruby 1410 scales? And do you think, if they go off to die, that they'll let me love Virtue—or rather that Virtue will be able to love me?

NEWPORT NEWS: (smiling, but pointedly) Didn't you try to negrify them? To graft Bambara lips and nostrils on them? To kink their hair? To reduce them to slavery? 1415

THE MISSIONARY: (roaring out) Off we go! And not another minute to waste. (to the VALET): Prepare the cloak and boots, a pound of cherries and Her Majesty's horse. (to the QUEEN): Madam, we must be off. It will be a long journey. (to the GOVERNOR): Do you have the umbrellas? 1420

THE GOVERNOR: (hurt) Ask Joseph. (to the VALET): Do you have the flask?

THE VALET: On getting out of bed, the Queen knighted me and gave me a title. And don't forget it. All the same, I have the umbrellas and the quinine tablets. I also have a flask of 1425 rum—full to the brim! Because it'll be hot.

THE MISSIONARY: During the trek, I authorize drinking to beguile fatigue, and let a Palestrina Mass be sung. Everyone ready? Then, forward . . . march!

(The entire COURT disappears, leaving the platform, where DIOUF, still masked, remains alone. At first, he hesitates, then, timidly, approaches the handrail and looks down.)

(The COURT remains off-stage for four or five minutes. The NEGROES below have gathered together, left. In front of the group stands NEWPORT NEWS. They are all waiting anxiously. BOBO raises her head. She sees DIOUF leaning over the rail and looking at them.)

BOBO: You! You, Mr. Diouf? 1430

(The NEGROES all raise their heads and look at DIOUF, who, still masked, nods "yes.")

Mr. Diouf, you're living a curious death. What's it like there?

DIOUF: (slowly removing his mask) The light there is rather queer.

BOBO: Tell us, Mr. Vicar General, what do you see there? Answer, Diouf. Seen through their eyes, what are their kings like? What do you see from the height of your blue eyes, from the height of those belvederes?

DIOUF: *(hesitating)* I see you — sorry — I see us as follows: I'm on high, and not on the ground. And I am perhaps experiencing the vision of God.

BOBO: Are you a white woman?

DIOUF: The first thing to tell you is that they lie or that they're mistaken. They're not white, but pink or yellowish.

BOBO: Then are you a pink woman?

DIOUF: I am. I move about in a light emitted by our faces which they reflect from one to another. We, that is, you, we're still suffocating in a heavy atmosphere. It all began when I had to leave your world. I was eaten with despair. But your insults and homage little by little exalted me. I was imbued with a new life. I felt Village's desires. His voice was so rough! And his gaze! Humble and triumphant. Before I knew it, I was with child by him.

BOBO: Are you proud?

DIOUF: Proud, no. Our cares and concerns no longer have meaning for me. New relationships come into being along with new things, and these things become necessary. *(pensively)* Indeed, necessity is a very curious novelty. The harmony thrills me. I had left the realm of gratuitousness where I saw you gesticulating. I could no longer see even our hatred, our hatred which rises up to them. I learned, for example, that they're able to perform true dramas and to believe in them.

NEWPORT NEWS: *(ironically)* You miss those days of the dead, don't you?

ARCHIBALD: Every actor knows that at a given time the curtain will fall. And that he almost always embodies a dead man or dead woman: Lady Macbeth, Don Giovanni, Antigone, Camille, Dr. Schweitzer . . .

(A long silence.)

(Footsteps are heard off-stage. DIOUF, *in a panic, puts on his mask again. The other* NEGROES *seem frightened. All of them, in a body, including* MRS. FELICITY, *go to the left side of the stage and huddle under the balcony where the* COURT *had been. The sound of footsteps becomes more distinct. At length, from the right wing, as if coming down a road, emerges first the* VALET, *walking backward. He is belching and staggering. He is obviously drunk.)*

THE VALET: *(facing the wing; belching)* Be careful with the nag! See that he doesn't stumble. The Queen's not going *(belches)* to arrive on a horse with broken knees. Oh, bishop-at-large, be careful that the train of the Queen's cloak and your *(belches)* white *(belches)* purple skirt don't get caught in the cactus. Damn it, what dust! Mouth's full of it! But you . . . *(belches)* Gives you a certain air! Watch out . . . watch out . . . there . . . there . . . *(He makes a gesture as if to indicate the road to take.)*

(Finally, also walking backward, appear the GOVERNOR, *the* MISSIONARY, *the* JUDGE, *and then, moving forward, the* QUEEN. *She seems very weary, as after a long journey. They are all drunk.)*

THE QUEEN: *(unsteady on her legs and advancing cautiously, looking about her)* Dust! Mouth's full of it, but it gives you a certain air! *(She belches and bursts out laughing.)* Look where it gets us, following old troopers under colonial skies. *(She takes the empty flask and throws it away.)* And not a drop left. *(belches)* *(suddenly noble)*: Thus do I set foot on my foreign possessions. *(laughs)*

THE GOVERNOR: *(hiccoughing after each word)* Stop in your tracks. Prudence, circumspection, mystery. All is swamp, quagmires, arrows, felines . . .

(Very softly at first, then more and more loudly, the NEGROES, *almost invisible under the balcony, utter sounds of the virgin forest: croaking at the toad, hoot of the owl, a hissing, very gentle roars, breaking of wood, moaning of the wind.)*

. . . here, from the skin of their bellies the snakes lay eggs from which blinded children take wing . . . the ants riddle you with vinegar or arrows . . . the creepers fall madly in love with you, kiss your lips and eat you . . . here the rocks float . . . the water is dry . . . the wind is a skyscraper . . . all is leprosy, sorcery, danger, madness . . .

THE QUEEN: *(wonderstruck)* And flowers!

THE JUDGE: *(hiccoughing)* Poisonous, Madam. Deadly. Sick. Drank too much rum. Leaden sky, Madam. Our pioneers tried grafts on our garden cabbage, on the Dutch peony, on rhubarb. Our plants died, madam, murdered by those of the tropics.

(The NEGROES *laugh with their orchestrated laugh, very softly. They start making their sounds again, cracking of branches, cries, caterwauling, etc.)*

THE QUEEN: I thought as much. Even their botany is wicked. Luckily we have our preserves.

THE GOVERNOR: And reserves of energy. Always fresh troops.

THE QUEEN: *(to the* GOVERNOR*)* Tell them their sovereign is with them in her heart . . . and . . . what about the gold? . . . the emeralds . . . the copper . . . the mother-of-pearl?

THE MISSIONARY: *(with a finger to his mouth)* In safe places. They'll be shown to you. Pounds of them. Stacks of them. Avalanches.

THE QUEEN: *(still moving forward)* If it's at all possible, before the sun sets behind the mountains I'd like to go down to a mine and row on the lake. *(Suddenly she notices the* VALET, *who is shivering.)* What's the matter? Scared?

THE VALET: Fever, Madam.

THE QUEEN: *(shaking the* VALET*)* Fever? Fever or liquor? You drank more than half the supply all by yourself.

THE VALET: I did it in order to sing better, and louder. I even danced.

THE QUEEN: *(to the* MISSIONARY*)* What about the dancing? Where's the dancing?

THE MISSIONARY: It takes place only at night . . .

THE QUEEN: Have the Night brought in!

THE GOVERNOR: It's coming, Madam! In quick time! One two! . . . One two!

(The jungle sounds made by the NEGROES *grow louder and louder.)*

THE MISSIONARY: *(timidly)* The dances take place only at night. Each and every one of them is danced for our destruction. Go no further. This is a dread region. Every thicket hides the grave of a missionary . . . *(belches)*

THE GOVERNOR: And of a captain. *(pointing with his arm)* There the north, there the east, the west, the south. On each of these shores, at the river's edge, on the plains, our soldiers have fallen. Don't go any closer, it's swamp . . . *(He holds back the QUEEN.)*

THE JUDGE: *(sternly)* The climate's no excuse for your laxity. I've lost none of my pride or daring. It was to punish a crime that I undertook the journey. Where are the Negroes, Mr. Governor?

(The NEGROES laugh as before, very softly, almost in a murmur. And the same rustling of leaves, moaning of wind, roars and other sounds that suggest the virgin forest.)

THE QUEEN: *(falling into the GOVERNOR's arms)* Did you hear? *(They all listen)* . . . and . . . and . . . what if they were . . . if they were really Blacks? And, what if they were alive?

THE MISSIONARY: Don't be afraid, Madam. They wouldn't dare . . . You are swathed in a gentle dawn that keeps them in awe.

THE QUEEN: *(trembling)* You think so? I haven't done anything bad, have I? Obviously, my soldiers have sometimes let themselves be carried away in their enthusiasm . . .

THE GOVERNOR: Madam, I'm in command here, and it's not the moment to pass judgment on ourselves . . . You're under my protection.

THE VALET: And I'm warrant of the fact that we have their welfare at heart. I've hailed their beauty in a poem that's become famous . . .

(The NEGROES have moved forward very softly. The COURT stops short. Then it moves back, as softly as the NEGROES moved forward, so that it is at the right, at the point where it entered, opposite the side where the NEGROES are, and facing them.)

FELICITY: *(to the NEGROES)* It's dawn! Take it, Absalom!

ARCHIBALD: *(imitating a cock)* Cock-a-doodle-doo!

FELICITY: *(still addressiing the NEGROES)* It's dawn, gentlemen. Since we've wanted to be guilty, let's be prepared. We must act and speak cautiously and with restraint.

THE GOVERNOR: *(to the VALET)* I'm going to see whether there's a possibility of our falling back. *(Exit, right, but reappearing immediately.)* Madam, the jungle has closed behind us.

THE QUEEN: *(frightened)* But we're in our native land, aren't we?

THE GOVERNOR: Madam, all the shutters are closed, the dogs are hostile, communications are cut off, the night is bitter cold. It was a trap. We must make a stand. It's dawn! *(to the VALET)* Take it!

THE VALET: Cock-a-doodle-doo!

THE QUEEN: *(gloomily)* Yes, it's dawn, and we're face to face with them. And they're black, just as I dreamt they were.

THE JUDGE: Let's set up the court of justice!

THE MISSIONARY: *(to the VALET)* The throne! And stop that absurd trembling. *(The VALET brings over FELICITY's gilded armchair. The QUEEN sits down on it.)*

(The NEGROES take a step forward, then remain still. NEWPORT NEWS goes to the catafalque and removes the sheet, which has been stretched over two chairs.)

THE QUEEN: My chairs!

THE VALET: They were there all the time! And I looked for them even under your skirts, Mr. Missionary!

(The VALET brings over the two chairs. The GOVERNOR and the MISSIONARY sit down in them. But first the COURT bows ceremoniously to the NEGROES, who, in like fashion, welcome the COURT. The dolls representing the COURT will remain on a kind of pedestal at the left until the curtain is drawn.)

DIOUF: And I who saw myself shut up in the case!

THE JUDGE: The Court is now ready. *(to the NEGROES)*: Lie down. You'll approach us on your bellies.

ARCHIBALD: *(to the COURT)* They're worn out, sir. If we may, we'll hear you on our haunches.

THE JUDGE: *(after exchanging glances of inquiry with the COURT)* Granted.

ARCHIBALD: *(to the NEGROES)* Squat. *(The NEGROES squat.)* *(to the JUDGE)*: May we whimper?

THE JUDGE: If you must. *(in a booming voice)* But first, tremble! *(The NEGROES tremble in orchestrated fashion.)* Harder! Tremble, come on, shake! Don't be afraid to bring down the coconuts that hang from your branches! Tremble, Negroes! *(The NEGROES, all together, tremble harder and harder.)* That'll do . . . That'll do . . . We'll overlook your impertinences, which would make us more severe. We've taken stock: although we're not missing the body of either a white woman, or white man, God has intimated to us that there's an extra soul on hand. What does that mean?

ARCHIBALD: Alas, what *does* it mean?

THE MISSIONARY: *(to the JUDGE)* Be careful. They're crafty, artful, cunning. They're fond of trials and theological discussions. They have a secret telegraph that flies over hill and dale.

THE JUDGE: *(to ARCHIBALD)* I'm not accusing *all* of Africa. That would be unjust, ungentlemanly . . .

(The QUEEN, the VALET, the MISSIONARY and the GOVERNOR applaud.)

THE QUEEN: Splendid! A fine and noble reply.

THE JUDGE: *(slyly)* No, one can't hold all of Africa responsible for the death of a white woman. Nevertheless, there's no denying the fact that one of you is guilty, and we've made the journey for the purpose of bringing him to trial. According to our statutes — naturally. He killed out of hatred. Hatred of the color white. That was tantamount to killing our entire race and killing us till doomsday. There was no one in the packing case . . . tell us why.

ARCHIBALD: *(sadly)* Alas, your Honor, there was no packing case either.

THE GOVERNOR: No packing case? No packing case either? They kill us without killing us and shut us up in no packing case either!

THE MISSIONARY: After that dodge, they won't be able to say they don't fake. They've been stringing us along. *(to the VALET)*: Don't laugh! Don't you see what they're doing with us?

THE JUDGE: *(to the NEGROES)* According to you, there's no crime since there's no corpse, and no culprit since there's no crime. But let's get things straight: one corpse, two, a battalion, a drove of corpses, we'll pile them high if that's what we need to avenge ourselves. But no corpse at all — why that could kill us. *(to ARCHIBALD)*: Do you want to be the death of us?

ARCHIBALD: We are actors and organized an evening's entertainment for you. We tried to present some aspect of our life that might interest you. Unfortunately, we haven't found very much.

THE MISSIONARY: Their dusky bodies were allowed to bear the Christian names of the Gregorian calendar. That was the first step.

THE VALET: (insidiously) Look at his mouth. You can see that their beauty can equal ours. Your Majesty, allow that beauty to be perpetuated . . .

THE JUDGE: For your pleasure? But my job is to seek out and judge a malefactor.

THE GOVERNOR: (in a single breath) And then I'll execute him: a bullet in his head and calves, spurts of saliva, bowie knives, bayonets, popguns, poisons of our Medicis . . .

THE JUDGE: He won't get out of it. I've got some tough laws, very sharp, very precise . . .

THE GOVERNOR: Puncturing of the abdomen, adrift in the eternal snows of our unconquered glaciers, Corsican blunderbuss, brass-knuckles, the guillotine, shoelaces, the itch, epilepsy . . .

THE JUDGE: Articles 280–8, 927–17, 18, 16, 5, 3, 2, 1, 0.

THE GOVERNOR: Tar and feathers, died like a rat, died like a dog; dyed in the wool, died in battle, hit the bottle, died in bed, cock-o'the-walk. Hemlock! . . .

THE MISSIONARY: Gentlemen, be calm. The monster won't escape us again. But first, I'll christen him. For it's a matter of executing a man, not of bleeding an animal. And if Her Majesty . . .

THE QUEEN: (gently) As usual. I'll be godmother.

THE MISSIONARY: And then I'll give absolution for his crimes. And after that, gentlemen, it'll be your turn. When it's over, we'll pray. But first, the christening.

ARCHIBALD: You're in Africa . . .

THE QUEEN: (ecstatically) Overseas! Capricorn! My islands! Coral!

ARCHIBALD: (slightly annoyed) By being obstinate you're courting danger. Be careful. If you make one of your signs, the waters of our lakes, of our streams and rivers and cataracts, the sap of our trees and even our saliva, may boil over . . . or freeze.

THE QUEEN: In exchange for a crime, we were bringing the criminal pardon and absolution.

VILLAGE: Madam, beware. You are a great queen, and Africa is unsafe.

FELICITY: (to the NEGROES) That'll do! Stand back! (She makes a sign, and all the NEGROES withdraw to the left of the stage. Then, at a sign from the QUEEN, the COURT withdraws to the right. The two women are face to face.)

THE QUEEN: (to FELICITY) Begin.

FELICITY: You begin!

THE QUEEN: (very courteously, as one behaves with humble folk) I assure you, I can wait . . .

FELICITY: Admit you don't know how to begin.

THE QUEEN: I can wait. I have eternity with me.

FELICITY: (with her hands on her hips; exploding) Oh, really? Well, then, Dahomey! Dahomey! Negroes, come back me up! And don't let the crime be glossed over. (to the QUEEN): No one could possibly deny it, it's sprouting, sprouting, my beauty, it's growing, bright and green, it's bursting into bloom, into perfume, and that lovely tree, that crime of mine, is all Africa! Birds have nested in it, and night dwells in its branches.

THE QUEEN: Every evening, and every single second, you engage, against me and mine—I know you do—in a preposterous and baleful rite. The odor of that tree's flowers spreads all the way to my country and tries to capture and destroy me.

FELICITY: (face to face with the QUEEN) You're a ruin!

THE QUEEN: But what a ruin! And I haven't finished sculpting myself, haven't finished carving and jagging and fashioning myself in the form of a ruin. An eternal ruin. It's not time that corrodes me, it's not fatigue that makes me forsake myself, it's death that's shaping me and that . . .

FELICITY: If you're death itself, then why, why do you reproach me for killing you?

THE QUEEN: And if I'm dead, why do you go on and on killing me, murdering me over and over in my color? Isn't my sublime corpse—which still moves—enough for you? Do you need the corpse of a corpse?

(Side by side, almost amicably, the two women move forward to the very front of the stage.)

FELICITY: I shall have the corpse of your corpse's ghost. You are pale, but you're becoming transparent. Fog that drifts over my land, you will vanish utterly. My sun . . .

THE QUEEN: But if all that remained of my ghost were a breath, and only the breath of that breath, it would enter through the orifices of your bodies to haunt you . . .

FELICITY: We'd let a fart and blow you out.

THE QUEEN: (infuriated) Governor! General! Bishop! Judge! Valet!

ALL: (gloomily and without moving) Coming.

THE QUEEN: Put them to the sword!

FELICITY: If you are the light and we the shade, so long as there is night into which day must sink . . .

THE QUEEN: I'm going to have you exterminated.

FELICITY: (ironically) You fool, just imagine how flat you'd be without that shade to set you off in high relief.

THE QUEEN: But . . .

FELICITY: (same tone) For this evening, until the end of the drama, let us therefore remain alive.

THE QUEEN: (turning to the COURT) Good God, good God, what's one to say to her . . .

(The GOVERNOR, JUDGE, MISSIONARY and VALET rush up to her and whisper encouragement.)

THE MISSIONARY: Speak of our concern for them . . . of our schools . . .

THE GOVERNOR: Bring up the white man's burden, quote some lines from Kipling . . .

THE QUEEN: (inspired) All the same, my proud beauty, I was more beautiful than you! Anyone who knows me can tell you that. No one has been more lauded than I. Or more courted, or more toasted. Or adorned. Clouds of heroes, young and old, have died for me. My retinues were famous. At the Emperor's ball, an African slave bore my train. And the Southern Cross was one of my baubles. You were still in darkness . . .

FELICITY: Beyond that shattered darkness, which was splintered into millions of Blacks who dropped to the jungle, we were Darkness in person. Not the darkness which is absence of light, but the kindly and terrible Mother who contains light and deeds.

1740 THE QUEEN: (*as if in a panic, to the* COURT) Well? What else . . .

THE GOVERNOR: Say that we have guns to silence them . . .

THE MISSIONARY: That's idiotic. No, be friendly . . . Mention Dr. Livingstone . . .

1745 FELICITY: Behold our gestures. Though now they're merely the mutilated arms of our ravaged rites, bogged down in weariness and time, before long you'll be stretching lopped-off stumps to heaven and to us . . .

THE QUEEN: (*to the* COURT) What should I answer?

1750 FELICITY: Look! Look, Madam. Here it comes, the darkness you were clamoring for, and her sons as well. They're her escort of crimes. To you, black was the color of priests and undertakers and orphans. But everything is changing. Whatever is gentle and kind and good and tender will be black. Milk will be 1755 black, sugar, rice, the sky, doves, hope, will be black. So will the opera to which we shall go, blacks that we are, in black Rolls Royces to hail black kings, to hear brass bands beneath chandeliers of black crystal . . .

THE QUEEN: But, after all, I haven't said my last word . . .

THE VALET: (*in her ear*) Sing a psalm!

1760 THE MISSIONARY: Can't be helped—show your legs!

FELICITY: Twelve hours of night. Our merciful mother will keep us in her house, huddled between her walls! Twelve hours of day, so that these fragments of darkness can perform for the sun ceremonies like those of this evening . . .

1765 THE QUEEN: (*very upset*) You fool! You see only the beauty of history. It's all well and good to come insulting us beneath our windows and to give birth every day to a hundred new heroes who put on an act . . .

1770 FELICITY: Before long you'll see what's hidden behind our display . . . You're exhausted, all of you . . . Your journey has worn you out. You're dropping with sleep . . . You're dreaming!

THE QUEEN: (*she and* FELICITY *now talk to each other like two women exchanging recipes*) Yes, that's so. But what about you?
1775 You're going to tire yourselves too. And don't expect me to suggest tonics. Your herbs won't do the trick.

FELICITY: I don't mind being dog-tired. Others will help me.

THE QUEEN: And what about your darkies? Your slaves? Where will you get them? . . . You'll need them, you know . . .

1780 FELICITY: (*timidly*) You might, perhaps . . . We'll be good negroes . . .

THE QUEEN: Oh no, not on your life! Governesses? Well, maybe . . .

THE MISSIONARY: If absolutely necessary, tutors for children . . .
1785 and even then . . .

FELICITY: It'll be hard, won't it?

THE QUEEN: (*leading her on*) Awful. But you'll be strong. And we, we'll be charmers. We'll be lascivious. We'll dance in order to be seductive. Just imagine what you're in for. Long
1790 labor on continents, for centuries, to carve yourself a sepulchre that may be less beautiful than mine . . . So let me manage things, won't you? No? You see how tired you are already. What is it you want? No, no, don't answer. Is it that you want your sons to be free of chains? Is that it? That's a
1795 noble wish, but listen to me . . . follow me . . . your sons— why, you don't know them yet . . . You do? Their feet are already riveted together? Your grandsons? They're unborn: so

they don't exist. Therefore you can't worry about their situation. What does freedom or slavery matter since they don't
1800 exist? Really . . . smile a little! . . . Really, my argument seems false? (*The* NEGROES *all look gloomy.*) Come, come, gentlemen. (*addressing her retinue*): Can I be wrong?

THE MISSIONARY: You are wisdom itself.

THE QUEEN: (*to* FELICITY) Your grandsons—who, bear in mind,
1805 do not exist—will have nothing to do. They'll serve us, no doubt, but we're not demanding. But think of the hardships for *us*. We'll have to *be*. And be radiant. (*A silence.*)

FELICITY: (*gently*) And you, think of the mosquitoes of our swamps. If they stung me, a grown Negro, fully armed, would
1810 spring from each abscess . . .

THE MISSIONARY: (*to the* QUEEN) Madam, I told you so. They're insolent, bitter, vindictive . . .

THE QUEEN: (*weeping*) But what have I done to them? I'm kind, and sweet, and beautiful!

1815 THE MISSIONARY: (*to the* NEGROES) You nasty things! Look at the state into which you've dared put the kindest, sweetest and most beautiful of women!

SNOW: The most beautiful?

THE MISSIONARY: (*embarrassed*) I meant the most beautiful in
1820 our country. Display a little good will. Look at how she got all dressed up to visit you, and think of all we've done for you. We've baptized you! All of you! What about the water it took to baptize you? And the salt? The salt on your tongues. Tons of salt, painfully extracted from mines. But here I am going
1825 on and on and in a moment I'll have to allow his Excellency the Governor to speak, and he'll be followed by His Honor the Judge. Why be massacred instead of recognizing . . .

THE JUDGE: Who's the culprit? (*Silence.*) You won't answer? I'm offering you one last chance. Now listen: it doesn't matter
1830 to us which of you committed the crime. We don't care whether it's X, Y or Z. If a man's a man, a Negro's a Negro, and all we need is two arms, two legs to break, a neck to put into the noose, and our justice is satisfied. Come, be decent about it.

(*Suddenly a firecracker explodes off-stage, followed by several more. The sparks of fireworks are seen against the black velvet of the set. Finally, everything grows quiet. The* NEGROES, *who were squatting behind* FELICITY, *stand up.*)

1835 NEWPORT NEWS: (*stepping forth*) I wish to inform you . . .

(*With a single movement, the members of the* COURT *solemnly remove their masks. The audience sees the five black faces.*)

VILLAGE: (*very anxiously*) Is he dead?

NEWPORT NEWS: He has paid. We shall have to get used to the responsibility of executing our own traitors.

THE ONE WHO PLAYED THE VALET: (*sternly*) Did everything go
1840 off with all due justice?

NEWPORT NEWS: (*deferentially*) Rest assured. Not only were the forms of justice applied, but the spirit as well.

THE ONE WHO PLAYED THE MISSIONARY: What about the defense?

NEWPORT NEWS: Perfect. Very eloquent. But it was unable to
1845 sway the jury. And execution followed almost immediately upon delivery of sentence.

(*A silence.*)

THE ONE WHO PLAYED THE QUEEN: And now?

NEWPORT NEWS: Now? While a court was sentencing the one who was just executed, a congress was acclaiming another. He's on his way. He's going off to organize and continue the fight. Our aim is not only to corrode and dissolve the idea they'd like us to have of them, we must also fight them in their actual persons, in their flesh and blood. As for you, you were present only for display. Behind . . .

THE ONE WHO PLAYED THE VALET: *(curtly)* We know. Thanks to us, they've sensed nothing of what's going on elsewhere.

(A silence.)

THE ONE WHO PLAYED THE QUEEN: And . . . you say he has already left?

NEWPORT NEWS: That's right. Everything was planned for his departure.

THE ONE WHO PLAYED THE QUEEN: And . . . what is he like?

NEWPORT NEWS: *(smiling)* Just as you imagine him. Exactly as he must be in order to spread panic by force and cunning.

ALL: *(speaking at the same time)* Describe him! . . . Show us parts of him! . . . Let's see his knee, his calf, his toe! . . . His eye! His teeth!

NEWPORT NEWS: *(laughing)* He's on his way. Let him go. He has our confidence. Everything has been planned and pre-pared so that he can count on us when he's away.

THE ONE WHO PLAYED THE GOVERNOR: What about his voice? What's his voice like?

NEWPORT NEWS: It's deep. Somewhat caressing. He'll first have to fascinate and then convince. Yes, he's also a charmer.

BOBO: *(suspiciously)* But . . . at least he's black?

(For a moment, they are all puzzled; then they burst out laughing.)

THE ONE WHO PLAYED THE MISSIONARY: We've got to hurry . . .

VILLAGE: Are you leaving?

THE ONE WHO PLAYED THE GOVERNOR: Everything has been planned for each of us. If we want to get things done, we haven't a minute to lose.

DIOUF: I . . .

THE ONE WHO PLAYED THE MISSIONARY: *(interrupting him very brusquely)* It'll be hard for the others too — especially in the early stages — to shake off the torpor of a whole continent. Hemmed in by vapors and flies, imprisoned in pollen . . .

DIOUF: *(whimpering)* I'm old . . . I may be forgotten . . . and besides, they draped me in such a pretty dress . . .

THE ONE WHO PLAYED THE VALET: *(sternly)* Keep it. If they've turned you into the image they want to have of us, then stay with them. You'd be a burden to us.

ARCHIBALD: *(to the* ONE WHO PLAYED THE VALET*)* But — is he still acting or is he speaking to himself? *(hesitating)* An Actor . . . a Negro . . . who wants to kill turns even his knife into something make-believe. *(to* DIOUF*)* Are you staying? *(A brief silence.* DIOUF *bows his head.)* Then stay.

SNOW: I've got to be going.

THE ONE WHO PLAYED THE VALET: Not before we finish the performance. *(to* ARCHIBALD*)* Resume the tone.

ARCHIBALD: *(solemnly)* As we could not allow the Whites to be present at a deliberation nor show them a drama that does not concern them, and as, in order to cover up, we have had to fabricate the only one that does concern them, we've got to finish this show and get rid of our judges . . . *(to the* ONE WHO PLAYED THE QUEEN*)* as planned.

THE ONE WHO PLAYED THE QUEEN: At last they'll know the only dramatic relationships we can have with them. *(to the four* NEGROES *of the* COURT*)*: Are you willing?

THE ONE WHO PLAYED THE JUDGE: We are.

THE ONE WHO PLAYED THE QUEEN: We masked our faces in order to live the loathsome life of the Whites and at the same time to help you sink into shame, but our roles as actors are drawing to a close.

ARCHIBALD: How far are you willing to go?

THE ONE WHO PLAYED THE GOVERNOR: To the bitter end.

VILLAGE: But . . . except for the flowers, we haven't provided anything . . . neither knives nor guns nor gallows nor rivers nor bayonets. Will we have to slit your throats in order to get rid of you?

THE ONE WHO PLAYED THE QUEEN: There's no need to. We're actors, our massacre will be lyrical. *(to the four* NEGROES *of the* COURT*)* Gentlemen, your masks.

(One after the other, they put on their masks again.)

(to ARCHIBALD*)*: As for you, all you need to do is give us our cues. All set?

ARCHIBALD: Begin.

THE QUEEN: You may start, Mr. Governor.

FELICITY: But, Madam, we haven't finished our oratorical con-test. Don't deprive me of the best part. There's still lots to be said against Negroes.

THE QUEEN: I have made the journey. It was a long one. Your warmth is inhuman, and I prefer to depart . . .

FELICITY: Nevertheless, you're going to hear what the color white will signify from now on.

THE QUEEN: Don't waste your time. We'll be off and away be-fore you've even finished your speech.

FELICITY: If we let you leave.

THE QUEEN: How simple-minded! You haven't realized that we're heading for death. We're going to it voluntarily, with a sneaking happiness.

FELICITY: Are you committing suicide? You? *(All the* NEGROES *and the members of the* COURT, *except the* QUEEN, *burst into loud, free laughter.)*

THE QUEEN: We choose to die so as to deprive you of pride of triumph. Unless you're going to boast of having conquered a people of shadows.

FELICITY: We'll always be able . . .

THE QUEEN: *(with great authority)* Be quiet. It's for me to speak and to give my orders. *(to the* GOVERNOR*)*: As I said, you may begin, Mr. Governor.

THE GOVERNOR: People usually draw lots in such circum-stances . . .

THE QUEEN: No explanations. Show these barbarians that we are great because of our respect for discipline, and show the Whites who are watching that we are worthy of their tears.

ARCHIBALD: No. No, please don't die. Mr. Governor, please stay! What we enjoyed was to kill you, to slaughter you down to your white powder, to your very soapsuds . . .

THE QUEEN: Ah, ah! I've got you. *(to the* GOVERNOR*)*: Gover-nor, lead off!

THE GOVERNOR: *(with resignation)* Very well! Colonially speaking, I've served my country well. *(he takes a swig of rum)*

I've been given a thousand nicknames, which proved the Queen's esteem and the savage's fear. So I'm going to die, but in an apotheosis, borne aloft by ten thousand lads leaner than Plague and Leprosy, exalted by anger and fury. *(At this point, the* GOVERNOR *takes a paper from his pocket, as he did at the beginning of the play, and reads.)* When I fall to earth, scurvily pierced by your spears, look closely, you will behold my ascension. My corpse will be on the ground, but my soul and body will rise into the air. You'll see them, and you'll die of fright. It is thus that I have chosen to conquer you and rid the earth of your shadows. First, you'll turn pale, then you'll fall, and you'll be dead. And I, great. *(He puts the paper back into his pocket.)* Sublime. Terrifying. *(Silence.)* Well, you won't speak? What? You say I'm trembling? You know very well it's military gout. *(Silence.)* Well, you won't speak? Oh, you're resentful because of the ten thousand lads who were crushed by my tanks? After all, can't a warrior make growing boys bite the dust? . . . *(He trembles more and more violently.)* No, I'm not trembling more and more violently, I'm sending alarm signals to my troops . . . All the same, you're not going to kill me for good? . . . You are? . . . You're not? . . . Well, all right, take aim at this indomitable heart. I die childless . . . but I'm counting on your sense of honor to donate by bloodstained uniform to the Army Museum. Ready, aim, fire!

*(*VILLAGE *points a revolver and shoots, but there is no sound of a shot. The* GOVERNOR *falls.)*

ARCHIBALD: *(indicating the middle of the stage)* No. Come and die here. *(With his heel,* ARCHIBALD *sets off a small cap, the kind children play with. The* GOVERNOR, *who has stood up, goes to the middle of the stage and falls there.)*

THE GOVERNOR: My liver bursting, my heart bleeding.

THE NEGROES: *(bursting into laughter and, in chorus, imitating the crowing of a cock)* Cock-a-doodle-doo!

ARCHIBALD: Off to Hell. *(to the* QUEEN*)*: Next.

*(*VILLAGE *and* VIRTUE *have stepped away from the group of* NEGROES *and come to the front of the stage, left.* VIRTUE *pretends to be flirting.)*

VILLAGE: When I come back, I'll bring you perfumes . . .

VIRTUE: And what else?

VILLAGE: Wild strawberries.

VIRTUE: You're silly. And who'll pick the strawberries? You? Squatting and looking for them under the leaves . . .

VILLAGE: I'm doing it to please you, and you . . .

VIRTUE: My pride? I want you to bring me . . .

(They continue flirting during the JUDGE's *speech.)*

THE JUDGE: *(standing up)* I understand. I won't use eloquence. I know all too well what that leads to. No, I've drafted a bill, the first paragraph of which reads as follows: Act of July 18th. Article 1. God being dead, the color black ceases to be a sin; it becomes a crime . . .

ARCHIBALD: You'll have your head sliced off, but sliced into slices.

THE JUDGE: You have no right . . . *(A shot is heard.)*

ARCHIBALD: Off to Hell!

(Slowly the JUDGE *falls upon the* GOVERNOR. *The moment he falls, the* NEGROES *cry out in chorus.)*

THE NEGROES: Cock-a-doodle-doo!

ARCHIBALD: Next.

VIRTUE: *(to* VILLAGE; *both of them are now at the extreme left of the stage)* I, too, for a long time didn't dare love you . . .

VILLAGE: You love me?

VIRTUE: I would listen. I would hear you striding along. I would run to the window and from behind the curtain would watch you go by . . .

VILLAGE: *(bantering tenderly)* You were wasting your time. I strolled by like an indifferent male, without a glance . . . but at night I would come and capture a beam of light from between your shutters. I would carry it off between my shirt and skin.

VIRTUE: And I, I was already in bed, with your image. Other girls may guard the image of their beloved in their heart or eyes. Yours was between my teeth. I would bite into it . . .

VILLAGE: In the morning, I would proudly display the marks of your bites.

VIRTUE: *(putting her hand over his mouth)* Be still.

THE MISSIONARY: *(standing up)* It was I who brought you knowledge of Hell. How dare you cast me into it? Why, that's preposterous. Hell obeys me. It opens or closes at a sign from my ringed hand. I have blessed brides and grooms, christened pickaninnies, ordained battalions of black priests, and I brought you the message of One who was crucified. I understand you—for if the Church speaks all languages, she likewise understands them all—you reproach Christ for his color. Let us bear in mind that no sooner was He born than a black prince, who was a bit of a sorcerer, came to adore Him . . . *(Suddenly, he breaks off. He looks at the motionless* NEGROES. *He is visibly frightened. Panicky.)* No, no! Gentlemen, gentlemen, don't do that! *(he trembles more and more violently)* Ladies, ladies, I beg of you! It would be too awful! In the name of the Heavenly Virgin, appeal to your husbands, your brothers, your lovers! Gentlemen, gentlemen, no, no, not that! In the first place, I don't believe in it. No, I don't believe in it. Hell, which I brought to you . . . I've mistreated your sorcerers—oh, I'm sorry! Not your sorcerers, gentlemen, your miracle-workers, your priests, your clergy . . . I've made jokes, I've blasphemed, I should be punished, but not that! . . . Gentlemen, gentlemen, I beg of you . . . Don't make the gesture . . . don't utter the formula . . . No, no . . . *(The* NEGROES *become more and more frozen, set, impassive. All at once, the* MISSIONARY *becomes calm. He no longer trembles. He breathes more easily. He seems relieved, almost smiling; suddenly he blurts out)*: Moo! . . . Moo! . . . *(Still mooing like a cow, he walks about on all fours, pretends to graze, and licks the feet of the* NEGROES, *who have stepped back, as if somewhat frightened.)*

ARCHIBALD: That'll do. To the slaughterhouse.

(The MISSIONARY *gets up and goes to fall on the* GOVERNOR *and* JUDGE.)*

THE MISSIONARY: *(screaming in a falsetto voice before falling)* Castrated! I've been castrated! I'll be canonized, high, stiff and firm.

ARCHIBALD: Next!

THE VALET: *(standing up and trembling)* Are you going to beat me? I can't stand physical pain, you know, for I was the artist. In a way, I was one of you, I too was a victim of the Governor

General and the established authorities. You say that I revered them? Yes and no. I was very disrespectful. You fascinated me far more than they did. In any case, this evening I'm no longer what I was yesterday, for I also know how to betray. If you like, though without quite going over to your side . . . I can . . .

THE QUEEN: (*to the* VALET) At least say to them that without us their revolt would be meaningless—and wouldn't even exist . . .

2075 THE VALET: (*still trembling*) They refuse to hear anything more. (*to the* NEGROES): I'll bring you trade secrets, plans . . .

(*The* NEGROES *clap their hands and stamp their feet as if to frighten him. The* VALET *runs away and falls on the heap formed by the* GOVERNOR, MISSIONARY *and* JUDGE. *Orchestrated laughter of the* NEGROES.)

ARCHIBALD: Off to Hell!

THE QUEEN: (*standing up solemnly*) Well, are you satisfied? Now am I alone. (*A shot.*) And dead. Beheaded, like my
2080 illustrious cousin. I too shall descend to Hell. I shall take with me my flock of corpses that you keep killing so that they may stay alive and that you keep alive in order to kill. But, be well assured, we had become unworthy only of you. It was easy for you to transform us into an allegory, but I had to live and
2085 suffer in order to become that image . . . and I have even loved . . . loved (*suddenly she changes her tone and, turning to* ARCHIBALD) but, tell me, sir, that Negro (*she points to* DIOUF) who served you as a prop for killing a corpse, and since it's customary, once they're dead, for those corpses to rise to
2090 Heaven and judge us . . .

SNOW: (*laughing*) And hurry down to Hell again!

THE QUEEN: I grant you that, young lady, but tell me at least, before I die, what has that one become in our Court? With what title have you adorned him, with what hatred have you
2095 charged him? What image has he become, what symbol?

(*They are all attentive, even the dead characters heaped on the ground raise their heads to listen.*)

THE GOVERNOR: (*lying on the ground*) Yes, who? What other prince? (*The* NEGROES *seem rather puzzled.*)

DIOUF: (*very gently*) Don't mind me, Mr. Archibald. I've reached the point where I can hear anything.

2100 ARCHIBALD: (*after a silence*) The collection would have been incomplete without the Mother. (*to* DIOUF): Tomorrow, and in the ceremonies to come, you'll represent the Worthy Mother of the heroes who died thinking they'd killed us, but who were devoured by our fury and our black ants.

(*The characters lying on the ground stand up and bow to* DIOUF, *who returns their bows. Then they lie down again in a heap, as if dead.*)

2105 DIOUF: (*to the* DEAD) Well then, I'm coming down to bury you, since that's indicated in the script. (*He leaves the balcony.*)

THE QUEEN: (*to* ARCHIBALD, *admiringly*) How well you hate! (*A pause.*) How I have loved! And now, I die—I must con-fess—choked by my desire for a Big Black Buck. Black nakedness, thou hast conquered me.   2110

SNOW: (*gently*) You've got to go, Madam. You're losing all your blood, and the stairway to death is interminable. And bright as day. Pale. White. Infernal.

THE QUEEN: (*to her* COURT) On your feet! (*All four stand up.*) Come with me to Hell. And mind your P's and Q's when we   2115
get there. (*She pushes them along like a flock.*)

ARCHIBALD: (*stopping her*) Just a moment. The performance is coming to an end and you're about to disappear. My friends, allow me first to thank you all. You've given an excellent per-formance. (*The five members of the* COURT *remove their masks*   2120
and bow.) You've displayed a great deal of courage, but you had to. The time has not yet come for presenting dramas about noble matters. But perhaps they suspect what lies be-hind this architecture of emptiness and words. We are what they want us to be. We shall therefore be it to the very end,   2125
absurdly. Put your masks on again before leaving. Have them escorted to Hell.

(*The five characters put their masks on.*)

THE QUEEN: (*turning to the* NEGROES) Farewell, and good luck to you. Decent girl that I am, I hope all goes well for you. As for us, we've lived a long time. We're now going to rest at last.   2130
(FELICITY *makes a gesture of impatience.*) We're going, we're going, but keep in mind that we shall lie torpid in the earth like larvae or moles, and if some day . . . ten thousand years hence . . .

(*Exeunt right, while the* NEGROES, *except* VIRTUE *and* VILLAGE, *leave quietly, left.* VILLAGE *and* VIRTUE *remain alone on the stage. They seem to be arguing.*)

VILLAGE: But if I take your hands in mine? If I put my arms   2135
around your shoulders—let me—if I hug you?

VIRTUE: All men are like you: they imitate. Can't you invent something else?

VILLAGE: For you I could invent anything: fruits, brighter words, a two-wheeled wheelbarrow, cherries without pits, a bed for   2140
three, a needle that doesn't prick. But gestures of love, that's harder . . . still, if you really want me to . . .

VIRTUE: I'll help you. At least, there's one sure thing: you won't be able to wind your fingers in my long golden hair . . .

(*The black backdrop rises. All the* NEGROES—*including those who constituted the* COURT *and who are without their masks—are standing about a white-draped catafalque like the one seen at the beginning of the play. Opening measures of the minuet from* Don Giovanni. *Hand in hand,* VILLAGE *and* VIRTUE *walk to-ward them, thus turning their backs to the audience. The curtain is drawn.*)

SLAWOMIR MROZEK

Born in 1930, the Polish playwright Slawomir Mrozek studied architecture and painting in Krakow before becoming a professional political cartoonist and journalist. Once his career as a writer was launched with the publication of several collections of short fiction, Mrozek devoted himself to writing full time. He lived in Poland until the Soviet invasion of Czechoslovakia in 1968, when his criticism of the invasion drew the displeasure of the Polish government and he was forced into exile. He currently lives in Paris. Mrozek's plays are often satirical political sketches, sometimes in the mode of theater of the absurd. His best-known play, *Tango* (1964), is a classic of the modern Polish theater. Mrozek's other plays include *Striptease* (1961), *The Policemen* (1961), *Emigres* (1974), and *Vatzlav* (1976).

Striptease

Striptease illustrates the difficulty of applying generic labels in the contemporary theater. Although the play takes place in the "noplace" of theater of the absurd, and concerns typically mysterious, absurd events and characters, the play invites us to take other kinds of interpretive possibilities into account as well. To many Eastern European playwrights — Vaclav Havel of Czechoslovakia, for example — the arbitrary authority of the "absurd" seems to be less an existential problem than an immediately political situation. Eastern European playwrights during the cold war found in absurdist drama a ready-made technique for an allegorical drama of life under a totalitarian political regime. In *Striptease*, as in other plays, this confluence of the politically neutral theater of the absurd with politically charged plays raises a typically Brechtian question: Which is the pretext for what? Are the techniques of the theater of the absurd being used as an allegory for the political situation, or are the authoritarian dynamics of the political situation somehow also contained in the theater of the absurd?

STRIPTEASE

Slawomir Mrozek

TRANSLATED BY LOLA GRUENTHAL

— CHARACTERS —

MR. I   THE HAND
MR. II   THE SECOND HAND

The stage is bare except for two chairs. Two doors, one stage left and one stage right, should be in clear view of the audience. When the curtain rises there is no one on stage. One can hear strange rattling and rumbling noises which may sound vaguely familiar but cannot be identified. The door on stage left opens and MR. I *comes rushing in. He is middle-aged, neatly but con-ventionally dressed, and carries a briefcase. Obviously he is not interested in his present environment but is rather preoccupied with something that has just happened outside. He should con-vey the impression that he has not entered the stage of his own will. He finally looks around and adjusts his suit. The door re-mains slightly ajar. A few moments later* MR. II *rushes in through the door on stage right. He looks like an exact replica of* MR. I *and also carries a briefcase. The second door is not completely closed either.*

MR. I: Extraordinary!

MR. II: Incredible!

MR. I: I was walking along as usual . . .

MR. II: Not a care in the world . . .

5   MR. I: When suddenly . . .

MR. II: Like a bolt from the sky . . .

MR. I: (*as though just becoming aware of the presence of* MR. II) How did you get here?

MR. II: Why don't you ask what brought me here, or who
10   brought me here?

MR. I: (*again following his own thoughts*) Outrageous!

MR. II: (*as though slightly mimicking* MR. I) Preposterous!

MR. I: I was simply walking, or perhaps, rather, hurrying along . . .

MR. II: Yes, that's right! You were certainly heading for a partic-
15   ular destination.

MR. I: How do you know?

MR. II: It's obvious. I was walking along too, or rather, hurrying along, heading for my destination.

MR. I: You took the words right out of my mouth. As I said, I was
20   heading for this destination when suddenly . . .

MR. II: And remember, this was a destination that you yourself had chosen.

MR. I: Exactly! And with conscious intent, mind you, with full conscious intent . . .

25   MR. II: Obeying the dictates of your conscience, motivated by faith and reason.

MR. I: You're reading my very thoughts. As I was saying, I fol-lowed the path most appropriate for my chosen destination when suddenly . . .

30   MR. II: (*confidentially*) They beat you?

MR. I: Oh, no! (*Also confidentially.*) And you?

MR. II: God forbid! I mean, I don't know a thing. That's all I can say.

MR. I: What was it then?

35   MR. II: That's hard to say for sure. It was like a gigantic elephant blocking the street. Or were there riots? First I had the impres-sion of a flood, then of a picnic. But being in such a fog . . .

MR. I: That's true! It's so foggy today you can hardly see a thing. Still, I was trying to reach my particular destination . . .

40   MR. II: Which you yourself had freely chosen . . .

MR. I: That's God's honest truth! Nothing was left to chance. I had prepared everything down to the last detail. My wife and I often spend long hours planning ahead, planning our entire lives.

MR. II: I also had it all mapped out in advance. Even as a 45 child . . .

MR. I: (*confidentially*) Did you hear a voice?

MR. II: I certainly did. There was a voice.

MR. I: Something like a saw . . . a persistent sound . . . no, actually an intermittent one. 50

MR. II: A gigantic buzz saw.

MR. I: But where the hell could a saw come from?

MR. II: Perhaps it wasn't a saw. Something threw me to the ground.

MR. I: But what? 55

MR. II: The worst part is this uncertainty. Was it really to the ground?

MR. I: Where else if not to the ground?

MR. II: But was I really thrown? What a jungle of riddles! I can't even tell if this was a "being-thrown" in the exact, classical 60 sense, deserving of the name. Though I had the sensation of being thrown down, lying on the ground; I was perhaps —

MR. I: (*tensely*) More overthrown than thrown down?

MR. II: Precisely! And to tell the truth, I really have no com-plaints. Did you see any people? 65

MR. I: Are there any at all?

MR. II: I suppose there are, but with all this fog . . . it doesn't seem likely.

MR. I: The worst of all is this lack of assurance.

MR. II: What color was it? 70

MR. I: What?

MR. II: It's so hard to figure out anything. It was something bright . . . a sort of rose color shot through with lead.

MR. I: Nonsense!

MR. II: (*moving over to* MR. I, *after a pause*) And still they hit 75 you in the jaw.

MR. I: Me?

MR. II: Me too.

(*Pause.*)

MR. I: Well, anyway, now I can't get there on time anymore.

MR. II: How about just walking out? Right now! As though noth- 80 ing had happened?

MR. I: No, no!

MR. II: Are you afraid?

MR. I: Me? Why should I be? I'm just a little nervous. I just can't
85   see . . .

MR. II: That's because of the fog.

MR. I: Did they say we must not leave the room?

MR. II: Who?

MR. I: Whom were you thinking of?

90   MR. II: Never mind!

MR. I: I've decided to stay put. The situation will clear up by
itself.

MR. II: But why? It may be quite possible for us to leave this
room, unimpeded, and to continue on our way. After all, we
95   can't really tell what's going on. Perhaps we ourselves went
astray.

MR. I: Are you blaming yourself? Us? We both knew where we
were going, each of us heading for his specific destination.

MR. II: Then it was not our own fault?

100   MR. I: No, unless . . .

MR. II: Unless?

MR. I: How do I know? Let's drop the subject! I, for one, feel
most strongly that we should not leave this room.

MR. II: If you're so sure about it . . .

105   MR. I: Definitely! We have to use sound reasoning in dealing
with this matter.

(Both sit down.)

MR. II: Perhaps you're right. *(Listens.)* There's nobody there.

MR. I: Actually, there's no cause for concern, is there?

MR. II: No obvious cause, I would say.

110   MR. I: Are you implying that there is a cause . . . an obscure
one?

MR. II: You have a mind of your own.

MR. I: Let's establish the facts.

MR. II: All right, go ahead.

115   MR. I: Very well, then: Each of us left his house according to
plan and walked, or rather hurried, as you observed correctly,
in the direction of his goal. The morning was brisk, the
weather fair, the existence of wife and children an established
fact. Each of us knew whatever there was to be known. Of
120   course, we had no exact idea about the kind of molecules, not
to speak of atoms, that our bedside tables are composed of,
but, after all, there are specialists who deal with such matters.
Basically, everything was perfectly clear. Well-shaved, carrying our practical and indispensable briefcases, we set out pur-
125   posefully toward our goal. The respective addresses had been
thoroughly committed to memory. But to be quite safe we
had also noted them down in our notebooks. Am I correct?

MR. II: On every point.

MR. I: Now listen carefully! At a certain moment, as we were
130   pursuing our course, a course that we had mapped out in
detail and that was, so to speak, the end result of all our rational calculations, something happened which . . . and this is a
point I must stress . . . came entirely from the outside, something separate in itself and independent of us.

135   MR. II: With regard to this point, I must register some doubt.
Since we are unable to define the exact nature of the occurrence, and since we cannot even agree as to its manifestations
. . . due to the fog or to whatever other causes . . . we are in no
position to state with any degree of certainty that this some-

thing came exclusively from the outside or that it was entirely   140
separate in itself and independent of us.

MR. I: You are discomposing me.

MR. II: I beg your pardon?

MR. I: You're interrupting my thoughts.

MR. II: I'm sorry.   145

MR. I: Unfortunately, we are not able to determine the exact
nature of the phenomenon, and . . .

MR. II: That's just what I said.

MR. I: If you wish to go on, don't mind me!

MR. II: The words just slipped out. It won't happen again.   150

MR. I: *(continuing)* We cannot even determine with any appropriate degree of accuracy what particular elements constituted this something. *(Pause.)* I beg your pardon?

MR. II: I didn't say anything.

MR. I: I, for instance, perceived something that seemed to have   155
the shape of an animal, but still I cannot be absolutely sure
that it was not at the same time a mineral. Actually, it seems
to me that it involved energy rather than matter. I think all
this may be best defined as a phenomenon hovering on the
borderline of dimensions and definitions, a connecting link   160
between color, form, smell, weight, length, and breadth,
shade, light, dark, and so on and so forth.

MR. II: Do you still feel any pain? Mine is almost all gone.

MR. I: Please don't reduce everything to its lowest level!

MR. II: I was just asking.   165

MR. I: *(continuing his train of thought)* This much is certain:
We were helpless in the face of the phenomenon, and, partly
of our own will, as we were looking for shelter, partly due to
external pressure, we happened to find ourselves in these
strange quarters which at that critical moment were close at   170
hand. Fortunately, we found the doors open. Needless to say,
our original intentions have thus been completely upset and,
as it were, arrested.

MR. II: I fully agree. What are your conclusions?

MR. I: This is just what I was coming to. Our main task now is to   175
preserve our calm and our personal dignity. Thus, it would
seem to me, we still remain in control of the situation. Basically, our freedom is in no way limited.

MR. II: You call this freedom, our sitting here?

MR. I: But we can walk out at any moment . . . the doors are   180
open.

MR. II: Then let's go! We've wasted too much time anyway.

(Again the same strange noise is heard as in the beginning.)

MR. I: What . . . ? What's that?

MR. II: I told you we should go.

MR. I: Right now?   185

MR. II: Are you afraid?

MR. I: Not at all.

MR. II: First you insist on preserving your personal dignity by
asserting your freedom, and then you don't even want to leave
while there is still time.   190

MR. I: If I left right now I would limit the idea of freedom.

MR. II: What do you mean?

MR. I: It's quite obvious. What is freedom? It is the capacity of
making a choice. As long as I am sitting here, knowing that I
can walk out of this door, I am free. But as soon as I get up and   195
walk out, I have already made my choice, I have limited the

possible courses of action, I have lost my freedom. I become the slave of my own locomotion.

200 MR. II: But your sitting here and not walking out is just another way of making a choice. You simply choose sitting rather than leaving.

MR. I: Wrong! While I'm sitting, I can still leave. If, however, I do leave, I preclude the alternative of sitting.

MR. II: And this makes you feel comfortable?

205 MR. I: Perfectly comfortable. Unlimited inner freedom, that is my answer to these strange happenings. (MR. II *gets up.*) What are you doing?

MR. II: I'm leaving. I don't like this.

MR. I: Are you joking?

210 MR. II: I'm not trying to. I believe in external freedom.

MR. I: And what about me?

MR. II: Goodbye.

MR. I: Please wait! Are you crazy? You don't even know what's out there!

(Both doors close slowly.)

215 MR. II: Hey! What's going on now?

MR. I: Don't close them! Don't close them!

MR. II: All because of your babbling! We should have made up our minds right away.

MR. I: You don't have to blame me. If you had sat still, the doors

220 wouldn't have closed. It was your fault.

MR. II: Now there's no way of finding out.

MR. I: It's all because of you. Thanks to your behavior we've lost our chance to get out.

(MR. II goes to one of the doors and tries unsuccessfully to open it.)

MR. II: Hey! Open up right now!

225 MR. I: Shh! Be quiet!

MR. II: Why should I be quiet?

MR. I: I don't know.

MR. II: *(goes to the other door, knocks, and listens)* Locked!

MR. I: Do me a favor and sit down!

230 MR. II: Well, where is it now, your precious freedom?

MR. I: I have nothing to blame myself for. My freedom remains unaffected.

MR. II: But there's no way to get out now, is there?

MR. I: The potential of my freedom has remained unchanged. I

235 have not made a choice, I have in no way confined myself. The doors were closed for external reasons. I am the same person that I was before. As you may have noticed, I did not even get up from my chair.

MR. II: These doors are upsetting me.

240 MR. I: My dear sir, while we are unable to influence external events, we must make every effort to preserve our dignity and our inner balance. And with regard to those, we command an unlimited field, even though the infinite variety of choices has been reduced to two alternatives. These, of course, exist

245 only as long as we do not choose either of them.

MR. II: What else could happen?

MR. I: Do you think it may get worse?

MR. II: I'll try to knock on the wall . . . perhaps somebody is there.

250 MR. I: It is regrettable that you have no regard for the inviolable nature of your personal freedom. I, too, could knock on the wall, but I won't. If I did, I would preclude other possibilities,

such as reading the papers I have in my briefcase or concentrating on last year's horse races.

(MR. II knocks on the wall several times and listens; he repeats this for a while. Then he takes off one shoe and bangs with it against the wall. One of the doors opens slowly, and in comes a HAND of supernatural size. It resembles the old-fashioned printer's symbol: HAND with pointing index finger and attached cuff. The palm should be brightly colored to make it stand out clearly against the scenery. With bent index finger the HAND makes a monotonously repeated gesture in the direction of MR. II, beckoning to him.)

MR. I: *(the first to notice the HAND)* Pssst! (MR. II *has not yet seen* 255 *the* HAND; *he keeps banging with his shoe and listening.)* Pssst! Stop it, please! Don't you see what's going on?

(MR. II turns around. MR. I points to the HAND.)

MR. II: Something new again!

(The HAND continues beckoning to him. MR. II walks over to it. The HAND points to the shoe he is holding, then it reaches out in an ambiguous gesture that may be either begging or demanding. Hesitantly, MR. II puts his shoe into the HAND. The HAND disappears and returns immediately without the shoe. MR. II takes off his other shoe and gives it to the HAND. The HAND leaves the room, returns, and repeatedly touches MR. II's stomach with its index finger. Guessing what this means, MR. II takes off his belt and hands it over. The HAND withdraws, returns without the belt, and begins to beckon to MR. I.)

MR. I: Me? *(He slowly walks over to the HAND, stopping at every other step. While he is talking, the HAND continually beckons* 260 *to him.)* But I didn't knock . . . There must be a misunderstanding . . . I didn't make a choice . . . no choice whatsoever . . . I did not knock, though I must admit that when my colleague knocked I was hoping that someone might hear it and come in, that the situation might be cleared up and that 265 we would be allowed to leave. This much I admit, but I didn't do any knocking. *(The HAND points to his shoes.)* I protest. I repeat once more: The knocking was not done by me. I don't understand why I should hand over my shoes. *(Bends down to untie the laces.)* I value my inner freedom. A little patience, 270 please! Can't the Hand see that there's a knot here? . . . Personally, I don't hold anything against the Hand, because my own conscience is clear. I am determined to save my inner freedom, even at the cost of my external freedom . . . quite the opposite to my colleague here. But I'm not holding any- 275 thing against him either, because, after all, what he does is his own business. I request only that we be treated as individuals, each according to his own views . . . Just a moment, I'm getting it. There's no fire, is there? *(Giving the HAND his shoes.)* Glad to oblige! *(The HAND points to his stomach.)* I'm 280 not wearing a belt . . . I prefer suspenders. All right, I'll give up the suspenders, too, if necessary. *(Takes off his jacket and unbuttons his suspenders.)* Peculiar methods they have here! All right, here they are . . . Somebody's fingernails could use a good cleaning, if I may venture an opinion. *(The HAND* 285 *disappears, the door closes slowly.)* At least I'm wearing a fresh pair of socks. I'm glad about that.

MR. II: Boot licker!

MR. I: Leave me alone! I'm not bothering you.

MR. II: What can I use now to knock with? 290

MR. I: That's your problem. I'm going to sit down. (*Returns to his chair.*)

MR. II: You're in good shape now with your inner freedom. You're losing your pants.

295 MR. I: What about yours? They won't stay up either without a belt.

MR. II: Well, what do you make of all this?

MR. I: I can only repeat what I said before: First the dear Hand interfered with my free movement in space and then with my

300 ability to wear trousers. This is true, and this I'm willing to admit. But what does it matter? All these are externals. Inwardly I have remained free. I have not become engaged in any action, I have not made any gesture. I haven't even moved a finger. Just sitting here I am still free to do whatever

305 lies in the realm of possibility. Not you, though. You did something . . . you made a choice . . . you knocked against the wall and made a fool of yourself. Slave!

MR. II: I could slap your face, but there are more important things to be done.

310 MR. I: Right. But why do they deal with us like this?

MR. II: It's always the first thing they do . . . take away your shoe laces, belts, and suspenders.

MR. I: What for?

MR. II: So you can't hang yourself.

315 MR. I: You must be joking! If I'm not even getting up from my chair, how can I hang myself? Of course, I could if I wanted to, but I won't. You know my views.

MR. II: I'm sick and tired of your views.

MR. I: That's your problem. But listen to this: If the dear Hand

320 doesn't want us to hang ourselves, this means that it wants to keep us alive. That's a good sign!

MR. II: This is just what bothers me. It means that the Hand thinks of us in terms of categories . . . Life and the other . . . what's it called?

325 MR. I: Death?

MR. II: You said it.

(*Pause.*)

MR. I: I am calm.

MR. II: Tell me, what could you do now, if you felt like doing something? Of course, taking into account the fact that you

330 had to relinquish your shoes and suspenders.

MR. I: Oh, quite a few things. I could, for instance, put on my jacket inside out, roll up the legs of my trousers, and pretend to be a fisherman.

MR. II: And what else?

335 MR. I: I could sing.

MR. II: That's enough. (*Turns up the legs of his trousers, puts on his jacket inside out, and takes off his socks.*)

MR. I: Are you crazy? What are you trying to do?

MR. II: I'm pretending to be a fisherman, and I'm going to sing,

340 too. In contrast to you, I want to explore all the possibilities of action. Maybe the Hand is partial to fishermen and lets them return to freedom. Who knows? One should not neglect any possibility. I've asked you because you have more imagination than I. For instance, I could never have thought up all those

345 things about inner freedom.

MR. I: It's all right with me. But please remember that I'm not moving from this chair.

MR. II: You don't have to. (*He climbs on the chair and sings Schubert's "The Trout." One of the doors slowly opens.*)

350 MR. I: (*who has been anxiously watching the door*) Now you've done it!

(*The* HAND *appears.*)

MR. II: How do you know? Perhaps I'll be allowed to go and you'll keep sitting. (*The* HAND *beckons to him.*) I'm coming, I'm coming. What's it all about? (*The* HAND *indicates that it wants his jacket.*) But I was just— Is there a law against fish- 355 ing? (*The* HAND *repeats its gesture.*) I was just pretending. I'm not really a fisherman. (*Gives the* HAND *his jacket. The* HAND *disappears, comes back, and now obviously requests his trousers.*) No, I won't give up the trousers! (*The* HAND *forms a fist and slowly rises.*) All right. (*He takes off his trousers.*) 360

MR. I: (*getting up*) Me too?

(*After waiting for an answer, which he does not receive,* MR. I *voluntarily removes his jacket. Meanwhile* MR. II *has given the* HAND *his trousers, and he now stands there in striped knee-length underpants. The* HAND *carries the trousers backstage, returns immediately and beckons to* MR. I.)

MR. I: All right, here it is. I'm not resisting, and I beg the Hand to take this into consideration. (*He gives his jacket to the* HAND, *which takes it out and returns immediately.*) I'm always willing to oblige . . . may I keep my trousers in re- 365 turn? (*The* HAND *makes a negative gesture.*) All right, I won't protest.

(*He takes off his trousers and stands up in his underpants, identical to those of* MR. II. *The* HAND *disappears, the door closes.*)

MR. I: You can go to hell with your idea about fishermen.

MR. II: It seems to me that it was your idea.

MR. I: But you carried it out. It's cold in here. 370

MR. II: It's quite possible that we might have been ordered to hand over our clothes anyway, idea or no idea.

MR. I: No! I'm convinced it was you who got us both into this predicament with your idiotic masquerade. It was you who attracted the Hand's attention to our clothing. If at least you 375 had not rolled up your trousers, they would not have caught its eye.

MR. II: But fishermen always roll up their trousers.

MR. I: What good does that do you now?

MR. II: You can't keep ignoring the fact that we differ in our 380 views. You do nothing so that you can feel free to do anything—of course, within the range of what is permitted— while I try to do everything I am permitted to do. But apparently wearing trousers is not permitted.

MR. I: You yourself have brought this down on your head. 385

MR. II: An anatomical inaccuracy! Besides, let me repeat this once more: We don't know whether the removal of our clothes was provoked by my action or whether it was part of a predetermined plan.

MR. I: At least now you should realize that my basic attitude is 390 superior to yours. Don't you see: I didn't knock, I didn't sing, I didn't roll up my trousers, and still, here I am, looking just like you. Even our stripes are the same.

MR. II: Where is your superiority then?

MR. I: No waste of energy; same results. Plus, of course, my 395 sense of inner freedom which . . .

MR. II: One more word about inner freedom and that will be the end of you.

MR. I: (*backing up*) You're unfair! After all, everyone has a right
to choose the philosophy that suits him best.

MR. II: Never mind! I can't stand this anymore!

MR. I: I'm warning you: I won't defend myself. Defending oneself involves making a choice, and for me this is out, in the
name of . . .

MR. II: What? Go on! In the name of what?

MR. I: (*hesitantly*) In the name of inner free— (MR. II *throws
himself at him.* MR. I *runs all over the stage.*) Keep your hands
off!

(*The door opens and the* HAND *reappears, beckoning to both.*
MR. I *and* MR. II *come to a sudden halt.*)

MR. II: Me?

MR. I: Or me?

MR. II: Maybe it's you . . .

MR. I: You started this fight. Now you'll get your just deserts.

MR. II: Why me? Do you still believe that your idiotic theory is
better?

MR. I: And you believe that your vulgar pragmatism, this lack of
any theory, will stand up to such a test?

(*The* HAND *beckons to both.*)

MR. II: We'd better go over! It wants something again.

MR. I: All right, let's go! We'll soon find out who is right.

(*They go over to the* HAND *which links them together with a pair
of handcuffs. The* HAND *disappears and the door closes.* MR. II
drags MR. I *along with him by the chain of the handcuffs and
collapses on his chair. Silence.*)

MR. I: What does this mean? (*Anxiously.*) Aren't you feeling
well? Do you believe that this time it's serious? Say something, please!

MR. II: I'm afraid . . .

MR. I: Of what?

MR. II: So far the Hand has limited only our freedom of movement in space. But what assurance is there that soon we won't
be limited in something even more essential?

MR. I: In what?

MR. II: In time. In our own duration.

(*Pause.*)

MR. I: I don't know either. (*Pedantically.*) You, of course, being
an activist, will exhaust your energies more rapidly. I, on the
other hand, conserve mine . . .

MR. II: (*imploringly*) Not again!

MR. I: I'm sorry. I didn't mean to hurt your feelings. Do you
have a plan?

MR. II: There is only one thing we can do now.

MR. I: What?

MR. II: Apologize to the Hand.

MR. I: Apologize? But what for? We haven't done anything to
the Hand. On the contrary, it should . . .

MR. II: This is completely irrelevant. We have to apologize all
the same . . . in general, for no reason. To save ourselves . . .
for whatever good it may do.

MR. I: No, I can't do that. I don't suppose I have to explain my
reasons.

MR. II: You're right, I know them by heart. To apologize to the
Hand would mean to make a choice, which again would limit
your freedom, and so on and so forth.

MR. I: Yes, that's how it is.

MR. II: Do as you please! In any case, I am going to apologize.
One has to abase oneself. Perhaps that is what it expects us
to do.

MR. I: I would like to join you, but my principles . . .

MR. II: I have nothing more to say.

MR. I: I think I can see a way out. You're going to force me to
apologize with you. In that case there is no question of choice
on my part. I'm simply going to be forced.

MR. II: All right, consider yourself forced.

(*The door opens.*)

MR. I: I think it's coming. (*The* HAND *appears.*) If only we had
some flowers! (*Whispering.*) You start!

(*Both run over to the* HAND. MR. II *clears his throat in preparation for his apology.*)

MR. II: Dear Hand! I mean, Dear and Most Honorable Hand!
Although well aware of the fact that the Hand is not here to
listen to us, we still beg permission to speak to the Hand from
the heart . . . I mean, we would like to hand the Hand a
confession, although somewhat belated, nevertheless with
full conscious awareness, we sincerely beg to apologize for
. . . for . . . (*Whispering to* MR. I.) For what?

MR. I: For walking, for going ahead, for everything in general . . .

MR. II: For walking, for going ahead, for . . . I'm expressing
myself poorly, but I simply wish to apologize in general . . .
for having been . . . for being . . . begging forgiveness from
the depth of my heart for whatever the Honorable Hand
knows that we don't know . . . for how are we to know what
there is to be known? Therefore, whatever the case may be, I
humbly apologize, I beg the Hand's forgiveness, I kiss the
Hand. (*He ceremoniously kisses the* HAND.)

MR. I: I wish to join my colleague, though only in a certain
sense, having been forced . . . The Hand knows my principles
. . . Therefore, though being forced, I nevertheless sincerely
apologize to the Hand on principle.

(*He ceremoniously kisses the* HAND. *Meanwhile the other door
opens and through it appears a* SECOND HAND, *completely covered by a red glove. It beckons to both.* MR. II *notices it first. Both
turn their backs to the* FIRST HAND.)

MR. II: There! Look!

MR. I: Another one!

MR. II: There are always two.

MR. I: It's calling us.

MR. II: Should we go? (*The* FIRST HAND *covers his head with a
conical cardboard hood.*) I can't see anything!

MR. I: It's calling us. (*The* FIRST HAND *covers his head with an
identical hood.*) It's dark.

MR. II: When you're called, you have to go.

(*Handcuffed to each other and blinded by the hoods, they move
toward stage center. Constantly stumbling and swerving, they
gradually come closer to the* SECOND HAND.)

MR. I: The briefcases! We forgot our briefcases!

MR. II: Right! My briefcase! Where's my briefcase?

(*They grope blindly for their briefcases, left standing next to the
chairs, then pick them up and follow the* SECOND HAND *through
the door. Blackout.*)

SAMUEL BECKETT

Samuel Beckett (1906–1989) is the most influential European dramatist of the postwar period. Born near Dublin, Ireland, Beckett was educated at Trinity College, Dublin, where he studied modern languages. Taking his B.A. in 1928, Beckett received an appointment as *lecteur* at l'École Normale Supérieure in Paris. While in Paris, Beckett met the Irish novelist James Joyce. Beckett assisted Joyce (who was nearly blind) in a variety of ways and became a close friend. Joyce also exerted a profound influence on Beckett's writing. Beckett contributed an essay entitled "Dante . . . Bruno . Vico . . Joyce" to a volume on Joyce's *Finnegans Wake* (1929). Throughout the 1930s, Beckett was associated with Joyce and with a variety of avant-garde movements in Paris. He wrote a series of poems — including the prize-winning "Whoroscope" — as well as a study of Proust (1931), the volume of short stories *More Pricks than Kicks* (1934), and the novel *Murphy* (1938). Although Beckett returned briefly to Ireland on a few occasions, he had settled permanently in Paris. During World War II, Beckett served in the French Resistance. He was discovered by the Nazis and forced to flee Paris in 1942. He worked in the unoccupied zone of southern France for the remainder of the war, where he wrote the novel *Watt* (1953). After the war, Beckett received the Croix de Guerre and the Médaille de la Résistance for his services. He began to write exclusively in French, starting work on a major trilogy of novels — *Molloy* (1951), *Malone Dies* (1951), and *The Unnameable* (1953).

Beckett had experimented with drama during the 1930s and 1940s, but his first staged play, *Waiting for Godot* (also written in French, as *En attendant Godot*), produced at the tiny Théâtre de Babylone in January of 1953, impelled him in a new direction. Although Beckett continued to write fiction — including *From an Abandoned Work* (1956), *How It Is* (1964), *Imagination Dead Imagine* (1965), and *Company* (1979) — his major writing of the 1960s, 1970s, and 1980s was for the theater. His second play, *Endgame,* also written in French, was produced in 1957 and was followed by a series of challenging works for the stage: *Krapp's Last Tape* (1958), *Happy Days* (1962), *Play* (1963), *Not I* (1972), *Footfalls* (1975), *Rockaby* (1981), and *Catastrophe* (1982). For his extraordinarily diverse and influential body of work, Beckett won the Nobel Prize for Literature in 1970. Beckett also wrote several plays for radio and television, as well as a film starring Buster Keaton, *Film* (1965). Beginning in the mid-1960s, Beckett directed productions of his plays, and several productions he directed in France and in Germany now have the status of classics — something like Elia Kazan's productions of Tennessee Williams's plays, or Stanislavsky's productions of Chekhov.

Beckett's impact on the contemporary theater can hardly be overestimated and can be seen in the work of Sam Shepard, Maria Irene Fornes, Harold Pinter, and many others. *Waiting for Godot* signaled new possibilities for stage action — or inaction — and developed the implications of Chekhov's static stage in a more symbolic direction. Each of Beckett's plays explores the nature and limitations of its medium in new and challenging ways. *Endgame* refigures the claustral box of realistic drama, for its characters are trapped in a room of endless — or possibly ending — routine. In *Play*, Beckett puts three urns onstage, from which three heads emerge to deliver, more or less simultaneously, a jarring, repetitive monologue of seduction and betrayal. Once the play has finished, Beckett directs his performers — and his audience — to "Repeat play," and so calls the relationship between actors and spectators, theater and reality into question: If we cannot leave the theater when the play is over, is it possible that there is no way out of the purgatory on the stage and in the auditorium? This sense that the self is always in flight is the theme of several of Beckett's later plays. In *Not I*, for instance, all that the audience sees is a Mouth eight feet above the stage, reciting an endless narrative in which she avoids claiming the speech as her own. In *Ohio Impromptu* (1981), an identical reader and listener relate a painful narrative of loss, in which it is unclear whether they are two individuals or parts of a single person. The power of Beckett's spare, minimalist theater, the beauty of his sculptural use of actors and stage space, and the harsh exigency of the action of his plays have transformed the stage of our time.

Happy Days

Beckett's work is among the most challenging and rewarding of the postwar canon: challenging because Beckett is a theatrical minimalist, working with little staging, few actors, and practically nothing in the way of action in the conventional sense; rewarding in that Beckett squeezes a rich world from these recalcitrant materials. In an early play, *Endgame*, Beckett conceived a post-tragic drama of stasis, and in his later plays, Beckett frequently designed his actors into abstract stage compositions. The most striking element of *Happy Days* in the theater is its visual design. In Act 1, the heroine, Winnie, is buried to her waist in a mound of earth, rattling on about her past, her relationship with Willie (briefly glimpsed behind the mound), and the contents of her capacious black bag. In Act 2, she is inexplicably buried to her neck and, again, talks her way through "another heavenly day."

Despite the mysterious "given circumstances" of the play, the action of *Happy Days* is in some ways familiar: a staging of the difficulty of getting through the day. In the course of her day, Winnie must be careful to pace herself, to parcel out her activities so as to give the day meaning. Even though the play's action is constricted to the sphere that Winnie can encompass with her arms, the action of the play is quite varied—Winnie reminisces about her youth; she examines the contents of her bag; she implores Willie to speak to her; she puts up her parasol (which bursts into flames). These are tiny events, but in many ways no less tiny than the ways we all construct our lives. Moreover, Winnie has other resources for interpreting her experience, for she frequently alludes to literature as a way of making sense of her situation. However, when Winnie quotes from *Hamlet* ("woe woe is me") or from *Romeo and Juliet* ("Ensign crimson") or from Milton's *Paradise Lost* ("fleeting joys"), her quotations have the fragmentary and incomplete quality of her other activities. Much like the miscellaneous junk in her bag, the history of literature has been reduced to a pile of tag-lines, the misremembered junk strewn about in Winnie's mind.

For all her resolute effort to pass the time, it is clear that time has altered for Winnie. The world of the play has been dislocated from our usual sense of time in which days proceed from one to the next, what Winnie calls "the old style." Winnie seems to exist in a kind of hellish theatrical purgatory, in which each day endlessly repeats the last one. Summoned to her performance by a bell (like the curtain bell in a theater that alerts the actors), Winnie must go through the script of her activities, remaining under the bright light until a certain time has passed. We might also find the dialectics of realistic theater literalized in Winnie's plight; she, too, is determined, hemmed in by her environment, a material world that she both struggles to resist and to interpret. As the play proceeds, Winnie's purgatorial suffering seems harsher, more painful, as the world presses in on her and reduces her experience to the mere fact of consciousness. This, too, seems a kind of schematic reduction of the dialectic between subject and object, self and things, character and environment that animates the realistic stage. In *Happy Days*, Beckett reduces the realistic theater—and the world it represents—to its essentials, presenting a brilliant allegory of the struggle to *be* in our indifferent and punitive world.

HAPPY DAYS

Samuel Beckett

— CHARACTERS —

WINNIE, *a woman about fifty*
WILLIE, *a man about sixty*

— ACT ONE —

Expanse of scorched grass rising centre to low mound. Gentle slopes down to front and either side of stage. Back an abrupter fall to stage level. Maximum of simplicity and symmetry.

Blazing light.

Very pompier trompe-l'oeil backcloth to represent unbroken plain and sky receding to meet in far distance.

Imbedded up to above her waist in exact centre of mound, WIN-NIE. *About fifty, well preserved, blond for preference, plump, arms and shoulders bare, low bodice, big bosom, pearl necklet. She is discovered sleeping, her arms on the ground before her, her head on her arms. Beside her on ground to her left a capacious black bag, shopping variety, and to her right a collapsible collapsed parasol, beak of handle emerging from sheath.*

To her right and rear, lying asleep on ground, hidden by mound, WILLIE.

Long pause. A bell rings piercingly, say ten seconds, stops. She does not move. Pause. Bell more piercingly, say five seconds. She wakes. Bell stops. She raises her head, gazes front. Long pause. She straightens up, lays her hands flat on ground, throws back her head and gazes at zenith. Long pause.

WINNIE: *(gazing at zenith.)* Another heavenly day. *(Pause. Head back level, eyes front, pause. She clasps hands to breast, closes eyes. Lips move in unaudible prayer, say ten seconds. Lips still. Hands remain clasped. Low.)* For Jesus Christ sake
5 Amen. *(Eyes open, hands unclasp, return to mound. Pause. She clasps hands to breast again, closes eyes, lips move again in inaudible addendum, say five seconds. Low.)* World without end Amen. *(Eyes open, hands unclasp, return to mound. Pause.)* Begin, Winnie. *(Pause.)* Begin your day, Winnie.
10 *(Pause. She turns to bag, rummages in it without moving it from its place, brings out toothbrush, rummages again, brings out flat tube of toothpaste, turns back front, unscrews cap of tube, lays cap on ground, squeezes with difficulty small blob of paste on brush, holds tube in one hand and brushes teeth with
15 other. She turns modestly aside and back to her right to spit out behind mound. In this position her eyes rest on* WILLIE. *She spits out. She cranes a little further back and down. Loud.)* Hoo-oo! *(Pause. Louder.)* Hoo-oo! *(Pause. Tender smile as she turns back front, lays down brush.)* Poor Willie —
20 *(examines tube, smile off)* — running out — *(looks for cap)* — ah well — *(finds cap)* — can't be helped — *(screws on cap)* — just one of those old things — *(lays down tube)* — another of those old things — *(turns towards bag)* — just can't be cured — *(rummages in bag)* — cannot be cured — *(brings out small
25 mirror, turns back front)* — ah yes — *(inspects teeth in mir-ror)* — poor dear Willie — *(testing upper front teeth with thumb, indistinctly)* — good Lord! — *(pulling back upper lip to inspect gums, do.)* — good God! — *(pulling back corner of mouth, mouth open, do.)* — ah well — *(other corner, do.)* — no worse — *(abandons inspection, normal speech)* — no better,
30 no worse — *(lays down mirror)* — no change — *(wipes fingers on grass)* — no pain — *(looks for toothbrush)* — hardly any — *(takes up toothbrush)* — great thing that — *(examines handle of brush)* — nothing like it — *(examines handle, reads)* — pure . . . what? — *(pause)* — what? — *(lays down brush)* — ah yes —
35 *(turns towards bag)* — poor Willie — *(rummages in bag)* — no zest — *(rummages)* — for anything — *(brings out spectacles in case)* — no interest — *(turns back front)* — in life — *(takes spectacles from case)* — poor dear Willie — *(lays down case)* — sleep for ever — *(opens spectacles)* — marvellous gift — *(puts
40 on spectacles)* — nothing to touch it — *(looks for toothbrush)* — in my opinion — *(takes up toothbrush)* — always said so — *(examines handle of brush)* — wish I had it — *(examines handle, reads)* — genuine . . . pure . . . what? — *(lays down brush)* — blind next — *(takes off spectacles)* — ah well — *(lays down spec-
45 tacles)* — seen enough — *(feels in bodice for handkerchief)* — I suppose — *(takes out folded handkerchief)* — by now — *(shakes out handkerchief)* — what are those wonderful lines — *(wipes one eye)* — woe woe is me — *(wipes the other)* — to see what I see — *(looks for spectacles)* — ah yes — *(takes up
50 spectacles)* — wouldn't miss it — *(starts polishing spectacles, breathing on lenses)* — or would I? — *(polishes)* — holy light — *(polishes)* — bob up out of dark — *(polishes)* — blaze of hellish light. — *(Stops polishing, raises face to sky, pause, head back level, resumes polishing, stops polishing, cranes back to her
55 right and down.)* Hoo-oo! *(Pause. Tender smile as she turns back front and resumes polishing. Smile off.)* Marvellous gift — *(stops polishing, lays down spectacles)* — wish I had it — *(folds handkerchief)* — ah well — *(puts handkerchief back in bodice)* — can't complain — *(looks for spectacles)* — no no —
60 *(takes up spectacles)* — mustn't complain — *(holds up spectacles, looks through lens)* — so much to be thankful for — *(looks through other lens)* — no pain — *(puts on spectacles)* — hardly any — *(looks for toothbrush)* — wonderful thing that — *(takes up toothbrush)* — nothing like it — *(examines handle of
65 brush)* — slight headache sometimes — *(examines handle, reads)* — guaranteed . . . genuine . . . pure . . . what? — *(looks closer)* — genuine pure . . . . — *(takes handkerchief from bodice)* — ah yes — *(shakes out handkerchief)* — occasional mild migraine — *(starts wiping handle of brush)* — it comes —
70 *(wipes)* — then goes — *(wiping mechanically)* — ah yes — *(wiping)* — many mercies — *(wiping)* — great mercies — *(stops wiping, fixed lost gaze, brokenly)* — prayers perhaps not for naught — *(pause, do.)* — first thing — *(pause, do.)* — last

771

75 thing—(*head down, resumes wiping, stops wiping, head up, calmed, wipes eyes, folds handkerchief, puts it back in bodice, examines handle of brush, reads*)—fully guaranteed . . . genuine pure . . .—(*looks closer*)—genuine pure . . .—(*Takes off spectacles, lays them and brush down, gazes before her.*) Old

80 things. (*Pause.*) Old eyes. (*Long pause.*) On, Winnie. (*She casts about her, sees parasol, considers it at length, takes it up and develops from sheath a handle of surprising length. Holding butt of parasol in right hand she cranes back and down to her right to hang over* WILLIE.) Hoo-oo! (*Pause.*) Willie!

85 (*Pause.*) Wonderful gift. (*She strikes down at him with beak of parasol.*) Wish I had it. (*She strikes again. The parasol slips from her grasp and falls behind mound. It is immediately restored to her by* WILLIE's *invisible hand.*) Thank you, dear. (*She transfers parasol to left hand, turns back front and examines right palm.*) Damp. (*Returns parasol to right hand, examines left palm.*) Ah well, no worse. (*Head up, cheerfully.*)

90 No better, no worse, no change. (*Pause. Do.*) No pain. (*Cranes back to look down at* WILLIE, *holding parasol by butt as before.*) Don't go off on me again now dear will you please, I may need you. (*Pause.*) No hurry, no hurry, just don't curl

95 up on me again. (*Turns back front, lays down parasol, examines palms together, wipes them on grass.*) Perhaps a shade off colour just the same. (*Turns to bag, rummages in it, brings out revolver, holds it up, kisses it rapidly, puts it back, rummages, brings out almost empty bottle of red medicine, turns

100 back front, looks for spectacles, puts them on, reads label.*) Loss of spirits . . . lack of keenness . . . want of appetite . . . infants . . . children . . . adults . . . six level . . . tablespoonfuls daily—(*head up, smile*)—the old style!—(*smile off, head

105 down, reads*)—daily . . . before and after . . . meals . . . instantaneous . . .—(*looks closer*)—improvement. (*Takes off spectacles, lays them down, holds up bottle at arm's length to see level, unscrews cap, swigs it off head well back, tosses cap and bottle away in* WILLIE's *direction. Sound of breaking

110 glass.*) Ah that's better! (*Turns to bag, rummages in it, brings out lipstick, turns back front, examines lipstick.*) Running out. (*Looks for spectacles.*) Ah well. (*Puts on spectacles, looks for mirror.*) Musn't complain. (*Takes up mirror, starts doing lips.*) What is that wonderful line? (*Lips.*) Oh fleeting joys—

115 (*lips*)—oh something lasting woe. (*Lips. She is interrupted by disturbance from* WILLIE. *He is sitting up. She lowers lipstick and mirror and cranes back and down to look at him. Pause. Top back of* WILLIE's *bald head, trickling blood, rises to view above slope, comes to rest.* WINNIE *pushes up her specta-*

120 *cles. Pause. His hand appears with handkerchief, spreads it on skull, disappears. Pause. The hand appears with boater, club ribbon, settles it on head, rakish angle, disappears. Pause.* WINNIE *cranes a little further back and down.*) Slip on your drawers, dear, before you get singed. (*Pause.*) No? (*Pause.*)

125 Oh I see, you still have some of that stuff left. (*Pause.*) Work it well in, dear. (*Pause.*) Now the other. (*Pause. She turns back front, gazes before her. Happy expression.*) Oh this is going to be another happy day! (*Pause. Happy expression off. She pulls down spectacles and resumes lips.* WILLIE *opens newspaper,*

130 *hands invisible. Tops of yellow sheets appear on either side of his head.* WINNIE *finishes lips, inspects them in mirror held a little further away.*) Ensign crimson. (WILLIE *turns page.* WINNIE *lays down lipstick and mirror, turns towards bag.*) Pale flag.

(WILLIE *turns page.* WINNIE *rummages in bag, brings out small ornate brimless hat with crumpled feather, turns back front, straightens hat, smoothes feather, raises it towards head, arrests gesture as* WILLIE *reads.*)

WILLIE: His Grace and Most Reverend Father in God Dr Carolus Hunter dead in tub. 135

(*Pause.*)

WINNIE: (*gazing front, hat in hand, tone of fervent reminiscence.*) Charlie Hunter! (*Pause.*) I close my eyes—(*she takes off spectacles and does so, hat in one hand, spectacles in other,* WILLIE *turns page*)—and am sitting on his knees again, in the 140 back garden at Borough Green, under the horse-beech. (*Pause. She opens eyes, puts on spectacles, fiddles with hat.*) Oh the happy memories!

(*Pause. She raises hat towards head, arrests gesture as* WILLIE *reads.*)

WILLIE: Opening for smart youth.

(*Pause. She raises hat towards head, arrests gesture, takes off spectacles, gazes front, hat in one hand, spectacles in other.*)

WINNIE: My first ball! (*Long pause.*) My second ball! (*Long 145 pause. Closes eyes.*) My first kiss! (*Pause.* WILLIE *turns page.* WINNIE *opens eyes.*) A Mr Johnson, or Johnston, or perhaps I should say Johnstone. Very bushy moustache, very tawny. (*Reverently.*) Almost ginger! (*Pause.*) Within a toolshed, though whose I cannot conceive. We had no toolshed and he 150 most certainly had no toolshed. (*Closes eyes.*) I see the piles of pots. (*Pause.*) The tangles of bast. (*Pause.*) The shadows deepening among the rafters.

(*Pause. She opens eyes, puts on spectacles, raises hat towards head, arrests gesture as* WILLIE *reads.*)

WILLIE: Wanted bright boy.

(*Pause.* WINNIE *puts on hat hurriedly, looks for mirror.* WILLIE *turns page.* WINNIE *takes up mirror, inspects hat, lays down mirror, turns towards bag. Paper disappears.* WINNIE *rummages in bag, brings out magnifying-glass, turns back front, looks for toothbrush. Paper reappears, folded, and begins to fan* WILLIE's *face, hand invisible.* WINNIE *takes up toothbrush and examines handle through glass.*)

WINNIE: Fully guaranteed . . . (WILLIE *stops fanning*) . . . genuine pure . . . (*Pause.* WILLIE *resumes fanning.* WINNIE *looks closer, reads.*) Fully guaranteed . . . (WILLIE *stops fanning*) . . . genuine pure . . . (*Pause.* WILLIE *resumes fanning.* WINNIE *lays down glass and brush, takes handkerchief from bodice, takes off and polishes spectacles, puts on spectacles, looks for 160 glass, takes up and polishes glass, lays down glass, looks for brush, takes up brush and wipes handle, lays down brush, puts handkerchief back in bodice, looks for glass, takes up glass, looks for brush, takes up brush and examines handle through glass.*) Fully guaranteed . . . (WILLIE *stops fanning*) 165 . . . genuine pure . . . (*pause,* WILLIE *resumes fanning*) . . . hog's (WILLIE *stops fanning, pause*) . . . setae. (*Pause.* WINNIE *lays down glass and brush, paper disappears,* WINNIE *takes off spectacles, lays them down, gazes front.*) Hog's setae. (*Pause.*) That is what I find so wonderful, that not a day goes 170 by—(*smile*)—to speak in the old style—(*smile off*)—hardly a

day, without some addition to one's knowledge however trifling, the addition I mean, provided one takes the pains.
(WILLIE's *hand reappears with a postcard which he examines*
close to eyes.) And if for some strange reason no further pains
are possible, why then just close the eyes — (*she does so*) — and
wait for the day to come — (*opens eyes*) — the happy day to
come when flesh melts at so many degrees and the night of
the moon has so many hundred hours. (*Pause*.) That is what I
find so comforting when I lose heart and envy the brute beast.
(*Turning towards* WILLIE.) I hope you are taking in — (*She*
sees postcard, bends lower.) What is that you have there,
Willie, may I see? (*She reaches down with hand and* WILLIE
hands her card. The hairy forearm appears above slope, raised
in gesture of giving, the hand open to take back, and remains
in this position till card is returned. WINNIE *turns back front*
and examines card.) Heavens what are they up to! (*She looks*
for spectacles, puts them on and examines card.) No but this is
just genuine pure filth! (*Examines card*.) Make any nice-
minded person want to vomit! (*Impatience of* WILLIE's *fingers.*
She looks for glass, takes it up and examines card through
glass. Long pause.) What does that creature in the background think he's doing? (*Looks closer*.) Oh no really! (*Impa-*
tience of fingers. Last long look. She lays down glass, takes
edge of card between right forefinger and thumb, averts head,
takes nose between left forefinger and thumb.) Pah! (*Drops*
card.) Take it away! (WILLIE's *arm disappears. His hand reap-*
pears immediately, holding card. WINNIE *takes off spectacles,*
lays them down, gazes before her. During what follows WILLIE
continues to relish card, varying angles and distance from his
eyes.) Hog's setae. (*Puzzled expression*.) What exactly is a
hog? (*Pause. Do*.) A sow of course I know, but a hog . . .
(*Puzzled expression off*.) Oh well what does it matter, that is
what I always say, it will come back, that is what I find so
wonderful, all comes back. (*Pause*.) All? (*Pause*.) No, not all.
(*Smile*.) No no. (*Smile off*.) Not quite. (*Pause*.) A part.
(*Pause*.) Floats up, one fine day, out of the blue. (*Pause*.)
That is what I find so wonderful. (*Pause. She turns towards*
bag. Hand and card disappear. She makes to rummage in
bag, arrests gesture.) No. (*She turns back front. Smile*.) No
no. *Smile off*.) Gently Winnie. (*She gazes front.* WILLIE's
hand reappears, takes off hat, disappears with hat.) What
then? (*Hand reappears, takes handkerchief from skull, disap-*
pears with handkerchief. Sharply, as to one not paying atten-
tion.) Winnie! (WILLIE *bows head out of sight*.) What is the
alternative? (*Pause*.) What is the al — (WILLIE *blows nose loud*
and long, head and hands invisible. She turns to look at him.
Pause. Head reappears. Pause. Hand reappears with hand-
kerchief, spreads it on skull, disappears. Pause. Hand reap-
pears with boater, settles it on head, rakish angle, disappears.
Pause.) Would I had let you sleep on. (*She turns back front.*
Intermittent plucking at grass, head up and down, to animate
following.) Ah yes, if only I could bear to be alone, I mean
prattle away with not a soul to hear. (*Pause*.) Not that I flatter
myself you hear much, no Willie, God forbid. (*Pause*.) Days
perhaps when you hear nothing. (*Pause*.) But days too when
you answer. (*Pause*.) So that I may say at all times, even when
you do not answer and perhaps hear nothing, Something of
this is being heard, I am not merely talking to myself, that is
in the wilderness, a thing I could never bear to do — for any
length of time. (*Pause*.) That is what enables me to go on, go

on talking that is. (*Pause*.) Whereas if you were to die —
(*smile*) — to speak in the old style — (*smile off*) — or go away
and leave me, then what would I do, what *could* I do, all day
long, I mean between the bell for waking and the bell for
sleep? (*Pause*.) Simply gaze before me with compressed lips.
(*Long pause while she does so. No more plucking*.) Not another word as long as I drew breath, nothing to break the
silence of this place. (*Pause*.) Save possibly, now and then,
every now and then, a sigh into my looking-glass. (*Pause*.) Or
a brief . . . gale of laughter, should I happen to see the old joke
again. (*Pause. Smile appears, broadens and seems about to*
culminate in laugh when suddenly replaced by expression of
anxiety.) My hair! (*Pause*.) Did I brush and comb my hair?
(*Pause*.) I may have done. (*Pause*.) Normally I do. (*Pause*.)
There is so little one *can* do. (*Pause*.) One does it all. (*Pause*.)
All one can. (*Pause*.) 'Tis only human. (*Pause*.) Human nature. (*She begins to inspect mound, looks up*.) Human weakness. (*She resumes inspection of mound, looks up*.) Natural
weakness. (*She resumes inspection of mound*.) I see no comb.
(*Inspects*.) Nor any hairbrush. (*Looks up. Puzzled expression.*
She turns to bag, rummages in it.) The comb is here. (*Back*
front. Puzzled expression. Back to bag. Rummages.) The
brush is here. (*Back front. Puzzled expression*.) Perhaps I put
them back, after use. (*Pause. Do*.) But normally I do not put
things back, after use, no, I leave them lying about and put
them back all together, at the end of the day. (*Smile*.) To
speak in the old style. (*Pause*.) The sweet old style. (*Smile*
off.) And yet . . . I seem . . . to remember . . . (*Suddenly*
careless.) Oh well, what does it matter, that is what I always
say, I shall simply brush and comb them later on, purely and
simply, I have the whole — (*Pause. Puzzled*.) Them? (*Pause*.)
Or it? (*Pause*.) Brush and comb it? (*Pause*.) Sounds improper
somehow. (*Pause. Turning a little towards* WILLIE.) What
would you say, Willie? (*Pause. Turning a little further*.) What
would you say, Willie, speaking of your hair, them or it?
(*Pause*.) The hair on your head, I mean. (*Pause. Turning a*
little further.) The hair on your head, Willie, what would you
say speaking of the hair on your head, them or it?

(*Long pause*.)

WILLIE: It.

WINNIE: (*turning back front, joyful*.) Oh you are going to talk to
me today, this is going to be a happy day! (*Pause. Joy off*.)
Another happy day. (*Pause*.) Ah well, where was I, my hair,
yes, later on, I shall be thankful for it later on. (*Pause*.) I have
my — (*raises hands to hat*) — yes, on, my hat on — (*lowers*
hands) — I cannot take it off now. (*Pause*.) To think there are
times one cannot take off one's hat, not if one's life were at
stake. Times one cannot put it on, times one cannot take it
off. (*Pause*.) How often I have said, Put on your hat now,
Winnie, there is nothing else for it, take off your hat now,
Winnie, like a good girl, it will do you good, and did not.
(*Pause*.) Could not. (*Pause. She raises hand, frees a strand of*
hair from under hat, draws it towards eye, squints at it, lets it
go, hand down.) Golden you called it, that day, when the last
guest was gone — (*hand up in gesture of raising a glass*) — to
your golden . . . may it never . . . (*voice breaks*) . . . may it
never . . . (*Hand down. Head down. Pause. Low*.) That day.
(*Pause. Do*.) What day? (*Pause. Head up. Normal voice*.)
What now? (*Pause*.) Words fail, there are times when even

290   they fail. (*Turning a little towards* WILLIE.) Is that not so,
Willie? (*Pause. Turning a little further.*) Is not that so, Willie,
that even words fail, at times? (*Pause. Back front.*) What is
one to do then, until they come again? Brush and comb the
hair, if it has not been done, or if there is some doubt, trim the
295   nails if they are in need of trimming, these things tide one
over. (*Pause.*) That is what I mean. (*Pause.*) That is all I
mean. (*Pause.*) That is what I find so wonderful, that not a
day goes by—(*smile*)—to speak in the old style—(*smile
off*)—without some blessing—(WILLIE *collapses behind
300   slope, his head disappears,* WINNIE *turns towards event*)—in
disguise. (*She cranes back and down.*) Go back into your hole
now, Willie, you've exposed yourself enough. (*Pause.*) Do as
I say, Willie, don't lie sprawling there in this hellish sun, go
back into your hole. (*Pause.*) Go on now, Willie. (WILLIE
305   *invisible starts crawling left towards hole.*) That's the man.
(*She follows his progress with her eyes.*) Not head first, stupid,
how are you going to turn? (*Pause.*) That's it . . . right round
. . . now . . . back in. (*Pause.*) Oh I know it is not easy, dear,
crawling backwards, but it is rewarding in the end. (*Pause.*)
310   You have left your vaseline behind. (*She watches as he crawls
back for vaseline.*) The lid! (*She watches as he crawls back
towards hole. Irritated.*) Not head first, I tell you! (*Pause.*)
More to the right. (*Pause.*) The *right*, I said. (*Pause. Irritated.*) Keep your tail down, can't you! (*Pause.*) Now.
315   (*Pause.*) There! (*All these directions loud. Now in her normal
voice, still turned towards him.*) Can you hear me? (*Pause.*) I
beseech you, Willie, just yes or no, can you hear me, just yes
or nothing.

(*Pause.*)

WILLIE: Yes.
320 WINNIE: (*turning front, same voice.*) And now?
WILLIE: (irritated.) Yes.
WINNIE: (*less loud.*) And now?
WILLIE: (*more irritated.*) Yes.
WINNIE: (*still less loud.*) And now? (*A little louder.*) And now?
325 WILLIE: (*violently*) Yes!
WINNIE: (*same voice.*) Fear no more the heat o' the sun. (*Pause.*)
Did you hear that?
WILLIE: (*irritated.*) Yes.
WINNIE: (*same voice.*) What? (*Pause.*) What?
330 WILLIE: (*more irritated.*) Fear no more.

(*Pause.*)

WINNIE: (*same voice.*) No more what? (*Pause.*) Fear no more
what?
WILLIE: (*violently.*) Fear no more!
WINNIE: (*normal voice, gabbled.*) Bless you Willie I do appreci-
335   ate your goodness I know what an effort it costs you, now you
may relax I shall not trouble you again unless I am obliged to,
by that I mean unless I come to the end of my own resources
which is most unlikely, just to know that in theory you can
hear me even though in fact you don't is all I need, just to feel
340   you there within earshot and conceivably on the qui vive is all
I ask, not to say anything I would not wish you to hear or
liable to cause you pain, not to be just babbling away on trust
as it is were not knowing and something gnawing at me.
(*Pause for breath.*) Doubt. (*Places index and second finger on

heart area, moves them about, brings them to rest.*) Here.
345 (*Moves them slightly.*) Abouts. (*Hand away.*) Oh no doubt
the time will come when before I can utter a word I must
make sure you heard the one that went before and then no
doubt another come another time when I must learn to talk to
myself a thing I could never bear to do such wilderness.
350 (*Pause.*) Or gaze before me with compressed lips. (*She does
so.*) All day long. (*Gaze and lips again.*) No. (*Smile.*) No no.
(*Smile off.*) There is of course the bag. (*Turns towards it.*)
There will always be the bag. (*Back front.*) Yes, I suppose so.
(*Pause.*) Even when you are gone, Willie. (*She turns a little
355 towards him.*) You *are* going, Willie, aren't you? (*Pause.
Louder.*) You *will* be going soon, Willie, won't you? (*Pause.
Louder.*) Willie! (*Pause. She cranes back and down to look at
him.*) So you have taken off your straw, that is wise. (*Pause.*)
You do look snug, I must say, with your chin on your hands
360 and the old blue eyes like saucers in the shadows. (*Pause.*)
Can you see me from there I wonder, I still wonder. (*Pause.*)
No? (*Back front.*) Oh I know it does not follow when two are
gathered together—(*faltering*)—in this way—(*normal*)—
that because one sees the other the other sees the one, life has
365 taught me that . . . too. (*Pause.*) Yes, life I suppose, there is no
other word. (*She turns a little towards him.*) Could you see
me, Willie, do you think, from where you are, if you were to
raise your eyes in my direction? (*Turns a little further.*) Lift up
your eyes to me, Willie, and tell me can you see me, do that
370 for me, I'll lean back as far as I can. (*Does so. Pause.*) No?
(*Pause.*) Well never mind. (*Turns back painfully front.*) The
earth is very tight today, can it be I have put on flesh, I trust
not. (*Pause. Absently, eyes lowered.*) The great heat possibly.
(*Starts to pat and stroke ground.*) All things expanding, some
375 more than others. (*Pause. Patting and stroking.*) Some less.
(*Pause. Do.*) Oh I can well imagine what is passing through
your mind, it is not enough to have to listen to the woman,
now I must look at her as well. (*Pause. Do.*) Well it is very
understandable. (*Pause. Do.*) Most understandable. (*Pause.
380 Do.*) One does not appear to be asking a great deal, indeed at
times it would seem hardly possible—(*voice breaks, falls to
a murmur*)—to ask less—of a fellow-creature—to put it
mildly—whereas actually—when you think about it—look
into your heart—see the other—what he needs—peace—to
385 be left in peace—then perhaps the moon—all this time—
asking for the moon. (*Pause. Stroking hand suddenly still.
Lively.*) Oh I say, what have we here? (*Bending head to
ground, incredulous.*) Looks like life of some kind! (*Looks for
spectacles, put them on, bends closer. Pause.*) An emmet! (*Re-
390 coils. Shrill.*) Willie, an emmet, a live emmet! (*Seizes magnifying-glass, bends to ground again, inspects through glass.*)
Where's it gone? (*Inspects.*) Ah! (*Follows its progress through
grass.*) Has like a little white ball in its arms. (*Follows progress. Hand still. Pause.*) It's gone in. (*Continues a moment to
395 gaze at spot through glass, then slowly straightens up, lays
down glass, takes off spectacles and gazes before her, spectacles
in hand. Finally.*) Like a little white ball.

(*Long pause. Gesture to lay down spectacles.*)

WILLIE: Eggs.
WINNIE: (*arresting gesture.*) What?
400

(*Pause.*)

WILLIE: Eggs. (*Pause. Gesture to lay down glasses.*) Formication.

WINNIE: (*arresting gesture.*) What?

(*Pause.*)

WILLIE: Formication.

(*Pause. She lays down spectacles, gazes before her. Finally.*)

405 WINNIE: (*murmur.*) God. (*Pause.* WILLIE *laughs quietly. After a moment she joins in. They laugh quietly together.* WILLIE *stops. She laughs on a moment alone.* WILLIE *joins in. They laugh together. She stops.* WILLIE *laughs on a moment alone. He stops. Pause. Normal voice.*) Ah well what a joy in any 410 case to hear you laugh again, Willie, I was convinced I never would, you never would. (*Pause.*) I suppose some people might think us a trifle irreverent, but I doubt it. (*Pause.*) How can one better magnify the Almighty than by sniggering with him at his little jokes, particularly the poorer ones? (*Pause.*) I 415 think you would back me up there, Willie. (*Pause.*) Or were we perhaps diverted by two quite different things? (*Pause.*) Oh well, what does it matter, that is what I always say, so long as one . . . you know . . . what is that wonderful line . . . laughing wild . . . something something laughing wild amid 420 severest woe. (*Pause.*) And now? (*Long pause.*) Was I lovable once, Willie? (*Pause.*) Was I ever lovable? (*Pause.*) Do not misunderstand my question, I am not asking you if you loved me, we know all about that, I am asking you if you found me lovable—at one stage. (*Pause.*) No? (*Pause.*) You can't? 425 (*Pause.*) Well I admit it is a teaser. And you have done more than your bit already, for the time being, just lie back now and relax, I shall not trouble you again unless I am compelled to, just to know you are there within hearing and conceivably on the semi-alert is . . . er . . . paradise enow. (*Pause.*) The day is 430 now well advanced. (*Smile.*) To speak in the old style. (*Smile off.*) And yet it is perhaps a little soon for my song. (*Pause.*) To sing too soon is a great mistake, I find. (*Turning towards bag.*) There is of course the bag. (*Looking at bag.*) The bag. (*Back front.*) Could I enumerate its contents? (*Pause.*) No. (*Pause.*) 435 Could I, if some kind person were to come along and ask, What all have you got in that big black bag, Winnie? give an exhaustive answer? (*Pause.*) No. (*Pause.*) The depths in particular, who knows what treasures. (*Pause.*) What comforts. (*Turns to look at bag.*) Yes, there is the bag. (*Back front.*) But 440 something tells me, Do not overdo the bag, Winnie, make use of it of course, let it help you . . . along, when stuck, by all means, but cast your mind forward, something tells me, cast your mind forward, Winnie, to the time when words must fail—(*she closes eyes, pause, opens eyes*)—and do not overdo 445 the bag. (*Pause. She turns to look at bag.*) Perhaps just one quick dip. (*She turns back front, closes eyes, throws out left arm, plunges hand in bag and brings out revolver. Disgusted.*) You again! (*She opens eyes, brings revolver front and contemplates it. She weighs it in her palm.*) You'd think the weight of 450 this thing would bring it down among the . . . last rounds. But no. It doesn't. Ever uppermost, like Browning. (*Pause.*) Brownie . . . (*Turning a little towards* WILLIE.) Remember Brownie, Willie? (*Pause.*) Remember how you used to keep on at me to take it away from you? Take it away, Winnie, take 455 it away, before I put myself out of my misery. (*Back front. Derisive.*) Your misery! (*To revolver.*) Oh I suppose it's a comfort to know you're there, but I'm tired of you. (*Pause.*) I'll leave you out, that's what I'll do. (*She lays revolver on ground to her right.*) There, that's your home from this day out. 460 (*Smile.*) The old style! (*Smile off.*) And now? (*Long pause.*) Is gravity what it was, Willie, I fancy not. (*Pause.*) Yes, the feeling more and more that if I were not held — (*gesture*) — in this way, I would simply float up into the blue. (*Pause.*) And that perhaps some day the earth will yield and let me go, the pull is 465 so great, yes, crack all round me and let me out. (*Pause.*) Don't you ever have that feeling, Willie, of being sucked up? (*Pause.*) Don't you have to cling on sometimes, Willie? (*Pause. She turns a little towards him.*) Willie.

(*Pause.*)

WILLIE: *Sucked* up?

WINNIE: Yes love, up into the blue, like gossamer. (*Pause.*) No? 470 (*Pause.*) You don't? (*Pause.*) Ah well, natural laws, natural laws, I suppose it's like everything else, it all depends on the creature you happen to be. All I can say is for my part is that for me they are not what they were when I was young and . . . foolish and . . . (*faltering, head down*) . . . beautiful . . . 475 possibly . . . lovely . . . in a way . . . to look at. (*Pause. Head up.*) Forgive me, Willie, sorrow keeps breaking in. (*Normal voice.*) Ah well what a joy in any case to know you are there, as usual, and perhaps awake, and perhaps taking all this in, some of all this, what a happy day for me . . . it will have 480 been. (*Pause.*) So far. (*Pause.*) What a blessing nothing grows, imagine if all this stuff were to start growing. (*Pause.*) Imagine. (*Pause.*) Ah yes, great mercies. (*Long pause.*) I can say no more. (*Pause.*) For the moment. (*Pause. Turns to look at bag. Back front. Smile.*) No no. (*Smile off. Looks at para-485 sol.*) I suppose I might — (*takes up parasol*) — yes, I suppose I might . . . hoist this thing now. (*Begins to unfurl it. Following punctuated by mechanical difficulties overcome.*) One keeps putting off—putting up—for fear of putting up—too soon— and the day goes by—quite by—without one's having put 490 up—at all. (*Parasol now fully open. Turned to her right she twirls it idly this way and that.*) Ah yes, so little to say, so little to do, and the fear so great, certain days, of finding oneself . . . left, with hours still to run, before the bell for sleep, and nothing more to say, nothing more to do, that the days go by, 495 certain days go by, quite by, the bell goes, and little or nothing said, little or nothing done. (*Raising parasol.*) That is the danger. (*Turning front.*) To be guarded against. (*She gazes front, holding up parasol with right hand. Maximum pause.*) I used to perspire freely. (*Pause.*) Now hardly at all. (*Pause.*) 500 The heat is much greater. (*Pause.*) The perspiration much less. (*Pause.*) That is what I find so wonderful. (*Pause.*) The way man adapts himself. (*Pause.*) To changing conditions. (*She transfers parasol to left hand. Long pause.*) Holding up wearies the arm. (*Pause.*) Not if one is going along. (*Pause.*) 505 Only if one is at rest. (*Pause.*) That is a curious observation. (*Pause.*) I hope you heard that, Willie, I should be grieved to think you had not heard that. (*She takes parasol in both hands. Long pause.*) I am weary, holding it up, and I cannot put it down. (*Pause.*) I am worse off with it up than with it 510 down, and I cannot put it down. (*Pause.*) Reason says, Put it down, Winnie, it is not helping you, put the thing down and get on with something else. (*Pause.*) I cannot. (*Pause.*) I cannot move. (*Pause.*) No, something must happen, in the

515 world, take place, some change, I cannot, if I am to move again. (*Pause.*) Willie. (*Mildly.*) Help. (*Pause.*) No? (*Pause.*) Bid me put this thing down, Willie, I would obey you instantly, as I have always done, honoured and obeyed. (*Pause.*) Please, Willie. (*Mildly.*) For pity's sake. (*Pause.*) No?

520 (*Pause.*) You can't? (*Pause.*) Well I don't blame you, no, it would ill become me, who cannot move, to blame my Willie because he cannot speak. (*Pause.*)Fortunately I am in tongue again. (*Pause.*) That is what I find so wonderful, my two lamps, when one goes out the other burns brighter. (*Pause.*)

525 Oh yes, great mercies. (*Maximum pause. The parasol goes on fire. Smoke, flames if feasible. She sniffs, looks up, throws parasol to her right behind mound, cranes back to watch it burning. Pause.*) Ah earth you old extinguisher. (*Back front.*) I presume this has occurred before, though I cannot recall it.

530 (*Pause.*) Can you, Willie? (*Turns a little towards him.*) Can you recall this having occurred before? (*Pause. Cranes back to look at him.*) Do you know what has occurred, Willie? (*Pause.*) Have you gone off on me again? (*Pause.*) I do not ask if you are alive to all that is going on, I merely ask if you have

535 not gone off on me again. (*Pause.*) Your eyes appear to be closed, but that has no particular significance we know. (*Pause.*) Raise a finger, dear, will you please, if you are not quite senseless. (*Pause.*) Do that for me, Willie please, just the little finger, if you are still conscious. (*Pause. Joyful.*) Oh

540 all five, you are a darling today, now I may continue with an easy mind. (*Back front.*) Yes, what ever occurred that did not occur before and yet . . . I wonder, yes, I confess I wonder. (*Pause.*) With the sun blazing so much fiercer down, and hourly fiercer, it is not natural things should go on fire never

545 known to do so, in this way I mean, spontaneous like. (*Pause.*) Shall I myself not melt perhaps in the end, or burn, oh I do not mean necessarily burst into flames, no, just little by little be charred to a black cinder, all this — (*ample gesture of arms*) — visible flesh. (*Pause.*) On the other hand, did I

550 ever know a temperate time? (*Pause.*) No. (*Pause.*) I speak of temperate times and torrid times, they are empty words. (*Pause.*) I speak of when I was not yet caught — in this way — and had my legs and had the use of my legs, and could seek out a shady place, like you, when I was tired of the sun, or a

555 sunny place when I was tired of the shade, like you, and they are all empty words. (*Pause.*) It is no hotter today than yesterday, it will be no hotter tomorrow than today, how could it, and so on back into the far past, forward into the far future. (*Pause.*) And should one day the earth cover my breasts, then

560 I shall never have seen my breasts, no one ever seen my breasts. (*Pause.*) I hope you caught something of that, Willie, I should be sorry to think you had caught nothing of all that, it is not every day I rise to such heights. (*Pause.*) Yes, something seems to have occurred, something has seemed to occur, and

565 nothing has occurred, nothing at all, you are quite right, Willie. (*Pause.*) The sunshade will be there again tomorrow, beside me on this mound, to help me through the day. (*Pause. She takes up mirror.*) I take up this little glass, I shiver it on a stone — (*does so*) — I throw it away — (*does so far behind

570 her*) — it will be in the bag again tomorrow, without a scratch, to help me through the day. (*Pause.*) No, one can do nothing. (*Pause.*) That is what I find so wonderful, the way things . . . (*voice breaks, head down*) . . . things . . . so wonderful. (*Long pause, head down. Finally turns, still bowed, to bag,

575 *brings out unidentifiable odds and ends, stuffs them back, fumbles, deeper, brings out finally musical-box, winds it up, turns it on, listens for a moment holding it in both hands, huddled over it, turns back front, straightens up and listens to tune, holding box to breast with both hands. It plays the* Waltz

580 Duet *"I love you so" from* The Merry Widow. *Gradually happy expression. She sways to the rhythm. Music stops. Pause. Brief burst of hoarse song without words — musical-box tune — from* WILLIE. *Increase of happy expression. She lays down box.*) Oh this will have been a happy day! (*She claps

585 hands.*) Again, Willie, again! (*Claps.*) Encore, Willie, please! (*Pause. Happy expression off.*) No? You won't do that for me? (*Pause.*) Well it is very understandable, very understandable. One cannot sing just to please someone, however much one loves them, no, song must come from the heart,

590 that is what I always say, pour out from the inmost, like a thrush. (*Pause.*) How often I have said, in evil hours, Sing now, Winnie, sing your song, there is nothing else for it, and did not. (*Pause.*) Could not. (*Pause.*) No, like the thrush, or the bird of dawning, with no thought of benefit, to oneself or

595 anyone else. (*Pause.*) And now? (*Long pause. Low.*) Strange feeling. (*Pause. Do.*) Strange feeling that someone is looking at me. I am clear, then dim, then gone, then dim again, then clear again, and so on, back and forth, in and out of someone's eye. (*Pause. Do.*) Strange? (*Pause. Do.*) No, here all is

600 strange. (*Pause. Normal voice.*) Something says, Stop talking now, Winnie, for a minute, don't squander all your words for the day, stop talking and do something for a change, will you? (*She raises hands and holds them open before her eyes. Apostrophic.*) Do something! (*She closes hands.*) What claws! (*She

605 turns to bag, rummages in it, brings out finally a nailfile, turns back front and begins to file nails. Files for a time in silence, then the following punctuated by filing.*) There floats up — into my thoughts — a Mr Shower — a Mr and perhaps a Mrs Shower — no — they are holding hands — his fiancée

610 then more likely — or just some — loved one. (*Looks closer at nails.*) Very brittle today. (*Resumes filing.*) Shower — Shower — does the name mean anything — to you, Willie — evoke any reality, I mean — for you, Willie — don't answer if you don't — feel up to it — you have done more — than your

615 bit — already — Shower — Shower. (*Inspects filed nails.*) Bit more like it. (*Raises head, gazes front.*) Keep yourself nice, Winnie, that's what I always say, come what may, keep yourself nice. (*Pause. Resumes filing.*) Yes — Shower — Shower — (*stops filing, raises head, gazes front, pause*) — or Cooker,

620 perhaps I should say Cooker. (*Turning a little towards* WILLIE.) Cooker, Willie, does Cooker strike a chord? (*Pause. Turns a little further. Louder.*) Cooker, Willie, does Cooker ring a bell, the name Cooker? (*Pause. She cranes back to look at him. Pause.*) Oh really! (*Pause.*) Have you no hand-

625 kerchief, darling? (*Pause.*) Have you no delicacy? (*Pause.*) Oh, Willie, you're not eating it! Spit it out, dear, spit it out! (*Pause. Back front.*) Ah well, I suppose it's only natural. (*Break in voice.*) Human. (*Pause. Do.*) What *is* one to do? (*Head down. Do.*) All day long. (*Pause. Do.*) Day after day.

630 (*Pause. Head up. Smile. Calm.*) The old style! (*Smile off. Resumes nails.*) No, done him. (*Passes on to next.*) Should have put on my glasses. (*Pause.*) Too late now. (*Finishes left hand, inspects it.*) Bit more human. (*Starts right hand. Following punctuated as before.*) Well anyway — this man

635 Shower—or Cooker—no matter—and the woman—hand in hand—in the other hands bags—kind of big brown grips—standing there gaping at me—and at last this man Shower—or Cooker—ends in er anyway—stake my life on that—What's she doing? he says—What's the idea? he says—stuck
640 up to her diddies in the bleeding ground—coarse fellow—What does it mean? he says—What's it meant to mean?—and so on—lot more stuff like that—usual drivel—Do you hear me? he says—I do, she says, God help me—What do you mean, he says, God help you? *(Stops filing, raises head,*
645 *gazes front.)* And you, she says, what's the idea of you, she says, what are you meant to mean? It is because you're still on your two flat feet, with your old ditty full of tinned muck and changes of underwear, dragging me up and down this fornicating wilderness, coarse creature, fit mate—*(with sudden*
650 *violence)*—let go of my hand and drop for God's sake, she says, drop! *(Pause. Resumes filing.)* Why doesn't he dig her out? he says—referring to you, my dear—What good is she to him like that?—What good is he to her like that—and so on—usual tosh—Good! she says, have a heart for God's
655 sake—Dig her out, he says, dig her out, no sense in her like that—Dig her out with what? she says—I'd dig her out with my bare hands, he says—must have been man and—wife. *(Files in silence.)* Next thing they're away—hand in hand—and the bags—dim—then gone—last human kind—to stray
660 this way. *(Finishes right hand, inspects it, lays down file, gazes front.)* Strange thing, time like this, drift up into the mind. *(Pause.)* Strange? *(Pause.)* No, here all is strange. *(Pause.)* Thankful for it in any case. *(Voice breaks.)* Most thankful. *(Head down. Pause. Head up. Calm.)* Bow and
665 raise the head, bow and raise, always that. *(Pause.)* And now? *(Long pause. Starts putting things back in bag, toothbrush last. This operation, interrupted by pauses as indicated, punctuates following.)* It is perhaps a little soon—to make ready—for the night—*(stops tidying, head up, smile)*—the old
670 style!—*(smile off, resumes tidying)*—and yet I do—make ready for the night—feeling it at hand—the bell for sleep—saying to myself—Winnie—it will not be long now, Winnie—until the bell for sleep. *(Stops tidying, head up.)* Sometimes I am wrong. *(Smile.)* But not often. *(Smile off.)* Some
675 times all is over, for the day, all done, all said, all ready for the night, and the day not over, far from over, the night not ready, far, far from ready. *(Smile.)* But not often. *(Smile off.)* Yes, the bell for sleep, when I feel it at hand, and so make ready for the night—*(gesture)*—in this way, sometimes I am wrong—
680 *(smile)*—but not often. *(Smile off. Resumes tidying.)* I used to think—I say I used to think—that all these things—put back into the bag—if too soon—put back too soon—could be taken out again—if necessary—if needed—and so on—indefinitely—back into the bag—back out of the bag—until
685 the bell—went. *(Stops tidying, head up, smile.)* But no. *(Smile broader.)* No no. *(Smile off. Resumes tidying.)* I suppose this—might seem strange—this—what shall I say—this what I have said—yes—*(she takes up revolver)*—strange—*(she turns to put revolver in bag)*—were it not—*(about to put*
690 *revolver in bag she arrests gesture and turns back front)*—were it not—*(she lays down revolver to her right, stops tidying, head up)*—that all seems strange. *(Pause.)* Most strange. *(Pause.)* Never any change. *(Pause.)* And more and more strange. *(Pause. She bends to mound again, takes up last object, i.e.*

695 *toothbrush, and turns to put it in bag when her attention is drawn to disturbance from* WILLIE. *She cranes back and to her right to see. Pause.)* Weary of your hole, dear? *(Pause.)* Well I can understand that. *(Pause.)* Don't forget your straw. *(Pause.)* Not the crawler you were, poor darling. *(Pause.)* No,
700 not the crawler I gave my heart to. *(Pause.)* The hands and knees, love, try the hands and knees. *(Pause.)* The knees! The knees! *(Pause.)* What a curse, mobility! *(She follows with eyes his progress towards her behind mound, i.e. towards place he occupied at beginning of act.)* Another foot, Willie, and
705 you're home. *(Pause as she observes last foot.)* Ah! *(Turns back front laboriously, rubs neck.)* Crick in my neck admiring you. *(Rubs neck.)* But it's worth it, well worth it. *(Turning slightly towards him.)* Do you know what I dream sometimes? *(Pause.)* What I dream sometimes, Willie. *(Pause.)* That
710 you'll come round and live this side where I could see you. *(Pause. Back front.)* I'd be a different woman. *(Pause.)* Unrecognizable. *(Turning slightly towards him.)* Or just now and then, come round this side just every now and then and let me feast on you. *(Back front.)* But you can't, I know. *(Head*
715 *down.)* I know. *(Pause. Head up.)* Well anyway—*(looks at toothbrush in her hand)*—can't be long now—*(looks at brush)*—until the bell. *(Top back of* WILLIE's *head appears above slope.* WINNIE *looks closer at brush.)* Fully guaranteed . . . *(head up)* . . . what's this it was? *(*WILLIE's *hand appears*
720 *with handkerchief, spreads it on skull, disappears.)* Genuine pure . . . fully guaranteed . . . *(*WILLIE's *hand appears with boater, settles it on head, rakish angle, disappears)* . . . genuine pure . . . ah! hog's setae. *(Pause.)* What is a hog exactly? *(Pause. Turns slightly towards* WILLIE.*)* What exactly is a hog,
725 Willie, do you know, I can't remember. *(Pause. Turning a little further, pleading.)* What is a hog, Willie, please!

(Pause.)

WILLIE: Castrated male swine. *(Happy expression appears on* WINNIE's *face.)* Reared for slaughter.

(Happy expression increases. WILLIE *opens newspaper, hands invisible. Tops of yellow sheets appear on either side of his head.* WINNIE *gazes before her with happy expression.)*

WINNIE: Oh this *is* a happy day! This will have been another happy day! *(Pause.)* After all. *(Pause.)* So far.
730

(Pause. Happy expression off. WILLIE *turns page. Pause. He turns another page. Pause.)*

WILLIE: Opening for smart youth.

(Pause. WINNIE *takes off hat, turns to put it in bag, arrests gesture, turns back front. Smile.)*

WINNIE: No. *(Smile broader.)* No no. *(Smile off. Puts on hat again, gazes front, pause.)* And now? *(Pause.)* Sing. *(Pause.)* Sing your song, Winnie. *(Pause.)* No? *(Pause.)* Then pray. *(Pause.)* Pray your prayer, Winnie.
735

(Pause. WILLIE *turns page. Pause.)*

WILLIE: Wanted bright boy.

(Pause. WINNIE *gazes before her.* WILLIE *turns page. Pause. Newspaper disappears. Long pause.)*

WINNIE: Pray your old prayer, Winnie.

(Long pause. Curtain.)

— ACT TWO —

Scene as before.

WINNIE *imbedded up to neck, hat on head, eyes closed. Her head, which she can no longer turn, nor bow, nor raise, faces front motionless throughout act. Movements of eyes as indicated.*

Bag and parasol as before. Revolver conspicuous to her right on mound.

Long pause.

Bell rings loudly. She opens eyes at once. Bell stops. She gazes front. Long pause.

WINNIE: Hail, holy light. *(Long pause. She closes her eyes. Bell rings loudly. She opens eyes at once. Bell stops. She gazes front. Long smile. Smile off. Long pause.)* Someone is looking at me still. *(Pause.)* Caring for me still. *(Pause.)* That is
5 what I find so wonderful. *(Pause.)* Eyes on my eyes. *(Pause.)* What is that unforgettable line? *(Pause. Eyes right.)* Willie. *(Pause. Louder.)* Willie. *(Pause. Eyes front.)* May one still speak of time? *(Pause.)* Say it is a long time now, Willie, since I saw you. *(Pause.)* Since I heard you. *(Pause.)* May one?
10 *(Pause.)* One does. *(Smile.)* The old style! *(Smile off.)* There is so little one can speak of. *(Pause.)* One speaks of it all. *(Pause.)* All one can. *(Pause.)* I used to think . . . *(pause)* . . . I say I used to think that I would learn to talk alone. *(Pause.)* By that I mean to myself, the wilderness. *(Smile.)* But no. *(Smile*
15 *broader.)* No no. *(Smile off.)* Ergo you are there. *(Pause.)* Oh no doubt you are dead, like the others, no doubt you have died, or gone away and left me, like the others, it doesn't matter, you are there. *(Pause. Eyes left.)* The bag is there too, the same as ever, I can see it. *(Pause. Eyes right. Louder.)* The
20 bag is there, Willie, as good as ever, the one you gave me that day . . . to go to market. *(Pause. Eyes front.)* That day. *(Pause.)* What day? *(Pause.)* I used to pray. *(Pause.)* I say I used to pray. *(Pause.)* Yes, I must confess I did. *(Smile.)* Not now. *(Smile broader.)* No no. *(Smile off. Pause.)* Then . . .
25 now . . . what difficulties here, for the mind. *(Pause.)* To have been always what I am — and so changed from what I was. *(Pause.)* I am the one, I say the one, then the other. *(Pause.)* Now the one, then the other. *(Pause.)* There is so little one can say, one says it all. *(Pause.)* All one can. *(Pause.)* And no
30 truth in it anywhere. *(Pause.)* My arms. *(Pause.)* My breasts. *(Pause.)* What arms? *(Pause.)* What breasts? *(Pause.)* Willie. *(Pause.)* What Willie? *(Sudden vehement affirmation.)* My Willie! *(Eyes right, calling.)* Willie! *(Pause. Louder.)* Willie! *(Pause. Eyes front.)* Ah well, not to know, not to know for
35 sure, great mercy, all I ask. *(Pause.)* Ah yes . . . then . . . now . . . beechen green . . . this . . . Charlie . . . kisses . . . this . . . all that . . . deep trouble for the mind. *(Pause.)* But it does not trouble mine. *(Smile.)* Not now. *(Smile broader.)* No no. *(Smile off. Long pause. She closes eyes. Bell rings loudly. She*
40 *opens eyes. Pause.)* Eyes float up that seem to close in peace . . . to see . . . in peace. *(Pause.)* Not mine. *(Smile.)* Not now. *(Smile broader.)* No no. *(Smile off. Long pause.)* Willie. *(Pause.)* Do you think the earth has lost its atmosphere, Willie! *(Pause.)* Do you, Willie? *(Pause.)* You have no opin
45 ion? *(Pause.)* Well that is like you, you never had any opinion about anything. *(Pause.)* It's understandable. *(Pause.)* Most. *(Pause.)* The earthball. *(Pause.)* I sometimes wonder. *(Pause.)* Perhaps not quite all. *(Pause.)* There always remains

something. *(Pause.)* Of everything. *(Pause.)* Some remains. *(Pause.)* If the mind were to go. *(Pause.)* It won't of course. 50 *(Pause.)* Not quite. *(Pause.)* Not mine. *(Smile.)* Not now. *(Smile broader.)* No no. *(Smile off. Long pause.)* It might be the eternal cold. *(Pause.)* Everlasting perishing cold. *(Pause.)* Just chance, I take it, happy chance. *(Pause.)* Oh yes, great mercies, great mercies. *(Pause.)* And now? *(Long pause.)* 55 The face. *(Pause.)* The nose. *(She squints down.)* I can see it . . . *(squinting down)* . . . the tip . . . the nostrils . . . breath of life . . . that curve you so admired . . . *(pouts)* . . . a hint of lip . . . *(pouts again)* . . . if I pout them out . . . *(sticks out tongue)* . . . the tongue of course . . . you so admired . . . if 60 I stick it out . . . *(sticks it out again)* . . . the tip . . . *(eyes up)* . . . suspicion of brow . . . eyebrow . . . imagination possibly . . . *(eyes left)* . . . cheek . . . no . . . *(eyes right)* . . . no . . . *(distends cheeks)* . . . even if I puff them out . . . *(eyes left, distends cheeks again)* . . . no . . . no damask. *(Eyes front.)* 65 That is all. *(Pause.)* The bag of course . . . *(eyes left)* . . . a little blurred perhaps . . . but the bag. *(Eyes front. Offhand.)* The earth of course and sky. *(Eyes right.)* The sunshade you gave me . . . that day . . . *(pause)* . . . that day . . . the lake . . . the reeds. *(Eyes front. Pause.)* What day? *(Pause.)* What 70 reeds? *(Long pause. Eyes close. Bell rings loudly. Eyes open. Pause. Eyes right.)* Brownie of course. *(Pause.)* You remember Brownie, Willie, I can see him. *(Pause.)* Brownie is there, Willie, beside me. *(Pause. Loud.)* Brownie is there, Willie. *(Pause. Eyes front.)* That is all. *(Pause.)* What would 75 I do without them? *(Pause.)* What would I do without them, when words fail? *(Pause.)* Gaze before me, with compressed lips. *(Long pause while she does so.)* I cannot. *(Pause.)* Ah yes, great mercies, great mercies. *(Long pause. Low.)* Sometimes I hear sounds. *(Listening expression. Normal voice.)* But not 80 often. *(Pause.)* They are a boon, sounds are a boon, they help me . . . through the day. *(Smile.)* The old style! *(Smile off.)* Yes, those are happy days, when there are sounds. *(Pause.)* When I hear sounds. *(Pause.)* I used to think . . . *(pause)* . . . I say I used to think they were in my head. *(Smile.)* But no. 85 *(Smile broader.)* No no. *(Smile off.)* That was just logic. *(Pause.)* Reason. *(Pause.)* I have not lost my reason. *(Pause.)* Not yet. *(Pause.)* Not all. *(Pause.)* Some remains. *(Pause.)* Sounds. *(Pause.)* Like little . . . sunderings, little falls . . . apart. *(Pause. Low.)* It's things, Willie. *(Pause. Normal* 90 *voice.)* In the bag, outside the bag. *(Pause.)* Ah yes, things have their life, that is what I always say, *things* have a life. *(Pause.)* Take my looking-glass, it doesn't need me. *(Pause.)* The bell. *(Pause.)* It hurts like a knife. *(Pause.)* A gouge. *(Pause.)* One cannot ignore it. *(Pause.)* How often . . . 95 *(pause)* . . . I say how often I have said, Ignore it, Winnie, ignore the bell, pay no heed, just sleep and wake, sleep and wake, as you please, open and close the eyes, as you please, or in the way you find most helpful. *(Pause.)* Open and close the eyes, Winnie, open and close, always that. *(Pause.)* But no. 100 *(Smile.)* Not now. *(Smile broader.)* No no. *(Smile off. Pause.)* What now? *(Pause.)* What now, Willie? *(Long pause.)* There is my story of course, when all else fails. *(Pause.)* A life. *(Smile.)* A long life. *(Smile off.)* Beginning in the womb, where life used to begin, Mildred has memories, she will 105 have memories, of the womb, before she dies, the mother's womb. *(Pause.)* She is now four or five already and has recently been given a big waxen dolly. *(Pause.)* Fully clothed, complete outfit. *(Pause.)* Shoes, socks, undies, complete set,

110 frilly frock, gloves. (*Pause.*) White mesh. (*Pause.*) A little
white straw hat with a chin elastic. (*Pause.*) Pearly necklet.
(*Pause.*) A little picture-book with legends in real print to go
under the arm when she takes her walk. (*Pause.*) China blue
eyes that open and shut. (*Pause. Narrative.*) The sun was not
115 well up when Milly rose, descended the steep . . . (*pause*) . . .
slipped on her nightgown, descended all alone the steep
wooden stairs, backwards on all fours, though she had been
forbidden to do so, entered the . . . (*pause*) . . . tiptoed down
the silent passage, entered the nursery and began to undress
120 Dolly. (*Pause.*) Crept under the table and began to undress
Dolly. (*Pause.*) Scolding her . . . the while. (*Pause.*) Suddenly a mouse—(*Long pause.*) Gently, Winnie. (*Long
pause. Calling.*) Willie! (*Pause. Louder.*) Willie! (*Pause.
Mild reproach.*) I sometimes find your attitude a little strange,
125 Willie, all this time, it is not like you to be wantonly cruel.
(*Pause.*) Strange? (*Pause.*) No. (*Smile.*) Not here. (*Smile
broader.*) Not now. (*Smile off.*) And yet . . . (*Suddenly anxious.*) I do hope nothing is amiss. (*Eyes right, loud.*) Is all
well, dear? (*Pause. Eyes front. To herself.*) God grant he did
130 not go in head foremost! (*Eyes right, loud.*) You're not stuck,
Willie? (*Pause. Do.*) You're not jammed, Willie? (*Eyes front,
distressed.*) Perhaps he is crying out for help all this time and I
do not hear him! (*Pause.*) I do of course hear cries. (*Pause.*)
But they are in my head surely. (*Pause.*) Is it possible that . . .
135 (*Pause. With finality.*) No no, my head was always full of
cries. (*Pause.*) Faint confused cries. (*Pause.*) They come.
(*Pause.*) Then go. (*Pause.*) As on a wind. (*Pause.*) That is
what I find so wonderful. (*Pause.*) They cease. (*Pause.*) Ah
yes, great mercies, great mercies. (*Pause.*) The day is now
140 well advanced. (*Smile. Smile off.*) And yet it is perhaps a little
soon for my song. (*Pause.*) To sing too soon is fatal, I always
find. (*Pause.*) On the other hand it is possible to leave it too
late. (*Pause.*) The bell goes for sleep and one has not sung.
(*Pause.*) The whole day has flown—(*smile, smile off*)—flown
145 by, quite by, and no song of any class, kind or description.
(*Pause.*) There is a problem here. (*Pause.*) One cannot sing
. . . just like that, no. (*Pause.*) It bubbles up, for some unknown reason, the time is ill chosen, one chokes it back.
(*Pause.*) One says, Now is the time, it is now or never, and
150 one cannot. (*Pause.*) Simply cannot sing. (*Pause.*) Not a
note. (*Pause.*) Another thing, Willie, while we are on this
subject. (*Pause.*) The sadness after song. (*Pause.*) Have you
run across that, Willie? (*Pause.*) In the course of your experience. (*Pause.*) No? (*Pause.*) Sadness after intimate sexual
155 intercourse one is familiar with of course. (*Pause.*) You would
concur with Aristotle there, Willie, I fancy. (*Pause.*) Yes, that
one knows and is prepared to face. (*Pause.*) But after song . . .
(*Pause.*) It does not last of course. (*Pause.*) That is what I find
so wonderful. (*Pause.*) It wears away. (*Pause.*) What are those
160 exquisite lines? (*Pause.*) Go forget me why should something
o'er that something shadow fling . . . go forget me . . . why
should sorrow . . . brightly smile . . . go forget me . . . never
hear me . . . sweetly smile . . . brightly sing . . . (*Pause. With
a sigh.*) One loses one's classics. (*Pause.*) Oh not all. (*Pause.*)
165 A part. (*Pause.*) A part remains. (*Pause.*) That is what I find
so wonderful, a part remains, of one's classics, to help one
through the day. (*Pause.*) Oh yes, many mercies, many mercies. (*Pause.*) And now? (*Pause.*) And now, Willie? (*Long
pause.*) I call to the eye of the mind . . . Mr. Shower—or
170 Cooker. (*She closes her eyes. Bell rings loudly. She opens her*

eyes. *Pause.*) Hand in hand, in the other hands bags. (*Pause.*)
Getting on . . . in life. (*Pause.*) No longer young, not yet old.
(*Pause.*) Standing there gaping at me. (*Pause.*) Can't have
been a bad bosom, he says, in its day. (*Pause.*) Seen worse
shoulders, he says, in my time. (*Pause.*) Does she feel her   175
legs? he says. (*Pause.*) Is there any life in her legs? he says.
(*Pause.*) Has she anything on underneath? he says. (*Pause.*)
Ask her, he says, I'm shy. (*Pause.*) Ask her what? she says.
(*Pause.*) Is there any life in her legs. (*Pause.*) Has she any-
thing on underneath. (*Pause.*) Ask her yourself, she says.   180
(*Pause. With sudden violence.*) Let go of me for Christ sake
and drop! (*Pause. Do.*) Drop dead! (*Smile.*) But no. (*Smile
broader.*) No no. (*Smile off.*) I watch them recede. (*Pause.*)
Hand in hand—and the bags. (*Pause.*) Dim. (*Pause.*) Then
gone. (*Pause.*) Last human kind—to stray this way. (*Pause.*)   185
Up to date. (*Pause.*) And now? (*Pause. Low.*) Help. (*Pause.
Do.*) Help, Willie. (*Pause. Do.*) No? (*Long pause. Narrative.*) Suddenly a mouse . . . (*Pause.*) Suddenly a mouse ran
up her little thigh and Mildred, dropping Dolly in her fright,
began to scream—(WINNIE *gives a sudden piercing scream*)—   190
and screamed and screamed—(WINNIE *screams twice*)—
screamed and screamed and screamed and screamed till all
came running, in their night attire, papa, mamma, Bibby
and . . . old Annie, to see what was the matter . . . (*pause*) . . .
what on earth could possibly be the matter. (*Pause.*) Too late.   195
(*Pause.*) Too late. (*Long pause. Just audible.*) Willie. (*Pause.
Normal voice.*) Ah well, not long now, Winnie, can't be long
now, until the bell for sleep. (*Pause.*) Then you may close
your eyes, then you *must* close your eyes—and keep them
closed. (*Pause.*) Why say that again? (*Pause.*) I used to think   200
. . . (*pause*) . . . I say I used to think there was no difference
between one fraction of a second and the next. (*Pause.*) I used
to say . . . (*pause*) . . . I say I used to say, Winnie, you are
changeless, there is never any difference between one fraction
of a second and the next. (*Pause.*) Why bring that up again?   205
(*Pause.*) There is so little one can bring up, one brings up all.
(*Pause.*) All one can. (*Pause.*) My neck is hurting me. (*Pause.
With sudden violence.*) My neck is hurting me! (*Pause.*) Ah
that's better. (*With mild irritation.*) Everything within reason. (*Long pause.*) I can do no more. (*Pause.*) Say no more.   210
(*Pause.*) But I must say more. (*Pause.*) Problem here.
(*Pause.*) No, something must move, in the world, I can't any
more. (*Pause.*) A zephyr. (*Pause.*) A breath. (*Pause.*) What
are those immortal lines? (*Pause.*) It might be the eternal
dark. (*Pause.*) Black night without end. (*Pause.*) Just chance,   215
I take it, happy chance. (*Pause.*) Oh yes, abounding mercies.
(*Long pause.*) And now? (*Pause.*) And now, Willie? (*Long
pause.*) That day. (*Pause.*) The pink fizz. (*Pause.*) The flute
glasses. (*Pause.*) The last guest gone. (*Pause.*) The last
bumper with the bodies nearly touching. (*Pause.*) The look.   220
(*Long pause.*) What day? (*Long pause.*) What look? (*Long
pause.*) I hear cries. (*Pause.*) Sing. (*Pause.*) Sing your old
song, Winnie.

(*Long pause. Suddenly alert expression. Eyes switch right.*
WILLIE's *head appears to her right round corner of mound. He is
on all fours, dressed to kill—top hat, morning coat, striped trousers, etc., white gloves in hand. Very long bushy white Battle of
Britain moustache. He halts, gazes front, smooths moustache.
He emerges completely from behind mound, turns to his left,
halts, looks up at* WINNIE. *He advances on all fours towards*

centre, halts, turns head front, gazes front, strokes moustache, straightens tie, adjusts hat, advances a little further, halts, takes off hat and looks up at WINNIE. *He is now not far from centre and within her field of vision. Unable to sustain effort of looking up he sinks head to ground.)*

WINNIE: *(mondaine.)* Well this is an unexpected pleasure!
225 *(Pause.)* Reminds me of the day you came whining for my hand. *(Pause.)* I worship you, Winnie, be mine. *(He looks up.)* Life a mockery without Win. *(She goes off into a giggle.)* What a get up, you do look a sight! *(Giggles.)* Where are the flowers? *(Pause.)* That smile today. *(Willie sinks head.)*
230 What's that on your neck, an anthrax? *(Pause.)* Want to watch that, Willie, before it gets a hold on you. *(Pause.)* Where were you all this time? *(Pause.)* What were you doing all this time. *(Pause.)* Changing? *(Pause.)* Did you not hear me screaming for you? *(Pause.)* Did you get stuck in your hole?
235 *(Pause. He looks up.)* That's right, Willie, look at me. *(Pause.)* Feast your old eyes, Willie. *(Pause.)* Does anything remain? *(Pause.)* Any remains? *(Pause.)* No? *(Pause.)* I haven't been able to look after it, you know. *(He sinks his head.)* You are still recognizable, in a way. *(Pause.)* Are you
240 thinking of coming to live this side now . . . for a bit maybe? *(Pause.)* No? *(Pause.)* Just a brief call? *(Pause.)* Have you gone deaf, Willie? *(Pause.)* Dumb? *(Pause.)* Oh I know you were never one to talk, I worship you Winnie be mine and then nothing from that day forth only titbits from Reynolds'
245 News. *(Eyes front. Pause.)* Ah well, what matter, that's what I always say, it will have been a happy day, after all, another happy day. *(Pause.)* Not long now, Winnie. *(Pause.)* I hear cries. *(Pause.)* Do you ever hear cries, Willie? *(Pause.)* No? *(Eyes back on Willie.)* Willie. *(Pause.)* Look at me again,
250 Willie. *(Pause.)* Once more, Willie. *(He looks up. Happily.)* Ah! *(Pause. Shocked.)* What ails you, Willie, I never saw such an expression! *(Pause.)* Put on your hat, dear, it's the sun, don't stand on ceremony, I won't mind. *(He drops hat and gloves and starts to crawl up mound towards her. Gleeful.)* Oh
255 I say, this is terrific! *(He halts, clinging to mound with one hand, reaching up with the other.)* Come on, dear, put a bit of jizz into it, I'll cheer you on. *(Pause.)* Is it me you're after,

Willie . . . or is it something else? *(Pause.)* Do you want to touch my face . . . again? *(Pause.)* Is it a kiss you're after,
260 Willie . . . or is it something else? *(Pause.)* There was a time when I could have given you a hand. *(Pause.)* And then a time before that again when I did give you a hand. *(Pause.)* You were always in dire need of a hand, Willie. *(He slithers back to foot of mound and lies with face to ground.)* Brrum!
(Pause. He rises to hands and knees, raises his face towards 265 *her.)* Have another go, Willie, I'll cheer you on. *(Pause.)* Don't look at me like that! *(Pause. Vehement.)* Don't look at me like that! *(Pause. Low.)* Have you gone off your head, Willie? *(Pause. Do.)* Out of your poor old wits, Willie?

(Pause.)

WILLIE: *(just audible.)* Win. 270

(Pause. WINNIE's *eyes front. Happy expression appears, grows.)*

WINNIE: Win! *(Pause.)* Oh this *is* a happy day, this will have been another happy day! *(Pause.)* After all. *(Pause.)* So far.

(Pause. She hums tentatively beginning of song, then sings softly, musical-box tune.)

> Though I say not
> What I may not
> Let you hear, 275
> Yet the swaying
> Dance is saying,
> Love me dear!
> Every touch of fingers
> Tells me what I know. 280
> Says for you,
> It's true, it's true,
> You love me so!

(Pause. Happy expression off. She closes her eyes. Bell rings loudly. She opens her eyes. She smiles, gazing front. She turns her eyes, smiling, to WILLIE, *still on his hands and knees looking up at her. Smile off. They look at each other. Long pause. Curtain.)*

HAROLD PINTER

Harold Pinter (b. 1930) has had an extensive career as an actor, playwright, and screenwriter, but is best-known for his strikingly disorienting stage plays. Pinter was born and raised in Hackney, a working-class neighborhood just beyond London's East End. He studied briefly at the Royal Academy of Dramatic Art and pursued a career as a stage and radio actor in the early 1950s before becoming a playwright. His early plays—notably *The Room* (1957), *The Birthday Party* (1958), and *The Dumb Waiter* (1960)—are inflected by the theater of the absurd in the indirect, often menacing, and finally inexplicable quality of their action. However, Pinter's drama is set in a much more recognizable locale than are many of Beckett's or Ionesco's plays; his plays often work by frustrating our "realistic" expectations of characters and their stage world. This is particularly true of Pinter's two major successes of the 1960s, *The Caretaker* (1960) and *The Homecoming* (1965). In both of these plays, a visitor disturbs the delicate balance of relations that bind a family together. What is characteristically "Pinteresque" about the action is the way that Pinter's spare and oblique dialogue makes the characters' motives and intentions nearly unreadable, often despite the violence with which they are expressed. If the poverty of language in most realistic drama tends to imply the emptiness of the characters, in Pinter's drama it seems most often to imply their explosive potential to erupt.

Pinter went through a period of profound writer's block in the late 1960s, writing only the short plays *Landscape* (1969) and *Silence* (1969). In the 1970s, though, he wrote a series of major dramas: *Old Times* (1971), *No Man's Land* (1975), *Betrayal* (1978). These plays take memory and the past as their subject, examining how, in the words of Anna in *Old Times*, "There are things I remember which may never have happened but as I recall them so they take place." More recently, Pinter has written *A Kind of Alaska* (1982), a play based on Oliver Sachs's *Awakenings*, and three plays on more political subjects, *One for the Road* (1984), *Mountain Language* (1988), and *Party Time* (1990). Pinter has also written a number of screenplays, both for his own plays, such as *Betrayal*, and for other projects, including *The French Lieutenant's Woman* and *Turtle Diary*.

The Homecoming

The Homecoming is typical of Pinter's earlier drama in that it provides us with a recognizable situation—Teddy, an American college professor, returns home to London with his wife Ruth to visit his family—that immediately twists in new and surprising directions. For much like the room onstage, with its missing upstage wall, something is missing in this family that determines the structure of their relationships. The most obvious missing element of family life here is the absent mother, Jessie, whose absence informs the relationships between the men of the play: Max, who does the cleaning and cooking, to everyone's ridicule; Sam, who is accused of homosexual prostitution; Lenny, the pimp; Joey, the macho boxer. When Ruth appears in this scenario, she seems suddenly to take the role vacated by Jessie, becoming the controlling figure in the house of crippled men. Ruth assumes the two roles attributed to Jessie—mother and whore. The question, as Max asks at the end, is will she prove "adaptable" to the men's fantasies or will she—as Ruth's independence suggests—adapt the men to her own designs?

The Homecoming clearly plays with the formalities and conventions of realistic drama. The secret that often motivates the action of an Ibsen play (Nora's forgery in *A Doll House*, for example) seems to be disclosed in the play by Sam—"MacGregor had Jessie in the back of my cab as I drove them along"—but finally this "secret" loses its power to explain. It is either already known or finally irrelevant to the characters. Indeed, the past in *The Homecoming* seems to be largely improvised or invented. The characters frequently seem to make up stories of the "past" that function more as maneuverings in the present than as reliable accounts of something that actually happened. Lenny's story of beating up a prostitute underneath an arch in Act 1, for instance, seems not really to have happened. It is instead an effort to intimidate the seductive Ruth, also a woman standing underneath an arch in the living room. The past in *The Homecoming* is one that the characters invent and reinvent as the action progresses. The past becomes a fantasy that the characters work to re-create in the present action of the play.

THE HOMECOMING

Harold Pinter

— CHARACTERS —

MAX, *a man of seventy*
LENNY, *a man in his early thirties*
SAM, *a man of sixty-three*
JOEY, *a man in his middle twenties*
TEDDY, *a man in his middle thirties*
RUTH, *a woman in her early thirties*

SUMMER: *An old house in North London.*

A large room, extending the width of the stage.

The back wall, which contained the door, has been removed. A square arch shape remains. Beyond it, the hall. In the hall a staircase, ascending upstage left, well in view. The front door upstage right. A coatstand, hooks, etc.

In the room a window, right. Odd tables, chairs. Two large arm-chairs. A large sofa, left. Against right wall a large sideboard, the upper half of which contains a mirror. Upstage left, a radiogram.

— ACT ONE —

(Evening.

LENNY *is sitting on the sofa with a newspaper, a pencil in his hand. He wears a dark suit. He makes occasional marks on the back page.*

MAX *comes in, from the direction of the kitchen. He goes to side-board, opens top drawer, rummages in it, closes it.*

He wears an old cardigan and a cap, and carries a stick.

He walks downstage, stands, looks about the room.)

MAX: What have you done with the scissors?

(Pause.)

I said I'm looking for the scissors. What have you done with them?

(Pause.)

Did you hear me? I want to cut something out of the paper.

5 LENNY: I'm reading the paper.
MAX: Not that paper. I haven't even read that paper. I'm talking about last Sunday's paper. I was just having a look at it in the kitchen.

(Pause.)

Do you hear what I'm saying? I'm talking to you! Where's the
10 scissors?
LENNY: *(looking up, quietly.)* Why don't you shut up, you daft prat?

(MAX lifts his stick and points it at him.)

MAX: Don't you talk to me like that. I'm warning you.

(He sits in large armchair.)

There's an advertisement in the paper about flannel vests. Cut
15 price. Navy surplus. I could do with a few of them.

(Pause.)

I think I'll have a fag. Give me a fag.

(Pause.)

I just asked you to give me a cigarette.

(Pause.)

Look what I'm lumbered with.

(He takes a crumpled cigarette from his pocket.)

I'm getting old, my word of honour.

(He lights it.)

You think I wasn't a tearaway? I could have taken care of you, 20
twice over. I'm still strong. You ask your Uncle Sam what I was. But at the same time I always had a kind heart. Always.

(Pause.)

I used to knock about with a man called MacGregor. I called him Mac. You remember Mac? Eh?

(Pause.)

Huhh! We were two of the worst hated men in the West End 25
of London. I tell you, I still got the scars. We'd walk into a place, the whole room'd stand up, they'd make way to let us pass. You never heard such silence. Mind you, he was a big man, he was over six foot tall. His family were all Mac-Gregors, they came all the way from Aberdeen, but he was 30
the only one they called Mac.

(Pause.)

He was very fond of your mother, Mac was. Very fond. He always had a good word for her.

(Pause.)

Mind you, she wasn't such a bad woman. Even though it made me sick just to look at her rotten stinking face, she 35
wasn't such a bad bitch. I gave her the best bleeding years of my life, anyway.
LENNY: Plug it, will you, you stupid sod, I'm trying to read the paper.
MAX: Listen! I'll chop your spine off, you talk to me like that! 40
You understand? Talking to your lousy filthy father like that!
LENNY: You know what, you're getting demented.

(Pause.)

What do you think of Second Wind for the three-thirty?

MAX: Where?

45 LENNY: Sandown Park.

MAX: Don't stand a chance.

LENNY: Sure he does.

MAX: Not a chance.

LENNY: He's the winner.

(LENNY *ticks the paper.*)

50 MAX: He talks to me about horses.

(*Pause.*)

I used to live on the course. One of the loves of my life. Epsom? I knew it like the back of my hand. I was one of the best-known faces down at the paddock. What a marvellous open-air life.

(*Pause.*)

55 He talks to me about horses. You only read their names in the papers. But I've stroked their manes, I've held them, I've calmed them down before a big race. I was the one they used to call for. Max, they'd say, there's a horse here, he's highly strung, you're the only man on the course who can calm him.

60 It was true. I had a . . . I had an instinctive understanding of animals. I should have been a trainer. Many times I was offered the job — you know, a proper post, by the Duke of . . . I forget his name . . . one of the Dukes. But I had family obligations, my family needed me at home.

(*Pause.*)

65 The times I've watched those animals thundering past the post. What an experience. Mind you, I didn't lose, I made a few bob out of it, and you know why? Because I always had the smell of a good horse. I could smell him. And not only the colts but the fillies. Because the fillies are more highly

70 strung than the colts, they're more unreliable, did you know that? No, what do you know? Nothing. But I was always able to tell a good filly by one particular trick. I'd look her in the eye. You see? I'd stand in front of her and look her straight in the eye, it was a kind of hypnotism, and by the look deep

75 down in her eye I could tell whether she was a stayer or not. It was a gift. I had a gift.

(*Pause.*)

And he talks to me about horses.

LENNY: Dad, do you mind if I change the subject?

(*Pause.*)

I want to ask you something. That dinner we had before, what

80 was the name of it? What do you call it?

(*Pause.*)

Why don't you buy a dog? You're a dog cook. Honest. You think you're cooking for a lot of dogs.

MAX: If you don't like it get out.

LENNY: I am going out. I'm going out to buy myself a proper

85 dinner.

MAX: Well, get out! What are you waiting for?

(LENNY *looks at him.*)

LENNY: What did you say?

MAX: I said shove off out of it, that's what I said.

LENNY: You'll go before me, Dad, if you talk to me in that tone

90 of voice.

MAX: Will I, you bitch?

(MAX *grips his stick.*)

LENNY: Oh, Daddy, you're not going to use your stick on me, are you? Eh? Don't use your stick on me, Daddy. No, please. It wasn't my fault, it was one of the others. I haven't done

95 anything wrong, Dad, honest. Don't clout me with that stick, Dad.

(*Silence.*

MAX *sits hunched.* LENNY *reads the paper.*

SAM *comes in the front door. He wears a chauffeur's uniform. He hangs his hat on a hook in the hall and comes into the room. He goes to a chair, sits in it and sighs.*)

Hullo, Uncle Sam.

SAM: Hullo.

LENNY: How are you, Uncle?

SAM: Not bad. A bit tired.

100 LENNY: Tired? I bet you're tired. Where you been?

SAM: I've been to London Airport.

LENNY: All the way up to London Airport? What, right up the M4?

SAM: Yes, all the way up there.

105 LENNY: Tch, tch, tch. Well, I think you're entitled to be tired, Uncle.

SAM: Well, it's the drivers.

LENNY: I know. That's what I'm talking about. I'm talking about the drivers.

110

SAM: Knocks you out.

(*Pause.*)

MAX: I'm here, too, you know.

(SAM *looks at him.*)

I said I'm here, too. I'm sitting here.

SAM: I know you're here.

(*Pause.*)

SAM: I took a Yankee out there today . . . to the Airport.   115

LENNY: Oh, a Yankee, was it?

SAM: Yes, I been with him all day. Picked him up at the Savoy at half past twelve, took him to the Caprice for his lunch. After lunch I picked him up again, took him down to a house in Eaton Square — he had to pay a visit to a friend there — and   120 then round about tea-time I took him right the way out to the Airport.

LENNY: Had to catch a plane there, did he?

SAM: Yes. Look what he gave me. He gave me a box of cigars.

(SAM *takes a box of cigars from his pocket.*)

MAX: Come here. Let's have a look at them.   125

(SAM *shows* MAX *the cigars.* MAX *takes one from the box, pinches it and sniffs it.*)

It's a fair cigar.

SAM: Want to try one?

(MAX *and* SAM *light cigars.*)

You know what he said to me? He told me I was the best chauffeur he'd ever had. The best one.

130 MAX: From what point of view?

SAM: Eh?

MAX: From what point of view?

LENNY: From the point of view of his driving, Dad, and his general sense of courtesy, I should say.

135 MAX: Thought you were a good driver, did he, Sam? Well, he gave you a first-class cigar.

SAM: Yes, he thought I was the best he'd ever had. They all say that, you know. They won't have anyone else, they only ask for me. They say I'm the best chauffeur in the firm.

140 LENNY: I bet the other drivers tend to get jealous, don't they, Uncle?

SAM: They do get jealous. They get very jealous.

MAX: Why?

(Pause.)

SAM: I just told you.

145 MAX: No, I just can't get it clear, Sam. Why do the other drivers get jealous?

SAM: Because (a) I'm the best driver, and because . . . (b) I don't take liberties.

(Pause.)

I don't press myself on people, you see. These big business-
150 men, men of affairs, they don't want the driver jawing all the time, they like to sit in the back, have a bit of peace and quiet. After all, they're sitting in a Humber Super Snipe, they can afford to relax. At the same time, though, this is what really makes me special . . . I do know how to pass the time of day
155 when required.

(Pause.)

For instance, I told this man today I was in the second world war. Not the first. I told him I was too young for the first. But I told him I fought in the second.

(Pause.)

So did he, it turned out.

(LENNY stands, goes to the mirror and straightens his tie.)

160 LENNY: He was probably a colonel, or something, in the American Air Force.

SAM: Yes.

LENNY: Probably a navigator, or something like that, in a Flying Fortress. Now he's most likely a high executive in a worldwide
165 group of aeronautical engineers.

SAM: Yes.

LENNY: Yes, I know the kind of man you're talking about.

(LENNY goes out, turning to his right.)

SAM: After all, I'm experienced. I was driving a dust cart at the age of nineteen. Then I was in long-distance haulage. I had ten
170 years as a taxi-driver and I've had five as a private chauffeur.

MAX: It's funny you never got married, isn't it? A man with all your gifts.

(Pause.)

Isn't it? A man like you?

SAM: There's still time.

MAX: Is there? 175

(Pause.)

SAM: You'd be surprised.

MAX: What you been doing, banging away at your lady customers, have you?

SAM: Not me.

MAX: In the back of the Snipe? Been have a few crafty reefs in a 180 layby, have you?

SAM: Not me.

MAX: On the back seat? What about the armrest, was it up or down?

SAM: I've never done that kind of thing in my car. 185

MAX: Above all that kind of thing, are you, Sam?

SAM: Too true.

MAX: Above having a good bang on the back seat, are you?

SAM: Yes, I leave that to others.

MAX: You leave it to others? What others? You paralysed prat! 190

SAM: I don't mess up my car! Or my . . . my boss's car! Like other people.

MAX: Other people? What other people?

(Pause.)

What other people?

(Pause.)

SAM: Other people. 195

(Pause.)

MAX: When you find the right girl, Sam, let your family know, don't forget, we'll give you a number one send-off, I promise you. You can bring her to live here, she can keep us all happy. We'd take it in turns to give her a walk around the park.

SAM: I wouldn't bring her here. 200

MAX: Sam, it's your decision. You're welcome to bring your bride here, to the place where you live, or on the other hand you can take a suite at the Dorchester. It's entirely up to you.

SAM: I haven't got a bride.

(SAM stands, goes to the sideboard, takes an apple from the bowl, bites into it.)

Getting a bit peckish. 205

(He looks out of the window.)

Never get a bride like you had, anyway. Nothing like your bride . . . going about these days. Like Jessie.

(Pause.)

After all, I escorted her once or twice, didn't I? Drove her round once or twice in my cab. She was a charming woman.

(Pause.)

All the same, she was your wife. But still . . . they were some 210 of the most delightful evenings I've ever had. Used to just drive her about. It was my pleasure.

MAX: (softly, closing his eyes.) Christ.

SAM: I used to pull up at a stall and buy her a cup of coffee. She was a very nice companion to be with. 215

(Silence.)

JOEY *comes in the front door. He walks into the room, takes his jacket off, throws it on a chair and stands.*

Silence.)

JOEY: Feel a bit hungry.

SAM: Me, too.

MAX: Who do you think I am, your mother? Eh? Honest. They walk in here every time of the day and night like bloody ani-
220 mals. Go and find yourself a mother.

(LENNY *walks into the room, stands.)*

JOEY: I've been training down at the gym.

SAM: Yes, the boy's been working all day and training all night.

MAX: What do you want, you bitch? You spend all the day sitting on your arse at London Airport, buy yourself a jamroll. You
225 expect me to sit here waiting to rush into the kitchen the moment you step in the door? You've been living sixty-three years, why don't you learn to cook?

SAM: I can cook.

MAX: Well, go and cook!

(Pause.)

230 LENNY: What the boys want, Dad, is your own special brand of cooking, Dad. That's what the boys look forward to. The spe-cial understanding of food, you know, that you've got.

MAX: Stop calling me Dad. Just stop all that calling me Dad, do you understand?

235 LENNY: But I'm your son. You used to tuck me up in bed every night. He tucked you up, too, didn't he, Joey?

(Pause.)

He used to like tucking up his sons.

(LENNY *turns and goes towards the front door.)*

MAX: Lenny.

LENNY: *(turning.)* What?

240 MAX: I'll give you a proper tuck up one of these nights, son. You mark my word.

(They look at each other.

LENNY *opens the front door and goes out.*

Silence.)

JOEY: I've been training with Bobby Dodd.

(Pause.)

And I had a good go at the bag as well.

(Pause.)

I wasn't in bad trim.

245 MAX: Boxing's a gentleman's game.

(Pause.)

I'll tell you what you've got to do. What you've got to do is you've got to learn how to defend yourself, and you've got to learn how to attack. That's your only trouble as a boxer. You don't know how to defend yourself, and you don't know how
250 to attack.

(Pause.)

Once you've mastered those arts you can go straight to the top.

(Pause.)

JOEY: I've got a pretty good idea . . . of how to do that.

(JOEY *looks round for his jacket, picks it up, goes out of the room and up the stairs.*

Pause.)

MAX: Sam . . . why don't you go, too, eh? Why don't you just go upstairs? Leave me quiet. Leave me alone.

SAM: I want to make something clear about Jessie, Max. I want 255 to. I do. When I took her out in the cab, round the town, I was taking care of her, for you. I was looking after her for you, when you were busy, wasn't I? I was showing her the West End.

(Pause.)

You wouldn't have trusted any of your other brothers. You 260 wouldn't have trusted Mac, would you? But you trusted me. I want to remind you.

(Pause.)

Old Mac died a few years ago, didn't he? Isn't he dead?

(Pause.)

He was a lousy stinking rotten loudmouth. A bastard uncouth sodding runt. Mind you, he was a good friend of yours. 265

(Pause.)

MAX: Eh, Sam . . .

SAM: What?

MAX: Why do I keep you here? You're just an old grub.

SAM: Am I?

MAX: You're a maggot. 270

SAM: Oh yes?

MAX: As soon as you stop paying your way here, I mean when you're too old to pay your way, you know what I'm going to do? I'm going to give you the boot.

SAM: You are, eh? 275

MAX: Sure. I mean, bring in the money and I'll put up with you. But when the firm gets rid of you—you can flake off.

SAM: This is my house as well, you know. This was our mother's house.

MAX: One lot after the other. One mess after the other. 280

SAM: Our father's house.

MAX: Look what I'm lumbered with. One cast-iron bunch of crap after another. One flow of stinking pus after another.

(Pause.)

Our father? I remember him. Don't worry. You kid yourself. He used to come over to me and look down at me. My old 285 man did. He'd bend right over me, then he'd pick me up. I was only that big. Then he'd dandle me. Give me the bottle. Wipe me clean. Give me a smile. Pat me on the bum. Pass me around, pass me from hand to hand. Toss me up in the air. Catch me coming down. I remember my father. 290

(Blackout.

Lights up. Night. TEDDY *and* RUTH *stand at the threshold of the room.*

They are both well dressed in light summer suits and light rain-coats. Two suitcases are by their side.

They look at the room. TEDDY *tosses the key in his hand, smiles.)*

TEDDY: Well, the key worked.

(Pause.)

They haven't changed the lock.

(Pause.)

RUTH: No one's here.

TEDDY: *(looking up.)* They're asleep.

(Pause.)

295 RUTH: Can I sit down?

TEDDY: Of course.

RUTH: I'm tired.

(Pause.)

TEDDY: Then sit down.

(She does not move.)

That's my father's chair.

300 RUTH: That one?

TEDDY: *(smiling.)* Yes, that's it. Shall I go up and see if my room's still there?

RUTH: It can't have moved.

TEDDY: No, I mean if my bed's still there.

305 RUTH: Someone might be in it.

TEDDY: No. They've got their own beds.

(Pause.)

RUTH: Shouldn't you wake someone up? Tell them you're here?

TEDDY: Not at this time of night. It's too late.

(Pause.)

Shall I go up?

(He goes into the hall, looks up the stairs, comes back.)

310 Why don't you sit down?

(Pause.)

I'll just go up . . . have a look.

(He goes up the stairs, stealthily.

RUTH *stands, then slowly walks across the room.*

TEDDY *returns.)*

It's still there. My room. Empty. The bed's there. What are you doing?

(She looks at him.)

Blankets, no sheets. I'll find some sheets. I could hear snores.
315 Really. They're all still here, I think. They're all snoring up there. Are you cold?

RUTH: No.

TEDDY: I'll make something to drink, if you like. Something hot.

320 RUTH: No, I don't want anything.

(TEDDY walks about.)

TEDDY: What do you think of the room? Big, isn't it? It's a big house. I mean, it's a fine room, don't you think? Actually

there was a wall, across there . . . with a door. We knocked it down . . . years ago . . . to make an open living area. The structure wasn't affected, you see. My mother was dead.   325

(RUTH sits.)

Tired?

RUTH: Just a little.

TEDDY: We can go to bed if you like. No point in waking anyone up now. Just go to bed. See them all in the morning . . . see my father in the morning . . .   330

(Pause.)

RUTH: Do you want to stay?

TEDDY: Stay?

(Pause.)

We've come to say. We're bound to stay . . . for a few days.

RUTH: I think . . . the children . . . might be missing us.

TEDDY: Don't be silly.   335

RUTH: They might.

TEDDY: Look, we'll be back in a few days, won't we?

(He walks about the room.)

Nothing's changed. Still the same.

(Pause.)

Still, he'll get a surprise in the morning, won't he? The old man. I think you'll like him very much. Honestly. He's a . . .   340
well, he's old, of course. Getting on.

(Pause.)

I was born here, do you realize that?

RUTH: I know.

(Pause.)

TEDDY: Why don't you go to bed? I'll find some sheets. I feel . . . wide awake, isn't it odd? I think I'll stay up for a bit. Are you   345
tired?

RUTH: No.

TEDDY: Go to bed. I'll show you the room.

RUTH: No, I don't want to.

TEDDY: You'll be perfectly all right up there without me. Really   350
you will. I mean, I won't be long. Look, it's just up there. It's the first door on the landing. The bathroom's right next door. You . . . need some rest, you know.

(Pause.)

I just want to . . . walk about for a few minutes. Do you mind?

RUTH: Of course I don't.   355

TEDDY: Well . . . Shall I show you the room?

RUTH: No, I'm happy at the moment.

TEDDY: You don't have to go to bed. I'm not saying you have to. I mean, you can stay up with me. Perhaps I'll make a cup of tea or something. The only thing is we don't want to make too   360
much noise, we don't want to wake anyone up.

RUTH: I'm not making any noise.

TEDDY: I know you're not.

(He goes to her.)

(Gently.) Look, it's all right, really. I'm here. I mean . . . I'm with you. There's no need to be nervous. Are you nervous?   365

RUTH: No.

TEDDY: There's no need to be.

(Pause.)

They're very warm people, really. Very warm. They're my family. They're not ogres.

(Pause.)

370   Well, perhaps we should go to bed. After all, we have to be up early, see Dad. Wouldn't be quite right if he found us in bed, I think. *(He chuckles.)* Have to be up before six, come down, say hullo.

(Pause.)

RUTH: I think I'll have a breath of air.

375   TEDDY: Air?

(Pause.)

What do you mean?

RUTH: *(standing.)* Just a stroll.

TEDDY: At this time of night? But we've . . . only just got here. We've got to go to bed.

380   RUTH: I just feel like some air.

TEDDY: But I'm going to bed.

RUTH: That's all right.

TEDDY: But what am I going to do?

(Pause.)

The last thing I want is a breath of air. Why do you want

385   a breath of air?

RUTH: I just do.

TEDDY: But it's late.

RUTH: I won't go far. I'll come back.

(Pause.)

TEDDY: I'll wait up for you.

390   RUTH: Why?

TEDDY: I'm not going to bed without you.

RUTH: Can I have the key?

(He gives it to her.)

Why don't you go to bed?

(He puts his arms on her shoulders and kisses her.

They look at each other, briefly. She smiles.)

I won't be long.

(She goes out of the front door.

TEDDY *goes to the window, peers out after her, half turns from the window, stands, suddenly chews his knuckles.*

LENNY *walks into the room from upstage left. He stands. He wears pyjamas and dressing-gown. He watches* TEDDY.

TEDDY *turns and sees him.*

Silence.)

395   TEDDY: Hullo, Lenny.

LENNY: Hullo, Teddy.

(Pause.)

TEDDY: I didn't hear you come down the stairs.

LENNY: I didn't.

(Pause.)

I sleep down here now. Next door. I've got a kind of study, workroom cum bedroom next door now, you see.   400

TEDDY: Oh. Did I . . . wake you up?

LENNY: No. I just had an early night tonight. You know how it is. Can't sleep. Keep waking up.

(Pause.)

TEDDY: How are you?

LENNY: Well, just sleeping a bit restlessly, that's all. Tonight,   405 anyway.

TEDDY: Bad dreams?

LENNY: No, I wouldn't say I was dreaming. It's not exactly a dream. It's just that something keeps waking me up. Some kind of tick.   410

TEDDY: A tick?

LENNY: Yes.

TEDDY: Well, what is it?

LENNY: I don't know.

(Pause.)

TEDDY: Have you got a clock in your room?   415

LENNY: Yes.

TEDDY: Well, maybe it's the clock.

LENNY: Yes, could be, I suppose.

(Pause.)

Well, if it's the clock I'd better do something about it. Stifle it in some way, or something.   420

(Pause.)

TEDDY: I've . . . just come back for a few days.

LENNY: Oh yes? Have you?

(Pause.)

TEDDY: How's the old man?

LENNY: He's in the pink.

(Pause.)

TEDDY: I've been keeping well.   425

LENNY: Oh, have you?

(Pause.)

Staying the night then, are you?

TEDDY: Yes.

LENNY: Well, you can sleep in your old room.

TEDDY: Yes, I've been up.   430

LENNY: Yes, you can sleep there.

*(*LENNY *yawns.)*

Oh well.

TEDDY: I'm going to bed.

LENNY: Are you?

TEDDY: Yes, I'll get some sleep.   435

LENNY: Yes, I'm going to bed, too.

*(*TEDDY *picks up the cases.)*

I'll give you a hand.

TEDDY: No, they're not heavy.

*(*TEDDY *goes into the hall with the cases.* LENNY *turns out the light in the room.*

The light in the hall remains on.

LENNY *follows into the hall.)*

LENNY: Nothing you want?
440 TEDDY: Mmmm?
LENNY: Nothing you might want, for the night? Glass of water, anything like that?
TEDDY: Any sheets anywhere?
LENNY: In the sideboard in your room.
445 TEDDY: Oh, good.
LENNY: Friends of mine occasionally stay there, you know, in your room, when they're passing through this part of the world.

(LENNY *turns out the hall light and turns on the first landing light.*

TEDDY *begins to walk up the stairs.)*

TEDDY: Well, I'll see you at breakfast, then.
450 LENNY: Yes, that's it. Ta-ta.

(TEDDY *goes upstairs.*

LENNY *goes off left.*

Silence.

The landing light goes out. Slight night light in the hall and room.

LENNY *comes back into the room, goes to the window and looks out.*

He leaves the window and turns on a lamp. He is holding a small clock.

He sits, places the clock in front of him, lights a cigarette and sits.
RUTH *comes in the front door.*

She stands still. LENNY *turns his head, smiles. She walks slowly into the room.)*

LENNY: Good evening.
RUTH: Morning, I think.
LENNY: You're right there.

(Pause.)

My name's Lenny. What's yours?
455 RUTH: Ruth.

(She sits, puts her coat collar around her.)

LENNY: Cold?
RUTH: No.
LENNY: It's been a wonderful summer, hasn't it? Remarkable.

(Pause.)

Would you like something? Refreshment of some kind? An
460 aperitif, anything like that?
RUTH: No, thanks.
LENNY: I'm glad you said that. We haven't got a drink in the house. Mind you, I'd soon get some in, if we had a party or something like that. Some kind of celebration . . . you know.

(Pause.)

465 You must be connected with my brother in some way. The one who's been abroad.
RUTH: I'm his wife.

LENNY: Eh listen, I wonder if you can advise me. I've been having a bit of a rough time with this clock. The tick's been keep-
ing me up. The trouble is I'm not all that convinced it was the 470 clock. I mean there are lots of things which tick in the night, don't you find that? All sorts of objects, which, in the day, you wouldn't call anything else but commonplace. They give you no trouble. But in the night any given one of a number of them is liable to start letting out a bit of a tick. Whereas you 475 look at these objects in the day and they're just common-place. They're as quiet as mice during the daytime. So . . . all things being equal . . . this question of me saying it was the clock that woke me up, well, that could very easily prove something of a false hypothesis. 480

(He goes to the sideboard, pours from a jug into a glass, takes the glass to RUTH.)

Here you are. I bet you could do with this.
RUTH: What is it?
LENNY: Water.

(She takes it, sips, places the glass on a small table by her chair.

LENNY *watches her.)*

Isn't it funny? I've got my pyjamas on and you're fully dressed? 485

(He goes to the sideboard and pours another glass of water.)

Mind if I have one? Yes, it's funny seeing my old brother again after all these years. It's just the sort of tonic my Dad needs, you know. He'll be chuffed to his bollocks in the morning, when he sees his eldest son. I was surprised myself when I saw Teddy, you know. Old Ted. I thought he was in 490 America.
RUTH: We're on a visit to Europe.
LENNY: What, both of you?
RUTH: Yes.
LENNY: What, you sort of live with him over there, do you? 495
RUTH: We're married.
LENNY: On a visit to Europe, eh? Seen much of it?
RUTH: We've just come from Italy.
LENNY: Oh, you went to Italy first, did you? And then he brought you over here to meet the family, did he? Well, the 500 old man'll be pleased to see you, I can tell you.
RUTH: Good.
LENNY: What did you say?
RUTH: Good.

(Pause.)

LENNY: Where'd you go to in Italy? 505
RUTH: Venice.
LENNY: Not dear old Venice? Eh? That's funny. You know, I've always had a feeling that if I'd been a soldier in the last war— say in the Italian campaign—I'd probably have found myself in Venice. I've always had that feeling. The trouble was I was 510 too young to serve, you see. I was only a child, I was too small, otherwise I've got a pretty shrewd idea I'd probably have gone through Venice. Yes, I'd almost certainly have gone through it with my battalion. Do you mind if I hold your hand?
RUTH: Why? 515
LENNY: Just a touch.

(He stands and goes to her.)

Just a tickle.

RUTH: Why?

(He looks down at her.)

LENNY: I'll tell you why.

(Slight pause.)

520   One night, not too long ago, one night down by the docks, I
was standing alone under an arch, watching all the men jib-
bing the boom, out in the harbour, and playing about with
the yardarm, when a certain lady came up to me and made
me a certain proposal. This lady had been searching for me
525   for days. She'd lost track of my whereabouts. However, the
fact was she eventually caught up with me, and when she
caught up with me she made me this certain proposal. Well,
this proposal wasn't entirely out of order and normally I
would have subscribed to it. I mean I would have subscribed
530   to it in the normal course of events. The only trouble was she
was falling apart with the pox. So I turned it down. Well, this
lady was very insistent and started taking liberties with me
down under this arch, liberties which by any criterion I
couldn't be expected to tolerate, the facts being what they
535   were, so I clumped her one. It was on my mind at the time to
do away with her, you know, to kill her, and the fact is, that as
killings go, it would have been a simple matter, nothing to it.
Her chauffeur, who had located me for her, he'd popped
around the corner to have a drink, which just left this lady and
540   myself, you see, alone, standing underneath this arch, watching all the steamers steaming up, no one about, all quiet on
the Western Front, and there she was up against the wall—
well, just sliding down the wall, following the blow I'd given
her. Well, to sum up, everything was in my favour, for a kill-
545   ing. Don't worry about the chauffeur. The chauffeur would
never have spoken. He was an old friend of the family. But . . .
in the end I thought . . . Aaah, why go to all the bother . . .
you know, getting rid of the corpse and all that, getting yourself into a state of tension. So I just gave her another belt in
550   the nose and a couple of turns of the boot and sort of left it at
that.

RUTH: How did you know she was diseased?

LENNY: How did I know?

(Pause.)

I decided she was.

(Silence.)

555   You and my brother are newly-weds, are you?

RUTH: We've been married six years.

LENNY: He's always been my favourite brother, old Teddy. Do
you know that? And my goodness we are proud of him here, I
can tell you. Doctor of Philosophy and all that . . . leaves
560   quite an impression. Of course, he's a very sensitive man, isn't
he? Ted. Very. I've often wished I was as sensitive as he is.

RUTH: Have you?

LENNY: Oh yes. Oh yes, very much so. I mean, I'm not saying
I'm not sensitive. I am. I could just be a bit more so, that's all.

565   RUTH: Could you?

LENNY: Yes, just a bit more so, that's all.

(Pause.)

I mean, I am very sensitive to atmosphere, but I tend to get
desensitized, if you know what I mean, when people make
unreasonable demands on me. For instance, last Christmas I
decided to do a bit of snow-clearing for the Borough Council,   570
because we had a heavy snow over here that year in Europe. I
didn't have to do this snow-clearing—I mean I wasn't financially embarrassed in any way—it just appealed to me, it appealed to something inside me. What I anticipated with a
good deal of pleasure was the brisk cold bite in the air in the   575
early morning. And I was right. I had to get my snowboots on
and I had to stand on a corner, at about five-thirty in the
morning, to wait for the lorry to pick me up, to take me to the
allotted area. Bloody freezing. Well, the lorry came, I
jumped on the tailboard, headlights on, dipped, and off we   580
went. Got there, shovels up, fags on, and off we went, deep
into the December snow, hours before cockcrow. Well, that
morning, while I was having my mid-morning cup of tea in a
neighboring cafe, the shovel standing by my chair, an old
lady approached me and asked me if I would give her a hand   585
with her iron mangle. Her brother-in-law, she said, had left it
for her, but he'd left it in the wrong room, he'd left it in the
front room. Well, naturally, she wanted it in the back room.
It was a present he'd given her, you see, a mangle, to iron out
the washing. But he'd left it in the wrong room, he'd left it in   590
the front room, well that was a silly place to leave it, it
couldn't stay there. So I took time off to give her a hand. She
only lived up the road. Well, the only trouble was when I got
there I couldn't move this mangle. It must have weighed
about half a ton. How this brother-in-law got it up there in the   595
first place I can't even begin to envisage. So there I was, doing
a bit of shoulders on with the mangle, risking a rupture, and
this old lady just standing there, waving me on, not even lifting a little finger to give me a helping hand. So after a few
minutes I said to her, now look here, why don't you stuff this   600
iron mangle up your arse? Anyway, I said, they're out of date,
you want to get a spin drier. I had a good mind to give her a
workover there and then, but as I was feeling jubilant with the
snow-clearing I just gave her a short-arm jab to the belly and
jumped on a bus outside. Excuse me, shall I take this ashtray   605
out of your way?

RUTH: It's not in my way.

LENNY: It seems to be in the way of your glass. The glass was
about to fall. Or the ashtray. I'm rather worried about the
carpet. It's not me, it's my father. He's obsessed with order and   610
clarity. He doesn't like mess. So, as I don't believe you're
smoking at the moment, I'm sure you won't object if I move
the ashtray.

(He does so.)

And now perhaps I'll relieve you of your glass.

RUTH: I haven't quite finished.   615

LENNY: You've consumed quite enough, in my opinion.

RUTH: No, I haven't.

LENNY: Quite sufficient, in my own opinion.

RUTH: Not in mine, Leonard.

(Pause.)

LENNY: Don't call me that, please.   620

RUTH: Why not?

LENNY: That's the name my mother gave me.

(Pause.)

Just give me the glass.

RUTH: No.

(Pause.)

625   LENNY: I'll take it, then.

RUTH: If you take the glass . . . I'll take you.

(Pause.)

LENNY: How about me taking the glass without you taking me?

RUTH: Why don't I just take you?

(Pause.)

LENNY: You're joking.

(Pause.)

630   You're in love, anyway, with another man. You've had a secret liaison with another man. His family didn't even know.
Then you come here without a word of warning and start to
make trouble.

(She picks up the glass and lifts it towards him.)

RUTH: Have a sip. Go on. Have a sip from my glass.

(He is still.)

635   Sit on my lap. Take a long cool sip.

(She pats her lap.

Pause. She stands, moves to him with the glass.)

Put your head back and open your mouth.

LENNY: Take that glass away from me.

RUTH: Lie on the floor. Go on. I'll pour it down your throat.

LENNY: What are you doing, making me some kind of proposal?

(She laughs shortly, drains the glass.)

640   RUTH: Oh, I was thirsty.

*(She smiles at him, puts the glass down, goes into the hall and up
the stairs.*

He follows into the hall and shouts up the stairs.)

LENNY: What was that supposed to be? Some kind of proposal?

(Silence.

He comes back into the room, goes to his own glass, drains it.

A door slams upstairs. The landing light goes on.

MAX *comes down the stairs, in pyjamas and cap. He comes into
the room.)*

MAX: What's going on here? You drunk?

(He stares at LENNY.*)*

What are you shouting about? You gone mad?

*(*LENNY *pours another glass of water.)*

Prancing about in the middle of the night shouting your head
645   off. What are you, a raving lunatic?

LENNY: I was thinking aloud.

MAX: Is Joey down here? You been shouting at Joey?

LENNY: Didn't you hear what I said, Dad? I said I was thinking
aloud.

650   MAX: You were thinking so loud you got me out of bed.

LENNY: Look, why don't you just . . . pop off, eh?

MAX: Pop off? He wakes me up in the middle of the night, I think
we got burglars here, I think he's got a knife stuck in him, I
come down here, he tells me to pop off.

*(*LENNY *sits down.)*

655   He was talking to someone. Who could he have been talking
to? They're all asleep. He was having a conversation with
someone. He won't tell me who it was. He pretends he was
thinking aloud. What are you doing, hiding someone here?

LENNY: I was sleepwalking. Get out of it, leave me alone, will
660   you?

MAX: I want an explanation, you understand? I asked you who
you got hiding here.

(Pause.)

LENNY: I'll tell you what, Dad, since you're in the mood for a bit
of a . . . chat, I'll ask you a question. It's a question I've been
665   meaning to ask you for some time. That night . . . you know
. . . the night you got me . . . that night with Mum, what was
it like? Eh? When I was just a glint in your eye. What was it
like? What was the background to it? I mean, I want to know
the real facts about my background. I mean, for instance, is it
a fact that you had me in mind all the time, or is it a fact that I
670   was the last thing you had in mind?

(Pause.)

I'm only asking this in a spirit of inquiry, you understand that,
don't you? I'm curious. And there's lots of people of my age
share that curiosity, you know that, Dad? They often rumi-
nate, sometimes singly, sometimes in groups, about the true
675   facts of that particular night — the night they were made in the
image of those two people *at it.* It's a question long overdue,
from my point of view, but as we happen to be passing the
time of day here tonight I thought I'd pop it to you.

(Pause.)

680   MAX: You'll drown in your own blood.

LENNY: If you prefer to answer the question in writing I've got no
objection.

*(*MAX *stands.)*

I should have asked my dear mother. Why didn't I ask my
dear mother? Now it's too late. She's passed over to the other
685   side.

*(*MAX *spits at him.*

LENNY *looks down at the carpet.)*

Now look what you've done. I'll have to Hoover that in the
morning, you know.

*(*MAX *turns and walks up the stairs.)*

LENNY *sits still.*

Blackout.

Lights up.

Morning.

JOEY *in front of the mirror. He is doing some slow limbering-up
exercises. He stops, combs his hair, carefully. He then shad-
owboxes, heavily, watching himself in the mirror.*

MAX *comes in from upstage left.*

Both MAX *and* JOEY *are dressed.* MAX *watches* JOEY *in silence.*
JOEY *stops shadowboxing, picks up a newspaper and sits.*

Silence.)

MAX: I hate this room.

(Pause.)

It's the kitchen I like. It's nice in there. It's cosy.

(Pause.)

690 But I can't stay in there. You know why? Because he's always
washing up in there, scraping the plates, driving me out of the
kitchen, that's why.
JOEY: Why don't you bring your tea in here?
MAX: I don't want to bring my tea in here. I hate it here. I want to
695 drink my tea in there.

(He goes into the hall and looks towards the kitchen.)

What's he doing in there?

(He returns.)

What's the time?
JOEY: Half past six.
MAX: Half past six.

(Pause.)

700 I'm going to see a game of football this afternoon. You want to
come?

(Pause.)

I'm talking to you.
JOEY: I'm training this afternoon. I'm doing six rounds with
Blackie.
705 MAX: That's not till five o'clock. You've got time to see a game of
football before five o'clock. It's the first game of the season.
JOEY: No, I'm not going.
MAX: Why not?

(Pause.

MAX *goes into the hall.)*

Sam! Come here!

*(*MAX *comes back into the room.*

SAM *enters with a cloth.)*

710 SAM: What?
MAX: What are you doing in there?
SAM: Washing up.
MAX: What else?
SAM: Getting rid of your leavings.
715 MAX: Putting them in the bin, eh?
SAM: Right in.
MAX: What point you trying to prove?
SAM: No point.
MAX: Oh yes, you are. You resent making my breakfast, that's
720 what it is, isn't it? That's why you bang round the kitchen like
that, scraping the frying-pan, scraping all the leavings into
the bin, scraping all the plates, scraping all the tea out of the
teapot . . . that's why you do that, every single stinking morn-

ing. I know. Listen, Sam. I want to say something to you.
From my heart.   725

(He moves closer.)

I want you to get rid of these feelings of resentment you've got
towards me. I wish I could understand them. Honestly, have I
ever given you cause? Never. When Dad died he said to me,
Max, look after your brothers. That's exactly what he said to
me.   730
SAM: How could he say that when he was dead?
MAX: What?
SAM: How could he speak if he was dead?

(Pause.)

MAX: Before he died, Sam. Just before. They were his last words.
His last sacred words, Sammy. A split second after he said   735
those words . . . he was a dead man. You think I'm joking?
You think when my father spoke—on his death-bed—I
wouldn't obey his words to the last letter? You hear that, Joey?
He'll stop at nothing. He's even prepared to spit on the memory of our Dad. What kind of a son were you, you wet wick?   740
You spent half your time doing crossword puzzles! We took
you into the butcher's shop, you couldn't even sweep the dust
off the floor. We took MacGregor into the shop, he could run
the place by the end of a week. Well, I'll tell you one thing. I
respected my father not only as a man but as a number one   745
butcher! And to prove it I followed him into the shop. I
learned to carve a carcass at his knee. I commemorated his
name in blood. I gave birth to three grown men! All on my
own bat. What have you done?

(Pause.)

What have you done? You tit!   750
SAM: Do you want to finish the washing up? Look, here's the
cloth.
MAX: So try to get rid of these feelings of resentment, Sam. After
all, we are brothers.
SAM: Do you want the cloth? Here you are. Take it.   755

*(*TEDDY *and* RUTH *come down the stairs. They walk across the
hall and stop just inside the room.*

The others turn and look at them. JOEY *stands.*

TEDDY *and* RUTH *are wearing dressing-gowns.*

Silence.

TEDDY *smiles.)*

TEDDY: Hullo . . . Dad . . . We overslept.

(Pause.)

What's for breakfast?

(Silence.

TEDDY *chuckles.)*

Huh. We overslept.

*(*MAX *turns to* SAM.)*

MAX: Did you know he was here?
SAM: No.   760

*(*MAX *turns to* JOEY.)*

MAX: Did you know he was here?

(Pause.)

I asked you if you knew he was here.
JOEY: No.
MAX: Then who knew?

(Pause.)

765   Who knew?

(Pause.)

I didn't know.
TEDDY: I was going to come down, Dad, I was going to . . . be
here, when you came down.

(Pause.)

How are you?

(Pause.)

770   Uh . . . look, I'd . . . like you to meet . . .
MAX: How long you been in this house?
TEDDY: All night.
MAX: All night? I'm a laughing-stock. How did you get in?
TEDDY: I had my key.

(MAX whistles and laughs.)

775   MAX: Who's this?
TEDDY: I was just going to introduce you.
MAX: Who asked you to bring tarts in here?
TEDDY: Tarts?
MAX: Who asked you to bring dirty tarts into this house?
780   TEDDY: Listen, don't be silly —
MAX: You been here all night?
TEDDY: Yes, we arrived from Venice —
MAX: We've had a smelly scrubber in my house all night. We've
had a stinking pox-ridden slut in my house all night.
785   TEDDY: Stop it! What are you talking about?
MAX: I haven't seen the bitch for six years, he comes home with-
out a word, he brings a filthy scrubber off the street, he shacks
up in my house!
TEDDY: She's my wife! We're married!

(Pause.)

790   MAX: I've never had a whore under this roof before. Ever since
your mother died. My word of honour. (To JOEY.) Have you
ever had a whore here? Has Lenny ever had a whore here?
They come back from America, they bring the slopbucket
with them. They bring the bedpan with them. (To TEDDY.)
795   Take that disease away from me. Get her away from me.
TEDDY: She's my wife.
MAX: (to JOEY.) Chuck them out.

(Pause.)

A Doctor of Philosophy. Sam, you want to meet a Doctor of
Philosophy? (To JOEY.) I said chuck them out.

(Pause.)

800   What's the matter? You deaf?
JOEY: You're an old man. (To TEDDY.) He's an old man.

(LENNY walks into the room, in a dressing-gown.

He stops.

They all look round. MAX turns back, hits JOEY in the stomach
with all his might.

JOEY contorts, staggers across the stage. MAX, with the exertion of
the blow, begins to collapse. His knees buckle. He clutches his
stick.

SAM moves forward to help him.

MAX hits him across the head with his stick.

SAM sits, head in hands.

JOEY, hands pressed to his stomach, sinks down at the feet of
RUTH.

She looks down at him. LENNY and TEDDY are still.

JOEY slowly stands. He is close to RUTH. He turns from RUTH,
looks round at

MAX. SAM clutches his head. MAX breathes heavily, very slowly
gets to his feet. JOEY moves to him.

They look at each other.

Silence.

MAX moves past JOEY, walks towards RUTH. He gestures with his
stick.)

MAX: Miss.

(RUTH walks toward him.)

RUTH: Yes?

(He looks at her.)

MAX: You a mother?
RUTH: Yes.
MAX: How many you got?   805
RUTH: Three.

(He turns to TEDDY.)

MAX: All yours, Ted?

(Pause.)

Teddy, why don't we have a nice cuddle and kiss, eh? Like the
old days? What about a nice cuddle and kiss, eh?   810
TEDDY: Come on, then.

(Pause.)

MAX: You want to kiss your old father? Want a cuddle with your
old father?
TEDDY: Come on, then.

(TEDDY moves a step towards him.)

Come on.   815

(Pause.)

MAX: You still love your old Dad, eh?

(They face each other.)

TEDDY: Come on, Dad. I'm ready for the cuddle.

(MAX begins to chuckle, gurgling.

He turns to the family and addresses them.)

MAX: He still loves his father!

(Curtain.)

— ACT TWO —

(Afternoon.

MAX, TEDDY, LENNY *and* SAM *are about the stage, lighting cigars.*

JOEY *comes in from upstage left with a coffee tray, followed by* RUTH. *He puts the tray down.* RUTH *hands coffee to all the men. She sits with her cup.* MAX *smiles at her.)*

RUTH: That was a very good lunch.
MAX: I'm glad you liked it. *(To the others.)* Did you hear that? *(To* RUTH.*)* Well, I put my heart and soul into it, I can tell you. *(He sips.)* And this is a lovely cup of coffee.
5 RUTH: I'm glad.

(Pause.)

MAX: I've got the feeling you're a first-rate cook.
RUTH: I'm not bad.
MAX: No, I've got the feeling you're a number one cook. Am I right, Teddy?
10 TEDDY: Yes, she's a very good cook.

(Pause.)

MAX: Well, it's a long time since the whole family was together, eh? If only your mother was alive. Eh, what do you say, Sam? What would Jessie say if she was alive? Sitting here with her three sons. Three fine grown-up lads. And a lovely daughter-
15 in-law. The only shame is her grandchildren aren't here. She'd have petted them and cooed over them, wouldn't she, Sam? She'd have fussed over them and played with them, told them stories, tickled them — I tell you she'd have been hysterical. *(To* RUTH.*)* Mind you, she taught those boys everything
20 they know. She taught them all the morality they know. I'm telling you. Every single bit of the moral code they live by — was taught to them by their mother. And she had a heart to go with it. What a heart. Eh, Sam? Listen, what's the use of beating round the bush? That woman was the backbone to
25 this family. I mean, I was busy working twenty-four hours a day in the shop, I was going all over the country to find meat, I was making my way in the world, but I left a woman at home with a will of iron, a heart of gold and a mind. Right, Sam?

(Pause.)

What a mind.

(Pause.)

30 Mind you, I was a generous man to her. I never left her short of a few bob. I remember one year I entered into negotiations with a top-class group of butchers with continental connections. I was going into association with them. I remember the night I came home, I kept quiet. First of all I gave Lenny a
35 bath, then Teddy a bath, then Joey a bath. What fun we used to have in the bath, eh, boys? Then I came downstairs and I made Jessie put her feet up on a pouffe — what happened to that pouffe, I haven't seen it for years — she put her feet up on the pouffe and I said to her, Jessie, I think our ship is going to
40 come home, I'm going to treat you to a couple of items, I'm going to buy you a dress in pale corded blue silk, heavily encrusted in pearls, and for casual wear, a pair of pantaloons in lilac flowered taffeta. Then I gave her a drop of cherry

brandy. I remember the boys came down, in their pyjamas,
45 all their hair shining, their faces pink, it was before they started shaving, and they knelt down at our feet, Jessie's and mine. I tell you, it was like Christmas.

(Pause.)

RUTH: What happened to the group of butchers?
MAX: The group? They turned out to be a bunch of criminals
50 like everyone else.

(Pause.)

This is a lousy cigar.

(He stubs it out.

He turns to SAM.*)*

What time you going to work?
SAM: Soon.
MAX: You've got a job on this afternoon, haven't you?
55 SAM: Yes, I know.
MAX: What do you mean, you know? You'll be late. You'll lose your job? What are you trying to do, humiliate me?
SAM: Don't worry about me.
MAX: It makes the bile come up in my mouth. The bile — you
60 understand. *(To* RUTH.*)* I worked as a butcher all my life, using the chopper and the slab, the slab, you know what I mean, the chopper and the slab! To keep my family in luxury. Two families! My mother was bedridden, my brothers were all invalids. I had to earn the money for the leading psychia-
65 trists. I had to read books! I had to study the disease, so that I could cope with an emergency at every stage. A crippled family, three bastard sons, a slutbitch of a wife — don't talk to me about the pain of childbirth — I suffered the pain, I've still got the pangs — when I give a little cough my back collapses —
70 and here I've got a lazy idle bugger of a brother won't even get to work on time. The best chauffeur in the world. All his life he's sat in the front seat giving lovely hand signals. You call that work? This man doesn't know his gearbox from his arse!
SAM: You go and ask my customers! I'm the only one they ever
75 ask for.
MAX: What do the other drivers do, sleep all day?
SAM: I can only drive one car. They can't all have me at the same time.
MAX: Anyone could have you at the same time. You'd bend over
80 for half a dollar on Blackfriars Bridge.
SAM: Me!
MAX: For two bob and a toffee apple.
SAM: He's insulting me. He's insulting his brother. I'm driving a man to Hampton Court at four forty-five.
85 MAX: Do you want to know who could drive? MacGregor! MacGregor was a driver.
SAM: Don't you believe it.

*(MAX *points his stick at* SAM.)*

MAX: He didn't even fight in the war. This man didn't even fight in the bloody war!
SAM: I did!
90 MAX: Who did you kill?

(Silence.

SAM *gets up, goes to* RUTH, *shakes her hand and goes out of the front door.*
MAX *turns to* TEDDY.)

Well, how you been keeping, son?
TEDDY: I've been keeping very well, Dad.
MAX: It's nice to have you with us, son.
95 TEDDY: It's nice to be back, Dad.

(Pause.)

MAX: You should have told me you were married, Teddy. I'd have sent you a present. Where was the wedding, in America?
TEDDY: No. Here. The day before we left.
MAX: Did you have a big function?
100 TEDDY: No, there was no one there.
MAX: You're mad. I'd have given you a white wedding. We'd have had the cream of the cream here. I'd have been only too glad to bear the expense, my word of honour.

(Pause.)

TEDDY: You were busy at the time. I didn't want to bother you.
105 MAX: But you're my own flesh and blood. You're my first born. I'd have dropped everything. Sam would have driven you to the reception in the Snipe, Lenny would have been your best man, and then we'd have all seen you off on the boat. I mean, you don't think I disapprove of marriage, do you? Don't be
110 daft. *(To* RUTH.) I've been begging my two youngsters for years to find a nice feminine girl with proper credentials — it makes life worth living. *(To* TEDDY.) Anyway, what's the difference, you did it, you made a wonderful choice, you've got a wonderful family, a marvellous career . . . so why don't we
115 let bygones be bygones?

(Pause.)

You know what I'm saying? I want you both to know that you have my blessing.
TEDDY: Thank you.
MAX: Don't mention it. How many other houses in the district
120 have got a Doctor of Philosophy sitting down drinking a cup of coffee?

(Pause.)

RUTH: I'm sure Teddy's very happy . . . to know that you're pleased with me.

(Pause.)

I think he wondered whether you would be pleased with me.
125 MAX: But you're a charming woman.

(Pause.)

RUTH: I was . . .
MAX: What?

(Pause.)

What she say?

(They all look at her.)

RUTH: I was . . . different . . . when I met Teddy . . . first.
130 TEDDY: No you weren't. You were the same.
RUTH: I wasn't.
MAX: Who cares? Listen, live in the present, what are you worrying about? I mean, don't forget the earth's about five thousand million years old, at least. Who can afford to live in the past?

(Pause.)

TEDDY: She's a great help to me over there. She's a wonderful 135 wife and mother. She's a very popular woman. She's got lots of friends. It's a great life, at the University . . . you know . . . it's a very good life. We've got a lovely house . . . we've got all . . . we've got everything we want. It's a very stimulating environment. 140

(Pause.)

My department . . . is highly successful.

(Pause.)

We've got three boys, you know.
MAX: All boys? Isn't that funny, eh? You've got three, I've got three. You've got three nephews, Joey. Joey! You're an uncle, do you hear? You could teach them how to box. 145

(Pause.)

JOEY: *(to* RUTH.) I'm a boxer. In the evenings, after work. I'm in demolition in the daytime.
RUTH: Oh?
JOEY: Yes. I hope to be full time, when I get more bouts.
MAX: *(to* LENNY.) He speaks so easily to his sister-in-law, do you 150 notice? That's because she's an intelligent and sympathetic woman.

(He leans to her.)

Eh, tell me, do you think the children are missing their mother?

(She looks at him.)

TEDDY: Of course they are. They love her. We'll be seeing them 155 soon.

(Pause.)

LENNY: *(to* TEDDY.) Your cigar's gone out.
TEDDY: Oh, yes.
LENNY: Want a light?
TEDDY: No. No. 160

(Pause.)

So has yours.
LENNY: Oh, yes.

(Pause.)

Eh, Teddy, you haven't told us much about your Doctorship of Philosophy. What do you teach?
TEDDY: Philosophy. 165
LENNY: Well, I want to ask you something. Do you detect a certain logical incoherence in the central affirmations of Christian theism?
TEDDY: That question doesn't fall within my province.
LENNY: Well, look at it this way . . . you don't mind my asking 170 you some questions, do you?
TEDDY: If they're within my province.
LENNY: Well, look at it this way. How can the unknown merit reverence? In other words, how can you revere that of which you're ignorant? At the same time, it would be ridiculous to 175 propose that what we *know* merits reverence. What we know merits any one of a number of things, but it stands to reason reverence isn't one of them. In other words, apart from the known and the unknown, what else is there?

(Pause.)

180 TEDDY: I'm afraid I'm the wrong person to ask.

LENNY: But you're a philosopher. Come on, be frank. What do you make of all this business of being and not-being?

TEDDY: What do you make of it?

LENNY: Well, for instance, take a table. Philosophically speak-

185 ing. What is it?

TEDDY: A table.

LENNY: Ah. You mean it's nothing else but a table. Well, some people would envy your certainty, wouldn't they, Joey? For instance, I've got a couple of friends of mine, we often sit

190 round the Ritz Bar having a few liqueurs, and they're always saying things like that, you know, things like: Take a table, take it. All right, I say, *take it, take* a table, but once you've taken it, what you going to do with it? Once you've got hold of it, where you going to take it?

195 MAX: You'd probably sell it.

LENNY: You wouldn't get much for it.

JOEY: Chop it up for firewood.

(LENNY looks at him and laughs.)

RUTH: Don't be too sure though. You've forgotten something. Look at me. I . . . move my leg. That's all it is. But I wear . . .

200 underwear . . . which moves with me . . . it . . . captures your attention. Perhaps you misinterpret. The action is simple. It's a leg . . . moving. My lips move. Why don't you restrict . . . your observations to that? Perhaps the fact that they move is more significant . . . than the words which come through

205 them. You must bear that . . . possibility . . . in mind.

(Silence.

TEDDY *stands.)*

I was born quite near here.

(Pause.)

Then . . . six years ago, I went to America.

(Pause.)

It's all rock. And sand. It stretches . . . so far . . . everywhere you look. And there's lots of insects there.

(Pause.)

210 And there's lots of insects there.

(Silence.

She is still.

MAX *stands.)*

MAX: Well, it's time to go to the gym. Time for your workout, Joey.

LENNY: *(standing).* I'll come with you.

(JOEY sits looking at RUTH.)

MAX: Joe.

(JOEY stands. The three go out.

TEDDY sits by RUTH, holds her hand. She smiles at him.

Pause.)*

215 TEDDY: I think we'll go back. Mmnn?

(Pause.)

Shall we go home?

RUTH: Why?

TEDDY: Well, we were only here for a few days, weren't we? We might as well . . . cut it short, I think.

RUTH: Why? Don't you like it here?   220

TEDDY: Of course I do. But I'd like to go back and see the boys now.

(Pause.)

RUTH: Don't you like your family?

TEDDY: Which family?

RUTH: Your family here.   225

TEDDY: Of course I like them. What are you talking about?

(Pause.)

RUTH: You don't like them as much as you thought you did?

TEDDY: Of course I do. Of course I . . . like them. I don't know what you're talking about.

(Pause.)

Listen. You know what time of the day it is there now, do you?   230

RUTH: What?

TEDDY: It's morning. It's about eleven o'clock.

RUTH: Is it?

TEDDY: Yes, they're about six hours behind us . . . I mean . . . behind the time here. The boys'll be at the pool . . . now . . .   235

swimming. Think of it. Morning over there. Sun. We'll go anyway, mmnn? It's so clean there.

RUTH: Clean.

TEDDY: Yes.

RUTH: Is it dirty here?   240

TEDDY: No, of course not. But it's cleaner there.

(Pause.)

Look, I just brought you back to meet the family, didn't I? You've met them, we can go. The fall semester will be starting soon.

RUTH: You find it dirty here?   245

TEDDY: I didn't say I found it dirty here.

(Pause.)

I didn't say that.

(Pause.)

Look. I'll go and pack. You rest for a while. Will you? They won't be back for at least an hour. You can sleep. Rest. Please.

(She looks at him.)

You can help me with my lectures when we get back. I'd love   250

that. I'd be so grateful for it, really. We can bathe till October. You know that. Here, there's nowhere to bathe, except the swimming bath down the road. You know what it's like? It's like a urinal. A filthy urinal!

(Pause.)

You liked Venice, didn't you? It was lovely, wasn't it? You had   255

a good week. I mean . . . I took you there. I can speak Italian.

RUTH: But if I'd been a nurse in the Italian campaign I would have been there before.

(Pause.)

TEDDY: You just rest. I'll go and pack.

(TEDDY *goes out and up the stairs.*

She closes her eyes.

LENNY *appears from upstage left. He walks into the room and sits near her.*

She opens her eyes.

Silence.)

260 LENNY: Well, the evenings are drawing in.
RUTH: Yes, it's getting dark.

(*Pause.*)

LENNY: Winter'll soon be upon us. Time to renew one's wardrobe.

(*Pause.*)

RUTH: That's a good thing to do.
LENNY: What?

(*Pause.*)

265 RUTH: I always . . .

(*Pause.*)

Do you like clothes?
LENNY: Oh, yes. Very fond of clothes.

(*Pause.*)

RUTH: I'm fond . . .

(*Pause.*)

What do you think of my shoes?
270 LENNY: They're very nice.
RUTH: No, I can't get the ones I want over there.
LENNY: Can't get them over there, eh?
RUTH: No . . . you don't get them there.

(*Pause.*)

I was a model before I went away.
275 LENNY: Hats?

(*Pause.*)

I bought a girl a hat once. We saw it in a glass case, in a shop.
I tell you what it had. It had a bunch of daffodils on it, tied
with a black satin bow, and then it was covered with a cloche
of black veiling. A cloche. I'm telling you. She was made for it.
280 RUTH: No . . . I was a model for the body. A photographic model
for the body.
LENNY: Indoor work?
RUTH: That was before I had . . . all my children.

(*Pause.*)

No, not always indoors.

(*Pause.*)

285 Once or twice we went to a place in the country, by train. Oh,
six or seven times. We used to pass a . . . a large white water
tower. This place . . . this house . . . was very big . . . the trees
. . . there was a lake, you see . . . we used to change and walk
down towards the lake . . . we went down a path . . . on stones
290 . . . there were . . . on this path. Oh, just . . . wait . . . yes . . .
when we changed in the house we had a drink. There was a
cold buffet.

(*Pause.*)

Sometimes we stayed in the house but . . . most often . . . we
walked down to the lake . . . and did our modelling there.

(*Pause.*)

Just before we went to America I went down there. I walked   295
from the station to the gate and then I walked up the drive.
There were lights on . . . I stood in the drive . . . the house was
very light.

(TEDDY *comes down the stairs with the cases. He puts them
down, looks at* LENNY.)

TEDDY: What have you been saying to her?

(*He goes to* RUTH.)

Here's your coat.   300

(LENNY *goes to the radiogram and puts on a record of slow jazz.*)

Ruth. Come on. Put it on.
LENNY: (*to* RUTH.) What about one dance before you go?
TEDDY: We're going.
LENNY: Just one.
TEDDY: No. We're going.   305
LENNY: Just one dance, with her brother-in-law, before she
goes.

(LENNY *bends to her.*)

Madam?

(RUTH *stands. They dance, slowly.*

TEDDY *stands, with* RUTH'S *coat.*

MAX *and* JOEY *come in the front door and into the room. They
stand.*

LENNY *kisses* RUTH. *They stand, kissing.*)

JOEY: Christ, she's wide open. Dad, look at that.

(*Pause.*)

She's a tart.   310

(*Pause.*)

Old Lenny's got a tart in here.

(JOEY *goes to them. He takes* RUTH'S *arm. He smiles at* LENNY.
He sits with RUTH *on the sofa, embraces and kisses her.*

He looks up at LENNY.)

Just up my street.

(*He leans her back until she lies beneath him. He kisses her. He
looks up at* TEDDY *and* MAX.)

It's better than a rubdown, this.

(LENNY *sits on the arm of the sofa. He caresses* RUTH'S *hair as*
JOEY *embraces her.*

MAX *comes forward, looks at the cases.*)

MAX: You going, Teddy? Already?

(*Pause.*)

Well, when you coming over again, eh? Look, next time you   315
come over, don't forget to let us know beforehand whether
you're married or not. I'll always be glad to meet the wife.
Honest. I'm telling you.

(JOEY *lies heavily on* RUTH.)

They are almost still.

LENNY *caresses her hair.*)

320   Listen, you think I don't know why you didn't tell me you
were married? I know why. You were ashamed. You thought
I'd be annoyed because you married a woman beneath you.
You should have known me better. I'm broadminded. I'm a
broadminded man.

(*He peers to see* RUTH's *face under* JOEY, *turns back to* TEDDY.)

325   Mind you, she's a lovely girl. A beautiful woman. And a
mother too. A mother of three. You've made a happy woman
out of her. It's something to be proud of. I mean, we're talking
about a woman of quality. We're talking about a woman of
feeling.

(JOEY *and* RUTH *roll off the sofa on to the floor.*

JOEY *clasps her.* LENNY *moves to stand above them. He looks
down on them. He touches* RUTH *gently with his foot.*

RUTH *suddenly pushes* JOEY *away.*

She stands up. JOEY *gets to his feet, stares at her.*)

RUTH: I'd like something to eat. (*to* LENNY.) I'd like a drink. Did
330   you get any drink?
LENNY: We've got drink.
RUTH: I'd like one, please.
LENNY: What drink?
RUTH: Whisky.
335 LENNY: I've got it.

(*Pause.*)

RUTH: Well, get it.

(LENNY *goes to the sideboard, takes out bottle and glasses.*

JOEY *moves towards her.*)

Put the record off.

(*He looks at her, turns, puts the record off.*)

I want something to eat.

(*Pause.*)

JOEY: I can't cook. (*Pointing to* MAX.) He's the cook.

(LENNY *brings her a glass of whisky.*)

340 LENNY: Soda on the side?
RUTH: What's this glass? I can't drink out of this. Haven't you got
a tumbler?
LENNY: Yes.
RUTH: Well, put it in a tumbler.

(*He takes the glass back, pours whisky into a tumbler, brings it to
her.*)

345 LENNY: On the rocks? Or as it comes?
RUTH: Rocks? What do you know about rocks?
LENNY: We've got rocks. But they're frozen stiff in the fridge.

(RUTH *drinks.*

LENNY *looks round at the others.*)

Drinks all round?

(*He goes to the sideboard and pours drinks.*

JOEY *moves closer to* RUTH.)

JOEY: What food do you want?

(RUTH *walks round the room.*)

RUTH: (*to* TEDDY.) Have your family read your critical works?   350
MAX: That's one thing I've never done. I've never read one of his
critical works.
TEDDY: You wouldn't understand them.

(LENNY *hands drinks all round.*)

JOEY: What sort of food do you want? I'm not the cook, anyway.
LENNY: Soda, Ted? Or as it comes?   355
TEDDY: You wouldn't understand my works. You wouldn't have
the faintest idea of what they were about. You wouldn't appreciate the points of reference. You're way behind. All of you.
There's no point in my sending you my works. You'd be lost.
It's nothing to do with the question of intelligence. It's a way   360
of being able to look at the world. It's a question of how far you
can operate on things and not in things. I mean it's a question
of your capacity to ally the two, to relate the two, to balance
the two. To see, to be able to *see*! I'm the one who can see.
That's why I can write my critical works. Might do you good   365
. . . have a look at them . . . see how certain people can view
. . . things . . . how certain people can maintain . . . intellectual equilibrium. Intellectual equilibrium. You're just objects. You just . . . move about. I can observe it. I can see what
you do. It's the same as I do. But you're lost in it. You won't   370
get me being . . . I won't be lost in it.

(*Blackout.*

Lights up.

Evening.

TEDDY *sitting, in his coat, the cases by him.* SAM.)

(*Pause.*)

SAM: Do you remember MacGregor, Teddy?
TEDDY: Mac?
SAM: Yes.
TEDDY: Of course I do.   375
SAM: What did you think of him? Did you take to him?
TEDDY: Yes. I liked him. Why?

(*Pause.*)

SAM: You know, you were always my favourite, of the lads.
Always.

(*Pause.*)

When you wrote to me from America I was very touched, you   380
know. I mean you'd written to your father a few times but
you'd never written to me. But then, when I got that letter
from you . . . well, I was very touched. I never told him. I
never told him I'd heard from you.

(*Pause.*)

(*Whispering.*) Teddy, shall I tell you something? You were   385
always your mother's favourite. She told me. It's true. You
were always the . . . you were always the main object of her
love.

(*Pause.*)

Why don't you stay for a couple more weeks, eh? We could
have a few laughs.   390

(LENNY *comes in the front door and into the room.*)

LENNY: Still here, Ted? You'll be late for your first seminar.

(*He goes to the sideboard, opens it, peers in it, to the right and the left, stands.*)

Where's my cheese-roll?

(*Pause.*)

Someone's taken my cheese-roll. I left it there (*To* SAM.) You been thieving?

395   TEDDY: I took your cheese-roll, Lenny.

(*Silence.*

SAM *looks at them, picks up his hat and goes out of the front door.*

Silence.)

LENNY: You took my cheese-roll?

TEDDY: Yes.

LENNY: I made that roll myself. I cut it and put the butter on. I sliced a piece of cheese and put it in between. I put it on a
400   plate and I put it in the sideboard. I did all that before I went out. Now I come back and you've eaten it.

TEDDY: Well, what are you going to do about it?

LENNY: I'm waiting for you to apologize.

TEDDY: But I took it deliberately, Lenny.

405   LENNY: You mean you didn't stumble on it by mistake?

TEDDY: No, I saw you put it there. I was hungry, so I ate it.

(*Pause.*)

LENNY: Barefaced audacity.

(*Pause.*)

What led you to be so . . . vindictive against your own brother? I'm bowled over.

(*Pause.*)

410   Well, Ted, I would say this is something approaching the naked truth, isn't it? It's a real cards on the table stunt. I mean, we're in the land of no holds barred now. Well, how else can you interpret it? To pinch your younger brother's specially made cheese-roll when he's out doing a spot of work, that's
415   not equivocal, it's unequivocal.

(*Pause.*)

Mind you, I will say you do seem to have grown a bit sulky during the last six years. A bit sulky. A bit inner. A bit less forthcoming. It's funny, because I'd have thought that in the United States of America, I mean with the sun and all that,
420   the open spaces, on the old campus, in your position, lecturing, in the centre of all the intellectual life out there, on the old campus, all the social whirl, all the stimulation of it all, all your kids and all that, to have fun with, down by the pool, the Greyhound buses and all that, tons of iced water, all the
425   comfort of those Bermuda shorts and all that, on the old campus, no time of the day or night you can't get a cup of coffee or a Dutch gin, I'd have thought you'd have grown more forthcoming, not less. Because I want you to know that you set a standard for us, Teddy. Your family looks up to you,
430   boy, and you know what it does? It does its best to follow the

example you set. Because you're a great source of pride to us. That's why we were so glad to see you come back, to welcome you back to your birthplace. That's why.

(*Pause.*)

No, listen, Ted, there's no question that we live a less rich life here than you do over there. We live a closer life. We're busy,   435
of course. Joey's busy with his boxing, I'm busy with my occupation, Dad still plays a good game of poker, and he does the cooking as well, well up to his old standard, and Uncle Sam's the best chauffeur in the firm. But nevertheless we do make up a unit, Teddy, and you're an integral part of it. When we   440
all sit round the backyard having a quiet gander at the night sky, there's always an empty chair standing in the circle, which is in fact yours. And so when you at length return to us, we do expect a bit of grace, a bit of je ne sais quoi, a bit of generosity of mind, a bit of liberality of spirit, to reassure us.   445
We do expect that. But do we get it? Have we got it? Is that what you've given us?

(*Pause.*)

TEDDY: Yes.

(JOEY *comes down the stairs and into the room, with a newspaper.*)

LENNY: (*to* JOEY.) How'd you get on?

JOEY: Er . . . not bad.

LENNY: What do you mean?   450

(*Pause.*)

What do you mean?

JOEY: Not bad.

LENNY: I want to know what you *mean*—by not bad.

JOEY: What's it got to do with you?   455

LENNY: Joey, you tell your brother everything.

(*Pause.*)

JOEY: I didn't get all the way.

LENNY: You didn't get all the way?

(*Pause.*)

(*With emphasis.*) You didn't get all the way?

But you've had her up there for two hours.   460

JOEY: Well?

LENNY: You didn't get all the way and you've had her up there for two hours!

JOEY: What about it?

(LENNY *moves closer to him.*)

LENNY: What are you telling me?   465

JOEY: What do you mean?

LENNY: Are you telling me she's a tease?

(*Pause.*)

She's a tease!

(*Pause.*)

What do you think of that, Ted? Your wife turns out to be a tease. He's had her up there for two hours and he didn't go the   470
whole hog.

JOEY: I didn't say she was a tease.

LENNY: Are you joking? It sounds like a tease to me, don't it to you, Ted?

475 TEDDY: Perhaps he hasn't got the right touch.

LENNY: Joey? Not the right touch? Don't be ridiculous. He's had more dolly than you've had cream cakes. He's irresistible. He's one of the few and far between. Tell him about the last bird you had, Joey.

(Pause.)

480 JOEY: What bird?

LENNY: The last bird? When we stopped the car . . .

JOEY: Oh, that . . . yes . . . well, we were in Lenny's car one night last week . . .

LENNY: The Alfa.

485 JOEY: And er . . . bowling down the road . . .

LENNY: Up near the Scrubs.

JOEY: Yes, up over by the Scrubs . . .

LENNY: We were doing a little survey of North Paddington.

JOEY: And er . . . it was pretty late, wasn't it?

490 LENNY: Yes, it was late. Well?

(Pause.)

JOEY: And then we . . . well, by the kerb, we saw this parked car . . . with a couple of girls in it.

LENNY: And their escorts.

JOEY: Yes, there were two geezers in it. Anyway . . .

(Pause.)

495 What we do then?

LENNY: We stopped the car and got out!

JOEY: Yes . . . we got out . . . and we told the . . . two escorts . . . to go away . . . which they did . . . and then we . . . got the girls out of the car . . .

500 LENNY: We didn't take them over the Scrubs.

JOEY: Oh, no. Not over the Shrubs. Well, the police would have noticed us there . . . you see. We took them over a bombed site.

LENNY: Rubble. In the rubble.

505 JOEY: Yes, plenty of rubble.

(Pause.)

Well . . . you know . . . then we had them.

LENNY: You've missed out the best bit. He's missed out the best bit!

JOEY: What bit?

510 LENNY: (to TEDDY.) His bird says to him, I don't mind, she says, but I've got to have some protection. I've got to have some contraceptive protection. I haven't got any contraceptive protection, old Joey says to her. In that case I won't do it, she says. Yes you will says Joey, never mind about the contracep-

515 tive protection.

(LENNY laughs.)

Even my bird laughed when she heard that. Yes, even she gave out a bit of a laugh. So you can't say old Joey isn't a bit of a knockout when he gets going, can you? And here he is upstairs with your wife for two hours and he hasn't even been

520 the whole hog. Well, your wife sounds like a bit of a tease to me, Ted. What do you make of it, Joey? You satisfied? Don't tell me you're satisfied without going the whole hog?

(Pause.)

JOEY: I've been the whole hog plenty of times. Sometimes . . . you can be happy . . . and not go the whole hog. Now and again . . . you can be happy . . . without going any hog. 525

(LENNY stares at him.

MAX and SAM come in the front door and into the room.)

MAX: Where's the whore? Still in bed? She'll make us all animals.

LENNY: The girl's a tease.

MAX: What?

LENNY: She's had Joey on a string.

MAX: What do you mean? 530

TEDDY: He had her up there for two hours and he didn't go the whole hog.

(Pause.)

MAX: My Joey? She did that to my boy?

(Pause.)

To my youngest son? Tch, tch, tch, tch. How you feeling, son? Are you all right? 535

JOEY: Sure I'm all right.

MAX: (to TEDDY.) Does she do that to you, too?

TEDDY: No.

LENNY: He gets the gravy.

MAX: You think so? 540

JOEY: No he don't.

(Pause.)

SAM: He's her lawful husband. She's his lawful wife.

JOEY: No he don't! He don't get no gravy! I'm telling you. I'm telling all of you. I'll kill the next man who says he gets the gravy. 545

MAX: Joey . . . what are you getting so excited about? (To LENNY.) It's because he's frustrated. You see what happens?

JOEY: Who is?

MAX: Joey. No one's saying you're wrong. In fact, everyone's saying you're right. 550

(Pause.

MAX turns to the others.)

You know something? Perhaps it's not a bad idea to have a woman in the house. Perhaps it's a good thing. Who knows? Maybe we should keep her.

(Pause.)

Maybe we'll ask her if she wants to stay.

(Pause.)

TEDDY: I'm afraid not, Dad. She's not well, and we've got to get 555 home to the children.

MAX: Not well? I told you, I'm used to looking after people who are not so well. Don't worry about that. Perhaps we'll keep her here.

(Pause.)

SAM: Don't be silly. 560

MAX: What's silly?

SAM: You're talking rubbish.

MAX: Me?

SAM: She's got three children.

565 MAX: She can have more! Here. If she's so keen.

TEDDY: She doesn't want any more.

MAX: What do you know about what she wants, eh, Ted?

TEDDY: (*smiling.*) The best thing for her is to come home with me, Dad. Really. We're married, you know.

(MAX *walks about the room, clicks his fingers.*)

570 MAX: We'd have to pay her, of course. You realize that? We can't leave her walking about without any pocket money. She'll have to have a little allowance.

JOEY: Of course we'll pay her. She's got to have some money in her pocket.

575 MAX: That's what I'm saying. You can't expect a woman to walk about without a few bob to spend on a pair of stockings.

(*Pause.*)

LENNY: Where's the money going to come from?

MAX: Well, how much is she worth? What we talking about, three figures?

580 LENNY: I asked you where the money's going to come from. It'll be an extra mouth to feed. It'll be an extra body to clothe. You realize that?

JOEY: I'll buy her clothes.

LENNY: What with?

585 JOEY: I'll put in a certain amount out of my wages.

MAX: That's it. We'll pass the hat round. We'll make a donation. We're all grown-up people, we've got a sense of responsibility. We'll all put a little in the hat. It's democratic.

LENNY: It'll come to a few quid, Dad.

(*Pause.*)

590 I mean, she's not a woman who likes walking around in second-hand goods. She's up to the latest fashion. You wouldn't want her walking about in clothes which don't show her off at her best, would you?

MAX: Lenny, do you mind if I make a little comment? It's not

595 meant to be critical. But I think you're concentrating too much on the economic considerations. There are other considerations. There are the human considerations. You understand what I mean? There are the human considerations. Don't forget them.

600 LENNY: I won't.

MAX: Well don't.

(*Pause.*)

Listen, we're bound to treat her in something approximating, at least, to the manner in which she's accustomed. After all, she's not someone off the street, she's my daughter-in-law!

605 JOEY: That's right.

MAX: There you are, you see. Joey'll donate, Sam'll donate. . . .

(SAM *looks at him.*)

I'll put in a few bob out of my pension, Lenny'll cough up. We're laughing. What about you, Ted? How much you going to put in the kitty?

610 TEDDY: I'm not putting anything in the kitty.

MAX: What? You won't even help to support your own wife? I thought he was a son of mine. You lousy stinkpig. Your mother would drop dead if she heard you take that attitude.

LENNY: Eh, Dad.

(LENNY *walks forward.*)

I've got a better idea.   615

MAX: What?

LENNY: There's no need for us to go to all this expense. I know these women. Once they get started they ruin your budget. I've got a better idea. Why don't I take her up with me to Greek Street?   620

(*Pause.*)

MAX: You mean put her on the game?

(*Pause.*)

We'll put her on the game. That's a stroke of genius, that's a marvellous idea. You mean she can earn the money herself— on her back?

LENNY: Yes.   625

MAX: Wonderful. The only thing is, it'll have to be short hours. We don't want her out of the house all night.

LENNY: I can limit the hours.

MAX: How many?

LENNY: Four hours a night.   630

MAX: (*dubiously.*) Is that enough?

LENNY: She'll bring in a good sum for four hours a night.

MAX: Well, you should know. After all, it's true, the last thing we want to do is wear the girl out. She's going to have her obligations this end as well. Where you going to put her in Greek 635
Street?

LENNY: It doesn't have to be right in Greek Street, Dad. I've got a number of flats all around that area.

MAX: You have? Well, what about me? Why don't you give me one?   640

LENNY: You're sexless.

JOEY: Eh, wait a minute, what's all this?

MAX: I know what Lenny's saying. Lenny's saying she can pay her own way. What do you think, Teddy? That'll solve all our problems.   645

JOEY: Eh, wait a minute. I don't want to share her.

MAX: What did you say?

JOEY: I don't want to share her with a lot of yobs!

MAX: Yobs! You arrogant git! What arrogance. (*To* LENNY.) Will you be supplying her with yobs?   650

LENNY: I've got a very distinguished clientèle, Joey. They're more distinguished than you'll ever be.

MAX: So you can count yourself lucky we're including you in.

JOEY: I didn't think I was going to have to share her!

MAX: Well, you *are* going to have to share her! Otherwise she 655
goes straight back to America. You understand?

(*Pause.*)

It's tricky enough as it is, without you shoving your oar in. But there's something worrying me. Perhaps she's not so up to the mark. Eh? Teddy, you're the best judge. Do you think she'd be up to the mark?   660

(*Pause.*)

I mean what about all this teasing? Is she going to make a habit of it? That'll get us nowhere.

(*Pause.*)

TEDDY: It was just love play . . . I suppose . . . that's all I suppose it was.

665 MAX: Love play? Two bleeding hours? That's a bloody long time for love play!

LENNY: I don't think we've got anything to worry about on that score, Dad.

MAX: How do you know?

670 LENNY: I'm giving you a professional opinion.

(LENNY *goes to* TEDDY.)

LENNY: Listen, Teddy, you could help us, actually. If I were to send you some cards, over to America . . . you know, very nice ones, with a name on, and a telephone number, very discreet, well, you could distribute them . . . to various par-

675 ties, who might be making a trip over here. Of course, you'd get a little percentage out of it.

MAX: I mean, you needn't tell them she's your wife.

LENNY: No, we'd call her something else. Dolores, or something.

MAX: Or Spanish Jacky.

680 LENNY: No, you've got to be reserved about it, Dad. We could call her something nice . . . like Cynthia . . . or Gillian.

(*Pause.*)

JOEY: Gillian.

(*Pause.*)

LENNY: No, what I mean, Teddy, you must know lots of pro-fessors, heads of departments, men like that. They pop over

685 here for a week at the Savoy, they need somewhere they can go to have a nice quiet poke. And of course you'd be in a position to give them inside information.

MAX: Sure. You can give them proper data. You know, the kind of thing she's willing to do. How far she'd be prepared to go

690 with their little whims and fancies. Eh, Lenny? To what ex-tent she's various. I mean if you don't know who does?

(*Pause.*)

I bet you before two months we'd have a waiting list.

LENNY: You could be our representative in the States.

MAX: Of course. We're talking in international terms! By the

695 time we've finished Pan-American'll give us a discount.

(*Pause.*)

TEDDY: She'd get old . . . very quickly.

MAX: No . . . not in this day and age! With the health service? Old! How could she get old? She'll have the time of her life.

(RUTH *comes down the stairs, dressed.*

She comes into the room.

She smiles at the gathering, and sits.

Silence.)

TEDDY: Ruth . . . the family have invited you to stay, for a little

700 while longer. As a . . . as a kind of guest. If you like the idea I don't mind. We can manage very easily at home . . . until you come back.

RUTH: How very nice of them.

(*Pause.*)

MAX: It's an offer from our heart.

705 RUTH: It's very sweet of you.

MAX: Listen . . . it would be our pleasure.

(*Pause.*)

RUTH: I think I'd be too much trouble.

MAX: Trouble? What are you talking about? What trouble? Lis-ten, I'll tell you something. Since poor Jessie died, eh, Sam?

710 we haven't had a woman in the house. Not one. Inside this house. And I'll tell you why. Because their mother's image was so dear any other woman would have . . . tarnished it. But you . . . Ruth . . . you're not only lovely and beautiful, but you're kin. You're kin. You belong here.

(*Pause.*)

715 RUTH: I'm very touched.

MAX: Of course you're touched. I'm touched.

(*Pause.*)

TEDDY: But Ruth, I should tell you . . . that you'll have to pull your weight a little, if you stay. Financially. My father isn't very well off.

720 RUTH: (*to* MAX.) Oh, I'm sorry.

MAX: No, you'd just have to bring in a little, that's all. A few pennies. Nothing much. It's just that we're waiting for Joey to hit the top as a boxer. When Joey hits the top . . . well . . .

(*Pause.*)

TEDDY: Or you can come home with me.

725 LENNY: We'd get you a flat.

(*Pause.*)

RUTH: A flat?

LENNY: Yes.

RUTH: Where?

LENNY: In town.

(*Pause.*)

730 But you'd live here, with us.

MAX: Of course you would. This would be your home. In the bosom of the family.

LENNY: You'd just pop up to the flat a couple of hours a night, that's all.

735 MAX: Just a couple of hours, that's all. That's all.

LENNY: And you make enough money to keep you going here.

(*Pause.*)

RUTH: How many rooms would this flat have?

LENNY: Not many.

RUTH: I would want at least three rooms and a bathroom.

740 LENNY: You wouldn't need three rooms and a bathroom.

MAX: She'd need a bathroom.

LENNY: But not three rooms.

(*Pause.*)

RUTH: Oh, I would. Really.

LENNY: Two would do.

745 RUTH: No. Two wouldn't be enough.

(*Pause.*)

I'd want a dressing-room, a rest-room, and a bedroom.

(*Pause.*)

LENNY: All right, we'll get you a flat with three rooms and a bathroom.

RUTH: With what kind of conveniences?

750 LENNY: All conveniences.

RUTH: A personal maid?

LENNY: Of course.

(*Pause.*)

We'd finance you, to begin with, and then, when you were established, you could pay us back, in instalments.

755 RUTH: Oh, no, I wouldn't agree to that.

LENNY: Oh, why not?

RUTH: You would have to regard your original outlay simply as a capital investment.

(*Pause.*)

LENNY: I see. All right.

760 RUTH: You'd supply my wardrobe, of course?

LENNY: We'd supply everything. Everything you need.

RUTH: I'd need an awful lot. Otherwise I wouldn't be content.

LENNY: You'd have everything.

RUTH: I would naturally want to draw up an inventory of every-
765 thing I would need, which would require your signatures in the presence of witnesses.

LENNY: Naturally.

RUTH: All aspects of the agreement and conditions of employment would have to be clarified to our mutual satisfaction
770 before we finalized the contract.

LENNY: Of course.

(*Pause.*)

RUTH: Well, it might prove a workable arrangement.

LENNY: I think so.

MAX: And you'd have the whole of your daytime free, of course.
775 You could do a bit of cooking here if you wanted to.

LENNY: Make the beds.

MAX: Scrub the place out a bit.

TEDDY: Keep everyone company.

(SAM *comes forward.*)

SAM: (*in one breath.*) MacGregor had Jessie in the back of my
780 cab as I drove them along.

(*He croaks and collapses.*

He lies still.

They look at him.)

MAX: What's he done? Dropped dead?

LENNY: Yes.

MAX: A corpse? A corpse on my floor? Get him out of here!
Clear him out of here!

(JOEY *bends over* SAM.)

785 JOEY: He's not dead.

LENNY: He probably was dead, for about thirty seconds.

MAX: He's not even dead!

(LENNY *looks down at* SAM.)

LENNY: Yes, there's still some breath there.

MAX: (*pointing at* SAM.) You know what that man had?
790 LENNY: Has.

MAX: Has! A diseased imagination.

(*Pause.*)

RUTH: Yes, it sounds a very attractive idea.

MAX: Do you want to shake on it now, or do you want to leave it
till later?

RUTH: Oh, we'll leave it till later.   795

(TEDDY *stands.*

He looks down at SAM.)

TEDDY: I was going to ask him to drive me to London Airport.

(*He goes to the cases, picks one up.*)

Well, I'll leave your case, Ruth. I'll just go up the road to the
Underground.

MAX: Listen, if you go the other way, first left, first right, you
remember, you might find a cab passing there.   800

TEDDY: Yes, I might do that.

MAX: Or you can take the tube to Piccadilly Circus, won't take you
ten minutes, and pick up a cab from there out to the Airport.

TEDDY: Yes, I'll probably do that.

MAX: Mind you, they'll charge you double fare. They'll charge   805
you for the return trip. It's over the six-mile limit.

TEDDY: Yes, Well, bye-bye, Dad. Look after yourself.

(*They shake hands.*)

MAX: Thanks, son. Listen. I want to tell you something. It's
been wonderful to see you.

(*Pause.*)

TEDDY: It's been wonderful to see you.   810

MAX: Do your boys know about me? Eh? Would they like to see a
photo, do you think, of their grandfather?

TEDDY: I know they would.

(MAX *brings out his wallet.*)

MAX: I've got one on me. I've got one here. Just a minute. Here
you are. Will they like that one?

TEDDY: (*taking it.*) They'll be thrilled.   815

(*He turns to* LENNY.)

Good-bye, Lenny.

(*They shake hands.*)

LENNY: Ta-ta, Ted. Good to see you. Have a good trip.

TEDDY: Bye-bye, Joey.

(JOEY *does not move.*)

JOEY: Ta-ta.   820

(TEDDY *goes to the front door.*)

RUTH: Eddie.

(TEDDY *turns.*)

(*Pause.*)

Don't become a stranger.

(TEDDY *goes, shuts the front door.*

Silence.

The three men stand.

RUTH *sits relaxed in her chair.* SAM *lies still.*

JOEY *walks slowly across the room. He kneels at her chair.*

She touches his head, lightly.

He puts his head in her lap.

MAX *begins to move above them, backwards and forwards.*

LENNY *stands still.* MAX *turns to* LENNY.*)*

MAX: I'm too old, I suppose. She thinks I'm an old man.

(Pause.)

I'm not such an old man.

(Pause.)

825   *(To* RUTH.*)* You think I'm too old for you?

(Pause.)

Listen. You think you're just going to get that big slag all the time? You think you're just going to have him . . . you're going to just have him all the time? You're going to have to work! You'll have to take them on, you understand?

(Pause.)

830   Does she realize that?

(Pause.)

Lenny, do you think she understands . . .

(He begins to stammer.)

What . . . what . . . what . . . we're getting at? What . . . we've got in mind? Do you think she's got it clear?

(Pause.)

I don't think she's got it clear.

(Pause.)

You understand what I mean? Listen, I've got a funny idea   835 she'll do the dirty on us, you want to bet? She'll use us, she'll make use of us, I can tell you! I can smell it! You want to bet?

(Pause.)

She won't . . . be adaptable!

(He falls to his knees, whimpers, begins to moan and sob. He stops sobbing, crawls past SAM's *body round her chair, to the other side of her.)*

I'm not an old man.

(He looks up at her.)

Do you hear me?   840

(He raises his face to her.)

Kiss me.

(She continues to touch JOEY's *head, lightly.*

LENNY *stands, watching.)*

(Curtain.)

ATHOL FUGARD, JOHN KANI, AND WINSTON NTSHONA

Born in 1932, the South African playwright Athol Fugard began his career in the theater in the 1950s, working with the Circle Players in Cape Town. As a mixed-race company, the Circle Players worked in violation of South Africa's apartheid laws. They brought the issue of apartheid to a head when Fugard—a white man—collaborated with the black actor Zakes Mokae in the play *The Blood Knot* (1961), a play about two brothers, one of whom is light-skinned enough to "pass" for white. The play's powerful indictment of apartheid and the brilliant performances of Fugard and Mokae were widely admired and gained Fugard a reputation as a dramatist outside South Africa. Yet, despite its notoriety, the play could hardly remove apartheid itself. Fugard and Mokae were still forced to travel separately, and the government passed new laws limiting interracial theater.

By the early 1970s, Fugard had written several of his best-known plays—*Hello and Goodbye* (1965), *Boesman and Lena* (1969)—when he became frustrated with his method of writing plays and decided to work collaboratively with a different company, the Serpent Players. Two of his collaborators, John Kani and Winston Ntshona, were prominent black actors in South Africa's township theaters and had suffered from the limitations of apartheid throughout their lives and careers. In fact, when they began to work with Fugard, they could perform legally only by being registered as his employees. Yet the plays they devised—*Sizwe Bansi is Dead* (1972) and *The Island* (1973)—are fully collaborative, for the three men improvised a variety of possible performances before setting them down in a final design. The opening monologue with the newspaper in *Sizwe Bansi is Dead*, for instance, is based on Kani's usual stand-up comedy routines. Fugard has gone on to write a number of plays about the effects of apartheid and racism on South African life, including *Master Harold . . . and the boys* (1982) and *My Children! My Africa!* (1989). Kani and Ntshona have come to enjoy considerable success in the theater and in films.

Sizwe Bansi is Dead

Sizwe Bansi is Dead opens in Styles's Photographic Studio, where Robert Zwelinzima arrives to have a picture-postcard taken to send to his wife in King William's Town. However, it soon emerges that "Robert Zwelinzima" is the man's assumed name. His real name is Sizwe Bansi, and he has left his home in the poverty-stricken Ciskei province—one of the black homelands created by the South African government—and walked the 150 miles to Port Elizabeth. Through an elegant flashback, we discover Sizwe Bansi's history in Port Elizabeth: how he was arrested in a raid and ordered to return to King William's Town. Indeed, much as Sizwe's new identity as "Robert Zwelinzima" is confirmed by the photo he has taken, so his old identity is also bound up in a photograph: the picture in his passbook. For Sizwe Bansi's passbook—which must be shown when required by white authorities, including employers—lacked the permit that would enable him to remain in Port Elizabeth and work. As "Sizwe Bansi," he was unable to work, to travel, or to survive.

Sizwe is caught in the terrible paradoxes of apartheid. If he destroys his passbook, he cannot work, for he can't be hired without his passbook and work permit. If he keeps his passbook, he cannot work in the city, for he does not have the proper authorization. At this moment, Sizwe and his friend Buntu stumble on a dead man, Robert Zwelinzima, and strike on a plan to subvert the passbook laws, for Zwelinzima has a work permit valid for the city in his passbook. Buntu and Sizwe steal the book and replace Zwelinzima's picture with Sizwe's—now Sizwe *is* Robert Zwelinzima. To work in South Africa, Sizwe must give up his identity, deny his wife and children, and assume the name and Native Identity Number of another man. The play concludes where it began, with "Robert" rehearsing his new identity, killing off "Sizwe," and having his photograph taken: the acts now necessary to his survival. Although the play is a realistic account of life in South Africa, it also has an allegorical dimension, for the word *sizwe* means "wide country" and *bansi* means "the difficult land." In dying in order to live, Sizwe Bansi must give up his identity and sacrifice his wide and difficult land as well. Losing his name, Sizwe Bansi dramatizes the loss of identity of all Africans under apartheid.

SIZWE BANSI IS DEAD

Athol Fugard, John Kani, and Winston Ntshona

— CHARACTERS —

STYLES
SIZWE BANSI
BUNTU

STYLES' *Photographic Studio in the African township of New Brighton, Port Elizabeth. Positioned prominently, the name-board:*

> STYLES PHOTOGRAPHIC STUDIO. REFERENCE BOOKS;
> PASSPORTS; WEDDINGS; ENGAGEMENTS; BIRTHDAY
> PARTIES AND PARTIES.
> PROP. — STYLES.

Underneath this a display of photographs of various sizes. Centre stage, a table and chair. This is obviously used for photographs because a camera on a tripod stands ready a short distance away.

There is also another table, or desk, with odds and ends of photographic equipment and an assortment of 'props' for photographs.

The setting for this and subsequent scenes should be as simple as possible so that the action can be continuous.

STYLES *walks on with a newspaper. A dapper, alert young man wearing a white dustcoat and bowtie. He sits down at the table and starts to read the paper.*

STYLES: (*reading the headlines.*) 'Storm buffets Natal. Damage in many areas . . . trees snapped like . . . what? . . . match-sticks. . . .'

(*He laughs.*)

They're having it, boy! And I'm watching it . . . in the paper.

(*Turning the page, another headline.*)

5 'China: A question-mark on South West Africa.' What's China want there? Yo! They better be careful. China gets in there. . . ! (*Laugh.*) I'll tell you what happens. . . .

(*Stops abruptly. Looks around as if someone might be eavesdropping on his intimacy with the audience.*)

No comment.

(*Back to his paper.*)

What's this? . . . Ag! American politics. Nixon and all his
10 votes. Means buggerall to us.

(*Another page, another headline.*)

'Car plant expansion. 1.5 million rand plan.' *Ja.* I'll tell you what *that* means . . . more machines, bigger buildings . . . never any expansion to the pay-packet. Makes me fed-up. I know what I'm talking about. I worked at Ford one time. We
15 used to read in the newspaper . . . big headlines! . . . 'So and so from America or London made a big speech: ". . . going to see to it that the conditions of their non-white workers in Southern Africa were substantially improved."' The talk ended in the bloody newspaper. Never in the pay-packet.
20 Another time we read: Mr Henry Ford Junior Number two or whatever the hell he is . . . is visiting the Ford Factories in South Africa!

(*Shakes his head ruefully at the memory.*)

But news for us, man! When a big man like that visited the plant there was usually a few cents more in the pay-packet at
25 the end of the week.

Ja, a Thursday morning. I walked into the plant . . . 'Hey! What's this?' . . . Everything was quiet! Those big bloody machines that used to make so much noise made my head go around. . . ? Silent! Went to the notice-board and read: Mr Ford's visit today!
30 The one in charge of us . . . (*laugh*) hey! I remember him. General Foreman Mr 'Baas' Bradley. Good man that one, if you knew how to handle him . . . he called us all together:

(STYLES *mimics Mr 'Baas' Bradley. A heavy Afrikaans accent.*)

'Listen, boys, don't go to work on the line. There is going to be a General Cleaning first.'
35 I used to like General Cleaning. Nothing specific, you know, little bit here, little bit there. But that day! Yessus . . . in came the big machines with hot water and brushes — sort of electric mop — and God alone knows what else. We started on the floors. The oil and dirt under the machines was thick,
40 man. All the time the bosses were walking around watching us:

(*Slapping his hands together as he urges on the 'boys'.*)

'Come on, boys! It's got to be spotless! Big day for the plant!' Even the *big* boss, the one we only used to see lunch-times, walking to the canteen with a big cigar in his mouth and his hands in his pocket . . . that day? Sleeves rolled up, running
45 around us:
'Come on! Spotless, my boys! Over there, John. . . .' I thought: What the hell is happening? It was beginning to feel like hard work, man. I'm telling you we cleaned that place — spot-checked after fifteen minutes! . . . like you would have
50 thought it had just been built.
First stage of General Cleaning finished. We started on the second. Mr. 'Baas' Bradley came in with paint and brushes. I watched.
W — h — i — t — e l — i — n — e
55

(*Mr 'Baas' Bradley paints a long white line on the floor.*)

What's this? Been here five years and I never seen a white line before. Then:

Note: Some words and phrases are explained in a brief glossary at the end of the play.

(Mr 'Baas' Bradley at work with the paint-brush.)

CAREFUL THIS SIDE. TOW MOTOR IN MOTION.

(STYLES laughs.)

60 It was nice, man. Safety-precautions after six years. Then another gallon of paint.
Y—e—l—l—o—w l—i—n—e—
NO SMOKING IN THIS AREA. DANGER!
Then another gallon:
G—r—e—e—n l—i—n—e—
65 I noticed that that line cut off the roughcasting section, where we worked with the rough engine blocks as we got them from Iscor. Dangerous world that. Big machines! One mistake there and you're in trouble. I watched them and thought: What's going to happen here? When the green line was finished, down they went on the floor—Mr 'Baas' Bradley, the
70 lot!—with a big green board, a little brush, and a tin of white paint. EYE PROTECTION AREA. Then my big moment:
'Styles!'
'Yes, sir!'
75 *(Mr 'Baas' Bradley's heavy Afrikaans accent)* 'What do you say in your language for this? Eye Protection Area.'
It was easy man!
'Gqokra Izi Khuselo Zamehlo Kule Ndawo.'
Nobody wrote it!
80 'Don't bloody fool me, Styles!'
'No, sir!'
'Then spell it . . . slowly.'

(STYLES has a big laugh.)

Hey! That was my moment, man. Kneeling there on the floor . . . foreman, general foreman, plant supervisor, plant man-
85 ager . . . and Styles? Standing!

(Folds his arms as he acts out his part to the imaginary figures crouched on the floor.)

'G—q—o—k—r—a' . . . and on I went, with Mr 'Baas' Bradley painting and saying as he wiped away the sweat:
'You're not fooling me, hey!'
After that the green board went up. We all stood and admired
90 it. Plant was looking nice, man! Colourful!
Into the third phase of General Cleaning.
'Styles!'
'Yes, sir!'
'Tell all the boys they must now go to the bathroom and wash
95 themselves clean.'
We needed it! Into the bathroom, under the showers . . . hot water, soap . . . on a Thursday! Before ten? Yo! What's happening in the plant? The other chaps asked me: What's going on, Styles? I told them: 'Big-shot cunt from America coming
100 to visit you.' When we finished washing they gave us towels . . . *(laugh).*
Three hundred of us, man! We were so clean we felt shy! Stand there like little ladies in front of the mirror. From there to the General Store.
105 Handed in my dirty overall.
'Throw it on the floor.'
'Yes, sir!'
New overall comes, wrapped in plastic. Brand new, man! I normally take a thirty-eight but this one was a forty-two. Then

next door to the tool room . . . brand new tool bag, set of 110
spanners, shifting spanner, torque wrench—all of them brand new—and because I worked in the dangerous hot test section I was also given a new asbestos apron and fire-proof gloves to replace the ones I had lost about a year ago. I'm telling you I walked back heavy to my spot. Armstrong on the 115
moon! Inside the plant it was general meeting again. General Foreman Mr 'Baas' Bradley called me.
'Styles!'
'Yes, sir.'
'Come translate.' 120
'Yes, sir!'

(STYLES pulls out a chair. Mr 'Baas' Bradley speaks on one side, STYLES translates on the other.)

'Tell the boys in your language, that this is a very big day in their lives.'
'Gentlemen, this old fool says this is a hell of a big day in our lives.' 125
The men laughed.
'They are very happy to hear that, sir.'
'Tell the boys that Mr Henry Ford the Second, the owner of this place, is going to visit us. Tell them Mr Ford is the big Baas. He owns the plant and everything in it.' 130
'Gentlemen, old Bradley says this Ford is a big bastard. He owns everything in this building, which means you as well.'
A voice came out of the crowd:
'Is he a bigger fool than Bradley?'
'They're asking, sir, is he bigger than you?' 135
'Certainly . . . *(blustering)* . . . certainly. He is a very big baas. He's a . . . *(groping for words)* . . . he's a Makulu Baas.'
I loved that one!
'Mr "Baas" Bradley says most certainly Mr Ford is bigger than him. In fact Mr Ford is the grandmother baas of them all . . . 140
that's what he said to me.'
'Styles, tell the boys that when Mr Henry Ford comes into the plant I want them all to look happy. We will slow down the speed of the line so that they can sing and smile while they are working.' 145
'Gentlemen, he says that when the door opens and his grandmother walks in you must see to it that you are wearing a mask of smiles. Hide your true feelings, brothers. You must sing. The joyous songs of the days of old before we had fools like this one next to me to worry about.' *(To Bradley.)* 'Yes, sir!' 150
'Say to them, Styles, that they must try to impress Mr Henry Ford that they are better than those monkeys in his own country, those niggers in Harlem who know nothing but strike, strike.'
Yo! I liked that one too. 155
'Gentlemen, he says we must remember, when Mr Ford walks in, that we are South African monkeys, not American monkeys. South African monkeys are much better trained. . . .'
Before I could even finish, a voice was shouting out of the crowd: 160
'He's talking shit!' I had to be careful!

(Servile and full of smiles as he turns back to Bradley.)

'No, sir! The men say they are much too happy to behave like those American monkeys.'

165 Right! Line was switched on nice and slow—and we started working.

(At work on the Assembly Line; singing.)

'Tshotsholoza . . . Tshotsholoza . . . kulezondawo. . . .'
We had all the time in the world, man! . . . torque wrench out . . . tighten the cylinder-head nut . . . wait for the next one. . . .
(Singing) 'Vyabaleka . . . vyabaleka . . . kulezondawo. . . .' I
170 kept my eye on the front office. I could see them—Mr 'Baas' Bradley, the line supervisor—through the big glass window, brushing their hair, straightening the tie. There was some General Cleaning going on there too.

(He laughs.)

We were watching them. Nobody was watching us. Even the
175 old Security Guard. The one who every time he saw a black man walk past with his hands in his pockets he saw another spark-plug walk out of the plant. Today? To hell and gone there on the other side polishing his black shoes.
Then, through the window, I saw three long black Galaxies
180 zoom up. I passed the word down the line: He's come!
Let me tell you what happened. The big doors opened; next thing the General Superintendent, Line Supervisor, General Foreman, Manager, Senior Manager, Managing Director . . . the bloody lot were there . . . like a pack of puppies!

(Mimics a lot of fawning men retreating before an important person.)

185 I looked and laughed! 'Yessus, Styles, they're all playing your part today!' They ran, man! In came a tall man, six foot six, hefty, full of respect and dignity . . . I marvelled at him! Let me show you what he did.
(Three enormous strides) One . . . two . . . three. . . . *(Cursory*
190 *look around as he turns and takes the same three strides back.)*
One . . . two . . . three . . . OUT! Into the Galaxie and gone! That's all. Didn't talk to me, Mr 'Baas' Bradley, Line Supervisor, or anybody. He didn't even look at the plant! And what did I see when those three Galaxies disappeared? The white
195 staff at the main switchboard.
'Double speed on the line! Make up for production lost!'
It ended up with us working harder that bloody day than ever before. Just because that big. . . . *(shakes his head.)*
Six years there. Six years a bloody fool.

(Back to his newspaper. A few more headlines with appropriate comment, then. . . .)

200 *(Reading)* 'The Mass Murderer! Doom!'

(Smile of recognition.)

'For fleas . . . Doom. Flies . . . Doom. Bedbugs . . . Doom. For cockroaches and other household pests. The household insecticide . . . Doom.' Useful stuff. Remember, Styles? *Ja.*
(To the audience.) After all that time at Ford I sat down one
205 day. I said to myself:
'Styles, you're a bloody monkey, boy!'
'What do you mean?'
'You're a monkey, man.'
'Go to hell!'
210 'Come on, Styles, you're a monkey, man, and you know it. Run up and down the whole bloody day! Your life doesn't

belong to you. You've sold it. For what, Styles? Gold wristwatch in twenty-five years time when they sign you off because you're too old for anything any more?'
I was right. I took a good look at my life. What did I see? A 215
bloody circus monkey! Selling most of his time on this earth to another man. Out of every twenty-four hours I could only properly call mine the six when I was sleeping. What the hell is the use of that?
Think about it, friend. Wake up in the morning, half-past six, 220
out of the pyjamas and into the bath-tub, put on your shirt with one hand, socks with the other, realize you got your shoes on the wrong bloody feet, and all the time the seconds are passing and if you don't hurry up you'll miss the bus. . . .
'Get the lunch, dear. I'm late. My lunch, please, darling! . . . 225
then the children come in . . . 'Daddy, can I have this? Daddy, I want money for that.' 'Go to your mother. I haven't got time. Look after the children, please, sweetheart!!' . . . grab your lunch . . . 'Bye Bye!!' and then run like I-don't-know-what for the bus stop. You call that living? I went back 230
to myself for another chat:
'Suppose you're right. What then?'
'Try something else.'
'Like what?'
Silly question to ask. I knew what I was going to say. Photog- 235
rapher! It was my hobby in those days. I used to pick up a few cents on the side taking cards at parties, weddings, big occasions. But when it came to telling my wife and parents that I wanted to turn professional . . . !!
My father was the worst. 240
'You call that work? Click-click with a camera. Are you mad?'
I tried to explain. 'Daddy, if I could stand on my own two feet and not be somebody else's tool, I'd have some respect for myself. I'd be a man.'
'What do you mean? Aren't you one already? You're circum- 245
cised, you've got a wife. . . .'
Talk about the generation gap!
Anyway I thought: To hell with them. I'm trying it.
It was the Christmas shutdown, so I had lots of time to look around for a studio. My friend Dhlamini at the Funeral Par- 250
lour told me about a vacant room next door. He encouraged me. I remember his words. 'Grab your chance, Styles. Grab it before somebody in my line puts you in a box and closes the lid.' I applied for permission to use the room as a studio. After some time the first letter back: 255
'Your application has been received and is being considered.'
A month later: 'The matter is receiving the serious consideration of the Board.' Another month: 'Your application is now on the director's table.' I nearly gave up, friends. But one day, a knock at the door—the postman—I had to sign for a regis- 260
tered letter. 'We are pleased to inform you. . . .'

(STYLES has a good laugh.)

I ran all the way to the Administration Offices, grabbed the key, ran all the way back to Red Location, unlocked the door, and walked in!
What I found sobered me up a little bit. Window panes were 265
all broken; big hole in the roof, cobwebs in the corners. I didn't let that put me off though. Said to myself: 'This is your chance, Styles. Grab it.' Some kids helped me clean it out. The dust! Yo! When the broom walked in the Sahara Desert

270 walked out! But at the end of that day it was reasonably clean.
I stood here in the middle of the floor, straight! You know
what that means? To stand straight in a place of your own? To
be your own . . . General Foreman, Mr 'Baas', Line Supervisor—the lot! I was tall, six foot six and doing my own in-
275 spection of the plant.
So I'm standing there—here—feeling big and what do I see
on the walls? Cockroaches. *Ja*, cockroaches . . . in *my* place. I
don't mean those little things that run all over the place when
you pull out the kitchen drawer. I'm talking about the big
280 bastards, the paratroopers as we call them. I didn't like them.
I'm not afraid of them but I just don't like them! All over. On
the floors, the walls. I heard the one on the wall say: 'What's
going on? Who opened the door?' The one on the floor answered: 'Relax. He won't last. This place is condemned.'
285 That's when I thought: Doom.
Out of here and into the Chinaman's shop. 'Good day, sir.
I've got a problem. Cockroaches.'
The Chinaman didn't even think, man, he just said: 'Doom!'
I said: 'Certainly.' He said: 'Doom, seventy-five cents a tin.'
290 Paid him for two and went back. Yo! You should have seen
me! Two-tin Charlie!

(His two tins at the ready, forefingers on the press-buttons,
STYLES *gives us a graphic re-enactment of what happened. There
is a brief respite to 'reload'—shake the tins—and tie a handkerchief around his nose after which he returns to the fight.*
STYLES *eventually backs through the imaginary door, still firing,
and closes it. Spins the tins and puts them into their holsters.)*

I went home to sleep. *I went to sleep.* Not them *(the cockroaches)*. What do you think happened here? General meeting under the floorboards. All the bloody survivors. The old
295 professor addressed them: 'Brothers, we face a problem of serious pollution . . . contamination! The menace appears to be
called Doom. I have recommended a general inoculation of
the whole community. Everybody in line, please. *(Inoculation proceeds.)* Next . . . next . . . next. . . .' While poor old
300 Styles is smiling in his sleep! Next morning I walked in. . . .
(He stops abruptly.) . . . What's this? Cockroach walking on
the floor? Another one on the ceiling? Not a damn! Doom did
it yesterday. Doom does it today. *(Whips out the two tins and
goes in fighting. This time, however, it is not long before they*
305 *peter out.)* Pssssssss . . . pssssss . . . pssss . . . pss *(a last
desperate shake, but he barely manages to get out a squirt.)*
Pss.
No bloody good! The old bastard on the floor just waved his
feelers in the air as if he was enjoying air-conditioning.
310 I went next door to Dhlamini and told him about my problem. He laughed. 'Doom? You're wasting your time, Styles.
You want to solve your problem, get a cat. What do you think
a cat lives on in the township? Milk? If there's any the baby
gets it. Meat? When the family sees it only once a week?
315 Mice? The little boys got rid of them years ago. Insects, man,
township cats are insect-eaters. Here. . . .'
He gave me a little cat. I'm . . . I'm not too fond of cats
normally. This one was called Blackie . . . I wasn't too fond of
that name either. But . . . Kitsy! Kitsy! Kitsy! . . . little Blackie
320 followed me back to the studio.
The next morning when I walked in what do you think I saw?
Wings. I smiled. Because one thing I do know is that no cockroach can take his wings off. He's dead!

(Proud gesture taking in the whole of his studio.)

So here it is!

(To his name-board.)

'Styles Photographic Studio. Reference Books; Passports; 325
Weddings; Engagements; Birthday Parties and Parties. Proprietor: Styles.'
When you look at this, what do you see? Just another photographic studio? Where people come because they've lost their
Reference Book and need a photo for the new one? That I sit 330
them down, set up the camera . . . 'No expression, please.' . . .
click-click . . . 'Come back tomorrow, please' . . . and then
kick them out and wait for the next? No, friend. It's more than
just that. This is a strong-room of dreams. The dreamers? My
people. The simple people, who you never find mentioned in 335
the history books, who never get statues erected to them, or
monuments commemorating their great deeds. People who
would be forgotten, and their dreams with them, if it wasn't
for Styles. That's what I do, friends. Put down, in my way, on
paper the dreams and hopes of my people so that even their 340
children's children will remember a man . . . 'This was our
Grandfather' . . . and say his name. Walk into the houses of
New Brighton and on the walls you'll find hanging the story
of the people the writers of the big books forget about.

(To his display-board.)

This one *(a photograph)* walked in here one morning. I was 345
just passing the time. Midweek. Business is always slow then.
Anyway, a knock at the door. Yes! I must explain something. I
get two types of knock here. When I hear . . . *(knocks solemnly on the table)* . . . I don't even look up, man. 'Funeral
parlour is next door.' But when I hear . . . *(energetic rap on the* 350
table . . . he laughs) . . . that's *my* sound, and I shout 'Come in!'
In walked a chap, full of smiles, little parcel under his arm.
I can still see him, man!

(STYLES *acts both roles.)*

'Mr Styles?'
I said: 'Come in!' 355
'Mr Styles, I've come to take a snap, Mr Styles.'
I said: 'Sit down! Sit down, my friend!'
'No, Mr Styles. I want to take the snap standing. *(Barely con-
taining his suppressed excitement and happiness)* Mr Styles,
take the card, please!' 360
I said: 'Certainly, friend.'
Something you mustn't do is interfere with a man's dream. If
he wants to do it standing, let him stand. If he wants to sit, let
him sit. Do exactly what they want! Sometimes they come in
here, all smart in a suit, then off comes the jacket and shoes 365
and socks . . . *(adopts a boxer's stance)* . . . 'Take it, Mr Styles.
Take it!' And I take it. No questions! Start asking stupid questions and you destroy that dream. Anyway, this chap I'm telling you about . . . *(laughing warmly as he remembers)* . . . I've
seen a lot of smiles in my business, friends, but that one gets 370
first prize. I set up my camera, and just as I was ready to go . . .
'Wait, wait, Mr Styles! I want you to take the card with this.'
Out of his parcel came a long piece of white paper . . . looked
like some sort of document . . . he held it in front of him.
(STYLES *demonstrates.)* For once I didn't have to say, 'Smile!' 375
Just: 'Hold it!' . . . and, click, . . . finished. I asked him what
the document was.

'You see, Mr Styles, I'm forty-eight years old. I work twenty-two years for the municipality and the foreman kept on saying to me if I want promotion to Boss-boy I must try to better my education. I didn't write well, Mr Styles. So I took a course with the Damelin Correspondence College. Seven years, Mr Styles! And at last I made it. Here it is. Standard Six Certificate, School Leaving, Third Class! I made it, Mr Styles. I made it. But I'm not finished. I'm going to take up for the Junior Certificate, then Matric . . . and you watch, Mr Styles. One day I walk out of my house, graduate, self-made! Bye-bye, Mr Styles,' . . . and he walked out of here happy man, self-made.

(Back to his display-board; another photograph.)

My best. Family Card. You know the Family Card? Good for business. Lot of people and they all want copies.
One Saturday morning. Suddenly a hell of a noise outside in the street. I thought: What's going on now? Next thing that door burst open and in they came! First the little ones, then the five- and six-year-olds. . . . I didn't know what was going on, man! Stupid children, coming to mess up my place. I was still trying to chase them out when the bigger boys and girls came through the door. Then it clicked. Family Card!

(Changing his manner abruptly.)

'Come in! Come in!'

(Ushering a crowd of people into his studio.)

. . . now the young men and women were coming in, then the mothers and fathers, uncles and aunties . . . the eldest son, a mature man, and finally . . .

(Shaking his head with admiration at the memory.)

the Old Man, the Grandfather! *(The 'old man' walks slowly and with dignity into the studio and sits down in the chair.)* I looked at him. His grey hair was a sign of wisdom. His face, weather-beaten and lined with experience. Looking at it was like paging the volume of his history, written by himself. He was a living symbol of Life, of all it means and does to a man. I adored him. He sat there — half smiling, half serious — as if he had already seen the end of his road.
The eldest son said to me: 'Mr Styles, this is my father, my mother, my brothers and sisters, their wives and husbands, our children. Twenty-seven of us, Mr Styles. We have come to take a card. My father. . . ,' he pointed to the old man, '. . . my father always wanted it.'
I said: 'Certainly. Leave the rest to me.' I went to work.

(Another graphic re-enactment of the scene as he describes it.)

The old lady here, the eldest son there. Then the other one, with the other one. On this side I did something with the daughters, aunties, and one bachelor brother. Then in front of it all the eight-to-twelves, standing, in front of them the four-to-sevens, kneeling, and finally right on the floor everything that was left, sitting. Jesus, it was hard work, but finally I had them all sorted out and I went behind the camera.

(Behind his camera.)

Just starting to focus . . .

(Imaginary child in front of the lens; STYLES chases the child back to the family group.)

'. . . Sit down! Sit down!'
Back to the camera, start to focus again. . . . Not One Of Them Was Smiling! I tried the old trick. 'Say cheese, please.' At first they just looked at me. 'Come on! Cheese!' The children were the first to pick it up.
(Child's voice.) 'Cheese. Cheese. Cheese.' Then the ones a little bit bigger — 'Cheese' — then the next lot — 'Cheese' — the uncles and aunties — 'Cheese' — and finally the old man himself — 'Cheese'! I thought the roof was going off, man! People outside in the street came and looked through the window. They joined in: 'Cheese.' When I looked again the mourners from the funeral parlour were there wiping away their tears and saying 'Cheese'. Pressed my little button and there it was — New Brighton's smile, twenty-seven variations. Don't you believe those bloody fools who make out we don't know how to smile!
Anyway, you should have seen me then. Moved the bachelor this side, sister-in-laws that side. Put the eldest son behind the old man. Reorganized the children. . . . *(Back behind his camera.)* 'Once again, please! Cheese!' Back to work . . . old man and old woman together, daughters behind them, sons on the side. Those that were kneeling now standing, those that were standing, now kneeling. . . . Ten times, friends! Each one different!

(An exhausted STYLES collapses in a chair.)

When they walked out finally I almost said Never Again! A week later the eldest son came back for the cards. I had them ready. The moment he walked through that door I could see he was in trouble. He said to me: 'Mr Styles, we almost didn't make it. My father died two days after the card. He will never see it.' 'Come on,' I said. 'You're a man. One day or the other everyone of us must go home. Here. . . .' I grabbed the cards. 'Here. Look at your father and thank God for the time he was given on this earth.' We went through them together. He looked at them in silence. After the third one, the tear went slowly down his cheek.
But at the same time . . . I was watching him carefully . . . something started to happen as he saw his father there with himself, his brothers and sisters, and all the little grandchildren. He began to smile. 'That's it, brother,' I said. 'Smile! Smile at your father. Smile at the world.'
When he left, I thought of him going back to his little house somewhere in New Brighton, filled that day with the little mothers in black because a man had died. I saw my cards passing from hand to hand. I saw hands wipe away tears, and then the first timid little smiles.
You must understand one thing. We own nothing except ourselves. This world and its laws, allows us nothing, except ourselves. There is nothing we can leave behind when we die, except the memory of ourselves. I know what I'm talking about, friends — I had a father, and he died.

(To the display-board.)

Here he is. My father. That's him. Fought in the war. Second World War. Fought at Tobruk. In Egypt. He fought in France so that this country and all the others could stay Free. When he came back they stripped him at the docks — his gun, his uniform, the dignity they'd allowed him for a few mad years because the world needed men to fight and be ready to sacrifice themselves for something called Freedom. In return they

let him keep his scoff-tin and gave him a bicycle. Size twenty-
eight. I remember, because it was too big for me. When he
died, in a rotten old suitcase amongst some of his old rags, I
485   found that photograph. That's all. That's all I have from him.

(The display-board again.)

Or this old lady. Mrs. Matothlana. Used to stay in Sangocha
Street. You remember! Her husband was arrested. . . .

(Knock at the door.)

Tell you about it later. Come in!

(A MAN *walks nervously into the studio. Dressed in an ill-fitting
new double-breasted suit. He is carrying a plastic bag with a hat
in it. His manner is hesitant and shy.* STYLES *takes one look at
him and breaks into an enormous smile.)*

490   *(An aside to the audience.)* A Dream!
       (To the man.) Come in, my friend.
MAN: Mr Styles?
STYLES: That's me. Come in! You have come to take a card?
MAN: Snap.
STYLES: Yes, a card. Have you got a deposit?
495 MAN: Yes.
STYLES: Good. Let me just take your name down. You see, you
       pay deposit now, and when you come for the card, you pay
       the rest.
MAN: Yes.
500 STYLES: *(to his desk and a black book for names and addresses.)*
       What is your name? *(The man hesitates, as if not sure of
       himself.)*
       Your name, please?

(Pause.)

Come on, my friend. You must surely have a name.
505 MAN: *(pulling himself together, but still very nervous.)* Robert
       Zwelinzima.
STYLES: *(writing.)* 'Robert Zwelinzima.' Address?
MAN: *(swallowing.)* Fifty, Mapija Street.
STYLES: *(writes, then pauses.)* 'Fifty, Mapija?'
510 MAN: Yes.
STYLES: You staying with Buntu?
MAN: Buntu.
STYLES: Very good somebody that one. Came here for his Wed-
       ding Card. Always helping people. If that man was white
515   they'd call him a liberal.

(Now finished writing. Back to his customer.)

All right. How many cards do you want?
MAN: One card.
STYLES: *(disappointed.)* Only one?
MAN: One.
520 STYLES: How do you want to take the card?

(The man is not sure of what the question means.)

You can take the card standing . . .

*(*STYLES *strikes a stylish pose next to the table.)*

sitting . . .

(Another pose . . . this time in the chair.)

anyhow. How do you want it?

MAN: Anyhow.
STYLES: Right. Sit down.   525

*(*ROBERT *hesitates.)*

Sit down!

*(*STYLES *fetches a vase with plastic flowers, dusts them off, and
places them on the table.* ROBERT *holds up his plastic bag.)*

What you got there?

(Out comes the hat.)

Aha! Stetson. Put it on, my friend.

*(*ROBERT *handles it shyly.)*

You can put it on, Robert.

*(*ROBERT *pulls it on.* STYLES *does up one of his jacket buttons.)*

What a beautiful suit, my friend! Where did you buy it?   530
MAN: Sales House.
STYLES: *(quoting a sales slogan.)* 'Where the Black world buys
       the best. Six months to pay. Pay as you wear.'

(Nudges ROBERT.*)*

. . . and they never repossess!

(They share a laugh.)

What are you going to do with this card?   535

*(Chatting away as he goes to his camera and sets it up for the
photo.* ROBERT *watches the preparations apprehensively.)*

MAN: Send it to my wife.
STYLES: Your wife!
MAN: Nowetu.
STYLES: Where's your wife?
MAN: King William's Town.   540
STYLES: *(exaggerated admiration.)* At last! The kind of man I
       like. Not one of those foolish young boys who come here to
       find work and then forget their families back home. A man,
       with responsibility!
       Where do you work?   545
MAN: Feltex.
STYLES: I hear they pay good there.
MAN: Not bad.

(He is now very tense, staring fixedly at the camera. STYLES
straightens up behind it.)

STYLES: Come on, Robert! You want your wife to get a card with
       her husband looking like he's got all the worries in the world 550
       on his back? What will she think? 'My poor husband is in
       trouble!' You must smile!

*(*ROBERT *shamefacedly relaxes a little and starts to smile.)*

That's it!

*(He relaxes still more. Beginning to enjoy himself. Uncertainly
produces a very fancy pipe from one of his pockets.* STYLES *now
really warming to the assignment.)*

Look, have you ever walked down the passage to the office
with the big glass door and the board outside: 'Manager—   555
Bestuurder.' Imagine it, man, you, Robert Zwelinzima, behind a desk in an office like that! It can happen, Robert.
Quick promotion to Chief Messenger. I'll show you what we do.

(STYLES *produces a Philips' class-room map of the world, which he hangs behind the table as a backdrop to the photo.*)

Look at it, Robert. America, England, Africa, Russia, Asia!

(*Carried away still further by his excitement.* STYLES *finds a cigarette, lights it, and gives it to* ROBERT *to hold. The latter is now ready for the 'card' . . . pipe in one hand and cigarette in the other.* STYLES *stands behind his camera and admires his handiwork.*)

560   Mr Robert Zwelinzima, Chief Messenger at Feltex, sitting in his office with the world behind him. Smile, Robert. Smile!

(*Studying his subject through the viewfinder of the camera.*)

Lower your hand, Robert . . . towards the ashtray . . . more . . . now make a four with your legs. . . .

(*He demonstrates behind the camera.* ROBERT *crosses his legs.*)

Hold it, Robert. . . . Keep on smiling . . . that's it. . . . (*presses
565   the release button — the shutter clicks.*)
Beautiful! All right, Robert.

(ROBERT *and his smile remain frozen.*)

Robert. You can relax now. It's finished!
MAN: Finished?
STYLES: Yes. You just want the one card?
570   MAN: Yes.
STYLES: What happens if you lose it? Hey? I've heard stories about those postmen, Robert. Yo! Sit on the side of the road and open the letters they should be delivering! 'Dear wife . . .' — one rand this side, letter thrown away. 'Dear wife . . .' —
575   another rand this side, letter thrown away. You want that to happen to you? Come on! What about a movie, man?
MAN: Movie?
STYLES: Don't you know the movie?
MAN: No.
580   STYLES: Simple! You just walk you see . . .

(STYLES *demonstrates; at a certain point freezes in mid-stride.*)

. . . and I take the card! Then you can write to your wife: 'Dear wife, I am coming home at Christmas. . . .' Put the card in your letter and post it. Your wife opens the letter and what does she see? Her Robert, walking home to her! She shows it
585   to the children. 'Look, children, your daddy is coming!' The children jump and clap their hands: 'Daddy is coming! Daddy is coming!'
MAN: (*excited by the picture* STYLES *has conjured up.*) All right!
STYLES: You want a movie?
590   MAN: I want a movie.
STYLES: That's my man! Look at this, Robert.

(STYLES *reverses the map hanging behind the table to reveal a gaudy painting of a futuristic city.*)

City of the Future! Look at it. Mr Robert Zwelinzima, man about town, future head of Feltex, walking through the City of the Future!
595   MAN: (*examining the backdrop with admiration. He recognizes a landmark*). OK.
STYLES: OK Bazaars . . . (*the other buildings*) . . . Mutual Building Society, Barclays Bank . . . the lot!
What you looking for, Robert?

MAN: Feltex.   600
STYLES: Yes . . . well, you see, I couldn't fit everything on, Robert. But if I had had enough space Feltex would have been here.

(*To his table for props.*)

Walking-stick . . . newspaper. . . .
MAN: (*diffidently*) I don't read.
STYLES: That is not important, my friend. You think all those   605
monkeys carrying newspapers can read? They look at the pictures.

(*After 'dressing'* ROBERT *with the props he moves back to his camera.*)

This is going to be beautiful, Robert. My best card. I must send one to the magazines.
All right, Robert, now move back. Remember what I showed   610
you. Just walk towards me and right in front of the City of the Future. I'll take the picture. Ready? Now come, Robert. . . .

(*Pipe in mouth, walking-stick in hand, newspaper under the other arm,* ROBERT *takes a jaunty step and then freezes, as* STYLES *had shown him earlier.*)

Come, Robert. . . .

(*Another step.*)

Just one more, Robert. . . .

(*Another step.*)

Stop! Hold it, Robert. Hold it!   615

(*The camera flash goes off; simultaneously a blackout except for one light on* ROBERT, *frozen in the pose that will appear in the picture. We are in fact looking at the photograph. It 'comes to life' and dictates the letter that will accompany it to* NOWETU *in King William's Town.*)

MAN: Nowetu . . .

(*Correcting himself.*)

Dear Nowetu,
I've got wonderful news for you in this letter. My troubles are over, I think. You won't believe it, but I must tell you. Sizwe Bansi, in a manner of speaking, is dead! I'll tell you what I can.   620
As you know, when I left the Railway Compound I went to stay with a friend of mine called Zola. A very good friend that, Nowetu. In fact he was even trying to help me find some job. But that's not easy, Nowetu, because Port Elizabeth is a big place, a very big place with lots of factories but also lots of   625
people looking for a job like me. There are so many men, Nowetu, who have left their places because they are dry and have come here to find work!
After a week with Zola, I was in big trouble. The headman came around, and after a lot of happenings which I will tell   630
you when I see you, they put a stamp in my passbook which said I must leave Port Elizabeth at once in three days time. I was very much unhappy, Nowetu. I couldn't stay with Zola because if the headman found me there again my troubles would be even bigger. So Zola took me to a friend of his called   635
Buntu, and asked him if I could stay with him until I decided what to do. . . .

(BUNTU's *house in New Brighton. Table and two chairs.* ROBERT, *in a direct continuation of the preceding scene, is already there, as* BUNTU, *jacket slung over his shoulder, walks in. Holds out his hand to* ROBERT.)

BUNTU: Hi. Buntu.

(They shake hands.)

MAN: Sizwe Bansi.

640 BUNTU: Sit down.

(They sit.)

Zola told me you were coming. Didn't have time to explain anything. Just asked if you could spend a few nights here. You can perch yourself on that sofa in the corner. I'm alone at the moment. My wife is a domestic . . . sleep-in at Kabega Park . . .
645 only comes home weekends. Hot today, hey?

(In the course of this scene BUNTU *will busy himself first by having a wash — basin and jug of water on the table — and then by changing from his working clothes preparatory to going out.* SIZWE BANSI *stays in his chair.)*

What's your problem, friend?

MAN: I've got no permit to stay in Port Elizabeth.

BUNTU: Where do you have a permit to stay?

MAN: King William's Town.

650 BUNTU: How did they find out?

MAN: *(tells his story with the hesitation and uncertainty of the illiterate. When words fail him he tries to use his hands.)* I was staying with Zola, as you know. I was very happy there. But one night . . . I was sleeping on the floor . . . I heard some
655 noises and when I looked up I saw torches shining in through the window . . . then there was a loud knocking on the door. When I got up Zola was there in the dark . . . he was trying to whisper something. I think he was saying I must hide. So I crawled under the table. The headman came in and looked
660 around and found me hiding under the table . . . and dragged me out.

BUNTU: Raid?

MAN: Yes, it was a raid. I was just wearing my pants. My shirt was lying on the other side. I just managed to grab it as they
665 were pushing me out. . . . I finished dressing in the van. They drove straight to the administration office . . . and then from there they drove to the Labour Bureau. I was made to stand in the passage there, with everybody looking at me and shaking their heads like they knew I was in big trouble. Later I was
670 taken into an office and made to stand next to the door. . . . The white man behind the desk had my book and he also looked at me and shook his head. Just then one other white man came in with a card. . . .

BUNTU: A card?

675 MAN: He was carrying a card.

BUNTU: Pink card?

MAN: Yes, the card was pink.

BUNTU: Record card. Your whole bloody life is written down on that. Go on.

680 MAN: Then the first white man started writing something on the card . . . and just then somebody came in carrying a. . . .

(demonstrates what he means by banging a clenched fist on the table.)

BUNTU: A stamp?

MAN: Yes, a stamp. *(Repeats the action.)* He was carrying a stamp.

BUNTU: And then?   685

MAN: He put it on my passbook.

BUNTU: Let me see your book?

*(*SIZWE *produces his passbook from the back-pocket of his trousers.* BUNTU *examines it.)*

Shit! You know what this is? *(The stamp.)*

MAN: I can't read.

BUNTU: Listen . . . *(reads).* 'You are required to report to the   690
Bantu Affairs Commissioner, King William's Town, within three days of the above-mentioned date for the. . . .' You should have been home yesterday! . . . 'for the purpose of repatriation to home district.' Influx Control.
You're in trouble, Sizwe.   695

MAN: I don't want to leave Port Elizabeth.

BUNTU: Maybe. But if that book says go, you go.

MAN: Can't I maybe burn this book and get a new one?

BUNTU: Burn that book? Stop kidding yourself, Sizwe! Anyway suppose you do. You must immediately go apply for a new   700
one. Right? And until that new one comes, be careful the police don't stop you and ask for your book. Into the Court-room, brother. Charge: Failing to produce Reference Book on Demand. Five rand or five days. Finally the new book comes. Down to the Labour Bureau for a stamp . . . it's got to   705
be endorsed with permission to be in this area. White man at the Labour Bureau takes the book, looks at it — doesn't look at you! — goes to the big machine and feeds in your number . . .

*(*BUNTU *goes through the motions of punching out a number on a computer.)*

. . . card jumps out, he reads: 'Sizwe Bansi. Endorsed to King William's Town. . . .' Takes your book, fetches that same   710
stamp, and in it goes again. So you burn that book, or throw it away, and get another one. Same thing happens.

*(*BUNTU *feeds the computer; the card jumps out.)*

'Sizwe Bansi. Endorsed to King William's Town. . . .' Stamp goes in the third time. . . . But this time it's also into a van and off to the Native Commissioner's Office; card around your   715
neck with your number on it; escort on both sides and back to King William's Town. They make you pay for the train fare too!

MAN: I think I will try to look for some jobs in the garden.

BUNTU: You? Job as a garden-boy? Don't you read the newspapers?

MAN: I can't read.   720

BUNTU: I'll tell you what the little white ladies say: 'Domestic vacancies. I want a garden-boy with good manners and a wide knowledge of seasons and flowers. Book in order.' Yours in order? Anyway what the hell do you know about seasons and flowers? *(After a moment's thought.)* Do you know any white   725
man who's prepared to give you a job?

MAN: No. I don't know any white man.

BUNTU: Pity. We might have been able to work something then. You talk to the white man, you see, and ask him to write a letter saying he's got a job for you. You take that letter from the   730
white man and go back to King William's Town, where you show it to the Native Commissioner there. The Native Com-missioner in King William's Town reads that letter from the

735 white man in Port Elizabeth who is ready to give you the job. He then writes a letter back to the Native Commissioner in Port Elizabeth. So you come back here with the two letters. Then the Native Commissioner in Port Elizabeth reads the letter from the Native Commissioner in King William's Town together with the first letter from the white man who is pre-
740 pared to give you a job, and he says when he reads the letters: Ah yes, this man Sizwe Bansi can get a job. So the Native Commissioner in Port Elizabeth then writes a letter which you take with the letters from the Native Commissioner in King William's Town and the white man in Port Elizabeth, to
745 the Senior Officer at the Labour Bureau, who reads all the letters. Then he will put the right stamp in your book and give you another letter from himself which together with the let-ters from the white man and the two Native Affairs Commis-sioners, you take to the Administration Office here in New
750 Brighton and make an application for Residence Permit, so that you don't fall victim of raids again. Simple.

MAN: Maybe I can start a little business selling potatoes and. . . .

BUNTU: Where do you get the potatoes and. . . ?

MAN: I'll buy them.

755 BUNTU: With what?

MAN: Borrow some money. . . .

BUNTU: Who is going to lend money to a somebody endorsed to hell and gone out in the bush? And how you going to buy your potatoes at the market without a Hawker's Licence?
760 Same story, Sizwe. You won't get that because of the bloody stamp in your book.
There's no way out, Sizwe. You're not the first one who has tried to find it. Take my advice and catch that train back to King William's Town. If you need work so bad go knock on
765 the door of the Mines Recruiting Office. Dig gold for the white man. That's the only time they don't worry about Influx Control.

MAN: I don't want to work on the mines. There is no money there. And it's dangerous, under the ground. Many black
770 men get killed when the rocks fall. You can die there.

BUNTU: (stopped by the last remark into taking possibly his first real look at SIZWE.) You don't want to die.

MAN: I don't want to die.

BUNTU: (stops whatever he is doing to sit down and talk to SIZWE
775 with an intimacy that was not there before.) You married, Sizwe?

MAN: Yes.

BUNTU: How many children?

MAN: I've got four children.

780 BUNTU: Boys? Girls?

MAN: I've got three boys and one girl.

BUNTU: Schooling?

MAN: Two are schooling. The other two stay at home with their mother.

785 BUNTU: Your wife is not working.

MAN: The place where we stay is fifteen miles from town. There is only one shop there. Baas van Wyk. He has already got a woman working for him. King William's Town is a dry place Mr Buntu . . . very small and too many people. That is why I
790 don't want to go back.

BUNTU: Ag, friend . . . I don't know! I'm also married. One child.

MAN: Only one?

BUNTU: Ja, my wife attends this Birth Control Clinic rubbish. The child is staying with my mother.
795 (Shaking his head.) Hai, Sizwe! If I had to tell you the trouble I had before I could get the right stamps in my book, even though I was born in this area! The trouble I had before I could get a decent job . . . born in this area! The trouble I had to get this two-roomed house . . . born in this area!

800 MAN: Why is there so much trouble, Mr Buntu?

BUNTU: Two weeks back I went to a funeral with a friend of mine. Out in the country. An old relative of his passed away. Usual thing . . . sermons in the house, sermons in the church, sermons at the graveside. I thought they were never
805 going to stop talking!
At the graveside service there was one fellow, a lay preacher . . . short man, neat little moustache, wearing one of those old-fashioned double-breasted black suits. . . . Haai! He was won-derful. While he talked he had a gesture with his hands . . .
810 like this . . . that reminded me of our youth, when we learnt to fight with kieries. His text was 'Going Home'. He handled it well, Sizwe. Started by saying that the first man to sign the Death Contract with God, was Adam, when he sinned in Eden. Since that day, wherever Man is, or whatever he does,
815 he is never without his faithful companion, Death. So with Outa Jacob . . . the dead man's name . . . he has at last accepted the terms of his contract with God.
But in his life, friends, he walked the roads of this land. He helped print those footpaths which lead through the bush and
820 over the veld . . . footpaths which his children are now walk-ing. He worked on farms from this district down to the coast and north as far as Pretoria. I knew him. He was a friend. Many people knew Outa Jacob. For a long time he worked for Baas van der Walt. But when the old man died his young son
825 Hendrik said: 'I don't like you. Go!' Outa Jacob picked up his load and put it on his shoulders. His wife followed. He went to the next farm . . . through the fence, up to the house. . . : 'Work, please, Baas.' Baas Potgieter took him. He stayed a long time there too, until one day there was trouble between
830 the Madam and his wife. Jacob and his wife were walking again. The load on his back was heavier, he wasn't so young any more, and there were children behind them now as well. On to the next farm. No work. The next one. No work. Then the next one. A little time there. But the drought was bad and
835 the farmer said: 'Sorry, Jacob. The cattle are dying. I'm mov-ing to the city.' Jacob picked up his load yet again. So it went, friends. On and on . . . until he arrived there. (The grave at his feet.) Now at last it's over. No matter how hard-arsed the boer on this farm wants to be, he cannot move Outa Jacob.
840 He has reached Home.

(Pause.)

That's it, brother. The only time we'll find peace is when they dig a hole for us and press our face into the earth.

(Putting on his coat.)

Ag, to hell with it. If we go on like this much longer we'll do the digging for them.

(Changing his tone.)

You know Sky's place, Sizwe?   845

MAN: No.

BUNTU: Come. Let me give you a treat. I'll do you there.

(*Exit* BUNTU.)

(*Blackout except for a light on* SIZWE. *He continues his letter to* NOWETU.)

MAN: Sky's place? (*Shakes his head and laughs.*) Hey, Nowetu! When I mention that name again, I get a headache . . . the same headache I had when I woke up in Buntu's place the next morning. You won't believe what it was like. You cannot! It would be like you walking down Pickering Street in King William's Town and going into Koekemoer's Café to buy bread, and what do you see sitting there at the smart table and chairs? Your husband, Sizwe Bansi, being served ice-cream and cool drinks by old Mrs Koekemoer herself. Such would be your surprise if you had seen me at Sky's place. Only they weren't serving cool drinks and ice-cream. No! First-class booze, Nowetu. And it wasn't old Mrs Koekemoer serving me, but a certain lovely and beautiful lady called Miss Nkonyemi. And it wasn't just your husband Sizwe sitting there with all the most important people of New Brighton, but *Mister* Bansi.

(*He starts to laugh.*)

Mister Bansi!

(*As the laugh gets bigger,* SIZWE *rises to his feet.*)

(*The street outside Sky's Shebeen in New Brighton. Our man is amiably drunk. He addresses the audience.*)

MAN: Do you know who I am, friend? Take my hand, friend. Take my hand. I am Mister Bansi, friend. Do you know where I come from? I come from Sky's place, friend. A most wonderful place. I met everybody there, good people. I've been drinking, my friends—brandy, wine, beer. . . . Don't you want to go in there, good people? Let's all go to Sky's place. (*Shouting.*) Mr Buntu! Mr Buntu!

(BUNTU *enters shouting goodbye to friends at the Shebeen. He joins* SIZWE. BUNTU, *though not drunk, is also amiably talkative under the influence of a good few drinks.*)

BUNTU: (*discovering the audience.*) Hey, where did you get all these wonderful people?

MAN: I just found them here, Mr Buntu.

BUNTU: Wonderful!

MAN: I'm inviting them to Sky's place, Mr Buntu.

BUNTU: You tell them about Sky's?

MAN: I told them about Sky's place, Mr Buntu.

BUNTU: (*to the audience.*) We been having a time there, man!

MAN: They know it. I told them everything.

BUNTU: (*laughing.*) Sizwe! We had our fun there.

MAN: Hey . . . hey. . . .

BUNTU: Remember that Member of the Advisory Board?

MAN: Hey. . . . Hey . . . Mr Buntu! You know I respect you, friend. You must call me nice.

BUNTU: What do you mean?

MAN: (*clumsy dignity.*) I'm not just Sizwe no more. He might have walked in, but Mr Bansi walked out!

BUNTU: (*playing along.*) I am terribly sorry, Mr Bansi. I apologize for my familiarity. Please don't be offended.

(*Handing over one of the two oranges he is carrying.*)

Allow me . . . with the compliments of Miss Nkonyeni.

MAN: (*taking the orange with a broad but sheepish grin.*) Miss Nkonyeni!

BUNTU: Sweet dreams, Mr Bansi.

MAN: (*tears the orange with his thumbs and starts eating it messily.*) Lovely lady, Mr Buntu.

BUNTU: (*leaves Sizwe with a laugh. To the audience.*) Back there in the Shebeen a Member of the Advisory Board hears that he comes from King William's Town. He goes up to Sizwe. 'Tell me, Mr Bansi, what do you think of Ciskeian Independence?'

MAN: (*interrupting.*) Ja, I remember that one. Bloody Mister Member of the Advisory Board. Talking about Ciskeian Independence!

(*To the audience.*)

I must tell you, friend . . . when a car passes or the wind blows up the dust, Ciskeian Independence makes you cough. I'm telling you, friend . . . put a man in a pondok and call that Independence? My good friend, let me tell you . . . Ciskeian Independence is shit!

BUNTU: Or that other chap! Old Jolobe. The fat tycoon man! (*to the audience*) Comes to me . . . (*pompous voice*) . . . 'Your friend, Mr Bansi, is he on an official visit to town?' 'No,' I said, 'Mr Bansi is on an official walkout!' (BUNTU *thinks this is a big joke.*)

MAN: (*stubbornly.*) I'm here to stay.

BUNTU: (*looking at his watch.*) Hey, Sizwe . . .

MAN: (*reproachfully.*) Mr Buntu!

BUNTU: (*correcting himself.*) Mr Bansi, it is getting late. I've got to work tomorrow. Care to lead the way, Mr Bansi?

MAN: You think I can't? You think Mr Bansi is lost?

BUNTU: I didn't say that.

MAN: You are thinking it, friend. I'll show you. This is Chinga Street.

BUNTU: Very good! But which way do we. . . ?

MAN: (*setting off.*) This way.

BUNTU: (*pulling him back.*) Mistake. You're heading for Site and Service and a lot of trouble with the Tsotsis.

MAN: (*the opposite direction.*) That way.

BUNTU: Lead on. I'm right behind you.

MAN: Ja, you are right, Mr Buntu. There is Newell High School. Now. . . .

BUNTU: Think carefully!

MAN: . . . when we were going to Sky's we had Newell in front. So when we leave Sky's we put Newell behind.

BUNTU: Very good!

(*An appropriate change in direction. They continue walking, and eventually arrive at a square, with roads leading off in many directions.* SIZWE *is lost. He wanders around, uncertain of the direction to take.*)

MAN: *Haai*, Mr Buntu . . . !

BUNTU: Mbizweni Square.

MAN: Yo! Cross-roads to hell, wait . . . (*Closer look at landmark.*) . . . that building . . . Rio Cinema! So we must. . . .

BUNTU: Rio Cinema? With a white cross on top, bell outside, and the big show on Sundays?

MAN: (sheepishly.) You're right, friend. I've got it, Mr Buntu. That way.

(He starts off. BUNTU watches him.)

BUNTU: Goodbye. King William's Town a hundred and fifty miles. Don't forget to write.
945 MAN: (hurried about-turn.) Haai . . . haii. . . .
BUNTU: Okay, Sizwe, I'll take over from here. But just hang on for a second I want to have a piss. Don't move!

(BUNTU disappears into the dark.)

MAN: Haai, Sizwe! You are a country fool! Leading Mr Buntu and Mr Bansi astray. You think you know this place New
950 Brighton? You know nothing!

(BUNTU comes running back.)

BUNTU: (urgently.) Let's get out of here.
MAN: Wait, Mr Buntu, I'm telling that fool Sizwe. . . .
BUNTU: Come on! There's trouble there . . . (pointing in the direction from which he has come) . . . let's move.
955 MAN: Wait, Mr Buntu, wait. Let me first tell that Sizwe. . . .
BUNTU: There's a dead man lying there!
MAN: Dead man?
BUNTU: I thought I was just pissing on a pile of rubbish, but when I looked carefully I saw it was a man. Dead. Covered in
960 blood. Tsotsis must have got him. Let's get the hell out of here before anybody sees us.
MAN: Buntu . . . Buntu. . . .
BUNTU: Listen to me, Sizwe! The Tsotsis might still be around.
MAN: Buntu. . . .
965 BUNTU: Do you want to join him?
MAN: I don't want to join him.
BUNTU: Then come.
MAN: Wait, Buntu.
BUNTU: Jesus! If Zola had told me how much trouble you were
970 going to be!
MAN: Buntu, . . . we must report that man to the police station.
BUNTU: Police Station! Are you mad? You drunk, passbook not in order . . . 'We've come to report a dead man, Sergeant.' 'Grab them!' Case closed. We killed him.
975 MAN: Mr Buntu, . . . we can't leave him. . . .
BUNTU: Please, Sizwe!
MAN: Wait. Let's carry him home.
BUNTU: Jst like that! Walk through New Brighton streets, at this hour, carrying a dead man. Anyway we don't know where he
980 stays. Come.
MAN: Wait Buntu, . . . listen. . . .
BUNTU: Sizwe!
MAN: Buntu, we can know where he stays. That passbook of his will talk. It talks, friend, like mine. His passbook will tell you.
985 BUNTU: (after a moment's desperate hesitation.) You really want to land me in the shit, hey.

(Disappears into the dark again.)

MAN: It will tell you in good English where he stays. My passbook talks good English too . . . big words that Sizwe can't read and doesn't understand. Sizwe wants to stay here in New
990 Brighton and find a job; passbook says, 'No! Report back.' Sizwe wants to feed his wife and children; passbook says, 'No. Endorsed out.' Sizwe wants to. . . .

(BUNTU reappears, a passbook in his hand. Looks around furtively and moves to the light under a lamp-post.)

They never told us it would be like that when they introduced it. They said: Book of Life! Your friend! You'll never get lost! 995 They told us lies.

(He joins BUNTU who is examining the book.)

BUNTU: Haai! Look at him (the photograph in the book, reading.) 'Robert Zwelinzima. Tribe: Xhosa. Native Identification Number. . . .'
MAN: Where does he stay, Buntu? 1000
BUNTU: (paging through the book.) Worked at Dorman Long seven years . . . Kilomet Engineering . . . eighteen months . . . Anderson Hardware two years . . . now unemployed. Hey, look, Sizwe! He's one up on you. He's got a work-seeker's permit. 1005
MAN: Where does he stay, Buntu?
BUNTU: Lodger's Permit at 42 Mdala Street. From there to Sangocha Street . . . now at. . . .

(Pause. Closes the book abruptly.)

To hell with it I'm not going there.
MAN: Where, Buntu? 1010
BUNTU: (emphatically.) I Am Not Going There!
MAN: Buntu. . . .
BUNTU: You know where he is staying now? Single Men's Quarters! If you think I'm going there this time of the night you got another guess coming. 1015

(SIZWE doesn't understand.)

Look, Sizwe . . . I stay in a house, there's a street name and a number. Easy to find. Ask anybody . . . Mapija Street? That way. You know what Single Men's Quarters is? Big bloody concentration camp with rows of things that look like train carriages. Six doors to each! Twelve people behind each door! You 1020 want me to go there now? Knock on the first one: 'Does Robert Zwelinzima live here?' 'No!' Next one: 'Does Robert . . . ?' 'Bugger off, we're trying to sleep!' Next one: 'Does Robert Zwelinzima . . . ?' They'll fuck us up, man! I'm putting this book back and we're going home. 1025
MAN: Buntu!
BUNTU: (half-way back to the alleyway.) What?
MAN: Would you do that to me, friend? If the Tsotsis had stabbed Sizwe, and left him lying there, would you walk away from him as well? 1030

(The accusation stops BUNTU.)

Would you leave me lying there, wet with your piss? I wish I was dead. I wish I was dead because I don't care a damn about anything any more.

(Turning away from BUNTU to the audience.)

What's happening in this world, good people? Who cares for who in this world? Who wants who? 1035
Who wants me, friend? What's wrong with me? I'm a man. I've got eyes to see. I've got ears to listen when people talk. I've got a head to think good things. What's wrong with me?

(Starts to tear off his clothes.)

1040 Look at me! I'm a man. I've got legs. I can run with a wheel-barrow full of cement! I'm strong! I'm a man. Look! I've got a wife. I've got four children. How many has he made, lady? *(The man sitting next to her.)* Is he a man? What has he got that I haven't . . . ?

(A thoughtful BUNTU *rejoins them, the dead man's reference book still in his hand.)*

BUNTU: Let me see your book?

*(*SIZWE *doesn't respond.)*

1045 Give me your book!

MAN: Are you a policeman now, Buntu?

BUNTU: Give me your bloody book, Sizwe!

MAN: *(handing it over.)* Take it, Buntu. Take this book and read it carefully, friend, and tell me what it says about me. Buntu, 1050 does that book tell you I'm a man?

*(*BUNTU *studies the two books.* SIZWE *turns back to the audience.)*

That bloody book . . . ! People, do you know? No! Wherever you go . . . it's that bloody book. You go to school, it goes too. Go to work, it goes too. Go to church and pray and sing lovely hymns, it sits there with you. Go to hospital to die, it lies there 1055 too!

*(*BUNTU *has collected* SIZWE's *discarded clothing.)*

BUNTU: Come!

*(*BUNTU's *house, as earlier. Table and two chairs.* BUNTU *pushes* SIZWE *down into a chair.* SIZWE *still muttering, starts to struggle back into his clothes.* BUNTU *opens the two reference books and places them side by side on the table. He produces a pot of glue, then very carefully tears out the photograph in each book. A dab of glue on the back of each and then* SIZWE's *goes back into* ROBERT's *book, and* ROBERT's *into* SIZWE's. SIZWE *watches this operation, at first uninterestedly, but when he realizes what* BUNTU *is up to, with growing alarm. When he is finished,* BUNTU *pushes the two books in front of* SIZWE.)*

MAN: *(shaking his head emphatically.)* Yo! *Haai, haai.* No, Buntu.

BUNTU: It's a chance.

1060 MAN: *Haai, haai, haai . . .*

BUNTU: It's your only chance!

MAN: No, Buntu! What's it mean? That me, Sizwe Bansi. . . .

BUNTU: Is dead.

MAN: I'm not dead, friend.

1065 BUNTU: We burn this book . . . (SIZWE's *original*) . . . and Sizwe Bansi disappears off the face of the earth.

MAN: What about the man we left lying in the alleyway?

BUNTU: Tomorrow the Flying Squad passes there and finds him. Check in his pockets . . . no passbook. Mount Road Mortu-1070 ary. After three days nobody has identified him. Pauper's Burial. Case closed.

MAN: And then?

BUNTU: Tomorrow I contact my friend Norman at Feltex. He's a boss-boy there. I tell him about another friend, Robert 1075 Zwelinzima, book in order, who's looking for a job. You roll up later, hand over the book to the white man. Who does Robert Zwelinzima look like? You! Who gets the pay on Friday? You, man!

MAN: What about all that shit at the Labour Bureau, Buntu?

BUNTU: You don't have to there. This chap had a workseeker's 1080 permit, Sizwe. All you do is hand over the book to the white man. *He* checks at the Labour Bureau. They check with their big machine. 'Robert Zwelinzima has the right to be employed and stay in this town.'

MAN: I don't want to lose my name, Buntu. 1085

BUNTU: You mean you don't want to lose your bloody passbook! You love it, hey?

MAN: Buntu. I cannot lose my name.

BUNTU: *(leaving the table.)* All right, I was only trying to help. As Robert Zwelinzima you could have stayed and worked in 1090 this town. As Sizwe Bansi . . . ? Start walking, friend. King William's Town. Hundred and fifty miles. And don't waste any time! You've got to be there by yesterday. Hope you enjoy it.

MAN: Buntu. . . .

BUNTU: Lots of scenery in a hundred and fifty miles. 1095

MAN: Buntu! . . .

BUNTU: Maybe a better idea is just to wait until they pick you up. Save yourself all that walking. Into the train with the escort! Smart stuff, hey. Hope it's not too crowded though. Hell of a lot of people being kicked out, I hear. 1100

MAN: Buntu! . . .

BUNTU: But once you're back! Sit down on the side of the road next to your pondok with your family . . . the whole Bansi clan on leave . . . for life! Hey, that sounds okay. Watching all the cars passing, and as you say, friend, cough your bloody 1105 lungs out with Ciskeian Independence.

MAN: *(now really desperate.)* Buntu!!!

BUNTU: What you waiting for? Go!

MAN: Buntu.

BUNTU: What? 1110

MAN: What about my wife, Nowetu?

BUNTU: What about her?

MAN: *(maudlin tears.)* Her loving husband, Sizwe Bansi, is dead!

BUNTU: So what! She's going to marry a better man. 1115

MAN: *(bridling.)* Who?

BUNTU: You . . . Robert Zwelinzima.

MAN: *(thoroughly confused.)* How can I marry my wife, Buntu?

BUNTU: Get her down here and I'll introduce you.

MAN: Don't make jokes, Buntu. Robert . . . Sizwe . . . I'm all 1120 mixed up. Who am I?

BUNTU: A fool who is not taking his chance.

MAN: And my children! Their father is Sizwe Bansi. They're registered at school under Bansi. . . .

BUNTU: Are you really worried about your children, friend, or 1125 are you just worried about yourself and your bloody name? Wake up, man! Use that book and with your pay on Friday you'll have a real chance to do something for them.

MAN: I'm afraid. How do I get used to Robert? How do I live as another man's ghost? 1130

BUNTU: Wasn't Sizwe Bansi a ghost?

MAN: No!

BUNTU: No? When the white man looked at you at the Labour Bureau what did he see? A man with dignity or a bloody pass-book with an N.I. number? Isn't that a ghost? When the 1135 white man sees you walk down the street and calls out, 'Hey, John! Come here' . . . to you, *Sizwe Bansi* . . . isn't that a ghost? Or when his little child calls you 'Boy' . . . you a man,

circumcised with a wife and four children . . . isn't that a
ghost? Stop fooling yourself. All I'm saying is be a real ghost,
if that is what they want, what they've turned us into. Spook
them into hell, man!

(SIZWE *is silenced.* BUNTU *realizes his words are beginning to
reach the other man. He paces quietly, looking for his next move.
He finds it.)*

Suppose you try my plan. Friday. Roughcasting section at
Feltex. Paytime. Line of men — non-skilled labourers. White
man with the big box full of pay-packets.
'John Kani!' 'Yes, sir!' Pay-packet is handed over. 'Thank you,
sir.'
Another one. (BANTU *reads the name on an imaginary pay-
packet.*) 'Winston Ntshona!' 'Yes, sir!' Pay-packet over.
'Thank you, sir!' Another one. 'Fats Bhokolane!' '*Hier is ek,
my baas!*' Pay-packet over. '*Dankie, my baas!*'
Another one. 'Robert Zwelinzima!'

(*No response from* SIZWE.)

'Robert Zwelinzima!'
MAN: Yes, sir.
BUNTU: (*handing him the imaginary pay-packet.*) Open it. Go on.

(*Takes back the packet, tears it open, empties its contents on the
table, and counts it.*)

Five . . . ten . . . eleven . . . twelve . . . and ninety-nine cents.
In *your* pocket!

(BUNTU *again paces quietly, leaving* SIZWE *to think. Eventually. . . .*)

Saturday. Man in overalls, twelve rand ninety-nine cents in
the back pocket, walking down Main Street looking for Sales
House. Finds it and walks in. Salesman comes forward to
meet him.
'I've come to buy a suit.' Salesman is very friendly.
'Certainly. Won't you take a seat. I'll get the forms. I'm sure
you want to open an account, sir. Six months to pay. But first
I'll need all your particulars.'

(BUNTU *has turned the table, with* SIZWE *on the other side, into
the imaginary scene at Sales House.*)

BUNTU: (*pencil poised, ready to fill in a form.*) Your name,
please, sir?
MAN: (*playing along uncertainly.*) Robert Zwelinzima.
BUNTU: (*writing.*) 'Robert Zwelinzima.' Address?
MAN: Fifty, Mapija Street.
BUNTU: Where do you work?
MAN: Feltex.
BUNTU: And how much do you get paid?
MAN: Twelve . . . twelve rand ninety-nine cents.
BUNTU: N.I. Number, please?

(SIZWE *hesitates.*)

Your Native Identity number please?

(SIZWE *is still uncertain.* BUNTU *abandons the act and picks up*
ROBERT ZWELINZIMA's *passbook. He reads out the number.*)

N—I—3—8—1—1—8—6—3.

Burn that into your head, friend. You hear me? It's more
important than your name.
N.I. number . . . three. . . .
MAN: Three.
BUNTU: Eight.
MAN: Eight.
BUNTU: One.
MAN: One.
BUNTU: One.
MAN: One.
BUNTU: Eight.
MAN: Eight.
BUNTU: Six.
MAN: Six.
BUNTU: Three.
MAN: Three.
BUNTU: Again. Three.
MAN: Three.
BUNTU: Eight.
MAN: Eight.
BUNTU: One.
MAN: One.
BUNTU: One.
MAN: One.
BUNTU: Eight.
MAN: Eight.
BUNTU: Six.
MAN: Six.
BUNTU: Three.
MAN: Three.
BUNTU: (*picking up his pencil and returning to the role of the
salesman.*) N.I. number, please.
MAN: (*pausing frequently, using his hands to remember.*) Three . . .
eight . . . one . . . one . . . eight . . . six . . . three. . . .
BUNTU: (*abandoning the act.*) Good boy.

(*He paces.* SIZWE *sits and waits.*)

Sunday. Man in a Sales House suit, hat on top, going to
church. Hymn book and bible under the arm. Sits down in
the front pew. Priest in the pulpit.

(BUNTU *jumps on to a chair in his new role.* SIZWE *kneels.*)

The Time has come!
MAN: Amen!
BUNTU: Pray, brothers and sisters. . . . Pray. . . . Now!
MAN: Amen.
BUNTU: The Lord wants to save you. Hand yourself over to him,
while there is still time, while Jesus is still prepared to listen to
you.
MAN: (*carried away by what he is feeling.*) Amen, Jesus!
BUNTU: Be careful, my brothers and sisters. . . .
MAN: Hallelujah!
BUNTU: Be careful lest when the big day comes and the pages of
the big book are turned, it is found that your name is missing.
Repent before it is too late.
MAN: Hallelujah! Amen.
BUNTU: Will all those who have not yet handed in their names for
membership of our burial society please remain behind.

(BUNTU *leaves the pulpit and walks around with a register.*)

Name, please, sir? Number? Thank you.
Good afternoon, sister. Your name, please.
Address? Number? God bless you.

(*He has reached* SIZWE.)

1235   Your name, please, brother?

MAN: Robert Zwelinzima.

BUNTU: Address?

MAN: Fifty, Mapija Street.

BUNTU: N.I. number.

1240   MAN: (*again tremendous effort to remember.*) Three . . . eight . . . one . . . one . . . eight . . . six . . . three. . . .

(*They both relax.*)

BUNTU: (*after pacing for a few seconds.*) Same man leaving the church . . . walking down the street.

(BUNTU *acts out the role while* SIZWE *watches. He greets other members of the congregation.*)

'God bless you, Brother Bansi. May you always stay within
1245   the Lord's mercy.'
'Greetings, Brother Bansi. We welcome you into the flock of Jesus with happy spirits.'
'God bless you, Brother Bansi. Stay with the Lord, the Devil is strong.'
1250   Suddenly. . . .

(BUNTU *has moved to behind* SIZWE. *He grabs him roughly by the shoulder.*)

Police!

(SIZWE *stands up frightened.* BUNTU *watches him carefully.*)

No, man! Clean your face.

(SIZWE *adopts an impassive expression.* BUNTU *continues as the policeman.*)

What's your name?

MAN: Robert Zwelinzima.

1255   BUNTU: Where do you work?

MAN: Feltex.

BUNTU: Book!

(SIZWE *hands over the book and waits while the policeman opens it, looks at the photograph, then* SIZWE, *and finally checks through its stamps and endorsements. While all this is going on* SIZWE *stands quietly, looking down at his feet, whistling under his breath. The book is finally handed back.*)

Okay.

(SIZWE *takes his book and sits down.*)

MAN: (*after a pause.*) I'll try it, Buntu.

1260   BUNTU: Of course you must, if you want to stay alive.

MAN: Yes, but Sizwe Bansi is dead.

BUNTU: What about Robert Zwelinzima then? That poor bastard I pissed on out there in the dark. So *he's* alive again. Bloody, miracle, man.

1265   Look, if someone was to offer me the things I wanted most in my life, the things that would make me, my wife, and my child happy, in exchange for the name Buntu . . . you think I wouldn't swop?

MAN: Are you sure, Buntu?

BUNTU: (*examining the question seriously.*) If there was just me . . .   1270
I mean, if I was alone, if I didn't have anyone to worry about or look after except myself . . . maybe then I'd be prepared to pay some sort of price for a little pride. But if I had a wife and four children wasting away their one and only life in the dust and poverty of Ciskeian Independence . . . if I had four chil-   1275
dren waiting for me, their father, to do something about their lives . . . *ag*, no, Sizwe. . . .

MAN: Robert, Buntu.

BUNTU: (*angry.*) All right! Robert, John, Athol, Winston. . . .
Shit on names, man! To hell with them if in exchange you   1280
can get a piece of bread for your stomach and a blanket in winter. Understand me, brother, I'm not saying that pride isn't a way for us. What I'm saying is shit on our pride if we only bluff ourselves that we are men.
Take your name back, Sizwe Bansi, if it's so important to you.   1285
But next time you hear a white man say 'John' to you, don't say '*Ja, Baas?*' And next time the bloody white man says to you, a man, 'Boy, come here,' don't run to him and lick his arse like we all do. Face him and tell him: 'White man. I'm a Man!' *Ag kak!* We're bluffing ourselves.   1290
It's like my father's hat. Special hat, man! Carefully wrapped in plastic on top of the wardrobe in his room. God help the child who so much as touches it! Sunday it goes on his head, and a man, full of dignity, a man I respect, walks down the street. White man stops him: 'Come here, kaffir!' What does   1295
he do?

(BUNTU *whips the imaginary hat off his head and crumples it in his hands as he adopts a fawning, servile pose in front of the white man.*)

'What is it, Baas?'
If that is what you call pride, then shit on it! Take mine and give me food for my children.

(*Pause.*)

Look, brother, Robert Zwelinzima, that poor bastard out   1300
there in the alleyway, if there *are* ghosts, he is smiling tonight.
He is here, with us, and he's saying: 'Good luck, Sizwe! I hope it works.' He's a brother, man.

MAN: For how long, Buntu?

BUNTU: How long? For as long as you can stay out of trouble.   1305
Trouble will mean police station, then fingerprints off to Pretoria to check on previous convictions . . . and when they do that . . . Siswe Bansi will live again and you will have had it.

MAN: Buntu, you know what you are saying? A black man stay out of trouble? Impossible, Buntu. Our skin is trouble.   1310

BUNTU: (*wearily.*) You said you wanted to try.

MAN: And I will.

BUNTU: (*picks up his coat.*) I'm tired, . . . Robert. Good luck. See you tomorrow.

(*Exit* BUNTU, SIZWE *picks up the passbook, looks at it for a long time, then puts it in his back pocket. He finds his walking-stick, newspaper, and pipe and moves downstage into a solitary light. He finishes the letter to his wife.*)

MAN: So Nowetu, for the time being my troubles are over.   1315
Christmas I come home. In the meantime Buntu is working a plan to get me a Lodger's Permit. If I get it, you and the chil-

dren can come here and spend some days with me in Port Elizabeth. Spend the money I am sending you carefully. If all goes well I will send some more each week.
I do not forget you, my dear wife.

Your loving Husband,
Sizwe Bansi.

(As he finishes the letter, SIZWE *returns to the pose of the photo. Styles Photographic Studio.* STYLES *is behind the camera.)*

STYLES: Hold it, Robert. Hold it just like that. Just one more. Now smile, Robert. . . . Smile. . . . Smile. . . .

(Camera flash and blackout.)

GLOSSARY

ag voetsek   go to hell

bioscope   cinema

brak   mongrel dog

broer   brother

Ciskei   (*adj.* Ciskeian) one of the Black 'homelands' created by the South African Government under its policy of Separate Development

dankie   thank you

gqokra izi khuselo zamehlo kule ndawo   put on safety glasses here

hai; haai   exclamation of surprise

hier is ek   here I am

ja   yes

kieries   fighting-sticks carried by young African men

lap; lappie   rag

makulu   grandmother

meester   schoolmaster

moer   literally, womb; used as a swear-word equivalent to 'fuck', 'fucking'

nyana we sizwe   brother of the land

ons was gemoer vandag   we were fucked up today

poes   cunt

pondok   shack, shanty

spruit   spring, stream

tshotsholoza kulezondawo, vyabaleka   opening phrase of an African work-chant; literally, work steady, the train is coming

tsotsis   Black hooligans

WOLE SOYINKA

Wole Soyinka was born in 1934 in Abeokuta, Nigeria. Educated at Government College in Ibadan, Soyinka then studied at Leeds University in England, where he worked with the notable Shakespearian scholar and actor G. Wilson Knight and took his B.A. in English in 1957. He remained in England working as play reader for the Royal Court Theater, before returning to Nigeria in 1959, where his first play, *The Lion and the Jewel*, was produced. In the course of the next decade, Soyinka wrote an important body of dramatic work, including the plays *The Invention* (1959), *A Dance of the Forests* (1960), *The Trials of Brother Jero* (1960), *Camwood on the Leaves* (radio play, 1960), *The Strong Breed* (1964), *Kongi's Harvest* (1964), and *The Road* (1965). He also taught at the universities of Ibadan, Ife, and Lagos, and founded two important theaters, the Orisun Theater and the 1960 Masks theater. Much of Soyinka's work is critical of authoritarian politics; he was arrested in 1967 and held as a political prisoner until 1969. Soyinka's memoir of imprisonment, *The Man Died*, was published in 1972 and was cited for excellence by Amnesty International. In the 1970s, Soyinka continued to write plays examining the tensions of tribal life in modern Africa: *Madmen and Specialists* (1970) and *Death and the King's Horseman* (1976). He also wrote plays more directly examining contemporary African politics: his rewriting of Brecht's *Threepenny Opera* as *Opera Wonyosi* (1977), and *A Play of Giants* (1985). He also wrote an adaptation of Euripides' *The Bacchae* (1973), placing the Greek narrative in a more explicitly tribal and ritualistic setting. Soyinka was awarded the Nobel Prize in 1986, the first African writer to receive the prize for literature.

Death and the King's Horseman

Soyinka is somtimes criticized by other African writers for being too oriented toward Europe. Not only are some of his plays adaptations or imitations of European works, but Soyinka has continued to write in English—the language of the colonial power, after all—rather than writing in his native language, Yoruba. It is precisely this tension between village and metropolis, between Africa and Europe, that provides the springboard for some of Soyinka's greatest work and dramatizes the challenges of cross-cultural interaction in the complex contemporary political environment.

Death and the King's Horseman is based on events that took place in the Yoruba city of Oyo in 1946. The play opens on the day the local African king is to be buried. According to custom, his Horseman, Elesin Oba, will die on this day as well, following his master in death as he followed him in life. It is clear from the scene in the marketplace that this ritual death is, however, a celebration. The village enacts a festive and playful marriage between Elesin and a new, young bride, so that he can procreate before he dies, bringing new life into the world even as he passes out of it.

In *Death and the King's Horseman*, indigenous African culture operates within the more restricted sphere of Britain's colonial values, laws, and institutions. The region's colonial administrator, Simon Pilkings, who is on his way to a masquerade to celebrate the arrival of the Prince, acts to stop Elesin's death. However, Pilkings and his wife are wearing African ceremonial costumes of the dead to the English masquerade, a decision that is not only offensive and irreligious to the Africans they meet, but that marks their complete incomprehension of the complex situation in which they find themselves. Wearing the costume also marks the Pilkings, and the colonial British as a whole, as figures of death, in contrast to the paradoxical life celebrated by Elesin.

Pilkings "saves" Elesin and brings about the play's tragic catastrophe. For Elesin's son Olunde—studying medicine in Britain—returns to perform funeral rites for his father. However, when Elesin is prevented from dying, it becomes clear that colonial intervention has destroyed what it attempted to protect. Olunde, too, is dishonored when his father remains alive and takes the only possible course of action.

In his note to the play, Soyinka criticizes the phrase "clash of cultures" to describe his work, for it "presupposes a potential equality *in every given situation* of the alien culture and the indigenous." In *Death and the King's Horseman*, the power vested in the colonial administration signals its ability to destroy the indigenous culture it claims, ironically, to govern.

— AUTHOR'S NOTE —

This play is based on events which took place in Oyo, ancient Yoruba city of Nigeria, in 1946. That year, the lives of Elesin (Olori Elesin), his son, and the Colonial District Officer intertwined with the disastrous results set out in the play. The changes I have made are in matters of detail, sequence and of course characterisation. The action has also been set back two or three years to while the war was still on, for minor reasons of dramaturgy.

The factual account still exists in the archives of the British Colonial Administration. It has already inspired a fine play in Yoruba (Oba Wàjà) by Duro Ladipo. It has also misbegotten a film by some German television company.

The bane of themes of this genre is that they are no sooner employed creatively than they acquire the facile tag of 'clash of cultures', a prejudicial label which, quite apart from its frequent misapplication, presupposes a potential equality *in every given situation* of the alien culture and the indigenous, on the actual soil of the latter. (In the area of misapplication, the overseas prize for illiteracy and mental conditioning undoubtedly goes to the blurb-writer for the American edition of my novel *Season of Anomy* who unblushingly declares that this work portrays the 'clash between old values and new ways, between western methods and African traditions'!) It is thanks to this kind of perverse mentality that I find it necessary to caution the would-be producer of this play against a sadly familiar reductionist tendency, and to direct his vision instead to the far more difficult and risky task of eliciting the play's threnodic essence.

One of the more obvious alternative structures of the play would be to make the District Officer the victim of a cruel dilemma. This is not to my taste and it is not by chance that I have avoided dialogue or situation which would encourage this. No attempt should be made in production to suggest it. The Colonial Factor is an incident, a catalytic incident merely. The confrontation in the play is largely metaphysical, contained in the human vehicle which is Elesin and the universe of the Yoruba mind — the world of the living, the dead and the unborn, and the numinous passage which links all: transition. *Death and the King's Horseman* can be fully realised only through an evocation of music from the abyss of transition.

Wole Soyinka

DEATH AND THE KING'S HORSEMAN

Wole Soyinka

— CHARACTERS —

PRAISE-SINGER
ELESIN, *Horseman of the King*
IYALOJA, *'Mother' of the market*
SIMON PILKINGS, *District Officer*
JANE PILKINGS, *his wife*
SERGEANT AMUSA
JOSEPH, *houseboy to the Pilkingses*

BRIDE
H.R.H. THE PRINCE
THE RESIDENT
AIDE-DE-CAMP
OLUNDE, *eldest son of Elesin*
DRUMMERS, WOMEN, YOUNG GIRLS, DANCERS *at the Ball*

The play should run without an interval. For rapid scene changes, one adjustable outline set is very appropriate.

— ONE —

A passage through a market in its closing stages. The stalls are being emptied, mats folded. A few women pass through on their way home, loaded with baskets. On a cloth-stand, bolts of cloth are taken down, display pieces folded and piled on a tray. ELESIN OBA *enters along a passage before the market, pursued by his* DRUMMERS *and* PRAISE-SINGERS. *He is a man of enormous vitality, speaks, dances and sings with that infectious enjoyment of life which accompanies all his actions.*

PRAISE-SINGER: Elesin o! Elesin Oba! Howu! What tryst is this the cockerel goes to keep with such haste that he must leave his tail behind?

5 ELESIN: *(slows down a bit, laughing)* A tryst where the cockerel needs no adornment.

PRAISE-SINGER: O-oh, you hear that my companions? That's the way the world goes. Because the man approaches a brand-new bride he forgets the long faithful mother of his children.

10 ELESIN: When the horse sniffs the stable does he not strain at the bridle? The market is the long-suffering home of my spirit and the women are packing up to go. That Esu-harrassed day slipped into the stewpot while we feasted. We ate it up with the rest of the meat. I have neglected my women.

15 PRAISE-SINGER: We know all that. Still it's no reason for shedding your tail on this day of all days. I know the women will cover you in damask and *alari* but when the wind blows cold from behind, that's when the fowl knows his true friends.

ELESIN: Olohun-iyo!

PRAISE-SINGER: Are you sure there will be one like me on the
20 other side?

ELESIN: Olohun-iyo!

PRAISE-SINGER: Far be it for me to belittle the dwellers of that place but, a man is either born to his art or he isn't. And I don't know for certain that you'll meet my father, so who is
25 going to sing these deeds in accents that will pierce the deafness of the ancient ones. I have prepared my going — just tell me: Olohun-iyo, I need you on this journey and I shall be behind you.

ELESIN: You're like a jealous wife. Stay close to me, but only on this side. My fame, my honour are legacies to the living; stay 30 behind and let the world sip its honey from your lips.

PRAISE-SINGER: Your name will be like the sweet berry a child places under his tongue to sweeten the passage of food. The world will never spit it out.

ELESIN: Come then. This market is my roost. When I come 35 among the women I am a chicken with a hundred mothers. I become a monarch whose palace is built with tenderness and beauty.

PRAISE-SINGER: They love to spoil you but beware. The hands of women also weaken the unwary. 40

ELESIN: This night I'll lay my head upon their lap and go to sleep. This night I'll touch feet with their feet in a dance that is no longer of this earth. But the smell of their flesh, their sweat, the smell of indigo on their cloth, this is the last air I wish to breathe as I go to meet my great forebears. 45

PRAISE-SINGER: In their time the world was never tilted from its groove, it shall not be in yours.

ELESIN: The gods have said No.

PRAISE-SINGER: In their time the great wars came and went, the little wars came and went; the white slavers came and went, 50 they took away the heart of our race, they bore away the mind and muscle of our race. The city fell and was rebuilt; the city fell and our people trudged through mountain and forest to found a new home but — Elesin Oba do you hear me?

ELESIN: I hear your voice Olohun-iyo. 55

PRAISE-SINGER: Our world was never wrenched from its true course.

ELESIN: The gods have said No.

PRAISE-SINGER: There is only one home to the life of a river-mussel; there is only one home to the life of a tortoise; there is 60 only one shell to the soul of man: there is only one world to the spirit of our race. If that world leaves its course and smashes on boulders of the great void, whose world will give us shelter?

ELESIN: It did not in the time of my forebears, it shall not in mine. 65

Note to this edition: Certain Yoruba words which appear in italics in the text are explained in a brief glossary at the end of the play.

PRAISE-SINGER: The cockerel must not be seen without his
    feathers.

ELESIN: Nor will the Not-I bird be much longer without his nest.

PRAISE-SINGER: (stopped in his lyric stride) The Not-I bird,
70   Elesin?

ELESIN: I said, the Not-I bird.

PRAISE-SINGER: All respect to our elders but, is there really such
    a bird?

ELESIN: What! Could it be that he failed to knock on your door?

75 PRAISE-SINGER: (smiling) Elesin's riddles are not merely the nut
    in the kernel that breaks human teeth; he also buries the ker-
    nel in hot embers and dares a man's fingers to draw it out.

ELESIN: I am sure he called on you, Olohun-iyo. Did you hide
    in the loft and push out the servant to tell him you were out?

(ELESIN executes a brief, half-taunting dance. The DRUMMER
moves in and draws a rhythm out of his steps. ELESIN dances
towards the market-place as he chants the story of the Not-I bird,
his voice changing dexterously to mimic his characters. He performs like a born raconteur, infecting his retinue with his humour
and energy. More women arrive during his recital, including
IYALOJA.)

80   Death came calling.
    Who does not know his rasp of reeds?
    A twilight whisper in the leaves before
    The great araba falls? Did you hear it?
    Not I! swears the farmer. He snaps
85   His fingers round his head, abandons
    A hard-worn harvest and begins
    A rapid dialogue with his legs.

    'Not I,' shouts the fearless hunter, 'but—
    It's getting dark, and this night-lamp
90   Has leaked out all its oil. I think
    It's best to go home and resume my hunt
    Another day.' But now he pauses, suddenly
    Lets out a wail: 'Oh foolish mouth, calling
    Down a curse on your own head! Your lamp
95   Has leaked out all its oil, has it?'
    Forwards or backwards now he dare not move.
    To search for leaves and make etutu
    On that spot? Or race home to the safety
    Of his hearth? Ten market-days have passed
100   My friends, and still he's rooted there
    Rigid as the plinth of Orayan.

    The mouth of the courtesan barely
    Opened wide enough to take a ha' penny robo
    When she wailed: 'Not I.' All dressed she was
105   To call upon my friend the Chief Tax Officer.
    But now she sends her go-between instead:
    'Tell him I'm ill: my period has come suddenly
    But not—I hope—my time.'

    Why is the pupil crying?
110   His hapless head was made to taste
    The knuckles of my friend the Mallam:
    'If you were then reciting the Koran
    Would you have ears for idle noises
    Darkening the trees, you child of ill omen?'
115   He shuts down school before its time
    Runs home and rings himself with amulets.

    And take my good kinsman Ifawomi.
    His hands were like a carver's, strong
    And true. I saw them
    Tremble like wet wings of a fowl   120
    One day he cast his time-smoothed opele
    Across the divination board. And all because
    The suppliant looked him in the eye and asked,
    'Did you hear that whisper in the leaves?'
    'Not I,' was his reply; 'perhaps I'm growing deaf— 125
    Good-day.' And Ifa spoke no more that day
    The priest locked fast his doors,
    Sealed up his leaking roof—but wait!
    This sudden care was not for Fawomi
    But for Osanyin, courier-bird of Ifa's   130
    Heart of wisdom. I did not know a kite
    Was hovering in the sky
    And Ifa now a twittering chicken in
    The brood of Fawomi the Mother Hen.

    Ah, but I must not forget my evening   135
    Courier from the abundant palm, whose groan
    Became Not I, as he constipated down
    A wayside bush. He wonders if Elegbara
    Has tricked his buttocks to discharge
    Against a sacred grove. Hear him   140
    Mutter spells to ward off penalties
    For an abomination he did not intend.
    If any here
    Stumbles on a gourd of wine, fermenting
    Near the road, and nearby hears a stream   145
    Of spells issuing from a crouching form.
    Brother to a sigidi, bring home my wine,
    Tell my tapper I have ejected
    Fear from home and farm. Assure him,
    All is well.   150

PRAISE-SINGER: In your time we do not doubt the peace of farm-
    stead and home, the peace of road and hearth, we do not
    doubt the peace of the forest.

ELESIN: There was fear in the forest too.
    Not-I was lately heard even in the lair   155
    Of beasts. The hyena cackled loud Not I,
    The civet twitched his fiery tail and glared:
    Not I. Not-I became the answering-name
    Of the restless bird, that little one
    Whom Death found nesting in the leaves   160
    When whisper of his coming ran
    Before him on the wind. Not-I
    Has long abandoned home. This same dawn
    I heard him twitter in the gods' abode.
    Ah, companions of this living world   165
    What a thing this is, that even those
    We call immortal
    Should fear to die.

IYALOJA: But you, husband of multitudes?

ELESIN: I, when that Not-I bird perched   170
    Upon my roof, bade him seek his nest again,
    Safe, without care or fear. I unrolled
    My welcome mat for him to see. Not-I
    Flew happily away, you'll hear his voice
    No more in this lifetime—You all know   175
    What I am.

PRAISE-SINGER: That rock which turns its open lodes
   Into the path of lightning. A gay
   Thoroughbred whose sudden disdains
180 To falter through an adder reared
   Suddenly in his path.
ELESIN: My rein is loosened.
   I am master of my Fate. When the hour comes
   Watch me dance along the narrowing path
185 Glazed by the soles of my great precursors.
   My soul is eager. I shall not turn aside.
WOMEN: You will not delay?
ELESIN: Where the storm pleases, and when, it directs
   The giants of the forest. When friendship summons
190 Is when the true comrade goes.
WOMEN: Nothing will hold you back?
ELESIN: Nothing. What! Has no one told you yet?
   I go to keep my friend and master company.
   Who says the mouth does not believe in
195 'No, I have chewed all that before?' I say I have.
   The world is not a constant honey-pot.
   Where I found little I made do with little.
   Where there was plenty I gorged myself.
   My master's hands and mine have always
200 Dipped together and, home or sacred feast,
   The bowl was beaten bronze, the meats
   So succulent our teeth accused us of neglect.
   We shared the choicest of the season's
   Harvest of yams. How my friend would read
205 Desire in my eyes before I knew the cause—
   However rare, however precious, it was mine.
WOMEN: The town, the very land was yours.
ELESIN: The world was mine. Our joint hands
   Raised houseposts of trust that withstood
210 The siege of envy and the termites of time.
   But the twilight hour brings bats and rodents—
   Shall I yield them cause to foul the rafters?
PRAISE-SINGER: Elesin Oba! Are you not that man who
   Looked out of doors that stormy day
215 The god of luck limped by, drenched
   To the very lice that held
   His rags together? You took pity upon
   His sores and wished him fortune.
   Fortune was footloose this dawn, he replied,
220 Till you trapped him in a heartfelt wish
   That now returns to you. Elesin Oba!
   I say you are that man who
   Chanced upon the calabash of honour
   You thought it was palm wine and
225 Drained its contents to the final drop.
ELESIN: Life has an end. A life that will outlive
   Fame and friendship begs another name.
   What elder takes his tongue to his plate,
   Licks it clean of every crumb? He will encounter
230 Silence when he calls on children to fulfill
   The smallest errand! Life is honour.
   It ends when honour ends.
WOMEN: We know you for a man of honour.
ELESIN: Stop! Enough of that!
235 WOMEN: (puzzled, they whisper among themselves, turning
   mostly to IYALOJA) What is it? Did we say something to give
   offense? Have we slighted him in some way?

ELESIN: Enough of that sound I say. Let me hear no more in that
   vein. I've heard enough.
IYALOJA: We must have said something wrong. (Comes forward 240
   a little.) Elesin Oba, we ask forgiveness before you speak.
ELESIN: I am bitterly offended.
IYALOJA: Our unworthiness has betrayed us. All we can do is ask
   your forgiveness. Correct us like a kind father.
ELESIN: This day of all days . . . 245
IYALOJA: It does not bear thinking. If we offend you now we have
   mortified the gods. We offend heaven itself. Father of us all,
   tell us where we went astray. (She kneels, the other women
   follow.)
ELESIN: Are you not ashamed? Even a tear-veiled 250
   Eye preserves its function of sight.
   Because my mind was raised to horizons
   Even the boldest man lowers his gaze
   In thinking of, must my body here
   Be taken for a vagrant's? 255
IYALOJA: Horseman of the King, I am more baffled than ever.
PRAISE-SINGER: The strictest father unbends his brow when the
   child is penitent, Elesin. When time is short, we do not spend
   it prolonging the riddle. Their shoulders are bowed with the
   weight of fear lest they have marred your day beyond repair. 260
   Speak now in plain words and let us pursue the ailment to the
   home of remedies.
ELESIN: Words are cheap. 'We know you for
   A man of honour.' Well tell me, is this how
   A man of honour should be seen?
   Are these not the same clothes in which 265
   I came among you a full half-hour ago?

(He roars with laughter and the WOMEN, relieved, rise and rush
into stalls to fetch rich cloths.)

WOMAN: The gods are kind. A fault soon remedied is soon for-
   given. Elesin Oba, even as we match our words with deed, let
   your heart forgive us completely. 270
ELESIN: You who are breath and giver of my being
   How shall I dare refuse you forgiveness
   Even if the offence were real.
IYALOJA: (dancing round him. Sings)

         He forgives us. He forgives us. 275
         What a fearful thing it is when
         The voyager sets forth
         But a curse remains behind.

WOMEN: For a while we truly feared
   Our hands had wrenched the world adrift 280
   In emptiness.
IYALOJA: Richly, richly, robe him richly
   The cloth of honour is *alari*
   Sanyan is the band of friendship
   Boa-skin makes slippers of esteem. 285
WOMEN: For a while we truly feared
   Our hands had wrenched the world adrift
   In emptiness.
PRAISE-SINGER: He who must, must voyage forth
   The world will not roll backwards 290
   It is he who must, with one
   Great gesture overtake the world.

WOMEN: For a while we truly feared
    Our hands had wrenched the world
295   In emptiness.
PRAISE-SINGER: The gourd you bear is not for shirking.
    The gourd is not for setting down
    At the first crossroad or wayside grove.
    Only one river may know its contents.
300 WOMEN: We shall all meet at the great market
    We shall all meet at the great market
    He who goes early takes the best bargains
    But we shall meet, and resume our banter.

(ELESIN *stands resplendent in rich clothes, cap, shawl, etc. His
sash is of a bright red* alari *cloth. The* WOMEN *dance round him.
Suddenly, his attention is caught by an object off-stage.*)

ELESIN: The world I know is good.
305 WOMEN: We know you'll leave it so.
ELESIN: The world I know is the bounty
    Of hives after bees have swarmed.
    No goodness teems with such open hands
    Even in the dreams of deities.
310 WOMEN: And we know you'll leave it so.
ELESIN: I was born to keep it so. A hive
    Is never known to wander. An anthill
    Does not desert its roots. We cannot see
    The still great womb of the world—
315   No man beholds his mother's womb—
    Yet who denies it's there? Coiled
    To the navel of the world is that
    Endless cord that links us all
    To the great origin. If I lose my way
320   The trailing cord will bring me to the roots.
WOMEN: The world is in your hands.

(*The earlier distraction, a beautiful young girl, comes along the
passage through which* ELESIN *first made his entry.*)

ELESIN: I embrace it. And let me tell you, women—
    I like this farewell that the world designed,
    Unless my eyes deceive me, unless
325   We are already parted, the world and I,
    And all that breeds desire is lodged
    Among our tireless ancestors. Tell me friends,
    Am I still earthed in that beloved market
    Of my youth? Or could it be my will
330   Has outleapt the conscious act and I have come
    Among the great departed?
PRAISE-SINGER: Elesin-Oba why do your eyes roll like a bush-rat
    who sees his fate like his father's spirit, mirrored in the eye of a
    snake? And all these questions! You're standing on the same
335   earth you've always stood upon. This voice you hear is mine,
    Oluhun-iyo, not that of an acolyte in heaven.
ELESIN: How can that be? In all my life
    As Horseman of the King, the juiciest
    Fruit on every tree was mine. I saw,
340   I touched, I wooed, rarely was the answer No.
    The honour of my place, the veneration I
    Received in the eye of man or woman
    Prospered my suit and
    Played havoc with my sleeping hours.
345   And they tell me my eyes were a hawk
    In perpetual hunger. Split an iroko tree

In two, hide a woman's beauty in its heartwood
    And seal it up again—Elesin, journeying by,
    Would make his camp beside that tree
    Of all the shades in the forest. 350
PRAISE-SINGER: Who would deny your reputation, snake-on-
    the-loose in dark passages of the market! Bed-bug who wages
    war on the mat and receives the thanks of the vanquished!
    When caught with his bride's own sister he protested—but I
    was only prostrating myself to her as becomes a grateful in- 355
    law. Hunter who carries his powder-horn on the hips and fires
    crouching or standing! Warrior who never makes that excuse
    of the whining coward—but how can I go to battle without
    my trousers?—trouserless or shirtless it's all one to him. Oka-
    rearing-from-a-camouflage-of-leaves, before he strikes the 360
    victim is already prone! Once they told him, Howu, a stallion
    does not feed on the grass beneath him: he replied, true, but
    surely he can roll on it!
WOMEN: Ba-a-a-ba O!
PRAISE-SINGER: Ah, but listen yet. You know there is the leaf- 365
    knibbling grub and there is the cola-chewing beetle; the leaf-
    nibbling grub lives on the leaf, the cola-chewing beetle lives
    in the colanut. Don't we know what our man feeds on when
    we find him cocooned in a woman's wrapper?
ELESIN: Enough, enough, you all have cause 370
    To know me well. But, if you say this earth
    Is still the same as gave birth to those songs,
    Tell me who was that goddess through whose lips
    I saw the ivory pebbles of Oya's river-bed.
    Iyaloja, who is she? I saw her enter 375
    Your stall; all your daughters I know well.
    No, not even Ogun-of-the-farm toiling
    Dawn till dusk on his tuber patch
    Not even Ogun with the finest hoe he ever
    Forged at the anvil could have shaped 380
    That rise of buttocks, not though he had
    The richest earth between his fingers.
    Her wrapper was no disguise
    For thighs whose ripples shamed the river's
    Coils around the hills of Ilesi. Her eyes 385
    Were new-laid eggs glowing in the dark.
    Her skin . . .
IYALOJA: Elesin Oba . . .
ELESIN: What! Where do you all say I am?
IYALOJA: Still among the living. 390
ELESIN: And that radiance which so suddenly
    Lit up this market I could boast
    I knew so well?
IYALOJA: Has one step already in her husband's home. She is
    betrothed. 395
ELESIN: (*irritated*) Why do you tell me that?

(IYALOJA *falls silent. The women shuffle uneasily.*)

IYALOJA: Not because we dare give you offence Elesin. Today is
    your day and the whole world is yours. Still, even those who
    leave town to make a new dwelling elsewhere like to be
    remembered by what they leave behind. 400
ELESIN: Who does not seek to be remembered?
    Memory is Master of Death, the chink
    In his armour of conceit. I shall leave
    That which makes my going the sheerest
    Dream of an afternoon. Should voyagers 405

Not travel light? Let the considerate traveller
Shed, of his excessive load, all
That may benefit the living.

410 WOMEN: *(relieved)* Ah Elesin Oba, we knew you for a man of
honour.

ELESIN: Then honour me. I deserve a bed of honour to lie upon.

IYALOJA: The best is yours. We know you for a man of honour.
You are not one who eats and leaves nothing on his plate for
children. Did you not say it yourself? Not one who blights the
415 happiness of others for a moment's pleasure.

ELESIN: Who speaks of pleasure? O women, listen!
Pleasure palls. Our acts should have meaning.
The sap of the plantain never dries.
You have seen the young shoot swelling
420 Even as the parent stalk begins to wither.
Women, let my going be likened to
The twilight hour of the plantain.

WOMEN: What does he mean Iyaloja? This language is the language of our elders, we do not fully grasp it.

425 IYALOJA: I dare not understand you yet Elesin.

ELESIN: All you who stand before the spirit that dares
The opening of the last door of passage,
Dare to rid my going of regrets! My wish
Transcends the blotting out of thought
430 In one mere moment's tremor of the senses.
Do me credit. And do me honour.
I am girded for the route beyond
Burdens of waste and longing.
Then let me travel light. Let
435 Seed that will not serve the stomach
On the way remain behind. Let it take root
In the earth of my choice, in this earth
I leave behind.

IYALOJA: *(turns to WOMEN)* The voice I hear is already touched
440 by the waiting fingers of our departed. I dare not refuse.

WOMAN: Buy Iyaloja . . .

IYALOJA: The matter is no longer in our hands.

WOMAN: But she is betrothed to your own son. Tell him.

IYALOJA: My son's wish is mine. I did the asking for him, the loss
445 can be remedied. But who will remedy the blight of closed
hands on the day when all should be openness and light? Tell
him, you say! You wish that I burden him with knowledge
that will sour his wish and lay regrets on the last moments of
his mind. You pray to him who is your intercessor to the other
450 world—don't set this world adrift in your own time; would
you rather it was my hand whose sacrilege wrenched it loose?

WOMAN: Not many men will brave the curse of a dispossessed
husband.

IYALOJA: Only the curses of the departed are to be feared. The
455 claims of one whose foot is on the threshold of their abode
surpasses even the claims of blood. It is impiety even to place
hindrances in their ways.

ELESIN: What do my mothers say? Shall I step
Burdened into the unknown?

460 IYALOJA: Not we, but the very earth says No. The sap in the
plantain does not dry. Let grain that will not feed the voyager
at his passage drop here and take root as he steps beyond this
earth and us. Oh you who fill the home from hearth to
threshold with the voices of children, you who now bestride
465 the hidden gulf and pause to draw the right foot across and

into the resting-home of the great forebears, it is good that
your loins be drained into the earth we know, that your last
strength be ploughed back into the womb that gave you being.

PRAISE-SINGER: Iyaloja, mother of multitudes in the teeming
470 market of the world, how your wisdom transfigures you!

IYALOJA: *(smiling broadly, completely reconciled)* Elesin, even at
the narrow end of the passage I know you will look back and
sigh a last regret for the flesh that flashed past your spirit in
flight. You always had a restless eye. Your choice has my
475 blessing. *(To the WOMEN.)* Take the good news to our daughter and make her ready. *(Some WOMEN go off.)*

ELESIN: Your eyes were clouded at first.

IYALOJA: Not for long. It is those who stand at the gateway of the
great change to whose cry we must pay heed. And then, think
480 of this—it makes the mind tremble. The fruit of such a union
is rare. It will be neither of this world nor of the next. Nor of
the one behind us. As if the timelessness of the ancestor world
and the unborn have joined spirits to wring an issue of the
elusive being of passage . . . Elesin!

485 ELESIN: I am here. What is it?

IYALOJA: Did you hear all I said just now?

ELESIN: Yes.

IYALOJA: The living must eat and drink. When the moment
comes, don't turn the food to rodents' droppings in their
490 mouth. Don't let them taste the ashes of the world when they
step out at dawn to breathe the morning dew.

ELESIN: This doubt is unworthy of you Iyaloja.

IYALOJA: Eating the awusa nut is not so difficult as drinking water afterwards.

495 ELESIN: The waters of the bitter stream are honey to a man
Whose tongue has savoured all.

IYALOJA: No one knows when the ants desert their home; they
leave the mound intact. The swallow is never seen to peck
holes in its nest when it is time to move with the season.
500 There are always throngs of humanity behind the leave-taker.
The rain should not come through the roof for them, the
wind must not blow through the walls at night.

ELESIN: I refuse to take offence.

IYALOJA: You wish to travel light. Well, the earth is yours. But be
505 sure the seed you leave in it attracts no curse.

ELESIN: You really mistake my person Iyaloja.

IYALOJA: I said nothing. Now we must go prepare your bridal
chamber. Then these same hands will lay your shrouds.

ELESIN: *(exasperated)* Must you be so blunt? *(Recovers.)* Well,
510 weave your shrouds, but let the fingers of my bride seal my
eyelids with earth and wash my body.

IYALOJA: Prepare yourself Elesin.

*(She gets up to leave. At that moment the women return, leading
the BRIDE. ELESIN's face glows with pleasure. He flicks the sleeves
of his agbada with renewed confidence and steps forward to meet
the group. As the girl kneels before IYALOJA, lights fade out on the
scene.)*

— TWO —

*The verandah of the District Officer's bungalow. A tango is play-
ing from an old hand-cranked gramophone and, glimpsed
through the wide windows and doors which open onto the forestage verandah are the shapes of SIMON PILKINGS and his wife,*

JANE, *tangoing in and out of shadows in the living-room. They were wearing what is immediately apparent as some form of fancy-dress. The dance goes on for some moments and then the figure of a 'Native Administration' policeman emerges and climbs up the steps onto the verandah. He peeps through and observes the dancing couple, reacting with what is obviously a long-standing bewilderment. He stiffens suddenly, his expression changes to one of disbelief and horror. In his excitement he upsets a flower-pot and attracts the attention of the couple. They stop dancing.*

PILKINGS: Is there anyone out there?
JANE: I'll turn off the gramophone.
PILKINGS: *(approaching the verandah)* I'm sure I heard something fall over. *(The constable retreats slowly, open-mouthed*
5 *as PILKINGS approaches the verandah.)* Oh it's you Amusa. Why didn't you just knock instead of knocking things over?
AMUSA: *(stammers badly and points a shaky finger at his dress)* Mista Pirinkin . . . Mista Pirinkin . . .
PILKINGS: What is the matter with you?
10 JANE: *(emerging)* Who is it dear? Oh, Amusa . . .
PILKINGS: Yes it's Amusa, and acting most strangely.
AMUSA: *(his attention now transferred to* MRS PILKINGS*)* Mam-madam . . . you too!
PILKINGS: What the hell is the matter with you man!
15 JANE: Your costume darling. Our fancy dress.
PILKINGS: Oh hell, I'd forgotten all about that. *(Lifts the face mask over his head showing his face. His wife follows suit.)*
JANE: I think you've shocked his big pagan heart bless him.
PILKINGS: Nonsense, he's a Moslem. Come on Amusa, you
20 don't believe in all this nonsense do you? I thought you were a good Moslem.
AMUSA: Mista Pirinkin, I beg you sir, what you think you do with that dress? It belong to dead cult, not for human being.
PILKINGS: Oh Amusa, what a let down you are. I swear by you at
25 the club you know—thank God for Amusa, he doesn't believe in any mumbo-jumbo. And now look at you!
AMUSA: Mista Pirinkin, I beg you, take it off. Is not good for man like you to touch that cloth.
PILKINGS: Well, I've got it on. And what's more Jane and I have
30 bet on it we're taking first prize at the ball. Now, if you can just pull yourself together and tell me what you wanted to see me about . . .
AMUSA: Sir, I cannot talk this matter to you in that dress. I no fit.
PILKINGS: What's that rubbish again?
35 JANE: He is dead earnest too Simon. I think you'll have to handle this delicately.
PILKINGS: Delicately my. . . ! Look here Amusa, I think this little joke has gone far enough hm? Let's have some sense. You seem to forget that you are a police officer in the service
40 of His Majesty's Government. I order you to report your business at once or face disciplinary action.
AMUSA: Sir, it is a matter of death. How can man talk against death to person in uniform of death? Is like talking against government to person in uniform of police. Please sir, I go
45 and come back.
PILKINGS: *(roars)* Now! *(AMUSA switches his gaze to the ceiling suddenly, remains mute.)*
JANE: Oh Amusa, what is there to be scared of in the costume? You saw it confiscated last month from those *egungun* men

who were creating trouble in town. You helped arrest the cult 50 leaders yourself—if the juju didn't harm you at the time how could it possibly harm you now? And merely by looking at it?
AMUSA: *(without looking down)* Madam, I arrest the ringleaders who make trouble but me I no touch *egungun*. That *egungun* inself, I no touch. And I no abuse 'am. I arrest ring- 55 leader but I treat *egungun* with respect.
PILKINGS: It's hopeless. We'll merely end up missing the best part of the ball. When they get this way there is nothing you can do. It's simply hammering against a brick wall. Write your report or whatever it is on that pad Amusa and take your- 60 self out of here. Come on Jane. We only upset his delicate sensibilities by remaining here.

*(*AMUSA *waits for them to leave, then writes in the notebook, somewhat laboriously. Drumming from the direction of the town wells up.* AMUSA *listens, makes a movement as if he wants to recall* PILKINGS *but changes his mind. Completes his note and goes. A few moments later* PILKINGS *emerges, picks up the pad and reads.)*

PILKINGS: Jane!
JANE: *(from the bedroom)* Coming darling. Nearly ready.
PILKINGS: Never mind being ready, just listen to this. 65
JANE: What is it?
PILKINGS: Amusa's report. Listen. 'I have to report that it come to my information that one prominent chief, namely, the Elesin Oba, is to commit death tonight as a result of native custom. Because this is criminal offence I await further in- 70 struction at charge office. Sergeant Amusa.'

*(*JANE *comes out onto the verandah while he is reading.)*

JANE: Did I hear you say commit death?
PILKINGS: Obviously he means murder.
JANE: You mean a ritual murder?
PILKINGS: Must be. You think you've stamped it all out but it's 75 always lurking under the surface somewhere.
JANE: Oh. Does it mean we are not getting to the ball at all?
PILKINGS: No-o. I'll have the man arrested. Everyone remotely involved. In any case there may be nothing to it. Just rumours.
JANE: Really? I thought you found Amusa's rumours generally 80 reliable.
PILKINGS: That's true enough. But who knows what may have been giving him the scare lately. Look at his conduct tonight.
JANE: *(laughing)* You have to admit he had his own peculiar logic. *(Deepens her voice.)* How can man talk against death to 85 person in uniform of death? *(Laughs.)* Anyway, you can't go into the police station dressed like that.
PILKINGS: I'll send Joseph with instructions. Damn it, what a confounded nuisance!
JANE: But don't you think you should talk first to the man, 90 Simon?
PILKINGS: Do you want to go to the ball or not?
JANE: Darling, why are you getting rattled? I was only trying to be intelligent. It seems hardly fair just to lock up a man—and a chief at that—simply on the er . . . what is that legal word 95 again?—uncorroborated word of a sergeant.
PILKINGS: Well, that's easily decided. Joseph!
JOSEPH: *(from within)* Yes master.
PILKINGS: You're quite right of course, I am getting rattled.

100   Probably the effect of those bloody drums. Do you hear how they go on and on?

JANE: I wondered when you'd notice. Do you suppose it has something to do with this affair?

PILKINGS: Who knows? They always find an excuse for making a
105   noise . . . (Thoughtfully.) Even so . . .

JANE: Yes Simon?

PILKINGS: It's different Jane. I don't think I've heard this particular —sound—before. Something unsettling about it.

JANE: I thought all bush drumming sounded the same.

110   PILKINGS: Don't tease me now Jane. This may be serious.

JANE: I'm sorry. (Gets up and throws her arms around his neck. Kisses him. The houseboy enters, retreats and knocks.)

PILKINGS: (wearily) Oh, come in Joseph! I don't know where you pick up all these elephantine notions of tact. Come over
115   here.

JOSEPH: Sir?

PILKINGS: Joseph, are you a christian or not?

JOSEPH: Yessir.

PILKINGS: Does seeing me in this outfit bother you?

120   JOSEPH: No sir, it has no power.

PILKINGS: Thank God for some sanity at last. Now Joseph, answer me on the honour of a christian—what is supposed to be going on in town tonight?

JOSEPH: Tonight sir? You mean that chief who is going to kill
125   himself?

PILKINGS: What?

JANE: What do you mean, kill himself?

PILKINGS: You do mean he is going to kill somebody don't you?

JOSEPH: No master. He will not kill anybody and no one will kill
130   him. He will simply die.

JANE: But why Joseph?

JOSEPH: It is native law and custom. The King die last month. Tonight is his burial. But before they can bury him, the Elesin must die so as to accompany him to heaven.

135   PILKINGS: I seem to be fated to clash more often with that man than with any of the other chiefs.

JOSEPH: He is the King's Chief Horseman.

PILKINGS: (in a resigned way) I know.

JANE: Simon, what's the matter?

140   PILKINGS: It would have to be him!

JANE: Who is he?

PILKINGS: Don't you remember? He's that chief with whom I had a scrap some three or four years ago. I helped his son get to a medical school in England, remember? He fought tooth
145   and nail to prevent it.

JANE: Oh now I remember. He was that very sensitive young man. What was his name again?

PILKINGS: Olunde. Haven't replied to his last letter come to think of it. The old pagan wanted him to stay and carry on
150   some family tradition or the other. Honestly I couldn't understand the fuss he made. I literally had to help the boy escape from close confinement and load him onto the next boat. A most intelligent boy, really bright.

JANE: I rather thought he was much too sensitive you know. The
155   kind of person you feel should be a poet munching rose petals in Bloomsbury.

PILKINGS: Well, he's going to make a first-class doctor. His mind is set on that. And as long as he wants my help he is welcome to it.

160   JANE: (after a pause) Simon.

PILKINGS: Yes?

JANE: This boy, he was his eldest son wasn't he?

PILKINGS: I'm not sure. Who could tell with that old ram?

JANE: Do you know, Joseph?

165   JOSEPH: Oh yes madam. He was the eldest son. That's why Elesin cursed master good and proper. The eldest son is not supposed to travel away from the land.

JANE: (giggling) Is that true Simon? Did he really curse you good and proper?

170   PILKINGS: By all accounts I should be dead by now.

JOSEPH: Oh no, master is white man. And good christian. Black man juju can't touch master.

JANE: If he was his eldest, it means that he would be the Elesin to the next king. It's a family thing isn't it, Joseph?

175   JOSEPH: Yes madam. And if this Elesin had died before the King, his eldest son must take his place.

JANE: That would explain why the old chief was so mad you took the boy away.

PILKINGS: Well it makes me all the more happy I did.

180   JANE: I wonder if he knew.

PILKINGS: Who? Oh, you mean Olunde?

JANE: Yes. Was that why he was so determined to get away? I wouldn't stay if I knew I was trapped in such a horrible custom.

PILKINGS: (thoughtfully) No, I don't think he knew. At least he
185   gave no indication. But you couldn't really tell with him. He was rather close you know, quite unlike most of them. Didn't give much away, not even to me.

JANE: Aren't they all rather close, Simon?

PILKINGS: These natives here? Good gracious. They'll open
190   their mouths and yap with you about their family secrets before you can stop them. Only the other day . . .

JANE: But Simon, do they really give anything away? I mean, anything that really counts. This affair for instance, we didn't know they still practised that custom did we?

195   PILKINGS: Ye-e-es, I suppose you're right there. Sly, devious bastards.

JOSEPH: (stiffly) Can I go now master? I have to clean the kitchen.

PILKINGS: What? Oh, you can go. Forgot you were still here.

(JOSEPH goes.)

200   JANE: Simon, you really must watch your language. Bastard isn't just a simple swear-word in these parts, you know.

PILKINGS: Look, just when did you become a social anthropologist, that's what I'd like to know.

JANE: I'm not claiming to know anything. I just happen to have
205   overheard quarrels among the servants. That's how I know they consider it a smear.

PILKINGS: I thought the extended family system took care of all that. Elastic family, no bastards.

JANE: (shrugs) Have it your own way.

(Awkward silence. The drumming increases in volume. JANE gets up suddenly, restless.)

210   That drumming Simon, do you think it might really be connected with this ritual? It's been going on all evening.

PILKINGS: Let's ask our native guide. Joseph! Just a minute Joseph. (JOSEPH re-enters.) What's the drumming about?

JOSEPH: I don't know master.

215 PILKINGS: What do you mean you don't know? It's only two years since your conversion. Don't tell me all that holy water nonsense also wiped out your tribal memory.

JOSEPH: (visibly shocked) Master!

JANE: Now you've done it.

220 PILKINGS: What have I done now?

JANE: Never mind. Listen Joseph, just tell me this. Is that drumming connected with dying or anything of that nature?

JOSEPH: Madam, this is what I am trying to say: I am not sure. It sounds like the death of a great chief and then, it sounds like the wedding of a great chief. It really mix me up.

225 PILKINGS: Oh get back to the kitchen. A fat lot of help you are.

JOSEPH: Yes master. (Goes.)

JANE: Simon . . .

PILKINGS: Alright, alright. I'm in no mood for preaching.

230 JANE: It isn't my preaching you have to worry about, it's the preaching of the missionaries who preceded you here. When they make converts they really convert them. Calling holy water nonsense to our Joseph is really like insulting the Virgin Mary before a Roman Catholic. He's going to hand in his

235 notice tomorrow you mark my word.

PILKINGS: Now you're being ridiculous.

JANE: Am I? What are you willing to bet that tomorrow we are going to be without a steward-boy? Did you see his face?

PILKINGS: I am more concerned about whether or not we will be

240 one native chief short by tomorrow. Christ! Just listen to those drums. (He strides up and down, undecided.)

JANE: (getting up) I'll change and make up some supper.

PILKINGS: What's that?

JANE: Simon, it's obvious we have to miss this ball.

245 PILKINGS: Nonsense. It's the first bit of real fun the European club has managed to organise for over a year, I'm damned if I'm going to miss it. And it is a rather special occasion. Doesn't happen every day.

JANE: You know this business has to be stopped Simon. And you

250 are the only man who can do it.

PILKINGS: I don't have to stop anything. If they want to throw themselves off the top of a cliff or poison themselves for the sake of some barbaric custom what is that to me? If it were ritual murder or something like that I'd be duty-bound to do

255 something. I can't keep an eye on all the potential suicides in this province. And as for that man—believe me it's good riddance.

JANE: (laughs) I know you better than that Simon. You are going to have to do something to stop it—after you've finished

260 blustering.

PILKINGS: (shouts after her) And suppose after all it's only a wedding. I'd look a proper fool if I interrupted a chief on his honeymoon, wouldn't I? (Resumes his angry stride, slows down.) Ah well, who can tell what those chiefs actually do on

265 their honeymoon anyway? (He takes up the pad and scribbles rapidly on it.) Joseph! Joseph! Joseph! (Some moments later JOSEPH puts in a sulky appearance.) Did you hear me call you? Why the hell didn't you answer?

JOSEPH: I didn't hear master.

270 PILKINGS: You didn't hear me! How come you are here then?

JOSEPH: (stubbornly) I didn't hear master.

PILKINGS: (controls himself with an effort) We'll talk about it in the morning. I want you to take this note directly to Sergeant Amusa. You'll find him at the charge office. Get on your

bicycle and race there with it. I expect you back in twenty 275 minutes exactly. Twenty minutes, is that clear?

JOSEPH: Yes master. (Going.)

PILKINGS: Oh er . . . Joseph.

JOSEPH: Yes master?

PILKINGS: (between gritted teeth) Er . . . forget what I said just 280 now. The holy water is not nonsense. I was talking nonsense.

JOSEPH: Yes master. (Goes.)

JANE: (pokes her head round the door) Have you found him?

PILKINGS: Found who?

JANE: Joseph. Weren't you shouting for him? 285

PILKINGS: Oh yes, he turned up finally.

JANE: You sounded desperate. What was it all about?

PILKINGS: Oh nothing. I just wanted to apologise to him. Assure him that the holy water isn't really nonsense.

JANE: Oh? And how did he take it? 290

PILKINGS: Who the hell gives a damn! I had a sudden vision of our Very Reverend Macfarlane drafting another letter of complaint to the Resident about my unchristian language towards his parishioners.

JANE: Oh I think he's given up on you by now. 295

PILKINGS: Don't be too sure. And anyway, I wanted to make sure Joseph didn't 'lose' my note on the way. He looked sufficiently full of the holy crusade to do some such thing.

JANE: If you've finished exaggerating, come and have something to eat. 300

PILKINGS: No, put it all way. We can still get to the ball.

JANE: Simon . . .

PILKINGS: Get your costume back on. Nothing to worry about. I've instructed Amusa to arrest the man and lock him up.

JANE: But that station is hardly secure Simon. He'll soon get his 305 friends to help him escape.

PILKINGS: A-ah, that's where I have out-thought you. I'm not having him put in the station cell. Amusa will bring him right here and lock him up in my study. And he'll stay with him till we get back. No one will dare come here to incite him to 310 anything.

JANE: How clever of you darling. I'll get ready.

PILKINGS: Hey.

JANE: Yes darling.

PILKINGS: I have a surprise for you. I was going to keep it until 315 we actually got to the ball.

JANE: What is it?

PILKINGS: You know the Prince is on a tour of the colonies don't you? Well, he docked in the capital only this morning but he is already at the Residency. He is going to grace the ball with 320 his presence later tonight.

JANE: Simon! Not really.

PILKINGS: Yes he is. He's been invited to give away the prizes and he has agreed. You must admit old Engleton is the best Club Secretary we ever had. Quick off the mark that lad. 325

JANE: But how thrilling.

PILKINGS: The other provincials are going to be damned envious.

JANE: I wonder what he'll come as.

PILKINGS: Oh I don't know. As a coat-of-arms perhaps. Anyway it won't be anything to touch this. 330

JANE: Well that's lucky. If we are to be presented I won't have to start looking for a pair of gloves. It's all sewn on.

PILKINGS: (laughing) Quite right. Trust a woman to think of that. Come on, let's get going.

335 JANE: (*rushing off*) Won't be a second. (*Stops.*) Now I see why
you've been so edgy all evening. I thought you weren't handling this affair with your usual brilliance—to begin with that is.
PILKINGS: (*his mood is much improved*) Shut up woman and get
your things on.
340 JANE: Alright boss, coming.

(PILKINGS *suddenly begins to hum the tango to which they were
dancing before. Starts to execute a few practice steps. Lights
fade.*)

— THREE —

A *swelling, agitated hum of women's voices rises immediately in
the background. The lights come on and we see the frontage of a
converted cloth stall in the market. The floor leading up to the
entrance is covered in rich velvets and woven cloth. The women
come on stage, borne backwards by the determined progress of
Sergeant* AMUSA *and his two constables who already have their
batons out and use them as a pressure against the women. At the
edge of the cloth-covered floor however the women take a determined stand and block all further progress of the men. They begin
to tease them mercilessly.*

AMUSA: I am tell you women for last time to commot my road. I
am here on official business.
WOMAN: Official business you white man's eunuch? Official
business is taking place where you want to go and it's a busi-
5 ness you wouldn't understand.
WOMAN: (*makes a quick tug at the constable's baton*) That
doesn't fool anyone you know. It's the one you carry under
your government knickers that counts. (*She bends low as if to
peep under the baggy shorts. The embarrassed constable
10 quickly puts his knees together. The* WOMEN *roar.*)
WOMAN: You mean there is nothing there at all?
WOMAN: Oh there was something. You know that handbell
which the whiteman uses to summon his servants . . . ?
AMUSA: (*he manages to preserve some dignity throughout*) I
15 hope you women know that interfering with officer in execution of his duty is criminal offence.
WOMAN: Interfere? He says we're interfering with him. You foolish man we're telling you there's nothing there to interfere with.
AMUSA: I am order you now to clear the road.
20 WOMAN: What road? The one your father built?
WOMAN: You are a Policeman not so? Then you know what they
call trespassing in court. Or—(*Pointing to the cloth-lined
steps.*)—do you think that kind of road is built for every kind
of feet.
25 WOMAN: Go back and tell the white man who sent you to come
himself.
AMUSA: If I go I will come back with reinforcement. And we will
all return carrying weapons.
WOMAN: Oh, now I understand. Before they can put on those
30 knickers the white man first cuts off their weapons.
WOMAN: What a cheek! You mean you come here to show
power to women and you don't even have a weapon.
AMUSA: (*shouting above the laughter*) For the last time I warn
you women to clear the road.
35 WOMAN: To where?
AMUSA: To that hut. I know he dey dere.

WOMAN: Who?
AMUSA: The chief who call himself Elesin Oba.
WOMAN: You ignorant man. It is not he who calls himself Elesin
Oba, it is his blood that says it. As it called out to his father 40
before him and will to his son after him. And that is in spite of
everything your white man can do.
WOMAN: Is it not the same ocean that washes this land and the
white man's land? Tell your white man he can hide our son
away as long as he likes. When the time comes for him, the 45
same ocean will bring him back.
AMUSA: The government say dat kin' ting must stop.
WOMAN: Who will stop it? You? Tonight our husband and father
will prove himself greater than the laws of strangers.
AMUSA: I tell you nobody go prove anyting tonight or anytime. Is 50
ignorant and criminal to prove dat kin' prove.
IYALOJA: (*entering, from the hut. She is accompanied by a group
of young girls who have been attending the* BRIDE) What is it
Amusa? Why do you come here to disturb the happiness of
others. 55
AMUSA: Madame Iyaloja, I glad you come. You know me. I no
like trouble but duty is duty. I am here to arrest Elesin for
criminal intent. Tell these women to stop obstructing me in
the performance of my duty.
IYALOJA: And you? What gives you the right to obstruct our 60
leader of men in the performance of his duty.
AMUSA: What kin' duty be dat one Iyaloja.
IYALOJA: What kin' duty? What kin' duty does a man have to his
new bride?
AMUSA: (*bewildered, looks at the women and at the entrance to* 65
the hut) Iyaloja, is it wedding you call dis kin' ting?
IYALOJA: You have wives haven't you? Whatever the white man
has done to you he hasn't stopped you having wives. And if he
has, at least he is married. If you don't know what a marriage
is, go and ask him to tell you. 70
AMUSA: This no to wedding.
IYALOJA: And ask him at the same time what he would have
done if anyone had come to disturb him on his wedding night.
AMUSA: Iyaloja, I say dis no to wedding.
IYALOJA: You want to look inside the bridal chamber? You want 75
to see for yourself how a man cuts the virgin knot?
AMUSA: Madam . . .
WOMAN: Perhaps his wives are still waiting for him to learn.
AMUSA: Iyaloja, make you tell dese women make den no insult
me again. If I hear dat kin' insult once more . . . 80
GIRL: (*pushing her way through*) You will do what?
GIRL: He's out of his mind. It's our mothers you're talking to, do
you know that? Not to any illiterate villager you can bully and
terrorise. How dare you intrude here anyway?
GIRL: What a cheek, what impertinence! 85
GIRL: You've treated them too gently. Now let them see what it is
to tamper with the mothers of this market.
GIRLS: Your betters dare not enter the market when the women
say no!
GIRL: Haven't you learnt that yet, you jester in khaki and starch? 90
IYALOJA: Daughters . . .
GIRL: No no Iyaloja, leave us to deal with him. He no longer
knows his mother, we'll teach him.

(*With a sudden movement they snatch the batons of the two
constables. They begin to hem them in.*)

GIRL: What next? We have your batons? What next? What are
95   you going to do?

(With equally swift movements they knock off their hats.)

GIRL: Move if you dare. We have your hats, what will you do
about it? Didn't the white man teach you to take off your hats
before women?
IYALOJA: It's a wedding night. It's a night of joy for us. Peace . . .
100   GIRL: Not for him. Who asked him here?
GIRL: Does he dare go to the Residency without an invitation?
GIRL: Not even where the servants eat the left-overs.
GIRLS: *(in turn. In an 'English' accent)* Well well it's Mister
Amusa. Were you invited? *(Play-acting to one another. The*
105   *older* WOMEN *encourage them with their titters.)*

—Your invitation card please?
—Who are you? Have we been introduced?
—And who did you say you were?
—Sorry, I didn't quite catch your name.
110   —May I take your hat?
—If you insist. May I take yours? *(Exchanging the police-
man's hats.)*
—How very kind of you.
—Not at all. Won't you sit down?
115   —After you.
—Oh no.
—I insist.
—You're most gracious.
—And how do you find the place?
120   —The natives are alright.
—Friendly?
—Tractable.
—Not a teeny-weeny bit restless?
—Well, a teeny-weeny bit restless.
125   —One might even say, difficult?
—Indeed one might be tempted to say, difficult.
—But you do manage to cope?
—Yes indeed I do. I have a rather faithful ox called Amusa.
—He's loyal?
130   —Absolutely.
—Lay down his life for you what?
—Without a moment's thought.
—Had one like that once. Trust him with my life.
—Mostly of course they are liars.
135   —Never known a native tell the truth.
—Does it get rather close around here?
—It's mild for this time of the year.
—But the rains may still come.
—They are late this year aren't they?
140   —They are keeping African time.
—Ha ha ha ha
—Ha ha ha ha
—The humidity is what gets me.
—It used to be whisky.
145   —Ha ha ha ha
—Ha ha ha ha
—What's your handicap old chap?
—Is there racing by golly?
—Splendid golf course, you'll like it.
150   —I'm beginning to like it already.

—And a European club, exclusive.
—You've kept the flag flying.
—We do our best for the old country.
—It's a pleasure to serve.
—Another whisky old chap?   155
—You are indeed too too kind.
—Not at all sir. Where is that boy? *(With a sudden bellow.)*
Sergeant!
AMUSA: *(snaps to attention)* Yessir!

(The WOMEN *collapse with laughter.)*

GIRL: Take your men out of here.   160
AMUSA: *(realising the trick, he rages from loss of face)* I'm give
you warning . . .
GIRL: Alright then. Off with his knickers! *(They surge slowly
forward.)*
IYALOJA: Daughters, please.   165
AMUSA: *(squaring himself for defence)* The first woman wey
touch me . . .
IYALOJA: My children, I beg of you . . .
GIRL: Then tell him to leave this market. This is the home of our
mothers. We don't want the eater of white left-overs at the   170
feast their hands have prepared.
IYALOJA: You heard them Amusa. You had better go.
GIRLS: Now!
AMUSA: *(commencing his retreat)* We dey go now, but make you
no say we no warn you.   175
GIRL: Before we read the riot act—you should know all about that.
AMUSA: Make we go. *(They depart, more precipitately.)*

(The WOMEN *strike their palms across in the gesture of wonder.)*

WOMEN: Do they teach you all that school?
WOMAN: And to think I nearly kept Apinke away from the place.
WOMAN: Did you hear them? Did you see how they mimicked   180
the white man?
WOMAN: The voices exactly. Hey, there are wonders in this world!
IYALOJA: Well, our elders have said it: Dada may be weak, but he
has a younger sibling who is truly fearless.
WOMAN: The next time the white man shows his face in this   185
market I will set Wuraola on his tail.

(A WOMAN *bursts into song and dance of euphoria—'Tani l'awa
o l'ogbeja? Kayi! A l'ogbeja. Omo Kekere l'ogbeja.' ['Who says we
haven't a defender? Silence! We have our defenders. Little children are our champions.'] The rest of the* WOMEN *join in, some
placing the girls on their back like infants, other dancing round
them. The dance becomes general, mounting in excitement.* ELE-
SIN *appears, in wrapper only. In his hands a white velvet cloth
folded loosely as if it held some delicate object. He cries out.)*

ELESIN: Oh you mothers of beautiful brides! *(The dancing stops.
They turn and see him, and the object in his hands.* IYALOJA
approaches and gently takes the cloth from him.) Take it. It is
no mere virgin stain, but the union of life and the seeds of   190
passage. My vital flow, the last from this flesh is intermingled
with the promise of future life. All is prepared. Listen! *(A
steady drum-beat from the distance.)* Yes. It is nearly time.
The King's dog has been killed. The King's favourite horse is
about to follow his master. My brother chiefs know their task   195
and perform it well. *(He listens again.)*

(The BRIDE *emerges, stands shyly by the door. He turns to her.)*

Our marriage is not yet wholly fulfilled. When earth and passage wed, the consummation is complete only when there are grains of earth on the eyelids of passage. Stay by me till then.
200 My faithful drummers, do me your last service. This is where I have chosen to do my leave-taking, in this heart of life, this hive which contains the swarm of the world in its small compass. This is where I have known love and laughter away from the palace. Even the richest food cloys when eaten days on
205 end; in the market, nothing ever cloys. Listen. *(They listen to the drums.)* They have begun to seek out the heart of the King's favourite horse. Soon it will ride in its bolt of raffia with the dog at its feet. Together they will ride on the shoulders of the King's grooms through the pulse centres of the town.
210 They know it is here I shall await them. I have told them. *(His eyes appear to cloud. He passes his hand over them as if to clear his sight. He gives a faint smile.)* It promises well; just then I felt my spirit's eagerness. The kite makes for wide spaces and the wind creeps up behind its tail; can the kite say less than—
215 thank you, the quicker the better? But wait a while my spirit. Wait. Wait for the coming of the courier of the King. Do you know friends, the horse is born to this one destiny, to bear the burden that is man upon its back. Except for this night, this night alone when the spotless stallion will ride in triumph on
220 the back of man. In the time of my father I witnessed the strange sight. Perhaps tonight also I shall see it for the last time. If they arrive before the drums beat for me, I shall tell him to let the Alafin know I follow swiftly. If they come after the drums have sounded, why then, all is well for I have gone
225 ahead. Our spirits shall fall in step along the great passage. *(He listens to the drums. He seems again to be falling into a state of semi-hypnosis; his eyes scan the sky but it is in a kind of daze. His voice is a little breathless.)* The moon has fed, a glow from its full stomach fills the sky and air, but I cannot
230 tell where is that gateway through which I must pass. My faithful friends, let our feet touch together this last time, lead me into the other market with sounds that cover my skin with down yet make my limbs strike earth like a thoroughbred. Dear mothers, let me dance into the passage even as I have
235 lived beneath your roofs. *(He comes down progressively among them. They make away for him, the* DRUMMERS *playing. His dance is one of solemn, regal motions, each gesture of the body is made with a solemn finality. The* WOMEN *join him, their steps a somewhat more fluid version of his. Beneath the*
240 PRAISE-SINGER's *exhortations the* WOMEN *dirge 'Alẹ lẹ lẹ, awo mi lọ'.)*
PRAISE-SINGER: Elesin Alafin, can you hear my voice?
ELESIN: Faintly, my friend, faintly.
PRAISE-SINGER: Elesin Alafin, can you hear my call?
245 ELESIN: Faintly my king, faintly.
PRAISE-SINGER: Is your memory sound Elesin?
Shall my voice be a blade of grass and
Tickle the armpit of the past?
ELESIN: My memory needs no prodding but
250 What do you wish to say to me?
PRAISE-SINGER: Only what has been spoken. Only what concerns
The dying wish of the father of all.
ELESIN: It is buried like seed-yam in my mind
This is the season of quick rains, the harvest
255 Is this moment due for gathering.

PRAISE-SINGER: If you cannot come, I said, swear
You'll tell my favourite horse. I shall
Ride on through the gates alone.
ELESIN: Elesin's message will be read
Only when his loyal heart no longer beats. 260
PRAISE-SINGER: If you cannot come Elesin, tell my dog.
I cannot stay the keeper too long
At the gate.
ELESIN: A dog does not outrun the hand
That feeds it meat. A horse that throws its rider 265
Slows down to a stop. Elesin Alafin
Trusts no beasts with messages between
A king and his companion.
PRAISE-SINGER: If you get lost my dog will track
The hidden path to me. 270
ELESIN: The seven-way crossroads confuses
Only the stranger. The Horseman of the King
Was born in the recesses of the house.
PRAISE-SINGER: I know the wickedness of men. If there is
Weight on the loose end of your sash, such weight 275
As no mere man can shift; if your sash is earthed
By evil minds who mean to part us at the last . . .
ELESIN: My sash is of the deep purple *alari*;
It is no tethering-rope. The elephant
Trails no tethering-rope; that king 280
Is not yet crowned who will peg an elephant—
Not even you my friend and King.
PRAISE-SINGER: And yet this fear will not depart from me
The darkness of this new abode is deep—
Will your human eyes suffice? 285
ELESIN: In a night which falls before our eyes
However deep, we do not miss our way.
PRAISE-SINGER: Shall I now not acknowledge I have stood
Where wonders met their end? The elephant deserves
Better than that we say 'I have caught 290
A glimpse of something.' If we see the tamer
Of the forest let us say plainly, we have seen
An elephant.
ELESIN: *(his voice is drowsy)* I have freed myself of earth and now
It's getting dark. Strange voices guide my feet. 295
PRAISE-SINGER: The river is never so high that the eyes
Of a fish are covered. The night is not so dark
That the albino fails to find his way. A child
Returning homewards craves no leading by the hand.
Gracefully does the mask regain his grove at the end of the 300
day . . .
Gracefully. Gracefully does the mask dance
Homeward at the end of day, gracefully . . .

*(*ELESIN's *trance appears to be deepening, his steps heavier.)*

IYALOJA: It is the death of war that kills the valiant,
Death of water is how the swimmer goes
It is the death of markets that kills the trader 305
And death of indecision takes the idle away
The trade of the cutlass blunts its edge
And the beautiful die the death of beauty.
It takes an Elesin to die the death of death . . .
Only Elesin . . . dies the unknowable death of death . . . 310

Gracefully, gracefully does the horseman regain
The stables at the end of day, gracefully . . .

PRAISE-SINGER: How shall I tell what my eyes have seen? The
Horseman gallops on before the courier, how shall I tell what
315   my eyes have seen? He says a dog may be confused by new
scents of beings he never dreamt of, so he must precede the
dog to heaven. He says a horse may stumble on strange boulders and be lamed, so he races on before the horse to heaven.
It is best, he says, to trust no messenger who may falter at the
320   outer gate; oh how shall I tell what my ears have heard? But
do you hear me still Elesin, do you hear your faithful one?

(ELESIN *in his motions appears to feel for a direction of sound,
subtly, but he only sinks deeper into his trance-dance.*)

Elesin Alafin, I no longer sense your flesh. The drums are
changing now but you have gone far ahead of the world. It is
not yet noon in heaven; let those who claim it is begin their
325   own journey home. So why must you rush like an impatient
bride: why do you race to desert your Olohun-iyo?

(ELESIN *is now sunk fully deep in his trance, there is no longer
sign of any awareness of his surroundings.*)

Does the deep voice of *gbedu* cover you then, like the passage
of royal elephants? Those drums that brook no rivals, have
they blocked the passage to your ears that my voice passes into
330   wind, a mere leaf floating in the night? Is your flesh lightened
Elesin, is that lump of earth I slid between your slippers to
keep you longer slowly sifting from your feet? Are the drums
on the other side now tuning skin to skin with ours in *osugbo*?
Are there sounds there I cannot hear, do footsteps surround
335   you which pound the earth like *gbedu*, roll like thunder
round the dome of the world? Is the darkness gathering in
your head Elesin? Is there now a streak of light at the end of
the passage, a light I dare not look upon? Does it reveal whose
voices we often heard, whose touches we often felt, whose
340   wisdoms come suddenly into the mind when the wisest have
shaken their heads and murmured: It cannot be done? Elesin
Alafin, don't think I do not know why your lips are heavy, why
your limbs are drowsy as palm oil in the cold of harmattan. I
would call you back but when the elephant heads for the jun-
345   gle, the tail is too small a handhold for the hunter that would
pull him back. The sun that heads for the sea no longer heeds
the prayers of the farmer. When the river begins to taste
the salt of the ocean, we no longer know what deity to call on,
the river-god or Olokun. No arrow flies back to the string, the
350   child does not return through the same passage that gave it
birth. Elesin Oba, can you hear me at all? Your eyelids are
glazed like a courtesan's, is it that you see the dark groom and
master of life? And will you see my father? Will you tell him
that I stayed with you to the last? Will my voice ring in your
355   ears awhile, will you remember Olohun-iyo even if the music
on the other side surpasses his mortal craft? But will they
know you over there? Have they eyes to gauge your worth,
have they the heart to love you, will they know what thoroughbred prances towards them in caparisons of honour? If
360   they do not Elesin, if any there cuts your yam with a small
knife, or pours you wine in a small calabash, turn back and
return to welcoming hands. If the world were not greater than
the wishes of Olohun-iyo, I would not let you go . . .

(*He appears to break down.* ELESIN *dances on, completely in a
trance. The dirge wells up louder and stronger.* ELESIN's *dance
does not lose its elasticity but his gestures become, if possible,
even more weighty. Lights fade slowly on the scene.*)

— FOUR —

*A Masque. The front side of the stage is part of a wide corridor
around the great hall of the Residency extending beyond vision
into the rear and wings. It is redolent of the tawdry decadence of
a far-flung but key imperial frontier. The couples in a variety of
fancy-dress are ranged around the walls, gazing in the same direction. The guest-of-honour is about to make an appearance. A
portion of the local police brass band with its white conductor is
just visible. At last, the entrance of Royalty. The band plays
'Rule Britannia', badly, beginning long before he is visible. The
couples bow and curtsey as he passes by them. Both he and his
companions are dressed in seventeenth century European costume. Following behind are the* RESIDENT *and his partner similarly attired. As they gain the end of the hall where the orchestra
dais begins the music comes to an end. The* PRINCE *bows to the
guests. The band strikes up a Viennese waltz and the* PRINCE
formally opens the floor. Several bars later the RESIDENT *and his
companion follow suit. Others follow in appropriate pecking order. The orchestra's waltz rendition is not of the highest musical
standard.*

Some time later the PRINCE *dances again into view and is settled
into a corner by the* RESIDENT *who then proceeds to select couples
as they dance past for introduction, sometimes threading his way
through the dancers to tap the lucky couple on the shoulder. Desperate efforts from many to ensure that they are recognised in
spite of, perhaps, their costume. The ritual of introductions soon
takes in* PILKINGS *and his wife. The* PRINCE *is quite fascinated by
their costume and they demonstrate the adaptations they have
made to it, pulling down the mask to demonstrate how the
egungun normally appears, then showing the various press-but-
ton controls they have innovated for the face flaps, the sleeves,
etc. They demonstrate the dance steps and the guttural sounds
made by the egungun, harrass other dancers in the hall,* MRS.
PILKINGS *playing the 'restrainer' to* PILKINGS' *manic darts. Everyone is highly entertained, the Royal Party especially who lead
the applause.*

*At this point a liveried footman comes in with a note on a salver
and is intercepted almost absent-mindedly by the* RESIDENT *who
takes the note and reads it. After polite coughs he succeeds in
excusing the* PILKINGSES *from the* PRINCE *and takes them aside.
The* PRINCE *considerately offers the* RESIDENT's *wife his hand
and dancing is resumed.*

On their way out the RESIDENT *gives an order to his* AIDE-DE-
CAMP. *They come into the side corridor where the* RESIDENT
hands the note to PILKINGS.

RESIDENT: As you see it says 'emergency' on the outside. I took
the liberty of opening it because His Highness was obviously
enjoying the entertainment. I didn't want to interrupt unless
really necessary.

5   PILKINGS: Yes, yes of course sir.

RESIDENT: Is it really as bad as it says? What's it all about?

PILKINGS: Some strange custom they have sir. It seems because the King is dead some important chief has to commit suicide.

RESIDENT: The King? Isn't it the same one who died nearly a
10   month ago?

PILKINGS: Yes sir.

RESIDENT: Haven't they buried him yet?

PILKINGS: They take their time about these things sir. The pre-burial ceremonies last nearly thirty days. It seems tonight is
15   the final night.

RESIDENT: But what has it got to do with the market women? Why are they rioting? We've waived that troublesome tax haven't we?

PILKINGS: We don't quite know that they are exactly rioting yet
20   sir. Sergeant Amusa is sometimes prone to exaggerations.

RESIDENT: He sounds desperate enough. That comes out even in his rather quaint grammar. Where is the man anyway? I asked my aide-de-camp to bring him here.

PILKINGS: They are probably looking in the wrong verandah. I'll
25   fetch him myself.

RESIDENT: No no you stay here. Let your wife go and look for them. Do you mind my dear . . . ?

JANE: Certainly not, your Excellency. (Goes.)

RESIDENT: You should have kept me informed Pilkings. You re-
30   alise how disastrous it would have been if things had erupted while His Highness was here.

PILKINGS: I wasn't aware of the whole business until tonight sir.

RESIDENT: Nose to the ground Pilkings, nose to the ground. If we all let these little things slip past us where would the em-
35   pire be eh? Tell me that. Where would we all be?

PILKINGS: (low voice) Sleeping peacefully at home I bet.

RESIDENT: What did you say Pilkings?

PILKINGS: It won't happen again sir.

RESIDENT: It mustn't Pilkings. It mustn't. Where is that damned
40   sergeant? I ought to get back to His Highness as quickly as possible and offer him some plausible explanation for my rather abrupt conduct. Can you think of one Pilkings?

PILKINGS: You could tell him the truth sir.

RESIDENT: I could? No no no no no Pilkings, that would never do.
45   What! Go and tell him there is a riot just two miles away from him? This is supposed to be a secure colony of His Majesty, Pilkings.

PILKINGS: Yes sir.

RESIDENT: Ah, there they are. No, these are not our native po-
50   lice. Are these the ring-leaders of the riot?

PILKINGS: Sir, these are my police officers.

RESIDENT: Oh, I beg your pardon officers. You do look a little . . . I say, isn't there something missing in their uniforms? I think they used to have some rather colourful sashes. If I remember
55   rightly I recommended them myself in my young days in the service. A bit of colour always appeals to the natives, yes. I remember putting that in my report. Well well well, where are we? Make your report man.

PILKINGS: (moves close to AMUSA, between his teeth) And let's
60   have no more superstitious nonsense from you Amusa or I'll throw you in the guardroom for a month and feed you pork!

RESIDENT: What's that? What has pork to do with it?

PILKINGS: Sir, I was just warning him to be brief. I'm sure you are most anxious to hear his report.

RESIDENT: Yes yes yes of course. Come on man, speak up. Hey,
65   didn't we give them some colourful fez hats with all those wavy things, yes, pink tassells . . .

PILKINGS: Sir, I think if he was permitted to make his report we might find that he lost his hat in the riot.

RESIDENT: Ah yes indeed. I'd better tell His Highness that. Lost
70   his hat in the riot, ha ha. He'll probably say well, as long as he didn't lost his head. (Chuckles to himself.) Don't forget to send me a report first thing in the morning young Pilkings.

PILKINGS: No sir.

RESIDENT: And whatever you do, don't let things get out of
75   hand. Keep a cool head and — nose to the ground Pilkings. (Wanders off in the general direction of the hall.)

PILKINGS: Yes sir.

AIDE-DE-CAMP: Would you be needing me sir?

PILKINGS: No thanks Bob. I think His Excellency's need of you is
80   greater than ours.

AIDE-DE-CAMP: We have a detachment of soldiers from the capital sir. They accompanied His Highness up here.

PILKINGS: I doubt if it will come to that but, thanks, I'll bear it in mind. Oh, could you send an orderly with my cloak.
85

AIDE-DE-CAMP: Very good sir. (Goes.)

PILKINGS: Now Sergeant.

AMUSA: Sir . . . (Makes an effort, stops dead. Eyes to the ceiling.)

PILKINGS: Oh, not again.

AMUSA: I cannot against death to dead cult. This dress get power
90   of dead.

PILKINGS: Alright, let's go. You are relieved of all further duty Amusa. Report to me first thing in the morning.

JANE: Shall I come Simon?

PILKINGS: No, there's no need for that. If I can get back later I
95   will. Otherwise get Bob to bring you home.

JANE: Be careful Simon . . . I mean, be clever.

PILKINGS: Sure I will. You two, come with me. (As he turns to go, the clock in the Residency begins to chime. PILKINGS looks at his watch then turns, horror-stricken, to stare at his wife.
100   The same thought clearly occurs to her. He swallows hard. An orderly brings his cloak.) It's midnight. I had no idea it was that late.

JANE: But surely . . . they don't count the hours the way we do. The moon, or something.
105

PILKINGS: I am . . . not so sure.

(He turns and breaks into a sudden run. The two constables follow, also at a run. AMUSA, who has kept his eyes on the ceiling throughout waits until the last of the footsteps has faded out of hearing. He salutes suddenly, but without once looking in the direction of the woman.)

AMUSA: Goodnight madam.

JANE: Oh. (She hesitates.) Amusa . . . (He goes off without seem-ing to have heard.) Poor Simon . . . (A figure emerges from the shadows, a young black man dressed in a sober western suit.
110   He peeps into the hall, trying to make out the figures of the dancers.) Who is that?

OLUNDE: (emerging into the light.) I didn't mean to startle you madam. I am looking for the District Officer.

JANE: Wait a minute . . . don't I know you? Yes, you are Olunde,
115   the young man who . . .

OLUNDE: Mrs Pilkings! How fortunate. I came here to look for your husband.

JANE: Olunde! Let's look at you. What a fine young man you've
  become. Grand but solemn. Good God, when did you return? Simon never said a word. But you do look well Olunde.
  Really!

OLUNDE: You are . . . well, you look quite well yourself Mrs
  Pilkings. From what little I can see of you.

JANE: Oh, this. It's caused quite a stir I assure you, and not all of
  it very pleasant. You are not shocked I hope?

OLUNDE: Why should I be? But don't you find it rather hot in
  there? Your skin must find it difficult to breathe.

JANE: Well, it is a little hot I must confess, but it's all in a good
  cause.

OLUNDE: What cause Mrs Pilkings?

JANE: All this. The ball. And His Highness being here in person
  and all that.

OLUNDE: (mildly) And that is the good cause for which you des-
  ecrate an ancestral mask?

JANE: Oh, so you are shocked after all. How disappointing.

OLUNDE: No I am not shocked Mrs Pilkings. You forget that I
  have now spent four years among your people. I discovered
  that you have no respect for what you do not understand.

JANE: Oh. So you've returned with a chip on your shoulder.
  That's a pity Olunde. I am sorry.

(An uncomfortable silence follows.)

  I take it then that you did not find your stay in England altogether edifying.

OLUNDE: I don't say that. I found your people quite admirable
  in many ways, their conduct and courage in this war for
  instance.

JANE: Ah yes the war. Here of course it is all rather remote.
  From time to time we have a black-out drill just to remind us
  that there is a war on. And the rare convoy passes through on
  its way somewhere or on manoeuvres. Mind you there is the
  occasional bit of excitement like that ship that was blown up
  in the harbour.

OLUNDE: Here? Do you mean through enemy action?

JANE: Oh no, the war hasn't come that close. The captain did it
  himself. I don't quite understand it really. Simon tried to explain. The ship had to be blown up because it had become
  dangerous to the other ships, even to the city itself. Hundreds
  of the coastal population would have died.

OLUNDE: Maybe it was loaded with ammunition and had
  caught fire. Or some of those lethal gases they've been experimenting on.

JANE: Something like that. The captain blew himself up with it.
  Deliberately. Simon said someone had to remain on board to
  light the fuse.

OLUNDE: It must have been a very short fuse.

JANE: (shrugs) I don't know much about it. Only that there was
  no other way to save lives. No time to devise anything else.
  The captain took the decision and carried it out.

OLUNDE: Yes . . . I quite believe it. I met men like that in England.

JANE: Oh just look at me! Fancy welcoming you back with such
  morbid news. Stale too. It was at least six months ago.

OLUNDE: I don't find it morbid at all. I find it rather inspiring. It
  is an affirmative commentary on life.

JANE: What is?

OLUNDE: That captain's self-sacrifice.

JANE: Nonsense. Life should never be thrown deliberately away.

OLUNDE: And the innocent people round the harbour?

JANE: Oh, how does one know? The whole thing was probably
  exaggerated anyway.

OLUNDE: That was a risk the captain couldn't take. But please
  Mrs Pilkings, do you think you could find your husband for
  me? I have to talk to him.

JANE: Simon? Oh. (As she recollects for the first time the full
  significance of OLUNDE's presence.) Simon is . . . there is a
  little problem in town. He was sent for. But . . . when did you
  arrive? Does Simon know you're here?

OLUNDE: (suddenly earnest) I need your help Mrs Pilkings. I've
  always found you somewhat more understanding than your
  husband. Please find him for me and when you do, you must
  help me talk to him.

JANE: I'm afraid I don't quite . . . follow you. Have you seen my
  husband already?

OLUNDE: I went to your house. Your houseboy told me you were
  here. (He smiles.) He even told me how I would recognise
  you and Mr Pilkings.

JANE: Then you must know what my husband is trying to do for
  you.

OLUNDE: For me?

JANE: For you. For your people. And to think he didn't even
  know you were coming back! But how do you happen to be
  here? Only this evening we were talking about you. We
  thought you were still four thousand miles away.

OLUNDE: I was sent a cable.

JANE: A cable? Who did? Simon? The business of your father
  didn't begin till tonight.

OLUNDE: A relation sent it weeks ago, and it said nothing about
  my father. All it said was, Our King is dead. But I knew I had
  to return home at once so as to bury my father. I understood
  that.

JANE: Well, thank God you don't have to go through that agony.
  Simon is going to stop it.

OLUNDE: That's why I want to see him. He's wasting his time.
  And since he has been so helpful to me I don't want him to
  incur the enmity of our people. Especially over nothing.

JANE: (sits down open-mouthed) You . . . you Olunde!

OLUNDE: Mrs Pilkings, I came home to bury my father. As soon
  as I heard the news I booked my passage home. In fact we
  were fortunate. We travelled in the same convoy as your
  Prince, so we had excellent protection.

JANE: But you don't think your father is also entitled to whatever
  protection is available to him?

OLUNDE: How can I make you understand? He has protection.
  No one can undertake what he does tonight without the deepest protection the mind can conceive. What can you offer
  him in place of his peace of mind, in place of the honour and
  veneration of his own people? What would you think of your
  Prince if he had refused to accept the risk of losing his life on
  this voyage? This . . . showing-the-flag tour of colonial
  possessions.

JANE: I see. So it isn't just medicine you studied in England.

OLUNDE: Yet another error into which your people fall. You believe that everything which appears to make sense was learnt
  from you.

JANE: Not so fast Olunde. You have learnt to argue I can tell
  that, but I never said you made sense. However cleverly you
  try to put it, it is still a barbaric custom. It is even worse — it's

feudal! The king dies and a chieftain must be buried with him. How feudalistic can you get!

OLUNDE: *(waves his hand towards the background. The* PRINCE *is dancing past again—to a different step—and all the guests are bowing and curtseying as he passes)* And this? Even in the midst of a devastating war, look at that. What name would you give to that?

JANE: Therapy, British style. The preservation of sanity in the midst of chaos.

OLUNDE: Others would call it decadence. However, it doesn't really interest me. You white races know how to survive; I've seen proof of that. By all logical and natural laws this war should end with all the white races wiping out one another, wiping out their so-called civilisation for all time and reverting to a state of primitivism the like of which has so far only existed in your imagination when you thought of us. I thought all that at the beginning. Then I slowly realised that your greatest art is the art of survival. But at least have the humility to let others survive in their own way.

JANE: Through ritual suicide?

OLUNDE: Is that worse than mass suicide? Mrs Pilkings, what do you call what those young men are sent to do by their generals in this war? Of course you have also mastered the art of calling things by names which don't remotely describe them.

JANE: You talk! You people with your long-winded, roundabout way of making conversation.

OLUNDE: Mrs Pilkings, whatever we do, we never suggest that a thing is the opposite of what it really is. In your newsreels I heard defeats, thorough, murderous defeats described as strategic victories. No wait, it wasn't just on your newsreels. Don't forget I was attached to hospitals all the time. Hordes of your wounded passed through those wards. I spoke to them. I spent long evenings by their bedside while they spoke terrible truths of the realities of that war. I know now how history is made.

JANE: But surely, in a war of this nature, for the morale of the nation you must expect . . .

OLUNDE: That a disaster beyond human reckoning be spoken of as a triumph? No. I mean, is there no mourning in the home of the bereaved that such blasphemy is permitted?

JANE: *(after a moment's pause)* Perhaps I can understand you now. The time we picked for you was not really one for seeing us at our best.

OLUNDE: Don't think it was just the war. Before that even started I had plenty of time to study your people. I saw nothing, finally, that gave you the right to pass judgement on other peoples and their ways. Nothing at all.

JANE: *(hesitantly)* Was it the . . . colour thing? I know there is some discrimination.

OLUNDE: Don't make it so simple, Mrs Pilkings. You make it sound as if when I left, I took nothing at all with me.

JANE: Yes . . . and to tell the truth, only this evening, Simon and I agreed that we never really knew what you left with.

OLUNDE: Neither did I. But I found out over there. I am grateful to your country for that. And I will never give it up.

JANE: Olunde, please. . . . promise me something. Whatever you do, don't throw away what you have started to do. You want to be a doctor. My husband and I believe you will make an excellent one, sympathetic and competent. Don't let anything make you throw away your training.

OLUNDE: *(genuinely surprised)* Of course not. What a strange idea. I intend to return and complete my training. Once the burial of my father is over.

JANE: Oh, please . . . !

OLUNDE: Listen! Come outside. You can't hear anything against that music.

JANE: What is it?

OLUNDE: The drums. Can you hear the change? Listen.

(The drums come over, still distant but more distinct. There is a change of rhythm, it rises to a crescendo and then, suddenly, it is cut off. After a silence, a new beat begins, slow and resonant.)

There. It's all over.

JANE: You mean he's . . .

OLUNDE: Yes Mrs Pilkings, my father is dead. His will-power has always been enormous; I know he is dead.

JANE: *(screams)* How can you be so callous! So unfeeling! You announce your father's own death like a surgeon looking down on some strange . . . stranger's body! You're just a savage like all the rest.

AIDE-DE-CAMP: *(rushing out)* Mrs Pilkings. Mrs Pilkings. *(She breaks down, sobbing.)* Are you alright, Mrs Pilkings?

OLUNDE: She'll be alright. *(Turns to go.)*

AIDE-DE-CAMP: Who are you? And who the hell asked your opinion?

OLUNDE: You're quite right, nobody. *(Going.)*

AIDE-DE-CAMP: What the hell! Did you hear me ask you who you were?

OLUNDE: I have business to attend to.

AIDE-DE-CAMP: I'll give you business in a moment you impudent nigger. Answer my question!

OLUNDE: I have a funeral to arrange. Excuse me. *(Going.)*

AIDE-DE-CAMP: I said stop! Orderly!

JANE: No no, don't do that. I'm alright. And for heaven's sake don't act so foolishly. He's a family friend.

AIDE-DE-CAMP: Well he'd better learn to answer civil questions when he's asked them. These natives put a suit on and they get high opinions of themselves.

OLUNDE: Can I go now?

JANE: No no don't go. I must talk to you. I'm sorry about what I said.

OLUNDE: It's nothing Mrs Pilkings. And I'm really anxious to go. I couldn't see my father before, it's forbidden for me, his heir and successor to set eyes on him from the moment of the king's death. But now . . . I would like to touch his body while it is still warm.

JANE: You will. I promise I shan't keep you long. Only, I couldn't possibly let you go like that. Bob, please excuse us.

AIDE-DE-CAMP: If you're sure . . .

JANE: Of course I'm sure. Something happened to upset me just then, but I'm alright now. Really.

(The AIDE-DE-CAMP *goes, somewhat reluctantly.)*

OLUNDE: I mustn't stay long.

JANE: Please, I promise not to keep you. It's just that . . . oh you saw yourself what happens to one in this place. The Resident's man thought he was being helpful, that's the way we all react. But I can't go in among that crowd just now and if I stay by myself somebody will come looking for me. Please,

350 just say something for a few moments and then you can go. Just so I can recover myself.

OLUNDE: What do you want me to say?

JANE: Your calm acceptance for instance, can you explain that? It was so unnatural. I don't understand that at all. I feel a need
355 to understand all I can.

OLUNDE: But you explained it yourself. My medical training perhaps. I have seen death too often. And the soldiers who returned from the front, they died on our hands all the time.

JANE: No. It has to be more than that. I feel it has to do with the
360 many things we don't really grasp about your people. At least you can explain.

OLUNDE: All these things are part of it. And anyway, my father has been dead in my mind for nearly a month. Ever since I learnt of the King's death. I've lived with my bereavement so
365 long now that I cannot think of him alive. On that journey on the boat, I kept my mind on my duties as the one who must perform the rites over his body. I went through it all again and again in my mind as he himself had taught me. I didn't want to do anything wrong, something which might jeopardise the
370 welfare of my people.

JANE: But he had disowned you. When you left he swore publicly you were no longer his son.

OLUNDE: I told you, he was a man of tremendous will. Sometimes that's another way of saying stubborn. But among our
375 people, you don't disown a child just like that. Even if I had died before him I would still be buried like his eldest son. But it's time for me to go.

JANE: Thank you. I feel calmer. Don't let me keep you from your duties.
380 OLUNDE: Goodnight Mrs Pilkings.

JANE: Welcome home. (*She holds out her hand. As he takes it footsteps are heard approaching the drive. A short while later a woman's sobbing is also heard.*)

PILKINGS: (*off*) Keep them here till I get back. (*He strides into
385 view, reacts at the sight of* OLUNDE *but turns to his wife.*) Thank goodness you're still here.

JANE: Simon, what happened?

PILKINGS: Later Jane, please. Is Bob still here?

JANE: Yes, I think so. I'm sure he must be.
390 PILKINGS: Try and get him out here as quietly as you can. Tell him it's urgent.

JANE: Of course. Oh Simon, you remember . . .

PILKINGS: Yes yes. I can see who it is. Get Bob out here. (*She runs off.*) At first I thought I was seeing a ghost.
395 OLUNDE: Mr Pilkings, I appreciate what you tried to do. I want you to believe that. I can only tell you it would have been a terrible calamity if you'd succeeded.

PILKINGS: (*opens his mouth several times, shuts it*) You . . . said what?
400 OLUNDE: A calamity for us, the entire people.

PILKINGS: (*sighs*) I see. Hm.

OLUNDE: And now I must go. I must see him before he turns cold.

PILKINGS: Oh ah . . . em . . . but this is a shock to see you. I mean er thinking all this while you were in England and
405 thanking God for that.

OLUNDE: I came on the mail boat. We travelled in the Prince's convoy.

PILKINGS: Ah yes, a-ah, hm . . . er well . . .

OLUNDE: Goodnight. I can see you are shocked by the whole

410 business. But you must know by now there are things you cannot understand — or help.

PILKINGS: Yes. Just a minute. There are armed policemen that way and they have instructions to let no one pass. I suggest you wait a little. I'll er . . . yes, I'll give you an escort.
415 OLUNDE: That's very kind of you. But do you think it could be quickly arranged.

PILKINGS: Of course. In fact, yes, what I'll do is send Bob over with some men to the er . . . place. You can go with them. Here he comes now. Excuse me a minute.
420 AIDE-DE-CAMP: Anything wrong sir?

PILKINGS: (*takes him to one side*) Listen Bob, that cellar in the disused annexe of the Residency, you know, where the slaves were stored before being taken down to the coast . . .

AIDE-DE-CAMP: Oh yes, we use it as a storeroom for broken
425 furniture.

PILKINGS: But it's still got the bars on it?

AIDE-DE-CAMP: Oh yes, they are quite intact.

PILKINGS: Get the keys please. I'll explain later. And I want a strong guard over the Residency tonight.
430 AIDE-DE-CAMP: We have that already. The detachment from the coast . . .

PILKINGS: No, I don't want them at the gates of the Residency. I want you to deploy them at the bottom of the hill, a long way from the main hall so they can deal with any situation long
435 before the sound carries to the house.

AIDE-DE-CAMP: Yes of course.

PILKINGS: I don't want His Highness alarmed.

AIDE-DE-CAMP: You think the riot will spread here?

PILKINGS: It's unlikely but I don't want to take a chance. I made
440 them believe I was going to lock the man up in my house, which was what I had planned to do in the first place. They are probably assailing it by now. I took a roundabout route here so I don't think there is any danger at all. At least not before dawn. Nobody is to leave the premises of course — the
445 native employees I mean. They'll soon smell something is up and they can't keep their mouths shut.

AIDE-DE-CAMP: I'll give instructions at once.

PILKINGS: I'll take the prisoner down myself. Two policemen will stay with him throughout the night. Inside the cell.
450 AIDE-DE-CAMP: Right sir. (*Salutes and goes off at the double.*)

PILKINGS: Jane. Bob is coming back in a moment with a detachment. Until he gets back please stay with Olunde.

(*He makes an extra warning gesture with his eyes.*)

OLUNDE: Please Mr Pilkings . . .

PILKINGS: I hate to be stuffy old son, but we have a crisis on our
455 hands. It has to do with your father's affair if you must know. And it happens also at a time when we have His Highness here. I am responsible for security so you'll simply have to do as I say. I hope that's understood. (*Marches off quickly, in the direction from which he made his first appearance.*)
460 OLUNDE: What's going on? All this can't be just because he failed to stop my father killing himself.

JANE: I honestly don't know. Could it have sparked off a riot?

OLUNDE: No. If he'd succeeded that would be more likely to start the riot. Perhaps there were other factors involved. Was
465 there a chieftancy dispute?

JANE: None that I know of.

ELESIN: (*an animal bellow from off*) Leave me alone! Is it not enough that you have covered me in shame! White man, take your hand from my body!

(OLUNDE stands frozen on the spot. JANE understanding at last, tries to move him.)

470   JANE: Let's go in. It's getting chilly out here.

PILKINGS: *(off)* Carry him.

ELESIN: Give me back the name you have taken away from me you ghost from the land of the nameless!

PILKINGS: Carry him! I can't have a disturbance here. Quickly!
475   stuff up his mouth.

JANE: Oh God! Let's go in. Please Olunde. *(OLUNDE does not move.)*

ELESIN: Take your albino's hand from me you . . .

(Sounds of a struggle. His voice chokes as he is gagged.)

OLUNDE: *(quietly)* That was my father's voice.

480   JANE: Oh you poor orphan, what have you come home to?

(There is a sudden explosion of rage from off-stage and powerful steps come running up the drive.)

PILKINGS: You bloody fools, after him!

(Immediately ELESIN, in handcuffs, comes pounding in the direction of JANE and OLUNDE, followed some moments afterwards by PILKINGS and the constables. ELESIN confronted by the seeming statue of his son, stops dead. OLUNDE stares above his head into the distance. The constables try to grab him. JANE screams at them.)

JANE: Leave him alone! Simon, tell them to leave him alone.

PILKINGS: All right, stand aside you. *(Shrugs.)* Maybe just as well. It might help to calm him down.

(For several moments they hold the same position. ELESIN moves a few steps forward, almost as if he's still in doubt.)

485   ELESIN: Olunde? *(He moves his head, inspecting him from side to side.)* Olunde! *(He collapses slowly at OLUNDE's feet.)* Oh son, don't let the sight of your father turn you blind!

OLUNDE: *(he moves for the first time since he heard his voice, brings his head slowly down to look on him).* I have no father,
490   eater of left-overs.

(He walks slowly down the way his father had run. Light fades out on ELESIN, sobbing into the ground.)

— FIVE —

A wide iron-barred gate stretches almost the whole width of the cell in which ELESIN is imprisoned. His wrists are encased in thick iron bracelets, chained together; he stands against the bars, looking out. Seated on the ground to one side on the outside is his recent BRIDE, her eyes bent perpetually to the ground. Figures of the two guards can be seen deeper inside the cell, alert to every movement ELESIN makes. PILKINGS now in a police officer's uniform enters noiselessly, observes him for a while. Then he coughs ostentatiously and approaches. Leans against the bars near a corner, his back to ELESIN. He is obviously trying to fall in mood with him. Some moments' silence.

PILKINGS: You seem fascinated by the moon.

ELESIN: *(after a pause)* Yes, ghostly one. Your twin-brother up there engages my thoughts.

PILKINGS: It is a beautiful night.

ELESIN: Is that so?   5

PILKINGS: The light on the leaves, the peace of the night . . .

ELESIN: The night is not at peace, District Officer.

PILKINGS: No? I would have said it was. You know, quiet . . .

ELESIN: And does quiet mean peace for you?

PILKINGS: Well, nearly the same thing. Naturally there is a sub-   10
tle difference . . .

ELESIN: The night is not at peace ghostly one. The world is not at peace. You have shattered the peace of the world for ever. There is no sleep in the world tonight.

PILKINGS: It is still a good bargain if the world should lose one   15
night's sleep as the price of saving a man's life.

ELESIN: You did not save my life District Officer. You destroyed it.

PILKINGS: Now come on . . .

ELESIN: And not merely my life but the lives of many. The end of the night's work is not over. Neither this year nor the next   20
will see it. If I wished you well, I would pray that you do not stay long enough on our land to see the disaster you have brought upon us.

PILKINGS: Well, I did my duty as I saw it. I have no regrets.

ELESIN: No. The regrets of life always come later.   25

(Some moments' pause.)

You are waiting for dawn white man. I hear you saying to yourself: only so many hours until dawn and then the danger is over. All I must do is keep him alive tonight. You don't quite understand it all but you know that tonight is when what ought to be must be brought about. I shall ease your mind   30
even more, ghostly one. It is not an entire night but a moment of the night, and that moment is past. The moon was my messenger and guide. When it reached a certain gateway in the sky, it touched that moment for which my whole life has been spent in blessings. Even I do not know the gateway. I   35
have stood here and scanned the sky for a glimpse of that door but, I cannot see it. Human eyes are useless for a search of this nature. But in the house of *osugbo*, those who keep watch through the spirit recognised the moment, they sent word to me through the voice of our sacred drums to prepare myself. I   40
heard them and I shed all thoughts of earth. I began to follow the moon to the abode of gods . . . servant of the white king, that was when you entered my chosen place of departure on feet of desecration.

PILKINGS: I'm sorry, but we all see our duty differently.   45

ELESIN: I no longer blame you. You stole from me my first-born, sent him to your country so you could turn him into something in your own image. Did you plan it all before-hand? There are moments when it seems part of a larger plan. He who must follow my footsteps is taken from me, sent   50
across the ocean. Then, in my turn, I am stopped from fulfill-ing my destiny. Did you think it all out before, this plan to push our world from its course and sever the cord that links us to the great origin?

PILKINGS: You don't really believe that. Anyway, if that was my   55
intention with your son, I appear to have failed.

ELESIN: You did not fail in the main thing ghostly one. We know the roof covers the rafters, the cloth covers blemishes; who

60 would have known that the white skin covered our future, preventing us from seeing the death our enemies had prepared for us. The world is set adrift and its inhabitants are lost. Around them, there is nothing but emptiness.

PILKINGS: Your son does not take so gloomy a view.

ELESIN: Are you dreaming now white man? Were you not present at my reunion of shame? Did you not see when the world reversed itself and the father fell before his son, asking forgiveness?

PILKINGS: That was in the heat of the moment. I spoke to him and . . . if you want to know, he wishes he could cut out his tongue for uttering the words he did.

ELESIN: No. What he said must never be unsaid. The contempt of my own son rescued something of my shame at your hands. You may have stopped me in my duty but I know now that I did give birth to a son. Once I mistrusted him for seeking the companionship of those my spirit knew as enemies of our race. Now I understand. One should seek to obtain the secrets of his enemies. He will avenge my shame, white one. His spirit will destroy you and yours.

PILKINGS: That kind of talk is hardly called for. If you don't want my consolation . . .

ELESIN: No white man, I do not want your consolation.

PILKINGS: As you wish. Your son anyway, sends his consolation. He asks your forgiveness. When I asked him not to despise you his reply was: I cannot judge him, and if I cannot judge him, I cannot despise him. He wants to come to you to say goodbye and to receive your blessing.

ELESIN: Goodbye? Is he returning to your land?

PILKINGS: Don't you think that's the most sensible thing for him to do? I advised him to leave at once, before dawn, and he agrees that is the right course of action.

ELESIN: Yes, it is best. And even if I did not think so, I have lost the father's place of honour. My voice is broken.

PILKINGS: Your son honours you. If he didn't he would not ask your blessing.

ELESIN: No. Even a thoroughbred is not without pity for the turf he strikes with his hoof. When is he coming?

PILKINGS: As soon as the town is a little quieter. I advised it.

ELESIN: Yes white man, I am sure you advised it. You advise all our lives although on the authority of what gods, I do not know.

PILKINGS: *(opens his mouth to reply, then appears to change his mind. Turns to go. Hesitates and stops again)* Before I leave you, may I ask just one thing of you?

ELESIN: I am listening.

PILKINGS: I wish to ask you to search the quiet of your heart and tell me — do you not find great contradictions in the wisdom of your own race?

ELESIN: Make yourself clear, white one.

PILKINGS: I have lived among you long enough to learn a saying or two. One came to my mind tonight when I stepped into the market and saw what was going on. You were surrounded by those who egged you on with song and praises. I thought, are these not the same people who say: the elder grimly approaches heaven and you ask him to bear your greetings yonder; do you really think he makes the journey willingly? After that, I did not hesitate.

(A pause. ELESIN sighs. Before he can speak a sound of running feet is heard.)

JANE: *(off)* Simon! Simon!

PILKINGS: What on earth . . ! *(Runs off.)*

(ELESIN turns to his new wife, gazes on her for some moments.)

ELESIN: My young bride, did you hear the ghostly one? You sit and sob in your silent heart but say nothing to all this. First I blamed the white man, then I blamed my gods for deserting me. Now I feel I want to blame you for the mystery of the sapping of my will. But blame is a strange peace offering for a man to bring a world he has deeply wronged, and to its innocent dwellers. Oh little mother, I have taken countless women in my life but you were more than a desire of the flesh. I needed you as the abyss across which my body must be drawn, I filled it with earth and dropped my seed in it at the moment of preparedness for my crossing. You were the final gift of the living to their emissary to the land of the ancestors, and perhaps your warmth and youth brought new insights of this world to me and turned my feet leaden on this side of the abyss. For I confess to you, daughter, my weakness came not merely from the abomination of the white man who came violently into my fading presence, there was also a weight of longing on my earth-held limbs. I would have shaken it off, already my foot had begun to lift but then, the white ghost entered and all was defiled.

(Approaching voices of PILKINGS and his wife.)

JANE: Oh Simon, you will let her in won't you?

PILKINGS: I really wish you'd stop interfering.

(They come in view. JANE is in a dressing-gown. PILKINGS is holding a note to which he refers from time to time.)

JANE: Good gracious, I didn't initiate this. I was sleeping quietly, or trying to anyway, when the servant brought it. It's not my fault if one can't sleep undisturbed even in the Residency.

PILKINGS: He'd have done the same if we were sleeping at home so don't sidetrack the issue. He knows he can get round you or he wouldn't send you the petition in the first place.

JANE: Be fair Simon. After all he was thinking of your own interests. He is grateful you know, you seem to forget that. He feels he owes you something.

PILKINGS: I just wish they'd leave this man alone tonight, that's all.

JANE: Trust him Simon. He's pledged his word it will all go peacefully.

PILKINGS: Yes, and that's the other thing. I don't like being threatened.

JANE: Threatened? *(Takes the note.)* I didn't spot any threat.

PILKINGS: It's there. Veiled, but it's there. The only way to prevent serious rioting tomorrow — what a cheek!

JANE: I don't think he's threatening you Simon.

PILKINGS: He's picked up the idiom alright. Wouldn't surprise me if he's been mixing with commies or anarchists over there. The phrasing sounds too good to be true. Damn! If only the Prince hadn't picked this time for his visit.

JANE: Well, even so Simon, what have you got to lose? You don't want a riot on your hands, not with the Prince here.

PILKINGS: *(going up to ELESIN.)* Let's see what he has to say. Chief Elesin, there is yet another person who wants to see you. As she is not a next-of-kin I don't really feel obliged to let her in. But your son sent a note with her, so it's up to you.

ELESIN: I know who that must be. So she found out your hiding-
place. Well, it was not difficult. My stench of shame is so
170   strong, it requires no hunter's dog to follow it.
PILKINGS: If you don't want to see her, just say so and I'll send
her packing.
ELESIN: Why should I not want to see her? Let her come. I have
no more holes in my rag of shame. All is laid bare.
175   PILKINGS: I'll bring her in. *(Goes off.)*
JANE: *(hesitates, then goes to* ELESIN) Please, try and understand. Everything my husband did was for the best.
ELESIN: *(he gives her a long strange stare, as if he is trying to
understand who she is)* You are the wife of the District
180   Officer?
JANE: Yes. My name, is Jane.
ELESIN: That is my wife sitting down there. You notice how still
and silent she sits? My business is with your husband.

(PILKINGS returns with IYALOJA.)

PILKINGS: Here she is. Now first I want your word of honour that
185   you will try nothing foolish.
ELESIN: Honour? White one, did you say you wanted my word
of honour?
PILKINGS: I know you to be an honourable man. Give me your
word of honour you will receive nothing from her.
190   ELESIN: But I am sure you have searched her clothing as you
would never dare touch your own mother. And there are
these two lizards of yours who roll their eyes even when I
scratch.
PILKINGS: And I shall be sitting on that tree trunk watching even
195   how you blink. Just the same I want your word that you will
not let her pass anything to you.
ELESIN: You have my honour already. It is locked up in that desk
in which you will put away your report of this night's events.
Even the honour of my people you have taken already; it is
200   tied together with those papers of treachery which make you
masters in this land.
PILKINGS: Alright. I am trying to make things easy but if you
must bring in politics we'll have to do it the hard way.
Madam, I want you to remain along this line and move no
205   nearer to that cell door. Guards! *(They spring to attention.)* If
she moves beyond this point, blow your whistle. Come on
Jane. *(They go off.)*
IYALOJA: How boldly the lizard struts before the pigeon when it
was the eagle itself he promised us he would confront.
210   ELESIN: I don't ask you to take pity on me Iyaloja. You have a
message for me or you would not have come. Even if it is the
curses of the world, I shall listen.
IYALOJA: You made so bold with the servant of the white king
who took your side against death. I must tell your brother
215   chiefs when I return how bravely you waged war against him.
Especially with words.
ELESIN: I more than deserve your scorn.
IYALOJA: *(with sudden anger)* I warned you, if you must leave a
seed behind, be sure it is not tainted with the curses of the
220   world. Who are you to open a new life when you dared not
open the door to a new existence? I say who are you to make
so bold? *(The* BRIDE *sobs and* IYALOJA *notices her. Her contempt noticeably increases as she turns back to* ELESIN.) Oh
you self-vaunted stem of the plantain, how hollow it all

proves. The pith is gone in the parent stem, so how will it   225
prove with the new shoot? How will it go with that earth that
bears it? Who are you to bring this abomination on us!
ELESIN: My powers deserted me. My charms, my spells, even
my voice lacked strength when I made to summon the powers
that would lead me over the last measure of earth into the   230
land of the fleshless. You saw it, Iyaloja. You saw me struggle
to retrieve my will from the power of the stranger whose
shadow fell across the doorway and left me floundering and
blundering in a maze I had never before encountered. My
senses were numbed when the touch of cold iron came upon   235
my wrists. I could do nothing to save myself.
IYALOJA: You have betrayed us. We fed your sweetmeats such as
we hoped awaited you on the other side. But you said No, I
must eat the world's left-overs. We said you were the hunter
who brought the quarry down; to you belonged the vital por-   240
tions of the game. No, you said, I am the hunter's dog and I
shall eat the entrails of the game and the faeces of the hunter.
We said you were the hunter returning home in triumph, a
slain buffalo pressing down on his neck, you said wait, I first
must turn up this cricket hole with my toes. We said yours was   245
the doorway at which we first spy the tapper when he comes
down from the tree, yours was the blessing of the twilight
wine, the purl that brings night spirits out of doors to steal
their portion before the light of day. We said yours was the
body of wine whose burden shakes the tapper like a sudden   250
gust on his perch. You said, No, I am content to lick the dregs
from each calabash when the drinkers are done. We said, the
dew on earth's surface was for you to wash your feet along the
slopes of honour. You said No, I shall step in the vomit of cats
and the droppings of mice; I shall fight them for the left-overs   255
of the world.
ELESIN: Enough Iyaloja, enough.
IYALOJA: We called you leader and oh, how you led us on. What
we have no intention of eating should not be held to the nose.
ELESIN: Enough, enough. My shame is heavy enough.   260
IYALOJA: Wait. I came with a burden.
ELESIN: You have more than discharged it.
IYALOJA: I wish I could pity you.
ELESIN: I need neither your pity nor the pity of the world. I need
understanding. Even I need to understand. You were present   265
at my defeat. You were part of the beginnings. You brought
about the renewal of my tie to earth, you helped in the binding of the cord.
IYALOJA: I gave you warning. The river which fills up before our
eyes does not sweep us away in its flood.   270
ELESIN: What were warnings beside the moist contact of living
earth between my fingers? What were warnings beside the
renewal of famished embers lodged eternally in the heart of
man. But even that, even if it overwhelmed one with a thou-
sandfold temptations to linger a little while, a man could   275
overcome it. It is when the alien hand pollutes the source of
will, when a stranger force of violence shatters the mind's
calm resolution, this is when a man is made to commit the
awful treachery of relief, commit in his thought the unspeakable blasphemy of seeing the hand of the gods in this alien   280
rupture of his world. I know it was this thought that killed me,
sapped my powers and turned me into an infant in the hands
of unnamable strangers. I made to utter my spells anew but
my tongue merely rattled in my mouth. I fingered hidden

285 charms and the contact was damp; there was no spark left to
sever the life-strings that should stretch from every finger-tip.
My will was squelched in the spittle of an alien race, and all
because I had committed this blasphemy of thought—that
there might be the hand of the gods in a stranger's intervention.

290 IYALOJA: Explain it how you will, I hope it brings you peace of
mind. The bush-rat fled his rightful cause, reached the market and set up a lamentation. 'Please save me!'—are these
fitting words to hear from an ancestral mask? 'There's a wild
beast at my heels' is not becoming language from a hunter.

295 ELESIN: May the world forgive me.

IYALOJA: I came with a burden I said. It approaches the gates
which are so well guarded by those jackals whose spittle will
from this day on be your food and drink. But first, tell me, you
who were once Elesin Oba, tell me, you who know so well

300 the cycle of the plantain: is it the parent shoot which withers
to give sap to the younger or, does your wisdom see it running
the other way?

ELESIN: I don't see your meaning Iyaloja?

IYALOJA: Did I ask you for a meaning? I asked a question. Whose

305 trunk withers to give sap to the other? The parent shoot or the
younger?

ELESIN: The parent.

IYALOJA: Ah. So you do know that. There are sights in this world
which say different Elesin. There are some who choose to

310 reverse this cycle of our being. Oh you emptied bark that the
world once saluted for a pith-laden being, shall I tell you what
the gods have claimed of you?

(In her agitation she steps beyond the line indicated by PILKINGS
and the air is rent by piercing whistles. The two GUARDS *also leap
forward and place safe-guarding hands on* ELESIN. IYALOJA
stops, astonished. PILKINGS *comes racing, followed by* JANE.)

PILKINGS: What is it? Did they try something?

GUARD: She stepped beyond the line.

315 ELESIN: *(in a broken voice)* Let her alone. She meant no harm.

IYALOJA: Oh Elesin, see what you've become. Once you had no
need to open your mouth in explanation because evil-smell-
ing goats, itchy of hand and foot had lost their senses. And it
was a brave man indeed who dared lay hands on you because

320 Iyaloja stepped from one side of the earth onto another. Now
look at the spectacle of your life. I grieve for you.

PILKINGS: I think you'd better leave. I doubt you have done him
much good by coming here. I shall make sure you are not
allowed to see him again. In any case we are moving him to a

325 different place before dawn, so don't bother to come back.

IYALOJA: We foresaw that. Hence the burden I trudged here to
lay beside your gates.

PILKINGS: What was that you said?

IYALOJA: Didn't our son explain? Ask that one. He knows what it

330 is. At least we hope the man we once knew as Elesin remembers the lesser oaths he need not break.

PILKINGS: Do you know what she is talking about?

ELESIN: Go to the gates, ghostly one. Whatever you find there,
bring it to me.

335 IYALOJA: Not yet. It drags behind me on the slow, weary feet of
women. Slow as it is Elesin, it has long overtaken you. It rides
ahead of your laggard will.

PILKINGS: What is she saying now? Christ! Must your people
forever speak in riddles?

340 ELESIN: It will come white man, it will come. Tell your men at
the gates to let it through.

PILKINGS: *(dubiously)* I'll have to see what it is.

IYALOJA: You will. *(Passionately.)* But this is one oath he cannot
shirk. White one, you have a king here, a visitor from your

345 land. We know of his presence here. Tell me, were he to die
would you leave his spirit roaming restlessly on the surface of
earth? Would you bury him here among those you consider
less than human? In your land have you no ceremonies of the
dead?

350 PILKINGS: Yes. But we don't make our chiefs commit suicide to
keep him company.

IYALOJA: Child, I have not come to help your understanding.
(Points to ELESIN.) This is the man whose weakened understanding holds us in bondage to you. But ask him if you wish.

355 He knows the meaning of a king's passage; he was not born
yesterday. He knows the peril to the race when our dead father, who goes as intermediary, waits and waits and knows he
is betrayed. He knows when the narrow gate was opened and
he knows it will not stay for laggards who drag their feet in

360 dung and vomit, whose lips are reeking of the left-overs of
lesser men. He knows he has condemned our king to wander
in the void of evil with beings who are enemies of life.

PILKINGS: Yes er . . . but look here . . .

IYALOJA: What we ask is little enough. Let him release our King

365 so he can ride on homewards alone. The messenger is on his
way on the backs of women. Let him send word through the
heart that is folded up within the bolt. It is the least of all his
oaths, it is the easiest fulfilled.

(The AIDE-DE-CAMP *runs in.)*

PILKINGS: Bob?

370 AIDE-DE-CAMP: Sir, there's a group of women chanting up the hill.

PILKINGS: *(rounding on* IYALOJA) If you people want trouble . . .

JANE: Simon, I think that's what Olunde referred to in his letter.

PILKINGS: He knows damned well I can't have a crowd here!
Damn it, I explained the delicacy of my position to him. I

375 think it's about time I got him out of town. Bob, send a car
and two or three soldiers to bring him in. I think the sooner he
takes his leave of his father and gets out the better.

IYALOJA: Save your labour white one. If it is the father of your
prisoner you want, Olunde, he who until this night we knew

380 as Elesin's son, he comes soon himself to take his leave. He
has sent the women ahead, so let them in.

(PILKINGS remains undecided.)

AIDE-DE-CAMP: What do we do about the invasion? We can still
stop them far from here.

PILKINGS: What do they look like?

385 AIDE-DE-CAMP: They're not many. And they seem quite peaceful.

PILKINGS: No men?

AIDE-DE-CAMP: Mm, two or three at the most.

JANE: Honestly, Simon, I'd trust Olunde. I don't think he'll deceive you about their intentions.

390 PILKINGS: He'd better not. Alright, let them in Bob. Warn them
to control themselves. Then hurry Olunde here. Make sure
he brings his baggage because I'm not returning him into town.

AIDE-DE-CAMP: Very good sir. *(Goes.)*

PILKINGS: *(to* IYALOJA*)* I hope you understand that if anything
395   goes wrong it will be on your head. My men have orders to
       shoot at the first sign of trouble.
IYALOJA: To prevent one death you will actually make other
       deaths? Ah, great is the wisdom of the white race. But have no
       fear. Your Prince will sleep peacefully. So at long last will
400   ours. We will disturb you no further, servant of the white
       king. Just let Elesin fulfil his oath and we will retire home and
       pay homage to our King.
JANE: I believe her Simon, don't you?
PILKINGS: Maybe.
405 ELESIN: Have no fear ghostly one. I have a message to send my
       King and then you have nothing more to fear.
IYALOJA: Olunde would have done it. The chiefs asked him to
       speak the words but he said no, not while you lived
ELESIN: Even from the depths to which my spirit has sunk, I find
410   some joy that this little has been left to me.

(The WOMEN *enter, intoning the dirge 'Alę lę lę' and swaying
from side to side. On their shoulders is borne a longish object
roughly like a cylindrical bolt, covered in cloth. They set it down
on the spot where* IYALOJA *had stood earlier, and form a semi-
circle round it. The* PRAISE-SINGER *and* DRUMMER *stand on the
inside of the semi-circle but the drum is not used at all. The*
DRUMMER *intones under the* PRAISE-SINGER's *invocations.)*

PILKINGS: *(as they enter)* What is *that?*
IYALOJA: The burden you have made white one, but we bring it
       in peace.
PILKINGS: I said *what* is it?
415 ELESIN: White man, you must let me out. I have a duty to
       perform.
PILKINGS: I most certainly will not.
ELESIN: There lies the courier of my King. Let me out so I can
       perform what is demanded of me.
420 PILKINGS: You'll do what you need to do from inside there or not
       at all. I've gone as far as I intend to with this business.
ELESIN: The worshipper who lights a candle in your church to
       bear a message to his god bows his head and speaks in a whis-
       per to the flame. Have I not seen it ghostly one? His voice
425   does not ring out to the world. Mine are no words for anyone's
       ears. They are not words even for the bearers of this load.
       They are words I must speak secretly, even as my father whis-
       pered them in my ears and I in the ears of my first-born. I
       cannot shout them to the wind and the open night-sky.
430 JANE: Simon . . .
PILKINGS: Don't interfere. Please!
IYALOJA: They have slain the favourite horse of the king and
       slain his dog. They have borne them from pulse to pulse cen-
       tre of the land receiving prayers for their king. But the rider
435   has chosen to stay behind. Is it too much to ask that he speak
       his heart to heart of the waiting courier? *(*PILKINGS *turns his
       back on her.)* So be it. Elesin Oba, you see how even the mere
       leavings are denied you. *(She gestures to the* PRAISE-SINGER.*)*
PRAISE-SINGER: Elesin Oba! I call you by that name only this
440   last time. Remember when I said, if you cannot come, tell
       my horse. *(Pause.)* What? I cannot hear you? I said, if you
       cannot come, whisper in the ears of my horse. Is your tongue
       severed from the roots Elesin? I can hear no response. I said,
       if there are boulders you cannot climb, mount my horse's
445   back, this spotless black stallion, he'll bring you over them.

(Pauses.) Elesin Oba, once you had a tongue that darted like a
drummer's stick. I said, if you get lost my dog will track a path
to me. My memory fails me but I think you replied: My feet
have found the path, Alafin.

(The dirge rises and falls.)

I said at the last, if evil hands hold you back, just tell my horse   450
there is weight on the hem of your smock. I dare not wait too
long.

(The dirge rises and falls.)

There lies the swiftest ever messenger of a king, so set me free
with the errand of your heart. There lie the head and heart of
the favourite of the gods, whisper in his ears. Oh my compan-   455
ion, if you had followed when you should, we would not say
that the horse preceded its rider. If you had followed when it
was time, we would not say the dog has raced beyond and left
his master behind. If you had raised your will to cut the thread
of life at the summons of the drums, we would not say your   460
mere shadow fell across the gateway and took its owner's place
at the banquet. But the hunter, laden with a slain buffalo,
stayed to root in the cricket's hole with his toes. What now is
left? If there is a dearth of bats, the pigeon must serve us for
the offering. Speak the words over your shadow which must   465
now serve in your place.
ELESIN: I cannot approach. Take off the cloth. I shall speak my
       message from heart to heart of silence.
IYALOJA: *(moves forward and removes the coverings)* Your cou-
       rier Elesin, cast your eyes on the favoured companion of the   470
       King.

*(Rolled up in the mat, his head and feet showing at either end is
the body of* OLUNDE.*)*

There lies the honour of your household and of our race.
Because he could not bear to let honour fly out of doors, he
stopped it with his life. The son has proved the father Elesin,
and there is nothing left in your mouth to gnash but infant   475
gums.
PRAISE-SINGER: Elesin, we placed the reins of the world in your
       hands yet you watched it plunge over the edge of the bitter
       precipice. You sat with folded arms while evil strangers tilted
       the world from its course and crashed it beyond the edge of   480
       emptiness—you muttered, there is little that one man can
       do, you left us floundering in a blind future. Your heir has
       taken the burden on himself. What the end will be, we are
       not gods to tell. But this young shoot has poured its sap into
       the parent stalk, and we know this is not the way of life. Our   485
       world is tumbling in the void of strangers, Elesin.

*(*ELESIN *has stood rock-still, his knuckles taut on the bars, his
eyes glued to the body of his son. The stillness seizes and paralyses
everyone, including* PILKINGS *who has turned to look. Suddenly*
ELESIN *flings one arm round his neck, once, and with the loop of
the chain, strangles himself in a swift, decisive pull. The guards
rush forward to stop him but they are only in time to let his body
down.* PILKINGS *has leapt to the door at the same time and struggles with the lock. He rushes within, fumbles with the handcuffs
and unlocks them, raises the body to a sitting position while he
tries to give resuscitation. The* WOMEN *continue their dirge, unmoved by the sudden event.)*

IYALOJA: Why do you strain yourself? Why do you labour at tasks for which no one, not even the man lying there would give you thanks? He is gone at last into the passage but oh, how late it all is. His son will feast on the meat and throw him bones. The passage is clogged with droppings from the King's stallion; he will arrive all stained in dung.

PILKINGS: (in a tired voice) Was this what you wanted?

IYALOJA: No child, it is what you brought to be, you who play with strangers' lives, who even usurp the vestments of our dead, yet believe that the stain of death will not cling to you. The gods demanded only the old expired plantain but you cut down the sap-laden shoot to feed your pride. There is your board, filled to overflowing. Feast on it. (She screams at him suddenly, seeing that PILKINGS is about to close ELESIN's staring eyes.) Let him alone! However sunk he was in debt he is no pauper's carrion abandoned on the road. Since when have strangers donned clothes of indigo before the bereaved cries out his loss?

(She turns to the BRIDE who has remained motionless throughout.)

Child.

(The GIRL takes up a little earth, walks calmly into the cell and closes ELESIN's eyes. She then pours some earth over each eyelid and comes out again.)

Now forget the dead, forget even the living. Turn your mind only to the unborn.

(She goes off, accompanied by the BRIDE. The dirge rises in volume and the WOMEN continue their sway. Lights fade to a black-out.)

GLOSSARY

alari   a rich, woven cloth, brightly coloured

egungun   ancestral masquerade

etutu   placatory rites or medicine

gbedu   a deep-timbred royal drum

opele   string of beads used in Ifa divination

osugbo   secret 'executive' cult of the Yoruba; its meeting place

robo   a delicacy made from crushed melon seeds, fried in tiny balls

sanyan   a richly valued woven cloth

sigidi   a squat, carved figure, endowed with the powers of an incubus

CARYL CHURCHILL

Caryl Churchill (b. 1938) was born in England and began her education in Canada during World War II; she returned to study at Oxford University, taking her B.A. in 1960. At Oxford, Churchill began her career as a playwright, producing several plays: *Downstairs* (1958), *Having a Wonderful Time* (1960), and *Early Death* (1962). During the 1960s, she wrote a series of brilliant radio plays. She also continued her study of radical politics and returned to the theater in the 1970s with a series of striking political dramas: *Owners* (1972), *Objections to Sex and Violence* (1975), and *A Light Shining in Buckinghamshire* (1976). In the mid-1970s, Churchill began to work more closely with experimental theater companies, collaborating with actors and directors in the writing of her plays. Working with the feminist theater company Monstrous Regiment (the name alludes to the Calvinist preacher John Knox's 1558 diatribe against Queen Mary of England, "The First Blast of the Trumpet against the Monstrous Regiment of Women"), she wrote *Vinegar Tom*, a play about witchcraft and sexual politics in seventeenth-century England. With the Joint Stock company, she investigated the politics of sexuality more extensively in *Cloud Nine* (1979), a pastiche of melodrama, Gilbert-and-Sullivan operetta, and modern realistic theater that uses CROSS-DRESSING and ROLE-DOUBLING to explore the relationship between colonial and sexual oppression in the nineteenth century and today. The history of gender oppression and the options for contemporary women are the subject of *Top Girls* (1982), and Churchill has continued to write challenging plays on the relationship between class, race, and gender in British social life, including *Fen* (1983) and *Serious Money* (1987). Her most recent play, *Mad Forest* (1990), concerns the revolution in Rumania.

Vinegar Tom

As she remarks in her preface, Churchill wanted to write "a play about witches with no witches in it." *Vinegar Tom* undertakes a revisionary history of seventeenth-century witchcraft in England, a history that sees witchcraft as part of the power relations of rural society. There are no witches in *Vinegar Tom*. "Witch" is a label that the politically and socially privileged—landowners, the middle class, the professional class—use to stigmatize and destroy those who are already impoverished and disempowered: the "old, poor, single, sexually unconventional." In *Vinegar Tom*, "witchcraft" arises in specific social and economic relationships. The witch hunt works both to legitimize the power of repressive social institutions like the church and the police—represented by the Puritan Packer—and to maintain the power and social prestige of the property-owning classes (Susan, John, Margery). More specifically, "witch" is a label used to scapegoat women, who are, as the play demonstrates, already deeply oppressed by the society in which they live. For the women in *Vinegar Tom*—Alice, seduced by the London aristocrat in Scene One; Betty, forced into an arranged marriage; Susan, constantly pregnant; Margery, doing Jack's drudgework while he tries to seduce Alice; the "cunning woman" Ellen, whose herbal medicine is being displaced by the new (male) physicians; poor, outcast Joan—are systematically depriviliged and dehumanized, both by specific individuals and by the structure of their society itself.

Moreover, Churchill also invites us to question the ways that we think about history, and uses the play's theatrical process to challenge our understanding of the relationship between the past and the present. Throughout the play, the action is punctuated with modern songs which should be performed in modern dress; when they sing, the actors should appear to be our contemporaries, singing about contemporary life, not the seventeenth-century characters of the play. Like Brecht, who used music in similar ways, Churchill uses this device to force the audience to negotiate between the past and the present. *Vinegar Tom* cuts abruptly between the situation of women in the seventeenth century and the songs about women's life today. This technique climaxes in the finale of Kramer and Sprenger, the medieval theologians who wrote the *Malleus Maleficarum* ("The Hammer of Witches") in 1498, but who appear onstage as contemporary song-and-dance men, to sing the song "Evil Women." Unlike most historical drama—Arthur Miller's *The Crucible*, for instance—which represents the past as a complete and finished event which has only analogous or allegorical significance for the presence, Churchill's play presents the past as something unfinished, a story we write at the same time that we write the narrative of our present history. The relationship between past and present, the dramatic scenes and the modern songs, is left open. It is up to the audience to decide how to understand the sharp discontinuities and appalling likenesses between the seventeenth century and our own era.

— PREFACE —

Early in 1976 I met some of the Monstrous Regiment, who were thinking they would like to do a play about witches; so was I, though it's hard now to remember what ideas I was starting from. I think I had already read *Witches, Midwives and Nurses* by Barbara Ehrenreich and Deirdre English. Certainly it had a strong influence on the play I finally wrote.

Soon I met the whole company to talk about working with them. They gave me a list of books they had read and invited me to a rehearsal of *Scum*. I left the meeting exhilarated. My previous work had been completely solitary — I never discussed my ideas while I was writing or showed anyone anything earlier than a final polished draft. So this was a new way of working, which was one of its attractions. Also a touring company, with a wider audience; also a feminist company — I felt briefly shy and daunted, wondering if I would be acceptable, then happy and stimulated by the discovery of shared ideas and the enormous energy and feeling of possibilities in the still new company.

I was about to do a play for Joint Stock, who excited me for some of the same reasons, some different. There wasn't a lot of time, and the two plays, *Vinegar Tom* and *Light Shining in Buckinghamshire*, overlapped both in time and ideas. All I knew at this point about the Joint Stock project was that it was going to be about the English Revolution in the 1640s, what people had wanted from it, and particularly the millenial expectations of the Ranters. A lot of what I was learning about the period, religion, class, the position of women, was relevant to both plays.

I rapidly left aside the interesting theory that witchcraft had existed as a survival of suppressed pre-Christian religions and went instead for the theory that witchcraft existed in the minds of its persecutors, that 'witches' were a scapegoat in times of stress like Jews and blacks. I discovered for the first time the extent of Christian teaching against women and saw the connections between medieval attitudes to witches and continuing attitudes to women in general. The women accused of witchcraft were often those on the edges of society, old, poor, single, sexually unconventional; the old herbal medical tradition of the cunning woman was suppressed by the rising professionalism of the male doctor. I didn't base the play on any precise historical events, but set it rather loosely in the seventeenth century, partly because it was the time of the last major English witchhunts, and partly because the social upheavals, class changes, rising professionalism and great hardship among the poor were the context of the kind of witchhunt I wanted to write about; partly of course because it was the period I was already reading about for Joint Stock. One of the things that struck me reading the detailed accounts of witch trials in Essex (*Witchcraft in Tudor and Stuart England*, Macfarlane) was how petty and everyday the witches' offences were, and how different the atmosphere of actual English witchhunts seemed to be from my received idea, based on slight knowledge of the European witchhunts and films and fiction, of burnings, hysteria and sexual orgies. I wanted to write a play about witches with no witches in it; a play not about evil, hysteria and possession by the devil but about poverty, humiliation and prejudice, and how the women accused of witchcraft saw themselves.

I met Monstrous Regiment again, talked over the ideas I had so far, and found the same aspects of witchcraft appealed to them too. Then I went off and wrote a first draft of the play, very quickly, in about three days. I may have written one or two songs at this stage but not all of them. The company were happy to accept this first draft and leave rewriting till after my work with Joint Stock, which was lucky as in May I started the Joint Stock workshop. In the autumn I met Monstrous Regiment again. Helen Glavin had been working on the music for the songs during the summer. I worked on the text again, expanding it slightly. It was only at this stage that Josefina Cupido joined the company and I wrote in the character of Betty, who didn't exist before and who filled a need that had come up in discussion for a character under pressure to make a conventional marriage. It was a very enjoyable co-operation with the company. My habit of solitary working and shyness at showing what I wrote at an early stage had been wiped out by the even greater self-exposure in Joint Stock's method of work. And our shared view of what the play was about and our commitment to it made rewriting precise and easy.

By the time *Traps* was done in January 1977 it seemed more than a year since I had written it. Though I still wanted to write alone sometimes, my attitude to myself, my work and others had been basically and permanently changed.

Caryl Churchill
1982

— PRODUCTION NOTE —

The songs, which are contemporary, should if possible be sung by actors in modern dress. They are not part of the action and not sung by the characters in the scenes before them. In the original company all the actors could sing so it was no problem for some members of the company to be out of costume at any time to be in the band. Obviously this may not always be possible. But it is essential that the actors are not in character when they sing the songs.

The first verse of 'Nobody Sings' was left out in the original production because the song seemed too long. I've put it back because I like the song being about a first period as well as about getting old. It could be left out again in performance, or verse 3 or 4 could be dropped instead.

The pricking scene is one of humiliation rather than torture and Packer is an efficient professional, not a sadistic maniac.

Kramer and Sprenger should be played by women. Originally they were played by Chris Bowler and Mary McCusker who, as Ellen and Joan, had just been hanged, which seems to be an ideal doubling. They played them as Edwardian music hall gents in top hats and tails, and some of the opening rhymes and jokes are theirs. The rest of the scene is genuine Kramer and Sprenger, from their handbook on witches and women, *Malleus Maleficarum, The Hammer of Witches*.

C.C.

VINEGAR TOM

CARYL CHURCHILL

— CHARACTERS —

ALICE, *a village girl, early 20s*
SUSAN, *her married friend, early 20s*
JOAN, *Alice's mother, a poor widow, 50*
MARGERY, *Joan's neighbour, a farmer's wife, 40*
JACK, *Margery's husband, a tenant farmer, 40*
BETTY, *the landowner's daughter, 16*
ELLEN, *a cunning woman, 35*
GOODY, *Packer's assistant, 45*
PACKER, *a witchfinder, 35*

MAN, *a gentleman, 30*
DOCTOR, *a professional, 50*
BELLRINGER, *a local, any age*
KRAMER and SPRENGER — *authors of the* Malleus Maleficarum, The Hammer of Witches, *a book highly thought of in the seventeenth century; they appear in top hat and tails as performers in a music hall*

The play takes place in and around a small village over a period of a few weeks in the seventeenth century. The songs take place in the present.

— SCENE ONE —

Roadside.

MAN: Am I the devil?

ALICE: What, sweet?

MAN: I'm the devil. Man in black, they say, they always say, a man in black met me in the night, took me into the thicket
5 and made me commit uncleanness unspeakable.

ALICE: I've seen men in black that's no devils unless clergy and gentlemen are devils.

MAN: Have I not got great burning eyes then?

ALICE: Bright enough eyes.

10 MAN: Is my body not rough and hairy?

ALICE: I don't like a man too smooth.

MAN: Am I not ice cold?

ALICE: In a ditch in November.

MAN: Didn't I lie on you so heavy I took your breath? Didn't the
15 enormous size of me terrify you?

ALICE: It seemed a fair size like other men's.

MAN: Didn't it hurt you? Are you saying I didn't hurt you?

ALICE: You don't need be the devil, I been hurt by men. Let me go now, you're hurting my shoulder.

20 MAN: What it is, you didn't see my feet.

ALICE: You never took off your shoes. Take off your shoes if your feet's cloven.

MAN: If you come with me and give me body and soul, you'll never want in this world.

25 ALICE: Are you saying that as a man?

MAN: Am I saying it as the devil?

ALICE: If you're saying it as a man I'll go with you. There's no one round here knows me going to marry me. There's no way I'll get money. I've a child, mind, I'll not leave the child.

30 MAN: Has it a father?

ALICE: No, never had.

MAN: So you think that was no sin we did?

ALICE: If it was I don't care.

MAN: Don't say that.

35 ALICE: You'd say worse living here. Any time I'm happy someone says it's a sin.

MAN: There's some in London say there's no sin. Each man has his own religion nearly, or none at all, and there's women speak out too. They smoke and curse in the tavern and they
40 say flesh is no sin for they are God themselves and can't sin.

The men and women lie together and say that's bliss and that's heaven and that's no sin. I believe it for there's such changes.

ALICE: I'd like to go to London and hear them.

MAN: But then I believe with Calvin that few are saved and I am
45 damned utterly. Then I think if I'm damned anyway I might as well sin to make it worthwhile. But I'm afraid to die. I'm afraid of the torture after. One of my family was burnt for a Catholic and they all changed to Protestant and one burnt for that too. I wish I was a Catholic and could confess my sins
50 and burn them away in candles. I believe it all in turn and all at once.

ALICE: Would you take me to London? I've nothing to keep me here except my mother and I'd leave her.

MAN: You don't think I'm sent you by the devil? Sometimes I
55 think the devil has me. And then I think there is no devil. And then I think the devil would make me think there was no devil.

ALICE: I'll never get away from here if you don't take me.

MAN: Will you do everything I say, like a witch with the devil her
60 master?

ALICE: I'll do like a wife with a husband her master and that's enough for man or devil.

MAN: Will you kiss my arse like the devil makes his witches?

ALICE: I'll do what gives us pleasure. Was I good just now?

65 MAN: In Scotland I saw a witch burnt.

ALICE: Did you? A real witch? Was she a real one?

MAN: She was really burnt for one.

ALICE: Did the spirits fly out of her like black bats? Did the devil make the sky go dark? I've heard plenty tales of witches and
70 I've heard some called witch, there's one in the next village some say and others say not, but she's nothing to see. Did she fly at night on a stick? Did you see her flying?

MAN: I saw her burnt.

ALICE: Tell then. What did she say?

75 MAN: She couldn't speak, I think. They'd been questioning her. There's wrenching the head with a cord. She came to the stake in a cart and men lifted her out, and the stake held her up when she was tied. She'd been in the boots you see that break the bones.

80 ALICE: And wood was put round? And a fire lit just like lighting a fire? Oh, I'd have shrieked, I cry the least thing.

MAN: She did shriek.

847

ALICE: I long to see that. But I might hide my face. Did you hide your face?

85 MAN: No, I saw it.

ALICE: Did you like seeing it then?

MAN: I may have done.

ALICE: Will you take me with you, to London, to Scotland? Nothing happens here.

90 MAN: Take you with me?

ALICE: Please, I'd be no trouble . . .

MAN: A whore? Take a whore with me?

ALICE: I'm not that.

MAN: What are you then? What name would you put to your-
95   self? You're not a wife or a widow. You're not a virgin. Tell me a name for what you are.

ALICE: You're not going? Stay a bit.

MAN: I've stayed too long. I'm cold. The devil's cold. Back to my warm fire, eh?

100 ALICE: Stay with me!

MAN: Get away, will you.

ALICE: Please.

MAN: Get away.

(He pushes her and she falls.)

ALICE: Go to hell then, go to the devil, you devil.

105 MAN: Cursing is it? I can outcurse you.

ALICE: You foul devil, you fool, bastard, damn you, you devil!

MAN: Devil take you, whore, whore, damned strumpet, suc-
       cubus, witch!

ALICE: But come back. I'll not curse you. Don't you curse. We
110   were friends just now.

MAN: You should have behaved better.

ALICE: Will I see you again?

MAN: Unless I see you first.

ALICE: But will I see you? How can I find you?

115 MAN: You can call on me.

ALICE: How? Where? How shall I call on you?

MAN: You know how to curse. Just call on the devil.

ALICE: Don't tease me, you're not the devil, what's your name?

MAN: Lucifer, isn't it, and Beelzebub.

120 ALICE: No, what's your name?

MAN: Darling was my name, and sweeting, till you called me
       devil.

ALICE: I'll not call you devil, come back, what's your name?

MAN: You won't need to know it. You won't be seeing me.

— SCENE TWO —

Inside JACK *and* MARGERY'S.

JACK: The river meadow is the one to get.

MARGERY: I thought the long field up the hill.

JACK: No, the river meadow for the cattle.

MARGERY: But Jack, for corn. Think of the long field full of
5   wheat.

JACK: He's had a bad crop two years. That's why he can't pay the
       rent.

MARGERY: No, but he's got no cattle. We'd be all right.

JACK: If we took both fields.

10 MARGERY: Could we? Both?

JACK: The more we have the more we can afford.

MARGERY: And we'll pray God sends us sunshine.

JACK: Who's that down by the river?

MARGERY: That Alice, is it, wandering about?

JACK: I'm surprised Mother Noakes can pay her rent.   15

MARGERY: Just a cottage isn't much.

JACK: I've been wondering if we'll see them turned out.

MARGERY: I don't know why she's let stay. If we all lived like her
       it wouldn't be the fine estate it is. And Alice . . .

JACK: You can't blame Alice.   20

MARGERY: You can blame her. You can't be surprised. She's just
       what I'd expect of a girl brought up by Joan Noakes.

JACK: If we rent both fields, we'll have to hire a man to help with
       the harvest.

MARGERY: Hire a man?   25

JACK: That's not Alice.

MARGERY: It's not Miss Betty out by herself again?

JACK: I wouldn't be her father, not even to own the land.

MARGERY: That's a fine idea, hire a man.

JACK: She's coming here.   30

MARGERY: What we going to do?

JACK: Be respectful.

MARGERY: No, but shall we take her home? She's not meant to.
       She's still shut up in her room, everyone says.

JACK: I won't be sorry to see her.   35

MARGERY: I love to see her. She was always so soft on your lap,
       not like ours all hard edges. I could sit all afternoon just to
       smell her hair. But she's not a child, now, you can have run in
       and out and touch her. She's in trouble at home and we
       shouldn't help her do wrong.   40

JACK: We can't stop her, can we, if she walks in?

(They wait and in a moment BETTY *does come in.)*

MARGERY: Miss Betty, how nice.

BETTY: I came to see you milking the cows.

JACK: We finished milking, miss. The cows are in.

BETTY: Is it that late?   45

MARGERY: You want to get home before dark.

BETTY: No, I don't. I want to be out in the dark. It's not late, it's
       dark in the day time. I could stay out for hours if it was summer.

JACK: If you want to come and see the farm, Miss Betty, you
       should ask your father to bring you one morning when he's   50
       inspecting the estate.

BETTY: I'm not let go where I like.

JACK: I've business with your father.

MARGERY: We're going to take on the river meadow for the
       cattle.   55

JACK: And the long field up the hill.

BETTY: I used to play here all day. Nothing's different. Have you
       still got Betty's mug?

MARGERY: That's right, she had her special mug.

BETTY: I milked the red cow right into it one day. I got milk in   60
       my eye.

JACK: She died, that red cow. But we've four new cows you've not
       seen.

MARGERY: Died last week. There's two or three cows died in the
       neighbourhood.   65

BETTY: I wish she hadn't.

JACK: That don't matter, losing one, we're doing well enough.

MARGERY: And you're doing well, I hear, miss.

BETTY: What?

70 MARGERY: I hear you're leaving us for better things.

BETTY: No.

MARGERY: I was only saying yesterday, our little Miss Betty that was and now to be a lady with her own house and . . .

BETTY: They lock me up. I said I won't marry him so they lock

75 me up. Don't you know that?

MARGERY: I had heard something.

BETTY: I get out the window.

MARGERY: Hadn't you better have him, Betty, and be happy? Everyone hopes so. Everyone loves a wedding.

80 BETTY: Margery, can I stay here tonight?

MARGERY: They'd worry for you.

BETTY: Can I? Please?

JACK: There's no bed fit for you, miss.

BETTY: On my way here I climbed a tree. I could see the whole

85 estate. I could see the other side of the river. I wanted to jump off. And fly.

MARGERY: Shall Jack walk home with you, miss, now it's getting dark?

— SCENE THREE —

Inside JOAN's.

JOAN: Alice?

ALICE: No need wake up, mum.

JOAN: You'll catch cold out all night in this weather.

ALICE: Don't wake up if it's only to moan at me.

5 JOAN: Who were you with?

ALICE: Did he wake up?

JOAN: No, not a sound.

ALICE: He's sleeping better. Not so much bad dreams.

JOAN: Come on, child, there's some broth left.

10 ALICE: I couldn't eat.

JOAN: You stay out half the night, you don't even enjoy it. You stay in with the boy. You sit by the fire with no one to talk to but old Vinegar Tomcat. I'll go out.

ALICE: You go out?

15 JOAN: Funny, isn't it? What would I do going out?

ALICE: I'll stay in if you like.

JOAN: Where would I go? Who wants an old woman?

ALICE: You want me to stay with you more?

JOAN: An old woman wandering about in the cold.

20 ALICE: Do you want some broth, mum?

JOAN: Who were you with this time? Anyone I know?

ALICE: Oh mum, I'm sick of myself.

JOAN: If we'd each got a man we'd be better off.

ALICE: You weren't better off, mum. You've told me often you're

25 glad he's dead. Think how he used to beat you.

JOAN: We'd have more to eat, that's one thing.

Nobody Sings

I woke up in the morning,
Blood was on the sheet,
I looked at all the women
30 When I passed them in the street.
   Nobody sings about it
   But it happens all the time.

I met an old old woman
Who made my blood run cold.
You don't stop wanting sex, she said,   35
Just because you're old.
   Oh nobody sings about it,
   But it happens all the time.

I could be glad of the change of life,
But it makes me feel so strange.   40
If your life is being wanted
Do you want your life to change?
   Oh nobody sings about it,
   But it happens all the time.

Do you want your skin to wrinkle   45
And your cunt get sore and dry?
And they say it's just your hormones
If you cry and cry and cry.
   Oh nobody sings about it,
   But it happens all the time.   50

Nobody ever saw me,
She whispered in a rage.
They were blinded by my beauty, now
They're blinded by my age.
   Oh nobody sings about it,   55
   But it happens all the time.

— SCENE FOUR —

JACK *and* MARGERY's *barn*.

MARGERY *is churning*.

JACK: Hurry up with that butter, woman.

MARGERY: Butter won't come.

JACK: There's other work to do.

MARGERY: Butter won't come.

JACK: You don't churn. You sit gossiping.   5

MARGERY: Who would I talk to?

JACK: I heard your voice now.

MARGERY: Mother Noakes.

JACK: Always hanging about.

MARGERY: Her girl's no better.   10

JACK: Was her girl here? No.

MARGERY: I told her be on her way. Mother Noakes.

JACK: You tell her.

MARGERY: I told her.

JACK: Get on now with the butter and don't be always gossiping.   15

(JACK *goes*. MARGERY *churns and sings very quietly*.)

MARGERY: Come butter come, come butter come. Johnny's standing at the gate waiting for a butter cake. Come butter come, come butter come. Johnny's standing at the gate waiting for a butter cake. Come butter come, come butter come. Johnny's standing at the gate . . .   20

(*She stops as she realises* JOAN NOAKES *has come in and is standing behind her*.)

JOAN: Just passing by.

MARGERY: Again.

JOAN: I wonder could you lend me a little yeast? I've no yeast, see. I'm fresh out of yeast. I've no bread in the house and I

25 thought, I thought . . . I'll do a little baking now and brew a
little beer maybe . . . and I went to get some yeast and I've no
yeast. Who'd have thought it? No yeast at all.

MARGERY: You'd be better without beer.

JOAN: I thought a little yeast as I was passing.

30 MARGERY: You get drunk. You should be ashamed.

JOAN: To bake a couple of little small loaves.

MARGERY: I've no yeast.

JOAN: A couple of little small loaves wouldn't take much yeast. A
woman comfortable off with a fine man and a nice field and

35 five cows and three pigs and plenty of apples that makes a
good cider, bless you, Margery, many's the time . . . you'd not
grudge a neighbour a little loaf? Many's the good times, eh,
Margery? I've my own flour, you know, I'm not asking for flour.

MARGERY: I gave you yeast last week.

40 JOAN: A little small crumb of yeast and God will bless you for
kindness to your poor old neighbour.

MARGERY: You're not so badly off, Joan Noakes. You're not on
the parish.

JOAN: If I was I'd be fed. I should be on relief, then I'd not trouble

45 you. There's some on relief, better off than me. I get nothing.

MARGERY: What money you get you drink.

JOAN: If you'd my troubles, Margery, you'd be glad of a drink,
but as you haven't, thank God, and lend me a little yeast like a
good woman.

50 MARGERY: I've no yeast.

JOAN: I know you, Margery.

MARGERY: What do you know?

JOAN: I know you've got yeast. My eyes are old, but I see through
you. You're a cold woman and getting worse and you'll die

55 without a friend in this parish when if you gave yeast to your
good neighbours everyone would bless you . . .

MARGERY: I've no yeast.

JOAN: But you don't give and they say what a mean bitter woman
and curse you.

60 MARGERY: There's nobody curses me. Now get out of my dairy.
Dirty old woman you are, smelling of drink, come in here day
after day begging, and stealing, too, I shouldn't wonder . . .

JOAN: You shouldn't say that.

MARGERY: . . . and your great ugly cat in here stealing the

65 cream. Get out of my dairy.

JOAN: You'll be sorry you spoke to me like that. I've always been
your friend, Margery, but now you'll find I'm not.

MARGERY: I've work to do. Now get out. I'm making my butter.

JOAN: Damn your butter to hell.

70 MARGERY: Will you get out?

JOAN: Devil take you and your man and your fields and your
cows and your butter and your yeast and your beer and your
bread and your cider and your cold face . . .

MARGERY: Will you go?

(JOAN goes. MARGERY churns.)

75 MARGERY: Come butter come, come butter come. Johnny's
standing at the gate waiting for a butter cake. Come butter . . .
It's not coming, this butter. I'm sick of it.

(JACK comes.)

JACK: What's all this? You're a lazy woman, you know that?
Times are bad enough. The little black calf don't look well.

80 MARGERY: Butter won't come. Mother Noakes said damn the
butter to hell.

JACK: Lazy slut, get on with it.

MARGERY: Come butter come. Come butter come. Come butter come. Come butter come. Come butter come. Come butter
. . . Mother Noakes come begging and borrowing. She still got 85
my big bowl I give her some eggs in that time she was poorly.
She makes out I've treated her bad. I've been a good neighbour
to that woman years out of mind and no return. We'll get that
bowl back off her. Jack, do you hear me? Go over Mother
Noakes and get my bowl. And we'll heat a horseshoe red hot and 90
put it in the milk to make the butter come.

— SCENE FIVE —

Outside JOAN's.

SUSAN: Don't always talk of men.

ALICE: He knew what he was doing.

SUSAN: You'll know what he was doing in a few months.

ALICE: No, it never happens. The cunning woman put a charm
inside me.   5

SUSAN: Take more than a charm to do me good.

ALICE: Not again? Does he know?

SUSAN: He wants it. I know the night it was. He said, 'Let's hope
a fine child comes of it.'

ALICE: And what did you say?   10

SUSAN: Devil take it.

ALICE: What he say to that?

SUSAN: He don't like me swearing.

ALICE: But the baby's not a year.

SUSAN: Two weeks late, so.   15

ALICE: But the baby's not weaned.

SUSAN: The boy wasn't weaned when I fell for the baby.

ALICE: You could go see the cunning woman.

SUSAN: What for?

ALICE: She's a good midwife.   20

SUSAN: I don't want a midwife. I got my mother, anyway. I don't
want to think about it. Nearly died last time. I was two days.

ALICE: Go and see the cunning woman. Just go see.

SUSAN: What for?

ALICE: She could say for certain.   25

SUSAN: I'm sure for certain.

ALICE: She could give you a charm.

SUSAN: They do say the pain is what's sent to a woman for her
sins. I complained last time after churching, and he said I
must think on Eve who brought the sin into the world that got 30
me pregnant. I must think on how woman tempts man, and
how she pays God with her pain having the baby. So if we try
to get round the pain, we're going against God.

ALICE: I hate my body.

SUSAN: You mustn't say that. God sent his son . . .   35

ALICE: Blood every month, and no way out of that but to be sick
and swell up, and no way out of that but pain. No way out of
all that till we're old and that's worse. I can't bear to see my
mother if she changes her clothes. If I was a man I'd go to
London and Scotland and never come back and take a girl   40
under a bush and on my way.

SUSAN: You could go to the cunning woman.

ALICE: What for?

SUSAN: Charm.

ALICE: What for?   45

SUSAN: Love charm bring him back.

ALICE: I don't want him back.

SUSAN: Did he look wonderful, more than anyone here, that he's got you so low?

50 ALICE: It was dark, I wouldn't know him again.

SUSAN: Not so much how he looked as how he felt?

ALICE: I could do with it now, I can tell you. I could do with walking across that field again and finding him there just the same. I want a man I can have when I want, not if I'm lucky

55 to meet some villain one night.

SUSAN: You always say you don't want to be married.

ALICE: I don't want to be married. Look at you. Who'd want to be you?

SUSAN: He doesn't beat me.

60 ALICE: He doesn't beat you.

SUSAN: What's wrong with me? Better than you.

ALICE: Three babies and what, two, three times miscarried and wonderful he doesn't beat you.

SUSAN: No one's going to marry you because they know you

65 here. That's why you say you don't want to be married— because no one's going to ask you round here, because they know you.

(They move apart. JACK has been lingering in the background a while, and now comes up to ALICE.)

JACK: It's not you I've come to see.

ALICE: Never thought it was.

70 JACK: You should have done then.

ALICE: Why?

JACK: You know why.

ALICE: You've come to see my mum, have you?

JACK: I've business with her, yes. That's why I came.

75 ALICE: She's somewhere around. I'll get her.

JACK: No hurry. Wait a bit. Never seem to talk.

ALICE: Nothing to talk about.

JACK: I'm forgetting. I brought something.

(He gives her two apples.)

ALICE: Thank you. What then?

80 JACK: Am I not handsome enough, is that it?

ALICE: I don't want trouble.

JACK: No one's to know.

ALICE: If I say you're not handsome enough, will you go away?

JACK: Alice, you must. I have dreams.

85 ALICE: You've a wife.

JACK: I'm no good to my wife. I can't do it. Not these three months. It's only when I dream of you or like now talking to you . . .

ALICE: Mum. There's someone to see you.

90 JACK: Alice, have some pity . . .

ALICE: Do you hear me? Mum? She'll be out to see you.

(She moves away. JOAN comes.)

JOAN: What's the matter?

JACK: I've come for the bowl.

JOAN: Bowl? Bowl?

95 JACK: Bowl my wife gave you some eggs in, you ungrateful old hag.

JOAN: You're asking for the bowl? You think I wouldn't give you back your bowl? You think I'm stealing your bowl? When have I ever kept anything? Have your bowl. I'll get your bowl and much good may it do you.

100 JACK: Then get it, damn you, and quick or you'll feel my hand.

(She goes.)

ALICE: Why treat her like that?

JACK: Don't speak to me. Let me get the bowl and go.

ALICE: And don't come back.

JACK: Alice, I'd be good to you. I'm not a poor man. I could give 105 you things for your boy . . .

ALICE: Go away to hell.

(JOAN comes back.)

JOAN: Here's your bowl, Jack, and the devil go with it. Get away home and I hope you've more trouble there than I have here.

JACK: I'll break your neck if you speak to me. 110

JOAN: You lift your hand to me, may it drop off.

ALICE: Go home away to hell, man.

(JACK goes.)

JOAN: Away to hell with him. Never liked the man. Never liked the wife.

ALICE: Don't think on them, mum. They're not worth your 115 time. Go in by the fire, go on, go in and be warm.

(JOAN goes. SUSAN approaches.)

Nobody likes my mother. That's what it is why nobody wants me.

SUSAN: I'm sorry for what I said, Alice.

ALICE: Going to see the cunning woman then? 120

SUSAN: Are you going for a love charm?

ALICE: It's something to do, isn't it? Better than waiting and waiting for something to happen. If I had a charm I could make him just appear in front of me now, I'd do anything. Will you come? 125

(ALICE gives SUSAN an apple.)

SUSAN: I'll keep you company then. Just tell her my trouble. There's no harm.

Oh Doctor

Oh, doctor, tell
me, make me well.
What's wrong with me 130
the way I am?
I know I'm sad.
I may be sick.
I may be bad.
Please cure me quick, 135
oh doctor.

— SCENE SIX —

The landowner's house.

BETTY *tied to a chair. The* DOCTOR *is about to bleed her arm.*

BETTY: Why am I tied? Tied to be bled. Why am I bled? Because I was screaming. Why was I screaming? Because I'm bad. Why was I bad? Because I was happy. Why was I happy? Because I ran out by myself and got away from them and—

5 Why was I screaming? Because I'm bad. Why am I bad? Because I'm tied. Why am I tied? Because I was happy. Why was I happy? Because I was screaming.

DOCTOR: Hysteria is a woman's weakness. Hysteron, Greek, the womb. Excessive blood causes an imbalance in the humours.
10 The noxious gases that form inwardly every month rise to the brain and cause behaviour quite contrary to the patient's real feelings. After bleeding you must be purged. Tonight you shall be blistered. You will soon be well enough to be married.

Oh Doctor

15   Where are you taking my skin?
     Where are you putting my bones?
     I shut my eyes and I opened wide,
     But why is my heart on the other side?
     Why are you putting my brain in my cunt?
20   You're putting me back all back to front.

     Stop looking up me with your metal eye.
     Stop cutting me apart before I die.
     Stop, put me back.
     Stop, put me back.
25   Put back my body.

     Who are you giving my womb?
     Who are you showing my breath?
     Tell me what you whisper to nurse,
     Whatever I've got, you're making it worse.
30   I'm wide awake, but I still can't shout.
     Why can't I see what you're taking out?

     Stop looking up me with your metal eye.
     Stop cutting me apart before I die.
     Stop, put me back.
35   Stop, put me back.
     Put back my body.

     Oh, doctor, tell
     me, wake me well.
     What's wrong with me
40   the way I am?
     I know I'm sad
     I may be sick.
     I may be bad.
     Please cure me quick,
45   oh doctor,
     What's wrong with me the way I am?
     What's wrong with me?
     I want to see myself.
     I want to see inside myself.
50   Give me back my head.
     I'll put my heart in straight.
     Let me out of bed now.
     I can't wait
     To see myself.
55   Give me back my body.
     I can see myself.
     Give me back my body.
     I can see myself.

— SCENE SEVEN —

JACK *and* MARGERY'S *barn.*

MARGERY: Jack, Jack, come quick — Jack.

JACK: What's the matter now?

MARGERY: The calves. Have you seen the calves?

JACK: What's the woman on about?

MARGERY: The calves are shaking and they've a terrible stench, 5
so you can't go near them and their bellies are swollen up. (JACK *goes off.*) There's no good running. There's nothing you can do for them. They'll die like the red cow. You don't love me. Damn this stinking life to hell. Calves stinking and shaking there. No good you going to see, Jack. Better stand and 10
curse. Everything dying on us. Aah. What's that? Who's there? Get out, you beast, get out. (*She throws her shoe.*) Jack, Jack.

JACK: Hold your noise.

MARGERY: That nasty old cat of Mother Noakes. I'll kill that cat 15
if I get it, stinking up my clean dairy, stealing my cream. Where's it gone?

JACK: Let it go.

MARGERY: What you think of those calves then? Nothing to be done is there? What can we do? Nothing. Nothing to be 20
done. Can't do nothing. Oh. Oh.

JACK: Now what is it?

MARGERY: Jack!

JACK: What is it? Don't frighten me, woman.

MARGERY: My head, oh, my stomach. Oh, Jack, I feel ill. 25

(*She sits on the ground.*)

JACK: Get up, woman. It's no time. There's things to do.

MARGERY: Nothing.

JACK: Lie there a bit then. You'll maybe feel better. I can hardly stir myself. What have I done to deserve it? Why me? Why my calves shaking? Why my wife falling down? 30

MARGERY: It's passing now.

JACK: Why me?

MARGERY: That was a terrible pain. I still feel it. I'm shaking, look.

JACK: Other people sin and aren't punished so much as we are.

MARGERY: We must pray to God. 35

JACK: We do pray to God, and he sends afflictions.

MARGERY: It must be we deserve it somehow, but I don't know how. I do my best. I do my best, Jack, God knows, don't I, Jack? God knows I do my best.

JACK: Don't other people sin? Is it just me? 40

MARGERY: You're not a bad man, Jack.

JACK: I must be the worst man.

MARGERY: No, dear.

JACK: Would God send all this to a good man? Would he? It's my sins those calves shaking and stinking and swelling up their 45
bellies in there.

MARGERY: Don't talk so.

JACK: My sins stinking and swelling up.

MARGERY: Unless it's not God.

JACK: How can I bear it? 50

MARGERY: If it's not God.

JACK: What?

MARGERY: If it's not God sends the trouble.

JACK: The devil?

55 MARGERY: One of his servants. If we're bewitched, Jack, that explains all.

JACK: If we're bewitched . . .

MARGERY: Butter not coming. Calves swelling. Me struck in the head.

60 JACK: Then it's not my sins. Good folk get bewitched.

MARGERY: Good folk like us.

JACK: It can happen to anyone.

MARGERY: Rich folk can have spells against them.

JACK: It's good people the witches want to hurt.

65 MARGERY: The devil can't bear to see us so good.

JACK: You know who it is?

MARGERY: Who?

JACK: The witch. Who it is.

MARGERY: Who?

70 JACK: You know who.

MARGERY: She cursed the butter to hell.

JACK: She cursed me when I got the bowl.

MARGERY: She said I'd be sorry I'd spoken to her.

JACK: She wished me trouble at home.

75 MARGERY: Devil take your man and your cows, she said that, and your butter. She cursed the calves see and she's made them shake. She struck me on the head and in the stomach.

JACK: I'll break her neck.

MARGERY: Be careful now, what she might do.

80 JACK: I'm not afraid of an old witch.

MARGERY: You should be. She could kill you.

JACK: I'll kill her first.

MARGERY: Wait, Jack. Let's meet cunning with cunning. What we must do is get the spell off.

85 JACK: She's not going to take it off for asking. She might for a few hard knocks.

MARGERY: No, wait, Jack. We can take the spell off and never go near her. Serve her right.

JACK: What we do then? Burn something?

90 MARGERY: Burn an animal alive, don't we? Or bury it alive. That takes witchcraft off the rest.

JACK: Burn the black calf then shall we? We'll get some straw and wood and put it in the yard and the calf on top and set it on fire.

MARGERY: Will it walk?

95 JACK: Or I'll carry it.

MARGERY: It stinks terrible.

JACK: Stink of witchcraft it is. Burn it up.

MARGERY: We must pray to God to keep us safe from the devil. Praying's strong against witches.

100 JACK: We'll pray God help us and help ourselves too.

MARGERY: She'll see the fire and smell it and she'll know we're fighting her back, stinking old witch, can't hurt us.

Something to Burn

What can we do, there's nothing to do,
about sickness and hunger and dying.
105 What can we do, there's nothing to do,
nothing but cursing and crying.
Find something to burn.
Let it go up in smoke.
Burn your troubles away.

110 Sometimes it's witches, or what will you choose?
Sometimes it's lunatics, shut them away.
It's blacks and it's women and often it's Jews.
We'd all be quite happy if they'd go away.
Find something to burn.
Let it go up in smoke. 115
Burn your troubles away.

— SCENE EIGHT —

ELLEN's *cottage.*

ELLEN: Take it or leave it, my dear, it's one to me. If you want to be rid of your trouble, you'll take it. But only you know what you want.

SUSAN: It's not what I came for.

ALICE: Of course it is. 5

SUSAN: I wanted to know for certain.

ALICE: You know for certain.

SUSAN: I want a charm against pain.

ELLEN: I'll come as your midwife if you send for me near the time and do what I can, if that's all you want. 10

ALICE: She wants to be rid of it. Well, do you want it?

SUSAN: I don't want it but I don't want to be rid of it. I want to be rid of it, but not do anything to be rid of it.

ELLEN: If you won't do anything to help yourself you must stay as you are. 15

SUSAN: I shall pray to God.

ALICE: It's no sin. You just give yourself the drink.

SUSAN: Oh, I don't know.

ELLEN: Let her go home. She can come back. You have your charm safe, Alice? I could do more if you could come at the 20 young man and give him a potion I'd let you have.

ALICE: If I could come at him he wouldn't need potion.

ELLEN: And you're sure you've nothing of his?

ALICE: He gave me nothing.

ELLEN: A few hairs or a drop of blood makes all the difference. 25 It's part of him and the powers can work on it to call him.

ALICE: I'll pull a few hairs out next time I've a lover. Come on, Susan.

ELLEN: For your heartache I'll give you these herbs to boil up in water and drink at night. Give you a sound sleep and think 30 less of him.

ALICE: Don't want to think less of him.

ELLEN: You have your sleep. There'll be other men along if not that one. Clever girl like you could think of other things.

ALICE: Like what? 35

ELLEN: Learn a trade.

ALICE: Nothing dangerous.

ELLEN: Where's the danger in herbs?

ALICE: Not just herbs.

ELLEN: Where's the danger in healing? 40

ALICE: Not just healing, is it?

ELLEN: There's powers, and you use them for healing or hurt. You use them how you like. There's no hurt if you're healing so where's the danger? You could use them. Not everyone can.

ALICE: Learn the herbs? 45

ELLEN: There's all kinds of wisdom. Bit by bit I'd teach you.

ALICE: I'd never thought.

ELLEN: There's no hurry. I don't want you unless it's what you want. You'll be coming by to leave a little something for me in

50   a few days, since I have to live and wouldn't charge you. You
      can tell me how you've got on with your young man and what
      you're thinking.
      ALICE: Yes, I'll be coming by. Goodnight then. What are you
      standing there for, Susan?
55   SUSAN: Maybe I'll take some potion with me. And see when I
      get home whether I take it.
      ELLEN: Don't be afraid if it makes you sick. It's to do you good.

— SCENE NINE —

ELLEN's *cottage.*

BETTY: I don't know what I'm here for. I've had so much treat-
      ment already. The doctor comes every day.
ELLEN: You know what you're here for.
BETTY: The doctor says people like you don't know anything. He
5   thinks he's cured me because I said I would get married to stop
      them locking me up. But I'll never do it.
ELLEN: Do you want a potion to make you love the man?
BETTY: I'd rather have one to make him hate me so he'd leave me
      alone. Or make him die.
10 ELLEN: The best I can do for you is help you sleep. I won't harm
      him for you, so don't ask. Get some sleep and think out what
      you want.
BETTY: Can I come again sometimes just to be here? I like it here.
ELLEN: Come when you like. I don't charge but you'll bring a
15   little present.
BETTY: I'll give you anything if you can help me.
ELLEN: Come when you like.

— SCENE TEN —

ELLEN's *cottage.*

ELLEN: I'm not saying I can't do anything. But if I can't, it's
      because you've left it too late.
JACK: Lift your hand to me, she said, may it drop off. Then next
      day it went stiff.
5   MARGERY: We want to be certain. I've talked to others and
      they've things against her too. She's cursed and scolded two or
      three, and one's lame and the other lost her hen. And while
      we were talking we thought of her great cat that's always in my
      dairy, stinking it up and stealing the cream. Ah what's that, I
10   said crying out, didn't I, and that was the cat, and I was struck
      down with a blow inside my head. That's her familiar sent her
      by Satan.
JACK: I've seen a rat run out of her yard into ours and I went for it
      with a pitchfork and the spikes were turned aside and nearly
15   went in my own foot by her foul magic. And that rat's another
      of her imps.
MARGERY: But you don't like to think it of your neighbour. Time
      was she was neighbourly enough. If you could tell us it was
      true, we could act against her more certain in our minds.
20 JACK: I shouted at her over the fence, I said I'll have you hanged
      you old strumpet, burnt and hanged, and she cursed me again.
MARGERY: We burnt a calf alive to save our calves but it was too
      late. If I knew for certain it was her I'd be easier.
ELLEN: I've a glass here, a cloudy glass. Look in the glass, so,
25   and see if any face comes into it.

(She gives them a mirror.)

MARGERY: Come on, Jack, don't be afraid.
JACK: I don't like it.
MARGERY: Come on, it's good magic to find a witch.
ELLEN: Look in the glass and think on all the misfortunes you've
      had and see what comes.   30
MARGERY: Nothing yet. Do you see anything?
JACK: No.
MARGERY: Nothing still.
JACK: Don't keep talking.
MARGERY: Look.   35
JACK: What?
MARGERY: Did something move in the glass? My heart's beating so.
JACK: It's too dark.
MARGERY: No. Look.
JACK: I did see something.   40
MARGERY: It's the witch.
JACK: It's her sure enough.
MARGERY: It is, isn't it, Jack? Mother Noakes, isn't it?
JACK: It was Mother Noakes in that glass.
ELLEN: There then. You have what you came for.   45
MARGERY: Proves she's a witch then?
ELLEN: Not for me to say one's a witch or not a witch. I give you
      the glass and you see in it what you see in it.
JACK: Saw Mother Noakes.
MARGERY: Proves she's a witch.   50
ELLEN: Saw what you come to see. Is your mind easy?

— SCENE ELEVEN —

ELLEN's *cottage.*

JACK: Want to ask you something private. It's about my . . . *(He
      gestures, embarrassed.)* It's gone. I can't do anything with it,
      haven't for some time. I accepted that. But now it's not even
      there, it's completely gone. There's a girl bewitched me. She's
      daughter of that witch. And I've heard how witches some-   5
      times get a whole boxful and they move and stir by themselves
      like living creatures and the witch feeds them oats and hay.
      There was one witch told a man in my condition to climb a
      tree and he'd find a nest with several in it and take which he
      liked, and when he took the big one she said no, not that one, 10
      because that one belongs to the parish priest. I don't want a
      big one, I want my own back, and this witch has it.
ELLEN: You'd better go and ask her nicely for it.
JACK: Is that all you can say? Can't you force her to give it me?
ELLEN: It's sure to come back. You ask the girl nicely, she'll give 15
      it you back. I'll give you a little potion to take.
JACK: Kill her else.

— SCENE TWELVE —

Outside JACK *and* MARGERY's.

JOAN: That's a foul stink. I don't know how you can stay there.
      Whatever is it?
MARGERY: Do you know why you've come?
JOAN: I was passing.
MARGERY: Why were you passing?   5

JOAN: Can't I pass by your door now? Time was it was always
open for me.
MARGERY: And what's that?
JOAN: A foul stink. Whatever are you making? I thought I'd
10 come and see you as I was passing. I don't want any trouble
between us. I thought, come and see her, make it all right.
MARGERY: You come to see me because of that. That's my piss
boiling. And two feathers of your chicken burning. It's a foul
stink brings a witch. If you come when I do that, proves
15 you've a spell on me. And now I'll get it off. You know how?
JOAN: Come and see you. Make it all right.
MARGERY: Blood you, that's how.

(MARGERY scratches JOAN's head.)

JOAN: Damn you, get away.
MARGERY: Can't hurt me now. And if that doesn't bring the spell
20 off I'll burn your thatch.

If Everybody Worked as Hard as Me

If everybody worked as hard as me,
if our children's shirts are white,
if their language is polite,
if nobody stays out late at night,
25 Oh, happy family.
Oh, the country's what it is because
the family's what it is because
the wife is what she is
to her man.
30 Oh I do all I can.
Yes, I do all I can.
I try to do what's right,
so I'll never be alone and afraid in the night.
And nobody comes knocking at my door in the night.
35 The horrors that are done will not be done to me.

Nobody loves a scold,
nobody loves a slut,
nobody loves you when you're old,
unless you're someone's gran.
40 Nobody loves you
unless you keep your mouth shut.
Nobody loves you
if you don't support your man.
Oh you can,
45 oh you can
have a happy family.

If everybody worked as hard as me,
sometimes you'll be bored,
you'll often be ignored,
50 but in your heart you'll know you are adored.
Oh, happy family.
Your dreams will all come true.
You'll make your country strong.
Oh the country's what it is because
55 the family's what it is because
the wife is what she is
to her man.
Oh please do all you can.
Yes, please do all you can
60 Oh, please don't do what's wrong,

so you'll never be alone and afraid in the night.
So nobody comes knocking at your door in the night.
So the horrors that are done will not be done to you.

Yes you can.
Yes you can. 65
Oh the country's what it is because
the family's what it is because
the wife is what she is
to her man.

— SCENE THIRTEEN —

Outside JACK *and* MARGERY's.

SUSAN: You're sure it was him? You said you wouldn't know him.
ALICE: I did when I saw him.
SUSAN: Riding? Couldn't see him close.
ALICE: Close enough to be spattered with his mud. He saw me.
SUSAN: But he didn't show he knew you. 5
ALICE: Pretended not to.
SUSAN: It wasn't him.
ALICE: It was him.
SUSAN: And you don't know the beautiful lady?
ALICE: I'll know her again. Scratch her eyes if I come at her. 10
SUSAN: What was she wearing?
ALICE: What was she wearing? How should I know? A fine rich
dress made her beautiful, I suppose. Are you trying to plague
me?
SUSAN: Was he in black still? 15
ALICE: Blue velvet jacket.
SUSAN: Blue velvet.
ALICE: Yes, damn you, I said that before. Are you stupid? (*Si-
lence.*) For God's sake, now what is it? Are you crying?
Shouldn't I be crying? 20
SUSAN: It's not your fault, Ally. I cry all the time.
ALICE: You're still weak, that's what it is. It's the blood you lost.
You should rest more.
SUSAN: I don't want him to know.
ALICE: Doesn't he know? 25
SUSAN: He may guess but I don't dare ask. He was out all day
that day and I said I'd been ill, but not why.
ALICE: It's done anyway.
SUSAN: Can't be undone.
ALICE: You're not sorry now? 30
SUSAN: I don't know.
ALICE: You'd be a fool to be sorry.
SUSAN: I am sorry. I'm wicked. You're wicked.

(*She cries.*)

ALICE: Oh, Susan, you're tired out, that's all. You're not wicked.
You'd have cried more to have it. All the extra work, another 35
baby.
SUSAN: I like babies.
ALICE: You'll have plenty more, God, you'll have plenty. What's
the use of crying?
SUSAN: You were crying for that lover. 40
ALICE: I'm not now. I'd sooner kill him. If I could get at him. If
thoughts could get at him he'd feel it.
SUSAN: I'm so tired, Ally.

ALICE: Do you think it's true thoughts can reach someone?

45 SUSAN: What are you thinking of?

ALICE: Like if I had something of his, I could bring him. Or harm him.

SUSAN: Don't try that.

ALICE: But I've nothing of his. I'd have to make a puppet.

50 SUSAN: Don't talk so. Oh, don't, Alice, when I'm so tired.

ALICE: Does it have to be like? Is it like just if you say it's like?

SUSAN: Alice!

ALICE: If I get this wet mud, it's like clay. There should be at least a spider or some ashes of bones, but mud will do. Here's a

55 man's shape, see, that's his head and that's arms and legs.

SUSAN: I'm going home. I'm too tired to move.

ALICE: You stay here and watch. This is the man. We know who though we don't know his name. Now here's a pin, let's prick him. Where shall I prick him? Between the legs first so he

60 can't get on with his lady.

SUSAN: Alice, stop.

ALICE: Once in the head to drive him mad. Shall I give him one in the heart? Do I want him to die yet? Or just waste till I please.

65 SUSAN: Alice . . .

(SUSAN *tries to get the mud man, it falls on the ground and breaks.*)

ALICE: Now look. You've broken him up. You've killed him.

SUSAN: I haven't.

ALICE: All in pieces. Think of the poor man. Come apart.

SUSAN: I didn't. Alice, I didn't. It was you.

70 ALICE: If it was me, I don't care.

SUSAN: Alice, what have you done? Oh Alice, Alice.

ALICE: It's not true, stupid. It's not him.

SUSAN: How do you know?

ALICE: It's a bit of mud.

75 SUSAN: But you said.

ALICE: That's just words.

SUSAN: But . . .

ALICE: No. I did nothing. I never do anything. Might be better if I did. (*They sit in silence.*) You're crying again. Here, don't cry.

(ALICE *holds* SUSAN *while she cries.*)

80 SUSAN: Little clay puppet like a tiny baby not big enough to live and we crumble it away.

(JACK *comes.*)

JACK: Witch.

ALICE: Are you drunk?

JACK: Give it back.

85 ALICE: What?

JACK: Give it back.

ALICE: What now, Jack?

JACK: Give it me back. You know. You took it from me these three months. I've not been a man since. You bewitched me.

90 You took it off me.

ALICE: Is he mad?

SUSAN: What is it?

ALICE: Susan's ill, will you leave us alone?

JACK: Everyone comes near you is ill. Give it back, come on,

95 give it back.

ALICE: How can I?

JACK: She said speak nicely to you. I would, Alice, if you were good to me. I never wanted this. Please, sweet good Alice, give it back.

ALICE: What? How can I?   100

JACK: Give it me.

(*He grabs her round the neck.* SUSAN *screams.*)

ALICE: Damn you!

SUSAN: You'll kill her.

JACK: Give it me.

SUSAN: Let her go, she'll give it you whatever it is, you'll kill her   105
Jack.

(JACK *lets go.*)

JACK: Give it me then. Come on.

SUSAN: Wait, she can't move, leave her alone.

JACK: Give it me.

(ALICE *puts her hand between his thighs.*)

ALICE: There. It's back.   110

JACK: It is. It is back. Thank you, Alice. I wasn't sure you were a witch till then.

(JACK *goes.*)

SUSAN: What you doing Alice? Alice? Alice?

(ALICE *turns to her.*)

ALICE: It's nothing. He's mad. Oh my neck, Susan. Oh, I'd laugh if it didn't hurt.   115

SUSAN: Don't touch me. I'll not be touched by a witch.

— SCENE FOURTEEN —

Public square.

BELLRINGER: Whereas if anyone has any complaint against any woman for a witch, let them go to the townhall and lay their complaint. For a man is in town that is a famous finder of witches and has had above thirty hanged in the country round and he will discover if they are or no. Whereas if anyone has   5
any complaint against any woman for a witch, let them go . . .

MARGERY: Stopped the butter.

JACK: Killed the calves.

MARGERY: Struck me in the head.

JACK: Lamed my hand.   10

MARGERY: Struck me in the stomach.

JACK: Bewitched my organ.

MARGERY: When I boiled my urine she came.

JACK: Blooded her and made my hand well.

MARGERY: Burnt her thatch.   15

JACK: And Susan, her friend, is like possessed screaming and crying and lay two days without speaking.

MARGERY: Susan's baby turned blue and its limbs twisted and it died.

JACK: Boy threw stones and called them witch, and after he vom-   20
ited pins and straw.

MARGERY: Big nasty cat she has in her bed and sends it to people's dairies.

JACK: A rat's her imp.

MARGERY: And the great storm last night brought a tree down in   25
the lane, who made that out of a clear sky?

PACKER: I thank God that he has brought me again where I am needed. Don't be afraid any more. You have been in great danger but the devil can never overcome the faithful. For God in his mercy has called me and shown me a wonderful way of finding out witches, which is finding the place on the body of the witch made insensitive to pain by the devil. So that if you prick that place with a pin no blood comes out and the witch feels nothing at all.

(PACKER and GOODY take JOAN, and GOODY holds her, while PACKER pulls up her skirts and pricks her legs. JOAN curses and screams throughout. PACKER and GOODY abuse her: a short sharp moment of great noise and confusion.)

GOODY: Hold still you old witch. Devil not help you now, no good calling him. Strong for your age, that's the devil's strength in her, see. Hold still, you stinking old strumpet.

PACKER: Hold your noise, witch, how can we tell what we're doing? Ah, ah, there's for you devil, there's blood, and there's blood, where's your spot, we'll find you out Satan.

JOAN: Damn you to hell, oh Christ help me! Ah, ah, you're hurting, let go, damn you, oh sweet God, oh you devils, oh devil take you.

PACKER: There, there, no blood here, Goody Haskins. Here's her spot. Hardly a speck here.

GOODY: How she cries the old liar, pretending it hurts her.

PACKER: There's one for hanging, stand aside there. We've others to attend to. Next please, Goody.

(GOODY takes ALICE. PACKER helps, and her skirts are thrown over her head while he pricks her. She tries not to cry out.)

GOODY: Why so much blood?

PACKER: The devil's cunning here.

GOODY: She's not crying much, she can't feel it.

PACKER: Have I the spot though? Which is the spot? There. There. There. No, I haven't the spot. Oh, it's tiring work. Set this one aside. Maybe there's others will speak against her and let us know more clearly what she is.

(ALICE is stood aside.)

PACKER: If anyone here knows anything more of this woman why she might be a witch, I charge them in God's name to speak out, or the guilt of filthy witchcraft will be on you for concealing it.

SUSAN: I know something of her.

PACKER: Don't be shy then girl, speak out.

ALICE: Susan, what you doing? Don't speak against me.

SUSAN: Don't let her at me.

ALICE: You'll have me hanged.

(SUSAN starts to shriek hysterically.)

GOODY: Look, she's bewitched.

MARGERY: It's Alice did it to her.

ALICE: Susan, stop.

SUSAN: Alice. Alice. Alice.

PACKER: Take the witch out and the girl may be quiet.

(GOODY takes ALICE off. SUSAN stops.)

MARGERY: See that.

JACK: Praise God I escaped such danger.

SUSAN: She met with the devil, she told me, like a man in black she met him in the night and did uncleanness with him, and ever after she was not herself but wanted to be with the devil again. She took me to a cunning woman and they made me take a foul potion to destroy the baby in my womb and it was destroyed. And the cunning woman said she would teach Alice her wicked magic, and she'd have powers and not everyone could learn that, but Alice could because she's a witch, and the cunning woman gave her something to call the devil, and she tried to call him, and she made a puppet, and stuck pins in, and tried to make me believe that was the devil, but that was my baby girl, and next day she was sick and her face blue and limbs all twisted up and she died. And I don't want to see her.

PACKER: These cunning women are worst of all. Everyone hates witches who do harm but good witches they go to for help and come into the devil's power without knowing it. The infection will spread through the whole country if we don't stop it. Yes, all witches deserve death, and the good witch even more than the bad one. Oh God, do not let your kingdom be overrun by the devil. And you, girl, you went to this good witch, and you destroyed the child in your womb by witchcraft, which is a grievous offence. And you were there when this puppet was stuck with pins, and consented to the death of your own baby daughter?

SUSAN: No, I didn't. I didn't consent. I never wished her harm. Oh if I was angry sometimes or cursed her for crying, I never meant it. I'd take it back if I could have her back. I never meant to harm her.

PACKER: You can't take your curses back, you cursed her to death. That's two of your children you killed. And what other harm have you done? Don't look amazed, you'll speak soon enough. We'll prick you as you pricked your babies.

— SCENE FIFTEEN —

Public square.

GOODY *takes* SUSAN *and* PACKER *pulls up her skirt.*

GOODY: There's no man finds more witches than Henry Packer. He can tell by their look, he says, but of course he has more ways than that. He's read all the books and he's travelled. He says the reason there's so much witchcraft in England is England is too soft with its witches, for in Europe and Scotland they are hanged and burned and if they are not penitent they are burnt alive, but in England they are only hanged. And the ways of discovering witches are not so good here, for in other countries they have thumbscrews and racks and the bootikens which is said to be the worst pain in the world, for it fits tight over the legs from ankle to knee and is driven tighter and tighter till the legs are crushed as small as might be and the blood and marrow spout out and the bones crushed and the legs made unserviceable forever. And very few continue their lies and denials then. In England we haven't got such thorough ways, our ways are slower but they get the truth in the end when a fine skilful man like Henry Packer is onto them. He's well worth the twenty shillings a time, and I get the same, which is very good of him to insist on and well worth it though some folk complain and say, 'what, the price of a cow, just to have a witch hanged?' But I say to them think of the expense a witch is to you in the damage she does to property,

such as a cow killed one or two pounds, a horse maybe four
pounds, besides all the pigs and sheep at a few shillings a
25 time, and chickens at sixpence all adds up. For two pounds
and our expenses at the inn, you have all that saving, besides
knowing you're free of the threat of sudden illness and death.
Yes, it's interesting work being a searcher and nice to do good
at the same time as earning a living. Better than staying home
30 a widow. I'd end up like the old women you see, soft in the
head and full of spite with their muttering and spells. I keep
healthy keeping the country healthy. It's an honour to work
with a great professional.

— SCENE SIXTEEN —

ELLEN's *cottage*.

BETTY: I'm frightened to come any more. They'll say I'm a witch.
ELLEN: Are they saying I'm a witch?
BETTY: They say because I screamed that was the devil in me.
And when I ran out of the house they say where was I going if
5   not to meet other witches. And some know I come to see you.
ELLEN: Nobody's said it yet to my face.
BETTY: But the doctor says he'll save me. He says I'm not a
witch, he says I'm ill. He says I'm his patient so I can't be a
witch. He says he's making me better. I hope I can be better.
10 ELLEN: You get married, Betty, that's safest.
BETTY: But I want to be left alone. You know I do.
ELLEN: Left alone for what? To be like me? There's no doctor
going to save me from being called a witch. Your best chance
of being left alone is marry a rich man, because it's part of his
15   honour to have a wife who does nothing. He has his big house
and rose garden and trout stream, he just needs a fine lady to
make it complete and you can be that. You can sing and sit on
the lawn and change your dresses and order the dinner. That's
the best you can do. What would you rather? Marry a poor
20   man and work all day? Or go on as you're going, go on
strange? That's not safe. Plenty of girls feel like you've been
feeling, just for a bit. But you're not one to go on with it.
BETTY: If it's true there's witches, maybe I've been bewitched. If
the witches are stopped, maybe I'll get well.
25 ELLEN: You'll get well, my dear, and you'll get married, and
you'll tell your children about the witches.
BETTY: What's going to happen? Will you be all right?
ELLEN: You go home now. You don't want them finding you here.

(BETTY *goes*.)

I could ask to be swum. They think the water won't keep a
30 witch in, for Christ's baptism sake, so if a woman floats she's a
witch. And if she sinks they have to let her go. I could sink.
Any fool can sink. It's how to sink without drowning. It's
whether they get you out. No, why should I ask to be half
drowned? I've done nothing. I'll explain to them what I do.
35 It's healing, not harm. There's no devil in it. If I keep calm
and explain it, they can't hurt me.

If You Float

If you float you're a witch.
If you scream you're a witch
If you sink, then you're dead anyway.
40 If you cure you're a witch

Or impure you're a witch
Whatever you do, you must pay.
Fingers are pointed, a knock at the door,
You may be a mother, a child or a whore.
If you complain you're a witch   45
Or you're lame you're a witch
Any marks or deviations count for more.
Got big tits you're a witch
Fall to bits you're a witch
He likes them young, concupiscent and poor.   50
Fingers are pointed, a knock at the door,
They're coming to get you, do you know what for?
So don't drop a stitch
My poor little bitch
If you're making a spell   55
Do it well
Deny it you're bad
Admit it you're mad
Say nothing at all
They'll damn you to hell.   60

— SCENE SEVENTEEN —

A *prison*.

ALICE *is tied up, sitting on the floor,* GOODY *is eating and
yawning.*

GOODY: You'd better confess, my dear, for he'll have you
watched night and day and there's nothing makes a body so
wretched as not sleeping. I'm tired myself. It's for your own
good, you know, to save you from the devil. If we let you stay
as you are, you'd be damned eternally and better a little pain   5
now than eternal . . . (*She realises* ALICE *is nodding to sleep
and picks up a drum and bangs it loudly. She gives it several
bangs to keep* ALICE *awake.* PACKER *comes in.*) She's an obstinate young witch, this one, on her second night. She tires a
body out.   10
PACKER: Go and sleep, Goody, I'll watch her a while.
GOODY: You're a considerate man, Mr Packer. We earn our
money.

(GOODY *goes*.)

PACKER: I'm not a hard man. I like to have my confession so I'm
easy in my mind I've done right.   15
ALICE: Where's my boy?
PACKER: Safe with good people.
ALICE: He wants me.
PACKER: He's safe from the devil, where you'll never come.
ALICE: I want him.   20
PACKER: Why won't you confess and make this shorter?
ALICE: It isn't true.
PACKER: Tell me your familiars. Tell me your imps' names. I
won't let them plague you for telling. God will protect you if
you repent.   25
ALICE: I haven't any. (PACKER *drums*.) I want my boy.
PACKER: Then you should have stayed home at night with him
and not gone out after the devil.
ALICE: I want him.

30 PACKER: How could a mother be a filthy witch and put her child in danger?

ALICE: I didn't.

PACKER: Night after night, it's well known.

ALICE: But what's going to happen to him? He's only got me.

35 PACKER: He should have a father. Who's his father? Speak up, who's his father?

ALICE: I don't know.

PACKER: You must speak.

ALICE: I don't know.

40 PACKER: You must confess.

(PACKER drums.)

ALICE: Oh my head. Please don't. Everything's drumming.

PACKER: I'll watch. Your imps will come to see you.

ALICE: Drumming.

(PACKER suddenly stops.)

PACKER: Ah. Ah. What's this? A spider. A huge black one. And
45 it ran off when it saw a godly man. Deny if you can that spider's one of your imps.

ALICE: No.

PACKER: Then why should it come? Tell me that.

ALICE: I want my boy.

50 PACKER: Why? Why do you keep on about the boy? Who's his father? Is the devil his father?

ALICE: No, no, no.

PACKER: I'll have the boy to see me in the morning. If he's not the devil's child he'll speak against you. (ALICE cries.) I'll
55 watch you. I've watched plenty of witches and hanged them all. I'll get that spider too if it comes back.

— SCENE EIGHTEEN —

A prison.

GOODY is shaving SUSAN under the arm.

GOODY: There, that's the second arm done, and no mark yet.
Devil hides his marks all kinds of places. The more secret the
better he likes it. Though I knew one witch had a great pink
mark on her shoulder and neck so everyone could see. And a
5 woman last week with a big lump in her breast like another
whole teat where she sucked her imps, a little black one she
had and a little white one and kept them in wool in a bottle.
And when I squeezed it first white stuff came out like milk
and then blood, for she fed those horrid creatures on milk and
10 blood and they sucked her secret parts in the night too. Now
let's see your secret parts and see what the devil does there.

(She makes SUSAN lie down, and pulls up her skirt to shave her.
PACKER comes in.)

PACKER: What devil's marks?

GOODY: No need to shave the other for she has three bigs in her
privates almost an inch long like great teats where the devil
15 sucks her and a bloody place on her side where she can't deny
she cut a lump off herself so I wouldn't find it.

PACKER: Such a stinking old witch I won't look myself. Is there
nothing here?

GOODY: She's clean yet but we'll shave her and see what shame-
20 ful thing's hidden.

PACKER: Though a mark is a sure sign of a witch's guilt having no
mark is no sign of innocence for the devil can take marks off.

JOAN: And the devil take you.

PACKER: You'll be with the devil soon enough.

25 JOAN: And I'll be glad to see him. I been a witch these ten years.
Boys was always calling after me and one day I said to a boy,
'Boy boy you call me witch but when did I make your arse to
itch.' And he ran off and I met a little grey kitling and the
kitling said, 'you must go with me' and I said, 'Avoid, Satan.'
30 And he said, 'You must give me your body and soul and you'll
have all happiness.' And I did. And I gave him my blood every
day, and that's my old cat Vinegar Tom. And he lamed John
Peter's son that's a cripple this day, that was ten years ago. And
I had two more imps sent me, crept in my bed in the night,
35 sucked my privy parts so sore they hurt me and wouldn't leave
me. And I asked them to kill Mary Johnson who crossed me
and she wasted after. And everyone knows Anne that had fits
and would gnash her teeth and took six strong men to hold
her. That was me sent those fits to her. My little imps are like
40 moles with four feet but no tails and a black colour. And I'd
send them off and they'd come back in the night and say they
did what I said. Jack is lucky I didn't bewitch him to death and
Margery, but she was kind to me long ago. But I killed their
cows like I killed ten cows last year. And the great storm and
45 tempest comes when I call it and strikes down trees. But now
I'm in prison my power's all gone or I'd call down thunder and
twist your guts.

PACKER: Is there any reason you shouldn't be hanged?

JOAN: I'm with child.

50 GOODY: Who'd believe that?

— SCENE NINETEEN —

Public square.

JOAN and ELLEN are hanged while MARGERY prays.

MARGERY: Dear God, thank you for saving us. Let us live safe
now. I have scrubbed the dairy out. You have shown your
power in destroying the wicked, and you show it in blessing
the good. You have helped me in my struggle against the
5 witches, help me in my daily struggle. Help me work harder
and our good harvests will be to your glory. Bless Miss Betty's
marriage and let her live happy. Bless Jack and keep him safe
from evil and let him love me and give us the land, amen.

— SCENE TWENTY —

Public square.

JOAN and ELLEN hanging.

SUSAN: Alice, how can you look? Your poor mother. You're not
even crying.

ALICE: She wasn't a witch. She wouldn't know how.

SUSAN: Alice, she was.

5 ALICE: The cunning woman was, I think. That's why I was
frightened of her.

SUSAN: I was a witch and never knew it. I killed my babies. I
never meant it. I didn't know I was so wicked. I didn't know I
had that mark on me. I'm so wicked. Alice, let's pray to God

10 we won't be damned. If we're hanged, we're saved, Alice, so
we mustn't be frightened. It's done to help us. Oh God, I
know now I'm loathsome and a sinner and Mr Packer has
shown me how bad I am and I repent I never knew that but
now I know and please forgive me and don't make me go to
15 hell and be burnt forever—

ALICE: I'm not a witch.

SUSAN: Alice, you know you are. God, don't hear her say that.

ALICE: I'm not a witch. But I wish I was. If I could live I'd be a
witch now after what they've done. I'd make wax men and
20 melt them on a slow fire. I'd kill their animals and blast their
crops and make such storms, I'd wreck their ships all over the
world. I shouldn't have been frightened of Ellen, I should
have learnt. Oh if I could meet with the devil now I'd give
him anything if he'd give me power. There's no way for us
25 except by the devil. If I only did have magic, I'd make them
feel it.

Lament for the Witches

Where have the witches gone?
Who are the witches now?
Here we are.

30 All the gentle witches' spells
blast the doctors' sleeping pills.
The witches hanging in the sky
haunt the courts where lawyers lie.
Here we are.

35 They were gentle witches
with healing spells
They were desperate witches
with no way out but the other side of hell.

A witch's crying in the night
40 switches out your children's light.
All your houses safe and warm
are struck at by the witches' storm.
Here we are.

Where have the witches gone?
45 Who are the witches now?
Here we are.

They were gentle witches
with healing spells.
They were desperate witches
50 with no way out but the other side of hell.
Here we are.

Look in the mirror tonight.
Would they have hanged you then?
Ask how they're stopping you now.
55 Where have the witches gone?
Who are the witches now?
Ask how they're stopping you now.
Here we are.

— SCENE TWENTY-ONE —

SPRENGER: He's Kramer.
KRAMER: He's Sprenger.
KRAMER/SPRENGER: Professors of Theology

KRAMER: delegated by letters apostolic
SPRENGER: (here's a toast, non-alcoholic).   5
KRAMER: Inquisitors of heretical pravities
SPRENGER: we must fill those moral cavities
KRAMER: so we've written a book
SPRENGER: *Malleus Maleficarum*
KRAMER: *The Hammer of Witches.*   10
SPRENGER: It works like a charm
KRAMER: to discover witches
SPRENGER: and torture with no hitches.
KRAMER: Why is a greater number of witches found in the frag-
ile feminine sex than in men?   15
SPRENGER: Why is a greater number of witches found in the
fragile feminine sex than in men?
KRAMER: 'All wickedness is but little to the wickedness of a
woman.' Ecclesiastes.
SPRENGER: Here are three reasons, first because   20
KRAMER: woman is more credulous and since the aim of the
devil is to corrupt faith he attacks them. Second because
SPRENGER: women are more impressionable. Third because
KRAMER: women have slippery tongues and cannot conceal
from other women what by their evil art they know.   25
SPRENGER: Women are feebler in both body and mind so it's not
surprising.
KRAMER: In intellect they seem to be of a different nature from
men—
SPRENGER: like children.   30
KRAMER: Yes.
SPRENGER: But the main reason is
KRAMER/SPRENGER: she is more carnal than a man
KRAMER: as may be seen from her many carnal abominations.
SPRENGER: She was formed from a bent rib   35
KRAMER: and so is an imperfect animal.
SPRENGER: Fe mina, female, that is fe faith minus without
KRAMER: so cannot keep faith.
SPRENGER: A defect of intelligence.
KRAMER: A defect of inordinate passions.   40
SPRENGER: They brood on vengeance.
KRAMER/SPRENGER: Wherefore it is no wonder they are witches.
KRAMER: Women have weak memories.
SPRENGER: Follow their own impulses.
KRAMER: Nearly all the kingdoms of the worlds have been over- 45
thrown by women.
SPRENGER: as Troy, etc.
KRAMER: She's a liar by nature
SPRENGER: vain
KRAMER: more bitter than death   50
SPRENGER: contaminating to touch
KRAMER: their carnal desires
SPRENGER: their insatiable malice
KRAMER: their hands are as bands for binding when they place
their hands on a creature to bewitch it with the help of the devil. 55
SPRENGER: To conclude.
KRAMER: All witchcraft
SPRENGER: comes from carnal lust
KRAMER: which is in woman
KRAMER/SPRENGER: insatiable.   60
KRAMER: It is no wonder there are more women than men found
infected with the heresy of witchcraft.
SPRENGER: And blessed be the Most High, which has so far pre-
served the male sex from so great a crime.

Evil Women

Evil women
Is that what you want?
Is that what you want to see?
On the movie screen
Of your own wet dream
Evil women.

If you like sex sinful, what you want is us.
You can be sucked off by a succubus.
We had this man, and afterwards he died.

Does she do what she's told or does she nag?
Are you cornered in the kitchen by a bitching hag?
Satan's lady, Satan's pride.
Satan's baby, Satan's bride,
A devil woman's not easily satisfied.

Do you ever get afraid
You don't do it right?
Does your lady demand it

Three times a night?
If we don't say you're big
Do you start to shrink?
We earn our own money   85
And buy our own drink.

Did you learn you were dirty boys, did you learn
Women were wicked to make you burn?

Satan's lady, Satan's pride,
Satan's baby, Satan's bride,   90
Witches were wicked and had to burn.

Evil women
Is that what you want?
Is that what you want to see?
In your movie dream   95
Do they scream and scream?
Evil women
Evil women
Women.

BRIAN FRIEL

Brian Friel (b. 1929) is perhaps the most prominent living Irish playwright, the heir of Ireland's brilliant modern dramatic tradition, the tradition of William Butler Yeats, John Millington Synge, and Sean O'Casey. Unlike these predecessors, who worked for the independence of the Republic of Ireland, Friel works in Northern Ireland, still a part of the United Kingdom. Educated in Derry and Belfast, Friel's concerns as a playwright have spanned the "troubles" of Northern Ireland, the poverty and depression of Derry in the 1930s, 1940s, and 1950s, and the installation of a British military presence and the open street warfare of the 1960s, 1970s, and 1980s. From his earliest success, *Philadelphia, Here I Come!* (1964), about a man's divided feelings concerning his emigration to the United States, Friel's drama has centered on the problems of Irish identity in the face of British rule. Many of his early plays and stories — *The Loves of Cass McGuire* (1966), *The Lovers* (1967) — are portraits of Irish life in the manner of Synge, and Friel's dramatization of the personal consequences of contemporary Irish life remains a prominent feature of fine plays like *Living Quarters* (1977) and *Faith Healer* (1979). However, Friel's drama has increasingly become more satirical — in *The Mundy Scheme* (1969) and *The Gentle Island* (1971) — and more politically concerned. In *The Freedom of the City* (1973), Friel dramatizes the fate of three people caught and killed by British soldiers in the 1972 "Bloody Sunday" riots in Derry. In *Volunteers* (1975), a crew of political prisoners are forced to work on an archaeological site, recovering the history of Celtic Ireland even as they are oppressed by British rule. In *Making History* (1988), Friel returns to the origins of Ireland's subjection to the British in the seventeenth and eighteenth centuries. In 1980, Friel and Stephen Rea founded the Field Day theater company in Derry, and its first production was the play generally taken to be Friel's masterpiece, *Translations*. Friel's most recent play, *Dancing at Lughnasa*, opened in 1990.

Translations

Translations is set in early nineteenth-century Ireland and concerns the mapping — both actual and cultural — of Ireland by the British. The play takes place at a local hedge-school, a subscription school run by a local master and attended by a variety of children and adults. This Ireland is already threatened by the British culture to the east: a national school — where, presumably, English will be the required language — is about to open, and the British army surveyors have arrived to map the region, part of the 1833 Survey of Ireland.

The play's politics are largely conveyed through the politics of language. Jimmy's Homeric Greek, for example, draws a parallel between Ireland and another lost civilization. The romance between Yolland and Maire bridges the barrier of language. They learn to communicate across this barrier, while the British army works to tear it down and destroy Irish cultural identity in the process. In mapping Ireland, the British convert local place names into English, either by translating them directly or by inventing some equivalent. As the relationship between Irish Owen and his British officers makes clear, English is the language of power; to map the landscape with English names is a figure for rewriting Ireland and its culture into submission and, finally, into nonexistence.

Although *Translations* may seem only indirectly about contemporary Irish politics, it dramatizes a struggle for national and cultural identity that continues to embroil Northern Ireland today. Throughout the play, for example, the mysterious and unseen Donnelly twins move around the edges of the action, guerrillas hindering the British progress through the country. Finally, when Yolland is missing, we learn the true consequences of the British mapping of Ireland. Mapping the land in English is the prelude to its occupation, as the army systematically destroys the village and countryside that they have made their own. At the play's close, we scent the sickly sweet smell of blighted potatoes, the sign of the impending famine that would weaken and disperse Friel's rural Irish population for good.

TRANSLATIONS

Brian Friel

— CHARACTERS —

MANUS	BRIDGET
SARAH	HUGH
JIMMY JACK	OWEN
MAIRE	CAPTAIN LANCEY
DOALTY	LIEUTENANT YOLLAND

The action takes place in a hedge-school in the townland of Baile Beag/Ballybeg, an Irish-speaking community in County Donegal.

ACT ONE   An afternoon in late August 1833.
ACT TWO   A few days later.
ACT THREE   The evening of the following day.
One interval — between the two scenes in Act Two.

— ACT ONE —

The hedge-school is held in a disused barn or hay-shed or byre. Along the back wall are the remains of five or six stalls — wooden posts and chains — where cows were once milked and bedded. A double door left, large enough to allow a cart to enter. A window right. A wooden stairway without a banister leads to the upstairs living-quarters (off) of the schoolmaster and his son. Around the room are broken and forgotten implements: a cart-wheel, some lobster-pots, farming tools, a battle of hay, a churn, etc. There are also the stools and bench-seats which the pupils use and a table and chair for the master. At the door a pail of water and a soiled towel. The room is comfortless and dusty and functional — there is no trace of a woman's hand.

When the play opens, MANUS *is teaching* SARAH *to speak. He kneels beside her. She is sitting on a low stool, her head down, very tense, clutching a slate on her knees. He is coaxing her gently and firmly and — as with everything he does — with a kind of zeal.*

MANUS *is in his late twenties/early thirties; the master's older son. He is pale-faced, lightly built, intense, and works as an unpaid assistant — a monitor — to his father. His clothes are shabby; and when he moves we see that he is lame.*

SARAH's *speech defect is so bad that all her life she has been considered locally to be dumb and she has accepted this: when she wishes to communicate, she grunts and makes unintelligible nasal sounds. She has a waiflike appearance and could be any age from seventeen to thirty-five.*

JIMMY JACK CASSIE — *known as the Infant Prodigy — sits by himself, contentedly reading Homer in Greek and smiling to himself. He is a bachelor in his sixties, lives alone, and comes to these evening classes partly for the company and partly for the intellectual stimulation. He is fluent in Latin and Greek but is in no way pedantic — to him it is perfectly normal to speak these tongues. He never washes. His clothes — heavy top coat, hat, mittens, which he wears now — are filthy and he lives in them summer and winter, day and night. He now reads in a quiet voice and smiles in profound satisfaction. For* JIMMY *the world of the gods and the ancient myths is as real and as immediate as everyday life in the townland of Baile Beag.*

MANUS *holds* SARAH's *hands in his and he articulates slowly and distinctly into her face.*

MANUS: We're doing very well. And we're going to try it once more — just once more. Now — relax and breathe in . . . deep . . . and out . . . in . . . and out . . .

(SARAH *shakes her head vigorously and stubbornly.*)

MANUS: Come on, Sarah. This is our secret.

(*Again vigorous and stubborn shaking of* SARAH's *head.*)

MANUS: Nobody's listening. Nobody hears you.   5
JIMMY: '*Ton d'emeibet epeita thea glaukopis Athene . . .*'
MANUS: Get your tongue and your lips working. 'My name —' Come on. One more try. 'My name is —' Good girl.
SARAH: My . . .
MANUS: Great. 'My name —'   10
SARAH: My . . . my . . .
MANUS: Raise your head. Shout it out. Nobody's listening.
JIMMY: '. . . *alla hekelos estai en Atreidao domois* . . .'
MANUS: Jimmy, please! Once more — just once more — 'My name —' Good girl. Come on now. Head up. Mouth open. 15
SARAH: My . . .
MANUS: Good.
SARAH: My . . .
MANUS: Great.
SARAH: My name . . .   20
MANUS: Yes?
SARAH: My name is . . .
MANUS: Yes?

(SARAH *pauses. Then in a rush.*)

SARAH: My name is Sarah.
MANUS: Marvellous! Bloody marvellous!   25

(MANUS *hugs* SARAH. *She smiles in shy, embarrassed pleasure.*)

    Did you hear that, Jimmy? — 'My name is Sarah' — clear as a bell. (*To* SARAH) The Infant Prodigy doesn't know what we're at. (SARAH *laughs at this.* MANUS *hugs her again and stands up.*) Now we're really started! Nothing'll stop us now! Nothing in the wide world!   30

(JIMMY, *chuckling at his text, comes over to them.*)

6 **Ton d'emeibet epeita thea glaukopis Athene** But the grey-eyed goddess Athene then replied to him (from Homer, *Odyssey,* XIII, 420)   13 **alla hekelos estai en Atreidao domois** . . . but he sits at ease in the halls of the Sons of Athens . . . (from Homer, *Odyssey,* XIII, 423–24)

JIMMY: Listen to this, Manus.

MANUS: Soon you'll be telling me all the secrets that have been in that head of yours all these years. Certainly, James — what is it? *(To* SARAH*)* Maybe you'd set out the stools?

*(*MANUS *runs up the stairs.)*

35 SARAH: Wait till you hear this, Manus.

MANUS: Go ahead. I'll be straight down.

JIMMY: '*Hos ara min phamene rabdo epemassat Athene* — ' 'After Athene had said this, she touched Ulysses with her wand. She withered the fair skin of his supple limbs and destroyed the
40 flaxen hair from off his head and about his limbs she put the skin of an old man . . .'! The divil! The divil!

*(*MANUS *has emerged again with a bowl of milk and a piece of bread.)*

JIMMY: And wait till you hear! She's not finished with him yet!

(As MANUS *descends the stairs he toasts* SARAH *with his bowl.)*

JIMMY: '*Knuzosen de oi osse* — ' 'She dimmed his two eyes that were so beautiful and clothed him in a vile ragged cloak be-
45 grimed with filthy smoke . . .'! D'you see! Smoke! Smoke! D'you see! Sure look at what the same turf-smoke has done to myself! *(He rapidly removes his hat to display his bald head.)* Would you call that flaxen hair?

MANUS: Of course I would.

50 JIMMY: 'And about him she cast the great skin of a filthy hind, stripped of the hair, and into his hand she thrust a staff and a wallet'! Ha-ha-ha! Athene did that to Ulysses! Made him into a tramp! Isn't she the tight one?

MANUS: You couldn't watch her, Jimmy.

55 JIMMY: You know what they call her?

MANUS: '*Glaukopis Athene.*'

JIMMY: That's it! The flashing-eyed Athene! By God, Manus, sir, if you had a woman like that about the house, it's not stripping a turf-bank you'd be thinking about — eh?

60 MANUS: She was a goddess, Jimmy.

JIMMY: Better still. Sure isn't our own Grania a class of a goddess and —

MANUS: Who?

JIMMY: Grania — Grania — Diarmuid's Grania.

65 MANUS: Ah.

JIMMY: And sure she can't get her fill of men.

MANUS: Jimmy, you're impossible.

JIMMY: I was just thinking to myself last night: if you had the choosing between Athene and Artemis and Helen of Troy —
70 all three of them Zeus's girls — imagine three powerful-looking daughters like that all in the one parish of Athens! — now, if you had the picking between them, which would you take?

MANUS: *(To* SARAH*)* Which should I take, Sarah?

JIMMY: No harm to Helen; and no harm to Artemis; and indeed
75 no harm to our own Grania, Manus. But I think I've no choice but to go bull-straight for Athene. By God, sir, them flashing eyes would fair keep a man jigged up constant!

(Suddenly and momentarily, as if in spasm, JIMMY *stands to attention and salutes, his face raised in pained ecstasy.* MANUS

laughs. So does SARAH. JIMMY *goes back to his seat, and his reading.)*

MANUS: You're a dangerous bloody man, Jimmy Jack.

JIMMY: 'Flashing-eyed'! Hah! Sure Homer knows it all, boy.
Homer knows it all.   80

*(*MANUS *goes to the window and looks out.)*

MANUS: Where the hell has he got to?

*(*SARAH *goes to* MANUS *and touches his elbow. She mimes rocking a baby.)*

MANUS: Yes, I know he's at the christening; but it doesn't take them all day to put a name on a baby, does it?

*(*SARAH *mimes pouring drinks and tossing them back quickly.)*

MANUS: You may be sure. Which pub?

*(*SARAH *indicates.)*

MANUS: Gracie's?   85

(No. Further away.)

MANUS: Con Connie Tim's?

(No. To the right of there.)

MANUS: Anna na mBreag's?

(Yes. That's it.)

MANUS: Great. She'll fill him up. I suppose I may take the class then.

*(*MANUS *begins to distribute some books, slates and chalk, texts, etc., beside the seats.* SARAH *goes over to the straw and produces a bunch of flowers she has hidden there. During this:)*

JIMMY: '*Autar o ek limenos prosebe* — ' 'But Ulysses went forth   90
from the harbour and through the woodland to the place where Athene had shown him he could find the good swineherd who — '*o oi biotoio malista kedeto*' — what's that, Manus?

MANUS: 'Who cared most for his substance'.   95

JIMMY: That's it! 'The good swineherd who cared most for his substance above all the slaves that Ulysses possessed . . .'

*(*SARAH *presents the flowers to* MANUS.*)*

MANUS: Those are lovely, Sarah.

(But SARAH *has fled in embarrassment to her seat and has her head buried in a book.* MANUS *goes to her.)*

MANUS: Flow-ers.

(Pause. SARAH *does not look up.)*

MANUS: Say the word: flow-ers. Come on — flow-ers.   100
SARAH: Flowers.

MANUS: You see? — you're off!

*(*MANUS *leans down and kisses the top of* SARAH's *head.)*

MANUS: And they're beautiful flowers. Thank you.

---

37 **Hos ara min phamene rabdo epemassat Athene** As she spoke Athene touched him with her wand (from Homer, *Odyssey*, XIII, 429) 43 **Knuzosen de oi osse** She dimmed his eyes (from Homer, *Odyssey*, XIII, 433) 56 **Glaukopis Athene** flashing-eyed Athene

90 **Autar o ek limenos prosebe** But he went forth from the harbour (from Homer, *Odyssey*, XIV, 1) 93 **o oi biotoio malista kedeto** he cared very much for his substance (from Homer, *Odyssey*, XIV, 3–4)

(MAIRE *enters, a strong-minded, strong-bodied woman in her twenties with a head of curly hair. She is carrying a small can of milk.*)

MAIRE: Is this all's here? Is there no school this evening?

105 MANUS: If my father's not back, I'll take it.

(MANUS *stands awkwardly, having been caught kissing* SARAH *and with the flowers almost formally at his chest.*)

MAIRE: Well now, isn't that a pretty sight. There's your milk. How's Sarah?

(SARAH *grunts a reply.*)

MANUS: I saw you out at the hay.

(MAIRE *ignores this and goes to* JIMMY.)

MAIRE: And how's Jimmy Jack Cassie?

110 JIMMY: Sit down beside me, Maire.

MAIRE: Would I be safe?

JIMMY: No safer man in Donegal.

(MAIRE *flops on a stool beside* JIMMY.)

MAIRE: Ooooh. The best harvest in living memory, they say; but I don't want to see another like it. (*Showing* JIMMY *her

115 hands.*) Look at the blisters.

JIMMY: *Esne fatigata?*

MAIRE: *Sum fatigatissima.*

JIMMY: *Bene! Optime!*

MAIRE: That's the height of my Latin. Fit me better if I had even

120 that much English.

JIMMY: English? I thought you had some English?

MAIRE: Three words. Wait — there was a spake I used to have off by heart. What's this it was? (*Her accent is strange because she is speaking a foreign language and because she does not under-

125 stand what she is saying.*) 'In Norfolk we besport ourselves around the maypool.' What about that!

MANUS: Maypole.

(*Again* MAIRE *ignores* MANUS.)

MAIRE: God have mercy on my Aunt Mary — she taught me that when I was about four, whatever it means. Do you know what

130 it means, Jimmy?

JIMMY: Sure you know I have only Irish like yourself.

MAIRE: And Latin. And Greek.

JIMMY: I'm telling you a lie: I know one English word.

MAIRE: What?

135 JIMMY: Bo-som.

MAIRE: What's a bo-som?

JIMMY: You know — (*He illustrates with his hands*) — bo-som — bo-som — you know — Diana, the huntress, she has two pow-erful bosom.

140 MAIRE: You may be sure that's the one English word you would know. (*Rises*) Is there a drop of water about?

(MANUS *gives* MAIRE *his bowl of milk.*)

MANUS: I'm sorry I couldn't get up last night.

MAIRE: Doesn't matter.

MANUS: Biddy Hanna sent for me to write a letter to her sister in Nova Scotia. All the gossip of the parish. 'I brought the cow to 145 the bull three times last week but no good. There's nothing for it now but Big Ned Frank.'

MAIRE: (*Drinking*) That's better.

MANUS: And she got so engrossed in it that she forgot who she was dictating to: 'The aul drunken schoolmaster and that 150 lame son of his are still footering about in the hedge-school, wasting people's good time and money.'

(MAIRE *has to laugh at this.*)

MAIRE: She did not!

MANUS: And me taking it all down. 'Thank God one of them new national schools is being built above at Poll na gCaorach.' 155 It was after midnight by the time I got back.

MAIRE: Great to be a busy man.

(MAIRE *moves away.* MANUS *follows.*)

MANUS: I could hear music on my way past but I thought it was too late to call.

MAIRE: (*To* SARAH) Wasn't your father in great voice last night? 160

(SARAH *nods and smiles.*)

MAIRE: It must have been near three o'clock by the time you got home?

(SARAH *holds up four fingers.*)

MAIRE: Was it four? No wonder we're in pieces.

MANUS: I can give you a hand at the hay tomorrow.

MAIRE: That's the name of a hornpipe, isn't it? — 'The Scholar 165 In The Hayfield' — or is it a reel?

MANUS: If the day's good.

MAIRE: Suit yourself. The English soldiers below in the tents, them sapper fellas, they're coming up to give us a hand. I don't know a word they're saying, nor they me; but sure that 170 doesn't matter, does it?

MANUS: What the hell are you so crabbed about?!

(DOALTY *and* BRIDGET *enter noisily. Both are in their twenties.* DOALTY *is brandishing a surveyor's pole. He is an open-minded, open-hearted, generous and slightly thick young man.* BRIDGET *is a plump, fresh young girl, ready to laugh, vain, and with a countrywoman's instinctive cunning.* DOALTY *enters doing his imitation of the master.*)

DOALTY: Vesperal salutations to you all.

BRIDGET: He's coming down past Carraig na Ri and he's as full as a pig! 175

DOALTY: *Ignari, stulti, rustici* — pot-boys and peasant whelps — semi-literates and illegitimates.

BRIDGET: He's been on the batter since this morning; he sent the wee ones home at eleven o'clock.

DOALTY: Three questions. Question A — Am I drunk? Question 180 B — Am I sober? (*Into* MAIRE's *face*) *Responde — responde!*

BRIDGET: Question C, Master — When were you last sober?

MAIRE: What's the weapon, Doalty?

BRIDGET: I warned him. He'll be arrested one of these days.

---

116 **Esne fatigata?** Are you tired?   117 **Sum fatigatissima** I am very tired.   118 **Bene! Optime!** Good! Excellent!

176 **Ignari, stulti, rustici** Ignoramuses, fools, peasants   181 **Responde — responde!** Answer — answer

185 DOALTY: Up in the bog with Bridget and her aul fella, and the
      Red Coats were just across at the foot of Croc na Mona, drag-
      ging them aul chains and peeping through that big machine
      they lug about everywhere with them — you know the name
      of it, Manus?
190 MAIRE: Theodolite.
    BRIDGET: How do you know?
    MAIRE: They leave it in our byre at night sometimes if it's raining.
    JIMMY: Theodolite — what's the etymology of that word, Manus?
    MANUS: No idea.
195 BRIDGET: Get on with the story.
    JIMMY: *Theo — theos* — something to do with a god. Maybe
      thea — a goddess! What shape's the yoke?
    DOALTY: 'Shape!' Will you shut up, you aul eejit you! Anyway,
      every time they'd stick one of these poles into the ground and
200   move across the bog, I'd creep up and shift it twenty or thirty
      paces to the side.
    BRIDGET: God!
    DOALTY: Then they'd come back and stare at it and look at their
      calculations and stare at it again and scratch their heads. And
205   cripes, d'you know what they ended up doing?
    BRIDGET: Wait till you hear!
    DOALTY: They took the bloody machine apart!

*(And immediately he speaks in gibberish — an imitation of two
very agitated and confused sappers in rapid conversation.)*

    BRIDGET: That's the image of them!
    MAIRE: You must be proud of yourself, Doalty.
210 DOALTY: What d'you mean?
    MAIRE: That was a very clever piece of work.
    MANUS: It was a gesture.
    MAIRE: What sort of gesture?
    MANUS: Just to indicate . . . a presence.
215 MAIRE: Hah!
    BRIDGET: I'm telling you — you'll be arrested.

(When DOALTY *is embarrassed — or pleased — he reacts physically. He now grabs* BRIDGET *around the waist.)*

    DOALTY: What d'you make of that for an implement, Bridget?
      Wouldn't that make a great aul shaft for your churn?
    BRIDGET: Let go of me, you dirty brute! I've a headline to do
220   before Big Hughie comes.
    MANUS: I don't think we'll wait for him. Let's get started.

*(Slowly, reluctantly they begin to move to their seats and specific
tasks.* DOALTY *goes to the bucket of water at the door and washes
his hands.* BRIDGET *sets up a hand-mirror and combs her hair.)*

    BRIDGET: Nellie Ruadh's baby was to be christened this morn-
      ing. Did any of yous hear what she called it? Did you, Sarah?

*(*SARAH *grunts: No.)*

    BRIDGET: Did you, Maire?
225 MAIRE: No.
    BRIDGET: Our Seamus says she was threatening she was going to
      call it after its father.
    DOALTY: Who's the father?
    BRIDGET: That's the point, you donkey you!
230 DOALTY: Ah.

    BRIDGET: So there's a lot of uneasy bucks about Baile Beag this
      day.
    DOALTY: She told me last Sunday she was going to call it Jimmy.
    BRIDGET: You're a liar, Doalty.
    DOALTY: Would I tell you a lie? Hi, Jimmy, Nellie Ruadh's aul   235
      fella's looking for you.
    JIMMY: For me?
    MAIRE: Come on, Doalty.
    DOALTY: Someone told him . . .
    MAIRE: Doalty!   240
    DOALTY: He heard you know the first book of the Satires of
      Horace off by heart . . .
    JIMMY: That's true.
    DOALTY: . . . and he wants you to recite it for him.
    JIMMY: I'll do that for him certainly, certainly.   245
    DOALTY: He's busting to hear it.

*(*JIMMY *fumbles in his pockets.)*

    JIMMY: I came across this last night — this'll interest you — in
      Book Two of Virgil's *Georgics.*
    DOALTY: Be God, that's my territory alright.
    BRIDGET: You clown you! *(To* SARAH*)* Hold this for me, would   250
      you? *(her mirror)*
    JIMMY: Listen to this, Manus. '*Nigra fere et presso pinguis sub
      vomere terra . . .*'
    DOALTY: Steady on now — easy, boys, easy — don't rush me,
      boys —   255

(He mimes great concentration.)

    JIMMY: Manus?
    MANUS: 'Land that is black and rich beneath the pressure of the
      plough . . .'
    DOALTY: Give *me* a chance!
    JIMMY: 'And with *cui putre* — with crumbly soil — is in the main   260
      best for corn.' There you are!
    DOALTY: There you are.
    JIMMY: 'From no other land will you see more wagons wending
      homeward behind slow bullocks.' Virgil! There!
    DOALTY: 'Slow bullocks'!   265
    JIMMY: Isn't that what I'm always telling you? Black soil for corn.
      That's what you should have in that upper field of yours —
      corn, not spuds.
    DOALTY: Would you listen to that fella! Too lazy be Jasus to wash
      himself and he's lecturing me on agriculture! Would you go   270
      and take a running race at yourself, Jimmy Jack Cassie!
      (Grabs SARAH*.)* Come away out of this with me, Sarah, and
      we'll plant some corn together.
    MANUS: All right — all right. Let's settle down and get some work
      done. I know Sean Beag isn't coming — he's at the salmon.   275
      What about the Donnelly twins? *(To* DOALTY*)* Are the Don-
      nelly twins not coming any more?

*(*DOALTY *shrugs and turns away.)*

      Did you ask them?
    DOALTY: Haven't seen them. Not about these days.

*(*DOALTY *begins whistling through his teeth. Suddenly the atmosphere is silent and alert.)*

---

196 **theos** a god   197 **thea** a goddess

252–253 **Nigra fere . . . vomere terra** Land that is black and rich beneath the pressure of the plough   260 **cui putre** crumbly soil

280 MANUS: Aren't they at home?
DOALTY: No.
MANUS: Where are they then?
DOALTY: How would I know?
285 BRIDGET: Our Seamus says two of the soldiers' horses were
found last night at the foot of the cliffs at Machaire Buidhe
and . . . (*She stops suddenly and begins writing with chalk on
her slate.*) D'you hear the whistles of this aul slate? Sure no-
body could write on an aul slippery thing like that.
MANUS: What headline did my father set you?
290 BRIDGET: 'It's easier to stamp out learning than to recall it.'
JIMMY: Book Three, the *Agricola* of Tacitus.
BRIDGET: God but you're a dose.
MANUS: Can you do it?
BRIDGET: There. Is it bad? Will he ate me?
295 MANUS: It's very good. Keep your elbow in closer to your side.
Doalty?
DOALTY: I'm at the seven-times table. I'm perfect, skipper.

(MANUS *moves to* SARAH.)

MANUS: Do you understand those sums?

(SARAH *nods:* Yes. MANUS *leans down to her ear.*)

MANUS: My name is Sarah.

(MANUS *goes to* MAIRE. *While he is talking to her the others swop
books, talk quietly, etc.*)

300 MANUS: Can I help you? What are you at?
MAIRE: Map of America. (*Pause.*) The passage money came last
Friday.
MANUS: You never told me that.
MAIRE: Because I haven't seen you since, have I?
305 MANUS: You don't want to go. You said that yourself.
MAIRE: There's ten below me to be raised and no man in the
house. What do you suggest?
MANUS: Do you want to go?
MAIRE: Did you apply for that job in the new national school?
310 MANUS: No.
MAIRE: You said you would.
MANUS: I said I might.
MAIRE: When it opens, this is finished: nobody's going to pay to
go to a hedge-school.
315 MANUS: I know that and I . . . (*He breaks off because he sees*
SARAH, *obviously listening, at his shoulder. She moves away
again.*) I was thinking that maybe I could . . .
MAIRE: It's £56 a year you're throwing away.
MANUS: I can't apply for it.
320 MAIRE: You *promised* me you would.
MANUS: My father has applied for it.
MAIRE: He has not!
MANUS: Day before yesterday.
MAIRE: For God's sake, sure you know he'd never—
325 MANUS: I couldn't—I can't go in against him.

(MAIRE *looks at him for a second. Then:—*)

MAIRE: Suit yourself. (*To* BRIDGET) I saw your Seamus heading
off to the Port fair early this morning.
BRIDGET: And wait till you hear this—I forgot to tell you this.
He said that as soon as he crossed over the gap at Cnoc na

Mona—just beyond where the soldiers are making the   330
maps—the sweet smell was everywhere.
DOALTY: You never told me that.
BRIDGET: It went out of my head.
DOALTY: He saw the crops in Port?
BRIDGET: Some.   335
MANUS: How did the tops look?
BRIDGET: Fine—I think.
DOALTY: In flower?
BRIDGET: I don't know. I think so. He didn't say.
MANUS: Just the sweet smell—that's all?   340
BRIDGET: They say that's the way it snakes in, don't they? First
the smell; and then one morning the stalks are all black and
limp.
DOALTY: Are you stupid? It's the rotting stalks makes the sweet
smell for God's sake. That's what the smell is—rotting stalks.   345
MAIRE: Sweet smell! Sweet smell! Every year at this time somebody comes back with stories of the sweet smell. Sweet God,
did the potatoes ever fail in Baile Beag? Well, did they ever—
ever? Never! There was never blight here. Never. Never. But
we're always sniffing about for it, aren't we?—looking for di-   350
saster. The rents are going to go up again—the harvest's going
to be lost—the herring have gone away for ever—there's
going to be evictions. Honest to God, some of you people
aren't happy unless you're miserable and you'll not be right
content until you're dead!   355
DOALTY: Bloody right, Maire. And sure St Colmcille prophesied
there'd never be blight here. He said:
     The spuds will bloom in Baile Beag
     Till rabbits grow an extra lug.
And sure that'll never be. So we're all right. Seven threes are   360
twenty-one; seven fours are twenty-eight; seven fives are forty-
nine—Hi, Jimmy, do you fancy my chances as boss of the
new national school?
JIMMY: What's that?—what's that?
DOALTY: Agh, g'way back home to Greece, son.   365
MAIRE: You ought to apply, Doalty.
DOALTY: D'you think so? Cripes, maybe I will. Hah!
BRIDGET: Did you know that you start at the age of six and you
have to stick at it until you're twelve at least—no matter how
smart you are or how much you know.   370
DOALTY: Who told you that yarn?
BRIDGET: And every child from every house has to go all day,
every day, summer or winter. That's the law.
DOALTY: I'll tell you something—nobody's going to go near
them—they're not going to take on—law or no law.   375
BRIDGET: And everything's free in them. You pay for nothing
except the books you use; that's what our Seamus says.
DOALTY: 'Our Seamus'. Sure your Seamus wouldn't pay anyway.
She's making this all up.
BRIDGET: Isn't that right, Manus?   380
MANUS: I think so.
BRIDGET: And from the very first day you go, you'll not hear one
word of Irish spoken. You'll be taught to speak English and
every subject will be taught through English and everyone'll
end up as cute as the Buncrana people.   385

(SARAH *suddenly grunts and mimes a warning that the master is
coming. The atmosphere changes. Sudden business. Heads
down.*)

DOALTY: He's here, boys. Cripes, he'll make yella meal out of me for those bloody tables.

BRIDGET: Have you any extra chalk, Manus?

MAIRE: And the atlas for me.

(DOALTY goes to MAIRE who is sitting on a stool at the back.)

390 DOALTY: Swop you seats.

MAIRE: Why?

DOALTY: There's an empty one beside the Infant Prodigy.

MAIRE: I'm fine here.

DOALTY: Please, Maire. I want to jouk in the back here.

(MAIRE rises.)

395   God love you. *(Aloud)* Anyone got a bloody table-book? Cripes, I'm wrecked.

(SARAH gives him one.)

God, I'm dying about you.

(In his haste to get to the back seat, DOALTY bumps into BRIDGET who is kneeling on the floor and writing laboriously on a slate resting on top of a bench-seat.)

BRIDGET: Watch where you're going, Doalty!

(DOALTY gooses BRIDGET. She squeals. Now the quiet hum of work: JIMMY reading Homer in a low voice; BRIDGET copying her headline; MAIRE studying the atlas; DOALTY, his eyes shut tight, mouthing his tables; SARAH doing sums. After a few seconds:—)

BRIDGET: Is this 'g' right, Manus? How do you put a tail on it?

400 DOALTY: Will you shut up! I can't concentrate!

(A few more seconds of work. Then DOALTY opens his eyes and looks around.)

False alarm, boys. The bugger's not coming at all. Sure the bugger's hardly fit to walk.

(And immediately HUGH enters. A large man, with residual dignity, shabbily dressed, carrying a stick. He has, as always, a large quantity of drink taken, but he is by no means drunk. He is in his early sixties.)

HUGH: *Adsum*, Doalty, *adsum*. Perhaps not in *sobrietate perfecta* but adequately *sobrius* to overhear your quip. Vesperal
405   salutations to you all.

(Various responses.)

JIMMY: *Ave*, Hugh.

HUGH: James. *(He removes his hat and coat and hands them and his stick to MANUS, as if to a footman.)* Apologies for my late arrival: we were celebrating the baptism of Nellie Ruadh's baby.

410 BRIDGET: *(Innocently)* What name did she put on it, Master?

HUGH: Was it Eamon? Yes, it was Eamon.

BRIDGET: Eamon Donal from Tor! Cripes!

HUGH: And after the *caerimonia nominationis*—Maire?

MAIRE: The ritual of naming.

415 HUGH: Indeed—we then had a few libations to mark the occasion. Altogether very pleasant. The derivation of the word 'baptize'?—where are my Greek scholars? Doalty?

DOALTY: Would it be—ah—ah—

HUGH: Too slow. James?

JIMMY: '*Baptizein*'—to dip or immerse.   420

HUGH: Indeed—our friend Pliny Minor speaks of the '*baptisterium*'—the cold bath.

DOALTY: Master.

HUGH: Doalty?

DOALTY: I suppose you could talk then about baptizing a sheep   425
at sheep-dipping, could you?

(Laughter. Comments.)

HUGH: Indeed—the precedent is there—the day you were appropriately named Doalty—seven nines?

DOALTY: What's that, Master?

HUGH: Seven times nine?   430

DOALTY: Seven nines—seven nines—seven times nine—seven times nine are—cripes, it's on the tip of my tongue, Master— I knew it for sure this morning—funny that's the only one that foxes me—

BRIDGET: *(Prompt)* Sixty-three.   435

DOALTY: What's wrong with me: sure seven nines are fifty-three, Master.

HUGH: Sophocles from Colonus would agree with Doalty Dan Doalty from Tulach Alainn: 'To know nothing is the sweetest life.' Where's Sean Beag?   440

MANUS: He's at the salmon.

HUGH: And Nora Dan?

MAIRE: She says she's not coming back any more.

HUGH: Ah. Nora Dan can now write her name—Nora Dan's education is complete. And the Donnelly twins?   445

(Brief pause. Then:—)

BRIDGET: They're probably at the turf. *(She goes to HUGH.)* There's the one-and-eight I owe you for last quarter's arithmetic and there's my one-and-six for this quarter's writing.

HUGH: *Gratias tibi ago. (He sits at his table.)* Before we commence our *studia* I have three items of information to impart   450
to you—*(To MANUS)* A bowl of tea, strong tea, black—

(MANUS leaves.)

Item A: on my perambulations today—Bridget? Too slow. Maire?

MAIRE: *Perambulare*—to walk about.

HUGH: Indeed—I encountered Captain Lancey of the Royal   455
Engineers who is engaged in the ordnance survey of this area. He tells me that in the past few days two of his horses have strayed and some of his equipment seems to be mislaid. I expressed my regret and suggested he address you himself on these matters. He then explained that he does not speak Irish.   460
Latin? I asked. None. Greek? Not a syllable. He speaks—on his own admission—only English; and to his credit he seemed suitably verecund—James?

JIMMY: *Verecundus*—humble.

HUGH: Indeed—he voiced some surprise that we did not speak   465
his language. I explained that a few of us did, on occasion— outside the parish of course—and then usually for the purposes of commerce, a use to which his tongue seemed particularly suited—*(Shouts)* and a slice of soda bread—and I went

---

403 **adsum** I am present   403 **sobrietate perfecta** with complete sobriety   404 **sobrius** sober   406 **Ave** hail   413 **caerimonia nominationis** ceremony of naming

420 **baptizein** to dip or immerse   421 **baptisterium** a cold bath, swimming pool   449 **Gratias tibi ago** I thank you   450 **studia** studies   454 **perambulare** to walk through   464 **verecundus** shame-faced, modest

470   on to propose that our own culture and the classical tongues made a happier conjugation—Doalty?

DOALTY: *Conjugo*—I join together.

(DOALTY *is so pleased with himself that he prods and winks at* BRIDGET.)

HUGH: Indeed—English, I suggested, couldn't really express us. And again to his credit he acquiesced to my logic. Acqui-
475   esced—Maire?

(MAIRE *turns away impatiently.* HUGH *is unaware of the gesture.*)

Too slow. Bridget?

BRIDGET: *Acquiesco.*

HUGH: *Procede.*

BRIDGET: *Acquiesco, acquiescere, acquievi, acquietum.*

480   HUGH: Indeed—and Item B . . .

MAIRE: Master.

HUGH: Yes?

(MAIRE *gets to her feet uneasily but determinedly. Pause.*)

Well, girl?

MAIRE: We should all be learning to speak English. That's what
485   my mother says. That's what I say. That's what Dan O'Con-
nell said last month in Ennis. He said the sooner we all learn to speak English the better.

(*Suddenly several speak together.*)

JIMMY: What's she saying? What? What?

DOALTY: It's Irish he uses when he's travelling around scroung-
490   ing votes.

BRIDGET: And sleeping with married women. Sure no woman's safe from that fella.

JIMMY: Who-who-who? Who's this? Who's this?

HUGH: *Silentium!* (*Pause.*) Who is she talking about?

495   MAIRE: I'm talking about Daniel O'Connell.

HUGH: Does she mean that little Kerry politician?

MAIRE: I'm talking about the Liberator, Master, as you well know. And what he said was this: 'The old language is a bar-rier to modern progress.' He said that last month. And he's
500   right. I don't want Greek. I don't want Latin. I want English.

(MANUS *reappears on the platform above.*)

I want to be able to speak English because I'm going to Amer-ica as soon as the harvest's all saved.

(MAIRE *remains standing.* HUGH *puts his hand into his pocket and produces a flask of whiskey. He removes the cap, pours a drink into it, tosses it back, replaces the cap, puts the flask back into his pocket. Then:—*)

HUGH: We have been diverted—*diverto*—*divertere*—Where were we?

505   DOALTY: Three items of information, Master. You're at Item B.

HUGH: Indeed—Item B—Item B—yes—On my way to the christening this morning I chanced to meet Mr George Alex-ander, Justice of the Peace. We discussed the new national school. Mr Alexander invited me to take charge of it when it
510   opens. I thanked him and explained that I could do that only

if I were free to run it as I have run this hedge-school for the past thirty-five years—filling what our friend Euripides calls the '*aplestos pithos*'—James?

JIMMY: 'The cask that cannot be filled'.

HUGH: Indeed—and Mr Alexander retorted courteously and 515
emphatically that he hopes that is how it will be run.

(MAIRE *now sits.*)

Indeed. I have had a strenuous day and I am weary of you all. (*He rises.*) Manus will take care of you.

(HUGH *goes towards the steps.* OWEN *enters.* OWEN *is the youn-ger son, a handsome, attractive young man in his twenties. He is dressed smartly—a city man. His manner is easy and charming: everything he does is invested with consideration and enthusi-asm. He now stands framed in the doorway, a travelling bag across his shoulder.*)

OWEN: Could anybody tell me is this where Hugh Mor O'Don-nell holds his hedge-school? 520

DOALTY: It's Owen—Owen Hugh! Look, boys—it's Owen Hugh!

(OWEN *enters. As he crosses the room he touches and has a word for each person.*)

OWEN: Doalty! (*Playful punch.*) How are you, boy? *Jacobe, quid agis?* Are you well?

JIMMY: Fine. Fine. 525

OWEN: And Bridget! Give us a kiss. Aaaaaah!

BRIDGET: You're welcome, Owen.

OWEN: It's not—? Yes, it *is* Maire Chatach! God! A young woman.

MAIRE: How are you, Owen? 530

(OWEN *is now in front of* HUGH. *He puts his two hands on his* FATHER's *shoulders.*)

OWEN: And how's the old man himself?

HUGH: Fair—fair.

OWEN: Fair? For God's sake you never looked better! Come here to me. (*He embraces* HUGH *warmly and genuinely.*) Great to see you, Father. Great to be back. 535

(HUGH's *eyes are moist—partly joy, partly the drink.*)

HUGH: I—I'm—I'm—pay no attention to—

OWEN: Come on—come on—come on—(*He gives* HUGH *his handkerchief.*) Do you know what you and I are going to do tonight? We are going to go up to Anna na mBreag's . . .

DOALTY: Not there, Owen. 540

OWEN: Why not?

DOALTY: Her poteen's worse than ever.

BRIDGET: They say she puts frogs in it!

OWEN: All the better. (*To* HUGH) And you and I are going to get footless drunk. That's arranged. 545

(OWEN *sees* MANUS *coming down the steps with tea and soda bread. They meet at the bottom.*)

And Manus!

MANUS: You're welcome, Owen.

OWEN: I know I am. And it's great to be here. (*He turns round, arms outstretched.*) I can't believe it. I come back after six

---

472 **conjugo** I join together   477 **acquiesco, acquiescere** to rest, to find comfort in   478 **procede** proceed   494 **Silentium!** Silence!   503 **diverto, divertere** to turn away

513 **aplestos pithos** unfillable cask   523–524 **Jacobe, quid agis?** James, how are you?

550 years and everything's just as it was! Nothing's changed! Not a thing! *(Sniffs.)* Even that smell—that's the same smell this place always had. What is it anyway? Is it the straw?

DOALTY: Jimmy Jack's feet.

(General laughter. It opens little pockets of conversation round the room.)

OWEN: And Doalty Dan Doalty hasn't changed either!

555 DOALTY: Bloody right, Owen.

OWEN: Jimmy, are you well?

JIMMY: Dodging about.

OWEN: Any word of the big day?

(This is greeted with 'ohs' and 'ahs'.)

Time enough, Jimmy. Homer's easier to live with, isn't he?

560 MAIRE: We heard stories that you own ten big shops in Dublin—is it true?

OWEN: Only nine.

BRIDGET: And you've twelve horses and six servants.

OWEN: Yes—that's true. God Almighty, would you listen to 565 them—taking a hand at me!

MANUS: When did you arrive?

OWEN: We left Dublin yesterday morning, spent last night in Omagh and got here half an hour ago.

MANUS: You're hungry then.

570 HUGH: Indeed—get him food—get him a drink.

OWEN: Not now, thanks; later. Listen—am I interrupting you all?

HUGH: By no means. We're finished for the day.

OWEN: Wonderful. I'll tell you why. Two friends of mine are waiting outside the door. They'd like to meet you and I'd like 575 you to meet them. May I bring them in?

HUGH: Certainly. You'll all eat and have . . .

OWEN: Not just yet, Father. You've seen the sappers working in this area for the past fortnight, haven't you? Well, the older man is Captain Lancey . . .

580 HUGH: I've met Captain Lancey.

OWEN: Great. He's the cartographer in charge of this whole area. Cartographer—James?

(OWEN begins to play this game—his father's game—partly to involve his classroom audience, partly to show he has not forgotten it, and indeed partly because he enjoys it.)

JIMMY: A maker of maps.

OWEN: Indeed—and the younger man that I travelled with from 585 Dublin, his name is Lieutenant Yolland and he is attached to the toponymic department—Father?—*responde—responde!*

HUGH: He gives names to places.

OWEN: Indeed—although he is in fact an orthographer—Dolty?—too slow—Manus?

590 MANUS: The correct spelling of those names.

OWEN: Indeed—indeed!

(OWEN laughs and claps his hands. Some of the others join in.)

Beautiful! Beautiful! Honest to God, it's such a delight to be back here with you all again—'civilized' people. Anyhow—may I bring them in?

595 HUGH: Your friends are our friends.

OWEN: I'll be straight back.

(There is general talk as OWEN goes towards the door. He stops beside SARAH.)

OWEN: That's a new face. Who are you?

(A very brief hesitation. Then:—)

SARAH: My name is Sarah.

OWEN: Sarah who?

SARAH: Sarah Johnny Sally. 600

OWEN: Of course! From Bun na hAbhann! I'm Owen—Owen Hugh Mor. From Baile Beag. Good to see you.

(During this OWEN—SARAH exchange.)

HUGH: Come on now. Let's tidy this place up. *(He rubs the top of his table with his sleeve.)* Move, Doalty—lift those books off the floor. 605

DOALTY: Right, Master; certainly, Master; I'm doing my best, Master.

(OWEN stops at the door.)

OWEN: One small thing, Father.

HUGH: *Silentium!*

OWEN: I'm on their pay-roll. 610

(SARAH, very elated at her success, is beside MANUS.)

SARAH: I said it, Manus!

(MANUS ignores SARAH. He is much more interested in OWEN now.)

MANUS: You haven't enlisted, have you?!

(SARAH moves away.)

OWEN: Me a soldier? I'm employed as a part-time, underpaid, civilian interpreter. My job is to translate the quaint, archaic tongue you people persist in speaking into the King's good 615 English.

(He goes out.)

HUGH: Move—move—move! Put some order on things! Come on, Sarah—hide that bucket. Whose are these slates? Somebody take these dishes away. *Festinate! Festinate!*

(MANUS goes to MAIRE who is busy tidying.)

MANUS: You didn't tell me you were definitely leaving. 620

MAIRE: Not now.

HUGH: Good girl, Bridget. That's the style.

MANUS: You might at least have told me.

HUGH: Are these your books, James?

JIMMY: Thank you. 625

MANUS: Fine! Fine! Go ahead! Go ahead!

MAIRE: You talk to me about getting married—with neither a roof over your head nor a sod of ground under your foot. I suggest you go for the new school; but no—'My father's in for that.' Well now he's got it and now this is finished and now 630 you've nothing.

MANUS: I can always . . .

MAIRE: What? Teach classics to the cows? Agh—

(MAIRE moves away from MANUS. OWEN enters with LANCEY and YOLLAND. CAPTAIN LANCEY is middle-aged; a small, crisp officer, expert in his field as cartographer but uneasy with people—especially civilians, especially these foreign civilians. His skill is with deeds, not words. LIEUTENANT YOLLAND is in his

619 **Festinate!** Hurry!

late twenties/early thirties. He is tall and thin and gangling, blond hair, a shy, awkward manner. A soldier by accident.)

OWEN: Here we are. Captain Lancey—my father.

635 LANCEY: Good evening.

(HUGH becomes expansive, almost courtly, with his visitors.)

HUGH: You and I have already met, sir.

LANCEY: Yes.

OWEN: And Lieutenant Yolland—both Royal Engineers—my father.

640 HUGH: You're very welcome, gentlemen.

YOLLAND: How do you do.

HUGH: *Gaudeo vos hic adesse.*

OWEN: And I'll make no other introductions except that these are some of the people of Baile Beag and—what?—well you're among the best people in Ireland now. *(He pauses to allow LANCEY to speak. LANCEY does not.)* Would you like to say a few words, Captain?

645

HUGH: What about a drop, sir?

LANCEY: A what?

650 HUGH: Perhaps a modest refreshment? A little sampling of our *aqua vitae?*

LANCEY: No, no.

HUGH: Later perhaps when—

LANCEY: I'll say what I have to say, if I may, and as briefly as possible. Do they speak *any* English, Roland?

655

OWEN: Don't worry. I'll translate.

LANCEY: I see. *(He clears his throat. He speaks as if he were addressing children—a shade too loudly and enunciating excessively.)* You may have seen me—seen me—working in this section—section?—working. We are here—here—in this place—you understand?—to make a map—a map—a map and—

660

JIMMY: *Nonne Latine loquitur?*

(HUGH holds up a restraining hand.)

HUGH: James.

665 LANCEY: *(To JIMMY)* I do not speak Gaelic, sir.

(He looks at OWEN.)

OWEN: Carry on.

LANCEY: A map is a representation on paper—a picture—you understand picture?—a paper picture—showing, representing this country—yes?—showing your country in miniature—a scaled drawing on paper of—of—of—

670

(Suddenly DOALTY sniggers. Then BRIDGET. Then SARAH. OWEN leaps in quickly.)

OWEN: It might be better if you *assume* they understand you—

LANCEY: Yes?

OWEN: And I'll translate as you go along.

LANCEY: I see. Yes. Very well. Perhaps you're right. Well. What we are doing is this. *(He looks at OWEN. OWEN nods reassuringly.)* His Majesty's government has ordered the first ever comprehensive survey of this entire country—a general triangulation which will embrace detailed hydrographic and topographic information and which will be executed to a scale of six inches to the English mile.

675

680

642 **Gaudeo vos hic adesse** Welcome   663 **Nonne Latine loquitur?** Does he not speak Latin?

HUGH: *(Pouring a drink)* Excellent—excellent.

(LANCEY looks at OWEN.)

OWEN: A new map is being made of the whole country.

(LANCEY looks to OWEN: Is that all? OWEN smiles reassuringly and indicates to proceed.)

LANCEY: This enormous task has been embarked on so that the military authorities will be equipped with up-to-date and accurate information on every corner of this part of the Empire.

685

OWEN: The job is being done by soldiers because they are skilled in this work.

LANCEY: And also so that the entire basis of land valuation can be reassessed for purposes of more equitable taxation.

OWEN: This new map will take the place of the estate agent's map so that from now on you will know exactly what is yours in law.

690

LANCEY: In conclusion I wish to quote two brief extracts from the white paper which is our governing charter: *(Reads)* 'All former surveys of Ireland originated in forfeiture and violent transfer of property; the present survey has for its object the relief which can be afforded to the proprietors and occupiers of land from unequal taxation.'

695

OWEN: The captain hopes that the public will cooperate with the sappers and that the new map will mean that taxes are reduced.

700

HUGH: A worthy enterprise—*opus honestum!* And Extract B?

LANCEY: 'Ireland is privileged. No such survey is being undertaken in England. So this survey cannot but be received as proof of the disposition of this government to advance the interests of Ireland.' My sentiments, too.

705

OWEN: This survey demonstrates the government's interest in Ireland and the captain thanks you for listening so attentively to him.

HUGH: Our pleasure, Captain.

710

LANCEY: Lieutenant Yolland?

YOLLAND: I—I—I've nothing to say—really—

OWEN: The captain is the man who actually makes the new map. George's task is to see that the place-names on this map are . . . correct. *(To YOLLAND.)* Just a few words—they'd like to hear you. *(To class.)* Don't you want to hear George, too?

715

MAIRE: Has he anything to say?

YOLLAND: *(To MAIRE)* Sorry—sorry?

OWEN: She says she's dying to hear you.

YOLLAND: *(To MAIRE)* Very kind of you—thank you . . . *(To class)* I can only say that I feel—I feel very foolish to—to—to be working here and not to speak your language. But I intend to rectify that—with Roland's help—indeed I do.

720

OWEN: He wants me to teach him Irish!

HUGH: You are doubly welcome, sir.

725

YOLLAND: I think your countryside is—is—is—is very beautiful. I've fallen in love with it already. I hope we're not too—too crude an intrusion on your lives. And I know that I'm going to be happy, very happy, here.

OWEN: He is already a committed Hibernophile—

730

JIMMY: He loves—

OWEN: All right, Jimmy—we know—he loves Baile Beag; and he loves you all.

702 **opus honestum** an honourable task

HUGH: Please . . . May I . . . ?

(HUGH *is now drunk. He holds on to the edge of the table.*)

735 OWEN: Go ahead, Father. (*Hands up for quiet.*) Please—please.
HUGH: And we, gentlemen, we in turn are happy to offer you our friendship, our hospitality, and every assistance that you may require. Gentlemen—welcome!

(*A few desultory claps. The formalities are over. General conversation. The soldiers meet the locals. MANUS and OWEN meet down stage.*)

OWEN: Lancey's a bloody ramrod but George's all right. How are
740 you anyway?
MANUS: What sort of a translation was that, Owen?
OWEN: Did I make a mess of it?
MANUS: You weren't saying what Lancey was saying!
OWEN: 'Uncertainty in meaning is incipient poetry'—who said
745 that?
MANUS: There was nothing uncertain about what Lancey said: it's a bloody military operation, Owen! And what's Yolland's function? What's 'incorrect' about the place-names we have here?
750 OWEN: Nothing at all. They're just going to be standardized.
MANUS: You mean changed into English?
OWEN: Where there's ambiguity, they'll be Anglicized.
MANUS: And they call you Roland! They both call you Roland!
OWEN: Shhhhh. Isn't it ridiculous? They seemed to get it wrong
755 from the very beginning—or else they can't pronounce Owen. I was afraid some of you bastards would laugh.
MANUS: Aren't you going to tell them?
OWEN: Yes—yes—soon—soon.
MANUS: But they . . .
760 OWEN: Easy, man, easy. Owen—Roland—what the hell. It's only a name. It's the same me, isn't it? Well, isn't it?
MANUS: Indeed it is. It's the same Owen.
OWEN: And the same Manus. And in a way we complement each other. (*He punches MANUS lightly, playfully and turns
765 to join the others. As he goes.*) All right—who has met whom? Isn't this a job for the go-between?

(MANUS *watches* OWEN *move confidently across the floor, taking* MAIRE *by the hand and introducing her to* YOLLAND. HUGH *is trying to negotiate the steps.* JIMMY *is lost in a text.* DOALTY *and* BRIDGET *are reliving their giggling.* SARAH *is staring at* MANUS.)

— ACT TWO —

SCENE I

The sappers have already mapped most of the area. YOLLAND's *official task, which* OWEN *is now doing, is to take each of the Gaelic names—every hill, stream, rock, even every patch of ground which possessed its own distinctive Irish name—and Anglicize it, either by changing it into its approximate English sound or by translating it into English words. For example, a Gaelic name like Cnoc Ban could become Knockban or—directly translated—Fair Hill. These new standardized names were entered into the Name-Book, and when the new maps appeared they contained all these new Anglicized names.* OWEN's

official function as translator is to pronounce each name in Irish and then provide the English translation.

The hot weather continues. It is late afternoon some days later.

Stage right: an improvised clothes-line strung between the shafts of the cart and a nail in the wall; on it are some shirts and socks.

A large map—one of the new blank maps—is spread out on the floor. OWEN *is on his hands and knees, consulting it. He is totally engrossed in his task which he pursues with great energy and efficiency.*

YOLLAND's *hesitancy has vanished—he is at home here now. He is sitting on the floor, his long legs stretched out before him, his back resting against a creel, his eyes closed. His mind is elsewhere. One of the reference books—a church registry—lies open on his lap.*

Around them are various reference books, the Name-Book, a bottle of poteen, some cups, etc.

OWEN *completes an entry in the Name-Book and returns to the map on the floor.*

OWEN: Now. Where have we got to? Yes—the point where that stream enters the sea—that tiny little beach there. George!
YOLLAND: Yes. I'm listening. What do you call it? Say the Irish name again?
OWEN: Bun na hAbhann.   5
YOLLAND: Again.
OWEN: Bun na hAbhann.
YOLLAND: Bun na hAbhann.
OWEN: That's terrible, George.
YOLLAND: I know. I'm sorry. Say it again.   10
OWEN: Bun na hAbhann.
YOLLAND: Bun na hAbhann.
OWEN: That's better. Bun is the Irish word for bottom. And Abha means river. So it's literally the mouth of the river.
YOLLAND: Let's leave it alone. There's no English equivalent for   15
a sound like that.
OWEN: What is it called in the church registry?

(*Only now does* YOLLAND *open his eyes.*)

YOLLAND: Let's see . . . Banowen.
OWEN: That's wrong. (*Consults text.*) The list of freeholders calls it Owenmore—that's completely wrong: Owenmore's   20
the big river at the west end of the parish. (*Another text.*) And in the grand jury lists it's called—God!—Binhone!—wherever they got that. I suppose we could Anglicize it to Bunowen; but somehow that's neither fish nor flesh.

(YOLLAND *closes his eyes again.*)

YOLLAND: I give up.   25
OWEN: (*At map*) Back to first principles. What are we trying to do?
YOLLAND: Good question.
OWEN: We are trying to denominate and at the same time describe that tiny area of soggy, rocky, sandy ground where that little stream enters the sea, an area known locally as Bun na   30
hAbhann . . . Burnfoot! What about Burnfoot?
YOLLAND: (*Indifferently*) Good, Roland, Burnfoot's good.
OWEN: George, my name isn't . . .
YOLLAND: B-u-r-n-f-o-o-t?
OWEN: Are you happy with that?   35

YOLLAND: Yes.

OWEN: Burnfoot it is then. (*He makes the entry into the Name-Book.*) Bun na hAbhann—B-u-r-n-

YOLLAND: You're becoming very skilled at this.

40 OWEN: We're not moving fast enough.

YOLLAND: (*Opens eyes again*) Lancey lectured me again last night.

OWEN: When does he finish here?

YOLLAND: The sappers are pulling out at the end of the week.
45 The trouble is, the maps they've completed can't be printed without these names. So London screams at Lancey and Lancey screams at me. But I wasn't intimidated.

(*MANUS emerges from upstairs and descends.*)

'I'm sorry, sir,' I said, 'But certain tasks demand their own tempo. You cannot rename a whole country overnight.' Your
50 Irish air has made me bold. (*To* MANUS) Do you want us to leave?

MANUS: Time enough. Class won't begin for another half-hour.

YOLLAND: Sorry—sorry?

OWEN: Can't you speak English?

(*MANUS gathers the things off the clothes-line.* OWEN *returns to the map.*)

55 OWEN: We now come across that beach . . .

YOLLAND: Tra—that's the Irish for beach. (*To* MANUS) I'm picking up the odd word, Manus.

MANUS: So.

OWEN: . . . on past Burnfoot; and there's nothing around here
60 that has any name that I know of until we come down here to the south end, just about here . . . and there should be a ridge of rocks there . . . Have the sappers marked it? They have. Look, George.

YOLLAND: Where are we?

65 OWEN: There.

YOLLAND: I'm lost.

OWEN: Here. And the name of that ridge is Druim Dubh. Put English on that, Lieutenant.

YOLLAND: Say it again.

70 OWEN: Druim Dubh.

YOLLAND: Dubh means black.

OWEN: Yes.

YOLLAND: And Druim means . . . what? a fort?

OWEN: We met it yesterday in Druim Luachra.

75 YOLLAND: A ridge! The Black Ridge! (*To* MANUS) You see, Manus?

OWEN: We'll have you fluent at the Irish before the summer's over.

YOLLAND: Oh, I wish I were. (*To* MANUS *as he crosses to go back upstairs*) We got a crate of oranges from Dublin today. I'll
80 send some up to you.

MANUS: Thanks. (*To* OWEN) Better hide that bottle. Father's just up and he'd be better without it.

OWEN: Can't you speak English before your man?

MANUS: Why?

85 OWEN: Out of courtesy.

MANUS: Doesn't he want to learn Irish? (*To* YOLLAND) Don't you want to learn Irish?

YOLLAND: Sorry—sorry? I—I—

MANUS: I understand the Lanceys perfectly but people like you
90 puzzle me.

OWEN: Manus, for God's sake!

MANUS: (*Still to* YOLLAND) How's the work going?

YOLLAND: The work?—the work? Oh, it's—it's staggering along—I think—(*To* OWEN)—isn't it? But we'd be lost without Roland.
95

MANUS: (*Leaving*) I'm sure. But there are always the Rolands, aren't there?

(*He goes upstairs and exits.*)

YOLLAND: What was that he said?—something about Lancey, was it?

OWEN: He said we should hide that bottle before Father gets his 100 hands on it.

YOLLAND: Ah.

OWEN: He's always trying to protect him.

YOLLAND: Was he lame from birth?

OWEN: An accident when he was a baby: Father fell across his 105 cradle. That's why Manus feels so responsible for him.

YOLLAND: Why doesn't he marry?

OWEN: Can't afford to, I suppose.

YOLLAND: Hasn't he a salary?

OWEN: What salary? All he gets is the odd shilling Father throws 110 him—and that's seldom enough. I got out in time, didn't I?

(*YOLLAND is pouring a drink.*)

Easy with that stuff—it'll hit you suddenly.

YOLLAND: I like it.

OWEN: Let's get back to the job. Druim Dubh—what's it called in the jury lists? (*Consults texts.*) 115

YOLLAND: Some people here resent us.

OWEN: Dramduff—wrong as usual.

YOLLAND: I was passing a little girl yesterday and she spat at me.

OWEN: And it's Drimdoo here. What's it called in the registry?

YOLLAND: Do you know the Donnelly twins? 120

OWEN: Who?

YOLLAND: The Donnelly twins.

OWEN: Yes. Best fishermen about here. What about them?

YOLLAND: Lancey's looking for them.

OWEN: What for? 125

YOLLAND: He wants them for questioning.

OWEN: Probably stolen somebody's nets. Dramduffy! Nobody ever called it Dramduffy. Take your pick of those three.

YOLLAND: My head's addled. Let's take a rest. Do you want a drink? 130

OWEN: Thanks. Now, every Dubh we've come across we've changed to Duff. So if we're to be consistent, I suppose Druim Dubh has to become Dromduff.

(*YOLLAND is now looking out the window.*)

You can see the end of the ridge from where you're standing. But D-r-u-m- or D-r-o-m-? (*Name-Book*) Do you remember—which did we agree on for Druim Luachra? 135

YOLLAND: That house immediately above where we're camped—

OWEN: Mm?

YOLLAND: The house where Maire lives.

OWEN: Maire? Oh, Maire Chatach. 140

YOLLAND: What does that mean?

OWEN: Curly-haired; the whole family are called the Catachs. What about it?

YOLLAND: I hear music coming from that house almost every
145 night.
OWEN: Why don't you drop in?
YOLLAND: Could I?
OWEN: Why not? We used D-r-o-m then. So we've got to call it
D-r-o-m-d-u-f-f—all right?
150 YOLLAND: Go back up to where the new school is being built
and just say the names again for me, would you?
OWEN: That's a good idea. Poolkerry, Ballybeg—
YOLLAND: No, no; as they still are—in your own language.
OWEN: Poll na gCaorach,

(YOLLAND *repeats the names silently after him.*)

155 Baile Beag, Ceann Balor, Lis Maol, Machaire Buidhe, Baile
na gGall, Carraig na Ri, Mullach Dearg—
YOLLAND: Do you think I could live here?
OWEN: What are you talking about?
YOLLAND: Settle down here—live here.
160 OWEN: Come on, George.
YOLLAND: I mean it.
OWEN: Live on what? Potatoes? Buttermilk?
YOLLAND: It's really heavenly.
OWEN: For God's sake! The first hot summer in fifty years and
165 you think it's Eden. Don't be such a bloody romantic. You
wouldn't survive a mild winter here.
YOLLAND: Do you think not? Maybe you're right.

(DOALTY *enters in a rush.*)

DOALTY: Hi, boys, is Manus about?
OWEN: He's upstairs. Give him a shout.
170 DOALTY: Manus! The cattle's going mad in that heat—Cripes,
running wild all over the place. (*To* YOLLAND) How are you
doing, skipper?

(MANUS *appears.*)

YOLLAND: Thank you for—I—I'm very grateful to you for—
DOALTY: Wasting your time. I don't know a word you're saying.
175 Hi, Manus, there's two bucks down the road there asking for
you.
MANUS: (*Descending*) Who are they?
DOALTY: Never clapped eyes on them. They want to talk to you.
MANUS: What about?
180 DOALTY: They wouldn't say. Come on. The bloody beasts'll end
up in Loch an Iubhair if they're not capped. Good luck, boys!

(DOALTY *rushes off.* MANUS *follows him.*)

OWEN: Good luck! What were you thanking Doalty for?
YOLLAND: I was washing outside my tent this morning and he
was passing with a scythe across his shoulder and he came up
185 to me and pointed to the long grass and then cut a pathway
round my tent and from the tent down to the road—so that
my feet won't get wet with the dew. Wasn't that kind of him?
And I have no words to thank him . . . I suppose you're right: I
suppose I couldn't live here . . . Just before Doalty came up to
190 me this morning, I was thinking that at that moment I might
have been in Bombay instead of Ballybeg. You see, my father
was at his wits end with me and finally he got me a job with
the East India Company—some kind of a clerkship. That was
ten, eleven months ago. So I set off for London. Unfor-

tunately I—I—I missed the boat. Literally. And since I   195
couldn't face Father and hadn't enough money to hang about
until the next sailing, I joined the army. And they stuck me
into the Engineers and posted me to Dublin. And Dublin
sent me here. And while I was washing this morning and
looking across the Tra Bhan, I was thinking how very, very   200
lucky I am to be here and not in Bombay.
OWEN: Do you believe in fate?
YOLLAND: Lancey's so like my father. I was watching him last
night. He met every group of sappers as they reported in. He
checked the field kitchens. He examined the horses. He in-   205
spected every single report—even examining the texture of
the paper and commenting on the neatness of the handwriting. The perfect colonial servant: not only must the job be
done—it must be done with excellence. Father has that
drive, too; that dedication; that indefatigable energy. He   210
builds roads—hopping from one end of the Empire to the
other. Can't sit still for five minutes. He says himself the longest time he ever sat still was the night before Waterloo when
they were waiting for Wellington to make up his mind to
attack.   215
OWEN: What age is he?
YOLLAND: Born in 1789—the very day the Bastille fell. I've often thought maybe that gave his whole life its character. Do
you think it could? He inherited a new world the day he was
born—The Year One. Ancient time was at an end. The   220
world had cast off its old skin. There were no longer any frontiers to man's potential. Possibilities were endless and exciting. He still believes that. The Apocalypse is just about to
happen . . . I'm afraid I'm a great disappointment to him. I've
neither his energy, nor his coherence, nor his belief. Do I   225
believe in fate? The day I arrived in Ballybeg—no, Baile
Beag—the moment you brought me in here, I had a curious
sensation. It's difficult to describe. It was a momentary sense
of discovery; no—not quite a sense of discovery—a sense of
recognition, of confirmation of something I half knew in-   230
stinctively; as if I had stepped . . .
OWEN: Back into ancient time?
YOLLAND: No, no. It wasn't an awareness of *direction* being
changed but of experience being of a totally different order. I
had moved into a consciousness that wasn't striving nor agi-   235
tated, but at its ease and with its own conviction and assurance. And when I heard Jimmy Jack and your father
swapping stories about Apollo and Cuchulainn and Paris and
Ferdia—as if they lived down the road—it was then that I
thought—I knew—perhaps I could live here . . . (*Now em-*   240
barrassed) Where's the pot-een?
OWEN: Poteen.
YOLLAND: Poteen—poteen—poteen. Even if I did speak Irish
I'd always be an outsider here, wouldn't I? I may learn the
password but the language of the tribe will always elude me,   245
won't it? The private core will always be . . . hermetic, won't it?
OWEN: You can learn to decode us.

(HUGH *emerges from upstairs and descends. He is dressed for the
road. Today he is physically and mentally jaunty and alert—
almost self-consciously jaunty and alert. Indeed, as the scene
progresses, one has the sense that he is deliberately parodying
himself. The moment* HUGH *gets to the bottom of the steps* YOL-
LAND *leaps respectfully to his feet.*)

HUGH: *(As he descends)*
  Quantumvis cursum longum fessumque moratur
250 *Sol, sacro tandem carmine vesper adest.*
  I dabble in verse, Lieutenant, after the style of Ovid. *(To* OWEN*)* A drop of that to fortify me.

YOLLAND: You'll have to translate it for me.

HUGH: *Let's see —*
255   No matter how long the sun may linger on his long and weary journey
    At length evening comes with its sacred song.

YOLLAND: Very nice, sir.

HUGH: English succeeds in making it sound . . . plebeian.

260 OWEN: Where are you off to, Father?

HUGH: An *expeditio* with three purposes. Purpose A: to acquire a testimonial from our parish priest — *(To* YOLLAND*)* a worthy man but barely literate; and since he'll ask me to write it myself, how in all modesty can I do myself justice? *(To* OWEN*)*
265 Where did this *(drink)* come from?

OWEN: Anna na mBreag's.

HUGH: *(To* YOLLAND*)* In that case address yourself to it with circumspection. *(And* HUGH *instantly tosses the drink back in one gulp and grimaces.)* Aaaaaaagh! *(Holds out his glass for a*
270 *refill.)* Anna na mBreag means Anna of the Lies. And Purpose B: to talk to the builders of the new school about the kind of living accommodation I will require there. I have lived too long like a journeyman tailor.

YOLLAND: Some years ago we lived fairly close to a poet — well,
275   about three miles away.

HUGH: His name?

YOLLAND: Wordsworth — William Wordsworth.

HUGH: Did he speak of me to you?

YOLLAND: Actually I never talked to him. I just saw him out
280   walking — in the distance.

HUGH: Wordsworth? . . . No. I'm afraid we're not familiar with your literature, Lieutenant. We feel closer to the warm Mediterranean. We tend to overlook your island.

YOLLAND: I'm learning to speak Irish, sir.

285 HUGH: Good.

YOLLAND: Roland's teaching me.

HUGH: Splendid.

YOLLAND: I mean — I feel so cut off from the people here. And I was trying to explain a few minutes ago how remarkable a
290   community this is. To meet people like yourself and Jimmy Jack who actually converse in Greek and Latin. And your place names — what was the one we came across this morning? — Termon, from Terminus, the god of boundaries. It — it — it's really astonishing.

295 HUGH: We like to think we endure around truths immemorially posited.

YOLLAND: And your Gaelic literature — you're a poet yourself —

HUGH: Only in Latin, I'm afraid.

YOLLAND: I understand it's enormously rich and ornate.

300 HUGH: Indeed, Lieutenant. A rich language. A rich literature. You'll find, sir, that certain cultures expend on their vocabularies and syntax acquisitive energies and ostentations entirely

---

249–250 **Quantumvis cursum . . . vesper adest** No matter how long the sun delays on his long weary course/At length evening comes with its sacred song   261 **expeditio** an expedition

---

lacking in their material lives. I suppose you could call us a spiritual people.

OWEN: *(Not unkindly; more out of embarrassment before* YOL- 305
LAND*)* Will you stop that nonsense, Father.

HUGH: Nonsense? What nonsense?

OWEN: Do you know where the priest lives?

HUGH: At Lis na Muc, over near . . .

OWEN: No, he doesn't. Lis na Muc, the Fort of the Pigs, has 310
become Swinefort. *(Now turning the pages of the Name-Book — a page per name.)* And to get to Swinefort you pass through Greencastle and Fair Head and Strandhill and Gort and Whiteplains. And the new school isn't at Poll na gCaorach — it's at Sheepsrock. Will you be able to find your 315
way?

*(*HUGH *pours himself another drink. Then: —)*

HUGH: Yes, it is a rich language, Lieutenant, full of the mythologies of fantasy and hope and self-deception — a syntax opulent with tomorrows. It is our response to mud cabins and a diet of potatoes; and our only method of replying to . . . inev- 320
itabilities. *(To* OWEN*)* Can you give me the loan of half-a-crown? I'll repay you out of the subscriptions I'm collecting for the publication of my new book. *(To* YOLLAND*)* It is entitled: 'The Pentaglot Preceptor or Elementary Institute of the English, Greek, Hebrew, Latin and Irish Languages; Partic- 325
ularly Calculated for the Instruction of Such Ladies and Gentlemen as may Wish to Learn without the Help of a Master'.

YOLLAND: *(Laughs)* That's a wonderful title!

HUGH: Between ourselves — the best part of the enterprise. Nor do I, in fact, speak Hebrew. And that last phrase — 'without 330
the Help of a Master' — that was written before the new national school was thrust upon me — do you think I ought to drop it now? After all you don't dispose of the cow just because it has produced a magnificent calf, do you?

YOLLAND: You certainly do not. 335

HUGH: The phrase goes. And I'm interrupting work of moment. *(He goes to the door and stops there.)* To return briefly to that other matter, Lieutenant. I understand your sense of exclusion, of being cut off from a life here; and I trust you will find access to us with my son's help. But remember that words are 340
signals, counters. They are not immortal. And it can happen — to use an image you'll understand — it can happen that a civilization can be imprisoned in a linguistic contour which no longer matches the landscape of . . . fact. Gentlemen. *(He leaves.)* 345

OWEN: 'An *expeditio* with three purposes': the children laugh at him: he always promises three points and he never gets beyond A and B.

YOLLAND: He's an astute man.

OWEN: He's bloody pompous. 350

YOLLAND: But so astute.

OWEN: And he drinks too much. Is it astute not to be able to adjust for survival? Enduring around truths immemorially posited — hah!

YOLLAND: He knows what's happening. 355

OWEN: What is happening?

YOLLAND: I'm not sure. But I'm concerned about my part in it. It's an eviction of sorts.

OWEN: We're making a six-inch map of the country. Is there something sinister in that? 360

YOLLAND: Not in —

OWEN: And we're taking place-names that are riddled with con-fusion and —

YOLLAND: Who's confused? Are the people confused?

365 OWEN: — and we're standardizing those names as accurately and as sensitively as we can.

YOLLAND: Something is being eroded.

OWEN: Back to the romance again. All right! Fine! Fine! Look where we've got to. (He drops on his hands and knees and

370 stabs a finger at the map.) We've come to this crossroads. Come here and look at it, man! Look at it! And we call that crossroads Tobair Vree. And why do we call it Tobair Vree? I'll tell you why. Tobair means a well. But what does Vree mean? It's a corruption of Brian — (Gaelic pronunciation)

375 Brian — an erosion of Tobair Bhriain. Because a hundred-and-fifty years ago there used to be a well there, not at the crossroads, mind you — that would be too simple — but in a field close to the crossroads. And an old man called Brian, whose face was disfigured by an enormous growth, got it into

380 his head that the water in that well was blessed; and every day for seven months he went there and bathed his face in it. But the growth didn't go away; and one morning Brian was found drowned in that well. And ever since that crossroads is known as Tobair Vree — even though that well has long since dried

385 up. I know the story because my grandfather told it to me. But ask Doalty — or Maire — or Bridget — even my father — even Manus — why it's called Tobair Vree; and do you think they'll know? I know they don't know. So the question I put to you, Lieutenant, is this: what do we do with a name like that? Do

390 we scrap Tobair Vree altogether and call it — what? — The Cross? Crossroads? Or do we keep piety with a man long dead, long forgotten, his name 'eroded' beyond recognition, whose trivial little story nobody in the parish remembers?

YOLLAND: Except you.

395 OWEN: I've left here.

YOLLAND: You remember it.

OWEN: I'm asking you: what do we write in the Name-Book?

YOLLAND: Tobair Vree.

OWEN: Even though the well is a hundred yards from the actual

400 crossroads — and there's no well anyway — and what the hell does Vree mean?

YOLLAND: Tobair Vree.

OWEN: That's what you want?

YOLLAND: Yes.

405 OWEN: You're certain?

YOLLAND: Yes.

OWEN: Fine. Fine. That's what you'll get.

YOLLAND: That's what you want, too, Roland.

(Pause.)

OWEN: (Explodes) George! For God's sake! My name is not

410 Roland!

YOLLAND: What?

OWEN: (Softly) My name is Owen.

(Pause.)

YOLLAND: Not Roland?

OWEN: Owen.

415 YOLLAND: You mean to say — ?

OWEN: Owen.

YOLLAND: But I've been —

OWEN: O-w-e-n.

YOLLAND: Where did Roland come from?

OWEN: I don't know.   420

YOLLAND: It was never Roland?

OWEN: Never.

YOLLAND: O my God!

(Pause. They stare at one another. Then the absurdity of the situation strikes them suddenly. They explode with laughter. OWEN pours drinks. As they roll about, their lines overlap.)

YOLLAND: Why didn't you tell me?

OWEN: Do I look like a Roland?   425

YOLLAND: Spell Owen again.

OWEN: I was getting fond of Roland.

YOLLAND: O my God!

OWEN: O-w-e-n.

YOLLAND: What'll we write —   430

OWEN: — in the Name Book?!

YOLLAND: R-o-w-e-n!

OWEN: Or what about Ol-

YOLLAND: Ol- what?

OWEN: Oland!   435

(And again they explode. MANUS enters. He is very elated.)

MANUS: What's the celebration?

OWEN: A christening!

YOLLAND: A baptism!

OWEN: A hundred christenings!

YOLLAND: A thousand baptisms! Welcome to Eden!   440

OWEN: Eden's right! We name a thing and — bang! — it leaps into existence!

YOLLAND: Each name a perfect equation with its roots.

OWEN: A perfect congruence with its reality. (To MANUS) Take a drink.   445

YOLLAND: Poteen — beautiful.

OWEN: Lying Anna's poteen.

YOLLAND: Anna na mBreag's poteen.

OWEN: Excellent, George.

YOLLAND: I'll decode you yet.   450

OWEN: (Offers drink) Manus?

MANUS: Not if that's what it does to you.

OWEN: You're right. Steady — steady — sober up — sober up.

YOLLAND: Sober as a judge, Owen.

(MANUS moves beside OWEN.)

MANUS: I've got good news! Where's Father?   455

OWEN: He's gone out. What's the good news?

MANUS: I've been offered a job.

OWEN: Where? (Now aware of YOLLAND.) Come on, man — speak in English.

MANUS: For the benefit of the colonist?   460

OWEN: He's a decent man.

MANUS: Aren't they all at some level?

OWEN: Please.

(MANUS shrugs.)

He's been offered a job.

YOLLAND: Where?   465

OWEN: Well — tell us!

MANUS: I've just had a meeting with two men from Inis Mead-hon. They want me to go there and start a hedge-school.

They're giving me a free house, free turf, and free milk; a rood
470 of standing corn; twelve drills of potatoes; and —

(He stops.)

OWEN: And what?
MANUS: A salary of £42 a year!
OWEN: Manus, that's wonderful!
MANUS: You're talking to a man of substance.
475 OWEN: I'm delighted.
YOLLAND: Where's Inis Meadhon?
OWEN: An island south of here. And they came looking for you?
MANUS: Well, I mean to say . . .

(OWEN punches MANUS.)

OWEN: Aaaaagh! This calls for a real celebration.
480 YOLLAND: Congratulations.
MANUS: Thank you.
OWEN: Where are you, Anna?
YOLLAND: When do you start?
MANUS: Next Monday.
485 OWEN: We'll stay with you when we're there. *(To* YOLLAND*)*
How long will it be before we reach Inis Meadhon?
YOLLAND: How far south is it?
MANUS: About fifty miles.
YOLLAND: Could we make it by December?
490 OWEN: We'll have Christmas together. *(Sings)* 'Christmas Day
on Inis Meadhon . . .'
YOLLAND: *(Toast)* I hope you're very content there, Manus.
MANUS: Thank you.

(YOLLAND holds out his hand. MANUS *takes it. They shake
warmly.)*

OWEN: *(Toast)* Manus.
495 MANUS: *(Toast)* To Inis Meadhon.

(He drinks quickly and turns to leave.)

OWEN: Hold on — hold on — refills coming up.
MANUS: I've got to go.
OWEN: Come on, man; this is an occasion. Where are you rushing to?
500 MANUS: I've got to tell Maire.

(MAIRE enters with her can of milk.)

MAIRE: You've got to tell Maire what?
OWEN: He's got a job!
MAIRE: Manus?
OWEN: He's been invited to start a hedge-school in Inis Meadhon.
505 MAIRE: Where?
MANUS: Inis Meadhon — the island! They're giving me £42 a
year and . . .
OWEN: A house, fuel, milk, potatoes, corn, pupils, what-not!
MANUS: I start on Monday.
510 OWEN: You'll take a drink. Isn't it great?
MANUS: I want to talk to you for —
MAIRE: There's your milk. I need the can back.

(MANUS takes the can and runs up the steps.)

MANUS: *(As he goes)* How will you like living on an island?
OWEN: You know George, don't you?
515 MAIRE: We wave to each other across the fields.
YOLLAND: Sorry-sorry?

OWEN: She says you wave to each other across the fields.
YOLLAND: Yes, we do; oh, yes; indeed we do.
MAIRE: What's he saying?
OWEN: He says you wave to each other across the fields. 520
MAIRE: That's right. So we do.
YOLLAND: What's she saying?
OWEN: Nothing — nothing — nothing. *(To* MAIRE*)* What's the
news?

(MAIRE moves away, touching the text books with her toe.)

MAIRE: Not a thing. You're busy, the two of you. 525
OWEN: We think we are.
MAIRE: I hear the Fiddler O'Shea's about. There's some talk of a
dance tomorrow night.
OWEN: Where will it be?
MAIRE: Maybe over the road. Maybe at Tobair Vree. 530
YOLLAND: Tobair Vree!
MAIRE: Yes.
YOLLAND: Tobair Vree! Tobair Vree!
MAIRE: Does he know what I'm saying?
OWEN: Not a word. 535
MAIRE: Tell him then.
OWEN: Tell him what?
MAIRE: About the dance.
OWEN: Maire says there may be a dance tomorrow night.
YOLLAND: *(To* OWEN*)* Yes? May I come? *(To* MAIRE*)* Would any- 540
body object if I came?
MAIRE: *(To* OWEN*)* What's he saying?
OWEN: *(To* YOLLAND*)* Who would object?
MAIRE: *(To* OWEN*)* Did you tell him?
YOLLAND: *(To* MAIRE*)* Sorry-sorry? 545
OWEN: *(To* MAIRE*)* He says may he come?
MAIRE: *(To* YOLLAND*)* That's up to you.
YOLLAND: *(To* OWEN*)* What does she say?
OWEN: *(To* YOLLAND*)* She says —
YOLLAND: *(To* MAIRE*)* What-what? 550
MAIRE: *(To* OWEN*)* Well?
YOLLAND: *(To* OWEN*)* Sorry-sorry?
OWEN: *(To* YOLLAND*)* Will you go?
YOLLAND: *(To* MAIRE*)* Yes, yes, if I may.
MAIRE: *(To* OWEN*)* What does he say? 555
YOLLAND: *(To* OWEN*)* What is she saying?
OWEN: Oh for God's sake! *(To* MANUS *who is descending with the
empty can.)* You take on this job, Manus.
MANUS: I'll walk you up to the house. Is your mother at home? I
want to talk to her. 560
MAIRE: What's the rush? *(To* OWEN*)* Didn't you offer me a drink?
OWEN: Will you risk Anna na mBreag?
MAIRE: Why not.

*(YOLLAND is suddenly intoxicated. He leaps up on a stool, raises
his glass and shouts.)*

YOLLAND: Anna na mBreag! Baile Beag! Inis Meadhon! Bom-
bay! Tobair Vree! Eden! And poteen — correct, Owen? 565
OWEN: Perfect.
YOLLAND: And bloody marvellous stuff it is, too. I love it!
Bloody, bloody, bloody marvellous!

*(Simultaneously with his final 'bloody marvellous' bring up very
loud the introductory music of the reel. Then immediately go to
black. Retain the music throughout the very brief interval.)*

SCENE II

The following night.

This scene may be played in the schoolroom, but it would be preferable to lose—by lighting—as much of the schoolroom as possible, and to play the scene down front in a vaguely 'outside' area.

The music rises to a crescendo. Then in the distance we hear MAIRE *and* YOLLAND *approach—laughing and running. They run on, hand-in-hand. They have just left the dance. Fade the music to distant background. Then after a time it is lost and replaced by guitar music.* MAIRE *and* YOLLAND *are now down front, still holding hands and excited by their sudden and impetuous escape from the dance.*

MAIRE: O my God, that leap across the ditch nearly killed me.
YOLLAND: I could scarcely keep up with you.
MAIRE: Wait till I get my breath back.
YOLLAND: We must have looked as if we were being chased.

(They now realize they are alone and holding hands—the beginnings of embarrassment. The hands disengage. They begin to drift apart. Pause.)

5 MAIRE: Manus'll wonder where I've got to.
YOLLAND: I wonder did anyone notice us leave.

(Pause. Slightly further apart.)

MAIRE: The grass must be wet. My feet are soaking.
YOLLAND: Your feet must be wet. The grass is soaking.

(Another pause. Another few paces apart. They are now a long distance from one another.)

YOLLAND: *(Indicating himself)* George.

*(*MAIRE *nods: Yes-yes. Then:—)*

10 MAIRE: Lieutenant George.
YOLLAND: Don't call me that. I never think of myself as Lieutenant.
MAIRE: What-what?
YOLLAND: Sorry-sorry? *(He points to himself again.)* George.

*(*MAIRE *nods: Yes-yes. Then points to herself.)*

15 MAIRE: Maire.
YOLLAND: Yes, I know you're Maire. Of course I know you're Maire. I mean I've been watching you night and day for the past—
MAIRE: *(Eagerly)* What-what?
20 YOLLAND: *(Points)* Maire. *(Points.)* George. *(Points both.)* Maire and George.

*(*MAIRE *nods: Yes-yes-yes.)*

I—I—I—
MAIRE: Say anything at all. I love the sound of your speech.
YOLLAND: *(Eagerly)* Sorry-sorry?

(In acute frustration he looks around, hoping for some inspiration that will provide him with communicative means. Now he has a thought: he tries raising his voice and articulating in a staccato style and with equal and absurd emphasis on each word.)

Every-morning-I-see-you-feeding-brown-hens-and-giving-   25
meal-to-black-calf—*(The futility of it)*—Oh my God.

*(*MAIRE *smiles. She moves towards him. She will try to communicate in Latin.)*

MAIRE: *Tu es centurio in—in—in exercitu Britannico—*
YOLLAND: Yes-yes? Go on—go on—say anything at all—I love the sound of your speech.
MAIRE: *—et es in castris quae—quae—quae sunt in agro—(The*   30
futility of it)—O my God. *(*YOLLAND *smiles. He moves towards her. Now for her English words.)* George—water.
YOLLAND: 'Water'? Water! Oh yes—water—water—very good—water—good—good.
MAIRE: Fire.   35
YOLLAND: Fire—indeed—wonderful—fire, fire, fire—splendid—splendid!
MAIRE: Ah . . . ah . . .
YOLLAND: Yes? Go on.
MAIRE: Earth.   40
YOLLAND: 'Earth'?
MAIRE: Earth. Earth. *(*YOLLAND *still does not understand.* MAIRE *stoops down and picks up a handful of clay. Holding it out.)* Earth.
YOLLAND: Earth! Of course—earth! Earth. Earth. Good Lord,   45
Maire, your English is perfect!
MAIRE: *(Eagerly)* What-what?
YOLLAND: Perfect English. English perfect.
MAIRE: George—
YOLLAND: That's beautiful—oh, that's really beautiful.   50
MAIRE: George—
YOLLAND: Say it again—say it again—
MAIRE: Shhh. *(She holds her hand up for silence—she is trying to remember her one line of English. Now she remembers it and she delivers the line as if English were her language—easily,*   55
fluidly, conversationally.) George, 'In Norfolk we besport ourselves around the maypoll.'
YOLLAND: Good God, do you? That's where my mother comes from—Norfolk. Norwich actually. Not exactly Norwich town but a small village called Little Walsingham close beside   60
it. But in our own village of Winfarthing we have a maypole too and every year on the first of May—*(He stops abruptly, only now realizing. He stares at her. She in turn misunderstands his excitement.)*
MAIRE: *(To herself)* Mother of God, my Aunt Mary wouldn't   65
have taught me something dirty, would she?

(Pause. YOLLAND *extends his hand to* MAIRE. *She turns away from him and moves slowly across the stage.)*

YOLLAND: Maire.

(She still moves away.)

Maire Chatach.

(She still moves away.)

---

27 **Tu es centurio in exercitu Britannico** You are a centurion in the British Army   30 **et es in castris quae sunt in agro** and you are in the camp in the field

Bun na hAbhann? *(He says the name softly, almost privately,*
70 *very tentatively, as if he were searching for a sound she might*
respond to. He tries again.) Druim Dubh?

(MAIRE stops. She is listening. YOLLAND is encouraged.)

Poll na gCaorach. Lis Maol.

(MAIRE turns towards him.)

Lis na nGall.
MAIRE: Lis na nGradh.

(They are now facing each other and begin moving—almost im-
perceptibly—towards one another.)

75 MAIRE: Carraig an Phoill.
YOLLAND: Carraig na Ri. Loch na nEan.
MAIRE: Loch an Iubhair. Machaire Buidhe.
YOLLAND: Machaire Mor. Cnoc na Mona.
MAIRE: Cnoc na nGabhar.
80 YOLLAND: Mullach.
MAIRE: Port.
YOLLAND: Tor.
MAIRE: Lag.

(She holds out her hands to YOLLAND. He takes them. Each now
speaks almost to himself/herself.)

YOLLAND: I wish to God you could understand me.
85 MAIRE: Soft hands; a gentleman's hands.
YOLLAND: Because if you could understand me I could tell you
how I spend my days either thinking of you or gazing up at
your house in the hope that you'll appear even for a second.
MAIRE: Every evening you walk by yourself along the Tra Bhan
90 and every morning you wash yourself in front of your tent.
YOLLAND: I would tell you how beautiful you are, curly-headed
Maire. I would so like to tell you how beautiful you are.
MAIRE: Your arms are long and thin and the skin on your shoul-
ders is very white.
95 YOLLAND: I would tell you . . .
MAIRE: Don't stop—I know what you're saying.
YOLLAND: I would tell you how I want to be here—to live
here—always—with you—always, always.
MAIRE: 'Always'? What is that word—'always'?
100 YOLLAND: Yes-yes; always.
MAIRE: You're trembling.
YOLLAND: Yes, I'm trembling because of you.
MAIRE: I'm trembling, too.

(She holds his face in her hand.)

YOLLAND: I've made up my mind . . .
105 MAIRE: Shhhh.
YOLLAND: I'm not going to leave here . . .
MAIRE: Shhhh—listen to me. I want you, too, soldier.
YOLLAND: Don't stop—I know what you're saying.
MAIRE: I want to live with you—anywhere—anywhere at all—
110 always—always.
YOLLAND: 'Always'? What is that word—'always'?
MAIRE: Take me away with you, George.

(Pause. Suddenly they kiss. SARAH enters. She sees them. She
stands shocked, staring at them. Her mouth works. Then almost
to herself.)

SARAH: Manus . . . Manus!

(SARAH runs off. Music to crescendo.)

— ACT THREE —

The following evening. It is raining.

SARAH *and* OWEN *alone in the schoolroom.* SARAH, *more waif-*
like than ever, is sitting very still on a stool, an open book across
her knee. She is pretending to read but her eyes keep going up to
the room upstairs. OWEN *is working on the floor as before, sur-*
rounded by his reference books, map, Name-Book, etc. But he
has neither concentration nor interest; and like SARAH *he glances*
up at the upstairs room.

After a few seconds MANUS *emerges and descends, carrying a*
large paper bag which already contains his clothes. His move-
ments are determined and urgent. He moves around the class-
room, picking up books, examining each title carefully, and
choosing about six of them which he puts into his bag. As he
selects these books:—

OWEN: You know that old limekiln beyond Con Connie Tim's
pub, the place we call The Murren?—do you know why it's
called The Murren?

(MANUS does not answer.)

I've only just discovered: it's a corruption of Saint Muranus. It
seems Saint Muranus had a monastery somewhere about   5
there at the beginning of the seventh century. And over the
years the name became shortened to the Murren. Very unat-
tractive name, isn't it? I think we should go back to the original—Saint Muranus. What do you think? The original's
Saint Muranus. Don't you think we should go back to that?   10

(No response. OWEN *begins writing the name into the Name-*
Book. MANUS *is now rooting about among the forgotten imple-*
ments for a piece of rope. He finds a piece. He begins to tie the
mouth of the flimsy, overloaded bag—and it bursts, the contents
spilling out on the floor.)

MANUS: Bloody, bloody, bloody hell!

(His voice breaks in exasperation: he is about to cry. OWEN *leaps*
to his feet.)

OWEN: Hold on. I've a bag upstairs.

(He runs upstairs. SARAH *waits until* OWEN *is off. Then:—)*

SARAH: Manus . . . Manus, I . . .

(MANUS hears SARAH but makes no acknowledgement. He
gathers up his belongings. OWEN *reappears with the bag he had*
on his arrival.)

OWEN: Take this one—I'm finished with it anyway. And it's supposed to keep out the rain.   15

(MANUS transfers his few belongings. OWEN *drifts back to his*
task. The packing is now complete.)

MANUS: You'll be here for a while? For a week or two anyhow?
OWEN: Yes.
MANUS: You're not leaving with the army?
OWEN: I haven't made up my mind. Why?
MANUS: Those Inis Meadhon men will be back to see why I   20
haven't turned up. Tell them—tell them I'll write to them as
soon as I can. Tell them I still want the job but that it might be
three or four months before I'm free to go.
OWEN: You're being damned stupid, Manus.
MANUS: Will you do that for me?   25

OWEN: Clear out now and Lancey'll think you're involved
somehow.

MANUS: Will you do that for me?

OWEN: Wait a couple of days even. You know George—he's a
30   bloody romantic—maybe he's gone out to one of the islands
and he'll suddenly reappear tomorrow morning. Or maybe the
search party'll find him this evening lying drunk somewhere
in the sandhills. You've seen him drinking that poteen—
doesn't know how to handle it. Had he drink on him last
35   night at the dance?

MANUS: I had a stone in my hand when I went out looking for
him—I was going to fell him. The lame scholar turned violent.

OWEN: Did anybody see you?

MANUS: (Again close to tears) But when I saw him standing
40   there at the side of the road—smiling—and her face buried
in his shoulder—I couldn't even go close to them. I just
shouted something stupid—something like, 'You're a bastard, Yolland.' If I'd even said it in English . . . 'cos he kept
saying 'Sorry-sorry?' The wrong gesture in the wrong
45   language.

OWEN: And you didn't see him again?

MANUS: 'Sorry?'

OWEN: Before you leave tell Lancey that—just to clear yourself.

MANUS: What have I to say to Lancey? You'll give that message
50   to the islandmen?

OWEN: I'm warning you: run away now and you're bound to be—

MANUS: (To SARAH) Will you give that message to the Inis
Meadhon men?

SARAH: I will.

(MANUS picks up an old sack and throws it across his shoulders.)

55   OWEN: Have you any idea where you're going?

MANUS: Mayo, maybe. I remember Mother saying she had
cousins somewhere away out in the Erris Peninsula. (He picks
up his bag.) Tell Father I took only the Virgil and the Caesar
and the Aeschylus because they're mine anyway—I bought
60   them with the money I got for that pet lamb I reared—do you
remember that pet lamb? And tell him that Nora Dan never
returned the dictionary and that she still owes him two-and-
six for last quarter's reading—he always forgets those things.

OWEN: Yes.

65   MANUS: And his good shirt's ironed and hanging up in the press
and his clean socks are in the butter-box under the bed.

OWEN: All right.

MANUS: And tell him I'll write.

OWEN: If Maire asks where you've gone . . . ?

70   MANUS: He'll need only half the amount of milk now, won't he?
Even less than half—he usually takes his tea black. (Pause.)
And when he comes in at night—you'll hear him; he makes a
lot of noise—I usually come down and give him a hand up.
Those stairs are dangerous without a banister. Maybe before
75   you leave you'd get Big Ned Frank to put up some sort of a
handrail. (Pause.) And if you can bake, he's very fond of soda
bread.

OWEN: I can give you money. I'm wealthy. Do you know what
they pay me? Two shillings a day for this—this—this—

(MANUS rejects the offer by holding out his hand.)

80   Goodbye, Manus.

(MANUS and OWEN shake hands. Then MANUS picks up his bag
briskly and goes towards the door. He stops a few paces beyond
SARAH, turns, comes back to her. He addresses her as he did in
Act One but now without warmth or concern for her.)

MANUS: What is your name? (Pause.) Come on. What is your
name?

SARAH: My name is Sarah.

MANUS: Just Sarah? Sarah what? (Pause.) Well?

SARAH: Sarah Johnny Sally.   85

MANUS: And where do you live? Come on.

SARAH: I live in Bun na hAbhann.

(She is now crying quietly.)

MANUS: Very good, Sarah Johnny Sally. There's nothing to stop
you now—nothing in the wide world. (Pause. He looks down
at her.) It's all right—it's all right—you did no harm—you   90
did no harm at all.

(He stoops over her and kisses the top of her head—as if in absolution. Then briskly to the door and off.)

OWEN: Good luck, Manus!

SARAH: (Quietly) I'm sorry . . . I'm sorry . . . I'm so sorry,
Manus . . .

(OWEN tries to work but cannot concentrate. He begins folding
up the map. As he does:—)

OWEN: Is there a class this evening?   95

(SARAH nods: yes.)

I suppose Father knows. Where is he anyhow?

(SARAH points.)

Where?

(SARAH mimes rocking a baby.)

I don't understand—where?

(SARAH repeats the mime and wipes away tears. OWEN is still
puzzled.)

It doesn't matter. He'll probably turn up.

(BRIDGET and DOALTY enter, sacks over their heads against the
rain. They are self-consciously noisier, more ebullient, more garrulous than ever—brimming over with excitement and gossip
and brio.)

DOALTY: You're missing the crack, boys! Cripes, you're missing   100
the crack! Fifty more soldiers arrived an hour ago!

BRIDGET: And they're spread out in a big line from Sean Neal's
over to Lag and they're moving straight across the fields towards Cnoc na nGabhar!

DOALTY: Prodding every inch of the ground in front of them with 105
their bayonets and scattering animals and hens in all
directions!

BRIDGET: And tumbling everything before them—fences,
ditches, haystacks, turf-stacks!

DOALTY: They came to Barney Petey's field of corn—straight   110
through it be God as if it was heather!

BRIDGET: Not a blade of it left standing!

DOALTY: And Barney Petey just out of his bed and running after
them in his drawers: 'You hoors you! Get out of my corn, you
hoors you!'   115

BRIDGET: First time he ever ran in his life.

DOALTY: Too lazy, the wee get, to cut it when the weather was good.

(SARAH *begins putting out the seats.*)

BRIDGET: Tell them about Big Hughie.

120 DOALTY: Cripes, if you'd seen your aul fella, Owen.

BRIDGET: They were all inside in Anna na mBreag's pub—all the crowd from the wake—

DOALTY: And they hear the commotion and they all come out to the street—

125 BRIDGET: Your father in front; the Infant Prodigy footless behind him!

DOALTY: And your aul fella, he sees the army stretched across the countryside—

BRIDGET: O my God!

130 DOALTY: And Cripes he starts roaring at them!

BRIDGET: 'Visigoths! Huns! Vandals!'

DOALTY: *'Ignari! Stulti! Rustici!'*

BRIDGET: And wee Jimmy Jack jumping up and down and shouting, 'Thermopylae! Thermopylae!'

135 DOALTY: You never saw crack like it in your life, boys. Come away on out with me, Sarah, and you'll see it all.

BRIDGET: Big Hughie's fit to take no class. Is Manus about?

OWEN: Manus is gone.

BRIDGET: Gone where?

140 OWEN: He's left—gone away.

DOALTY: Where to?

OWEN: He doesn't know. Mayo, maybe.

DOALTY: What's on in Mayo?

OWEN: (*To* BRIDGET) Did you see George and Maire Chatach

145 leave the dance last night?

BRIDGET: We did. Didn't we, Doalty?

OWEN: Did you see Manus following them out?

BRIDGET: I didn't see him going out but I saw him coming in by himself later.

150 OWEN: Did George and Maire come back to the dance?

BRIDGET: No.

OWEN: Did you see them again?

BRIDGET: He left her home. We passed them going up the back road—didn't we, Doalty?

155 OWEN: And Manus stayed till the end of the dance?

DOALTY: We know nothing. What are you asking us for?

OWEN: Because Lancey'll question me when he hears Manus's gone. (*Back to* BRIDGET.) That's the way George went home? By the back road? That's where you saw him?

160 BRIDGET: Leave me alone, Owen. I know nothing about Yolland. If you want to know about Yolland, ask the Donnelly twins.

(*Silence.* DOALTY *moves over to the window.*)

(*To* SARAH) He's a powerful fiddler, O'Shea, isn't he? He told our Seamus he'll come back for a night at Hallowe'en.

(OWEN *goes to* DOALTY *who looks resolutely out the window.*)

OWEN: What's this about the Donnellys? (*Pause.*) Were they

165 about last night?

DOALTY: Didn't see them if they were.

(*Begins whistling through his teeth.*)

OWEN: George is a friend of mine.

DOALTY: So.

OWEN: I want to know what's happened to him.

DOALTY: Couldn't tell you. 170

OWEN: What have the Donnelly twins to do with it? (*Pause.*) Doalty!

DOALTY: I know nothing, Owen—nothing at all—I swear to God. All I know is this: on my way to the dance I saw their boat beached at Port. It wasn't there on my way home, after I 175 left Bridget. And that's all I know. As God's my judge. The half-dozen times I met him I didn't know a word he said to me; but he seemed a right enough sort . . . (*With sudden excessive interest in the scene outside.*) Cripes, they're crawling all over the place! Cripes, there's millions of them! Cripes, 180 they're levelling the whole land!

(OWEN *moves away.* MAIRE *enters. She is bareheaded and wet from the rain; her hair in disarray. She attempts to appear normal but she is in acute distress, on the verge of being distraught. She is carrying the milk-can.*)

MAIRE: Honest to God, I must be going off my head. I'm halfway here and I think to myself, 'Isn't this can very light?' and I look into it and isn't it empty.

OWEN: It doesn't matter. 185

MAIRE: How will you manage for tonight?

OWEN: We have enough.

MAIRE: Are you sure?

OWEN: Plenty, thanks.

MAIRE: It'll take me no time at all to go back up for some. 190

OWEN: Honestly, Maire.

MAIRE: Sure it's better you have it than that black calf that's . . . that . . . (*She looks around.*) Have you heard anything?

OWEN: Nothing.

MAIRE: What does Lancey say? 195

OWEN: I haven't seen him since this morning.

MAIRE: What does he *think*?

OWEN: We really didn't talk. He was here for only a few seconds.

MAIRE: He left me home, Owen. And the last thing he said to me—he tried to speak in Irish—he said, 'I'll see you yester- 200 day'—he meant to say 'I'll see you tomorrow.' And I laughed that much he pretended to get cross and he said 'Maypoll! Maypoll!' because I said that word wrong. And off he went, laughing—laughing, Owen! Do you think he's all right? What do *you* think? 205

OWEN: I'm sure he'll turn up, Maire.

MAIRE: He comes from a tiny wee place called Winfarthing. (*She suddenly drops on her hands and knees on the floor— where* OWEN *had his map a few minutes ago—and with her finger traces out an outline map.*) Come here till you see. 210 Look. There's Winfarthing. And there's two other wee villages right beside it; one of them's called Barton Bendish—it's there; and the other's called Saxingham Nethergate—it's about there. And there's Little Walsingham—that's his mother's townland. Aren't they odd names? Sure they make 215 no sense to me at all. And Winfarthing's near a big town called Norwich. And Norwich is in a county called Norfolk. And Norfolk is in the east of England. He drew a map for me on the wet strand and wrote the names on it. I have it all in my head now: Winfarthing—Barton Bendish—Saxingham 220 Nethergate—Little Walsingham—Norwich—Norfolk. Strange sounds, aren't they? But nice sounds; like Jimmy Jack reciting his Homer. (*She gets to her feet and looks around; she*

225 *is almost serene now. To* SARAH) You were looking lovely last
night, Sarah. Is that the dress you got from Boston? Green
suits you. *(To* OWEN) Something very bad's happened to him,
Owen. I know. He wouldn't go away without telling me.
Where is he, Owen? You're his friend—where is he? *(Again
she looks around the room; then sits on a stool.)* I didn't get a
230 chance to do my geography last night. The master'll be angry
with me. *(She rises again.)* I think I'll go home now. The wee
ones have to be washed and put to bed and that black calf has
to be fed . . . My hands are that rough; they're still blistered
from the hay. I'm ashamed of them. I hope to God there's no
235 hay to be saved in Brooklyn. *(She stops at the door.)* Did you
hear? Nellie Ruadh's baby died in the middle of the night. I
must go up to the wake. It didn't last long, did it?

*(*MAIRE *leaves. Silence. Then.)*

OWEN: I don't think there'll be any class. Maybe you should . . .

*(*OWEN *begins picking up his texts.* DOALTY *goes to him.)*

DOALTY: Is he long gone?—Manus?
240 OWEN: Half an hour.
DOALTY: Stupid bloody fool.
OWEN: I told him that.
DOALTY: Do they know he's gone?
OWEN: Who?
245 DOALTY: The army.
OWEN: Not yet.
DOALTY: They'll be after him like bloody beagles. Bloody,
bloody fool, limping along the coast. They'll overtake him
before night for Christ's sake.

*(*DOALTY *returns to the window.* LANCEY *enters—now the commanding officer.)*

250 OWEN: Any news? Any word?

*(*LANCEY *moves into the centre of the room, looking around as he
does.)*

LANCEY: I understood there was a class. Where are the others?
OWEN: There was to be a class but my father—
LANCEY: This will suffice. I will address them and it will be their
255 responsibility to pass on what I have to say to every family in
this section.

*(*LANCEY *indicates to* OWEN *to translate.* OWEN *hesitates, trying
to assess the change in* LANCEY's *manner and attitude.)*

I'm in a hurry, O'Donnell.
OWEN: The captain has an announcement to make.
LANCEY: Lieutenant Yolland is missing. We are searching for
him. If we don't find him, or if we receive no information as
260 to where he is to be found, I will pursue the following course
of action. *(He indicates to* OWEN *to translate.)*
OWEN: They are searching for George. If they don't find him—
LANCEY: Commencing twenty-four hours from now we will
shoot all livestock in Ballybeg.

*(*OWEN *stares at* LANCEY.)*

265 At once.
OWEN: Beginning this time tomorrow they'll kill every animal in
Baile Beag—unless they're told where George is.
LANCEY: If that doesn't bear results, commencing forty-eight
hours from now we will embark on a series of evictions and
270 levelling of every abode in the following selected areas—

OWEN: You're not—!
LANCEY: Do your job. Translate.
OWEN: If they still haven't found him in two days time they'll
begin evicting and levelling every house starting with these
townlands. 275

*(*LANCEY *reads from his list.)*

LANCEY: Swinefort.
OWEN: Lis na Muc.
LANCEY: Burnfoot.
OWEN: Bun na hAbhann.
LANCEY: Dromduff. 280
OWEN: Druim Dubh.
LANCEY: Whiteplains.
OWEN: Machaire Ban.
LANCEY: Kings Head.
OWEN: Cnoc na Ri. 285
LANCEY: If by then the lieutenant hasn't been found, we will
proceed until a complete clearance is made of this entire
section.
OWEN: If Yolland hasn't been got by then, they will ravish the
whole parish. 290
LANCEY: I trust they know exactly what they've got to do. *(Point-
ing to* BRIDGET.) I know you. I know where you live. *(Point-
ing to* SARAH.) Who are you? Name!

*(*SARAH's *mouth opens and shuts, opens and shuts. Her face becomes contorted.)*

What's your name?

(Again SARAH *tries frantically.)*

OWEN: Go on, Sarah. You can tell him. 295

(But SARAH *cannot. And she knows she cannot. She closes her
mouth. Her head goes down.)*

OWEN: Her name is Sarah Johnny Sally.
LANCEY: Where does she live?
OWEN: Bun na hAbhann.
LANCEY: Where?
OWEN: Burnfoot. 300
LANCEY: I want to talk to your brother—is he here?
OWEN: Not at the moment.
LANCEY: Where is he?
OWEN: He's at a wake.
LANCEY: What wake? 305

*(*DOALTY, *who has been looking out the window all through* LAN-
CEY's *announcements, now speaks—calmly, almost casually.)*

DOALTY: Tell him his whole camp's on fire.
LANCEY: What's your name? *(To* OWEN) Who's that lout?
OWEN: Doalty Dan Doalty.
LANCEY: Where does he live?
OWEN: Tulach Alainn. 310
LANCEY: What do we call it?
OWEN: Fair Hill. He says your whole camp is on fire.

*(*LANCEY *rushes to the window and looks out. Then he wheels on*
DOALTY.)*

LANCEY: I'll remember you, Mr Doalty. *(To* OWEN) You carry a
big responsibility in all this.

(He goes off.)

315 BRIDGET: Mother of God, does he mean it, Owen?

OWEN: Yes, he does.

BRIDGET: We'll have to hide the beasts somewhere—our Seamus'll know where. Maybe at the back of Lis na nGradh—or in the caves at the far end of Tra Bhan. Come

320 on, Doalty! Come on! Don't be standing about there!

(DOALTY does not move. BRIDGET runs to the door and stops suddenly. She sniffs the air. Panic.)

The sweet smell! Smell it! It's the sweet smell! Jesus, it's the potato blight!

DOALTY: It's the army tents burning, Bridget.

BRIDGET: Is it? Are you sure? Is that what it is? God, I thought

325 we were destroyed altogether. Come on! Come on!

(She runs off. OWEN goes to SARAH who is preparing to leave.)

OWEN: How are you? Are you all right?

(SARAH nods: Yes.)

OWEN: Don't worry. It will come back to you again.

(SARAH shakes her head.)

OWEN: It will. You're upset now. He frightened you. That's all's wrong.

(Again SARAH shakes her head, slowly, emphatically, and smiles at OWEN. Then she leaves. OWEN busies himself gathering his belongings. DOALTY leaves the window and goes to him.)

330 DOALTY: He'll do it, too.

OWEN: Unless Yolland's found.

DOALTY: Hah!

OWEN: Then he'll certainly do it.

DOALTY: When my grandfather was a boy they did the same

335 thing. *(Simply, altogether without irony)* And after all the trouble you went to, mapping the place and thinking up new names for it. *(OWEN busies himself. Pause. DOALTY almost dreamily.)* I've damned little to defend but he'll not put me out without a fight. And there'll be others who think the same

340 as me.

OWEN: That's a matter for you.

DOALTY: If we'd all stick together. If we knew how to defend ourselves.

OWEN: Against a trained army.

345 DOALTY: The Donnelly twins know how.

OWEN: If they could be found.

DOALTY: If they could be found. *(He goes to the door.)* Give me a shout after you've finished with Lancey. I might know something then.

(He leaves.)

(OWEN picks up the Name-Book. He looks at it momentarily, then puts it on top of the pile he is carrying. It falls to the floor. He stoops to pick it up—hesitates—leaves it. He goes upstairs. As OWEN ascends, HUGH and JIMMY JACK enter. Both wet and drunk. JIMMY is very unsteady. He is trotting behind HUGH, trying to break in on HUGH's declamation. HUGH is equally drunk but more experienced in drunkenness: there is a portion of his mind which retains its clarity.)

350 HUGH: There I was, appropriately dispositioned to proffer my condolences to the bereaved mother . . .

JIMMY: Hugh—

HUGH: . . . and about to enter the *domus lugubris*—Maire Chatach?

JIMMY: The wake house.

355

HUGH: Indeed—when I experience a plucking at my elbow: Mister George Alexander, Justice of the Peace. 'My tidings are infelicitous,' said he—Bridget? Too slow. Doalty?

JIMMY: *Infelix*—unhappy.

HUGH: Unhappy indeed. 'Master Bartley Timlin has been ap-

360 pointed to the new national school.' 'Timlin? Who is Timlin?' 'A schoolmaster from Cork. And he will be a major asset to the community: he is also a very skilled bacon-curer!'

JIMMY: Hugh—

HUGH: Ha-ha-ha-ha-ha! The Cork bacon-curer! *Barbarus hic*

365 *ego sum quia non intelligor ulli*—James?

JIMMY: Ovid.

HUGH: *Procede.*

JIMMY: 'I am a barbarian in this place because I am not under-

stood by anyone.'

370

HUGH: Indeed—*(Shouts)* Manus! Tea! I will compose a satire on Master Bartley Timlin, schoolmaster and bacon-curer. But it will be too easy, won't it? *(Shouts)* Strong tea! Black!

(The only way JIMMY can get HUGH's attention is by standing in front of him and holding his arms.)

JIMMY: Will you listen to me, Hugh!

HUGH: James. *(Shouts)* And a slice of soda bread.

375

JIMMY: I'm going to get married.

HUGH: Well!

JIMMY: At Christmas.

HUGH: Splendid.

JIMMY: To Athene.

380

HUGH: Who?

JIMMY: Pallas Athene.

HUGH: *Glaukopis Athene?*

JIMMY: Flashing-eyed, Hugh, flashing-eyed!

(He attempts the gesture he has made before: standing to atten-tion, the momentary spasm, the salute, the face raised in pained ecstasy—but the body does not respond efficiently this time. The gesture is grotesque.)

HUGH: The lady has assented?

385

JIMMY: She asked *me*—I assented.

HUGH: Ah. When was this?

JIMMY: Last night.

HUGH: What does her mother say?

JIMMY: Metis from Hellespont? Decent people—good stock.

390

HUGH: And her father?

JIMMY: I'm meeting Zeus tomorrow. Hugh, will you be my best man?

HUGH: Honoured, James; profoundly honoured.

JIMMY: You know what I'm looking for, Hugh, don't you? I

395 mean to say—you know—I—I—I joke like the rest of them—you know?—*(Again he attempts the pathetic routine but abandons it instantly.)* You know yourself, Hugh—don't you?—you know all that. But what I'm really looking for, Hugh—what I really want—companionship, Hugh—at my

400

353 **domus lugubris** house of mourning   359 **infelix** unlucky, un-happy   365–366 **Barbarus hic ego . . . ulli** I am a barbarian here be-cause I am not understood by anyone

time of life, companionship, company, someone to talk to. Away up in Beann na Gaoithe — you've no idea how lonely it is. Companionship — correct, Hugh? Correct?

HUGH: Correct.

405 JIMMY: And I always liked her, Hugh. Correct?

HUGH: Correct, James.

JIMMY: Someone to talk to.

HUGH: Indeed.

JIMMY: That's all, Hugh. The whole story. You know it all now,
410 Hugh. You know it all.

(As JIMMY *says those last lines he is crying, shaking his head, trying to keep his balance, and holding a finger up to his lips in absurd gestures of secrecy and intimacy. Now he staggers away, tries to sit on a stool, misses it, slides to the floor, his feet in front of him, his back against the broken cart. Almost at once he is asleep.* HUGH *watches all of this. Then he produces his flask and is about to pour a drink when he sees the Name-Book on the floor. He picks it up and leafs through it, pronouncing the strange names as he does. Just as he begins,* OWEN *emerges and descends with two bowls of tea.*)

HUGH: Ballybeg. Burnfoot. King's Head. Whiteplains. Fair Hill. Dunboy. Green Bank.

(OWEN *snatches the book from* HUGH.)

OWEN: I'll take that. (*In apology.*) It's only a catalogue of names.

HUGH: I know what it is.

415 OWEN: A mistake — my mistake — nothing to do with us. I hope that's strong enough (*tea*). (*He throws the book on the table and crosses over to* JIMMY.) Jimmy. Wake up, Jimmy. Wake up, man.

JIMMY: What — what-what?

420 OWEN: Here. Drink this. Then go on away home. There may be trouble. Do you hear me, Jimmy? There may be trouble.

HUGH: (*Indicating Name-Book*) We must learn those new names.

OWEN: (*Searching around*) Did you see a sack lying about?

HUGH: We must learn where we live. We must learn to make
425 them our own. We must make them our new home.

(OWEN *finds a sack and throws it across his shoulders.*)

OWEN: I know where I live.

HUGH: James thinks he knows, too. I look at James and three thoughts occur to me: A — that it is not the literal past, the 'facts' of history, that shape us, but images of the past embod-
430 ied in language. James has ceased to make that dis-crimination.

OWEN: Don't lecture me, Father.

HUGH: B — we must never cease renewing those images; because once we do, we fossilize. Is there no soda bread?

435 OWEN: And C, Father — one single, unalterable 'fact': if Yolland is not found, we are all going to be evicted. Lancey has issued the order.

HUGH: Ah. *Edictum imperatoris.*

OWEN: You should change out of those wet clothes. I've got to
440 go. I've got to see Doalty Dan Doalty.

HUGH: What about?

OWEN: I'll be back soon.

(As OWEN *exits.*)

438 **edictum imperatoris** the decree of the commander

HUGH: Take care, Owen. To remember everything is a form of madness. (*He looks around the room, carefully, as if he were about to leave it forever. Then he looks at* JIMMY, *asleep*
445 *again.*) The road to Sligo. A spring morning. 1798. Going into battle. Do you remember, James? Two young gallants with pikes across their shoulders and the *Aeneid* in their pockets. Everything seemed to find definition that spring — a congruence, a miraculous matching of hope and past and
450 present and possibility. Striding across the fresh, green land. The rhythms of perception heightened. The whole enterprise of consciousness accelerated. We were gods that morning, James; and I had recently married *my* goddess, Caitlin Dubh Nic Reactainn, may she rest in peace. And to leave her and
455 my infant son in his cradle — that was heroic, too. By God, sir, we were magnificent. We marched as far as — where was it? — Glenties! All of twenty-three miles in one day. And it was there, in Phelan's pub, that we got homesick for Athens, just like Ulysses. The *desiderium nostrorum* — the need for
460 our own. Our *pietas*, James, was for older, quieter things. And that was the longest twenty-three miles back I ever made. (*Toasts* JIMMY.) My friend, confusion is not an ignoble condition.

(MAIRE *enters.*)

MAIRE: I'm back again. I set out for somewhere but I couldn't
465 remember where. So I came back here.

HUGH: Yes, I will teach you English, Maire Chatach.

MAIRE: Will you, Master? I must learn it. I need to learn it.

HUGH: Indeed you may well be my only pupil.

(*He goes towards the steps and begins to ascend.*)

MAIRE: When can we start?
470
HUGH: Not today. Tomorrow, perhaps. After the funeral. We'll begin tomorrow. (*Ascending*) But don't expect too much. I will provide you with the available words and the available grammar. But will that help you to interpret between priva-cies? I have no idea. But it's all we have. I have no idea at all.
475
(*He is now at the top.*)

MAIRE: Master, what does the English word 'always' mean?

HUGH: *Semper — per omnia saecula.* The Greeks called it '*aei*'. It's not a word I'd start with. It's a silly word, girl.

(*He sits.* JIMMY *is awake. He gets to his feet.* MAIRE *sees the Name-Book, picks it up, and sits with it on her knee.*)

MAIRE: When he comes back, this is where he'll come to. He told me this is where he was happiest.
480
(JIMMY *sits beside* MAIRE.)

JIMMY: Do you know the Greek word *endogamein*? It means to marry within the tribe. And the word *exogamein* means to marry outside the tribe. And you don't cross those borders casually — both sides get very angry. Now, the problem is this: Is Athene sufficiently mortal or am I sufficiently godlike for
485 the marriage to be acceptable to her people and to my people? You think about that.

460 **desiderium nostrorum** longing/need for our things/people   461 **pietas** piety   477 **Semper — per omnia saecula** Always — for all time 477 **aei** always   481 **endogamein** to marry within the tribe   482 **exogamein** to marry outside the tribe

HUGH: *Urbs antiqua fuit* — there was an ancient city which, 'tis
said, Juno loved above all the lands. And it was the goddess's
490   aim and cherished hope that here should be the capital of all
nations — should the fates perchance allow that. Yet in truth
she discovered that a race was springing from Trojan blood to
overthrow some day these Tyrian towers — a people *late regem
belloque superbum* — kings of broad realms and proud in war
495   who would come forth for Lybia's downfall — such was —
such was the course — such was the course ordained —

488 **Urbs antiqua fuit** there was an ancient city   493–494 **late regem
belloque superbum** kings of broad realms and proud in war

ordained by fate . . . What the hell's wrong with me? Sure I
know it backways. I'll begin again. *Urbs antiqua fuit* — there
was an ancient city which, 'tis said, Juno loved above all the
lands.   500

(Begin to bring down the lights.)

And it was the goddess's aim and cherished hope that here
should be the capital of all nations — should the fates
perchance allow that. Yet in truth she discovered that a race
was springing from Trojan blood to overthrow some day these
Tyrian towers — a people kings of broad realms and proud in   505
war who would come forth for Lybia's downfall . . .

(Blackout.)

MANUEL PUIG

Manuel Puig (1932–1990) was raised in provincial Argentina and moved to Buenos Aires for his secondary and university education. Although he entered the University of Buenos Aires as an architecture student in 1950, he quickly changed to the study of philosophy, taking his degree in 1955 and leaving Argentina for Europe, where he spent the late 1950s. Living mainly in Rome and London, Puig worked as a language teacher and applied his skill with language to writing movie subtitles as well. He also worked as an assistant director on several films. Puig returned several times to Argentina, but lived mainly in New York and Brazil, where he wrote several important novels: *Betrayed by Rita Hayworth* (1968), *Heartbreak Tango* (1973), and *The Buenos Aires Affair* (1973), among others. The novel *The Kiss of the Spider Woman* was first published in 1976. Puig then wrote a stage adaptation of the novel, which was produced in Spain in 1981, and subsequently in South America. The film version of *Kiss of the Spider Woman*, published in 1987, was directed by the Argentine director Hector Barbenco, with a screenplay by Leonard Schrader.

The Kiss of the Spider Woman

The Kiss of the Spider Woman is one of many contemporary films dramatizing the brutality of Latin American military regimes. Puig's narrative, however, focuses more immediately on how the imprisonment of its two central characters—Valentin, the guerrilla leader of a political resistance group, and Molina, a gay man—forges a bond of solidarity between the prisoners. In the novel, Puig uses a variety of devices—the characters' dialogue, police reports, popular music—as narrative frames for the action. In the film, these layers are also important to our understanding of the action. Throughout the film, for instance, Molina entertains Valentin by telling him the story of a Nazi spy thriller. Through this device he gains Valentin's confidence, which he will use to gain information about Valentin's political activities to tell to the authorities. However, the relationship of gay man and guerrilla, weak and strong, betrayer and betrayed, becomes more complex as the two characters' relationship grows to include respect, love, and sex. Molina, having poisoned Valentin, persuades the prison authorities to provide better food, while refusing to give them any real information. In the end, it is Valentin's desire to make contact with his political cell that betrays his comrades and Molina to the authorities. The politics of *Kiss of the Spider Woman* extend beyond a critique of the Argentine government and its apparatus of torture and surveillance to embrace a more subtle and complex treatment of the politics of identity: political identity, sexual identity, and human identity in the face of an omnipotent police state.

Today, the great bulk of dramatic scripts are written for film and television. As Leonard Schrader's screenplay of *Kiss of the Spider Woman* demonstrates, screenwriting requires the writer not only to construct dialogue and action for the characters, but also to outline the camera work that determines how we will view the scene. The camera allows us to move quickly from scene to scene, and as a result the pacing of drama on the screen often seems more rapid and abrupt than the pacing of stage drama. Moreover, films tend to tell the story visually, using the visual element of the events to construct a narrative. For this reason, the verbal texture of screenplays is usually leaner than the dialogue of stage plays, which rely much more exclusively on dialogue to establish the narrative of events. Of course, the boundaries between dramatic modes—film, television, stage—are permeable. The style, language, and form of film and television drama have pervasively influenced our expectations of dramatic action on the stage.

KISS OF THE SPIDER WOMAN PRO-vides the opportunity to observe how a story's production—as a novel and as a film—shapes its effect on us. In his original novel, Puig uses a variety of narrative techniques. Dialogue between the characters, internal monologues, excerpts from news and police reports, descriptions of films are all interwoven to tell the story of Molina and Valentin. This variety of textures confronts the reader of the novel with a characteristically postmodern problem: how to sort the "story" out from the means of its telling. For each of these ways of narrating events tells the story of Valentin and Molina from a different perspective, and so in effect writes a different story. The reader is forced to move between the competing surfaces of the novel, to reconstruct the narrative that lies between the ways in which the story is told.

The film version of *Kiss*, however, is able to depict events that are only narrated in the novel. Although the film develops several visual narratives that approximate the several "voices" of the novel, film places a premium on realistic detail, on showing the audience a complete and full environment. Film is able to "show" the scene of *Kiss* in an immediacy and detail that go far beyond the scope of either the novel or the stage play. Yet at the same time, this immediacy can seem to literalize the story, to fill in the gaps between the narratives that are one of the novel's chief achievements.

Here is an excerpt of the final moments from the original novel, *Kiss of the Spider Woman*. The novel con-cludes with an extensive police report, written as a journal documenting the surveillance placed on Molina after his release from the prison. The final chapter is written as a dialogue between Valentin and a sympathetic doctor giving him morphine after he has been brutally tortured, and concludes with Valentin's interior monologue, his thoughts while dying. The film, on the other hand, is able to depict these events rapidly and clearly, moving instantly between the prison and the outside world; and between reality, dreams, and death. In this sense, the film gains in compression what it may lose in formal complexity, as Molina's meeting with the revolutionaries, his surveillance by the police agent Pedro, his death, and the morphine-induced dream (and death) of Valentin are visualized for us on the screen. The visual power of the film is striking and rich; what the film loses of the novel's narrative variety it gains in the force of the images themselves.

FROM PAGE *to* SCREEN

EXCERPT FROM THE NOVEL *KISS OF THE SPIDER WOMAN*
TRANSLATED BY THOMAS COLCHIE
CHAPTER 15
. . .

24. *Thursday*. According to separate report, subject withdrew total savings from bank, leaving only minimum deposit required in order not to close account. Money withdrawn had been deposited at intervals prior to term of imprisonment. At notary public's office, "José Luis Neri Castro," subject left sealed envelope in the name of the mother, containing only the above savings, this according to sworn declaration of named executive of said enterprise. Subject's activities minimal, left for work at regular morning hour, ate lunch at work, with coffee, which subject drank continuously on and off throughout day, there on premises. Arrived home directly, at 8:10 P.M. We also note, as per decision at command level, cancellation of project to leak to press imaginary confession, by Arregui to Molina, along with the latter's supposed undercover work as intelligence agent. Cancellation based upon the probability of pending or possible imminent contact between subject and partisans of Arregui.

25. *Friday*. Subject arrived at place of employment in the morning, left 12:30 P.M., and went to have lunch, alone, a few blocks away, at a pizzeria, number 2476 on Las Heras. Subject first spoke by public phone at same location, after dialing three times and hanging up immediately, as on previous occasion. Talked for a few minutes. Then ate by himself, or rather had a bite or two, leaving the plate almost untouched. Returned to work. Left there at 6:40 P.M., at Callao caught a bus to Congreso, where then went by subway as far as José Maria Moreno station. Walked to Riglos and Formosa. Waited there approximately thirty minutes, which is to say the amount of time allotted by Central Bureau until subject was to be picked up, if he had not been met by party or parties

beforehand, and then taken away for interrogation. Therefore, two agents of the CISL, already in close contact with our patrol unit, proceeded to make the arrest. Subject demanded to see credentials. At that moment, however, several shots were fired from a passing automobile, wounding CISL agent Joaquin Perrone, along with subject, both of whom immediately fell to the ground. The arrival of our patrol unit, minutes later, was too late for pursuit of extremist vehicle. Of the wounded, Molina expired before arriving patrol unit could administer first aid. The above agent, Perrone, suffered thigh wounds plus serious contusions caused by his fall. The impression of other members of the patrol unit is that the extremists preferred to eliminate Molina to avoid the possibility of a confession. In fact, the recent activities of the subject, the matter of the bank account, etc., suggest that he himself feared something might actually occur. Furthermore, if he was in fact aware of our continued surveillance, his plan—in the event of being surprised in an incriminating position—may in fact have been one of the following: either he expected to escape with the extremists, or he was ready to be eliminated by same.

The present compilation of reports has been typed up in quadruplicate, for distribution only to authorized personnel, with the original to remain in this office permanently on file.

CHAPTER 16

—Which part of your body hurts you the most?

—Agh . . . aghhh . . . aghhh . . .

—Don't try to talk, Arregui . . . if it hurts you that much.

—Ov- . . . over . . . here . . .

—Third-degree burns, what animals.

—Aiee . . . Agh, no . . . please . . .

—And how many days since you had any food?

—Th- . . . thr- . . . ee . . .

—Bastards . . .

— . . .

—Listen . . . you won't tell anyone, promise me.

— . . .

—Nod your head whether you want it or not. God, what they did to you it's barbaric, you'll be in a lot of pain for quite a few days . . . Listen to me. Nobody's around here in first aid right now, so I can take a chance and give you some morphine, that way you'll be able to rest. If you want it, nod your head. But you're never to tell anyone, because they'll throw me right out of here.

— . . .

—Okay, you'll get some relief in just a minute.

— . . .

—There, just a little pinch, and now you'll start feeling less pain.

— . . .

—Count to forty.

—One, two, three, four, five, six, seven, eight, nine, ten, eleven, twelve, thirteen, fourteen, fifteen . . .

—The way they've worked you over is unbelievable. Those burns in the groin . . . It will take weeks to heal up. But don't tell about this or I'm finished. By tomorrow it'll begin to hurt less.

—. . . twenty-nine, thirty, thirty-one, thirty-two, thirty-th- . . . thirty-three, th- . . . what number am I on? don't hear any steps anymore, is it somehow possible they're not following me anymore? if it weren't for your knowing the way out of here, doctor, and leading me, I couldn't go on, I'd be afraid of falling into some hole, and is it possible that I've covered such a long stretch if I'm so exhausted? from not eating? it must be, and since I keep falling off to sleep, how is it possible that I go on walking without stumbling? "Don't be afraid, Valentin, the intern is a kind person and he's going to take care of you," Marta . . . where are you? when did you get here? I can't open my eyes because I'm asleep, but please come closer to me, Marta . . . don't stop speaking to me, can't you touch me? "Don't be afraid, I'm listening, but only on one condition, Valentin," what's that? "That you don't hide anything of what you're thinking, because the moment you do that, even though I want to listen to you I won't be able to anymore," no one can overhear us? "No one," Marta, I've been in terrible pain . . . "I want to know how you are now," and no one could be listening? someone waiting for me to denounce my comrades? "No," Marta, darling, I hear you speaking inside of me, "Because I'm inside of you," is that really true? and will it be that way always? "No, that can be only as long as I don't keep any secrets from you, just as you're not going to keep any from me," then I'll tell you everything, because this very kind intern is leading me to some way out of here through this long, long tunnel, "Is it very dark?" yes, and he told me that at the end there'll be a light, very far away, but I don't know if it's true because I'm asleep and hard as I try, I can't seem to open my eyes, "What are you thinking about this very minute?" my eyelids are so heavy that it's impossible to open them, I'm so very sleepy, "I hear water running, and you?" water when it runs over stones is always clean and if I could reach over to where the water is with my hand, I could wet the tips of my fingers and then moisten my eyelashes to unseal them, but I'm afraid, Marta, "You're afraid of waking up and finding yourself in your cell," then it's not certain that someone is going to help me to escape? I can't remember, but this warmth that I'm beginning to feel in my hands and on my face is like the sun's, "It's possible that it's beginning to be light," I don't know if the water is clean, do I dare take a sip? "Moving ahead in the direction of the water, surely it'll be possible to get to wherever it empties," it's true, but it looks like what I see is really a desert, there are no trees, or houses, nothing more than the dunes that follow each other as far as the eye can see, "Instead of a desert, couldn't it be the sea?" yes, it is the sea, and there's a stretch of very hot sand, I have to run so that I don't burn the soles of my feet, "What else can you see?" from one end of the coast to the other there's no sign of that painted ship made of cardboard, "And what is it that you hear there?" nothing, you don't hear any maracas, the pounding of the waves and nothing else, sometimes the waves are so big they crash on the shore and reach up as far as where the palm trees begin, Marta . . . it looks like a flower fell in the sand, "A wild orchid?" if the waves reach it they'll carry it out too far, and is it possible for the wind to carry it off just as I was about to pick it up? and carry it way far out to sea, and it doesn't matter if it disappears because I can swim and I'll dive in, but right in the place where I'm sure that the flower sank . . . what you see now is a woman, a native girl, I could reach her if she didn't try to escape me by swimming so fast, I don't reach her though, Marta, and it's impossible to shout under the water and tell her not to be afraid, "Underwater you hear whatever one is thinking," she looks at me unafraid, a man's shirt is tied across her chest, but I'm so tired already, I have no more oxygen left in my lungs after such a long swim underwater, but Marta, the native takes my hand and lifts me up to the surface, she puts a finger to her lips as a sign that I shouldn't speak, the wet knot is tied so tightly that she can't undo it without my help, and while I untie the knot she looks the other

way . . . I didn't remember that I was naked and I'm brushing against her, the island girl flushed with embarrassment now puts her arms around me, my hand is warm and I touch her and it dries her right away, I touch her face, her long hair down to the waist, her hips, her navel, her breasts, her shoulders, her back, her tummy, her legs, her feet, and again her tummy, "Can I ask you to pretend that she's me?" yes, "But don't tell her anything, don't be critical of her, let her think she is me, even if she fails in some way," with a finger to her lips the native signals me not to say a word, but to you, Marta, I'll tell everything, since I feel the same as I felt with you, because you're with me, and soon this jet will spurt out of me, white and warm from my insides and I'm going to flood her, oh, Marta, such joy, yes I will tell you everything so that you won't go away then, so that you'll be with me every minute, especially now, in this instant, don't think of leaving me, this precise instant! the most beautiful of all, now, yes, don't move, it's better quiet, now, now, and later on, in a while, I'll also tell you that the native is closing her eyes because she's sleepy, she wants to rest, and if I close my eyes, who knows when I'll be able to open them again? my eyelids are so heavy, when it gets dark I'm not going to be able to tell be cause my eyes are closed, "And you're not cold? it's night and you're sleeping out in the open, the sea air is cool, didn't you feel cold during the night? tell me," no, I didn't feel cold, my back touched this sheet that's so smooth and warm on which I slept every night since I came to the island, and I don't know how to explain it, my love, but the sheet seems like . . . like in reality it's very smooth and warm skin, of a woman, and you don't see anything more in this place than that skin which reaches as far as the eye can see, you don't see anything else but the skin of a woman lying down, I'm like a grain of sand in the

palm of her hand, she's lying in the sea and she lifts her hand and from up here I can see that the island is a woman, "The native?" I can't make out the face, it's too far, "And the sea?" just the same as always, I keep swimming underwater and you can't see the bottom it's so very deep but underwater my mother hears every word I'm thinking and we're talking, do you want me to tell you what she's asking? "Yes," well . . . she's asking me if it's true all that stuff in the papers, that my cellmate died, in a shootout, and she's asking if it was my fault, and if I'm not ashamed of having brought him such awful luck, "What did you answer her?" that yes, it was my fault, and that yes, I am very sad, but that there's no point in being so sad because the only one who knows for sure is him, if he was sad or happy to die that way, sacrificing himself for a just cause, be cause he's the only one who will ever have known, and let's hope, Marta, how much I wish it with all my heart, let's hope that he may have died happily, "For a just cause? hmmm . . . I think he let himself be killed because that way he could die like some heroine in a movie, and none of that business about a just cause," that's something only he can know, and it's possible that even he never knew, but in my cell I can't sleep anymore because he got me used to listening to him tell films every night, like lullabies, and if I ever get out of here sometime I'm not going to be able to call him and invite him over to dinner, he who had invited me so many times, "And what would you like to have most to eat this minute?" I'm swimming with my head above the water now so that way I won't lose sight of the island coast, and I'm very tired by the time I reach the sand, it doesn't burn anymore because the sun isn't so strong anymore and before it starts to get dark I have to look for some fruit, you don't know how beautiful it is here with this mixture of palm trees, and

lianas, at night it's all silvery, because the film is in black and white, "And the music in the background?" very soft maracas, and drums, "Isn't that a sign of danger?" no, it's the music that announces, when they switch on a strong spotlight, the appearance of such a strange woman, with a long dress on, that's shining, "Silver lamé, that fits her like a glove?" yes, "And her face?" she's wearing a mask, it's also silver, but . . . poor creature . . . she can't move, there in the deepest part of the jungle she's trapped in a spider's web, or no, the spiderweb is growing out of her own body, the threads are coming out of her waist and her hips, they're part of her body, so many threads that look hairy like ropes and disgust me, even though if I were to touch them they might feel as smooth as who knows what, but it makes me queasy to touch them, "Doesn't she speak?" no, she's crying, or no, she isn't, she's smiling but a tear rolls out from beneath the mask, "A tear that shines like a diamond?" yes, and I ask her why she's crying and in a close-up that covers the whole screen at the end of the film she answers me that that's just what can never be known, because the ending is enigmatic, and I answer her that it's good this way, that it's the very best part of the film because it signifies . . . and at that point she didn't let me go on, she said that I wanted to find an explanation for everything, but that in reality

I was just talking from hunger although I didn't have the courage to admit it, and she was looking at me, but every minute she seemed sadder and sadder, and more and more tears fell, "Mmm, more diamonds," and I didn't know what to do to get rid of her unhappiness, "I know what you did, and I'm not jealous, because you're never going to see her again in your whole life," it's just that she was so sad, don't you see? "But you enjoyed it, and I shouldn't forgive you for that," but I'm never going to see her again in my whole life, "And is it true that you're very hungry?" yes, it's true, and the spider woman pointed out to me the way through the forest with her finger, and so I don't know where to even begin to eat so many things I've found now, "Are they very tasty?" yes, a leg of roast chicken, crackers with big chunks of fresh cheese and little rolled up slices of cooked ham, and a delicious piece of glazed fruit, it's pumpkin, and later with a spoon I get to eat all the guava paste I want to, without worrying about finishing it all because there's so much, and I'm getting so sleepy, Marta, you can't imagine how much I just feel like sleeping after eating all that food I found thanks to the spider woman, and after I have one more spoonful of this guava paste and after I sleep . . . "You want to wake up already?" no, much, much later, because after eating all these rich foods

such a heavy sleep has come over me, and I'll just go on talking with you in my sleep, will it be possible? "Yes, this is a dream and we're talking together, so even if you fall asleep you don't have to be afraid, and I think now that nothing is ever going to separate us again, because we've realized the most difficult thing of all," what's the most difficult thing of all to realize? "That I live deep inside your thoughts and so I'll always remain with you, you'll never be alone," of course that's it, that's what I can never let myself forget, if the two of us think the same then we're together, even if I can't see you, "Yes, that's it," so when I wake up on the island you're going to go away with me, "Don't you want to stay forever in such a beautiful place?" no, it's been so good up to now, but enough resting, once I've eaten everything up and after some sleep I'm going to be strong again, because my comrades are waiting for me to resume the age-old fight, "That's the only thing that I don't ever want to know, the name of your comrades," Marta, oh how much I love you! that was the only thing I couldn't tell you, I was so afraid you were going to ask me that and then I was going to lose you forever, "No, Valentin, beloved, that will never take place, because this dream is short but this dream is happy."

THE KISS OF THE
SPIDER WOMAN

Screenplay by Leonard Schrader

BASED ON THE NOVEL BY MANUEL PUIG

— CHARACTERS —

MOLINA	A JUDGE
VALENTIN	A CALLER
MICHELLE	MARTA
CLUBFOOT	AMERICO
LENI	PEDRO
A MESSENGER	A WARDEN
A GUARD	A LEADER
WERNER	A MOTHER
A FLUNKY	A TELLER
GRETA	LYDIA
GABRIEL	AN INTERN
A DOCTOR	

The screen is black. We hear a "woman's" VOICE.

VOICE OF MOLINA: She, uh. Well, something a little strange, that's what you notice, that she's not a woman like all the others.

(pause)

She seems all wrapped up in herself. Lost in a world she carries deep inside her. But surrounded by a world of luxury.

(fade to:)

Int. prison cell — night

(We pan a stark cell and discover a woman's touch — glamor magazines, earrings, clothesline, pin-ups of Lana Turner and Rita Hayworth.)

VOICE OF MOLINA: A sumptuous boudoir. Her bed all quilted satin. Chiffon drapes. From her window you can see the Eiffel Tower.

(pause)

Suddenly her maid brings in a gift-wrapped box, a token from an admirer. She's a cabaret star, of the highest rank. She opens the box, it's a diamond bracelet, but she sends it back.

(pause)

Men are really at her feet. She's known a few; but not the one she's been waiting for all her life — a real man.

(The camera finds the PRISONER *who is speaking. He is* LUIS MOLINA, *41, his red-tinted hair no longer hiding the gray. He has the seasoned face of a man who has seen it all, and been hurt by most of it.)*

MOLINA: Her maid has prepared her a foam bath. The star takes a towel and wraps it around her hair like a turban. Her fingernails painted a rosy peach, she unfastens her taffeta night gown and lets it slide smoothly down her thighs to the tile floor.

*(*MOLINA, *playing the role, wraps a red towel around his head and sashays toward the other bunk.)*

MOLINA: Her skin glistens, her petite ankle slips into the perfumed water, then her sensuous legs, until finally her whole body is caressed with foam.

(The CELL-MATE *glances over his shoulder. He is* VALENTIN AR-REGUI, *34, his arms marked by torture. He has the intense look of a man who has been hurt in more ways than one.)*

VALENTIN: I told you. — No erotic descriptions.

*(*MOLINA *hides his delight at having evoked a response.)*

MOLINA: Whatever, but she's a ravishing woman, do you know what I mean? I mean the most ravishing woman in the world.

VALENTIN: Yeah, sure.

MOLINA: She really is — perfect figure, classical features, but with these big green eyes.

(We drift into the movie he describes. A glamorous STAR *in a lavish bathtub caresses her skin with foam.* VALENTIN's *voice wrenches us back to the cell.)*

VALENTIN: They're black.

MOLINA: I'm the one who saw the movie, but if that's what you want — big black eyes.

(resumes)

Kind eyes, tender eyes, but beware. They can see everything.

(pause)

There's nothing you can hide from them.

(Another movie flash. The STAR *steps from the foamy water and gazes into a mirror with big sad eyes.)*

MOLINA: No matter how lonely she may be, she keeps men at a distance.

VALENTIN: *(laughs)* She's probably got bad breath or something.

MOLINA: If you're going to crack jokes about a film I happen to be fond of, there's no reason to go on.

(MOLINA *glares at him.* VALENTIN *turns away, too weak to care one way or the other.*)

VALENTIN: Alright, alright. Go ahead.

MOLINA: Suddenly we're in Paris! Troops are marching right un-
40   derneath the Arc de Triomphe. Really handsome soldiers, and the French girls are applauding as they pass by.

(*pause*)

Then we're on this typical Parisian back-street, dead end, sort of looking up a hill.

(*Another flash.* TWO FRENCHMEN *with yarmulkes unload a truck in the dark. The images resemble a slapdash Nazi propaganda film.*)

MOLINA: And these really weird-looking Frenchmen, not the
45   typical ones with the berets, are unloading a truck. It's war-time, of course, and the boxes contain contraband delicacies. Like canned meat . . . the best cheeses . . . peaches in syrup—

VALENTIN: (*sitting up*) Don't talk about food.

50   MOLINA: Not to mention the hams, and the pates—

(VALENTIN *struggles to the shit-bucket in the corner and, exhausted, leans against the wall as he urinates.*)

MOLINA: You still feeling dizzy?

VALENTIN: It's my back.

MOLINA: You've been bleeding again. Look at your shirt, it's all wet.

55   VALENTIN: It's just sweat. I had another fever break.

MOLINA: What do you think so far?

(*pause*)

Isn't it fabulous?

VALENTIN: It helps pass the time.

(VALENTIN *hobbles toward his bunk. His shirtback is streaked with old bloodstains.*)

MOLINA: Does that mean you like it?

60   VALENTIN: Doesn't help any great cause, but I guess it's alright.

MOLINA: Blessed Mary, is that all you can talk about? You must've studied Political Philosophies in school.

VALENTIN: The phrase is Political *Science*, and the answer is no, I studied Journalism.

65   MOLINA: Ah! So you *can* appreciate a good story.

VALENTIN: And easily spot a cheap one.

MOLINA: Well, I know it's nothing terribly intellectual like you must be used to. It's just a romance, but it's so beautiful.

(*pause*)

Now. Suddenly this military convoy rushes forward.

(*Cut to:*)

Ext. Paris back-street—night (Nazi movie)

(*Spotlights hit the* FRENCHMEN *unloading the truck. German* TROOPS *grab them. A handsome* LIEUTENANT *shoves one against the truck.*)

70   VOICE OF MOLINA: Marvelous German soldiers catch those weird smugglers in the act and arrest them all.

(*A small truck lurks in the shadows.*)

VOICE OF MOLINA: But watching nearby is this small truck, with these two French thugs from the Resistance who are spying on the Germans. — This hulking Clubfoot and his
75   half-deaf Flunky.

(*Cut to:*)

Int. cell—night

(VALENTIN *sits up on his bunk.*)

VALENTIN: Wait a minute. Those weird guys the Germans arrested?

MOLINA: Yes?

VALENTIN: What do you mean, they didn't look French?

MOLINA: They didn't look French. They looked, uh, Turkish.
80   I'm not sure, they had like these caps on their heads—like these, like these, uh . . . Turkish. Like fezzes.

VALENTIN: Those caps are yarmulkes. Can't you see this is a fucking anti-Semitic film?

MOLINA: Oh, come on!
85
VALENTIN: Wait. This must've been a German movie, right?

MOLINA: I don't know, it was from years ago. — Look. I don't explain my movies. It just ruins the emotion.

VALENTIN: This must've been a Nazi propaganda film done dur-
90   ing the war.

MOLINA: I don't know, that's just the background. This is where the important part begins, the part about the lovers. It's divine.

(*Cut to:*)

Int. Paris cabaret—night (Nazi movie)

(*Deco doors swing open. Elegant waiters move along dimly-lit tables.*)

VOICE OF MOLINA: Every night the chic set flocks to this exclusive club—with lovers at every table, spies in every corner. And the top officers of the German High Command.
95

(*pause*)

One of them is Werner. Werner, so distant, so divine. And the Chief of Counter-Intelligence for all France.

(*pause*)

And Michelle with her angel face, the cigarette girl who really is working for the—well, you'll see.

(MICHELLE *leaves the table of the handsome blond* WERNER. *Musical fanfare. Dancing couples sit and applaud.*)

VOICE OF MOLINA: And then, the moment they're all waiting   100
for.

(*Cut to:*)

Int. cell—night

(MOLINA *opens his clothesline towels like a stage curtain and strikes a grandiose pose.*)

MOLINA: Stepping into the spotlight is that legendary star, that ravishing chanteuse—Leni La Maison!

(*Cut to:*)

Int. cabaret—night (Nazi movie)

(LENI *turns to the crowd in a deco pose and, singing, glides and swirls among the hushed tables.* WERNER *can't take his eyes off her.* MICHELLE *hurries backstage and picks up the phone.*)

MICHELLE: Yes?

105 CLUBFOOT: (on phone) Did you get the map?

MICHELLE: No, there was no time.

CLUBFOOT: (hanging up) Just get it. Nothing else matters. Vive La France.

(LENI, still singing, passes WERNER's table with a haughty glance and concludes with a flourish, then sees him gazing at her. Wild applause.)

VOICE OF MOLINA: Werner's eyes begin to burn into her soul.
110 Eyes like the claws of an eagle—inescapable.

(LENI clutches her pounding heart and dashes away from his piercing eyes.)
(Cut to:)

Int. cell—night

(VALENTIN muffles his scornful laughter. MOLINA, miffed, plunks down on his bunk.)

MOLINA: What are you laughing at?

(more laughter)

    Well, it must be something.

(VALENTIN stares straight at MOLINA.)

VALENTIN: At you.

(looks away)

    And me.

(MOLINA blows out his candle. The two men sit in silence on opposite ends of the dark cell.)
(Cut to:)

Ext. prison corridor—night

(TWO GUARDS drag an old HOODED PRISONER into a cell across the courtyard. His shirt is covered with bloodstains.)
(Cut to:)

Int. cell—night

(VALENTIN watches through the food slot in the door. MOLINA wakes up and rubs his eyes.)

115 MOLINA: What's going on?

VALENTIN: (tense whisper) Quiet! They're bringing in someone new.

MOLINA: What time is it anyway?

VALENTIN: He's really bleeding.

120 MOLINA: Is it a political prisoner?

VALENTIN: They don't treat you like that for stealing bananas.

MOLINA: You know him?

(VALENTIN, deeply disturbed, says nothing.)
(Cut to:)

Int. prison corridor—dawn

(GUARDS conduct the morning bedcheck. Prisoners bark out their names.)

VALENTIN: Valentin Arregui!

MOLINA: Luis Molina!

(VALENTIN strains to see the hooded prisoner across the courtyard. The GUARD shoves him in his cell.)
(Cut to:)

Int. cell—day

(MOLINA finishes shaving and offers the razor.)

MOLINA: Do you want to shave?   125

VALENTIN: (turns away) Shit.

MOLINA: Well, I didn't mean your legs.

(VALENTIN looks out the crack in the metal wall plates.)

MOLINA: What is the matter?

VALENTIN: I don't understand why they stopped my interrogation. It's been almost a week.   130

MOLINA: Why couldn't they give me that handsome leading blond man to keep me company—instead of you.

VALENTIN: What the hell are you talking about?

MOLINA: Afraid to talk about sex?

VALENTIN: You really wanna know, Molina? I find you boring.   135

MOLINA: Darling, you don't know page one. You know I'm a faggot? Well, congratulations. You know I corrupted a minor? Well, that's even on TV, film at eleven.

VALENTIN: You really like those Nazi blonds, don't you?

MOLINA: Well, no, you see I detest politics but I'm mad about the leading man. He's so romantic.   140

(pause)

    Should I be shot for that?

VALENTIN: Your Nazis are about as romantic as the fucking warden and his torture room.

MOLINA: I can imagine.   145

VALENTIN: (hard) No. You can't.

(VALENTIN stares into his eyes. MOLINA, chagrined, looks away.)
(Cut to:)

Int. cell—night

(VALENTIN, unable to sleep, climbs up to the barred window and stares at the city lights in the dark. MOLINA, drowsy, sits up on his bunk.)

MOLINA: You can't sleep?

(pause)

    Mind if I tell my picture?

(VALENTIN stares out the window.)

MOLINA: After the show, Leni changes into a satin evening-gown that makes her look heavenly. Firm breasts. Thin waist. Smooth hips.   150

VALENTIN: Is this propaganda or porno?

MOLINA: Just listen, you'll see.

(Cut to:)

Int. cabaret dressing room—night (Nazi movie)

(Knock on the door. MICHELLE, upset, enters LENI's ornate dressing room.)

MICHELLE: Excuse me. Leni.

LENI: What is it, Michelle?   155

MICHELLE: (near tears) Leni, I'm a traitor. A traitor to France.

LENI: What do you mean?

MICHELLE: I'm going to have a baby. But the father is a young Lieutenant of the Occupation Army.

LENI: Is that so? My poor Michelle.   160

MICHELLE: But he loves me. And wants to get married as soon as he can get permission.

LENI: I really can't understand. How could you fall in love with an enemy of our France?

165 MICHELLE: Love has no country, Leni.

(pause)

But there's something else you don't know. I'm working for the Resist—

(Another knock. MICHELLE *gasps.)*

LENI: Come in!

(A MESSENGER *enters with a bouquet of flowers. The* TWO WOMEN *sigh with relief.)*

MESSENGER: For you, Madame.

(Cut to:)

Int. cell—night

*(*VALENTIN *shakes his head in disgust.)*

170 VALENTIN: How can you remember all this crap? You must be making it up.

MOLINA: No, I'm not, I swear. Well, I embroider a little, so you can see it the way I did.

VALENTIN: God help me.

175 MOLINA: You atheists never stop talking about God.

VALENTIN: And you gays never face facts. Fantasies are no escape.

MOLINA: If you've got the keys to that door, I will gladly follow. Otherwise I'll escape in my own way, thank you.

180 VALENTIN: Then your life is as trivial as your movies.—I'm going to sleep.

MOLINA: Tell the truth, Valentin. Who do you identify with the most—the Clubfoot patriot or the handsome Werner?

VALENTIN: Who do *you* identify with?

185 MOLINA: Oh, the singer. She's the star. I'm always the heroine.

(Cut to:)

Int. cell—day

(Sunlight streams through the bars. MOLINA *slices an avocado and offers it to* VALENTIN.*)*

MOLINA: Have some, it's delicious.

VALENTIN: No thanks.

MOLINA: What's wrong, you don't like it?

VALENTIN: Sure I like it, but no thanks.

190 MOLINA: Well, then go ahead and have some. It's a long time till lunch.

VALENTIN: Can't afford to get spoiled.

MOLINA: Do you really think eating this avocado will make you spoiled and weak? Enjoy what life offers you.

195 VALENTIN: What life "offers" me is the struggle. When you're dedicated to that, pleasure becomes secondary.

MOLINA: Does your girlfriend think the same thing?

VALENTIN: *(suspicious)* How do you know I have a girl?

MOLINA: *(shrugs)* It's the normal thing. Does she avoid pleasure

200 too?

VALENTIN: She knows what really counts. That the most important thing is serving a cause that is noble.

MOLINA: What kind of cause is that, one that doesn't let you eat an avocado?

205 VALENTIN: *(turns away)* Molina, you would never understand.

MOLINA: Well, I understand one thing. I offer you half of my precious avocado and you throw it back in my face!

VALENTIN: Don't act like that. You sound just like a—

MOLINA: Like a what? Say it. Like a woman, you mean.

*(*VALENTIN *shrugs yes.)*

210 MOLINA: What's wrong with being like a woman? Why do only women get to be sensitive? Why not a man, a dog, or a faggot? If more men acted like women, there wouldn't be so much violence.—Like that!

*(*MOLINA *points at the welts on* VALENTIN'S *face.)*

(Cut to:)

Ext. prison corridor—day

(A GUARD *walks down the corridor and unlocks their door.)*

VALENTIN: *(o.s.)* Maybe you have a point, a flimsy one but still—

MOLINA: *(o.s.)* Oh nice! Maybe I have a point! 215

(Cut to:)

Int. cell—day

(The fat GUARD *steps into their cell.)*

GUARD: Molina, today's yer lucky day. The Warden wanna talk to ya.

*(*MOLINA *is led away.)*

(Cut to:)

Int. cell—night

*(*MOLINA *mends a shirt with needle and thread.* VALENTIN *cleans his teeth with a damp rag.)*

VALENTIN: Why did the Warden want to see you?

MOLINA: My lawyer called. Parole seems out of the question.

(sighs)

For a while, at least. 220

VALENTIN: How'd he treat you, the Warden?

MOLINA: Like a faggot, same as always.

(lights out)

Oh, no. Shit.

(Curfew buzzer. MOLINA *lights a candle and places it near the photo of his mother.)*

MOLINA: He told me something else. My mother's not doing too well. She has high blood-pressure, and her heart is kind of 225 weak.

VALENTIN: People can go on forever like that.

MOLINA: *(melancholy)* Sure, but not if you upset them. Can you imagine the shame of having a son in prison?

(pause)

And the reason. 230

VALENTIN: Go to sleep, you'll feel better.

MOLINA: No, only one thing can help.

VALENTIN: *(grudgingly)* Sure, man. Go ahead.

MOLINA: Man! Is there a man in here? Don't let him go!

(looks under bed)

Did he get away? 235

VALENTIN: *(exasperated smile)* Okay, cut the crap and tell your movie.

(MOLINA, beaming, spins his web of romantic intrigue.)

MOLINA: And now, waiting in the moonlight behind the cabaret is Werner's limousine.

(Cut to:)

Ext. cabaret back door — night (Nazi movie)

(WERNER watches LENI say goodbye to MICHELLE.)

240 VOICE OF MOLINA: Werner's eyes are locked on the backstage exit. "La sortie des artistes." He signals his chauffeur to open the door for her. Maybe because Leni sees a chance to help Michelle, or maybe because Leni wants to know what kind of a man is hidden inside this enemy invader — she decides to
245 join him for the evening.

(LENI descends the stairs. WERNER offers his hand.)

WERNER: Madame.

(With a haughty glance, she enters his limousine.)

(Cut to:)

Int. nightclub — night (Nazi movie)

(LENI and WERNER lift champagne glasses. Their eyes meet.)

WERNER: *(clicks glasses)* To a great artiste.

(Cut to:)

Ext. Paris street — night (Nazi movie)

(MICHELLE walks along a dark neighborhood street.)

VOICE OF MOLINA: Michelle hurries to meet her secret love. But dark forces have already decided the fate of this sweet girl.
250 This girl from the French Resistance in love with a German Lieutenant. Because . . .

(The CLUBFOOT and his FLUNKY watch her hurry past their parked truck.)

CLUBFOOT: Her time is up.
FLUNKY: *(grips hearing aid)* What?

(MICHELLE approaches an elegant apartment building.)

VOICE OF MOLINA: Because . . . love is a luxury a spy cannot
255 afford.

(She calls up to the balcony.)

MICHELLE: Hanschen!

(The German LIEUTENANT appears on the balcony, smiles and tosses down his key. It lands in the street. MICHELLE stoops down to pick it up. Suddenly the truck hurtles toward her at full speed. Turning in horror, she sees the CLUBFOOT at the wheel. The truck races into the night, leaving MICHELLE sprawled across the dark pavement.)

(Cut to:)

Int. cell — night

(VALENTIN is deep in thought. MOLINA approaches and snaps his fingers.)

MOLINA: Valentin, are you listening?

(pause)

How can you leave me chattering to myself like some silly parrot?
VALENTIN: Strange. When Michelle was killed, I — it was 260 chilling.

(MOLINA, touched by the compliment, sits on the floor beside his bunk.)

MOLINA: It's just a movie, Valentin. One of Mother's many stories.
VALENTIN: Yeah, but I keep thinking about — someone I know.
MOLINA: Your girlfriend. Tell me about her. My lips are sealed.
VALENTIN: It's just that I'm so helpless in here, with no way to 265 protect her.
MOLINA: So you have a heart after all.
VALENTIN: Mm.
MOLINA: Write to her. Tell her to stop taking chances.

(VALENTIN snaps out of his reverie.)

VALENTIN: If you think like that, you'll never change anything 270 in this world.
MOLINA: *(amused)* Now look who's living a fantasy.

(VALENTIN angrily lifts his shirt, displaying the torture welts on his torso.)

VALENTIN: You call this a fantasy?
MOLINA: — I'm so sorry.
VALENTIN: Some day the struggle will be won. 275
MOLINA: Don't worry, Valentin. You'll have your day, I'm sure.

(Cut to:)

Ext. prison corridor — day

(Both men stand outside their door for morning bed-check.)

VALENTIN: Valentin Arregui.
MOLINA: Luis Molina.

(Cut to:)

Int. cell — day

(MOLINA leans on his bunk, humming LENI's song. VALENTIN paces for exercise. Two tin plates are pushed through the food slot in the door.)

VALENTIN: Great. I'm starving. — Here.
MOLINA: No, you take this one. It has twice as much. 280
VALENTIN: Sure, because those bastards want us to fight over it. Take it.
MOLINA: No, you need it more than I do. Please, please, to build your strength.
VALENTIN: Don't argue. Take it. 285

(MOLINA reluctantly accepts the larger portion.)

MOLINA: *(snide)* May I have a spoon?

(VALENTIN obliges)

Thanks.

(VALENTIN sits on his bunk and eats the black beans, then notices MOLINA toying with his food.)

VALENTIN: What's the matter? Afraid of getting fat?
MOLINA: No.
VALENTIN: This glue is not so bad today. 290

(MOLINA *hesitantly swallows another spoonful.*)

MOLINA: Valentin.

(*pause*)

When I said you should write your girlfriend, I also meant you should tell her you love her. It's so nice to get a letter from someone you love.

295 VALENTIN: Are you crazy? A letter would be like denouncing her to them. The only reason I'm still alive is because they want information from me. And if anyone tries to save me, they'd hide my arrest by killing me on the spot.

MOLINA: (*upset*) Valentin, please don't say things like that.

300 VALENTIN: The same thing could be happening to her. Right now.

MOLINA: (*melancholy*) You love her very much, don't you. Love should always come first.

VALENTIN: That's great.

(*turns away*)

Now I'd like to eat in peace.

305 MOLINA: Don't worry, I won't disturb you.

(MOLINA *bursts into muffled sobs.*)

VALENTIN: (*annoyed*) What is it now?

MOLINA: (*weepy moans*) It's my mother. She must really be in bad shape or she'd come visit me with groceries. This happened once before.

310 VALENTIN: (*cold*) Sorry to hear that.

(MOLINA *moans more.* VALENTIN *keeps eating and tries to ignore him.* MOLINA *moans louder, then says:*)

MOLINA: Yeah, well, I told you she was sick, but of course you weren't paying any attention.

(*pause*)

But that's not what I'm crying about.

VALENTIN: (*very annoyed*) So what is it, for Chrissake?

315 MOLINA: (*wipes tears*) Because it's so beautiful when lovers are together for a lifetime. Why is it so impossible?

VALENTIN: You gotta be crazy, crying about something like that.

MOLINA: I will cry about whatever I want to.

(*stops crying*)

Valentin, do you think you're the only one who's suffered?
320 You think it's easy to find a real man? One who's humble, and yet has dignity?

(*pause*)

How many years have I been searching? How many nights? How many faces filled with scorn and deceit?

(*Cut to:*)

Ext. store window — day (flashback)

(*The window contains two mannequins dressed as bride and groom.* MOLINA *meticulously adjusts the fluffy bridal gown.*)

VOICE OF MOLINA: You know, working as a window dresser, en-
325 joyable as it is, sometimes at the end of the day you wonder what it's all about. And you feel kind of empty inside.

(*pause*)

Then, one night. . . .

(*Cut to:*)

Int. restaurant — night (flashback)

(MOLINA *takes a table with two effeminate friends. One is black. The other is* GRETA, *31, babbling with chit-chat.*)

GRETA: It's something new she just invented herself. She calls it La Chika-Chaka and she goes chika-chaka, chika-chaka. And she's an overnight sensation, the next day she's in *all* the news-
330 papers, and her husband becomes so jealous because he thinks—

(MOLINA's *eyes are riveted on* GABRIEL, *34, a handsome waiter in a white tunic.*)

GABRIEL: Good evening, gentlemen. Would you care for the daily special? Or would you like to order a la carte?

MOLINA: I haven't decided yet.   335

(GABRIEL *offers a menu and leaves.*)

VOICE OF MOLINA: My heart was pounding . . . so afraid that I would be hurt once again.

(*Cut to:*)

Int. restaurant — night (flashback)

(MOLINA *sits alone, impeccably dressed, immaculately groomed.*)

GABRIEL: Are you ready for me, sir?

MOLINA: What do you suggest?

GABRIEL: Perhaps the lasagna and antipasto.   340

MOLINA: Don't you think the lasagna might be fattening?

GABRIEL: Then perhaps the steak and onion soup.

MOLINA: (*returning to the menu*) Sounds wonderful.

(GABRIEL *goes to place the order.* MOLINA *can't take his eyes off him.*)

VOICE OF MOLINA: His white tunic, the way he moved, his sad smile. Everything seemed so perfect, like in the movies.   345

(*Cut to:*)

Int. restaurant — night (flashback)

(*The restaurant is closed.* GABRIEL *mops the floor. The only customer is* MOLINA, *still in his chair, waiting.*)

VOICE OF MOLINA: You have no idea how much trouble I went through, month after month, just to get him to go for a walk. But little by little I made him see I respected him.

(*Cut to:*)

Int. cell — night

(MOLINA *sits on the floor, hugging his knees.*)

MOLINA: Anyway, after more than a year, we finally became friends.   350

VALENTIN: Jesus, did it take another year to get him in the sack?

MOLINA: Are you out of your mind? Nothing at all happened. Ever!

VALENTIN: You gotta be kidding.

MOLINA: Don't you know anything at all? He's straight. He's   355
married. I said to him, let's do it just once. But he never wanted to.

VALENTIN: I don't believe this. Here I am, staying up all night, thinking about your boyfriend.

(pause)

360   Sounds like a real bind, Molina. All you can do is take it like a man.

MOLINA: I take it like a woman. Always. That's why I want a husband who's the boss.

(MOLINA stretches across the floor toward VALENTIN's bunk. VALENTIN awkwardly changes the subject.)

VALENTIN: Uh, did you ever meet his wife?

365   MOLINA: No, but when they were on the verge of splitting up — God, such illusions I had.

VALENTIN: Like what?

MOLINA: That he might come home to live with me, with my mother and me. And I would take care of him and help him

370   lose that sadness of his forever.

(Cut to:)

Ext. bar district — night (flashback)

(MOLINA and GABRIEL stroll up the narrow street. Most of the garish bars are dark. Male and female HOOKERS stand in shadowy doorways.)

GABRIEL: (shrugs) That's life, Molina.

MOLINA: No, it's a shame. With your looks and charm, you should work in a chic restaurant in a luxury hotel. Making three times what you get in that stinkhole.

375   GABRIEL: It's not so easy.

MOLINA: I know someone who works in a big hotel on the Coast. He could talk to the manager and presto, a new life.

GABRIEL: And be what, a busboy in a snob joint? I'd make less money than now.

380   MOLINA: I could help you with a loan. With your poise, you'd be a waiter in six months.

GABRIEL: I don't know.

MOLINA: Of course you do. And in a year, a maitre d'. In a tuxedo! You could pay me back in no time.

385   GABRIEL: Maybe. Anyway, I appreciate your offer. I'll think about it.

(leaving)

I gotta get my bus, I'm gonna be late. See you tomorrow, Molina.

MOLINA: Goodnight, Gabriel. Kiss the children for me.

(MOLINA watches the bus leave, then heads back down the dark street toward the male HOOKERS. A teenage BOY asks for a light. MOLINA responds and they walk off together.)

390   VOICE OF MOLINA: And then it's over . . . again . . . my dreams disappear . . . into the darkness. And I wake up alone.

(Cut to:)

Int. cell — night)

(MOLINA, stretched out on the floor, looks up at VALENTIN.)

MOLINA: Waiting as always. Waiting and waiting. Waiting and waiting and waiting.

VALENTIN: Waiting for what?

MOLINA: A man. A real man. But that can't happen because a   395
real man, what he wants is a real woman.

VALENTIN: (stands up) Can I ask you a question? What is a real man in your terms?

MOLINA: Well, to be marvelous looking and strong. Without making any fuss about it. And walking very tall. Like my waiter.   400

VALENTIN: He just gives you that impression, but inside it's another story. In this society, without power behind you, no one walks tall.

MOLINA: Don't be jealous.

VALENTIN: Don't be stupid.   405

MOLINA: You see how you react? There's just no talking about a guy with another guy without getting into a fuss.

VALENTIN: (hard) Look, just keep it on a certain level, okay? Or let's not talk at all.

MOLINA: Okay, you tell me what a real man is.   410

VALENTIN: (caught off guard) I don't know.

MOLINA: Sure you do. Go ahead, tell me.

VALENTIN: Well, not taking any crap from anyone, not even the powers-that-be. That's not the most important thing; what really makes a man has to do with not humiliating anybody.   415
It's not letting the people around you feel degraded.

MOLINA: That sounds like a saint.

VALENTIN: Forget it.

(MOLINA suddenly grabs his stomach and doubles over, groaning in pain.)

VALENTIN: What's wrong?

MOLINA: (drops to floor) — My stomach.   420

VALENTIN: Maybe it's your appendix?

MOLINA: No, I had mine out.

(grimacing)

God, it hurts, it hurts!

VALENTIN: You feel like throwing up?

MOLINA: No, it's below there. It's in my guts.   425

(VALENTIN pulls MOLINA to his feet and helps him hobble to his bunk.)

VALENTIN: The food didn't do anything to me.

MOLINA: (lays down) I don't know, maybe it's my ulcer.

(writhing in pain)

I — I don't like this!

VALENTIN: Why don't you go on with your movie?

MOLINA: God, I never felt a pain like this.   430

VALENTIN: Go ahead and tell it.

(Cut to:)

Ext. LENI's apartment — night (Nazi movie)

(LENI stands at her window, waving goodbye to WERNER in his limousine.)

VOICE OF MOLINA: Leni lingers at the window, so sad, so alone, so afraid that she will fall in love.

(Suddenly a hand reaches from the shadows and muffles her scream. It's the half-deaf FLUNKY.)

(Cut to:)

Int. LENI's apartment — night (Nazi movie)

(The FLUNKY *flings* LENI *onto a sofa. She sees the* CLUBFOOT *in her armchair.)*

CLUBFOOT: Tonight the invaders murdered your friend Michelle.

435 LENI: *(shocked)* No.

CLUBFOOT: You must complete her mission and find the secret map to the German arsenal. The Chief of Counter-Intelligence is in love with you.

LENI: I could never get involved with such a thing.

440 CLUBFOOT: *(approaching)* Nonsense, nothing could be safer. Do you love France?

LENI: Of course I do.

CLUBFOOT: That Kraut can't keep his hands off you. Next time he touches you like this—

(fondling her)

445   —and like this, think of your country. And get the map.

*(*LENI *has grasped a statuette of "Justice." She hammers his skull and dashes out the door. The* CLUBFOOT *tumbles to the carpet and shouts at his* FLUNKY.*)*

CLUBFOOT: Stop her, you idiot!

(Cut to:)

Ext. Paris street—night (Nazi movie)

*(*LENI *runs across dark cobblestones, turns a corner and sees a taxi in the distance.)*

LENI: Taxi! Taxi!

(The bleeding CLUBFOOT *lumbers around the corner.)*

VOICE OF MOLINA: Leni, desperate, runs along this dark empty street. The furious Clubfoot hobbles after her, when

450   suddenly—

(Cut to:)

Int. cell—night

*(*MOLINA, *hunched over the edge of his bed, clutches his stomach and whispers:)*

MOLINA: —this girl is finished.

VALENTIN: What girl?

MOLINA: Me, stupid.

*(*MOLINA, *passing out, slumps onto the floor.* VALENTIN *pounds the cell door.)*

VALENTIN: Guard! *Guard!*

(Cut to:)

Int. prison infirmary—night

*(*MOLINA *sleeps on an infirmary cot.)*

(Cut to:)

Int. cell—night

*(*VALENTIN *looks under* MOLINA's *bunk and finds his crucifix neck-chain. He places the gold chain on* MOLINA's *pillow.)*

(Cut to:)

Int. prison infirmary—day

*(*MOLINA, *in bed, reaches for his missing crucifix and looks up at the prison* DOCTOR.*)*

DOCTOR: You're strong enough to go back to your cell. Your 455 diarrhea will stop tomorrow. Till then, no food. Only water. Clean water. If you can find it.

MOLINA: Doctor, I need to see the Warden. Right away.

DOCTOR: *(leaving)* That's what they all say.

(Cut to:)

Int. cell—night

*(*VALENTIN *does pushups on the floor.* MOLINA *pages through glamor magazines on his bunk.)*

VALENTIN: I don't understand how you can pass out from an ulcer. 460

MOLINA: I'm no spring chicken, darling. I'm getting dizzy just looking at these pictures.

*(*MOLINA *sighs for attention.* VALENTIN *says nothing.)*

MOLINA: God, wouldn't it be wonderful if you told me a movie for a change. One that I haven't seen.

VALENTIN: I don't remember any. 465

MOLINA: Don't be like that. Come on, tell me one.

(pause)

   Please.

VALENTIN: Don't be such a cry-baby.

MOLINA: Valentin. Have you ever loved someone you didn't *want* to love? 470

VALENTIN: *(wary)* What do you mean?

MOLINA: Leni didn't want to fall in love with Werner, but what could she do? She steps through his doorway like a goddess. Her slim graceful figure trembles at the sight of Werner descending the marble staircase. Their eyes meet. Leni says— 475

(Cut to:)

Int. chateau—night (Nazi movie)

*(*WERNER *descends his marble stairs.* LENI *stands beside the* BUTLER *in the vestibule.)*

LENI: My best friend has been killed. I need a place to stay.

WERNER: *(to* BUTLER*)* Prepare the guest room.

LENI: This music is magical. I feel like I'm floating on air.

(Wagnerian music fills the baroque chateau. WERNER *leads* LENI *inside.)*

VOICE OF MOLINA: But her heart is saying, Oh Werner, you seem like a god, but your tears— 480

(Cut to:)

Int. cell—night

*(*MOLINA *savors his sad reverie.)*

MOLINA: —your tears are proof you have the feelings of a man.

VALENTIN: Quiet! I can't hear.

*(*VALENTIN *peers through the wall plate and sees two* GUARDS *returning the* HOODED PRISONER *in blood-stained underpants. His skin is covered with welts and burns.*

VALENTIN *bangs the door with his metal cup.)*

VALENTIN: Murderers! Fascist murderers. Fascist murderers!

(More prisoners join the protest. The GUARDS *use clubs to crush the outbreak.*

VALENTIN *sees a* GUARD's *shoes facing his cell. Suddenly a stream of urine splashes onto* VALENTIN. *Sound of* GUARDS *laughing.*)

VALENTIN: Motherfucker. Motherfucker!

485 MOLINA: I'll clean it up.

(VALENTIN, *furious, spins around and hurls his metal cup at* MOLINA's *head.* MOLINA *ducks.* VALENTIN *stalks forward.*)

VALENTIN: You son of a bitch! They're killing one of my brothers and what am I doing? Listening to your fucking Nazi movie!

(MOLINA *clutches his ragdoll to his chest.*)

VALENTIN: Don't you know what the Nazis did to people — Jews, Marxists, Catholics? Homosexuals!

490 MOLINA: Of course I know. What do you take me for, an even dumber broad than I am?

(VALENTIN *grabs* MOLINA *and hurls him headfirst across the cell, then fires the doll at his face.* MOLINA *cowers on the floor.* VALENTIN *clenches his fist and approaches.*)

VALENTIN: You don't know shit. You wouldn't know reality if it was stuck up your ass.

MOLINA: (*terrified*) Why should I think about reality in a stink-
495 hole like this? Why should I get more depressed than I already am?

(MOLINA *shrinks back into the corner.* VALENTIN, *seething, kneels down and rips off* MOLINA's *earrings.*)

VALENTIN: You're worse than I thought. You just use these movies to jerk yourself off.

MOLINA: (*bursts into tears*) If you don't stop, I will never speak to
500 you again.

VALENTIN: Stop crying! You sound just like an old woman.

MOLINA: (*sobbing*) That's what I am, that's what I am.

(MOLINA *looks down, whimpering.* VALENTIN *violently wrenches apart* MOLINA's *knees.*)

VALENTIN: What's this between your legs? Huh? Tell me, "lady"!

MOLINA: It's an accident. If I had the courage, I'd cut if off.

(MOLINA *struggles to regain his dignity.* VALENTIN *moves in for the kill.*)

505 VALENTIN: You'd still be a man! A man in prison, just like the faggots the Nazis shoved in the ovens.

MOLINA: (*pleading*) Don't. Don't look at me like that.

(MOLINA, *sobbing, looks up at the barred window.*)

(*Cut to:*)

Int. courtroom — day (flashback)

(MOLINA *stands beside his* LAWYER, *facing the massive oak desk. The* JUDGE *glowers down at him.*)

JUDGE: . . . Luis Alberto Molina. You shall endure the full weight of the law and not one day less. You will be confined
510 without chance of parole for a period of not less than eight years.

(MOLINA *turns from the* JUDGE *to gaze forlornly at his* MOTHER. *She pulls a handkerchief from her purse. As their eyes meet, she smiles warmly through her tears.*)

VOICE OF MOLINA: Poor Mama. Her eyes full of tears as if someone had died. A life full of humiliation and then the

humiliation of a son steeped in vice, but she never gave me that black look. Her heart broken by too much suffering, too much forgiving. Because of me she could die. 515

(*Cut to:*)

Int. cell — day

(MOLINA's *red eyes are stark and determined.*)

MOLINA: If he ever says one unkind word about her, I'll strangle the son of a bitch. Him and his filthy words and his piss-ass revolution.

(*Lightning flashes through the barred window.*)

(*Cut to:*)

Int. cell — night

(*Two plates are shoved through the food slot.* MOLINA, *still angry, plops one on* VALENTIN's *bunk and goes to eat by the window. Lightning flashes.*

Suddenly VALENTIN *clutches his stomach and groans in pain.* MOLINA *rushes to his side.*)

VALENTIN: My stomach. It's like a bomb exploding.

MOLINA: The same thing I had. 520

VALENTIN: (*grimacing*) I think it's the food.

MOLINA: You gotta go to the Infirmary right now. — Guard!

(MOLINA *hurries to the door.* VALENTIN *lunges forward and grabs him.*)

VALENTIN: No! Wait. Stop.

MOLINA: Why?

VALENTIN: I'm a political prisoner. 525

MOLINA: Don't be ridiculous. This is no time for your damn discipline.

VALENTIN: Get away from the door.

MOLINA: They gave me a shot, and I'm better already.

VALENTIN: Are you crazy? That's just what they want. They get 530 me hooked on those shots, and I'll tell them everything.

MOLINA: What else can we do?

(VALENTIN, *groaning, returns to his bunk and mutters:*)

VALENTIN: Leave me alone.

(MOLINA *thinks, then gets a scarf and says:*)

MOLINA: What about my movie? It might help you forget the pain.

(*Cut to:*)

Ext. chateau — night (Nazi movie)

(LENI *and* WERNER *slowly waltz among billowing white curtains.*)

VOICE OF MOLINA: Later that night, on the moonlit veranda, 535 Leni feels so safe, so secure in Werner's arms.

(*music stops*)

Even when the phonograph stops, they continue dancing . . . dancing.

(*Cut to:*)

Int. cell — night

(MOLINA *dances with the scarf as if his empty arms held* WERNER.)

MOLINA: To the music of the evening breezes, whooh, whoooh.

(MOLINA *sees* VALENTIN *shivering in his sleep, drenched with sweat. He kneels down and wipes* VALENTIN's *fevered forehead with the scarf.*)

540   VALENTIN: (*asleep*) Marta . . . Marta.

(*opens eyes*)

. . . who are you?

MOLINA: It's okay. Try to rest.

(VALENTIN *closes his weary eyes.* MOLINA *tenderly adjusts the blanket.*)

Int. cell — night

(*Both men are eating.* MOLINA *watches* VALENTIN *reading a letter.*)

MOLINA: You shouldn't eat this garbage while you're sick.
VALENTIN: (*keeps eating*) I have to get my strength back.
545   MOLINA: It'll only make you worse.
VALENTIN: Tastes like dog piss.
MOLINA: (*shakes his head*) My poor little Valentina.
VALENTIN: Don't call me Valentina. I'm not a woman.
MOLINA: (*leans forward*) Well, I've never seen proof to the
550   contrary.
VALENTIN: And you never will.
MOLINA: Now, the Clubfoot told —

(VALENTIN *grimaces in disgust.*)

MOLINA: You'll like this part, wait and see.

(*Cut to:*)

Int. WERNER's *bedroom — day (Nazi movie)*

(LENI *wakes in a lavish antique bed, reaches for* WERNER *and discovers he is gone.*)

VOICE OF MOLINA: The Clubfoot told Leni that her sweet lover
555   was ordering the execution of her countrymen everyday. But she refused to believe it. She only wanted to live this love, to feel his touch, to hear his voice.

(*The phone rings.* LENI *eavesdrops on* WERNER.)

WERNER'S VOICE: It's a difficult decision.
CALLER'S VOICE: Ja, Herr Commandant.

(*Cut to:*)

Int. WERNER's *study — day (Nazi movie)*

(WERNER, *in uniform, stands at a desk piled with documents.*)

560   CALLER'S VOICE: We captured ten of them. They're all French, but their activities prove they are enemies of the people.
WERNER: They call themselves patriots, but in fact they are common criminals.

(*Cut to:*)

Int. WERNER's *bedroom — day (Nazi movie)*

(LENI *sits up in shock.*)

WERNER'S VOICE: Let the execution take place at dawn.

(*Cut to:*)

Int. cell — night

(MOLINA *looks at his fingers.*)

MOLINA: Her fingers tremble with the agony of betraying the   565
man she loves.

(VALENTIN *suddenly curls up with pain.*)

VALENTIN: It's like a nail in my gut.

(*pause*)

That's better. Do me a favor and stop all this crap about beautiful women in tears.

(MOLINA *goes to the corner for coconut shells and returns, clutching them to his chest under his robe.*)

MOLINA: Leni's heart was beating so fast that her swelling breasts   570
leapt out of her low-cut gown. Like luscious hors d'oeuvres on a silver platter.

(VALENTIN *chokes with laughter.*)

VALENTIN: Don't make me laugh. It hurts.

(MOLINA *opens his robe, revealing the coconut-shell breasts.*)

MOLINA: Here, have a nice juicy tit. Have another. The best
places serve them in pairs.   575

(VALENTIN *laughs out loud. Suddenly, his eyes snap open in pain. Trying to sit up, he clutches his pants and points to the shit-bucket.*)

VALENTIN: The bucket! Quick!

(MOLINA *dashes to the bucket.* VALENTIN *struggles to his feet and tugs his zipper. Diarrhea fills his trousers.* VALENTIN *collapses on the floor, covering his face in shame.*)

VALENTIN: Oh, no.
MOLINA: Christ, what a smell.
VALENTIN: (*groaning*) I'm sorry. You don't know how much it
hurts.   580
MOLINA: Let it all out. It can't smell any worse than it already does.
VALENTIN: God, I can't stand this.

(VALENTIN *trembles on the floor.* MOLINA *pulls the sheet from his own bed and grabs some rags.*)

MOLINA: You've been through worse. Much worse.
VALENTIN: I'm so ashamed.
MOLINA: Aren't you the one always saying take it like a man? So   585
what's this business about being embarrassed?
VALENTIN: I can't stand it. I can't stand myself like this.

(VALENTIN *lifts his hand to hide his tears.* MOLINA *kneels down with maternal concern.*)

MOLINA: Take off your pants. Cover yourself with this. Why do
you always have to pick on yourself so much?

(MOLINA *tosses the soiled trousers and underpants beside the bucket, then grabs the rags.*)

MOLINA: Wipe yourself off.   590
VALENTIN: No, it's yours.
MOLINA: No, it's ours. Wipe yourself. There's a little more here,
and here.

(VALENTIN *struggles to remove the glop from his buttocks.* MOLINA *wipes the brown liquid from his ankles.*

Despondent, VALENTIN *gives up.* MOLINA, *taking over, cleans his thighs and buttocks like a mother cleaning a child.*)

VALENTIN: *(turning away)* Jesus, aren't you disgusted?
595 MOLINA: No, it breaks my heart to see you like this. There, almost finished. Good. Now take off your shirt.
VALENTIN: No, it's alright.
MOLINA: The shirt-tails are soiled. Please.

(VALENTIN *removes his shirt. Tossing it,* MOLINA *feels a letter in the pocket and keeps it.*)

MOLINA: Okay, now try and stand up.

(MOLINA, *tenderly insistent, helps him to his feet and puts the bedsheet around his shoulders.*)

600 VALENTIN: No, it'll stink.
MOLINA: My weekly shower is tomorrow. I'll have it all clean by noon. There we go. All wrapped up like a little papoose.

(MOLINA *wraps the bedsheet around him like a toga and helps him crawl back in bed.*)

VALENTIN: It doesn't disgust you?
MOLINA: Lie down. Don't want you to catch a chill. What a
605 shame I have no talcum left. Are you comfortable now?
VALENTIN: Yes, but I'm so cold.
MOLINA: I'll make you a nice hot cup of tea.

(VALENTIN, *deeply touched, watches him pour a cup.*)

MOLINA: This will work wonders.

(hands cup)

It's hot, you'll burn yourself.

(VALENTIN *takes a sip.*)

610 VALENTIN: You're very kind, honestly, I don't know what to say.
MOLINA: Don't burn yourself.

(MOLINA *finishes cleaning the floor, then pulls out the hidden letter.*)

MOLINA: Oh, uh, this fell out of your shirt.
VALENTIN: Go ahead, read it. I know you've been curious.
MOLINA: No, I only read love letters. I don't want to know any
615 thing about your politics.
VALENTIN: It's from my girlfriend. Her name is Lydia.
MOLINA: —What about Marta?
VALENTIN: *(bolts upright)* How do you know about Marta?
MOLINA: You mumbled her name in your sleep.
620 VALENTIN: *(worried)* What else did I mumble?
MOLINA: Nothing.
VALENTIN: The letter's from Lydia. She's my girlfriend in the movement.

(MOLINA *opens the pages and scans the letter.*)

MOLINA: Her handwriting is like a child's.
625 VALENTIN: —She hasn't had much of an education.

(VALENTIN *lays back down with a sigh.*)

VALENTIN: I'm going to tell you the truth. During torture, whenever I felt close to death, it was Marta I would think about, and she would save me. My whole body ached to hold her.
630 MOLINA: What's she like?

VALENTIN: She's upper-class. Pure bourgeoisie. She's got everything. Money, looks, education, freedom. I'm such a hypocrite. Just like all those class-conscious pigs.

(pause)

I must admit it was convenient, a safe place to stay when I was forced to hide. Until one day I had to tell her about my other 635
life.

(Cut to:)

Int. high-rise apartment—day (flashback)

(MARTA, 29, *puts out a cigarette and listens.*)

VOICE OF VALENTIN: She just listened in silence like she knew already. Then she asked me to leave the movement. But how could I do nothing when my friends were disappearing every day? I sensed that she was right but I had no choice. So once 640
again I didn't know what to say.

(MARTA *steps onto the balcony and looks at the city. Her strong eyes brim with tears.* VALENTIN *approaches.*)

VALENTIN: Things are what they are. I'll be back in a few days. Same as always.
MARTA: I can't take it any more. Always waiting, watching the phone. Always alone. 645

(VALENTIN *brushes back her long black hair and kisses her cheek. She makes no response. He turns to leave.*)

MARTA: *(fights back tears)* Valentin. If you leave, don't come back. Please, don't come back.

(VALENTIN *hesitates, then leaves.*)

(Cut to:)

Int. train—day (flashback)

(VALENTIN, *deep in thought, stares out the train window at the passing slums.*)

VOICE OF VALENTIN: I no longer believed in violence, but I had to do something. As a journalist, I was always hearing about the illegal arrests and secret torture, then leaking this infor 650
mation abroad.

(Cut to:)

Ext. train station—day (flashback)

(*The train pulls into a station.* VALENTIN *steps onto the platform.*)

VOICE OF VALENTIN: My assignment was to meet one of the last surviving members of the original movement. His code name was Americo. He needed my passport to leave the country.

(VALENTIN *approaches an old man.* AMERICO, 62, *walks with a cane toward a railing.* VALENTIN *stops beside him.*)

VALENTIN: Are you all right? 655
AMERICO: A little tired.
VALENTIN: You should have left long ago, Doctor Americo.
AMERICO: *(points down)* This is where I'm needed.
VALENTIN: I keep wondering if it's all worth it—when nothing really changes. 660

(VALENTIN *tugs the passport from his pocket and slides it along the railing.*)

VALENTIN: Well, good luck. Here's your passport. Take care of yourself.

AMERICO: Thank you.

(AMERICO *walks away.* VALENTIN *stays at the railing.*)

VOICE OF VALENTIN: He had accomplished almost nothing,
665   but I was glad I could help him.

(*Cut to:*)

Ext. station entrance—day (flashback)

(*Reaching street level,* VALENTIN *steps off the escalator and enters the turnstyle. Suddenly three* PLAIN-CLOTHES AGENTS *surround him with guns.*)

Their burly leader, PEDRO, *44, black, spins* VALENTIN *around and jams an automatic pistol in the back of his head.*)

PEDRO: Freeze! Stop!

(*frisks him*)

   Open your legs.

(*handcuffs him*)

   Move!

(PEDRO *shoves* VALENTIN *toward a black car.*)

VOICE OF MOLINA: What happened to Marta?

(*Cut to:*)

Int. cell—night

(VALENTIN, *tormented, lays on his bunk in the sheet.* MOLINA *sits at the foot of the bed.*)

670   VALENTIN: I don't know anything for sure. Except that I'll never see her again.

MOLINA: Don't say that.

VALENTIN: (*writhing*) I don't deserve to die in this cell. I only confessed some code names they already knew. I can't stand
675   being a martyr, it infuriates me. I don't *want* to be a martyr.

(*deeply depressed*)

   My whole life . . . a mistake.

MOLINA: No.

(VALENTIN, *fighting despair, extends his hand.*)

VALENTIN: Give me your hand.

(MOLINA *grips his hand tightly.* VALENTIN *whispers:*)

VALENTIN: I don't want to die, Molina. I don't want to die.
680   Don't let me die.

MOLINA: (*grips tighter*) Of course not.

(*Cut to:*)

Int. WARDEN'S *office—day*

(*The* WARDEN, *60, gray-haired in a business suit, leans forward at his large desk.*)

WARDEN: You look thin, Molina, what's the matter?

MOLINA: It's nothing, sir. I was sick, but I'm better now.

WARDEN: So stop trembling. There's nothing to be afraid of.

(*pause*)

685   Arregui doesn't suspect anything, does he?

MOLINA: No, sir.

WARDEN: What has he told you?

MOLINA: Uhh. Nothing yet. He, uh, I feel I should proceed very cautiously.

(*Stepping from the adjoining bathroom is* PEDRO, *the Secret Agent who arrested* VALENTIN. *Wearing a three-piece suit, he adjusts his tie and measures* MOLINA *with ice-cold eyes.*)

PEDRO: Molina, you are lying. What are you hiding?   690

MOLINA: Nothing.

(*to* WARDEN)

   How can you accuse me when I almost died for you? He insisted I eat the bowl with the poison.

(*The* WARDEN *pushes back from his desk and rolls around front in a wheelchair.*)

WARDEN: Why? You made a mistake there.

MOLINA: One plate had twice as much as the other one, so he   695
insisted I eat the larger portion. Sir, you told me the poisoned food would be in a new tin plate, but they loaded it up so much I had no choice. I had to eat it myself, or he would've become suspicious.

WARDEN: Poor Molina. I'm sorry for the mix-up. I commend   700
you. Sit down here. Please.

(MOLINA *takes a seat. The* WARDEN *wheels closer, treating him like a child.*)

WARDEN: Your mother's feeling much better since she learned you may be paroled.

MOLINA: Really?

WARDEN: Of course. So stop crying. You should be pleased.   705

MOLINA: It's from happiness, sir.

(PEDRO *takes the chair beside* MOLINA *and says curtly:*)

PEDRO: What did Valentin say about his cadre?

MOLINA: (*puzzled*) His what?

PEDRO: His group—who they are, where they meet.

MOLINA: Nothing, sir. He is very sick. If he has anymore poison,   710
I don't know *what* will happen.

PEDRO: His girlfriend, what'd he say about her?

MOLINA: He says personal things are secondary to revolution, he thinks everything else is trash, so I think he's warming up to talking about it.   715

(*the* WARDEN *hands him a cup of coffee.*)

MOLINA: For me? Thank you.

PEDRO: What did he say about the new prisoner? The one across the hall.

MOLINA: The one who's all messed up? He said that no crime justifies that kind of punishment.   720

(*takes a sip*)

   This coffee really hits the spot.

PEDRO: Did he tell you his name?

MOLINA: (*puzzled*) Of course, sir. It's Valentin Arregui.

PEDRO: No, you idiot! The name of the new prisoner.

MOLINA: (*frightened*) Of course not. He's always wearing a hood.   725

(PEDRO, *furious, glances at the* WARDEN.)

PEDRO: Who put a hood on him?

WARDEN: (*worried*) It's routine. He's political.

PEDRO: How do you expect him to talk if he can't even see the bastard's face?

730   WARDEN: It won't happen again.

(PEDRO *looks at his "female" prisoner. He's not sure if this "actress" is really naive—or just pretending.*)

PEDRO: Molina, we gotta know everything they're planning.

(*pause*)

As soon as he sees that new prisoner's face, he'll spill his guts. Remember every damn word he says.

MOLINA: Yes, sir.

735   PEDRO: The quicker he talks, the quicker you get out. Now get back to work.

(MOLINA *stands up to leave, then hesitates.*)

MOLINA: Uh, Warden, one more thing. He heard the guard say my mother was coming. And I told him that, uh, she always brings me a bag full of groceries. I don't want him to get
740   suspicious.

WARDEN: Okay, dictate what she brings.

MOLINA: To you, sir?

WARDEN: Yes, to me! And make it quick. I'm busy.

MOLINA: Um. Two roast chickens in butter, egg salad, canned
745   peaches, condensed milk. Two boxes of tea—one regular, one camomile. A jar of pickled herring, four bars of toilet soap. What else?

(PEDRO, *disgusted, watches the* WARDEN *write it down.* MOLINA *nervously taps his teeth, watching from the corner of his eye, pushing them to the limit.*)

MOLINA: Blessed Mary, my mind's a blank. Let me think. Rye bread. Sugar, I need. Uhh.

(*The* WARDEN, *exasperated, eyes the ceiling.*)

(*Cut to:*)

Int. cell—day

(VALENTIN *struggles to sit up in bed.* MOLINA, *victorious, unpacks two bags of groceries.*)

750   MOLINA: Roast chickens! Canned peaches! Cheddar cheese! Rye bread!

VALENTIN: What happened?

MOLINA: Look at this. Two roast chickens, *two*! How about that. Just watch how fast you get better now.

755   VALENTIN: Your mother came.

MOLINA: Yes! Tea, sugar, and—

(*proud chuckle*)

cigarettes.

VALENTIN: That's great. How is she?

MOLINA: Oh, she's much better, thank you. And look at all she
760   brought me. I mean *us*.

VALENTIN: Well, really that's all meant for you.

MOLINA: No, you have to stop eating that damn prison chow, and you'll feel better in no time.

VALENTIN: You think so?

765   MOLINA: You're damn right I do. Starting today a new life begins. Oh, I took a chance and left the sheets out to dry, and no

one walked away with them. So tonight we both have clean sheets.

(*He tosses the sheets.* VALENTIN *catches them and smiles.*)

VALENTIN: Nice going.

MOLINA: (*lights the burner*) Let me get this started and presto, in   770
a few minutes you'll be licking your fingers. I expect you to eat all of those chickens, *both* of them.

VALENTIN: But what about you? I'm not gonna let you just sit around and drool.

MOLINA: No, I've gotta keep an eye on my girlish figure. At least   775
what's left of it.

(VALENTIN *reaches for the peaches.* MOLINA *slaps his hand.*)

MOLINA: Not yet, that's for dessert.

(*time cut:*)

Spread across the floor is a picnic blanket of leftovers. VALENTIN *relaxes with a cigarette.* MOLINA *stretches.*)

MOLINA: Would you like some more peaches?

VALENTIN: No thanks. I'm stuffed.

(*rubs stomach*)

Good food, good cigarette. I don't remember when I felt so   780
good. There's only one thing missing.

MOLINA: Christ! And I thought I was supposed to be the one who's the degenerate around here.

VALENTIN: (*laughs*) No, I mean a good movie.

MOLINA: Of course! Jeez, why didn't I think of that?   785

VALENTIN: Your Nazi movie, how does it end?

MOLINA: I thought you hated it.

VALENTIN: Yeah, but I'm curious to see how it turns out.

MOLINA: (*stands up*) Well, let's see.

(*Cut to:*)

Int. WERNER's *dining room—night (Nazi movie)*

(LENI *and* WERNER *sit at a magnificent table.*)

VOICE OF MOLINA: They are dining at the majestic table in   790
Werner's chateau. As Werner begins to notice Leni's cold distance, she suddenly—

(LENI *stands up with a crystal goblet.* INSERT: *In the cell,* MOLINA *flings his tin cup at the wall. In the chateau, his tin cup turns into her crystal goblet.*)

VOICE OF MOLINA: —impulsively, hurls her wine glass across the room and says—

LENI: I refuse to love a man who is the butcher of my country.   795

WERNER: (*stands up*) Oh, my love. Come with me and you'll understand.

(*Cut to:*)

Int. cell—day

(MOLINA *and* VALENTIN *sit side-by-side against the wall. In the fading daylight,* MOLINA *spins his delicate web.*)

MOLINA: Werner takes her to this government archive, filled with photos and documents about famine throughout the world.   800

(Cut to:)

Int. projection room—day (Nazi movie)

(Slides show the tragedy of famine. LENI wipes a teardrop.)

VOICE OF MOLINA: He shows her how the elite create false shortages to enslave the masses. Leni is deeply moved and begins to see things through Werner's eyes.

(Cut to:)

Ext. government archive—day (Nazi movie)

(LENI and WERNER walk arm-in-arm along a corridor of columns.)

VOICE OF MOLINA: From that moment on, Leni understood
805   Werner's mission. To liberate humanity from injustice and domination. As they leave the baroque archive, Leni feels the anguish in her heart being transformed back to her previous admiration, but this time with the depth of a love reborn.

(LENI stops on the balustrade and looks into his eyes.)

LENI: My love, how could I ever have doubted you.

(Cut to:)

Int. cell—night

(In the darkened cell MOLINA quietly says:)

810   MOLINA: She begs him to forgive her and promises to help ensnare his enemies.

(Cut to:)

Int. car—night (Nazi movie)

(The FLUNKY drives an old sedan with LENI in the backseat.)

VOICE OF MOLINA: She arranges this secret meeting with the head of the Resistance by telling him that she will give the map—remember the map?—only to him.

(Cut to:)

Ext. castle—night (Nazi movie)

(The sedan stops beside a dark castle. LENI runs up the stone steps and enters an underground tunnel. The FLUNKY waits at the entrance.)

(Cut to:)

Int. castle—night (Nazi movie)

(LENI enters an underground chamber and sees the Resistance LEADER in the shadows.)

815   LENI: *(offers map)* I believe this is what you want.
LEADER: Yes, well done. So often I was tempted to steal it from him myself. But some things are best done by a woman. A woman who betrays the man she loves.

(The LEADER steps from the shadows with a lecherous grin.)

LEADER: And there is something else I have wanted almost as
820   much as the map.
LENI: What?

(Taking the map, the LEADER backs LENI against the wall and nuzzles her neck.)

LEADER: You know very well. I've prepared a lavish banquet for two.

LENI: I'm not hungry.
LEADER: I am. For you.   825

(He paws her. LENI, struggling, spots a steak knife on the banquet table. Pretending to submit, she maneuvers him sideways and grabs the knife.

Kissing him, she plunges the blade into his back. The LEADER moans and topples to the floor.

LENI grabs the map and dashes into the dark tunnel.)

(Cut to:)

Ext. castle—night (Nazi movie)

(Rushing outside, LENI is grabbed by the FLUNKY. She elbows his throat and starts down the stone stairs.

He pulls a handgun and aims at her but, suddenly, is shot in the chest and drops to the ground.

WERNER stands at the foot of the stairway with a smoking pistol. LENI, smiling, rushes into his embrace and kisses him.

The dying FLUNKY raises his gun and fires. LENI slumps back and dies in WERNER's arms.)

VOICE OF MOLINA: Werner hears her sing. She sings like never before. She sings of her eternal love for him and—

(Cut to:)

Int. cell—night

(They sit side-by-side in the dark. VALENTIN is wrapped in his blanket. MOLINA is rapt in his web.)

MOLINA: —begs him not to cry, because her sacrifice was not in vain.

(sighs)

The End.   830

(pause)

What did you think?
VALENTIN: *(shrugs)* You told it well. Next time tell one I like.
MOLINA: Come off it, the love story was divine. Forget about the rest. It's so perfect when Leni—

(corridor noise)

What's going on?   835

(VALENTIN jumps up)

What is it?

(VALENTIN peers through the wall plate and sees two GUARDS dragging the HOODED PRISONER to his cell. He has no hood.)

VALENTIN: *(stunned)* That guy is Americo.
MOLINA: Who?
VALENTIN: The man with my passport.

(looks down)

They don't know he's here.   840
MOLINA: Who doesn't know?

(VALENTIN, depressed, turns to the wall.)

MOLINA: Please, Valentin. Maybe I can help.

(VALENTIN says nothing.)

(Cut to:)

Ext. prison courtyard—day

(A prison WORK CREW *cleans out* AMERICO's *empty cell. They toss his bloody shirt in a trash can.)*

(Cut to:)

Int. cell—day

*(*MOLINA *watches through the wall plate, then hears* VALENTIN *waking up.)*

MOLINA: Good morning. Did you sleep well?
VALENTIN: *(glances down)* Turn the other way, will you?
845   MOLINA: Why?
VALENTIN: Because you'll laugh.
MOLINA: At what?
VALENTIN: Something on any healthy man, that's all.
MOLINA: A hard-on. Well, that *is* healthy.

(turns away)

850   Should I close my eyes too?

*(*VALENTIN *grins and wraps a towel around his waist.)*

VALENTIN: Hey, I missed breakfast. Why didn't you wake me?
MOLINA: I told the guard not to bring anything as long as our food holds out.
VALENTIN: Dammit, Molina, stop running my life for me.

*(*MOLINA *nods an apology.* VALENTIN *moves toward the crack in the wall plate.)*

855   MOLINA: They already took him away. I didn't want to wake you. The water's almost hot if you want some tea.

*(*VALENTIN *stares at dead* AMERICO's *cell.* MOLINA *unwraps some baked goods.)*

MOLINA: Have some cake.
VALENTIN: You eat it.
MOLINA: *(offers cake)* Come on, let me spoil you a little bit.
860   VALENTIN: *(turns, glares)* Back off, Molina.
MOLINA: It's not my fault they killed your friend.
VALENTIN: Shut up!

(slaps cake)

You damn faggot!

(Cut to:)

Ext. prison corridor—day

(Two GUARDS *escort* MOLINA *across the courtyard and open his cell door. He carries two new bags of groceries.)*

(Cut to:)

Int. cell—day

*(*MOLINA *puts down the bags and pulls out a red heart-shaped box of candy.)*

MOLINA: Look at the wonderful things Mama brought me. And
865   there's a special treat. Assorted bonbons.

*(*VALENTIN *watches in silence from his bunk, his hands folded around his knee.* MOLINA *sits near him with the candy box.)*

MOLINA: What's the matter? You don't like candy?

VALENTIN: About this morning . . . about my temper, I'm really sorry.
MOLINA: Oh, nonsense.
VALENTIN: It wasn't even you I was mad at.   870

(pause)

But I've been thinking. Maybe I *am* mad at you.
MOLINA: Why?
VALENTIN: Because you're so kind. I don't want to feel obligated to treat you the same way.
MOLINA: *(sing-song)* "Unable to take, unable to give."   875

*(*MOLINA *opens the candy box and slides it toward* VALENTIN.*)*

VOICE OF MOLINA: Every day he opens up more and more with me.

*(*NOTE: *We leave and return to the candy in the cell as* MOLINA *recalls his latest meeting with the* WARDEN *and* PEDRO.*)*

(Cut to:)

Ext. prison rooftop—day

*(*MOLINA *faces them on the prison roof.)*

MOLINA: *(continues)* Just give me a few more days. I'm sure he'll talk.
PEDRO: If he don't, he'll be interrogated again. And thoroughly   880
this time.
MOLINA: But he's too weak to be tortured. If he drops dead, we all lose out.

(Cut to:)

Int. cell—dusk

*(*VALENTIN *sits on the floor beside the half-empty candy box.)*

VALENTIN: I can't take someone being nice to me without asking anything in return.   885
MOLINA: Well, if I'm nice to you, it's because I want your friendship and, why not say it? . . . your affection.

(offers cigarette)

The same way I try to be nice to my mother who's never harmed anyone, and who accepts me for what I am and loves me. It's like a gift from heaven, and the only thing that keeps   890
me going, the only thing.

(lights cigarette)

And you too are a very good person.

*(*VALENTIN, *embarrassed, moves to the wall and smokes the cigarette.)*

MOLINA: Very selfless and devoted, risking your life for your ideals, ready to die even in here for what you believe in. Am I embarrassing you?   895
VALENTIN: *(shrugs)* No.

(Cut to:)

Ext. prison rooftop—day

*(*MOLINA *turns to the* WARDEN.*)*

MOLINA: Well, sir, there might be a way to speed this up. I'm not sure but I'm—it's just a hunch.
WARDEN: *(exasperated)* Say it straight, Molina.

900 MOLINA: You know inmates, sir. When a cell-mate leaves, they feel all sentimental and helpless. Well, he's gotten a bit attached to me, so if he thought that I was being released, he's bound to open up and talk. Get a few things off his chest.

WARDEN: *(to* PEDRO*)* What do you think?

(Cut to:)

Int. cell — night

(VALENTIN *still leans against the wall with his cigarette.* MOLINA *watches from the bunk.)*

905 MOLINA: So that's why I respect you and like you, and hope that you feel the same way about me. So I want us always to be friends.

VALENTIN: Sure.

MOLINA: The reason I wanted to get this in the open is because I
910 may be leaving, since I just heard from the Warden that I may be paroled soon.

VALENTIN: — When?

(Cut to:)

Ext. prison rooftop — day

(PEDRO *removes his suitcoat, revealing a shoulder holster.)*

PEDRO: Tell him you're up for parole, that we're gonna move you to another cell in 24 hours.

915 MOLINA: Yes, sir.

WARDEN: And this is your last chance, so get going. You got 24 hours.

MOLINA: One thing, sir. You can't catch a fish without bait. I need more food. This time, sir, I prepared a list.

(MOLINA *hands him a long list.)*

(Cut to:)

Int. cell — night

(MOLINA *still sits on* VALENTIN*'s bunk.)*

920 MOLINA: They'll probably move me to another cell in 24 hours. My lawyer says that's the procedure.

(VALENTIN *turns away.* MOLINA *walks back to his own bunk.)*

MOLINA: I don't want to get my hopes up too high. Do you want an apple?

VALENTIN: No, thanks. I guess I should be happy for you, but
925 uh — I don't know.

MOLINA: Yes, all I wanted in life was to get out of here and take care of my mother. Nothing else mattered, but now that my wish might be —

VALENTIN: Be happy, dammit. I'd give anything to get out.

930 MOLINA: But is it fair?

VALENTIN: What?

MOLINA: That I always end up with nothing. That I don't have anything truly my own in life.

VALENTIN: You've got your mother.

935 MOLINA: Yes, but listen though. She's had a life and lived it. She had a husband and a son, but I'm still waiting.

VALENTIN: At least she's still alive.

MOLINA: But so am I. When is my life supposed to begin?

(pause)

When do I strike it lucky and have something for my own?

VALENTIN: *(approaches)* Right now. You just *got* lucky. Take ad-   940
vantage of it. You're getting out.

MOLINA: And do what? Hang out with my friends, a bunch of silly old queens like me? Tell a few jokes until I can't stand the sight of them, because they're a bunch of mirrors that send me running for my life? My life of waiting for nothing.   945

VALENTIN: Tell a movie. You'll feel better.

(Curfew buzzer. The dim light bulb goes out. VALENTIN *moves to his bunk.*

Alone in the dark, MOLINA *turns to the moonlit window and spins another web.)*

MOLINA: Once upon a time, on a tropical island far away, there lived a strange woman.

(pause)

She wore a long gown of black lamé that fit her like a glove. But the poor thing, she was caught in a giant spider web that   950
grew from her own body.

(Cut to:)

Ext. tropical beach — night (Spider movie)

(The masked SPIDER WOMAN *stands silhouetted against the moonlit ocean, waiting and waiting inside a huge silvery spider web. Gliding from the web, she moves across the sandy beach and slowly approaches the body of a* MAN *washed onto her island shore.)*

VOICE OF MOLINA: One day a shipwrecked man drifted onto the beach.

(She kneels in the sand beside him. Insert: VALENTIN *leans against the cell wall, listening in the candlelight.)*

VOICE OF MOLINA: She fed him and cared for his wounds. She nourished him with love and brought him back to life.   955

(The SHIPWRECKED MAN *opens his eyes.)*

VOICE OF MOLINA: When he awoke, he gazed up at the Spider Woman and saw a perfect tear-drop slide from under her mask.

(Cut to:)

Int. cell — night

(Misty-eyed, MOLINA *steps into the candlelight and approaches* VALENTIN. *Insert: The* SHIPWRECKED MAN *lifts his head for a closer look at the* SPIDER WOMAN.*)*

VOICE OF VALENTIN: Why is she crying?

*(MOLINA *answers with a lump in his throat.)*

MOLINA: I don't know. Why do you always need explanations?

(sad sigh)

Valentin, I'm tired. Tired of suffering. You're not the only   960
one they've hurt. You don't know, I hurt so much inside.

VALENTIN: Where does it hurt you?

MOLINA: In my neck and shoulders. Why does the sadness always jam up in the same spot?

*(VALENTIN *places a sympathetic hand on his shoulder.* MOLINA *tightens up and pulls away.)*

965 MOLINA: Please. Don't touch me.
VALENTIN: Can't a friend even pat your back?
MOLINA: *(sits on bunk)* It only makes it worse.
VALENTIN: Why?

(MOLINA, *dropping his many masks, speaks with stark vulnerability.*)

MOLINA: Because I've fallen in love with you.

(pause)

970   I'm sorry, Valentin, I wish it hadn't happened.
VALENTIN: *(looks away)* I understand.

(looks back)

   Don't be ashamed.

(VALENTIN *moves to* MOLINA's *bunk and tentatively sits down.* MOLINA, *motionless, keeps looking away.* VALENTIN *clears his throat and says:*)

VALENTIN: Can I touch you?
MOLINA: *(looking away)* If it doesn't disgust you.

(pause)

975   I'd like you to.

(VALENTIN *wraps a friendly arm around his shoulders.* MOLINA *shudders, then turns and looks apprehensively into his eyes.*)

MOLINA: Can I touch your scar?
VALENTIN: *(shrugs)* Sure.

(MOLINA *gently caresses the scar near* VALENTIN's *eyebrow, then rests his head on* VALENTIN's *chest and whispers:*)

MOLINA: Do what you want with me, because that's what I want.

(pause)

   If it doesn't disgust you.
980 VALENTIN: *(hesitant)* Okay.

(MOLINA *trembles.* VALENTIN *holds him against his chest like a father comforting a child.* MOLINA *looks up and says:*)

MOLINA: You are so kind to me.
VALENTIN: No. You're the one who's kind.

(VALENTIN *straightens up and removes his shirt, then leans forward and blows out the candle.*

The cell is dark. The camera lingers on the candle-spark amid whisps of smoke.)

MOLINA: *(O.S.)* Wait. I'm squeezed against the wall. That's better.

(pause)

   No, wait. Let me lift my legs.

(*The spark fades. The screen is black.*)

(Cut to:)

Int. cell—day

(MOLINA, *radiant, looks at the morning sunlight.*)

985 MOLINA: You know when I woke up, I put my hand to my eyebrow, to feel my scar like—
VALENTIN: You don't have one.
MOLINA: —like I wasn't me anymore. As if somehow I was you.

(pause)

   Look, let's not talk about this. Let's not talk about anything at all. Just for this morning I'm asking. Aren't you going to ask 990 me why?
VALENTIN: Why?
MOLINA: Because I'm happy, I'm really happy, and I don't want to spoil it.

(sad smile)

   The nicest thing about feeling happy is that you think you'll 995 never feel unhappy again.

(Cut to:)

Int. Warden's office—day

(PEDRO, *seething, leans into* MOLINA's *face.*)

PEDRO: You shit-faced motherfuck. Talk!

(MOLINA *looks down in fear. The* WARDEN *wheels forward and motions* PEDRO *away.*)

WARDEN: Let me handle this.

(wheels closer)

   Look at me, Molina. What's the matter? You're afraid his group will kill you, is that it? 1000
MOLINA: No sir. I *want* to help.
WARDEN: So what did he say?
MOLINA: Nothing. Wouldn't it be worse if I told you something that wasn't true?
WARDEN: I'll have to move you to another cell, Molina. 1005
MOLINA: No sir, please. Don't do that. As long as I'm with him, there's still a chance that he might talk.

(PEDRO *leans around the* WARDEN *into* MOLINA's *face.*)

PEDRO: You faggot piece of shit! You fell in love with that bastard.
WARDEN: Okay, Molina. You can go.

(MOLINA *stands up. The* WARDEN *reaches in his pocket.*)

WARDEN: Get your things ready. You're leaving today. 1010

(hands document)

   Here, the Ministry approved your parole.

(MOLINA *kisses the* WARDEN's *hand.*)

MOLINA: Thank you, sir.
WARDEN: And no more hanky-panky with the little boys.
MOLINA: Oh no, sir. I swear.

(MOLINA *leaves.*)

(Cut to:)

Int. cell—day

(MOLINA *pulls his mother's photo from the wall and packs his suitcase.* VALENTIN *stoops beside him.*)

VALENTIN: They, they would never suspect you. I mean really, 1015 there's no risk at all.
MOLINA: Sorry, I can't do it. I, uh, I'm just too afraid.
VALENTIN: All you have to do is give them a message. From any public phone.
MOLINA: No. No names, no phone numbers, nothing. I'm terrified of the police. 1020

VALENTIN: Okay. I guess I shouldn't drag you into this.

(VALENTIN *moves to the far corner.* MOLINA *watches him.*)

MOLINA: I swear, Valentin. My only desire is to stay here with you.
VALENTIN: Take care of yourself.
1025   MOLINA: Valentin, I've only loved two people in my life. My
          mother and you.
VALENTIN: I'm gonna miss you, Molina.
MOLINA: At least the movies.
VALENTIN: (*smiles*) Yeah, whenever I go to sleep, I'll probably be
1030   thinking of you and your crazy movies.
MOLINA: And whenever I see bonbons, I'll be thinking of you.

(*pause*)

   Valentin, there's something I'd like to ask you, although we've
   done much more.

(*pause*)

   A kiss.
1035   VALENTIN: Okay. But first promise me something.
MOLINA: I told you, I can't. I'm so sorry.
VALENTIN: No, no, no.

(*approaches*)

   Promise you'll never let anybody humiliate you again, that
   you'll make them respect you. Promise me you'll never let
1040   anybody exploit you again. Nobody has the right to do that to
   anybody.
MOLINA: (*deeply moved*) I promise. Thank you.

(*pause*)

   Valentin?
VALENTIN: What? The kiss?
1045   MOLINA: No. The uhh. The phone number.

(VALENTIN, *overwhelmed, hugs him.* MOLINA, *surprised, returns
the embrace.*)

VALENTIN: Wait a few days. Dial two times and hang up. The
   third time . . .

(VALENTIN *whispers in his ear.* MOLINA *nods twice. Their eyes
meet.* VALENTIN *grips his shoulders and kisses him on the mouth.
The* GUARD *unlocks the door, then steps inside and says:*)

GUARD: Molina, let's go.

(MOLINA *picks up his suitcase and moves toward the door.*)

VALENTIN: Wait.

(VALENTIN *holds out the heart-shaped box.* MOLINA, *touched,
takes it and looks deep into his eyes.*)

1050   VALENTIN: Good luck, Molina.

(MOLINA *nods with a sad smile. The* GUARD *pushes him outside.*)

GUARD: Come on.

(*The door is slammed shut on* VALENTIN.)

(*Cut to:*)

Ext. prison courtyard — day

(*The* GUARD *escorts* MOLINA *across the courtyard to the gate.*)

(*Cut to:*)

Int. cell — day

(VALENTIN, *alone, paces the empty cell, then sits down and
stares at* MOLINA's *bunk.*)

(*Cut to:*)

Ext. prison gate — day

(MOLINA *crosses the busy street to a bus stop, then turns to the
nearby counter of an open cafe.*)

MOLINA: A beer.

(*The* WAITER *uncaps a beer bottle.*)

(*Cut to:*)

Int. WARDEN's office — day

(PEDRO *opens the venetian blinds and watches* MOLINA *sipping
beer at the bus stop. We hear him typing a Secret Police report.*)

VOICE OF PEDRO: Subject was granted a special parole by the
   Minister of Justice, on orders from the Department of Political Surveillance. The Department believes he will lead our   1055
   agents to the cadre of Valentin Arregui.

(*The bus arrives.* MOLINA *tosses his bottle in a trash can and
climbs on board.*)

(*Cut to:*)

Int. bus — day

(MOLINA *watches the passing city with sad and empty eyes.*)

(*Cut to:*)

Int. MOLINA's apartment — day

(MOLINA *opens the door, moves quietly down the hallway and
sees her at the sewing machine, unspooling thread with the quiet
precision of a spider.*)

MOLINA: — Mama.
MOTHER: (*surprised*) Ahhh.

(*She hurries into his waiting arms. He wraps her in a warm
embrace.*)

(*Cut to:*)

Int. cabaret — night

(MOLINA, *wearing a leopard pullover, crosses a smoke-filled cabaret to a table of* MIDDLE-AGED HOMOSEXUALS. *They flatter
him with campy flair.*)

GROUP OF VOICES: — Luisa! So nice to see you! — You look
   great! Ten years younger, darling. Doesn't she? — The return   1060
   of the Leopard Woman.

(MOLINA's *transvestite friend* GRETA *finishes a song on the small
stage and approaches the microphone.*)

GRETA: (*rowdy applause*) Oh shut up, you bunch of faggots.

(*indicates* MOLINA)

   I'd like to welcome home a cherished sister who sacrificed
   Lord-knows-how-many precious nights to pay a stupid debt to
   a hypocritical society.   1065

(*throws a kiss*)

   This is for you, lovely Luisa.

(*He sings in a feminine voice.* MOLINA, *touched, nods.*)

(Cut to:)

Int. MOLINA's *apartment — night*

(MOLINA, *motionless, sits in the bay window. His stark sad eyes gaze across the city lights at the prison on the dark horizon.*)

(Cut to:)

Ext. MOLINA's *apartment — night*

(PEDRO *waits in a car parked in the shadows. His piercing eyes are fixed on* MOLINA *in the bay window. We hear him file a police report.*)

VOICE OF PEDRO: Surveillance reveals subject has not returned to work and almost never leaves home. He spends his evenings staring out the window for no apparent reason.

(Cut to:)

Int. restaurant — day

(MOLINA *sips coffee alone at a table.* GABRIEL *approaches.*)

1070   GABRIEL: You sure you won't eat something?
MOLINA: Just coffee.
GABRIEL: You wanna talk, Molina? Is something wrong?
MOLINA: No, I'm just not gonna see you for awhile. I'm going away.
1075   GABRIEL: With another boy?

(sad smile)

That's good. Don't get arrested again. You're too old for it.

(Cut to:)

Int. MOLINA's *apartment — night*

(MOLINA *sits with his arm around his frail mother. They are bathed in the blue radiance of a late movie on TV.*)

(Cut to:)

Int. MOLINA's *bedroom — night*

(MOLINA *slumps in bed in the robe he wore in prison. A red lamp illumines his poster of Rita Hayworth.*
His sad eyes stare at the red box in his lap. His fingers trace the heart-shaped edges.)

(Cut to:)

Int. bay window — night

(MOLINA *sits in the bay window with his head in his hands, then lifts his head and gazes across the rooftops at the distant prison. Wearing a yellow satin jacket, he is dressed to go out but remains seated. Finally he sighs and moves to the door.*)

(Cut to:)

Int. subway station — night

(MOLINA *enters an empty subway station, glances around and approaches a row of futuristic phones.*
He dials twice and hangs up, then dials a third time and nervously brushes back his red-tinted hair.)

MOLINA: I have a message from Valentin Arregui.

(short pause)

Yes, a pay phone.

(short pause)

Excuse me, is that really necessary?

(long pause)

Alright. I'll be wearing a red scarf.   1080

(Cut to:)

Int. bank — day

(*The* BANK TELLER *hands* MOLINA *a thick wad of money.*)

TELLER: You don't have to close your account. There's no penalty if you maintain a minimum balance of—
MOLINA: Thank you. Do you have an envelope please?

(MOLINA *slips the money in the envelope and leaves.*)

(Cut to:)

Ext. park — day

(MOLINA *sits on a park bench with* GRETA *and hands him the envelope.*)

MOLINA: This is for Mama. To take care of her while I'm gone. Please.   1085
GRETA: All right, I'll handle it.

(pause)

Wherever you're going, it's probably for the best.

(Cut to:)

Int. MOTHER's *bedroom — night*

(MOLINA *tiptoes into his* MOTHER's *bedroom and whispers:*)

MOLINA: Mama, you look so beautiful.

(*She is asleep. He gently kneels beside her.*)

MOLINA: You remember, Mama, when I was little and you used to come into my room to kiss me goodnight. I always pretended to be asleep, but I was always waiting for your kiss.   1090

(pause)

Although you're sleeping now, I know you understand me. It's time for me to take care of my own life. You understand, don't you, Mama?

(pause)

Don't be sad.   1095

(*He kisses her forehead.*)

(Cut to:)

Int. MOLINA's *bedroom — day*

(MOLINA *steps to his bedroom mirror and, expressionless, ties a red scarf around his neck. Rita Hayworth watches over his shoulder.*)

(Cut to:)

Ext. city streets — day

(MOLINA, *tense, jockeys his way through a street jammed with pedestrians. Glancing up, he spots* PEDRO *and three* SECRET AGENTS *on an overpass.*

Frightened, MOLINA *plunges into the crowd.* PEDRO *sprints down the overpass and barges through the crowd, his* AGENTS *right behind him.* MOLINA *turns a corner into a shopping arcade and, hurrying, glances back. He sees* PEDRO *round the corner and stare into his eyes.*

MOLINA *desperately elbows through the shoppers.* PEDRO *keeps a safe distance.*

Struggling, MOLINA *weaves his way inside a dense cluster of pedestrians, then darts down a narrow alley.*

PEDRO *scans the four alleys.* MOLINA *is gone.)*

PEDRO: Go that way. Hurry.

(The AGENTS *split into two groups and go the wrong way.)*

(Cut to:)

Ext. Cathedral Square—day

*(*MOLINA *steps from an alley into an open square. Fingering his red scarf, he searches the crowd for* SECRET POLICE.

Relieved, he crosses the square to the cathedral and stops beside a BEGGAR *playing an accordion. Pretending to listen, he scrutinizes the street and nervously taps his teeth.*

A white taxi slowly approaches the cathedral steps. The YOUNG WOMAN *beside the driver nervously eyes* MOLINA.

He hesitantly stoops down and sees a pistol half-hidden by a newspaper on her lap. She leans out the window.)

LYDIA: —Who are you?
MOLINA: I have a message from Valentin. Are you Lydia?
LYDIA: Yes, get in. Quick.

*(*MOLINA *reaches for the door handle.)*

1100   PEDRO: Get 'em!

(Suddenly an AGENT *slams* MOLINA *aside and thrusts a revolver in the window.* LYDIA *rapid-fires two shots and blasts the* AGENT *to the pavement.*

The taxi roars away. MOLINA *runs.* PEDRO *and two* AGENTS *bolt forward, firing at the taxi careening through the terrified crowd. Turning,* PEDRO *sprints after* MOLINA *disappearing into a dark alley. The two* AGENTS *follow at top speed, firing warning shots in the air.)*

(Cut to:)

Ext. plaza—day

*(*MOLINA, *gasping, races along the dark alley toward the sunlit plaza across a busy avenue.*

PEDRO *barrels around the corner with his automatic pistol and charges down the alley. Bystanders run for cover.)*

PEDRO: Molina! Stop!

*(*MOLINA *rushes toward the plaza when, suddenly, the white taxi skids to a stop on the avenue directly ahead.* LYDIA *rapid-fires three shots out the window.*

MOLINA, *twisted sideways, grabs his bleeding chest. The taxi screeches away.* MOLINA *lurches across the avenue into the plaza. Bystanders scream and scatter.* PEDRO *reaches the corner and fires at the fleeing taxi, then aims at* MOLINA *and strides into the plaza.* MOLINA, *clutching his blood-stained shirt, staggers into a flock of pigeons.* AGENTS *surround him with aimed handguns.* MOLINA *turns and faces them, then drops to his knees.*

The pigeons scatter. PEDRO *motions to an* AGENT.)

PEDRO: Get the car. Move, hurry.

(The AGENT *runs.* PEDRO *steps forward and slowly circles behind* MOLINA, *then jams the automatic against the back of his head and frisks him.*

The car pulls up. PEDRO *jerks* MOLINA *to his feet.)*

PEDRO: Get up. Move! Get in the car.

*(*PEDRO *hurls* MOLINA *into the backseat, climbs in and slams the door. The car speeds away.)*

(Cut to:)

Int. PEDRO's *car—day*

*(*MOLINA *lies stretched out on the backseat.* PEDRO *straddles his waist and sticks the automatic in his face.)*

PEDRO: The number. Tell me the phone number and you go to
    the hospital.   1105

*(*MOLINA *spits up foamy blood, then calmly gazes at* PEDRO.)

PEDRO: Talk! You fucking fag!

*(*MOLINA's *eyes slowly close. His head slumps sideways.)*

(Cut to:)

Ext. slum—day

(The car turns off a busy street into a shanty-town slum and stops beside a pile of garbage.

PEDRO *drags* MOLINA's *body from the backseat and dumps it on the garbage.)*

VOICE OF PEDRO: Subject was shot to death by the extremists.
    His recent activities, such as closing his bank account, sug-
    gest that he planned to escape with them. Also, the way he
    was shot seems to indicate he had agreed, if necessary, to be   1110
    eliminated by them.

(pause)

In any case, it appears he was more deeply involved than we
suspected.

(Cut to:)

Int. prison infirmary—day

*(*VALENTIN, *dying, lies on a cot. His face is swollen with bloody bruises. His chest is disfigured by electric burns.
A prison* INTERN *takes out a hypodermic needle.)*

INTERN: This is morphine. So you can get some rest, okay?

*(*VALENTIN *nods feebly. The* INTERN *injects the needle.)*

INTERN: My God, the way they worked you over.   1115

(removes needle)

Just don't tell about this or I'll lose my job. Count to forty and
you'll be asleep.

*(*VALENTIN *takes two deep breaths and falls sound asleep. A woman's dream-like hand slowly reaches out and touches his wrist.)*

VOICE OF VALENTIN: . . . Marta . . .

*(*VALENTIN *turns in his sleep and sees the beaming smile of his love.* MARTA, *vibrant in a pure white dress, caresses his battered head and tenderly tugs him to his feet.)*

MARTA: Come, Valentin, come with me. Don't be afraid. You won't wake up in the cell.

(Cut to:)

Ext. prison courtyard—day (dream)

(Running hand-in-hand, MARTA *leads* VALENTIN *across the dark courtyard toward the gate. The* GUARDS *and* PRISONERS *cannot see them.* VALENTIN, *bleeding, stops and looks back.)*

VOICE OF VALENTIN: —What about Molina?

VOICE OF MARTA: Come, my love. Only he knows if he died happy or sad.

(She takes his hand and opens the prison gate, revealing a burst of sunlight.)

(Cut to:)

Ext. tropical island—day (dream)

(Smiling in the sunshine, they run toward the ocean across a sandy beach—the same beach in MOLINA's *movie about the* SPIDER WOMAN.

VALENTIN, *radiant, has no scars or wounds. Stopping at the shoreline, he brushes back her hair and looks into her eyes.)*

VOICE OF VALENTIN: I love you so much. That's the one thing I never said, because I was afraid of losing you forever.

(They kiss warmly. MARTA *caresses his healed face and looks into his loving eyes.)*

VOICE OF MARTA: That can never happen now. This dream is short, but this dream is happy.

(Holding hands, they wade into the water and climb into a wooden rowboat. Taking the oars, VALENTIN *rows farther and farther toward the sparkling horizon.)*

✠ CRITICAL CONTEXTS ✠

ANTONIN ARTAUD

(1896–1948)

FROM *The Theater and Its Double*

(1938)

TRANSLATED BY MARY CAROLINE RICHARDS

The Theater and Culture

AN EARLY MEMBER OF the surrealist movement in Paris, Antonin Artaud was well-known between the wars as an actor, playwright, and essayist of the avant-garde theater, and he is one of the formative influences on the modern European theater. Artaud is most often associated with the "theater of cruelty," his label for a theater that would assault the representational dynamics of traditional theater and break the boundaries between actor and audience, stage and spectacle. Artaud was declared insane and committed to a mental hospital in 1937. He remained institutionalized for most of the remainder of his life.

Never before, when it is life itself that is in question, has there been so much talk of civilization and culture. And there is a curious parallel between this generalized collapse of life at the root of our present demoralization and our concern for a culture which has never been coincident with life, which in fact has been devised to tyrannize over life.

Before speaking further about culture, I must remark that the world is hungry and not concerned with culture, and that the attempt to orient toward culture thoughts turned only toward hunger is a purely artificial expedient.

What is most important, it seems to me, is not so much to defend a culture whose existence has never kept a man from going hungry, as to extract, from what is called culture, ideas whose compelling force is identical with that of hunger.

We need to live first of all; to believe in what makes us live and that something *makes* us live — to believe that whatever is produced from the mysterious depths of ourselves need not forever haunt us as an exclusively digestive concern.

I mean that if it is important for us to eat first of all, it is even more important for us not to waste in the sole concern for eating our simple power of being hungry.

If confusion is the sign of the times, I see at the root of this confusion a rupture between things and words, between things and the ideas and signs that are their representation.

Not, of course, for lack of philosophical systems; their number and contradictions characterize our old French and European culture: but where can it be shown that life, our life, has ever been affected by these systems? I will not say that philosophical systems must be applied directly and immediately: but of the following alternatives, one must be true:

Either these systems are within us and permeate our being to the point of supporting life itself (and if this is the case, what use are books?), or they do *not* permeate us and therefore do not have the capacity to support life (and in this case what does their disappearance matter?).

We must insist upon the idea of culture-in-action, of culture growing within us like a new organ, a sort of second breath; and on civilization as an applied culture controlling even our subtlest actions, a *presence of mind*; the distinction between culture and civilization is an artificial one, providing two words to signify an identical function.

A civilized man judges and is judged according to his behavior, but even the term "civilized" leads to confusion: a cultivated "civilized" man is regarded as a person instructed in systems, a person who thinks in forms, signs, representations — a monster whose faculty of deriving thoughts from acts, instead of identifying acts with thoughts, is developed to an absurdity.

If our life lacks brimstone, i.e., a constant magic, it is because we choose to observe our acts and lose ourselves in considerations of their imagined form instead of being impelled by their force.

And this faculty is an exclusively human one. I would even say that it is this infection of the human which contaminates ideas that should have remained divine; for far from believing that man invented the supernatural and the divine, I think it is man's age-old intervention which has ultimately corrupted the divine within him.

All our ideas about life must be revised in a period when nothing any longer adheres to life; it is this painful cleavage which is responsible for the revenge of *things*; the poetry which is no longer within us and which we no longer succeed in finding in things suddenly appears on their wrong side: consider the unprecedented number of crimes whose perverse gratuitousness is explained only by our powerlessness to take complete possession of life.

If the theater has been created as an outlet for our repressions, the agonized poetry expressed in its bizarre corruptions of the facts of life demonstrates that life's intensity is still intact and asks only to be better directed.

But no matter how loudly we clamor for magic in our lives, we are really afraid of pursuing an existence entirely under its influence and sign.

Hence our confirmed lack of culture is astonished by certain grandiose anomalies; for example, on an island without any contact with modern civilization, the mere passage of a ship carrying only healthy passengers may provoke the sudden outbreak of diseases unknown on that island but a specialty of nations like our own: shingles, influenza, grippe, rheumatism, sinusitis, polyneuritis, etc.

Similarly, if we think Negroes smell bad, we are ignorant of the fact that anywhere but in Europe it is we whites who "smell bad." And I would even say that we give off an odor as white as the gathering of pus in an infected wound.

As iron can be heated until it turns white, so it can be said that everything excessive is white; for Asiatics white has become the mark of extreme decomposition.

This said, we can begin to form an idea of culture, an idea which is first of all a protest.

A protest against the senseless constraint imposed upon the idea of culture by reducing it to a sort of inconceivable Pantheon, producing an idolatry no different from the image-worship of those religions which relegate their gods to Pantheons.

A protest against the idea of culture as distinct from life — as if there were culture on one side and life on the other, as if true culture were not a refined means of understanding and *exercising* life.

The library at Alexandria can be burnt down. There are forces above and beyond papyrus: we may temporarily be deprived of our ability to discover these forces, but their energy will not be suppressed. It is good that our excessive facilities are no longer available, that forms fall into oblivion: a culture without space or time, restrained only by the capacity of our own nerves, will reappear with all the more energy. It is right that from time to time cataclysms occur which compel us to return to nature, i.e., to rediscover life. The old totemism of animals, stones, objects capable of discharging thunderbolts, costumes impregnated with bestial essences — everything, in short, that might determine, disclose, and direct the secret forces of the universe — is for us a dead thing, from which we derive nothing but static and aesthetic profit, the profit of an audience, not of an actor.

Yet totemism is an actor, for it moves, and has been created in behalf of actors; all true culture relies upon the barbaric and primitive means of totemism whose savage, i.e., entirely spontaneous, life I wish to worship.

What has lost us culture is our Occidental idea of art and the profits we seek to derive from it. Art and culture cannot be considered together, contrary to the treatment universally accorded them!

True culture operates by exaltation and force, while the European ideal of art attempts to cast the mind into an attitude distinct from force but addicted to exaltation. It is a lazy, unserviceable notion which engenders an imminent death. If the Serpent Quetzalcoatl's multiple twists and turns are harmonious, it is because they express the equilibrium and fluctuations of a sleeping force; the intensity of the forms is there only to seduce and direct a force which, in music, would produce an insupportable range of sound.

The gods that sleep in museums: the god of fire with his incense burner that resembles an Inquisition tripod; Tlaloc, one of the manifold Gods of the Waters, on his wall of green granite; the Mother Goddess of Waters, the Mother Goddess of Flowers; the immutable expression, echoing from beneath many layers of water, of the Goddess robed in green jade; the enraptured, blissful expression, features crackling with incense, where atoms of sunlight circle — the countenance of the Mother Goddess of Flowers; this world of obligatory servitude in which a stone comes alive when it has been properly carved, the world of organically civilized men whose vital organs too awaken from their slumber, this human world enters into us, participating in the dance of the gods without turning round or looking back, on pain of becoming, like ourselves, crumbled pillars of salt.

In Mexico, since we are talking about Mexico, there is no art: things are made for use. And the world is in perpetual exaltation.

To our disinterested and inert idea of art an authentic culture opposes a violently egoistic and magical, i.e., *interested* idea. For the Mexicans seek contact with the *Manas*, forces latent in every form, unreleased by contemplation of the forms for themselves, but springing to life by magic identification with these forms. And the old Totems are there to hasten the communication.

How hard it is, when everything encourages us to sleep, though we may look about us with conscious, clinging eyes, to wake and yet look about us as in a dream, with eyes that no longer know their function and whose gaze is turned inward.

This is how our strange idea of disinterested action originated, though it is action nonetheless, and all the more violent for skirting the temptation of repose.

Every real effigy has a shadow which is its double; and art must falter and fail from the moment the sculptor believes he has liberated the kind of shadow whose very existence will destroy his repose.

Like all magic cultures expressed by appropriate hieroglyphs, the true theater has its shadows too, and, of all languages and all arts, the theater is the only one left whose shadows have shattered their limitations. From the beginning, one might say its shadows did not tolerate limitations.

Our petrified idea of the theater is connected with our petrified idea of a culture without shadows, where, no matter which way it turns, our mind (*esprit*) encounters only emptiness, though space is full.

But the true theater, because it moves and makes use of living instruments, continues to stir up shadows where life has never ceased to grope its way. The actor does not make the same gestures twice, but he makes gestures, he moves; and although he brutalizes forms, nevertheless behind them and through their destruction he rejoins that which outlives forms and produces their continuation.

The theater, which is in *no thing*, but makes use of everything—gestures, sounds, words, screams, light, darkness—rediscovers itself at precisely the point where the mind requires a language to express its manifestations.

And the fixation of the theater in one language—written words, music, lights, noises—betokens its imminent ruin, the choice of any one language betraying a taste for the special effects of that language; and the dessication of the language accompanies its limitation.

For the theater as for culture, it remains a question of naming and directing shadows: and the theater, not confined to a fixed language and form, not only destroys false shadows but prepares the way for a new generation of shadows, around which assembles the true spectacle of life.

To break through language in order to touch life is to create or recreate the theater; the essential thing is not to believe that this act must remain sacred, i.e., set apart—the essential thing is to believe that not just anyone can create it, and that there must be a preparation.

This leads to the rejection of the usual limitations of man and man's powers, and infinitely extends the frontiers of what is called reality.

We must believe in a sense of life renewed by the theater, a sense of life in which man fearlessly makes himself master of what does not yet exist, and brings it into being. And everything that has not been born can still be brought to life if we are not satisfied to remain mere recording organisms.

Furthermore, when we speak the word "life," it must be understood we are not referring to life as we know it from its surface of fact, but to that fragile, fluctuating center which forms never reach. And if there is still one hellish, truly accursed thing in our time, it is our artistic dallying with forms, instead of being like victims burnt at the stake, signaling through the flames.

✢   ✢   ✢

No More Masterpieces

One of the reasons for the asphyxiating atmosphere in which we live without possible escape or remedy—and in which we all share, even the most revolutionary among us—is our respect for what has been written, formulated, or painted, what has been given form, as if all expression were not at last exhausted, were not at a point where things must break apart if they are to start anew and begin fresh.

We must have done with this idea of masterpieces reserved for a self-styled elite and not understood by the general public; the mind has no such restricted districts as those so often used for clandestine sexual encounters.

Masterpieces of the past are good for the past: they are not good for us. We have the right to say what has been said and even what has not been said in a way that belongs to us, a way that is immediate and direct, corresponding to present modes of feeling, and understandable to everyone.

It is idiotic to reproach the masses for having no sense of the sublime, when the sublime is confused with one or another of its formal manifestations, which are moreover always defunct manifestations. And if for example a contemporary public does not understand *Oedipus Rex*, I shall make bold to say that it is the fault of *Oedipus Rex* and not of the public.

In *Oedipus Rex* there is the theme of incest and the idea that nature mocks at morality and that there are certain unspecified powers at large which we would do well to beware of, call them *destiny* or anything you choose.

There is in addition the presence of a plague epidemic which is a physical incarnation of these powers. But the whole in a manner and language that have lost all touch with the rude and epileptic rhythm of our time. Sophocles speaks grandly perhaps, but in a style that is no longer timely. His language is too refined for this age, it is as if he were speaking beside the point.

However, a public that shudders at train wrecks, that is familiar with earthquakes, plagues, revolutions, wars; that is sensitive to the disordered anguish of love, can be affected by all these grand notions and asks only to become aware of them, but on condition that it is addressed in its own language, and that its knowledge of these things does not come to it through adulterated trappings and speech that belong to extinct eras which will never live again.

Today as yesterday, the public is greedy for mystery: it asks only to become aware of the laws according to which destiny manifests itself, and to divine perhaps the secret of its apparitions.

Let us leave textual criticism to graduate students, formal criticism to esthetes, and recognize that what has been said is not still to be said; that an expression does not have the same value twice, does not live two lives; that all words, once spoken, are dead and function only at the moment when they are uttered, that a form, once it has served, cannot be used again and asks only to be replaced by another, and that the theater is the only place in the world where a gesture, once made, can never be made the same way twice.

If the public does not frequent our literary masterpieces, it is because those masterpieces are literary, that is to say, fixed; and fixed in forms that no longer respond to the needs of the time.

Far from blaming the public, we ought to blame the formal screen we interpose between ourselves and the public, and this new form of idolatry, the idolatry of fixed masterpieces which is one of the aspects of bourgeois conformism.

This conformism makes us confuse sublimity, ideas, and things with the forms they have taken in time and in our minds—in our snobbish, precious, aesthetic mentalities which the public does not understand.

How pointless in such matters to accuse the public of bad taste because it relishes insanities, so long as the public is not shown a valid spectacle; and I defy anyone to show me *here* a spectacle valid— valid in the supreme sense of the theater—since the last great romantic melodramas, i.e., since a hundred years ago.

The public, which takes the false for the true, has the sense of the true and always responds to it when it is manifested. However it is not upon the stage that the true is to be sought nowadays, but in the street; and if the crowd in the street is offered an occasion to show its human dignity, it will always do so.

If people are out of the habit of going to the theater, if we have all finally come to think of theater as an inferior art, a means of popular distraction, and to use it as an outlet for our worst instincts, it is because we have learned too well what the theater has been, namely, falsehood and illusion. It is because we have been accustomed for four hundred years, that is since the Renaissance, to a purely descriptive and narrative theater—storytelling psychology; it is because every possible ingenuity has been exerted in bringing to life on the stage plausible but detached beings, with the spectacle on one side, the public on the other—and because the public is no longer shown anything but the mirror of itself.

Shakespeare himself is responsible for this aberration and decline, this disinterested idea of the theater which wishes a theatrical performance to leave the public intact, without setting off one image that will shake the organism to its foundations and leave an ineffaceable scar.

If, in Shakespeare, a man is sometimes preoccupied with what transcends him, it is always in order to determine the ultimate consequences of this preoccupation within him, i.e., psychology.

Psychology, which works relentlessly to reduce the unknown to the known, to the quotidian and the ordinary, is the cause of the theater's abasement and its fearful loss of energy, which seems to me to have reached its lowest point. And I think both the theater and we ourselves have had enough of psychology.

I believe furthermore that we can all agree on this matter sufficiently so that there is no need to descend to the repugnant level of the modern and French theater to condemn the theater of psychology.

Stories about money, worry over money, social careerism, the pangs of love unspoiled by altruism, sexuality sugar-coated with an eroticism that has lost its mystery have nothing to do with the theater, even if they do belong to psychology. These torments, seductions, and lusts before which we are nothing but Peeping Toms gratifying our cravings, tend to go bad, and their rot turns to revolution: we must take this into account.

But this is not our most serious concern.

If Shakespeare and his imitators have gradually insinuated the idea of art for art's sake, with art on one side and life on the other, we can rest on this feeble and lazy idea only as long as the life outside endures. But there are too many signs that everything that used to sustain our lives no longer does so, that we are all mad, desperate, and sick. And I call for *us* to react.

This idea of a detached art, of poetry as a charm which exists only to distract our leisure, is a decadent idea and an unmistakable symptom of our power to castrate.

Our literary admiration for Rimbaud, Jarry, Lautréamont, and a few others, which has driven two men to suicide, but turned into café gossip for the rest, belongs to this idea of literary poetry, of detached art, of neutral spiritual activity which creates nothing and produces nothing; and I can bear witness that at the very moment when that kind of personal poetry which involves only the man who creates it and only at the moment he creates it broke out in its most abusive fashion, the theater was scorned more than ever before by poets who have never had the sense of direct and concerted action, nor of efficacy, nor of danger.

We must get rid of our superstitious valuation of texts and *written* poetry. Written poetry is worth reading once, and then should be destroyed. Let the dead poets make way for others. Then we might even come to see that it is our veneration for what has already been created, however beautiful and valid it may be, that petrifies us, deadens our responses, and prevents us from making contact with that underlying power, call it thought-energy, the life force, the determinism of change, lunar menses, or anything you like. Beneath the poetry of the texts, there is the actual poetry, without form and without text. And just as the efficacy of masks in the magic practices of certain tribes is exhausted — and these masks are no longer good for anything except museums — so the poetic efficacy of a text is exhausted; yet the poetry and the efficacy of the theater are exhausted least quickly of all, since they permit the *action* of what is gesticulated and pronounced, and which is never made the same way twice.

It is a question of knowing what we want. If we are prepared for war, plague, famine, and slaughter we do not even need to say so, we have only to continue as we are; continue behaving like snobs, rushing en masse to hear such and such a singer, to see such and such an admirable performance which never transcends the realm of art (and even the Russian ballet at the height of its splendor never transcended the realm of art), to marvel at such and such an exhibition of painting in which exciting shapes explode here and there but at random and without any genuine consciousness of the forces they could rouse.

This empiricism, randomness, individualism, and anarchy must cease.

Enough of personal poems, benefitting those who create them much more than those who read them.

Once and for all, enough of this closed, egoistic, and personal art.

Our spiritual anarchy and intellectual disorder is a function of the anarchy of everything else — or rather, everything else is a function of this anarchy.

I am not one of those who believe that civilization has to change in order for the theater to change; but I do believe that the theater, utilized in the highest and most difficult sense possible, has the power to influence the aspect and formation of things: and the encounter upon the stage of two passionate manifestations, two living centers, two nervous magnetisms is something as entire, true, even decisive, as, in life, the encounter of one epidermis with another in a timeless debauchery.

That is why I propose a theater of cruelty. —With this mania we all have for depreciating everything, as soon as I have said "cruelty," everybody will at once take it to mean "blood." But "*theater of cruelty*" means a theater difficult and cruel for myself first of all. And, on the level of performance, it is not the cruelty we can exercise upon each other by hacking at each other's bodies, carving up our personal anatomies, or, like Assyrian emperors, sending parcels of human ears, noses, or neatly detached nostrils through the mail, but the much more terrible and necessary cruelty which things can exercise against us. We are not free. And the sky can still fall on our heads. And the theater has been created to teach us that first of all.

Either we will be capable of returning by present-day means to this superior idea of poetry and poetry-through-theater which underlies the Myths told by the great ancient tragedians, capable once more of entertaining a religious idea of the theater (without meditation, useless contemplation, and vague dreams), capable of attaining awareness and a possession of certain dominant forces, of certain notions that control all others, and (since ideas, when they are effective, carry their energy with them) capable of recovering within ourselves those energies which ultimately create order and increase the value of life, or else we might as well abandon ourselves now, without protest, and recognize that we are no longer good for anything but disorder, famine, blood, war, and epidemics.

Either we restore all the arts to a central attitude and necessity, finding an analogy between a gesture made in painting or the theater, and a gesture made by lava in a volcanic explosion, or we must stop painting, babbling, writing, or doing whatever it is we do.

I propose to bring back into the theater this elementary magical idea, taken up by modern psychoanalysis, which consists in effecting a patient's cure by making him assume the apparent and exterior attitudes of the desired condition.

I propose to renounce our empiricism of imagery, in which the unconscious furnishes images at random, and which the poet arranges at random too, calling them poetic and hence hermetic images, as if the kind of trance that poetry provides did not have its reverberations throughout the whole sensibility, in every nerve, and as if poetry were some vague force whose movements were invariable.

I propose to return through the theater to an idea of the physical knowledge of images and the means of inducing trances, as in Chinese medicine which knows, over the entire extent of the human anatomy, at what points to puncture in order to regulate the subtlest functions.

Those who have forgotten the communicative power and magical mimesis of a gesture, the theater can reinstruct, because a gesture carries its energy with it, and there are still human beings in the theater to manifest the force of the gesture made.

To create art is to deprive a gesture of its reverberation in the organism, whereas this reverberation, if the gesture is made in the conditions and with the force required, incites the organism and, through it, the entire individuality, to take attitudes in harmony with the gesture.

The theater is the only place in the world, the last general means we still possess of directly affecting the organism and, in periods of neurosis and petty sensuality like the one in which we are immersed, of attacking this sensuality by physical means it cannot withstand.

If music affects snakes, it is not on account of the spiritual notions it offers them, but because snakes are long and coil their length upon the earth, because their bodies touch the earth at almost every point; and because the musical vibrations which are communicated to the earth affect them like a very subtle, very long massage; and I propose to treat the spectators like the snakecharmer's subjects and conduct them *by means of their organisms* to an apprehension of the subtlest notions.

At first by crude means, which will gradually be refined. These immediate crude means will hold their attention at the start.

That is why in the "theater of cruelty" the spectator is in the center and the spectacle surrounds him.

In this spectacle the sonorisation is constant: sounds, noises, cries are chosen first for their vibratory quality, then for what they represent.

Among these gradually refined means light is interposed in its turn. Light which is not created merely to add color or to brighten, and which brings its power, influence, suggestions with it. And the light of a green cavern does not sensually dispose the organism like the light of a windy day.

After sound and light there is action, and the dynamism of action: here the theater, far from copying life, puts itself whenever possible in communication with pure forces. And whether you accept or deny them, there is nevertheless a way of speaking which gives the name of "forces" to whatever brings to birth images of energy in the unconscious, and gratuitous crime on the surface.

A violent and concentrated action is a kind of lyricism: it summons up supernatural images, a bloodstream of images, a bleeding spurt of images in the poet's head and in the spectator's as well.

Whatever the conflicts that haunt the mind of a given period, I defy any spectator to whom such violent scenes will have transferred their blood, who will have felt in himself the transit of a superior action, who will have seen the extraordinary and essential movements of his thought illuminated in extraordinary deeds — the violence and blood having been placed at the service of the violence of the thought — I defy that spectator to give himself up, once outside the theater, to ideas of war, riot, and blatant murder.

So expressed, this idea seems dangerous and sophomoric. It will be claimed that example breeds example, that if the attitude of cure induces cure, the attitude of murder will induce murder. Everything depends upon the manner and the purity with which the thing is done. There is a risk. But let it not be forgotten that though a theatrical gesture is violent, it is disinterested; and that the theater teaches precisely the uselessness of the action which, once done, is not to be done, and the superior use of the state unused by the action and which, *restored*, produces a purification.

I propose then a theater in which violent physical images crush and hypnotize the sensibility of the spectator seized by the theater as by a whirlwind of higher forces.

A theater which, abandoning psychology, recounts the extraordinary, stages natural conflicts, natural and subtle forces, and presents itself first of all as an exceptional power of redirection. A theater that induces trance, as the dances of Dervishes induce trance, and that addresses itself to the organism by precise instruments, by the same means as those of certain tribal music cures which we admire on records but are incapable of originating among ourselves.

There is a risk involved, but in the present circumstances I believe it is a risk worth running. I do not believe we have managed to revitalize the world we live in, and I do not believe it is worth the trouble of clinging to; but I do propose something to get us out of our marasmus, instead of continuing to complain about it, and about the boredom, inertia, and stupidity of everything.

MARTIN ESSLIN

FROM *The Theatre of the Absurd*
(1961)

IN HIS SEMINAL STUDY OF THE POSTWAR THEATER OF EUGÈNE IONESCO, SAMUEL BECKETT, *Harold Pinter, and other playwrights, Martin Esslin coined the phrase "theater of the absurd" to describe the disorienting quality of their plays. The book has been widely influential and provided the first generation of postwar theatergoers with a way of understanding the new drama. Esslin has written several books on modern drama and theater, including* Brecht: A Choice of Evils *(1959),* Pinter: A Study of His Plays *(1976), and* An Anatomy of Drama *(1976). He has also worked for the British Broadcasting Corporation and has taught drama at Stanford University and elsewhere.*

On 19 November 1957, a group of worried actors were preparing to face their audience. The actors were members of the company of the San Francisco Actors' Workshop. The audience consisted of fourteen hundred convicts at the San Quentin penitentiary. No live play had been performed at San Quentin since Sarah Bernhardt appeared there in 1913. Now, forty-four years later, the play that had been chosen, largely because no woman appeared in it, was Samuel Beckett's *Waiting for Godot.*

No wonder the actors and Herbert Blau, the director, were apprehensive. How were they to face one of the toughest audiences in the world with a highly obscure, intellectual play that had produced near riots among a good many highly sophisticated audiences in Western Europe? Herbert Blau decided to prepare the San Quentin audience for what was to come. He stepped on to the stage and addressed the packed, darkened North Dining Hall — a sea of flickering matches that the convicts tossed over their shoulders after lighting their cigarettes. Blau compared the play to a piece of jazz music 'to which one must listen for whatever one may find in it.' In the same way, he hoped, there would be some meaning, some personal significance for each member of the audience in *Waiting for Godot.*

The curtain parted. The play began. And what had bewildered the sophisticated audiences of Paris, London, and New York was immediately grasped by an audience of convicts. As the writer of 'Memos of a first-nighter' put it in the columns of the prison paper, the *San Quentin News*:

> The trio of muscle-men, biceps overflowing, . . . parked all 642 lbs on the aisle and waited for the girls and funny stuff. When this didn't appear they audibly fumed and audibly decided to wait until the house lights dimmed before escaping. They made one error. They listened and looked two minutes too long—and stayed. Left at the end. All shook . . .[1]

Or as the writer of the lead story of the same paper reported, under the headline, 'San Francisco Group Leaves S.Q. Audience Waiting for Godot':

> From the moment Robin Wagner's thoughtful and limbo-like set was dressed with light, until the last futile and expectant handclasp was hesitantly activated between the two searching vagrants, the San Francisco company had its audience of captives in its collective hand. . . . Those that had felt a less controversial vehicle should be attempted as a first play here had their fears allayed a short five minutes after the Samuel Beckett piece began to unfold.[2]

A reporter from the San Francisco *Chronicle* who was present noted that the convicts did not find it difficult to understand the play. One prisoner told him, 'Godot is society.' Said another: 'He's the outside.'[3] A teacher at the prison was quoted as saying, 'They know what is meant by waiting . . . and they knew if Godot finally came, he would only be a disappointment.'[4] The leading article of the prison paper showed how clearly the writer had understood the meaning of the play:

> It was an expression, symbolic in order to avoid all personal error, by an author who expected each member of his audience to draw his own conclusions, make his own errors. It asked nothing in point, it forced no dramatized moral on the viewer, it held out no specific hope. . . . We're still waiting for Godot, and shall continue to wait. When the scenery gets too drab and the action too slow, we'll call each other names and swear to part forever—but then, there's no place to go![5]

It is said that Godot himself, as well as turns of phrase and characters from the play, have since become a permanent part of the private language, the institutional mythology of San Quentin.

Why did a play of the supposedly esoteric avant-garde make so immediate and so deep an impact on an audience of convicts? Because it confronted them with a situation in some ways analogous to their own? Perhaps. Or perhaps because they were unsophisticated enough to come to the theatre without any preconceived notions and ready-made expectations, so that they avoided the mistake that trapped so many established critics who condemned the play for its lack of plot, development, characterization, suspense, or plain common sense. Certainly the prisoners of San Quentin could not be suspected of the sin of intellectual snobbery, for which a sizeable proportion of the audiences of *Waiting for Godot* have often been reproached; of pretending to like a play they did not even begin to understand, just to appear in the know.

The reception of *Waiting for Godot* at San Quentin, and the wide acclaim given to plays by Ionesco, Adamov, Pinter, and others, testify that these plays, which are so often superciliously dismissed as nonsense or mystification, *have* something to say and *can* be understood. Most of the incomprehension with which plays of this type are still being received by critics and theatrical reviewers, most of the bewilderment they have caused and to which they still give rise, come from the fact that they are part of a new, and still developing stage convention that has not yet been generally understood and has hardly ever been defined. Inevitably, plays written in this new convention will, when judged by the standards and criteria of another, be regarded as impertinent and outrageous

---

[1]*San Quentin News*, San Quentin, Calif., 28 November 1957.
[2]ibid.
[3]*Theatre Arts*, New York, July 1958.
[4]ibid.
[5]*San Quentin News*, 28 November 1957.

impostures. If a good play must have a cleverly constructed story, these have no story or plot to speak of; if a good play is judged by subtlety of characterization and motivation, these are often without recognizable characters and present the audience with almost mechanical puppets; if a good play has to have a fully explained theme, which is neatly exposed and finally solved, these often have neither a beginning nor an end; if a good play is to hold the mirror up to nature and portray the manners and mannerisms of the age in finely observed sketches, these seem often to be reflections of dreams and nightmares; if a good play relies on witty repartee and pointed dialogue, these often consist of incoherent babblings.

But the plays we are concerned with here pursue ends quite different from those of the conventional play and therefore use quite different methods. They can be judged only by the standards of the Theatre of the Absurd, which it is the purpose of this book to define and clarify.

It must be stressed, however, that the dramatists whose work is here discussed do not form part of any self-proclaimed or self-conscious school or movement. On the contrary, each of the writers in question is an individual who regards himself as a lone outsider, cut off and isolated in his private world. Each has his own personal approach to both subject-matter and form; his own roots, sources, and background. If they also, very clearly and in spite of themselves, have a good deal in common, it is because their work most sensitively mirrors and reflects the preoccupations and anxieties, the emotions and thinking of many of their contemporaries in the Western world.

This is not to say that their works are representative of mass attitudes. It is an oversimplification to assume that any age presents a homogeneous pattern. Ours being, more than most others, an age of transition, it displays a bewilderingly stratified picture: medieval beliefs still held and overlaid by eighteenth-century rationalism and mid-nineteenth-century Marxism, rocked by sudden volcanic eruptions of prehistoric fanaticisms and primitive tribal cults. Each of these components of the cultural pattern of the age finds its own artistic expression. The Theatre of the Absurd, however, can be seen as the reflection of what seems to be the attitude most genuinely representative of our own time.

The hallmark of this attitude is its sense that the certitudes and unshakable basic assumptions of former ages have been swept away, that they have been tested and found wanting, that they have been discredited as cheap and somewhat childish illusions. The decline of religious faith was masked until the end of the Second World War by the substitute religions of faith in progress, nationalism, and various totalitarian fallacies. All this was shattered by the war. By 1942, Albert Camus was calmly putting the question why, since life had lost all meaning, man should not seek escape in suicide. In one of the great, seminal heart-searchings of our time, *The Myth of Sisyphus*, Camus tried to diagnose the human situation in a world of shattered beliefs:

> A world that can be explained by reasoning, however faulty, is a familiar world. But in a universe that is suddenly deprived of illusions and of light, man feels a stranger. His is an irremediable exile, because he is deprived of memories of a lost homeland as much as he lacks the hope of a promised land to come. This divorce between man and his life, the actor and his setting, truly constitutes the feeling of Absurdity.[6]

'Absurd' originally means 'out of harmony', in a musical context. Hence its dictionary definition: 'out of harmony with reason or propriety; incongruous, unreasonable, illogical'. In common usage, 'absurd' may simply mean 'ridiculous', but this is not the sense in which Camus uses the word, and in which it is used when we speak of the Theatre of the Absurd. In an essay on Kafka, Ionesco defined his understanding of the term as follows: 'Absurd is that which is devoid of purpose. . . . Cut off from his religious, metaphysical, and transcendental roots, man is lost; all his actions become senseless, absurd, useless.'[7]

This sense of metaphysical anguish at the absurdity of the human condition is, broadly speaking, the theme of the plays of Beckett, Adamov, Ionesco, Genet, and the other writers discussed in this

---

[6]Albert Camus, *Le Mythe de Sisyphe* (Paris: Gallimard, 1942), p. 18.
[7]Eugène Ionesco, *'Dans les armes de la ville'*, *Cahiers de la Compagnie Madeleine Renaud–Jean-Louis Barrault*, Paris, no. 20, October 1957.

book. But it is not merely the subject-matter that defines what is here called the Theatre of the Absurd. A similar sense of the senselessness of life, of the inevitable devaluation of ideals, purity, and purpose, is also the theme of much of the work of dramatists like Giraudoux, Anouilh, Salacrou, Sartre, and Camus himself. Yet these writers differ from the dramatists of the Absurd in an important respect: they present their sense of the irrationality of the human condition in the form of highly lucid and logically constructed reasoning, while the Theatre of the Absurd strives to express its sense of the senselessness of the human condition and the inadequacy of the rational approach by the open abandonment of rational devices and discursive thought. While Sartre or Camus express the new content in the old convention, the Theatre of the Absurd goes a step further in trying to achieve a unity between its basic assumptions and the form in which these are expressed. In some senses, the *theatre* of Sartre and Camus is less adequate as an expression of the *philosophy* of Sartre and Camus — in artistic, as distinct from philosophic, terms — than the Theatre of the Absurd.

If Camus argued that in our disillusioned age the world has ceased to make sense, he did so in the elegantly rationalistic and discursive style of an eighteenth-century moralist, in well-constructed and polished plays. If Sartre argues that existence comes before essence and that human personality can be reduced to pure potentiality and the freedom to choose itself anew at any moment, he presents his ideas in plays based on brilliantly drawn characters who remain wholly consistent and thus reflect the old convention that each human being has a core of immutable, unchanging essence — in fact, an immortal soul. And the beautiful phrasing and argumentative brilliance of both Sartre and Camus in their relentless probing still, by implication, proclaim a tacit conviction that logical discourse can offer valid solutions, that the analysis of language will lead to the uncovering of basic concepts — Platonic ideas.

This is an inner contradiction that the dramatists of the Absurd are trying, by instinct and intuition rather than by conscious effort, to overcome and resolve. The Theatre of the Absurd has renounced arguing *about* the absurdity of the human condition; it merely *presents* it in being — that is, in terms of concrete stage images. This is the difference between the approach of the philosopher and that of the poet; the difference, to take an example from another sphere, between the *idea* of God in the works of Thomas Aquinas or Spinoza and the *intuition* of God in those of St John of the Cross or Meister Eckhart — the difference between theory and experience.

It is this striving for an integration between the subject-matter and the form in which it is expressed that separates the Theatre of the Absurd from the Existentialist theatre.

It must also be distinguished from another important, and parallel, trend in the contemporary French theatre, which is equally preoccupied with the absurdity and uncertainty of the human condition: the 'poetic avant-garde' theatre of dramatists like Michel de Ghelderode, Jacques Audiberti, Georges Neveux, and, in the younger generation, Georges Schehadé, Henri Pichette, and Jean Vauthier, to name only some of its most important exponents. This is an even more difficult dividing line to draw, for the two approaches overlap a good deal. The 'poetic avant-garde' relies on fantasy and dream reality as much as the Theatre of the Absurd does; it also disregards such traditional axioms as that of the basic unity and consistency of each character or the need for a plot. Yet basically the 'poetic avant-garde' represents a different mood; it is more lyrical, and far less violent and grotesque. Even more important is its different attitude toward language: the 'poetic avant-garde' relies to a far greater extent on consciously 'poetic' speech; it aspires to plays that are in effect poems, images composed of a rich web of verbal associations.

The Theatre of the Absurd, on the other hand, tends toward a radical devaluation of language, toward a poetry that is to emerge from the concrete and objectified images of the stage itself. The element of language still plays an important part in this conception, but what *happens* on the stage transcends, and often contradicts, the *words* spoken by the characters. In Ionesco's *The Chairs*, for example, the poetic content of a powerfully poetic play does not lie in the banal words that are uttered but in the fact that they are spoken to an ever-growing number of empty chairs.

The Theatre of the Absurd is thus part of the 'anti-literary' movement of our time, which has found its expression in abstract painting, with its rejection of 'literary' elements in pictures; or in the 'new novel' in France, with its reliance on the description of objects and its rejection of empathy and anthropomorphism. It is no coincidence that, like all these movements and so many of the efforts to create new forms of expression in all the arts, the Theatre of the Absurd should be centred in Paris. . . .

FREDRIC JAMESON

FROM

*"Postmodernism and
Consumer Society"*
(1983)

*FREDRIC JAMESON IS PROBABLY THE MOST PROMINENT MARXIST CULTURAL CRITIC WRITING IN THE
United States today and is the author of several important books, including* Marxism and Form
(1971), The Prison-House of Language *(1972), and* The Political Unconscious *(1988). This section is
from one of Jameson's many essays on postmodern art, culture, and society. Jameson uses the term*
pastiche *to characterize the problematic ways contemporary arts invoke the imagery and style of earlier
historical eras, paradoxically erasing "history" in the process.*

. . . One of the most significant features or practices in postmodernism today is pastiche. I must first
explain this term, which people generally tend to confuse with or assimilate to that related verbal
phenomenon called parody. Both pastiche and parody involve the imitation or, better still, the mimicry of other styles and particularly of the mannerisms and stylistic twitches of other styles. It is obvious
that modern literature in general offers a very rich field for parody, since the great modern writers have
all been defined by the invention or production of rather unique styles: think of the Faulknerian long
sentence or of D. H. Lawrence's characteristic nature imagery; think of Wallace Stevens's peculiar way
of using abstractions; think also of the mannerisms of the philosophers, of Heidegger for example, or
Sartre; think of the musical styles of Mahler or Prokofiev. All of these styles, however different from
each other, are comparable in this: each is quite unmistakable; once one is learned, it is not likely to
be confused with something else.

Now parody capitalizes on the uniqueness of these styles and seizes on their idiosyncrasies and
eccentricities to produce an imitation which mocks the original. I won't say that the satiric impulse is
conscious in all forms of parody. In any case, a good or great parodist has to have some secret
sympathy for the original, just as a great mimic has to have the capacity to put himself/herself in the
place of the person imitated. Still, the general effect of parody is—whether in sympathy or with
malice—to cast ridicule on the private nature of these stylistic mannerisms and their excessiveness
and eccentricity with respect to the way people normally speak or write. So there remains somewhere
behind all parody the feeling that there is a linguistic norm in contrast to which the styles of the great
modernists can be mocked.

But what would happen if one no longer believed in the existence of normal language, of
ordinary speech, of the linguistic norm (the kind of clarity and communicative power celebrated by
Orwell in his famous essay, say)? One could think of it in this way: perhaps the immense fragmentation and privatization of modern literature—its explosion into a host of distinct private styles and
mannerisms—foreshadows deeper and more general tendencies in social life as a whole. Supposing
that modern art and modernism—far from being a kind of specialized aesthetic curiosity—actually
anticipated social developments along these lines; supposing that in the decades since the emergence
of the great modern styles society has itself begun to fragment in this way, each group coming to speak
a curious private language of its own, each profession developing its private code or idiolect, and
finally each individual coming to be a kind of linguistic island, separated from everyone else? But
then in that case, the very possibility of any linguistic norm in terms of which one could ridicule
private languages and idiosyncratic styles would vanish, and we would have nothing but stylistic
diversity and heterogeneity.

That is the moment at which pastiche appears and parody has become impossible. Pastiche is,
like parody, the imitation of a peculiar or unique style, the wearing of a stylistic mask, speech in a
dead language: but it is a neutral practice of such mimicry, without parody's ulterior motive, without
the satirical impulse, without laughter, without that still latent feeling that there exists something
normal compared to which what is being imitated is rather comic. Pastiche is blank parody, parody
that has lost its sense of humor: pastiche is to parody what that curious thing, the modern practice of a
kind of blank irony, is to what Wayne Booth calls the stable and comic ironies of, say, the 18th
century.

But now we need to introduce a new piece into this puzzle, which may help explain why
classical modernism is a thing of the past and why postmodernism should have taken its place. This
new component is what is generally called the "death of the subject" or, to say it in more conventional
language, the end of individualism as such. The great modernisms were, as we have said, predicated
on the invention of a personal, private style, as unmistakable as your fingerprint, as incomparable as

your own body. But this means that the modernist aesthetic is in some way organically linked to the conception of a unique self and private identity, a unique personality and individuality, which can be expected to generate its own unique vision of the world and to forge its own unique, unmistakable style.

Yet today, from any number of distinct perspectives, the social theorists, the psychoanalysts, even the linguists, not to speak of those of us who work in the area of culture and cultural and formal change, arc all exploring the notion that that kind of individualism and personal identity is a thing of the past; that the old individual or individualist subject is "dead"; and that one might even describe the concept of the unique individual and the theoretical basis of individualism as ideological. There are in fact two positions on all this, one of which is more radical than the other. The first one is content to say: yes, once upon a time, in the classic age of competitive capitalism, in the heyday of the nuclear family and the emergence of the bourgeoisie as the hegemonic social class, there was such a thing as individualism, as individual subjects. But today, in the age of corporate capitalism, of the so-called organization man, of bureaucracies in business as well as in the state, of demographic explosion — today, that older bourgeois individual subject no longer exists.

Then there is a second position, the more radical of the two, what one might call the poststructuralist position. It adds: not only is the bourgeois individual subject a thing of the past, it is also a myth; it *never* really existed in the first place; there have never been autonomous subjects of that type. Rather, this construct is merely a philosophical and cultural mystification which sought to persuade people that they "had" individual subjects and possessed this unique personal identity.

For our purposes, it is not particularly important to decide which of these positions is correct (or rather, which is more interesting and productive). What we have to retain from all this is rather an aesthetic dilemma: because if the experience and the ideology of the unique self, an experience and ideology which informed the stylistic practice of classical modernism, is over and done with, then it is no longer clear what the artists and writers of the present period are supposed to be doing. What is clear is merely that the older models — Picasso, Proust, T.S. Eliot — do not work any more (or are positively harmful), since nobody has that kind of unique private world and style to express any longer. And this is perhaps not merely a "psychological" matter: we also have to take into account the immense weight of seventy or eighty years of classical modernism itself. There is another sense in which the writers and artists of the present day will no longer be able to invent new styles and worlds — they've already been invented; only a limited number of combinations are possible; the most unique ones have been thought of already. So the weight of the whole modernist aesthetic tradition — now dead — also "weighs like a nightmare on the brains of the living," as Marx said in another context.

Hence, once again, pastiche: in a world in which stylistic innovation is no longer possible, all that is left is to imitate dead styles, to speak through the masks and with the voices of the styles in the imaginary museum. But this means that contemporary or postmodernist art is going to be about art itself in a new kind of way; even more, it means that one of its essential messages will involve the necessary failure of art and the aesthetic, the failure of the new, the imprisonment in the past.

As this may seem very abstract, I want to give a few examples, one of which is so omnipresent that we rarely link it with the kinds of developments in high art discussed here. This particular practice of pastiche is not high-cultural but very much within mass culture, and it is generally known as the "nostalgia film" (what the French neatly call *la mode rétro* — retrospective styling). We must conceive of this category in the broadest way: narrowly, no doubt, it consists merely of films about the past and about specific generational moments of that past. Thus, one of the inaugural films in this new "genre" (if that's what it is) was Lucas's *American Graffiti*, which in 1973 set out to recapture all the atmosphere and stylistic peculiarities of the 1950s United States, the United States of the Eisenhower era. Polanski's great film *Chinatown* does something similar for the 1930s, as does Bertolucci's *The Conformist* for the Italian and European context of the same period, the fascist era in Italy; and so forth. We could go on listing these films for some time: why call them pastiche? Are they not rather work in the more traditional genre known as the historical film — work which can more simply be theorized by extrapolating that other well-known form which is the historical novel?

I have my reasons for thinking that we need new categories for such films. But let me first add some anomalies: supposing I suggested that *Star Wars* is also a nostalgia film. What could that mean? I presume we can agree that this is not a historical film about our own intergalactic past. Let me put it somewhat differently: one of the most important cultural experiences of the generations that grew up from the '30s to the '50s was the Saturday afternoon serial of the Buck Rogers type—alien villains, true American heroes, heroines in distress, the death ray or the doomsday box, and the cliffhanger at the end whose miraculous resolution was to be witnessed next Saturday afternoon. *Star Wars* reinvents this experience in the form of a pastiche: that is, there is no longer any point to a parody of such serials since they are long extinct. *Star Wars*, far from being a pointless satire of such now dead forms, satisfies a deep (might I even say repressed?) longing to experience them again: it is a complex object in which on some first level children and adolescents can take the adventures straight, while the adult public is able to gratify a deeper and more properly nostalgic desire to return to that older period and to live its strange old aesthetic artifacts through once again. This film is thus *metonymically* a historical or nostalgia film: unlike *American Graffiti*, it does not reinvent a picture of the past in its lived totality; rather, by reinventing the feel and shape of characteristic art objects of an older period (the serials), it seeks to reawaken a sense of the past associated with those objects. *Raiders of the Lost Ark*, meanwhile, occupies an intermediary position here: on some level it is *about* the '30s and '40s, but in reality it too conveys that period metonymically through its own characteristic adventure stories (which are no longer ours).

Now let me discuss another interesting anomaly which may take us further towards understanding nostalgia film in particular and pastiche generally. This one involves a recent film called *Body Heat*, which, as has abundantly been pointed out by the critics, is a kind of distant remake of *The Postman Always Rings Twice* or *Double Indemnity*. (The allusive and elusive plagiarism of older plots is, of course, also a feature of pastiche.) Now *Body Heat* is technically not a nostalgia film, since it takes place in a contemporary setting, in a little Florida village near Miami. On the other hand, this technical contemporaneity is most ambiguous indeed: the credits—always our first cue—are lettered and scripted in a '30s Art-Deco style which cannot but trigger nostalgic reactions (first to *Chinatown*, no doubt, and then beyond it to some more historical referent). Then the very style of the hero himself is ambiguous: William Hurt is a new star but has nothing of the distinctive style of the preceding generation of male superstars like Steve McQueen or even Jack Nicholson, or rather, his persona here is a kind of mix of their characteristics with an older role of the type generally associated with Clark Gable. So here too there is a faintly archaic feel to all this. The spectator begins to wonder why this story, which could have been situated anywhere, is set in a small Florida town, in spite of its contemporary reference. One begins to realize after a while that the small town setting has a crucial strategic function: it allows the film to do without most of the signals and references which we might associate with the contemporary world, with consumer society—the appliances and artifacts, the high rises, the object world of late capitalism. Technically, then, its objects (its cars, for instance) are 1980s products, but everything in the film conspires to blur that immediate contemporary reference and to make it possible to receive this too as nostalgia work—as a narrative set in some indefinable nostalgic past, an eternal '30s, say, beyond history. It seems to me exceedingly symptomatic to find the very style of nostalgia films invading and colonizing even those movies today which have contemporary settings: as though, for some reason, we were unable today to focus our own present, as though we have become incapable of achieving aesthetic representations of our own current experience. But if that is so, then it is a terrible indictment of consumer capitalism itself—or at the very least, an alarming and pathological symptom of a society that has become incapable of dealing with time and history.

So now we come back to the question of why nostalgia film or pastiche is to be considered different from the older historical novel or film (I should also include in this discussion the major literary example of all this, to my mind the novels of E. L. Doctorow—*Ragtime*, with its turn-of-the-century atmosphere, and *Loon Lake*, for the most part about our 1930s. But these are, to my mind, historical novels in appearance only. Doctorow is a serious artist and one of the few genuinely Left or radical novelists at work today. It is no disservice to him, however, to suggest that his narratives do not represent our historical past so much as they represent our ideas or cultural stereotypes about that past). Cultural production has been driven back inside the mind, within the monadic subject: it can no longer look directly out of its eyes at the real world for the referent but must, as in Plato's cave, trace its mental images of the world on its confining walls. If there is any realism left here, it is a "realism" which springs from the shock of grasping that confinement and of realizing that, for whatever peculiar reasons, we seem condemned to seek the historical past through our own pop images and stereotypes about that past, which itself remains forever out of reach. . . .

LYNDA HART IS A *scholar who writes frequently on feminism and theater. This selection is taken from the introduction to her excellent anthology,* Making a Spectacle: Feminist Essays in Contemporary Women's Theatre.

LYNDA HART

FROM *"Performing Feminism"*
(1989)

> *She is providing words, emotions, and an imaginative structure for others to inhabit and create anew onstage. A playwright — in this theoretical sense — thus makes other people speak and act — . . . . No wonder, then, that even the woman playwright with the mildest of messages is bound to be seen as an anomaly, if not an actual threat. Who knows what she will say once she gives voice?*
>
> — MICHELENE WANDOR

The above quotation is from Michelene Wandor's valuable study of British women's theatre which bears the telling title *Carry on, Understudies*.[1] An understudy is one who learns the part of another and waits prepared to appear as a substitute. It thus evokes the voices of women who are suppressed, heard only when unforeseen circumstances make it necessary for them to speak onstage, and then only as ventriloquists for the "real" actors. But in its negativity it announces their existence, creating knowledge of their presence and urging them out of the shadows.

It also points to the critical neglect of women's theatre, clearly the genre that has received the least scholarly attention. In 1975, Elaine Showalter said that "feminist criticism has allowed us to see meaning in what previously has been empty space."[2] But over a decade later, an abundance of books are now available about women poets and prose writers, while feminist critics still have much ground to break in our explorations of women's theatre. This book's contribution to filling the still sparsely occupied critical space is "making a spectacle," in defiance of the warning generally given to women to avoid having attention drawn to themselves, a prohibition against being publicly seen and heard. This collection of essays celebrates the intersection of feminism and theatre; we write to disregard that injunction, appropriating the stage to assert our own images and dismantle what seems to be the last bastion of male hegemony in the literary arts.

Spectacle derives from the Latin *spectare*, "to behold." The power of the spectator, and of those who create the spectacles, is discovered in the dormant meaning of *see*, "a seat of authority, especially a throne." Seeing is also the root of *theatre*, from *theoria*, "a looking at," a speculation. The *theatron*, the place of viewing, has rendered the woman playwright anomalistic, deviant when visible. As a form, the drama is more public and social than the other literary arts. The woman playwright's voice reaches a community of spectators in a public place that has historically been regarded as a highly subversive, politicized environment. The theatre is the sphere most removed from the confines of domesticity, thus the woman who ventures to be heard in this space takes a greater risk than the woman poet or novelist, but it may also offer her greater potential for effecting social change. Wandor sees in the theatre an "extraordinary range of potential voice and subject matter which makes the advent of women writers into theatre both so necessary and so exciting."[3] The latter half of the twentieth century has seen an emergence of women playwrights in numbers equal to the entire history of their dramatic foremothers. The power inherent in this collective confrontation challenges the very structures of "reality" that have kept women behind the scenes.

With a subversive twist, Marilyn Frye playfully appropriates the Ur-metaphor for the drama, *theatrum mundi*, the world as stage, refocusing our attention on the power of the background and implicitly calling the woman as "stagehand" to emerge center stage:

> All eyes, all attention, all attachment must be focused on the play, which is Phallocratic Reality. Any notice of the stagehands must be oblique and filtered through interest in the play. Anything which threatens the fixation of attention on the play threatens a cataclysmic dissolution of Reality into Chaos. Even the thought of the possibility of distraction is a distraction. The ever-present potential for cosmological disaster lies with the background. . . . There is nothing in the nature of the background that disposes it to be appropriately tame.[4]

In Frye's analogy, Reality is shaped and fixed, like stage realism's *mise en scène*. The unified foreground is constructed to pass for what is essential, objective, actual. Feminist adjustment of the lens to the background reveals the singular perspective that has placed women outside of representation—hidden, offstage, invisible—while representation has nonetheless been grounded in women. Frye's stagehands and Wandor's understudies metonymically capture the paradoxical positioning of women in dramatic discourse that Teresa de Lauretis articulates: ". . . while culture originates from woman and is founded on the dream of her captivity, women are all but absent from history and cultural process."[5]

Feminist theory of dramatic representation simultaneously addresses the absence of women from conventional theatre while it struggles to construct alternative ways of seeing. In a genre laden with famous male-created female heroines, from Antigone, to Portia, to Nora, the feminist seer nonetheless recognizes the absence of women's experience in the tradition. Playwright and theorist Hélène Cixous tells us that she stopped going to the theatre because "it was like going to [her] own funeral." In the theatre she found "the horror of the murder scene repeated and intensified with more violence even than fiction," and declared that "a woman must die before the play can begin."[6]

Jeannette Savona points out that Cixous's "murder scene," which confronts the minimalization or depletion of women "by all historical, anthropological, or psychological theories of humankind and by all philosophical or linguistic systems of thought," was written shortly after Cixous's own debut as a playwright.[7] After producing five plays herself, Cixous's profound skepticism shifted into a recognition of the power inherent in feminist theatrical articulations. According to Savona, Cixous began to see "the playwright's miraculous power to unite and disturb her audience, and perhaps even change them."[8] Such a transformation in attitude signals the emergence of strategies for foregrounding women's reality on the stage. By appropriating certain dramatic conventions and methods, subverting their customary usage and turning the lens of "objectivity" to re-present women through their own looking glasses, the women playwrights discussed in this book and the authors who call attention to their disruptions are canceling and deforming the structures that have held women framed, stilled, embedded, revoking the forms that have misrepresented women and "killed them into art."[9]

If the feminist writer's first efforts were investigations of the male-inscribed literary tradition, a second and ongoing effort has been to document women's realities as constructed by women writers. A shift in the last decade has been toward rigorous exploration of the language of representation itself. The constitutive dramatic aesthetic, the "mirror held up to nature," is a particularly pernicious concept for the feminist critic of the theatre, firmly entrenched as it has been by the Aristotelian directive which has had a powerful and lasting hold on the drama, dictating a linear structure that "imitates an action" embedded in conflict, climaxes, recognitions, and resolutions.[10] As feminist criticism has taught us, Woman and Nature have been equated in patriarchal discourses, thus woman becomes the screen onto which men project their fantasies of women, or rather of Woman—the monolithic Other. This aesthetic of mimesis has maintained the hegemony of realism in the drama which effectively masks the *re-creational* power of mimesis. The drama then must be challenged not only on the basis of what it represents but how it reproduces meaning through representation.

The assumption of objectivity which informs mimetic theory presupposes a division of experience, encoding differences as Difference grounded in gender polarity. The supposed objectivity of the artist must have something to look at, something that is Other than itself. As the subject/author records nature, eschewing selectively structured representations that are shaped by the personal experience and historical specificity of the perceiver, there is the persistent denial that "objectivity" is simply one lens among many. The feminist critic must seek ways out of this discourse to bring about change, for this is the master's way of seeing, and as Toril Moi reminds us "as long as the master's scopophilia, love of looking, remains satisfied, his domination is secure."[11] . . .

Notes

Since this introduction was written, two major books in the field have been published: Sue-Ellen Case, *Feminism in Theatre* (London: Methuen, 1988), and Jill Dolan, *The Feminist Spectator as Critic* (Ann Arbor: UMI Research Press, 1988).

1. Michelene Wandor, *Carry On, Understudies: Theatre and Sexual Politics* (London and New York: Routledge and Kegan Paul, 1986), p. 128.

2. Elaine Showalter, "Review Essay," *Signs* I, no. 2 (Winter 1975): 435.

3. *Understudies*, p. 128.

4. Marilyn Frye, *The Politics of Reality: Essays in Feminist Theory* (New York: The Crossing Press, 1983), p. 170.

5. Teresa de Lauretis, *Alice Doesn't: Feminism, Semiotics, Cinema* (Bloomington, Ind.: Indiana University Press, 1984), p. 13.

6. Hélène Cixous, "Aller à la mer," trans. Barbara Kerslake, *Modern Drama* 27, no. 4 (December 1984): 546.

7. Jeannette Laillou Savona, "French Feminism and Theatre: An Introduction," *Modern Drama* 27, no. 4 (December 1984): 541–42.

8. Ibid., p. 542.

9. Sandra Gilbert and Susan Gubar, *The Madwoman in the Attic* (New Haven: Yale University Press, 1979), p. 17.

10. For further discussion of the significance of Aristotle's *Poetics* and its implications for the feminist theatre critic, see Nancy S. Reinhardt, "New Directions for Feminist Criticism in the Theatre and the Related Arts," in *A Feminist Perspective in the Academy: The Difference It Makes*, ed. Elizabeth Langland and Walter Gove, pp. 25–51 (Chicago: University of Chicago Press, 1981). See also Sue-Ellen Case, *Feminism and Theatre* (New York: Methuen, 1988) for a more extended analysis.

11. Toril Moi, *Sexual/Textual Politics: Feminist Literary Criticism* (New York: Methuen, 1985), p. 132.

VII

DRAMA AND THEATER TODAY:
POPULAR ARTS AND THE
CANON(S) OF THEATER

CONTEMPORARY THEATER

has received most of its important innovations from outside the commercial mainstream. Sometimes — as in the case of Wole Soyinka's plays or the Asian theater admired by Antonin Artaud — these innovations have been imported into the Western theater from beyond its borders. Much as the early twentieth-century theater was influenced by small, independent theaters on the fringes of the "legitimate" stage, so today's avant-garde movements are often socially, politically, and artistically marginal. Black theater, Chicano theater, women's theater, gay and lesbian theater, workers' theater, the British "fringe" theater, off-off-Broadway theater, and the world's many resistance and underground theaters are — like the absurdist theater of Samuel Beckett and Jean Genet in the 1950s — the source of much that is new and exciting in theater and drama today. In theater studies and in other disciplines, the contribution of the once-unregarded perspectives represented by such theaters has excited considerable interest, debate, and even hostility as "new" works and "new" voices jostle to take their places in long-standing literary, dramatic, and cultural traditions.

This excitement is usually described as a debate over the CANON, the list, so to speak, of texts, objects, or ideas — in this case, plays — that are generally accepted to represent a common culture. Previous units have conveyed some of this excitement by including plays and playwrights that implicitly question what "generally accepted" and "common culture" might mean. *The Tempest*, for example, has long been part of the established canon of Shakespeare's work and of English literary studies. Some recent criticism, however, contends that this "canonical" status depends in part on how the play represents colonial subjects. Aphra Behn's *The Rover* arguably provides a different perspective on the rakish Restoration heroes than do plays by Behn's male contemporaries, William Wycherley and Sir George Etherege. Susan Glaspell's *Trifles* similarly questions the relationship between realism, interpretive authority, and gender. Many of the plays in this book present marginalized racial, ethnic, and class perspectives, while also implicitly questioning the idea of "the canon." How does Ntozake Shange's "theater piece," for example, change our understanding of what a canonical dramatic text should look like? How is it that the plays of Athol Fugard and Wole Soyinka — written in English — are already part of the canon of *world* drama, though they are not always considered part of the canon *English* drama?

This unit raises the question of canon in a particular way, narrowing the focus to the contemporary American stage in order to clarify some of the issues involved in forming a dramatic canon. The term *canon* originates in Biblical scholarship, but is most often used today to mean the "traditional" texts of Western culture, texts like *Oedipus Rex* or *King Lear* that are widely recognized as "classics." However, canons necessarily reflect the ideas, tastes, and politics both of the historical period when the works were created and of the institutions that have transmitted them to the present day. In this view, the dominant role played by a patriarchal, white European culture in the formation of a "common" literary and cultural tradition has resulted in a canon that reflects the values and attitudes of socially empowered groups in that culture. Such a tradition, it is argued, systematically undervalues or discriminates against other voices and other perspectives, commonly dismissing them as "minor," of "lesser artistic value," as "primitive," or as "irrelevant."

The idea that there is a single canon, though, oversimplifies a complex and important problem. Only superficially a list of works, a canon is actually a list of implied interpretations. What is canonical is not the texts themselves, but how they are interpreted. Herman

Melville's novel *Moby-Dick*, for example, is now regarded as a classic, part of the traditional canon of American literature. However, *Moby-Dick* has had this status only since the 1930s or so, when the novel was rediscovered by scholars, discussed in new ways, and newly taught in colleges and universities. When first published in 1851, it was a failure and remained relatively unknown — and certainly uncanonical — throughout the rest of the nineteenth century. The novel became part of established tradition only when it was seen to embody certain attitudes and techniques that — by the 1930s and 1940s — had come to seem "typical" of American literature at its best. Paradoxically, now that *Moby-Dick* is part of the canon, it is sometimes taken to represent eternal American values, "canonical" values that would not have been recognized by Melville's contemporaries. The history of *Moby-Dick* suggests that what makes a work canonical is how we read it, what kinds of value we learn to find in it.

If canons are really sets of implied interpretations, rather than lists of texts, then presumably works can become canonical for different reasons, or occupy a place in a number of different, competing canons. Canonical texts can even be read in ways that make them seem inimical to the values that once made them appear canonical. Shakespeare's *The Tempest* is again a good example. Although now-entrenched ideas of Shakespeare's canonicity largely prevent modern directors and producers from rewriting his plays, earlier eras had different values and companies often rewrote the plays to bring them into line with their tastes. In the late seventeenth century, William Davenant and John Dryden added a second pair of lovers, music, and other effects in their production of *The Tempest*. This may sound like heresy to modern readers — how could the play still be Shakespeare's if it was rewritten? — but we have to recognize that every time we interpret a play (or produce it on the stage) we "rewrite" it in a sense and bring its action into line with our own critical biases and perspectives. For this reason, even canonical works like *Moby-Dick* and *The Tempest* can seem oddly disruptive of the traditional values that are usually said to inform "the canon." *The Tempest* can be read as a play about the power of art and civilization to reform humankind: as a "traditional" play about the humanistic virtues of Western culture. *The Tempest* also can be read — as the Cuban critic Roberto Fernandez Retamar does in his essay *Caliban* — as a parable of colonialism, a critique of how the arts of Western civilization deform, exploit, and destroy indigenous cultures like Caliban's. A work that is capable of sustaining both of these readings raises the question of canonicity in different terms. How can these two *Tempests* be part of the same canon?

Drama poses special problems to the idea of a single literary canon. As popular entertainments, plays have not always been regarded as having literary merit. Plays were not generally published in Shakespeare's era for this reason, and even today few publishers have much commitment to keeping contemporary plays in publication — which makes it particularly difficult for contemporary drama to become part of *any* literary canon. More important, plays are produced under very different conditions than novels and poems. Plays are made to be meaningful in a specific theater. Their "literary" impact on readers is secondary to their original purpose, which is to make a theatrical impact on a given body of spectators. Dramatic texts, particularly in the modern period, sometimes lack the verbal complexity associated with canonical "literature." The language of drama, for example, often depends on the conventions of acting and theatrical speech. Set beside poetry, the language of drama sometimes seems prosaic, simple, not "complex" enough. Moreover, the author of a play has a different relation to his or her work than a novelist or a poet does, in that plays are written in collaborative circumstances. We know that Shakespeare revised *King Lear*, possibly in response to a changed sense of how the play worked on the stage. He "collaborated," in a sense, with the actors and with the audiences of the play to come up with a second version of the play. Like Shakespeare, Molière conceived his dramatic characters as roles for the specific members of his company and in this sense collaborated with members of the cast in constructing his plays. Even playwrights like O'Neill or Beckett—who did not collaborate with directors or actors, or work with a company when writing their plays—imagined a certain kind of production for their plays even in the process of composition. Dramatic texts also incorporate material from rehearsals and stage productions as part of the text, ideas suggested to the playwright and added to the script, or silently added to the dramatist's script by the publisher (as is sometimes the case with stage directions). Drama sometimes seems noncanonical because it does not have a single "author" in the traditional sense, and the sense that the dramatic text may contain only part of the play—the rest of it is waiting to be produced onstage—makes dramatic texts seem "open" in ways that frustrate the sense of closure implied by the conception of a "canon."

This book is relatively "canonical" in the selection of plays gathered here, though it implies some ways in which these plays are susceptible to new and challenging readings, or to being rearranged in new combinations with other works (think of *The Bacchae* and *Major Barbara* as commentaries on one another; or *Doctor Faustus*, *The Crucible*, and *Vinegar Tom*; or *Death and the King's Horseman* and *The Tempest*). The canon of modern and contemporary drama is particularly open to negotiation, in part because there is no firm tradition to protect or displace. The final two units of this book include a wide selection of the kinds of plays now being written and performed, plays not only challenging in subject matter but in their dramatic style, in the kind of theater they provide, and in their attitude toward contemporary life. Indeed, perhaps the most significant question about the canon of contemporary drama is whether we can define a canon of contemporary drama as fundamentally "literary" at all.

The question of canonicity is characteristic of contemporary arts of any kind, where there is no great weight of tradition to guide our thinking and interpretation, no fixed notion of how or where these works should fit into our lives. The plays included in this unit raise the question of the relationship between several arenas of production—the avant-garde, Broadway, Hollywood—and the process of canon formation. Today, this dichotomy is sometimes cast as a contest between "high art" and "entertainment," and the point is sometimes made that in Shakespeare's or Molière's theater, plays that we now regard as art were once regarded as mere entertainment. However, this dichotomy is in most ways a false one, for it is not a work's origin that determines its canonicity, any more than its themes, its value, or its style. Canonical status arises from a complex of factors that determine *how* a work will be read. The discovery or invention of those means is what makes contemporary art so liberating and exciting. These works are *our* contemporaries and they pose questions of interpretation with real immediacy. Would *you* have liked *King Lear* if you had been in Shakespeare's audience at its first performance? How would *you* have responded to *A Doll House* at its premiere? Or *Happy Days*?

The previous units of this book raised the issues of cultural authority with some urgency, and suggested a variety of approaches even to canonical plays. This unit contains four plays written within the past decade that have been popular for a variety of reasons, and at a variety of theatrical venues. *Mud* has been an influential play in the avant-garde and feminist theaters; *As Is* demonstrates the use of quasi-Brechtian techniques to render the politics of AIDS immediate to an audience; *M. Butterfly* was a huge Broadway success by an Asian-American dramatist; *Speed-the-Plow* is a recent play by an established playwright. In different ways, each of these plays evaluates and criticizes contemporary social life and raises important questions about the "canons" of value informing American culture today.

MARIA IRENE FORNES

Maria Irene Fornes was born in Cuba in 1930 and emigrated to the United States in 1945. She toured Europe in the mid-1950s studying to be a painter and in Paris saw Roger Blin's production of Beckett's *Waiting for Godot*. Fornes was impressed both by its power and by its severe visual imagery onstage, and when she returned to the United States in 1957, she returned as a playwright. Fornes has had a distinguished career in the avant-garde theater, experimenting in a variety of theatrical modes. She has produced brilliant absurdist plays like *There! You Died* (1963; revised as *Tango Palace* in 1964) and *Dr. Kheal* (1968); a successful musical, *Promenade* (1965, music by Al Carmines); and a moving, ritual-participatory play, *A Vietnamese Wedding* (1967). More recently, her plays have taken a more serious — though no less experimental — turn, examining women's identity in *Fefu and Her Friends* (1977), the relationship between politics, language, and love in *The Danube* (1982), and military and sexual oppression in Latin America in *The Conduct of Life* (1985). In 1986, she wrote another musical, with Tito Puente, *Lovers and Keepers*. Fornes has won several prestigious awards, including an Obie for Sustained Achievement in the Theater in 1982. *Mud* was first performed in 1983.

Mud

Mud's relation to the canon of American drama is complex, in that the play responds to both the thematic and the formal traditions of American domestic realism. On the thematic level, the play's depiction of domestic life treats the issues of gender and power much more explicitly than, say, Tennessee Williams's *The Glass Menagerie*. In terms of form, the play's abrupt and discontinuous plotting, its fragmentary characterization, and its disorienting MISE-EN-SCÈNE — the constricted room of realism perched on a dirt pile — all challenge the interpretive conventions we usually apply to realistic plays.

M U D

Maria Irene Fornes

— CHARACTERS —

MAE: *A spirited young woman. She is single-minded and determined, a believer. She is mid-twenties.*

LLOYD: *A simple and good-hearted young man. He is ungainly and unkempt. His shoulders slope, his stomach protrudes, some of his teeth are missing. At the start of the play, illness contributes to his poor appearance. He is mid-twenties.*

HENRY: *A large man. He has a natural sense of dignity, a philosophical mind. He can barely read. He is mid-fifties.*

The set is a wooden room which sits on an earth promontory. The promontory is five feet high and covers the same periphery as the room. The wood has the color and texture of bone that has dried in the sun. It is ashen and cold. The earth in the promontory is red and soft and so is the earth around it. There is no greenery. Behind the promontory there is a vast blue sky. On the back wall of the room there is an oversized fireplace which is the same color and texture as the walls and floor. On each side of the fireplace there are narrow doors. The door to the right leads to the exterior. There is a blue sky. The one to the left leads to a dark corridor. In the center of the room there is a kitchen table. There is a chair on each end. Down right there is an ironing board. There is an iron on it and a pair of trousers. Against the back wall on the left there is another chair. After the first scene these three chairs will always be placed around the table and will be referred to as right, center,

and left. Against the right wall there is a bench. On it there is a pile of unpressed trousers. On the table there is a pile of pressed trousers. Under the bench, there is a bundle of women's clothes and a pair of old, flat women's shoes. Inside the fireplace there are two cardboard boxes. One is full and tied with a string, the other is empty. On the mantelpiece there are, from right to left: a brown paper bag with a pamphlet in it, a pot with three metal plates and three spoons stacked upon it, a plate with broken bread, a pitcher with milk, a textbook, a notebook and pencil, a dish with string beans, a folded newspaper and a box with pills. Between the fireplace and the door to the left there are an ax and a rifle.

Offstage there is an empty box the same size as the box tied with a string. The following props are carried by the actors as they enter to perform the scene:

MAE: *2 bundles of clothes and a loose clean rag.*

LLOYD: *3 coins, a prescription note and a cup with oatmeal and a spoon.*

HENRY: *lipstick wrapped in paper, a small mirror, a notebook, bills and pencil, loose coins, a tin cup of milk, and a wad of bills.*

At the end of each scene a freeze is indicated. These freezes will last eight seconds which will create the effect of a still photograph. When the freeze is broken, the actors will make the necessary set changes and proceed to perform the following scene.

— ACT ONE —

SCENE I

LLOYD *sits left. He is unwashed and unshaven. He has a fever. He is clumsy and badly coordinated.* MAE *is at the ironing board. She is unkempt.*

LLOYD: You think you learn a lot at school?
MAE: I do.
LLOYD: What do you learn?
MAE: Subjects.
5 LLOYD: What is subjects?
MAE: Different things.
LLOYD: What things?
MAE: You want to know?
LLOYD: What are they?
10 MAE: Arithmetic.
LLOYD: Big deal arithmetic. I know arithmetic.
MAE: I'll bet.
LLOYD: Don't talk back to me. I'll kick your ass.
MAE: Fuck you, Lloyd. I'm telling you about arithmetic and you
15   talk to me like that? You're a moron. I won't tell you anything.
LLOYD: Oh, no?
MAE: No.
LLOYD: So what's arithmetic?
MAE: Fuck you. I'm not telling you.

LLOYD: *(Moving toward her.)* I'll fuck you till you're blue in the 20
    face! *(He stops and starts back to the chair.)* I don't even want
    to fuck you.
MAE: You can't, that's why. You can't get it up.
LLOYD: Oh yeah? I got it up yesterday!
MAE: When! 25
LLOYD: Afternoon!
MAE: Never saw it.
LLOYD: You weren't here.
MAE: Where was I?
LLOYD: At school. You missed it. I got it up. 30
MAE: Who with?
LLOYD: Fuck you. I'm not telling you.
MAE: Who with?
LLOYD: With myself. —I don't need someone. I got it up right
    here. *(Pointing to the wall.)* See that? I did that! From here. I 35
    didn't give it to you or anyone. *(Pantomiming an erection and
    ejaculation.)* I held it as long as I wanted. Then I gave it to the
    wall. *(Pointing to a spot on the wall.)* See. Fuck you, Mae.
MAE: Fuck you, Lloyd.
LLOYD: So tell me! 40
MAE: Tell you what.
LLOYD: What's arithmetic?

MAE: It's numbers.

LLOYD: Oh yeah!

45 MAE: Yeah!

LLOYD: Why didn't you say it's numbers! — I know numbers.

MAE: You don't know numbers.

LLOYD: Yes I do. *(He stands.)* I'm Lloyd. I have two pigs. My mother died. I was seven. My father left. He is dead. *(He gets*

50 *three coins from his pocket.)* This is money. It's mine. It's three nickels. I'm Lloyd. That's arithmetic.

MAE: That is not arithmetic.

LLOYD: Why not?

MAE: It isn't.

55 LLOYD: *(He returns to the chair.)* It's numbers!

MAE: Arithmetic is more!

LLOYD: What more!

MAE: A lot more! — Multiplication!

LLOYD: Come here! *(She puts the iron down.)*

60 MAE: What for!

LLOYD: I'm going to show you something.

MAE: *(She walks to him.)* What!

LLOYD: *(In one move he takes her hand, crosses his left leg, and puts her hand on his crotch.)* Feel it!

65 MAE: What?

LLOYD: It! It! Touch it!

MAE: I'm touching it!

LLOYD: Do something to it!

MAE: What!

70 LLOYD: Anything, stupid!

MAE: Let go of my hand!

LLOYD: *(Pressing her tighter.)* What hand?

MAE: Let go, you jerk! You stink! You smell bad!

LLOYD: So what!

75 MAE: You're disgusting!

LLOYD: No kidding!

MAE: Let go! *(She steps on his foot.)*

LLOYD: Shit! *(She goes back to the ironing board.)* I'll kick your ass! *(He feels his genitals.)* Shit, it's gone!

80 MAE: What's gone! You can't get it up! You have some sickness there! *(Short pause.)* You should go to a doctor.

LLOYD: Didn't I say I got it up yesterday!

MAE: Yes. You did.

LLOYD: OK! So I did! — So where's dinner!

85 MAE: I don't know where's dinner.

LLOYD: You know where's dinner!

MAE: You know where's dinner!

LLOYD: Yeah, where's dinner! Dinner's in a pot on the stove! Dinner's on the table! It's in the cupboard! It's dried up in the

90 pot! Dinner is somewhere! It's spilled on the floor! Where's dinner! *(There is a pause.)* Where's dinner! *(She continues ironing.)* Come here!

MAE: Fuck you.

LLOYD: You're a whore!

95 MAE: I'm pressing, jerk! What are you doing! I'm pressing. What are you doing! *(He looks away.)* I'm pressing what are you doing! *(She continues ironing.)* I work. See, I work. I'm working. I learned to work. I wake up and I work. I work. What do you do! Yeah,

100 what do you do! — Work!

LLOYD: So what. *(He sits in a corner on the floor.)*

MAE: What do you do when you open your eyes. I work, jerk. You're a pig. You'll die like a pig in the mud. You'll rot there in the mud. No one will bury you. Your skin will bloat. In the 105 mud. Then, it will get blue like rotten meat and it will bloat even more. And you will get so rotten that the dogs will puke when they come near you. Even flies won't go near you. You'll just lay there and rot. *(She irons.)* I'm going to die in a hospital. In white sheets. You hear? *(She looks front.)* Clean 110 feet. Injections. That's how I'm going to die. I'm going to die clean. I'm going to school and I'm learning things. You're stupid. I'm not. When I finish school I'm leaving. You hear that? You can stay in the mud. *(She irons.)* Did you pick the corn?

115 LLOYD: What corn?

MAE: The corn I told you to pick.

LLOYD: There is no corn.

MAE: How come there is no corn.

LLOYD: The groundhog ate it.

120 MAE: You let him eat it.

LLOYD: I didn't.

MAE: You didn't watch it.

LLOYD: I came in to sleep. I had to sleep.

MAE: You can sleep in the field.

125 LLOYD: It's wet there! It's cold! I'm sick! You sleep there!

MAE: I work here, not in the field.

LLOYD: I'll work here. You work there.

MAE: *(Harshly.)* I wish you went to the doctor. — You're not going to get well if you don't. When I leave you'll starve.

130 LLOYD: I'll find food.

MAE: Where?

LLOYD: Anywhere. There's food.

MAE: Where.

LLOYD: There's pigslop.

135 MAE: What pigslop? There won't be any pigslop. Not if you don't grow something to put in it!

(Pause.)

LLOYD: I did it to Betsy.

MAE: You did.

LLOYD: Yeah. — I felt bad. — My head hurt. — I went to her. She's nice. She lets me eat her food. — I did it to her. — I got it 140 up. I got it in her all the way. — It didn't hurt.

MAE: No kidding.

LLOYD: It didn't hurt.

MAE: You don't fuck pigs.

LLOYD: She liked it.

145 MAE: I'll bet.

LLOYD: What do you mean?

MAE: Did you get clean before you did it?

LLOYD: What for? I'm clean.

MAE: No you're not. You stink.

150 LLOYD: She didn't mind.

MAE: *(She places the ironing board alongside the right wall and places the garment she has pressed on top of the other pressed clothes.)* I'm taking these up now. We'll walk to the clinic. You have to see a doctor. *(She starts putting on her shoes.)* Put 155 on your shoes, Lloyd. — I'll walk there with you. I know you won't get there if I don't go with you. Get moving, Lloyd. *(She takes the clothes and goes to the door.)* Come on. *(He*

doesn't move.) Let's go, Lloyd. (He stands and goes for the ax.
160   He holds the ax as he waits for her to exit.) You're not going to
the clinic with an ax.
LLOYD: (He goes to the chair still holding the ax and sits.) Why
not.
MAE: You can't.
165 LLOYD: I'll take my knife, then.
MAE: You can't take your knife either.
LLOYD: I won't go then.

(They freeze.)

SCENE II

MAE takes a brown paper bag from the mantelpiece, opens the
right door, steps on the threshold and turns front as if she had just
come from the outside. She has an air of serenity. LLOYD sits on
the left. His appearance has worsened.

MAE: I went to the clinic, Lloyd. And I told them what you have.
LLOYD: What did you tell them?
MAE: (Stepping into the room.) I told them you're sick. And I
told them what you have.
5   LLOYD: What did they say?
MAE: They said you have to go there. (As she gets the chair from
the left corner and places it center.) You have to go to the
clinic. They won't give you medicine till you go.
LLOYD: I'm not going.
10 MAE: They have to give you a test. They can't give you medicine
till they find out what you have. They said you may have
something bad.
LLOYD: What.
MAE: (She sits.) They didn't say. (She takes a pamphlet out of the
15   paper bag.) They gave me this book.
LLOYD: What does it say?
MAE: (She places the paper bag on the mantelpiece.) I couldn't
read it. I tried to read it but I can't. I got Henry to read it for
you. He's outside.
20 LLOYD: Why can't you read it?
MAE: It's too difficult.
LLOYD: All that time at school and you can't read.
MAE: I tried to read it and it was too difficult. That's why I got
Henry to read it because it was too difficult for me. It is ad-
25   vanced. I'm not advanced yet. I'm intermediate. I can read a
lot of things but not this. —I'm going to let Henry in.
LLOYD: (Reproachfully.) I wish you could have read it.
MAE: Me too. I wish I could have read it. (She opens the door
and walks to the left of the center chair.) Come in, Henry.
30   (HENRY enters and stands by the fireplace. He places his left
hand on the mantelpiece.) Sit down, Henry. (HENRY sits on
the center chair. MAE closes the door.) Here's Henry, Lloyd.
He's going to read for you.
HENRY: Are you drunk, Lloyd? You look drunk.
35   MAE: (Sitting on the right.) He's sick. He has a fever.
HENRY: Has he been drinking?
LLOYD: I am not drunk.
HENRY: What's wrong with him?
MAE: He's sick.
40 HENRY: Remember Ron, what happened to him.
LLOYD: What happened to him?

HENRY: He died. —And what did he die of?
LLOYD: He drank till he died.
MAE: His liver failed him.
HENRY: Why did his liver fail him? Alcohol. —Why did he   45
drink? He drank because he owned alcohol. And why did he
own alcohol? He owned alcohol because he owned a pharmacy. And why did that lead a man to drinking? Because he
kept alcohol in the pharmacy. —There you have two things:
alcohol and time to do nothing. So what happens? You drink   50
yourself to death. —So, you have alcohol, you drink it. You
don't have alcohol, you don't drink it. You have money to buy
alcohol, you buy it. You don't have money to buy it, you
don't buy it. —Does Lloyd have alcohol, Mae?
MAE: He has no money to buy it.   55
HENRY: If Lloyd had money he would drink. He'd be a drunk.
MAE: Yes, he would.
HENRY: If he's not a drunk it's because he's poor.
MAE: He is. —This is the book, Henry.
HENRY: (HENRY puts on his glasses. He reads each section first to   60
himself in a low voice. Then he reads it out loud stumbling
through the words at a high speed.) Prostatitis and Prostatosis.
Acute and chronic bacterial infection of the prostrate gland:
symptoms, diagnosis, and treatment. (He wets his finger and
turns the page.) Common symptoms of acute prostatitis and   65
bacterial prostatosis are: febrile illness, back pains, perineal
pain, irritative voiding, aching of the perineum, sexual pain,
sexual impotency, painful ejaculation, and intermittent dis-
ureah, or bloody ejaculation.
LLOYD: What does that mean?   70
HENRY: I don't know what it means, Lloyd. These are medical
terms. It needs study. This may require the use of a dictionary—a special dictionary. One that has medical terms—
technical terms—probably a dictionary that would have all
kinds of technical terms—from hardware and construction   75
terms to scientific terms—like physics. There are such dictionaries. (Short pause.) You look swollen, Lloyd.
MAE: He is swollen.
HENRY: And your color is poor.
MAE: Show him your tongue, Lloyd. His tongue is white and his   80
breath smells bad.

(LLOYD opens his mouth. HENRY looks at LLOYD's tongue.)

HENRY: What is wrong with you?
MAE: I want him to go to the doctor but he won't.
HENRY: Why won't you go to the doctor, Lloyd.
LLOYD: I don't want to go.   85
MAE: He will stay here and rot.
LLOYD: I won't rot. I said I'd go. You said I couldn't go.
MAE: He wanted to go up with an ax. He's an animal. You don't
go to the clinic with an ax. You can't do that.
HENRY: Why would you do that, Lloyd?   90
LLOYD: I didn't do it. I never went.
HENRY: He does smell bad.
MAE: He's rotting away and he won't do anything about it. You
better dig your grave while you can, Lloyd. Because I'm not
going to do it for you. I told him to find a spot and dig it. It   95
takes a strong person to dig that deep. I can't do it. I wouldn't,
even if I could. (Pause.) Would you like some bread, Henry? I
got some butter.

HENRY: Yes, thank you.

100 MAE: Would you like some dinner? We have soup.

HENRY: Yes, thank you.

MAE: Stay then, I haven't started it yet.

HENRY: I will, thank you.

(They freeze.)

SCENE III

MAE *places the pamphlet on the mantelpiece, then takes the pot, plates and spoons and places them on the table. They each take a spoon and plate, then they pass them to* MAE, *who holds the plates in her hands as if she were about to put them away.* LLOYD *lies on the floor, under the table, facing front.* HENRY *moves his chair slightly to the left. He and* MAE *have been talking. They both speak with philosophical objectivity.*

HENRY: Soon everything will be used only once. We will use things once. We will need to do that as our time will be of value and it will not be feasible to spend it caring for things: washing them, mending them, repairing them. We will use a

5   car till it breaks down. Then, we will discard it. A radio or any machine or appliance will be discarded as soon as it breaks down. We will make a call on the telephone and a new one will be delivered. Already we see places that use paper cups, paper plates, paper towels. — Our time will not be wasted and

10   we will choose how to spend it.

MAE: I don't think I'll be wanted in such a world.

HENRY: Why not?

MAE: Oh. *(Pause.)* In such a world a person must be of value.

HENRY: Oh?

15 MAE: I feel I am hollow . . . and offensive. *(As* MAE *places the dishes on the mantelpiece.)*

HENRY: Why is that?

MAE: I think most people are.

HENRY: What do you mean? — Explain what you mean.

20 MAE: I don't think I can.

HENRY: I am not offensive. I don't think I am offensive. I think I am a decent man.

MAE: You are decent, Henry. I know you are, and so is Lloyd in his own way.

25 HENRY: Then, what do you mean when you say we are offensive?

MAE: I mean that we are base, and that we spend our lives with small things.

HENRY: I don't feel I do that.

MAE: Don't be offended, Henry. You are not base. Of all the

30   people I know you are the finest. You are the person I respect and I feel most proud to know. — *(She begins to look at him fixedly, possessed by fervor.)* I have no one to talk to. And sometimes I feel hollow and base. And I feel I don't have a mind. But when I talk to you I do. I feel I have a mind. Why is

35   that? *(She moves closer to him.)* Why is it that some people make you feel stupid and some people make you feel smart. Not smart, because I am not smart. But some people make you feel that you have something inside you. Inside your head. *(She moves closer.)* Why is it that you can talk, Henry,

40   and Lloyd cannot talk? Why is that? What I'm saying, Henry, is that I want you. That I want you here with me. That I love you.

HENRY: Mae, this is unexpected.

MAE: It is unexpected, Henry.

HENRY: I have nothing to offer you.   45

MAE: Yes, you do. I want you.

HENRY: Me?

MAE: *(She starts to move her head toward him slowly and intensely.)* I want your mind.

HENRY: . . . My mind?   50

MAE: *(Still moving her head toward him.)* I want it. *(She kisses him intensely. They look at each other.)*

HENRY: Did you feel my mind?

MAE: Yes, I did. *(She kisses him again.)* I did. I want you here.

HENRY: Here?   55

MAE: I want you here.

HENRY: To live here?

MAE: If you will.

(They freeze.)

SCENE IV

HENRY *exits.* MAE *places the spoons and pot on the mantelpiece. Then, she takes off her shoes, places a pair of trousers on the ironing board and puts out the ironing board.* LLOYD *gets the box with the string from the fireplace and stands down left holding it.* MAE *irons.*

MAE: Just put it down. *(He stands still. She continues ironing.)* Put it down Lloyd. *(He stands still.)* Henry is going to stay here with us. He is going to live here. He needs a place and I want him to stay here. You can learn from Henry. If you want to, he can teach you how to read. Put the box down. I'll take it   5 up to the bedroom. Henry's going to sleep in the bedroom. He has a bad back and he needs to sleep in the bed. You can sleep here. — Get papers from the shed and lay them on the floor. I'll get you a blanket. — I'll take it up now. *(She takes the box from* LLOYD *and exits left. He is distraught. He sits on the   10 chair on the left and cries. He puts his head on the table and freezes.)*

SCENE V

MAE *places the ironing board against the wall.* LLOYD *places the pitcher of milk and the plate with bread on the table.* MAE *gets the plates and spoons. She places the spoons in the center and lays each plate in front of her.* HENRY *enters and sits center.* LLOYD *sits left.* LLOYD *and* HENRY *take a spoon each.* MAE *serves bread onto the plates, pours milk on the bread and passes two plates to* HENRY, *who passes one to* LLOYD *and keeps the second for himself.* MAE *sits. They start eating.*

MAE: Do you say grace before a meal, Henry?

HENRY: I do sometimes.

MAE: Would you say grace?

HENRY: I will, if you want me to.

MAE: I do.   5

HENRY: *(Crosses his hands.)* Oh, give thanks unto the Lord, for he is good: for his mercy endures forever. For he satisfies the longing soul, and fills the hungry soul with goodness.

MAE: We never said grace in this house. My father never did and I never learned how and neither did Lloyd. — Lloyd did you   10

hear that? Henry said grace. I feel grace in my heart. I feel fresh inside as if a breeze had just gone inside my heart. What was it you said, Henry? What were these words. I don't retain the words. I never do. I find it hard to retain words I learn. It is
15 hard for me to do the work at school. I can work on my feet all day at the ironing board. I can make myself do it, even if I am tired. But I cannot make myself retain what I learn. I have no memory. The teacher says I have no memory. And it's true I don't. I don't remember the things I learn too well. Not
20 enough to pass the test. But I rejoice with the knowledge that I get. Not everything, but most things, make me feel joyful. Do you feel that way, Henry?
HENRY: I am not sure. I like to know things. But if I didn't remember what I learned, I don't think I would feel any plea-
25 sure. — If I didn't remember things, I would feel that I don't know them. I like to learn things so I can live according to them, according to my knowledge. What would be the use of knowing things if they don't serve you, if they don't help you shape your life. — Lloyd, do you take pleasure in learning if
30 you forget what you have learned?

(LLOYD *looks at* MAE, *then at* HENRY *again.*)

MAE: Lloyd doesn't like learning things.
LLOYD: I like learning things.
MAE: Why don't you then?
LLOYD: What is it I haven't learned?

(MAE *and* HENRY *look at each other.*)

35 Henry, would you say grace again?
HENRY: Again?
MAE: Is that wrong?
HENRY: No. Oh, give thanks unto the Lord, for he is good: for his mercy endures forever. For he satisfies the longing soul,
40 and fills the hungry soul with goodness. (MAE *sobs.*) Why are you crying?
MAE: I am a hungry soul. I am a longing soul. I am an empty soul. (*She cries.*) I cry with joy. It satisfies me to hear words that speak so lovingly to my soul. (MAE *eats.* LLOYD *eats.*
45 HENRY *watches* MAE.) Don't be afraid to eat from our dishes, Henry. They are clean.

(*They freeze.*)

SCENE VI

LLOYD *places his plate and spoon over* HENRY'S. HENRY *places the pitcher and bread plate on the mantelpiece and exits.* MAE *places the plates and spoons on the mantelpiece and gets the textbook. She sits center and reads with difficulty. She follows the written words with the fingers of both hands. Her reading is inspired.* LLOYD *listens to her and stares at the book.*

MAE: The starfish is an animal, not a fish. He is called a fish because he lives in the water. The starfish cannot live out of the water. If he is moist and in the shade he may be able to live out of the water for a day. Starfish eat old and dead sea ani-
5 mals. They keep the water clean. A starfish has five arms like a star. That is why it is called a starfish. Each of the arms of the starfish has an eye in the end. These eyes do not look like our eyes. A starfish's eye cannot see. But they can tell if it is night or day. If a starfish loses an arm he can grow a new one.

This takes about a year. A starfish can live five or ten years or 10 perhaps more, no one really knows.

(LLOYD *slaps the book off the table.* MAE *slaps* LLOYD. *They freeze.*)

SCENE VII

LLOYD *picks up the book and places it on the down-left corner of the table. He places the left chair against the wall and sits.* MAE *takes a notebook and pencil from the mantelpiece. She takes the book and stands on the up-right side of the table copying from the book.* HENRY *enters and stands on the up-left corner.*

HENRY: What is Lloyd to you? (*There is a pause.*) He's a man and he's not a blood relative. So what is he to you?
MAE: Lloyd? (*Pause.*) He is like family.
HENRY: But he is not. — Everyone knows he is not. What is he?
MAE: I don't know what you call what he is. If I were to ask 5 myself I would not know what to answer. — He is not with me. You know he is not. He sleeps down here.
HENRY: I feel I am offending him. And he is offending me. So what is he.
MAE: (*Sitting on the right facing front.*) What can I do, Henry, I 10 don't want you to be offended. There's nothing I can do and there's nothing you can do and there is nothing Lloyd can do. He's always been here, since he was little. My dad brought him in. He said that Lloyd was a good boy and that he could keep me company. He said he was old and tired and he didn't 15 understand what a young person like me was like. That he had no patience left and he was weary of life and he had no more desire to make things work. He didn't want to listen to me talk and he felt sorry to see me sad and lonely. He didn't want to be mean to me, but he didn't have the patience. He 20 was sick. My dad was good but he was sad and hopeless and when my mom died he went to hell with himself. He got sick and died and he left Lloyd here and Lloyd and I took care of each other. I don't know what we are. We are related but I don't know what to call it. We are not brother and sister. We 25 are like animals who grow up together and mate. We were mates till you came here, but not since then. I could not be his mate again, not while you are here. I am not an animal. I care about things, Henry, I do. I know some things that I never learned. It's just that I don't know what they are. I can- 30 not grasp them. (*She goes on her knees as her left shoulder leans on the corner of the table.*) I don't want to live like a dog. (*Pause.*) Lloyd is good, Henry. And this is his home. (*Pause. She looks up.*) When you came here I thought heaven had come to this place, and I still feel so. How can there be of- 35 fense here for you?

(*They freeze.*)

SCENE VIII

LLOYD *places his chair by the table and exits.* MAE *places the notebook, pencil and textbook on the mantelpiece. She places the dish with string beans center and sits. She snaps beans.* HENRY *walks behind* MAE *and covers her eyes. He takes a small package from his pocket and puts it in the bowl.*

MAE: What is it? (*He uncovers her eyes. She unwraps the package. It is a lipstick.*) Lipstick . . . (HENRY *pushes the lipstick out of the tube. He takes a mirror out of his pocket and holds it in front of her.*) A mirror. (*She holds the mirror and puts on lipstick. She puckers her lips. He kisses her.*) Oh, Henry.

(*They freeze.*)

SCENE IX

MAE *places the lipstick, mirror, and dish with string beans on the mantelpiece. She places the textbook center and sits.* HENRY *places the paper and lipstick cover on the mantelpiece. He takes the newspaper, turns the left chair toward the down-left corner and sits to read, leaning his elbow on the table.* LLOYD *sits on the floor, down of the right chair with his arm leaning on it.*

MAE: (*Reading.*) This is a hermit crab. He is called a hermit because he lives in empty shells that once belonged to other animals. When he is little he likes to crawl into the shells of water snails. When he grows larger he finds a larger shell. Often he tries several shells before he finds the one that fits. Sometimes he wants the shell of another hermit crab and then there is a fight. Sometimes the owner is pulled out. Sometimes the owner wins and stays.

(LLOYD *lifts himself up to look at* HENRY. *He mouths a curse.* MAE *turns to look at* LLOYD, *then looks at* HENRY. HENRY *turns to look at* MAE, *then he looks at* LLOYD. *They freeze.*)

— ACT TWO —

SCENE X

HENRY *enters left carrying a notebook, pencil and a few bills. He sits left. He transfers figures from the bills to the ledger.* LLOYD *enters right. He stands up-center. He reaches into his pocket for a medical prescription and stretches his arm in* HENRY's *direction. He sits to the right. The italicized words represent a stuttering.*

LLOYD: They gave me *this.*

HENRY: (*Reads what's on the paper while still in* LLOYD's *hand. He returns to his papers.*) That's the prescription for your medicine.

5 LLOYD: They said I should buy *this.* (*Pause.*) They said I should *buy* it.

HENRY: Did you?

LLOYD: No.

HENRY: Why not.

10 LLOYD: I went to the *clinic.*

HENRY: (*Without looking at him.*) I'm glad you did.

LLOYD: It took a *while.* I thought they *kept* me a long time. I went *early* and just came back.

HENRY: How do you feel?

15 LLOYD: I don't feel *better.* — I feel *worse.*

HENRY: Why is that?

LLOYD: They have *instruments* there. They *stuck instruments* in me.

HENRY: What did they say?

20 LLOYD: I have to take *medicine* — *pills.* I have to *buy* them. They said I have to *swallow* the pills.

HENRY: I'm glad you went.

LLOYD: (*Stretches his arm to show* HENRY *the prescription.*)

They gave me *this.* They said I should *buy* this. (*He puts the prescription on the table.*) They said I should *buy* it.

25 HENRY: (*With contained anger.*) You should get the medicine, Lloyd. You should take it and get it over with. You should take the medication and get well. You should not walk around with an illness that's eating your insides. Get the medicine. Do as you are told.

30 (*They freeze.*)

SCENE XI

HENRY *exits.* LLOYD *takes the box of pills from the mantelpiece and empties it on the table. He sits center.* MAE *enters right, wiping her wet hands with her skirt. She sits right.* LLOYD *puts a pill in his mouth. A moment later he spits it.*

MAE: What are they?

LLOYD: Pills.

MAE: Lloyd . . . What are you doing? (*He cleans his tongue.*) Does it taste bad?

5 LLOYD: Yeah.

MAE: (*She picks up the pill and sits.*) Try it again. (*He puts it in his mouth.*) Swallow it. (*He swallows and chokes. She stands by him and pushes the pill down his throat. She looks at him.*) Did you swallow it? (*She looks at him.*) What do you feel? (*He makes a face. She sits and puts the pills in the box.*) How did 10 you get them?

LLOYD: (*Defensively.*) I bought them. — I took the money. — From Henry. — From his trousers. — I took the money from his trousers. — I don't care. — He owes me money. — For rent. — For my bed. — He took my bed. — Like a crab. — He 15 got into my bed like a crab. — I took it. — I didn't steal it, because it belonged to me. — Because I needed to get my medicine. — And he never gave me what he owed me. — I had to ask him for it. — And he never gave it to me. — I asked him. — And he never gave it to me. — And he came here only 20 to take things from me. — Like a crab.

(HENRY *enters left. He is in his underwear. He carries his pants over his left arm. He holds a change purse in his right hand. He walks down left and stands there. He is stunned.*)

HENRY: Someone took money from my purse. — There is less money here than I should have. — Some of the money I had is gone.

MAE: Lloyd took it. 25

HENRY: (*He sits.*) Well, tell him to give it back.

MAE: He took it for his medicine.

HENRY: He went to my purse and took it?

MAE: He needed money for his medicine. (*Pause.*) Would you let Lloyd have that money? 30

HENRY: Have Lloyd have my money?

(*Pause.*)

MAE: He'll pay it back.

HENRY: How will he pay it back?

MAE: (*To* LLOYD.) . . . Lloyd. . . ? (LLOYD *looks at* MAE.)

HENRY: How will he pay it back? How will Lloyd get money to 35 pay me back? (*Pause.*) How much money did he take?

MAE: . . . Lloyd. . . ?

LLOYD: I don't know how much I took.

HENRY: How will he pay it back if he doesn't know how much he
40   took? *(Pause.)* Tell him I want to know how much he took.
LLOYD: I went to the clinic. — And they put those instruments in
me. — And they said I had to buy that medicine. — And I
couldn't find someone to help me buy that medicine. — I
went to the pharmacy. — And they said I had to pay for it. —
45   And Henry had money but he wouldn't pay for it. — And he
took my bed. — And he can take anything he wants from
me. — And I had to buy that medicine. — So I took the money
from him.
HENRY: Ask him when he took it.
50 LLOYD: I took it while he slept.
HENRY: How much did he take?

(Pause.)

MAE: Lloyd can't count, Henry.
HENRY: *(He takes money out of the purse, puts it on the table and
counts it. He does mental subtraction.)* Tell him he took one
55   fifty four. (MAE *looks at* LLOYD.) Is that what he spent? Does
he still have any of that money? (LLOYD *reaches into his
pocket.)* Tell him to put it on the table. (LLOYD *does.* HENRY
counts the money, then does mental subtraction. He puts the
coins in the purse and goes to the door.) Tell him he owes me
60   one thirty eight. And tell him I wish he'll pay it back. *(He
exits.* MAE *goes to the door and looks in the direction* HENRY
has walked. They freeze.)*

SCENE XII

MAE *puts a pair of trousers on the ironing board and puts the
ironing board out.* LLOYD *places the box of pills on the mantelpiece and stands on top of the table.*

LLOYD: There is a reason why it happened to him and not to me.
MAE: I wish it had happened to you.
LLOYD: Ha! — It couldn't have happened to me. I'm strong. He's
weak and old. That's why he fell. *(Doing an exaggerated dem-
5   onstration of someone walking on dangerous ground.)* I can
walk on wet stones and I don't fall. Look. I can run on wet
stones. I can stand on my own two feet. Look! *(He jumps to
the floor and stands with his feet apart.)* Try and push me. Go
on. Push me. *(She ignores him. He jumps on the table in a
10   prone position with his legs crossed and his hands under his
head.)* I wish he had drowned. I wish he had fallen in the
water and drowned. He's old. His legs couldn't hold him.
That's why he fell. *(He jumps to the floor and runs across
jumping up in the air making sounds as he goes up and down.
15   He does this several times, then holds an athletic pose.)* Can he
do that?
MAE: *(Still ironing.)* No, he can't. He's paralyzed. He may be a
cripple. You know he can't do that!
LLOYD: *(Lies on the table with his hands under his head.)* He
20   couldn't do it before he fell. That's why he fell. He's old. He
was falling apart. That's why he fell. Now he can't even
move. — Look! *(He does several cartwheels.)* Can he do that?
MAE: No, he can't.
LLOYD: *(Sits on the table with his arms and legs in a body-
25   builder's pose.)* He has no muscle. I wouldn't fall if I had to
walk on wet stones. I can run on wet stones. Like this. *(He
demonstrates.)* I wish he had fell in the water. I wish he had

drowned. So now he can't walk. *(Short pause.)* Who's going
to take care of him?
MAE: We are.   30

(LLOYD *exits right. The sound of vomiting is heard. She freezes.)*

SCENE XIII

MAE *puts the ironing board alongside the wall.* LLOYD *enters left
with the cup with oatmeal and the spoon. He places the right
chair away from the table.* HENRY *enters. He sits on the chair to
the right. His left side is paralyzed and deformed. His trousers are
rolled to his knees. He is bare-chested and wears a kitchen towel
as a bib. He wears a necktie under the towel. He holds a tin cup
of milk in his left hand.* LLOYD *is perched against the table next
to* HENRY. *He feeds oatmeal to him.* HENRY *moves the oatmeal
around his mouth, then he lets it dribble out or he spits it.*
HENRY'S *speech is incomprehensible.*

LLOYD: Stop it! *(Scooping the spilled oatmeal from* HENRY'S *chin
and bib and putting it back in his mouth.)* Stop doing that. —
Don't do that. (HENRY *lets the oatmeal out.)* You just quit
that. — Chew it. — Swallow it. (HENRY *lets the oatmeal out.
LLOYD starts scooping it.)* Stop that! Stop doing that! You   5
better stop that, Henry. — (HENRY *lets the oatmeal out.)* Quit
that. You just quit that. (HENRY *slaps the cup of milk and
spills it on the floor.)* That is it, Henry. *(Taking* HENRY'S *bib
off.)* You get your own food.
HENRY: It spilled!   10
LLOYD: You did it on purpose.
HENRY: It spilled.
LLOYD: No, it didn't. You spilled it.
HENRY: Clean it!
LLOYD: No, I won't. You clean it. I saw you do it. You clean it.   15
HENRY: Clean it!
LLOYD: I won't clean it. You clean it.
HENRY: Clean it!
LLOYD: You clean it!
HENRY: Mae. . . ! *(Pause.)* Mae. . . ! *(Pause.)* Mae. . . !   20
MAE: *(Enters. She carries a bundle of clothes and a cleaning
rag.)* What is it?
HENRY: *(Pointing to the milk.)* Look!
MAE: What happened? (MAE *puts the clothes on the bench and
stands by* HENRY *with the rag.)*   25
HENRY: He spilled it!
LLOYD: I didn't spill it! He spilled it!
MAE: So clean it up!
HENRY: Clean it!
LLOYD: I'm going to kill him.   30
MAE: Kill him if you want. — He can't talk straight any more.
(She starts wiping the oatmeal off HENRY.) Clean up the milk!
HENRY: Clean it!

(LLOYD *takes* HENRY'S *bib and starts wiping the milk.)*

MAE: Did you feed the pigs?
LLOYD: Yeah.   35
MAE: Did Henry eat?
LLOYD: He spilled the milk.
MAE: Did he eat! (LLOYD *doesn't answer.)* Did he eat! *(Pause.)*
Did you eat, Henry?

40 HENRY: I ate.
   MAE: He ate. Why didn't you say he ate. (MAE *walks to the left
     door and opens it.*)
   LLOYD: I'm going to kill him.
   MAE: (*Stands on the threshold and turns to* LLOYD.) So kill him.

(*They freeze.*)

SCENE XIV

MAE *exits.* LLOYD *places the bib, the oatmeal cup and spoon,
and the tin cup on the mantelpiece. He takes the textbook and
sits center. He attempts to read. He first makes the sound of the
letter. Then, he speaks the name of the letter and traces it with his
finger on the table. Then, he puts the sounds of the letters together.* HENRY *sits to the right facing front. He mimics* LLOYD's
effort and laughs in silent convulsions.

   LLOYD: S.
   HENRY: S.
   LLOYD: T. St.
   HENRY: T. St.
5 LLOYD: A.
   HENRY: A.
   LLOYD: Stop that!
   HENRY: A.
   LLOYD: Stop it, Henry!
10 HENRY: A.
   LLOYD: R. Ar.
   HENRY: R. Ar.
   LLOYD: Sta.
   HENRY: Sta.
15 LLOYD: Star.

(*The left door opens.* MAE *stands outside and looks in.*)

   HENRY: Star.
   LLOYD: F.
   HENRY: F.
   LLOYD: I. Fi.
20 HENRY: I. Fi.
   LLOYD: S. Fis.
   HENRY: S. Fis.
   LLOYD: Stop it. Cut it out. Fish.
   HENRY: Fish.

(MAE *enters left. She carries a bundle of clothes.*)

25 LLOYD: Fish.
   HENRY: Fish.
   MAE: Someone took my money. Who did? (*Neither looks at
     her.*) Who did! —Did you Lloyd!
   LLOYD: I didn't. Fish.
30 HENRY: Fish.
   MAE: Did Henry? Did you take the money, Henry? (*She closes
     the door.*) Answer me. Did you take the money! Someone
     took it! You took it, Lloyd. Hand it over.
   LLOYD: I didn't take it.
35 MAE: Hand it over.
   LLOYD: I didn't take it!
   MAE: Who took it then!
   LLOYD: Henry took it.
   MAE: (*To* LLOYD.) He didn't take it. He can't walk.

   LLOYD: Yes, he can. You know he can. Walk, Henry. Show Mae 40
     how you can walk. Walk! He can walk.
   MAE: (*Enraged.*) Walk!
   HENRY: I can't walk.
   LLOYD: You can walk!
   MAE: Don't say he can walk, Lloyd. He can't walk. He didn't 45
     take the money. (*She notices the book.*) What are you doing
     with my book? (*He lowers his head. She is perplexed.*) What
     are you doing? (*She takes the book and holds it protectively.*)
     Don't mess my book.
   HENRY: He was messing it. (*He laughs.*) 50
   MAE: Shut up, Henry.
   HENRY: He was saying "Fish." (*He laughs.*)
   MAE: Everything turns bad for me.

(*They freeze.*)

SCENE XV

LLOYD *exits.* MAE *places the book on the mantelpiece and stands
by the down-right corner of the table.* HENRY *walks to the left and
sits. His hand is inside his fly. He handles himself.*

   HENRY: Mae. I still feel desire. —I am sexual. —I have not lost
     my sexuality. —Mae, make love to me. (MAE *doesn't answer.
     He continues touching himself.*) You are my wife. I want you.
     I feel the same desires. I feel the same needs. I have not
     changed. (*He holds on to the table and begins to stand.*) Mae, 5
     I have not stopped wanting you. —I can make love to you. —I
     can satisfy you. (*Supporting himself on the table, he slides
     toward her.*) I am potent. —I can make you happy. Kiss me,
     Mae. —(*He grabs her wrist.*) Tell me you still love me. Kiss
     me. Let me feel you close to me. —You think a cripple has no 10
     feelings. —I'm not crippled in my parts. —It gets hard. (*He
     puts his right arm around her waist.*) Mae, I love you. (*He
     holds her tighter. He starts moving his pelvis against her.*) I'm
     coming. . . . (*He starts sliding down to the floor.*) I'm coming.
     . . . I'm coming. . . . I'm coming. . . . I'm coming. . . . (*He 15
     collapses. She falls on the chair. She stands and leans against
     the table.*)
   MAE: You can walk, Henry. You took my money.

(*They freeze.*)

SCENE XVI

MAE *exits left.* HENRY *is on the floor trying to sit on the chair.*
LLOYD *enters right. He helps* HENRY *up and closes his fly.* MAE
enters with HENRY's *box and lifts it up in the air.*

   HENRY: Don't Mae.
   MAE: (*Throwing the box at him.*) Get out!

(LLOYD *exits right.*)

   HENRY: Don't throw things at me, Mae!
   MAE: You took the money!
   HENRY: You hurt me, Mae! You threw that box at me and hurt 5
     me!
   MAE: You took the money!
   HENRY: I didn't take it!
   MAE: You took it! Where is it? (*She moves toward him.*)
   HENRY: I didn't take it! 10

(MAE *reaches in his right pocket. She pulls out a wad of bills. She grabs his necktie, turns it back and pulls it down.* LLOYD *puts his head in through the left door and begins to enter.* MAE *and* LLOYD *speak the following speeches at the same time.*)

MAE: I feed you and I take care of you! And you steal from me? You eat my food and you sleep in my bed and you steal from me! You're a pig, Henry. You're worse than Lloyd!	LLOYD: Kill him, Mae! Kill him! Kill him! (*He climbs on the table on all fours.*) He's no good! Kill him, Mae! He's no good! He's a thief!

(HENRY *falls off the chair.* MAE *falls on her knees next to him.* LLOYD *jumps off the table. He lets out a hysterical laugh.*)

LLOYD: Look he's bleeding! (*He chants and dances.*) Henry's bleeding! Henry's bleeding! Henry's bleeding!

MAE: Shut up, Lloyd.

(*There is silence.*)

HENRY: It was my money. Lloyd never paid me. He never paid me. He never paid me what he owed me.

MAE: You could have let him have it. Just because he takes care of you. You could have let him have your money. He takes care of you.

HENRY: He never paid me.

MAE: (*She looks up to the sky.*) Can't I have a decent life? (*There is a pause.*)

LLOYD: But I love you, Mae.

HENRY: I love you, Mae.

(*They freeze.*)

SCENE XVII

LLOYD *places the box inside the fireplace. He closes the left door.* MAE *gets the empty box from the fireplace and places it on the right chair. She places the bundle of women's clothes from under the bench on the table. She is packing clothes in the box.* LLOYD *stands up-left. He watches her.* HENRY *sits left.*

MAE: (*As she packs.*) I'm leaving, Lloyd. I'm going somewhere else. I'm leaving you and Henry. Both of you are no good. I got rotten luck. I work too hard and the two of you keep sucking my blood. I'm going to look for a better place to be. (LLOYD *sits on the chair upstage of the table.*) Just a place where the two of you are not sucking my blood. I'm going to find myself a job. And a room to live in. Far away from you. Where I don't have my blood sucked.

LLOYD: Don't go, Mae.

HENRY: Don't go.

MAE: I'm going and that's that.

LLOYD: Where are you going?

MAE: I don't know, Lloyd. I'm just going.

LLOYD: I'll do what you say.

MAE: I don't care what you do. (*Closing the box.*) You do what you want. Henry too. I don't care what he does.

LLOYD: Stay, Mae.

HENRY: Please.

MAE: I'm going. You take care of Henry, Lloyd. (*She goes to the door.*)

LLOYD: Don't go, Mae.

HENRY: Please.

MAE: Goodbye.

(*She exits through the right door and closes the door.* LLOYD *is still for a few seconds. He then runs to the door, knocking down his chair. He exits.*)

LLOYD: (*Shouting.*) Mae. . . ! (HENRY *makes a plaintive sound.*) Mae. . . !

HENRY: Mae. . . !

LLOYD: (*Offstage.*) Mae. . . ! (HENRY *makes a plaintive sound.*) Stop, Mae!

HENRY: Stop!

(LLOYD *enters running. He takes the rifle.* HENRY *makes incoherent sounds.* LLOYD *exits running.*)

LLOYD: Mae. . . ! Stop. . . . ! Stop, Mae!

HENRY: Mae. . . !

LLOYD: Mae, stop. . . !

HENRY: Mae. . . !

LLOYD: Mae! Mae! Mae!

(*A shot is heard. There is silence. Another shot is heard.*)

HENRY: (*Plaintively*) . . . Mae . . .

(LLOYD *appears in threshold carrying* MAE. *She is drenched in blood and unconscious.* LLOYD *turns to* HENRY.)

LLOYD: She's not leaving, Henry.

(HENRY *lets out a whimper.* LLOYD *places* MAE *on the table.* MAE *begins to move.*)

MAE: Like the starfish, I live in the dark and my eyes see only a faint light. It is faint and yet it consumes me. I long for it. I thirst for it. I would die for it. Lloyd, I am dying.

(MAE *collapses.* LLOYD *sobs.* HENRY *lets out a plaintive cry. They freeze.*)

WILLIAM M. HOFFMAN

William M. Hoffman was born in New York in 1939. He took his B.A. from City College of New York in 1960 and then worked for a series of publishers as an editor. Hoffman's earlier plays gained notoriety in New York's off-off Broadway theater scene, and he has been invited to serve as a guest artist at several colleges and universities, including Hofstra University and the University of Massachusetts at Amherst. Hoffman has won Guggenheim and National Endowment for the Arts grants for playwriting. He also has written the book and lyrics for several musicals and the libretto for an opera—*A Figaro for Antonia*, music by John Corigliano—which was commissioned by the Metropolitan Opera. His best-known plays include *Thank-You Miss Victoria* (1965), *Saturday Night at the Movies* (1966), *Good Night, I Love You* (1966), *Luna* (1970), and *As Is* (1985). The text of *As Is* published here was revised by the author for the play's 1987 revival.

As Is

As Is is perhaps the best-known American play of the 1980s to examine the impact of AIDS on the lives of the people who contract it, and on their friends, lovers, and families. In this sense, *As Is* is a play that is "local" in its meanings, challenging the notion of "canonicity" by raising an issue that seems immediate to a particular moment in history, rather than claiming a more abstract or "universal" significance. *As Is* reminds us that plays we take as universal once were similarly local in the issues they raised for their first audiences. *King Lear*, for example, may have seemed most immediately about domestic politics in the early 1600s, *The Crucible* about communist witch hunts in the 1950s.

The theatrical style of *As Is* is also striking, since Hoffman avoids the documentary realism often used to dramatize contemporary events. Instead, *As Is* takes the form of ritual improvisation. The director of the 1985 production, Marshall W. Mason, worked to keep the cast onstage throughout the duration of the play, watching the dramatic action not as other "characters" but as real people, as themselves. The cast formed a live community onstage to bear witness to Rich's life—a "real" community that reflected and extended the community of the theater audience. This device is reminiscent of Brecht's use of DEMONSTRATION. (By keeping the audience aware that the actors are not identified with the characters, only playing them, Brecht had used such demonstration himself in the Berliner Ensemble's famous production of *Antigone*.) Its purpose is to "alienate" or "estrange" the audience, to force it out of the role of passive observer. Much as the actors must acknowledge the reality of AIDS, so the audience is invited to see AIDS as a live danger, something they share with the actors and the characters on the stage. The character of the Hospice Worker is key in this regard, for in speaking to the audience she implies that the story of Rich's life and death is being staged for the audience's benefit. It is not the characters in the play who need to understand more about AIDS, it is the silent, spectatorial public that needs to be enlightened. In this sense, *As Is* "alienates" the conventions of realistic theater—the absent, voyeuristic audience pretending not to be there while it watches the drama onstage—to criticize the broader social milieu in which the drama of AIDS takes place. In the theater, at least, the audience witnesses the complicity of its own silence and inaction in prolonging the AIDS crisis.

AS IS

William M. Hoffman

— CHARACTERS —

SAUL
RICH

Depending on the budget and the skills and aptitudes of the performers, at least four other men and two women play the following:

HOSPICE WORKER
CHET
BROTHER
BUSINESS PARTNER
LILY
TV ANNOUNCER *(Prerecorded)*
DOCTORS (5)
BARTENDER
PICKUPS (2)
MARTY
VINNIE
CLONES (3)
PEOPLE WITH AIDS (4)
AVERAGE PEOPLE (6)
HOTLINE COUNSELORS (2)
NURSE
HOSPITAL WORKER
DRUG DEALERS AND CUSTOMERS (5)

Except for short exits, the actors remain onstage for the whole play. There is no intermission.

TIME
The present.

SETTING
New York City.

— PRODUCTION NOTE —

In approaching the original production of *As Is*, I felt it was important to find a visual stage life for the play that permitted the freedom of time and place that the text suggests. David Potts, the designer, and I came up with an open stage that suggested simultaneously the stature of the classical Greek theater and the frankness of Brecht, and still allowed the audience, with a little imagination, to see the realistic studio/apartment of a New York photographer. I feel it is important that the actors remain on stage as much as possible, to witness as a community the events of the play in which they do not participate as characters. The audience must be kept from feeling "safe" from this subject, so the actors of the "chorus" must act as a bridge between the fictional characters and the real theater event, and also as an unconventional kind of "threat" — keeping the audience aware that entertaining as the play may be, the subject is deadly. The desired effect is to assist the audience in a catharsis, as they are required to contemplate our common mortality.

—Marshall W. Mason

— IN MEMORY OF: —

Stage right is SAUL's *fashionable loft space, suggested by a sofa, Barcelona chair, bench, and area rug. Upstage center is a bar; stage left, a bench.*

The HOSPICE WORKER, *a dowdy middle-aged woman, walks downstage center and addresses the audience.*

HOSPICE WORKER: Mother Superior always used to say, "Watch out for the religious cranks, Sister Veronica." When I started working for the hospice I had a touch of the crank about me. I think maybe that's why they gave me the old heave-ho from the convent. But I've kept my vow of chastity and I've made a 5
pilgrimage to Lourdes

My job is to ease the way for those who are dying. I've done this for the last couple of years. I work mainly here at St. Vincent's. During the day I have a boring secretarial job, which is how I support my career as a saint. 10

I was much more idealistic when I started. I had just left the convent. I guess I thought working with the dying would give me spiritual gold stars. I thought I'd be able to impart my great wisdom to those in need of improvement. I wanted to bear

15 witness to dramatic deathbed conversions, see shafts of light emanating from heaven, multicolored auras hovering above the heads of those in the process of expiring. I always imagined they would go out expressing their gratitude for all I had done.

20   A quick joke: Did you hear about the man who lost his left side? . . . He's all *right* now. All right now. (*She laughs.*) We tell a lot of jokes in my line of work.

(*She takes her seat. Lights come up on two casually dressed men in their thirties seated in the living area.*)

RICH: You take Henry.
SAUL: Cut him in half.
25 RICH: You can keep him.
SAUL: What are we going to do about him?
RICH: I said he's yours.
SAUL: You found him.
RICH: I don't want him.
30 SAUL: Chet doesn't like cats?
RICH: I knew this would happen. Don't start in.
SAUL: We gotta get things settled.
RICH: Then let's. How 'bout if we simplify things: sell everything and split the cash.
35 SAUL: Even the cobalt glass?
RICH: Yes.
SAUL: And Aunt Billie's hooked rug? Say, how's she doing?
RICH: She's on medication. Sell the rug.
SAUL: I will not sell the manikin heads. I don't care what you
40   say.
RICH: Then take them.
SAUL: And the chromium lamp? I love that lamp.
RICH: Take it.
SAUL: And the Barcelona chair?
45 RICH: The Barcelona chair is *mine!* (*Beat.*) Fuck it. Take it. Take everything. I won't be Jewish about it. (*He rises to go.*)
SAUL: Why didn't you warn me we were going to play Christians and Jews today? I would have worn my yellow star.
RICH: I've gotta go. (RICH *is leaving.*)
50 SAUL: Where're you going?
RICH: I'm not feeling so hot. Let's make it another day.
SAUL: (*blocking his way*) Sit down.
RICH: (*pushing his hand away*) Don't push me.
SAUL: Sorry. I don't like this any more than you, but we gotta do
55   it. It's been six months. (*Lightening things up.*) A divorce is not final until the property settlement.
RICH: Saul . . .? (*He's about to say something important.*)
SAUL: What, Rich? (*He waits expectantly.*) What?
RICH: Never mind.
60 SAUL: What? . . . What? . . . You always do that!
RICH: I want the chair.
SAUL: You can have the fucking Barcelona chair if Chet wants it so bad! . . . What about the paintings? Do you want to sell the Paul Cadmus?
65 RICH: Yes.
SAUL: You love the Cadmus. (*Silence.*) And who's going to buy the Burgess drawings? Did you hear that Kenny had a heart attack?
RICH: We'll donate them to the Metropolitan.
70 SAUL: Just what they always wanted: the world's largest collection of Magic Marker hustler portraits. (RICH *nods.*)

RICH: They're yours.
SAUL: But you commissioned them. We'll split them up: I get the blonds and you get the blacks—or vice versa.
75 RICH: All yours.
SAUL: Then you get the Mickey Mouse collection.
RICH: Sell it.
SAUL: You don't sell collectibles. Not right now. What's with this money mania? Between the book and the catering, I thought
80   you were doing well.
RICH: I want to build a swimming pool.
SAUL: You don't swim.
RICH: I want a Mercedes.
SAUL: You don't drive. It's Chet—he'll bankrupt you! (*Beat.*) I
85   don't believe I said that . . . (*Sincerely.*) Your book is beautiful.
RICH: I never thanked you for the cover photograph.
SAUL: (*shrugging off the compliment*) How's it selling?
RICH: Not bad—for short stories. Everyone mentions your
90   photo. Ed White said—
SAUL: Your book is terrific. Really.
RICH: I'm glad you like it.
SAUL: One minor thing.
RICH: What's that?
95 SAUL: I thought the dedication was a bit much.
RICH: Why are you doing this?
SAUL: Don't you think quoting Cavafy in Greek is a little coy?
RICH: Please!
SAUL: Why didn't you just say, "To Chet, whose beautiful buns
100   inspired these tales"?
RICH: Jesus Christ!
SAUL: I'm sorry!

(*Silence.*)

RICH: I sold the IBM stock. You were right about it. You have always been right about money. (*He hands* SAUL *a check.*)
105   This includes the thousand I borrowed for the periodontist.
SAUL: You sure?
RICH: Take it.
SAUL: I'm not desperate for it.
RICH: It's yours.
110 SAUL: I don't want it.
RICH: Damn it!
SAUL: (*taking the check*) Okay.
RICH: That makes us even now.
SAUL: (*examining the check*) Clouds and trees.
115 RICH: Let's get on with this.
SAUL: Is he waiting for you downstairs? You could have told him to come up.
RICH: Shit. No! Can it. (*Beat.*) I won't be wanting the copper pots.
120 SAUL: Why not? When you and Chet move to your space you'll want to cook again.
RICH: I just don't want them! People change. (*Silence.*) I'm eating out a lot.
SAUL: Chet can't cook?
125 RICH: (*deciding not to respond with a bitchy comment*) You keep the rowing machine.
SAUL: Have you lost weight?
RICH: And the trampoline.

SAUL: There's some Black Forest cake in the fridge. (SAUL *goes*
130 *toward the kitchen to get the cake.*)
RICH: Stop it.
SAUL: Stop what?
RICH: Just stop.
SAUL: I can't.
135 RICH: We're almost through.
SAUL: I have feelings.
RICH: You have only one feeling.
SAUL: He won't make you happy.
RICH: Here we go again. (RICH *gets up to go.*)
140 SAUL: Don't!
RICH: Keep everything.
SAUL: I'm not myself.
RICH: Nothing is worth this.
SAUL: I've been upset.
145 RICH: I mean it.
SAUL: Don't go. Please. (RICH *sits. Long pause.*) I visited Teddy
today at St. Vincent's. It's very depressing . . . He's lying there
in bed, out of it. He's been out of it since the time we saw him.
He's not in any pain, snorting his imaginary cocaine, doing
150 his poppers. Sometimes he's washing his mother's floor, and
he's speaking to her in Spanish. Sometimes he's having sex.
You can see him having sex right in front of you. He doesn't
even know you're there. (*Pause. Both men look down at their
feet.*) Jimmy died, as you must have heard. I went out to San
155 Francisco to be with him the last few weeks. You must have
heard that, too. He was in a coma for a month. Everybody
wanted to pull the plug, but they were afraid of legal complications. I held his hand. He couldn't talk, but I could see his
eyelids flutter. I swear he knew I was with him. (*Pause.*) Harry
160 has K.S., and Matt has the swollen glands. He went for tests
today . . . I haven't slept well for weeks. Every morning I
examine my body for swellings, marks. I'm terrified of every
pimple, every rash. If I cough I think of Teddy. I wish he
would die. He *is* dead. He might as well be. Why can't he die?
165 I feel the disease closing in on me. All my activities are life
and death. Keep up my Blue Cross. Up my reps. Eat my
vegetables.
    Sometimes I'm so scared I go back on my resolutions: I
drink too much, and I smoke a joint, and I find myself at the
170 bars and clubs, where I stand around and watch. They remind me of accounts of Europe during the Black Plague: coupling in the dark, dancing till you drop. The New Wave is the
corpse look. I'm very frightened and I miss you. Say something, damn it. (*Beat.*)
175 RICH: I have it.

(*Immediately the lights come up on the left side of the stage.*)

CHET: (*a handsome, boyish man in his early twenties*) You what?
LILY: (*a beautiful woman, thirtyish*) You have what?
BROTHER: (*to his wife, whom we don't see*) He has AIDS.
SAUL: I don't think that's funny.
180 PARTNER: Don't be ridiculous.
RICH: That's the bad news.
PARTNER: You ran the god-
    damned marathon.   LILY: Darling!
RICH: The good news is that I have only the swollen glands.

(*Two doctors appear in white gowns.*)

DOCTOR 1: We call it a "Pre-   185
    AIDS Condition"
                                  DOCTOR 2: "AIDS-related
                                      Complex."
RICH: And I've lost some weight.
SAUL: I'm in a state of shock.

LILY: Move in with me. Chet   190
    doesn't know how to take
    care of you.
                                  RICH: I tire easily. My tem-
                                      perature goes up and down.

DOCTOR 1: Your suppressor cells outnumber your helper cells.
BROTHER: I don't care what he has, Betty, he's my brother.   195
CHET: You're my lover.
LILY: You're my buddy.

PARTNER: Rich and I started
    the business about a year
    ago. But now word got out   200
    that Rich has this disease. I
    tried to explain: he doesn't   BROTHER: I'm not in the habit
    touch the food; I do all the   of kissing my brother. I
    cooking. But they won't   touched him on the back
    listen.   when I arrived and when I
                                       left.   205

PARTNER: Why would they? I wonder if I'd use a caterer who had
    AIDS.
SAUL: Doctors make mistakes all the time.

DOCTOR 2: There a number of
    highly experimental treat-   DOCTOR 1: Of highly experi-   210
    ments.   mental treatments.

LILY: I got this job.
CHET: If you don't mind, I'll sleep on the couch tonight. You've
been sweating a lot.

LILY: I can't turn it down. The   215
    work is pure dreck, and
    who wants to tour Canada   BROTHER: When he offered
    in January, but they're pay-   me a cup of coffee I told
    ing a fortune. I'll be back in   him I'd have a can of beer.
    four weeks.   PARTNER: I can understand   220
                                         what he's going through.
                                         Myself, I've been wrestling
                                         with cancer for a while.

SAUL: Remember when they
    told my niece she had skin   225
    cancer? It turned out to be
    dry skin.   PARTNER: I'm winning.

CHET: I hope you don't mind, but I'll use the red soap dish and
you'll use the blue.
RICH: Christ! I've been putting   230
    the blocks to you nightly for   BROTHER: Christ, I didn't
    months and now you're   even use the bathroom,
    worried about sharing the   even though I had to take a
    fucking soap dish?   leak so bad I could taste it.
                                         Now, that's paranoid.   235
PARTNER: I wonder if it's safe
    to use the same telephone,
    or whether I'm being
    paranoid.

240   CHET: I know I'm being
      paranoid.

      LILY: They're flying me out to
      the Coast.
      I hate that place.   RICH: Chet, you've been out
245   every night this week. Do
                                             you have to go out again?

      BROTHER: I know you're scared, Betty, but I will not tell my own
         brother he's not welcome in my house.
      CHET: Need something from outside?
250   BROTHER: He's spent every Christmas with us since we got mar-
         ried, and this year will be no exception.
      RICH: Forget I said anything: just don't wake me up when you
         get in.
      BROTHER: You're forcing me to choose between you and my
255   brother.
      CHET: See you later.

      LILY: I've been dating this guy
         Mick—can you imagine
         me dating? Well, he's very
260   nice, and he's got a lot of
         money, and he's not im-
         pressed with my life in the   CHET: You know I'd do any-
         theater and he's straight—   thing for you?
         and that's why I haven't   RICH: You're walking out on
265   been up to see you. Rich?   me.

      BROTHER: We're going to Betty's mother's for Christmas.
      CHET: I need more space to get my head together.
      SAUL: What did you expect?
      RICH: Chet, please, I need you!

      (RICH *tries to put his arms around* CHET. *Everyone except* SAUL
      pulls back terrified.)

270   CHET, BROTHER, LILY, PARTNER, DOCTORS: Don't touch me!
         (*Beat.*)
      LILY: Please forgive me!
      CHET: This thing has me blown away.
      BROTHER: If it weren't for the kids.
275   PARTNER: I don't know what the hell we're going to do.
      SAUL: Bastards!

      (CHET, BROTHER, PARTNER, *and* LILY *put on white gowns and
      become* DOCTORS.)

      RICH: (*to* DOCTOR 1) Doctor,   TV COMMENTATOR: (*pre-
         tell me the truth. What are   recorded*) Since 1981,
         my chances?   nearly 32,000 Americans
280   have been diagnosed with
      DOCTOR 1: I don't know.   AIDS [use current fatality
                                         figures] and about sixty per-
      RICH: (*to* DOCTOR 2) Doctor,   cent of them have died.
         tell me the truth. What are   Scientists project that by
285   my chances?   1991, some 54,000 people
                                         will be dead. So far, nine
      DOCTOR 2: I don't know.   out of ten patients have
                                         been homosexual or bisex-
      RICH: (*to* DOCTOR 3) What   ual men or intravenous
290   are my chances?   drug users. Experts esti-
                                         mate that from four to

      DOCTOR 3: I just don't know.   seven percent of all adult
                                         patients were infected
      RICH: (*to* DOCTORS 4 *and* 5)   through heterosexual inter-
         Am I going to make it, doc-   course. When will science   295
         tors, yes or no?!   conquer this dreaded
                                         plague? We don't know. We
      DOCTORS 4 and 5: I'm sorry,   don't know. We simply
         we just don't know.   don't know. Don't know.
                                         (*Etc.*)   300
      SAUL: Rich?

      DOCTORS: We don't know.
      SAUL: And for three months you kept this from me.

      (*The* DOCTORS *exit. We're back in* SAUL's *apartment.*)

      RICH: I don't want your pity.
      SAUL: You're my friend. You'll stay with me till you feel better.   305
      RICH: Aren't you afraid I'll infect you?
      SAUL: Maybe you already have.
      RICH: And maybe I haven't.
      SAUL: Maybe I gave it to you.
      RICH: Maybe you did.   310
      SAUL: We'll take precautions.
      RICH: Paper plates, Lysol, face masks—no, I'd prefer to live
         alone, thank you.
      SAUL: You need me.
      RICH: Besides, if I live with you, where am I going to bring my   315
         tricks?
      SAUL: You pick up people?
      RICH: (*standing at the bar*) I go to bars . . . I pick up guys . . . but
         I give them a medical report before we leave . . . (*Without a
         pause, we're in a bar.* RICH *is talking to a stranger.*) I should   320
         tell you something.
      PICKUP 1: You like something kinky. Whips? Golden showers?
         Fist?
      RICH: It's not like that.
      PICKUP 1: I once picked up a guy who liked to be yelled at in   325
         German. The only German I know is the "Ode to Joy" from
         Beethoven's Ninth. (*Yelling like an enraged Nazi.*) "O
         Freude, schöner Götterfunken, Schweinehund, Tochter aus
         Elysium, Dummkopf!"
      RICH: I have a very mild case of lymphadenopathy.   330
      PICKUP 1: What's that?
      RICH: An AIDS-related condition.
      PICKUP 1: Oh, shit.
      RICH: Just the swollen glands—
      PICKUP 1: No way. Uh-uh . . . Good luck . . . Oh, man . . .   335

      (PICKUP 1 *exits. We're back with* RICH *and* SAUL)

      RICH: So I stopped telling them.
      SAUL: You mean you take them home and don't tell them?
      RICH: We do it there in the bar.
      SAUL: How can you?
      RICH: I lurk in dark corners where they can't see my lumps. I'm   340
         like a shark or a barracuda, and I snap them up and infect
         them.
      SAUL: How can you joke about this?
      RICH: I don't care. I'm going to die! I'll take as many as I can with
         me. And I've pissed in the Croton Reservoir. I'm going to   345
         infect the whole fucking city! Wheeeee!

SAUL: No fucking around, give me a straight answer. Do you still pick up people?

RICH: Maybe I ought to wear a sign around my neck and ring a
350 bell: "AIDS, I've got AIDS, stand clear!" Would that make you happy? Or maybe I should dig a hole in the ground, douse myself with kerosene, and have a final cigarette. No muss, no fuss. Is that what you want?

SAUL: Forgive me for not trusting you. It's just that I'm fright-
355 ened of it. I don't know what I'm saying half the time.

RICH: How the fuck do you think I feel? My lover leaves me; my family won't let me near them; I lose my business; I can't pay my rent. How the fuck do you think I feel?

SAUL: You'll stay here with me.

360 RICH: Till death do us part.

SAUL: I love you.

RICH: I don't want your love!

SAUL: Take what you can . . . [get]! I didn't mean that. I love you. I always have. You have nowhere to go. You've got to
365 stay with me.

RICH: Shit shit shit.

SAUL: You were kidding about picking up people.

RICH: What do you think? What would you do in my place?

SAUL: I wouldn't . . . I'd . . . Therapy! . . . I don't know what I'd do.

(We're back in the bar.)

370 PICKUP 2: Jesus, I've told you all about myself. I've really spilled my guts to you. I *needed* to do that. Maybe I shouldn't say this, but, Christ, you know something? I like you very much. Even though you *are* a writer . . . Would you like to come home with me?

375 RICH: I'd like to very much . . . *(he checks his watch)* but I have an appointment.

PICKUP 2: Then tomorrow, how about tomorrow? I don't want to lose track of you. I don't know when I've had such a good time. I can *talk* to you.

380 RICH: I've enjoyed myself, too.

PICKUP 2: Then maybe we'll have dinner, maybe go to the movies. Do you like movies? There's an Alfred Hitchcock festival at the Regency. Or maybe we could see the new Mark Morris—

385 RICH: Thanks, but I have to tell you something. I have—

PICKUP 2: You have a lover. I knew it. You're too nice to be unattached.

RICH: I have . . . I have . . . I have a lover.

(We're back with SAUL.)

SAUL: You have a lover.

390 RICH: I don't even know where he is.

SAUL: I don't mean Chet. I mean me. *(RICH turns away. He's back in the bar with another stranger, CLONE 1, who is wearing a leather jacket and reflecting aviator glasses. SAUL continues to plead to RICH's back.)* What about me? *(RICH tries in
395 vain to get CLONE 1's attention.)*

RICH: Pardon me.

SAUL: What about me?

RICH: Yo. Yoo-hoo. Hello.

SAUL: What about *me*?!

400 RICH: *(to CLONE 1)* What about me?!

CLONE 1: What about you?

RICH: I'm a very interesting guy. You look like a very interesting guy. Let's talk. And if you don't want to talk, let's go back there and let's . . . *(RICH stares CLONE 1 straight in the face.)* I'll do
405 anything you want. Anything.

CLONE 1: I want you to get the fuck out of my face. Can't you see I'm cruising that dude over there? *(We notice for the first time an identically dressed man standing across the room.)*

RICH: Well, fuck you.

410 CLONE 1: What's that, buddy?

(RICH turns his back on CLONE 1 and starts talking loudly to the bartender.)

RICH: Gimme a Jack Daniels straight up—*no* ice—make it a double, and a Heineken chaser.

BARTENDER: Double Jack up, Heinie back.

(CLONE 2 has moseyed on over to CLONE 1. They stand side by side, facing the audience, feigning indifference to each other.)

CLONE 2: Your name Chip?

415 RICH: No ice!

BARTENDER: No ice.

CLONE 1: Chuck.

RICH: Hate ice.

CLONE 2: *(extending his hand)* Chad. *(The clones shake hands.)*

420 RICH: *(to the bartender)* Put 'er there, Chet—I mean Chump. You come here often? *(He downs the shot and beer as quickly as he can.)*

CLONE 2: Thought you were this guy, Chip, I met here on Jock-strap Night.

425 CLONE 1: Haven't been here since the Slave Auction.

CLONE 2: Look familiar. *(With synchronized actions the clones turn to look at each other, then turn away.)*

CLONE 1: Go to the Spike?

CLONE 2: Been there.

430 RICH: *(to the bartender)* Quiet for a Friday . . .

CLONE 1: I know where.

RICH: Not much action.

CLONE 2: Palladium?

RICH: *(offering his glass)* Same . . .

435 CLONE 1: Nah.

RICH: Probably's this disease thing.

CLONE 1: Bookstore on Christopher. Ever go there?

CLONE 2: Stopped going since this disease thing.

CLONE 1: Gotta be real careful.

440 RICH: No use getting hysterical.

CLONE 2: Right. Me, I'm HIV negative.

CLONE 1: Can you prove it? *(He punches CLONE 2 on the arm.)* Kidding.

CLONE 2: Gotta be real careful. Run six miles a day.

445 RICH: My philosophy is: you've got it, you've got it. Nothing you can do about it. *(He offers his glass.)* Same.

CLONE 1: *(tweaking CLONE 2's nipple)* So what're you up for?

CLONE 2: Come right to the point, don't you?

(The clones perform a macho mating ritual of arm wrestling, punching, and ass grabbing to determine who is the "top man.")

450 RICH: Poor bastards that got it: cancer, pneumonia, herpes all over. I mean, I'd kill myself if I had to go through all that shit. Get a gun and perform fellatio on it . . .

CLONE 2: What're you up for, Daddy?

RICH: Slash my wrists *with* the grain . . .

CLONE 1: Me top.

455 RICH: Subway tracks?

CLONE 1: Got some beautiful . . . *(He snorts deeply to indicate cocaine.)*

CLONE 2: Ever do opium?

CLONE 1: I have a water pipe. We'll smoke it through some
460   Southern Comfort.

RICH: Or maybe I'd mix myself a Judy Garland: forty reds and a quart of vodka. *(He hands his glass to the bartender.)* Fuck the beer!

CLONE 1: We're roommates now. What about you?

465 RICH: *(the ecstatic drunken poet)* "Glory be to God for dappled things . . ."

CLONE 2: I'm free, white, and twenty-four.

RICH: "For skies of couple-colour as a brinded cow . . ."

SAUL: I know it sounds stupid, but take care of your health.

470 RICH: "For rose-moles all in stipple upon trout that swim . . ."

CLONE 2: In bed, I mean.

RICH: I don't care what anybody says, I believe that somewhere, you know, *deep* down. *(He holds out his glass.)*

CLONE 1: I'll do anything you want.

475 RICH: Beyond all this incredible pain and confusion, anxiety, fear, terror . . . *(He holds out his glass.)*

BARTENDER: No ice.

CLONE 2: Anything?

RICH: I believe that there might be . . . *(searching for words to
480   describe the Supreme Being)* that there could be . . . that there is —

CLONE 1: Safe sex!

SAUL: You're drinking too much.

RICH: I believe in a perfect . . . *(He is having a booze-fueled
485   vision of the Godhead.)*

CLONE 2: Mirrors . . .

RICH: Shining . . .

CLONE 1: Chains . . .

RICH: Powerful . . .

490 SAUL: Vitamins . . .

RICH: Pure . . .

(A third clone appears.)

CLONE 3: Condom . . .

CLONE 1: Dildo . . .

SAUL: Diet . . .

495 RICH: Free . . .

CLONE 2: Dungeon . . .

SAUL: Acupuncture . . .

RICH: Truthful . . .

CLONE 3: Ten inches . . .

500 SAUL: AZT . . .

RICH: Beautiful . . .

CLONE 3: *(approaching the bar, to the BARTENDER)* Beer! *(He accidentally spills beer on RICH.)*

CLONE 2: Watersports.

505 RICH: *(raging drunkenly)* Asshole!

CLONE 1: Hey!

RICH: I'll kill ya, faggot!

SAUL: *(intervening)* Hey! . . . He's been drinking.

BARTENDER: Get that jerk outta here!

510 RICH: What's a matter, can't you fight like a man?

SAUL: *(gently but firmly)* Rich.

RICH: Fuck all that shit!

SAUL: Rich.

RICH: Let Him cure me!

SAUL: *(trying to distract him)* Did you hear the one about the   515
faggot, the black, and the Jew?

RICH: *(to God in the sky, shaking his fist)* You hear me, motherfucker?

SAUL: How did that go?

RICH: Cure me!   520

(They are out on the street by now.)

SAUL: C'mon, keep moving.

RICH: I'm a very bad person.

SAUL: You're an asshole.

RICH: I wanted to go to bed with that guy.

SAUL: I practically beg you to move in —   525

RICH: I wasn't going to tell him about me or anything.

SAUL: And what do you do?

RICH: But you want to know something?

SAUL: You disappear for two weeks.

RICH: I wouldn't do that. I would *never* do that.   530

SAUL: I almost called the cops.

RICH: You believe me?

SAUL: Believe what?

RICH: I never never never would ever do that.

SAUL: Do you remember the one about the Polish Lesbian?   535

RICH: Never.

SAUL: She liked men. *(The joke pretty much sobers RICH up.)*

RICH: You asshole.

SAUL: You schmuck.

RICH: You prick.   540

SAUL: God, I miss talking dirty.

RICH: Talking dirty makes it feel like spring. *(He is the super-stud.)* Suck my dick, faggot.

SAUL: *(superstud)* Kiss my ass, cocksucker.

RICH: Sit on it, punk.   545

SAUL: Lick boot, fruit.

RICH: God, how I used to love sleaze: the whining self-pity of a rainy Monday night in a leather bar in early spring; five o'clock in the morning in the Mineshaft, with the bathtubs full of men dying to get pissed on and whipped; a subway john   550
full of horny high school students; Morocco — getting raped on a tombstone in Marrakesh. God, how I miss it.

SAUL: I miss my filthy old ripped-up, patched button-fly jeans that I sun-bleached on myself our first weekend on the Island. Remember? It was Labor Day —   555

RICH: Memorial Day.

SAUL: And we did blotter acid. Remember acid before they put the speed in it? And we drank muscadet when we got thirsty.

RICH: Which we did a lot.

SAUL: Remember?   560

RICH: Remember Sunday afternoons blitzed on beer?

SAUL: And suddenly it's Sunday night and you're getting fucked in the second-floor window of the Hotel Christopher and you're being cheered on by a mob of hundreds of men.

RICH: And suddenly it's Friday a week later, and he's moved in,   565
sleeping next to you, and you want him to go because you've met his brother Rod or Lance —

SAUL: *(practically sighing)* Miles.

RICH: — late of the merchant marines, who's even humpier.

570 SAUL: Orgies at the baths —

RICH: Afternoons at the Columbus Avenue bookstore. (*They are in the back room of a gay porno shop, or "bookstore." They play their favorite bookstore habitués.*) More! *Give* it to me.

SAUL: Give it to *you*? Give it to *me*! Get out of my way, he's mine!

575 RICH: No, he's mine! Keep your hands *off* my wallet!

SAUL: (*a black queen*) Sistuhs, theyuh's plenty heah fo' ivrybody.

RICH: (*a tough New York queen*) Hey, Mary, the line forms at the rear.

SAUL: And whose rear might that be, sugar?

(*Two other men appear in the bookstore.*)

580 MARTY: Hey, Vinnie?

VINNIE: Marty?

MARTY: What are you doing here? You said you were gonna buy the papers.

VINNIE: You said you were gonna walk the dogs.

585 MARTY: You trash! (*They exit, bickering.*)

SAUL: I always knew when you were fucking around.

RICH: You did your share.

SAUL: *Moi?*

RICH: I knew why Grand Union wouldn't deliver to our house. (*They have returned to the loft.*)

590 SAUL: God, I used to love promiscuous sex.

RICH: Not "promiscuous," Saul, nondirective, noncommitted, nonauthoritarian —

SAUL: Free, wild, rampant —

595 RICH: Hot, sweaty, steamy, smelly —

SAUL: Juicy, funky, hunky —

RICH: Sex.

SAUL: Sex. God, I miss it. (*RICH lowers his eyes. SAUL nods and goes to RICH. He takes RICH's face in both hands and tries to kiss him square on the mouth. RICH pulls away frantically.*)

600 RICH: NO!

SAUL: It's safe!

RICH: You don't know what you're doing!

SAUL: It's my decision!

605 RICH: (*shaking his head*) No. Uh-uh. NO! (*SAUL sits on the sofa. RICH tries to take SAUL's hand, but SAUL pulls it away. Beat.*) The best times for me were going out with you on shoots.

SAUL: I thought you found them boring.

RICH: I enjoyed them.

610 SAUL: I was always afraid of boring you.

RICH: Remember staying up all night shooting the harvest moon at Jake's place?

SAUL: My fingers got so cold I could barely change film.

RICH: It was almost as bright as daylight. Remember the apple tree stuck out in the middle of the pasture, how the moonlight drained it of color?

615

SAUL: I remember the smell of the blanket we took from the barn.

RICH: Remember, I bet you I could find five constellations?

620 SAUL: You found six . . . I never wanted us to break up.

RICH: Passive aggression.

SAUL: I wanted things to always remain the same. I'm still like that. I even like eating the same things day after day.

RICH: Pork chops, French fries —

625 SAUL: No change. I used to love our routine together. I'd go to work and then you'd be there when I got home, writing —

RICH: Drinking.

SAUL: I'd do this and you'd do that, and then we'd . . . (*he makes a graceful gesture to indicate making love*) for a while — while *Mission Impossible*'d be on low in the background.

630

RICH: And then *Star Trek*.

SAUL: I never got tired of the same —

RICH: We were stagnating.

SAUL: —day after day the same, so we'd have a structure to fall back on when life dealt us its wild cards or curve balls. I want to be just half awake, like at the seashore, watching the waves roll in late in the afternoon, hypnotized by the glare of the sun, smelling the sea breeze and suntan lotion. (*Beat.*)

635

Mom is what? She's lying there next to Dad on the Navaho blanket, with white gunk on her nose, and my baby sister has finally stopped screaming and is sucking on the ear of her dollie. And Aunt Ellie — the one who said she thought I had good taste when she met you — is snoring next to husband number three. Her bazooms are going up and down, up and down, almost popping out of her bathing suit. It's so peaceful. (*Long pause.*)

640

645

I was at the St. Mark's baths soaking in the hot tub when I first heart about AIDS. It was how many years ago? My friend Brian — remember him? — was soaking, too, and he told me about a mutual friend who had died the week before. It was "bizarre," he said . . .

650

(*A group enters, quietly talking.*)

1ST MAN: The first person I knew who had AIDS was George. I had just seen him at the movies — *Mommie Dearest* — and we had a big laugh together. I remember he had a little cough. I ran into his mother it couldn't have been a week later and she told me he had died. It was absurd. I had just seen George.

655

660

1ST WOMAN: The first time it really hit me was when my boss got ill. When Roger got out of the hospital I didn't know what to say. I said, "You look so much taller." He said, "Well, I've lost about forty-five pounds."

665

670

It hit home after that.

2ND WOMAN: The first time I heard about it I was standing in my kitchen. I was about to go out shopping for my youngest's birthday party. The phone rang. It was this doctor calling me about my son Bernard. He used all these words I can't

675

680

685 pronounce. And then he said, "Do you understand what I've told you?" I said yes. Right before he hung up he said, "So you know he has AIDS." That's the 690 first time I heard that word.

I turned white.

3RD MAN (*a cop*): The word 710 never really registered in my mind until they transferred this guy with AIDS to our unit. Maybe I 715 thought AIDS was like Legionnaire's Disease

or Toxic Shock Syndrome—one of those rare diseases you read about in the papers. Anyway, the 720 guys on the job were up in arms that they were going to expose us to it. I didn't know what to think. I got used to Bobby though. He 725 wanted to keep working very badly.
I think he had a lot of courage.

730

2ND WOMAN: He was in the theater.

735 3RD MAN: I couldn't figure it out.

1ST MAN: Do you understand what I've told you?

1ST WOMAN: So you know he has AIDS.

JOHN: The first time I heard about AIDS was in 1980. I was on the seven A.M. shuttle to Boston, trying to make a nine o'clock appointment in Cambridge. I was looking over the shoulder of the man next to me, at his newspaper, and I caught the words "cancer," "promiscuous," "homosexual."

1ST and 2ND MEN: I think he had a lot of courage.

4TH MAN: The first memorial service I went to was on the set of *Oh Calcutta!* It was for Bill. He was in the theater. They filled the house. He had hidden the fact that he was ill for a year. A while

1ST WOMAN: . . . Fortunato

3RD MAN: . . . Stephen . . .

4TH MAN: . . .Phil . . .

1ST WOMAN: . . . Arthur . . .

2ND WOMAN: . . . Neil . . .

1ST WOMAN: . . . John . . .

2ND WOMAN: . . . Julie . . .

3RD MAN: . . . Luis . . . Larry and his lover Danny . . . Stuart . . . J.J. . . . Maria . . . Jamal . . .

2ND WOMAN: . . . David . . . Stuart . . . J.J. . . . Maria . . . Jamal . . .

before he asked me if I wanted his dog—a beautiful huskie. I couldn't figure 740 it out. He loved that dog. . . . Since that time I've been to how many memorial services? Seth . . . Robby . . .

2ND WOMAN: . . . Francis . . . 745

2ND MAN: . . . Greg . . .

2ND WOMAN: . . . Freddie . . . 750

1ST MAN: . . . Tom . . .

2ND MAN: . . . André . . .

3RD MAN: . . . Glen . . . 755

1ST and 4TH MAN and 1ST WOMAN: . . . Russell . . . Luis . . . Larry and his lover Danny . . . David . . . 760 Stuart . . . J.J. . . . Maria . . . Jamal . . .

2ND MAN: . . . Larry . . . David . . . Stuart . . . J.J. . . . 765 Maria . . . Jamal . . . Charles . . .

(THE GROUP *exits.*)

SAUL: . . . and he told me about a mutual friend who had died the week before. It was "bizarre," he said. Brian died last week of the same thing. And he and I once soaked in the same hot 770 tub, making a kind of human soup. . . . That's all I ever wanted to do was relax. (*Long pause.*) You'll stay with me. I won't bother you.
RICH: Just until I feel better.
SAUL: I understand: you're not coming back to be my lover. 775
RICH: Right. Is that okay?
SAUL: Schmuck. (*Mimicking him.*) Is that okay? Is that okay? It's *okay*! Asshole. Who the fuck wants you anyhow? And when I have guests stay the night, you disappear into your room. Right? 780
RICH: Right. Understood. (*Offhand.*) You seeing somebody?
SAUL: I said when I have guests.
RICH: You planning an orgy?
SAUL: Just so we understand each other.
RICH: I should mention one thing. 785
SAUL: No, you do not have to spend Passover with the tribe.
RICH: I miss your father.
SAUL: Then go live with him. He *likes* you. The two of you could be very happy together.
RICH: One thing. 790
SAUL: He's never really liked me.
RICH: Saul.
SAUL: He's always been polite but—

RICH: Are you finished?

795 SAUL: No, I will not bring you coffee in bed. I only do that for lovers. Besides, I broke your blue mug.

RICH: Saul, please.

SAUL: On purpose.

RICH: One thing. I'm embarrassed. I'm just about broke. The
800 doctors. Tests.

SAUL: I thought you were insured.

RICH: They're pulling a fast one.

SAUL: We'll sue. I'll call Craig. He'll know what—

RICH: Craig told me not to have high hopes.

805 SAUL: We'll get by. You'll see.

RICH: I'll keep track of every cent you spend on me. You'll get it all back when I can work. I swear.

SAUL: Not to worry, I'll take it out in trade.

RICH: Saul, I'm frightened! (SAUL *takes him in his arms.*)

810 SAUL: We'll be okay, we'll be okay . . .

(*They hold each other.* LILY *walks into the scene with* CHET. *She's dressed in evening wear and is carrying a number of accessories, including a mirror and a shawl.* CHET *is dressed in cutoffs and a sweatshirt. We are in a flashback.*)

LILY: Rich, congratulations! It's fantastic that they're going to publish your book.

(SAUL *tries to break from the clinch, but* RICH *holds him back.*)

RICH: No autographs, please.

LILY: It's wonderful, it really is, but can you guys celebrate later?

815 SAUL: (*to* RICH) Let me go. (*To* CHET) How do you do? I'm Saul.

LILY: Shit. Saul, Rich—my cousin Chet.

SAUL: (*trying to shake hands*) Hi, Chet. (*To* RICH) You're strangling me.

CHET: Hi.

820 RICH: (*to* SAUL) It's your last chance to kiss the author before he becomes famous and goes straight.

SAUL: Straight to the bars. (*To* CHET) So how do you like New York?

CHET: I only got here yesterday. Lily's taking me to a show
825 tonight.

RICH: Do you think success will change me?

SAUL: God, I hope so.

LILY: I know I'm being a pig, but I need head shots by six o'clock. (*She lowers a roller of colored background paper.*) It's a daz-
830 zling role for me and (*to* SAUL) you're such an artist.

SAUL: Rich is the "artiste" in the family.

LILY: Chet, be an angel and bring Saul his camera. It's by the bar. (CHET *looks for the camera.*)

SAUL: (*to* CHET) Don't let your cousin push you around the way
835 she does me.

LILY: Come on, Saul, make click-click.

SAUL: Unless you like that sort of thing.

RICH: That's all I get?

LILY: (*to* RICH, *about* SAUL) Leave the boy alone.

840 RICH: A hug and a bitchy remark?

SAUL: (*to* RICH) That and a subway token.

RICH: (*to* SAUL) No "Gee, Rich, I'm so proud of you"?

SAUL: (*smiling falsely*) Gee, Rich, I'm so proud of you.

RICH: I finally have some good news and he's annoyed.

845 CHET: (*to* LILY, *holding the camera*) What should I do with this?

SAUL: Well, your brother called, while you were out guzzling lunch with your agent, Dr. Mengele. Call him back.

RICH: What'd he have to say?

SAUL: Call him and ask him. I'm not your secretary.

850 RICH: (*imitating him*) I'm not your—

SAUL: He forgot my fucking name again. How long we been together?

RICH: Too long. Forget my brother. It's my first fucking book. Let's celebrate.

855 SAUL: You celebrate.

LILY: I'll throw a party.

RICH: What'll you serve, organic cabbage juice?

SAUL: (*to* LILY) His brother's a scumbag.

RICH: He likes you, too.

860 CHET: (*to* SAUL, *still holding the camera*) Do you want this?

SAUL: (*to* CHET) Thanks, Chuck.

CHET: Chet. (SAUL *accepts the camera from* CHET, *but ignores the correction.*)

LILY: (*fondly, to* RICH) You're such a lush.

865 RICH: Whatever happened to my old drinking buddy?

LILY: Did you know they have gay A.A. meetings? (RICH *makes a face.*)

SAUL: (*to* RICH, *trying to be nice*) It's great news, babes, really.

RICH: You really don't give a fuck.

870 SAUL: Just how many copies you think a book of "fairy tales" will sell?

LILY: I picked a fine day to have my picture taken.

SAUL: If you only knew how much I love doing head shots.

RICH: (*to* SAUL) Ah, fuck it, I guess I'm being childish.

875 SAUL: I shouldn't have said that. I'm thoughtless. (RICH *shrugs.*)

LILY: And I'm Sneezy. No, really, I'm selfish. But I want that role so bad. I play the ghost of Marie Antoinette. (*To* SAUL, *throwing the scarf around her neck and taking a tits-and-ass pose:*) How do you like this, hon? "Let them eat . . ." (*She
880 drops the pose immediately as* SAUL *starts to photograph her.*)

SAUL: Move your head a little to the . . . (*She moves her head.*) Good. (SAUL *snaps her.*)

RICH: (*going to the living area, followed by* CHET) I'm going running. (RICH *changes into jogging clothes.*)

885 CHET: How far do you run?

RICH: Depends. I'm in training for the marathon.

CHET: The marathon! Hey, that's great. I run, too.

RICH: Oh, yeah? (LILY *and* SAUL *are busy taking pictures in the other side of the loft. They can see* RICH *and* CHET, *but they
890 can't easily hear them.*)

LILY: How's this?

CHET: Congratulations on the book.

RICH: Thanks.

SAUL: That's right.

895 LILY: I forget the director's name. He's Lithuanian.

CHET: That poem of yours that Lily has hung up in her kitchen, I read it. I think it's great.

SAUL: Great.

RICH: You don't much look like the poetry type.

900 LILY: Bulgarian.

CHET: I'm not. I just love your poem.

RICH: Are you a student?

CHET: Just graduated from San Francisco State.

LILY: Everybody in the play is dead.

905 SAUL: Your cousin's hot. Is he gay?

LILY: I don't know. I'll ask him. (Yelling to CHET.) Chet, are you gay?

SAUL: Christ.

RICH: That's what I call tact.

910 LILY: Well?

CHET: (loud, to LILY) Yes.

LILY: Thanks, hon.

SAUL: Give us a little more cheek . . .

CHET: There's a line of your poem I don't understand.

915 RICH: Only one? I have no idea what any of it means.

CHET: "The final waning moon . . ."

SAUL: Don't smile.

RICH: "And the coming of the light."

CHET: I love the way it sounds.

920 SAUL: Smile.

CHET: "The final waning moon/And the coming of the light."

SAUL: (indicating to LILY that he wants a sexy pose) He loves you.

CHET: Oh, I get it.

RICH: Lily tells me you're looking for a place to stay.

925 CHET: New York is so expensive.

SAUL: He lusts for you.

RICH: A friend of mine wants someone to take care of his loft while he's in L.A.

SAUL: He wants to ravage you.

930 CHET: I'll do it.

RICH: He has eight cats.

CHET: Eight tigers, I don't care.

LILY: I love that play.

RICH: It's in Tribeca.

935 SAUL: (yelling to RICH) I apologize about the book.

(RICH and CHET ignore SAUL.)

CHET: Where's Tribeca?

SAUL: Did you hear me?

RICH: On the isle of Manhattan.

CHET: We're on the isle of Manhattan.

940 RICH: We are.

LILY: The main characters are all ghosts.

CHET: I know that.

SAUL: I'll throw him a party.

RICH: That's about all you have to know.

945 SAUL: A big bash.

CHET: Is it?

LILY: We'll do it together.

RICH: I'll tell you a few more things.

CHET: Will you?

950 SAUL: I'll even invite his brother.

RICH: You bet your ass I will.

SAUL: (snapping up the roller of background paper—) Finished.

(LILY, RICH, and CHET leave. SAUL goes to the sofa. The HOSPICE WORKER comes forward.)

HOSPICE WORKER: A woman is told by her doctor that she has cancer and has only a month to live. "Now wait just one

955 minute," she tells the doctor. "I'll be wanting a second opinion." To which the doctor replies, "Okay, you're ugly, too."

David told me that one. He was an old Jewish man who had survived the Lodz ghetto in World War II. He'd seen everything in his life, and when the time came for him to go,

he accepted it. The doctors wanted to go to obscene lengths to 960 keep his body alive, but he refused. I loved him.

But most of my people are more like Margaret. She was in her nineties. She half accepted the fact that she was dying. One moment she'd be talking to you about which nephew she was definitely going to cross out of her will, and the next she'd 965 be telling you about the summer vacation she was planning in Skibbereen. She had terminal cancer! But I always go along with what they have to say. My job is not to bring enlightenment, only comfort.

Which reminds me: Margaret's family saw her as some 970 kind of prophet. The whole clan was in the room waiting to hear her last words. She had developed a distinct dislike for her family, so I was sitting closest to her when she went, and therefore I could hear what the poor soul was whispering. After it was all over, they asked me what prayer she had been 975 uttering. I told them the Lord's Prayer. I didn't have the heart to tell them that what she was saying was "Oh, shit, oh, shit, oh, shit."

I've worked with thirty-five people altogether. About a third of them had AIDS. It is the Village. 980

(She exits. Lights come up on left area. An AIDS support group is in session.)

PERSON WITH AIDS 1: Funny thing is, I wasn't at all promiscuous.

PWA 2: Oh, please.

PWA 1: I swear. And I never drank much—once in a while a 985 beer with Mexican food—and I don't smoke, and drugs, forget . . . I met Jerry in my sophomore year—we shared the same dorm room at Hofstra—and we fell in love, and that was it for me. When the sex revolution thing happened, I remember I felt retarded. Everybody was doing all those wild things. Me, I was going to the opera a lot. As far as I know, Jerry 990 didn't screw around. He swore he didn't. But then . . . he's not around for me to cross-examine. He left me.

RICH: Well, I . . .

PWA 3: What?

RICH: No. 995

PWA 4: (a young housewife, eight months pregnant) At least when I come here I don't have to lie. Like "Bernie's doing better. I'm fine." I can even crack up if I want to. Don't worry, I won't do it two weeks in a row. I mean, who's there to talk to in Brewster? These things don't happen in Brewster. Police 1000 officers don't shoot up heroin, cops don't come down with the "gay plague"—that's what they call it in Brewster. I can't talk to Bernie. I'll never forgive him. Have a chat with the minister? "Well, Reverend Miller, I have this little problem. My husband has AIDS, and I have AIDS, and I'm eight months 1005 pregnant, and I . . ." You guys know what I mean. You're the only people in this world who know what I mean.

PWA 5: I know what you guys are going to tell me: I'm suffering the homophobia that an oppressive society blah blah blah. I never felt good about being gay. 1010

PWA 2: Oh, Mary.

PWA 5: Gay was grim. It was something I did because I had to. Like a dope fiend needs his fix. It always left me feeling like shit afterward. And that's the truth. I felt guilty. I still feel that way. 1015

(PWA 4 *leans over to put a consoling hand on him. He pulls away.*)

PWA 2: I was part of a team trying to teach robots how to use language. (*He moves and talks like a robot.*) "I'm Harris, your android model 3135X. I can vacuum the floors, cook cheeseburgers, play the piano." It's much harder to teach robots to understand. (*Instructing a backward robot.*) "Joke." (*The robot responds dutifully.*) "Noun: a clash of values or levels of reality, producing laughter. Example: Have you heard about the disease attacking Jewish American princesses? It's called MAIDS. You die if you *don't* get it. Ha. Ha." My co-workers asked me to leave. They were afraid of contracting AIDS through the air, or by my looking at them. You see, they are scientists. My last act before I left was programming one final robot. (*He behaves like a robot again.*) "Good morning. This is Jack — (*he suddenly becomes a flamboyantly gay robot*) but you can call me Jackie — your *fabulous* new android model 1069. If you wish to use me — and I *love* being used — press one of those cunning little buttons on my pecs. Go on, press one — (*he switches from a campy tone to an almost angry, accusatory one*) or are you afraid of me, too?" That was my stab at immortality.

RICH: I'm not sure I have it anymore. I feel guilty saying this, like somehow I'm being disloyal to the group. I'm getting better, I know it. I just have these lumps, which for some reason won't go away, and a loss of weight, which has made me lighter than I've been for years.

PWA 3: Lose weight the AYDS way!

RICH: But anyway, I feel great. I feel the disease disappearing in me. Only a small percentage of those with the swollen glands come down with the rest. I'm going to *not* come here next week. I'm sorry.

PWA 3: Rich?

SAUL: (*calling to* RICH *as if he were in the next room, while feeling the glands in his neck and armpits*) Rich?

RICH: (*still to group*) Why do I keep on apologizing?

SAUL: Rich?

RICH: If I *really* thought that I was coming down with it . . . We all have *options*.

PWA 2: Rich?

SAUL: Rich.

RICH: (*entering* SAUL'S *area*) What?

SAUL: Here, feel my glands.

RICH: You are such a hypochondriac.

SAUL: Do you think they're swollen?

RICH: (*placing his hands around* SAUL'S *neck*) They feel okay to me. (*Transylvanian accent.*) But your neck — eet is grotesquely meesshapen. (*Suddenly mock-strangling* SAUL.) Here, let me feex it. (*They start wrestling on the sofa.*)

SAUL: Not fair!

RICH: You're such a hypochondriac.

SAUL: Ow! *I'm* such a hypochondriac. You and your vitamins!

RICH: You and your yoga!

SAUL: You and your yoghurt!

RICH: It's working. My ratio's up.

SAUL: All right! (*To the tune of* "New York, New York.")

> T-cells up,
> The suppressors are down.
> New York, New York . . .

RICH: Hey, I love you! You know that?

SAUL: If you love me, get off my chest!

RICH: I don't dare. You'd try and get even. You're that way.

SAUL: We'll call a truce. One, two, three . . .

RICH and SAUL: Truce. (*As* RICH *climbs off* SAUL'S *chest,* SAUL *pulls him down, lifting his shirt, and gets him in a hammerlock.*)

SAUL: You were right. You never should have trusted me.

RICH: Unfair . . . foul . . . most unfair!

SAUL: Fuck fair. The winner gets his way with the loser. (*They tussle until* RICH *gives up.*) Having vanquished the good ship *Socrates*, the savage pirate chief Bigmeat takes the first mate as his captive.

RICH: (*in falsetto*) No, Captain Bigmeat, no!

SAUL: I've had my eye on ye since that time we met in Bangalore. Ye can't escape me now, matey. I shall ravish ye fer sure. (SAUL *tickles* RICH)

RICH: No! . . . I'm pure of blood and noble born! (*Gradually their play turns more and more sexual, which* RICH *resists at first.*) No! . . . No! . . . (*Relents.*) Perhaps . . . Please!

SAUL: Now I got ye, boy-o . . . boy-o . . . boy-o . . . Oh, boy! (*Finally* RICH *stops struggling.* RICH *and* SAUL *are close together, panting, exhausted.* SAUL *is about to make love to* RICH *when he notices a mark on his back.*)

RICH: What? (SAUL *ignores him and looks at the mark carefully.*) What? You seduce me, you finally succeed in getting me hot and bothered, and what do you do as I lie here panting? You look at my birthmark.

(SAUL *looks at* RICH'S *back. He touches some marks.*)

RICH: What is it?

SAUL: Nothing.

RICH: What is it? Tell me!

SAUL: I'm sure it's nothing!

RICH: What! WHAT! WHAT! . . .

(*Immediately, the* HOSPICE WORKER *draws a curtain that surrounds the entire living area of* SAUL'S *loft, hiding it from view. Overlapping the closing of the curtain, we hear the ringing of two telephones. Lights up on two men sitting side by side, answering multiline telephones.*)

PAT: Hotline, Pat speaking.

BARNEY: Hotline. This is Barney. (*To* PAT, *covering the phone*) Oh, no, it's her again.

PAT: Are you a gay man?

BARNEY: Didn't we speak a few days ago? (*To* PAT, *covering the phone:*) She doesn't stop.

PAT: We're all worried.

BARNEY: Is he bisexual?

PAT: Calm down, first of all. (*The third line rings.*)

BARNEY: Is he an IV drug user?

PAT: It's not all that easy to get it — *if* you take a few precautions. (*To* BARNEY *covering the phone:*) Okay, I'll get it. (*He speaks into the phone.*) Please hold on. (*He presses a button.*)

BARNEY: It wasn't my intention to insult you.

PAT: Hotline . . . Shit. (*To* BARNEY, *pressing a button:*) Lost him. Fucking phone.

BARNEY: So what makes you think he has AIDS?

PAT: (*to phone*) Hello.

BARNEY: He is what?

1125 PAT: The disease is spread through the blood and the semen.

BARNEY: American Indians are *not* a risk group. (*To* PAT, *covering the phone:*) American Indians?

PAT: So wear a condom.

BARNEY: There's half a zillion diseases he has symptoms of.

1130 PAT: Make *him* wear a condom. (*The phone rings.*)

BARNEY: Please hold. (*He presses a button.*)

PAT: Kissing is acceptable.

BARNEY: Hotline . . . (*In response to a hate call.*) And your mother eats turds in hell! . . . Thank you. (*He presses a*

1135 *button.*)

PAT: Myself, I don't do it on the first date.

BARNEY: I would definitely check it out with a physician.

BARNEY: Spots? I'm not a doctor. . . . Go to a doctor.	PAT: Stroking, holding, rubbing, mirrors, whips, chains, jacking off, porno — use your imagination.

1140

BARNEY: I'm sorry you're lonely.

PAT: Our motto is: "On me, not in me."

BARNEY: Madam, we're busy here. I can't stay on the line with

1145 you all day.

PAT: You have a nice voice, too, but I'm seeing someone.

BARNEY: Hello?

PAT: Thanks.

BARNEY: (*to* PAT) Thank God.

1150 PAT: Good luck. (*They hang up at the same time.*)

BARNEY: Spots. I love it.

PAT: (*to himself*) I am not seeing anyone.

BARNEY: What are you talking about?

PAT: I was saying how much I love being celibate. (*He kisses his*

1155 *palm.*) So how the fuck are you?

BARNEY: Tired, broke, depressed, and Tim is moving out this afternoon. Well, you asked. I hear you have a new PWA.

PAT: Sorry about Tim. Yes, I have a new baby, a writer. Why do I get all the tough customers?

1160 BARNEY: Because you're so tough.

PAT: So butch.

BARNEY: So mean.

PAT: Weathered by life like the saddle under a cowboy's ass.

BARNEY: Ooooh. I could never be a CMP. Where do you get

1165 your energy?

PAT: Drugs. I don't do that anymore either. What *do* I do? I wait tables, answer phones, and work with ingrates like Rich. Boy, is he pissed. He calls me Miss Nightingale or Florence and throws dishes and curses his roommate and won't cooperate

1170 with the doctor and won't see his shrink and isn't interested in support groups *and he shit in the fucking bathtub!* He shit —

BARNEY: Is he incontinent?

PAT: Fuck, no. He ain't that sick yet. He said it was "convenient." I don't know why he shit in the tub.

1175 BARNEY: A real sweetheart.

PAT: I'm going out of my mind. Thank God they put him in the hospital.

BARNEY: First time?

PAT: Yep.

1180 BARNEY: I'd probably be a real bastard.

PAT: I wouldn't take it lying down.

BARNEY: You'd take it any way you can get it.

PAT: Go on, girlfriend.

BARNEY: Me, if I learned I had it, I'd shove a time bomb up my tush and drop in on Timmy for tea and meet his new lover: 1185 Jimmy.

PAT: Jimmy?

BARNEY: I swear: Jimmy. (*Visiting* TIMMY *and* JIMMY *for high tea.*) "Timmy has told me so much about you. I've been *dying* to meet you." And kaboom! There goes Timmy and 1190 Jimmy.

PAT: Timmy and Jimmy? (*The telephone rings.*)

BARNEY: Ain't it a gas?

PAT: Gag me, for sure.

BARNEY: For sure. 1195

PAT: (*answering the phone*) Hotline. Pat speaking.

BARNEY: (*raging*) When are we going to get some more help around here??!! I'm going out of my mind! (*Suddenly, sweet and sultry as he answers the phone.*) Hotline, Barney speaking. 1200

PAT: Are you a gay man?

BARNEY: Are you a gay man?

(*The lights quickly fade on the two men. The curtain opens, revealing a hospital room, with bed, chair, and bed table. The loft space and bar have disappeared.* RICH *is in bed.* LILY, SAUL, *and a* NURSE *are standing nearby.*)

NURSE: Temperature and blood pressure, Mr. Farrell.

LILY: Can you come back later?

SAUL: He's had some bad news. 1205

NURSE: He's last on my rounds.

RICH: (*to* SAUL) You lied to me.

SAUL: I didn't know.

LILY: He didn't know. I swear.

NURSE: It'll just take a minute. 1210

RICH: What other little details are you keeping from me? They let him lie there like a dog. What else? (*A* Hispanic hospital worker *comes in to empty the waste basket.*) You! *Váyase!* Get the wetback out of here! *Váyase!*

HOSPITAL WORKER: I not do nothing! He crazy. 1215

RICH: You, get out of here before I breathe on you! *Ahora! Ahora! Váyase!*

NURSE: Mr. Farrell, please.

SAUL: Come back later. *Más tarde, por favor.*

RICH: Go back to your picket line. (*To* SAUL) They want a wage 1220 hike, no less. He tried to get me to bribe him to clean my room —

HOSPITAL WORKER: *Qué coño estás diciendo?* [What the fuck are you saying?]

NURSE: Please cooperate. 1225

LILY: He didn't say anything.

RICH: He won't go near my bed, but he's not afraid to touch my money.

SAUL: You misunderstood him.

RICH: *El dinero está limpio, ah? Tu madre.* [Money is clean, 1230 huh, motherfucker?]

HOSPITAL WORKER: *Maricón.* [Faggot.]

RICH: (*to* SAUL) They're unionizing primates now.

LILY: (*to* RICH) Sh!

HOSPITAL WORKER: *No entiendo.* [I don't understand.] I going. 1235 (*He exits.*)

LILY: (*aside to* SAUL) I shouldn't have told him about Chet.

SAUL: (*aside to* LILY) Better you than someone else.

1240 RICH: (*imitating* LILY *and* SAUL) Bzzz bzzz bzzz.
NURSE: (*trying to put a blood pressure cuff on* RICH's *arm*) Will you be still a moment so I can check your blood pressure?
RICH: Are you a union member, too?
NURSE: (*to* SAUL) What shall I do?
LILY: A good friend of his just passed away.
1245 NURSE: AIDS? (*She resumes struggling with the cuff.*)
RICH: The undertakers' union. Go away, I'm on strike, too; I refuse to participate in the documentation of my own demise.
SAUL: She's only trying to help you.
RICH: (*to the nurse, ripping off the cuff*) Go find another statistic
1250 for the Center for Disease Control.
NURSE: (*to* SAUL) I'm a patient woman, but he wants me to lose it. I swear that's what he's after.
RICH: Lady, fuck off!
SAUL: (*to the* NURSE) Please. Can't you see he's upset?
1255 NURSE: (*to* RICH) Okay, you win. I'm losing it. Are you happy? I'm *angry*, angry, Mr. Farrell.
LILY: Will you please go!
NURSE: A person can take only so much. I give up. I don't have to put up with this shit. I'm gonna speak to my supervisor.
1260 (*The* NURSE *exits.*)
RICH: (*applauding*) Three gold stars for self-assertion!
LILY: (*to* SAUL) I should have kept my mouth shut.
RICH: Having brought Romeo the news that Juliet is dead, Balthasar makes a tearful exit.
1265 LILY: I don't know what to say. (LILY *looks at* RICH, *then* SAUL.)
RICH: I said: Balthasar makes a tearful exit.
LILY: I know how you're feeling.
RICH: No matter. Get thee gone and hire those horses.
LILY: I loved Chet, too.
1270 RICH: Tush, thou art deceived.
NURSE: He told me he was sorry for the way he treated you.
RICH: Do the thing I bid thee.
LILY: He didn't belong in New York. He thought he was so sophisticated, but he was just a kid from Mendocino. I'm sorry I
1275 let him go home.
RICH: The messenger must go. The hero wishes to be alone with his confidant. (RICH *turns his back on* SAUL *and* LILY.)
LILY: I'll be back tomorrow. (*Aside to* SAUL) I've got half a crown roast from Margo. She went vegetarian. I'll be up. I have to
1280 have a talk with Mick. He's irrational on the subject of AIDS. He can go to hell. If he's so afraid, let him move out. (*To* RICH) I won't let him come between us. You're my buddy. (SAUL *indicates that* LILY *should leave. She gathers up her belongings, mimes dialing a telephone, and blows* SAUL *a*
1285 *kiss.*) Rich? (SAUL *shakes his head no. She leaves.* SAUL *tries to think of something to say to* RICH. *He abandons the effort and picks up the Sunday* New York Times *crossword puzzle.*)
SAUL: "African quadruped." (*Writing.*) G-n-u . . . "Hitler's father." (*Counting on his fingers.*) One, two . . . five letters.
1290 Let's see: Herman? Herman Hitler? (*Counting.*) That's six . . . Otto? . . . Werner? . . . Rudi? . . . Putzi? (*He shrugs.*) Fuck. (*He reads on.*) Thank God: "Jewish rolls." Starts with a *b*, six letters: bagels. (*He starts to write it in.*) Shit, that won't work. I need a *y*.
1295 RICH: (*without turning*) Bialys.
SAUL: B-i-a-l-y-s.
RICH: Short for Bialystok, a large industrial city in eastern Poland . . . (*turning to* SAUL) hometown of Ludwig Zamenhof,

inventor of Esperanto, an artificial international language. Alois Hitler! A-l-o— 1300
SAUL: (*putting down the puzzle*) Outclassed again. Why do I bother? He knows everything.
RICH: When I was a kid I used to spend all my time in libraries. My childhood was—
SAUL: If I had a father like yours I would have done the same thing. 1305
RICH: But thanks to that son of a bitch I could tell you how many metric tons of coal the Benelux countries produced per annum, and the capital city of the Grand Duchy of Liechtenstein.
SAUL: I give up. 1310
RICH: Vaduz.
SAUL: Miss Trivial Pursuit.
RICH: I knew to which great linguistic family the Telegu language of South India belongs.
SAUL: Telegu? Isn't that the national dish of Botswana? 1315
RICH: (*ignoring him*) The Dravidian. (SAUL *straightens up the bed table.*) I've always loved words . . . I wrote poetry when I was a kid. My brother used to make fun of me . . .

Winter, winter,
How you glinter, 1320
With holidays' array.
And the snow
We all know
Is here all day.

(SAUL *smiles*)

I was eight, nine when I wrote that. I had just come in from 1325
sledding down Indian Hill—a steep road that connects Jefferson Heights to the valley.
SAUL: You showed it to me on our grand tour of West Jersey.
RICH: It was a late afternoon just before sundown and the sky was intensely blue and intensely cold and you could see the stars 1330
already. For some reason nobody was home when I came back, so I stood there at the stamped enamel-top kitchen table dripping in my frozen corduroys and wrote that poem.
SAUL: Are you comfortable? (RICH *shrugs.* SAUL *fixes his pillows.*) 1335
RICH: I was a good kid, but I was lonely and scared all the time. I was so desperate to find people like myself that I looked for them in the indexes of books—under *H*. I eventually found them—
SAUL: But not in books. 1340
RICH: The next thing you know I moved to the city and was your typical office-worker-slash-writer. I hated my job, so I grew a beard and wore sandals, hoping they would fire me and give me permanent unemployment. I wanted to stay at home in my rent-controlled apartment and drink bourbon and write 1345
poems. I did that for a period. I loved it. The apartment got filthy and I did, too, and I'd go out only at night—to pick up guys. And then I found you—in a porno theater—(*he takes* SAUL's *hand*) and we semi-settled down and you took my picture and I started to jog. We bought a loft— 1350
SAUL: And raised a cat—
RICH: —and loved each other. But that wasn't enough for me. I don't think you ever understood this. you weren't my muse, you were . . . (*he searches for the word*) Saul. (SAUL *rises and*

1355 *looks out the window.)* I loved you but I wanted someone to write poems to. During our marriage I had almost stopped writing and felt stifled even though our loft had appeared in *New York* magazine. And then I met Chet and left you in the lurch and lived with him at the Chelsea Hotel. He was shal-

1360 low, callow, and selfish, and I loved him, too.

We did a lot of coke and I wrote a lot of poetry and the catering was booming and the *New Yorker* published a story of mine and I ran in the marathon. I was on a roll. *(With mounting excitement as he relives the experience.)* I remember

1365 training on the East River Drive for the first time. I didn't realize how narrow and dark the city streets were until I got to the river and all of a sudden there was the fucking river. The sky was the same color as that twilight when I was a kid. I came from the darkness into the light. I'm running downtown

1370 and I make this bend and out of nowhere straight up ahead is the Manhattan Bridge and then the Brooklyn Bridge, one after another, and my earphones are playing Handel's *Royal Fireworks Music.* It can't get better than this, I know it. I'm running and crying from gratitude. I came from the darkness

1375 into the light. I'm running and telling God I didn't know He was *that* good or *that* big, thank you, Jesus, thanks, thanks . . . *(He slumps back, exhausted from the effort.)*

The next morning I woke up with the flu and stayed in bed for a couple of days and felt much better. But my throat stayed

1380 a little sore and my glands were a little swollen . . . *(Long silence. Casually.)* Saul, I want you to do something for me. Will you do something for me, baby?

SAUL: Sure, babe.

RICH: Now listen. I want you to go out of here and go to the

1385 doctor and tell him you aren't sleeping so hot—

SAUL: I'm sleeping okay.

RICH: Sh! Now listen: you tell him you want something to make you sleep and Valium doesn't work on you, but a friend once gave you some Seconal—

1390 SAUL: *No!* I won't do it!

RICH: *(pressuring* SAUL *relentlessly)* I tried hoarding the pills here, but every night the nurse stays to watch me swallow them down.

SAUL: I can't do that.

1395 RICH: I don't want to end up like Chet.

SAUL: I won't listen.

RICH: If you love me, you'll help me. I have something that's eating me up. I don't want to go on. I'm scared to go on.

SAUL: Don't do this to me! I can't handle it. I'll go out the win-

1400 dow, I swear, don't do this—

RICH: Don't you see, it's the only way. Just get the pills.

SAUL: No!

RICH: Just have them around. You'll get used to the idea. And when the lesions spread above my neck so that I don't look the

1405 same, you'll want me to have them.

SAUL: Help me, help me!

RICH: It's all right. Not now.

SAUL: No.

RICH: Tomorrow.

1410 SAUL: No.

RICH: The day after.

SAUL: No.

RICH: We'll see.

(RICH's brother, wearing a surgical mask, gown, and gloves and carrying a small shopping bag, tiptoes in, stopping when he notices RICH *and* SAUL.*)*

SAUL: Oh, my God. I think it's your brother.

BROTHER: I'll come back later. 1415

SAUL: *(pulling himself together)* No, I was just going.

BROTHER: It's all right, really.

SAUL: I've been here for a while.

BROTHER: I'm interrupting.

SAUL: Really. 1420

RICH: *(to his* BROTHER*)* Unless you're planning to come into intimate contact with me or my body fluids, none of that shit you have on is necessary.

BROTHER: The sign says—

RICH: But please restrain your brotherly affection for my sake; 1425 who knows what diseases you might have brought in with you? *(The* BROTHER *removes the mask, gown, and gloves.)*

SAUL: You two haven't seen each other for a while, so why don't I just—

RICH: By all means. You need a break, kid. Think about what I 1430 said.

SAUL: It stopped raining. I'll take a walk.

RICH: Have a nice walk.

BROTHER: Good seeing ya . . .? *(He has forgotten* SAUL's *name.)*

SAUL: Saul. Yeah. 1435

(SAUL exits. Beat.)

BROTHER: I owe you an apology . . . *(RICH won't help him.)* I was very frightened . . . I'm afraid I panicked . . . Please forgive me.

RICH: Nothing to forgive.

BROTHER: *(brightly)* Betty sends her love. She sent along a tin of butter crunch. *(He offers* RICH *a tin, which* RICH *ignores.)* 1440 You're not on any special diet? I told Betty I thought maybe you'd be on one of those macrobiotic diets. I read in the papers that it's helped some people with . . .

RICH: AIDS.

BROTHER: Yes. I keep a file of clippings on all the latest medical 1445 developments. *(He takes a clipping out of his wallet.)* Looks like they're going to have a vaccine soon. The French—

RICH: That's to *prevent* AIDS. I already *have* AIDS.

BROTHER: They have this new drug, AZT.

RICH: That's for the pneumonia. I don't have pneumonia. 1450

BROTHER: Right . . . So how are you doing?

RICH: *(smiling cheerfully)* I have Kaposi's sarcoma, a hitherto rare form of skin cancer. It's spreading. I have just begun chemotherapy. It nauseates me. I expect my hair will fall out. I also have a fungal infection of the throat called candidiasis, or 1455 thrush. My life expectancy is . . . I have a greater chance of winning the lottery. Otherwise I'm fine. How are you?

BROTHER: I'm sorry . . . *(Brightly again, after a long pause.)* Mary Pat sends her love. She won her school swimming competition and I registered her for the South Jersey champion- 1460 ship. Oh, I forgot, she made this for you . . . *(He takes a large handmade fold-out card from the shopping bag. It opens downward a full two feet.)*

RICH: Say, have you heard about the miracle of AIDS?

BROTHER: What? 1465

RICH: It can turn a fruit into a vegetable. What's the worst thing about getting AIDS? (*The* BROTHER *lets the card fall to the floor.*)

BROTHER: Stop it!

1470 RICH: Trying to convince your parents that you're Haitian. Get it?

BROTHER: I came here to see if I could help you.

RICH: Skip it. So what do you want?

BROTHER: I don't want anything.

RICH: Everything I own is going to Saul—

1475 BROTHER: I don't want anything.

RICH: Except for the stuff Mom left us. I told Saul that it's to go to you. Except for the Barcelona chair—

BROTHER: I don't care about—

RICH: I'm leaving Saul the copyright to my book—

1480 BROTHER: Why are you doing this to me?

RICH: So you don't want my worldly possessions, such as they are; you want me to relieve your guilt.

BROTHER: Stop it.

RICH: (*making the sign of the cross over his* BROTHER, *chanting*) I

1485 hereby exonerate you of the sin of being ashamed of your queer brother and being a coward in the face of—

BROTHER: Stop! Don't! (*The* BROTHER *grabs* RICH's *hand.*)

RICH: No!

BROTHER: Richard, don't! . . . (*He attempts to hug* RICH, *who*

1490 *resists with all his strength.*) I don't care . . . I don't care! . . . Rich! . . . Richie . . . Richie . . . (RICH *relents. They hug.*)

RICH: I'm so . . . [frightened]

BROTHER: Forgive me. Forgive me.

RICH: I don't want to . . . [die]

1495 BROTHER: It's all right. I'm here . . . I'm here . . .

(*They hold each other close for a beat. The* HOSPITAL WORKER *rushes into the room.*)

HOSPITAL WORKER: Psst. Oye. Psst.

(RICH *and his* BROTHER *notice the* WORKER.)

RICH: What do you want now?

HOSPITAL WORKER: (*shakes his head no*) Viene. Viene. He come. He come. (*He pulls the* BROTHER *from* RICH.)

1500 RICH: Who come?

HOSPITAL WORKER: Su amigo. Your freng. He no like.

BROTHER: What's he saying?

(RICH *starts to laugh. Enter* SAUL. *The* WORKER *starts sweeping and whistling with an air of exuberant nonchalance. The following is overlapping.*)

RICH: (*laughing*) He . . . he . . .

SAUL: What's going on?

1505 BROTHER: Richie, what's so damned funny?

RICH: He thought we . . . (*he breaks up*) that he and I were cheating on you.

BROTHER: He thought that you and I were . . . (*He laughs.*)

RICH: He came in to warn me that you were coming! (*He*

1510 *laughs. To the worker:*) Gracias! Muchas gracias!

SAUL: He thought you two were . . . (*He laughs.*)

HOSPITAL WORKER: (*to* RICH) De nada. [You're welcome.] Why you laugh? (*The* WORKER *laughs.*) Como hay maricones. [What a bunch of faggots.]

RICH: Es mi hermano. [He's my brother.]   1515

HOSPITAL WORKER: Coño. [Fuck.]

RICH: Perdona por lo que dije antes. Yo (*pointing to himself*) era mucho estupido. [Forgive me for what I said to you before. I was being very stupid.]

HOSPITAL WORKER: De nada. Somos todos estúpidos, chico.   1520
[We're all stupid, my friend.] (*He exits. The giggles subside.*)

BROTHER: (*checking watch, stiffening his spine*) I've got to be going now.

RICH: I'm glad you came by.

BROTHER: I'll be back tomorrow with Mary Pat. She's been   1525
dying—wanting to come by. She's been writing poetry and—

RICH: I'd love to see her. And tell Betty thanks for the . . .?

BROTHER: Butter crunch. (*Exiting, shaking hands with* SAUL.)
Good seeing ya . . .?(*He has forgotten* SAUL's *name again.*)

SAUL: Saul.   1530

BROTHER: Sorry. Bye. (*He exits.*)

SAUL: I won't get upset. I won't get upset.

RICH: What's the matter?

SAUL: It's *my* problem.

RICH: What?   1535

SAUL: Rich, I've thought about things.

RICH: What?

SAUL: (*suddenly exploding*) Goddamn it! That prick doesn't know my name after—how many years are we together?

RICH: *Were* together.   1540

SAUL: Pardon me, I forgot we got an annulment from the pope. Fuck it, I won't get upset.

RICH: (*overlapping*) My brother finds it hard to deal with the fact that—

SAUL: I said fuck it.   1545

RICH: Don't you see, it was a big step for him—

SAUL: Your brother hates my fucking guts. Haven't you ever told him I didn't turn you queer?

RICH: My brother—

SAUL: I didn't give you AIDS either.   1550

RICH: My brother—

SAUL: Why're you always defending him? What about me?

RICH: My brother's got a few feelings, too, even if he isn't a card-carrying member of the lavender elite.

SAUL: Let's hear it for our working-class hero.   1555

RICH: You've never tried talking to him. You're so self-centered that it never occurred to you—

SAUL: I'm self—Now wait one minute! I'm so self-centered that I was willing to buy the pills for you.

RICH: You have the pills?   1560

(*The other actors create the sleazy atmosphere of Christopher Street near the Hudson River.*)

DEALER 1: Yo, my man.

SAUL: I was willing to go down to Christopher Street, where all the drug dealers hang out.

DEALER 2: What's 'attenin', what's 'attenin'?

(SAUL *turns his back to* RICH *and immediately he is on Christopher Street.*)

SAUL: (*to* DEALER 2) Nice night.   1565

RICH: I told you to go to the doctor's.

DEALER 1: Smoke 'n' acid,   DEALER 2: Smoke 'n' coke,
  MDA 'n' speed, Smoke 'n'   smoke 'n' coke, smoke 'n'
  acid, MDA 'n' speed . . .   coke . . .

1570 SAUL: (to DEALER 1) I said, "Nice night."
DEALER 1: Real nice. What's shakin', babe?
RICH: All you would've had to say to the doctor was "My room-
  mate has AIDS and I'm not sleeping well."
SAUL: (to DEALER 1) I'm not sleeping well.
1575 DEALER 1: I have just the thing. Step right into my office.
DEALER 3: Speed, acid, mesc, ups, downs, crack . . .
SAUL: I'll take one hundred.
DEALER 1: Two dollars a cap.
RICH: Forty's enough.
1580 SAUL: I wanted enough for both of us.
DEALER 1: You got the cash, I got the stash.
RICH: Tristan and Isolde.
DEALER 1: Hey, man, you want them or not?
SAUL: You don't understand anything!
1585 DEALER 1: Look, man, I can't handle all that emotiating.
SAUL: (near the breaking point) You've never understood anything!
DEALER 1: Gimme the greens, I'll give you the reds.
RICH: The widow throws herself on her husband's funeral pyre.
SAUL: (hitting the bed with his fists. If RICH were the bed he'd be
1590 dead) SHIT! SHIT! SHIT! You selfish bastard!
RICH: What stopped you?
SAUL: From hitting you?
RICH: From buying the pills.
SAUL: The pills? Nothing stopped me. I bought them.
1595 RICH: Thank you. Where are they?
SAUL: I threw them away.
RICH: Why?
SAUL: Let me help you live!
RICH: What's so hot about living when you're covered with le-
1600 sions and you're coming down with a new infection every
  day? . . . If it gets too bad, I want to be able to quietly
  disappear.
SAUL: I won't argue the logic of it. I can't do what you want me
  to do.
1605 RICH: I just want them around. You keep them for me—just in
  case.
SAUL: I won't.
RICH: Then I'll get them myself. I'll go out of here and get them.
  (He climbs out of bed. He's shaky.)
1610 SAUL: You're crazy.
RICH: I don't need you to do my dirty work. (He takes a few steps.)
  Where're my clothes? Where'd they put them?
SAUL: Get back in bed!
RICH: I want to get out of here! (He puts on his robe.) This place
1615 is a death machine! (He starts to leave but collapses on the floor.)
SAUL: (rushing to his aid) You idiot.
RICH: (catching his breath) Well, here we are again. (SAUL tries
  to help him back to bed.) No. Let me sit . . . Fuck . . . (He sits
  in chair.) "Dependent": from the Late Latin "to hang from."
1620 SAUL: I tried to do what you asked me to do. Just like always.
RICH: You don't have to apologize.
SAUL: I want you to understand something.
RICH: I understand.
SAUL: It's important. Listen. I had made up my mind to give you

half of the pills and keep the other half for myself. I was walk- 1625
  ing past Sheridan Square. It was starting to drizzle again.
  You've never seen Sheridan Square look grungier: a drunk
  was pissing on the pathetic little flowers. And that crazy
  lady—you know the one that sings off-key at the top of her
  lungs—she was there, too. And my favorite, the guy with his 1630
  stomach out to here—
RICH: I get the picture.
SAUL: There I was walking with the pills in my pocket, contemplating our suicides. And I was getting wet and cold. As I
  passed the square, Seconal seemed too slow to me. You don't 1635
  have a monopoly on pain.
RICH: I never thought—
SAUL: Shut up. Anyway, I had stopped in front of the Pleasure
  Chest. I looked up and there in the window were sex toys and
  multicolored jockstraps, lit by a red neon sign. I said, "Help 1640
  me, God." Which is funny coming from an atheist, let me tell
  you . . . I said it out loud.
RICH: And you could walk again.
SAUL: Well, it wasn't exactly a miracle.
RICH: Thank God. 1645
SAUL: Anyway, there I was in front of a sex shop, and I looked
  down and there was a puddle. Now this'll sound stupid.
RICH: Couldn't sound stupider than the rest.
SAUL: In this dirty little puddle was a reflection of the red neon
  sign. It was beautiful. And the whole street was shining with 1650
  the incredible colors. They kept changing as the different
  signs blinked on and off . . . I don't know how long I stood
  there. A phrase came to my head: "The Lord taketh and the
  Lord giveth."
RICH: You blew your punch line. 1655
SAUL: It's the other way around. Anyway, there went two hun-
  dred bucks down the sewer.
RICH: Take it off your taxes.
SAUL: Don't you see, I just don't have the right to take your life
  or mine. 1660
RICH: The Miracle of the Pleasure Chest.
SAUL: Hang in there, Rich.
RICH: Our Lady of Christopher Street.
SAUL: Maybe I'm being selfish, but I want you here. I need you.
RICH: My future isn't exactly promising. 1665
SAUL: I'll take you as is.
RICH: But what happens when it gets worse? It's gonna get worse.
SAUL: I'll be here for you no matter what happens.
RICH: Will you?
SAUL: I promise. 1670
RICH: Shit.
SAUL: What do you want me to say?
RICH: You're so goddamned noble.
SAUL: How do you want me to be?
RICH: I can't afford to be noble. The only thing holding me to- 1675
  gether is rage. It's not fair! Why me?
SAUL: Why not you? Maybe I'm next. No one knows.
RICH: I reserve the right to put an end to all this shit.
SAUL: All right, but if you kill yourself they won't bury you in
  hallowed ground and you'll go to hell with all us Jews. 1680
RICH: I bet they have a separate AIDS section in the cemetery so
  I don't infect the other corpses. (Beat, then suddenly he speaks
  fiercely.) Do you promise to stick with me no matter what
  happens?

1685 SAUL: I do.

RICH: *Do you?* (*He searches* SAUL's *face for the answer.*) I need you. (*Long silence. He releases* SAUL.) Paradise in a puddle.

SAUL: You couldn't resist that, could you?

RICH: Prodigies and signs, why not? It's the end of an era.

1690 SAUL: What do you think'll come next?

RICH: Next? After I'm gone?

SAUL: Don't be maudlin. You know I didn't mean that.

RICH: I know you didn't . . . I've been wondering what happens after I die . . . Do you think things go on and on? I don't know.

1695 Is this all the time I have? I hope not . . . Do you think anywhere out there is a place as sweet as this one? I like it here—even though right now I am going through a lot of . . . (*searching for the word*) difficulty. (*He goes back to bed.*) And if we get to come back, where do we get to come back to? I

1700 don't feature leaving here and going to a goddamned naphtha swamp in the Z sector of some provincial galaxy to live as some kind of weird insect . . . But if life is a kind of educational process in which each piece of the universe eventually gets to discover its own true divine nature, if it is, then a

1705 methane bog on Jupiter might serve just as well as a meadow in the Berkshires . . . I want to be cremated and I want my ashes to fertilize the apple tree in the middle of Jake's pasture. When you take a bite of an apple from that tree, think of me.

SAUL: You'd be the worm in it.

1710 RICH: Saul?

SAUL: What, Rich?

RICH: There's a café way over by Tompkins Square Park, off of B. It holds maybe ten tables and has the scuzziest art on the walls.

1715 SAUL: What about it?

RICH: I want to read my work there.

SAUL: You turned down the Y.

RICH: People go there, gay, straight, with their weird hair and their ears pierced ninety-nine different ways, they go there

1720 late in the evening, and there's a guitarist, and they sit there politely and listen. They look newborn, but slightly depraved. I want to read there when I get out of here. And you'll take pictures. Okay?

SAUL: Sounds okay. Sounds good to me.

1725 RICH: Forgive me for being such a fuck.

SAUL: You really are a fuck.

RICH: I'm a real prick.

SAUL: You're an asshole.

RICH: You're a faggot.

1730 SAUL: You're a fruit.

RICH: You know, if we took precautions . . .

SAUL: If what? What? You always do that.

RICH: I don't know.

SAUL: Would you like to?

1735 RICH: If we're careful. Do you want to?

SAUL: I'd love to. What do you think?

RICH: I think it'd be okay.

SAUL: What'll we do?

RICH: I don't know. Something safe.

1740 SAUL: We'll think of something.

RICH: Close the curtain.

SAUL: Do you think we should?

RICH: Well, we can't do it like this.

SAUL: Right.

RICH: Right.   1745

SAUL: What if someone comes in?

RICH: So what?

SAUL: Right. (SAUL *doesn't move.*)

RICH: So what are you waiting for?

SAUL: I'm scared.   1750

RICH: So am I. Do you think we should?

SAUL: God, I want to.

RICH: Well, close the fucking curtain! (*The* HOSPICE WORKER *ends the impasse by closing the curtain.*) Thanks.

SAUL: Thanks.   1755

(*When the curtain is completely shut, the* HOSPICE WORKER *walks down center.*)

HOSPICE WORKER: I have a new AIDS patient. Richard. He still has a lot of denial about his condition. Which is normal. I think most of us would go crazy if we had to face our own deaths squarely. He's a wonderful man. He writes extraordinarily funny poems about the ward. His lover's there all the   1760 time, and he's got a lot of friends visiting, and both families. I only hope it keeps up. It's only his second time in the hospital. They get a lot of support at first, but as the illness goes on, the visitors stop coming—and they're left with only me.

But something tells me it's not going to happen in his case.   1765 You should see how his lover takes care of him. God forbid they treat Rich badly, Saul swoops down and lets them have it. He's making a real pain in the ass of himself, which is sometimes how you have to be in this situation.

Rich should be out of the hospital again in a week or so.   1770 For a while. He's a fighter . . . The angry phase is just about over and the bargaining phase is beginning. If he behaves like a good little boy, God will do what Rich tells Him to do . . . I certainly hope that God does.

I don't know anymore. Sometimes I think I'm an atheist.   1775 No. Not really. It's more that I'm angry at God: how can He do this? (*Pause.*) I have a lot of denial, *I* am angry, and *I* bargain with God. I have a long way to go towards acceptance. Maybe it's time for me to resign. Maybe I'm suffering from burnout.   1780

But what would I do if I didn't go to St. Vincent's? And it's a privilege to be with people when they are dying. Sometimes they tell you the most amazing things. The other night Jean-Jacques—he's this real queen, there's no other word for it—he told me what he misses most in the hospital is his corset   1785 and high heels. I mean he weighs all of ninety pounds and he's half-dead. But I admire his spirit. The way they treat him. Sometimes they won't even bring the food to his bed. And I'm afraid to complain for fear they take it out on him! Damn them! . . . I've lost some of my idealism, as I said. Last   1790 night I painted his nails for him. (*She shows the audience her vividly painted fingernails.*) Flaming red. He loved it.

DAVID HENRY HWANG

David Henry Hwang was born in Los Angeles in 1957. He graduated with a B.A. in English from Stanford University in 1979 and studied at the Yale School of Drama 1980–1981. In the 1980s, Hwang wrote a series of powerful plays concerning the cultural and political experience of Asian Americans in the United States. His first play, *F.O.B.* ("fresh off the boat"), dramatizes the tensions that arise between Chinese immigrants to the United States and their assimilated friends and relatives. The play won an Obie award in 1980. Hwang addressed similar issues in *The Dance of the Railroad* (1981) and in *Rich Relations* (1986), and he collaborated with composer Philip Glass on *1000 Airplanes on the Roof* (1988). Hwang's Tony Award-winning *M. Butterfly* (1988) is a brilliant critique of Western attitudes toward Asia, epitomized by one of Western culture's most powerful and seductive images of the Orient: Puccini's opera, *Madame Butterfly*.

M. Butterfly

In *M. Butterfly*, Hwang traces the relationship between the "Orient" of the Western imagination and the political realities that such images help to foster. The play's central character, the diplomat Gallimard, conducts his relationship with China in terms of Puccini's *Madame Butterfly*. In Puccini's 1904 opera, the naval officer Pinkerton marries the Japanese geisha girl Butterfly. He leaves for the United States, promising to return, and Butterfly waits for him, meanwhile bearing his child. When Pinkerton sends his wife from America to collect his child, Butterfly realizes that he will never return. She commits suicide.

As Hwang has remarked, Butterfly has become a cultural stereotype of East-West relations — "speaking of an Asian woman, we would sometimes say, 'She's pulling a Butterfly,' which meant playing the submissive Oriental number." This sexist and racist stereotype, Hwang argues, pervades not only Western men's fantasies about Asian women — as the mail-order business in Asian wives suggests, Western men see Asian women as obedient, submissive, and sexually self-sacrificing — but also conditions the political relationship between Asia and the West as well.

M. Butterfly fuses this erotic and political desire for domination in the character of Gallimard, a French diplomat who falls in love with Song Liling, an opera singer whom he first sees singing the death aria from *Madame Butterfly*. However, the play develops a fascinating twist, for Song is in fact a man, who plays female roles in the Beijing Opera, and who — as a woman — develops a love affair with Gallimard in order to spy for the Chinese government. *M. Butterfly* compacts a complex reading of the politics of race, gender, and sexuality in a brilliantly theatrical drama.

M. BUTTERFLY

David Henry Hwang

— CHARACTERS —

KUROGO	GIRL IN MAGAZINE	*The action of the play takes place in a Paris prison in the present,*
RENE GALLIMARD	COMRADE CHIN	*and in recall, during the decade 1960 to 1970 in Beijing, and*
SONG LILING	SUZUKI	*from 1966 to the present in Paris.*
MARC	SHU FANG	
MAN #2	HELGA	
CONSUL SHARPLESS	M. TOULON	
RENEE	MAN #1	
WOMAN AT PARTY	JUDGE	

— ACT ONE —

SCENE I

M. GALLIMARD's *prison cell. Paris. Present.*

Lights fade up to reveal RENE GALLIMARD, *65, in a prison cell. He wears a comfortable bathrobe, and looks old and tired. The sparsely furnished cell contains a wooden crate upon which sits a hot plate with a kettle, and a portable tape recorder.* GALLIMARD *sits on the crate staring at the recorder, a sad smile on his face.*

Upstage SONG, *who appears as a beautiful woman in traditional Chinese garb, dances a traditional piece from the Peking Opera, surrounded by the percussive clatter of Chinese music.*

Then, slowly, lights and sound cross-fade; the Chinese opera music dissolves into a Western opera, the "Love Duet" from Puccini's Madame Butterfly. SONG *continues dancing, now to the Western accompaniment. Though her movements are the same, the difference in music now gives them a balletic quality.*

GALLIMARD *rises, and turns upstage towards the figure of* SONG, *who dances without acknowledging him.*

GALLIMARD: Butterfly, Butterfly . . .

(He forces himself to turn away, as the image of SONG *fades out, and talks to us.)*

GALLIMARD: The limits of my cell are as such: four-and-a-half meters by five. There's one window against the far wall; a door, very strong, to protect me from autograph hounds. I'm responsible for the tape recorder, the hot plate, and this charming coffee table.

When I want to eat, I'm marched off to the dining room — hot, steaming slop appears on my plate. When I want to sleep, the light bulb turns itself off — the work of fairies. It's an enchanted space I occupy. The French — we know how to run a prison.

But, to be honest, I'm not treated like an ordinary prison. Why? Because I'm a celebrity. You see, I make people laugh.

I never dreamed this day would arrive. I've never been considered witty or clever. In fact, as a young boy, in an informal poll among my grammar school classmates, I was voted "least likely to be invited to a party." It's a title I managed to hold onto for many years. Despite some stiff competition.

But now, how the tables turn! Look at me: the life of every social function in Paris. Paris? Why be modest? My fame has spread to Amsterdam, London, New York. Listen to them! In the world's smartest parlors. I'm the one who lifts their spirits!

(With a flourish, GALLIMARD *directs our attention to another part of the stage.)*

SCENE II

A party. Present.

Lights go up on a chic-looking parlor, where a well-dressed trio, two men and one woman, make conversation. GALLIMARD *also remains lit; he observes them from his cell.*

WOMAN: And what of Gallimard?

MAN 1: Gallimard?

MAN 2: Gallimard!

GALLIMARD: *(To us)* You see? They're all determined to say my name, as if it were some new dance.

WOMAN: He still claims not to believe the truth.

MAN 1: What? Still? Even since the trial?

WOMAN: Yes. Isn't it mad?

MAN 2: *(Laughing)* He says . . . it was dark . . . and she was very modest!

(The trio break into laughter.)

MAN 1: So — what? He never touched her with his hands?

MAN 2: Perhaps he did, and simply misidentified the equipment. A compelling case for sex education in the schools.

WOMAN: To protect the National Security — the Church can't argue with that.

MAN 1: That's impossible! How could he not know?

MAN 2: Simple ignorance.

MAN 1: For twenty years?

MAN 2: Time flies when you're being stupid.

WOMAN: Well, I thought the French were ladies' men.

MAN 2: It seems Monsieur Gallimard was overly anxious to live up to his national reputation.

WOMAN: Well, he's not very good-looking.

MAN 1: No, he's not.

MAN 2: Certainly not.

WOMAN: Actually, I feel sorry for him.

MAN 2: A toast! To Monsieur Gallimard!

WOMAN: Yes! To Gallimard!
MAN 1: To Gallimard!
30   MAN 2: Vive la différence!

(They toast, laughing. Lights down on them.)

SCENE III

M. GALLIMARD's *cell.*

GALLIMARD: *(Smiling)* You see? They toast me. I've become patron saint of the socially inept. Can they really be so foolish?
Men like that—they should be scratching at my door, begging to learn my secrets! For I, Rene Gallimard, you see, I
5   have known, and been loved by . . . the Perfect Woman.
   Alone in this cell, I sit night after night, watching our story
play through my head, always searching for a new ending,
one which redeems my honor, where she returns at last to my
arms. And I imagine you—my ideal audience—who come
10   to understand and even, perhaps just a little, to envy me.

*(He turns on his tape recorder. Over the house speakers, we hear
the opening phrases of* Madame Butterfly.*)*

GALLIMARD: In order for you to understand what I did and why,
I must introduce you to my favorite opera: *Madame Butterfly.*
By Giacomo Puccini. First produced at La Scala, Milan, in
1904, it is now beloved throughout the Western world.

(As GALLIMARD *describes the opera, the tape seques in and out to
sections he may be describing.)*

15   GALLIMARD: And why not? Its heroine, Cio-Cio-San, also
known as Butterfly, is a feminine ideal, beautiful and brave.
And its hero, the man for whom she gives up everything, is—
*(He pulls out a naval officer's cap from under his crate, pops it
on his head, and struts about)*—not very good-looking, not
20   too bright, and pretty much a wimp: Benjamin Franklin
Pinkerton of the U.S. Navy. As the curtain rises, he's just
closed on two great bargains: one on a house, the other on a
woman—call it a package deal.
   Pinkerton purchased the rights to Butterfly for one hundred
25   yen—in modern currency, equivalent to about . . . sixty-six
cents. So, he's feeling pretty pleased with himself as Sharpless, the American consul, arrives to witness the marriage.

(MARC, wearing an official cap to designate SHARPLESS, *enters
and plays the character.)*

SHARPLESS/MARC: Pinkerton!
PINKERTON/GALLIMARD: Sharpless! How's it hangin'? It's a great
30   day, just great. Between my house, my wife, and the rickshaw
ride in from town, I've saved nineteen cents just this morning.
SHARPLESS: Wonderful. I can see the inscription on your tombstone already: "I saved a dollar, here I lie." *(He looks around)*
Nice house.
35   PINKERTON: It's artistic. Artistic, don't you think? Like the way
the shoji screens slide open to reveal the wet bar and disco
mirror ball? Classy, huh? Great for impressing the chicks.
SHARPLESS: "Chicks"? Pinkerton, you're going to be a married
man!
40   PINKERTON: Well, sort of.
SHARPLESS: What do you mean?

PINKERTON: This country—Sharpless, it is okay. You got all
these geisha girls running around—
SHARPLESS: I know! I live here!
PINKERTON: Then, you know the marriage laws, right? I split for   45
one month, it's annulled!
SHARPLESS: Leave it to you to read the fine print. Who's the
lucky girl?
PINKERTON: Cio-Cio-San. Her friends call her Butterfly. Sharp-
less, she eats out of my hand!   50
SHARPLESS: She's probably very hungry.
PINKERTON: Not like American girls. It's true what they say
about Oriental girls. They want to be treated bad!
SHARPLESS: Oh, please!
PINKERTON: It's true!   55
SHARPLESS: Are you serious about this girl?
PINKERTON: I'm marrying her, aren't I?
SHARPLESS: Yes—with generous trade-in terms.
PINKERTON: When I leave, she'll know what it's like to have
loved a real man. And I'll even buy her a few nylons.   60
SHARPLESS: You aren't planning to take her with you?
PINKERTON: Huh? Where?
SHARPLESS: Home!
PINKERTON: You mean, America? Are you crazy? Can you see
her trying to buy rice in St. Louis?   65
SHARPLESS: So, you're not serious.

(Pause.)

PINKERTON/GALLIMARD: *(As* PINKERTON*)* Consul, I am a sailor
in port. *(As* GALLIMARD*)* They then proceed to sing the famous duet, "The Whole World Over."

(The duet plays on the speakers. GALLIMARD, *as* PINKERTON,
lip-syncs his lines from the opera.)

GALLIMARD: To give a rough translation: "The whole world   70
over, the Yankee travels, casting his anchor wherever he
wants. Life's not worth living unless he can win the hearts of
the fairest maidens, then hotfoot it off the premises ASAP."
(He turns towards MARC*)* In the preceding scene, I played
Pinkerton, the womanizing cad, and my friend Marc from   75
school . . . *(MARC* bows grandly for our benefit*)* played Sharpless, the sensitive soul of reason. In life, however, our positions were usually—no, always—reversed.

SCENE IV

Ecole Nationale. Aix-en-Provence. 1947.

GALLIMARD: No, Marc, I think I'd rather stay home.
MARC: Are you crazy?! We are going to Dad's condo in Mar-
seille! You know what happened last time?
GALLIMARD: Of course I do.
MARC: Of course you don't! You never know. . . . They stripped,   5
Rene!
GALLIMARD: Who stripped?
MARC: The girls!
GALLIMARD: Girls? Who said anything about girls?
MARC: Rene, we're a buncha university guys goin' up to the   10
woods. What are we gonna do—talk philosophy?
GALLIMARD: What girls? Where do you get them?

MARC: Who cares? The point is, they come. On trucks. Packed in like sardines. The back flips open, babes hop out, we're ready to roll.

GALLIMARD: You mean, they just—?

MARC: Before you know it, every last one of them—they're stripped and splashing around my pool. There's no moon out, they can't see what's going on, their boobs are flapping, right? You close your eyes, reach out—it's grab bag, get it? Doesn't matter whose ass is between whose legs, whose teeth are sinking into who. You're just in there, going at it, eyes closed, on and on for as long as you can stand. (Pause) Some fun, huh?

GALLIMARD: What happens in the morning?

MARC: In the morning, you're ready to talk some philosophy. (Beat) So how 'bout it?

GALLIMARD: Marc, I can't . . . I'm afraid they'll say no—the girls. So I never ask.

MARC: You don't have to ask! That's the beauty—don't you see? They don't have to say yes. It's perfect for a guy like you, really.

GALLIMARD: You go ahead . . . I may come later.

MARC: Hey, Rene—it doesn't matter that you're clumsy and got zits—they're not looking!

GALLIMARD: Thank you very much.

MARC: Wimp.

(MARC walks over to the other side of the stage, and starts waving and smiling at women in the audience.)

GALLIMARD: (To us) We now return to my version of Madame Butterfly and the events leading to my recent conviction for treason.

(GALLIMARD notices MARC making lewd gestures.)

Marc, what are you doing?

MARC: Huh? (Sotto voce) Rene, there're a lotta great babes out there. They're probably lookin' at me and thinking, "What a dangerous guy."

GALLIMARD: Yes—how could they help but be impressed by your cool sophistication?

(GALLIMARD pops the SHARPLESS cap on MARC's head, and points him offstage. MARC exits, leering.)

SCENE V

M. GALLIMARD's cell.

GALLIMARD: Next, Butterfly makes her entrance. We learn her age—fifteen . . . but very mature for her years.

(Lights come up on the area where we saw SONG dancing at the top of the play. She appears there again, now dressed as MADAME BUTTERFLY, moving to the "Love Duet." GALLIMARD turns upstage slightly to watch, transfixed.)

GALLIMARD: But as she glides past him, beautiful, laughing softly behind her fan, don't we who are men sigh with hope? We, who are not handsome, nor brave, nor powerful, yet somehow believe, like Pinkerton, that we deserve a Butterfly. She arrives with all her possessions in the folds of her sleeves, lays them all out, for her man to do with as he pleases. Even her life itself—she bows her head as she whispers that she's

not even worth the hundred yen he paid for her. He's already given too much, when we know he's really had to give nothing at all.

(Music and lights on SONG out. GALLIMARD sits at his crate.)

GALLIMARD: In real life, women who put their total worth at less than sixty-six cents are quite hard to find. The closest we come is in the pages of these magazines. (He reaches into his crate, pulls out a stack of girlie magazines, and begins flipping through them.) Quite a necessity in prison. For three or four dollars, you get seven or eight women.

I first discovered these magazines at my uncle's house. One day, as a boy of twelve. The first time I saw them in his closet . . . all lined up—my body shook. Not with lust—no, with power. Here were women— a shelfful—who would do exactly as I wanted.

(The "Love Duet" creeps in over the speakers. Special comes up, revealing, not SONG this time, but a pinup girl in a sexy negligee, her back to us. GALLIMARD turns upstage and looks at her.

GIRL: I know you're watching me.

GALLIMARD: My throat . . . it's dry.

GIRL: I leave my blinds open every night before I go to bed.

GALLIMARD: I can't move.

GIRL: I leave my blinds open and the lights on.

GALLIMARD: I'm shaking. My skin is hot, but my penis is soft. Why?

GIRL: I stand in front of the window.

GALLIMARD: What is she going to do?

GIRL: I toss my hair, and I let my lips part . . . barely.

GALLIMARD: I shouldn't be seeing this. It's so dirty. I'm so bad.

GIRL: Then, slowly, I lift off my nightdress.

GALLIMARD: Oh, god. I can't believe it. I can't—

GIRL: I toss it to the ground.

GALLIMARD: Now, she's going to walk away. She's going to—

GIRL: I stand there, in the light, displaying myself.

GALLIMARD: No. She's—why is she naked?

GIRL: To you.

GALLIMARD: In front of a window? This is wrong. No—

GIRL: Without shame.

GALLIMARD: No, she must . . . like it.

GIRL: I like it.

GALLIMARD: She . . . she wants me to see.

GIRL: I want you to see.

GALLIMARD: I can't believe it! She's getting excited!

GIRL: I can't see you. You can do whatever you want.

GALLIMARD: I can't do a thing. Why?

GIRL: What would you like me to do . . . next?

(Lights go down on her. Music off. Silence, as GALLIMARD puts away his magazines. Then he resumes talking to us.)

GALLIMARD: Act Two begins with Butterfly staring at the ocean. Pinkerton's been called back to the U.S., and he's given his wife a detailed schedule of his plans. In the column marked "return date," he's written "when the robins nest." This failed to ignite her suspicions. Now, three years have passed without a peep from him. Which brings a response from her faithful servant, Suzuki.

(COMRADE CHIN enters, playing SUZUKI.)

60 SUZUKI: Girl, he's a loser. What'd he ever give you? Nineteen cents and those ugly Day-Glo stockings? Look, it's finished! Kaput! Done! And you should be glad! I mean, the guy was a woofer! He tried before, you know—before he met you, he went down to geisha central and plunked down his spare change in front of the usual candidates—everyone else 65 gagged! These are hungry prostitutes, and they were not interested, get the picture? Now, stop slathering when an American ship sails in, and let's make some bucks—I mean, yen! We are broke!

70   Now, what about Yamadori? Hey, hey—don't look away— the man is a prince—figuratively, and, what's even better, literally. He's rich, he's handsome, he says he'll die if you don't marry him—and he's even willing to overlook the little fact that you've been deflowered all over the place by a foreign devil. What do you mean, "But he's Japanese?" You're Japa- 75 nese! You think you've been touched by the whitey god? He was a sailor with dirty hands!

(SUZUKI stalks offstage.)

GALLIMARD: She's also visited by Consul Sharpless, sent by Pinkerton on a minor errand.

(MARC enters, as SHARPLESS.)

SHARPLESS: I hate this job.
80 GALLIMARD: This Pinkerton—he doesn't show up personally to tell his wife he's abandoning her. No, he sends a government diplomat . . . at taxpayer's expense.
SHARPLESS: Butterfly? Butterfly? I have some bad—I'm going to be ill. Butterfly, I came to tell you—
85 GALLIMARD: Butterfly says she knows he'll return and if he doesn't she'll kill herself rather than go back to her own peo- ple. *(Beat)* This causes a lull in the conversation.
SHARPLESS: Let's put it this way . . .
GALLIMARD: Butterfly runs into the next room, and returns
90   holding—

(Sound cue: a baby crying. SHARPLESS, "seeing" this, backs away.)

SHARPLESS: Well, good. Happy to see things going so well. I suppose I'll be going now. Ta ta. Ciao. *(He turns away. Sound cue out)* I hate this job. *(He exits)*
GALLIMARD: At that moment, Butterfly spots in the harbor an
95   American ship—the *Abramo Lincoln!*

(Music cue: "The Flower Duet." SONG, still dressed as BUTTER- FLY, changes into a wedding kimono, moving to the music.)

GALLIMARD: This is the moment that redeems her years of wait- ing. With Suzuki's help, they cover the room with flowers—

(CHIN, as SUZUKI, trudges onstage and drops a lone flower with- out much enthusiasm.)

GALLIMARD: —and she changes into her wedding dress to pre- pare for Pinkerton's arrival.

(SUZUKI helps BUTTERFLY change. HELGA enters, and helps GALLIMARD change into a tuxedo.)

100 GALLIMARD: I married a woman older than myself—Helga.
HELGA: My father was ambassador to Australia. I grew up among criminals and kangaroos.
GALLIMARD: Hearing that brought me to the altar—

(HELGA exits.)

GALLIMARD: —where I took a vow renouncing love. No fantasy woman would ever want me, so, yes, I would settle for a quick 105 leap up the career ladder. Passion, I banish, and in its place— practicality!
    But my vows had long since lost their charm by the time we arrived in China. The sad truth is that all men want a beauti- ful woman, and the uglier the man, the greater the want. 110

(SUZUKI makes final adjustments of BUTTERFLY's costume, as does GALLIMARD of his tuxedo.)

GALLIMARD: I married late, at age thirty-one. I was faithful to my marriage for eight years. Until the day when, as a junior- level diplomat in puritanical Peking, in a parlor at the Ger- man ambassador's house, during the "Reign of a Hundred Flowers," I first saw her . . . singing the death scene from 115 *Madame Butterfly.*

(SUZUKI runs offstage.)

SCENE VI

German ambassador's house. Beijing. 1960.

The upstage special area now becomes a stage. Several chairs face upstage, representing seating for some twenty guests in the par- lor. A few "diplomats"—RENEE, MARC, TOULON—in formal dress enter and take seats.

GALLIMARD *also sits down, but turns towards us and continues to talk. Orchestral accompaniment on the tape is now replaced by a simple piano.* SONG *picks up the death scene from the point where* BUTTERFLY *uncovers the hara-kiri knife.*

GALLIMARD: The ending is pitiful. Pinkerton, in an art of great courage, stays home and sends his American wife to pick up Butterfly's child. The truth, long deferred, has come up to her door.

(SONG, playing BUTTERFLY, sings the lines from the opera in her own voice—which, though not classical, should be decent.)

SONG: "Con onor muore / chi non puo serbar / vita con onore." 5
GALLIMARD: *(Simultaneously)* "Death with honor / Is better than life / Life with dishonor."

(The stage is illuminated; we are now completely within an ele- gant diplomat's residence. SONG *proceeds to play out an abbrevi- ated death scene. Everyone in the room applauds.* SONG, *shyly, takes her bows. Others in the room rush to congratulate her.* GAL- LIMARD *remains with us.)*

GALLIMARD: They say in opera the voice is everything. That's probably why I'd never before enjoyed opera. Here . . . here was a Butterfly with little or no voice—but she had the grace, 10 the delicacy . . . I believed this girl. I believed her suffering. I wanted to take her in my arms—so delicate, even I could protect her, take her home, pamper her until she smiled.

(Over the course of the preceding speech, SONG *has broken from the upstage crowd and moved directly upstage of* GALLIMARD.)*

SONG: Excuse me. Monsieur. . . ?

(GALLIMARD turns upstage, shocked.)

GALLIMARD: Oh! Gallimard. Mademoiselle. . . ? A beautiful . . . 15

SONG: Song Liling.
GALLIMARD: A beautiful performance.
SONG: Oh, please.
GALLIMARD: I usually—
20 SONG: You make me blush. I'm no opera singer at all.
GALLIMARD: I usually don't like *Butterfly*.
SONG: I can't blame you in the least.
GALLIMARD: I mean, the story—
SONG: Ridiculous.
25 GALLIMARD: I like the story, but . . . what?
SONG: Oh, you like it?
GALLIMARD: I . . . what I mean is, I've always seen it played by huge women in so much bad makeup.
SONG: Bad makeup is not unique to the West.
30 GALLIMARD: But, who can believe them?
SONG: And you believe me?
GALLIMARD: Absolutely. You were utterly convincing. It's the first time—
SONG: Convincing? As a Japanese woman? The Japanese used
35 hundreds of our people for medical experiments during the war, you know. But I gather such an irony is lost on you.
GALLIMARD: No! I was about to say, it's the first time I've seen the beauty of the story.
SONG: Really?
40 GALLIMARD: Of her death. It's a . . . a pure sacrifice. He's unworthy, but what can she do? She loves him . . . so much. It's a very beautiful story.
SONG: Well, yes, to a Westerner.
GALLIMARD: Excuse me?
45 SONG: It's one of your favorite fantasies, isn't it? The submissive Oriental woman and the cruel white man.
GALLIMARD: Well, I didn't quite mean . . .
SONG: Consider it this way: what would you say if a blonde homecoming queen fell in love with a short Japanese busi-
50 nessman? He treats her cruelly, then goes home for three years, during which time she prays to his picture and turns down marriage from a young Kennedy. Then, when she learns he has remarried, she kills herself. Now, I believe you would consider this girl to be a deranged idiot, correct? But
55 because it's an Oriental who kills herself for a Westerner— ah!—you find it beautiful.

(*Silence.*)

GALLIMARD: Yes . . . well . . . I see your point . . .
SONG: I will never do Butterfly again, Monsieur Gallimard. If you wish to see some real theatre, come to the Peking Opera
60 sometime. Expand your mind.

(SONG *walks offstage.*)

GALLIMARD: (*To us*) So much for protecting her in my big Western arms.

SCENE VII

M. GALLIMARD's *apartment. Beijing. 1960.*

GALLIMARD *changes from his tux into a casual suit.* HELGA *enters.*

GALLIMARD: The Chinese are an incredibly arrogant people.
HELGA: They warned us about that in Paris, remember?

GALLIMARD: Even Parisians consider them arrogant. That's a switch.
HELGA: What is it that Madame Su says? "We are a very old 5 civilization." I never know if she's talking about her country or herself.
GALLIMARD: I walk around here, all I hear every day, everywhere is how *old* this culture is. The fact that "old" may be synonymous with "senile" doesn't occur to them. 10
HELGA: You're not going to change them. "East is east, west is west, and . . ." whatever that guy said.
GALLIMARD: It's just that—silly. I met . . . at Ambassador Koening's tonight—you should've been there.
HELGA: Koening? Oh god, no. Did he enchant you all again 15 with the history of Bavaria?
GALLIMARD: No. I met, I suppose, the Chinese equivalent of a diva. She's a singer in the Chinese opera.
HELGA: They have an opera, too? Do they sing in Chinese? Or maybe—in Italian? 20
GALLIMARD: Tonight, she did sing in Italian.
HELGA: How'd she manage that?
GALLIMARD: She must've been educated in the West before the Revolution. Her French is very good also. Anyway, she sang the death scene from *Madame Butterfly*. 25
HELGA: *Madame Butterfly*! Then I should have come. (*She begins humming, floating around the room as if dragging long kimono sleeves*) Did she have a nice costume? I think it's a classic piece of music.
GALLIMARD: That's what *I* thought, too. Don't let her hear you 30 say that.
HELGA: What's wrong?
GALLIMARD: Evidently the Chinese hate it.
HELGA: She hated it, but she performed it anyway? Is she perverse? 35
GALLIMARD: They hate it because the white man gets the girl. Sour grapes if you ask me.
HELGA: Politics again? Why can't they just hear it as a piece of beautiful music? So, what's in their opera?
GALLIMARD: I don't know. But, whatever it is, I'm sure it must 40 be *old*.

(HELGA *exits.*)

SCENE VIII

Chinese opera house and the streets of Beijing. 1960.

The sound of gongs clanging fills the stage.

GALLIMARD: My wife's innocent question kept ringing in my ears. I asked around, but no one knew anything about the Chinese opera. It took four weeks, but my curiosity overcame my cowardice. This Chinese diva—this unwilling Butterfly—what did she do to make her so proud? 5
  The room was hot, and full of smoke. Wrinkled faces, old women, teeth missing—a man with a growth on his neck, like a human toad. All smiling, pipes falling from their mouths, cracking nuts between their teeth, a live chicken pecking at my foot—all looking, screaming, gawking . . . at 10 her.

(*The upstage area is suddenly hit with a harsh white light. It has become the stage for the Chinese opera performance. Two dancers enter, along with* SONG. GALLIMARD *stands apart, watching.* SONG *glides gracefully amidst the two dancers. Drums suddenly slam to a halt.* SONG *strikes a pose, looking straight at* GALLIMARD. *Dancers exit. Light change. Pause, then* SONG *walks right off the stage and straight up to* GALLIMARD.)

SONG: Yes. You. White man. I'm looking straight at you.
GALLIMARD: Me?
SONG: You see any other white men? It was too easy to spot you.
15   How often does a man in my audience come in a tie?

(SONG *starts to remove her costume. Underneath, she wears simple baggy clothes. They are now backstage. The show is over.*)

SONG: So, you are an adventurous imperialist?
GALLIMARD: I . . . thought it would further my education.
SONG: It took you four weeks. Why?
GALLIMARD: I've been busy.
20 SONG: Well, education has always been undervalued in the West, hasn't it?
GALLIMARD: (*Laughing*) I don't think it's true.
SONG: No, you wouldn't. You're a Westerner. How can you objectively judge your own values?
25 GALLIMARD: I think it's possible to achieve some distance.
SONG: Do you? (*Pause.*) It stinks in here. Let's go.
GALLIMARD: These are the smells of your loyal fans.
SONG: I love them for being my fans, I hate the smell they leave behind. I too can distance myself from my people. (*She looks*
30 *around,* then whispers in his ear) "Art for the masses" is a shitty excuse to keep artists poor. (*She pops a cigarette in her mouth*) Be a gentleman, will you? And light my cigarette.

(GALLIMARD *fumbles for a match.*)

GALLIMARD: I don't . . . smoke.
SONG: (*Lighting her own.*) Your loss. Had you lit my cigarette, I
35 might have blown a puff of smoke right between your eyes. Come.

(*They start to walk about the stage. It is a summer night on the Beijing streets. Sounds of the city play on the house speakers.*)

SONG: How I wish there were even a tiny cafe to sit in. With cappuccinos, and men in tuxedos and bad expatriate jazz.
GALLIMARD: If my history serves me correctly, you weren't even
40 allowed into the clubs in Shanghai before the Revolution.
SONG: Your history serves you poorly, Monsieur Gallimard. True, there were signs reading "No dogs and Chinamen." But a woman, especially a delicate Oriental woman—we always go where we please. Could you imagine it otherwise? Clubs
45 in China filled with pasty, big-thighed white women, while thousands of slender lotus blossoms wait just outside the door? Never. The clubs would be empty. (*Beat*) We have always held a certain fascination for you Caucasian men, have we not?
50 GALLIMARD: But . . . that fascination is imperialist, or so you tell me.
SONG: Do you believe everything I tell you? Yes. It is always imperialist. But sometimes . . . sometimes, it is also mutual. Oh—this is my flat.
55 GALLIMARD: I didn't even—
SONG: Thank you. Come another time and we will further expand your mind.

(SONG *exits.* GALLIMARD *continues roaming the streets as he speaks to us.*)

GALLIMARD: What was that? What did she mean, "Sometimes . . . it is mutual?" Women do not flirt with me. And I normally can't talk to them. But tonight, I held up my end of the 60 conversation.

SCENE IX

GALLIMARD's *bedroom. Beijing. 1960.*

HELGA *enters.*

HELGA: You didn't tell me you'd be home late.
GALLIMARD: I didn't intend to. Something came up.
HELGA: Oh! Like what?
GALLIMARD: I went to the . . . to the Dutch ambassador's home.
HELGA: Again? 5
GALLIMARD: There was a reception for a visiting scholar. He's writing a six-volume treatise on the Chinese revolution. We all gathered that meant he'd have to live here long enough to actually write six volumes, and we all expressed our deepest sympathies. 10
HELGA: Well, I had a good night too. I went with the ladies to a martial arts demonstration. Some of those men—when they break those thick boards—(*She mimes fanning herself*) whoo-whoo!

(HELGA *exits. Lights dim.*)

GALLIMARD: I lied to my wife. Why? I've never had any reason 15 to lie before. But what reason did I have tonight? I didn't do anything wrong. That night, I had a dream. Other people, I've been told, have dreams where angels appear. Or dragons, or Sophia Loren in a towel. In my dream, Marc from school appeared. 20

(MARC *enters, in a nightshirt and cap.*)

MARC: Rene! You met a girl!

(GALLIMARD *and* MARC *stumble down the Beijing streets. Night sounds over the speakers.*)

GALLIMARD: It's not that amazing, thank you.
MARC: No! It's so monumental, I heard about it halfway around the world in my sleep!
GALLIMARD: I've met girls before, you know. 25
MARC: Name one. I've come across time and space to congratulate you. (*He hands* GALLIMARD *a bottle of wine*)
GALLIMARD: Marc, this is expensive.
MARC: On those rare occasions when you become a formless spirit, why not steal the best? 30

(MARC *pops open the bottle, begins to share it with* GALLIMARD.)

GALLIMARD: You embarrass me. She . . . there's no reason to think she likes me.
MARC: "Sometimes, it is mutual"?
GALLIMARD: Oh.
MARC: "Mutual"? "Mutual"? What does that mean? 35
GALLIMARD: You heard!
MARC: It means the money is in the bank, you only have to write the check!
GALLIMARD: I am a married man!

40 MARC: And an excellent one too. I cheated after . . . six months. Then again and again, until now—three hundred girls in twelve years.

GALLIMARD: I don't think we should hold that up as a model.

MARC: Of course not! My life—it is disgusting! Phooey! Phooey!
45 But, you—you are the model husband.

GALLIMARD: Anyway, it's impossible. I'm a foreigner.

MARC: Ah, yes. She cannot love you, it is taboo, but something deep inside her heart . . . she cannot help herself . . . she must surrender to you. It is her destiny.

50 GALLIMARD: How do you imagine all this?

MARC: The same way you do. It's an old story. It's in our blood. They fear us, Rene. Their women fear us. And their men— their men hate us. And, you know something? They are all correct.

(They spot a light in a window.)

55 MARC: There! There, Rene!

GALLIMARD: It's her window.

MARC: Late at night—it burns. The light—it burns for you.

GALLIMARD: I won't look. It's not respectful.

MARC: We don't have to be respectful. We're foreign devils.

(Enter SONG, in a sheer robe. The "One Fine Day" aria creeps in over the speakers. With her back to us, SONG mimes attending to her toilette. Her robe comes loose, revealing her white shoulders.)

60 MARC: All your life you've waited for a beautiful girl who would lay down for you. All your life you've smiled like a saint when it's happened to every other man you know. And you see them in magazines and you see them in movies. And you wonder, what's wrong with me? Will anyone beautiful ever want me?
65 As the years pass, your hair thins and you struggle to hold onto even your hopes. Stop struggling, Rene. The wait is over. *(He exits)*

GALLIMARD: Marc? Marc?

(At that moment, SONG, her back still towards us, drops her robe. A second of her naked back, then a sound cue: a phone ringing, very loud. Blackout, followed in the next beat by a special up on the bedroom area, where a phone now sits. GALLIMARD stumbles across the stage and picks up the phone. Sound cue out. Over the course of his conversation, area lights fill in the vicinity of his bed. It is the following morning.)

GALLIMARD: Yes? Hello?

70 SONG: *(Offstage)* Is it very early?

GALLIMARD: Why, yes.

SONG: *(Offstage)* How early?

GALLIMARD: It's . . . it's 5:30. Why are you—?

SONG: *(Offstage)* But it's light outside. Already.

75 GALLIMARD: It is. The sun must be in confusion today.

(Over the course of SONG's next speech, her upstage special comes up again. She sits in a chair, legs crossed, in a robe, telephone to her ear.)

SONG: I waited until I saw the sun. That was as much discipline as I could manage for one night. Do you forgive me?

GALLIMARD: Of course . . . for what?

SONG: Then I'll ask you quickly. Are you really interested in the
80 opera?

GALLIMARD: Why, yes. Yes I am.

SONG: Then come again next Thursday. I am playing *The Drunken Beauty*. May I count on you?

GALLIMARD: Yes. You may.

SONG: Perfect. Well, I must be getting to bed. I'm exhausted. It's 85 been a very long night for me.

(SONG hangs up; special on her goes off. GALLIMARD begins to dress for work.)

SCENE X

SONG LILING's *apartment. Beijing. 1960.*

GALLIMARD: I returned to the opera that next week, and the week after that . . . she keeps our meetings so short—perhaps fifteen, twenty minutes at most. So I am left each week with a thirst which is intensified. In this way, fifteen weeks have gone by. I am starting to doubt the words of my friend Marc. 5 But no, not really. In my heart, I know she has . . . an interest in me. I suspect this is her way. She is outwardly bold and outspoken, yet her heart is shy and afraid. It is the Oriental in her at war with her Western education.

SONG: *(Offstage)* I will be out in an instant. Ask the servant for 10 anything you want.

GALLIMARD: Tonight, I have finally been invited to enter her apartment. Though the idea is almost beyond belief, I believe she is afraid of me.

(GALLIMARD looks around the room. He picks up a picture in a frame, studies it. Without his noticing, SONG enters, dressed elegantly in a black gown from the twenties. She stands in the doorway looking like Anna May Wong.)

SONG: That is my father. 15

GALLIMARD: *(Surprised)* Mademoiselle Song . . .

(She glides up to him, snatches away the picture.)

SONG: It is very good that he did not live to see the Revolution. They would, no doubt, have made him kneel on broken glass. Not that he didn't deserve such a punishment. But he is my father. I would've hated to see it happen. 20

GALLIMARD: I'm very honored that you've allowed me to visit your home.

(SONG curtsys.)

SONG: Thank you. Oh! Haven't you been poured any tea?

GALLIMARD: I'm really not—

SONG: *(To her offstage servant)* Shu-Fang! Cha! Kwai-lah! *(To 25 GALLIMARD.)* I'm sorry. You want everything to be perfect—

GALLIMARD: Please.

SONG: —and before the evening even begins—

GALLIMARD: I'm really not thirsty.

SONG: —it's ruined. 30

GALLIMARD: *(Sharply)* Mademoiselle Song!

(SONG sits down.)

SONG: I'm sorry.

GALLIMARD: What are you apologizing for now?

(Pause; SONG starts to giggle.)

SONG: I don't know!

(GALLIMARD laughs.)

35   GALLIMARD: Exactly my point.
SONG: Oh, I am silly. Lightheaded. I promise not to apologize
     for anything else tonight, do you hear me?
GALLIMARD: That's a good girl!

(SHU-FANG, *a servant girl, comes out with a tea tray and starts
to pour.*)

SONG: *(To* SHU-FANG) No! I'll pour myself for the gentleman!

(SHU-FANG, *staring at* GALLIMARD, *exits.*)

40   SONG: No, I . . . I don't even know why I invited you up.
GALLIMARD: Well, I'm glad you did.

(SONG *looks around the room.*)

SONG: There is an element of danger to your presence.
GALLIMARD: Oh?
SONG: You must know.
45   GALLIMARD: It doesn't concern me. We both know why I'm here.
SONG: It doesn't concern me either. No . . . well perhaps . . .
GALLIMARD: What?
SONG: Perhaps I am slightly afraid of scandal.
GALLIMARD: What are we doing?
50   SONG: I'm entertaining you. In my parlor.
GALLIMARD: In France, that would hardly—
SONG: France. France is a country living in the modern era.
     Perhaps even ahead of it. China is a nation whose soul is
     firmly rooted two thousand years in the past. What I do, even
55   pouring the tea for you now . . . it has . . . implications. The
     walls and windows say so. Even my own heart, strapped in-
     side this Western dress . . . even it says things—things I don't
     care to hear.

(SONG *hands* GALLIMARD *a cup of tea.* GALLIMARD *puts his
hand over both the teacup and* SONG's *hand.*)

GALLIMARD: This is a beautiful dress.
60   SONG: Don't.
GALLIMARD: What?
SONG: I don't even know if it looks right on me.
GALLIMARD: Believe me—
SONG: You are from France. You see so many beautiful women.
65   GALLIMARD: France? Since when are the European women—?
SONG: Oh! What am I trying to do, anyway?!

(SONG *runs to the door, composes herself, then turns towards*
GALLIMARD.)

SONG: Monsieur Gallimard, perhaps you should go.
GALLIMARD: But . . . why?
SONG: There's something wrong about this.
70   GALLIMARD: I don't see what.
SONG: I feel . . . I am not myself.
GALLIMARD: No. You're nervous.
SONG: Please. Hard as I try to be modern, to speak like a man, to
     hold a Western woman's strong face up to my own . . . in the
75   end, I fail. A small, frightened heart beats too quickly and
     gives me away. Monsieur Gallimard, I'm a Chinese girl. I've
     never . . . never invited a man up to my flat before. The
     forwardness of my actions makes my skin burn.
GALLIMARD: What are you afraid of? Certainly not me, I hope.
80   SONG: I'm a modest girl.
GALLIMARD: I know. And very beautiful. (*He touches her hair*)
SONG: Please—go now. The next time you see me, I shall again
     be myself.

GALLIMARD: I like you the way you are right now.
SONG: You are a cad.   85
GALLIMARD: What do you expect? I'm a foreign devil.

(GALLIMARD *walks downstage.* SONG *exits.*)

GALLIMARD: (*To us*) Did you hear the way she talked about
     Western women? Much differently than the first night. She
     does— she feels inferior to them—and to me.

SCENE XI

The French embassy. Beijing. 1960.

GALLIMARD *moves towards a desk.*

GALLIMARD: I determined to try an experiment. In *Madame
     Butterfly*, Cio-Cio-San fears that the Western man who
     catches a butterfly will pierce its heart with a needle, then
     leave it to perish. I began to wonder: had I, too, caught a
     butterfly who would writhe on a needle?   5

(MARC *enters, dressed as a bureaucrat, holding a stack of papers.
As* GALLIMARD *speaks,* MARC *hands papers to him. He peruses,
then signs, stamps or rejects them.*)

GALLIMARD: Over the next five weeks, I worked like a dynamo. I
     stopped going to the opera, I didn't phone or write her. I knew
     this little flower was waiting for me to call, and, as I wickedly
     refused to do so, I felt for the first time that rush of power—
     the absolute power of a man.   10

(MARC *continues acting as the bureaucrat, but he now speaks as
himself.*)

MARC: Rene! It's me!
GALLIMARD: Marc—I hear your voice everywhere now. Even in
     the midst of work.
MARC: That's because I'm watching you—all the time.
GALLIMARD: You were always the most popular guy in school.   15
MARC: Well, there's no guarantee of failure in life like happiness
     in high school. Somehow I knew I'd end up in the suburbs
     working for Renault and you'd be in the Orient picking exotic
     women off the trees. And they say there's no justice.
GALLIMARD: That's why you were my friend?   20
MARC: I gave you a little of my life, so that now you can give me
     some of yours. (*Pause*) Remember Isabelle?
GALLIMARD: Of course I remember! She was my first experience.
MARC: We all wanted to ball her. But she only wanted me.
GALLIMARD: I had her.   25
MARC: Right. You balled her.
GALLIMARD: You were the only one who ever believed me.
MARC: Well, there's a good reason for that. (*Beat*) C'mon. You
     must've guessed.
GALLIMARD: You told me to wait in the bushes by the cafeteria   30
     that night. The next thing I knew, she was on me. Dress up in
     the air.
MARC: She never wore underwear.
GALLIMARD: My arms were pinned to the dirt.
MARC: She loved the superior position. A girl ahead of her time. 35
GALLIMARD: I looked up, and there was this woman . . . bounc-
     ing up and down on my loins.
MARC: Screaming, right?
GALLIMARD: Screaming, and breaking off the branches all
     around me, and pounding my butt up and down into the dirt. 40

MARC: Huffing and puffing like a locomotive.

GALLIMARD: And in the middle of all this, the leaves were getting into my mouth, my legs were losing circulation, I thought, "God. So this is *it*?"

45 MARC: You thought that?

GALLIMARD: Well, I was worried about my legs falling off.

MARC: You didn't have a good time?

GALLIMARD: No, that's not what I—I had a great time!

MARC: You're sure?

50 GALLIMARD: Yeah. Really.

MARC: 'Cuz I wanted you to have a good time.

GALLIMARD: I did.

(Pause.)

MARC: Shit. *(Pause)* When all is said and done, she was kind of a lousy lay, wasn't she? I mean, there was a lot of energy there,

55 but you never knew what she was doing with it. Like when she yelled "I'm coming!"—hell, it was so loud, you wanted to go "Look, it's not that big a deal."

GALLIMARD: I got scared. I thought she meant someone was actually coming. *(Pause)* But, Marc?

60 MARC: What?

GALLIMARD: Thanks.

MARC: Oh, don't mention it.

GALLIMARD: It was my first experience.

MARC: Yeah. You got her.

65 GALLIMARD: I got her.

MARC: Wait! Look at that letter again!

(GALLIMARD picks up one of the papers he's been stamping, and rereads it.)

GALLIMARD: *(To us)* After six weeks, they began to arrive. The letters.

(Upstage special on SONG, as MADAME BUTTERFLY. The scene is underscored by the "Love Duet.")

SONG: Did we fight? I do not know. Is the opera no longer of

70 interest to you? Please come—my audiences miss the white devil in their midst.

(GALLIMARD looks up from the letter, towards us.)

GALLIMARD: *(To us)* A concession, but much too dignified. *(Beat; he discards the letter)* I skipped the opera again that week to complete a position paper on trade.

(The bureaucrat hands him another letter.)

75 SONG: Six weeks have passed since last we met. In this your practice—to leave friends in the lurch? Sometimes I hate you, sometimes I hate myself, but always I miss you.

GALLIMARD: *(To us)* Better, but I don't like the way she calls me "friend." When a woman calls a man her "friend," she's call-

80 ing him a eunuch or a homosexual. *(Beat; he discards the letter)* I was absent from the opera for the seventh week, feeling a sudden urge to clean out my files.

(Bureaucrat hands him another letter.)

SONG: Your rudeness is beyond belief. I don't deserve this cruelty. Don't bother to call. I'll have you turned away at the door.

85 GALLIMARD: *(To us)* I didn't. *(He discards the letter; bureaucrat hands him another.)* And then finally, the letter that concluded my experiment.

SONG: I am out of words. I can hide behind dignity no longer. What do you want? I have already given you my shame.

(GALLIMARD gives the letter back to MARC, slowly. Special on SONG fades out.)

90 GALLIMARD: *(To us)* Reading it, I became suddenly ashamed. Yes, my experiment had been a success. She was turning on my needle. But the victory seemed hollow.

MARC: Hollow? Are you crazy?

GALLIMARD: Nothing, Marc. Please go away.

95 MARC: *(Exiting, with papers)* Haven't I taught you anything?

GALLIMARD: "I have already given you my shame." I had to attend a reception that evening. On the way, I felt sick. If there is a God, surely he would punish me now. I had finally gained power over a beautiful woman, only to abuse it cruelly. There

100 must be justice in the world. I had the strange feeling that the ax would fall this very evening.

SCENE XII

AMBASSADOR TOULON's *residence. Beijing. 1960.*

Sound cue: party noises. Light change. We are now in a spacious residence. TOULON, the French ambassador, enters and taps GALLIMARD on the shoulder.

TOULON: Gallimard? Can I have a word? Over here.

GALLIMARD: *(To us)* Manuel Toulon. French ambassador to China. He likes to think of us all as his children. Rather like God.

5 TOULON: Look, Gallimard, there's not much to say. I've liked you. From the day you walked in. You were no leader, but you were tidy and efficient.

GALLIMARD: Thank you, sir.

TOULON: Don't jump the gun. Okay, our needs in China are

10 changing. It's embarrassing that we lost Indochina. Someone just wasn't on the ball there. I don't mean you personally, of course.

GALLIMARD: Thank you, sir.

TOULON: We're going to be doing a lot more information-gath-

15 ering in the future. The nature of our work here is changing. Some people are just going to have to go. It's nothing personal.

GALLIMARD: Oh.

TOULON: Want to know a secret? Vice-Consul LeBon is being

20 transferred.

GALLIMARD: *(To us)* My immediate superior!

TOULON: And most of his department.

GALLIMARD: *(To us)* Just as I feared! God has seen my evil heart—

TOULON: But not you.

25 GALLIMARD: *(To us)*—and he's taking her away just as . . . *(To TOULON)* Excuse me, sir?

TOULON: Scare you? I think I did. Cheer up, Gallimard. I want you to replace LeBon as vice-consul.

GALLIMARD: You—? Yes, well, thank you, sir.

30 TOULON: Anytime.

GALLIMARD: I . . . accept with great humility.

TOULON: Humility won't be part of the job. You're going to coordinate the revamped intelligence division. Want to know a secret? A year ago, you would've been out. But the past few

35 months, I don't know how it happened, you've become this new aggressive confident . . . thing. And they also tell me you

get along with the Chinese. So I think you're a lucky man, Gallimard. Congratulations.

(They shake hands. TOULON *exits. Party noises out.* GALLIMARD *stumbles across a darkened stage.)*

40 GALLIMARD: Vice-consul? Impossible! As I stumbled out of the party, I saw it written across the sky: There is no God. Or, no—say that there is a God. But that God . . . understands. Of course! God who creates Eve to serve Adam, who blesses Solomon with his harem but ties Jezebel to a burning bed—that God is a man. And he understands! At age thirty-nine, I

45 was suddenly initiated into the way of the world.

SCENE XIII

SONG LILING's *apartment. Beijing. 1960.*

SONG *enters, in a sheer dressing gown.*

SONG: Are you crazy?
GALLIMARD: Mademoiselle Song—
SONG: To come here—at this hour? After . . . after eight weeks?
GALLIMARD: It's the most amazing—
5 SONG: You bang on my door? Scare my servants, scandalize the neighbors?
GALLIMARD: I've been promoted. To vice-consul.

(Pause.)

SONG: And what is that supposed to mean to me?
GALLIMARD: Are you my Butterfly?
10 SONG: What are you saying?
GALLIMARD: I've come tonight for an answer: are you my Butterfly?
SONG: Don't you know already?
GALLIMARD: I want you to say it.
15 SONG: I don't want to say it.
GALLIMARD: So, that is your answer?
SONG: You know how I feel about—
GALLIMARD: I do remember one thing.
SONG: What?
20 GALLIMARD: In the letter I received today.
SONG: Don't.
GALLIMARD: "I have already given you my shame."
SONG: It's enough that I even wrote it.
GALLIMARD: Well, then—
25 SONG: I shouldn't have it splashed across my face.
GALLIMARD: —if that's all true—
SONG: Stop!
GALLIMARD: Then what is one more short answer?
SONG: I don't want to!
30 GALLIMARD: Are you my Butterfly? *(Silence; he crosses the room and begins to touch her hair)* I want from you honesty. There should be nothing false between us. No false pride.

(Pause.)

SONG: Yes, I am. I am your Butterfly.
GALLIMARD: Then let me be honest with you. It is because of
35 you that I was promoted tonight. You have changed my life forever. My little Butterfly, there should be no more secrets: I love you.

(He starts to kiss her roughly. She resists slightly.)

SONG: No . . . no . . . gently . . . please, I've never . . .
GALLIMARD: No?
SONG: I've tried to appear experienced, but . . . the truth is . . . 40
no.
GALLIMARD: Are you cold?
SONG: Yes. Cold.
GALLIMARD: Then we will go very, very slowly.

(He starts to caress her; her gown begins to open.)

SONG: No . . . let me . . . keep my clothes . . . 45
GALLIMARD: But . . .
SONG: Please . . . it all frightens me. I'm a modest Chinese girl.
GALLIMARD: My poor little treasure.
SONG: I am your treasure. Though inexperienced, I am not . . . ignorant. They teach us things, our mothers, about pleasing 50
a man.
GALLIMARD: Yes?
SONG: I'll do my best to make you happy. Turn off the lights.

(GALLIMARD gets up and heads for a lamp. SONG, *propped up on one elbow, tosses her hair back and smiles.)*

SONG: Monsieur Gallimard?
GALLIMARD: Yes, Butterfly? 55
SONG: "Vieni, vieni!"
GALLIMARD: "Come, darling."
SONG: "Ah! Dolce notte!"
GALLIMARD: "Beautiful night."
SONG: "Tutto estatico d'amor ride il ciel!" 60
GALLIMARD: "All ecstatic with love, the heavens are filled with laughter."

(He turns off the lamp. Blackout.)

— ACT TWO —

SCENE I

M. GALLIMARD's *cell. Paris. Present.*

Lights up on GALLIMARD. *He sits in his cell, reading from a leaflet.*

GALLIMARD: This, from a contemporary critic's commentary on *Madame Butterfly:* "Pinkerton suffers from . . . being an obnoxious bounder whom every man in the audience itches to kick." Bully for us men in the audience! Then, in the same note: "Butterfly is the most irresistibly appealing of Puccini's 5
'Little Women.' Watching the succession of her humiliations is like watching a child under torture." *(He tosses the pamphlet over his shoulder.)* I suggest that, while we men may all want to kick Pinkerton, very few of us would pass up the opportunity to *be* Pinkerton. 10

(GALLIMARD moves out of his cell.)

SCENE II

GALLIMARD *and* BUTTERFLY's *flat. Beijing. 1960.*

We are in a simple but well-decorated parlor. GALLIMARD *moves to sit on a sofa, while* SONG, *dressed in a chong sam, enters and curls up at his feet.*

GALLIMARD: *(To us)* We secured a flat on the outskirts of Peking. Butterfly, as I was calling her now, decorated our "home" with Western furniture and Chinese antiques. And there, on a few stolen afternoons or evenings each week, Butterfly commenced her education.

SONG: The Chinese men—they keep us down.

GALLIMARD: Even in the "New Society"?

SONG: In the "New Society," we are all kept ignorant equally. That's one of the exciting things about loving a Western man. I know you are not threatened by a woman's education.

GALLIMARD: I'm no saint, Butterfly.

SONG: But you come from a progressive society.

GALLIMARD: We're not always reminding each other how "old" we are, if that's what you mean.

SONG: Exactly. We Chinese—once, I suppose, it is true, we ruled the world. But so what? How much more exciting to be part of the society ruling the world today. Tell me—what's happening in Vietnam?

GALLIMARD: Oh, Butterfly—you want me to bring my work home?

SONG: I want to know what you know. To be impressed by my man. It's not the particulars so much as the fact that you're making decisions which change the shape of the world.

GALLIMARD: Not the world. At best, a small corner.

(TOULON enters, and sits at a desk upstage.)

SCENE III

French embassy. Beijing. 1961.

GALLIMARD *moves downstage, to* TOULON's *desk.* SONG *remains upstage, watching.*

TOULON: And a more troublesome corner is hard to imagine.

GALLIMARD: So, the Americans plan to begin bombing?

TOULON: This is very secret, Gallimard: yes. The Americans don't have an embassy here. They're asking us to be their eyes and ears. Say Jack Kennedy signed an order to bomb North Vietnam, Laos. How would the Chinese react?

GALLIMARD: I think the Chinese will squawk—

TOULON: Uh-huh.

GALLIMARD: —but, in their hearts, they don't even like Ho Chi Minh.

(Pause.)

TOULON: What a bunch of jerks. Vietnam was *our* colony. Not only didn't the Americans help us fight to keep them, but now, seven years later, they've come back to grab the territory for themselves. It's very irritating.

GALLIMARD: With all due respect, sir, why, should the Americans have won our war for us back in '54 if we didn't have the will to win it ourselves?

TOULON: You're kidding, aren't you?

(Pause.)

GALLIMARD: The Orientals simply want to be associated with whoever shows the most strength and power. You live with the Chinese, sir. Do you think they like Communism?

TOULON: I live in China. Not with the Chinese.

GALLIMARD: Well, I—

TOULON: *You* live with the Chinese.

GALLIMARD: Excuse me?

TOULON: I can't keep a secret.

GALLIMARD: What are you saying?

TOULON: Only that I'm not immune to gossip. So, you're keeping a native mistress. Don't answer. It's none of my business. *(Pause.)* I'm sure she must be gorgeous.

GALLIMARD: Well . . .

TOULON: I'm impressed. You have the stamina to go out into the streets and hunt one down. Some of us have to be content with the wives of the expatriate community.

GALLIMARD: I do feel . . . fortunate.

TOULON: So, Gallimard, you've got the inside knowledge— what *do* the Chinese think?

GALLIMARD: Deep down, they miss the old days. You know, cappuccinos, men in tuxedos—

TOULON: So what do we tell the Americans about Vietnam?

GALLIMARD: Tell them there's a natural affinity between the West and the Orient.

TOULON: And that you speak from experience?

GALLIMARD: The Orientals are people too. They want the good things we can give them. If the Americans demonstrate the will to win, the Vietnamese will welcome them into a mutually beneficial union.

TOULON: I don't see how the Vietnamese can stand up to American firepower.

GALLIMARD: Orientals will always submit to a greater force.

TOULON: I'll note your opinions in my report. The Americans always love to hear how "welcome" they'll be. *(He starts to exit)*

GALLIMARD: Sir?

TOULON: Mmmm?

GALLIMARD: This . . . rumor you've heard.

TOULON: Uh-huh?

GALLIMARD: How . . . widespread do you think it is?

TOULON: It's only widespread within this embassy. Where nobody talks because everybody is guilty. We were worried about you, Gallimard. We thought you were the only one here without a secret. Now you go and find a lotus blossom . . . and top us all. *(He exits)*

GALLIMARD: *(To us)* Toulon knows! And he approves! I was learning the benefits of being a man. We form our own clubs, sit behind thick doors, smoke—and celebrate the fact that we're still boys. *(He starts to move downstage, towards* SONG.*)* So, over the—

(Suddenly COMRADE CHIN *enters.* GALLIMARD *backs away.)*

GALLIMARD: *(To* SONG*)* No! Why does she have to come in?

SONG: Rene, be sensible. How can they understand the story without her? Now, don't embarrass yourself.

*(*GALLIMARD *moves down center.)*

GALLIMARD: *(To us)* Now, you will see why my story is so amusing to so many people. Why they snicker at parties in disbelief. Please—try to understand it from my point of view. We are all prisoners of our time and place. *(He exits)*

SCENE IV

GALLIMARD *and* BUTTERFLY's *flat. Beijing. 1961.*

SONG: *(To us)* 1961. The flat Monsieur Gallimard rented for us. An evening after he has gone.

CHIN: Okay, see if you find out when the Americans plan to start
bombing Vietnam. If you can find out what cities, even
5 better.
SONG: I'll do my best, but I don't want to arouse his suspicions.
CHIN: Yeah, sure, of course. So, what else?
SONG: The Americans will increase troops in Vietnam to
170,000 soldiers with 120,000 militia and 11,000 American
10 advisors.
CHIN: (Writing) Wait, wait. 120,000 militia and —
SONG: — 11,000 American —
CHIN: — American advisors. (Beat) How do you remember so
much?
15 SONG: I'm an actor.
CHIN: Yeah. (Beat) Is that how come you dress like that?
SONG: Like what, Miss Chin?
CHIN: Like that dress! You're wearing a dress. And every time I
come here, you're wearing a dress. Is that because you're an
20 actor? Or what?
SONG: It's a . . . disguise, Miss Chin.
CHIN: Actors, I think they're all weirdos. My mother tells me
actors are like gamblers or prostitutes or —
SONG: It helps me in my assignment.

(Pause.)

25 CHIN: You're not gathering information in any way that violates
Communist Party principles, are you?
SONG: Why would I do that?
CHIN: Just checking. Remember: when working for the Great
Proletarian State, you represent our Chairman Mao in every
30 position you take.
SONG: I'll try to imagine the Chairman taking my positions.
CHIN: We all think of him this way. Good-bye, comrade. (She
starts to exit) Comrade?
SONG: Yes?
35 CHIN: Don't forget: there is no homosexuality in China!
SONG: Yes, I've heard.
CHIN: Just checking. (She exits)
SONG: (To us) What passes for a woman in modern China.

(GALLIMARD sticks his head out from the wings.)

GALLIMARD: Is she gone?
40 SONG: Yes, Rene. Please continue in your own fashion.

SCENE V

Beijing. 1961–63.

GALLIMARD *moves to the couch where* SONG *still sits. He lies
down in her lap, and she strokes his forehead.*

GALLIMARD: (To us) And so, over the years 1961, '62, '63, we
settled into our routine, Butterfly and I. She would always
have prepared a light snack and then, ever so delicately, and
only if I agreed, she would start to pleasure me. With her
5 hands, her mouth . . . too many ways to explain, and too sad,
given my present situation. But mostly we would talk. About
my life. Perhaps there is nothing more rare than to find a
woman who passionately listens.

(SONG *remains upstage, listening, as* HELGA *enters and plays a
scene downstage with* GALLIMARD.)

HELGA: Rene, I visited Dr. Bolleart this morning.
GALLIMARD: Why? Are you ill?   10
HELGA: No, no. You see, I wanted to ask him . . . that question
we've been discussing.
GALLIMARD: And I told you, it's only a matter of time. Why did
you bring a doctor into this? We just have to keep trying — like
a crapshoot, actually.   15
HELGA: I went, I'm sorry. But listen: he says there's nothing
wrong with me.
GALLIMARD: You see? Now, will you stop —?
HELGA: Rene, he says he'd like you to go in and take some tests.
GALLIMARD: Why? So he can find there's nothing wrong with   20
both of us?
HELGA: Rene, I don't ask for much. One trip! One visit! And
then, whatever you want to do about it — you decide.
GALLIMARD: You're assuming he'll find something defective!
HELGA: No! Of course not! Whatever he finds — if he finds   25
nothing, we decide what to do about nothing! But go!
GALLIMARD: If he finds nothing, we keep trying. Just like we do
now.
HELGA: But at least we'll know! (Pause) I'm sorry. (She starts to
exit)   30
GALLIMARD: Do you really want me to see Dr. Bolleart?
HELGA: Only if you want a child, Rene. We have to face the fact
that time is running out. Only if you want a child. (She exits)
GALLIMARD: (To SONG) I'm a modern man, Butterfly. And yet,
I don't want to go. It's the same old voodoo. I feel like God   35
himself is laughing at me if I can't produce a child.
SONG: You men of the West — you're obsessed by your odd de-
sire for equality. Your wife can't give you a child, and you're
going to the doctor?
GALLIMARD: Well, you see, she's already gone.   40
SONG: And because this incompetent can't find the defect, you
now have to subject yourself to him? It's unnatural.
GALLIMARD: Well, what is the "natural" solution?
SONG: In Imperial China, when a man found that one wife was
inadequate, he turned to another — to give him his son.   45
GALLIMARD: What do you —? I can't . . . marry you, yet.
SONG: Please. I'm not asking you to be my husband. But I am
already your wife.
GALLIMARD: Do you want to . . . have my child?
SONG: I thought you'd never ask.   50
GALLIMARD: But, your career . . . your —
SONG: Phooey on my career! That's your Western mind, twist-
ing itself into strange shapes again. Of course I love my ca-
reer. But what would I love most of all? To feel something
inside me — day and night — something I know is yours.   55
(Pause) Promise me . . . you won't go to this doctor. Who is
this Western quack to set himself as judge over the man I love?
I know who is a man, and who is not. (She exits)
GALLIMARD: (To us) Dr. Bolleart? Of course I didn't go. What
man would?   60

SCENE VI

Beijing. 1963.

Party noises over the house speakers. RENEE *enters, wearing a
revealing gown.*

GALLIMARD: 1963. A party at the Austrian embassy. None of us could remember the Austrian ambassador's name, which seemed somehow appropriate. (*To* RENEE) So, I tell the Americans, Diem must go. The U.S. wants to be respected by the Vietnamese, and yet they're propping up this nobody seminarian as her president. A man whose claim to fame is his sister-in-law imposing fanatic "moral order" campaigns? Oriental women—when they're good, they're very good, but when they're bad, they're Christians.

RENEE: Yeah.

GALLIMARD: And what do you do?

RENEE: I'm a student. My father exports a lot of useless stuff to the Third World.

GALLIMARD: How useless?

RENEE: You know. Squirt guns, confectioner's sugar, hula hoops . . .

GALLIMARD: I'm sure they appreciate the sugar.

RENEE: I'm here for two years to study Chinese.

GALLIMARD: Two years?

RENEE: That's what everybody says.

GALLIMARD: When did you arrive?

RENEE: Three weeks ago.

GALLIMARD: And?

RENEE: I like it. It's primitive, but . . . well, this is the place to learn Chinese, so here I am.

GALLIMARD: Why Chinese?

RENEE: I think it'll be important someday.

GALLIMARD: You do?

RENEE: Don't ask me when, but . . . that's what I think.

GALLIMARD: Well, I agree with you. One hundred precent. That's very farsighted.

RENEE: Yeah. Well of course, my father thinks I'm a complete weirdo.

GALLIMARD: He'll thank you someday.

RENEE: Like when the Chinese start buying hula hoops?

GALLIMARD: There're a billion bellies out there.

RENEE: And if they end up taking over the world—well, then I'll be lucky to know Chinese too, right?

(*Pause.*)

GALLIMARD: At this point, I don't see how the Chinese can possibly take—

RENEE: You know what I *don't* like about China?

GALLIMARD: Excuse me? No—what?

RENEE: Nothing to do at night.

GALLIMARD: You come to parties at embassies like everyone else.

RENEE: Yeah, but they get out at ten. And then what?

GALLIMARD: I'm afraid the Chinese idea of a dance hall is a dirt floor and a man with a flute.

RENEE: Are you married?

GALLIMARD: Yes. Why?

RENEE: You wanna . . . fool around?

(*Pause.*)

GALLIMARD: Sure.

RENEE: I'll wait for you outside. What's your name?

GALLIMARD: Gallimard. Rene.

RENEE: Weird. I'm Renee too. (*She exits*)

GALLIMARD: (*To us*) And so, I embarked on my first extra-extra-marital affair. Renee was picture perfect. With a body like those girls in the magazines. If I put a tissue paper over my eyes, I wouldn't have been able to tell the difference. And it was exciting to be with someone who wasn't afraid to be seen completely naked. But is it possible for a woman to be *too* uninhibited, *too* willing, so as to seem almost too . . . masculine?

(CHUCK BERRY *blares from the house speakers, then comes down in volume as* RENEE *enters, toweling her hair.*)

RENEE: You have a nice weenie.

GALLIMARD: What?

RENEE: Penis. You have a nice penis.

GALLIMARD: Oh. Well, thank you. That's very . . .

RENEE: What—can't take a compliment?

GALLIMARD: No, it's very . . . reassuring.

RENEE: But most girls don't come out and say it, huh?

GALLIMARD: And also . . . what did you call it?

RENEE: Oh. Most girls don't call it a "weenie," huh?

GALLIMARD: It sounds very—

RENEE: Small, I know.

GALLIMARD: I was going to say, "young."

RENEE: Yeah. Young, small, same thing. Most guys are pretty, uh, sensitive about that. Like, you know, I had a boyfriend back home in Denmark. I got mad at him once and called him a little weeniehead. He got so mad! He said at least I should call him a great big weeniehead.

GALLIMARD: I suppose I just say "penis."

RENEE: Yeah. That's pretty clinical. There's "cock," but that sounds like a chicken. And "prick" is painful, and "dick" is like you're talking about someone who's not in the room.

GALLIMARD: Yes. It's a . . . bigger problem than I imagined.

RENEE: I—I think maybe it's because I really don't know what to do with them—that's why I call them "weenies."

GALLIMARD: Well, you did quite well with . . . mine.

RENEE: Thanks, but I mean, really *do* with them. Like, okay, have you ever looked at one? I mean, really?

GALLIMARD: No, I suppose when it's part of you, you sort of take it for granted.

RENEE: I guess. But, like, it just hangs there. This little . . . flap of flesh. And there's so much fuss that we make about it. Like, I think the reason we fight wars is because we wear clothes. Because no one knows—between the men, I mean—who has the bigger . . . weenie. So, if I'm a guy with a small one, I'm going to build a really big building or take over a really big piece of land or write a really long book so the other men don't know, right? But, see, it never really works, that's the problem. I mean, you conquer the country, or whatever, but you're still wearing clothes, so there's no way to prove absolutely whose is bigger or smaller. And that's what we call a civilized society. The whole world run by a bunch of men with pricks the size of pins. (*She exits*)

GALLIMARD: (*To us*) This was simply not acceptable.

(A *high-pitched chime rings through the air.* SONG, *dressed as* BUTTERFLY, *appears in the upstage special. She is obviously distressed. Her body swoons as she attempts to clip the stems of flowers she's arranging in a vase.*)

GALLIMARD: But I kept up our affair, wildly, for several months. Why? I believe because of Butterfly. She knew the secret I was

trying to hide. But, unlike a Western woman, she didn't confront me, threaten, even pout. I remembered the words of
110 Puccini's *Butterfly*:
SONG: "Noi siamo gente avvezza/ alle piccole cose/ umili e silenziose."
GALLIMARD: "I come from a people/ Who are accustomed to little/ Humble and silent." I saw Pinkerton and Butterfly, and
115 what she would say if he were unfaithful . . . nothing. She would cry, alone, into those wildly soft sleeves, once full of possessions, now empty to collect her tears. It was her tears and her silence that excited me, every time I visited Renee.
TOULON: *(Offstage)* Gallimard!

(TOULON enters. GALLIMARD turns towards him. During the next section, SONG, up center, begins to dance with the flowers. It is a drunken dance, where she breaks small pieces off the stems.)

120 TOULON: They're killing him.
GALLIMARD: Who? I'm sorry? What?
TOULON: Bother you to come over at this late hour?
GALLIMARD: No . . . of course not.
TOULON: Not after you hear my secret. Champagne?
125 GALLIMARD: Um . . . thank you.
TOULON: You're surprised. There's something that you've wanted, Gallimard. No, not a promotion. Next time. Something in the world. You're not aware of this, but there's an informal gossip circle among intelligence agents. And some of ours
130 heard from some of the Americans—
GALLIMARD: Yes?
TOULON: That the U.S. will allow the Vietnamese generals to stage a coup . . . and assassinate President Diem.

(The chime rings again. TOULON freezes. GALLIMARD turns upstage and looks at BUTTERFLY, who slowly and deliberately clips a flower off its stem. GALLIMARD turns back towards TOULON.)

GALLIMARD: I think . . . that's a very wise move!

(TOULON unfreezes.)

135 TOULON: It's what you've been advocating. A toast?
GALLIMARD: Sure. I consider this a vindication.
TOULON: Not exactly. "To the test. Let's hope you pass."

(They drink. The chime rings again. TOULON freezes. GALLIMARD turns upstage, and SONG clips another flower.)

GALLIMARD: *(To TOULON)* The test?
TOULON: *(Unfreezing)* It's a test of everything you've been say-
140 ing. I personally think the generals probably will stop the Communists. And you'll be a hero. But if anything goes wrong, then your opinions won't be worth a pig's ear. I'm sure that won't happen. But sometimes it's easier when they don't listen to you.
145 GALLIMARD: They're your opinions too, aren't they?
TOULON: Personally, yes.
GALLIMARD: So we agree.
TOULON: But my opinions aren't on that report. Yours are. Cheers.

(TOULON turns away from GALLIMARD and raises his glass. At that instant SONG picks up the vase and hurls it to the ground. It shatters. SONG sinks down amidst the shards of the vase, in a calm, childlike trance. She sings softly, as if reciting a child's nursery rhyme.)

150 SONG: *(Repeat as necessary)* "The whole world over, the white man travels, setting anchor, wherever he likes. Life's not worth living, unless he finds, the finest maidens, of every land . . ."

(GALLIMARD turns downstage towards us. SONG continues singing.)

GALLIMARD: I shook as I left his house. That coward! That worm! To put the burden for his decisions on my shoulders! 155
I started for Renee's. But no, that was all I needed. A schoolgirl who would question the role of the penis in modern society. What I wanted was revenge. A vessel to contain my humiliation. Though I hadn't seen her in several weeks, I headed for Butterfly's. 160

(GALLIMARD enters SONG's apartment.)

SONG: Oh! Rene . . . I was dreaming!
GALLIMARD: You've been drinking?
SONG: If I can't sleep, then yes, I drink. But then, it gives me these dreams which—Rene, it's been almost three weeks since you visited me last. 165
GALLIMARD: I know. There's been a lot going on in the world.
SONG: Fortunately I am drunk. So I can speak freely. It's not the world, it's you and me. And an old problem. Even the softest skin becomes like leather to a man who's touched it too often. I confess I don't know how to stop it. I don't know how to 170 become another woman.
GALLIMARD: I have a request.
SONG: Is this a solution? Or are you ready to give up the flat?
GALLIMARD: It may be a solution. But I'm sure you won't like it.
SONG: Oh well, that's very important. "Like it?" Do you think I 175 "like" lying here alone, waiting, always waiting for your return? Please—don't worry about what I may not "like."
GALLIMARD: I want to see you . . . naked.

(Silence.)

SONG: I thought you understood my modesty. So you want me to—what—strip? Like a big cowboy girl? Shiny pasties on my 180 breasts? Shall I fling my kimono over my head and yell "yahoo" in the process? I thought you respected my shame!
GALLIMARD: I believe you gave me your shame many years ago.
SONG: Yes—and it is just like a white devil to use it against me. I can't believe it. I thought myself so repulsed by the passive 185 Oriental and the cruel white man. Now I see—we are always most revolted by the things hidden within us.
GALLIMARD: I just mean—
SONG: Yes?
GALLIMARD: —that it will remove the only barrier left between us. 190
SONG: No, Rene. Don't couch your request in sweet words. Be yourself—a cad—and know that my love is enough, that I submit—submit to the worst you can give me. *(Pause)* Well, come. Strip me. Whatever happens, know that you have willed it. Our love, in your hands. I'm helpless before my 195 man.

(GALLIMARD starts to cross the room.)

GALLIMARD: Did I not undress her because I knew, somewhere deep down, what I would find? Perhaps. Happiness is so rare that our mind can turn somersaults to protect it.
At the time, I only knew that I was seeing Pinkerton stalk- 200 ing towards his Butterfly, ready to reward her love with his

lecherous hands. The image sickened me, pulled me to my knees, so I was crawling towards her like a worm. By the time I reached her, Pinkerton . . . had vanished from my heart. To be replaced by something new, something unnatural, that flew in the face of all I'd learned in the world—something very close to love.

(He grabs her around the waist; she strokes his hair.)

GALLIMARD: Butterfly, forgive me.
SONG: Rene . . .
GALLIMARD: For everything. From the start.
SONG: I'm . . .
GALLIMARD: I want to—
SONG: I'm pregnant. *(Beat)* I'm pregnant. *(Beat)* I'm pregnant.

(Beat.)

GALLIMARD: I want to marry you!

SCENE VII

GALLIMARD *and* BUTTERFLY'S *flat. Beijing. 1963.*

Downstage, SONG *paces as* COMRADE CHIN *reads from her note-pad. Upstage,* GALLIMARD *is still kneeling. He remains on his knees throughout the scene, watching it.*

SONG: I need a baby.
CHIN: *(From pad)* He's been spotted going to a dorm.
SONG: I need a baby.
CHIN: At the Foreign Language Institute.
SONG: I need a baby.
CHIN: The room of a Danish girl . . . What do you mean, you need a baby?!
SONG: Tell Comrade Kang—last night, the entire mission, it could've ended.
CHIN: What do you mean?
SONG: Tell Kang—he told me to strip.
CHIN: *Strip?!*
SONG: Write!
CHIN: I tell you, I don't understand nothing about this case anymore. Nothing.
SONG: He told me to strip, and I took a chance. Oh, we Chinese, we know how to gamble.
CHIN: *(Writing)* ". . . told him to strip."
SONG: My palms were wet, I had to make a split-second decision.
CHIN: Hey! Can you slow down?!

(Pause.)

SONG: You write faster, I'm the artist here. Suddenly, it hit me—"All he wants is for her to submit. Once a woman submits, a man is always ready to become 'generous.'"
CHIN: You're just gonna end up with rough notes.
SONG: And it worked! He gave in! Now, if I can just present him with a baby. A Chinese baby with blond hair—he'll be mine for life!
CHIN: Kang will never agree! The trading of babies has to be a counterrevolutionary act.
SONG: Sometimes, a counterrevolutionary act is necessary to counter a counterrevolutionary act.

(Pause.)

CHIN: Wait.
SONG: I need one . . . in seven months. Make sure it's a boy.

CHIN: This doesn't sound like something the Chairman would do. Maybe you'd better talk to Comrade Kang yourself.
SONG: Good. I will.

(CHIN gets up to leave.)

SONG: Miss Chin? Why, in the Peking Opera, are women's roles played by men?
CHIN: I don't know. Maybe, a reactionary remnant of male—
SONG: No. *(Beat)* Because only a man knows how a woman is supposed to act.

(CHIN exits. SONG *turns upstage, towards* GALLIMARD.*)*

GALLIMARD: *(Calling after* CHIN*)* Good riddance! *(To* SONG*)* I could forget all that betrayal in an instant, you know. If you'd just come back and become Butterfly again.
SONG: Fat chance. You're here in prison, rotting in a cell. And I'm on a plane, winging my way back to China. Your President pardoned me of our treason, you know.
GALLIMARD: Yes, I read about that.
SONG: Must make you feel . . . lower than shit.
GALLIMARD: But don't you, even a little bit, wish you were here with me?
SONG: I'm an artist, Rene. You were my greatest . . . acting challenge. *(She laughs)* It doesn't matter how rotten I answer, does it? You still adore me. That's why I love you, Rene. *(She points to us)* So—you were telling your audience about the night I announced I was pregnant.

*(GALLIMARD *puts his arms around* SONG's *waist. He and* SONG *are in the positions they were in at the end of Scene 6.)*

SCENE VIII

Same.

GALLIMARD: I'll divorce my wife. We'll live together here, and then later in France.
SONG: I feel so . . . ashamed.
GALLIMARD: Why?
SONG: I had begun to lose faith. And now, you shame me with your generosity.
GALLIMARD: Generosity? No, I'm proposing for very selfish reasons.
SONG: Your apologies only make me feel more ashamed. My outburst a moment ago!
GALLIMARD: Your outburst? What about my request?!
SONG: You've been very patient dealing with my . . . eccentricities. A Western man, used to women freer with their bodies—
GALLIMARD: It was sick! Don't make excuses for me.
SONG: I have to. You don't seem willing to make them for yourself.

(Pause.)

GALLIMARD: You're crazy.
SONG: I'm happy. Which often looks like crazy.
GALLIMARD: Then make me crazy. Marry me.

(Pause.)

SONG: No.
GALLIMARD: What?
SONG: Do I sound silly, a slave, if I say I'm not worthy?
GALLIMARD: Yes. In fact you do. No one has loved me like you.
SONG: Thank you. And no one ever will. I'll see to that.

25 GALLIMARD: So what is the problem?

SONG: Rene, we Chinese are realists. We understand rice, gold, and guns. You are a diplomat. Your career is skyrocketing. Now, what would happen if you divorced your wife to marry a Communist Chinese actress?

30 GALLIMARD: That's not being realistic. That's defeating yourself before you begin.

SONG: We must conserve our strength for the battles we can win.

GALLIMARD: That sounds like a fortune cookie!

SONG: Where do you think fortune cookies come from?

35 GALLIMARD: I don't care.

SONG: You do. So do I. And we should. That is why I say I'm not worthy. I'm worthy to love and even to be loved by you. But I am not worthy to end the career of one of the West's most promising diplomats.

40 GALLIMARD: It's not that great a career! I made it sound like more than it is!

SONG: Modesty will get you nowhere. Flatter yourself, and you flatter me. I'm flattered to decline your offer. *(She exits)*

GALLIMARD: *(To us)* Butterfly and I argued all night. And, in

45 the end, I left, knowing I would never be her husband. She went away for several months—to the countryside, like a small animal. Until the night I received her call.

(A baby's cry from offstage. SONG *enters, carrying a child.)*

SONG: He looks like you.

GALLIMARD: Oh! *(Beat; he approaches the baby)* Well, babies

50 are never very attractive at birth.

SONG: Stop!

GALLIMARD: I'm sure he'll grow more beautiful with age. More like his mother.

SONG: "Chi vide mai / a bimbo del Giappon . . ."

55 GALLIMARD: "What baby, I wonder, was ever born in Japan"— or China, for that matter—

SONG: ". . . occhi azzurrini?"

GALLIMARD: "With azure eyes"—they're actually sort of brown, wouldn't you say?

60 SONG: "E il labbro."

GALLIMARD: "And such lips!" *(He kisses* SONG.*)* And such lips.

SONG: "E i ricciolini d'oro schietto?"

GALLIMARD: "And such a head of golden"—if slightly patchy— "curls?"

65 SONG: I'm going to call him "Peepee."

GALLIMARD: Darling, could you repeat that because I'm sure a rickshaw just flew by overhead.

SONG: You heard me.

GALLIMARD: "Song Peepee"? May I suggest Michael, or Ste-

70 phan, or Adolph?

SONG: You may, but I won't listen.

GALLIMARD: You can't be serious. Can you imagine the time this child will have in school?

SONG: In the West, yes.

75 GALLIMARD: It's worse than naming him Ping Pong or Long Dong or—

SONG: But he's never going to live in the West, is he?

(Pause.)

GALLIMARD: That wasn't my choice.

SONG: It is mine. And this is my promise to you: I will raise him,

80 he will be our child, but he will never burden you outside of China.

GALLIMARD: Why do you make these promises? I want to be burdened! I want a scandal to cover the papers!

SONG: *(To us)* Prophetic.

GALLIMARD: I'm serious. 85

SONG: So am I. His name is as I registered it. And he will never live in the West.

*(*SONG *exits with the child.)*

GALLIMARD: *(To us)* It is possible that her stubbornness only made me want her more. That drawing back at the moment of my capitulation was the most brilliant strategy she could 90 have chosen. It is possible. But it is also possible that by this point she could have said, could have done . . . anything, and I would have adored her still.

SCENE IX

Beijing. 1966.

A driving rhythm of Chinese percussion fills the stage.

GALLIMARD: And then, China began to change. Mao became very old, and his cult became very strong. And, like many old men, he entered his second childhood. So he handed over the reins of state to those with minds like his own. And children ruled the Middle Kingdom with complete caprice. The 5 doctrine of the Cultural Revolution implied continuous anarchy. Contact between Chinese and foreigners became impossible. Our flat was confiscated. Her fame and my money now counted against us.

(Two dancers in Mao suits and red-starred caps enter, and begin crudely mimicking revolutionary violence, in an agitprop fashion.)

GALLIMARD: And somehow the American war went wrong too. 10 Four hundred thousand dollars were being spent for every Viet Cong killed; so General Westmoreland's remark that the Oriental does not value life the way Americans do was oddly accurate. Why weren't the Vietnamese people giving in? Why were they content instead to die and die and die again? 15

*(*TOULON *enters.)*

TOULON: Congratulations, Gallimard.

GALLIMARD: Excuse me, sir?

TOULON: Not a promotion. That was last time. You're going home.

GALLIMARD: What? 20

TOULON: Don't say I didn't warn you.

GALLIMARD: I'm being transferred . . . because I was wrong about the American war?

TOULON: Of course not. We don't care about the Americans. We care about your mind. The quality of your analysis. In 25 general, everything you've predicted here in the Orient . . . just hasn't happened.

GALLIMARD: I think that's premature.

TOULON: Don't force me to be blunt. Okay, you said China was ready to open to Western trade. The only thing they're trading 30 out there are Western heads. And, yes, you said the Americans would succeed in Indochina. You were kidding, right?

GALLIMARD: I think the end is in sight.

TOULON: Don't be pathetic. And don't take this personally. You were wrong. It's not your fault. 35

GALLIMARD: But I'm going home.
TOULON: Right. Could I have the number of your mistress? (*Beat*) Joke! Joke! Eat a croissant for me.

(TOULON *exits*. SONG, *wearing a Mao suit, is dragged in from the wings as part of the upstage dance. They "beat" her, then lampoon the acrobatics of the Chinese opera, as she is made to kneel onstage.*)

GALLIMARD: (*Simultaneously*) I don't care to recall how Butter-
40   fly and I said our hurried farewell. Perhaps it was better to end our affair before it killed her.

(GALLIMARD *exits*. COMRADE CHIN *walks across the stage with a banner reading: "The Actor Renounces His Decadent Profession!" She reaches the kneeling* SONG. *Percussion stops with a thud. Dancers strike poses.*)

CHIN: Actor-oppressor, for years you have lived above the common people and looked down on their labor. While the farmer ate millet—
45   SONG: I ate pastries from France and sweetmeats from silver trays.
CHIN: And how did you come to live in such an exalted position?
SONG: I was a plaything for the imperialists!
CHIN: What did you do?
SONG: I shamed China by allowing myself to be corrupted by a
50   foreigner . . .
CHIN: What does this mean? The People demand a full confession!
SONG: I engaged in the lowest perversions with China's enemies!
CHIN: What perversions? Be more clear!
55   SONG: I let him put it up my ass!

(*Dancers look over, disgusted.*)

CHIN: Aaaa-ya! How can you use such sickening language?!
SONG: My language . . . is only as foul as the crimes I committed . . .
CHIN: Yeah. That's better. So—what do you want to do now?
SONG: I want to serve the people.

(*Percussion starts up, with Chinese strings.*)

60   CHIN: What?
SONG: I want to serve the people!

(*Dancers regain their revolutionary smiles, and begin a dance of victory.*)

CHIN: What?!
SONG: I want to serve the people!!

(*Dancers unveil a banner: "The Actor Is Rehabilitated!"* SONG *remains kneeling before* CHIN, *as the dancers bounce around them, then exit. Music out.*)

SCENE X

A commune. Hunan Province. 1970.

CHIN: How you planning to do that?
SONG: I've already worked four years in the fields of Hunan, Comrade Chin.
CHIN: So? Farmers work all their lives. Let me see your hands.

(SONG *holds them out for her inspection.*)

5   CHIN: Goddamn! Still so smooth! How long does it take to turn you actors into good anythings? Hunh. You've just spent too many years in luxury to be any good to the Revolution.

SONG: I served the Revolution.
CHIN: Serve the Resolution? Bullshit! You wore dresses! Don't
10   tell me—I was there. I saw you! You and your white vice-consul! Stuck up there in your flat, living off the People's Treasury! Yeah, I knew what was going on! You two . . . homos! Homos! Homos! (*Pause; she composes herself.*) Ah! Well . . . you will serve the people, all right. But not with the
15   Revolution's money. This time, you use your own money.
SONG: I have no money.
CHIN: Shut up! And you won't stink up China anymore with your pervert stuff. You'll pollute the place where pollution begins—the West.
20   SONG: What do you mean?
CHIN: Shut up! You're going to France. Without a cent in your pocket. You find your consul's house, you make him pay your expenses—
SONG: No.
25   CHIN: And you give us weekly reports! Useful information!
SONG: That's crazy. It's been four years.
CHIN: Either that, or back to rehabilitation center!
SONG: Comrade Chin, he's not going to support me! Not in France! He's a white man! I was just his plaything—
30   CHIN: Oh yuck! Again with the sickening language. Where's my stick?
SONG: You don't understand the mind of a man.

(*Pause.*)

CHIN: Oh no? No I don't? Then how come I'm married, huh? How come I got a man? Five, six years ago, you always tell me those kinds of things, I felt very bad. But not now! Because
35   what does the Chairman say? He tells us *I'm* now the smart one, you're now the nincompoop! *You're* the blackhead, the harebrain, the nitwit! You think you're so smart? You understand "The Mind of a Man"? Good! Then *you* go to France
40   and be a pervert for Chairman Mao!

(CHIN *and* SONG *exit in opposite directions*)

SCENE XI

Paris. 1968–70.

GALLIMARD *enters.*

GALLIMARD: And what was waiting for me back in Paris? Well, better Chinese food than I'd eaten in China. Friends and relatives. A little accounting, regular schedule, keeping track of traffic violations in the suburbs. . . . And the indignity of
5   students shouting the slogans of Chairman Mao at me—in French.
HELGA: Rene? Rene? (*She enters, soaking wet*) I've had a . . . a problem. (*She sneezes.*)
GALLIMARD: You're wet.
10   HELGA: Yes, I . . . coming back from the grocer's. A group of students, waving red flags, they—

(GALLIMARD *fetches a towel.*)

HELGA: —they ran by, I was caught up along with them. Before I knew what was happening—

(GALLIMARD *gives her the towel.*)

HELGA: Thank you. The police started firing water cannons at
15   us. I tried to shout, to tell them I was the wife of a diplomat,

but—you know how it is . . . (Pause) Needless to say, I lost the groceries. Rene, what's happening to France?

GALLIMARD: What's—? Well, nothing, really.

HELGA: Nothing? The storefronts are in flames, there's glass in
20   the streets, buildings are toppling—and I'm wet!

GALLIMARD: Nothing! . . . that I care to think about.

HELGA: And is that why you stay in this room?

GALLIMARD: Yes, in fact.

HELGA: With the incense burning? You know something? I hate
25   incense. It smells so sickly sweet.

GALLIMARD: Well, I hate the French. Who just smell—period!

HELGA: And the Chinese were better?

GALLIMARD: Please—don't start.

HELGA: When we left, this exact same thing, the riots—
30   GALLIMARD: No, no . . .

HELGA: Students screaming slogans, smashing down doors—

GALLIMARD: Helga—

HELGA: It was all going on in China, too. Don't you remember?!

GALLIMARD: Helga! Please! (Pause) You have never understood
35   China, have you? You walk in here with these ridiculous
ideas, that the West is falling apart, that China was spitting in
our faces. You come in, dripping of the streets, and you leave
water all over my floor. (He grabs HELGA's towel, begins mopping up the floor)

40   HELGA: But it's the truth!

GALLIMARD: Helga, I want a divorce.

(Pause; GALLIMARD continues, mopping the floor.)

HELGA: I take it back. China is . . . beautiful. Incense, I like
incense.

GALLIMARD: I've had a mistress.

45   HELGA: So?

GALLIMARD: For eight years.

HELGA: I knew you would. I knew you would the day I married
you. And now what? You want to marry her?

GALLIMARD: I can't. She's in China.

50   HELGA: I see. You want to leave. For someone who's not here, is
that right?

GALLIMARD: That's right.

HELGA: You can't live with her, but still you don't want to live
with me.

55   GALLIMARD: That's right.

(Pause.)

HELGA: Shit. How terrible that I can figure that out. (Pause) I
never thought I'd say it. But, in China, I was happy. I knew,
in my own way, I knew that you were not everything you
pretended to be. But the pretense—going on your arm to the
60   embassy ball, visiting your office and the guards saying,
"Good morning, good morning, Madame Gallimard"—the
pretense . . . was very good indeed. (Pause) I hope everyone is
mean to you for the rest of your life. (She exits)

GALLIMARD: (To us) Prophetic.

(MARC enters with two drinks.)

65   GALLIMARD: (To MARC) In China, I was different from all other
men.

MARC: Sure. You were white. Here's your drink.

GALLIMARD: I felt . . . touched.

MARC: In the head? Rene, I don't want to hear about the Oriental love goddess. Okay? One night—can we just drink and   70
throw up without a lot of conversation?

GALLIMARD: You still don't believe me, do you?

MARC: Sure I do. She was the most beautiful, et cetera, et cetera, blasé blasé.

(Pause.)

GALLIMARD: My life in the West has been such a disappointment.   75

MARC: Life in the West is like that. You'll get used to it. Look,
you're driving me away. I'm leaving. Happy, now? (He exits,
then returns) Look, I have a date tomorrow night. You wanna
come? I can fix you up with—

GALLIMARD: Of course. I would love to come.   80

(Pause.)

MARC: Uh—on second thought, no. You'd better get ahold of
yourself first.

(He exits; GALLIMARD nurses his drink.)

GALLIMARD: (To us) This is the ultimate cruelty, isn't it? That I
can talk and talk and to anyone listening, it's only air—too
rich a diet to be swallowed by a mundane world. Why can't   85
anyone understand? That in China, I once loved, and was
loved by, very simply, the Perfect Woman.

(SONG enters, dressed as BUTTERFLY in wedding dress.)

GALLIMARD: (To SONG) Not again. My imagination is hell. Am
I asleep this time? Or did I drink too much?

SONG: Rene?   90

GALLIMARD: God, it's too painful! That you speak?

SONG: What are you talking about? Rene—touch me.

GALLIMARD: Why?

SONG: I'm real. Take my hand.

GALLIMARD: Why? So you can disappear again and leave me   95
clutching at the air? For the entertainment of my neighbors
who—?

(SONG touches GALLIMARD.)

SONG: Rene?

(GALLIMARD takes SONG's hand. Silence.)

GALLIMARD: Butterfly? I never doubted you'd return.

SONG: You hadn't . . . forgotten—?   100

GALLIMARD: Yes, actually, I've forgotten everything. My mind,
you see—there wasn't enough room in this hard head—not
for the world and for you. No, there was only room for one.
(Beat) Come, look. See? Your bed has been waiting, with
the Klimt poster you like, and—see? The xiang lu [incense   105
burner] you gave me?

SONG: I . . . I don't know what to say.

GALLIMARD: There's nothing to say. Not at the end of a long
trip. Can I make you some tea?

SONG: But where's your wife?   110

GALLIMARD: She's by my side. She's by my side at last.

(GALLIMARD reaches to embrace SONG. SONG sidesteps, dodging
him.)

GALLIMARD: Why?

SONG: (To us) So I did return to Rene in Paris. Where I found—

GALLIMARD: Why do you run away? Can't we show them how
115   we embraced that evening?

SONG: Please. I'm talking.

GALLIMARD: You have to do what I say! I'm conjuring you up in
    my mind!

SONG: Rene, I've never done what you've said. Why should it be
120   any different in your mind? Now split — the story moves on,
    and I must change.

GALLIMARD: I welcomed you into my home! I didn't have to,
    you know! I could've left you penniless on the streets of Paris!
    But I took you in!

125 SONG: Thank you.

GALLIMARD: So . . . please . . . don't change.

SONG: You know I have to. You know I will. And anyway, what
    difference does it make? No matter what your eyes tell you,
    you can't ignore the truth. You already know too much.

(GALLIMARD *exits.* SONG *turns to us.*)

130 SONG: The change I'm going to make requires about five min-
    utes. So I thought you might want to take this opportunity to
    stretch your legs, enjoy a drink, or listen to the musicians. I'll
    be here, when you return, right where you left me.

(SONG *goes to a mirror in front of which is a wash basin of water.
She starts to remove her makeup as stagelights go to half and
houselights come up.*)

— ACT THREE —

SCENE I

A courthouse in Paris. 1986.

As he promised, SONG *has completed the bulk of his transformation, onstage by the time the houselights go down and the stagelights come up full. He removes his wig and kimono, leaving
them on the floor. Underneath, he wears a well-cut suit.*

SONG: So I'd done my job better than I had a right to expect.
    Well, give him some credit, too. He's right — I was in a fix
    when I arrived in Paris. I walked from the airport into town,
    then I located, by blind groping, the Chinatown district. Let
5   me make one thing clear: whatever else may be said about the
    Chinese, they are stingy! I slept in doorways three days until I
    could find a tailor who would make me this kimono on credit.
    As it turns out, maybe I didn't even need it. Maybe we
    would've been happy to see me in a simple shift and mascara.
10   But . . . better safe than sorry.
       That was 1970, when I arrived in Paris. For the next fifteen
    years, yes, I lived in a very comfy life. Some relief, believe
    me, after four years on a fucking commune in Nowheresville,
    China. Rene supported the boy and me, and I did some dem-
15   onstrations around the country as part of my "cultural ex-
    change" cover. And then there was the spying.

(SONG *moves upstage, to a chair.* TOULON *enters as a judge,
wearing the appropriate wig and robes. He sits near* SONG. *It's
1986, and* SONG *is testifying in a courtroom.*)

SONG: Not much at first. Rene had lost all his high-level con-
    tacts. Comrade Chin wasn't very interested in parking-ticket

statistics. But finally, at my urging, Rene got a job as a courier, handling sensitive documents. He'd photograph them 20
for me, and I'd pass them on to the Chinese embassy.

JUDGE: Did he understand the extent of his activity?

SONG: He didn't ask. He knew that I needed those documents,
    and that was enough.

JUDGE: But he must've known he was passing classified 25
    information.

SONG: I can't say.

JUDGE: He never asked what you were going to do with them?

SONG: Nope.

(Pause.)

JUDGE: There is one thing that the court — indeed, that all of 30
    France — would like to know.

SONG: Fire away.

JUDGE: Did Monsieur Gallimard know you were a man?

SONG: Well, he never saw me completely naked. Ever.

JUDGE: But surely, he must've . . . how can I put this? 35

SONG: Put it however you like. I'm not shy. He must've felt
    around?

JUDGE: Mmmmm.

SONG: Not really. I did all the work. He just laid back. Of course
    we did enjoy more . . . complete union, and I suppose he 40
    might have wondered why I was always on my stomach, but.
    . . . But what you're thinking is, "Of course a wrist must've
    brushed . . . a hand hit . . . over twenty years!" Yeah. Well,
    Your Honor, it was my job to make him think I was a woman.
    And chew on this: it wasn't all that hard. See, my mother was 45
    a prostitute along the Bundt before the Revolution. And, uh,
    I think it's fair to say she learned a few things about Western
    men. So I borrowed her knowledge. In service to my country.

JUDGE: Would you care to enlighten the court with this secret
    knowledge? I'm sure we're all very curious. 50

SONG: I'm sure you are. *(Pause)* Okay, Rule One is: Men always
    believe what they want to hear. So a girl can tell the most
    obnoxious lies and the guys will believe them every time —
    "This is my first time" — "That's the biggest I've ever seen" —
    or *both*, which, if you really think about it, is not possible in a 55
    single lifetime. You've maybe heard those phrases a few times
    in your own life, yes, Your Honor?

JUDGE: It's not my life, Monsieur Song, which is on trial today.

SONG: Okay, okay, just trying to lighten up the proceedings.
    Tough room. 60

JUDGE: Go on.

SONG: Rule Two: As soon as a Western man comes into contact
    with the East — he's already confused. The West has sort of an
    international rape mentality towards the East. Do you know
    rape mentality? 65

JUDGE: Give us your definition, please.

SONG: Basically, "Her mouth says no, but her eyes say yes."
       The West thinks of itself as masculine — big guns, big in-
    dustry, big money — so the East is feminine — weak, delicate,
    poor . . . but good at art, and full of inscrutable wisdom — the 70
    feminine mystique.
       Her mouth says no, but her eyes say yes. The West believes
    the East, deep down, *wants* to be dominated — because a
    woman can't think for herself.

JUDGE: What does this have to do with my question? 75

SONG: You expect Oriental countries to submit to your guns, and you expect Oriental women to be submissive to your men. That's why you say they make the best wives.

JUDGE: But why would that make it possible for you to fool Mon-
80 sieur Gallimard? Please—get to the point.

SONG: One, because when he finally met his fantasy woman, he wanted more than anything to believe that she was, in fact, a woman. And second, I am an Oriental. And being an Oriental, I could never be completely a man.

(Pause.)

85 JUDGE: Your armchair political theory is tenuous, Monsieur Song.

SONG: You think so? That's why you'll lose in all your dealings with the East.

JUDGE: Just answer my question: did he know you were a man?

(Pause.)

90 SONG: You know, your Honor, I never asked.

SCENE II

Same.

Music from the "Death Scene" from Butterfly *blares over the house speakers. It is the loudest thing we've heard in this play.*

GALLIMARD *enters, crawling towards* SONG's *wig and kimono.*

GALLIMARD: Butterfly? Butterfly?

(SONG remains a man, in the witness box, delivering a testimony we do not hear.)

GALLIMARD: *(To us)* In my moment of greatest shame, here, in this courtroom—with that . . . person up there, telling the world. . . . What strikes me especially is how swallow he is,
5   how glib and obsequious . . . completely . . . without sub-
stance! The type that prowls around discos with a gold medal-
lion stinking of garlic. So little like my Butterfly.
        Yet even in this moment my mind remains agile, flip-flop-
ping like a man on a trampoline. Even now, my picture dis-
10 solves, and I see that . . . witness . . . talking to me.

(SONG suddenly stands staight up in his witness box, and looks at GALLIMARD.)

SONG: Yes. You. White man.

*(SONG steps out of the witness box, and moves downstage to-
wards GALLIMARD. Light change.)*

GALLIMARD: *(To SONG)* Who? Me?

SONG: Do you see any other white men?

GALLIMARD: Yes. There're white men all around. This is a
15   French courtroom.

SONG: So you are an adventurous imperialist. Tell me, why did it take you so long? To come back to this place?

GALLIMARD: What place?

SONG: This theatre in China. Where we met many years ago.

20 GALLIMARD: *(To us)* And once again, against my will, I am transported.

(Chinese opera music comes up on the speakers. SONG begins to do opera moves, as he did the night they met.)

SONG: Do you remember? The night you gave your heart?

GALLIMARD: It was a long time ago.

SONG: Not long enough. A night that turned your world upside
    down.   25

GALLIMARD: Perhaps.

SONG: Oh, be honest with me. What's another bit of flattery when you've already given me twenty years' worth? It's a wonder my head hasn't swollen to the size of China.

GALLIMARD: Who's to say it hasn't?   30

SONG: Who's to say? And what's the shame? In pride? You think I could've pulled this off if I wasn't already full of pride when we met? No, not just pride. Arrogance. It takes arrogance, really—to believe you can will, with your eyes and your lips, the destiny of another. *(He dances)* C'mon. Admit it. You still 35
want me. Even in slacks and a button-down collar.

GALLIMARD: I don't see what the point of—

SONG: You don't Well maybe, Rene, just maybe—I want you.

GALLIMARD: You do?

SONG: Then again, maybe I'm just playing with you. How can   40
you tell? *(Reprising his feminine character, he sidles up to* GALLIMARD*)* "How I wish there were even a small cafe to sit in. With men in tuxedos, and cappuccinos, and bad expatriate jazz." Now you want to kiss me, don't you?

GALLIMARD: *(Pulling away)* What makes you—?   45

SONG: —so sure? See? I take the words from your mouth. Then I wait for you to come and retrieve them. *(He reclines on the floor)*

GALLIMARD: Why? Why do you treat me so cruelly?

SONG: Perhaps I *was* treating you cruelly. But now—I'm being   50
nice. Come here, my little one.

GALLIMARD: I'm not your little one!

SONG: My mistake. It's I who am *your* little one, right?

GALLIMARD: Yes, I—

SONG: So come get your little one. If you like. I may even let you 55
strip me.

GALLIMARD: I mean, you were! Before . . . but not like this!

SONG: I was? Then perhaps I still am. If you look hard enough.
    (He starts to remove his clothes)

GALLIMARD: What—what are you doing?   60

SONG: Helping you to see through my act.

GALLIMARD: Stop that! I don't want to! I don't—

SONG: Oh, but you asked me to strip, remember?

GALLIMARD: What? That was years ago! And I took it back!

SONG: No. You postponed it. Postponed the inevitable. Today,   65
the inevitable has come calling.

(From the speakers, cacophony: BUTTERFLY *mixed in with Chinese gongs.)*

GALLIMARD: No! Stop! I don't want to see!

SONG: Then look away.

GALLIMARD: You're only in my mind! All this is in my mind! I order you! To stop!   70

SONG: To what? To strip? That's just what I'm—

GALLIMARD: No! Stop! I want you—!

SONG: You want me?

GALLIMARD: To stop!

SONG: You know something, Rene? Your mouth says no, but   75
your eyes say yes. Turn them away. I dare you.

GALLIMARD: I don't have to! Every night, you say you're going to strip, but then I beg you and you stop!

SONG: I guess tonight is different.

80 GALLIMARD: Why? Why should that be?

SONG: Maybe I've become frustrated. Maybe I'm saying "Look at me, you fool!" Or maybe I'm just feeling . . . sexy. (*He is down to his briefs*)

GALLIMARD: Please. This is unnecessary. I know what you are.

85 SONG: Do you? What am I?

GALLIMARD: A—a man.

SONG: You don't really believe that.

GALLIMARD: Yes I do! I knew all the time somewhere that my happiness was temporary, my love a deception. But my mind

90 kept the knowledge at bay. To make the wait bearable.

SONG: Monsieur Gallimard—the wait is over.

(SONG *drops his briefs. He is naked. Sound cue out. Slowly, we and* SONG *come to the realization that what we had thought to be* GALLIMARD's *sobbing is actually his laughter.*)

GALLIMARD: Oh god! What an idiot! Of course!

SONG: Rene—what?

GALLIMARD: Look at you! You're a man! (*He bursts into laugh-*

95 *ter again*)

SONG: I fail to see what's so funny!

GALLIMARD: "You fail to see—!" I mean, you never did have much of a sense of humor, did you? I just think it's ridiculously funny that I've wasted so much time on just a man!

100 SONG: Wait. I'm not "just a man."

GALLIMARD: No? Isn't that what you've been trying to convince me of?

SONG: Yes, but what I mean—

GALLIMARD: And now, I finally believe you, and you tell me it's

105 not true? I think you must have some kind of identity problem.

SONG: Will you listen to me?

GALLIMARD: Why?! I've been listening to you for twenty years. Don't I deserve a vacation?

110 SONG: I'm not just any man!

GALLIMARD: Then, what exactly are you?

SONG: Rene, how can you ask—? Okay, what about this?

(*He picks up* BUTTERFLY's *robes, starts to dance around. No music.*)

GALLIMARD: Yes, that's very nice. I have to admit.

(SONG *holds out his arm to* GALLIMARD.)

SONG: It's the same skin you've worshiped for years. Touch it.

115 GALLIMARD: Yes, it does feel the same.

SONG: Now—close your eyes.

(SONG *covers* GALLIMARD's *eyes with one hand. With the other,* SONG *draws* GALLIMARD's *hand up to his face.* GALLIMARD, *like a blind man, lets his hands run over* SONG's *face.*)

GALLIMARD: This skin, I remember. The curve of her face, the softness of her cheek, her hair against the back of my hand . . .

SONG: I'm your Butterfly. Under the robes, beneath everything,

120 it was always me. Now, open your eyes and admit it—you adore me. (*He removes his hand from* GALLIMARD's *eyes*)

GALLIMARD: You, who knew every inch of my desires—how could you, of all people, have made such a mistake?

SONG: What?

GALLIMARD: You showed me your true self. When all I loved

125 was the lie. A perfect lie, which you let fall to the ground— and now, it's old and soiled.

SONG: So—you never really loved me? Only when I was playing a part?

GALLIMARD: I'm a man who loved a woman created by a man.

130 Everything else—simply falls short.

(*Pause.*)

SONG: What am I supposed to do now?

GALLIMARD: You were a fine spy, Monsieur Song, with an even finer accomplice. But now I believe you should go. Get out of

135 my life!

SONG: Go where? Rene, you can't live without me. Not after twenty years.

GALLIMARD: I certainly can't live with you—not after twenty years of betrayal.

SONG: Don't be so stubborn! Where will you go?

140 GALLIMARD: I have a date . . . with my Butterfly.

SONG: So, throw away your pride. And come . . .

GALLIMARD: Get away from me! Tonight, I've finally learned to tell fantasy from reality. And, knowing the difference, I choose fantasy.

145 SONG: *I'm* your fantasy!

GALLIMARD: You? You're as real as hamburger. Now get out! I have a date with my Butterfly and I don't want your body polluting the room! (*He tosses* SONG's *suit at him*) Look at these—you dress like a pimp.

150 SONG: Hey! These are Armani slacks and—! (*He puts on his briefs and slacks*) Let's just say . . . I'm disappointed in you, Rene. In the crush of your adoration, I thought you'd become something more. More like . . . a woman.

But no. Men. You're like the rest of them. It's all in the way

155 we dress, and make up our faces, and bat our eyelashes. You really have so little imagination!

GALLIMARD: You, Monsieur Song? Accuse me of too little imagination? You, if anyone, should know—I am pure imagination. And in imagination I will remain. Now get out!

160

(GALLIMARD *bodily removes* SONG *from the stage, taking his kimono.*)

SONG: Rene! I'll never put on those robes again! You'll be sorry!

GALLIMARD: (*To* SONG) I'm already sorry! (*Looking at the kimono in his hands*) Exactly as sorry . . . as a Butterfly.

SCENE III

M. GALLIMARD's *prison cell. Paris. Present.*

GALLIMARD: I've played out the events of my life night after night, always searching for a new ending to my story, one where I leave this cell and return forever to my Butterfly's arms.

Tonight I realize my search is over. That I've looked all

5 along in the wrong place. And now, to you, I will prove that my love was not in vain—by returning to the world of fantasy where I first met her.

(*He picks up the kimono; dancers enter.*)

GALLIMARD: There is a vision of the Orient that I have. Of slender women in chong sams and kimonos who die for the love

10 of unworthy foreign devils. Who are born and raised to be the perfect women. Who take whatever punishment we give them, and bounce back, strengthened by love, unconditionally. It is a vision that has become my life.

(Dancers bring the wash basin to him and help him make up his face.)

GALLIMARD: In public, I have continued to deny that Song Lil-
15 ing is a man. This brings me headlines, and is a source of great embarrassment to my French colleagues, who can now be sent into a coughing fit by the mere mention of Chinese food. But alone, in my cell, I have long since faced the truth.
    And the truth demands a sacrifice. For mistakes made over
20 the course of a lifetime. My mistakes were simple and absolute — the man I loved was a cad, a bounder. He deserved nothing but a kick in the behind, and instead I gave him . . . all my love.
    Yes — love. Why not admit it all? That was my undoing,
25 wasn't it? Love warped my judgment, blinded my eyes, rearranged the very lines on my face . . . until I could look in the mirror and see nothing but . . . a woman.

(Dancers help him put on the BUTTERFLY *wig.)*

GALLIMARD: I have a vision. Of the Orient. That, deep within its almond eyes, there are still women. Women willing to sacrifice themselves for the love of a man. Even a man whose 30 love is completely without worth.

(Dancers assist GALLIMARD *in donning the kimono. They hand him a knife.)*

GALLIMARD: Death with honor is better than life . . . life with dishonor. *(He sets himself center stage, in a seppuku position)* The love of a Butterfly can withstand many things — unfaithfulness, loss, even abandonment. But how can it face 35 the one sin that implies all others? The devastating knowledge that, underneath it all, the object of her love was nothing more, nothing less than . . . a man. *(He sets the tip of the knife against his body)* It is 19__. And I have found her at last. In a prison on the outskirts of Paris. My name is Rene Galli- 40 mard — also known as Madame Butterfly.

*(*GALLIMARD *turns upstage and plunges his knife into his body, as music from the "Love Duet" blares over the speakers. He collapses into the arms of the dancers, who lay him reverently on the floor. The image holds for several beats. Then a tight special up on* SONG, *who stands as a man, staring at the dead* GALLIMARD. *He smokes a cigarette; the smoke filters up through the lights. Two words leave his lips.)*

SONG: Butterfly? Butterfly?

(Smoke rises as lights fade slowly to black.)

DAVID MAMET

David Mamet (b. 1947) is one of the best-known playwrights working in the United States today. Born and raised in Chicago, Mamet took his B.A. at Goddard College in 1969 and then pursued a career as a writer. His first success, *American Buffalo* (1975), established Mamet as a major voice in the contemporary American theater, and it framed the distinctive features of Mamet's theater: the slangy, sleazy world of masculine power, bonding, and betrayal. Although Mamet has written several successful films — most recently *Homicide* (1991) — his reputation in the theater rests on plays like *Sexual Perversity in Chicago* (1974), *Lakeboat* (1970), *Edmond* (1982), *Glengarry Glen Ross* (which won the Pulitzer Prize for Drama in 1983), and *Speed-the-Plow* (1988).

Speed-the-Plow

Taking his title from Thomas Morton's famous nineteenth-century melodrama of rivalry and reunion in a provincial English family, Mamet moves his *Speed-the-Plow* to Hollywood. He uses the Hollywood "buddy film" to investigate the relationship between entertainment, art, and gender politics. Two men, the film producer Gould and the agent Fox, have to choose between making Fox's film (a prison "buddy film" with a famous, bankable star, Doug Brown) and an "art film." Yet while Fox and Gould are involved in negotiating the "buddy film," Mamet suggests that *their* relationship is itself modeled on the stereotypes of that genre. Although they are initially wary of one another, for example, Fox and Gould develop a kind of comradeship between them as they work together on the film. It's Fox and Gould against the world: "We're gonna kick the ass of a lot of them fucken' people." The "buddy film" — and the men's relationship — emerges as a complex ballet of fear and aggression, a relationship that soon develops a third term: the exploitation of women. Gould bets Fox that he can not only date his temporary secretary, Karen, but that "I can get her to my house, that I can screw her." Gould attracts Karen by giving her the "art film" to read, inviting her to his house for a final discussion of her opinion, and he finally does seduce her. However, when he decides to make the "art film" instead of the "buddy film," the real dynamics of "buddy" relationships become clear. Fox explodes, savagely attacking Gould for falling in love with Karen, and he reveals to Karen that Gould seduced her on a bet. The "buddy play" — *Speed-the-Plow* included — is a genre that uses women as a means to develop men's relationships, a token of exchange in the economy of male bonding. The play raises the question of women's exploitation as an inherent feature of male relationships and of their representation in the "buddy film." Does the play valorize Gould and Fox, confirming their "buddy film" bonding as just the kind of thing men do? Or does the play take a more critical view toward Gould and Fox, buddy films, and men's relationships by asking whether the exploitation and exchange of women finally provide the means of their empowerment?

SPEED-THE-PLOW

David Mamet

— CHARACTERS —

BOBBY GOULD ⎫
CHARLIE FOX ⎬ *two men around forty*
KAREN *a woman in her twenties*

— ACT ONE —

GOULD's *office. Morning. Boxes and painting materials all around.* GOULD *is sitting, reading,* FOX *enters.*

GOULD: When the gods would make us mad, they answer our prayers.

FOX: Bob . . .

GOULD: I'm in the midst of the wilderness.

5 FOX: Bob . . .

GOULD: If it's not quite "Art" and it's not quite "Entertainment," it's here on my desk. I have inherited a monster.

FOX: . . . Bob . . .

GOULD: Listen to this . . . (*Reads:*) "How are things made
10 round? Was there one thing which, originally, was round . . . ?"

FOX: . . . Bob . . .

GOULD: (*leafing through the book he is reading, reads*) "A certain frankness came to it . . ." (*He leafs.*) "The man, downcast, then met the priest, under the bridge, beneath that
15 bridge which stood for so much, where so much had transpired *since* the radiation."

FOX: . . . yeah, Bob, that's great . . .

GOULD: Listen to this: "and with it brought grace. But still the questions persisted . . . that of the Radiation. That of the
20 growth of animalism, the decay of the soil. And it said, 'Beyond terror. Beyond grace' . . . and caused a throbbing . . . machines in the void . . ." (*He offers the book to* FOX.) Here: take a page.

FOX: I have to talk to you.

25 GOULD: Chuck, Chuck, Chuck, *Charles:* you get too old, too busy to have 'fun' in this business; to have 'fun,' then what are you . . . ?

FOX: . . . Bob . . .

GOULD: What are you?

30 FOX: What am I . . . ?

GOULD: Yes.

FOX: What am I when?

GOULD: What are you, I was saying, if you're just a slave to commerce?

35 FOX: If I'm just a slave to commerce?

GOULD: Yes.

FOX: I'm nothing.

GOULD: No.

FOX: You're absolutely right.

40 GOULD: You got to have fun. You know why?

FOX: Okay: why?

GOULD: Because, or else you'll die, and people will say "he never had any fun."

FOX: How close are you to Ross?

45 GOULD: How close am I to Ross . . . ? I don't know. How close should I be?

FOX: I have to ask you something.

GOULD: (*pause*) Go ahead, Charl.

FOX: You wanna' greenlight a picture? What's your deal, what's your new deal?

50 GOULD: What's my new deal, that's all you can talk about?

FOX: What's your new deal?

GOULD: Alright. Over ten mil I need Ross's approval. Under ten mil, I can greenlight it. So what. (*Pause.*)

FOX: This morning, Bob.

55 GOULD: . . . Yes . . . ?

FOX: This morning a man came to me.

GOULD: . . . a man came to you. Whaddayou, already, you're here to "Promote" me . . . ?

FOX: Bob . . .

60 GOULD: You here to promote me? Charl? Because, Charl, one thing I don't need . . .

FOX: Bob.

GOULD: When everybody in this jolly *town* is tryin' to promote me, do you wanna see my messages . . . ?

65 FOX: Bob.

GOULD: "Get Him While He's Hot" . . .

FOX: Yes, yes, but . . .

GOULD: My good, my "good" friend, Charles Fox . . .

FOX: Bob . . .

70 GOULD: That's why we have "channels."

FOX: Uh huh.

GOULD: All these "little" people out there, that we see. Y'unnerstand? Fellow asks "what are they *there* for?" Well, Charl, We Don't Know. But we *think*, you give the thing to *your* boy,
75 gives it to *my* boy, these people get to *eat*, they don't have to go *beg*, and get in everybody's face the *airport* the whole time. This morning the phone won't stop ringing. Do you know who's calling? Everybody says they met me in *Topeka*, 1962, and do I want to make their movie. Guys want me to do
80 remakes of films haven't been made yet.

FOX: . . . Huh, huh . . .

GOULD: I'm drowning in "coverage." (*He picks up a script and reads:*) "The Story of a Horse and the Horse Who Loved Him." (*He drops script.*) . . . Give me a breather from all
85 those fine folk suddenly see what a great "man" I am. N'when I *do* return my calls, Charl, do you know what I'll tell those people?

FOX: No.

GOULD: I'm going to tell them "Go through Channels." This
90 protects me from them. And from folk, fine as they are, like you, Charl, when you come to me for favors. Or did you come up here to congratulate me on my new promotion?

FOX: Congratulations.

986

95 GOULD: Do I deserve it?
FOX: Yes. You do, Bob.
GOULD: Why?
FOX: Because you're a prince among men and you're Yertle the
Turtle.
100 GOULD: Alright then, that's enough. What did you bring me?
FOX: This morning, Bob.
GOULD: Yes?
FOX: This morning Doug Brown came to me.
GOULD: . . . Doug Brown.
105 FOX: *(pause)* He came to my *house* Bob. How would you *like* . . .
How would you like for Doug Brown to "cross the street" to do
a picture for us? *(Pause.)* Bob? How would you *like*, a script
that I got him. He's *nuts* for it, he's *free*, we could start to
shoot next *month*, I have his word and he'll come to the stu-
110 dio, and do the film for us. Doug Brown will cross the street
and do a film for us next month.
GOULD: *(picks up phone)* Get me Ross. *(Pause.)*
FOX: . . . do you see what I'm telling you?
GOULD: . . . he came to your house . . .
115 FOX: . . . can you believe what I'm saying to you . . . ?
GOULD: Douggie Brown. *(Into phone:)* Ross *(pause)* *Richard
Ross* . . . no, no, no, *don't* look in the book . . . there's a
button on the console . . . Richard R . . . just push the button
on the . . . *(Pause.)* There's a button on the console . . .
120 Richard Ross . . . just . . . *Thank* you. *(Hangs up the phone.
Pause.)* Are you alright?
FOX: I'm fine. I'm fine, I just need coffee.
GOULD: We'll get it for you. Tell mmm . . .
FOX: Alright, I, this is some time ago.
125 GOULD: . . . uh huh . . .
FOX: That I get the script to Brown . . .
GOULD: What script . . . ?
FOX: You don't know it, a prison script . . .
GOULD: *(simultaneously with "script")* One of ours . . . ?
130 FOX: I found it in the file. I *loved* it . . . all the time I'm thinking . . .
GOULD: Uh huh . . .
FOX: How to do this script, I, one day . . .
GOULD: Uh huh . . .
FOX: . . . so . . .
135 GOULD: So, you give the script to Brown . . .
FOX: Not "him," his . . .
GOULD: Uh huh . . .
FOX: . . . his . . .
GOULD: . . . I know . . .
140 FOX: His "guy."
GOULD: Yes.
FOX: *Gives* Douggie the script . . . *(Phone rings.* GOULD *picks up
the phone.)*
GOULD: *(into phone)* Yes. Thank you. *(Hangs up.)* Ross'll get
145 back to us . . .
FOX: . . . His guy *gives* Douggie the scri . . .
GOULD: He gives Douggie the script.
FOX: Yes.
GOULD: Mmm . . .
150 FOX: *Months* ago, alright? *I* don't know. *Today,* alright . . . ?
Today. *(Pause.)* I'm having coffee . . .
GOULD: Umm hmmm . . .
FOX: Who drives up?
GOULD: . . . coffee at your house . . .

155 FOX: Who drives up?
GOULD: Douggie Brown.
FOX: Douglas Brown drives up to my house. *(Pause.)* He says "I
Want To Do Your Script. I've got this other thing to deal with,
and we'll settle it tomorrow. Call me ten o'clock tomorrow
160 morning. I'll come in and sign *up*." *(Phone rings.)*
GOULD: *(into phone)* Hello . . . who? No calls. *No* calls. Just
Richard Ross. And we need coffee . . . okay? *Got it* . . . ?
(Hangs up.)
FOX: . . . cross the street to shoot it . . . ? And he says "why not."
165 *(Pause.)*
GOULD: . . . huh . . .
FOX: *Huh* . . . ?
GOULD: . . . He'd come over here to shoot it . . .
FOX: Sonofabitch like out of some damn fairytale.
170 GOULD: . . . he drove to your house . . .
FOX: . . . I'm looking out the window . . .
GOULD: . . . son of a bitch . . .
FOX: . . . Douglas Brown drives up . . .

(The phone rings. GOULD *picks it up.)*

GOULD: *(into phone)* Hello. Yes. *Richard* . . . *(Pause.)* Yes. Put
175 him . . . Hello, *Richard.* Fine, just fine. They're painting it.
Well, thank you. Thank you. Listen Richard. Do you need
some good news . . . ? *(Pause.)* Well, it's a surprise that I've got
for you. No, I want to tell you in person. Do you have five mi
. . . *(Checks watch.)* We'll be there. *(Pause.)* Charlie Fox . . .
180 *Charlie* came in with a . . . *(Pause.)* Right. Right. We'll be
there. Right. *(Hangs up.)* Well. We see him in ten minutes.
FOX: *Yessir.* I need some coffee.
GOULD: Oh, Jesus, what's the . . .
FOX: What . . . ?
185 GOULD: The, what's the story? Tell me the . . .
FOX: *I* can tell it. No, you're right. *You* tell it.
GOULD: Gimme the broad outl . . .
FOX: Yes, yes.
GOULD: Just sketch me the broad . . .
190 FOX: Yes, yes, the *thing*, of course, is . . .
GOULD: Douggie, Brown, of course, the thing . . .
FOX: "A Douggie Brown picture" . . .
GOULD: A Douggie Brown picture . . .
FOX: Eh? A buddy . . .
195 GOULD: A *Buddy* Picture.
FOX: Douggie and . . .
GOULD: "Watch this space," I got it . . .
FOX: Right.
GOULD: The Flavor of the Month . . . okay, now, what's the
200 story?
FOX: Doug's in prison.
GOULD: . . . prison . . .
FOX: Right. These guys, they want to get him.
GOULD: *Black* guys . . .
205 FOX: Black guys in the prison.
GOULD: *(into phone)* Coffee, quickly, can you get some coffee in
here? *(Hangs up.)*
FOX: And the black guys going to rape his ass.
GOULD: Mmm.
210 FOX: Okay. Now. "Now, you could," he goes, "you could have
your 'way' with me, all of you . . ."
GOULD: Uh huh, what? ten or twenty guys . . .

FOX: ". . . and you could *do* that. But I'd have to, you see? Here's the *thing* of it. Unless you *killed* me, I would . . ."

215 GOULD: Uh huh . . .

FOX: ". . . have to come back and *retaliate*, sometime, somehow, because . . ."

GOULD: . . . okay . . .

FOX: "I couldn't . . ."

220 GOULD: . . . uh huh . . .

FOX: ". . . *live* with that."

GOULD: . . . The degradation . . .

FOX: "So whyn't you skip all the *middle* shit, kill me right now."

GOULD: . . . he throws it in their face.

225 FOX: You got it.

GOULD: . . . uh huh . . .

FOX: "*Or.*" (*Pause.*) Or . . .

GOULD: . . . yes . . .

FOX: "If you could use a *friend*, why not allow me this? To *be*

230   your friend . . ."

GOULD: He teams up with the guys . . .

FOX: "To *side* with you . . ."

GOULD: Yes.

FOX: "and, *together* . . ."

235 GOULD: . . . and . . .

FOX: . . . they become friends, they teach him the . . .

GOULD: . . . he learns the Prison Ways . . .

FOX: They blah blah, *so on* . . .

GOULD: Uh huh . . .

240 FOX: *Now.* Eh? Now. With his, his knowledge of *computers*, so on, with his *money* . . .

GOULD: . . . yeah . . .

FOX: His Links to the Outside . . .

GOULD: A girl . . . ?

245 FOX: Ah. Now that's the *great* part, I'm telling you, when I saw this script . . .

GOULD: . . . I don't know how it got past us . . .

FOX: When they get out of *prison*, the Head Convict's Sister . . .

GOULD: . . . a buddy film, a prison film, Douggie Brown, blah,

250   blah, some girl . . .

FOX: Action, a social . . .

GOULD: Action, blood, a social theme . . .

FOX: (*simultaneously with "theme"*) That's what I'm *saying*, an offbeat . . .

255 GOULD: Good. Good. Good. Alright. Now: Now: when we go in . . .

FOX: That's what I'm saying Bob.

GOULD: Don't even say it.

FOX: Bob:

260 GOULD: I understand.

FOX: . . . I wanted to say . . .

GOULD: I know what you wanted to say, and you're right. I know what you're going to ask, and I'm going to see you get it. Absolutely right: You go on this package as the co-producer.

265   (*Pause.*) The name above the title. This is your . . .

FOX: . . . thank you . . .

GOULD: *Thank* me?

FOX: Thank you, Bob.

GOULD: *Hey:* You came in here.

270 FOX: . . . thank you . . .

GOULD: Hey, Charl, it's *right* . . .

FOX: No, but the thing is that you *thought* of it. You thought of me. You thought to *say* it.

GOULD: I should be thanking you and I *do* thank you.

FOX: Thank you, Bob.   275

GOULD: This is your thing and you should get a bump.

FOX: Thank you.

GOULD: Because. *Charlie:* Don't thank me. You start me off here with a bang. I know that you could have Gone Across the Street . . .   280

FOX: I wouldn't have done that.

GOULD: But you could.

FOX: I wouldn't . . .

GOULD: But you *could*. And that's the point, Charl. That you absolutely *could*. And it was "loyalty" kept you with us . . .   285

FOX: Hey, hey, it's only common sense.

GOULD: You stuck with the Home Store.

FOX: Hey, you've been good for me, to put it bluntly, all the years . . .

GOULD: . . . you stuck with the Old Firm, Charl, you stuck with   290   your friends.

FOX: It's where I work, Bob, it's what I *do*, and my relationship with you . . . we were all happy for you, Bob, you got bumped up, and I feel that I'm lucky . . .

GOULD: *I'm* the lucky one, Charl . . .   295

FOX: Hey, Bullshit, to have somebody I could *come* to . . .

GOULD: (*simultaneously with "come"*) Because you *could* have gone Across the Street. Who would have blamed you?

FOX: Yeah, but I wouldn't of done it.

GOULD: Who would of blamed you, Charl? You get a Free Op-   300   tion on a Douggie Brown film, guys would walk in here, hold a guy up . . .

FOX: I work here, Bob. And my loyalty has always been to you. (*Pause.*)

GOULD: Well, I'm one lucky son of a bitch . . .   305

FOX: That you are.

GOULD: And what I do is "owe you."

FOX: No, no, Bob. Bull*shit* . . . The times you've . . .

GOULD: I'm just doing my job.

FOX: No, I know, I know . . . and I know at times, that it was   310   *difficult* for you . . .

GOULD: No.

FOX: I, and I hesitate to *ask* it, to ask for the credit . . .

GOULD: . . . Don't *have* to ask it.

FOX: 'Cause I know, anybody was to *come* in here, *exploit* you . . .   315   this thing . . .

GOULD: . . . *Forget* . . .

FOX: . . . your new "position," all, I even hesitate . . .

GOULD: Don't hesitate about a goddamn thing, *forget* it, Charl: *You Brought Me Gold.* You're gonna be co-producer. What   320   the fuck are you *talkin'* about . . . ?

FOX: I just, I wanted to say . . .

GOULD: (*simultaneously with "say"*) I'm grateful to *you*, pal. For *this* n'for all that you've been, over the years . . .

FOX: Now . . . *you* know . . .   325

GOULD: Hey, hey, hey (GOULD *checks his watch.*) Let's go make some money. (*He rises.*)

FOX: I, I need a cuppa coffee . . .

GOULD: You get it in Ross's office. Here's how we play it: we get in . . .   330

FOX: . . . yes . . .

GOULD: We get in, get out and we give it to him *in one sentence.* Let *me* talk, no disrespect . . .

FOX: No.

335 GOULD: But it's courtesy . . .

FOX: I understand.

GOULD: One sentence. "Doug Brown, Buddy Film." *(Phone rings. Into phone:)* Whoever it is, we'll be with Mr. Rrr . . . *(Pause.)* Yes? Put him on . . . Hello: *Richard.* . . . Yes . . . ?

340 Yes, well, how long will you bbb . . . *(Pause.)* I see . . . Absolutely. *(Pause.)* No problem whatsoever . . . you'll be *back* by then . . . ? *(Pause.)* Absolutely so. Thank you. *(He hangs up. Pause. To* FOX:*)* Ross just got called to New York. He's going on the Gulfstream, turn around and come right

345 back. So we got pushed to tomorrow morning, ten o'clock.

FOX: *(pause)* Aha. *(Pause.)*

GOULD: No help for it.

FOX: I've got, Douggie only gave me until . . .

GOULD: . . . I'm sorry . . .

350 FOX: Doug Brown only gave me until ten tomorrow morn . . .

GOULD: No, I know, we've only got 'til ten to tie . . .

FOX: We got to come up with a Pay or Play to *tie* him to this thing by ten o'clock to . . .

GOULD: No problem. Ross'll be back for tomorrow morning, if

355 he *doesn't* . . .

FOX: . . . if he doesn't . . .

GOULD: . . . yes . . .

FOX: . . . then . . .

GOULD: . . . Then we'll raise him on the *phone* . . .

360 FOX: . . . I'm saying . . .

GOULD: Wherever he is, we'll pull him *out* of *it* . . .

FOX: Wherever he is.

GOULD: Yup.

FOX: Because I only got the option until ten o'clock tomorrow.

365 Doug Brown told me . . .

GOULD: Yeah. I'm *saying.* Ten o'clock tomorrow. Ross: he'll be here, one chance in a *quillion* he isn't, then we go Condition Red, we get him on the . . .

FOX: . . . because . . .

370 GOULD: Yeah, yeah, yeah, I'm *with* you.

FOX: Be . . .

GOULD: . . . You understand . . . I wanted to do . . .

FOX: . . . I understand . . .

GOULD: I wanted to do it in *person* . . .

375 FOX: Yes.

GOULD: . . . 'Cause you're gonna be the Bringer of Good *News* . . .

FOX: No, no, you're absolutely right.

GOULD: Do it in *person* . . .

FOX: . . . yes . . .

380 GOULD: And forge that bond.

FOX: It's just . . .

GOULD: Don't worry.

FOX: Not me. It's just, you move up to *the big league* . . . *(Pause.)*

385 GOULD: Charlie. Your ship has come in . . .

FOX: *(pause)* . . . all I'm saying . . . *Ross* . . .

GOULD: What's Ross going to say . . . "No"? It's *done.*

FOX: Lord, I believe, aid thou my unbelief . . . the sucker walked in, said "I love the script."

390 GOULD: Oh yes, Charlie, for we're now the *Fair*-haired boys.

FOX: I couldn't believe it, you talk, talk about, talk, what is the . . . "watersheds."

GOULD: That's right.

FOX: And, that is one of them.

395 GOULD: And why *shouldn't* it be — you understand . . . ?

FOX: *I* don't know.

GOULD: 'Cause you . . .

FOX: . . . I, I don't know . . .

GOULD: . . . You *worked* for it . . . you know, you know . . .

FOX: "I'm going to be rich and I can't believe it." 400

GOULD: Rich, are you kidding me? We're going to have to hire someone just to figure out the *things* we want to buy . . .

FOX: I mean, I mean, you think about a concept, all your life . . .

GOULD: . . . I'm with you . . .

FOX: "Wealth." 405

GOULD: Yes. Wealth.

FOX: Then it comes *down* to you . . .

GOULD: Uh huh . . .

FOX: All you can think of . . . "*This* is what that means . . ."

GOULD: And that *is* what it means. *(Pause.)* 410

FOX: How, how, figuring up the rentals, tie in, foreign, air, the . . .

GOULD: Uh huh . . .

FOX: Over the course . . .

GOULD: . . . don't forget the sequels.

FOX: Do we . . . we're tied in to that . . . ? 415

GOULD: Are we tied in to that, Charl? Welcome to the world.

FOX: Hhhhh. How . . . *(Pause.)*

GOULD: The question, your crass question: how much money could we stand to make . . . ?

FOX: Yes. 420

GOULD: I think the operative concept here is "lots and lots . . ."

FOX: Oh, maan . . .

GOULD: Great big jolly *shitloads* of it.

FOX: Oh, maan . . .

GOULD: But money . . . 425

FOX: Yeah.

GOULD: Money, Charl . . .

FOX: Yeah . . .

GOULD: Money is not the important thing.

FOX: No. 430

GOULD: Money is not Gold.

FOX: No.

GOULD: What can you do with Money?

FOX: Nothing.

GOULD: Nary a goddamn thing. 435

FOX: . . . I'm gonna be rich.

GOULD: "Buy" things with it.

FOX: Where would I *keep* them?

GOULD: What would you *do* with them?

FOX: Yeah. 440

GOULD: Take them out and *dust* them, time to time.

FOX: Oh yeah.

GOULD: I piss on money.

FOX: I know that you do. I'll help you.

GOULD: *Fuck* money. 445

FOX: Fuck it. Fuck "things" too . . .

GOULD: Uh huh. But don't fuck "people."

FOX: No.

GOULD: 'Cause, people, Charlie . . .

FOX: People . . . yes. 450

GOULD: Are what it's All About.

FOX: I know.

GOULD: And it's a People Business.

FOX: That it is.

GOULD: It's *full* of fucken' people . . . 455

FOX: And we're gonna kick some ass, Bob.

GOULD: That we are.

FOX: We're gonna kick the ass of a lot of them fucken' people.

GOULD: That's right.

460 FOX: We get rolling, Bob. It's "up the ass with gun and camera."

GOULD: Yup.

FOX: 'Cause when you spend twenty years in the barrel . . .

GOULD: . . . I know . . .

FOX: No, you *don't* know, you've forgotten. Due respect.

465 GOULD: . . . may be . . .

FOX: But, but . . . oh maan . . . I'm gonna settle some fucken' scores.

GOULD: Better things to do . . .

FOX: If there are, *show* them to me, man . . . A bunch of cock-

470 suckers out there. Gimme' a cigarette. Oh, Man, I can't come down.

GOULD: No need to. Huh . . . ?

FOX: Ross, Ross, Ross isn't going to fuck me out of this . . . ?

GOULD: No. Absolutely not. You have my word.

475 FOX: I don't need your word, Bob. I know *you* . . . Drives right to my house. I need a cup of coffee.

GOULD: *(into phone)* Could we get a cup . . . well, where did you try? Why not try the *coffee mach* . . . well, it's right down at the . . . down the, no, it's unmarked, just go . . . that's right.

480 *(Hangs up.)*

FOX: What, you got a new broad, go with the new job . . .

GOULD: No. Cathy's just out sick.

FOX: Cute broad, the new broad.

GOULD: What? She's cute? The broad out there is cute? Baby,

485 she's nothing. You wait 'til we make this film.

FOX: She's nothing?

GOULD: Playing in this league? I'm saying, it's Boy's Choice: Skate in One Direction Only. *(Pause.)*

FOX: Oh, man, what am I going to *do* today?

490 GOULD: Go to a movie, get your hair done.

FOX: I'm jumping like a leaf.

GOULD: It's a done deal. We walk in *tomorrow* . . .

FOX: *(picks up the book)* What's this, what's the thing you're reading I come in?

495 GOULD: This thing?

FOX: Uh huh . . .

GOULD: From the East. An Eastern Sissy Writer. *(Passes the book to* FOX.*)*

FOX: *(reads)* "The Bridge: or, Radiation and the Half-Life of

500 Society. A Study of Decay."

GOULD: A Novel.

FOX: Great.

GOULD: A cover note from Richard Ross: "Give this a Courtesy Read."

505 FOX: *(reads)* "The wind against the Plains, but not a wind of change . . . a wind like that one which he'd been foretold, the rubbish of the world — swirling, swirling . . . two thousand years . . ." Hey I wouldn't just give it a *courtesy* read, I'd *make* this sucker.

510 GOULD: Good idea.

FOX: Drop a dime on western civilization.

GOULD: . . . 'Bout time.

FOX: Why don't you do that? *Make* it.

GOULD: I think that I will.

515 FOX: Yeah. Instead of our Doug, Doug Brown's *Buddy* film.

GOULD: Yeah. *I* could do that. You know why? Because my job, my new job is one thing: the capacity to make decisions.

FOX: I know that it is.

GOULD: Decide, decide, decide . . .

FOX: It's lonely at the top. 520

GOULD: But it ain't crowded.

(KAREN, the secretary, comes in with a tray of coffee.)

KAREN: I'm sorry, please, but how do you take your coffee . . . ?

FOX: He takes his coffee like he makes his movies: nothing in it.

GOULD: Very funny.

FOX: 'Cause he's an Old Whore. 525

GOULD: . . . that's right . . .

FOX: Bobby Gould . . .

GOULD: . . . Huh . . .

FOX: You're just an Old Whore.

GOULD: Proud of it. Yes, yes. 530

FOX: They kick you upstairs and you're still just some old whore.

GOULD: You're an old whore, too.

FOX: I never said I wasn't. Soon to be a *rich* old whore.

GOULD: That's right.

FOX: And I deserve it. 535

GOULD: That you do, Babe, that you do.

FOX: Because, Miss, lemme tell you something, I've been *loyal* to this guy, you know, you know . . . *what's* your name?

KAREN: Karen . . .

FOX: Karen, lemme tell you: since the *mail* room . . . you know? 540 Step-by-step. Yes, in his shadow, yes, why not. Never forgot him, and he never forgot me.

GOULD: That's absolutely right.

FOX: You know why I never forgot him?

KAREN: . . . I . . . 545

FOX: . . . Because the shit of his I had to eat, how *could* I forget him?

GOULD: . . . huh . . .

FOX: Yes, but the Wheel Came Around. And here we are. Two Whores. *(To* GOULD:*)* You're gonna decorate your office. 550 Make it a bordello. You'll feel more at home.

GOULD: *You,* you sonofabitch . . .

FOX: . . . and come to work in a soiled nightgown.

GOULD: Hey, after the Doug Brown thing, I come to work in that same nightgown, I say "kiss the hem," then every swing- 555 ing dick in this man's studio will kiss that hem.

FOX: They will.

GOULD: They'll *french* that jolly jolly hem.

FOX: Uh huh, uh huh . . . *you,* you, you fucken' whore, on his deathbed, St. Peter'll come for him, his dying words, "Just let 560 me turn One More Trick . . ."

GOULD: I'm a whore and I'm proud of it. But I'm a *secure* whore. Yes, and you get *ready,* now: you get ready 'cause they're going to plot, they're going to plot against you . . . *(To* KAREN:*)* Karen. My friend's stepping up in class . . . *(To* FOX:*)* 565 They're going to plot against you, Charlie, like they plotted against me. They're going to go back in their Tribal Caves and say "Chuck Fox, that *hack* . . ."

FOX: "That powerful hack . . ."

GOULD: Let's go and steal his job . . . 570

KAREN: Sir . . . ?

FOX: Black, two sugars, thank you.

GOULD: To your face they'll go, "Three bags full." And behind your back they'll say, "let's tear him down — let's tear Charlie Fox down . . ." 575

FOX: Behind my back. Yes, but in Public . . . ? They'll say: "I waxed Mr. Fox's car. He seemed pleased."

KAREN: *(serving coffee)* Black, two sugars.

FOX: "I blew his poodle. He gave me a smile." *(Of coffee:)* Thank
580 you.

GOULD: This is Charlie Fox. This is . . . *Karen* . . .

FOX: Yes. Good morning.

KAREN: Good morning, sir.

GOULD: Please put me down. Tomorrow. Richard Ross. His of-
585 fice. Ten A.M. Whatever you find in the book, call back and
cancel it. And leave a note for Cathy, should she be back . . .

KAREN: I'm told that she'll be back tomorrow.

GOULD: . . . draw her attention to our meeting with Ross.

KAREN: Yessir.

590 FOX: Karen, as Mr. Gould moves on up the ladder, will you go
with him?

KAREN: Sir?

FOX: When . . .

KAREN: I'm just a temporary . . .

595 GOULD: That's right, she's just here for a . . .

FOX: Well, would you like to stay on, if . . .

GOULD: Hey, what are you? The Master of the Revels?

KAREN: I'm just, I'm on a temporary . . .

FOX: Hey, everything's temporary 'til it's "not" . . .

600 KAREN: No, this is just a temporary job.

GOULD: It's just a temporary job — so leave the girl alone.

FOX: Karen: yeah: Karen, this seem like a good place to work?

KAREN: Sir?

FOX: Call me Charlie. This seem like a good place to work?

605 KAREN: Here?

FOX: Mr. Gould's office.

KAREN: I'm sure that it is.

FOX: She's "sure that it is." How wonderful to be so sure. How
wonderful to have such certainty in this wonderful world.
610 Hey, Bobby . . . ? Your boss tells you "take initiative," you best
guess right — and you *do*, then you get no credit. Day-in, . . .
smiling, smiling, just a cog.

GOULD: Mr. Fox is talking about his own self.

FOX: You *bet* I am. But my historical self, Bob, for I am a cog no
615 more.

GOULD: Karen, you come here at an auspicious time.

FOX: *Give* this man a witness.

GOULD: Because in this sinkhole of slime and depravity, something is about to work out.

620 FOX: . . . singing a song, rolling along.

GOULD: . . . and all that garbage that we put up with is going to
pay off. *(Pause.)*

KAREN: . . . why is it garbage . . . ? *(Pause.)*

GOULD: It's not all garbage, but most of it is.

625 KAREN: Why?

GOULD: Why. That's a good . . . *(To FOX:)* Why? *(Pause.)*

FOX: Because.

GOULD: *(to KAREN)* Because.

FOX: Life in the movie business is like the, is like the beginning
630 of a new love affair: it's full of surprises, and you're constantly
getting fucked.

KAREN: But why should it all be garbage?

FOX: Why? Why should nickels be bigger than dimes? That's the
way it is.

635 GOULD: It's a business, with its own unchanging rules. Isn't that
right, Charlie?

FOX: Yes, it is. The *one* thing is: nobody pays off on work.

GOULD: That is the truth.

FOX: Everybody says "Hey, I'm a maverick."

GOULD: That's it . . .   640

FOX: But what do they do? Sit around like, hey, Pancho-the-
dead-whale . . .

GOULD: . . . huh . . .

FOX: Waiting for the . . .

GOULD: . . . mmm . . .   645

FOX: Yeah . . . ? The Endorsement of their Superiors . . .

GOULD: Uh huh. Listen to the guy. He's telling you.

FOX: You wanna *do* something out here, it better be one of The
Five Major Food Groups.

GOULD: Uh huh.   650

FOX: Or your superiors go napsy — bye. The *upside* of which,
though, a guy . . .

GOULD: . . . that's right . . .

FOX: The *upside* . . .

GOULD: Hmm.   655

FOX: The *upside*, though . . .

GOULD: . . . Hmm.

FOX: The one time you *do* get support . . .

GOULD: . . . hey . . .

FOX: If you *do* have a relationship . . .   660

GOULD: Hey, Charl, kidding aside, that is what I'm here for . . .

FOX: Then, you can do something. *(To KAREN, of GOULD:)* This
guy, Karen, this guy . . . the last eleven years.

GOULD: *Forget* it . . .

FOX: Forget? Bullshit. This man, my friend . . .   665

GOULD: Now we're even.

FOX: Oh, you Beauty . . . what's it like being Head of Production? I mean, is it more fun than miniature golf?

GOULD: You put as much energy in your job as you put into
kissing my ass . . .   670

FOX: My job *is* kissing your ass.

GOULD: And don't you forget it.

FOX: Not a chance. *(Pause.)*

KAREN: Sir:

GOULD: Yes.   675

KAREN: *(pause)* I feel silly saying it.

GOULD: What?

KAREN: I . . .

GOULD: Well, whatever it is, say it.

KAREN: *(pause)* I don't know what to do. *(Pause.)* I don't know   680
what I'm supposed to do. *(Pause.)*

GOULD: Well, that was very frank of you. I tell you what: don't
do anything.

KAREN: Sir . . . ?

GOULD: We'll call it a Bank Holiday. *(To FOX:)* Huh? Let's get   685
out of here.

FOX: Good, let's get out of here.

GOULD: Huh?

FOX: Well done.

GOULD: And let's get out of here. *(To KAREN:)* Look in my book,   690
and *cancel* whatever I've got today. Anybody calls, call me
tomorrow. I'll be in tomorrow for my ten A.M. meeting with
Ross.

FOX: Young America at WORK and PLAY.

GOULD: You get done cancelling my stuff, you can go home.   695

FOX: Where we going for lunch?

GOULD: Well, I figured we'd drop by the commissary, get the

tuna sandwich, then go swishing by Laura Ashley and pick out some cunning prints for my new office.

700 FOX: Whyn't you just paint it with broken capillaries, decorate it like the inside of your nose.

GOULD: I may. I just may. So, lunch, the Coventry, in half an hour. (To KAREN:) Call the Coventry. Table for two, at One. Thank you. (She exits. Pause. He sighs.) First in war. First in

705 peace. First in the hearts of Pee Wee Reese.

FOX: Lunch at the Coventry.

GOULD: That's right.

FOX: Thy will be done.

GOULD: You see, all that you got to do is eat my doo doo for

710 eleven years, and eventually the wheel comes round.

FOX: Pay back time.

GOULD: You brought me the Doug Brown script.

FOX: Glad I could do it.

GOULD: You son of a *bitch* . . .

715 FOX: Hey.

GOULD: Charl, I just hope.

FOX: What?

GOULD: The shoe was on the other foot, I'd act in such a . . .

FOX: . . . hey . . .

720 GOULD: Really, princely way toward *you*.

FOX: I *know* you would, Bob, because lemme tell you: experiences like this, *films* like this . . . these are the films . . .

GOULD: . . . Yes . . .

FOX: *These* are the films, that whaddayacallit . . . (long pause)

725 that make it all worthwhile.

GOULD: . . . I think you're going to find a *lot* of things now, make it all worthwhile. I think *conservatively*, you and me, we build ourselves in to split, minimally, ten percent. (Pause.)

730 FOX: Of the net.

GOULD: Char, Charlie: permit me to tell you: two things I've learned, twenty-five years in the entertainment industry.

FOX: What?

GOULD: The two things which are always true.

735 FOX: One:

GOULD: The first one is: there is no net.

FOX: Yeah . . . ? (Pause.)

GOULD: And I forgot the second one. Okay, I'm gonna meet you at the Coventry in half an hour. We'll talk about boys and

740 clothes.

FOX: Whaddaya gonna do the interim?

GOULD: I'm gonna Work . . . (Indicating his figures on the pad.)

FOX: Work . . . ? You never did a day's work in your life.

GOULD: Oooh, Oooh, . . . the Bitching Lamp is Lit.

745 FOX: You never did a fucken' day's work in your life.

GOULD: That true?

FOX: Eleven years I've known you, you're either scheming or you're ziggin' and zaggin', hey, I *know* you, Bob.

GOULD: Oh yes, the scorn of the impotent . . .

750 FOX: I know you, Bob. I know you from the *back*. I know what you're staying for.

GOULD: You do?

FOX: Yes.

GOULD: What?

755 FOX: You're staying to Hide the Afikomen.

GOULD: Yeah?

FOX: You're staying to put those moves on your new secretary.

GOULD: I am?

FOX: Yeah, and it *will* not work.

GOULD: It will not work, what are you saying . . . ? 760

FOX: No, I was just saying that she . . .

GOULD: . . . she wouldn't go for me.

FOX: That she won't go for you.

GOULD: (pause) Why?

FOX: Why? (Pause.) I don't know. 765

GOULD: What do you see . . . ?

FOX: I think . . . I think . . . you serious?

GOULD: Yes.

FOX: I don't want to pee on your parade.

GOULD: No . . . 770

FOX: I mean, I'm sorry that I took the edge off it.

GOULD: I wasn't *going* to hit on her.

FOX: Hmmm.

GOULD: I was gonna . . .

FOX: You were gonna work. 775

GOULD: Yes.

FOX: Oh.

GOULD: (pause) But tell me what you see.

FOX: What I see, what I *saw*, just an observation . . .

GOULD: . . . yes . . . 780

FOX: It's not important.

GOULD: Tell me what you see. Really.

FOX: I just thought, I just thought she falls between two stools.

GOULD: And what would those stools be?

FOX: That she is not, just some, you know, a "floozy" . . . 785

GOULD: A "floozy" . . .

FOX: . . . on the other hand, I think I'd have to say, I don't think she is so *ambitious* she would schtup you just to get ahead. (Pause.) That's all. (Pause.)

GOULD: What if she just "liked" me? (Pause.) 790

FOX: If she just "liked" you?

GOULD: Yes.

FOX: Ummm. (Pause.)

GOULD: Yes.

FOX: You're saying, if she just . . . *liked* you . . . (Pause.) 795

GOULD: You mean nobody loves me for myself.

FOX: No.

GOULD: No?

FOX: Not in *this* office . . .

GOULD: And she's neither, what, vacant nor ambitious enough 800 to go . . .

FOX: . . . I'm not saying you don't *deserve* it, you *do* deserve it. Hey, . . . I think you're worth it.

GOULD: Thank you. You're saying that she's neither, what, dumb, nor ambitious enough, she would go to bed with me. 805

FOX: . . . she's too, she's too . . .

GOULD: She's too . . . High-line . . . ?

FOX: No, she's, she's too . . .

GOULD: She's too . . .

FOX: . . . yes. 810

GOULD: Then what's she doing in this office?

FOX: She's a *Temporary* Worker.

GOULD: You're full of it, Chuck.

FOX: Maybe. And I didn't mean to take the *shine* off our . . .

GOULD: Hey, hey, he sends the cross, he sends the strength to 815 bear it. Go to, go to lunch, I'll meet you at . . .

FOX: I didn't mean to imply . . .

GOULD: Imply. Naaa. Nobody Loves Me. Nobody loves me for myself. Hey, Big Deal, don't go mopin' on me here. We'll go and celebrate. A Douglas Brown Film. Fox and Gould . . .

FOX: . . . you're very kind . . .

GOULD: . . . you brought the guy in. Fox and Gould Present:

FOX: I'll see you at lunch . . . (*Starts to exit.*)

GOULD: But I bet she would go, I bet she *would* go out with me.

FOX: I bet she would, too.

GOULD: No, No. I'm saying, I think that she "likes" me.

FOX: Yeah. I'm sure she does.

GOULD: No, joking apart, Babe. My *perceptions* . . . Say I'm nuts, I don't *think* so — she likes me, and she'd go out with me.

FOX: How much?

GOULD: How much? Seriously . . . ? (*Pause.*)

FOX: Yeah.

GOULD: . . . that she would . . . ?

FOX: Yeah. That she would *anything*. (*Pause.*) That she would anything. (*Pause.*) That she would deal with you in any other than a professional way. (*Pause.*)

GOULD: Well, my, my, my, my, my.

FOX: What can I tell you, "*Bob.*"

GOULD: That I can get her on a date, that I can get her to my house, that I can screw her.

FOX: I don't think so.

GOULD: How much? (*Pause.*)

FOX: A hundred bucks.

GOULD: That's enough?

FOX: Five hundred bucks that you can't.

GOULD: Five hundred? That's enough?

FOX: A gentleman's bet.

GOULD: Done. Now get out of here, and let me work . . . the Coventry at One. I need . . .

FOX: The script, the budget, chain of ownership . . .

GOULD: Good.

FOX: I'll swing by my, I'll bring it to lunch.

GOULD: Good. Char . . . (*Pause.*)

FOX: What?

GOULD: Thank you.

FOX: Hey. Fuck you. (*Exits.*)

(GOULD *sits alone for a moment, writing.* KAREN *enters.*)

KAREN: Mr. Gould . . .

GOULD: Bobby.

KAREN: Sir. (*Pause.*) I was not able to get you a table at the Coventry. But I tentatively booked you at . . .

GOULD: Whoa, whoa, whoa, whoa. (*Pause.*) It's alright. I'm going to tell you what you did, and it's alright you did it. Sit down. You called up the Coventry and asked them for a table for two at one o'clock. And they told you they had absolutely nothing. That right?

KAREN: Yes. (*Pause.*) I . . . I . . . I'm so sorry. Of course. I should have mentioned your name.

GOULD: It's alright.

KAREN: It was very . . . it was *naïve* of me.

GOULD: It's alright.

KAREN: I had . . . no: you're right. I had a thought, when I was hanging up, then I thought: "You forgot to . . ."

GOULD: . . . . it's alright.

KAREN: "You forgot to 'tell' them," then I thought: "what difference does it make? If they don't have a *table* . . ."

GOULD: It's alright.

KAREN: If they didn't have a table, what difference who called up? But, of *course*, they have a table for *you* . . . I'm sorry. It was naïve of me.

GOULD: Listen, there's nothing wrong with being naïve, with learning . . .

KAREN: (*simultaneously with "learning"*) And I'm sure . . . I'm sorry.

GOULD: No, go on.

KAREN: . . . I was going to say . . .

GOULD: . . . yes . . . ?

KAREN: I was going to say that I'm sure that much of a job like this, a job like this, is learning to think in a . . .

GOULD: Yes.

KAREN: To think in a . . . business fashion.

GOULD: That's what makes the life exciting, *addictive*, you know what I'm talking about, you want a *thrill* in your life?

KAREN: . . . a thrill . . . ?

GOULD: To *make* something, to *do* something, to be a *part* of something. Money, art, a chance to Play at the Big Table . . . Hey, you're here, and you want to participate in it. (*Pause.*)

KAREN: Yes.

GOULD: Well, of course you do. And it *is* an exciting world.

KAREN: I'm sure it is.

GOULD: Sudden changes all the time. You want to *know* some of it. Now, you want to know a secret?

KAREN: Yes.

GOULD: I'll *tell* you one. Siddown. (KAREN *sits.*) Charlie Fox comes in and he's formed a relationship with Doug Brown. Doug will leave his studio and do a film with us. Charlie Fox brought it to us, brought it to *me* really. And in the Highest Traditions of the Motion Picture Industry, we're actually going to make a movie.

KAREN: Is it a good film?

GOULD: I'm sorry.

KAREN: Is it a good film?

GOULD: Well, it's a commodity. And I admire you for not being ashamed to ask the question. Yes, it's a good question, and I don't *know* if it is a good film. "What about Art?" I'm not an artist. Never said I was, and nobody who sits in this chair can be. I'm a businessman. "Can't we try to make good films?" Yes. We try. I'm going to try to make a good film of this prison film. The question: Is there such a thing as a good film which loses money? In general, of course. But, really, not. For *me*, 'cause if the films I make lose money, then I'm back on the streets with a sweet and silly smile on my face, they lost money 'cause nobody saw them, it's my fault. A tree fell in the forest, what did I accomplish? Yes. You *see*? There is a way things are. Some people are elected, try to change the world, this job is not that job. Somebody, somebody . . . in this job, in the job I have, somebody is always trying to "promote" you: to use *something*, some "hook" to get you to do something in their own best interest. You follow me?

KAREN: Of course.

GOULD: 'Cause this *desk* is a position to *advance*, y'understand? It's a *platform* to *aid*, to push someone along. But I Can't Do It, Why? That's not my business. My business is to make decisions for the studio. Means I have to be *blunt*, to say "no," much, most of the time, that's my job. And I think it's a *good* job: 'cause it's a job of *responsibility*. Pressure, many rewards.

One of them, one time in a billion years, someone was loyal to me, and I'm talking about Charlie Fox, stuck *with* me, comes in here, let's face it, does a favor for me . . . he could of took the script across the street, no, but he came to me, now — I can throw in with him and we rise together. That's what the job is. It's a job, all the bullshit aside, deals with *people. (He hunts on his desk, picks up a copy of the book he was reading from earlier.)* Look here. Agent gives his client's book to Ross: "The Bridge or, Radiation and the Half-Life of Society": Now, *who* is Mister Ross, now . . . ?

KAREN: He is the Head of the Studio.

GOULD: And he has a button on my console. That's right. Author's agent gave this book to Ross. A novel. Written by a Very Famous Eastern Writer. What's this book about? "The End of the World." Great. Now: Ross, no dummy, says, of course, he'll read the book. Gives *me* the book to read, so when he tells the author "how he loved the book but it won't make a movie," he can say something intelligent about it. You get it? This, in the business, is called "a courtesy read."

KAREN: A courtesy read.

GOULD: Yes. No one has any intention of making the book, but we read it, as a courtesy. Does this mean that we're depraved? No. It's just business . . . how business is done, you see?

KAREN: I think.

GOULD: A business. Start to close.

KAREN: But what if there is something in the book?

GOULD: In the book?

KAREN: Yes. *(Pause.)*

GOULD: It's a novel about the historical effects of radiation . . .

KAREN: Yes, but . . .

GOULD: I mean, I mean, the author's crazy as a fucken' June bug.

KAREN: But, but.

GOULD: . . . what if . . . ?

KAREN: Yes.

GOULD: What if, after everything . . .

KAREN: . . . yes . . .

GOULD: Hope against hope, there is *something* in the book.

KAREN: Yes.

GOULD: *Something* in the book, that . . .

KAREN: Yes. *(Pause.)*

GOULD: Well, I'd be delighted. No. You're right. You're right. I'll tell you. *(Pause.)* You're making my point. Absolutely. This job corrupts you. You start to think, all the time "what do these people want from me?" *(Pause.)* And everything becomes a task. *(Pause.)*

KAREN: Does it have to be that?

GOULD: Can we keep ourselves pure? Hey, I prayed to be pure.

KAREN: You prayed? To be pure?

GOULD: I did, I said God give me the job as Head of Production. Give me a platform to be "good," and I'll be good. They gave me the job, I'm here one day and *look* at me: a Big Fat Whore. A book, it may be a *fine, fine* book by a well-respected writer. And because this writer's got the reputation being "artsy" . . . artsy, you understand . . . I'm ready, everybody backs me up in this, to assume that his book is unsuitable for the screen, so I look on it as a "courtesy read."

KAREN: Do you enjoy your work?

GOULD: Excuse me?

KAREN: Do, if I'm being too frank . . .

GOULD: . . . do I enjoy my work? Yes. Very much. *(Pause.)* Don't you think *you* would enjoy it?

KAREN: Yes, I think I would enjoy it.

GOULD: You do? Good for you. What of it would you enjoy?

KAREN: The making decisions.

GOULD: Then good for you.

KAREN: Because . . .

GOULD: . . . yes . . . ?

KAREN: Perhaps I'm naïve, but I would think that if you could keep your values straight, if you had *principles* to *refer* to, then . . .

GOULD: Hmmm.

KAREN: I know it's naïve . . .

GOULD: Yes it is naïve, and it's also correct.

KAREN: You think it is?

GOULD: Yes, I do. Now, we could talk about purity or we could turn the page. What do you want to do?

KAREN: Talk about purity.

GOULD: Okay. *(Pause.)* If you don't have *principles*, whatever they are . . . then each day is hell, you haven't got a compass. All you've got is "good taste"; and you can shove good taste up your ass and fart "The Carnival of Venice." Good taste will not hack it. 'Cause each day the pressure just gets worse. It gets more difficult. *(Pause.)* I want you to do me a favor. Read that book for me.

KAREN: *I* should read it . . . ?

GOULD: Yes.

KAREN: The Radiation Book?

GOULD: Let's be frank: it's probably, it's almost definitely unsuitable, it probably *is* artsy. But as you said, maybe it isn't. *You* read it, you'll tell me, and I'll tell Mr. Ross.

KAREN: . . . I . . .

GOULD: . . . and then, you're right, and then at least we looked.

KAREN: I'd be flattered to read it.

GOULD: *Good.*

KAREN: Thank you.

GOULD: Not at all. I thank *you.* I'll need a report on it . . .

KAREN: . . . of course.

GOULD: By tonight. How long will it take you to . . .

KAREN: Well, I won't be able to start reading it 'til after work . . .

GOULD: *(simultaneously with "work")* Fine. Tonight, I'm going to be home. When you're finished, you bring the report to me and we'll discuss it.

KAREN: Absolutely. Thank you.

GOULD: Not at all. Now, I've . . . Please call the Coventry. Tell them, a table for Mr. Fox and me, twenty minutes . . .

KAREN: Yes, I will.

GOULD: I'm going to clean up here before I go. Call Mr. Fox's girl up on the phone, get her to *page* him or to try him in the car.

KAREN: Uh huh.

GOULD: . . . and tell him that I'll be ten minutes late.

KAREN: Of course . . .

GOULD: . . . and tell him he owes me five hundred bucks.

— ACT TWO —

GOULD's *apartment. Night.* GOULD *and* KAREN. KAREN *is reading from the book.*

KAREN: He puts his hand on the child's chest, and he says "heal," as if he felt he had the power to heal him, he calls on God . . . it's in here . . . something to the effect that if *ever* in his life he had the power, any power, that now is the time . . . list . . . *(She reads:)* " . . . in that lonely place, the low place, the tramp, under the bridge, he finds him. Faced with his troubles, and pours out his heart." We hear the rain, and we see, in his misery, it is forgotten, wet, cold . . . and the problems which assaulted him: *they do not disappear*, but they are

10 forgotten. He says: years later: it did not occur to him 'til then that this was happiness. That the thing which he lacked, he says, was *courage*. What does the Tramp say? "All fears are one fear. Just the fear of death. And we accept it, and then we are at peace." And so, you see, and so all of the *events* . . . the

15 *stone*, the *instrument*, the *child* which he met, *led* him there.

GOULD: They led him.

KAREN: . . . in his . . . yes, you see — I know that you see — and that's, that's to me, that's the perfection of the story, when I *read* it . . . I almost, I wanted to sit, I saw, I almost couldn't

20 come to you, the *weight* of it . . . *(Pause.)* You know what I mean. He says that the radiation . . . *all* of it, the planes, the televisions, clocks, all of it *is to the one end*. To *change us* — to, to *bring about a change* — all radiation has been sent by God. To change us. Constantly.

25 GOULD: To change us.

KAREN: Yes.

GOULD: How?

KAREN: To this new thing. And that we needn't feel frightened. That it comes from God. And I felt empowered. *(Pause.)* Em-

30 powered. *(Pause.)*

GOULD: Empowered . . .

KAREN: You've felt that, I hope you've felt that, when something made sense, you'd heard it for the longest time and finally you, you know what it means. So . . . so . . . it's not *courage*,

35 it's *greater* than courage. Perhaps it *is* courage. You've felt like that.

GOULD: I have.

KAREN: Yes.

GOULD: Felt like . . .

40 KAREN: Like they say in *stories*: where, where one thing changes you.

GOULD: . . . have I felt like that? I don't know.

KAREN: . . . and that it puts you at Peace. And I'll tell you: like books you find at an Inn, or in a bookshop, when, you know,

45 when you go in, that you'll *find* something there, something. Old, or, or scraps of *paper* . . . have you had this . . . ? In a pocket, or, or even on the ground, a phrase . . . something that *changes* you. And you were drawn to it. *Just* like the man. Beneath the bridge. "What was it that you feared?" he

50 says "*Embrace* it . . ." Well! *(Pause.)* And like my coming here. Why? A temporary job. But I thought, who can say I knew, but I thought I knew, I thought: I would find something. *(Pause.)* Too much. It all came at once. So much. May I have another drink? (GOULD *pours drink.*) Do you

55 know, and he says, the *radiation*, in all things: not just in bombs, in microwaves, in *power*, in *air* travel . . . and the *purpose* of this radiation . . . well, I've *said* it . . .

GOULD: Thank you.

KAREN: No, I thank *you*. Do you know what he's talking about?

60 Fear. A life lived in fear, and he says, It Says In The Book, it doesn't have to *be* so; that those things we have *seen* . . . *you* know, and you think "I, am I the only one on the whole planet who knows how *bad* it is . . . that it's *coming* . . . that it's sure to come." What . . . don't you see? What can I do . . . ?

65 And you *can't* join a convent, or "cut off your hair," or, or, or, you see, this is our pain, I think, we *can't* embrace Jesus. He,

you see, and he says, "I know. And you don't have to be afraid." And I realized: I haven't *breathed*. How long? In *years*. From, I don't know. From terror, perhaps ever. And

70 you say, how can you say it? Is our life so bad? No. No. But that it's ending. That our life is ending. Yes. It's true. And he says that, that these are the Dark Ages. *(Pause.)* They aren't to come, the Dark Ages — they are now. We're living them. *(Reads:)* "In the waning days . . . in the last days" . . . "Yes,"

75 he says, it's *true*, and you needn't deny it . . . and I felt such *fear*, because, of course, he's right. Then he says: "do not be afraid." The story . . . when you, when you read it, the story itself. Down below the bridge, I'll tell you: written with such love . . . *(Pause.)* Such love . . . *(Pause.)* God. A thing to be

80 thankful for. Such love.

GOULD: You've done a fantastic job.

KAREN: I have?

GOULD: Yes.

KAREN: I have? Doing what?

85 GOULD: On the book. *(Pause.)*

KAREN: I . . . ?

GOULD: In your report on the book. It means something, it means a lot, I want to tell you, if you want to "do" something out here. A *freshness*, you said a *naïveté*, but call it a "fresh-

90 ness," and a capacity to get involved . . . I think that it's fantastic. And, you know, you dream about making a connection; but I feel I've *done* it.

KAREN: You've made a connection . . .

GOULD: Yes. And you reached out to *me*.

95 KAREN: I did . . .

GOULD: You shared this thing with me.

KAREN: . . . the book . . .

GOULD: You did it. Someone does something . . . *totally* . . .

KAREN: . . . yes . . .

100 GOULD: And you say "yes" . . . "*That's* . . . that's what I've been missing."

KAREN: . . . you're saying . . .

GOULD: That's what I've been missing. I'm saying, you come *alive*, and you see everyone's been holding their *breath* in this

105 town, twenty years, forever, *I* don't know . . . and then . . .

KAREN: Yes . . .

GOULD: So rare, someone shows, shows some *enthusiasm* . . . it becomes, it becomes *simple*. You know what I mean . . .

KAREN: Yes. I do.

110 GOULD: N'I want to thank you. *(Pause.)*

KAREN: Um . . . it's nothing.

GOULD: *(simultaneously with "nothing")* It's something. No. Let, let, let, let me *help* you. That's what I want to do.

KAREN: *(pause)* I'm confused.

115 GOULD: I'm saying I *thank* you; I want to do something for you.

KAREN: No, no . . .

GOULD: And, whatever, I'm saying, if I can, that you would like to do, in, in the *Studio*, if you would like to do it, if I can help you with it, then I would like to help you.

120 KAREN: Yes. *Thank* you. *(Pause.)* I absolutely do. You *know* what I want to do.

GOULD: I . . . ?

KAREN: I want to work on the film.

GOULD: Alright. If we can. The *Prison* film . . .

125 KAREN: No. On this. *This* film. The Radiation film and I don't care. I don't care in what capacity, well, why *should* I, 'cause I don't have any skills . . . *that's* presumptuous, of *course*, in

any way I could. But I'd just like, it would be so important to me, to *be* there. To help. *(Pause.)* If you could just help me
130 with that. And, seriously, I'll get coffee, I don't care, but if you could do that for me, I would be . . . *(Pause.)*

GOULD: Hmmm.

KAREN: I've put you on the spot.

GOULD: No. Yes, a little.

135 KAREN: I'm serious. I'd do *anything* . . .

GOULD: *(pause)* Look . . . *(Pause.)* This was a "courtesy read."

KAREN: I know that, but . . .

GOULD: As I told you, the chances were, were astronomically slim that it would . . .

140 KAREN: Of course, but you said, you, you wanted to *investigate* . . .

GOULD: . . . yes . . .

KAREN: . . . "because once in a while" . . .

GOULD: . . . yes.

KAREN: And once in a while one finds a pearl . . .

145 GOULD: Yes . . .

KAREN: And *this* book . . . I'm *telling* you, when you *read* it . . .

GOULD: Karen, it's about the End of the World.

KAREN: That's what I'm *saying*. That's why it . . .

GOULD: It's about the End of the World.

150 KAREN: Uh huh, uh huh. *(Pause.)* This book . . . *(Pause.)* This book . . . *(Pause.)* But you said someone's job was to read the manuscripts. *(Pause.)*

GOULD: Someone reads the manuscripts. Yes.

KAREN: . . . that come in . . .

155 GOULD: . . . yes. *(Pause.)* We have readers.

KAREN: Now: why do the readers read them?

GOULD: *(simultaneously with "read")* I get it. I get it. Yes. As I said. Yes. Once in a while, in a great while, yes, that . . .

KAREN: Why not this? I'm telling you . . .

160 GOULD: Look: I'm going to pay you the compliment of being frank. *(Pause.)* I'm going to talk to you. *(Pause.)* Power, people who are given a slight power, tend to think, they think that they're the only one that has these ideas, pure ideas, whatever, no matter. And, listen to me. Listen. I'm going to tell
165 you. This book. Your book. On The End of the World which has meant so much to you, as I see that it has: Won't Make A Good Movie. Okay? I could tell you many things to influence you. But why? I have to respect your enthusiasm. And I *do* respect it. But this book, you want us to make, won't Get The
170 Asses In The Seats. Sounds crass? Whatever the thing just may be. My job: my job, my new job . . . is not even to "make," it is to "suggest," to "push," to champion . . . good work, I hope . . . choosing *from* Those Things Which the Public Will Come In To See. If they don't come to see it,
175 what's the point? You understand? *(Pause.)* This is what I do. You said a certain kind of courage to embrace a fact? *(Pause.)* This is the fact here.

KAREN: Why do you . . . *(Pause.)* Your job is to make movies people will come see.

180 GOULD: That's right.

KAREN: Why do you think they won't come see this one? *(Pause.)* Are you ever wrong? Do you see what I'm asking? Just because you think it is "too good" . . . I . . . I . . . I think they would come see it. *(Pause.)* I would. It's about . . . it's
185 about what we feel. *(Pause.)*

GOULD: It is?

KAREN: Yes.

GOULD: Which is . . .

KAREN: Everyone is frightened.

GOULD: Everyone is frightened.   190

KAREN: Everything is breaking down.

GOULD: It is.

KAREN: Yes.

GOULD: It is?

KAREN: Yes. It's over . . .   195

GOULD: It . . .

KAREN: I believe it is.

GOULD: . . . the . . .

KAREN: . . . things as we know them.

GOULD: Are over?   200

KAREN: Of course they are. Do you see? We don't have to *deny* it . . . The *power* that this thought will release . . . in, in, in *everyone*. Something which speaks to them . . . this book spoke to *me*. It *changed* me . . . I . . .

GOULD: Yes, but quite frankly the fact that it changed *you*, that   205
you like it, that you'd like to see it "go" is not sufficient reason for the studio to pay fifteen million dollars to put it up there.

KAREN: A sufficient reason.

GOULD: Yes.

KAREN: To make the film.   210

GOULD: Yes. *(Pause.)*

KAREN: Someone, someone makes a decision to, someone can make a decision to . . .

GOULD: Richard Ross.

KAREN: You're going to see him tomorrow, you could . . . look.   215
Look, I *read* the script. Mister Fox's script, the prison film. That's, that's just *degradation*, that's the same old . . . it's despicable, it's . . . It's degrading to the human spirit . . . it . . .

GOULD: It *what* . . . ?

KAREN: Of course; this rage . . . it's killing people, meaningless   220
. . . the sex, the titillation, violence . . . people don't want, they don't *want*, they . . . they don't want this.

GOULD: Of course they do, that's what we're in business *to* do, don't you underst . . . that's what we're in business to do. *Make the thing everyone made last year. Make that image*   225
people want to see. That *is* what they, it's more than what they want. It is what they require. And it's my job. That's my job . . . when I tell Ross about the Douglas Brown film, he's going to fall upon my neck and *kiss* me. *You* know that. *You* know that I can't make this book.   230

KAREN: I *don't* know that.

GOULD: I *told* you . . .

KAREN: You held out a hope to me, this morning . . .

GOULD: . . . I held out a hope . . .

KAREN: . . . that what I said . . .   235

GOULD: Aha! You see? That what *you* said . . . We all, as I said, everyone has feelings, *everyone* would like to "make a difference." Everyone says "I'm a maverick" but we're, *you* know that, just one part of the whole, nobody's a maverick.

KAREN: But . . .   240

GOULD: Now: what I told you was: it was a "courtesy read."

KAREN: . . . I, I don't like to be naïve . . .

GOULD: . . . I told you what the chances were . . .

KAREN: . . . I don't think it's attractive, and I don't think it's right. To be naïve. But . . .   245

GOULD: I *told* you what the deal was. Don't you understand?

KAREN: But I . . .

GOULD: But *you*. Yes. Everyone Is Trying To "Promote" Me . . .
Don't you *know* that? Don't you *care*? Don't you *care*? *Every*
250 *move I make*, do you understand? Everyone *wants* something
from me.
KAREN: *(pause)* Yes. I understand that.
GOULD: You understand that?
KAREN: Yes, I do.
255 GOULD: Well, if you understand that, then *how can you act this*
way?
KAREN: To come here . . .
GOULD: Yes.
KAREN: . . . you asked me here. *(Pause.)* I knew what the deal
260 was. I know you wanted to sleep with me. You're right, I came
anyway; you're right.
GOULD: . . . to sleep with you . . .
KAREN: Didn't you?
GOULD: No . . .
265 KAREN: Why lie? You don't have to lie.
GOULD: But you're wrong.
KAREN: But I'm *not* wrong. This is what I'm saying. Are we so
poor . . . that we can't have those simple things: we want love,
why should we deny it. Why should you? You could of asked
270 me, you *did* ask me. I know what you meant. That's why I
came.
GOULD: You came to . . . ?
KAREN: I said why not? I'm weak, too. We all need companionship, the things we want . . . I wanted them. You're right. I
275 shouldn't act as though I was naïve. I shouldn't act as though I
believed you. You're . . . but but but:
GOULD: I asked you here to sleep with me?
KAREN: Then I read the book. I, I, I've been depraved, too, I've
been frightened, I know that you're frightened. I *know* what
280 you are. You see. That's what I'm telling you.
GOULD: *I'm* frightened . . .
KAREN: I know that you are. I would have come here anyway. Is
that depraved? *I* know what it is to be bad. I've been bad, I
know what it is to be lost, I know you're lost. *I know* that . . .
285 How we are afraid . . . to "*ask*," to even "*ask*," and say in jest,
"Yes. I prayed to be pure" . . . but it was not an accident. That
I came here. Sometimes it reaches for us. And we say "show
me a sign." And when it reaches us, then we see we *are* the
sign. And we find the answers. In the book . . .
290 GOULD: Why did you say you would come here anyway . . .
KAREN: . . . listen to me: The Tramp said "Radiation." Well,
whatever it had been, it makes no difference . . . Listen *(she*
reads) "What was coming was a return to the self, which is to
say, a return to God. It was round. He saw all things were
295 round. And the man saw that it all had been devoted to one
end. That the diseases in the body were the same diseases in the
world. That things were ending. *Yes*. That things *must* end.
And that vouchsafed to him a vision of infinity . . ." You see?
GOULD: No.
300 KAREN: No?
GOULD: No, I don't understand.
KAREN: You don't understand.
GOULD: No.
KAREN: Would you like to understand? *(Pause.)* The things
305 you've hoped for. The reason you asked me here.
GOULD: I don't understand you.
KAREN: You wanted something—you were frightened.

GOULD: I was frightened?
KAREN: That forced you to lie. I forgive you.
GOULD: . . . you forgive me . . . ?   310
KAREN: You know how I can? Because we're just the same. You
said you prayed to be pure.
GOULD: I said that . . .
KAREN: This morning.
GOULD: I was joking.   315
KAREN: I looked in your heart. I saw you. And people can need
each other. That's what the book says. You understand? We
needn't be afraid.
GOULD: I don't understand.
KAREN: You can if you wish to. In the world. Dying. We prayed   320
for a sign. A temporary girl. You asked read the book. I read
the book. Do you know what it says? It says that you were put
here to make stories people need to see. To make them less
afraid. It says in *spite* of our transgressions—that we could do
something. Which would bring us alive. So that we needn't   325
feel ashamed. *(Pause.)* We needn't feel frightened. The wild
animal dies with pride. He didn't make the world. God made
the world. You say that you prayed to be pure. What if your
prayers were answered? You asked me to come. Here I am.

— ACT THREE —

GOULD's *office. The next morning.* GOULD *is sitting behind his
desk.* FOX *enters.*

FOX: Okay. The one, the one, the one thing, I was up all night;
I'm sorry, I should be better at these things, I don't know how
to say it, you know how you do? You stand and think, you
think, and, the only thing, one hand you say: "Am I worthy to
be rich?" The other hand, you, you know, you feel *greedy*; so   5
it's hard to know what's rightfully yours . . . Bob: when we
said, when we said: *yesterday*: we were talking, when you said
"producer"; what we *meant*, what we were talking about was,
I understand it, that we were to "share" above-the-title, we
would co-produce, because . . . that's right, isn't it? And the 10
other thing; I'm sure you thought of this; to *say* to Ross, to,
that we, as a team, you and I, this is only the *beginning*, for, if
we brought *this* (I'm sure you thought of this) it's fairly limitless, we can bring *more* . . . those two things, only, what I
wanted to say to you . . .   15
GOULD: I'm not going to do the film.
FOX: Which film?
GOULD: The Douglas Brown film.
FOX: . . . you're not . . .
GOULD: I'm not going to greenlight the Doug Brown prison   20
film.
FOX: I don't blame you. It's a piece of shit. I were you, I'd do the
film on Radiation. That's the project I would do. "A Story of
Love, a Story of Hope." That's what I would do; and then
spend the rest of my life in a packing crate. I can't get over   25
those guys. Why do they waste our time? A talky piece of
puke. Prestige and all, *okay*, but why, we should just say, "Sir,
Sir, *you* go to the movies . . . if *you* saw a movie of this shit,
would you sit through it?" Eastern Office sent the coverage to
me—listen to this . . . *(He hunts through his papers. Reads.)*   30

"The Bridge; or, Radiation, Half-Life and Decay of Society,"
the Blah Blah . . . set in novel form, The Growth of Radiation, as . . . "What is this? the device of *God*, in all things, to
prepare the world for its final decay." Yeah. It's a *Summer*
35 picture. (*Pause. Reads again.*) "The author seems to think
that radio and television, aircraft travel and microwaves were
invented solely to irradiate the world and so bring about genetic change in humankind." Great. And Scene Two, he
comes out of the bar to find that his horse is gone and he has
40 to go steal the sheriff's nag to ride for help. I'm sorry. I need a
drink. Ten o'clock in the morning and I need a drink. You
know, you look forward to something and you think it's never
going to happen—and you *really* think, bullshit aside, it's
never going to happen, and I've got to say, it's *over*, now, yeah,
45 *yeah*, I felt a certain amount of *jealousy*, toward you, here we
started out together, and I always said, someday I'll, you
know, I'll get something for myself, and it'll be a Brand New
Ballgame. I'll sit up there *with* Bobby Gould . . . *over* him . . .
you know how we think. Deep inside, I never thought I
50 would. (*Pause.*) And the *other* thing, talk about envy, is, a
certain extent, I was riding, several years, on your *coattails* . . .
don't say "no," I know I was, and I want to thank you, that you
were *man* enough, that you were *friend* enough, you never
brought it *up*, you never rubbed it in. And I'm *glad* I can pay
55 it back. Speaking of paying it back. Do I owe you, for sure, the
five c? Fess up. (*Pause.*)
GOULD: Five c?
FOX: The broad come to your house?
GOULD: The broad?
60 FOX: You fuck the temporary girl? You fuck her. (*Pause.*)
GOULD: I'm going to go see Ross myself.
FOX: You're going to see him yourself. (*Pause.*) Without me,
you're saying. (*Pause.*) Do you think that . . . (*Pause.*) Do you
think that that's the . . . I mean . . . it was . . . if you think that
65 that's the thing, then that's it. If you think that that's the thing,
but, we should, we should, I think we should *talk* about it
Bob. Don't you . . . (*Pause.*) It was, um, um, uh (*Pause.*) I
brought you the picture, Bob.
GOULD: I know you did.
70 FOX: You see what . . . (*Pause.*) I, I, *I* think that we should go in
there together. (*Pause.*) Babe. If this is truly a collaborative
thing. (*Pause.*) But if you think that . . .
GOULD: I'm not going to take him the Prison Film.
FOX: . . . if you think that that's the . . .
75 GOULD: . . . are you listening to me? I'm not going to greenlight
the pris . . .
FOX: . . . sure, sure, sure . . . I understand that, but listen to
what I'm asking you. Since I "brought" . . . which, I was
saying, since, since I *brought* you the film and since, you say,
80 we're going to split the credit. Because, because what I was
saying, Bob, to to, finally get a position where I can be *equal*;
where *I* brought *you* the film, it means a lot to me, and,
frankly, um, um, I think . . .
GOULD: I'm not going to recommend the prison picture.
85 FOX: Okay. (*Pause.*) Is there . . . you're not . . .
GOULD: No. (*Pause.*)
FOX: I don't understand.
GOULD: I'm not going to recommend the Doug Brown film.
(*Pause.*)
90 FOX: Because . . . hold on a second . . . hold on a second, before

we get to that. You told me yesterday that we were going to go
to Ross to greenlight it.
GOULD: Yes.
FOX: You promised me.
GOULD: I know.   95
FOX: I know that you know. Do you know *why* . . . ? Because you
did it.
GOULD: I know that I did.
FOX: You're joking, right?
GOULD: No. (*Pause.*)   100
FOX: Huh. (*Pause.*) Because, um, you know, I had the package,
Doug gave me one day, Doug Brown gave me the one day to
have the package, I could have, I could have *took* the thing
across the street, you know that? Walked right across the
street, As People Do In This Town, and I'd done it *yesterday*,   105
I'd been Executive Producer of a Doug *Brown* film. *Yesterday.*
Yesterday. Which is what comes up when you tell me that
you aren't going to . . . This is a joke. Right? I'm sorry . . . *I'm*
sorry. Bob: When you take the film to Ross . . .
GOULD: I'm not going to take the film to Ross.   110
FOX: (*pause*) Can you tell me why you're not?
GOULD: I'm going to greenlight the book.
FOX: What book?
GOULD: The Radiation book.
FOX: No, you aren't.   115
GOULD: Yes. If I can I am.
FOX: I have to siddown. (*Pause.*) Hold on a second, Bob, you're
seeing Ross when . . . ?
GOULD: Twenty minutes.
FOX: I'm not upset with you. (*Pause.*) Alright. (*Pause.*) Bob   120
(*pause*) Now, listen to me: when you walk in his door, Bob,
what you're paid to do . . . now, listen to me now: is make
films that make money—you are paid to *make films people
like*. And so gain for yourself a *fortune* every day. This is what
Ross *pays* us for. This is the thing he and the stockholders   125
want from us. This is what the, listen to me now, 'cause I'm
going to "say" it, Movie Going Public wants from us, excuse
me, I'm talking to you like some Eastern Fruit, but *this*, what
I've just told you, is your job. You *cannot* make the radiation
book.   130
GOULD: I'm going to try.
FOX: Shut up, I'm not done speaking, when it's your turn you
can speak—because Ross will not do it and he will not *let* you
do it.
GOULD: I have it in my contract. I can greenlight one picture a   135
year under ten mil, at my discretion, without his prior approval or consent.
FOX: You will find your contract's shit.
GOULD: I don't think so.
FOX: Think so or not, you will find it's a *sucker* clause. You will 140
find that if you insist on it you're going to become a
laughingstock, and no one will *hire* you. Bob . . . You'll be
"off the Sports List." *Why?* Because they will not understand
why you did what you did. You follow me . . . ? That is the
worst pariah. Your best *friend* won't hire you. *I* won't hire   145
you. Because I won't understand why you did the thing that
you did, and tried to make a movie that no one will watch.
Are you *insane?* What the fuck's *wrong* with you . . . ? Have
you read this book?
GOULD: Have you?   150

FOX: I read the coverage. What do you want from me? Blood? List . . . list . . . listen to this . . . (FOX *hunts on the desk for the book, opens it, reads:*) "'. . . the world is dying,' he said, 'there is nothing we can do for that,' as he stood on the bridge. 'It all

155 proliferates. Faster and faster. It begets itself, until it's time to die. The economy will collapse. The reactors *will* explode, because that's what they're meant to do. We will die, because that's what *we're* meant to do. The radiation, which has grown over the years, faster and faster.'" (*He puts the book

160 down.*)

GOULD: We have different ideas, Charlie.

FOX: We do? Since when . . . ?

GOULD: (*simultaneously with "when"*) I was up all night thinking.

165 FOX: Were you?

GOULD: Yes.

FOX: Thinking about what?

GOULD: The . . .

FOX: Yes? (*Pause.*)

170 GOULD: The . . . why I was called to my new job.

FOX: Why you, uh huh . . .

GOULD: The notion, yes the notion that our life is *short* . . . The . . . that, in some way . . .

FOX: Go on.

175 GOULD: I . . . I believe in the ideas that are contained in the book.

FOX: Hey, I believe in the Yellow Pages, Bob, but I don't want to *film* it. Bobby. Bobby. Why are you doing this? Why are you doing this to me?

GOULD: You, *you* can take the prison film to Ross.

180 FOX: I take Ross the film, he'll make the film, and he'll give me a "thank you." You know that. I need *you*. I need your *protection* . . .

GOULD: I . . .

FOX: You're going toidy over my whole life.

185 GOULD: I . . .

FOX: Have, Bob, have you always hated me?

GOULD: No.

FOX: Some secret . . .

GOULD: No.

190 FOX: Doubted my loyalty, my . . .

GOULD: No.

FOX: Then, then why are you doing this?

GOULD: I think . . .

FOX: I'm listening to you.

195 GOULD: . . . that we have few chances . . .

FOX: I'm listening to you.

GOULD: To do something which is right.

FOX: To do something which is right? To someth . . . ?

GOULD: I want to read you something. (*Hunts in book. Reads:*)

200 "'Is it true,' she asked, 'that we are always in the same state of growth, the same state of decay as the world in which we live? If it is true is it not true that the world is then a dream, and delusion?' All this being true, then what remained to him was this: Nothing." (*Pause.*) "Nothing but God." (*Pause.*) I've

205 wasted my life, Charlie. My life is a sham, it's true. But I think I found something.

FOX: Bob, what's happened to you . . . ?

GOULD: . . . And I think your prison movie has a place . . . and I respect your . . .

210 FOX: I don't want your respect. Your respect *stinks*: You know

why? You've proved yourself insane. You're gonna buy a piece of shit . . . you're gonna spend ten million dollars for a piece of *pussy*, you were "up all night . . ." You were up all night boffing the *broad*. Are you getting *old*? What is this? *Meno-*

215 *pause*? Your "life is a sham"? Two days in the new job, you can't stand the strain . . . ? They're going to invalid you out, your name will be a *punchline* in this town . . .

GOULD: . . . if the film doesn't *work* out here . . .

FOX: If the film . . .

220 GOULD: The radiation film.

FOX: Did you miss your *wake* up call . . . ? If the film doesn't work out here, you know what you got? Little Lambsy Divey. No One Will Touch You, do you understand . . . ? You're throwing your life away. (*Pause.*) Listen to me: Bob (*pause*):

225 Bob (*pause*): I have to tell you something . . . It's the secretary. She, what did she do to you . . . ?

GOULD: She did nothing to me.

FOX: What is she, a witch?

GOULD: She did nothing, we, we talked . . .

230 FOX: You talked and you decided to throw your career away . . . ? And my, and my, and *my* chances with it . . .

GOULD: . . . I don't want . . .

FOX: *Bullshit* what you want. *Bullshit*. I Could Of Gone Across the Street.

235 GOULD: . . . I don't . . .

FOX: *Fuck* you . . . *Fuck* you (*He hits* GOULD.) *Fuck* you. Get up. (*He hits him again.*) I'll fucken' kill you right here in this office. All this bullshit; you *wimp*, you *coward* . . . now you got the job, and now you're going to *run* all over everything,

240 like something broke in the *shopping* bag, you *fool*—your fucken' sissy film—you squat to pee. You old *woman* . . . all of my life I've been eating your shit and taking your leavings . . . *Fuck* you, the Head of Production. Job I could of done ten *times* better'n you, the *press*, the *money*, all this time, and

245 now you're going to be some fucken' *wimp*, cost me my, my, my . . . *fortune*? Not In This Life, Pal. Your Writ Has Run. You hear me . . . ? (*Pause.*) Bob . . . ? (*Pause.*) Do you hear me . . . ? You want somebody to take charge? I'll take charge. Do you hear me, mister . . . ? You need an excuse to cop out,

250 I'll give you your fucken' excuse. (*Pause.*) We have a meeting. Can you fix yourself up?

GOULD: No. (*Pause.*)

FOX: What's the matter?

GOULD: Nothing.

255 FOX: You have another shirt . . . ? Can you get through the meeting with Ross?

GOULD: I'm going to greenlight the radiation book.

FOX: It's alright, Bob. It's okay. I see it now. It's okay. Everything is okay. Listen to me, it's alright. I'll explain it to you: a beauti-

260 ful, a beautiful and an ambitious woman comes to . . .

GOULD: I want you to be careful what you say about her.

FOX: It's only words, unless they're true. It's alright, now. I'm sorry I got frightened. Forgive me. I'll explain it to you. (*Pause.*) A beautiful and an ambitious woman comes to town.

265 Why? Why does *anyone* come here . . . ? You follow my argument? (*Pause.*) Everyone wants power. How do we get it? Work. How do they get it? Sex. The End. She's different? Nobody's different. *You* aren't, *I'm* not, why should she? The broad wants power. How do I *know*? Look: She's out with

270 Albert Schweitzer working in the jungle? No: she's here in

movieland, Bob, and she trades the one thing that she's got, her *looks*, get into a position of authority—through you. Nobody likes to be promoted; it's ugly to see, but that's what happened, babe. I'm sorry. She lured *you* in. "Come up to my house, read this script . . ." She doesn't know what that *means*? Bob: that's why she's here.

GOULD: . . . A woman . . .

FOX: . . . Hey, pay me the courtesy . . . how *lonely* you must be. How hard the world is. You complain to her. "No one understands me . . ." "*I* understand you" . . . she says.

GOULD: She *does* understand me.

FOX: Hey, that's *first-rate*.

GOULD: She *does* understand me . . . she knows what I suffer.

FOX: "What You Suffer . . ."? "What you suffer . . ."? You're a *whore* . . . Bob. You're a *chippy* . . . you're a fucken' bought-and-paid-for *whore*, and you think you're a ballerina cause you work with your legs? You're a whore. You want some sympathy? You don't get none. You—you think you can let down. You *cannot* let down. That's what they pay the big bucks for. This is what you put up with you wanna have two homes. Okay? Bob, let's speak frankly, eh? This broad *just took you down.*

GOULD: . . . she came to me.

FOX: Why did she come to you? Cause you're the Baal Shem Tov? You stupid shit, I'm talking to you . . . Why does she come to you? 'Cause you're so good looking? She *wants* something from you. You're nothing to her but what you can *do* for her.

GOULD: You're full of shit.

FOX: Uh huh. I know I am.

GOULD: What does she want from me?

FOX: If I'm so smart? She wants you to greenlight this radiation book.

GOULD: Why?

FOX: The fuck should *I* know. *I* don't know. It's not important. Is she Head of Production? *You're* Head of Production. Read the new plaque on your door. Can she greenlight a film? No. *You* can. Now: what does she want from you? Hearth and Home? No. What? Love? Huh? Children? . . . To greenlight a film. To greenlight some bizarre idea . . .

GOULD: It's not a bizarre idea.

FOX: It's not a bizarre idea . . . ? *Tell* it to me . . . Come on. You can't tell it to me in one sentence, they can't put it in T.V. Guide. What is this movie that you're going to make? Come on, "A Boy Joins the Cattle Drive and Learns to Be a Man . . ."? "A Couple Finds a Million Dollars Buried in Their Yard . . ."? Come on, come on . . . what is this movie . . . ? *(Pause.)*

GOULD: We are . . .

FOX: Tell me the story.

GOULD: We . . . I'm *telling* it to you, and I don't think that we have to mock the possibility that someone could find something that meant something to them. You understand me?

FOX: Tell me the film, Bob.

GOULD: We . . . I'll *tell* you the film. Alright? We are frightened . . . *(Pause.)* Because the World is Ending. Uh . . . *(Pause.)* A man gives up everything . . . wait. *(Pause.)* A man, to find happiness . . . *(Pause.)*

FOX: *(picks up the book, reads)* "A gross infection rampant in the world, they spied, and thought they were the messengers of cure, when they were the disease" . . . *(Turns page and reads again:)* "That silver is more powerful than gold; and the circle than the square or the triangle. He thought of architecture . . ." *(He throws the book down.)* Are you kidding me . . . ? *(Pause.)* Are you kidding me . . . ? I wouldn't believe this shit if it was *true* . . . the fuck *happened* to you? Let your dick run your *office*? What kind of a man . . .

GOULD: Okay, Okay. That's enough.

FOX: I beg your pardon.

GOULD: I said that's enough. Get out.

FOX: Fuck you.

GOULD: Fuck me. Fuck me in *hell*. Fuck me in hell, pal. *You* read the plaque on my door. I am your superior. Now, I've made my decision. I'm sorry it hurt you.

FOX: It hurt me? You ruined my life.

GOULD: Be that as it may.

FOX: I see.

GOULD: Now, I have a meeting.

FOX: Would you tell me why?

GOULD: I told you why. Because I've found something that's right.

FOX: I can't buy that.

GOULD: Then "why" is because I say so.

FOX: And eleven years down the drain.

GOULD: I'm sorry. *(Pause.)*

FOX: How sorry are you?

GOULD: What?

FOX: One question . . .

GOULD: It won't change my mind.

FOX: Well then, just say it's a boon, and grant it to me to assuage your guilt. I want to ask your girl one question. Then I swear I'll go.

GOULD: Alright—ask it.

FOX: *(pushes the intercom button; into intercom)* Dear, could you come in here for one moment, please . . . ?

(KAREN enters.)

KAREN: *(to GOULD)* What *happened* to you?

FOX: Where's *Cathy* . . . ?

KAREN: What happened to you, Bob . . . are you alr . . .

FOX: Where's Cathy, honey? She still sick . . . ?

GOULD: It's alright, Karen.

FOX: I have one question for you, and then I'll leave you alone. I understand . . .

KAREN: I have to . . . *(Starts to exit.)*

FOX: No, no, no, no, no . . . No, no. It's alright. You alright, Bob?

GOULD: Yes.

FOX: Are you, really, though, *tell* us, now . . .

GOULD: I'm fine. We'll be done here in one minute.

KAREN: What's going on?

GOULD: Just answer him.

FOX: I understand. Karen. I *understand* . . . that things have been *occurring* . . . large decisions . . . do you follow me . . . ? *(Pause.)* Do you follow what I'm going to say?

KAREN: What do you want?

FOX: Well, Dear, I want to ask you something. *(Pause.)*

KAREN: Alright.

FOX: You went to Mister Gould's last night? *(Pause.)*

KAREN: Yes.

FOX: You discussed certain things?

KAREN: Yes. We did.

FOX: You talked about . . . his new job, you . . .

390 KAREN: You know what we talked about. We *talked* about . . . we talked about not being frightened. We talked about the ability to make a difference.

FOX: To make a difference. Yes.

KAREN: To make a film . . .

395 FOX: To make a film that makes a difference. Yes, I know. Now: listen: I'm not going to talk to you of what gives you the "insight" to, or the experience to know what will make a good film. (*Pause.*) I'm not going to ask you, I'm not going to ask you what, what brought you to this job . . .

400 KAREN: . . . it was a temporary job . . .

FOX: Uh huh . . . I'm almost there, bear with me. Now: I understand, last night, that you and Bob became intimate.

KAREN: I think you should leave.

FOX: I know you do, but this is something more than your life,

405 honey, you're at the Big Table, and, I'm done, then *Bob*, the Head of Production, is going to say what's what. I have one question. Now, then, you and Bob, you became "Lovers."

GOULD: Leave her alone.

FOX: I don't think so. Do you owe me this? Do you *owe* me this?

410 For all the years I spent with you? You became *lovers*. (*Pause.*)

KAREN: Bob? No? Alright. Then, yes. We did.

FOX: You talked of love.

KAREN: Is that . . .

FOX: Did . . . ?

415 KAREN: Is that so impossible . . . ?

FOX: It's not impossible. No. Not at all. You were drawn to him. You were drawn to a man. It's not impossible, I think that we would say it happens all the time; you "said" things to each other. (*Pause.*) Things occurred. And this is serious. Forgive

420 me if my words seem to belie that, but I'm doing all I can, 'cause I love this guy, too. My *question*: you answer me frankly, as I know you will: you came to his house with the preconception, you wanted him to greenlight the book. (*Pause.*)

425 KAREN: Yes.

FOX: If he had said "No," would you have gone to bed with him?

KAREN: (*pause*) I don't think that I'll answer you.

FOX: No?

KAREN: I don't think you have the right to ask it. Bob . . .

430 GOULD: *I* would like to know the answer.

KAREN: You would.

GOULD: Yes. I would. (*Pause.*)

KAREN: Bob. Bob: the man I could respect . . .

GOULD: Without the bullshit. Just tell me. You're living in a

435 World of Truth. Would you of gone to bed with me, I didn't do your book. (*Pause.*)

KAREN: No. (*Pause.*) No.

GOULD: Oh, God, now I'm lost.

FOX: Bob . . .

440 GOULD: Please be quiet for one moment.

KAREN: Bob. Bob, we have the opportunity . . .

FOX: "We"? "We" . . . ? I know who *he* is, who are *you*? Some broad from the Temporary Pool. A Tight Pussy wrapped around Ambition. That's who *you* are, Pal. Now you listen to

445 me, Bob . . .

GOULD: Charlie. Please . . .

KAREN: We talked last night, Bob . . .

GOULD: You told me to Be a Man . . .

FOX: "Be a Man"? "Be a Man"? What right do you have? You

know what this man has *done* . . . ? (*Phone rings*, FOX *picks it* 450 *up. Into phone:*) Yes. One moment. Please . . . (*Hangs up.*)

GOULD: Oh, God. I don't know what to do.

FOX: You know the right thing to do.

KAREN: Bob, Bob. You reached out to me . . .

FOX: He reached out to you? He fucked you on a bet. 455

KAREN: I don't care.

FOX: You don't "care"?

KAREN: Bob, perfect love . . .

GOULD: Yes. Alright. Alright. Alright. Alright. Perfect Love. Alright. Just *stop* for a moment, will you? Will you? Will you 460 just fucken' stop taking a *piece* of me for a moment. *Everyone*. Just *stop*. I need one moment, please.

KAREN: Bob, we decided last *night*.

GOULD: Yes. I'm *lost*, do you hear me, I'm *lost*. I have to think, I . . . 465

KAREN: We decided last night.

GOULD: We what?

KAREN: We decided last night.

FOX: Bob: I need you.

GOULD: I have to think. 470

FOX: I need you to remember me.

GOULD: I have to stop. I have to *think* now.

KAREN: Bob . . .

GOULD: . . . No.

KAREN: Bob, we have a meeting. (*Pause.*) 475

FOX: I rest my case. (*Pause.*)

KAREN: Did I say something wrong . . . ?

FOX: No. We have a meeting, that's true. Thank you, honey.

KAREN: Did I say something wrong . . . ?

FOX: Not at all. (*Picks up phone. Dials.*) Yes. Charlie Fox. Call- 480 ing for Bob Gould. Mr. Gould and I have a . . . Yes. Mr. Ross is back from . . . ? Fine. Would you tell him we'll be just two, three minutes late? Thank you. (*Hangs up.*)

GOULD: I have to change my shirt.

KAREN: I don't understand. 485

GOULD: We're rather busy now. You'll excuse me. Mr. Fox will show you out.

KAREN: No. No. Listen to me. One moment. One moment, Bob. Wait, Bob. The things we said last night. You called for help. Bob, you remember? Listen to me. (*She picks up the* 490 *book and starts to read:*) "One bell was 'showers about us': two bells was 'showers across the Lake'; three bells was 'showers across the Ocean'; and four bells was 'showers across the World.' And he wondered how they had obtained that conces- sion to rehearse the bells for the benefit of this instruction." 495 No, that's the wrong bit. That's not the part . . . (GOULD *exits to the washroom. She looks up.*) Bob . . . ?

FOX: That was a close one. Don't you think?

KAREN: I think I'm being punished for my wickedness.

FOX: Yeah, I do, too. You got a lot of nerve, Babe. And I'll tell 500 you something else, that's why you're *stupid*, is you made your move on something wasn't *ever* going to make a movie. Cause the people wouldn't come. (*He picks up the book, reads:*) "The Earth burned. But the last man had a vision . . ."

KAREN: I don't belong here. 505

FOX: Well, I can help you out on that. You ever come on the lot again, I'm going to have you killed. Goodbye. See you at the A and P.

KAREN: Goodbye.

510 FOX: I heard you. *(Pause.)*

KAREN: What did I say . . . ?

FOX: . . . Uh huh . . .

KAREN: I don't understand.

FOX: I'll send you the coverage. *(Pause.)* Goodbye. You've said

515 your piece. Now go away. *(Pause.)*

KAREN: I hope . . .

FOX: We *all* hope. It's what keeps us alive. *(Pause. KAREN exits. He picks up the book, throws it out after her.)* And take this with you. *(To himself:)* How are things made round . . .

520 *(GOULD reenters, tucking in his clean shirt. Pause. GOULD looks at FOX.)* Well, Bob, you're human. You think I don't know? I know. We wish people would like us, huh? To Share Our Burdens. But it's not to be.

GOULD: . . . I suppose not.

525 FOX: You're goddamn right, not. And what *if* this fucken' "grace" exists? It's not for you. You know that, Bob. You know that. You have a different thing.

GOULD: She told me I was a good man.

FOX: How would *she* know? You *are* a good man. Fuck *her.*

GOULD: I only wanted . . . 530

FOX: I know what you wanted, Bob.

GOULD: I only wanted . . .

FOX: I know what you wanted, Bob. You wanted to do good.

GOULD: Yes. *(Pause.)* Thank you.

FOX: Hey, what'd you want me to say, Bob, you "Owe" me . . . ? 535 *(Phone rings, FOX answers it. Into phone:)* We're coming . . . *(Hangs up.)* Because we joke about it, Bob, we joke about it, but it *is* a "People Business," what else is there . . . ?

GOULD: I wanted to do Good . . . But I became foolish.

FOX: Well, so we learn a lesson. But we aren't here to "pine," 540 Bob, we aren't put here to *mope.* What are we here to do *(pause)* Bob? After everything is said and done. What are we put on earth to do?

GOULD: We're here to make a movie.

FOX: Whose name goes above the title? 545

GOULD: Fox and Gould.

FOX: Then how bad can life be?

WENDELL V. HARRIS IS A prominent scholar of literary and philosophical traditions and is the author of Interpretive Acts: In Search of Meaning *(1990). "Canonicity" carefully describes both the history of our ideas of literary canons and many of the uses that canons can have. As Harris argues, there is never a single canon, but a multiplicity of canons vying for our attention, canons which are distinguished largely by the different interpretive values and practices that produce them.*

WENDELL V. HARRIS

"Canonicity"

(1991)

The canonical facts about the canons of English and American literature are, first, that there are no canons and never have been; second, that there have necessarily always been canons; and third, that canons are made up of readings, not of disembodied texts. What is contradictory in that statement results from play on different connotations of the word *canon* — a critical strategy that is constantly, though often more subtly, in use. As with many another critical term, the first step in understanding *canon* is to unpack its meanings. The "canon question" then proves much more complex than contemporary ideological criticism admits.

The well-known core meaning of the Greek *kanon* is "rule" or "measure" and, by extrapolation, "correct" or "authoritative." As Rudolph Pfeiffer has pointed out, the first application of the word to selections of authors — by David Ruhnken in 1768 — was catachrestic (207). A more nearly precise word than *selection* was so much needed that *canon* quickly became almost indispensable, despite its entanglement with concepts of authority and rule not necessarily relevant to literary canons. Not surprisingly, the normative sense of the term has clung alongside its elective sense: selections suggest norms, and norms suggest an appeal to some sort of authority. However, the criteria for selecting literary texts are derived not from authority but from chosen functions.

The Inappropriateness of the Biblical Parallel

 The normative sense of *canon* has been strongly reinforced by the application of the term to the accepted books of the Bible, though there is no agreement on the original force of the word even in this application.[1] The processes by which specific collections of Jewish and Christian writings became closed canons in the first century B.C. and the fourth century A.D., respectively, are not only too complicated for useful summary here but, more important, largely irrelevant to the question of the literary canon. In fact, considerable confusion has resulted from the seductive apparent parallel between the creation and closing of the biblical canons and the formation of lists of literary works that, since Ruhnken, have been called "canons." Chapter 14 of Ernst Robert Curtius's *European Literature and the Latin Middle Ages*, a chapter frequently cited in discussions of literary canons, considers early catalogs of authors, aspects of the ever-renewed conflict between ancients and moderns, canon formation in the church, the medieval canon, and finally modern canons. The section on the church and the Bible seems to have encouraged Curtius to use *canon* for the authorized literary lists, whose variations from period to period and country to country he learnedly surveys. But the section on modern canon formation essentially considers the relations among the works that Italy, France, Germany, and Spain defined as "classical" — an issue that, for Curtius, depends not on degrees of authoritative sponsorship but largely on the degree of romanticism in the literature of each country. It has not been sufficiently noted that this chapter is titled "Classicism," not "The Canon," and that it primarily concerns the question of how works somehow come to be regarded as "classic."

 Though there have been many lists of approved authors through the centuries and across Europe, they have differed widely; not even Aristotle has been canonical in the sense of the biblical texts. This is not to deny that there were traditions — usefully traced by Bruce Kimball — in which authors were regarded as "standard" because they seemed to inculcate the right moral and intellectual principles or to demonstrate a mastery of accurate thinking.[2] But the catalogs identifying especially valuable works not only varied considerably, they did not fence others out. The texts that one ought to have read differed from others in degree; they were not absolutely distinct like the biblical books, which very quickly came to be regarded as different in kind. Obviously the very entelechy of the process of biblical canonizing was toward closure, whereas literary canons have always implicitly allowed for at least the possibility of adding new or revalued works.

Though the sense of "unquestionably and uniquely authoritative" that belongs to the biblical canon (and to the theologically derived endorsements and prohibitions churches enforce on members of their faith) continually colors the debate over the modern literary canon, the analogy is more dramatic than helpful. Frank Kermode, whose essay on the subject has become an almost obligatory citation, is among those who use the biblical canon as a model: "The desire to have a canon, more or less unchanging, and to protect it against the charges of inauthenticity or low value (as the Church protected Hebrews, for example, against Luther) is an aspect of the necessary conservatism of a learned institution" (77). The point is unarguable, but despite the assumption in "the profession of English" that some texts are better and some interpretations more reasonable than others, admission into the profession hardly requires the candidate to accept any list of texts as uniquely necessary to the academic equivalent of salvation.[3] The most conservative of our colleagues do not demand that a candidate take, say, Johnson, Coleridge, Arnold, and Eliot as "articles of faith" and abjure Wharton, Dallas, Gosse, and Fish. Nor have universities wielded full authority over the canon since they separated themselves from the medieval church. Until then, of course, the following excerpt from a bishop's condemnation of heresy in the records of the University of Paris was not untypical:

> Let the body of master Amaury be removed from the cemetery and cast into unconsecrated ground, and the same be excommunicated by all the churches of the entire province. . . . The writings of David of Dinant are to be brought to the bishop of Paris before the Nativity and burned.
> Neither the books of Aristotle on natural philosophy nor their commentaries are to be read at Paris in public or secret, and this we forbid under penalty of excommunication. He in whose possession the writings of David of Dinant are found after Nativity shall be considered a heretic.
> (Thorndike 26–27)

The most cogent portion of Kermode's essay is his suggestion that certain texts somehow become "licensed" for exegesis and are thereafter subject to "interminable" explication (83). What Kermode so aptly describes, however, is canon formation not through a work's acceptance into a severely limited set of authoritative texts but through its introduction into an ongoing critical colloquy. The analogy with a colloquy or conversation functions in several ways. In a given time and place there are events and topics that everyone presumably knows about. Some of these have been of continuous interest, or at least have had a place in a society's cultural discourse from generation to generation; others have recently gained attention and will quickly fade. What proves interesting in general conversation will depend on what the conversationalists are at that time accustomed to discussing. There are topics that sustain no more than a few moments' talk, but the cleverness with which a subject is introduced has a great deal to do with whether it is taken up. While there are conversational unfortunates who wrap everything they say in dullness, others do the opposite, using wit, an ability to see unexpected significances, and intriguing modes of argument to lend at least momentary interest to whatever topic they initiate. Precisely the same distinctions operate within the critical colloquy.

On this analogy, the historical resonance of a text (the degree to which it explicitly relates to other texts), the possible multiplication of its significances (the degree to which it is multivalent),[4] the skill with which it is brought into the critical colloquy (the degree to which it finds fortunate sponsorship), and the congruence between its possible significances and critics' current preoccupations (the degree to which it proves malleable)—all these interact to determine how much interest the text can sustain over how long a period. Instead of stamping works with authority, literary canons propose entries into a culture's critical colloquy. This colloquy is nothing but a corner of that "unending conversation" Kenneth Burke so memorably describes:

> Imagine that you enter a parlor. You come late. When you arrive, others have long preceded you, and they are engaged in a heated discussion, a discussion too heated for them to pause and tell you exactly what it is about. In fact, the discussion had already begun long before any of them got there, so that no one present is qualified to retrace for you all the steps that had gone before. You listen for a while, until you decide that you have caught the tenor of the argument; then you put in your oar. Someone answers; you answer him. . . . However, the discussion is interminable. The hour grows late, you must depart. And you do depart, with the discussion vigorously in progress.
> (94–96)

Alastair Fowler's discrimination of six kinds of canons has met with general acceptance. The *potential* canon "comprises the entire written corpus, together with all surviving oral literature." The *accessible* canon is that portion of the potential canon available at a given time. Lists of authors and texts — as in anthologies, syllabi, and reviewers' choices — are *selective* canons. What Fowler calls the *official* canon is, I take it, a blending of such lists. What individual readers "know and value" are *personal* canons. And, finally, the *critical* canon is made up of those works or parts of works that are repeatedly treated in critical articles and books (98–99). As useful as these distinctions are, it is equally useful to recognize the variety of the principles defining them, the looseness of the resulting definitions, and the need for additional classifications. Fowler's potential canon, for instance, is defined by total inclusivity, but the degree to which what it includes goes beyond traditional definitions of literature will depend on one's critical allegiances. The accessible canon is also inclusive, but only for a single location; perhaps further, it varies with the sophistication of each reader. Personal canons seem made up of an indeterminate interaction between all the works individuals have read and those they prefer to some degree or other. Since official and critical canons are precipitated out of the mass of selective canons, the only canons produced by systematic choice are the innumerable and heterogeneous selective ones.

Additional distinctions suggest themselves as useful, though like Fowler's they rest on no systematic taxonomic principle and therefore overlap at various points. The term *canon* as applied to a closed, uniquely authoritative body of texts, such as the Bible, fits nowhere in his six classifications; it represents a seventh kind (canon$_7$). If we take Fowler's official canon to mean something like all the authors and titles in whatever reasonably comprehensive literary histories are standard at a given time and if we accept his definition of the critical canon as the texts most written about at that time, the list of works commonly taught in high school and undergraduate classes will be not only much shorter than the official canon but also unlikely to correspond exactly to the critical. Thus there is theoretical space for a *pedagogical* canon (canon$_8$).

What of the numerous authors who are given special recognition in selection after selection over centuries or at least decades? Or those contemporary authors who have high visibility? In a haphazard way these tend to be grouped together — in the 1990s a person interested in literature presumably knows not only Ovid, Milton, and Arnold but Ozick, Morrison, and Ashbery. But the glacially changing core is a kind of *diachronic* canon (canon$_9$), to be distinguished from a rapidly changing periphery that could be called the *nonce* canon (canon$_{10}$), only a minuscule part of which will eventually become part of the diachronic canon.[5] I leave open the question whether the academy's hegemony is such that there are no longer truly popular canons rivaling the diachronic and nonce canons of the literary professoriat.[6]

What makes it easy to think of a continuing monolithic canon, to confuse the diachronic and something of the nonce canon with the biblical analogue, is the smoothness with which certain new writers enter the diachronic canon and certain texts and authors move within it from the accepted center to the doubtful periphery (and occasionally back again). That smoothness is born of an interwoven set of processes. What a generation is taught depends on the tastes and interests of the previous generation and on the anthologies and texts created in response to the demands that issue from those tastes and interests. To the selection that it has inherited, each generation adds those works given visibility by either fortunate sponsorship or malleability to current interests. What one generation transmits to the next, however, can hardly be the sum of these two — there is only so much time in any degree curriculum, only so much time for anyone to read. Something has to give. Still, as has frequently been noticed, authors once a part of the diachronic canon generally retain at least a minimal cachet; they may be relegated to a canonical attic but rarely to the trash can. Perhaps, therefore, the diachronic canon is actually divided into two subcanons, a canonical haven and a canonical limbo.

Further perspective comes from recognizing that, until the Renaissance, selective canons in literature were generally of little importance, that selective canons of European vernacular literature blossomed only in the eighteenth century (see Curtius 264–72), and that selective canons of English and American literature are more recent still. The only nonecclesiastical canons that have carried even local authority have been the lists of required readings for specific educational endeavors. In the medieval period, given the aleatory availability of Greek and Latin texts and the practice of studying the ancient poets largely as part of the process of learning the classical languages and acquiring rhetorical skills, the literary works prescribed vary considerably. Knowledge of literature was in any case wholly ancillary for centuries, having little directly to do with the requirements for the bachelor-of-arts degree, which from the twelfth century to the sixteenth were almost wholly in logic.[7]

In contrast, the breadth of learning that a Renaissance humanist like Erasmus expected of teachers was less a canon than a summons to universal knowledge: at one point or another, *De Ratione Studii* mentions Pliny, Macrobius, Gellius, Athenaeus, Plato, Aristotle, Theophrastus, Plotinus, Origen, Chrysostom, Basil, Jerome, Homer, Hesiod, Ovid, Boccaccio, Pomponius Mela, Ptolemy, Strabo, Lucian, Demosthenes, Herodotus, Cicero, Quintilian, Horace, Caesar, Sallust, Aristophanes, Euripides, Terence, and Donatus. The formalization of curricula after the Renaissance, of course, tended to produce a selective canon in each university. At least in the United States and England, the prescribed literary and humanistic texts remained wholly classical until at least the latter half of the nineteenth century. Thus the Dartmouth "Course of Study" for 1852–53 lists the following more or less literary readings over the four years: Livy, Homer's *Iliad*, Coleridge's *Introductions to the Greek Classic Poets*, Ovid, Horace, Felton's *Selections from the Greek Historians*, Aeschylus's *Prometheus*, Tacitus, Sophocles's *Ajax*, Demosthenes, Cicero, Plato's *Gorgias*, Juvenal, and Terence's *Andria*. Vernacular literature did not enter the university curriculum until the nineteenth century. English became a school at Oxford only in 1893, a tripos at Cambridge only in 1917, and a major at most American universities still later; thus academic canons of English literature developed at about the same time as those of American literature and have gone through parallel twentieth-century revisions.

Comparison of anthologies—a popular academic pastime at present—is informative in several ways. Alan C. Golding's "History of American Poetry Anthologies" surveys the range of criteria used in anthologies from Elihu Hubbard Smith's 1793 *American Poems, Selected and Original* to the 1975 *Norton Anthology of American Literature*. As Golding points out, an anthologist like Smith, gathering poems from periodicals and newspapers,[8] seeks to preserve, to increase the Fowlerian accessible canon. But what an editor deems worthy of preservation is already a selection. The criteria Golding finds in the earlier anthologies are the promotion of political values, the celebration of an American sense of nationhood, and the provision of moral inspiration; after the middle of the nineteenth century the primary consideration is the maintenance of a formal and conservative tradition; this is followed by the urge to undermine genteel values, and today the most important challengers are feminist, ethnic, and political (primarily Marxist) concerns.

A glance at Victorian poetry collections is particularly useful, since the selection processes are recent. E. C. Stedman's *Victorian Anthology* (1895), apparently intended for the general reader as well as the student, offers poems by 329 poets, including George Darley, Barry Cornwall (Bryan Procter), C. J. Wells, William Maginn, William James Linton, Sara Coleridge, Mary Howitt, Eliza Cook, Roden Noel, Cosmo Monkhouse, Dinah Craik, Gerald Griffin, Robert Gilfillan, and Eugene Lee-Hamilton. Given the volume's date and anticipated readership, Stedman was altogether reasonable in casting a broad net "to make a truthful exhibit of the course of song during the last sixty years, as shown by the poets of Great Britain in the best of their shorter productions" (ix). Who could know which poets of the preceding sixty years would maintain readers' interest?

Seventeen years later another anthology not intended specifically for the classroom, Arthur Quiller-Couch's *Oxford Book of Victorian Verse*, omits about seventy-five of Stedman's poets, while adding a few American writers. Christopher Ricks's *New Oxford Book of Victorian Verse*, published seventy-five years after Quiller-Couch's, offers only 113 poets. Granted that neither the editors' intentions nor the publishing exigencies can have been quite the same for these volumes, a two-thirds reduction in the number of poets is nonetheless a dramatic winnowing.

Editors of classroom texts have found the pressures for reduction of the number of authors even greater. Assigning three hundred, two hundred, or even fifty poets to an undergraduate class would be a daunting and probably an unfruitful undertaking. Thus a true textbook like George Benjamin Woods's *Victorian Poetry* (1930) offers only sixty-nine poets for instructors to choose from. That number was cut to fifty-four in the 1955 edition of *Victorian Poetry* and to forty-seven for the 1965 edition. (The three editions do not greatly differ in the number of lines of poetry they contain; additional poems by the poets who have been retained take up the space.) Bowyer and Brooks's *Victorian Age: Prose, Poetry, and Drama* (1954) offers poems by forty-nine writers; Bloom and Trilling's *Victorian Prose and Poetry* (1973) by just twenty-one (including only one poet, John Davidson, who does not appear in Bowyer and Brooks). Among the forces driving textbook anthologists to restrict their selections is what can be called "the principle of academic recirculation." Academics tend to teach what they have been taught, what is easily available in print, what others are writing interestingly about, and what they themselves are writing about; what is easily available in print tends to be what is being taught and written about; what is written about tends to be what one is teaching or others are writing about.

*Selective Canons:
Criteria and
Functions*

Sorting the criteria used in drawing up selective canons requires as much attention as sorting the definitions of the term *canon* itself. The criteria also tend to overlap, and it is difficult to imagine a selection truly being made on one alone. Any editor of a collection titled "Writing by American Women, 1990" would clearly have to apply criteria beyond those stated in the title. Moreover, unrecognized assumptions underlie both explicit criteria and unacknowledged intentions. Thus the New Critical argument that poems cannot be paraphrased was developed into the claim that poetry has no propositional meaning; the ultimate implication of that position is the futility of critical discussion. Similarly, as R. S. Crane points out, the tension valued in New Criticism all too easily passed over into the automatic ascription of universal oppositions to any text the critic valued.[9] In explicitly seeking "the best that is known and thought," Arnold intended either to impose the uniform moral and social values of his own class (a common interpretation today) or (as it is possible to argue) to set in motion a constant process of revaluation, behind which lay assumptions grounded in a belief in the necessity of a hierarchical society (now the usual view) or (as it is also possible to argue) the necessity of breaking through the class structure.[10]

To some extent one can avoid the problem of differentiating specific criteria and basic assumptions in a critic's or theorist's work by investigating the functions a particular selection was apparently intended to perform. Barbara Herrnstein Smith argues that all evaluations of literary texts are actually judgments of how well the texts in question satisfy the changing needs of individuals and societies, that is, how well they fulfill particular functions. To analyze the criteria on which a selection appears to have been made, critics must seek such functions, always keeping in mind that they recognize these through processes that reflect their own changing needs.

Arnold having been mentioned, it is appropriate to begin with his influential effort to disentangle the evaluative criteria—the kinds of "estimates," in his terms—on which selections are made. The two against which Arnold warns can easily be defined by their functions. The "personal" estimate attempts to achieve congruence with individual needs and experiences (an aim that presumably represents the evaluative component of Fowler's personal canon). The "historical" estimate, by which Arnold means the literary-historical, seeks to provide signposts to mark forks and turns in the historical development of genres, new subject matter, and formal features. In urging the "real" estimate, however, Arnold begs the question by looking for hallmarks rather than functions; perhaps he intuitively knew that if he looked for functions he would find all too many for his purposes.

The personal and literary-historical estimates are but two among countless others. While an exhaustive list of the functions of selective canons would probably not be either possible or useful, it is easy to suggest a sufficient range of examples to caution against reductive generalizations.

Providing Models, Ideals, and Inspiration. Though the furnishing of examples is one of the oldest functions of selection, there are evidently models of many different kinds. The Alexandrians chose texts demonstrating the best grammatical usage, while the Ciceronian and Quintilian concepts of the orator-leader required texts embodying various social virtues. Models of belief and conduct are of course constantly shifting. What serves as a model of morality for most readers in one period may at another time be regarded as a model of self-righteousness; one person's inspirational clarion is another's intolerable cant. Golding describes Rufus Griswold's *Poets and Poetry of America* as based on "the conviction that American poetry should be represented by specimens of the utmost moral purity, that poetry's function is inspirational" (288), but the challenge to the poetry that Griswold assumed filled that function—and the rather similar poetry anthologized by Bryant, Emerson, and Whittier—came primarily from Whitman, whose champions could equally describe him as moral and inspirational. *Moralizing* and *inspiring* are currently rather out of fashion as honorific adjectives for literature, but the functions they designate are still fully operative. Marxist and feminist arguments are no less appeals to assumed moral values than are Pope's, Wordsworth's, or Holmes's; the working-class writers sponsored by Paul Lauter in "Caste, Class, and Canon" offer no less a commentary on how the world should be than do the writers honored by the New Critics.

Transmitting the Heritage of Thought.   Another canonical function is the provision of what is regarded as the basic cultural knowledge necessary to interpret past texts, see current issues in historical perspective, and orient oneself to the aesthetic achievements, social and political changes, and philosophical debates that have gone on for centuries. The Philology of Martianus Capella's fifth-century *Marriage of Philology and Mercury* is the bride who brings this ability to Mercury (eloquence). At one level the goal is "cultural literacy" in the specific sense of the ability to read texts written by writers who have assumed such literacy—as most serious writers have.[11] Harry Levin's more ambitious description of knowledge as "our most valued patrimony, our collective memory," expresses the use of such knowledge.

> Higher education, across the centuries, has constituted a continuous dialogue between the minds of ancestors and contemporaries. If we, the latter, know any more than the former, it is because we have learned so much from them. As T. S. Eliot remarked, "They are that which we know." Naturally we may react against them, and the reactions would not prove unproductive if they pointed towards a dialectical synthesis.   (362)

In fact, what appear to be efforts to overthrow the present canon are often endeavors to expand it, to enlarge our patrimony and enrich the "collective memory," that is, communal knowledge and awareness.

Creating Common Frames of Reference.   It is possible to argue not that any particular canon is justified but rather that *some* canon is necessary to provide common reference points. If it is true that all interpretation of texts depends on a community's sharing interpretive strategies, it may be equally true that, as Howard Felperin argues, "the institutional study of [literature] is inconceivable without a canon. Without a canon, a corpus or cynosure of exemplary texts, there can be no interpretive community, no more than there can be a faith-community without a gospel" (46). This conception of the function of the canon does not directly offer criteria for text selection, but it tends to favor a limited selection from the diachronic canon.

Logrolling.   Writers have gained entrance into the nonce canon not only by the power of their writing (for "power" one may read "appeal to extant societal or critical interests") but by their active espousal of texts or criteria congenial to their own aims. Wordsworth does this transparently enough in the 1802 Preface to the *Lyrical Ballads*; Arnold was creating a place for his own poetry even in condemning his "Empedocles on Etna." Writing about the Victorian canon, G. Robert Stange states that

> the principal agents of canon formation are the poets themselves who alter the poetic tradition by disvaluing some accepted "classics," giving authority to certain earlier art that has special meaning for them, or redefining in the interests of their own practice . . . the nature and responsibilities of poetic language.   (159)

Alan Golding reminds us that "Bryant, Emerson, and Whittier all agree that the six most important poets in America are themselves, Longfellow, Lowell, and Holmes" (292). Hugh Kenner comments, "The Modernist canon has been made . . . chiefly . . . by the canonized themselves, who were apt to be aware of a collective enterprise, and repeatedly acknowledged one another" (374); and, of course, Eliot's championship of Donne was no less strategic than sincere.

Legitimating Theory.   The New Critics provide a dramatic instance of the influence of critical theory on selection: while the function of their explication was presumably to exhibit meaning as fully as possible, their selection of works to be explicated had the implicit function of exhibiting the power of their approach. Deconstructionists, it hardly needs to be said, prefer texts with almost invisible seams that can be pried open to suggest gaping contradictions, while neo-Marxists, including most of the new historicists, are partial to texts that can be shown to reveal unsuspected workings of political power. Practiced New Critics, deconstructionists, and Marxists can, of course, read almost any text in a way that supports their own allegiances, but the texts each group is most likely to select are those for which it can provide the fullest, most dramatic, and most convincing readings.

Historicizing.   Literary texts have been so traditionally thought to cast light on the periods in which they were written — and historical and contemporary events to affect the proper interpretation of texts — that arguments over the relation of literature to history have primarily involved questions of emphasis. How fully are Chaucer's pilgrims representative of fourteenth-century England? How reductive, how much confined to a single class, is the "world picture" Tillyard found in the Elizabethans? While one of the accepted values of literature, one reason for selecting older works, has been to convey a sense of how the world was *then*, recent "historicizing" has shifted this emphasis to an analysis of the unconscious assumptions of earlier writers (as revealed by the conscious psychological or political assumptions of the critic)[12] or — as Annette Kolodny writes, citing Jane Tomkins — to an analysis of "'how and why specific texts have power in the world' (or do not attain power, as the case may be) at any given moment" (304).

Pluralizing.   Though the attention given to literature written by, or representing the experience of, women and ethnic minorities may seem especially characteristic of the 1970s and 1980s, there was a better balance at the turn of the century than now. The 1890s in England were a strongly pluralizing time in which writers expressing the points of view of the Irish, the Scots, women, and the poor were selected precisely because they represented perspectives outside the dominant one. Stedman's 1895 anthology includes, for instance, sections for poets of Australasia and Canada and, among those who would now be called poets of the people, Thomas Cooper, Ebenezer Elliott, and Ebenezer Jones. A full third of the poets included are women. By contrast, in Quiller-Couch's 1912 *Oxford Book of Victorian Verse* only a sixth of the poets are women (a fraction maintained in Christopher Ricks's 1987 *New Oxford Book of Victorian Verse*), Irish poets are less frequent, and Indian and Australian poets have largely disappeared. In "Race and Gender in the Shaping of the American Literary Canon" Paul Lauter notes a similar phenomenon in anthologies of American literature, with the percentages of black and women writers declining markedly between 1919 and 1950. Though Lauter elsewhere sees the invisible hand of monopoly capitalism in canon selection, he here lists the causes as "the eastern male elite's professionalization of the teaching of literature," the formalist aesthetic, and the "historiographic organization of literature into conventional 'periods' and 'themes'" (440).

At present, pluralization appears to have real, if unstated, limits. For instance, there has been no rush to defend the sentimental description and inspirational storytelling that delighted our grandparents. The generation educated early in this century still happily quoted "Little Orphant Annie," "Excelsior," "Curfew Must Not Ring Tonight," "Casabianca," and "The Good Time Coming," but the antielitist impulse has yet to rehabilitate Mrs. Hemans or Charles Mackay.

Whatever the functions governing selections, it is important to recognize that although a canon is nominally made up of texts, it is actually made up not of texts in themselves but of texts as read. When the church found ways of accommodating pagan authors to Christian belief, what it admitted to its selection of Greek and Roman philosophers and poets were particular readings of the texts. Augustine thus compares the acceptable teachings of the pagans to the "vases and ornaments of gold and silver and clothing which the Israelites took with them secretly when they fled, as if to put them to a better use" (75).

Leaping to the present, one can cite *The Catcher in the Rye*, which owes its continuing place in the nonce canon to its mimetic function as a portrait of adolescence but which can be selected, according to Richard Ohmann's reading, as a neo-Marxist text that intends to reveal the omnipresence of capitalist ideology. Again, as Annette Kolodny argues more clearly and explicitly than most other critics seeking to expand the canon, the reading of unfamiliar literary texts and unfamiliar types of criticism should not merely make one comfortable with new texts but defamiliarize the texts in the current critical and pedagogical canons. While her already influential 1985 essay argues for expansion and pluralization of the official canon, it implies as well that future selections should include only those works from the present critical and pedagogical canons whose texts as read after defamiliarization meet whatever selection criteria are applied.

The Selection of Texts as the Selection of Readings

The Ultimate
Function of Canons
Is to Compete

If we have not one canon of literature but many, no canon formation but, rather, constant processes of text selection, no selection based on a single criterion, and no escape from the necessity of selection, to attack The Canon is to misconceive the problem. Similarly, to attribute all selection processes to the influence of power is radically simplistic, unless *power* and *influence* are defined so broadly that they include all social motivation. The dominant conventions in a particular society at a particular time obviously derive their power from some source. But the possible sources are many — political, economic, moral, aesthetic, metaphysical, religious, and psychological — and since they appear to be closely intertwined, the question of which, if any, underlies all the others remains moot. One can argue that all human choices are at root political, or economic, or moral, or aesthetic, or metaphysical, or psychological, but little is illuminated by this tactic. [13]

Whatever the motivation of canon selection, it remains important to contest the constrictive tendencies of the critical and pedagogical lists. Given the forces generating the professional recirculation of texts, we risk intellectual stagnation if we do not champion new selections based on new criteria. It is something else, however, to read as an ideological censor. Much contemporary commentary on the diachronic canon seems intended to discredit any text that arguably supports authority, elitism, or capitalism. But simply to emphasize the "elitist" and "capitalist" assumptions of older texts seems designed more to invoke magical exorcism than to do anything else. As Murray Krieger writes:

> To reject our revered masterpieces, then, is really to reject the political institutions at work in the cultures that produced them. It is as if, by turning against an aesthetic monument . . . the anti-elitist critics somehow can wish out of existence the reactionary political context that may have been thriving when the work was created. (155)

Charles Altieri similarly questions "the hermeneutics of suspicion": "It is a mistake to read cultural history only as a tawdry melodrama of interests pursued and ideologies produced" (37).

Though ideologically oriented critics frequently cite the relativity of "truth," they must, of course, assume that their own social and political beliefs are, if not absolute, a great deal less relative than others. In contrast, those of a somewhat more consistent indeterminizing persuasion hold that, since there are no absolute truths, or at least no way to discover them if they do exist, no text is to be preferred for its presumed truth-value. Such a position is perennially open to the objection that it must accept as absolute the relativity of all truths and values or fall into a version of the liar paradox (all beliefs are relative, including the belief that all beliefs are relative), but it has a long history, beginning no later than Heraclitus and given sanction by Socrates, who is forever seeking, not promulgating, truth. [14] What Bruce Kimball calls the "philosophical" (as opposed to the "oratorical") tradition of liberal education is based precisely on this argument, asserting itself against any standard selection of authors (*auctores*) on the ground that there can be no authorities since there can be no final truth. Nevertheless, critics, however relativist, must choose what texts they wish to talk about, just as readers must choose what ones to read.

At the practical level, there will always be competing canons: it is impossible to avoid the question of which texts one wishes to share or discuss in one's anthology, or critical article, or syllabus, or polemic. Recent textbook anthologies have fattened noticeably in their editors' attempts to represent greater cultural diversity, but the length of semesters has unfortunately remained the same. As teachers of literature we have thus again had to become more consciously selective. This is all to the good to the extent that it makes us recognize the clarification of a literary text's functions as the necessary prolegomenon to the process of selection. Critics continue to agree with Bacon, if one can judge from what they write, that two of the primary activities of criticism are providing "brief censure and judgment of authors; that men may make some election unto themselves what books to read" and setting an order of studies so "that men may know in what order or pursuit to read" (86, 182); the requisite qualification is that "judgment and censure" and the preferable order of reading depend on criteria that depend on purposes.

None of the functions I have outlined is either nefarious or trivial. It is well to have some knowledge of major literary-historical influences on texts and some familiarity with the sources of the literary and philosophical allusions authors have expected their educated readers to share. It is well to bring some historical perspective to contemporary debates: to see the scandals of television evangelism against the background of the Pardoner's Tale, contemporary theological disputes against Pope's *Essay on Man*, questions of the limits of individual freedom against Mill's *On Liberty*, and arguments over corporate responsibility for the environment against Ruskin's essays on political economy. It is well to recognize that much of our literature assumes male, Anglo-Saxon, competitively individualistic biases. It is well to encounter models of prose that persuasively use traditionally effective rhetorical devices and well to encounter individualistic, countercultural prose. But no selection of texts that can be fitted into the one literature course, or perhaps the two or three, taken by the average undergraduate—or into the dozen or so literature courses taken by the baccalaureate major—can adequately provide all that background. We need more than ever, then, to be honest with ourselves and with our students about the limited purposes both of individual courses and of the requirements for our degrees—to be honest about what *our* selection of texts and *our* approach to them does *not* accomplish. If The Canon no longer lives, the reason is that it never did; there have been and are only selections with purposes. If anything has been clarified by the last twenty years of critical alarms and excursions, it is the multiplicity of possible purposes.

Notes

[1] Under the heading "canon" in the eleventh edition of the *Encyclopaedia Britannica*, Samuel Davidson summarizes three opinions: in ecclesiastical use *canon* originally meant a list of "the books publicly read in Christian assemblies," or one that was canonical in the sense of "excellent as a model," or one that embodied a regulative principle.

[2] Kimball's *Orators and Philosophers* is a masterly survey of the tensions and later confusions between the "oratorical" (*artes liberales*) tradition that sought to imbue leaders of society with the proper virtues and the "philosophical" tradition underlain by a skepticism that required an unending search for ever-elusive truths. Isocrates, Cicero, and Quintilian are key figures in the first tradition; Plato, Socrates, and Aquinas in the second.

[3] By way of comparison, the sixth of the thirty-nine Articles of Religion of the Anglican Church reads, "Holy Scripture containeth all things necessary to salvation: so that whatsoever is not read therein, nor may be proved thereby, is not to be required of any man, that it should be believed as an article of the Faith, or be thought requisite or necessary to salvation. In the name of Holy Scripture we do understand those canonical Books of the Old and New Testament, of whose authority was never any doubt in the Church."

[4] I am using *significance* to contrast with intentional *meaning*, following the distinction developed by E. D. Hirsch in *Validity in Interpretation*.

[5] Older works that had not become part of, or had dropped out of, the diachronic canon may of course enter it belatedly if they are fortunate in their sponsorship—Eliot's sponsorship of Donne is the standard example—and sufficiently malleable to be linked to current cultural and critical interests.

[6] There seems at least a short-term popular canon in the area of fiction and nonfiction: Harriet Doerr's *Stones for Ibarra*, Tony Hillerman's Navajo mysteries, Gerald Durrell's autobiographical stories of animal collecting, and Cleveland Amory's tale *The Cat That Came for Christmas* are perhaps examples of more or less recent books that, though appropriately advertised, came to be known primarily through the recommendations of one reader to another.

[7] As stated in 1252 by "the masters of the English nation, teaching in Paris," the requirements for the bachelor-of-arts degree were attendance in "lectures in arts for five years or four at least at Paris continually or elsewhere in a university of arts," at which the student should have heard lectures on a large portion of Aristotle—the *Praedicamenta*, the *Periarmeniae*, the *Topics*, the *Divisions*, the *Elenci*, the *Prior Analytics*, the *Posterior Analytics*, and *De anima*—together with the *Sex Principia*, the eighteen books of Priscian's grammar, and the *Barbarismus* of Donatus (Thorndike 53–54).

[8] It is worth noting that E. C. Stedman similarly drew on ephemeral publications in compiling his *Victorian Anthology* a hundred years later.

[9] Gerald Graff's chapter "What Was New Criticism" in his *Literature against Itself* succinctly sums up the contradictions within the New Critical program. Examples of the "all-embracing dichotomies" Crane cites are "good and evil, love and hate, harmony and strife, order and disorder, eternity and time, reality and appearance." Crane comments, "Of such universal contraries, not restricted in their applicability to any kind of work, whether lyric, narrative, or dramatic, it will be easy enough for us to acquire an adequate supply, and once we have them . . . it will seldom be hard to discover their presence in poems as organizing principles of symbolic content" (123–24).

[10] For a presentation of the second set of views of Arnold, see Harris.

[11] It is instructive to note how frequently arguments against the possibility of a shared culture nevertheless rely on one. Clifford Geertz, for instance, argues that the "enormous multiplicity" and the "radical variousness of the way we think now" make the transmission of a core of shared cultural knowledge impossible (161). What gives his article depth, however, is the multiplicity of his own allusions to the presumed knowledge of the educated reader. He appears to expect appropriate responses, for instance, when he mentions Copernicus, Freud, Bach, Ptolemy, Einstein, Malinowski, Boas, Whorf, the Tewas language, Bertrand Russell, Kant, Berkeley's *Esse est percipi*, the Pyrenees, William James, Henry James, Yeats, C. P. Snow, mandarins, and Eden.

[12] For instance, Jonathan Dollimore writes in the foreword to *Political Shakespeare*: "Finally, cultural materialism does not pretend to political neutrality. . . . Cultural materialism does not, like much established literary criticism, attempt to mystify its perspective as the natural, obvious, or right interpretation of

an allegedly given textual fact. On the contrary, it registers its commitment to the transformation of a social order which exploits people on grounds of race, gender and class" (viii).

[13]In one sense, whatever exists, including all cultural beliefs, conventions, artifacts, and conditions, can be described as demonstrating the triumph of one force or power over another: the power of tradition, education, religion, political structures, science, logic, capitalism, socialism, selfishness, hatred, ignorance, benevolence, self-interest, advertising, propaganda, personal experience, the press, the constitution of the human mind and body, the knowledge of the brevity of life, the need for love and approval — the list is endless. All the powers or forces influencing human decisions interact to produce the total social structure of any given moment. The canonical status of a literary text — like the economic status of a rock musician, the repu-

tation of a painter, the purity of the air and water, the desirability of consumer goods, or the majority positions on taxes, abortion, and nuclear power — can only be understood as the result of multiple causes. To attribute any cultural phenomenon to a single "power" — that of capitalism, or male prejudice, or political corruption, or economic greed, or moral idealism — is as naive as to think such powers can be ignored.

[14]See Bruce Kimball's tracing of this "philosophical" orientation from Plato to the present. The second part of the seventh chapter of Walter Pater's *Plato and Platonism* emphasizes (and perhaps magnifies) this aspect of Plato's thought, carefully outlining the "dialectic method, this continuous discourse with one's self" (185), and the spirit "which to the last will have its diffidence and reserve, its scruples and second thoughts" (196).

Works Cited

Altieri, Charles. "An Idea and Ideal of a Literary Canon." *Critical Inquiry* 10 (1983): 37–60.

Augustine, Bishop of Hippo. *On Christian Doctrine*. Trans. D. W. Robertson, Jr. Indianapolis: Bobbs, 1958.

Bacon, Francis. *The Advancement of Learning*. Ed. W. A. Wright. Oxford: Clarendon–Oxford UP, 1900.

Bloom, Harold, and Lionel Trilling. *Victorian Prose and Poetry*. New York: Oxford UP, 1973.

Bowyer, John Wilson, and John Lee Brooks. *The Victorian Age: Prose, Poetry, and Drama*. New York: Appleton, 1954.

Burke, Kenneth. *The Philosophy of Literary Form*. 1941. New York: Vintage, 1957.

Crane, R. S. *The Language of Criticism and the Structure of Poetry*. Toronto: U of Toronto P, 1953.

Curtius, Ernst Robert. *European Literature and the Latin Middle Ages*. Trans. Willard R. Trask. Bollingen Series 36. Princeton: Princeton UP, 1953.

Dollimore, Jonathan, and Alan Sinfield, eds. *Political Shakespeare: New Essays in Cultural Materialism*. Manchester, Eng.: Manchester UP, 1985.

Erasmus, Desiderius. *De Ratione Studii. Concerning the Aim and Method of Education*. Ed. and trans. William Harrison Woodward. New York: Teachers Coll. P, 1964.

Felperin, Howard. *Beyond Deconstruction: The Uses and Abuses of Literary Theory*. Oxford: Clarendon–Oxford UP, 1985.

Fowler, Alastair. "Genre and the Literary Canon." *New Literary History* 11 (1979): 97–119.

Geertz, Clifford. "The Way We Think Now: Toward an Ethnography of Modern Thought." *Local Knowledge: Further Essays in Interpretive Anthropology*. New York: Basic, 1983. 147–63.

Golding, Alan C. "A History of American Poetry Anthologies." *Canons*. Ed. Robert von Hallberg. Chicago: U of Chicago P, 1984. 279–307.

Graff, Gerald. *Literature against Itself*. Chicago: U of Chicago P, 1979.

Harris, Wendell V. "The Continuously Creative Function of Arnoldian Criticism." *Victorian Poetry* 26 (Spring-Summer 1988): 117–33.

Hirsch, E. D., Jr. *Validity in Interpretation*. New Haven: Yale UP, 1967.

Kenner, Hugh. "The Making of the Modernist Canon."

Canons. Ed. Robert von Hallberg. Chicago: U of Chicago P, 1984. 363–75.

Kermode, Frank. "Institutional Control of Interpretation." *Salmagundi* 43 (1979): 72–86.

Kimball, Bruce. *Orators and Philosophers: A History of the Idea of Liberal Education*. New York: Teachers Coll. P, 1986.

Kolodny, Annette. "The Integrity of Memory: Creating a New Literary History of the United States." *American Literature* 57 (1985): 291–307.

Krieger, Murray. *Words about Words about Words: Theory, Criticism, and the Literary Text*. Baltimore: Johns Hopkins UP, 1988.

Lauter, Paul. "Caste, Class, and Canon." *A Gift of Tongues*. Ed. Marie Harris and Kathleen Aguerro. Athens: U of Georgia P, 1987. 51–82.

——. "Race and Gender in the Shaping of the American Literary Canon: A Case Study from the Twenties." *Feminist Studies* 9 (1983): 435–65.

Levin, Harry. "Core, Canon, Curriculum." *College English* 43 (1981): 352–62.

Ohmann, Richard, with Carol Ohmann. "A Case Study in Canon Formation: Reviewers, Critics, and *The Catcher in the Rye*." *Politics or Letters*. By Richard Ohmann. Middletown: Wesleyan UP, 1987. 45–67.

Pater, Walter. *Plato and Platonism*. London: Macmillan, 1910.

Pfeiffer, Rudolf. *History of Classical Scholarship from the Beginning to the End of the Hellenistic Age*. Oxford: Clarendon–Oxford UP, 1968.

Quiller-Couch, Arthur, ed. *The Oxford Book of Victorian Verse*. Oxford: Clarendon–Oxford UP, 1912.

Ricks, Christopher, ed. *The New Oxford Book of Victorian Verse*. Oxford: Oxford UP, 1987.

Smith, Barbara Herrnstein. "Contingencies of Value." *Critical Inquiry* 10 (1983): 1–35.

Stange, G. Robert. "1887 and the Making of the Victorian Canon." *Victorian Studies* 25 (1987): 151–68.

Stedman, E. C. *A Victorian Anthology, 1837–1895*. Boston: Houghton, 1895.

Thorndike, Lynn. *University Records and Life in the Middle Ages*. New York: Columbia UP, 1944.

Woods, George Benjamin, ed. *Poetry of the Victorian Period*. Chicago: Scott, 1930. 2nd and 3rd eds. with Jerome Hamilton Buckley. 1955, 1965.

IN THE CONTEMPORARY theater, questions of canonicity often first arise on the occasion of the play's production onstage. In these reviews, theater critics make the first effort to characterize a play's significance, both as a text and as a performance.

MUD WAS WRITTEN AND DIRECTED BY MARIA IRENE FORNES AND PRESENTED BY THE THEATER *for the New City, New York. The review, "Clearer than Anything," appeared in the* Village Voice, *November 29, 1983.*

MICHAEL FEINGOLD

REVIEW OF *Mud*

Maria Irene Fornes's *Mud* is just what one would expect from such a multifaceted talent: a brilliant, devastating surprise. This time, the surprise is a naturalistic play. At first it seems to be of the old-fashioned low-life-of-rural-illiterates kind, but Fornes's staging, demonically precise, makes it clear that something else is going on: the reality seems to have had its details airbrushed out; the actions happen with the hypnotic slowness of a dream, unnerving you, making you restless, and finally eating into the mind like etchers' acid. Diann E. Duthie's austere set is a bare hardwood box perched at a distance from the audience atop a hill of the titular substance; it's lit by Anne Militello with a harsh whiteness that zeroes in on the characters, rather than softening, for a change of mood. The language is like a hand-to-hand combat between Fornes's usual, comically digressive way with words and the knot-hard, uncouth terseness of a Mamet or a Kroetz.

The story Fornes tells with this amazing array of techniques turns out to be a variant on *Ethan Frome*, with the sexes reversed. (She's never read Wharton's novella.) Dirt-poor Mae lives with Lloyd, a foundling her late father took in who's grown up to be her lover. Lloyd has become impotent, through an illness which he won't go to the clinic about; he ridicules Mae's attempts to learn reading and mathematics. Mae brings educated Henry into the house to persuade Lloyd to see a doctor; before long she's abandoned Lloyd and married Henry. Lloyd, cured, is rambunctious; Henry, unused to the farm (it seems to be a farm), falls and is crippled. When Mae attempts to leave them both, a duly tragic end is precipitated.

The bareness of this narrative conveys very little about the meanings Fornes's artistry reads into it. When not being terse with each other, the characters explode into wonderful long speeches in which the human capacity for seizing a small detail and riding it is heightened into a revelatory poem. These flashes, along with the dreamlike movement and the absence of explanatory details, give a simple genre painting the nightmare quality of a Magritte. The fact that *Mud* comes directly after last year's *The Danube,* in which a nuclear holocaust was depicted, suggests that Fornes's lowlifes and their strange ailments are some kind of post-nuclear survivors, though this is never stated and may be a pure projection on my part. Certainly a feminist moral about women suffering under the brutish and warlike tendencies of men is being played out, though this again is never signaled or underlined in any dogmatic way.

As in the best Renaissance painting, the iconography is there in Fornes's picture, not to offer a cut-and-dried meaning, but to allow meanings to interpenetrate in an image that means more than they can sum up in words. Similarly, the fact that one is half encouraged to laugh nearly all the way through, and can't because of the hypnotic quality of the event, is a summation: the piece is both a tragic image of human life and a sardonic goof on it; the two are inseparable. It's hard to accept while watching, but utterly unshakable once you've seen it. Apart from the designers, Fornes gets excellent help from her actors, with a performance of particular distinction by Patricia Mattick as the woman in the case.

AS IS WAS WRITTEN BY WILLIAM M. HOFFMAN AND DIRECTED BY MICHAEL WARREN POWELL. IT *was presented by Circle Repertory Company, New York. The review appeared in the* New York Times, *April 27, 1987.*

WALTER GOODMAN

REVIEW OF *As Is*

Since the original production of "As Is" a little more than two years ago, public concern over the AIDS epidemic has grown along with the number of deaths and predictions of worse to come. The worthy revival of William M. Hoffman's affecting play, which opened last night at the Circle Repertory Company, where it was originally staged, is, unfortunately, as timely as it was in 1985.

Mr. Hoffman focuses on a pair of lovers, Rich and Saul, whom we meet on the verge of breaking up, dividing their possessions in humorously testy exchanges so that Rich can go off to live with another, younger man. "You weren't my Muse," Rich later tells the admittedly conventional Saul. But then comes the revelation that Rich has acquired immune deficiency syndrome, and the play deepens into an exploration of love in extremis even as it broadens to explore a community that suddenly finds itself in panicked mourning.

Alan Feinstein, as Saul, and Steve Bassett, as Rich, give strong performances; for all the manner and mannerisms of the Christopher Street set, which Mr. Hoffman evidently knows well and which the two sport most engagingly in their banter, they are never anything but manly. Their embraces are natural; they are sexy together as they indulge in Mr. Hoffman's entertainingly dirty talk.

Saul rises to meet tragedy; as others desert Rich, he moves ever closer. The ideal of "nondirective, noncommitted, nonauthoritarian sex" is exposed as paltry. Rich, stricken just as his career as a writer seemed to have begun in earnest, goes from denial to bitterness ("The only thing holding me together is rage") to a dependence on Saul's love.

Mr. Hoffman can be soft. Saul is undeviatingly giving; the reconciliation between Rich and his brother, though moving, is a bit easy. But there is also a streetwise side to the play, evident in the brief episodes—a leather bar, a therapy group, an AIDS hotline—that capture the reactions to what is soon labeled "the gay plague." A hospice worker tells us that of the 35 dying people whom she tries to comfort, one-third have AIDS: "This is the Village." A community develops, united by grief and fear.

Briskly directed by Michael Warren Powell, these scenes capture the solidarity and the nervousness, the frankness and the reticence of people at risk. The cast, including several actors from the original production who take two or three roles apiece, is generally admirable.

The first reaction, of homosexuals and heterosexuals alike, to the bad news is, "Don't touch me!" But on this stage, at least, the spirit changes into some sort of reaching out. Everyone is helped by a healthy humor that enables even mourners to cope and gives "As Is" its light feeling despite its grim subject. In one brief scene, the chorus simply recites the names of friends who have died, and the play's program offers a memorial to about 30 real people, presumably victims of the disease. "As Is" itself stands as a fine memorial.

FRANK RICH

REVIEW OF
M. Butterfly

M. BUTTERFLY WAS WRITTEN BY DAVID HENRY HWANG AND DIRECTED BY JOHN DEXTER. IT WAS *presented by Stuart Ostrow and David Geffen at the Eugene O'Neill Theater, New York. The review,* "'M. Butterfly,' A Story of a Strange Love, Conflict and Betrayal," *appeared in the* New York Times, *March 21, 1988.*

It didn't require genius for David Henry Hwang to see that there were the makings of a compelling play in the 1986 newspaper story that prompted him to write "M. Butterfly." Here was the incredible true-life tale of a career French foreign service officer brought to ruin — conviction for espionage — by a bizarre 20-year affair with a Beijing Opera diva. Not only had the French diplomat failed to recognize that his lover was a spy; he'd also failed to figure out that "she" was a he in drag. "It was dark, and she was very modest," says Gallimard (John Lithgow), Mr. Hwang's fictionalized protagonist, by half-joking way of explanation. When we meet him in the prison cell where he reviews his life, Gallimard has become, according to his own understatement, "the patron saint of the socially inept."

But if this story is a corker, what is it about, exactly? That's where Mr. Hwang's imagination, one of the most striking to emerge in the American theater in this decade, comes in, and his answer has nothing to do with journalism. This playwright, the author of "The Dance and the Railroad" and "Family Devotions," does not tease us with obvious questions such as is she or isn't she?, or does he know or doesn't he? Mr. Hwang isn't overly concerned with how the opera singer, named Song Liling (B. D. Wong), pulled his hocus-pocus in the boudoir, and he refuses to explain away Gallimard by making him a closeted, self-denying homosexual. An inversion of Puccini's "Madama Butterfly," "M. Butterfly" is also the inverse of most American plays. Instead of reducing the world to an easily digested cluster of sexual or familial relationships, Mr. Hwang cracks open a liaison to reveal a sweeping, universal meditation on two of the most heated conflicts — men versus women, East versus West — of this or any other time.

As a piece of playwriting that manages to encompass phenomena as diverse as the origins of the Vietnam War and the socio-economic code embedded in Giorgio Armani fashions, "M. Butterfly" is so singular that one hates to report that a visitor to the Eugene O'Neill Theater must overcome a number of obstacles to savor it. Because of some crucial and avoidable lapses — a winning yet emotionally bland performance from Mr. Lithgow and inept acting in some supporting roles — the experience of seeing the play isn't nearly as exciting as thinking about it after the curtain has gone down. The production only rises to full power in its final act, when the evening's triumphant performance, Mr. Wong's mesmerizing account of the transvestite diva, hits its own tragic high notes. Until then, one must settle for being grateful that a play of this ambition has made it to Broadway, and that the director, John Dexter, has realized as much of Mr. Hwang's far-ranging theatricality as he has.

As usual, Mr. Hwang demands a lot from directors, actors and theatergoers. A 30-year-old Chinese-American writer from Los Angeles, he has always blended Oriental and Western theater in his work, and "M. Butterfly" does so on an epic scale beyond his previous plays, let alone such similarly minded Western hybrids as "Pacific Overtures" or "Nixon in China." While ostensibly constructed as a series of Peter Shafferesque flashbacks narrated by Gallimard from prison, the play is as intricate as an infinity of Chinese boxes. Even as we follow the narrative of the lovers' affair, it is being refracted through both overt and disguised burlesque deconstructions of "Madama Butterfly." As Puccini's music collides throughout with a percussive Eastern score by Lucia Hwong, so Western storytelling and sassy humor intermingle with flourishes of martial-arts ritual, Chinese opera (Cultural Revolution Maoist agitprop included) and Kabuki. Now and then, the entire mix is turned inside out, Genet and Pirandello style, to remind us that fantasy isn't always distinguishable from reality and that actors are not to be confused with their roles.

The play's form — whether the clashing and blending of Western and Eastern cultures or of male and female characters — is wedded to its content. It's Mr. Hwang's starting-off point that a cultural icon like "Madama Butterfly" bequeaths the sexist and racist roles that burden Western men: Gallimard believes he can become "a real man" only if he can exercise power over a beautiful and submissive woman, which is why he's so ripe to be duped by Song Liling's impersonation of a shrinking butterfly. Mr. Hwang broadens his message by making Gallimard an architect of the Western foreign policy in Vietnam. The diplomat disastrously reasons that a manly display of American might can bring the Viet Cong to submission as easily as he or Puccini's Pinkerton can overpower a Madama Butterfly.

Lest that ideological leap seem too didactic, the playwright shuffles the deck still more, suggesting that the roles played by Gallimard and Song Liling run so deep that they cross the boundaries of nations, cultures, revolutions and sexual orientations. That Gallimard was fated to love "a woman created by a man" proves to be figuratively as well as literally true: we see that the male culture that inspired his "perfect woman" is so entrenched that the attitudes of "Madama Butterfly" survive in his cherished present-day porno magazines. Nor is the third world, in Mr. Hwang's view, immune from adopting the roles it condemns in foreign devils. We're sarcastically told that men continue to play women in Chinese opera because "only a man knows how a woman is supposed to act." When Song Liling reassumes his male "true self," he still must play a submissive Butterfly to Gallimard — whatever his or Gallimard's actual sexual persuasions — unless he chooses to play the role of aggressor to a Butterfly of his own.

Mr. Hwang's play is not without its repetitions and its overly explicit bouts of thesis mongering. When the playwright stops trusting his own instinct for the mysterious, the staging often helps out. Using Eiko Ishioka's towering, blood-red Oriental variant on the abstract sets Mr. Dexter has employed in "Equus" and the Metropolitan Opera "Dialogues of the Carmelites," the director stirs together Mr. Hwang's dramatic modes and settings until one floats to a purely theatrical imaginative space suspended in time and place. That same disorienting quality can be found in Mr. Wong's Song Liling — a performance that, like John Lone's in the early Hwang plays, finds even more surprises in the straddling of cultures than in the blurring of genders.

But Mr. Dexter's erratic handling of actors, also apparent in his Broadway "Glass Menagerie" revival, inflicts a serious toll. John Getz and Rose Gregorio, as Gallimard's oldest pal and wife, are wildly off-key, wrecking the intended high-style comedy of the all-Western scenes. Mr. Lithgow, onstage virtually throughout, projects intelligence and wit, and his unflagging energy drives and helps unify the evening. Yet this engaging, ironic Gallimard never seems completely consumed by passion, whether the eroticism of imperialism or of the flesh, and the performance seems to deepen more in pitch than despair from beginning to end. Though "M. Butterfly" presents us with a visionary work that bridges the history and culture of two worlds, the production stops crushingly short of finding the gripping human drama that merges Mr. Hwang's story with his brilliant play of ideas.

FRANK RICH

REVIEW OF
Speed-the-Plow

SPEED-THE-PLOW WAS WRITTEN BY DAVID MAMET AND DIRECTED BY GREGORY MOSHER. IT WAS *presented by Lincoln Center Theater, New York. The review, "Mamet's Dark View of Hollywood As a Heaven for the Virtueless," appeared in the* New York Times, *May 4, 1988.*

Hell hath no fury like a screenwriter scorned, and American culture is all the livelier for it. Out of the rage of embittered novelists and playwrights in studio backlots has come an enduring literature, nearly all of it practicing the same scorched-earth policy toward Hollywood that Nathanael West first apotheosized in "The Day of the Locust." While the theater has made many contributions of its own to the genre in the six decades since Kaufman and Hart mocked the early talking-picture industry in "Once in a Lifetime," David Mamet's new play, "Speed-the-Plow," may be the most cynical and exciting yet.

What we have at the Royale is not merely another screenwriter's bitchy settling of scores. Even as Mr. Mamet savages the Hollywood he calls a "sinkhole of slime and depravity," he pitilessly implicates the society whose own fantasies about power and money keep the dream factory in business. "Speed-the-Plow" refuses to hold out the sentimental hope that art might someday triumph over commerce. Mr. Mamet takes the darker view that show business titans know all too well whereof they speak when they claim to make "the stories people need to see."

By turns hilarious and chilling — and, under Gregory Mosher's exhilarated direction, wire-taut from start to finish — "Speed-the-Plow" is the culmination of this playwright's work to date. Bobby Gould (Joe Mantegna) and Charlie Fox (Ron Silver), the movie-industry sharpies at center stage, are tribal hustlers in the prize tradition of the penny-ante thieves of "American Buffalo," the lowlife real-estate salesmen of "Glengarry Glen Ross" and the poker-playing conmen of Mr. Mamet's film "House of Games." This time the scam is "entertainment." Charlie, a producer, is asking Bobby, a newly anointed head of production, to get approval for a "package": a big star will do a prison melodrama sure to make a zillion, provided that within 24 hours the studio gives the project the green light.

No one, of course, actually cares what this commodity is. The movie's plot, outlined in buzz words, is a riotous morass of action- and message-picture clichés that finally must be boiled down to the single phrase needed to sell it to the studio chief: "buddy film." But Mr. Mamet, like his moguls, is not concerned with the substance of the movie so much as the games that attend the making of the deal. As Charlie and Bobby, longtime pals who started out in the mail room together, fantasize about how much money they can make ("The operative concept is lots and lots"), they engage in a sub rosa power struggle — a warped, Pinteresque buddy movie of their own. The supplicant Charlie literally as well as figuratively kisses Bobby's behind to enlist his support with higherups at the other end of the phone. Though the men frequently and proudly label themselves whores, they are sentimental whores who boast of their brotherly loyalty and describe Hollywood as a "people business" even as they stab anyone handy in the back.

If "Speed-the-Plow" were only the story of these two men scheming to get a movie made, it would still be a worthwhile, funny evening. Exhaustively mined as the territory is, Mr. Mamet has come up with fresh Hollywood gags and newly minted Goldwynisms ("It's only words unless they're true"). His pungent, scatological dialogue skyrockets with the addition of such industry locutions as "net" and "coverage." Yet "Speed-the-Plow" contains a third character and a second film project — forces that collide to push Mr. Mamet's drama and themes well beyond parochial show-biz satire.

The catalytic character is a temporary secretary named Karen (Madonna), a naïve young woman who is so unused to thinking in "a business fashion" that she can hardly fetch coffee, let alone adopt the proper phone attitude required to secure a lunch reservation for her boss at a trendy industry restaurant. The play's second, much-discussed potential film property is "The Bridge, or Radiation and the Halflife of Society," a book by an "Eastern sissy writer" that an agent has submitted to Bobby's boss. "The Bridge" is the sort of artsy tome anathema to Hollywood — an allegorical tale of apocalypse rife with allusions to grace, the fear of death and the decay of Western civilization. Bobby has promised to give the book "a courtesy read" before rejecting it, and he also wouldn't mind taking his temporary secretary to bed. To accomplish both missions as expeditiously as possible, he gives Karen the task of preparing a reader's report on "The Bridge," with the hint that the assignment might advance her career to "the big table."

It would be unfair to divulge anything else that happens. Mr. Mamet had developed into a more inventive storyteller than most people working in the movies, and his new play is full of the unexpected twists that have distinguished "Glengarry Glen Ross" and "House of Games" from much of his earlier work. In "Speed-the-Plow," the spiraling plot not only pays off in a violent catharsis reminiscent of "American Buffalo," but also gives the drama the hallucinatory mood of "The Water Engine," Mr. Mamet's spectral radio play about an idealistic inventor who is silenced and destroyed by nightmarish forces of industry during the 1930's.

As "The Water Engine" was haunted by the recital of a mysterious chain letter, so the frequently cited preachments by the anonymous author of "The Bridge" percolate elliptically through "Speed-the-Plow." The more fun is poked at "The Bridge" and its lofty warnings about the end of the world, the more it seems that a religious vision of salvation may be presenting itself to one of the hardened moguls, prompting him to change the world and maybe even to make better movies. Or is God Himself just another exploitable concept — or con — in the greedy machinations of American commerce? Mr. Mamet certainly gives full sway to the consideration that religion might be the last refuge of whores.

Although her role is the smallest, Madonna is the axis on which the play turns — an enigma within an enigma, in the manner of the Lindsay Crouse heroine in "House of Games." It's a relief to report that this rock star's performance is safely removed from her own Hollywood persona. Madonna serves Mr. Mamet's play much as she did the Susan Seidelman film "Desperately Seeking Susan," with intelligent, scrupulously disciplined comic acting. She delivers the shocking transitions essential to the action and needs only more confidence to relax a bit and fully command her speaking voice.

The men could not be better. Mr. Silver gives the performance of his career as the producer who has waited too long for his big break and will now stop at nothing to keep it from eluding his grasp. While one expects this actor to capture Charlie's cigar-chomping vulgarity, Mr. Silver's frightening eruptions of snarling anger and crumpled demeanor in the face of defeat make what could be another Beverly Hills caricature into a figure of pathos. Just as brilliant is Mr. Mantegna, whose reptilian head of production is a distinct creation from his past Mamet lowlifes. The actor is very funny when he demonstrates Bobby's delight in his new decision-making authority by barking "Decide! Decide! Decide!" into a phone. But when unforeseen circumstances suddenly force this self-assured Machiavelli to declare "I'm lost," Mr. Mantegna evinces just the ashen, glassy-eyed pallor needed to convey the vertigo-inducing moral void that Mr. Mamet has opened up before him and the audience.

"Speed-the-Plow," not so incidentally, cannot be opened up by the movies. A two-set, three-person play that leaves no room for expansion, it would probably make terrible cinema. Perhaps that's another part of Mr. Mamet's revenge on Hollywood — to torture the studios to death with a script that is this entertaining and yet so far out of their reach. In "Speed-the-Plow," Mr. Mamet has created riveting theater by mastering the big picture that has nothing to do with making films.

APPENDIX

WRITING ABOUT DRAMA AND THEATER

IN MOST WAYS, WRITING
about drama and theater is like other kinds of analytical and argumentative writing. The best work is clear in its claims, tenacious in its analysis, rich and skillful in its discussion of detail. This section presents a brief outline of some of the techniques and practices of effective writing and some of the special concerns particular to writing about drama.

WHY WRITE?

On one level, this is an easy question to answer. You are writing because the instructor has assigned a paper as one of the requirements of the class. Most instructors assign papers — rather than merely assigning quizzes or examinations — because they believe that writing plays a unique role in teaching and in learning. Writing is active, a means of producing learning. When you write, you explore a particular problem or issue, thinking about it in a variety of ways, and teaching yourself something about it in the process. By writing, you also present an argument that attempts to persuade your audience to view the problem in the way that you do. In effect, you become a teacher yourself. Writing forces you to make the subject your own. It forces you to explore it and to consider how you can best represent the results of your thinking. Indeed, in the act of writing you may well discover what it is you have to say.

THE WRITING PROCESS

Most college-level writing about drama asks you to construct an interpretation of some aspect of a play or plays. The kind of interpretation you will perform, though, has much in common with persuasive argument — your paper should make an assertion about the play, a *claim* that you will develop in the course of the essay. First, a good claim is not simply a description of the work, a statement of what's already self-evident. To say, for example, that Ibsen's play *A Doll House* is about conflicted gender and marital relations is merely to state the obvious; it leaves you nothing to argue. Nor is a good claim merely a personal opinion about the work, a statement that invites agreement without persuasion or evidence. To say that *A Doll House* is a bad play, or that Nora is an unbelievable character, is an opinion-statement of this kind. Argumentative writing requires you to consider a fundamentally *problematic* issue, a question about which there could be some important disagreement — disagreement regarding the interpretation of the play itself. Writing is, after all, a form of communication. It is important that you have something worthwhile to say and that your way of saying it can be made persuasive to others.

For most people, writing an effective analytical argument has three basic phases that work to transform thoughts into an effective piece of writing. The first phase is the *invention* phase, when you consider the issues you want to raise. This is the time to ask yourself very general and stimulating questions that will lead to a commitment — a *claim* — about the work. If the choice of the paper is up to you, you might ask which of the plays you have read you liked the most. What aspects of the play seem most important, impressive, or unusual to you? If a paper topic has been assigned, you still need to make it your own. You might ask yourself how the topic seems to interpret the play, what problems or questions the topic seems to raise about your understanding of the play. It is at this point that most students come up with the *topic* of their papers; but a topic is only a first step. In order for a topic to be transformed into an argumentative claim, you have to think about it as a *problem*. A topic is inert while a problem is controversial — an idea about which there can be disagreement. For example, this is a topic: "Nora Helmer is a good mother in *A Doll House*."

Although this statement does make a claim, the claim is vague and underdeveloped. Its importance and consequences are not yet made clear. To transform the topic into a problem, we might ask how this claim could be seen as controversial, to involve us in a specific kind of interpretation of the play. One way to transform this topic into a problem is to imply an alternative perspective as part of the claim: "Although Nora Helmer leaves her children at the end of the play, she is really a good mother." This is a more problematic claim, precisely because it raises the possibility that Nora could be seen in two ways. This claim could be made more effective by suggesting how resolving this problem is central to an understanding of the play: "Although Nora Helmer leaves her children at the end of *A Doll House*, the play presents her as a good mother. Nora herself must become a free adult, must discover who she really is, before she can raise her children." This claim raises several complex issues and suggests a particular perspective on them. Your audience would expect you to discuss Nora's accomplishments as a mother in the play and relate those accomplishments to her difficult decision to leave her family at the end of the play.

This process — transforming a topic into a problem — usually marks the end of the first phase of writing, at which you come up with the major claim of your paper, a provisional *thesis*. This claim is still only provisional, because you will probably have to modify it in the next phase of the writing process: organizing your argument, developing your evidence, and drafting the paper. Now that you have a sense of what you want to claim in the essay, you will want to consider how to present your claim effectively. This usually means choosing some elements of the play to examine in detail. In this case, for instance, you might choose to discuss the scenes in which Nora interacts with her children; or the scenes in which she refuses to see them; or the scenes in which she discusses her children with others, like Mrs. Linde and Torvald. Of course, none of these scenes explicitly answers your claim: Ibsen never tells his audience "Nora is a good mother in this scene." It's your task to *interpret* the scene, suggest how we — your audience — should look at it in order to see it as you do. Generating detail of this kind — scenes, characters, speeches, language — to discuss is often one of the most challenging parts of the writing process. One way to help yourself here (and as a writer) is to take some notes on the play after you have read it. What scenes do you think are important or memorable? Why? What do you make of the major characters? These notes can help to provide some of the initial material you will discuss as part of your drafting of the essay.

Having considered what aspects of the play you want to address, you will want to make an outline, a map of your approach. Most students learn to make a formal outline — with major headings, subheadings, and so on — in high school, and some college and university classes require you to submit the outline as part of your writing process. Most writers use a more informal outlining strategy; they make a list of the issues or evidence they want to treat in the paper, as a way of putting main points and main pieces of evidence in order. Once you begin writing, you may well need to revise your outline, as what you have already written suggests new directions for the rest of the essay. Having outlined your approach, the next step is the writing itself. Instead of trying to get everything right in the first draft, most writers use the writing process to generate ideas and develop some prose. There will be plenty of opportunity to shape, develop, and revise the writing later. So, when you begin the paper, do your best to get your argument into a clear order. Write as much as it occurs to you to say on each point, giving yourself a lot of leeway to improvise ideas that may need to be clarified in revision. If important new evidence occurs to you, put it down in the draft, making a note to return to it. The important factor at this stage is to get as many of your thoughts down in order as you can.

The final phase — or phases, since most good papers take several revisions — is the process of revision. Revising is where the process of your thinking is transformed into an effective argument. Through revision your thinking is reshaped to become effective written communication. Written communication is sequential; your audience can only process information one piece at a time. For that reason, it's important to clarify your claims at the outset, tell your audience where the argument is going, and why. It's also important to tell the audience how each section of the argument is helping to substantiate that claim, and why it is important that we've accompanied you so far. A major objective of revision is to make the outlines of the argument — its major phases — explicit in this way. When revising, one useful trick is to read over your text — a paragraph, for instance — and then ask yourself, "What's the point of this paragraph? How does it contribute to my overall argument?" If you cannot answer that question, then you need to consider whether the paragraph — in this form — belongs in the paper at all. If you can answer it, then look to see that your answer is actually written down in the paragraph somewhere, made explicit to your readers, who, after all, are probably not thinking about the problem in exactly the way that you are.

Of course, these are the large-scale revisions; you will also want to ask similar questions of more local matters. Have I presented enough evidence on this point? Have I interpreted the evidence fully for the reader? How are my mechanics — sentence clarity, structure, variety, spelling?

APPROACHES TO WRITING

Writing about drama and theater is not essentially different from writing about other literary, historical, or cultural subjects, and the skills and habits of effective writing will serve well in writing about drama, too. However, writing about drama and theater also follows some of its own conventions. First, papers are generally written in the present verb tense, as though the play were actually taking place now, in front of us. It's up to you, of course, whether you want to write from the point of view of the reader or the point of view of the theater audience, but you will have to adopt a consistent perspective throughout and recognize that each perspective can help to make certain features of the play more clearly visible.

Second, many papers about drama begin by taking issue with one of Aristotle's categories of dramatic structure: the play's plot (how does its sequence of events contribute to its overall meaning?), its characters (how are the characters constructed; how do the conventions of characterization represent "real" people?), its thought or themes (how does the play generate its "themes"?), its language (are there patterns of language, images, or ways of speaking that contribute to your sense of its action?), and its spectacle (are there explicit features of its action onstage that help to realize the play's meaning?). These topics can be expanded through reference to the specific forms of drama in a given period or theater. To talk about the plot structure of a Shakespearean play, after all, is to talk about something very different from the plot of a Beckett play. It's important to realize that these features of the drama can provide a good starting point for your discussion, but that each will need to be specified in terms of your particular argument.

Another approach that's often useful in thinking about drama is to consider the play's staging, either in terms of effects that are described or made explicit in the text (the times that Prospero appears "aloft" in *The Tempest*; the confining single room of *A Doll House*), or in terms of the actual production choices made in a given staging. Thinking about how a production you have seen interpreted the text and how it used acting, movement, set design, costuming to provide the audience with a given perspective on the play is another standard approach to writing about drama and theater.

CITATION AND DOCUMENTATION

There are a few mechanical conventions specific to writing about drama. As you can see from the essays included in this volume, there are several forms you can use for citing secondary sources. The two main approaches are to use footnotes for all citations (see Sue-Ellen Case's article in unit 1), or to put the page numbers in parentheses in the text and add a list of Works Cited at the end of the paper, saving notes only for further explanation

THIS ESSAY ON RACINE'S PHAEDRA WAS written by an undergraduate student in a class on tragedy at the University of Texas at Austin. In the essay, Heather E. Brand uses Georges Bataille's discussion of eroticism to analyze and discuss the stages of Phaedra's moral progress through the play. Several aspects of this essay seem particularly successful: Brand's definition of the problem in the opening paragraph, her arrangement of the paper's series of ideas around Bataille's phases of erotic transgression, and her interpretation of scenes and passages from Phaedra to substantiate her claims about the play. Although different papers will require different conceptual and organizational strategies, this paper suggests one concise, effective, and detailed way of comparing the action of a play to a critical or theoretical text.

TRAGIC EROTICISM

Heather E. Brand
English 379M
Professor Worthen
30 April 1991

Human existence is founded on a dichotomy—the conflict between the discontinuous order of society and the continuous chaos of the natural world. While social order is defended by a system of taboos and boundaries, human desire aims at transcending these taboos through transgression. However, once the transgression occurs, the transgressor is forever excluded from the realm of society and is either driven to exile or to death. Between the mutually exclusive realms of nature and society lies the domain of eroticism. As Georges Bataille argues, the erotic is the means by which "we are incessantly trying to get at continuity, which implies that the boundaries have been crossed, without actually crossing the boundaries of the discontinuous life. We want to get across without taking the final step, while remaining cautiously on the hither side" (Bataille 141). The tragic theater shares with the erotic this form of voyeurism—a means of envisioning social transgression without its nullifying repercussions. Jean Racine utilizes this tragic eroticism in *Phaedra* as a tool for denouncing erotic fulfillment as detrimental to social morality. In this particular instance, Racine uses the character of Phaedra to portray the destructive and tragic phases of erotic fulfillment.

Bataille's theory of eroticism involves three phases: attraction, transgression, and sacrifice. Phaedra enacts this process throughout the course of the play. Phaedra is simultaneously confronted by her desire to uphold the order of society in the absence of Theseus, and her incentuous attraction to Hippolytus. The incest taboo is historically grounded in the attempt to deny our animal nature in favor of forming the social order of the family, the foundation of the social structure. "The horror of incest thus embodies a factor which makes humans of us and the problem it poses is the problem of man himself as far as he adds the human element to animal nature. In consequence all that we are is at stake in our decision to eschew the loose freedom of sexual conduct and the natural and unformulated life of the animals" (Bataille 198).

Phaedra's transgressive urges are characterized by her inconsistent behavior in the beginning of the play; Racine presents her in the throes of erotic anxiety. For example, she is rendered practically incapable of making the slightest decision, such as the styling of her hair or whether or not to venture into the sunlight. Oenone recognizes this interior struggle:

> How all her wishes war among
>   themselves!
> Yourself, condemning your unlawful
>   plans,
> A moment past, bade us adorn your
>   brow;
> Yourself, summoning your former
>   strength,
> Wished to come forth and see the light
>   again.
> Scarce have you seen it than you long
>   to hide;
> You hate the daylight you came forth
>   to see. (Racine 155)

In order to impress the maddening agony of erotic passion upon the audience, Racine reduces Phaedra to a state of social withdrawal and mental

(see Lynda Boose's article in unit 2). Your instructor may well have a preference here and will help you to use secondary citations. The purpose of citing secondary works you may use in writing your essay is twofold: first, to give credit to your sources, to the other writers whose work you may have used in coming to your own conclusions; second, to direct your readers to other material that may be interesting or helpful to them. At most colleges and

division as she wavers between taboo and transgression.

Phaedra's submission to erotic fulfillment constitutes the second phase of her erotic destruction. Although she never actually commits the crime of incest, her confession of her desire is enough to render her culpable in the eyes of society. In the preface to the play, Racine comments that, "The very thought of crime is regarded with as much horror as the crime itself" (Racine 146). Her admission of erotic attraction is a transgression in itself; her guilt is confounding. In submitting to this animal desire, Phaedra irrevocably dissolves her social bonds and becomes a self-proclaimed "monster," continuous with the irrational chaos of nature. Her feeble attempt to realign herself with order by falsely accusing Hippolytus of her own crime only serves to magnify her monstrosity. When approached with the possible leadership of the state, she recognizes the irreconcilable contradictions of her position:

I reign? I bring a State beneath my
    rule?
When reason reigns no longer over
    me;
When I have lost my self-dominion;
    when
Beneath a shameful sway I scarcely
    breathe;
When I am dying? (Racine 180–181)

In this passage, Phaedra realizes that her only prospect is to submit to nature entirely, to submit to death. The tragic transgression of taboo, instigated by eroticism, leads her to no other possibility than that of self-destruction.

Yet, the act of transgression is not only fatal to the transgressor but also to the erotic object. The death of the erotic object, in this instance the death of Hippolytus, marks the third and final phase of eroticism. Since Hippolytus' death is the result of a false accusation, we must regard it as a sacrifice that restores moral and social order. Bataille suggests that the sacrificial process is an "extravagance of nature ending in the profusion of death" (Bataille 88); this "profusion" or "chaos" of death signifies the utter dissolution of the human body into the continuity of nature, just as Hippolytus' body, in death, is no longer a singular object, but a part of nature itself. Theramenes is left with the task of relaying Hippolytus' corporeal explosion:

The traces of his blood showed us the
    way.
The rocks were stained with it, the
    cruel thorns
Dripped with the bleeding remnants
    of his hair . . .
. . . And then he passed away,
And in my arms lay a disfigured
    corpse,
A tribute to the anger of the gods.

The death of Hippolytus is a sacrificial appeal to social order because it inspires the communal response of disgust and nausea among the spectators. More important, in dying Hippolytus becomes continuous with nature, one with the rocks, thorns, and bushes that bear the traces of his body. His grotesque return to nature is Racine's reminder of the horrible consequences of the erotic. This scene also serves to unite the audience in a feeling of pathos: pity for the innocent, and fear of transgression. In this manner, Racine justifies the moral importance of maintaining social taboos.

Racine employs these three phases of eroticism (the attraction, transgression, and sacrifice) as a means of ordering the erotic into a plot of destruction. In inducing the audience to identify the erotic attraction of the tragic theater with that of Phaedra's attraction to Hippolytus, the play invites the audience to undergo a sympathetic process of erotic fulfillment. However, Racine then proceeds to play upon this desire by presenting his audience with the destructive nature of erotic fulfillment and its negative social implications. Racine, conscious that "eroticism springs from an alternation of fascination and horror, of affirmation and denial," fosters tragic eroticism as a tool for encouraging the denial of eroticism itself (Bataille 211). He relies on a classical pathos to act as a purging mechanism for our own erotic desire. In centering his tragedy upon the crux of eroticism, Racine allows the spectator to experience the continuous chaos beyond taboo without actually becoming committed to it. The method of theatrical voyeurism, then, assigns its eroticism to the ordered domain of theatrical language and form; Racine's play guards against any actual social transgression by inviting us, finally, to reorder erotic transgression within moral terms. This edifying morality of tragic eroticism is what Racine claims as "the real purpose of tragedy" (Racine 147).

Works Cited

Bataille, Georges. *Eroticism*. San Francisco: City Lights Books, 1986.
Racine, Jean. *Iphigenia/Phaedra/Athaliah*. New York: Viking Penguin, 1970.

universities, plagiarism—submitting someone else's work as your own—is an extremely serious offense, and careful attention to citations protects you as well as informing your readers.

Writing about drama uses several conventions to identify quotations from plays. Classical Greek plays are usually cited by line number, and the citation follows the quotation:

Clytaemnestra's effect on Agamemnon is complete when he steps on to the blood-red carpet, saying, "I feel such shame — to tread the life of the house" (ll. 945–46).

Notice that "ll." is the abbreviation for the word "lines" and is used to identify the line numbers of the quotation, and that the citation follows the close-quotation mark and precedes the period. The citation is part of the sentence, so it's included inside the sentence, before the period.

A different convention is followed for plays from the Renaissance, Restoration, and Neoclassical periods, which are commonly written in verse and usually are divided into acts and scenes. Here, the citation includes act, scene, and line numbers, separated by a period. Some people prefer using Roman numerals (IV.iii.21–22) — for Act Four, Scene 3, Lines 21–22 — but many people now use Arabic numerals (4.3.21–22) as follows:

Prospero finally accepts his own role in creating Caliban at the end of *The Tempest*, when he says, "this thing of darkness I/Acknowledge mine" (5.1.305–6).

When the play is written in verse, the lineation of the original text is preserved with a slash (/) between the lines, and the capitalization of each new line is preserved as above. Usually, quotations of more than three lines are set off as a separate quotation.

Since modern plays are not consistently divided into acts and scenes, and are not written in verse lines, it's common to identify the section (act and scene) of the play you are discussing as part of your prose, and then to cite the page number:

The most chilling moment in Shaw's *Major Barbara* occurs at the end of the second act of the play, when Cusins claims, "Dionysus Undershaft has descended. I am possessed!" (478).

The mechanics of quotation are easy to learn and lend your work an air of competence and credibility. For additional information, ask your instructor to recommend a handbook, or consult *The MLA Handbook for Writers of Research Papers*, ed. Joseph Gibaldi and Walter S. Achtert, 3rd ed. (New York, Modern Language Association of America, 1988). It contains extensive material on how and when to use footnotes, the preparation of works cited, and more specialized questions of style and mechanics.

✢ GLOSSARY ✢

Absurd *See* **Theater of the Absurd.**

Académie Française An academy founded by Cardinal Richelieu in 1635 to resolve the critical debate surrounding Corneille's play *The Cid* and to regularize the French language.

actos Short satirical plays devised by Luis Valdez and El Teatro Campesino in the late 1960s to dramatize the conditions of farmworkers in California.

afterpiece A short play — usually a pantomime or farce — that followed the main play on the evening's bill; common in England in the eighteenth and nineteenth centuries.

agora The marketplace in ancient Green towns; the agora was often used for dramatic performance.

alienation effect A stage technique developed by Bertolt Brecht in the 1920s and 1930s for "estranging" the action of the play. By making characters and their actions seem remarkable, alien, or unusual, Brecht encouraged the audience to question the social realities that produced such events, the political and ideological background of the drama and of its stage production.

allegory A literary or dramatic technique that uses actual characters, places, and actions to represent more abstract political, moral, or religious ideas. *See Everyman.*

amphitheater A semicircular theater design, consisting of a playing area faced by rising tiers of seats; often used outdoors, this was the design of classical Greek theaters.

anachronism Using people, places, or things that are chronologically out of keeping with the rest of the fictive world of a play or narrative; for example, using medieval English shepherds to attend the birth of Christ in medieval cycle plays.

anagnorisis Greek term for a character's "recognition" of something previously not known in the play. In the *Poetics*, Aristotle links *anagnorisis* with *peripeteia*, the "reversal" in the action of the play.

antagonist The force or character that opposes the main character ("protagonist") of a play.

antiphonal performance Alternative or responsive singing between individuals or groups; in the Middle Ages, it commonly involved two choirs.

apron The section of the stage that extends toward the auditorium beyond the proscenium.

archon A magistrate in classical Athens; each year, an *archon* was assigned the responsibility for organizing the City Dionysia.

Atellan farce Improvised comic skits in ancient Rome featuring stock characters performed by masked actors.

avant-garde Literally the "advance group," the term usually refers to the most innovative, experimental, or unorthodox artists in a given historical period. Used almost exclusively of late nineteenth- and twentieth-century movements.

benefit In the English theater of the seventeenth, eighteenth, and nineteenth centuries, a performance whose profits were assigned to a single performer or to the playwright.

biomechanics An experimental technique for actor training and performance devised by the Russian director Vsevolod Meyerhold after the Russian Revolution (1917). The technique emphasized the actor's physical training, stressing acrobatic and choreographic elements in production.

blank verse   An English verse meter consisting of unrhymed iambic pentameter lines (ten syllables with alternating stress, the first stress falling on the second syllable).

box   Box seating first appeared in theaters in the late seventeenth century; boxes were arranged around the side of the stage and the sides of the auditorium for the private accommodation of small numbers of people. Boxes were more expensive than pit or gallery seats.

box set   First devised in the 1830s, a set consisting of three practical walls enclosing the stage in a roomlike way.

cabaret performance   Stage performances in restaurants serving food and drink; especially popular in Europe after World War I, cabarets often were used for innovative kinds of performance.

canon   An authorized body of texts, such as the "canon" of Shakespeare's known plays; also commonly used to mean a "traditional" body of texts.

Capitano   The braggart soldier of *commedia dell' arte*.

catastrophe   The turning point in the plot of a classical tragedy.

catharsis   Literally the "purging" that Aristotle discusses as the effect of tragedy in his *Poetics*. Catharsis has been variously described as an emotional release on the part of the spectators, or as the recognition and purging of wrongdoing in the action of the play.

character   A fictional "person" appearing in a play or other work of fiction; usually conventionalized to some degree.

choregos   An important citizen in ancient Athens given the responsibility for financing, assembling, and training the chorus of Greek tragedy.

chorus   A masked group of young men who sang and danced as a group in Greek tragedy and comedy; larger choruses also performed dithyrambs.

City Dionysia   Annual spring festival honoring the god Dionysus; one of four festivals held between December and April. Sometimes called the "Great Dionysia," it included dramatic competitions and other public displays and rituals.

Comédie Française   The official national theater of France, devoted to the staging of the classics. Founded and chartered by Louis XIV in 1680 when Molière's company and the Marais company were united.

comedy   Traditionally a humorous literary form, comedy typically concerns the trials of love, and/or ridicules the failings of certain members of society. *See* **comedy of manners, new comedy, old comedy, romantic comedy.**

comedy of manners   Comic drama that takes the manners of high society as its subject; in comedy of manners, the dialogue is often witty or epigrammatic.

commedia dell' arte   Improvised comic plays performed by itinerant companies; it originated in Italy in the sixteenth century and then spread throughout Europe. Actors each played a stock character type and improvised the action according to a shared outline plot.

Constructivist theater   A movement in the Soviet theater after World War I and often associated with the director Vsevolod Meyerhold. Adapted from the visual arts, Constructivist theater resisted the use of representational sets, using more abstract "constructions" onstage.

cross-dressing   One of the conventions of cross-gendered acting, in which women play male characters in male costume, and men play female characters in female costume.

cycle plays   A series of plays dramatizing Christian history from the Creation to the Last Judgment, devised and performed in the Middle Ages by craft-guilds called "mysteries"; the cycles are sometimes also called "mystery cycles" or "mystery plays." They were performed outside the church on the Feast of Corpus Christi.

Dada A nonsense term adopted as the name of a literary and theatrical movement in Europe after World War I; Dada developed an esthetic of random and irrational art. Dada performances became popular in cabarets of Paris, Zurich, and Berlin in the 1920s.

decorum The notion, associated with neoclassicism, that the action and subject matter (idealized), language (heightened), and moral propriety (elevated), should be stylistically integrated and unified.

demonstration Describing "alienation effects," Bertolt Brecht urged his actors to "demonstrate" the roles they played, rather than identifying with them in the mode of Stanislavskian acting. Acting-as-demonstration keeps the audience aware of both the actor *and* the "character" at the same time.

deus ex machina Literally "god from the machine," the term refers to the practice of using a crane to lower the character of a god to the stage at the end of a classical Greek tragedy, usually to resolve the action of the play. Modern usage takes the term to refer to any dramatic device that suddenly resolves the action of a play.

dithyramb Choral hymns sung and danced to honor Dionysus as part of the City Dionysia. Choruses of fifty men or fifty boys drawn from each tribe performed dithyrambs prior to the tragedy competition; Aristotle thought tragedy originated in these dithyrambic performances.

Dottore The "doctor" or old pedant of *commedia dell' arte*; usually a friend of Pantalone.

drama A literary composition, usually in dialogue form, and centering on the actions of fictional characters.

emotion memory A term developed by the Russian director Constantin Stanislavsky to describe an actor's "work on himself" in acting. After considering a character's circumstances in the play, and his past life leading up to the action of the play, the actor tries to connect the character's situation with important events in his or her own life. This emotional or affectual connection can make the character's display of emotion onstage seem realistic and immediate.

Environmental theater A term coined by Richard Schechner in the late 1960s to describe performances that do not distinguish between the playing area and the audience; the performance takes place throughout the theatrical environment.

Epic theater A term associated with the German director Erwin Piscator and theorized by Bertolt Brecht in the late 1920s and 1930s, Epic theater uses episodic dramatic action, nonrepresentational staging, and alienation effects to demonstrate the political, social, and economic factors governing the lives of the dramatic characters. In the theater, Brecht advocated the use of placards to announce the action, visible lighting, film screens on the stage, and other devices to produce this epic effect.

episode Originally a dramatic scene in a classical Greek tragedy, as distinct from the choral odes; now usually refers to any incident or event in a play. Plays that are episodic tend not to subordinate episodes to a causal plot, but simply to arrange them in a series.

exodos The final scene and exit of the characters and chorus in a classical Greek play.

Expressionist theater An early twentieth-century movement challenging the verisimilitude of realistic theater by staging individual emotional, unconscious states of mind directly. In Expressionist plays, the action is usually abrupt and intense; the characters are usually generalized; the plot is typically symbolic or allegorical.

extravaganza Visual spectacle popular in nineteenth century theater.

Fabian society   A late nineteenth-century English socialist political society; Marxist in its orientation to social change, the Fabian society advocated a policy of gradual reform rather than revolution.

farce   Usually a short comic play, often relying on a highly coincidental plot.

film noir   A genre of black-and-white detective films popular in the 1940s, which frequently used shadowy, nighttime settings to establish an aura of menace and foreboding.

folio   A large-format printed volume, in which only four pages (two per side) are printed on each sheet of paper; the paper is folded once to from four pages.

fourth-wall   Refers to the style of realistic theater since the late nineteenth century, in which the stage is treated as a room with one wall missing. The audience is not acknowledged or addressed by the actors, but overlooks the scene as a silent, invisible observer.

gallery   In seventeenth-, eighteenth-, and nineteenth-century theaters, ascending rows of bench seating usually located opposite the stage on the third level of the auditorium; generally the most inexpensive seats in the theater.

genre   Literally "kind" or "type," genre in literary and dramatic studies refers to the main types of literary form, principally tragedy and comedy. The term can also refer to forms that are more specific to a given historical era, such as "revenge tragedy," or to more specific sub-genres of tragedy and comedy, such as comedy of manners.

given circumstances   Term used by Constantin Stanislavsky to describe the situation a character finds himself or herself in at the opening of the play, which the actor must construct as his first step in building the character toward performance.

grave trap   A trap door in the floor of the stage, often in the center.

hamartia   A term used by Aristotle in the *Poetics* to describe the tragic hero's decisive act, the "error" or "mistake" that brings about the tragedy. Sometimes mistranslated as "tragic flaw," a translation that mistakenly changes the meaning of the term from the description of an action to a feature of the character's moral makeup or personality.

Harlequin   The main character of *commedia dell' arte*, and later of English pantomime. Usually a wily schemer, Harlequin was originally played in a patched costume, which became conventionalized as the familiar diamond-covered costume. Harlequin was usually masked and carried a flat bat or paddle.

heroic tragedy   A seventeenth-century genre, usually on the theme of love *vs.* honor; associated with Dryden in England, Corneille in France, Calderón de la Barca in Spain.

iambic pentameter   English verse meter consisting of ten-syllable lines with alternating stressed and unstressed syllables, the first stress falling on the second syllable.

ideology   A complex term first used in the eighteenth century to categorize political beliefs and attitudes. Used to mean 1) a body of beliefs, a doctrine; 2) a body of illusory beliefs, a false doctrine; 3) a socially grounded system for producing beliefs and values, a way of producing meanings or doctrines.

Independent Theater Movement   A late nineteenth-century movement in Europe, in which small theaters gambled on the production of new and unconventional plays—by Ibsen, Shaw, Chekhov—for a small audience, usually outside the theatrical mainstream.

Innamorata/o   The attractive young lovers of *commedia dell' arte*; played without masks.

interlude   A short play, usually comic, performed during courtly feasts at the English court in the sixteenth century.

komos A procession and dance in ancient Greece, sometimes thought to be the origin of comic drama.

language One of the six elements of drama defined by Aristotle in the *Poetics*; the words spoken in the play.

line of business A conventional or stock character type that is the specialty of a given actor; his or her "line of business" might be old men, heavy villains, comic heroines, etc.

Little Negro Theater Movement A movement in the U.S. theater in the 1920s to develop theaters owned and operated by African Americans, playing a dramatic repertory by African-American writers.

Little Theater Movement A movement in the American theater in the early twentieth century akin to the Independent Theater Movement in Europe. Little Theaters offered new or noncommercial plays to smaller audiences.

liturgical drama Short dramatized sections of the Catholic Mass performed as part of the service; may have inspired the more elaborate, nonliturgical cycle plays.

machina The Greek term for the crane used in the ancient theater to raise and lower characters, particularly the gods.

machine plays Term used principally in seventeenth-century French theater to describe spectacular special-effects extravaganzas, in which the dramatic action—usually drawn from mythological subjects—was merely a pretext for the use of stage machinery.

magic if Term developed by Constantin Stanislavsky to describe the actor's attitude toward a role; to play "as if I were in this situation."

mansions Structures placed at several locations inside medieval churches as settings for liturgical plays.

masque A brief, usually symbolic, mythological or allegorical play, with elaborate scenic effects performed at the English court during the sixteenth and seventeenth centuries; performed both by actors and by courtiers.

melodrama First used in the late eighteenth century, the term originally referred to highly charged, popular plays using music to reinforce their clear-cut moral action; now refers more generally to plays with a schematic opposition between good and evil, in which good usually prevails.

metatheater A term used to describe plays that self-consciously comment on the process of theater, and so treat the relationship between theater and life. Such plays sometimes use the play-within-the-play device.

Method acting A technique of acting developed by Constantin Stanislavsky at the turn of the twentieth century, which teaches actors to use emotion memory to enact the character's feelings persuasively and realistically in performance; Method acting became especially popular in the United States in the 1930s, 1940s, and 1950s.

mimesis Greek word for "imitation" used by Aristotle in *Poetics* to describe the function of art.

mise-en-scène The "putting onstage" of a play, including the setting, scenery, direction, and action.

mitos Lyrical plays on Mexican-American life devised by Luis Valdez and El Teatro Campesino in the late 1960s and 1970s.

monopoly The right to exclusive production of the drama.

montage A technique used in film consisting of a rapid sequence of images.

morality drama A late medieval dramatic form using allegorical characters to dramatize moral and ethical problems involved in leading a Christian life.

music   Element of drama defined by Aristotle in *Poetics*; Aristotle refers to flute-music that accompanied Greek theater performance.

mystery cycles   *See* **cycle plays.**

Naturalism   A late nineteenth-century movement that attempted to achieve an objective verisimilitude in art—chiefly in theater and literature—by adopting a "scientific" attitude toward its subject matter. Thematically, naturalism emphasizes the role of society, history, and personality in determining the actions of its characters, usually expressed as a conflict between the characters and their environment.

nautical shows   A type of melodrama popular in England in the eighteenth and nineteenth centuries on seafaring subjects; in aquatic dramas, the stage was actually flooded.

neoclassical drama   Drama written under the influence of **neoclassicism**; see below.

neoclassicism   A movement throughout Europe in the sixteenth through eighteenth centuries to revive the forms and values of art exemplified by ancient literature; associated with the recovery of Aristotle's *Poetics* and its translation into prescriptions for the stage.

new comedy   A form originating in the fourth and third centuries B.C., first in Greece and then in Rome. In the plays of Plautus, for instance, new comedy generally concerns a romantic plot involving a conflict between young lovers, an old man, and a tricky servant.

Noh drama   Japanese classical theater dating from the fourteenth century; the plays are highly poetic dramas given extremely formal production onstage. Noh drama was admired by Yeats and by other modern playwrights.

ode   In Greek drama, a song performed by the chorus while dancing.

old comedy   Satiric social comedy of fifth-century B.C. Athens; Aristophanes' plays are the only surviving examples.

orchestra   Literally the "dancing place," the circular area before the skene where the chorus performed in ancient Greek theater.

pageant wagons   Wagons carrying the sets for productions of medieval cycle plays, on which the plays were performed.

Pantalone   Foolish old man in *commedia dell' arte*; played masked.

pantomime   In general, silent acting using gesture and facial expression. English pantomime is a spoken form, in which spectacular fairy-tale extravaganzas are performed with music and dance during the Christmas season.

parabasis   A choral speech in ancient Greek comedy in which the chorus comments on contemporary social issues.

parados   The entrance song of the chorus in Greek tragedy.

parterre   The standing area in the auditorium of late seventeenth-century Parisian theaters; the pit.

pastiche   Term used by Fredric Jameson to describe the toneless quotation of earlier artistic styles in contemporary (or postmodern) works.

patents   License given by the crown permitting a company to give dramatic performances; often it would give a company or a small number of companies a **monopoly** on dramatic performance.

patent theaters   Theaters given patents (or licenses) by the crown for dramatic performance, sometimes holding a monopoly on performances. Charles II of England granted two patents and gave their owners a monopoly on dramatic performance.

peripeteia   A term used by Aristotle in *Poetics* to describe the "reversal" in the action of a tragedy.

phallus   A leather phallus worn by male characters in Greek comedy.

pit   Floor area immediately in front of the stage in seventeenth- and eighteenth-century theaters.

plot   The sequence of events in a play or narrative; differs from the "story," which encompasses earlier events. Some works have several plots.

pointing   Common practice in the eighteenth-century theater of delivering a famous speech directly to the audience, from a downstage position; to "make a point."

polis   A city-state in ancient Greece.

political theater   In conventional usage, theater that seems to question the inequities and injustices of contemporary society. Bertolt Brecht developed a more searching critique of political theater, however, in which the ideology of theatrical representation itself could be seen as the theater's "politics."

postmodern   A term used to characterize the complex relationship between some contemporary works of art and their modernist forebears. Postmodern works are generally characterized by stylistic "quotation," an invocation and disengagement from history, and the fragmentation of artistic surface.

private theaters   In Renaissance England, indoor theaters serving a more privileged audience. Often located on lands within the city limits that were not under city jurisdiction, such as Blackfriars.

prologue   In Greek drama, an introductory scene preceding the entrance of the chorus. In later usage, an introductory scene not directly part of the main action.

proscenium   An arch over the front of the stage that was first used in European theaters in the Renaissance. Throughout the eighteenth and nineteenth centuries, theater design gradually eliminated the apron that extended in front of the proscenium and decorated the proscenium arch itself, emphasizing its framelike quality.

protagonist   Literally the "first contestant" in the ancient Greek theater, the term referred to the "first" or main actor competing for a prize. In modern usage, refers to the play's main character.

public theaters   In Renaissance England, large outdoor theaters, usually polygonal or round in shape, consisting of three-story galleries surrounding an open standing pit and a thrust stage.

quarto   A small-size book format, in which eight pages are printed on a single sheet of paper; the paper is folded twice to make eight pages.

raked stage   A stage that is elevated in the back and lower in the front; common in Europe after the seventeenth century. The raked stage gave rise to the terms "upstage" (toward the back, which was higher) and "downstage" (toward the front, which was lower).

Realism   A literary and theatrical practice valuing direct imitation or verisimilitude. Often associated with Naturalism, modern realism is sometimes described as the inheritor of naturalism. In practice, realism is usually more concerned with psychological motives, the "inner reality," and less committed to achieving a superficial verisimilitude alone.

repertory   A company that performs several plays in rotation throughout a season is a repertory company; the term also refers to a set of plays.

revenge tragedy   A tragic genre popular in the English Renaissance, usually involving a complicated intrigue plot in which the hero is forced to commit murder in order to avenge himself; madness and supernatural agents (ghosts) are also a common feature. Shakespeare's *Hamlet* is the most well-known example.

role-doubling   The practice of using one actor to play more than one part.

romance   A modern term used to define idealized narratives and sometimes applied to the idealized comedies written by Shakespeare late in his career, especially *The Winter's Tale* and *The Tempest*.

romantic comedy   Comic form centering on the romance between two lovers, or between several sets of lovers. Romantic comedy typically begins with some unreasonable impediment to the lovers' union, and when after a complicated series of events the obstacle is overcome, the play ends in marriage.

satyr play   A brief, rugged comedy performed by actors in satyr costumes (half-man, half-goat) after the performance of a tragic trilogy at the City Dionysia; usually about mythological subjects.

scaena   Three-story stage house behind the stage in the Roman theater, facing the audience. Elaborately decorated with columns, panels, and porticos.

scenic unity   The practice of harmonizing acting style, costumes, and sets to create the illusion of a single, unified environment on the stage.

sharers   Actors and playwrights in the English Renaissance theater who, as investors in the company, took a share of the profits; they were responsible for building or leasing a theater and were legally liable for the company's actions.

skene   A low building behind the orchestra in the Greek theater facing the audience; possibly used for changing costumes or storage.

social realism   A form of modern realistic drama emphasizing social messages and themes; social realism was the official genre approved by the Communist Party in the Soviet Union after the Russian Revolution.

sociétaires   Leading actors and shareholders in the Comédie Française; upon serving 20 years, *sociétaires* were entitled to a pension.

soliloquy   A speech delivered by a character alone onstage, speaking to himself or herself, or to the audience.

soubrette   A stock character in drama: a young, pert female character.

spectacle   Aristotle's term for the visual element of theatrical performance in the *Poetics*.

subtext   A term first elaborated by Constantin Stanislavsky, "subtext" refers to the unspoken motive for a given line or speech, what the character wants to get or to do by saying the line. It is sometimes now used more generally to suggest a text's underlying sense or meaning.

Surrealist theater   A movement originating in Paris in the 1920s attempting to represent subconscious experience directly in art.

Symbolist theater   A European movement of the late nineteenth and early twentieth century in reaction to realism and naturalism. Symbolist theater attempted to dramatize more poetic or metaphorical situations, often using unusual stage settings and ethereal dramatic action and language.

Syndicate   A group of investors who developed a massive organization for theatrical production in the United States in the late nineteenth century.

tableau/tableaux (pl.)   A motionless grouping of actors to represent a "picture" of a dramatic scene; sometimes called *tableau vivant*, a "living picture."

tableaux vivants   *See* **tableau.**

theater   A structure built for the performance of drama; also refers to the institution of dramatic performance.

theater-in-the-round   The presentation of a play in an arena setting, in which the audience sits on all sides of the stage area, but is separate from the playing space itself.

Theater of Cruelty   Term used by Antonin Artaud to describe his nonrepresentational, mystical, mythological theater.

Theater of the Absurd   A type of late twentieth-century theater and drama, characterized by a relatively abstract setting and by arbitrary and illogical action. It is sometimes said to express the "human condition" in a basic or "existential" way. The term was first coined by Martin Esslin.

theme   A term used to describe a consistent kind of meaning asserted by a work of literature.

tiring house   A structure at the rear of the stage in the Renaissance English public theater, where actors would change costumes (attire themselves) and from which they would enter the stage.

tragedy   Originating in the classical Greek theater, tragedy generally refers to serious drama, taking a central character's conflict with himself or herself, with society, or with a god as its subject. Aristotle first described tragedy in his *Poetics*, and tragedy has undergone almost continual redefinition.

tragicomedy   In the English Renaissance, a term describing a dramatic form: a play beginning like a tragedy, but ending happily, like a comedy. In modern usage, the term refers most often to a play's tone or attitude: a play that is ironic, both serious and absurd, leaning toward black comedy or tragic farce.

trilogy   Three tragedies produced in sequence as part of the tragic competition in the City Dionysia of ancient Greece. Plays were not necessarily on the same subject.

trope   An enlargement on Catholic liturgy, through song or dramatic performance.

verisimilitude   Verisimilitude refers to the extent to which the drama or stage setting appears to copy the superficial appearance of life offstage.

well-made play   A form of drama popularized in the nineteenth century, especially in France. The plot usually turns on the revelation of a secret and includes a character who explains and moralizes the action of the play to others; the plot is often relentlessly coincidental, often mechanically so.

wings and backdrop   Scenic practice developed in Italy and exported to France and England in the seventeenth century, using staggered painted flats in a receding series and a painted central backcloth to depict the setting of the play.

Zanni   Wily and clever comic characters, usually clowns or servants, in *commedia dell' arte*; played masked.

✛ BIBLIOGRAPHY ✛

READINGS ON DRAMA AND THEATER

Barish, Jonas. *The Antitheatrical Prejudice*. Berkeley, CA: University of California Press, 1981.

Beckerman, Bernard. *Dynamics of Drama*. New York: Drama Book Specialists, 1979.

Bennett, Susan. *Theatre Audiences: A Theory of Production and Reception*. London: Routledge, 1990.

Bentley, Eric. *The Life of the Drama*. New York: Atheneum, 1964.

Brockett, Oscar G. *History of the Theatre*. Boston: Allyn and Bacon, 1987.

Carlson, Marvin. *Theories of the Theatre: A Historical and Critical Survey, from the Greeks to the Present*. Ithaca, NY: Cornell University Press, 1984.

Case, Sue-Ellen. *Feminism and Theatre*. New York: Methuen, 1988.

Case, Sue-Ellen, ed. *Performing Feminisms: Feminist Critical Theory and Theatre*. Baltimore: Johns Hopkins University Press, 1990.

Clark, Barrett H. *European Theories of the Drama*. New York: Crown, 1965.

Dukore, Bernard F. *Dramatic Theory and Criticism: Greeks to Grotowski*. New York: Holt, Rinehart and Winston, 1974.

Elam, Keir. *The Semiotics of Theatre and Drama*. London: Methuen, 1980.

Frye, Northrop. *Anatomy of Criticism*. Princeton, NJ: Princeton University Press, 1957.

Goldman, Michael. *The Actor's Freedom*. New York: Viking, 1975.

Leacroft, Richard, and Helen Leacroft. *Theatre and Playhouse: An Illustrated Survey of Theatre Building from Ancient Greece to the Present Day*. New York: Methuen, 1984.

Nagler, Alois M. *Sources of Theatrical History*. New York: Dover, 1952.

States, Bert O. *Great Reckonings in Little Rooms: On the Phenomenology of Theater*. Berkeley, CA: University of California Press, 1985.

States, Bert O. *Irony and Drama*. Ithaca, NY: Cornell University Press, 1971.

Turner, Victor. *From Ritual to Theatre: The Human Seriousness of Play*. New York: Performing Arts Journal Publications, 1982.

Worthen, William B. *The Idea of the Actor: Drama and the Ethics of Performance*. Princeton, NJ: Princeton University Press, 1984.

UNIT 1: DRAMA AND THEATER IN CLASSICAL ATHENS

Arnott, Peter D. *Greek Scenic Conventions in the Fifth Century, B.C.* Oxford: Oxford University Press, 1962.

Beare, William. *The Roman Stage*. London: Methuen, 1969.

Bieber, Margarete. *The History of the Greek and Roman Theatre*. Princeton, NJ: Princeton University Press, 1961.

Else, Gerald F. *The Origin and Early Form of Greek Tragedy*. New York: Norton, 1972.

Hamilton, Edith. *The Greek Way*. New York: Norton, 1983.

Knox, Bernard M. *Word and Action: Essays on the Ancient Theater*. Baltimore: Johns Hopkins University Press, 1979.

Konstan, David. *Roman Comedy*. Ithaca, NY: Cornell University Press, 1983.

Pickard-Cambridge, A. W. *Dithyramb, Tragedy, and Comedy*. Oxford: Oxford University Press, 1962.

Pickard-Cambridge, A. W. *The Dramatic Festivals of Athens*. Oxford: Oxford University Press, 1968.

Pickard-Cambridge, A. W. *The Theatre of Dionysus in Athens*. Oxford: Oxford University Press, 1945.

Segal, Erich, ed. *Greek Tragedy: Modern Essays in Criticism*. New York: Harper and Row, 1983.

Taplin, Oliver. *Greek Tragedy in Action*. Berkeley, CA: University of California Press, 1978.

Vince, Ronald W. *Ancient and Medieval Theatre: A Historiographical Handbook*. Westport, CT: Greenwood, 1984.

Webster, T. B. L. *Greek Theater Production*. London: Methuen, 1970.

Winkler, John J., and Froma I. Zeitlin, eds. *Nothing to Do with Dionysus? Athenian Drama in Its Social Context*. Princeton, NJ: Princeton University Press, 1990.

Gagarin, Michael. *Aeschylean Drama*. Berkeley, CA: University of California Press, 1976.

Knox, B. M. W., "Aeschylus and the Third Actor." In Bernard M. Knox. *Word and Action: Essays on the Ancient Theater*. Baltimore: Johns Hopkins University Press, 1979.

Lloyd-Jones, Hugh. "The Guilt of Agamemnon." In Erich Segal, ed. *Greek Tragedy: Modern Essays in Criticism*. New York: Harper and Row, 1983.

Rosenmeyer, Thomas G. *The Art of Aeschylus*. Berkeley, CA: University of California Press, 1982.

Taplin, Oliver. *The Stagecraft of Aeschylus*. Oxford: Oxford University Press, 1977.

Deardon, C. W. *The Stage of Aristophanes*. London: Athlone, 1976.

Dover, K. J. *Aristophanic Comedy*. Berkeley, CA: University of California Press, 1972.

Harriott, Rosemary. *Aristophanes: Poet and Dramatist*. Baltimore: Johns Hopkins University Press, 1986.

Ussher, Robert Glenn. *Aristophanes*. Oxford: Oxford University Press, 1979.

Dodds, E. R. *The Greeks and the Irrational*. Berkeley, CA: University of California Press, 1951.

Foley, Helene P. *Ritual Irony: Poetry and Sacrifice in Euripides*. Ithaca, NY: Cornell University Press, 1985.

Michelini, Ann N. *Euripides and the Tragic Tradition*. Madison, WI: University of Wisconsin Press, 1987.

Rosenmeyer, Thomas G. "Tragedy and Religion: *The Bacchae*." In Erich Segal, ed. *Greek Tragedy: Modern Essays in Criticism*. New York: Harper and Row, 1983.

Dodds, E. R., "On Misunderstanding the *Oedipus Rex*." In Erich Segal, ed. *Greek Tragedy: Modern Essays in Criticism*. New York: Harper and Row, 1983.

Fergusson, Francis. *The Idea of a Theater*. Princeton, NJ: Princeton University Press, 1947.

Knox, B. M. W. *Oedipus at Thebes*. New York: Norton, 1971.

Segal, Charles. *Tragedy and Civilization: An Interpretation of Sophocles*. Cambridge, MA: Harvard University Press, 1981.

Whitman, C. H. *Sophocles: A Study in Heroic Humanism*. Cambridge, MA: Cambridge University Press, 1951.

Winnington-Ingram, R. P. *Sophocles: An Interpretation*. New York: Cambridge University Press, 1980.

Bentley, Gerald Eades. *The Jacobean and Caroline Stage*. 5 vols. Oxford: Oxford University Press, 1941–56.

Bentley, Gerald Eades. *The Profession of Dramatist in Shakespeare's Time, 1590–1642*. Princeton, NJ: Princeton University Press, 1971.

Bentley, Gerald Eades. *The Profession of Player in Shakespeare's Time, 1590–1642*. Princeton, NJ: Princeton University Press, 1984.

Bevington, David. *From Mankind to Marlowe: Growth in Structure in the Popular Drama of Tudor England*. Cambridge, MA: Harvard University Press, 1962.

Bevington, David. *Medieval Drama*. Boston: Houghton, 1975.

Aeschylus

Aristophanes

Euripides

Sophocles

UNIT 2: DRAMA AND THEATER IN MEDIEVAL AND RENAISSANCE ENGLAND

Chambers, E. K. *The Elizabethan Stage*. 4 vols. Oxford: Oxford University Press, 1923.

Chambers, E. K. *The Medieval Stage*. 2 vols. London: Oxford University Press, 1967.

Greenblatt, Stephen, ed. *Representing the English Renaissance*. Berkeley, CA: University of California Press, 1988.

Gurr, Andrew. *The Shakespearean Stage, 1574–1642*. Cambridge, MA: Cambridge University Press, 1970.

Hardison, O. B., Jr. *Christian Rite and Christian Drama in the Middle Ages*. Baltimore: Johns Hopkins University Press, 1965.

Kolve, V. A. *The Play Called Corpus Christi*. Stanford, CA: Stanford University Press, 1966.

Orgel, Stephen. *The Illusion of Power: Political Theatre in the English Renaissance*. Berkeley, CA: University of California Press, 1975.

Vince, Ronald W. *Ancient and Medieval Theatre: A Historiographical Handbook*. Westport, CT: Greenwood, 1984.

Wickham, Glynne. *The Medieval Theatre*. New York: Cambridge University Press, 1987.

Woolf, Rosemary. *The English Mystery Plays*. Berkeley, CA: University of California Press, 1972.

Everyman

Bevington, David. *From Mankind to Marlowe: Growth in Structure in the Popular Drama of Tudor England*. Cambridge, MA: Harvard University Press, 1962.

Garner, Stanton B., Jr. "Theatricality in *Mankind* and *Everyman*." *Studies in Philology* 84 (1987): 272–85.

Christopher Marlowe

Bevington, David. *From Mankind to Marlowe: Growth in Structure in the Popular Drama of Tudor England*. Cambridge, MA: Harvard University Press, 1962.

Cole, Douglas. *Suffering and Evil in the Plays of Christopher Marlowe*. Princeton, NJ: Princeton University Press, 1962.

Kernan, Alvin B., ed. *Two Renaissance Mythmakers: Christopher Marlowe and Ben Jonson*. Baltimore: Johns Hopkins University Press, 1977.

Leech, Clifford, ed. *Marlowe: A Collection of Critical Essays*. Englewood Cliffs, NJ: Prentice-Hall, 1964.

Levin, Harry. *The Overreacher: A Study of Christopher Marlowe*. Boston: Beacon, 1964.

William Shakespeare

Bamber, Linda. *Comic Women, Tragic Men: A Study of Gender and Genre in Shakespeare*. Stanford, CA: Stanford University Press, 1982.

Barber, C. L. *Shakespeare's Festive Comedy*. Princeton, NJ: Princeton University Press, 1968.

Barker, Francis, and Peter Hulme. "Nymphs and Reapers Heavily Vanish: The Discursive Con-texts of *The Tempest*." In John Drakakis, ed. *Alternative Shakespeares*. New York: Methuen, 1985.

Bradley, A. C. *Shakespearean Tragedy*. New York: Meridian, 1955.

Brown, Paul. "'This thing of darkness I acknowledge mine': *The Tempest* and the Discourse of Colonialism." In Jonathan Dollimore and Alan Sinfield, eds. *Political Shakespeare: New Essays in Cultural Materialism*. Ithaca, NY: Cornell University Press, 1985.

Bullough, Geoffrey, ed. *Narrative and Dramatic Sources of Shakespeare*. 8 vols. New York: Columbia University Press, 1957–75.

Cavell, Stanley. "The Avoidance of Love: A Reading of *King Lear*." In *Must We Mean What We Say?* Cambridge, MA: Cambridge University Press, 1976.

Danson, Lawrence, ed. *On King Lear*. Princeton, NJ: Princeton University Press, 1981.

Dollimore, Jonathan, and Alan Sinfield, eds. *Political Shakespeare: New Essays in Cultural Materialism*. Ithaca, NY: Cornell University Press, 1985.

Drakakis, John, ed. *Alternative Shakespeares*. New York: Methuen, 1985.

Greenblatt, Stephen. *Shakespearean Negotiations*. Berkeley, CA: University of California Press, 1988.

Howard, Jean E., and Marion F. O'Connor, eds. *Shakespeare Reproduced: The Text in History and Ideology.* London: Methuen, 1987.

Jardine, Lisa. *Still Harping on Daughters: Women and Drama in the Age of Shakespeare.* Totowa, NJ: Barnes and Noble, 1983.

Kernan, Alvin B., ed. *Modern Shakespearean Criticism.* New York: Harcourt, Brace & World, 1970.

Kernan, Alvin B. *The Playwright as Magician.* New Haven, CT: Yale University Press, 1979.

Kott, Jan. *Shakespeare Our Contemporary.* New York: Norton, 1974.

Mack, Maynard. *King Lear in Our Time.* Berkeley, CA: University of California Press, 1972.

Orgel, Stephen. "Prospero's Wife." In Stephen Greenblatt, ed., *Representing the English Renaissance.* Berkeley, CA: University of California Press, 1988.

Parker, Patricia, and Geoffrey Hartman, eds. *Shakespeare and the Question of Theory.* London: Methuen, 1985.

Schoenbaum, S. *Shakespeare: A Documentary Life.* New York: Oxford University Press, 1975.

Schwartz, Murray M., and Coppélia Kahn, eds. *Representing Shakespeare: New Psychoanalytic Essays.* Baltimore: Johns Hopkins University Press, 1981.

Taylor, Gary, and Michael Warren, eds. *The Division of the Kingdoms: Shakespeare's Two Versions of King Lear.* Oxford: Oxford University Press, 1983.

Thompson, Marvin, and Ruth Thompson, eds. *Shakespeare and the Sense of Performance.* Newark, NJ: University of Delaware Press, 1989.

Holland, Norman N. *The First Modern Comedies: The Significance of Etheredge, Wycherley, and Congreve.* Cambridge, MA: Harvard University Press, 1959.

Kirsch, Arthur C. *Dryden's Heroic Drama.* Princeton, NJ: Princeton University Press, 1965.

Lancaster, H. C. *A History of French Dramatic Literature in the Seventeenth Century.* 5 vols. Baltimore: Johns Hopkins University Press, 1929–1942.

Loftis, John. *The Politics of Drama in Augustan England.* Oxford: Oxford University Press, 1963.

Loftis, John, Richard Southern, Marion Jones, and A. H. Scouten, eds. *The Revels History of Drama in English.* Vol. 5: 1660–1750. London: Methuen, 1976.

Staves, Susan. *Players' Scepters: Fictions of Authority in the Restoration.* Lincoln, NE: University of Nebraska Press, 1979.

Styan, J. L. *Restoration Comedy in Performance.* Cambridge: Cambridge University Press, 1986.

Waith, Eugene. *The Herculean Hero.* New York: Columbia University Press, 1962.

Waith, Eugene. *Ideas of Greatness.* London: Routledge and Kegan Paul, 1971.

Wiley, W. L. *The Early Public Theatre in France.* Cambridge, MA: Harvard University Press, 1920.

UNIT 3: DRAMA AND THEATER IN THE LATE SEVENTEENTH CENTURY: RESTORATION ENGLAND AND LOUIS XIV'S FRANCE

Diamond, Elin. "Gestus and Signature in Aphra Behn's *The Rover.*" *ELH* 56 (1989): 519–39.

Duffy, Maureen. *The Passionate Shepherdess: Aphra Behn, 1640–89.* London: Methuen, 1977.

Aphra Behn

Gaines, James F. *Molière's Theater.* Columbus, OH: Ohio State University Press, 1984.

Gossman, L. *Men and Masks: A Study of Molière.* Baltimore: Johns Hopkins University Press, 1963.

Gross, Nathan. *From Gesture to Idea: Esthetics and Ethics in Molière's Comedy.* New York: Columbia University Press, 1982.

Guicharnaud, Jacques. *Molière: A Collection of Critical Essays.* Englewood Cliffs, NJ: Prentice-Hall, 1964.

Molière

Barthes, Roland. *On Racine.* Trans. Richard Howard. New York: Hill and Wang, 1964.

Cook, A. S. *French Tragedy: The Power of Enactment.* Chicago: University of Chicago Press, 1980.

Goldmann, Lucien. *Racine.* Trans. Alastair Hamilton. London: Writers and Readers, 1981.

Jean Racine

UNIT 4: DRAMA AND THEATER IN MODERN EUROPE

Antoine, André. *Memories of the Théâtre Libre*. Trans. Marvin Carlson. Coral Gables, FL: University of Miami Press, 1964.

Bennett, Benjamin. *Modern Drama and German Classicism: Renaissance from Lessing to Brecht*. Ithaca, NY: Cornell University Press, 1979.

Bennett, Benjamin. *Theater as Problem: Modern Drama and Its Place in Literature*. Ithaca, NY: Cornell University Press, 1990.

Bentley, Eric. *The Playwright as Thinker: A Study of Drama in Modern Times*. New York: Harcourt, 1946.

Braun, Edward. *Meyerhold on Theatre*. New York: Hill and Wang, 1969.

Brockett, Oscar G., and Robert R. Findlay. *Century of Innovation: A History of European and American Theatre and Drama Since 1870*. Englewood Cliffs, NJ: Prentice-Hall, 1973.

Brustein, Robert. *The Theatre of Revolt*. Boston: Little, Brown, 1964.

Cole, Toby, ed. *Directors on Directing*. Indianapolis, IN: Bobbs-Merrill, 1963.

Cole, Toby, ed. *Playwrights on Playwriting*. New York: Hill and Wang, 1960.

Davis, Tracy C. *Actresses as Working Women: Their Social Identity in Victorian Culture*. London: Routledge, 1991.

Driver, Tom. *Romantic Quest and Modern Query: A History of the Modern Theatre*. New York: Delacorte, 1970.

Finney, Gail. *Women in Modern Drama: Freud, Feminism, and European Theater at the Turn of the Century*. Ithaca, NY: Cornell University Press, 1989.

Gilman, Richard. *The Making of Modern Drama*. New York: Farrar, Straus & Giroux, 1974.

Hunt, Hugh, et al., eds. *The Revels History of Drama in English*. Vol. 7: 1880 to the Present Day. London: Methuen, 1979.

Jones, David Richard. *Great Directors at Work*. Berkeley, CA: University of California Press, 1986.

Peter, John. *Vladimir's Carrot: Modern Drama and the Modern Imagination*. Chicago: University of Chicago Press, 1987.

Quigley, Austin. *The Modern Stage and Other Worlds*. London: Methuen, 1985.

Seltzer, Daniel, ed. *The Modern Theatre: Readings and Documents*. Boston: Little, Brown, 1967.

Stanislavski, Constantin. *An Actor Prepares*. Trans. Elizabeth Reynolds Hapgood. New York: Theatre Arts, 1936.

Stanislavski, Constantin. *Building a Character*. Trans. Elizabeth Reynolds Hapgood. New York: Theatre Arts, 1949.

Stanislavski, Constantin. *Creating a Role*. Trans. Elizabeth Reynolds Hapgood. New York: Theatre Arts, 1961.

Stanislavski, Constantin. *My Life in Art*. Trans. J. J. Robbins. Boston: Little, Brown, 1924.

Styan, J. L. *The Dark Comedy*. Cambridge: Cambridge University Press, 1968.

Styan, J. L. *Modern Drama in Theory and Practice*. 3 vols. Cambridge: Cambridge University Press, 1980.

Whitaker, Thomas R. *Fields of Play in Modern Drama*. Princeton, NJ: Princeton University Press, 1977.

Wiles, Timothy J. *The Theater Event: Modern Theories of Performance*. Chicago: University of Chicago Press, 1980.

Williams, Raymond. *Drama from Ibsen to Brecht*. London: Hogarth, 1987.

Williams, Raymond. *Modern Tragedy*. Stanford, CA: Stanford University Press, 1966.

Worthen, W. B. *Modern Drama and the Rhetoric of Theater*. Berkeley, CA: University of California Press, 1992.

Bertolt Brecht

Benjamin, Walter. *Understanding Brecht*. Trans. Anna Bostock. London: NLB, 1973.

Bentley, Eric. *The Brecht Commentaries 1943–1980*. New York: Grove, 1981.

Brecht, Bertolt. *Brecht on Theatre: The Development of an Aesthetic*. Ed. and Trans. John Willett. New York: Hill and Wang, 1964.

Brecht, Bertolt. *The Messingkauf Dialogues*. Trans. John Willett. London: Methuen, 1965.

Dickson, Keith A. *Towards Utopia: A Study of Brecht*. Oxford: Oxford University Press, 1978.

Esslin, Martin. *Brecht: The Man and His Work*. Garden City, NJ: Doubleday, 1971.

Ewen, Frederick. *Bertolt Brecht: His LIfe, His Art and His Times*. New York: Citadel, 1967.

Fuegi, John. *Bertolt Brecht: Chaos According to Plan*. Cambridge: Cambridge University Press, 1987.

Lyon, James K. *Bertolt Brecht in America*. Princeton, NJ: Princeton University Press, 1980.

Wright, Elizabeth. *Postmodern Brecht: A Re-Presentation*. London: Routledge, 1989.

Anton Chekhov

Chekhov, Anton. *Letters of Anton Chekhov*. Trans. Michael Henry Heim and Simon Karlinsky. New York: Harper and Row, 1973.

Gottleib, Vera. *Chekhov and the Vaudeville*. Cambridge: Cambridge University Press, 1982.

Hingley, Ronald. *Chekhov: A Biographical and Critical Study*. New York: Barnes and Noble, 1966.

Magarshack, David. *Chekhov the Dramatist*. New York: Hill and Wang, 1960.

Peace, Richard. *Chekhov: A Study of the Four Major Plays*. New Haven, CT: Yale University Press, 1983.

Pitcher, Henry. *The Chekhov Play*. London: Chatto and Windus, 1973.

Rayfield, Donald. *Chekhov: The Evolution of His Art*. London: Paul Elek, 1975.

Styan, J. L. *Chekhov in Performance*. Cambridge: Cambridge University Press, 1971.

Henrik Ibsen

Cima, Gay Gibson. "Discovering Signs: The Emergence of the Critical Actor in Ibsen," *Theatre Journal* 35 (1983): 5–22.

Egan, Michael, ed. *Ibsen: The Critical Heritage*. London: Routledge and Kegan Paul, 1972.

Hardwick, Elizabeth. "A Doll's House." In *Seduction and Betrayal*. New York: Random House, 1970.

Lyons, Charles R. *Henrik Ibsen: The Divided Consciousness*. Carbondale, IL: Southern Illinois University Press, 1972.

Marker, Frederick J., and Lise-Lone Marker. *Ibsen's Lively Art: A Performance Study of the Major Plays*. Cambridge: Cambridge University Press, 1989.

Meyer, Michael. *Henrik Ibsen: A Biography*. Garden City, NJ: Doubleday, 1971.

Northam, John. *Ibsen: A Critical Study*. Cambridge: Cambridge University Press, 1973.

Northam, John. *Ibsen's Dramatic Method: A Study of the Prose Dramas*. London: Faber and Faber, 1953.

Shaw, Bernard. *The Quintessence of Ibsenism*. New York: Hill and Wang, 1957.

Sprinchorn, Evert, ed. *Ibsen: Letters and Speeches*. New York: Hill and Wang, 1964.

Luigi Pirandello

Bassnet-McGuire, Susan. *Luigi Pirandello*. New York: Grove, 1983.

Bentley, Eric. *The Pirandello Commentaries*. Evanston, IL: Northwestern University Press, 1986.

Guidice, Gaspare. *Pirandello: A Biography*. Trans. Alastair Hamilton. Oxford: Oxford University Press, 1975.

Kennedy, Andrew K. "Six Characters: Pirandello's Last Tape." *Modern Drama* 12 (1969): 1–9.

Oliver, Roger W. *Dreams of Passion: The Theater of Luigi Pirandello*. New York: New York University Press, 1979.

Paolucci, Anne. *Pirandello's Theater*. Carbondale, IL: Southern Illinois University Press, 1974.

Pirandello, Luigi. *On Humor.* Trans. Antonio Illiano and Daniel P. Testa. Chapel Hill, NC: University of North Carolina Press, 1974.

Sogluizzo, A. Richard. *Luigi Pirandello, Director: The Playwright in the Theatre.* Metuchen, NJ: Scarecrow, 1982.

Bernard Shaw

Bentley, Eric. *Bernard Shaw.* New York: Norton, 1976.

Berst, Charles A. *Bernard Shaw and the Art of Drama.* Urbana, IL: University of Illinois Press, 1973.

Compton, Louis. *Shaw the Dramatist.* Lincoln, NE: University of Nebraska Press, 1969.

Evans, T. F., ed. *Shaw: The Critical Heritage.* London: Routledge and Kegan Paul, 1976.

Goldman, Michael. "Shaw and the Marriage in Dionysus." In *The Play and Its Critic: Essays for Eric Bentley.* Ed. Michael Bertin. New York: University Presses of America, 1986.

Holroyd, Michael. *Bernard Shaw.* 3 vols. New York: Random House, 1988–1991.

Meisel, Martin. *Shaw and the Nineteenth-Century Theater.* Princeton, NJ: Princeton University Press, 1963.

Peters, Margot. *Bernard Shaw and the Actresses.* Garden City, NJ: Doubleday, 1980.

Turco, Alfred, Jr. *Shaw's Moral Vision: The Self and Salvation.* Ithaca, NY: Cornell University Press, 1976.

Wisenthal, J. L. *The Marriage of Contraries: Bernard Shaw's Middle Plays.* Cambridge, MA: Harvard University Press, 1974.

August Strindberg

Carlson, Harry G. *Strindberg and the Poetry of Myth.* Berkeley, CA: University of California Press, 1982.

Lucas, F. L. *The Drama of Ibsen and Strindberg.* London: Cassell, 1962.

Reinert, Otto, ed. *Strindberg: A Collection of Critical Essays.* Englewood Cliffs, NJ: Prentice-Hall, 1971.

Sprinchorn, Evert. *Strindberg as Dramatist.* New Haven, CT: Yale University Press, 1982.

Strindberg, August. *From an Occult Diary.* Trans. Mary Sandbach. New York: Hill and Wang, 1965.

Strindberg, August. *Open Letters to the Intimate Theater.* Trans. Walter Johnson. Seattle, WA: University of Washington Press, n.d.

Törnqvist, Egil. *Strindbergian Drama.* Atlantic Highlands, NJ: Humanities Press, 1982.

William Butler Yeats

Donoghue, Denis. *The Third Voice: Modern British and American Verse Drama.* Princeton, NJ: Princeton University Press, 1959.

Ellmann, Richard. *Yeats: The Man and the Masks.* New York: Norton, 1978.

Flannery, James W. *W. B. Yeats and the Idea of a Theatre.* New Haven, CT: Yale University Press, 1976.

Frazier, Adrian. *Behind the Scenes: Yeats, Horniman, and the Struggle for the Abbey Theatre.* Berkeley, CA: University of California Press, 1990.

Friedman, Barton R. *Adventures in the Deeps of the Mind.* Princeton, NJ: Princeton University Press, 1977.

Hunt, Hugh. *The Abbey: Ireland's National Theatre, 1904–1979.* New York: Columbia University Press, 1979.

Jeffares, A. Norman, and A. S. Knowland. *A Commentary on the Collected Plays of W. B. Yeats.* London: Macmillan, 1975.

Miller, Liam. *The Noble Drama of W. B. Yeats.* Dublin: Dolmen Press, 1977.

O'Driscoll, Robert, ed. *Theatre and Nationalism in Twentieth-Century Ireland.* Toronto: University of Toronto Press, 1971.

Ure, Peter. *Yeats the Playwright.* London: Routledge and Kegan Paul, 1963.

Worth, Katharine. *The Irish Drama of Europe from Yeats to Beckett*. London: Athlone, 1978.

Yeats, W. B. *Autobiographies*. London: Macmillan, 1955.

Yeats, W. B. *Essays and Introductions*. New York: Macmillan, 1961.

Yeats, W. B. *Explorations*. New York: Macmillan, 1962.

Bigsby, C. W. E. *A Critical Introduction to Twentieth-Century American Drama*. 3 vols. Cambridge: Cambridge University Press, 1982–85.

Bronner, Edwin, ed. *The Encyclopedia of the American Theatre 1900–1975*. New York: A. S. Barnes, 1980.

Chinoy, Helen Krich, and Linda Walsh Jenkins, eds. *Women in American Theatre*. New York: Crown, 1981.

Clurman, Harold. *The Fervent Years: The Story of the Group Theatre and the Thirties*. New York: Knopf, 1945.

Cohn, Ruby. *New American Dramatists, 1960–1980*. New York: Grove, 1982.

Coven, Brenda, ed. *American Women Dramatists of the Twentieth Century: A Bibliography*. Metuchen, NJ: Scarecrow, 1982.

Downer, Alan S., ed. *American Drama and Its Critics*. Chicago: University of Chicago Press, 1965.

Flanagan, Hallie. *Arena*. New York: Duell, Sloan and Pearce, 1949.

Garza, Roberto, ed. *Contemporary Chicano Theatre*. Notre Dame, IN: University of Notre Dame Press, 1976.

Harrison, Paul Carter. *The Drama of Nommo*. New York: Grove, 1972.

Hatch, James V., ed. *Black Theatre USA: Forty-Five Plays by Black Americans 1847–1974*. New York: Macmillan, 1974.

Hill, Errol, ed. *The Theatre of Black Americans*. 2 vols. Englewood Cliffs, NJ: Prentice-Hall, 1980.

Huerta, Jorge A. *Chicano Theater: Themes and Forms*. Ypsilanti, MI: Bilingual Press, 1982.

Kanellos, Nicolás. *Hispanic Theatre in the United States*. Houston: Arte Público Press, 1984.

Kernan, Alvin B. *The Modern American Theater: A Collection of Critical Essays*. Englewood Cliffs, NJ: Prentice-Hall, 1967.

Marker, Lise-Lone. *David Belasco: Naturalism in the American Theatre*. Princeton, NJ: Princeton University Press, 1975.

Perkins, Kathy A. *Black Female Playwrights: An Anthology of Plays Before 1950*. Bloomington, IN: Indiana University Press, 1989.

Rabkin, Gerald. *Drama and Commitment: Politics in the American Theatre of the Thirties*. Bloomington, IN: Indiana University Press, 1964.

Shank, Ted. *American Alternative Theatres*. New York: Grove, 1982.

Shewey, Don, ed. *Out Front: Contemporary Gay and Lesbian Plays*. New York: Grove, 1988.

Baraka, Imamu Amiri. *The Autobiography of LeRoi Jones/Amiri Baraka*. New York: Freundlich, 1984.

Baraka, Imamu Amiri. "Exaugural Address." *Kulchur* 3:3 (Winter 1964).

Baraka, Imamu Amiri. *Selected Plays and Prose of Amiri Baraka/LeRoi Jones*. New York: William Morrow, 1979.

Bentson, Kimberly W., ed. *Imamu Amiri Baraka (LeRoi Jones): A Collection of Critical Essays*. Englewood Cliffs, NJ: Prentice-Hall, 1978.

Richards, Sandra. "Negative Forces and Positive Non-Entities: Images of Women in the Drama of Amiri Baraka." *Theatre Journal* 32 (1985): 233–40.

UNIT 5: DRAMA AND THEATER IN THE UNITED STATES

Amiri Baraka/ LeRoi Jones

Smith, David. "Amiri Baraka and the Politics of Popular Culture." In *Politics and the Muse: Studies in the Politics of Recent American Literature.* Ed. Adam Sorkin. Bowling Green, OH: Popular, 1989.

Sollors, Werner. *Amiri Baraka/LeRoi Jones: The Quest for a "Populist Modernism."* New York: Columbia University Press, 1978.

Susan Glaspell

Ben-Zvi, Linda. "Susan Glaspell's Contributions to Contemporary Women Playwrights." In *Feminine Focus: The New Women Playwrights.* Ed. Enoch Brater. New York: Oxford University Press, 1989.

Dymkowski, Christine. "On the Edge: The Plays of Susan Glaspell." *Modern Drama* 31 (1988): 91–105.

Kolodny, Annette. "A Map for Rereading: Gender and the Interpretation of Literary Texts." In *The New Feminist Criticism: Essays on Women, Literature, and Theory.* Ed. Elaine Showalter. New York: Pantheon, 1985.

Stein, Karen F. "The Women's World of Glaspell's *Trifles.*" In Helen Krich Chinoy and Linda Walsh Jenkins, eds. *Women in American Theatre.* New York: Crown, 1981.

Arthur Miller

Carson, Neil. *Arthur Miller.* New York: Grove, 1982.

Corrigan, Robert W., ed. *Arthur Miller: A Collection of Critical Essays.* Englewood Cliffs, NJ: Prentice-Hall, 1969.

Martin, Robert A., ed. *Arthur Miller: New Perspectives.* Englewood Cliffs, NJ: Prentice-Hall, 1982.

Miller, Arthur. *The Theater Essays of Arthur Miller.* Ed. Robert Martin. New York: Viking, 1978.

Miller, Arthur. *Timebends: A Life.* New York: Grove, 1987.

Eugene O'Neill

Bogard, Travis. *Contour in Time: The Plays of Eugene O'Neill.* Oxford: Oxford University Press, 1988.

Cargill, Oscar, N. Bryllion Fagin, and William J. Fisher, eds. *O'Neill and His Plays: Four Decades of Criticism.* New York: New York University Press, 1961.

Chothia, Jean. *Forging a Language: A Study of the Plays of Eugene O'Neill.* Cambridge: Cambridge University Press, 1979.

Floyd, Virginia, ed. *Eugene O'Neill at Work: Newly Released Ideas for Plays.* New York: Ungar, 1981.

Gelb, Arthur, and Barbara Gelb. *O'Neill.* New York: Harper and Row, 1973.

Sheaffer, Louis. *O'Neill: Son and Playwright.* Boston: Little, Brown, 1968.

Wainscott, Ronald H. *Staging O'Neill: The Experimental Years, 1920–1934.* New Haven, CT: Yale University Press, 1988.

Ntozake Shange

Cronacher, Karen. "Unmasking the Minstrel Mask's Black Magic: Ntozake Shange's *spell #7.*" *Theatre Journal* 44 (1992): 177–93.

Shange, Ntozake. *See No Evil: Prefaces, Essays, and Accounts 1976–1983.* San Francisco: Momo's Press, 1984.

Shange, Ntozake. *Three Pieces: spell #7, A Photograph: Lovers in Motion, Boogie Woogie Landscapes.* New York: Penguin, 1982.

Sam Shepard

King, Kimball. *Sam Shepard: A Casebook.* New York: Garland, 1988.

Marranca, Bonnie, ed. *American Dreams: The Imagination of Sam Shepard.* New York: Performing Arts Journal Publications, 1981.

Mottram, Ron. *Inner Landscapes: The Theater of Sam Shepard.* Columbia, MO: University of Missouri Press, 1984.

Oumano, Ellen. *Sam Shepard: The Life and Work of an American Dreamer.* New York: St. Martin's, 1986.

Broyles González, Yolanda. "Toward a Re-Vision of Chicano Theatre History: The Women of El Teatro Campesino." In Lynda Hart, ed. *Making a Spectacle: Feminist Essays on Contemporary Women's Theatre*. Ann Arbor, MI: University of Michigan Press, 1989.

Huerta, Jorge A. *Chicano Theater: Themes and Forms*. Ypsilanti, MI: Bilingual Press, 1982.

Kanellos, Nicolás. *Hispanic Theatre in the United States*. Houston: Arte Público, 1984.

Morton, Carlos. "The Teatro Campesino." *Tulane Drama Review* 18:4 (December 1974): 71–6.

von Bardeleben, Renate, ed. *Missions in Conflict: Essays on U.S.–Mexican Relations and Chicano Culture*. Tübingen, Germany: G. Narr, 1986.

Valdez, Luis. *Pensamiento Serpentino*. El Centro Campesino Cultural, CA: Cucaracha, 1973.

Valdez, Luis, and El Teatro Campesino. *Actos*. San Juan Bautista, CA: Menyah Productions, 1971.

Boxill, Roger. *Tennessee Williams*. New York: St. Martin's, 1987.

Devlin, Albert J., ed. *Conversations with Tennessee Williams*. Jackson, MS: University of Mississippi Press, 1986.

Leavitt, Richard Freeman, ed. *The World of Tennessee Williams*. New York: Putnam, 1978.

Spoto, Donald. *The Kindness of Strangers: The Life of Tennessee Williams*. Boston: Little, Brown, 1985.

Stanton, Stephen, ed. *Tennessee Williams: A Collection of Critical Essays*. Englewood Cliffs, NJ: Prentice-Hall, 1977.

Williams, Tennessee. *Memoirs*. Garden City, NJ: Doubleday, 1975.

Artaud, Antonin. *The Theater and Its Double*. Trans. Mary Caroline Richards. New York: Grove, 1958.

Bentley, Eric. *Theatre of War*. New York: Viking, 1972.

Betsko, Kathleen, and Rachel Koenig, eds. *Interviews with Contemporary Women Playwrights*. New York: Beech Tree, 1987.

Bigsby, C. W. E. "The Language of Crisis in British Theatre: The Drama of Cultural Pathology." In *Contemporary English Drama*. Ed. C. W. E. Bigsby. New York: Holmes and Meier, 1981.

Blau, Herbert. *Eve of the Prey: Subversions of the Postmodern*. Bloomington, IN: Indiana University Press, 1987.

Bradby, David. *Modern French Drama, 1940–1980*. New York: Grove, 1984.

Brater, Enoch, ed. *Feminine Focus: The New Women Playwrights*. New York: Oxford University Press, 1989.

Brook, Peter. *The Empty Space*. New York: Avon, 1968.

Calandra, Denis. *New German Dramatists*. New York: Grove, 1983.

Case, Sue-Ellen. "Toward a Butch-Femme Aesthetic." In Lynda Hart, ed. *Making a Spectacle: Feminist Essays on Contemporary Women's Theatre*. Ann Arbor, MI: University of Michigan Press, 1989.

Chinweizu, Onwuchekwa Jemie, and Ihechukwu Madubuike. *Toward the Decolonization of African Literature*. Vol. 1. Washington, DC: Howard University Press, 1983.

Cohn, Ruby. *From Desire to Godot: Pocket Theater of Postwar Paris*. Berkeley, CA: University of California Press, 1987.

de Lauretis, Teresa. "Sexual Indifferentiation and Lesbian Representation." *Theatre Journal* 40 (1988): 155–77.

Dolan, Jill. *The Feminist Spectator as Critic*. Ann Arbor, MI: UMI Research Press, 1988.

Elsom, John. *Post-War British Theatre*. London: Routledge and Kegan Paul, 1976.

Esslin, Martin. *The Theatre of the Absurd*. New York: Doubleday, 1969.

Grotowski, Jerzy. *Towards a Poor Theatre*. New York: Simon & Schuster, 1968.

Luis Valdez

Tennessee Williams

**UNIT 6:
DRAMA AND
THEATER
TODAY: THE
WORLD STAGE**

Hart, Lynda, ed. *Making a Spectacle: Feminist Essays on Contemporary Women's Theatre*. Ann Arbor, MI: University of Michigan Press, 1989.

Marranca, Bonnie, ed. *The Theatre of Images*. New York: Drama Book Specialists, 1977.

Ndlovu, Duma. *Woza Afrika! An Anthology of South African Plays*. New York: Braziller, 1986.

Ngugi wa Thiong'o. *Decolonising the Mind: The Politics of Language in African Literature*. London: James Currey, 1986.

Rosen, Carol. *Plays of Impasse: Contemporary Drama Set in Confining Institutions*. Princeton, NJ: Princeton University Press, 1983.

Schechner, Richard. *Environmental Theater*. New York: Hawthorn, 1973.

Taylor, John Russell. *Anger and After*. London: Methuen, 1969.

Taylor, John Russell. *The Second Wave: British Drama of the Sixties*. London: Eyre Methuen, 1978.

Worth, Katharine. *Revolutions in Modern English Drama*. London: G. Bell and Sons, 1972.

Samuel Beckett

Acheson, James, and Kateryna Arthur, eds. *Beckett's Later Fiction and Drama: Texts for Company*. New York: St. Martin's, 1987.

Bair, Deirdre. *Samuel Beckett: A Biography*. New York: Harcourt Brace Jovanovich, 1978.

Beckett, Samuel. *Happy Days: The Production Notebook of Samuel Beckett*. Ed. James Knowlson. New York: Grove, 1985.

Brater, Enoch, ed. *Beckett at 80/Beckett in Context*. Oxford: Oxford University Press, 1986.

Brater, Enoch. *Beyond Minimalism: Beckett's Late Style in the Theater*. Oxford: Oxford University Press, 1987.

Cohn, Ruby. *Just Play: Beckett's Theater*. Princeton, NJ: Princeton University Press, 1980.

Cohn, Ruby. *Samuel Beckett: The Comic Gamut*. New Brunswick, NJ: Rutgers University Press, 1962.

Gontarski, S. E. *Beckett's Happy Days: A Manuscript Study*. Columbus, OH: Ohio University Libraries, 1977.

Gontarski, S. E. *On Beckett: Essays and Criticism*. New York: Grove, 1986.

Graver, Lawrence, and Raymond Federman, eds. *Samuel Beckett: The Critical Heritage*. London: Routledge and Kegan Paul, 1979.

Kalb, Jonathan. *Beckett in Performance*. Cambridge: Cambridge University Press, 1989.

Kenner, Hugh. *Samuel Beckett*. Berkeley, CA: University of California Press, 1968.

Worth, Katharine. *The Irish Drama of Europe from Yeats to Beckett*. London: Athlone, 1978.

Caryl Churchill

Churchill, Caryl. "The Common Imagination and the Individual Voice." *New Theatre Quarterly* 4 (February 1988): 3–16.

Diamond, Elin. "Brechtian Theory/Feminist Criticism: Toward a Gestic Feminist Criticism." *Drama Review* 32:1 (Spring 1988): 82–94.

Diamond, Elin. "(In)Visible Bodies in Churchill's Theatre." *Theatre Journal* 40 (1988): 188–204.

Diamond, Elin. "Refusing the Romanticism of Identity: Narrative Interventions in Churchill, Benmussa, Duras." *Theatre Journal* 37 (1985): 273–86.

Quigley, Austin E. "Stereotype and Prototype: Character in the Plays of Caryl Churchill." In Enoch Brater, ed. *Feminine Focus: The New Women Playwrights*. New York: Oxford University Press, 1989.

Randall, Phyllis R., ed. *Caryl Churchill: A Casebook*. New York: Garland, 1989.

Brian Friel

Dantanus, Ulf. *Brian Friel: A Study*. London: Faber and Faber, 1988.

Deane, Seamus. *Celtic Revivals: Essays in Modern Irish Literature, 1880–1980*. Winston-Salem, NC: Wake Forest University Press, 1987.

Maxwell, D. E. S. *Brian Friel*. Lewisburg, PA: Bucknell University Press, 1973.

O'Brien, Lance. *Brian Friel*. Boston: Twayne, 1990.

Pine, Richard. *The Diviner: The Art of Brian Friel*. Mullingar, Ireland: Lilliput Press, 1988.

Fugard, Athol. *Notebooks 1960–1977*. New York: Knopf, 1983.

Gray, Stephen, ed. *Athol Fugard*. Johannesburg, South Africa: McGraw, 1982.

Kavanagh, Robert Mshengu. *Theatre and Cultural Struggle in South Africa*. London: Zed, 1985.

Vandenbroucke, Russell. *Truths the Hand Can Touch: The Theatre of Athol Fugard*. New York: Theatre Communications Group, 1985.

Walder, Dennis. *Athol Fugard*. New York: Grove, 1985.

Athol Fugard, John Kani, Winston Ntshona

Brooks, Peter, and Joseph Halpern, eds. *Genet: A Collection of Critical Essays*. Englewood Cliffs, NJ: Prentice-Hall, 1979.

Chaudhuri, Una. *No Man's Stage: A Semiotic Study of Jean Genet's Major Plays*. Ann Arbor, MI: UMI Research Press, 1986.

Coe, Richard N. *The Vision of Jean Genet*. New York: Grove, 1968.

Genet, Jean. *Reflections on the Theatre and Other Writings*. Trans. Richard Seaver. London: Faber and Faber, 1972.

Sartre, Jean-Paul. *Saint Genet: Actor and Martyr*. Trans. Bernard Frechtman. New York: Pantheon, 1963.

Solich, W. F. "Genet's *The Blacks* and *The Screens*: Dialectic of Refusal and Revolutionary Consciousness." *Comparative Drama* 10 (1969): 216–34.

Jean Genet

Czerwinski, E. J. *Contemporary Polish Theater and Drama (1956–1984)*. Westport, CT: Greenwood, 1988.

Gerould, Daniel, ed. *Twentieth-Century Polish Avant-Garde Drama: Plays, Scenarios, Critical Documents*. Ithaca, NY: Cornell University Press, 1977.

Slawomir Mrozek

Diamond, Elin. *Pinter's Comic Play*. Lewisburg, PA: Bucknell University Press, 1985.

Esslin, Martin. *Pinter*. New York: Norton, 1976.

Ganz, Arthur, ed. *Pinter: A Collection of Critical Essays*. Englewood Cliffs, NJ: Prentice-Hall, 1972.

Postlewait, Thomas. "Pinter's *The Homecoming*: Displacing and Repeating Ibsen." *Comparative Drama* 15 (1981): 195–212.

Quigley, Austin E. *The Pinter Problem*. Princeton, NJ: Princeton University Press, 1975.

Harold Pinter

Kerr, Lucille. *Suspended Fictions: A Reading of Novels by Manuel Puig*. Urbana, IL: University of Illinois Press, 1987.

Gallagher, D. P. *Modern Latin American Literature*. Oxford: Oxford University Press, 1973.

MacAdam, Alfred J. *Modern Latin American Narratives: The Dreams of Reason*. Chicago: University of Chicago Press, 1977.

Tittler, Jonathan. *Narrative Irony in the Contemporary Spanish-American Novel*. Ithaca, NY: Cornell University Press, 1984.

Manuel Puig

Gibbs, James. *Wole Soyinka*. London: Macmillan, 1986.

Gibbs, James, ed. *Critical Perspectives on Wole Soyinka*. Washington, DC: Three Continents, 1980.

Gibbs, James, Ketu H. Katrak, and Henry Louis Gates, Jr., eds. *Wole Soyinka: A Bibliography of Primary and Secondary Sources*. Westport, CT: Greenwood, 1986.

Gugelberger, Georg M., ed. *Marxism and African Literature*. London: James Currey, 1985.

Wole Soyinka

Jones, Eldred Durosimi. *The Writings of Wole Soyinka*. London: James Currey, 1988.

Nazareth, Peter. *An African View of Literature*. Evanston, IL: Northwestern University Press, 1974.

Ogunba, Oyin. *The Movement of Transition: A Study of the Plays of Wole Soyinka*. Ibadan, Nigeria: Ibadan University Press, 1975.

Soyinka, Wole. "The Fourth Stage." In *The Morality of Art: Essays Presented to G. Wilson Knight by his Colleagues and Friends*. Ed. D. W. Jefferson. New York: Barnes and Noble, 1969.

Soyinka, Wole. *The Man Died*. London: Rex Collings, 1972.

UNIT 7: DRAMA AND THEATER TODAY: POPULAR ARTS AND THE CANON(S) OF THEATER

Further reading on the question of canons:

Altieri, Charles. "An Idea and Ideal of a Literary Canon." *Critical Inquiry* 10 (1983): 37–60.

Fish, Stanley. *Is There a Text in This Class? The Authority of Interpretive Communities*. Cambridge, MA: Harvard University Press, 1980.

Fowler, Alastair. "Genre and the Literary Canon." *New Literary History* 11 (1979): 97–119.

Hirsch, E. D. *Cultural Literacy: What Every American Needs to Know*. Boston: Houghton Mifflin, 1987.

Kermode, Frank. "Institutional Control of Interpretation." *Salmagundi* 43 (1979): 72–86.

Lauter, Paul. "Race and Gender in the Shaping of the American Literary Canon: A Case Study from the Twenties." *Feminist Studies* 9 (1983): 435–65.

Levin, Harry. "Core, Canon, Curriculum." *College English* 43 (1981): 352–62.

von Hallberg, Robert. *Canons*. Chicago: University of Chicago Press, 1984.

Maria Irene Fornes

Cummings, Scott. "Seeing with Clarity: The Visions of Maria Irene Fornes." *Theater* (Yale) 17:1 (Winter 1985): 51–56.

Fornes, Maria Irene. "Interview." *Performing Arts Journal* 2:3 (Winter 1978): 106–11.

Marranca, Bonnie. "The Real Life of Maria Irene Fornes." In *Theatrewritings*. New York: PAJ Publications, 1984.

Worthen, W. B. "*Still playing games*: Ideology and Performance in the Theater of Maria Irene Fornes." In *Feminine Focus: The New Women Playwrights*. Ed. Enoch Brater. Oxford: Oxford University Press, 1989.

William M. Hoffman

Gevisser, Mark. "Gay Theater Today." *Theater* 21:3 (Summer–Fall 1990) 46–51.

Sedgwick, Eve Kosofsky. *Epistemology of the Closet*. Berkeley, CA: University of California Press, 1990.

Wallace, Robert. "To Become: The Ideological Function of Gay Theatre." *Canadian Theatre Review* 59 (1989): 5–10.

David Henry Hwang

Hwang, David Henry. "Afterword." In *M. Butterfly*. New York: New American Library, 1988.

Hwang, David Henry. *F.O.B.* In *New Plays USA 1*. New York: Theatre Communications Group, 1982.

Moy, James S. "David Henry Hwang's *M. Butterfly* and Philip Kan Gotanda's *Yankee Dawg You Die*: Repositioning Chinese American Marginality on the American Stage." *Theatre Journal* 42 (1990): 48–56.

David Mamet

Carroll, Dennis. *David Mamet*. New York: Grove, 1987.

Dean, Anne. *David Mamet: Language as Dramatic Action*. Rutherford, NJ: Fairleigh Dickinson University Press, 1990.

Aeschylus, *Agamemnon*
> VHS. 1983. National Theatre of Great Britain production. Director: Peter Hall. Films for the Humanities.

Aristophanes, *Lysistrata*
> Sound Recording. 1966. Director: Howard Sackler. Cast includes Hermione Gingold and Stanley Holloway. Caedmon Records.

Sophocles, *Oedipus Rex*
> VHS. 1959. Distributed by Encyclopedia Brittanica Educational Corp.
> Film. 1967. Director: Philip Saville. Cast includes Christopher Plummer and Orson Welles.
> VHS. 1975. *The Rise of Greek Tragedy.* Director: Howard Mantell. Cast includes James Mason, Claire Bloom. Set in outdoor amphitheater, using masks. Films for the Humanities, 1982.

UNIT 1

Anonymous, *Everyman*
> Film. 1971. Distributed by Paul Lewison.
> Sound Recording. Cast includes Burgess Meredith. Caedmon Records.

Christopher Marlowe, *Doctor Faustus*
> VHS. 1968. Cast includes Richard Burton, Elizabeth Taylor.

William Shakespeare, *King Lear*
> Film. 1970. Director: Peter Brook. Cast includes Paul Scofield, Irene Worth.
> Film. 1970. Director: Grigori Kozintzev. Made in USSR.
> VHS. 1983. The BBC-TV Shakespeare Plays. Cast includes Michael Hordern.
> VHS. 1983. Cast includes Laurence Olivier, John Hurt. Films for the Humanities.

William Shakespeare, *The Tempest*
> VHS. 1983. The BBC-TV Shakespeare Plays. Cast includes Michael Hordern.
> VHS. Director: George Schaefer. Cast includes Maurice Evans, Roddy McDowell, Richard Burton, Lee Remick. Films for the Humanities.

UNIT 2

Molière, *Tartuffe*
> Sound Recording. 1968. Stratford National Theatre of Canada. Director: Jean Gascon. Caedmon Records.

UNIT 3

Anton Chekhov, *The Cherry Orchard*
> Film. 1967. Distributed by Encyclopedia Britannica Educational Corp.
> Sound Recording. Director: Tyrone Guthrie. Cast includes Jessica Tandy. Caedmon Records.

Henrik Ibsen, *A Doll House*
> VHS. 1959. Director: Barry A. Brown. Cast includes Christopher Plummer, Julie Harris, Richard Thomas.
> VHS. 1973. Director: Joseph Losey. Cast includes Jane Fonda, Trevor Howard.
> VHS. 1973. Director: Patrick Garland. Cast includes Claire Bloom, Ralph Richardson, Anthony Hopkins.

Luigi Pirandello, *Six Characters in Search of an Author*
> VHS. 1978. Miami Dade Community College.

UNIT 4

George Bernard Shaw, *Major Barbara*
> VHS. 1941. Director: Gabriel Pascal, in consultation with George Bernard Shaw. Cast includes Wendy Hiller, Rex Harrison, Sybil Thorndike.

August Strindberg, *Miss Julie*
> VHS. 1951. Director: Alf Sjöberg. Cast includes Max Von Sydow, Anita Bjork, Ulf Palme.

UNIT 5

Amiri Baraka/LeRoi Jones, *Dutchman*
> Film. 1966. Director: Anthony Harvey. Cast includes Al Freeman, Jr., Shirley Knight.

Arthur Miller, *The Crucible*
> Film. 1958. Director: Raymond Rouleau. Cast includes Simone Signoret, Yves Montand.

Eugene O'Neill, *The Emperor Jones*
> VHS. 1933. Director: Dudley Murphey. Cast includes Paul Robeson, Dudley Digges.

Sam Shepard, *True West*
> VHS. 1984. Director: Allan Goldstein. Cast includes John Malkovich and Gary Sinise.

Tennessee Williams, *The Glass Menagerie*
> Film. 1950. Director: Irving Rippen. Cast includes Jane Wyman, Kirk Douglas, Arthur Kennedy.
> Film. 1973. Director: Anthony Harvey. Cast includes Katharine Hepburn, Sam Waterston, Joanna Miles, Michael Moriarty.
> VHS. 1987. Director: Paul Newman. Cast includes John Malkovich, Joanne Woodward, Karen Allen.

UNIT 6

Samuel Beckett, *Happy Days*
> Sound Recording. Cast includes Irene Worth and George Voscovec. Caedmon Records.

Harold Pinter, *The Homecoming*
> Film. 1973. Director: Peter Hall. Cast includes Cyril Cusac, Ian Holm, Vivian Merchant.

Manuel Puig, *The Kiss of the Spider Woman*
> VHS. 1985. Director: Hector Babenco. Cast includes William Hurt, Raul Julia, Sonia Braga.

UNIT 7

William M. Hoffman, *As Is*
> VHS. 1986. Director: Michael Lindsay-Hogg. Cast includes Robert Carradine, Colleen Dewhurst.

✤ ILLUSTRATIONS ✤

p. 133 Reproduced by permission of the Marquess of Bath, Longleat House, Warminster, Wiltshire, Great Britain.

p. 267 HISTORY OF THE THEATRE , by Oscar G. Brockett (Boston: Allyn and Bacon, Figure 9.23) © 1987, Allyn and Bacon.
p. 269 THEATRE AND PLAYHOUSE by Richard and Helen Leacroft (London, New York: Methuen, 1984, p. 73) © 1984 by Richard and Helen Leacroft. Reprinted by permission of Methuen London.
p. 271 Public Domain.

p. 374 THEATRE AND PLAYHOUSE by Richard and Helen Leacroft (London, New York: Methuen, 1984, p. 157) © 1984 by Richard and Helen Leacroft. Reprinted by permission of Methuen London.
p. 375 THEATRE AND PLAYHOUSE by Richard and Helen Leacroft (London, New York: Methuen, 1984, p. 158) © 1984 by Richard and Helen Leacroft. Reprinted by permission of Methuen London.
p. 734 THEATRE AND PLAYHOUSE by Richard and Helen Leacroft (London, New York: Methuen, 1984, p. 187) © 1984 by Richard and Helen Leacroft. Reprinted by permission of Methuen London.

✦ PHOTO ESSAYS ✦

ESSAY I

© D. A. Harissiadis.
Photo: Rick Adams.
Richard Feldman.
Billy Rose Theatre Collection, The New York Public Library for the Performing Arts. Astor, Lenox and Tilden Foundations.
© 1992 Martha Swope.
© 1992 Martha Swope.
© 1992 Martha Swope.

ESSAY II

Photo: Bill Reid.
© 1992 Martha Swope.
© 1980 Gerry Goodstein.
MIRAMAX Film Release © 1991.

ESSAY III

© 1992 Martha Swope.
Richard Feldman / American Repertory Theatre.
Photo by Joan Marcus.
© 1992 Martha Swope.
© 1992 Martha Swope.
Richard Feldman.